KT-382-829

13 50
N

WITHDRAWN

N 0097052 2

THE OXFORD
RUSSIAN-ENGLISH
DICTIONARY

BY

MARCUS WHEELER

General Editor

B. O. UNBEGAUN

WITH THE ASSISTANCE OF

D. P. COSTELLO *and* W. F. RYAN

REFERENCE ONLY

NEWMAN COLLEGE
BARTLEY GREEN
BIRMINGHAM, 32.

CLASS 491.7
ACCESSION 71015
AUTHOR OXF

OXFORD
AT THE CLARENDON PRESS

Oxford University Press, Walton Street, Oxford OX2 6DP

OXFORD LONDON GLASGOW
NEW YORK TORONTO MELBOURNE WELLINGTON
KUALA LUMPUR SINGAPORE HONG KONG TOKYO
DELHI BOMBAY CALCUTTA MADRAS KARACHI
NAIROBI DAR ES SALAAM CAPE TOWN

ISBN 0 19 864111 7

© Oxford University Press 1972

First published 1972
Reprinted with corrections 1978, 1980

All rights reserved. No part of this publication may be reproduced,
stored in a retrieval system, or transmitted, in any form or by any
means, electronic, mechanical, photocopying, recording, or otherwise,
without the prior permission of Oxford University Press

Printed in Great Britain
at the University Press, Oxford
by Eric Buckley
Printer to the University

LIST OF ABBREVIATIONS

a.	accusative	hist.	history
abbr.	abbreviation	hort.	horticulture
abstr.	abstract		
act.	active	i.	instrumental
adj.	adjective	imp.	imperative
adv.	adverb	impers.	impersonal
aeron.	aeronautics	impf.	imperfective
agric.	agriculture	indecl.	indeclinable
anat.	anatomy	indet.	indeterminate
anthrop.	anthropology	inf.	infinitive
approx.	approximately	inst.	instantaneous
arch.	archaic	interj.	interjection
archaeol.	archaeology	interrog.	interrogative
archit.	architecture	intrans.	intransitive
as opp. to	as opposed to	in var. senses	in various senses
astron.	astronomy		
		joc.	jocular
bibl.	biblical		
biol.	biology	leg.	legal
bot.	botany	ling.	linguistics
		lit.	literature
chem.	chemistry		
coll.	colloquial	m.	masculine
collect.	collective	math.	mathematics
comm.	commercial	med.	medicine
comp.	comparative	meteor.	meteorology
concr.	concrete	mil.	military
conj.	conjunction	min.	mineral(ogy)
cul.	culinary	mus.	music
		myth.	mythology
d.	dative		
det.	determinate	n.	neuter
dial.	dialectal	n.-a.	nominative-accusative
dim.	diminutive	naut.	nautical
dipl.	diplomacy	neg.	negative
		nom.	nominative
eccl.	ecclesiastical	**N.S.**	New Style (of calendar)
econ.	economics		
electr.	electrical	obs.	obsolete
esp.	especially	onomat.	onomatopeia
ethnol.	ethnology	opt.	optics
euph.	euphemism	orn.	ornithology
exc.	except	**o.s.**	Old Style (of calendar)
f.	feminine	p.	prepositional (case)
fig.	figurative	part.	participle
fin.	financial	pass.	passive
freq.	frequentative	pejor.	pejorative
		pf.	perfective
g.	genitive	pharm.	pharmaceutical
geod.	geodesy	philol.	philology
geogr.	geography	philos.	philosophy
geol.	geology	phys.	physics
gram.	grammar	physiol.	physiology

pl.	plural	sl.	slang
poet.	poetry	superl.	superlative
polit.	politics		
p.p.p.	past participle passive	tech.	technical
pred.	predicate	text.	textiles
prep.	preposition	theatr.	theatre
pres.	present	theol.	theology
pron.	pronoun	trans.	transitive
psych.	psychology	typ.	typography
rel.	religion	usu.	usually
relat.	relative (pronoun)		
rhet.	rhetorical	var.	various
		voc.	vocative
		vulg.	vulgar
sc.	scilicet		
sing.	singular	zool.	zoology

The Russian -н. in illustrative phraseology within entries stands for the enclitic -нибудь (in the words кто-нибудь, что-нибудь, etc.).

ACKNOWLEDGEMENTS

THE Author and Editors gratefully acknowledge the assistance of scholars in the field of Russian studies, in particular that of Mr. I. P. Foote, Mr. M. Hayward, and Mr. J. Sullivan, who read the Dictionary in proof, and of Dr. S. Utechin, who checked a substantial part of the manuscript. Valuable suggestions concerning selection of vocabulary and treatment of individual entries were made also by Mrs. B. Costello, Dr. V. Du Feu, Mrs. M. Stokes, Mr. J. S. G. Simmons and Mme. H. Unbegaun; by Professor S. Konovalov, who encouraged the project from its inception; and by members of the staff of the former Joint Services School for Linguists. A number of scholars in fields other than Russian gave help in elucidating specialist terms. Mention should also be made of the friendly interest shown in the project by professional lexicographers and others in the Soviet Union, from a number of whom the Author received generous advice. Among dictionaries used in compiling the present work, a particular debt is due to D. N. Ushakov's *Tolkovyi slovar' russkogo yazyka* (Moscow, 1935–9), to the *Slovar' russkogo yazyka* compiled under the auspices of the Russian Language Institute of the U.S.S.R. Academy of Sciences (Moscow, 1957–61), and to A. I. Smirnitsky's *Russko-angliiskii slovar'* (3rd edition, under general editorship of Professor O. S. Akhmanova, Moscow, 1958).

The Author and Editors wish to record their appreciation of the important contribution made by the late Professor D. P. Costello to the production of this Dictionary. At the time of his death, in 1964, he had worked through nearly half the manuscript draft. A large number of entries in this part of the work were improved in detail thanks to his criticisms and suggestions, and the whole Dictionary benefited by his enthusiasm and by his wide knowledge both of Russian literature and of the contemporary colloquial Russian language.

Thanks are due, finally, to the Clarendon Press for invaluable editorial and technical expertise.

NOTE TO THE SECOND IMPRESSION

THE Author wishes to record his gratitude to all the many users who have reported errata or submitted comments or suggestions, but especially to Mr. S. Marder (Victoria University of Wellington, New Zealand) for his comprehensive orthographic analysis of the entire work. More substantial corrections will be incorporated when a second, revised edition is published.

INTRODUCTION

This work is intended as a general-purpose dictionary of Russian as it is written and spoken. It is designed primarily, though not exclusively, for the use of those whose native language is English.

A separate head-word is given for each entry, and there is a separate entry for each word. The entries include a substantial quantity of idiomatic and illustrative phraseology, but no literary quotations.

The following devices are used to economise space in the dictionary:

(i) The first letter of the head-word, followed by a full point, represents the whole head-word, thus:

това́рный ... т. соста́в (= това́рный соста́в)

(ii) The tilde sign, in conjunction with a vertical stroke, represents that part of the head-word which is to the left of the vertical stroke, thus:

роди́м|ый ... ~ое пятно́ (= роди́мое пятно́)

exceptions: the tilde is not used in indicating the genitive singular of nouns or the 1st and 2nd persons singular of the present tense of verbs with unchanged stress (for examples, see below: *Nouns* and *Verbs*); and, in cross-references from the imperfective to the perfective verbal aspect, it may, when preceded by a prefix, represent the entire head-word, thus:

ста́р|ить, ю, ишь, *impf.* (*of* со~) ... (= *of* соста́рить)

Pronunciation

The Russian alphabet and orthography are to a large extent phonetically accurate and phonetic symbols have not been employed in this dictionary. Stress, however, is indicated for every word. A stress mark above the tilde, where this sign represents two or more syllables, indicates shift of stress to the syllable immediately preceding the vertical stroke dividing the head-word, thus:

запи|са́ть, шу́, ~шешь ... (= запишу́, запи́шешь)

Conversely, a stress mark above a syllable to the right of the tilde indicates shift of stress away from the syllable(s) represented by the tilde, thus:

ва́хтер, а, *pl.* ~а́ ... (= вахтера́)

Where a variant stress is permissible, both variants are shown, thus:

скобл|и́ть, ю́, ~и́шь ... (= ско́блишь *or* скобли́шь)

Phraseology

Idiomatic phrases are in many cases duplicated in entries for the component words. Phrases consisting of adjective and noun, however, are normally entered under the adjective component.

Meaning

Separate meanings of a Russian word are marked off by Arabic numerals, thus:

гада́тельный . . . 1. pertaining to divination. 2. based on conjecture, problematical

Shades of meaning, represented by translations not considered strictly synonymous, are marked off by a semi-colon: translations considered synonymous—by a comma, thus:

га́дкий . . . ugly, repulsive; vile, nasty.

Homonyms are indicated by repetition of the head-word as a separate entry, followed by a raised Arabic numeral, thus:

газ¹, а, *m.* gas.
газ², а, *m.* gauze.

It should be noted that there is no accepted all-embracing criterion for differentiating homonymy from polysemy (plurality of meanings of a single word) or 'meaning' from 'shade of meaning'.

Explanation

This dictionary presents translations, not definitions. Where necessary for the avoidance of ambiguity, however, explanatory glosses are given in brackets in italic type, thus:

интерпрета́тор, а, *m.* interpreter (*expounder*). [i.e. *not* translator]

This device is used in particular in the case of words denoting specifically Russian or Soviet concepts (e.g. да́ча, ка́ша; микрорайо́н, толка́ч). This makes it possible to use one-word transliterations rather than clumsy paraphrases as a substitute for a translation.

Indications of style or usage are given, where appropriate, in brackets, thus: (*coll.*), (*dial.*); (*fig.*), (*joc.*); (*agric.*), (*polit.*), etc.

GRAMMAR

This dictionary is not a substitute for a grammar, but users familiar with the bases of Russian grammar will, it is hoped, profit from the grammatical indications supplied.

Nouns

The genitive singular ending and gender of all nouns are shown, thus:

мо́лот, а, *m.* hammer.
мо́лни|я, и, *f.* lightning.
молок|о́, а́, *n.* milk.

Other case endings are shown where declension or stress is, in relation to generally accepted systems of classification, irregular, thus:

> англича́н|ин, ина, *pl.* ~е, ~, *m.* Englishman.
> бор|ода́, оды́, *a.* ~оду, *pl.* ~оды, ~о́д, *d.* ~ода́м, *f.* beard.

(But the inserted vowel in the genitive plural ending of numerous feminine nouns with nominative singular ending -ка is not regarded as irregular, e.g. англича́нка, *g. pl.* англича́нок.)

Variant genitive case endings of certain *pluralia tantum* are indicated by a hyphen, thus:

> вы́молот|ки, ~ок-ков, *no sing.* . . . (= вы́молоток or вы́молотков).

Nouns ending -ость derived from adjectives have not been included where an appropriate English rendering can be obtained by adding *-ness* to the corresponding adjective (e.g., зо́ркий . . . sharpsighted . . . зо́ркость . . . sharpsightedness . . .).

Adjectives

Only the masculine nominative singular of the full form of the adjective is shown. Endings of the short forms, where these are found, are shown in brackets, thus:

> глу́п|ый (~, ~а́, ~о) . . .

The neuter short form ending is omitted where stress is as for the feminine, thus:

> нау́ч|ный (~ен, ~на) . . .

Verbs

Endings are shown of the 1st and 2nd persons singular of the present tense (or of the 1st person only of verbs with infinitive ending -ать, -овать, -ять, -еть which retain stem and stress unchanged throughout the present tense), thus:

> говор|и́ть, ю́, и́шь, . . .
> чита́|ть, ю, . . .

Other endings of the present tense and endings of the past tense are shown where formation or stress are irregular, thus:

> ид|ти́, у́, ёшь, *past* шёл, шла, шло . . .
> стере́|чь, гу́, жёшь, гу́т, *past* ~г, ~гла́, ~гло́ . . .

Participles and gerunds, and forms of the passive voice, are not shown unless having special semantic or syntactical features.

Verbal aspects: the imperfective aspect is normally treated as the basic form of the simple verb, a cross-reference to the relevant perfective form being shown in brackets, thus:

> чита́|ть, ю, *impf.* (*of* про~) . . .

The corresponding entry is:

> прочита́|ть, ю, *pf. of* чита́ть.

In the case, however, of compound verbs formed by means of a prefix, the perfective aspect is treated as the basic form, thus:

зачит|а́ть, а́ю, *pf. (of* ~ывать) . . .

Since, in a number of cases, a correspondence cannot, for semantic or other reasons, be firmly established (e.g. иска́ть-сыска́ть), the absence of a corresponding aspect is not necessarily noted.

Meanings and phraseology are shown under the basic form in each case unless peculiar to the other aspect.

Prefixes

A number of prefixes—verbal and other, and also truncated elements of words functioning as prefixes—are shown as separate entries, thus:

до- [verbal prefix]
гидро- hydro-
сов- *abbr. of* ~е́тский

Numerous compounded words, the meaning of which is judged sufficiently clear from a knowledge of the meaning of the prefix and root-word, have, to economise space, been excluded from the dictionary.

а¹, *conj.* **1.** and; while; вот ма́рки, а вот три рубля́ сда́чи here are the stamps and here is three roubles change; иди́те напра́во, пото́м нале́во, а пото́м ещё раз напра́во turn right, then left, (and) then right again; моя́ жена́ лю́бит е́здить в теа́тр, а я предпочита́ю кино́ my wife likes going to the theatre, while I prefer the cinema; а и́менно namely; to be exact. **2.** but; yet (*or not translated*); пора́ идти́ — а мы то́лько что пришли́! 'It's time to go.' 'But we've only just come!'; хотя́ ты и не хо́чешь посове́товаться с врачо́м, а на́до you may not want to see a doctor but you must; я иду́ не в кино́, а в теа́тр I am going to the theatre, not to the cinema. **3.** а то or (else), otherwise; спеши́, а то мы опозда́ем hurry up or we'll be late.

а², *interrog. particle* (*coll.*) eh?

а³, *interj.* (*expressing surprise, annoyance, pain, etc.; coll.*) ah, oh; а ну его́! oh, to hell with him!

абажу́р, а, *m.* lampshade.

аба́к|а, и, *f.* (*and* ∼, ∼а, *m.*) (*archit.*) abacus.

абба́т, а, *m.* abbot; (Roman Catholic) priest.

аббати́с|а, ы, *f.* abbess.

абба́тств|о, а, *n.* abbey.

аббревиату́р|а, ы, *f.* abbreviation.

аберра́ци|я, и, *f.* (*opt. and fig.*) aberration.

абза́ц, а, *m.* **1.** (*typ.*) indention; сде́лать а. to indent; нача́ть с но́вого ∼а to begin a new line, new paragraph. **2.** paragraph.

абисси́н|ец, ца, *m.* Abyssinian, Ethiopian.

абисси́нк|а, и, *f.* Abyssinian (woman), Ethiopian (woman).

абисси́нский, *adj.* Abyssinian, Ethiopian.

абитурие́нт, а, *m.* pupil taking school-leaving examination; leaver.

абляти́в, а, *m.* (*gram.*) ablative.

абонеме́нт, а, *m.* subscription; season ticket; сверх ∼а beyond the terms of agreement.

абоне́нт, а, *m.* subscriber.

абони́р|овать, ую, *impf. and pf.* to subscribe (to); to take out a booking (for), reserve a seat (for) (*a season at a theatre, a series of concerts, etc.*).

абони́р|оваться, уюсь, *impf. and pf.* **1.** (на+*a.*) to subscribe (to); to take out a booking (for). **2.** *pass. of* ∼овать.

аборда́ж, а, *m.* (*naut.*) boarding; взять на а. to board.

аборда́жный, *adj.* boarding; а. крюк (*naut.*) grapnel.

абориге́н, а, *m.* aboriginal.

або́рт, а, *m.* **1.** abortion, miscarriage; сде́лать себе́ а. to have an abortion. **2.** failure, cancellation.

аборти́вн|ый, *adj.* **1.** *adj. of* або́рт; ∼ые сре́дства means for procuring abortion. **2.** (*biol.*) abortive.

абракада́бр|а, ы, *f.* abracadabra.

абре́к, а, *m.* abrek (*member of Caucasian mountain bands who fought the Russians in the 19th century*).

абрико́с, а, *m.* **1.** apricot. **2.** apricot-tree.

абрико́совый, *adj.* apricot.

абрикоти́н, а, *m.* apricot liqueur.

а́брис, а, *m.* contour(s); outline.

абсе́нт, а, *m.* absinthe.

абсентеи́зм, а, *m.* absenteeism (*esp. from meetings, voting, etc.*).

абсенте́ист, а, *m.* absentee (*esp. from meetings, voting, etc.*).

абси́да = апси́да.

абсолю́т, а, *m.* (*philos.*) the absolute.

абсолюти́зм, а, *m.* (*polit.*) absolutism.

абсолюти́ст, а, *m.* (*polit.*) absolutist.

абсолю́т|ный (∼ен, ∼на), *adj.* absolute; а. слух (*mus.*) perfect ear.

абсорби́р|овать, ую, *impf. and pf.* to absorb.

абсо́рбци|я, и, *f.* absorption.

абстраги́р|овать, ую, *impf. and pf.* to abstract.

абстра́кт|ный (∼ен, ∼на), *adj.* abstract.

абстракциони́зм, а, *m.* abstract art.

абстракциони́ст, а, *m.* abstract artist.

абстра́кци|я, и, *f.* abstraction.

абсу́рд, а, *m.* absurdity; довести́ до ∼а to carry to the point of absurdity.

абсу́рдност|ь, и, *f.* absurdity.

абсу́рд|ный (∼ен, ∼на), *adj.* absurd.

абсце́сс, а, *m.* abscess.

абсци́сс|а, ы, *f.* (*math.*) abscissa.

абха́з|ец, ца, *m.* Abkhazian (*inhabitant of Abkhazia in the Caucasus*).

абха́зк|а, и, *f.* Abkhazian (woman).

абха́зский, *adj.* Abkhazian.

а́бцуг, а, *m.* (*obs.*) only in phrases с пе́рвого ∼а, по пе́рвому ∼у right from the start, from the first go-off.

аванга́рд, а, *m.* advance-guard, van; vanguard (*also fig.*).

аванпо́рт, а, *m.* outer harbour.

аванпо́ст, а, *m.* (*mil.*) outpost; forward position (*also fig.*).

ава́нс, а, *m.* **1.** advance (*of money*); получи́ть а. to receive an advance (*of wages*). **2.** (*pl. only; fig.*) advances, overtures.

аванси́р|овать, ую, *impf. and pf.* to advance (*money*).

ава́нсом, *adv.* in advance, on account.

авансце́н|а, ы, *f.* (*theatr.*) proscenium.

авантя́ж|ный (~ен, ~на), *adj.* (*obs., coll.*) fine, showing to advantage.

авантю́р|а, ы, *f.* 1. (*pejor.*) adventure; venture, escapade; пусти́ться в ~ы to embark on adventures. 2. (*coll.*) shady enterprise.

авантюри́зм, а, *m.* disposition to engage in adventures, ventures.

авантюри́ст, а, *m.* (*pejor.*) adventurer.

авантюр|исти́ческий, *adj.* of ~и́зм.

авантю́р|ный (~ен, ~на), *adj.* adventurous; а. рома́н (*lit.*) adventure story.

ава́р, а, *m.* (*hist.*) Avar.

ава́р, а, *m.* Avar (*member of ethnic group inhabiting Caucasus*).

авари́йност|ь, и, *f.* accidents, accident rate.

авари́йн|ый, *adj.* 1. *adj.* of ава́рия; ~ая маши́на breakdown van; (*aeron.*) ~ая кома́нда crash crew; ~ая поса́дка crash landing; а. сигна́л distress signal. 2. emergency, spare.

ава́ри|я, и, *f.* 1. damage; wreck, crash, accident; breakdown; (*fig., iron.*) misfortune; потерпе́ть ~ю to crash, have an accident. 2. (*leg.*) damages, average.

ава́р|ка, ки, *f.* of ~ and ~ец.

ава́р|ский, *adj.* of ~ and ~ец.

авгу́р, а, *m.* augur; язы́к ~ов esoteric language.

а́вгуст, а, *m.* August.

августе́йший, *adj.* (*as title of emperors*) most august.

августи́н|ец, ца, *m.* Augustinian, Austin friar.

а́вгуст|овский, *adj.* of ~.

а́виа (= авиапо́чтой) 'by air mail'.

авиа- air-, aero-.

авиаба́з|а, ы, *f.* air base.

авиаконстру́ктор, а, *m.* aircraft designer.

авиама́тк|а, и, *f.* aircraft-carrier.

авиамодели́зм, а, *m.* model aircraft construction.

авиамодели́ст, а, *m.* model aircraft constructor, model aircraft enthusiast.

авиамоде́л|ь, и, *f.* model aircraft.

авиамоде́ль|ный, *adj.* of ~.

авиано́с|ец, ца, *m.* aircraft carrier.

авиапо́чт|а, ы, *f.* air mail.

авиасъёмк|а, и, *f.* air photography, aerial surveying.

авиацио́нн|ый, *adj.* of авиа́ция; ~ая промы́шленность aircraft industry; ~ая шко́ла flying school.

авиа́ци|я, и, *f.* 1. aviation. 2. (*collect.*) aircraft; бомбардиро́вочная а. bomber force.

авиача́ст|ь, и, *f.* air force unit.

ави́зо, *indecl., n.* 1. (*comm.*) letter of advice.

2. (*naut.*) aviso, advice-boat.

аво́сь, *adv.* perhaps; на а. on the off-chance.

аво́сь|ка, и, *f.* (*coll.*) string (shopping) bag.

авра́л, а, *m.* (*naut.*) work involving all hands; (*as interj.*) all hands on deck!; (*fig.*) all hands to the pump!

авра́л|ьный, *adj.* of ~; ~ьная рабо́та emergency job.

авро́ра, ы, *f.* (*poet.*) aurora, dawn.

австрали́|ец, йца, *m.* Australian.

австрали́йк|а, и, *f.* Australian (woman).

австрали́йский, *adj.* Australian.

австри́|ец, йца, *m.* Austrian.

австри́йк|а, и, *f.* Austrian (woman).

австри́йский, *adj.* Austrian.

австрия́к, а, *m.* (*coll., obs.*) Austrian.

австрия́чк|а, и, *f.* (*coll., obs.*) Austrian (woman).

автарки́|я, и, *f.* (*econ., philos.*) self-sufficiency, autarky.

автенти́чный, *adj.* = аутенти́чный

авто́, *indecl., n.* (*coll.*) (motor-)car.

авто- 1. self-. 2. auto-, automatic. 3. motor-.

автоба́з|а, ы, *f.* motor-transport depot.

автобиографи́ческий, *adj.* autobiographical.

автобиографи́чност|ь, и, *f.* autobiographical nature, character.

автобиогра́фи|я, и, *f.* autobiography.

автоблокиро́вк|а, и, *f.* (*railways*) automatic block system.

авто́бус, а, *m.* (motor) 'bus, omnibus.

автоге́нный, *adj.* (*tech.*) autogenous.

авто́граф, а, *m.* (*in var. senses*) autograph.

автодро́м, а, *m.* 1. vehicle testing point. 2. motor-racing circuit.

автожи́р, а, *m.* autogyro.

автозаво́д, а, *m.* motor-car factory.

автока́р, а, *m.* motor trolley.

автокефа́льный, *adj.* (*eccl.*) autocephalous.

автокла́в, а, *m.* (*tech.*) autoclave.

автокра́т, а, *m.* autocrat.

автократи́ческий, *adj.* autocratic.

автокра́ти|я, и, *f.* autocracy.

автомагистра́л|ь, и, *f.* motorway.

автома́т, а, *m.* 1. automatic machine, slot-machine; биле́тный а. ticket machine; телефо́н-а. public telephone, call-box; (*fig.*) automaton, robot. 2. (*mil.*) sub-machine-gun, tommy-gun.

автоматиза́ци|я, и, *f.* automation.

автоматизи́р|овать, ую, *impf. and pf.* 1. to render automatic. 2. to introduce automation (into); to automate.

автомати́зм, а, *m.* automatism.

автомати́ческ|ий, *adj.* 1. (*tech.*) automatic, self-acting; ~ая винто́вка automatic (rifle); ~ая ру́чка fountain-pen. 2. (*fig.*) automatic, involuntary.

автомати́ч|ный(~ен, ~на), *adj.* = ~еский 2.

автома́т|ный, *adj. of* ~ 2.
автома́тчик, а, *m.* (*mil.*) sub-machine-gunner, tommy-gunner.
автомаши́н|а, ы, *f.* motor vehicle.
автомобили́зм, а, *m.* motoring.
автомобили́ст, а, *m.* motorist.
автомоби́л|ь, я, *m.* (motor-)car, motor vehicle; управля́ть ~ем to drive a (motor-)car.
автомоби́льный, *adj. of* ~; а. заво́д motor-car factory; а. спорт motoring.
автоно́ми|я, и, *f.* autonomy.
автоно́м|ный (~ен, ~на), *adj.* autonomous.
автопортре́т, а, *m.* self-portrait.
а́втор, а, *m.* author; composer; а. предло-же́ния, резолю́ции mover of resolution.
автореферат, а, *m.* abstract (*of dissertation, etc.*).
авториза́ци|я, и, *f.* authorization.
авториз|о́ванный, *p.p.p. of* ~ова́ть *and adj.* authorized.
авториз|ова́ть, у́ю, *impf. and pf.* to authorize.
авторита́р|ный (~ен, ~на), *adj.* authoritarian.
авторите́т, а, *m.* authority; по́льзоваться ~ом to enjoy authority, have prestige; счита́ться ~ом to be considered an authority.
авторите́тност|ь, и, *f.* authoritativeness; trustworthiness.
авторите́т|ный (~ен, ~на), *adj.* authoritative; trustworthy; а. исто́чник an authoritative source (of information).
а́втор|ский, *adj. of* ~; а. лист (*typ.*) unit of 40,000 ens (*used in calculating author's royalties*); ~ское пра́во copyright; *as noun* ~ские, ~ских royalties.
а́вторств|о, а, *n.* authorship.
авторучк|а, и, *f.* (*coll.*) fountain-pen.
автосто́п, а, *m.* 1. (*railways*) automatic braking gear. 2. (*coll.*) hitch-hiking.
автостра́д|а, ы, *f.* motorway, motor highway; trunk-road.
автосце́пк|а, и, *f.* (*railways*) automatic coupling.
автоти́пи|я, и, *f.* (*typ.*) autotype.
автотра́нспорт, а, *m.* motor transport.
автохто́н, а, *m.* autochthon, aboriginal.
автохто́нный, *adj.* autochthonous.
ага́, *interj.* (*expressing* (*i*) *comprehension,* (*ii*) *malicious pleasure*) ah!, aha!
ага́в|а, ы, *f.* (*bot.*) agave.
агаря́н|ин, ина, *pl.* ~е, ~, *m.* (*coll., obs.*) Hagarite.
ага́т, а, *m.* (*min.*) agate.
ага́т|овый, *adj. of* ~.
агглютинати́вный, *adj.* (*ling.*) agglutinative.
агглютин|и́рующий, *adj.* = ~ати́вный.
аге́нт, а, *m.* (*in var. senses*) agent.
аге́нтств|о, а, *n.* agency.

агенту́р|а, ы, *f.* 1. secret service; занима́ться ~ой to be an agent. 2. (*collect.*) agents.
агиогра́фи|я, и, *f.* hagiography.
агит-, *abbr. of* ~ацио́нный.
агита́тор, а, *m.* (*polit.*) agitator; canvasser.
агитацио́н|ный (~ен, ~на), *adj.* (*polit.*) agitation.
агита́ци|я, и, *f.* (*polit.*) agitation; drive; вести́ ~ю to campaign, conduct a drive.
агити́р|овать, ую, *impf.* 1. (*impf. only*) (*polit.*) to agitate, carry on agitation, campaign. 2. (*pf.* с~) (*coll.*) to try to persuade.
аги́тк|а, и, *f.* (*polit.*) item of propaganda (*plays, posters, etc.*).
агитпро́п, а, *m.* (*abbr. of* отде́л агита́ции и пропага́нды) agitation and propaganda section (*of central and local committees of the Communist Party of the Soviet Union*).
а́глицкий, *adj.* (*coll., obs.*) English.
а́гн|ец, ца, *m.* 1. (*eccl.*) lamb (*Agnus Dei*). 2. *fig. of a meek person*: прики́нуться ~цем to feign meekness, play the innocent.
агно́стик, а, *m.* agnostic.
агностици́зм, а, *m.* agnosticism.
агности́ческий, *adj.* agnostic.
агонизи́р|овать, ую, *impf. and pf.* to be in one's death agony.
аго́ни|я, и, *f.* (*med.*) death agony, death-pangs; (*fig.*) last struggle.
агра́ри|й, я, *m.* (*hist.*) landowner.
агра́рный, *adj.* agrarian.
агрега́т, а, *m.* 1. (*tech.*) unit, assembly. 2. aggregate.
агресси́в|ный (~ен, ~на), *adj.* aggressive.
агре́сси|я, и, *f.* aggression (*of one State against another*).
агре́ссор, а, *m.* aggressor.
агрикульту́р|а, ы, *f.* agriculture.
агрикульту́рный, *adj.* agricultural.
агро- agro-, agricultural, farm.
агроно́м, а, *m.* agronomist.
агроно́ми|я, и, *f.* agronomics; agricultural science.
агу́, *interj. used to make a baby smile.*
ад, а, *m.* hell; (*fig.*) bedlam; душе́вный а. mental torment, anguish.
ада́мов, *adj.*; ~о я́блоко Adam's apple.
ада́жио, *adv. and noun indecl., n.* (*mus.*) adagio.
ада́птер, а, *m.* 1. (*tech.*) adapter 2. (*mus.*) pick-up.
адвока́т, а, *m.* barrister; (*fig.*) advocate.
адвокату́р|а, ы, *f.* 1. the profession of barrister. 2. (*collect.*) the Bar, the legal profession.
адеква́т|ный (~ен, ~на), *adj.* identical, coincident; adequate.
адено́ид, а, *m.* (*med.*) adenoid.

адéпт, а, *m.* adherent, disciple.

аджáр|ец, ца, *m.* Adzharian.

аджáрк|а, и, *f.* Adzharian (woman).

аджáрский, *adj.* Adzharian.

административн|ый, *adj.* administrative; в ~ом порядке administratively, by administrative means.

администрáтор, а, *m.* administrator; (hotel) manager.

администрáци|я, и, *f.* administration.

администрир|овать, ую, *impf.* to administer; (*pejor.*) to run (an organization, *etc.*) by means of orders and decrees.

адмирáл, а, *m.* admiral.

адмиралтéй|ский, *adj. of* ~ство.

адмиралтéйств|о, а, *n.* (*obs.*) **1.** naval dockyard. **2.** The Admiralty.

адмирáл|ьский, *adj. of* ~; а. корáбль flagship; а. чин, ~ьское звáние flag rank; а. час (*joc., obs.*) midday drinking time.

адмирáльш|а, и, *f.* admiral's wife.

áдрес, а, *pl.* ~á, ~óв, *m.* (*in var. senses*) address; не по ~y (*fig.*) mistakenly, at the wrong door, to the wrong quarter; áта критика напрáвлена не по ~y these criticisms are misdirected.

адресáнт, а, *m.* sender (*of mail*).

адресáт, а, *m.* addressee; в случае ненахождéния ~а 'if undelivered'; за ненахождéнием ~а 'not known' (*on letters*).

áдрес-календáр|ь, я, *m.* (*obs.*) directory.

áдрес|ный, *adj. of* ~; ~ная книга directory; а. стол address bureau.

áдрес|овáть, ую, *impf. and pf.* to address, direct.

áдрес|овáться, уюсь, *impf. and pf.* (к + *dat.*) to address oneself (to).

áдски, *adv.* (*coll.*) infernally, terribly, fearfully; я а. зáнят I am terribly busy.

áдск|ий, *adj.* infernal, diabolical; (*fig.*) hellish, intolerable; ~ая скука infernal bore; ~ая машина infernal machine.

áдов, *adj.* (*rel. and fig., coll.*) of ад.

адсóрбци|я, и, *f.* (*chem.*) adsorption.

адъюнкт, а, *m.* **1.** (*obs.*) junior scientific assistant. **2.** advanced student in military academy.

адъютáнт, а, *m.* (*mil.*) aide-de-camp; стáрший а. adjutant.

адюльтéр, а, *m.* adultery.

адюльтéр|ный, *adj. of* ~.

аж, *adv. and conj.* (*coll.*) **1.** (*adv.*) аж до right up to; аж на (+ *a.*) right on to. **2.** (*conj.*) so that, until; онá так закричáла, аж сéрдце похолодéло she cried enough to break one's heart.

áжио, *indecl., n.* (*comm.*) agio.

ажиотáж, а, *m.* **1.** (*comm.*) stock-jobbing. **2.** (*fig.*) stir, hullabaloo.

ажитáци|я, и, *f.* (*obs.*) agitation, excite-

ment; быть в ~и to be agitated, het up, in a state.

ажýр¹, а, *m.* open-work.

ажýр², *adv.* (*comm.*) up to date.

ажýрн|ый, *adj.* open-work; (*fig.*) delicate, fine; ~ые чулки open-work stockings; ~ая рабóта open-work; (*archit.*) tracery.

аз, á, *m.* **1.** az (*Slavonic name of the letter A*). **2.** (*usu. pl.; coll.*) ABC; elements, rudiments; начинáть с ~óв to begin at the beginning; ни ~á не знать (о + *p.*) not to know the first thing (about).

азáли|я, и, *f.* (*bot.*) azalea.

азáрт, а, *m.* heat; excitement; fervour; войти в а. to grow heated, excited.

азáрт|ный (~ен, ~на), *adj.* heated; venturesome; ~ная игрá game of chance.

азбéст, *see* асбéст.

áзбук|а, и, *f.* alphabet; the ABC (*also fig.*); а. Мóрзе Morse code.

áзбучн|ый, *adj.* alphabetical; ~ая истина truism.

азербайджáн|ец, ца, *m.* Azerbaijani(an).

азербайджáнк|а, и, *f.* Azerbaijani(an) (woman).

азербайджáнский, *adj.* Azerbaijani.

азиáт, а, *m.* **1.** Asiatic. **2.** (*fig., obs.*) barbarous person.

азиáтский, *adj.* **1.** Asiatic. **2.** (*fig., obs.*) barbarous.

азиáтчин|а, ы, *f.* (*obs.*) barbarous manners, way of life.

áзимут, а, *m.* (*astron.*) azimuth.

азóт, а, *m.* (*chem.*) nitrogen; óкись ~а nitric oxide.

азотистокислый, *adj.* (*chem.*) nitrite.

азóтистый, *adj.* (*chem.*) nitrous.

азотнокислый, *adj.* (*chem.*) nitrate.

азóтн|ый, *adj.* (*chem.*) nitric; ~ая кислотá nitric acid.

áист, а, *m.* (*zool.*) stork.

ай, *interj.* (*expressing (i) fear, (ii) surprise and/or pleasure*) oh!; ай да (*expressing approval*) what а . . . !; ай да молодéц! well done!

айв|á, ы, *f.* **1.** quince. **2.** quince-tree.

айвóвый, *adj.* quince.

айдá, *interj.* (*coll.*) come along!, let's go!

áйсберг, а, *m.* iceberg.

айсóр, а, *m.* Aysor.

айсóрк|а, и, *f.* Aysor (woman).

академизм, а, *m.* academic manner.

академик, а, *m.* **1.** academician (*member of an Academy*). **2.** (*coll., obs.*) student of an academy.

академический, *adj.* academic(al).

академич|ный (~ен, ~на), *adj.* academic, theoretical.

академи|я, и, *f.* academy.

áкань|е, я, *n.* akanie (*pronunciation of unstressed 'o' as 'a'*).

а́ка|ть, ю, *impf.* to pronounce unstressed 'o' as 'a' in Russian words.

ака́фист, а, *m.* (*eccl.*) acathistus (*series of doxological prayers*).

ака́ци|я, и, *f.* (*bot.*) acacia.

аквамари́н, а, *m.* (*min.*) aquamarine.

акварели́ст, а, *m.* water-colour painter.

акваре́л|ь, и, *f.* water-colour; писа́ть ~ью to paint in water-colours.

акваре́льный, *adj.* water-colour.

аква́риум, а, *m.* aquarium.

аквато́ри|я, и, *f.* (*defined*) area of water.

акведу́к, а, *m.* aqueduct.

акклиматиза́ци|я, и, *f.* acclimatization.

акклиматизи́р|овать, ую, *impf. and pf.* to acclimatize.

акклиматизи́р|оваться, уюсь, *impf. and pf.* to become acclimatized.

аккомпанеме́нт, а, *m.* (*mus.*) accompaniment (*also fig.*); под а. (+*g.*) to the accompaniment of.

аккомпаниа́тор, а, *m.* (*mus.*) accompanist.

аккомпани́р|овать, ую, *impf.* (+*d.*, на+*p.*; *mus.*) to accompany; а. певцу́ на роя́ле to accompany a singer on the piano.

акко́рд, а, *m.* (*mus.*) chord; заключи́тельный а. (*fig.*) finale; взять а. to strike a chord (*on the piano*).

аккордео́н, а, *m.* accordion.

акко́рдн|ый, *adj.* ~ая пла́та payment by the job; ~ая рабо́та job paid for as a whole.

аккредити́в, а, *m.* (*fin.*) letter of credit.

аккредит|ова́ть, у́ю, *impf. and pf.* to accredit.

аккумули́р|овать, ую, *impf. and pf.* to accumulate.

аккумуля́тор, а, *m.* (*tech.*) accumulator.

аккумуля́ци|я, и, *f.* accumulation.

аккура́т, *adv.* (*coll.*) only in phrases в а. exactly, precisely; в ~e properly.

аккура́тност|ь, и, *f.* 1. exactness, thoroughness. 2. tidiness, neatness.

аккура́т|ный (~ен, ~на), *adj.* 1. exact, thorough. 2. tidy, neat.

акмеи́зм, а, *m.* (*lit.*) acmeism.

акмеи́ст, а, *m.* (*lit.*) acmeist.

акони́т, а, *m.* (*bot.*) aconite.

акри́д|ы, ~, *no sing.*, only in phrase пита́ться ~ами и ди́ким мёдом to live on locusts and wild honey (*i.e. to live meagrely*).

акроба́т, а, *m.* acrobat.

акроба́тик|а, и, *f.* acrobatics.

акробати́ческий, *adj.* acrobatic.

акро́пол|ь, я, *m.* (*hist.*) acropolis.

акрости́х, а, *m.* acrostic.

аксельба́нт, а, *m.* aiguillette.

аксессуа́р, а, *m.* 1. accessory. 2. (*theatr.*) properties.

аксио́м|а, ы, *f.* axiom.

акт, а, *m.* 1. act. 2. (*theatr.*) act. 3. (*leg.*) deed, document; обвини́тельный а. indictment. 4. (*obs.*) speech-day (*in schools*).

актёр, а, *m.* actor (*also fig., pejor.*).

актёр|ский, *adj.* of ~.

актёрств|о, а, *n.* acting; (*fig.*) affectation, posing.

акти́в[1], а, *m.* (*fin.*) assets; (*fig.*) asset, advantage.

акти́в[2], а, *m.* (*polit.*) most active members; парти́йный а. most active members of a party.

активиза́ци|я, и, *f.* activization.

активизи́р|овать, ую, *impf. and pf.* to make more active, stir up.

активи́ст, а, *m.* (*polit.*) activist (*active member of political or social organization*).

акти́в|ный (~ен, ~на), *adj.* active, energetic.

а́ктов|ый, *adj.* (*obs.*) ~ая бума́га official paper; а. зал assembly hall.

актри́с|а, ы, *f.* actress.

актуа́льност|ь, и, *f.* 1. (*tech.*) actuality. 2. topicality.

актуа́л|ьный (~ен, ~ьна), *adj.* 1. (*tech.*) actual. 2. topical; а. вопро́с pressing question, topical question.

аку́л|а, ы, *f.* (*zool.*) shark (*also fig.*).

аку́стик|а, и, *f.* acoustics.

акусти́ческий, *adj.* acoustic.

акушёр, а, *m.* obstetrician.

акуше́рк|а, и, *f.* midwife.

акуше́рский, *adj.* obstetric(al).

акуше́рств|о, а, *n.* obstetrics; midwifery.

акце́нт, а, *m.* accent.

акценти́р|овать, ую, *impf. and pf.* to accent, accentuate.

акце́пт, а, *m.* (*comm.*) acceptance.

акцепт|ова́ть, у́ю, *impf. and pf.* (*comm.*) to accept.

акци́з, а, *m.* (excise-)duty; обложи́ть ~ом to excise.

акционе́р, а, *m.* shareholder.

акционе́р|ный, *adj.* of ~; ~ное о́бщество joint-stock company.

а́кци|я[1], и, *f.* (*fin.*) share; а. на предъяви́теля ordinary share; именна́я а. nominal share; привилегиро́ванная а. preference share; (*fig., coll.; pl. only*) stock; его́ ~и си́льно поднима́ются his stock is rising rapidly.

а́кци|я[2], и, *f.* action, démarche (*particularly in diplomacy*).

албан|ец, ца, *m.* Albanian.

алба́нк|а, и, *f.* Albania n (woman).

алба́нский, *adj.* Albanian.

а́лгебр|а, ы, *f.* algebra.

алгебраи́ческий, *adj.* algebraic(al).

алеба́рд|а, ы, *f.* (*hist.*) halberd.

алеба́стр, а, *m.* alabaster.

александри́йский, *adj.* (*geogr.*) Alexandrian; а. лист (*med.*) senna; а. стих (*lit.*) Alexandrine (verse).

александри́т, а, *m.* (*min.*) alexandrite.

але|́ть, ю, *impf.* (of за~) 1. to redden, flush. 2. to show red.

алеу́т, а, *m.* Aleutian.

алеу́тк|а, и, *f.* Aleutian (woman).

Алеу́тск|ий, *adj.* ~ие острова́ the Aleutian Islands.

алжи́р|ец, ца, *m.* Algerian.

алжи́рк|а, и, *f.* Algerian (woman).

алжи́рский, *adj.* Algerian.

а́ли (*coll.*) = и́ли.

а́либи, *indecl., n.* (*leg.*) alibi; установи́ть а. to establish an alibi.

алиме́нтщик, а, *m.* (*coll.*) person paying alimony.

алиме́нтщиц|а, ы, *f.* (*coll.*) woman in receipt of alimony.

алиме́нт|ы, ов, *no sing.* (*leg.*) alimony, maintenance.

ал|ка́ть, ⌣чу, ⌣чешь, *impf.* (+*g.*; *poet.*) to hunger (for), crave (for).

алкоголи́зм, а, *m.* alcoholism.

алкого́лик, а, *m.* alcoholic; (*coll.*) drunkard.

алкоголи́ческий, *adj.* alcoholic.

алкого́л|ь, я, *m.* alcohol.

алкого́льный, *adj.* alcoholic.

Алла́х, а, *m.* Allah; А. его́ ве́дает God knows; одному́ ~у изве́стно God alone knows.

аллегори́ч|еский, *adj.* allegorical.

аллегори́ч|ный (~ен, ~на), *adj.* = ~еский.

аллего́ри|я, и, *f.* allegory.

алле́гро, *adv. and noun, indecl., n.* (*mus.*) allegro.

алле́|я, и, *f.* avenue.

аллига́тор, а, *m.* alligator.

аллилу́йщик, а, *m.* (*pejor.*) eulogist of the status quo.

аллилу́йщин|а, ы, *f.* (*pejor.*) disposition to eulogize the status quo.

аллилу́йя, *indecl., n. and as interj.* alleluia, hallelujah.

аллитера́ци|я, и, *f.* alliteration.

алло́, *interj.* (*on lifting telephone receiver or in course of telephone conversation*) hullo!

аллопа́т, а, *m.* (*med.*) allopath(ist).

аллопа́ти|я, и, *f.* (*med.*) allopathy.

аллопати́ческий, *adj.* (*med.*) allopathic.

аллювиа́льный, *adj.* (*geol.*) alluvial.

аллю́ви|й, я, *m.* (*geol.*) alluvium.

аллю́р, а, *m.* pace, gait (*of horses*).

алма́з, а, *m.* (uncut) diamond.

ало́э, *indecl., n.* (*bot.*) aloe; (*med.*) aloes.

алта́р|ь, я́, *m.* 1. (*eccl.*) altar; возложи́ть, принести́ на а. (+*g.*) to sacrifice (to). 2. (*eccl.*) chancel; sanctuary.

алты́н, а, *m.* (*obs.*) three-kopeck piece.

алты́нник, а, *m.* (*obs., coll.*) skinflint.

алфави́т, а, *m.* alphabet.

алфави́тный, *adj.* alphabetical; а. указа́тель index.

алхи́мик, а, *m.* alchemist.

алхи́ми|я, и, *f.* alchemy.

а́лчност|ь, и, *f.* greed, avidity, cupidity.

а́лч|ный (~ен, ~на), *adj.* greedy, grasping.

а́лчущий, *pres. part. of* алка́ть; ~ие и жа́ждущие (+*g.*) those that hunger and thirst (after).

а́л|ый (~, ~а), *adj.* scarlet.

алыч|а́, и́, *f.* cherry-plum (*kind of small plum:* Prunus divaricata).

аль (*coll.*) = и́ли.

альбатро́с, а, *m.* albatross.

альбини́зм, а, *m.* (*med.*) albinism.

альбино́с, а, *m.* (*med.*) albino.

альбо́м, а, *m.* album.

алько́в, а, *m.* alcove.

алько́в|ный, *adj.* 1. *adj. of* ~. 2. erotic, pornographic.

альмана́х, а, *m.* 1. literary miscellany. 2. (*obs.*) almanac.

альпака́¹, *indecl., n.* alpaca.

альпака́², *indecl., n.* (*min.*) German silver.

альпа́ри, *adv.* (*comm.*) at par.

альпи́йский, *adj.* alpine.

альпини́зм, а, *m.* mountaineering.

альпини́ст, а, *m.* mountain-climber.

альт, а́, *pl.* ~ы́, *m.* (*mus.*) 1. alto (*voice or singer*). 2. viola.

альтера́ци|я, и, *f.* (*mus.*) change in pitch of notes (*by a tone or semitone*); зна́ки ~и accidentals.

альтернати́в|а, ы, *f.* alternative.

альтернати́в|ный (~ен, ~на), *adj.* alternative.

альти́ст, а, *m.* viola-player.

альт|о́вый, *adj. of* ~; ~о́вая па́ртия alto part.

альтруи́зм, а, *m.* altruism.

альтруи́ст, а, *m.* altruist.

альтруисти́ческий, *adj.* altruistic.

а́льф|а, ы, *f.* alpha; от ~ы до оме́ги from A to Z.

альфо́нс, а, *m.* (*pejor.*) gigolo.

алюми́ниевый, *adj.* aluminium.

алюми́ни|й, я, *m.* aluminium.

аляпова́т|ый (~, ~а), *adj.* tasteless; tastelessly painted; crudely constructed.

амазо́нк|а, и, *f.* 1. (*myth.*) Amazon. 2. horsewoman. 3. riding-habit.

амальга́м|а, ы, *f.* (*chem. and fig.*) amalgam.

амальгами́р|овать, ую, *impf. and pf.* (*chem. and fig.*) to amalgamate.

амана́т, а, *m.* (*dial.*) hostage.

а́мба, *interj.* (*sl.*) kaput!, it's all up!

амба́р, а, *m.* barn, granary; warehouse, storehouse.

амба́рго = эмба́рго.

амба́р|ный, *adj. of* ~.

амби́ци|я, и, *f.* (*obs.*) pride; arrogance; челове́к с ~ей arrogant man; вломи́ться в ~ю to take offence.

а́мбр|а, ы, *f.* amber; се́рая а. ambergris.

амбразу́р|а, ы, *f.* (*mil., archit.*) embrasure.

амбре́, *indecl., n.* scent, smell, fragrance (*now usu. iron.*).

амбро́зи|я, и, *f.* ambrosia.

амбулато́ри|я, и, *f.* (*med.*) out-patients department (*of hospital*); (*general practioner's*) surgery.

амбулато́р|ный, *adj. of* ~ия; а. больно́й out-patient, walking patient; а. приём out-patient reception hours; surgery hours.

амбушю́р, а, *m.* (*mus.*) mouthpiece.

амво́н, а, *m.* (*eccl.*) ambo, pulpit.

амёб|а, ы, *f.* (*zool.*) amoeba.

америка́н|ец, ца, *m.* American.

американи́зм, а, *m.* 1. (*ling.*) Americanism. 2. American methods (of work).

американи́стик|а, и, *f.* American studies.

америка́нк|а, и, *f.* 1. American (woman). 2. (*agric.*) amerikanka (*variety of spring wheat*). 3. snack bar. 4. two-wheeled cart.

америка́нск|ий, *adj.* American; ~ие го́ры switchback (*at fairs*); а. дя́дюшка 'rich uncle' (*character, esp. in comedies, from whom a legacy is hoped for*); а. замо́к Yale lock; ~ая мастерска́я 'while-you-wait' shoe repair shop; а. оре́х Brazil nut.

амети́ст, а, *m.* (*min.*) amethyst.

амети́ст|овый, *adj. of* ~.

ампи́р|ный, *adj. of* ~.

амикошо́нств|о, а, *n.* (*coll.*) hail-fellow-well-met attitude.

аминокислот|а́, ы́, *f.* (*chem.*) aminoacid.

ами́нь, *particle* (*eccl.*) amen.

аммиа́к, а, *m.* (*chem.*) ammonia.

аммиа́чный, *adj.* (*chem.*) ammoniac.

аммо́ни|й, я, *m.* (*chem.*) ammonium.

амнисти́р|овать, ую, *impf. and pf.* to amnesty.

амни́сти|я, и, *f.* amnesty.

аморали́зм, а, *m.* (*philos.*) amoralism.

амора́льность|ь, и, *f.* amorality; immorality.

амора́л|ьный (~ен, ~ьна), *adj.* amoral; immoral.

амортиза́тор, а, *m.* (*tech.*) shock-absorber.

амортиза́ци|я, и, *f.* 1. (*econ.*) amortization. 2. (*tech.*) shock-absorption.

амортизи́р|овать, ую, *impf. and pf.* to amortize.

аморф|ный (~ен, ~на), *adj.* amorphous.

ампе́р, а, *g. pl.* **а.,** *m.* (*phys.*) ampere.

ампи́р, а, *m.* Empire style (*of furniture, etc.*).

ампи́р|ный, *adj. of* ~.

амплиту́д|а, ы, *f.* amplitude.

амплифика́ци|я, и, *f.* (*lit.*) amplification, inflation.

амплуа́, *indecl., n.* (*theatr.*) type; (*fig.*) role.

а́мпул|а, ы, *f.* ampoule.

ампута́ци|я, и, *f.* (*med.*) amputation.

ампути́р|овать, ую, *impf. and pf.* (*med.*) to amputate.

амуле́т, а, *m.* amulet.

амуни́ци|я, и, *f.* (*collect.*) ammunition.

Аму́р, а, *m.* 1. (*myth.*) Cupid. 2. аму́ры (*pl. only*) (*coll.*) intrigues, love affairs.

аму́р|иться, юсь, *impf.* (с+*i*; *coll.*) to flirt (with), have an affair (with).

аму́рн|ый, *adj.* (*coll.*) love; amorous; ~ые дела́ love affairs; ~ые пи́сьма love letters.

амфи́би|я, и, *f.* (*zool., bot.*) amphibian.

амфибра́хи|й, я, *m.* (*lit.*) amphibrach.

амфитеа́тр, а, *m.* (*hist.*) amphitheatre; (*theatr.*) circle.

ан, *conj.* (*dial.*) on the contrary; but in fact.

анабапти́зм, а, *m.* Anabaptism.

анабапти́ст, а, *m.* Anabaptist.

анабио́з, а, *m.* (*biol.*) anabiosis.

анагра́мм|а, ы, *f.* anagram.

анаколу́ф, а, *m.* (*lit.*) anacoluthon.

анакреонти́ческий, *adj.* (*lit.*) anacreontic.

ана́лиз, а, *m.* analysis; а. кро́ви blood test.

анализи́р|овать, ую, *impf.* to analyse.

анали́тик, а, *m.* analyst.

анали́тик|а, и, *f.* (*math.*) analytic geometry.

аналити́ческий, *adj.* analytic(al).

ана́лог, а, *m.* analogue.

аналоги́ческ|ий, *adj.* analogical; ~ое рассужде́ние reasoning by analogy.

аналоги́ч|ный (~ен, ~на), *adj.* analogous; ~ные слу́чаи analogous cases.

аналоги|я, и, *f.* analogy; по ~и (с+*i*.) by analogy (with), on the analogy (of); проводи́ть ~ю to draw an analogy.

анало́|й, я, *m.* (*eccl.*) lectern.

ана́льный, *adj.* anal.

анана́с, а, *m.* pineapple.

анана́с|ный, *adj. of* ~.

анана́с|овый, *adj. of* ~; а. сок pineapple juice.

ана́пест, а, *m.* (*lit.*) anapaest.

анархи́зм, а, *m.* (*polit.*) anarchism.

анархи́ст, а, *m.* (*polit.*) anarchist.

анархи́ческий, *adj.* anarchic(al).

ана́рхи|я, и, *f.* anarchy.

ана́рхо-синдикали́зм, а, *m.* (*polit.*) anarcho-syndicalism.

ана́рхо-синдикали́ст, а, *m.* (*polit.*) anarcho-syndicalist.

ана́том, а, *m.* anatomist.

анатоми́р|овать, ую, *impf. and pf.* (*med.*) to dissect.

анатоми́ческий, *adj.* anatomic(al); а. теа́тр dissecting room.

анатоми́чк|а, и, *f.* (*coll.*) dissecting room.

анато́ми|я, и, *f.* anatomy.

ана́фем|а, ы, *f.* 1. (*eccl.*) anathema;

excommunication; (*fig.*) преда́ть ∼e to anathematize. **2.** (*coll.*) accursed fellow.

анафема́тств|овать, ую, *impf.* (*eccl.*) to excommunicate.

ана́фемский, *adj.* (*coll.*) accursed.

анахоре́т, а, *m.* hermit, anchorite; (*fig.*) recluse.

анахрони́зм, а, *m.* anachronism.

анахрони́ческий, *adj.* anachronistic.

ангажеме́нт, а, *m.* (*theatr.*) engagement.

ангажи́р|овать, ую, *impf. and pf.* (*theatr.*) to engage.

анга́р, а, *m.* (*aeron.*) hangar.

а́нгел, а, *m.* angel; а.-храни́тель guardian angel; а. во пло́ти (*coll.*) (an absolute) angel; день ∼а name-day.

а́нгельск|ий, *adj.* angelic (*also fig.*); ∼ое терпе́ние angelic patience; а. о́браз (*obs.*) monk's habit.

ангидри́д, а, *m.* (*chem.*) anhydride.

ангидри́т, а, *m.* (*chem.*) anhydrite.

анги́н|а, ы, *f.* (*med.*) quinsy; tonsillitis.

англизи́р|овать, ую, *impf. and pf.* to anglicize.

англи́йск|ий, *adj.* **1.** English; ∼ая боле́знь rickets; ∼ая була́вка safety-pin; а. рожо́к (*mus.*) cor anglais, alto oboe; ∼ая соль Epsom salts; *as noun* **а.,** ∼ого, *m.* Baskerville (type). **2.** British.

англика́нский, *adj.* (*eccl.*) Anglican.

англи́ст, а, *m.* specialist in English philology *or* English studies.

англи́стик|а, и, *f.* English philology, English studies.

англици́зм, а, *m.* (*lit.*) anglicism; (*ling.*) English loan-word.

англича́н|ин, ина, *pl.* ∼е, ∼, *m.* Englishman.

англича́нк|а, и, *f.* English woman.

англома́н, а, *m.* anglomane.

англоса́кс, а, *m.* Anglo-Saxon.

англосаксо́нский, *adj.* Anglo-Saxon.

англофи́л, а, *m.* anglophile.

англофи́льств|о, а, *n.* anglophilia.

англофо́б, а, *m.* anglophobe.

англофо́бств|о, а, *n.* anglophobia.

анго́рск|ий, *adj.* Angora; ∼ая ко́шка Angora cat, Persian cat; ∼ая шерсть Angora wool.

анда́нте, *adv.* (*mus.*) andante.

андре́евский, *adj.* а. крест St. Andrew's cross; а. флаг ensign of Imperial Russian Navy.

анекдо́т, а, *m.* **1.** anecdote, story. **2.** funny thing.

анекдоти́ческий, *adj.* anecdotal.

анекдоти́ч|ный (∼ен, ∼на), *adj.* improbable; humorous.

анеми́ческий, *adj.* anaemic.

анеми́ч|ный (∼ен, ∼на), *adj.* anaemic, pale.

анеми́|я, и, *f.* anaemia.

анемо́н, а, *m.* (*bot.*) anemone.

анеро́ид, а, *m.* aneroid.

анестези́р|овать, ую, *impf. and pf.* (*med.*) to anaesthetize; ∼ующее сре́дство anaesthetic.

анестези́|я, и, *f.* (*med.*) anaesthesia.

анили́н, а, *m.* (*chem.*) aniline.

анимали́ст, а, *m.* animal painter.

аними́зм, а, *m.* animism.

аними́ст, а, *m.* animist.

ани́с, а, *m.* (*bot.*) **1.** anise. **2.** anise apples.

ани́совк|а, и, *f.* (*coll.*) anisette.

ани́с|овый, *adj.* of ∼; ∼овое се́мя aniseed; ∼овая во́дка anisette.

а́нкер, а, *m.* **1.** (*tech.*) crutch (*in watch*). **2.** (*archit.*) anchor.

анке́т|а, ы, *f.* questionnaire; poll, survey.

анна́л|ы, ов, *no sing.* annals.

аннекси́р|овать, ую, *impf. and pf.* (*polit.*) to annex.

анне́кси|я, и, *f.* (*polit.*) annexation.

аннота́ци|я, и, *f.* annotation.

анноти́р|овать, ую, *impf. and pf.* to annotate.

аннули́р|овать, ую, *impf. and pf.* to annul; nullify; to cancel; to abrogate.

аннуля́ци|я, и, *f.* annulment; cancellation; abrogation.

ано́д, а, *m.* (*phys.*) anode.

анома́ли|я, и, *f.* anomaly.

анома́л|ьный (∼ен, ∼ьна), *adj.* anomalous.

анони́м, а, *m.* anonymous author.

анони́мк|а, и, *f.* (*coll.*) anonymous letter.

анони́м|ный (∼ен, ∼на), *adj.* anonymous.

ано́нс, а, *m.* announcement, notice.

анонси́р|овать, ую, *impf. and pf.* (+*a.* or о+*p.*) to announce.

анорма́л|ьный (∼ен, ∼ьна), *adj.* abnormal.

анса́мбл|ь, я, *m.* **1.** harmony. **2.** (*mus., theatr.*) ensemble, company.

антаблеме́нт, а, *m.* (*archit.*) entablature.

антагони́зм, а, *m.* antagonism.

антагони́ст, а, *m.* antagonist.

антаркти́ческий, *adj.* antarctic.

анте́нн|а, ы, *f.* **1.** (*zool.*) antenna. **2.** (*tech.*) aerial; ра́мочная а. loop aerial.

анте́нн|ый, *adj.* of ∼а.

антибио́тик, а, *m.* (*med.*) antibiotic.

анти́к, а, *m.* (*monument, work of art, etc.*) antique.

антиква́р, а, *m.* antiquary.

антиквариа́т, а, *m.* antique-shop.

антиква́ри|й, я, *m.* (*obs.*) antiquary.

антиква́рный, *adj.* antiquarian.

антило́п|а, ы, *f.* (*zool.*) antelope.

антими́нс, а, *m.* (*eccl.*) communion cloth.

антимо́ни|я¹, и, *f.* (*min.; obs.*) antimony.

антимо́ни|а², и, *f.* only in phrase разводи́ть ∼и (*coll.*) to indulge in trivialities, idle chat.

антиноми|я, и, *f.* antinomy.
антипати́ч|ный (~ен, ~на), *adj.* antipathetic.
антипа́ти|я, и, *f.* antipathy.
антипо́д, а, *m.* antipode.
антисеми́т, а, *m.* anti-Semite.
антисемити́зм, а, *m.* anti-Semitism.
антисеми́тский, *adj.* anti-Semitic.
антисе́птик|а, и, *f.* 1. antisepsis. 2. (*collect.*) antiseptics.
антисепти́ческий, *adj.* antiseptic.
антите́з|а, ы, *f.* antithesis.
антите́зис, а, *m.* (*philos.*) antithesis.
антитети́ческий, *adj.* antithetical.
антицикло́н, а, *m.* (*meteor.*) anti-cyclone.
анти́чност|ь, и, *f.* antiquity; (*hist.*) classical antiquity.
анти́чный, *adj.* ancient; classical; а. мир the ancient world; а. про́филь classical profile.
антологи́ческий, *adj.* (*lit.*) anthological.
антоло́ги|я, и, *f.* (*lit.*) anthology.
анто́ним, а, *m.* antonym.
анто́нов, *adj.* а. ого́нь gangrene.
анто́новк|а, и, *f.* antonovka (*kind of winter apples*).
анто́новск|ий, *adj.* ~ие я́блоки = анто́новка.
антра́кт, а, *m.* 1. (*theatr.*) interval. 2. (*mus.*) entr'acte.
антраци́т, а, *m.* (*min.*) anthracite.
антраша́, *indecl.*, *n.* entrechat; выде́лывать а. (*coll.*) to cut capers.
антреко́т, а, *m.* entrecôte, steak.
антрепренёр, а, *m.* impresario.
антрепри́з|а, ы, *f.* (*theatr.*) private theatrical concern.
антресо́л|ь, и, *f.* (*usually pl.*) 1. mezzanine. 2. shelf.
антропо́лог, а, *m.* anthropologist.
антропологи́ческий, *adj.* anthropological.
антрополо́ги|я, и, *f.* anthropology.
антропоме́три|я, и, *f.* anthropometry.
антропоморфи́зм, а, *m.* anthropomorphism.
антропоморфи́ческий, *adj.* anthropomorphic.
антропомо́рфный, *adj.* anthropoid.
антропофа́г, а, *m.* cannibal.
антропофа́ги|я, и, *f.* cannibalism.
антура́ж, а, *m.* environment; (*collect.*) entourage, associates.
анфа́с, *adv.* full face.
анфила́д|а, ы, *f.* suite (of rooms).
анча́р, а, *m.* (*bot.*) upas-tree (*Antiaris toxicaria*).
анчо́ус, а, *m.* anchovy.
аншла́г, а, *m.* notice; (*theatr.*) full house; спекта́кль идёт с ~ом the show is sold out, the house is full.
аню́тины: а. гла́зки (*bot.*) pansy.

аóрт|а, ы, *f.* (*anat.*) aorta.
апарта́мен|ты, ов, *sing.* ~, ~а, *m.* apartment.
апати́т, а, *m.* (*min.*) apatite.
апати́ч|ный (~ен, ~на), *adj.* apathetic.
апа́ти|я, и, *f.* apathy.
апа́ш, а, *m.* apache.
апелли́р|овать, ую, *impf. and pf.* to appeal.
апелля́нт, а, *m.* (*leg.*) appellant.
апелл|яцио́нный, *adj.* of ~я́ция; а. суд Court of Appeal.
апелля́ци|я, и, *f.* (*leg.*) appeal.
апельси́н, а, *m.* 1. orange. 2. orange-tree.
апельси́н|ный, *adj.* of ~.
апельси́нов|ый, *adj.* orange; ~ое варе́нье orange marmelade.
аппелике́, *indecl.*, *adj.* plated.
аплоди́р|овать, ую, *impf.* (+*d.*) to applaud.
аплодисме́нт|ы, ов, *sing.* а., ~а, *m.* applause; бу́рные а. loud cheers, storm of applause.
апло́мб, а, *m.* aplomb, assurance.
апоге́|й, я, *m.* (*astron*). apogee; (*fig.*) climax.
Апока́липсис, а, *m.* (*bibl.*) Revelation.
апокалипти́ческий, *adj.* apocalyptic.
апо́криф, а, *m.* an apocryphal work, story.
апокриф|и́ческий, *adj.* of апо́криф.
апокрифи́ч|ный (~ен, ~на), *adj.* (*coll.*) apocryphal.
аполити́зм, а, *m.* (*polit.*) political indifference; abstention from participation in politics.
аполити́ч|ный (~ен, ~на), *adj.* apolitical; politically indifferent.
апологе́т, а, *m.* apologist.
апологе́тик|а, и, *f.* apologetics.
аполо́ги|я, и, *f.* apologia.
апоплекси́ческий, *adj.* (*med.*) apoplectic.
апопле́кси|я, и, *f.* (*med.*) apoplexy.
апо́рт¹, а, *m.* Oporto apples.
апо́рт², *interj.* fetch! (*command to dog*)
апостерио́ри, *adv.* (*philos.*) a posteriori.
апостерио́рный, *adj.* (*philos.*) a posteriori.
апо́стол, а, *m.* 1. apostle (*also fig.*). 2. (*eccl., lit.*) Books of the Apostles (*the Acts of the Apostles and the Epistles*).
апо́стольский, *adj.* apostolic.
апостро́ф, а, *m.* apostrophe.
апофео́з, а, *m.* apotheosis.
аппара́т, а, *m.* apparatus; instrument; organs; госуда́рственный а. machinery of State; дыха́тельный а. respiratory system; фотографи́ческий а. camera.
аппарату́р|а, ы, *f.* (*tech., collect.*) apparatus, gear.
аппара́тчик, а, *m.* 1. (machine) operative. 2. (*polit.*) apparatchik (*member of party or governmental machine*).
аппе́ндикс, а, *m.* (*anat.*) appendix.
аппендици́т, а, *m.* (*med.*) appendicitis.
аппети́т, а, *m.* appetite; прия́тного ~а! bon appétit!

аппети́т|ный (~ен, ~на), *adj.* appetizing.
аппликату́р|а, ы, *f.* (*mus.*) fingering.
аппликаци|я, и, *f.* (*tech.*) appliqué work.
аппрету́р|а, ы, *f.* (*tech.*) dressing.
апре́л|ь, я, *m.* April.
апре́ль|ский, *adj. of* ~.
априо́ри, *adv.* (*philos.*) a priori.
априо́р|ный (~ен, ~на), *adj.* (*philos.*) a priori.
апроба́ци|я, и, *f.* approbation.
апроби́р|овать, ую, *impf. and* ¹*pf.* to approve.
апро́ш, а, *m.* (*typ.*) space left between words.
апси́д|а, ы, *f.* (*archit.*) apse.
апте́к|а, и, *f.* chemist's (shop); как в ~e (*coll., joc.*) just so, exactly right.
апте́карский, *adj.* chemist's; pharmaceutical; a. магази́н non-dispensing chemist's (shop).
апте́кар|ша, ши, *f.* 1. (*coll.*) chemist's wife. 2. *f. of* ~ь.
апте́кар|ь, я, *m.* chemist.
апте́чк|а, и, *f.* first-aid set; medicine chest.
ар, а, *m.* are (*unit of land measurement*).
ара́б, а, *m.* Arab, Arabian.
арабе́ск, а, *m.* arabesque.
арабе́ск|а, и, *f.* = ~.
араби́ст, а, *m.* Arabic scholar, Arabist.
ара́бк|а, и, *f.* Arab (woman); Arabian (woman).
ара́бск|ий, *adj.* Arab; Arabian; Arabic; a. восто́к the Arab countries (of the Near and Middle East); ~ая ло́шадь Arab (horse); ~ие ци́фры arabic numerals; a. язы́к Arabic.
арави́йский, *adj.* Arabian, of Arabia.
ара́к, а, *m.* arrack (*rice or palm-sap spirit*).
аракче́евский, *adj.* 'Arakcheyevan', despotic.
аракче́евщин|а, ы, *f.* (*hist.*) the Arakcheyev regime; (*fig.*) despotism.
араме́йский, *adj.* Aramaic.
аранжи́р|овать, ую, *impf. and pf.* (*mus.*) to arrange.
аранжиро́вк|а, и, *f.* (*mus.*) arrangement.
ара́п, а, *m.* 1. (*coll., obs.*) negro. 2. (*sl.*) cheat, swindler; на ~a by bluffing.
ара́пник, а, *m.* whip.
ара́п|ский, *adj. of* ~; ~ские шту́чки (*coll.*) tricks.
араука́ри|я, и, *f.* araucaria, monkey-puzzle tree.
арб|а́, ы́, *pl.* ~ы, *f.* bullock-cart.
арбале́т, а, *m.* arbalest, crossbow.
арби́тр, а, *m.* arbiter, arbitrator; umpire, referee.
арбитра́ж, а, *m.* arbitration.
арбу́з, а, *m.* water-melon.
аргама́к, а, *m.* argamak (*Central Asian breed of race-horses*).

аргенти́н|ец, ца, *m.* Argentinian.
аргенти́н|ка, ки, *f.* Argentinian (woman).
аргенти́нский, *adj.* Argentine.
арго́, *indecl., n.* argot, slang.
арго́н, а, *m.* (*chem.*) argon.
арготи́ческий, *adj. of* арго́.
аргуме́нт, а, *m.* argument.
аргумента́ци|я, и, *f.* reasoning, argumentation.
аргументи́р|овать, ую, *impf. and pf.* to argue; (*pf. only*) to prove.
А́ргус, а, *m.* (*myth.*) Argus; (*fig.*) watchful guardian.
ареа́л, а, *m.* (*bot. and zool.*) natural habitat.
аре́н|а, ы, *f.* arena, ring.
аре́нд|а, ы, *f.* lease; сдать в ~y to rent, lease (*of owner, landlord*); взять в ~y to rent, lease (*of tenant*).
аренда́тор, а, *m.* tenant, lessee.
аре́нд|ный, *ddj. of* ~a; ~ная пла́та rent.
аренд|ова́ть, у́ю, *impf. and pf.* to rent, lease (*of tenant*).
аре́ст, а, *m.* arrest; сиде́ть, находи́ться под ~ом to be under arrest, in custody; a. иму́щества seizure, sequestration.
ареста́нт, а, *m.* (*obs.*) prisoner.
ареста́нт|ский, *adj. of* ~; ~ская ро́та (*obs.*) penal battalion; *as noun* ~ская, ~ской, *f.* lock-up, cells.
арест|ова́ть, у́ю, *pf.* (*of* ~о́вывать) to arrest; to sequestrate.
аресто́выва|ть, ю, *impf. of* арестова́ть.
ари́|ец, йца, *m.* Aryan.
ари́йский, *adj.* Aryan.
аристокра́т, а, *m.* aristocrat.
аристократ|и́ческий, *adj.*, aristocratic.
аристокра́ти|я, и, *f.* aristocracy.
аритми́ч|ный (~ен, ~на), *adj.* unrhythmical.
арифме́тик|а, и, *f.* arithmetic.
арифмети́ческий, *adj.* arithmetical.
арифмо́граф, а, *m.* automatic calculating machine.
арифмо́метр, а, *m.* calculating machine.
а́ри|я, и, *f.* (*mus.*) aria.
а́рк|а, и, *f.* arch.
арка́д|а, ы, *f.* (*archit.*) arcade.
арка́н, а, *m.* lasso.
арка́н|ить, ю, ишь, *impf.* (*pf.* за~) to lasso.
аркти́ческий, *adj.* arctic.
арлеки́н, а, *m.* harlequin.
арлекина́д|а, ы, *f.* harlequinade.
арма́д|а, ы, *f.* armada.
армату́р|а, ы, *f.* (*collect.*) fittings; (*tech.*) armature; steel *or* ferro-concrete reinforcement.
армату́р|ный, *adj. of* ~a.
армату́рщик, а, *m.* (*tech.*) fitter.
арме́|ец, йца, *m.* 1. soldier. 2. (*obs.*) member of line regiment.

армéйский, *adj.* of áрмия.

áрми|я, и, *f.* 1. army; A. Спасéния Salvation Army; дéйствующая а. front-line forces. 2. (*obs.*) line regiments.

армя́|к, á, *m.* armyak (*peasant's coat of heavy cloth*).

армя́н|ин, и́на, *pl.* ~e, ~, *m.* Armenian.

армя́нк|а, и, *f.* Armenian (woman).

армя́нский, *adj.* Armenian.

áрник|а, и, *f.* (*bot., med.*) arnica.

аромáт, а, *m.* scent, odour, aroma.

аромати́ч|ный (~ен, ~на), *adj.* aromatic, fragrant.

áрочный, *adj.* arched, vaulted.

арпéдж|ио, (*mus.*) 1. *adv.* 2. *noun*; *sing. indecl.*, *pl.* ~ии, ~ий, *n.* arpeggio.

арсенáл, а, *m.* arsenal.

арт-, *abbr.* of артилл|éрия, ~ерийский.

артáч|иться, усь, ишься, *impf.* (*coll.*) to jib, be restive.

артезиáнский, *adj.* а. колóдец artesian well.

артéл|ь, и, *f.* artel (*co-operative association of workmen or peasants*).

артéль|ный, *adj.* of ~; (*coll.*) common, collective; на ~ных началах on collective principles.

артéльщик, а, *m.* 1. member of an artel. 2. collector of money(s). 3. (*obs.*) porter.

артериáльный, *adj.* (*anat.*) arterial.

артериосклерóз, а, *m.* (*med.*) arteriosclerosis.

артéри|я, и, *f.* artery.

арти́кл|ь, я, *m.* (*gram.*) article.

арти́кул, а, *m.* вóинский а. (*hist.*) Articles of War.

артикýл, а, *m.* (*mil.*; *obs.*) firearms exercises; выки́дывать а. (*obs., coll.*) to play tricks.

артикули́р|овать, ую, *impf.* (*ling.*) to articulate.

артикуля́ци|я, и, *f.* (*ling.*) articulation.

артиллери́йск|ий, *adj.* (*mil.*) artillery; а. обóз artillery-train; ~ая подготóвка artillery preparation, preparatory bombardment; а. склад ordnance depot.

артиллéри|я, и, *f.* artillery.

арти́ст, а, *m.* 1. artist(e); óперный а. opera singer; а. балéта ballet dancer; а. дрáмы actor; а. кинó film actor. 2. artist (= painter). 3. (*fig.*) artist, expert; он ~ своегó дéла he is a real artist (at his job).

артисти́ческ|ий, *adj.* artistic; *as noun* ~ая, ~ой, *f.* green-room, dressing-room.

арти́стк|а, и, *f.* 1. artiste. 2. (*fig.*) artist, expert (*woman*).

артишóк, а, *m.* (*bot.*) artichoke.

артри́т, а, *m.* (*med.*) arthritis.

áрф|а, ы, *f.* harp.

арфи́ст, а, *m.* harpist.

архаи́зм, а, *m.* archaism.

архаи́ческий, *adj.* archaic.

архаи́ч|ный (~ен, ~на), *adj.* archaic.

архáнгел, а, *m.* 1. archangel. 2. (*obs., iron.*) policeman.

архáнгельский, *adj.* archangelic.

архáров|ец, ца, *m.* (*coll.*) ruffian.

археографи́ческий, *adj.* of археогрáфия.

археогрáфи|я, и, *f.* study (and publication) of early texts.

археóлог, а, *m.* archaeologist.

археологи́ческий, *adj.* archaeological.

археолóги|я, и, *f.* archaeology.

архи- arch-.

архи́в, а, *m.* archives; сдать в а. (*coll.*) to shelve, throw out, leave out of account.

архивáриус, а, *m.* keeper of archives.

архиви́ст, а, *m.* archivist.

архи́в|ный, *adj.* of ~; ~ная кры́са (*coll.*) employee in the archives.

архидья́кон, а, *m.* archdeacon.

архиепи́скоп, а, *m.* archbishop.

архиерé|й, я, *m.* member of higher orders of clergy (*bishop, archbishop or metropolitan*).

архимандри́т, а, *m.* (*eccl.*) archimandrite.

архимиллионéр, а, *m.* multi-millionaire.

архипелáг, а, *m.* archipelago.

архитектóник|а, и, *f.* (*geol. and fig.*) architectonics.

архитéктор, а, *m.* architect.

архитектýр|а, ы, *f.* architecture.

архитектýрный, *adj.* architectural.

архитрáв, а, *m.* (*archit.*) architrave.

арши́н, а, *m.* 1. arshin (*Russian measure, equivalent to 28 inches or 71 cm*). 2. rule one arshin in length; мéрить на свой а. to measure by one's own bushel; как бýдто а. проглоти́л (*coll.*) as stiff as a poker.

ары́к, а, *m.* irrigation canal (*in Central Asia*).

арьергáрд, а, *m.* (*mil.*) rearguard.

арьергáрдный, *adj.* (*mil.*) rearguard.

ас, а, *m.* (air) ace.

асéптик|а, и, *f.* (*med.*) asepsis.

асбéст, а, *m.* asbestos.

асбéстовый, *adj.* asbestos.

асепти́ческий, *adj.* (*med.*) aseptic.

асéссор, а, *m.* (*obs.*) assessor; коллéжский а. collegiate assessor (*8th grade in tsarist Russian civil service, equivalent to rank of major in the army*).

асимметри́ческий, *adj.* asymmetrical.

асимметри́ч|ный (~ен, ~на), *adj.* asymmetrical.

асимметри́|я, и, *f.* asymmetry.

аскéт, а, *m.* ascetic.

аскети́зм, а, *m.* asceticism.

аскети́ческий, *adj.* ascetic.

асоциáльный, *adj.* anti-social.

аспéкт, а, *m.* aspect, perspective.

áспид¹, а, *m.* (*zool.*) asp; (*fig.*) viper.

áспид², а, *m.* (*min.*) slate.

а́спид|ный, *adj. of* ~²; ~ная доска́ slate.

аспира́нт, а, *m.* post-graduate student.

аспиранту́р|а, ы, *f.* **1.** post-graduate study. **2.** (*collect.*) post-graduate students.

аспири́н, а, *m.* (*med.*) aspirin; табле́тка ~a an aspirin.

ассамбле́|я, и, *f.* **1.** assembly. **2.** (*hist.*) ball.

ассенизацио́нный, *adj.* а. обо́з (*collect.*) sewage-disposal men.

ассениза́ци|я, и, *f.* sewage disposal.

ассигна́ци|я, и, *f.* (*obs.*) banknote.

ассигнова́ни|е, я, *n.* (*fin.*) assignation, appropriation, allocation.

ассигн|ова́ть, у́ю, *impf. and pf.* (*fin.*) to assign, appropriate, allocate.

ассигно́вк|а, и, *f.* (*fin.*) assignment; grant (*of funds*).

ассимили́р|овать, ую, *impf. and pf.* to assimilate.

ассимиля́ци|я, и, *f.* assimilation.

ассири́|ец, йца, *m.* **1.** Assyrian. **2.** Aysor.

ассири́|йка, йки, *f. of* ~ец.

ассири́йский, *adj.* Assyrian.

ассири́ян|ин, ина, *pl.* ~e, ~, *m.* (*obs.*) Assyrian.

ассири́ян|ка, ки, *f. of* ~ин.

ассисте́нт, а, *m.* **1.** assistant. **2.** (*in university, etc.*) junior member of teaching *or* research staff.

ассисти́р|овать, ую, *impf.* (+*d.*) to assist.

ассона́нс, а, *m.* assonance.

ассортиме́нт, а, *m.* assortment; range (of goods).

ассоциа́ци|я, и, *f.* association.

ассоции́р|овать, ую, *impf. and pf.* (с+*i.*; *philos.*) to associate (with).

астеро́ид, а, *m.* (*astron.*) asteroid.

астигмати́зм, а, *m.* (*med.*) astigmatism.

а́стм|а, ы, *f.* (*med.*) asthma.

астма́тик, а, *m.* (*med.*) asthmatic.

астмати́ческий, *adj.* (*med.*) asthmatic.

а́стр|а, ы, *f.* (*bot.*) aster.

астра́льный, *adj.* astral.

астро́лог, а, *m.* astrologer.

астрологи́ческий, *adj.* astrological.

астроло́ги|я, и, *f.* astrology.

астроля́би|я, и, *f.* astrolabe; circumferentor.

астроно́м, а, *m.* astronomer.

астрономи́ческий, *adj.* astronomic(al).

астроно́ми|я, и, *f.* astronomy.

астрофи́зик|а, и, *f.* astrophysics.

асфа́льт, а, *m.* asphalt.

асфальти́р|овать, ую, *impf. and pf.* (*pf. also* за~) (*tech.*) to asphalt.

асфа́льтовый, *adj.* asphalt.

асфи́кси|я, и, *f.* (*med.*) asphyxia.

ась, *interj.* (*coll.*) what? eh?

атави́зм, а, *m.* atavism.

атависти́ческий, *adj.* atavistic.

ата́к|а, и, *f.* attack.

атак|ова́ть, у́ю, *impf. and pf.* to attack, charge, assault; а. с ты́ла to take in rear; а. с фла́нга to take in flank.

атама́н, а, *m.* **1.** (*hist.*) ataman (*Cossack chieftain*). **2.** (*coll.*) (gang-)leader, (robber) chief.

атеи́зм, а, *m.* atheism.

атеи́ст, а, *m.* atheist.

атеисти́ческий, *adj.* atheistic.

ателье́, *indecl.*, *n.* studio; а. мод fashion house.

а́тлас, а, *m.* atlas.

атла́с, а, *m.* satin.

атла́систый, *adj.* satiny.

атла́сный, *adj.* satin.

атле́т, а, *m.* athlete.

атле́тик|а, и, *f.* athletics.

атлети́ческий, *adj.* athletic.

атмосфе́р|а, ы, *f.* atmosphere.

атмосфери́ческий, *adj.* atmospheric.

атмосфе́рн|ый, *adj.* atmospheric; ~ые оса́дки atmospheric precipitation, rainfall.

ато́лл, а, *m.* atoll.

а́том, а, *m.* atom.

атомисти́ческий, *adj.* atomistic.

а́томник, а, *m.* (*coll.*) atomic scientist.

а́томност|ь, и, *f.* (*chem.*) atomicity.

а́томн|ый, *adj.* atomic; ~ая бо́мба atomic bomb; а. вес (*chem.*) atomic weight.

атомохо́д, а, *m.* atomic-powered vessel.

атони́|я, и, *f.* (*med.*) atony.

атрибу́т, а, *m.* attribute.

атропи́н, а, *m.* (*med.*) atropin.

атрофи́р|оваться, уюсь, *impf. and pf.* to atrophy.

атрофи́|я, и, *f.* atrophy.

атташе́, *indecl.*, *m.* (*dipl.*) attaché.

аттеста́т, а, *m.* testimonial; certificate; pedigree; а. зре́лости school-leaving certificate; дать дурно́й а. to give a bad character.

аттестацио́нн|ый, *adj.* ~ая коми́ссия examination board.

аттеста́ци|я, и, *f.* **1.** attestation. **2.** testimonial.

аттест|ова́ть, у́ю, *impf. and pf.* to attest, recommend.

аттракцио́н, а, *m.* (*theatr.*) attraction.

ату́, *interj.* (*hunting*) tally-ho!, halloo!

ау́, *interj.* **1.** hi! halloo! **2.** (*coll.*) it's all up!, it's done for!

аудие́нци|я, и, *f.* audience.

ауди́тор, а, *m.* (*obs.*) auditor.

аудито́ри|я, и, *f.* **1.** auditorium; lecture-hall. **2.** (*collect.*) audience.

ау́ка|ть, ю, *impf.* to halloo, shout 'hi'.

ау́к|аться, аюсь, *impf.* (*of* ~нуться), to halloo to one another.

ау́к|нуть, ну, нешь, *pf. of* ~ать.

ау́к|нуться, нусь, *pf. of* ~аться; как ~нется,

так и откли́кнется serves you, *etc.*, right; do as you would be done by.

аукцио́н, а, *m.* auction; продава́ть с ~а to sell by auction.

аукцио́н|ный, *adj. of* ~; а. зал auction room.

ау́л, а, *m.* aul (*mountain village in Caucasus*).

ауспи́ци|и, й, *no sing.* auspices.

а́ут, а, *m.* (*sport*) out (*also as interj.*).

аутенти́ч|ный (~ен, ~на), *adj.* authentic.

аутодафе́, *indecl., n.* auto-da-fé.

афа́зи|я, и, *f.* (*med.*) aphasia.

афга́н|ец, ца, *m.* Afghan.

афга́нк|а, и, *f.* Afghan (woman).

афга́нский, *adj.* Afghan.

афе́р|а, ы, *f.* (*coll.*) speculation; trickery.

афери́ст, а, *m.* speculator; trickster.

афи́нск|ий, *adj.* Athenian; ~ие вечера́, ~ие но́чи orgies.

афи́нян|ин, ина, *pl.* ~е, ~, *m.* Athenian.

афиня́нк|а, и, *f.* Athenian (woman).

афи́ш|а, и, *f.* poster, placard.

афиши́р|овать, ую, *impf.* to parade, advertise.

афори́зм, а, *m.* aphorism.

афористи́ческий, *adj.* aphoristic.

афористи́ч|ный (~ен, ~на), *adj.* aphoristic.

африка́н|ец, ца, *m.* African.

африка́нк|а, и, *f.* African (woman).

африка́нск|ий, *adj.* African; ~ие стра́сти (*coll.*) unbridled passions.

афро́нт, а, *m.* (*obs.*) insult.

аффе́кт, а, *m.* (*psych., leg.*) temporary insanity.

аффекта́ци|я, и, *f.* affectation.

аффекти́рованный, *adj.* affected.

ах, *interj.* ah! oh!; *as noun* а́х|и, ~ов, *no sing.*, exclamations of 'ah!', 'oh!'

а́хань|е, я, *n.* (*coll.*) sighing.

а́ха|ть, ю, *impf.* (*coll.*) to sigh, to exclaim 'ah!', 'oh!'

ахилле́сов, *adj.* ~а пята́ Achilles heel; ~о сухожи́лие (*anat.*) Achilles tendon.

ахине́|я, и, *f.* (*coll.*) nonsense; нести́ ~ю to talk nonsense.

ах|нуть, ну, нешь, *pf.* **1.** *pf. of* ~ать; он и а. не успе́л before he knew where he was. **2.** (*coll.*) to bang.

а́ховый, *adj.* (*coll.*) **1.** breath-taking; он па́рень а. he is a terrific chap. **2.** rotten.

ахромати́зм, а, *m.* achromatism.

ахромати́ческий, *adj.* achromatic.

ахтерште́в|ень, ня, *m.* (*naut.*) stern-post.

ахти́, *interj.* (*coll.*) alas!; а. мне! woe is me!; не а. как, не а. како́й not particularly, not particularly good; он был студе́нтом не а. каки́м he was not a very bright student.

ацетиле́н, а, *m.* (*chem.*) acetylene.

ацето́н, а, *m.* (*chem.*) acetone.

ацте́к, а, *m.* Aztec.

ашу́г, а, *m.* ashug (*folk poet and singer in the Caucasus*).

аэра́ри|й, я, *m.* (*med.*) aerarium.

аэро- aero-; air-, aerial.

аэровокза́л, а, *m.* airport building.

аэродина́мик|а, и, *f.* aerodynamics.

аэродро́м, а, *m.* aerodrome.

аэрозо́л|ь, я, *m.* aerosol.

аэрона́вт, а, *m.* aeronaut.

аэрона́втик|а, и, *f.* aeronautics.

аэропла́н, а, *m.* (*obs.*) aeroplane.

аэропо́рт, а, *m.* airport.

аэропо́чт|а, ы, *f.* (*obs.*) air mail.

аэроса́н|и, е́й, *no sing.* aero-sleigh.

аэросе́в, а, *m.* aerial sowing.

аэроста́т, а, *m.* balloon; а. загражде́ния barrage balloon.

аэроста́тик|а, и, *f.* aerostatics.

аэросъёмк|а, и, *f.* aerial photograph.

аэрохо́д, а, *m.* hovercraft.

Б

б, *particle* = бы (*after words ending in vowel*).

ба, *interj.* (*coll.*) hullo! well! (*expressing surprise*).

ба́б|а¹, ы, *f.* **1.** married peasant woman. **2.** (*coll. or dial.*) wife, old woman; (*pl.*) womenfolk. **3.** (*coll.*) woman; бой-б. (*coll.*) virago; ка́менная б. stone image; сне́жная б. snowman. **4.** (*coll.*) 'old woman' (*said of a man*).

ба́б|а², ы, *f.* (*tech.*) ram (*of pile-driver*).

ба́б|а³, ы, *f.* baba (*cylindrical cake*); ро́мовая б. rum-baba.

ба́ба-яга́, ба́бы-яги́, *f.* Baba-Yaga (*witch in Russian folk-tales*).

баба́х, *interj.* (*expressing noise of heavily falling object*) bang!

бабахн|у́ть, у, ешь, *pf.* (*coll.*) to bang; ~уло (*impers.*) there was a bang.

babbit, а, *m.* (*tech.*) babbit.

бабёнк|а, и, *f.* (*coll.*) wench.

ба́б|ий, *adj.* (*coll.*) women's; womanish; ~ье ле́то Indian summer; ~ьи ска́зки old wives' tales.

ба́бк|а¹, и, *f.* **1.** (*coll., obs.*) grandmother. **2.** (*повива́льная*) б. midwife.

ба́бк|а², и, *f.* **1.** (*anat.*) pastern. **2.** knuckle-bone; ~и (*pl.*) babki (*Russian children's game*). **3.** (*tech.*) mandrel.

ба́бк|а³, и, *f.* (*dial.*) shock, stook (*of corn*).

ба́бник, а, *m.* (*coll.*) ladies' man.

ба́бнича|ть, ю, *impf.* **1.** (*dial.*) to be a midwife. **2.** (*coll.*) to be a ladies' man.

ба́бочк|а, и, *f.* butterfly; ночна́я б. moth.

бабу́ин, а, *m.* (*zool.*) baboon.

ба́бушк|а, и, *f.* grandmother; (*coll.*) grandma, grannie (*as mode of address to old woman*); б. на́двое сказа́ла we shall see!

ба́бушкин, *adj.* grandmother's.

бабь|ё, я́, *n.* (*collect.*) womenfolk.

бава́р|ец, ца, *m.* Bavarian.

бава́рк|а, и, *f.* Bavarian (woman).

бава́рский, *adj.* Bavarian.

бага́ж, а́, *m.* luggage; сдать свои́ ве́щи в б. to register one's luggage.

бага́жник, а, *m.* luggage carrier, rack; boot (*of motor-car*).

бага́ж|ный, *adj. of* ~; б. ваго́н luggage van; ~ная квита́нция luggage receipt.

баг|о́р, ра́, *m.* boat-hook.

ба́грен|ье, я, *n.* gaffing.

багре́ц, а́, *m.* crimson, purple.

ба́гр|ить, ю, ишь, *impf.* **1.** to gaff. **2.** (*sl.*) to steal; pilfer.

багр|и́ть, ю́, и́шь, *impf.* to paint purple, crimson; to incarnadine.

багрове́|ть, ю, *impf.* (*of* по~) to turn crimson, purple.

багро́в|ый (~, ~а), *adj.* crimson, purple.

багря́н|ец, ца, *m.* crimson, purple.

багряни́ц|а, ы, *f.* (*hist.*) purple (mantle).

багря́нник, а, *m.* (*bot.*) Judas-tree.

багря́н|ый (~, ~а), *adj.* (*poet.*) crimson, purple.

багу́льник, а, *m.* (*bot.*) Labrador tea, wild rosemary (*Ledum*).

бад|ья́, ьи́, *g. pl.* ~е́й, *f.* tub.

ба́з|а, ы, *f.* **1.** (*in var. senses*) base; depot; centre. **2.** basis; на ~е (+*g.*) on the basis (of); подвести́ ~у (под+*a.*) to give good grounds (for).

база́льт, а, *m.* basalt.

база́льтовый, *adj.* basaltic.

база́р, а, *m.* market; bazaar; пти́чий б. bird-colony on sea-shore; (*fig., coll.*) row, din; что за б.! what a row!

база́р|ный, *adj. of* ~; (*coll.*) of the market-place, rough, crude; ~ная ба́ба noisy woman, fishwife; б. день market-day; ~ная ру́гань billingsgate.

базе́дов, *adj.* (*med.*) ~а боле́знь exophthalmic goitre (Basedow's disease).

базили́к|а, и, *f.* (*archit.*) basilica.

бази́р|овать, ую, *impf.* (на+*p.*) to base (on).

бази́р|оваться, уюсь, *impf.* (на+*p.*) **1.** to be based (on), to rest (on); все его́ мне́ния ~уются на газе́тах all his opinions are based on what he reads in the newspapers. **2.** (*mil.*) to base oneself (on), be based (on).

ба́зис, а, *m.* base; basis.

ба́иньки = бай-ба́й.

ба|й, я, *m.* bai (*rich landowner in Central Asia*).

бай-ба́й, *interj.* bye-byes; пора́ б.! time for bye-byes!

байба́к, а́, *m.* (*zool.*) steppe marmot; (*fig.*) lazybones.

байда́рк|а, и, *f.* (Aleutian) canoe.

байда́р|очный, *adj. of* ~ка; ~очная гре́бля (canoe-)paddling.

ба́йк|а¹, и, *f.* flannelette.

ба́йк|а², и, *f.* (*dial.*) story.

ба́йковый, *adj.* flannelette.

байрони́ческий, *adj.* Byronic.

бак¹, а, *m.* cistern; tank.

бак², а, *m.* (*naut.*) forecastle.

бакала́вр, а, *m.* bachelor (*holder of bachelor's degree*).

бакале́йн|ый, *adj.* grocery; ~ая ла́вка grocer's shop.

бакале́йщик, а, *m.* grocer.

бакале́|я, и, *f.* **1.** (*collect.*) groceries. **2.** grocer's shop.

ба́кан, а, *m.* (*naut.*) buoy.

бака́ут, а, *m.* (*bot.*) lignum vitae, guaiacum.

ба́кен = ба́кан.

бакенба́рд|ы, ~, *sing.* ~а, ~ы, *f.* side-whiskers.

ба́кенщик, а, *m.* buoy-keeper.

ба́кен|ы, ов, *sing.* ~, ~а, *m.* (*obs.*) side-whiskers.

ба́к|и, ~, *no sing.* = бакенба́рды.

баки́нский, *adj.* of Baku.

баккара́¹, *indecl., n.* (Baccarat) cut glass.

баккара́², *indecl., n.* baccarat (*card-game*).

бакла́г|а, и, *f.* flask, water-bottle.

баклажа́н, а, *m.* (*bot.*) aubergine, egg-plant.

бакла́н, а, *m.* (*zool.*) cormorant.

баклу́ши, now only in phrase (*coll.*) бить б. to idle, fritter away one's time.

баклу́шнича|ть, ю, *impf.* (*coll.*) to idle.

ба́к|овый, *adj. of* ~²; bow; б. гребе́ц bow oarsman.

бактериа́льный, *adj.* bacterial.

бактери́йный, *adj.* bacterial.

бактерио́лог, а, *m.* bacteriologist.

бактериологи́ческ|ий, *adj.* bacteriological; ~ая война́ bacteriological, germ warfare.

бактериоло́ги|я, и, *f.* bacteriology.

бакте́ри|я, и, *f.* bacterium.

бакши́ш, а, *m.* bakshish; tip; bribe.

бал, а, о ~е, на ~у́, *pl.* ~ы́, *m.* ball, dance; ко́нчен б.! it's all over, that's that.

балабо́лк|а, и, *m. and f.* (*coll.*) **1.** (*f.*) pendant. **2.** (*f.*) (*child's*) rattle. **3.** (*m. and f.*) chatterbox.

балага́н, а, *m.* **1.** booth (*at fairs*). **2.** low farce; (*fig.*) farce.

балага́н|ить, ю, ишь, *impf.* (*coll.*) to play the fool.

балага́н|ный, *adj. of* ~; farcical.
балага́нщик, а, *m.* (*coll.*) 1. showman. 2. clown, joker.
балагу́р, а, *m.* joker, clown.
балагу́р|ить, ю, ишь, *impf.* to jest, joke.
балагу́рств|о, а, *n.* foolery, buffoonery.
бала́ка|ть, ю, *impf.* (*dial.*) to chatter, natter.
балала́ечник, а, *m.* balalaika-player.
балала́|ечный, *adj. of* ~йка.
балала́йк|а, и, ƒ. balalaika.
баламу́т, а, *m.* (*coll.*) trouble-maker.
баламу́|тить, чу, тишь, *impf.* (*of* вз~) (*coll.*) to stir up, trouble (*water*); (*fig.*) to disturb, upset.
бала́нда, ы, ƒ. (*sl.*) bad soup (*in prison or camp*).
бала́нс¹, а, *m.* (*econ.*) balance; платёжный б. balance of payment; торго́вый б. balance of trade.
бала́нс², а, *m.* pulpwood.
балансёр, а, *m.* tightrope-walker.
баланси́р, а, *m.* (*tech.*) 1. bob, (balance) beam, equalizer; rocking beam, rocking shaft. 2. balance-wheel (*in clock*).
баланси́р|овать, ую, *impf.* 1. (*impf. only*) to keep one's balance, balance. 2. (*pf.* с~) (*bookkeeping*) to balance.
балахо́н, а, *m.* loose overall; (*coll.*) shapeless garment.
балбе́с, а, *m.* (*coll.*) booby.
балбе́снича|ть, ю, *impf.* (*coll.*) to idle away one's time.
балд|а́, ы́, ƒ. 1. (*tech.*) heavy hammer, sledge-hammer. 2. (*dial.*) knob, knur. 3. (*m. and ƒ.*) (*fig., coll.*) blockhead.
балдахи́н, а, *m.* canopy.
балери́н|а, ы, ƒ. ballerina.
бале́т, а, *m.* ballet.
балетме́йстер, а, *m.* ballet-master.
бале́т|ный, *adj. of* ~.
балетома́н, а, *m.* balletomane.
балетома́ни|я, и, ƒ. balletomania.
ба́лк|а¹, и, ƒ. beam, girder; а́нкерная б. tie-beam; попере́чная б. cross-beam; решётчатая б. lattice girder; клёпаные ~и riveted girders; прока́тные ~и rolled girders.
ба́лк|а², и, ƒ. (*dial.*) gully.
балка́нский, *adj.* Balkan.
балко́н, а, *m.* balcony.
балл, а, *m.* 1. (*meteor.*) number; ве́тер в пять ~ов wind force 5; о́блачность в семь ~ов 7/10ths cloud. 2. mark (*in school*); о́бщий б. total mark(s); проходно́й б. pass mark.
балла́д|а, ы, ƒ. 1. ballad. 2. (*mus.*) ballade.
балла́ст, а, *m.* ballast (*also fig.*).
балли́стик|а, и, ƒ. ballistics.
баллисти́ческий, *adj.* ballistic.
ба́лл|овый, *adj. of* ~ 1.

балло́н, а, *m.* 1. balloon (*vessel*); container (*of glass, metal, or rubber*); carboy; б. с кисло́родом oxygen cylinder. 2. (*motor-car, etc.*) balloon tyre.
баллоти́р|овать, ую, *impf.* to ballot (for), vote (for).
баллоти́р|оваться, уюсь, *impf.* 1. (в+*a.*, на+*a.*) to stand (for), be a candidate (for); б. на до́лжность секретаря́ па́ртии to stand for secretary of the party. 2. (*pass. of* ~овать) to be put to the vote.
баллотиро́вк|а, и, ƒ. 1. vote, ballot, poll. 2. voting, balloting, polling.
баллотиро́в|очный, *adj. of* ~ка; б. бюлле́тень ballot paper.
ба́лл|ьный, *adj. of* ~ 2.
балóв|анный, *p.p.p. of* ~а́ть *and adj.* (*coll.*) spoiled.
бал|ова́ть, у́ю, *impf.* (*of* из~). 1. to spoil, indulge; to pet, pamper. 2. (*coll.*) to play about; to play up; мото́р ~у́ет the engine is playing up. 3. (+*i.*; *coll.*) to play (with), amuse oneself (with), toy (with). 4. (*coll., obs., or dial.*) to get up to monkey business (*sc.* to engage in brigandage, practise immorality, *etc.*).
бал|ова́ться, у́юсь, *impf.* 1. to play about; to get up to monkey tricks. 2. (+*i.*; *coll.*) to play (with), amuse oneself (with), toy (with). 3. (*coll.*) to indulge in. 4. = ~ова́ть 4.
ба́лов|ень, ня, *m.* 1. spoilt child; pet, favourite; б. судьбы́ favourite of fortune. 2. naughty child.
баловни́к, а́, *m.* (*coll.*) 1. naughty child; mischievous person. 2. pet; favourite. 3. (*obs.*) one who spoils someone.
баловств|о́, а́, *n.* (*coll.*) 1. spoiling, over-indulgence; petting, pampering. 2. mischievousness; monkey tricks.
ба́л|очный, *adj.* (*tech.*) *of* ~ка¹.
балти́|ец, йца, *m.* sailor of the (Soviet) Baltic Fleet.
балти́йский, *adj.* Baltic.
балы́к, а́, *m.* balyk (*cured fillet of sturgeon, etc.*).
бальза́м, а, *m.* balsam; (*fig.*) balm.
бальзами́н, а, *m.* (*bot.*) balsam.
бальзами́р|овать, ую, *impf.* (*of* на~) to embalm.
бальзамиро́вк|а, и, ƒ. embalming.
бальзамиро́вщик, а, *m.* embalmer.
бальзами́ческ|ий, *adj.* (*bot.*) balsam, balsamic; (*fig.*) balmy; ~ая пи́хта balsam fir; б. во́здух balmy air.
бальнео́лог, а, *m.* (*med.*) balneologist.
бальнеологи́ческий, *adj.* (*med.*) balneological.
бальнеоло́ги|я, и, ƒ. (*med.*) balneology.
бальнеотерапи́|я, и, ƒ. medicinal bathing.
ба́льник, а, *m.* (*school sl.*; *obs.*) report.

бáл|ьный, *adj. of* ~; ~ьное плáтье ball-dress.

балюстрáд|а, ы, *f.* (*archit.*) balustrade.

баля́син|а, ы, *f.* baluster.

баля́снича|ть, ю, *impf.* (*coll.*) to jest.

баля́с|ы, ~, *no sing.* banister; точи́ть б. (*fig., coll.*) to jest.

бамбу́к, а, *m.* bamboo.

бамбу́ков|ый, *adj.* bamboo; ~ое положéние (*coll.*) awkward position.

банáльност|ь, и, *f.* 1. banality. 2. banal remark; platitude.

банáл|ьный (~ен, ~ьна), *adj.* banal, trite.

банáн, а, *m.* banana.

банáн|овый, *adj. of* ~.

бáнд|а, ы, *f.* band, gang.

бандáж, á, *m.* 1. bandage; грыжевóй б. truss. 2. (*tech.*) tyre, band (*of metal*).

бандерóл|ь, и, *f.* 1. wrapper (*for dispatching newspapers, etc., by post*). 2. 'printed matter', 'book post'; отправля́ть ~ью to send as printed matter, by book post. 3. label (*certifying payment of tax, etc.*).

банди́т, а, *m.* bandit, brigand; gangster.

бандити́зм, а, *m.* brigandage; gangsterism.

банди́т|ский, *adj. of* ~.

банду́р|а, ы, *f.* (*mus.*) bandura (*Ukrainian string instrument similar to large mandoline*).

бандури́ст, а, *m.* (*mus.*) bandura-player.

банк, а, *m.* (*fin.*) bank (*also in card-games*). 2. faro (*card-game*).

бáнк|а¹, и, *f.* jar; (*med.*) cupping-glass; аптéчная б. gallipot.

бáнк|а², и, *f.* (*naut.*) thwart; bank.

бáнк|а³, и, *f.* bank, shoal.

банкабрóш, а, *m.* (*tech., text.*) flyer frame.

банкéт¹, а, *m.* banquet.

банкéт², а, *m.* bank (*of earth or stones*), embankment.

банки́р, а, *m.* banker.

банки́р|ский, *adj. of* ~; б. дом banking--house.

банкнóт, а, *m.* (*fin.*) bank-note.

банкнóт|а, ы, *f.* = ~.

бáнк|овский, *adj. of* ~; б. билéт bank-note; ~овская кни́жка passbook, bank-book.

бáнк|овый, *adj. of* ~; б. аккредити́в circular note; б. билéт bank-note; б. слу́жащий bank clerk.

банкомёт, а, *m.* banker (*at cards*); croupier.

банкрóт, а, *m.* bankrupt; объявля́ть ~ом to declare bankrupt.

банкрó|титься, чусь, ти́шься, *impf.* (*of* о~) to become bankrupt (*also fig.*).

банкрóтств|о, а, *n.* bankruptcy.

бáнник, а, *m.* (*mil.*) cleaning rod, rammer.

бáн|ный, *adj. of* ~я; б. вéник besom used in Russian baths; (он) пристáл как б. лист (*coll.*) (he) sticks like a leech.

бант, а, *m.* bow; завязáть ~ом to tie in a bow.

бáнтик, а, *m.* *dim. of* бант; гу́бки ~ом Cupid's bow.

бáнщик, а, *m.* bath-house attendant.

бáн|я, и, *f.* (*Russian*) baths; bath-house; задáть ~ю (+*d.*; *coll.*) to give it (someone) hot; кровáвая б. blood-bath.

баобáб, а, *m.* (*bot.*) baobab.

бапти́зм, а, *m.* the doctrine of Baptists.

бапти́ст, а, *m.* Baptist.

бапти́стский, *adj.* Baptist.

бар¹, а, *m.* (*snack-*)bar.

бар², а, *m.* (*naut.*) (sand-)bar.

бар³, а, *m.* (*phys.*) bar (*unit of atmospheric pressure*).

барабáн, а, *m.* drum (*also tech.*).

барабáн|ить, ю, ишь, *impf.* to drum, play the drum(s); (*fig., coll.*) to patter, gabble; дождь ~ил в óкна the rain was drumming on the windows; б. на роя́ле to drum on the piano.

барабáн|ный, *adj. of* ~; ~ная дробь drum-roll; ~ная перепóнка (*anat.*) ear-drum, tympanum.

барабáнщик, а, *m.* drummer.

барáк, а, *m.* wooden barrack; hut (*mil.*; *also in hospitals, esp. as infectious diseases ward*).

барáн, а, *m.* ram; sheep; смóтрит, как б. на нóвые ворóта (*coll.*) he looks quite lost.

барáн|ий, *adj.* 1. sheep's; согну́ть в б. рог (*coll.*) to make (someone) knuckle under. 2. sheepskin; б. полушу́бок sheepskin coat. 3. mutton; ~ья котлéта mutton chop.

барáнин|а, ы, *f.* mutton.

барáнк|а, и, *f.* 1. baranka (*ring-shaped roll*). 2. (*coll.*) steering-wheel.

барахл|и́ть, ю, и́шь, *impf.* (*coll.*) 1. to pink (*of an engine*). 2. to talk nonsense.

барахл|ó, á, *n.* (*collect.*; *coll.*) 1. old clothes; jumble; goods and chattels, odds and ends; торгóвец ~óм second-hand dealer. 2. trash, junk.

барахóлк|а, и, *f.* (*coll.*) second-hand goods market, stall.

барах|óльный, *adj. of* ~лó.

барахóльщик, а, *m.* (*coll.*) second-hand dealer.

барáхта|ться, юсь, *impf.* (*coll.*) to flounder; to wallow.

барá|чный, *adj. of* ~к.

барáш|ек, ка, *m.* 1. young ram; lamb; б. в бумáжке (*iron.*) bribe. 2. lambskin. 3. (*pl.*) 'white horses' (*on surface of sea, etc.*). 4. (*pl.*) fleecy clouds. 5. small curls; зави́ться~ком to have one's hair done in small curls. 6.(*tech*) wing nut, thumbscrew. 7. (*bot.*) catkin.

барáшковый, *adj.* lambskin.

барбари́с, а, *m.* barberry.

барбóс, а, *m.* 'Barbos' (*name given to house-dogs*; *fig. of* coarse, rude person).

барви́н|ок, ка, *m.* (*bot.*) periwinkle (*Vinca minor*).

бард, а, *m.* bard.

бард|а́, ы́, *f.* distillery waste.

барда́к, а́, *m.* (*coll.*) brothel; настоя́щий б. (*fig.*) complete chaos.

барелье́ф, а, *m.* bas-relief.

баре́тк|а, и, *f.* (*coll., obs.*) (woman's) shoe, slipper.

ба́рж|а, и, *f.* barge.

барж|а́, и́, *g. pl.* ~е́й = ба́ржа.

ба́ри|й, я, *m.* (*chem.*) barium.

ба́р|ин, а, *pl.* ~е *and* ~ы, ~, *m.* barin (*member of landowning gentry*); landowner; gentleman; master; (*as mode of address employed by peasants, servants, etc.*) sir; оде́т ~ином dressed like a gentleman; жить ~ином to live like a lord.

бари́т, а, *m.* (*min.*) barytes.

барито́н, а, *m.* baritone.

ба́рич, а, *m.* barin's son; (*coll., pejor.*) = ба́рин.

ба́рк|а, и, *f.* wooden barge.

баркаро́л|а, ы, *f.* (*mus.*) barcarole.

барка́с, а, *m.* launch; long boat.

ба́рмен, а, *m.* barman.

ба́рм|ы, ~, *no sing.* (*hist.*) small shoulder mantle (*worn by Moscow princes*).

баро́граф, а, *m.* barograph, self-recording barometer.

баро́кко, *indecl., n.* baroque.

баро́метр, а, *m.* barometer.

барометри́ческий, *adj.* barometric.

баро́н, а, *m.* baron.

бароне́сс|а, ы, *f.* baroness.

баро́нский, *adj.* baronial.

баро́нств|о, а, *n.* barony.

ба́рочник, а, *m.* bargee.

ба́р|очный, *adj. of* ~ка.

баро́чный, *adj.* baroque.

баррика́д|а, ы, *f.* barricade.

баррикади́р|овать, ую, *imperf.* (*of* за~) to barricade.

баррика́д|ный, *adj. of* ~а.

барс, а, *m.* (*zool.*) ounce, snow leopard (*Uncia uncia*).

ба́рск|ий, *adj. of* ба́рин; б. дом manor-house; жить на ~ую но́гу to live like a lord.

ба́рс|овый, *adj. of* ~.

ба́рственный, *adj.* lordly, grand.

ба́рств|о, а, *n.* 1. lordliness. 2. (*collect.*) gentry.

ба́рств|овать, ую, *impf.* to live in idleness and plenty.

барсу́к, а́, *m.* badger.

барсу́чий, *adj.* 1. *adj. of* барсу́к. 2. badgerskin.

бархáн, а, *m.* (sand-)dune (*in steppe or desert*).

ба́рхат, а, *m.* velvet.

бархати́ст|ый (~, ~а), *adj.* velvety.

ба́рхатк|а, и, *f.* piece of velvet; velvet ribbon.

ба́рхатный, *adj.* 1. velvet; б. сезо́н autumn season, autumn months. 2. (*fig.*) velvety.

ба́рхат|цы, цев, *sing.* ~ец, ~ца, *m.* (African) marigold (*Tagetes*).

бархо́тк|а, и, *f.* velvet ribbon.

барч|о́нок, о́нка, *pl.* ~а́та, ~а́т, *m.* barin's son.

барчу́к, а́, *m.* (*coll.*) barin's son.

ба́рщин|а, ы, *f.* (*hist.*) corvée.

ба́рын|я, и, *f.* barin's wife; lady; mistress; (*as term of address employed by peasants, servants, etc.*) madam.

бары́ш, а́, *m.* profit.

бары́шник, а, *m.* 1. profiteer; speculator (*esp. in theatre tickets*). 2. horse-dealer.

бары́шнича|ть, ю, *impf.* to profiteer; (+*i.*) to speculate (in).

бары́шничеств|о, а, *n.* profiteering; speculation.

ба́рыш|ня, ни, *g. pl.* ~ень, *f.* 1. girl of gentry family; (*as term of address employed by peasants, servants, etc.*) miss. 2. (*coll.*) girl, young lady. 3. (*coll., obs.*) female assistant; телефо́нная б. (*female*) telephone operator.

барье́р, а, *m.* barrier (*also fig.*); (*sport*) hurdle; взять б. to clear a hurdle; поста́вить кого́-н. к ~у to make someone fight a duel.

бас, а, *pl.* ~ы́, *m.* (*mus.*) bass.

ба́с|енный, *adj. of* ~ня.

баси́ст|ый (~, ~а), *adj.* (*coll.*) bass.

ба|си́ть, шу́, си́шь, *impf.* (*coll.*) to speak (*or* sing) in a deep voice.

баск, а, *m.* Basque.

баскетбо́л, а, *m.* (*sport*) basket-ball.

баскетболи́ст, а, *m.* basket-ball player.

баско́нк|а, и, *f.* Basque (woman).

ба́скский, *adj.* Basque.

басма́ч, а́, *m.* (*hist.*) basmach (*member of anti-Soviet movement in Central Asia*).

басма́честв|о, а, *n.* basmachestvo (*anti-Soviet movement in Central Asia*).

баснопи́с|ец, ца, *m.* (*lit.*) writer of fables.

баснослови|е, я, *n.* (*obs.*) 1. mythology. 2. (*collect.*) fabulous stories, fabrications.

баснослов|ный (~ен, ~на), *adj.* 1. mythical, legendary. 2. (*fig., coll.*) fabulous.

ба́с|ня, ни, *g. pl.* ~ен, *f.* 1. fable. 2. (*fig., coll.*) fable, fabrication.

бас|о́вый, *adj. of* ~; б. ключ (*mus.*) bass clef.

бас|о́к, ка́, *m.* (*mus.*) bass-string.

басо́н, а, *m.* braid.

бассе́йн, а, *m.* 1. (*man-made*) pool; reservoir; б. для пла́вания swimming-pool. 2. (*geogr.*) basin; каменноу́гольный б. coalfield.

ба́ста, *interj.* (*coll.*) that's enough! that'll do!

бастио́н, а, *m.* (*mil. and fig.*) bastion.

баст|ова́ть, у́ю, *impf.* to strike, go on strike; to be on strike.

бастр, а, *m.* brown sugar.

баст|у́ющий, *pres. part.* of ~ова́ть *and adj.* striking; *as noun* б., ~у́ющего, *m.* striker.

басурма́н, а, *m.* (*obs.*) infidel (*esp. Mohammedan*).

баталёр, а, *m.* (*naut.*) storeman; petty officer in charge of stores.

балали́ст, а, *m.* painter of battle-pieces.

бата́ли|я, и, *f.* **1.** (*obs.*) battle. **2.** (*coll.*) fight; row, squabble.

бата́л|ьный, *adj.* of ~ия; ~ьная карти́на battle-piece.

батальо́н, а, *m.* (*mil.*) battalion; стрелко́вый б. rifle battalion; б. свя́зи signal battalion.

батальо́н|ный, *adj.* of ~; б. команди́р battalion commander; *as noun* б., ~ного, *m.* = б. команди́р.

батаре́|ец, йца, *m.* (*mil.; coll.*) gunner.

батаре́йк|а, и, *f.* (*electric*) battery.

батаре́|йный, *adj.* of ~я; ~йная па́луба (*naut.*) gun deck; б. приёмник (*radio*) battery set.

батаре́|я, и, *f.* (*mil. and tech.*) battery; б. парово́го отопле́ния (central heating) radiator; б. сухи́х элеме́нтов dry battery; аккумуля́торная б. storage battery.

ба́теньк|а, и, *m.* (*coll.*) (*familiar mode of address*) old chap!

бати́ст, а, *m.* cambric, lawn.

бати́ст|овый, *adj.* of ~.

батисфе́р|а, ы, *f.* bathysphere.

бато́г, а́, *m.* (*obs. or dial.*) **1.** rod, cudgel; не жале́ть ~о́в not to spare the rod. **2.** walking-stick.

бато́н, а, *m.* **1.** long loaf. **2.** stick (*of confectionery*).

батра́к, а́, *m.* farm-labourer.

батра́|цкий, *adj.* of ~к.

батра́честв|о, а, *n.* **1.** farm work. **2.** (*collect.*) farm-labourers.

батра́ч|ить, у, ишь, *impf.* to work as a farm-labourer.

батра́чк|а, и, *f.* woman farm-labourer.

бату́т, а, *m.* (*sport*) trampoline.

ба́тьк|а, и, *m.* (*coll. or dial.*) = ба́тюшка 1.

ба́тюшк|а, и, *m.* **1.** (*coll.*) father; как вас по ~е? what is your patronymic? **2.** (*as mode of address to priests*) father. **3.** (*coll.*) old chap! my dear fellow!

ба́тюшки, *interj.* б. (мой)! good gracious!

ба́т|я, и, *m.* (*dial.*) = ~юшка.

ба́ул, а, *m.* trunk.

бах, *interj.* bang!

ба́ха|ть, ю, *impf.* of ба́хнуть.

ба́ха|ться, юсь, *impf.* of ба́хнуться.

бахва́л, а, *m.* (*coll.*) braggart, boaster.

бахва́л|иться, юсь, ишься, *impf.* (*coll.; +i.*) to brag (of).

бахва́льств|о, а, *n.* (*coll.*) bragging.

ба́хн|уть, у, ешь, *pf.* (*coll.*) **1.** to bang; to bark (*of gunfire*). **2.** to bang, slap; б. кого́-н. по спине́ to slap someone on the back.

ба́хн|уться, усь, ешься, *pf.* (*coll.*) to bang, bump (oneself); (*+i.*) б. голово́й о стол to bang one's head on the table.

бахром|а́, ы́, *f.* fringe.

бахро́мчатый, *adj.* fringed.

бахч|а́, и́, *f.* (water-)melon plantation; pumpkin (gourd) field.

бахчево́дств|о, а, *n.* melon-growing.

бахч|ево́й, *adj.* of ~а́; ~евы́е культу́ры melons and gourds.

бац, *interj.* = бах.

ба́ца|ть, ю, *impf.* **1.** *impf.* of ба́цнуть. **2.** (*coll.*) to tap-dance.

баци́лл|а, ы, *f.* bacillus.

бациллоноси́тел|ь, я, *m.* (bacillus-)carrier.

ба́цн|уть, у, ешь, *pf.* (*coll.*) = ба́хнуть.

ба́шенк|а, и, *f.* turret.

ба́ш|енный, *adj.* of ~ня; ~енные часы́ tower clock.

башибузу́к, а, *m.* bashi-bazouk; Turkish irregular (soldier); (*fig.*) desperado.

башк|а́, и́, *no g. pl., f.* (*coll.*) head; pate; глу́пая б. blockhead.

башки́р, а, *m.* Bashkir.

башки́р|ец, ца, *m.* (*obs.*) Bashkir.

башки́рк|а, и, *f.* Bashkir (woman).

башки́рский, *adj.* Bashkir.

башкови́т|ый (~, ~а), *adj.* (*coll.*) brainy.

башлы́к, а́, *m.* hood.

башма́к, а́, *m.* shoe (*also tech.*); (*tech.*) chock; быть под ~о́м у кого́-н. to be under someone's thumb.

башма́чник, а, *m.* shoemaker, cobbler.

башма́|чный, *adj.* of ~к.

ба́ш|ня, ни, *g. pl.* ~ен, *f.* tower; turret.

башта́н, а, *m.* = бахча́.

ба|шу́, сишь, *see* ~си́ть.

баю́ка|ть, ю, *impf.* to sing lullabies (to).

ба́юшки-баю́, *interj.* lullaby.

баяде́р|а, ы, *f.* = ~ка.

баяде́рк|а, и, *f.* bayadère.

бая́н, а, *m.* (*mus.*) bayan (*kind of accordion*).

баяни́ст, а, *m.* (*mus.*) bayan-player.

ба́|ять, ю, ешь, *impf.* (*coll., obs. or dial.*) to say, talk.

бде́ни|е, я, *n.* vigil; всено́щное б. (*eccl.*) all-night vigil.

бд|еть, *1st sing. not used,* ~ишь, *impf.* (*obs.*), to keep watch, keep vigil; б. (о+p.) to watch (over).

бди́тельност|ь, и, *f.* vigilance, watchfulness.

бди́тел|ьный (~ен, ~ьна), *adj.* vigilant, watchful.

бебе́, *indecl.*, *n.* (*coll.*) baby.

бебе́шк|а, и, *m.* and *f.* (*coll.*) baby; наряжа́ться ~ой to dress like a little girl.

бег, а, о ~е, на ~у́, *pl.* **~а́, ~о́в,** *m.* **1.** run, running; ~о́м, на ~у́ at the double; на всём ~у́ at full speed; б. на ме́сте running on the spot; marking time (*also fig.*). **2.** (*sport*) race; б. на коро́ткие диста́нции sprint. **3.** (*pl.*) the races (*for horses harnessed, not ridden*); trotting races; быть на ~а́х to be at the races. **4.** быть в ~а́х to be on the run; яви́ться из ~о́в to come out of hiding.

бе́га|ть, ю, *impf.* (*indet. of* бежа́ть) **1.** to run (about); (за+*i.*; *coll.*) to run (after), chase (after). **2.** (*of someone's eyes*) to rove, roam.

бегемо́т, а, *m.* hippopotamus.

бегле́ц, а́, *m.* fugitive.

бе́глост|ь, и, *f.* fluency; dexterity.

бе́гл|ый, *adj.* **1.** (*obs.*) fugitive. **2.** fluent, quick. **3.** superficial; cursory; б. взгляд fleeting glance; ~ое замеча́ние passing remark; б. звук unstable sound; б. осмо́тр cursory inspection. **4.** б. гла́сный (*gram.*) mobile vowel. **5.** б. ого́нь (*mil.*) volley fire.

бегля́нк|а, и, *f.* of бегле́ц.

бег|ово́й, *adj.* of ~; ~ова́я доро́жка race-track, running-track; ~ова́я ло́шадь race-horse.

бего́м, *adv.* running; at the double.

бего́ни|я, и, *f.* (*bot.*) begonia.

беготн|я́, и́, *f.* (*coll.*) running about; bustle.

бе́гств|о, а, *n.* flight; escape; обрати́ть в б. to put to flight; обрати́ться в б., спаса́ться ~ом to take to flight.

бе|гу́, ~жи́шь, *see* ~жа́ть.

бегу́н, а́, *m.* runner (*also tech.*); (ме́льничные) ~ы́ runners, millstones.

бегун|о́к, ка́, *m.* **1.** (*tech.*) runner. **2.** (*pl.*) small front wheels (*of locomotive*). **3.** (*pl. only*) sulky. **4.** (*coll.*) clearance chit, loan slip.

бед|а́, ы́, *pl.* **~ы,** *f.* **1.** misfortune; calamity; на ~у́ unfortunately; на свою́ ~у́ to one's cost; б. в том, что the trouble is (that); пришла́ б. — отворя́й воро́та (*prov.*) it never rains but it pours; семь ~ — оди́н отве́т (*prov.*) in for a penny, in for a pound. **2.** (the) trouble, the matter; (*as pred.*) it is awful!; it is a trouble; б. в том, что the trouble is (that); про́сто б.! it's simply awful!; б. мне с ним (*coll.*) he's an awful trouble; не б.! it doesn't matter; что за б.! what does it matter!, so what! **3.** (*coll.*) an awful lot. **4.** б. (как) (*as adv.*; *coll.*) awfully, terribly.

бе́декер, а, *m.* guide-book, Baedeker.

бедла́м, а, *m.* bedlam.

бедне́|ть, ю, *impf.* (*of* о~) (+*i.*) to grow poor (in).

бе́дност|ь, и, *f.* poverty (*also fig.*); indigence.

беднот|а́, ы́, *f.* **1.** (*collect.*) the poor; дере́венская б. poor peasants. **2.** (*coll.*) poverty.

бе́д|ный (~ен, ~на́, ~но), *adj.* poor; meagre; (*fig.*) barren, jejune.

бедня́г|а, и, *m.* (*coll.*) poor fellow; poor devil.

бедня́жк|а, и, *m.* and *f.* (*coll.*) **1.** *dim.* of бедня́га. **2.** *f.* of бедня́га.

бедня́к, а́, *m.* **1.** poor man. **2.** poor peasant.

бедня́|цкий, *adj.* of ~к.

бедня́честв|о, а, *n.* (*collect.*) poor peasants.

бедня́чк|а, и, *f.* poor peasant woman.

бедо́в|ый (~, ~а), *adj.* (*coll.*) sharp, lively; mischievous; daredevil.

бедоку́р, а, *m.* (*coll.*) mischief-maker; joker.

бедоку́р|ить, ю, ишь, *impf.* (*of* на~) (*coll.*) to get up to mischief, play jokes.

бе́дренный, *adj.* (*anat.*) femoral.

бед|ро́, ра́, *pl.* **~ра, ~ер, ~рам,** *n.* **1.** thigh; hip. **2.** (*joint of meat*) leg.

бе́дствен|ный (~, ~на), *adj.* disastrous, calamitous.

бе́дстви|е, я, *n.* calamity, disaster; сигна́л ~я distress signal.

бе́дств|овать, ую, *impf.* to live in poverty.

бедуи́н, а, *m.* bedouin.

бедуи́н|ский, *adj.* of ~.

беж, *indecl.*, *adj.* beige.

бе|жа́ть, гу́, жи́шь, гу́т, *impf.* (*det. of* бе́гать) **1.** to run; (*fig.*) to run, fly; to boil over; горя́чая вода́ ~жи́т из э́того кра́на hot water runs from this tap; вре́мя ~жи́т time flies. **2.** (*impf. and pf.*) to escape.

бе́жевый, *adj.* beige.

бе́жен|ец, ца, *m.* refugee.

бе́жен|ка, ки, *f.* of ~ец.

бе́женский, *adj.* refugee.

бе́женств|о, а, *n.* **1.** flight, exodus, refuge-seeking. **2.** (*collect.*) refugees.

без, *prep.*+*g.* without; in the absence of; minus, less; не б. not without, not devoid (of); б. вас in your absence; б. пяти́ (мину́т) три five (minutes) to three; б. че́тверти час a quarter to one; б. ма́лого (*coll.*) almost, all but; быть б. ума́ (от) to be crazy (about); не б. того́ (*coll.*) that's about it, it can't altogether be denied.

без- in-, un-, -less.

безава́ри́йный, *adj.* accident-free.

безала́берност|ь, и, *f.* disorder; lack of system.

безала́бер|ный (~ен, ~на), *adj.* disorderly; slovenly.

безала́берщин|а, ы, *f.* (*coll.*) muddle; slovenliness.

безалкого́льный, *adj.* non-alcoholic; б. напи́ток non-alcoholic drink, soft drink.

безапелляцио́н|ный (~ен, ~на), *adj.* peremptory, categorical.

безбéд|ный (~ен, ~на), *adj.* well-to-do, comfortable.

безбилéтный, *adj.* ticketless; б. пассажи́р passenger travelling without ticket; (*on ship*) stowaway.

безбóжи|е, я, *n.* atheism.

безбóжник, а, *m.* atheist.

безбóжно, *adv.* (*coll.*) shamelessly, scandalously; здесь б. деру́т they fleece you shamelessly here.

безбóжн|ый, *adj.* 1. irreligious, anti-religious. 2. (*coll.*) shameless, scandalous; ~ые цéны outrageous prices.

безболéзнен|ный (~, ~на), *adj.* painless.

безборóдый, *adj.* beardless (*also fig.*).

безбоя́знен|ный (~, ~на), *adj.* fearless.

безбрáчи|е, я, *n.* celibacy.

безбрáчный, *adj.* celibate.

безбрéж|ный (~ен, ~на), *adj.* boundless.

безбрóвый, *adj.* eyebrow-less.

безбýр|ный (~ен, ~на), *adj.* calm, peaceful.

безвéри|е, я, *n.* unbelief.

безвéстност|ь, и, *f.* obscurity.

безвéст|ный (~ен, ~на), *adj.* unknown; obscure; ~ное отсýтствие absence in place unknown.

безвéтренный, *adj.* calm.

безвéтри|е, я, *n.* calm.

безви́н|ный (~ен, ~на), *adj.* guiltless.

безвкýси|е, я, *n.* lack of taste.

безвкýсиц|а, ы, *f.* lack of taste; что за б.! what bad taste!

безвкýс|ный (~ен, ~на), *adj.* tasteless (*also fig.*)

безвлáсти|е, я, *n.* anarchy.

безвлáст|ный (~ен, ~на), *adj.* powerless.

безвóд|ный (~ен, ~на), *adj.* 1. arid; waterless. 2. (*chem.*) anhydrous.

безвóдь|е, я, *n.* aridity.

безвозврáт|ный (~ен, ~на), *adj.* irrevocable; ~ная ссýда permanent loan.

безвоздýшный, *adj.* airless.

безвозмéздный, *adj.* gratuitous, free of charge; б. труд unpaid work.

безвóли|е, я, *n.* lack of will; weak will.

безволóсый, *adj.* hairless, bald.

безвóл|ьный (~ен, ~ьна), *adj.* weak-willed.

безврéд|ный (~ен, ~на), *adj.* harmless.

безврéменн|ый, *adj.* untimely, premature; ~ая кончи́на untimely decease.

безврéмень|е, я, *n.* (*obs.*) 1. hard times. 2. period of (social) stagnation.

безвы́ездно, *adv.* uninterruptedly, without a break.

безвы́ездн|ый, *adj.* uninterrupted; ~ое пребывáние continuous residence.

безвы́ходно, *adv.* uninterruptedly, without a break.

безвы́ход|ный (~ен, ~на), *adj.* 1. hopeless,

desperate; быть в ~ном положéнии to be in a desperate position. 2. uninterrupted.

безглагóльный, *adj.* 1. (*gram.*) without a verb. 2. (*fig., poet.*) silent, dumb.

безглáзый, *adj.* eyeless.

безглáс|ный (~ен, ~на), *adj.* (*fig.*) silent, dumb.

безголóв|ый (~, ~а), *adj.* 1. headless; (*iron.*) brainless. 2. (*fig., coll.*) forgetful, scatter-brained.

безголóсный, *adj.* (*ling.*) unvoiced.

безголóс|ый, *adj.* weak (*of voice*); voiceless; он стал совсéм ~ым his voice is quite ruined.

безгрáмотност|ь, и, *f.* illiteracy.

безгрáмот|ный (~ен, ~на), *adj.* illiterate (*also fig.*); ignorant.

безграни́ч|ный (~ен, ~на), *adj.* infinite, limitless, boundless; (*fig.*) extreme, extraordinary.

безгрéшност|ь, и, *f.* innocence.

безгрéш|ный (~ен, ~на), *adj.* innocent, sinless.

бездáрност|ь, и, *f.* 1. lack of talent. 2. person without talent.

бездáр|ный (~ен, ~на), *adj.* talentless, undistinguished.

бездáр|ь (*and* бéздар|ь), **и,** *f.* (*coll.*) person without talent.

бездéйствен|ный (~, ~на), *adj.* inactive.

бездéйстви|е, я, *n.* inactivity, inertia, idleness; (*leg.*) (criminal) negligence.

бездéйств|овать, ую, *impf.* to be inactive; to lie idle; not to work (*of a machine, etc.*).

бездéлиц|а, ы, *f.* trifle, bagatelle; такáя сýмма для негó б. for him such a sum is a trifle.

бездéлк|а, и, *f.* (*coll.*) 1. trifle, bagatelle. 2. knick-knack.

безделýшк|а, и, *f.* knick-knack.

бездéль|е, я, *n.* idleness.

бездéльник, а, *m.* 1. idler, loafer. 2. ne'er-do-well.

бездéльниц|а, ы, *f.* of бездéльник.

бездéльнича|ть, ю, *impf.* to idle, loaf.

бездéл|ьный (~ен, ~ьна), *adj.* (*coll.*) idle.

безденéжный, *adj.* 1. impecunious. 2. (*econ.*) non-monetary.

безденéжь|е, я, *n.* lack of money, impecuniousness.

бездéтност|ь, и, *f.* childlessness.

бездéт|ный (~ен, ~на), *adj.* childless.

бездефици́тный, *adj.* (*econ.*) entailing no deficit; self-supporting.

бездéятельност|ь, и, *f.* inactivity, inertia.

бездéятел|ьный (~ен, ~ьна), *adj.* inactive; sluggish.

бéздн|а, ы, *f.* 1. abyss, chasm. 2. (*coll.*) a huge number; б. хлопóт a multitude, sea of troubles; б. премýдрости (*joc.*) a mine of information.

бездо́ждь|е, я, *n.* dry weather, drought.

бездоказа́тел|ьный (~ен, ~ьна), *adj.* unsubstantiated.

бездо́м|ный (~ен, ~на), *adj.* homeless.

бездо́нный, *adj.* bottomless; (*fig.*, *poet.*) fathomless.

бездоро́ж|ный (~ен, ~на), *adj.* without roads.

бездоро́жь|е, я, *n.* 1. absence of roads. 2. bad condition of roads; season when roads are impassable.

бездохо́д|ный (~ен, ~на), *adj.* (*econ.*) unprofitable.

безду́м|ный, (~ен, ~на), *adj.* unthinking; feckless.

безду́ши|е, я, *n.* heartlessness, callousness.

безду́ш|ный (~ен, ~на), *adj.* 1. heartless, callous. 2. inanimate; (*fig.*) soulless.

безды́мный, *adj.* smokeless; **б. по́рох** (*mil.*) smokeless powder.

бездыха́н|ный (~ен, ~на), *adj.* lifeless.

безе́, *indecl.*, *n.* meringue.

безжа́лост|ный (~ен, ~на), *adj.* ruthless, pitiless.

безжи́знен|ный (~, ~на), *adj.* lifeless, inanimate; (*fig.*) spiritless.

беззабо́т|ный (~ен, ~на), *adj.* carefree, light-hearted; careless.

беззаве́т|ный (~ен, ~на), *adj.* selfless, wholehearted; **~ная хра́брость** selfless courage.

беззако́ни|е, я, *n.* 1. lawlessness. 2. unlawful action.

беззако́нннича|ть, ю, *impf.* (*coll.*) to transgress, break the law.

беззако́н|ный (~ен, ~на), *adj.* 1. illegal, unlawful. 2. (*poet.*) lawless, wayward.

беззапре́тн|ый, *adj.* 1. permitted; **~ая су́мма иностра́нной валю́ты** permitted amount of foreign currency. 2. unrestrained.

беззасте́нчив|ый (~, ~а), *adj.* shameless; **б. лгун** brazen, unblushing liar; **~ая ложь** barefaced lie.

беззащи́т|ный (~ен, ~на), *adj.* defenceless, unprotected.

беззвёзд|ный (~ен, ~на), *adj.* starless.

беззву́ч|ный (~ен, ~на), *adj.* soundless, noiseless.

безземе́ль|е, я, *n.* lack of land.

безземе́льный, *adj.* landless.

беззло́би|е, я, *n.* good nature, mildness.

беззло́б|ный (~ен, ~на), *adj.* mild, good-natured.

беззу́б|ый, *adj.* 1. toothless; (*fig.*) impotent, harmless; **~ая зло́ба** impotent rage. 2. (*zool.*) edentate.

безле́с|ный (~ен, ~на), *adj.* woodless; treeless.

безле́сь|е, я, *n.* 1. woodless tract. 2. absence of forest.

безли́кий, *adj.* featureless.

безли́ственный, *adj.* leafless.

безли́ч|ие, ия, *n.* = **~ность.**

безли́чност|ь, и, *f.* lack of personality; impersonality.

безли́ч|ный (~ен, ~на), *adj.* 1. without personality, characterless, impersonal. 2. (*gram.*) impersonal.

безлоша́дный, *adj.* not possessing a horse.

безлу́н|ный (~ен, ~на), *adj.* moonless.

безлю́д|ный (~ен, ~на), *adj.* uninhabited; sparsely populated; solitary, unfrequented.

безлю́дь|е, я, *n.* 1. deficiency of population; absence of human life; **в дере́вне бы́ло по́лное б.** the village was completely deserted. 2. lack of suitable company, lack of the right people; **на б. и Фома́ дворяни́н** (*prov.*) in the land of the blind the one-eyed is king.

безме́н, а, *m.* bismar; steelyard.

безме́р|ный (~ен, ~на), *adj.* immense, excessive.

безмо́зглый, *adj.* (*coll.*) brainless.

безмо́лви|е, я, *n.* silence; **цари́т б.** silence reigns.

безмо́лв|ный (~ен, ~на), *adj.* silent, mute, speechless; **~ное согла́сие** tacit consent.

безмо́лвств|овать, ую, *impf.* to keep silence.

безмото́рный, *adj.* engineless.

безмяте́жность, и, *f.* serenity, placidity.

безмяте́ж|ный (~ен, ~на), *adj.* serene, placid.

безнадёж|ный (~ен, ~на), *adj.* hopeless; despairing; **больно́й ~ен** the patient's case is hopeless.

безнадзо́рност|ь, и, *f.* neglect.

безнадзо́рный, *adj.* neglected.

безнака́занно, *adv.* with impunity; **э́то ему́ не пройдёт б.** he won't get away with this.

безнака́занност|ь, и, *f.* impunity.

безнака́зан|ный (~, ~на), *adj.* unpunished.

безнали́чный, *adj.* without cash transfer; **б. расчёт** (*fin.*) clearing.

безнача́ли|е, я, *n.* anarchy.

безнача́льный, *adj.* without beginning, from eternity.

безно́гий, *adj.* 1. legless; one-legged. 2. deprived of the use of one's legs. 3. (*zool.*) apod.

безно́сый, *adj.* noseless; **б. ча́йник** spoutless teapot.

безнра́вственност|ь, и, *f.* immorality.

безнра́вствен|ный (~, ~на), *adj.* immoral.

безо, *prep.* (*before g. of* **весь** *and* **вся́кий**) = **без.**

безоби́д|ный (~ен, ~на), *adj.* inoffensive.

безо́блачност|ь, и, *f.* cloudlessness; (*fig.*) serenity.

безо́блач|ный (~ен, ~на), *adj.* cloudless; (*fig.*) serene, unclouded.

безобра́зи|е, я, n. 1. ugliness. 2. outrage; (pl.) disgraceful things, shocking things. 3. (as pred.; coll.) it is disgraceful; э́то про́сто б.! it's simply disgraceful, scandalous.

безобра́|зить, жу, зишь, impf. (of о~) 1. to disfigure, mutilate. 2. (coll.) to make a nuisance of oneself, make a disturbance.

безобра́зник, а, m. (coll.) 1. hooligan. 2. naughty child.

безобра́знича|ть, ю, impf. (coll.) to carry on disgracefully, outrageously; to make a nuisance of oneself; to get up to mischief.

безо́браз|ный (~ен, ~на), adj. 1. unadorned; not employing images. 2. vague.

безобра́з|ный (~ен, ~на), adj. 1. ugly. 2. disgraceful, scandalous, outrageous, shocking.

безогово́рочн|ый (~а, ~о), adj. unconditional, unreserved.

безопа́сност|ь, и, f. safety, security; Сове́т Безопа́сности Security Council.

безопа́с|ный (~ен, ~на), adj. safe, secure; ~ная бри́тва safety razor.

безору́ж|ный (~ен, ~на), adj. unarmed.

безоснова́тел|ьный (~ен, ~ьна), adj. groundless.

безостано́вочный, adj. unceasing; non-stop.

безотве́т|ный (~ен, ~на), adj. 1. (rare) unanswered. 2. meek; dumb.

безотве́тственност|ь, и, f. irresponsibility.

безотве́тствен|ный (~, ~на), adj. irresponsible.

безотгово́рочн|ый (~а, ~о), adj. unquestioning, implicit.

безотка́зный, adj. unfailing; without hitches.

безотка́тный, adj. (mil.) non-recoil.

безотлага́тельный, adj. urgent.

безотло́жный, adj. = безотлага́тельный.

безотлу́чно, adv. continually; она́ нахо́дится б. до́ма she is tied to the home, she never gets out.

безотлу́ч|ный (~ен, ~на), adj. ever-present; continuous.

безотноси́тельно, adv. (к) irrespective (of); б. к его́ пла́нам я пое́ду за́втра в Ло́ндон irrespective of his plans I shall go to London tomorrow.

безотноси́тел|ьный (~ен, ~ьна), adj. absolute, valid absolutely.

безотра́д|ный (~ен, ~на), adj. cheerless.

безотры́вн|ый, adj. ~ое обуче́ние workers' education (not involving taking time off from work).

безотчётност|ь, и, f. 1. absence of control. 2. unaccountableness; instinctiveness.

безотчёт|ный, (~ен, ~на), adj. 1. not liable to account, not subject to control. 2. unaccountable, inexplicable; unreasoning, instinctive.

безошибоч|ный (~ен, ~на), adj. correct; faultless, infallible; ~ное предсказа́ние unerring prediction.

безрабо́тиц|а, ы, f. unemployment.

безрабо́тн|ый, adj. unemployed; as noun ~ые, ~ых pl. the unemployed.

безра́дост|ный (~ен, ~на), adj. joyless; dismal.

безразде́л|ьный (~ен, ~ьна), adj. undivided; ~ьная власть complete sway; ~ьное иму́щество indivisible property.

безразли́чи|е, я, n. indifference.

безразли́чно (adv.) indifferently; относи́ться б. (к) to be indifferent (to); б. кто, где no matter who, where.

безразли́ч|ный (~ен, ~на), adj. indifferent; мне ~но it's all the same to me.

безразме́р|ный (~ен, ~на), adj. one-size (nylon, etc.); ~ные носки́ stretch socks.

безрассве́т|ный (~ен, ~на), adj. continuous (of night in polar regions).

безрассу́д|ный (~ен, ~на), adj. reckless; foolhardy.

безрассу́дств|о, а, n. recklessness; foolhardiness.

безрасчёт|ный (~ен, ~на), adj. uneconomical.

безрезульта́тност|ь, и, f. futility; failure.

безрезульта́т|ный (~ен, ~на), adj. futile; unsuccessful.

безре́льсов|ый, adj. railless; б. тра́нспорт motor transport; ~ая доро́га road.

безрессо́рный, adj. unsprung.

безро́г|ий, adj. hornless; ~ое живо́тное pollard.

безро́д|ный (~ен, ~на), adj. 1. without kith or kin. 2. (obs.) of humble origin. 3. (fig.) homeless, stateless.

безро́пот|ный (~ен, ~на), adj. uncomplaining, resigned; submissive.

безрука́вк|а, и, f. sleeveless jacket or blouse.

безру́кий, adj. 1. armless. 2. one-armed. 3. (fig.) clumsy.

безры́бь|е, я, n. absence of fish; на б. и рак ры́ба (prov.) in the land of the blind the one-eyed is king.

безубы́точ|ный (~ен, ~на), adj. (comm.) not entailing loss.

безуда́р|ный (~ен, ~на), adj. (ling.) unaccented, unstressed.

безуде́рж|ный (~ен, ~на), adj. unrestrained; impetuous.

безуе́здный, adj. б. го́род (hist.) town, not being principal town of uyezd, but possessing its own administration.

безукори́знен|ный (~, ~на), adj. irreproachable; impeccable.

безу́м|ец, ца, m. madman.

безу́ми|е, я, n. 1. madness, insanity. 2. (fig.) madness; folly; довести́ до ~я to drive crazy; люби́ть до ∼я to love to distraction.

безу́мно, *adv.* madly, crazily; terribly, dreadfully; я б. за́нят I am terribly busy.

безу́м|ный (∼ен, ∼на), *adj.* 1. mad, insane. 2. (*fig.*) mad, crazy, senseless. 3. (*coll.*) terrible; ∼ные це́ны absurd prices.

безумо́лч|ный (∼ен, ∼на), *adj.* incessant (*of noise*).

безу́мств|о, а, *n.* madness; foolhardiness.

безу́мств|овать, ую, *impf.* to behave like a madman; to rave.

безупре́ч|ный (∼ен, ∼на), *adj.* irreproachable.

безуря́диц|а, ы, *f.* disorder, confusion.

безусло́вно, *adv.* 1. unconditionally, absolutely. 2. (*coll.*) of course, it goes without saying, undoubtedly.

безусло́вност|ь, и, *f.* certainty.

безусло́в|ный (∼ен, ∼на), *adj.* 1. unconditional, absolute. 2. undoubted, indisputable.

безуспе́ш|ный (∼ен, ∼на), *adj.* unsuccessful.

безуста́нный, *adj.* tireless, indefatigable.

безу́сый, *adj.* having no moustache; (*fig.*) callow, immature, 'beardless'.

безуте́ш|ный (∼ен, ∼на), *adj.* inconsolable.

безу́хий, *adj.* 1. earless. 2. one-eared.

безуча́сти|е, я, *n.* apathy, unconcern, neutrality.

безуча́стност|ь, и, *f.* = безуча́стие.

безуча́ст|ный (∼ен, ∼на), *adj.* apathetic, unconcerned, neutral.

безъязы́кий, *adj.* dumb, without a tongue.

безъязы́ч|ный (∼ен, ∼на), *adj.* dumb, speechless.

безыде́йност|ь, и, *f.* lack of principle(s); lack of ideals; lack of ideological content.

безыде́|йный (∼ен, ∼йна), *adj.* unprincipled; lacking ideals; lacking ideological content.

безызве́стност|ь, и, *f.* 1. uncertainty. 2. obscurity.

безызве́ст|ный (∼ен, ∼на), *adj.* unknown, obscure.

безым|ённый, *adj.* = ∼я́нный.

безымя́нн|ый, *adj.* nameless; anonymous; б. па́лец third finger, ring-finger; ∼ая неде́ля the third week in Lent.

безынициати́в|ный (∼ен, ∼на), *adj.* lacking initiative.

безынтере́с|ный (∼ен, ∼на), *adj.* 1. uninteresting. 2. (*obs.*) disinterested.

безыску́сствен|ный (∼, ∼на), *adj.* artless, ingenuous.

безысхо́д|ный (∼ен, ∼на), *adj.* irreparable; interminable; perpetual.

бе|й, я, *m.* bey (*Turkish title*).

бей(те), *imp. of* бить.

бейдеви́нд, *adv.* (*naut.*) close-hauled.

бейсбо́л, а, *m.* baseball.

бейсболи́ст, а, *m.* baseball player.

бек, а, *m.* (*sport; obs.*) back.

бека́р, а, *m.* (*also as indecl. adj.*) (*mus.*) natural; до б. C natural.

бека́с, а, *m.* (*orn.*) snipe.

бекаси́нник, а, *m.* small shot.

бекаси́ный, *adj. of* бека́с.

беке́ш|а, и, *f.* (*knee-length*) winter overcoat.

беко́н, а, *m.* bacon.

беко́нный, *adj.* bacon.

белемни́т, а, *m.* (*geol.*) belemnite.

белен|а́, ы́, *f.* (*bot.*) henbane; что ты, ∼ы́ объе́лся? have you gone crazy?

беле́ни|е, я, *n.* bleaching.

белёный, *adj.* bleached.

белесова́т|ый (∼, ∼а), *adj.* whitish.

белёсый, *adj.* whitish.

беле́|ть, ю, *impf.* (*of* по∼) 1. to grow white. 2. (*no pf.*) to show up white.

беле́|ться, юсь, *impf.* to show up white.

бел|е́ц, ьца́, *m.* (*eccl.*) novice.

бел|и, ей, *no sing.* (*med.*) leucorrhoea.

белиберд|а́, ы́, *f.* (*coll.*) nonsense, rubbish.

белизн|а́, ы́, *f.* whiteness.

бели́л|а, ∼, *no sing.* 1. whitewash; свинцо́вые б. white lead; ци́нковые б. zinc white. 2. ceruse.

бели́льный, *adj.* bleaching.

бели́л|ьня, ьни, *g. pl.* ∼ен, *f.* bleaching works, bleachery.

бел|и́ть, ю́, ∼ишь, *impf.* 1. (*pf.* по∼) to whitewash. 2. (*pf.* на∼) to whiten (*one's face, etc.*). 3. (*pf.* вы́∼) to bleach.

бел|и́ться, ю́сь, ∼ишься, *impf.* 1. *pass. of* ∼и́ть. 2. (*pf.* на∼) to whiten one's face.

бели́ц|а, ы, *f.* (*eccl.*) female novice.

бел|и́чий, *adj. of* ∼ка¹; б. мех squirrel (fur).

бе́лк|а¹, и, *f.* squirrel; верте́ться, кружи́ться как б. в колесе́ to put in much work without visible result, run round in small circles.

бе́лк|а², и, *f.* (*coll.*) bleaching.

белкови́н|а, ы, *f.* (*chem.*) albumen.

белко́вый, *adj.* (*chem.*) albuminous.

белладо́нн|а, ы, *f.* (*bot.*) belladonna.

беллетри́ст, а, *m.* fiction writer.

беллетри́стик|а, и, *f.* (*lit.*) fiction.

беллетристи́ческий, *adj.* (*lit.*) fictional.

бело- white-.

белобры́с|ый (∼, ∼а), *adj.* (*coll.*) tow-haired.

белова́т|ый (∼, ∼а), *adj.* whitish.

белови́к, а́, *m.* fair copy (*of MS.*).

белово́й, *adj.* clean, fair; б. экземпля́р fair copy.

белогварде́|ец, йца, *m.* (*polit.*) White Guard.

белогварде|йский, *adj. of* ~ец.

белоголо́вый, *adj.* 1. white-haired. 2. fair (-haired).

бел|о́к¹, ка́, *m.* (*biol., chem.*) albumen; protein.

бел|о́к², ка́, *m.* white (of egg); glair.

бел|о́к³, ка́, *m.* white (of the eye).

белока́менн|ый, *adj.* (*folk poet.*) built of white stone (*esp. as epithet of Moscow*).

белокро́ви|е, я, *n.* (*med.*) leucaemia.

белоку́р|ый (~, ~a), *adj.* blond(e), fair (-haired).

белоли́ц|ый (~, ~a), *adj.* pale, white-faced.

белоподкла́дочник, а, *m.* (*hist.*) student of aristocratic appearance and reactionary views.

белору́с, а, *m.* Byelorussian (*formerly* White Russian).

белору́ск|а, и, *f.* Byelorussian (woman).

белору́сский, *adj.* Byelorussian (*formerly* White Russian).

белору́чк|а, и, *m. and f.* (*coll., pejor.*) person shirking rough *or* dirty (physical) work.

белоры́биц|а, ы, *f.* white salmon.

Белосне́жк|а, и, *f.* Snow-White.

белосне́ж|ный (~ен, ~на), *adj.* snow-white.

белоте́л|ый (~, ~a), *adj.* fair-skinned.

белошве́йк|а, и, *f.* seamstress.

белошве́йн|ый, *adj.* linen; ~ая мастерска́я seamstress's workshop.

белоэмигра́нт, а, *m.* (*polit.*) White Russian emigré.

белу́г|а, и, *f.* 1. beluga, white sturgeon (*Huso huso*). 2. (*dial.*) white whale; реве́ть ~ой to bellow.

белу́|жий, *adj. of* ~га.

белу́жин|а, ы, *f.* (*meat of*) white sturgeon.

белу́х|а, и, *f.* white whale (*Delphinapterus leucus*).

бе́л|ый (~, ~а́, ~o), *adj.* 1. white; ~ая бере́за silver birch; б. медве́дь polar bear; ~ая сова́ snowy owl. 2. (*as opp. to dark and in var. fig. senses*) white; fair; б. биле́т (*obs.*) 'white chit' (*certificate of exemption from military service*); ~oe вино́ white wine; ~oe духове́нство secular clergy; ~oe зо́лото 'white gold' (= *cotton*); ~oe кале́ние white heat, incandescence; ~ые кровяны́е ша́рики white blood corpuscles; ~oe мя́со white meat; ~ые но́чи 'white nights', 'midnight sun'; б. у́голь 'white coal' (= *water power*); б. хлеб white bread, wheatmeal bread; на ~ом све́те in all the world; средь ~а дня in broad daylight; э́то ши́то ~ыми ни́тками it is all too obvious, it is quite transparent; *as noun* ~ые, ~ых, *pl.* white-skinned people, white men. 3. clean; blank (= *unused*; *fig.* unadorned); б. лист clean sheet (of paper); ~ая страни́ца blank page (*in book*); ~ые стихи́ blank

verse. 4. (= of superior quality, of high class, *etc.*) б. гриб (edible) boletus (*mushroom*); ~ая кость (*iron.*) blue blood; ~ая куха́рка (*obs.*) head cook. 5. ~ая горя́чка (*med.*) delirium tremens. 6. (*polit.*) White (*also as noun*).

бельведе́р, а, *m.* belvedere.

бельги́|ец, йца, *m.* Belgian.

бельги́йк|а, и, *f.* Belgian (woman).

бельги́йский, *adj.* Belgian.

бель|ё, я́, *n.* (*collect.*) linen; ни́жнее б. underclothes; посте́льное б. bed-linen; столо́вое б. table-linen.

бель|ево́й, *adj. of* ~ё; б. шкаф linen cupboard; ~ева́я прище́пка clothes-peg.

бельме́с, а, *m.* ни ~a (*coll.*) nothing; он ни ~a не понима́ет he hasn't a clue.

бельм|о́, а́, *pl.* ~a, *n.* 1. (*med.*) cataract; как б. на глазу́ (*fig.*) a thorn in the flesh; bête noire. 2. (*pl. only*; *also* ~ы; *coll.*) eyes.

бельэта́ж, а, *m.* 1. first floor. 2. (*theatr.*) dress circle.

беля́к, а́, *m.* white hare.

беля́н|а, ы, *f.* (*obs.*) barge (*of unpainted wood, used on Volga and Kama rivers*).

беля́нк|а, и, *f.* 1. blonde woman, girl. 2. cabbage butterfly. 3. white mushroom.

бемо́л|ь, я, *m.* (*also as indecl. adj.*) (*mus.*) flat; ре б. D flat.

бе́мск|ий, *adj.* ~oe стекло́ Bohemian glass.

бенга́льский, *adj.* Bengal; б. ого́нь Bengal light; б. язы́к Bengali.

бенедикти́н, а, *m.* benedictine (*liqueur*).

бенедикти́н|ец, ца, *m.* (*eccl.*) member of Benedictine order.

бенедикти́нский, *adj.* (*eccl.*) Benedictine.

бенефи́с, а, *m.* (*theatr.*) benefit performance; устро́ить б. (+*d.*; *sl.*) to give someone what for.

бенефи́с|ный, *adj. of* ~; б. спекта́кль benefit performance.

бенефициа́нт, а, *m.* (*theatr.*) artist for whom benefit performance is given.

бенефи́ци|я, и, *f.* (*eccl.*) living, benefice.

бензи́н, а, *m.* benzine; petrol.

бензи́н|овый, *adj. of* ~; petrol; ~овая коло́нка petrol pump.

бензиноме́р, а, *m.* petrol gauge.

бензинопрово́д, а, *m.* petrol pipe.

бензоба́к, а, *m.* petrol tank.

бензоколо́нк|а, и, *f.* petrol pump.

бензо́л, а, *m.* (*chem.*) benzol, benzene.

бензохрани́лищ|е, а, *n.* petrol tank.

бенуа́р, а, *m.* (*theatr.*) boxes (*on level of the stalls*).

бербе́р, а, *m.* Berber.

бербе́рк|а, и, *f.* Berber (woman).

бербе́рский, *adj.* Berber.

бергамо́т, а, *m.* bergamot (*kind of pear*).

бердáнк|а, и, *f.* (*obs.*) Berdan rifle.
бёрд|о, а, *n.* (*tech.*) reed (*of loom*).
бердьíш, á, *m.* (*hist.*) pole-axe.
бéрег, а, о ~е, на ~ý, *pl.* ~á, *m.* bank; shore; на ~ý мóря at the seaside; вьíброситься нá берег to run aground; вьíйти из ~óв to burst its banks; сойтú на б. to go ashore.
бер|ёг, ~еглá, *see* берéчь.
берегов|óй, *adj.* coastal; waterside; б. вéтер offshore wind, land-wind; ~áя оборóна coastal defence; ~óе прáво (*leg.*) right of salvage; ~óе судохóдство coastal shipping; ~áя лáсточка sand-martin.
бере|гý, ~жёшь, ~гýт, *see* берéчь.
бере|дúть, жý, дúшь, *impf.* (*of* раз~) (*coll.*) to irritate; б. стáрые рáны (*fig.*) to re-open old wounds.
бережён|ый, *adj.* (*coll.*) guarded, preserved; ~ая копéйка рубль бережёт (*prov.*) take care of the pennies, the pounds will take care of themselves; ~ого и Бог бережёт God helps those who help themselves.
бережлúвост|ь, и, *f.* thrift, economy.
бережлúв|ый (~, ~а), *adj.* thrifty, economical.
бéрежност|ь, и, *f.* care; caution; solicitude.
бéреж|ный (~ен, ~на), *adj.* careful; cautious; solicitous.
берёз|а, ы, *f.* birch.
берéзник, á, *no pl.*, *m.* birch grove.
березня́к, á, *no pl.*, *m.* 1. birch grove. 2. birch-wood.
берёзовик, а, *m.* brown mushroom (*Boletus scaber*).
берёз|овый, *adj.* of ~а; ~овая кáша (*coll.*) the birch; a flogging.
берéйтор, а, *m.* riding-master.
берéмене|ть, ю, ешь, *impf.* (*of* за~) (*coll.*) to become pregnant.
берéме|нная (~нна), *adj.* (+*i.*) pregnant (with).
берéменност|ь, и, *f.* pregnancy; gestation; быть на пя́том мéсяце ~и to be in the fifth month (of pregnancy).
берём|я, ени, *n.* (*dial.*) armful; bundle.
берёст|а, ы, *no pl.*, *f.* birch-bark.
берёст|овый, *adj.* of ~а.
берестяно́й, *adj.* = берёстовый.
берéт, а, *m.* beret.
бер|éчь, егý, ежёшь, егýт, *past* ~ёг, ~еглá, *impf.* 1. to take care (of), look after; to keep, guard; б. кáждую копéйку to count every penny; б. своё врéмя not to waste one's time; б. тáйну to keep a secret. 2. to spare; to spare the feelings (of).
бер|éчься, егýсь, ежёшься, егýтся, *past* ~ёгся, ~еглáсь, *impf.* 1. to be careful, take care. 2. (+*g.* or +*inf.*) to beware (of); ~егúтесь воро́в! beware of pickpockets!;

~егúтесь переедáть! mind you don't eat too much! 3. *pass. of* ~éчь.
берúлл, а, *m.* (*min.*) beryl.
берúлли|й,я, *m.* (*chem.*) beryllium,glucinium.
бéрков|ец, ца, *m.* (*obs.*) berkovets (*weight equivalent to 10 poods or 360 lb. avoirdupois*).
бéркут, а, *m.* golden eagle.
берлúнск|ий, *adj.* Berlin; ~ая лазýрь Prussian blue.
берлóг|а, и, *f.* den, lair.
бертолéтов, *adj.* ~а соль potassium chlorate (Berthollet's salt).
бер|ý, ёшь, *see* брать.
берцóв|ый, *adj.* (*anat.*) большáя ~ая кость shin-bone, tibia; мáлая ~ая кость fibula.
бес, а, *m.* demon, evil spirit; рассыпáться мéлким ~ом (пéред+*i.*; *coll.*) to fawn (on), ingratiate oneself (with).
бесéд|а, ы, *f.* 1. talk, conversation. 2. discussion; провестú ~у to give a talk; б. по прочúтанному discussion of what one has read (*in school, etc.*).
бесéдк|а, и, *f.* summer-house.
бесéд|овать, ую, *impf.* (с+*i.*) to talk, converse (with).
бесéдчик, а, *m.* (*coll.*) discussion-leader.
бесён|ок, ка, *pl.* ~я́та, ~я́т, *m.* imp, little devil (*also fig.*).
бе|сúть, шý, ~сишь, *impf.* (*of* вз~) (*coll.*) to enrage, madden, infuriate.
бе|сúться, шýсь, ~сишься, *impf.* (*of* вз~) 1. to go mad (*of animals*). 2. (*fig.*) to rage, be furious; с жúру б. (*coll.*) to grow fastidious, fussy; to be too well off.
бесклáссовый, *adj.* classless.
бескозы́рк|а, и, *f.* peakless cap; матрóсская б. sailor's cap.
бескозы́рный, *adj.* (*cards*) without trumps.
бесконéчно, *adv.* infinitely, endlessly; (*coll.*) extremely; я б. рад вáшему успéху I am extremely pleased about your success; б. мáлый (*math.*) infinitesimal.
бесконéчност|ь, и, *f.* endlessness; infinity; до ~и endlessly.
бесконéч|ный (~ен, ~на), *adj.* endless; infinite; interminable; ~ная дробь (*math.*) recurring decimal; б. винт (*tech.*) endless screw; б. ряд (*math.*) infinite series.
бесконтрóл|ьный (~ен, ~ьна), *adj.* uncontrolled; unchecked.
бескóрмиц|а, ы, *f.* fodder shortage.
бескорóвный, *adj.* not possessing a cow.
бескорь́сти|е, я, *n.* disinterestedness.
бескорь́ст|ный (~ен, ~на), *adj.* disinterested; unselfish.
бескóстный, *adj.* boneless.
бескрáйний, *adj.* boundless.
бескрóв|ный (~ен, ~на), *adj.* 1. anaemic, pale. 2. bloodless; ~ная револю́ция bloodless revolution.

бескро́вный², *adj.* (*obs.*) roofless; homeless.

бескры́лый, *adj.* wingless; (*fig.*) uninspired.

бескульту́рь|е, я, *n.* lack of culture.

беснова́ни|е, я, *n.* frenzy; raging.

беснова́тый, *adj.* possessed; raging, raving.

бесн|ова́ться, у́юсь, *impf.* to be possessed; to rage, rave.

бесо́вский, *adj.* devilish, diabolical.

беспа́лубный, *adj.* without decks.

беспа́лый, *adj.* lacking one *or* more fingers *or* toes.

беспа́мят|ный (~ен, ~на), *adj.* (*coll.*) forgetful.

беспа́мятств|о, а, *n.* **1.** unconsciousness; впасть в б. to lose consciousness. **2.** frenzy; delirium; быть в ~е to be beside oneself; to be delirious.

беспардо́нный, *adj.* shameless, brazen.

беспарти́йн|ый, *adj.* non-party; *as noun* б., ~ого, *m., and* ~ая, ~ой, *f.* non-party man, woman.

беспа́спортный, *adj.* not having a passport.

беспате́нтный, *adj.* unlicensed.

бесперебо́йный, *adj.* uninterrupted; regular.

беспереса́дочный, *adj.* direct; б. по́езд through train.

бесперспекти́в|ный (~ен, ~на), *adj.* having no prospects; hopeless.

беспеча́л|ьный (~ен, ~ьна), *adj.* carefree.

беспе́чност|ь, и, *f.* carelessness, unconcern.

беспе́ч|ный (~ен, ~на), *adj.* careless, unconcerned; carefree.

беспи́сьменный, *adj.* having no written language.

беспла́новост|ь, и, f. absence of plan.

беспла́новый, *adj.* planless.

беспла́тно, *adv.* free of charge, gratis.

беспла́т|ный (~ен, ~на), *adj.* free, gratuitous; б. биле́т free ticket, complimentary ticket.

бесплацка́ртный, *adj.* without reserved seat(s); б. по́езд train with unreserved seats only; б. пассажи́р passenger travelling without reserving a seat.

беспло́ди|е, я, *n.* sterility, barrenness.

беспло́дност|ь, и, f. fruitlessness, futility.

беспло́д|ный (~ен, ~на), *adj.* **1.** sterile, barren. **2.** (*fig.*) fruitless, futile.

беспло́тный, *adj.* (*rel.*; *poet.*) incorporeal.

бесповоро́тност|ь, и, f. irrevocability, finality.

бесповоро́тн|ый (~а, ~о), *adj.* irrevocable, final; ~ое реше́ние final decision.

бесподо́б|ный (~ен, ~на), *adj.* matchless; incomparable; superlative; ~но! *interj.* superb!, splendid!

беспозвоно́чн|ый, *adj.* (*zool.*) invertebrate; *as noun* ~ое, ~ого, *n.* invertebrate.

беспоко́|ить, ю, ишь, *impf.* **1.** (*pf.* о~) to disturb, bother. **2.** (*pf.* по~) to disturb, worry.

беспоко́|иться, юсь, ишься, *impf.* **1.** (*pf.* о~) (о+*p.*) to worry, be worried *or* anxious (about). **2.** (*pf.* по~) (*coll.*) to worry, put oneself out; не ~йтесь! don't trouble!, don't worry!

беспоко́|йный (~ен, ~йна), *adj.* **1.** agitated; anxious; uneasy; ~йное состоя́ние a state of agitation. **2.** disturbing; restless, fidgety; б. ребёнок fidgety child.

беспоко́йств|о, а, *n.* **1.** agitation; anxiety; unrest; с ~ом anxiously. **2.** disturbance; причини́ть б. (+*d.*) to disturb.

бесполе́з|ный (~ен, ~на), *adj.* useless.

беспо́л|ый, *adj.* sexless; ~ое размноже́ние asexual reproduction.

беспоме́стный, *adj.* (*hist.*) not possessing an estate.

беспо́мощ|ный (~ен, ~на), *adj.* helpless, powerless; (*fig.*) feeble; б. ум feeble intellect.

беспоро́д|ный (~ен, ~на), *adj.* not thoroughbred, not pedigree; ~ная соба́ка mongrel.

беспоро́ч|ный (~ен, ~на), *adj.* blameless, irreproachable; immaculate; ~ное зача́тие (*rel.*) the Immaculate Conception; ~ная слу́жба irreproachable service.

беспоря́д|ок, ка, *m.* disorder, confusion; (*pl. only*; *polit.*) disturbances, riots.

беспоря́доч|ный (~ен, ~на), *adj.* disorderly; untidy.

беспоса́дочный, *adj.* б. перелёт non-stop flight.

беспо́чвен|ный (~, ~на), *adj.* groundless; unsound.

беспо́шлинн|ый, *adj.* (*econ.*) duty-free; ~ая торго́вля free trade.

беспоща́д|ный (~ен, ~на), *adj.* merciless, relentless.

бесправи|е, я, *n.* **1.** lawlessness; arbitrariness. **2.** state of possessing no rights.

беспра́вност|ь, и, f. = беспра́вие 2.

беспра́в|ный (~ен, ~на), *adj.* without rights; deprived of rights.

беспреде́л|ьный (~ен, ~ьна), *adj.* boundless; infinite.

беспредме́тник, а, *m.* supporter of abstract art.

беспредме́тн|ый, *adj.* **1.** aimless. **2.** ~ая жи́вопись abstract painting.

беспрекосло́в|ный (~ен, ~на), *adj.* unquestioning, absolute; он тре́бует ~ного повинове́ния he demands unquestioning obedience.

беспрепя́тствен|ный (~, ~на), *adj.* free, clear, unimpeded.

беспреры́вно, *adv.* continuously; uninterruptedly; дождь шёл б. в течение трёх дней it rained for three days on end.

беспрерыв|ный (~ен,~на), *adj.* continuous; uninterrupted.

беспрестанно, *adv.* continually, incessantly.

беспрестан|ный (~ен, ~на), *adj.* continual; incessant.

беспрецедент|ный (~ен, ~на), *adj.* unprecedented.

беспри́был|ьный (~ен, ~ьна), *adj.* profitless.

беспривет|ный (~ен, ~на), *adj.* unwelcoming.

бесприданниц|а, ы, *f.* girl without dowry.

беспризорник, а, *m.* besprizornik; waif, homeless child.

беспризорн|ый, *adj.* 1. neglected. 2. stray, homeless; *as noun* б., ~ого, *m.* waif, homeless child.

беспример|ный (~ен, ~на), *adj.* unexampled, unparalleled; ~ная храбрость unexampled bravery.

беспримесный, *adj.* unalloyed.

беспринцип|ный (~ен, ~на), *adj.* unscrupulous, unprincipled.

беспристрасти|е, я, *n.* impartiality.

беспристрастност|ь, и, *f.* impartiality.

беспристраст|ный (~ен, ~на), *adj.* impartial, unbiassed.

беспричин|ный, *adj.* causeless; pointless.

бесприют|ный (~ен, ~на), *adj.* homeless; not affording shelter; ~ная жизнь life spent in roaming.

беспробуд|ный (~ен, ~на), *adj.* 1. deep, heavy (*of sleep*); спать ~ным сном to be in a deep sleep. 2. unrestrained (*of drunkenness*).

беспроволочный, *adj.* wireless; б. телеграф wireless.

беспроигрышн|ый, *adj.* safe; without risk of loss; ~ая лотерея lottery in which no competitor loses.

беспросвет|ный (~ен, ~на), *adj.* 1. pitch-dark; ~ная тьма thick darkness. 2. (*fig.*) cheerless, hopeless; ~ное горе unrelieved misery.

беспроцентный, *adj.* (*fin.*) bearing no interest.

беспутиц|а, ы, *f.* 1. absence of roads. 2. bad condition of roads. 3. season when roads are impassable.

беспутник, а, *m.* (*coll.*) debauchee.

беспутнича|ть, ю, *impf.* (*coll.*) to lead a dissipated life, be a debauchee.

беспут|ный (~ен, ~на), *adj.* dissipated, dissolute.

беспутств|о, а, *n.* dissipation, debauchery.

бессвязност|ь, и, *f.* incoherence.

бессвяз|ный (~ен, ~на), *adj.* incoherent.

бессемейный, *adj.* having no family.

бессеменн|ый, *adj.* 1. (*obs.*) seedless. 2. (*rel.*) ~ое зачатие the Virgin Birth (*of Christ*).

бессеменодо́льный, *adj.* (*bot.*) acotyledonous.

бессемерова́ни|е, я, *n.* (*tech.*) Bessemer process.

бессеме́ровский, *adj.* (*tech.*) Bessemer.

бессемянный, *adj.* seedless.

бессердечи|е, ия, *n.* = ~ность.

бессердечност|ь, и, *f.* heartlessness; callousness.

бессердеч|ный (~ен, ~на), *adj.* heartless; callous.

бессили|е, я, *n.* impotence; debility; (*fig.*) feebleness.

бессил|ьный (~ен, ~ьна), *adj.* impotent, powerless.

бессистемност|ь, и, *f.* unsystematic character, lack of system.

бессистем|ный (~ен, ~на), *adj.* unsystematic.

бесслави|е, я, *n.* infamy.

бесслав|ить, лю, ишь, *impf.* (*of* о~) to defame.

бесслав|ный (~ен, ~на), *adj.* infamous; inglorious.

бесследно, *adv.* without leaving a trace; completely, utterly.

бесследн|ый, *adj.* without leaving a trace; ~ое исчезновение complete disappearance.

бессловес|ный (~ен, ~на), *adj.* dumb, speechless; (*fig.*) silent; ~ные животные dumb animals; (*theatr.*) ~ная роль silent part.

бессмен|ный (~ен, ~на), *adj.* permanent; continuous.

бессмерти|е, я, *n.* immortality.

бессмертник, а, *m.* (*bot.*) immortelle.

бессмерт|ный (~ен, ~на), *adj.* immortal; undying.

бессмыслен|ный (~, ~на), *adj.* senseless; foolish; meaningless, nonsensical; б. поступок senseless act; ~ная фраза meaningless sentence.

бессмыслиц|а, ы, *f.* nonsense.

бесснежный, *adj.* snowless.

бессовест|ный (~ен, ~на), *adj.* unscrupulous, dishonest.

бессодержа́тел|ьный (~ен, ~ьна), *adj.* empty; tame; dull.

бессозна́тел|ьный (~ен, ~ьна), *adj.* 1. unconscious. 2. involuntary.

бессонниц|а, ы, *f.* insomnia, sleeplessness.

бессонный, *adj.* sleepless.

бесспорно, *adv.* indisputably; undoubtedly.

бесспор|ный (~ен, ~на), *adj.* indisputable, incontrovertible.

бессре́бреник, а, *m.* disinterested person.

бессро́чн|ый, *adj.* without time-limit; б. о́тпуск indefinite leave; ~ое тюре́мное заключе́ние imprisonment for life, life term.

бесстра́ст|ный (~ен, ~на), *adj.* impassive.

бесстра́ши|е, я, *n.* fearlessness, intrepidity.

бесстра́ш|ный (~ен, ~на), *adj.* fearless, intrepid.

бессты́дник, а, *m.* shameless person.

бессты́дниц|а, ы, *f.* shameless woman, hussy.

бессты́д|ный (~ен, ~на), *adj.* shameless.

бессты́дств|о, а, *n.* shamelessness.

бессты́жий, *adj.* (*coll.*) shameless; brazen.

бессубъе́кт|ный, *adj.* ~ное предложе́ние (*gram.*) sentence not containing subject.

бессу́дный, *adj.* arbitrary, summary.

бессчётный, *adj.* innumerable.

беста́ктност|ь, и, *f.* 1. tactlessness. 2. tactless action.

беста́кт|ный (~ен, ~на), *adj.* tactless.

бестала́н|ный (~ен, ~на), *adj.* 1. untalented. 2. (*folk poet.*) ill-starred, luckless; ~ная голо́вушка poor devil.

бестеле́с|ный (~ен, ~на), *adj.* incorporeal.

бе́сти|я, и, *f.* (*coll.*) rogue; то́нкая б. sly rogue.

бестова́рь|е, я, *n.* shortage of goods.

бестолко́вщин|а, ы, *f.* (*coll.*) disorder, confusion.

бестолко́в|ый (~, ~а), *adj.* 1. slow-witted; muddle-headed. 2. disconnected, incoherent.

бе́столоч|ь, и, *f.* (*coll.*) 1. confusion. 2. muddle-headed person (*also collect.*).

бестре́пет|ный (~ен, ~на), *adj.* (*poet.*) dauntless.

бесту́жевск|ий, *adj.* ~ие ку́рсы (*hist.*) 'Bestuzhev courses' (*higher education courses for women established in St. Petersburg in 1879; named after the first director, K. N. Bestuzhev-Ryumin*).

бесту́жевк|а, и, *f.* (*coll.*) member of 'Bestuzhev courses'.

бесфо́рмен|ный (~, ~на), *adj.* shapeless, formless.

бесхара́ктер|ный (~ен, ~на), *adj.* lacking in character; weak-willed.

бесхво́ст|ый, *adj.* tailless; *as noun* ~ое, ~ого, *n.* (*zool.*) ecaudate.

бесхи́трост|ный (~ен, ~на), *adj.* artless; unsophisticated; ingenuous.

бесхле́биц|а, ы, *f.* (*coll.*) corn shortage; bread shortage.

бесхо́з|ный, *adj.* ownerless; ~ое иму́щество property in abeyance.

бесхозя́йный, *adj.* (*obs.*) ownerless.

бесхозя́йственност|ь, и, *f.* thriftlessness; bad management.

бесхозя́йствен|ный (~, ~на), *adj.* thriftless; improvident.

бесхребе́т|ный (~ен, ~на), *adj.* (*fig.*) spineless, weak.

бесцве́т|ный (~ен, ~на), *adj.* colourless; (*fig.*) colourless, insipid.

бесце́л|ьный (~ен, ~ьна), *adj.* aimless; idle; ~ьная болтовня́ idle chat.

бесце́н|ный (~ен, ~на), *adj.* 1. priceless, invaluable. 2. (*obs.*) valueless.

бесце́н|ок, ка, *m.* (*coll.*) *only in phrase* за б. very cheaply; купи́ть за б. to buy for a song.

бесцеремо́н|ный (~ен, ~на), *adj.* unceremonious; familiar.

бесчелове́чност|ь, и, *f.* inhumanity.

бесчелове́ч|ный (~ен, ~на), *adj.* inhuman.

бесче́|стить, щу, стишь, *impf.* (*of* о~) to dishonour, disgrace.

бесче́ст|ный (~ен, ~на), *adj.* dishonourable; disgraceful.

бесче́сть|е, я, *n.* dishonour; disgrace.

бесчи́нный, *adj.* (*obs.*) unseemly, scandalous.

бесчи́нств|о, а, *n.* excess; enormity.

бесчи́нств|овать, ую, *impf.* to commit excesses.

бесчи́сленност|ь, и, *f.* innumerable quantity.

бесчи́слен|ный (~, ~на), *adj.* innumerable.

бесчу́вственност|ь, и, *f.* 1. insensibility. 2. insensitivity.

бесчу́вствен|ный (~, ~на), *adj.* 1. insensible. 2. insensitive, unfeeling.

бесчу́встви|е, я, *n.* 1. loss of consciousness; пья́ный до ~я dead drunk; бить до ~я to knock insensible. 2. insensitivity.

бесшаба́ш|ный (~ен, ~на), *adj.* (*coll.*) reckless.

бесшёрстный, *adj.* hairless, woolless.

бесшёрст|ый, *adj.* = ~ный.

бесшо́вный, *adj.* (*tech.*) seamless; jointless.

бесшу́м|ный (~ен, ~на), *adj.* noiseless.

бе́тел|ь, я, *m.* betel.

бето́н, а, *m.* (*tech.*) concrete.

бетони́ровани|е, я, *n.* (*tech.*) concreting.

бетони́р|овать, ую, *impf.* (*tech.*) to concrete.

бето́нный, *adj.* (*tech.*) concrete.

бетономеша́лк|а, и, *f.* (*tech.*) concrete mixer.

бето́нщик, а, *m.* concrete worker.

беф-стро́ганов, *indecl.*, *m.* (*cul.*) bœuf Stroganov.

бечев|а́, ы́, *no pl.*, *f.* tow-rope.

бечёвк|а, и, *f.* string, twine.

бечевни́к, а́, *m.* tow-path.

бечев|о́й, *adj. of* ~а́; ~а́я тя́га towing; *as noun* ~а́я, ~о́й, *f.* tow-path.

бешаме́л|ь, и, *f.* (*cul.*) Bechamel sauce.

бе́шенств|о, а, *n.* 1. (*med.*) hydrophobia; rabies. 2. fury, rage; довести́ до ~а to enrage. 3. б. ма́тки (*med.*) nymphomania.

бе́шен|ый, *adj.* **1.** rabid, mad; ~ая соба́ка mad dog. **2.** furious; violent; ~ая ско́рость furious pace; ~ые це́ны (*coll.*) exorbitant prices. **3.** ~ые де́ньги (*obs.*) easy money. **4.** б. огуре́ц 'squirting' cucumber (*Ecballium elaterium*).

бешме́т, а, *m.* beshmet (*kind of quilted coat*).

бзик, а, *m.* (*coll.*) quirk, oddity.

бибабо́, *indecl., n.* glove puppet.

библе́йский, *adj.* biblical.

библио́граф, а, *m.* bibliographer.

библиографи́ческий, *adj.* bibliographical.

библиогра́фи|я, и, *f.* bibliography.

библиоте́к|а, и, *f.* (*in var. senses*) library; б. с вы́дачей книг на́ дом lending-library; б.-чита́льня reading-room.

библиоте́кар|ша, ши, *f. of* ~ь.

библиоте́кар|ь, я, *m.* librarian.

библиотекове́дени|е, я, *n.* librarianship.

библиоте́|чный, *adj. of* ~ка.

библиофи́л, а, *m.* bibliophil.

би́бли|я, и, *f.* bible; the Bible.

бива́к, а, *m.* (*mil.*) bivouac, camp; стоя́ть ~ом, на ~ах to bivouac, camp.

бива́|чный, *adj. of* ~к; б. пункт (*mil.*) bivouacking site, camping site.

би́в|ень, ня, *pl.* ~ни, ~ней, *m.* tusk.

бивуа́к, а, *m.* (*obs.*) = бива́к.

бигуд|и́, е́й, *no sing.* (*also indecl.*) (hair) curlers.

бидо́н, а, *m.* can, churn; б. для молока́ milk-can.

бие́ни|е, я, *n.* beating; throb; б. се́рдца heartbeat; б. пу́льса pulse.

биза́н|ь, и, *f.* (*naut.*) mizzen; б.-ма́чта mizzen-mast.

бизо́н, а, *m.* (*zool.*) bison.

бикарбона́т, а, *m.* (*chem.*) bicarbonate.

биквадра́т, а, *m.* (*math.*) biquadrate.

биквадра́тный, *adj.* (*math.*) biquadratic.

бикфо́рдов, *adj.* б. шнур (*tech.*) Bickford (safety) fuse.

билабиа́льный, *adj.* (*ling.*) bilabial.

биле́т, а, *m.* ticket; card; входно́й б. entrance ticket, permit; жёлтый б. (*obs.*) prostitute's passport; креди́тный б. bank-note; обра́тный б. return ticket; отпускно́й б. (*mil.*) leave-pass; парти́йный б. Party-membership card; почётный б. complimentary ticket; пригласи́тельный б. invitation card; экзаменацио́нный б. examination question (-paper) (*at oral examination*).

биле́тёр, а, *m.* ticket-collector.

билетёр|ша, ши, *f. of* ~; (*in cinema, etc.*) usherette.

биллиа́рд, а, *m.* = билья́рд.

биллио́н, а, *m.* billion (= *a 1000 millions*).

билло́н, а, *no pl., m.* (*tech.*) billon (*debased silver*).

билл|ь, я, *m.* (*polit.*) bill.

би́л|о, а, *n.* **1.** (*tech.*) beater. **2.** gong.

бильбоке́, *indecl., n.* cup and ball (*toy*).

бильдаппара́т, а, *m.* (*tech.*) telephote, photograph transmitter.

билья́рд, а, *m.* **1.** billiard-table. **2.** billiards; игра́ть в б. to play billiards; па́ртия в б., на ~е game of billiards.

билья́рд|ный, *adj. of* ~; б. шар billiard ball; *as noun* ~ная, ~ной, *f.* billiards room.

биметалли́зм, а, *m.* (*econ.*) bimetallism.

бимс, а, *m.* (*naut.*) beam, transom.

бино́кл|ь, я, *m.* binoculars; полево́й б. field glasses; театра́льный б. opera glasses.

бинокуля́рный, *adj.* binocular.

бино́м, а, *m.* (*math.*) binomial; б. Нью́тона binomial theorem.

бинт, а́, *m.* bandage.

бинт|ова́ть, у́ю, *impf.* to bandage.

бинто́вк|а, и, *f.* bandaging.

био́граф, а, *m.* **1.** biographer. **2.** (*obs.*) cinematograph.

биографи́ческий, *adj.* biographical.

биогра́фи|я, и, *f.* biography.

био́лог, а, *m.* biologist.

биологи́ческий, *adj.* biological.

биоло́ги|я, и, *f.* biology.

биоста́нци|я, и, *f.* biological research station.

биосфе́р|а, ы, *f.* biosphere.

биохими́ческий, *adj.* biochemical.

биохи́ми|я, и, *f.* biochemistry.

бипла́н, а, *m.* biplane.

биполя́рност|ь, и, *f.* (*phys.*) bipolarity.

биполя́рный, *adj.* (*phys.*) bipolar.

би́рж|а, и, *f.* **1.** exchange; фо́ндовая б. stock-exchange; чёрная б. black market (*in currency*); б. труда́ labour exchange. **2.** изво́зчичья б. (*obs.*) cabstand, cab-rank.

биржеви́к, а́, *m.* **1.** stockbroker. **2.** (*obs.*) cabby.

бирж|ево́й, *adj. of* ~а; б. ма́клер stock-broker; ~ева́я сде́лка stock-exchange deal.

би́рк|а, и, *f.* **1.** (*obs.*) tally (*notched stick*). **2.** name-plate; label-tag.

бирма́н|ец, ца, *m.* Burmese, Burman.

бирма́нк|а, и, *f.* Burmese (woman).

бирма́нский, *adj.* Burmese.

бирюз|а́, ы́, *no pl., f.* turquoise.

бирюзо́вый, *adj.* turquoise (**1.** *made of turquoise.* **2.** *of turquoise colour*).

бирю́к, а́, *m.* (*dial.*) lone wolf; (*fig.*) lone wolf, unsociable person; смотре́ть ~о́м (*coll.*) to look gloomy, morose.

бирю́льк|а, и, *f.* spillikin; игра́ть в ~и to play at spillikins; (*fig.*) to occupy oneself with trifles.

бирю́ч, а́, *m.* (*hist.*) crier, herald.

бис, *interj.* encore; сыгра́ть, спеть на б. to play, sing an encore.

би́сер, а, *no pl., m.* beads; мета́ть б. пе́ред свиньями (*fig.*) to cast pearls before swine.

би́серин|а, ы, *f.* bead.

би́сер|ный, *adj. of* ~; (*fig.*) minute; б. по́черк minute handwriting.

биси́р|овать, ую, *impf. and pf.* to repeat, give an encore.

бискви́т, а, m. 1. sponge-cake. **2.** (*tech.*) biscuit (*unglazed pottery*).

бискви́т|ный, *adj. of* ~; б. руле́т Swiss roll.

биссектри́с|а, ы, *f.* (*math.*) bisector.

бисульфа́т, а, m. (*chem.*) bisulphate.

бит|а́, ы́, *f.* (*sport*) bat.

би́тв|а, ы, *f.* battle; б. за Атланти́ческий океа́н, на Ма́рне, под Полта́вой, при Трафа́льгаре Battle of the Atlantic, of the Marne, of Poltava, of Trafalgar.

би́тенг, а, *no pl., m.* (*naut.*) bitts.

битко́м, *adv. only in phrase* б. наби́ть (*coll.*) to pack, crowd; авто́бус был б. наби́т the bus was packed, crammed.

бит|о́к, ка́, m. rissole, hamburger.

биту́м, а, m. (*min.*) bitumen.

битумино́зный, *adj.* (*min.*) bituminous.

би́т|ый (~, ~а), *p.p.p. of* ~ь *and adj.*; ~ая посу́да два ве́ка живёт (*prov.*) cracked pots last the longest; б. час (*coll.*) a full hour, a good hour; ~ые сли́вки whipped cream; ~ое стекло́ broken glass.

бить, бью, бьёшь, *impf.* **1.** (*pf.* по~) to beat (*a person, an animal, etc.*). **2.** (*pf.* по~) to beat, defeat (*in war, sports or games*); (*impf. only*) б. ка́рту (*cards*) to cover a card. **3.** (уда́рить *used in place of pf.*) to strike, hit; б. кнуто́м to whip, flog; б. себя́ в грудь to thump one's chest; б. в лицо́ to strike, hit in the face (*also fig.*). **4.** (*impf. only*) to strike, hit; to beat, thump, bang; б. в бараба́н to beat a drum; б. в ладо́ши to clap one's hands; б. по столу́ to bang on the table; б. за́дом to kick (*of a horse*); б. чело́м (*i*) (*hist.*) to present a petition, (*ii*) (+*d.*) to take off one's hat (to) (*fig.*). **5.** (*impf. only*) to kill, slaughter (*animals*); б. гарпуно́м to harpoon; б. ры́бу острого́й to spear fish. **6.** (*pf.* с~) б. ма́сло to churn butter. **7.** (*impf. only*) to break, smash (*crockery, etc.*). **8.** (уда́рить *used in place of pf.*) to combat, fight (against), wage war (on); to damage, injure; б. по хулига́нству to combat hooliganism; б. по чьему́-н. самолю́бию to wound someone's vanity; б. по карма́ну to cost one a pretty penny. **9.** (*pf.* про~) to strike, sound; б. (в) наба́т to sound the alarm; б. отбо́й to beat a retreat (*also fig.*); часы́ бьют пять the clock is striking five; бьёт пять (*impers.*) it is striking five. **10.** (*impf. only*) to spurt, gush; б. ключо́м to gush out, well up; (*fig.*) to be in full swing. **11.** (*impf. only*) to shoot, fire; (*with fire-arms*; *also fig.*) to hit; to have a range (of); б. из духово́го ружья́ to fire an air-gun; б. в цель to hit the target (*also fig.*); б. наверняка́ (*fig.*) to take no chances; б. на́ два киломе́тра to have a range of two kilometres. **12.** (*impf. only*; на+*a.*) to strive (for, after); б. на эффе́кт to strive after effect.

бить|ё, я́, *n.* (*coll.*) beating, flogging; smashing.

би́ться, бьюсь, бьёшься, *impf.* **1.** (с+*i.*) to fight (with, against); б. на поеди́нке to fight a duel. **2.** (*of the heart*) to beat; се́рдце его́ переста́ло б. his heart stopped beating. **3.** (о+*a.*) to knock (against), hit (against), strike; б. голово́й об сте́ну to be up against a blank wall; б., как ры́ба об лёд to struggle desperately. **4.** to writhe, struggle; б. в исте́рике to writhe in hysterics. **5.** (над+*i.*; *fig.*) to struggle (with), exercise oneself (over); б. над зада́чей to rack one's brains over a problem; как бы он ни би́лся however hard he tried. **6.** (*of crockery, etc.*) to break, smash; легко́ б. to be very fragile. **7.** б. об закла́д to bet, wager.

битю́г, а́, m. bityug (*Russian breed of cart-horse*); (*fig.*) strong man; он настоя́щий б. he is strong as a horse.

бифурка́ци|я, и, *f.* bifurcation.

бифште́кс, а, m. beefsteak.

би́цепс, а, m. (*anat.*) biceps.

бич, а́, m. whip, lash; (*fig.*) scourge.

бичева́ = бечева́.

бичева́ние, я, *n.* flogging; flagellation.

бич|ева́ть, у́ю, *impf.* to flog; (*fig.*) to lash, castigate.

бичёвка = бечёвка.

бишь, *particle* (*expressing effort to recall name, etc.*; *coll.*) now (*or not translated*); как б. его́ зову́т? what is his name?, what was the name now?; то б. that is to say.

бла́г|о¹, а, *n.* good, the good; blessing; о́бщее б. the common weal; жела́ю вам всех благ! I wish you every happiness; всех благ! (*coll.*) all the best! ни за каки́е ~а not for the world.

бла́го², conj. (*coll.*) since; seeing that; скажи́те ему́ сейча́с, б. он здесь tell him now since he is here.

благове́рн|ый, *now used only facetiously as noun*; б., ~ого, *m.* husband; ~ая, ~ой, *f.* wife.

бла́говест, а, m. ringing of church bell(s).

бла́гове|стить, щу, стишь, *impf.* **1.** (*pf.* от~) to ring for church. **2.** (*pf.* раз~) (*coll.*, *iron.*) to publish, spread news.

Благове́щени|е, я, *n.* (*eccl.*) the Annunciation.

благове́щен|ский, *adj. of* ~ие.

благови́д|ный (~ен, ~на), *adj.* **1.** (*obs.*) comely. **2.** specious, plausible; б. предло́г specious excuse.

благоволе́ни|**е, я,** *n.* goodwill, kindness; favour; по́льзоваться чьим-н. ~ем to be in favour with someone.

благовол|**и́ть, ю, и́шь,** *impf.* (к+*d.*) to be favourably disposed (toward), favour; ~и́те (+*inf.*) have the kindness (to); ~и́те отве́тить на э́то письмо́ kindly answer this letter.

благово́ни|**е, я,** *n.* fragrance, aroma.

благово́нный, *adj.* fragrant.

благовоспи́танност|**ь, и,** *f.* good manners; good breeding.

благовоспи́тан|**ный** (~, ~на), *adj.* well--mannered; well brought up.

благовре́мени|**е, я,** *n. only in phrase* во ~и (*obs.*) opportunely.

благовре́менный, *adj.* (*obs.*) timely.

благоглу́пост|**ь, и,** *f.* pompous triviality.

благогове́|**йный** (~ен, ~йна), *adj.* reverential.

благогове́ни|**е, я,** *n.* reverence; veneration.

благогове́|**ть, ю,** *impf.* (пе́ред+*i.*) to have a reverential attitude (towards).

благодар|**и́ть, ю, и́шь,** *impf.* (*of* по~) to thank; ~ю́ вас (за+*a.*) thank you (for).

благода́рност|**ь, и,** *f.* 1. gratitude; не сто́ит ~и don't mention it. 2. (*usually pl.*) thanks, acknowledgement of thanks. 3. (*coll.*) bribe.

благода́р|**ный** (~ен, ~на), *adj.* 1. grateful. 2. rewarding; worth-while.

благода́рственн|**ый,** *adj.* (*obs.*) expressing thanks; б. моле́бен thanksgiving service; ~ое письмо́ letter of thanks.

благода́рств|**овать, ую,** *impf.* (*obs.*) *only used in forms* ~ую, ~уем, ~уй(те) thank you.

благодаря́, *prep.*+*d.* thanks to, owing to, because of; б. тому́, что owing to the fact that; б. хоро́шему кли́мату он ско́ро попра́вился thanks to the good climate he soon recovered.

благода́т|**ный** (~ен, ~на), *adj.* beneficial; abundant; б. край land of plenty.

благода́т|**ь, и,** *f.* 1. plenty, abundance. 2. (*rel.*) grace; Сло́во о зако́не и ~и (*hist.*) Sermon on Law and Grace.

благоде́нственный, *adj.* (*obs.*) prosperous.

благоде́нстви|**е, я,** *n.* (*obs.*) prosperity.

благоде́нств|**овать, ую,** *impf.* to prosper, flourish.

благоде́тел|**ь, я,** *m.* benefactor.

благоде́тельниц|**а, ы,** *f.* benefactress.

благоде́тел|**ьный** (~ен, ~ьна), *adj.* beneficial.

благоде́тельств|**овать, ую,** *impf.* (+*d.*) to be a benefactor (to).

благодея́ни|**е, я,** *n.* good deed; blessing, boon.

благоду́шеств|**овать, ую,** *impf.* (*coll.*) to take life easily.

благоду́ши|**е, я,** *n.* placidity, equability; good humour.

благоду́ш|**ный** (~ен, ~на), *adj.* placid, equable; good-humoured.

благожела́тел|**ь, я,** *m.* well-wisher.

благожела́тел|**ьный** (~ен, ~ьна), *adj.* well-disposed; benevolent; б. приём a friendly, cordial reception; ~ьная реце́нзия favourable review.

благожела́тельност|**ь, и,** *f.* goodwill; benevolence.

благозву́чи|**е, я,** *n.* euphony.

благозву́чност|**ь, и,** *f.* euphony.

благозву́ч|**ный** (~ен, ~на), *adj.* euphonious; melodious.

благ|**о́й**[1], *adj.* good; ~а́я мысль a happy thought; ~и́е наме́рения good intentions; избра́ть ~у́ю часть (*often iron.*) to choose the better part.

благ|**о́й**[2], *adj.* (*dial.*) crazy, cranky; ~и́м ма́том (*coll.*) at the top of one's voice.

благоле́пи|**е, я,** *n.* (*obs.*) grandeur.

благомы́слящий, *adj.* (*obs.*) right-thinking.

благонадёжност|**ь, и,** *f.* reliability, trustworthiness; loyalty; свиде́тельство о ~и (*obs.*) certificate of loyalty.

благонадёж|**ный** (~ен, ~на), *adj.* reliable, trustworthy; loyal.

благонаме́ренност|**ь, и,** *f.* (*obs.*) loyalty.

благонаме́рен|**ный** (~, ~на), *adj.* (*obs.*) loyal.

благонра́ви|**е, я,** *n.* good behaviour.

благонра́в|**ный** (~ен, ~на), *adj.* well-behaved.

благообра́зи|**е, я,** *n.* good looks; noble appearance.

благообра́з|**ный** (~ен, ~на), *adj.* good-looking; fine, fine-looking.

благополу́чи|**е, я,** *n.* well-being; prosperity.

благополу́чно, *adv.* well, all right; happily; safely; всё ко́нчилось б. everything turned out happily.

благополу́ч|**ный** (~ен, ~на), *adj.* successful; safe; б. коне́ц happy ending.

благоприобре́тени|**е, я,** *n.* (*obs.*) acquisition.

благоприобре́тенн|**ый,** *adj.* acquired; всё иму́щество у него́ ~ое, не насле́дственное his property is entirely acquired, not inherited.

благопристо́йност|**ь, и,** *f.* decency, decorum.

благопристо́|**йный** (~ен, ~йна), *adj.* (*obs.*) decent, decorous.

благоприя́т|**ный** (~ен, ~на), *adj.* favourable; propitious; ~ные ве́сти good news.

благоприя́тств|**овать, ую,** *impf.* (+*d.*) to favour; наибо́лее ~уемая держа́ва (*econ.*) most favoured nation.

благоразу́ми|**е, я,** *n.* prudence; sense.

благоразу́м|ный (~ен, ~на), *adj.* prudent; sensible.

благорасположе́ни|е, я, *n.* (*obs.*) favour.

благорасполо́жен|ный (~, ~на), *adj.* (*obs.*) favourably disposed.

благораствори́|е, я, *n.* б. возду́хов (*eccl.*; *often joc.*) healthful climate.

благоро́ди|е, я, *n.* (*obs.*) ва́ше б. (*term of address to officers of rank up to and including that of captain*) your Honour.

благоро́д|ный (~ен, ~на), *adj.* noble; б. газ noble gas; б. мета́лл precious metal; на ~ном расстоя́нии at a decent distance.

благоро́дств|о, а, *n.* nobleness; nobility.

благоскло́нность|ь, и, *f.* favour; по́льзоваться чье́й-н. ~ью to be in someone's good graces.

благоскло́н|ный (~ен, ~на), *adj.* favourable; gracious.

благослове́ни|е, я, *n.* (*eccl. and fig.*) blessing; benediction; подойти́ под б. (+*d.*) to ask a blessing (from); с ~я (+*g.*) with the blessing (of), with the consent (of).

благослове́н|ный (~, ~на), *adj.* (*eccl., poet.*) blessed, blest.

благослов|и́ть, лю́, и́шь, *pf.* (*of* ~ля́ть) 1. to bless; to give one's blessing (to). 2. to be grateful to; б. свою́ судьбу́ to thank one's stars.

благослов|и́ться, лю́сь, и́шься, *pf.* (*of* ~ля́ться) (*coll.*) 1. (у+*g.*) to receive the blessing (of). 2. to cross oneself.

благослов|ля́ть(ся), ля́ю(сь), *impf. of* ~и́ть(ся).

благосостоя́ни|е, я, *n.* well-being, welfare.

благотвори́тел|ь, я, *m.* philanthropist.

благотвори́тельност|ь, и, *f.* charity, philanthropy.

благотвори́тельный, *adj.* charitable, philanthropic; б. спекта́кль charity performance.

благотво́р|ный (~ен, ~на), *adj.* beneficial; wholesome, salutary.

благоусмотре́ни|е, я, *n.* (*obs.*) consideration; отда́ть на чье́-н. б. to submit for someone's consideration.

благоустра́ива|ть, ю, *impf. of* благоустро́ить.

благоустро́ен|ный (~, ~на), *p.p.p. of* благоустро́ить *and adj.* well-equipped, improved; comfortable; б. дом house with all modern conveniences.

благоустро́|ить, ю, ишь, *pf.* (*of* благоустра́ивать) to equip with services and utilities; to improve.

благоустро́йств|о, а, *n.* equipping with services and utilities; improvement; отде́л ~а department of public services and utilities; б. се́льских посёлков improvement of rural settlements.

благоуха́ни|е, я, *n.* fragrance.

благоуха́нный, *adj.* fragrant, sweet-smelling.

благоуха́|ть, ю, *impf.* to be fragrant, to smell sweet.

благочести́в|ый (~, ~а), *adj.* pious, devout.

благоче́сти|е, я, *n.* piety.

благочи́ни|е, я, *n.* 1. (*sing. only*) decency, decorum. 2. (*eccl.*) deanery.

благочи́нн|ый, *adj.* 1. (*obs.*) decent, decorous. 2. (*as noun eccl.*) б., ~ого, *m.* rural dean.

блаже́н|ный (~, ~на), *adj.* 1. blessed, blissful; (*eccl.*) the Blessed; ~ной па́мяти of blessed memory; ~ое состоя́ние (state of) bliss. 2. *as noun* б., ~ого, *m.* simple person.

блаже́нств|о, а, *n.* bliss, felicity; на верху́ ~а in perfect bliss.

блаже́нств|овать, ую, *impf.* to be in a state of bliss.

блаж|и́ть, у́, и́шь, *impf.* (*coll.*) to be capricious; to indulge whims; to be eccentric.

блажно́й, *adj.* (*coll.*) capricious; eccentric.

блаж|ь, и, *f.* (*coll.*) whim, caprice.

бла́нжевый, *adj.* (*obs.*) flesh-coloured.

бланк, а, *m.* form; анке́тный б. questionnaire; б. зака́за на кни́гу order slip for book (*in library*); запо́лнить б. to fill in a form.

бла́нк|овый, *adj.* of ~; ~овая на́дпись endorsement.

бланманже́, *indecl., n.* blancmange.

блат, а, *m.* (*sl.*) 1. crime. 2. pull, protection, influence; получи́ть по ~у to get on the quiet, come by through influence. 3. thieves' cant, thieves' Latin.

блатме́йстер, а, *m.* (*sl.*) racketeer.

блатн|о́й, *adj.* (*sl.*) criminal; ~а́я му́зыка thieves' cant, thieves' Latin.

блатня́г|а, и, *m.* (*sl.*) racketeer.

бл|ева́ть, юю, юёшь, *impf.* (*vulg.*) to puke.

блево́тин|а, ы, *f.* (*vulg.*) 1. vomit. 2. (*fig.*) filth.

бледне́|ть, ю, ешь, *impf.* (*of по~*) to grow pale; to pale.

бледноли́ц|ый, *adj.* pale; *as noun* б., ~ого, *m.* paleface.

бле́дност|ь, и, *f.* paleness, pallor.

бле́д|ный (~ен, ~на́, ~но), *adj.* pale, pallid; б. как полотно́ white as a sheet; (*fig.*) colourless, insipid; ~ная не́мочь (*med.*) chlorosis.

блёкл|ый, *adj.* faded; wan; ~ая руда́ (*min.*) tetrahedrite.

блёк|нуть, ну, нешь, *past* ~, ~ла, *impf.* (*of по~*) to fade; to wither.

блéнноррé|я, и, *f.* (*med.*) blennorrhoea.

блеск, а, *m.* 1. brightness, brilliance, shine; splendour, magnificence; б. наря́да finery;

б. остроу́мия brilliance of wit; б. со́лнца brightness of the sun; во всём ∼е in all (one's) glory; прида́ть б. to add lustre (to); игра́ть с ∼ом на роя́ле to play the piano brilliantly. **2.** (*min.*) желе́зный б. haematite; свинцо́вый б. galena.

блесн|а́, ы́, *f.* spoon-bait.

блесн|у́ть, у́, ёшь, *pf.* to flash; to shine; у меня́ ∼у́ла мысль a thought flashed across my mind; у нас ∼у́ла наде́жда we saw a ray of hope.

бле|сте́ть, щу́, сти́шь and ∼ще́шь, *impf.* to shine (*also fig.*); to glitter; to sparkle; её глаза́ ∼сте́ли ра́достью her eyes shone with joy; он не ∼щет умо́м he is not over-blessed with intelligence, he does not shine.

блёстк|а, и, *f.* **1.** sparkle; ∼и остроу́мия flashes of wit. **2.** spangle, sequin; усе́янный ∼ами spangled.

блестя́щ|ий (∼, ∼а, ∼е), *pres. part. of* блесте́ть and *adj.* shining, bright; (*fig.*) brilliant; б. ум brilliant mind.

блеф, а, *m.* bluff; его́ угро́зы оказа́лись чи́стым ∼ом his threats turned out to be pure bluff.

блеф|ова́ть, у́ю, *impf.* (*coll.*) to bluff.

бле|щу́, ∼ще́шь, *see* ∼сте́ть.

бле́яни|е, я, *n.* bleat(ing).

бле́|ять, ю, ешь, *impf.* to bleat.

ближа́йш|ий, *superl. of* бли́зкий nearest; next; immediate; в ∼ем бу́дущем in the near future; б. друг closest friend; б. нача́льник immediate superior; б. по́вод (*leg., philos.*) proximate cause, immediate cause; б. ро́дственник next of kin; при ∼ем рассмотре́нии on closer examination; ∼ее уча́стие personal participation.

бли́|же, *comp. of* ∼зкий, ∼зко nearer; (*fig.*) closer.

ближневосто́чный, *adj.* Near-Eastern.

бли́жн|ий, *adj.* **1.** near; neighbouring. **2.** (*mil.*) short range, close range, close; б. ого́нь close (range) fire. **3.** near, close (*of kinship*); *as noun* б., ∼его, *m.* (*fig.*) one's neighbour; люби́ть ∼его to love one's neighbour.

близ, *prep.*+*g.* near, close to, by.

бли́|зиться, жусь, зишься, *impf.* to approach, draw near.

бли́з|кий (∼ок, ∼ка́, ∼ко), adj. 1. near, close; на ∼ком расстоя́нии at a short distance, a short way off; at close range. **2.** (*of time*) near; imminent; ∼кое бу́дущее the near future. **3.** intimate, close, near; б. ро́дственник near relation; быть ∼ким с кем-н. to be on intimate terms with someone; быть ∼ким (+*d.*) to be dear (to); *as noun* ∼кие, ∼ких one's nearest and dearest, one's people. **4.** (к) like; similar (to); close (to); б. нам по ду́ху челове́к

kindred spirit; ∼кая ко́пия faithful copy; ∼кая те́ма congenial topic.

бли́зко, *adv.* **1.** (от) near, close (to); close by. **2.** (*fig., coll.*) nearly, closely; б. каса́ться (+*g.*) to concern nearly; б. познако́миться (с+*i.*) to become closely acquainted (with). **3.** *as pred.* it is not far; ему́ б. ходи́ть he has not far to go.

близлежа́щий, *adj.* neighbouring, near-by.

близне́ц, а́, *m.* twin (*also* triplet, *etc.*); Близнецы́ (*astron.*) Gemini.

близору́к|ий (∼, ∼a), *adj.* short-sighted (*also fig.*).

близору́кост|ь, и, *f.* short-sightedness; (*med.*) myopia (*also fig.*).

бли́зост|ь, и, *f.* nearness, closeness, proximity; intimacy.

блик, а, *m.* speck, patch of light; light, highlight; со́лнечный б. patch of sunlight; ∼и на карти́не lights in a picture.

блин, а́, *m.* blin (*kind of pancake*); пе́рвый б. ко́мом (*prov.*) practice makes perfect!; пло́ский как б. flat as a pancake.

блинда́ж, а́, *m.* (*mil.*) dug-out.

блиндир|ова́ть, у́ю, *impf. and pf.* (*mil.*) to blind.

бли́н|чатый, *adj. of* ∼; б. пиро́г pancake pie (*made with pancakes, eggs and kasha*).

бли́нчик, а, *m.* pancake; fritter.

блиста́тельност|ь, и, *f.* brilliance, splendour.

блиста́тел|ьный (∼ен, ∼ьна), *adj.* brilliant, splendid.

блиста́|ть ю, *impf.* to shine; б. отсу́тствием (*iron.*) to be conspicuous by one's absence.

блок¹, а, *m.* (*tech.*) block, pulley, sheave.

блок², а, *m.* (*polit.*) bloc.

блока́д|а, ы, *f.* blockade; снять ∼у to raise the blockade; прорва́ть ∼у to run the blockade.

блок-аппара́т, а, *m.* (*railways*) signal-box.

блокга́уз, а, *m.* (*mil.*) blockhouse.

блоки́р|овать, ую, *impf. and pf.* **1.** to blockade. **2.** (*railways*) to block.

блоки́р|оваться, уюсь, *impf. and pf.* **1.** *pass. of* ∼ова́ть. **2.** (с+*i.*; *polit.*) to form a bloc with.

блокиро́вк|а, и, *f.* (*railways*) block system, signal system.

блокиро́в|очный, *adj. of* ∼ка.

блокно́т, а, *m.* notebook, small writing-pad.

блокпо́ст, а, *m.* (*railways*) blockhouse.

блок-уча́ст|ок, ка, *m.* (*railways*) block section.

бло́нд|а, ы, *f.* (*usu. pl.*) white silk lace.

блонди́н, а, *m.* fair-haired man.

блонди́нист|ый (∼, ∼a), *adj.* (*coll.*) blonde, fair.

блонди́нк|а, и, *f.* blonde, fair woman.

блох|а́, и́, *pl.* ~и, ~а́м, *f.* flea.

бло|ши́ный, *adj. of.* ~ха́; б. уку́с flea-bite.

бло́ш|ки, ек, *f.* tiddly-winks; игра́ть в б. to play tiddly-winks.

блуд, а, *m.* lechery, fornication.

блу|ди́ть[1], жу́, ди́шь, *impf.* to lecher, fornicate.

блу|ди́ть[2], жу́, ~ди́шь, *impf.* (*coll.*) to wander, roam.

блудли́в|ый (~, ~а), *adj.* 1. lascivious, lecherous. 2. mischievous, roguish; thievish; ~ как кот, трусли́в как за́яц thievish as a cat, timid as a hare.

блу́дн|и, ей, *no sing.* (*coll.*) 1. debauchery, lechery. 2. getting up to mischief.

блудни́к, а́, *m.* (*obs.*) lecher, fornicator.

блудни́ц|а, ы, *f.* (*obs.*) 1. fornicatress, loose woman. 2. whore.

блу́д|ный, *adj. of* ~; б. сын (*eccl. and fig.*) prodigal son.

блужда́ни|е, я, *n.* wandering, roaming.

блужда́|ть, ю, *impf.* to roam, wander; to rove; б. по у́лицам to roam the streets.

блужда́|ющий, *pres. part. of* ~ть; б. взгляд vague, wandering expression; ~ющие звёзды (*obs.*) the planets; б. нерв (*anat.*) vagus (nerve); б. огонёк will-o'-the-wisp; ~ющая по́чка (*med.*) floating kidney.

блу́з|а, ы, *f.* (working) blouse; smock.

блу́зк|а, и, *f.* blouse (*worn only by women*).

блу́зник, а, *m.* (*coll., obs.*) labourer.

блу́минг = блю́минг.

блю́деч|ко, ка, *pl.* ~ки, ~ек, ~кам, *n.* saucer; small dish; б. для варе́нья jam plate.

блю́д|о, а, *n.* dish (*concr. and abstr.*); обе́д из трёх ~ three-course dinner; вку́сное б. a tasty dish; как на ~е (*of visibility of objects situated on even, open ground*) as on the palm of one's hand.

блюдоли́з, а, *m.* (*coll.*) sponger.

блю́|ду́, дёшь, *see* ~сти́.

блю́д|це, ца, *g. pl.* ~ец, *n.* saucer.

блю́минг, а, *m.* (*tech.*) blooming (mill).

блю|сти́, ду́, дёшь, *past* ~л, ~ла́, *impf.* (*obs.*) to guard, watch over; to observe; б. зако́ны to abide by the law; б. поря́док to keep order.

блюсти́тел|ь, я, *m.* keeper, guardian; б. поря́дка (*coll., iron.*) arm of the law.

блю́|ю, ёшь, *see* блева́ть.

бля́д|ский, *adj. of* ~ь.

бляд|ь, и, *f.* (*vulg.*) whore (*especially as term of abuse, also used as interj.*).

бля́х|а, и, *f.* 1. name plate; number plate. 2. ме́дная б. (*as ornament on harness*) horse brass.

боа́, *indecl.* 1. (*m.*) (*zool.*) boa, boa-constrictor. 2. (*n.*) boa; мехово́е б. fur (boa).

боб, а́, *m.* bean; туре́цкий б. kidney bean, haricot; ~ы́ разводи́ть (*coll.*) to talk nonsense; оста́ться, сиде́ть на ~а́х (*coll.*) to get nothing for one's pains.

боб|ёр, ра́, *m.* 1. (*sing. only*) beaver (fur). 2. (*pl. only*) beaver collar.

боби́н|а, ы, *f.* (*tech.*) bobbin.

бобк|и́, о́в, *no sing.* (*bot.*) bayberries.

бобко́в|ый, *adj.* bay; ~ое ма́сло bay-oil.

боб|о́вый 1. *adj. of* ~; б. стручо́к bean-pod. 2. *as noun* ~о́вые, ~о́вых leguminous plants.

бобр, а́, *m.* beaver; уби́ть ~а́ to come off well, be in luck (*also iron.*).

бо́брик, а, *m.* (*text.*) beaver, castor; во́лосы ~ом (*coll.*) French crop; crew cut; постри́чься ~ом to have a French crop, crew cut.

бобр|о́вый, *adj. of* ~; beaver; beaver-fur; ~о́вая струя́ (*med.*) castoreum.

бобы́л|ь, я́, *m.* 1. (*obs.*) poor, landless peasant. 2. solitary, lonely man; жить ~ём to lead a solitary, lonely existence.

Бог, а, *vocative sing.* Бо́же, *m.* God; god; Бо́же мой! good God!, my God!; Б. зна́ет! Б. весть! God knows!; Б. его́ зна́ет who knows!; не дай Б.! God forbid!; ра́ди ~а! for God's sake!; с ~ом! (*obs.*) good luck!; сла́ва ~у! thank God!; как Б. на́ душу поло́жит anyhow, at random; Б. с ним let it pass; good luck to him (*iron.*); обе́дать чем Б. посла́л to take pot luck; а он дава́й Б. но́ги he took to his heels.

богаде́лк|а, и, *f.* alms-woman.

богаде́л|ьня, ьни, *g. pl.* ~ен, *f.* almshouse, workhouse.

богар|а́, ы́, *f.* dry-farming (*in Central Asia*); dry-farming land.

бога́р|ный, *adj. of* ~а́.

богате́|й, я, *m.* (*coll.*) rich man.

богате́|ть, ю, ешь, *impf.* (*of* раз~) to grow rich.

бога́тств|о, а, *n.* 1. riches, wealth; есте́ственные ~а natural resources. 2. (*fig.*) richness, wealth.

бога́т|ый (~, ~а), *adj.* (+*i.*) rich (in), wealthy; страна́, ~ая го́рными проду́ктами a country rich in mineral products; ~ая расти́тельность luxuriant vegetation; б. переплёт a luxurious binding; б. о́пыт wide experience; чем ~ы, тем и ра́ды you are welcome to whatever we have; *as noun* б., ~ого, *m.* rich man.

богаты́р|ский, *adj. of* ~ь; heroic; (*fig.*) powerful, mighty, Herculean; б. э́пос the Russian folk-epic; ~ское сложе́ние powerful physique; б. сон profound sleep.

богаты́рств|о, а, *n.* 1. heroic qualities. 2. (*collect.*) bogatyrs.

богаты́р|ь, я́, *m.* 1. bogatyr (*hero in Russian folklore*). 2. (*fig.*) Hercules; hero.

богáч, á, *m.* rich man; ~и́ (*collect.*) the rich.

богдыхáн, a, *m.* (*hist.*) Chinese emperor.

богéм|a, ы, *f.* (*fig.*) Bohemia; Bohemianism.

богéм|ный, *adj. of* ~a.

богéмский, *adj.* (*geogr.*) Bohemian.

боги́н|я, и, *f.* goddess (*also fig.*).

богобóр|ец, ца, *m.* theomachist.

богобóр|ческий, *adj. of* ~ец.

богобоя́знен|ный (~, ~на), *adj.* god-fearing.

богоискáтел|ь, я, *m.* 'God-seeker'.

богомáз, a, *m.* (*coll.*) icon-dauber.

Богомáтер|ь, и, *f.* Mother of God.

богомéрзкий, *adj.* (*obs.*) 1. impious. 2. (*coll.*) hideous, repulsive.

богомóл, a, *m.* (*zool.*) praying mantis.

богомóл|ец, ьца, *m.* 1. devout person. 2. pilgrim. 3. one who prays (for someone else).

богомóл|ка, ки, *f.* 1. (*zool.*) = ~. 2. *f. of* ~ец.

богомóль|е, я, *n.* pilgrimage.

богомóль|ный (~ен, ~ьна), *adj.* religious, devout.

богонóс|ец, ца, *m.* bearer of religious mission; нарóд-б. the Chosen People.

богоотстýпник, a, *m.* apostate.

богоотстýпничеств|о, a, *n.* apostasy.

богоподóб|ный (~ен, ~на), *adj.* god-like.

богопроти́в|ный (~ен, ~на), *adj.* 1. (*obs.*) impious. 2. (*coll.*) hideous, repulsive.

Богорóдиц|а, ы, *f.* the Virgin, Our Lady; сидéть ~ей (*coll., iron.*) to sit with arms folded.

богорóдич|ен, на, *m.* (*eccl.*) hymn in praise of the Virgin.

богослóв, a, *m.* theologian.

богослóви|е, я, *n.* theology.

богослóвский, *adj.* theological.

богослужé|бный, *adj. of* ~ние; liturgical; ~бная кни́га prayer-book.

богослужéни|е, я, *n.* divine service, worship; liturgy.

богоспасáемый, *adj.* blessed (*usu. iron.*).

боготвор|и́ть, ю, и́шь, *impf.* 1. to worship, idolize. 2. to deify.

богоугóд|ный (~ен, ~на), *adj.* (*obs.*) pleasing to God; ~ное заведéние charitable institution.

богохýльник, a, *m.* blasphemer.

богохýльный, *adj.* blasphemous.

богохýльств|о, a, *n.* blasphemy.

богохýльств|овать, ую, *impf.* to blaspheme.

богочеловéк, a, *m.* (*theol.*) 'God-Man', God incarnate.

Богоявлéни|е, я, *n.* (*eccl.*) Epiphany.

бодá|ть, ю, *impf.* (*of* за~) to butt.

бодá|ться, юсь, *impf.* to butt (*intrans.*).

бодли́вост|ь, и, *f.* disposition to butt.

бодли́в|ый (~, ~a), *adj.* given to butting; ~ая корóва a cow that butts.

бодн|ýть, ý, ёшь, *pf.* to butt, give a butt.

бодр|и́ть, ю́, и́шь, *impf.* to stimulate, invigorate; здéшний вóздух óчень ~и́т it is very bracing here.

бодр|и́ться, ю́сь, и́шься, *impf.* to try to keep one's spirits up, try to be cheerful.

бóдрост|ь, и, *f.* cheerfulness; courage; good spirits.

бóдрствовани|е, я, *n.* keeping awake; vigilance.

бóдрств|овать, ую, *impf.* to be awake, stay awake; to keep awake, keep vigil; ей пришлóсь б. всю ночь при больнóм she had to sit up all night with the sick man.

бóдр|ый (~, ~á, ~o), *adj.* cheerful, bright; hale and hearty.

бодр|я́щий, *pres. part. of* ~и́ть *and adj.* invigorating, bracing.

бодя́г|а, и, *f.* fresh-water sponge.

боеви́к, á, *m.* 1. (*obs.*) member of revolutionary fighting group. 2. (*coll.*) hit; б. сезóна the hit of the season.

боев|óй, *adj.* 1. fighting, battle; ~ы́е дéйствия operations; б. дух fighting spirit; в б. готóвности prepared for action, cleared for action; ~óе крещéние baptism of fire; б. патрóн live cartridge; б. поря́док battle formation; ~ы́е припáсы (live) ammunition; ~áя пружи́на mainspring (*of gun*). 2. urgent; ~áя задáча urgent task. 3. (*coll.*) militant; energetic; pushing; ~áя бáба virago. 4. б. механи́зм striking mechanism (*of clock*).

боеголóвк|а, и, *f.* (*mil.*) warhead.

бо|ёк, йкá, *m.* (*tech.*) firing-pin.

боеприпáс|ы, ов, *no sing.* ammunition.

боеспосóбност|ь, и, *f.* (*mil.*) fighting efficiency, fighting value.

боеспосóб|ный (~ен, ~на), *adj.* (*mil.*) efficient, battle-worthy.

бо|éц, йцá, *m.* 1. fighter; private soldier; ~йцы́ пéрвой áрмии the men of the First Army; петýх-б. fighting-cock. 2. butcher; slaughterman.

божб|á, ы́, *f.* swearing.

Бóже, *see* Бог.

бóжеск|ий, *adj.* 1. (*obs.*) divine. 2. (*coll.*) fair, just; ~ая ценá a fair price.

божéственност|ь, и, *f.* divinity; divine nature.

божéствен|ный (~, ~на), *adj.* divine (*also fig.*); б. гóлос divine voice.

божеств|ó, á, *n.* deity, divine being.

бóж|ий, *adj.* God's; б. человéк simple, otherworldly person; я́сно, как б. день it is as clear as noonday; ~ья корóвка (*zool.*) ladybird.

бож|и́ться, у́сь, ~ишься, *impf.* (*of* по~) to swear.

божни́ц|а, ы, *f.* **1.** icon-case. **2.** (*dial.*) chapel.

бож|о́к, ка́, *m.* idol (*also fig.*).

бо|й¹, я, *pl.* **~й, ~ёв,** *m.* **1.** battle, fight, action, combat; **~й** fighting; **в ~ю́** in action; **без ~я** without striking a blow; **взять с ~я** to take by force; **кула́чный б.** fisticuffs; **петуши́ный б.** cock-fight; **б. быко́в** bullfight. **2.** beating; **бить сме́ртным ~ем** to thrash within an inch of one's life. **3.** striking, strike (*of a clock*); **часы́ с ~ем** striking clock; **бараба́нный б.** drum-beat. **4.** killing, slaughtering; **б. кито́в** whaling; **б. тюле́ней** sealing. **5.** breakage; broken objects; **в после́дней па́ртии посу́ды бы́ло мно́го ~я** in the last consignment of crockery there were many breakages. **6.** accuracy (*of fire-arm*); **винто́вка с хоро́шим ~ем** accurate rifle.

бо|й², я, *pl.* **~и, ~ев,** *m.* message-boy; office-boy.

бой³-, *as indecl. adj. in compounds* lively, energetic; **б.-ба́б|а, ы,** *f.* virago; **б.-де́вк|а, и,** *f.* tomboy.

бо́|йкий (~ек, ~йка́, ~йко), *adj.* **1.** bold, spry, smart; **б. ум** ready wit; **б. язы́к** glib tongue. **2.** lively, animated; **~йкая торго́вля** brisk trade; **~йкая у́лица** busy street.

бо́йкост|ь, и, *f.* (*coll.*) **1.** smartness; glibness. **2.** liveliness, animation.

бойко́т, а, *m.* boycott; **объяви́ть б.** (+*d.*) to declare a boycott (of).

бойкоти́р|овать, ую, *impf.* to boycott.

бойни́ц|а, ы, *f.* loop-hole, embrasure.

бо́йн|я, и, *g. pl.* **бо́ен,** *f.* slaughter-house, abattoir; (*fig.*) slaughter, butchery, carnage.

бойска́ут, а. *m.* Boy Scout.

бойскаути́зм, а, *m.* scouting; the Boy Scout movement.

бойцо́вый, *adj.* fighting; **б. пету́х** fighting-cock.

бо́йче, *comp. of* **бо́йк|ий, ~о.**

бок, а, о ~е, на ~у́, *pl.* **~а́,** *m.* side; flank; **в б.** sideways; **взять за ~а́** to put the screw on; **схвати́ться за ~а́** (**от сме́ха**) to split one's sides (with laughter); **на́ б.** sideways, to the side; **на ~у́** on one side; **б. о́ б.** side by side; **по́ ~у** away with; **по́ ~у уче́ние!** (we've done) enough studying!; **под ~ом** near by, close at hand; **с ~у** from the side, from the flank; **с ~у на́ б.** from side to side.

бока́л, а, *m.* glass, goblet; **подня́ть б.** (**за**+*a.*) to drink the health (of), raise one's glass (to).

боков|о́й, *adj.* side, flank, lateral, sidelong;

~а́я ка́чка (*naut.*) rolling; **~а́я ли́ния** collateral line; **~а́я у́лица** side-street; **отпра́виться на ~у́ю** (*coll.*) to go to bed, turn in.

бо́ком, *adv.* **1.** sideways; **ходи́ть б.** to sidle. **2. вы́йти б.** (*coll.*) to turn out badly, give trouble.

бокс¹, а, *m.* (*sport*) boxing.

бокс², а, *m.* (*tech.*) boxcalf.

бокс³, а, *m.* boxer cut (*masculine hair-style, with hair short or shaved back and sides*).

бокс⁴, а, *m.* box (*isolation compartment in hospital*).

боксёр, а, *m.* (*sport*) boxer.

бокси́р|овать, ую, *impf.* (*sport*) to box.

бокси́т, а, *m.* (*min.*) bauxite.

бо́ксовый, *adj.* boxcalf.

болва́н, а, *m.* (*coll.*) **1.** blockhead, dolt. **2.** block (*esp. for shaping headgear*). **3.** (*in card-games*) dummy. **4.** (*obs.*) idol.

болва́нк|а, и, *f.* **1.** (*tech.*) pig (*of iron, etc.*); **желе́зо в ~ax** pig-iron. **2.** block (*for shaping headgear*).

болга́р|ин, ина, *pl.* **~ы, ~,** *m.* Bulgarian.

болга́рк|а, и, *f.* Bulgarian (woman).

болга́рский, *adj.* Bulgarian.

бо́ле (*obs.*) = **бо́лее.**

болев|о́й, *adj.* of **боль;** **~о́е ощуще́ние** sensation of pain.

бо́лее, *adv.* more; **б. ро́бкий** more timid; **б. то́лстый** thicker; **б. и б.** more and more; **он всё б. и б. слабе́л** he was growing gradually weaker and weaker; **б. и́ли ме́нее** more or less; **не б. и не ме́нее, как** neither more nor less than; **б. всего́** most of all; **тем б., что** especially as.

боле́зненност|ь, и, *f.* **1.** sickliness; abnormality, morbidity. **2.** painfulness.

боле́знен|ный (~, ~на), *adj.* **1.** sickly; unhealthy; **б. румя́нец** unhealthy flush; (*fig.*) abnormal, morbid; **~ное любопы́тство** morbid curiosity. **2.** painful.

болезнетво́рный, *adj.* (*med.*) morbific.

боле́зный, *adj.* (*dial.*) piteous; **мой б.!** poor thing!; my dear one!

боле́зн|ь, и, *f.* illness; disease; (*fig.*) abnormality; **б. ро́ста** growing pains.

боле́льщик, а, *m.* (*coll.*) fan, supporter.

болеро́, *indecl., n.* (*Spanish dance or woman's jacket*) bolero.

боле́|ть¹, ю, ешь, *impf.* **1.** (+*i.*) to be ill, to be down (with); (*intrans.*) to ail; **она́ с де́тства ~ет а́стмой** she has suffered from asthma ever since she was a child; **б. душо́й** (о+*p.*) to be worried (about). **2.** (**за**+*a.*; *coll.*) to be a fan (of), support.

бол|е́ть², 1st and 2nd persons not used, ~и́т, *impf.* to ache, hurt; **у меня́ зу́бы ~я́т** I have toothache; **у него́ ~и́т в у́хе** he has ear-ache; **у меня́ душа́ ~и́т** (о+*p.*) my heart bleeds (for, over).

болеутоля́ющ|ий, *adj.* soothing, analgesic; ~ее сре́дство (*med.*) anodyne, analgesic.

боливи́|ец, йца, *m.* Bolivian.

боливи́йк|а, и, *f.* Bolivian (woman).

боливи́йский, *adj.* Bolivian.

болиголо́в, а, *m.* (*bot.*) hemlock.

боли́д, а, *m.* (*astron.*) fireball.

боло́нк|а, и, *f.* lap-dog.

боло́тист|ый (~, ~а), *adj.* marshy, boggy, swampy.

боло́тн|ый, *adj.* marsh; ~ая вода́ stagnant water; б. газ marsh gas; ~ая лихора́дка marsh fever, malaria.

боло́т|о, а, *n.* marsh, bog, swamp; торфяно́е б. peatbog; (*fig.*) mire, slough.

болт, а́, *m.* (*tech.*) bolt; нарезно́й б. screw-bolt; скрепля́ть ~а́ми to bolt.

болта́нк|а, и, *f.* (*aeron.; coll.*) bumps.

болта́|ть¹, ю, *impf.* **1.** to stir; to shake; б. ло́жкой в ча́шке ча́ю to stir one's tea with a spoon. **2.** (+*i.*) to dangle (*arms or legs*).

болта́|ть², ю, *impf.* (*coll.*) to chatter, jabber, natter; б. глу́пости to drivel; б. по-неме́цки, по-францу́зски, *etc.*, to jabber German, French, *etc.*; б. языко́м to wag one's tongue.

болта́|ться¹, юсь, *impf.* (*coll.*) **1.** to dangle, swing; to hang loosely; он так похуде́л, вся оде́жда ~ется на нём he has grown so thin that this clothes all hang on him. **2.** to hang about, loaf; чего́ вы тут весь день ~етесь? why do you hang about here all day?

болта́|ться², ется, *impf.* (*coll.*) *pass. of* ~ть²; здесь ~ется мно́го вздо́ру a lot of nonsense is being talked here.

болтли́вост|ь, и, *f.* garrulity, talkativeness.

болтли́в|ый (~, ~а), *adj.* garrulous, talkative; indiscreet.

болтн|у́ть¹, у́, ёшь, *pf.* to give a stir, give a shake.

болтн|у́ть², у́, ёшь, *pf.* to blurt out.

болтн|у́ться, ~ётся, *pf.* to work loose; to come off.

болтовн|я́, и́, *f.* (*coll.*) talk; chatter; gossip; пуста́я б. idle talk.

болторе́зный, *adj.* (*tech.*) б. стано́к bolt-screwing machine.

болту́н¹, а́, *m.* (*coll.*) **1.** talker, chatterer; chatterbox. **2.** gossip.

болту́н², а́, *m.* addled egg.

болту́н|ья, ьи, *g. pl.* ~ий, *f. of* ~¹.

болту́шк|а, и, *f.* (*coll.*) **1.** = болту́нья. **2.** scrambled eggs. **3.** swill, mash. **4.** whisk.

бол|ь, и, *f.* pain; ache; б. в боку́ stitch; зубна́я б. toothache; душе́вная б. mental anguish.

больни́ц|а, ы, *f.* hospital; лечь в ~у to go to hospital; лежа́ть в ~е to be in hospital; вы́писаться из ~ы to be discharged from hospital.

больни́|чный, *adj. of* ~ца; ~чная ка́сса hospital fund, club; б. листо́к medical certificate.

бо́льно¹, *adv.* **1.** painfully, badly; б. уши́биться to be badly bruised. **2.** *as pred.* it is painful (*also fig.*); мне б. дыша́ть it hurts me to breathe; б., что мы должны́ расста́ться I am sorry that we have to part.

бо́льно², *adv.* (*coll.*) very, exceedingly, badly; он б. хитёр he is exceedingly wily; мне б. уж хо́чется пить I badly want a drink.

бол|ьно́й (~ен, ~ьна́), *adj.* ill, sick; diseased; sore (*also fig.*); ~ьны́е дёсны sore gums; б. зуб bad tooth; он тяжело́ ~ен he is seriously ill; б. вопро́с sore subject; ~ьно́е ме́сто sore spot; свали́ть с б. головы́ на здоро́вую, *see* голова́; *as noun* б., ~ьно́го, *m.*; ~ьна́я, ~ьно́й, *f.* patient, invalid; амбулато́рный б. out-patient; стациона́рный б. in-patient.

больша́к, а́, *m.* (*dial.*) **1.** head of the family. **2.** high road.

бо́льше 1. (*comp. of* большо́й *and* вели́кий) bigger, larger; greater; Ло́ндон б. Пари́жа London is larger than Paris. **2.** (*comp. of* мно́го) more; чем б... тем б. the more ... the more; б. того́ and what is more; б. не no more, no longer; он б. не живёт на той у́лице he does not live in that street any longer; б. не бу́ду! I won't do it again!; б. нет вопро́сов? any more questions? **3.** *adv.* (*coll.*) for the most part.

большевиза́ци|я, и, *f.* bolshevization.

большевизи́р|овать, ую, *impf. and pf.* to bolshevize.

большеви́зм, а, *m.* Bolshevism.

большеви́к, а́, *m.* Bolshevik.

большеви́стский, *adj.* Bolshevik, Bolshevist.

большеголо́вый, *adj.* with a large head; macrocephalous.

бо́льш|ий, *comp. of* ~о́й *and* вели́кий; greater, larger; ~ей ча́стью, по ~ей ча́сти for the most part; са́мое ~ee at most; съезд бу́дет продолжа́ться са́мое ~ee три дня the congress will last at most three days.

большинств|о́, а́, *n.* majority; most (of); в ~е́ слу́чаев in most cases; б. голосо́в a majority vote.

больш|о́й, *adj.* big, large; great; large-scale; (*coll.*) grown-up; ~а́я бу́ква capital (letter); ~а́я доро́га high road; ~ое знако́мство wide range of acquaintance; б. па́лец thumb; б. па́лец ноги́ big toe; на б. па́лец (*coll.*) in first-rate fashion, top-hole; ~о́й ско́ростью (*railways*) by fast goods (train); б. свет haut monde, society; когда́ я бу́ду б. when I grow up.

большу́х|а, и, *f.* (*dial.*) mistress (of the house).

большу́щий, *adj.* (*coll.*) huge.
боля́чк|а, и, *f.* sore; scab; (*fig.*) defect.
бол|я́щий, *pres. part. of* ~еть²; *as noun* б., ~я́щего, *m.* (*usu. joc.*) the patient.
бо́мб|а, ы, *f.* bomb.
бомбарди́р, а, *m.* 1. (*mil., hist.*) bombardier. 2. (*aeron.*) bomb-aimer. 3. (*zool.*) bombardier (*beetle*).
бомбарди́р|ова́ть, у́ю, *impf.* to bombard; б. про́сьбами (*fig.*) to bombard with requests.
бомбардиро́вк|а, и, *f.* bombardment.
бомбардиро́вочный, *adj.* bombing.
бомбардиро́вщик, а, *m.* 1. bomber; пики́рующий б. dive-bomber; сре́дний б. medium bomber. 2. (*coll.*) bomber pilot.
бомбёжк|а, и, *f.* (*coll.*) bombing.
бомб|и́ть, лю́, и́шь, *impf.* to bomb.
бомбово́з, а, *m.* bomber.
бо́мб|овый, *adj. of* ~а; б. люк bomb-bay door (*on aircraft*); ~овая нагру́зка bomb-load; б. уда́р thud of exploding bomb.
бомбодержа́тел|ь, я, *m.* bomb-rack.
бомбомёт, а, *m.* (*mil.*) 1. (*naut.*) depth-charge gun. 2. (*obs.*) bomb-thrower.
бомбомета́ни|е, я, *n.* bomb-dropping, bomb-release.
бомбосбра́сывател|ь, я, *m.* bomb-release gear.
бомбоубе́жищ|е, а, *n.* air-raid shelter, bomb-proof shelter.
бом-бра́мсел|ь, я, *m.* (*naut.*) royal (sail).
бом-брам-сте́ньг|а, и, *f.* (*naut.*) royal mast.
бомо́нд, а, *m.* (*obs.*) beau monde, society.
бон, а, *m.* (*naut.*) boom.
бонапарти́зм, а, *m.* (*hist.*) Bonapartism.
бонапарти́ст, а, *m.* (*hist.*) Bonapartist.
бонбонье́рк|а, и, *f.* bonbonnière.
бонвива́н, а, *m.* bon vivant.
бонда́р|ить, ю, ишь, *impf.* (*dial.*) to cooper.
бонда́р|ный, *adj. of* ~ство; ~ное ремесло́ the cooper's craft.
бонда́р|ня, ни, *g. pl.* ~ен, *f.* cooperage.
бо́ндарств|о, а, *n.* coopering, cooperage.
бо́ндар|ь, я/я́, *m.* cooper.
бо́нз|а, ы, *g. pl.* ~, *m.* bonze (*Buddhist priest*); (*fig.*) superior, distant person.
бонмо́, *indecl., n.,* bon mot, witticism.
бонмоти́ст, а, *m.* wit.
бо́нн|а, ы, *f.* nursery-governess.
бонто́н, а, *m.* (*coll., obs.*) bon ton.
бо́н|ы, ~, *sing.* ~а, ~ы, *f.* 1. cheques; vouchers, tokens. 2. emergency paper money.
бор¹, а, о ~е, на ~у́, *pl.* ~ы́, ~о́в, *m.* coniferous forest; с ~у да с со́сенки, с ~у по со́сенке chosen at random; (я ви́жу), отку́да сыр б. загоре́лся (I see) how it all started.
бор², а, *m.* (*chem.*) boron.

бор|а́, ы́, *f.* bora (*NE. wind blowing in Black Sea and Adriatic*).
бу́ргес, а, *m.* (*typ.*) bourgeois.
борде́л|ь, я, *m.* (*coll.*) brothel.
бордо́ 1. *indecl., n.* claret. **2.** *as adj.* claret-coloured.
бордо́вый, *adj.* claret-coloured.
бордю́р, а, *m.* border (*of fabric*).
боре́ни|е, я, *n.* (*rhet.*) struggle, fight.
бор|е́ц, ца́, *m.* 1. (за+а.) fighter (for). 2. (*sport*) wrestler.
боржо́м, а (у), *m.* Borzhomi water; буты́лка ~у bottle of Borzhomi water.
борз|а́я, о́й, *f.* borzoi (*dog*).
борз|о́й, *adj. of* ~а́я.
борзопи́с|ец, ца, *m.* (*iron.*) hack writer.
бо́рзый, *adj.* (*obs. or poet.*) swift, fleet.
бормаши́н|а, ы, *f.* (dentist's) drill.
бормота́ни|е, я, *n.* muttering.
бормо|та́ть, чу́, ~чешь, *impf.* to mutter.
бормоту́н, а́, *m.* (*coll.*) 1. mutterer. 2. (*breed of pigeons*) drummer.
борм|очу́, о́чешь, *see* ~ота́ть.
бо́рн|ый, *adj.* (*chem.*) boric, boracic; ~ая кислота́ boric, boracic acid.
бо́ров¹, а, *m.* hog; (*fig.*) obese man.
бо́ров², а, *pl.* ~а́, *m.* (*tech.*) horizontal flue.
борови́к, а́, *m.* (*dial.*) (edible) boletus (*kind of mushroom*).
борови́нк|а, и, *f.* borovinka (*kind of winter apple*).
бор|ово́й, *adj. of* ~¹.
бор|ода́, оды́, *а.* ~оду, *pl.* ~оды, ~о́д, ~ода́м, *f.* 1. beard; отпусти́ть ~оду to grow a beard; смея́ться в ~оду to laugh into one's beard. 2. wattles (*of bird*).
борода́вк|а, и, *f.* wart.
борода́вчатый, *adj.* warty.
борода́ст|ый, *adj.* (*coll.*) long-bearded, heavily bearded.
борода́т|ый (~, ~а), *adj.* bearded.
борода́ч, а́, *m.* 1. (*coll.*) bearded man. 2. (*bot.*) beard grass. 3. (*orn.*) bearded vulture, lammergeyer.
боро́дк|а¹, и, *f.* small beard, tuft.
боро́дк|а², и, *f.* (*tech.*) key-bit.
бор|озда́, озды́, *а.* ~озду and ~озду́, *pl.* ~озды, ~о́зд, ~озда́м, *f.* furrow; (*anat.*) fissure.
бороз|ди́ть, жу́, ди́шь, *impf.* 1. (*pf.* вз~) to furrow; to leave a furrow behind one; (*fig.*) to leave a wake. 2. (*pf.* из~) to cover with furrows; морщи́ны ~ди́ли его́ лоб (*fig.*) wrinkles furrowed his brow; б. океа́ны (*poet.*) to plough, furrow the seas.
борозди́к|а, и, *f.* furrow; groove.
борозди́чатый, *adj.* furrowed; grooved.
бор|она́, оны́, *а.* ~ону, *pl.* ~оны, ~о́н, ~она́м, *f.* (*agric.*) harrow.

борон|и́ть, ю́, и́шь, *imp.* (*of* вз~) (*agric.*) to harrow.

борон|ова́ть, у́ю, *impf.* (*of* вз~) = ~и́ть.

бороньб|а́, ы́, *f.* (*agric.*) harrowing.

бор|о́ться, ю́сь, ~ешься, *impf.* (с+*i.*; за+*a.*; про́тив+*g.*) to wrestle; (*fig.*) to struggle, fight (with; for; against); б. с суеве́рием to struggle against superstition; б. со свое́й со́вестью to wrestle with one's conscience.

борт, а, о ~е, на ~у́, *pl.* ~а́, ~о́в, *m.* 1. side (*of a ship*); пра́вый б. starboard side; ле́вый б. port side; на ~у́ on board (*ship or aircraft*); б.-о́-б. broadside to broadside; вы́бросить за б. to throw overboard (*also fig.*); челове́к за ~ом! man overboard! 2. coat-breast. 3. cushion (*billiards*).

борт|ево́й, *adj.* *of* ~ь.

бортмеха́ник, а, *m.* (*aeron.*) flight engineer.

бо́ртник, а, *m.* wild-honey farmer.

бо́ртничеств|о, а, *n.* wild-honey farming.

борт|ово́й, *adj.* *of* ~; б. журна́л (ship's) log--book; ~ова́я ка́чка (*naut.*) rolling.

бортпроводни́к, а́, *m.* air steward.

бортпроводни́ц|а, ы, *f.* stewardess; air hostess.

бортради́ст, а, *m.* radio operator (*aircraft*).

борт|ь, и, *f.* hive of wild bees.

борщ, а́, *m.* borshch (*soup made of beetroot and cabbage*).

борщ|о́к, ка́, *m.* (clear) beetroot soup.

борьб|а́, ы́, *f.* 1. (*sport*) wrestling. 2. (*fig.*) (с+*i.*; за+*a.*; про́тив+*g.*) struggle, fight (with; for; against); conflict; кла́ссовая б. the class struggle; душе́вная б. mental strife.

босико́м, *adv.* barefoot; ходи́ть б. to go barefoot.

боске́т, а, *m.* spinney, copse.

бос|о́й (~, ~а́, ~о), *adj.* barefooted; на ~у́ но́гу with bare feet, barefoot.

босоно́гий, *adj.* barefooted.

босоно́жк|а, и, *f.* 1. barefoot dancer. 2. (*pl.*) sandals; mules.

босто́н, а, *m.* Boston (1. *card-game.* 2. *kind of wool cloth.* 3. *name of dance*).

бося́к, а́, *m.* tramp; down-and-out.

бося́|цкий, *adj.* *of* ~к.

бот, а, *m.* (*obs.*) boat.

ботанизи́рк|а, и, *f.* (*coll.*) plant-collecting box.

ботанизи́р|овать, ую, *impf.* to collect plants (*for study*).

бота́ник, а, *m.* botanist.

бота́ник|а, и, *f.* botany.

ботани́ческий, *adj.* botanical; б. сад botanical gardens.

ботв|а́, ы́, *f.* leafy tops of root vegetables (*esp. beet leaves*).

ботви́нь|я, и, *f.* botvinia (*cold soup of fish, pot-herbs, and kvass*).

бо́тик, а, *m.* (*obs.*) small boat.

бо́тик|и, ов, *sing.* ~, ~а, *m.* high (women's) over-shoes.

боти́н|ок, ка, *g. pl.* б. *m.* (ankle-high) boot.

ботфо́рт|ы, ов, *sing.* ~, ~а, *m.* (*obs.*) jack-boots, Hessian boots.

бо́т|ы, ов, *sing.* ~, ~а, *m.* high overshoes.

бо́цман, а, *m.* (*naut.*) boatswain.

боча́г, а́, *m.* (*dial.*) pool.

боча́р, а́, *pl.* ~ы́, *m.* cooper.

боча́р|ный, *adj.* *of* ~; coopering.

боча́р|ня, ни, *g. pl.* ~ен, *f.* (*dial.*) cooperage.

бо́чк|а, и, *f.* 1. barrel, cask; (*fig.*) плати́ть де́ньги на ~у to pay on the nail. 2. barrel (*liquid measure about 108 gallons*). 3. (*aeron.*) roll.

бочко́м, *adv.* sideways; пробира́ться б. to sidle.

боч|о́к, ка́, *m.* (*coll.*) flank.

бочо́н|ок, ка, *m.* small barrel, keg.

боязли́вост|ь, и, *f.* timidity, timorousness.

боязли́в|ый (~, ~а), *adj.* timid, timorous.

боя́зно, *adv. as pred.* (+*d.*; *coll.*) to be afraid, frightened; ей б. остава́ться одно́й по вечера́м she is frightened of being left alone in the evening.

боя́зн|ь, и, *f.* (+*g. or* пе́ред+*i.*) fear (of), dread of; б. темноты́ fear of the dark; б. простра́нства (*med.*) agoraphobia; из ~и for fear of, lest; он перемени́л фами́лию из ~и, что бу́дут смея́ться над ним he changed his name for fear of being laughed at.

боя́р|ин, ина, *pl.* ~е, ~, *m.* (*hist.*) boyar.

боя́р|ский, *adj.* *of* ~; ~ские де́ти (*hist.*) small landowners.

боя́рств|о, а, *n.* (*collect.*; *hist.*) the boyars, the nobility.

боя́рын|я, и, *f.* (*hist.*) boyar's wife.

боя́рышник, а, *m.* (*bot.*) hawthorn.

боя́рышниц|а, ы, *f.* pierid butterfly (*Aporia crataegi*).

боя́рыш|ня, ни, *g. pl.* ~ень, *f.* (*hist.*) (un-married) daughter of a boyar.

бо|я́ться, ю́сь, и́шься, *impf.* (+*g.*) 1. to fear, be afraid (of); она́ ~и́тся темноты́ she is afraid of the dark; он ~и́тся пойти́ к врачу́ he is afraid to go to the doctor; ~ю́сь, что он (не) прие́дет I am afraid that he will (not) come; ~ю́сь, как бы (что́бы) он не прие́хал I am afraid that he may come; ~ю́сь сказа́ть I would not like to say. 2. to be afraid of, suffer from; э́ти расте́ния ~ятся хо́лода these plants do not like the cold.

бра, *indecl.* *n.* sconce; lamp-bracket.

брава́д|а, ы, *f.* bravado.

брави́р|овать, ую, *impf.* (+*i.*) to brave, defy; б. опа́сностью to defy danger.

бра́во, *interj.* bravo!

браву́р|ный (~ен, ~на), *adj.* (*mus.*) bravura.

бра́вый, *adj.* gallant; manly.

бра́г|а, и, *f.* home-brewed beer.

брадобре́|й, я, *m.* (*obs. or joc.*) barber.

бра́жник, а, *m.* (*obs.*) reveller.

бра́жнича|ть, ю, *impf.* (*obs.*) to revel, carouse.

бразд|а́, ы́, *f.* (*poet., obs.*) furrow.

бразд|ы́, ~, now only in phrase б. правле́ния the reins of government.

брази́л|ец, ьца, *m.* Brazilian.

брази́льский, *adj.* Brazilian.

бразилья́нк|а, и, *f.* Brazilian (woman).

брак¹, а, *m.* marriage; matrimony; гражда́нский б. civil marriage; (*obs.*) cohabitation; свиде́тельство о ~е certificate of marriage; б. по расчёту marriage of convenience; рождённый вне ~а born out of wedlock.

брак², а, *m.* waste; defective products, rejects.

бракёр, а, *m.* (*tech.*) inspector.

бракера́ж, а, *m.* (*tech.*) certification, inspection.

брако́ван|ный (~, ~а), *p.p.p.* of бракова́ть and *adj.* rejected; defective.

брак|ова́ть, у́ю, *impf.* (*of* за~) to reject (*manufactured articles; also fig.*).

брако́вк|а, и, *f.* rejection (*of defective articles*).

брако́вщик, а, *m.* sorter (*of manufactured articles*).

брако́вщиц|а, ы, *f. of* брако́вщик.

бракоде́л, а, *m.* (*coll.*) bad workman.

браконье́р, а, *m.* poacher.

браконье́рств|о, а, *n.* poaching.

бракоразво́дный, *adj.* divorce; б. проце́сс divorce suit.

бракосочета́ни|е, я, *n.* wedding, nuptials.

брам- (*naut.*) top-.

брама́н, а, *m.* = брами́н.

брами́н, а, *m.* Brahmin.

брам-ре́|й, я, *m.* (*naut.*) topgallant yard.

бра́мсел|ь, я, *m.* (*naut.*) topsail.

брам-сте́ньг|а, и, *f.* (*naut.*) topgallant (mast).

брандахлы́ст, а, *m.* (*coll.*) 1. slops; swipes. 2. (*fig.*) worthless person.

брандва́хт|а, ы, *f.* guard-ship.

бра́ндер, а, *m.* 1. (*hist.*) fire-ship; запусти́ть, подпусти́ть б. (*fig.*) to put the cat among the pigeons. 2. block-ship.

брандмайо́р, а, *m.* (*obs.*) chief of the fire brigade.

брандма́уэр, а, *m.* fire-proof wall.

брандме́йстер, а, *m.* (*obs.*) chief fireman.

брандспо́йт, а, *m.* 1. fire-pump. 2. nozzle.

бран|и́ть, ю́, и́шь, *impf.* (*of* вы~) to reprove; to scold; to abuse, curse (*coll.*).

бран|и́ться, ю́сь, и́шься, *impf.* 1. (*of* по~) (с+*i*) to quarrel (with). 2. to swear, curse (*intrans.*).

бра́нн|ый¹, *adj.* abusive; ~ое сло́во swearword.

бра́нный², *adj.* (*obs., poet.*) martial.

бранч(л)и́в|ый (~, ~а), *adj.* (*coll.*) quarrelsome.

бра́ный, *adj.* (*text.; obs.*) embroidered.

бран|ь¹, и, *f.* swearing; abuse; bad language.

бран|ь², и, *f.* (*obs., poet.*) по́ле ~и field of battle.

брас, а, *m.* (*naut.*) brace.

брасле́т, а, *m.* bracelet.

брас|ова́ть, у́ю, *impf.* (*naut.*) to brace.

брасс, а, *m.* (*sport*) breast stroke.

брат, а, *pl.* ~ья, ~ьев, *m.* 1. brother; моло́чный б. foster-brother; сво́дный б. stepbrother; единокро́вный б. half-brother (*by father*); единоутро́бный б. half-brother (*by mother*); двою́родный б. cousin. 2. (*fig.*) brother; comrade; ~ья-писа́тели fellow-writers; наш б. (*coll.*) we, the likes of us; ваш б. (*coll.*) you, you and your sort. 3. *as familiar or patronising term of address* old man; my lad; (*pl.*) friends, lads. 4. (*eccl.*) lay brother; (*as style*) Brother, Friar; б. милосе́рдия male nurse. 5. на ~а (*coll.*) a head; по два я́блока на ~а two apples a head.

брата́нь|е, я, *n.* fraternization.

брата́|ться, ю́сь, *impf.* (*of* по~) (с+*i*.) to fraternize (with).

братв|а́, ы́, *f.* (*collect.; coll.*) comrades; chaps, lads.

бра́т|ец, ца, *m.* affectionate or patronising dim. of ~; (*as term of address*) old man, old chap; boy.

брати́н|а, ы, *f.* (*hist.*) winebowl.

брати́ш|ка, ки, *g. pl.* ~ек, *m.* (*coll.*) 1. little brother. 2. = брат 2.

бра́ти|я, и, *g. pl.* ~й, *f.* (*collect.*) brotherhood, fraternity (*also fig.*); доминика́нская б. Dominican community; актёрская б. the acting fraternity.

бра́тнин, *adj.* (*coll.*) brother's, belonging to one's brother.

брат|о́к, ка́, *m.* (*coll.*) = брат 2.

братоуби́йственный, *adj.* fratricidal (*also fig.*).

братоуби́йств|о, а, *n.* fratricide (*act*).

братоуби́йц|а, ы, *m.* fratricide (*agent*).

бра́тск|ий, *adj.* brotherly, fraternal; б. приве́т fraternal greetings; ~ая моги́ла communal grave (*esp. of war dead*).

бра́тств|о, а, *n.* (*abstr. and concr.*) brotherhood, fraternity.

брату́ш|ка, ки, *g. pl.* ~ек, *m.* dim. of брат; ~ки (*hist.; coll.*) 'the Little Brothers' (= the Southern Slavs).

бра|ть, беру́, берёшь, past ~л, ~ла́, ~ло, *impf.* (*of* взять). 1. (*in var. senses*) to take; б. наза́д, б. обра́тно to take back; б. курс (на+*a.*) to make (for), head (for); б. нача́ло (в+p.) to originate (in); б. но́ту to sing, play a note; б. поруче́ние to undertake a commission; б. приме́р (с+g.) to follow the example (of); б. сло́во to take the floor; б. в ско́бки to place in brackets; б. в плен to take prisoner; б. на букси́р to take in tow; б. на пору́ки (*leg*.) to go bail (for); б. на себя́ to take upon oneself; б. под аре́ст to put under arrest; б. кого́-н. по́д руку to take someone's arm. **2.** to take; to get, obtain; to book; to hire; б. биле́ты to take, book tickets; б. верх to get the upper hand; б. такси́ to take a taxi; б. своё to get one's way; to make itself felt; го́ды беру́т своё age tells; б. взаймы́ to borrow; б. в аре́нду to rent; б. на прока́т to hire. **3.** (в+n.–a.) to take (as); б. в жёны to take to wife; б. в свиде́тели to call to witness. **4.** to seize; to grip; б. власть to seize power; его́ берёт страх he is in the grip of fear; б. за се́рдце to move deeply. **5.** to exact; to take (= to demand, require); б. штраф to exact a fine; б. сло́во с кого́-н. to get someone's word; б. вре́мя to take time. **6.** to take; to surmount; б. барье́р to clear a hurdle. **7.** (+i.) to succeed (by means of, by dint of); она́ берёт такти́чностью the secret of her success is tact. **8.** (*usu.*+*neg.*; *coll.*) to work, operate; to be effective; (на+a.; *of a fire-arm*) to have a range (of); э́ти но́жницы не беру́т these scissors don't cut; э́та винто́вка берёт на пятьсо́т ме́тров this rifle has a range of, is effective at, five hundred metres. **9.** (+*adv. of place*; *coll.*) to bear; б. вле́во to bear left. **10.** (*dial.*) to gather, collect. **11.** (*impf. only*) (*coll.*) to take bribes.

бра́|ться, беру́сь, берёшься, *past* ~лся, ~ла́сь, ~ло́сь, *impf.* (*of* взя́ться). **1.** *pass. of* ~ть. **2.** (за+a.) to touch, lay hands (upon); не бери́сь за то́рмоз! don't touch the brake!; б. за́ руки to link arms. **3.** (за+a.) to take up; to get down (to); б. за де́ло to get down to business, get down to brass tacks; б. за перо́ to take up the pen; б. за чте́ние to get down to reading. **4.** (за+a. *or* +*inf.*) to undertake; to take upon oneself; б. за поруче́ние to undertake a commission; б. вы́полнить рабо́ту to undertake a job; не беру́сь суди́ть I do not presume to judge. **5.** (*3rd person only*) (*coll.*) to appear, arise; не зна́ю, отку́да у них де́ньги беру́тся I don't know where they get their money from. **6.** б. за ум (*coll.*) to come to one's senses. **7.** б. нарасхва́т to sell like hot cakes.

бра́т|ья¹, *see* ~ья.
бра́ть|я², и, *f.* = бра́тия.
бра́унинг, а, *m.* Browning (*automatic pistol*).

брахицефа́л, а, *m.* (*anthrop.*) brachycephalous person.
брахицефа́ли|я, и, *f.* (*anthrop.*) brachycephaly.
брахма́н, а, *m.* = брами́н.
бра́чн|ый, *adj.* marriage; conjugal; ~ое свиде́тельство marriage certificate; б. наря́д (*zool.*) breeding-dress; ~ое опере́ние (*zool.*) breeding plumage.
бра́чущ|иеся, ихся, *no sing.* parties to a marriage.
бра́шпил|ь, я, *m.* (*naut.*) windlass, capstan.
бреве́нчатый, *adj.* log, made of logs.
брев|но́, на́, *pl.* ~на, ~ен, ~нам, *n.* log, beam; (*fig.*) dullard, insensitive person.
брег, а, *pl.* ~а́, *m.* (*poet., arch.*) = бе́рег.
брегет, а, *m.* (*obs.*) Bréguet (watch).
бред, а, о ~е, **в** ~у́, *m.* delirium; ravings; (*fig.*) gibberish; быть в ~у́ to be delirious.
бред|ень, ня, *m.* drag-net.
бре́|дить, жу, дишь, *impf.* to be delirious, rave; (+i.; *fig.*) to rave about, be mad about; он ~дит джа́зом he is crazy about jazz.
бре́|диться, дится, *impf.* (*impers.*+d.) (*coll.*) to dream (of); ему́ всё ~дилось, что он па́дает в про́пасть he was always dreaming that he was falling down a precipice.
бре́дн|и, ей, *no sing.* ravings; fantasies.
бредово́й, *adj.* **1.** delirious. **2.** (*fig.*) fantastic, nonsensical.
бре|ду́, дёшь, *see* ~сти́.
бре́|жу, дишь, *see* ~дить.
брезг|ать, аю, аешь, *impf.* (*of* по~) (+i.) to be squeamish, fastidious (about); он ~ает есть немы́тые фру́кты he is squeamish about eating unwashed fruit; тако́й ниче́м бы не ~ал he is the sort of person who would balk at nothing.
брезгли́в|ец, ца, *m.* squeamish, fastidious person.
брезгли́вост|ь, и, *f.* squeamishness, fastidiousness; disgust.
брезгли́в|ый (~, ~а), *adj.* squeamish, fastidious; ~ое чу́вство feeling of disgust.
брезе́нт, а, *m.* tarpaulin.
брезе́нтовый, *adj.* tarpaulin, canvas.
бре́зж|ить(ся), ~ит(ся), *impf.* to dawn; to glimmer; ~ила заря́ dawn was breaking.
брейд-вы́мпел, а, *m.* (*naut.*) broad pennant.
брёл, а́, *see* брести́.
брело́к, а, *m.* (bracelet) charm.
бремен|и́ть, ю, и́шь, *impf.* (*obs.*) to burden.
бре́мсберг, а, *m.* (*tech.*) gravity roadway.
бре́м|я, ~ени, ~енем, ~ени, *n.* burden; load; разреши́ться от ~ени to be delivered (of a child).
бре́нн|ый (~а, ~о), *adj.* transitory; perishable; ~ые оста́нки mortal remains.
бренч|а́ть, у́, и́шь, *impf.* **1.** (+i.) to jingle

сль́шно бы́ло, как ~а́ли шпо́ры the jingling of spurs could be heard; он всё ~а́л моне́тами в карма́не he was always jingling coins in his pocket. 2. (*coll.*) to strum; б. на роя́ле to strum on the piano.

бр|ести́, еду́, едёшь, *past* ~ёл, ~ела́, *impf.* 1. to shuffle; to drag oneself along. 2. to amble, stroll pensively.

брете́льк|а, и, *f.* shoulder-strap.

брете́р, а, *m.* (*obs.*) duellist, swashbuckler, bully.

брете́р|ский, *adj. of* ~.

брето́н|ец, ца, *m.* Breton.

брето́нк|а, и, *f.* Breton (woman).

брето́нский, *adj.* Breton.

бре|ха́ть, шу́, ~шешь, *impf.* (*coll.*) 1. to yelp, bark. 2. (*fig.*) to tell lies.

брехн|я́, й, *no pl.*, *f.* (*coll.*) lies; nonsense.

бреху́н, а́, *m.* (*coll.*) liar.

брехун|е́ц, ца́, *m.* (*coll.*) liar; (*fig.*, *iron.*) lawyer.

бреш|у́, ~ешь, *see* бреха́ть.

бреш|ь, и, *f.* breach; проби́ть б. (в+*p.*) to breach; (*fig.*) flaw, gap, deficit.

бре́|ю, ешь, *see* бри́ть.

бре́ющий, *pres. part. of* брить; б. полёт hedge-hopping flight.

бриг, а, *m.* brig.

брига́д|а, ы, *f.* 1. (*mil.*) brigade; (*naut.*) subdivision. 2. brigade, team; поездна́я б. train crew; уда́рная б. shock brigade.

бригади́р, а, *m.* 1. (*mil.*; *obs.*) brigadier. 2. brigade-leader; team-leader; foreman.

бригади́рш|а, и, *f.* (*obs.*) brigadier's wife.

брига́дник, а, *m.* member of a brigade, team.

брига́д|ный, *adj. of* ~а.

бриганти́н|а, ы, *f.* brigantine.

бридж, а, *m.* bridge (*card-game*).

бри́дж|и, ей, *no sing.* breeches.

бриз, а, *m.* breeze.

бриза́нтн|ый, *adj.* high explosive; ~ые вещества́ high explosives; б. снаря́д high explosive shell.

брике́т, а, *m.* briquette.

брил|лиа́нт, а *and* ~ья́нт, а, *m.* (cut) diamond, brilliant.

бриллиа́нт|овый, *adj. of* ~.

брил|ья́нт = ~лиа́нт.

брил|ья́нтовый = ~лиа́нтовый.

брита́н|ец, ца, *m.* Briton.

брита́нк|а, и, *f.* Briton (*woman*).

брита́нский, *adj.* British; б. мета́лл Britannia metal.

бри́тв|а, ы, *f.* razor; безопа́сная б. safety razor.

бри́твенн|ый, *adj.* shaving; ~ые принадле́жности shaving things; б. реме́нь (razor-) strop.

бритт, а, *m.* (ancient) Briton.

бри́т|ый (~, ~а), *p.p.p. of* ~ь *and adj.* clean-shaven.

бр|ить, е́ю, е́ешь, *impf.* (*pf.* по~) to shave.

бри́ть|ё, я́, *n.* shave; shaving.

бр|и́ться, е́юсь, е́ешься, *impf.* to shave, have a shave.

бри́чк|а, и, *f.* (*obs.*) britzka (*light carriage*).

бро́вк|а, и, *f.* 1. *dim. of* бровь. 2. edge (*of running track*).

бров|ь, и, *pl.* ~и, ~е́й, *f.* eyebrow; brow; ~и дуго́й arched eyebrows; хму́рить ~и to knit one's brows, frown; он и ~ью не повёл he did not turn a hair; попа́сть не в б., а (пря́мо) в глаз (*prov.*) to hit the nail on the head.

брод, а, *m.* ford; не зна́я ~у, не су́йся в во́ду (*prov.*) look before you leap.

броди́льный, *adj.* (*tech.*) fermentative; б. чан fermenting vat; б. ферме́нт fermenting-agent.

бро|ди́ть¹, жу́, ~дишь, *impf.* to wander, roam; to amble, stroll; б. по у́лицам to roam the streets; б. в потёмках (*fig.*) to be in the dark, not to know one's way about; (*fig.*) улы́бка ~ди́ла на её лице́ a smile played about her face.

бро|ди́ть², ~дит, *impf.* to ferment.

бродя́г|а, и, *m.* tramp, vagrant; down-and-out.

бродя́жнича|ть, ю, *impf.* to be a tramp, be on the road.

бродя́жничеств|о, а, *n.* vagrancy.

бродя́ч|ий, *adj.* vagrant; wandering, roving; (*fig.*) restless; ~ие племена́ nomadic tribes; ~ая соба́ка stray dog.

броже́ни|е, я, *n.* fermentation; б. умо́в (*fig.*) intellectual ferment.

бро|жу́, ~дишь, *see* ~ди́ть.

бром, а, *m.* (*chem.*) bromine; (*med.*) bromide.

бро́мистый, *adj.* (*chem.*) bromide; б. на́трий sodium bromide.

бро́м|овый, *adj. of* ~.

броне- (*mil.*) armoured-.

бронеавтомоби́л|ь, я, *m.* armoured car.

бронебо́йк|а, и, *f.* (*coll.*) anti-tank rifle.

бронебо́йный, *adj.* armour-piercing.

бронебо́йщик, а, *m.* anti-tank rifleman.

броневи́к, а́, *m.* armoured car.

бронев|о́й, *adj.* armoured; ~ые пли́ты (*mil.*) armour plating.

броненос|ец, ца, *m.* (*naut.*) battleship; ironclad.

броненос|ец², ца, *m.* (*zool.*) armadillo.

бронено́сный, *adj.* armoured.

бронепо́езд, а, *m.* armoured train.

бронеси́л|ы, ~, *no sing.* armoured forces.

бронета́нков|ый, *adj.* (*mil.*) armoured; ~ые ча́сти armoured units.

бронетранспортёр, а, *m.* armoured troop carrier.

бро́нз|а, ы, *f.* **1.** bronze. **2.** (*collect.*) bronzes.

бронзи́р|ова́ть, у́ю, *impf. and pf.* to bronze.

бронзиро́вк|а, и, *f.* bronzing.

бронзиро́вщик, а, *m.* bronzer.

бронзовщи́к, а́, *m.* worker in bronze.

бро́нзов|ый, *adj.* bronze; bronzed, tanned; ~ая боле́знь (*med.*) Addison's disease; б. век (*archeol.*) the Bronze Age; б. зага́р sunburn, sun-tan.

брони́рова|нный, *p.p.p. of* ~ть *and adj.* reserved.

брониро́в|анный, *p.p.p. of* ~а́ть *and adj.* armoured.

брони́р|овать, ую, *impf.* (*of* за~) to reserve, book.

бронир|ова́ть, у́ю, *impf. and pf.* to armour.

бронх, а, *m.* (*anat.*) bronchial tube.

бронхиа́льный, *adj.* (*anat.*) bronchial.

бронхи́т, а, *m.* (*med.*) bronchitis.

бро́н|я, и, *f.* reservation; commandeering; получи́ть ме́сто по ~е to have a seat reserved.

броня́, й, *f.* armour; armour-plating.

броса́|ть, ю, *impf.* (*of* бро́сить). **1.** to throw, cast, fling; б. взгляд to dart a glance; б. обвине́ния to hurl accusations; б. тень to cast a shadow; (на + *a.*; *fig.*) to cast aspersions (on); б. я́корь to drop anchor; б. на ве́тер to throw away, waste; б. запасны́е войска́ в бой to fling reserves into the battle; (*impers.*) его́ ~ет то в жар, то в хо́лод he keeps going hot and cold. **2.** to leave, abandon, desert; б. му́жа to desert one's husband; б. ору́жие to lay down one's arms; б. рабо́ту to give up, throw up one's work. **3.** (+ *inf.*) to give up, leave off; он всё ~л кури́ть he was always trying to give up smoking.

брос|а́ться, а́юсь, *impf.* **1.** (*impf. only*) (+ *i.*) to throw at one another, pelt one another (with); по пути́ в шко́лу мы ~а́лись снежка́ми we used to pelt one another with snowballs on the way to school. **2.** (*impf. only*) (+ *i.*) to throw away; б. деньга́ми to throw away, squander one's money. **3.** (*pf.* ~иться) (на, в + *a.*) to throw oneself (on, upon), rush (to); б. на еду́ to fall upon one's food; б. на коле́ни to fall on one's knees; б. в объя́тия (+ *d.*) to fall into the arms (of); б. на по́мощь to rush to assistance; б. на ше́ю (+ *d.*) to fall on the neck (of); кровь ~а́лась ей в лицо́ the blood was rushing to her face. **4.** (*pf.* ~иться) б. в глаза́ to be striking, arrest attention. **5.** (*pf.* ~иться) (+ *inf.*) to begin, start.

бро́|сить, шу, сишь, *pf. of* ~са́ть; ~сь(те)! stop it!; хоть ~сь (*coll.*) it is no good.

бро́|ситься, шусь, сишься, *pf. of* ~са́ться.

бро́с|кий (~ок, ~ка́, ~ко), *adj.* (*coll.*) bright, loud, garish; б. га́лстук loud tie.

броско́м, *adv.* (*coll.*) **1.** with one throw. **2.** with a spurt.

бро́совый, *adj.* **1.** worthless; low-grade. **2.** б. э́кспорт (*econ.*) dumping.

брос|о́к, ка́, *m.* (*coll.*) **1.** throw. **2.** bound; spurt; он пришёл пе́рвым в го́нке благодаря́ после́днему ~ку́ he came in first in the race by making a final spurt.

бро́шк|а, и, *f.* brooch.

бро́|шу, сишь, *see* ~сить.

брош|ь, и, *f.* brooch.

брошир- (~ова́ть, *etc.*) = брошюр-.

брошю́р|а, ы, *f.* pamphlet, brochure.

брошюр|ова́ть, у́ю, *impf.* (*of* с~) (*tech.*) to stitch.

брошюро́вк|а, и, *f.* (*tech.*) stitching.

брошюро́вочн|ая, ой, *f.* book-stitching shop.

брошюро́вщик, а, *m.* (*tech.*) stitcher.

бру́дер, а, *m.* brooder (*for poultry*).

брудерша́фт, а, *m. only in phrase* вы́пить (на) б. to drink 'Bruderschaft'.

брульо́н, а, *m.* (*obs.*) rough copy.

брус, а, *pl.* ~ья, ~ьев, *m.* squared beam; паралле́льные ~ья (*sport*) parallel bars.

бруско́в|ый, *adj.* bar, bar-shaped; ~ое желе́зо bar-iron; ~ое мы́ло bar soap.

брусни́к|а, и, *f.* red whortleberry (*Vaccinium vitis idaea*).

брусни́|чный, *adj. of* ~ка.

брус|о́к, ка́, *m.* bar; ingot; б. мы́ла bar of soap; точи́льный б. whetstone.

бру́ствер, а, *m.* (*mil.*) breastwork, parapet.

бру́тто, *indecl., adj.* gross; вес б. gross weight.

брыже́йк|а, и, *f.* (*anat.*) mesentery.

брыж|и́, е́й, *no sing.* ruff, frill.

бры́з|гать, жу, жешь, *impf.* (*of* ~нуть) (+ *i.*) **1.** to splash, spatter; to gush, spurt; б. гря́зью (на + *a.*) to splash mud (on to), spatter with mud. **2.** (*pres.* ~жу *or* ~гаю) to sprinkle.

бры́зга|ться, юсь, *impf.* (*coll.*) to splash; to splash oneself, one another; соба́ки лю́бят б. в лу́жах the dogs enjoy splashing in the puddles; б. духа́ми to spray oneself with scent.

брызг|и, ~, *no sing.* **1.** spray, splashes (*of liquids*). **2.** fragments (*of stone, glass, etc.*).

брыз|жу, жешь, *see* ~гать.

брыз|нуть, ну, нешь, *pf. of* ~гать; кровь ~нула из ра́ны blood spurted from the wound.

брык|а́ть, а́ю, *impf.* (*of* ~ну́ть) to kick.

брыка́|ться, юсь, *impf.* to kick; (*fig.*) to kick, rebel.

брыкли́в|ый (~, ~а), *adj.* (*coll.*) inclined to kick.

брык|ну́ть, ну́, нёшь, *pf. of* ~а́ть.

брыку́н, а́, *m.* (*coll., dial.*) kicker.

бры́нз|а, ы, *f.* brynza (*sheep's milk cheese*).

брысь, *interj.* shoo! (*to a cat*).

брюзг|а́, и́, *m. and f.* grumbler.

брюзгли́в|ый (~, ~a), *adj.* grumbling, peevish.

брюзжа́ни|е, я, *n.* grumbling.

брюзж|а́ть, у́, и́шь, *impf.* to grumble.

брю́кв|а, ы, *f.* (*bot.*) swede.

брю́кв|енный, *adj. of* ~a.

брю́к|и, ~, *no sing.* trousers.

брюне́т, а, *m.* dark-haired man.

брюне́тк|а, и, *f.* brunette.

брю́ссельск|ий, *adj.* Brussels; ~ая капу́ста Brussels sprouts; ~ие кружева́ Brussels lace.

брюха́ст|ый (~, ~a), *adj.* (*coll.*) big-bellied.

брюха́|тить, чу, тишь, *impf.* (*vulg.*) to get with child.

брюха́т|ый, *adj.* (*coll.*) = брюха́стый; ~ая big with child.

брюх|о, а, *pl.* ~и, *n.* (*coll.*) belly; paunch; ходи́ть с ~ом (*vulg.*) to be big with child.

брюхоно́г|ие, их, (*zool.*) gasteropods.

брюши́н|а, ы, *f.* (*anat.*) peritoneum; воспале́ние ~ы (*med.*) peritonitis.

брюшк|о́, а́, *pl.* ~и́, ~о́в, *n.* 1. abdomen; (*coll.*) paunch. 2. belly-pieces [(*i*) *of fur-bearing animals*, (*ii*) *of fish as food*].

брюшно́й, *adj.* abdominal; б. тиф typhoid (fever).

бряк, *interj.* bang!, crash!

бря́кань|е, я, *n.* (*coll.*) clatter.

бря́к|ать, аю, *impf.* (*of* ~нуть) (*coll.*) 1. (+*i.*) to clatter; б. посу́дой to clatter crockery. 2. to let fall with a bang; (*fig.*) to drop a clanger.

бря́к|аться, аюсь, *impf.* (*of* ~нуться) (*coll.*) to crash, fall heavily.

бря́к|нуть(ся), ну(сь), нешь(ся), *pf. of* ~ать(ся).

бряца́ни|е, я, *n.* 1. rattling. 2. rattle; clang; clank, clanking; б. шпор the rattle of spurs; б. ору́жием sabre-rattling.

бряца́|ть, ю, *impf.* (+*i. or* на+*p.*) to rattle; to clang; to clank; б. цимба́лами to clash cymbals; б. ору́жием (*fig.*) to rattle the sabre; кимва́л ~ющий (*iron.*) 'tinkling cymbal'.

бу́б|ен, на, *g. pl.* ~ен, *m.* tambourine.

бубен|е́ц, ца́, *m.* little bell; колпа́к с ~ца́ми cap and bells.

бубе́нчик, а, *m.* 1. *dim. of* бубене́ц. 2. (*bot.*) harebell, campanula.

бу́блик, а, *m.* boublik (*thick, ring-shaped bread roll*).

бу́б|на, ны, *g. pl.* ~ён, *f.* (*cards*) 1. (*pl.*) diamonds; ходи́ть с ~ён to lead diamonds; дво́йка ~ён the two of diamonds. 2. a diamond.

бубн|и́ть, ю́, и́шь, *impf.* (*of* про~) (*coll.*) to grumble; to mutter.

бубно́вк|а, и, *f.* (*cards*; *coll.*) diamond.

бубно́вый, *adj.* (*cards*) diamond; б. туз ace

of diamonds; (*hist.*; *fig.*) diamond-shaped patch on convict's coat.

бу́б|ны¹, ен, *see* ~ен.

бу́б|ны², ён, *see* ~на.

бубо́н, а, *m.* (*med.*) bubo.

бубо́н|ный, *adj. of* ~; ~ная чума́ (*med.*) bubonic plague.

буга́|й, я, *m.* (*dial.*) bull (*also fig.*).

бу́гел|ь, я, *m.* 1. (*naut.*) hoop. 2. (*electr.*) bow-collector.

буг|о́р, ра́, *m.* mound, knoll; bump, lump.

бугор|о́к, ка́, *m.* 1. *dim. of* ~; knob, protuberance. 2. (*med.*) tubercle.

бугорча́тк|а, и, *f.* (*med.*; *obs.*) tuberculosis.

буго́рчатый, *adj.* 1. covered with lumps. 2. (*med.*) tuberculous. 3. (*bot.*) tuberous.

бугри́ст|ый (~, ~a), *adj.* hilly; bumpy.

бугшпри́т = бушпри́т.

будди́зм, а, *m.* Buddhism.

будди́йский, *adj.* Buddhist.

будди́ст, а, *m.* Buddhist.

бу́де, *conj.* (*obs.*) if, provided that.

буде́новк|а, и, *f.* (*hist.*) budyonovka (*pointed helmet worn by Red Army men during period 1918–21*).

бу́дет 1. *3rd sing. fut. of* быть; б. ему́ за э́то! he'll catch it. 2. *as pred.* (*coll.*) that's enough, that'll do; б. с вас э́того? will that do?; вы́пьем ещё одну́ буты́лку и б. we'll drink one more bottle and call it a day; уже́ за́ полночь, б. вам писа́ть it's past midnight, it's time you stopped writing.

буди́льник, а, *m.* alarmclock.

буди́р|овать, ую, *impf.* (*obs.*) to sulk.

бу|ди́ть, жу́, ~дишь, *impf.* 1. (*pf.* раз~) to wake, awaken, call. 2. (*pf.* про~) (*fig.*) to rouse, arouse; to stir up; б. мысль to set (one) thinking, give food for thought.

бу́дк|а, и, *f.* box, booth; stall; железнодоро́жная б. (railway) trackman's hut, crossing-keeper's hut; карау́льная б. sentry-box; соба́чья б. dog kennel; суфлёрская б. prompt-box; телефо́нная б. telephone booth.

бу́д|ни, ней, *sing.* (*obs. or coll.*) ~ень, ~ня, *m.* 1. weekdays; working days, workdays; по ~ням on weekdays. 2. humdrum life; colourless existence.

бу́дний, *adj.* б. день weekday.

бу́дничн|ый, *adj.* 1. б. день weekday; ~ое расписа́ние weekday timetable. 2. everyday; dull, humdrum.

бу́днишний, *adj.* = бу́дничный.

будора́ж|ить, у, ишь, *impf.* (*of* вз~) (*coll.*) to disturb; to excite.

бу́дочник, а, *m.* 1. (*obs.*) policeman on duty. 2. railway trackman; crossing-keeper.

бу́дто 1. *conj.* as if, as though; он верну́лся с таки́м ви́дом, б. его́ изби́ли he came

back looking as if he had been beaten up.
2. *conj.* that (*implying doubt as to the truth of a reported affirmation*); он утвержда́ет, б. говори́т свобо́дно на десяти́ языка́х he says that he speaks, he claims to speak ten languages fluently. **3.** (*also* б. бы, как б.) *particle* (*coll.*) apparently; allegedly, ostensibly; она́ б. должна́ уха́живать за отцо́м apparently she has to look after her father. **4.** *interrog. particle* (*coll.*) really?; уж б. он так умён? is he really all that clever?

бу́д|у, ешь, *future of* быть.

будуа́р, а, *m.* boudoir.

будуа́р|ный, *adj. of* ~.

бу́дучи, *pres. gerund of* быть being.

бу́дущ|ий, *adj.* future; next; ~ее вре́мя (*gram.*) future tense; в ~ем году́ next year; в б. раз next time; *as noun* ~ее, ~его, *n.* (*i*) the future; в ближа́йшем ~ем in the near future, (*ii*) (*gram.*) future tense.

бу́дущност|ь, и, *f.* future; ему́ предстои́т блестя́щая б. a brilliant future lies before him.

бу́дь(те), *imp. of* быть (*sing. also used in place of* е́сли+*main verb to form protasis of conditional sentences*) бу́дьте добры́, б. любе́зны (+*inf. or imp.*) please; would you be good enough (to), kind enough (to); будь, что бу́дет come what may; не будь вас, всё бы пропа́ло but for you all would have been lost; будь он бога́т, будь он бе́ден, мне всё равно́ be he rich or be he poor, it is all one to me.

бу|ёк, йка́, *m.* (*naut.*) anchor-buoy, life-buoy.

бу́ер, а, *pl.* ~а́, *m.* **1.** ice-yacht, land-yacht. **2.** (*obs.*) small sailing-boat.

буера́к, а, *m.* (*dial.*) gully; coombe.

буж, á, *m.* (*med.*) probe.

бужени́н|а, ы, *f.* boiled salted pork.

бу|жу́, ~дишь, *see* ~ди́ть.

буз|а́¹, ы́, *f.* (*dial.*) bouza (*fermented beverage made from millet, buckwheat or barley*).

буз|а́², ы́, *f.* (*coll.*) row; подня́ть ~у́ to kick up a row.

бузин|а́, ы́, *f.* (*bot.*) elder.

бузи́нник, а, *m.* (*bot.*) elder grove, elder-bush.

бузи́н|ный, *adj. of* ~а́.

бузи́|ть (*1st person not used*), ~шь, *impf.* (*coll.*) to kick up a row.

буз|ова́ть, у́ю, *impf.* (*coll.*) to beat.

бузотёр, а, *m.* (*coll.*) rowdy.

бузотёрств|о, а, *n.* (*coll.*) rowdyism.

бузу́н¹, á, *m.* salt-lumps (*precipitated in salt lakes*).

бузу́н², á, *m.* (*coll.*) rowdy.

бу́|й, я, *pl.* ~и́, ~ёв, *m.* buoy.

бу́йвол, а, *m.* (*zool.*) buffalo.

бу́йвол|овый, *adj. of* ~; ~овая ко́жа buff.

бу́|йный (~ен, ~йна́, ~йно), *adj.* **1.** wild; violent, turbulent; tempestuous; ungovernable; б. сумасше́дший violent, dangerous lunatic; б. хара́ктер ungovernable character. **2.** luxuriant, lush; б. рост luxuriant growth.

бу́йств|о, а, *n.* unruly, riotous conduct.

бу́йств|овать, ую, *impf.* (*coll.*) to create uproar; to behave violently.

бук, а, *m.* beech.

бу́к|а, и, *m. and f.* (*coll.*) **1.** bogy(man), bugbear. **2.** (*fig.*) misanthrope, unsociable person; surly person; смотре́ть ~ой to look surly.

бука́шк|а, и, *f.* small insect.

бу́кв|а, ы, *g. pl.* ~, *f.* letter (of the alphabet); б. в ~у literally; б. зако́на (*fig.*) the letter of the law.

буква́льно, *adv.* literally; word for word.

буква́льн|ый, *adj.* literal; ~ое значе́ние literal meaning; б. перево́д word-for-word translation.

буква́р|ь, я́, *m.* ABC; primer.

бу́квиц|а, ы, *f.* (*bot.*) wood betony.

бу́квенный, *adj.* in letters.

буквое́д, а, *m.* pedant.

буквое́дств|о, а, *n.* pedantry.

буке́т, а, *m.* **1.** bouquet; bunch of flowers, posy. **2.** bouquet; aroma.

букини́ст, а, *m.* second-hand bookseller.

букинисти́ческий, *adj.* б. магази́н second--hand bookshop.

бу́кл|я, и, *f.* curl; ringlet.

бу́ковый, *adj.* beechen; б. жёлудь beech nut.

буко́лик|а, и, *f.* (*lit.*) bucolic literature.

буколи́ческий, *adj.* bucolic, pastoral.

букс, а, *m.* (*bot.*) box.

бу́кс|а, ы, *f.* (*tech.*) axle-box.

букси́р, а, *m.* **1.** tug, tugboat. **2.** tow-rope; взять на б. to take in tow; (*fig.*) to give a helping hand; тяну́ть на ~е to have in tow.

букси́р|ный, *adj. of* ~; б. парохо́д steam tug.

букси́р|овать, ую, *impf.* to tow, have in tow.

букси́ровк|а, и, *f.* towing.

буксова́ни|е, я, *n.* skidding, wheel-spin.

букс|ова́ть, у́ю, *impf.* to skid (*of wheels of locomotive, etc., to revolve on the spot without moving forward*).

бу́кс|овый, *adj. of* ~.

булав|а́, ы́, *f.* mace.

була́вк|а, и, *f.* pin; англи́йская б. safety--pin; де́ньги на ~и pin-money.

була́вочник, а, *m.* **1.** pincushion, pin-box. **2.** pin-maker.

була́в|очный, *adj. of* ~ка.

була́ный, *adj.* Isabel(la), dun (*colour of horse*).

була́т, а, *m.* (*hist.*) damask steel; (*fig.*) sword.

була́т|ный, *adj. of* ~; (*hist., poet.*; *conventional epithet of sword*).

булга́ч|ить, у, ишь, *impf.* (*coll.*) to stir up, excite.

бу́лин|ь, я, *m.* (*naut.*) bowline.

бу́лк|а, и, *f.* small loaf; white bread; сдо́бная б. bun.

бу́лл|а, ы, *f.* (Papal) bull.

бу́лочн|ая, ой, *f.* bakery; baker's shop.

бу́лочник, а, *m.* baker.

булты́х, *interj.* plop! (*also as pred.*) де́вочка б. в во́ду the little girl fell plop into the water.

булты́х|а́ть, а́ю, *impf.* (*of* ~ну́ть) (*coll.*) 1. to slop. 2. to drop with a plopping noise (*into liquid*).

булты́х|а́ться, а́юсь, *impf.* (*coll.*) 1. (*pf.* ~ну́ться) to fall plop. 2. (*impf. only*) to flounder (about).

булты́х|ну́ть, ну-ну́, нешь-нёшь, *pf. of* ~а́ть.

булты́х|ну́ться, нусь-ну́сь, нешься-нёшься, *pf. of* ~а́ться.

булы́жник, а, *m.* cobble-stone (*also collect.*).

бульва́р, а, *m.* avenue; boulevard.

бульва́р|ный, *adj. of* ~; ~ная пре́сса gutter press; б. рома́н cheap novel.

бульдо́г, а, *m.* bulldog.

бульдо́зер, а, *m.* bulldozer.

бу́лькань|е, я, *n.* gurgling.

бу́лька|ть, ю, *impf.* to gurgle.

бульо́н, а, *m.* broth.

бум[1], а, *m.* (*coll.*) 1. (*econ.*) boom. 2. newspaper sensation.

бум[2], а, *m.* (*sport*) beam.

бум[3], *interj.* boom!

бума́г|а[1], и, *f.* 1. paper; газе́тная б. newsprint; б. в кле́тку squared paper. 2. document; (*pl.*) (official) papers; це́нные ~и (*fin.*) securities.

бума́г|а[2], и, *f.* (хлопча́тая) б. cotton; шерсть с ~ой wool and cotton.

бумагодержа́тел|ь[1], я, *m.* (*fin.*) holder of securities, bondholder.

бумагодержа́тел|ь[2], я, *m.* paper-clip.

бумагомара́ни|е, я, *n.* (*coll.*) scrawl.

бумагомара́тел|ь, я, *m.* (*coll.*) scribbler.

бумагопряде́ни|е, я, *n.* cotton-spinning.

бумагопряди́льн|ый, *adj.* cotton-spinning; ~ая фа́брика cotton mill.

бумагопряди́л|ьня, ьни, *g. pl.* ~ен, *f.* cotton mill.

бума́жк|а, и, *f.* 1. *dim. of* бума́га scrap of paper. 2. note; (paper) money.

бума́жник[1], а, *m.* wallet.

бума́жник[2], а, *m.* paper-maker.

бума́|жный[1], *adj. of* ~га[1]; (*fig.*) (existing only on) paper; ~жная волоки́та red tape; ~жные де́ньги paper money; б. змей kite; ~жная фа́брика paper-mill.

бума́|жный[2], *adj. of* ~га[2]; ~жная пря́жа cotton yarn; ~жная ткань cotton fabric.

бумажо́нк|а, и, *f.* (*coll.*) scrap of paper.

бумазе́йный, *adj.* fustian.

бумазе́|я, и, *f.* fustian.

бумера́нг, а, *m.* boomerang.

бу́нкер, а, *m.* (*tech.*) bunker.

бункер|ова́ть, у́ю, *impf. and pf.* to bunker.

бункер|ова́ться, у́юсь, *impf. and pf.* (*naut.*) to coal.

бункеро́вк|а, и, *f.* coaling.

бунт[1], а, *pl.* ~ы́, *m.* revolt; riot; mutiny.

бунт[2], а́, *m.* bale; packet; bundle.

бунта́рский, *adj.* 1. seditious; mutinous. 2. (*fig.*) rebellious; turbulent; б. дух rebellious spirit.

бунта́рств|о, а, *n.* rebelliousness.

бунта́р|ь, я́, *m.* 1. rebel (*also fig.*); insurgent; mutineer; rioter; он б. в душе́ he is a rebel at heart. 2. inciter to mutiny, rebellion.

бунт|ова́ть, у́ю, *impf.* 1. (*pf.* взбунтова́ться) to revolt, rebel; to mutiny; to riot; (*fig.*) to rage, go berserk. 2. (*pf.* вз~) to incite to revolt, mutiny.

бунт|ова́ться, у́юсь, *impf.* = ~ова́ть 1.

бунт|ово́й, *adj. of* ~[2].

бунтовско́й, *adj.* rebellious, mutinous.

бунтовщи́к, а́, *m.* rebel, insurgent; mutineer; rioter.

бунчу́к, а́, *m.* (*hist.*) staff of Cossack hetman.

бур[1], а, *m.* (*tech.*) auger.

бур[2], а, *m.* Boer.

бур|а́, ы́, *f.* (*chem.*) borax.

бура́в, а́, *pl.* ~а́, *m.* (*tech.*) auger; gimlet.

бура́в|ить, лю, ишь, *impf.* to bore, drill.

бура́вчик, а, *m.* gimlet.

бура́к, а́, *m.* 1. (*dial.*) beetroot. 2. (*dial.*) cylindrical birch-bark box. 3. cascade (*kind of firework*).

бура́н, а, *m.* snow-storm (*in steppes*).

бурбо́н, а, *m.* (*coll., obs.*) coarse fellow; upstart.

бургоми́стр, а, *m.* burgomaster.

бурго́нское = бургу́ндское.

бургу́ндск|ий, *adj.* Burgundian; *as noun* ~ое, ~ого, *n.* burgundy (*wine*).

бурд|а́, ы́, *f.* slops.

бурдю́к, а́, *m.* wineskin, water-skin.

буреве́стник, а, *m.* stormy petrel.

бур|ево́й, *adj. of* ~я; stormy.

бурело́м, а, *m.* wind-fallen trees.

буре́ни|е, я, *n.* (*tech.*) boring, drilling; о́пытное б. test boring; уда́рное б. percussion drilling.

буре́|ть, ю, ешь, *impf.* (*of* по~) to grow brown.

буржуа́, *indecl., m.* bourgeois.

буржуази́|я, и, *f.* bourgeoisie; ме́лкая б. petty bourgeoisie.

буржуа́з|ный (~ен, ~на), *adj.* bourgeois.

буржу́|й, я, *m.* (*coll.*) bourgeois.
буржу́й|ка, ки, *f.* 1. *f. of* ~. 2. (*coll.*) small stove.
буржу́йский, *adj.* (*coll.*) bourgeois.
бури́льный, *adj.* (*tech.*) boring.
бури́льщик, а, *m.* borer; driller, drill-operator.
бур|и́ть, ю́, и́шь, *impf.* (*tech.*) to bore; to drill.
бу́рк|а¹, и, *f.* (*folk poet.*) chestnut horse.
бу́рк|а², и, *f.* felt cloak (*worn in Caucasus*).
бу́ркал|ы, ~, *no sing.* (*coll.*) eyes.
бу́рк|ать, аю, *impf.* (*of* ~нуть) (*coll.*) to mutter, growl out.
бу́рк|нуть, ну, нешь, *pf. of* ~ать.
бурла́к, а́, *m.* barge hauler.
бурла́|цкий, *adj. of* ~к.
бурла́честв|о, а, *n.* trade of barge hauler.
бурла́ч|ить, у, ишь, *impf.* to be a barge hauler.
бурли́в|ый (~, ~а), *adj.* turbulent; seething.
бурл|и́ть, ю́, и́шь, *impf.* to seethe, boil up (*also fig.*).
бурми́стр, а, *m.* (*hist.*) bailiff.
бурну́с, а, *m.* burnous.
бу́р|ный (~ен, ~на́), *adj.* 1. stormy, rough; impetuous; ~ные аплодисме́нты loud cheers, stormy applause. 2. rapid; energetic; б. рост rapid growth.
буровик, а́, *m.* (*tech.*) boring, drilling technician.
буров|о́й, *adj.* boring; ~а́я вы́шка derrick; ~а́я сква́жина bore, bore-hole, well.
бу́рс|а, ы, *f.* (*hist.*) seminary.
бурса́к, а́, *m.* (*hist.*) seminarist.
бурса́|цкий, *adj. of* ~к.
бу́рский, *adj.* Boer.
бу́ртик, а, *m.* (*tech., naut.*) fender.
буру́н, а́, *m.* breaker; bow-wave.
бурунду́к, а́, *m.* (*zool.*) chipmunk.
бурча́ни|е, я, *n.* (*coll.*) grumbling; (stomach-)rumbling.
бурч|а́ть, у́, и́шь, *impf.* (*of* про~) (*coll.*) 1. to mumble, mutter; to grumble. 2. (*impf. only*) to rumble; to bubble; (*impers.*) в котле́ ~и́т the cauldron is bubbling; у меня́ ~и́т в животе́ my stomach is rumbling.
бу́р|ый (~, ~а, ~о), *adj.* brown; б. медве́дь brown bear; ~ая лиси́ца red fox.
бурья́н, а, *m.* tall weeds.
бу́р|я, и, *f.* storm (*also fig.*); б. в стака́не воды́ storm in a teacup; б. и на́тиск (*hist., lit.*) 'Sturm und Drang'.
буря́т, а, *g. pl.* ~, *m.* Buryat.
буря́тк|а, и, *f.* Buryat (woman).
буря́тский, *adj.* Buryat.
бу́син|а, ы, *f.* bead.
буссо́л|ь, и, *f.* surveying compass.
бу́с|ы, ~, *no sing.* beads.
бут, а, *m.* (*tech.*) rubble, quarry-stone.

бутафо́р, а, *m.* (*theatr.*) property-man.
бутафо́ри|я, и, *f.* (*theatr.*) properties; dummies (*in shop window*); (*fig.*) window-dressing, sham.
бутафо́р|ский, *adj. of* ~ия; (*fig.*) sham, mock-; illusory.
бутербро́д, а, *m.* slice of bread and butter; sandwich.
бути́л, а, *m.* (*chem.*) butyl.
бутиле́н, а, *m.* (*chem.*) butylene.
бу|ти́ть, чу́, ти́шь, *impf.* (*of* за~) (*tech.*) to fill with rubble.
бу́товый, *adj.* rubble.
буто́н, а, *m.* 1. bud. 2. (*coll.*) pimple.
бутонье́рк|а, и, *f.* buttonhole, posy.
бу́тс|ы, ~, *sing.* ~а, ы, *f.* football boots.
буту́з, а, *m.* (*coll.*) chubby lad.
буту́|зить, жу, зишь, *impf.* (*coll.*) to punch.
буты́лк|а, и, *f.* bottle.
буты́лочк|а, и, *f.* small bottle; vial, phial.
буты́лочник, а, *m.* glass-blower.
буты́л|очный, *adj. of* ~ка; ~очного цве́та bottle-green.
буты́л|ь, и, *f.* large bottle; carboy.
бу́фер, а, *pl.* ~а́, *m.* buffer.
бу́фер|ный, *adj. of* ~; ~ное госуда́рство (*polit.*) buffer state.
буфе́т, а, *m.* 1. sideboard. 2. buffet, refreshment room; (refreshment) bar, counter.
буфе́тн|ая, ой, *f.* pantry.
буфе́т|ный, *adj. of* ~.
буфе́тчик, а, *m.* barman, bartender.
буфе́тчиц|а, ы, *f.* barmaid.
буфф, *indecl.*, *adj.* comic, buffo; о́пера-б. comic opera; теа́тр-б. comedy.
буффо́н, а, *m.* (*theatr.*) buffoon; (*fig.*) buffoon, clown.
буффона́д|а, ы, *f.* (*theatr.*) buffoonery, slapstick; (*fig.*) buffoonery.
бу́ф|ы, ~, *no sing.* gathers, puffs; б. на рукава́х puff sleeves.
бух, *interj.* (*also as pred.*) bang!; plonk!; plop!; он б. на зе́млю he fell to the ground with a thud.
буха́нк|а, и, *f.* loaf.
буха́рский, *adj.* б. ковёр Bokhara carpet.
бу́х|ать, аю, *impf.* (*of* ~нуть) 1. to thump, bang; б. кулако́м в дверь to bang on the door with one's fist. 2. to let fall with a thud. 3. to thud, thunder; слы́шно бы́ло, как вдали́ ~али пу́шки the thunder of cannon could be heard in the distance. 4. (*fig., coll.*) to blurt out.
бу́х|аться, аюсь, *impf.* (*of* ~нуться) (*coll.*) to fall heavily; to plonk oneself down.
бухга́лтер, а, *pl.* ~ы, *m.* book-keeper, accountant.
бухгалте́ри|я, и, *f.* 1. book-keeping; двойна́я б. double-entry book-keeping. 2. counting-house.

бухга́лтерск|ий, *adj.* book-keeping, account; ~ая кни́га account book.

бу́х|нуть¹, ну, нешь, *past* ~нул, *pf. of* ~ать.

бу́х|нуть², ну, нешь, *past* ~, ~ла, *impf.* to swell, expand.

бу́х|нуться, нусь, нешься, *pf. of* ~аться.

бухо́й, *adj.* (*sl.*) sozzled (= *drunk*).

бу́хт|а¹, ы, *f.* (*geogr.*) bay, bight.

бу́хт|а², ы, *f.* coil (*of rope*).

бу́хточк|а, и, *f.* creek, cove, inlet.

бу́хты-бара́хты, *only in phrase* (*coll.*) с б.-б. offhand; off the cuff; suddenly.

бу́цы=бу́тсы.

бу́ч|а, и, *f.* (*coll.*) row.

бу́чени|е, я, *n.* (*tech.*) washing in lye.

бу́ч|ить, у, ишь, *impf.* (*tech.*) to wash in lye.

бу|чу́, ти́шь, *see* ~ти́ть.

бу́ч|у, ишь, *see* ~ить.

буш|ева́ть, у́ю, *impf.* to rage; (*fig.*) to rage, storm.

бу́шел|ь, я, *m.* bushel.

бушла́т, а, *m.* (*naut.*) pea-jacket.

бушпри́т, а, *m.* (*naut.*) bowsprit.

буя́н¹, а, *m.* (*coll.*) rowdy, brawler.

буя́н², а, *m.* (*obs.*) wharf.

буя́н|ить, ю, ишь, *impf.* (*coll.*) to make a row; to brawl.

буя́нств|о, а, *n.* (*coll.*) rowdyism, brawling.

бы (*abbr.* б), *particle* **1.** *indicates hypothetical sentence* (*see also* е́сли): я мог бы об э́том догада́ться I might have guessed it; бы́ло бы о́чень прия́тно вас ви́деть it would be very nice to see you. **2.** (+ни) *forms indefinite pronouns*: кто бы ни whoever; что бы ни whatever; как бы ни however; кто бы ни пришёл whoever comes; что бы ни случи́лось whatever happens; как бы то ни́ было however that may be, be that as it may. **3.** *expresses wish*: я бы вы́пил пи́ва I should like a drink of beer. **4.** *expresses polite suggestion or exhortation*: вы бы отдохну́ли you should take a rest.

быва́|ло **1.** *see* ~ть. **2.** *particle indicating repetition of an action in past time*: моя́ мать б. ча́сто пе́ла э́ту пе́сню my mother would often sing this song.

быва́л|ый, *adj.* **1.** experienced; worldly-wise. **2.** (*coll.*) habitual, familiar; э́то де́ло ~ое this is nothing new. **3.** (*obs.*) former.

быва́|ть, ю, *impf.* **1.** to happen; to take place; заседа́ния горсове́та ~ют раз в неде́лю the town council meets once a week; ~ет, что поезда́ с се́вера опа́здывают trains from the north are apt to be late, are sometimes late; э́тому не б.! this must not occur!; I forbid it! **2.** to be; to be present; to frequent; он ~ет ка́ждый день в кабине́те с девяти́ часо́в утра́ he is in his office every day from nine a.m.; они́ ре́дко ~ют в теа́тре they seldom go to the theatre;

он ~ет у нас he comes to see us. **3.** to be inclined to be, tend to be; он ~ет раздражи́телен he is inclined to be irritable. **4.** как ни в чём не ~ло (*coll.*) as if nothing had happened; as if nothing were wrong; как не ~ло (+g.) to have completely disappeared; головно́й бо́ли у меня́ как не ~ло my headache has completely gone.

бы́вш|ий, *past part. of* быть *and adj.* former, ex-; ci-devant; б. президе́нт former president; ~ие лю́ди déclassés; го́род Ку́йбышев, ~ая Сама́ра Kuibyshev, formerly (called) Samara.

бы́дл|о, а, *n.* (*collect.*; *dial.*; *also fig.*) cattle.

бык¹, а́, *m.* **1.** bull; ox; рабо́чий б. draught ox; бой ~о́в bullfight; взять ~а́ за рога́ (*fig.*) to take the bull by the horns; здоро́в, как б. as strong as a horse; упере́ться, как б. to be as stubborn as an ox. **2.** male (*of certain horned animals*); оле́ний б. stag. **3.** (*pl.*) the Bovidae.

бык², а́, *m.* pier (*of a bridge*).

был|ево́й, *adj. of* ~и́на.

были́н|а, ы, *f.* (*lit.*) bylina (*Russian traditional heroic poem*).

были́нк|а, и, *f.* blade of grass.

были́н|ный, *adj. of* ~a; epic.

бы́ло, *particle* **1.** *indicates cancellation of projected or impending action*: nearly, on the point of; он пое́хал б. с ни́ми, но заболе́л he would have gone with them, but he fell ill; чуть б. не very nearly; я чуть б. не забы́л I very nearly forgot; они́ чуть б. не уби́ли его́ they all but killed him. **2.** *indicates cessation of action already, but only just, commenced*: он отпра́вился б. с ни́ми, но верну́лся he started out with them but turned back.

был|о́й, *adj.* former, past, bygone; в ~ы́е времена́ in days of old; *as noun* ~о́е, ~о́го, *n.* (*poet.*) the past, olden time; Было́е и ду́мы 'My Past and Thoughts' (*title of work by Alexander Herzen*).

был|ь, и, *f.* **1.** (*obs.*) fact. **2.** true story.

был|ё, я́, *n.* (*obs.*) grass; *now only in phrase* ~ём поросло́ long forgotten.

быстрин|а́, ы́, *pl.* ~ы, *f.* (*geogr.*) rapid(s).

быстрогла́з|ый (~, ~a), *adj.* saucy, sprightly, busybodyish.

быстроно́гий, *adj.* (*poet.*) fleet of foot.

быстрот|а́, ы́, *f.* rapidity, quickness; speed.

быстроте́кущий, *adj.* (*poet.*, *obs.*) swift-flowing.

быстроте́ч|ный (~ен, ~на), *adj.* fleeting, transient.

быстрохо́д|ный (~ен, ~на), *adj.* fast, high-speed; б. танк (*mil.*) cruiser tank.

бы́стр|ый (~, ~а́, ~о), *adj.* rapid, fast, quick; prompt.

быт, а, о ~е, в ~у́, *no pl.*, *m.* way of life;

life; дома́шний б. family life; солда́тский б. army life; слу́жба ~а consumer services.

быти|е́, я́, n. (*philos.*) being, existence, objective reality; б., по слова́м Ма́ркса, определя́ет созна́ние existence, according to Marx, determines consciousness; кни́га ~я́ (*bibl.*) Genesis.

бы́тност|ь, и, f. *only in phrase* в б. during a given period; в б. мою́ студе́нтом in my student days; в б. его́ в Ри́ме during his stay in Rome, in his Rome days.

быт|ова́ть, у́ет, *impf.* to occur, be current; были́ны ещё ~у́ют на се́вере byliny still exist in the North.

бытови́к, а́, m. (*coll.*) writer *or* artist treating themes from everyday life.

быт|ово́й, adj. *of* ~; social; ~ова́я жи́вопись genre painting; ~ова́я пье́са play on theme of everyday life; ~ово́е револю́ция social revolution; ~ово́е явле́ние everyday occurrence; комбина́т ~ово́го обслу́живания consumer service establishment (*multiple enterprise comprising hair-dressing, dry-cleaning, household appliance repair services, etc.*).

бытописа́ни|е, я, n. (*obs.*) annals, chronicles.

бытописа́тел|ь, я, m. 1. (*obs.*) historian, annalist. **2.** writer on social themes.

быть, *pres.* not used exc. *3rd sing.* есть and (*obs.*) *3rd pl.* **суть, *fut.* бу́ду, бу́дешь, *past* был, была́, бы́ло (не́ был, не была́, не́ было),** *imp.* **бу́дь(те)** (*see also* бу́дет, бу́дь(те), бы́ло, есть).

I. **1.** to be (= to exist); есть таки́е лю́ди there are such people, such people do exist. **2.** б. у (*see also* есть) to be in the possession (of); у них была́ прекра́сная да́ча they had a lovely dacha. **3.** to be (= to be situated, be located); (к) to come (to), be present (at); здесь был тракти́р there used to be an inn here; где вы бы́ли вчера́? where were you yesterday?; он тут был не при чём he had nothing to do with it; они́ бу́дут к нам за́втра they are coming (to see us) tomorrow; на ней была́ ро́зовая ко́фточка she had on a pink blouse. **4.** to

be, happen, take place; э́того не мо́жет б.! it cannot be!; что с ним бы́ло? what happened to him?; б. беде́ there's sure to be trouble; как б.? what is to be done?; так и б. so be it, all right, very well, have it your own way; б. по сему́ (*obs.*) be it so enacted.

II. *as auxiliary verb* to be.

быть|ё, я́, n. (*obs.*) mode of life.

быча́ч|ий, adj. *of* бык¹; ~ья ко́жа oxhide; ~ья ше́я bull neck.

бы́чий, adj. = быча́чий.

быч|о́к¹, ка́, m. steer.

быч|о́к², ка́, m. Gobius (*small fish found in Black Sea*).

быч|о́к³, ка́, m. (*coll.*) cigarette butt.

бьеф, а, m. reach; ве́рхний б. head water; ни́жний б. tail water.

бью, бьёшь, *see* бить.

бюва́р, а, m. blotting-pad.

бюве́т, а, m. pump-room.

бюдже́т, а, m. budget.

бюдже́тный, adj. budgetary; б. год fiscal year.

бюллете́н|ь, я, m. 1. bulletin. **2.** (избира́тельный) б. voting-paper. **3.** (больни́чный) б. medical certificate; быть на ~е (*coll.*) to be on sick-leave, be on the sick-list.

бю́ргер, а, m. burgher; (*fig., iron.*) philistine.

бюре́тк|а, и, f. (*tech.*) burette.

бюро́, *indecl.*, n. 1. bureau, office; б. нахо́док lost-property office; спра́вочное б. inquiry office. **2.** bureau, writing-desk.

бюрокра́т, а, m. bureaucrat.

бюрократи́зм, а, m. bureaucracy; red tape.

бюрократи́ческий, adj. bureaucratic.

бюрокра́ти|я, и, f. bureaucracy (*also collect.*).

бюст, а, m. bust; bosom.

бюстга́льтер, а, m. brassière.

бя́з|евый, adj. *of* ~ь.

бяз|ь, и, f. coarse calico.

бя́к|а, и, f. (*in children's speech*) nasty thing; nasty man.

бя́ша, *interj.* (*dial.*; *onomat.*) baa!

В

в, *prep.*

I. +*a.* and *p.* **1.** (+*a.*) into, to; (+*p.*) in, at; пое́хать в Москву́ to go to Moscow; роди́ться в Москве́ to be born in Moscow; сесть в ваго́н to get into the carriage; сиде́ть в ваго́не to be in the carriage; оде́ться в смо́кинг to put on a dinner-jacket; быть в смо́кинге to be in a dinner-jacket; разби́ть в куски́ to smash to pieces; са́хар в куска́х sugar in lumps; привести́ в восто́рг to delight, enrapture; быть в восто́рге to be delighted, be in raptures. **2.** *in reference to external attributes*: руба́шка в кле́тку check(ed) shirt; лицо́ в весну́шках freckled face. **3.** (+*n.–a. pl.* and *p. pl.*) *in reference to occupation*: пойти́ в стенографи́стки to become a shorthand-typist; служи́ть в куха́рках to be a cook. **4.** *in reference to calendar units and periods of time*: в понеде́льник on Monday; в январе́ in January; в 1899-ом году́ in 1899; в двадца́том ве́ке in the twentieth century; в четы́ре часа́ at four o'clock; в четвёртом часу́ between three and four; в на́ши дни in our day; в тече́ние (+*g.*) during, in the course (of).

II. +*a.* **1.** *in reference to objects through which vision is directed*: смотре́ть в окно́ to look out of the window; смотре́ть в бино́кль to look through binoculars. **2.** *in attribution of resemblance*: быть в кого́-н. to take after someone; она́ вся в тётю she is the image of her aunt. **3.** *indicating aim or purpose*: for, as; сказа́ть в шу́тку to say for a joke; привести́ в доказа́тельство to adduce as proof. **4.** *in specification of quantitative attributes*: моро́з в де́сять гра́дусов ten degrees of frost; высото́й в три ме́тра three metres high; ве́сом в пять килогра́ммов weighing five kilograms. **5.** (+*раз and comp. adv.*) *indicates comparison in numerical terms*: в два ра́за бо́льше twice as big, twice the size; в два ра́за ме́ньше half as big, half the size. **6.** *of time*: in, within; наде́юсь ко́нчить чернови́к в ме́сяц I hope to finish the rough draft in a month. **6.** *indicates game or sport played*: игра́ть в ка́рты, ша́хматы, те́ннис, футбо́л to play cards, chess, tennis, football.

III. +*p.* **1.** at a distance of; в трёх киломе́трах от го́рода three kilometres from the town; они́ живу́т в десяти́ мину́тах ходьбы́ отсю́да they live ten minutes' walk from here. **2.** in; of (= consisting of, amounting to); пье́са в трёх де́йствиях play in three acts; ра́зница в двух копе́йках a difference of two kopecks.

ва-ба́нк, *adv.* (*cards*) игра́ть, идти́ ва-б. to stake everything; (*fig.*) to stake one's all.

ва́б|ить, лю, ишь, *impf.* to lure, decoy.

вавило́нск|ий, *adj.* Babylonian; ～ое столпотворе́ние babel; ～ая ба́шня the tower of Babel.

вавило́н|ы, ов, *no sing.* (*coll.*) **1.** (*archit.*) scrolls. **2.** flourishes (*in handwriting*), scrawl; выводи́ть, писа́ть в. (*fig.*) to stagger, lurch (*of a drunken person*).

ва́г|а, и, *f.* (*tech.*) **1.** weighing-machine. **2.** splinter-bar; swingle-tree. **3.** lever.

ваго́н, а, *m.* **1.** carriage, coach; мя́гкий, жёсткий в. soft-seated, hard-seated carriage; бага́жный в. luggage van; в.-рестора́н dining-car, restaurant car; спа́льный в. sleeping-car; това́рный в. goods wagon, goods truck; трамва́йный в. tram-car;

в.-цисте́рна tank truck. **2.** wagon-load; (*fig., coll.*) loads, lots; игру́шек у него́ в. he has loads of toys; вре́мени у нас в. we have masses of time.

вагоне́тк|а, и, *f.* truck; trolley.

вагоне́тчик, а, *m.* truck-, trolley-operator.

ваго́нник, а, *m.* carriage-building worker.

ваго́н|ный, *adj.* of ～; ～ная ось carriage axle; в. парк rolling-stock.

вагоновожа́т|ый, ого, *m.* tram-driver.

вагоностро́ени|е, я, *n.* carriage-building.

вагоностро́ительный, *adj.* carriage-building; в. заво́д carriage(-building) works.

вагра́нк|а, и, *f.* (*tech.*) cupola furnace.

ва́женк|а, и, *f.* (*dial.*) female reindeer.

важне́цк|ий, *adj.* (*coll.*) good, good-quality; вот у вас ～ие боти́нки that's a good pair of boots you have on.

ва́жничани|е, я, *n.* airs and graces.

ва́жнича|ть, ю, *impf.* (*coll.*) to give oneself airs, get a swelled head; (+*i.*) to plume oneself (on).

ва́жност|ь, и, *f.* **1.** importance; significance; де́ло большо́й ～и a matter of great importance, of great moment; не велика́ в. (*coll.*) it's of no consequence; э́ка в.! (*coll.*) what does it matter! **2.** pomposity, pretentiousness.

ва́ж|ный (～ен, ～на́, ～но), *adj.* **1.** important; weighty, consequential; са́мое ～ое узна́ть, отку́да они́ прие́хали the (important) thing is to discover where they have come from; в свое́й стране́ он дово́льно в. челове́к in his own country he is a man of some consequence; ～ная ши́шка (*coll.*) bigwig, big knob. **2.** pompous, pretentious.

ва́з|а, ы, *f.* vase, bowl; в. для цвето́в flower vase; ночна́я в. chamber-pot.

вазели́н, а, *m.* vaseline.

вазели́н|овый, *adj.* of ～; ～овое ма́сло (*med.*) liquid paraffin.

вазомото́рный, *adj.* (*med.*) vasomotor.

вазо́н, а, *m.* (flower-)pot.

ва́и|я, и, *g. pl.* ～й, *f.* **1.** (*bot.*) fern-branch. **2.** palm(-branch); неде́ля ～й (*eccl.*) Palm Sunday.

ва́йя = ва́ия.

вака́нси|я, и, *f.* vacancy; бу́дут две ～и в шта́те в бу́дущем году́ there will be two vacancies on the staff next year.

вака́нт|ный (～ен, ～на), *adj.* vacant (*of posts in an institution*).

вака́ци|я, и, *f.* (*obs.*) vacation.

ва́кс|а, ы, *f.* (shoe) polish; blacking.

ва́к|сить, шу, сишь, *impf.* (*of* на～) to black, polish.

ва́куум, а, *m.* (*tech.*) vacuum; в.-маши́на, в.-насо́с vacuum pump.

вакхана́ли|я, и, *f.* **1.** (*usu. pl.*; *hist.*) bacchanalia. **2.** (*fig.*) orgy. **3.** (*fig.*) confusion, disorder.

вакха́нк|а, и, *f.* **1.** Bacchante, maenad. **2.** (*fig.*) bawd, hussy.

вакхи́ческий, *adj.* Bacchic.

вакци́н|а, ы, *f.* vaccine.

вакцина́ци|я, и, *f.* vaccination.

ва́к|шу, сишь, *see* ~сить.

вал¹, а, *pl.* ~ы́, *m.* billow, roller; девя́тый в. 'ninth wave' (*according to superstition, fatal to sailors*).

вал², а, *pl.* ~ы́, *m.* bank, earthen wall; (*mil.*) rampart; (*geol.*) swell.

вал³, а, *pl.* ~ы́, *m.* (*tech.*) shaft.

вал⁴, а, *m.* (*econ.*) **1.** gross output (*as indicator of industrial efficiency, by contrast with profit*). **2.** = план ~ово́й проду́кции (*see* ~ово́й).

вала́нда|ться, юсь, *impf.* (*coll.*) **1.** to loiter, hang about. **2.** (c+*i.*) to dawdle (over), mess about (with).

вала́нсьен, *indecl.,* *adj.* (*text.*) кружева́ в. Valenciennes lace.

вале́жник, а, *no pl., m.* (*collect.*) windfallen trees, branches.

вал|ёк, ька́, *m.* (*tech.*) **1.** battledore. **2.** swingle-tree. **3.** (*typ., etc.*) roller. **4.** (*agric.*) (threshing-)flail. **5.** (*naut.*) loom (*of an oar*).

ва́лен|ки, ок *and* **ков,** *sing.* ~ок, ~ка, *m.* valenki (*felt boots*).

вале́нтност|ь, и, *f.* (*chem.*) valency.

ва́леный, *adj.* = валя́ный.

валерья́н|а, ы, *f.* (*bot.*) valerian.

валерья́нк|а, и, *f.* (*coll.*) tincture of valerian.

валерья́нов|ый, *adj.* (*med.*) ~ые ка́пли tincture of valerian.

вале́т, а, *m.* (*cards*) knave, jack.

ва́лик, а, *m.* **1.** (*tech.*) roller, cylinder; spindle, shaft. **2.** bolster.

вал|и́ть¹, ю, ~ишь, *impf.* **1.** (*pf.* по~ *and* c~) to throw down, bring down, send toppling; to overthrow; в. кого́-н. с ног to knock someone off his feet; в. дере́вья to fell trees; нас всех ~и́л грипп we were all being laid low by the 'flu. **2.** (*pf.* c~) to heap up, pile up; в. всё в одну́ ку́чу to lump everything together (*also fig.*); в. вину́ (на+*a.*) to lump the blame (on).

вал|и́ть², и́т, *impf.* (*coll.*) **1.** to flock, throng, pour; вало́м в. to throng, go en masse; лю́ди ~и́ли на стадио́н people were flocking to the stadium; снег ~и́т кру́пными хло́пьями the snow is coming down in large flakes; дым ~и́л из трубы́ smoke was belching from the chimney; ему́ уж давно́ ~и́т сча́стье he has had a long run of luck. **2.** ~й(те)! go on!, have a go!; ~й, беги́! be off with you!

вал|и́ться, ю́сь, ~ишься, *impf.* (*of* по~ *and* c~) to fall, collapse; to topple; в. от уста́лости to drop from tiredness; у него́ всё

из рук ~ится (*coll.*) he is all fingers and thumbs; де́ло у него́ ~ится и́з рук his heart is not in the matter, he cannot put his mind to the matter; на бе́дного Мака́ра все ши́шки ~ятся (*prov.*) an unfortunate man would be drowned in a teacup.

ва́лк|а¹, и, *f.* felling.

ва́лк|а², и, *f.* (*text.*) fulling.

ва́л|кий (~ок, ~ка́, ~ко), *adj.* unsteady, shaky; (*naut.*) crank; ни ша́тко, ни ~ко middling; neither good nor bad.

ва́лкост|ь, и, *f.* (*naut.*) crankness.

валли́|ец, йца, *m.* Welshman.

валли́йк|а, и, *f.* Welshwoman.

валли́йский, *adj.* Welsh.

валло́н, а, *m.* Walloon.

валло́нк|а, и, *f.* Walloon (woman).

валло́нский, *adj.* Walloon.

валово́й, *adj.* **1.** (*econ.*) gross; wholesale; в. дохо́д gross revenue; в. сбор gross yield; план в. проду́кции gross output plan. **2.** general, mass (*of migration of birds*).

вало́м, *see* вали́ть².

вало́ш|ить, у, ишь, *impf.* to castrate, geld.

валто́рн|а, ы, *f.* (*mus.*) French horn.

валу́|й, я́, *m.* mushroom (*Russula foetens*).

валу́н, а́, *m.* boulder.

ва́льдшнеп, а, *m.* (*zool.*) woodcock.

вальс, а, *m.* waltz.

вальси́р|овать, ую, *impf.* to waltz.

вальц|ева́ть, у́ю, *impf.* (*tech.*) to roll.

вальцо́вк|а, и, *f.* (*tech.*) **1.** rolling. **2.** rolling press.

вальцо́вщик, а, *m.* (*tech.*) operative of rolling-mill, roller.

вальцо́в|ый, *adj.* (*tech.*); ~ая ме́льница rolling-mill.

вальц|ы́, о́в, *no sing.* (*tech.*) rolling press.

ва́льщик, а, *m.* (*dial.*) woodcutter.

валья́жный, *adj.* (*coll.*) weighty, impressive; handsome; вид у него́ в. he has an impressive presence; в. переплёт handsome binding.

валю́т|а, ы, *f.* (*fin., econ.*) **1.** currency; курс ~ы rate of exchange. **2.** (*collect.*) foreign currency.

валю́т|ный, *adj.* of ~a; currency.

валю́тчик, а, *m.* (*coll.*) speculator in foreign currency.

валя́льный, *adj.* fulling.

валя́л|ьня, ьни, *g. pl.* ~ен, *f.* fulling-mill.

валя́льщик, а, *m.* fuller.

валя́ни|е, я, *n.* (*tech.*) fulling, milling.

ва́ляный, *adj.* felt.

валя́|ть, ю, *impf.* **1.** (*impf. only*) to drag; в. по́ полу to drag along the floor. **2.** (*pf.* вы́~) to roll, drag; в. в грязи́ to drag in the mire. **3.** (*pf.* c~) to knead. **4.** (*pf.* c~) to full; to felt. **5.** (*pf.* на~) (*coll.*) to botch, bungle; to muck about. **6.** в. дурака́ (*coll.*) to play the fool. **7.** ~й(те)! (*coll.*) go ahead!, carry on!

валя́|ться, юсь, *impf.* **1.** to roll. **2.** (*coll.*) to lie about, loll; весь день он ~ется в хала́те he lies about in his dressing-gown all day; её оде́жда ~лась везде́ по ко́мнате her clothes lay scattered all over the room; в. в нога́х у кого́-н. (*fig.*) to fall down at someone's feet.

вам, *d. of* вы.

ва́ми, *i. of* вы.

вампи́р, а, *m.* **1.** vampire (*also fig.*). **2.** (*zool.*) vampire-bat.

вана́ди|й, я, *m.* (*chem.*) vanadium.

ванда́л, а, *m.* (*hist. and fig.*) Vandal; vandal.

вандали́зм, а, *m.* vandalism.

ванили́н, а, *m.* vanillin.

вани́л|ь, и, *f.* vanilla.

вани́ль|ный, *adj. of* ~.

ва́нн|а, ы, *f.* bath; сидя́чая в. hip-bath; со́лнечная в. sun-bath; фотографи́ческая в. photographic bath; взять ~у, приня́ть ~у to take a bath.

ва́нночк|а, и, *f. dim. of* ва́нна; (*phot.*) developing tray; глазна́я в. eye-bath.

ва́нн|ый, *adj. of* ~а; *as noun* ~ая, ~ой, *f.* bathroom.

ва́нт|а, ы, *f.* (*naut.*) shroud.

ва́ньк|а, и, *m.* (*obs.*) cabby (*nickname of poor droshky-drivers*).

ва́нька-вста́нька, **ва́ньки-вста́ньки**, *m.* cork-tumbler (*doll with weight attached to its base which causes it always to recover standing position*); (*fig.*) *of person never discouraged by misfortune*).

вапориза́тор, а, *m.* (*tech.*) vaporizer.

вапориза́ци|я, и, *f.* (*tech.*) vaporization.

вар, а, *m.* **1.** pitch; cobbler's wax. **2.** (*dial.*) boiling water.

вара́кушк|а, и, *f.* (*orn.*) bluethroat.

вара́н, а, *m.* (*zool.*) giant lizard.

ва́рвар, а, *m.* barbarian.

варвари́зм, а, *m.* (*ling., lit.*) barbarism.

ва́рварский, *adj.* barbarian; (*fig.*) barbaric.

ва́рварств|о, а, *n.* barbarity; vandalism.

варга́н|ить, ю, ишь, *impf.* (*coll.*) to botch, bungle.

ва́рев|о, а, *n.* (*coll., pejor.*) broth; slop.

ва́режк|а, и, *f.* mitten (*glove with thumb but no fingers*).

варен|е́ц, ца́, *m.* fermented boiled milk.

варе́ние = ва́рка.

варе́ник, а, *m.* varenik (*curd or fruit dumpling*).

варёный, *adj.* **1.** boiled. **2.** (*coll.*) limp.

варе́нь|е, я, *n.* preserve(s) (*containing whole fruit*), jam.

вариа́нт, а, *m.* reading, variant; version; расска́з был распространён во мно́гих ~ах many versions of the story were circulated.

вариацио́нн|ый, *adj.* variant; ~ое исчисле́ние (*math.*) calculus of variations.

вариа́ци|я, и, *f.* variation; те́ма с ~ями (*mus.*) theme and variations.

варико́зный, *adj.* (*anat.*) varicose.

вар|и́ть, ю́, ~ишь, *impf.* (*of* с~) **1.** to boil; to cook; в. карто́фель to boil potatoes; в. обе́д to cook dinner; в. глинтве́йн to mull wine; в. пи́во to brew beer. **2.** (*of the stomach*) to digest. **3.** to found (*steel*).

вар|и́ться, ю́сь, ~ишься, *impf.* (*of* с~) **1.** to boil (*intrans.*); to cook (*intrans.*); карто́фель уже́ полчаса́ ~ится the potatoes have been on for half an hour already; в. в со́бственном соку́ (*coll.*) to keep to oneself. **2.** *pass. of* ~и́ть.

ва́рк|а, и, *f.* boiling; cooking; в. варе́нья preserve-making; в. желе́за iron-founding; в. пи́ва brewing.

ва́р|кий (~ок, ~ка́, ~ко), *adj.* **1.** heat-giving; ~кая печь hot stove. **2.** tender (*of meat, etc.*).

варна́к, а́, *m.* (*dial.*) (escaped) convict.

ва́рниц|а, ы, *f.* **1.** saltworks. **2.** saltpan.

варра́нт, а, *m.* (*comm.*) custom-house license; warehouse warrant.

варша́вский, *adj.* (of) Warsaw.

варьете́, *indecl.*, *n.* variety (show); теа́тр-в. music-hall.

варьи́р|овать, ую, *impf.* to vary, modify.

варя́г, а, *m.* (*hist.*) Varangian.

варя́жский, *adj.* (*hist.*) Varangian.

вас, *g., a., and p. of* вы.

васил|ёк, ька́, *m.* (*bot.*) cornflower.

васили́ск, а, *m.* basilisk.

васил|ько́вый, *adj. of* ~ёк; cornflower blue.

васса́л, а, *m.* vassal, liege(-man).

васса́ль|ный, *adj.* vassal; ~ая зави́симость vassalage.

ва́т|а, ы, *f.* cotton wool; wadding; пальто́ на ~е wadded coat.

вата́г|а, и, *f.* band, gang.

ватерклозе́т, а, *m.* water-closet.

ватерли́ни|я, и, *f.* (*naut.*) water-line; грузова́я в. load water-line.

ва́тер-маши́н|а, ы, *f.* (*text.*) water frame.

ватерпа́с, а, *m.* (*tech.*) water-level, spirit-level.

ватер-по́ло, *indecl.*, *n.* (*sport*) water polo.

вати́н, а, *m.* sheet wadding.

ва́тман, а, *m.* Whatman paper.

ва́тник, а, *m.* quilted jacket.

ва́тн|ый, *adj.* wadded, quilted; ~ое одея́ло quilt.

ватру́шк|а, и, *f.* curd tart; cheese-cake.

ватт, а, *g. pl.* в. *m.* (*electr.*) watt.

ва́ттност|ь, и, *f.* (*electr.*) wattage.

ва́фельниц|а, ы, *f.* waffle-iron.

ва́фельщик, а, *m.* waffle-maker; waffle--vendor.

ва́ф|ля, ли, *g. pl.* ~ель, *f.* waffle.

вахла́к, а́, *m.* (*coll.*) lout; sloven.

ва́хмистр, а, *m.* (*obs.*) cavalry sergeant-major.

ва́хт|а, ы, *f.* 1. (*naut.*) watch; стоя́ть на ~е to keep watch. 2. (*fig.*) special (collective) effort, special stint (*of Soviet workers on anniversary of October revolution, etc.*).

ва́хт|енный, *adj.* of ~а (*naut.*); в. журна́л log(-book); в. команди́р officer of the watch; *as noun* в., ~енного, *m.* watch.

ва́хтер, а, *pl.* ~а́, *m.* (*obs.*) senior watchman.

вахтёр, а, *m.* janitor, porter.

вахтпара́д, а, *m.* (*obs.*) changing of the guard.

ваш, ~его; *f.* ~а, ~ей; *n.* ~е, ~его; *pl.* ~и, ~их, *possessive pron.* your(s); э́то в. каранда́ш this is your pencil; э́тот каранда́ш в. this pencil is yours; ~его мне не ну́жно (*coll.*) I don't want anything of yours; он зна́ет бо́льше ~его (*coll.*) he knows more than you; не ~е де́ло it is none of your business; *as noun* ~и, ~их your people, your folk.

ва́шгерд, а, *m.* (*tech.*) buddle.

вая́ни|е, я, *n.* (*obs.*) sculpture.

вая́тел|ь, я, *m.* (*obs.*) sculptor.

вая́|ть, ю, *impf.* (*of* из~) (*obs.*) to sculpture; to carve, chisel.

вбега́|ть, ю, *impf.* (в+*a.*) to run (into).

вбе|жа́ть, гу́, жи́шь, гу́т, *pf. of* ~га́ть.

вбер|у́, ёшь, *see* вобра́ть.

вбива́|ть, ю, *impf. of* вбить.

вби́вк|а, и, *f.* knocking-in.

вбира́|ть, ю, *impf. of* вобра́ть.

вбить, вобью́, вобьёшь, *pf.* (*of* вбива́ть) to drive in, hammer in; (*sport*) в. мяч to score a goal; (*coll.*) в. в го́лову (+*d.*; *fig.*) to knock into someone's head; в. себе́ в го́лову to get into one's head.

вблизи́, *adv.* (*ot*) close by; not far (from); они́ живу́т где́-то в. they live somewhere near here; в. был слы́шен водопа́д the sound of a waterfall could be heard near by; в. от библиоте́ки not far from the library; рассма́тривать в. to examine closely.

вбок, *adv.* sideways, to one side.

вбра́сывани|е, я, *n.* в. (мяча́) throw-in (*in football*).

вбра́сыва|ть, ю, *impf. of* вбро́сить.

вброд, *adv.* переходи́ть в. to wade; to ford.

вбро́|сить, шу, сишь, *pf.* (*of* вбра́сывать) to throw in(to).

вва́лива|ть, ю, *impf. of* ввали́ть.

вва́лива|ться, юсь, *impf. of* ввали́ться.

ввал|и́ть, ю́, ~ишь, *pf.* to hurl, heave into.

ввал|и́ться, ю́сь, ~ишься, *pf.* 1. (*coll.*) to tumble into, sink into. 2. (*fig., coll.*) to burst into. 3. to become hollow, sunken; с ~и́вшимися щека́ми hollow-cheeked.

введе́ни|е, я, *n.* 1. leading in(to); в. в заблужде́ние leading into temptation; В. (во храм) (*eccl.*) Feast of the Presentation of the Blessed Virgin. 2. introduction; preamble; в. в языкозна́ние introduction to philology.

вве|ду́, дёшь, *see* ~сти́.

ввез|ти́, у́, ёшь, *past* ~, ~ла́, *pf.* (*of* ввози́ть) to import.

ввек, *adv.* (*now only used before neg.*) ever; я э́того в. не забу́ду I shall not forget it as long as I live.

вверг|а́ть, а́ю, *impf. of* ~нуть.

вве́рг|нуть, ну, нешь, *past* ~, ~ла, *pf.* (*of* ~а́ть) (в+*a.*; *obs.*) to cause to fall (into); to reduce (to); в. в тюрьму́ to cast into gaol; в. в нищету́ to bring to ruin; в. в отча́яние to drive to despair.

вве́р|ить, ю, ишь, *pf.* (*of* ~я́ть) to entrust; в. та́йну кому́-н. to confide a secret in someone.

вве́р|иться, юсь, ишься, *pf.* (*of* ~я́ться) (+*d.*) to trust (in), put one's faith (in), put oneself in the hands of.

вверн|у́ть, у́, ёшь, *pf.* (*of* вве́ртывать) 1. to screw in, insert. 2. (*fig., coll.*) to insert, put in; в. замеча́ние to insert a comment; ему́ не удало́сь в. ни слове́чка he could not get a word in.

вверста́|ть, ю, *pf.* (*of* вверсты́вать) (*typ.*) to inset.

вверсты́ва|ть, ю, *impf. of* вверста́ть.

ввер|те́ть, чу́, ~тишь, *pf.* (*of* ~ты́вать) (*coll.*) to screw in.

вве́ртыва|ть, ю, *impf. of* вверну́ть *and* ввертеть.

вверх, *adv.* up, upward(s); идти́ в. по ле́стнице to go upstairs; в. по тече́нию upstream; в. дном upside down; topsy-turvy; в. нога́ми head over heels.

вверху́, *adv. and prep.*+*g.* above, overhead; в. над кры́шами домо́в above the roofs of the houses; в. страни́цы at the top of the page.

ввер|чу́, ~тишь, *see* ~те́ть.

вверя́|ть(ся), ю(сь), *impf. of* вве́рить(ся).

вве|сти́, ду́, дёшь, *past* ~л, ~ла́, *pf.* (*of* вводи́ть) to introduce, bring in; в. мо́ду to introduce a fashion; в. су́дно в га́вань to bring a ship into harbour; в. во владе́ние (*leg.*) to put in possession; в. в заблужде́ние to mislead; в. в искуше́ние to lead into temptation; в. в курс чего́-н. to acquaint with the facts of something; в. в расхо́д to put to expense; (*math.*) to interpolate.

вве́черу́, *adv.* (*obs.*) in the evening.

ввива́|ть, ю, *impf. of* ввить.

ввиду́, *prep.+g.* in view (of); в. тума́на полёт не состои́тся in view of the fog the flight will not take place; в. того́, что as; в. того́, что вы прие́хали as you have come.

ввин|ти́ть, чу́, ти́шь, *pf. (of* ~чивать (в+*a.*) to screw (in); в. што́пор в про́бку to insert a corkscrew into a cork.

вви́нчива|ть, ю, *impf. of* ввинти́ть.

ввить, вовью́, вовьёшь, *pf. (of* ввива́ть) to weave in.

ввод, а, *m.* 1. bringing in; в. в бой (*mil.*) throwing into battle; в. во владе́ние (*leg.*) putting in possession. 2. (*electr.*) lead-in.

вво|ди́ть, жу́, ~дишь, *impf. of* ввести́.

вво́дн|ый, *adj.* introductory; (*gram.*) ~ое предложе́ние parenthetic clause; ~ое сло́во parenthetic word, parenthesis; в. тон (*mus.*) leading note.

вво|жу́[1], ~дишь, *see* вводи́ть.

вво|жу́[2], ~зишь, *see* ввози́ть.

ввоз, а, *no pl.*, *m.* 1. importation. 2. import; (*collect.*) imports.

вво|зи́ть, жу́, ~зишь, *impf. of* ввезти́.

вво́зн|ый, *adj.* imported; import; ~ые континге́нты quota of imports; ~ая по́шлина import duty.

ввола́кива|ть, ю, *impf. of* вволо́чь.

вволо́|чь, ку́, чёшь, ку́т, *past* ~к, ~кла́, *pf.* (*coll.*) to drag in.

вво́лю, *adv.* (*coll.*) to one's heart's content, ad lib.; нае́сться в. to eat one's fill.

вво́сьмеро, *adv.* eight times; в. бо́льше eight times as much.

ввосьмеро́м, *adv.* eight together; они́ в. сде́лали рабо́ту eight of them did the job together.

ввысь, *adv.* up, upward(s).

ввя|за́ть, жу́, ~жешь, *pf. (of* ~зывать) to knit in; (*fig.*) to involve.

ввя|за́ться, жу́сь, ~жешься, *pf.* (в+*a.*; *coll.*) to meddle (in); to get involved (in); mixed up (in); в. в неприя́тную исто́рию to get mixed up in a nasty business; в. в бой (*mil.*) to become engaged.

ввя́зыва|ть(ся), ю(сь), *impf. of* ввяза́ть(ся).

вгиб, а, *m.* bend inwards.

вгиба́|ть, ю, *impf. of* вогну́ть.

вглубь, *adv. and prep.+g.* deep down; deep into, into the depths; в. лесо́в into the heart of the forest; в. страны́ far inland.

вгля|де́ться, жу́сь, ди́шься, *pf. (of* ~ды-ваться) (в+*a.*) to peer (at).

вгля́дыва|ться, юсь, *impf. of* вгляде́ться.

вгоня́|ть, ю, *impf. of* вогна́ть.

вгрыз|ться, у́сь, ёшься, *pf.* (*coll.*) to get one's teeth into (*of animals*).

вда|ва́ться, ю́сь, ёшься, *impf. of* ~ться.

вдав|и́ть, лю́, ~ишь, *pf. (of* ~ливать) to press in.

вда́влива|ть, ю, *impf. of* вдави́ть.

вда́лблива|ть, ю, *impf. of* вдолби́ть.

вдалеке́, *adv.* in the distance; в. от a long way from.

вдали́, *adv.* in the distance, far off; в. от го́рода a long way from the city; держа́ться в. to keep aloof, keep one's distance; исчеза́ть в. to vanish into thin air.

вдаль, *adv.* afar, at a distance; гляде́ть в. to look into the distance.

вд|а́ться, а́мся, а́шься, а́стся, ади́мся, ади́тесь, аду́тся, *pf. (of* вдава́ться) (в+*a.*) to jut out (into); в. в подро́бности to go into details; в. в то́нкости to split hairs.

вдвига́|ть(ся), ю(сь), *impf. of* вдви́нуть(ся).

вдвижно́й, *adj.* insertable.

вдви́|нуть, ну, нешь, *pf. (of* ~га́ть) to push in(to).

вдви́|нуться, нусь, нешься, *pf. (of* ~га́ться) to push in, squeeze in.

вдво́е, *adv.* twice; double; в. бо́льше twice as much, twice as big; в. ста́рше double the age; сложи́ть в. to fold double.

вдвоём, *adv.* the two together; они́ в. написа́ли статью́ the two of them together wrote the article.

вдвойне́, *adv.* twice, double; doubly (*also fig.*); плати́ть в. to pay double; он в. винова́т he is doubly to blame.

вдева́|ть, ю, *impf. of* вдеть.

вде́вятеро, *adv.* nine times.

вдевятеро́м, *adv.* nine together.

вдёжк|а, и, *f.* 1. threading (*of a needle*). 2. thread.

вде́л|ать, аю, *pf. (of* ~ывать) (в+*a.*) to fit (into), set (into); в. ка́мень в кольцо́ to set a stone into a ring.

вде́лыва|ть, ю, *impf. of* вде́лать.

вде́н|у, ешь, *see* вдеть.

вдёргива|ть, ю, *impf. of* вдёрнуть.

вдёржк|а, и, *f.* 1. bodkin. 2. threading.

вдёрн|уть, у, ешь, *pf. (of* вдёргивать) to pull through; to thread; в. ни́тку в иглу́ to thread a needle.

вде́сятеро, *adv.* ten times; в. бо́льше ten times as much.

вдесятеро́м, *adv.* ten together; мы в. ten of us.

вде|ть, ~ну, ~нешь, *pf. (of* ~ва́ть) (в+*a.*) to put in(to); в. ни́тку в иглу́ to thread a needle.

вдоба́вок, *adv.* in addition; moreover; into the bargain.

вдов|а́, ы́, *pl.* ~ы, *f.* widow; соло́менная в. (*coll.*) grass widow.

вдове́|ть, ю, *impf. (of* о~) to be a widow(er); to be widowed.

вдов|е́ц, ца́, *m.* widower; соло́менный в. grass widower.

вдо́в|ий, *adj. of* ~á; ~ья часть насле́дства (*leg.*) dower, jointure.

вдови́ц|а, ы, *f.* (*obs.*) widow.

вдо́воль, *adv.* (*coll.*) **1.** in abundance; у нас вся́кого ро́да фру́ктов в. we have abundance of every kind of fruit. **2.** enough; он нае́лся в. he ate his fill.

вдовств|о́, а́, *n.* widowhood; widowerhood.

вдо́вств|овать, ую, *impf.* (*obs.*) to be a widow, a widower; ~у́ющая императри́ца the Dowager Empress.

вдо́в|ый (~), *adj.* widowed.

вдого́нку, *adv.* after, in pursuit of; бро́ситься вдого́нку (за+*i.*) to rush (after).

вдолб|и́ть, лю́, и́шь, *pf.* (*of* вда́лбливать) (*coll.*) в. кому́-н. в го́лову to drum, din into someone's head.

вдоль 1. *prep.* (+*g.* *or* по+*d.*) along; в. бе́рега along the bank; я поплы́л в. по реке́ I sailed down the river. **2.** *adv.* lengthwise, longways; разреза́ть мате́рию в. to cut material lengthwise; в. и поперёк in all directions, far and wide; он изъе́здил всю Росси́ю в. и поперёк he has travelled the length and breadth of Russia; (*fig.*) minutely, in detail; он зна́ет Шекспи́ра в. и поперёк he knows Shakespeare inside out.

вдо́сталь, *adv.* **1.** (*coll.*) in plenty. **2.** (*obs.*) completely.

вдох, а, *m.* (*coll.*) breath; сде́лать глубо́кий в. to take a deep breath.

вдохнове́ни|е, я, *n.* inspiration.

вдохнове́нный, *adj.* inspired.

вдохнови́тел|ь, я, *m.* inspirer; inspiration (*of persons*); он — наш в. he is an inspiration to us.

вдохнови́тельн|ый, *adj.* (*obs.*) inspiring; ~ая речь an inspiring speech.

вдохнов|и́ть, лю́, и́шь, *pf.* (*of* ~ля́ть) (+*a.* *or* на+*a.*) to inspire (to); его́ слова́ ~и́ли меня́ his words inspired me; казнь бра́та ~и́ла его́ на борьбу́ his brother's execution inspired him to struggle.

вдохновля́|ть, ю, *impf. of* вдохнови́ть.

вдохн|у́ть, у́, ёшь, *pf.* (*of* вдыха́ть) (в+*a.*) **1.** to breathe in, inhale; в. све́жий во́здух в лёгкие to breathe fresh air into one's lungs. **2.** to inspire (with), instil (into); в. му́жество в кого́-н. to inspire someone with courage, instil courage into someone.

вдре́безги, *adv.* to pieces, to smithereens; разби́ть в. to smash to smithereens; в. пьян (*coll.*) dead drunk.

вдруг, *adv.* **1.** suddenly, all of a sudden; все в. all together; не говори́те все в. don't all speak at once. **2.** *as interrog. particle* (*coll.*) what if, suppose; а в. они́ узна́ют? but suppose they find out?

вдры́зг, *adv.* (*coll.*) completely; в. пьян dead drunk.

вдува́ни|е, я, *n.* inflation, blowing up; (*med.*) pneumothorax.

вдува́|ть, ю, *impf. of* вдуть.

вду́м|аться, аюсь, *pf.* (*of* ~ываться) (в+*a.*) to think over, ponder, meditate (on).

вду́мчив|ый (~, ~а), *adj.* pensive, meditative; thoughtful.

вду́мыва|ться, юсь, *impf. of* вду́маться.

вду́н|уть, у, ешь, *pf.* = вдуть.

вду|ть, ~ю, ~ешь, *pf.* (*of* ~ва́ть) to blow into; в. во́здух в ши́ну to inflate, blow up a tyre.

вдыха́ни|е, я, *n.* inhalation.

вдыха́тельный, *adj.* (*med.*) respiratory.

вдыха́|ть, ю, *impf. of* вдохну́ть.

вегетариа́н|ец, ца, *m.* vegetarian.

вегетариа́нский, *adj.* vegetarian.

вегетариа́нств|о, а, *n.* vegetarianism.

вегетати́вный, *adj.* (*biol.*) vegetative.

вегетацио́нный, *adj.* (*biol.*) vegetation; в. пери́од vegetation period.

вегета́ци|я, и, *f.* vegetation.

ве́да|ть, ю, *impf.* **1.** (*obs.*) to know. **2.** (+*i.*) to manage, be in charge of.

ве́дени|е, я, *n.* authority; быть в ~и (+*g.*) (*leg.*) to be under the jurisdiction (of); э́то вне моего́ ~я this is outside my province.

веде́ни|е, я, *n.* conducting; conduct; в. де́ла conduct of an affair, transaction.

ве́дерный, *adj.* **1.** of a bucket, pail. **2.** holding a bucketful, pailful. **3.** holding one vedro (*see* ведро́ 2).

ведовств|о́, а́, *n.* (*obs.*) sorcery.

ве́дома, *only in phrases* без в., с в.; без моего́ в. unknown to me; с моего́ в. with my knowledge, with my consent.

ве́домост|ь, и, *pl.* ~и, ~е́й, *f.* **1.** list, register; плате́жная в. pay-roll; в. расхо́дов expense-sheet. **2.** (*pl. only*) gazette (*as name of newspaper*); Моско́вские ~и Moscow Gazette.

ве́домственный, *adj.* departmental.

ве́домств|о, а, *n.* department; Вое́нное в. War Department.

ве́дом|ый (~, ~а), *adj.* (*obs.*) known; вам э́то ~о? did you know about it?

ведо́м|ый (~, ~а), *pres. part. pass. of* вести́ (*obs.*) driven.

ве́дренный, *adj. of* ведро́ (*obs., coll.*); в. день a fine day.

вёдр|о, а, *n.* (*obs., coll.*) fine weather.

вед|ро́, ра́, *pl.* ~ра, ~ер, *n.* **1.** bucket, pail; по́лное в. a pailful. **2.** (*liquid measure*) vedro (*approx. twenty-one pints or 12 litres*).

вед|у́, ёшь, *see* вести́.

веду́щ|ий, *pres. part. act. of* вести́ *and adj.* leading; (*tech.*) ~ее колесо́ driving-wheel; *as noun* в., ~его, *m.* (*aeron.*) leader (*of flight*).

ведь, *conj.* **1.** you see, you know (*but often requires no translation*); она́ всё покупа́ет но́вые пла́тья — в. она́ о́чень бога́та she is always buying new dresses—she is very rich, you know; но в. э́то всем изве́стно but everyone knows about this. 2. is it not?; is it?; в. э́то пра́вда? it's the truth, isn't it?

ве́дьм|а, ы, *f.* 1. witch. 2. (*coll.*) hag, harridan.

ведьм|овско́й, *adj. of* ~а.

ве́ер, а, *pl.* ~а́, *m.* fan (*also fig.*); обма́хиваться ~ом to fan oneself; рассы́паться ~ом (*mil., etc.*) to fan out.

веерообра́зный, *adj.* fan-shaped; в. свод (*archit.*) fan tracery.

ве́жд|ы, ~, *sing.* ~а, ~ы, *f.* (*obs., poet.*) eyelids.

ве́жливост|ь, и, *f.* politeness, courtesy, civility.

ве́жлив|ый (~, ~а), *adj.* polite, courteous, civil.

везде́, *adv.* everywhere; в. и всю́ду here, there and everywhere.

вездесу́щ|ий (~, ~а), *adj.* ubiquitous, omnipresent (*initially as epithet of God*).

вездехо́д, а, *m.* landrover; (*mil.*) cross-country vehicle.

везе́ни|е, я, *n.* luck.

вез|ти́, у́, ёшь, *past* ~, ~ла́, *impf.* (*of* по~) (*det. of* вози́ть) 1. to cart, convey, carry (*of beasts of burden or mechanical transport*). 2. (*coll.*) (*impers.+d.*), to have luck; ему́ не ~ёт в ка́рты he has no luck at cards.

везу́чий, *adj.* (*coll.*) lucky.

вей[1], *imp. of* вить.

вей[2], *imp. of* ве́ять.

век, а, о ~е, на ~у́, *pl.* ~а́ (*obs.* ~и), *m.* 1. century. 2. age; ка́менный в. Stone Age; сре́дние ~а́ the Middle Ages; испоко́н ~о́в from time immemorial; отжи́ть свой в. to have had one's day, go out of fashion; в ко́и-то ~и once in a blue moon; во ~и ~о́в for all time; на ~и ве́чные for ever; в. живи́ — в. учи́сь! (*prov.*) live and learn! 3. life, lifetime; на моём ~у́ in my lifetime. 4. *as adv.* for ages; мы с ва́ми в. не вида́лись we have not seen each other for ages.

ве́к|о, а, *pl.* ~и, ~, *n.* eyelid.

век|ова́ть, у́ю, у́ешь, *impf., usu. in phrase* век в. (*folk poet.*) to pass a lifetime.

векове́чный, *adj.* eternal, everlasting.

вековой, *adj.* ancient, age-old.

векселеда́тел|ь, я, *m.* (*comm.*) drawer (*of a bill*).

векселедержа́тел|ь, я, *m.* (*comm.*) payee, holder (*of a bill*).

ве́ксел|ь, я, *pl.* ~я́, *m.* promissory note; bill of exchange; в. на заграни́цу foreign bill; уплати́ть по ~ю to meet a bill; учи́тывать в. to discount a bill.

ве́ксель|ный, *adj. of* ~; в. курс rate of exchange.

ве́кш|а, и, *f.* (*dial.*) squirrel.

вёл, ~а́, *see* вести́.

веле́невый, *adj.* vellum.

веле́ни|е, я, *n.* (*obs.*) command, behest.

велеречи́в|ый (~, ~а), *adj.* (*obs. or iron.*) bombastic, magniloquent.

вел|е́ть, ю́, и́шь, *impf. and pf.* (+*d. and inf.* or чтобы) 1. to order; я ~е́л ему́ сде́лать э́то *or* чтобы он сде́лал э́то I ordered him to do this; де́лайте, как вам ~ено do as you are told. 2. не в. to forbid.

велика́н, а, *m.* giant.

велика́нский, *adj.* (*coll.*) gigantic.

велика́нш|а, и, *f.* (*coll.*) giant(ess).

вели́к|ий (~, ~а́, ~о́), *adj.* 1. (*short form* ~а, ~о) great; ~ие держа́вы the Great Powers; Екатери́на Вели́кая Catherine the Great; в. князь grand prince, grand duke; ~ая седми́ца Passion Week; В. четве́рг Maundy Thursday. 2. (*short form* ~а́, ~о́, *pl.* ~и́), big, large; но́ги у неё о́чень ~и́ she has very big feet; от ма́ла до ~а (*coll.*) young and old. 3. (*short form only*; ~а́, ~о́, *pl.* ~и́) (+*d. or* для) too big; э́ти брю́ки мне ~и́ these trousers are too big for me.

великова́т|ый (~, ~а), *adj.* (*coll.*) rather large, big; э́ти боти́нки мне ~ы these boots are rather big for me.

великовозра́ст|ный (~ен, ~на), *adj.* overgrown.

великодержа́вный, *adj.* great-power.

великоду́ши|е, я, *n.* magnanimity, generosity.

великоду́шнича|ть, ю, *impf.* to affect magnanimity, generosity.

великоду́ш|ный (~ен, ~на), *adj.* magnanimous, generous.

великокня́жеский, *adj.* grand-ducal.

великоле́пи|е, я, *n.* splendour, magnificence.

великоле́п|ный (~ен, ~на), *adj.* 1. splendid, magnificent; в. дворе́ц a magnificent palace. 2. excellent; э́то — ~ная иде́я that's an excellent idea; ~но! (*interj.*) splendid!, excellent!

великому́ченик, а, *m.* great martyr.

великопо́стный, *adj.* (*eccl.*) Lenten.

великоро́дный, *adj.* (*obs.*) of noble birth.

велико|ро́сс = ~ру́с.

великору́с, а, *m.* Great Russian.

великору́сский, *adj.* Great Russian.

великосве́тск|ий, *adj.* fashionable, society; ~ая жизнь high life.

велича́вост|ь, и, *f.* stateliness, majesty.

велича́в|ый (~, ~а), *adj.* stately, majestic.

велича́йш|ий, *adj.* (*superl. of* вели́кий) greatest, extreme, supreme; де́ло ~ей ва́жности a matter of extreme importance; с ~им удово́льствием with the greatest pleasure.

велича́ни|е, я, *n.* 1. glorification, extolling. 2. songs of praise (*eccl.*; *also in honour of living persons*).

величá|ть, ю, *impf.* **1.** (*coll., dial.*) to call by patronymic; как вас ~ют? what is your patronymic? **2.** (+*a. and i.*; *obs. and iron.*) to call, dignify by the name of; в. писáку гéнием to dignify a hack by the name of genius. **3.** (*folk poet.*) to honour with songs.

величá|ться, юсь, *impf.* **1.** *pass. of* ~ть. **2.** (+*i.*; *coll.*) to glory (in), plume oneself (on).

величéственност|ь, и, *f.* majesty, grandeur.

величéствен|ный (~, ~на), *adj.* majestic, grand.

величеств|о, а, *n.* majesty; вáше в. Your Majesty.

величи|е, я, *n.* greatness; grandeur; мáния ~я megalomania.

величин|á, ы́, *pl.* ~ы, ~áм, *f.* **1.** size; дом срéдней ~ы́ a house of average size; ~óю с человéческую рýку about the size of a man's hand. **2.** (*math.*) quantity, magnitude; value; в. подъéма up gradient; в. уклóна down gradient; постоя́нная ~. constant. **3.** great figure; литератýрная в. an eminent literary figure.

вело- bicycle-, cycle-.

велодрóм, а, *m.* cycle track.

велосипéд, а, *m.* bicycle; cycle.

велосипедúст, а, *m.* cyclist; cyclist.

велосипéд|ный, *adj. of* ~.

вельбóт, а, *m.* whale-boat, whaler.

вельвéт, а, *m.* velveteen; в. в рýбчик corduroy.

вельвéтовый, *adj.* velveteen.

вельмú, *adv.* (*obs. or iron.*) very.

вельмóж|а, и, *m.* (*obs. or iron.*) grandee.

вельмóж|ный, *adj. of* ~а.

веля́рный, *adj.* (*ling.*) velar.

вéн|а, ы, *f.* (*anat.*) vein; воспалéние ~ phlebitis; расширéние ~ varicose veins.

венгéр|ец, ца, *m.* Hungarian.

венгéрк|а, и, *f.* **1.** Hungarian (woman). **2.** Hungarian dance. **3.** dolman (*jacket*).

венгéрск|ий, *adj.* Hungarian; *as noun* ~ое, ~ого, *n.* Hungarian wine.

венгр, а, *m.* = венгéрец.

венéрик, а, *m.* (*coll.*) venereal patient.

венéрин, *adj.* of Venus; в. волосóк (*bot.*) maidenhair; в. холм (*palmistry*) mount of Venus.

венерúческий, *adj.* (*med.*) venereal.

венерóлог, а, *m.* specialist in venereal diseases.

венерологи|я, и, *f.* science of venereal diseases.

вéн|ец, ца, *m.* Viennese.

вен|éц, цá, *m.* **1.** crown; (*fig.*) completion, consummation. **2.** (*fig.*) wedding; вести под в. to marry, lead to the altar; под ~цóм during the wedding. **3.** (*poet.*) wreath, garland. **4.** (*astron.*) corona. **5.** (*eccl.*) halo. **6.** row of beams (*in a house*).

венециáн|ец, ца, *m.* Venetian.

венециáнк|а, и, *f.* Venetian (woman).

венециáнск|ий, *adj.* Venetian; ~ая ярь verdigris.

венéчный, *adj.* **1.** (*anat.*) coronal, coronary. **2.** *adj. of* венéц.

вéнзел|ь, я, *pl.* ~я́, ~éй, *m.* monogram; ~я́ писáть (*coll.*) to walk unsteadily (*of a drunken person*).

вéник, а, *m.* besom.

вéнк|а, и, *f.* Viennese (woman).

вéн|о, а, *n.* (*hist.*) bride-price.

вен|óзный, *adj. of* ~a; venous.

вен|óк, кá, *m.* wreath, garland.

вéнский, *adj.* Viennese; в. стул bentwood chair.

вентилúр|овать, ую, *impf.* (*of* про~) to ventilate (*also fig.*).

вéнтил|ь, я, *m.* (*tech.*) valve; (*mus.*) mute.

вентиля́тор, а, *m.* ventilator.

вентиля́ци|я, и, *f.* ventilation.

венценóс|ец, ца, *m.* (*epithet of monarch*; *rhet.*) wearer of crown, crowned head.

венчá|льный, *adj. of* ~ние; ~льное кольцó wedding ring; в. наря́д wedding dress.

венчáни|е, я, *n.* **1.** в. на цáрство coronation. **2.** wedding ceremony.

венчá|ть, ю, *impf.* **1.** (*pf.* в. *and* у~) to crown. **2.** (*pf.* у~) (*fig.*) to crown; конéц ~ет дéло all's well that ends well. **3.** (*pf.* об~ *and* по~) to marry (*of officiating priest*).

венчá|ться, юсь, *impf.* **1.** (*pf.* об~ *and* по~) to be married, marry. **2.** *pass. of* ~ть.

вéнчик, а, *m.* **1.** halo, nimbus. **2.** (*bot.*) corolla. **3.** edge, rim (*of vessel*). **4.** (*anat.*) crown (*of tooth*). **5.** (*tech.*) ring, bolt. **6.** (*eccl.*) paper band placed on forehead of dead person.

вепр|ь, я, *m.* wild boar.

вéр|а, ы, *f.* (в+*a.*) faith, belief (in); trust, confidence; приня́ть на ~у to take on trust; дать ~у (+*d.*) to give credence (to); сúмвол ~ы (*eccl.*) the Creed.

верáнд|а, ы, *f.* veranda.

вéрб|а, ы, *f.* willow; willow branch.

вербáльн|ый, *adj.* verbal; ~ая нóта (*dipl.*) note verbale.

вербéн|а, ы, *f.* (*bot.*) verbena.

верблю́д, а, *m.* camel; одногóрбый в. Arabian camel, dromedary; двугóрбый в. Bactrian camel.

верблю́диц|а, ы, *f.* female camel.

верблю́жáтник, а, *m.* camel driver.

верблю́|жий, *adj. of* ~д; ~жья шерсть camel's hair; ~жье сукнó camel-hair cloth.

верблю́жин|а, ы, *f.* camel-meat.

верблюж|óнок, óнка, *pl.* ~áта, ~áт, *m.* young of camel.

вéрб|ный, *adj. of* ~а; ~ное воскресéнье

(*eccl.*) Palm Sunday; в. база́р Palm Sunday fair.

верб|ова́ть, у́ю, *impf.* (*of* за~ *and* на~) to recruit, enlist; (*fig.*) to win over.

вербо́вк|а, и, *f.* recruiting.

вербо́вщик, а, *m.* recruiter.

ве́рбов|ый, *adj.* willow; osier; ~ая корзи́на wicker basket.

верди́кт, а, *m.* verdict.

верёвк|а, и, *f.* cord, rope; string; (*fig.*) noose; в. для белья́ clothes-line; свя́зывать ~ой to rope, cord, tie up.

верёв|очный, *adj. of* ~ка.

ве́ред, а, *m.* (*dial.*) boil, abscess.

вере|ди́ть, жу́, ди́шь, *impf.* (*of* раз~) (*coll.*) to knock, irritate (*a sore place; also fig.*).

верезж|а́ть, у́, и́шь, *impf.* (*coll.*) to squeal.

верени́ц|а, ы, *f.* row, file, line; в. лошаде́й a string of horses; в. иде́й a series of ideas.

ве́реск, а, *m.* (*bot.*) heather.

ве́реск|овый, *adj. of* ~; *as pl. noun* ~овые, ~овых (*bot.*) Ericaceae.

веретёниц|а, ы, *f.* (*zool.*) slow-worm.

веретён|ный, *adj. of* ~о́; ~ное ма́сло (*tech.*) axle grease; spindle oil.

веретен|о́, а́, *pl.* веретёна, веретён, *n.* 1. spindle; shank (*of an anchor*). 2. (*tech.*) axle.

вере́ть|е, я, *no pl.*, *n.* (*dial.*) sacking.

верещ|а́ть, у́, и́шь, *impf.* (*coll.*) to squeal; to chirp (*of a cricket, etc.*).

вере|я́[1], й, *f.* (*dial.*) gate-post.

вере|я́[2], й, *f.* (*naut.*) wherry.

верзи́л|а, ы, *m. and f.* (*coll.*) lanky person.

вери́г|и, ~, *sing.* ~а, ~и, *f.* chains, fetters (*worn by ascetics; also fig.*).

вери́тельн|ый, *adj.* ~ая гра́мота (*dipl.*) letters of credence, credentials.

ве́р|ить, ю, ишь, *impf.* (*of* по~) (+*d. or* в+*a.*) to believe, have faith (in); to trust (in), rely (upon); в. в Бо́га to believe in God; в. в прогре́сс to believe in progress; в. в привиде́ния to believe in ghosts; э́тому челове́ку никто́ не ~ит no one believes that man; он не ~ит свое́й жене́ he does not trust his wife; в. на́ слово to take on trust; я не ~ил свои́м уша́м, свои́м глаза́м I could not believe my ears, eyes.

ве́р|иться, ится, *impf.* (*impers.*+*d.*) мне ~ится с трудо́м I find it hard to believe; ему́ не ~ится, что лю́ди мо́гут быть соверше́нны he cannot believe in the perfectibility of man.

вермише́л|ь, и, *f.* vermicelli.

верн|е́е, *adv.* (*comp. of* ~о) rather; писа́тель и́ли, в., писа́ка a writer or, rather, a hack.

верниса́ж, а, *m.* (*art*) 1. private viewing. 2. opening-day (*of an exhibition*).

ве́рн|о, *adv. of* ~ый; *as particle* (*coll.*) probably, I suppose; вы, в., уже́ слыха́ли но́вости you have probably already heard the news.

вернопо́дданический, *adj.* (*obs. or iron.*) loyal, faithful.

вернопо́дданств|о, а, *n.* (*obs. or iron.*) loyalty, allegiance.

вернопо́дданн|ый, *adj.* (*obs. or iron.*) loyal, faithful; *as noun* в., ~ого, *m.* loyal subject.

ве́рност|ь, и, *f.* 1. faithfulness, loyalty. 2. truth, correctness.

верн|у́ть, у́, ёшь, *pf.* (*of* возвраща́ть) 1. to give back, return. 2. to get back, recover, retrieve; в. здоро́вье to recover one's health; в. поте́рянное вре́мя to make up for lost time. 3. (*coll.*) to make come back.

верн|у́ться, у́сь, ёшься, *pf.* (*of* возвраща́ться) to return, revert (*also fig.*); в. домо́й to return home; в. к пре́жней рабо́те to return to one's old job.

ве́р|ный (~ен, ~на́, ~но), *adj.* 1. faithful, loyal, true; в. свои́м убежде́ниям true to one's convictions. 2. true, correct; в. слух a good ear; ~ны ли ва́ши часы́? is your watch right?; ~но́ли, что вы уезжа́ете? is it true that you are going away? 3. sure, reliable; в. исто́чник reliable source; ~ная ко́пия faithful copy; в. при́знак sure sign. 4. certain, sure; ~ная смерть certain death.

ве́ровани|е, я, *n.* belief, creed; ~я дре́вних египтя́н the beliefs of the ancient Egyptians.

ве́р|овать, ую, *impf.* (в+*a.*) to believe (in).

вероисповеда́ни|е, я, *n.* creed; denomination; свобо́да ~я freedom of religion.

вероло́м|ный (~ен, ~на), *adj.* treacherous, perfidious.

вероло́мств|о, а, *n.* treachery, perfidy.

верона́л, а, *m.* (*med.*) veronal.

верони́к|а, и, *f.* (*bot.*) speedwell, veronica.

вероотсту́пник, а, *m.* apostate.

вероотсту́пничеств|о, а, *n.* apostasy.

вероподо́би|е, я, *n.* (*obs.*) likelihood.

вероподо́б|ный (~ен, ~на), *adj.* (*obs.*) likely.

веротерпи́мост|ь, и, *f.* (*rel.*) toleration.

веротерпи́м|ый (~, ~а), *adj.* (*rel.*) tolerant.

вероуче́ни|е, я, *n.* (*rel.*) dogma.

вероучи́тел|ь, я, *m.* religious teacher, apologist.

вероя́ти|е, я, *n.* probability, likelihood; по всему́ ~ю, по всем ~ям in all probability; сверх вся́кого ~я beyond all expectation.

вероя́тно, *adv.* probably; он, в., бо́лен probably he is ill; он, в., прие́дет ночны́м по́ездом he is likely to come, he will probably come by the night train.

вероя́тност|ь, и, *f.* probability; по всей ~и in all probability; тео́рия ~и (*math.*) theory of probability.

вероя́т|ный (~ен, ~на), *adj.* probable, likely; э́то вполне́ ~но it is highly probable; в. насле́дник heir presumptive.

версифика́тор, а, *m.* versifier; (*also pejor.*) он не поэ́т, а в. he is not a poet but a versifier.

версифика́ци|я, и, *f.* versification.

ве́рси|я, и, *f.* version; есть ра́зные ~и э́того собы́тия there are various versions of this story.

верст|а́, ы́, *a.* ~у́ *and* ~у, *pl.* ~ы, ~, *f.* verst (*3500 English feet or* 1·06 *km*); verst-post; за́ ~y (*coll.*) far off; ме́рить ~ы (*coll.*) to travel a long way; коло́менская в. (*coll.*) lanky person.

верста́к, а́, *m.* (*tech.*) joiner's *or* locksmith's bench.

верста́тк|а, и, *f.* (*typ.*) composing-stick.

верста́|ть¹, ю, *impf.* (*of* с~) (*typ.*) to impose, make up into pages.

верста́|ть², ю, *impf.* (*of* по~) (*hist.*) 1. to arrange in line; (c+*i.*; *fig.*) to rank (with), compare (with). 2. (+*a. and i.*) to assign (to); в. кого́-н. поме́стьем to assign an estate to someone. 3. (в+*n.-a.*) to recruit (for), conscript (for).

ве́рстк|а, и, *f.* (*typ.*) 1. imposing, imposition. 2. forme; made-up matter.

верст|ово́й, adj. of ~а́; в. столб milestone.

ве́ртел, а, *m.* spit; skewer.

верте́п, а, *m.* 1. cave, den (*of thieves, etc.*). 2. (*theatr.*) puppet-show of the Nativity; Nativity Play.

вер|те́ть, чу́, ~тишь, *impf.* (+*a. or i.*) to twirl, turn round and round; в. тро́стью to twirl a cane; она́ ~тит им, как хо́чет she can twist him round her little finger; как ни ~ти́, нам придётся заплати́ть there is nothing for it, we shall have to pay.

вер|те́ться, чу́сь, ~тишься, *impf.* 1. to rotate, turn (round), resolve (*also fig.*); разгово́р у них всё ~тится о́коло войны́ conversation with them always turns on the war; его́ фами́лия весь день ~те́лась у меня́ на ко́нчике языка́ his name was on the tip of my tongue all day; в. под нога́ми, пе́ред глаза́ми (*coll.*) to be under one's feet, in the way. 2. (*coll.*) to move (among), mix (with); он бо́льшей ча́стью ~тится среди́ иностра́нцев he mixes mostly with foreigners. 3. (*coll.*) to fidget. 4. (*coll.*) to prevaricate; отве́ть на вопро́с пря́мо, не ~ти́сь answer the question directly and don't prevaricate.

вертиголо́вк|а, и, *f.* = вертише́йка.

вертика́л, а, *m.* (*astron.*) vertical.

вертика́л|ь, и, *f.* vertical line; file (*on chessboard*); down (*in crossword*).

вертика́льный, adj. (*math.*) vertical.

вертихво́стк|а, и, *f.* (*coll.*) flirt, coquette.

вертише́йк|а, и, *f.* (*orn.*) wryneck.

ве́рт|кий (~ок, ~ка́, ~ко), *adj.* (*coll.*) nimble, agile.

вертлю́г, а́, *m.* 1. (*anat.*) head of the femur. 2. (*tech.*) swivel.

вертлю́|жный, adj. of ~г.

вертля́в|ый (~, ~а), *adj.* (*coll.*) 1. restless, fidgety. 2. flighty, frivolous.

вертогра́д, а, *m.* (*obs.*) garden.

вертодро́м, а, *m.* heliport.

вертолёт, а, *m.* helicopter.

вертопра́х, а, *m.* (*coll.*) frivolous person.

вертопра́шнича|ть, ю, *impf.* (*coll.*) to behave in a frivolous way.

верту́н, а́, *m.* (*coll.*) 1. fidget; restless person. 2. tumbler-pigeon.

верту́шк|а, и, *f.* (*coll.*) 1. revolving object (*e.g. door, bookcase*). 2. whirligig, teetotum (*toy*). 3. flirt, coquette.

ве́р|ующий, pres. part. act. of ~овать; *as noun* в., ~ующего, *m.* believer.

верф|ь, и, *f.* dockyard; shipyard.

верх, а, *pl.* ~й, *m.* 1. top, summit (*also fig.*); совеща́ние на ~а́х (*polit.*) summit conference; в. глу́пости the height of folly. 2. upper part, upper side; bonnet, hood (*of vehicle*); (*fig.*) ~й (*pl. only*) upper crust (*of society*); (*mus.*) high notes; взять, одержа́ть в. (над) to gain the upper hand (over). 3. outside, top; right side (*of material*); хвата́ть ~й, нахвата́ться ~о́в (*fig., coll.*) to get a smattering (of), acquire a superficial knowledge (of); скользи́ть по ~а́м to touch lightly on the surface.

ве́рхн|ий, adj. upper; ~яя оде́жда overcoat; outer clothing; ~яя пала́та (*polit.*) upper chamber; в. реги́стр (*mus.*) highest register; ~ее тече́ние (реки́) upper reaches (of river); в. я́щик top drawer.

верхове́нств|о, а, *n.* (*obs.*) leadership.

верхо́вн|ый, adj. supreme; ~ое кома́ндование high command; В. Сове́т Supreme Soviet.

верхово́д, а, *m.* (*coll.*) boss, leader.

верхово́|дить, жу, дишь, *impf.* (+*i.; coll.*) to lord it over, boss over; он ~дит все́ми в четвёртом кла́ссе he rules the fourth form.

верх|ово́й¹, adj. of ~о́м; ~ова́я езда́ riding; ~ова́я ло́шадь saddle-horse; *as noun* в., ~ово́го, *m.* rider.

верхово́й², adj. up-river.

верхо́вь|е, я, *g. pl.* ~ев, *n.* upper reaches.

верхогля́д, а, *m.* (*coll.*) superficial person.

верхогля́днича|ть, ю, *impf.* (*coll.*) to be superficial.

верхогля́дств|о, а, *n.* (*coll.*) superficiality.

верхола́з, а, *m.* steeplejack.

ве́рхом, adv. 1. on high ground. 2. quite

full, brim-full; нали́ть стака́н в. to pour out a full glass.

верхо́м, *adv.* astride; on horseback; е́здить в. to ride.

верху́шк|а, и, *f.* **1.** top, summit; apex. **2.** (*fig., coll.*) bosses; профсою́зная в. trade-union bosses.

ве́рченый, *adj.* (*coll., pejor.*) flighty, frivolous.

вер|чу́, ~тишь, *see* ~те́ть.

ве́рш|а, и, *f.* fish-trap (*made of osiers*).

верши́н|а, ы, *f.* **1.** top, summit; peak; (*fig.*) peak, acme; он дости́г ~ы сла́вы he had reached the summit of his fame. **2.** (*math.*) vertex; apex.

верш|и́ть, у́, и́шь, *impf.* **1.** (+*i.*) to manage, control; в. все́ми дела́ми to run the whole show. **2.** (*dial.*) to top; в. стог to top a rick. **3.** (+*a.*) to decide.

вершко́вый, *adj.* one vershok long.

верш|о́к, ка́, *m.* vershok (*measure of length equivalent to $1\frac{3}{4}$ inches or 4·4 cm*); (*fig.*) smattering, superficial knowledge; хвата́ть ~ки́ (+*g.*) to get a smattering (of).

вес, а, *pl.* ~а́, *m.* **1.** weight; (*fig.*) weight, authority; на в. by weight; ~ом в сто фу́нтов weighing a hundred pounds; на ~у́ balanced, hanging, suspended; держа́ться на ~у́ to be balanced; приба́вить, уба́вить в ~е to put on, lose weight; быть на в. зо́лота to be worth one's weight in gold; име́ть в. to carry weight. **2.** system of weights; апте́карский в. apothecaries' weight. **3.** уде́льный в. specific gravity.

веселе́|ть, ю, *impf.* (*of* по~) to become gay, become bright.

весел|и́ть, ю́, и́шь, *impf.* (*of* по~) to cheer, gladden; to amuse.

весел|и́ться, ю́сь, и́шься, *impf.* (*of* по~) to enjoy oneself; to amuse oneself.

ве́село, *adv.* gaily, merrily; *as pred.* (+*d.*) to enjoy oneself; нам тут о́чень в. we very much enjoy being here; мне в. бы́ло смотре́ть на вас I enjoyed seeing you.

весёлост|ь, и, *f.* **1.** gaiety; cheerfulness. **2.** (*pl. only*); *obs.*) merry-making.

весёл|ый (ве́сел, ~а́, ве́село), *adj.* gay, merry; cheerful; у него́ ~ое настрое́ние сего́дня he is in good spirits today.

весе́л|ье, ья, *g. pl.* ~ий, *n.* **1.** gaiety, merriment. **2.** (*pl. only*); *obs.*) merry-making.

вес|е́льный, *adj.* of ~ло́; ~е́льная ло́дка rowing-boat.

весельча́к, а́, *m.* (*coll.*) convivial fellow.

вес|е́нний, *adj.* of ~на́; ~е́ннее равноде́нствие vernal equinox.

ве́|сить, шу, сишь, *impf.* **1.** to weigh (*intrans.*); ~сит три то́нны it weighs three tons. **2.** (*obs., coll.*) to weigh (*trans.*).

ве́с|кий (~ок, ~ка), *adj.* weighty.

вес|ло́, ла́, *pl.* ~ла, ~ел, ~лам, *n.* oar; scull;

paddle; завяза́ть в. to catch a crab; подня́ть ~ла to rest on one's oars.

вес|на́, ны́, *pl.* ~ны, ~ен, ~нам, *f.* spring (*season*).

весну́ш|ки, ек, *sing.* ~ка, ~ки, *f.* freckles.

весну́шчатый, *adj.* freckled.

весня́нк|а, и, *f.* **1.** (*zool.*) mayfly. **2.** (*ethnol.*) spring-song.

вес|ово́й, 1. *adj.* of ~. **2.** sold by weight.

весовщи́к, а́, *m.* weigher; checkweighman.

весо́мост|ь, и, *f.* (*phys.*) ponderability.

весо́м|ый (~, ~а), *adj.* (*phys.*) ponderable; (*fig.*) weighty; heavy.

вест, а, *m.* (*naut.*) **1.** west. **2.** west wind.

веста́лк|а, и, *f.* vestal (virgin).

ве|сти́, ду́, дёшь, *past* ~л, ~ла́, *impf.* (*det. of* води́ть) **1.** (*pf.* по~) to lead; to conduct; to take; в. слепо́го to lead a blind man. **2.** (*pf.* про~) (+*i.* по +*d.*) to run (over), pass (over, across); в. смычко́м по стру́нам to run one's bow over the strings. **3.** (*pf.* про~) to conduct; to carry on; в. войну́ to wage war; в. обще́ственную рабо́ту to do social work; в. ого́нь (по+*d.*) to fire (on); в. перегово́ры to carry on negotiations; в. перепи́ску (с+*i.*) to correspond (with); в. пра́вильный о́браз жи́зни to lead a regular life; в. проце́сс to carry on a lawsuit. **4.** (*impf. only*) to drive; в. кора́бль to navigate a ship; в. самолёт to pilot an aircraft. **5.** (*impf. only*) to conduct, direct, run; в. де́ло to run a business; в. собра́ние to preside at a meeting; в. хозя́йство to keep house. **6.** (*impf. only*) to keep, conduct; в. дневни́к to keep a diary; в. кни́ги to keep books, keep accounts; в. протоко́л to keep minutes. **7.** (*impf. only*) в. себя́ to behave, conduct oneself. **8.** (*impf. only*) (к) to lead (to) (*also fig.*); куда́ ~дёт э́та доро́га? where does this road lead (to)?; э́то ни к чему́ не ~дёт this is leading nowhere. **9.** (*impf. only*) в. своё нача́ло (от) to originate (in), take rise (in); в. свой род (от) to be descended (from). **10.** и у́хом не в. (*coll.*) to pay no heed.

вестибю́л|ь, я, *m.* hall, lobby.

вести́мо, *adv.* (*dial.*) of course, certainly.

ве|сти́сь, ду́сь, дёшься, *past* вёлся, ~ла́сь, *impf.* (*of* по~) **1.** *pass. of* ~сти́. **2.** (*usu. impers.*; *coll.*) to be observed (*of customs, etc.*); так ~дётся уже́ три́ста лет this has been the custom for three hundred years. **3.** to multiply (*of domestic animals*).

ве́стник, а, *m.* messenger, herald; (*also in title of publications*) bulletin.

ве́стниц|а, ы, *f.* of ве́стник.

вестов|о́й, *adj.* (*obs.*) signal; ~а́я раке́та signal-rocket; *as noun* в., ~о́го, *m.* orderly.

вестовщи́к, а́, *m.* (*coll., obs.*) newsmonger, gossip.

вéсточк|а, и, *f.* (*coll.*) news; дáйте о себé ~у, как тóлько приéдете let me hear from you as soon as you arrive.

вест|ь[1], и, *pl.* ~и, ~éй, *f.* news; piece of news; пропáсть бéз ~и (*mil.*) to be missing.

весть[2], *only in phrases* Бог в. God knows; не в. что goodness knows, heaven knows what; не (Бог) в. какóй trifling, insignificant.

вес|ы́, óв, *no sing.* 1. scales, balance; мостовы́е в. weighbridge; пружи́нные в. spring balance; брóсить на в. (*fig.*) to throw into the balance. 2. В. the Scales, Libra (*sign of the Zodiac*).

весь[1], вся, всё, *g.* **всегó, всей, всегó,** *pl.* **все, всех,** *pron.* all; весь день all day; вся Фрáнция the whole of France; он весь в отцá he is the (very) image of his father; весь в лохмóтьях all in rags; вы́йти весь to be used up; бумáга вся вы́шла the paper is all used up, there is no paper left; во в. гóлос at the top of one's voice; во всю мочь with all one's might; от всегó сéрдца from the bottom of one's heart, with all one's heart; по всемý гóроду all over the town; во-всю (*coll.*) like anything; прéжде всегó before all, first and foremost; при всём том for all that, moreover; вот и всё that's all; всегó (хорóшего)! good-bye!, all the best!; всё и вся (*coll.*) all and everything; *as noun* **всё, всегó,** *n.* everything; **все, всех** all, everyone; всем, всем, всем! attention, everyone!

вес|ь[2], и, *f.* (*obs.*) village.

весьмá, *adv.* very, highly; в. успéшный óпыт highly successful experiment.

ветви́ст|ый (~, ~а), *adj.* branchy, spreading.

ветв|ь, и, *pl.* ~и, ~éй, *f.* branch, bough; (*fig.*) branch.

вét|ер, ра, *m.* 1. wind; крéпкий в. (*naut.*) half a gale; óчень крéпкий в. fresh gale; ти́хий в. light air; по ~ру before the wind, down wind; держáть нос по ~ру (*fig.*) to trim one's sails to the wind; под ~ром leeward; прóтив ~ра close to the wind, in the teeth of the wind; в. с бéрега off-shore wind; (*fig.*) брóсать словá на в. to talk idly; у негó в. в головé he is a thoughtless fellow; подби́тый ~ром (*coll.*) (*i*) empty--headed, (*ii*) light, flimsy. 2. ~ры (*med.*) wind, flatulence.

ветерáн, а, *m.* veteran.

ветеринáр, а, *m.* veterinary surgeon.

ветеринáри|я, и, *f.* veterinary science; veterinary medicine.

ветеринáрный, *adj.* veterinary.

ветер|óк, кá, *m.* breeze.

вéтк|а, и, *f.* branch; twig; железнодорóжная в. branch-line.

вет|лá, лы́, *pl.* ~лы, ~ел, *f.* (*bot.*) white willow.

вéто, *indecl., n.* veto; наложи́ть в. (на + *a.*) to veto.

вéточк|а, и, *f.* twig, sprig, shoot.

ветóшник, а, *m.* (*obs.*) old clothes dealer.

ветóш|ь, и, *f.* old clothes, rags.

ветр = вéтер.

ветрене́|ть, ет, *impf.* (*impers.*; *coll.*) to become windy.

вéтреник, а, *m.* (*coll.*) empty-headed, frivolous person.

ветрени|ца[1], цы, *f.* *of* ~к.

ветрени́ц|а[2], ы, *f.* (*bot.*) anemone.

вéтреност|ь, и, *f.* empty-headedness, instability.

вéтрен|ый (~, ~а), *adj.* 1. windy; зáвтра бýдет ~о it will be windy tomorrow. 2. (*fig.*) empty-headed, unstable.

ветри́л|о, а, *n.* (*poet.*) sail.

ветробó|й, я, *no pl., m.* (*dial., collect.*) 1. wind--fallen wood. 2. windfalls (*fruit*).

ветровóй, *adj.* *of* вéтер.

ветрогóн, а, *m.* 1. (*tech.*) fan. 2. = вéтреник.

ветрогóнный, *adj.* (*med.*) carminative.

ветромéр, а, *m.* (*phys.*) anemometer.

ветросиловóй, *adj.* wind-powered.

ветроуказáтел|ь, я, *m.* (*aeron.*) drogue, wind cone, wind sock.

ветроулови́тел|ь, я, *m.* (*aeron.*) rudder air scoop.

ветрочёт, а, *m.* (*aeron.*) course and speed computer.

ветря́к, á, m. 1. (*tech.*) wind turbine. 2. (*coll.*) windmill.

ветря́нк|а, и, *f.* (*coll.*) 1. windmill. 2. chicken-pox.

ветрян|óй, *adj.* wind(-powered); ~áя мéльница windmill.

вéтрян|ый, *adj.* ~ая óспа chicken-pox.

вéтх|ий (~, ~á, ~о), *adj.* old, ancient; dilapidated, tumbledown; decrepit; В. завéт the Old Testament.

ветхозавéтный, *adj.* Old Testament; (*fig.*) antiquated.

вéтхост|ь, и, *f.* decrepitude; dilapidation.

ветчин|á, ы́, *no pl., f.* ham.

ветчи́н|ный, *adj.* *of* ~á.

ветшá|ть, ю, *impf.* (*of* об~) to decay; to become dilapidated; to become decrepit.

вéх|а, и, *f.* landmark (*also fig.*); (*naut.*) spar--buoy; смéна ~ (*polit.*) volte-face; смени́ть ~и to execute a volte-face.

вéч|е, а, *n.* (*hist.*) veche (*popular assembly in medieval Russian towns*).

вечевóй, *adj.* *of* вéче.

вéчер, а, *pl.* ~á, *m.* 1. evening; по ~áм in the evenings; под в., к ~у towards evening. 2. party; evening, soirée; музыкáльный в. musical evening; вчерá был в. у Ивáновых the Ivanovs had a party last night; в.

па́мяти Че́хова Chekhov commemoration meeting.

вечере́|ть, ет, *impf.* (*impers.*) to grow dark; ~ет night is falling.

вечери́нк|а, и, *f.* (evening-)party.

вечерко́м, *adv.* (*coll.*) in the evening.

вече́рн|ий, *adj.* of ве́чер; ~яя заря́ twilight, dusk; в. звон vesper chimes; ~ие ку́рсы evening classes; ~ее пла́тье evening dress; ~яя шко́ла night-school.

вече́рник, а, *m.* (*coll.*) night-school student.

вече́р|ня, ни, *pl. g.* ~ен, *f.* (*eccl.*) vespers.

ве́чером, *adv.* in the evening.

ве́чер|я, и, *f.* (*obs.*) supper; Та́йная в. (*bibl.*) the Last Supper.

ве́чник, а, *m.* (*sl.*) lifer (*convict serving life sentence*).

ве́чно, *adv.* for ever, eternally; always; они́ в. ссо́рятся they are always quarrelling.

вечнозелёный, *adj.* (*bot.*) evergreen.

ве́чност|ь, и, *f.* eternity; ка́нуть в в. to sink into oblivion; це́лую в. (*coll.*) for ages, for an age; он не приходи́л сюда́ це́лую в. he has not been here for ages.

ве́ч|ный (~ен, ~на), *adj.* **1.** eternal, everlasting; ~ная мерзлота́ permafrost; засну́ть ~ным сном to take one's last sleep. **2.** endless; perpetual; ~ное владе́ние possession in perpetuity; ~ное перо́ fountain-pen.

вечо́р, *adv.* (*coll., obs.*) yesterday evening.

вечёрк|а, и, *f.* (*coll.*) evening paper.

ве́шалк|а, и, *f.* **1.** peg, rack, stand. **2.** tab (*on clothes for hanging on pegs*). **3.** cloak-room.

ве́ша|ть¹, ю, *impf.* (*of* пове́сить) to hang; в. бельё на верёвку to hang washing on a line; в. уби́йцу to hang a murderer; в. соба́к (на+*a. or* на ше́ю+*d.*; *coll.*) to pin accusations (upon).

ве́ша|ть², ю, *impf.* (*of* взве́сить) to weigh, weigh out; в. фунт ко́фе to weigh out a pound of coffee.

ве́ша|ться¹, юсь, *impf.* (*of* пове́ситься) **1.** *pass. of* ~ть¹; to be hung; to be hanged. **2.** to hang oneself; **3.** в. на ше́ю кому́-н. (*coll.*) to run after; она́ всё ~ется молоды́м офице́рам на ше́ю she is always running after young officers.

ве́ша|ться², юсь, *impf.* (*of* с~) (*coll.*) to weigh oneself.

веш|и́ть, у́, и́шь, *impf.* (*of* про~) (*geod.*) to mark out.

ве́шк|а, и, *f.* landmark; surveying rod.

ве́шний, *adj.* (*poet.*) vernal.

ве́|шу, сишь, *see* ~сить.

веш|у́, и́шь, *see* ~и́ть.

веща́ни|е, я, *n.* **1.** prophesying. **2.** (*radio*) broadcasting.

веща́|ть, ю, *impf.* **1.** (*obs.*) to prophesy.

2. (*coll.*) to pontificate, play the oracle, lay down the law. **3.** (*radio*) to broadcast.

вещ|ево́й, *adj.* of ~ь; ~ево́е дово́льствие payment in kind; (*mil.*) clothing, kit; в. мешо́к hold-all; kit-bag; в. склад storage warehouse, store; (*mil.*) stores.

веще́ственност|ь, и, *f.* substantiality, materiality.

веще́ственн|ый, *adj.* substantial, material; ~ые доказа́тельства material evidence.

вещество́, а́, *n.* substance; matter; взры́вчатое в. explosive; отравля́ющее в. poison-gas; се́рое в. grey matter.

ве́щий, *adj.* (*poet.*) prophetic.

вещ|и́ца, и́цы, *f.* *dim.* of ~ь; little thing; bagatelle.

**вещ|но́й, **adj.* of ~ь; ~ное пра́во (*leg.*) law of estate.

вещу́н, а́, *m.* (*obs.*) soothsayer.

вещ|ь, и, *pl.* ~и, ~е́й, *f.* **1.** (*in var. senses*) thing; пе́рвая любо́вь — чуде́сная в. first love is a marvellous thing; э́то в.! (*expressing approval*; *coll.*) that's quite something!; вот кака́я в.: президе́нт собира́ется посети́ть наш го́род do you know what? the President is going to visit our town. **2.** (*pl.*) things (= (*i*) belongings; baggage, (*ii*) clothes); ва́ши ли э́ти ~и? are these things yours?; тебе́ сле́дует носи́ть бо́лее тёплые ~и you ought to be wearing warmer things; со все́ми ~а́ми bag and baggage. **3.** (*of artistic productions*) work; piece, thing; его́ лу́чшие ~и ещё не переведены́ his best things have not yet been translated.

вея́лк|а, и, *f.* (*agric.*) winnowing-fan; winnowing-machine.

вея́ни|е, я, *n.* **1.** (*agric.*) winnowing. **2.** breathing, blowing (*of wind*). **3.** (*fig.*) current (*of opinion*), tendency, trend; в. вре́мени spirit of the times.

ве́|ять, ю, ешь, *impf.* **1.** (*agric.*) to winnow. **2.** (*intrans.*) to blow (*of wind*); ~ял прохла́дный ветеро́к a cool breeze was blowing; (*impers.*, +*i.*) ~ет весно́й spring is in the air; ~ет но́выми иде́ями new ideas are in the air. **3.** to wave, flutter; знамёна ~яли по ве́тру banners were fluttering in the wind.

вжива́|ться, юсь, *impf.* of вжи́ться.

вжи́|ться, ву́сь, вёшься, *pf.* (в+*a.*; *coll.*) to get used (to), grow accustomed (to); он с трудо́м ~вётся в вое́нную жизнь he will find it hard to get used to army life.

взад, *adv.* (*coll.*) back; в. и вперёд backwards and forwards, to and fro; ни в. ни вперёд neither backwards nor forwards; он не мог дви́нуться ни в. ни вперёд he could not budge an inch.

взаи́мност|ь, и, *f.* reciprocity; return (*of affection*); отвеча́ть кому́-н. ~ью to reciprocate someone's feelings, return someone's love; любо́вь без ~и unrequited love.

взаи́м|ный (~ен, ~на), adj. mutual, reciprocal; ~ная по́мощь mutual aid; в. глаго́л (gram.) reciprocal verb.

взаимоде́йстви|е, я, n. interaction; (mil.) co-operation, co-ordination.

взаимоде́йств|овать, ую, impf. to interact; (mil.) to co-operate.

взаимоотноше́ни|е, я, n. interrelation.

взаимопо́мощ|ь, и, f. mutual aid; ка́сса ~и mutual benefit; догово́р о ~и mutual assistance pact.

взаймы́, adv. взять в. to borrow; дать в. to lend, loan.

взалка́|ть, ю, pf. (obs.) to hunger (for) (+g. or +inf.; fig., now usu. iron.).

взаме́н, prep.+g. instead (of); in return (for), in exchange (for).

взаперти́, adv. 1. under lock and key; сиде́ть в. to be locked up. 2. in seclusion.

взапра́вду, adv. (coll.) in truth, indeed.

вза́пуски, adv. бе́гать в. to chase one another.

взасо́с, adv. целова́ться в. (coll.) to exchange long-drawn-out kisses.

взатя́жку, adv. кури́ть в. (coll.) to inhale (in smoking).

вза́шей, adv. (coll.) вы́гнать в. to chuck out; to throw out (on one's neck).

взбадрива|ть, ю, impf. of взбодри́ть.

взбаламу́|тить, чу, тишь, pf. of баламу́тить.

взбалмо́шный, adj. (coll.) unbalanced, eccentric.

взба́лтывани|е, я, n. shaking (up).

взба́лтыва|ть, ю, impf. of взболта́ть.

взбега́|ть, ю, impf. (of взбежа́ть) to run up; в. на́ гору to run up a hill; в. по ле́стнице to run upstairs.

взбе|жа́ть, гу́, жи́шь, гу́т, pf. of ~га́ть.

взбелен|и́ться, ю́сь, и́шься, pf. (на+a.; coll.) to become enraged (with).

взбе|си́ть(ся), шу́(сь), ~си́шь(ся), pf. of беси́ть(ся).

взбива́|ть, ю, impf. of взбить.

взбира́|ться, юсь, impf. of взобра́ться.

взби́т|ый (~, ~а), p.p.p. of ~ь; ~ые сли́вки whipped cream.

вз|бить, обью, обьёшь, pf. (of ~бива́ть) 1. to beat up; в. сли́вки to whip cream; в. я́ичные белки́ to beat up white of egg. 2. to shake up, fluff up.

взбодр|и́ть, ю́, и́шь, pf. (of взба́дривать) to cheer up; to encourage.

взболта́|ть, ю, pf. (of взба́лтывать) to shake (up) (liquids); пе́ред приёмом в. миксту́ру shake the bottle before taking.

взбороз|ди́ть, жу́, ди́шь, pf. of борозди́ть 1.

взборон|и́ть, ю́, и́шь, pf. of борони́ть.

взбра́сыва|ть, ю, impf. of взбро́сить.

взбреда́|ть, ю, impf. of взбрести́.

взбре|сти́, ду́, дёшь, past взбрёл, ~ла́, pf. (of ~да́ть) (на+a.; coll.) to mount with difficulty; в. в го́лову, на ум to come into one's head; ему́ ~ло́ на ум, что все его́ ненави́дят he got it into his head that everyone hated him.

взбро́|сить, шу, сишь, pf. (of взбра́сывать) (coll.) to throw up, toss up.

взбры́згива|ть, ю, impf. of взбры́знуть.

взбры́з|нуть, ну, нешь, pf. (of ~гивать) (coll.) to sprinkle, spatter.

взбудора́жива|ть, ю, impf. of взбудора́жить.

взбудора́ж|ить, у, ишь, pf. (coll.) to agitate, work up.

взбунт|ова́ть(ся), у́ю(сь), pf. of бунтова́ть(ся).

взбух|а́ть, а́ю, impf. of ~нуть.

взбу́х|нуть, ну, нешь, past ~, ~ла, pf. (of ~а́ть) to swell out.

взбу́ч|ить, у, ишь, pf. (coll.) 1. to thrash, beat. 2. to reprimand.

взбу́чк|а, и, f. (coll.) 1. thrashing, beating. 2. reprimand; получи́ть ~у to be hauled over the coals.

взва́лива|ть, ю, impf. of взвали́ть.

взвал|и́ть, ю́, ~ишь, pf. (of ~ивать) to load, lift (onto); в. мешо́к на́ спину to hoist a pack onto one's back; всю рабо́ту ~и́ли на но́вого учи́теля (coll.) the new teacher was loaded with all the work; всю вину́ ~и́ли на него́ he was made to shoulder all the blame.

взвар, а, m. (cul.) stewed fruit and berries.

взве́|сить, шу, сишь, pf. (of ~шивать and ве́шать) to weigh; (fig.) to weigh, consider; в. возмо́жные после́дствия посту́пка to weigh the possible consequences of an action.

взве|сти́, ду́, дёшь, past ~л, ~ла́, pf. (of взводи́ть) 1. to lead up, take up; в. куро́к (ружья́) to cock (a gun). 2. (на+a.) to impute (to); на генера́ла ~ли́ обвине́ние в пораже́нии blame for the defeat was laid at the general's door.

взвес|ь, и, f. (chem.) suspension.

взве́шен|ный (~, ~а), 1. p.p.p. взве́сить. 2. (chem.) suspended; ~ое состоя́ние suspension.

взве́шивани|е, я, n. weighing.

взве́шива|ть, ю, impf. of взве́сить.

взвива́|ть, ю, impf. of взвить.

взвива́|ться, юсь, impf. of взви́ться.

взви́|деть, жу, дишь, pf. only in phrase све́та не в. (coll.) to see stars.

взвизг, а, m. (coll.) scream; yelp (of a dog).

взви́згива|ть, ю, impf. and freq. of взви́згнуть.

взви́згн|уть, у, ешь, pf. to scream, cry out; to yelp (of a dog); соба́ка жа́лобно ~ула the dog let out a piteous yelp.

взвин|ти́ть, чу́, ти́шь, *pf.* (*of* взви́нчивать) (*coll.*) to excite, work up; в. це́ны to inflate prices.

взви́нчен|ный (~, ~a), *p.p.p. of* взвинти́ть *and adj.* excited, worked up; highly-strung, nervy; не́рвы у него́ всегда́ ~ы he is always on edge; ~ные це́ны inflated prices.

взви́нчива|ть, ю, *impf. of* взвинти́ть.

взвить, взовью́, взовьёшь, *pf.* (*of* взвива́ть) to raise.

взви́ться, взовью́сь, взовьёшься, *pf.* (*of* взвива́ться) to rise; to fly up, soar (*of birds*); to be raised, go up (*of flags, etc.*); за́навес взви́лся ро́вно в во́семь часо́в the curtain went up at eight o'clock exactly.

взвод¹, a, *m.* (*mil.*) platoon.

взвод², a, *m.* (cocking) notch (*of guns*); боево́й в., второ́й в. full bent; на боево́м ~е cocked; на пе́рвом ~е at half-cock; предохрани́тельный в. safety notch; на предохрани́тельном ~е at safety; быть на ~е (*coll.*) to be in one's cups.

взво|ди́ть, жу́, ~ди́шь, *impf. of* взвести́.

взвод|но́й, *adj. of* ~²; ~на́я ру́чка cocking handle.

взво́д|ный, *adj. of* ~¹; *as noun* в., ~ного, *m.* platoon commander.

взволно́ван|ный (~, ~a), *p.p.p. of* взволнова́ть *and adj.* agitated, disturbed; anxious, worried; у неё в. вид she has a worried look.

взволн|ова́ть, у́ю, *pf. of* волнова́ть.

взволн|ова́ться, у́юсь, *pf. of* волнова́ться.

взво́|ю, ешь, *see* взвыть.

взвыва́|ть, ю, *impf. of* взвыть.

взв|ыть, о́ю, о́ешь, *pf.* (*of* ~ыва́ть) to howl, set up a howl.

взгляд, a, *m.* 1. look; glance; gaze, stare; бро́сить в. (на+*a.*) to glance (at); на в. to judge from appearances; на пе́рвый в., с пе́рвого ~a at first sight. 2. view; opinion; на мой в. in my opinion, as I see it.

взгля́дыва|ть, ю, *impf. of* взгляну́ть.

взгля́н|у́ть, у́, ~ешь, *pf.* (на+*a.*) to look (at); to cast a glance (at); в. на что-н. серьёзно (*fig.*) to take a serious view of something.

взговор|и́ть, ю́, и́шь, *pf.* (*folk poet.*) to say.

взго́рь|е, я, *n.* (*dial.*) hillock.

взгре|ть, ю, ешь, *pf.* (*coll.*) to thrash; (*fig.*) to give it hot.

взгромозжда́|ть, ю, *impf. of* взгромозди́ть.

взгромозжда́|ться, юсь, *impf. of* взгромозди́ться.

взгромоз|ди́ть, жу́, ди́шь, *pf.* (*coll.*) to pile up.

взгромоз|ди́ться, жу́сь, ди́шься, *pf.* (*coll.*) to clamber up.

взгрустн|у́ть, у́, ёшь, *pf.* (*coll.*) to feel sad, depressed.

взгрустн|у́ться, ётся, *pf.* (*impers.*+*d.*; *coll.*) to feel sad, depressed; ему́ ~у́лось he feels depressed.

вздва́ива|ть, ю, *impf. of* вздво́ить.

вздв|о́ить, о́ю, о́ишь, *pf.* (*of* ~а́ивать) в. ряды́ (*mil.*) to form fours.

вздёргива|ть, ю, *impf. of* вздёрнуть.

вздёрнут|ый (~, ~a), *p.p.p. of* ~ь; в. нос snub nose.

вздёрн|уть, у, ешь, *pf.* (*coll.*) 1. to hitch up; to jerk up; в. нос to become proud. 2. to hang.

вздор, a, *no pl., m.* (*coll.*) nonsense; городи́ть, моло́ть в. to talk nonsense.

вздо́р|ить, ю, ишь, *impf.* (*of* по~) (*coll.*) to squabble.

вздо́р|ный (~ен, ~на), *adj.* (*coll.*) 1. foolish, stupid. 2. cantankerous, quarrelsome.

вздорожа́ни|е, я, *n.* rise in price.

вздорожа́|ть, ю, *pf. of* дорожа́ть.

вздох, a, *m.* sigh; deep breath; испусти́ть после́дний в. to breathe one's last.

вздохн|у́ть, у́, ёшь, *pf.* (*of* вздыха́ть) 1. to sigh. 2. (*coll.*) to take breath, have a breathing-space; дава́йте ~ём! let's pause for breath!

вздра́гива|ть, ю, *impf.* (*of* вздро́гнуть) to shudder, quiver.

вздремн|у́ть, у́, ёшь, *pf.* (*coll.*) to have a nap, doze.

вздремн|у́ться, ётся, *pf.* (*impers.*+*d.*; *coll.*); как раз по́сле еды́ ему́ ~у́лось immediately after the meal he dozed off.

вздро́гн|уть, у, ешь, *pf.* (*of* вздра́гивать) to start; to wince, flinch.

вздрю́ч|ить, у, ишь, *pf.* (*coll.*) to thrash, beat; to reprimand.

вздува́|ть, ю, *impf. of* вздуть¹.

вздума́|ть, ю, *pf.* (+*inf.*; *coll.*) to take it into one's head; она́ ~ла носи́ть чёрные ве́щи she took it into her head to wear black; не ~й(те) mind you don't; не ~йте ныря́ть здесь! mind you don't dive in here!, don't try to dive in here!

вздума́|ться, ется, *pf.* (*impers.*+*d.*; *coll.*) to take it into one's head; ему́ ~лось пое́хать в Аме́рику he took it into his head to go to America; как ~ется at one's own sweet will.

вздути́|е, я, *n.* (*med.*) swelling; в. цен (*fig.*) inflation of prices.

взду́т|ый¹ (~, ~a), *p.p.p. of* ~ь¹ *and adj.* swollen.

взду́т|ый² (~, ~a), *p.p.p. of* ~ь².

взду́|ть¹, ю, ешь, *pf.* (*of* вздува́ть) 1. to blow up, inflate. 2. (*dial.*) to light (*a fire*).

взду́|ть², ю, ешь, *pf.* (*coll.*) to thrash, give a thrashing (to).

взду́|ться, юсь, ешься, *pf.* to swell (*intrans.*).

вздыма́|ть, ю, *impf.* to raise.

вздыма́|ться, юсь, *impf.* to rise; ~лась мгла над о́зером mist was rising over the lake.

вздыха́ни|е, я, *n.* (*obs.*) 1. sighing. 2. (*pl. only*) love-sickness.

вздыха́тел|ь, я, *m.* (*coll., obs.*) admirer.

вздыха́|ть, ю, *impf.* (*of* вздохну́ть) 1. to) breathe; to sigh. 2. (о, по+*p.*) to pine (for; to long, sigh (for).

взима́ни|е, я, *n.* levy, collection.

взима́|ть, ю, *impf.* to levy, collect, raise (*taxes*).

взира́|ть, ю, *impf.* (на+*a.*) 1. (*obs.*) to look (at), gaze (at). 2. не ~я на in spite of, notwithstanding; не ~я на ли́ца without respect of persons.

взла́мыва|ть, ю, *impf. of* взлома́ть.

взлеза́|ть, ю, *impf. of* взлезть.

взлез|ть, у, ешь, *past* ~, ~ла, *pf.* (*of* ~а́ть) to climb up.

взлеле́|ять, ю, ешь, *pf. of* леле́ять.

взлёт, а, *m.* (upward) flight (*also fig.*); (*aeron.*) take-off; в. фанта́зии flight of fancy.

взлета́|ть, ю, *impf. of* взлете́ть.

взле|те́ть, чу́, ти́шь, *pf.* (*of* ~та́ть) to fly up; to take off; в. по ле́стнице to fly upstairs; в. на во́здух to explode, blow up (*also fig.*); в тече́ние еди́ного дня мечты́ всей жи́зни ~те́ли на во́здух the dreams of a lifetime exploded in a day.

взлёт|ный, *adj. of* ~; (*aeron.*) ~ная доро́жка runway; ~но-поса́дочная площа́дка landing strip.

взли́з|а, ы, (*coll.*) bald patch (*above the temples*).

взли́з|ина, ины, *f.* = ~а.

взлом, а, *m.* breaking open, breaking in; кра́жа со ~ом house-breaking.

взлома́|ть, ю, *pf.* (*of* взла́мывать) to break open, force; to smash; в. замо́к to force a lock; в. неприя́тельскую оборо́ну to force the enemy's defences.

взло́мщик, а, *m.* burglar, house-breaker.

взлохма́|тить, чу, тишь, *pf. of* лохма́тить *and* ~чивать.

взлохма́|ченный (~чен, ~чена), *p.p.p. of* ~тить *and adj.* tousled; dishevelled.

взлохма́чива|ть, ю, *impf.* to tousle.

взлюб|и́ть, лю́, ~ишь, *pf., only with neg.*; не в. с пе́рвого взгля́да to take an instant dislike (to).

взмах, а, *m.* wave (*of hand*); flap, flapping (*of wings*); stroke (*of oars, etc.*); одни́м ~ом at one stroke.

взма́хива|ть, ю, *impf. of* взмахну́ть.

взмахн|у́ть, у́, ёшь, *pf.* (+*i.*) to wave, flap; в. платко́м to wave a handkerchief.

взметн|у́ть, у́, ёшь, *pf.* (*of* взмётывать) (+*i.*) to throw up, fling up; в. рука́ми to fling up one's hands.

взметн|у́ться, у́сь, ёшься, *pf.* 1. to leap up, fly up; и́скры ~у́лись из-под копы́т коня́ sparks flew up'from the horse's hoofs. 2. (на+*a.* (*obs.*)) to leap (upon), fly (at); соба́ки ~у́лись на бродя́гу the dogs flew at the tramp.

взмётыва|ть, ю, *impf. of* взметну́ть.

взмётыва|ться, юсь, *impf. of* взметну́ться.

взмол|и́ться, ю́сь, ~ишься, *pf.* (о+*p.*) to beg (for); to beseech; в. о поща́де to beg for mercy.

взмо́рь|е, я, *n.* sea-shore; seaside.

взмо|сти́ться, щу́сь, сти́шься, *pf.* (*coll.*) (на+*a.*) to perch (on).

взму|ти́ть, чу́, ти́шь, *pf. of* мути́ть.

взмыва́|ть, ю, *impf. of* взмыть.

взмы́лива|ть(ся), ю(сь), *impf. of* взмы́лить(ся).

взмы́л|ить, ю, ишь, *pf.* to cause to foam, lather.

взмы́л|иться, юсь, ишься, *pf.* to foam (*intrans.*), froth.

взм|ыть, о́ю, о́ешь, *pf.* (*of* ~ыва́ть) to shoot upwards (*of a bird*).

взнос, а, *m.* payment; fee, dues; subscription; вступи́тельный в. entrance fee; очередно́й в. instalment; профсою́зный в. trade-union dues; чле́нский в. membership fee.

взнузда́|ть, ю, *pf.* to bridle.

взну́здыва|ть, ю, *impf. of* взнузда́ть.

взобра́|ться, взберу́сь, взберёшься, *past* ~лся, ~ла́сь, *pf.* (*of* взбира́ться) (на+*a.*) to climb (up), clamber (up); им пришло́сь в. на склон холма́ на четвере́ньках they had to clamber up the slope on all fours.

взобь|ю́, ёшь, *see* взбить.

взовь|ю́, ёшь, *see* взвить.

взо|йти́, йду́, йдёшь, *past* ~шёл, ~шла́, *past part.* ~ше́дший, *pf.* (*of* восходи́ть) (на+*a.*) 1. to mount, ascend; to rise; в. на трибу́ну to mount the platform; со́лнце ~шло́ в пять часо́в сего́дня the sun rose at five o'clock today; посе́вы уже́ ~шли́ the crops are already standing; те́сто не ~шло́ the dough would not rise. 2. (*obs., coll.*) to enter.

взор, а, *m.* look; glance; обрати́ть на себя́ ~ы пу́блики to come into the public eye; устреми́ть ~ы (на+*a.*) to fasten one's eyes (on).

взорв|а́ть, у́, ёшь, *pf.* (*of* взрыва́ть) 1. to blow up; to detonate. 2. (*fig.*) to exasperate, madden; его́ ~а́ло, когда́ они́ сообщи́ли о свое́й помо́лвке (*impers.*) he exploded when they announced their engagement.

взорв|а́ться, у́сь, ёшься, *pf.* (*of* взрыва́ться) to blow up, burst, explode (*also fig.*).

взо|шёл, шла́, *see* ~йти́.

взра|стить, щу́, сти́шь, *pf.* to grow, cultivate; to bring up, nurture.

взра́щива|ть, ю, *impf. of* взрасти́ть.

взра|щу́, сти́шь, *see* ~сти́ть.

взрев|е́ть, у́, ёшь, *pf.* to let out a roar.

взре́ж|у, ешь, *see* взре́зать.

взре́|зать, жу, жешь, *pf.* to cut open.

взреза́|ть, ю, *impf. of* взре́зать.

взре́зыва|ть, ю = взреза́ть.

взро́сл|ый, *adj.* grown-up, adult; *also as noun* в., ~ого, *m.*; ~ая, ~ой, *f.*

взрыв, а, *m.* explosion; (*fig.*) burst, outburst; в. аплодисме́нтов burst of applause; в. негодова́ния outburst of indignation.

взрыва́|ть¹, ю, *impf. of* взорва́ть.

взрыва́|ть², *impf. of* взрыть.

взрыва́|ться, юсь, *impf. of* взорва́ться.

взрывн|о́й, *adj.* **1.** explosive; ~а́я волна́ blast. **2.** (*ling.*) plosive.

взрывча́тк|а, и, *f.* (*coll.*) explosive.

взры́вчат|ый, *adj.* explosive; ~ое вещество́ explosive.

взр|ы́ть, о́ю, о́ешь, *pf.* (*of* ~ыва́ть²) to plough up, turn up.

взрыхл|и́ть, ю́, и́шь, *pf.* to loosen, break up.

взрыхля́|ть, ю, *impf. of* взрыхли́ть.

взъеда́|ться, юсь, *impf. of* взъе́сться.

взъезжа́|ть, ю, *impf. of* взъе́хать.

взъерепе́н|иться, юсь, ишься, *pf. of* ерепе́ниться.

взъеро́шен|ный (~, ~а), *p.p.p. of* взъеро́шить *and adj.* tousled, dishevelled.

взъеро́шива|ть(ся), ю(сь), *impf. of* взъеро́шить(ся).

взъеро́ш|ить, у, ишь, *pf.* (*of* ~ивать) (*coll.*) to tousle, rumple.

взъеро́ш|иться, усь, ишься, *pf.* (*of* ~иваться) (*coll.*) to rumple one's hair; to become dishevelled.

взъ|е́сться, е́мся, е́шься, е́стся, еди́мся, еди́тесь, едя́тся, *past* ~е́лся, *pf.* (*of* ~еда́ться) (на+*a.*; *coll.*) to pitch into, go for (*fig.*).

взъе́|хать, ду, дешь, *pf.* (*of* ~зжа́ть) to mount, ascend (*in a vehicle or on an animal*).

взыва́|ть, ю, *impf. of* воззва́ть.

взыгра́|ть, ю, *pf.* **1.** to leap (for joy); се́рдце во мне ~ло my heart leapt up. **2.** to become disturbed; мо́ре ~ло the sea grew rough.

взыска́ни|е, я, *n.* **1.** penalty; punishment; подве́ргнуться ~ю to incur a penalty. **2.** exaction; prosecution; пода́ть на кого́-н. ко ~ю (*leg.*) to proceed against someone (*for recovery of debt, etc.*).

взыска́тел|ьный (~ен, ~ьна), *adj.* exacting; demanding; severe.

взы|ска́ть¹, щу́, ~щешь, *pf.* (*of* ~скивать) **1.** to exact; to recover; в. долг (с+*g.*) to recover a debt (from). **2.** to call to account,

make answer (for); за неуда́чу в бою́ ~ска́ли с генера́лов the generals were called to account for their failure in battle; не ~щи́(те)! (*coll.*) please forgive (me)!, don't be hard on (me)!

взы|ска́ть², щу́, ~щешь, *pf.* (*of* ~скивать) (+*i.*; *obs.*) to confer (on); to reward (with); в. ми́лостями to load with favours.

взы́скива|ть, ю, *impf. of* взыска́ть.

взыску́ющ|ий, его, m. (*lit.*) 'seeker'.

взы|щу́, ~щешь, *see* ~ска́ть.

взя́ти|е, я, *n.* taking; capture.

взя́тк|а, и, f. 1. bribe; ~и гла́дки, *see* гла́дкий. **2.** (*cards*) trick.

взя́т|ок, ка, m. honey-gathering.

взя́точник, а, m. bribe-taker.

взя́точничеств|о, а, n. bribery, bribe-taking, corruption.

взя|ть, возьму́, возьмёшь, *past* ~л, ~ла́, ~ло, *pf.* (*of* брать) **1.** *see* брать. **2.** (*coll.*) to conclude, suppose; с чего́ вы ~ли, что он не́мец? what gave you the idea that he is a German? **3.** в. да, в. и, в. да и... (*coll.*) to do something suddenly; он ~л да убежа́л he up and ran; он возьми́ да скажи́ he up and spoke; возьми́ да скажи́ speak up, speak your mind. **4.** чёрт возьми́! (*coll.*) devil, deuce take it! **5.** ни дать ни в. (*coll.*) exactly, neither more nor less.

взя|ться, возьму́сь, возьмёшься, *past* ~лся, ~ла́сь, ~ло́сь, *pf.* (*of* бра́ться) отку́да ни возьми́сь (*coll.*) from nowhere, out of the blue; отку́да ни возьми́сь налете́ла саранча́ out of the blue the locusts appeared.

виаду́к, а, m. viaduct.

вибра́тор, а, m. (*electr.*) vibrator; (*radio*) oscillator.

вибра́ци|я, и, f. vibration.

вибрио́н, а, m. (*med.*) vibrio.

вибри́р|овать, ую, *impf.* to vibrate; to oscillate.

виве́р, а, m. (*coll., obs.*) bon vivant.

виве́рр|а, ы, f. (*zool.*) civet.

вивисе́кци|я, и, f. vivisection.

виг, а, m. (*hist.*) whig.

вигва́м, а, m. wigwam.

виго́н|ь, и, f. vicuña; vicuña wool.

вид¹, а, m. 1. air, look; appearance; aspect; у вас хоро́ший в. you look well; име́ть мра́чный в. to look gloomy, have a gloomy air; приня́ть пра́здничный в. to assume a festive air; сде́лать в., бу́дто to make it appear that, pretend that; для ~у for the sake of appearances; на в., с ~у in appearance; знать по ~у to know by sight; под ~ом (+*g.*) under the guise (of); ни под каки́м ~ом on no account. **2.** shape, form; в любо́м ~е in any shape or form; в тре́звом ~е in a sober state; в хоро́шем ~е in good condition, in good shape. **3.** view; ко́мната с ~ом на го́ры room with a view of the mountains; в. сбо́ку side-view; откры́тка с ~ом picture postcard. **4.** (*pl.*) prospect; ~ы на бу́дущее prospects for the future. **5.** sight; потеря́ть из ~у to lose sight (of); упусти́ть из ~у (*fig.*) to lose sight (of), fail to take into account; поста́вить на в. кому́-н. что-н. to reprimand someone for something; быть на ~у to be in the public eye; при ~е (+*g.*) at the sight (of); в ~у́ (+*g.*) in sight (of); в ~у́ того́, что as, since, seeing that; име́ть в ~у́ (*i*) to plan, intend, (*ii*) to mean; что вы име́ли в ~у́, говоря́ э́то? what did you mean when you said that?, (*iii*) to bear in mind; име́й(те) в ~у́ bear in mind, don't forget; име́ться в ~у́ (*i*) to be intended, be envisaged, (*ii*) to be meant.

вид², **а**, *m.* **1.** (*biol.*) species. **2.** kind, sort. **3.** (*gram.*) aspect; соверше́нный, несоверше́нный в. perfective, imperfective aspect.

вид³, **а**, *m.* в. на жи́тельство residence permit; identity card.

ви́дан|ный (~, ~а), *p.p.p.* of вида́ть; ~ное ли э́то де́ло? have you ever heard of such a thing?

вида́|ть, **ю**, *impf.* (*of* у~) (*coll.*) to see; его́ не в. he is not to be seen; ничего́ подо́бного я не ~л I have never seen such a thing; он ~л ви́ды he has seen, knocked about, the world.

вида́|ться, **юсь**, *impf.* (*of* по~) (с+*i.*; *coll.*) to meet; to see one another; мы с жено́й три го́да не ~лись my wife and I had not seen one another for three years.

ви́дени|е, **я**, *n.* sight, vision.

виде́ни|е, **я**, *n.* vision, apparition.

ви́|деть, **жу**, **дишь**, *impf.* (*of* у~) to see; в. кого́-н. наскво́зь to see through someone; в. во сне to dream (of); его́ то́лько и ~дели (*coll.*) he was gone in a flash; ~дишь (ли)?, ~дите (ли)? (*coll.*) you see?, do you see?

ви́|деться, **жусь**, **дишься**, *impf.* **1.** to see one another; (с+*i.*) to see. **2.** (*pf.* при~) to appear; ему́ ~делся стра́шный сон he had a terrifying dream; Га́млету ~делась тень отца́ на валу́ the ghost of his father appeared to Hamlet on the rampart.

ви́димо, *adv.* **1.** (*obs.*) visibly. **2.** evidently; он, в., чу́вствовал себя́ оскорблённым evidently he was offended.

ви́димо-неви́димо, *adv.* (*coll.*) in immense quantity; наро́ду бы́ло в.-н. there was an immense crowd.

ви́димост|ь, **и**, *f.* **1.** visibility. **2.** outward appearance; для ~и for show, for appearances. **3.** по (всей) ~и to all appearances.

ви́дим|ый (~, ~а), *p.p.p.* of ви́деть *and adj.*

1. visible. **2.** apparent, evident; без ~ой причи́ны with no apparent cause. **3.** apparent, seeming.

видне́|ться, **юсь**, **ешься**, *impf.* to be visible; на горизо́нте ~лись огни́ корабля́ a ship's lights could be seen on the horizon.

ви́дно 1. *adv.* obviously, evidently; она́, в., уста́ла obviously she is tired; *as pred.* it is obvious, it is evident, it is apparent; всем бы́ло в., что он лжёт it was obvious to everyone, everyone could see that he was lying; как в. из ска́занного as is clear from the statement. **2.** *adv. as pred.* visible; in sight; бе́рега ещё не́ бы́ло в. the coast was not yet visible; конца́ ещё не в. the end is not yet in sight; бы́ло хорошо́ в. visibility was good.

вид|ный, *adj.* **1.** (~ен, ~на́, ~но) visible; conspicuous. **2.** distinguished, prominent. **3.** (*coll.*) portly, stately; в. мужчи́на fine figure of a man.

видово́й¹, *adj.* of вид¹; в. объекти́в (*phot.*) landscape lens; в. фильм travel film, travelogue.

видово́й², *adj.* (of вид²) **1.** (*biol.*) specific. **2.** (*gram.*) aspectual.

видоизмене́ни|е, **я**, *n.* **1.** modification, alteration. **2.** modification; variety.

видоизмен|и́ть, **ю**, **и́шь**, *pf.* (*of* ~я́ть) to modify, alter.

видоизмен|и́ться, **ю́сь**, **и́шься**, *pf.* (of ~я́ться) **1.** to alter (*intrans.*). **2.** *pass.* of ~я́ть.

видоизмен|я́ть(ся), **я́ю(сь)**, *impf.* of ~и́ть(ся).

видоиска́тел|ь, **я**, *m.* (*phot.*) view-finder.

видообразова́ни|е, **я**, *n.* (*biol.*) formation of species.

ви́дыва|ть, **ю**, *freq.* of ви́деть (*coll.*) to see.

ви́|жу, **дишь**, *see* ~деть.

ви́з|а, **ы**, *f.* **1.** visa. **2.** official stamp.

визави́ 1. *adv.* opposite; они́ сиде́ли в. they sat opposite one another. **2.** *indecl. noun*, *m. and f.* the person opposite, facing; мы с мои́м в. завяза́ли разгово́р I entered into conversation with the person facing me.

византи́|ец, **йца**, *m.* Byzantine.

византи́йский, *adj.* Byzantine.

византини́ст, **а**, *m.* Byzantine scholar, Byzantinist.

визг, **а**, *m.* scream; squeal; yelp.

визгли́в|ый (~, ~а), *adj.* **1.** shrill. **2.** given to screaming, squealing, yelping.

визготн|я́, **и́**, *f.* (*coll.*) screaming; squealing; yelping.

визж|а́ть, **у́**, **и́шь**, *impf.* to scream; to squeal; to yelp.

визи́г|а, **и**, *no pl.*, *f.* viziga (*foodstuff prepared from gristle of fish of sturgeon family*).

визионе́р, **а**, *m.* visionary, mystic.

визионе́рств|о, **а**, *n.* mystical propensities.

визи́р, а, *m.* **1.** (*mil.*) sight; навигацио́нный в. (*aeron.*) drift sight. **2.**(*phot.*) view-finder.

визи́р|овать¹, ую, *impf. and pf.* (*pf. also* за~) to visa, visé (*passport*).

визи́р|овать², ую, *impf. and pf.* to sight; to take a sight (on).

визи́р|ь, я, *m.* vizier.

визи́т, а, *m.* visit; call; нанести́ в. to make an (official) visit; отда́ть в. to return a visit, call; прийти́ с ~ом к кому́-н. to visit someone, pay someone a call.

визита́ци|я, и, *f.* **1.** call; round (*of doctor*). **2.** search (*for contraband goods*).

визитёр, а, *m.* (*obs.*) visitor, caller.

визити́р|овать, ую, *impf.* **1.** (*obs.*) to pay a visit. **2.** to make a round (*of doctor*).

визи́тк|а, и, *f.* morning coat.

визи́т|ный, *adj. of* ~; ~ная ка́рточка visiting card.

ви́к|а, и, *no pl.*, *f.* vetch, tares.

вика́ри|й, я, *m.* (*eccl.*) vicar; suffragan.

вика́рный, *adj.* (*eccl.*) suffragan.

вико́нт, а, *m.* viscount.

виктори́н|а, ы, *f.* quiz.

викто́ри|я, и, *no pl.*, *f.* pine strawberries.

ви́лк|а, и, *f.* **1.** fork. **2.** (*electr.*) штéпсельная в. two-pin plug. **3.** (*mil.*) bracket.

ви́лл|а, ы, *f.* villa.

ви́ллис, а, *m.* (*mil.*) jeep.

вил|о́к, ка́, *m.* (*dial.*) head of cabbage.

вилообра́з|ный (~ен, ~на), *adj.* forked.

ви́л|ы, ~, *no sing.*, pitchfork; э́то ещё ~ами на воде́ пи́сано (*fig.*) it is still in the air.

вильн|у́ть, у́, ёшь, *pf.* **1.** *pf. of* виля́ть. **2.** to glide away; to turn off sharply, sidetrack.

виля́ни|е, я, *n.* **1.** wagging. **2.**(*fig.*) prevarication; evasions.

виля́|ть, ю, *impf.* (*of* вильну́ть) **1.** to wag; в. хвосто́м to wag one's tail; хвост у соба́ки всё вре́мя ~л the dog's tail was wagging the whole time. **2.** (*fig.*) to prevaricate; to be evasive.

вин|а́, ы́, *pl.* ~ы, *f.* fault, guilt; blame; моя́ в. it is my fault; не по их ~é through no fault of theirs; поста́вить кому́-н. в ~у́ to accuse someone of, reproach someone with; свали́ть ~у́ (на+*a.*) to lay the blame (on).

винегре́т, а, *m.* Russian salad; (*fig.*) medley, farrago.

ви́н|и, éй, *no sing.* (*coll.*) spades (*cards*).

вини́тельный, *adj.* (*gram.*) в. паде́ж accusative case.

вин|и́ть, ю́, и́шь, *impf.* (в+*p.*) to accuse (of); (за+*a.*; *obs., coll.* (to reproach (for).

вин|и́ться, ю́сь, и́шься, *impf.* (*of* по~) (в+*p.*; *coll.*) to confess (to).

вини́щ|е, а, *n.* (*coll.*) spirit *or* wine.

ви́нкел|ь, я, *pl.* ~я, *m.* (*tech.*) set-square.

виннока́менн|ый, *adj.* (*chem.*) ~ая кислота́ tartaric acid.

ви́нн|ый, *adj.* wine; winy; vinous; в. ка́мень (*chem.*) tartar; ~ая кислота́ tartaric acid; в. спирт ethyl alcohol; ~ая я́года dried figs.

вин|о́, а́, *pl.* ~а, *n.* **1.** wine. **2.** (*sing. only*; *coll.*) vodka.

винова́т|ый (~, ~а), *adj.* guilty; to blame; мы все ~ы в э́том we are all to blame for this; ~! sorry!; без вины́ ~ый innocent victim.

вино́вник, а, *m.* author, initiator; culprit; в. преступле́ния perpetrator of a crime; в. побе́ды architect of victory.

вино́вност|ь, и, *f.* guilt.

вино́в|ный (~ен, ~на), *adj.* (в+*p.*) guilty (of); объявля́ть ~ным to bring in a verdict of guilty; призна́ть себя́ ~ным to plead guilty.

виногра́д, а (у), *m.* **1.** vine. **2.** (*collect.*) grapes; зéлен в.! sour grapes!

виногра́дарств|о, а, *n.* viticulture; wine-growing.

виногра́дар|ь, я, *m.* wine-grower.

виногра́дин|а, ы, *f.* (*coll.*) grape.

виногра́дник, а, *m.* vineyard.

виногра́д|ный, *adj. of* ~; ~ная лоза́ vine; в. сезо́н vintage; ~ное су́сло must.

виноде́л, а, *m.* wine-grower.

виноде́ли|е, я, *n.* wine-making.

винокур, а, *m.* distiller.

винокуре́ни|е, я, *n.* distillation.

винокур|енный, *adj. of* ~е́ние; в. заво́д distillery.

винокур|ня, ни, *g. pl.* ~ен, *f.* (*obs.*) distillery.

виноторго́в|ец, ца, *m.* wine-merchant.

виноторго́вл|я, и, *f.* **1.** wine-trade. **2.** wine-shop.

виноче́рпи|й, я, *m.* (*hist.*) cup-bearer.

винт¹, а́, *m.* **1.** screw; подъёмный в. jack-screw; упо́рный в. stop screw; установо́чный в. adjusting set screw. **2.** screw, propeller; дать ~á (*sl.*) to take to one's heels, scarper. **3.** spiral; ле́стница ~о́м spiral staircase.

винт², а́, *m.* vint (*card-game*).

винт³, а́, *m.* (*sl.*) rifle.

ви́нт|ик, а, *m. dim. of* ~¹; у него́ ~а не хвата́ет (*coll.*) he has a screw loose somewhere.

вин|ти́ть¹, чу́, ти́шь, *impf.* to screw up.

вин|ти́ть², чу́, ти́шь, *impf.* (*coll.*) to play vint.

винтова́льн|ый, *adj.* ~ая доска́ (*tech.*) screw plate.

винто́вк|а, и, *f.* rifle.

винт|ово́й, *adj. of* ~¹; spiral; ~ова́я ле́стница spiral staircase; ~ова́я наре́зка thread (*of screw*); в. парохо́д screw steamer; ~ова́я переда́ча (*tech.*) helical gear.

винтообра́з|ный (∼ен, ∼на), *adj.* spiral.

винторе́зный, *adj.* (*tech.*) screw-cutting.

вин|чу́, ти́шь, *see* ∼ти́ть.

виньетк|а, и, *f.* vignette.

виол|а, ы, *f.* viol; viola.

виолончели́ст, а, *m.* (violon)cellist.

виолончел|ь, и, *f.* (violon)cello.

ви́ра¹, *interj.* (*dockers' sl.*) lift!

ви́р|а², ы, *f.* (*hist.*) wergeld.

вира́ж|, а, *m.* (*phot.*) intensifier; в.-фикса́ж tone-fixing bath.

вира́ж², á, *m.* **1.** turn; круто́й в. steep turn. **2.** bend, curve (*of road, racing-track, etc.*).

вири́р|овать, ую, *impf. and pf.* (*phot.*) to intensify.

виртуа́л|ьный (∼ен, ∼ьна), *adj.* virtual.

виртуо́з, а, *m.* virtuoso.

виртуо́зност|ь, и, *f.* virtuosity.

виртуо́з|ный (∼ен, ∼на), *adj.* masterly.

вируле́нт|ный (∼ен, ∼на), *adj.* (*med.*) virulent.

ви́рус, а, *m.* (*med.*) virus.

ви́рус|ный, *adj. of* ∼.

ви́рш|и, ей, *no sing.* **1.** (*lit.*) (syllabic) verses (*based on Polish form*). **2.** (*coll.*) doggerel.

вис, а, *m.* (*sport*) hanging (on the pole).

ви́селиц|а, ы, *f.* gallows, gibbet.

ви́сельник, а, *m.* **1.** hanged man. **2.** (*coll.*) gallows-bird.

ви|се́ть, шу́, си́шь, *impf.* to hang; to be hanging, be suspended; в. на волоске́ to hang by a thread; в. в во́здухе (*i*) to be in the air, (*ii*) to be unfounded.

ви́ски, *indecl., n.* whisky.

виско́з|а, ы, *f.* **1.** (*tech.*) viscose. **2.** (*coll.*) rayon.

вислоу́х|ий (∼, ∼а), *adj.* lop-eared.

ви́смут, а, *m.* (*chem.*) bismuth.

ви́сн|уть, у, ешь, *impf.* (на+*p.*) to hang (on); to droop; в. у кого́-н. на ше́е (*fig., coll.*) to hang on someone's neck.

вис|о́к, ка́, *m.* (*anat.*) temple.

високо́сный, *adj.* в. год leap-year.

висо́чный, *adj.* (*anat.*) temporal.

вист, а, *m.* whist (*card-game*).

висю́льк|а, и, *f.* (*coll.*) pendant.

вися́чий, *adj.* hanging, pendent; в. замо́к padlock; в. мост suspension bridge.

витали́зм, а, *m.* (*philos.*) vitalism.

витали́ст, а, *m.* (*philos.*) vitalist.

витами́н, а, *m.* vitamin.

витами́нный, *adj.* vitaminous.

витамин|о́зный = ∼ный.

вита́|ть, ю, *impf.* (*lit.*) to be; to wander (*of thoughts*); to hover; он ∼ет в ми́ре фанта́зий he inhabits a world of fantasy; он всё ещё говори́л, но мы́сли у него́ ∼ли далеко́ he went on speaking but his thoughts were far away; в. в облака́х to be up in the clouds; смерть ∼ла над ней death was hovering over her.

витиева́т|ый (∼, ∼а), *adj.* flowery, ornate, rhetorical.

вити́йств|о, а, *n.* (*obs.*) oratory, rhetoric.

вити́йств|овать, ую, *impf.* (*obs.*) to orate.

вити́|я, и, *m.* (*coll., iron.*) orator.

вит|о́й, *adj.* twisted; spiral; ∼а́я ле́стница spiral staircase.

вит|о́к, ка́, *m.* **1.** (*tech.*) spire. **2.** circuit (*of planet by space vehicle*).

витра́ж, а, *m.* stained-glass window.

витри́н|а, ы, *f.* **1.** (shop-)window. **2.** show-case.

ви|ть, вью, вьёшь, *past* ∼л, ∼ла́, ∼ло, *impf.* (*of* с∼) to twist, wind; в. венки́ to weave garlands; в. гнездо́ to build a nest; в. верёвки из кого́-н. (*coll.*) to twist round one's little finger.

ви|ться, вьюсь, вьёшься, *past* ∼лся, ∼ла́сь, ∼ло́сь, *impf.* (*of* с∼) **1.** to wind, twine. **2.** to curl, wave (*of hair*). **3.** to hover, circle (*of birds*). **4.** to writhe, twist (*of reptiles*).

витю́т|ень, ня, *m.* wood-pigeon.

ви́тяз|ь, я, *m.* (*poet., arch.*) knight; hero.

вихля́|ть, ю, *impf.* (*coll.*) to reel.

вихля́|ться, юсь, *impf.* (*coll.*) to wobble.

вих|о́р, ра́, *m.* forelock.

вихра́ст|ый (∼, ∼а), *adj.* (*coll.*) shaggy; shock-headed.

вихрево́й, *adj.* (*phys.*) vortical.

вихр|ь, я, *m.* **1.** whirlwind; сне́жный в. blizzard. **2.** (*fig.*) vortex.

ви́це- vice-.

вице-адмира́л, а, *m.* vice-admiral.

вице-коро́л|ь, я́, *m.* viceroy.

вицмунди́р, а, *m.* uniform (*of civil servants*).

ви́ши, *indecl., n.* Vichy (water).

вишнёвк|а, и, *f.* cherry brandy.

вишнёвый, *adj.* **1.** cherry; в. сад cherry orchard. **2.** cherry-coloured.

ви́ш|ня, ни, *g. pl.* ∼ен, *f.* **1.** cherry-tree. **2.** cherry; (*collect.*) cherries.

вишь (*contraction of* ви́дишь; *coll.*) look!, just look!; в. что сде́лал! look what he's done!

вка́лыва|ть, ю, *impf.* **1.** *impf. of* вколо́ть. **2.** *impf. only* (*sl.*) to work hard.

вка́п|ать, аю, *pf.* (*of* ∼ывать¹) (*coll.*) to pour in.

вка́пыва|ть¹, ю, *impf. of* вка́пать.

вка́пыва|ть², ю, *impf. of* вкопа́ть.

вка|ти́ть, чу́, ∼тишь, *pf.* (*of* ∼тывать) **1.** to roll into, onto; to wheel in, into; в. бо́чку в подва́л to roll a barrel into a cellar. **2.** (*fig., coll.*) to administer; to put in, on; в. пощёчину (+*d.*) to slap in the face; в. в спи́сок to place in a list.

вка|ти́ться, чу́сь, ∼тишься, *pf.* (*of* ∼тываться) to roll in (*intrans.*); (*coll.*) to run in.

вка́тыва|ть(ся), ю(сь), *impf. of* вкати́ть-(ся).

вклад, а, *m.* **1.** (*fin.*) deposit; investment. **2.** endowment; (*fig.*) contribution; внести́ ва́жный в. в нау́ку to make an important contribution to learning.

вкла́дк|а, и, *f.* supplementary sheet.

вклад|но́й **1.** *adj. of* ~. **2.** supplementary, inserted; в. лист loose leaf.

вкла́дчик, а, *m.* depositor; investor.

вкла́дыва|ть, ю, *impf. of* вложи́ть.

вкла́д|ыш, а, *m.* **1.** = ~ка. **2.** (*tech.*) bush, bearing brass.

вкле́ива|ть, ю, *impf. of* вклеи́ть.

вкле|и́ть, ю́, ~и́шь, *pf.* (*of* ~и́вать) to stick in; в. сло́во в разгово́р (*fig.*, *coll.*) to put in a word.

вкле́йк|а, и, *f.* **1.** sticking in. **2.** inset (*in a book*).

вклеп|а́ть, а́ю, *pf.* (*of* ~ывать) **1.** to rivet in. **2.** (*fig.*, *coll.*) to mix up (in), involve (in).

вклеп|а́ться, а́юсь, *pf.* (*of* ~ываться) **1.** to be riveted in. **2.** (*fig.*, *coll.*) to be mixed up in.

вклёпыв|ать(ся), аю(сь), *impf. of* вклепа́ть-(ся).

вкли́нива|ть(ся), ю(сь), *impf. of* вклини́ть-(ся).

вклин|и́ть, ю́, ~и́шь, *pf.* to wedge in; в. сло́во (*fig.*, *coll.*) to put a word in.

вклин|и́ться, ю́сь, ~и́шься, *pf.* **1.** *pass.* of ~и́ть. **2.** (в+а.) to edge one's way into; (*mil.*) to drive a wedge (into).

включа́тел|ь, я, *m.* switch.

включ|а́ть(ся), а́ю(сь), *impf. of* ~и́ть(ся).

включа́|я, *pres. gerund of* ~ть; *as prep.+a.* including, inclusive; вы́ставка откры́та ка́ждый день, в. воскресе́нье the exhibition is open every day including Sundays.

включе́ни|е, я, *n.* **1.** inclusion, insertion; со ~ем (+*g.*) including. **2.** (*tech.*) switching on, turning on.

включи́тельно, *adv.* inclusive; с пя́того по девя́тое в. from the 5th to the 9th inclusive.

включ|и́ть, у́, и́шь, *pf.* (*of* ~а́ть) **1.** (в+а.) to include (in); to insert (in); в. в себя́ to include, comprise, take in; в. в пове́стку дня to enter on the agenda; в. в спи́сок to enter on a list. **2.** (*tech.*) to switch on, turn on; to plug in; в. ра́дио to put the wireless on; в. ско́рость to engage a gear; в. сцеп-ле́ние to let in the clutch.

включ|и́ться, у́сь, и́шься, *pf.* (*of* ~а́ться) **1.** (в+а.) to join (in), enter (into); в. в за́говор to enter into a conspiracy. **2.** *pass.* *of* ~и́ть.

вкола́чива|ть, ю, *impf. of* вколоти́ть.

вкол|оти́ть, очу́, ~о́тишь, *pf.* (*of* ~а́чи-вать) to knock in, hammer in (*also fig.*); в. в го́лову (+*d.*; *coll.*) to knock into some-

one's head; в. себе́ в го́лову to get it into one's head.

вкол|о́ть, ю́, ~ешь, *pf.* (*of* вка́лывать) (в+*a.*) to stick (in, into).

вкол|очу́, ~о́тишь, *see* ~оти́ть.

вконе́ц, *adv.* (*coll.*) completely, absolutely.

вко́пан|ный (~, ~а), *p.p.p. of* вкопа́ть; как в. rooted to the ground.

вкопа́|ть, ю, *pf.* to dig in.

вкорен|и́ть, ю́, и́шь, *pf.* (*of* ~я́ть) to incul-cate.

вкорен|и́ться, ю́сь, и́шься, *pf.* (*of* ~я́ться) to be inculcated; to take root.

вкореня́|ть(ся), ю(сь), *impf. of* вкорени́ть(ся).

вкоротке́, *adv.* (*coll.*, *obs.*). **1.** shortly. **2.** in brief.

вкось, *adv.* obliquely; slantwise; вкривь и в., *see* вкривь.

вкрад|у́сь, ёшься, *see* вкра́сться.

вкра́дчив|ый (~, ~а), *adj.* insinuating, in-gratiating.

вкра́дыва|ться, юсь, *impf. of* вкра́сться.

вкра́п|ить, лю, ишь, *pf.* (*of* ~ливать) to sprinkle (with); (*fig.*) to intersperse (with); он ~ил в речь цита́ты he interspersed his speech with quotations.

вкра́пленник, а, *m.* (*geol.*) phenocryst, por-phyritic crystal.

вкра́плива|ть, ю, *impf. of* вкра́пить.

вкрапл|я́ть, я́ю, *impf.* = ~ивать.

вкра́|сться, ду́сь, дёшься, *past* ~лся, *pf.* (*of* ~дываться) to steal in, creep in; в текст ~лось мно́го оши́бок many mistakes have crept into the text; в. в дове́рие к кому́-н. to worm oneself, insinuate oneself into someone's confidence.

вкра́тце, *adv.* briefly; succinctly.

вкривь, *adv.* aslant; (*fig.*) wrongly, per-versely; всё, что говорю́, он понима́ет в. he misinterprets everything I say; в. и вкось all over the place; (*fig.*, *coll.*) indis-criminately.

вкруг = вокру́г.

вкругову́ю, *adv.* (*coll.*) round; пусти́ть ча́шу в. to send the cup round (*at banquets*).

вкру|ти́ть, чу́, ~тишь, *pf.* (*of* ~чивать) to twist in.

вкруту́ю, *adv.* (*coll.*) яйцо́ в. hard-boiled egg; свари́ть яйцо́ в. to hard-boil an egg.

вкру́чива|ть, ю, *impf. of* вкрути́ть.

вкру|чу́, ~тишь, *see* ~ти́ть.

вку́пе, *adv.* (*obs.*) together.

вкус, а, *m.* **1.** taste (*also fig.*); про́бовать на в. to taste; войти́ во в. (+*g.*) to begin to en-joy, develop a taste (for); на в. и цвет товари́ща нет (*prov.*) tastes differ; э́то де́ло ~а it is a matter of taste; челове́к со ~ом a man of taste. **2.** manner, style; во ~е Ренеса́нса in the Renaissance style.

вку|си́ть, шу́, ~сишь, *pf.* (*of* ~ша́ть) **1.**

(*obs.*) to taste, partake (of). 2. (*fig.*, *poet.*) to taste, savour, experience.

вку́с|ный (~ен, ~на́, ~но), *adj.* good, nice (*to taste*); appetizing, tasty.

вкусов|о́й, *adj.* gustatory; ~ы́е вещества́ flavouring substances; ~ы́е о́рганы organs of taste.

вкуша́|ть, ю, *impf. of* вкуси́ть.

вку|шу́, ~сишь, *see* ~си́ть.

влаг|а́, и, *no pl.*, *f.* moisture, liquid.

влага́лищ|е, а, *n.* (*anat.*, *bot.*) vagina.

влага́|ть, ю, *impf. of* вложи́ть.

влагоме́р, а, *m.* hygrometer.

владе́л|ец, ьца, *m.* owner; proprietor.

владе́ни|е, я, *n.* 1. ownership; possession; вступи́ть во в. иму́ществом to take possession of property. 2. property, possession; domain, estate; колониа́льные ~я colonial possessions.

владе́тел|ь, я, *m.* possessor; sovereign.

владе́тельный, *adj.* sovereign.

владе́|ть, ю, ешь, *impf.* (+*i.*) 1. to own, possess. 2. to control; to be in possession (of); в. собо́й to control oneself; им ~ют стра́сти he is at the mercy of his passions. 3. (*fig.*) to have (a) command (of); to have the use (of); в. перо́м to wield a skilful pen; она́ ~ет шестью́ языка́ми she has a command of six languages; он не ~ет пра́вой руко́й he has not the use of his right arm.

Влади́мирк|а, и, *f.* (*coll.*) the Vladimir road (*the road to Siberia*); идти́ по ~е to be exiled, be going into exile.

владь́к|а, и, *m.* 1. master, sovereign. 2. member of higher orders of clergy (*bishop*, *archbishop, or metropolitan*).

владь́честв|о, а, *n.* dominion, sway.

владь́честв|овать, ую, *impf.* (над+*i.*) to hold sway, exercise dominion (over).

владь́чиц|а, ы, *f.* 1. mistress, sovereign. 2. В. (*eccl.*) Our Lady.

влажне́|ть, ю, ешь, *impf.* (*of* по~) to become damp, humid.

вла́жност|ь, и, *f.* humidity, dampness.

вла́ж|ный (~ен, ~на́, ~но), *adj.* humid, damp; moist.

вла́мыва|ться, юсь, *impf. of* вломи́ться.

вла́ств|овать, ую, *impf.* (над+*i.*) to rule, hold sway (over).

властели́н, а, *m.* (*usu. fig.*) ruler; lord; master.

власти́тел|ь, я, *m.* sovereign, potentate; в. дум dominant influence.

вла́ст|ный (~ен, ~на), *adj.* 1. imperious, commanding; masterful. 2. (в+*p.*; *leg.*) authoritative, competent; я не ~ен в э́том де́ле I have no competence to deal with this matter.

властолюби́в|ый (~, ~а), *adj.* power-loving; power-seeking.

властолюби́|е, я, *n.* love of power; lust for power.

власт|ь, и, *pl.* ~и, ~е́й, *f.* 1. power; во ~и (+*g.*) at the mercy (of), in the power (of); прийти́ к ~и to come to power; у ~и in power. 2. power, authority; (*pl.*) authorities; ме́стная в., в. на места́х local authority; сове́тская в. the Soviet régime; в. предержа́щая the powers that be. 3. ва́ша в. (*coll.*) as you like, please yourself.

власяни́ц|а, ы, *f.* hair shirt.

влач|и́ть, у́, и́шь, *impf.* (*obs.*, *poet.*) to drag; в. жа́лкое существова́ние to drag out a miserable existence.

влач|и́ться, у́сь, и́шься, *impf.* (*obs.*, *poet.*) to drag oneself along.

вле́во, *adv.* (от+*g.*) to the left (of).

влеза́|ть, ю, *impf. of* влезть.

влез|ть, у, ешь, *past* ~, ~ла, *pf.* (*of* ~а́ть) 1. to climb in, into, up; to get in, into; в. на де́рево to climb up a tree; ей пришло́сь в. в окно́ she had to get in by the window; в. в долги́ (*fig.*) to get into debt; в. в ду́шу (+*g.*) to worm oneself into someone's confidence; to worm confidences out of someone. 2. (*coll.*) to get on, board; в. в авто́бус to get on the bus. 3. (*coll.*) to fit in, go in, go on; все э́ти ве́щи не ~ут в мою́ су́мку these things will not all go into my bag; сапоги́ мне не ~ли my boots would not go on; ско́лько ~ет (*i*) as much as possible, (*ii*) as much as you like.

влеп|и́ть, лю́, ~ишь, *pf.* to stick in, fasten in; (*coll.*) в. пощёчину кому́-н. to slap someone's face; в. пу́лю в лоб кому́-н. to put a bullet in someone's brain.

влепля́|ть, ю, *impf. of* влепи́ть.

влет|а́ть, а́ю, *impf. of* ~е́ть.

вле|те́ть, чу́, ти́шь, *pf.* (*of* ~та́ть) to fly in, into; (*fig.*, *coll.*) to rush in, into; в. в исто́рию to get into trouble; (*impers.*) ему́ опя́ть ~те́ло he is in trouble again.

влече́ни|е, я, *n.* (к) attraction (to); bent (for); он чу́вствует си́льное в. к Восто́ку he is strongly drawn to the East; сле́довать своему́ ~ю to follow one's bent.

вле|чь, ку́, чёшь, ку́т, *past* влёк, ~кла́, *impf.* to draw; to attract; в. за собо́й to involve, entail.

вле́|чься, ку́сь, чёшься, ку́тся, *past* ~кся, ~кла́сь, *impf.* 1. (к) to be drawn (to); to be attracted (by). 2. *pass. of* ~чь.

влива́ни|е, я, *n.* infusion; (*med.*) внутриве́нное в. intravenous administration.

влива́|ть, ю, *impf. of* влить.

влипа́|ть, ю, *impf. of* влипнуть.

вли́п|нуть, ну, нешь, *past* ~, ~ла, *pf.* (*coll.*) to get into a mess; to put one's foot in it; to get caught.

вли|ть, волью́, вольёшь, *past* ~л, ~ла́, ~ло, *pf.* (*of* ~ва́ть) 1. to pour in; в. по ка́пле to instil, administer drops; (*med.*) to infuse; (*fig.*) to instil; в. наде́жду в кого́-н. to instil hope into someone. 2. (*mil.*) to bring in; в. пополне́ния в часть to reinforce a unit.

влия́ни|е, я, *n.* influence; по́льзоваться ~ем to have influence, be influential.

влия́тел|ьный (~ен, ~ьна), *adj.* influential.

влия́|ть, ю, *impf.* (*of* по~) (на+*a.*) to influence, have an influence on, affect.

вложе́ни|е, я, *n.* 1. enclosure; со ~ем 'enclosure' (*on letters*). 2. (*fin.*) investment.

влож|и́ть, у́, ~ишь, *pf.* (*of* вкла́дывать *and* влага́ть) 1. to put in, insert; to enclose (*with a letter*); он ~и́л всю свою́ ду́шу в рабо́ту (*fig.*) he put his whole soul into his work; в. в уста́ кому́-н. to put into someone's mouth. 2. (*fin.*) to invest.

влом|и́ться, люсь, ~ишься, *pf.* (*of* вла́мываться) to break in, into; в. в амби́цию (*coll.*) to take offence.

вло́па|ться, юсь, *pf.* (*coll.*) 1. to get into an awkward situation. 2. to fall in love.

влюб|и́ть, лю́, ~ишь, *pf.* (*of* ~ля́ть) (в+*a.*) to make fall in love (with).

влюб|и́ться, лю́сь, ~ишься, *pf.* (*of* ~ля́ться) (в+*a.*) to fall in love (with).

влюблённост|ь, и, *f.* love; being in love.

влюблён|ный (~, ~а́), *p.p.p. of* влюби́ть *and adj.* 1. (*p.p.p.*) in love; в. по́ уши head over ears in love. 2. (*adj.*) loving; tender.

влюбля́|ть, ю, *impf. of* влюби́ть.

влюбля́|ться, юсь, *impf. of* влюби́ться.

влю́бчив|ый (~, ~а), *adj.* (*coll.*) amorous, susceptible.

вля́па|ться, юсь, *pf.* (*coll.*) to plunge into; (*fig.*) в. в исто́рию to get into a mess.

вма́|зать, жу, жешь, *pf.* to cement, putty in.

вма́зыва|ть, ю, *impf. of* вма́зать.

вмен|и́ть, ю́, и́шь, *pf.* (*of* ~я́ть) (*d.*+в+*a.*) 1. to regard (as); в. в вину́ to lay to the charge of; в. в заслу́гу to regard as a merit; в. в обя́занность to impose as a duty; он ~и́л себе́ в обя́занность чте́ние всех газе́т he imposed on himself the duty of reading all the newspapers. 2. to impute.

вменя́емост|ь, и, *f.* (*leg.*) responsibility; liability.

вменя́ем|ый (~, ~а), *adj.* (*leg.*) responsible, liable; of sound mind.

вменя́|ть, ю, *impf. of* вмени́ть.

вме|си́ть, шу́, ~сишь, *pf.* (*of* ~шивать²) to knead in.

вме́сте, *adv.* together; at the same time; в. с тем at the same time, also.

вмести́лищ|е, а, *n.* receptacle.

вмести́мост|ь, и, *f.* capacity.

вмести́тел|ьный (~ен, ~ьна), *adj.* capacious; spacious, roomy.

вме|сти́ть, щу́, сти́шь, *pf. of* ~ща́ть.

вме́сто, *prep.*+*g.* instead of; in place of.

вмеша́тельств|о, а, *n.* interference; intervention; хирурги́ческое в. surgical operation.

вмеша́|ть, ю, *pf.* (*of* вме́шивать¹) (в+*a.*) 1. to mix in. 2. (*coll.*, *fig.*) to mix up (in), implicate (in).

вмеш|а́ться, а́юсь, *pf.* (*of* ~иваться) (в+*a.*) to interfere (in), meddle (with); to intervene (in); в. в чужу́ю жизнь to meddle with other people's lives; полице́йский ~а́лся в дра́ку a policeman intervened in the fight.

вме́шива|ть¹, ю, *impf. of* вмеша́ть.

вме́шива|ть², ю, *impf. of* вмеси́ть.

вме́шива|ться, юсь, *impf. of* вмеша́ться.

вмеща́|ть, ю, *impf.* (*of* вмести́ть) 1. to contain; to hold; to accommodate; э́та бо́чка ~ет пятьдеся́т ли́тров this barrel holds fifty litres; зал ~ет пятьсо́т челове́к the hall can seat five hundred. 2. (в+*a.*) to put, place (in, into).

вмеща́|ться, юсь, *impf.* (*of* вмести́ться) 1. to go in; ва́ши башмаки́ не ~ются в мой чемода́н your shoes will not go into my case. 2. *pass. of* ~ть 2.

вмиг, *adv.* in an instant; in a flash.

вмина́|ть, ю, *impf. of* вмять.

вмя́тин|а, ы, *f.* dent.

вмять, вомну́, вомнёшь, *pf.* (*of* вмина́ть) to press in.

внаём, внаймы́, *adv.* отда́ть в. to let, hire out, rent; взять в. to hire, rent; сдаётся в. 'to let'.

внаки́дку, *adv.* (*coll.*) носи́ть в. to wear thrown over the shoulders.

внакла́де, *adv.* (*coll.*) оста́ться в. to be the loser, come off loser; не оста́ться в. (от+*g.*) to be none the worse off (for).

внакла́дку, *adv.* пить чай в. to drink tea with sugar in (*as opp. to* вприку́ску).

внача́ле, *adv.* at first, in the beginning.

вне, *prep.*+*g.* outside; out of; в. зако́на without the law; объяви́ть в. зако́на to outlaw; в. ко́нкурса hors concours; в. о́череди out of turn; в. пла́на over and above the plan; в. себя́ beside oneself; в. вся́ких сомне́ний beyond any doubt.

вне- extra-.

внебра́чный, *adj.* extra-marital; в. ребёнок illegitimate child.

вневойскови́к, а́, *m.* civilian receiving military training.

вневойсков|о́й, *adj.* ~а́я подгото́вка military training for civilians.

вневре́менный, *adj.* timeless.

внедре́ни|е, я, *n.* **1.** introduction; inculcation; indoctrination. **2.** (*geol.*) intrusion.

внедр|и́ть, ю́, и́шь, *pf.* (*of* ~я́ть) **1.** to inculcate, instil; в. в молоды́х привы́чку к чистоте́ to inculcate habits of cleanliness into the young. **2.** to introduce; в. но́вые ме́тоды to introduce new methods.

внедр|и́ться, ю́сь, и́шься, *pf.* (*of* ~я́ться) to take root.

внедря́|ть(ся), ю(сь), *impf. of* внедри́ть(ся).

внеза́пно, *adv.* suddenly, all of a sudden.

внеза́пност|ь, и, *f.* **1.** suddenness. **2.** (*obs.*) unexpected event.

внеза́пный, *adj.* sudden.

внекла́сс|ый, *adj.* out of school (hours); extra-curricular; ~ые заня́тия out of school activities.

внекла́ссовый, *adj.* (*polit.*) non-class.

внема́точный, *adj.* (*med.*) extra-uterine.

внемл|ю, ешь, *see* внима́ть.

внеочередн|о́й, *adj.* **1.** out of turn; зада́ть в. вопро́с to ask a question out of order. **2.** extraordinary; extra; в. съезд extraordinary congress; ~а́я сме́на extra shift.

внепарти́йный, *adj.* (*polit.*) non-party.

внепла́новый, *adj.* (*econ.*) not provided for by the plan; extraordinary.

внесе́ни|е, я, *n.* **1.** bringing in, carrying in. **2.** paying in, deposit (*of money*). **3.** entry, insertion (*into an agreement, etc.*). **4.** moving, submission (*of a resolution*).

внеслуже́бный, *adj.* leisure-time.

внес|ти́, у́, ёшь, *past* ~, ~ла́, *pf.* (*of* вноси́ть) **1.** to bring in, carry in; в. ра́неных to bring in the wounded. **2.** (*fig.*) to introduce, put in; в. я́сность в де́ло to clarify a matter; в. свой вклад в де́ло to do one's bit. **3.** to pay in, deposit. **4.** to bring in, move, table; в. законопрое́кт to bring in a bill; в. предложе́ние to move, table a resolution. **5.** to insert, enter; в. попра́вки в текст ре́чи to emend the text of a speech; в. в спи́сок to enter on a list. **6.** to bring about, cause; в. раздо́ры to cause bad feeling.

внестуди́йный, *adj.* (*of radio or television transmission*) outside.

внешко́льник, а, *m.* adult education specialist.

внешко́льн|ый, *adj.* ~ое образова́ние adult education.

вне́шне, *adv.* outwardly.

вне́шн|ий, *adj.* **1.** outer, exterior; outward, external; outside; в. вид outward appearance; в. у́гол (*math.*) external angle; в. лоск surface polish. **2.** foreign; ~яя поли́тика foreign policy; ~яя торго́вля foreign trade.

вне́шност|ь, и, *f.* exterior; surface; appearance; суди́ть по ~и to judge by appearances.

внешта́тный, *adj.* not on permanent staff; not established.

вниз, *adv.* down, downwards; в. голово́й head first; идти́ в. по ле́стнице to go downstairs; в. по тече́нию downstream; в. по Во́лге down the Volga.

внизу́, *adv.* below; downstairs; *prep.+g.* в. страни́цы at the foot of the page.

вник|а́ть, а́ю, *impf. of* ~нуть.

вни́к|нуть, ну, нешь, *past* ~, ~ла, *pf.* (*of* ~а́ть) (в+*a.*) to go carefully (into), investigate thoroughly; в. в обстоя́тельства уби́йства to investigate the circumstances of a murder.

внима́ни|е, я, *n.* **1.** attention; heed; notice, note; обраща́ть в. (на+*a.*) (i) to pay attention, give heed (to), take note (of) (ii) to draw attention (to); он весь в. he is all ears; принима́я во в. taking into account. **2.** attention(s); kindness, consideration; оказа́ть в. to do a kindness; по́льзоваться ~ем to be the object of attentions. **3.** (*interj.*) в.! look out! mind out!; в. на старт! (*sport*) get set!

внима́тельност|ь, и, *f.* **1.** attentiveness. **2.** thoughtfulness, consideration.

внима́тел|ьный (~ен, ~ьна), *adj.* **1.** attentive. **2.** (к+*d.*) thoughtful, considerate (towards).

внима́|ть, ю *and* вне́млю, *impf.* (*of* внять) (+*d.*; *poet.*, *obs.*) to hear (*fig.*); to heed; в. моли́тве to hear prayer.

вничью́, *adv.* (*sport*) drawn; па́ртия око́нчилась в. the game ended in a draw; на́ша хокке́йная кома́нда сыгра́ла сего́дня в. our hockey team drew today.

вно́ве, *adv. as pred.* new, strange; всё во францу́зском быту́ ей бы́ло в. everything about life in France was new to her.

вновь, *adv.* **1.** afresh, anew; again. **2.** newly; в. прибы́вший newcomer.

вно|си́ть, шу́, ~сишь, *impf. of* внести́.

вно|шу́, ~сишь, *see* ~си́ть.

внук, а, *m.* grandson; grandchild (*also fig.*).

вну́к|а, и, *f.* (*obs.*) granddaughter.

вну́тренн|ий, *adj.* **1.** inner, interior; internal; intrinsic; ~ие боле́зни internal diseases; в. мир inner life, private world; ~ие причи́ны intrinsic causes; ~ее сгора́ние internal combustion; в. смысл inner meaning. **2.** home, inland; ~ие дохо́ды inland revenue; Министе́рство ~их дел Ministry of Internal Affairs.

вну́тренност|ь, и, *f.* **1.** interior. **2.** (*pl. only*) entrails, intestines; internal organs; (*anat.*) viscera.

внутри́, *adv. and prep.+g.* inside, within; в. до́ма inside the house.

внутри́- intra-.

внутриве́нный, *adj.* (*med.*) intravenous.

внутрипарти́йный, *adj.* within the Party, inner-Party.

внутрь, *adv. and prep.*+*g.* within, inside; inwards; открыва́ться в. to open inwards; войти́ в. до́ма to go inside the house.

внуча́тный, *adj.* в. брат second cousin; в. племя́нник great-nephew.

внуча́т|ый = ~ный.

вну́чк|а, и, *f.* granddaughter.

внуч|о́нок, о́нка, *pl.* ~а́та, ~а́т, *m.* grandson; (*pl.*) grandchildren.

внуша́емост|ь, и, *f.* suggestibility.

внуш|а́ть, а́ю, *impf. of* ~и́ть.

внуше́ни|е, я, *n.* 1. (*psych.*) suggestion. 2. reproof, reprimand.

внуши́тел|ьный (~ен, ~ьна), *adj.* inspiring, impressive; (*coll.*) imposing, striking; ~ьное зда́ние imposing edifice; ~ьное зре́лище inspiring sight.

внуш|и́ть, у́, и́шь, *pf.* (*of* ~а́ть) (+*a. and d.*) to inspire (with); to instil; to suggest; его́ вид ~и́л мне страх the sight of him inspired me with fear; в. уве́ренность в себе́ to instil self-confidence; он уме́л в. слу́шателям, что он всегда́ прав he had the power of suggesting to his audience that he was always right.

внюха́|ться, юсь, *pf.* (в+*a.*; *coll.*) to take a sniff (at) (*also fig.*).

внюхива|ться, юсь, *impf. of* внюха́ться.

вня́т|ный (~ен, ~на), *adj.* 1. distinct. 2. (*obs.*) intelligible.

вня|ть, *future not used, past* ~л, ~ла́, ~ло, *imp.* вонми́(те), *pf. of* внима́ть.

во¹, *prep.* = в.

во², *interj.* (*coll.*) = вот.

во́бл|а, ы, *f.* vobla (*Caspian roach*).

вобр|а́ть, вберу́, вберёшь, *past* ~а́л, ~ала́, ~а́ло, *pf.* (*of* вбира́ть) to absorb, suck in; to inhale.

вобь|ю́, ёшь, *see* вбить.

вове́к(и), *adv.* (*obs.*) for ever; в. веко́в for ever and ever.

вовлека́|ть, ю, *impf. of* вовле́чь.

вовл|е́чь, еку́, ечёшь, еку́т, *past* ~ёк, ~екла́, *pf.* to draw in, involve; to inveigle.

вовне́, *adv.* outside.

вовну́трь, *adv. and prep.*+*g.* (*coll.*) inside.

во́-время, *adv.* at the proper time, at the normal time; in time; говори́ть не в. to speak out of turn.

во́все, *adv.* (+*neg.*; *coll.*) at all; он в. не бога́тый челове́к he is not at all a rich man; вы в. не по́няли, в чём де́ло you have completely failed to grasp the point.

вовсю́, *adv.* to its (one's) utmost; with might and main; бежа́ть в. to run as fast as one's legs will carry one.

во-вторы́х, *adv.* secondly, in the second place.

вогна́|ть, вгоню́, вго́нишь, *past* ~л, ~ла́, ~ло, *pf.* (*of* вгоня́ть) to drive in; в. гвоздь в сте́ну to drive a nail into the wall; в. в гроб to be the death of; в. в кра́ску to put to the blush; в. кого́-н. в пот to make someone go hot and cold.

во́гнут|ый (~, ~а), *p.p.p. of* ~ь *and adj.* concave.

вогн|у́ть, у́, ёшь, *pf.* (*of* вгиба́ть) to bend, curve inwards.

вод|а́, ы́, *а.* ~у, *pl.* ~ы, ~а́м, *f.* 1. water; е́хать ~о́й, по ~е́ to go by water; жёлтая в. (*med.*; *coll.*) glaucoma; тёмная в. (*med.*) amaurosis; ~о́й не разольёшь as thick as thieves; выводи́ть на чи́стую ~у to show up, unmask; и концы́ в во́ду none will be the wiser; как две ка́пли ~ы похо́жи as like as two peas; как с гу́ся в. like water off a duck's back; мно́го ~ы утекло́ much water has flowed under the bridges; он ~ы́ не замути́т he could not hurt a fly; как в ~у опу́щенный downcast, dejected; чи́стой, чисте́йшей ~ы (*tech. and fig.*) of the first water. 2. (*pl.*) the waters; watering-place, spa.

водворе́ни|е, я, *n.* settlement; establishment.

водвор|и́ть, ю́, и́шь, *pf.* 1. to settle, install, house. 2. to establish; в. мир и споко́йствие to introduce peace and quiet.

водворя́|ть, ю, *impf. of* водвори́ть.

водеви́л|ь, я, *m.* (*theatr.*) musical comedy; comic sketch.

води́тел|ь, я, *m.* 1. driver. 2. (*obs.*) leader.

води́тельств|о, а, *n.* (*obs.*) leadership.

во|ди́ть, жу́, ~дишь, *impf.* (*indet. of* вести́) 1. (*see also* вести́) to lead; to conduct; to drive. 2. (*see also* вести́) в. дру́жбу (с+*i.*) to be friends (with); в. знако́мство (с+*i.*) to keep up an acquaintance (with). 3. (+*i.*, по+*d.*; *see also* вести́) to pass (over, across); в. глаза́ми (по+*d.*) to cast one's eye (over) (*only* в. *used in this phrase*). 4. (*coll.*) to keep (*animals, birds, etc.*); в. пчёл to keep bees.

во|ди́ться, жу́сь, ~дишься, *impf.* 1. (с+*i.*) to associate (with); to play (with); он с на́ми бо́льше не ~дится he will not play with us any more. 2. to be, be found; в э́той реке́ ~дятся ло́соси salmon abounds in this river; львы не ~дятся в Евро́пе lions are not found in Europe; (*fig.*) у него́ де́нег никогда́ не ~дится he never has any money. 3. to be the custom; to happen; так у нас ~дится it is the custom here; э́то за ни́ми ~дится (*pejor.*) they are always doing this.

води́ц|а, ы, *f.* dim. of вода́.

во́дк|а, и, *f.* vodka; дать на ~у to tip; кре́пкая в. (*chem.*) aqua fortis; ца́рская в. (*chem.*) aqua regis.

водник, а, *m.* water-transport worker.
водн|ый, *adj.* 1. water; watery; ~ое поло water polo; в. путь waterway; в. спорт aquatic sports. 2. (*chem.*) aqueous; ~ое соединение hydrate.
водобоязн|ь, и, *f.* (*med.*) hydrophobia.
водовместилищ|е, а, *n.* reservoir.
водовоз, а, *m.* water-carrier.
водоворот, а, *m.* whirlpool; maelstrom (*also fig.*).
водогрейк|а, и, *f.* water-heater.
водоём, а, *m.* reservoir (*natural or artificial*).
водоизмещени|е, я, *n.* (*naut.*) displacement; судно ~ем в шесть тысяч тонн a vessel of six thousand tons displacement.
водокачк|а, и, *f.* water-tower.
водолаз¹, а, *m.* diver.
водолаз², а, *m.* Newfoundland (dog).
водолаз|ный, *adj. of* ~¹; в. костюм diving-suit.
водоле|й, я, *m.* 1. (water-)bailer. 2. (*coll.*) spouter. 3. В. (*astron.*) Aquarius.
водолечебниц|а, ы, *f.* hydropathic establishment.
водолечебный, *adj.* hydropathic.
водолечени|е, я, *n.* hydropathic treatment; water-cure.
водолив, а, *m.* 1. (water-)bailer, water-pumper. 2. chief bargee.
водомер, а, *m.* (*tech.*) water-gauge.
водомер|ный, *adj. of* ~; в. кран gauge-cock; ~ное стекло gauge-glass; ~ная трубка gauge-tube.
водомёт, а, *m.* (*poet., obs.*) fountain.
водомоин|а, ы, *f.* gully, ravine (*formed by running water*).
водонапор|ный, *adj. only in phrase* ~ая башня water-tower.
водонепроница́ем|ый (~, ~а), *adj.* watertight; waterproof; ~ая переборка (*naut.*) watertight bulkhead.
водонос, а, *m.* 1. water-carrier. 2. (*dial.*) yoke (*for carrying water-buckets*).
водонос|ный (~ен, ~на), *adj.* (*geol.*) water-bearing.
водоотвод, а, *m.* drainage system.
водоотводн|ый, *adj.* drainage; ~ая канава draining ditch; ~ая трубка waste-pipe.
водоотливн|ый, *adj.* discharge; в. насос hydrant; ~ая система (*naut.*) bilge system.
водоочистительный, *adj.* water-purifying.
водопад, а, *m.* waterfall.
водоплавающ|ий, *adj.* ~ие птицы water-fowl; ~ая машина amphibious vehicle.
водопо|й, я, *m.* 1. watering-place; water-trough; pond. 2. watering (*of animals*).
водополь|е, я, *n.* (*dial.*) spring floods.
водопровод, а, *m.* 1. water-pipe. 2. water-supply; дом с ~ом house with running water.

водопровод|ный, *adj. of* ~; ~ная магистраль water-main; ~ная сеть water-supply; ~ная станция waterworks.
водопроводчик, а, *m.* plumber.
водопроница́ем|ый (~, ~а), *adj.* permeable to water.
водораздел, а, *m.* (*geogr.; fig.*) watershed.
водораспределител|ь, я, *m.* water-distributor.
водорез, а, *m.* (*naut.*) cutwater.
водород, а, *m.* (*chem.*) hydrogen.
водородистый, *adj.* (*chem.*) hydrogen; hydride (of).
водород|ный, *adj.* hydrogen; ~ая бомба hydrogen bomb.
водоросл|ь, и, *f.* (*bot.*) alga; морская в. seaweed.
водосбор, а, *m.* 1. (*natural or artificial*) reservoir (*used for water-supply, irrigation, etc.*). 2. (*tech.*) (*water-collecting*) header.
водосборн|ый, *adj.* 1. ~ая площадь (*geogr.*) basin. 2. (*tech.*) water-collecting.
водослив, а, *m.* (*tech.*) waste-gate; sluice.
водоснабжени|е, я, *n.* water-supply.
водоспуск, а, *m.* floodgate.
водосток, а, *m.* drain; gutter.
водосто|чный, *adj. of* ~к; ~чная труба drain-pipe.
водотруб|ный, *adj.* в. котёл (*tech.*) water-tube boiler.
водоупор|ный (~ен, ~на), *adj.* water-proof.
водоходн|ый, *adj.* amphibious; ~ая авто-машина (*mil.*) amphibious vehicle, DUKW.
водохранилищ|е, а, *n.* reservoir; cistern, tank.
водочерпалк|а, и, *f.* water-engine.
водочерпательный, *adj.* (*tech.*) water-lifting.
водочк|а, и, *f.* (*coll.*) dim. of водка.
водоч|ный, *adj. of* ~ка.
водружа|ть, ю, *impf. of* водрузить.
водру|зить, жу, зишь, *pf.* (*of* ~жать) to hoist, erect.
водяне|ть, ю, *impf.* to grow watery.
водяник, а, *m.* (*dial.*) water-sprite.
водянист|ый (~, ~а), *adj.* watery; (*fig., coll.*) wishy-washy.
водянк|а, и, *f.* (*med.*) dropsy.
водян|ой¹, *adj.* 1. *adj. of* вода. 2. water, aquatic; ~ые птицы waterfowl; ~ые растения aquatic plants. 3. water-driven, water-operated; ~ая мельница water-mill; ~ое отопление hot-water heating. 4. в. знак watermark.
водян|ой², ого, *m.* water-sprite.
водя́н|очный, *adj. of* ~ка.
во|евать, юю, юешь, *impf.* (c+*i.*) 1. to wage war (with), make war (upon); to be at war. 2. (*coll.*) to quarrel (with).

воево́д|а, ы, *m.* **1.** (*hist.*) voivode (*commander of an army in medieval Russia; also, in Muscovite period, governor of a town or province*). **2.** governor of province (*in Poland*).

воево́дств|о, а, *n.* **1.** (*hist.*) office of voivode. **2.** province (*in Poland*).

воеди́но, *adv.* together; собра́ть в. to bring together.

воен- military.

военача́льник, а, *m.* commander; leader in war.

воениза́ци|я, и, *f.* militarization.

военизи́р|овать, ую, *impf. and pf.* to militarize; to place on a war footing.

военко́м, а, *m.* (*abbr. of* вое́нный комисса́р) military commissar.

военкома́т, а, *m.* (*abbr. of* вое́нный комиссариа́т) military registration and enlistment office.

военко́р, а, *m.* (*abbr. of* вое́нный корреспонде́нт) war correspondent.

вое́нно- military.

вое́нно-возду́шн|ый, *adj.* ~ые си́лы Air Force(s).

вое́нно-морско́й, *adj.* naval; в. флот the Navy.

военнообя́занн|ый, ого, *m.* man liable for call-up (*including reservists*).

военноплённ|ый, ого, *m.* prisoner of war.

вое́нно-полево́й, *adj.* (*mil.*) field; в. суд court-martial.

военнослу́жащ|ий, его, *m.* serviceman.

вое́нно-уче́бный, *adj.* military training.

вое́нн|ый, *adj.* military; war; army; в. врач (army) medical officer; ~ое вре́мя wartime; в. заво́д munitions factory; в. коммуни́зм (*hist.*) War Communism; в. мини́стр Minister of War; В~ое министе́рство War Ministry, War Office; на ~ую но́гу on a war footing; в. о́круг Command, military district; ~ое положе́ние martial law; ~ое учи́лище military college; *as noun* в., ~ого, *m.* soldier, serviceman; ~ые (*collect.*) the military.

военру́к, а, *m.* (*abbr. of* вое́нный руководи́тель) military instructor.

вое́нщин|а, ы, *f.* (*coll., pejor.*) **1.** (*collect.; obs.*) soldiery. **2.** militarists, military clique. **3.** military outlook.

вожа́к, а́, *m.* **1.** guide; в. медве́дя, в. с медве́дем bearleader; в. слепо́го blind man's guide. **2.** leader. **3.** leader (*of herd, flock*).

вожа́т|ый, ого, *m.* **1.** guide. **2.** leader (*of youth organization*). **3.** (*coll.*) tram-driver. **4.** (*agric.*) leader (*of herd*).

вожделе́ни|е, я, *n.* desire, lust (*also fig.*).

вожделе́нн|ый, *adj.* (*poet., obs.*) desired, longed-for; ~ое здра́вие perfect health.

вожделе́|ть, ю, ешь, *impf.* (к+*d.*) **1.** to long (for). **2.** (*obs.*) to lust (after).

вожде́ни|е, я, *n.* leading; driving; в. корабля́ navigation; в. самолёта flying, piloting.

вожд|ь, я́, *m.* leader; chief.

вожжа́|ться, ю́сь, *impf.* (c+*i.*; *coll.*) to bother oneself (with), trouble oneself (over).

во́жж|и, е́й, *sing.* ~а́, ~и́, *f.* reins; отпусти́ть в. to give a horse the reins; (*fig.*) to slacken the reins; ему́ ~а́ под хвост попа́ла (*coll.*) he has taken to acting capriciously.

во|жу́[1]**, ~дишь,** *see* ~ди́ть.

во|жу́[2]**, ~зишь,** *see* ~зи́ть.

воз, а, о ~е, на ~у́, *pl.* ~ы́, *m.* **1.** cart, waggon; что с ~а упа́ло, то пропа́ло (*prov.*) it is no use crying over spilt milk. **2.** cartload. **3.** (*fig., coll.*) load(s), heap(s); в. вре́мени loads of time.

возблагодар|и́ть, ю́, и́шь, *pf.* (*obs.*) to give thanks to.

возбран|и́ть, ю́, и́шь, *pf.* to prohibit, forbid; в. вход подро́сткам не дости́гшим восемна́дцати лет to prohibit entry to young people under the age of eighteen.

возбран|я́ть, я́ю, *impf. of* ~и́ть.

возбран|я́ться, я́ется, *impf.* to be prohibited, be forbidden; купа́ться тут не ~я́ется swimming is permitted here.

возбуди́мост|ь, и, *f.* excitability.

возбуди́м|ый (~, ~а), *adj.* excitable.

возбуди́тел|ь, я, *m.* **1.** agent; stimulus; (*fig.*) instigator; дро́жжи — в. броже́ния yeast is an agent of fermentation. **2.** (*med.*) в. боле́зни pathogenic organism. **3.** (*tech.*) exciter.

возбу|ди́ть, жу́, ди́шь, *pf.* (*of* ~жда́ть) **1.** to excite, rouse, arouse; в. аппети́т to whet the appetite; в. любопы́тство to excite, stimulate curiosity. **2.** (про́тив+*g.*) to stir up (against), incite (against), instigate (against). **3.** (*leg.*) to institute; в. де́ло (про́тив+*g.*) to institute proceedings (against), bring an action (against); в. иск (про́тив+*g.*) to bring a suit (against); в. хода́тайство (о+*p.*) to submit a petition (for).

возбужда́емост|ь, и, *f.* excitability.

возбужда́|ть, ю, *impf. of* возбуди́ть.

возбужда́|ющий, *pres. part. act. of* ~ть; ~ющее сре́дство (*med.*) stimulant.

возбу|жу́, ди́шь, *see* ~ди́ть.

возбужде́ни|е, я, *n.* excitement; в состоя́нии кра́йнего ~я in a state of extreme excitement.

возбу|жде́нный, *p.p.p. of* ~ди́ть *and adj.* excited.

возведе́ни|е, я, *n.* **1.** raising; erection. **2.** в. во втору́ю, в тре́тью сте́пень (*math.*) rais-

ing to the second, third power. **3.** в. обви-
не́ния bringing of an accusation.

возведу́|**у́, ёшь**, *see* возвести́.

возвели́чива|**ть, ю**, *impf. of* возвели́чить.

возвели́ч|**ить, у, ишь**, *pf.* (*of* ~ивать) (*obs.*)
to extol.

возве|**сти́, ду́, дёшь**, *past* ~л, ~ла́, *pf.* (*of*
возводи́ть) **1.** to elevate; в. в сан патриа́р-
ха to elect to the patriarchate; в. на
престо́л to elevate to the throne. **2.** to
raise, erect, put up; в. высо́тный дом to
erect a skyscraper. **3.** (*math.*) to raise; в.
во втору́ю сте́пень to raise to the second
power; в. в куб to cube. **4.** to bring, advance, level (*a charge, an accusation, etc.*); в.
клевету́ на кого́-н. to cast aspersions on
someone. **5.** (к+*d.*) to trace (to), derive
(from); в. происхожде́ние к норма́ннам
to trace one's ancestry to the Northmen.

возве|**сти́ть, щу́, сти́шь**, *pf.* (*of* ~ща́ть) to
proclaim, announce; в. побе́ду to pro-
claim a victory.

возвеща́|**ть, ю**, *impf. of* возвести́ть.

возве|**щу́, сти́шь**, *see* ~сти́ть.

возво|**ди́ть, жу́, ~дишь**, *impf. of* возвести́.

возво|**жу́, ~дишь**, *see* ~ди́ть.

возвра́т, а, *m.* return; repayment, reim-
bursement; в. боле́зни relapse; в. со́лнца
(*astron.*) solstice.

возвра|**ти́ть, щу́, ти́шь** *pf.* (*of* ~ща́ть) **1.** to
return, give back; to pay back; в. иму́-
щество to restore property. **2.** to recover,
retrieve; в. де́ньги, о́тданные взаймы́ to
recover a loan. **3.** to make return.

возвра|**ти́ться, щу́сь, ти́шься**, *pf.* (*of*
~ща́ться) to return; (*fig.*) to revert; в. ко
всем ста́рым привы́чкам to revert to all
one's old habits.

возвра́т|**ный**, *adj.* **1.** *adj. of* ~; на ~ном
пути́ on the way back. **2.** (*med.*) recurring.
3. (*gram.*) reflexive. **4.** ~ная по́шлина
drawback (duty).

возвраща́|**ть(ся), ю(сь)**, *impf. of* возвра-
ти́ть(ся) *and* верну́ть(ся).

возвраще́ни|**е, я**, *n.* return; его в. бы́ло
отло́жено без сро́ка his return was post-
poned indefinitely; он настоя́л на неме́д-
ленном ~и кольца́ he insisted on immediate
return of the ring.

возвра|**щу́, ти́шь**, *see* ~ти́ть.

возвы́|**сить, шу, сишь**, *pf.* (*of* ~ша́ть) **1.** to
raise, elevate; в. в обще́ственном мне́нии
to raise in public opinion. **2.** в. го́лос to
raise one's voice.

возвы́|**ситься, шусь, сишься**, *pf.* (*of*
~ша́ться) (*in var. senses*) to raise, go up;
они́ ~сились в на́шем мне́нии they have
risen in our estimation.

возвыша́|**ть, ю**, *impf.* **1.** *impf. of* возвы́сить.
2. (*impf. only*) to elevate, ennoble.

возвыша́|**ться, юсь**, *impf.* **1.** *impf. of* воз-
вы́ситься. **2.** (*impf. only*) (над+*i.*) to tower
(above) (*also fig.*); за́мок ~ется над го́ро-
дом the castle towers above the city; он
~ется умо́м над това́рищами he towers
above his fellows in intellect.

возвыше́ни|**е, я**, *n.* **1.** rise; raising; в.
Моско́вской Руси́ the rise of Muscovite
Russia. **2.** eminence; raised place.

возвы́шенност|**ь, и**, *f.* **1.** (*geogr.*) height;
eminence. **2.** loftiness, sublimity.

возвы́шен|**ный**, *p.p.p. of* возвы́сить *and adj.*
1. high; elevated. **2.** lofty, sublime, elevated; ~ные идеа́лы lofty ideals; в. стиль
elevated style.

возвы́|**шу, сишь**, *see* ~сить.

возгла́в|**ить, лю, ишь**, *pf.* (*of* ~ля́ть) to
head, be at the head of.

возглавля́|**ть, ю**, *impf. of* возгла́вить.

во́зглас, а, *m.* **1.** cry, exclamation; в.
удивле́ния cry of astonishment; в. с ме́ста
exclamation from the audience. **2.** (*eccl.*)
concluding words of prayer (*pronounced in
a loud voice*).

возгла|**си́ть, шу́, си́шь**, *pf.* (*of* ~ша́ть) to
proclaim.

возглаша́|**ть, ю**, *impf. of* возгласи́ть.

возглаше́ни|**е, я**, *n.* **1.** proclamation. **2.** ex-
clamation. **3.** = во́зглас 2.

возгна́|**ть, возгоню́, возго́нишь**, *past* ~л,
~ла́, ~ло, *pf. of* возгоня́ть.

возго́нк|**а, и**, *f.* (*chem.*) sublimation.

возгон|**ю́, ~ишь**, *see* возгна́ть.

возгоня́|**ть, ю**, *impf.* (*chem.*) to subli-
mate.

возгора́емост|**ь, и**, *f.* inflammability.

возгора́емый, *adj.* inflammable.

возгора́ни|**е, я**, *n.* (*tech.*) inflammation, ig-
nition; то́чка ~я flash-point.

возгора́|**ться, юсь**, *impf. of* возгоре́ться.

возгор|**ди́ться, жу́сь, ди́шься**, *pf.* to be-
come proud; (+*i.*) to begin to pride oneself (on).

возгор|**е́ться, ю́сь, и́шься**, *pf.* **1.** to flare
up (*also fig.*); внеза́пно ~е́лась ссо́ра
ме́жду ни́ми suddenly there flared up a
quarrel between them. **2.** (+*i.*) to be in-
flamed (with); она́ ~е́лась стра́стью к
кино́ she was seized with a passion for the
cinema.

возда|**ва́ть, ю́, ёшь**, *impf. of* возда́ть.

возда|**м, шь, ст**, *see* ~ть.

возда́|**ть, м, шь, ст, ди́м, ди́те, ду́т**, *past* ~л,
~ла́, ~ло, *pf.* (*of* ~ва́ть) to render; в.
кому́-н. до́лжное to give someone his due;
в. кому́-н. по заслу́гам to reward someone
according to his deserts.

воздая́ни|**е, я**, *n.* (*obs.*) recompense; retri-
bution.

воздвига́|**ть, ю**, *impf.* to raise, erect; в.

гонéние (на+a.; *obs.*) to raise a hue-and-
-cry (after).

воздвигá|ться, юсь, *impf.* 1. *pass. of* ~ть.
2. to rear (up) (*intrans.*).

воздвиг|нуть, ну, нешь, *past* ~, ~ла, *pf. of*
~áть.

воздвиг|нуться, нусь, нешься, *past* ~ся,
~лась, *pf. of* ~áться.

Воздвижени|е, я, *n.* (*eccl.*) Exaltation of the
Cross (*Christian festival celebrated on 14 Sep-
tember O.S.*).

воздевá|ть, ю, *impf. of* воздéть.

воздéйстви|е, я, *n.* influence; оказáть
морáльное в. (на+a.) to bring moral pressure to bear (upon); он э́то сдéлал под
физи́ческим ~ем he did it under coercion.

воздéйств|овать, ую, *impf. and pf.* (на+a.)
to influence, affect; to exert influence,
bring influence to bear (upon); to bring
pressure to bear (upon); в. на когó-н.
си́лой примéра to influence someone by
one's example; страсть к приключéниям
~овала на егó решéние сдéлаться моря-
кóм love of adventure influenced his decision to become a sailor.

воздéл|ать, аю, *pf.* (*of* ~ывать) to cultivate,
till.

воздéлыва|ть, ю, *impf. of* воздéлать.

воздержáвш|ийся, *past part. of* воздер-
жáться; *as noun* в., ~егося, *m.* abstainer;
предложéние бы́ло при́нято при трёх
~ихся the motion was carried with three
abstentions.

воздержáни|е, я, *n.* 1. abstinence. 2. ab-
stention.

воздéржанност|ь, и, *f.* abstemious-
ness; temperance.

воздéржан|ный (~, ~на), *adj.* abstemious;
temperate.

воздерж|áться, у́сь, *pf.* (*of* ~ивáться) (от
+g.) 1. to restrain oneself, keep oneself
(from); to abstain (from); to refrain (from);
в. от мя́са to abstain from meat; я дóлее не
мог в. от гнéва I could no longer contain
my rage. 2. to abstain (*from voting*). 3. to
withhold acceptance (of).

воздéржива|ться, юсь, *impf. of* воздер-
жáться.

воздéржност|ь, и, *f.* = воздéржанность.

воздéрж|ный (~ен, ~на), *adj.* = ~анный.

воздé|ть, ну, нешь, *pf.* (*of* ~вáть) *only in
phrase* в. ру́ки (*obs.*) to lift up one's
hands.

вóздух¹, а, *no pl.*, *m.* air; на (откры́том) ~е
out of doors; вы́йти на в. to go out of doors;
в ~е (*fig.*) in the air; в ~е носи́лось чу́вство
предстоя́щей беды́ a sense of impending
disaster was in the air; *as interj.* в.! (enemy)
aircraft approaching!

вóздух², а, *pl.* ~и, *m.* (*eccl.*) paten.

воздуходу́вк|а, и, *f.* (*tech.*) blast-engine;
blower.

воздуходу́вный, *adj.* (*tech.*) blast.

воздухомéр, а, *m.* (*phys.*) aerometer.

воздухоохлажда́емый, *adj.* air-cooled.

воздухоплáвани|е, я, *n.* aeronautics.

воздухоплáватель, я, *m.* 1. aeronaut.
2. balloonist.

воздухоплáвательный, *adj.* 1. aeronautic.
2. (*mil.*) balloon.

возду́ш|ный, *adj.* 1. air, aerial; ~ная
желéзная доро́га overhead railway; ~ные
зáмки castles in the air; в. змей kite; ~ная
ли́ния airline; послáть ~ные поцелу́и to
blow kisses; ~ная прово́дка overhead
cable; ~ное сообщéние aerial communication; ~ная трево́га air-raid warning; в.
шар balloon; ~ная я́ма air-pocket. 2. air-
-driven, air-operated; в. насо́с air-pump.
3. (~ен, ~на), airy, light; flimsy; в. пиро́г
soufflé; ~ное плáтье flimsy dress.

воздыхáни|е, я, *n.* (*obs.*) lamentation; com-
plaint.

воздыхá|ть, ю, *impf.* (*obs.*) = вздыхáть.

воз|жгу́, жжёшь, жгу́т, *see* ~жéчь.

воз|жéчь, жгу́, жжёшь, жгу́т, *past* ~жёг,
~жглá, *pf.* (*of* ~жигáть) (*obs.*) to light,
kindle (*also fig.*).

возжигá|ть, ю, *impf. of* возжéчь.

воззвáни|е, я, *n.* appeal; в. к шахтёрам
appeal to miners.

возз|вáть, ову́, овёшь, *past* ~вáл, ~валá,
~вáло, *pf* (*of* взывáть) (к+d., о+p.) to
appeal (to), call (for); он ~вáл к избирá-
телям о поддéржке he appealed to the
electors for their support.

возз|ову́, овёшь, *see* ~вáть.

воззрéни|е, я, *n.* view, opinion, outlook.

воззр|éть, ю́, и́шь, *pf. of* взирáть.

воззр|и́ться, ю́сь, и́шься, *pf.* (на+a.; *coll.*)
to stare (at).

во|зи́ть, жу́, ~зишь, *impf.* (*indet. of* везти́)
1. to cart, convey; to carry; to draw (*of
beasts of burden or mechanical transport*); э́тот
парово́з ~зит до тридцати́ ваго́нов this
engine draws up to thirty coaches. 2. (+i.,
по+d.; *coll.*) to pass (over), run (over).
3. (*coll.*) to beat, flog.

во|зи́ться, жу́сь, ~зишься, *impf.* 1. to play
noisily, romp (*of children*). 2. (с +i, над
+i.) to take trouble (over), spend time
(on), busy oneself (with); (*coll.*) to potter; to
tinker (with), fiddle about (with); он мно́го
~зится над лéкциями he takes much
trouble over the preparation of his lectures;
он лю́бит в. в саду́ he likes pottering about
in the garden.

вóзк|а, и, *f.* (*coll.*) carting, carriage.

возлагá|ть, ю, *impf. of* возложи́ть.

вóзле, *adv. and prep.*+g. by, near; past; он

стоя́л в. he was standing near-by; ка́ждый день он хо́дит в. моего́ до́ма he walks up and down past my house every day.

возлеж|а́ть, у́, и́шь, *impf.* (*of* возле́чь) (*obs.*) to recline.

возл|е́чь, я́гу, я́жешь, я́гут, *imp.* ~**я́г,** *past* ~**ёг,** ~**егла́,** *pf. of* ~**ежа́ть.**

возлик|ова́ть, у́ю, *pf.* to rejoice.

возлия́ни|е, я, *n.* 1. libation. 2. (*coll.*) drinking-bout.

возлож|и́ть, у́, ~**ишь,** *pf.* (*of* возлага́ть) to lay on (*also fig.*); в. вено́к на моги́лу to lay a wreath on a grave; наро́д ~и́л все наде́жды на но́вого президе́нта the people had placed all their hopes on the new president.

возлюб|и́ть, лю́, ~**ишь,** *pf.* (*obs.*) to love.

возлюбленн|ый, *adj.* beloved; *as noun* (i) **в.,** ~**ого,** *m.* 1. boy-friend. (ii) ~**ая,** ~**ой,** *f.* 1. girl-friend, sweetheart. 2. mistress.

возля́|гу, жешь, гут, *see* возле́чь.

возме́зди|е, я, *n.* retribution; requital.

возме|сти́ть, щу́, сти́шь, *pf.* (*of* ~ща́ть) to compensate, make up (for); to replace; в. поте́рянное вре́мя to make up for lost time; в. расхо́ды to refund expenses.

возмечта́|ть, ю, *pf.* 1. to dream, start dreaming. 2. в. о себе́ (*coll.*) to form a high opinion of oneself, become conceited.

возмеща́|ть, ю, *impf. of* возмести́ть.

возмеще́ни|е, я, *n.* 1. compensation, indemnity; (*leg.*) damages; получи́ть в. убы́тков по суду́ to be awarded damages. 2. replacement; refund, reimbursement.

возме|щу́, сти́шь, *see* ~сти́ть.

возмо́жно, *adv.* 1. possibly; (+*comp.*) as . . . as possible; в. лу́чше as well as possible; иди́те в. скоре́е go as soon as possible. 2. *as pred.* it is possible; в., что мы за́втра уе́дем we may possibly go away tomorrow.

возмо́жност|ь, и, *f.* 1. possibility; по (ме́ре) ~и as far as possible; до после́дней ~и to the uttermost. 2. opportunity; ему́ да́ли в. пое́хать в Росси́ю he has been given an opportunity of going to Russia; при пе́рвой ~и at the first opportunity, at one's earliest convenience. 3. (*pl.*) means, resources; у него́ больши́е ~и he has great potentialities.

возмо́ж|ный (~**ен,** ~**на),** *adj.* 1. possible; врач сде́лал для неё всё ~ное the doctor did all in his power for her. 2. the greatest possible; с ~ной то́чностью with the greatest possible accuracy, as accurately as possible.

возмо́|чь, гу́, жешь, гут, *past* ~**г,** ~**гла́,** *pf.* (*obs.*) to be able.

возмужа́лост|ь, и, *f.* maturity; manhood.

возмужа́лый, *adj.* mature; grown up.

возмужа́|ть, ю, *pf.* 1. to grow up. 2. to gain in strength, become stronger.

возмути́тел|ьный (~**ен,** ~**ьна),** *adj.* 1. disgraceful, scandalous. 2. (*obs.*) seditious, subversive.

возму|ти́ть, щу́, ти́шь, *pf.* 1. (*obs.*) to disturb, trouble. 2. (*fig., obs.*) to stir up, incite. 3. to anger, rouse the indignation (of).

возму|ти́ться, щу́сь, ти́шься, *pf.* 1. to be indignant (at); to be exasperated (by); все ~ти́лись его́ заявле́нием all were filled with indignation by his announcement. 2. (*obs.*) to rebel, rise in revolt.

возмуща́|ть, ю, *impf. of* возмути́ть.

возмуща́|ться, юсь, *impf. of* возмути́ться.

возмуще́ни|е, я, *n.* 1. indignation. 2. (*obs.*) revolt, rebellion. 3. (*astron.*) perturbation. 4. магни́тное в. (*phys.*) magnetic disturbance.

возмущён|ный (~**,** ~**а́),** *p.p.p. of* возмути́ть *and adj.* (+*i.*) indignant (at).

возму|щу́, ти́шь, *see* ~ти́ть.

вознагра|ди́ть, жу́, ди́шь, *pf.* to reward; to recompense; to compensate, make up (for); его́ ~ди́ли за заслу́ги золоты́ми часа́ми he was rewarded for his services with a gold watch.

вознагражда́|ть, ю, *impf. of* вознагради́ть.

вознагражде́ни|е, я, *n.* 1. reward, recompense; compensation. 2. fee, remuneration.

вознаме́рива|ться, юсь, *impf. of* вознаме́риться.

вознаме́р|иться, юсь, ишься, *pf.* (+*inf.*) to conceive a design, idea; она́ ~илась сде́латься актри́сой she conceived the idea of going on the stage.

вознегод|ова́ть, у́ю, *pf.* to become indignant.

возненави|деть, жу, дишь, *pf.* to conceive hatred (for), come to hate.

вознесе́ни|е, я, *n.* ascent; В. (*eccl.*) Ascension (Day).

вознес|ти́, у́, ёшь, *past* ~́, ~**ла́,** *pf.* (*of* возноси́ть) (*poet.*) to raise, lift up; в. моли́тву to offer up a prayer.

вознес|ти́сь, у́сь, ёшься, *past* ~́ся, ~**ла́сь,** *pf.* (*of* возноси́ться) 1. (*poet.*) to rise; to ascend. 2. (*coll.*) to become conceited.

возник|а́ть, а́ю, *impf.* (*of* ~нуть) to arise, spring up; на на́ших глаза́х ~а́л но́вый го́род a new town was springing up before our eyes; у меня́ ~а́ет мысль the thought occurs to me.

возникнове́ни|е, я, *n.* rise, beginning, origin.

возник|нуть, ну, нешь, *past* ~, ~**ла,** *pf. of* ~**а́ть.**

возни́ц|а, ы, *m.* coachman, driver.

возни́ч|ий, его, *m.* 1. (*obs.*) coachman, driver. 2. В. (*astron.*) Auriga.

возно|си́ть, шу́, ~**сишь,** *impf. of* вознести́.

возно|си́ться, шу́сь, ⌣си́шься, *impf. of* вознести́сь.

возноше́ни|е, я, *n.* (*obs.*) raising, elevation; в. даро́в (*eccl.*) elevation (of the host).

возно|шу́, ⌣си́шь, *see* ⌣си́ть.

возн|я́, и́, *no pl., f.* (*coll.*) **1.** row, noise; мыши́ная в. (*fig.*) petty intrigues. **2.** bother, trouble; у него́ мно́го ⌣и́ с автомоби́лем he has a lot of trouble with his car.

возблада́|ть, ю, *pf.* (над+*i.*) to prevail (over).

возобнов|и́ть, лю́, и́шь, *pf.* (*of* ⌣ля́ть) **1.** to renew, resume. **2.** to restore.

возобновле́ни|е, я, *n.* renewal, resumption; revival (*of a play*).

возобновля́|ть, ю, *impf. of* возобнови́ть.

воз|о́к, ка́, *m.* closed sleigh.

возомн|и́ть, ю, и́шь, *pf.* в. о себе́ (*iron.*) to get a false idea of one's own importance; в. себя́ авторите́том to consider oneself (*falsely*) an authority.

возоп|и́ть, лю́, и́шь, *pf.* (*obs.*) to cry out.

возра́д|оваться, уюсь, *pf.* (+*d.*; *obs.*) to be delighted (at).

возража́|ть, ю, *impf. of* возрази́ть; не ⌣ю I have no objection; вы не ⌣ете? have you any objection(s)?, do you mind?

возраже́ни|е, я, *n.* **1.** objection; retort; без ⌣й! don't argue! **2.** (*leg.*) answer.

возра|зи́ть, жу́, зи́шь, *pf.* (*of* ⌣жа́ть) (про́тив+*g. or* на+*a.*) **1.** to object, raise an objection (to); to take exception (to); to retort; про́тив э́того не́чего в. nothing can be said against it. **2.** to say.

во́зраст, а, *m.* age; одного́ ⌣а of the same age; о́троческий в. boyhood; преде́льный в. age-limit; быть на ⌣е to be of age; вы́йти из ⌣а to pass the age, exceed the age-limit; он вы́шел из ⌣а для вое́нной слу́жбы he is over the age for military service; прекло́нный в. declining years.

возраст|а́ть, а́ю, *impf. of* ⌣и́; ⌣а́ющая ско́рость (*phys.*) accelerated velocity.

возраст|и́, у́, ёшь, *past* возро́с, возросла́, *pf.* (*of* ⌣а́ть) to grow, increase.

возраст|но́й, *adj. of* во́зраст; ⌣на́я гру́ппа age group.

возро|ди́ть, жу́, ди́шь, *pf.* (*of* ⌣жда́ть) to regenerate; to revive; его́ слова́ ⌣ди́ли в ней во́лю к жи́зни his words revived in her the will to live.

возро|ди́ться, жу́сь, ди́шься, *pf.* (*of* ⌣жда́ться) to revive (*intrans.*).

возрожда́|ть, ю, *impf. of* возроди́ть.

возрожда́|ться, юсь, *impf. of* возроди́ться.

возрожде́ни|е, я, *n.* rebirth; revival; эпо́ха Возрожде́ния Renaissance.

возроп|та́ть, щу́, ⌣щешь, *pf.* (*obs.*) to cry out (*in protest*).

во́зчик, а, *m.* carter, carrier.

возыме́|ть, ю, ешь, *pf.* to conceive (*wish intention, etc.*); больно́й ⌣л жела́ние пое́сть фру́ктов the invalid conceived a desire for fruit; в. де́йствие to take effect; ва́ши предупрежде́ния наконе́ц ⌣ли де́йствие your warnings have at last taken effect; в. си́лу to come into force.

возьм|у́(сь), ёшь(ся), *see* взя́ть(ся).

во́ин, а, *m.* warrior; fighter.

во́инск|ий, *adj.* **1.** military; ⌣ая пови́нность liability for military service; в. по́езд troop-train. **2.** martial, warlike.

во́инствен|ный (⌣, ⌣на), *adj.* warlike; bellicose.

во́инств|о, а, *n.* (*collect.*; *obs.*) host, army.

во́инствующ|ий, *adj.* militant; ⌣ая це́рковь the church militant; Сою́з ⌣их безбо́жников (*hist.*) League of Militant Atheists.

во́истину, *adv.* (*obs.*) indeed; verily; (Христо́с) в. воскре́с! (*response at Orthodox Easter service*) He (Christ) is risen indeed!

во́ител|ь, я, *m.* **1.** (*poet.*) warrior. **2.** (*coll.*) rowdy.

во́ительниц|а, ы, *f.* **1.** (*poet.*) female warrior, Amazon. **2.** (*coll.*) shrew, termagant.

во|й, я, *no pl., m.* howl, howling; wail, wailing.

вой|ду́, дёшь, *see* ⌣ти́.

во́йлок, а, *m.* felt; strip of felt.

во́йлочный, *adj.* felt.

войн|а́, ы́, *pl.* ⌣ы, *f.* war; warfare; вести́ ⌣у́ to wage war; объяви́ть ⌣у́ to declare war.

во́йск|а, ⌣, *sing.* ⌣о, ⌣а, *n.* **1.** troops; forces; наёмные в. mercenaries. **2.** (*sing.*) army; (*hist.*) host (*of Cossacks*); запоро́жское ⌣о the Zaporozhian host. **3.** (*sing.*; *fig.*) host, multitude.

войсково́|й, *adj.* **1.** military. **2.** (*hist.*) of the host; в. круг Cossack assembly; в. старшина́ Lieutenant-Colonel (*of Cossack troops*).

во|йти́, йду́, йдёшь, *past* ⌣шёл, ⌣шла́, *pf.* (*of* входи́ть) (в.+*a.*) to enter; to go in(to); to come in(to); в. в аза́рт to grow heated; в. в дове́рие к кому́-н. to be taken into someone's confidence; в. в исто́рию to go down in history; в. в колею́ to carry on as normal; в. в ле́та to get on (in years); в. в мо́ду to become fashionable; в. в погово́рку to pass into a proverb; в. в роль to (begin to) feel one's feet.

вока́бул|ы, ⌣, *no sing.* (*obs.*) foreign words (*as object of study*).

вокали́з, а, *m. and* вокали́з|а, ы, (*obs.*) *f.* exercise in vocalization.

вокализа́ци|я, и, *f.* (*ling., mus.*) vocalization.

вокали́зм, а, *m.* (*ling.*) vowel-system.

вокали́ст, а, *m.* (*mus.*) teacher of singing.

вока́льный, *adj.* vocal; в. ве́чер sing-song.

вокза́л, а, *m.* (large) station; station building; железнодоро́жный в. railway (*esp. main or terminus*) station; морско́й в. port arrival and departure building; речно́й в. river-boat station.

вокза́л|ьный, *adj. of* ~ station.

вокру́г, *adv. and prep.*+*g.* round, around, about; путеше́ствие в. све́та voyage round the world; верте́ться в. да о́коло (*coll.*) to beat about the bush.

ВОКС, а, *m.* (*abbr. of* Всесою́зное о́бщество культу́рной свя́зи с заграни́цей) (*hist.*) All-Union Society for Cultural Relations with Foreign Countries.

вол, а́, *m.* ox, bullock.

вола́н, а, *m.* 1. flounce (*on woman's skirt*). 2. shuttlecock; игра́ в в. badminton; battledore and shuttlecock.

Волапю́к, а, *m.* Volapuk (*artificial international language*).

волга́р|ь, я́, *m.* (*coll.*) native of Volga region.

волдыр|ь, я́, *m.* blister; bump.

волево́й, *adj.* 1.(*psych.*) volitional. 2. strong-willed; tough.

волеизъявле́ни|е, я, *n.* will, pleasure; command; по короле́вскому ~ю at the king's pleasure, by royal command.

волейбо́л, а, *m.* (*sport*) volley-ball.

волейболи́ст, а, *m.* volley-ball player.

во́лей-нево́лей, *adv.* (*coll.*) willy-nilly.

волжа́н|ин, ина, *pl.* ~е, ~, *m.* native of Volga region.

волжа́н|ка, ки, *f. of* ~ин.

во́лжский, *adj.* Volga, of the Volga.

волк, а, *pl.* ~и, ~о́в, *m.* wolf; морско́й в. (*coll.*) old salt; смотре́ть ~ом (*fig.*) to scowl; в. вове́чьей шку́ре wolf in sheep's clothing; хоть ~ом вы́ть (*coll.*) it's enough to make you despair; с ~а́ми жить, по-во́лчьи выть (*prov.*) when in Rome do as the Romans do; сде́лать так, чтоб и в. был сыт и о́вцы це́лы (*prov.*) to run with the hare and hunt with the hounds.

волк-маши́н|а, ы, *f.* (*text.*) willow, willy.

волкода́в, а, *m.* wolf-hound.

волн|а́¹, ы́, *pl.* ~ы, ~а́м, *f.* (*in var. senses*) wave; breaker.

волн|а́², ы́, *f.* (*dial.*) wool.

волне́ни|е, я, *n.* 1. choppiness (*of water*). 2. (*fig.*) agitation, disturbance; emotion; прийти́ в в. to become agitated, excited. 3. (*usu. pl.*; *polit.*) disturbance(s); unrest.

волни́ст|ый (~, ~а), *adj.* wavy; watered (*of stuffs*); ~ое желе́зо corrugated iron; ~ая ме́стность undulating ground.

волн|ова́ть, у́ю, *impf.* (*of* вз~) to disturb, agitate (*also fig.*); to excite; to worry; его́

всё ~у́ет he is easily excited; не ну́жно в. больно́го the patient must not be disturbed.

волн|ова́ться, у́юсь, *impf.* 1. (*of water, etc.*) to be agitated, choppy; to ripple, wave. 2. to be disturbed, agitated; to worry, be nervous; to be excited; она́ ~у́ется о де́тях she worries about her children; он всегда́ ~у́ется пе́ред экза́меном he is always nervous before an examination. 3. (*polit.*; *obs.*) to be in a state of ferment, of unrest; наро́д всё бо́лее ~ова́лся popular unrest was increasing.

волново́д, а, *m.* (*electr.*) wave-guide.

волнов|о́й, *adj.* wave, undulatory; ~а́я тео́рия (*phys.*) wave theory.

волноло́м, а, *m.* breakwater.

волноме́р, а, *m.* (*tech.*) wave-meter.

волнообра́з|ный (~ен, ~на), *adj.* undulatory; wavy, undulating.

волноре́з, а, *m.* breakwater.

волноуказа́тел|ь, я, *m.* (*radio*) wave detector.

волну́шк|а, и, *f.* coral milky cap (*mushroom*).

волн|у́ющий, *pres. part. act. of* ~ова́ть *and adj.* disturbing, worrying; exciting, thrilling, stirring; ~у́ющие изве́стия disturbing, exciting news; ~у́ющая по́весть thrilling, exciting story.

вол|о́вий, *adj. of* ~; (*fig.*) very strong; ~о́вья шку́ра oxhide; у него́ ~о́вья си́ла he is as strong as an ox.

во́лок, а, *m.* portage; перепра́вить ~ом to portage.

воло́к(ся), ла́(сь), *see* волочь(ся).

волоки́т|а¹, ы, *f.* (*coll.*) red tape.

волоки́т|а², ы, *m.* (*coll.*) ladies' man; philanderer.

волоки́тств|о, а, *n.* (*coll.*) philandering.

волоки́тчик, а, *m.* (*coll.*) red-tape merchant, red-tape monger.

волокни́ст|ый (~, ~а), *adj.* fibrous; stringy.

волок|но́, на́, *pl.* ~на, ~он, ~нам, *n.* fibre, filament.

волонтёр, а, *m.* (*obs.*) volunteer.

воло́окий, *adj.* (*poet.*) ox-eyed.

во́лос, а, *pl.* ~ы (*and coll.* ~а́), воло́с, ~а́м, *m.* 1. hair; (*pl.*) hair (*of the head*); рвать на себе́ ~ы to tear one's hair; схвати́ть за́ ~ы to take by the hair; при ви́де тру́па ~ы у меня́ ста́ли ды́бом the sight of the corpse made my hair stand on end; э́то притя́нуто за́ волосы it is far fetched; ни на́ волос not a bit; у него́ ни на́ волос ума́ he has not a grain of sense. 2. hair (*as material*); подкла́дка из ко́нского ~а horsehair lining.

волоса́тик, а, *m.* (*zool.*) hair-worm.

волоса́т|ый (~, ~а), *adj.* hairy; hirsute; pilose.

волоси́стый, *adj.* (*min.*) fibrous.

волосн|о́й, *adj.* (*phys.*) capillary; ~ы́е сосу́ды (*anat.*) capillaries.

волосност|ь, и, *f.* (*phys.*) capillarity.

волос|о́к, ка́, *m.* 1. *dim. of* во́лос; на в. (от +*g.*) within a hairbreadth (of); висе́ть, держа́ться на ~ке́ to hang by a thread; я не тро́нул ~ка́ у неё I did not touch a hair of her head. 2. hair-spring. 3. (*electr.*) filament.

волостно́й, *adj.* volost.

во́лост|ь, и, *pl.* ~и, ~е́й, *f.* (*hist.*) volost (*smallest administrative division of tsarist Russia*).

волосяно́й, *adj.* hair, of hair; в. покро́в (*anat.*) scalp.

волоче́ни|е, я, *n.* dragging; (*tech.*) в. про́волоки wire-drawing.

волочи́льн|ый, *adj.* (*tech.*) wire-drawing; ~ая доска́ draw-plate.

волочи́льщик, а, *m.* (*tech.*) wire-drawer.

волоч|и́ть, у́, ~и́шь, *impf.* 1. to drag; в. но́гу to drag one's foot; в. но́ги to shuffle one's feet; е́ле но́ги в. to be hardly able to drag one's legs along; в. де́ло to drag out an affair. 2. (*tech.*) to draw.

волоч|и́ться, у́сь, ~и́шься, *impf.* 1. *pass. of* ~и́ть. 2. to drag (*intrans.*), trail. 3. (за+*i.*; *coll.*) to run after; три ме́сяца он уже́ ~и́тся за ней he has been running after her for three months.

вол|о́чь, оку́, очёшь, оку́т, *past* ~о́к, ~окла́, *impf.* (*coll.*) to drag.

вол|о́чься, оку́сь, очёшься, оку́тся, *past* ~о́кся, ~окла́сь, *impf.* (*coll.*) 1. to drag (*intrans.*), trail. 2. to drag (oneself) along; to shuffle.

воло́шский, *adj.* (*hist.*) Wallachian; в. оре́х (*obs.*) walnut.

волхв, а́, *m.* magician, sorcerer; soothsayer; три ~а́ the Three Wise Men, the Magi.

волхв|ова́ть, у́ю, *impf.* to practise magic, sorcery.

волча́нк|а, и, *f.* (*med.*) lupus.

волч|а́та, *see* ~о́нок.

волч|е́ц, ца́, *m.* (*bot.*) thistle.

во́лч|ий, *adj. of* волк; wolf, lupine; в. аппети́т (*coll.*) voracious appetite; в. па́спорт (*hist., coll.*) passport (*in tsarist Russia*) with note of political unreliability of holder; у него́ в. па́спорт he is a marked man; ~ья пасть cleft palate; ~ья я́года (*bot.*) spurge-flax; ~ья я́ма (*mil.*) trou-de-loup.

волчи́х|а, и, *f.* (*coll.*) she-wolf.

волчи́ц|а, ы, *f.* she-wolf.

волч|о́к¹, ка́, *m.* 1. top (*toy*); верте́ться ~ко́м to spin like a top. 2. (*tech.*) gyroscope.

волч|о́к², ка́, *m.* judas (*in door of prison cell*).

волч|о́нок, о́нка, *pl.* ~а́та, ~а́т, *m.* wolf-cub.

волше́бник, а, *m.* magician; wizard.

волше́бниц|а, ы, *f.* enchantress.

волше́б|ный (~ен, ~на), *adj.* 1. magical; в. жезл, ~ная па́лочка magic wand; ~ное ца́рство fairyland; в. фона́рь magic lantern. 2. (*fig.*) bewitching, enchanting.

волшебств|о́, а́, *n.* magic; (*fig.*) magic, enchantment.

волы́н|ить, ю, ишь, *impf.* (*coll.*) to dawdle, delay, be dilatory, slack.

волы́нк|а¹, и, *f.* bagpipes.

волы́нк|а², и, *f.* dawdling, delay, dilatoriness, slacking; hold-up; тяну́ть ~у to dawdle, delay, be dilatory.

волы́нщик¹, а, *m.* piper.

волы́нщик², а, *m.* (*coll.*) dawdler, slacker.

вольго́тный, *adj.* (*coll.*) free, free-and-easy, carefree.

во́льн|ая, ой, *f.* (*hist.*) letter of enfranchisement (*given to freed serf*); дать кому́-н. ~ую to give someone his freedom.

во́льниц|а, ы, *m. and f.* 1. (*f.*; *collect.*; *hist.*) freemen; outlaws (*runaway serfs, Cossacks, etc., in Muscovite Russia*). 2. (*m. and f.*; *coll.*) self-willed person, child.

во́льнича|ть, ю, *impf.* (*pejor.*) to take liberties, make free.

во́льн|о, *adv. of* ~ый; (*as mil. command*) в.! stand at ease!

вольно́, *as pred.*+*d. and inf.* (*coll.*; *addressed to person complaining of misfortune*) в. тебе́ it's of your own choosing; ты простуди́лась? в. ж тебе́ бы́ло вы́йти без пальто́ have you caught cold? well, you *would* go out without a coat.

вольноду́м|ец, ца, *m.* free-thinker.

вольноду́м|ный (~ен, ~на), *adj.* free-thinking.

вольноду́мств|о, а, *n.* free-thinking.

вольнолюби́в|ый (~, ~а), *adj.* freedom-loving.

вольнонаёмн|ый, *adj.* 1. civilian (*employed in or for military establishment*); в э́том ла́гере нет ~ого соста́ва in this camp there are no civilian staff. 2. (*obs.*) hired; free-lance.

вольноопределя́ющ|ийся, егося, *m.* (*hist.*) 'volunteer' (*person with secondary education serving term in tsarist Russian army on privileged conditions*).

вольноотпу́щенник, а, *m.* (*hist.*) freedman; emancipated serf.

вольноотпу́щенн|ый, *adj.* (*hist.*) freed, emancipated; *as noun* в., ~ого, *m.* = ~ик.

вольнопракти́ку́ющий, *adj.* conducting a private practice (*of doctors, etc.*).

вольнослу́шател|ь, я, *m.* 'lecturegoer' (*permitted to attend university, etc., lecture courses without having the formal status of student*).

во́льност|ь, и, *f.* 1. freedom, liberty; поэти́ческая в. poetic license; позволя́ть себé ~и to take liberties. 2. (*usu. pl.*; *hist.*) liberties, rights.

вóл|ьный, *adj.* 1. free; в. гóрод free city; в. казáк, ~ьная птúца one's own master. 2. (*econ.*) free, unrestricted; в. рýнок free market; ~ьная продáжа unrestricted sale. 3. (*obs.*) private; жить на ~ьной квартúре (*mil.*) to live out (*as opp. to* in barracks); служúть по ~ьному нáйму to work by private agreement. 4. (*of clothing*) free, loose. 5. в. перевóд (*lit.*) free translation; ~ьные стихú vers libre. 6. (*sport*) free, free-style; ~ьная борьбá free-style wrestling; в. стиль (*in swimming*) free-style; в. удáр free kick; ~ьные упражнéния free exercises. 7. постáвить на в. дух, на в. жар, на в. пар (*cul.*) to leave to cook (*after source of heat has been removed or switched off*). 8. в. кáменщик Freemason. 9. (~ен, ~ьнá), free, familiar (*in behaviour*). 10. (~ен, ~ьнá, *pl.* ~ьнú), (*full form not used*) free, at liberty; ты ~ен дéлать, что хóчешь you are a free agent, you are at liberty to do as you wish.

вольт¹, а, *g. pl.* ~, *m.* (*electr.*) volt.

вольт², а, о ~е, на ~ý, *m.* 1. (*sport*) vault. 2. volte (*in fencing*). 3. (*sl.*) cheating (*at cards*); вýкинуть в. (*fig., coll.*) to play a trick.

вольтáж, а, *m.* (*electr.*) voltage.

вольтáметр, а, *m.* (*electr.*) voltameter.

вольтерья́н|ец, ца, *m.* (*hist.*) Voltairian, free-thinker.

вольтерья́нств|о, а, *n.* (*hist.*) Voltairianism, free-thinking.

вольтижёр, а, *m.* (*sport*) trick-rider, equestrian acrobat.

вольтижúр|овать, ую, *impf.* (*sport*) to do acrobatics on horseback.

вольтировóвк|а, и, *f.* (*sport*) acrobatics on horseback.

вольтмéтр, а, *m.* (*electr.*) voltmetre.

вóльтов, *adj.* (*electr.*) voltaic.

вольфрáм, а, *m.* (*chem.*) tungsten.

вольфрамúт, а, *m.* (*min.*) wolframite.

вольфрáм|овый, *adj. of* ~; ~овая лáмпочка tungsten lamp; ~овая рудá wolfram.

воль|ю́, ёшь, *see* влить.

волюнтарúзм, а, *m.* (*philos.*) libertarianism.

волюнтарúст, а, *m.* (*philos.*) libertarian.

волю́т|а, ы, *f.* (*archit.*) volute, scroll.

вóл|я, и, *no pl.*, *f.* 1. (*in var. senses*) will; volition; wish(es); послéдняя в. last will; свобóдная в. free will; в. к жúзни will to live; сúла ~и will-power; человéк с сúльной ~ей strong-willed person; ~ею судéб as the fates decree, as fate has willed; считáться с ~ей избирáтелей to take into account the wishes of the voters; в. вáша (*coll.*) as you please, as you like; в своéй ~е in one's power; по дóброй ~е freely, of

one's own free will; не по своéй ~е against one's will. 2. freedom, liberty; вýпустить, отпустúть на ~ю to set at liberty; на ~е at liberty; at large; с ~и (*prison sl.*) from outside; дать ~ю (+*d.*) to give free play (to), give free rein (to), give vent (to); дать ~ю рукáм (*coll.*) to be free with one's hands, fists.

вон¹, *adv.* out; off, away; вýйти в. to go away; в. отсю́да! get out!; в. егó! out with him!; из рук в. плóхо wretchedly; пьéса былá сýграна из рук в. плóхо the play was wretchedly played; из ря́да в. выходя́щий outstanding; у меня́ э́то из умá в. (*coll.*) it went right out of my mind.

вон², *particle* there, over there; в. он идёт there he goes; кудá вы положúли газéту? — на стол, в. тáм where have you put the paper? — over there, on the table; в. он кто! so that's who he is!; в. онó что (*coll.*) so that's it!

вóна, *particle* (*coll., dial.*) 1. = вон². 2. *as interj.* в. so that's it!

вон|жу́, зúшь, *see* ~зúть.

вонзá|ть, ю, *impf. of* вонзúть.

вонзá|ться, юсь, 1. *impf. of* вонзúться. 2. *pass. of* ~ть.

вон|зúть, жу́, зúшь, *pf.* (*of* ~зáть) 1. (в+*a.*) to plunge, thrust (into). 2. (*sl.*) to drink.

вон|зúться, жу́сь, зúшься, *pf.* (*of* ~зáться) 1. to pierce, penetrate; стрелá ~зúлась ему́ в сéрдце the arrow pierced his heart. 2. *pass. of* ~зúть.

вонúщ|а, и, *f.* (*coll.*) stink, stench.

вонмú, *see* внять.

вон|ь, и, *no pl.*, *f.* stink, stench.

воню́ч|ий (~, ~а), *adj.* stinking, fetid.

воню́чк|а, и, *f.* (*coll.*) stinker; (*zool.*) skunk.

воня́|ть, ю, *impf.* 1. (+*i.*) to stink, reek (of); весь дом ~ет чеснокóм the whole house reeks of garlic. 2. (*pf.* на~) (*vulg.*) to fart.

воображá|емый, *pres. part. pass. of* ~ть *and adj.* imaginary; fictitious.

воображá|ть, ю, *impf.* (*of* вообразúть) 1. to imagine, fancy; в. жизнь в кáменном вéке to imagine life in the Stone Age; он ~ет, что слýшит гóлос своегó умéршего отцá he imagines that he can hear the voice of his dead father; ~ю, как вы чýвствуете себя́ I can imagine how you feel. 2. (*coll.*) в. о себé to fancy oneself; он слúшком ~ет о себé he thinks too much of himself.

воображá|ться, юсь, *impf.* 1. (+*i.*; *obs.*) to imagine oneself; ему́ ~ется, бýдто он велúкий учёный (*impers.*) he imagines that he is a great scholar. 2. *pass. of* ~ть.

воображéни|е, я, *n.* imagination; fancy; у неё живóе в. she has a lively imagination; э́то однó твоё в. it's just your imagination.

вообрази́м|ый (~, ~а), *pres. part. pass. of* вообрази́ть *and adj.* imaginable.

вообра|зи́ть, жу́, зи́шь, *pf. of* ~жа́ть; ~зи́(те)! fancy!, (just) imagine!

вообра|зи́ться, жу́сь, зи́шься, *pf. of* ~жа́ться.

вообще́, *adv.* **1.** in general; on the whole; в. говоря́, я не люблю́ рабо́тать по нача́м generally speaking I do not like working at night; он сейча́с за́нят, но в. он лени́вый челове́к he is busy at the moment but on the whole he is a lazy man. **2.** always; altogether; она́ вы́глядит бле́дной в., а не то́лько сего́дня she always looks pale, not just today.

воодушев|и́ть, лю́, и́шь, *pf. (of* ~ля́ть*)* to inspire, rouse; to inspirit, hearten; его́ речь ~и́ла всю страну́ his speech was an inspiration to the whole nation.

воодушевле́ни|е, я, *n.* **1.** rousing; inspiriting. **2.** animation; enthusiasm, fervour; говори́ть с больши́м ~ем to speak with great fervour.

воодушевлён|ный (~, ~á), *p.p.p. of* воодушеви́ть *and adj.* animated; enthusiastic, fervent.

воодушевля́|ть, ю, *impf. of* воодушеви́ть.

вооруж|а́ть(ся), а́ю(сь), *impf. of* ~и́ть(ся).

вооруже́ни|е, я, *n.* **1.** arming. **2.** arms, armament; в., состоя́щее из пу́шек и пулемётов an armament consisting of cannon and machine-guns. **3.** equipment; па́русное в. (*naut.*) rig.

вооружён|ный (~, ~á), *p.p.p. of* вооружи́ть *and adj.* armed; в. до зубо́в armed to the teeth; в. но́выми све́дениями armed with fresh information; ~ные си́лы armed forces.

вооруж|и́ть, у́, и́шь, *pf. (of* ~а́ть*)* **1.** (+*i.*) to arm; to equip (with) (*also fig.*); в. кора́бль (*obs.*) to fit out a ship. **2.** (про́тив+*g.*) to set (against), instigate (against).

вооруж|и́ться, у́сь, и́шься, *pf. (of* ~а́ться*)* **1.** to arm oneself, take up arms; (*fig.*) to equip oneself, provide oneself; в. ули́ками to provide oneself with evidence; в. терпе́нием to arm oneself with patience. **2.** *pass. of* ~и́ть.

воо́чию, *adv.* **1.** with one's own eyes, for oneself; я в. убеди́лся в том, что он небре́жно пра́вил маши́ной I could see for myself that he was driving carelessly. **2.** clearly, plainly; показа́ть в. to show clearly.

во-пе́рвых, *adv.* first, first of all, in the first place.

воп|и́ть, лю́, и́шь, *impf. (coll.)* to cry out; to howl; to wail.

вопи́|ющий, *pres. part. act. of* ~я́ть *and adj.* scandalous; crying; ~ющее безобра́зие crying shame; ~ющее противоре́чие glar-

ing contradiction; глас ~ющего в пусты́не, *see* глас.

вопи|я́ть, ю, е́шь, *impf. (obs.)* to cry out, clamour; в. об отмще́нии to cry out for vengeance.

во́пленищ|а, ы, *f.* (*dial.*) (professional) mourner.

вопло|ти́ть, щу́, ти́шь, *pf. (of* ~ща́ть*)* to embody, incarnate; в. в себе́ to be the embodiment (of), incarnation (of); Ле́вин, в «А́нне Каре́нине» Толсто́го, ~ти́л в себе́ тип «ка́ющегося дворяни́на» Levin, in Tolstoy's *Anna Karenina*, embodied the type of the 'repentant nobleman'.

воплоща́|ть, ю, *impf. of* воплоти́ть.

воплоще́ни|е, я, *n.* embodiment, incarnation; он — в. здоро́вья he is the picture of health; в. Христа́ the Incarnation.

воплощён|ный (~, ~á), *p.p.p. of* воплоти́ть *and adj.* incarnate; personified; он — ~ная добросо́вестность he is conscientiousness personified.

вопл|ь, я, *m.* cry, wail; wailing, howling.

вопреки́, *prep.*+*d.* despite, in spite of; against, contrary to, in the teeth of; он вы́шел в. предписа́нию врача́ he went out against doctor's orders; в. предупрежде́ниям regardless of warnings; в. сове́ту contrary to advice.

вопро́с, а, *m.* **1.** question; зада́ть в. to put, pose a question; ко́свенный в. (*gram.*) indirect question. **2.** question, problem; matter; подня́ть, поста́вить в. (о+*p.*) raise the question (of); поста́вить под в. to call in question; возмо́жность сверхзвуково́го полёта бо́льше не под ~ом the possibility of supersonic flight is no longer in question; в. жи́зни и сме́рти matter of life and death; спо́рный в. moot point; что за в.! what a question!, of course!; (*sometimes does not require translation*) како́е ва́ше мне́ние по вопро́су национализа́ции земли́? what is your opinion about nationalization of the land?

вопроси́тельный, *adj.* interrogative; interrogatory; в. знак question-mark; в. взгляд inquiring look.

вопро|си́ть, шу́, си́шь, *pf. (of* ~ша́ть*) (obs.)* to question, inquire (of).

вопро́сник, а, *m.* questionnaire.

вопро́сный, *adj.* containing questions; в. лист question-paper; form.

вопроша́|ть, ю, *impf. of* вопроси́ть; ~ющий взгляд inquiring look.

вопр|у́, ёшь, *see* впере́ть.

вопь|ю́, ёшь, *see* впить.

вор, а, *pl.* ~ы́, ~о́в, *m.* **1.** thief; карма́нный в. pickpocket; магази́нный в. shoplifter. **2.** (*hist.*) criminal (*esp. one guilty of high treason*); ту́шинский в. (*hist.*) 'the impostor of Tushino' (*the second pseudo-Dmitri*).

во́рван|ь, и, *f.* train-oil; blubber.

ворв|а́ться, у́сь, ёшься, *past* ~а́лся, ~ала́сь, *pf.* (*of* врыва́ться²) to burst (into); он ~а́лся ко мне в ко́мнату he burst into my room.

вори́шк|а, и, *m.* petty thief.

ворк|ова́ть, у́ю, *impf.* (*of pigeons*) to coo; (*fig.*) to bill and coo.

воркотн|я́, и́, *f.* (*coll.*) grumbling.

вороб|е́й, ья́, *m.* sparrow; ста́рый в., стре́ляный в. (*fig.*) old hand; ста́рого ~ья́ на мяки́не не проведёшь (*prov.*) an old bird is not caught with chaff.

вороб|ьи́ный, *adj. of* ~е́й; ~ьи́ная ночь 1. short summer night. 2. night of continuous thunder and/or summer-lighting.

воро́ваный, *adj.* stolen.

ворова́т|ый (~, ~а), *adj.* thievish; furtive; в. взгляд furtive glance.

вор|ова́ть, у́ю, *impf.* 1. (*pf.* с~) to steal; в. де́ньги у кого́-н. to steal money from someone. 2. *impf. only* to be a thief; с са́мых ра́нних лет он ~у́ет he has been a thief from his earliest years.

воро́вк|а, и, *f. of* вор.

воровски́, *adv.* (*coll.*) furtively.

воровск|о́й, *adj.* 1. of thieves; в. язы́к, ~о́е арго́ thieves' Latin, thieves' cant. 2. (*hist.*) illegal; ~и́е де́ньги counterfeit money.

воровств|о́, а́, *n.* stealing; theft; литерату́рное в. plagiarism.

во́рог, а, *m.* (*folk poet.*) 1. foe. 2. fiend.

ворожб|а́, ы́, *no pl., f.* sorcery; fortune-telling.

вороже|я́, и́, *f.* sorceress; fortune-teller.

ворож|и́ть, у́, и́шь, *impf.* (*of* по~) to practise sorcery; to tell fortunes; ему́ ба́бушка ~и́т (*coll.*) (*i*) he holds good cards, (*ii*) he has a friend at court.

во́рон, а, *m.* raven.

воро́н|а, ы, *f.* 1. crow; бе́лая в. rara avis (*of someone outstanding*); в. в павли́ньих пе́рьях daw in peacock's feathers; ни па́ва, ни в. neither one thing nor another; пу́ганая в. куста́ бои́тся (*prov.*) a burnt child dreads the fire. 2. (*fig.*) gaper, loafer, Johnny-head-in-air; ~ счита́ть (*coll.*) to be a gaper, loafer, Johnny-head-in-air.

вороне́н|ый, *adj.* (*tech.*) blued; ~ая сталь blue steel, burnished steel.

воро́н|ий, ий, *adj. of* ~а.

воро́н|ить, ю, ишь, *impf.* (*tech.*) to blue, burnish.

воро́нк|а, и, *f.* 1. funnel (*for pouring liquids*). 2. (*mil.*) crater.

**во́рон|ов, , adj. of* ~; only in phrase цвет ~ова крыла́ raven (*of hair, etc.*).

ворон|о́й, *adj.* black (*of horses*); прокати́ть на ~ы́х (*coll.*) to blackball.

**воронь|ё, я́, *n.* (*collect.*) carrion-crows (*also fig.*).

воро́т¹, а, *pl.* ~ы, *m.* collar (*of garment*); neckband; схвати́ть за́ в. to seize by the collar, collar.

воро́т², а, *m.* (*tech.*) winch; windlass.

**воро́т|а (*coll.* ~а́), ~, *no sing.* 1. gate, gates; gateway; шлю́зные в. lock-gate; въе́хать в в. to enter the gates; стоя́ть в ~ах to stand in the gateway; пришла́ беда́, отворя́й ~а́ (*prov.*) misfortunes never come singly. 2. (*sport*) goal, goal-posts.

вороти́л|а, ы, *m.* (*coll.*) bigwig, big noise.

воро|ти́ть¹, чу́, ~ти́шь, *pf.* (*coll.*) 1. to bring back; to get back; to call back; сде́ланного не ~ти́шь what's done can't be undone. 2. to turn aside, back.

воро|ти́ть², ти́шь, *impf.* (*coll.*) (+*i.*) to be in charge (of), run; он тут всем ~тит he runs the whole show here. 2. нос, ры́ло в. (от) (*coll.*) to turn up one's nose (at); (*impers.*) (с души́) меня́ ~тит от э́того де́ла this business makes me sick.

воро|ти́ться, чу́сь, ~ти́шься, *pf.* (*coll.*) to return.

воротни́к, а́, *m.* collar; отложно́й в. turn-down collar; стоя́чий в. stand-up collar.

воротнич|о́к, ка́, *m.* collar.

воро́т|ный, *adj. of* ~а; в. ство́р gate-post; (*med.*) ~ная ве́на portal vein.

во́рох, а, *pl.* ~а́, *m.* heap, pile; (*fig., coll.*) heaps, masses, lots; мне на́до в. пи́сем написа́ть I have lots of letters to write; в. новосте́й lots of news.

воро́ча|ть, ю, *impf.* (*coll.*) 1. to turn, move; в. глаза́ми to roll one's eyes. 2. (+*i.*; *fig.*) to have control (of); в. ты́сячами, в. миллио́нами to be rolling (*in money*).

воро́ча|ться, юсь, *impf.* (*coll.*) to turn, move (*intrans.*); в. с бо́ку на́ бок to toss and turn; ~йтесь! (*coll.*) get a move on!

воро|чу́(сь), ~ти́шь(ся), *see* ~ти́ть(ся).

вороши́|ть, у́, и́шь, *impf.* (*of* раз~) 1. в. се́но to turn, ted hay. 2. (*fig., coll.*) to stir up.

вороши́|ться, у́сь, и́шься, *impf.* (*coll.*) to move about, stir.

ворс, а, *no pl., m.* pile; nap; по ~у with the pile, nap.

ворси́льн|ый, *adj.* (*text.*) ~ая маши́на teaser; ~ая ши́шка teasel.

ворси́нк|а, и, *f.* 1. (*text.*) hair. 2. (*physiol., bot.*) fibre.

ворси́ст|ый (~, ~а), *adj.* 1. (*text.*) fleecy, with thick pile. 2. (*bot.*) lanate.

ворсова́льн|ый, *adj.* ~ая маши́на (*text.*) teaser.

ворс|ова́ть, у́ю, *impf.* (*of* на~) (*text.*) to tease.

ворсянк|а, и, *f.* (*bot.*) teasel.

ворчань|е, я, *n.* grumbling; growling.

ворч|а́ть, у́, и́шь, *impf.* (на+*a.*) to grumble (at); to growl (at); в. себе́ под нос to mutter (into one's beard); эти соба́ки ~а́т на всех чужих люде́й these dogs always growl at strangers.

ворчли́в|ый (~, ~a), *adj.* querulous.

ворчу́н, а́, *m.* (*coll.*) grumbler.

восвоя́си, *adv.* (for) home; он уже́ отпра́вился в. he has already set out for home.

восемна́дцатый *adj.* eighteenth.

восемна́дцат|ь, и, *num.* eighteen.

вос|емь, ьми́, ьмью́, *and* **емью́,** *num.* eight.

вос|емьдесят, ьми́десяти, *num. eighty.*

вос|емьсо́т, ьмисо́т, ьмиста́ми, *num.* eight hundred.

во́семью, *adv.* eight times (*in multiplication*).

воск, а, *m.* wax, beeswax; го́рный в. (*min.*) ozocerite.

воскли́кн|уть, у, ешь, *pf.* to exclaim.

восклица́ни|е, я, *n.* exclamation.

восклица́тельный, *adj.* exclamatory; в. знак exclamation mark.

восклица́|ть, ю, *impf.* (*of* воскли́кнуть) to exclaim.

воско́вк|а, и, *f.* wax-paper; stencil (*for use in duplicating machine, etc.*).

восков|о́й, *adj.* wax, waxen; ~а́я свеча́ wax candle; ~о́е лицо́ waxen complexion.

воскрес|а́ть, а́ю, *impf.* (*of* ~ну́ть) to rise again, rise from the dead; (*fig.*) to revive.

воскресе́ни|е, я, *n.* resurrection.

воскресе́нь|е, я, *n.* Sunday.

воскре|си́ть, шу́, си́шь, *pf.* (*of* ~ша́ть) to raise from the dead, resurrect; (*fig.*) to resurrect, revive; о́тдых ~си́л его́ си́лы the rest revived his energies; в. ста́рый обы́чай to resurrect an old custom.

воскре́сник, а, *m.* voluntary Sunday work.

воскре́с|нуть, ну, нешь, *past* ~, ~ла, *pf. of* ~а́ть.

воскре́сн|ый, *adj.* Sunday.

воскреша́|ть, ю, *impf. of* воскреси́ть.

воскреше́ни|е, я, *n.* raising from the dead, resurrection; (*fig.*) revival.

воскре|шу́, си́шь, *see* ~си́ть.

воскур|и́ть, ю́, ~ишь, *pf.* (*of* ~я́ть) (*obs.*) to burn (*incense*); в. фимиа́м кому́-н. to sing one's praises.

воскур|я́ть, я́ю, *impf. of* ~и́ть.

вослед = вслед.

воспале́ни|е, я, *n.* (*med.*) inflammation; в. брюши́ны peritonitis; в. кишо́к enteritis; в. лёгких pneumonia; в. по́чек nephritis; ро́жистое в. erysipelas.

воспалён|ный (~, ~а́), *p.p.p. of* воспали́ть *and adj.* sore; inflamed (*also fig.*); ~ное воображе́ние fevered imagination.

воспали́тельный, *adj.* (*med.*) inflammatory; в. проце́сс inflammation.

воспал|и́ть, ю́, и́шь, *pf.* (*of* ~я́ть) to inflame.

воспал|и́ться, ю́сь, и́шься, *pf.* (*of* ~я́ться) to become inflamed; (+*i.*; *obs.*) to become inflamed (with), be on fire (with); в. гне́вом to flare up with rage.

воспал|я́ть(ся), я́ю(сь), *impf. of* ~и́ть(ся).

воспар|и́ть, ю́, и́шь, *pf.* (*of* ~я́ть) (*poet.*) to soar; в. ду́хом (*iron.*) to be carried away.

воспаря́|ть, ю, *impf. of* воспари́ть.

воспева́|ть, ю, *impf. of* воспе́ть.

восп|е́ть, ою́, оёшь, *pf.* (*of* ~ева́ть) (*poet.*) to sing (of), hymn; в. по́двиги наро́дных геро́ев to sing of the deeds of national heroes.

воспита́ни|е, я, *n.* 1. education; upbringing. 2. (good) breeding.

воспита́нник, а, *m.* 1. pupil; в. сре́дней шко́лы secondary schoolboy. 2. ward (*a minor*).

воспи́танност|ь, и, *f.* (good) breeding.

воспи́танный, *p.p.p. of* воспита́ть *and adj.* well brought up.

воспита́тел|ь, я, *m.* tutor, educator.

воспита́тельниц|а, ы, *f.* governess.

воспита́тельный, *adj.* educational; в. дом foundling hospital.

воспит|а́ть, а́ю, *pf.* (*of* ~ывать) 1. to educate, bring up. 2. to cultivate, foster; в. са́мые хоро́шие накло́нности в ком-н. to bring out the best in someone. 3. (из+*g.*) to make (of); в. солда́т из сбро́да to make an army of a rabble.

воспи́тыва|ть, ю, *impf. of* воспита́ть.

воспламене́ни|е, я, *n.* ignition.

воспламен|и́ть, ю́, и́шь, *pf.* (*of* ~я́ть) to kindle, ignite; (*fig.*) to fire, inflame; его́ слова́ ~и́ли воображе́ние his words fired the imagination of the audience.

воспламен|и́ться, ю́сь, и́шься, *pf.* (*of* ~я́ться) to catch fire, ignite; (*fig.*) to take fire, flare up.

воспламеня́емост|ь, и, *f.* inflammability.

воспламеня́емый, *adj.* inflammable.

воспламеня́|ть(ся), ю(сь), *impf. of* воспламени́ть(ся).

воспо́лн|ить, ю, ишь, *pf.* to fill in; в. пробе́лы свои́х зна́ний to fill in the gaps in one's knowledge.

восполня́|ть, ю, *impf. of* воспо́лнить.

воспо́льз|оваться, уюсь, *pf. of* по́льзоваться.

воспомина́ни|е, я, *n.* 1. recollection, memory; жить ~ями to live on memories; от его́ иму́щества оста́лось одно́ в. of his possessions nothing is left. 2. *pl.* (*lit.*) memoirs; reminiscences.

воспосле́д|овать, ую, *pf.* (*obs.*) to follow, ensue; ~овал це́лый ряд несча́стных слу́чаев a whole chapter of accidents ensued.

восп|ою́, оёшь, *see* ~**е́ть.**

зоспрепя́тств|овать, ую, *pf. of* препя́тствовать.

зоспрети́тельный, *adj.* prohibitive.

зоспре|ти́ть, щу́, ти́шь, *pf.* (*of* ~**ща́ть**) (+*a. or inf.*) to forbid, prohibit; в. вход to prohibit entry; в. разгова́ривать за столо́м to forbid talking at meals.

зоспреща́|ть, ю, *impf. of* воспрети́ть.

зоспреща́|ться, юсь, *impf.* to be prohibited; кури́ть ~ется no smoking; посторо́нним вход ~ется unauthorized persons not admitted.

зоспреще́ни|е, я, *n.* prohibition.

восприе́мник, а, *m.* godfather.

восприе́мниц|а, ы, *f.* godmother.

восприи́мчив|ый (~, ~а), *adj.* 1. receptive; impressionable. 2. susceptible; он о́чень ~ к на́сморку he is very susceptible to colds.

восприм|у́, ~ешь, *see* восприня́ть.

воспринима́ем|ый (~, ~а), *adj.* perceptible.

воспринима́|ть, ю, *impf. of* восприня́ть.

воспри|ня́ть, му́, ~мешь, *past* ~нял, ~няла́, ~няло, *pf.* (*of* ~нима́ть) 1. to perceive, apprehend; to grasp, take in. 2. to take (for), interpret; в. молча́ние как знак согла́сия to take silence as a mark of consent. 3. в. от купе́ли (*eccl.*) to stand godfather, godmother (to).

восприя́ти|е, я, *n.* (*philos., psych.*) perception.

воспроизведе́ни|е, я, *n.* reproduction; в. челове́ческого ро́да reproduction of the human species; ве́рное в. карти́ны Ру́бенса faithful reproduction of a painting by Rubens.

воспроизве|сти́, ду́, дёшь, *past* ~л, ~ла́, *pf.* (*of* воспроизводи́ть) (*in var. senses*) to reproduce; в. в па́мяти to recall; в. по́длинный докуме́нт to reproduce an original document; он то́лько ~л утвержде́ния профе́ссора he merely echoed the professor's statements.

воспроизводи́тельный, *adj.* reproductive.

воспроизво|ди́ть, жу́, ~дишь, *impf. of* воспроизвести́.

воспроизво́дств|о, а, *n.* (*econ.*) reproduction.

воспроти́в|иться, люсь, ишься, *pf. of* проти́виться.

воспря́н|уть, у, ешь, *pf.* 1. (*obs.*) to leap up. 2. (*coll.*) to cheer up; в. ду́хом to take heart.

воспыла́|ть, ю, *pf.* (+*i.*) to be inflamed (with); to blaze (with); в. гне́вом to blaze with anger; в. любо́вью (к+*d.*) to be smitten with love (for).

воссеца́|ть, ю, *impf. of* воссе́сть.

восс|е́сть, я́ду, я́дешь, *past* ~е́л, *pf.* to sit

(*in state, formally*); в. на престо́л to mount the throne.

восслáв|ить, лю, ишь, *pf.* (*of* ~ля́ть) (*obs.*) to hymn, praise.

восславля́|ть, ю, *impf. of* восслáвить.

воссоедине́ни|е, я, *n.* reunion, reunification.

воссоедин|и́ть, ю́, и́шь, *pf.* (*of* ~я́ть) to reunite.

воссоединя́|ть, ю, *impf. of* воссоедини́ть.

воссозда|ва́ть, ю́, ёшь, *impf. of* ~ть.

воссозда́ни|е, я, *n.* reconstruction.

воссоз|да́ть, да́м, да́шь, да́ст, дади́м, дади́те, даду́т, *past* ~да́л, ~дала́, ~да́ло, *pf.* (*of* ~дава́ть) to reconstruct, reconstitute; он ~да́л в кни́ге собы́тия Троя́нской войны́ in his book he has reconstructed the events of the Trojan War.

восста|ва́ть, ю́, ёшь, *impf. of* ~ть.

восстáв|ить, лю, ишь, *pf.* (*obs.*) to set up, erect; в. перпендикуля́р (*math.*) to raise a perpendicular.

восставля́|ть, ю, *impf. of* восстáвить.

восстанáвлива|ть, ю, *impf. of* восстанови́ть.

восстáни|е, я, *n.* rising, insurrection.

восстанови́тел|ь, я, *m.* 1. renovator, restorer. 2. restorative (*for hair*).

восстанови́тельный, *adj.* of restoration, reconstruction.

восстанов|и́ть, лю́, ~ишь, *pf.* (*of* восстанáвливать) 1. to restore, renew; to rehabilitate; в. мир to restore peace; в. хозя́йство страны́ to restore the economy of a country; в. в па́мяти to recall, recollect; в. кого́-н. в права́х to restore someone's rights, rehabilitate; его́ ~и́ли в до́лжности заве́дующего he has been reinstated as manager. 2. (про́тив+*g.*) to set (against); они́ ~и́ли сосе́дей про́тив себя́ свое́й гру́бостью they have set their neighbours against them by their rudeness. 3. (*chem.*) to reduce.

восстановле́ни|е, я, *n.* 1. restoration, renewal; rehabilitation; в. в права́х restoration of rights, rehabilitation; в. в до́лжности reinstatement. 2. (*chem.*) reduction.

восстановля́|ть, ю, *impf.* 1. *impf. of* восстанови́ть. 2. (*chem.*) to reduce.

восстá|ть, ну, нешь, *imp.* ~нь, *pf.* (*of* ~ва́ть) 1. (*obs.*) to rise (up). 2. (на+*a.*, про́тив +*g.*) to rise (against); (*fig.*) to be up in arms (against), fly in the face (of); всё дереве́нское населе́ние ~ло на врага́ the whole countryside rose against the enemy; вы ~ли про́тив здра́вого смы́сла you are flying in the face of the dictates of common sense.

воссыла́|ть, ю, *impf.* (*obs.*) to offer up, send up.

восто́к, а, *m.* 1. east; на в., с ~а to, from the east. 2. В. the East; Бли́жний В. the

Near East; Сре́дний В. the Middle East; Да́льний В. the Far East.

востокове́д, а, m. orientalist.

востокове́ди|е, я, n. oriental studies.

востокове́дный, adj. of oriental studies.

востокове́д|ческий, adj. = ~ный.

восто́рг, а, m. delight; rapture; быть в ~е (от+g.) to be delighted (with); приходи́ть в в. (от+g.) to go into raptures (over).

восторга́|ть, ю, impf. to delight, enrapture.

восторга́|ться, юсь, impf. (+i.) to be delighted (with); to go into, be in raptures (over); она́ ~ется бале́том she goes into raptures over the ballet.

восто́рженност|ь, и, f. 1. enthusiasm. **2.** proneness to enthusiasm.

восто́ржен|ный (~, ~на), adj. enthusiastic, full of lofty enthusiasm; ~ная голова́ exalté; в. приём enthusiastic reception; его́ нове́йшая пье́са получи́ла ~ные о́тзывы his latest play has received enthusiastic comment.

восторжеств|ова́ть, у́ю, pf. of торжество-ва́ть.

восто́чник, а, m. (coll.) orientalist.

восто́чн|ый, adj. east, eastern; oriental; ~ая це́рковь the Eastern Church.

востре́бовани|е, я, n. claiming; demand; до ~я to be called for, on demand; посла́ть паке́т до ~я to send a parcel to be called for, send a parcel poste restante.

востре́б|овать, ую, pf. to claim, call for (from post-office, etc.).

вострепе|та́ть, щу́, ~щешь, pf. (obs.) to begin to tremble.

востро́, adv. (coll.) держа́ть у́хо в. to keep a sharp look-out.

вострогла́зый, adj. (coll.) sharp-eyed; bright-eyed.

востроно́сый, adj. (coll.) sharp-nosed.

во́ст|рый (~ёр, ~pá, ~po), adj. (dial.) sharp.

восхвале́ни|е, я, n. eulogy.

восхвал|и́ть, ю́, ~ишь, pf. (of ~я́ть) to laud, extol, eulogize.

восхваля́|ть, ю, impf. of восхвали́ть.

восхити́тел|ьный (~ен, ~ьна), adj. entrancing, ravishing; delightful; delicious; ~ьная пе́сня an entrancing song; из рестора́на нёсся в. за́пах a delicious smell came from the restaurant.

восхи|ти́ть, щу, тишь, pf. (poet., obs.) to carry away.

восхи|ти́ть, щу́, ти́шь, pf. (fig.) to carry away, delight, enrapture; красота́ италья́нских озёр его́ ~ти́ла he was carried away by the beauty of the Italian lakes.

восхи|ти́ться, щу́сь, ти́шься, pf. (+i.) to be carried away (by); to admire; все ~ти́лись его́ хра́бростью his courage was the admiration of all.

восхища́|ть(ся, ю(сь), impf. of восхити́ть-(ся).

восхище́ни|е, я, n. delight, rapture; admiration.

восхищён|ный (~, ~á), p.p.p. of восхити́ть and adj. rapt; admiring; в. взгляд rapt gaze.

восхи́|щу, тишь, see ~тить.

восхи|щу́(сь), ти́шь(ся), see ~ти́ть(ся).

восхо́д, а, m. 1. rising; в. со́лнца sunrise. **2.** (obs.) the east.

восхо|ди́ть, жу́, ~дишь, impf. 1. impf. of взойти́. **2.** (impf. only) (к) to go back (to), date (from); в. к дре́вности to go back to antiquity.

восход|я́щий, pres. part. of ~и́ть and adj. ~я́щая звезда́, ~я́щее свети́ло (fig.) rising star; ~я́щее поколе́ние rising generation; ~я́щая интона́ция (ling.), ~я́щее ударе́ние (mus.) rising intonation.

восхожде́ни|е, я, n. ascent; в. на Монбла́н the ascent of Mont Blanc.

восчу́вств|овать, ую, pf. (obs. or iron.) to feel.

восше́стви|е, я, n. (на престо́л) accession (to the throne).

восьм|а́я, see ~о́й.

восьмери́чн|ый, adj. eightfold; и ~ое name of letter 'и' in old Russian orthography.

восьмёрк|а, и, f. 1. (coll.) eight; number eight (of 'buses, etc.). **2.** (cards) eight; в. черве́й eight of hearts. **3.** eight (boat). **4.** figure of eight.

во́сьмер|о, ы́х, num. 1. eight; нас бы́ло в. there were eight of us; в. сане́й eight sledges. **2.** eight pairs; в. перча́ток eight pairs of gloves.

восьми- eight-, octo-.

восьмивесе́льный, adj. eight-oared.

восьмигра́нник, а, m. (math.) octahedron.

восьмидесятиле́тний, adj. 1. of eighty years; в. юбиле́й eightieth anniversary. **2.** eighty-year-old.

восьмидеся́тник, а, m. 'man of the eighties' (of nineteenth century).

восьмидеся́тый, adj. eightieth.

восьмикла́ссник, а, m. pupil of eighth form.

восьмикла́ссни|ца, ы, f. f. of восьмикла́ссник.

восьмикра́тный, adj. eightfold; octuple.

восьмиле́тний, adj. 1. eight-year. **2.** eight--year-old.

восьмино́г, а, m. (zool.) octopus.

восьмисо́тый, adj. eight-hundredth.

восьмисти́ши|е, я, n. (lit.) octave, octet.

восьмисто́пный, adj. (lit.) eight-foot, octo-narian.

восьмиуго́льник, а, m. (math.) octagon.

восьмиуго́льный, adj. octagonal.

восьмичасово́й, *adj.* eight-hour; в. рабо́чий день eight-hour (working-)day.

восьм|о́й, *adj.* eighth; *as noun* ~а́я, ~о́й, *f.* (*in var. senses*) an eighth.

восьму́шк|а, и, *f.* **1.** (*coll.*) eighth of a pound (*in weight*). **2.** octavo; писа́ть на ~е to write on octavo.

вот, *particle* **1.** here (is), there (is); this is; в. мой дом here is my house, this is my house; в. авто́бус here's, there's the 'bus; в. авто́бус идёт here comes the 'bus; в. и я here I am; в. мы пришли́ here we are; в. где я живу́ this is where I live. **2.** (*emphasizing pronouns; unstressed*) в. э́ти ту́фли ей нра́вились these are the shoes she liked; в. ему́ я бы э́того не поруча́л I would not trust *him* with this. **3.** (*in exclamations; always stressed*) here's a . . . , there's a . . . (for you); в́. тип! there's a character (for you)!; в́. так исто́рия! here's a pretty kettle of fish!; (*expressing surprise*) в́. как!, в́. что! really? you don't mean to say so!; слы́шали ли вы но́вость? коро́ль у́мер. В. как! have you heard the news? the king is dead. No! (not) really?; в. так та́к!, в. тебе́ на́! well!; well, I never!; говоря́т, что Пётр обручи́лся с Ли́зой. В. так та́к! they say Peter and Elizabeth are engaged. Well!; (*surprise and disapproval*) в́. ещё! indeed!; what(ever) next!; good heavens!; не да́шь ли мне пять фу́нтов взаймы́? ну, в́. ещё! will you lend me five pounds? well, what next!; (*approval and/or encouragement*) в. та́к!, в.-в.! that's right!; that's it!; (*accompanying blows*) в́. тебе́! take that!; в́. тебе́, в. тебе́! take that, and that!; (*expressing disagreeable surprise at non-occurrence of expected event*) вот тебе́ и . . . so much for . . . ; вот тебе́ и пое́здка в Пари́ж! so much for the trip to Paris!, we've (you've, *etc.*) had the trip to Paris!

вот-во́т, *adv.* just, on the point of; вода́ в.-в. закипи́т the water is just boiling, is on the boil; по́езд в.-в. придёт the train is just coming.

воти́р|овать, ую, *impf. and pf.* to vote (for); в. увеличе́ние дота́ций студе́нтам to vote an increase of students' grants.

вотиро́вк|а, и, *f.* voting.

вотк|а́ть, у́, ёшь, *past* ~а́л, ~ала́, ~а́ло, *pf.* to interweave.

воткн|у́ть, у́, ёшь, *pf.* (*of* втыка́ть) (в+*a.*) to stick (into), drive (into); в. кол в зе́млю to drive a stake into the ground; она́ ~у́ла ему́ гвозди́ку в петли́цу she stuck a carnation in his buttonhole.

вотр|у́, ёшь, *see* втере́ть.

во́тский, *adj.* Votyak.

во́тум, а, *no pl.*, *m.* vote; в. (не)дове́рия (+*d.*) vote of (no) confidence (in).

во́тчин|а, ы, *f.* (*hist.*) inherited estate, lands; allodium, patrimony (*in Muscovite Russia as opp. to* поме́стье).

во́тчинник, а, *m.* (*hist.*) great landowner (*in Muscovite Russia*).

во́тчинный, *adj.* (*hist.*) allodial, patrimonial.

вотще́, *adv.* (*obs.*) in vain, to no purpose.

вотя́к, а́, *m.* Votyak.

вотя́цкий, *adj.* = во́тский.

вотя́чк|а, и, *f.* Votyak (woman).

воцаре́ни|е, я, *n.* accession (to the throne).

воцар|и́ться, ю́сь, и́шься, *pf.* (*of* ~я́ться) **1.** to come to the throne. **2.** (*fig.*) to set in; в лесу́ ~и́лась тишина́ in the forest silence fell.

воцаря́|ться, ю́сь, *impf. of* воцари́ться.

вочелове́чени|е, я, *n.* (*theol.*) incarnation.

вочелове́ч|иться, усь, ишься, *pf.* (*theol.*) to become man, be incarnate.

вош|ёл, ла́, *see* войти́.

во́шк|а, и, *f.* (*coll.*) louse.

вошь, вши, *i.* ~ю, *pl.* вши, вшей, *f.* louse.

вощанк|а, и, *f.* **1.** wax-paper; waxed cloth. **2.** cobbler's wax.

вощано́й, *adj.* wax.

вощёный, *adj.* waxed.

вощи́н|а, ы, *f.* **1.** (*collect.*) empty honeycomb. **2.** unrefined beeswax.

вощ|и́ть, у́, и́шь, *impf.* (*of* на~) to wax; to polish with wax.

во́|ю, ешь, *see* выть.

вою́|ю, ешь, *see* воева́ть.

воя́ж, а, *m.* (*obs. or iron.*) journey, travels.

вояжёр, а, *m.* **1.** (*obs. or iron.*) traveller. **2.** commercial traveller.

воя́к|а, и, *m.* (*coll., iron.*) warrior; fire-eater.

впада́|ть, ю, *impf.* **1.** *impf. of* впасть. **2.** *impf. only* (*of rivers*) to fall (into), flow (into); Ока́ ~ет в Во́лгу the Oka flows into the Volga. **3.** *impf. only* (в+*a.*) to verge (on), approximate (to).

впаде́ни|е, я, *n.* confluence; mouth (*of rivers*).

впа́дин|а, ы, *f.* cavity, hollow; глазна́я в. eye-socket.

впад|у́, ёшь, *see* впасть.

впа́ива|ть, ю, *impf. of* впая́ть.

впа́йк|а, и, *f.* **1.** soldering-in. **2.** soldered-in piece.

впа́л|ый, *adj.* hollow, sunken; ~ые щёки hollow cheeks.

впа|сть, ду́, дёшь, *pf.* (*of* ~да́ть) **1.** (в+*a.*) to fall (into), lapse (into), sink (into); в. в бе́дность to fall into penury; в. в грех to lapse into sin; в. в де́тство to sink into dotage; в. в неми́лость to fall into disgrace. **2.** (*of eyes, cheeks*) to fall in, sink.

впа|я́ть, я́ю, *pf.* (*of* ~ивать) to solder in.

впервинку, *adv.* (*coll.*) for the first time;

ему́ не в. е́хать в Росси́ю it is not the first time he has been to Russia.

впере|о́й, *adv.* (*coll.*) = ~ы́е.

впервы́е, *adv.* for the first time, first; семи́десяти лет он в. полете́л на самолёте at the age of seventy he went in an aeroplane for the first time; когда́ в. я прие́хал в Ло́ндон when I first came to London.

впере

ва́лку, *adv.* (*coll.*) ходи́ть в. to waddle.

вперего́нки, *adv.* (*coll.*) бе́гать в. to run races.

вперёд, *adv.* 1. forward(s), ahead; (*of clocks and watches*) fast; взад и в. back and forth; большо́й шаг в. (*fig.*) a big step forward; ра́зве ва́ши часы́ не иду́т в.? surely your watch is fast?; в.! (*mil. command*) forward! 2. in future, henceforward; в. будь осторо́жнее be more careful in future. 3. in advance; заплати́ть в. to pay in advance; дать очки́ в. (*sport*) to give points; дав мне пять очко́в в., он всё-таки вы́играл he gave me five points and still won.

впереди́ 1. *adv.* in front, ahead. 2. *adv.* in (the) future; ahead. 3. *prep.+g.* in front of, before; лейтена́нт марширова́л в. взво́да the lieutenant marched at the head of the platoon.

вперемёжку, *adv.* (*coll.*) alternately; на пара́де солда́ты и моряки́ шли в. soldiers and sailors alternated in the parade.

вперемешку, *adv.* (*coll.*) pell-mell, higgledy-piggledy; in confusion; все его́ ве́щи лежа́ли в. на полу́ ко́мнаты all his things lay in confusion on the floor of the room.

впер|е́ть, вопру́, вопрёшь, *past* ~, ~ла, *pf.* (*of* впира́ть) (*coll.*) 1. to barge in; он про́сто ~ в дом, не дожда́вшись приглаше́ния he simply barged into the house without waiting to be invited. 2. to shove in, thrust in.

впер|е́ться, вопру́сь, вопрёшься, *past* ~ся, ~лась, *pf.* (*of* впира́ться) (*coll.*) to barge in.

впер|и́ть, ю́, и́шь, *pf.* (*of* ~я́ть) (в+*a.*) to direct (upon); в. взор to fasten one's gaze (upon).

впер|и́ться, ю́сь, и́шься, *pf.* (*of* ~я́ться) (*coll.*) to stare (at), fasten one's eyes (upon).

вперя́|ть(ся), ю(сь), *impf. of* впери́ть(ся).

впечатле́ни|е, я, *n.* impression; ~я де́тства childhood impressions; произвести́ в. (на +*a.*) to make an impression (upon); его́ речь произвела́ в. на всех his speech made an impression on all; у меня́ созда́лось в., что она́ недово́льна I formed the impression that she was dissatisfied.

впечатли́тельност|ь, и, *f.* impressionability.

впечатли́тел|ьный (~ен, ~ьна), *adj.* impressionable.

впечатля́ющий, *adj.* impressive.

впива́|ть, ю, *impf.* 1. *impf. of* впить. 2. *impf. only* to drink in, enjoy (*esp. olfactory sensations*).

впива́|ться[1], юсь, *impf. of* впи́ться[1].

впива́|ться[2], юсь, *impf. of* впи́ться[2].

впира́|ть(ся), ю(сь), *impf. of* впере́ть(ся).

впи́санный, *p.p.p. of* вписа́ть *and adj.* (*math.*) inscribed.

впи|са́ть, шу́, ~шешь, *pf.* (*of* ~сывать) 1. to enter; to insert; в. своё имя в спи́сок to enter one's name on a list; в. фра́зу в ру́копись статьи́ to insert a sentence into the manuscript of an article. 2. (*math.*) to inscribe.

впи|са́ться, шу́сь, ~шешься, *pf.* (*of* ~сываться) (*coll.*) to be enrolled, join.

впи́ск|а, и, *f.* (*coll.*) 1. entry. 2. insertion; страни́ца была́ полна́ впи́сок the page was full of insertions.

впи́сыва|ть(ся), ю(сь), *impf. of* вписа́ть(ся).

впит|а́ть, а́ю, *pf.* (*of* ~ывать) to absorb; (*fig.*) to absorb, take in; за удиви́тельно коро́ткий срок он ~а́л в себя́ всю филосо́фию Ка́нта in an amazingly short time he had absorbed the whole of Kant's philosophy.

впит|а́ться, а́юсь, *pf.* (*of* ~ываться) (в+*a.*) to soak (into).

впи́тыва|ть(ся), ю(сь), *impf. of* впита́ть(ся).

впи|ть, вопью́, вопьёшь, *past* ~л, ~ла́, ~ло, *pf.* (*of* ~ва́ть) to imbibe, absorb.

впи|ться[1], вопью́сь, вопьёшься, *past* ~лся, ~ла́сь, *pf.* (*of* ~ва́ться) (в+*a.*) 1. to stick (into); to bite; to sting; ко́шка ~ла́сь в неё когтя́ми the cat stuck its claws into her; ва́ша соба́ка ~ла́сь мне в но́гу your dog has bitten me in the leg; гвоздь ~лся мне в но́гу a nail stuck into my foot. 2. в. взо́ром, глаза́ми to fix, fasten one's eyes (upon).

впи|ться[2], вопью́сь, вопьёшься, *past* ~лся, ~ла́сь, *pf.* (*coll.*) to become hardened to drink.

впих|а́ть, а́ю, *pf.* (*coll.*) = ~ну́ть.

впи́хива|ть, ю, *impf. of* впиха́ть *and* впихну́ть.

впих|ну́ть, ну́, нёшь, *pf.* (*of* ~ивать) to stuff in, cram in; to shove; в. кого́-н. в ко́мнату to shove someone into a room.

вплавь, *adv.* swimming; каки́м о́бразом перепра́вился он че́рез ре́ку? в. how did he get across the river? he swam it.

впле|сти́, ту́, тёшь, *past* ~л, ~ла́, *pf.* (*of* ~та́ть) (в+*a.*) to plait (into), intertwine; (*fig.*, *coll.*) to involve (in); вы ~ли́ меня́ в хоро́шенькое де́ло you have got me into a fine mess.

вплета́|ть, ю, *impf. of* вплести́.

впле|ту́, тёшь, *see* ~сти́.

вплотну́ю, *adv.* close; (*fig.*) in (real) earnest;

поста́вить стол в. к стене́ to put the table right against the wall; приня́ться за де́ло в. to get to grips with the matter, tackle the matter in real earnest.

вплоть, *adv.* **1.** в. до (right) up to; он шути́л в. до моме́нта ка́зни he was joking right up to the moment of his execution; мы танцева́ли в. до утра́ we danced till morning; всё живо́е исче́зло, в. до крыс every living thing had vanished, even the rats. **2.** в. (к+*d.*) right against, right up to; толпа́ подошла́ в. к воро́там the crowd came right up to the gates.

вплыва́|ть, ю, *impf. of* вплыть.

вплы|ть, ву́, вёшь, *past* ~л, ~ла́, ~ло, *pf.* (*of* ~ва́ть) to swim in; to sail in, steam in.

вповалку, *adv.* (*coll.*) side by side (*in prone position*; *only of human beings*).

вполгла́за, *adv.* (*coll.*) спать в. to sleep with one eye open.

вполго́лоса, *adv.* in an undertone, under one's breath.

вполз|а́ть, а́ю, *impf. of* ~ти́.

вполз|ти́, у́, ёшь, *past* ~, ~ла́, *pf.* (*of* ~а́ть) to creep in, crawl in; to creep up, crawl up.

вполне́, *adv.* fully, entirely; quite; э́то в. доста́точно that is quite enough; он в. знако́м с пра́вилами игры́ he is perfectly familiar with the rules of the game; он в. понима́ет, в како́й он опа́сности he is quite aware of his danger.

вполоборо́та, *adv.* half-turned; (*of a portrait, etc.*) half-face.

вполови́ну, *adv.* (*coll.*) by half; за две неде́ли коли́чество прису́тствующих уменьши́лось в. after two weeks the attendance had dropped by half.

вполпья́на́, *adv.* (*coll.*) half seas over.

впопа́д, *adv.* (*coll.*) to the point; opportunely; вы спроси́ли о́чень в. your question was very much to the point.

впопыха́х, *adv.* (*coll.*) **1.** in a hurry, hastily. **2.** in one's haste; в. я оста́вил мой зо́нтик в по́езде in my haste I left my umbrella on the train.

впо́ру, *adv.* (*coll.*) **1.** at the right time, opportunely; его́ прие́зд был о́чень в. his arrival was very opportune. **2.** just right, exactly; быть, прийти́сь в. to fit; э́тот костю́м мне соверше́нно в. this suit fits me perfectly; бе́дному да во́ру вся́кое пла́тье в. (*prov.*) beggars cannot be choosers. **3.** *as pred.* it is possible; так поступа́ть в. лишь дураку́ only a fool would behave like that; тут в. двои́м спра́виться there is enough work here for two.

впорхн|у́ть, у́, ёшь, *pf.* (*of birds or butterflies*) to flit in(to), flutter in(to); (*fig.*) to fly (into).

впосле́дствии, *adv.* subsequently; afterwards.

впотьма́х, *adv.* (*coll.*) in the dark; (*fig.*) броди́ть в. to be in the dark.

вправду, *adv.* (*coll.*) really, in reality.

впра́ве, *as pred.* быть в. (+*inf.*) to have a right (to); он был в. серди́ться на вас he had a right to be angry with you.

вправ|ить, лю, ишь, *pf.* (*of* ~ля́ть) **1.** (*med.*) to set, reduce (*fractured or dislocated bone*). **2.** to tuck in (*shirt, trousers*).

вправк|а, и, f. (*med.*) setting, reduction.

вправля́|ть, ю, *impf. of* впра́вить.

впра́во, *adv.* (от+*g.*) to the right (of).

впредь, *adv.* in future, henceforward; в. до until; в. до конца́ ме́сяца until the end of the month; в. до распоряже́ния until further notice.

впригля́дку, *adv.* (*coll., joc.*) *only in phrase* пить чай в. to have tea without sugar.

вприку́ску, *adv.* (*coll.*) *only in phrase* пить чай в. to drink unsweetened tea while holding a piece of loaf sugar in the mouth (*as opp. to* внакла́дку).

вприпры́жку, *adv.* (*coll.*) skipping; hopping.

вприси́дку, *adv.* пляса́ть в. to dance squatting.

впро́голодь, *adv.* half-starving.

впрок, *adv.* **1.** for future use; заготови́ть в. to lay in, store; to preserve, put by; загото́вить я́йца в. to put down eggs. **2.** to advantage; э́то не пойдёт ему́ в. it will not profit him, he will do no good by it; ху́до на́житое в. не идёт (*prov.*) ill-gotten wealth never thrives.

впроса́к, *adv.* (*coll.*); попа́сть в. to make a fool of oneself.

впросо́нках, *adv.* (*coll.*) half asleep.

впро́чем, *conj.* **1.** however, but; он у́мный челове́к, в. он ча́сто ошиба́ется he is a clever man, but he often makes mistakes. **2.** (*expressing indecisiveness, revision of opinion*) or rather; приезжа́йте за́втра, в. лу́чше бы́ло бы послеза́втра come tomorrow, or rather, the day after would be better.

впры́гива|ть, ю, *impf. of* впры́гнуть.

впры́г|нуть, ну, нешь, *pf.* (*of* ~ивать) (в, на+*a.*) to jump (into, on).

впры́скивани|е, я, n. injection.

впры́скива|ть, ю, *impf. of* впры́снуть.

впры́сн|уть, у, ешь, *pf.* (*of* впры́скивать) to inject.

впряга́|ть(ся), ю(сь), *impf. of* впря́чь(ся).

впрямь, *adv.* (*coll.*) really, indeed.

впря|чь, гу́, жёшь, гу́т, *past* впряг, ~гла́, ~гло́, *pf.* (*of* ~га́ть) (в+*a.*) to harness (to), put (to).

впря́|чься, гу́сь, жёшься, гу́тся, *past* впря́гся, ~гла́сь, *pf.* (*of* ~га́ться) **1.** (в+*a.*) to harness oneself (to). **2.** *pass. of* ~чь.

впуск, а, m. admission, admittance.

впуска́|ть, ю, *impf. of* впусти́ть.

впускн|ой, *adj.* admittance; inlet; ~áя трубá inlet pipe.

впýсте, *adv.* (*obs.*) fallow; лежáть в. to lie fallow.

впу|стить, щý, ~стишь, *pf.* (*of* ~скáть) to admit, let in.

впустýю, *adv.* (*coll.*) for nothing, to no purpose.

впýт|ать, аю, *pf.* (*of* ~ывать) to twist in; (*fig.*) to entangle, involve, implicate.

впýт|аться, аюсь, *pf.* (*of* ~ываться) *pass. of* ~ать; (*fig.*) to get mixed up (in).

впýтыва|ть(ся), ю(сь), *impf. of* впýтать(ся).

впу|щý, ~стишь, *see* ~стить.

впятеро, *adv.* five times; в. бóльше five times as much.

впятерóм, *adv.* five (together); в э́ту игрý мóжно игрáть в. five can play this game.

враг, á, *m.* **1.** enemy; (*collect.*) the enemy. **2.** (*obs.*) the Fiend, the Devil.

вражд|á, ы́, *f.* enmity, hostility.

враждéб|ный (~ен, ~на), *adj.* hostile.

вражд|овáть, ýю, *impf.* (с+*i.* *and* мéжду собóю) to be at enmity, at odds (with).

врáжеский, *adj.* (*mil.*) enemy.

врáж|ий, *adj.* (*folk poet.*) enemy; hostile; ~ья сила (*obs.*) Satan, the Devil.

враз, *adv.* (*coll.*) all together, simultaneously.

вразби́вку, *adv.* (*coll.*) at random.

вразбрóд, *adv.* (*coll.*) separately; in disunity.

вразбрóс, *adv.* (*coll.*) separately; сéять в. (*agric.*) to sow broadcast.

вразвáлку, *adv.* (*coll.*) ходи́ть в. to waddle.

вразнóс, *adv.* (*coll.*) торговáть в. to peddle.

вразрéз, *adv.*, *only in phrase* идти́ в. (с+*i.*) to go against; э́то идёт в. с мои́ми интерéсами it goes against my own interests.

вразря́дку, *adv.* (*typ.*) набрáть в. to space.

вразуми́тел|ьный (~ен, ~ьна), *adj.* **1.** intelligible; perspicuous. **2.** instructive.

вразум|и́ть, лю́, и́шь, *pf.* (*of* ~лять) to teach, make understand; ничéм их не ~и́шь they will never learn.

вразумля́|ть, ю, *impf. of* вразуми́ть.

врáк|и, ~, *no sing.* (*coll.*) nonsense, rubbish.

врал|ь, я́, *m.* (*coll.*) liar; chatterbox.

врань|ё, я́, *n.* (*coll.*) lies; nonsense.

врасплóх, *adv.* unexpectedly, unaware; застáть, захвати́ть, засти́гнуть в. to take unawares.

врассыпнýю, *adv.* in all directions; helter-skelter.

врастáни|е, я, *n.* growing in.

враст|áть, áю, *impf.* (*of* ~и́) to grow in(to); ~áющий нóготь ingrowing nail.

враст|и́, ý, ёшь, *past* врос, вросла́, *pf. of* ~áть.

врастя́жку, *adv.* (*coll.*) **1.** at full length; упáсть в. to fall flat. **2.** говори́ть в. to drawl.

врат|á, ~, *no sing.* (*poet.*, *obs.*) = ворóта.

вратáр|ь, я́, *m.* **1.** (*sport*) goalkeeper. **2.** (*obs.*) gate-keeper.

вр|ать, у, ёшь, *past* ~ал, ~ала́, ~áло, *impf.* (*of* на~ *and* со~) (*coll.*) **1.** to lie, tell lies. **2.** to talk nonsense.

врач, á, *m.* doctor, physician; зубнóй в. dentist.

врачéбный, *adj.* medical.

врач|евáть, ýю, *impf.* (*of* у~) (*obs.*) to doctor, treat; (*fig.*) to heal.

вращáтельный, *adj.* rotary.

вращá|ть, ю, *impf.* to revolve, rotate; в. глазáми to roll one's eyes.

вращá|ться, юсь, *impf.* to revolve, rotate (*intrans.*); он ~ется в худóжественных кругáх he moves in artistic circles.

вращéни|е, я, *n.* rotation; revolution.

вред, á, *no pl.*, *m.* harm, hurt, injury; damage; без ~á (для+*g.*) without detriment (to).

вреди́тел|ь, я, *m.* **1.** (*agric.*) pest; vermin. **2.** (*polit.*) wrecker, saboteur.

вреди́тель|ский, *adj. of* ~ 2.

вреди́тельств|о, а, *n.* **1.** wrecking, sabotage. **2.** act of sabotage.

вре|ди́ть, жý, ди́шь, *impf.* (*of* по~) (+*d.*) to injure, harm, hurt; в. здорóвью to be injurious to health.

врéдно, *adv. as pred.* it is harmful, it is injurious; в. для торгóвли it is bad for trade.

врéд|ный (~ен, ~на́, ~но), *adj.* harmful, injurious; unhealthy.

врé|жу(сь), жешь(ся), *see* ~зать(ся).

вре|жý, ди́шь, *see* ~ди́ть.

врé|зать, жу, жешь, *pf.* (*of* ~зáть) to cut in; to set in, socket.

врез|áть, áю, *impf. of* ~ать.

врé|заться, жусь, жешься, *pf.* (*of* ~зáться) (в+*a.*) **1.** to cut (into); to force one's way (into); в. в зéмлю to dig into the ground; в. в толпý to run into a crowd. **2.** to be engraved (on); черты́ её лица́ ~зались в егó па́мять her features were engraved on his memory. **3.** (*pf. only*) (*coll.*) to fall in love (with).

врез|áться, áюсь, *impf. of* ~áться.

врéзыва|ть(ся), ю(сь), *impf.* = врезáть(ся).

временáми, *adv.* at times, now and then, now and again.

временни́к, á, *m.* chronicle, annals.

временнóй, *adj.* **1.** (*philos.*) temporal. **2.** (*gram.*) tense. **3.** (*tech.*) time.

врéменн|ый, *adj.* temporary; provisional; В~ое прави́тельство (*hist.*) the Provisional Government (*of Russia, March–November 1917*).

временщи́к, á, *m.* (*hist.*) favourite (*enjoying position of trust or power*).

врéм|я, ени, енем, ени, *pl.* ~енá, ~ён,

~енам, n. 1. time; times; во в. оно (arch. or joc.) in the old days; в данное в. at present, at the present moment; в мирное в. in peace-time; (в) первое в. at first; (в) последнее в. lately, of late; в своё в. (i) (in ref. to past) in one's time, once, at one time, (ii) (in ref. to future) in due course; in one's own time; в скором ~ени in the near future, shortly, before long; в то же (самое) в. at the same time, on the other hand; до ~ени for the time being; за последнее в. lately, of late; на в. for a while; на первое в. for the initial period, initially; по средне-европейскому ~ени by Central European time; с незапамятных ~ён from time immemorial, time out of mind; с течением ~ени in the course of time; всё в. all the time, continually; раньше ~ени prematurely; самое в. (+inf. or +d.; coll.) just the time (to, for); the (right) time (to, for); апрель — самое в. побывать в Париже April is the (right) time to be in Paris; теперь — самое в. сливам now is the time for plums; сколько ~ени? what is the time?; тем ~енем meanwhile. 2. в. года season. 3. (gram.) tense. 4. в то в. как while, whereas.

времяисчислени|е, я, n. calendar (system of reckoning time).

времянк|а, и, f. (coll.) small stove.

времяпрепровождение, я, n. way of spending one's time.

вретищ|е, а, n. (obs.) sackcloth.

врид, а, m. (abbr. of временно исполняющий должность) acting (director, manager, etc.).

вровень, adv. (с+i.) level (with); в. с краями to the brim.

вроде 1. prep.+g. like; у него есть галстук в. моего he has a tie like mine; нечто в. (coll.) a sort of, a kind of; оркестр начал играть нечто в. фокстрота the band began to play some sort of foxtrot. **2.** particle such as, like; весь его разговор состоит из односложных слов. «да» и «нет» his entire conversation consists of monosyllables such as 'yes' and 'no'.

врождён|ный (~, ~а), adj. innate; congenital.

врознь, adv. (obs.) = врозь.

врозь, adv. separately, apart.

врó|ю(сь), ~ешь(ся), see врыть(ся).

вруб, а, m. (mining) cut.

вруб|ать(ся), аю(сь), impf. of ~ить(ся).

вруб|ить, лю, ~ишь, pf. (of ~ать) to cut in(to).

вруб|иться, люсь, ~ишься, pf. (of ~аться) (в+a.) to cut one's way (into), hack one's way (through).

врубов|ый, adj. ~ая машина coal-cutter.

врукопашную, adv. hand to hand; схватиться в. to come to grips.

врун, á, m. (coll.) liar.

врунь|я, и, f. of врун.

вруч|ать, аю, impf. of ~ить.

вручéни|е, я, n. handing, delivery; в. солдату медали investiture of a soldier with a medal; (leg.) service (of summons, etc.).

вруч|ить, ý, ишь, pf. (of ~ать) to hand, deliver; to entrust; в. судебную повестку to serve a subpoena.

вручител|ь, я, m. bearer (of message, writ, etc.).

вручную, adv. by hand.

врыва|ть, ю, impf. of врыть.

врыва|ться¹, юсь, impf. of врыться.

врыва|ться², юсь, impf. of ворваться.

вр|ыть, óю, óешь, pf. (of ~ывать) to dig in(to), bury (in).

вр|ыться, óюсь, óешься, pf. (of ~ываться¹) to dig oneself (into), bury oneself (in).

вряд (ли), adv. (coll.) hardly, scarcely (expressing doubt); в. ли стоит it is hardly worth it; в. ли они уже придут they will scarcely come now.

вса|дить, жý, ~дишь, pf. (of ~живать) **1.** to thrust, plunge (into); в. нож в спину (+d.) to stab in the back (also fig.); в. пулю в лоб кому-н. to put a bullet in someone's brains. **2.** (coll.) to put, sink (into); он ~дил весь свой капитал в одно рискованное предприятие he has sunk all his capital in one doubtful venture.

всадник, а, m. **1.** rider, horseman. **2.** (hist.) knight.

всадниц|а, ы, f. horsewoman.

всажива|ть, ю, impf. of всадить.

вса|жý, ~дишь, see ~дить.

всасывани|е, я, n. suction; absorption.

всасыва|ть(ся), ю(сь), impf. of всосать(ся).

все- all-, omni-, pan-.

всё 1. pron., see весь. **2.** adv. always; all the time; он в. отвечает одно и то же he always gives the same answer; он в. ругается he swears all the time. **3.** (ещё) still; дождь в. (ещё) идёт it is still raining; дождь в. (ещё) шёл it kept on raining. **4.** (coll.) only, all; он провалился на экзамене,— в. из-за тебя! he has failed his examination—all because of you! **5.** as conj. however, nevertheless; как ни стараюсь, в. не разбираю, что он говорит however hard I try, I cannot make out what he says. **6.** as particle (strengthening comparative) в. более и более more and more; он в. толстеет he is becoming fatter and fatter.

всеведени|е, я, n. omniscience.

всеведущий, adj. omniscient.

всевидящий, adj. all-seeing.

всевласти|е, я, n. absolute power.

всевла́стный, *adj.* all-powerful.

всево́буч, а, *m.* (*abbr. of* всео́бщее вое́нное обуче́ние) universal military training.

всевозмо́жный, *adj.* various; all kinds of; every possible; в. това́р goods of all kinds.

всево́лновый, *adj.* (*radio*) all-wave.

всевы́шний, *adj.* (*rel.*) the Most High (*also as noun*).

всегда́, *adv.* always; как в. as ever.

всегда́шний, *adj.* usual, customary, wonted.

всего́, *adv.* **1.** in all, all told; в. упла́чено две ты́сячи рубле́й in all two thousand roubles has been paid. **2.** only; в.-на́всего all in all; нас бы́ло в. пя́теро there were only five of us; в. ничего́ (*coll.*) practically nothing; то́лько и в. (*coll.*) that's all.

вседержи́тел|ь, я, *m.* (*rel.*) the Almighty.

вседне́вный, *adj.* (*obs.*) daily, everyday.

всезна́йк|а, и, *m. and f.* (*coll., iron.*) know-all.

всезна́йств|о, а, *n.* (*coll., iron.*) knowingness; behaviour of a know-all.

вселе́ни|е, я, *n.* installation, quartering; moving in.

вселе́нн|ая, ой, *no pl., f.* universe.

вселе́нский, *adj.* universal; (*eccl.*) ecumenical; в. собо́р ecumenical council.

всел|и́ть, ю́, и́шь, *pf.* (*of* ~я́ть) **1.** to install, quarter (in). **2.** (*fig., rhet.*) to inspire (in); в. страх (в+*a.*) to strike fear (into).

всел|и́ться, ю́сь, и́шься, *pf.* (*of* ~я́ться) (в+*a.*) **1.** to move in(to). **2.** (*fig.*) to be implanted (in); to seize.

вселя́|ть(ся), ю(сь), *impf. of* всели́ть(ся).

всеме́рный, *adj.* utmost, with all the means at one's disposal.

все́меро, *adv.* seven times.

всемеро́м, *adv.* seven (together).

всеми́лостивейший, *adj.* (*hist.*) most gracious.

всеми́рный, *adj.* world; world-wide.

всемогу́ществ|о, а, *n.* omnipotence.

всемогу́щ|ий (~, ~а), *adj.* omnipotent, all--powerful; (*of God*) Almighty.

всенаро́дн|ый, *adj.* national; nation-wide; ~ая пе́репись general census.

всенаро́дно, *adv.* **1.** throughout the nation. **2.** publicly.

всенижа́йший, *adj.* most humble.

всено́щн|ая, ой, *f.* (*eccl.*) night service (*vespers and matins*).

всео́буч, а, *m.* (*abbr. of* всео́бщее обуче́ние) universal education.

всео́бщ|ий, *adj.* general; universal; ~ая во́инская пови́нность universal military service; ~ая забасто́вка general strike.

всеобъе́млющ|ий (~, ~а), *adj.* all-embracing, comprehensive.

всеору́жи|е, я, *n. only in phrase* во ~и fully armed; во ~и све́дений in full possession of the facts.

всепоглоща́ющий, *adj.* all-consuming (*also fig.*).

всепо́дданейш|ий, *adj.* (*obs.*) loyal, humble; ~ее проше́ние humble petition.

всепожира́ющий, *adj.* all-consuming.

всеросси́йский, *adj.* All-Russian.

всерьёз, *adv.* seriously, in earnest.

всеси́л|ьный (~ен, ~ьна), *adj.* all-powerful.

всеславя́нский, *adj.* pan-Slav(ic).

всесожже́ни|е, я, *n.* holocaust.

всесосло́вный, *adj.* of all classes.

всесою́зный, *adj.* All-Union (*esp. in designations of institutions, associations, etc., as opp. to those of individual republics of the Soviet Union*).

всесторо́нний, *adj.* all-round; thorough, detailed.

всё-таки, *conj. and particle* for all that, still, all the same.

всеуслы́шани|е, я, *n. only in phrase* во в. publicly, for all to hear; объяви́ть во в. to announce publicly.

всецело́, *adv.* completely; exclusively.

всеча́сный, *adj.* (*obs.*) hourly.

всея́дный, *adj.* omnivorous.

вска́кива|ть, ю, *impf. of* вскочи́ть.

вска́пыва|ть, ю, *impf. of* вскопа́ть.

вскара́бк|аться, аюсь, *pf.* (*of* кара́бкаться *and* ~иваться) (на+*a.*; *coll.*) to scramble (up, on to), clamber (up, on to).

вскара́бкива|ться, юсь, *impf. of* вскара́бкаться.

вска́рмлива|ть, ю, *impf. of* вскорми́ть.

вскачь, *adv.* at a gallop.

вски́дыва|ть(ся), ю(сь), *impf. of* вски́нуть(ся).

вски́|нуть, ну, нешь, *pf.* (*of* ~дывать) to throw up; в. на пле́чи to shoulder; в. глаза́ми to look up suddenly.

вски́|нуться, нусь, нешься, *pf.* (*of* ~дываться) (на+*a.*; *coll.*) **1.** to leap up (on to). **2.** (*fig.*) to turn (on), go (for).

вскипа́|ть, ю, *impf. of* вскипе́ть.

вскип|е́ть, лю́, и́шь, *pf.* (*of* ~а́ть) **1.** to boil up. **2.** (*fig.*) to flare up, fly into a rage; в. негодова́нием to flare with indignation.

вскипя|ти́ть, чу́, ти́шь, *pf. of* кипяти́ть.

вскипя|ти́ться, чу́сь, ти́шься, *pf.* **1.** *pass. of* вскипяти́ть **2.** (*coll.*) to flare up, fly into a rage.

всклоко́чен|ный (~, ~а), *p.p.p. of* всклоко́чить *and adj.* (*coll.*) dishevelled, tousled.

всклоко́чива|ть, ю, *impf. of* всклоко́чить.

всклоко́ч|ить, у, ишь, *pf.* (*of* ~ивать) (*coll.*) to dishevel, tousle.

всклочива|ть, ю, *impf. of* всклочить.

всклоч|ить, у, ишь, *pf.* (*of* ~ивать) (*coll.*) to dishevel, tousle.

всколыхн|у́ть, у́, ёшь, *pf.* to stir; to rock; (*fig.*) to stir up.

вско́лыхн|у́ться, у́сь, ёшься, *pf.* to rock (*intrans.*); (*fig.*) to be roused.

вско́льзь, *adv.* slightly; in passing; упомяну́ть в. to mention in passing.

вскопа́|ть, ю, *pf.* (*of* вска́пывать) to dig up.

вско́ре, *adv.* soon, shortly after.

вскорм|и́ть, лю́, ⌐ишь, *pf.* (*of* вска́рмливать) to rear.

вскоч|и́ть, у́, ⌐ишь, *pf.* (*of* вска́кивать) 1. (в, на+*a.*, с+*g.*) to leap up (into, on to; from). 2. (*coll.*) to come up (*of bumps, boils, etc.*). 3. в. (в копе́ечку) (+*d.*; *coll.*) to cost dear.

вскри́кива|ть, ю, *impf. of* вскри́кнуть.

вскри́к|нуть, ну, нешь, *pf.* (*of* ⌐ивать) to cry out.

вскрич|а́ть, у́, и́шь, *pf.* to exclaim.

вскро́|ю, ешь, *see* вскрыть.

вскруж|и́ть, у́, ⌐и́шь, *pf.* only in phrase в. го́лову кому́-н. to turn someone's head.

вскрыва́|ть(ся), ю(сь), *impf. of* вскры́ть(ся).

вскры́ти|е, я, *n.* 1. opening, unsealing. 2. (*fig.*) revelation, disclosure. 3. (*geogr.*) opening (*of rivers after break-up of ice*). 4. (*med.*) lancing. 5. (*med.*) dissection; post-mortem (examination).

вскр|ы́ть, о́ю, о́ешь, *pf.* (*of* ⌐ыва́ть) 1. to open, unseal. 2. (*fig.*) to reveal, disclose; в. ко́зыря (*cards*) to turn up a trump. 3. (*med.*) to lance, open. 4. (*med.*) to dissect.

вскр|ы́ться, о́юсь, о́ешься, *pf.* (*of* ⌐ыва́ться) 1. to come to light, be revealed. 2. (*geogr.*) to become clear (of ice; *of rivers*); become open. 3. (*med.*) to break, burst.

всласть, *adv.* (*coll.*) to one's heart's content.

вслед 1. *adv.* (за+*i.*) after; посла́ть письмо́ в. to forward a letter. 2. *prep.*+*d.* after; смотре́ть в. to follow with one's eyes.

всле́дствие, *prep.*+*g.* in consequence of, owing to; в. дождя́ па́ртия в те́ннис не состоя́лась owing to the rain the game of tennis did not take place.

вслепу́ю, *adv.* 1. blindly. 2. blindfold.

вслух, *adv.* aloud.

вслу́ш|аться, аюсь, *pf.* (*of* ⌐иваться) (в+*a.*) to listen attentively (to).

вслу́шива|ться, юсь, *impf. of* вслу́шаться.

всма́трива|ться, юсь, *impf. of* всмотре́ться.

всмотр|е́ться, ю́сь, ⌐ишься, *pf.* (*of* всма́триваться) (в+*a.*) to peer (at); to scrutinize.

всмя́тку, *adv.* яйцо́ в. soft-boiled, lightly-boiled egg; сапоги́ в. (*coll.*) nonsense; все его́ мы́сли — про́сто сапоги́ в. all his ideas are quite half-baked.

вс|ова́ть, ую́, уёшь, *pf.* (*of* ⌐о́вывать) (*coll.*) to put in, stick in; to slip in.

всо́выва|ть, ю, *impf. of* всова́ть *and* всу́нуть.

всос|а́ть, у́, ёшь, *pf.* (*of* вса́сывать) to suck in; (*fig.*) to absorb, imbibe; в. с молоко́м

ма́тери to imbibe with one's mother's milk.

всос|а́ться, у́сь, ёшься, *pf.* (*of* вса́сываться) (в+*a.*) 1. to fasten upon (*with mouth, lips, etc.*). 2. to soak through (into).

вспа́ива|ть, ю, *impf. of* вспои́ть.

вспа́рива|ть, ю, *impf. of* вспа́рить.

вспа́р|ить, ю, ишь, *pf.* (*of* ⌐ивать) 1. (*dial.*) to steam. 2. (*coll.*) to put into a sweat. 3. (*coll.*) to thrash.

вспа́рхива|ть, ю, *i mpf. of* вспорхну́ть.

вспа́рыва|ть, ю, *impf. of* вспоро́ть.

вспа|сть, ду́, дёшь, *past* ⌐л, *pf.* (*obs.*) *only in phrases* в. на ум, на мысль (+*d.*) to occur to one.

вспа|ха́ть, шу́, ⌐шешь, *pf.* (*of* ⌐хивать) to plough up.

вспа́хива|ть, ю, *impf. of* вспаха́ть.

вспа́шк|а, и, *f.* ploughing.

вспашу́, ⌐ешь, *see* вспаха́ть.

вспе́нива|ть(ся), ю(сь), *impf. of* вспе́нить(ся).

вспе́н|ить, ю, ишь, *pf.* (*of* ⌐ивать) to make foam, make froth, make lather; в. коня́ to get one's horse into a lather.

вспе́н|иться, юсь, ишься, *pf.* (*of* ⌐иваться) to froth; to lather (*intrans.*).

вспетуш|и́ться, у́сь, и́шься, *pf. of* петуши́ться.

вспла́кн|у́ть, у́, ёшь, *pf.* to shed a few tears, have a little cry.

всплеск, а, *m.* splash.

вспле́скива|ть, ю, *impf. of* всплесну́ть.

всплес|ну́ть, ну́, нёшь, *pf.* (*of* ⌐кивать) to splash; в. рука́ми to clasp one's hands (*under stress of emotion*).

всплыва́|ть, ю, *impf. of* всплы́ть.

всплы|ть, ву́, вёшь, *past* ⌐л, ⌐ла́, ⌐ло, *pf.* (*of* ⌐ва́ть) to rise to the surface, surface; (*fig.*) to come to light, be revealed; ⌐ли но́вые све́дения об обстоя́тельствах уби́йства new evidence has come to light about the circumstances of the murder; э́тот вопро́с ⌐вёт вероя́тно на сле́дующем собра́нии this question will probably come up at the next meeting.

вспо|и́ть, ю́, и́шь, *pf.* (*of* вспа́ивать) to nurse; to rear в.-вскорми́ть (*fig., coll.*) to bring up.

вспола́скива|ть, ю, *impf. of* всполосну́ть.

всполосн|у́ть, у́, ёшь, *pf.* (*of* всполаскивать) to rinse.

вспо́лох, а, *m.* (*obs.*) alarm.

вспо́лох|и, ов, *no sing.* 1. (flashes of) summer lightning; (*collect.*) flashes, glow (*from fire, explosion, etc.*). 2. (*dial.*) Northern lights.

всполош|и́ть, у́, и́шь, *pf.* (*of* полоши́ть) (*coll.*) to rouse; to alarm.

всполош|и́ться, у́сь, и́шься, *pf.* (*of* полоши́ться) (*coll.*) to take alarm.

вспомина́|ть(ся), ю(сь), *impf. of* вспо́м-
нить(ся).

вспо́м|нить, ню, нишь, *pf.* (*of* ~ина́ть) to
remember, recall, recollect.

вспо́м|ниться¹, нюсь, нишься, *pf.* (*of* ~и-
на́ться) (*impers.*+*d.*) мне, *etc.*, ~ни́лось I,
etc., remembered.

вспо́мн|иться², юсь, ишься, *pf.* (*obs.*) to
collect oneself.

вспомога́тельный, *adj.* auxiliary; sub-
sidiary, branch; в. глаго́л (*gram.*) auxiliary
verb.

вспомоществова́ни|е, я, *n.* (*obs.*) relief,
assistance.

вспомян|у́ть, у́, ~ешь, *pf.* (+*a.* or o+*p.*;
coll.) to remember.

вспор|о́ть, ю́, ~ешь, *pf.* (*of* вспа́рывать)
(*coll.*) to rip open.

вспорхн|у́ть, у́, ёшь, *pf.* to take wing.

вспоте́|ть, ю, *pf.* (*of* поте́ть) to come out in
a sweat; to mist over (*of spectacles, etc.*).

вспры́гива|ть, ю, *impf. of* вспры́гнуть.

вспры́г|нуть, ну, нешь, *pf.* (*of* ~ивать)
(на+*a.*) to jump up (on to), spring up (on
to).

вспры́скивани|е, я, *n.* (*med.*) injection.

вспры́скива|ть, ю, *impf. of* вспры́снуть.

вспры́с|нуть, ну, нешь, *pf.* (*of* ~кивать)
1. to sprinkle; (*fig., coll.*) to celebrate; в.
сде́лку to wet a bargain. **2.** (*med.*) to
inject.

вспу́гива|ть, ю, *impf. of* вспугну́ть.

вспуг|ну́ть, ну́, нёшь, *pf.* (*of* ~ивать) to
scare away; to put up (*birds*).

вспух|а́ть, а́ю, *impf. of* ~нуть.

вспу́х|нуть, ну, нешь, *pf.* (*of* ~а́ть) to swell
up.

вспу́чива|ть, ю, *impf. of* вспу́чить.

вспу́ч|ить, у, ишь, *pf.* (*of* ~ивать) (*usu.*
impers.) to distend; у него́ живо́т ~ило his
abdomen is distended.

вспыл|и́ть, ю́, и́шь, *pf.* to flare up; в.
(на+*a.*) to fly into a rage (with).

вспы́льчив|ый (~, ~а), *adj.* hot-tempered;
irascible.

вспы́хива|ть, ю, *impf. of* вспы́хнуть.

вспы́х|нуть, ну, нешь, (*of* ~ивать) **1.** to
burst into flame, blaze up; to flash out;
(*fig.*) to flare up; to break out; на грани́це
~нули бои́ fighting flared up on the frontier. **2.** to blush.

вспы́шк|а, и, *f.* flash; (*fig.*) outburst, burst;
outbreak (*of epidemic, etc.*).

вспять, *adv.* (*obs.*) back(wards).

встава́ни|е, я, *n.* rising; почти́ть ~ем to
stand in honour (of).

встава́|ть, ю́, ёшь, *impf. of* ~ть.

вста́в|ить, лю, ишь, *pf.* (*of* ~ля́ть) to put in,
insert; в. в ра́му to frame; в. себе́ зу́бы to
have a set of (false) teeth made; в. шпо́ны

(*typ.*) to interline; в. перо́ (+*d.*; *obs., vulg.*)
to give the sack, give the boot.

вста́вк|а, и, *f.* **1.** fixing, insertion; framing,
mounting. **2.** inset. **3.** interpolation.

вставля́|ть, ю, *impf. of* вста́вить.

вставн|о́й, *adj.* inserted; ~ы́е зу́бы false
teeth; ~ы́е ра́мы double window-frames.

встарь, *adv.* of old, in olden time(s).

вста́скива|ть, ю, *impf. of* встащи́ть.

вста|ть, ну, нешь, *pf.* (*of* ~ва́ть) **1.** to get
up, rise; to stand up; он ра́но ~л сего́дня
у́тром he got up early this morning; он
вчера́ ~л впервы́е со дня несча́стного
слу́чая he got up yesterday for the first
time since his accident; в. с ле́вой ноги́ to
get out of bed on the wrong side; в. из-за
стола́ to rise from table; (*fig.*) в. на свои́
но́ги to stand on one's own feet; в. гру́дью
за (+*a.*) to stand up for. **2.** to stand; в. на
рабо́ту to start work. **3.** (в+*a.*) to go (into),
fit (into); большо́й шкаф не ~нет в э́ту
ко́мнату the large cupboard will not go
into this room. **4.** (*fig.*) to arise, come up;
тот же са́мый вопро́с ~л на про́шлом
собра́нии the same question arose at the
last meeting. **5.** (*coll.*) to get out, get off
(*means of conveyance*).

встащ|и́ть, у́, ~ишь, *pf.* (*of* встаскивать)
(*coll.*) to pull up.

встрева́|ть, ю, *impf. of* встрять.

встрево́жен|ный (~, ~на), *p.p.p. of* встре-
во́жить *and adj.* anxious.

встрево́ж|ить, у, ишь, *pf. of* трево́жить.

встрёпанный, *p.p.p. and adj.* (*coll.*) dishevelled; как в. full of beans.

встреп|а́ть, лю́, ~лешь, *pf.* (*of* ~ывать)
(*coll.*) to dishevel.

встрепен|у́ться, у́сь, ёшься, *pf.* **1.** to rouse
oneself, start (up). **2.** to begin to beat
faster (*of heart*).

встрёпк|а, и, *f.* (*coll.*) **1.** scolding. **2.** shock.

встрёпыва|ть, ю, *impf. of* встрепа́ть.

встре́|тить, чу, тишь, *pf.* (*of* ~ча́ть) **1.** to
meet (with), encounter; в. сопротивле́ние
to encounter resistance. **2.** to greet, receive;
в. аплодисме́нтами to greet with cheers;
в. Но́вый год to see the New Year in.

встре́|титься, чусь, тишься, *pf.* (*of* ~ча́ться)
(c+*i.*) **1.** to meet (with), encounter, come
across; в. с затрудне́ниями to encounter
difficulties. **2.** to be found, occur.

встре́ч|а, и, *f.* **1.** meeting, encounter; recep-
tion; в. Но́вого го́да New Year's Eve party.
2. (*sport*) match, meeting.

встреча́|ть, ю, *impf. of* встре́тить.

встреча́|ться, юсь, ишься, *impf.* **1.** *impf. of* встре́-
титься. **2.** *impf. only* to be found, be met
with; в Шотла́ндии ещё ~ются ди́кие
ко́шки wild cats are still to be found in
Scotland.

встре́чный, adj. **1.** proceeding from opposite direction; в. ве́тер head wind; as noun пе́рвый в. the first person you meet, anyone; (ка́ждый) в. и попере́чный every Tom, Dick, and Harry. **2.** counter; в. иск (leg.) counter-claim; в. план counter-plan; в. бой (mil.) encounter battle; (naut.) action on opposite courses.

вструхн|у́ть, у́, ёшь, pf. (coll.) to be alarmed.

встря́ск|а, и, f. (coll.) **1.** shaking; он получи́л си́льную ~y he has been badly shaken up, he has received a severe shock. **2.** real telling off.

встря́|ть, ну, нешь, pf. (of встрева́ть) (в+a.; coll.) to get mixed up (in).

встря́хива|ть(ся), ю(сь), impf. of встряхну́ть(ся).

встря́х|ну́ть, ну́, нёшь, pf. (of ~ивать) to shake; (fig.) to shake up, rouse.

встря́х|ну́ться, ну́сь, нёшься, pf. (of ~иваться) **1.** to shake oneself. **2.** (fig.) to rouse oneself; to cheer up; ~ни́тесь! pull yourself together! **3.** (coll.) to have a fling.

вступа́|ть(ся), ю(сь), impf. of вступи́ть(ся).

вступи́тельн|ый, adj. introductory; в. взнос entrance fee; ~ая ле́кция inaugural lecture.

вступ|и́ть, лю́, ~ишь, pf. (of ~а́ть) **1.** (в+a.) to enter (into), join (in); в. в бой to join battle; в. в де́йствие to come into force; в. в брак to marry; в. в свои́ права́ to come into one's own. **2.** (на+a.) to mount, go up; в. на престо́л to ascend the throne.

вступ|и́ться, лю́сь, ~ишься, pf. (of ~а́ться) **1.** (за+a.) to stand up (for), take (someone's) part. **2.** (coll.) to intervene.

вступле́ни|е, я, n. **1.** entry, joining. **2.** prelude, opening, introduction, preamble.

всу́е, adv. (obs.) in vain; призва́ть в. и́мя Бо́жье to take the name of God in vain.

всу́н|уть, у, ешь, pf. (of всо́вывать) to stick in; to slip in.

всухомя́тку, adv. (coll.) есть в. to live on, eat cold food without liquids.

всу́чива|ть, ю, impf. of всучи́ть.

всуч|и́ть, у́, ~ишь, pf. (of ~ивать) **1.** to entwine. **2.** (+d.; fig., coll., pejor.) to foist (on), palm off (on).

всхли́п|нуть, ну, нешь, pf. (of ~ывать) to sob.

всхли́пыванъ|е, я, n. sobbing; sobs.

всхли́пыва|ть, ю, impf. of всхли́пнуть.

всхо|ди́ть, жу́, ~дишь, impf. of взойти́.

всхо́д|ы, ов, no sing. (corn-)shoots.

всхо́жест|ь, и, f. (agric.) germinating capacity.

всхо́жий, adj. (agric.) capable of germinating.

всхрап|ну́ть, ну́, нёшь, pf. **1.** pf. of ~ывать. **2.** (coll.) to have a nap.

всхра́пыва|ть, ю, impf. (of всхрапну́ть) to snore; to snort (of a horse).

всы́п|ать, лю, лешь, pf. (of ~а́ть) **1.** (в+a.) to pour (into). **2.** (+d.; coll.) to swear at; to beat; в. по пе́рвое число́ to knock into the middle of next week.

всыпа́|ть, ю, impf. of всы́пать.

всы́пк|а, и, f. rating; beating, drubbing.

всю́ду, adv. everywhere.

вся, see весь[1].

всяк, short form (obs.) of ~ий; as pron. (obs.) everyone.

вся́к|ий, adj. **1.** any; без ~ого сомне́ния beyond any doubt; во ~ом слу́чае in any case, at any rate; as pron. anyone. **2.** all sorts of; every; на в. слу́чай against every eventuality; to be on the safe side; тут мно́го ~их моше́нников here are all sorts of rogues.

вся́чески, adv. (coll.) in every way possible; в. стара́ться to try one's hardest, try all ways.

вся́ческ|ий, adj. (coll.) all kinds of; все и ~ие уло́вки every sort and kind of trick.

вся́чин|а, ы, f. (coll.) вся́кая в. all kinds of things; odds and ends.

вся́чинк|а, и, f. (coll.) жить со ~ой to have one's ups and downs.

втайне, adv. secretly, in secret.

вта́лкива|ть, ю, impf. of втолкну́ть.

вта́птыва|ть, ю, impf. of втопта́ть.

вта́скива|ть(ся), ю(сь), impf. of втащи́ть(ся).

втач|а́ть, а́ю, pf. (of ~ивать) (в+a.) to stitch in(to).

вта́чива|ть, ю, impf. of втача́ть.

вта́чк|а, и, f. **1.** stitching in. **2.** patch.

втащ|и́ть, у́, ~ишь, pf. (of вта́скивать) (в+a., на+a.) to drag (into, on to).

втащ|и́ться, у́сь, ~ишься, pf. (of вта́скиваться) (coll.) to drag oneself.

втека́|ть, ю, impf. of втечь.

втёмную, adv. without seeing one's cards; (fig.) blindly, in the dark; де́йствовать в. to take a leap in the dark.

втемя́ш|ить, у, ишь, pf. (+d.; coll.) to impress (upon); в. что-н. кому́-н. в башку́ to get something into someone's skull.

втемя́ш|иться, усь, ишься, pf. (+d.; coll.) to get into one's head.

втер|е́ть, вотру́, вотрёшь, past ~, ~ла, pf. (of втира́ть) (в+a.) to rub in(to); в. очки́ кому́-н. (fig., coll.) to bluff, pull the wool over someone's eyes.

втер|е́ться, вотру́сь, вотрёшься, past ~ся, ~ла́сь, pf. (of втира́ться) **1.** (в+a.; coll.) to insinuate oneself, worm oneself into; ему́ удало́сь в. в дове́рие к премье́р-мини́стру he succeeded in worming his way into the confidence of the Prime Minister. **2.** to sink in(to), soak in(to).

вте|са́ться, шу́сь, ~шешься, *pf.* (*of* ~сыва́ться) (в+*a.*; *coll.*) to insinuate oneself in(to), brazen one's way in(to).

втёсыва|ться, юсь, *impf.* *of* втеса́ться.

вте|чь, ку́, чёшь, ку́т, *past* ~к, ~кла́, *pf.* (*of* ~ка́ть) to flow in(to).

втира́ни|е, я, *n.* 1. rubbing in. 2. embrocation, liniment.

втира́|ть(ся), ю(сь), *impf.* *of* втере́ть(ся).

вти́скива|ть(ся), ю(сь), *impf.* *of* вти́снуть(ся).

вти́с|нуть, ну, нешь, *pf.* (*of* ~кивать) (в+*a.*) to squeeze in(to).

вти́с|нуться, нусь, нешься, *pf.* (*of* ~киваться) (*coll.*) to squeeze (oneself) in(to).

втихомо́лку, *adv.* (*coll.*) surreptitiously; on the quiet, on the sly.

втих|у́ю, *adv.* (*coll.*) = ~омо́лку.

втолкн|у́ть, у́, ёшь, *pf.* (*of* вта́лкивать) (в+*a.*) to push in(to), shove in(to).

втолк|ова́ть, у́ю, *pf.* (*of* ~о́вывать) (+*d.*; *coll.*) to din (into), ram (into).

втолко́выва|ть, ю, *impf.* *of* втолкова́ть.

втоп|та́ть, чу́, ~чешь, *pf.* (*of* вта́птывать) to trample in; в. в грязь (*fig.*) to drag in the mire.

вто́р|а, ы, *f.* (*mus.*) second voice; second violin.

вторачива|ть, ю, *impf.* *of* второчи́ть.

вторг|а́ться, а́юсь, *impf.* *of* ~нуться.

вто́рг|нуться, нусь, нешься, *past* ~ся, ~лась, *pf.* (*of* ~а́ться) (в+*a.*) to invade; to encroach (upon), trespass (on), intrude (in); (*also fig.*).

вторже́ни|е, я, *n.* invasion; intrusion.

вто́р|ить, ю, ишь, *impf.* (+*d.*) 1. (*mus.*) to play, sing second part (to). 2. (*fig., pejor.*) to echo, repeat; он про́сто ~ит отцо́вским мне́ниям he simply echoes his father's opinions.

втори́чн|ый, *adj.* 1. second; ~ое предупрежде́ние second warning. 2. secondary; ~ые половы́е при́знаки secondary sexual characteristics.

вто́рник, а, *m.* Tuesday.

вто́рни|чный, *adj.* *of* ~к.

второбра́чный, *adj.* (*obs.*) (born) of second marriage.

второго́дник, а, *m.* pupil remaining in same form for second year.

Второзако́ни|е, я, *n.* (*bibl.*) Deuteronomy.

втор|о́й, *adj.* 1. second; ~а́я мо́лодость second youth; ~а́я скри́пка second violin; (*fig.*) second fiddle; в. час (it is) past one; из ~ы́х рук (at) second hand. 2. *as noun* ~о́е, ~о́го, *n.* second course (*of meal*). 3. *as particle* ~о́е (*coll.*) in the second place.

второкла́ссник, а, *m.* second-form boy.

второкла́ссниц|а, ы, *f.* second-form girl.

второкла́ссный, *adj.* second-class; (*pejor.*) second-rate.

второку́рсник, а, *m.* second-year student.

второочередно́й, *adj.* secondary.

второпя́х, *adv.* 1. hurriedly, in haste. 2. in one's hurry.

второразря́дный, *adj.* second-rate.

второсо́ртный, *adj.* second-quality; inferior.

второстепе́нный, *adj.* secondary; minor.

второ́ч|ить, у́, и́шь, *pf.* (*of* второ́чивать) to strap to one's saddle.

втрав|и́ть, лю́, ~ишь, *pf.* (*of* ~ливать) (в+*a.*) to inveigle (into).

втра́влива|ть, ю, *impf.* *of* втрави́ть.

втре́ска|ться, юсь, *pf.* (в+*a.*; *coll.*) to fall (for), fall in love (with).

в-тре́тьих, *adv.* thirdly, in the third place.

втри́дешева, *adv.* (*coll.*) three times as cheap; excessively cheaply; прода́ть в. to sell for a song.

втри́дорога, *adv.* (*coll.*) triple the price; extremely dear(ly); плати́ть в. to pay through the nose.

втро́е, *adv.* three times; treble.

втроём, *adv.* three (together); мы пое́хали в Ло́ндон в. the three of us went to London.

втройне́, *adv.* three times as much, treble.

втуз, а, *m.* (*abbr. of* вы́сшее техни́ческое уче́бное заведе́ние) technical college.

вту́лк|а, и, *f.* 1. (*tech.*) bush. 2. plug; bung.

вту́не, *adv.* (*obs.*) in vain.

втыка́|ть, ю, *impf.* *of* воткну́ть.

вты́чк|а, и, *f.* (*coll.*) 1. sticking in. 2. plug, bung.

втю́р|иться, юсь, ишься, *pf.* (в+*a.*; *coll.*) to fall in love (with).

втя́гива|ть(ся), ю(сь), *impf.* *of* втяну́ть(ся).

втяжно́й, *adj.* (*tech.*) suction.

втя|ну́ть, ну́, ~нешь, *pf.* (*of* ~гивать) 1. to draw (in, into, up), pull (in, into, up); to absorb, take in; в. живо́т to pull in one's stomach; в. жи́дкость to take in a liquid. 2. (*fig.*) to draw (into), involve (in); в. в спор to draw into an argument.

втя|ну́ться, ну́сь, ~нешься, *pf.* (*of* ~гиваться) (в+*a.*) 1. to draw (into), enter; коло́нна ~ну́лась в уще́лье the column entered the defile. 2. (*of cheeks*) to sag, fall in. 3. (*coll.*) to get accustomed (to), used (to); вы ско́ро ~нетесь в рабо́ту you will soon get used to the work. 4. to become keen (on); он о́чень ~ну́лся в игру́ в те́ннис he has become very keen on tennis.

втя́па|ться, юсь, *pf.* (в+*a.*; *coll.*) to get involved (in); to get into a mess.

вуале́тк|а, и, *f.* veil.

вуали́р|овать, ую, *impf.* (*of* за~) to veil, draw a veil (over).

вуа́л|ь, и, *f.* veil.

вуз, а, *m.* (*abbr. of* вы́сшее уче́бное заведе́ние) institution of higher education.

ву́зов|ец, ца, *m.* student (*at any institution of higher education*).

ву́зов|ка, ки, *f. of* ~ец.

ву́з|овский, *adj. of* ~.

вулка́н, а, *m.* volcano; де́йствующий, поту́хший в. active, extinct volcano; жить (как) на ~е (*fig.*) to be living on the edge of a volcano.

вулканиза́ци|я, и, *f.* (*tech.*) vulcanization.

вулканизи́р|овать, ую, *impf. and pf.* (*tech.*) to vulcanize.

вулкани́зм, а, *m.* (*geol.*) vulcanism.

вулканиз|ова́ть, у́ю = ~и́ровать.

вулкани́ческий, *adj.* volcanic (*also fig.*).

вульгариза́тор, а, *m.* vulgarizer.

вульгариза́ци|я, и, *f.* vulgarization.

вульгаризи́р|овать, ую, *impf. and pf.* to vulgarize.

вульгари́зм, а, *m.* (*ling.*) vulgarism.

вульга́рност|ь, и, *f.* vulgarity.

вульга́р|ный (~ен, ~на), *adj.* (*in var. senses*) vulgar; в. маркси́зм vulgar Marxism.

вундерки́нд, а, *m.* infant prodigy.

вурдала́к, а, *m.* werewolf; vampire.

вход, а, *m.* 1. entry. 2. entrance.

вхо|ди́ть, жу́, ~дишь, *impf. of* войти́.

вход|но́й, *adj. of* ~; ~на́я пла́та entrance fee.

входя́щий, *pres. part. of* ~и́ть *and adj.* incoming; в. журна́л book of entries; в. у́гол (*math.*) re-entrant angle; *as noun* ~я́щая, ~я́щей, *f.* incoming paper.

вхожде́ни|е, я, *n.* entry.

вхо́ж|ий (~, ~а), *adj.* (*coll.*) быть ~им (в+а., к) to be (well) received (at); to be well in (with).

вхолосту́ю, *adv.* (*tech.*) рабо́тать в. to run idle.

вцеп|и́ться, лю́сь, ~ишься, *impf.* (*of* ~ля́ться) (в+а.) to seize hold of (by).

вцепля́|ться, юсь, *impf. of* вцепи́ться.

вчера́, *adv.* yesterday.

вчера́|шний, *adj. of* ~; есть у вас ~шняя «Пра́вда»? have you yesterday's *Pravda*?; иска́ть ~шнего дня to waste time on a hopeless quest.

вчерне́, *adv.* in rough; я написа́л свою́ ле́кцию в. I have made a rough draft of my lecture.

вчер|ти́ть, чу́, ~тишь, *pf.* (*of* ~чивать) (*math.*) to inscribe.

вче́рчива|ть, ю, *impf. of* вчерти́ть.

вче́тверо, *adv.* four times; four times as much; сложи́ть в. to fold in four.

вчетверо́м, *adv.* four (together).

в-четвёртых, *adv.* fourthly, in the fourth place.

вчин|и́ть, ю́, и́шь, *pf.* (*of* ~я́ть) (*leg.*; *obs.*) в. иск to bring an action.

вчиня́|ть, ю, *impf. of* вчини́ть.

вчисту́ю, *adv.* (*coll.*, *obs.*) 1. finally, definitively; он был уво́лен в. he was pensioned off. 2. completely.

вчит|а́ться, а́юсь, *pf.* (*of* ~ываться) (в+а.) to get a grasp (of) (*a text*).

вчи́тыва|ться, юсь, *impf.* 1. *impf. of* вчита́ться. 2. *impf. only* to try to grasp the meaning (of).

вчу́же, *adv.* disinterestedly, vicariously; я в. любова́лся его́ успе́хом his success gave me vicarious pleasure.

вше́стеро, *adv.* six times; six times as much.

вшестеро́м, *adv.* six (together).

вшива́|ть, ю, *impf. of* вшить.

вши́ве|ть, ю, *impf.* (*of* за~ *and* обо~) to become lice-ridden.

вши́вк|а, и, *f.* (*coll.*) 1. sewing in. 2. patch.

вшивно́й, *adj.* sewn in.

вши́в|ый (~, ~а), *adj.* lousy, lice-ridden.

вширь, *adv.* in breadth.

вшить, вошью́, вошьёшь, *pf.* (*of* вшива́ть) (в+а.) to sew in(to).

въеда́|ться, юсь, *impf. of* въе́сться.

въе́длив|ый (~, ~а), *adj.* (*coll.*) corrosive; (*fig.*) acid; ~ое замеча́ние acid remark; в. челове́к caustic person.

въе́дчив|ый (~, ~а), *adj.* = въе́дливый.

въезд, а, *m.* 1. entry. 2. entrance.

въезд|но́й, *adj. of* ~; ~на́я ви́за entry visa.

въезжа́|ть, ю, *impf. of* въе́хать.

въе́|сться, мся, шься, стся, ди́мся, ди́тесь, дя́тся, *past* ~лся, *pf.* (*of* ~да́ться) (в+а.) to eat (into).

въе́|хать, ду, дешь, *pf.* (*of* ~зжа́ть) (в+а.) to enter, ride in(to), drive in(to); to ride, drive up; в. в мо́рду, в ры́ло (+d.; *vulg.*) to slap in the face.

въя́в|е, *adv.* = ~ь.

въявь, *adv.* (*obs.*) 1. openly; ви́деть в. to see with one's own eyes. 2. in reality; и в. случи́лось так, как я сказа́л it really did happen as I said.

вы, вас, вам, ва́ми, вас, *pron.* (*pl. and formal mode of address to one person*) you; быть на в. (с+i.) to be on formal terms (with).

вы- *prefix indicating* 1. motion outwards. 2. action directed outwards. 3. acquisition (*as outcome of a series of actions*). 4. completion of a process.

выба́лтыва|ть, ю, *impf. of* вы́болтать.

выбега́|ть, ю, *impf. of* вы́бежать.

вы́бега|ться, юсь, *pf.* 1. (*coll.*) to wear oneself out with running. 2. to become sterile (*of livestock*).

вы́бе|жать, гу, жишь, гут, *pf.* (*of* ~га́ть) to run out.

вы́бел|ить, ю, ишь, *pf. of* бели́ть 3.

вы́белк|а, и, *f.* bleaching; whitening.

вы́бер|у, ешь, *see* вы́брать.

выбива́|ть(ся), ю(сь), *impf. of* вы́бить(ся).

выбира́|ть(ся), ю(сь), *impf. of* вы́брать(ся).

вы́б|ить, ью, ьешь, *pf.* (*of* ~ива́ть) **1.** to knock out; to dislodge; в. из седла́ to unseat, unhorse; в. из коле́й (*fig.*) to unsettle, upset; в. дурь из кого́-н. to knock the nonsense out of someone. **2.** to beat (clean); в. ковёр to beat a carpet. **3.** to beat; to stamp; to print (*fabrics*); в. медь to beat copper; в. меда́ль to strike a medal. **4.** to beat down; град ~ил посе́вы the hail had beaten down the crops. **5.** to beat out; to drum; в. бараба́нную дробь to beat a tattoo.

вы́б|иться, ьюсь, ьешься, *pf.* (*of* ~ива́ться) **1.** to get out; to break loose (from); в. из коле́й to go off the rails; в. в лю́ди to make one's way in the world; в. из сил to strain oneself to breaking point, wear oneself out. **2.** to come out, show (*intrans.*; *usually of hair, from under hat*).

вы́боин|а, ы, *f.* **1.** rut, pot-hole. **2.** dent; groove.

вы́бойк|а, и, *f.* **1.** beating (*of metals*). **2.** (*text.*) print.

вы́бойчатый, *adj.* (*text.*) printed.

вы́болта|ть, ю, *pf.* (*of* выба́лтывать) (*coll.*) to let out, blurt out.

выболта́|ться, юсь, *pf.* (*coll.*) **1.** to talk oneself to a standstill. **2.** to talk (*to let out secrets*).

вы́бор, а, *m.* **1.** choice; option. **2.** selection; assortment; в э́том магази́не име́ется большо́й в. конфе́т this shop has a large selection of sweets. **3.** (*pl. only*) election(s); дополни́тельные в. by-election.

вы́борк|а, и, f. **1.** selection. **2.** (*coll.*) excerpt.

вы́борност|ь, и, f. appointment by election.

вы́борн|ый, *adj.* **1.** elective. **2.** electoral; в. бюллете́нь ballot-paper. **3.** elected; *as noun* **в., ~ого,** *m.* delegate.

вы́борочный, *adj.* selective.

вы́борщик, а, m. **1.** elector (*in indirect elections*). **2.** selector.

вы́бор|ы, ов, *see* ~.

вы́бран|ить, ю, ишь, *pf. of* брани́ть.

выбра́сывател|ь, я, m. ejector (*in firearms*).

выбра́сыва|ть(ся), ю(сь), *impf. of* вы́бро-сить(ся).

вы́б|рать, еру, ерешь, *pf.* (*of* ~ира́ть) **1.** to choose, select, pick out. **2.** to elect. **3.** в. пате́нт (*leg.*) to take out a patent. **4.** to take (everything) out. **5.** (*naut.*) to haul in.

вы́б|раться, ерусь, ерешься, *pf.* (*of* ~ира́ться) **1.** to get out; в. из затрудне́ний to get out of a difficulty. **2.** to move (house). **3.** (*coll.*) to (manage to) get to; несмотря́

на боле́знь, мать всё-таки ~ра́лась це́рковь in spite of being ill mother man aged to get to church.

выбива́|ть(ся), ю(сь), *impf. of* вы́брить(ся)

вы́бр|ить, ею, еешь, *pf.* (*of* ~ива́ть) t shave.

вы́бр|иться, еюсь, еешься, *pf.* (*of* ~ива́тьс to shave, have a shave.

вы́бро|сить, шу, сишь, *pf.* (*of* выбра́сыват **1.** to throw out; в. за борт to throw ove board (*also fig.*); в. на у́лицу to throw on t the street. **2.** to reject, discard, throw away в. зря to waste; в. из головы́ to put out (one's head, dismiss. **3.** (*in var. senses*) to pu out; в. флаг to hoist a flag; в. ло́зунг to pu out, launch a slogan.

вы́бро|ситься, шусь, сишься, *pf.* (*of* вы бра́сываться) to throw oneself out, lea out; (*naut.*) в. на мель, на́ берег to ru aground; в. с парашю́том из самолёта t bale out of an aircraft.

выбыва́|ть, ю, *impf. of* вы́быть.

выбы́ти|е, я, n. departure; за ва́шим ~е письмо́ бы́ло возвращено́ отправи́телю i view of your having gone away the lette was returned to the sender.

вы́б|ыть, уду, удешь, *pf.* (*of* ~ыва́ть) (и to leave, quit; в. из стро́я (*mil.*) (*i*) to leav the ranks (*ii*) to become a casualty.

выва́лива|ть(ся), ю(сь), *impf. of* вы́валит (ся).

вы́вал|ить, ю, ишь, *pf.* (*of* ~ивать) **1.** t throw out. **2.** (*coll.*) to pour out (*intrans.*; (*a crowd*).

вы́вал|иться, юсь, ишься, *pf.* (*of* ~иваться to fall out, tumble out.

вы́валя|ть, ю, *pf.* (*of* валя́ть 2) to drag (i through) (*mud, snow, etc.*).

вы́валя|ться, юсь, *pf.* (в+*p.*) to get covere (*in mud, snow, etc.*).

выва́рива|ть, ю, *impf. of* вы́варить.

вы́вар|ить, ю, ишь, *pf.* (*of* ~ивать) **1.** t boil down; to extract by boiling; в. соль и морско́й воды́ to extract salt from se water. **2.** to boil thoroughly. **3.** to remov (*stains, etc.*) by boiling.

вы́варк|а, и, f. decoction, extraction.

вы́вед|ать, аю, *pf.* (*of* ~ывать) to find out в. секре́т у кого́-н. to worm a secret out (someone.

выведе́н|ец, ца, m. (*hist.*) peasant forcibl removed to different area.

выведе́ни|е, я, n. **1.** leading out, bringin out. **2.** deduction, conclusion. **3.** hatchin (out); growing (*of plants*); breeding, raising **4.** putting up, erection. **5.** getting ou removal (*of stains*); extermination (*of pest*

вы́ведр|ить, ит, *pf.* (*impers.*; *dial.*) to be come fine, clear up (*of weather*).

вывё́дыва|ть, ю, *impf.* **1.** *impf. of* вы́ведат

2. *impf. only* to investigate, try to find out; в. чьи-н. наме́рения to sound out someone's intentions.

вы́вез|ти, у, ешь, *past* ~, ~ла, *pf. (of* вывозить) **1.** to take out, remove; to bring out. **2.** (*econ.*) to export. **3.** (*coll.*) to save, rescue; счастли́вый слу́чай ~ меня́ a lucky chance saved me. **4.** в. в свет to bring out (into society).

вы́вер|ить, ю, ишь, *pf. (of* ~я́ть) to adjust; to regulate (*clocks and watches*).

вы́верк|а, и, *f.* adjustment; regulation (*of clocks and watches*).

вы́вер|нуть, ну, нешь, *pf. (of* ~тывать) **1.** to unscrew; to pull out. **2.** (*coll.*) to twist, wrench. **3.** (*coll.*) to dislocate. **4.** to turn (inside) out.

вы́вер|нуться, нусь, нешься, *pf. (of* ~тываться) **1.** to come unscrewed. **2.** (*coll.*) to slip out. **3.** (*coll.*) to get out (of), extricate oneself (from). **4.** (*coll.*) to appear, emerge (*from behind something, from round a corner*). **5.** (*coll.*) to be dislocated.

вы́верт, а, *m.* (*coll.*) **1.** caper; танцева́ть с ~ами to caper. **2.** mannerism; affectation; челове́к с ~ом eccentric.

вы́вер|теть, чу, тишь, *pf.* (*coll.*) to unscrew.

вывёртыва|ть(ся), ю(сь), *impf. of* вы́вернуть(ся).

вывёрчива|ть, ю, *impf. of* вы́вертеть.

выверя́|ть, ю, *impf. of* вы́верить.

вы́ве|сить[1], шу, сишь, *pf. (of* ~шивать) **1.** to put up; to post up. **2.** to hang out (*linen, flags, etc.*).

вы́ве|сить[2], шу, сишь, *pf. (of* ~шивать) to weigh.

вы́веск|а, и, *f.* **1.** sign, signboard. **2.** (*fig.*) screen, pretext; он обману́л её под ~ой любе́зности he deceived her under the mask of kindness. **3.** (*sl.*) mug (= *face*).

вы́ве|сти, ду, дешь, *past* ~л, ~ла, *pf. (of* выводи́ть) **1.** to lead out, bring out; в. самолёт из што́пора to pull an aeroplane out of a spin; в. кого́-н. в лю́ди to help someone on in life; в. из заблужде́ния to undeceive; в. кого́-н. из себя́ to drive someone out of his wits; в. из стро́я to disable, put out of action (*also fig.*); в. из терпе́ния to exasperate; в. кого́-н. на доро́гу (*fig.*) to set someone on the right path; в. на чи́стую во́ду to expose, show up. **2.** to turn out, force out; в. из соста́ва прези́диума to remove from the presidium. **3.** to remove (*stains*); to exterminate (*pests*). **4.** to deduce, conclude. **5.** to hatch (out); to grow (*plants*); to breed, raise. **6.** to put up, erect. **7.** to depict, portray (*in a lit. work*). **8.** to write, draw, trace out painstakingly. **9.** в. балл, в. отме́тку to give a mark.

вы́ве|стись, дусь, дешься, *pf. (of* выводи́ться) **1.** to go out of use; to lapse. **2.** to disappear; to come out (*of stains*); to become extinct. **3.** to hatch out (*intrans.*).

выве́тривани|е, я, *n.* **1.** airing. **2.** (*geol.*) weathering.

выве́трива|ть(ся), ю(сь), *impf. of* вы́ветрить(ся).

вы́ветр|ить, ю, ишь, *pf. (of* ~ивать) **1.** to air; to ventilate; to remove (by ventilation); в. дурно́й за́пах to remove a bad smell. **2.** (*fig.*) to remove. **3.** (*impers.*; *geol.*) to weather.

вы́ветр|иться, юсь, ишься, *pf. (of* ~иваться) **1.** (*geol.*) to weather. **2.** to disappear (*by action of wind or fresh air*; *also fig.*); в. из па́мяти to be effaced from memory.

выве́шива|ть, ю, *impf. of* вы́весить.

вы́вин|тить, чу, тишь, *pf. (of* ~чивать) to unscrew.

вы́вин|титься, чусь, тишься, *pf. (of* ~чиваться) to come unscrewed.

вывинчива|ть(ся), ю(сь), *impf. of* вы́винтить(ся).

вы́вих, а, *m.* **1.** dislocation; dislocated part. **2.** (*fig.*, *coll.*) kink; oddity, quirk.

вывихива|ть, ю, *impf. of* вы́вихнуть.

вы́вих|нуть, ну, нешь, *pf. (of* ~ивать) to dislocate, put out (of joint); он ~нул себе́ но́гу he has dislocated his foot.

вы́вод, а, *m.* **1.** deduction, conclusion. **2.** (*electr.*) outlet; leading-out wire. **3.** leading out, bringing out. **4.** hatching (out); growing (*of plants*); breeding, raising.

выво|ди́ть(ся), жу́(сь), ~дишь(ся), *impf. of* вы́вести(сь).

вы́водк|а, и, *f.* **1.** removal (*of stains*). **2.** exercising (*of horses*).

выводно́й, *adj.* **1.** (*tech.*) discharge. **2.** (*anat.*) excretory.

вы́вод|ок, ка, *m.* brood (*also fig.*); hatch; litter.

выво|жу́[1], ~дишь, *see* ~ди́ть.

выво|жу́[2], ~зишь, *see* ~зи́ть.

вы́воз, а, *m.* **1.** export. **2.** removal.

выво|зи́ть, жу, зишь, *pf.* (в+*p.*; *coll.*) to cover (*in mud, snow, etc.*).

выво|зи́ть, жу́, ~зишь, *impf. of* вы́везти.

вы́возк|а, и, *f.* (*coll.*) carting out.

вывозно́й, *adj.* export.

вывола́кива|ть, ю, *impf. of* вы́волочь.

вы́волочк|а, и, *f.* (*coll.*) **1.** dragging out. **2.** beating. **3.** dressing-down.

вы́воло|чь, ку, чешь, кут, *past* ~к, ~кла *pf. (of* вывола́кивать) (*coll.*) to drag out.

вывора́чива|ть, ю, *impf. of* вы́воротить.

вы́воро|тить, чу, тишь, *pf. (of* вывора́чивать) (*coll.*) **1.** to pull out, shake loose. **2.** to twist, wrench. **3.** to turn (inside) out. **4.** to overturn.

выгад|ать, аю, *pf.* (*of* ∼ывать) to gain; to save, economize; что вы ∼али на э́том? what did you gain by it?

выга́дыва|ть, ю, *impf. of* вы́гадать.

вы́гарк|и, ов, *no sing.* slag.

вы́гиб, а, *m.* curve; curvature.

выгиба́|ть(ся), ю(сь), *impf. of* вы́гнуть(ся).

вы́гла|дить, жу, дишь, *pf. of* гла́дить 1.

вы́гля|деть[1], жу, дишь, *pf.* (*coll.*) to discover; to spy out.

вы́гля|деть[2], жу, дишь, *impf.* to look (like); он ∼дит о́чень молоды́м he looks very young; он ∼дит грузи́ном he looks like a Georgian; она́ пло́хо ∼дит she does not look well.

выгля́дыва|ть, ю, *impf. of* вы́глянуть.

вы́гля|нуть, ну, нешь, *pf.* (*of* ∼дывать) 1. to look out. 2. to peep out, emerge, become visible; из-за туч ∼нуло со́лнце the sun peeped out from behind the clouds.

вы́г|нать, оню, онишь, *pf.* (*of* ∼оня́ть) 1. to drive out; to expel; в. со слу́жбы (*coll.*) to sack. 2. to distil. 3. (*coll.*) to make (*a sum of money, etc.*).

выгнива́|ть, ю, *impf. of* вы́гнить.

вы́гни|ть, ю, ешь, *pf.* (*of* ∼ва́ть) to rot away; to rot at the core.

вы́гнут|ый (∼, ∼a), *p.p.p. of* ∼ь *and adj.* curved; convex.

вы́гн|уть, у, ешь, *pf.* (*of* выгиба́ть) to bend; в. спи́ну to arch the back.

вы́гн|уться, усь, ешься, *pf.* (*of* выгиба́ться) to bend (*intrans.*).

выгова́рива|ть, ю, *impf.* 1. *impf. of* вы́говорить. 2. *impf. only* (+*d.*; *coll.*) to reprimand, tell off.

вы́говор, а, *m.* 1. accent; pronunciation. 2. reprimand; rebuke; dressing-down, ticking-off.

вы́говор|ить, ю, ишь, *pf.* (*of* выгова́ривать) 1. to articulate, speak. 2. (*leg.*) to reserve; to stipulate; в. себе́ пра́во расторже́ния контра́кта to reserve the right of annulment of contract.

вы́говор|иться, юсь, ишься, *pf.* (*coll.*) to speak out.

вы́год|а, ы, *f.* advantage, benefit; profit, gain; interest.

вы́годно, *adv.* 1. advantageously. 2. *as pred.* it is profitable, it pays.

вы́год|ный (∼ен, ∼на), *adj.* advantageous, beneficial; profitable.

вы́гон, а, *m.* pasture; common.

вы́гонк|а, и, *f.* distillation.

выгоня́|ть, ю, *impf. of* вы́гнать.

выгора́жива|ть, ю, *impf. of* вы́городить.

выгора́|ть, ет, *impf. of* вы́гореть.

вы́гор|еть[1], ит, *pf.* (*of* ∼а́ть) 1. to burn down, burn out (*intrans.*). 2. to fade.

вы́гор|еть[2], ит, *pf.* (*of* ∼а́ть) (*3rd person only or impers.*; *coll.*) to succeed, come off.

вы́горо|дить, жу, дишь, *pf.* (*of* выгора́живать) 1. to fence off. 2. (*fig.*, *coll.*) to shield, screen.

вы́гравир|овать, ую, *pf. of* гравирова́ть.

вы́гра́нива|ть, ю, *impf. of* вы́гранить.

вы́гран|ить, ю, ишь, *pf.* (*of* ∼ивать) (*tech.*) to cut (*crystal, glass*).

вы́греб[1], а, *m.* 1. raking out; clearing away. 2. cesspool.

вы́гре|б[2], *see* ∼сти.

выгреба́|ть, ю, *impf. of* вы́грести.

выгребн|о́й, *adj.* refuse; ∼а́я я́ма cesspool.

вы́гре|сти[1], бу, бешь, *past* ∼б, ∼бла, *pf.* (*of* ∼ба́ть) to rake out; to clear away.

вы́гре|сти[2], бу, бешь, *past* ∼б, ∼бла, *pf.* (*of* ∼ба́ть) to row (out), pull (out).

выгружа́|ть(ся), ю(сь), *impf. of* вы́грузить(ся).

вы́гру|зить, жу, зишь, *pf.* (*of* ∼жа́ть) to unload, unlade; to disembark.

вы́гру|зиться, жусь, зишься, *pf.* (*of* ∼жа́ться) to disembark; (*mil.*) to detrain, debus.

вы́грузк|а, и, *f.* unloading; disembarkation.

вы́грузчик, а, *m.* unloader; stevedore.

выгрыза́|ть, ю, *impf. of* вы́грызть.

вы́грыз|ть, у, ешь, *past* ∼, ∼ла, *pf.* (*of* ∼а́ть) to gnaw out.

выда|ва́ть(ся), ю(сь), ёшь(ся), *impf. of* вы́дать(ся).

вы́дав|ить, лю, ишь, *pf.* (*of* ∼ливать) 1. to press out, squeeze out (*also fig.*); в. улы́бку to force a smile. 2. to break, knock out.

выда́влива|ть, ю, *impf. of* вы́давить.

выда́ива|ть, ю, *impf. of* вы́доить.

выда́лблива|ть, ю, *impf. of* вы́долбить.

вы́дань|е, я, *n.* only in phrase (*coll.*, *obs.*) на в. marriageable.

вы́да|ть, м, шь, ст, дим, дите, дут, *pf.* (*of* ∼ва́ть) 1. to give (out), issue, produce; в. ве́ксель to draw a bill; в. зарпла́ту to pay out wages; в. про́пуск to issue a pass; в. кого́-н. за́муж (за+*a.*) to give someone in marriage (to); в. на-гора́ (*tech.*) to hoist, wind (to the surface); в. у́голь на-гора́ to produce coal. 2. to give away, betray; to deliver up, extradite; в. голово́й to betray. 3. (за+*a.*) to pass off (as), give out to be; (себя́) to pose (as); в. себя́ за свяще́нника to pose as a clergyman.

вы́да|ться, мся, шься, стся, димся, дитесь, дутся, *pf.* (*of* ∼ва́ться) 1. to protrude, project, jut out; (*fig.*) to stand out, be conspicuous. 2. (*coll.*) to happen; как то́лько ∼лся хоро́ший денёк, мы пое́хали в дере́вню on the first fine day that came along we went into the country.

вы́дач|а, и, f. 1. issuing. 2. issue; payment. 3. extradition.

выдаю́щийся, *pres. part. of* выдава́ться *and adj.* prominent, salient; (*fig.*) eminent, outstanding; prominent.

выдвига́|ть(ся), ю(сь), *impf. of* вы́двинуть(ся).

выдвиже́н|ец, ца, m. worker promoted to an administrative post.

выдвиже́ни|е, я, n. 1. nomination. 2. promotion, advancement.

выдвиже́н|ка, ки, f. *of* ~ец.

выдвиже́нчеств|о, а, n. system of promotion of workers to positions of responsibility and authority.

выдвижно́й, adj. sliding; (*tech.*) telescopic.

вы́дви|нуть, ну, нешь, pf. (*of* ~га́ть) 1. to move out, pull out. 2. (*fig.*) to bring forward, advance; в. обвине́ние to bring an accusation. 3. to promote; в. на до́лжность секретаря́ to promote to the post of secretary. 4. to nominate, propose; в. чью-н. кандидату́ру, кого́-н. в кандида́ты to propose someone as candidate.

вы́дви|нуться, нусь, нешься, pf. (*of* ~га́ться) 1. to move forward, move out; to slide in and out (*of a drawer, etc.*). 2. to rise, get on (in the world). 3. *pass. of* ~нуть.

вы́двор|ить, ю, ишь, pf. (*of* ~я́ть) (*coll. and leg.; obs.*) to evict; (*fig.*) to throw out.

выдворя́|ть, ю, *impf. of* вы́дворить.

вы́дел, а, m. apportionment.

вы́дел|ать, аю, pf. (*of* ~ывать) 1. to manufacture; to process. 2. to dress, curry (*leather*).

выделе́ни|е, я, n. 1. (*physiol.*) secretion; excretion. 2. (*chem.*) isolation. 3. apportionment.

выдели́тельный, adj. (*physiol.*) secretory; excretory.

вы́дел|ить, ю, ишь, pf. (*of* ~я́ть) 1. to pick out, single out; (*mil.*) to detach, detail; (*typ.*) в. курси́вом to italicize. 2. to assign, earmark; to allot. 3. (*physiol.*) to secrete; to excrete. 4. (*chem.*) to isolate.

вы́дел|иться, юсь, ишься, pf. (*of* ~я́ться) 1. to take one's share (*of a legacy*). 2. (+*i.*) to stand out (for); to make a mark (by); он ~ился остроу́мием he was noted for his wit. 3. to ooze out, exude. 4. *pass. of* ~ить.

вы́делк|а, и, f. 1. manufacture. 2. workmanship. 3. dressing, currying.

выде́лыва|ть, ю, *impf. of* вы́делать; что ты тепе́рь ~ешь? (*coll.*) what are you up to now?

выделя́|ть(ся), ю(сь), *impf. of* вы́делить(ся).

выдёргива|ть, ю, *impf. of* вы́дернуть.

вы́держанност|ь, и, f. 1. consistency. 2. self-possession; firmness.

вы́держа|нный (~н, ~на), p.p.p. of ~ть *and adj.* 1. consistent; ~нная поли́тика consistent policy. 2. self-possessed; firm. 3. mature; seasoned (*of wine, cheese, wood, etc.*).

вы́держ|ать, у, ишь, pf. (*of* ~ивать) 1. to bear, hold; лёд вас не ~ит the ice will not hold you. 2. (*fig.*) to bear, stand (up to), endure; to contain oneself; не в. to give in, break down; я не мог э́того бо́льше в. I could not stand it no longer; ва́ши мне́ния не ~ат кри́тики your opinions will not stand up to criticism; выраже́ние лица́ у него́ бы́ло тако́е коми́чное, что я не ~ал his expression was so funny that I could not contain myself. 3. в. экза́мен to pass an examination. 4. в. не́сколько изда́ний to run into several editions. 5. to keep, lay up; to mature; to season. 6. в. под аре́стом to keep in custody. 7. to maintain, sustain; в. роль to keep up a part, sustain an act; в. хара́ктер to stand firm; в. па́узу to pause.

выде́ржива|ть, ю, *impf. of* вы́держать.

вы́держк|а¹, и, f. 1. endurance; self-possession. 2. (*phot.*) exposure.

вы́держк|а², и, f. excerpt, quotation.

вы́дер|нуть, ну, нешь, pf. (*of* ~гивать) to pull out.

выдира́|ть, ю, *impf. of* вы́драть¹.

выдира́|ться, юсь, *impf. of* вы́драться.

вы́до|ить, ю, ишь, pf. (*of* выда́ивать) 1. to milk (dry). 2. to obtain (by milking).

вы́долб|ить, лю, ишь, pf. (*of* выда́лбливать) 1. to hollow out, gouge out. 2. (*coll.*) to learn by rote.

вы́дох, а, m. exhalation.

вы́дохн|уть, у, ешь, pf. (*of* выдыха́ть) to breathe out.

вы́дохн|уться, усь, ешься, pf. (*of* выдыха́ться) to have lost fragrance, smell; (*of wines, etc.*) to be flat; (*fig.*) to be past one's best, to be played out.

вы́др|а, ы, f. otter (*also fig., coll., of a thin, unattractive woman*).

вы́д|рать¹, еру, ерешь, pf. (*of* ~ира́ть) to tear out.

вы́д|рать², еру, ерешь, pf. (*of* драть 4) (*coll.*) to thrash, flog.

вы́д|раться, ерусь, ерешься, pf. (*of* ~ира́ться) (*coll.*) to extricate oneself.

вы́дрессир|овать, ую, pf. *of* дрессирова́ть.

вы́дуб|ить, лю, ишь, pf. *of* дуби́ть.

выдува́льщик, а, m. glass-blower.

выдува́|ть, ю, *impf. of* вы́дуть.

вы́дувк|а, и, f. (*tech.*) (glass-)blowing.

выдувно́й, adj. blown (*of glass*).

вы́думан|ный (~, ~а), p.p.p. of вы́думать *and adj.* made-up, fabricated; ~ная исто́рия fabrication, fiction.

вы́дум|ать, аю, pf. (*of* ~ывать) to invent; to

make up, fabricate; он пороха не ~ает he will not set the Thames on fire; не выдумай напиться! mind you don't get drunk!

вы́думк|а, и, *f.* 1. invention; idea (*discovery, device*); голь на ~и хитра (*prov.*) necessity is the mother of invention. 2. (*coll.*) inventiveness. 3. (*coll.*) invention, fabrication (*lie*).

вы́думщик, а, *m.* (*coll.*) 1. inventor. 2. fabricator (*liar*).

выду́мыва|ть, ю, *impf. of* вы́думать; не ~й (*coll.*) don't argue; делай то, что тебе велено, а не ~й do what you are told and don't argue.

вы́ду|ть, ю, ешь, *pf.* (*of* ~ва́ть) 1. to blow out. 2. (*impf.* дуть) (*tech.*) to blow. 3. в огонь (*coll.*) to blow up a fire. 4. (*impf.* дуть) (*coll.*) to drain, toss off (*drink*).

выдыха́ни|е, я, *n.* exhalation.

выдыха́|ть(ся), ю(сь), *impf. of* вы́дохнуть-(ся).

выеда́|ть, ю, *impf. of* вы́есть.

вы́еденн|ый, *p.p.p. of* вы́есть; не стоит ~ого яйца it is not worth a brass farthing.

вы́езд, а, *m.* 1. departure. 2. exit (*concr.*). 3. (*obs.*) turn-out, equipage. 4. (*obs.*) going out (*to balls, theatres, etc.*).

вы́ез|дить, жу, дишь, *pf.* (*of* ~жа́ть) to break(-in); to train (*horses*).

вы́ездк|а, и, *f.* breaking-in; training (*of horses*).

выезд|ной, *adj. of* вы́езд; ~на́я сессия суда assizes; в. матч (*sport*) away match; в. лакей (*obs.*) footman; ~но́е платье (*obs.*) evening dress; party dress.

выезжа́|ть, ю, *impf. of* вы́ездить *and* вы́-ехать.

вы́емк|а, и, *f.* 1. taking out; collection (*of letters from letter-box*); в. документов seizure of documents. 2. excavation. 3. hollow; groove; (*archit.*) fluting. 4. (*railways*) cutting. 5. (*tailoring*) cut, cutting.

вы́е|сть, м, шь, ст, дим, дите, дят, *pf.* (*of* ~да́ть) to eat away; (*coll.*) to corrode.

вы́е|хать, ду, дешь, *pf.* (*of* ~зжа́ть) 1. to go out, depart (*in or on a vehicle or on an animal*); to drive out; to ride out. 2. to leave, move (*from dwelling-place*). 3. (на+ *p.*) (*fig., coll.*) to make use (of), exploit, take advantage (of).

выжа́рива|ть, ю, *impf. of* вы́жарить.

вы́жар|ить, ю, ишь, *pf.* (*of* ~ивать) (*coll.*) 1. to heat up. 2. to roast to a turn; to fry up.

вы́ж|ать¹, му, мешь, *pf.* (*of* ~има́ть) 1. to press out, wring (out); to squeeze out; в. последние силы из кого-н. to squeeze the last ounce of effort out of someone; ~атый лимон (*fig.*) a has-been. 2. (*sport*) to lift (*weights*).

вы́ж|ать², ну, нешь, *pf.* (*of* ~ина́ть) to reap clean.

вы́жд|ать, у, ешь, *pf.* (*of* выжида́ть) (+*g.*) to wait (for); to bide one's time.

вы́ж|ечь, гу, жешь, *pf.* (*of* ~ига́ть) 1. to burn down; to burn out; to scorch. 2. (*med.*) to cauterize. 3. to make a mark, *etc.*, by burning; в. клеймо (на+*p.*) to brand.

вы́жжен|ный, *p.p.p. of* вы́жечь *and adj.* ~ная земля scorched earth.

выжива́ни|е, я, *n.* survival; в. наиболее приспособленных (*biol.*) survival of the fittest.

выжива́|ть, ю, *impf. of* вы́жить.

вы́жиг|а, и, *m. and f.* (*coll.*) cunning rogue; skinflint.

выжига́ни|е, я, *n.* 1. scorching; в. по дереву poker-work. 2. (*med.*) cauterization.

выжига́|ть, ю, *impf. of* вы́жечь; в. по дереву to do poker-work.

выжида́ни|е, я, *n.* waiting; temporizing.

выжида́тельн|ый, *adj.* waiting; temporizing; занима́ть ~ую позицию to temporize, play a waiting game.

выжида́|ть, ю, *impf. of* вы́ждать.

вы́жим, а, *m.* (*sport*) press-up.

выжима́л|а, ы, *m. and f.* (*sl.*) exploiter.

выжима́ни|е, я, *n.* 1. squeezing; wringing. 2. (*sport*) (weight-)lifting.

выжима́|ть, ю, *impf. of* вы́жать¹.

вы́жимк|и, ов, *no sing.* husks, marc; льняные в. linseed-cake.

выжина́|ть, ю, *impf. of* вы́жать².

вы́жи|ть, ву, вешь, *pf.* (*of* ~ва́ть) 1. to survive; to live through. 2. (*coll.*) to live on in spite of something, hold out, stick it out; они три месяца ~ли на плавучей льдине they stuck it out for three months on an ice-floe. 3. в. из ума to lose possession of one's faculties. 4. (*coll.*) to drive out, hound out; to get rid of.

вы́жлец, а, *m.* (*hunting*) hound.

выжля́тник, а, *m.* (*hunting*) whipper-in.

вызва́нива|ть, ю, *impf. of* вы́звонить.

вы́з|вать, ову, овешь, *pf.* (*of* ~ыва́ть) 1. to call (out); to send for; в. актёра to call for an actor; в. врача́ to call a doctor, send for a doctor; в. ученика́ to call out a pupil; в. по телефо́ну to ring up; в. в суд (*leg.*) to summon(s), subpoena. 2. to challenge; в. на дуэль to challenge to a duel, call out; в. на откровенность to draw out. 3. to call forth, provoke; to cause; to stimulate, rouse; в. любопытство to provoke curiosity; в. пожа́р to cause a fire.

вы́з|ваться, овусь, овешься, *pf.* (*of* ~ы-ва́ться) (+*inf. or* в+*a.*) to volunteer; to offer; в. помочь to offer to help; в. в экспедицию to volunteer for an expedition.

вы́звезд|ить, ит, *pf. impers.* ~ит, ~ило, the stars are (were) out, it is (was) a starlit night.

вы́звол|ить, ю, ишь, *pf.* (*of* ~я́ть) (*coll.*) to help out; в. из беды́ to get out of trouble.

вызволя́|ть, ю, *impf. of* вы́зволить.

вы́звон|ить, ю, ишь, *pf.* (*of* вызва́нивать) **1.** to ring (out) (*of bells*). **2.** (*fig.*) to ring, jingle.

выздора́влива|ть, ю, *impf. of* вы́здороветь.

вы́здорове|ть, ю, ешь, *pf.* (*of* выздора́вливать) to recover, get better.

выздоровле́ни|е, я, *n.* recovery; convalescence.

вы́зов, а, *m.* **1.** call; в. по телефо́ну telephone call. **2.** summons. **3.** challenge; бро́сить в. to throw down a challenge.

вы́золо|тить, чу, тишь, *pf. of* золоти́ть.

вы́золочен|ный (~, ~а), *p.p.p. of* вы́золотить *and adj.* gilt.

вызрева́|ть, ю, *impf. of* вы́зреть.

вы́зре|ть, ю, ешь, *pf.* (*of* ~ва́ть) to ripen.

вы́зубр|ить, ю, ишь, *pf.* (*of* зубри́ть²) (*coll.*) to learn by heart.

вызыва́|ть(ся), ю(сь), *impf. of* вы́звать(ся).

вызыва́|ющий, *pres. part. act. of* ~ть *and adj.* defiant; provocative.

вы́игр|ать, аю, *pf.* (*of* ~ывать) to win; to gain; в. вре́мя to gain time; он ~ал в моём мне́нии he has gone up in my estimation.

вы́игрыва|ть, ю, *impf. of* вы́играть.

вы́игрыш, а, *m.* **1.** win; winning. **2.** gain, winnings; prize; быть в ~е to be winner; (*fig.*) to be the gainer, stand to gain.

вы́игрышн|ый, *adj.* **1.** winning; в. ход winning move; в. заём premium bonds (issue); в. биле́т lottery ticket. **2.** advantageous; effective; ~ое положе́ние advantageous position; ~ая нару́жность winsome appearance.

вы́и|скать, щу, щешь, *pf.* to light upon, track down, run to earth.

вы́и|скаться, щусь, щешься, *pf.* (*coll., iron.*) to turn up, put in an appearance.

вы́искива|ть, ю, *impf.* to seek out, try to trace.

вы́|йти, йду, йдешь, *past* ~шел, ~шла, *pf.* (*of* ~ходи́ть) **1.** to go out; to come out; она́ вчера́ ~шла в пе́рвый раз по́сле боле́зни she went out yesterday for the first time since her illness; в. в лю́ди to get on in the world; в. в отста́вку to retire; в. в офице́ры to be commissioned, get a commission; в. в тира́ж (*of a bond, etc.; fin.*) to be drawn; (*fig.*) to take a back seat; в. в фина́л (*sport*) to reach the final; в. из берего́в to overflow its banks; в. из бо́я (*mil.*) to disengage; в. из ваго́на to alight from a carriage; в. из во́зраста to pass the age limit; в. из головы́, из па́мяти, из ума́ (*coll.*) to go out of one's head; в. из грани́ц (+*g.*), из

преде́лов (+*g.*) (*fig.*) to exceed the bounds (of); в. из долго́в to get out of debt; в. из игры́ to go out of a game; в. из положе́ния to get out of a (tight) spot; в. из себя́ to lose one's temper; в. из терпе́ния to lose patience; в. на вы́зовы (*theatr.*) to take a call; в. на прогу́лку to go out for a walk; в. на сце́ну to come on to the stage. **2.** (в свет) (*of publications*) to come out, appear. **3.** (*of photographs or persons photographed*) to come out; вы хорошо́ ~шли на э́том сни́мке you have come out well in this photo. **4.** в., в. за́муж (за + *a.*) (*of a woman*) to marry. **5.** to come (out) (*also impers.*); to ensue; не в. (+*i. of noun; coll.*) to be lacking (in); в. победи́телем to come out victor; из него́ ~шел бы хоро́ший лётчик he would have made a good pilot; из э́того куска́ мате́рии ~шла хоро́шенькая блу́зка that piece of material has made a pretty blouse; из э́того ничего́ не ~йдет nothing will come of it; ~шло, (что) он ни одного́ сло́ва не по́нял it turned out that he did not understand a single word; как бы чего́ не ~шло (*coll.*) it will come to no good; ро́стом не ~шел (*coll.*) he has not grown; умо́м не ~шел (*coll.*) he is not too bright. **6.** to be by origin; она́ ~шла из крестья́н she is of peasant origin, she comes of peasant stock. **7.** to be used up; (*of a period of time*) to have expired; горчи́ца вся ~шла the mustard is used up; срок уже́ ~шел time is up. **8.** го́да ~шли (+*d. or g.*; *coll.*) (*i*) to be of age, (*ii*) to be over the age (for).

вы́ка|зать, жу, жешь, *pf.* (*of* ~зывать) (*coll.*) to manifest, display (*abstract qualities*).

выка́зыва|ть, ю, *impf. of* вы́казать.

выка́лива|ть, ю, *impf. of* вы́калить.

вы́кал|ить, ю, ишь, *pf.* (*of* ~ивать) (*tech.*) to fire.

выка́лыва|ть, ю, *impf. of* вы́колоть.

выка́пчива|ть, ю, *impf. of* вы́коптить.

выка́пыва|ть(ся), ю(сь), *impf. of* вы́копать(ся).

вы́карабк|аться, аюсь, *pf.* (*of* ~иваться) to scramble out; (*fig., coll.*) to get (oneself) out; в. из боле́зни to get over an illness.

выкара́бкива|ться, юсь, *impf. of* вы́карабкаться.

выка́рмлива|ть, ю, *impf. of* вы́кормить.

вы́кат|ать, аю, *pf.* (*of* ~ывать¹) **1.** to roll out. **2.** (*impf.* ката́ть) to smooth out; to mangle (*linen*). **3.** (*coll.*) to roll (in).

вы́кат|аться, аюсь, *pf.* (*of* ~ываться¹) (*coll.*) **1.** *pass. of* ~ать. **2.** to roll (*intrans.*).

вы́ка|тить, чу, тишь, *pf.* (*of* ~тывать²) **1.** to roll out; to wheel out. **2.** (*coll.*) to come rolling out, come bowling out; (*fig.*) to hare out. **3.** в. глаза́ (*coll.*) to open one's eyes wide, stare.

вы́ка|титься, чусь, тишься, *pf.* (*of* ~ты-
ваться²) to roll out (*intrans.*).
вы́катк|а¹, и, *f.* mangling.
вы́катк|а², и, *f.* rolling out.
выка́тыва|ть(ся)¹, ю(сь), *impf. of* выка-
тать(ся).
выка́тыва|ть(ся)², ю(сь), *impf. of* выка-
тить(ся); ~йся (*coll.*) be off! get out!
вы́ка|ть, ю, *impf.* (*coll.*) to address formally,
address as 'вы'.
вы́кач|ать, аю, *pf.* (*of* ~ивать) to pump out;
(*fig., coll.*) to extort.
выка́чива|ть, ю, *impf. of* вы́качать.
вы́качк|а, и, *f.* pumping out; (*fig., coll.*)
extortion.
выка́шива|ть, ю, *impf. of* вы́косить.
выка́шлива|ть(ся), ю(сь), *impf. of* вы́ка-
шлять(ся).
вы́кашл|ять, яю, *pf.* (*of* ~ивать) to cough
up.
вы́кашл|яться, яюсь, *pf.* (*of* ~иваться) to
clear one's throat.
выки́дыва|ть, ю, *impf. of* вы́кинуть.
вы́кидыш, а, *m.* (*med.*) 1. miscarriage; abortion. 2. foetus (*after miscarriage or abortion*).
вы́ки|нуть, ну, нешь, *pf.* (*of* ~дывать) 1. to
throw out, reject. 2. to put out; в. флаг to
hoist a flag. 3. (*med.*) to have a miscarriage;
to have an abortion. 4. (*coll.*) в. но́мер,
шту́ку, фо́кус to play a trick.
выкипа́|ть, ет, *impf. of* вы́кипеть.
вы́кип|еть, ит, *pf.* (*of* ~а́ть) to boil away.
вы́кипя|тить, чу, тишь, *pf.* to boil out, boil
through.
вы́кладк|а, и, *f.* 1. laying-out; lay-out.
2. (*tech.*) facing; в. кирпичо́м bricking.
3. (*mil.*) kit; в по́лной ~e in full marching
order. 4. (*math.*) computation.
выкла́дыва|ть, ю, *impf. of* вы́ложить.
вы́кл|евать, юю, юешь, *pf.* (*of* ~ёвывать)
1. to peck out. 2. to peck up.
вы́кл|еваться, ююсь, юешься, *pf.* (*of*
~ёвываться) to hatch out (*of birds*).
выклёвыва|ть(ся), ю(сь), *impf. of* вы́кле-
вать(ся); пока́ что ничего́ не ~ется (*coll.*)
at the moment nothing is happening, there
are no bites.
выкле́ива|ть, ю, *impf. of* вы́клеить.
вы́кле|ить, ю, ишь, *pf.* (*of* ~ивать) (*coll.*)
to paste up; в. обо́ями to paper.
выклика́|ть, ю, *impf. of* вы́кликнуть.
вы́клик|нуть, ну, нешь, *pf.* (*of* ~ать) to call
out; в. по спи́ску to call over the roll.
выключа́тел|ь, я, *m.* switch.
выключа́|ть, ю, *impf. of* вы́ключить.
вы́ключ|ить, у, ишь, *pf.* (*of* ~а́ть) 1. to
turn off, switch off. 2. to remove, exclude;
в. кого́-н. из спи́ска to take someone's
name off a list. 3. (*typ.*) to justify.

выклянчива|ть, ю, *impf.* 1. *impf. of* вы́клян-
чить. 2. *impf. only* в. что-н. у кого́-н. to try
to get something out of someone.
вы́клянч|ить, у, ишь, *pf.* (*of* ~ивать) (у+
g.; *coll.*) to cadge (from, off), get (out of).
вы́к|овать, ую, уешь, *pf.* (*of* ~о́вывать) to
forge (*also fig.*).
выко́выва|ть, ю, *impf. of* вы́ковать.
выковы́рива|ть, ю, *impf. of* вы́ковырять.
вы́ковыр|ять, яю, *pf.* (*of* ~ивать) to pluck
out, pick out; (*coll.*) to hunt out.
выкола́чива|ть, ю, *impf. of* вы́колотить.
вы́коло|тить, чу, тишь, *pf.* (*of* выкола́чи-
вать) 1. to knock out, beat out. 2. to beat
(*a carpet, etc.*). 3. (*coll.*) to extort, wring out.
4. (*coll.*) to make (*money*).
вы́кол|оть, ю, ешь, *pf.* (*of* выка́лывать) 1. to
thrust out; в. глаза́ кому́-н. to put out
someone's eyes; хоть глаз ~и, *see* глаз. 2. to
tattoo.
вы́колуп|ать, аю, *pf.* (*of* ~ывать) (*coll.*) to
pick out.
выколу́пыва|ть, ю, *impf. of* вы́колупать.
вы́копа|ть, ю, *pf.* (*of* выка́пывать) 1. to dig;
в. я́му to dig a hole. 2. (*impf. also* копа́ть)
to dig up, dig out; to exhume; (*fig., coll.*)
to unearth.
вы́копа|ться, юсь, *pf.* (*of* выка́пываться)
(*coll.*) to dig oneself out.
вы́коп|тить, чу, тишь, *pf.* (*of* выка́пчи-
вать) to smoke (*trans.*).
вы́корм|ить, лю, ишь, *pf.* (*of* выка́рмли-
вать) to rear, bring up.
вы́корм|ок, ка, *m.* (*coll.*) fosterling; (*fig.*)
protégé; (*pejor.*) creature.
вы́кормыш, а, *m.* = вы́кормок.
вы́корч|евать, ую, *pf.* (*of* ~ёвывать) to up-
root; (*fig.*) to root out, extirpate.
выкорчёвыва|ть, ю, *impf. of* вы́корчевать.
вы́ко|сить, шу, сишь, *pf.* (*of* выка́шивать)
to mow clean.
выкра́дыва|ть(ся), ю(сь), *impf. of* вы́-
красть(ся).
выкра́ива|ть, ю, *impf. of* вы́кроить.
вы́кра|сить, шу, сишь, *pf.* (*of* ~шивать) to
paint; to dye.
вы́кра|сть, ду, дешь, *past* ~л, *pf.* (*of* ~ды-
вать) to steal; (*fig.*) to plagiarize.
вы́кра|сться, дусь, дешься, *past* ~лся, *pf.*
(*of* ~дываться) (*coll.*) to steal away, steal
out.
выкра́шива|ть, ю, *impf. of* вы́красить.
вы́крест, а, *m.* (*coll.*) convert (*to Christianity,
esp. of Jews*).
вы́кре|стить, щу, стишь, *pf.* (*coll.*) to con-
vert (*to Christianity*).
вы́крик, а, *m.* cry, shout; yell.
выкри́кива|ть, ю, *impf. of* вы́крикнуть.
вы́крик|нуть, ну, нешь, *pf.* (*of* ~ивать) to
cry out; to yell.

вы́кристаллиз|оваться, уюсь, *pf.* (*of* ~о́вы-ваться) to crystallize (*also fig.*).

выкристаллизо́выва|ться, юсь, *impf. of* вы́кристаллизоваться.

вы́кро|ить, ю, ишь, *pf.* (*of* выкра́ивать) **1.** (*tailoring*) to cut out. **2.** (*fig.*) to find; **в.** вре́мя to make, find time.

вы́кройк|а, и, *f.* pattern; снять ~у to cut out a pattern.

выкрута́с|ы, ов, *no sing.* (*coll.*) intricate movements, figures; flourishes (*in hand-writing*); (*fig.*) peculiarities, idiosyncracies; говори́ть с ~ами to speak affectedly; челове́к с ~ами eccentric.

вы́кру|тить, чу, тишь, *pf.* (*of* ~чивать) **1.** to unscrew. **2.** (*tech.*) to twist; **в.** верёвку to twist a rope; (*coll.*) ему́ ~тили ру́ку they twisted his arm.

вы́кру|титься, чусь, тишься, *pf.* (*of* ~чи-ваться) **1.** to come unscrewed. **2.** (*fig.*, *coll.*) to extricate oneself, get oneself out (of); ему́ удало́сь в. из беды́ he has managed to get himself out of the mess.

выкру́чива|ть(ся), ю(сь), *impf. of* вы́кру-тить(ся).

выкувы́ркива|ть, ю, *impf. of* вы́кувырнуть.

вы́кувыр|нуть, ну, нешь, *pf.* (*of* ~кивать) (*coll.*) to overturn.

вы́куп, а, *m.* **1.** (*leg.*) redemption. **2.** ran-som; redemption-fee, redemption-dues.

выкупа́|ть(ся), ю(сь), *pf. of* купа́ть(ся).

выкупа́|ть, а́ю, *impf. of* вы́купить.

вы́куп|ить, лю, ишь, *pf.* (*of* ~а́ть) **1.** to ran-som. **2.** to redeem; **в.** из-под зало́га to get out of pawn.

выкупно́й, *adj.* redemption.

вы́кури|ва|ть, ю, ишь, *pf.* (*of* ~ивать) **1.** to smoke; to finish smoking; пойдёмте, — но, пре́жде всего́, ~ите ва́шу папиро́су! let's go, but first of all finish your cigarette. **2.** to smoke out; (*fig.*, *coll.*) to drive out. **3.** to distil.

вы́ку|сить, шу, сишь, *pf.* (*of* ~сывать) to bite through; на́кось, ~си! (*coll.*) you'll get nothing out of me!; you shan't have it!

выку́сыва|ть, ю, *impf. of* вы́кусить.

вы́куша|ть, ю, *pf.* (*obs.*) to drink.

вы́ку|шу, сишь, *see* ~сить.

вы́ку|ю, ешь, *see* вы́ковать.

выла́влива|ть, ю, *impf. of* вы́ловить.

вы́лаз, а, *m.* (*coll.*) opening (*in animal's burrow, etc.*).

вы́ла|зить, жу, зишь, *pf.* (*coll.*) to climb all over.

выла́|зить, жу, зишь, *impf.* (*dial.*) to fall out, come out.

вы́лазк|а, и, *f.* **1.** (*mil.*) sally, sortie (*also fig.*). **2.** ramble, excursion, outing.

вы́лака|ть, ю, *pf.* (*of* лака́ть) to lap up.

выла́мыва|ть, ю, *impf. of* вы́ломать *and* вы́ломить.

выла́щива|ть, ю, *impf. of* вы́лощить.

вы́леж|ать, у, ишь, *pf.* (*of* ~ивать) (*coll.*) to remain lying down; to stay in bed, keep one's bed.

вы́леж|аться, усь, ишься, *pf.* (*of* ~иваться) (*coll.*) **1.** to have a thorough rest. **2.** to ripen; to mature (*of tobacco, etc.*).

вылёжива|ть(ся), ю(сь), *impf. of* вы́ле-жать(ся).

вылеза́|ть, ю, *impf. of* вы́лезть.

вы́лезт|и = ~ь.

вы́лез|ть, у, ешь, *past* ~, ~ла, *pf.* (*of* ~ать) **1.** to crawl out; to climb out; (*coll.*) to get out, alight. **2.** to fall out, come out; по́сле боле́зни у него́ ~ли почти́ все во́лосы almost all his hair fell out after his illness. **3.** (c+*i.*; *coll.*, *pejor.*) to come out with; он, должно́ быть, ~ет с каки́м-н. глу́пым замеча́нием he is sure to come out with some fatuous remark.

вы́леп|ить, лю, ишь, *pf. of* лепи́ть.

вы́лет, а, *m.* flight (*of birds*); (*aeron.*) take--off, commencement of flight.

вылета́|ть, ю, *impf. of* вы́лететь.

вы́ле|теть, чу, тишь, *pf.* (*of* ~та́ть) **1.** to fly out; (*aeron.*) to take off; (*fig.*, *coll.*) to rush out, dash out; **в.** пу́лей to go like a shot from a gun; не дожда́вшись отве́та, он ~тел из ко́мнаты without waiting for an answer he rushed from the room; **в.** из головы́ to escape one; его́ сообще́ние ~тело у меня́ из головы́ I clean forgot his message; **в.** в трубу́ (*coll.*) to become bank-rupt, go broke. **2. в.** со слу́жбы (*fig.*, *coll.*) to be given the sack.

вы́ле́чива|ть(ся), ю(сь), *impf. of* вы́ле-чить(ся).

вы́леч|ить, у, ишь, *pf.* (*of* ~ивать) (от) to cure (of) (*also fig.*).

вы́леч|иться, усь, ишься, *pf.* (*of* ~иваться) (от) to recover (from), be cured (of); to get over (*also fig.*); он ~ился от наркома́-нии he has been cured of his drug--addiction.

вы́леч|у[1], ишь, *see* ~ить.

вы́ле|чу[2], тишь, *see* ~теть.

вылива́|ть(ся), ю(сь), *impf. of* вы́лить(ся).

вы́ли|зать, жу, жешь, *pf.* (*of* ~зывать) to lick clean, lick up.

вы́ли́зыва|ть, ю, *impf. of* вы́лизать.

вы́линя|ть, ю, *pf. of* линя́ть.

вы́лит|ый (~, ~а), *p.p.p. of* ~ь; (*fig.*, *coll.*; *long form only*) он — в. оте́ц he is the (spit and) image of his father, the very spit of his father.

вы́л|ить, ью, ьешь, *pf.* (*of* ~ива́ть) **1.** to pour out; to empty (out). **2.** (*tech.*) to cast, found; to mould.

вы́л|иться, ьюсь, ьешься, *pf.* (*of* ~ива́ться) 1. to run out, flow out; (*fig.*) to flow (from), spring (from); её жа́лобы ~ились пря́мо из се́рдца her complaints came straight from the heart. 2. (в+*a.* or в фо́рму +*g.*) to take the form (of); to be expressed, express itself (in); никто́ не знал, во что ~ется его́ восто́рг no one knew how his feeling of delight would express itself.

вы́лов|ить, лю, ишь, *pf.* (*of* выла́вливать) 1. to fish out; уто́пленника наконе́ц ~или из реки́ the drowned man has at last been fished out of the river. 2. to draw out (*catch all the fish in a stream, etc.*); в. всю ры́бу в пруду́ to draw out a pond.

вы́лож|ить, у, ишь, *pf.* (*of* выкла́дывать) 1. to lay out, spread out; (*fig., coll.*) to tell; to reveal, make an exposé (of). 2. (+*i.*) to cover, lay (with); в. дёрном to turf; в. ка́мнем to face with masonry, revet; (*tailoring*) to decorate, embellish (with). 3. (*dial.*) to geld.

вы́лом, а, *m.* 1. breaking open; breaking off. 2. breach.

вы́лома|ть, ю, *pf.* (*of* выла́мывать) to break open; to break off.

вы́лом|ить, лю, ишь, *pf.* (*coll.*) = вы́ломать.

вы́ломк|а, и, *f.* breaking off.

вы́лощен|ный (~, ~а), *p.p.p. of* вы́лощить *and adj.* 1. glossy. 2. (*coll., fig.*) polished, smooth.

вы́лощ|ить, у, ишь, *pf.* (*of* выла́щивать) to polish; (*fig., coll.*) to make polished, sophisticated.

вы́лу|дить, жу, дишь, *pf.* (*of* ~живать) to tin(-plate).

вы́лужива|ть, ю, *impf. of* вы́лудить.

вы́лу|жу, дишь, *see* ~дить.

вы́луп|ить, лю, ишь, *pf.* (*of* ~ля́ть) (*coll.*) to peel; to shell; в. глаза́ to goggle.

вы́луп|иться, люсь, ишься, *pf.* (*of* ~ля́ться) to hatch (out); не счита́й утя́т, пока́ не ~ились (*prov.*) don't count your chickens before they are hatched.

вылупля́|ть(ся), ю(сь), *impf. of* вы́лупить(ся).

вы́лущива|ть, ю, *impf. of* вы́лущить.

вы́лущ|ить, у, ишь, *pf.* (*of* ~ивать) 1. to shell (*peas*). 2. (*med.*) to remove (*by surgical operation*).

вы́л|ью, ьешь, *see* ~ить.

вы́ма|зать, жу, жешь, *pf.* (*of* ма́зать 2 *and* ~зывать) (+*i.*) to smear (with), daub (with); (*coll.*) to dirty; в. свои́ па́льцы в черни́лах to make one's fingers inky.

вы́ма|заться, жусь, жешься, *pf.* (*of* ма́заться 1 *and* ~зываться) (*coll.*) to get dirty, make oneself dirty.

выма́зыва|ть(ся), ю(сь), *impf. of* вы́мазать(ся).

выма́лива|ть, ю, *impf.* 1. *impf. of* вы́молить. 2. *impf. only* to beg for.

выма́лыва|ть, ю, *impf. of* вы́молоть.

выма́нива|ть, ю, *impf. of* вы́манить.

вы́ман|ить, ю, ишь, *pf.* (*of* ~ивать) 1. (у+ *g.*) to cheat, swindle (out of); to wheedle (out of); у него́ ~или поже́ртвование they wheedled a contribution out of him. 2. (из+*g.*) to entice (from), lure (out of, from).

вы́мар|ать, аю, *pf.* (*of* ~ывать) (*coll.*) 1. to soil, dirty. 2. to strike out, cross out.

выма́рива|ть, ю, *impf. of* вы́морить.

вы́марк|а, и, *f.* striking out, crossing out, deletion.

выма́рыва|ть, ю, *impf. of* вы́марать.

выма́тыва|ть, ю, *impf. of* вы́мотать.

вы́махн|уть, у, ешь, *pf.* (*coll.*) to fly out; to leap out.

выма́чива|ть, ю, *impf. of* вы́мочить.

выма́щива|ть, ю, *impf. of* вы́мостить.

вы́межева|ть, ю, *pf.* (*of* вымежёвывать) (*agric.*) to measure out (*strips of land*).

вымежёвыва|ть, ю, *impf. of* вы́межевать.

вы́м|ени, енем, *see* ~я.

вы́менива|ть, ю, *impf. of* вы́менять.

вы́мен|ять, яю, *pf.* (*of* ~ивать) (на+*a.*) to receive in exchange, barter (for); в. проду́кты на оде́жду to barter produce for clothing.

вы́м|ереть, ру, решь, *past* ~ер, ~ерла, *pf.* (*of* ~ира́ть) 1. to die out, become extinct. 2. to become desolate, deserted.

вымерз|а́ть, а́ю, *impf. of* вы́мерзнуть.

вы́мерз|нуть, ну, нешь, *past* ~, ~ла, *pf.* (*of* ~а́ть) 1. to be killed by frost. 2. to freeze (right through).

выме́рива|ть, ю, *impf. of* вы́мерить.

вы́мер|ить, ю, ишь, *pf.* (*of* ~ивать) to measure.

вы́мер|ший, *past part. of* ~еть *and adj.* extinct.

вы́меря|ть, ю = вы́мерить.

вымеря́|ть, ю = выме́ривать.

вы́ме|сти, ту, тешь, *past* ~л, *pf.* (*of* ~та́ть) 1. to sweep out; to sweep clean; в. сор to sweep out refuse; в. ко́мнату to sweep a room clean. 2. (*coll.*) to throw out, chuck out.

вы́ме|стить, щу, стишь, *pf.* (*of* ~ща́ть) 1. (+*d.*; *obs.*) to retaliate, take reprisals (against). 2. (на+*p.*) to vent; в. злобу на ком-н. to vent one's anger on someone.

вы́мет|ать¹, аю, *pf.* (*of* ~ывать) 1. to put out, cast out (*a net, etc.*). 2. в. икру́ to spawn.

вы́мет|ать², аю, *pf.* (*of* ~ывать) в. пе́тли to make buttonholes.

вымета́|ть, ю, *impf. of* вы́мести.

вымета́|ться, юсь, *impf.* (*coll.*) to clear out, clear off (*intrans.*).

вымётыва|ть, ю, *impf. of* вы́метать.

вымеща́|ть, ю, *impf. of* вы́местить.

вы́ме|щу, стишь, *see* ~стить.

вымина́|ть, ю, *impf. of* вы́мять.

вымира́|ть, ю, *impf. of* вы́мереть.

вы́м|ну, нешь, *see* ~ять.

вымога́тел|ь, я, *m.* extortioner.

вымога́тельский, *adj.* extortionate.

вымога́тельств|о, а, *n.* extortion.

вымога́|ть, ю, *impf.* to extort; to wring (out); угро́зами он неред́ко ~л у неё обеща́ния he frequently wrung promises out of her by means of threats.

вы́моин|а, ы, *f.* (*dial.*) gully.

вымока́|ть, ю, *impf. of* вы́мокнуть.

вы́мок|нуть, ну, нешь, *past* ~, ~ла, *pf* (*of* ~а́ть) **1.** (*of crops, foodstuffs, etc.*) to rot, ret; to become soggy. **2.** to be drenched, be soaked; мы ~ли до ни́тки we are soaked to the skin.

вымола́чива|ть, ю, *impf. of* вы́молотить.

вы́молв|ить, лю, ишь, *pf.* to say, utter (*usually with neg.*); за весь ве́чер он сло́ва не ~ил he did not say a word all evening.

вы́мол|ить, ю, ишь, *pf.* (*of* выма́ливать) to obtain by asking, by entreaties; to beg (for) and obtain; (у Бо́га) to obtain by prayer.

вы́молот, а, *m.* **1.** threshing. **2.** grain (obtained by threshing).

вы́моло|тить, чу, тишь, *pf.* (*of* вымола́чивать) to thresh (out).

вы́молот|ки, ок-ков, *no sing.* (*dial.*) chaff.

вы́м|олоть, елю, елешь, *pf.* (*of* выма́ливать) (*coll.*) to obtain by grinding.

вымора́жива|ть, ю, *impf. of* вы́морозить.

вы́мор|ить, ю, ишь, *pf.* (*of* мори́ть¹ *and* выма́ривать, to exterminate; го́лодом в. to starve out.

вы́моро|зить, жу, зишь, *pf.* (*of* вымора́живать) **1.** to cool; to air, give an airing (to). **2.** to freeze out; to freeze to death (*trans.*).

вы́морочн|ый, *adj.* (*leg.*) escheated; ~ое иму́щество escheat.

вы́мо|стить, щу, стишь, *pf.* (*of* мости́ть *and* выма́щивать) to pave.

вы́мота|ть, ю, *pf.* (*of* выма́тывать) (*coll.*) **1.** to wind (*wool*). **2.** to wind off, use up (*wool*); (*fig.*) to use up; to exhaust; в. ду́шу to annoy, wear out; они́ ~ли не́рвы друг дру́гу they got on one another's nerves.

вы́мота|ться, юсь, *pf.* (*of* выма́тываться) (*coll.*) **1.** *pass. of* ~ть. **2.** to be worn out.

вы́моч|ить, у, ишь, *pf.* (*of* выма́чивать) **1.** to soak, drench. **2.** to ret (*flax, hemp*); to steep, macerate.

вы́мо|щу, стишь, *see* ~стить.

вы́м|ою, оешь, *see* ~ыть.

вы́мпел, а, *m.* **1.** pendant, pennant. **2.** (*naut.*) unit; эска́дра в соста́ве двадцати́ ~ов a squadron consisting of twenty units.

3. (*aeron.*) message bag (*used for messages dropped by air*).

вы́мр|у, ешь, *see* вы́мереть.

вы́мучен|ный (~, ~а), *p.p.p. of* вы́мучить *and adj.* forced; (*lit.*) laboured.

вы́мучива|ть, ю, *impf. of* вы́мучить.

вы́муч|ить, у, ишь, *pf.* (*of* ~ивать) (из+*g.*) to extort (from), force (out of); он наконе́ц ~ил согла́сие у отца́ at last he extorted his father's consent.

вы́муштр|овать, ую, *pf. of* муштрова́ть.

вымыва́|ть(ся), ю(сь), *impf. of* вы́мыть(ся).

вы́мыс|ел, ла, *m.* **1.** invention, fabrication. **2.** fantasy, flight of imagination.

вы́мы|слить, слю, слишь, *pf.* (*of* ~шля́ть) (*obs.*) to think up, invent; to imagine.

вы́м|ыть, ою, оешь, *pf.* (*of* мыть *and* ~ыва́ть) **1.** to wash; to wash out, off; в. го́лову кому́-н. to give someone a dressing-down. **2.** to wash away.

вы́м|ыться, оюсь, оешься, *pf.* (*of* мы́ться *and* ~ыва́ться) to wash oneself.

вы́мышлен|ный (~, ~а), *p.p.p. of* вы́мыслить *and adj.* fictitious, imaginary.

вымышля́|ть, ю, *impf. of* вы́мыслить.

вы́м|я, ени, ени, енем, ени, *pl.* ~ена́, ~ён, ~ена́м, *n.* udder.

вы́м|ять, ну, нешь, *pf.* (*of* ~ина́ть) **1.** to knead, work (*clay*). **2.** (*dial.*) to trample down.

вына́шива|ть, ю, *impf. of* вы́носить.

вынесе́ни|е, я, *n.* в. пригово́ра (*leg.*) pronouncement of sentence.

вы́нес|ти, у, ешь, *pf.* (*of* выноси́ть) **1.** to carry out, take out; to take away; (*of sea or river current, etc.*) to carry away; в. поко́йника to carry out a body for burial; в. на бе́рег to wash ashore; в. ле́вую но́гу to step off with the left foot; в. на поля́ to enter in the margin (*of a book*); в. под строку́ to make a footnote; в. сор из избы́ to wash one's dirty linen in public. **2.** (*fig.*) to take away, carry away, derive; в. прия́тное впечатле́ние to be favourably impressed. **3.** в. вопро́с (на собра́ние, на обсужде́ние) to put, submit a question (to a meeting, for discussion). **4.** в. на свои́х плеча́х (*fig.*) to shoulder, take the full weight (of), bear the full brunt (of). **5.** to bear, stand, endure; не в. to be unable to stand, be unable to take, be allergic (to) (*diet, treatment, etc.*). **6.** в. благода́рность to express gratitude, return thanks; в. пригово́р (+*d.*) to pass sentence (on), pronounce sentence (on); в. реше́ние to decide; (*leg.*) to pronounce judgement.

вы́нес|тись, усь, ешься, *past* ~ся, ~лась, *pf.* (*of* выноси́ться) (*coll.*) to fly out, rush out.

вы́ни|зать, жу, жешь, *pf.* (*of* ‿зыва́ть) (*obs.*) to decorate, adorn (*with string of beads, pearls, etc.*).

вынизыва|ть, ю, *impf. of* вы́низать.

вынима́|ть, ю, *impf. of* вы́нуть.

вынима́|ться, ется, *impf.* (*of* вы́нуться) (*coll.*) to come out; э́тот я́щик не ‿ется this drawer does not come out.

вы́нос, а, *m.* 1. (из це́ркви) bearing-out, carrying-out (*of bier, at funerals*). 2. trace; ло́шадь под ‿ом trace-horse.

вы́но|сить, шу, сишь, *pf.* (*of* вына́шивать) to bear, bring forth (*a child at full term*); в. мысль (*fig.*) to give birth to an idea.

выно|си́ть, шу́, ‿сишь, *impf.* 1. *impf. of* вы́нести. 2. *impf. only* (+*neg.*) to be unable to bear, be unable to stand; я его́ не ‿шу́ I can't stand him. 3. хоть святы́х ‿си́ (*coll.*) it is intolerable.

вы́носк|а, и, *f.* 1. taking out, carrying out. 2. marginal note; footnote.

выно́сливост|ь, и, *f.* (powers of) endurance; staying-power.

выно́слив|ый (‿, ‿а), *adj.* hardy (*also hort.*).

выносн|о́й, *adj.* 1. inserted in footnote. 2. ‿а́я ло́шадь trace-horse.

вы́ношен|ный (‿, ‿а), *p.p.p. of* выноси́ть *and adj.*; в. ребёнок child born at full term; в. прое́кт (*fig.*) mature project.

вы́но|шу, сишь, *see* ‿сить.

выно|шу́, ‿сишь, *see* ‿си́ть.

вы́ну|дить, жу, дишь, *pf.* (*of* ‿жда́ть) 1. (+*inf.*) to force, compel; его́ ‿дили уе́хать из страны́ he was forced to leave the country. 2. (у+*g.*) to extort, force (from, out of); они́ ‿дили у него́ призна́ние в свое́й вине́ they have extorted an admission of guilt from him.

вынужда́|ть, ю, *impf. of* вы́нудить.

вы́нужден|ный (‿, ‿а), *p.p.p. of* вы́нудить *and adj.* forced, compulsory; ‿ная поса́дка (*aeron.*) forced landing.

вы́н|уть, у, ешь, *pf.* (*of* ‿има́ть) 1. to take out; to pull out, extract; to draw out (*money from bank, etc.*). 2. ‿ь да поло́жь (*coll.*) here and now, on the spot; there and then; он тре́бует шампа́нского — ‿ь да поло́жь he demands champagne here and now.

выны́рива|ть, ю, *impf. of* вы́нырнуть.

вы́ныр|нуть, ну, нешь, *pf.* (*of* ‿ивать) to come up, come to the surface (*of diver*); (*fig., coll.*) to turn up; как для него́ характе́рно — он опя́ть ‿ул без гроша́ how like him to turn up without a farthing again!

вы́нюх|ать, аю, *pf.* (*of* ‿ивать) (*coll.*) to sniff up; (*fig.*) to nose out, sniff out; в формулиро́вке предложе́ния он ‿ал что-то недо́брое he smelled a rat in the wording of the offer.

вынюхива|ть, ю, *impf. of* вы́нюхать.

вынянчива|ть, ю, *impf. of* вы́нянчить.

вы́нянч|ить, у, ишь, *pf.* (*of* ‿ивать) (*coll.*) to bring up, nurse.

вы́пад, а, *m.* 1. (*fig.*) attack. 2. (*sport*) lunge, thrust.

выпада́|ть, ю, *impf. of* вы́пасть.

выпаде́ни|е, я, *n.* 1. falling out. 2. (*med.*) prolapsus.

выпа́ива|ть, ю, *impf. of* вы́поить.

выпа́лива|ть, ю, *impf. of* вы́палить.

вы́пал|ить, ю, ишь, *pf.* (*of* ‿ивать) (*coll.*) 1. (в+*a.*) to shoot, fire (at). 2. (*fig.*) to blurt out. 3. (*dial.*) to fire (*trans.*), burn up.

выпа́лыва|ть, ю, *impf. of* вы́полоть.

выпа́рива|ть, ю, *impf. of* вы́парить.

вы́пар|ить, ю, ишь, *pf.* (*of* ‿ивать) 1. to steam; to clean, disinfect (by steaming). 2. (*chem.*) to evaporate. 3. to clean (*in a steam-bath*).

вы́парк|а, и, *f.* (*coll.*) 1. steaming. 2. evaporation.

выпарно́й, *adj.* (*tech.*) evaporation.

выпа́рхива|ть, ю, *impf. of* вы́порхнуть.

выпа́рыва|ть, ю, *impf. of* вы́пороть¹.

вы́пас, а, *m.* pasture.

вы́па|сть, ду, дешь, *past* ‿л, *pf.* (*of* ‿да́ть) 1. to fall out. 2. to fall (*of rain, snow, etc.*); но́чью ‿ло мно́го сне́гу there was a heavy fall of snow in the night. 3. to befall, fall (to); им ‿ло тяжёлое испыта́ние a severe test has befallen them; ему́ ‿л жре́бий стоя́ть на карау́ле в день Рождества́ it fell to his lot to be on guard on Christmas Day. 4. to occur, turn out; ночь ‿ла звёздная it turned out a starry night. 5. (*sport*) lunge, thrust.

вы́па|хать, шу, шешь, *pf.* (*of* ‿хивать) 1. to exhaust (*soil*). 2. to turn up with the plough.

выпа́хива|ть, ю, *impf. of* вы́пахать.

вы́пачка|ть, ю, *pf.* to soil, dirty; to stain.

вы́пачка|ться, юсь, *pf.* to make oneself dirty.

вы́па|шу, шешь, *see* ‿хать.

вы́пе|к, *see* ‿чь.

выпека́|ть, ю, *impf. of* вы́печь.

вы́п|ереть, ру, решь, *past* ‿ер, ‿ерла, *pf.* (*of* ‿ира́ть) 1. to push out, shove out. 2. to stick out, bulge out, protrude. 3. (*sl.*) to throw out, kick out, sling out.

вы́пест|овать, ую, *pf. of* пе́стовать.

вы́печк|а, и, *f.* 1. baking. 2. batch (*of loaves, etc.*).

вы́пе|чь, ку, чешь, кут, *past* ‿к, ‿кла, *pf.* (*of* ‿ка́ть) to bake.

выпива́л|а, ы, *m. and f.* (*coll.*) tippler.

выпива́|ть, ю, *impf.* 1. *impf. of* вы́пить. 2. (*impf. only; coll.*) to be fond of the bottle.

вы́пивк|а, и, *f.* (*coll.*) 1. drinking-bout. 2. (*collect.*) drinks.

выпивóх|а, и, *m. and f.* (*sl.*) tippler; boozer.

вы́пи|вши, *past gerund of* ~ть; (*coll.*) drunk (*also used as predicative adjective*).

выпи́лива|ть, ю, *impf. of* вы́пилить.

вы́пил|ить, ю, ишь, *pf.* (*of* ~ивать) to saw, saw up, saw off; в. ра́мку ло́бзиком to make a fretwork frame.

вы́пилк|а, и, *f.* 1. sawing. 2. sawn-up, sawn-off object.

выпира́|ть, ю, *impf. of* вы́переть.

вы́пи|сать, шу, шешь, *pf.* (*of* ~сывать) 1. to copy out; to excerpt. 2. to delineate scrupulously; to trace out. 3. to write out; в. квита́нцию to write out a receipt. 4. to order; to subscribe (to); to send for (*in writing*); в. кни́гу to order a book; е́сли ей ста́нет ху́же, вам придётся в. её сы́на if she gets worse you will have to send for her son. 5. to strike off the list; в. из больни́цы to discharge from hospital.

вы́пи|саться, шусь, шешься, *pf.* (*of* ~сы-ваться) 1. to leave (*on discharge*); to be dis-charged; он уже́ ~са́лся из больни́цы he is already out of hospital. 2. (*obs.*) to write oneself out.

вы́писк|а, и, *f.* 1. copying, excerpting. 2. writing out. 3. extract, excerpt; ~и из газе́т newspaper extracts. 4. ordering; subscription. 5. discharge.

выпи́сыва|ть(ся), ю(сь), *impf. of* вы́пи-сать(ся).

вы́пис|ь, и, *f.* extract, copy; метри́ческая в. birth certificate.

вы́п|ить, ью, ьешь, *pf.* (*of* выпива́ть *and* пить) to drink; to drink up, off.

выпи́хива|ть, ю, *impf. of* вы́пихнуть.

вы́пих|нуть, ну, нешь, *pf.* (*of* ~ивать) (*coll.*) to shove out, bundle out.

вы́пи|шу, шешь, *see* ~сать.

вы́плав|ить, лю, ишь, *pf.* (*of* ~ля́ть) to smelt.

вы́плавк|а, и, *f.* 1. smelting. 2. smelted metal.

выплавля́|ть, ю, *impf. of* вы́плавить.

вы́пла|кать, чу, чешь, *pf.* 1. (*coll., folk poet.*) to sob out. 2. (*coll.*) to obtain by weeping, by tearful entreaties. 3. (*coll., folk poet.*) в. (все) глаза́ to cry one's eyes out.

вы́пла|каться, чусь, чешься, *pf.* (*coll.*) to have a good cry, have one's cry out.

вы́плат|а, ы, *f.* 1. payment. 2. (*coll.*) pay-ment by instalments; купи́ть на ~у to pur-chase by instalments.

вы́пла|тить, чу, тишь, *pf.* (*of* ~чивать) 1. to pay (out). 2. to pay off (*debts*).

выпла́чива|ть, ю, *impf. of* вы́платить.

вы́пла|чу¹, тишь, *see* ~тить.

вы́пла|чу², чешь, *see* ~кать.

выплёвыва|ть, ю, *impf. of* вы́плюнуть.

вы́пле|скать, щу, щешь, *pf.* (*of* ~скивать) to splash out.

выплёскива|ть, ю, *impf. of* вы́плескать *and* вы́плеснуть.

вы́плес|нуть, ну, нешь, *pf.* (*of* ~кивать) to splash out; в. с водо́й и ребёнка (*fig.*) to throw out the baby with the (bath-)water.

вы́пле|сти, ту, тешь, *pf.* (*of* ~та́ть) 1. to undo, untie. 2. to weave.

выплета́|ть, ю, *impf. of* вы́плести.

выплыва́|ть, ю, *impf. of* вы́плыть.

вы́плы|ть, ву, вешь, *pf.* (*of* ~ва́ть) 1. to swim out; (*fig.*) она́ ~ла из ко́мнаты she sailed out of the room. 2. to come to the surface, come up; (*fig., coll.*) to emerge; to appear; to crop up; пре́жнее недоразуме́-ние сно́ва ~ло the old misunderstanding has cropped up again.

вы́плюн|уть, у, ешь, *pf.* (*of* выплёвывать) to spit out.

вы́по|ить, ю, ишь, *pf.* (*of* выпа́ивать) to feed (*livestock*).

выпола́скива|ть, ю, *impf. of* вы́полоскать.

выполза́|ть, ю, *impf. of* вы́ползти.

вы́полз|ок, ка, *m.* (*dial.*) 1. slough. 2. worm.

вы́полз|ти, у, ешь, *past* ~, ~ла, *pf.* (*of* ~а́ть) (из+*g.*) to crawl out, creep out (from).

вы́полир|овать, ую, *pf.* (*coll.*) to polish (up).

выполне́ни|е, я, *n.* execution, carrying-out; fulfilment.

выполни́м|ый (~, ~а), *pres. part. pass. of* вы́полнить *and adj.* practicable, feasible.

вы́полн|ить, ю, ишь, *pf.* (*of* ~я́ть) to exe-cute, carry out; to fulfil; в. свои́ обя́зан-ности to discharge one's obligations, do one's duty; в. приказа́ние to carry out an order.

выполня́|ть, ю, *impf. of* вы́полнить.

вы́поло|скать, щу, щешь, *pf.* (*of* выпо-ла́скивать) to rinse out.

вы́пол|оть, ю, ешь, *pf.* (*of* выпа́лывать) to weed out.

вы́порот|ок, ка, *m.* unborn animal (*re-moved from female for fur*).

вы́пор|оть¹, ю, ешь, *pf.* (*of* выпа́рывать) (*coll.*) to rip out, rip up.

вы́пор|оть², ю, ешь, *pf. of* поро́ть².

вы́порхн|уть, у, ешь, *pf.* (*of* выпа́рхивать) to flit out (*of birds*); (*fig., coll.*) to dart out.

вы́поте|ть, ю, ешь, *pf.* (*coll.*) to sweat out.

вы́потрош|ить, у, ишь, *pf. of* потроши́ть.

вы́прав|ить, лю, ишь, *pf.* (*of* ~ля́ть) 1. to straighten (out). 2. to correct; to improve. 3. (*coll.*) to get, obtain (*documents*); в. па́с-порт to get a passport.

вы́прав|иться, люсь, ишься, *pf.* (*of* ~ля́ться) 1. to become straight. 2. to im-prove (*intrans.*).

вы́правк|а, и, *f.* 1. bearing. 2. (*typ.*) correc-tion.

выправля́|ть(ся), ю(сь), *impf. of* вы́править(ся).

выпра́стыва|ть(ся), ю(сь), *impf. of* вы́простать(ся).

выпра́шива|ть, ю, *impf.* 1. *impf. of* вы́просить. 2. *impf. only* to solicit, try to get; он всё ~ет разрешéние на вы́езд he is always trying to get permission to go abroad.

выпрева́|ть, ю, *impf. of* вы́преть.

вы́пре|ть, ю, ешь, *pf.* (*of* ~ва́ть) (*coll., dial.*) to rot (*of crops*).

выпрова́жива|ть, ю, *impf. of* вы́проводить.

вы́прово|дить, жу, дишь, *pf.* (*of* выпрова́живать) (*coll.*) to send packing; to show the door (to).

вы́про|сить, шу, сишь, *pf.* (*of* выпра́шивать) (у+*g.*) to get (out of), obtain, elicit (by begging); наконе́ц он ~сил разреше́ние на вы́езд at last he elicited permission to go abroad.

вы́проста|ть, ю, *pf.* (*of* выпра́стывать) (*coll.*) 1. to free, work loose. 2. to empty.

вы́проста|ться, юсь, *pf.* (*of* выпра́стываться) (*coll.*) 1. to free oneself, work (oneself) free. 2. to defecate.

вы́про|шу, сишь, *see* ~сить.

вы́п|ру, решь, *see* ~ереть.

выпры́гива|ть, ю, *impf. of* вы́прыгнуть.

вы́прыг|нуть, ну, нешь, *pf.* (*of* ~ивать) to jump out, spring out.

выпряга́|ть, ю, *impf. of* вы́прячь.

выпрями́тел|ь, я, *m.* (*electr.*) rectifier.

вы́прям|ить, лю, ишь, *pf.* (*of* ~ля́ть) 1. to straighten (out). 2. (*electr.*) to rectify.

вы́прям|иться, люсь, ишься, *pf.* (*of* ~ля́ться) 1. to become straight; в. во весь рост to draw oneself up to one's full height.

выпрямля́|ть(ся), ю(сь), *impf. of* вы́прямить(ся).

вы́пря|чь, гу, жешь, гут, *past* ~г, ~гла, *pf.* (*of* ~га́ть) to unharness.

выпу́гива|ть, ю, *impf. of* вы́пугнуть.

вы́пуг|нуть, ну, нешь, *pf.* (*of* ~ивать) to scare off; to start (*game*).

вы́пукло-во́гнутый, *adj.* (*phys.*) convexo-concave.

вы́пуклост|ь, и, *f.* 1. protuberance; prominence, bulge. 2. (*phys.*) convexity. 3. relief (*in sculpture, etc.*). 4. (*sing. only*; *fig.*) clarity, distinctness.

вы́пуклый, *adj.* 1. protuberant; prominent, bulging. 2. (*phys.*) convex. 3. in relief. 4. (*fig.*) clear, distinct.

вы́пуск, а, *m.* 1. output; issue; discharge (*of steam, gases, etc.*); в. из печа́ти publication. 2. part, number, instalment (*of serial publication*). 3. leavers; graduates (*those who complete studies at the same time*); он — са́мый блестя́щий из прошлого́днего ~а

по хи́мии he is the most brilliant of those who graduated in chemistry last year. 4. cut, omission. 5. (*obs.*) edging, piping. 6. брю́ки на в. *see* навы́пуск.

выпуска́|ть, ю, *impf. of* вы́пустить.

выпуска́|ющий, *pres. part. act. of* ~ть; *as noun* в., ~ющего, *m.* person responsible for seeing newspaper *or* journal through press.

выпускни́к, а́, *m.* final-year student.

выпускн|о́й, *adj. of* вы́пуск; в. кла́пан (*tech.*) exhaust valve; в. кран (*tech.*) discharge cock; ~а́я труба́ (*tech.*) exhaust pipe; ~а́я цена́ (*econ.*) market price; в. экза́мен final examination, finals; *as noun* в., ~но́го, *m.*, ~на́я, ~но́й, *f.* final-year student.

вы́пу|стить, щу, стишь, *pf.* (*of* ~ска́ть) 1. to let out; to release; в. во́ду из ва́нны to let the water out of a bath; в. из тюрьмы́ to release from prison; в. (пулемётную) о́чередь (*mil.*) to fire a burst. 2. to put out, issue; to turn out, produce; в. в прода́жу to put on the market; в. заём to float a loan; в. офице́ров to turn out officers; в. кинокарти́ну to release a film. 3. to cut (out), omit. 4. (*tailoring*) to let out, let down. 5. to show; в. свои́ ко́гти to show one's claws. 6. (*typ.*) to see through the press.

вы́пут|ать, аю, *pf.* (*of* ~ывать) to disentangle.

вы́пут|аться, аюсь, *pf.* (*of* ~ываться) to disentangle oneself, extricate oneself (*also fig.*).

вы́путыва|ть(ся), ю(сь), *impf. of* вы́путать(ся).

вы́пуч|енный, *p.p.p. of* ~ить *and adj.*; (*coll.*) с ~енными глаза́ми wide-eyed, goggle-eyed.

выпу́чива|ть, ю, *impf. of* вы́пучить.

вы́пуч|ить, у, ишь, *pf.* (*of* ~ивать) в. глаза́ (*coll.*) to open one's eyes wide.

вы́пушк|а, и, *f.* edging, braid, piping.

вы́пыт|ать, аю, *pf.* (*of* ~ывать) (у+*g.*) to elicit, extort (*information, secrets, etc., from*).

вы́пытыва|ть, ю, *impf.* 1. *impf. of* вы́пытать. 2. *impf. only* to try to discover (*by interrogation*); в. секре́т у кого́-н. to try to get a secret out of someone.

вы́п|ь, и, *f.* bittern (*bird*).

выпя́лива|ть, ю, *impf. of* вы́пялить.

вы́пял|ить, ю, ишь, *pf.* (*of* ~ивать) (*coll.*) to stick out; в. глаза́ to open one's eyes wide, stare.

вы́пя|тить, чу, тишь, *pf.* (*of* ~чивать) (*coll.*) 1. to stick out; в. грудь to stick out one's chest. 2. (*fig.*) to over-emphasize.

вы́пя|титься, чусь, тишься, *pf.* (*of* ~чиваться) (*coll.*) to stick out (*intrans.*), protrude.

выпя́чива|ть(ся), ю(сь), *impf. of* вы́пятить(ся).

выраба́тыва|ть, ю, *impf. of* вы́работать.

вы́работа|ть, ю, *pf. (of* выраба́тывать) **1.** to manufacture; to produce, make. **2.** to work out, draw up; в. пове́стку дня для заседа́ния to draw up an agenda for a meeting; в. хоро́ший стиль to work up a good style; в. си́лу хара́ктера to develop, acquire strength of character. **3.** (*coll.*) to earn, make. **4.** (*tech.*) to work out (*a mine*).

вы́работк|а, и, *f.* **1.** manufacture; production, making. **2.** working-out, drawing-up. **3.** output, yield. **4.** (*coll.*) make; хоро́шей ~и well-made. **5.** (*tech.*) (mine-)working.

выра́внивани|е, я, *n.* smoothing-out, levelling; equalization; alignment.

выра́внива|ть(ся), ю(сь), *impf. of* вы́ровнять(ся).

выража́|ть, ю, *impf. of* вы́разить.

выража́|ться, юсь, *impf.* **1.** *impf. of* вы́разиться; мя́гко ~ясь to put it mildly. **2.** (*coll.*) to swear, use swear-words.

выраже́ни|е, я, *n.* (*in var. senses*) expression.

вы́ражен|ный (~, ~а), *p.p.p. of* вы́разить *and adj.* pronounced, marked; он говори́т по-англи́йски, но с ре́зко ~ным неме́цким акце́нтом he speaks English, but with a very pronounced German accent.

вырази́тел|ь, я, *m.* one who expresses; exponent, spokesman; он был еди́нственным в исто́рии страны́ ~ем стремле́ний всего́ наро́да he was the only man in the country's history who had expressed the aspirations of the entire people.

вырази́тел|ьный (~ен, ~ьна), *adj.* expressive; significant; ~ьное чте́ние elocution.

выра|зить, жу, зишь, *pf. (of* ~жа́ть) to express; to convey; to voice; его́ докла́д ~зил взгля́ды прису́тствующих на ми́тинге his report conveyed the views of the meeting.

вы́ра|зиться, жусь, зишься, *pf. (of* ~жа́ться) **1.** to express oneself. **2.** (в+*p.*) to manifest itself (in). **3.** (в+*p.*) to amount to, come to; изде́ржки ~зились в шести́ рубля́х the costs came to six roubles.

вы́разуме|ть, ю, *pf.* (*obs.*) to understand.

выраста́|ть, ю, *impf. of* вы́расти.

вы́р|асти, асту, астешь, *past* ~ос, ~осла, *pf. (of* ~аста́ть) **1.** to grow (up). **2.** (в+*a.*) to grow (into), develop (into), become; их дру́жба ~осла в любо́вь their friendship grew into love. **3.** (из+*g.*) to grow (out of) (*clothing*). **4.** to increase; населе́ние за пять лет ~осло на два́дцать проце́нтов in five years the population had increased by twenty per cent. **5.** to appear, rise up; пе́ред на́шими глаза́ми ~ос Арара́т Mount Ararat rose up before our eyes. **6.** в. в чьих-н. глаза́х to rise in someone's estimation.

вы́ра|стить, щу, стишь, *pf. (of* ~́щивать) to bring up (*children*); to rear, breed (*livestock*); to grow, cultivate (*plants*).

выра́щива|ть, ю, *impf. of* вы́растить.

вы́рв|ать¹, у, ешь, *pf. (of* вырыва́ть¹) **1.** to pull out, tear out; в. зуб to pull out a tooth; в. себе́ зуб (у врача́) to have a tooth out; он ~ал кни́гу у меня́ из рук he snatched the book out of my hands. **2.** (*fig.*) to extort, wring; в. призна́ние у кого́-н. to wring a confession out of someone.

вы́рв|ать², у, ешь, *pf. of* рвать².

вы́рв|аться, усь, ешься, *pf. (of* вырыва́ться) **1.** (из+*g.*) to tear oneself away (from); to break out (from), break loose (from), break free (from); to get away (from); в. из чьих-н. объя́тий to tear oneself away from someone's embrace; в. из чьих-н. рук to break loose from someone's grip; едва́ ли мне уда́стся до ле́та в. из Москвы́ I shall hardly manage to get away from Moscow before the summer. **2.** to come loose, come out; не́сколько страни́ц ~алось из э́той кни́ги several pages have come out of this book. **3.** (*of a sound, a remark, etc.*) (из, у+*g.*) to break (from), burst (from), escape; из груди́ старика́ ~ался стон a groan broke from the old man. **4.** to shoot up, shoot out; пла́мя ~алось из трубы́ a flame shot up from the chimney; четвёртая маши́на вдруг ~алась вперёд на пе́рвое ме́сто the fourth car suddenly shot ahead into first place.

вы́рез, а, *m.* cut; notch; пла́тье с больши́м ~ом low-necked dress; покупа́ть (арбу́з) на в. (*coll.*) to buy (a water-melon) on trial.

вы́ре|зать, жу, жешь, *pf. (of* ~за́ть) **1.** to cut out; to excise. **2.** to cut, carve; to engrave. **3.** (*fig.*) to slaughter, butcher.

выреза́|ть, ю, *impf. of* вы́резать.

вы́резк|а, и, *f.* **1.** cutting-out, excision; carving; engraving. **2.** газе́тная в. press-cutting. **3.** fillet steak.

вырезно́й, *adj.* **1.** cut; carved. **2.** low-necked, décolleté.

вы́резывани|е, я, *n.* cutting-out; excision; carving; engraving.

вы́резыва|ть, ю, *impf.* = вырезать.

вы́реш|ить, у, ишь, *pf.* (*coll.*) to decide finally.

вы́рис|овать, ую, *pf. (of* ~о́вывать) to draw carefully, draw in detail.

вы́рис|оваться, уется, *pf. (of* ~о́вываться) to appear (in outline); to stand out; на горизо́нте ~ова́лась го́рная цепь a mountain chain stood out against the horizon.

вырисо́выва|ть(ся), ю(сь), *impf. of* вы́рисовать(ся).

вы́ровня|ть, ю, *pf. (of* выра́внивать) **1.** to smooth (out), level; в. доро́гу to level a road; в. шаг to regulate one's pace. **2.** to equalize; to align. **3.** (*mil.*) to draw up in line; в. ряды́ to dress ranks. **4.** в. самолёт to straighten out an aeroplane.

вы́ровня|ться, юсь, *pf.* (*of* выра́вниваться) **1.** to become level; to become even; (*mil.*) to form up; to dress, take up dressing; (*sport*) to equalize. **2.** (*fig.*) to catch up, draw level; несмотря́ на боле́знь ему́ удало́сь в. с други́ми ученика́ми кла́сса despite his illness he has managed to catch up with the rest of the class. **3.** (*fig.*) to improve, get better; (*coll.*) to become more equable.

вы́род|иться, ится, *pf.* (*of* вырожда́ться) to degenerate.

вы́род|ок, ка, *m.* (*coll.*) degenerate; он — в. в на́шей семье́ he is the black sheep of our family.

вырожда́|ться, юсь, *impf. of* вы́родиться.

вырожде́н|ец, ца, *m.* degenerate.

вырожде́ни|е, я, *n.* degeneration.

вы́рон|ить, ю, ишь, *pf.* to drop.

вы́рост, а, *no pl.*, *m.* **1.** growth, excrescence; offshoot. **2.** шить на в. to make (*clothes*) with room for growth.

вы́ростковый, *adj.* calf(-leather).

вы́рост|ок, ка, *m.* year-old calf; calf--leather.

вы́р|ою, оешь, *see* ∼ыть.

выруба́|ть(ся), ю(сь), *impf. of* вы́рубить(ся).

вы́руб|ить, лю, ишь, *pf.* (*of* ∼а́ть) **1.** to cut down, fell; to hew out. **2.** to cut out; в. дыру́ to make a hole. **3.** to carve (out).

вы́руб|иться, люсь, ишься, *pf.* (*of* ∼а́ться) to cut one's way out.

вы́рубк|а, и, *f.* **1.** cutting down, felling; hewing out. **2.** (*dial.*) clearing (*in forest*).

вы́руга|ть(ся), ю(сь), *pf. of* руга́ть(ся).

вы́рулива|ть, ю, *impf. of* вы́рулить.

вы́рул|ить, ю, ишь, *pf.* (*of* ∼ивать) (*aeron.*) to taxi.

выруча́|ть, ю, *impf. of* вы́ручить.

вы́руч|ить, у, ишь, *pf.* (*of* ∼а́ть) **1.** to rescue; to come to the help, aid (of). **2.** to gain; to make (*coll.*); он ∼ил мно́го де́нег от прода́жи свои́х карти́н he has made a lot of money from the sale of his pictures; в. затра́ченное to recover one's expenses.

вы́ручк|а, и, *f.* **1.** rescue, assistance; прийти́ на ∼у to come to the rescue; gain; proceeds, receipts; earnings.

вырыва́ни|е[1], я, *n.* **1.** pulling out; extraction (*of teeth, etc.*). **2.** uprooting.

вырыва́ни|е[2], я, *n.* digging (up).

вырыва́|ть[1], ю, *impf. of* вы́рвать[1].

вырыва́|ть[2], ю, *impf. of* вы́рыть.

вырыва́|ться, юсь, *impf. of* вы́рваться.

вы́р|ыть, ою, оешь, *pf.* (*of* ∼ыва́ть[2]) to dig up, dig out, unearth; в. труп to exhume

a corpse; где вы ∼ыли э́ту ру́копись? (*fig.*, *coll.*) where did you dig up this manuscript?

вы́ря|дить, жу, дишь, *pf.* (*coll.*) to dress up (*trans.*).

вы́ря|диться, жусь, дишься, *pf.* (*coll.*) to dress up (*intrans.*).

выряжа́|ть(ся), ю(сь), *impf. of* вы́ря-дить(ся).

вы́са|дить, жу, дишь, *pf.* (*of* ∼живать) **1.** to set down; to help down; to make alight; в. на бе́рег to put ashore; в. деса́нт (*mil.*) to make a landing; пья́ницу ∼дили из авто́-буса the drunken man was made to get off the 'bus. **2.** (*hort.*) to transplant. **3.** (*coll.*) to smash; to break in.

вы́са|диться, жусь, дишься, *pf.* (*of* ∼жи-ваться) (из, с+*g.*) to alight (from), get off; в. (с су́дна) to land, disembark; в. (с самолёта) to land.

вы́садк|а, и, *f.* **1.** debarkation, disembarkation; landing. **2.** (*hort.*) transplanting.

выса́жива|ть(ся), ю(сь), *impf. of* вы́са-дить(ся).

вы́са|жу, дишь, *see* ∼дить.

выса́сыва|ть, ю, *impf. of* вы́сосать.

вы́свата|ть, ю, *pf.* (*coll.*, *obs.*) to make a match, arrange a marriage (with).

высва́тыва|ть, ю, *impf.* **1.** *impf. of* вы́-сватать. **2.** *impf. only* to try to make a match, arrange a marriage (with); to seek in marriage.

высве́рлива|ть, ю, *impf. of* вы́сверлить.

вы́сверл|ить, ю, ишь, *pf.* to drill, bore.

вы́сви|стать, щу, щешь, *pf.* (*of* ∼стывать) (*coll.*) **1.** to whistle; в. мело́дию to whistle a tune. **2.** to whistle for, whistle up.

вы́сви|стеть, щу, стишь, *pf.* = ∼стать.

высви́стыва|ть, ю, *impf. of* вы́свистать.

вы́свобо|дить, жу, дишь, *pf.* **1.** to free, liberate; to disentangle, disengage. **2.** (*coll.*) to help (to) escape; не́которые ме́стные жи́тели ∼дили заключённых some of the local inhabitants helped the prisoners escape.

высвобожда́|ть, ю, *impf. of* вы́свободить.

вы́сев|ки, ок, *no sing.* bran, siftings.

высе́ива|ть, ю, *impf. of* вы́сеять.

высека́|ть, ю, *impf. of* вы́сечь[2].

вы́се|ку, чешь, *see* ∼чь.

выселе́н|ец, ца, *m.* evacuee.

выселе́ни|е, я, *n.* eviction.

вы́сел|ить, ю, ишь, *pf.* (*of* ∼я́ть) **1.** to evict. **2.** to evacuate, move.

вы́сел|иться, юсь, ишься, *pf.* (of ∼я́ться) to move (*from one dwelling-place to another*).

вы́сел|ок, ка, *m.* settlement.

вы́сел|ять(ся), ю(сь), *impf. of* вы́селить(ся).

вы́семен|иться, ится, *pf.* (*agric.*) to go to seed.

вы́сечк|а, и, *f.* carving; hewing.

вы́се|чь¹, ку, чешь, кут, *past* ∼к, ∼кла, *pf.* (*of* сечь¹) to beat, flog.

вы́се|чь², ку, чешь, кут, *past* ∼к, ∼кла, *pf.* (*of* ∼ка́ть) to cut (out); to carve, sculpture; to hew; в. огóнь to strike fire (*from a flint*).

вы́се|ять, ю, *pf.* (*of* ∼ивать) (*agric.*) to sow.

вы́си|деть, жу, дишь, *pf.* (*of* ∼живать) 1. to hatch (out) (*of birds; also fig.*). 2. to stay; to sit out (*trans.*); мы ∼дели до концá лéкции we sat the lecture out.

вы́сидк|а, и, *f.* (*coll.*) 1. incubation. 2. imprisonment.

вы́сижива|ть, ю, *impf. of* вы́сидеть.

вы́|ситься, шусь, сишься, *impf.* to tower (up), rise.

вы́скáблива|ть, ю, *impf. of* вы́скоблить.

вы́ска|зать, жу, жешь, *pf.* (*of* ∼зывать) to express; to state; в. мнéние to advance an opinion; в. предположéние to suggest, come out with a suggestion.

вы́ска|заться, жусь, жешься, *pf.* (*of* ∼зываться) 1. to speak out; to speak one's mind; to have one's say. 2. to speak (for *or* against); никто́ не ∼зался про́тив законопроéкта no one spoke against the bill.

вы́скáзывани|е, я, *n.* 1. utterance. 2. pronouncement; opinion.

вы́скáзыва|ть(ся), ю(сь), *impf. of* вы́сказать(ся).

вы́скáкива|ть, ю, *impf. of* вы́скочить.

вы́скáльзыва|ть, ю, *impf. of* вы́скользнуть.

вы́скобл|ить, ю, ишь, *pf.* (*of* выскáбливать) to scrape out; to erase; (*med.*) to remove.

вы́скользн|уть, у, ешь, *pf.* (*of* выскáльзывать) to slip out (*also fig.*); арестáнт ∼ул из рук охрáны (*coll.*) the prisoner slipped through his escort's fingers.

вы́скоч|ить, у, ишь, *pf.* (*of* выскáкивать) 1. to jump out; to leap out, spring out; (*fig.*, *coll.*) to butt in, come out (with); он ∼ил с крáйне неумéстным замечáнием he came out with an extremely uncalled-for remark. 2. (*of a boil, etc.*) (*coll.*) to come up. 3. (*coll.*) to drop out, fall out. 4. в. в лю́ди (*fig.*, *coll.*) to fall on one's feet.

вы́скочк|а, и, *m. and f.* (*coll.*) upstart, parvenu.

вы́скребá|ть, ю, *impf. of* вы́скрести.

вы́скре|сти, бу, бешь, *past* ∼б, ∼бла, *pf.* 1. to scrape out, scrape off. 2. to rake out.

вы́слан|ный (∼, ∼а), *p.p.p. of* вы́слать; *as noun* в., ∼ного, *m.*, ∼ная, ∼ной, *f.* exile, deportee.

вы́|слать, шлю, шлешь, *pf.* (*of* ∼сылáть) 1. to send, send out, dispatch. 2. (*polit.*) to exile; to deport.

вы́сле|дить, жу, дишь, *pf.* to trace; to track down.

вы́слéжива|ть, ю, *impf.* 1. *impf. of* вы́следить. 2. *impf. only* to be on the track of; to shadow.

вы́сле|жу, дишь, *see* ∼дить.

вы́слуг|а, и, *f.* period of service; за ∼у лет for long service, for meritorious service; за ∼ой двадцати́ лет on the expiry of twenty years' service.

вы́слу́жива|ть(ся), ю(сь), *impf. of* вы́служить(ся).

вы́служ|ить, у, ишь, *pf.* 1. to qualify for, obtain (*as result of service*); он ∼ил повышéние he has qualified for promotion. 2. to serve (out); он ∼ил двáдцать пять лет на Да́льнем Востóке he has completed twenty-five years' service in the Far East.

вы́служ|иться, усь, ишься, *pf.* 1. to gain promotion, be promoted. 2. (*coll.*, *pejor.*) to gain favour (with), get in (with); он ∼ился пéред бригади́ром he is well in with the foreman.

вы́слуша|ть, ю, *pf.* (*of* выслу́шивать) 1. to hear out. 2. (*med.*) to sound; to listen to.

вы́слу́шивани|е, я, *n.* (*med.*) auscultation.

вы́слу́шива|ть, ю, *impf. of* вы́слушать.

вы́смáтрива|ть, ю, *impf. of* вы́смотреть.

вы́смéива|ть, ю, *impf. of* вы́смеять.

вы́сме|ять, ю, ешь, *pf.* (*of* ∼ивать) to deride, ridicule.

вы́смол|ить, ю, ишь, *pf. of* смоли́ть.

вы́сморка|ть(ся), ю(сь), *pf. of* сморкáть(ся).

вы́смотр|еть, ю, ишь, *pf.* (*of* высмáтривать) 1. to scrutinize, look through. 2. to spy out; to locate (*by eye*). 3. (*coll.*) в. глазá to tire one's eyes out.

вы́сóвыва|ть(ся), ю(сь), *impf. of* вы́сунуть(ся).

высóк|ий (∼, ∼á, ∼ó), *adj.* (*in var. senses*) high; tall; lofty; elevated, sublime; (*mus.*) high, high-pitched; ∼ая водá high water, high tide; в. стиль elevated style; я о нём ∼ого мнéния I have a high opinion of him; в ∼ой стéпени highly; ∼ие договáривающиеся стóроны, *see* договáриваться.

высóкó, *adv.* 1. high (up); лежáть в. над у́ровнем мóря to be high above sea level. 2. *as pred.* it is high (up); it is a long way up; окнó бы́ло в. от земли́ the window was high up off the ground.

высóко- high-, highly-.

высокоблагорóди|е, я, *n.* (вáше) в. (your) Honour, (your) Worship (*title, in tsarist Russia, of civil servants of the eighth to the sixth classes and of officers from the rank of captain to that of colonel*).

высокогóрный, *adj.* Alpine, mountain.

высококáчественный, *adj.* high-quality.

высококвалифици́рованный, *adj.* highly qualified; в. рабо́тник (highly) skilled workman.

высокомéри|е, я, *n.* haughtiness, arrogance.

высокомéрнича|ть, ю, *impf.* (*coll.*) to behave haughtily, arrogantly.

высокоме́р|ный (~ен, ~на), *adj.* haughty, arrogant.

высокомолекуля́рный, *adj.* (*phys.*) high--molecular.

высокопа́р|ный (~ен, ~на), *adj.* (*lit.*) high--flown, stilted; bombastic, turgid.

высокопоста́вленный, *adj.* of high rank.

высокопревосходи́тельств|о, а, *n.* (ва́ше) в. (your) Excellency (*title, in tsarist Russia, of officers and civil servants of the first and second class*).

высокопреосвяще́нств|о, а, *n.* (ва́ше) в. (your) Eminence, (your) Grace (*title of archbishops and metropolitans of the Orthodox Church*).

высокопреподо́бби|е, я, *n.* (ва́ше) в. (your) Reverence (*title of archimandrites, abbots, and archpriests of the Orthodox Church*).

высокопро́б|ный (~ен, ~на), *adj.* sterling, standard; (*fig.*) sterling, of high quality.

высокоро́ди|е, я, *n.* (ва́ше) в. (your) Honour, (your) Worship (*title, in tsarist Russia, of civil servants of the fifth class*).

высокосо́ртный, *adj.* high-grade.

высокоторже́ственный, *adj.* solemn.

высокоуважа́емый, *adj.* (*obs.*; *mode of address in letters*) honoured (*Sir*), respected (*Sir*).

высокоу́м|ный (~ен, ~на), *adj.* (*iron.*) clever, brainy.

высокочасто́тный, *adj.* (*electr.*) high-frequency.

высокочти́мый, *adj.* (*obs.*) highly esteemed.

вы́сол|ить, ю, ишь, *pf.* (*coll.*) to salt well.

вы́сос|ать, у, ешь, *pf.* (*of* выса́сывать) 1. to suck out, suck dry. 2. (*fig., coll.*) to get out (of); extort (from); в. все со́ки из то exhaust, wear out; в. из па́льца to invent, fabricate; всё э́то из па́льца ~ано it is an entire fabrication.

высот|а́, ы́, *pl.* ~ы, ~, *f.* 1. height, altitude; (*mus.*) pitch; го́род нахо́дится на ~é ты́сячи фу́тов над у́ровнем мо́ря the town is a thousand feet above sea level; набра́ть ~у́ (*aeron.*) to gain altitude. 2. height, eminence (*concr.*); кома́ндные ~ы commanding heights (*also fig.*). 3. high level; high quality. 4. (*fig.*) на до́лжной ~é up to the mark; быть, оказа́ться на ~é положе́ния to rise to the occasion; быть на ~é зада́чи to be equal to a task. 5. (*math.*) в. треуго́льника altitude of a triangle.

высо́тник, а, *m.* 1. workman employed on construction of skyscrapers. 2. high-altitude flier.

высо́тн|ый, *adj.* 1. high-altitude. 2. ~ое зда́ние high-rise building, tower block.

высотоме́р, а, *m.* 1. (*aeron.*) altimeter. 2. (*mil.*) height-finder.

вы́сох|нуть, ну, нешь, *past* ~, ~ла, *pf.* (*of*

высыха́ть) 1. to dry (out); to dry up (*o rivers, etc.*). 2. to wither, fade; (*fig.*) t waste away, fade away.

вы́сох|ший, *past part. act. of* ~нуть *and adj* dried-up; shrivelled; wizened.

высоча́йш|ий, *adj.* 1. *superl. of* высо́кий 2. (*epithet of tsar or emperor*) imperial, royal проше́ние на ~ее и́мя petition to His Im perial Majesty.

высоче́нный, *adj.* (*coll.*) very high, ver tall.

высо́честв|о, а, *n.* (ва́ше) в. (your) High ness.

вы́сп|аться, люсь, ишься, *pf.* (*of* высыпа́ть ся²) (*coll.*) to have a good sleep; to have one's sleep out.

выспева́|ть, ю, *impf. of* вы́спеть.

вы́спе|ть, ю, *pf.* (*coll.*) to ripen.

выспра́шива|ть, ю, *impf. of* вы́спросить.

вы́спренний, *adj.* high-flown; bombastic.

вы́спро|сить, шу, сишь, *pf.* (*of* выспра́шивать) (*coll.*) 1. to inquire. 2. to inquire of interrogate; to pump посла́ ~сили о поли́тике прави́тельства его́ страны́ the ambassador was pumped about his government's policy; ~сили у посла́ наме́рения его́ прави́тельства the ambassador wa pumped about his government's intentions.

вы́став|ить, лю, ишь, *pf.* (*of* ~ля́ть) 1. tc bring out, bring forward; to display, exhibit; в. на прода́жу to display for sale; в. на свет to expose to the light; в. напока́з tc show off, parade. 2. (*mil.*) to post (*guard etc.*). 3. (+*i.*) to represent (as), make out (as); в. в плохо́м све́те to represent in an unfavourable light; в. в смешно́м ви́де tc make a laughing-stock (of); его́ ~или тру́сом he was made out to be a coward. 4. to put forward; to adduce; в. свою́ кандидату́ру to come forward as a candidate; в. до́воды to adduce arguments. 5. to put down, set down (*in writing*); в. отме́тки to put down marks; в. число́ на письме́ to date a letter. 6. to take out, remove; в. око́нную ра́му to take out a window frame. 7. (*coll.*) to send out, turn out, throw out; в. из ко́мнаты to send out of the room; в. со слу́жбы to sack.

вы́став|иться, люсь, ишься, *pf.* (*of* ~ля́ться) (*coll.*) to lean out; to thrust oneself forward; (*fig., pejor.*) to show off.

вы́ставк|а, и, *f.* 1. exhibition, show; display. 2. (show-)window, (shop-)window.

выставля́|ть, ю, *impf. of* вы́ставить.

выставля́|ться, юсь, *impf.* 1. *impf. of* вы́ставиться. 2. *impf. only* to exhibit (*intrans.*; *of an artist*).

выставно́й, *adj.* removable.

вы́став|очный, *adj. of* ~ка; в. комите́т exhibition committee.

выстáива|ть(ся), ю(сь), *impf. of* вы́стоять-(ся).

вы́стега|ть¹, ю, *pf. of* стегáть².

вы́стега|ть², ю, *pf.* (*coll.*) to thrash, flog.

вы́стёгива|ть, ю, *impf. of* вы́стегнуть.

вы́стегн|уть, у, ешь, *pf.* (*coll.*) to flick out.

вы́стел|ить, ю, ешь, *pf.* = вы́стлать.

вы́ст|елю, елешь, *see* ~лать.

выстилá|ть, ю, *impf. of* вы́стлать *and* вы́сте-лить.

вы́стира|ть, ю, *pf. of* стирáть².

вы́ст|лать, елю, елешь, *pf.* to cover; to pave; они́ ~лали лино́леумом пол во всех ко́мнатах they have covered all their floors with linoleum.

вы́сто|ять, ю, ишь, *pf.* (*of* выстáивать) 1. to stand; нам пришло́сь в. весь путь we had to stand the whole way. 2. to stand one's ground.

вы́сто|яться, юсь, ишься, *pf.* (of выстáи-ваться) 1. to mature, ripen. 2. to become stale, flat. 3. to rest (*of horses*).

выстрáгива|ть, ю, *impf. of* вы́строгать.

вы́страда|ть, ю, *pf.* 1. to suffer; to go through. 2. to gain, achieve through suffering.

выстрáива|ть(ся), ю(сь), *impf. of* вы́-строить(ся).

выстрáчива|ть, ю, *impf. of* вы́строчить.

вы́стрел, а, *m.* shot; report; произвести́ в. to fire a shot; разда́лся в. a shot rang out; на в. (от+*g.*) (*coll.*) within gunshot (of).

выстрéлива|ть, ю, *impf. of* выстрелять.

вы́стрел|ить, ю, ишь, *pf.* to shoot, fire; я ~ил в него́ три ра́за I fired three shots at him.

вы́стреля|ть, ю, *pf.* (*of* выстрéливать) (*coll.*) 1. to use up in shooting; мы ~ли все патро́ны we had used up all our cartridges. 2. to kill off (*by shooting*).

вы́стри|г, гу, жешь, *see* ~чь.

вы́стригá|ть, ю, *impf. of* вы́стричь.

вы́стри|чь, гу, жешь, гут, *past* ~г, ~гла, *pf.* to cut, clip out; to shear.

вы́строга|ть, ю, *pf.* (*of* строгáть *and* выстрá-гивать) (*tech.*) to plane, shave.

вы́стро|ить, ю, ишь, *pf.* (*of* выстрáивать) 1. to build. 2. to draw up, order, arrange; (*mil.*) to form up.

вы́стро|иться, юсь, ишься, *pf.* (*of* выстрáи-ваться) 1. (*mil.*) to form up (*intrans.*). 2. *pass. of* ~ить.

вы́строч|ить, у, ишь, *pf.* (*of* выстрáчивать) to hemstitch.

вы́струга|ть, ю, *pf.* = вы́строгать.

вы́сту|дить, жу, дишь, *pf.* (*coll.*) to cool; дом ~дило (*impers.*) the house had grown cold.

выстýжива|ть, ю, *impf. of* вы́студить.

вы́сту|жу, дишь, *see* ~дить.

вы́стука|ть, ю, *pf.* (*of* выстýкивать) (*coll.*) 1. (*med.*) to tap. 2. to tap out; в. мело́дию to tap out a tune; в. сообщéние to tap out a message (*prison sl.*); to type out.

выстýкивани|е, я, *n.* percussion; tapping.

выстýкива|ть, ю, *impf. of* вы́стукать.

вы́ступ, а, *m.* 1. protuberance, projection, ledge; в. фро́нта (*mil.*) salient. 2. (*tech.*) lug.

выступá|ть, ю, *impf.* 1. *impf. of* выступить. 2. (*impf. only*) to project, jut out, stick out. 3. (*impf. only*) to strut, pace.

вы́ступ|ить, лю, ишь, *pf.* 1. to come for-ward; to come out; герои́ня ~ила из-за кули́с the heroine came forward from the wings; в. в похо́д (*mil.*) to take the field; сыпь ~ила у неё на рука́х a rash has come out on her arms. 2. (из+*g.*) to go beyond; в. из берего́в to overflow its banks. 3. to appear (*publicly*); to come out (with, as); в. в печа́ти to appear in print; в. за предло-же́ние to come out in favour of a proposal; в. защи́тником (*leg.*) to appear for the defence; в. с ре́чью to make a speech; в. по ра́дио с докла́дом to give a broadcast talk, give a talk on the radio.

выступлéни|е, я, *n.* 1. appearance (*in public*); speech. 2. setting out.

выстывá|ть, ю, *impf. of* вы́стыть.

вы́сты|ть, ну, нешь, *pf.* (*coll.*) to cool off, become cold.

вы́су|дить, жу, дишь, *pf.* (*coll.*) to obtain by court decision.

высýжива|ть, ю, *impf. of* вы́судить.

вы́су|жу, дишь, *see* ~дить.

вы́сун|уть, у, ешь, *pf.* (*of* высо́вывать) to put out, thrust out; в. язы́к to put one's tongue out; бежа́ть ~я язы́к (*coll.*) to run without pausing for breath; нельзя́ но́су в. (из дому) (*coll.*) one can't show one's face (outside).

вы́сун|уться, усь, ешься, *pf.* (*of* высо́вы-ваться) to show oneself, thrust oneself for-ward; в. в окно́ to lean out of the window.

высýшива|ть, ю, *impf. of* вы́сушить.

вы́суш|ить, у, ишь, *pf.* 1. to dry (out). 2. (*coll.*) to emaciate. 3. (*coll., fig.*) to make callous, make hard.

вы́счита|ть, ю, *pf.* 1. to calculate, com-pute; to reckon out. 2. (*coll.*) to deduct.

высчи́тыва|ть, ю, *impf. of* вы́считать.

вы́с|ший, *adj.* (*comp. and superl. of* высо́кий) highest; supreme; high; higher; ~шего ка́чества of the highest quality; ~шая ме́ра наказа́ния supreme penalty; (*leg.*) capital punishment; суд ~шей инста́нции High Court; ~шее образова́ние higher educa-tion; ~шее о́бщество (high) society; ~шее учёбное заведе́ние higher education esta-blishment; ~шая шко́ла university; в ~шей сте́пени in the highest degree.

высыла́|ть, ю, *impf. of* вы́слать.
вы́сылк|а, и, *f.* 1. sending, dispatching. 2. expulsion; exile.
вы́сып|ать, лю, лешь, *pf.* 1. to pour out; to empty (out); to spill; (*fig.*, *coll.*) to pour out, tell; в. все свои́ забо́ты to pour out all one's troubles; ну, ~айте всё! come on, spill the beans! 2. (*coll.*) to pour out (*intrans.*) 3. to break out (*of a rash, etc.*); (*impers.*) у него́ ~ало на всем те́ле he has come out in a rash all over.
высыпа́|ть, ю, *impf. of* вы́сыпать.
вы́сып|аться, люсь, лешься (*coll.* ~ешься), *pf.* 1. *pass. of* ~ать. 2. to pour out; to spill (*intrans.*).
высыпа́|ться¹, юсь, *impf. of* вы́сыпаться.
высыпа́|ться², юсь, *impf. of* вы́спаться.
вы́сыпк|а, и, *f.* 1. (*coll.*) pouring out, spilling. 2. (*hunting*) descent (*of birds, etc.*).
высыха́|ть, ю, *impf. of* вы́сохнуть.
выс|ь, и, *f.* height; (*usu. pl.*) summit; (*fig.*) the world of fantasy; он всё вита́ет в заоблачной ~и he lives in the clouds.
выта́лкива|ть, ю, *impf. of* вы́толкать *and* вы́толкнуть.
вы́танц|евать(ся), ует(ся), *pf. of* вытанцо́вывать(ся).
вытанцо́выва|ть, ю, *impf.* (*coll.*) to execute assiduously (*steps of a dance*).
вытанцо́выва|ться, ется, *impf.* (*coll.*) to succeed, come off; де́ло не ~ется it is not coming off.
выта́плива|ть, ю, *impf. of* вы́топить.
выта́птыва|ть, ю, *impf. of* вы́топтать.
вытара́щива|ть, ю, *impf. of* вы́таращить.
вы́таращ|ить, у, ишь, *pf.* (*coll.*) в. глаза́ to open one's eyes wide.
выта́ска|ть, ю, *pf.* (*coll.*) to drag out, fish out.
выта́скива|ть, ю, *impf. of* вы́таскать *and* вы́тащить.
вы́тача|ть, ю, *pf. of* тача́ть.
выта́чива|ть, ю, *impf. of* вы́точить.
вы́тачк|а, и, *f.* tuck, dart.
вы́тащ|ить, у, ишь, *pf.* (*of* выта́скивать) 1. to drag out; to pull out, extract; (*coll.*) в. кого́-н. to drag someone out, drag someone off; они́ ~или его́ в кино́ they have dragged him off to the cinema; в. кого́-н. из беды́ to help someone out of trouble. 2. (*coll.*) to steal, pinch; у меня́ ~или бума́жник I have had my wallet stolen.
вы́твер|дить, жу, дишь, *pf.* (*coll.*) to get by heart.
вытве́ржива|ть, ю, *impf. of* вы́твердить.
вытворя́|ть, ю, *impf.* (*coll.*) to get up to, be up to; что ты тепе́рь ~ешь? what are you up to now?
вытека́|ть, ю, *impf.* 1. *impf. of* вы́течь. 2. (*impf. only*) to flow (from, out of) (*of a river*). 3. (*impf. only*) (*fig.*) to result, follow (from);

отсю́да ~ет, что вы ошибли́сь from this it follows that you are mistaken.
вы́те|ку, чешь, кут, *see* ~чь.
вы́т|ереть, ру, решь, *past* ~ер, ~ерла, *pf.* (*of* ~ира́ть) 1. to wipe (up); to dry, rub dry; в. но́ги to wipe one's feet; в. посу́ду to dry the crockery; в. пыль со стола́ to dust the table. 2. (*coll.*) to wear out, wear threadbare.
вы́терп|еть, лю, ишь, *pf.* to bear, endure; to suffer; я е́ле ~ел, когда́ он сказа́л э́то I could hardly stand it when he said that.
вы́терт|ый (~, ~а), *p.p.p. of* вы́тереть *and adj.* threadbare.
вы́те|сать, шу, шешь, *pf.* to square off.
вытесне́ни|е, я, *n.* 1. ousting; supplanting. 2. (*phys.*) displacement.
вы́тесн|ить, ю, ишь, *pf.* 1. to crowd out; to force out; (*fig.*) to oust; to supplant. 2. (*phys.*) to displace.
вытесня́|ть, ю, *impf. of* вы́теснить.
вытёсыва|ть, ю, *impf. of* вы́тесать.
вы́те|чь, ку, чешь, кут, *past* ~к, ~кла, *pf.* (*of* ~ка́ть) to flow out, run out; у него́ глаз ~к he has lost an eye.
вы́те|шу, шешь, *see* ~сать.
вытира́|ть, ю, *impf. of* вы́тереть.
вы́тисн|ить, ю, ишь, *pf.* to stamp, imprint, impress.
вы́тисн|уть, у, ешь, *pf.* = ~ить.
вытисня́|ть, ю, *impf. of* вы́тиснить.
вы́тк|ать, у, ешь, *pf.* 1. to weave, finish weaving; в. ковёр to weave a carpet; в. цветы́ на ковре́ to weave a flower pattern on a carpet.
вы́толка|ть, ю, *pf.* (*of* выта́лкивать) (*coll.*) to throw out; его́ ~ли в ше́ю (*sl.*) he was thrown out on his neck.
вы́толкн|уть, у, ешь, *pf.* (*of* выта́лкивать) 1. to throw out. 2. (*coll.*) to push out, force out.
вы́топ|ить, лю, ишь, *pf.* (*of* выта́пливать) 1. (*coll.*) to heat. 2. to melt (down).
вы́топ|тать, чу, чешь, *pf.* (*of* выта́птывать) to trample down.
вытора́чива|ть, ю, *impf. of* вы́торочить.
вы́торг|овать, ую, *pf.* 1. to gain, obtain (*by bargaining, haggling*); to get a reduction (of); он ~овал де́сять рубле́й из цены́ э́тих сапо́г he got a reduction of ten roubles on the price of these boots, he got these boots reduced by ten roubles; (*fig.*, *coll.*) to manage to get; он ~овал отсро́чку для оконча́ния диссерта́ции he has managed to get an extension of time to finish his dissertation. 2. (*coll.*) to make (a profit of); to net, clear.
выторго́выва|ть, ю, *impf.* 1. *impf. of* вы́торговать. 2. to try to get (*by bargaining*); to haggle over.

вы́тороч|ить, у, ишь, *pf.* (*of* вытора́чивать) to unstrap from the saddle.

вы́точен|ный (~, ~a), *p.p.p. of* вы́точить *and adj.* сло́вно в. chiselled (*of facial features*); perfect, perfectly-formed (*of bodies*).

вы́точ|ить, у, ишь, *pf.* (*of* выта́чивать) **1.** to turn (*tech.*) **2.** (*coll.*) to sharpen. **3.** (*coll.*) to gnaw through.

вы́трав|ить, лю, ишь, *pf.* (*of* трави́ть¹ *and* ~ля́ть) **1.** to exterminate, destroy. **2.** to remove, get out (*by chemical action*); в. пятно́ to remove a stain. **3.** to etch. **4.** (*of cattle, etc.*) to trample down (*crops, etc.*).

вытра́влива|ть, ю, *impf.* (*coll.*) = вытравля́ть.

вытравля́|ть, ю, *impf. of* вы́травить.

вытравно́й, *adj.* corrosive, erosive.

вытра́ива|ть, ю, *impf. of* вы́троить.

вытра́лива|ть, ю, *impf. of* вы́тралить.

вы́трал|ить, ю, ишь, *pf.* (*mil.*) to sweep (*mines*).

вы́треб|овать, ую, *pf.* **1.** to obtain on demand. **2.** to send for, summon(s); в. кого́-н. в суд пове́сткой to summons somebody.

вытрезви́тел|ь, я, *m.* 'sobering-up' station (*in U.S.S.R.*)

вы́трезв|ить, лю, ишь, *pf.* to sober.

вы́трезв|иться, люсь, ишься, *pf.* (*coll.*) to sober up (*intrans.*).

вытрезвля́|ть(ся), ю(сь), *impf. of* вы́трезвить(ся).

вы́тро|ить, ю, ишь, *pf.* (*of* вытра́ивать) (*dial., tech.*) **1.** to distil three times. **2.** to plough up three times.

вы́т|ру, решь, *see* ~ереть.

вы́тру|сить, шу, сишь, *pf.* (*coll.*) to drop, let fall; to spill.

вытряса́|ть, ю, *impf. of* вы́трясти.

вы́тряс|ти, у, ешь, *past* ~, ~ла, *pf.* **1.** to shake out. **2.** to clean;by shaking out; в. ковёр to shake out a carpet.

вытряха́|ть, ю, *impf.* (*dial., coll.*) = вытря́хивать.

вытря́хива|ть, ю, *impf. of* вы́тряхнуть.

вы́тряхн|уть, у, ешь, *pf.* to drop, let fall; to shake out.

вытури́ва|ть, ю, *impf. of* вы́турить.

вы́тур|ить, ю, ишь, *pf.* (*coll.*) to throw out, chuck out.

выть, во́ю, во́ешь, *impf.* to howl (*of animals, the wind, etc.*); (*fig., coll.*) to howl, wail.

выть|ё, я́, *no pl., n.* (*coll.*) howling; wailing.

вы́тяга|ть, ю, *pf.* (*obs.*) to win (by a lawsuit).

вытя́гива|ть(ся), ю(сь), *impf. of* вы́тянуть(ся).

вытяже́ни|е, я, *n.* stretching.

вытя́жк|а, и, f.* **1. drawing out, extraction. **2.** (*chem., med.*) extract. **3.** stretching, ex-

tension; на ~у, *see* навы́тяжку.

вытяжн|о́й, *adj.* for extracting, for drawing out; в. пла́стырь drawing plaster; ~а́я труба́ ventilating pipe; в. шкаф fume cupboard.

вы́тянут|ый (~, ~a), *p.p.p. of* ~ь *and adj.* stretched; ~ое лицо́ (*fig.*) a long face.

вы́тян|уть, у, ешь, *pf.* (*of* вытя́гивать) **1.** to stretch (out); to extend. **2.** to draw out, extract (*also fig.*); (*impers.*) газ ~уло в окно́ the gas had escaped through the window; (*fig., coll.*) в. всю ду́шу (+*d. or* у+*g.*) to wear (someone) out; в. все жи́лы (у, из+*g.*) to exhaust. **3.** (*coll.*) to endure, stand, stick; он до́лго не ~ет при тако́м кли́мате he won't stick it for long in a climate like that. **3.** (*coll.*) to weigh. **5.** (*coll.*) to flog.

вы́тян|уться, усь, ешься, *pf.* (*of* вытя́гиваться) **1.** to stretch (*intrans.*); to stretch oneself (out); он засну́л ~увшись на полу́ he fell asleep stretched out on the floor; лицо́ у неё ~улось (*coll.*) her face lengthened, her face fell. **2.** (*coll.*) to grow, shoot up. **3.** to stand erect; в. в стру́нку, в. во фронт (*mil.*) to stand at attention.

вы́у|дить, жу, дишь, *pf.* **1.** to catch. **2.** (*fig., pejor.*) to extract.

выу́жива|ть, ю, *impf. of* вы́удить.

вы́утюж|ить, у, ишь, *pf. of* утю́жить.

выу́ченик, а, *m.* pupil (*of a craftsman*); disciple, follower.

выу́чива|ть, ю, *impf. of* вы́учить.

вы́уч|ить, у, ишь, *pf.* (*of* учи́ть 4 *and* ~ивать) **1.** to learn. **2.** (+*a.* and *d. or* +*inf.*) to teach; он ~ил нас испа́нскому языку́ he taught us Spanish; он ~ил её пра́вить маши́ной he has taught her to drive (a car).

вы́уч|иться, усь, ишься, *pf.* (+*d. or inf.*) to learn.

**вы́учк|а, и, f.* teaching, training; отда́ть на ~у (+*d.*) to apprentice (to); он прошёл хоро́шую ~у he has had a sound schooling; боева́я в. (*mil.*) battle training.

выха́жива|ть, ю, *impf. of* вы́ходить.

вы́харка|ть, ю, *pf.* (*coll.*) to hawk (up).

выха́ркива|ть, ю, *impf. of* вы́харкать.

вы́харк|нуть, ну, нешь, *pf.* = ~ать.

выхва́лива|ть, ю, *impf. of* вы́хвалить.

вы́хвал|ить, ю, ишь, *pf.* to praise.

выхваля́|ть, ю, *impf.* = выхва́ливать.

выхваля́|ться, юсь, *impf.* **1.** (*coll.*) to sing one's own praises, blow one's own trumpet. **2.** *pass. of* ~ть.

вы́хва|тить, чу, тишь, *pf.* **1.** to snatch out, snatch away from; он про́сто ~тил газе́ту из-под моего́ но́са he simply snatched up the newspaper from under my nose. **2.** to pull out, draw; в. нож to draw a knife. **3.** to pull out, take out, pick up (*at random*); он ~тил кни́гу из ку́чи и на́чал чита́ть he picked up a book from the pile and began to read; в. цита́ту (*fig.*) to quote at random.

выхва́тыва|ть, ю, *impf. of* вы́хватить.

вы́хвачен|ный (~, ~а), *p.p.p. of* вы́хватить; ~ из жи́зни true to life, taken from the life.

вы́хва|чу, тишь, *see* ~тить.

вы́хлеба|ть, ю, *pf.* (*coll.*) to eat up.

вы́хлеб|нуть, ну, нешь, *pf.* = ~ать.

выхлёбыва|ть, ю, *impf. of* вы́хлебать.

вы́хлеста|ть, ю, *pf.* (*coll.*) **1.** to flog, lash. **2.** to flick out. **3.** (*sl.*) to drink off, drain.

вы́хлестн|уть, у, ешь, *pf.* (*coll.*) **1.** to flick out. **2.** to splash out.

выхлёстыва|ть, ю, *impf. of* вы́хлестнуть.

вы́хлоп, а, *m.* (*tech.*) exhaust.

выхлопа́тыва|ть, ю, *impf. of* вы́хлопотать.

выхлопно́й, *adj.* (*tech.*) exhaust.

вы́хлопо|тать, чу, чешь, *pf.* (*of* выхлопа́тывать) to obtain (after much trouble).

вы́ход, а, *m.* **1.** going out; leaving, departure; в. за́муж marriage (*of woman*); в. в отста́вку retirement. **2.** way out, exit; outlet; из э́того положе́ния ~а не́ было (*fig.*) there was no way out of this situation; дать в. (+*d.*) to give vent (to); знать все хо́ды и ~ы (*coll.*) to know all the ins and outs. **3.** appearance (*of a publication*); (*theatr.*) entrance. **4.** (*econ.*) output; yield. **5.** (*geol.*) outcrop. **6.** (*eccl.*) вели́кий, ма́лый в. great, little entrance. **7.** быть на ~а́х (*theatr.*) to play a supernumerary part.

вы́ход|ец, ца, *m.* **1.** emigrant; immigrant; он роди́лся в США, а роди́тели бы́ли ~цами из Гре́ции he was born in the United States but his parents were emigrants from Greece; в. с того́ све́та apparition, ghost. **2.** person springing from different social group; он — в. из крестья́н he is of peasant origin.

вы́хо|дить¹, жу, дишь, *pf.* (*of* выха́живать) (*coll.*) **1.** to tend, nurse. **2.** to rear, bring up; to grow (*plants*).

вы́хо|дить², жу, дишь, *pf.* (*of* выха́живать) (*coll.*) to pass (through); go all over.

выхо|ди́ть, жу́, ~дишь, *impf.* **1.** *impf. of* вы́йти. **2.** (*impf. only*) to look out (on), give (on), face; его́ ко́мната ~дит о́кнами на у́лицу his room looks onto the street. **3.** не в. из головы́, из ума́ to be unforgettable, stick in one's mind. **4.** *as pred.* ~дит (*coll.*) it turns out.

вы́ходк|а, и, *f.* **1.** (*pejor.*) trick; escapade. **2.** (*coll.*) initial step of a dance.

выходни́к, а́, *m.* (*coll.*) person working on day off.

выходн|о́й, *adj.* **1.** exit; ~а́я дверь street door. **2.** в. день day off, free day, rest-day; ~а́я оде́жда 'best' clothes, walking-out clothes; ~о́е пла́тье party dress; *as noun* (*i*) в., ~о́го, *m.* = в. день, (*ii*) в., ~о́го, *m.*,

~а́я, ~о́й, *f.* person having day off; он сего́дня в. it is his day off today. **3.** ~о́е посо́бие (*also as noun* ~ы́е, ~ы́х) gratuity on discharge. **4.** (*theatr.*) ~а́я роль supernumerary part. **5.** (*typ.*) в. лист title-page; ~ы́е све́дения imprint.

выход|я́щий, *pres. part. of* ~и́ть; из ря́да вон ~я́щий outstanding; *as noun* в., ~я́щего, *m.* (*chess, cards*) extra player, bye; в пе́рвом ту́ре он был ~я́щим he had a bye in the first round.

выхо|жу́, дишь, *see* ~ди́ть.

выхо|жу́, ~дишь, *see* ~ди́ть.

выхола́жива|ть, ю, *impf. of* вы́холодить.

выхола́щива|ть, ю, *impf. of* вы́холостить.

вы́хол|енный, *p.p.p. of* ~ить *and adj.* well-cared-for; well-groomed.

вы́хол|ить, ю, ишь, *pf.* to care for, tend.

вы́холо|дить, жу, дишь, *pf.* (*of* выхола́живать) to cool.

вы́холо|стить, щу, стишь, *pf.* (*of* выхола́щивать) to castrate, geld; (*fig.*) to emasculate.

вы́холо|щенный, *p.p.p. of* ~стить *and adj.* castrated; gelded; (*fig.*) emasculated; ~щенная ло́шадь gelding.

вы́хухолевый, *adj.* musquash.

вы́хухол|ь, я, *m.* **1.** desman, musk-rat. **2.** (*fur*) musquash.

вы́цапа|ть, ю, *pf.* (у+*g.*; *coll.*) to seize, grasp.

вы́царапа|ть, ю, *pf.* (*coll.*) **1.** to scratch; (+*a. and d.*) to scratch out; они́ почти́ ~ли друг дру́гу глаза́ they almost scratched each other's eyes out. **2.** (*fig.*) to extract, get (out of); он ~л у отца́ ещё де́сять рубле́й he has got another ten roubles out of his father.

выцара́пыва|ть, ю, *impf. of* вы́царапать.

вы́цве|сти (*coll.* ~сть), ту, тешь, *past* ~л, *pf.* to fade.

выцвета́|ть, ю, *impf. of* вы́цвести.

вы́цве|тший, *past part. of* ~сти *and adj.* faded.

вы́це|дить, жу, дишь, *pf.* **1.** to filter, rack (off); to decant. **2.** (*fig., coll.*) to drink off, drain.

выце́жива|ть, ю, *impf. of* вы́цедить.

вычали́ва|ть, ю, *impf. of* вы́чалить.

вы́чал|ить, ю, ишь, *pf.* to haul up, beach (*a boat*).

вычека́нива|ть, ю, *impf. of* вы́чеканить.

вы́чекан|ить, ю, ишь, *pf.* to mint; to strike; в. меда́ль to strike a medal.

вы́ч|ел, ла, *see* ~есть.

вычёркива|ть, ю, *impf. of* вы́черкнуть.

вы́черкн|уть, у, ешь, *pf.* to cross out, strike out; to expunge, erase; в. кого́-н. из спи́ска живы́х to give up as dead.

вы́черпа|ть, ю, *pf.* (из+*g.*) to take out (*fluids*); to bail (out); в. во́ду из ло́дки to bail out a boat.

вычёрпыва|ть, ю, *impf. of* вы́черпать.
вы́чер|тить, чу, тишь, *pf.* to draw; to trace.
вы́черчен|ный (~, ~a), *p.p.p. of* вы́чертить *and adj.* finely-drawn; ~ные бро́ви pencilled eyebrows.
вычёрчива|ть, ю, *impf. of* вы́чертить.
вы́чер|чу, тишь, *see* ~тить.
вы́че|сать, шу, шешь, *pf.* (*of* ~сывать) to comb out.
вы́ческ|а, и, *no pl., f.* combing out.
вы́чес|ки, ок, *no sing.* (*text.*) combings.
вы́ч|есть, ту, тешь, *past* ~ел, ~ла, *pres. gerund* ~тя, *pf.* (*of* ~ита́ть) 1. (*math.*) to subtract. 2. to deduct, keep back; пять проце́нтов из ва́шего жа́лованья ~ли на страхова́ние five per cent. of your salary has been kept back for insurance.
вычёсыва|ть, ю, *impf. of* вы́чесать.
вы́чет, а, *m.* deduction; за ~ом (+*g.*) except; less, minus, allowing for; он зараба́тывает две́сти рубле́й в ме́сяц за ~ом нало́гов he earns two hundred roubles a month less taxes.
вы́че|шу, шешь, *see* ~сать.
вычисле́ни|е, я, *n.* calculation.
вычисли́тел|ь, я, *m.* 1. calculator. 2. (*mil.*) plotter. 3. calculating-machine.
вычисли́тельн|ый, *adj.* calculating, computing; ~ая маши́на computer.
вычисл|ить, ю, ишь, *pf.* to calculate, compute.
вычисля́|ть, ю, *impf. of* вы́числить.
вы́чи|стить, щу, стишь, *pf.* (*of* чи́стить *and* ~ща́ть) 1. to clean (up, out). 2. (*fig.*) to purge; to expel; его́ ~стили из па́ртии he has been expelled from the party.
вычита́ем|ое, ого, *n.* (*math.*) subtrahend.
вычита́ни|е, я, *n.* (*math.*) subtraction.
вы́чита|ть, ю, *pf.* (*of* вычи́тывать) 1. (*coll.*) to find (*by reading, perusing*); я ~л сообще́ние о его́ сме́рти в одно́й из вчера́шних газе́т I found a report of his death in one of yesterday's newspapers. 2. (*typ.*) to read (*manuscripts, proofs*).
вычита́|ть, ю, *impf. of* вы́честь.
вы́читк|а, и, f. (*typ.*) reading.
вычи́тыва|ть¹, ю, *impf. =* вычита́ть.
вычи́тыва|ть², ю, *impf.* 1. *impf. of* вы́читать. 2. *impf. only* to reprimand, tell off.
вычища́|ть, ю, *impf. of* вы́чистить.
вы́чи|щу, стишь, *see* ~стить.
вы́ч|ту, тешь, *see* ~есть.
вы́чур|ы, ~, sing. ~а, ~ы, *f.* 1. fancy; mannerism; (*lit.; obs.*) conceit. 2. (*obs.*) intricate pattern (*on fabrics*).
вы́чур|ный (~ен, ~на), *adj.* fanciful; mannered; precious.
вы́шага|ть, ю, *pf.* (*coll.*) to pace out.
вы́ша́рива|ть, ю, *impf. of* вы́шарить.

вы́шар|ить, ю, ишь, *pf.* (*coll.*) to rummage out, ferret out.
вышвы́рива|ть, ю, *impf. of* вы́швырнуть *and* вы́швырять.
вы́швырн|уть, у, ешь, *pf.* to throw out, hurl out; (*fig., coll.*) to chuck out.
вы́швыря|ть, ю, *pf.* (*coll.*) to throw out.
вы́ше 1. *comp. of* высо́кий *and* высоко́; higher, taller. 2. *prep.*+*g.* above, beyond; over; э́то в. моего́ понима́ния it is beyond my comprehension, it passes my understanding; в. свои́х сил beyond one's powers, beyond one; зада́ча оказа́лась в. его́ сил the task proved to be beyond him; быть в. (+*g.*) to rise superior (to); в по́лдень температу́ра подняла́сь в. восьми́десяти гра́дусов by midday the temperature had risen to over eighty degrees; дере́вня на Во́лге, в. Сара́това a village on the Volga, above Saratov. 3. *adv.* (*lit.*) above; смотри́ в. *vide supra*.
вы́ше- above-, afore-.
вышеизло́женный, *adj.* foregoing.
вы́|шел, шла, *see* ~йти.
вы́шелу́шива|ть, ю, *impf. of* вы́шелушить.
вы́шелуш|ить, у, ишь, *pf.* to peel; to shell.
вышена́званный, *adj.* afore-named.
вышеозна́ченный, *adj.* aforesaid, above-mentioned.
вышеприведённый, *adj.* above-cited; в. приме́р the above-cited example, the example above.
вышере́ченный, *adj.* (*obs., now iron.*) afore-mentioned.
вышеска́занный, *adj.* aforesaid.
вышестоя́щ|ий, *adj.* higher; (*polit.*) ~ие о́рганы вла́сти the higher organs of power.
вышеука́занный, *adj.* foregoing.
вышеупомя́нутый, *adj.* afore-mentioned.
вышиба́л|а, ы, m. 1. (*sl.*) chucker-out. 2. (*coll.*) rude fellow.
вышиба́|ть, ю, *impf. of* вы́шибить.
вы́шиб|ить, у, ешь, *past* ~, ~ла, *pf.* (*coll.*) 1. to knock out; в. ду́шу, в. дух (из+*g.*) to bump off, beat to death. 2. to chuck out.
вышива́льный, *adj.* embroidery.
вышива́льщиц|а, ы, f. needle-woman.
вышива́ни|е, я, *n.* embroidery, needle-work.
вышива́|ть, ю, *impf. of* вы́шить.
вы́шивк|а, и, f. embroidery, needle-work.
вышивно́й, *adj.* embroidered.
вышин|а́, ы́, pl. ~ы, *f.* height; в ~е́ aloft, high up; ~о́й в ты́сячу ме́тров a thousand metres high, up.
вы́ш|ить, ью, ьешь, *imp.* ~ей, *pf.* (*of* ~ива́ть) to embroider (on; with); в. узо́р на пла́тье to embroider a pattern on a dress; в. узо́р гла́дью to embroider a pattern in satin-stitch.

вы́шк|а, и, *f.* **1.** turret. **2.** (watch-)tower; диспе́тчерская в. (*aeron.*) control tower; сторожева́я в. watch-tower; бурова́я в. derrick.

вы́школ|ить, ю, ишь, *pf. of* шко́лить.

вы́шлиф|овать, ую, *pf.* **1.** (*tech.*) to polish. **2.** (*fig., coll.*) to polish, give a polish to; to smarten up.

вышлифо́выва|ть, ю, *impf. of* вы́шлифовать.

вы́|шлю, шлешь, *see* ~сла́ть.

вышмы́гива|ть, ю, *impf. of* вы́шмыгнуть.

вы́шмыгн|уть, у, ешь, *pf.* (*coll.*) to slip out.

вы́шн|ий, *adj.* heavenly, divine; ~яя си́ла the power of the Most High.

вышны́рива|ть, ю, *impf. of* вы́шмырнуть *and* вы́шнырять.

вы́шнырн|уть, у, ешь, *pf.* (*coll.*) to jump out.

вы́шныря|ть, ю, *pf.* (*coll.*) **1.** to rush all round. **2.** to smell out, scent out (*information*).

вышпа́рива|ть, ю, *impf. of* вы́шпарить.

вы́шпар|ить, ю, ишь, *pf.* (*coll.*) to smoke out; to scald out (*insects, etc.*).

выштукату́рива|ть, ю, *impf. of* вы́штукату-рить.

вы́штукатур|ить, ю, ишь, *pf.* to stucco.

вы́шу|тить, чу, тишь, *pf.* to laugh at, make fun of; to poke fun at.

вышу́чива|ть, ю, *impf. of* вы́шутить.

выщела́чива|ть, ю, *impf. of* вы́щелочить.

выщёлкива|ть, ю, *impf.* (*coll.*) (*of nightingales, etc.*) to warble forth; (*fig.; of horses' hoofs*) to clatter.

вы́щелоч|ить, у, ишь, *pf.* (*of* выщела́чивать) **1.** (*chem.*) to leach, lixiviate. **2.** to steep, soak (*linen*) in lye.

вы́щерб|ить, лю, ишь, *pf.* (*coll.*) to dent; to jag.

выщербля́|ть, ю, *impf. of* вы́щербить.

вы́щип|ать, лю, лешь, *pf.* to pull out, pull up; в. пе́рья у ку́рицы to pluck a hen.

вы́щипн|уть, у, ешь, *pf.* to pull out; to pluck out.

вы́щи́пыва|ть, ю, *impf. of* вы́щипать *and* вы́щипнуть.

вы́щупа|ть, ю, *pf.* **1.** (*med.*) to find (*by probing*). **2.** (*coll.*) to run one's hands over; to ransack.

выщу́пыва|ть, ю, *impf. of* вы́щупать.

вы́|я, и, *f.* (*obs. or rhet.*) neck.

вы́яв|ить, лю, ишь, *pf.* (*of* ~ля́ть) **1.** to display, reveal. **2.** to bring out; to make known. **3.** (*pejor.*) to show up, expose.

вы́яв|иться, люсь, ишься, *pf.* (*of* ~ля́ться) to appear, come to light, be revealed.

выявле́ни|е, я, *n.* revelation; showing up, exposure.

выявля́|ть(ся), ю(сь), *impf. of* вы́явить(ся).

выясне́ни|е, я, *n.* elucidation; explanation.

вы́ясн|ить[1], ю, ишь, *pf.* to elucidate; to clear up, explain.

вы́ясн|ить[2], ит, *pf.* (*impers.; dial.*) to clear up (*of weather*).

вы́ясн|иться, ится, *pf.* to become clear; to turn out, prove (*intrans.*); как ~илось, он лгал всё вре́мя he was lying all the time as it turned out.

выясня́|ть(ся), яю(сь), *impf. of* вы́яснить(ся).

вью, вьёшь, *see* вить.

вью́г|а, и, *f.* snow-storm, blizzard.

вью́|жный, *adj. of* ~га.

вьюк, а, *m.* pack; load.

вьюн, а́, *m.* **1.** loach (*fish*). **2.** (*fig., coll.*) restless, mobile person; верте́ться ~о́м, ви́ться ~о́м о́коло кого́-н. to be all over someone, try to get round someone.

вьюн|о́к, ка́, *m.* (*bot.*) bindweed, convolvulus.

вьюр|о́к, ка́, *m.* (*orn.*) mountain finch, brambling.

вью́ч|ить, у, ишь, *impf.* (*of* на~) to load (up).

вью́чн|ый, *adj.* pack; ~ое живо́тное beast of burden; ~ое седло́ pack-saddle.

вью́шк|а, и, *f.* damper.

вью́щ|ийся, *pres. part. of* ви́ться *and adj.*; ~иеся во́лосы curly hair; ~ееся расте́ние (*bot.*) creeper, climber; в. плющ tree ivy.

вя|жу́, ~жешь, *see* ~за́ть.

вя́жущий, *pres. part. act. of* вяза́ть *and adj.* **1.** astringent. **2.** (*tech.*) binding, cementing.

вяз, а, *m.* elm(-tree).

вяза́льн|ый, *adj.* knitting; в. крючо́к crochet hook; ~ая спи́ца knitting-needle.

вяза́льщик, а, *m.* **1.** knitter. **2.** binder.

вяза́ни|е, я, *n.* **1.** knitting. **2.** binding, tying.

вяза́нк|а, и, *f.* (*coll.*) knitted garment (*jumper, jacket, etc.*).

вяза́нк|а, и, *f.* bundle; truss.

вя́заный, *adj.* knitted.

вяза́нь|е, я, *n.* knitting (*object in process of being knitted*).

вя|за́ть, жу́, ~жешь, *impf.* **1.** (*pf.* с~) to tie, bind; (*tech.*) to tie, clamp; в. кому́-н. ру́ки to tie someone's hands. **2.** (*pf.* с~) to knit. **3.** (*impf. only*) to be astringent; (*impers.*) у меня́ ~жет во рту my mouth feels constricted.

вя|за́ться, жу́сь, ~жешься, *impf.* (с+*i.*) to accord, agree (with); to fit in, be in keeping (with), tally; ва́ше предположе́ние о причи́не ава́рии не ~жется с э́тими све́дениями your theory as to the cause of the crash does not fit in with this evidence; его́ вычисле́ния никогда́ не ~за́лись с мои́ми his calculations never tallied with mine; де́ло не ~за́лось, пока́ вы не прие́хали the business was making no progress until you came.

вязи́га = визи́га.

вя́зк|а, и, *f.* 1. tying, binding. 2. knitting. 3. bunch, string; в. ключе́й bunch of keys.

вя́з|кий (~ок, ~ка́, ~ко), *adj.* 1. viscous, sticky; boggy. 2. (*tech.*) ductile, malleable; tough. 3. (*coll.*) astringent.

вя́зкост|ь, и, *f.* 1. viscosity, stickiness; bogginess. 2. (*tech.*) ductility, malleability; toughness.

вя́зн|уть, у, ешь, *impf.* (в+*p.*) to stick, get stuck (in); to sink (into); в. в грязи́ to stick in the mud.

вя́зовый, *adj.* elm.

вя́з|че, *comp. of* ~кий *and* ~ко.

вя́зчик, а, *m.* binder.

вязь|, и, *no pl.*, *f.* 1. (*philol.*) ornamental ligatured script. 2. interwoven ornament (*in pattern*).

вя́ка|ть, ю, *impf.* (*coll.*, *dial.*) to speak in-

distinctly; to talk nonsense, blather.

вял, *see* вя́нуть.

вя́лени|е, я, *n.* (*of meat, fish, etc.*) drying; dry-curing, jerking.

вя́леный, *adj.* dried.

вя́л|ить, ю, ишь, *impf.* (*of* про~) to dry (*in the sun*); to dry-cure, jerk (*meat, fish, etc.*).

вя́лост|ь, и, *f.* flabbiness; limpness; (*fig.*) sluggishness; inertia; slackness.

вя́л|ый, *adj.* 1. faded. 2. (~, ~а́, ~о) flabby, flaccid; limp; (*fig.*) sluggish; inert; slack; ~ое настрое́ние sluggish disposition; в. ры́нок (*econ.*) slack market.

вя́н|уть, у, ешь, *past* ~ул, ~ула *and* вял, вя́ла, *impf.* (*of* за~) to fade, wither; (*fig.*) to droop, flag; у́ши ~ут от тако́го разгово́ра it makes one sick to listen to such talk.

вя́хир|ь, я, *m.* wood-pigeon.

вя́щ|ий, *adj.* (*obs. or joc.*) greater; к ~ему несча́стью to crown the misfortune; для ~ей предосторо́жности to make assurance doubly sure.

Г

га, *indecl.*, *n.*, *abbr. of* гекта́р.

габарди́н, а, *m.* gaberdine.

габари́т, а, *m.* (*tech.*) 1. (*railways*) clearance. 2. size, dimension (*of a machine*).

габари́т|ный, *adj. of* ~; ~ные воро́та (*railways*) clearance gauge; ~ная высота́ overall height; overhead clearance.

гава́нн|а, ы, *f.* (*coll.*) Havana (*tobacco or cigar*).

гава́н|ский, *adj. of* ~ь.

га́ван|ь, и, *f.* harbour.

га́вка|ть, ю, *impf.* (*coll.*) to bark.

га́врик, а, *m.* (*sl.*) 1. petty crook. 2. mate.

га́г|а, и, *f.* eider-duck.

гага́ка|ть, ет, *impf.* (*dial. or coll.*; *onomat.*, *of geese*) to cackle.

гага́р|а, ы, *f.* (*orn.*) loon, diver.

гага́рк|а, и, *f.* (*orn.*) razorbill.

гага́т, а, *m.* (*min.*) jet.

гага́чий, *adj. of* га́га; г. пух eiderdown.

гад, а, *m.* 1. (*obs.*) amphibian, reptile. 2. (*fig.*, *coll.*) repulsive person; (*pl.*) vermin.

гада́лк|а, и, *f.* fortune-teller.

гада́ни|е, я, *n.* 1. divination, fortune-telling; г. на ка́ртах card-reading, cartomancy; г. по руке́ palmistry. 2. guess-work.

гада́тел|ьный (~ен, ~ьна), *adj.* problematic, conjectural, hypothetical; ~ьная кни́га fortune-telling book.

гада́|ть, ю, *impf.* 1. (*pf.* по~) (на+*p.* or по+*d.*) to tell fortunes (by); г. на кофе́йной

гу́ще to make wild guesses. 2. *impf. only* (о+*p.*) to guess, conjecture, surmise.

га́дин|а, ы, *f.* (*fig.*) reptile; (*coll.*) repulsive person; (*pl.*) vermin.

га́|дить, жу, дишь, *impf.* (*of* на~) 1. (*of animals*) to defecate. 2. (на+*a.* or *p.*, в+*p.*) to foul, defile. 3. (+*d.*; *coll.*) to play dirty tricks (on).

га́д|кий (~ок, ~ка́, ~ко), *adj.* nasty, vile, repulsive; г. утёнок ugly duckling.

га́дк|о¹, *adv. of* ~ий.

га́дко², *as pred.* мне, *etc.*, г. I, *etc.*, loathe (it); I, *etc.*, am repelled.

гадли́вост|ь, и, *f.* aversion, disgust.

гадли́в|ый (~, ~а), *adj.* ~ое чу́вство (feeling of) disgust.

га́дост|ный (~ен, ~на), *adj.* disgusting; (*coll.*) poor, bad.

га́дост|ь, и, *f.* 1. (*coll.*) filth, muck. 2. dirty trick; он спосо́бен на вся́кую г. he is capable of the lowest trick; говори́ть ~и to say foul things.

гадю́к|а, и, *f.* 1. adder, viper. 2. (*coll.*) repulsive person.

га́ер, а, *m.* (*obs.*) buffoon, clown.

га́ерств|о, а, *n.* (*obs.*) buffoonery, tomfoolery.

га́ерств|овать, ую, *impf.* (*obs.*, *pejor.*) to play the buffoon; to clown.

га́ечный, *adj. of* га́йка; г. ключ spanner, wrench.

гáже, *comp. of* гáдкий.

газ¹, а, *m.* **1.** gas. **2.** (*coll.*) на пóлном ⁓е (⁓ý) at top speed; дать г. to step on the gas, step on it; сбáвить г. to reduce speed. **3.** (*pl.*; *med.*) wind; скоплéние ⁓ов flatulence, wind.

газ², а, *no pl., m.* gauze.

газáн|ýть, ý, ёшь, *pf.* (*sl.*) **1.** to accelerate (*in a car*). **2.** to scram.

газáци|я, и, *f.* aeration.

газгóльдер, а, *m.* gasholder.

газéл|ь¹, и, *f.* (*zool.*) gazelle.

газéл|ь², и, *f.* (*lit.*) ghazal (*Arabic verse form*).

газéт|а, ы, *f.* newspaper.

газéт|ный, *adj. of* ⁓а; ⁓ная бумáга news-print; г. стиль journalese.

газéтчик, а, *m.* **1.** newspaper-seller; newspaper-boy. **2.** (*coll.*) journalist.

гáзик, а, *m.* 'Gazik' (*small lorry produced by Gorky motor-vehicle works*).

газирóванный, *adj.* aerated.

газир|овáть, ую, *impf.* to aerate.

газирóвк|а, и, *f.* **1.** aeration. **2.** (*coll.*) aerated water.

газификáци|я, и, *f.* **1.** supplying with gas. **2.** gasification.

газифици́р|овать, ую, *impf. and pf.* **1.** to supply with gas; to install gas (in). **2.** (*tech.*) to extract gas (from).

газбалло́н, а, *m.* gas cylinder.

газовщи́к, а́, *m.* gas-works employee; gas-man.

гáзов|ый¹, *adj. of* газ¹; ⁓ая коло́нка geyser; ⁓ая плита́ gas cooker, gas-stove; г. рожо́к gas-burner; gas bracket; ⁓ая сва́рка оху-acetylene welding; г. счётчик gas-meter; ⁓ая ата́ка (*mil.*) gas attack; ⁓ая ка́мера gas chamber.

гáзовый², *adj. of* газ².

газогенера́тор, а, *m.* (*tech.*) gas generator, gas producer.

газокали́льн|ый, *adj.* г. колпачо́к gas mantle; ⁓ая ла́мпа incandescent gas-lamp.

газоли́н, а, *m.* gasolene.

газоме́р, а, *m.* gas-meter.

газомёт, а, *m.* (*mil.*) gas projector.

газомото́р, а, *m.* (*tech.*) gas-engine.

газо́н, а, *m.* grass-plot, lawn; по ⁓ам ходи́ть воспреща́ется keep off the grass.

газонепроница́емый, *adj.* gas-proof, gas-tight.

газонокоси́лка, и, *f.* lawn-mower.

газообра́з|ный (⁓ен, ⁓на), *adj.* (*phys.*) gaseous, gasiform.

газопрово́д, а, *m.* gas pipeline; gas-main.

газопрово́д|ный, *adj. of* ⁓; ⁓ная труба́ gas-pipe.

газоубе́жищ|е, а, *n.* gas-proof shelter.

газохрани́лищ|е, а, *n.* gas-holder; gasometer.

гайдама́к, а, *m.* (*hist.*) haydamak (*Ukrainian Cossack; also member of anti-Bolshevik Ukrainian cavalry detachment in 1918*).

гайдама́|цкий, *adj. of* ⁓к.

гайду́к, а́, *m.* (*hist.*) hayduck (**1.** *rebel against Turkish domination in Balkans.* **2.** *footman in house of wealthy landowner*).

га́йк|а, и, *f.* nut, female screw; у него́ в голове́ не хвата́ет ⁓и (*coll.*) he's got a screw loose.

гаймори́т, а, *m.* (*med.*) antritis.

га́йморов, *adj.* ⁓а по́лость (*anat.*) antrum of Highmore.

гак¹, а, *m.* (*naut.*) hook.

гак², а, *m.* (*coll.*) superfluity; часа́ три с ⁓ом about three hours or more.

гала́, *indecl. adj.* gala; г.-представле́ние gala performance.

гала́ктик|а, и, *f.* (*astron.*) galaxy.

галантере́йност|ь, и, *f.* (*obs., coll.*) urbanity, gallantry.

галантере́|йный, *adj.* **1.** *adj. of* ⁓я; г. магази́н haberdashery, fancy-goods shop. **2.** (*obs., coll.*) urbane, gallant.

галантере́|я, и, *f.* haberdashery, fancy goods.

галанти́р, а, *m.* galantine.

гала́нтност|ь, и, *f.* gallantry (= *courtliness*).

гала́нт|ный (⁓ен, ⁓на, ⁓но), *adj.* gallant (= *courtly*).

гал|дёж, а́, *m.* (*coll.*) din, racket.

галд|е́ть, 1st pers. not used, и́шь, *impf.* (*coll.*) to make a din, racket.

гале́р|а, ы, *f.* galley.

галере́|я, и, *f.* (*in var. senses*) gallery.

галёрк|а, и, *f.* (*theatr.*; *coll.*) **1.** gallery, 'the gods'. **2.** 'the gods' (= *those occupying gallery seats*).

галёр|ный, *adj. of* ⁓а.

гале́т|а, ы, *f.* (ship's) biscuit.

га́лечник, а, *m.* (*collect.*) pebbles, shingle.

га́лечный, *adj.* pebble, shingle; pebbly, shingly.

галима́ть|я́, и́, *f.* (*coll.*) rubbish, nonsense.

галифе́, *indecl., n.* riding-breeches, jodhpurs.

галици́йский, *adj.* Galician.

га́лк|а, и, *f.* daw, jackdaw; счита́ть га́лок (*i*) to stand gaping, gawp (*ii*) to loaf.

галл, а, *m.* Gaul.

га́лли|й, я, *m.* (*chem.*) gallium.

галлици́зм, а, *m.* Gallicism.

галлома́ни|я, и, *f.* gallomania.

галло́н, а, *m.* gallon.

галлофо́би|я, и, *f.* gallophobia.

га́лльский, *adj.* Gallic.

галлюцина́ци|я, и, *f.* hallucination.

галлюцини́р|овать, ую, *impf.* to have hallucinations.

галоге́н, а, *m.* (*chem.*) halogen.

галóид, а, *m.* (*chem.*) haloid.

галóп, а, *m.* **1.** gallop; ~ом at a gallop; лёгкий г. canter; скакáть ~ом to gallop; подня́ть в г. to put into a gallop. **2.** galop (*dance*).

галопи́р|овать, ую, *impf.* to gallop.

гáл|очий, *adj. of* ~ка.

галóш|а, и, *f.* galosh; сесть в ~у (*coll.*) to get into a fix, into a spot.

галóш|ный, *adj. of* ~а.

галс, а, *m.* (*naut.*) tack; пра́вым (ле́вым) ~ом on the starboard (port) tack.

гáлстук, а, *m.* (neck)tie, cravat; заложи́ть, зали́ть за г. (*coll.*) to booze.

галу́н, á, *m.* lace, galloon.

галу́шк|а, и, *f.* (*cul.*) dumpling.

гальваниза́ци|я, и, *f.* (*phys.*) galvanization.

гальванизи́р|овать, ую, *impf. and pf.* (*phys.*) to galvanize.

гальвани́ческий, *adj.* (*phys.*) galvanic.

гальвáно, *indecl., n.* (*typ.*) electrotype.

гальванóметр, а, *m.* (*phys.*) galvanometer.

гальванопла́стик|а, и, *f.* electroplating.

гáл|ька, ьки, *f.* **1.** (*g. pl.* ~ек) pebble. **2.** (*collect.*) pebble, shingle.

галью́н, а, *m.* (*naut.*) (the) heads.

гам, а, *m.* (*coll.*) din, uproar.

гамадри́л, а, *m.* (*zool.*) hamadryad (*baboon*).

гамáк, á, *m.* hammock.

гамáш|а, и, *f.* gaiter, legging.

гáмм|а¹, ы, *f.* (*mus.*) scale; gamut (*also fig.*).

гáмм|а², ы, *f.* gamma (*letter of Greek alphabet*); г.-лучи́ (*phys.*) gamma-rays.

гáнгли|й, я, *m.* (*anat.*) ganglion.

гангрéн|а, ы, *f.* gangrene.

гангренóзный, *adj.* gangrenous.

гáнгстер, а, *m.* gangster.

гандикáп, а, *m.* (*sport*) handicap.

ганзéйский, *adj.* (*hist.*) Hanseatic.

гантéл|ь, и, *f.* (*sport*) dumb-bell.

гарáж, á, *m.* garage.

гарáнт, а, *m.* (*leg.*) guarantor.

гаранти́йный, *adj.* guarantee.

гаранти́р|овать, ую, *impf. and pf.* **1.** to guarantee, vouch for. **2.** (от+*g.*) to guarantee (against).

гарáнти|я, и, *f.* guarantee.

гардемари́н, а, *m.* (*hist.*) **1.** naval cadet. **2.** (корабéльный) г. midshipman.

гардерóб, а, *m.* **1.** wardrobe (*article of furniture*). **2.** cloakroom. **3.** (*collect.*) wardrobe (*clothes belonging to one person*).

гардерóбн|ая, ой, *f.* cloakroom.

гардерóбщик, а, *m.* cloakroom attendant.

гардерóбщи|ца, цы, *f. of* ~к.

гарди́н|а, ы, *f.* curtain.

гар|евóй, *adj. of* ~ь; ~евáя доро́жка cinder path.

гарéм, а, *m.* harem.

гáрк|ать, аю, *impf. of* ~нуть.

гáрк|нуть, ну, нешь, *pf.* (*of* ~ать) (*coll.*) to bark (out), bawl (out); г. на кого́-н. to bark at someone.

гармониза́ци|я, и, *f.* (*mus.*) harmonization.

гармонизи́р|овать, ую, *impf. and pf.* (*mus.*) to harmonize (*trans.*).

гармóник|а, и, *f.* **1.** accordion, concertina; губнáя г. mouth organ. **2.** ~ой, в ~у *as adv.* pleated; concertina'ed.

гармони́р|овать, ую, *impf.* (с+*i.*) to harmonize (*intrans.*) (with), go (with); to tone (with).

гармони́ст¹, а, *m.* accordion player, concertina player.

гармони́ст², а, *m.* (*mus.*) specialist in harmony.

гармони́ческий, *adj.* (**1.** (*mus.*) harmonic. **2.** harmonious. **3.** (*tech.*) rhythmic.

гармони́ч|ный (~ен, ~на, ~но), *adj.* harmonious.

гармóни|я¹, и, *f.* **1.** (*mus.*) harmony. **2.** (*fig.*) harmony, concord.

гармóни|я², и, *f.* (*coll.*) accordion, concertina.

гармóн|ь, и, *f.* (*coll.*) accordion, concertina.

гармóшк|а, и, *f.* = гармóнь.

гáрн|ец, ца, *m.* (*obs.*) garnets (*Russian dry measure* = 3·28 *litres*).

гарнизóн, а, *m.* garrison.

гарнизóн|ный, *adj. of* ~; ~ная слу́жба garrison duty.

гарни́р, а, *m.* (*cul.*) trimmings, garnish.

гарниту́р, а, *m.* set; suite.

гáрн|ый, *adj.* (*obs.*); ~ое мáсло lamp oil.

гáрпи|я, и, *f.* harpy.

гарпу́н, á, *m.* harpoon.

гарпу́н|ный, *adj. of* ~; ~ная пу́шка harpoon-gun.

гарт, а, *m.* type-metal; printer's pie.

гáрус, а, *m.* worsted (yarn); вы́шивка ~ом worsted work.

гарц|евáть, у́ю, *impf.* to caracole, prance.

гар|ь, и, *f.* **1.** burning; пáхнет ~ю there's a smell of burning. **2.** cinders, ashes.

гаси́льник, а, *m.* (*obs.*) extinguisher.

гаси́тел|ь, я, *m.* extinguisher; (*fig.*) suppressor; г. просвеще́ния obscurantist.

га|си́ть, шу́, ~сишь, *impf.* (*of* по~) **1.** (*pf. also* за~) to put out, extinguish; г. свет to put out the light. **2.** г. и́звесть to slake lime. **3.** (*fig.*) to suppress, stifle. **4.** to cancel; г. долг to liquidate a debt; г. почтóвую мáрку to frank a postage stamp.

гáс|нуть, ну, нешь, *past* ~, ~ла, *impf.* (*of* по~) to be extinguished, go out; to grow feeble; он ~нет не по дням, а по часáм he is sinking hourly.

гастри́т, а, *m.* gastritis.

гастри́ческий, *adj.* gastric.

гастролёр, а, *m.* **1.** artiste on tour. **2.** (*coll.*) casual worker.

гастроли́р|овать, ую, *impf.* to tour, be on tour (*of an artiste*).

гастро́л|ь, и, *f.* tour; temporary engagement (*of artiste*).

гастро́льный, *adj.* touring (*of artistes*).

гастроно́м¹, а, *m.* gastronome, gourmet.

гастроно́м², а, *m.* = ~оми́ческий магази́н.

гастрономи́ческий, *adj.* **1.** gastronomical. **2.** г. магази́н grocer's (shop), provision shop.

гастроно́ми|я, и, *f.* **1.** connoisseur's taste in food. **2.** provisions, delicatessen.

га|ти́ть, чу́, ти́шь, *impf.* to make a road (of brushwood) across (*marshy ground*).

гат|ь, и, *f.* road of brushwood; бреве́нчатая г. corduroy road.

га́убиц|а, ы, *f.* (*mil.*) howitzer.

га́уб|ичный, *adj. of* ~ица.

гауптва́хт|а, ы, *f.* (*mil.*) guardhouse, guardroom.

га́ч|и, ей (*sing.* ~а, ~и)*, f.* (*dial.*) **1.** trousers. **2.** haunches (*of an animal*).

гаше́ни|е, я, *n.* extinguishing; slaking.

гашён|ый, *p.p.p. of* гаси́ть *and adj.*; ~ая и́звесть slaked lime.

гаше́тк|а, и, *f.* trigger.

гаши́ш, а, *m.* hashish.

гвалт, а, *m.* (*coll.*) row, uproar, rumpus.

гварде́|ец, йца, *m.* (*mil.*) guardsman.

гварде́йский, *adj.* (*mil.*) Guards'; г. миномёт multi-rail rocket launcher.

гва́рди|я, и, *f.* (*mil.*) Guards; ~и (*preceding* капита́н, *etc., in titles of rank*) Guards.

гво́здик, а, *m.* tack (*small nail*).

гвозди́к|а¹, и, *f.* (*bot.*) pink(s); пе́ристая г. carnation(s); туре́цкая г., борода́тая г. sweet-william.

гвозди́к|а², и, *f.* (*collect.*) cloves.

гвозди́льный, *adj.* nail, nail-making.

гвоз|ди́ть, жу́, ди́шь, *impf.* (*coll.*) **1.** to bang, bash; to bang away. **2.** to repeat, keep on.

гвозди́|чный¹, *adj. of* ~ка¹.

гвозди́|чный², *adj. of* ~ка²; ~чное ма́сло oil of cloves.

гвозд|ь, я́, *pl.* ~и, ~ей, *m.* **1.** nail; tack; peg; пове́сить шля́пу на г. to hang one's hat on a peg; ~ём засе́сть (*fig.*) to become firmly fixed. **2.** (+*g.*; *fig.*, *coll.*) the crux (of); the pièce de résistance (of); highlight (of); г. вопро́са the crux of the matter; г. ве́чера the highlight of the evening; г. сезо́на the hit of the season. **3.** (и) никаки́х ~ей! (*coll.*) and that's that!, and that's the end of it!

где, *adv.* **1.** (*interrog. and relat. adv.*) where; г. бы ни wherever; г. бы то ни́ было по matter where. **2.** (*coll.*) somewhere; any-

where. **3.** г. ..., г. ... (*coll.*) in one place ..., in another .... **4.** г. (уж) (+*d. and inf.*)(*coll.*) how should one, how is one to; г. мне знать? how should I know?

где́-либо, *adv.* anywhere.

где́-нибудь, *adv.* somewhere; anywhere.

где́-то, *adv.* somewhere.

гебра́ист, а, *m.* Hebraist.

гегелья́н|ец, ца, *m.* Hegelian.

гегелья́нств|о, а, *n.* Hegelianism.

гегемо́н, а, *m.* leader.

гегемони́зм, а, *m.* (*polit.*) 'hegemonism'.

гегемо́ни|я, и, *f.* hegemony, supremacy.

гедони́зм, а, *m.* hedonism.

гедони́ст, а, *m.* hedonist.

гедонисти́ческий, *adj.* hedonistic.

гей, *interj.* hi!

ге́йзер, а, *m.* geyser.

гекато́мб|а, ы, *f.* hecatomb.

гекза́метр, а, *m.* hexameter.

гекса́эдр, а, *m.* (*math.*) hexahedron.

гекта́р, а, *m.* hectare.

гекто- hecto-.

гекто́граф, а, *m.* hectograph (*duplicating machine*).

ге́ли|й, я, *m.* (*chem.*) helium.

геликопте́р, а, *m.* (*obs.*) = вертолёт.

гелио́граф, а, *m.* heliograph.

гелиотро́п, а, *m.* (*bot. and min.*) heliotrope.

гелиоцентри́ческий, *adj.* heliocentric.

гельминтоло́ги|я, и, *f.* helminthology.

ге́мм|а, ы, *f.* stone with engraved design.

гемоглоби́н, а, *m.* (*physiol.*) haemoglobin.

геморроида́льн|ый, *adj.* (*med.*) haemorrhoidal; ~ая ши́шка pile.

геморро́|й, я, *m.* (*med.*) haemorrhoids, piles.

гемофили́|я, и, *f.* (*med.*) haemophilia.

ген- (*abbr. of* генера́льный) general.

ген, а, *m.* (*physiol.*) gene.

генеалоги́ческий, *adj.* genealogical.

генеало́ги|я, и, *f.* genealogy.

ге́незис, а, *m.* origin, source, genesis.

генера́л, а, *m.* general; г.-майо́р major-general; г.-лейтена́нт lieutenant-general; г.-полко́вник colonel-general; г.-губерна́тор governor-general.

генера́л-ба́с, а, *m.* (*mus.*) figured bass.

генерали́ссимус, а, *m.* generalissimo.

генералите́т, а, *m.* (*collect.*) the generals; the top brass.

генера́льн|ый, *adj.* (*in var. senses*) general; г. констру́ктор chief designer; ~ая ли́ния па́ртии (*polit.*) Party general line; ~ая репети́ция dress rehearsal; ~ое сраже́ние decisive battle; г. штаб general staff.

генера́льский, *adj.* general's; г. чин rank of general.

генера́льш|а, и, *f.* (*coll.*) general's wife.

генера́тор, а, *m.* (*tech.*) generator; г. колеба́ний oscillator; г. то́ка current generator.

генера́тор|ный, *adj. of* ~; г. газ producer gas.

генера́ци|я, и, *f.* generation.

генетик|а, и, *f.* genetics.

генети́ческий, *adj.* genetic.

гениа́льность|ь, и, *f.* genius; greatness.

гениа́л|ьный (ен, ьна), *adj.* of genius, great; brilliant; ~ьная иде́я a stroke of genius.

ге́ни|й, я, *m.* genius; a genius; злой г. evil genius.

геншта́б, а, *m.* general staff.

генштаби́ст, *m.* (*coll.*) general staff officer.

гео- geo-.

гео́граф, а, *m.* geographer.

географи́ческий, *adj.* geographical.

геогра́фи|я, и, *f.* geography.

геодези́ст, а, *m.* land-surveyor.

геодези́ческий, *adj.* geodesic, geodetic.

геоде́зи|я, и, *f.* geodesy, (land-)surveying.

гео́лог, а, *m.* geologist.

геологи́ческий, *adj.* geological.

геоло́ги|я, и, *f.* geology.

гео́метр, а, *m.* geometrician.

геометри́ческий, *adj.* geometric(al).

геоме́три|я, и, *f.* geometry.

георги́н, а, *m.* (*bot.*) dahlia.

георги́н|а, ы, *f.* = ~.

геофи́зик|а, и, *f.* geophysics.

геофизи́ческий, *adj.* geophysical.

гепа́рд, а, *m.* cheetah.

гера́льдик|а, и, *f.* heraldry.

геральди́ческий, *adj.* heraldic.

гера́н|ь, и, *f.* geranium.

герб, а́, *m.* arms, coat of arms.

гербари|й, я, *m.* herbarium.

гербо́вник, а, *m.* armorial.

ге́рбо|вый, *adj.* 1. heraldic. 2. bearing a coat of arms; ~ая бума́га stamped paper; ~ая ма́рка duty stamp. 3. г. сбор stamp--duty.

геркуле́с, а, *m.* 1. (a) Hercules (*strong man*). 2. (*sing. only*) rolled oats; porridge.

геркуле́совский, *adj.* Herculean.

герма́н|ец, ца, *m.* 1. Teuton; ancient German; ~цы the Germanic, Nordic peoples. 2. (*coll.*) German.

германиза́ци|я, и, *f.* Germanization.

германизи́р|овать, ую, *impf. and pf.* to Germanize.

германи́зм, а, *m.* Germanism.

герма́ни|й, я, *m.* (*chem.*) germanium.

германи́ст, а, *m.* specialist in Germanic studies.

германи́стик|а, и, *f.* Germanic studies.

германофи́л, а, *m.* Germanophile.

германофо́б, а, *m.* Germanophobe.

герма́нск|ий, *adj.* 1. Germanic; Teutonic; ~ие языки́ Germanic languages. 2. (*coll.*) German.

гермафроди́т, а, *m.* hermaphrodite.

гермети́чески, *adv.* г. закры́тый hermetically sealed.

гермети́ческ|ий, *adj.* 1. hermetic, sealed; air-tight; water-tight; ~ая каби́на (*aeron.*) pressurized cabin. 2. hermetic, secret.

геройзм, а, *m.* heroism.

геро́ик|а, и, *f.* heroics; heroic spirit; heroic style.

герои́н|я, и, *f.* heroine.

герои́ческ|ий, *adj.* heroic; ~ие ме́ры heroic measures.

геро́|й, я, *m.* hero.

геро́йский, *adj.* heroic.

геро́йств|о, а, *n.* heroism.

геро́льд, а, *m.* (*hist.*) herald.

геру́нди́в, а, *m.* (*gram.*) gerundive.

геру́нди|й, я, *m.* (*gram.*) gerund.

герц, а, *g. pl.* г. *m.* (*phys.*) hertz, cycle per second.

ге́рцог, а, *m.* duke.

герцоги́н|я, и, *f.* duchess.

ге́рцогский, *adj.* ducal.

ге́рцогств|о, а, *n.* duchy.

геста́по, *indecl., n.* Gestapo.

гете́р|а, ы, *f.* hetaera.

гетероге́нный, *adj.* heterogeneous.

ге́тман, а, *m.* (*hist.*) hetman.

ге́тр|ы, гетр, *sing.* ~а, ~ы, *f.* gaiters.

ге́тто, *indecl., n.* ghetto.

гешёфт, а, *m.* (*coll.*) deal, speculation.

гиаци́нт, а, *m.* 1. (*bot.*) hyacinth. 2. (*min.*) jacinth.

ги́бел|ь, и, *f.* 1. death; destruction, ruin; loss; wreck; downfall. 2. (+*g.*; *coll.*) masses (of), swarms (of), hosts (of).

ги́бел|ьный (~ен, ~ьна), *adj.* disastrous, fatal.

ги́б|кий (~ок, ~ка́, ~ко), *adj.* 1. flexible, pliant; lithe, lissom; г. стан slender build. 2. adaptable, versatile. 3. tractable.

ги́бкост|ь, и, *f.* 1. flexibility, pliancy. 2. versatility, resourcefulness.

ги́бл|ый, *adj.* (*coll.*) bad, rotten, good-for--nothing; ~ое де́ло a bad job.

ги́б|нуть, ну, нешь, *past* ~, ~ла, *impf.* (*of* по~) to perish.

гибри́д, а, *m.* hybrid, mongrel.

гибридиза́ци|я, и, *f.* hybridization.

гига́нт, а, *m.* giant.

гига́нтский, *adj.* gigantic.

гигие́н|а, ы, *f.* hygiene, hygienics.

гигиени́ческ|ий, *adj.* hygienic, sanitary; ~ая повя́зка sanitary towel; ~ая бума́га toilet paper.

гигро́метр, а, *m.* hygrometer.

гигроско́п, а, *m.* hygroscope.

гигроскопи́ческий, *adj.* hygroscopic.

гид, а, *m.* guide.

гида́льго, *indecl., m.* hidalgo.

ги́др|а, ы, *f.* (*myth., zool.*; *fig.*) hydra.

гидра́влик|а, и, *f.* hydraulics.

гидравли́ческий, *adj.* hydraulic.

гидра́т, а, *m.* (*chem.*) hydrate.

гидро- hydro-.

гидроавиа́ци|я, и, *f.* hydroaviation.

гидро́граф, а, *m.* **1.** hydrograph. **2.** hydrographer.

гидрографи́ческий, *adj.* hydrographic.

гидрогра́фи|я, и, *f.* hydrography.

гидродина́мик|а, и, *f.* hydrodynamics.

гидро́лиз, а, *m.* (*chem.*) hydrolysis.

гидроло́ги|я, и, *f.* hydrology.

гидроме́три|я, и, *f.* hydrometry.

гидроо́кис|ь, и, *f.* hydroxide.

гидропа́ти|я, и, *f.* hydropathy.

гидропу́льт, а, *m.* stirrup pump.

гидросамолёт, а, *m.* seaplane.

гидроста́нци|я, и, *f.* hydro-electric (power-) station.

гидроста́тик|а, и, *f.* hydrostatics.

гидросульфи́т, а, *m.* (*chem.*) hydrosulphite.

гидротерапи́|я, и, *f.* hydrotherapy.

гидроте́хник, а, *m.* hydraulic engineer.

гидроте́хник|а, и, *f.* hydraulic engineering.

гидроустано́вк|а, и, *f.* (*tech.*) hydro-electric power-plant.

гидрофо́н, а, *m.* (*naut.*) hydrophone.

гидроэлектри́ческий, *adj.* hydro-electric.

гидроэлектроста́нци|я, и, *f.* hydro-electric power-station.

гие́н|а, ы, *f.* hyena.

гик, а, *m.* (*coll.*) whoop.

ги́к|ать, аю, *impf.* (*of* ~нуть) (*coll.*) to whoop.

ги́к|нуть, ну, нешь, *pf.* (*of* ~ать) to whoop.

гил|ь, и, *f.* (*obs., coll.*) nonsense.

гильде́йский, *adj.* *of* ги́льдия.

ги́льди|я, и, *f.* (*hist.*) guild; class, order (*of merchants in tsarist Russia*).

ги́льз|а, ы, *f.* case, empty; патро́нная г. cartridge-case; папиро́сная г. cigarette-wrapper; г. цили́ндра (*tech.*) cylinder sleeve.

гильоти́н|а, ы, *f.* guillotine.

гильотини́р|овать, ую, *impf. and pf.* to guillotine.

гимн, а, *m.* hymn; госуда́рственный г. national anthem.

гимнази́ст, а, *m.* grammar-school boy.

гимнази́стк|а, и, *f.* grammar-school girl.

гимна́зи|я, и, *f.* grammar school, high school.

гимна́ст, а, *m.* gymnast.

гимнастёрк|а, и, *f.* soldier's blouse.

гимна́стик|а, и, *f.* gymnastics.

гимнасти́ческ|ий, *adj.* gymnastic; г. зал gymnasium; ~ие снаря́ды gymnastic apparatus.

гинеко́лог, а, *m.* gynaecologist.

гинекологи́ческий, *adj.* gynaecological.

гинеколо́ги|я, и, *f.* gynaecology.

гине́|я, и, *f.* guinea.

гипе́рбол|а, ы, *f.* **1.** hyperbole. **2.** (*math.*) hyperbola.

гиперболи́ческий, *adj.* **1.** hyperbolical. **2.** (*math.*) hyperbolic.

гиперболи́ч|ный (~ен, ~на), *adj.* exaggerated.

гипертони́|я, и, *f.* (*med.*) hypertonia, high blood-pressure.

гипертрофи́рованный, *adj.* (*biol.*) hypertrophied.

гипертрофи́|я, и, *f.* (*biol.*) hypertrophy.

гипно́з, а, *m.* hypnosis.

гипнотизёр, а, *m.* hypnotist.

гипнотизи́р|овать, ую, *impf.* (*of* за~) to hypnotize.

гипноти́зм, а, *m.* hypnotism.

гипноти́ческий, *adj.* hypnotic.

гипосульфи́т, а, *m.* (*chem.*) hyposulphite.

гипо́тез|а, ы, *f.* hypothesis.

гипотену́з|а, ы, *f.* (*math.*) hypotenuse.

гипотети́ческий, *adj.* hypothetical.

гиппопота́м, а, *m.* hippopotamus.

гипс, а, *m.* **1.** (*min.*) gypsum, plaster of Paris. **2.** plaster cast. **3.** (*med.*) plaster.

гипс|ова́ть, у́ю, *impf.* (*of* за~) to plaster; to gypsum.

ги́псовый, *adj.* **1.** gypseous. **2.** plaster; г. слéпок plaster-cast.

гиреви́к, а́, *m.* (*sport*) weight-lifter.

гир|ево́й, *adj. of* ~я́.

гирля́нд|а, ы, *f.* garland, wreath.

гироко́мпас, а, *m.* gyrocompass.

гироско́п, а, *m.* gyroscope.

гироскопи́ческий, *adj.* gyroscopic.

ги́р|я, и, *f.* weight; г. для гимна́стики dumb-bells.

гисто́лог, а, *m.* histologist.

гистологи́ческий, *adj.* histological.

гистоло́ги|я, и, *f.* histology.

гита́р|а, ы, *f.* guitar.

гитари́ст, а, *m.* guitarist.

гитлери́зм, а, *m.* Hitlerism; Naz(i)ism.

ги́тлеров|ец, ца, *m.* Hitlerite, Nazi; German soldier (*in Second World War*).

ги́тлеровский, *adj.* Hitlerite, Nazi.

ги́чк|а, и, *f.* (*naut.*) gig.

глав- (*abbr. of* гла́вный) chief, main.

глав|а́[1], ы́, *pl.* ~ы, *f.* **1.** (*obs. or rhet.*) head. **2.** (*m. and f.*) head, chief; г. делега́ции head of a delegation; быть во ~é (+*g.*) to be at the head (of), lead; во ~é (с+*i.*) under the leadership (of), led (by). **3.** поста́вить во ~у́ угла́ to regard as of paramount importance. **4.** (*archit.*) cupola (*of a church*).

глав|а́[2], ы́, *pl.* ~ы, *f.* chapter (*of a book*).

глава́р|ь, я́, *m.* leader; ringleader.

главе́нств|о, а, *n.* supremacy.

главе́нств|овать, ую, *impf.* (в+*p.*, над+*i.*) to have command (over), hold sway (over).

главк, a, *m.* (*abbr. of* гла́вный комите́т) central directorate (*department of Ministry controlling either branch of industry falling within competence of Ministry or establishments in a particular area*).

главнокома́ндующ|ий, его, *m.* commander-in-chief; верхо́вный г. supreme commander.

гла́вн|ый, *adj.* chief, main, principal; head, senior; г. врач head physician; г. инжене́р chief engineer; ~ая кварти́ра (*mil.*; *obs.*) headquarters; ~ая кни́га ledger; ~ое предложе́ние main clause; ~ое управле́ние main directorate, central directorate; ~ым о́бразом chiefly, mainly, for the most part; *as noun* ~ое, ~ого, *n.* the chief thing, the main thing; the essentials.

глаго́л, a, *m.* 1. (*gram.*) verb. 2. (*arch.*) word.

глаго́лиц|а, ы, *f.* (*ling.*) the Glagolitic alphabet.

глаголи́ческий, *adj.* (*ling.*) Glagolitic.

глаго́льный, *adj.* verbal.

гладиа́тор, a, *m.* gladiator.

гладиа́торский, *adj.* gladiatorial.

гради́льн|ый, *adj.* ironing; ~ая доска́ ironing-board.

гла́|дить, жу, дишь, *impf.* (*of* по~[1]) 1. (*pf. also* вы́~) to iron, press. 2. to stroke; г. по голо́вке (*coll.*) to pat on the back; г. про́тив ше́рсти to rub the wrong way.

гла́д|кий (~ок, ~ка́, ~ко), *adj.* 1. smooth; (*of hair*) straight; (*of fabrics*) plain, unfigured; с него́ взя́тки ~ки (*coll.*) you'll get nothing out of him. 2. fluent, facile. 3. (*coll.*) sleek, well-nourished.

гла́д|ко, *adv. of* ~кий; smoothly, swimmingly; де́ло сошло́ г. the affair went off smoothly; г. вы́бритый clean-shaven.

гладкоство́льный, *adj.* (*of firearms*) smooth-bore.

глад|ь[1], и, *f.* smooth surface (*of water*); тишь да г. (*coll.*) peace and quiet.

глад|ь[2], и, *f.* satin-stitch; вышива́ть ~ью to satin-stitch.

гла́же, *comp. of* гла́дкий, гла́дко.

гла́жень|е, я, *n.* ironing.

гла́жу, *see* гла́дить.

глаз, a, о ~е, в ~у́, *pl.* ~а́, ~, ~а́м, *m.* eye; eyesight; дурно́й г. evil eye; невооружённый г. naked eye; не в бровь, а в г. (*coll.*) to hit the mark, strike home; в ~а́ to one's face; я его́ в ~а́ не вида́л I have never seen him; в ~а́х (+*g.*) in the eyes (of); он был геро́ем в ~а́х ма́тери he was a hero in his mother's eyes; за ~а́ (*i*) in absence; руга́ть кого́-н. за ~а́ to abuse someone behind his back, (*ii*) (*coll.*) enough, more than enough; на ~а́, на ~а́х before one's eyes; не попа-

да́йся мне на ~а́! keep out of my sight!; дитя́ вы́росло на роди́тельских ~а́х the child grew before its parents' eyes; на г. approximately, by eye; с ~у на г. tête-à-tête, cheek-by-jowl; с г. доло́й out of sight; убира́йся с г. доло́й! get out of my sight!; с г. доло́й — из се́рдца вон out of sight, our of mind; не спуска́ть с г., г. с+*g.* not to let out of one's sight; с пья́ных г. in a drunken condition, drunk; смотре́ть во все ~а́ to be all eyes; хоть г. вы́коли it's pitch dark; закрыва́ть ~а́ (на+*a.*) to close one's eyes (to), connive (at); открыва́ть кому́-н. ~а́ (на+*a.*) to open someone's eyes (to); премье́р-мини́стр откры́л нам ~а́ на неизбе́жность войны́ the Prime Minister opened our eyes to the fact that war was inevitable; идти́ куда́ ~а́ гляди́т to follow one's nose.

глаза́ст|ый (~, ~а), *adj.* (*coll.*) big-eyed; quick-sighted.

глазена́п|ы, ов, *no sing.* (*coll.*, *joc.*) eyes.

глазе́т, a, *m.* brocade.

глазе́|ть, ю, *impf.* (*of* по~) (на+*a.*; *coll.*) to stare (at), gawk (at).

глазир|о́ванный, *p.p.p. of* ~ова́ть *and adj.* glazed; glossy; (*cul.*) iced, glacé.

глазир|ова́ть, у́ю, *impf. and pf.* to glaze; (*cul.*) to ice.

глазиро́вк|а, и, *f.* glazing; icing; торт с ~ой iced cake.

глазни́к, а́, *m.* (*coll.*) oculist.

глазни́ц|а, ы, *f.* eye-socket.

глазн|о́й, *adj. of* глаз; г. врач oculist; г. нерв optic nerve; ~о́е я́блоко eyeball.

глаз|о́к, ка́, *pl.* ~ки́, ~ок *and* ~ки́, ~ко́в, *m.* 1. (*pl.* ~ки) *dim. of* ~; одни́м ~ко́м with half an eye; де́лать, стро́ить ~ки кому́-н. to make eyes at someone; аню́тины ~ки (*bot.*) pansy. 2. (*pl.* ~ки́) pigmented spot (*on some birds and insects*). 3. (*pl.* ~ки́) (*coll.*) peephole; inspection hole; glory hole (*of furnace*); head (*of periscope*). 4. (*pl.* ~ки́) bud; eye (*of potato*). 5. (*pl.* ~ки́) (*tech.*) eye, eyelet.

глазоме́р, a, *m.* 1. measurement by eye. 2. ability to judge by eye; хоро́ший г. good eye.

глазоме́р|ный, *adj. of* ~; ~ное определе́ние estimation by eye.

глазу́н|ья, ьи, *g. pl.* ~ий, *f.* fried eggs.

глазу́р|ь, и, *f.* 1. glaze (*on pottery*). 2. (*cul.*) icing.

гла́нд|а, ы, *f.* (*anat.*) tonsil; удали́ть ~ы to take out tonsils.

глас, a, *m.* 1. (*obs.*) voice; г. вопию́щего в пусты́не the voice of one crying in the wilderness. 2. (*eccl.*) tune.

гла|си́ть, шу́, си́шь, *impf.* 1. (*obs.*) to announce. 2. to say, run; докуме́нт ~си́т сле́дующее the paper runs as follows; как ~си́т погово́рка as the saying goes.

гла́сно¹, *adv.* openly, publicly.

гла́сно², *as pred.* (*obs.*) it is well known.

гла́сност|ь, и, *f.* publicity; преда́ть ~и to give publicity (to), make known, publish.

гла́сный¹, *adj.* open, public; г. суд public trial.

гла́сн|ый², *adj.* vowel, vocalic; *as noun* г., ~ого, *m.* vowel.

гла́сн|ый³, ого, *m.* (*hist.*) (*town, province, etc.*) councillor.

глауко́м|а, ы, *f.* (*med.*) glaucoma.

глаша́та|й, я, *m.* 1. (*hist.*) town crier, public crier. 2. (*fig., rhet.*) herald.

гле́тчер, а, *m.* glacier.

гли́н|а, ы, *f.* clay; валя́льная г. fuller's earth; жи́рная г. loam; огнеупо́рная г. fire-clay; фарфо́ровая г. china clay, porcelain clay; ма́зать ~ой to clay.

гли́нист|ый, *adj.* clayey, argillaceous; ~ая по́чва loam.

глиноби́тный, *adj.* pisé (*of clay, mixed with straw, gravel, etc.*).

глинозём, а, *m.* (*chem.*) alumina.

глинтве́йн, а, *m.* mulled wine; де́лать г. to mull wine.

гли́нян|ый, *adj.* 1. clay; earthenware; ~ая посу́да earthenware crockery. 2. clayey.

гли́ссер, а, *m.* (*naut.*) speed-boat.

глист, а́, *m.* (intestinal) worm.

глистого́нный, *adj.* (*med.*) vermifuge.

глицери́н, а, *m.* glycerine.

гло́бус, а, *m.* globe.

гло|да́ть, жу́, ~жешь, *impf.* to gnaw (*also fig.*)

глота́|ть, ю, *impf.* to swallow.

гло́тк|а, и, *f.* 1. (*anat.*) gullet. 2. (*coll.*) throat.

глот|о́к, ка́, *m.* gulp, mouthful; drink.

гло́х|нуть, ну, нешь, *past* ~, ~ла, *impf.* 1. (*pf.* о~) to become deaf. 2. (*pf.* за~) to die away, subside (*of noise*). 3. (*pf.* за~) to become wild, go to seed.

глу́б|же, *comp. of* ~о́кий *and* ~око́.

глубин|а́, ы́, *pl.* ~ы, *f.* 1. depth. 2. (*pl.*) (the) depths, deep places. 3. heart, interior (*also fig.*); в ~е́ ле́са in the heart of the forest; в ~е́ веко́в in ancient times; в ~е́ души́ at heart, in one's heart of hearts; от ~ы́ души́ with all one's heart. 4. (*fig.*) depth, profundity; intensity.

глуби́нн|ый, *adj.* 1. deep; deep-laid; deep--sea; ~ая бо́мба depth charge; г. лов ры́бы deep-sea fishing. 2. remote, out-of-the-way.

глубо́к|ий (~, ~а́, ~о́), *adj.* 1. (*in var. senses*) deep; ~ая вспа́шка deep ploughing; г. сон deep sleep; ~ая таре́лка soup-plate; ~ая оборо́на defence in depth; в ~ом тылу́ (*mil.*) deep in the rear; г. вира́ж (*aeron.*) steep turn. 2. profound; thorough,

thoroughgoing; considerable, serious; ~ие зна́ния thorough knowledge; ~ая оши́бка serious error. 3. (*of time, age, seasons*) late; advanced; extreme; до ~ой но́чи (until) far into the night; ~ая дре́вность extreme antiquity; ~ая ста́рость extreme old age; ~ая стару́ха a very old woman; наступи́ла ~ая зима́ it was mid-winter. 4. (*fig.*; *of feelings, etc.*) deep, profound, intense; с ~им приско́рбием (*in obituary formula*) with deep regret.

глубоко́¹, *adv.* deep; (*fig.*) deeply, profoundly; г. сиде́ть в воде́ (*of a vessel*) to draw much water.

глубоко́², *as pred.* it is deep.

глубоково́д|ный (~ен, ~на), *adj.* 1. deep--water. 2. deep-sea.

глубокомы́сленный, *adj.* thoughtful; serious.

глубокомы́сли|е, я, *n.* profundity; perspicacity.

глубокоуважа́емый, *adj.* much-esteemed; (*in formal letters*) dear.

глубоме́р, а, *m.* depth gauge.

глубоча́йший, *superl. of* глубо́кий.

глуб|ь, и, *f.* depth; г. реки́ the river--bottom.

глум|и́ться, лю́сь, и́шься, *impf.* (над+*i.*) to mock (at); to desecrate.

глумле́ни|е, я, *n.* mockery; gibe; desecration.

глумли́вый, *adj.* (*coll.*) mocking; gibing.

глупе́|ть, ю, *impf.* (*of* по~) to grow stupid.

глуп|е́ц, ца́, *m.* fool, blockhead.

глуп|и́ть, лю́, и́шь, *impf.* (*of* с~) to make a fool of oneself; to do something foolish.

глупова́т|ый (~, ~а), *adj.* silly; rather stupid.

глу́пост|ь, и, *f.* 1. foolishness, stupidity. 2. foolish, stupid action; foolish, stupid thing. 3. (*usu. pl.*) nonsense; ~! (stuff and) nonsense!

глу́п|ый (~, ~а́, ~о), *adj.* foolish, stupid; silly; (*coll.*) она́ ещё ~а́ she is still young and innocent.

глупы́ш, а́, *m.* (*coll.*) silly; silly little thing.

глупы́ш², а́, *m.* (*orn.*) fulmar.

глуха́р|ь, я́, *m.* 1. (*orn.*) capercailzie, wood-grouse. 2. (*coll.*) deaf person. 3. (*tech.*) propeller (*with hexahedral or square head*).

глухо́¹, *adv. of* глухо́й; (*coll.*) = на́глухо.

глухо́², *as pred.* it is lonely, deserted.

глухова́т|ый (~, ~а), *adj.* somewhat deaf, hard of hearing.

глух|о́й (~, ~а́, ~о), *adj.* 1. deaf (*also fig.*); он был ~ к на́шим мольба́м he was deaf to our entreaties; *as noun* г., ~о́го, *m.* deaf man; ~а́я, ~о́й, *f.* deaf woman. 2. (*of sound*) muffled, confused, indistinct. 3. indistinct, obscure; ~а́я молва́ vague rumours. **4.** (*ling.*) voiceless. **5.** thick, dense; wild; г. лес dense forest. **6.** remote, out-of-the-way; god-forsaken; в ~о́й провинции in the depths of the country; ~а́я у́лица lonely street. **7.** sealed; blank, blind; ~а́я стена́ blind wall. **8.** (*of clothing*) buttoned-up, done up; not open. **9.** г. ряд (*mil.*) blank file. **10.** (*of times or seasons*) dead; late; ~а́я ночь dead of night; ~а́я пора́ slack period; г. сезо́н dead season.

глухома́н|ь, и, *f.* (*coll.*) out-of-the-way place, backwoods.

глухонем|о́й, *adj.* deaf and dumb; *as noun* **г., ~о́го,** *m.* deaf mute.

глухот|а́, ы́, *f.* deafness.

глу́|ше, *comp. of* ~хо́й *and* ~хо.

глуши́тел|ь, я, *m.* **1.** (*tech.*) silencer, muffler. **2.** (*fig.*) suppressor.

глуш|и́ть, у́, ~и́шь, *impf.* **1.** (*pf.* о~) to stun, stupefy; г. ры́бу to stun fish (*by means of explosives*). **2.** (*pf.* за~) to muffle (*sounds*); г. боль to dull pain; г. мото́р to stop the engine; г. радиопереда́чи to jam broadcasts. **3.** (*pf.* за~) (*coll.*) to put out (*a fire, etc.*). **4.** (*pf.* за~) to choke, stifle (*growth*). **5.** (*pf.* за~) (*fig.*) to suppress, stifle; г. кри́тику to suppress criticism. **6.** (*impf. only*) (*sl.*) to soak up (= to drink in large quantities).

глуш|ь, и́, *f.* overgrown part (*of forest or garden*); backwoods (*also fig.*).

глы́б|а, ы, *f.* clod; lump, block.

глюко́з|а, ы, *f.* glucose, grape sugar, dextrose.

гля|де́ть, жу́, ди́шь, *impf.* (*of* по~) **1.** (на+*a.*) to look (at); to peer (at); to gaze (upon); г. ко́со (на+*a.*) to take a poor view (of); г. в о́ба to be on one's guard; г. в гроб to have one foot in the grave; г. сквозь па́льцы (на+*a.*) to wink (at), shut one's eyes (to), turn a blind eye (to); идти́ куда́ глаза́ ~дя́т to follow one's nose. **2.** (на+*a.*; *coll.*) to look to (= to take as an example). **3.** (на+*a.*) to heed, mark; не́чего на них г. don't take any notice of them. **4.** (*coll.*) to look for, seek (*with one's eyes*). **5.** (*impf. only*) to show, appear. **6.** (*impf. only*) (на+*a.*) to look (on to), face, give (on to). **7.** (*impf. only*) (+*i. or adv.*; *coll.*) to look, look like, appear; она́ ~ди́т пла́ксой she looks a cry-baby. **8.** (за+*i.*; *coll.*) to look after, see to. **9.** ~ди́(те) (*expressing warning or threat*) mind (out); ~ди́ не (+*imp.*) mind you don't . . . **10.** того́ и ~ди́ (*coll.*) it looks as if; I'm afraid; того́ и ~ди́ бу́дет бу́ря I'm afraid there's going to be a storm. **11.** ~дя (по+*d.*, *coll.*) depending (on).

гля|де́ться, жу́сь, ди́шься, *impf.* (*of* по~) (в+*a.*) to look at oneself (in).

глядь, *interj.* lo and behold!, hey presto!

гля́н|ец, ца, *m.* gloss, lustre.

гля́|нуть, ну, нешь, *pf.* (на+*a.*) glance (at).

глянцеви́т|ый (~, ~а), *adj.* glossy, lustrous.

гм, *interj.* hm!

гна|ть, гоню́, го́нишь, *past* ~л, ~ла́, ~ло, *impf.* **1.** (*det. of* гоня́ть) to drive. **2.** to urge (on); to whip up (*an animal*); (*coll.*) to drive (*a vehicle*) hard. **3.** (*coll.*) to dash, tear. **4.** to hunt, chase; (*fig.*) to persecute. **5.** to turn out, turf out. **6.** to distil. **7.** (*usu. imp.*; *coll.*) to give. **8.** (*dial.*) to raft (*timber*).

гна́|ться, гоню́сь, го́нишься, *past* ~лся, ~ла́сь, ~ло́сь, *impf.* (*indet. of* гоня́ться) (за+*i.*) to pursue; to strive (for, after); (*fig.*) to keep up with.

гнев, а, *m.* anger, rage, wrath; не во гнев будь ска́зано if you don't mind me saying so.

гне́ва|ться, юсь, *impf.* (*of* раз~) (на+*a.*; *obs.*) to be angry (with).

гнев|и́ть, лю́, и́шь, *impf.* (*of* про~) (*obs.*) to anger, enrage.

гневли́в|ый (~, ~а), *adj.* (*obs.*) irascible.

гне́в|ный (~ен, ~на́, ~но), *adj.* angry, irate.

гнедо́й, *adj.* bay (*colour of horse*).

гнез|ди́ться, жу́сь, ди́шься, *impf.* **1.** to nest, build one's nest; to roost. **2.** (*fig.*) to have its seat; to be lodged.

гнезд|о́, а́, *pl.* **гнёзда,** *n.* **1.** nest; eyrie. **2.** den, lair (*also fig.*); г. сопротивле́ния (*mil.*) pocket of resistance. **3.** brood (*also fig.*). **4.** (*bot., med.*) nidus; cluster. **5.** (*tech.*) socket; seat; housing. **6.** (*ling.*) 'nest' (*group of words of same root*).

гнездова́ни|е, я, *n.* nesting; пора́ ~я nesting season.

гнездово́й, *adj. of* гнездо́.

гнейс, а, *m.* (*min.*) gneiss.

гне|сти́, ту́, тёшь, *impf.* to oppress, weigh down; to press; его́ ~ту́т забо́ты he is weighed down by cares.

гнёт, а, *m.* **1.** (*obs.*) press; weight. **2.** oppression.

гнету́щий, *pres. part. act. of* гнести́ *and adj.* oppressive.

гни́д|а, ы, *f.* nit.

гние́ни|е, я, *n.* decay, putrefaction, rot.

гнил|о́й (~, ~а́, ~о), *adj.* **1.** rotten (*also fig.*); decayed; putrid; corrupt. **2.** (*of weather*) damp, muggy.

гнилокро́ви|е, я, *n.* (*med.*) septicaemia.

гни́лостный, *adj.* **1.** putrefactive. **2.** putrid.

гни́лост|ь, и, *f.* rottenness (*also fig.*); putridity.

гнилу́шк|а, и, *f.* piece of rotten wood; (*coll.*) rotten stump (*of tooth*).

гнил|ь, и, *f.* **1.** rotten stuff. **2.** mould.

гнилье́, я́, *n.* (*collect.*) rotten stuff.

гнильц|а́, ы́, *f.* (*coll.*) rottenness; с ~о́й slightly rotten.

гни|ть, ю, ёшь, *impf.* (*of* с~) to rot, decay; to decompose.

гноекро́ви|е, я, *n.* (*med.*) pyaemia.

гное́ни|е, я, *n.* suppuration.

гноетече́ни|е, я, *n.* suppuration.

гно|и́ть, ю, и́шь, *impf.* (*of* с~) to let rot, allow to decay; г. наво́з to ferment manure; г. в тюрьме́ to leave to rot in prison.

гно|и́ться, ю́сь, и́шься, *impf.* to suppurate, discharge matter.

гно́ищ|е, а, *n.* (*obs.*) garbage dump.

гно|й, я, в ~е *or* в ~ю́, *m.* pus, matter.

гнойни́к, а́, *m.* abscess; ulcer.

гно́йный, *adj.* purulent.

гном, а, *m.* gnome.

гно́м|а, ы, *f.* maxim, aphorism.

гноми́ческий, *adj.* gnomic.

гно́мон, а, *m.* gnomon, sun-dial.

гносеоло́ги|я, и, *f.* (*philos.*) gnosiology; theory of knowledge.

гно́стик, а, *m.* gnostic.

гностици́зм, а, *m.* gnosticism.

гнус, а, *m.* (*collect.*) midges.

гнуса́в|ить, лю, ишь, *impf.* to speak through one's nose.

гнуса́вост|ь, и, *f.* twang; nasal intonation.

гнуса́в|ый (~, ~а), *adj.* nasal.

гну́сност|ь, и, *f.* 1. vileness, foulness. 2. vile, foul action.

гну́с|ный (~ен, ~на́, ~но), *adj.* vile, foul.

гну́т|ый, *p.p.p.* of гнуть *and adj.* bent; ~ая ме́бель bent-wood furniture.

гнуть, гну, гнёшь, *impf.* (*of* со~) 1. to bend, bow (*trans.*); г. спи́ну, ше́ю (пе́ред+*i.*) (*coll.*) to cringe (before), kow-tow (to); г. свою́ ли́нию to have it one's own way. 2. (*coll.*) to drive at; aim at; я не понима́ю, куда́ ты гнёшь I don't know what you are driving at.

гнуть|ё, я́, *n.* bending.

гну́ться, гнусь, гнёшься, *impf.* (*of* со~) 1. to bend (*intrans.*), be bowed; to stoop. 2. (*impf. only*) to bend (*intrans.*), be flexible.

гнуш|а́ться, а́юсь, *impf.* (*of* по~) 1. (+*g.* *or i.*) to abhor, have an aversion (to). 2. (+*inf.*) to disdain (to).

гобеле́н, а, *m.* gobelin, tapestry.

гобои́ст, а, *m.* (*mus.*) oboist.

гобо́|й, я, *m.* oboe.

гова́рива|ть (*pres. tense not used*), *impf.* (*freq.* of говори́ть; *coll.*); он ~л he often used to say, he would often say.

гове́нь|е, я, *n.* fasting (*as preparation for Communion*).

гов|е́ть, е́ю, е́ешь, *impf.* (*eccl.*) to prepare for Communion (*by fasting*); (*coll.*) to fast, go without food.

говн|о́, а́, *n.* (*vulg.*) shit.

го́вор, а, *m.* 1. sound of voices (*usu. human,* but also *fig.*); г. волн the murmur of the waves. 2. (*coll.*) talk, rumour. 3. mode of speech, accent. 4. dialect.

говори́л|ьня, ьни, *g. pl.* ~ен, *f.* (*coll., pejor.*) talking-shop.

говор|и́ть, ю́, и́шь, *impf.* 1. (*impf. only*) to (be able to) speak, talk; он ещё не ~и́т he can't speak yet; г. по-францу́зски to speak French. 2. (*pf.* сказа́ть) to say; to tell; to speak, talk; г. пра́вду to tell the truth; г. де́ло to talk sense; ~я́т they say, it is said; ~я́т тебе́! (*emphasizing command*) do you hear?; что вы ~и́те? (*expressing incredulity*) you don't mean to say so!; ~и́т Москва́! (*introducing radio programme*) this is Radio Moscow!; не́чего (и) г. it goes without saying, needless to say; что и г. (*coll.*) it cannot be denied; что ни ~и́ say what you like; и не ~и́! certainly!, of course!; ина́че ~я́ in other words; со́бственно ~я́ strictly speaking; не ~я́ уже́ (о+*p.*) not to mention. 3. (*pf.* по~) (о+*p.*) to talk (about), discuss. 4. (*impf. only*) to mean, convey, signify; э́ти карти́ны мне ничего́ не ~я́т these pictures convey nothing to me. 5. (*impf. only*) (о+*p.*) to point (to), indicate, betoken, testify (to); всё ~и́т о том, что он ко́нчил самоуби́йством everything points to his having committed suicide. 6. (*impf. only*) г. в по́льзу (+*g.*) to tell in favour (of); to support, back.

говор|и́ться, и́тся, *impf. pass.* of ~и́ть; как ~и́тся as they say, as the saying goes.

говорли́вост|ь, и, *f.* garrulity, talkativeness.

говорли́в|ый (~, ~а), *adj.* garrulous, talkative.

говор|о́к, ка́, *m.* (*coll.*) 1. sound of voices; hum of conversation. 2. accent, speech.

говору́н, а́, *m.* (*coll.*) talker, chatterer.

говору́н|ья, ьи, *g. pl.* ~ий, *f.* of ~.

говя́дин|а, ы, *f.* beef.

говя́жий, *adj.* beef.

го́гол|ь, я, *m.* (*orn.*) golden-eye (*Clangula bucephala*); ходи́ть ~ем to strut.

го́голь-мо́гол|ь *and* го́гель-мо́гел|ь, я, *m.* egg-flip.

го́гот, а, *m.* cackle (*of geese*); (*coll.*) loud laughter.

гогота́нь|е, я, *n.* cackling.

гого|та́ть, чу́, ~чешь, *impf.* 1. to cackle (*of geese*). 2. (*coll.*) to cackle, roar with laughter.

год, а, в ~у́, о ~е, *pl.* ~ы *and* ~а́, *g.* ~о́в *and* лет, *m.* 1. (*g. pl.* лет) year; високо́сный г. leap-year; кру́глый г. (*as adv.*) the whole year round; в бу́дущем, про́шлом ~у́ next, last year; в теку́щем ~у́ during the current year; в г. a year, per annum; из ~а в г. year in, year out; г. о́т ~у every year; спустя́ три ⁓а three years later; чéрез три ⁓а in three years' time; бéз ⁓у недéля (*coll.*) only a few days; мы ⁓ы не видáлись we have not met for years; встречáть Нóвый г. to see the New Year in; ей пошёл пятнáдцатый г. she is in her fifteenth year. **2.** двадцáтые, тридцáтые, *etc.*, ⁓ы (*g.* ⁓óв) the twenties, the thirties, *etc.* **3.** ⁓á and ⁓ы, ⁓óв (*pl. only*) years, age, time; шкóльные ⁓á schooldays; в ⁓ы (+*g.*) in the days (of), during; в те ⁓ы in those days; в ⁓áх advanced in years; не по ⁓áм beyond one's years, precocious(ly).

годáми, *adv.* for years (*on end*).

годúн|а, ы, *f.* **1.** (*rhet.*) time, period; г. войны war-time; тяжёлая г. hard times. **2.** (*arch.*) year.

го|дúть, жу́, дúшь, *impf.* (*coll.*) to wait, loiter.

го|дúться, жу́сь, дúшься, *impf.* **1.** (на+*a.*, для+*g.*, *or* +*d.*) to be fit (for), be suited (for), do (for), serve (for); э́та матéрия ни на что, никудá не ⁓дúтся this material is no good (for anything); не ⁓дúтся it's no good, it won't do. **2.** (в+*n.–a.*) to serve (as), be suited to be; он не ⁓дúтся в офицéры he is not cut out to be an officer. **3.** (в+*n.–a.*) to be old enough to be; онá ⁓дúтся тебé в мáтери she is old enough to be your mother. **4.** не ⁓дúтся (+*inf.*) it does not do (to), one should not.

годúчн|ый, *adj.* **1.** lasting a year; ⁓ое путешéствие a year's journey. **2.** annual, yearly; г. съезд annual conference; ⁓ые кóльца (*bot.*) annual rings.

гóдност|ь, и, *f.* fitness, suitability; validity.

гóд|ный (⁓ен, ⁓нá, ⁓но), *adj.* fit, suitable, valid; г. к воéнной слу́жбе fit for military service; г. к плáванию seaworthy; билéт гóден три мéсяца the ticket is valid for three months.

годовáлый, *adj.* one year óld, yearling.

годовúк, á, *m.* (*dial.*) yearling (*animal*).

годовóй, *adj.* annual, yearly; г. дохóд annual revenue.

годовщúн|а, ы, *f.* anniversary.

гой[1], *interj.* (*folk poet.*) hail!

го|й[2], я, *m.* goy, gentile.

гол, а, *m.* (*sport*) goal; забúть г. to score a goal.

голáвл|ь, я, *m.* chub (*fish*).

гóлб|ец, ца, *m.* (*dial.*) store-room, cellar.

голгóф|а, ы, *f.* Calvary (*also fig.*)

голенáстый, *adj.* **1.** (*coll.*) long-legged. **2.** *as pl. noun* (*zool.*) waders, Grallatores.

голенúщ|е, а, *n.* top (*of a boot*).

гóлен|ь, и, *f.* shin.

гол|éц, ьцá, *m.* loach (*fish*).

голизн|á, ы́, *f.* nakedness.

голúк, á, *m.* **1.** (*dial.*) besom. **2.** (*naut.*) sea-mark.

голкú|пер, а, *m.* (*sport*; *obs.*) goal-keeper.

голлáнд|ец, ца, *m.* Dutchman.

голлáндк|а[1], и, *f.* Dutchwoman.

голлáндк|а[2], и, *f.* **1.** tiled stove. **2.** animal (*cow, hen, etc.*) of Dutch breed. **3.** (*naut.*) jumper.

голлáндск|ий, *adj.* Dutch; ⁓ая печь tiled stove; ⁓ое полотнó holland (*cloth*); г. сыр Dutch cheese.

голов|á, ы́, *a.* гóлову, *pl.* гóловы, голóв, ⁓áм, *f.* **1.** head (*also fig.*); г. в гóлову (*mil.*) shoulder to shoulder; на свéжую гóлову while one is fresh; быть ⁓óй, нá голову вы́ше когó-н. (*fig.*) to be head and shoulders above someone; с ⁓ы́ до ног from head to foot; с ⁓óй погрузúться, окуну́ться, уйтú (во что-н.) (*fig.*) to throw oneself (into something), plunge (into something), get up to one's neck (in something); свалúть с больнóй ⁓ы́ на здорóвую to lay the blame on someone else; чéрез чью-н. гóлову (*fig.*) behind someone's back; у неё г. шла кру́гом her head was going round and round; у меня́ г. кру́жится I feel giddy; у них г. кру́жится от успéхов they are giddy with success; вы́дать ⁓óй (*obs.*) to give away, betray; вы́мыть, намы́лить кому́-н. гóлову to give someone a dressing-down; гóлову повéсить to hang one's head. **2.** head (*of cattle*). **3.** (*fig.*) head (*as unit of calculation*); с ⁓ы́ per head. **4.** (*fig.*) head; brain, mind; wits; он пáрень с ⁓óй he's a bright lad; ломáть гóлову to rack one's brains; не теря́ть ⁓ы́ to keep one's head; ей пришлá в гóлову мысль it occurred to her, it struck her, the thought crossed her mind. **5.** (*fig.*) head (= *person*); горя́чая г. hothead; смéлая г. bold spirit. **6.** (*fig.*) head, life; на свою́ гóлову to one's cost, to one's misfortune; заплатúть, поплатúться за что-н. ⁓óй to pay for something with one's life; отвечáть, ручáться ⁓óй за что-н. to stake one's life on something. **7.** (*m. and f.*) (*fig.*) head; person in charge; городскóй г. (*obs.*) mayor; сам себé г. one's own master. **8.** (*fig.*) head, van; в ⁓áх at the head of the bed. **9.** г. сáхару sugar-loaf; г. сы́ру a cheese; г. капу́сты head of cabbage. **10.** в пéрвую гóлову in the first place, first and foremost.

головáстик, а, *m.* tadpole.

головéшк|а, и, *f.* brand, smouldering piece of wood.

головúзн|а, ы́, *f.* jowl (*of sturgeon*).

головк|а, и, *f.* **1.** *dim. of* головá. **2.** head, cap, nose; tip; г. поршня piston head; г. лу́ка an onion, onion bulb; спúчечная г. match-head. **3.** (*collect.*; *coll.*) heads, big shots. **4.** (*pl.*) vamp (*of boot*). **5.** (*obs.*)

head-scarf (*worn by married peasant or merchant-class women*).

головн|óй, *adj.* **1.** *adj. of* головá; ∼áя боль headache; г. платóк head-scarf; г. убóр headgear, head-dress. **2.** (*anat.*) encephalic; г. мозг brain, cerebrum. **3.** (*obs.*) brain, cerebral; ∼áя рабóта brain work. **4.** г. гóлос (*mus.*) head-voice, falsetto. **5.** (*fig.*) head, leading; ∼áя железнодорóжная стáнция railhead; г. отря́д (*mil.*) vanguard, leading detachment; ∼áя похóдная застáва (*mil.*) advance party.

головн|я́¹, й, *g. pl.* ∼éй, *f.* charred log.

головн|я́², й, *g. pl.* ∼éй, *f.* blight, smut, rust (*disease of crops*).

головокружéни|е, я, *n.* giddiness, dizziness (*also fig.*); vertigo.

головокружи́тельн|ый, *adj.* dizzy, giddy (*also fig.*); ∼ая высотá dizzy height; ∼ые перспекти́вы breath-taking prospects.

головолóмк|а, и, *f.* puzzle, conundrum.

головолóмный, *adj.* puzzling.

головомóйк|а, и, *f.* (*coll.*) reprimand, dressing-down.

головонóг|ие, их, *sing.* ∼ое, ∼ого, *n.* (*zool.*) cephalopoda.

головорéз, а, *m.* (*coll.*) **1.** cutthroat; bandit. **2.** blackguard, rascal.

головотя́п, а, *m.* (*coll.*) bungler, muddler.

головотя́пств|о, а, *n.* (*coll.*) bungling.

голóвушк|а, и, *f.* **1.** *affect. dim. of* головá; пропáла моя́ г. it's all up with me, I've had it. **2.** (*folk poet.*; *coll.*) fellow, chap; бéдная г. poor wretch.

гóлод, а (у), *m.* **1.** hunger; starvation; вóлчий г. ravenous appetite; умирáть с ∼у to die of starvation; мори́ть ∼ом to starve (*trans.*). **2.** famine. **3.** dearth, acute shortage; шерстянóй г. wool shortage.

голодáни|е, я, *n.* **1.** starvation. **2.** fasting.

голод|áть, áю, *impf.* **1.** to hunger, starve. **2.** to fast, go without food.

голодá|ющий, *pres. part. act. of* ∼ть *and adj.* starving, hungry, famished; *as noun* г., ∼ющего, *m.*; ∼ющая, ∼ющей, *f.* starving person.

голóд|ный (гóлоден, ∼á, ∼но), *adj.* **1.** hungry; г. как собáка, как волк hungry as a hunter. **2.** (*caused by*) hunger, starvation; ∼ные бóли hunger-pangs; г. похóд hunger-march; ∼ная смерть starvation. **3.** (*of food, food supplies, etc.*) meagre, scanty, poor; г. год lean year; г. край barren country; г. паёк starvation rations.

голодóвк|а, и, *f.* **1.** starvation. **2.** hunger-strike; объяви́ть ∼у to go on hunger-strike.

голодрá|нец, нца, *m.* (*coll.*) beggar.

голодýх|а, и, *f.* (*coll.*) hunger.

гололéдиц|а, ы, *f.* ice-covered ground, icy condition of roads

голонóгий, *adj.* bare-legged; bare-foot.

гóлос, а, *pl.* ∼á, *m.* **1.** voice; во весь г. at the top of one's voice; быть в ∼е to be in good voice; с ∼а by ear. **2.** (*mus.*) voice, part; фýга на четы́ре ∼а four-part fugue. **3.** (*fig.*) voice, word, opinion; в оди́н г. with one accord, unanimously; имéть свой г. to have one's say. **4.** vote; прáво ∼а the vote, suffrage, franchise; подáть г. (за + *a.*) to vote (for), cast one's vote (for); победи́ть большинствóм ∼ов to outvote.

голосемя́нный, *adj.* (*bot.*) gymnospermous.

голоси́ст|ый (∼, ∼а), *adj.* loud-voiced; vociferous; loud.

голо|си́ть, шý, си́шь, *impf.* **1.** (*coll.*) to sing loudly; to cry. **2.** (*obs.*) to wail; to keen; г. по покóйнику to keen a dead person.

голослóвно, *adv.* without adducing any proof.

голослóв|ный (∼ен, ∼на), *adj.* unsubstantiated, unfounded; unsupported by evidence.

голосовáни|е, я, *n.* voting; poll; всеóбщее г. universal suffrage; постáвить на г. to put to the vote.

голос|овáть, ýю, *impf.ʳ (of* про∼) **1.** (за + *a.*, прóтив + *g.*) to vote (for; against). **2.** to put to the vote, vote on. **3.** (*sl.*) to (try to) hitch a lift.

голосоведéни|е, я, *n.* (*mus.*) harmonisation of themes.

голосов|óй, *adj.* vocal; (*anat.*) ∼ые свя́зки vocal chords; ∼áя щель glottis.

голоýсый, *adj.* (*coll.*) clean-shaven; (*fig.*) young, immature.

голоштáнник, а, *m.* (*coll.*) ragamuffin.

голубевóдств|о, а, *n.* pigeon breeding.

голубегрáмм|а, ы, *f.* (*mil.*) pigeon(-carried) message.

голубестáнци|я, и, *f.* (postal-)pigeon loft.

голубé|ть, ю, *impf.* (*of* по∼) to show blue; to turn blue.

голуб|éц¹, ца́, *m.* (*min.*) mountain-blue, azurite.

голуб|éц², ца́, *m.* (*usually pl.*) golubets (*rissole rolled in cabbage-leaves*)

голубизн|á, ы́, *f.* blueness.

голуби́к|а, и, *f.* great bilberry, bog whortle-berry (*Vaccinium uliginosum*).

голуби́н|ый, *adj.* **1.** *adj. of* гóлубь; ∼ая пóчта pigeon post. **2.** (*fig.*) dove-like.

голý|бить, блю, бишь, *impf.* (*of* при∼) to caress, fondle.

голуби́ц|а¹, ы, *f.* = голуби́ка.

голуби́ц|а², ы, *f.* **1.** female pigeon, dove. **2.** (*fig.*; *of a girl*) innocent creature.

голýбк|а, и, *f.* **1.** female pigeon, dove. **2.** (*fig.*; *as term of endearment*) (my) dear, (my) darling.

голубогла́з|ый (∼, ∼a), *adj.* blue-eyed.
голуб|о́й, *adj.* pale blue, sky-blue; ∼а́я кровь (*fig.*) blue blood; г. песе́ц blue fox; ∼о́е то́пливо 'blue fuel' (= natural gas).
голуб|о́к, ка́, *m.* 1. *dim. of* го́лубь; *fig.* = голу́бчик. 2. (*bot.*) columbine, aquilegia.
голу́бушк|а, и, *f.* 1. (*coll.*; *as mode of address*) (my) dear. 2. *affect. dim. of* голу́бка 1.
голу́бчик, а, *m.* (*coll.*; *as mode of address*) 1. my dear; dear friend; dear (so and so). 2. (*iron.*) my friend.
го́луб|ь, я, *g. pl.* ∼е́й, *m.* 1. pigeon, dove; г. свя́зи (*mil.*) carrier-pigeon. 2. (*fig.*; *as mode of address to man*) = голу́бчик.
голубя́тник, а, *m.* 1. pigeon-fancier. 2. pigeon-hawk.
голубя́т|ня, ни, *g. pl.* ∼ен, *f.* dovecot(e), pigeon loft.
го́л|ый (∼, ∼а́, ∼o), *adj.* 1. naked, bare (*also fig.*); ∼ая голова́ (*i*) bare head, (*ii*) bald head; г. про́вод naked wire; ∼ыми рука́ми with one's bare hands; (*fig.*) without a hand's turn. 2. (*coll.*) poor; ∼ как соко́л poor as a church mouse. 3. (*coll.*) unmixed, pure, neat; г. спирт pure spirit. 4. (*fig.*, *coll.*) bare, pure, unadorned; ∼ые ци́фры bare figures.
голытьб|а́, ы́, *f.* (*collect.*; *coll.*) the poor.
го́лыш, а́, *m.* 1. (*coll.*) naked child; naked person. 2. (*obs.*) pauper. 3. round flat stone.
гол|ь, и, *no pl.*, *f.* 1. (*collect.*) the poor; г. перека́тная the down-and-outs, the utterly destitute; г. на вы́думки хитра́ necessity is the mother of invention. 2. (*obs.*) bare place, barren place.
голь|ё, я́, *n.* 1. (*cul.*) tripe. 2. raw hide.
гольём, *adv.* (*coll.*) 1. bare, clean. 2. neat, unmixed.
гольф, а, *m.* 1. golf; игро́к в г. golfer. 2. ∼ы (*coll.*) plus-fours; knee-length stockings.
голя́к, а́, *m.* (*coll.*) beggar, tramp.
гомеопа́т, а, *m.* homoeopath(ist).
гомеопати́ческий, *adj.* 1. homoeopathic. 2. (*fig.*) minute, very small.
гомеопати|я, и, *f.* homoeopathy.
гомери́ческий, *adj.* Homeric (= *on heroic scale*); г. смех Homeric laughter.
гоме́ровский, *adj.* Homeric (= *pertaining to Homer*); г. вопро́с the Homeric question.
гоминда́н, а, *m.* (*polit.*) Kuomintang.
гоминда́нов|ец, ца, *m.* member, supporter of Kuomintang.
гоминда́новский, *adj.* Kuomintang.
гомоге́нный, *adj.* homogeneous.
го́мон, а, *m.* (*coll.*) hubbub.
гомон|и́ть, ю́, и́шь, *impf.* (*coll.*) to talk noisily, shout (*of large number of people*).
гомосексуали́зм, а, *m.* homosexuality.

гомосексуали́ст, а, *m.* homosexual.
гомосексуа́льный, *adj.* homosexual.
гон, а, *m.* 1. dash, rush. 2. hunt, chase, pursuit. 3. (*area of*) hunt. 4. (*of animals*) heat; во вре́мя ∼a (when) on heat. 5. (*agric.*) row.
гондо́л|а, ы, *f.* 1. gondola. 2. (*aeron.*) car (*of balloon*); (*tech.*) nacelle. 3. (*railways*) gondola.
гондолье́р, а, *m.* gondolier.
гоне́ни|е, я, *n.* persecution.
гон|е́ц, ца́, *m.* courier; (*fig.*) herald, harbinger.
гонио́метр, а, *m.* (*phys.*) goniometer.
гони́тел|ь, я, *m.* persecutor.
го́нк|а, и, *f.* 1. dashing, rushing. 2. (*coll.*) haste, hurry. 3. (*sport*) race; гребны́е ∼и boat race; г. вооруже́ний arms race. 4. (*coll.*, *obs.*) scolding, dressing-down. 5. (*dial.*) floatage, raftage.
го́н|кий (∼ок, ∼ка́, ∼ко), *adj.* 1. fast; ∼кая соба́ка hound. 2. (*of trees*) fast-growing.
гоноко́кк, а, *m.* (*med.*) gonococcus.
го́нор, а, *m.* (*coll.*) arrogance, conceit.
гонора́р, а, *m.* fee, honorarium; а́вторский г. royalties.
гоноре́|я, и, *f.* gonorrhoea.
го́ночный, *adj. of* го́нка; г. автомоби́ль racing car.
гонт, а, *m.* (*collect.*; *tech.*) shingles.
гонто́в|ый, *adj. of* гонт; ∼а́я кры́ша shingle roof.
гонча́р, а́, *m.* potter.
гонча́рн|ый, *adj.* potter's; ∼ые изде́лия pottery; г. круг potter's wheel.
го́нч|ая, ей, *f.* hound.
го́нщик, а, *m.* 1. racer; велосипеди́ст-г. racing cyclist. 2. drover. 3. rafter.
гоню́(сь), го́нишь(ся), *see* гнать(ся).
гоня́|ть, ю, *impf.* 1. (*indet. of* гнать) to drive. 2. (*coll.*) to make run errands. 3. (по + *d.*; *coll.*) to make run over, grill (on) (*something learnt, read, etc.*). 4. г. голубе́й to race pigeons. 5. г. ло́дыря, соба́к (*coll.*) to idle, kick one's heels.
гоня́|ться, юсь, *impf.* 1. (*indet. of* гна́ться) (за + *i.*) to chase, pursue, hunt. 2. (с + *i.*; *obs.*) to race.
гоп, *interj.* hup!, jump!
гопа́к, а́, *m.* hopak (*Ukrainian dance*).
го́пля, *interj.* hup!, jump!
гор- *abbr. of* 1. городско́й; горко́м = городско́й комите́т. 2. го́рный; горпромы́шленность = го́рная промы́шленность.
гор|а́, ы́, *a.* ∼у, *pl.* ∼ы, *a.* ∼а́м, *f.* 1. mountain; hill; г. с плеч a load off one's mind; ката́ться с ∼ы́ to toboggan; в ∼у uphill; идти́ в ∼у to go uphill; (*fig.*) to go up in the world; не за ∼а́ми (*fig.*) not far off; под ∼у downhill (*also fig.*); пир ∼о́й lavish,

riotous feast; надéяться на когó-н. как на кáменную ~y to place implicit faith in someone; стоя́ть за когó-н. ~óй to be solidly behind someone. **2.** (*fig.*) heap, pile, mass.

горáзд (~а, ~о), *pred. adj.* (+*inf. or* на+*a.*; *coll.*) good (at), clever (at); он на всё г. he's a Jack of all trades; кто во что г. each in his own way; он г. вы́пить he is no mean drinker.

горáздо, *adv.* (+*comp. adjs. and advs.*) much, far, by far; г. лýчше far better.

горб, á, о ~é, на ~ý, *m.* **1.** hump; (*dial.*) back; свои́м ~óм by the sweat of one's brow; испытáть на своём ~ý to learn by bitter experience. **2.** protuberance, bulge; ~óм (*as adv.*) sticking out.

горбáт|ый (~, ~а), *adj.* humpbacked, hunchbacked, gibbous; г. мост humpback bridge; г. нос hooked nose; ~ого могúла испрáвит (*prov.*) can the leopard change his spots?

горбúнк|а, и, *f.* small protuberance; нос с ~ой aquiline nose.

гóрб|ить, лю, ишь, *impf.* (*of* с~) to arch, hunch; г. спи́ну to arch one's back.

гóрб|иться, люсь, ишься, *impf.* (*of* с~) to stoop, become bent.

горбонóс|ый (~, ~а), *adj.* hook-nosed.

горбýн, á, *m.* hunchback.

горбýш|а¹, и, *f.* hunchback salmon.

горбýш|а², и, *f.* sickle.

горбýшк|а, и, *f.* crust (*of loaf*).

горбы́л|ь, я́, *m.* (*tech.*) slab.

горделúвост|ь, и, *f.* haughtiness, pride.

горделúв|ый (~, ~а), *adj.* haughty, proud.

гордéц, á, *m.* arrogant man.

гóрдиев, *adj.*; г. ýзел Gordian knot.

гор|ди́ться, жу́сь, ди́шься, *impf.* **1.** (+*i.*) to be proud (of), pride oneself (on). **2.** to put on airs, be haughty.

гóрдост|ь, и, *f.* (*in var. senses*) pride.

гóрд|ый (~, ~á, ~о, ~ы́), *adj.* (*in var. senses*) proud.

горды́н|я, и, *f.* arrogance; aloofness.

гордя́чк|а, и, *f.* arrogant woman.

гóр|е, я, n. **1.** grief, sorrow, woe; на своé г. to one's sorrow. **2.** misfortune, trouble; г. в том, что... the trouble is that... **3.** (*as pred.*, +*d.*; *coll.*) woe (unto), woe betide.

гóре- (*in compounds*) sorry, woeful; apology for a ...; г.-поэ́т poetaster; г.-войскá a Fred Karno's army.

горé, *adv.* (*arch.*) on high; upwards; г. сердцá (*eccl.*) sursum corda.

гор|евáть, ю́ю, ю́ешь, *impf.* **1.** (о+*p.*) to grieve (for). **2.** (*coll. or dial*). to be in need, be penurious.

горевóй, *adj.* (*coll. or dial.*) piteous, unhappy.

горéлк|а¹, и, *f.* burner; г. Бýнзена Bunsen burner; прúмусная г. Primus stove.

горéлк|а², и, *f.* (*dial.*) vodka.

горéл|ки, ок, *no sing.* (*game of*) catch.

горéл|ый, *adj.* **1.** burnt; пáхло ~ым there was a smell of burning. **2.** rotten, decomposed (*of skins*).

горельéф, а, *m.* (*art*) high relief.

горемы́к|а, и, *m. and f.* (*coll.*) unlucky individual, victim of misfortune.

горемы́ч|ный (~ен, ~на), *adj.* hapless, ill-starred; down on one's luck.

горéни|е, я, n. burning, combustion; (*fig.*) enthusiasm.

гóрест|ный (~ен, ~на), *adj.* sad, sorrowful; pitiful, mournful.

гóрест|ь, и, *f.* **1.** sorrow, grief. **2.** (*pl.*) afflictions, misfortunes, troubles.

гор|éть, ю́, и́шь, *impf.* **1.** to burn, be on fire. **2.** to burn, be alight; в кýхне у них ~éл свет the lights were burning in their kitchen; ~и́т ли пéчка? is the stove alight?; дéло ~и́т things are going like a house on fire; земля́ ~éла у негó под ногáми (*i*) he went like greased lightning, (*ii*) the place was getting too hot for him, (*iii*) he was impatient to be off. **3.** (+*i.*; *fig.*) to burn (with); г. желáнием (+*inf.*) to burn with the desire (to), be impatient (to). **4.** to glitter, shine. **5.** to rot, ferment.

гóр|ец, ца, *m.* mountain-dweller, highlander.

гóреч|ь, и, *f.* **1.** bitter taste. **2.** bitter stuff. **3.** bitterness.

гóрж|а, и, *f.* (*mil.*) gorge.

горжéтк|а, и, *f.* boa, throat-wrap.

горизóнт, а, *m.* **1.** horizon (*also fig.*), skyline. **2.** г. воды́ (*tech.*) water-level.

горизонтáл|ь, и, *f.* **1.** horizontal; по ~и (*in crossword*) across. **2.** (*geogr.*) contour line.

горизонтáл|ьный (~ен, ~ьна), *adj.* horizontal; г. полёт (*aeron.*) horizontal flight, level flight.

горúлк|а, и, *f.* = горéлка².

горúлл|а, ы, *f.* gorilla.

горúст|ый (~, ~а), *adj.* mountainous, hilly.

горихвóстк|а, и, *f.* redstart (*bird*).

горицвéт, а, *m.* (*bot.*) lychnis; ragged robin.

гóрк|а, и, *f.* **1.** hillock. **2.** cabinet, stand. **3.** (*aeron.*) steep climb. **4.** крáсная г. (*coll.*) the week following Easter week.

гóркн|уть, у, ешь, *impf.* (*of* про~) to turn rancid.

горкóм, а, *m.* (*abbr. of* городскóй комитéт) town, city committee.

горлáн, а, *m.* (*coll.*) bawler.

горлáн|ить, ю, ишь, *impf.* (*coll.*) to bawl.

горлáст|ый (~, ~а), *adj.* (*coll.*) noisy, loud-mouthed.

гóрлинк|а, и, *f.* = гóрлица.

гóрлиц|а, ы, *f.* **1.** turtle-dove. **2.** (*obs.*) = голýбка.

го́рл|о, а, *n.* 1. throat; дыха́тельное г. windpipe; драть г. to bawl; во всё г. at the top of one's voice; по г. up to the neck (*also fig.*); сыт по г. full up; (*fig.*) fed up; приста́ть с ножо́м к ~у (+*d.*) to press, importune; приста́вить нож к чьему́-н. ~у to hold a knife to one's throat; промочи́ть г. (*coll.*) to wet one's whistle; слова́ застря́ли у меня́ в ~е the words stuck in my throat; схвати́ть за г. to catch, take by the throat. 2. neck (*of a vessel*). 3. narrow entrance to a gulf, bay.

горлови́к, а́, *m.* (*coll.*) throat specialist.

горлови́н|а, ы, *f.* mouth, orifice; manhole hatch; г. вулка́на crater.

горлово́й, *adj.* 1. *adj. of* го́рло; throat; guttural. 2. raucous.

горлодёр, а, *m.* (*coll.*) 1. bawler. 2. табак-г. rough shag.

го́рлыш|ко, ка, *g. pl.* ~ек, *n.* 1. *dim. of* го́рло. 2. neck (*of a bottle*).

гормо́н, а, *m.* (*physiol.*) hormone.

гормона́льный, *adj.* hormone(-containing).

горн¹, а, *m.* furnace, forge.

горн², а, *m.* bugle.

го́рн|ий, *adj.* 1. (*arch., poet.*) heavenly, celestial; lofty. 2. ~ее ме́сто (*eccl.*) east end (*of church, part behind altar*).

горни́л|о, а, *n.* 1. (*obs.*) hearth, furnace. 2. (*fig.*) crucible.

горни́ст, а, *m.* bugler.

го́рниц|а, ы, *f.* 1. (*obs.*) chamber. 2. (*dial.*) clean part of peasant's hut.

го́рничн|ая, ой, *f.* (house)maid; stewardess (*on ship*).

горнов|о́й, *adj. of* горн¹; *as noun* г., ~о́го, *m.* furnace-worker.

горнозаво́дский, *adj.* mining and metallurgical.

горнозаво́дчик, а, *m.* owner of a mine *or* foundry.

горнопромы́шленност|ь, и, *f.* mining industry.

горнопромы́шленный, *adj.* mining.

горнорабо́ч|ий, его, *m.* miner.

горноста́евый, *adj.* ermine.

горноста́|й, я, *m.* 1. (*zool.*) ermine, stoat. 2. ermine (*fur*).

го́рн|ый, *adj.* 1. *adj. of* гора́; mountain; mountainous; ~ая боле́знь mountain sickness; ~ая цепь mountain range; ~ая артилле́рия (*mil.*) mountain artillery. 2. mineral; г. лён asbestos; ~ая поро́да rock; г. хруста́ль rock crystal. 3. mining; ~ое де́ло mining; г. институ́т College of Mines. 4. ~ое со́лнце artificial sunlight.

горня́к, а́, *m.* (*coll.*) 1. miner. 2. mining engineer; mining student.

горня́|цкий, *adj. of* ~к 1.

го́род, а, *pl.* ~а́, *m.* 1. town; city; вы́ехать за́ г. to go out of town; жить за́ ~ом to live out of town, in the suburbs; ни к селу́, ни к ~у (*coll.*) for no reason at all, inappropriate(ly). 2. (*sports and games*) base; home.

гор|оди́ть, ожу́, о́дишь, *impf.* to enclose, fence; огоро́д г. to make unnecessary fuss; г. чепуху́, чушь to talk nonsense.

городи́ш|ко, ка, *g. pl.* ~ек, *m.* small, provincial town.

городи́щ|е, а, *n.* 1. very large town. 2. (*archaeol.*) site of ancient settlement.

город|ки́, ко́в, *sing.* ~о́к, ~а́, *m.* gorodki (*game similar to skittles*).

городни́ч|ий, его, *m.* (*hist.*) governor of a town.

городов|о́й¹, *adj.* (*obs.*) *of* го́род; ~о́е положе́ние municipal statutes.

городов|о́й², о́го, *m.* (*hist.*) policeman.

город|о́к, ка́, *m.* 1. small town; вое́нный г. cantonment; университе́тский г. campus. 2. block of wood (*in game* городки́).

городск|о́й, *adj.* urban; city; municipal; (*coll.*) *as noun* г., ~о́го, *m.* city-dweller, town-dweller.

городьб|а́, ы́, *f.* 1. fencing, enclosure. 2. fence, hedge.

горожа́н|ин, ина, *pl.* ~е, ~, *m.* city-dweller, town-dweller; townsman.

горожа́н|ка, ки, *f. of* ~ин; townswoman.

гороско́п, а, *m.* horoscope.

горо́х, а (у), *no pl.*, *m.* 1. pea. 2. (*collect.*) peas; как об сте́ну, в сте́ну, от стены́ г. (*coll.*) like being up against a brick wall; при царе́ Горо́хе in days of yore.

горо́хов|ый, *adj.* 1. pea. 2. greenish-khaki; ~ое пальто́ (*hist.*; *coll.*) agent of secret police; чу́чело ~ое scarecrow; шут г. buffoon, laughing-stock.

горо́ш|ек, ка, *m.* 1. *dim. of* горо́х; души́стый г. (*bot.*) sweet peas; ме́лким ~ком рассыпа́ться (пе́ред+*i.*) to cringe (before). 2. (*collect.*) spots, spotted design (*on material*).

горо́шин|а, ы, *f.* a pea.

го́рский, *adj. of* го́рец; mountain, highland.

горсове́т, а, *m.* (*abbr. of* городско́й сове́т) town, city soviet.

го́рсточк|а, и, *f.* handful.

горст|ь, и, *g. pl.* ~е́й, *f.* 1. cupped hand; держа́ть ру́ку ~ью to cup one's hand. 2. handful (*also fig.*).

горта́нный, *adj.* 1. (*anat.*) laryngeal. 2. (*ling.*) guttural.

горта́н|ь, и, *f.* larynx; у него́ язы́к прили́п к ~и he was struck dumb; he was tongue-tied.

горте́нзи|я, и, *f.* hydrangea.

го́рче, *comp. of* го́рький.

горч|и́ть, и́т, *impf.* (*impers.*) to have a bitter taste.

горчи́ц|а, ы, *f.* mustard.

горчи́чник, а, *m.* mustard-poultice.

горчи́чниц|а, ы, *f.* mustard-pot.

горчи́чн|ый, *adj. of* горчи́ца; г. газ mustard gas; ~ое се́мя mustard seed.

го́рше, *comp. of* го́рький.

горше́чник, а, *m.* potter.

горше́чный, *adj.* pottery; г. това́р pottery, earthenware.

го́рший (*obs.*) *comp. of* го́рький; more bitter (*fig.*).

горш|о́к, ка́, *m.* pot; jug; vase; ночно́й г. chamber-pot.

го́рьк|ая, ой, *f.* vodka; пить ~ую (*coll.*) to hit the bottle.

го́р|ький (~ек, ~ька́, ~ько), *adj.* 1. (*comp.* ~че) bitter; ~ькое ма́сло rancid butter. 2. (*comp.* ~ше, ~ший) (*fig.*) bitter; hard; ~ькие слёзы bitter tears; ~ьким о́пытом узна́ть to learn by bitter experience. 3. (*coll.*) hapless, wretched. 4. г. пья́ница (*coll.*) inveterate drunkard.

го́рько[1], *adv.* bitterly.

го́рько[2], *as pred.* 1. мне г. во рту I have a bitter taste in my mouth. 2. it is bitter; мне г. I am sorry, I am grieved.

горю́н, а́, *m.* (*coll.*) unfortunate.

горю́н|ья, ьи, *g. pl.* ~ий, *f. of* ~.

горю́ч|ее, его, *n.* fuel.

горю́чест|ь, и, *f.* combustibility; inflammability.

горю́ч|ий, *adj.* 1. combustible, inflammable. 2. (*folk poet.*) burning; ~ие слёзы bitter tears.

го́рюшк|о, а, *n.* (*coll.*) grief, affliction; а ему́ и ~а ма́ло he does not care a jot.

горячело́мкий, *adj.* (*tech.*) hot-short.

горя́ч|ечный, *adj. of* ~ка; feverous; г. бред delirium; ~ечная руба́шка strait-jacket.

горя́ч|ий (~, ~а́, ~о́), *adj.* 1. hot (*also fig.*); по ~им следа́м (*i*) (+*g.*) hot on the heels (of), (*ii*) (*fig.*) forthwith; под ~ую ру́ку in the heat of the moment. 2. passionate, ardent, fervent. 3. hot-tempered; mettlesome; ~ая голова́ hothead. 4. heated; impassioned; г. спор heated argument. 5. busy; ~ее вре́мя busy season. 6. (*tech.*) high-temperature; ~ая обрабо́тка heat treatment.

горячи́тельн|ый, *adj.* (*obs.*) hot, warming; ~ые напи́тки strong drink.

горяч|и́ть, у́, и́шь, *impf.* (*of* раз~) to excite, irritate.

горяч|и́ться, у́сь, и́шься, *impf.* (*of* раз~) to get excited, become impassioned.

горя́чк|а, и, *f.* 1. fever (*also fig.*). 2. feverish activity; feverish haste; поро́ть ~у (*coll.*) to act impetuously, in the heat of the moment. 3. (*m. and f.*; *coll.*) hothead; firebrand.

горя́чност|ь, и, *f.* zeal, fervour, enthusiasm; impulsiveness.

горячо́[1], *adv.* hot.

горячо́[2], *as pred.* it is hot.

гос- (*abbr. of* госуда́рственный) State; Госизда́т State Publishing House; Госпла́н State Planning Commission; Госстра́х National Insurance.

госпитализа́ци|я, и, *f.* hospitalization.

го́спитал|ь, я, *m.* hospital (*esp. military*).

госпита́льный, *adj. of* го́спиталь.

госпо́д|ень, ня, не, *adj.* (*eccl.*) the Lord's; моли́тва ~ня the Lord's Prayer.

го́споди, *interj.* good heavens!, good Lord!, good gracious!;

господ|и́н, и́на, *pl.* ~а́, ~, ~а́м, *m.* 1. master; сам себе́ г. one's own master; г. своего́ сло́ва a man of one's word. 2. gentleman; э́ти ~а́ (*often iron.*) these gentlemen. 3. (*as style*) Mr.; ~а́ (*as form of address*) (*i*) gentlemen, (*ii*) ladies and gentlemen; (*as style*) Messrs.

госпо́дский, *adj.* seigniorial, manorial; г. дом manor-house.

госпо́дств|о, а, *n.* 1. supremacy, dominion, mastery. 2. predominance.

госпо́дств|овать, ую, *impf.* 1. to hold sway, exercise dominion. 2. to predominate, prevail. 3. (над+*i.*) to command, dominate; to tower (above).

госпо́дств|ующий, *pres. part. act. of* ~овать *and adj.* 1. ruling; г. класс ruling class. 2. predominant, prevailing. 3. (*of physical features*) commanding.

Госпо́дь, Го́спода, *voc.* Го́споди, *m.* God, the Lord; г. его́ зна́ет! (the) Lord knows!

госпож|а́, и́, *f.* 1. mistress. 2. lady. 3. (*as style*) Mrs.; Miss.

госпожи́н|ки, ок, *no sing.* (*dial.*) fast before the feast of the Assumption.

гостево́й, *adj.* guest, guests'.

гостеприи́м|ный (~ен, ~на), *adj.* hospitable.

гостеприи́мств|о, а, *n.* hospitality.

гости́н|ая, ой, *f.* 1. drawing-room, sitting-room. 2. drawing-room suite.

гости́н|ец, ца, *m.* (*coll.*) present.

гости́ниц|а, ы, *f.* hotel, inn.

гости́н|ичный, *adj. of* ~ица.

гостинодво́|рец, рца, *m.* (*obs.*) shopkeeper (*in a bazaar*).

гости́ный, *adj.*; г. двор arcade, bazaar.

гости́ть, гощу́, гости́шь, *impf.* (у) to stay (with), be on a visit (to).

гост|ь, я, *g. pl.* ~е́й, *m.* guest, visitor; пойти́ в ~и (к+*d.*) to visit; быть в гостя́х (у) to be a guest (at, of), be visiting; в гостя́х хорошо́, а до́ма лу́чше there's no place like home.

гост|ья, ьи, *g. pl.* ~ий, *f. of* ~ь.

госуда́рственност|ь, и, *f.* State system.

госуда́рственн|ый, *adj.* State, public; г.

переворо́т coup d'état; ∼ая изме́на high treason; ∼ое пра́во public law; ∼ая слу́жба public service; г. слу́жащий civil servant; ∼ые экза́мены final examinations (*in higher education institutions*).

госуда́рств|о, а, *n.* State.

госуда́рын|я, и, *f.* **1.** sovereign; Г. (*as form of address*) Your Majesty. **2.** (*obs.*) mistress; ми́лостивая г. (*as form of address*) madam.

госуда́р|ь, я, *m.* **1.** sovereign; Г. (*as form of address*) Your Majesty, Sire. **2.** (*obs.*) master; ми́лостивый г. (*as form of address*) sir.

гот, а, *m.* (*hist.*) Goth.

го́тик|а, и, *f.* (*archit.*) Gothic style.

готи́ческий, *adj.* (*art*) Gothic; г. шрифт Gothic script, black-letter.

готова́л|ьня, ьни, *g. pl.* ∼**ен,** *f.* case of drawing instruments.

гото́в|ить, лю, ишь, *impf.* **1.** to prepare, make ready; to train. **2.** to cook. **3.** to lay in, store. **4.** (+*d.*; *fig.*) to have in store (for).

гото́в|иться, люсь, ишься, *impf.* **1.** (к+*d.* or +*inf.*) to get ready (for, to); to prepare oneself (for), make preparations (for). **2.** (*impf. only*) to be at hand, be in the offing, be impending, be imminent; ∼ятся кру́пные собы́тия great events are in the offing.

гото́вност|ь, и, *f.* **1.** readiness, preparedness; в боево́й ∼и ready for action; (*naut.*) cleared for action. **2.** readiness, willingness.

гото́во, *as pred.*; и г. (*coll.*) and that's that.

гото́в|ый (∼, ∼a), *adj.* **1.** (к+*d.*) ready (for), prepared (for); г. к де́йствию ready for action; я не ∼ I'm not ready; г. к услу́гам (*epistolary formula*) yours faithfully. **2.** (на+ *a.* or +*inf.*) ready (for, to), prepared (for, to); willing (to); мы ∼ы на всё we are prepared for anything; она́ не ∼а идти́ she is not willing to go. **3.** (+*inf.*) on the point (of), on the verge (of), ready (to); он ∼ был ка́ждую мину́ту расхохота́ться he was on the verge of bursting out laughing. **4.** ready-made, finished; ∼ое пла́тье ready--made dress; ∼ые изде́лия finished articles. **5.** на всём ∼ом with all found; на ∼ых харча́х with full board and lodging. **6.** (*short form only*; *coll.*) (*i*) finished (= *dead*), (*ii*) tight, plastered (= *drunk*).

го́тский, *adj.* Gothic (*of the Goths and Gothic language*).

гофма́ршал, а, *m.* (*hist.*) Marshal of the (Imperial) Court.

гофме́стер, а, *m.* (*hist.*) steward of the household.

гофриро́ванн|ый, *p.p.p.* of гофрирова́ть *and adj.*; ∼ое желе́зо corrugated iron; ∼ые во́лосы waved hair; ∼ая ю́бка pleated skirt; ∼ый воротни́к goffered collar.

гофрир|ова́ть, у́ю, *impf. and pf.* **1.** to corrugate; to wave; to crimp. **2.** to goffer.

гофриро́вк|а, и, *no pl., f.* **1.** corrugation; goffering; waving. **2.** waves (*of hair*).

граб, а, *m.* (*bot.*) hornbeam.

гра́бар|ь, я, *m.* (*dial.*) navvy.

грабёж, а́, *m.* robbery (*also fig., coll.*).

граби́тел|ь, я, *m.* robber.

граби́тельский, *adj.* **1.** predatory. **2.** extortionate, exorbitant (*of prices*).

граби́тельств|о, а, *n.* (*obs.*) robbery.

граб|ить[1], лю, ишь, *impf.* (*of* o∼) to rob, pillage; (*fig.*) to rob.

граб|ить[2], лю, ишь, *impf.* to rake.

гра́блени|е, я, *n.* raking.

гра́блен|ый, *adj.* stolen.

гра́бл|и, лей *or* ∼**ель,** *no sing.* rake.

гра́б|овый, *adj.* of ∼.

граве́р, а, *m.* engraver.

гравёр|ный, *adj.* of ∼; ∼ное иску́сство engraving.

гра́ви|й, я, *m.* gravel.

грави́йн|ый, *adj.* of гра́вий; ∼ые карье́ры gravel pits.

гравирова́льн|ый, *adj.* engraving; ∼ая доска́ steel plate, copper plate; ∼ая игла́ etching needle.

гравир|ова́ть, у́ю, у́ешь, *impf.* (*of* вы́∼) to engrave.

гравиро́вк|а, и, *f.* engraving.

гравиро́вщик, а, *m.* engraver.

гравитацио́нный, *adj.* gravitation(al).

гравита́ци|я, и, *f.* (*phys.*) gravitation.

гравю́р|а, ы, *f.* engraving, print; etching; г. на де́реве woodcut; г. на лино́леуме linocut; г. на ме́ди copper-plate engraving.

град[1], а, *m.* **1.** hail. **2.** (*fig.*) hail, shower, torrent; volley.

град[2], а, *m.* (*arch. or poet.*) city, town.

града́ци|я, и, *f.* gradation, scale.

градие́нт, а, *m.* gradient.

гра́дин|а, ы, *f.* (*coll.*) hailstone.

гради́р|ня, ни, *g. pl.* ∼**ен,** *f.* **1.** salt-pan. **2.** (water-)cooling tower.

гради́р|овать, ую, *impf. and pf.* to evaporate, graduate (*salt*).

градоби́ти|е, я, *n.* damage done by hail.

градово́й, *adj.* of град[1].

гра́дом, *adv.* thick and fast; уда́ры посы́пались г. blows showered down, rained down.

градонача́льник, а, *m.* (*hist.*) town governor (*of a town independent administratively of its province*).

градонача́льств|о, а, *n.* (*hist.*) **1.** town, borough (*independent administratively of province*). **2.** town governor's office.

градострои́тел|ь, я, *m.* town-planner.

градострои́тельный, *adj.* town-planning.
градострои́тельств|о, а, *n.* town-planning.
градуи́р|овать, ую, *impf. and pf.* **1.** to graduate (*to mark with lines to indicate degrees, etc.*). **2.** to grade.
гра́дус, а, *m.* **1.** degree (*unit of measurement*); у́гол в 40 ~ов angle of 40 degrees; сего́дня 20 ~ов тепла́, моро́за it is twenty degrees above, below zero today. **2.** (*fig.*) degree, pitch; stage; в после́днем ~е in the final stage (*of an illness*). **3.** под ~ом (*coll.*) under the weather, one over the eight.
гра́дусник, а, *m.* thermometer.
гра́дус|ный, *adj.* of ~; ~ная се́тка (*geogr.*) grid.
граждани́н, а, *pl.* гра́ждане, гра́ждан, *m.* **1.** citizen; пото́мственный почётный г. (*hist.*) hereditary honorary citizen (*title conferred in tsarist Russia on persons not of gentle birth for services*). **2.** person.
гражда́нк|а¹, и, *f.* citizeness.
гражда́нк|а², и, *f.* (*coll.*) **1.** = гражда́нская а́збука. **2.** the Civil War (*in Russia 1917–1921*).
гражда́нск|ий, *adj.* **1.** (*leg., etc.*) civil; citizen's; civic; г. иск civil suit; предъяви́ть г. иск (к+*d.*) to bring a civil suit (against); г. ко́декс civil code; ~ое пра́во civil law; ~ая смерть deprivation of civil rights. **2.** civil, secular (*as opp. to ecclesiastical*); г. брак (*i*) civil marriage, (*ii*) (*coll., obs.*) cohabitation, free union; ~ая панихи́да civil funeral rite. **3.** civilian (*as opp. to military*); ~ое пла́тье civilian clothes, civvies, mufti. **4.** civic, befitting a citizen; ~ие доброде́тели civic virtues. **5.** (*of poetry, etc.*) civic, having social content. **6.** ~ая война́ civil war. **7.** ~ая а́збука, ~ая печа́ть Russian type (*introduced by Peter the Great in place of Church Slavonic*).
гражда́нственност|ь, и, *f.* **1.** civilization; civil society. **2.** civic spirit.
гражда́нств|о, а, *n.* **1.** citizenship, nationality; права́ ~а civic rights; получи́ть права́ ~а to be granted civic rights; (*fig.*) to achieve general recognition. **2.** (*collect.; obs.*) citizenry.
грамза́пис|ь, и, *f.* gramophone recording.
грамм, а, *m.* gramme, gram.
грамма́тик, а, *m.* grammarian.
грамма́тик|а, и, *f.* **1.** grammar. **2.** grammar(-book).
граммати́ческий, *adj.* grammatical.
граммофо́н, а, *m.* gramophone (*with loudspeaker horn*).
граммофо́н|ный, *adj.* of ~; ~ная пласти́нка gramophone record.
гра́мот|а, ы, *f.* **1.** reading and writing, ability to read and write. **2.** official document; deed.

грамоте́|й, я, *m.* (*coll.*) **1.** one who can read and write. **2.** scholar.
гра́мотк|а, и, *f.* (*coll.*) letter, note.
гра́мотност|ь, и, *f.* **1.** literacy (*also fig.*). **2.** grammatical correctness. **3.** competence.
гра́мот|ный (~ен, ~на), *adj.* **1.** literate; able to read and write. **2.** grammatically correct. **3.** competent. **4.** полити́чески г. politically aware.
грампласти́нк|а, и, *f.* gramophone record.
гран, а, *m.* grain (*unit of weight*); в э́том нет ни ~а и́стины there is not a grain of truth in it.
грана́т¹, а, *m.* **1.** pomegranate. **2.** pomegranate tree.
грана́т², а, *m.* (*min.*) garnet.
грана́т|а, ы, *f.* (*mil.*) shell, grenade; ручна́я г. hand-grenade.
грана́тник, а, *m.* pomegranate tree.
грана́т|ный, *adj.* of ~а; г. ого́нь shell-fire.
грана́товый¹, *adj.* pomegranate.
грана́т|овый² **1.** *adj.* of ~². **2.** rich red.
гранатомёт, а, *m.* (*mil.*) grenade cup discharger, grenade thrower.
гранатомётчик, а, *m.* grenade-thrower, grenadier.
гранд, а, *m.* grandee (*Spanish nobleman*).
грандио́зност|ь, и, *f.* grandeur; immensity.
грандио́з|ный (~ен, ~на), *adj.* grandiose; mighty; vast.
гране́ни|е, я, *n.* cutting (*of precious stones, glass*).
гранёный, *adj.* **1.** cut, faceted; ~ое стекло́ cut glass. **2.** cut-glass.
грани́льный, *adj.* lapidary; diamond-cutting.
грани́л|ьня, ьни, *g. pl.* ен, *f.* lapidary workshop; г. алма́зов diamond-cutting shop.
грани́льщик, а, *m.* lapidary; г. алма́зов diamond-cutter.
грани́т, а, *m.* granite.
грани́тный, *adj.* granite.
гран|и́ть, ю́, и́шь, *impf.* to cut, facet; (*coll.*) г. мостову́ю to loaf, saunter, promenade.
грани́ц|а, ы, *f.* **1.** frontier, border; за ~ей abroad; е́хать за ~у to go abroad. **2.** (*fig.*) boundary, limit; вы́йти из ~ to overstep the limits, overstep the mark; перейти́ все ~ы to pass all bounds; в ~ах прили́чия within the bounds of decency.
грани́ч|ить, у, ишь, *impf.* (с+*i.*) **1.** to border (upon), be contiguous (with). **2.** (*fig.*) to border (on), verge (on); э́то ~ит с изме́ной it borders on treason.
гра́нк|а, и, *f.* (*typ.*) slip, galley-proof.
грануди́р|овать, ую, *impf. and pf.* to granulate.
грануля́ци|я, и, *f.* (*tech., astron., med.*) granulation.

гран|ь, и, *f.* **1.** border, verge; на ∾и сумасше́ствия on the verge of insanity; «поли́тика на ∾и войны́» brinkmanship. **2.** side, facet; edge. **3.** (*math.*) period.

грасси́р|овать, ую, *impf.* to pronounce one's *r*'s in the French manner.

грат, а, *m.* (*tech.*) barb, burr.

граф, а, *m.* count.

граф|а́, ы́, *f.* (*book-keeping, etc.*) column (*of a table or page*).

гра́фик[1], а, *m.* **1.** graph; chart. **2.** schedule; то́чно по ∾у according to schedule.

гра́фик[2], а, *m.* draughtsman.

гра́фик|а, и, *f.* **1.** (*art*) drawing. **2.** script.

графи́н, а, *m.* carafe; decanter.

графи́н|я, и, *f.* countess.

графи́т, а, *m.* **1.** (*min.*) graphite, black-lead. **2.** pencil-lead.

графи́т|ный, *adj.* = ∾овый.

графи́товый, *adj.* graphite.

граф|и́ть, лю́, и́шь, *impf.* (*of* раз∾) to rule (*paper*).

графи́ческий, *adj.* graphic.

графлёный, *adj.* (vertically) ruled.

графо́лог, а, *m.* graphologist.

графоло́ги|я, и, *f.* graphology.

графома́н, а, *m.* graphomaniac; (*fig.*) pulp-writer, hack.

графома́ни|я, и, *f.* graphomania.

гра́фский, *adj. of* граф.

гра́фств|о, а, *n.* **1.** title of count. **2.** county.

грацио́з|ный (∾ен, ∾на), *adj.* graceful.·

гра́ци|я, и, *f.* **1.** gracefulness. **2.** Г. (*myth.*) Grace; (*fig.*) beauty.

грач, а́, *m.* (*orn.*) rook.

грач|и́ный, *adj. of* ∾.

грач|о́нок, о́нка, *pl.* ∾а́та, ∾а́т, *m.* (*orn.*) young rook.

гребёнк|а, и, *f.* **1.** comb; стричь под ∾у to crop close; стричь всех под одну́ ∾у to treat all alike, reduce all to the same level. **2.** (*tech.*) rack; (*text.*) hackle.

гребе́нчатый, *adj.* **1.** (*zool.*) cristate; pectinate. **2.** comb-shaped; г. подши́пник (*tech.*) collar thrust bearing.

греб|ень, ня, *m.* **1.** comb. **2.** (*tech.*) comb; (*text.*) hackle. **3.** (*of bird*) comb, crest; петуши́ный г. cock's comb. **4.** crest (*of hill or wave*). **5.** (*archit.*) ridge-piece, roof-tree. **6.** (*agric.*) ridge.

греб|е́ц, ца́, *m.* rower, oarsman.

гребеш|о́к, ка́, *m.* = гре́бень.

гребл|я́[1], и, *f.* **1.** rowing. **2.** (*dial.*) raking.

гребл|я́[2], и, *f.* (*dial.*) dyke.

гребневи́д|ный (∾ен, ∾на), *adj.* comb-shaped, pectinate.

гребнечеса́льн|ый, *adj.*; ∾ая маши́на (*text.*) hackling machine, comber.

гребни́ст|ый (∾, ∾а), *adj.* (high-)crested.

гребн|о́й, *adj.* **1.** rowing; г. спорт rowing.

2. г. вал propeller shaft; г. винт propeller screw; ∾о́е колесо́ paddle wheel.

греб|о́к, ка́, *m.* **1.** stroke (*in rowing*). **2.** blade (*of a mill-wheel or paddle-wheel*).

грегориа́нский, *adj.*, = григориа́нский.

грёз|а, ы, *f.* day-dream, reverie.

гре́|зить, жу, зишь, *impf.* to dream; г. наяву́ to day-dream.

гре́|зиться, жусь, зишься, *impf.* (*of* при∾) (*impers.*, +*d.*) to dream; мне ∾зилось, что... I used to dream that...

гре́|жу, *see* ∾зить.

гре́йдер, а, *m.* (*tech.*) **1.** grader. **2.** (*coll.*) earth road (*levelled but unmetalled*).

гре́йдер|ный, *adj. of* ∾; ∾ная доро́га grader road.

гре́йпфрут, а, *m.* grapefruit.

гре́йфер, а, *m.* (*tech.*) grab (*of crane*).

грек, а, *m.* Greek.

гре́лк|а, и, *f.* hot-water bottle.

грем|е́ть, лю́, и́шь, *impf.* to thunder, roar; peal; rattle; (*fig.*) to resound, ring out; и́мя его́ ∾е́ло по всей Евро́пе his name resounded throughout Europe.

грему́ч|ий, *adj.* roaring; г. газ detonating-gas; ∾ая змея́ rattlesnake; ∾ая ртуть (*chem.*) fulminate of mercury; г. сту́день nitrogelatine, blasting gelatine.

грему́шк|а, и, *f.* **1.** rattle (*child's toy*). **2.** sleigh-bell.

гре́н|а, ы, *f.* (*collect.*) silkworm eggs.

гренаде́р, а, *m.* grenadier.

гренаде́р|ский, *adj. of* ∾; г. полк Grenadiers.

грен|о́к, ка́, *m.* (finger of) toast; (*cul.*) croûton.

гре|сти́, бу́, бёшь, *past* ∾б, ∾бла́, *impf.* **1.** to row. **2.** to rake; г. лопа́той де́ньги (*coll.*) to rake in the shekels.

греть, гре́ю, гре́ешь, *impf.* **1.** (*intrans.*) to give out warmth. **2.** (*trans.*) to warm, heat; г. (себе́) ру́ки to warm one's hands; (*fig., coll., pejor.*) to be on to a good thing.

гре́|ться, юсь, ешься, *impf.* **1.** to warm oneself. **2.** *pass. of* греть.

грех, а́, *m.* **1.** (*rel. or fig.*) sin; приня́ть на себя́ г. to take the blame upon oneself; не́чего ∾а́ таи́ть it must be owned; есть тако́й г. I own it; пода́льше от ∾а́ get out of harm's way; как на г. as ill-luck would have it. **2.** (*as pred.* +*inf.*; *coll.*) it is a sin, it is sinful; не г. (+*inf.*) it does not, would not hurt (to); there is no harm (in); не г. вы́пить рю́мочку-две there is no harm in (drinking) a glass or two. **3.** с ∾о́м пополáм (only) just; мы с ∾о́м пополáм расшифрова́ли твой по́черк we just managed to decipher your handwriting.

грехо́в|ный (∾ен, ∾на), *adj.* sinful.

греховóдник, а, *m.* (*coll., obs.*) sinner; (*of a child*) naughty boy.

грехово́дниц|а, ы, *f. of* грехово́дник.

грехово́днича|ть, ю, *impf.* (*coll.*, *obs.*) to be a sinner.

грехопаде́ни|е, я, *n.* (*bibl.*) the Fall; (*fig.*) fall.

гре́цкий, *adj.*; г. оре́х walnut.

гре́ч|а, и, *f.* (*coll.*) buckwheat.

греча́нк|а, и, *f.* Greek woman.

гре́ческий, *adj.* Greek; Grecian.

гречи́х|а, и, *f.* buckwheat.

гре́чнев|ый, *adj.* buckwheat; ~ая ка́ша buckwheat porridge.

греш|и́ть, у́, и́шь, *impf.* 1. (*pf.* co~) to sin. 2. (*pf.* по~) (про́тив+*g.*; *fig.*) to sin (against).

гре́шник, а, *m.* sinner.

гре́шниц|а, ы, *f. of* гре́шник.

гре́ш|ный (~ен, ~на́), *adj.* sinful; culpable; г. челове́к (*parenth.*) I am ashamed to say; ~ным де́лом (*parenth.*) much as I regret it, I am ashamed to say.

греш|о́к, ка́, *m.* peccadillo.

гриб, а́, *m.* fungus, mushroom; съедо́бный г. mushroom, edible fungus; несъедо́бный г. toadstool; уче́ние о ~а́х (*bot.*) mycology; г. съесть (*obs.*) to be unsuccessful, meet with failure; расти́ как ~ы́ to spring up like mushrooms.

грибко́вый, *adj.* fungoid.

грибни́ц|а, ы, *f.* 1. mushroom spawn. 2. (*coll.*) mushroom soup.

грибн|о́й, *adj. of* гриб; fungoid; mushroom; г. дождь rain during sunshine; ~а́я похлёбка mushroom soup.

гриб|о́к, ка́, *m.* 1. *dim. of* гриб. 2. (*biol.*) fungus, microorganism. 3. mushroom (*for darning stockings*).

гри́в|а, ы, *f.* 1. mane. 2. wooded ridge. 3. (*dial.*) shoal.

грива́ст|ый (~, ~a), *adj.* with a long mane.

гри́венник, а, *m.* (*coll.*) ten-kopeck piece.

гри́вн|а, ы, *f.* 1. (*hist.*) grivna (*unit of currency in medieval Russia*). 2. (*obs.*) ten kopecks. 3. (*hist.*) pendant.

гривуа́з|ный (~ен, ~на), *adj.* obscene, indecent.

григориа́нск|ий, *adj.* Gregorian; г. кале́ндарь, ~ое летосчисле́ние Gregorian Calendar.

гри́дниц|а, ы, *f.* (*hist.*) quarters of body-guard.

грид|ь, и, *f.* (*collect.*; *hist.*) (*prince's*) body-guard.

грим, а, *m.* make-up (*theatr. only*); grease-paint.

грима́с|а, ы, *f.* grimace; де́лать ~ы to make, pull faces.

грима́сник, а, *m.* grimacer.

грима́снича|ть, ю, *impf.* to grimace; to make, pull faces.

гримёр, а, *m.* (*theatr.*) make-up man.

гримир|ова́ть, у́ю, *impf.* 1. (*theatr.*) (*pf.* на~) to make up. 2. (*pf.* за~) (+*i.*) to make up (as); (+*i. or* под+*a.*; *fig.*) to make to appear, make out (as); г. Наполео́на геро́ем, под геро́я to paint Napoleon as a hero.

гримир|ова́ться, у́юсь, *impf.* (*of* за~) (*theatr.*) to make up (*intrans.*); (+*i. or* под +*a.*; *fig.*) to make oneself out, seek to appear; г. патрио́том, под патрио́та to make oneself out a patriot.

гримиро́вк|а, и, *f.* (*theatr.*) making-up.

грипп, а, *m.* influenza.

гриппо́зный, *adj.* influenzal.

гриф¹, а, *m.* 1. (*myth.*) gryphon. 2. (*zool.*) vulture.

гриф², а, *m.* (*mus.*) finger-board (*of stringed instruments*).

гриф³, а, *m.* seal, stamp.

гриф⁴, а, *m.* (*sport*) grip (*in wrestling*).

гри́фел|ь, я, *m.* slate-pencil.

гри́фельн|ый, *adj.* slate; ~ая доска́ slate; г. сла́нец (*geol.*) grapholite.

грифо́н, а, *m.* 1. (*myth., archit.*) gryphon. 2. griffon (*dog*).

гроб, а, о ~е, в ~у́, *pl.* ~ы́ *and* ~а́, *m.* 1. coffin; идти́ за ~ом to follow the coffin. 2. (*obs.*) grave, burial-place. 3. (*fig.*) the grave (= *death*); вогна́ть в г. to drive to the grave; до ~а, по г. жи́зни (*coll.*) until death, as long as one shall live; стоя́ть одно́й ного́й в ~у́ to have one foot in the grave.

гроб|и́ть, лю, ишь, *impf.* (*sl.*) to destroy; to ruin.

гробни́ц|а, ы, *f.* tomb, sepulchre.

гробов|о́й, *adj.* 1. *adj. of* гроб; ~а́я доска́ (*fig.*) the grave; ве́рный до ~о́й доски́ faithful unto death. 2. sepulchral, deathly; г. го́лос sepulchral voice; ~ое молча́ние deathly silence.

гробовщи́к, а́, *m.* coffin-maker; undertaker.

гробокопа́тел|ь, я, *m.* (*obs.*) gravedigger (*iron.* = dry-as-dust historian, etc.).

грог, а, *m.* grog.

гроз|а́, ы́, *pl.* ~ы, *f.* 1. (thunder)storm. 2. calamity, disaster. 3. (*fig.*; *of a person or thing*) terror. 4. (*obs.*) threats.

гроздь|ь, и, *pl.* ~и, ~е́й, *f. and* ~ья, ~ьев, *m.* cluster, bunch (*of fruit or flowers*).

гро|зи́ть, жу́, зи́шь, *impf.* 1. (*pf.* при~) (+*d. and i. or* + *inf.*) to threaten; он ~зи́л мне револьве́ром he was threatening me with a revolver; г. уби́ть кого́-н. to threaten to kill someone. 2. (*pf.* по~) (+*i.*) to make threatening gestures; г. кулако́м кому́-н. to shake one's fist at someone. 3. (*no pf.*) to threaten; ему́ ~зи́т банкро́тство he is threatened with bankruptcy; дом ~зи́т паде́нием the house threatens to collapse.

гро|зи́ться, жу́сь, зи́шься, *impf.* (*of* по~) (*coll.*) **1.** (+*inf.*) to threaten. **2.** to make threatening gestures.

гро́з|ный (~ен, ~на́, ~но), *adj.* **1.** menacing, threatening. **2.** dread, terrible; formidable; ~ная опа́сность terrible danger. **3.** (*coll.*) stern, severe.

гроз|ово́й, *adj. of* ~а́; ~ова́я ту́ча storm-cloud, thundercloud.

гром, а, *pl.* ~ы, ~о́в, *m.* thunder (*also fig.*); уда́р ~а thunderclap; г. среди́ я́сного не́ба a bolt from the blue; мета́ть ~ы и мо́лнии (*fig.*) to fulminate.

грома́д|а¹, ы, *f.* mass, bulk, pile; (+*g.*) a mass (of), heaps (of).

грома́д|а², ы, *f.* (*hist.*) gromada (*rural commune or assembly in Ukraine and Byelorussia*).

грома́дин|а, ы, *f.* (*coll.*) vast object.

грома́д|ный (~ен, ~на), *adj.* huge, vast, enormous, colossal.

громи́л|а, ы, *m.* (*coll.*) **1.** burglar. **2.** thug.

гром|и́ть, лю́, и́шь, *impf.* (*of* раз~) **1.** to destroy; (*mil.*) to smash, rout. **2.** (*fig.*) to thunder against, fulminate against.

гро́м|кий (~ок, ~ка́, ~ко), *adj.* **1.** loud. **2.** famous; notorious; ~кое поведе́ние infamous conduct. **3.** fine-sounding, specious; ~кие слова́ (*iron.*) big words.

гро́мко, *adv.* loud(ly); aloud.

громкоговори́тел|ь, я, *m.* loud-speaker.

громоголо́сый, *adj.* loud-voiced.

громове́рж|ец, ца, *m.* the thunderer (*epithet of Zeus; myth. and fig.*).

громов|о́й, *adj.* **1.** *adj. of* гром; ~ы́е раска́ты peals of thunder. **2.** thunderous, deafening; ~ы́е рукоплеска́ния thunderous applause. **3.** crushing, smashing.

громогла́сно, *adv.* **1.** loudly. **2.** out loud, publicly.

громогла́с|ный (~ен, ~на), *adj.* **1.** loud; loud-voiced. **2.** public, open.

громозву́ч|ный (~ен, ~на), *adj.* (*obs.*) **1.** loud. **2.** (*fig.*) triumphal; highflown.

громоз|ди́ть, жу́, ди́шь, *impf.* (*of* на~) to pile up, heap up.

громоз|ди́ться, жу́сь, ди́шься, *impf.* **1.** to tower. **2.** (*coll.*) to clamber up.

громо́зд|кий (~ок, ~ка), *adj.* cumbersome, unwieldy.

громоотво́д, а, *m.* lightning-conductor (*also fig.*).

громоподо́б|ный (~ен, ~на), *adj.* thunderous.

гро́м|че, *comp. of* ~кий *and* ~ко.

громыха́|ть, ю, *impf.* (*coll.*) to rumble.

гросс, а, *m.* gross.

гро́ссбух, а, *m.* ledger.

гроссме́йстер, а, *m.* **1.** grand master (*at chess*). **2.** (*hist.*) Grand Master (*of order of knights in Middle Ages*).

грот¹, а, *m.* grotto.

грот², а, *m.* mainsail.

грот- (*naut.*) main-.

гроте́ск, а, *m.* (*art*) grotesque.

гроте́скный, *adj.* grotesque.

грох|ать(ся), аю(сь), *impf. of* ~нуть(ся).

гро́хн|уть, у, ешь, *pf.* (*coll.*) **1.** to crash, bang. **2.** (*trans.*) to drop with a crash, bang down.

гро́хн|уться, усь, ешься, *pf.* (*coll.*) to fall with a crash.

гро́хот¹, а, *m.* crash, din; thunder.

гро́хот², а, *m.* (*tech., agric.*) riddle, screen, sifter.

грохота́нь|е, я, *n.* crashing; rumbling.

грох|ота́ть, очу́, о́чешь, *impf.* **1.** to crash; roll, rumble; roar. **2.** (*coll.*) to roar (with laughter).

грохо|ти́ть, чу́, ти́шь, *impf.* (*of* про~) (*tech., agric.*) to riddle, sift, screen.

грош, а́, *m.* **1.** half-kopeck piece. **2.** grosz (*Polish unit of currency*). **3.** *pl.* ~и́, ~е́й (*fig., coll.*) penny, farthing; э́тому г. ме́дный, ло́маный цена́; э́то ~а́ ме́дного, ло́маного не сто́ит it's not worth a brass farthing; ни в г. не ста́вить not to give a brass farthing (for); купи́ть за ~й to buy for a song. **4.** *pl.* ~и́, ~е́й (*sl.*) brass (= *money*).

грошо́вый, *adj.* (*coll.*) **1.** dirt-cheap; (*fig.*) cheap, shoddy. **2.** insignificant, trifling.

грубе́|ть, ю, ешь, *impf.* (*of* о~) to grow coarse, rude.

груб|и́ть, лю́, и́шь, *impf.* (*of* на~) (+*d.*) to be rude (to).

грубия́н, а, *m.* (*coll.*) boor.

грубия́н|ить, ю, ишь, *impf.* (*of* на~) (+*d.; coll.*) to be rude (to); to behave boorishly.

гру́бо, *adv.* **1.** coarsely, roughly. **2.** crudely. **3.** rudely. **4.** roughly (= *approximately*); г. говоря́ roughly speaking.

грубова́т|ый (~, ~а), *adj.* rather coarse, rude.

гру́бост|ь, и, *f.* **1.** rudeness; coarseness; grossness. **2.** rude remark; coarse action; говори́ть ~и to be rude.

грубошёрстный, *adj.* (*of cloth, etc.*) coarse.

гру́б|ый (~, ~а́, ~о), *adj.* **1.** coarse, rough; ~ое сукно́ coarse fabric; г. го́лос gruff voice. **2.** (*of workmanship, etc.*) crude, rude. **3.** gross, flagrant; г. обма́н gross deception. **4.** rude; coarse, crude; ~ое сло́во rude, coarse word. **5.** rough (= *approximate*); в ~ых черта́х in rough outline.

гру́д|а, ы, *f.* heap, pile.

груда́ст|ый (~, ~а), *adj.* broad-chested; big-breasted, big-bosomed.

груди́н|а, ы, *f.* (*anat.*) breastbone.

груди́нк|а, и, *f.* brisket; breast (*of lamb, etc.*).

грудни́ц|а, ы, *f.* (*med.*) mastitis.

грудн|о́й, *adj.* **1.** breast; chest; г. го́лос chest-voice; ~а́я жа́ба (*med.*) angina pectoris; ~а́я железа́ (*anat.*) mammary gland; ~а́я кле́тка (*anat.*) thorax. **2.** at the breast; г. ребёнок infant in arms. **3.** г. мох (*bot.*) Iceland moss.

грудобрю́шн|ый, *adj.*; ~ая прегра́да (*anat.*) diaphragm.

груд|ь, и, о ~и, в ~й, *pl.* ~и, ~е́й, *f.* **1.** breast, chest; стоя́ть ~ью (за+*a.*) to stand up (for), champion; г. с ~ью, г. на́ г. би́ться to fight hand to hand. **2.** (*female*) breast; bosom, bust; корми́ть ~ью to breast-feed; отня́ть от ~и to wean. **3.** (shirt-)front.

гружёный, *adj.* loaded, laden.

груз, а, *m.* **1.** weight; load, cargo, freight. **2.** (*fig.*) weight, burden. **3.** (*pendulum*) bob.

грузд|ь, я́, *pl.* ~и, ~е́й, *m.* milk-agaric (*mushroom*).

грузи́л|о, а, *n.* sinker.

грузи́н, а, *m.* Georgian.

грузи́нк|а, и, *f.* Georgian (woman).

грузи́нский, *adj.* Georgian.

гру|зи́ть, жу́, ~зи́шь, *impf.* **1.** (*pf.* за~ *and* на~) to load; to lade, freight; г. су́дно to lade a ship. **2.** (*pf.* по~) (в, на+*a.*) to load; г. това́р на су́дно to put a cargo aboard a ship.

гру|зи́ться, жу́сь, ~зи́шься, *impf.* (*of* по~) to load (*intrans.*), take on cargo.

гру́зк|а, и, *f.* lading.

грузне́|ть, ю, ешь, *impf.* (*of* по~) to grow heavy, corpulent.

гру́зност|ь, и, *f.* weightiness, bulkiness; unwieldiness; corpulence.

гру́зн|уть, у, ешь, *impf.* to go down, sink.

гру́з|ный (~ен, ~на́, ~но), *adj.* weighty, bulky; unwieldy; corpulent.

грузови́к, а́, *m.* lorry.

грузовладе́л|ец, ьца, *m.* owner of freight.

грузов|о́й, *adj.* goods, cargo, freight; ~о́е движе́ние goods traffic; ~о́е су́дно cargo boat, freighter.

грузооборо́т, а, *m.* turnover of goods.

грузоотправи́тел|ь, я, *m.* consignor of goods.

грузоподъёмност|ь, и,*f.* payload capacity; freight-carrying capacity.

грузоподъёмный, *adj.*; г. кран (loading) crane.

грузополуча́тел|ь, я, *m.* consignee.

грузопото́к, а, *m.* goods traffic.

грузотакси́, *indecl.*, *n.* 'taxi-lorry' (*lorry operated for hire from taxi-station*).

гру́зчик, а, *m.* docker, stevedore.

грум, а, *m.* groom.

грунт, а, *m.* **1.** soil, earth; bottom; пересади́ть в г. to plant out. **2.** priming, prime coating (*of a picture*).

грунт|ова́ть, у́ю, *impf.* (*of* за~) (*art*) to prime.

грунто́вк|а, и,f.* priming, first coat (*of paint*).

грунтов|о́й, *adj. of* грунт; ~ые во́ды subsoil waters; ~а́я доро́га dirt road, earth road.

гру́пп|а, ы,f.* (*in var. senses*) group; г. кро́ви (*med.*) blood group.

группир|ова́ть, у́ю, *impf.* (*of* с~) to group; to classify.

группир|ова́ться, у́ется, *impf.* (*of* с~) to group, form groups.

группиро́вк|а, и,f.* **1.** grouping, classification; г. сил (*mil.*) distribution of forces. **2.** group, grouping.

группово́д, а, *m.* group leader.

группов|о́й, *adj.* group; ~ые заня́тия group study, group work; ~ые и́гры team games; г. полёт formation flying; г. сни́мок group photograph.

группово́щин|а, ы, *f.* clique-formation, cliquishness.

гру|сти́ть, щу́, сти́шь, *impf.* to grieve, mourn; (по+*d.*) to pine (for).

гру́стно[1], *adv.* sadly, sorrowfully.

гру́стно[2], *as pred.* it is sad; ей г. she feels sad; нам г. узна́ть, что we are sorry to hear that...

гру́ст|ный (~ен, ~на́, ~но), *adj.* **1.** sad, melancholy. **2.** sad(-making); (*coll.*) grievous, distressing.

груст|ь, и,*f.* sadness, melancholy.

гру́ш|а, и,f.* **1.** pear. **2.** pear-tree. **3.** земляна́я г. Jerusalem artichoke. **4.** pear-shaped object.

грушеви́д|ный (~ен, ~на), *adj.* pear-shaped.

гру́шевый, *adj.* pear; г. компо́т stewed pears.

грушо́вк|а, и,f.* **1.** pear liqueur. **2.** grushovka (*kind of apple-tree*).

гры́ж|а, и,f.* (*med.*) hernia, rupture.

грыжево́й *and* **гры́жевый**, *adj.* hernial; г. банда́ж truss.

гры́зл|о, а, *n.* bit (*of bridle*).

грызн|я́, и́,*f.* (*coll.*) **1.** fight (*of animals*). **2.** squabble.

гры́з|ть, у́, ёшь, *past* ~, ~ла, *impf.* **1.** to gnaw; to nibble; г. но́гти to bite one's nails. **2.** (*coll.*) to nag (at). **3.** (*fig.*) to devour, consume; нас ~ло любопы́тство we were consumed with curiosity.

гры́з|ться, у́сь, ёшься, *past* ~ся, ~лась, *impf.* **1.** to fight (*of animals*). **2.** (*coll.*) to squabble, bicker.

грызу́н, а́, *m.* rodent.

гры́мз|а, ы, *m. and f.* (*coll.*) grumbler.

грю́ндер, а, *m.* company promoter.

грю́ндерств|о, а, *n.* company promotion.

гряд|а́, ы́, *pl.* ~ы, ~, ~а́м,*f.* **1.** ridge. **2.** bed (*in garden*). **3.** row, series.

грядил|ь, я, *m.* plough-beam.
грядк|а¹, и, *f. dim. of* грядá.
грядк|а², и, *f.* edge (*of cart or sledge*).
грядков|ый, *adj. of* грядка¹; ~ая культу́ра (*hort.*) growing in beds.
грядовóй, *adj.* (*hort.*) growing, grown in beds.
грядýщ|ий *pres. part. act. of* грясти́ (*obs.*) and *adj.* (*rhet.*) coming, future; ~ие дни days to come; на сон г. (*coll.*) at bedtime, before going to bed; *as noun* ~ee, ~его, *n.* the future.
грязев|óй, *adj.* mud; ~ая вáнна mud-bath.
грязелечéбниц|а, ы, *f.* institution for mud--cures, therapeutic mud-baths.
грязелечéни|е, я, *n.* mud-cure.
грязнé|ть, ю, *impf.* to get covered in mud, become dirty.
грязн|и́ть, ю́, и́шь, *impf.* (*of* на~) 1. to make dirty, soil; (*fig.*) to sully, besmirch. 2. to litter.
грязн|и́ться, ю́сь, и́шься, *impf.* to become dirty.
грязн|о¹, *adv. of* ~ый.
грязно², *as pred.* it is dirty.
грязнýл|я, и, *m. and f.* (*coll.*) guttersnipe; slut.
грязн|уть, у, ешь, *impf.* to sink in the mire (*also fig.*).
гряз|ный (~ен, ~нá, ~но), *adj.* 1. muddy, mud-stained. 2. dirty; ~ное бельё dirty washing (*also fig.*). 3. untidy; slovenly; ~ная тетрáдь untidy copy-book. 4. (*fig.*) dirty, filthy; ~ное дéло dirty business. 5. mud-grey. 6. refuse, garbage; ~ное ведрó refuse-pail, garbage-pail, slop-pail.
гряз|ь, и, о ~и, в ~и́, *f.* 1. mud (*also fig.*); меси́ть г. (*coll.*) to wade through mud; забросáть ~ью, смешáть с ~ью; втоптáть, затоптáть в г. (*fig.*) to sling mud (at). 2. (*pl.*) (*therapeutic*) mud; mud-baths; mud-cure. 3. dirt, filth (*also fig.*).
гря́н|уть, у, ешь, *pf.* 1. (*of sounds and fig.*) to burst out, crash out; ~ул гром there was a clap of thunder; ~ул вы́стрел a shot rang out. 2. to strike up (*a song, etc.*).
гря́н|уться, усь, ешься, *pf.* to crash.
гря|сти́, дý, дёшь, *impf.* (*obs.*) to approach.
гуáно, *indecl., n.* guano.
гуáш|ь, и, *f.* (*art*) gouache; gouache painting.
губ|á¹, ы́, *pl.* ~ы, ~áм, *f.* 1. lip; надýть ~ы to pout; по ~áм комý-н. помáзать (*coll.*) to raise false hopes in someone; у негó губá не дýра (*coll.*) he knows which side his bread is buttered; молокó на ~áх не обсóхло he is still green. 2. (*pl.*) pincers.
губ|á², ы́, *pl.* ~ы, ~áм, *f.* bay, inlet, firth (*in N. Russia*).
губ|á³, ы́, *pl.* ~ы, ~áм, *f.* tree-fungus.

губ|á⁴, ы́, *pl.* ~ы, ~áм, *f.* (*hist.*) guba (*administrative division of Muscovite Russia, corresponding to later uyezd*).
губáст|ый (~, ~а), *adj.* (*coll.*) thick-lipped.
губернáтор, а, *m.* governor.
губернáторск|ий, *adj.* of a governor; (*joc.*) положéние хýже ~ого a critical situation, a tight spot.
губернáторств|о, а, *n.* governorship.
губернáторш|а, и, *f.* (*coll.*) governor's wife.
губéрни|я, и, *f.* (*hist.*) guberniya, province; пошлá писáть г. (*joc.*) everything is in commotion.
губéрн|ский, *adj. of* ~ия; г. гóрод principal town of province.
губи́тел|ь, я, *m.* destroyer.
губи́тел|ьный (~ен, ~ьна), *adj.* destructive, ruinous; baneful, pernicious.
губ|и́ть, лю́, ~ишь, *impf.* (*of* по~) to destroy; to be the undoing (of); to ruin, spoil.
губ|и́ться, ~ится, *impf.* (*of* по~) to be destroyed; to be wasted.
губ|ка¹, ки, *f. dim. of* губá¹.
губк|а², и, *f.* sponge; мыть ~ой to sponge.
губн|óй¹, *adj.* 1. lip; ~ая помáда lipstick. 2. (*ling.*) labial.
губн|óй², *adj. of* ~á⁴.
губошлёп, а, *m.* (*coll.*) 1. mumbler. 2. lout.
губчат|ый, *adj.* porous, spongy; ~ое желéзо sponge iron, porous iron; г. каучýк foam rubber.
гувернáнтк|а, и, *f.* governess.
гувернёр, а, *m.* tutor.
гугенóт, а, *m.* (*hist.*) Huguenot.
гугни́в|ый (~, ~а), *adj.* (*coll.*) speaking through the nose.
гу-гý *only used in phrase* ни г.! not a word!; об э́том ни г.! don't let it go any further!
гуд, а, *m.* (*coll.*) buzzing; drone; hum.
гудéни|е, я, *n.* buzzing; drone; hum; honk (*of a motor-car horn, etc.*).
гу|дéть, жý, ди́шь, *impf.* 1. to buzz; to drone; to hum; у меня́ ~дéло в ушáх (*impers.*) there was a buzzing in my ears. 2. (*of a factory whistle, steamer's siren, etc.*) to hoot; to honk. 3. (*coll.*) to ache.
гуд|óк, кá, *m.* 1. hooter, siren, horn, whistle. 2. hoot(ing); honk; toot; по ~кý when the whistle blows.
гудрóн, а, *m.* tar.
гудрони́р|овать, ую, *impf. and pf.* to tar.
гудрóн|ный, *adj. of* ~; ~ое шоссé tarred highroad.
гуж, á, *m.* 1. tug (*part of harness*); взя́лся за г., не говори́, что не дюж (*prov.*) in for a penny in for a pound. 2. cartage.
гужев|óй, *adj.* 1. *adj. of* гуж. 2. cart; ~áя дорóга cart-track; г. трáнспорт cartage, animal-drawn transport.

гужо́м, *adv.* **1.** by cartage; вози́ть г. to cart. **2.** (*dial.*) in file.

гу́зк|а, и, *f.* rump (*of a bird*).

гу́зн|о, а, *n.* (*vulg.*) arse, buttocks.

гул, а, *m.* rumble; hum; boom.

гу́л|кий, (~ок, ~ка́, ~ко), *adj.* **1.** resonant. **2.** booming, rumbling.

гулли́в|ый (~, ~а), *adj.* (*coll.*) gadabout.

гульб|а́, ы́, *f.* (*coll.*) idling; revelry.

гу́льбищ|е, а, *n.* **1.** (*obs.*) promenade. **2.** (*coll.*) revels, carousal.

гу́льден, а, *m.* **1.** (*hist.*) gulden (*coin*). **2.** guilder (*Dutch unit of currency*).

гульн|у́ть, у́, ёшь, *pf.* (*coll.*) to make merry.

гу́л|я, и, *m. and f.* (*coll.*) dove, pigeon.

гуля́к|а, и, *m. and f.* (*coll.*) idler; flâneur; playboy.

гуля́нк|а, и, *f.* (*coll.*) **1.** fête; outdoor party. **2.** feast.

гуля́н|ье, ья, *g. pl.* **~ий,** *n.* **1.** walking; (going for a) walk. **2.** fête; outdoor party. **3.** (*obs. or dial.*) pleasure-ground.

гуля́|ть, ю, *impf.* (*of* по~) **1.** to walk, stroll; to take a walk, go for a walk; г. по рука́м to pass from hand to hand. **2.** (*impf. only*) (*coll.*) not to be working; (*of land*) to be untilled; мы сего́дня ~ем we have got the day off today. **3.** (*coll.*) to make merry, have a good time; to carouse, go on the spree. **4.** (с+*i.*; *coll.*) to go (with) (= *have a sexual relationship with*). **5.** (*of a baby*; *coll.*) to lie awake.

гуля́ш, а, *m.* (*cul.*) goulash.

гуля́щ|ий, *adj.* (*coll.*) idle; *as noun* **~ая, ~ей,** *f.* streetwalker.

гумани́зм, а, *m.* **1.** humanism. **2.** (*hist.*) the revival of learning.

гумани́ст, а, *m.* humanist.

гуманисти́ческий, *adj.* humanist.

гуманита́рн|ый, *adj.* **1.** pertaining to the humanities; ~ые нау́ки the humanities, the Arts (*as opp. to natural sciences*). **2.** humane.

гума́нност|ь, и, *f.* humanity, humaneness.

гума́н|ный (~ен, ~на), *adj.* humane.

гумённый, *adj. of* гумно́.

гуме́нц|е, а, *n.* **1.** *dim. of* гумно́. **2.** (*eccl.*) tonsure.

гу́мка|ть, ю, *impf.* (*coll.*) to repeat frequently 'hm!'.

гу́мм|а, ы, *f.* (*med.*) gumma (*kind of tumour*).

гу́мми, *indecl., n.* gum.

гуммиара́бик, а, *m.* gum arabic.

гуммигу́т, а, *m.* gamboge.

гуммила́стик, а, *m.* india-rubber.

гумми́р|овать, ую, *impf. and pf.* to stick (with) gum.

гуммо́зный, *adj.* (*med.*) gummatous.

гум|но́, на́, *pl.* **~на, ~ен** *and* **~ён, ~нам,** *n.* **1.** threshing-floor. **2.** barn.

гу́мус, а, *m.* (*agric.*) humus.

гундо́|сить, шу, сишь, *impf.* (*coll.*) to speak through one's nose.

гунн, а, *m.* (*hist.*) Hun.

гу́нтер, а, *m.* hunter (*horse*).

гу́н|я, и, *f.* (*obs. or dial.*) old rags.

гури́|ец, йца, *m.* Gurian (*inhabitant of western districts of Georgia*).

гури́йк|а, и, *f.* Gurian (woman).

гури́йский, *adj.* Gurian.

гу́ри|я, и, *f.* houri.

гурма́н, а, *m.* gourmet, epicure.

гурма́нств|о, а, *n.* connoisseurship (*of food and drink*).

гурт¹, а, *m.* herd, drove; flock.

гурт², а, *m.* **1.** milling (*of a coin*). **2.** frieze.

гуртовщи́к, а́, *m.* **1.** herdsman; drover. **2.** (*obs.*) cattle-dealer.

гурто́м, *adv.* (*coll.*) **1.** wholesale; in bulk. **2.** together; in a body, en masse.

гурьб|а́, ы́, *f.* crowd, gang.

гуса́к, а́, *m.* gander.

гуса́р, а, *m.* hussar.

гуса́рский, *adj.* hussar.

гус|ёк, ька́, *m.* goose.

гу́с|ельный, *adj. of* ~ли.

гу́сениц|а, ы, *f.* **1.** (*zool.*) caterpillar. **2.** (caterpillar) track.

гу́сеничн|ый, *adj.* (*zool., tech.*) caterpillar; ~ая ле́нта (*tech.*) caterpillar track; г. тра́ктор caterpillar tractor; г. ход caterpillar drive.

гус|ёнок, ёнка, *pl.* **~я́та,** *m.* gosling.

гуси́н|ый, *adj.* goose; ~ая ко́жа goose-flesh; ~ые ла́пки crow's feet; ~ое перо́ goose-quill.

гуси́т, а, *m.* (*hist.*) Hussite.

гу́сл|и, ей, *no sing.* (*mus.*) psaltery, gusli.

гусля́р, а́-а, *m.* psaltery player.

густе́|ть, ет, *impf.* (*of* по~) to thicken, get thicker, get denser.

гу|сти́ть, щу́, сти́шь, *impf.* to thicken (*trans.*).

гу́сто¹, *adv.* thickly, densely.

гу́сто², *as pred.* (*coll.*) there is much, there is plenty; у меня́ де́нег не г. I'm a bit hard up, a bit pushed.

густоволо́сый, *adj.* thick-haired, shaggy.

густ|о́й (~, ~а́, ~о), *adj.* **1.** (*in var. senses*) thick, dense; ~а́я листва́ thick foliage; г. тума́н dense fog; ~о́е населе́ние dense population; ~ы́е бро́ви bushy eyebrows. **2.** (*of sound or colour*) deep, rich.

густоли́ственный, *adj.* with thick foliage, leafy.

густонаселённый, *adj.* densely populated.

густопсо́вый, *adj.* **1.** a breed of borzoi. **2.** (*fig.*) out-and-out.

густот|а́, ы́, *f.* **1.** thickness, density. **2.** (*of sound or colour*) deepness, richness.

гусы́н|я, и, *f.* goose.

гус|ь, я, *pl.* **⁓и, ⁓е́й,** *m.* goose; как с ⁓я вода́ like water off a duck's back; хоро́ш гусь! (*iron.*) a fine fellow indeed!

гусько́м, *adv.* in (single) file, in crocodile.

гуся́тин|а, ы, *f.* goose(-meat).

гуся́тник, а, *m.* **1.** goose-pen, goose-run. **2.** goshawk.

гу́т|а, ы, *f.* (*obs.*) glass-foundry.

гутали́н, а, *m.* shoe-polish.

гути́р|овать, ую, *impf.* (*obs.*) to savour.

гуто́р|ить, ю, ишь, *impf.* (*dial.*) to natter.

гуттапе́рч|а, и, *f.* gutta percha.

гуттапе́рч|евый, *adj. of* ⁓a.

гуцу́л, а, *m.* Huzul (*Ukrainian inhabitant of Carpathian region*).

гуцу́лк|а, и, *f.* Huzul (woman).

гуцу́льский, *adj.* Huzul.

гу́щ|а, и, *f.* **1.** dregs, lees, grounds, sediment; кофе́йная г. coffee grounds. **2.** thicket; (*fig.*) thick, centre, heart; в са́мой ⁓е собы́тий in the thick of things.

гу́ще, *comp. of* густо́й, гу́сто.

гущин|а́, ы́, *f.* (*coll.*) **1.** thickness. **2.** thicket.

гэ́льский, *adj.* Gaelic.

гю́йс, а, *m.* (*naut.*) jack.

гяу́р, а, *m.* giaour.

Д

да¹, *particle* **1.** yes. **2.** (*interrog.*) yes?, is that so?, really?, indeed?; он мно́го лет прожива́л в Пари́же. — Да? а я и не знал he lived in Paris for many years. Really? I didn't know. **3.** (*emphatic*) why; well; да не мо́жет быть! why, that's impossible!; да в чём де́ло? well, what's it all about? **4.** *emphasizes predicate*: когда́-н. да ко́нчится it must end some time; э́то что́-н. да зна́чит there's something behind this. **5.** (вот) э́то да! (*coll.*) splendid!, super!

да², *particle* (+3rd *person pres. or fut. of verb*) да здра́вствует..! long live . . . !

да³, *conj.* **1.** (*mainly in conventional phrases*) and; день да ночь day and night; ко́жа да ко́сти skin and bone. **2.** (да и, да ещё) and (besides); and what is more; бы́ло за́ полночь, да и снег шёл it was past midnight and (what is more) it was snowing; принеси́те мне во́дки, да поскоре́е! bring me some vodka, and quick about it!; он занима́лся, занима́лся, да и провали́лся на экза́мене he studied and studied and then he (went and) failed his exam. **3.** да и то́лько and that's all, and no more; она́ ворчи́т, да и то́лько she does nothing but grouse. **4.** but; я охо́тно проводи́л бы тебя́, да вре́мени не́ту I would gladly come with you but I haven't the time.

дабы́, *conj.* (*obs.*) in order (to, that).

дава́й(те), *as particle* **1.** (+*inf. or* 1st *plur. of fut. tense*) let's; дава́йте приостано́вимся мину́точку-две let's pause for a minute or two; дава́йте заку́рим let's light up. **2.** (+*imp.*; *coll.*) come on; дава́й, расскажи́ что-н. come on, tell us a story. **3.** (+*inf.*; *coll.*) *expresses inception of action*: а он дава́й бежа́ть he just took to his heels.

да|ва́ть, ю́, ёшь, *impf. of* дать.

да|ва́ться, ю́сь, ёшься, *impf.* (*of* ⁓ться) **1.** *pass. of* дава́ть. **2.** to let oneself be caught;

не д. (+d.) to dodge, evade. **3.** легко́ д. to come easily, naturally; ру́сский язы́к ему́ легко́ даётся Russian comes easily to him.

да́веча, *adv.* (*coll.*) lately, recently.

да́вешний, *adj.* (*coll.*) recent; late.

дави́л|о, а, *n.* press.

дави́льный, *adj.*; д. пресс winepress.

дави́л|ьня, ьни, *g. pl.* ⁓ен, *f.* winepress.

дави́льщик, а, *m.* presser, treader.

дав|и́ть, лю́, ⁓ишь, *impf.* **1.** (*also* на+*a.*) to press (upon); (*fig.*) to oppress, weigh (upon), lie heavy (on); се́рдце ⁓ит (*impers.*) (my) heart is heavy. **2.** to crush; to trample. **3.** to squeeze (*juice out of fruit, etc.*).

дав|и́ться, лю́сь, ⁓ишься, *impf.* (*of* по⁓) **1.** (+*i. or* от) to choke (with); д. от ка́шля to choke with coughing. **2.** (*pf.* у⁓) (*coll.*) to hang oneself. **3.** *pass. of* ⁓и́ть.

да́вка, и, *f.* (*coll.*) **1.** crushing, squeezing. **2.** throng, crush.

давле́ни|е, я, *n.* pressure (*also fig.*); под ⁓ем (+*g.*) under pressure (of); through stress (of).

да́вленый, *adj.* pressed, crushed.

давне́нько, *adv.* (*coll.*) for quite a long time.

да́вн|ий, *adj.* **1.** ancient. **2.** of long standing; с ⁓их пор, времён of old, for a long time.

давни́шний, *adj.* (*coll.*) = да́вний.

давно́, *adv.* **1.** long ago; он д. у́мер he died long ago; д. бы так (*expressing approval of someone's action*) not before (it was) time. **2.** for a long time (*up to and including the present moment*); long since; мы д. живём в дере́вне we have been living in the country for a long time.

давнопрошéдш|ий, *adj.* remote (*in time*); ⁓ее вре́мя (*gram.*) pluperfect tense.

да́вност|ь, и, *f.* **1.** antiquity; remoteness. **2.** long standing. **3.** (*leg.*) prescription.

давны́м-давно́, *adv.* (*coll.*) very long ago, ages (and ages) ago.

дагерроти́п, а, *m.* daguerrotype.

дагерроти́пный, *adj.* daguerrotype.

дагеста́н|ец, ца, *m.* Dagestani.

дагеста́нк|а, и, *f.* Dagestani (woman).

дагеста́нский, *adj.* Dagestani.

да́же, *particle* even; е́сли д. even if; о́чень д. пло́хо extremely bad.

да́к|ать, аю, *impf.* (*coll.*) to keep saying 'yes'.

дактили́ческий, *adj.* (*lit.*) dactylic.

дактилоло́ги|я, и, *f.* finger-speech.

дактилоско́пи|я, и, *f.* identification by means of finger-prints; taking of finger-prints.

да́ктил|ь, я, *m.* (*lit.*) dactyl.

далай-ла́м|а, ы, *m.* Dalai Lama.

да́лее, *adv.* further; не д., как вчера́, он был здесь he was here only yesterday; и так д. (*abbr.* и т. д.) and so on, etcetera.

далёк|ий (~, ~а́, ~о́, *and* ~о), *adj.* 1. (*in var. senses*) distant, remote; far(away); д. путь long journey; ~ое про́шлое distant past; д. от и́стины wide of the mark; я ~ от того́, что́бы жела́ть I am far from wishing. 2. (*only with neg.*; *coll.*) clever, bright; она́ не о́чень ~а́ she is not awfully bright.

далеко́ *and* далёко[1], *adv.* 1. far, far off; (от) far (from); д. зайти́ (*fig.*) to go too far, burn one's boats; д. пойти́ (*fig.*) to go far (= *to be a success*). 2. far, by a long way, by much; д. за (*of time*) long after; д. не far from; она́ д. не краса́вица she is far from beautiful.

далеко́ *and* далёко[2], *as pred.* it is far, it is a long way; (+*d.* до; *fig.*) to be far (from), be much inferior (to); ему́ д. до соверше́нства he is far from perfect.

дале́че, *adv.* (*obs. or dial.*) = далеко́.

дал|ь, и, о ~и, в ~й, *f.* 1. distance; distant prospect. 2. (*coll.*) distant spot. 3. така́я д.! (*coll.*) it is so far, such a long way!

дальневосто́чный, *adj.* Far Eastern.

дальне́йш|ий, *adj.* further, furthest; в ~ем (*i*) in future, henceforth, (*ii*) below, herein-after.

да́льн|ий, *adj.* 1. distant, remote; Д. Восто́к the Far East; ~ее пла́вание long voyage; ~его де́йствия long-range; ~его сле́дования (*of a train*) long-distance. 2. (*of kinship*) distant. 3. без ~их слов without more ado.

дальнобо́йност|ь, и, *f.* (*mil.*) long range.

дальнобо́йный, *adj.* (*mil.*) long-range.

дальнови́дени|е, я, *n.* (*obs.*) television.

дальнови́дност|ь, и, *f.* foresight.

дальнови́д|ный (~ен, ~на), *adj.* far-sighted.

дальнозо́р|кий (~ок, ~ка), *adj.* long-sighted.

дальнозо́ркост|ь, и, *f.* long sight.

дальноме́р, а, *m.* range-finder.

дальноме́рщик, а, *m.* range-finder operator.

да́льност|ь, и, *f.* distance; range; д. полёта снаря́да range of a missile.

дальтони́зм, а, *m.* colour-blindness, Daltonism.

дальто́ник, а, *m.* colour-blind person.

да́льше, *adj. and adv.* 1. *comp. of* далёкий. 2. (*adv.*) farther; ти́ше е́дешь, д. бу́дешь (*prov.*) more haste, less speed; д. не́куда (*coll.*) that's the limit. 3. (*adv.*) further; расска́зывать д. to go on (telling a story); д.! go on! 4. (*adv.*) then, next; они́ не зна́ли, что д. де́лать they did not know what to do next. 5. (*adv.*) longer; ждать д. нельзя́ бы́ло it was impossible to wait any longer.

да́м|а, ы, *f.* 1. lady. 2. partner (*in dancing*). 3. (*cards*) queen.

дама́сск|ий, *adj.*; ~ая сталь Damascus steel.

да́мб|а, ы, *f.* dike.

да́мк|а, и, *f.* king (*at draughts*).

да́м|ский, *adj. of* ~a; ~ская су́мка ladies' handbag; д. кавале́р, д. уго́дник ladies' man.

да́нник, а, *m.* (*hist.*) tributary.

да́нн|ые, ых 1. data; facts, information. 2. qualities, gifts, potentialities. 3. grounds.

да́нн|ый, *p.p.p. of* дать *and adj.* given; present; in question; в д. моме́нт at the present moment, at present; в ~ом слу́чае in this case, in the case in question; ~ая (величина́) (*math.*) datum.

данти́ст, а, *m.* dentist.

дан|ь, и, *f.* 1. (*hist.*) tribute; обложи́ть ~ью to lay under tribute. 2. (*fig.*) tribute; debt; отда́ть д. (+*d.*) to appreciate, recognize.

дар, а, *pl.* ~ы́, *m.* 1. gift, donation; grant. 2. (+*g.*) gift (of); д. сло́ва (*i*) the gift of the gab, (*ii*) speech, ability to speak. 3. (*pl.*) (*eccl.*) the sacraments (*of bread and wine*).

дарвини́зм, а, *m.* Darwinism.

дарвини́ст, а, *m.* Darwinist.

даре́ни|е, я, *n.* donation.

дарёный, *adj.* received as a present; ~ому коню́ в зу́бы не смо́трят (*prov.*) one should not look a gift horse in the mouth.

дари́тел|ь, я, *m.* donor.

дар|и́ть, ю́, ~ишь, *impf.* (*of* по~) 1. (+*d. of person*) to give, make a present. 2. (+*a. of person and i.*) to favour (with), bestow (upon); д. кого́-н. улы́бкой to bestow a smile upon someone.

дармое́д, а, *m.* (*coll.*) parasite, sponger, scrounger.

дармое́днича|ть, ю, *impf.* (*coll.*) to sponge, scrounge.

дармое́дств|о, а, *n.* (*coll.*) parasitism, sponging, scrounging.

дарова́ни|е, я, *n.* (**1.** *obs.*) donation, giving. **2.** gift, talent.

дар|ова́ть, у́ю, *impf. and pf.* to grant, confer.

дарови́тост|ь, и, *f.* giftedness.

дарови́т|ый (~, ~а), *adj.* gifted, talented.

даровóй, *adj.* free (of charge), gratuitous.

даровщи́нк|а, и, *f.*; **на ~у** (*coll.*) for nothing, for free.

да́ром, *adv.* **1.** free (of charge), gratis; **э́то вам д. не пройдёт** you'll pay for this. **2.** in vain, to no purpose; **пропа́сть д.** to be wasted. **3.** *as conj.*; **д. что** (*coll.*) although.

дароно́сиц|а, ы, *f.* (*eccl.*) pyx.

дарохрани́тельниц|а, ы, *f.* (*eccl.*) tabernacle.

да́рственн|ый, *adj.* **1.** (*obs.*) received as a present. **2.** confirming a gift; **~ая на́дпись** dedicatory inscription; **~ая за́пись** (*leg.*) settlement, deed.

да́т|а, ы, *f.* date.

да́тельный, *adj.* (*gram.*) dative.

дати́р|овать, ую, *impf. and pf.* to date (= (*i*) *affix a date to,* (*ii*) *establish the date of*).

да́тский, *adj.* Danish.

датча́н|ин, ина, *pl.* **~е, ~,** *m.* Dane.

датча́нк|а, и, *f.* Danish woman.

дать, дам, дашь, даст, дади́м, дади́те, даду́т, *past* **дал, дала́, да́ло, да́ли,** *pf.* (*of* **дава́ть**) **1.** to give; **д. взаймы́** to lend (*money*); **д. на во́дку, на чай** to tip; **д. обе́д** to give a dinner; **д. уро́ки** to give lessons; **д. показа́ния** to testify, depose. **2.** to give, administer; **д. лека́рство** to give medicine; **д. кому́-н. пощёчину** (*coll.*) to box someone's ears. **3.** (**по**+*d.,* **в**+*a.*; *coll.*) to give (it); to hit; **д. кому́-н. по́ уху** to clip someone on the ear-hole; **я те дам!** (*coll.*; *expressing vague threat*) I'll give you what-for!, I'll teach you! **4.** (*fig.*) to give; **д. кля́тву** to take an oath; **д. нача́ло** (+*d.*) to give rise (to); **д. сло́во** to pledge one's word; **д. себе́ труд** (+*inf.*) to put oneself to the trouble (of). **5.** (*fig.*) to give, grant; **д. во́лю** (+*d.*) to give (free) rein (to), give vent (to); **д. газ** (*coll.*) to open the throttle; **д. доро́гу** (+*d.*) to make way (for); **д. но́гу** (*aeron.*) to give (it) rudder; **не д. поко́я** (+*d.*) to give no peace; **д. кому́-н. сло́во** to give someone the floor (*at a meeting*); **д. ход** (+*d.*) to set in motion, get going; **д. ход кому́-н.** (*coll.*) to help someone on, give someone a leg-up. **6.** +*certain nouns expresses action related to meaning of noun*: **д. залп** to fire a volley; **д. звоно́к** to ring (*a bell*); **д. отбо́й** to ring off (*on telephone*); **д. отпо́р** (+*d.*) to repulse; **д. течь** to spring a leak; **д. тре́щину** to crack. (+*inf.*) to let; **д. поня́ть** to give to understand; **д. себя́ знать, д. себя́ почу́вствовать** to make oneself (itself) felt; **да́йте ему́ говори́ть** let

him speak. **8.** **дай**+*1st person of fut. tense expresses decision to take some action*: **дай вы́купаюсь** I think I'll take a bath. **9.** **ни д. ни взять** (*i*) exactly the same, neither more nor less, (*ii*) as like as two peas.

да́ться, да́мся, да́шься, *etc.,* *past* **да́лся, дала́сь,** *pf.* **1.** *pf.* of **дава́ться. 2.** (+*d.*) to have become an obsession (with).

да́ч|а¹, и, *f.* **1.** giving. **2.** helping, portion.

да́ч|а², и, *f.* **1.** dacha (*holiday cottage in the country in environs of city or large town*). **2.** **быть на ~е** to be in the country; **поéхать на ~у** to go to the country.

да́ч|а³, и, *f.* (*forestry*) (piece of) woodland.

дачевладе́л|ец, ьца, *m.* owner of a dacha.

дачевладе́л|ица, ицы, *f.* of **~ец.**

да́чник, а, *m.* (holiday) visitor (in the country).

да́ч|ный, *adj.* **о, ~а²;** **д. о́тдых** country holiday; **д. по́езд** suburban train.

дашна́к, а, *m.* (*hist.*) Dashnak (*member of Armenian nationalist movement*).

дая́ни|е, я, *n.* (*rhet.*; *obs. or iron.*) donation, contribution.

два (*f.* **две), двух, двум, двумя́, о двух,** *num.* two; **два-три, две-три** two or three, a couple; **ни д. ни полтора́** (*coll.*) neither one thing nor another; **в двух слова́х** briefly, in short; **в д. счёта** in no time, in two ticks; **в двух шага́х** a short step away; **ка́ждые д. дня** every other day, on alternate days.

двадцати- twenty-.

двадцатигра́нник, а, *m.* (*math.*) icosahedron.

двадцатиле́ти|е, я, *n.* **1.** period of twenty years. **2.** twentieth anniversary.

двадцатиле́тний, *adj.* **1.** twenty-year, of twenty years. **2.** twenty-year-old.

двадцатипятиле́ти|е, я, *n.* **1.** period of twenty-five years. **2.** twenty-fifth anniversary.

двадца́т|ый, *adj.* twentieth; **одна́ ~ая** a twentieth; **~ое января́** the twentieth of January; **~ые го́ды** the twenties.

два́дцат|ь, и, *i.* **ью,** *num.* twenty; **д. оди́н,** *etc.,* twenty-one, *etc.*; **д. одно́** (*card-game*) vingt-et-un.

два́дцатью, *adv.* twenty times.

два́жды, *adv.* twice; **я́сно как д. два четы́ре** as plain as a pikestaff.

дванадеся́тый and двунадеся́тый, *adj.*; **д. пра́здник** (*eccl.*) major festival (*each of the twelve major festivals of the Orthodox Church*).

двенадцатипёрстн|ый, *adj.*; **~ая кишка́** (*anat.*) duodenum.

двенадцатисло́жный, *adj.* dodecasyllabic.

двена́дцатый, *adj.* twelfth.

двена́дцат|ь, и, *adj.* twelve.

двер|но́й, *adj.* of **~ь; д. проём** doorway; **~ная ру́чка** door-handle.

двéр|ца, ы, *g. pl.* ~ец, *f.* door (*of car, cupboard, etc.*).

двер|ь, и, о ~и, в ~й, *pl.* ~и, ~éй, *i.* ~ями *and* ~ьми, *f.* door; в ~ях in the doorway; у ~éй close at hand; при закрытых ~ях behind closed doors, in camera.

двéсти, двухсóт, двумстáм, двумястáми, о двухстáх, *num.* two hundred.

двигатель|ь, я, *m.* motor, engine; (*fig.*) mover, motive force.

двигательн|ый, *adj.* **1.** motive; ~ая сила moving force, impetus. **2.** (*anat.*) motor.

двига|ть, ю *and* **движу,** *impf.* (*of* двинуть) **1.** (~ю) to move. **2.** (~ю) (+*i.*) to move (*part of the body*); to make a movement (of). **3.** (движу) to set in motion, get going (*also fig.*); д. вперёд (*fig.*) to advance, further.

двига|ться, юсь *and* **движусь** *impf.* (*of* двинуться) **1.** to move (*intrans.*); д. вперёд to advance (*also fig.*). **2.** to start, get going. **3.** *pass. of* ~ть.

движéни|е, я, *n.* **1.** (*in var. senses*) movement; motion; д. вперёд forward movement, advance; привести в д. to set in motion. **2.** (*physical*) movement, exercise. **3.** traffic; д. в одном направлéнии one-way traffic; правила уличного ~я traffic regulations. **4.** д. по службе promotion, advancement. **5.** impulse.

движимост|ь, и, *f.* movables, chattels; personal property.

движим|ый, *pres. part. pass. of* двигать *and adj.* **1.** (*part.*) moved, prompted, activated. **2.** (*adj.*) movable; ~ое имущество movable, personal property.

движител|ь, я, *m.* (*tech.*) mover.

движ|óк, ка, *m.* **1.** (*tech.*) slide, runner. **2.** (wooden) shovel. **3.** (*coll.*) (small) engine, motor.

движущ|ий, *pres. part. act. of* двигать *and adj.*; ~ие силы driving force.

дви|нуть, ну, нешь, *pf.* **1.** *pf. of* ~гать. **2.** (*coll.*) to hit, cosh.

дви|нуться, нусь, нешься, *pf. of* ~гаться.

двóе, двойх, *num.* **1.** (+*m.* *nouns denoting persons, personal pronouns in pl. or nouns used only in pl.*) two; д. сыновéй two sons; нас было д. there were two of us; д. санéй two sledges; д. суток forty-eight hours. **2.** (+*nouns denoting objects usually found in pairs*) two pairs; д. глаз two pairs of eyes; д. чулóк two pairs of stockings; на свойх (на) двойх on Shanks's pony.

двоебрáчи|е, я, *n.* bigamy.

двоевлáсти|е, я, *n.* diarchy.

двоедуши|е, я, *n.* duplicity.

двоедуш|ный (~ен, ~на), *adj.* two-faced.

двоежéн|ец, ца, *m.* bigamist (*of a man*).

двоежéнств|о, а, *n.* bigamy (*of man*).

двоемужи|е, я, *n.* bigamy (*of woman*).

двоемужниц|а, ы, *f.* bigamist (*of a woman*).

двоетóчи|е, я, *n.* (*gram.*) colon.

дво|йть, ю, йшь, *impf.* **1.** to double. **2.** to divide in two. **3.** (*chem.*) to rectify, distil. **4.** to plough a second time.

дво|йться, юсь, йшься, *impf.* **1.** to divide in two (*intrans.*). **2.** to appear double; у негó ~йлось в глазáх he saw (objects) double.

двойчн|ый, *adj.* (*math.*) binary; ~ая автоматическая вычислительная машина binary computer; ~ая цифра binary digit, bit.

двóйк|а, и, *f.* **1.** (*figure*) two. **2.** (*coll.*) No. 2 (*bus, tram, etc.*). **3.** 'two' (*out of five, according to marking system used in Russian educational establishments*). **4.** (*cards*) two; д. треф two of clubs. **5.** pair-oar (*boat*).

двойник, á, *m.* **1.** (a person's) double. **2.** (*coll.*) twin.

двойн|óй, *adj.* double, twofold, binary; д. подбородок double chin; ~áя бухгалтéрия double-entry book-keeping; вести ~ую игру to play a double game.

двó|йня, йни, *g. pl.* ~ен, *f.* twins.

двойняшк|а, и, *f.* **1.** (*coll.*) twin. **2.** twin, double (*e.g. two trees growing together*).

двóйственност|ь, и, *f.* **1.** duality. **2.** duplicity.

двóйствен|ный (~, ~на), *adj.* **1.** dual; ~ное числó (*gram.*) dual number. **2.** two-faced. **3.** bipartite.

двойчáтк|а, и, *f.* twin kernel, philippine.

двор, á, *m.* **1.** yard, court, courtyard. **2.** (peasant) homestead. **3.** скотный д. farmyard; птичий д. poultry-yard. **4.** на ~é out of doors, outside; по ~áм, ко ~áм (*obs.*) to one's home, home(wards); со ~á (*obs.*) from home. **5.** (royal) court; при ~é at court. **6.** быть ко ~у to be (found) suitable; быть не ко ~у not to be wanted.

двор|éц, ца, *m.* palace; Д. бракосочетáния Wedding Palace.

дворéцк|ий, ого, *m.* butler, major-domo.

двóрник, а, *m.* **1.** dvornik; yardman. **2.** (*coll.*) windscreen-wiper.

двóрницк|ий, *adj. of* дворник 1; *as noun* ~ая, ~ой, *f.* dvornik's lodge.

двóрничих|а, и, *f.* (*coll.*) **1.** wife of dvornik. **2.** yardwoman.

двóрн|я, и, *f.* (*collect.*) servants, menials (*before 1861*).

дворня́г|а, и, *f.* (*coll.*) mongrel (dog).

дворня́жк|а, и, *f.* = дворня́га.

дворóв|ый, *adj.* **1.** *adj. of* двор 1, 2; ~ые постройки outbuildings, farm buildings; ~ая собáка watch-dog. **2.** ~ые люди house-serfs; *as noun* д., ~ого, *m.*; ~ая, ~ой, *f.* house-serf.

дворцóв|ый, *adj. of* дворéц; д. переворóт palace revolution.

дворян|йн, йна, *pl.* **~е, ~,** *m.* nobleman, member of the gentry.

дворян|ка, ки, *f. of* дворянйн.

дворянск|ий, *adj.* of the nobility; of the gentry; **~ое звание** the rank of gentleman.

дворянств|о, а, *n.* (*collect.*) nobility, gentry.

двоюродный, *adj.* related through grandparent; **д. брат** (first) cousin (*male*); **д. дядя** (first) cousin once removed.

двоякий, *adj.* double, two-fold.

двояко, *adv.* in two ways.

двояковогнутый, *adj.* (*phys.*) concavo-concave.

двояковыпуклый, *adj.* (*phys.*) convexo-convex.

дву-, двух- bi-, di-, two-, double-.

двубортный, *adj.* double-breasted.

двуглав|ый, *adj.* two-headed; **~ая мышца** (*anat.*) biceps; **д. орёл** double-headed eagle.

двуглас|ный, ого, *m.* (*gram.*) diphthong.

двугорбый, *adj.* having two humps.

двугранный, *adj.* two-sided; dihedral.

двугривенн|ый, ого, *m.* (*coll.*) twenty-kopeck piece.

двудольный, *adj.* **1.** two-part. **2.** (*bot.*) dicotyledonous.

двудомный, *adj.* (*bot.*) diclinous.

двужильный, *adj.* **1.** (*coll.*) strong; hardy, tough. **2.** (*tech.*) twin-core.

двузначный, *adj.* two-digit.

двузубый, *adj.* two-prong, two-tine.

двуколк|а, и, *f.* two-wheeled cart.

двуконный, *adj.* two-horse.

двукопытный, *adj.* cloven-footed.

двукратный, *adj.* twofold, double; reiterated.

двукрыл|ый, *adj.* dipterous; *as noun* **~ые, ~ых** (*zool.*) Diptera.

двулик|ий (~, ~а), *adj.* two-faced (*also fig.*).

двуличи|е, я, *n.* double-dealing, duplicity.

двуличност|ь, и, *f.* duplicity.

двулич|ный (~ен, ~на), *adj.* (*fig.*) two-faced; hypocritical.

двунадесятый = **дванадесятый.**

двуногий, *adj.* two-legged, biped.

двуокис|ь, и, *f.* (*chem.*) dioxide.

двуперсти|е, я, *n.* (*eccl.*) making the sign of the cross with two fingers (*as done by the Old Believers*).

двуперст(н)ый, *adj.* (*eccl.*) two-fingered; with two fingers (*of making the sign of the cross*).

двупланный, *adj.* two-dimensional.

двуполый, *adj.* bisexual.

двуполь|е, я, *n.* (*agric.*) two-field rotation of crops.

двурог|ий, *adj.* two-horned; **~ая луна** crescent moon.

двуручный, *adj.* two-handed; two-handled.

двурушник, а, *m.* double-dealer.

двурушнича|ть, ю, *impf.* to play a double game.

двурушничеств|о, а, *n.* double dealing.

двусветный, *adj.* with two tiers of windows.

двускат|ый, *adj.* with two sloping surfaces; **~ая крыша** gable roof.

двусложный, *adj.* disyllabic.

двусменный, *adj.* in two shifts, two-shift.

двусмысленност|ь, и, *f.* **1.** ambiguity. **2.** ambiguous expression, double entendre.

двусмыслен|ный (~, ~на), *adj.* ambiguous.

двуспальный, *adj.* double (*of beds*).

двуствол|а, и, *f.* double-barrelled gun.

двуствольный, *adj.* double-barrelled.

двустворчат|ый, *adj.* bivalve; **~ые двери** folding doors.

двустиши|е, я, *n.* (*lit.*) distich, couplet.

двустопный, *adj.* (*lit.*) of two feet (*verse*).

двусторон|ий, *adj.* **1.** double-sided; **~ее воспаление лёгких** double pneumonia. **2.** two-way. **3.** bilateral; **~ее соглашение** bilateral agreement.

двутавров|ый, *adj.*; **~ая балка** I-beam.

двууглекисл|ый, *adj.* (*chem.*) bicarbonate; **д. натр, ~ая сода** sodium bicarbonate.

двуутроб|а, и, *f.* (*zool.*) marsupial.

двухатомный, *adj.* diatomic.

двухвёрстк|а, и, *f.* (*coll.*) map on scale of two versts to the inch.

двухвёрстный, *adj.* **1.** two versts in length. **2.** in proportion of two versts to the inch.

двухвесельный, *adj.* pair-oar.

двухгодичный, *adj.* of two years' duration.

двухгодовалый, *adj.* two-year-old.

двухдневный, *adj.* of two days.

двухдюймовый, *adj.* two-inch.

двухквартирный, *adj.* containing two flats.

двухколейный, *adj.* (*railways*) double-track.

двухколёсный, *adj.* two-wheeled.

двухкрасочный, *adj.* two-tone.

двухлемешный, *adj.*; **д. плуг** two-share plough.

двухлетний, *adj.* **1.** of two years' duration. **2.** two-year-old. **3.** (*bot.*) biennial.

двухлетник, а, *m.* (*bot.*) biennial.

двухмачтовый, *adj.* two-masted.

двухместн|ый, *adj.* two-seater; **~ая каюта** two-berth cabin.

двухмесячный, *adj.* **1.** of two months' duration. **2.** two-month-old. **3.** (*of periodicals, etc.*) appearing every two months.

двухмоторный, *adj.* twin-engined.

двухнедельник, а, *m.* (*coll.*) fortnightly (*magazine, etc.*).

двухнедельный, *adj.* **1.** of two weeks' duration. **2.** two-week-old. **3.** (*of publications*) fortnightly.

двухпалатный, *adj.* (*polit.*) bicameral, two-chamber.

двухпалубный, *adj.* (*naut.*) having two decks.

двухпарти́йный, *adj.* (*polit.*) two-party.

двухря́дный, *adj.* double-row.

двухсо́тенный, *adj.* (*coll.*) costing two hundred roubles.

двухсотле́ти|е, я, *n.* bicentenary.

двухсотле́тний, *adj.* 1. of two hundred years' duration. 2. bicentenary.

двухсо́тый, *adj.* two-hundredth.

двухстепе́нн|ый, *adj.*; ~ые вы́боры indirect elections.

двухсу́точный, *adj.* forty-eight-hour.

двухта́ктный, *adj.* (*tech.*) two-stroke.

двухто́мник, а, *m.* (*coll.*) two-volume book, work.

двухты́сячный, *adj.* 1. two-thousandth. 2. costing two thousand roubles.

двухцве́тный, *adj.* two-coloured.

двухчасово́й, *adj.* 1. two-hour. 2. (*coll.*) two o'clock.

двухъя́русный, *adj.* two-tier(ed).

двухэта́жный, *adj.* two-storeyed; double--deck.

двучле́н, а, *m.* (*math.*) binomial.

двучле́нный, *adj.* (*math.*) binomial.

двуязы́чи|е, я, *n.* bilingualism.

двуязы́ч|ный (~ен, ~на), *adj.* bilingual.

де (*coll.*) *enclitic particle indicating attribution of utterance to another speaker*: они́-де не мо́гут прийти́ (they say) they can't come.

дебаркаде́р, а, *m.* 1. landing-stage. 2. (*obs.*) platform (*on railway station*).

дебати́р|овать, ую, *impf.* to debate.

деба́т|ы, ов, *no sing.* debate.

дебе́л|ый (~, а), *adj.* (*coll.*) plump, corpulent.

де́бет, а, *m.* debit.

дебет|ова́ть, у́ю, *impf. and pf.* to debit.

деби́т, а, *m.* (*tech.*) yield, output (*of oil, etc.*).

дебито́р, а, *m.* debtor.

деблоки́р|овать, ую, *impf. and pf.* (*mil.*) to relieve, raise the blockade (of).

дебо́ш, а, *m.* (*coll.*) riot; uproar, shindy.

дебоши́р, а, *m.* (*coll.*) rowdy, brawler.

дебоши́р|ить, ю, ишь, *impf.* (*coll.*) to kick up a row, create a shindy.

дебоши́рств|о, а, *n.* (*coll.*) rowdyism.

де́бр|и, ей, *no sing.* 1. jungle; thickets. 2. the wilds. 3. (*fig.*) maze, labyrinth; запу́таться в ~ях (+*g.*) to get bogged down in.

дебю́т, а, *m.* 1. début. 2. (*chess*) opening.

дебюта́нт, а, *m.* débutant.

дебюта́нтк|а, и, *f.* débutante.

дебюти́р|овать, ую, *impf. and pf.* to make one's début.

дебю́т|ный, *adj.* of ~; д. спекта́кль (*theatr.*) début, first performance; д. ход (*chess*) opening move.

де́в|а, ы, *f.* 1. (*obs.*) girl, maiden; unmarried girl; ста́рая д. (*coll.*) old maid. 2. Д. (*rel.*) the Virgin. 3. Д. (*astron.*) Virgo.

девалориза́ци|я, и, *f.* debunking.

девальва́ци|я, и, *f.* (*econ.*) devaluation.

дева́|ть, ю 1. *impf. of* деть. 2. (*in past tense =* деть) to put, do (with); куда́ ты ~л письмо́? what have you done with the letter?

дева́|ться, юсь 1. *impf. of* де́ться; она́ не зна́ла, куда́ д. от смуще́ния she did not know where to put herself for embarrassment. 2. (*in past tense =* де́ться) to get to, disappear; куда́ ~лись мои́ часы́? where has my watch got to?

де́вер|ь, я, *pl.* ~ья́, ~ей *and* ~ьёв (*coll.*) brother-in-law (*husband's brother*).

девиа́ци|я, и, *f.* (*tech.*) deviation.

деви́з, а, *m.* motto; device (*in heraldry*).

деви́з|а, ы, *f.* bill of exchange (*cheque, etc.*) payable in foreign currency.

деви́ц|а, ы, *f.* (*obs.*) unmarried woman, spinster; girl; в ~ах unmarried, before marriage.

деви́ческий = де́вичий.

деви́честв|о, а, *n.* girlhood; spinsterhood.

де́ви́ч|ий, *adj.* girlish; maidenly; ~ья фами́лия maiden name; ~ья па́мять (*joc.*) a memory like a sieve; ~ья ко́жа (*pharm.*) althea paste.

деви́чник, а, *m.* (*ethnol.*) party for girls given by a bride on the eve of her wedding.

де́вичь|я, ей, *f.* (*obs.*) maid-servants' work--room.

де́вк|а, и, *f.* 1. (*coll. and dial.*) girl, wench, lass; засиде́ться в ~ах to remain a long time unmarried; оста́ться в ~ах to become an old maid. 2. (*coll.*) tart, whore.

Девома́тер|ь, и, *f.* (*rel.*) the Virgin Mother.

дево́н, а, *m.* (*geol.*) Devonian period.

дево́нский, *adj.* (*geol.*) Devonian.

де́вочк|а, и, *f.* (little) girl.

де́вственник, а, *m.* virgin.

де́вственниц|а, ы, *f.* virgin.

де́вственност|ь, и, *f.* virginity; chastity; обе́т ~и vow of chastity.

де́вствен|ный (~, ~на), *adj.* 1. virgin; ~ная плева́ (*anat.*) hymen. 2. virginal, innocent. 3. (*fig.*) virgin; д. лес virgin forest.

де́вств|о, а, *n.* spinsterhood.

де́вушк|а, и, *f.* 1. (*unmarried*) girl. 2. (*obs.*) maid. 3. (*coll.; as mode of address to shop-assistant, etc.*) miss.

девча́т|а, ~, *no sing.* (*coll.*) girls.

девчо́нк|а, и, *f.* (*coll.*) 1. slut. 2. kid; slip of a girl.

девчу́рк|а, и, *f.* (*coll.*) little girl.

девчу́шк|а, и, *f.* (*coll.*) little girl.

девяно́ст|о, *g., d., i. and p.* а, *num.* ninety.

девяно́стый, *adj.* ninetieth.

девятерно́й, *adj.* ninefold.

де́вятер|о, ы́х, *num.* 1. (+*m. nouns denoting*

persons, personal pronouns in pl. or nouns used only in pl.) nine. **2.** (+*nouns denoting objects usually found in pairs*) nine pairs.

девятидесятый (*obs.*) = девяностый.

девятикратный, *adj.* ninefold.

девятилетний, *adj.* **1.** nine-year; of nine years' duration. **2.** nine-year-old.

девятисотый, *adj.* nine-hundredth.

девятк|а, **и**, *f.* **1.** (*figure*) nine. **2.** (*coll.*) No. 9 (*bus, tram, etc.*). **3.** (*coll.*) group of nine objects. **4.** (*cards*) nine.

девятнадцатый, *adj.* nineteenth.

девятнадцат|ь, **и**, *num.* nineteen.

девятый, *adj.* ninth; д. вал 'the ninth wave' (*symbol of impending danger*).

девят|ь, **и́**, *i.* **ью́**, *num.* nine.

девятьсот, **девятисот**, **девятистам**, **девятьюстами**, **о девятистах**, *num.* nine hundred.

девятью, *adv.* nine times.

дегазатор, **а**, *m.* decontaminator.

дегазационн|ый, *adj.* of дегазация; ~ая часть decontamination unit.

дегазаци|я, **и**, *f.* decontamination.

дегази́р|овать, **ую**, *impf. and pf.* to decontaminate.

дегенерат, **а**, *m.* degenerate.

дегенеративност|ь, **и**, *f.* degeneracy.

дегенерати́в|ный (~ен, ~на), *adj.* degenerate.

дегенераци|я, **и**, *f.* degeneration.

дегенери́р|овать, **ую**, *impf. and pf.* to degenerate.

дёг|оть, **тя**, *no pl.*, *m.* tar; ложка ~тя в бочке мёда a fly in the ointment.

деградаци|я, **и**, *f.* degradation.

деградир|овать, **ую**, *impf. and pf.* to become degraded.

дегтярн|ый, *adj.* tar; ~ая вода (*pharm.*) tar water; ~ое мыло coal-tar soap.

дегустатор, **а**, *m.* taster.

дегустаци|я, **и**, *f.* tasintg; д. вин wine-tasting.

дегусти́р|овать, **ую**, *impf. and pf.* to carry out a tasting (of).

дед, **а**, *m.* **1.** grandfather; (*pl.*; *fig.*) grandfathers, forefathers. **2.** (*coll.*; *as mode of address to an old man*) grand-dad, grandpa. **3.** д.-мороз Father Christmas, Santa Claus.

дедовский, *adj.* **1.** grandfather's. **2.** old-world; old-fashioned.

дедукти́вный, *adj.* deductive.

деду́кци|я, **и**, *f.* deduction.

дедуци́р|овать, **ую**, *impf. and pf.* to deduce.

дедушк|а, **и**, *m.* grandfather.

деепричасти|е, **я**, *n.* (*gram.*) gerund (*e.g.* читая, читавши).

деепричаст|ный, *adj.* of ~ие.

дееспособност|ь, **и**, *f.* **1.** energy, activity. **2.** (*leg.*) capability.

дееспособ|ный (~ен, ~на), *adj.* **1.** energetic, active. **2.** (*leg.*) capable.

деж|а́, **и́**, *pl.* ~и, ~ей, *f.* (*dial.*) vat.

дежу́р|ить, **ю**, **ишь**, *impf.* **1.** to be on duty. **2.** to be in constant attendance, not to leave one's post.

дежу́рк|а, **и**, *f.* **1.** duty room. **2.** pilot flame.

дежу́рн|ый, *adj.* **1.** duty; on duty; д. офицер (*mil.*) orderly officer; д. пункт (*mil.*) guard-room; ~ая аптека chemist's shop open after normal closing hour or on holiday. **2.** ~ое блюдо plat du jour. **3.** *as noun* д., ~ого, *m.*, ~ая, ~ой, *f.* man, woman on duty; кто д.? who is on duty?; д. по школе teacher on duty; д. по полётам (*aeron.*) duty pilot. **4.** *as noun* ~ая, ~ой, *f.* duty room.

дежу́рств|о, **а**, *n.* (being on) duty; расписание ~а rota, (*mil.*) roster; смениться с ~а to come off duty, be relieved.

дезабилье́, *indecl.*, *n.* déshabillé.

дезавуи́р|овать, **ую**, *impf. and pf.* to repudiate, disavow.

дезерти́р, **а**, *m.* deserter.

дезерти́р|овать, **ую**, *impf. and pf.* to desert.

дезерти́рств|о, **а**, *n.* desertion.

дезинсекционн|ый, *adj.* of дезинсекция; ~ые средства insecticides.

дезинсекци|я, **и**, *f.* insecticide.

дезинфекционный, *adj.* of дезинфекция.

дезинфекци|я, **и**, *f.* disinfection; (*coll.*) disinfectant.

дезинфици́р|овать, **ую**, *impf. and pf.* to disinfect.

дезинформаци|я, **и**, *f.* misinformation.

дезинформи́р|овать, **ую**, *impf. and pf.* to misinform.

дезодоратор, **а**, *m.* deodorant.

дезодораци|я, **и**, *f.* deodorization.

дезорганизаци|я, **и**, *f.* disorganization.

дезорганиз|овать, **у́ю**, *impf. and pf.* to disorganize.

дезориентаци|я, **и**, *f.* disorientation.

дезориенти́р|овать, **ую**, *impf. and pf.* to disorient; to cause to lose one's bearings, confuse.

дезориенти́р|оваться, **уюсь**, *impf. and pf.* to to lose one's bearings.

деи́зм, **а**, *m.* deism.

деи́ст, **а**, *m.* deist.

действенност|ь, **и**, *f.* efficacy; effectiveness.

действен|ный (~, ~на), *adj.* efficacious; effective.

действи|е, **я**, *n.* **1.** action, operation; activity; ввести в д. to bring into operation, bring into force. **2.** functioning (*of a machine etc.*). **3.** effect; action; под ~ем (+*g.*) under the influence (of); не оказывать никакого ~я to have no effect.

4. action (*of a story, etc.*); д. происходит во время первой мировой войны the action takes place during the First World War. **5.** act (*of a play*). **6.** (*math.*) operation.

действи́тельно, *adv.* really; indeed.

действи́тельност|ь, и, *f.* **1.** reality. **2.** realities; conditions, life; совреме́нная кита́йская д. present-day conditions in China; в ~и in reality, in fact. **3.** validity (*of a document*). **4.** efficacy (*of a medicine, etc.*).

действи́тел|ьный (~ен, ~ьна), *adj.* **1.** real, actual; true, authentic; ~ьное положе́ние веще́й the true state of affairs; э́то бы́ли его́ ~ьные слова́ these were his actual words; ~ьная слу́жба (*mil.*) active service; ~ьное число́ (*math.*) real number; д. член Акаде́мии нау́к (full) member of the Academy of Sciences. **2.** valid; удостовере́ние ~ьно на шесть ме́сяцев the licence is valid for six months. **3.** efficacious (*of a medicine, etc.*). **4.** (*tech.*) effective. **5.** д. зало́г (*gram.*) active voice.

де́йств|овать, ую, *impf.* **1.** (*impf. only*) to act; to work, function; to operate; телефо́н не ~ует the telephone is not working, is out of order; ~ует ли у больно́го кише́чник? are the patient's bowels open? **2.** (*pf.* по~) (на+*a.*) to affect, have an effect (upon), act (upon); лека́рство ~ует the medicine is taking effect; д. кому́-н. на не́рвы to get on someone's nerves. **3.** (*impf. only*) (+*i.*; *coll.*) to work, operate; to use; д. локтя́ми to use one's elbows.

де́йствующ|ий, *pres. part. act. of* де́йствовать *and adj.*; ~ая а́рмия army in the field; д. вулка́н active volcano; ~ее лицо́ (*i*) (*theatr., lit.*) character, (*ii*) active participant; ~ие ли́ца (*theatr.*) dramatis personae.

дека~ deca~.

де́к|а, и, *f.* (*mus.*) sounding-board.

декабри́ст, а, *m.* (*hist.*) Decembrist.

декабри́ст|ский, *adj. of* ~.

декабр|ь, я́, *m.* December.

дека́брь|ский, *adj. of* ~.

дека́д|а, ы, *f.* **1.** ten-day period. **2.** (ten-day) festival; д. молда́вской литерату́ры и иску́сства (Ten-day) Festival of Moldavian Literature and Art.

декада́нс, а, *m.* decadence.

декаде́нт, а, *m.* decadent.

декаде́нтский, *adj.* decadent.

декаде́нтств|о, а, *n.* decadence.

дека́дник, а, *m.* (*polit.*) ten-day campaign.

дека́д|ный, *adj. of* ~а.

декали́тр, а, *m.* decalitre.

декальки́р|овать, ую, *impf. and pf.* (*art*) to transfer.

декалькома́ни|я, и, *f.* transfer-making; transfer (*of a design on to glass, pottery, etc.*).

декаме́тр, а, *m.* decametre.

дека́н, а, *m.* dean (*of university*).

декана́т, а, *m.* **1.** office of dean (*of university*). **2.** dean's office (*building*).

дека́нств|о, а, *n.* (*of university*) duties of dean, deanship.

декатир|ова́ть, у́ю, *impf. and pf.* (*text.*) to sponge (*woollen cloth, to prevent shrinking*).

дека́э|др, а, *m.* (*math.*) decahedron.

деквалифика́ци|я, и, *f.* loss of professional skill.

де́кел|ь, я, *m.* (*typ.*) tympan.

декла́ма́тор, а, *m.* reciter, declaimer.

декла́ма́ци|я, и, *f.* recitation, declamation.

деклами́р|овать, ую, *impf.* (*of* про~) **1.** to recite, declaim. **2.** (*pejor.*) to rant.

деклара́ти́вност|ь, и, *f.* (*pejor.*) tendency to make pronouncements for effect, pretentiousness.

деклара́ти́в|ный (~ен, ~на), *adj.* **1.** declaratory; solemn. **2.** (*pejor.*) made for effect, pretentious.

деклара́ци|я, и, *f.* declaration.

деклари́р|овать, ую, *impf. and pf.* to declare, proclaim.

декласси́рованный, *adj.* déclassé.

декови́льк|а, и, *f.* (*tech.*) tub (*on colliery railway, etc.*).

деко́кт, а, *m.* (*med.*; *obs.*) decoction.

декольте́, *indecl., n.* décolleté (*also as adj.*); décolletage.

декольти́рованный, *adj.* **1.** décolleté. **2.** bare(d).

декорати́в|ный (~ен, ~на), *adj.* decorative, ornamental.

декора́тор, а, *m.* decorator; scene-painter.

декора́ци|я, и, *f.* **1.** scenery, décor. **2.** (*fig.*) window-dressing.

декори́р|овать, ую, *impf. and pf.* to decorate.

деко́рум, а, *m.* decorum.

декре́т, а, *m.* decree.

декрети́р|овать, ую, *impf. and pf.* to decree.

декре́т|ный, *adj. of* ~; д. о́тпуск maternity leave.

декстри́н, а, *m.* (*chem.*) dextrine.

де́ланност|ь, и, *f.* artificiality; affectation.

де́ланный, *p.p.p. of* де́лать *and adj.* artificial, forced, affected.

де́ла|ть, ю, *impf.* (*of* с~) **1.** to make (= *to construct, produce*). **2.** to make (= *to cause to become*); д. кого́-н. несча́стным to make someone unhappy; д. из кого́-н. посме́шище to make a laughing-stock of someone. **3.** to do; д. не́чего there is nothing for it, it can't be helped; от не́чего д. for want of anything better to do; д. под себя́ to foul *or* wet one's bed. **4.** (+*var. nouns*) to make, do, give; д. вид to pretend, feign; д. вы́воды to draw conclusions; д. вы́говор (+*d.*) to reprimand; д. гла́зки

($+d$.; *coll.*) to make eyes (at); д. докла́д to give a report; д. комплиме́нт ($+d$.) to pay a compliment; д. предложе́ние ($+d$.) to propose (*marriage*) (to); д. уси́лия to make an effort; д. честь ($+d$.) (*i*) to honour, (*ii*) to do credit. **5.** (*of distance covered*) to do, make; д. два́дцать узло́в (*naut.*) to make twenty knots.

де́ла|ться, юсь, *impf.* (*of* с~) **1.** to become, get, grow. **2.** to happen; что там ~ется? what is going on?; что с ней ~ется? what is the matter with her? **3.** (*coll.*) to break out, appear.

делега́т, а, *m.* delegate.

делега́т|ский, *adj.* of ~.

делега́ци|я, и, *f.* delegation; group.

делеги́р|овать, ую, *impf. and pf.* to delegate.

делёж, а́, *m.* sharing, division; partition.

делёж|ка, ки, *f.* (*coll.*) = ~.

деле́ни|е, я, *n.* **1.** (*in var. senses*) division; д. кле́ток (*biol.*) cell-fission; знак ~я (*math.*) division sign. **2.** (*on graduated scale*) point, degree, unit.

дел|е́ц, ьца́, *m.* (*pejor.*) smart operator, person on the make.

деликате́с, а, *m.* dainty; delicacy.

делика́тнича|ть, ю, *impf.* (*coll.*) to be overnice; (с+*i*.) to treat unnecessarily softly, be too soft with someone.

делика́тност|ь, и, *f.* (*in var. senses*) delicacy.

делика́т|ный (~ен, ~на), *adj.* (*in var. senses*) delicate.

дели́м|ое, ого, *n.* (*math.*) dividend.

дели́мост|ь, и, *f.* divisibility.

дели́тел|ь, я, *m.* divisor.

дел|и́ть, ю́, ~ишь, *impf.* **1.** (*pf.* раз~) to divide; д. поровну to divide into equal parts; д. шесть на́ три to divide six by three. **2.** (*pf.* по~) (с+*i*.) to share (with); д. с кем-н. го́ре и ра́дость to share someone's sorrows and joys.

дел|и́ться, ю́сь, ~ишься, *impf.* **1.** (*pf.* раз~) (на+*a*.) to divide (into). ` **2.** (*impf. only*) (на+*a*.) to be divisible (by). **3.** (*pf.* по~) (+*i*., с+*i*.) to share (with); to communicate (to), impart (to); д. куско́м хле́ба с кем-н. to share a crust of bread with someone; д. ве́стью с кем-н. to impart news to someone; д. впечатле́ниями с кем-н. to compare notes with someone.

де́л|о, а, *pl.* ~а́, ~, ~а́м, *n.* **1.** business, affair(s); ме́жду ~ом (*coll.*) at odd moments, between times; по ~у, по ~а́м on business; э́то моё д. that is my affair; име́ть д. (с+*i*.) to have to do (with), deal (with); не вме́шивайтесь не в своё д. mind your own business; как (ва́ши) д.? how are things going (with you)?, how are you getting on?; за чем д. ста́ло? what's holding things up?; привести́ свои́ ~а́ в поря-

док to put one's affairs in order; без ~а не входи́ть no entry except on business; таки́е-то ~а́! (*coll.*) so that's how it is!; д. в шля́пе (*coll.*) it's in the bag; говори́ть д. to talk sense; вот э́то д.! (*coll.*) now you're talking!; д. за ва́ми it's up to you; како́е мне до э́того д.? what has this to do with me?; что тебе́ за д.? what does it matter to you?; пе́рвым ~ом in the first instance, first of all. **2.** cause; д. ми́ра the cause of peace; э́то д. его́ жи́зни it's his life's work. **3.** (+*adj.*) occupation; (*obs.*) business, concern; вое́нное д. soldiering; military science; го́рное д. mining. **4.** matter; point; д. вку́са matter of taste; д. привы́чки matter of habit; д. че́сти point of honour; д. в том, что... the point is that...; в то́м-то и д. that's (just) the point; не в э́том д. that's not the point; совсе́м друго́е д. quite another matter. **5.** fact, deed; thing; на са́мом ~е in actual fact, as a matter of fact; и на слова́х и на ~е in word and deed; на слова́х..., на ~е же in theory, nominally . . . but actually; в са́мом ~е really, indeed. **6.** (*leg.*) case; cause; вести́ д. to plead a cause; возбуди́ть д. (про́тив) to bring an action (against), institute proceedings (against). **7.** file, dossier; ли́чное д. personal file; приложи́ть к ~у to file. **8.** battle, fighting. **9.** *idiomatic phrases*: то и д. continually, time and again; то ли д. (*coll.*) what a difference (*how much better*).

делови́тост|ь, и, *f.* business-like character, efficiency.

делови́т|ый (~, ~а), *adj.* business-like, efficient.

делов|о́й, *adj.* **1.** business; work; ~о́е письмо́ business letter; ~а́я пое́здка business trip; ~о́е вре́мя working time. **2.** business-like.

делопроизводи́тел|ь, я, *m.* chief clerk; д. шко́лы school secretary.

делопроизво́дств|о, а, *n.* office work, clerical work; record keeping.

де́льн|о, *adv. of* ~ый; говори́ть д. to talk sense.

де́льн|ый, *adj.* **1.** business-like, efficient. **2.** sensible, practical; ~ое предложе́ние sensible suggestion.

де́льт|а, ы, *f.* delta.

дельтови́дн|ый, *adj.* delta-shaped; д. самолёт delta-wing aircraft; ~ая мы́шца (*anat.*) deltoid muscle.

дельфи́н, а, *m.* dolphin.

де́льц|е, а, *n.* (*dim. of* де́ло) job.

деля́г|а, и, *m.* **1.** (*coll.*) person pursuing his own interests. **2.** (*obs.*) good worker.

деля́нк|а, и, *f.* plot (of land); piece (of woodland).

деля́ческий, *adj.* narrow-minded, narrowly pragmatic (*not related to moral or philosophical principle*).

деля́честв|о, а, *n.* narrow-mindedness, narrowly pragmatic attitude.

демаго́г, а, *m.* demagogue.

демагоги́ческий, *adj.* demagogic.

демаго́ги|я, и, f. demagogy.

демаркацио́нн|ый, *adj.*; ~ая ли́ния line of demarcation.

демарка́ци|я, и, f. demarcation.

демаски́р|овать, ую, *impf. and pf.* (*mil.*) to unmask.

демикото́н, а, *m.* (*text.*) jean.

демилитариза́ци|я, и, f. demilitarization.

демилитаризи́р|овать, ую, *impf. and pf.* to demilitarize.

демисезо́нн|ый, *adj.*; ~ое пальто́ light overcoat (*for spring and autumn wear*).

демиу́рг, а, *m.* demiurge, creator.

демобилизацио́нный, *adj.* demobilization.

демобилиза́ци|я, и, f. demobilization.

демобилиз|ова́ть, у́ю, *impf. and pf.* to demobilize.

демогра́фи|я, и, f. demography.

демокра́т, а, *m.* 1. democrat. 2. plebeian.

демократиза́ци|я, и, f. democratization.

демократизи́р|овать, ую, *impf. and pf.* to democratize.

демократи́зм, а, *m.* democratism.

демократи́ческий, *adj.* 1. democratic. 2. plebeian.

демокра́ти|я, и, f. democracy; стра́ны наро́дной ~и the People's Democracies. 2. the common people, lower classes.

де́мон, а, *m.* demon.

демони́ческий, *adj.* demonic, demoniacal.

демоноло́ги|я, и, f. demonology.

демонстра́нт, а, *m.* (*polit.*) demonstrator.

демонстрати́в|ный (~ен, ~на), *adj.* 1. demonstrative, done for effect. 2. demonstration; ~ная ле́кция demonstration lecture. 3. (*mil.*) feint, decoy.

демонстра́тор, а, *m.* demonstrator.

демонстра́ци|я, и, f. 1. (*in var. senses*) demonstration. 2. (public) showing (*of a film, etc.*). 3. (*mil.*) feint, manœuvre.

демонстри́р|овать, ую, *impf. and pf.* 1. to demonstrate, make a demonstration. 2. (*pf. also* про~) to show, display; to give a demonstration (of); д. но́вый кинофи́льм to show a new film.

демонта́ж, а, *m.* (*tech.*) dismantling.

демонти́р|овать, ую, *impf. and pf.* (*tech.*) to dismantle.

деморализа́ци|я, и, f. demoralization.

деморализ|ова́ть, у́ю, *impf. and pf.* to demoralize.

де́мос, а, *m.* (*hist.*) the people, plebs.

де́мпинг, а, *m.* (*econ.*) dumping.

де́мпфер, а, *m.* (*tech.*) damper; shock absorber.

денатурализа́ци|я и, f. (*leg.*) denaturalization.

денатурализ|ова́ть, у́ю, *impf. and pf.* (*leg.*) to denaturalize.

денатура́т, а, *m.* methylated spirits.

денатури́р|овать, ую, *impf. and pf.* (*chem.*) to denature.

денационализа́ци|я, и, f. 1. (*polit.*) denationalization. 2. loss *or* suppression of national characteristics.

денационализи́р|овать, ую, *impf. and pf.* (*polit.*) to denationalize.

денацифика́ци|я, и, f. denazification.

денацифици́р|овать, ую, *impf. and pf.* to denazify.

де́нди, *indecl., m.* dandy.

дендри́т, а, *m.* (*anat., min.*) dendrite.

дендроло́ги|я, и, f. dendrology.

де́нежк|а, и, f. 1. (*obs.*) half-kopeck coin. 2. *usu. pl.* (*coll.*) money; пла́кали на́ши ~и that's our money down the drain.

де́нежный, *adj.* 1. monetary; money; д. знак bank-note; д. перево́д money order; д. ры́нок money-market; д. штраф fine; д. я́щик strong-box. 2. (*coll.*) moneyed; д. челове́к a man of means.

ден|ёк, ька́, m., *dim. of* день.

денни́к, а́, *m.* (*dial.*) loose box.

денни́ц|а, ы, f. (*poet.*) 1. dawn. 2. morning star.

де́нно, *adv.*; д. и но́щно day and night.

денно́й, *adj.* (*obs.*) day, daylight.

деномина́ци|я, и, f. (*econ.*) denomination.

денонса́ци|я, и, f. (*dipl.*) denouncement.

денонси́р|овать, ую, *impf. and pf.* (*dipl.*) to denounce.

денти́н, а, *m.* (*anat.*) dentine.

денщи́к, а́, *m.* (*mil.*) batman.

день, дня, *m.* 1. day; afternoon; в 4 ч. дня at 4 p.m.; днём in the afternoon; д.-деньско́й all day long; д. рожде́ния birthday; д. откры́тых двере́й open day; д. за д. day by day; д. ото дня with every passing day, day by day; в оди́н прекра́сный д. one fine day; во дни о́ны in those days; изо дня в д. day after day; на друго́й, сле́дующий д. next day; на дню (*obs.*) in the course of the day; на днях (i) the other day, (ii) one of these days, any day now; не по дням, а по часа́м hourly, fast, rapidly; со дня на́ д. daily, from day to day; че́рез д. every other day, on alternate days. 2. (*pl.*) days (= (i) *time, period,* (ii) *life*); его́ дни сочтены́ his days are numbered.

ден|ьги, ег, ьгам *or* **ьга́м,** *sing.* (*coll.*) ~ьга́, ~ьги́, f. money; ме́лкие д. small change; нали́чные д. cash, ready money; при ~ьга́х in funds; не при ~ьга́х hard up.

деньжа́т|а, ~, *no sing.* (*coll.*) money, cash.
деньжо́н|ки, ок, *no sing.* (*coll.*) money, cash.
департа́мент, а, *m.* department.
депе́ш|а, и, *f.* 1. dispatch. 2. (*obs.*) telegram.
депо́, *indecl.*, *n.* (*railways*) depot; shed, roundhouse; пожа́рное д. fire-station.
депо́в|ец, ца, *m.* engine-shed worker.
депо́вский, *adj. of* депо́.
депози́т, а, *m.* (*fin.*) deposit.
депози́тор, а, *m.* (*fin.*) depositor.
деполяриза́ци|я, и, *f.* (*phys.*) depolarization.
депоне́нт, а, *m.* (*fin.*) depositor.
депони́р|овать, ую, *impf. and pf.* (*fin.*, *leg.*) to deposit.
депресси́вн|ый, *adj. of* депре́ссия; д. пери́од (*econ.*) depression, slump; ~ое состоя́ние (*econ. and psych.*) depression.
депре́сси|я, и, *f.* 1. (*econ.*) depression, slump. 2. (*psych.*) depression.
депута́т, а, *m.* deputy; delegate; пала́та ~ов Chamber of Deputies.
депута́ци|я, и, *f.* deputation.
дёр, у, *m.* (за)да́ть ~у (*coll.*) to take to one's heels.
дератиза́ци|я, и, *f.* rodent control.
де́рби, *indecl.*, *n.* (*sport*) Derby.
де́рвиш, а, *m.* dervish.
дёрга|ть, ю, *impf.* (*of* дёрнуть) 1. to pull, tug; д. кого́-н. за рука́в to tug at someone's sleeve, pluck by the sleeve. 2. to pull out; д. зу́бы (*i*) to pull out teeth, (*ii*) to have teeth out (*at the dentist's*); д. лён to pull flax. 3. (*impf. only*) to harass, pester. 4. (*impf. only*) (*coll.*) to cause to twitch; (*impers.*) to twitch; его́ всего́ ~ло he was twitching all over. 5. (*impf. only*) (+*i.*; *coll.*) to move sharply, jerk; д. плеча́ми to shrug one's shoulders.
дёрга|ться, юсь, *impf.* (*of* дёрнуться) 1. *pass. of* ~ть. 2. to twitch; рот у него́ непреста́нно ~ется his mouth twitches incessantly.
дерга́ч[1], а́, *m.* (*orn.*) landrail, corncrake.
дерга́ч[2], а́, *m.* (*tech.*) nail extractor.
деревене́|ть, ю, *impf.* (*of* о~) to grow stiff, numb.
дереве́нский, *adj.* 1. village. 2. rural, country.
дереве́нщин|а, ы, *m. and f.* (*coll.*) (country) bumpkin.
дере́в|ня, ни, *g. pl.* ~е́нь, *f.* 1. village. 2. (the) country (*as opp. to the town*).
де́рев|о, а, *pl.* ~ья, ~ьев, *n.* 1. tree; за ~ьями ле́са не ви́деть not to see the wood for the trees. 2. (*sing. only*) wood (*as material*).
де́рево-земляно́й, *adj.* (*mil.*) earth-and-timber.
деревообде́лочник, а, *m.* woodworker.

деревообде́лочный, *adj.* wood-working.
деревообрабо́тк|а, и, *f.* woodworking (industry).
дереву́шк|а, и, *f.* hamlet.
де́ревц|е, а *and* деревц|о́, а́, *n.* sapling.
деревяни́ст|ый (~, ~а), *adj.* 1. ligneous. 2. hard (*of fruit, etc.*).
деревя́нн|ый, *adj.* 1. wood; wooden. 2. (*fig.*) wooden; expressionless, dead; dull; ~ое выраже́ние лица́ wooden expression; д. го́лос expressionless voice. 3. ~ое ма́сло lamp-oil (*low-grade olive oil*).
деревя́шк|а, и, *f.* 1. piece of wood. 2. (*coll.*) wooden leg.
держа́в|а, ы, *f.* 1. (*polit.*) power; вели́кие ~ы the Great Powers. 2. (*hist.*) orb (*as emblem of monarchy*).
держа́вный, *adj.* 1. holding supreme power, sovereign. 2. powerful.
держа́лк|а, и, *f.* (*coll.*) handle.
де́ржаный, *adj.* (*coll.*) used, worn, second-hand.
держа́тел|ь, я, *m.* 1. (*fin.*) holder. 2. bracket; socket; holder.
держ|а́ть, у́, ~ишь, *impf.* 1. to hold; to hold on to; ~и́те во́ра! stop thief! 2. to hold up, support. 3. (*in var. senses*) to keep, hold; д. в посте́ли to keep in bed; д. банк (*card-games*) to be banker; д. курс (на+*a.*) to hold course (for), head (for); (*fig.*) to head (for), make (for); д. пари́ to bet; д. чью́-н. сто́рону to take someone's side; д. язы́к за зуба́ми to hold one's tongue; д. в ку́рсе to keep posted; д. в неве́дении to keep in the dark; д. в плену́ to hold prisoner. 4. to keep (= *to own, possess*); д. лошаде́й to keep horses. 5. д. себя́ to behave. 6. +*certain nouns* = to carry out: д. корректу́ру to read proofs; д. речь to make a speech; д. экза́мен to sit, take an examination.
держ|а́ться, у́сь, ~ишься, *impf.* 1. (за+*a.*) to hold (on to); ~и́тесь за пери́ла hold on to the banister. 2. (на+*p.*) to be held up (by), be supported (by); д. на ни́точке to hang by a thread (*also fig.*). 3. to keep, stay, be; д. вме́сте to stick together; д. в стороне́ to hold aloof. 4. to hold oneself; (*fig.*) to behave. 5. to last; to hold together; у неё всё ещё ~ится америка́нский акце́нт she still retains her American accent; э́тот стол у вас е́ле ~ится this table of yours is on its last legs. 6. to hold out, stand firm; to hold one's ground. 7. (+*g.*) to keep (to); д. ле́вой стороны́ to keep to the left; д. бе́рега to hug the shore. 8. (+*g.*) to adhere (to), stick (to); д. те́мы to stick to the subject; д. убежде́ний to have the courage of one's convictions. 9. то́лько ~и́сь! (*interj.*) and how!

дерза́ни|е, я, *n*. daring.

дерз|а́ть, а́ю, *impf.* (*of* ~ну́ть) to dare.

дерз|и́ть, (у́), и́шь, *impf.* (*of* на~) (+*d.*; *coll.*) to be impertinent (to), cheek.

дёрз|кий (~ок, ~ка́, ~ко), *adj.* 1. impertinent, cheeky. 2. daring, audacious.

дерзнове́ни|е, я, *n*. (*obs.*) audacity.

дерзнове́н|ный (~ен, ~на), *adj.* 1. (*obs.*) impertinent, insolent. 2. daring, audacious.

дерзн|у́ть, у́, ёшь, *pf. of* дерза́ть.

де́рзост|ный (~ен, ~на), *adj.* (*obs.*) = дёрзкий.

де́рзост|ь, и, *f*. 1. impertinence; cheek; rudeness; говори́ть ~и to be impertinent, cheeky, rude. 2. daring, audacity.

дерива́т, а, *m*. (*tech.*) derivative.

дерива́ци|я, и, *f*. 1. (*mil.*) drift. 2. (*math.*) derivation. 3. canalization.

дермати́н, а, *m*. leatherette.

дермати́т, а, *m*. dermatitis.

дермато́лог, а, *m*. dermatologist.

дерматоло́ги|я, и, *f*. dermatology.

дёрн, а, *m*. turf.

дерни́н|а, ы, *f*. (a) turf, sod.

дерни́ст|ый (~, ~а), *adj.* turfy.

дерн|ова́ть, у́ю, *impf.* to cover with turf; to make a turf edging round.

дерно́вый, *adj. of* дёрн.

дёрн|уть, у, ешь, *pf.* 1. *pf. of* дёргать; чёрт ~ет (~ул), нелёгкая ~ет (~ула) *or* (*impers.*) ~ет (~уло) кого́-н. (+*inf.*; *coll.*) to be possessed (to do something); чёрт меня́ ~ул дать сло́во I don't know what possessed me to promise. 2. to get going, get cracking. 3. (*coll.*) to go off. 4. (*coll.*) to drink up; to take a swig. 5. (*coll.*) to start vigorously to do something; д. плясову́ю to strike up a (dance) tune.

дёрн|уться, усь, ешься, *pf.* (*of* дёргаться) to start up (with a jerk), to dart.

дер|у́, ёшь, *see* драть.

дерьм|о́, а́, *n*. (*vulg.*) dung, muck (*also fig.*).

дерю́г|а, и, *f*. sackcloth, sacking.

дерю́жный, *adj.* sackcloth.

деря́бн|уть, у, ешь, *pf.* (*sl.*) 1. to make (= *to acquire by sharp practice*). 2. to drink up.

деса́нт, а, *m*. (*mil.*) 1. (*airborne or amphibious*) landing; д. с бо́ем opposed landing. 2. landing force.

деса́нтный, *adj.* (*mil.*) landing.

дёсенный, *adj.* (*anat.*) gingival.

десе́рт, а, *m*. dessert.

десе́рт|ный, *adj. of* ~; ~ная ло́жка dessert spoon; ~ное вино́ sweet wine.

де́скать, *particle indicating reported speech* (*coll.*): она́, д., ничего́ подо́бного не хоте́ла сказа́ть she said she had not meant anything of the kind.

десн|а́, ы́, *pl.* ~ы, дёсен, *f*. (*anat.*) gum.

десни́ц|а, ы, *f*. (*obs. or poet.*) right hand.

де́спот, а, *m*. despot.

деспоти́зм, а, *m*. despotism.

деспоти́ческий, *adj.* despotic.

деспоти́ч|ный (~ен, ~на), *adj.* despotic.

деспоти́|я, и, *f*. despotism.

дест|ь, и, *g. pl.* ~е́й, *f*. quire (*of paper*) (ру́сская д. = 24 sheets; метри́ческая д. = 50 sheets).

десятери́к, а́, *m*. measure *or* object containing ten units.

десятери́чн|ый, *adj.* (*obs.*) tenfold; и ~ое name of letter 'i' in old Russian orthography.

десятерно́й, *adj.* tenfold.

де́сятер|о, ы́х, *num.* 1. (+*m. nouns denoting persons, personal pronouns in pl. or nouns used only in pl.*) ten. 2. (+*nouns denoting objects usually found in pairs*) ten pairs.

десятигра́нник, а, *m*. decahedron.

десятидне́вк|а, и, *f*. ten-day period.

десятизу́б|ый, *adj.*; ~ые ко́шки (*mountaineering*) crampons.

десятикилометро́вк|а, и, *f*. (*coll.*) map on scale of ten kilometres to the centimetre.

десятикра́тный, *adj.* tenfold.

десятиле́ти|е, я, *n*. 1. decade. 2. tenth anniversary.

десятиле́тк|а, и, *f*. ten-year (secondary) school.

десятиле́тний, *adj.* 1. ten-year, decennial. 2. ten-year-old.

десяти́н|а, ы, *f*. 1. desyatina (*land measure equivalent to* 2·7 *acres*). 2. tithe.

десятирублёвк|а, и, *f*. (*coll.*) ten-rouble note.

десятисло́жный, *adj.* (*lit.*) decasyllabic.

десятиуго́льник, а, *m*. (*math.*) decagon.

десяти́чн|ый, *adj.* decimal; ~ая дробь decimal fraction.

деся́тк|а, и, *f*. 1. (*figure*) ten. 2. (*coll.*) No. 10 (*bus, tram, etc.*). 3. (*coll.*) group of ten objects. 4. (*cards*) ten. 5. (*coll.*) ten-rouble note. 6. ten-oared boat.

деся́тник, а, *m*. (*obs.*) foreman.

деся́т|ок, ка, *m*. 1. ten. 2. ten years, decade (*of life*). 3. (*pl.*) (*math.*) tens. 4. (*pl.*) tens. 5. неро́бкого ~ка no coward.

деся́тск|ий, ого, *m*. (*hist.*) peasant policeman.

деся́т|ый, *num.* tenth; расска́зывать из пя́того в ~ое, с пя́того на ~ое to relate inconsequentially; э́то де́ло ~ое (*coll.*) it is of no consequence.

де́сят|ь, и́, ью́, *num.* ten.

де́сять, *adv.* ten times (*in multiplication*).

дет- *abbr. of* де́тский.

детализа́ци|я, и, *f*. working out in detail.

детализи́р|овать, ую *and* детализ|ова́ть, у́ю, *impf. and pf.* to work out in detail.

дета́л|ь, и, *f.* 1. detail. 2. part, component (*of a machine, etc.*).

дета́л|ьный (~ен, ~ьна), *adj.* detailed; minute.

детвор|а́, ы́, *no pl.*, *f.* (*collect.*; *coll.*) children.

детдо́м, а, *m.* (*abbr. of* де́тский дом) children's home.

детекти́в, а, *m.* 1. detective. 2. detective story.

детекти́вный, *adj.*; д. рома́н detective story.

дете́ктор, а, *m.* (*tech.*) detector; spark indicator.

детёныш, а, *m.* young (*of animals*; whelp, cub, calf, *etc.*).

детермини́зм, а, *m.* determinism.

детермини́ст, а, *m.* determinist.

дет|и, ~е́й, ~ям, ~ьми́, о ~ях, *sing.* дитя́, children; д. боя́рские, *see* боя́рский.

дети́н|а, ы, *m.* (*coll.*) big fellow, hefty chap.

дети́н|ец, ца, *m.* (*hist.*) citadel.

де́тищ|е, а, *g. pl.* ~, *n.* child, offspring; (*fig.*) child, creation.

де́тный, *adj.* (*coll.*) having children.

детона́тор, а, *m.* (*tech.*) detonator.

детона́ци|я, и, *f.* (*tech.*) detonation.

детони́р|овать¹, ую, *impf.* (*tech.*) to detonate.

детони́р|овать², ую, *impf.* to sing, play out of tune.

деторо́дный, *adj.* genital.

деторожде́ни|е, я, *n.* procreation.

детоуби́йств|о, а, *n.* infanticide (*action*).

детоуби́йц|а, ы, *m. and f.* infanticide (*agent*).

детри́т, а, *m.* 1. (*physiol.*) detritus. 2. vaccine.

детса́д, а, *m.* (*abbr. of* де́тский сад) kindergarten, nursery school.

де́тск|ая, ой, *f.* nursery.

де́тск|ий, *adj.* 1. child's, children's; д. дом children's home; д. сад kindergarten, nursery school; ~ая сме́ртность infantile mortality; ~ая ко́мната (*i*) = ~ая, (*ii*) room for mothers and children (*at railway station, etc.*), (*iii*) juvenile delinquents' room (*at police station*); ~ая коло́ния reformatory (school). 2. childish. 3. ~ое ме́сто (*anat.*) placenta.

де́тскост|ь, и, *f.* childishness.

де́тств|о, а, *n.* childhood; с ~а from childhood, from a child; впада́ть в д. to lapse into dotage.

деть, де́ну, де́нешь, *pf.* (*of* дева́ть) to put, do (with); куда́ ты дел моё перо́? what have you done with my pen?; не знать, куда́ глаза́ д. not to know where to look; э́того никуда́ не де́нешь there's no getting away from it, there's no disputing it.

де́|ться, нусь, нешься, *pf.* (*of* дева́ться) to get to, disappear.

де-фа́кто, *adv.* de facto.

дефе́кт, а, *m.* defect.

дефекти́в|ный (~ен, ~на), *adj.* defective; handicapped; д. ребёнок (mentally)

defective *or* (physically) handicapped child.

дефе́ктный, *adj.* imperfect, faulty.

дефекто́лог, а, *m.* specialist on mental defects and physical handicaps (*in children*).

дефектол|оги́ческий, *adj. of* ~о́гия.

дефектоло́ги|я, и, *f.* study of mental defects and physical handicaps (*in connexion with education of blind, spastic, etc., children*).

дефектоско́п, а, *m.* (*tech.*) fault detector.

дефектоскопи́|я, и, *f.* (*tech.*) fault detection.

дефиле́, *indecl.*, *n.* (*mil.*) defile.

дефили́р|овать, ую, *impf.* (*of* про~) to march past, go in procession.

дефини́ци|я, и, *f.* definition.

дефи́с, а, *m.* hyphen.

дефици́т, а, *m.* 1. (*econ.*) deficit. 2. shortage, deficiency; д. в то́пливе fuel shortage.

дефици́т|ный (~ен, ~на), *adj.* 1. (*econ.*) showing a loss. 2. in short supply; scarce.

дефля́ци|я, и, *f.* 1. (*econ.*) deflation. 2. (*geol.*) deflation, wind erosion.

деформа́ци|я, и, *f.* deformation.

деформи́р|овать, ую, *impf. and pf.* to deform; to transform.

деформи́р|оваться, уюсь, *impf. and pf.* to change one's shape; to become deformed.

дехка́н|ин, ина, *pl.* ~е, ~, *m.* peasant (*in Uzbekistan and Tadzhikistan*).

дехка́н|ский, *adj. of* ~ин.

децентрализа́ци|я, и, *f.* decentralization.

децентрализ|ова́ть, у́ю, *impf. and pf.* to decentralize.

деци- deci-.

децили́тр, а, *m.* decilitre.

децима́льный, *adj.* decimal.

дециме́тр, а, *m.* decimetre.

дешеве́|ть, ю, *impf.* (*of* по~) to fall in price, become cheaper.

дешеви́зн|а, ы́, *f.* cheapness; low price.

дешев|и́ть, лю́, и́шь, *impf.* (*coll.*) to underprice.

дешёвк|а, и, *f.* 1. low price; купи́ть по ~е to buy cheap. 2. sale at reduced prices; купи́ть на ~е (*coll.*) to buy at a sale. 3. (*fig.*) cheap stuff; worthless object.

деше́вле, *comp. of* дешёвый *or* дёшево; д. па́реной ре́пы dirt-cheap.

дёшево, *adv.* cheap, cheaply; (*fig.*) cheaply, lightly; д. да гни́ло cheap and nasty; д. и серди́то cheap but good; д. отде́латься to get off lightly; э́то вам д. не пройдёт this will cost you dear; д. остри́ть to make cheap jokes; д. сто́ить to be of no account.

дешёв|ый (дёшев, дешева́, дёшево), *adj.* 1. cheap. 2. (*fig.*) cheap; empty, worthless; ~ая острота́ cheap witticism.

дешифри́р|овать, ую, *impf. and pf.* to decipher, decode.

дешифро́вк|а, и, *f.* decipherment, de-ciphering, decoding.

де-ю́ре, *adv.* de jure.

дея́ни|е, я, *n.* (*obs. or rhet.*) act; action; Дея́ния апо́столов the Acts of the Apostles.

де́ятел|ь, я, *m.* agent; госуда́рственный д. statesman; обще́ственный д. public figure; заслу́женный д. иску́сства, нау́ки Honoured Artist, Scientist (*honorific title in U.S.S.R.*).

де́ятельност|ь, и, *f.* 1. activity, activities; work; обще́ственная д. public work; педагоги́ческая д. educational work, teaching. 2. (*physiol., psych., etc.*) activity, operation; д. се́рдца operation of the heart.

де́ятел|ьный (~ен, ~ьна), *adj.* active, energetic.

де́|яться, ется, *impf.* (*coll.*) to happen; что там ~ется? what's going on?

джаз, а, *m.* 1. jazz band. 2. jazz music.

джаз-ба́нд, а, *m.* jazz band.

джа́зовый, *adj.* jazz.

джем, а, *m.* jam.

дже́мпер, а, *m.* jumper.

джентльме́н, а, *m.* gentleman.

джентльме́нск|ий, *adj.* gentlemanly; ~ое соглаше́ние gentlemen's agreement.

джентльме́нств|о, а, *n.* gentlemanliness.

джерсе́ *and* дже́рси, *indecl., adj.* jersey (*material*).

джиги́т, а, *m.* Dzhigit (*Caucasian horseman*).

джигит|ова́ть, у́ю, *impf.* to engage in trick riding.

джигито́вк|а, и, *f.* trick riding (*originally by Caucasian horsemen*).

джин¹, а, *m.* gin (*liquor*).

джин², а, *m.* (*tech.*) (cotton-)gin.

джингои́зм, а, *m.* jingoism.

джи́у-джи́тсу, *indecl., n.* ju-jutsu.

джо́нк|а, и, *f.* junk (*Chinese sailing vessel*).

джо́ул|ь, я, *g. pl.* ~ей, *m.* (*phys.*) joule.

джу́нгл|и, ей, *no sing.,* jungle.

джут, а, *m.* jute.

джу́т|овый, *adj. of* ~.

дзот, а, *m.* (*abbr. of* де́рево-земляна́я огнева́я то́чка) (*mil.*) earth-and-timber pill-box.

диабе́т, а, *m.* diabetes.

диабе́тик, а, *n.* diabetic.

диа́гноз, а, *n.* diagnosis.

диагно́ст, а, *m.* diagnostician.

диагно́стик|а, и, *f.* diagnostics.

диагности́р|овать, ую, *impf. and pf.* to diagnose.

диагона́л|ь, и, *f.* diagonal; по ~и diagonally.

диагона́л|ьный (~ен, ~ьна), *adj.* diagonal.

диагра́мм|а, ы, *f.* diagram.

диаде́м|а, ы, *f.* diadem.

диа́кон, а, *m.* = дья́кон.

диакони́сс|а, ы, *f.* deaconess.

диакрити́ческий, *adj.*; д. знак (*ling.*) diacritical mark.

диале́кт, а, *m.* dialect.

диалекта́льный, *adj.* dialectal.

диалекти́зм, а, *m.* dialect word, expression.

диале́ктик, а, *m.* (*philos.*) dialectician.

диале́ктик|а, и, *f.* (*philos.*) dialectics.

диалекти́ческий¹, *adj.* (*philos.*) dialectical.

диалекти́ческий², *adj.* (*ling.*) dialectal.

диале́ктный, *adj.* (*ling.*) dialectal.

диалектологи́ческий, *adj.* (*ling.*) dialectological.

диалектоло́ги|я, и, *f.* (*ling.*) dialectology.

диало́г, а, *m.* dialogue.

диалоги́ческий, *adj.* having dialogue form.

диама́нт, а, *m.* (*obs.*) diamond.

диама́т, а, *m.* (*abbr. of* диалекти́ческий материали́зм) dialectical materialism.

диа́метр, а, *m.* diameter.

диаметра́льно, *adv.*; д. противополо́жный diametrically opposite.

диаметра́льный, *adj.* 1. diametral. 2. diametrical.

диапазо́н, а, *m.* 1. (*mus.*) diapason, range. 2. (*fig.*) range, compass; у него́ о́чень большо́й д. интере́сов he has a very wide range of interests. 3. (*tech.; fig.*) range; д. волн (*radio*) wave band; д. скоросте́й (*aeron.*) air speed bracket.

диапозити́в, а, *m.* (*phot.*) slide, transparency.

диатерми́|я, и, *f.* (*med.*) diathermy.

диатри́б|а, ы, *f.* diatribe.

диафра́гм|а, ы, *f.* 1. diaphragm. 2. (*phys.*) stop; (*phot.*) aperture.

ди́в|а, ы, *f.* (*obs.*) diva, prima donna.

дива́н¹, а, *m.* divan (*couch*); sofa.

дива́н², а, *m.* 1. (*hist.*) divan (*Turkish Council of State*). 2. (*lit.*) divan (*Persian name for collection of lyric poetry*).

дива́н|ный, *adj. of* ~¹; (*obs.*) *as noun* ~ная, ~ной, *f.* divan-room.

диверса́нт, а, *m.* saboteur.

диве́рси|я, и, *f.* 1. (*mil.*) diversion. 2. sabotage.

дивертисме́нт, а, *m.* (*theatr.*) variety show, music-hall entertainment; divertissement (*ballet programme*).

дивиде́нд, а, *m.* dividend.

дивизио́н, а, *m.* (*mil.*) 1. battalion (*of artillery or cavalry*). 2. division (*of small warships*).

дивизио́н|ный, *adj.* 1. *adj. of* диви́зия; д. кома́ндный пункт division command post. 2. *adj. of* ~.

диви́зи|я, и, *f.* (*mil.*) division.

див|и́ть, лю́, и́шь, *impf.* (*coll.*) to amaze.

див|и́ться, лю́сь, и́шься, *impf.* (*of* по~) (+*d.*) to be surprised, wonder, marvel (at); (на+*a.*) to look upon with wonder.

ди́в|ный (~ен, ~на), *adj.* 1. amazing; что тут ~ного? what's extraordinary about that? 2. marvellous, wonderful.

ди́в|о, а, n. wonder, marvel; ~у да́ться to wonder, marvel; что за д.! how extraordinary!; на д. marvellously. 2. as pred. it is amazing; не д. it is no wonder.

дидакти́ческий, adj. didactic.

дие́з, а, m. (and as indecl. adj.) (mus.) sharp; ре-д. D sharp.

дие́т|а, ы, f. diet; посади́ть на ~у to place on a diet; соблюда́ть ~у to keep to a diet.

диете́тик|а, и, f. dietetics.

диете́ти́ческий, adj. dietetic; д. магази́н health food shop; д. проду́кт dietetic foodstuff.

диза́йн, а, m. design.

диза́йнер, а, m. designer.

ди́зел|ь, я, m. diesel engine.

ди́зельный, adj. diesel.

дизентери́|я, и, f. dysentery.

дика́р|ский, adj. of ~ь.

дика́рств|о, а, n. shyness.

дика́р|ь, я́, m. 1. savage; (fig.) barbarian. 2. (fig., coll.) shy, unsociable person. 3. (coll.) non-official holiday-maker.

ди́к|ий (~, ~а́, ~о), adj. 1. wild (as opp. to tame, cultivated); ~ая ко́шка wild cat; ~ое по́ле (hist.) steppe frontier region; ~ое я́блоко crab-apple. 2. savage (= pertaining to primitive society; also as noun д., ~ого, m.). 3. wild (= unrestrained); ~ие кри́ки wild cries; д. восто́рг wild delight. 4. queer, absurd; fantastic, preposterous, ridiculous; ~ое предложе́ние fantastic suggestion. 5. shy; unsociable. 6. (obs.) dark-grey. 7. ~ое мя́со (med.) proud flesh. 8. not officially organized.

ди́к|о¹, adv. 1. adv. of ~ий; д. расти́ to grow wild. 2. in fright; startled; д. озира́ться to look around wildly.

ди́ко², as pred. it is absurd, it is ridiculous; д. задава́ть таки́е вопро́сы it is ridiculous to ask such questions.

дикобра́з, а, m. porcupine.

дико́вин|а, ы and ~ка, ~ки, f. (coll.) marvel, wonder; э́то мне не в ~(к)у it is not familiar to me.

дико́винный, adj. strange, unusual, remarkable.

дикорасту́щий, adj. wild.

ди́кост|ь, и, f. 1. wildness; savagery. 2. shyness; unsociableness. 3. absurdity, queerness; э́то соверше́нная д. it is quite absurd.

дикта́нт, а, m. dictation.

дикта́т, а, m. (polit.) diktat.

дикта́тор, а, m. dictator.

дикта́торский, adj. dictatorial.

дикта́торств|о, а, n. 1. dictatorship. 2. (coll.) dictatorial attitude.

диктату́р|а, ы, f. dictatorship; д. пролета-риа́та dictatorship of the proletariat.

дикт|ова́ть, у́ю, у́ешь, impf. (of про~) to dictate.

дикто́вк|а, и, f. dictation; под чью-н. ~у to someone's dictation; (fig.) at someone's bidding.

ди́ктор, а, m. (radio-)announcer.

диктофо́н, а, m. dictophone.

ди́кци|я, и, f. diction; enunciation.

диле́мм|а, ы, f. dilemma.

дилета́нт, а, m. dilettante, dabbler.

дилета́нтств|о, а, n. dilettantism.

дилижа́нс, а, m. stage-coach.

динами́зм, а, m. dynamism.

дина́мик, а, m. loudspeaker.

дина́мик|а, и, f. 1. dynamics. 2. (fig.) dynamics; movement, action; в пье́се ма́ло ~и there is little action in the play.

динами́т, а, m. dynamite.

динами́тчик, а, m. 1. dynamiter. 2. (coll.) terrorist.

динами́ческий, adj. dynamic.

дина́мо, indecl., n., and дина́мо-маши́н|а, ы, f. dynamo.

дина́р, а, m. dinar (unit of currency in Iraq, Tunisia, and Yugoslavia).

династи́ческий, adj. dynastic.

дина́сти|я, и, f. dynasty.

ди́нго, indecl., m. (zool.) dingo.

диноза́вр, а, m. dinosaur.

диора́м|а, ы, f. diorama.

дипкурье́р, а, m. (abbr. of дипломати́ческий курье́р) diplomatic courier.

дипло́м, а, m. 1. diploma; degree (certificate). 2. (coll.) degree work, research. 3. pedigree.

диплома́т, а, m. diplomat, diplomatist.

диплома́тик|а, и, f. (philol.) diplomatic(s).

дипломати́ческий, adj. diplomatic; д. ко́рпус corps diplomatique; д. курье́р diplomatic courier; Queen's Messenger.

дипломати́ч|ный (~ен, ~на), adj. (fig.) diplomatic.

диплома́ти|я, и, f. diplomacy.

дипломи́рованный, adj. graduate; professionally qualified, certificated.

дипло́мник, а, m. student engaged on degree thesis.

дипло́м|ный, adj. of ~; ~ная рабо́та degree work, degree thesis.

директи́в|а, ы, f. directive; instruction.

дире́ктор, а, pl. ~а́, m. director, manager; д. шко́лы head (master, mistress); principal.

дире́кторств|о, а, n. (coll.) directorship.

директри́с|а¹, ы, f. (obs.) head mistress.

директри́с|а², ы, f. 1. (math.) directrix. 2. (mil.) д. стрельбы́ base line.

дире́кци|я, и, f. management; board (of directors).

дирижа́бл|ь, я, m. airship, dirigible.

дирижёр, а, *m.* conductor (*of band or orchestra*).

дирижёр|ский, *adj.* of ~; ~ская па́лочка conductor's baton.

дирижи́р|овать, у́ю, *impf.* (+*i.*; *mus.*) to conduct.

дисгармони́р|овать, у́ю, *impf.* 1. (*mus.*) to be out of tune. 2. (*fig.*) to clash, jar; to be out of keeping.

дисгармо́ни|я, и, *f.* (*mus. and fig.*) disharmony; discord.

диск, а, *m.* 1. disk; **д.** номеронабира́теля telephone dial. 2. (*sport*) discus. 3. (cartridge-)drum (*of automatic weapon*).

ди́скант, а, *m.* (*mus.*) treble.

дисквалифика́ци|я, и, *f.* disqualification.

дисквалифици́р|овать, у́ю, *impf. and pf.* to disqualify.

дискобо́л, а, *m.* discus-thrower.

диск|ова́ть, у́ю, *impf.* (*agric.*) to disc-harrow.

ди́сков|ый, *adj.* disc-shaped; ~ая борона́ disc-harrow.

диско́нт, а, *m.* (*fin.*) discount.

дисконти́р|овать, у́ю, *impf. and pf.* (*fin.*) to discount.

ди́скос, а, *m.* (*eccl.*) paten.

дискредити́р|овать, у́ю, *impf. and pf.* to discredit.

дискримина́ци|я, и, *f.* discrimination.

дискримини́р|овать, у́ю, *impf. and pf.* to discriminate against; to deprive of equality of rights; **д.** национа́льные меньшинства́ to discriminate against national minorities.

дискуссио́нн|ый, *adj.* 1. *adj.* of дискуссия; в ~ом поря́дке as a basis for discussion. 2. debatable, open to question.

дискусси|я, и, *f.* discussion.

дискути́р|овать, у́ю, *impf. and pf.* (+*a.* or о+*p.*) to discuss.

дислока́ци|я, и, *f.* 1. (*mil.*) stationing, distribution (*of troops*). 2. (*geol.*) displacement. 3. (*med.*) dislocation.

дислоци́р|овать, у́ю, *impf. and pf.* (*mil.*) to station (*troops*).

диспансе́р, а, *m.* (*med.*) clinic, (health) centre (*for treatment and prevention of disease*).

диспансериза́ци|я, и, *f.* clinic system, health centre system.

диспепси|я, и, *f.* dyspepsia.

диспе́тчер, а, *m.* controller (*of movement of transport, etc.*); (*aeron.*) flying control officer.

диспе́тчер|ский, *adj.* of ~; (*aeron.*) ~ская вы́шка control tower; ~ская слу́жба flying control organization; *as noun* ~ская, ~ской, *f.* controller's office; (*aeron.*) control tower.

диспози́ци|я, и, *f.* (*mil.*) disposition.

ди́спут, а, *m.* disputation, debate; public defence of dissertation.

диссерта́нт, а, *m.* author of dissertation.

диссерта́ци|я, и, *f.* dissertation, thesis.

диссиде́нт, а, *m.* (*rel.*) nonconformist.

диссимиля́ци|я, и, *f.* dissimilation.

диссона́нс, а, *m.* (*mus. and fig.*) dissonance, discord.

диссони́р|овать, у́ю, *impf.* to strike a discordant note, be discordant.

диссоциа́ци|я, и, *f.* dissociation.

дистанцио́нн|ый, *adj.*; **д.** взрыва́тель, ~ая тру́бка time fuse; ~ое управле́ние remote control.

диста́нци|я, и, *f.* 1. distance; на большо́й, ма́лой ~и at a great, short distance. 2. (*sport*) distance; сойти́ с ~и to withdraw, scratch. 3. (*mil.*) range. 4. (*railways*) division, region.

дистилли́р|овать, у́ю, *impf. and pf.* to distil.

дистилля́ци|я, и, *f.* distillation.

дистрофи́|я, и, *f.* (*med.*) dystrophia.

дисципли́н|а, ы, *f.* (*in var. senses*) discipline.

дисциплина́рный, *adj.* disciplinary; **д.** батальо́н penal battalion.

дисциплини́рова|нный, *p.p.p.* of ~ть and *adj.* disciplined.

дисциплини́р|овать, у́ю, *impf. and pf.* to discipline.

дитя́, *g. and d.* ~ти, *i.* ~тею, *p.* о ~ти, *pl.* де́ти, *n.* child; baby.

дифира́мб, а, *m.* 1. dithyramb. 2. (*fig.*) eulogy; петь ~ы (+*d.*) to sing the praises (of), extol, eulogize.

дифтер|и́йный, *adj.* of ~и́я; diphtheritic.

дифтер|и́т, а, *m.* = ~и́я.

дифтер|и́тный, *adj.* = ~и́йный.

дифтери́|я, и, *f.* diphtheria.

дифто́нг, а, *m.* diphthong.

диффама́ци|я, и, *f.* (*leg.*) defamation, libel.

дифференциа́л, а, *m.* 1. (*math.*) differential. 2. (*tech.*) differential gear.

дифференциа́льн|ый, *adj.* differential; ~ое исчисле́ние (*math.*) differential calculus.

дифференци́р|овать, у́ю, *impf. and pf.* to differentiate.

диффу́зи|я, и, *f.* (*phys.*) diffusion.

дича́|ть, ю, *impf.* (*of* о~) to run wild, become wild; (*fig.*) to become unsociable.

дичи́н|а, ы, *f.* (*coll.*) game.

дич|и́ться, у́сь, и́шься, *impf.* (+*g.*; *coll.*) to be shy (of); to avoid.

дич|о́к, ка́, *m.* 1. wilding (*wild fruit-bearing plant*). 2. (*fig.*) shy person.

дич|ь, и, *f.* 1. (*collect.*) game; wildfowl. 2. wilderness, wilds. 3. (*coll.*) nonsense; поро́ть д. to talk nonsense.

диэле́ктрик, а, *m.* (*phys.*) dielectric, non-conductor.

длан|ь, и, *f.* (*arch. or poet.*) palm (*of hand*).

длин|а́, ы́, *f.* length; в ~у́ longwise, lengthwise; во всю ~у́ at full length; ме́ры ~ы́ long measures; ~ой в шесть métров six metres long.

длинно- long-.

длинноволно́вый, *adj.* (*radio*) long-wave.

длиннот|а́, ы́, *pl.* ~ы, *f.* **1.** (*obs. or coll.*) length. **2.** (*pl.*) longueurs, prolixities.

длинну́щий, *adj.* (*coll.*) (terribly) long.

дли́н|ный (~ен, ~на́, ~но), *adj.* long; lengthy; д. рубль (*coll.*) easy money, quick money; у него́ д. язы́к he has a long tongue.

дли́тельност|ь, и, *f.* duration.

дли́тел|ьный (~ен, ~ьна), *adj.* long, protracted, long-drawn-out; ~ьная боле́знь lingering illness.

дл|и́ться, и́тся, *impf.* (*of* про~) to last.

для, *prep.*+*g.* **1.** for (the sake of); э́то д. тебя́ this is for you. **2.** (*expressing purpose*) for; маши́на д. выка́чивания воды́ machine for pumping out water; я э́то сде́лал то́лько д. ви́ду I only did it for appearances' sake; д. того́, что́бы... in order to... **3.** for, to (= *in relation to, in respect of*); д. нас не сто́ит for us it is not worth while; вре́дно д. дете́й bad for children; непроница́емый д. воды́ waterproof. **4.** for, to (= *in relation to a stated norm*); он о́чень высо́к д. свои́х лет he is very tall for his age; э́то поведе́ние типи́чно д. них such behaviour is typical of them.

дневáльн|ый, ого, *m.* (*mil.*) orderly, fatigue man.

дневáть, дню́ю, дню́ешь, *impf.* to spend the day; д. и ночевáть to spend all one's time.

днёвк|а, и, *f.* day's rest.

дневни́к, á, *m.* diary, journal; вести́ д. to keep a diary.

дневн|о́й, *adj.* **1.** day; в ~о́е вре́мя during daylight hours; д. свет daylight; ~áя сме́на day shift; д. спектáкль matinée. **2.** day's, daily; ~áя зарплáта day's pay.

днём, *adv.* **1.** in the day-time, by day. **2.** in the afternoon; сего́дня д. this afternoon.

дни, *see* день.

дни́щ|е, а, *n.* bottom (*of vessel or barrel*).

дно, дна, *pl.* до́нья, до́ньев, *n.* **1.** bottom (*of sea, river, etc.*); идти́ ко дну to go to the bottom, sink; золото́е 'д. (*fig.*) gold-mine **2.** bottom (*of vessel*); вверх дном upside down; пить до дна to drink to the dregs; ни дна ему́ ни покры́шки! (*coll.*) bad cess to him!

дноуглуби́тел|ь, я, *m.* dredger.

до, *prep.*+*g.* **1.** (*of place or indicating length, etc.*) to, up to; as far as; от Ленингра́да до Москвы́ from Leningrad to Moscow; дое́хать до Кали́нина to go as far as Kalinin; ю́бка до коле́н knee-length skirt. **2.** (*of time*) to, up to; until, till; до шести́ часо́в till six o'clock; рабо́тать от девяти́ (часо́в) до шести́ to work from nine

(o'clock) to six; до сих пор up to now, till now, hitherto; до тех пор till then, before; до тех пор, пока́ until; до свида́ния! good-bye!, au revoir! **3.** before; до войны́ before the war; до на́шей э́ры (до н. э.) before Christ (в.с.); до того́, как before. **4.** (*expressing degree or limiting point*) to, up to, to the point of; до бо́ли until it hurt(s); до того́..., что to the point where; мы до того́ уста́ли, что и засну́ть не удало́сь we were too tired even to be able to sleep. **5.** under, up to (= *not over, not more than*); де́ти до пяти́ лет children under five, under-fives; зараба́тывать до ты́сячи рубле́й to earn up to a thousand roubles. **6.** about, approximately; у нас в больни́це до двух ты́сяч ко́ек in our hospital there are about two thousand beds. **7.** with regard to, concerning; что до меня́ as far as I am concerned; у меня́ до тебя́ де́ло (*coll.*) I want (to see) you, I want a word with you; не быть охо́тник до not to be keen on, not to like; мне, *etc.*, не до (*coll.*) I, *etc.*, don't feel like, am not in the mood for; мне не до разгово́ра I am not in a mood for talk.

до- *prefix* I. (*of verbs*) **1.** *expresses completion of action*: дочита́ть кни́гу to finish (reading) a book. **2.** *indicates that action is carried to a certain point*: дочита́ть до страни́цы 270 to read as far as page 270. **3.** *expresses supplementary action*: докупи́ть to buy in addition. **4.** (+*reflexive vbs.*) *expresses eventual attainment of object*: дозвони́ться to ring until one gets an answer. **5.** (+*reflexive vbs.*) *expresses continuation of action with injurious consequences*: доигра́ться до беды́ (*coll.*) to carry on until one gets into a mess. II. (*of adjectives*) *indicates priority in chronological sequence* (pre-): дово́енный pre-war; де́ти дошко́льного во́зраста children under school age.

доба́в|ить, лю, ишь, *pf.* (*of* ~ля́ть) (+*a. or g.*) to add.

доба́вк|а, и, *f.* **1.** addition. **2.** second helping.

добавле́ни|е, я, *n.* addition; appendix, addendum; extra.

добавля́|ть, ю, *impf. of* доба́вить.

доба́вочн|ый, *adj.* additional, supplementary; accessory; ~ое вре́мя (*sport*) extra time; д. нало́г surtax; ~ая труба́ (*tech.*) extension pipe.

доба́лтыва|ться, юсь, *impf. of* доболта́ться.

добега́|ть, ю, *impf. of* добежа́ть.

добега́|ться, юсь, *pf.* (до+*g.*) to run oneself (to the point of); д. до уста́лости to tire oneself out running.

добе|жа́ть, гу́, жи́шь, гу́т, *pf.* (*of* ~га́ть) (до+*g.*) to run (to, as far as); to reach (*also fig.*).

добела́, *adv.* **1.** to white heat; раскалённый

д. white-hot. 2. clean, white; чёрного кобеля́ не отмо́ешь д. (*prov.*) the leopard can't change his spots.

добива́|ть, ю, *impf. of* доби́ть.

добива́|ться, юсь, *impf.* **1.** *impf. of* доби́ться. **2.** (+*g.*) to try to get, strive (for), aim (at).

добира́|ть, ю, *impf. of* добра́ть.

добира́|ться, юсь, *impf. of* добра́ться.

до|би́ть, бью, бьёшь, *pf.* (*of* ~бива́ть) to finish off, do for, deal the final blow (*also in var. senses corresponding to meanings of prefix and simple verb*).

до|би́ться, бью́сь, бьёшься, *pf.* (*of* добива́ться) (+*g.*) to get, obtain, secure; д. своего́ to get one's way; не д. то́лку от кого́-н. to be unable to get any sense out of someone.

до́блест|ный (~ен, ~на), *adj.* valiant, valorous.

до́блест|ь, и, *f.* valour, prowess; за трудо-ву́ю д. (*honour conferred in U.S.S.R.*) 'For Labour Prowess'.

доболта́|ться, юсь, *pf.* (*of* доба́лтываться) (*coll.*) to talk oneself (into trouble).

до|бра́ть, беру́, берёшь, *past* ~бра́л, ~брала́, ~бра́ло, *pf.* (*of* ~бира́ть) **1.** to finish gathering. **2.** (*typ.*) to finish setting up.

до|бра́ться, беру́сь, берёшься, *past* ~бра́л-ся, ~брала́сь, ~бра́ло́сь, *pf.* (*of* ~бира́ться) **1.** (до+*g.*) to get (to), reach. **2.** (*coll.*) to get, deal with; я до тебя́ ~беру́сь! I'll get you!

добре|сти́, ду́, дёшь, *past* ~л, ~ла́, *pf.* (до+ *g.*) to get (to), reach (*slowly or with difficulty*).

добре́|ть¹, ю, ешь, *impf.* (*of* по~) to become kinder.

добре́|ть², ю, ешь, *impf.* (*of* раз~)(*coll.*) to become corpulent, put on weight.

добр|о́¹, á, n. 1. good; good deed; жела́ю вам ~á I wish you well; от ~á ~á не и́щут let well alone; нет ху́да без ~á every cloud has a silver lining; э́то не к ~у́ it is a bad omen, it bodes ill; помина́ть ~о́м to speak well (of), remember kindly. **2.** (*collect.; coll.*) goods, property.

добро́², particle (*coll.*) good; all right.

добро́³; д. пожа́ловать! welcome!

добро́⁴, as conj. (+бы) it would be a different matter if, there would be some excuse if.

доброво́л|ец, ьца, *m.* volunteer.

доброво́льно, *adv.* voluntarily, of one's own free will.

доброво́л|ьный (~ен, ~ьна), *adj.* voluntary.

доброво́льческий, *adj.* volunteer.

доброде́тел|ь, и, *f.* virtue.

доброде́тел|ьный (~ен, ~ьна), *adj.* virtuous.

добродуши|е, я, *n.* good-nature.

добродуш|ный (~ен, ~на), *adj.* good--natured; genial.

доброжела́тел|ь, я, *m.* well-wisher.

доброжела́тел|ьный (~ен, ~ьна), *adj.* benevolent.

доброка́чествен|ный (~, ~на), *adj.* **1.** of good quality. **2.** (*med.*) benign.

добро́м, *adv.* (*coll.*) of one's own free will, voluntarily.

добронра́в|ный (~ен, ~на), *adj.* (*obs.*) well-behaved.

добропоря́доч|ный (~ен, ~на), *adj.* re-spectable.

добросерде́ч|ный (~ен, ~на), *adj.* good--hearted.

добросо́вест|ный (~ен, ~на), *adj.* con-scientious.

добрососе́дский, *adj.* neighbourly; friendly.

доброт|á, ы́, f. goodness, kindness.

добро́тност|ь, и, f. (good) quality; д. сукна́ quality of cloth.

добро́т|ный (~ен, ~на), *adj.* of good, high quality; durable.

доброхо́т, а, m. (*obs.*) well-wisher.

доброхо́т|ный (~ен, ~на), *adj.* (*obs.*) **1.** benevolent. **2.** voluntary.

до́бр|ый (~, ~á, ~о, ~ы́), *adj.* **1.** (*in var. senses*) good; ~ое и́мя good name; д. конь good horse; д. знако́мый good friend; д. ма́лый decent chap; ~ое у́тро! good morn-ing!; всего́ ~ого! good-bye!, all the best!; в д. час! good luck!; по ~у́ по здоро́ву while the going is (was) good. **2.** kind, good; бу́дьте ~ы́ (+*imper.*) please, would you be so kind as to. **3.** (*coll.*) a good (= *fully, not less than*); оста́лось нам идти́ ~ых пять км we had still a good five kilometres to go. **4.** по ~ой во́ле of one's own free will. **5.** чего́ ~ого (*introducing expression of antici-pation of unpleasant eventuality*) who knows; it may be.

добря́к, á, m. (*coll.*) good-natured person.

добу|ди́ться, жу́сь, ~дишься, *pf.* (*coll.*) to wake, succeed in waking.

добыва́|ть, ю, *impf. of* добы́ть.

добы́тчик, а, m. (*coll.*) **1.** getter (*of minerals, etc.*). **2.** bread-winner.

до|бы́ть, бу́ду, бу́дешь, *past* ~бы́л, ~была́, ~бы́ло, *pf.* (*of* ~быва́ть) **1.** to get, obtain, procure. **2.** to extract, mine, quarry.

добы́ч|а, и, f. 1. extraction (*of minerals*), mining, quarrying. **2.** booty, spoils, loot. **3.** (*hunting*) bag; catch (*of fish*). **4.** mineral products; output.

дова́рив|ать, аю, *impf. of* довари́ть.

довар|и́ть, ю́, ~ишь, *pf.* (*of* ~ивать) **1.** to finish cooking; to do to a turn. **2.** to cook a little longer.

довЕ́да|ться, юсь, *pf.* (*obs. or coll.*) to find out by inquiry.

довез|ти́, у́, ёшь, *past* ‿, ‿ла́, *pf.* (*of* довози́ть¹) to take (to).

дове́ренност|ь, и, *f.* 1. warrant, power of attorney; получи́ть де́ньги по ‿и to obtain money by proxy. 2. (*obs.*) trust.

дове́р|енный, *p.p.p. of* ‿ить *and adj.* trusted; ‿енное лицо́; *also as noun* д., ‿енного, *m.* agent, proxy; person empowered to act for someone.

довери|е, я, *n.* trust, confidence; по́льзоваться чьим-н. ‿ем to enjoy someone's confidence; поста́вить вопро́с о ‿и to call for a vote of confidence.

довери́тел|ь, я, *m.* principal (*person empowering another to act for him*).

довери́тельный, *adj.* 1. confiding. 2. (*obs.*) confidential (= *classified; of documents*). 3. (*obs.*) empowering to act for one.

дове́р|ить, ю, ишь, *pf.* (*of* ‿я́ть) (+*d.*) to entrust (to).

дове́р|иться, юсь, ишься, *pf.* (*of* ‿я́ться) (+*d.*) to trust (in), confide (in).

до́верху, *adv.* to the top; to the brim.

дове́рчивост|ь, и, *f.* trustfulness, credulity.

дове́рчив|ый (‿, ‿а), *adj.* trustful, credulous.

доверш|а́ть, а́ю, *impf. of* ‿и́ть.

доверше́ни|е, я, *n.* completion, consummation; в д. всего́ to crown all, on top of it all.

доверш|и́ть, у́, и́шь, *pf.* (*of* ‿а́ть) to complete.

довер|я́ть, я́ю, *impf.* 1. *impf. of* ‿ить. 2. (*impf. only*) (+*d.*) to trust, confide (in).

довер|я́ться, я́юсь, *impf. of* ‿иться.

довес|о́к, ка, *m.* makeweight.

дове|сти́, ду́, дёшь, *past* ‿л, ‿ла́, *pf.* (*of* доводи́ть) 1. (до+*g.*) to lead (to), take (to), accompany (to). 2. (до+*g.*) to bring (to); to drive (to), reduce (to); д. до соверше́нства to perfect; д. до сумасше́ствия to drive mad; д. до слёз to reduce to tears; д. до све́дения (+*g.*) to inform, let know, bring to the notice (of).

дове|сти́сь, дётся, *past* ‿ло́сь, *pf.* (*of* доводи́ться) (*impers.*+*d.*; *coll.*) to have occasion (to); to manage (to); to happen (to); нам ‿ло́сь заста́ть его́ до́ма we happened to catch him in.

довин|ти́ть, чу́, ти́шь, *pf.* (*of* ‿чивать) to screw up.

дови́нчива|ть, ю, *impf. of* довинти́ть.

довле́|ть, ет, *impf.* 1. (*obs.*) to suffice; д. себе́ to be self-sufficient; ‿ет дне́ви зло́ба еро́ sufficient unto the day is the evil thereof. 2. (над+*i.*; *vulg.*) to dominate, prevail over).

до́вод, а, *m.* argument.

дово|ди́ть, жу́, ‿дишь, *impf. of* довести́.

дово|ди́ться, жу́сь, ‿дишься, *impf.* 1. *impf. of* довести́сь. 2. (+*d. and i.*) to be

related (to as); он ‿дится ей племя́нником he is her nephew.

дово́дк|а, и, *f.* (*tech.*) finishing; lapping.

дово́енный, *adj.* pre-war.

дово|зи́ть, жу́, ‿зишь, *impf. of* довезти́.

дово|зи́ть², жу́, ‿зишь, *pf.* (*coll.*) to finish carrying.

дово́льно¹, *adv.* 1. enough; *as pred.* it is enough; с нас э́того д. we've had enough of this; д. спо́рить stop arguing. 2. quite, fairly; rather, pretty; д. хоро́ший фильм quite a good film; д. глу́пый челове́к rather a stupid person.

дово́льно², *adv.* contentedly.

дово́л|ьный (‿ен, ‿ьна), *adj.* 1. contented, satisfied; д. вид contented expression. 2. (+*i.*) content (with), satisfied (with), pleased (with); д. собо́й pleased with oneself, self-satisfied; он не осо́бенно ‿ен но́вой рабо́той he does not like his new job very much. 3. (*obs.*) considerable.

дово́льстви|е, я, *n.* (*mil.*) allowance (*of money, food or clothing*).

дово́льств|о, а, *n.* 1. content, contentment. 2. (*coll.*) ease, prosperity.

дово́льств|овать, ую, *impf.* 1. (*obs.*) to satisfy, make content. 2. (*mil.*) to supply, maintain.

дово́льств|оваться, уюсь, *impf.* (*of* у‿) 1. (+*i.*) to be content (with), be satisfied (with). 2. *pass. of* ‿овать.

довре́менный, *adj.* (*obs.*) premature.

довы́бор|ы, ов, *no sing.* by-election.

дог, а, *m.* Great Dane.

догад|а́ться, а́юсь, *pf.* (*of* ‿ываться) to guess; to have the sense to.

дога́дк|а, и, *f.* 1. surmise, conjecture; теря́ться в ‿ах to be lost in conjecture. 2. (*coll.*) imagination; прояви́ть ‿у to be on the spot.

дога́длив|ый (‿, ‿а), *adj.* quick-witted, shrewd.

дога́дыва|ться, юсь, *impf.* 1. *impf. of* догада́ться. 2. (*impf. only*) to suspect.

догля|де́ть, жу́, ди́шь, *pf.* (*coll.*) 1. to watch to the end, see through. 2. to keep an eye out; (за+*i.*) to keep an eye (on).

до́гм|а, ы, *f.* 1. dogma, dogmatic assertion. 2. (*pl.*) foundations, bases (*of a theory, inteltectual discipline, etc.*).

до́гмат, а, *m.* 1. (*rel.*) doctrine, dogma; д. непогреши́мости па́пы the doctrine of the infallibility of the Pope. 2. tenet, foundation; одни́м из ‿ов ло́гики явля́ется зако́н тожде́ственности the law of identity is one of the foundations of logic.

догмати́зм, а, *m.* dogmatism (*in general, also in Marxist polit. jargon, as a deviation opp. to revisionism*).

догма́тик, а, *m.* 1. dogmatic person. 2.

'dogmatist' (in Marxist polit. jargon, as opp. to revisionist).

догмати́ческий, adj. dogmatic.

до|гна́ть, гоню́, го́нишь, past ~гна́л, ~гнала́, ~гна́ло, pf. (of ~гоня́ть) 1. to catch up (with) (also fig.); д. и перегна́ть За́пад (polit. slogan) to catch up with and pass the West. 2. (до+g.) to drive (to); (fig., coll.) to raise (to).

догова́рива|ть, ю, impf. of договори́ть.

догова́рива|ться, юсь, impf. 1. impf. of договори́ться. 2. (impf. only) (o+p.) to negotiate (about), treat (for); Высо́кие ~ющиеся сто́роны (dipl.) the High Contracting Parties.

догово́р, а and (coll.) до́говор, pl. ~а́, m. agreement; (polit.) treaty, pact; заключи́ть ми́рный д. to conclude a peace treaty.

договорённост|ь, и, f. agreement, understanding.

договор|и́ть, ю́, и́шь, pf. (of догова́ривать) to finish saying; to finish telling.

договор|и́ться, ю́сь, и́шься, pf. (of догова́риваться) 1. (o+p.) to come to an agreement, understanding (about); to arrange. 2. (до+g.) to come (to); to talk (to the point of).

догово́рник, а, m. (coll.) worker under contract for a particular job.

догово́рн|ый, adj. 1. agreed; contractual; ~ая цена́ agreed price. 2. fixed by treaty.

догола́, adv. stark naked; разде́ться д. to strip to the skin.

догоня́л|ки, ок, no sing. (children's game) 'he'.

догоня́|ть, ю, impf. of догна́ть.

догор|а́ть, а́ю, impf. of ~е́ть.

догор|е́ть, ю́, и́шь, pf. (of ~а́ть) to burn down, burn out.

догружа́|ть, ю, impf. of догрузи́ть.

догру|зи́ть, жу́, ~зи́шь, pf.(of ~жа́ть) 1. to finish loading. 2. to load in addition.

догу́лива|ть, ю, impf. of догуля́ть.

догуля́|ть, ю, pf. (of догу́ливать) (coll.) to spend in pleasure (the remainder of); дава́йте ~ем о́тпуск let's make the most of what's left of the holidays.

дода|ва́ть, ю́, ёшь, impf. of ~ть.

дода́|ть, м, шь, ст, ди́м, ди́те, ду́т, past до́дал, ~ла́, до́дало, pf. (of ~ва́ть) to make up (the rest of); to pay up.

доде́л|ать, аю, pf. (of ~ывать) to finish.

доде́лыва|ть, ю, impf. of доде́лать.

доду́м|аться, аюсь, pf. (of ~ываться) (до+ g.) to hit (upon) (afterthought).

доду́мыва|ться, юсь, impf. of доду́маться.

доеда́|ть, ю, impf. of дое́сть.

доезжа́|ть, ю, impf. of дое́хать.

доезжа́ч|ий, его, m. whipper-in.

дое́ни|е, я, n. milking.

до|е́сть, е́м, е́шь, е́ст, еди́м, еди́те, едя́т, pf. (of ~еда́ть) to eat up, finish eating.

до|е́хать, е́ду, е́дешь, pf. (of ~езжа́ть) 1. (до+g.) to reach, arrive (at). 2. (fig., coll.) to wear out.

дож, а, m. (hist.) doge.

дожа́рива|ть, ю, impf. of дожа́рить.

дожа́р|ить, ю, ишь, pf. (of ~ивать) to finish roasting, frying; to roast, fry to a turn.

дожд|а́ться, у́сь, ёшься, past ~а́лся, ~ала́сь, ~ало́сь, pf. 1. (+g.) to wait (for); д. конца́ спекта́кля to wait until the end of the show. 2. д. того́, что to end up (by); он ~а́лся того́, что ему́ показа́ли дверь he ended up by being shown the door.

дождева́льный, adj.; д. аппара́т (agric.) water-sprinkler.

дождева́ни|е, я, n. (agric.) irrigation by sprinkling.

дождеви́к, а́, m. 1. (coll.) raincoat. 2. puff-ball (Lycoperdon giganteum).

дождев|о́й, adj. of дождь; ~а́я ка́пля rain-drop; ~о́е о́блако rain-cloud, nimbus; ~о́е пла́тье oilskins.

дождеме́р, а, m. rain-gauge.

до́ждик, а, m. shower.

дожди́нк|а, и, f. (coll.) rain-drop.

дожд|и́ть, и́т, impf. (impers.; coll.) to rain, be raining.

дождли́в|ый (~, ~а), adj. rainy.

дожд|ь, я, m. 1. rain (also fig.); под ~ём in the rain; ме́лкий д. drizzle; проливно́й д. downpour; д. идёт it is raining; д. льёт как из ведра́ it is raining cats and dogs. 2. (fig.) rain, hail, cascade; д. искр cascade of sparks; д. руга́тельств torrent of abuse; сы́паться ~ём to rain down, cascade.

дожива́|ть, ю, impf. 1. impf. of дожи́ть. 2. (impf. only) to live out; д. свой век to live out one's days.

дожида́|ться, юсь, impf. (of дожда́ться) (+g.) to wait (for).

дожи́н|ки, ок, no sing. (dial.) harvest festival.

до|жи́ть, живу́, живёшь, past ~жи́л, ~жила́, ~жило, pf. (of ~жива́ть) 1. (до+g.) to live (till); to attain the age (of); она́ ~жила́ до конца́ войны́ she lived to see the end of the war. 2. (до+g.) to come (to), be reduced (to); до чего́ мы ~жили! what have we come to! 3. (coll.) to stay, spend (the rest of); я доживу́ ле́то в Пари́же I shall spend the rest of the summer in Paris.

до́з|а, ы, f. dose.

доза́тор, а, m. measure, measuring hopper.

до|зва́ться, зову́сь, зовёшься, past ~зва́лся, ~звала́сь, ~звало́сь, pf. (coll.) to call until one gets an answer, его́ не ~зовёшься he never comes when he is called.

дозволе́ни|е, я, n. (obs.) permission.

дозво́л|енный, p.p.p.of ~ить and adj.permitted.

дозво́л|ить, ю, ишь, *pf.* (*of* ~я́ть) (*obs. or coll.*) to permit, allow.

дозвол|я́ть, я́ю, *impf. of* ~и́ть.

дозвон|и́ться, ю́сь, и́шься, *pf.* (*coll.*) (до+ *g.*, к+*d.*) to ring (*at doorbell, on telephone*) until one gets an answer; to get through (*on telephone*); я не мог к тебе́ д. I rang you but could get no reply, could not get through.

дозву́ковый, *adj.* subsonic.

дози́р|овать, ую, *impf. and pf.* to measure out (in doses).

дозиро́вк|а, и, *f.* dosage.

дозна|ва́ться, ю́сь, ёшься, *impf.* 1. *impf. of* ~ться. 2. (*impf. only*) (о+*p.*) to inquire (about).

дозна́ни|е, я, *n.* (*leg.*) inquiry; inquest.

дозн|а́ться, а́юсь, *pf.* (*of* ~ава́ться) to find out, ascertain.

дозо́р, а, *m.* patrol.

дозо́р|ный, *adj. of* ~; ~ная шлю́пка patrol boat; *as noun* д., ~ного, *m.* (*mil.*) scout.

дозрева́|ть, ю, *impf. of* дозре́ть.

дозре́лый, *adj.* fully ripe.

дозр|е́ть, е́ю, *pf.* (*of* ~ева́ть) to ripen.

доигр|а́ть, а́ю, *pf.* (*of* ~ывать) to finish (playing).

доигр|а́ться, а́юсь, *pf.* (*of* ~ываться) (до+ *g.*) to play (until); (*fig.*) to get oneself (into), land oneself (in); вот и ~а́лся! now you've (he's, *etc.*) done it!

доигрыва|ть(ся), ю(сь), *impf. of* доигра́ть-(ся).

дойльн|ый, *adj.*; ~ая маши́на milking machine.

дойльщица, ы, *f.* = доя́рка.

до|иска́ться, ищу́сь, и́щешься, *pf.* (*of* ~и́скиваться) (*coll.*) 1. (+*g.*) to find, discover. 2. to find out, ascertain.

дойскива|ться, юсь, *impf.* 1. *impf. of* доиска́ться. 2. (*impf. only*) to try to find out.

доистори́ческий, *adj.* prehistoric.

до|и́ть, ю, ~и́шь, (*of* по~) to milk; (*fig.*) to milk (*of money*).

до|и́ться, ~и́тся, *impf.* 1. to give milk; хорошо́ д. to be a good milker. 2. *pass. of* ~и́ть.

до́йк|а, и, *f.* milking.

до́йн|ый, *adj.* milch; ~ая коро́ва milch cow (*also fig.*).

до|йти́, йду́, йдёшь, *past* ~шёл, ~шла́, *pf.* (*of* ~ходи́ть) 1. (до+*g.*) (*in var. senses*) to reach; письмо́ ~шло́ до меня́ то́лько сего́дня the letter only reached me today; слух ~шёл до нас a rumour reached us; д. до све́дения (+*g.*) to come to the notice (of), come to the ears (of); д. до того́, что... to reach a point where...; ру́ки не ~шли́ (до+*g.*) I, *etc.*, had no time (for). 2. (*coll.*) (до+*g.*) to make an impression (upon), get through (to), penetrate (to), touch; его́

про́поведь про́сто не ~шла́ до слу́шателей his homily left his audience quite unmoved. 3. (*impers.*; *also* де́ло ~йдёт, ~шло́ до+*g.*) to come (to), be a matter (of); де́ло ~шло́ до проце́сса it came to a court case. 4. (*coll.*) to be done (= *to be cooked*); to be ripe.

док, а, *m.* dock.

до́к|а, и, *m. and f.* (*coll.*) expert, authority.

доказа́тел|ьный (~ен, ~ьна), *adj.* demonstrative, conclusive.

доказа́тельств|о, а, *n.* 1. proof, evidence. 2. (*math.*) demonstration.

док|аза́ть, ажу́, а́жешь, *pf.* (*of* ~а́зывать) 1. to demonstrate, prove; счита́ть ~а́занным to take for granted; что и тре́бова-лось д. (*math.*) quod erat demonstrandum (Q.E.D.). 2. (*coll.*) д. на кого́-н. to inform on someone.

доказу́ем|ый (~, ~а), *adj.* demonstrable.

дока́зыва|ть, ю, *impf.* 1. *impf. of* доказа́ть. 2. (*impf. only*) to argue, try to prove.

дока́нчива|ть, ю, *impf. of* доко́нчить.

дока́пыва|ться, юсь, *impf. of* докопа́ться.

док|ати́ться, ачу́сь, а́тишься, *pf.* (*of* ~а́ты-ваться) 1. (до+*g.*) to roll (to). 2. (*of sounds*) to roll, thunder, boom. 3. (*fig., coll.*) (до+*g.*) to sink (into), come (to); д. до преступле́ния to sink into crime.

дока́тыва|ться, юсь, *impf. of* докати́ться.

до́кер, а, *m.* docker.

докла́д, а, *m.* 1. report; lecture; paper; talk, address; чита́ть д. to give a report, read a paper. 2. announcement (*of arrival of guest, etc.*); войти́ без ~а to enter unannounced.

докладн|о́й, *adj.*; ~а́я запи́ска report, memorandum; *as noun* ~а́я, ~о́й, *f.* = ~а́я запи́ска.

докла́дчик, а, *m.* speaker, lecturer; reader of a report.

докла́дыва|ть(ся), ю(сь), *impf. of* доло-жи́ть(ся).

доко́ле (*and* **доко́ль**), *adv.* (*obs.*) 1. (*interrog.*) how long. 2. (*relat.*) as long as; until.

докона́|ть, ю, *pf.* (*coll.*) to finish off, be the end (of).

доко́нч|ить, у, ишь, *pf.* (*of* дока́нчивать) to finish, complete.

докопа́|ться, юсь, *pf.* (*of* дока́пываться) (до+*g.*) 1. to dig down (to). 2. (*fig.*) to get to the bottom (of); to find out, discover.

до́красна́, *adv.* to redness; to red heat; раскалённый д. red-hot.

докрич|а́ться, у́сь, и́шься, *pf.* 1. to shout until one is heard. 2. д. до хрипоты́, to shout oneself hoarse,

до́ктор, а, *pl.* á, *m.* doctor.

доктора́льный, *adj.* didactic.

доктора́нт, а, *m.* person working for degree of doctor.

до́ктор|ский, *adj. of* ~; ~ская диссерта́ция thesis for degree of doctor.

до́кторш|а, и, *f.* (*coll.*) 1. doctor's wife. 2. woman-doctor.

доктри́н|а, ы, *f.* doctrine.

доктринёр, а, *m.* doctrinaire.

доктринёрский, *adj.* doctrinaire.

доктринёрств|о, а, *n.* doctrinaire attitude.

доку́да, *adv.* (*coll.*) 1. (*interrog.*) how far. 2. (*relat.*) as far as.

доку́к|а, и, *f.* (*obs. or coll.*) tiresome request.

докуме́нт, а, *m.* 1. document, paper; предъяви́ть ~ы to produce one's papers. 2. (*leg.*) deed; instrument.

документа́льный, *adj.* documentary; д. фильм documentary (film).

документа́ци|я, и, *f.* 1. documentation. 2. (*collect.*) documents, papers.

документи́р|овать, ую, *impf. and pf.* to document.

докуп|а́ть¹, а́ю, *impf. of* ~и́ть.

докупа́|ть², ю, *pf.* to finish bathing (*trans.*).

докуп|и́ть, лю́, ~ишь, *pf.* (*of* ~а́ть¹) to buy in addition.

докуча́|ть, ю, *impf.* (+*d. and i.*; *coll.*) to bother (with), pester (with), plague (with).

доку́члив|ый (~, ~а), *adj.* (*coll.*) tiresome; importunate.

доку́ч|ный (~ен, ~на), *adj.* (*coll.*) tiresome, boring.

дол, а, *m.* (*poet.*) dale, vale; за гора́ми, за ~а́ми far and wide; по гора́м, по ~а́м up hill and down dale.

долбёжк|а, и, *f.* (*sl.*) swotting; учи́ться в ~у to learn by rote.

долб|и́ть, лю́, и́шь, *impf.* 1. to hollow; to chisel, gouge. 2. (*coll.*) to repeat, say over and over. 3. (*sl.*) to swot (up); to learn by rote.

долг, а, о ~е, в ~у́, *pl.* ~и́, *m.* 1. duty; по ~у слу́жбы in the performance of one's duty. 2. debt; в д. on credit; войти́, влезть в ~и́ to get into debt; быть у кого́-н. в ~у́ to be indebted to someone; отда́ть после́дний д. to pay the last honours; д. платежо́м кра́сен one good turn deserves another.

до́л|гий (~ог, ~га́, ~го), *adj.* long, of long duration; ~гая пе́сня (*fig.*) a long story; отложи́ть в д. я́щик to shelve, put off.

до́лго, *adv.* 1. long, a long time. 2. д. ли (+*inf. or* до+*g.*) one may easily, it can easily happen that; д. ли до беды́ accidents will happen.

долгове́ч|ный (~ен, ~на), *adj.* lasting; long-lived.

долгово́|й, *adj. of* долг 2; ~о́е обяза́тельство promissory note; ~о́е отделе́ние (*hist.*) debtor's prison.

долговре́менн|ый, *adj.* of long duration; ~ая огнева́я то́чка, ~ое огнево́е сооруже́ние (*mil.*) pillbox (*of reinforced concrete*).

долговя́з|ый (~, ~а), *adj.* (*coll.*) lanky.

долгоде́нстви|е, я, *n.* (*obs.*) long life.

долгоигра́ющ|ий, *adj.*; ~ая пласти́нка long-playing (gramophone) record.

долголе́ти|е, я, *n.* longevity.

долголе́тний, *adj.* of many years; of many years' standing, long-standing.

долгоно́сик, а, *m.* weevil.

долгосро́чный, *adj.* long-term; of long duration.

долгот|а́, ы́, *pl.* ~ы, *f.* 1. (*sing. only*) duration. 2. longitude.

долготерпели́в|ый (~, ~а), *adj.* long-suffering.

долготерпе́ни|е, я, *n.* long-suffering.

долгун|е́ц, ца́, *m.* (лён-)д. long-stalked flax (*commercial brand*).

долево́й¹, *adj.* lengthwise.

долев|о́й², *adj. of* до́ля; ~о́е отчисле́ние royalty.

до́лее, *comp. of* до́лго.

долет|а́ть, а́ю, *impf. of* ~е́ть.

доле|те́ть, чу́, ти́шь, *pf.* (*of* ~та́ть) (до+*g.*) 1. to fly (to, as far as). 2. to reach (*also fig.*); to be wafted (to).

долж|а́ть, ю, *impf.* (*of* за~) (*obs.*) (у+*g.*) to borrow (from).

до́лж|ен (~на́, ~но́), *pred. adj.* 1. owing; он д. мне три рубля́ he owes me three roubles. 2. (+*inf.*) *expresses obligation*: я д. идти́ I must go, I have to go; он д. был отказа́ться he had to refuse. 3. (+*inf.*) *expresses probability or expectation*; она́ ~на́ ско́ро прийти́ she should be here soon; ~но́ быть probably; вы с ним, ~но́ быть, уже́ знако́мы you must have met him; you probably met him.

долженств|ова́ть, у́ю, *impf.* (+*inf.*; *obs.*) to be obliged (to); to be intended (to).

должни́к, а́, *m.* debtor.

до́лжно, *pred.* (+*inf.*) one should, one ought (to).

должностн|о́й, *adj.* official; ~о́е лицо́ official, functionary, public servant; ~о́е преступле́ние malfeasance in office.

до́лжност|ь, и, *g. pl.* ~е́й, *f.* post, appointment, office; duties.

до́лж|ный, *adj.* due, fitting, proper; ~ым о́бразом properly; *as noun* ~ое, ~ого, *n.* due, воздава́ть д. (+*d.*) to do justice.

долива́|ть, ю, *impf. of* доли́ть.

доли́вк|а, и, *f.* refilling, replenishment; refuelling.

доли́н|а, ы, *f.* valley.

дол|и́ть, ью́, ьёшь, *past* ~и́л, ~ила́, ~и́ло, *pf.* (*of* ~ива́ть) 1. to add; to pour in addition. 2. to fill (up); to refill.

до́ллар, а, *m.* dollar.

доло́ж|и́ть¹, у́, ~ишь, *pf.* (*of* докла́дывать) 1. (+*a. or* о+*p.*) to report; to give a report (on). 2. (о+*p.*) to announce (*a guest, etc.*).

доло́ж|и́ть², у́, ~ишь, *pf.* (*of* докла́дывать) to add.

доло́ж|и́ться, у́сь, ~и́шься, *pf.* (*of* докла́дываться) to announce one's arrival.

доло́й, *adv.* (+*a.*; *coll.*) down (with), away (with); д. изме́нников! down with the traitors!; уйди́ с глаз д.! out of my sight! 2. off (with); ша́пки д.! hats off!

доло́т|о́, а́, *pl.* ~а́, ~, *n.* chisel.

до́лу, *adv.* (*poet.*) down, downwards.

до́льк|а, и, *f.* segment, clove.

до́льний, *adj.* (*poet.*) 1. valley. 2. earthly, terrestrial.

до́льше, *adv.* longer.

до́л|я, и, *g. pl.* ~е́й, *f.* 1. part, portion; share; quota, allotment; войти́ в ~ю (с+*i.*) to go shares (with); в его́ слова́х не́ было и ~и и́стины there was not a grain of truth in his words; кни́га в четвёртую, восьму́ю ~ю листа́ quarto, octavo. 2. (*anat., bot.*) lobe. 3. lot, fate; вы́пасть на чью-н. ~ю to fall to someone's lot. 4. (*obs.*) *unit of weight equivalent to 44 mg.*

дом, а (у), *pl.* ~а́, *m.* 1. (*in var. senses*) building, house; Д. культу́ры Palace of Culture; д. о́тдыха rest home, holiday home; Д. Сове́тской А́рмии Soviet Army Club; д. терпи́мости brothel. 2. home; house, household; вести́ д. to keep house, run the house; хлопота́ть по ~y to busy oneself with housework, with domestic chores; на ~у́ at home; брать рабо́ту на́ д. to take work home; тоска́ по ~y homesickness. 3. house (= *dynasty*), lineage; family; д. Рома́новых the House of Romanov.

до́ма, *adv.* at home, in; быть как д. to feel at home; бу́дьте как д. make yourself at home; у него́ не все д. he's not all there.

домаркси́стский, *adj.* pre-Marxist.

домаха́|ть, ю, *pf.* (*coll.*) (до+*g.*) to get (to).

дома́шн|ий, *adj.* 1. house; home; domestic; д. а́дрес home address; ~ие забо́ты household chores; ~ее пла́тье house dress; ~яя рабо́тница domestic servant; ~яя хозя́йка housewife; под ~им аре́стом under house arrest. 2. home-made; homespun; home-brewed. 3. tame (*as opp. to* wild); domestic; ~ие живо́тные domestic animals; ~ие пти́цы poultry. 4. *as noun* ~ие, ~их one's people, one's family.

дома́шност|ь, и, *f.* (*coll. or dial.*) 1. housekeeping. 2. household equipment.

доме́н, а, *m.* (*hist.*) domain, state lands.

до́менн|ый, *adj.* of до́мна; ~ая печь blast furnace.

до́менщик, а, *m.* blast-furnace operator.

до́мик, а, *m. dim. of* дом.

домина́нт|а, ы, *f.* 1. (*mus.*) dominant. 2. (*fig.*) leitmotiv.

доминика́н|ец, ца, *m.* Dominican (monk).

доминио́н, а, *m.* dominion (*member of British Commonwealth*).

домини́р|овать, ую, *impf.* 1. to dominate, prevail (*fig.*). 2. (*geogr.*) (над+*i.*) to dominate, command.

домино́, *indecl., n.* 1. dominoes (*game*). 2. domino (*costume*).

до́миш|ко, а, *pl.* ~ки, ~ек, ~кам, *m.* (*coll.*) small, wretched house; hovel.

домкра́т, а, *m.* (*tech.*) jack.

до́мн|а, ы, *f.* blast furnace.

домови́н|а, ы, *f.* (*dial.*) coffin.

домови́т|ый (~, ~а), *adj.* thrifty, economical; ~ая хозя́йка good housewife.

домовладе́л|ец, ьца, *m.* house-owner; landlord.

домовни́ц|а, ы, *f.* (*coll. or dial.*) housekeeper.

домовни́ча|ть, ю, *impf.* (*coll. or dial.*) to keep house.

домово́дств|о, а, *n.* (art of) housekeeping; household management.

домов|о́й, о́го, *m.* (*folklore*) house-spirit.

домо́в|ый, *adj.* 1. house; household; ~ая кни́га house register, register of tenants; ~ая конто́ра house-manager's office; д. пау́к house-spider. 2. housing; д. трест housing trust.

домога́тельств|о, а, *n.* 1. solicitation, importunity. 2. demand, bid; д. госпо́дства bid for power.

домога́|ться, юсь, *impf.* (+*g.*) to seek (after), solicit, covet.

домоде́льный, *adj.* home-made.

домо́й, *adv.* home, homewards; нам пора́ д. it's time for us to go home.

домоправи́тел|ь, я, *m.* (*obs.*) steward.

домоправле́ни|е, я, *n.* (*obs.*) household management.

доморо́щенный, *adj.* 1. home-bred. 2. (*fig.*) crude; primitive; homespun.

домосе́д, а, *m.* stay-at-home.

домостро́ени|е, я, *n.* house-building.

домостро́ительный, *adj.* house-building.

домотка́ный, *adj.* home-spun.

домоуправле́ни|е, я, *n.* house management (committee).

домохозя́|ин, ина, *pl.* ~ева, ~ев, *m.* householder. 2. (*obs.*) head of peasant household.

домохозя́йк|а, и, *f.* housewife.

домоча́д|ец, ца, *m.* (*obs.*) member of household.

до́мр|а, ы, *f.* (*mus.*) domra (*Russian stringed instrument similar to mandoline*).

домрабо́тниц|а, ы, *f.* domestic servant, maid.

домраче́|й, я, *m.* (*obs.*) = домри́ст.

домри́ст, а, *m.* domra-player.

домýшник, а, *m.* (*sl.*) burglar, housebreaker.

домч|áть, ý, и́шь, *pf.* (*coll.*) to bring quickly (*in a vehicle, etc.*).

домч|áться, ýсь, и́шься, *pf.* (*coll.*) to reach quickly (*at a run or gallop*).

дóмыс|ел, ла, *m.* conjecture.

дон, *interj.* (*onomat.*) ding-dong.

донагá, *adv.* stark naked.

донáшива|ть, ю, *impf. of* доноси́ть[1].

донéльзя, *adv.* to the utmost; in the extreme; он д. упря́м he is obstinate in the extreme.

донесéни|е, я, *n.* dispatch, report, message; д. о боевы́х потéрях casualty report.

донес|ти́[1], ý, ёшь, *past* ~, ~лá, *pf.* (*of* доноси́ть[2]) (до+*g.*) to carry (to, as far as); to carry, bear (*a sound or smell*).

донес|ти́[2], ý, ёшь, *past* ~, ~лá, *pf.* (*of* доноси́ть[3]) 1. to report, announce; (+*d.*) to inform. 2. (на+*a.*) to inform (on, against), denounce.

донес|ти́сь, ýсь, ёшься, *past* ~ся, ~лáсь, *pf.* (*of* доноси́ться[2]) 1. (*of sounds or smells, also of news, etc.*) to reach; до нас ужé ~ся слух a rumour had already reached us. 2. (*coll.*) to reach quickly.

дон|éц, цá, *m.* Don Cossack.

донжуáн, а, *m.* Don Juan, philanderer.

донжуáнств|о, а, *n.* philandering.

дóнизу, *adv.* to the bottom; свéрху д. from top to bottom.

донимá|ть, ю, *impf. of* доня́ть.

донкихóтский, *adj.* quixotic.

донкихóтств|о, а, *n.* quixotry.

дóнн|а, ы, *f.* donna.

дóнник, а, *m.* (*bot.*) melilot, sweet clover.

дóнный, *adj. of* дно; д. лёд ground ice; д. заря́д (*mil.*) base charge.

дóнор, а, *m.* (blood-)donor.

донóс, а, *m.* denunciation, information, delation.

дон|оси́ть[1], ошý, ~óсишь, *pf.* (*of* донáшивать) 1. to finish carrying. 2. to wear out. 3. д. ребёнка to bear at full term.

дон|оси́ть[2, 3], ошý, ~óсишь, *impf. of* донести́[1, 2].

дон|оси́ться[1], ~óсится, *pf.* to wear out, be worn out.

дон|оси́ться[2], ~óсится, *impf. of* донести́сь.

донóсчик, а, *m.* informer.

донскóй, *adj.* (of the river) Don; д. казáк Don Cossack.

дóнц|е, а, *n. dim. of* дно.

доны́не, *adv.* (*rhet.*.) hitherto.

до|ня́ть, йму́, ймёшь, *past* ~ня́л, ~няля́, ~ня́ло, *pf.* (*of* ~нимáть) (*coll.*) to weary, tire out, exasperate.

дообéденный, *adj.* pre-prandial.

дооктя́брьский, *adj.* pre-October (*before the Russian Revolution of October 1917*).

допекá|ть, ю, *impf. of* допéчь.

допетрóвский, *adj.* pre-Petrine, before Peter the Great.

допé|чь, кý, чёшь, кýт, *past* ~к, ~клá, *pf.* (*of* ~кáть) 1. to bake until done; to finish baking. 2. (*fig., coll.*) to wear out, plague, pester.

допивá|ть, ю, *impf. of* допи́ть.

допи|сáть, шý, ~шешь, *pf.* (*of* ~сывать) 1. to finish writing. 2. to add.

допи́сыва|ть, ю, *impf. of* дописáть.

доп|и́ть, ью́, ьёшь, *past* ~и́л, ~илá, ~и́ло, *pf.* (*of* ~ивáть) to drink (up).

доплáт|а, ы, *f.* additional payment; excess fare.

допл|ати́ть, ачý, ~áтишь, *pf.* (*of* ~áчивать) to pay in addition, in excess.

доплáчива|ть, ю, *impf. of* доплати́ть.

доплывá|ть, ю, *impf. of* доплы́ть.

доплы́|ть, вý, вёшь, *past* ~л, ~лá, ~ло, *pf.* (*of* ~вáть) (до+*g.*) to swim (to, as far as); to sail (to, as far as); (*fig.*) to reach.

допóдлинно, *adv.* (*coll.*) for certain.

допóдлинный, *adj.* (*coll.*) authentic, genuine.

дополнéни|е, я, *n.* 1. supplement, addition; addendum. 2. (*gram.*) object; прямóе д. direct object; кóсвенное д. indirect object.

дополни́тельно, *adv.* in addition.

дополни́тельн|ый, *adj.* supplementary, additional, extra; д. оклáд extra pay; д. ýгол (*math.*) supplement; ~ые цветá complementary colours.

дополн|ить, ю, ишь, *pf.* (*of* ~я́ть) to supplement, add to; (*fig.*) to embellish (*a story, etc.*); д. друг дрýга to complement one another.

дополн|я́ть, я́ю, *impf. of* ~ить.

допотóпный, *adj.* antediluvian.

допрáшива|ть, ю, *impf. of* допроси́ть.

допризы́вник, а, *m.* youth undergoing pre-conscription military training.

допризы́вный, *adj.* pre-conscription.

допрóс, а, *m.* (*leg.*) interrogation, examination; перекрёстный д. cross-examination.

допр|оси́ть, ошý, оси́шь, *pf.* (*of* ~áшивать) (*leg.*) to interrogate, question, examine.

допр|оси́ться, ошýсь, ~óсишься, *pf.* (*coll.*) 1. to obtain, find out by asking; у негó ничегó не ~óсишься one cannot get anything out of him. 2. (+*g. or inf.*) to make, get (*to do something*).

дóпуск, а, *m.* 1. right of entry, admittance. 2. (*tech.*) tolerance.

допускá|ть, ю, *impf. of* допусти́ть.

допусти́м|ый (~, ~а), *adj.* permissible, admissible; ~ая нагрýзка permissible load.

допу|сти́ть, щý, ~сти́шь, *pf.* (*of* ~скáть) 1. (до+*g.*, к+*d.*) to admit (to); д. к кóнкурсу to allow to compete. 2. to allow permit; to tolerate. **3.** to grant, assume; ⌣стим let us suppose, let us assume. **4.** to commit.

допущéни|е, я, *n.* assumption.

допыт|áться, áюсь, *pf.* (*of* ⌣ываться) to find out.

допы́тыва|ться, юсь, *impf. of* допытáться; (*impf. only*) to try to find out, try to elicit.

дóпьяна́, *adv.* (*coll.*) dead drunk; напои́ть д. to make dead drunk.

дораст|áть, áю, *impf. of* ⌣и́.

дораст|и́, у́, ёшь, *past* дорóс, доросла́, *pf.* (*of* дорастáть) **1.** (до+g.) to grow (to); (*fig.*) to attain (to), come up (to). **2.** не д. чтóбы (+inf.) not to be old enough (to); она́ ещё не доросла́, чтóбы éздить на велосипéде she is not old enough yet to ride a bicycle.

дорв|áться, у́сь, ёшься, *past* ⌣áлся, ⌣ала́сь, ⌣áлóсь, *pf.* (до; *coll.*) to fall upon, seize upon.

дореволюциóнный, *adj.* pre-revolutionary.

дорефóрменный, *adj.* before the reform(s) (*esp. with reference to the emancipation of serfs and other reforms in Russia in the 1860s*).

дори́ческий, *adj.* (*ling., archit.*) Doric, Dorian.

дорóг|а, и, f. **1.** road, way (*also fig.*); желéзная д. railway(s); д. пéрвого клáсса first--class road; д. государственного значéния national highway; вы́йти на ⌣y to get on, succeed; дать, уступи́ть комý-н. ⌣y to let someone pass, make way for someone (*also fig.*); идти́ своéй ⌣ой to go one's own way; перебежáть, переби́ть комý-н. ⌣y to steal a march on someone; пойти́ по плохóй ⌣е to be on the downward path; стать комý-н. ⌣и to stand in someone's way; тудá емý и д. (*coll.*) it serves him right; скáтертью д.! good riddance! **2.** journey; отпрáвиться в ⌣y to set out; запасти́ прови́зии на ⌣y to lay in supplies for the journey; в ⌣е on the journey, en route; с ⌣и after the journey, from the road. **3.** (the) way, route; показáть ⌣y to show the way, direct; сби́ться с ⌣и to lose one's way; нам с ни́ми бы́ло по ⌣е we went the same way; нам с ни́м дáльше нé было по ⌣е our ways parted (*also fig.*).

дóрого, *adv.* dear, dearly; д. обойти́сь (+d.) to cost one dear; д. бы я дал, чтóбы... (*coll.*) I would give anything to . . .

дороговизн|а, ы́, f. dearness, expensiveness.

дорóгой, *adv.* on the way, en route.

дорог|óй (дóрог, дорогá, дóрого), *adj.* **1.** dear, expensive; costly; по ⌣óй ценé at a high price; ⌣áя побéда dearly-bought victory. **2.** dear; precious; *as noun* д., ⌣óго, *m.*, ⌣áя, ⌣óй, f. (my) dear.

дорóд|ный (⌣ен, ⌣на), *adj.* portly, burly.

дорóдств|о, а, *n.* **1.** portliness, burliness. **2.** (*obs.*) courage, prowess.

дорожá|ть, ет, *impf.* (*of* вз⌣ *and* по⌣) to rise (in price), go up.

дорóже, *comp. of* дорогóй *and* дóрого.

дорож|и́ть, у́, и́шь, *impf.* (+i.) to value; to prize, set store (by).

дорож|и́ться, у́сь, и́шься, *impf.* (*coll.*) to ask too high a price, overcharge.

дорóжк|а, и, f. **1.** path, walk. **2.** (*sport*) track; lane. **3.** (*aeron.*) runway. **4.** strip (*of carpet, linoleum or fabric*); runner.

дорóжник, а, *m.* road-worker.

дорóжн|ый, *adj.* **1.** *adj. of* дорóга; д. знак road sign; д. отдéл highways department; ⌣ое строи́тельство road-building. **2.** travel, travelling; ⌣ые расхóды travelling expenses. **3.** *as noun* д., ⌣ого, *m.* (*obs.*) traveller.

дорсáльный, *adj.* dorsal.

дортуáр, а, *m.* (*obs.*) dormitory.

досáд|а, ы, f. vexation, disappointment, spite; какáя д.! what a nuisance!, what a pity!

доса|ди́ть[1], жý, ди́шь, *pf.* (*of* ⌣ждáть) (+d.) to annoy, vex.

доса|ди́ть[2], жý, ⌣ди́шь, *pf.* to finish planting.

досáдлив|ый (⌣, ⌣а), *adj.* expressing vexation, irritation, disappointment; д. жест a gesture of vexation.

досáдно, *as pred.* it is vexing, annoying; it is a nuisance.

досáд|ный (⌣ен, ⌣на), *adj.* vexing, annoying; disappointing.

досáд|овать, ую, *impf.* (на+a.) to be annoyed (with), be vexed (with).

досаждá|ть, ю, *impf. of* досади́ть[1].

досéле, *adv.* (*obs.*) up to now.

доси|дéть, жý, ди́шь, *pf.* (*of* ⌣живать) (до +g.) to sit (until), stay (until).

доси́жива|ть, ю, *impf. of* досидéть.

доск|á, и́, а. ⌣у, *pl.* ⌣и, *g.* досóк, *d.* ⌣áм, *f.* **1.** board, plank; д. для объявлéний notice-board; д. почёта board of honour (*with photographs and names of outstanding workers*); как д. (худóй) thin as a rake; прочéсть от ⌣й до ⌣й to read from cover to cover; стáвить на однý ⌣у (c+i.) to put on a level (with); пьян в ⌣у (*sl.*) dead drunk. **2.** slab; plaque, plate.

досконáл|ьный (⌣ен, ⌣ьна), *adj.* thorough.

до|слáть, шлю, шлёшь, *pf.* (*of* ⌣сылáть) **1.** to send in addition; to send the remainder. **2.** (*mil.*) to seat, chamber (*a cartridge, etc.*).

дослéдовани|е, я, *n.* (*leg.*) supplementary examination, further inquiry; напрáвить дéло на д. to remit a case for further inquiry.

дослед|овать, ую, *impf. and pf.* (*leg.*) to submit to supplementary examination, further inquiry.

дословно, *adv.* verbatim, word for word.

дословный, *adj.* literal, verbatim; **д. перевод** literal translation.

дослужива|ть(ся), ю(сь), *impf. of* дослужить(ся).

дослуж|ить, у, ~ишь, *pf.* (*of* ~ивать) (до+ g.) to serve (until); to finish a period of service.

дослуж|иться, усь, ~ишься, *pf.* (*of* ~иваться) to obtain as a result of service; **д. до чина майора** to rise to the rank of major; **д. до пенсии** to qualify for a pension.

досматрива|ть, ю, *impf. of* досмотреть.

досмотр, а, *m.* examination (*at Customs, etc.*).

досмотр|еть, ю, ~ишь, *pf.* (*of* досматривать) **1.** (до+g.) to watch, look at (to, as far as); **мы ~ели пьесу до третьего акта** we saw the play as far as the third act. **2. не д.** to overlook, to allow to escape one's notice.

досмотрщик, а, *m.* inspector, examiner.

досоветский, *adj.* pre-Soviet.

доспева|ть, ю, *impf. of* доспеть.

доспе|ть, ю, ешь, *pf.* (*of* ~вать) to ripen, mature; **время ~ло** (*obs.*) the time has come.

доспех|и, ов, *sing.* ~, ~а, *m.*, armour.

досрочный, *adj.* ahead of schedule, early.

доста|вать(ся), ю(сь), ёшь(ся), *impf. of* ~ть(ся).

достав|ить, лю, ишь, *pf.* (*of* ~лять) **1.** to deliver, convey; to supply, furnish. **2.** to give, cause; **д. случай** to afford an opportunity; **д. удовольствие** to give pleasure.

доставк|а, и, *f.* delivery, conveyance (*of goods, etc.*).

доставля|ть, ю, *impf. of* доставить.

доставщик, а, *m.* delivery man, roundsman.

достаива|ть, ю, *impf. of* достоять.

достат|ок, ка, *m.* **1.** sufficiency. **2.** prosperity; **жить в ~ке** to be comfortably off. **3.** (*pl. only*) income.

достаточно¹, *adv.* sufficiently, enough.

достаточно², *as pred.* it is enough; **д. сказать** suffice it to say; **д. было одного взгляда** one glance was enough.

достаточност|ь, и, f. **1.** sufficiency. **2.** (*obs.*) easy circumstances.

достаточ|ный (~ен, ~на), *adj.* **1.** sufficient. **2.** (*coll.*) prosperous, well-to-do.

доста|ть, ну, нешь, *pf.* (*of* ~вать) **1.** to fetch; to take out; **д. платок из кармана** to take a handkerchief out of one's pocket. **2.** (+g. *or* до+g.) to touch; to reach; **д. рукой до потолка** to touch the ceiling. **3.** to get, obtain. **4.** (*impers.*+g.; *coll.*) to suffice.

доста|ться, нусь, нешься *pf.* (*of* ~ваться)

(+d.) **1.** to pass (to) (by inheritance); **ему ~лось большое имение** he came into a large estate. **2.** to fall to one's lot. **3.** (*impers.*; *coll.*) **ему, etc., ~нется** he, *etc.*, will catch it.

достига|ть, ю, *impf. of* достигнуть *and* достичь.

достиг|нуть, ну, нешь, *past* ~, ~ла, *pf.* (*of* ~ать) **1.** (+g. *or* до+g.) to reach; **д. гавани** to reach harbour; **д. старости** to reach old age; **слух ~ до наших ушей** a rumour had come to our ears. **2.** (+g.) to attain, achieve.

достижени|е, я, *n.* achievement, attainment.

достижим|ый (~, ~а), *adj.* accessible; attainable.

достичь = достигнуть.

достоверност|ь, и, f. authenticity; trustworthiness.

достовер|ный (~ен, ~на), *adj.* authentic, trustworthy.

достодолжный, *adj.* (*obs.*) due, just.

достоевщин|а, ы, f. **1.** mental imbalance (*as exemplified especially by characters in the novels of Dostoevsky*). **2.** analysis of character in the manner of Dostoevsky.

достоинств|о, а, *n.* **1.** merit, virtue. **2.** (*sing. only*) dignity; **чувство собственного ~а** self-respect. **3.** (*econ.*) value; **монеты малого ~а** coins of small denomination. **4.** (*obs.*) rank, title.

достойно, *adv.* **1.** suitably, fittingly, adequately, properly. **2.** (*obs.*) with dignity.

досто|йный (~ин, ~йна), *adj.* **1.** (+g.) worthy (of), deserving; **д. внимания** worthy of note; **д. похвалы** praiseworthy. **2.** deserved; fitting, adequate; **~йная награда** deserved reward. **3.** suitable, fit. **4.** worthy.

достопамят|ный (~ен, ~на), *adj.* memorable.

достопочтённый, *adj.* (*obs.*) venerable; (*iron.*) worthy.

достопримечательност|ь, и, f. sight; place, object of note; **осматривать ~и** to go sight-seeing, see the sights.

достопримечател|ьный (~ен, ~ьна), *adj.* remarkable, notable.

достояни|е, я, *n.* property.

досто|ять, ю, ишь, *pf.* (*of* достаивать) to wait standing (until).

достука|ться, юсь, *pf.* (*coll.*) to get what one had been asking for, get the punishment one deserves.

доступ, а, *m.* **1.** entrance. **2.** access, admission, admittance.

доступ|ный (~ен, ~на), *adj.* **1.** accessible; easy of access. **2.** (для+g.) open (to); available (to). **3.** simple; easily understood;

intelligible. **4.** (*of prices*) moderate, reasonable. **5.** affable, approachable. **6.** ~ная жéнщина (*obs.*) loose woman, woman of easy virtue.

достуЧ|а́ться, у́сь, и́шься, *pf.* (*coll.*) to knock until one is heard.

досу́г, а, *m.* **1.** leisure, leisure-time; на ~е at leisure, in one's spare time. **2.** (*as pred.*; +d. and *inf.*; *coll.*) to have time (to, for); где мне д. чита́ть? what time have I for reading?

досу́ж|ий, *adj.* (*coll.*) **1.** leisure; ~ее врéмя leisure-time, spare time. **2.** idle; ~ие разгово́ры idle talk.

до́суха, *adv.* (until) dry; вы́тереть д. to rub dry.

досчита́|ть, ю, *pf.* (*of* досчи́тывать) **1.** to finish counting. **2.** (до+g.) to count (up to); д. до ста to count up to a hundred.

досчи́тыва|ть, ю, *impf. of* досчита́ть.

досыла́|ть, ю, *impf. of* досла́ть.

досы́п|ать, лю, лешь, *pf.* (*of* ~а́ть) to pour in, fill up.

досы́п|а́ть, а́ю, *impf. of* ~ать.

до́сы́та, *adv.* (*coll.*) to satiety.

досьé, *indecl.,* *n.* dossier, file.

досю́да, *adv.* (*coll.*) as far as here, up to here.

досяга́емост|ь, и, *f.* reach; (*mil.*) range; вне предéлов ~и beyond reach.

досяга́ем|ый (~, ~а), *adj.* attainable, accessible.

дот, а, *m.* (*abbr. of* долговрéменная огневáя то́чка) (*mil.*) (*reinforced concrete*) pill-box.

дота́скива|ть(ся), ю(сь), *impf. of* дотащи́ть-(ся).

дота́ци|я, и, *f.* (State) grant, subsidy.

дотащ|и́ть, у́, ~ишь, *pf.* (*of* дота́скивать) (*coll.*) (до+g.) to carry, drag (to).

дотащ|и́ться, у́сь, ~ишься, *pf.* (*of* дота́скиваться) (*coll.*) to drag oneself; рáненый едвá ~и́лся до свои́х пози́ций the wounded man hardly managed to drag himself to his lines.

дотемна́, *adv.* until it gets (got) dark.

дотла́, *adv.* utterly, completely; разорён д. razed to the ground; сгорéть д. to burn to the ground.

дото́ле, *adv.* (*obs.*) until then, hitherto.

дото́шный, *adj.* (*coll.*) meticulous.

дотра́гива|ться, юсь, *impf. of* дотро́нуться.

дотро́н|уться, усь, ешься, *pf.* (*of* дотра́гиваться) (до+g.) to touch.

дотя́гива|ть(ся), ю(сь), ешь(ся), *impf. of* дотяну́ть(ся).

дотян|у́ть, у́, ~ешь, *pf.* (*of* дотя́гивать) (до +g.) **1.** to draw, drag, haul (to, as far as). **2.** (*coll.*) to reach, make. **3.** to stretch out (to, as far as). **4.** (*coll.*) to hold out (till); to live (till); он до утра́ не ~ет he won't last till morning. **5.** (*coll.*) to put off (till).

дотян|у́ться, у́сь, ~ешься, *pf.* (*of* дотя́гиваться) (до+g.) **1.** to reach; to touch. **2.** (*coll.*) to stretch (to), reach; о́чередь ~у́лась до конца́ у́лицы the queue stretched to the end of the street. **3.** (*coll.*; *of time*) to drag by (until).

доу́чива|ть(ся), ю(сь), *impf. of* доучи́ть(ся).

доуч|и́ть, у́, ~ишь, *pf.* (*of* ~ивать) **1.** to finish teaching; (до+g.) to teach (up to). **2.** to finish learning; (до+g.) to learn (up to, as far as).

доуч|и́ться, у́сь, ~ишься, *pf.* (*of* ~иваться) **1.** to complete one's studies, finish one's education. **2.** (до+g.) to study (up to, till).

дох|á, и́, *pl.* ~и, *f.* fur-coat (*with fur on both sides*).

до́хлый, *adj.* **1.** dead (*of animals*). **2.** (*coll.*) sickly; weakly (*of human beings*).

дохля́тин|а, ы (*coll.*) **1.** *f.* carcase; (*collect.*) carrion. **2.** *m. and f.* feeble, sickly person.

дох|нуть, ну, нешь, *past* ~, ~ла, *impf.* (*of* по~) to die (*of animals*).

дохн|у́ть, у́, ёшь, *pf.* **1.** to breathe (*of a single breath*); тут д. нéгде there is no room to breathe here. **2.** to blow.

дохо́д, а, *m.* income; receipts; revenue.

дохо|ди́ть, жу́, ~дишь, *impf. of* дойти́.

дохо́дност|ь, и, *f.* profitableness; income.

дохо́д|ный (~ен, ~на), *adj.* **1.** profitable, lucrative, paying. **2.** *adj. of* ~.

дохо́дчив|ый (~, ~а), *adj.* intelligible, easy to understand.

дохристиа́нский, *adj.* pre-Christian.

доцéнт, а, *m.* senior lecturer, (university) reader.

доценту́р|а, ы, *f.* post of senior lecturer, (university) reader. **2.** (*collect.*) = доцéнты.

до́чери, до́черью, *see* дочь.

до́черин = дочéрнин.

дочéрн|ий, *adj.* **1.** daughter's. **2.** daughter; branch; ~ее предприя́тие (*comm.*) branch (establishment).

дочéрнин, *adj.* (*coll.*) daughter's.

до́чиста, *adv.* **1.** clean; вы́мыть д. to wash clean. **2.** (*fig.*, *coll.*) clean, completely; егó обыгра́ли д. they cleaned him out (*at cards*).

дочит|а́ть, а́ю, *pf.* (*of* ~ывать) **1.** to finish reading. **2.** (до+g.) to read (to, as far as).

дочит|а́ться, а́юсь, *pf.* (*of* ~ываться) (*coll.*) (до+g.) to read (to the point of).

дочи́тыва|ть(ся), ю(сь), *impf. of* дочита́ть(ся).

до́чк|а, и, *f.* (*coll.*) = дочь.

дочу́рк|а, и, *f.* (*coll.*) dim. of дочь.

дочь, ~ери, i. ~ерью, *pl.* ~ери, ~ерéй, ~еря́м, о ~еря́х, *f.* daughter.

дошко́льник, а, *m.* **1.** child under school age. **2.** specialist on training of pre-school-age children.

дошко́льный, adj. pre-school.

до́шлый, adj. (coll.) cunning, shrewd.

доща́ник, а, m. flat-bottomed boat.

доща́тый, adj. made of planks, boards; д. насти́л duckboards.

доще́чк|а, и, f. 1. dim. of доска́. 2. door--plate, name-plate.

доя́рк|а, и, f. milkmaid.

дра́г|а, и, f. (tech.) drag, dredge.

драги́р|овать, ую, impf. and pf. (tech.) to drag, dredge.

драго́й, adj. (obs. or poet.) dear, precious.

драгома́н, а, m. dragoman.

драгоце́нност|ь, и, f. 1. jewel; gem; precious stone; (pl.) jewelry. 2. object of great value; (pl.) valuables.

драгоце́н|ный (~ен, ~на), adj. precious (also fig.); ~ные ка́мни precious stones.

драгу́н, а, g. pl. ~, m. dragoon.

дража́йш|ий, superl. of дорого́й; ~ая поло-ви́на 'better half'.

драже́, indecl., n. dragée; шокола́дное д. chocolate drop.

дразн|и́ть, ю́, ~ишь, impf. 1. to tease; его́ ~и́ли тру́сом they used to mock him by calling him a coward. 2. to excite; to tantalize.

дра́|ить, ю, ишь, impf. (naut.) to polish; to swab.

драйв, а, m. drive (in tennis).

дра́к|а, и, f. fight; у них дошло́ до ~и they came to blows.

драко́н, а, m. 1. dragon. 2. (heraldry) wyvern.

драко́новский, adj. Draconian.

дра́ла, as pred. (coll.) (he) ran off, made off; встал да и д. he got up and made off; дать д. to take to one's heels.

дра́м|а, ы, f. 1. drama. 2. (fig.) tragedy, calamity.

драматиза́ци|я, и, f. dramatization.

драматизи́р|овать, ую, impf. and pf. to dramatize.

драмати́зм, а, m. 1. (theatr.) dramatic effect. 2. (fig.) dramatic character, quality; tension.

драмати́ческ|ий, adj. 1. dramatic; drama, theatre; ~ое иску́сство dramatic art, art of the theatre; д. теа́тр theatre (as opp. to cinema, ballet, opera). 2. dramatic, theatrical; ~им то́ном in a dramatic tone. 3. (fig.) dramatic; tense. 4. (mus.) strong (of a voice).

драмати́ч|ный (~ен, ~на), adj. (fig.) dramatic.

драмату́рг, а, m. playwright, dramatist.

драматурги́|я, и, f. 1. dramatic art. 2. (collect.) plays, drama; д. Че́хова the plays of Chekhov. 3. dramatic theory, drama.

драмкруж|о́к, ка́, m. dramatic circle.

драндуле́т, а, m. (coll., joc.) old, dilapidated conveyance.

драни́ц|а, ы, f. (dial.)= дра́нка.

дра́нк|а, и, f. (tech.) 1. lathing, shingle. 2. lath.

дра́ночный, adj. of дра́нка.

дра́ный, adj. (coll.) tattered, ragged.

дран|ь, и, f. (collect.; tech.) lathing, shingle.

драп, а, m. thick woollen cloth.

драпа́н|уть, у́, ёшь, pf. of дра́пать.

дра́па|ть, ю, impf. (of ~нуть) (sl.) to clear out, scarper.

драпир|ова́ть, у́ю, impf. to drape.

драпир|ова́ться, у́юсь, impf. 1. (в+a. or +i.) to drape oneself (in); (fig.) to affect, make a parade (of). 2. pass. of ~ова́ть.

драпиро́вк|а, и, f. 1. draping. 2. curtain; hangings.

драпиро́вщик, а, m. upholsterer.

дра́п|овый, adj. of ~.

драпри́, indecl., n. 1. draperies. 2. hangings, curtains.

дра́тв|а, ы, f. waxed thread.

дра|ть, деру́, дерёшь, past ~л, ~ла́, ~ло, impf. 1. (impf. only) to tear (up, to pieces); д. го́рло (coll.) to bawl; д. нос (coll.) to turn up one's nose, put on airs; д. на себе́ во́лосы (fig.) to tear one's hair. 2. (pf. со~) to tear off; д. лы́ко (с лип) to bark (lime--trees); д. шку́ру to flay. 3. (pf. за~) to kill (of wild animals). 4. (pf. вы́~) (coll.) to beat, flog, thrash; to tear out; д. зу́бы to pull out teeth. 5. (pf. со~) (с+g.; fig., coll.) to fleece; to sting; д. с живо́го и мёртвого to fleece unmercifully. 6. (pf. по~) чёрт его́ (по)дери́! damn him! 7. (impf. only) (coll.) to sting, irritate; д. у́ши (+d.) to jar (on); у меня́ в го́рле дерёт (impers.) I have a sore throat. 8. (impf. only) (coll.) to run away, make off; д. во все лопа́тки, со всех ног to run as fast as one's legs can carry one.

дра́|ться, деру́сь, дерёшься, past ~лся, ~ла́сь, ~ло́сь, impf. 1. (с+i.) to fight (with); д. на дуэ́ли to fight a duel. 2. (fig.) (за+a.) to fight, struggle (for). 3. to hit, to give a hiding.

дра́хм|а, ы, f. 1. drachma (Greek unit of currency). 2. dram (apothecaries' weight).

драце́н|а, ы, f. (bot.) club palm, cabbage--tree (Cordyline australis).

драч¹, а́, m. (tech.) plane.

драч², а́, m. (coll.) flayer, knacker.

драчли́вост|ь, и, f. pugnacity.

драчли́в|ый (~, ~а), adj. pugnacious.

драчу́н, а́, m. (coll.) pugnacious, quarrelsome fellow.

драчу́н|ья, и, g. pl. ~ий, (coll.) f. of ~.

дребеде́н|ь, и, f. (coll.) nonsense; сплошна́я д. absolute rubbish.

дрéбезг, а, *m.* (*coll.*) 1. tinkling sound (*as of breaking glass, etc.*). 2. (*pl. only*) разби́ть(ся) в (мéлкие) ~и to smash to smithereens.

дребезжáни|е, я, *n.* jingle, tinkle.

дребезж|áть, и́т, *impf.* to jingle, tinkle.

древеси́н|а, ы, *f.* 1. wood (*substance*); wood-pulp. 2. timber.

древéсниц|а, ы, *f.* (*zool.*) 1. tree-frog. 2. leopard moth.

древéсн|ый, *adj.* of дéрево; ~ая мáсса wood-pulp; д. сáхар wood sugar, xylose; д. спирт wood alcohol; д. у́голь charcoal; д. у́ксус (*chem.*) wood vinegar, pyroligneous acid.

дрéвк|о, а, *pl.* ~и, ~ов, *n.* pole; staff; shaft (*of spear, etc.*); д. знáмени flagstaff.

древлехрани́лищ|е, а, *n.* (*obs.*) archive.

древнегрéческий, *adj.* ancient Greek.

древнееврéйский, *adj.* Hebrew.

древнеру́сский, *adj.* Old Russian.

древнецеркóвнославя́нский, *adj.* (*ling.*) Old Church Slavonic.

дрéв|ний (~ен, ~ня), *adj.* 1. ancient; ~няя истóрия ancient history; ~ние языки́ classical languages; *as noun* ~ние, ~них, the ancients. 2. very old, aged.

дрéвност|ь, и, *f.* 1. (*sing. only*) antiquity. 2. (*pl.; archaeol.*) antiquities.

дрéв|о, а, *pl.* ~есá, ~éс, ~есáм, *n.* (*poet.*) tree; д. познáния добрá и злá the tree of the knowledge of good and evil.

древови́д|ный (~ен, ~на), tree-like; д. пáпоротник tree-fern.

древонасаждéни|е, я, *n.* 1. tree-plantation. 2. planting of trees.

дреднóут, а, *m.* (*naut.*) dreadnought.

дрези́н|а, ы, *f.* (*railways*) trolley, hand car.

дрейф, а, *m.* (*naut.*) drift, leeway; лечь в д. to heave to; лежáть в ~е to lie to.

дрейф|ить, лю, ишь, *impf.* (*of* с~) (*coll.*) to be a coward, funk.

дрейф|овáть, у́ю, *impf.* (*naut.*) to drift; ~у́ющий лёд drift ice; научная ~у́ющая стáнция drift-ice research unit.

дрек, а, *m.* (*naut.*) grapnel.

дрекóль|е, я, *n.* (*collect.*) staves (*as weapon*).

дрел|ь, и, *f.* (*tech.*) (hand-)drill.

дрем|á, ы́ (*and* дрём|а, ы), *f.* (*poet.*) drowsiness, sleepiness.

дрем|áть, лю́, ~лешь, *impf.* to doze; to slumber; не д. (*also fig.*) to be watchful; to be wide awake.

дрем|áться, ~лется, *impf.* (*impers.* +*d.*) to feel sleepy, drowsy.

дремóт|а, ы, *f.* drowsiness, sleepiness, somnolence.

дремóтный, *adj.* drowsy, sleepy, somnolent.

дрему́ч|ий (~, ~а), *adj.* (*poet.*) thick, dense (*of a forest*).

дренáж, а, *m.* 1. (*tech. and med.*) drainage. 2. (*med.*) drainage-tube.

дренажи́р|овать, ую, *impf. and pf.* (*med.*) to drain.

дренáж|ный, *adj.* of ~; ~ная трубá drain-pipe.

дрени́р|овать, ую, *impf. and pf.* to drain.

дресв|á, ы́, *f.* gravel.

дрессирóванн|ый, *p.p.p.* of дрессировáть *and adj.*; ~ые живóтные performing animals.

дрессир|овáть, у́ю, *impf.* (*of* вы́~) to train (*animals*); (*fig.*) to school.

дрессирóвк|а, и, *f.* training.

дрессирóвщик, а, *m.* trainer.

дриáд|а, ы, *f.* (*myth.*) dryad.

дроби́лк|а, и, *f.* (*tech.*) crusher.

дроби́льн|ый, *adj.* (*tech.*) crushing; ~ая маши́на crusher.

дроби́н|а, ы, *f.* pellet.

дроб|и́ть, лю́, и́шь, *impf.* (*of* раз~) 1. to break up, crush, smash (to pieces). 2. (*fig.*) to subdivide, split up.

дроб|и́ться, и́тся, *impf.* (*of* раз~) 1. to break to pieces, smash, smash to pieces. 2. to divide, split up.

дроблéни|е, я, *n.* 1. crushing, breaking up. 2. (*fig.*) subdivision, splitting up. 3. (*biol.*) cell-division.

дроблёный, *adj.* splintered, crushed, ground.

дробни́ц|а, ы, *f.* ammunition-pouch.

дрóб|ный (~ен, ~на), *adj.* 1. separate; subdivided, split up; minute. 2. staccato, abrupt; д. стук staccato knocking; д. дождь fine rain. 3. (*math.*) fractional.

дробови́к, á, *m.* shot-gun.

дроб|ь, и, *pl.* ~и, ~éй, *f.* 1. (*collect.*) small shot. 2. drumming; tapping; trilling. 3. (*math.*) fraction. 4. oblique stroke.

дров|á, ~, ~áм, *no sing.* firewood; наколóть д. to chop firewood; кто в лес, кто по дровá (*fig.*) at sixes and sevens, inharmoniously.

дрóвн|и, ~éй, *no sing.* (*peasant*) wood-sledge.

дровокóл, а, *m.* (*obs.*) woodcutter.

дровосéк, а, *m.* 1. woodcutter. 2.(*pl.*) (*zool.*) Cerambycidae.

дровяни́к, á, *m.* 1. (*obs.*) firewood merchant. 2. (*coll.*) woodshed.

дров|янóй, *adj.* of ~á; д. сарáй woodshed; д. склад wood pile, wood store.

дрог|á, и́, *a.* ~у, *pl.* ~и, *f.* centre pole (*of cart*).

дрóг|и, ~, *no sing.* 1. dray cart. 2. hearse.

дрóг|нуть[1], ну, нешь, *past* ~, ~ла, *impf.* to be chilled, freeze.

дрóгн|уть[2], у, ешь, *past* ~ул, ~ула, *pf.* 1. to shake, move; to quaver; to flicker. 2. to waver, falter; у меня́ рукá не ~ет (+*inf.*) I shall not hesitate to . . .

дрожа́ни|е, я, *n.* trembling, vibration.

дрожа́тельный, *adj.* tremulous, shivery; д. парали́ч (*med.*) shaking palsy, Parkinson's disease.

дрож|а́ть, у́, и́шь, *impf.* 1. to tremble; to shiver, shake; to quiver; to vibrate; to quaver; to flicker; д. от хо́лода, испу́га to shiver with cold, with fright. 2. (за+*a.* or пе́ред+*i.*; *fig.*) to tremble (for; before). 3. (над+*i.*) to grudge; д. над ка́ждой копе́йкой to count every penny.

дрожж|ево́й, *adj.* of ∼и; ∼евы́е грибки́ (*bot.*) Ascomycetes.

дро́жж|и, е́й, *no sing.* yeast, leaven; ста́вить на ∼а́х to leaven; пивны́е д. barm, brewer's yeast.

дро́ж|ки, ∼ек, ∼кам, *no sing.* droshky.

дрож|ь, и, *f.* 1. shivering, trembling; tremor, quaver. 2. (varied) tints.

дрозд, а́, *m.* thrush; пе́вчий д. song-thrush; чёрный д. blackbird.

дрок, а, *m.* (*bot.*) gorse.

дромаде́р, а, *m.* (*zool.*) dromedary.

дро́ссел|ь, я, *m.* (*tech.*) throttle, choke.

дро́тик, а, *m.* javelin.

дрочён|а, ы, *f.* (*cul.*) batter.

друг¹, а, *pl.* друзья́, друзе́й, *m.* friend; д. до́ма friend of the family.

друг² (*short form of* ∼о́й) д. ∼а each other, one another; д. за ∼ом one after another; д. с ∼ом with each other.

друг|о́й, *adj.* 1. other, another; different; и тот и д. both; ни тот ни д. neither; никто́ д. none other; э́то ∼о́е де́ло that is another matter; ∼и́ми слова́ми in other words; с ∼о́й стороны́ on the other hand; на д. день the next day; *as noun* ∼и́е, ∼и́х others. 2. second. 3. (*coll.*) the odd.

дру́жб|а, ы, *f.* friendship; не в слу́жбу, а в ∼у out of friendship.

дружелю́би|е, я, *n.* friendliness.

дружелю́б|ный (∼ен, ∼на), *adj.* friendly, amicable.

дру́жеск|ий, *adj.* friendly; быть на ∼ой ноге́ (c+*i.*) to be on friendly terms (with).

дру́жественн|ый, *adj.* friendly, amicable; ∼ая держа́ва friendly power.

дру́жеств|о, а, *n.* (*obs.*) friendship.

дружи́н|а, ы, *f.* 1. (*hist.*) (prince's) armed force. 2. militia unit, detachment (*in tsarist Russia*); боева́я д. (*hist.*) armed workers' detachment. 3. squad, team; доброво́льная наро́дная д. voluntary people's (militia) patrol (*as organized in U.S.S.R. since 1958 to assist police in maintaining public order, combatting hooliganism, etc.*).

дружи́нник, а, *m.* 1. (*hist.*) member of (prince's) armed force. 2. (*hist.*) member of militia detachment; member of armed band. 3. member of voluntary people's (militia) patrol, vigilante; д. противовоздушной оборо́ны air-raid warden.

друж|и́ть, у́, ∼и́шь, *impf.* 1. (c+*i.*) to be friends (with), on friendly terms (with). 2. (*obs.*) to make friends, unite.

друж|и́ться, у́сь, ∼и́шься, *impf.* (*of* по∼) (c+*i.*) to make friends (with).

дру́жищ|е, а, *m.* (*coll.*) old chap (*as mode of address*).

дру́жк|а¹, и, *m.* (*ethnol.*) best man (*at wedding*).

дру́жк|а²: друг ∼у, *etc.* (*coll.*) = друг дру́га, *etc.*

дру́жно, *adv.* 1. harmoniously, in concord. 2. simultaneously, in concert; раз, два, ∼! heave-ho!, all together! 3. rapidly, smoothly (*of coming of spring, thawing of snow, etc.*).

дру́ж|ный (∼ен, ∼на́, ∼но), *adj.* 1. amicable; harmonious. 2. simultaneous, concerted; ∼ные уси́лия concerted efforts. 3. ∼ная весна́ spring with rapid, uninterrupted thawing of snow.

друж|о́к, ка́, *m.* (*coll.*) pal; (*as mode of address*) my dear.

друзья́, *see* друг.

друммо́ндов, *adj.*; д. свет (*theatr.*) limelight.

дры́г|ать, аю, *impf.* (*of* ∼нуть) (+*i.*; *coll.*) to jerk, twitch.

дры́г|нуть, ну, нешь, *pf. of* ∼ать.

дрых|нуть, ну, нешь, *past* ∼ *and* ∼нул, ∼ла, *impf.* (*coll.*) to sleep.

дря́бл|ый (∼, ∼а́, ∼о), *adj.* flabby (*also fig.*); flaccid; sluggish.

дря́бн|уть, у, ешь, *impf.* (*coll.*) to become flabby.

дря́гил|ь, я, *m.* (*obs.*) carrier, porter.

дря́зг, а (у), *m.* (*collect.*; *obs. or dial.*) refuse, rubbish.

дря́зг|и, ∼, *no sing.* (*coll.*) squabbles; annoyances, unpleasantnesses.

дрянно́й, *adj.* (*coll.*) worthless, rotten; good-for-nothing.

дрян|ь, и, *f.* (*coll.*) 1. trash, rubbish. 2. *as pred.* it is rotten, it is no good; пого́да ∼. the weather is awful. 3. (*of a person*) a bad lot, a good-for-nothing.

дряхле́|ть, ю, *impf.* (*of* о∼) to grow decrepit.

дря́хлост|ь, и, *f.* decrepitude, senile infirmity.

дря́хл|ый (∼, ∼а́, ∼о), *adj.* decrepit, senile.

дуали́зм, а, *m.* (*philos.*) dualism.

дуб, а, *pl.* ∼ы́, *m.* 1. oak. 2. (*coll.*) blockhead, numskull.

дуба́|сить, шу, сишь, *impf.* (*coll.*) 1. to cudgel. 2. (по+*d.*, в+*a.*) to bang (on).

дуби́льн|ый, *adj.* tanning, tannic; ∼ое вещество́ tannin; ∼ая кислота́ tannic acid.

дуби́л|ьня, ьни, *g. pl.* ∼ен, *f.* tannery.

дуби́льщик, а, *m.* tanner.

дуби́н|а, ы, *f.* 1. club, cudgel. 2. (*coll.*) blockhead, numskull.

дуби́нк|а, и, *f.* truncheon, baton.

дуб|и́ть, лю́, йшь, *impf.* (*of* вы́~) to·tan.

дублёный, *adj.* tanned (*also fig.* = weather-
-beaten).

дублёр, а, *m.* (*theatr.*) understudy; (*cinema*)
actor dubbing a part.

дубле́т, а, *m.* duplicate.

дублика́т, а, *m.* duplicate.

дубли́р|овать, ую, *impf.* 1. to duplicate; д.
роль (*theatr.*) to understudy a part. 2.
(*cinema*) to dub.

дубня́к, а́, *m.* wood of oak-trees.

дубова́т|ый (~, ~а), *adj.* (*coll.*) coarse;
stupid, thick.

дубо́в|ый, *adj.* 1. oak; д. лист oak-leaf; д.
гроб oak coffin. 2. (*fig., coll.*) coarse; thick;
~ая голова́ blockhead, numskull. 3. (*fig.,
coll.*) hard (= inedible).

дуб|о́к, ка́, *m.* oakling.

дубра́в|а, ы, *f.* (*poet.*) leafy grove.

дубь|ё, я́, *no pl., n.* (*collect.; coll.*) 1. cudgels.
2. fools, blockheads.

дува́н, а, *m.* (*dial. or obs.*) division of spoils;
д. ~ить to divide the spoils.

дуг|а́, и́, *pl.* ~и, *f.* 1. shaft-bow (*part of
harness*). 2. arc, arch; бро́ви ~о́й arched
brows; согну́ть в ~у́, в три ~и́ (*coll.*) to
bring under, compel to submit.

дуг|ово́й, *adj. of* ~а́; ~ова́я ла́мпа arc-lamp;
~ова́я сва́рка arc welding.

дугообра́з|ный (~ен, ~на), *adj.* arched,
bow-shaped.

дуд|е́ть, *1st person not used,* и́шь, *impf.* (*coll.*)
to play the pipe, fife.

ду́дк|а, и, *f.* pipe, fife; пляса́ть под чью-н.
~у (*fig.*) to dance to someone's tune.

ду́дки, *interj.* (*coll.*) not if I know it!, not on
your life!

ду́жк|а, и, *f.* 1. *dim. of* дуга́. 2. hoop (*at
croquet*). 3. handle.

дука́т, а, *m.* ducat.

ду́л|о, а, *n.* muzzle, barrel (*of firearms*); д.
без наре́зки smooth bore.

ду́л|ьный, *adj. of* ~о; ~ьная ско́рость
muzzle velocity.

ду́л|ьце, ьца, *g. pl.* ~ец, *n.* 1. *dim. of* ~о.
2. (*mus.*) mouthpiece (*of wind instruments*).

ду́м|а, ы, *f.* 1. thought, meditation; (*folk
poet.*) ду́мать ~у to meditate, brood. 2.
duma (*Ukrainian folk ballad*). 3. (*hist.*) duma, council, representative assembly; Госу-
да́рственная Д. the State Duma.

ду́ма|ть, ю, *impf.* (*of* по~) 1. (о+*p. or* над+
i.) to think (about); to be concerned (about);
мно́го о себе́ д. to have a high opinion of
oneself. 2. (*impf. only*) д. что... to think,
suppose that...; я ~ю! of course!, I should
think so! 3. (+*inf.*) to think of, intend; он
~ет пое́хать в Ло́ндон he is thinking of
going to London; и не ~ю (+*inf.*) I do not

dream (of); и д. не смей (+*inf.*) don't
dare (to). 4. (+*indirect question*) to wonder.

ду́ма|ться, ется, *impf.* (*impers.*+*d.*) to seem;
мне ~ется I think, I fancy; ~ется it seems.

ду́м|ец, ца, *m.* (*hist.*) member of duma;
councillor.

ду́мк|а, и, *f.* 1. *dim. of* ду́ма 1. 2. (*coll.*)
small pillow. 3. dumka (*Ukrainian folk-
-lyric*).

ду́мный, *adj.* (*hist.*) of the Boyars' Council.

ду́м|ский, *adj. of* ~а 3; ~ские де́ньги credit
notes (*issued by the Provisional Government in
1917*).

дунове́ни|е, я, *n.* puff, breath (*of wind*).

ду́н|уть, у, ешь, *pf.* to blow.

ду́пел|ь, я, *pl.* ~я́, *m.* (*orn.*) great snipe.

дупле́т, а, *m.* doublet (*at billiards*).

дупли́ст|ый (~, ~а), *adj.* hollow.

дупл|о́, а́, *pl.* ~а, ду́пел, *n.* 1. hollow (*in
tree-trunk*). 2. cavity (*in a tooth*).

-дур, *indecl. adj.,* (*mus.*) major.

ду́р|а, ы, *f. of* дура́к.

дура́к, а́, *m.* 1. (*hist.*) jester, fool. 2. fool,
ass; д. ~о́м an utter fool; не д. (+*inf.*) (to
be) expert (at); оста́вить в ~а́х to make a
fool of; оста́ться в ~а́х to be fooled, make
a fool of oneself; валя́ть, лома́ть ~а́ to play
the fool; to make a fool of oneself; на ~а́
for fun, for a joke; ~а́м зако́н не пи́сан
(*prov.*) fools rush in where angels fear to
tread; нашёл ~а́! not likely!, no thanks!

дурале́|й, я, *m.* = дура́к 2.

дура́цкий, *adj.* (*coll.*) stupid, foolish, idiotic;
д. колпа́к dunce's cap.

дура́честв|о, а, *n.* folly, absurdity; foolish
trick.

дура́ч|ить, у, ишь, *impf.* (*of* о~) to fool,
dupe.

дура́ч|иться, усь, ишься, *impf.* to play the
fool.

дурач|о́к, ка́, *m.* 1. *affectionate dim. of* дура́к.
2. (*coll.*) idiot, imbecile.

дура́шлив|ый (~, ~а), *adj.* (*coll.*) stupid.

ду́р|ень, ня, *m.* (*coll.*) fool, simpleton.

дуре́|ть, ю, *impf.* (*of* о~) to become stupid.

дур|и́ть, ю́, и́шь, *impf.* (*coll.*) 1. to be
naughty (*of children*); to play tricks. 2. to be
obstinate (*esp. of horses*).

дурма́н, а, *m.* 1. (*bot.*) thorn-apple (*Datura
stramonium*). 2. (*coll.*) drug, narcotic; in-
toxicant.

дурма́н|ить, ю, ишь, *impf.* (*of* о~) to stupefy.

дурне́|ть, ю, *impf.* (*of* по~) to grow ugly.

ду́рно, *adv. of* дурно́й.

ду́рно, *as pred.* (*impers.*+*d.*) мне, *etc.,* д. I,
etc., feel faint, bad, queer.

дур|но́й (~ен, ~на́, ~но), *adj.* 1. (*in var.
senses*) bad, evil; nasty; д. вкус nasty taste;
д. глаз the evil eye; ~ны́е мы́сли evil
thoughts; ~ны́е привы́чки bad habits; д.

сон bad dream. 2. (собою) ugly. 3. (coll.) foolish, stupid. 4. ~на́я боле́знь (coll.) venereal disease.

дурнот|а́, ы́, f. (coll.) faintness; nausea; чу́вствовать ~у́ to feel faint, sick.

дурну́шк|а, и, f. (coll.) plain girl, plain Jane.

ду́рост|ь, и, f. (coll.) folly, stupidity.

дуршла́г, а, m. colander.

дур|ь, и, f. (coll.) foolishness, stupidity; вы́бить, вы́колотить д. (из) to knock the nonsense (out of).

ду́с|я, и, f. (coll., affect. mode of address) darling.

ду́т|ый, p.p.p. of ~ь and adj. 1. hollow. 2. inflated; ~ые ши́ны pneumatic tyres. 3. (fig.) inflated, exaggerated; ~ые ци́фры exaggerated figures.

дуть, ду́ю, ду́ешь, impf. 1. (pf. по~) to blow; сего́дня ду́ет ве́тер с за́пада there is a west wind today; от окна́ ду́ет there is a draught from the window; в ус не ду́ет (coll.) he does not give a damn. 2. (pf. вы́~) to blow (glassware). 3. (pf. от~) (coll.) to thrash; д. и в хвост и в гри́ву to urge on, drive relentlessly. 4. (pf. вы́~) (coll.) to drink deep. 5. (coll.) to rush. 6. (coll.) to do something (e.g., to play a musical instrument) with abandon, energetically.

дуть|ё, я́, n. 1. (tech.) blowing, blast; про́ба че́рез д. bubble test. 2. (glass-)blowing.

ду́|ться, юсь, ешься, impf. (coll.) 1. (на+a.) to grumble (at), pout (at). 2. (в+a.) to play with abandon.

дух, а, m. 1. (rel., philos., and fig.) spirit; Свято́й Д. the Holy Spirit, the Holy Ghost; д. ве́ка Zeitgeist (spirit of the age). 2. spirit(s); heart; mind; настрое́ние ~а, расположе́ние ~а mood, temper, humour; быть в ~е to be in good (high) spirits; не в ~е in low spirits; па́дать ~ом to lose heart, become despondent; собра́ться с ~ом to take heart, pluck up one's courage; прису́тствие ~а presence of mind; хва́тит ~у (на+a.) to have the strength (for); у меня́ ~у не хвата́ет (+inf.) I have not the heart (to); э́то не в моём ~е it is not to my taste; что́-то в э́том ~е something of the sort. 3. breath; (coll.) air; перевести́ д. to take breath; испусти́ть д. (fig.) to give up the ghost; во весь д. (coll.) at full speed, flat out; одни́м ~ом in one breath; (fig.) at one go, at a stretch; о нём ни слу́ху ни ~у nothing is heard of him. 4. spectre, ghost. 5. (coll.) smell.

духа́н, а, m. dukhan (inn in Caucasus).

дух|и́, о́в, no sing., perfume, scent.

духобо́р, а, m. Dukhobor.

духобо́рств|о, а, n. the Dukhobor religious sect.

ду́хов, adj.; Д. день (eccl.) Whit Monday.

духове́нств|о, а, n. (collect.) clergy, priesthood.

духови́д|ец, ца, m. clairvoyant; medium.

духови́т|ый (~, ~а), adj. (coll., dial.) aromatic.

духо́вк|а, и, f. oven.

духовни́к, а́, m. (eccl.) confessor.

духо́вност|ь, и, f. spirituality.

духо́вн|ый, adj. 1. spiritual; inner, inward; ~ые запро́сы spiritual demands; д. мир inner world; д. о́блик spiritual make-up. 2. ecclesiastical; church; religious; ~ое лицо́ ecclesiastic; ~ая му́зыка church music, sacred music; д. оте́ц confessor, spiritual director; д. сан holy orders. 3. ~ое завеща́ние (last) will, testament. 4. ~ое о́ко (the) mind's eye.

духов|о́й, adj. 1. (mus.) wind; д. инструме́нт wind instrument; д. орке́стр brass band. 2. (hot-)air; ~ое отопле́ние hot-air heating; ~а́я печь oven; ~о́е ружьё air-gun; д. утю́г steam iron. 3. (cul.) steamed.

духот|а́, ы́, f. stuffiness, closeness; stuffy heat.

душ, а, m. shower-bath; приня́ть д. to take a shower(-bath).

душ|а́, и́, a. ~у, pl. ~и, f. 1. soul; (fig.) heart; без ~и́ (от; obs.) beside oneself (with); д. в ~у at one, in harmony; в ~е́ (i) inwardly, secretly, (ii) at heart; для ~и́ for one's private satisfaction; за ~ой to one's name; у него́ за ~ой ни гроша́ he hasn't a penny to his name; от ~и́ from the heart; от всей ~и́ with all one's heart; по ~е́ (+d.) to one's liking; по ~а́м говори́ть (с+i.) to have a heart-to-heart talk (with); вложи́ть ~у (в+a.) to put one's heart (into); изли́ть, отвести́ ~у to pour out one's heart; ~й не ча́ять (в+p.) to worship, adore; ско́лько ~е уго́дно to one's heart's content; ~о́й и те́лом heart and soul; ни ~о́й, ни те́лом in no wise, in no respect. 2. feeling, spirit; говори́ть с ~о́й to speak with feeling. 3. (fig.) (the) soul; moving spirit; inspiration; д. о́бщества the life and soul of the party. 4. (fig.) spirit (= person); сме́лая д. a bold spirit. 5. (fig.) soul (= person); на ~у per head; ни (живо́й) ~и́ not a (living) soul. 6. (моя́) (coll.; affectionate mode of address) my dear, darling.

душев|а́я, о́й, f. shower-bath.

душевнобольн|о́й, adj. insane; suffering from mental illness; as noun д., ~о́го, m. ~а́я, ~о́й, f. insane person; mental patient.

душе́вн|ый, adj. 1. mental, psychical; ~ая боле́знь mental illness; ~ое потрясе́ние nervous shock. 2. sincere, cordial, heartfelt; ~ая бесе́да friendly chat; д. челове́к understanding person.

душев|о́й¹, *adj.* per head; ~о́е потребле́ние consumption per head.

душево́й², *adj.* of душ.

душегре́йк|а, и, *f.* (*woman's*) sleeveless jacket (*usu. wadded or fur-lined*).

душегу́б, а, *m.* (*coll.*) murderer.

душегу́б|ка, ки, *f.* **1.** *f.* of ~. **2.** dugout (*canoe*).

душегу́бств|о, а, *n.* (*coll.*) murder.

ду́шеньк|а, и, *m. and f.* (*obs., coll.*) darling (*affectionate mode of address*).

душеполе́з|ный (~ен, ~на), *adj.* (*obs.*) edifying.

душеприка́зчик, а, *m.* (*leg.; obs.*) executor.

душеприка́зчиц|а, ы, *f.* (*leg.; obs.*) executrix.

душераздира́ющий, *adj.* heart-rending.

душеспаси́тел|ьный (~ен, ~ьна), *adj.* (*eccl. or iron.*) salutary, edifying.

ду́шечк|а, и, *m. and f.* = ду́шенька.

души́ст|ый (~, ~а), *adj.* fragrant, sweet-scented.

души́тел|ь, я, *m.* strangler, suffocator; (*fig.*) suppressor.

душ|и́ть¹, у́, ~ишь, *impf.* (*of* за~) **1.** to strangle; to stifle, smother, suffocate; (*fig.*) to stifle, suppress; д. поцелу́ями to smother with kisses. **2.** (*impf. only*) to choke; его́ ~и́л ка́шель, гнев he choked with coughing, with rage.

душ|и́ть², у́, ~ишь, *impf.* (*of* на~) to scent, perfume.

душ|и́ться¹, у́сь, ~ишься, *impf., pass. of* ~и́ть¹.

душ|и́ться², у́сь, ~ишься, *impf.* (*of* на~) (+*i.*) to perfume oneself (with); она́ всегда́ ~ится францу́зскими духа́ми she always uses French perfume.

ду́шк|а, и, *m. and f.* (*coll.*) dear (person); он тако́й д., она́ така́я д. he, she is such a dear.

душни́к, а́, *m.* vent (*in stove*).

ду́шно, *as pred.* it is stuffy; it is stifling, suffocating; мне ста́ло д. I felt suffocated.

душ|ный (~ен, ~на́, ~но), *adj.* stuffy, close, sultry; stifling.

душ|о́к, ка́, *m.* (*coll.*) **1.** smell (*esp. of decaying matter*); с ~ко́м high, tainted. **2.** (*fig.*) smack, taint; tinge; газе́та с либера́льным ~ко́м (*pejor.*) newspaper with a liberal tinge.

дуэли́ст, а, *m.* duellist.

дуэл|ь, и, *f.* duel; вы́звать на д. to challenge; дра́ться на ~и to fight a duel.

дуэля́нт, а, *m.* = дуэли́ст.

дуэ́н|ья, ьи, *g. pl.* ~ий, *f.* duenna.

дуэ́т, а, *m.* duet.

дыб|а, ы, *f.* (*hist.*) rack (*instrument of torture*).

дыб|и́ться, ится, *impf.* **1.** to stand on end. **2.** (*of a horse*) to rear, prance.

ды́бом, *adv.* on end; во́лосы у него́ вста́ли д. his hair stood on end.

дыбы́; на д. on to the hind legs; станови́ться на д. to rear, prance; (*fig.*) to kick, resist.

дылд|а, ы, *m. and f.* (*coll.*) lanky fellow, girl.

дым, а (у), о ~е, в ~у́, *pl.* ~ы́, *m.* **1.** smoke; в д. (*coll.*) completely; там д. коромы́слом (*coll.*) it's a bedlam there. **2.** (*hist.*) household, hearth (*as unit for taxation*).

дым|и́ть, лю́, и́шь, *impf.* (*of* на~) to smoke (*intrans.*), emit smoke.

дым|и́ться, и́тся, *impf.* to smoke (*intrans.*); (*of fog*) to billow.

дымк|а, и, *f.* **1.** haze (*also fig.*). **2.** (*obs.*) gauze.

ды́мный, *adj.* smoky; д. по́рох black powder, gunpowder.

дымов|о́й, *adj.* of дым; ~а́я заве́са (*mil.*) smoke-screen; ~а́я ма́ска (anti-)smoke mask; д. снаря́д (*mil.*) smoke-shell; ~а́я труба́ flue, chimney; funnel, smoke-stack.

дымога́рн|ый, *adj.*; д. котёл fire-tube boiler; ~ая труба́ flue, fire tube.

дым|о́к, ка́, *m.* puff of smoke.

дымомёт, а, *m.* (*mil.*) smoke projector.

дымохо́д, а, *m.* flue.

ды́мчат|ый (~, ~а), *adj.* smoke-coloured.

ды́нный, *adj.* of ды́ня.

ды́н|я, и, *f.* melon.

дыр|а́, ы́, *pl.* ~ы, *f.* **1.** hole; заткну́ть ~у́ (*fig.*) to stop a gap. **2.** (*fig., coll.*) hole (= remote place). **3.** (*pl. only*) gaps, shortcomings.

дыроко́л, а, *m.* hole-puncher, punch.

дыря́в|ить, лю, ишь, *impf.* (*coll.*) to make a hole (in).

дыря́в|ый (~, ~а), *adj.* full of holes, holey.

дыха́ни|е, я, *n.* breathing; breath; иску́сственное д. artificial respiration.

дыха́тельн|ый, *adj.* respiratory; ~ое го́рло (*anat.*) windpipe; ~ые пути́ respiratory tract.

дыш|а́ть, у́, ~ишь, *impf.* (+*i.*) to breathe; д. ме́стью to breathe vengeance; е́ле д. to be at one's last gasp; (*fig.*) to be on one's last legs.

ды́шл|о, а, *n.* shaft, pole, beam (*attached to front axle of cart, etc., drawn by two horses*).

дья́вол, а, *m.* devil; како́го ~а?, за каки́м ~ом?, на кой ~? (*coll.*) why the devil?, why the deuce?

дьяво́л|ёнок, ёнка, *pl.* ~я́та, ~я́т, *m.* (*coll.*) imp.

дья́вольский, *adj.* devilish, diabolical; (*coll.*) damnable.

дья́вольщина, ы, *f.* (*coll.*) devilment; что за д.! what the hell's going on?, what a fearful mess!

дьяк, а́, *m.* (*hist.*) **1.** (prince's) scribe. **2.** clerk, secretary.

дья́кон, а, *pl.* ~а́, ~о́в, *m.* (*eccl.*) deacon.

дья́кониц|а, ы, *f.* (*coll.*) deacon's wife.

дья́констВ|о, а, *n.* (*eccl.*) diaconate.

дьяч|о́к, ка́, *m.* (*eccl.*) sacristan, sexton; reader.

дю́же, *adv.* (*coll. or dial.*) terribly, awfully.

дю́ж|ий, (~, ~а́, ~е), *adj.* (*coll.*) sturdy, hefty, robust.

дю́жин|а, ы, *f.* dozen; чёртова д. baker's dozen.

дю́жинный, *adj.* ordinary, commonplace.

дюйм, а, *m.* inch.

дюймо́вк|а, и, *f.* (*coll.*) 1. inch(-thick) plank. 2. one-inch nail.

дюймо́вый, *adj.* one-inch.

дю́н|а, ы, *f.* dune.

дюра́л|ь, я, *m.* = ~юми́ний.

дюралюми́ни|й, я, *m.* (*tech.*) duralumin.

дюше́с, а, *m.* Duchess pear.

дя́гил|ь, я, *m.* (*bot.*) angelica.

дя́деньк|а, и, *m.* *affectionate form of* дя́дя.

дя́дин, *adj.* uncle's.

дя́дьк|а, и, *m.* 1. *pejor. form of* дя́дя. 2. (*coll.*) = дя́дя 2. 3. (*obs.*) tutor (*in noble families*); usher (*in boys' private schools*).

дя́дюшк|а, и, *m.* (*coll.*) *affectionate form of* дя́дя.

дя́д|я, и, *pl.* ~и, ~ей, *and* ~ья́, ~ьёв, *m.* 1. uncle. 2. (*coll.*) uncle (*as term of address by children to any male of mature age*).

дя́т|ел, ла, *m.* woodpecker.

Е

еб|а́ть, у́, ёшь, *impf.* (*of* уе́ть) (*vulg.*) to fuck.

ев- (*in words derived from Greek*) eu-.

Ева́нгели|е, я, *n.* (*collect.*) the Gospels; е. gospel (*also fig.*).

ева́нгелик, а, *m.* (an) evangelical.

евангели́ст, а, *m.* 1. Evangelist. 2. (an) evangelical.

евангели́ческ|ий, *adj.* evangelical; ~ая це́рковь Evangelical Church

ева́нгельский, *adj.* gospel.

евге́ник|а, и, *f.* eugenics.

евкали́пт(овый), = эвкали́пт(овый).

е́внух, а, *m.* eunuch.

евразийский, *adj.* (*geogr.*) Eurasian.

евразийстВ|о, а, *n.* Eurasianism (*theory asserting special character of Russian and related Eastern cultures*).

евре́|й, я, *m.* Jew; Hebrew.

евре́йк|а, и, *f.* Jewess.

евре́йский, *adj.* Jewish.

евре́йстВ|о, а, *n.* 1. (*collect.*) Jewry, the Jews. 2. Jewishness.

европе́|ец, йца, *m.* European.

европеиза́ци|я, и, *f.* Europeanization.

европеизи́р|овать, ую, *impf. and pf.* to europeanize.

европе́йск|ий, *adj.* European; Western.

евста́хиев, *adj.*; ~а труба́ (*anat.*) Eustachian tube.

евфеми́зм, а, *m.* euphemism.

евхаристи́ческий, *adj.* (*eccl.*) eucharistal.

евхари́сти|я, и, *f.* (*eccl.*) Eucharist.

егермейстер, а, *m.* (*obs.*) master of the hunt.

е́гер|ский, *adj. of* ~ь; е. полк regiment of chasseurs.

е́гер|ь, я, *pl.* ~и, ~ей *and* ~я́, ~е́й, *m.* 1. huntsman. 2. (*mil.*) chasseur.

еги́петск|ий, *adj.* Egyptian; (*fig.*) severe, hard; ~ая тьма pitch darkness; ~ая синь Egyptian blue (*a copper pigment*).

египто́лог, а, *m.* Egyptologist.

египтоло́ги|я, и, *f.* Egyptology.

египтя́н|ин, ина, *pl.* ~е, ~, *m.* Egyptian.

египтя́н|ка, ки, *f. of* ~ин.

его́ 1. *g. and a. sing. of* он; *g. sing. of* оно́. 2. (*possessive adj.*) his; its.

егоз|а́, ы́, *m. and f.* (*coll.*) fidget.

его|зи́ть, жу́, зи́шь, *impf.* (*coll.*) 1. to fidget. 2. (перед+*i.*) to fawn (upon).

егозли́в|ый (~, ~а), *adj.* (*coll.*) fidgety.

ед|а́, ы́, *f.* 1. food. 2. meal; во вре́мя ~ы́ at meal-times, during a meal, while eating.

еда́|ть, *no pres., past* ~л, ~ла, (*coll.*) *freq. of* есть[1].

едва́, *adv. and conj.* 1. (*adv.*) hardly, barely, only just (= *with difficulty*); мы е. попа́ли на по́езд we only just caught the train. 2. (*adv.*) hardly, scarcely, barely, only just (= *only slightly*); печь е. гори́т the fire is barely alight. 3. едва́-едва́ *emphatic variant of* е. 1, 2. 4. е. ли (*adv.*) hardly, scarcely (*in judgements of probability*); е. ли он отка́жется от тако́го соблазни́тельного предложе́ния he will hardly refuse such a tempting offer. 5. е. (ли) не (*adv.*) nearly, almost, all but; я е. не по́мер со́ смеху I nearly died laughing; э́та оши́бка е. ли не грубе́йшая из заме́ченных мно́ю that is perhaps (= I am inclined to think) the worst howler I have ever seen. 6. (*conj.*) hardly, scarcely, barely; е...., как scarcely . . . when,; no sooner . . . than; е. самолёт взлете́л, как оди́н из мото́ров зае́ло no sooner had the plane taken off than one of the engines seized up.

ед|и́м, и́те, я́т, *see* есть[1].

едине́ни|е, я, *n.* unity.

един|и́ть, ю, и́шь, *impf.* (*obs.*) to unite.

едини́ц|а, ы, *f.* **1.** one; figure 1; (*math.*) unity. **2.** (*in var. senses*) unit; е. мо́щности unit of power; ~ы вое́нно-морско́го фло́та naval units. **3.** 'one' (*lowest mark in Russian university and school marking system*). **4.** individual; (то́лько) ~ы only a few, only a handful.

едини́чност|ь, и, *f.* singleness; single occurrence.

едини́чн|ый, *adj.* **1.** single, unitary; е. слу́чай solitary instance; ~ые слу́чаи isolated cases. **2.** individual; ~ое се́льское хозя́йство farming on an individual basis.

единобо́жи|е, я, *n.* monotheism.

единобо́рств|о, а, *n.* (*rhet.*) single combat.

единобра́чи|е, я, *n.* monogamy.

единобра́чный, *adj.* monogamous; (*bot.*) monogamian, monogynous.

единове́р|ец, ца, *m.* **1.** co-religionist. **2.** member of Edinoverie (*see* ~ие).

единове́ри|е, я, *n.* **1.** community of religion. **2.** Edinoverie (*an Old Believer sect which reached an organizational compromise with the official Orthodox Church*).

единове́р|ный (~ен, ~на), *adj.* (+*d.* or с+*i.*) of the same faith (as).

единове́р|ческий, *adj. of* ~ие 2.

единовла́сти|е, я, *n.* autocracy, absolute rule.

единовла́ст|ный (~ен, ~на), *adj.* autocratic; dictatorial; е. прави́тель absolute ruler.

единовре́менно, *adv.* **1.** but once, once only. **2.** simultaneously.

единовре́менн|ый, *adj.* **1.** extraordinary, unique; ~ое посо́бие extraordinary grant. **2.** (+*d.* or с+*i.*) simultaneous (with).

единогла́си|е, я, *n.* unanimity.

единогла́сно, *adv.* unanimously; при́нято е. carried unanimously.

единогла́сный, *adj.* unanimous.

единодержа́ви|е, я, *n.* (*obs.*) monarchy, autocracy.

единодержа́в|ный (~ен, ~на), *adj.* (*obs.*) having autocratic powers, unlimited powers.

единоду́ши|е, я, *n.* unanimity.

единоду́ш|ный (~ен, ~на), *adj.* unanimous.

еди́ножды, *adv.* (*obs.*) once; е. три — три three ones are three.

единокро́в|ный (~ен, ~на), *adj.* **1.** (*obs.*) consanguineous; е. брат half-brother. **2.** of the same stock.

единоли́чник, а, *m.* individual peasant--farmer (*working his own holding*).

единоли́чн|ый, *adj.* individual; personal; ~ое реше́ние individual decision; ~ое хозя́йство individual peasant holding.

единомы́сли|е, я, *n.* agreement of opinion; like-mindedness.

единомы́шленник, а, *m.* **1.** person who holds the same views; like-minded person; мы с ним ~и по вопро́сам вне́шней поли́тики we agree, we think the same way on matters of foreign policy. **2.** confederate, accomplice.

единонасле́ди|е, я, *n.* (*leg.*) primogeniture.

единонача́ли|е, я, *n.* one-man management; unified management; combined (military and political) command.

единонача́льник, а, *m.* **1.** combined (military and political) commander. **2.** sole director.

единообра́зи|е, я, *n.* uniformity.

единообра́з|ный (~ен, ~на), *adj.* uniform.

единоплеме́нник, а, *m.* member of the same tribe; fellow-countryman.

единоплеме́нный, *adj.* of the same tribe; of the same nationality.

единоро́г, а, *m.* **1.** (*myth.*) unicorn. **2.** (*hist.*) 'unicorn' (*name of kind of cannon*). **3.** (*zool.*) narwhal.

единоро́дный, *adj.* (*obs.*) only-begotten; е. сын only son.

единосу́щност|ь, и, *f.* (*theol.*) consubstantiality.

единосу́щный, *adj.* (*theol.*) (+*d.*) consubstantial (with).

единоутро́б|ный (~ен, ~на), *adj.* (*obs.*) uterine; е. брат half-brother, uterine brother.

еди́нственно, *adv.* only, solely; е. возмо́жный ход the only possible move; она́ прису́тствовала е. из любопы́тства she came solely from curiosity.

еди́нственн|ый, *adj.* **1.** only, sole; one and only; е. сын only son; он е. пережи́л кораблекруше́ние he was the sole survivor of the shipwreck; е. в своём ро́де the only one of its kind, unique specimen; ~ое число́ (*gram.*) singular (number). **2.** (*obs.*) unique, unequalled.

еди́нств|о, а, *n.* (*in var. senses*) unity.

еди́н|ый (~, ~а), *adj.* **1.** one; single, sole; не́ было там ни ~ой души́ there was not a soul there; всё ~о (*coll.*) it's all one; все до ~ого to a man. **2.** united, unified; е. и недели́мый one and indivisible. **3.** common, single; ~ая во́ля single will, purpose.

éд|кий (~ок, ~ка́, ~ко), *adj.* **1.** caustic; acrid, pungent; е. натр (*chem.*) caustic soda; е. за́пах pungent smell. **2.** (*fig.*) caustic, sarcastic.

éдкост|ь, и, *f.* **1.** causticity; pungency; (*fig.*) sarcasm. **2.** sarcasm, sarcastic remark.

едо́к, а́, *m.* **1.** mouth; head; у него́ в семье́ де́сять ~о́в he has ten mouths to feed; на ~а́ per head. **2.** (*coll.*) (big) eater; плохо́й е. a poor eater.

éд|у, ешь, *see* éхать.

еду́н, á, *m.* (*coll.*) mouth (= едо́к 2).

е́дучи, *pres. gerund* (*coll.*) *of* éхать.

éд|че, *comp. of* ~кий.

её 1. *g. and a. of* oná. **2.** (*possessive adj.*) her.

ёж, ежá, *m.* hedgehog (*also mil.* = *obstruction of barbed wire entangled with stakes or iron bars*).

éж|а, и, *f.* (*agric.*) orchard grass (*Dactylis*).

ежеви́к|а, и, *f.* **1.** (*collect.*) blackberries. **2.** bramble, blackberry bush.

ежеви́|чный, *adj. of* ~ка; ~чное варéнье bramble preserves.

ежего́дник, а, *m.* annual, year-book.

ежего́дный, *adj.* annual, yearly.

ежедне́вн|ый, *adj.* daily; everyday; ~ая лихора́дка quotidian fever.

éжели, *conj.* (*obs. or coll.*) if.

ежеме́сячник, а, *m.* monthly (magazine).

ежеме́сячный, *adj.* monthly.

ежемину́тный, *adj.* **1.** occurring every minute, at intervals of a minute; у нас есть е. автóбусный рейс в гóрод we have a one-minute bus service to town. **2.** incessant, continual.

еженеде́льник, а, *m.* weekly (newspaper, magazine).

еженеде́льный, *adj.* weekly.

ежено́щный, *adj.* nightly.

ежесеку́ндный, *adj.* **1.** occurring every second. **2.** (*coll.*) incessant, continual.

ежесу́точный, *adj.* daily (= *occurring every 24 hours*).

ежеча́сный, *adj.* hourly.

ёжик, а, *m.* **1.** *dim. of* ёж. **2.** стри́чься ~ом to have one's hair cut en brosse. **3.** brush (*for cleaning Primus stove, etc.*).

ёж|иться, усь, ишься, *impf.* (*of* съ~) **1.** to shiver, huddle oneself up (*from cold, fever, etc.*). **2.** (*fig., coll.*) to shrink (*from fear, shyness, etc.*).

ежи́х|а, и, *f.* female hedgehog.

ежо́в|ый, *adj. of* ёж; держáть в ~ых рукави́цах (*coll.*) to rule with a rod of iron.

езд|á, ы́, *f.* **1.** ride, riding; drive, driving; going; е. на велосипе́де bicycling. **2.** *in phrases indicating distance from one point to another*: journey; отсю́да до óзера — дóбрых три часá ~ы́ from here to the lake is a good three hours' journey.

éз|дить, жу, дишь, *impf.* **1.** (*indet. of* éхать) to go (*in or on a vehicle or on an animal*); to ride, drive; е. верхóм to ride (on horseback). **2.** to (be able to) ride, drive. **3.** (к) to visit (*habitually*). **4.** (*coll.*) to slip.

езд|ово́й, *adj. of* ~á; ~овы́е собáки draught-dogs; *as noun* е., ~овóго, *m.* (*mil.*) driver.

ездо́к, á, *m.* **1.** rider; horseman. **2.** тудá я бóльше не е. I am not going there again.

езжá|ть, *no pres., past* ~л, ~ла, (*coll.*), *freq. of* éздить; ~й(те) (*as imper. of* éхать) go!, get going!

éзжен|ый, *adj.*; ~ая дорóга beaten track; (*coll.*) ~ая лóшадь broken-in horse.

езóп, ~овский, *see* эзóп.

ей, *d. and i. of* oná.

ей-Бóгу, *interj.* (*coll.*) truly!, really and truly!

ей-éй, *interj.* (*coll.*) truly!, in very truth!

ёк|ать, аю, *impf.* (*of* ~нуть) (+сéрдце) (*coll.*) to miss a beat; to go pit-a-pat.

ёкн|уть, у, ешь, *pf. of* ёкать.

ектен|ья́, ьи́, *g. pl.* ~и́й, *f.* (*eccl.*) ektenia (*part of Orthodox liturgy consisting of versicles and responses*).

ел, éла, *see* есть[1].

éле, *adv.* **1.** hardly, barely, only just (= *with difficulty*); егó речь былá е. слышнá his speech was hardly audible. **2.** hardly, scarcely, barely, only just (= *only slightly*); пóезд е. дви́гался the train was scarcely moving. **3.** éле-éле *emphatic variant of* е.; он е.-е. спáсся he had a very narrow escape.

éловый, *adj.* (*bot.*) fir, spruce.

еле́|й, я, *m.* (*eccl.*) anointing oil; unction; (*fig.*) unction; balm.

еле́й|ный, *adj.* **1.** (*eccl.*) *adj. of* ~. **2.** unctuous.

елеосвяще́ни|е, я, *n.* (*eccl.*) extreme unction.

ел|е́ц, ьцá, *m.* dace (*fish*).

ели́ко, *adv.* (*obs.*) as far as, as much as; е. возмóжно as far as possible.

ёлк|а, и, *f.* fir(-tree), spruce; рождéственская е. Christmas-tree; зажéчь ~у to light up the Christmas-tree; быть на ~е (*coll.*) to be at a Christmas, New Year's party.

ел|óвый, *adj. of* ~ь; ~óвые ши́шки fir-cones; головá ~óвая (*coll.*) blockhead, numskull.

ело́|зить, жу, зишь, *impf.* (*coll.*) to crawl.

ёлочк|а, и, *f.* **1.** *dim. of* ёлка. **2.** herring-bone (pattern); он нóсит зелёный пиджáк ~ой, в ~у he wears a green herring-bone jacket.

ёлочн|ый, *adj. of* ёлка; ~ые украшéния Christmas-tree decorations.

ел|ь, и, *f.* spruce (*Picea*); fir(-tree); (*comm.*) white wood; обыкновéнная е. Norway spruce, common spruce (*Picea abies*).

éльник, а, *m.* **1.** fir-grove, fir-plantation. **2.** (*collect.*) fir-wood; fir-twigs.

ем, ешь, ест, *see* есть[1].

ём|кий (~ок, ~кá), *adj.* capacious.

ёмкост|ь, и, *f.* capacity, cubic content; ё. цистéрны tankage; мéры ~и measures of capacity; ё. ры́нка (*econ.*) market capacity.

éмл|ю, ешь, *see* имáть.

ему́, *d. of* он, онó.

ендов|á, ы́, *f.* (*hist.*) flagon (*large copper or earthenware vessel with spout formerly used in Russia for pouring out wine, beer, mead, etc.*).

енот, а, *m.* **1.** (*zool.*) raccoon. **2.** raccoon (fur).

енот|овый, *adj. of* ~; ~овая шуба raccoon coat, coonskin coat.

епанч|а, й, *g. pl.* ~ей, *f.* (*hist.*) cloak, mantle.

епархиалк|а, и, *f.* (*hist.*; *coll.*) church secondary schoolgirl.

епархиальн|ый, *adj.* (*eccl.*) diocesan; ~ое училище (*obs.*)church secondary school for girls (*mainly for children of the Orthodox clergy*).

епархи|я, и, *f.* (*eccl.*) diocese, see; bishopric; eparchy (*in Orthodox Church*).

епископ, а, *m.* bishop.

епископальный, *adj.* (*eccl.*) episcopalian.

епископский, *adj.* episcopal.

епископств|о, а, *n.* episcopate.

епитим|ья, ьй, *g. pl.* ~ий, *f.* (*eccl.*) penance.

епитрахил|ь, и, *f.* (*eccl.*) stole.

ер, а, *m.* (hard) yer (*name of Russian letter* 'ъ').

ералаш, а, *m.* **1.** (*coll.*) jumble, confusion; у него в голове полный е. his thoughts are in complete confusion. **2.** mixture of preserved fruits. **3.** eralash (*card-game*).

ерепен|иться, юсь, ишься, *impf.* (*of* взъ~) (*coll.*) to bristle (*fig.*).

ерес|ь, и, *pl.* ~и, ~ей, *f.* **1.** heresy. **2.** (*coll.*) городить е. to talk nonsense.

еретик, а, *m.* heretic.

еретический, *adj.* heretical.

ёрза|ть, ю, *impf.* (*coll.*) to fidget.

ермолк|а, и, *f.* skull-cap.

ерош|ить, у, ишь, *impf.* (*coll.*) to rumple, ruffle; to dishevel.

ерош|иться, ится, *impf.* (*coll.*) to bristle, stick up.

ерунд|а, ы, *f.* (*coll.*) **1.** nonsense, rubbish; говорить ~у to talk nonsense. **2.** trifle, trifling matter; child's play.

ерундистик|а, и, *f.* (*coll.*) nonsense.

ерунд|ить, *1st sing. not used, ~ишь,** *impf.* (*coll.*) to talk nonsense; to play the fool.

ерундов|ский, *adj.* = ~ый.

ерундовый, *adj.* (*coll.*) **1.** foolish. **2.** trifling.

ёрш¹, ерша, *m.* **1.** (*fish*) ruff. **2.** (lamp--chimney) brush. **3.** notched nail *or* spike. **4.** hair sticking up; ~ом (*as adv.*) sticking up, on end.

ёрш², ерша, *m.* (*coll.*) mixture of beer and vodka.

ершист|ый (~, ~а), *adj.* (*coll.*) **1.** bristling; sticking up. **2.** (*fig.*) obstinate; unyielding.

ерш|иться, усь, йшься, *impf.* (*coll.*) **1.** to stick up. **2.** to grow heated, fly into a rage.

ершовый, *adj. of* ёрш¹ 1.

еры, *indecl., *n.* yery (*name of Russian letter* 'ы').

ер|ь, я, *m.* (soft) yer (*name of Russian letter* 'ь').

есаул, а, *m.* (*hist.*) esaul (*Cossack captain*).

если, *conj.* if; е. не unless; е. только provided; е. бы не but for, if it were not for;

е. бы не ты, он мог бы кончить самоубийством but for you he might have committed suicide; (о,) е. бы (*in exclamations*) if only; что е...? what if...?; (а) что, е. бы (*introducing suggestion of course of action*) what about, how about.

ессентук|и, ов, *no sing.* Essentuki (water).

ест, *see* есть¹.

естественник, а, *m.* (*obs.*) **1.** scientist. **2.** science student.

естественно¹, *adv.* **1.** naturally. **2.** *as particle* naturally, of course.

естественно², *as pred.* it is natural.

естествен|ный (~, ~на), *adj.* (*in var. senses*) natural; ~ые богатства natural resources; ~ное закрытие (*mil.*) natural cover; ~ная надобность, ~ная потребность (*euph.*) needs of nature; ~ные науки natural sciences; е. отбор (*biol.*) natural selection.

естеств|о, а, *n.* **1.** nature; essence; е. вопроса the nature of the question. **2.** (*obs.*) Nature.

естествовед, а, *m.* **1.** (natural) scientist. **2.** (natural) science teacher.

естествоведени|е, я, *n.* natural history, (natural) science.

естествознани|е, я, *n.* (natural) science.

естествоиспытател|ь, я, *m.* (natural) scientist.

есть¹, ем, ешь, ест, едим, едите, едят, *past* **ел, ела,** *imper.* **ешь,** *impf.* (*of* съ~) **1.** to eat; е. глазами to devour with one's eyes. **2.** (*impf. only*) to corrode, eat away. **3.** (*impf. only*) to sting, cause to smart. **4.** (*impf. only*) (*coll.*) to torment; to nag.

есть² **1.** *3rd sing.* (*also, rarely, substituted for all persons*) *pres. of* быть; и е. (*coll.*) yes, indeed; как е. (*coll.*) entirely, completely. **2.** there is, there are; у меня, его, *etc.*, е. I have, he has, *etc.*; е. такое дело (*coll.*) all right, O.K.

есть³, *interj.* (*mil.*; *in acknowledgement of a superior's order*) yes, sir; (*naut.*) aye-aye, very good.

ети = еть.

еть, ебу, ебёшь, *past* **ёб, ебли,** *impf.* = ебать.

ефрейтор, а, *m.* (*mil.*) lance-corporal.

ехать, еду, едешь, *impf.* (*of* по~) (*det. of* ездить) to go (*in or on a vehicle or on an animal*); to ride, drive; е. верхом to ride (on horseback); е. поездом, на поезде to go by train; е. на пароходе to go by boat; е. в Ригу (*vulg.*) to puke, spew; дальше е. некуда (*coll.*) that's the end, that's the last straw.

ехидн|а, ы, *f.* **1.** (*zool.*) echidna. **2.** Australian viper. **3.** (*fig., coll.*) viper, snake.

ехиднича|ть, ю, *impf.* (*of* съ~) (*coll.*) to employ malicious innuendo; to be malicious.

ехид|ный (~ен, ~на), *adj.* (*coll.*) malicious, spiteful; (*fig.*) venomous.

ехи́дств|о, а, *n.* (*coll.*) malice, spite; innuendo.

ехи́дств|овать, ую, *impf.* (*coll.*) = ехи́дничать.

ешь, *see* есть[1].

ещё, *adv.* **1.** still; yet; е. не, нет е. not yet; всё е. still; пока́ е. for the present, for the time being; э́то е. ничего́! that's nothing! **2.** some more; any more; yet, further; again; мо́жно нали́ть е. (вина́, *etc.*)? may I pour you some more (wine, *etc.*)?; есть ли е. хлеб? is there any more bread?; е. оди́н one more, yet another; е. раз (*i*) once more, again, (*ii*) *as interj.* encore!; наде́юсь, е. приду́ I hope I shall come again. **3.** already; as long ago as, as far back as; е. в 1900-ом году́ in 1900 already, as long ago as 1900; что тут но́вого? е. Маркс э́то дока́зывал what is new in this? (Why,) Marx argued thus. **4.** (+*comp.*) still, yet, even; е. гро́мче even louder; е. и е. more and more. **5.** (+*pronouns and adverbs*) *as emphatic particle*: кого́ е. мы не спра́шивали? whomever did we not ask? ты ви́дел инду́са? — како́го е. инду́са? have you seen the Indian?—What Indian, for heaven's sake? **6.** е. бы (*i*) yes, rather!, and how!, I'll say!, (*ii*) it would be surprising if . . .; е. бы вы с ни́ми не сошли́сь it would be surprising if you and they didn't get on. **7.** а е. *expresses reproach or sarcastic criticism*: тепе́рь ворчи́шь, а е. сам предложи́л you grumble now, but it was you who suggested it.

е́ю, *i. of* она́.

ея́, *g. of* она́ *in pre-1918 orthography*.

Ж

ж = же.

жа́б|а[1], ы, *f.* (*zool.*) toad.

жа́б|а[2], ы, *f.* (*med.*) quinsy; грудна́я ж. angina pectoris.

жа́берный, *adj.* (*zool.*) branchiate.

жа́б|ий, *adj. of* ~а[1].

жабо́, *indecl.*, *n.* jabot.

жа́бр|ы, ~, *sing.* ~а, ~ы, *f.* (*zool.*) gills; branchia; взять за ж. (*fig.*, *coll.*) to bring pressure to bear upon.

жаве́лев, *adj.*; ~а вода́ liquid bleach.

жаве́л|ь, я, *m.* = ~ева вода́.

жа́воронок, ка, *m.* (*orn.*) lark; лесно́й ж. wood lark; хохла́тый ж. crested lark.

жа́дин|а, ы, *m. and f.* (*coll.*) greedy person.

жадне́|ть, ю, *impf.* (*coll.*) to become greedy.

жа́днича|ть, ю, *impf.* (*coll.*) to be greedy; to be mean.

жа́дност|ь, и, *f.* **1.** greed; greediness; avidity. **2.** avarice, meanness.

жа́д|ный (~ен, ~на́, ~но), *adj.* **1.** (к+*d.*) greedy (for); avid (for); он всегда́ был ~ным к но́вым ощуще́ниям he was always greedy for new sensations. **2.** avaricious, mean.

жа́жд|а, ы, *no pl.*, *f.* thirst; (+*g.*; *fig.*) thirst, craving (for); ж. зна́ний thirst for knowledge.

жа́жд|ать, у, *impf.* (*obs.*) to be thirsty; (+*g. or inf.*; *fig.*) to thirst (for, after); а́лчущие и ~ущие, *see* а́лчущий.

жаке́т, а, *m.* **1.** (*obs.*) morning coat. **2.** (*ladies'*) jacket.

жаке́тк|а, и, *f.* (*coll.*) jacket.

жакт, а, *m.* (*abbr. of* жили́щно-аре́ндное кооперати́вное това́рищество) housing lease co-operative society (*up to 1937*).

жа́кт|овский, *adj. of* ~.

жале́йк|а, и, *f.* (*mus.*; *dial.*) zhaleyka (*kind of pipe played by peasants, made from cow's horn or birchbark*).

жале́|ть, ю, *impf.* (*of* по~) **1.** to pity, feel sorry (for). **2.** (о+*p.* or +*g.*; что) to regret, be sorry (for, about); ~ю об утра́ченном вре́мени I regret the waste of time; ~ю, что не оста́лся до конца́ ма́тча I am sorry I did not stay till the end of the match. **3.** (+*a.* or *g.*) to spare; to grudge; не ~я сил not sparing oneself, unsparingly.

жа́л|ить, ю, ишь, *impf.* (*of* у~) to sting; to bite.

жа́л|иться[1], юсь, ишься, *impf.* (*coll.*) to sting; to bite.

жа́л|иться[2], юсь, ишься, *impf.* (*dial.*) to complain.

жа́л|кий (~ок, ~ка́, ~ко), *adj.* pitiful, pitiable, pathetic, wretched (= (*i*) *arousing pity*, (*ii*) *arousing contempt*); име́ть ж. вид to be a sorry sight.

жа́лк|о[1], *adv. of* ~ий.

жа́лко[2], *as pred.* (*impers.*) **1.** (+*d. and g.*) to pity, feel sorry (for); ей ж. бы́ло себя́ she felt sorry for herself. **2.** (it is) a pity, a shame; (+*d. and g. or a.*) it grieves (me, *etc.*); to regret, feel sorry; мне ста́ло ж. да́нного обеща́ния I began to regret giving a promise. **3.** (+*g. or* +*inf.*) to grudge.

жа́л|о, а, *n.* **1.** sting (*also fig.*). **2.** point (*of pin, needle, etc.*).

жа́лоб|а, ы, *f.* complaint; пода́ть ~у (на+ *a.*) to make, lodge a complaint (about).

жа́лоб|ный (~ен, ~на), *adj.* **1.** plaintive; doleful, mournful. **2.** *adj. of* ~a; ~ная кни́га complaints book.

жа́лобщик, а, *m.* **1.** person lodging complaint. **2.** (*leg.*) plaintiff.

жа́лова|нный, *p.p.p. of* ~ть *and adj.* (*hist.*) granted, received as grant; ~нная гра́мота letters patent, charter.

жа́лованье, я, *n.* **1.** salary. **2.** (*obs.*) reward; donation.

жа́л|овать, ую, *impf.* (*of* по~) **1.** (+*a. and i.* or +*d. and a.*) to grant (to); to bestow, confer (on); to reward (with); ж. сторо́нников землёй, ж. сторо́нникам зе́млю to grant land to one's supporters, reward one's supporters with (grants of) land. **2.** (*coll.*) to favour, regard with favour. **3.** (к; *obs.*) to visit, come to see.

жа́л|оваться, уюсь, *impf.* (*of* по~) (на+*a.*) to complain (of, about); он всё ~уется офице́рам на харчи́ he is always complaining to officers about the food; ж. в суд to go to law.

жалоно́сный, *adj.* (*zool.*) stinging, possessing a sting.

жа́лостлив|ый (~, ~a), *adj.* (*coll.*) **1.** compassionate, sympathetic. **2.** pitiful.

жа́лост|ный (~ен, ~на), *adj.* (*coll.*) **1.** piteous; doleful, mournful. **2.** compassionate, sympathetic.

жа́лост|ь, и, *f.* pity, compassion; из ~и (к) out of pity (for); кака́я ж.! what a pity!

жаль, *as pred.* (*impers.*) **1.** (+*d. and a. or g.*) to pity, feel sorry (for); мне ж. тебя́ I pity you. **2.** (it is) a pity; (+*d.*) it grieves (me, *etc.*); to regret, feel sorry; ж., что вас там не бу́дет it is a pity that you will not be there; нам ж. бы́ло расстава́ться it grieved us to part. **3.** (+*g. or* +*inf.*) to grudge. **4.** *as adv.* unfortunately.

жа́л|ьче, (*coll.*) *comp. of* ~ко.

жалюзи́, *indecl.*, *n.* Venetian blind, jalousie.

жанда́рм, а, *m.* gendarme.

жандарме́ри|я, и, *f.* (*collect.*) gendarmerie.

жанда́рм|ский, *adj. of* ~.

жанр, а, *m.* **1.** genre. **2.** genre-painting.

жанри́ст, а, *m.* genre-painter.

жа́нр|овый, *adj. of* ~.

жанти́льнича|ть, ю, *impf.* (*coll.*) to behave in an affected way, put on airs.

жанти́л|ьный (~ен, ~ьна), *adj.* (*coll.*) affected.

жар, а (у), о ~е, в ~у́, *no pl. m.* **1.** heat; heat of the day; hot place; в ~у́ (+*g.*) in the heat (of). **2.** (*coll.*) embers; как ж. горе́ть to gleam, glitter; чужи́ми рука́ми ж. загреба́ть to use others to pull one's chestnuts out of the fire. **3.** fever; (high) temperature. **4.** (*fig.*) heat, ardour;

с ~ом приня́ться за что-н. to set about something with a will.

жар|а́, ы́, *f.* heat; hot weather.

жарго́н, а, *m.* **1.** jargon; slang, cant (*of a particular social or occupational group*). **2.** (*obs.*) Yiddish (language).

жарго́н|ный, *adj. of* ~.

жардинье́рк|а, и, *f.* flower-stand, jardinière.

жа́рев|о, а, *n.* (*collect.; coll.*) roast *or* fried food.

жа́рен|ое, ого, *n.* (*coll.*) roast meat.

жа́реный, *adj.* roast, broiled; fried; grilled.

жа́р|ить, ю, ишь, *impf.* **1.** (*pf.* за~ *or* из~) (на огне́) to roast, broil; (на сковоро́де) to fry; (на решётке) to grill. **2.** (*of the sun*) to burn, scorch. **3.** (*coll.*) *used as substitute for other verbs to emphasize speed of action or vigour of performance*: ~ь за по́мощью! run for help as fast as you can!; ж. на гармо́шке to bash out a tune on the accordion.

жа́р|иться, юсь, ишься, *impf.* **1.** (*pf.* за~ *or* из~) to roast, fry (*intrans.*). **2.** ж. на со́лнце (*coll.*) to roast, grill (oneself), bask in the sun. **3.** *pass. of* ~ить.

жа́р|кий (~ок, ~ка́, ~ко), *adj.* **1.** hot; torrid; tropical; ж. по́яс (*geogr.*) torrid zone. **2.** (*fig.*) hot, heated; ardent; passionate; ж. спор heated argument.

жа́р|ко[1], *adv. of* ~кий.

жа́рко[2], *as pred.* it is hot; мне, *etc.*, ж. I am, *etc.*, hot.

жарк|о́е, о́го, *n.* roast (meat).

жаро́в|ня, ни, *g. pl.* ~ен, *f.* brazier.

жарово́й, *adj.* **1.** *adj. of* жар 1. **2.** caused by heat; ж. уда́р heat-stroke.

жар|о́к, ка́, *m.* (*coll.*) fever; (slight) temperature.

жаропонижа́ющ|ий, *adj.* (*med.*) febrifugal; *as noun* ~ее, ~его, *n.* febrifuge.

жаросто́йкий, *adj.* (*tech.*) heat-resisting, heatproof.

жаротру́бный, *adj.*; ж. котёл (*tech.*) fire-tube boiler, flue boiler.

жароупо́рный = жаросто́йкий.

Жар-пти́ц|а, ы, *f.* (*folklore*) the Fire-bird.

жа́р|че, *comp. of* ~кий *and* ~ко.

жары́н|ь, и, *f.* (*coll.*) intense heat (*of atmosphere*); very hot weather.

жасми́н, а, *m.* jasmin(e), jessamin(e).

жа́тв|а, ы, *no pl.*, *f.* reaping, harvesting; harvest (*also fig.*).

жа́тв|енный, *adj. of* ~a; ~енная маши́на binder, harvester, reaping-machine.

жа́тк|а, и, *f.* binder, harvester, reaping-machine.

жать[1], жму, жмёшь, *impf.* (*no pf.*) **1.** to press, squeeze; ж. ру́ку to shake (someone) by the hand. **2.** to press out, squeeze out. **3.** to pinch, be tight (*of shoes or clothing*); в плеча́х жмёт (*impers.*) it is tight on the shoulders. **4.** (*fig., coll.*) to oppress.

жать², жну, жнёшь, *impf.* (*of* с~) to reap, cut, mow.

жа́ться, жму́сь, жмёшься, *impf.* 1. to huddle up; ж. в у́гол to skulk in a corner. 2. (к) to press close (to), draw closer (to). 3. (*coll.*) to hesitate, vacillate. 4. (*coll.*) to stint oneself; to be stingy.

жбан, а, *m.* (wooden) jug.

жва́чк|а, и, *f.* chewing, rumination. 2. cud; жева́ть ~у to chew the cud, ruminate; (*fig.*) to repeat something monotonously. 3. (*coll.*) chewing-gum.

жва́чн|ый, *adj.* (*zool.*) ruminant; *as noun* ~ое, ~ого, *n.* ruminant.

жгу, жжёшь, жгут, *see* жечь.

жгут, а́, *m.* 1. plait; braid; wisp. 2. (*med.*) tourniquet.

жгу́тик, а, *m.* (*zool.*) flagellum.

жгу́чест|ь, и, *f.* burning heat.

жгу́ч|ий (~, ~а, ~е), *adj.* burning hot (*also* fig.); ~ая боль smart, smarting pain; ж. брюне́т person with jet-black hair and eyes; ж. вопро́с burning question.

ждать, жду, ждёшь, *past* ждал, ждала́, жда́ло, *impf.* 1. (+*g.*) to wait (for); to await; заста́вить ж. to keep waiting; не заста́вить себя́ ж. to come quickly; ж. не дожда́ться (*coll.*) to wait impatiently, be on tenterhooks; что нас ждёт? what is in store for us?; того́ и жди (*coll.*) any time now, any minute. 2. (+*g.*) to expect (= to hope for). 3. (+что) to expect; мы жда́ли, что вы пойдёте на ми́тинге we expected you to come to the meeting.

же¹, *conj.* 1. but; иди́, е́сли тебе́ охо́та, я же оста́нусь здесь you go, if you feel like it, but I shall stay here. 2. (*introducing clause elucidating or modifying preceding clause*) and; с тех пор как я его́ зна́ю, зна́ю же я его́ два́дцать лет, я всегда́ ве́рил ему́ ever since I have known him, and I have known him for twenty years, I have always trusted him; Ока́ впада́ет в Во́лгу, Во́лга же в Каспи́йское мо́ре the Oka flows into the Volga, and the Volga flows into the Caspian Sea. 3. after all; расскажи́ ей — она́ же твоя́ мать tell her—she's your mother, after all.

же², *emphatic particle*: когда́ же они́ прие́дут? whenever will they come?; что же ты де́лаешь? whatever are you doing, what *are* you doing?; сего́дня же он собира́лся прие́хать it was today that he intended to come.

же³, *particle expressing identity*: тот же, тако́й же the same, idem; тогда́ же at the same time; там же in the same place, ibidem; Петрося́н, он же Петро́в Petrosyan, alias Petrov.

жева́ни|е, я, *n.* mastication; rumination.

жёваный *adj.* (*coll.*) chewed up; crumpled.

жева́тельн|ый, *adj.* masticatory, manducatory; ~ая рези́нка chewing gum.

жева́ть, жую́, жуёшь, *impf.* to chew, masticate; to ruminate; ж. губа́ми to munch; (*fig.*) ж. жва́чку, *see* жва́чка; ж. вопро́с to chew over a question.

жёг, жгла, *see* жечь.

жезл, а́, *m.* 1. rod; staff (of office); baton; (*eccl.*) crozier; (*hist.*) warder. 2. staff (*token of authority to proceed on single-line railways*). 3. Jacob's staff (*used by surveyors*).

жезлов|о́й, *adj.*; ~а́я систе́ма staff system (*on single-line railways*).

жела́ни|е, я, *n.* 1. (+*g.*) wish (for), desire (for); бу́дет по ва́шему ~ю it shall be as you wish; я всегда́ стара́юсь счита́ться с ва́шими ~ями I always try to consult your wishes; при всём ~и with the best will in the world. 2. desire, lust.

жела́|нный, *p.p.p. of* ~ть *and adj.* wished for, longed for, desired, beloved; ж. гость welcome visitor.

жела́тельно¹, *adv.* preferably.

жела́тельно², *as pred.* it is desirable; it is advisable, preferable; ж., что́бы вы прису́тствовали it is desirable that you should be present, your presence is desirable.

жела́тел|ьный (~ен, ~ьна), *adj.* 1. desirable; advisable, preferable. 2. ~ьное наклоне́ние (*gram.*) optative mood.

желати́н, а, *no pl.*, *m.* gelatin(e).

желати́новый, *adj.* gelatinous.

жела́|ть, ю, *impf.* (*of* по~) 1. (+*g.*) to wish (for), desire. 2. (что́бы *or* +*inf.*) to wish, want; я ~ю, что́бы вы при́няли уча́стие в игре́ I want you to join in the game; ~ете ли вы познако́миться с ним? do you wish to meet him? 3. (+*d. and g. or inf.*) to wish (*someone something*); ~ю вам вся́ких благ (*coll.*) I wish you every happiness; ~ю вам успе́ха good luck!; э́то оставля́ет ж. лу́чшего, мно́гого it leaves much to be desired.

жела́|ющий, *pres. part. act. of* ~ть; ~ющие persons interested, those who so desire.

желва́к, а́, *m.* (*med.*) tumour; (*fig.*) moving knot of muscle.

желе́, *indecl.*, *n.* jelly.

желез|а́, ы́, *pl.* же́лезы, ~, ~а́м, *f.* (*anat.*) gland *pl.*; (*coll.*) tonsils; же́лезы вну́тренней секре́ции endocrine glands.

желе́зистый¹, *adj.* (*anat.*) glandular.

желе́зист|ый² (~, ~а), *adj.* ferriferous; (*chem.*) ferrocyanide (of); ferruginous; chalybeate (*of water*); ж. препара́т iron preparation.

желе́зк|а, и, *f.* (*coll.*) 1. piece of iron. 2. (*obs.*) railway. 3. chemin-de-fer (*card-game*).

желёзк|а, и, *f.* (*anat.*) glandule.

железнéни|е, я, *n.* (*tech.*) iron plating.

железнодорóжник, а, *m.* railwayman.

железнодорóжн|ый, *adj.* rail, railway; ~ая ветка branch line; ~ая перевóзка rail transport; ~ое полотнó permanent way; ж. путь (railway) track; ж. ýзел (railway) junction.

желéзн|ый, *adj.* 1. iron (*also fig.*); (*chem.*) ferric, ferrous; ж. блеск (*min.*) haematite; ж. век the Iron Age; ~ое дéрево (*bot.*) lignum vitae (*Guaiacum officinale*); ж. зáнавес the 'Iron Curtain'; ~ая кислотá ferric acid; ж. колчедáн (*min.*) iron pyrites; ~ая кóмната strong-room; ж. купорóс (*min.*) green vitriol; ж. лом scrap iron; ~ые опилки iron filings; за ~ой решёткой (*coll.*) behind bars; ~ая рудá iron-stone, iron-ore; ~ые товáры ironmongery, hardware; ~ая травá (*bot.*) vervain. 2. ~ая дорóга railway(s); по ~ой дорóге by rail; ~ая дорóга мéстного значéния local line. 3. (*sl.*) reliable, dependable.

железнáк, á, *m.* (*min.*) iron-stone, iron clay.

желéз|о, а, *pl.* (*obs. or poet.*) ~ы, *n.* 1. iron; ж. в болвáнках pig-iron; óкись ~а (*chem.*) ferric oxide. 2. (*collect.*) iron; hardware. 3. (*pl.*) (*obs.*) fetters, irons.

желéзо- iron-, ferro-.

железобетóн, а, *m.* (*tech.*) reinforced concrete, ferro-concrete.

железобетóн|ный, *adj.* of ~.

железоплавúльный, *adj.*; ж. завóд (*tech.*) iron foundry.

железопрокáтный, *adj.*; ж. завóд (*tech.*) rolling mill.

жёлоб, а, *pl.* ~á, ~óв, *m.* gutter; trough; chute.

желоб|óк, кá, *m.* (*tech.*) groove, channel, flute.

желóбчатый, *adj.* (*tech.*) channelled, fluted.

желóнк|а, и, *f.* (*tech.*) sludge pump, sand pump.

желтé|ть, ю, *impf.* 1. (*pf.* по~) to turn yellow. 2. (*impf. only*) to be yellow, show up yellow.

желтé|ться, ется, *impf.* to be yellow, show up yellow.

желтизн|á, ы́, *f.* yellowness; yellow spot; sallow complexion.

желтúнк|а, и, *f.* (*coll.*) yellow spots; yellow shade.

жел|тúть, чý, тúшь, *impf.* to colour yellow.

желтовáт|ый (~, ~а), *adj.* yellowish; sallow.

желт|óк, кá, *m.* yolk.

желтокóжий, *adj.* yellow-skinned.

желтолúц|ый (~, ~а), *adj.* sallow.

желторóт|ый (~, ~а), *adj.* 1. yellow-beaked. 2. (*fig.*) inexperienced, green.

желтофиóл|ь, и, *f.* (*bot.*) wallflower.

желтоцвéт, а, *m.* (*bot.*) golden rod.

желт|óчный, *adj.* of ~óк.

желтýх|а, и, *f.* (*med.*) jaundice.

желтý|шный, *adj.* of ~ха; jaundiced.

жёлт|ый (~, ~á, ~о and ~ó), *adj.* yellow; ж. билéт (*hist., coll.*) 'yellow ticket' (*prostitute's passport in tsarist Russia*); ~ая водá (*med.*) glaucoma; ж. дом (*coll., obs.*) lunatic asylum; ~ая лихорáдка yellow fever; ~ая прéсса the yellow press.

желт|ь, и, *f.* yellow (paint).

желудёвый, *adj.* of жёлудь; ж. кóфе acorn coffee.

желýд|ок, ка, *m.* stomach; несварéние ~ка indigestion.

желýдоч|ек, ка, *m.* (*anat.*) ventricle.

желýдочный, *adj.* stomach; stomachic, gastric; ж. зонд stomach pump; ж. сок gastric juice.

жёлуд|ь, я, *g. pl.* ~éй, *m.* acorn.

жёлч|ный (~ен, ~на), *adj.* 1. bilious; ж. кáмень gall-stone; ж. пузы́рь gall-bladder. 2. (*fig.*) peevish, irritable; atrabilious.

жёлч|ь (*coll.* желчь), и, *no pl.*, *f.* bile, gall (*also fig.*); разлúтие ~и (*med.*) jaundice.

жемáн|иться, юсь, ишься, *impf.* (*coll.*) to attitudinize, behave with false modesty.

жемáнниц|а, ы, *f.* (*coll.*) affected creature.

жемáннича|ть, ю, *impf.* (*coll.*) to behave affectedly.

жемáн|ный (~ен, ~на), *adj.* affected.

жемáнств|о, а, *n.* affectedness.

жéмчуг, а, *pl.* ~á, *m.* pearl(s); мéлкий ж. seed-pearls.

жемчýжин|а, ы, *f.* pearl (*also fig.*).

жемчýжниц|а, ы, *f.* 1. pearl-oyster. 2. pearl disease.

жемчýжн|ый, *adj.* of жéмчуг; (*fig.*) pearly (-white); ~ая болéзнь pearl disease; ~ое ожерéлье pearl necklace.

жен- *abbr.* of жéнский.

жен|á, ы́, *pl.* ~ы, ~, ~ам, *f.* 1. wife; быть у ~ы́ под башмакóм to be henpecked. 2. (*poet., obs.*) woman.

женáт|ый (~), *adj.* married; ж. (на+*p.*) married (to; *of man*).

жéнин, *adj.* (*obs.*) wife's.

жен|úть, ю, ~ишь, *impf. and pf.* (*pf. also* по~) to marry (off); без меня меня ~úли (*fig., coll.*) I was roped in without being consulted.

женúтьб|а, ы, *no pl.*, *f.* marriage.

жен|úться, юсь, ~ишься, *impf. and pf.* (на+*p.*) (*of man*) to marry, get married (to).

женúх, á, *m.* 1. fiancé; смотрéть ~óм (*coll.*) to look happy. 2. bridegroom. 3. suitor. 4. eligible bachelor.

жениха́|ться, юсь, *impf.* (*coll. or dial.*) to be engaged; to be courting.

женихо́вский, *adj.* (*coll.*) of жени́х.

женихо́вств|о, а, *n.* (*coll.*) engagement; courting(-days).

жёнк|а, и, *f.* (*coll.*) 1. *affect. form of* жена́. 2. (*obs. or dial.*) woman.

женолю́б, а, *m.* ladies' man.

женолюби́в|ый (~), *adj.*; ж. челове́к ladies' man.

женолюби|е, я, *n.* fondness for women.

женоненави́стник, а, *m.* misogynist.

женоненави́стнический, *adj.* misogynous.

женоненави́стничеств|о, а, *n.* misogyny.

женоподо́б|ный (~ен, ~на), *adj.* effeminate.

женотде́л, а, *m.* (*hist.*) women's section (*section of Communist party committees dealing with political work among women*).

жен-премье́р, а, *m.* (*theatr.*) jeune premier.

же́нск|ий, *adj.* 1. woman's; female; feminine; ~ое зва́ние, ~ая на́ция, ~ое сосло́вие (*obs.*) the female sex; ж. вопро́с the question of women's rights; ~ое ца́рство petticoat government. 2. (*gram.*) feminine. 3. *as noun* ~ое, ~ого, *n.* (*coll.*) menstruation.

же́нственност|ь, и, *f.* femininity; (*pejor.*) effeminacy.

же́нствен|ный (~, ~на), *adj.* feminine, womanly; (*pejor.*) womanish, effeminate.

жёнушк|а, и, *f.* *affect. form of* жена́.

же́нщин|а, ы, *f.* woman.

женьше́н|ь, я, *m.* (*bot., med.*) ginseng.

жёрдочк|а, и, *f.* (*coll.*) pole; perch (*in bird-cage*).

жерд|ь, и, *pl.* ~и, ~е́й, *f.* pole; stake; худо́й, как ж. (*coll.*) thin as a lath.

жереб|ая (~а), *adj.* in foal.

жереб|ёнок, ёнка, *pl.* ~я́та, ~я́т, *m.* foal, colt.

жеребе́|ц, ца́, *m.* stallion.

жереби́|ться, и́тся, *impf.* (*of* о~) to foal.

жеребчик, а, *m.* *dim. of* жеребе́ц; мыши́ный ж. (*obs.*) old lecher.

жеребьёвк|а, и, *f.* casting of lots, sortition.

жереб|я́чий, *adj.* *of* ~ёнок; ж. смех (*coll.*) horse-laugh.

же́рех, а, *m.* chub (*fish*).

жерли́ц|а, ы, *f.* kind of fishing tackle (*for catching pike, etc.*).

жерл|о́, а́, *pl.* ~а, ~, *n.* mouth, orifice; muzzle (*of gun*); ж. вулка́на crater.

жёрнов, а, *pl.* ~а́, ~о́в, *m.* millstone.

же́ртв|а, ы, *f.* 1. sacrifice (*also fig.*); принести́ ~у (+*d.*) to make a sacrifice (to); принести́ в ~у to sacrifice. 2. victim; пасть ~ой (+*g.*) to fall victim (to).

же́ртвенник, а, *m.* 1. sacrificial altar. 2. (*eccl.*) credence table.

же́ртвенный, *adj.* sacrificial.

же́ртвовател|ь, я, *m.* donor.

же́ртв|овать, ую, *impf.* (*of* по~) 1. to make

a donation (of), present. 2. (+*i.*) to sacrifice, give up.

жертвоприноше́ни|е, я, *n.* sacrifice; oblation.

жест, а, *m.* gesture (*also fig.*).

жестикули́р|овать, ую, *impf.* to gesticulate.

жестикуля́ци|я, и, *f.* gesticulation.

жёст|кий (~ок, ~ка́, ~ко), *adj.* hard; tough; (*fig.*) rigid, strict; ж. ваго́н hard-seated carriage, 'hard' carriage; ~кая вода́ hard water; ~кие во́лосы wiry hair.

жёст|ко¹, *adv. of* ~кий.

жёстко², *as pred.* it is hard.

жесткокры́л|ые, ых, *sing.* ~ое, ~ого, *n.* (*zool.*) Coleoptera.

жесто́к|ий (~, ~а́, ~о), *adj.* cruel; brutal; (*fig.*) severe, sharp.

жестокосе́рд|ный (~ен, ~на), *adj.* hard-hearted.

жестокосе́рд|ый = ~ный.

жесто́кост|ь, и, *f.* cruelty, brutality.

жесто|ча́йший, *superl. of* ~кий.

жёст|че, *comp. of* ~кий *and* ~ко.

жест|ь, и, *f.* tin-plate.

жестя́ник, а, *m.* tinman, tin-smith.

жестя́нк|а, и, *f.* 1. tin, can; ж. из-под сарди́нок sardine tin. 2. (*coll.*) piece of tin.

жест|яно́й, *adj. of* ~ь; ~яна́я посу́да tin-ware.

жестя́нщик, а, *m.* tinman, tin-smith.

жето́н, а, *m.* 1. medal. 2. counter.

жечь, жгу, жжёшь, жгут, *past* жёг, жгла, *impf.* 1. (*pf.* с~) to burn (up, down); ж. му́сор to burn up refuse. 2. (*impf. only*) to burn, sting; от э́того ликёра жжёт го́рло (*impers.*) this liqueur burns one's throat.

же́чься, жгусь, жжёшься, жгу́тся, *past* жёгся, жглась, *impf.* 1. to burn, sting (*intrans.*). 2. (*coll.*) to burn oneself.

жжёни|е, я, *n.* 1. burning. 2. burning pain; heartburn.

жжёнк|а, и, *f.* hot punch.

жжёный, *adj.* burnt, scorched; ж. ко́фе roasted coffee.

жжёшь, *see* жечь.

жива́ть, *no pres.* (*coll.*) *freq. of* жить.

жив|е́й, *see* ~о 5.

живе́те, *indecl.*, *n.*, old name of letter ж.

жив|е́ц¹, ца́, *m.* live bait, sprat.

жив|е́ц², ца́, *m.* (*obs., coll.*) member of Living Church.

живи́тел|ьный (~ен, ~ьна), *adj.* life-giving; bracing; ~ьная вла́га (*coll.*) intoxicating liquor.

жив|и́ть, лю́, и́шь, *impf.* to give life to, animate; to brace.

жив|и́ться, лю́сь, и́шься, *impf.* (+*i.*; *obs.*) to live (on), make a living (by).

живи́ц|а, ы, *f.* soft resin.

жи́вност|ь, и, *no pl.*, *f.* (*collect.*; *coll.*) poultry, fowl.

жи́в|о, *adv.* 1. vividly. 2. with animation. 3. keenly; extremely, exceedingly; он ж. чу́вствовал оскорбле́ние he felt deeply insulted. 4. (*coll.*) quickly, promptly. 5. ж.!, ∼е́й! (*coll.*) make haste!, look lively!

живодёр, а, *m.* knacker; (*fig.*) fleecer, flay-flint; profiteer.

живодёр|ня, ни, *g. pl.* ∼ен, *f.* (*coll.*) knacker's yard.

живодёрств|о, а, *n.* (*coll.*) cruelty.

жив|о́й (∼, ∼á, ∼о), *adj.* 1. living, live, alive; он ещё в ∼ы́х he is still alive; оста́ться в ∼ы́х to survive, escape with one's life; ∼ (и) здоро́в (*coll.*) safe and sound; ни ∼ ни мёртв (*coll.*) petrified (*with fright, astonishment*); ж. вес live weight; ∼áя вода́ (*folklore*) water of life; ∼áя и́згородь (quickset) hedge; ж. инвента́рь livestock; ∼ые карти́ны tableaux (vivants); шить на ∼у́ю ни́тку to tack; на ∼у́ю ни́тку (*coll.*) hastily, anyhow; стоя́ть в ∼о́й о́череди to queue in person; ж. портре́т (+*g.*) the living image (of); ∼áя ра́на open wound; ∼áя си́ла (*mil.*) men and beasts (*as opp. to* matériel); ∼ым сло́вом рассказа́ть to tell by word of mouth; ж. уголо́к nature corner (*in schools*); ∼ые цветы́ natural flowers; не́ было ви́дно ни (одно́й) ∼о́й души́ there was not a living soul to be seen; на нём не́ было ∼о́го ме́ста he was all battered and bruised; забра́ть, заде́ть за ∼о́е to touch, sting to the quick. 2. lively; keen; brisk; animated; ж. ум lively mind; проявля́ть ж. интере́с (к) to take a keen interest (in); принима́ть ∼о́е уча́стие (в+*p.*) to take an active part (in); to feel keen sympathy with. 3. lively, vivacious; bright; ∼ые глаза́ bright eyes. 4. keen, poignant. 5. (*short form only*; +*i.*) expresses raison d'être: он ∼ одни́ми ша́хматами he lives for chess alone; чем она́ ∼á? what makes her tick?

жи́вокост|ь, и, *f.* (*bot.*) larkspur.

живопис|а́ть, у́ю, *impf. and pf.* (*obs.*) to describe vividly, paint a vivid picture (of).

живопи́с|ец, ца, *m.* painter; ж. вы́весок sign-painter.

живопи́с|ный (∼ен, ∼на), *adj.* 1. pictorial. 2. picturesque (*also fig.*).

жи́вопис|ь, и, *f.* 1. painting. 2. (*collect.*) paintings; италья́нская ж. paintings of the Italian school; стенна́я ж. murals.

живородя́щий, *adj.* (*zool.*) viviparous.

живорожде́ни|е, я, *n.* (*zool.*) viviparity.

живоры́бный, *adj.*; ж. садо́к fishpond.

жи́вост|ь, и, *f.* liveliness, vivacity; animation.

живо́т, á, *m.* 1. abdomen, belly; stomach; (*coll.*) у него́ ж. подво́дит he feels hungry; же́нщина с ∼о́м (*coll.*) pregnant woman. 2. (*arch.*) life; не на ж., а на смерть to the death; не щадя́ ∼á своего́ not counting the cost. 3. (*obs. or dial.*) animals, beasts; (*pl.*) goods and chattels.

животвор|и́ть, ю́, и́шь, *impf.* (*of* о∼) to revive.

животво́р|ный (∼ен, ∼на), *adj.* life-giving.

животвор|я́щий, *pres. part. act. of* ∼и́ть *and adj.* (*obs. or poet.*) life-giving; ж. крест (*theol.*) the life-giving cross.

живо́тик, а, *m.* (*coll.*) tummy.

животи́н|а, ы, *f.* (*coll.*) domestic animal; (*fig.*) beast.

животново́д, а, *m.* cattle-breeder.

животново́дств|о, а, *n.* stock-raising, animal husbandry.

животново́дческий, *adj.* cattle-breeding, stock-raising.

живо́тно|е, го, *n.* animal; (*fig.*, *pejor.*) beast, brute.

живо́тный, *adj.* 1. animal; ж. жир animal fat; ж. у́голь animal charcoal; ж. э́пос (*lit.*) bestiary. 2. bestial, brute.

животрепе́щущий, *adj.* 1. topical; stirring, exciting. 2. lively, full of life. 3. (*joc.*) unsound, unstable.

живу́чест|ь, и, *f.* 1. vitality, tenacity of life. 2. (*fig.*) firmness, stability.

живу́ч|ий (∼, ∼a), *adj.* 1. tenacious of life; (*bot.*) hardy; он ∼ как ко́шка he has nine lives like a cat. 2. (*fig.*) firm, stable.

жи́вчик, а, *m.* 1. (*coll.*) lively person. 2. (*biol.*) spermatozoon. 3. (*coll.*) perceptible pulsing of artery on temple *or* twitching of eyelid.

живь|ё, я́, *n.* (*collect.*; *dial.*) live things.

живьём, *adv.* 1. (*coll.*) alive; постара́йтесь схвати́ть его́ ж. try to catch him alive. 2. (*dial.*) anyhow; in rough and ready fashion.

жиган|у́ть, у́, ёшь, *pf.* (*coll.*) to lash.

жид, á, *m.* (*obs. or pejor.*) 1. (*obs.*) Jew. 2. (*pejor. and vulg.*) Yid.

жи́д|кий (∼ок, ∼ка́, ∼ко), *adj.* 1. liquid; fluid; ∼кое то́пливо liquid fuel, fuel oil. 2. watery; (*of liquids*) weak, thin; ж. чай weak tea. 3. sparse, scanty; ∼кая борода́ straggly beard. 4. (*coll.*; *of voice or sound*) weak, thin. 5. (*fig.*) weak, feeble.

жи́дкостный, *adj.* (*tech.*) liquid; fluid.

жи́дкост|ь, и, *f.* 1. liquid; fluid. 2. wateriness; weakness, thinness (*also fig.*).

жидо́вк|а, и, *f.* (*obs. or pejor.*) Jewess.

жидо́вск|ий, *adj.* (*obs. or pejor.*) Jewish; ∼ая смола́ (*min.*) Jew's pitch.

жи́ж|а, и, *no pl.*, *f.* liquid; swill; slush.

жи́|же, *comp. of* ∼дкий.

жи́жиц|а, ы, f. (coll.) dim. of жи́жа.

жизнеде́ятельност|ь, и, f. 1. (biol.) vital activity. 2. (obs.) life's work.

жизнеде́ятел|ьный (~ен, ~ьна), adj. 1. (biol.) active. 2. lively; energetic.

жи́зненност|ь, и, f. 1. vitality. 2. closeness to life; (art) lifelikeness.

жи́знен|ный (~, ~на), adj. 1. life; (biol.) vital; ~ные отправле́ния vital functions; ж. путь life; ~ные си́лы vitality, sap; ж. у́ровень standard of living. 2. close to life; lifelike. 3. (fig.) vital, vitally important; ж. вопро́с question of vital importance; ~ные це́нтры страны́ nerve-centres of a country.

жизнеописа́ни|е, я, n. biography.

жизнера́достност|ь, и, f. joie de vivre; cheerfulness.

жизнера́дост|ный (~ен, ~на), adj. full of joie de vivre; cheerful.

жизнеспосо́бност|ь, и, f. (biol.) viability; (fig.) vitality.

жизнеспосо́б|ный (~ен, ~на), adj. capable of living; (biol.) viable; (fig.) vigorous, flourishing.

жизнесто́|йкий (~ек, ~йка), adj. tenacious of life; tough, durable.

жизн|ь, и, f. life; existence; ж. моя́! my dear!; зарабо́тать на ж. to earn one's living; как ж.? (coll.) how are you?; лиши́ть себя́ ~и to take one's life; не на ж., а на смерть to the death; ни в ж. never, not for anything; о́браз ~и way of life; вести́ широ́кий о́браз ~и to live in style; по ж. for life; провести́ что-н. в ж. to put something into practice; проже́чь ж. to dissipate one's life, fritter away one's life; ~и не рад (coll.) upset, distressed, miserable; из-за э́того он и ~и не рад he is very vexed about it.

жиклёр, а, m. (tech.) (carburettor) jet.

жил- abbr. of ~и́щный, ~о́й.

жи́л|а¹, ы, f. 1. vein; tendon, sinew; тяну́ть ~ы (из; coll.) to torment, rack. 2. (min.) vein, lode. 3. filament, strand (of cable).

жи́л|а², ы, m. and f. (coll., pejor.) skinflint.

жиле́т, а, m. waistcoat.

жиле́тк|а, и, f. (coll.) waistcoat; пла́кать в ~у (+d.) to cry on someone's shoulder.

жиле́т|ный, adj. of ~; ж. карма́н waistcoat pocket, vest-pocket.

жил|е́ц, ьца́, m. 1. lodger; tenant. 2. (obs.) inhabitant; он не ж. (на бе́лом све́те) (coll.) he is not long for this world.

жи́лист|ый (~, ~а), adj. 1. having prominent veins. 2. sinewy; (fig.) wiry; ~ое мя́со stringy meat.

жи́л|ить, ю, ишь, impf. (у; coll.) to swindle.

жи́л|иться¹, юсь, ишься, impf. (coll.) to heave, strain.

жи́л|иться², юсь, ишься, impf. (pejor., coll.) to stint; to be miserly.

жили́ц|а, ы, f. of жиле́ц.

жили́чк|а, и, f. (coll.) = жили́ца.

жили́щ|е, а, n. 1. dwelling, abode; habitation. 2. lodging; (living) quarters.

жили́щ|ный, adj. of ~е; ~ные усло́вия housing conditions; ~но-бытовы́е усло́вия living conditions.

жи́лк|а, и, f. 1. (anat., geol.) vein; (zool., bot.) fibre, rib (of insect's wing or of leaf). 2. (fig.) vein, streak; bent; артисти́ческая ж. artistic streak; попа́сть в ~у (obs.) to do something opportunely.

жилкова́ни|е, я, n. (zool., bot.) nervation.

жи́л|о, а, n. (obs. or dial.) habitation.

жилова́т|ый (~, ~а), adj. (coll.) with prominent veins.

жил|о́й, adj. 1. dwelling; residential; inhabited; ж. дом dwelling house, block of flats (as opp. to office block, etc.); ж. кварта́л residential area; ~ые ко́мнаты rooms lived in; ~а́я пло́щадь (i) floor space, (ii) housing, accommodation (= available dwelling space). 2. habitable, fit to live in.

жилотде́л, а, m. (abbr. of жили́щный отде́л) housing department (of local Soviet).

жилпло́щад|ь, и, f. (abbr. of жила́я пло́щадь) see жило́й.

жилстрои́тельств|о, а, n. (abbr. of жили́щное строи́тельство) house building.

жилфо́нд, а, m. (abbr. of жили́щный фонд) housing, accommodation.

жиль|ё, я́, n. 1. habitation; dwelling; мы не нашли́ никако́го при́знака ~я́ we could find no sign of life. 2. lodging; (living) accommodation. 3. (obs.) storey, floor.

жи́льн|ый, adj. venous; ~ая поро́да (geol.) veinstone, matrix, gangue.

жим, а, m. (sport) press (in weight-lifting).

жи́молост|ь, и, f. (bot.) honeysuckle.

жи́нк|а, и, f. (dial.) = жёнка.

жир, а (у), о ~е, в ~у́, pl. ~ы́, m. fat; grease.

жира́ф, а, m. giraffe.

жира́ф|а, ы, f. = ~.

жире́|ть, ю, impf. (of о~ and раз~) to grow fat, stout, plump.

жирномоло́чный, adj. (agric.) giving milk with high fat content.

жи́р|ный (~ен, ~на́, ~но), adj. 1. fatty; (chem.) aliphatic; rich (of food); greasy; ~ная кислота́ fatty acid, aliphatic acid; ~ное пятно́ grease stain. 2. fat, plump. 3. rich (of soil); lush (of vegetation); ~ная земля́ loam. 4. (typ.) bold, heavy; ж. шрифт bold (-face) type. 5. (coll.) ж. кусо́к fat sum (of money); ~но бу́дет! that's too much!

жи́ро, indecl., n. (fin.) endorsement.

жир|ова́ть¹, у́ю, impf. to lubricate, oil, grease.

жир|овáть², ýет, *impf.* to fatten (*intrans.*).

жировúк, á, *m.* 1. (*med.*) fatty tumour. 2. (*min.*) steatite, soapstone.

жиров|óй, *adj.* 1. fatty, aliphatic; (*anat.*) adipose; ~áя ткань adipose tissue; ~óe перерождéние (*med.*) fatty degeneration. 2. ~áя промышленность fat-products industry. 3. ~óe яйцó wind-egg.

жировóск, a, *m.* (*physiol.*) adipocere.

жиропóт, a, *m.* (*tech.*) suint, yolk (*of wool*).

жироприкáз, a, *m.* (*fin.*) (banking) order.

жироскóп, a, *m.* (*phys.*) gyroscope.

житéйск|ий, *adj.* 1. worldly; of life, of the world; ~ая мýдрость worldly wisdom; ~oe мóре the ups and downs of life. 2. everyday; дéло ~oe (*coll.*) there's nothing extraordinary in that.

жúтел|ь, я, *m.* inhabitant; dweller.

жúтельств|о, а, *n.* residence; вид на ж. residence permit; мéсто ~a residence, domicile; мéсто постоянного ~a permanent address.

жúтельств|овать, ую, *impf.* (*obs.*) to reside, dwell.

жити|é, я, *n.* 1. life, biography; ~я святых Lives of the Saints. 2. (*obs.*) life, existence.

житúйн|ый, *adj. of* житиé; ~ая литератýра hagiology, hagiography.[1]

жúтниц|а, ы, *f.* granary (*also fig.*).

жúтный, *adj.* cereal; ж. двор (*obs.*) granary.

жúт|о, a, *no pl., n.* (unground) corn (*denotes rye in Ukraine, barley in N. Russia, spring-sown cereals in general in E. Russia*).

жить, живý, живёшь, *past* жил, жилá, жúло (нé жил, не жилá, нé жило), *impf.* 1. to live; ж. в Москвé to live in Moscow; ж. вéсело to have a good time; ж. припевáючи to be in clover; ж. на широкую нóгу to live in style; ж. со дня нá день to live from hand to mouth; ж. да ж. бы емý (*of a person untimely dead*) he should have lived to see another day; жил-был once upon a time there lived . . . (*formula for opening of fairy-tale*). 2. (+*i. or* на+*a.*) to live (on); (+*i.*; *fig.*) to live (in, for); нам нéчем ж. we have nothing to live on; ж. на свой срéдства to support oneself, live on one's own means; ж. надéждами to live in hopes; ж. искýсством to live for art. 3. (в+*p.*; *of domestic servants*) to work (as); ж. в прислýгах (у) to be a maid (at), work as a maid (for).

жить|ё, я, *n.* (*coll.*) 1. life; existence; ~я тут нет от мух the flies make life here impossible. 2. habitation, residence; квартúра готóва для ~я the flat is ready for habitation.

житьё-бытьё, житья-бытья, *n.* (*coll.*) life; existence.

жúться, живётся, *past* жилóсь, *impf.* (*impers.*+*d.*; *coll.*) to live, get on; ей вéсело живётся she leads a gay life; как вам жилóсь в Амéрике? how did you get on in America?

жмот, a, *m.* (*coll.*) miser.

жму, жмёшь, *see* жать¹.

жмýр|ить, ю, ишь, *impf.* (*of* за~) ж. глазá to screw up one's eyes, narrow one's eyes.

жмýр|иться, юсь, ишься, *impf.* (*of* за~) to screw up one's eyes, narrow one's eyes.

жмýр|ки, ок, *no sing.* blind man's buff.

жмых|й, óв, *sing.* ~, ~á, *m.* (*agric.*) oil-cake.

жнéйк|а, и, *f.* (*agric.*) binder, harvester reaping-machine.

жнец, á, *m.* reaper.

жне|я, á, *f.* (*obs. or dial.*) 1. *f. of* ~ц. 2. reaping-machine.

жнúв|о, а, *n.* (*dial.*) = ~ьё.

жнивь|ё, я, *pl.* ~я, *n.* 1. stubble-field. 2. (*sing. only*) stubble. 3. (*sing. only*) (*dial.*) harvest, harvest-time.

жнитв|ó, á, *n.* (*dial.*) 1. stubble. 2. harvest, harvest-time.

жнúц|а, ы, *f. of* жнец.

жну, жнёшь, *see* жать².

жокé|й, я, *m.* jockey.

жокéйк|а, и, *f.* (*coll.*) jockey cap.

жокéй|ский, *adj. of* ~.

жóлоб = жёлоб.

жóлудь = жёлудь.

жом, a, *m.* 1. (*tech.*) press. 2. (*sing. (collect.*) husks, marc.

жонглёр, a, *m.* juggler.

жонглёрств|о, а, *n.* sleight-of-hand; juggling (*also fig.*).

жонглúр|овать, ую, *impf.* (+*i.*) to juggle (with) (*also fig.*); он любит ж. цúфрами he likes juggling with figures.

жóп|а, ы, *f.* (*vulg.*) arse; arsehole.

жóрнов = жёрнов.

жох, a, *m.* (*coll.*) rogue.

жрань|ё, я, *n.* (*vulg.*) guzzling, hogging.

жратв|á, ы, *f.* (*vulg.*) 1. guzzling, hogging. 2. (*sl.*) grub.

жр|ать, ý, ёшь, *past* ~áл, ~алá, ~áло, *impf.* (*of* со~) 1. (*of animals*) to eat. 2. (*vulg.*) to guzzle, gobble.

жрéби|й, я, *m.* 1. lot; бросáть, метáть ж. to cast lots; вынуть, тянýть ж. to draw lots. 2. (*fig.*) lot, fate, destiny; ж. брóшен the die is cast.

жрец, á, *m.* priest (*of heathen religious cult*); (*fig.*) devotee.

жрéческий, *adj.* priestly.

жрéчеств|о, а, *n.* priesthood.

жрúц|а, ы, *f.* priestess; ж. любвú woman of easy virtue.

жýжелиц|а, ы, *f.* (*zool.*) ground beetle.

жужжáни|е, я, *n.* hum, buzz, drone; humming, buzzing, droning.

жужж|а́ть, у́, и́шь, *impf.* to hum, buzz, drone; to whizz (*of projectiles*).

жуи́р, а, *m.* playboy.

жуи́р|овать, ую, *impf.* to lead a life of idleness and ease.

жук, а́, *m.* **1.** beetle; ма́йский ж. may-bug, cockchafer. **2.** (*coll.*) rogue.

жу́лик, а, *m.* petty thief; cheat, swindler; (card-)sharper.

жулик|ова́т|ый (∼, ∼а), adj. (*coll.*) roguish.

жуль|ё, я́, n. (*collect.; coll.*) rogues.

жу́льнича|ть, ю, *impf.* (*of с∼*) (*coll.*) to cheat; to swindle.

жу́льнический, adj. (*coll.*) roguish; underhand, dishonest.

жу́льничеств|о, а, n. (*coll.*) **1.** cheating (*at games*). **2.** underhand, dishonest action; sharp practice.

жупа́н, а, *m.* (*hist.*) zhupan (*kind of jerkin worn by Poles and Ukrainians*).

жу́пел, а, *m.* **1.** bugbear, bogy. **2.** (*rel.*) brimstone.

журавл|и́ный, adj. of ∼ь; ∼и́ные но́ги spindle shanks.

журавл|ь, я́, m. **1.** (*orn.*) crane; не сули́ ∼я́ в не́бе, а дай сини́цу в ру́ки (*prov.*) a bird in the hand is worth two in the bush. **2.** (*well*) sweep, shadoof.

жур|и́ть, ю́, и́шь, *impf.* (*coll.*) to reprove, take to task.

журна́л, а, *m.* **1.** magazine; periodical; journal. **2.** journal, diary; register; ж. заседа́ний minutes, minute-book.

журнали́ст, а, *m.* **1.** journalist. **2.** ledger-clerk.

журнали́стик|а, и, f. **1.** journalism. **2.** (*collect.*) periodical press.

журнали́стский, adj. journalistic.

журна́л|ьный, adj. of ∼; ∼ьная статья́ magazine article.

журфи́кс, а, *m.* (*obs.*) at-home.

журча́ни|е, я, n. purling, babbling, murmur.

журч|а́ть, у́, и́шь, *impf.* to purl, babble, murmur (*of water; also fig., poet.*).

жу́т|кий (∼ок, ∼ка́, ∼ко), adj. terrible, terrifying; awe-inspiring, eerie.

жу́тко[1], adv. terrifyingly; (*coll.*) terribly, awfully.

жу́тко[2], as pred. (*impers.+d.*) мне, etc., ж. I, etc., am terrified, feel awestruck.

жут|ь, и, f. **1.** terror; awe; воспомина́ния о де́тстве для него́ — пря́мо ж. memories of childhood simply terrify him. **2.** *as pred.* = ∼ко[2].

жу́хл|ый (∼, ∼а), adj. withered, dried-up; hardened; tarnished.

жу́х|нуть, нет, *past* ∼, ∼ла, *impf.* to dry up; to become hard; to become tarnished.

жу́ч|ить, у, ишь, *impf.* (*coll.*) to scold.

жу́чк|а, и, f. (*coll.*) house-dog (*from name 'Zhuchka', very frequently given to mongrel dogs*).

жуч|о́к, ка́, m. **1.** *dim. of* жук. **2.** (*coll.*) wood-engraver (*insect*).

жу|ю́, ёшь, *see* жева́ть.

жюри́, indecl. **1.** *n.* (*collect.*) judges (*of competition, etc.*). **2.** *m.* (*obs.*) umpire, referee.

З

за, prep. I. +*a.* and *i.* (+*a.*: *indicates motion or action;* +*i.*: *indicates rest or state*). **1.** behind; за крова́ть, за крова́тью behind the bed. **2.** beyond; across, the other side of; за боло́то, за боло́том beyond the marsh; за́ борт, за бо́ртом overboard; за́ угол, за угло́м round the corner; за́ городом out of town; за рубежо́м abroad. **3.** at; сесть за роя́ль to sit down at the piano; сиде́ть за роя́лем to be at the piano. **4.** (*denoting occupation*) at, to (*or translated by participle*); приня́ться за рабо́ту to set to work, get down to work; заста́ть кого́-н. за рабо́той to find someone at work, working; сесть за кни́гу to sit down with a book, get down to reading; проводи́ть всё своё вре́мя за чте́нием to spend all one's time reading. **5.** вы́йти за́муж за (+*a.*) (*of a woman*) to

marry; (быть) за́мужем за (+*i.*) (to be) married (to).

II. +*a.* **1.** after (*of time*); over (*of age*); далеко́ за́ полночь long after midnight; ему́ уже́ за́ сорок he is already over forty. **2.** *expresses distance in space or time:* самолёт разби́лся за ми́лю от дере́вни the aeroplane crashed a mile from the village; за два дня до его́ сме́рти two days before his death; за час an hour before, an hour early. **3.** during, in the space of; за́ ночь during the night, overnight; за су́тки in the space of twenty-four hours; за после́днее вре́мя recently, lately, of late. **4.** (+*verbs having sense of* to take hold of, *etc.*) by; вести́ за́ руку to lead by the hand. **5.** (*in var. senses*) for; плати́ть за биле́т to pay for a ticket; подписа́ть за дире́ктора to sign for the

director; боя́ться, ра́доваться за кого́-н. to
fear, be glad for someone; слыть за знатока́
to pass for an expert; есть за трои́х to eat
(enough) for three; за ва́ше здоро́вье! your
health!, cheers!
III. +*i.* **1.** after; друг за дру́гом one
after another; год за го́дом year after year;
сле́довать за кем-н. to follow someone.
2. (*fig.*) after; следи́ть за детьми́ to look
after children; уха́живать за больны́м to
look after a sick person; волочи́ться за
же́нщиной (*coll.*) to run after a woman.
3. for (= in order to fetch, obtain); идти́
за молоко́м to go for milk; посла́ть за
до́ктором to send for a doctor; зайти́ за
кем-н. to call for someone. **4.** at, during;
за за́втраком at breakfast. **5.** for, on
account of, because of; за неиме́нием,
недоста́тком (+*g.*) for want of; за тем-
ното́й for the darkness, on account of the
darkness; за чем де́ло ста́ло? what's up?
6. (+*pronouns*) (*i*) *ascribes habits, qualities,*
(*ii*) *imputes responsibility*: за ним во́дятся
стра́нности he has his peculiarities; за
тобо́й пять рубле́й you are owing five
roubles; о́чередь за ва́ми it is your turn.
7. *indicates provenance of a document, etc.*: пись-
мо́ за по́дписью гла́вного реда́ктора a
letter signed by the editor-in-chief.
за- *prefix* I. (*of verbs*) **1.** *indicates commencement
of action*: зала́ять to start barking. **2.** *indicates direction of action beyond given point*: за-
верну́ть за́ угол to turn a corner. **3.** *indicates
continuation of action to excess*: закорми́ть to
overfeed. **4.** *forms perfective aspect of some verbs.*
II. (*of nouns and adjs.*) trans-; Закавка́зье
Transcaucasia; заатланти́ческий transatlantic.

заадрес|ова́ть, у́ю, *pf.* (*coll.*) to address,
write the address (on).

заале́|ть, ет, *pf. of* але́ть.

заале́|ться, ется = ~ть.

зааплоди́р|овать, ую, *pf.* to break out into
applause, start clapping.

зааренд|ова́ть, у́ю, *pf.* (*of* ~о́вывать) to
rent, lease.

заарендо́outbound|ть, ю, *impf. of* заарендова́ть.

заарка́н|ить, ю, ишь, *pf. of* арка́нить.

заарта́ч|иться, усь, ишься, *pf.* (*coll.*) to
become restive, stubborn.

заасфальти́р|овать, ую, *pf. of* асфальти́ро-
вать.

заатланти́ческий, *adj.* transatlantic.

заа́ха|ть, ю, *pf.* (*coll.*) to begin to sigh,
begin to groan.

заба́в|а, ы, *f.* **1.** game; pastime. **2.** amuse-
ment, fun; он э́то сде́лал для ~ы he did it
for fun.

забавля́|ть, ю, *impf.* to amuse, entertain,
divert.

забавля́|ться, юсь, *impf.* to amuse oneself.

заба́вник, а, *m.* (*coll.*) amusing chap, entertaining person; humorist.

заба́вн|о¹, *adv. of* ~ый.

заба́вно², *as pred.* it is amusing, funny; мне
з. I find it amusing, funny; з.! how
funny!

заба́в|ный (~ен, ~на), *adj.* amusing;
funny.

забаллоти́р|овать, ую, *pf.* to blackball,
reject, fail to elect.

заба́лтыва|ть, ю, *impf. of* заболта́ть¹ 2.

забараба́н|ить, ю, ишь, *pf.* to begin to
drum.

забаррикади́р|овать, ую, *pf. of* баррикади́-
ровать.

забаст|ова́ть, у́ю, *pf.* to go, come out on
strike.

забасто́вк|а, и, *f.* strike; всео́бщая з.
general strike; италья́нская з. sit-down
strike.

забасто́в|очный, *adj. of* ~ка.

забасто́вщик, а, *m.* striker.

забве́ни|е, я, *n.* **1.** oblivion; преда́ть ~ю to
consign to oblivion. **2.** (*obs.*) unconscious-
ness; drowsiness.

забве́нный, *adj.* (*obs.*) forgotten.

забе́г, а, *m.* (*sport*) heat, race.

забега́ловк|а, и, *f.* (*coll.*) snack bar.

забе́га|ть, ю, *pf.* **1.** to start running. **2.** to
assume a shifty expression.

забега́|ть, ю, *impf. of* забежа́ть.

забе́га|ться, юсь, *pf.* (*coll.*) to run oneself
to a standstill.

забе|жа́ть, гу́, жи́шь, гу́т, *pf.* (*of* ~га́ть)
1. to run up. **2.** (к; *coll.*) to drop in (to see).
3. to run off; to stray. **4.** з. вперёд to run
ahead; (*fig., coll.*) to anticipate.

забеле́|ть, ет, *pf.* to begin to turn white.

забел|и́ть, ю́, ~и́шь, *pf.* **1.** to whiten, paint
white. **2.** (*coll.*) to add milk, cream (to);
з. чай молоко́м to put milk in tea.

забе́лк|а, и, *f.* (*coll.*) **1.** whitening. **2.** milk
or cream added to tea, *etc.*

забере́мене|ть, ю, *pf.* (*of* бере́менеть) to be-
come pregnant.

забеспоко́|иться, юсь, ишься, *pf.* to begin
to worry.

забива́ни|е, я, *n.* (*coll.*) jamming (*of radio
transmissions*).

забива́|ть(ся), ю(сь), *impf. of* заби́ть(ся)¹.

заби́вк|а, и, *f.* (*coll.*) driving in; blocking
up, stopping up.

забинт|ова́ть, у́ю, *pf.* (*of* ~о́вывать) to
bandage.

забинт|ова́ться, у́юсь, *pf.* (*of* ~о́вываться)
to bandage oneself.

забинто́outbound|ть(ся), аю(сь), *impf. of* забин-
това́ть(ся).

забира́|ть(ся), ю(сь), *impf. of* забра́ть(ся).

заби́т|ый (~, ~а), *p.p.p. of* ~ь *and adj.* cowed, downtrodden.

заб|и́ть¹, ью, ьёшь, *pf.* (*of* ~ива́ть) **1.** to drive in, hammer in, ram in; з. себе́ в го́лову to get (it) firmly fixed in one's head. **2.** (*sport*) to score; з. мяч to kick the ball into the goal; з. гол to score a goal. **3.** to seal, stop up, block up; з. ще́ли па́клей to caulk up cracks with oakum. **4.** to obstruct; (*of plants*) to choke; (*coll.*) to jam (*radio transmissions*). **5.** (+*i.*; *coll.*) to cram, stuff (with). **6.** to beat up, knock senseless; (*fig.*) to render defenceless. **7.** (*coll.*) to beat (*at something*); to outdo, surpass. **8.** to slaughter (*cattle*).

заб|и́ть², ью, ьёшь, *pf.* (*in var. senses*; *trans. and intrans.*) to begin to beat (*in some cases forms perfective aspect of* бить); з. трево́гу to sound the alarm; у нас из сква́жины ~и́ла нефть we have struck oil.

заб|и́ться¹, ью́сь, ьёшься, *pf.* (*of* ~ива́ться) **1.** (в+*a.*) to hide (in), take refuge (in). **2.** (в+*a.*) to get (into), penetrate. **3.** (+*i.*) to become cluttered (with), clogged (with).

заб|и́ться², ью́сь, ьёшься, *pf.* to begin to beat (*intrans.*).

забия́к|а, и, *m. and f.* (*coll.*) squabbler; trouble-maker; bully.

заблаговре́менно, *adv.* in good time; well in advance; з. предупреди́ть to warn in advance.

заблаговре́менный, *adj.* timely, done in good time.

заблагорассу́|дить, жу, дишь, *pf.* (*obs.*) to think fit.

заблагорассу́д|иться, ится, *pf.* (*impers.*) to like, think fit; to come into one's head; он придёт, когда́ ему́ ~ится he will come when he thinks fit, when he feels so disposed.

забле|сте́ть, щу́, сти́шь *and* ~щешь, *pf.* to begin to shine, glitter, glow.

забле́|ять, ю, ешь, *pf.* to begin to bleat.

заблу|ди́ться, жу́сь, ~дишься, *pf.* to lose one's way, get lost; з. в трёх со́снах not to be able to see beyond the end of one's own nose.

заблу́дш|ий, *adj.* (*obs.*) lost, stray; ~ая овца́ a lost sheep.

заблужда́|ться, юсь, *impf.* to be mistaken.

заблужде́ни|е, я, *n.* error; delusion; ввести́ в з. to delude, mislead; впасть в з. to be deluded.

забода́|ть, ю, *pf. of* бода́ть.

забо́|й¹, я, *m.* (*mining*) (pit-)face.

забо́|й², я, *m.* slaughtering.

забо́йник, а, *m.* (*tech.*) beetle, rammer.

забо́йщик, а, *m.* face-worker, (coal-)hewer, getter (*in mine*).

заболачива|ть(ся), ет(ся), *impf. of* заболо́тить(ся).

заболева́емост|ь, и, *f.* sickness rate; number of cases; з. полиомиели́том утро́илась за про́шлую неде́лю the number of cases of infantile paralysis has tripled during the last week.

заболева́ни|е, я, *n.* **1.** sickness, illness. **2.** falling sick, falling ill.

заболева́|ть¹, ю, *impf. of* заболе́ть¹.

заболева́|ть², ет, *impf. of* заболе́ть².

заболе́|ть¹, ю, ешь, *pf.* (*of* ~ва́ть¹) to fall ill, fall sick; (+*i.*) to be taken ill (with), go down (with).

забол|е́ть², и́т, *pf.* (*of* ~ева́ть²) to (begin to) ache, hurt; у меня́ ~е́л зуб I have toothache.

за́болон|ь, и, *f.* (*bot.*) alburnum, sap-wood.

заболо́|тить, чу, тишь, *pf.* (*of* заболо́чивать) to swamp, turn into swamp. (*intrans.*)

заболо́|титься, тится, *pf.* (*of* заболо́чиваться) to turn into swamp. (*intrams.*)

заболта́|ть¹, ю, *pf.* **1.** (+*i.*) to begin to swing. **2.** (*impf.* заба́лтывать) to mix (in).

заболта́|ть², ю, *pf.* (*coll.*) to start chattering, nattering.

заболта́|ться¹, юсь, *pf.* (*coll.*) to begin to swing.

заболта́|ться², юсь, *pf.* (*coll.*) to become engrossed in conversation.

забо́р¹, а, *m.* fence.

забо́р², а, *m.* **1.** taking away. **2.** obtaining on credit.

забо́рист|ый (~, ~а), *adj.* (*coll.*) **1.** strong (*of liquor, tobacco, etc.*). **2.** (*fig.*) з. анекдо́т risqué story; з. моти́в racy tune.

забо́р|ный¹, *adj.* **1.** *adj. of* ~¹. **2.** coarse, indecent; risqué; ~ная литерату́ра pornography.

забо́р|ный², *adj. of* ~²; ~ная кни́жка (*i*) ration book, (*ii*) account (*book in which purchases obtained on credit are entered*).

забо́ртный, *adj.* (*naut.*) outboard; з. дви́гатель outboard engine; з. кла́пан (*tech.*) seacock; з. трап companion ladder.

забо́т|а, ы, *f.* **1.** cares, trouble(s); без ~ carefree; (*coll.*) вот не́ было ~ы! there was trouble enough already; ему́ ма́ло ~ы what does he care? **2.** care, attention(s); concern; з. о челове́ке concern for people's welfare.

забо́|тить, чу, тишь, *impf.* to trouble, worry, cause anxiety.

забо́|титься, чусь, тишься, *impf.* (*of* по~) (о+*p.*) **1.** to worry, be troubled (about). **2.** to take care (of); to take trouble (about); to care (about); она́ всё ~тится о де́тях she is always thinking of the children; он ни о чём не ~тится he does not care about anything.

забо́тливост|ь, и, *f.* solicitude, care, thoughtfulness.

забо́тлив|ый (~, ~а), *adj.* solicitous, thoughtful.

забрако́в|анный, *p.p.p. of* ~а́ть; з. това́р rejects.

забрак|ова́ть, у́ю, *pf. of* бракова́ть.

забра́л|о, а, *n.* visor; с откры́тым ~ом openly, frankly.

забра́сыва|ть, ю, *impf. of* заброса́ть *and* забро́сить.

забра́|ть¹, заберу́, заберёшь, *past* ~л, ~ла́, ~ло, *pf. (of* забира́ть) 1. to take (*in one's hands*); to take (with one); з. во́жжи to take the reins; з. с собо́й ве́щи to take one's things with one; з. себе́ в го́лову to take it into one's head; з. за живо́е to touch to the quick. 2. to take away; to seize, appropriate. 3. (*of emotions; coll.*) to come over, seize; его́ ~ла́ охо́та пое́хать в Аме́рику he was seized with a desire to go to America. 4. to take in (*part of a garment, etc.*). 5. to turn off, aside. 6. (*tech.*) to catch; (*of an anchor*) to bite.

забра́|ть², заберу́, заберёшь, *past* ~л, ~ла́, ~ло, *pf. (of* забира́ть) to stop up, block up.

забра́|ться, заберу́сь, заберёшься, *past* ~лся, ~ла́сь, ~ло́сь, *pf. (of* забира́ться) 1. (в+*a.*) to get (into); (в, на+*a.*) to climb (into, on to); з. в чужо́й дом to get into someone else's house. 2. to get to; to hide out, go into hiding; куда́ они́ ~ли́сь? where have they got to?

забре́|дить, жу, дишь, *pf.* to become delirious.

забре́зж|ить, ит, *pf.* to begin to dawn; to begin to appear; чуть ~ил свет it was barely light; ~ило (*impers.*) it is just beginning to get light.

забре|сти́, ду́, дёшь, *past* ~л, ~ла́, *pf.* (*coll.*) 1. to drop in. 2. to go astray, wander off.

забр|и́ть, е́ю, е́ешь, *pf.* (*obs.*) to call up (into the army); з. лоб (+*d.*) = з.

заброни́р|овать, ую, *pf. (of* брони́ровать) to reserve.

забронир|ова́ть, у́ю, *pf. (of* бронирова́ть) to armour.

забро́с, а, *m.*; в ~е (*coll.*) in a state of neglect.

заброса́|ть, ю, *pf. (of* забра́сывать) (+*i.*) 1. to fill (up) (with); з. я́му золо́й to fill up a hole with ashes. 2. to shower (with), bespatter (with); з. кого́-н. гря́зью to sling mud at someone (*also fig.*); з. кого́-н. бла́нками to deluge someone with forms.

забро́|сить, шу, сишь, *pf. (of* забра́сывать) 1. to throw (*with force or to a distance*); to cast (*also fig.*); кто ~сил мя́чик в окно́? who threw a ball through the window?; вое́нная слу́жба ~сила его́ на Да́льний Восто́к military service took him to the Far East. 2. to throw (*a part of the body, etc.*); з. го́лову наза́д to throw one's head back. 3. (*pf.*

only) to mislay. 4. to throw up, give up, abandon; to neglect, let go; з. иссле́дования to throw up one's research; з. дете́й to neglect children. 5. to take, bring (*to a certain place*). 6. to leave behind (*somewhere*).

забро́шенност|ь, и, *f.* 1. neglect. 2. desertion.

забро́|шенный, *p.p.p. of* ~сить *and adj.* 1. neglected. 2. deserted, desolate.

забры́зг|ать¹, аю, *pf. (of* ~ивать) (+*i.*) to splash; to bespatter (with).

забры́з|гать², жет, *pf.* to begin to play (*of a fountain*).

забры́згива|ть, ю, *impf. of* забры́згать¹.

забубённ|ый, *adj.* (*coll.*) reckless; wild; ~ая голо́вушка desperate fellow, reprobate.

заб|у́ду, у́дешь, *see* ~ы́ть.

забукси́р|овать, ую, *pf.* to take in tow.

забулды́г|а, и, *m.* (*coll.*) debauchee, profligate.

забу|ти́ть, чу́, ти́шь, *pf. (of* бути́ть) to fill with rubble; (+*i.*) to fill in (with).

забуха́|ть, ет, *impf. of* забу́хнуть.

забу́х|нуть, нет, *past* ~, ~ла, *pf.* to swell; to become stuck.

забуя́н|ить, ю, ишь, *pf.* to become unruly, get out of hand.

забыва́|ть(ся), ю(сь), *impf. of* забы́ть(ся).

забы́вчив|ый (~, ~а), *adj.* forgetful; absent-minded.

заб|ы́ть, у́ду, у́дешь, *pf. (of* ~ыва́ть) 1. (+*a.*, +*p. or inf.*) to forget; и ду́мать ~у́дь! (*coll.*) get it out of your head!; себя́ не з. to take care of oneself. 2. to leave behind, forget (to bring); вы опя́ть ~ы́ли биле́ты you have forgotten the tickets again.

забыть|ё, я́, в ~и́, *n.* 1. drowsy state. 2. half-conscious state, oblivion. 3. (state of) distraction; в ~и́ distractedly.

заб|ы́ться, у́дусь, у́дешься, *pf. (of* ~ыва́ться) 1. to doze off, drop off. 2. to become unconscious, lose consciousness. 3. to sink into a reverie. 4. to forget oneself. 5. *pass. of* ~ы́ть.

зав, а, *m.* (*abbr. of* ~е́дующий) (*coll.*) manager; chief, head.

зав, *abbr. of* 1. заве́дующий. 2. заво́дский.

зава́л, а, *m.* obstruction, blockage.

зава́лива|ть(ся), ю(сь), *impf. of* завали́ть(ся).

зава́линк|а, и, *f.* zavalinka (*mound of earth round a Russian peasant hut serving as protection from the weather and often used for sitting out*).

завал|и́ть, ю́, ~ишь, *pf. (of* ~ивать) 1. to block up, obstruct; to fill (*so as to block up*); з. вход мешка́ми с песко́м to block up the entrance with sandbags. 2. (+*i.*; *coll.*) to pile (with); to fill cram-full (with); (*fig.*) to overload (with); прила́вок ⌐ен коро́бками the stall is piled high with boxes; реда́кция ⌐ена рабо́той the editors are snowed under with work. **3.** (*coll.*) to throw back; to tip up, cant. **4.** (*coll.*) to knock down, demolish. **5.** (*fig.*, *coll.*) to make a mess (of), muck up. **6.** (*impers.*; *coll.*) to block up, stuff up; у меня́ у́хо ⌐и́ло my ear feels blocked up.

завал|и́ться, ю́сь, ⌐и́шься, *pf.* (*of* ⌐ива́ться) **1.** to fall; to collapse; нож ⌐и́лся за шкаф the knife has fallen behind the cupboard. **2.** (*coll.*) to lie down; з. спать to fall into bed. **3.** (*coll.*) to overturn, tip up. **4.** (*fig.*, *coll.*) to miscarry, come to grief; (*of a person*) to slip up.

зава́лк|а, и, *f.* **1.** filling up. **2.** (*tech.*) (furnace) charge.

за́вал|ь, и, *f.* (*collect.*; *coll.*) shop-soiled goods; trash.

заваля́|ться, ется, *pf.* (*coll.*) **1.** to be still on hand; э́тот това́р ⌐ется these goods will not sell. **2.** to remain without attention; to be shelved.

зава́лящий, *adj.* (*coll.*) long unsold, shop-soiled; worthless, useless.

зава́рива|ть(ся), ет(ся), *impf. of* завари́ть(ся).

завар|и́ть, ю́, ⌐ишь, *pf.* (*of* ⌐ива́ть) **1.** to make (*drinks, etc., by pouring on boiling water*); з. чай to brew tea; з. ка́шу (*fig.*) to start trouble; ну и ⌐и́л ка́шу! now the fat's in the fire! **3.** (*tech.*) to weld. **4.** (*coll.*) to start, initiate.

завар|и́ться, ⌐ится, *pf.* (*of* ⌐ива́ться) **1.** (*of drinks*) to have brewed. **2.** (*coll.*) to start; ⌐и́лось большо́е де́ло there's big trouble brewing.

зава́рк|а, и, *f.* **1.** brewing (*of tea, etc.*). **2.** scalding. **3.** (*tech.*) welding. **4.** (*coll.*) enough tea for one brew.

заварно́й, *adj.* (*cul.*) boiled.

завару́х|а, и, *f.* (*coll.*) commotion, stir.

заведе́ни|е, я, *n.* **1.** establishment, institution. **2.** (*obs.*) custom, habit; здесь уж тако́е з. it is the custom here.

заве́д|овать, ую, *impf.* (+*i.*) to manage, superintend; to be in charge (of).

заве́домо, *adv.* wittingly; (+*adj.*) known to be; з. зна́я being fully aware; переда́ть з. необосно́ванный слух to pass on a rumour known to be unfounded.

заве́домый, *adj.* notorious; undoubted.

заве|ду́, дёшь, *see* ⌐сти́.

заве́дующ|ий, его, *m.* (+*i.*) manager; head; person in charge (of); з. уче́бной ча́стью director of studies; з. отде́лом head of a department.

завез|ти́, у́, ёшь, *past* ⌐, ⌐ла́, *pf.* (*of* заво-зи́ть) **1.** to convey, deliver; з. запи́ску по доро́ге домо́й to deliver a note on the way

home. **2.** to take (to a distance *or* out of one's way).

заверб|ова́ть, у́ю, *pf. of* вербова́ть.

заве́рени|е, я, *n.* assurance; protestation.

завери́тел|ь, я, *m.* witness (*to a signature, etc.*).

заве́р|ить, ю, ишь, *pf.* (*of* ⌐я́ть) **1.** (в+*p.*) to assure (of). **2.** to certify; з. по́дпись to witness a signature.

заве́рк|а, и, *f.* certification.

заверн|у́ть, у́, ёшь, *pf.* (*of* завёртывать) **1.** (в+*a.*) to wrap (in); ⌐и́те его́ в одея́ло wrap him in a blanket. **2.** to tuck up, roll up (*sleeve, etc.*). **3.** to turn (*intrans.*); з. напра́во to turn to the right. **4.** (*coll.*) to drop in, call in. **5.** to screw tight; to turn off (*by screwing*); з. га́йку to screw a nut tight; з. кран to turn off a tap; з. во́ду to turn the water off. **6.** (*of weather conditions*; *coll.*) to come on, come down.

заверн|у́ться, у́сь, ёшься, *pf.* (*of* завёрты-ваться) **1.** (в+*a.*) to wrap oneself up (in), muffle oneself (in). **2.** *pass. of* ⌐у́ть.

заверт|е́ть, чу́, ⌐тишь, *pf.* **1.** to begin to twirl. **2.** з. кого́-н. (*fig.*, *coll.*) to turn some-one's head.

заверт|е́ться, чу́сь, ⌐тишься, *pf.* **1.** to begin to turn, begin to spin. **2.** (*coll.*) to become flustered; to lose one's head.

завёртк|а, и, *f.* **1.** wrapping up. **2.** (*coll.*) package.

завёртыва|ть(ся), ю(сь), *impf. of* завер-ну́ть(ся).

заверш|а́ть, а́ю, *impf. of* ⌐и́ть.

заверше́ни|е, я, *n.* completion; end; в з. in conclusion.

заверш|и́ть, у́, и́шь, *pf.* (*of* ⌐а́ть) to com-plete, conclude, crown.

завер|я́ть, я́ю, *impf. of* ⌐ить.

заве́с|а, ы, *f.* (*obs.*) curtain; дымова́я з. (*mil.*) smoke-screen; (*fig.*) veil, screen; при-подня́ть ⌐y to lift the veil.

заве́|сить, шу, сишь, *pf.* (*of* ⌐шивать) to curtain (off).

заве|сти́, ду́, дёшь, *past* ⌐л, ⌐ла́, *pf.* (*of* заводи́ть[1]) **1.** to take, bring (*to a place*); to leave, drop off (*at a place*). **2.** to take (to a distance *or* out of one's way). **3.** to set up; to start; з. де́ло (*coll.*) to set up in business; з. птицефе́рму to start a poultry farm; з. перепи́ску с кем-н. to start up a correspondence with someone. **4.** to acquire. **5.** to institute, introduce (*as a custom*); з. привы́чку (+*inf.*) to get into the habit (of); у нас так ⌐дено́ this is our custom. **6.** to wind (up), start (*a mechan-ism*); з. часы́ to wind up a clock; з. мото́р to crank an engine; как ⌐дённый (*coll.*) like a machine.

заве|сти́сь, ду́сь, дёшься, *past* ⌐лся, ⌐ла́сь,

pf. (*of* заводи́ться) **1.** to be; to appear; в погребе ~ли́сь кры́сы there are rats in the cellar. **2.** to be established, be set up; ~лось обыкнове́ние it has become a habit. **3.** (+*i.*; *coll.*) to acquire; з. свои́м до́мом to acquire a home of one's own. **4.** (*of a mechanism*) to start (*intrans.*).

завéт, а, *m.* **1.** (*rhet.*) behest, bidding, ordinance. **2.** Ве́тхий, Но́вый з. the Old, the New Testament.

завéтн|ый, *adj.* cherished; intimate; secret, hidden; стать кинозвездо́й — её ~ая мечта́ her secret dream is to become a film--star.

завéтренный, *adj.* leeward.

завéш|ать, аю, *pf.* (*of* ~ивать) (+*a. and i.*) to hang (all over); он ~ал сте́ны своего́ кабине́та фотогра́фиями he has hung the walls of his study with photographs.

завéшива|ть, ю, *impf. of* заве́сить *and* заве́шать.

завеща́ни|е, я, *n.* will, testament.

завеща́тел|ь, я, *m.* (*leg.*) testator.

завеща́тельниц|а, ы, *f.* (*leg.*) testatrix.

завеща́|ть, ю, *impf. and pf.* (+*a. and d.*) to leave (to), bequeath (to); (*leg.*) to devise (to).

заве́|ять, ет, *pf.* **1.** to begin to blow (*of the wind*). **2.** (*of blizzard, etc.*) to cover.

завзя́тый, *adj.* (*coll.*) inveterate, out-and--out, downright; incorrigible.

завива́|ть(ся), ю(сь), *impf. of* зави́ть(ся).

зави́вк|а, и, *f.* **1.** waving; curling; сде́лать себе́ ~у to have one's hair waved. **2.** (hair-) wave.

зави́|деть, жу, дишь, *pf.* (*coll.*) to catch sight of.

зави́д|ки, ок, *no sing.* (*coll.*); меня́, *etc.*, беру́т з. I, *etc.*, feel envious.

зави́дно, *as pred.* (*impers.*+*d.*) to feel envious.

зави́д|ный (~ен, ~на), *adj.* enviable.

зави́д|овать, ую, *impf.* (*of* по~) (+*d.*) to envy.

завиду́щий, *adj.* (*coll.*) envious, covetous.

завизж|а́ть, у́, и́шь, *pf.* to begin to scream, squeal.

завизи́р|овать, ую, *pf. of* визи́ровать.[1]

завин|ти́ть, чу́, ти́шь, *pf.* (*of* ~чивать) to screw up.

завин|ти́ться, чу́сь, ти́шься, *pf.* (*of* ~чиваться) to screw up (*intrans.*).

зави́нчива|ть(ся), ю(сь), *impf. of* завинти́ть(ся).

завира́льный, *adj.* (*coll.*) false; nonsensical.

завира́|ться, юсь, *impf. of* завра́ться.

завиру́х|а, и, *f.* (*dial.*) **1.** snow-storm. **2.** (*coll.*) bother, fuss.

зависа́|ть, ю, *impf.* (*aeron.*) to hover.

зави́|сеть, шу, сишь, *impf.* (от) **1.** to de-

pend (on). **2.** to lie in the power (of); я помогу́ тебе́, наско́лько от меня́ ~сит I will help you as far as in me lies.

зави́симост|ь, и, *f.* dependence; в ~и (от) depending (on), subject (to).

зави́сим|ый (~, ~а), *adj.* (от) dependent (on).

зави́стлив|ый (~, ~а), *adj.* envious.

зави́стник, а, *m.* envious person.

за́вист|ь, и, *f.* envy.

завит|о́й ~ый (зави́т, ~а́, зави́то), *adj.* curled; waved.

завит|о́к, ка́, *m.* **1.** curl, lock. **2.** flourish (*in handwriting*). **3.** (*archit.*) volute, scroll. **4.** (*bot.*) tendril. **5.** (*anat.*) helix.

зав|и́ть, ью́, ьёшь, *past* ~и́л, ~ила́, ~и́ло, *pf.* (*of* ~ива́ть) to curl; to wave; to twist, wind; з. го́ре верёвочкой (*coll.*) to pack up one's troubles.

зав|и́ться, ью́сь, ьёшься, *past* ~и́лся, ~ила́сь, *pf.* (*of* ~ива́ться) **1.** to curl, wave, twine (*intrans.*). **2.** to curl, wave one's hair; to have one's hair curled, waved.

завко́м, а, *m.* (*abbr. of* заводско́й комите́т) factory committee.

завладева́|ть, ю, *impf. of* завладе́ть.

завладе́|ть, ю, *pf.* (*of* ~ва́ть) (+*i.*) to take possession (of); to seize, capture (*also fig.*); свои́м красноре́чием он ~л внима́нием слу́шателей he gripped the audience with his eloquence.

завлека́тел|ьный (~ен, ~ьна), *adj.* (*coll.*) alluring; fascinating, captivating.

завлека́|ть, ю, *impf. of* завле́чь.

завле́|чь, ку́, чёшь, ку́т, *past* ~к, ~кла́, *pf.* (*of* ~ка́ть) **1.** to lure, entice. **2.** to fascinate, captivate.

заво́д[1], а, *m.* **1.** factory, mill; works. **2.** (ко́нский) з. stud(-farm).

заво́д[2], а, *m.* **1.** winding up. **2.** winding mechanism; игру́шка с ~ом clockwork toy. **3.** period of running (*of clock, etc.*); часы́ с су́точным ~ом twenty-four-hour clock.

заво́д[3], а, *m. only in phrase* э́того (и) в ~е нет (*coll.*) it has never been the custom.

заводи́л|а, ы, *m. and f.* (*coll.*) instigator; live--wire.

заво|ди́ть[1], жу́, ~дишь, *impf. of* завести́.

заво|ди́ть[2], жу́, ~дишь, *pf.* (*coll.*) to walk off one's feet.

заво|ди́ться, ~дится, *impf. of* завести́сь.

заво́дк|а, и, *f.* winding up; starting.

заводн|о́й, *adj.* **1.** clockwork. **2.** (*tech.*) winding, starting; ~а́я рукоя́тка, ру́чка starting crank.

заводоуправле́ни|е, я, *n.* works management.

заво́д|ский, *adj. of* ~[1]; ~ская ло́шадь stud--horse; *as noun* з., ~ского, *m.* factory worker.

заво́д|ско́й = ~ский.

заво́дчик¹, а, *m.* 1. factory-owner, mill-owner.

заво́дчик², а, *m.* (*coll., obs.*) instigator, author.

за́вод|ь, и, *f.* creek, backwater.

завоева́ни|е, я, *n.* 1. winning. 2. conquest; (*fig.*) achievement, gain; нове́йшие ~я те́хники the latest achievements of technology.

завоева́тел|ь, я, *m.* conqueror.

завоева́тельн|ый, *adj.* aggressive; ~ая война́ war of conquest.

заво|ева́ть, ю́ю, ю́ешь, *pf.* (*of* ~ёвывать) to conquer; (*fig.*) to win, gain; з. о́бщие симпа́тии to gain general sympathy.

завоёвыва|ть, ю, *impf. of* завоева́ть; to try to get.

заво|жу́, ~дишь, *see* ~ди́ть.

заво|жу́, ~зишь, *see* ~зи́ть.

заво́з, а, *m.* delivery; carriage.

заво|зи́ть¹, жу́, ~зишь, *impf. of* завезти́.

заво|зи́ть², жу́, ~зишь, *pf.* (*coll.*) to dirty, soil.

заво|зи́ться¹, жу́сь, ~зишься, *impf., pass. of* ~зи́ть¹.

заво|зи́ться², жу́сь, ~зишься, *pf.* (*coll.*) to begin to play about.

заво́зный, *adj.* brought in; imported.

завола́кива|ть(ся), ю(сь), *impf. of* заволо́чь(ся).

заво́лжск|ий, *adj.* (situated, living) on the left bank of the Volga; ~ие ста́рцы (*hist.*) trans-Volga monks (*adherents of 'non-possessor' doctrine of Nil Sorsky*).

заволн|ова́ться, у́юсь, *pf.* to become agitated.

заволо́|чь, ку́, чёшь, ку́т, *past* ~к, ~кла́, *pf.* (*of* завола́кивать) to cloud; to obscure; тума́н ~к со́лнце the sun was obscured by fog; её глаза́ ~кло́ слеза́ми her eyes were clouded with tears.

заволо́|чься, чётся, ку́тся, *past* ~кся, ~кла́сь, *pf.* (*of* завола́киваться) to cloud over, become clouded.

завоп|и́ть, лю́, и́шь, *pf.* (*coll.*) to cry out, yell; to give a cry.

завора́жива|ть, ю, *impf. of* заворожи́ть.

завора́чива|ть¹, ю, *impf.* = заве́ртывать.

завора́чива|ть², ю, *impf.* 1. *impf. of* завороти́ть. 2. (*impf. only*) (+*i.*; *coll.*) to be boss (of).

заворож|и́ть, у́, и́шь, *pf.* (*of* завора́живать) to cast a spell (over); bewitch; (*fig.*) to fascinate.

за́воро́т, а, *m.*; з. кишо́к (*med.*) volvulus.

заворо́т, а, *m.* (*coll.*) 1. turn, turning. 2. bend (*in road, river, etc.*).

завор|оти́ть, очу́, о́тишь, *pf.* (*of* завора́чивать²) 1. to turn. 2. to turn in; to drop in. 3. to roll up; to tuck up.

заворо́шк|а, и, *f.* (*coll.*) complication(s).

завр|а́ться, у́сь, ёшься, *past* ~а́лся, ~ала́сь, *pf.* (*of* завира́ться) (*coll.*) to become entangled in lies; to become an inveterate liar.

завсегда́, *adv.* (*coll.*) always.

завсегда́та|й, я, *m.* habitué.

за́втра, *adv.* tomorrow; до з.! see you tomorrow!; не ны́нче-з. (*coll.*) any day now.

за́втрак, а, *m.*; breakfast; lunch(eon); корми́ть ~ами (*coll.*) to feed with empty hopes.

за́втрака|ть, ю, *impf.* (*of* по~) to (have) breakfast; to (have) lunch.

за́втрашн|ий, *adj.* tomorrow's; з. день tomorrow; забо́титься о ~ем дне to take thought for the morrow.

завуали́рован|ный, *p.p.p. of* ~ать *and adj.* (*phot.*) fogged.

завуали́р|овать, ую, *pf. of* вуали́ровать.

за́вуч, а, *m.* (*abbr. of* заве́дующий уче́бной ча́стью) director of studies.

завхо́з, а, *m.* (*abbr. of* заве́дующий хозя́йством) bursar, steward.

завши́ве|ть, ю, *pf. of* вши́веть.

завши́вленный, *adj.* (*coll.*) lousy, lice--ridden.

завыва́|ть, ю, *impf.* to howl; to sough.

завы́|сить, шу, сишь, *pf.* (*of* ~ша́ть) to raise too high; з. отме́тку на экза́мене to give too high a mark in an examination.

завы́|ть, о́ю, о́ешь, *pf.* to begin to howl.

завыша́|ть, ю, *impf. of* завы́сить.

завя|за́ть¹, жу́, ~жешь, *pf.* (*of* ~зывать) 1. to tie (up); to knot; з. шнурки́ боти́нок to tie up one's shoe-laces. 2. to bind (up). 3. (*fig.*) to start; з. бой to join battle; з. перепи́ску to start a correspondence.

завя|за́ть², ю, *impf. of* завя́знуть.

завя|за́ться, ~жется, *pf.* (*of* ~зываться) 1. *pass. of* ~за́ть. 2. to start; to arise. 3. (*bot.*) to set.

завязи́|ть, ть, *no 1st person,* шь, *pf.* (*coll.*) to get stuck (*trans.*).

завя́зк|а, и, *f.* 1. string, lace, band. 2. beginning, start; opening (*of novel, etc.*).

завя́з|нуть, ну, нешь, *past* ~, ~ла, *pf.* to stick, get stuck; з. в долга́х to be over head and ears in debt.

завя́зыва|ть(ся), ет(ся), *impf. of* завяза́ть-(ся).

завя́з|ь, и, *f.* (*bot.*) ovary.

завя́лый, *adj.* (*obs.*) withered, faded.

завя́|нуть, ну, нешь, *past* ~л, *pf. of* вя́нуть.

загад|а́ть, а́ю, *pf.* (*of* ~ывать) 1. з. зага́дки to ask riddles. 2. to guess one's fortune; to decide, settle (*by tossing a coin, etc.*). 3. to think of (= to select arbitrarily, at random); ~а́йте число́ think of a number. 4. to plan ahead, look ahead.

загá|дить, жу, дишь, *pf.* (*of* ~живáть) (*coll.*) to soil, dirty, befoul.

загáдк|а, и, *f.* riddle; enigma; mystery.

загáдоч|ный (~ен, ~на), *adj.* enigmatic; mysterious.

загáдыва|ть, ю, *impf. of* загадáть.

загáжива|ть, ю, *impf. of* загáдить.

загáр, а, *m.* sunburn, (sun-)tan.

загасá|ть, ет, *impf. of* загáснуть.

зага|сить, шý, ~сишь, *pf. of* гасить 1.

загáс|нуть, нет, *past* ~, ~ла, *pf.* (*of* ~áть) (*coll.*) to go out.

загвоз|дить, жý, дишь, *pf.* 1. (*obs.*) to spike (*a gun*). 2. (*coll.*) to pose, set (*a problem, etc.*).

загвóздк|а, и, *f.* (*coll.*) snag, obstacle; вот в чём з.! there's the rub!

загиб, а, *m.* 1. fold; bend. 2. (*coll.*) exaggeration; (*polit.*) deviation.

загибá|ть(ся), ю(сь), *impf. of* загнýть(ся).

загибщик, а, *m.* (*polit.; coll.*) deviationist.

загипнотизир|овать, ую, *pf. of* гипнотизировать.

загипс|овáть, ýю, *pf. of* гипсовáть.

заглáви|е, я, *n.* title; heading; под ~ем entitled, headed.

заглáв|ный, *adj. of* ~ие; з. лист title-page; ~ная бýква capital letter; ~ные бýквы initials; ~ная роль (*theatr.*) title-role, name-part.

заглá|дить, жу, дишь, *pf.* (*of* ~живать) 1. to iron (out), press. 2. (*fig.*) to make up (for), make amends (for); з. грехи to expiate one's sins.

заглá|диться, дится, *pf.* (*of* ~живаться) 1. to iron out (*intrans.*); to become smooth. 2. (*fig.*) to fade.

заглáжива|ть, ю, *impf. of* заглáдить.

заглáжива|ться, ется, *impf. of* заглáдиться.

заглáзно, *adv.* (*coll.*) in someone's absence, behind someone's back.

заглáзн|ый, *adj.* (*coll.*) done, said in someone's absence, behind someone's back; ~ое решéние (*leg.*) judgment by default; ~ая клеветá scandal uttered about someone behind his back.

заглáтыва|ть, ю, *impf. of* заглотáть.

заглотá|ть, ю, *pf.* (*of* заглáтывать) to swallow.

заглóхн|уть, у, ешь, *pf. of* глóхнуть 2, 3.

заглуш|áть, áю, *impf. of* ~ить.

заглуш|ить, ý, ишь, *pf.* (*of* глушить *and* ~áть) 1. to drown, deaden, muffle (*sound*). 2. to jam (*radio transmissions*). 3. (*of plants*) to choke. 4. (*fig.*) to suppress, stifle. 5. to alleviate, soothe.

заглýшк|а, и, *f.* (*tech.*) choke, plug, stopper.

заглядéнь|е, я, *n.* (*coll.*) lovely sight; э́то прóсто з.! isn't that lovely?, what a beautiful sight!

загля|дéться, жýсь, дишься, *pf.* (*of* ~дываться) (на + *a.*; *coll.*) to stare (at); to be unable to take one's eyes off; to be lost in admiration (of).

заглядыва|ть, ю, *impf. of* заглянýть.

заглядыва|ться, юсь, *impf. of* заглядéться.

заглян|ýть, ý, ~ешь, *pf.* (*of* заглядывать) 1. to peep; to glance; онá ~ýла в окнó и увидела, что дéти заснýли she peeped in at the window and saw that the children had gone to sleep; з. в газéты to glance at the newspapers. 2. (*coll.*) to look in, drop in; ~ите к нам, пожáлуйста! please, look in (to see us)!

загнáива|ть(ся), ю(сь), *impf. of* загноить-(ся).

зáгнанный, *p.p.p. of* загнáть *and adj.* 1. tired out, exhausted; (*of a horse*) winded; как з. зверь at the end of one's tether. 2. downtrodden, cowed.

загнá|ть, загоню́, загóнишь, *past* ~л, ~лá, ~ло, *pf.* (*of* загоня́ть[1]) 1. to drive in; з. корóв в хлев to drive the cows into the shed, get the cows in; з. мяч в ворóта (*sport*) to score, shoot a goal. 2. to drive (off). 3. to tire out, exhaust; to override (*a horse*). 4. (*coll.*) to drive home; з. свáи в зéмлю to drive piles into the ground. 5. (*sl.*) to flog (= to sell). 6. з. копéйку (*sl.*) to make (some) money.

загнивáни|е, я, *n.* rotting, putrescence; (*fig.*) decay; (*med.*) suppuration.

загнивá|ть, ю, *impf. of* загнить.

загни|ть, ю́, ёшь, *past* ~л, ~лá, ~ло, *pf.* (*of* ~вáть) to begin to rot; to rot, decay (*also fig.*); (*med.*) to fester.

загно|ить, ю́, ишь, *pf.* (*of* загнáивать) (*coll.*) 1. to allow to fester. 2. to allow to rot, allow to decay.

загно|иться, ится, *pf.* (*of* загнáиваться) to fester.

загн|ýть, ý, ёшь, *pf.* (*of* загибáть) 1. to turn up, turn down; to bend, fold; to crease; з. страницу to dog-ear a page. 2. to turn (*intrans.*); з. зá угол to turn a corner. 3. (*coll.*) to utter (*a swear-word or vulgarism*); ну и словéчко ~ýл! (*iron.*) what language! 4. (*coll.*) to ask (*an exorbitant price*).

загн|ýться, ýсь, ёшься, *pf.* (*of* загибáться) 1. to turn up, stick up; to turn down. 2. (*sl.*) to turn up one's toes (= to die).

заговáрива|ть, ю, *impf. of* заговорить[1].

заговáрива|ться, юсь, *impf.* (*of* заговориться) 1. to be carried away by a conversation. 2. (*impf. only*) to rave; to ramble (*in speech*); говори, да не ~йся! talk sense!

зáговень|е, я, *n.* (*eccl.*) last day before fast.

заговé|ться, юсь, *pf.* (*eccl.*) to eat meat for the last time (*before a fast*).

зáговор, а, *m.* 1. plot, conspiracy. 2. charm, spell.

заговор|и́ть[1], **ю́, и́шь**, *pf.* (*of* заговáривать) **1.** (*coll.*) to talk someone's head off; to tire out with much talk. **2.** to cast a spell (over); (от) to put on a spell (against); to exorcize; з. зýбы комý-н. (*coll.*) to get round someone, talk someone into something.

заговор|и́ть[2], **ю́, и́шь**, *pf.* **1.** to begin to speak. **2.** to (be able to) speak; to learn to speak.

заговор|и́ться, ю́сь, и́шься, *pf. of* загова́риваться.

заговóрщик, а, *m.* conspirator, plotter.

заговóрщицкий, *adj.* (*coll.*) conspiratorial.

загог|отáть, очý, óчешь, *pf.* to begin to cackle; (*coll.*) to begin to guffaw.

загогýлин|а, ы, *f.* (*coll.*) flourish.

зáгодя, *adv.* (*coll.*) in good time.

загол|и́ть, ю́, и́шь, *pf.* (*of* ~я́ть) to bare.

заголóв|ок, ка, *m.* **1.** title; heading. **2.** headline.

заголя́|ть, ю, *impf. of* заголи́ть.

загóн, а, *m.* **1.** driving in; rounding-up. **2.** enclosure (*for cattle*); pen. **3.** strip (*of ploughed land*). **4.** быть в ~е (*fig.*) to be kept down; у когó-н. в ~е under someone's thumb. **5.** в ~е (*sl.*) to one's credit, 'chalked up'; у негó в ~е три дня he has three days' (work) to his credit.

загóнщик, а, *m.* (*hunting*) beater.

за|гоню́, гóнишь, *see* ~гна́ть.

загоня́|ть[1], **ю,** *impf. of* загна́ть.

загоня́|ть[2], **ю,** *pf.* (*coll.*) **1.** to tire out; to work to death. **2.** (*sl.*) to grill (*with questions*).

загора́жива|ть(ся), ю(сь), *impf. of* загороди́ть(ся).

загорá|ть(ся), ю(сь), *impf. of* загорéть(ся).

загóрб|ок, ка, *m.* (*coll.*) upper part of the back (*between shoulder-blades*).

загор|ди́ться, жýсь, ди́шься, *pf.* (*coll.*) to become proud, become stuck-up.

загорéлый, *adj.* sunburnt; brown, bronzed.

загор|éть, ю́, и́шь, *pf.* (*of* ~а́ть) to become sunburnt, become brown; to acquire a tan.

загор|éться, ю́сь, и́шься, *pf.* (*of* ~а́ться) **1.** to catch fire; to begin to burn; в библиотéке ~éлось (*impers.*) a fire broke out in the library. **2.** (+*i.*; от) to blaze (with), burn (with) (*fig.*); егó глазá ~éлись от гнéва his eyes blazed with anger; онá ~éлась от смущéния she went red with embarrassment. **3.** (*impers.*+*d.*; *coll.*) to want very much; to have a burning desire; ей ~éлось ви́деть Рим she had a burning desire to see Rome. **4.** (*fig.*) to break out, start; ~éлась дра́ка a fight broke out.

загоро|ди́ть, жý, ~ди́шь, *pf.* (*of* загора́живать) **1.** to enclose, fence in. **2.** to barricade; to obstruct; з. комý-н. свет to stand in someone's light.

загоро|ди́ться, жýсь, ~ди́шься, *pf.* (*of* загора́живаться) **1.** to barricade oneself; з. ши́рмой to screen oneself off. **2.** *pass. of* ~ди́ть.

загорóдк|а, и, *f.* (*coll.*) **1.** fence. **2.** enclosure.

зáгородн|ый, *adj.* out-of-town; country; ~ая экскýрсия excursion into the country.

заго|сти́ться, щýсь, сти́шься, *pf.* (*coll.*) to outstay one's welcome.

заготови́тел|ь, я, *m.* official in charge of (State) procurements.

заготов|и́тельный, *adj. of* ~ка; з. аппара́т official organization in charge of (State) procurements; з. пункт storage place; ~и́тельная ценá (*econ.*) fixed price (*for purchases by State*).

заготóв|ить, лю, ишь, *pf.* (*of* ~ля́ть) **1.** to lay in; to make a stock (of), stockpile, store. **2.** to prepare.

заготóвк|а, и, *f.* **1.** (State) procurement (*of agricultural products, timber, etc.*). **2.** laying in; stocking up, stockpiling. **3.** half-finished product; (*tech.*) blank, billet.

заготовля́|ть, ю, *impf. of* заготóвить.

заготóвщик, а, *m.* = заготови́тель.

заграбáст|ать, аю, *pf.* (*of* ~ывать) (*coll., pejor.*) to seize; to make off with.

заграбáстыва|ть, ю, *impf. of* заграбáстать.

заграб|ить, лю, ишь, *pf.* (*coll.*) to seize; to plunder.

загради́тел|ь, я, *m.* (*naut.*) minelayer.

загради́тельный, *adj.* (*mil.*) barrage; (*naut.*) mine-laying; з. аэроста́т barrage balloon; з. огóнь defensive fire.

загра|ди́ть, жý, ди́шь, *pf.* (*of* ~жда́ть) to block, obstruct; з. путь to bar the way.

загражда́|ть, ю, *impf. of* загради́ть.

загражде́ни|е, я, *n.* **1.** blocking, obstruction. **2.** obstacle, barrier, obstruction.

заграни́ц|а, ы, *f.* (*coll.*) foreign countries (*see also* грани́ца).

заграни́чный, *adj.* foreign (**1.** = of foreign make, *etc.* **2.** = for foreign travel, *etc.*; з. па́спорт foreign passport).

загребá|ть, ю, *impf. of* загрести́[1]; чужи́ми рука́ми жар з., *see* жар.

загрёбистый *adj.* (*coll.*) greedy.

загребн|óй, *adj.*; ~óе веслó stroke oar; *as noun* з., ~óго, *m.* stroke (*rower*).

загребýщий, *adj.* (*coll.*) greedy.

загрем|éть[1], **лю, и́шь,** *pf.* (*coll.*) to crash down.

загрем|éть[2], **лю, и́шь,** *pf.* to begin to thunder.

загре|сти́[1], **бý, бёшь,** *past* ~б, ~блá, *pf.* (*of* ~бáть) (*coll.*) to rake up, gather; (*fig.*) to rake in; з. жар to bank up the fire; з. дéньги to rake in the shekels.

загре|сти́[2], **бý, бёшь,** *past* ~б, ~блá, *pf.* to begin to row.

загри́в|ок, ка, *m.* **1.** withers (*of horse*). **2.** (*coll.*) nape (of the neck).

загримир|ова́ть(ся), у́ю(сь), *pf. of* гримирова́ть(ся).

загро́бн|ый, *adj.* **1.** beyond the grave; ～ая жизнь the future life. **2.** sepulchral (*of voice*).

загроможда́|ть, ю, *impf. of* загромозди́ть.

загромоз|ди́ть, жу́, ди́шь, *pf.* (*of* загроможда́ть) to block up, encumber; (*fig.*) to pack, cram; з. расска́з подро́бностями to cram a story with detail.

загрох|ота́ть, очу́, о́чешь, *pf.* to begin to rumble, begin to rattle.

загрубе́лый, *adj.* coarsened, callous.

загрубе́|ть, ю, *pf.* to become coarsened; to become callous (*also fig.*).

загружа́|ть, ю, *impf. of* загрузи́ть 2, 3.

загру́женност|ь (*and* **загружённост|ь**)**, и,** *f.* **1.** utilised capacity (*of transport services, etc.*). **2.** programme (*of work*), commitment.

загр|узи́ть, ужу́, у́зишь, *pf.* **1.** (*impf.* грузи́ть) to load. **2.** (*impf.* ～ужа́ть) (*tech.*) to feed, charge, prime; з. то́пливо в печь to stoke a furnace. **3.** (*impf.* ～ужа́ть) (*coll.*) to keep fully occupied, provide with a full--time job; to fill out (a period of time) with occupations.

загру|зи́ться, жу́сь, зи́шься, *pf.* (*of* ～жа́ться) **1.** (+*i.*) to load up (with), take on. **2.** (*coll.*) to take on a job, a commitment.

загру́зк|а, и, *f.* **1.** loading. **2.** (*tech.*) feeding, charging, priming. **3.** capacity (*of work*), load; заво́д рабо́тает при по́лной ～е the factory is working at full capacity.

загру́з|очный, *adj. of* ～ка; з. ковш, я́щик hopper; з. лото́к feed chute, loading chute.

загрунт|ова́ть, у́ю, *pf. of* грунтова́ть.

загру|сти́ть, щу́, сти́шь, *pf.* to grow sad.

загрыза́|ть, ю, *impf. of* загры́зть.

загры́з|ть, у́, ешь, *past* ～, ～ла, *pf.* (*of* ～а́ть) **1.** to bite to death; (*fig.*) to worry the life out of, worry to death. **2.** to tear to pieces.

загрязне́ни|е, я, *n.* soiling; pollution; contamination.

загрязн|и́ть, ю́, и́шь, *pf.* (*of* ～я́ть) to soil, make dirty; to pollute.

загрязн|и́ться, ю́сь, и́шься, *pf.* (*of* ～я́ться) to make oneself dirty, become dirty.

загрязня́|ть(ся), ю(сь), *impf. of* загрязни́ть(ся).

загс, а, *m.* (*abbr. of* отде́л за́писи а́ктов гражда́нского состоя́ния) registry office.

загси́р|оваться, уюсь, *impf. and pf.* (*coll.*) to be married (in a registry office).

загуб|и́ть, лю́, ～ишь, *pf.* **1.** to ruin; з. чей-н. век, з. чью-н. жизнь to make someone's life a misery. **2.** (*coll.*) to squander.

загу́л, а, *m.* (*coll.*) drinking(-bout).

загуля́|ть, ю, *pf.* (*coll.*) to take to drink, start drinking.

загусте́|ть, ю, *pf.* to thicken (*intrans.*).

зад, а, о ～**е, на** ～**у́,** *pl.* ～**ы́,** *m.* **1.** back; ～ом наперёд back to front. **2.** hind quarters; buttocks; croup, rump; бить ～ом to kick (*of animal*). **3.** (*pl.*) = задво́рки 1. **4.** повтори́ть ～ы́ (*coll.*) to repeat what one has learned before; to pass on stale news.

зада́брива|ть, ю, *impf. of* задо́брить.

зада|ва́ть, ю́, ёшь, *impf. of* ～ть.

зада|ва́ться¹, ю́сь, ёшься, *impf. of* ～ться.

зада|ва́ться², ю́сь, ёшься, *impf.* (*coll.*) to give oneself airs, put on airs.

задав|и́ть, лю́, ～ишь, *pf.* to crush; to run over, knock down.

зада́ни|е, я, *n.* task, job.

зада́рива|ть, ю, *impf. of* задари́ть.

задар|и́ть, ю́, ～ишь, *pf.* (*of* ～ивать) **1.** to load with presents. **2.** to bribe.

зада́ром, *adv.* (*coll.*) **1.** for nothing: very cheaply; купи́ть з. to buy for a song. **2.** in vain, to no purpose.

зада́тк|и, ов, *no sing.* instincts, inclinations.

зада́т|ок, ка, *m.* deposit, advance.

за|да́ть, да́м, да́шь, *past* ～да́л, ～дала́, ～дало,** *pf.* (*of* ～дава́ть) to set; to give; з. уро́к to set a lesson; з. вопро́с to put a question; з. бал to give a dance; з. корм коро́вам to feed the cows; з. тон to set the tone; з. тя́гу to take to one's heels; з. стра́ху (+*d.*) to strike terror (into); я ему́ ～да́м! (*coll.*) I'll give him what-for!

за|да́ться, да́мся, да́шься, *past* ～да́лся, ～дала́сь,** *pf.* (*of* ～дава́ться¹) **1.** з. це́лью, мы́слью (+*inf.*) to set oneself (to), make up one's mind (to). **2.** (*coll.*) to turn out (well); to work out, succeed; пое́здка не ～дала́сь the trip was not a success.

зада́ч|а, и, *f.* **1.** (*math., etc.*) problem. **2.** task; mission.

зада́чник, а, *m.* book of (mathematical) problems.

задвига́|ть, ю, *pf.* to begin to move.

задвига́|ть, ю, *impf. of* задви́нуть.

задвига́|ться, юсь, *impf.* **1.** *impf. of* задви́нуться. **2.** (*impf. only*) to be drawable, be slidable.

задви́жк|а, и, *f.* bolt; catch, fastening; (*tech.*) slide-valve.

задвижно́й, *adj.* sliding.

задви́н|уть, у, ешь, *pf.* (*of* задвига́ть) **1.** to push; з. задви́жку to shoot a bolt. **2.** to bolt; to bar; to close; з. за́навес to draw a curtain (across).

задви́н|уться, усь, ешься, *pf.* (*of* задвига́ться) to shut; to slide (*intrans.*).

задво́р|ки, ок, *no sing.* **1.** backyard; (*fig.*) out--of-the-way place, backwoods. **2.** быть на ～ках (*fig.*) to take a back seat.

задева́|ть¹, ю, *impf. of* заде́ть.

задева́|ть², ю, *pf.* (*coll.*) to mislay; куда́ ~л мои́ очки́? where did I put my spectacles?

задева́|ться¹, юсь, *impf., pass. of* ~ть¹.

задева́|ться², юсь, *pf.* (*coll.*) to disappear; куда́ ты ~лся? where did you get to?

заде́л, а, *m.* (*coll.*) **1.** undertaking (*begun but not completed*). **2.** (*tech.*) surplus (*of goods or products*).

заде́л|ать, аю, *pf.* (*of* ~ывать) to do up; to block up, close up; з. посы́лку to do up a parcel; (*naut.*) з. течь to stop a leak.

заде́ла|ться¹, юсь, *pf., pass. of* ~ть.

заде́л|аться², аюсь, *pf.* (*of* ~ываться) (*coll.*) to become; to turn; он ~ался литературове́дом he has turned literary critic.

заде́лк|а, и, *f.* doing up; blocking up, stopping up.

заде́лыва|ть(ся), ю(сь), *impf. of* заде́лать(ся).

задёрга|ть¹, ю, *pf.* (+*a. or i.*) to begin to tug.

задёрга|ть², ю, *pf.* to wear out (*by tugging on the reins*); (*fig., coll.*) to break the spirit of (*by nagging, etc.*).

задёргива|ть, ю, *impf. of* задёрнуть.

задеревене́лый, *adj.* numb(ed), stiff.

задеревене́|ть, ю, *pf.* (*coll.*) to become numb, become stiff.

задержа́ни|е, я, *n.* **1.** detention; arrest. **2.** (*med.*) з. мочи́ retention of urine. **3.** (*mus.*) suspension.

задерж|а́ть, у́, ~ишь, *pf.* (*of* ~ивать) **1.** to detain; to delay; до́ждик ~а́л нача́ло ма́тча the start of the match was delayed by a shower. **2.** to withhold, keep back; to retard; з. зарпла́ту to stop wages; з. дыха́ние to hold one's breath. **3.** to detain, arrest.

задерж|а́ться, у́сь, ~ишься, *pf.* (*of* ~иваться) **1.** to stay too long; to linger. **2.** *pass. of* ~а́ть.

заде́ржива|ть(ся), ю(сь), *impf. of* задержа́ть(ся).

заде́ржк|а, и, *f.* delay; hold-up.

задёрн|уть, у, ешь, *pf.* (*of* задёргивать) **1.** to pull; to draw; з. за́навески to draw the curtains. **2.** to cover; to curtain off.

заде́т|ый (~, ~а), *p.p.p. of* ~ь; **1.** з. насме́шками stung by taunts. **2.** (*med.; coll.*) affected; пра́вое лёгкое у него́ ~о he has a spot on his right lung.

заде́|ть, ну, нешь, *pf.* (*of* ~ва́ть¹) **1.** to touch, brush (against), graze; (*fig.*) to offend, wound; его́ ~ло за живо́е he was stung to the quick. **2.** to catch (on, against).

за́дешево, *adv.* (*coll.*) very cheaply.

задир|а, ы, *m. and f.* (*coll.*) bully; trouble-maker.

задира́|ть(ся)¹, ю(сь), *impf. of* задра́ть(ся).

задира́|ться², юсь, *impf.* (*coll.*) to pick a quarrel.

задненёбный, *adj.* (*ling.*) velar.

заднепрохо́дный, *adj.* (*anat.*) anal.

заднеязы́чный, *adj.* (*ling.*) velar, back.

за́дн|ий, *adj.* back, rear; hind; ~яя мысль ulterior motive; з. план background; з. прохо́д (*anat.*) anus; ~им умо́м кре́пок (*coll.*) wise after the event; з. ход (*tech.*) backward movement; (*naut.*) stern-board; дать з. ход to back; поме́тить ~им число́м to antedate; быть без ~их ног (*coll.*) to be falling off one's feet; ходи́ть на ~их ла́пках (пе́ред) (*coll.*) to dance attendance on).

за́дник, а, *m.* **1.** back, counter (*of shoe*). **2.** (*theatr.*) back drop.

за́дниц|а, ы, *f.* (*vulg.*) arse, buttocks.

задо́бр|ить, ю, ишь, *pf.* (*of* задо́бривать) to cajole; to coax; to win over (*by bribes, etc.*).

зад|о́к, ка́, *m.* back (*of conveyance or furniture*).

задолб|и́ть, лю́, и́шь, *pf.* **1.** to begin to peck. **2.** (*coll.*) to learn off by rote; з. себе́ to get it into one's head.

задо́лго, *adv.* long before; он ко́нчил рабо́ту з. до ве́чера he finished the work long before evening.

задолжа́|ть, ю, *pf. of* должа́ть.

задолжа́|ться, юсь, *pf.* (*coll.*) to run into debt.

задо́лженност|ь, и, *f.* debts; погаси́ть з. to pay off one's debts.

задо́р, а, *m.* fervour, ardour; passion; temper.

задо́ринк|а, и, *f.* unevenness, roughness; (*fig., coll.*) без сучка́, без ~и *or* ни сучка́, ни ~и without a hitch.

задо́р|иться, юсь, ишься, *impf.* (*coll.*) to become provocative.

задо́р|ный (~ен, ~на), *adj.* **1.** fervent, ardent; impassioned. **2.** provocative; quick-tempered.

задох|ну́ться, ну́сь, нёшься, *past* ~ся, ~ла́сь *and* ~ну́лся, ~ну́лась, *pf.* (*of* задыха́ться) **1.** to suffocate; to choke; (*fig.*) з. от гне́ва to choke with anger. **2.** to pant; to gasp for breath.

задра́знива|ть, ю, *impf. of* задразни́ть.

задразн|и́ть, ю́, ~ишь, *pf.* (*coll.*) to tease unmercifully.

задра́ива|ть, ю, *impf. of* задра́ить.

задра́|ить, ю, ишь, *pf.* (*naut.*) to batten down.

задрапир|ова́ть, у́ю, *pf.* (+*a. and i.*) to drape (with).

задрапир|ова́ться, у́юсь, *pf.* (+*i. or* в+*a.*) to drape oneself (with), wrap oneself up (in).

задрапиро́выва|ть(ся), ю(сь), *impf. of* задрапирова́ть(ся).

зад|ра́ть, еру́, ерёшь, *past* ~ра́л, ~рала́, ~ра́ло, *pf.* (*of* ~ира́ть) **1.** to tear to pieces; to kill (*of wolves, etc.*). **2.** (*coll.*) to lift up; to pull up; з. го́лову to crane one's neck; з. нос (*fig.*) to cock one's nose. **3.** to break (*finger-nail, etc.*); з. ко́жу на па́льце to split a finger. **4.** (*coll.*) to insult; to provoke.

зад|ра́ться, ерётся, *past* ~ра́лся, ~рала́сь, ~ра́лось, *pf.* (*of* ~ира́ться) **1.** to break (*intrans.*; *finger-nail, etc.*); to split (*intrans.*). **2.** (*coll.*) to ride up (*of clothing*). **3.** *pass. of* ~ра́ть.

задрем|а́ть, лю́, ~лешь, *pf.* to doze off, begin to nod.

задри́пан|ный (~, ~a), *adj.* (*coll.*) bedraggled.

задрож|а́ть, у́, и́шь, *pf.* to begin to tremble; to begin to shiver.

за́друг|а, и, *f.* (*ethnol.*) zadruga (*patriarchal commune among the Southern Slav peoples*).

задры́га|ть, ю, *pf.* (*coll.*) to begin to jerk, begin to twitch.

задува́|ть, ю, *impf. of* заду́ть.

заду́ма|ть, ю, *pf.* (*of* заду́мывать) **1.** (+*a.* or *inf.*) to plan; to intend; to conceive the idea (of). **2.** з. число́ to think of a number.

заду́ма|ться, юсь, *pf.* to become thoughtful, pensive; to fall to thinking; о чём вы ~лись? what are you thinking about?

заду́мчивост|ь, и, *f.* thoughtfulness, pensiveness; reverie.

заду́мчив|ый (~, ~a), *adj.* thoughtful, pensive.

заду́мыва|ть, ю, *impf. of* заду́мать.

заду́мыва|ться, юсь, *impf.* to be thoughtful, be pensive; to meditate; to ponder; не ~ясь, он согласи́лся he agreed without a moment's thought.

задур|и́ть, ю́, и́шь, *pf.* (*coll.*) to start playing the fool; он мне едва́ не ~и́л го́лову he nearly drove me crazy.

заду́|ть, ю, ешь, *pf.* (*of* ~ва́ть) **1.** to blow out. **2.** (*tech.*) з. до́мну to blow in a blast-furnace. **3.** to begin to blow.

задушёв|ный (~ен, ~на), *adj.* sincere; cordial; intimate.

задуш|и́ть, у́, ~ишь, *pf. of* души́ть[1].

зад|ы́[1], *see* ~.

зад|ы́[2] = ~во́рки.

задым|и́ть, лю́, и́шь, *pf.* **1.** to begin to (emit) smoke. **2.** to blacken with smoke. **3.** (*mil.*) to lay a smoke-screen.

задым|и́ться, и́тся, *pf.* **1.** to begin to (emit) smoke. **2.** to be blackened with smoke.

задымля́|ть, ю, *impf. of* задыми́ть 2, 3.

задыха́|ться, юсь, *impf. of* задохну́ться.

задыш|а́ть, у́, ~ишь, *pf.* to begin to breathe.

заеда́ни|е, я, *n.* (*tech.*) jamming.

заеда́|ть(ся), ю(сь), *impf. of* зае́сть(ся).

заезд, а, *m.* **1.** calling in (*en route*). **2.** (*sport*) lap, round, heat.

зае́з|дить, жу, дишь, *pf.* to override (*a horse*); (*fig.*) to wear out; to work too hard.

заезжа́|ть, ю, *impf. of* зае́хать.

зае́зженный, *adj.* (*coll.*) **1.** hackneyed, trite. **2.** worn out.

зае́зж|ий, *adj.* visiting; ~ая тру́ппа touring company; он здесь з. челове́к he is a stranger, he is passing through; з. двор (*obs.*) wayside inn.

заём, за́йма, *m.* loan.

заёмн|ый, *adj.* loan; ~ое письмо́ (*leg.*) acknowledgement of debt.

заёмщик, а, *m.* borrower, debtor.

заёрза|ть, ю, *pf.* (*coll.*) **1.** to begin to fidget. **2.** to dirty, wear out as a result of fidgeting.

зае́|сть[1], м, шь, ст, ди́м, ди́те, дя́т, *past* ~л, *pf.* (*of* ~да́ть) **1.** to bite to death; (*fig.*) to torment, oppress; его́ ~ла тоска́ he fell a prey to melancholy. **2.** (*impers.*; *tech.*) to jam; (*naut.*) to foul; кана́т ~ло the cable has fouled. **3.** (*dial.*) to seize, appropriate.

зае́|сть[2], м, шь, ст, ди́м, ди́те, дя́т, *past* ~л, *pf.* (*of* ~да́ть) (+*a. and i.*) to take (with); он ~л пилю́лю са́харом he took the pill with sugar.

зае́|сться, мся, шься, стся, ди́мся, ди́тесь, дя́тся, *past* ~лся, *pf.* (*of* ~да́ться) (*coll.*) to become fastidious, become fussy.

зае́|хать, ду, дешь, *pf.* (*of* ~зжа́ть) **1.** (к) to call in (at); (в+*a.*) to enter, ride into, drive into; (за+*a.*) to go beyond, past; (за+*i.*) to call for; to fetch. **2.** to go too far (*also fig.*); он ~хал в кана́ву he landed in the ditch; ведь куда́ он ~хал со свои́м хвастовство́м! look where he got himself with his boasting! **3.** (+*d.* в+*a.*; *coll.*) to strike; я ~хал ему́ в мо́рду I gave him a sock on the jaw.

зажа́р|ить(ся), ю(сь), ишь(ся), *pf. of* жа́рить(ся).

заж|а́ть, му́, мёшь, *pf.* (*of* ~има́ть) to squeeze; to press; to clutch; з. в руке́ to grip; з. рот кому́-н. (*fig.*) to stop someone's mouth; з. кри́тику to suppress criticism.

заж|гу́, жёшь, гу́т, *see* ~е́чь.

зажд|а́ться, у́сь, ёшься, *past* ~а́лся, ~ала́сь, ~а́лось, *pf.* (*coll.*) to be tired of waiting (for).

зажелте́|ть, ю, ешь, *pf.* **1.** to turn yellow. **2.** to begin to appear, begin to show up yellow.

зажел|ти́ть, чу́, ти́шь, *pf.* (*coll.*) to paint yellow; to stain yellow.

заж|е́чь, гу́, жёшь, гу́т, *past* ~ёг, ~гла́, *pf.* (*of* ~ига́ть) to set fire to; to kindle, light; з. спи́чку to strike a match; (*fig.*, *rhet.*) to kindle; to inflame.

заж|е́чься, гу́сь, жёшься, гу́тся, *past*

зажёгся, зажглáсь, *pf.* (*of* ~игáться) to catch fire; to light up; (*fig.*) to flame up.

заживá|ть(ся), ю(сь), *impf. of* зажи́ть(ся).

зажив|и́ть, лю́, и́шь, *pf.* to heal.

заживля́|ть, ю, *impf. of* заживи́ть.

зáживо, *adv.* alive; з. погребённый buried alive.

зажигáлк|а, и, f. 1. (cigarette) lighter. **2.** (*coll.*) incendiary (bomb).

зажигáтел|ьный (~ен, ~ьна), *adj.* inflammatory (*also fig.*); incendiary; ~ьная бóмба incendiary (bomb); ~ьная речь inflammatory speech.

зажигá|ть(ся), ю(сь), *impf. of* зажéчь(ся).

зажи́л|ить, ю, ишь, *pf.* (*coll.*) to fail to return (*something borrowed*).

зажи́лива|ть, ю, *impf. of* зажи́лить.

зажи́м, а, m. 1. (*tech.*) clamp; clutch; clip. **2.** (*electr.*) terminal. **3.** (*fig.*) suppression; clamping down.

зажимá|ть, ю, *impf. of* зажáть.

зажи́мист|ый (~, ~a), *adj.* (*coll.*) **1.** strong, powerful; у негó ~ая рукá he has a strong grip. **2.** tight-fisted, stingy.

зажимнóй, *adj.* (*coll.*) tight-fisted.

зажи́мный, *adj.* (*tech.*) clamping; з. винт clamping screw.

зажи́мщик, а, m. (*coll.*) suppressor.

зажирéлый, , *adj.* (*dial.*) excessively stout, overweight.

зажирé|ть, ю, *pf.* (*coll.*) to put on weight to excess.

зажит|óй, p.p.p. of ~ь **and** *adj.* earned; *as noun* ~óe, ~óго, n. (*coll.*) earned income.

зажи́точност|ь, и, f. prosperity; easy circumstances.

зажи́точ|ный (~ен, ~на), *adj.* well-to-do; prosperous.

зáжит|ый = ~óй.

зажи́|ть, ву́, вёшь, past зáжил, ~лá, зáжило, *pf.* (*of* ~вáть) **1.** to heal (*intrans.*); to close up (*of wound*). **2.** to begin to live; з. по-нóвому to begin a new life; з. семéйной жи́знью to settle down; з. трудовóй жи́знью to begin to earn one's own living.

зажи́|ться, ву́сь, вёшься, past ~лся, ~лáсь, *pf.* (*of* ~вáться) (*coll.*) to live to a great age; to exceed one's allotted span.

зажму́р|ить(ся), ю(сь), ишь(ся), *pf. of* жму́рить(ся).

зажужж|áть, у́, и́шь, *pf.* to begin to buzz; to begin to drone.

зажу́лива|ть, ю, *impf. of* зажу́лить.

зажу́л|ить, ю, ишь, *pf.* (*coll.*) to obtain by fraud.

зажу́хлый, *adj.* (*coll.*) tarnished, dull; dry, stiff (*of leather, etc.*).

заз|вáть, ову́, овёшь, past ~вáл, ~валá, ~вáло, *pf.* (*of* ~ывáть) (*coll.*) to press (to come); to press an invitation on.

зазвен|éть, и́т, *pf.* to begin to ring.

зазвóнист|ый (~, ~a), *adj.* (*coll.*) loud.

зазвон|и́ть, ю́, и́шь, *pf.* to begin to ring.

зазвуч|áть, у́, и́шь, *pf.* to begin to sound; to begin to resound.

заздрáвный, *adj.* to the health (of), in honour (of); они́ вы́пили з. тост за послá they drank the ambassador's health.

зазевá|ться, ю́сь, *pf.* (на+a.; *coll.*) to stand gaping (at); to gape (at).

зазеленé|ть, ю, *pf.* to turn green.

зазелен|и́ть, ю́, и́шь, *pf.* (*coll.*) to paint green; to colour green.

заземлéни|е, я, n. (*electr.*)|**1.** earthing. **2.** earth.

заземл|и́ть, ю́, и́шь, *pf.* (*electr.*) to earth.

заземл|я́ть, я́ю, *impf. of* ~и́ть.

зазим|овáть, у́ю, *pf.* to winter; to pass the winter.

зази́м|ок, ка, m. (*dial.*) **1.** first snow. **2.** first frost(s). **3.** fresh sledge track.

зазна|вáться, ю́сь, ёшься, *impf. of* ~ться.

зазнáйств|о, a, n. (*coll.*) conceit.

зазнá|ться, ю́сь, *pf.* (*of* ~вáться) (*coll.*) to give oneself airs, become conceited.

зазнóб|а, ы, f. 1. (*folk poet.*) passion. **2.** (*coll.*) sweetheart.

зазнóб|и́ть, лю́, и́шь, *pf.* (*coll.*) **1.** to be frozen; to get shivery. **2.** (*impers.*) егó ~и́ло he is beginning to be feverish.

зазнóбушк|а, и, f. (*folk poet.*) sweetheart.

заз|овý, овёшь, *see* ~вáть.

зазóр[1], а, m. (*coll.*) shame, disgrace.

зазóр[2], а, m. gap; (*tech.*) clearance; (*mil.*) windage.

зазóр|ный (~ен, ~на), *adj.* (*coll.*) shameful, disgraceful.

зазрéни|е, я, n.; без ~я (сóвести) (*coll.*) without a twinge of conscience.

зáзр|ить, ит, *pf., only in phrase* сóвесть ~ит, ~и́ла (*coll.*) conscience forbids, forbade (it).

зазýбрен|ный (~, ~a), p.p.p. of зазубри́ть[1] *and adj.* notched, jagged, serrated.

зазýбрива|ть, ю, *impf. of* зазубри́ть.

зазýбрин|а, ы, f. notch, jag.

зазубр|и́ть[1], ю́, и́шь, *pf.* (*of* зубри́ть *and* ~ивать) to notch, serrate.

зазубр|и́ть[2], ю́, ~и́шь, *pf.* (*of* зубри́ть *and* ~ивать) (*sl.*) **1.** to learn by rote. **2.** to start cramming.

зазы́в, а, m. (*coll.*) pressing invitation.

зазывá|ть, ю, *impf. of* зазвáть.

зазя́б|нуть, ну, нешь, past ~, ~ла, *pf.* (*coll.*) **1.** to become frozen. **2.** (*hort.*) to die of frost.

заигрá|ть, ю, *pf.* **1.** to begin to play; з. весёлый моти́в to strike up a lively tune. **2.** to begin to sparkle. **3.** to wear out (*cards, etc.*); з. пьéсу to stage a play so often that it becomes stale.

заѝгрыва|ть¹, ю, *impf. of* заигра́ть.

заѝгрыва|ть², ю, *impf.* (c+*i.*; *coll.*) to flirt (with); to make advances (to) (*also fig.*).

заѝк|а, и, *m. and f.* stammerer, stutterer.

заика́ни|е, я, *n.* stammer(ing), stutter(ing).

заика́|ться, юсь, *impf.* **1.** to stammer, stutter. **2.** (o+*p.*; *coll.*) to hint (at), to mention in passing; он никогда́ не ~ется о свое́й про́шлой жи́зни he never breathes a word about his past life.

заикн|у́ться, у́сь, ёшься, *pf. of* заика́ться 2.

за́имк|а, и, *f.* (*hist.*) **1.** squatting (*on land*). **2.** squatter's holding. **3.** isolated arable field.

заимода́в|ец, ца, *m.* creditor, leader.

заимообра́зно, *adv.* on credit, on loan.

заимообра́з|ный (~ен, ~на), *adj.* **1.** borrowed, taken on credit. **2.** lent, loaned.

заи́мствовани|е, я, *n.* borrowing.

заи́мствован|ный (~, ~а), *p.p.p. of* заи́мствовать; ~ное сло́во (*ling.*) loan-word.

заи́мств|овать, ую, *impf.* (*of* по~) to borrow.

заѝндеве|ть, ет, *pf.* (*of* и́ндеветь) (*coll.*) to be covered with hoar-frost.

заинтересо́ван|ный (~, ~а), *p.p.p. of* заинтересова́ть *and adj.* (в+*p.*) interested (in); он ~ в возмо́жности торго́вых сноше́ний с Да́льним Восто́ком he is interested in the possibility of trade relations with the Far East; ~ная сторона́ interested party.

заинтерес|ова́ть, у́ю, *pf.* to interest; to excite the curiosity (of).

заинтерес|ова́ться, у́юсь, *pf.* (+*i.*) to become interested; to take an interest (in).

заинтриг|ова́ть, у́ю, *pf. of* интригова́ть 2.

заѝскива|ть, ю, *impf.* (у *or* пе́ред) to try to ingratiate oneself (with).

заѝскива|ющий, *pres. part. act. of* ~ть *and adj.* ingratiating.

заѝскр|иться, юсь, ишься, *pf.* to begin to sparkle.

зай|ду́, дёшь, *see* ~ти́.

за́ймищ|е, а, *n.* (*dial.*) water-meadow.

займодержа́тел|ь, я, *m.* loan-holder.

займ|у́, ёшь, *see* заня́ть.

за|йти́, йду́, йдёшь, *past* ~шёл, ~шла́, *pf.* (*of* ~ходи́ть¹) **1.** (к, в+*a.*) to call (on); to look in (at); по пути́ домо́й я ~шёл к Ива́новым I dropped in at the Ivanovs on the way home; не забу́дьте з. в апте́ку don't forget to look in at the chemist's. **2.** (за+*i.*) to call for, fetch. **3.** (в+*a.*) to get (*to a place*); to find oneself (*in a place*); мы ~шли́ в во́ду по го́рло we got up to our necks in water; разгово́р ~шёл о выступле́нии президе́нта по ра́дио the conversation turned on the President's broadcast; з. на цель (*aeron.*) to be over the target; з. в тыл врага́ (*mil.*) to take the enemy

in the rear. **4.** (за+*a.*) to go behind; to turn; to go on, continue (after); to set (*of sun, etc.*); (*fig., obs.*) to wane; з. за́ угол to turn a corner; з. плечо́м (*mil.*) to wheel; заседа́ние ~шло́ далеко́ за́ полночь the meeting went on until long after midnight; з. сли́шком далеко́ (*fig.*) to go too far.

за́йчик, а, *m.* (*coll.*) **1.** *affect. dim. of* за́яц. **2.** reflection of a sunray. **3.** catkin.

за́йчих|а, и, *f.* doe-hare.

за́йч|онок, о́нка, *pl.* ~а́та, ~а́т, *m.* leveret.

закабал|и́ть, ю́, и́шь, *pf.* to enslave.

закабал|и́ться, ю́сь, и́шься, *pf.* **1.** (+*d.*) to tie oneself in slavery (to). **2.** *pass. of* ~и́ть.

закабал|я́ть(ся), я́ю(сь), *impf. of* ~и́ть(ся).

закавка́зский, *adj.* Trans-Caucasian.

закавы́ч|ить, у, ишь, *pf.* (*coll.*) to place in inverted commas.

закавы́чк|а, и, *f.* (*coll.*) **1.** obstacle, hitch. **2.** inuendo.

закады́чный, *adj.*; з. друг (*coll.*) bosom friend.

зака́з¹, а, *m.* order; ваш з. ещё не гото́в your order is not ready yet; на з. to order; мне де́лают костю́м на з. I am having a suit made to measure; социа́льный з. (*polit.*) demand formulated by a social class.

зака́з², а, *m.* (*obs.*) prohibition.

зака|за́ть¹, жу́, ~жешь, *pf.* (*of* ~зывать) to order; to reserve.

зака|за́ть², жу́, ~жешь, *pf.* (+*inf. or a.*; *obs. or coll.*) to forbid.

зака́зник, а, *m.* (game) reserve.

зака́зн|о́й, *adj.* **1.** made to order; made to measure. **2.** ~о́е письмо́ registered letter; посла́ть письмо́ ~ы́м to send a letter registered; *as noun* ~о́е, ~о́го, *n.* registered postal packet.

зака́зчик, а, *m.* customer, client.

зака́зыва|ть, ю, *impf. of* заказа́ть.¹

зака́ива|ться, юсь, *impf. of* зака́яться.

зака́л, а, *m.* **1.** (*tech.*) temper; (*fig.*) stamp, cast; он челове́к ста́рого ~а he is one of the old school. **2.** (*fig.*) strength of character; guts, backbone.

закалён|ный (~, ~а́), *p.p.p. of* закали́ть *and adj.* hardened, hard; з. в боя́х battle-hardened.

зака́лива|ть, ю, *impf. of* закали́ть.

закал|и́ть, ю́, и́шь, *pf.* (*of* ~ивать *and* ~я́ть) (*tech.*) to temper; to case-harden; (*fig.*) to temper, harden; to make hard, make hardy.

зака́лк|а, и, *f.* tempering; hardening.

зака́лыва|ть, ю, *impf. of* заколо́ть.

закаля́|ть, ю, *impf. of* закали́ть.

закаменѐлый, *adj.* (*coll.*) hard as stone.

закаменѐ|ть, ю, *pf.* (*coll.*) to turn to stone, become petrified.

закáнчива|ть, ю, *impf. of* закóнчить.

закáп|ать, аю (*obs.* ~лю, ~лешь), *pf.*
1. to begin to drip; дождь ~ал it began to
spot with rain. **2.** (*impf.* ~ывать) to spot;
вот ты ~ала себе плáтье черни́лами look,
you have spotted your dress with ink.

закáпыва|ть(ся), ю(сь), *impf. of* закопа́ть(ся) *and* закáпать 2.

закáрмлива|ть, ю, *impf. of* закорми́ть.

закаспи́йский, *adj.* Trans-Caspian.

закáт, а, *m.* setting; з. (сóлнца) sunset; он
пришёл на ~е he came at sunset; (*fig.*) decline; на ~е дней in one's declining years.

закатá|ть, ю, *pf.* (*of* закáтывать) **1.** to
begin to roll. **2.** (в+*a.*) to roll up (in). **3.**
to roll out. **4.** з. в тюрьмý (*sl.*) to throw
into prison.

закáтист|ый (~, ~а), *adj.* (*coll.*) rolling;
з. смех peals of laughter.

закá|ти́ть, чý, ~ти́шь, *pf.* (*of* ~тывать)
(*coll.*) to roll; з. глазá to screw up one's eyes
(*in pain*); онá ~ти́ла емý пощёчину she
slapped his face; з. истéрику to go off into
hysterics; з. сцéну to make a scene.

закá|ти́ться, чýсь, ~ти́шься, *pf.* (*of* ~ты-
ва́ться) **1.** to roll (*intrans.*); мáльчик плáкал,
потомý что мяч ~ти́лся под стол the
little boy was crying because the ball
had rolled under the table. **2.** to set (*of
heavenly bodies*); (*fig.*) to wane; to vanish,
disappear; егó слáва давнó ~ти́лась his
fame had long since waned; моя́ звездá
~ти́лась my luck is out. **3.** (*coll.*) to go off;
он ~ти́лся на недéлю в Лóндон he went
off to London for a week; з. смéхом to go
off into peals of laughter.

закáтный, *adj.* sunset.

закáтыва|ть, ю, *impf. of* закатáть *and* за-
кати́ть.

закáтыва|ться, юсь, *impf. of* закати́ться.

закачá|ть, ю, *pf.* **1.** to begin to shake, begin
to swing; он ~л головóй he began shaking
his head. **2.** to rock (to sleep). **3.** (*impers.*) to
make feel sick by rocking; я собирáюсь в
каю́ту: меня́ ~ло I am going to my cabin;
I feel sick.

закачá|ться, юсь, *pf.* to begin to rock
(*intrans.*), begin to sway.

закáшива|ть, ю, *impf. of* закоси́ть.

закáшля|ться, юсь, *pf.* to have a fit of
coughing.

закá|яться, юсь, ешься, *pf.* (*of* ~ивáться)
(+*inf.*; *coll.*) to forswear; to swear to give
up; он ~я́лся кури́ть he has sworn that he
will give up smoking.

заквá|сить, шу, сишь, *pf.* (*of* ~шивать) to
ferment; to leaven.

заквáск|а, и, *f.* ferment; leaven; (*fig.*, *coll.*)
у негó хорóшая з. he promises well, he has
received a good start in life.

заквáшива|ть, ю, *impf. of* заквáсить.

закидá|ть, ю, *pf.* (*coll.*) **1.** (+*a. and i.*) to be-
spatter (with); to shower (with); з. камня́-
ми to stone; кандидáтов ~ли вопрóсами
the candidates were plied with questions;
з. гря́зью (*fig.*) to sling mud (at). **2.** to fill
up (with); to cover (with).

заки́дыва|ть, ю, *impf. of* закидáть *and* заки́-
нуть.

заки́дыва|ться, юсь, *impf. of* заки́нуться.

заки́н|уть, у, ешь, *pf.* to throw (out, away);
to cast, toss; з. нóгу нá ногу to cross one's
legs; з. винтóвку зá спину to sling a rifle on
one's back; з. ýдочку (*fig.*, *coll.*) to put out
a feeler; з. словéчко (о+*p.*) (*coll.*) to throw
out a hint (about); ~ьте словéчко за меня́
put in a word for me.

заки́н|уться, усь, ешься, *pf.* **1.** to fall back.
2. to jib, shy (*of a horse*).

закипá|ть, ю, *impf. of* закипéть.

закип|éть, лю́, и́шь, *pf.* to begin to boil; to
be on the boil; (*fig.*) to be in full swing.

закисá|ть, ю, *impf. of* заки́снуть.

заки́с|нуть, ну, нешь, *past* ~, ~ла, *pf.* **1.** to
turn sour. **2.** (*fig.*, *coll.*) to become apathe-
tic.

за́кис|ь, и, *f.* (*chem.*) protoxide; з. азóта
nitrous oxide; з. желéза ferrous oxide.

заклáд, а, *m.* (*obs.*) **1.** pawning; mortgaging;
мои́ часы́ в ~е my watch is in pawn. **2.**
bet, wager; би́ться об з. to bet, wager.

заклáдк|а¹, и, *f.* laying (*of bricks, etc.*).

заклáдк|а², и, *f.* bookmark.

закладн|áя, óй, *f.* (*leg.*, *obs.*) mortgage
(-deed).

заклад|нóй¹, *adj. of* ~ка¹; ~нáя рáма fixed
frame.

заклад|нóй², *adj. of* ~; ~нáя квитáнция
pawn-ticket.

заклáдчик, а, *m.* (*obs*) pawner; mortgagor.

заклáдыва|ть, ю, *impf. of* заклáсть *and*
заложи́ть.

заклáни|е, я, *n.* immolation, sacrifice;
идти́ (как) на з. to go to the slaughter.

заклá|сть, дý, дёшь, *past* ~л, ~лá, ~ло, *pf.*
(*coll.*) to fill up; to block up; to pile.

зак|лáть, олю́, óлешь, *past* ~лáл, *pf.* (*obs.*)
to sacrifice, immolate.

закл|евáть, юю́, юёшь, *pf.* **1.** to begin to
peck; to begin to bite (*of fish*). **2.** to peck to
death; (*fig.*, *coll.*) to go for.

заклёвыва|ть, ю, *impf. of* заклевáть.

заклéива|ть(ся), ю(сь), *impf. of* заклéить-
(ся).

заклé|ить, ю, ишь, *pf.* to glue up; to stick
up; з. конвéрт to seal an envelope.

заклé|иться, ится, *pf.* to stick (*intrans.*).

заклейм|и́ть, лю́, и́шь, *pf. of* клейми́ть.

заклепá|ть, ю, *pf.* (*of* заклёпывать) (*tech.*) to
rivet.

заклёпк|а, и, *f.* (*tech.*) **1.** riveting. **2.** rivet.

заклёпник, а, *m.* (*tech.*) riveting hammer.

заклёпыва|ть, ю, *impf. of* заклепа́ть.

заклина́ни|е, я, *n.* **1.** incantation; spell. **2.** exorcism.

заклина́тел|ь, я, *m.* exorcist; з. змей snake-charmer.

заклина́|ть, ю, *impf.* (*of* закля́сть) **1.** to conjure; to invoke. **2.** to exorcize (*by means of incantation*). **3.** to enchant, endow with magical powers. **4.** to conjure, adjure; to entreat.

закли́нива|ть, ю, *impf. of* заклини́ть.

заклин|и́ть, ю́, и́шь, *pf.* **1.** to wedge ,fasten with a wedge. **2.** to jam.

заключа́|ть, ю, *impf. of* заключи́ть.

заключ|а́ться, а́юсь, *impf.* (*of* ~и́ться) **1.** *pass. of* ~а́ть. **2.** (*impf. only*) (в+*p.*) to consist of); to lie (in); гла́вное затрудне́ние ~а́ется в недоста́тке де́нежных средств the principal difficulty consists in the lack of funds. **3.** з. в монастырь to enter a monastery. **4.** з. в монастырь to enter a monastery.

заключе́ни|е, я, *n.* **1.** conclusion, end; в з. in conclusion. **2.** conclusion, inference. **3.** з. догово́ра conclusion of a treaty. **4.** (*leg.*) resolution, decision; переда́ть на з. to submit for a decision. **5.** confinement, detention; тюре́мное з. imprisonment.

заключён|ный (~, ~а́, ~о́), *p.p.p. of* заключи́ть; *as noun* з., ~ного, *m. and* ~ная, ~ной, *f.* (*leg.*) prisoner, convict.

заключи́тельн|ый, *adj.* final, concluding; з. акко́рд (*mus.*) finale; ~ое сло́во concluding remarks.

заключ|и́ть, у́, и́шь, *pf.* (*of* ~а́ть) **1.** (+*i.*) to conclude, end (with). **2.** to conclude, infer. **3.** to conclude, enter into; з. брак to contract marriage; з. догово́р to conclude a treaty; з. сде́лку to strike a bargain. **4.** з. в себе́ to contain, enclose; to comprise; з. в ско́бки to enclose in brackets. **5.** to confine; з. в тюрьму́ to imprison; з. под стра́жу to take into custody.

заключ|и́ться, у́сь, и́шься, *pf. of* ~а́ться.

закля|сть, ну́, нёшь, *past* ~л, ~ла́, ~ло, *pf. of* заклина́ть.

закля|сться, ну́сь, нёшься, *past* ~лся, ~ла́сь, ~ло́сь, *pf.* (*obs.*) to swear to give up.

закля́ти|е, я, *n.* (*obs.*) **1.** incantation. **2.** oath, pledge.

закля́тый, *adj.* **1.** (*coll.*) passionate; inveterate; з. враг sworn enemy. **2.** enchanted, bewitched; з. дом haunted house.

зак|ова́ть, ую́, уёшь, *pf.* **1.** to chain; з. в кандалы́ to shackle, put in irons; (*fig., obs.*) to chain, bind, hold down; (*poet.*) моро́з ~ова́л зе́млю the land was in the grip of frost. **2.** to begin to forge. **3.** to injure in shoeing (*a horse*).

заковыва́|ть, ю, *impf. of* закова́ть.

заковыля́|ть, ю, *pf.* (*coll.*) to begin to hobble.

заковы́рист|ый (~, ~а), *adj.* (*coll.*) subtle, complicated; odd.

заковы́чк|а, и, *f.* = закавы́чка.

зако́л, а, *m.* weir.

закола́чива|ть, ю, *impf. of* заколоти́ть.

заколдо́ван|ный (~, ~а), *p.p.p. of* заколдова́ть *and adj.* bewitched, enchanted; spellbound; (*fig.*) з. круг vicious circle.

заколд|ова́ть, у́ю, *pf.* to bewitch, enchant; to lay a spell (on).

заколдо́выва|ть, ю, *impf. of* заколдова́ть.

заколеб|а́ться, ~лю́сь, ~ле́шься, *pf.* to begin to shake; (*fig.*) to begin to waver, begin to vacillate.

зако́лк|а, и, *f.* **1.** stabbing. **2.** pinning. **3.** hairpin.

заколо́д|ить, ит, *pf.* (*impers.+d.; dial.*) to stand in the way (of), impede; почему́ он не прие́хал? ~ило ему́, что ли? why hasn't he come? has he been held up?

заколо|ти́ть, чу́, ~тишь, *pf.* (*of* закола́чивать) (*coll.*) **1.** to board up; to nail up. **2.** to knock in, drive in. **3.** to beat the life out of; to knock insensible. **4.** to begin to knock; в дверь ~ти́ли there was a knocking on the door.

заколо|ти́ться, чу́сь, ~тишься, *pf.* (*coll.*) **1.** *pass. of* ~ти́ть. **2.** to begin to beat; се́рдце у неё ~ти́лось her heart began to thump.

закол|о́ть, ю́, ~ешь, *pf.* (*of* зака́лывать *and* коло́ть²) **1.** to stab (to death), spear, stick. **2.** to pin (up). **3.** to begin to chop. **4.** (*impers.*) у меня́, *etc.*, ~о́ло в боку́ I, *etc.*, have a stitch in my side.

закол|о́ться, ю́сь, ~ешься, *pf.* to stab oneself.

заколы|ха́ться, ~шется, *pf.* to begin to sway; to begin to wave, begin to flutter.

закольц|ева́ть, у́ю, у́ешь, *pf. of* кольцева́ть.

зако́н, а, *m.* law; свод ~ов code, statute book; объяви́ть вне ~а to outlaw; з. Бо́жий (*as school subject, etc.*) scripture, divinity.

зако́нник, а, *m.* (*coll.*) **1.** one versed in law, lawyer. **2.** one who keeps to letter of the law.

законнорождённый, *adj.* legitimate (*child*).

зако́нност|ь, и, *f.* lawfulness, legality.

зако́н|ный (~ен, ~на, ~но), *adj.* lawful, legal; legitimate, rightful; з. брак lawful wedlock; з. владе́лец rightful owner.

законове́д, а, *m.* **1.** jurist. **2.** tutor in law.

законове́дени|е, я, *n.* jurisprudence, law.

законода́тел|ь, я, *m.* legislator; lawgiver.

законода́тельный, *adj.* legislative.

законода́тельств|о, а, *n.* legislation.

закономе́рност|ь, и, *f.* regularity; conformity with a law; normality.

закономе́р|ный (~ен, ~на), *adj.* **1.** regular, natural. **2.** *as pred.* ~но it is in order.

законопа́|тить, чу, тишь, *pf.* **1.** to caulk up; з. у́ши (*fig., coll.*) to block up one's ears. **2.** (*fig., coll.*) to coop up; pack off (to).

законопа́|титься, чусь, тишься, *pf.* (*coll.*) to box oneself up, shut oneself up.

законопа́чива|ть(ся), ю(сь), *impf.* of законопа́тить(ся).

законоположе́ни|е, я, *n.* (*leg.*) statute.

законопослу́шный, *adj.* (*obs.*) law-abiding.

законопрое́кт, а, *m.* (*polit., leg.*) bill.

законосовеща́тельн|ый, *adj.* (*polit., leg.*) concerned with discussion and/or preparation of bills; ~ая коми́ссия consultative commission.

законоуче́ни|е, я, *n.* (*obs.*) religious instruction.

законоучи́тел|ь, я, *m.* (*obs.*) religious teacher.

законсерви́р|овать, ую, *pf.* of консерви́ровать.

законспири́р|овать, ую, *pf.* (*of* конспири́ровать) to keep secret, keep dark.

законтракт|ова́ть, у́ю, *pf.* (*of* контрактова́ть) to contract (for), enter into a contract (for).

законтракт|ова́ться, у́юсь, *pf.* (*of* контрактова́ться) to contract to work (for); to hire oneself out (to).

законфу́|зиться, жусь, зишься, *pf.* to show embarrassment.

зако́нченност|ь, и, *f.* finish; completeness.

зако́нчен|ный (~, ~a), *p.p.p.* of зако́нчить *and adj.* finished; complete; (*coll.*) consummate; он явля́ется ~ным проза́иком he is a finished prose-writer; з. лгун a consummate liar.

зако́нч|ить, у, ишь, *pf.* (*of* зака́нчивать) to end, finish.

зако́нч|иться, усь, ишься, *pf.* (*of* зака́нчиваться) to end, finish (*intrans.*).

закопа́|ть, ю, *pf.* (*of* зака́пывать) **1.** to begin to dig. **2.** to bury.

закопа́|ться, юсь, *pf.* (*of* зака́пываться) (*coll.*) **1.** to begin to rummage. **2.** to bury oneself. **3.** (*mil.*) to dig in.

закопёрщик, а, *m.* **1.** foreman pile-driver. **2.** (*fig., coll.*) ringleader.

закопте́лый, *adj.* (*coll.*) sooty; smutty.

закопт|е́ть, и́т, *pf.* (*of* копте́ть¹) to become covered with soot.

закоп|ти́ть, чу́, ти́шь, *pf.* (*of* копти́ть) **1.** to smoke. **2.** to blacken with smoke.

закоп|ти́ться, чу́сь, ти́шься, *pf.* **1.** to be smoked. **2.** to become covered with soot.

закорене́лый, *adj.* deep-rooted; ingrained; inveterate.

закорене́|ть, ю, ешь, *pf.* **1.** (*fig.*) to take root. **2.** (в+*p.*) to become steeped (in); он ~л

в греха́х he became an inveterate sinner.

зако́р|ки, ок, *no sing.* (*coll.*) back, shoulders; он перенёс де́вочку че́рез реку́ на ~ках carried the little girl across the river on his shoulders.

закорм|и́ть, лю́, ~ишь, *pf.* (*of* зака́рмливать) to overfeed; to stuff.

закорю́чк|а, и, *f.* (*coll.*) **1.** hook; flourish (*in handwriting*). **2.** (*fig., dial.*) hitch, snag.

зако|си́ть, шу́, ~сишь, *pf.* (*of* зака́шивать) (*agric.*) **1.** to begin to mow, begin to scythe. **2.** to mow up, scythe up.

закосне́лый, *adj.* incorrigible, inveterate.

закосне́|ть, ю, *pf.* of косне́ть.

закостене́лый, *adj.* ossified; stiff.

закостене́|ть, ю, *pf.* to ossify; (*fig.*) он ~л от хо́лода he became stiff with cold.

закостыля́|ть, ю, *pf.* (*coll.*) to hobble, limp.

закоу́л|ок, ка, *m.* **1.** back street, (dark) alley. **2.** (*coll.*) secluded corner; обыска́ть все углы́ и ~ки to search in every nook and cranny; знать все ~ки (*fig.*) to know all the ins and outs.

закочене́лый, *adj.* numb with cold.

закочене́|ть, ю, ешь, *pf.* of кочене́ть.

закра́дыва|ться, юсь, *impf.* of закра́сться.

закра́ива|ть, ю, *impf.* of закро́йть.

закра́ин|а, ы, *f.* **1.** (*geogr.*) zakraina (*water at edge of frozen river, lake, etc.*). **2.** (*tech.*) flange.

закра́па|ть, ю, *pf.* **1.** to begin to fall (*of raindrops*). **2.** to spot.

закра́пыва|ть, ю, *impf.* of закра́пать 2.

закра́|сить, шу, сишь, *pf.* (*of* ~шивать) **1.** to paint over, paint out. **2.** to begin to paint.

закрасне́|ть, ю, ешь, *pf.* to begin to show red.

закрасне́|ться, юсь, ешься, *pf.* **1.** to begin to show red. **2.** to blush.

закра́|сться, ду́сь, дёшься, *past* ~лся, *pf.* (*of* ~дываться) to steal in, creep in; (*fig.*) у меня́ ~лось подозре́ние a suspicion creeped into my mind.

закра́шива|ть, ю, *impf.* of закра́сить.

закре́п|а, ы, *f.* catch; fastener.

закрепи́тел|ь, я, *m.* (*chem., phot.*) fixing agent, fixer.

закрепи́тельный, *adj.*; з. тало́н voucher.

закреп|и́ть, лю́, и́шь, *pf.* **1.** to fasten, secure; (*naut.*) to make fast; (*phot.*) to fix. **2.** (*fig.*) to consolidate; мы ~и́ли прошлого́дние успе́хи we have consolidated last year's successes. **3.** (+*a.* за+*i.*) to allot, assign (to); to appoint, attach (to); з. за собо́й to secure; за на́ми ~и́ли одну́ из но́вых кварти́р we have been assigned one of the new flats; он ~и́л за собо́й места́ на за́втрашнее представле́ние в Большо́м теа́тре he has secured seats for tomorrow's performance at the Bolshoi Theatre. **4.** (*impers.*; *coll.*) его́, *etc.*, ~и́ло he, *etc.*, has got over his diarrhoea.

закреп|и́ться, лю́сь, и́шься, *pf.* **1.** *pass. of* ~и́ть. **2.** (на + *a.*) to consolidate one's hold (on).

закрепля́|ть(ся), ю(сь), *impf. of* закрепи́ть(ся).

закрепо|сти́ть, щу́, сти́шь, *pf.* to enslave; to make a serf.

закрепоща́|ть, ю, *impf. of* закрепости́ть.

закрепоще́ни|е, я, *n.* **1.** enslaving. **2.** slavery; serfdom.

закрив|и́ть, лю́, и́шь, *pf.* **1.** to bend; to fold. **2.** (*coll.*) to begin to bend.

закрив|и́ться, лю́сь, и́шься, *pf.* **1.** to become crooked. **2.** (*coll.*) to begin to bend (*intrans.*).

закривля́|ть(ся), ю(сь), *impf. of* закриви́ть(ся).

закристаллиз|ова́ться, у́юсь, *pf. of* кристаллизова́ться.

закрич|а́ть, у́, и́шь, *pf.* **1.** to cry out. **2.** to begin to shout; to give a shout.

закро|и́ть, ю́, и́шь, *pf.* (*of* закра́ивать) **1.** to cut out. **2.** (*tech.*) to groove.

закро́|й, я, *m.* **1.** cutting out. **2.** cut; style (*of dress*). **3.** (*tech.*) groove.

закро́йны|й, *adj.* for cutting clothes; ~е но́жницы cutting-out scissors.

закро́йщик, а, *m.* cutter.

за́кром, а, *pl.* ~а́, *m.* corn-bin; (*fig., rhet.*) granary.

закругле́ни|е, я, *n.* **1.** rounding, curving. **2.** curve; curvature. **3.** (*lit.*) well-rounded period.

закруглён|ный (~, ~а́), *p.p.p. of* закругли́ть *and adj.* rounded; (*lit.*) well-rounded.

закругл|и́ть, ю́, и́шь, *pf.* to make round; з. фра́зу to round off a sentence.

закругл|и́ться, ю́сь, и́шься, *pf.* to become round.

закругля́|ть(ся), ю(сь), *impf. of* закругли́ть(ся).

закруж|и́ть, у́, ~и́шь, *pf.* **1.** to begin to whirl (*trans. and intrans.*); з. кому́-н. го́лову (*fig., coll.*) to turn someone's head. **2.** to make giddy, make dizzy; она́ его́ совсе́м ~и́ла (*fig., coll.*) she has swept him off his feet. **3.** (*dial.*) to lead astray.

закруж|и́ться, у́сь, ~и́шься, *pf.* **1.** to begin to whirl, begin to go round; у меня́ голова́ ~и́лась my head began to swim. **2.** *pf. of* кружи́ться.

закрута́с|ы, ов, *no sing.* (*coll., obs.*) flourishes.

закру|ти́ть, чу́, ~тишь, *pf.* **1.** to twist; to twirl; to wind round; они́ ~ти́ли ему́ ру́ки за́ спину they twisted his arms behind his back. **2.** to turn; to screw in; (*fig.*) з. сло́вечко to make a caustic remark. **3.** (*fig., coll.*) to turn someone's head. **4.** (*coll., dial.*) to go drinking.

закру|ти́ться, чу́сь, ~тишься, *pf.* **1.** to

twist; to twirl; to wind round (*intrans.*). **2.** to begin to whirl.

закру́чива|ть(ся), ю(сь), *impf. of* закрути́ть(ся).

закрыва́|ть(ся), ю(сь), *impf. of* закры́ть(ся).

закры́ти|е, я, *n.* **1.** closing; shutting. **2.** (*mil.*) cover.

закры́т|ый (~, ~а), *p.p.p. of* ~ь *and adj.* closed, shut; private; с ~ыми глаза́ми (*fig.*) blindly; ~ое голосова́ние secret ballot; при ~ых дверя́х behind closed doors, in private; ~ое заседа́ние private meeting; з. ко́нкурс closed competition; ~ое мо́ре inland sea; ~ое пла́тье high-necked dress; в ~ом помеще́нии indoors; з. просмо́тр private view; з. распредели́тель store closed to non-members; ~ое уче́бное заведе́ние (private) boarding-school.

закр|ы́ть, о́ю, о́ешь, *pf.* (*of* ~ыва́ть) **1.** to close, shut; з. глаза́ to pass away; я ему́ ~ы́л глаза́ I attended him on his death-bed; з. глаза́ (на + *a.*) to shut one's eyes (to); з. ско́бки to close brackets; з. счёт to close an account. **2.** to shut off, turn off. **3.** to close down, shut down. **4.** to cover.

закр|ы́ться, о́юсь, о́ешься, *pf.* (*of* ~ыва́ться) **1.** to close, shut; to end; to close down; (*intrans.*). **2.** to cover oneself; to take cover; они́ ~лись от дождя́ зонто́м they took cover from the rain beneath the awning. **3.** *pass. of* ~ы́ть.

закули́сный, *adj.* (occurring) behind the scenes; (*fig.*) secret; underhand, under-cover.

за́куп, а, *m.* (*hist.*) zakup (*peasant in Kievan Russia repaying loan by means of labour*).

закупа́|ть, ю, *impf. of* закупи́ть.

закупа́|ться¹, юсь, *impf., pass. of* ~ть.

закупа́|ться², юсь, *pf.* (*coll.*) to bathe excessively.

закуп|и́ть, лю́, ~ишь, *pf.* (*of* ~а́ть) **1.** to buy up (wholesale). **2.** to lay in; to stock up with. **3.** (*obs.*) to bribe.

заку́пк|а, и, *f.* purchase.

закупно́й, *adj.* bought, purchased.

заку́порива|ть, ю, *impf. of* закупорить.

заку́пор|ить, ю, ишь, *pf.* **1.** to cork; to stop up. **2.** (*fig., coll.*) to shut up; coop up.

заку́порк|а, и, *f.* **1.** corking. **2.** (*med.*) embolism, thrombosis.

заку́п|очный, *adj. of* ~ка; ~очная цена́ purchase price.

заку́пщик, а, *m.* purchaser; buyer.

заку́рива|ть(ся), ю(сь), *impf. of* закури́ть(ся).

закур|и́ть, ю́, ~ишь, *pf.* **1.** to light up (*cigarette, pipe, etc.*). **2.** to begin to smoke; ещё не ко́нчив шко́лу он ~и́л he began to smoke before he had left school. **3.** (*dial.*) to begin to distil.

закур|и́ться, ю́сь, ~ишься, *pf.* **1.** to begin to smoke (*intrans.*). **2.** (*coll.*) to smoke excessively; to make oneself ill by excessive smoking.

заку|си́ть¹, шу́, ~сишь, *pf.* (*of* ~сывать) to bite; (*fig.*) з. удила́ to take the bit between the teeth; з. язы́к to hold one's tongue; to shut up.

заку|си́ть², шу́, ~сишь, *pf.* (*of* ~сывать) **1.** to have a snack, have a bite; з. на́скоро to snatch a hasty bite. **2.** (+*a. and i.*) to take (with); з. во́дку ры́бкой to drink vodka with fish hors-d'œuvres.

заку́ск|а, и, *f.* (*usu. pl.*) hors-d'œuvre; snack; на ~y for a titbit; (*fig., coll.*) as a special treat.

заку́с|очный, *adj. of* ~ка; *as noun* ~очная, ~очной, *f.* snack bar.

заку́сыва|ть, ю, *impf. of* закуси́ть.

заку́т, а, *m.* (*dial.*) **1.** storeroom. **2.** kennel; (pig-)sty.

заку́та|ть, ю, *pf.* (*of* заку́тывать) to wrap up, muffle; з. в одея́ло to tuck up (in bed).

заку́та|ться, юсь, *pf.* (*of* заку́тываться) to wrap oneself up, muffle oneself.

заку|ти́ть, чу́, ~тишь, *pf.* to begin to drink; to go drinking.

заку|ти́ться, чу́сь, ~тишься, *pf.* (*coll.*) to spend (all) one's time drinking.

заку́тк|а, и, *f.* (*dial.*) **1.** *dim. of* заку́т. **2.** chimney-corner (*in peasant's hut*).

заку́тыва|ть(ся), ю(сь), *impf. of* заку́тать(ся).

зал, а, *m.* hall; з. ожида́ния waiting-room.

за́л|а, ы, *f.* (*obs. or coll.*) = ~.

зала́в|ок, ка, *m.* (*dial.*) chest, locker.

зала́|дить, жу, дишь, *pf.* (*coll.*) **1.** (+*inf.*) to take to; он ~дил заходи́ть к нам по вечера́м he has taken to calling in on us in the evening. **2.** з. одно́ и то́ же to harp on the same string.

залакир|ова́ть, у́ю, *pf.* to varnish over; (*fig.*) to make shiny.

зала́мыва|ть, ю, *impf. of* заломи́ть.

залата́|ть, ю, *pf. of* лата́ть.

зал|га́ться, гу́сь, жёшься, гу́тся, *past* ~га́лся, ~гала́сь, ~гало́сь, *pf.* (*coll.*) to become an inveterate liar.

залега́ни|е, я, *n.* (*geol.*) **1.** bedding. **2.** bed, seam.

залега́|ть, ю, *impf. of* зале́чь.

заледене́лый, *adj.* **1.** covered with ice; ice-bound. **2.** ice-cold, icy.

заледене́|ть, ю, *pf.* (*of* леденеть) (*coll.*) **1.** to be covered with ice; to freeze up, ice up. **2.** to become cold as ice; to become numb.

залежа́лый, *adj.* (*coll.*) **1.** stale. **2.** long unused.

залеж|а́ться, у́сь, и́шься, *pf.* **1.** to lie too long; to lie idle a long time. **2.** (*econ.*) to

find no market **3.** become stale.

залёжива|ться, юсь, *impf. of* залежа́ться.

за́леж|ь, и, *f.* **1.** (*geol.*) deposit, bed, seam; **2.** (*agric.*) fallow land. **3.** (*sing. only*; *collect.*; *coll.*) stale goods.

залеза́|ть, ю, *impf. of* зале́зть.

зале́з|ть, у, ешь, *past* ~, ~ла, *pf.* **1.** (на+*a.*) to climb (up, on to). **2.** (в+*a.*; *coll.*) to get (into); to creep (into); з. кому́-н. в карма́н to pick someone's pocket; з. в во́ду по го́рло to get up to one's neck in water; он ~ в отцо́вские сапоги́ he got into his father's boots; з. в долги́ to run into debt.

залени́ться, ю́сь, ~ишься, *pf.* (*coll.*) to grow lazy.

залепе|та́ть, чу́, ~чешь, *pf.* (*coll.*) to begin to babble.

залеп|и́ть, лю́, ~ишь, *pf.* (+*a. and i.*) to paste up, paste over; to glue up; всю сте́ну ~и́ли афи́шами the whole wall had been pasted over with bills; глаза́ у него́ ~и́ло сне́гом his eyes were stuck up with snow; з. кому́-н. пощёчину (*vulg.*) to slap someone's face.

залепля́|ть, ю, *impf. of* залепи́ть.

залета́|ть¹, ю, *pf.* (*coll.*) to begin to fly.

залета́|ть², ю, *impf. of* залете́ть.

зале|те́ть, чу́, ти́шь, *pf.* **1.** (в+*a.*) to fly (into); (за+*a.*) to fly (over, beyond); пти́ца ~те́ла в ко́мнату a bird flew into the room; мы ~те́ли за Се́верный по́люс we flew over the North Pole. **2.** (в+*a.*) to fly (into), land (*on the way*); нам пришло́сь з. в Стокго́льм за горю́чим we had to land at Stockholm to refuel. **3.** (*fig., coll.*) з. высоко́, з. далеко́ to go up in the world.

залётн|ый, *adj.* (*coll.*) ~ая пти́ца bird of passage (*also fig.*); з. гость unexpected visitor.

зале́чива|ть, ю, *impf. of* залечи́ть.

залеч|и́ть, у́, ~ишь, *pf.* **1.** to heal; to remedy. **2.** (*coll.*) з. до́ смерти to doctor to death; to murder (*by unskilful treatment*).

залеч|и́ться, и́тся, *pf.* (*coll.*) to heal (up).

зал|е́чь, я́гу, я́жешь, я́гут, *past* ~ёг, ~егла́, *pf. of* ~ега́ть) **1.** to lie down; to lie low; to lie in wait. **2.** (*geol.*) to lie, be deposited; здесь руда́ ~егла́ на глубине́ ста ме́тров there is a deposit of ore here at a depth of a hundred metres. **3.** (*fig.*) to take root; to become ingrained. **4.** (*med.*) to become blocked; нос у него́ ~ёг, у него́ в носу́ ~егло́ his nose is blocked.

зали́в, а, *m.* bay; gulf; creek, cove.

залива́|ть¹, ю, *impf.* (*coll.*) to lie, tell lies.

залива́|ть²(ся), ю(сь), *impf. of* зали́ть(ся).

зали́вист|ый (~, ~а), *adj.* (*of sound*) modulating.

зали́вк|а, и, *f.* mending; stopping up, filling in (*with liquid substance*).

заливн|о́е, о́го, *n.* fish *or* meat in aspic.

заливн|о́й, *adj.* **1.** з. луг water-meadow. **2.** for pouring; ~а́я труба́ funnel. **3.** (*folk poet.*) trilling. **4.** jellied; ~а́я ры́ба fish in aspic.

зали|за́ть, жу́, ~жешь, *pf.* **1.** to lick clean. **2.** з. у себя́ во́лосы to sleek down one's hair.

зали́зыва|ть, ю, *impf. of* зализа́ть.

зал|и́ть, ью́, ьёшь, *past* ~и́л, ~ила́, ~и́ло, *pf.* (*of* ~ива́ть) **1.** to flood, inundate; (*fig.*) ко́мнату ~и́ло све́том the room was flooded with light; толпа́ ~ила́ у́лицы the crowd filled the streets to overflowing. **2.** (+*a. and i.*) to pour (over); to spill (on); кто ~и́л но́вую ска́терть черни́лами? who has spilled ink on the new table-cloth?; з. кра́ской to give a wash of paint; з. ту́шью to ink in. **3.** to quench, extinguish (*with water*); з. пожа́р to put out a fire; з. го́ре (вино́м) to drown one's sorrows. **4.** to stop up (*with liquid substance, as putty, rubber solution, etc.*); з. гало́ши to mend galoshes. **5.** to begin to pour (*intrans.*).

зал|и́ться, ью́сь, ьёшься, *past* ~и́лся, ~ила́сь, *pf.* (*of* ~ива́ться) **1.** to be flooded, inundated. **2.** to pour; to spill (*intrans.*); вода́ ~ила́сь мне за воротни́к water has gone down my neck. **3.** to spill on oneself; ты весь ~и́лся су́пом you have spilled soup all over yourself. **4.** (+*i.*) to break into, burst into; соба́ка ~ила́сь ла́ем the dog began to bark furiously; з. пе́сней to break into a song; з. слеза́ми to burst into tears, dissolve in tears. **5.** to set (*of jellies*).

залихва́тск|ий, *adj.* (*coll.*) devil-may-care; ~ая пе́сня rollicking song.

зало́г¹, а, *m.* **1.** deposit; pledge; security; под з. (+ *g.*) on the security of; отда́ть в з. to pawn; to mortgage; вы́купить из ~а to redeem; to pay off mortgage (on). **2.** (*fig.*) pledge, token.

зало́г², а, *m.* (*gram.*) voice.

зало́г|овый, *adj. of* ~; ~овое свиде́тельство mortgage-deed.

залогода́тел|ь, я, *m.* depositor; mortgagor.

залогодержа́тел|ь, я, *m.* pawnee.

залож|и́ть, у́, ~ишь, *pf.* (*of* закла́дывать) **1.** to put (behind); он ~и́л ру́ки за́ спину he put his hands behind his back. **2.** to lay (the foundation of). **3.** (*coll.*) to mislay. **4.** (+*i.*) to pile up, heap up (with); to block up (with); (*impers.*+*d.*) мне нос ~и́ло my nose is blocked, is stuffed up. **5.** to mark, put a marker in; я ~и́л страни́цу девяно́сто I have put a marker in at page ninety. **6.** to pawn; to mortgage. **7.** to harness. **8.** to lay in, store, put by.

зало́жник, а, *m.* hostage.

залом|и́ть, лю́, ~ишь, *pf.* (*of* зала́мывать) **1.** to break off. **2.** (*coll.*) з. це́ну to ask an exorbitant price; з. ша́пку to cock one's hat.

залосн|и́ться, и́тся, *pf.* (*coll.*) to become shiny.

залп, а, *m.* volley; salvo; вы́стрелить ~ом to fire a volley, salvo; ~ом (*fig., coll.*) without pausing for breath; вы́пить ~ом to drain at one draught.

залуп|и́ть, лю́, ~ишь, *pf.* (*coll.*) **1.** to peel off; to tear off. **2.** to ask an exorbitant price for. **3.** to begin to beat. **4.** to beat up.

залуп|и́ться, ~ится, *pf.* (*coll.*) to peel off, flake off.

залупля́|ть(ся), ет(ся), *impf. of* залупи́ть(ся).

залуча́|ть, ю, *impf. of* залучи́ть.

залуч|и́ть, у́, и́шь, *pf.* (*coll.*) to entice, lure.

заль|сти́ть, щу́, сти́шь, *pf.* (*coll.*) **1.** (+*d.*) to begin to flatter. **2.** (*dial.*) to win over by flattery.

залюб|ова́ться, у́юсь, *pf.* (+*i.*) to be lost in admiration (of).

заля́па|ть, ю, *pf.* (*coll.*) to make dirty.

зам, а, *m.* *abbr. of* ~ести́тель.

зам-, *prefix* = ~ести́тель.

зама́|зать, жу, жешь, *pf.* (*of* ма́зать *and* ~зывать) **1.** to paint over; to efface; (*fig.*) to slur over. **2.** to putty; to lute. **3.** to daub, smear; to soil.

зама́|заться, жусь, жешься, *pf.* (*of* ма́заться *and* ~зываться) to smear oneself; to get dirty.

зама́зк|а, и, *f.* **1.** putty. **2.** closing up with putty, luting.

зама́зыва|ть(ся), ю(сь), *impf. of* зама́зать(ся).

зама́й, *only in phrase* не з. (*dial.*) don't touch, leave alone.

зама́лива|ть, ю, *impf. of* замоли́ть.

зама́лчива|ть, ю, *impf. of* замолча́ть.

зама́нива|ть, ю, *impf. of* замани́ть.

заман|и́ть, ю́, ~ишь, *pf.* to entice, lure; to decoy.

зама́нчив|ый (~, ~а), *adj.* tempting, alluring.

замара́|ть, ю, *pf.* (*of* мара́ть 1) **1.** to soil, dirty; (*fig.*) to disgrace; з. свою́ репута́цию to sully one's reputation. **2.** to blot out, efface.

замара́|ться, юсь, *pf. of* мара́ться 1.

замара́шк|а, и, *m. and f.* (*coll.*) slut, sloven; grubby child.

зама́рива|ть, ю, *impf. of* замори́ть.

замарин|ова́ть, у́ю, *pf. of* маринова́ть.

замаскир|ова́ть, у́ю, *pf.* to mask; to disguise; to camouflage; з. свои́ чу́вства (*fig.*) to conceal one's feelings.

замаскир|ова́ться, у́юсь, *pf.* to disguise oneself.

замаскиро́выва|ть(ся), ю(сь), *impf. of* замаскирова́ть(ся).

зама́слива|ть(ся), ю(сь), *impf. of* зама́слить(ся).

замасл|ить, ю, ишь, *pf.* **1.** to oil, grease. **2.** to make oily, make greasy. **3.** (*fig.*, *sl.*) to butter up.

замасл|иться, юсь, ишься, *pf.* to become oily, become greasy.

заматерелый, *adj.* hardened, inveterate.

заматере|ть, ю, *pf.* to become hardened.

замат|орелый = ~ерелый.

заматыва|ть(ся), ю(сь), *impf. of* замотать(ся).

замах, а, *m.* threatening gesture.

зама|хать, шу, ~шешь, *pf.* to begin to wave.

замахива|ться, юсь, *impf. of* замахнуться.

замахн|уться, усь, ёшься, *pf.* (+*i.*) to raise threateningly; он даже ~улся рукой на беззащитную старуху he even lifted up his hand against a defenceless old woman.

замачива|ть, ю, *impf. of* замочить.

замашк|а, и, *f.* (*coll.*, *pejor.*) way, manner.

замащива|ть, ю, *impf. of* замостить.

зама|ять, ю, ешь, *pf.* (*coll.*) to tire out, wear out.

зама|яться, юсь, ешься, *pf.* (*coll.*) to be tired out, exhausted.

замаяч|ить, у, ишь, *pf.* to loom; вдали ~или огни гавани the lights of the harbour loomed up in the distance.

замедлени|е, я, *n.* **1.** slowing down, deceleration; (*mus.*) ritardando. **2.** delay; без ~я without delay, at once.

замедленн|ый, *p.p.p. of* замедлить *and adj.* retarded; delayed; бомба ~ого действия delayed-action bomb.

замедл|ить, ю, ишь, *pf.* **1.** to slow down, retard; з. шаг to slacken one's pace; з. ход to reduce speed. **2.** (+*inf.* or +*i.* or с+*i.*) to delay (in); to be long (in); ответ не ~ил прийти the answer was not long in coming; з. (с) ответом to delay in answering.

замедл|иться, ится, *pf.* **1.** to slow down; to slacken, become slower. **2.** *pass of* ~ить.

замедля|ть(ся), ет(ся), *impf. of* замедлить(ся).

замел|ить, ю, ишь, *pf.* (*coll.*) to chalk over.

замен|а, ы, *f.* **1.** substitution; replacement; з. смертной казни тюремным заключением commutation of death sentence to imprisonment. **2.** substitute.

замени|мый, *pres. part. pass. of* ~ть *and adj.* replaceable.

заменитель, я, *m.* (+*g.*) substitute; з. кожи leather substitute.

замен|ить, ю, ~ишь, *pf.* **1.** (+*a. and i.*) to replace (by), substitute (for); мы ~или керосин электричеством we have replaced oil by electricity; з. масло маргарином to use margarine instead of butter. **2.** to take the place of; она ~ила ребёнку мать she was (like) a mother to the child; трудно будет з. его it will be hard to replace him.

замен|ять, яю, *impf. of* ~ить.

зам|ереть, ру, рёшь, *past* ~ер ~ерла, ~ерло, *pf.* (*of* ~ирать) **1.** to stand still; to freeze, be rooted to the spot; to die (*fig.*); сердце моё ~ерло, когда дверь открылась my heart stopped beating when the door opened. **2.** to die down, die away; к полуночи стрельба ~ерла towards midnight firing died down.

замерзани|е, я, *n.* freezing; точка ~я freezing point; на точке ~я (*fig.*) at a standstill.

замерза|ть, ю, *impf. of* замёрзнуть.

замёрз|нуть, ну, нешь, *past* ~, ~ла, *pf.* (*of* ~ать) to freeze (up); to freeze to death; to be killed by frost.

замертво, *adv.* **1.** like one dead; она упала з. she collapsed in a dead faint. **2.** (*coll.*) dead drunk.

заме|сить, шу, ~сишь, *pf.* (*of* ~шивать) to mix; з. тесто to knead dough.

заме|сти, ту, тёшь, *past* ~л, ~ла, *pf.* (*of* ~тать) **1.** to sweep up. **2.** to cover (up); (*impers.*) дорогу ~ло снегом the road is covered with snow; (*fig.*) з. следы to cover up one's traces.

заместитель, я, *m.* substitute; deputy; з. директора deputy director; з. президента vice-president; быть ~ем (+*g.*) to stand proxy (for), substitute (for).

заместительств|о, а, *n.* position of deputy; acting tenure of office; по ~y by proxy.

заме|стить, щу, стишь, *pf.* (*of* ~щать) **1.** (+*a. and i.*) to replace (by); to substitute (for). **2.** (+*a. and i.*) to appoint (to); они ~стили кафедру психологии немцем they have appointed a German to the chair of psychology. **3.** to deputize for, act for; to serve in place of.

замета|ть¹, ю, *impf. of* замести.

замета|ть², ю, *pf.* (*of* заметывать) to tack, baste; *p.p.p. as pred.* (*coll.*) замётано! all right!, agreed!

заме|таться, чусь, ~чешься, *pf.* to begin to rush about; to begin to toss.

заме|тить, чу, тишь, *pf.* (*of* ~чать) **1.** to notice, remark; ~тили ли вы, что он часто повторяется? have you noticed that he often repeats himself?; я ~тил за ним склонность повторяться I have noticed that he has a tendency to repeat himself. **2.** to take notice (of); to make a note (of). **3.** to remark, observe; «совершенно верно» — ~тил он 'perfectly true', he remarked.

заметк|а, и, *f.* **1.** mark. **2.** note; ~и на полях marginal notes; взять на ~y (*coll.*) to make a note (of). **3.** notice; paragraph; ни одна газета не удостоила выставки ~ой not a single newspaper gave the exhibition a notice.

заме́т|ный (~ен, ~на), *adj.* **1.** noticeable; appreciable; ме́жду ни́ми есть ~ная ра́зница в во́зрасте there is an appreciable difference in age between them; ~но (*as pred.*) it is noticeable; ~но, как он не лю́бит говори́ть о де́тстве it is noticeable that he does not like talking about his childhood. **2.** outstanding.

заме́тыва|ть, ю, *impf. of* замета́ть².

замеча́ни|е, я, *n.* **1.** remark, observation. **2.** reprimand; reproof; он у меня́ на ~и (*obs.*) he is in my bad books.

замеча́тел|ьный (~ен, ~ьна), *adj.* remarkable; splendid, wonderful.

замеча́|ть, ю, *impf. of* заме́тить.

заме́чен|ный (~, ~а), *p.p.p. of* заме́тить; з. (в+*p.*) discovered, noticed, detected (in); он был неоднокра́тно ~ во взя́точничестве he was several times discovered taking bribes.

замечта́|ться, юсь, *pf.* to give oneself up to day-dreaming; to fall into a reverie; он опя́ть ~лся he is day-dreaming again.

замеша́тельств|о, а, *n.* confusion; embarrassment; привести́ в з. to throw into confusion; прийти́ в з. to be confused, be embarrassed.

замеша́|ть, ю, *pf.* (в+*a.*) to mix up, entangle (in).

замеша́|ться, юсь, *pf.* (в+*a.*) **1.** to become mixed up, entangled (in). **2.** to mix (with), mingle (in, with); з. в толпу́ to mingle with the crowd.

заме́шива|ть(ся), ю(сь), *impf. of* замеси́ть *and* замеша́ть(ся).

заме́шк|а, и, *f.* (*coll.*) delay.

заме́шка|ться, юсь, *pf.* (*coll.*) to linger, tarry.

замеща́|ть, ю, *impf. of* замести́ть.

замеще́ни|е, я, *n.* **1.** substitution. **2.** appointment; бу́дет ко́нкурс на з. вака́нтной до́лжности there will be a competition to fill the vacancy.

замина́|ть, ю, *impf. of* замя́ть.

зами́нк|а, и, *f.* (*coll.*) **1.** hitch. **2.** hesitation (*in speech*).

замира́ни|е, я, *n.* dying out, dying down; он ждал с ~ем се́рдца he waited with a sinking heart.

замира́|ть, ю, *impf. of* замере́ть.

замире́ни|е, я, *n.* peace-making.

замир|и́ть, ю́, и́шь, *pf.* (*obs.*) to pacify; to reconcile.

замир|и́ться, ю́сь, и́шься, *pf.* (с+*i.*; *obs.*) to make peace (with).

замиря́|ть(ся), ю(сь), *impf. of* замири́ть(ся).

за́мкнут|ый (~, ~а), *adj.* **1.** exclusive. **2.** reserved; адмира́л — о́чень з. челове́к the admiral is a very reserved person; вести́ ~ую жизнь to lead an unsociable life.

замкн|у́ть, у́, ёшь, *pf.* (*of* замыка́ть) to lock; to close; з. ше́ствие, з. коло́нну to bring up the rear; з. цепь (*electr.*) to close the circuit.

замкн|у́ться, у́сь, ёшься, *pf.* (*of* замыка́ться) **1.** *pass. of* ~у́ть. **2.** to shut oneself up; з. в круг to form a circle; (*fig.*) з. в себя́ to become reserved, retire into oneself.

замле́|ть, ю, *pf.* (*coll.*) to become numb; to go to sleep (*of a limb*).

зам|ну́, нёшь, *see* ~я́ть.

замоги́льный, *adj.* sepulchral (*of voice*).

за́м|ок, ка, *m.* castle; возду́шные ~ки castles in the air.

зам|о́к, ка́, *m.* **1.** lock; америка́нский з. Yale lock; вися́чий з. padlock; под ~ко́м under lock and key; за семью́ ~ка́ми well and truly hidden. **2.** (*archit.*) keystone. **3.** bolt (*of fire-arm*). **4.** clasp (*of necklace, etc.*); clip (*of ear-ring*).

замока́|ть, ет, *impf. of* замо́кнуть.

замо́кн|уть, ет, *pf.* to become drenched, become soaked.

замо́лв|ить, лю, ишь, *pf.* (*coll.*); з. слове́чко за (+*a.*) to put in a word (for); прошу́ вас з. слове́чко за меня́ у нача́льства will you, please, put in a word for me with the authorities.

замол|и́ть, ю́, ~ишь, *pf.* (*of* зама́ливать); з. грехи́ to atone for one's sins by prayer.

замо́лка|ть, ю, *impf. of* замо́лкнуть.

замо́лк|нуть, ну, нешь, *past* ~, ~ла, *pf.* to fall silent; to stop, cease (*speaking, etc.*); внеза́пно пе́ние ~ло suddenly the singing ceased.

замолч|а́ть¹, у́, и́шь, *pf.* to fall silent; (*fig.*), to cease corresponding.

замолч|а́ть², у́, и́шь, *pf.* (*of* зама́лчивать) (*coll.*) to keep silent about; to hush up.

замора́живани|е, я, *n.* freezing; з. зарпла́ты wage-freezing.

замора́жива|ть, ю, *impf. of* заморо́зить.

заморд|ова́ть, у́ю, *pf.* (*coll.*) to torment.

замор|и́ть, ю́, и́шь, *pf.* (*of* зама́ривать) (*coll.*) **1.** to overwork; з. ло́шадь to founder a horse. **2.** to underfeed; з. червячка́ to have a bite, have a snack.

заморо́|женный, *p.p.p. of* ~зить *and adj.* frozen; iced; ~женное мя́со frozen meat; ~женное шампа́нское iced champagne.

заморо́|зить, жу, зишь, *pf.* (*of* замора́живать) to freeze; to ice.

за́морозк|и, ов, *no sing.* (light) frosts.

замо́рский, *adj.* oversea(s).

замо́рыш, а, *m.* (*coll.*) weakling; runt.

замо|сти́ть, щу́, сти́шь, *pf.* (*of* мости́ть *and* зама́щивать) to pave.

замота́|ть, ю, *impf.* (*of* зама́тывать) **1.** to wind, twist; to roll up. **2.** (*fig.*) to tire out. **3.** (*sl.*) to pinch, whip. **4.** (+*i.*) to begin to shake; з. голово́й to begin to shake one's head; з. хвосто́м to begin to wag its tail.

замота́|ться, ю́сь, *pf.* (*of* зама́тываться) (*coll.*) **1.** to wind round. **2.** to be tired out, be fagged out. **3.** to begin to shake; to begin to swing (*intrans.*).

замоч|и́ть, у́, ~ишь, *pf.* (*of* зама́чивать) to wet; to soak; з. лён to ret (rate, rait) flax.

замо́чник, а, *m.* locksmith.

замо́чн|ый, *adj. of* замо́к; ~ая сква́жина keyhole.

за́муж, *adv.*; вы́йти з. за кого́-н. to marry someone (*of woman*); вы́дать кого́-н. з. (за +*a.*) to give someone in marriage (to); она́ вы́шла з. за моряка́, несмотря́ на то́, что её оте́ц всё мечта́л вы́дать её за врача́ she has married a sailor despite the fact that her father always dreamed of marrying her to a doctor.

за́мужем, *adv.*; быть з. (за +*i.*) to be married (to) (*of woman*).

заму́жеств|о, а, *n.* marriage (*of woman*); у неё о́чень счастли́вое з. she is very happily married.

заму́жняя, *adj.* married (*of woman*).

замундшту́чива|ть, ю, *impf. of* замундшту́чить.

замундшту́ч|ить, у, ишь, *pf.* to bit.

замур|ова́ть, у́ю, *pf.* to brick up; to immure.

замуро́выва|ть, ю, *impf. of* замурова́ть.

заму́сл|ить, ю, ишь, *pf.* = замусо́лить.

замусо́лива|ть, ю, *impf. of* замусо́лить.

замусо́л|ить, ю, ишь, *pf.* to beslobber.

заму|ти́ть, чу́, ~ти́шь, *pf. of* мути́ть; он воды́ не ~ти́т he won't cause any trouble.

замухры́шк|а, и, *m. and f.* (*coll., pejor.*) poor specimen.

заму́чива|ть, ю, *impf. of* заму́чить.

заму́ч|ить, у, ишь, *pf.* (*of* му́чить *and* ~ивать) to torment; to wear out; to plague the life out of; to bore to tears.

заму́ч|иться, усь, ишься, *pf. of* му́читься.

за́мш|а, и, *f.* chamois (leather); suede.

за́мш|евый, *adj. of* ~а.

замше́лый, *adj.* mossy, moss-covered.

замше́|ть, ет, *pf.* to be overgrown with moss.

замыва́|ть, ю, *impf. of* замы́ть.

замы́зга|ть, ю, *pf.* (*coll.*) to wear out, ruin; to make dirty.

замыка́ни|е, я, *n.* locking; коро́ткое з. (*electr.*) short circuit.

замы́ка|ться, юсь, *pf.* (*coll.*) to be tired out.

замыка́|ть(ся), ю(сь), *impf. of* замкну́ть(ся).

за́мыс|ел, ла, *m.* project, plan; design, scheme; idea; его́ но́вая пье́са осно́вана на о́чень оригина́льном ~ле his new play is based on a very original idea; зло́е ~лы evil designs.

замы́сл|ить, ю, ишь, *pf.* (*of* замышля́ть)

(+*a. or inf.*) to plan; to contemplate, meditate; он ~ил самоуби́йство he contemplated suicide; они́ ~или убежа́ть под покро́вом темноты́ had planned to escape under cover of darkness.

замыслова́т|ый (~, ~а), *adj.* intricate, complicated.

зам|ы́ть, о́ю, о́ешь, *pf.* (*of* ~ыва́ть) to wash off, wash out.

замышля́|ть, ю, *impf. of* замы́слить.

зам|я́ть, ну́, нёшь, *pf.* (*of* ~ина́ть) (*coll.*) to put a stop to; з. разгово́р to change the subject.

зам|я́ться, ну́сь, нёшься, *pf.* (*coll.*) to stumble; to stop short (*in speech*).

за́навес, а, *m.* curtain; под з. (*theatr.*) near the end of an act.

занаве́|сить, шу, сишь, *pf.* (*of* ~шивать) to curtain; to cover.

занаве́с|ка, ки, *f.* curtain (*of light material*).

занаве́шива|ть, ю, *impf. of* занаве́сить.

занаво́|зить, жу, зишь, *pf.* **1.** (*dial.*) to manure. **2.** (*coll.*) to befoul.

зана́шива|ть, ю, *impf. of* заноси́ть².

зане́, *conj.* (*arch.*) since, because.

занеме́|ть, ю, *pf.* (*coll.*) to grow numb.

занемога́|ть, ю, *impf. of* занемо́чь.

занемо́|чь, гу́, жешь, гут, *past* ~г, ~гла́, *pf.* to fall ill, be taken ill.

занес|ти́, у́, ёшь, *past* ~, ~ла́, *pf.* (*of* заноси́ть¹) **1.** to bring import. **2.** to raise, lift; з. но́гу в стре́мя to raise one's foot into the stirrup. **3.** to note down; з. в протоко́л to enter in the minutes. **4.** (*coll.*) to carry (away); куда́ его́ нелёгкая ~ла́? where the devil has he got to?; (*impers.*) каки́м ве́тром вас сюда́ ~ло́? what wind blows you here? **5.** (*impers.*) з. сне́гом to cover with snow; доро́гу ~ло́ сне́гом the road is snowed up.

занес|ти́сь, у́сь, ёшься, *past* ~ся, ~ла́сь, *pf.* (*of* заноси́ться¹) (*coll., pejor.*) to be carried away (*fig.*).

занима́тел|ьный (~ен, ~ьна), *adj.* entertaining, diverting; absorbing.

занима́|ть¹, ю, *impf.* (*of* заня́ть) **1.** to occupy; з. го́род to occupy a city; з. кварти́ру to occupy a flat; крова́ть ~ет мно́го ме́ста the bed takes up a lot of room; он ~ет высо́кое положе́ние (*fig.*) he occupies a high post. **2.** to occupy; to interest; она́ ника́к не могла́ з. дете́й she simply could not keep the children occupied; его́ ~ют бо́льше всего́ вопро́сы филосо́фии his chief interest is in philosophy. **3.** to take (*of time*); э́то ~ет мно́го вре́мени this takes a lot of time. **4.** (*impers.; coll.*) дух ~ет it takes your breath away!

занима́|ть², ю, *impf.* (*of* заня́ть) to borrow.

занима́|ться¹, юсь, *impf.* (*of* заня́ться) (+*i.*) **1.** to be occupied (with), be engaged (in);

to work (at, on); to study; чем вы ~лись
вчера́? what were you doing yesterday?;
он ~ется подгото́вкой но́вой экспеди́ции
he is engaged in preparations for a new expedition; до заму́жества она́ ~лась му́зы-
кой before her marriage she was studying
music. 2. to busy oneself (with); to devote
oneself (to); з. собо́й to devote attention to
one's appearance. 3. (c+i.) to assist; to
attend to.

занима́|ться², *impf.* (*of* заня́ться) to catch
fire; ~лась заря́ day was breaking.

за́ново, *adv.* anew.

зано́з|а, ы, *f.* 1. splinter. 2. *m. and f.* (*fig.*,
coll.) thorn in the flesh; nagger.

зано́зист|ый (~, ~а), *adj.* (*coll.*) splintery;
(*fig.*) nagging.

зано|зи́ть, жу́, зи́шь, *pf.* to get a splinter
into.

зано́с¹, а, *m.* snow-drift.

зано́с², а, *m.* 1. bringing, importing, import. 2. raising, lifting.

зано|си́ть¹, шу́, ~сишь, *impf. of* занести́.

зано|си́ть², шу́, ~сишь, *pf.* (*of* зана́шивать)
to wear out.

зано|си́ться¹, шу́сь, ~сишься, *impf. of*
занести́сь.

зано|си́ться², ~сится, *pf.* to be worn out;
to wear out (*intrans.*).

зано́сный, *adj.* alien, imported.

зано́счив|ый (~, ~а), *adj.* arrogant,
haughty.

заноч|ева́ть, у́ю, *pf.* (*coll.*) to stay for the
night.

занумер|ова́ть, у́ю, *pf.* (*of* нумерова́ть) to
number.

заня́нч|ить, у, ишь, *pf.* (*coll.*) 1. to begin to
nurse. 2. to distress by unskilful nursing.

заня́ти|е, я, *n.* 1. occupation; pursuit. 2.
(*pl.*) studies; work; часы́ ~й working hours.

заня́т|ный (~ен, ~на), *adj.* (*coll.*) enter-
taining, amusing.

заня́той, *adj.* busy.

за́нятост|ь, и, *f.* being busy; у нас в э́ту
неде́лю больша́я з. we are very busy this
week; (*econ.*) по́лная з. full employment.

за́нят|ый (~, ~а́, ~о), *p.p.p. of* ~ь *and adj.*
1. occupied; здесь ~o this place is taken;
~o engaged (*of telephone number*); на э́том
заво́де ~o свы́ше ты́сячи рабо́чих over a
thousand people are employed in this
factory; быть ~ым собо́й to be self-centred.
2. busy.

зан|я́ть(ся), займу́(сь), займёшь(ся), *past*
~я́л(ся́), ~яла́(сь), ~я́ло(сь), *pf. of* занн-
ма́ть(ся); у кого́-н. дух ~я́ло (*impers.; coll.*)
to be out of breath; (*fig.*) to be breathless.

заобла́чн|ый, *adj.* (*poet., fig.*) beyond the
clouds; ~ая высь, *see* высь.

заодно́, *adv.* 1. in concert, at one; де́йство-

вать з. to act in concert; насчёт э́того
мужчи́ны — з. с же́нщинами on this the
men are in agreement with the women.
2. (*coll.*) at the same time; купи́те з. и
апельси́нов buy some oranges at the same
time.

заозёрный, *adj.* situated on the other side
of the lake.

заокеа́нский, *adj.* transoceanic.

заор|а́ть, у́, ёшь, *pf.* (*coll.*) to begin to bawl,
begin to yell.

заострённост|ь, и, *f.* pointedness, sharp-
ness.

заострённый, *p.p.p. of* заостри́ть *and adj.*
pointed, sharp.

заостр|и́ть, ю́, и́шь, *pf.* to sharpen; (*fig.*)
to stress, emphasize; з. внима́ние (на+a.)
to stimulate an interest (in).

заостр|и́ться, и́тся, *pf.* to become sharp;
to become pointed.

заостр|я́ть(ся), я́ет(ся), *impf. of* ~и́ть(ся).

зао́чник, а, *m.* student taking correspondence course; external student.

зао́чно, *adv.* 1. in one's absence. 2. by correspondence course, externally.

зао́чн|ый, *adj.* 1. (*leg.*) з. пригово́р judg-
ment by default. 2. з. курс correspondence
course; ~ое обуче́ние postal tuition.

за́пад, а, *m.* 1. west. 2. the West; the Occi-
dent.

запада́|ть, ю, *impf. of* запа́сть.

за́падник, а, *m.* Westernizer, Westernist.

за́падничеств|о, а, *n.* Westernism.

за́падный, *adj.* west, western; westerly.

**западн|я́, и́, g. pl.* ~е́й, *f.* trap, snare; по-
па́сть в ~ю́ to fall into a trap (*also fig.*).

запа́здывани|е, я, *n.* 1. lateness, being late.
2. (*tech.*) lag.

запа́здыва|ть, ю, *impf. of* запозда́ть; (*impf.
only; tech.*) to lag.

запа́ива|ть, ю, *impf. of* запая́ть.

**запа́йк|а, и, f.* soldering.

запак|ова́ть, у́ю, *pf.* to pack (up); to wrap
up, do up.

запако́выва|ть, ю, *impf. of* запакова́ть.

запа́ко|стить, щу, стишь, *pf. of* па́костить 1.

запа́л¹, а, *m.* fuse; touchhole.

запа́л², а, *m.* heaves; broken wind.

запа́лива|ть, ю, *impf. of* запали́ть.¹

запал|и́ть¹, ю́, и́шь, *pf.* (*coll.*) to set fire to,
kindle; to light.

запал|и́ть², ю́, и́шь, *pf.* (*dial.*) 1. to water
(*a horse*) when overheated. 2. to override
(*a horse*).

запал|и́ть³, ю́, и́шь, *pf.* (*coll.*) 1. to open
fire. 2. (+i.) to hurl.

запа́л|ьный, *adj. of* ~¹; ~ьная свеча́ spark-
ing plug.

**запа́льчивост|ь, и, f.* (quick) temper.

запа́льчив|ый, (~а), *adj.* quick-tempered.

запа́мят|овать, ую, *pf.* (*obs.*, *coll.*) to forget.

запанибра́та, *adv.*; (*coll.*) быть з. с кем-н. to be hail-fellow-well-met with someone.

запанибра́тский, *adj.* (*coll.*) hail-fellow- -well-met.

запанибра́тств|о, а, *n.* (*coll.*, *obs.*) hail- -fellow-well-met terms.

запа́рива|ть(ся), ю(сь), *impf. of* запа́рить- (ся).

запа́р|ить, ю, ишь, *pf.* 1. (*coll.*) to put into a sweat. 2. to stew; to bake.

запа́р|иться, юсь, ишься, *pf.* 1. (*coll.*) to get into a sweat. 2. to be worn out.

запарши́ве|ть, ю, *pf. of* парши́веть.

запа́рыва|ть, ю, *impf. of* запоро́ть.

запа́с, а, *m.* 1. supply, stock; reserve; з. това́ров stock-in-trade; прове́рить з. to take stock; про з. for emergency; отло- жи́ть про з. to put by; истощи́ть з. терпе́ния (*fig.*) to exhaust one's reserves of patience; приобрести́ большо́й з. слов to acquire a large vocabulary. 2. (*mil.*) re- serve; его́ уво́лили в з. he has been trans- ferred to the reserve. 3. hem; вы́пустить з. to let out.

запаса́|ть(ся), ю(сь), *impf. of* запасти́(сь).

запа́слив|ый (~, ~а), *adj.* thrifty; provident.

запа́сник, а, *m.* (*coll.*) reservist.

запасн|о́й, *adj.* 1. spare; reserve; з. вы́ход emergency exit; з. путь siding; з. батальо́н (*mil.*) depot battalion; ~а́я часть spare part; з. я́корь (*naut.*) sheet anchor, spare bower anchor. 2. *as noun* з., ~о́го, *m.* reservist.

запа́сн|ый, *adj.* = ~о́й.

запас|ти́, у́, ёшь, *past* ~, ~ла́, *pf.* (*of* ~а́ть) (+*a. or g.*) to stock, store; to lay in a stock of.

запас|ти́сь, у́сь, ёшься, *past* ~ся, ~ла́сь, *pf.* (*of* ~а́ться) (+*i.*) to provide oneself (with); to stock up (with); з. терпе́нием (*fig.*) to arm oneself with patience.

запа́|сть, ду́, дёшь, *past* ~л, *pf.* (*of* ~да́ть) to fall (behind); to sink down; слова́ его́ ~ли мне в ду́шу (*fig*). his words are im- printed in my mind.

запат|ова́ть, у́ю, *pf. of* патова́ть.

за́пах, а, *m.* smell.

запа|ха́ть, шу́, ~шешь, *pf.* (*agric.*) 1. to plough in. 2. to begin to plough.

запа́хива|ть¹(ся), ю(сь), *impf. of* запахну́ть- (ся).

запа́хива|ть², ю, *impf. of* запаха́ть.

запахн|у́ть, у, ешь, *pf.* to begin to emit a smell.

запахн|у́ть, у́, ёшь, *pf.* (*of* запа́хивать¹) 1. to wrap over (*folds of a garment*). 2. (*coll.*) з. за́навеску to draw the curtain.

запахн|у́ться, у́сь, ёшься, *pf.* (в+*a.*) to wrap oneself tighter (into).

запа́чка|ть, ю, *pf. of* па́чкать 1.

запа́шк|а, и, *f.* 1. ploughing up. 2. plough- -land, arable land.

запаш|о́к, ка́, *m.* (*coll.*) faint smell.

запая́|ть, ю, *pf.* (*of* запа́ивать) 1. to solder. 2. (*coll.*) з. кому́-н. в у́хо to box someone's ears.

запе́в, а, *m.* introduction (*to song*); solo part.

запева́л|а, ы, *m.* leader (of choir); precen- tor; (*fig.*, *coll.*) leader, instigator.

запева́|ть, ю, *impf.* (*of* запе́ть) to lead the singing, set the tune.

запека́нк|а, и, *f.* 1. baked pudding. 2. spiced brandy.

запека́|ть(ся), ю(сь), *impf. of* запе́чь(ся).

запелена́|ть, ю, *pf. of* пелена́ть.

запе́н|ить, ю, ишь, *pf.* to froth up.

запе́н|иться, юсь, ишься, *pf.* to begin to froth up, begin to foam (*intrans.*).

зап|ере́ть, ру́, рёшь, *past* ~ер, ~ерла́, ~ерло, *pf.* (*of* ~ира́ть) 1. to lock; з. на засо́в to bolt. 2. to lock in; to shut up. 3. to bar; to block up.

зап|ере́ться, ру́сь, рёшься, *past* ~ерся́, ~ерла́сь, ~ерло́сь, *pf.* (*of* ~ира́ться) 1. to lock oneself in. 2. (в+*p.*; *coll.*) to refuse to admit; to refuse to speak (about); to shut up (*intrans.*).

зап|е́ть, ою́, оёшь, *pf.* 1. *pf. of* ~ева́ть. 2. to begin to sing; з. пе́сню to break into a song; з. друго́е (*fig.*) to change one's tune. 3. (*coll.*) з. пе́сню to plug a song.

запеча́т|ать, аю, *pf.* (*of* ~ывать) to seal.

запечатлева́|ть(ся), ю(сь), *impf. of* запеча- тле́ть(ся).

запечатле́|ть, ю, *pf.* to imprint, impress, engrave; з. что-н. в па́мяти (*fig.*) to im- print something on one's memory.

запечатле́|ться, юсь, *pf.* (*fig.*) to imprint itself, stamp itself, impress itself; черты́ его́ лица́ ~лись у де́вочки в па́мяти his fea- tures stamped themselves in the little girl's memory.

запеча́тыва|ть, ю, *impf. of* запеча́тать.

запе́|чь, чь, ку́, чёшь, ку́т, *past* ~к, ~кла́, *pf.* (*of* ~ка́ть) to bake.

запе́|чься, чётся, ку́тся, *past* ~кся, ~кла́сь, *pf.* (*of* ~ка́ться) 1. to bake (*intrans.*). 2. to clot, coagulate. 3. to become parched.

запива́|ть, ю, *impf. of* запи́ть.

запина́|ться, юсь, *impf.* (*of* запну́ться) to hesitate; to stumble, halt (*in speech*); to stammer; з. ного́й to trip up; з. о ка́мень to strike against a stone.

запи́нк|а, и, *f.* hesitation (*in speech*).

запира́тельств|о, а, *n.* (*pejor.*) denial, dis- avowal.

запира́|ть(ся), ю(сь), *impf. of* запере́ть(ся).

запи|са́ть, шу́, ~шешь, *pf.* (*of* ~сывать) 1.

to note, make a note (of); to take down (in writing); to record (*with sound-recording apparatus*); з. ле́кцию to take notes of a lecture. **2.** to enter, register, enrol; ~ши́те меня́ пожа́луйста на приём к врачу́ please, make an appointment with the doctor for me. **3.** (+*a.* на+*a.*; *leg.*) to make over (to); он ~са́л всю со́бственность на свою́ племя́нницу he made over all his property to his niece. **4.** (*coll.*) to begin to write, begin to correspond.

запи|са́ться, шу́сь, ~шешься, *pf.* (*of* ~сы́ваться) **1.** to register, enter one's name, enrol; з. в клуб to join a club; з. к врачу́ to make an appointment with the doctor. **2.** to forget the time in writing. **3.** *pass. of* ~са́ть.

запи́ск|а, и, *f.* **1.** note; дипломати́ческая з., делова́я з. memorandum, minute. **2.** ~и (*pl.*) notes; memoirs; (*as title of learned journals*) transactions.

записно́|й¹, *adj.*; ~а́я кни́жка notebook.

записно́й², *adj.* (*coll.*) inveterate; regular.

запи́сыва|ть(ся), ю(сь), *impf. of* записа́ть(ся).

за́пис|ь, и, *f.* **1.** writing down; recording. **2.** entry; record; (*leg.*) deed; метри́ческая з. registration of vital statistics.

зап|и́ть, ью́, ьёшь, *past* ~и́л, ~ила́, ~и́ло, *pf.* (*of* ~ива́ть) **1.** (*coll.*; *past* ~и́л) to take to drink; to go on a blind. **2.** (*past* ~и́л; +*a.* and *i.*) to wash down (with); to take (with, after); з. пилю́лю водо́й to take a pill with water.

запиха́|ть, ю, *pf.* (*coll.*) to cram into.

запи́хива|ть, ю, *impf. of* запиха́ть.

запих|ну́ть, ну́, нёшь, *pf.* (*coll.*) = ~а́ть.

запи́чка|ть, ю, *pf.* (*coll.*) to stuff, cram.

запи|шу́, ~шешь, *see* ~са́ть.

запла́кан|ный (~, ~a), *adj.* tear-stained; in tears.

запла́|кать, чу, чешь, *pf.* to begin to cry.

заплани́р|овать, ую, *pf. of* плани́ровать¹.

запла́т|а, ы, *f.* patch (*in garments*); наложи́ть ~y (на+*a.*) to patch.

заплата́|ть, ю, *pf.* (*of* плата́ть) (*coll.*) to patch.

запла|ти́ть, чу́, ~тишь, *pf.* to pay.

запла́чк|а, и, *f.* (*anthrop.*; *dial.*) lamentation (*of bride, in course of wedding rite; at funerals*).

запла́|чу, чешь, *see* ~кать.

запла|чу́, ~тишь, *see* ~ти́ть.

заплёван|ный (~, ~a), *p.p.p. of* заплева́ть *and adj.* bespattered (with spittle); dirty.

запл|ева́ть, юю́, юёшь, *pf.* (*coll.*) to spit on; to spit at; (*fig.*) to rain curses on.

заплёвыва|ть, ю, *impf. of* заплева́ть.

запле|ска́ть, ска́ю, *and* ~щу́, ~щешь, *pf.* **1.** to splash. **2.** to begin to splash.

заплёскива|ть, ю, *impf. of* заплеска́ть *and* заплесну́ть.

заплёсневелый, *adj.* mouldy, mildewed.

заплёсневе|ть, ю, *pf. of* пле́сневеть.

заплесн|у́ть, у́, ёшь, *pf.* (*of* заплёскивать) (*coll.*) to splash into; to swamp.

запле|сти́, ту́, тёшь, *past* ~л, ~ла́, *pf.* to braid, plait.

запле|сти́сь, ту́сь, тёшься, *past* ~лся, ~ла́сь, *pf.* **1.** (*coll.*) to stumble, be unsteady on one's legs; to falter (*in speech*). **2.** (*dial.*) to wind (*intrans.*). **3.** *pass. of* ~сти́.

заплета́|ть(ся), ю(сь), *impf. of* заплести́(сь).

заплечный, *adj.* over the shoulders; з. мешо́к rucksack; з. ма́стер (*obs.*) executioner.

заплеч|ье, ья, *g. pl.* ~ий *and* ~ьев, *n.* shoulder-blade.

запломбир|ова́ть, у́ю, *pf.* (*of* пломбирова́ть *and* ~о́вывать) **1.** з. зуб to stop, fill a tooth. **2.** to seal.

запломбиро́выва|ть, ю, *impf. of* запломбирова́ть.

заплута́|ться, юсь, *pf.* (*coll.*) to lose one's way, stray.

запль́в, а, *m.* round, heat (*of water sports*).

заплыва́|ть, ю, *impf. of* заплы́ть.

заплы́|ть¹, ву́, вёшь, *past* ~л, ~ла́, ~ло, *pf.* to swim far out; to sail away.

заплы́|ть², ву́, вёшь, *past* ~л, ~ла́, ~ло, *pf.* to be swollen; to be bloated; ~вшие жи́ром глаза́ bloated eyes.

запн|у́ться, у́сь, ёшься, *pf. of* запина́ться.

запове́да|ть, ю, *pf.* (*of* запове́дывать) (*rhet.*) to command.

запове́дник, а, *m.* reserve; preserve; госуда́рственный з. national park.

запове́дн|ый, *adj.* **1.** prohibited; з. лес forest reserve; ~ое име́ние entailed estate. **2.** (*poet.*) precious.

запове́дыва|ть, ю, *impf. of* запове́дать.

за́повед|ь, и, *f.* precept; (*rel. and fig.*) commandment; де́сять ~ей the Ten Commandments.

запода́зрива|ть, ю, *impf. of* заподо́зрить.

заподо́зр|ить, ю, ишь, *pf.* **1.** (+*a.* в+*p.*) to suspect (of); его́ ~или в прича́стности к за́говору he was suspected of complicity in the plot. **2.** (*obs.*) to suspect, be suspicious of; з. чьи-н. наме́рения to suspect someone's intentions.

запо́ем, *adv.*; пить з. to be a heavy drinker; (*fig., coll.*) heavily, unrestrainedly; чита́ть з. to read avidly; кури́ть з. to smoke like a chimney.

запозда́лый, *adj.* belated.

запозда́|ть, ю, *pf.* (*of* запа́здывать) (с+*i.*) to be late (with); он ~л с упла́той аре́нды he is late in paying his rent.

запо|и́ть, ю́, и́шь, *pf.* (*coll., dial.*) to give too much to drink (to).

запо́|й, я, *m.* (addiction to periodical) hard drinking; пить ~ем, *see* ~ем; страда́ть ~ем to have a weakness for the bottle.

запо́й|ный, *adj. of* ~; з. пери́од drunken bout; з. пья́ница chronic drunkard.

запола́скива|ть, ю, *impf. of* заполоска́ть *and* заполоснуть.

запо́лза|ть, ю, *pf.* to begin to crawl.

заполза́|ть, ю, *impf. of* заползти́.

заполз|ти́, у́, ёшь, *past* ~, ~ла́, *pf.* (в, под+*a.*) to creep, crawl (into, under).

запо́лн|ить, ю, ишь, *pf.* (*of* ~я́ть) to fill in, fill up; чем вы ~или вре́мя? how did you fill in the time?; з. бла́нк to fill in a form; з. пробе́л to fill a gap.

заполня́|ть, ю, *impf. of* запо́лнить.

заполон|и́ть, ю́, и́шь, *pf.* (*folk poet. and arch.*) to take captive; (*fig.*) to captivate, enthrall.

заполон|я́ть, я́ю, *impf. of* ~и́ть.

заполо|ска́ть, щу́, ~щешь, *pf.* (*of* запола́скивать) (*coll.*) 1. to begin to rinse. 2. to rinse out.

заполо|ска́ться, щу́сь, ~щешься, *pf.* (*coll.*) 1. to begin to paddle. 2. to enjoy paddling.

заполосн|у́ть, у́, ёшь, *pf.* (*of* запола́скивать) (*coll.* to rinse out.

заполуч|а́ть, а́ю, *impf. of* ~и́ть.

заполуч|и́ть, у́, ~ишь, *pf.* (*coll.*) to get hold of, pick up; я мог бы з. биле́ты на представле́ние в суббо́ту I could get tickets for Saturday's performance; з. на́сморк to pick up a cold.

заполя́рный, *adj.* (*geogr.*) 1. polar (*situated within one or other of the polar circles*). 2. trans-polar; з. возду́шный путь trans-polar air route.

заполя́рь|е, я, *n.* (*geogr.*) polar regions.

запомина́|ть(ся), ю(сь), *impf. of* запо́мнить(ся); ~ющее устро́йство computer memory.

запо́мн|ить, ю, ишь, *impf. and pf.* 1. (*pf.*) to memorize. 2. (*pf.*) (+*neg.*; *coll.*) to remember; никто́ не ~ит тако́й жары́ в ма́е ме́сяце no one remembers such heat in May.

запо́мн|иться, юсь, ишься, *pf.* to be retained, stick in one's memory; ему́ ~ился день землетрясе́ния the day of the earthquake is stuck in his memory.

за́понк|а, и, *f.* cuff-link; stud.

запо́р¹, а, *m.* 1. bolt; lock; на ~(e) locked; bolted (and barred). 2. (*coll.*) closing; locking; bolting.

запо́р², а, *m.* constipation.

запора́шива|ть, ет, *impf. of* запороши́ть.

запоро́ж|ец, ца, *m.* (*hist.*) Zaporozhian Cossack.

запоро́жский, *adj.* (*hist.*) Zaporozhian.

запор|о́ть, ю́, ~ешь, *pf.* (*of* запа́рывать)

(*coll.*) 1. to flog to death. 2. to begin to talk (nonsense).

запорош|и́ть, и́т, *pf.* (*of* запора́шивать) 1. (+*i.*) to powder (with); (*impers.*) доро́гу ~и́ло сне́гом the road was powdered with snow; глаза́ мой ~и́ло пы́лью there is dust in my eyes. 2. to begin to powder.

запорхн|у́ть, у́, ёшь, *pf.* (*coll.*) to flutter (away, in).

запо|сти́ться, щу́сь, сти́шься, *pf.* (*coll.*) 1. to begin to fast. 2. to make oneself weak by fasting.

запотева́|ть, ю, *impf. of* запоте́ть.

запоте́лый, *adj.* misted; dim; (*from perspiration*).

запоте́|ть, ю, *pf.* (*of* поте́ть *and* ~ва́ть) to mist over.

запо́тч|евать, ую, *pf.* (*coll.*) to tire with entertainment.

започива́|ть, ю, *pf.* (*obs.*) to retire (*for the night*).

зап|ою́, оёшь, *see* ~е́ть.

запра́вдашный (*coll., dial.*) true, authentic.

заправи́л|а, ы, *m.* (*coll.*) boss.

запра́в|ить, лю, ишь, *pf.* (*of* ~ля́ть) 1. to insert; з. брю́ки в сапоги́ to tuck one's trousers into one's boots. 2. to prepare; to adjust; з. ла́мпу to trim a lamp; з. автомоби́ль бензи́ном to fill a car up with petrol. 3. (+*i.*) to mix in; to season (with); з. со́ус муко́й to thicken a sauce with flour.

запра́в|иться, люсь, ишься, *pf.* (*of* ~ля́ться) 1. (*coll.*) to satisfy hunger; to eat one's fill. 2. з. (горю́чим) to refuel (*intrans.*).

запра́вк|а, и, *f.* 1. seasoning. 2. refuelling.

заправля́|ть(ся), ю(сь), *impf. of* запра́вить(ся).

запра́вский, *adj.* (*coll.*) real, true; thorough; он — з. моря́к he is a real sailor.

запра́шива|ть, ю, *impf. of* запроси́ть.

запреде́льный, *adj.* (*obs.*) 1. lying beyond the bounds (of). 2. fantastic; other-worldly.

запресто́льный, *adj.* (*eccl.*) situated behind the altar; з. о́браз altar-piece.

запре́т, а, *m.* prohibition, ban; наложи́ть з. (на+*a.*) to place a ban (on); быть под запре́том to be banned.

запрети́тельн|ый, *adj.* prohibitive; prohibitory; (*econ.*) ~ая по́шлина prohibitive duty.

запре|ти́ть, щу́, ти́шь, *pf.* (*of* ~ща́ть) to prohibit, forbid, ban; врач ~ти́л мне кури́ть, врач ~ти́л мне куре́ние the doctor has forbidden me to smoke; з. пье́су to ban a play.

запре́тн|ый, *adj.* forbidden; ~ая зо́на (*mil.*) restricted area.

запреща́|ть, ю, *impf. of* запрети́ть.

запреща́|ться, ется, *impf.* to be forbidden, to be prohibited; (*in official notices, etc.*) вход ~ется no entry; кури́ть ~ется no smoking.

запрещёни|е, я, *n.* prohibition; (*leg.*) з. на
иму́щество distraint, arrest on property;
суде́бное з. injunction.

заприме́|тить, чу, тишь, *pf.* (*coll.*) 1. to
notice, perceive. 2. to recognize, spot; я
~тил его́ в толпе́ по кра́сной руба́шке I
spotted him in the crowd by his red shirt.

заприхо́д|овать, ую, *pf. of* приходовать.

запрода|ва́ть, ю, ёшь, *impf. of* ~ть.

запрода́ж|а, и, *f.* (*comm.*) forward contract,
provisional sale.

запрода́ж|ный, *adj. of* ~a; ~ная за́пись
document concerning sale.

запрод|а́ть, а́м, а́шь, а́ст, ади́м, ади́те,
аду́т, *past* ~а́л, ~ала́, ~а́ло, *pf.* (*of* ~ава́ть)
(*comm.*) to conclude a forward contract (on),
sell on part-payment; to agree to sell.

запроекти́р|овать, ую, *pf. of* проекти́ро-
вать¹ I.

запроки́дыва|ть, ю, *impf. of* запроки́нуть.

запроки́н|уть, у, ешь, *pf.* (*coll.*) to throw
back; он захохота́л ~ув го́лову he threw
back his head and guffawed.

запроки́н|уться, усь, ешься, *pf.* (*coll.*) to
~ack, slump back.

~апропада́|ть, ю, *impf. of* запропа́сть.

запропа|сти́ть, щу́, сти́шь, *pf.* (*coll.*) to
mislay.

запропа|сти́ться, щу́сь, сти́шься, *pf.* (*coll.*)
to get lost, disappear; куда́ ты ~сти́лся?
where on earth did you get to?

запропа́|сть, ду́, дёшь, *past* ~л, *pf.* (*of*
~да́ть) (*coll.*) to get lost, disappear.

запро́с, а, *m.* 1. inquiry; (*polit.*) question.
2. overcharging; це́ны без ~a fixed prices.
3. (*pl. only*) spiritual needs.

запро|си́ть, шу́, ~сишь, *pf.* (*of* запра́ши-
вать) 1. (o+*p.*) to inquire (about); (+*a.*)
to inquire (of), question; мини́стра ~си́ли
o его́ расхо́дах the Minister was questioned
about his expenditure. 2. з. сли́шком вы-
со́кую це́ну to ask an exorbitant price.

за́просто, *adv.* (*coll.*) without ceremony,
without formality.

запротоколи́р|овать, ую, *pf.* to enter in the
minutes.

запротоко́л|ить, ю, ишь, *pf.* (*coll.*) = ~и́ро-
вать.

запро|шу́, ~сишь, *see* ~си́ть.

зап|ру́, рёшь, *see* ~ере́ть.

запру́д|а, ы, *f.* 1. dam, weir 2. mill-pond.

запру́|дить, жу́, ~дишь, *pf.* 1. (~дишь) to
dam. 2. (~ди́шь) (*fig., coll.*) to block (up);
to fill to overflowing.

запружа́|ть, ю, *impf. of* запруди́ть.

запру́жива|ть, ю, *impf.,* = запружа́ть.

запры́га|ть, ю, *pf.* to begin to jump; (*coll.*)
се́рдце у неё ~ло her heart began to
thump.

запры́гива|ть, ю, *impf. of* запры́гнуть.

запры́гн|уть, у, ешь, *pf.* (за+*a.*; *coll.*) to
leap (over).

запры́ска|ть, ю, *pf.* (*coll.*) 1. to begin to
sprinkle. 2. to besprinkle.

запры́скива|ть, ю, *impf. of* запры́скать.

запря́|г, гла́, *see* ~чь.

запряга́|ть, ю, *impf. of* запря́чь.

запря|гу́, жёшь, гу́т, *see* ~чь.

запря́жк|а, и, *f.* 1. harnessing. 1. equipage.

запря́|тать, чу, чешь, *pf.* (*coll.*) to hide.

запря́|таться, чусь, чешься, *pf.* (*coll.*) to
hide oneself.

запря́тыва|ть(ся), ю(сь), *impf. of* запря́-
тать(ся).

запря́|чь, гу́, жёшь, гу́т, *past* ~г, ~гла́, *pf.*
(*of* ~га́ть) to harness (*also fig.*); з. воло́в to
yoke oxen.

запря́|чься, гу́сь, жёшься, гу́тся, *past* ~гся,
~гла́сь, *pf.* 1. *pass. of* ~чь. 2. (*fig., coll.*) to
harness oneself; to buckle to, get down to.

запу́ганный *p.p.p. of* запуга́ть *and adj.*
broken-spirited.

запуга́|ть, ю, *pf.* to intimidate, cow.

запу́гива|ть, ю, *impf. of* запуга́ть.

запу́дрива|ть, ю, *impf. of* запу́дрить.

запу́др|ить, ю, ишь, *pf.* to powder.

запузы́рива|ть, ю, *impf.* (*sl.*) to do some-
thing vigorously; з. на фортепья́но to
knock out a tune on the piano.

запул|и́ть, ю́, и́шь, *pf.* (+*a. or i.*; *coll., dial.*)
to sling, chuck; з. ка́мнем в окно́ to sling a
stone at a window.

запус|ка́ть, ка́ю, *impf. of* ~ти́ть.

запусте́лый, *adj.* neglected; desolate.

запусте́ни|е, я, *n.* neglect; desolation.

запусте́|ть, ет, *pf.* to fall into neglect; to
become desolate.

запу|сти́ть, щу́, ~стишь, *pf.* (*of* ~ска́ть)
1. (+*i.* в+*a.*; *coll.*) to throw (at), fling (at);
он ~сти́л кирпичо́м в окно́ he flung a brick
at the window. 2. (в+*a.*) to thrust (*hands,
etc.,* into); ко́шка ~сти́ла ко́гти в мышь the
cat dug its claws into the mouse; з. ко́гти,
ла́пы, ру́ки (в+*a.*; *fig.*) to get one's hands
on; з. глаза́ (*pejor.*) to let one's eyes roam.
3. to start (up) (*mechanism*); з. мото́р to
start up the engine; з. раке́ту to launch
a rocket. 4. (в+*a.*) (*coll.*) to put (into), let
loose (in); з. коро́в в луг to let cows loose
in a meadow.

запу|сти́ть², щу́, ~стишь, *pf.* (*of* ~ска́ть)
1. to neglect, allow to fall into neglect; з.
дела́ to neglect one's affairs; з. сад to
neglect a garden. 2. to allow to develop
unchecked; он ~сти́л на́сморк и тепе́рь
заболе́л бронхи́том he neglected his cold
and now he is ill with bronchitis.

запу́тан|ный, *p.p.p. of* запу́тать *and adj.*
tangled; (*fig.*) intricate, involved; з. вопро́с
knotty question.

запу́та|ть, ю, *pf.* **1.** to tangle (up). **2.** (*fig.*) to confuse; to complicate; to muddle; его́ сообще́ние ~ло де́ло his statement has complicated matters; тако́го ро́да вопро́сы то́лько ~ют кандида́тов questions of this kind will only confuse the candidates. **3.** (в+*a.*; *fig.*) to involve (in).

запу́та|ться, юсь, *pf.* **1.** to become entangled; to foul (*intrans.*); (в+*p.*; *fig.*) to entangle oneself (in), be caught (in). **2.** (в+*p.*; *fig.*) to become entangled (in), become involved (in); to become complicated; з. в долга́х to become involved in debts; докла́дчик ~лся в слова́х the lecturer became tied up in knots.

запу́тыва|ть(ся), ю(сь), *impf.* of запу́тать(ся).

запуш|и́ть, и́т *pf.* to cover lightly (*of snow or frost*).

запу́щен|ный, *p.p.p.* of запусти́ть² and *adj.* neglected.

запча́ст|ь, и, *f.* spare part.

запыла́|ть, ю, *pf.* to blaze up, flare up.

запыл|и́ть, ю́, и́шь, *pf.* (*of* пыли́ть) to cover with dust, make dusty.

запыл|и́ться, ю́сь, и́шься, *pf.* (*of* пыли́ться) to become dusty.

запыха́|ться, юсь, *impf.* (*coll.*) to puff, pant.

запы́ха|ться, юсь, *pf.* (*coll.*) to be out of breath.

запьяне́|ть, ю, *pf.* (*coll.*) to get drunk.

запья́нств|овать, ую, *pf.* to take to drink.

запя́сть|е, я, *n.* **1.** wrist; (*anat.*) carpus. **2.** (*poet.*) bracelet.

запя́т|а́я, о́й, *f.* **1.** comma. **2.** (*coll.*) difficulty, snag.

запя́т|ки, ок, *no sing.* footboard (*at back of carriage*).

запятна́|ть, ю, *pf.* of пятна́ть.

зараба́тыва|ть(ся), ю(сь), *impf.* of зарабо́тать(ся).

зарабо́та|ть, ю, *pf.* **1.** to earn. **2.** to begin to work; to start (up).

зарабо́та|ться, юсь, *pf.* (*coll.*) **1.** to overwork, tire oneself out with work. **2.** to work late; он вчера́ ~лся далеко́ за́ полночь he went on working long after midnight last night.

за́работн|ый, *adj.*; ~ая пла́та wages, pay, salary.

за́работ|ок, ка, *m.* **1.** earnings; лёгкий з. easy money. **2.** (*pl. only*) (seasonal) labour, work.

зара́внива|ть, ю, *impf.* of заровня́ть.

заража́емост|ь, и, *f.* susceptibility to infection.

заража́|ть(ся), ю(сь), *impf.* of зарази́ть(ся).

зараже́ни|е, я, *n.* infection.

зара|жу́, зи́шь, *see* ~зи́ть.

зара́з, *adv.* (*coll.*) at once; at a sitting; at one fell swoop.

зара́з|а, ы, *f.* **1.** infection, contagion. **2.** (*fig.*, *coll.*) pest, plague (*of person*).

зарази́тел|ьный (~ен, ~ьна), *adj.* infectious; catching; (*fig.*) з. смех infectious laughter.

зара|зи́ть, жу́, зи́шь, *pf.* (*of* ~жа́ть) (+*i.*) to infect (with); (*also fig.*) з. свои́м приме́ром to infect with one's example.

зара|зи́ться, жу́сь, зи́шься, *pf.* (*of* ~жа́ться) (+*i.*) to be infected (with); catch (*also fig.*).

зара́з|ный (~ен, ~на), *adj.* **1.** infectious; contagious. **2.** of *or* for infectious diseases; з. бара́к infectious diseases ward; з. больно́й patient suffering from infectious disease, infectious case; *as noun* з., ~ного, *m.*, ~ная, ~ной, *f.* infectious case.

зара́не, *adv.* (*obs.*) = ~е.

зара́нее, *adv.* beforehand; in good time; заплати́ть з. to pay in advance; преступле́ние с з. обду́манным наме́рением premeditated crime; ра́доваться з. (+*d.*) to look forward (to).

зарапорт|ова́ться, у́юсь, *pf.* (*coll.*) to let one's tongue run away with one.

зараста́|ть, ю, *impf.* of зарасти́.

зараст|и́, у́, ёшь, *past* заро́с, заросла́, *pf.* **1.** (+*i.*) to be overgrown (with). **2.** (*of a wound*) to heal, skin over.

зарв|а́ться, у́сь, ёшься, *past* ~а́лся, ~ала́сь, ~а́ло́сь, *pf.* (*of* зарыва́ться) (*coll.*) to go too far; to overstep the mark.

зарде́|ть, ю, *pf.* (*poet.*) = ~ться I.

зарде́|ться, юсь, *pf.* **1.** (*poet.*) to redden, grow red. **2.** to blush.

за́рев|о, а, *n.* glow; з. (от) пожа́ра the glow of a fire.

зар|ево́й, *adj.* of ~ево.

зарегистри́р|овать, ую, *pf.* (*of* регистри́ровать) to register.

зарегистри́р|оваться, уюсь, *pf.* (*of* регистри́роваться) **1.** to register oneself. **2.** (*coll.*) to register one's marriage. **3.** *pass.* of ~овать.

зарегистр|ова́ть(ся), у́ю(сь), *pf.*, = ~и́ровать(ся).

заре́з, а, *m.* **1.** (*coll.*) disaster; до ~у extremely, badly, urgently; мне до ~у нужны́ пять рубле́й I badly need five roubles. **2.** (*dial.*) killing, slaughtering.

заре́|зать, жу, жешь, *pf.* **1.** to murder; to knife; з. свинью́ to stick a pig; (*of a wolf*) to devour, kill; хоть заре́жь (*coll.*) extremely, urgently; come what may. **2.** (*fig.*) to undo, be the undoing of; to do for; без ножа́ з. to do for; to make mincemeat of.

зареза́|ть(ся), ю(сь), *impf.* of заре́зать(ся).

заре́|заться, жусь, жешься, *pf.* (*coll.*) cut one's throat.

заре́зыва|ть(ся), ю(сь), *impf.*, = заре́за́ть(ся).

зарека́|ться, ю́сь, *impf. of* заре́чься.

зареко́менд|ова́ть, у́ю, *pf. only in phrase* з. себя́ (+*i.*) to prove oneself, show oneself (to be); хорошо́ з. себя́ to show to advantage.

зарекомендо́выва|ть, ю, *impf. of* зарекомендова́ть.

заре|ку́сь, чёшься, ку́тся, *see* ~чься.

заре́чный, *adj.* situated on the other side of the river.

заре́чь|е, я, *n.* part of town, *etc.*, on the other side of a river.

заре́|чься, ку́сь, чёшься, ку́тся, *past* ~кся, ~кла́сь, *pf. (of* ~ка́ться) (+*inf.*; *coll.*) to renounce; to promise to give up, vow to give up; он ~кся кури́ть he has promised to give up smoking.

заржа́ве|ть, ет, *pf. (of* ржа́веть) to rust; to have got rusty.

заржа́влен|ный (~, ~а), *adj.* rusty.

зарис|ова́ть, у́ю, *pf. (of* ~о́вывать) to sketch.

зарис|ова́ться, у́юсь, *pf. (of* ~о́вываться) (*coll.*) to spend too much time in drawing.

зарисо́вк|а, и, *f.* 1. sketching. 2. sketch.

зарисо́выва|ть(ся), ю(сь), *impf. of* зарисова́ть(ся).

за́р|иться, юсь, ишься, *impf. (of* по~) (на+*a.*; *coll.*) to hanker (after).

зарни́ц|а, ы, *f.* summer lightning.

заровня́|ть, ю, *pf. (of* зара́внивать) to level, even up; з. я́му to fill up a hole.

заро|ди́ть, жу́, ди́шь, *pf. (of* ~жда́ть) to generate, engender (*also fig.*).

заро|ди́ться, жу́сь, ди́шься, *pf. pass. of* ~ди́ть; (*fig.*) to arise; у него́ ~ди́лось сомне́ние a doubt arose in his mind.

заро́дыш, а, *m.* (*biol.*) foetus; (*bot.*) bud; (*fig.*) embryo, germ; подави́ть в ~е to nip in the bud.

заро́дышевый, *adj.* embryonic.

зарожда́|ть(ся), ю(сь), *impf. of* зароди́ть(ся).

зарожде́ни|е, я, *n.* conception; (*fig.*) origin.

заро|жу́, ди́шь, *see* ~ди́ть.

заро́к, а, *m.* 1. (solemn) promise, vow, pledge, undertaking; дать з. to pledge oneself, give an undertaking. 2. (*dial.*) charm, incantation.

зарон|и́ть, ю́, ~ишь, *pf.* 1. (*coll.*) to drop (behind); to let fall. 2. (*fig.*) to excite, arouse; з. сомне́ния to give rise to doubts.

зарон|и́ться, ю́сь, ~ишься, *pf.* (в+*a.*; *obs.*) to sink in, make an impression (on).

зароня́|ть, ю, *impf. of* зарони́ть.

за́росл|ь, и, *f.* brake; thicket.

зар|о́ю, о́ешь, *see* ~ы́ть.

зарпла́т|а, ы, *f.* (*abbr. of* за́работная пла́та) wages, pay, salary.

заруба́|ть, ю, *impf. of* заруби́ть.

зарубе́жный, *adj.* foreign.

заруб|и́ть, лю́, ~ишь, *pf. (of* ~а́ть) 1. to kill (*with sabre, axe, etc.*). 2. to notch, make an incision (on); ~и́ э́то себе́ на носу́, на лбу, на стене́ (*coll.*) put that in your pipe and smoke it. 3. (*tech.*) to hew.

зару́бк|а, и, *f.* 1. notch; incision. 2. (*tech.*) hewing.

зарубц|ева́ться, у́ется, *pf. (of* рубцева́ться *and* ~о́вываться) to cicatrize.

зарубцо́выва|ться, ется, *impf. of* зарубцева́ться.

зару́бщик, а, *m.* (coal-)hewer.

заруга́|ть, ю, *pf.* (*coll.*) to abuse, scold.

зарумя́нива|ть(ся), ю(сь), *impf. of* зарумя́нить(ся).

зарумя́н|ить, ю, ишь, *pf.* to redden.

зарумя́н|иться, юсь, ишься, *pf.* 1. to redden (*intrans.*); to blush, colour. 2. (*coll.*) to brown, bake brown.

заруч|а́ться, а́юсь, *impf. of* ~и́ться.

заруч|и́ться, у́сь, и́шься, *pf.* 1. (+*i.*) to secure; з. подде́ржкой to enlist support; з. согла́сием to obtain consent. 2. (*sl.*) to secure oneself (*in a suit at cards*).

зару́чк|а, и, *f.* (*coll.*) pull, protection.

зарыва́|ть, ю, *impf. of* зары́ть.

зарыва́|ться¹, юсь, *impf. of* зары́ться.

зарыва́|ться², юсь, *impf. of* зарва́ться.

зарыда́|ть, ю, *pf.* to begin to sob.

зар|ы́ть, о́ю, о́ешь, *pf. (of* ~ыва́ть) to bury; з. тала́нт в зе́млю (*fig.*) to bury one's talent, hide one's light under a bushel.

зар|ы́ться, о́юсь, о́ешься, *pf. (of* ~ыва́ться) 1. to bury oneself; з. лицо́м в поду́шку to bury one's head in the pillow; з. в дере́вне (*fig., coll.*) to bury oneself in the country; з. в кни́ги to bury oneself in one's books. 2. (*mil.*) to dig in. 3. (*dial.*) to become fussy.

зар|я́, и́, *a.* ~ю́ *and* (*rare*) зо́рю, *pl.* зо́ри, зорь, ~я́м, *and* зо́рям, *f.* 1. (*a.* ~ю́) dawn, daybreak; на ~е́ at dawn, at daybreak; встать с ~ей to rise at crack of dawn; что ты встал ни свет ни з.? what made you get up at this unearthly hour? 2. (*a.* ~ю́) (вече́рняя) з. sunset, evening glow; от ~и́ до ~и́ from night to morning, all night long. 3. (*a.* ~ю́) (*fig.*) start, outset; dawn, threshold. 4. (*a.* зо́рю, *d. pl.* зо́рям) (*mil.*) reveille; retreat; бить зо́рю to beat retreat.

заря́д, а, *m.* 1. charge (*also electr.*), cartridge; холосто́й з. blank cartridge; (*fig., coll.*) round (*of drinks*). 2. (*fig.*) fund, supply.

заря|ди́ть¹, жу́, ~ди́шь, *pf. (of* ~жа́ть) 1. to load (*fire-arm*). 2. (*electr.*) to charge.

заря|ди́ть², жу́, ди́шь, *pf.* (*coll.*) to keep on, persist in; с утра́ ~ди́л дождь it has kept on raining since the morning; он ~ди́л одно́ и то же he keeps saying the same thing over and over again.

заря|ди́ться, жу́сь, ～ди́шься, *pf.* (*of* ～жа́ться) **1.** to be loaded; (*electr.*) to be charged. **2.** (*fig., coll.*) to cheer oneself up, revive oneself.

заря́дк|а, и, *f.* **1.** loading (*of fire-arms*); (*electr.*) charging. **2.** exercises; drill.

заря́д|ный, *adj. of* ～; з. я́щик ammunition wagon.

заряжа́|ть(ся), ю(сь), *impf. of* заряди́ть(ся).

заряжа́|ющий, *pres. part. act. of* ～ть; *as noun* з., ～ющего, *m.* (*mil.*) loader.

заря|жу́, ～ди́шь, *see* ～ди́ть.

заса́д|а, ы, *f.* ambush.

заса|ди́ть, жу́, ～дишь, *pf.* (*of* ～жива́ть) **1.** (+*a. and i.*) to plant (with); з. сад плодо́выми дере́вьями to plant a garden with fruit-trees. **2.** (+*a.* в+*a.; coll.*) to plant (into), plunge (into), drive (into). **3.** (*coll.*) to shut in, confine; to keep in; з. (в тюрьму́) to put in prison, lock up; боле́знь на це́лый ме́сяц ～ди́ла меня́ в го́спиталь illness kept me in hospital for a whole month. **4.** (+*a.* за+*a.; coll.*) to set (to); его́ ～ди́ли за изуче́ние ру́сского языка́ he was set to learn Russian. **5.** (в+*a.*) get (*a knife, axe, etc.*) stuck (in).

заса́дк|а, и, *f.* planting.

заса́жива|ть, ю, *impf. of* засади́ть.

заса́жива|ться, юсь, *impf.* **1.** *impf. of* засе́сть. **2.** *pass. of* ～ть.

заса|жу́, ～дишь, *see* ～ди́ть.

заса́лива|ть¹, ю, *impf. of* заса́лить.

заса́лива|ть², ю, *impf. of* засоли́ть.

заса́л|ить, ю, ишь, *pf.* (*of* ～ивать¹) to soil, make greasy.

заса́рива|ть, ю, *impf. of* засори́ть.

заса́сыва|ть, ю, *impf. of* засоса́ть.

заса́харен|ный, *p.p.p. of* заса́харить *and adj.* candied; ～ные фру́кты crystallized fruits, candied fruits.

заса́харива|ть, ю, *impf. of* заса́харить.

заса́хар|ить, ю, ишь, *pf.* (*of* ～ивать) to candy.

засверка́|ть, ю, *pf.* to begin to sparkle, begin to twinkle.

засве|ти́ть, чу́, ～ти́шь, *pf.* **1.** to light. **2.** (+*d.* в+*a.; coll.*) to strike, hit; з. кому́-н. в физионо́мию кулако́м to stick one's fist in someone's face.

засве|ти́ться, ～тится, *pf.* to light up (*also fig.*).

засветле́|ть, ю, *pf.* to show up.

за́светло, *adv.* (*coll.*) before nightfall, before dark.

засве|чу́, ～тишь, *see* ～ти́ть.

засвиде́тельств|овать, ую, *pf. of* свиде́тельствовать 2.

засви|ста́ть, щу́, ～щешь = ～сте́ть.

засви|сте́ть, щу́, сти́шь, *pf.* **1.** to begin to whistle.

засда|ва́ться, ю́сь, ёшься, *impf. of* ～ться.

засда́|ться, мся, шься, стся, ди́мся, ди́тесь, ду́тся, *past* ～лся, ～ла́сь, *pf.* (*sl.*) to misdeal.

засе́в, а, *m.* **1.** sowing. **2.** seed, seed-corn. **3.** sown area.

засева́|ть, ю, *impf. of* засе́ять.

заседа́ни|е, я, *n.* meeting; conference; session, sitting.

заседа́тел|ь, я, *m.* assessor; прися́жный з. juryman.

заседа́|ть, ю, *impf.* to sit; to meet.

засе́ива|ть, ю, *impf. of* засе́ять.

засе́|к, кла, *see* ～чь.

засе́к|а, и, *f.* abat(t)is.

засека́|ть(ся), ет(ся), *impf. of* засе́чь(ся).

засекре́|тить, чу, тишь, *pf.* **1.** to place on secret list; to classify as secret, restrict. **2.** to give access to secret documents; admit to secret work.

засекре́ченный, *p.p.p.* of засекре́тить *and adj.* hush-hush, secret.

засекре́чива|ть, ю, *impf. of* засекре́тить.

засе|ку́, чёшь, ку́т, *see* ～чь.

засе́|л, ла, *see* ～сть.

заселе́ни|е, я, *n.* settlement; colonization.

заселённый, *p.p.p. of* засели́ть *and adj.* populated; inhabited; ре́дко з. sparsely populated.

засел|и́ть, ю́, и́шь, *pf.* (*of* ～я́ть) to settle; colonize; to populate; з. но́вый дом to occupy a new house.

засел|я́ть, я́ю, *impf. of* ～и́ть.

засемен|и́ть, ю́, и́шь, *pf.* to begin to mince (*of gait*).

зас|е́сть, я́ду, я́дешь, *past* ～е́л, *pf.* (*o* ～а́живаться) (*coll.*) **1.** (за+*a.* or +*inf.*) to sit down (to). **2.** to sit firm, sit tight; to ensconce oneself; з. в тюрьму́ to go to prison. **3.** (в+*p.*) to lodge (in), stick (in); пу́ля ～е́ла у него́ в боку́ a bullet had lodged in his side; моти́в ～е́л у меня́ в голове́ (*fig.*) the tune has stuck in my head.

засе́чк|а, и, *f.* **1.** notch, mark. **2.** (*geogr.*) intersection. **3.** (*med.*) canker.

засе́|чь, ку́, чёшь, ку́т, *past* ～к, ～кла, *pf.* (*of* ～ка́ть) **1.** to flog to death. **2.** to notch. **3.** (*geogr.*) to determine by intersection.

засе́|чься, чётся, ку́тся, *past* ～кся, ～кла́сь, *pf.* (*of* ～ка́ться) to overreach itself, cut, hitch (*of horse*).

засе́|ять, ю, ешь, *pf.* (*of* ～ва́ть *and* ～ивать) to sow.

заси|де́ть, ди́т, *pf.* (*of* ～жива́ть) (*coll.*) to fly-spot.

заси|де́ться, жу́сь, ди́шься, *pf.* (*of* ～жива́ться) (*coll.*) to sit too long, stay too long; to sit up late; to stay late; з. за рабо́той to sit up late working; з. в де́вках, *see* де́вка.

заси́женный, *p.p.p.* of засиде́ть *and adj.* (*coll.*) з. (му́хами) fly-blown.

заси́жива|ть(ся), ю(сь), *impf.* of заси-де́ть(ся).

заси́лье|е, я, *no pl.*, *n.* (*pejor.*) domination, sway.

заси́м, *adv.* (*obs.*) hereafter, after this.

засине́|ть(ся), ю(сь), *pf.* to become blue; to appear blue (in the distance).

заси́нива|ть, ю, *impf.* of засини́ть.

засин|и́ть, ю́, и́шь, *pf.* (*of* ⁓ива́ть) 1. to over-blue (*in laundering*). 2. to cover with blue paint.

засин|я́ть, я́ю, = ⁓ива́ть.

засия́|ть, ю, *pf.* 1. to begin to shine, begin to beam. 2. to appear, come out; ме́сяц ⁓л из-за туч the moon appeared from behind the clouds.

заска|ка́ть, чу́, ⁓чешь, *pf.* 1. to begin to jump; to break into a gallop. 2. (*impf.* ⁓кивать) (в+*a.*) to gallop (away to, up to).

заска|ка́ться, чу́сь, ⁓чешься, *pf.* (*coll.*) to gallop until exhausted.

заска́кива|ть, ю, *impf.* of заскака́ть 2 *and* заскочи́ть.

заскво|зи́ть, зи́т, *pf.* to begin to show light through.

заскирд|ова́ть, у́ю, *pf.* of скирдова́ть.

заскоб|и́ть, лю́, и́шь, *pf.* (*coll.*) to place in brackets.

заско́к, а, *m.* (*coll.*) 1. leap, jump. 2. crazy idea; э́то у тебя́ з.? have you gone crazy?, are you out of your mind?

заскору́злый, *adj.* 1. hardened, calloused. 2. (*fig.*) coarsened, callous. 3. (*fig.*) backward, retarded.

заскору́з|нуть, ну, нешь, *past* ⁓, ⁓ла, *pf.* 1. to harden, coarsen, become callous; (*also fig.*). 2. (*fig.*) to stagnate; to become retarded.

заскоч|и́ть, у́, ⁓ишь, *pf.* (*of* заска́кивать) 1. (за+*a.*, на+*a.*) to jump, spring (behind, onto). 2. (в+*a.*; *fig.*) to drop in (to, at).

засла|сти́ть, щу́, сти́шь, *pf.* (*of* ⁓щивать) 1. to take (*medicine, etc.*) with something sweet. 2. to sweeten, put sugar into.

за|сла́ть, шлю́, шлёшь, *pf.* (*of* ⁓сыла́ть) to send, despatch; з. не по а́дресу to send to the wrong address; з. шпио́на to send out a spy.

засла́щива|ть, ю, *impf.* of засласти́ть.

засле|ди́ть, жу́, ди́шь, *pf.* (*of* ⁓живать) (*coll.*) to leave dirty foot-marks on.

засле́жива|ть, ю, *impf.* of заследи́ть.

засле|зи́ться, зи́тся, *pf.* to begin to water.

заслеп|и́ть, лю́, и́шь, *pf.* (*of* ⁓ля́ть) (*coll.*) to blind.

заслепля́|ть, ю, *impf.* of заслепи́ть.

засло́н, а, *m.* 1. screen, barrier. 2. (*mil.*) covering force.

заслон|и́ть, ю́, и́шь *and* (*coll.*) ⁓ишь, *pf. and* (*of* ⁓я́ть) 1. to hide, cover; to shield, screen. 2. (*fig.*) to push into the background.

заслон|и́ться, ю́сь, и́шься *and* (*coll.*) ⁓ишь-ся, *pf.* (*of* ⁓я́ться) 1. (от) to shield oneself, screen oneself (from). 2. *pass.* of ⁓и́ть.

засло́нк|а, и, *f.* oven-door; stove-door.

заслон|я́ть(ся)[1], я́ю(сь), *impf.* of ⁓и́ть(ся).

заслоня́|ться[2], ю́сь, *impf.* (*coll.*) to begin to pace up and down.

заслу́г|а, и, *f.* merit, desert; service; их наказа́ли по ⁓ам they have been punished according to their deserts; у него́ больши́е ⁓и пе́ред родны́м го́родом he has rendered great services to his home town.

заслу́женно, *adv.* deservedly; according to (one's) deserts.

заслу́жен|ный (*and* ⁓ный), *p.p.p.* of заслу-жи́ть *adj.* 1. deserved, merited. 2. meritorious, of merit; (*as honorific in U.S.S.R.*) Honoured. 3. ⁓ный профе́ссор professor emeritus. 4. (*fig.*, *joc.*) time-honoured; good old.

заслу́жива|ть, ю, *impf.* (*of* заслужи́ть) (+*g.*) to deserve, merit.

заслу́жива|ться, юсь, *impf.* 1. *impf.* of за-служи́ться. 2. *pass.* of ⁓ть.

заслуж|и́ть, у́, ⁓ишь, *pf.* (*of* ⁓ивать) (+*a.*) 1. to deserve, merit; win, earn. 2. (*coll.*, *obs.*) to repay, pay back. 3. (*dial.*) to atone for, make up for.

заслуж|и́ться, у́сь, ⁓ишься, *pf.* (*of* ⁓ивать-ся) (*coll.*) to serve for too long.

заслу́ш|ать, аю, *pf.* (*of* ⁓ивать) to hear, listen to (*a public or official pronouncement*).

заслу́ш|аться, аюсь, *pf.* (*of* ⁓иваться) (+*g.*) to listen spellbound (to).

заслу́шива|ть(ся), ю(сь), *impf.* of заслу́-шать(ся).

заслы́ш|ать, у, ишь, *pf.* 1. to hear, catch. 2. (*coll.*) to smell; з. за́пах to detect a smell.

заслы́ш|аться, ится, *pf.* (*coll.*) to begin to be audible; to be able to be heard.

заслю́нива|ть, ю, *impf.* of заслюни́ть.

заслюн|и́ть, ю́, и́шь, *pf.* (*of* слюни́ть *and* ⁓ивать) (*coll.*) to slobber over.

засма́ли|ть, ю, *impf.* of засмоли́ть.

засма́ркива|ть, ю, *impf.* of засморка́ть.

засма́трива|ть, ю, *impf.* (в+*a.*; *coll.*) to look (into); to peep (into); з. в окно́ к кому́-н. to look in at someone's window.

засма́трива|ться, юсь, *impf.* of засмот-ре́ться.

засме́ива|ть, ю, *impf.* of засмея́ть.

засме|я́ть, ю́, ёшь, *pf.* (*coll.*) to ridicule.

засме|я́ться, ю́сь, ёшься, *pf.* to begin to laugh.

засмол|и́ть, ю́, и́шь, *pf.* to tar; to caulk.

засмо́рканный, *p.p.p. of* засморка́ть *and adj.* (*coll.*) snotty.

засморка́|ть, ю, ю, *pf.* (*coll.*) to make snotty.

засмотр|е́ться, ю́сь, ~ишься, *pf.* (*of* засма́триваться) (на+*a.*) to be lost in contemplation (of), be carried away (by the sight of).

засне́женный, *adj.* snow-covered.

заснима́|ть, ю, *impf. of* засня́ть.

засн|иму́, и́мешь, *see* ~я́ть.

засн|у́ть, у́, ёшь, *pf.* (*of* засыпа́ть¹) to go to sleep, fall asleep; (*fig.*) to die down; (*rhet.*) з. ве́чным сном to go to one's eternal rest.

засн|я́ть, иму́, и́мешь, *past* ~я́л, ~яла́, ~я́ло, *pf.* (*of* ~има́ть) to photograph, snap (*coll.*); (*cinema sl.*) to shoot.

засо́в, а, *m.* bolt, bar.

засове|сти́ться, щусь, сти́шься, *pf.* (+*inf.*; *coll.*) to feel ashamed (to).

засо́выва|ть, ю, *impf. of* засу́нуть.

засо́л, а, *m.* salting; pickling.

засол|и́ть, ю́, ~и́шь, *pf.* (*of* заса́ливать²) to salt; to pickle.

засо́льщик, а, *m.* salter, pickler.

засоре́ни|е, я, *n.* littering, obstruction, clogging up.

засор|и́ть, ю́, и́шь, *pf.* (*of* заса́ривать *and* ~я́ть) 1. to clog, block up, stop. 2. to litter; to get dirt into; (*fig.*) з. чью-н. ду́шу to poison someone's mind.

засор|и́ться, ю́сь, и́шься, *pf.* (*of* заса́риваться *and* ~я́ться) to become obstructed, blocked up.

засоря́|ть(ся), ю(сь), *impf. of* засори́ть(ся).

засо́с, а, *m.* sucking in.

засос|а́ть, у́, ёшь, *pf.* (*of* заса́сывать) 1. to suck in, engulf, swallow up (*also fig.*) 2. (*coll.*) to exhaust by sucking. 3. to begin to suck.

засо́х|нуть, ну, нешь, *past* ~, ~ла, *pf.* (*of* засыха́ть) 1. to dry (up). 2. to wither.

за́спанный, *p.p.p. of* заспа́ть *and adj.* (*coll.*) sleepy.

засп|а́ть, лю́, и́шь, *past* ~а́л, ~ала́, ~а́ло, *pf.* (*of* засыпа́ть²) (*dial.*) to smother (a baby) in one's sleep, overlie.

засп|а́ться, лю́сь, и́шься, *past* ~а́лся, ~ала́сь, ~ а́лось, *pf.* (*of* засыпа́ться¹) (*coll.*) to oversleep.

заспирт|ова́ть, у́ю, *pf.* (*of* ~о́вывать) to preserve in alcohol.

заспирто́выва|ть, ю, *impf. of* заспиртова́ть.

засп|лю́, и́шь, *see* ~а́ть.

заспо́р|ить, ю, ишь, *pf.* to begin to argue.

заспо́р|иться, юсь, ишься, *pf.* (*coll.*) to get carried away by argument.

заспор|и́ться, ю́сь, и́шься, *pf.* (*coll.*) to go well; to be a success.

засрам|и́ть, лю́, и́шь, *pf.* (*coll.*) to put to shame.

заста́в|а, ы, *f.* 1. gate (*of town*). 2. (*hist., mil.*) barrier. 3. (*mil.*) picket; outpost.

заста|ва́ть, ю́, ёшь, *impf. of* ~ть.

заста́в|ить¹, лю, ишь, *pf.* (*of* ~ля́ть¹) 1. to cram, fill; з. ко́мнату ме́белью to cram a room with furniture. 2. to block up, obstruct. 3. (*library sl.*) з. кни́гу to put a book in the wrong place.

заста́в|ить², лю, ишь, *pf.* (*of* ~ля́ть²) (+*a.* *and inf.*) to compel, force, make; он ~ил нас ждать себя́ два часа́ he kept us waiting for two hours; они́ не ~или до́лго проси́ть себя́ they agreed with alacrity.

заста́вк|а, и, *f.* illumination (*in book or MS.*).

заставля́|ть¹, ², ю, *impf. of* заста́вить¹, ².

заста́в|очный, *adj. of* ~ка.

заста́ива|ться, юсь, *impf. of* застоя́ться.

заста́|ну, нешь, *see* ~ть.

застарева́|ть, ю, *impf. of* застаре́ть.

застаре́лый, *adj.* inveterate; chronic.

застаре́|ть, ю, *pf.* (*of* ~ва́ть) (*coll.*) to become inveterate; to become chronic.

заста́|ть, ну, нешь, *pf.* (*of* ~ва́ть) to find; ~ли ли вы его́ до́ма? did you find him in?; я ~л его́ ещё спя́щим I found him still asleep; з. враспло́х to catch napping; з. на ме́сте преступле́ния to catch red-handed.

заста́|ю, ёшь, *see* ~ва́ть.

застега́|ть, ю, *pf.* (*coll.*) 1. to begin to flog. 2. з. до́ смерти to flog to death.

застёгива|ть, ю, *impf. of* застегну́ть.

застёгива|ться, юсь, *impf.* 1. *impf. of* застегну́ться. 2. *pass. of* ~ть. 3. to fasten, do up (*intrans.*); во́рот ~ется на пу́говицу the collar does up with a button.

застег|ну́ть, ну́, нёшь, *pf.* (*of* ~ивать) to fasten, do up; з. (на пу́говицы) to button up.

застег|ну́ться, ну́сь, нёшься, *pf.* (*of* ~иваться) to button oneself up; з. на все пу́говицы to do up all one's buttons.

застёжк|а, и, *f.* fastening; clasp, buckle, hasp; з.-мо́лния zip fastener.

застекл|и́ть, ю́, и́шь, *pf.* (*of* ~я́ть) to glaze, fit with glass; з. портре́т to frame a portrait.

застекл|я́ть, я́ю, *impf. of* ~и́ть.

застел|и́ть, ю́, ~ешь, *pf.*, = застла́ть 1.

засте́н|ок, ка, *m.* torture-chamber.

засте́нчив|ый (~, ~а), *adj.* shy; bashful.

засти́|г, гла, *see* ~чь.

засти|га́ть, га́ю, *impf. of* ~гнуть *and* ~чь.

засти́|гнуть = ~чь.

застила́|ть, ю, *impf. of* застла́ть.

засти́лк|а, и, *f.* 1. covering. 2. floor-covering.

застир|а́ть, а́ю, *pf.* (*of* ~ывать) (*coll.*) 1. to wash off. 2. to ruin by washing. 3. (*rare*) to begin to wash.

застира́рыва|ть, ю, *impf. of* застира́ть.

за́|стить, щу, стишь, *impf.* (*coll.*) з. свет to stand in the light.

засти́|чь, гну, гнешь, *past* ~г, ~гла, *pf.* (*of* ~га́ть) to catch; to take unawares; нас ~гла гроза́ we were caught by the storm.

заст|ла́ть, елю́, е́лешь, *pf.* (*of* ~ила́ть) 1. (+*i.*) to cover (with); з. ковро́м to carpet, lay a carpet (over). 2. (*fig.*) to hide from view; to cloud; облака́ ~ла́ли со́лнце clouds obscured the sun; слёзы ~ла́ли её глаза́ tears dimmed her eyes.

засто́|й, я, m. stagnation (*fig.*); в ~е at a standstill; (*econ.*) depression; з. кро́ви (*med.*) haemostasia.

засто́йный, *adj.* stagnant (*fig.*); (*econ.*) unwanted, idle as result of depression.

засто́льн|ый, *adj.* table-, occurring at table; ~ая бесе́да table-talk; ~ая пе́сня drinking-song; ~ая речь after-dinner speech.

засто́порива|ть(ся), ю(сь), *impf. of* засто́порить(ся).

засто́пор|ить, ю, ишь, *pf.* (*of* ~ивать) (*tech.*) to stop; (*fig., coll.*) to bring to a standstill.

засто́пор|иться, юсь, ишься, *pf.* (*of* ~иваться) (*tech.*) to stop (*of a machine*); (*fig., coll.*) to come to a standstill.

засто|я́ться, ю́сь, и́шься, *pf.* (*of* заста́иваться) 1. to stand too long. 2. to stagnate. 3. (*coll.*) to linger.

застрога́́ива|ть, ю, *impf. of* застрога́ть 2.

застра́ива|ть, ю, *impf. of* застро́ить.

застрахо́ван|ный, *p.p.p. of* застрахова́ть *and* *adj.* insured; *as noun* з., ~ного, *m.* insured person.

застрах|ова́ть, у́ю, *pf.* (*of* страхова́ть *and* ~о́вывать) (от) to insure (against).

застрах|ова́ться, у́юсь, *pf.* (*of* страхова́ться *and* ~о́вываться) to insure oneself.

застрахо́выва|ть(ся), ю(сь), *impf. of* застрахова́ть(ся).

застра́чива|ть, ю, *impf. of* застрочи́ть.

застраща́|ть, ю, *pf.* (*coll.*) to frighten, intimidate.

застра́щива|ть, ю, *impf. of* застраща́ть.

застрева́|ть, ю, *impf. of* застря́ть.

застре́лива|ть(ся), ю(сь), *impf. of* застре-ли́ть(ся).

застрел|и́ть, ю́, ~ишь, *pf.* (*of* ~ивать) to shoot (dead).

застрел|и́ться, ю́сь, ~ишься, *pf.* (*of* ~иваться) to shoot oneself; to blow one's brains out.

застре́льщик, а, m. 1. (*mil.*) skirmisher, tirailleur. 2. (*fig.*) pioneer, leader.

застреля́|ть, ю, *pf.* (*coll.*) to begin to shoot, begin to fire.

застре́х|а, и, f. (*dial.*) eaves.

застрига́|ть, ю, *impf. of* застри́чь 2.

застри́|чь, гу́, жёшь, гу́т, *past* ~г, ~гла, *pf.*

(*coll.*) 1. to begin to cut. 2. (*impf.* ~га́ть) to cut (nails) too short.

застрога́|ть, ю, *pf.* 1. to begin to plane. 2. (*pf. of* застра́гивать) to plane (down).

застро́|ить, ю, ишь, *pf.* (*of* застра́ивать) 1. to build (over, on, up). 2. to begin to build.

застро́йк|а, и, f. building; пра́во ~и building permit.

застро́йщик, а, m. person building (or having built for him) his own house.

застроч|и́ть, у́, ~и́шь, *pf.* 1. (*impf.* застра́чивать) to sew up, stitch up. 2. (*coll.*) to begin to scribble, dash off (*a letter, etc.*). 3. (*coll.*) to rattle away (*of or with automatic weapons*).

застру́га|ть, ю, *pf.* = застрога́ть.

застру́гива|ть, ю, *impf. of* застругать.

застря́|ну, нешь, *see* ~ть.

застря́па|ться, юсь, *pf.* (*coll.*) to devote too much time to cooking.

застря́|ть, ну, нешь, *pf.* (*of* застрева́ть) 1. to stick; з. в грязи́ to get stuck in the mud; слова́ ~ли у него́ в го́рле the words stuck in his throat. 2. (*fig., coll.*) to be held up; to become bogged down.

засту|ди́ть, жу́, ~ди́шь, *pf.* (*of* ~жива́ть) (*coll.*) to expose to cold; to aggravate by exposure to cold.

засту|ди́ться, жу́сь, ~ди́шься, *pf.* (*of* ~жива́ться) (*coll.*) to catch cold, catch a chill.

засту́жива|ть(ся), ю(сь), *impf. of* застуди́ть(ся).

засту|жу́, ~дишь, *see* ~ди́ть.

за́ступ, а, m. spade.

заступа́|ть(ся), ю(сь), *impf. of* заступи́ть-(ся).

заступ|и́ть, лю́, ~ишь, *pf.* (*of* ~а́ть) 1. to take the place of; з. отца́ сироте́ to become a father to an orphan. 2. (на пост) to take up (a post).

заступ|и́ться, лю́сь, ~ишься, *pf.* (за+*a.*) to stand up for; to take someone's part; to plead (for).

засту́пник, а, m. defender, protector.

засту́пничеств|о, а, n. protection.

застыва́|ть, ю, *impf. of* засты́ть.

засты|ди́ть, жу́, ди́шь, *pf.* (*coll.*) to shame, cause to feel shame.

засты|ди́ться, жу́сь, ди́шься, *pf.* (*coll.*) to feel shame; to become confused.

засты|жу́, ди́шь, *see* ~ди́ть.

засты́лый, *adj.* (*coll.*) congealed; stiff.

засты́|ну, нешь, *see* ~ть.

засты́|нуть = ~ть.

засты́|ть *and* ~нуть, **ну, нешь,** *pf.* (*of* ~ва́ть) 1. to thicken, set; to harden; to congeal, coagulate. 2. (*coll.*) to become stiff; (*fig.*) з. от у́жаса to be paralyzed with fright. 3. (*coll.*) to freeze (*also fig.*).

засу|ди́ть, жу́, ～дишь, *pf.* (*of* ～жива́ть) (*coll.*) to condemn.

засуе|ти́ться, чу́сь, ти́шься, *pf.* **1.** to begin to bustle about, begin to fuss. **2.** to wear oneself out with fussing.

засу́жива|ть, ю, *impf. of* засуди́ть.

засу́|жу́, ～дишь, *see* ～ди́ть.

засу́н|уть, у, ешь, *pf.* (*of* засо́вывать) to shove in, thrust in; to tuck in; з. ру́ки в карма́н to thrust one's hands into one's pockets.

засу́сл|ить, ю, ишь, *pf. of* су́слить.

засусо́л|ить, ю, ишь, *pf. of* сусо́лить.

за́сух|а, и, *f.* drought.

засухоусто́йчив|ый (～, ～а), *adj.* (*agric.*) drought-resisting.

засу́чива|ть, ю, *impf. of* засучи́ть.

засуч|и́ть, у́, ～ишь, *pf.* (*of* ～ивать) (рукава́, *etc.*) to roll up (*sleeves, etc.*).

засу́шива|ть(ся), ю(сь), *impf. of* засуши́ть(ся).

засуш|и́ть, у́, ～ишь, *pf.* (*of* ～ивать) to dry up (*plants; also fig.*).

засуш|и́ться, у́сь, ～ишься, *pf.* (*of* ～иваться) to dry up (*intrans.*), shrivel.

засу́шлив|ый (～, ～а), *adj.* droughty, dry.

засчит|а́ть, а́ю, *pf.* (*of* ～ывать) to take into consideration; з. в упла́ту до́лга to reckon towards payment of a debt.

засчи́тыва|ть, ю, *impf. of* засчита́ть.

засыла́|ть, ю, *impf. of* засла́ть.

засы́лк|а, и, *f.* sending, despatching.

засы́п|ать[1], лю, лешь, *pf.* (*of* ～а́ть[3]) **1.** to fill up. **2.** (+*i.*) to cover (with), strew (with); за одну́ ночь доро́жка была́ ～ана опа́вшими ли́стьями in a single night the path was strewn with fallen leaves. **3.** (+*i.*; *fig., coll.*) з. вопро́сами to bombard with questions; з. поздравле́ниями to shower congratulations (on). **4.** (+*a. or g.* в+*a.*; *coll.*) to put (into), add (to); з. овса́ в я́сли to pour oats into the manger.

засы́п|ать[2], лю, лешь, *pf.* (*of* ～а́ть[4]) (*sl.*) to give away, betray.

засыпа́|ть[1], ю, *impf. of* засну́ть.

засыпа́|ть[2], ю, *impf. of* заспа́ть.

засыпа́|ть[3, 4], ю, *impf. of* засы́пать[1, 2].

засы́п|аться[1], люсь, лешься, *pf.* (*of* ～а́ться[2]) **1.** to get into; песо́к ～ался мне в башмаки́ I have got sand into my shoes. **2.** (+*i.*) *pass. of* ～ать[1].

засы́п|аться[2], люсь, лешься, *pf.* (*of* ～а́ться[3]) (*coll.*) **1.** to be caught; (*sl.*) to be nabbed. **2.** to come to grief, slip up.

засыпа́|ться[1], юсь, *impf. of* заспа́ться.

засыпа́|ться[2, 3], юсь, *impf. of* засы́паться[1, 2].

засы́пк|а, и, *f.* **1.** filling up; covering, strewing. **2.** pouring in, putting in.

засыха́|ть, ю, *impf. of* засо́хнуть.

зас|я́ду, я́дешь, *see* ～е́сть.

затавр|и́ть, ю́, и́шь, *pf.* (*of* таври́ть) to brand (*cattle, etc.*).

затаён|ный, *p.p.p. of* затаи́ть *and adj.* secret; suppressed; ～ная мечта́ secret dream.

зата́ива|ть(ся), ю(сь), *impf. of* затаи́ть(ся).

зата|и́ть, ю́, и́шь, *pf.* (*of* ～ивать) **1.** to conceal; to suppress; з. дыха́ние to hold one's breath. **2.** to harbour, cherish; з. оби́ду (на+*a.*) to nurse a grievance (against).

зата|и́ться, ю́сь, и́шься, *pf.* (*of* ～иваться) (*coll.*) to hide (*intrans.*); з. в себе́ (*fig.*) to become reserved, retire into oneself.

зата́лкива|ть, ю, *impf. of* затолка́ть *and* затолкну́ть.

затанц|ева́ться, у́юсь, *pf.* (*coll.*) to dance until exhausted.

зата́плива|ть[1, 2], ю, *impf. of* затопи́ть[1, 2].

зата́птыва|ть, ю, *impf. of* затопта́ть.

зата́сканный, *p.p.p. of* затаска́ть *and adj.* worn; threadbare; (*fig.*) hackneyed, trite.

затаск|а́ть, а́ю, *pf.* (*of* ～ивать[1]) (*coll.*) **1.** to wear out; to make dirty (with wear); (*fig.*) to make hackneyed, make trite. **2.** to drag about; з. по суда́м to drag through the courts. **3.** to begin to drag.

затаск|а́ться, а́юсь, *pf.* (*of* ～иваться) (*coll.*) to wear out, become worn out; to become dirty (with wear).

зата́скива|ть[1], ю, *impf. of* затаска́ть.

зата́скива|ть[2], ю, *impf. of* затащи́ть.

зата́скива|ться, юсь, *impf. of* затаска́ться.

зата́чива|ть, ю, *impf. of* заточи́ть[1].

затащ|и́ть, у́, ～ишь, *pf.* (*of* зата́скивать[2]) (*coll.*) to drag off, drag away; (*fig.*) они́ ～и́ли его́ в теа́тр they have dragged him off to the theatre.

затвердева́|ть, ю, *impf. of* затверде́ть.

затверде́лост|ь, и, *f.* = затверде́ние.

затверде́лый, *adj.* hardened.

затверде́ни|е, я, *n.* **1.** hardening. **2.** (*med.*) induration, callosity. **3.** (*med.*) callus.

затверде́|ть, ю, *pf.* (*of* ～ва́ть) to harden, become hard; to set.

затвер|ди́ть, жу́, ди́шь, *pf.* (*of* ～жива́ть) (*coll.*) **1.** to learn by rote. **2.** з. одно́ и то же to harp on one string.

затве́ржива|ть, ю, *impf. of* затверди́ть.

затво́р, а, *m.* **1.** shutting; bolting. **2.** bolt, bar; breech-block (*of fire-arm*); water-gate, flood-gate; (*phot.*) shutter. **3.** (*eccl.*) cell; seclusion, solitude.

затвор|и́ть, ю́, ～ишь, *pf.* (*of* ～я́ть) to shut, close.

затвор|и́ться, ю́сь, ～ишься, *pf.* (*of* ～я́ться) **1.** to shut, close (*intrans.*). **2.** to shut oneself in, lock oneself in. **3.** (*eccl.*) to become a recluse; з. в монасты́рь, в монастыре́ to go into a monastery, become a monk.

затво́рник, а, *m.* hermit, anchorite, recluse;

он живёт совершённым ∼ом (*fig.*) he is a complete recluse.

затворни|ческий, *adj.* *of* ∼к, solitary; ∼ческая жизнь the life of a recluse.

затворничеств|о, а, *n.* (*eccl.*) seclusion, solitary life.

затвор|я́ть(ся), я́ю(сь), *impf. of* ∼и́ть(ся).

затева́|ть, ю, *impf. of* затея́ть.

затейлив|ый (∼, ∼а), *adj.* **1.** intricate, involved; ∼ая речь involved discourse; ∼ое украше́ние intricate ornament. **2.** ingenious, original; inventive; ∼ая игру́шка ingenious toy.

затейник, а, *m.* **1.** practical joker; humorist. **2.** entertainer; organizer (of entertainments).

зате́|йный (∼ен, ∼йна), *adj.* (*coll.*) = ∼йливый.

затейщик, а, *m.* (*coll.*) instigator.

затёк, ла́, *see* затёчь.

затека́|ть, ю, *impf. of* затёчь.

зате|ку́, чёшь, ку́т, *see* ∼чь.

зате́м, *adv.* **1.** after that, thereupon, then, next. **2.** for that reason; з. что because, since, as; зачём ты приёхала? з., что слыха́ла, что ты заболёл why have you come? because I heard that you had been taken ill; з. чтобы in order that; она́ приёхала з., чтобы уха́живать за тобо́й she has come (in order) to look after you.

затемнёни|е, я, *n.* **1.** darkening; obscuring (*also fig.*). **2.** (*med.*) dark patch. **3.** (*mil.*) black-out. **4.** (*psych.*) black-out.

затемн|и́ть, ю́, и́шь, *pf.* (*of* ∼я́ть) **1.** to darken; to obscure (*also fig.*). **2.** (*mil.*) to black-out.

затемн|и́ться, ю́сь, и́шься, *pf.* (*of* ∼я́ться) to become dark; to become obscure; (*fig.*) to become obscured, become clouded.

за́темно, *adv.* (*coll.*) before daybreak.

затемн|я́ть(ся), я́ю(сь), *impf. of* ∼и́ть(ся).

затен|и́ть, ю́, и́шь, *pf.* (*of* ∼я́ть) to shade.

затен|я́ть, я́ю, *impf. of* ∼и́ть.

затёплива|ть(ся), ю(сь), *impf. of* затёплить(ся).

затёпл|ить, ю, ишь, *pf.* (*of* ∼ивать) (*obs., folk poet.*) to light (*candle, etc.*).

затёпл|иться, юсь, ишься, *pf.* (*of* ∼иваться) (*obs., folk poet.*) to begin to gleam.

зат|ере́ть, ру́, рёшь, *past* ∼ёр, ∼ёрла, *pf.* (*of* ∼ира́ть) **1.** to rub out. **2.** to block, jam; (*impers.*) су́дно ∼ёрло льда́ми the ship was ice-bound; (*fig., coll.*) з. кого́-н. to keep someone down, impede someone's career. **3.** (*coll.*) to make dirty, soil.

зат|ере́ться, ру́сь, рёшься, *past* ∼ёрся, ∼ёрлась, *pf.* (*of* ∼ира́ться) (*coll.*) **1.** (в+*a.*) to get (into), worm one's way (into). **2.** to begin to rub oneself.

затёрива|ть(ся), ю(сь), *impf. of* затеря́ть(ся).

затёрпн|уть, ет, *pf. of* тёрпнуть.

затёрянный, *p.p.p. of* затеря́ть *and adj.* forgotten, forsaken.

затер|я́ть, я́ю, *pf.* (*of* ∼ивать) (*coll.*) to lose, mislay.

затер|я́ться, я́юсь, *pf.* (*of* ∼иваться) to be lost, be mislaid; (*fig.*) to become forgotten; моё перо́ ∼я́лось (*coll.*) my pen has vanished; з. в толпё to be lost in a crowd.

зате|са́ть, шу́, ∼шешь, *pf.* (*of* ∼сывать) to rough-hew; to sharpen (*stake, etc.*).

зате|са́ться, шу́сь, ∼шешься, *pf.* (*of* ∼сываться) (*coll.*) to worm one's way in, intrude.

затесн|и́ть, ю́, и́шь, *pf.* (*of* ∼я́ть) (*coll.*) **1.** to jostle, press. **2.** (*fig.*) to oppress, persecute.

затесн|и́ться, ю́сь, и́шься, *pf.* (*of* ∼я́ться) (*coll.*) to begin to crowd.

затесн|я́ть(ся), я́ю(сь), *impf. of* ∼и́ть(ся).

затёсыва|ть(ся), ю(сь), *impf. of* затеса́ть(ся).

зате́|чь, ку́, чёшь, ку́т, *past* ∼к, ∼кла́, *pf.* (*of* ∼ка́ть) **1.** (в+*a.*; за+*a.*) to pour, flow, leak (into; behind). **2.** to swell up. **3.** to become numb; у меня́ нога́ ∼кла́ I have pins and needles in my foot.

зате́|я, и, *f.* **1.** undertaking, enterprise, venture. **2.** (*usually pl.*) piece of fun; escapade; practical joke. **3.** (*pl., obs.*) embellishment, ornament; (*lit.*) conceit; жить без ∼й to live simply, unpretentiously.

зате́|ять, ю, *pf.* (*of* ∼ва́ть) (*coll.*) to undertake, venture; to organize; з. дра́ку to start a fight.

затира́|ть(ся), ю(сь), *impf. of* затере́ть(ся).

зати́ск|ать, аю, *pf.* (*of* ∼ивать) (*coll.*) to smother with caresses.

зати́скива|ть(ся), ю(сь), *impf. of* зати́скать *and* зати́снуть(ся).

зати́с|нуть, ну, нешь, *pf.* (*of* ∼кивать) (*coll.*) to squeeze in.

зати́с|нуться, нусь, нешься, *pf.* (*of* ∼киваться) (*coll.*) to squeeze (oneself) in.

затих|а́ть, а́ю, *impf. of* ∼нуть.

зати́х|нуть, ну, нешь, *past* ∼, ∼ла, *pf.* (*of* ∼а́ть) to die down, abate; to die away, fade (*of noise*).

зати́шь|е, я, *n.* calm; lull.

затк|а́ть, у́, ёшь, *past* ∼а́л, ∼ала́, ∼а́ло, *pf.* (+*a. and i.*) to cover all over with a woven pattern.

заткн|у́ть, у́, ёшь, *pf.* (*of* затыка́ть) **1.** (+*a. and i.*) to stop up; to plug; з. буты́лку про́бкой to cork a bottle; з. рот, гло́тку кому́-н. (*coll.*) to shut someone up; ∼и́ гло́тку! shut your mouth! **2.** to stick, thrust; з. кого́-н. за по́яс (*fig., coll.*) to outdo someone.

заткн|у́ться, у́сь,-ёшься, *pf.* (*coll.*) to shut up; **~и́сь!** shut up!

затмева́|ть, ю, *impf. of* затми́ть.

затме́ни|е, я, *n.* **1.** (*astron.*) eclipse. **2.** (*fig., coll.*) black-out, mental derangement.

затм|и́ть, и́шь, *pf.* (*of* **~ева́ть**) **1.** to darken. **2.** (*fig.*) to eclipse; to overshadow.

зато́, *conj.* (*coll.*) but then, but on the other hand; but to make up for it; **до́рого, з. хоро́шая вещь** it is expensive, but then it is good.

затова́ренност|ь, и, *f.* (*econ.*) glut.

затова́ренный, *p.p.p. of* затова́рить *and adj.* (*econ.*) surplus.

затова́ривани|е, я, *n.* glutting; overstocking.

затова́рива|ть(ся), ю(сь), *impf. of* затова́рить(ся).

затова́р|ить, ю, ишь, *pf.* (*of* **~ивать**) (*econ.*) to accumulate (excess stock of), overstock.

затова́р|иться, юсь, ишься, *pf.* (*of* **~иваться**) (*econ.*) **1.** to be over-stocked. **2.** (*coll.*) to have a surplus.

затолка́|ть, ю, *pf.* (*of* зата́лкивать) to jostle (*to the point of discomfort*).

затолкн|у́ть, у́, ёшь, *pf.* (*of* зата́лкивать) (*coll.*) to shove in.

зато́н, а, *m.* **1.** backwater. **2.** (river-)boat yard. **3.** dam, weir.

затон|у́ть, у́, ~ешь, *pf.* to sink (*intrans.*).

затоп|и́ть, лю́, ~ишь, *pf.* (*of* зата́пливать) to light (*a stove*); to turn on the heating.

затоп|и́ть², лю́, ~ишь, *pf.* (*of* **~ля́ть**) **1.** to flood; to submerge. **2.** to sink; **з. кора́бль** to scuttle a ship.

зато́пк|а, и, f. **1.** fire-lighting. **2.** kindling (-wood).

затопля́|ть, ю, *impf. of* затопи́ть².

затоп|та́ть, чу́, ~чешь, *pf.* (*of* зата́птывать) to trample (down, in); to trample underfoot.

затоп|чу́, ~чешь, *see* **~та́ть.**

зато́р¹, а, *m.* blocking, obstruction; **з. у́личного движе́ния** traffic-jam, congestion.

зато́р², а, *m.* mash (*in brewing and distilling*).

затормо|зи́ть, жу́, зи́шь, *pf. of* тормози́ть.

затормош|и́ть, у́, и́шь, *pf.* (*coll.*) to pester.

зато́р|ный, *adj. of* **~².**

заточ|а́ть, а́ю, *impf. of* **~и́ть².**

заточе́ни|е, я, *n.* confinement; incarceration, captivity.

заточ|и́ть¹, у́, ~ишь, *pf.* (*of* зата́чивать) to sharpen.

заточ|и́ть², у́, ~и́шь, *pf.* (*of* **~а́ть**) to confine, shut up; to incarcerate.

затравене́|ть, ет, *pf. of* травене́ть.

затрав|и́ть, лю́, ~ишь, *pf.* (*of* трави́ть¹ *and* **~ливать**) to hunt down, bring to bay; (*fig., coll.*) to persecute; to badger; to worry the life out of.

затра́вк|а, и, f. **1.** (*tech.*) priming-tube. **2.** touchhole.

затра́влива|ть, ю, *impf. of* затрави́ть.

затра́вник, а, *m.* (*tech.*) priming-tube.

затра́гива|ть, ю, *impf. of* затро́нуть.

затрапе́з|ный¹, *adj.* taking place in the refectory, at table; **~ная бесе́да** table-talk.

затрапе́зный², *adj.* (*obs.*) working-, everyday- (*of dress*).

затра́т|а, ы, f. expense; outlay.

затра́|тить, чу, тишь, *pf.* (*of* **~чивать**) to expend, spend.

затра́чива|ть, ю, *impf. of* затра́тить.

затре́б|овать, ую, *pf.* to request, require; to ask for.

затреп|а́ть, лю́, ~лешь, *pf.* (*of* **~ывать**) **1.** to wear out; to make dirty (with wear). **2.** (*fig.*) to wear out; **з. чьё-н. и́мя** to give someone a bad name. **3.** to begin to scutch.

затреп|а́ться, лю́сь, ~лешься, *pf.* (*of* **~ываться**) **1.** to wear out (*intrans.*), be worn out. **2.** (*fig.*) **я совсе́м ~а́лся** (*coll.*) I have stayed gossiping too long. **3.** to begin to flutter.

затрёпыва|ть(ся), ю(сь), *impf. of* затрепа́ть(ся).

затре́щин|а, ы, f. (*coll.*) box on the ears.

затро́н|уть, у, ешь, *pf.* (*of* затра́гивать) **1.** to affect; to touch, graze. **2.** (*fig.*) to touch (on); **з. вопро́с** to broach a question; **з. чьё-н. самолю́бие** to wound someone's self-esteem.

затрудне́ни|е, я, *n.* difficulty.

затруднённый, *p.p.p. of* затрудни́ть *and adj.* laboured.

затрудни́тельност|ь, и, f. difficulty; straits.

затрудни́тел|ьный (~ен, ~ьна), *adj.* difficult; embarrassing.

затрудн|и́ть, ю́, и́шь, *pf.* (*of* **~я́ть**) **1.** to trouble; to cause trouble (to); to embarrass. **2.** to make difficult; to hamper.

затрудн|и́ться, ю́сь, и́шься, *pf.* (*of* **~я́ться**) (+*inf. or i.*) to find difficulty (in); **з. отве́том** to find difficulty in replying; **он ~и́лся испо́лнить мою́ про́сьбу** he found difficulty in complying with my request.

затрудн|я́ть(ся), я́ю(сь), *impf. of* **~и́ть(ся).**

затума́н|ивать(ся), иваю(сь), иваешь(ся), *impf. of* **~ить(ся).**

затума́н|ить, ю, ишь, *pf.* (*of* **~ивать**) **1.** to befog; to cloud, dim; (*impers.*) **~ило горизо́нт** the horizon was obscured by fog; **слёзы ~или её глаза́** tears dimmed her eyes. **2.** (*fig.*) to obscure.

затума́н|иться, юсь, ишься, *pf.* (*of* **~иваться**) **1.** to grow foggy, become clouded (with). **2.** (*fig.*) to grow sad. **3.** (*fig.*) to become obscure.

затуп|и́ть, лю́, ~ишь, *pf.* (*of* **~ля́ть**) to blunt; to dull.

затуп|и́ться, лю́сь, ~ишься, *pf.* (*of* ~ля́ться) to become blunt(ed).

затупля́|ть(ся), ю(сь), *impf. of* затупи́ть(ся).

зату́рка|ть, ю, *pf.* (*coll.*) to nag.

затуха́ни|е, я, *n.* extinction; (*tech.*) damping; fading.

затух|а́ть, а́ет, *impf. of* ~нуть.

зату́х|нуть, нет, *past* ~, ~ла, *pf.* (*of* ~а́ть) 1. to go out, be extinguished. 2. (*fig.*, *coll.*) to die away (*of sounds*); (*tech.*) to damp; to fade.

затуш|ева́ть, у́ю, *pf.* (*of* ~ёвывать) 1. to shade. 2. (*fig.*, *coll.*) to conceal; to draw a veil over.

затушёвыва|ть, ю, *impf. of* затушева́ть.

затуш|и́ть, у́, ~ишь, *pf.* to put out, extinguish; (*fig.*) to suppress.

за́тхлый, *adj.* mouldy, musty; stuffy; (*fig.*) stagnant.

затыка́|ть, ю, *impf. of* заткну́ть.

заты́л|ок, ка, *m.* 1. back of the head; (*anat.*) occiput; scrag (*cut of meat*). 2. станови́ться в з. to form up in file.

заты́лочный, *adj.* (*anat.*) occipital.

заты́чк|а, и, *f.* (*coll.*) 1. stopping up; plugging. 2. stopper; plug; spigot; (*fig.*) stopgap.

затя́гива|ть(ся), ю(сь), *impf. of* затяну́ть(ся).

затяжеле́|ть, ю, *pf.* (*coll.*, *dial.*) to become pregnant.

затя́жк|а, и, *f.* 1. inhaling (*in smoking*). 2. prolongation; (*coll.*) dragging out. 3. delaying, putting off. 4. (*tech.*) tie-beam.

затяжн|о́й, *adj.* long drawn-out; ~а́я боле́знь lingering illness.

затя́нут|ый, *p.p.p. of* ~ь and *adj.* tightly buttoned, corseted.

затя|ну́ть, ну́, ~нешь, *pf.* (*of* ~гивать) 1. to tighten; (*naut.*) to haul taut. 2. to cover; to close; (*impers.*) не́бо ~ну́ло ту́чами it has clouded over; ра́ну ~ну́ло the wound has closed. 3. (*coll.*) to drag down, drag in; (*fig.*) to inveigle. 4. (*coll.*) to drag out, spin out. 5. з. пе́сню (*coll.*) to strike up a song.

затя|ну́ться, ну́сь, ~нешься, *pf.* (*of* ~гиваться) 1. to lace oneself up; з. по́ясом to tighten one's belt. 2. to be covered; to close (*intrans.*), skin over (*of a wound*). 3. (*coll.*) to be delayed; to linger; to be dragged out, drag on (*intrans.*); вечери́нка ~ну́лась до по́лночи the party dragged on till midnight. 4. to inhale (*in smoking*).

зау́л|ок, ка, *m.* (*coll.*) back street.

зау́мн|ый, *adj.* unintelligible; з. язы́к a kind of futuristic language (*based on arbitrary usage and invented words having no objective reference*).

за́ум|ь, и, *no pl.*, *f.* = ~ный язы́к.

зауны́в|ный (~ен, ~на), *adj.* doleful.

заупоко́йн|ый, *adj.* for the repose of the soul (*of the dead*); ~ая слу́жба requiem.

заупря́м|иться, люсь, ишься, *pf.* to begin to be obstinate, turn obstinate.

зауря́д, а, *m.* (*obs.*) 1. acting rank, brevet rank. 2. (*fig.*, *coll.*) mediocrity.

зауря́д- (*obs.*) acting-, brevet-.

зауря́д|ный (~ен, ~на), *adj.* ordinary, commonplace; mediocre.

заусе́ниц|а, ы, *f.* 1. agnail, hangnail. 2. (*tech.*) wire-edge.

за́утра, *adv.* (*poet.*, *obs.*) on the morrow.

за́утрен|я, и, *f.* (*eccl.*) matins.

заутю́жива|ть, ю, *impf. of* заутю́жить.

заутю́ж|ить, у, ишь, *pf.* to iron (out).

зау́ченный, *p.p.p. of* заучи́ть *and adj.* studied.

зау́чива|ть(ся), ю(сь), *impf. of* заучи́ть(ся).

зау|чи́ть, чу́, ~чишь, *pf.* (*of* ~чивать) 1. to learn by heart. 2. (*coll.*) to din learning into.

зауч|и́ться, у́сь, ~ишься, *pf.* (*of* ~иваться) (*coll.*) to overstudy.

зауша́тельский, *adj.* disparaging, abusive.

зауша́тельств|о, а, *n.* disparagement, abuse.

зауш|а́ть, а́ю, *impf. of* ~и́ть.

зауше́ни|е, я, *n.* box on the ears; (*fig.*) slap in the face, insult.

зауш|и́ть, у́, и́шь, *pf.* (*of* ~а́ть) (*obs.*) to box on the ears; (*fig.*) to insult.

зау́шниц|а, ы, *f.* (*med.*) mumps.

зау́шный, *adj.* behind the ears; (*med.*) parotid.

зафикси́р|овать, ую, *pf. of* фикси́ровать.

зафрахт|ова́ть, у́ю, *pf.* (*of* фрахтова́ть *and* ~о́вывать) to charter, freight.

зафрахто́выва|ть, ю, *impf. of* зафрахтова́ть.

заха́жива|ть, ю, *freq. of* заходи́ть[1]; он часте́нько к нам ~л he often used to drop in (to see us).

заха́п|ать, аю, *pf.* (*of* ~ывать) (*coll.*) to grab, lay hold of.

заха́пыва|ть, ю, *impf. of* заха́пать.

захва́лива|ть, ю, *impf. of* захвали́ть.

захвал|и́ть, ю́, ~ишь, *pf.* (*coll.*) to praise to excess; to spoil by flattery.

захва́т, а, *m.* 1. seizure, capture; usurpation. 2. (*tech.*) claw.

захва́танный *p.p.p. of* захвата́ть *and adj.* soiled by handling, thumbed; (*fig.*, *coll.*) trite, hackneyed.

захват|а́ть, а́ю, *pf.* (*of* ~ывать[2]) (*coll.*) to make dirty by handling; to thumb.

захва|ти́ть, чу́, ~тишь, *pf.* (*of* ~тывать[1]) 1. to take; з. горсть ви́шен to take a handful of cherries; они́ ~ти́ли с собо́й дете́й they have taken the children with them. 2. to seize; to capture; з. власть to seize power; мы ~ти́ли три́ста пле́нных we took three hundred prisoners. 3. (*fig.*) to carry away; to thrill, excite; кни́га меня́ ~ти́ла I was thrilled by the book. **4.** (*coll.*) to catch; з. после́дний по́езд to catch the last train; я успе́л з. его́ в кабине́те I managed to catch him in his office; ~ти́ла ли тебя́ гроза́? were you caught by the storm? **5.** to stop (*an illness, etc.*) in time. **6.** (*impers.*) от э́того у меня́ дух ~ти́ло it took my breath away.

захва́тнический, *adj.* (*pejor.*) aggressive.

захва́тчик, а, *m.* invader; aggressor.

захва́тыва|ть¹, ю, *impf. of* захвати́ть.

захва́тыва|ть², ю, *impf. of* захвата́ть.

захва́тыва|ющий, *pres. part. act. of* ~ть¹ and *adj.* (*fig.*) gripping; слу́шать но́вости с ~ющим интере́сом to listen to news with keen interest.

захвора́|ть, ю, *pf.* (*coll.*) to be taken ill.

захиле́|ть, ю, *pf. of* хиле́ть.

захире́лый, *adj.* faded; ailing.

захире́|ть, ю, *pf. of* хире́ть.

захлеб|ну́ть, ну́, нёшь, *pf.* (*of* ~ывать) (*coll.*) **1.** to swallow, take a mouthful of. **2.** (+а. *and* i.) to take (with), wash down (with).

захлеб|ну́ться, ну́сь, нёшься, *pf.* (*of* ~ываться) **1.** to choke (*intrans.*); to swallow the wrong way. **2.** (*fig., coll.*) з. от восто́рга to be transported with delight; ата́ка ~ну́лась (*mil.*) the attack misfired.

захлёбыва|ть, ю, *impf. of* захлебну́ть.

захлёбыва|ться, юсь, *impf.* (*of* захлебну́ться) to choke (*intrans.*); (*fig.*) з. от сме́ха to choke with laughter; говори́ть ~ющимся го́лосом to speak in a voice choked with emotion.

захлест|а́ть, а́ю, *pf.* (*of* ~ывать²) (*coll.*) **1.** to flog to death. **2.** to begin to pour (*of rain*).

захлест|ну́ть, ну́, нёшь, *pf.* (*of* ~ывать¹) **1.** to fasten, secure. **2.** to flow over, swamp, overwhelm; (*fig.*) её ~ну́ла волна́ сча́стья a wave of happiness flowed over her.

захлёстыва|ть¹, ю, *impf. of* захлеста́ть.

захлёстыва|ть², ю, *impf. of* захлестну́ть.

захло́п|нуть, ну, нешь, *pf.* (*of* ~ывать) **1.** to slam. **2.** to shut in.

захло́п|нуться, нусь, нешься, *pf.* (*of* ~ываться) to slam to; to close with a bang.

захлопо|та́ться, чу́сь, ~чешься, *pf.* (*coll.*) to be worn out (with bustling about).

захло́пыва|ть(ся), ю(сь), *impf. of* захло́пнуть(ся).

захлороформи́р|овать, ую, *pf. of* хлороформи́ровать.

захмеле́|ть, ю, *pf. of* хмеле́ть.

захо́д, а, *m.* **1.** (со́лнца) sunset. **2.** stopping (at), calling (at), putting in (at); э́тот парохо́д пришёл из Аме́рики без ~а в Шербу́р this ship has arrived from America without calling at Cherbourg.

захо|ди́ть¹, жу́, ~дишь, *impf. of* зайти́.

захо|ди́ть², жу́, ~дишь, *pf.* to begin to walk; он ~ди́л по ко́мнате he began to pace up and down the room.

захо|ди́ться, жу́сь, ~дишься, *pf.* (*coll.*) to tire oneself out with walking, walk oneself off one's feet.

захо́жий, *adj.* (*coll.*) newly-arrived; он — з. челове́к he is a stranger.

захо|жу́, ~дишь, *see* ~ди́ть.

захолоде́|ть, ю, *pf.* (*coll.*) to become cold; (*impers.*) to turn cold.

захолу́стный, *adj.* remote; з. быт (*fig.*) provincial life.

захолу́ст|ье, ья, *g. pl.* ~ий (*coll.* ~ьев), *n.* out-of-the-way place.

захороне́ни|е, я, *n.* burial.

захорон|и́ть, ю́, ~ишь, *pf.* (*of* хорони́ть) **1.** to bury. **2.** (*dial.*) to hide.

захо|те́ть(ся), чу́(сь), ~чешь(ся), ти́м(ся), ти́те(сь), тя́т(ся), *pf. of* хоте́ть(ся).

захребе́тник, а, *m.* (*dial.*) parasite.

захуда́лый, *adj.* impoverished, decayed.

заца́п|ать, ую, *pf.* (*of* ~ывать) (*coll.*) to grab; to lay hold of.

заца́пыва|ть, ю, *impf. of* заца́пать.

зацве|сти́, ту́, тёшь, *past* ~л, ~ла́, *pf.* (*of* ~та́ть) to break into blossom.

зацвета́|ть, ю, *impf. of* зацвести́.

зацве|ту́, тёшь, *see* ~сти́.

зацел|ова́ть, у́ю, *pf.* (*coll.*) to smother with kisses, rain kisses on.

зацеп|и́ть, лю́, ~ишь, *pf.* (*of* ~ля́ть) **1.** to hook. **2.** (за+а.) to catch (on); з. ного́й за ка́мень to catch one's foot on a stone; (*tech.*) to engage (*gears*); (*fig.*) to sting.

зацеп|и́ться, лю́сь, ~ишься, *pf.* (*of* ~ля́ться) (за+а.) **1.** to catch (on); чуло́к у неё ~и́лся за гвоздь her stocking caught on a nail. **2.** to catch hold (of).

заце́пк|а, и, *f.* (*coll.*) **1.** peg, hook. **2.** hooking. **3.** (*fig.*) pull, protection. **4.** hitch, catch (*fig.*).

зацепля́|ть(ся), ю(сь), *impf. of* зацепи́ть(ся).

зачаро́ванный, *p.p.p. of* зачарова́ть *and adj.* spell-bound.

зачар|ова́ть, у́ю, *pf.* (*of* ~о́вывать) to bewitch, enchant, captivate.

зачаро́выва|ть, ю, *impf. of* зачарова́ть.

зача|сти́ть, щу́, сти́шь, *pf.* (*coll.*) **1.** (+*inf.*) to take (to); он ~сти́л игра́ть в те́ннис по вечера́м he has taken to playing tennis in the evening; они́ ~сти́ли к нам в го́сти they have taken to visiting us, they have become regular visitors at our house. **2.** to begin to go fast; докла́дчик ~сти́л так, что переводи́ть его́ слова́ ста́ло невозмо́жно the lecturer began to go so fast that it was impossible to translate; дождь ~сти́л it began to rain cats and dogs.

зачасту́ю, *adv.* (*coll.*) often, frequently.

зача́ти|е, я, *n.* (*physiol.*) conception.

зача́т|ок, ка, *m.* **1.** embryo. **2.** rudiment (*biol.*). **3.** (*usually pl.*; *fig.*) beginning, germ.

зача́точн|ый, *adj.* rudimentary; в ~ом состоя́нии in embryo.

зач|а́ть, ну́, нёшь, *past* ~а́л, ~ала́, ~а́ло, *pf.* (*of* ~ина́ть) **1.** to conceive (*trans. and intrans.*). **2.** (+*a.* or *inf.*) (*coll.*) to begin.

зача́х|нуть, ну, нешь, *past* ~нул and ~, ~ла, *pf. of* ча́хнуть.

зача́|щу, сти́шь, *see* ~сти́ть.

зач|ёл, ла́, *see* ~е́сть.

зачéм, *interrog. and relat. adv.* why; what for; з. ты пришла́? why did you come?; вот з. пришла́ that's why I came.

зачéм-то, *adv.* for some reason or other.

зачёркива|ть, ю, *impf. of* зачеркну́ть.

зачерк|ну́ть, ну́, нёшь, *pf.* (*of* ~ивать) to cross out, strike out.

зачернé|ть, ю, *pf.* to show black.

зачернé|ться, юсь, *pf.* to turn black.

зачерн|и́ть, ю́, и́шь, *pf.* (*of* черни́ть 1 and ~я́ть) to blacken, paint black.

зачерн|я́ть, я́ю, *impf. of* ~и́ть.

зачерп|а́ть, а́ю, *pf.* to begin to ladle.

зачерп|ну́ть, ну́, нёшь, *pf.* (*of* ~ывать) to draw up, scoop; to ladle.

зачéрпыва|ть, ю, *impf. of* зачерпну́ть.

зачерствéлый, *adj.* stale; (*fig.*) hard-hearted.

зачерствé|ть, ю, *pf. of* черстве́ть 1.

зачер|ти́ть, чу́, ~ти́шь, *pf.* (*of* ~чивать) **1.** to cover with pencil-strokes. **2.** to sketch.

зачéрчива|ть, ю, *impf. of* зачерти́ть.

зачер|чу́, ~ти́шь, *see* ~ти́ть.

заче|са́ть, шу́, ~шешь, *pf.* **1.** to begin to scratch. **2.** (*impf.* ~сывать) to comb back.

заче|са́ться, шу́сь, ~шешься, *pf.* (*coll.*) **1.** to begin to scratch oneself. **2.** to begin to itch.

зач|е́сть, ту́, тёшь, *past* ~ёл, ~ла́, *pf.* (*of* ~и́тывать[1]) **1.** to take into account, reckon as, credit; з. де́сять рубле́й в упла́ту до́лга to account ten roubles towards payment of a debt; з. проведённый на вое́нной слу́жбе год за два го́да to reckon a year spent on war service as two years. **2.** (+*d.* and *a.*) to pass (*trans.*); мы ~ли́ ему́ перево́д с францу́зского we passed him in French translation.

зачёсыва|ть, ю, *impf. of* зачеса́ть.

зачёт, а, *m.* **1.** reckoning; в з. пла́ты in payment. **2.** test (*in school, etc.*); получи́ть з., сдать з. (по+*d.*) to pass a test (in); поста́вить (+*d.*) з. (по+*d.*) to pass (in); поста́вили мне з. по исто́рии they have passed me in history.

зачёт|ный, *adj. of* ~. **1.** ~ная квита́нция receipt. **2.** ~ная кни́жка (student's) record

book; ~ная се́ссия test period; ~ная стрельба́ classification shoot.

зачехл|и́ть, ю́, и́шь, *pf. of* чехли́ть.

зач|ешу́, ~е́шешь, *see* ~еса́ть.

зачи́н, а, *m.* (*lit.*) beginning; introduction (*of folk-tale, etc.*).

зачина́тел|ь, я, *m.* (*rhet.*) author, founder.

зачина́|ть, ю, *impf. of* зача́ть.

зачи́нива|ть, ю, *impf. of* зачини́ть.

зачин|и́ть, ю́, ~ишь, *pf.* (*of* ~ивать) (*coll.*) to mend; to patch; to sharpen (*a pencil*).

зачи́нщик, а, *m.* (*pejor.*) instigator, ring-leader.

зачи́сл|ить, ю, ишь, *pf.* (*of* ~я́ть) **1.** to include; з. в счёт to enter in an account. **2.** to enrol, enlist; з. в штат to take on the staff, on the strength.

зачи́сл|иться, юсь, ишься, *pf.* (*of* ~я́ться) (в+*a.*). **1.** to join, enter. **2.** *pass. of* ~ить.

зачисл|я́ть(ся), я́ю(сь), *impf. of* ~и́ть(ся).

зачи́|стить, щу, стишь, *pf.* (*of* ~ща́ть) **1.** to smooth out. **2.** to clean up, clean out.

зачит|а́ть, а́ю, *pf.* (*of* ~ывать[2]) (*coll.*) **1.** to read out. **2.** to borrow and fail to return to its owner, take and keep (*a book*). **3.** to exhaust (*by continual reading aloud*). **4.** (*university sl.*) to exceed one's allotted time (*in lecturing*). **5.** (*no impf.*) to begin to read.

зачит|а́ться, а́юсь, *pf.* (*of* ~ываться) **1.** to become engrossed in reading; to go on reading; вчера́ я ~а́лся далеко́ за́ полночь last night I went on reading until long after midnight. **2.** (*coll.*) to make oneself stale by excessive reading.

зачи́тыва|ть[1], ю, *impf. of* зачесть.

зачи́тыва|ть[2], ю, *impf. of* зачита́ть.

зачи́тыва|ться, юсь, *impf.* **1.** *impf. of* зачита́ться. **2.** *pass. of* ~ть[2].

зачища́|ть, ю, *impf. of* зачи́стить.

зачи́|щу, стишь, *see* ~стить.

зач|ну́, нёшь, *see* ~а́ть.

зачтён|ный (~, ~а́), *p.p.p. of* зачесть.

зач|ту́, тёшь, *see* ~е́сть.

зачумлённый, *adj.* infected with plague.

зачу́|ять, ю, ешь, *pf.* (*coll.*) to scent, smell.

зашáрка|ть, ю, *pf.* (*coll.*) **1.** (*impf.* зашáрки-вать) to scratch (*with one's feet*). **2.** to begin to scrape (one's feet).

зашáркива|ть, ю, *impf. of* зашáркать 1.

зашварт|ова́ть, у́ю, *pf.* (*of* ~о́вывать) (*naut.*) to moor, tie up.

зашварт|ова́ться, у́юсь, *pf.* (*of* ~о́вываться) (*naut.*) to moor, tie up (*intrans.*).

зашварто́выва|ть(ся), ю(сь), *impf. of* зашвартова́ть(ся).

зашвы́рива|ть, ю, *impf. of* зашвырну́ть *and* зашвыря́ть.

зашвыр|ну́ть, ну́, нёшь, *pf.* (*of* ~ивать) (*coll.*) to throw, fling (away).

зашвыр|я́ть, я́ю, *pf.* (*of* ~ива́ть) (+*a. and i.*; *coll.*) to shower (with); з. кого́-н. ка́мнями to stone someone, throw stones at someone.

зашелохн|у́ть, у́, ёшь, *pf.* (*obs.*) to ripple.

зашиб|а́ть, а́ю, *impf.* (*coll.*) **1.** *impf. of* ~и́ть. **2.** to drink (*intrans.*).

зашиб|а́ться, а́юсь, *impf. of* ~и́ться.

зашиб|и́ть, у́, ёшь, *past* ~, ~ла, *pf.* (*of* ~а́ть) (*coll.*) **1.** to bruise, knock, hurt; он ~ себе́ коле́но he has bruised his knee. **2.** з. деньгу́ (*sl.*) to coin money.

зашиб|и́ться, у́сь, ёшься, *past* ~ся, ~лась, *pf.* (*of* ~а́ться) (*coll.*) to bruise oneself, knock oneself.

зашива́ть, ю, *impf. of* заши́ть.

заш|и́ть, ью́, ьёшь, *pf.* (*of* ~ива́ть) **1.** to mend. **2.** to sew up; з. посы́лку в холст to sew up a parcel in sacking. **3.** (*med.*) to put (a) stitch(es) in.

зашифр|ова́ть, у́ю, *pf.* (*of* шифрова́ть *and* ~о́вывать) to encipher, put into code.

зашифро́выва|ть, ю, *impf. of* зашифрова́ть.

за|шлю́, шлёшь, *see* ~сла́ть.

зашнур|ова́ть, у́ю, *pf.* (*of* шнурова́ть *and* ~о́вывать) to lace up.

зашнуро́выва|ть, ю, *impf. of* зашнурова́ть.

зашпакл|ева́ть, ю́ю, *pf.* (*of* шпаклева́ть *and* ~ёвывать) to putty (*woodwork, etc., before painting*).

зашпаклёвыва|ть, ю, *impf. of* зашпаклева́ть.

зашпи́л|ить, ю, ишь, *pf.* (*of* ~ивать) to pin up, fasten with a pin.

зашпи́лива|ть, ю, *impf. of* зашпи́лить.

зашта́тный, adj. (*obs.*) supernumerary, extra; з. чино́вник official not on permanent staff; з. го́род unimportant town (*not being, or having ceased to be, the administrative centre of an uyezd*).

заштемпелева́|ть, ю, *pf.* (*of* штемпелева́ть) to stamp, postmark.

заштопа|ть, ю, *pf.* (*of* што́пать) to darn.

заштрих|ова́ть, у́ю, *pf. of* штрихова́ть.

заштукату́рива|ть, ю, *impf. of* заштукату́рить.

заштукату́р|ить, ю, ишь, *pf.* (*of* ~ивать) to plaster.

защеко|та́ть, чу́, ~чешь, *pf.* (*coll.*) **1.** to torment by tickling. **2.** to begin to tickle.

защёлк|а, и, *f.* click, latch (*of lock*); catch, pawl.

защёлкива|ть, ю, *impf. of* защёлкнуть.

защёлк|нуть, ну, нешь, *pf.* (*of* ~ивать) (*coll.*) to latch.

защем|и́ть, лю́, и́шь, *pf.* (*of* ~ля́ть) **1.** to pinch, jam, nip; з. па́лец to pinch one's finger. **2.** (*impers.; coll.*) у неё ~и́ло се́рдце her heart aches.

защемля́|ть, ю, *impf. of* защеми́ть.

защип|ну́ть, ну́, нёшь, *pf.* (*of* ~ывать)

to take (*with pincers, tongs, etc.*); to nip, tweak; to curl (*hair*); to punch (*tickets*).

защи́пыва|ть, ю, *impf. of* защипну́ть.

защи́т|а, ы, *no pl., f.* defence; protection; (*collect.*) the defence (*leg. and sport*); в ~у (+*g.*) in defence (of); под ~ой (+*g.*) under the protection (of); свиде́тели ~ы witnesses for the defence.

защи|ти́ть(ся), щу́(сь), ти́шь(ся), *pf. of* ~ща́ть(ся).

защи́тник, а, *m.* **1.** defender, protector; (*leg.*) counsel for the defence; колле́гия ~ов the Bar. **2.** (*sport*) (full-)back; ле́вый, пра́вый з. left, right back.

защи́тн|ый, adj. protective; ~ая окра́ска (*zool.*) protective coloration; ~ые очки́ goggles; з. цвет khaki.

защища́|ть, ю, *impf.* **1.** (*impf. of* защити́ть) to defend, protect. **2.** (*no pf.*) to defend (*leg.*); to stand up for; з. диссерта́цию to defend a thesis (*before examiners*).

защища́|ться, ю́сь, *impf.* (*of* защити́ться) **1.** to defend oneself, protect oneself. **2.** *pass. of* ~ть.

за|щу́, сти́шь, *see* ~сти́ть.

заяви́тел|ь, я, *m.* (*leg.*) declarant, deponent.

заяв|и́ть, лю́, ~ишь, *pf.* (*of* ~ля́ть) **1.** (+*a.*, о+*p. or* что) to announce, declare; з. свои́ права́ (на+*a.*) to claim one's rights (to); з. об ухо́де со слу́жбы to announce one's retirement. **2.** (*obs.*) to certify, attest.

заяв|и́ться, лю́сь, ~ишься, *pf.* (*coll.*) to appear, turn up.

зая́вк|а, и, *f.* (на+*a.*) claim (for); demand (for).

заявле́ни|е, я, *n.* **1.** statement, declaration. **2.** application; пода́ть з. to put in an application.

заявля́|ть, ю, *impf. of* заяви́ть.

зая́длый, adj. (*coll.*) inveterate.

за́|яц, йца, *m.* **1.** hare; (*prov.*) одни́м уда́ром уби́ть двух ~йцев to kill two birds with one stone. **2.** (*coll.*) stowaway; gate-·crasher; е́хать ~йцем to travel without paying for a ticket.

зая́|чий, adj. *of* ~ц; ~чья губа́ (*med.*) hare-lip; (*bot.*) ~чья ла́пка hare's foot; з. щаве́ль wood sorrel.

збру́|я, и = сбру́я.

зва́ни|е, я, *n.* **1.** (*obs.*) profession, calling. **2.** rank; title.

зва́ный, adj. **1.** invited. **2.** with invited guests; з. ве́чер guest-night; з. обе́д banquet.

зва́тельный, adj. (*gram.*) з. паде́ж vocative case.

зва|ть, зову́, зовёшь, *past* ~л, ~ла́, ~ло, *impf.* (*of* по~) **1.** to call; з. на по́мощь to call for help. **2.** to ask, invite. **3.** (*impf.*

only) to call; как вас зову́т? what is your name? меня́ зову́т Влади́мир my name is Vladimir, I am called Vladimir.

зва́|ться, зову́сь, зовёшься, *past* ⁀лся́, ⁀ла́сь, ⁀ло́сь, *impf.* (+*i.*; *coll.*) to be called; её сестра́ ⁀ла́сь Татья́ной her sister was called Tatyana.

звезд|а́, ы́, *pl.* ⁀ы, ⁀, ⁀а́м, *f.* 1. star; (*fig.*) з. экра́на film star; ве́рить в свою́ ⁀у́ to believe in one's lucky star; роди́ться под счастли́вой ⁀о́й to be born under a lucky star; он ⁀ с не́ба не хвата́ет (*coll., iron.*) he won't set the Thames on fire. 2. (*zool.*) морска́я з. starfish.

звёзд|ный, *adj.* of ⁀а́; ⁀ная ка́рта celestial map; ⁀ная ночь starlit night.

звездообра́з|ный (⁀ен, ⁀на), *adj.* star-shaped; з. дви́гатель (*tech.*) radial engine.

звездочёт, а, *m.* (*obs.*) astrologer.

звёздочк|а, и, *f.* 1. *dim. of* звезда́. 2. asterisk.

звен|е́ть, ю́, и́шь, *impf.* 1. to ring; у неё ⁀е́ло в уша́х there was a ringing in her ears. 2. (+*i.*) з. моне́тами to jingle coins; з. стака́нами to clink glasses.

звен|о́, а́, *pl.* ⁀ья, ⁀ьев, *n.* 1. link (*of a chain; also fig.*). 2. (*fig.*) team, section (*in agriculture, etc.*); (*aeron.*) flight. 3. row (*of logs*).

звен|ьево́й, *adj.* of ⁀о́; *as noun* з., ⁀ьево́го, *m.* team leader; section leader (*of Pioneers*).

звер|ёк, ька́, *m. dim. of* ⁀ь.

зверёныш, а, *m.* (*coll.*) young of wild animal.

звере́|ть, ю, ешь, *impf.* (*of* о⁀) to become brutalized.

звери́н|ец, ца, *m.* menagerie.

звер|и́ный, *adj.* of ⁀ь; of wild animals; ⁀и́ное число́ (*bibl.*) number of the Beast.

зверобо́|й¹, я, *m.* hunter, trapper.

зверобо́|й², я, *m.* (*bot.*) St. John's wort.

зверово́дств|о, а, *n.* breeding of animals for furs.

зверово́дческий, *adj.* fur-breeding.

звероло́в, а, *m.* hunter, trapper.

звероло́в|ный, *adj.* of ⁀; з. про́мысел hunting, trapping.

звероподо́б|ный (⁀ен, ⁀на), *adj.* beast-like; bestial.

зве́рски, *adv.* 1. brutally, bestially. 2. (*coll.*) terribly, awfully; я з. уста́л I am terribly tired.

зве́рский, *adj.* 1. brutal, bestial. 2. (*coll.*) terrific, tremendous; у него́ з. аппети́т he has a tremendous appetite.

зве́рств|о, а, *n.* brutality; atrocity; ⁀а atrocities (*in war, etc.*).

зве́рств|овать, ую, *impf.* to behave with brutality; to commit atrocities.

звер|ь, я, *pl.* ⁀и, ⁀е́й, *m.* 1. wild animal, wild beast; пушно́й з. fur-bearing animal. 2. (*fig.*) brute, beast; смотре́ть ⁀ем to look (very) savage, look (very) fierce.

зверь|ё, я́, *no pl., n.* (*collect.*) wild animals, wild beasts; (*fig.*) brutes, beasts.

звон, а, *m.* 1. (ringing) sound, peal; з. моне́т chinking of coins; з. стака́нов clinking of glasses; слы́шал з., да не зна́ет, где он he does not know what he is talking about. 2. (*fig., coll.*) rumour; gossip.

звона́р|ь, я́, *m.* 1. bell-ringer. 2. (*fig., coll.*) rumour-monger; gossip.

звон|и́ть, ю́, и́шь, *impf.* 1. (*pf. of* по⁀) (в+*a.*) to ring; з. кому́-н. (по телефо́ну) to telephone someone, ring someone up; вы не туда́ ⁀и́те you've got the wrong number; ⁀я́т someone is ringing; з. во все колокола́ (*fig.*) to set all the bells a-ringing. 2. (о+*p.*) to gossip (about).

звон|и́ться, ю́сь, и́шься, *impf.* (*of* по⁀) to ring (*a doorbell*).

зво́н|кий (⁀ок, ⁀ка́, ⁀ко), *adj.* 1. ringing, clear; ⁀кая моне́та hard cash, coin. 2. (*ling.*) voiced.

звон|ко́вый, *adj.* of ⁀о́к.

зво́нниц|а, ы, *f.* belfry (*of old Russian churches*).

звон|о́к, ка́, *m.* bell; дать з. to ring; з. по телефо́ну telephone call; встава́ть по ⁀ку́ to get up when the bell goes.

зво́н|че and (*coll.*) ⁀чée, *comp. of* ⁀кий and ⁀ко.

звук, а, *m.* sound; пусто́й звук (*fig.*) (mere) name, empty phrase; я звал её, а она́ ни ⁀а I kept calling her but she never uttered a sound; (*ling.*) гла́сный з. vowel; согла́сный з. consonant.

звукови́к, а́, *m.* (*mil., coll.*) member of sound-locating *or* sound-ranging unit.

звук|ово́й, *adj.* of ⁀; ⁀ова́я волна́ sound wave; ⁀ово́е измене́ние (*ling.*) sound change; ⁀ово́е кино́, з. фильм sound-film(s), talkie(s).

звукоза́пис|ь, и, *f.* sound recording.

звуконепроница́емый, *adj.* sound-proof.

звукоопера́тор, а, *m.* sound producer (*in film industry*).

звукоподража́ни|е, я, *n.* onomatopoeia.

звукоподража́тельный, *adj.* onomatopoeic.

звукопрово́дный, *adj.* (*phys.*) sound-conducting.

звукоря́д, а, *m.* (*mus.*) scale.

звукоснима́тел|ь, я, *m.* (*radio*) pick-up.

звукоула́вливател|ь, я, *m.* (*mil.*) sound-locator.

звукоулови́тел|ь, я, *m.* = звукоула́вливатель.

звуча́ни|е, я, *n.* 1. (*ling.*) phonation. 2. sound(s).

звуч|а́ть, у́, и́шь, *impf.* (*of* про⁀) 1. to be heard; to sound; вдали́ ⁀а́ли голоса́ voices could be heard in the distance;

э́тот пасса́ж ~и́т прекра́сно (*mus.*) this passage sounds splendid. **2.** (+*adv. or i.*; *fig.*) to sound; to express, convey; з. трево́гой to sound a note of alarm; з. и́скренно to ring true.

зву́ч|ный (~ен, ~на́, ~но), *adj.* sonorous.

звя́кань|е, я, *n.* jingling; tinkling.

звя́к|ать, аю, *impf. of* ~нуть.

звя́к|нуть, ну, нешь, *pf.* (*of* ~ать) **1.** (+*i.*) to jingle; to tinkle. **2.** (+*d.*) з. по телефо́ну (*coll.*) to ring up.

зга, *only in phrase* ни зги не ви́дно it is pitch dark.

зда́ни|е, я, *n.* building, edifice.

здесь, *adv.* **1.** (*of place*) here; (*on letters*) local. **2.** (*coll.*) here, at this point (*of time*); in this; з. мы засмея́лись here we burst out laughing; з. нет ничего́ смешно́го there is nothing funny in this.

зде́шний, *adj.* local; of this place; вы з. жи́тель? нет, я не з. are you a resident of this place? no, I am a stranger here.

здоро́ва|ться, юсь, *impf.* (*of* по~) (с+*i.*) to greet; to pass the time of day (with); з. за́ руку to shake hands (*in greeting*).

здорове́нн|ый, *adj.* (*coll.*) robust, muscular; big, strong; ~ая ба́ба muscular woman; з. го́лос powerful voice.

здорове́|ть, ю, ешь, *impf.* (*of* по~) (*coll.*) to become stronger.

здо́рово (*coll.*) **1.** (*adv.*) splendidly, magnificently; ты з. порабо́тал you have worked splendidly. **2.** (*adv.*) very, very much; вчера́ они́ з. вы́пили they had a great deal to drink yesterday. **3.** (*interj.*) well done!

здоро́во¹, *interj.* (*coll.*) hullo.

здоро́в|о², *adv. of* ~ый¹; healthily, soundly; (за) з. живёшь for nothing, without rhyme or reason.

здоро́в|ый¹ (~, ~а), *adj.* **1.** healthy; бу́дь(те) ~(ы)! (*on parting*) good luck!; (*to someone sneezing*) (God) bless you! **2.** health-giving, wholesome; (*fig.*) sound, healthy; з. кли́мат healthy climate; ~ая иде́я sound idea.

здоро́в|ый² (~, ~а́, ~о́), *adj.* (*coll.*) **1.** robust, sturdy. **2.** strong, powerful; sound; з. моро́з sharp frost; ~ая трёпка sound thrashing. **3.** (*short form* +*inf.*) clever (at), good (at), expert; он ~ льстить же́нщинам he is expert at flattering women.

здоро́вь|е, я, *no pl., n.* health; пить за чьё-н. з. to drink someone's health; за ва́ше з.! your health!; как ва́ше з.? how are you?; на з. to your heart's content, as you please.

здоровя́к, а́, *m.* (*coll.*) person in the pink of health.

здрав- (*abbr. of* ~оохране́ние) health(-).

здра́ви|е, я, *n.* (*obs.*) health; ~я жела́ю! *soldiers' reply to senior officer's greeting.*

здра́виц|а, ы, *f.* toast; провозгласи́ть ~у за (+*a.*) to propose a toast to.

здра́вниц|а, ы, *f.* sanatorium.

здравомы́слящий, *adj.* sensible, judicious.

здравоохране́ни|е, я, *n.* (care of) public health; Министе́рство ~я Ministry of Health; о́рганы ~я (public) health services.

здравоохрани́тельный, *adj.* public health.

здравотде́л, а, *m.* health department (*of local authority*).

здра́вств|овать, ую, *impf.* to be healthy; to thrive, prosper; ~уй(те)! how do you do; how are you; да ~ует! long live!

здра́в|ый (~, ~а), *adj.* **1.** sensible; з. смысл common sense. **2.** (*obs.*) healthy; ~ и невреди́м safe and sound; быть в ~ом уме́ to be in one's right mind.

зе́бр|а, ы, *f.* (*zool.*) zebra.

зе́бр|овый, *adj. of* ~a.

зе́бу, *indecl., m.* (*zool.*) zebu.

зев, а, *m.* **1.** (*anat.*) pharynx; воспале́ние ~а (*med.*) pharyngitis. **2.** (*obs.*) jaws.

зева́к|а, и, *m. and f.* idler, gaper.

зев|а́ть, а́ю, *impf.* **1.** (*pf.* ~ну́ть) to yawn. **2.** (*no pf.*) (*coll.*) to gape, stand gaping; не ~а́й! keep your wits about you! **3.** (*pf.* про~) (*coll.*) to miss opportunities, let chances slip through one's fingers. **4.** (*no pf.*) (*dial.*) to shout, bawl.

зева́|ться, ется, *impf.* (*impers.*+*d.*) (*coll.*) to have an urge to yawn; мне сего́дня ~ется I can't stop yawning today.

зев|ну́ть, ну́, нёшь, *pf. of* ~а́ть 1.

зев|о́к, ка́, *m.* yawn.

зево́т|а, ы, *f.* (fit of) yawning.

зелёненьк|ая, ой, *f.* (*coll., obs.*) three-rouble note.

зелене́|ть, ю, *impf.* **1.** (*pf.* по~) to turn green; come out green. **2.** to show green.

зелен|и́ть, ю́, и́шь, *impf.* (*of* по~) to make green, paint green.

зеленн|о́й, *adj.*; ~а́я ла́вка greengrocer's (shop).

зеленова́т|ый (~, ~а), *adj.* greenish.

зеленогла́з|ый (~, ~а), *adj.* green-eyed.

зеленщи́к, а́, *m.* greengrocer.

зелён|ый (зе́лен, ~ а́, зе́лено), *adj.* green (*of colour; of vegetation; unripe; also fig.*); ~ое вино́ (*folk poet. or coll.*) vodka; з. горо́шек green peas; ~ые насажде́ния (plantations of) trees and shrubs; ~ая ску́ка intolerable boredom; ~ое я́блоко green apple; з. ю́нец greenhorn; ~ая у́лица go (*of traffic signals*); прогна́ть по ~ой у́лице (*hist.*) to make to run the gauntlet.

зе́лен|ь, и, *no pl., f.* **1.** green colour. **2.** (*collect.*) verdure. **3.** (*collect.*) greens (*green vegetables*).

зело́, *adv.* (*arch.*) very.

зе́л|ье, ья, *g. pl.* ~ий, *n.* **1.** potion; приворо́тное з. philtre. **2.** (*fig.*) poison; з. замо́рское (*obs.*) tobacco. **3.** (*fig., coll.*) venomous person; pest (*sl.*).

земе́льн|ый, *adj.* land; з. банк (*hist.*) Land Bank; з. наде́л allotment; ~ая ре́нта ground-rent; ~ая со́бственность (property in) land.

зе́м|ец, ца, *m.* member of zemstvo.

землеве́дени|е, я, *n.* physical geography.

землевладе́л|ец, ьца, *m.* landowner.

землевладе́л|ьческий, *adj.* of ~ец.

землевладе́ни|е, я, *n.* land-ownership.

земледе́л|ец, ьца, *m.* (peasant) farmer.

земледе́ли|е, я, *n.* agriculture, farming.

земледе́льческий, *adj.* agricultural, farming.

землеко́п, а, *m.* navvy.

землеме́р, а, *m.* land-surveyor.

землеме́ри|е, я, *n.* land-surveying, geodesy.

землеме́рный, *adj.* geodetic; з. шест Jacob's staff.

землепа́шеств|о, а, *n.* (*obs.*) tillage.

землепа́ш|ец, ца, *m.* (*obs.*) tiller, ploughman.

землепо́льзовани|е, я, *n.* land-tenure.

землепрохо́д|ец, ца, *m.* (*obs.*) explorer.

землеро́йк|а, и, *f.* (*zool.*) shrew.

землетрясе́ни|е, я, *n.* earthquake.

землеустро́йств|о, а, *n.* land-tenure regulations.

землечерпа́лк|а, и, *f.* (*tech.*) dredger, excavator.

землечерпа́ни|е, я, *n.* (*tech.*) dredging.

земли́ст|ый (~, ~а), *adj.* earthy; sallow (*of complexion*).

зем|ля́, ли́, *a.* ~лю, *pl.* ~ли, ~е́ль, ~ля́м, *f.* **1.** earth; (dry) land; уви́деть ~лю to sight land; упа́сть на ~лю to fall to the ground. **2.** land; soil (*fig.*); поме́щичья з. (*collect.*) landed estates; на чужо́й ~ле́ on foreign soil. **3.** earth, soil.

земля́к, а́, *m.* fellow-countryman, person from same district.

земляни́к|а, и, *no pl.*, *f.* (*collect.*) wild strawberries.

земляни́|чный, *adj.* of ~ка.

земля́нк|а, и, *f.* dug-out; adobe cottage.

земля́н|о́й, *adj.* **1.** earthen, of earth; ~ые рабо́ты excavations. **2.** earth-; ~а́я гру́ша Jerusalem artichoke; з. оре́х peanut; з. червь earth-worm.

земля́честв|о, а, *n.* **1.** friendly society of persons coming from same district. **2.** national group (*of foreign students at Soviet universities*).

земля́чк|а, и, *f.* of земля́к.

зе́мно, *adv.*, *only in phrase* з. кла́няться (*obs.*) to bow to the ground.

земново́дн|ый, *adj.* amphibious; *as noun* (*zool.*) ~ые, ~ых, amphibia; *sing.* ~ое, ~ого, *n.* amphibian.

земн|о́й, *adj.* **1.** earthly; terrestrial; ~а́я кора́ (earth-)crust; з. шар the globe; ~ы́е вое́нные си́лы land forces; з. покло́н bow to the ground. **2.** (*fig.*) mundane.

землоро́дный, *adj.* (*poet., rhet.*) earth-born, mortal.

зе́м|ский, *adj.* **1.** of ~ля́ 2; (*hist.*) ~ское ополче́ние militia; з. собо́р Assembly of the Land. **2.** of ~ство.

зе́мств|о, а, *n.* **1.** zemstvo (*elective district council in Russia, 1864–1917*). **2.** zemstvo system (*of local administration*).

зе́мщин|а, ы, *f.* (*hist.*) **1.** populace. **2.** zemshchina (*boyar domains, as opp. to* oprichnina, *under Tsar Ivan IV*).

зени́т, а, *m.* zenith (*also fig.*).

зени́тк|а, и, *f.* (*mil.; coll.*) anti-aircraft gun.

зени́тн|ый, *adj.* **1.** (*astron.*) zenithal; ~ое расстоя́ние zenith-distance. **2.** (*mil.*) anti-aircraft.

зени́тчик, а, *m.* (*mil.*) anti-aircraft gunner.

зени́ц|а, ы, *f.* (*arch.*) pupil (*of the eye*); бере́чь как ~у о́ка to keep as the apple of one's eye.

зе́ркал|о, а, *pl.* ~а́, зерка́л, ~а́м, *n.* looking-glass; mirror (*also fig.*); криво́е з. distorting mirror.

зерка́льн|ый, *adj.* of зе́ркало; (*fig.*) smooth; ~ое стекло́ plate glass; ~ое окно́ plate-glass window; ~ое изображе́ние looking-glass reflection; ~ая пове́рхность smooth surface; з. карп (*zool.*) mirror carp.

зерни́ст|ый (~, ~а), *adj.* granular; ~ая икра́ unpressed caviar(e).

зер|но́, на́, *pl.* ~на, ~ен, ~нам, *n.* **1.** grain; seed; (*fig.*) grain; kernel, core; горчи́чное з. mustard seed; жемчу́жное з. pearl; ко́фе в ~нах coffee beans; з. и́стины grain of truth. **2.** (*collect., sing. only*) grain, corn.

зернови́д|ный (~ен, ~на), *adj.* granular.

зерново́з, а, *m.* grain carrier (*ship*).

зернов|о́й, *adj.* grain, corn; ~ы́е зла́ки cereals; ~а́я торго́вля grain trade.

зернодроби́лк|а, и, *f.* (*agric.*) corn-crusher.

зерносовхо́з, а, *m.* State grain farm.

зерносуши́лк|а, и, *f.* (*agric.*) grain dryer.

зернохрани́лищ|е, а, *n.* granary.

зёрныш|ко, ка, *pl.* ~ки, ~ек, ~кам, *n., dim.* of зерно́ 1.

зерца́л|о, а, *n.* **1.** (*arch.*) looking-glass. **2.** (*pl. only*; *hist.*) breastplate.

зефи́р, а, *m.* **1.** З. (*poet.*) Zephyr. **2.** zephyr (*material*).

зигза́г, а, *m.* zigzag.

зижди́тел|ь, я, *m.* (*obs. or rhet.*) founder, author; (*rel.*) the Creator.

зижди́тельный, *adj.* (*obs.*) creative.

зи́жд|иться, ется, *impf.* (на+*p.*; *obs. or rhet.*) to be founded (on), based (on).

зил, а, *m.* Zil (*motor-vehicle produced by Likhachev factory*).

зим, а, *m.* Zim (*motor-vehicle produced by former Molotov factory*).

зим|а́, ы́, *a.* ~у, *pl.* ~ы, *d.* ~ам, *f.* winter; на́ ~у for the winter; всю ~у all winter; ско́лько лет, ско́лько ~, *see* ле́то.

зи́м|ний, *adj.* of ~а́; winter; wintry.

зим|ова́ть, у́ю, *impf.* (*of* пере~ *and* про~) to winter, pass the winter; to hibernate; знать, где ра́ки ~у́ют, *see* рак.

зимо́вк|а, и, *f.* **1.** wintering, hibernation; оста́ться на ~y to stay for the winter. **2.** polar station.

зимо́вщик, а, *m.* winterer.

зимо́вь|е, я, *n.* winter quarters, winter hut.

зимо́й, *adv.* in winter.

зиморо́д|ок, ка, *m.* (*orn.*) kingfisher.

зипу́н, а́, *m.* homespun coat.

зис, а, *m.* Zis (*motor-vehicle produced by former Stalin factory*).

зия́ни|е, я, *n.* **1.** gaping, yawning. **2.** (*ling.*) hiatus.

зия́|ть, ю, *impf.* to gape, yawn; ~ющая бе́здна yawning abyss.

злак, а, *m.* (*bot.*) grass; хле́бные ~и cereals.

зла́т|о, а, *n.* (*arch.*; *poet.*) gold.

златове́рхий, *adj.* (*folk poet.*) with roof(s) of gold.

златогла́вый, *adj.* gold-domed; with gold cupolas.

златоку́дрый, *adj.* (*poet.*) golden-haired.

зла́чн|ый, *adj.* (*obs.*) lush; (*coll.*) ~ое ме́сто haunt of vice.

зле́йший, *superl. of* злой.

зл|ить, ю, ишь, *impf.* (*of* обо~ *and* разо~) to anger; to vex; to irritate.

зл|и́ться, юсь, и́шься, *impf.* (*of* обо~ *and* разо~) **1.** (на+*a.*) to be in a bad temper; to be angry (with). **2.** (*fig.*, *poet.*) to rage (*of a storm*).

зло¹, зла, *no pl. except g.* зол, *n.* **1.** evil; harm; отплати́ть ~м за добро́ to repay good with evil. **2.** evil, misfortune, disaster; из двух зол вы́брать ме́ньшее to choose the lesser of two evils; жела́ть кому́-н. зла to bear someone malice. **3.** (*sing. only*) malice, spite; vexation; э́то сде́лал то́лько со зла he did it purely from malice, out of spite; меня́ з. берёт it vexes me, it annoys me, I feel vexed, annoyed.

зло², *adv. of* ~й; з. подшути́ть над кем-н. to play a spiteful trick on someone.

зло́б|а, ы, *f.* malice; spite; anger; по ~e out of spite; со ~ой maliciously; з. дня topic of the day, latest news; довле́ет дне́ви з. его́ (*arch.*) sufficient unto the day is the evil thereof.

зло́б|иться, люсь, ишься, *impf.* (на+*a.*; *coll.*) to feel malice (towards); to be in a bad temper (with).

зло́б|ный (~ен, ~на), *adj.* malicious, spiteful; bad-tempered.

злободне́вност|ь, и, *f.* topical interest, topical character.

злободне́вн|ый, *adj.* topical; ~ые вопро́сы burning topics of the day.

злоб|ствовать, ую, *impf.* to bear malice; (на+*a.*) to have it in (for).

злове́щ|ий (~, ~а), *adj.* ominous, ill--omened; sinister.

злово́ни|е, я, *n.* stink, stench.

злово́н|ный (~ен, ~на), *adj.* fetid, stinking.

зловре́д|ный (~ен, ~на), *adj.* pernicious; noxious.

злоде́|й, я, *m.* **1.** villain, scoundrel (*also joc.*) **2.** (*theatr.*; *obs.*) villain.

злоде́йский, *adj.* villainous.

злоде́йств|о, а, *n.* **1.** villainy. **2.** crime, evil deed.

злоде́йств|овать, ую, *impf.* to act villainously.

злодея́ни|е, я, *n.* crime, evil deed.

зложела́тельный, *adj.* (*obs.*) malevolent.

злой (зол, зла, зло), *adj.* **1.** evil; bad; з. ге́ний evil genius. **2.** wicked; malicious; malevolent; vicious; зла́я улы́бка malevolent smile; со злым у́мыслом with malicious intent; (*leg.*) of malice prepense. **3.** (*short form only*) angry; быть злым (на+*a.*) to be angry (with). **4.** (*of animals*) fierce, savage; « зла́я соба́ка » 'beware of the dog!' **5.** dangerous; severe; з. моро́з severe frost. **6.** (*coll.*) bad, nasty; з. ка́шель bad cough. **7.** (*sl.*) terrible (= keen, *enthusiastic*).

злока́чественн|ый, *adj.* (*med.*) malignant; ~ая о́пухоль malignant tumour; ~ое малокро́вие pernicious anaemia.

злоключе́ни|е, я, *n.* mishap, misadventure.

злоко́зненный, *adj.* (*obs.*) crafty, wily; perfidious.

злонаме́рен|ный (~, ~на), *adj.* ill-intentioned.

злонра́ви|е, я, *n.* (*obs.*) bad character; depravity.

злонра́в|ный (~ен, ~на), *adj.* (*obs.*) having a bad character; depraved.

злопа́мятност|ь, и, *f.* = злопа́мятство.

злопа́мят|ный (~ен, ~на), *adj.* rancorous, unforgiving.

злопа́мятств|о, а, *n.* rancour, unforgivingness.

злополу́ч|ный (~ен, ~на), *adj.* unlucky, ill-starred.

злопыха́тел|ь, я, *m.* (*coll.*) disingenuous, spiteful critic.

злопыха́тельский, *adj.* (*coll.*) disingenuously spiteful, malevolent; ranting.

злопыха́тельств|о, а, n. (coll.) malevolence; ranting.

злора́дный, adj. gloating, maliciously rejoicing at others' misfortune.

злора́дств|о, а, n. Schadenfreude (malicious delight in others' misfortunes).

злора́дств|овать, ую, impf. to rejoice at, gloat over, others' misfortunes.

злосло́ви|е, я, n. scandal, backbiting.

злосло́в|ить, лю, ишь, impf. to say spiteful things.

зло́ст|ный (~ен, ~на), adj. 1. malicious. 2. conscious, intentional; ~ное банкро́тство fraudulent bankruptcy; з. неплате́льщик persistent defaulter (in payment of debt). 3. inveterate, hardened.

зло́ст|ь, и, f. malice, spite; их з. берёт на него́ they are furious with him.

злосча́ст|ный (~ен, ~на), adj. ill-fated, ill-starred.

злот|ый, ого, m. zloty (Polish currency).

злоумы́шленник,а,m.(obs.);plotter;criminal.

злоумы́шленный, adj. (obs.) with criminal intent.

злоумышля́|ть, ю, impf. (obs.) to plot.

злоупотреб|и́ть, лю́, и́шь, pf. (of ~ля́ть) (+i.) to abuse; to indulge in to excess; to overdo; з. вла́стью to abuse power; з. чьим-н. внима́нием to take up too much of someone's time.

злоупотребле́ни|е, я, n. (+i.) abuse (of); з. дове́рием breach of confidence.

злоупотреб|ля́ть, ля́ю, impf. of ~и́ть.

злоязы́чи|е, я, n. (obs.) slander, back-biting.

злоязы́ч|ный (~ен, ~на), adj. (obs.) slanderous.

злы́д|ень, ня, m. (dial.) 1. (obs.) rogue, rascal. 2. wicked person; wicked creature.

злю́к|а, и, m. and f. (coll.) bad-tempered person; (f.) shrew.

злю́чк|а, и, m. and f. = злю́ка.

злю́щий, adj. (coll.) furious.

змееви́д|ный (~ен, ~на), adj. serpentine; sinuous, snaky.

змееви́к, á, m. 1. (tech.) coil(-pipe). 2. (min.) serpentine, ophite.

змеёныш, а, m. young snake.

зме|и́ный, adj. 1. adj. of ~я́; ~и́ная ко́жа snake-skin. 2. cunning, crafty; wicked.

змей|тый (~, ~а), adj. serpentine, sinuous.

зме|и́ться, и́тся, impf. to wind, coil; (fig., poet., pejor.) to glide; по её лицу́ ~и́лась улы́бка a smile stole across her face.

змей, змея́, m. 1. (obs. or coll.) = змея́. 2. dragon. 3. (бума́жный) з. kite; запусти́ть змея́ to fly a kite.

зме́йк|а, и, f. 1. dim. of змея́; бежа́ть ~ой to glide. 2. (mil.) broken file.

зме́йковый, adj.; з. аэроста́т kite balloon.

зме|я́, и́, pl. ~и, ~й, f. snake (also fig.);

отогре́ть, пригре́ть ~ю́ на свое́й груди́ to cherish a snake in one's bosom.

зми|й, я, m. (arch.) serpent, dragon; the Serpent (Old Testament representation of the Devil); напи́ться до зелёного ~я (coll.) to drink oneself into delirium tremens.

знава́ть, pres. not used, impf. (coll.) freq. of знать.

знак, а, m. 1. (in var. senses) sign; mark; token, symbol; ~и препина́ния stops, punctuation marks; ~и отли́чия decorations (and medals); ~и разли́чия (mil.) badges of rank, insignia; в з. (+g.) as a mark (of), as a token (of), to show. 2. omen. 3. signal; пода́ть з. to give a signal.

знако́м|ить, лю, ишь, impf. (of по~) (+a. c+i.) to acquaint (with); to introduce (to).

знако́м|иться, люсь, ишься, impf. (of по~) (c+i.) 1. to meet, make the acquaintance (of a person). 2. to introduce oneself; ~ьтесь! (informal mode of introduction) may I introduce you? 3. to become acquainted (with), familiarize oneself (with); to study, investigate; з. с ме́стностью to get to know a locality; з. с тео́рией относи́тельности to go into the theory of relativity.

знако́мств|о, а, n. 1. (c+i.) acquaintance (with). 2. acquaintances; (collect.) acquaintance; у него́ большо́е з. he has a wide circle of acquaintances; по ~у by exploiting one's personal connexions, by pulling strings. 3. (c+i.) knowledge (of).

знако́м|ый (~, ~а), adj. 1. familiar; его́ лицо́ мне ~о his face is familiar. 2. (c+i.) familiar (with); быть ~ым (c+i.) to be acquainted (with), know; я с ней ~ с де́тства I have known her since childhood. 3. as noun з., ~ого, m.; ~ая, ~ой, f. acquaintance, friend.

знамена́тел|ь, я, m. (math.) denominator; о́бщий з. common denominator; привести́ к одному́ ~ю (fig.) to reduce to a common denominator.

знамена́тел|ьный (~ен, ~ьна), adj. 1. significant, important. 2. (gram.) principal (as opp. to subordinate).

зна́м|ени, енем, etc., see ~я.

зна́мени|е, я, n. sign; ~я вре́мени signs of the times.

знамени́тост|ь, и, f. celebrity.

знамени́т|ый (~, ~а), adj. 1. celebrated, famous, renowned. 2. (coll.) outstanding, superlative.

знамен|ова́ть, у́ю, impf. to signify, mark.

знамено́с|ец, ца, m. standard-bearer (also fig.).

знамёнщик; а, m. (mil.) colour bearer.

зна́мо, as pred. (coll. or dial.) it is well known.

зна́м|я, g., d., and p. ~ени, i. ~енем, pl. ~ёна, ~ён, n. banner; standard; под ~енем (+g.; fig., rhet.) in the name of;

высо́ко держа́ть з. свобо́ды to keep the flag of freedom flying.

зна́ни|е, я, *n.* **1.** knowledge; тео́рия ~я (*philos.*) theory of knowledge; у него́ хоро́шее з. сце́ны he has a good knowledge of the stage; со ~ем де́ла capably, competently. **2.** (*pl. only*) learning; accomplishments.

зна́т|ный (~ен, ~на́, ~но), *adj.* **1.** (*adj. of* ~ь²) in an exalted station. **2.** outstanding, distinguished; ~ные лю́ди celebrities, leading figures. **3.** (*coll.*) splendid; ~ные бли́нчики splendid pancakes; ~ная су́мма a splendid sum (*of money*).

знато́к, а́, *m.* expert; connoisseur.

зна|ть¹, ю, *impf.* to know, have a knowledge of; ⌐ете ли вы Алекса́ндрова? do you know Alexandrov?; з. в лицо́ to know by sight; з. своё де́ло to know one's job; з. своё ме́сто to know one's place; з. ме́ру to know when to stop; не з. поко́я to know no peace; з. толк (в+*p.*) to be knowledgeable (about); з. уро́к to know a lesson; он хорошо́ ⌐ет Пу́шкина he has a good knowledge of Pushkin; з. себе́ це́ну to know one's own value; они́ не ⌐ли о на́ших наме́рениях they were unaware of our intentions; дать кому́-н. з. to let someone know; да́йте мне з. о вас let me hear from you; дать себя́ з. to make itself felt; он з. не хо́чет he won't listen; ~й (себе́) unconcerned; она́ ~й себе́ пе́ла she was singing away quite unconcerned; то и ~й (*coll.*) continually; как з., почём з.? who can tell?, how should I know?; кто его́ ⌐ет, Бог его́ ⌐ет, чёрт его́ ⌐ет (*coll.*) goodness knows!, God knows!, the devil (only) knows!; ⌐ешь (ли), ⌐ете (ли) (*coll.*) you know, do you know what.

знат|ь², и, *no pl., f.* (*collect.*) the nobility, the aristocracy.

знать³, *as pred.* (*coll.*) evidently, it seems.

зна́|ться, юсь, *impf.* (с+*i.*; *coll.*) to associate (with).

зна́хар|ка, ки, *f. of* ~ь.

зна́хар|ь, я, *m.* sorcerer, witch-doctor; quack(-doctor).

знач|ащий, *pres. part. act. of* ~и́ть *and adj.* significant, meaningful.

значе́ни|е, я, *n.* **1.** meaning, significance. **2.** importance, significance; прида́ть большо́е з. (+*d.*) to attach great importance (to); э́то не име́ет ~я it is of no importance. **3.** (*math.*) value.

зна́чимост|ь, и, *f.* significance.

зна́чимый, *adj.* significant.

зна́чит (*coll.*) so, then; well then; он у́мер до войны́? з., вы не́ были с ним знако́мы he died before the war? then you didn't know him.

значи́тел|ьный (~ен, ~ьна), *adj.* **1.** considerable, sizeable; в ~ьной сте́пени to a considerable extent. **2.** important; игра́ть ~ьную роль to play an important part. **3.** significant, meaningful.

зна́ч|ить, у, ишь, *impf.* **1.** to mean, signify. **2.** to mean, have significance, be of importance; ничего́ не ~ит it is of no importance; получи́ть приглаше́ние на бал о́чень мно́го ~ит для неё to be invited to a dance means a great deal to her.

зна́ч|иться, усь, ишься, *impf.* to be; to be mentioned, appear; з. в отпуску́ to be on leave; з. в спи́ске to appear on a list.

знач|о́к, ка́, *m.* **1.** badge. **2.** mark (*in margin of book, etc.*).

зна́|ющий, *pres. part. act. of* ~ть *and adj.* expert; learned, erudite.

зноб|и́ть, и́т, *impf.* **1.** (*coll.*) to chill. **2.** (*impers.*) меня́, *etc.*, ~и́т I, *etc.*, feel shivery, feverish.

зноб|кий (~ок, ~ка́, ~ко), *adj.* (*dial.*) **1.** sensitive to cold. **2.** chilly.

зно|й, я, *m.* intense heat; sultriness.

зно́|йный (~ен, ~йна), *adj.* hot, sultry; burning (*also fig.*).

зоб, а, *pl.* ~ы́, ~о́в, *m.* **1.** crop, craw (*of birds*). **2.** (*med.*) goitre.

зоба́ст|ый (~, ~а), *adj.* (*coll.*) **1.** with a large crop (*of birds*). **2.** goitrous.

зов, а, *m.* **1.** call, summons. **2.** (*coll.*) invitation.

зов|у́, ёшь, *see* звать.

зодиа́к, а, *m.* (*astron.*) zodiac; зна́ки ~а signs of the zodiac.

зодиака́льный, *adj.* (*astron.*) zodiacal, of the zodiac.

зо́дчес|кий, *adj. of* ~тво.

зо́дчеств|о, а, *n.* architecture.

зо́дч|ий, его, *m.* (*obs.*) architect.

зол¹, *see* злой.

зол², *g. pl. of* зло¹.

зол|а́, ы́, *no pl., f.* ashes, cinders.

золо́вк|а, и, *f.* sister-in-law (*husband's sister*).

золота́рник, а, *m.* (*bot.*) golden rod.

золоти́льщик, а, *m.* gilder.

золоти́ст|ый (~, ~а), *adj.* golden (*of colour*).

золо|ти́ть, чу́, ти́шь, *impf.* (*of* вы~ *and* по~) to gild.

золо|ти́ться, ти́тся, *impf.* **1.** to become golden. **2.** to shine (*of something golden*).

золотни́к¹, а́, *m.* zolotnik (*old Russian measure of weight, equivalent to* $\frac{1}{96}$ *of Russian pound*); мал з., да до́рог (*coll.*) small but precious.

золотни́к², а́, *m.* (*tech.*) slide valve; цилиндри́ческий з. piston valve.

золотнико́вый, *adj. of* золотни́к²; з. дви́гатель pusher-type engine; з. приво́д eccentric drive.

зо́лот|о, а, *no pl., n.* gold; (*collect.*) gold (*coins, ware*); плати́ть ~ом to pay in gold; есть на ~е to eat off gold plate. **2.** (*fig.*) она́ настоя́щее з. she is pure gold, a treasure; не всё то з., что блести́т (*prov.*) all is not gold that glitters; на вес ~а worth its weight in gold.

золотоволо́сый, *adj.* golden-haired.

золотоиска́тел|ь, я, m. gold-prospector; gold-digger.

золот|о́й, *adj.* **1.** gold; golden (*also fig.*); ~ы́х дел*~*ма́стер goldsmith; з. песо́к gold-dust; з. запа́с (*econ.*) gold reserves; ~а́я ры́бка goldfish; ~о́е руно́ (*myth.*) golden fleece; з. век the Golden Age; ~о́е дно (*fig.*) gold-mine; ~а́я молодёжь jeunesse dorée, gilded youth; ~ые ру́ки skilful fingers; ~а́я середи́на golden mean; ~о́е сече́ние (*math.*) golden section. **2.** (*coll.*) invaluable, precious; мой з.! my precious!, my darling! **3.** *as noun* з., ~о́го *m.* gold coin; ten-rouble piece.

золотоно́сный, *adj.* gold-bearing; з. райо́н gold-field.

золотопромы́шленник, а, m. owner of gold-mines.

золотопромы́шленност|ь, и, f. gold-mining.

золоторо́т|ец, ца, m. (*obs., coll.*) tramp, down-and-out.

золототы́сячник, а, m. (*bot.*) centaury.

золотошве́йный, *adj.* of gold embroidery.

золоту́х|а, и, f. (*med.*) scrofula.

золоту́шный, *adj.* (*med.*) scrofulous.

золоче́ни|е, я, n. gilding.

золочёный, *adj.* gilded, gilt.

Зо́лушк|а, и, f. Cinderella.

зо́льник, а, m. (*tech.*) ashpit.

зо́н|а, ы, f. **1.** zone; area, belt; з. де́йствий (*mil.*) zone of operations; з. досяга́емости (*mil.*) field of fire; з. пораже́ния (*mil.*) area under fire. **2.** (*geol.*) stratum, layer.

зона́льный, *adj.* zone; regional.

зонд, а, m. 1. (*med.*) probe. **2.** (*geol.*) bore. **3.** weather-balloon, sonde.

зонди́р|овать, ую, *impf.* (*med. and fig.*) to sound, probe; з. по́чву (*fig.*) to explore the ground.

зо́н|ный, *adj.* of ~а; (*railways*) regional.

зонт, а́, m. 1. umbrella. **2.** awning.

зо́нтик, а, m. 1. umbrella; sunshade. **2.** (*bot.*) umbel.

зо́нти|чный, *adj.* of ~к; (*bot.*) umbellate, umbelliferous.

зоо́лог, а, m. zoologist.

зоологи́ческий, *adj.* **1.** zoological; з. парк, з. сад zoological garden(s). **2.** (*fig.*) brutish, bestial.

зооло́ги|я, и, f. zoology.

зоопа́рк, а, m. zoological gardens, zoo.

зооте́хник, а, m. livestock specialist.

зо́ри, *see* заря́.

зо́р|кий (~ок, ~ка́, ~ко), adj. 1. sharp-sighted. **2.** (*fig.*) perspicacious, penetrating; vigilant.

зо́рьк|а, и, (*folk poet.*) *affect. form of* заря́.

зо́рю, *see* заря́.

зра́з|ы, ~, *sing.* (*rare*) ~а, ~ы, f. (*cul.*) zrazy (*meat cutlets stuffed with rice, buckwheat kasha, etc.*).

зрач|о́к, ка́, m. pupil (*of the eye*).

зре́лищ|е, а, n. 1. sight. **2.** spectacle; show; pageant.

зре́лищ|ный, *adj.* of ~е; ~ные предприя́тия places of entertainment.

зре́лост|ь, и, f. ripeness; maturity (*also fig.*); полова́я з. puberty; аттеста́т ~и school-leaving certificate.

зре́л|ый (~, ~а́, ~о), adj. ripe; mature (*also fig.*); дости́гнуть ~ого во́зраста to reach maturity; з. ум a mature mind; по ~ом размышле́нии on reflection, on second thoughts.

зре́ни|е, я, n. (eye)sight; по́ле ~я (*phys.*) field of vision; обма́н ~я optical illusion; то́чка ~я point of view; под э́тим угло́м ~я from this standpoint.

зре|ть¹, ю, ешь, *impf.* (*of* со~) to ripen; to mature (*also fig.*); у нас ~ет план our plans are maturing.

зреть², зрю, зришь, *impf.* (*of* у~) (*obs.*) **1.** to behold. **2.** (на+*a.*) to gaze (upon).

зри́м|ый (~, ~а), p.p.p. *of* зреть² *and adj.* visible.

зри́тел|ь, я, m. spectator, observer; быть ~ем to look on.

зри́тельн|ый, *adj.* **1.** visual; optic; з. нерв optic nerve; ~ая па́мять visual memory; ~ая труба́ telescope. **2.** з. зал hall, auditorium.

зря, *adv.* (*coll.*) to no purpose, for nothing; болта́ть з. to chatter idly; рабо́тать з. to plough the sand.

зря́чий, *adj.* sighted (*as opp. to* blind).

зуа́в, а, m. zouave.

зуб, а, m. 1. (*pl.* ~ы, ~о́в) tooth; з. му́дрости wisdom tooth; вооружённый до ~о́в armed to the teeth; име́ть з. (про́тив), точи́ть ~ы (на+*a.*; *coll.*) to have one's knife into someone; положи́ть ~ы на по́лку (*coll.*) to tighten one's belt; он по-неме́цки ни в з. толкну́ть (*coll.*) he does not know a word of German; не по ~а́м beyond one's capacity; (*coll.*) э́та пробле́ма мне не по ~а́м I cannot get my teeth into this problem; э́то у меня́ в ~а́х навя́зло (*coll.*) it sticks in my gullet, I am sick and tired of it; у тебя́ з. на́ з. не попада́ет your teeth are chattering; хоть ви́дит о́ко, да з.

неймёт (*coll.*) there's many a slip 'twixt the cup and lip; ∼ы заговори́ть, *see* заговори́ть[1]; держа́ть язы́к за ∼а́ми to hold one's tongue. **2.** (*pl.* ∼ья, ∼ьев) tooth, cog.

зуба́ст|ый (∼, ∼a), *adj.* (*coll.*) large-toothed; (*fig.*) sharp-tongued.

зуб|е́ц, ца́, *m.* **1.** tooth, cog; з. ви́лки prong. **2.** merlon (*of wall*). **3.** (*radar*) blip.

зуби́л|о, a, *n.* (*tech.*) point-tool, chisel.

зу́бно-губно́й, *adj.* (*ling.*) labio-dental.

зубн|о́й, *adj.* **1.** dental; ∼а́я боль toothache; з. врач dentist; ∼а́я па́ста toothpaste; з. порошо́к tooth-powder; ∼а́я щётка tooth-brush. **2.** (*ling.*) dental.

зубо́вн|ый, *adj., only in phrases* скре́жет з. gnashing of teeth; де́лать что-н. со скре́жетом ∼ым to do something with extreme unwillingness.

зубоврачебн|ый, *adj. of* зубно́й врач; з. кабине́т dental surgery; ∼ая шко́ла dental school.

зубоврачева́ни|е, я, *n.* dentistry.

зуб|о́к, ка́, *pl.* ∼ки́, *m.* **1.** (*g. pl.* ∼о́к) *dim. of* ∼; подари́ть на з. (*coll.*) to bring a present for a (new-born) baby; вы́учить на з. (*coll.*) to learn by rote; попа́сть на з. кому́-н. (*coll., fig.*) to be torn to pieces by someone. **2.** (*g. pl.* ∼ко́в) bit (*of coal-cutting machine*).

зуболече́бниц|а, ы, *f.* dental surgery.

зубоска́л|ить, ю, ишь, *impf.* (*coll.*) to scoff, mock.

зубоска́льств|о, a, *n.* (*coll.*) scoffing, mocking.

зуботы́чин|а, ы, *f.* (*vulg.*) sock on the jaw.

зубочи́стк|а, и, *f.* toothpick.

зубр, a, *m.* **1.** (*zool.*) (European) bison. **2.** (*fig.*) die-hard.

зубрёжк|а, и, *f.* (*coll.*) cramming.

зубри́л|а, ы, *m. and f.* (*coll.*) crammer.

зубр|и́ть[1], ю́, ∼и́шь, *impf.* (*of* за∼) to notch, serrate.

зубр|и́ть[2], ю́, ∼ и́шь, *impf.* (*of* вы́∼ *and* за∼) (*coll.*) to cram.

зубро́вк|а, и, *f.* **1.** sweet grass, holy grass. **2.** zubrovka (*sweet-grass vodka*).

зубча́тк|а, и, *f.* (*tech.*) rack-wheel.

зубча́т|ый, *adj.* **1.** (*tech.*) toothed, cogged; ∼ая желе́зная доро́га rack-railway; ∼ое колесо́ rack-wheel, cogwheel, pinion; з. насо́с gear pump; ∼ая ре́йка rack. **2.** jagged, indented.

зуд, a, *m.* itch; (*fig.*) itch, urge; писа́тельский з. the urge to write, to be a writer.

зуд|а́, ы́, *m. and f.* (*coll.*) bore (*person*).

зуд|е́ть, и́т, *impf.* **1.** (*coll.*) to itch (*intrans.*). **2.** (*fig.*) to itch, feel an itch (*to do something*).

зу|ди́ть, жу́, ди́шь, *impf.* (*coll.*) **1.** to nag at. **2.** to cram.

зу|ёк, йка́, *m.* (*orn.*) plover.

зулу́с, a, *m.* Zulu.

зулу́сский, *adj.* Zulu.

зу́ммер, a, *m.* (*tech.*) buzzer.

зурн|а́, ы́, *f.* (*mus.*) zurna (*kind of clarinet*).

зы́б|иться, лется (*past and 1st and 2nd persons of pres. not used*) *impf.* (*obs.*) to be ruffled (*of the sea*); to toss (*intrans.*).

зы́бк|а, и, *f.* (*dial.*) cradle.

зы́б|кий (∼ок, ∼ка́, ∼ко), *adj.* unsteady, shaky; (*fig.*) vacillating.

зыбу́н, а́, *m.* marshy ground; bog.

зыбу́ч|ий, *adj.* unsteady, unstable; ∼ие пески quicksands.

зыб|ь, и, *pl.* ∼и, ∼е́й, *f.* (*on water*) rippling, ripple; мёртвая з. swell; (*poet.*) lop.

зык, a, *m.* (*coll.*) loud voice; loud cry.

зы́ч|ный (∼ен, ∼на), *adj.* (*coll.*) loud, stentorian.

зюйд, a, *m.* (*naut.*) **1.** south. **2.** southerly wind.

зюйдве́стк|а, и, *f.* sou'wester (*hat*).

зэк, a, *m.* (*sl.*) prisoner, convict.

зя́б|кий (∼ок, ∼ка́, ∼ко), *adj.* chilly, sensitive to cold.

зя́б|левый, *adj. of* ∼ь; ∼левая вспа́шка autumn ploughing.

зя́блик, a, *m.* chaffinch.

зя́блый, *adj.* (*coll. or dial.*) frozen, killed by frost (*of plants*).

зя́б|нуть, ну, нешь, *past* ∼, ∼ла, *impf.* to suffer from cold, feel the cold.

зяб|ь, и, *f.* (*agric.*) land ploughed in autumn for spring sowing.

зят|ь, я, *pl.* ∼ья́, ∼ье́в, *m.* **1.** son-in-law. **2.** brother-in-law (*sister's husband or husband's sister's husband*).

И

и[1], *conj.* **1.** and; добро́ и зло good and evil; *indicating temporal sequence*: я встал и вы́мылся и побри́лся I got up and washed and shaved; *introducing narrative*: и наста́ло у́тро and then came the morning; *emphasizing questions*: и ра́зве э́то не пра́вда? and is it not the truth?; *adversative*: мужчи́на, и пла́чет! a man, and crying!; и так да́лее, и про́чее (*abbr.* и т. д., и пр.) etcetera, and so on, and so forth. **2.** и …и both … and; и тот и друго́й both. **3.** too; (*with negation*) either; она́ сказа́ла, что и муж придёт she

said that her husband would come too;
и он не знал he did not know either. **4.**
even; и знато́к ошиба́ется even an expert
may be mistaken; я не мог бы и поду́мать
об э́том I would not (even) think of it.
5. (*emphatic*) в то́м-то и де́ло that is the
whole point. **6.** и... да (*concessive*): я и
пое́хал бы, да не́когда (*coll.*) I should like to
go, but I have not time; и рад э́то сде́лать,
но не могу́ as much as I should like to, I can't.

и², *interj.* (*expressing disagreement*; *coll.*) oh!;
и, по́лно! that's quite enough!; (*iron.*) you
don't say (so)!

ибери́йский, *adj.* Iberian.

и́бис, а, *m.* (*orn.*) ibis.

и́бо, *conj.* for.

и́в|а, ы, *f.* willow; корзи́ночная и. osier;
плаку́чая и. weeping willow.

Ива́н, а, *m.* John; И. Купа́л|а, ы (*and* ~о,
~а), *no pl.*, St. John Baptist's Day (*24 June
O.S.*); ночь на Ива́на Купа́лу Midsummer
Night.

ива́н-да-ма́рья, ива́н-да-ма́рьи, *no pl.*, *f.*
(*bot.*) **1.** cow-wheat (*Melampyrum nemorosum*).
2. heart's ease (*Viola tricolor*).

Ива́нов, *adj.*; И. день St. John's Day, Midsummer Day (*24 June O.S.*).

ива́новск|ий¹, *adj.* only in phrase во всю ~ую
(*coll.*) with all one's might; extremely
loudly; крича́ть во всю ~ую to shout at
the top of one's voice; скака́ть во всю ~ую
to go hell-for-leather.

ива́новский², *adj.*; и. червя́к (*dial.*) glow-
-worm.

ива́н-ча́й, ива́н-ча́я, *no pl.*, *m.* (*bot.*) rose-
-bay, willow-herb.

иваси́, *indecl.*, *f.* iwashi (*kind of sardine fished in
Far Eastern waters*).

ивня́к, á, *no pl.*, *m.* **1.** osier-bed. **2.** (*collect.*)
osier(s).

и́в|овый, *adj.* of ~а.

и́волг|а, и, *f.* (*orn.*) oriole.

игл|á, ы́, *pl.* ~ы, ~, *f.* **1.** needle. **2.** (*bot.*)
needle; thorn, prickle; ело́вая и. fir-needle.
3. quill, spine (*of porcupine, etc.*).

игли́ст|ый (~, ~а), *adj.* prickly; covered
with quills; и. скат thornback (*fish*).

иглова́т|ый (~, ~а), *adj.* (*coll.*) prickly.

игло́ви́д|ный (~ен, ~на), *adj.* needle-
-shaped.

иглодержа́тел|ь, я, *m.* needle-holder.

иглоко́ж|ие, их, *sing.* ~ее, ~его, *n.* (*zool.*)
Echinodermata.

иглообра́з|ный (~ен, ~на), *adj.* needle-
-shaped.

и́глу, *indecl.*, *n.* igloo.

игнори́р|овать, ую, *impf. and pf.* to ignore;
to disregard.

и́г|о, а, *n.* yoke (*fig.*); тата́рское и. the
Tatar yoke.

иго́лк|а, и, *f.* needle; сиде́ть как на ~ах
to be on thorns, on tenterhooks; каблуки́
на ~ах stiletto heels.

иго́лочк|а, и, *f.* dim. of иго́лка; (*coll.*) оде́-
тый с ~и spick and span; костю́м с ~и
brand-new suit.

иго́льник, а, *m.* needle-case.

иго́льн|ый, *adj.* of игла́; ~ое у́шко eye of a
needle.

иго́льчат|ый, *adj.* **1.** needle-shaped; ~ые
каблуки́ stiletto heels. **2.** (*min.*) needle
(-shaped), acicular; ~ые криста́ллы acicular crystals; ~ая руда́ needle ore. **3.** (*tech.*)
needle; и. кла́пан needle valve.

иго́рный, *adj.* playing, gaming; и. дом
gaming-house; и. прито́н gambling-den;
и. стол gaming-table.

игр|á, ы́, *pl.* ~ы, *f.* **1.** play (*action*), playing;
у скрипа́чки была́ блестя́щая и. the violin-
ist's performance was brilliant; и. све́та на
стене́ the play of light on the wall; и. слов
play upon words; биржева́я и. stock exchange speculation; и. приро́ды freak,
sport of nature. **2.** game; аза́ртная и.
game of chance; ко́мнатные ~ы indoor
games, party games; олимпи́йские ~ы
Olympic games; (*fig.*) опа́сная и. dangerous game; и. не сто́ит свеч the game is not
worth the candle; игра́ть, вести́ большу́ю,
кру́пную ~у́ to play for high stakes;
раскры́ть чью-н. ~у́ to uncover someone's
game. **3.** (*sport, cards*) game (*part of set,
match, etc.*); взять ~у́ при свое́й пода́че to
win one's service. **4.** (*cards*) hand; сдать
хоро́шую ~у́ to deal a good hand. **5.** turn
(to play); сейча́с твоя́ и. it is your turn
now.

игра́лищ|е, а, *n.* (*obs., rhet.*) plaything.

игра́льн|ый, *adj.* playing; ~ые ка́рты play-
ing cards; ~ые ко́сти dice.

и́граный, *adj.* (*coll.*) (already) used.

игра́|ть, ю, *impf.* (*of* сыгра́ть) **1.** to play;
и. пье́су to put on a play; и. роль to play a
part; и. Ле́ди Ма́кбет to play, take the
part of, Lady Macbeth; э́то не ~ет ро́ли
it is of no importance, it does not signify;
и. коме́дию to act (*fig.*); и. симфо́нию to
play a symphony; и. пе́рвую, втору́ю
скри́пку (*fig.*) to play first, second fiddle;
и. кому́-н. в ру́ку (*fig.*) to play into someone's hand; и. глаза́ми to flash one's eyes;
и. слова́ми to play upon words; и. ферзём
to move the queen (*at chess*); и. в ка́рты,
те́ннис, футбо́л, ша́хматы, *etc.*, to play
cards, tennis, football, chess, *etc.*; и. в
зага́дки to talk in riddles; и. в пря́тки to
play hide-and-seek; (*fig.*) to be secretive;
и. в скро́мность to feign modesty; и. на
роя́ле, скри́пке, *etc.*, to play the piano, the
violin, *etc.*; и. на билья́рде to play billiards;

и. на би́рже to speculate on the Stock Exchange; и. на (+*p.*) to play on (*fig.*); и. на чу́вствах толпы́ to play on the emotions of a crowd. 2. (*impf. only*) (+*i.* or с+*i.*) to play with, toy with, trifle with (*also fig.*); и. чьи́ми-н. чу́вствами to trifle with someone; и. с огнём (*fig.*) to play with fire. 3. (*impf. only*) to play; to sparkle (*of wine, jewellery, etc.*); улы́бка ∼ла на её лице́ a smile played on her face.

игра́|ющий, *pres. part. act. of* ∼ть; *as noun* и., ∼ющего, *m.* player.

и́грек, а, *m.* (the letter) у; (*math.*) у (*second unknown quantity*).

игре́невый, *adj.* skewbald.

игре́н|ий, *adj.* = ∼евый.

игре́ц, а́, *m.* 1. (*obs.*) musician, strolling player. 2. (*coll.*) player; швец и жнец, и в ду́ду и. jack-of-all-trades.

игри́в|ый (∼, ∼а), *adj.* playful; skittish (*of a woman*); (*coll.*) naughty, ribald.

игри́ст|ый (∼, ∼а), *adj.* sparkling (*of wine*).

игро́к, а́, *m.* 1. (в+*a.*, на+*p.*) player (of); и. в футбо́л football-player; хоро́ший и. на балала́йке a good balalaika player. 2. gambler.

игроте́к|а, и, *f.* collection of children's games; games store.

игру́шечный, *adj.* 1. toy; и. магази́н toyshop; и. парово́з toy engine. 2. (*coll.*) tiny.

игру́шк|а, и, *f.* toy; (*fig.*) plaything.

и́гр|ывать, *pres. not used; freq. of* ∼а́ть (*coll.*).

игуа́н|а, ы, *f.* (*zool.*) iguana.

игу́мен, а, *m.* (*eccl.*) Father Superior (*of monastery*).

игу́мен|ья, ьи, *g. pl.* ∼ий, *f.* (*eccl.*) Mother Superior (*of a convent*).

идеа́л, а, *m.* ideal.

идеализи́р|овать, ую, *impf. and pf.* to idealize.

идеали́зм, а, *m.* (*in var. senses*) idealism.

идеали́ст, а, *m.* (*in var. senses*) idealist.

идеалисти́ческий, *adj.* (*philos.*) idealist(ic).

идеалисти́ч|ный (∼ен, ∼на), *adj.* idealistic.

идеа́л|ьный (∼ен, ∼ьна), *adj.* 1. (*philos.*) ideal. 2. (*coll.*) ideal, perfect.

иде́йк|а, и, *f.* (*pejor.*) *dim. of* иде́я; paltry idea.

иде́йност|ь, и, *f.* 1. ideological content. 2. 'progressive' character (*of work of art, etc.—from Marxist point of view*). 3. principle, integrity (*from Marxist point of view*).

иде́|йный (∼ен, ∼йна), *adj.* 1. ideological. 2. expressing an idea *or* ideas; ∼йная пье́са play of ideas. 3. 'progressive' (*from Marxist point of view*); ∼йное иску́сство 'progressive' art. 4. high-principled, acting on principle (*from Marxist point of view*).

идентифика́ци|я, и, *f.* identification.

идентифици́р|овать, ую, *impf. and pf.* to identify.

иденти́ч|ный (∼ен, ∼на), *adj.* identical.

идеогра́мм|а, ы, *f.* (*ling.*) ideogram.

идеогра́фи|я, и, *f.* (*ling.*) ideography.

идео́лог, а, *m.* ideologist; (*coll.*) idea-monger.

идеологи́ческий, *adj.* ideological.

идеоло́ги|я, и, *f.* ideology.

идёт (*3rd sing. pres. of* идти́) *as interj.* (*coll.*) (all) right!

иде́|я, и, *f.* 1. idea (*also coll.*); notion, concept; (*philos.*) Idea; боро́ться за ∼ю to fight for an idea; пода́ть ∼ю to suggest, make a suggestion; навя́зчивая и. obsession, idée fixe; счастли́вая и. happy thought. 2. point, purport (*of a work of art, of fiction, etc.*).

идилли́ческий, *adj.* idyllic.

иди́лли|я, и, *f.* idyll (*lit. and fig.*).

идио́м|а, ы, *f.* (*and* ∼, ∼а, *m.*) idiom.

идиомати́зм, а, *m.* idiom.

идиома́тик|а, и, *f.* (*ling.*) 1. study of idiom(s). 2. (*collect.*) idiom, idiomatic expressions.

идиомати́ческий, *adj.* idiomatic.

идиосинкрази́|я, и, *f.* 1. idiosyncrasy. 2. (*med.*) allergy.

идио́т, а, *m.* idiot, imbecile (*med. and coll.*).

идиоти́зм[1], а, *m.* idiocy, imbecility (*med. and coll.*).

идиоти́зм[2], а, *m.* (*ling.*) idiom.

идиоти́ческий, *adj.* idiotic, imbecile.

идио́тский, *adj.* idiotic, imbecile.

и́диш, *indecl., m.* Yiddish (*language*).

и́дол, а, *m.* 1. idol (*also fig.*); стоя́ть, сиде́ть ∼ом to stand, sit like a stone image. 2. (*coll., pejor.*) callous *or* obtuse person.

идолопокло́нник, а, *m.* idolater.

идолопокло́ннический, *adj.* idolatrous.

идолопокло́нств|о, а, *n.* idolatry.

ид|ти́ (итти́), у́, ёшь, *past* шёл, шла, *impf.* (*of* пойти́; *det. of* ходи́ть) 1. to go; (*impf. only*) to come; и. в го́ру to go uphill; авто́бус ∼ёт the bus is coming; кто ∼ёт? who goes there?; и. гуля́ть to go for a walk; и. в прода́жу to go for sale, be up for sale; и. в но́гу to keep in step (*also fig.*); и. на охо́ту to go hunting; и. на сме́ну (+*d.*) to take the place (of), succeed. 2. (на+*a.*) to enter; (в+*n.-a.*) to become; и. на госуда́рственную слу́жбу to enter Government service; и. в лётчики to become an airman. 3. (в+*a.*) to be used (for); (на+*a.*) to go to make; и. в корм to be used for fodder; и. в лом to go for scrap; и. на ю́бку to go to make a skirt. 4. (из, от) to come (from), proceed (from); из трубы́ шёл чёрный дым black smoke was coming from the chimney. 5. (*of news, etc.*) to go round; шла мо́лва, что... word went round that..., rumour had it that... 6. (*coll.*) to sell, be sold; хорошо́ и. to be selling well; и.

за бесцéнок to go for a song. **7.** (*of machines, machinery, etc.*) to go, run, work. **8.** (*of rain, etc.*) to fall; дождь, снег ~ёт it is raining, snowing. **9.** (*of time*) to pass; шли гóды years passed; ей ~ёт тридцáтый год she is in her thirtieth year. **10.** to go on, be in progress; (*of entertainments*) to be on, be showing; переговóры ~ýт negotiations are in progress; сегóдня ~ёт « Ревизóр » 'The Government Inspector' is on tonight. **11.** (+*d.* or к) to suit, become; э́та шля́па ей не ~ёт this hat does not become her. **12.** (в, на+*a.*; *coll.*) to go (in, on). **13.** (+*i.* or с+*g.*) to play, lead, move (*at chess, cards, etc.*); и. ферзём to move one's queen; и. с червéй to lead a heart. **14.** (о+*p.*; *of a discussion, etc.*) to be (about); речь ~ёт о том, что... the point is that . . ., it is a matter of . . .

йд|ы, ~, *no sing.* (*hist.*) Ides.

иезуúт, а, *m.* (*eccl.*) Jesuit.

иезуúтский, *adj.* (*eccl.*) Jesuit; (*fig.*) jesuitical.

иéн|а, ы, *f.* yen (*Japanese currency*).

иерáрх, а, *m.* hierarch.

иерархúческий, *adj.* hierarchic(al).

иерáрхи|я, и, *f.* hierarchy.

иератúческ|ий, *adj.* hieratic; ~ое письмó (*ling.*) hieratic script.

иерé|й, я, *m.* priest.

иерéйский, *adj.* priestly.

иерéйств|о, а, *n.* priesthood.

иеремиáд|а, ы, *f.* jeremiad.

иерóглиф, а, *m.* hieroglyph.

иероглифúческий, *adj.* hieroglyphic.

иждивéн|ец, ца, *m.* dependant.

иждивéни|е, я, *n.* **1.** maintenance; на чьём-н. ~и at someone's expense; жить на своём ~и to maintain oneself, keep oneself; жить на ~и родúтелей to live on one's parents. **2.** (*obs.*) means, funds.

иждивéнчеств|о, а, *n.* dependence.

úже, *relat. pron.* (*arch.*) who, which; *now only used in phrase* и úже с ним(и) (and others) of that ilk, and company.

úжиц|а, ы, *f.* 'v' (*last letter of Church Slavonic and pre-1918 Russian alphabet*); от азá до ~ы (*fig.*) from A to Z; прописáть ~y (+*d.*) (*obs. or joc.*) to lecture, bring to book; to give a lesson (to); с ногáми ~ей (*coll.*) knock-kneed.

из (изо), *prep.*+*g.* from, out of; of. **1.** *indicates place of origin of action, source, etc.*: приéхать из Лóндона to come from London; пить из чáшки to drink out of a cup; узнáть из газéт to learn from the newspapers; из достовéрных истóчников from reliable sources, on good authority; вы́йти из себя́ to be beside oneself; вы́йти из употреблéния to pass out of use, become obsolete; он из крестья́н he is of peasant

origin. **2.** *with numeral or in partitive sense*: одúн из её поклóнников one of her admirers; ни одúн из ста not one in a hundred; млáдший из всех the youngest of all; главнéйшие собы́тия из истóрии Россúи the principal events in the history of Russia; трус из трýсов a craven. **3.** *indicates material*: из чегó э́то сдéлано? what is it made of?; варéнье из абрикóсов apricot jam; обéд из трёх блюд a three-course dinner; лóжки из серебрá silver spoons; букéт из крáсных гвоздúк bouquet of carnations; (*fig.*; *of human potential*) из негó вы́йдет хорóший трубáч he will make a good trumpet-player. **4.** *indicates agency*: изо всех сил with all one's might; из послéдних срéдств with one's last penny. **5.** *indicates cause, motive*: из благодáрности in gratitude; из лúчных вы́год for private gain; из рéвности from jealousy; мнóго шýму из ничегó a lot of fuss about nothing.

из- (*also* **изо-, изъ-**, *and* **ис-**) *verbal prefix indicating*: **1.** motion outwards. **2.** action over entire surface of object, in all directions. **3.** expenditure of instrument *or* object in course of action; continuation *or* repetition of action to extreme point; exhaustiveness of action.

изб|á, ы́, *a.* ~ý, *pl.* ~ы, *f.* **1.** izba (*peasant's hut or cottage*); и.-читáльня, ~ы-читáльни, *f.* village reading-room. **2.** (*hist.*) government office (*in Muscovite Russia*).

избáб|иться, люсь, ишься, *pf.* (*coll.*) to become womanish, effeminate.

избавúтел|ь, я, *m.* deliverer.

избáв|ить, лю, ишь, *pf.* (*of* ~ля́ть) (от) to save, deliver (from); ~ьте меня́ от вáших замечáний spare me your remarks; ~ьте меня́! leave me alone!; ~и Бог! God forbid!

избáв|иться, люсь, ишься, *pf.* (*of* ~ля́ться) (от) to be saved (from), escape; to get out (of); to get rid (of); и. от привы́чки to get out of a habit.

избавлéни|е, я, *n.* deliverance.

избавля́|ть(ся), ю(сь), *impf. of* избáвить(ся).

избáлованный, *p.p.p. of* избаловáть *and adj.* spoilt.

избал|овáть, ýю, *pf.* (*of* баловáть *and* ~óвывать) to spoil (*a child, etc.*).

избал|овáться, ýюсь, *pf.* (*of* ~óвываться) to become spoilt.

избалóвыва|ть(ся), ю(сь), *impf. of* избаловáть(ся).

избáч, á, *m.* village librarian.

избéга|ть, ю, *pf.* (*coll.*) to run about, run all over.

избег|áть, áю, *impf.* (*of* ~нуть *and* избежáть) (+*g.* or *inf.*) to avoid; (*impf. only*) to

shun; to escape, evade; и. встреча́ться с
кем-н. to avoid meeting someone; и.
штра́фа to evade a penalty.

избега́|ться, юсь, *pf.* (*coll.*) **1.** to exhaust
oneself by running (about). **2.** to get out
of hand (*of an undisciplined child*).

избег|ну́ть, ну, нешь, *past* ~ну́л *and* ~, ~ла,
pf. of ~а́ть.

избежа́ни|е, я, *n.*; во и. (+*g.*) in order to
avoid.

избе|жа́ть, гу́, жи́шь, гу́т, *pf. of* ~га́ть.

избива́|ть(ся), ю(сь), *impf. of* изби́ть(ся).

избие́ни|е, я, *n.* **1.** slaughter, massacre; и.
младе́нцев (*bibl.*; *also fig. of persecutions*)
Massacre of the Innocents. **2.** (*leg.*) assault
and battery.

избира́тел|ь, я, *m.* elector, voter.

избира́тельност|ь, и, *f.* (*radio*) selectivity.

избира́тельн|ый, *adj.* **1.** electoral; и. бюл-
лете́нь voting-paper; ~ая кампа́ния elec-
tion campaign; и. о́круг electoral district;
~ое пра́во suffrage; franchise; и. спи́сок
electoral roll, register of voters; ~ая у́рна
ballot-box; и. уча́сток polling station; и.
ценз voting qualification. **2.** (*tech.*) selective.

избира́|ть, ю, *impf. of* избра́ть.

изби́т|ый, *p.p.p. of* ~ь *and adj.*; (*fig.*) hack-
neyed, trite.

из|би́ть, обью́, обьёшь, *pf.* (*of* ~бива́ть)
1. to beat unmercifully, beat up. **2.** to
slaughter, massacre. **3.** (*coll.*) to wear down,
ruin.

из|би́ться, обью́сь, обьёшься, *pf.* (*of*
~бива́ться) (*coll.*) **1.** to bruise oneself. **2.** to
be worn out, be ruined.

избл|ева́ть, юю, юёшь, *pf.* (*of* ~ёвывать)
1. (*obs.*) to bring up, throw up; (*fig.*) to bring
out (*coarse or vituperative language*). **2.** (*coll.*)
to vomit over.

изблёвыва|ть, ю, *impf. of* изблева́ть.

изб|но́й, *adj. of* ~а́.

избо́ин|а, ы, *no pl., f.* (*agric.*) oilcake.

изболе́|ть(ся), ю(сь), *pf.* (*coll.*) to be in tor-
ment.

избо́рник, а, *m.* (*hist., lit.*) miscellany, an-
thology.

избороз|ди́ть, жу́, ди́шь, *pf. of* борозд-
ди́ть 2.

избоче́н|иваться, иваюсь, *impf. of* ~иться.

избоче́н|иться, юсь, ишься, *pf.* (*of* ~ивать-
ся) (*coll.*) to stand in a challenging pose
(with one hip forward and one hand on it).

избра́ни|е, я, *n.* election.

избра́нник, а, *m.* (*rhet.*) elect, chosen one;
favoured one, darling.

избра́нн|ица, ицы, *f. of* ~ик.

и́збран|ный, *p.p.p. of* избра́ть *and adj.* **1.**
selected; ~ные сочине́ния Пу́шкина se-
lected works of Pushkin. **2.** select; *as noun*
~ные, ~ных, *no sing.*, élite.

из|бра́ть, беру́, берёшь, *past* ~бра́л, ~бра-
ла́, ~бра́ло, *pf.* (*of* ~бира́ть) (+*a. and i.*)
to elect (as, for); to choose; его́ ~бра́ли
чле́ном парла́мента, he has been elected
a Member of Parliament.

и́збура- brownish-; и.-жёлтый brownish-
-yellow.

избу́шк|а, и, *f. dim. of* изба́.

избы́т|ок, ка, *m.* surplus, excess; abun-
dance, plenty; в ~ке in plenty; от ~ка
се́рдца, от ~ка чувств out of the fullness
of the heart.

избы́точ|ный (~ен, ~на), *adj.* **1.** surplus.
2. abundant, plentiful.

из|бы́ть, бу́ду, бу́дешь, *past* ~бы́л, ~была́,
~бы́ло, *pf.* (*of* ~быва́ть) (*obs.*) to rid oneself
of.

изб|яно́й, *adj. of* ~а́.

изва́яни|е, я, *n.* statue, sculpture; graven
image.

изва́я|ть, ю, *pf. of* вая́ть.

изве́д|ать, аю, *pf.* (*of* ~ывать) to come to
know, learn the meaning of; и. го́ре to taste,
have the taste of, grief.

изве́дыва|ть, ю, *impf. of* изве́дать.

изве́ка, *adv.* (*obs.*) of old.

и́зверг, а, *m.* monster, cruel person; и. ро́да
челове́ческого scum of the earth.

изверг|а́ть, а́ю, *impf.* (*of* ~нуть) to throw
out, disgorge; (*physiol.*) to excrete; (*fig.*) to
eject, expel.

изверг|а́ться, а́юсь, *impf.* (*of* ~нуться) **1.** to
erupt (*of volcanoes*). **2.** *pass. of* ~а́ть.

изве́рг|нуть(ся), ну(сь), нешь(ся), *past*
~(ся) *and* ~нул(ся), ~ла(сь), *pf. of*
~а́ть(ся).

изверже́ни|е, я, *n.* **1.** eruption (*of volcano*).
2. ejection, expulsion; (*physiol.*) excretion.
3. (*pl. only*; *obs.*) excreta, ordure.

изве́рженный, *p.p.p. of* изве́ргнуть *and adj.*
(*geol.*) igneous, eruptive, volcanic.

изве́рива|ться, юсь, *impf. of* изве́риться.

изве́р|иться, юсь, ишься, *pf.* (*of* ~иваться)
(в+*a. or p.*) to lose faith (in), lose confidence
(in); и. в людей, и. в людях to lose faith
in people.

извер|ну́ться, ну́сь, нёшься, *pf.* (*of* ~ты-
ваться[1] *and* извора́чиваться) (*coll.*) to dodge,
take evasive action (*also fig.*); и. при отве́те
to give an evasive answer.

извер|те́ться, чу́сь, ~тишься, *pf.* (*of* ~ты-
ваться[2]) (*coll.*) **1.** to wear out (*intrans.*) as
a result of turning (*of propeller, etc.*). **2.** (*no
impf.*; *fig.*) to become flighty; to go to the
bad.

изве́ртыва|ться[1], юсь, *impf. of* извер-
ну́ться.

изве́ртыва|ться[2], юсь, *impf. of* изверте́ться.

изве|сти́, ду́, дёшь, *past* ~л, ~ла́, *pf.* (*of*

изводи́ть) (*coll.*) **1.** to spend, use up; to waste. **2.** to destroy, exterminate. **3.** to vex, exasperate; to torment.

изве́сти|е, я, *n.* **1.** (o+*p.*) news (of); intelligence; information; после́дние ~я the latest news. **2.** (*pl. only*; *as title of periodicals*) proceedings, transactions; ~я Акаде́мии нау́к Proceedings of the Academy of Sciences.

изве|сти́сь, ду́сь, дёшься, *past* ~лся, ~ла́сь, *pf.* (*of* изводи́ться) (*coll.*) **1.** to consume oneself, eat one's heart out; to exhaust oneself, wear oneself out; и. от за́висти to consume oneself with envy. **2.** to perish, disappear. **3.** *pass. of* ~сти́.

изве|сти́ть, щу́, сти́шь, *pf.* (*of* ~ща́ть) to inform, notify.

изве́стк|а, и, *f.* (slaked) lime.

известк|ова́ть, у́ю, *impf. and pf.* (*agric.*) to lime.

известко́вый, *adj. of* и́звесть.

изве́стно 1. *as pred.* it is (well) known; как и. as is well known; наско́лько мне и. as far as I know. **2.** (*as particle*; *coll.*) of course, certainly.

изве́стност|ь, и, *f.* **1.** fame, reputation; repute; notoriety; приноси́ть и. (+*d.*) to bring fame (to); по́льзоваться гро́мкой ~ью to be far-famed. **2.** publicity; привести́ в и. to make known, make public; поста́вить кого́-н. в и. to inform, notify. **3.** (*coll.*) notability, prominent figure.

изве́ст|ный (~ен, ~на), *adj.* **1.** (+*d.*) well-known (to); (+*i.*) (well-)known (for); (за+ *a.*) (well-)known (as); он ~ен свое́й бо́дростью he is well known for his cheerfulness; челове́к, и. как пья́ница a well-known drunkard. **2.** notorious. **3.** (a) certain; ~ным о́бразом in a certain way; в ~ных слу́чаях in certain cases; до ~ной сте́пени, в ~ной ме́ре to a certain extent. **4.** *as noun* ~ное, ~ного, *n.* (*math.*) the known.

известня́к, а́, *m.* limestone.

известняко́вый, *adj.* limestone.

и́звест|ь, и, *f.* lime; гашёная и. slaked lime; негашёная и. quicklime; хло́рная и. chloride of lime; раство́р ~и mortar, grout; whitewash; преврати́ть в и. to calcify.

изве́т, а, *m.* (*obs.*) denunciation, delation.

изве́тчик, а, *m.* (*obs.*) informer, delator.

изветша́лый, *adj.* (*obs.*) dilapidated.

изветша́|ть, ет, *pf.* (*obs.*) to become completely dilapidated.

извеща́|ть, ю, *impf. of* извести́ть.

извеще́ни|е, я, *n.* notification, notice; (*comm.*) advice; ~я морепла́вателям Instructions to Mariners.

изви́в, а, *m.* winding, bend.

извива́|ть, ю, *impf. of* изви́ть.

извива́|ться, юсь, *impf.* (*of* изви́ться) **1.** to coil (*intrans.*); to wriggle. **2.** (*impf. only*) to twist, wind (*intrans.*); to meander.

изви́лин|а, ы, *f.* bend, twist; ~ы мо́зга (*anat.*) convolutions of the brain.

изви́лист|ый (~, ~a), *adj.* winding; tortuous; sinuous; (*of river*) meandering.

извине́ни|е, я, *n.* **1.** excuse. **2.** apology; приня́ть ~я to accept an apology. **3.** pardon; прошу́ ~я I beg your pardon, I apologize.

извини́тел|ьный (~ен, ~ьна), *adj.* **1.** excusable, pardonable. **2.** apologetic.

извин|и́ть, ю́, и́шь, *pf.* (*of* ~я́ть) **1.** to excuse (= *to pardon*); ~и́те (меня́)! I beg your pardon, excuse me!, (I'm) sorry!; ~и́те, что я опозда́л sorry I'm late; прошу́ и. меня́ за беста́ктное замеча́ние I apologize for my tactless remark; ~и́те за выраже́ние (*coll.*) if you will excuse the expression; уж ~и́(те)! (*coll.*; *expresses disagreement*) excuse me! **2.** to excuse (= *to justify*); э́то ниче́м нельзя́ и. this is inexcusable.

извин|и́ться, ю́сь, и́шься, *pf.* (*of* ~я́ться) **1.** (пе́ред) to apologize (to); ~и́тесь за меня́ present my apologies, make my excuses. **2.** (+*i.*) to excuse oneself (on account of, on the ground of); to make excuses.

извин|я́ть, я́ю, *impf. of* ~и́ть.

извин|я́ться, я́юсь, *impf. of* ~и́ться; ~я́юсь (*coll.*) I apologize, (I'm) sorry!

извиня́|ющийся, *pres. part. of* ~ться *and adj.* apologetic.

из|ви́ть, овью́, овьёшь, *past* ~ви́л, ~вила́, ~ви́ло, *pf.* (*of* ~вива́ть) to coil, twist, wind (*trans.*).

из|ви́ться, овью́сь, овьёшься, *past* ~ви́лся, ~вила́сь, *pf. of* ~вива́ться.

извлека́|ть(ся), ю(сь), *impf. of* извле́чь(ся).

извлече́ни|е, я, *n.* **1.** extraction; (*math.*) и. ко́рня extraction of root, evolution. **2.** extract, excerpt.

извле́|чь, ку́, чёшь, ку́т, *past* ~к, ~кла́, *pf.* (*of* ~ка́ть) to extract; (*fig.*) to derive, elicit; и. уро́к (из) to learn a lesson (from); и. дохо́д, по́льзу, удово́льствие (из) to derive profit, benefit, pleasure (from); и. ко́рень (*math.*) to find the root.

извле́|чься, ку́сь, чёшься, ку́тся, *past* ~кся, ~кла́сь, *pf.* (*of* ~ка́ться) to come out (*to be extracted*).

извне́, *adv.* from without.

изво́д¹, а, *m.* (*coll.*) **1.** waste. **2.** vexation.

изво́д², а, *m.* (*lit.*) recension, text (*of a manuscript document*).

изво|ди́ть(ся), жу́(сь), ~дишь(ся), *impf. of* извести́(сь).

изво́з, а, *m.* (*hist.*) carrying (*on horse-drawn carts*); промышля́ть ~ом to be a carrier (*by trade*).

изво|зи́ть, жу́, ~зишь, *pf.*; **и. в грязи́** (*coll.*) to drag through the mud.

изво́знича|ть, ю, *impf.* to be a carrier.

изво́з|ный, *adj. of* ~; **и. про́мысел** carrier's trade.

изво́зчик, а, *m.* **1.** carrier; (легково́й) и. cabman, cabby; (ломово́й) и. carter, drayman. **2.** (*coll.*) cab; е́хать на ~е to go in a cab.

изво́зчи|чий, *adj. of* ~к; ~чья би́ржа cabstand, cab-rank.

изволе́ни|е, я, *n.* (*obs.*) will, pleasure; по ~ю Бо́жию Deo volente.

изво́л|ить, ю, ишь, *impf.* **1.** (+*inf. or g.*; *obs. or iron. except in imp.*) to wish, desire; чего́ ~ите? what can I do for you?; ~ь(те) (*coll.*) if you wish, all right; with pleasure; ~ь, я оста́нусь all right, I will stay; да́йте мне папиро́су. — ~ьте give me a cigarette. —with pleasure! **2.** (+*inf.*; *expresses respectful attention* (*obs.*) *or ironical disapproval*) to deign, be pleased (*often equivalent to polite form of indicative of following verb*); ба́рин ~ит спать the master is asleep; а как вы ~ите пожива́ть? and, pray, how are you?; ~ь(те) kindly, please be good enough; ~ьте молча́ть! kindly be quiet!

изво́льнича|ться, юсь, *pf.* (*coll.*) to become wayward, get out of hand.

извора́чива|ться, юсь, *impf. of* изверну́ться.

изворо́т, а, *m.* **1.** bend, twist. **2.** (*pl.*; *fig.*) tricks, wiles.

изворо́тист|ый (~, ~а), *adj.* (*coll.*) = изворо́тливый.

изворо́тлив|ый (~, ~а), *adj.* versatile, resourceful; wily, shrewd.

извра|ти́ть, щу́, ти́шь, *pf.* (*of* ~ща́ть) **1.** to pervert. **2.** to misinterpret, misconstrue; и. и́стину to distort the truth; и. чью-н. мысль to misinterpret someone.

извраща́|ть, ю, *impf. of* изврати́ть.

извраще́ни|е, я, *n.* **1.** perversion. **2.** misinterpretation, distortion (*fig.*).

извращённый, *p.p.p. of* изврати́ть *and adj.* perverted; unnatural.

изга́|дить, жу, дишь, *pf.* (*of* ~живать) (*coll.*) **1.** to befoul, soil. **2.** (*fig.*) to make a mess of.

изга́|диться, жусь, дишься, *pf.* (*of* ~живаться) (*coll.*) to turn nasty (*of weather*); to go to the bad.

изга́жива|ть(ся), ю(сь), *impf. of* изга́дить(ся).

изги́б, а, *m.* **1.** bend, twist; winding. **2.** inflexion (*of voice*); nuance.

изгиба́|ть(ся), ю(сь), *impf. of* изогну́ть(ся).

изгла́|дить, жу, дишь, *pf.* (*of* ~живать) to efface, wipe out (*also fig.*); и. из па́мяти to blot out of one's memory.

изгла́жива|ть, ю, *impf. of* изгла́дить.

изгна́ни|е, я, *n.* **1.** banishment; expulsion. **2.** exile.

изгна́нник, а, *m.* exile (*person*).

из|гна́ть, гоню́, го́нишь, *past* ~гна́л, ~гнала́, ~гна́ло, *pf.* (*of* ~гоня́ть) to banish, expel; to exile; и. из употребле́ния to prohibit the use of, ban; и. плод (*med.*) to procure an abortion.

изго́|й, я, *m.* (*hist.*) déclassé person (*person in Kievan Russian society having lost status*; *e.g. illiterate son of priest, ruined merchant, etc.*); (*fig.*) social odd man out.

изголо́вь|е, я, *n.* head of the bed; сиде́ть у ~я to sit at the bedside; служи́ть ~ем to serve as a pillow.

изголода́|ться, юсь, *pf.* **1.** to be famished, starve. **2.** (по+*d.*) to yearn (for).

из|голо́дать, *see* ~гна́ть.

изгоня́|ть, ю, *impf. of* изгна́ть.

изго́рб|иться, люсь, ишься, *pf.* (*coll.*) **1.** to arch the back (*of cat, etc.*). **2.** to warp (*intrans.*).

и́згород|ь, и, *f.* fence; жива́я и. hedge.

изгота́влива|ть, ю, *impf.* = изготовля́ть.

изгото́в|ить, лю, ишь, *pf.* (*of* ~ля́ть) **1.** to manufacture. **2.** (*obs.*) to prepare; и. ружьё (*mil.*) to come to the ready. **3.** (*obs.*) to cook.

изгото́в|иться, люсь, ишься, *pf.* (*of* ~ля́ться) **1.** to get ready, place oneself in readiness. **2.** *pass. of* ~ить.

изгото́в|ка, ки, *f.* = ~ле́ние; взять ружьё на ~ку (*mil.*) to come to the ready.

изготовле́ни|е, я, *n.* **1.** manufacture. **2.** (*mil.*) preparation; 'ready' position.

изготовля́|ть(ся), ю(сь), *impf. of* изгото́вить(ся).

изгрыза́|ть, ю, *impf. of* ~ть.

изгрыз|ть, у́, ёшь, *past* ~, ~ла, *pf.* (*of* ~а́ть) to gnaw to shreds.

изда|ва́ть, ю́, ёшь, *impf. of* ~ть.

изда|ва́ться, ётся, *impf. of* ~ться.

и́здавна, *adv.* for a long time; from time immemorial.

издал|ека́ (*more rarely* ~ёка), *adv.* from afar; from a distance; го́род ви́ден и. the town is visible from afar; прие́хать и. to come from a distance; говори́ть и. (*coll.*) to speak in a roundabout way.

и́здал|и, *adv.* = ~ека́.

изда́ни|е, я, *n.* **1.** publication; promulgation (*of law*). **2.** edition; пе́рвое и. first edition; испра́вленное и. revised edition.

изда́тел|ь, я, *m.* publisher.

изда́тель|ский, *adj. of* ~ *and* ~ство; ~ское де́ло publishing; ~ская фи́рма publishing house.

изда́тельств|о, а, *n.* publishing house.

изда́|ть, м, шь, ст, ди́м, ди́те, ду́т, *past* ~л, ~ла́, ~ло, *pf.* (*of* ~ва́ть) **1.** to publish; и.

зако́н to promulgate a law; и. ука́з to issue an edict. **2.** to produce, emit (*a smell*); to let out (*a sound*); и. крик to let out a cry.

изда́|ться, стся, *past* ∼лся, ∼ла́сь, ∼лось, *pf.* to be published.

издева́тельский, *adj.* mocking.

издева́тельств|о, а, *n.* **1.** mocking, scoffing. **2.** mockery; taunt, insult.

издева́|ться, юсь, *impf.* (над) to mock (at), scoff (at).

издёвк|а, и, *f.* (*coll.*) taunt, insult.

изде́ли|е, я, *n.* **1.** (*sing. only*) make; куста́рного ∼я hand-made; фабри́чного ∼я factory-made. **2.** (manufactured) article; (*pl.*) wares.

издёрган|ный, *p.p.p.* of издёргать *and adj.* harassed; overstrained; ∼ные не́рвы shattered nerves.

издёрг|ать, аю, *pf.* (*of* ∼ивать) (*coll.*) **1.** to pull to pieces. **2.** to harass; to overstrain.

издёрг|аться, аюсь, *pf.* (*of* ∼иваться) (*coll.*) **1.** *pass. of* ∼ать. **2.** to become overwrought, become unhinged.

издёргива|ть(ся), ю(сь), *impf.* of издёргать(ся).

издерж|а́ть, у́, ∼ишь, *pf.* (*of* ∼ивать) to spend; to expend.

издерж|а́ться, у́сь, ∼ишься, *pf.* (*of* ∼иваться) (*coll.*) **1.** to have spent all one has, be spent up. **2.** *pass. of* ∼а́ть.

изде́ржива|ть(ся), ю(сь), *impf.* of издержа́ть(ся).

изде́рж|ки, ек, *sing.* ∼ка, ∼ки, *f.* expenses; суде́бные и. (*leg.*) costs; и. произво́дства production costs.

издира́|ть, ю, *impf. of* изодра́ть.

издо́льщин|а, ы, *f.* (*hist.,* econ.) share-
-cropping.

издо́х|нуть, ну, нешь, *past* ∼, ∼ла, *pf.* (*of* издыха́ть) to die (*of animals*); (*sl.*; *of human beings*) to peg out, kick the bucket.

издре́вле, *adv.* (*obs.*) from the earliest times.

издроб|и́ть, лю́, и́шь, *pf.* to pulverize, granulate.

издыха́ни|е, я, *n.* (one's) last breath; до после́днего ∼я to one's last breath; при после́днем ∼и at one's last gasp.

издыха́|ть, ю, *impf.* of издо́хнуть.

изжа́р|ить(ся), ю(сь), ишь(ся), *pf.* of жа́рить(ся) 1, 2.

изжёванный, *p.p.p.* of изжева́ть *and adj.* (*coll.*) **1.** crumpled. **2.** (*fig.*) hackneyed.

изж|ева́ть, ую́, уёшь, *pf.* (*of* ∼ёвывать) (*coll.*) to chew up.

изжёвыва|ть, ю, *impf.* of изжева́ть.

и́зжелта- yellowish-.

из|же́чь, жгу́, жжёшь, ожгу́т, *past* ∼жёг, ∼ожгла́, *pf.* (*of* ∼жига́ть) (*coll.*) **1.** to burn all over; to burn holes in; она́ ∼ожгла́ ру́ки

утюго́м she has burned her hands all over on the iron. **2.** to use up (*fuel, by burning*).

из|же́чься, ожгу́сь, ожжёшься, ожгу́тся, *past* ∼жёгся, ∼ожгла́сь, *pf.* (*of* ∼жига́ться) (*coll.*) **1.** to burn oneself all over; to be covered with burns; но́ги у неё ∼ожгли́сь от кислоты́ her legs were all covered with burns from the acid. **2.** to be burned up, be used up (*of fuel*).

изжива́|ть, ю, *impf.* of изжи́ть.

изжига́|ть(ся), ю(сь), *impf.* of изже́чь(ся).

изжи́ти|е, я, *n.* elimination.

изжи́|ть, ву́, вёшь, *past* ∼л, ∼ла́, ∼ло, *pf.* (*of* ∼ва́ть) **1.** to eliminate. **2.** (*obs.*) to overcome (gradually); и. разочарова́ние to get over a disappointment. **3.** и. себя́ to become obsolete.

изжо́г|а, и, *f.* heartburn.

из-за, *prep.*+*g.* **1.** from behind; из-за две́ри from behind the door; встать из-за стола́ to rise from the table; прие́хать из-за мо́ря to come from oversea(s); (*fig.*) спле́тничать о ком-н. из-за угла́ to gossip about someone behind his back. **2.** because of, through; не засыпа́ть из-за шу́ма to be unable to get to sleep because of the noise; ссо́риться из-за пустяко́в to fall out over trifles; то́лько из-за тебя́ мы опозда́ли it was all because of you that we were late. **3.** for; жени́ться из-за де́нег to marry for money.

и́ззелена- greenish-.

иззя́б|нуть, ну, нешь, *past* ∼, ∼ла, *pf.* (*coll.*) to feel frozen, feel chilled to the marrow.

излага́|ть, ю, *impf. of* изложи́ть.

изла́мыва|ть(ся), ю(сь), *impf.* of излома́ть(ся).

излени́ва|ться, юсь, *impf.* of излени́ться.

излен|и́ться, ю́сь, ∼ишься, *pf.* (*of* ∼иваться) (*coll.*) to grow incorrigibly lazy, become a lazybones.

излёт, а, *m.* (*tech.*) end of trajectory; пу́ля на ∼е spent bullet.

излече́ни|е, я, *n.* **1.** medical treatment; он был на ∼и в Москве́ he was undergoing medical treatment in Moscow; отпра́вить в го́спиталь на и. to send to hospital for treatment. **2.** recovery.

изле́чива|ть(ся), ю(сь), *impf.* of излечи́ть(ся).

излечи́м|ый (∼**,** ∼**а),** *adj.* curable.

излеч|и́ть, у́, ∼ишь, *pf.* (*of* ∼ивать) to cure.

излеч|и́ться, у́сь, ∼ишься, *pf.* (*of* ∼ива́ться) (от) to make a complete recovery (from); (*fig.*) to rid oneself (of), shake off.

излива́|ть(ся), ю(сь), *impf.* of изли́ть(ся).

из|ли́ть, олью́, ольёшь, *past* ∼ли́л, ∼лила́, ∼ли́ло, *pf.* (*of* ∼лива́ть) **1.** (*obs.*) to pour out, shed. **2.** (*fig.*) to pour out, give vent to; и. свой гнев на (+*a*.) to vent one's anger (on); и. ду́шу to unbosom oneself.

из|ли́ться, олью́сь, ольёшься, *past* ~ли́лся, ~лила́сь, ~ли́ло́сь, *pf.* (*of* ~лива́ться) **1.** (*obs. or poet.*) to stream, pour out (*intrans.*); ~лили́сь слёзы tears welled up. **2.** (в+*p.*) to find expression (in). **3.** (в+*p.*) to give vent to one's feelings (in); (на+*a.*) to vent itself (on); его́ гнев ~ли́лся на всех окружа́ющих his anger vented itself on all about him.

изли́ш|ек, ка, *m.* **1.** surplus; remainder. **2.** excess; нам э́того хва́тит с ~ком we have more than enough, enough and to spare; и. осторо́жности excessive caution.

изли́шеств|о, а, *n.* excess; over-indulgence.

изли́шеств|овать, ую, *impf.* to go to excess, over-indulge oneself.

изли́шн|е, *adv.* excessively; unnecessarily, superfluously.

изли́ш|ний (~ен, ~ня, ~не), *adj.* excessive; unnecessary, superfluous.

излия́ни|е, я, *n.* outpouring, effusion (*fig.*).

излов|и́ть, лю́, ~ишь, *pf.* (*coll.*) to catch.

изловч|и́ться, у́сь, и́шься, *pf.* (*coll.*) to contrive, manage; он ~и́лся и вы́бил ору́жие из руки́ проти́вника he contrived to knock his opponent's weapon out of his hand; он ~и́лся попа́сть в цель he managed to hit the target.

изложе́ни|е, я, *n.* exposition, account.

излож|и́ть, у́, ~ишь, *pf.* (*of* излага́ть) to expound, state; to set forth; to word, draft; и. на бума́ге to commit to paper.

изло́жниц|а, ы, *f.* (*tech.*) mould.

изло́м, а, *m.* **1.** break, fracture; sharp bend. **2.** душе́вный и. mental unbalance.

изло́ман|ный, *p.p.p. of* изломать *and adj.* **1.** broken. **2.** winding, tortuous. **3.** (*fig.*) unbalanced, unhinged; warped.

излома́|ть, ю, *pf.* (*of* изла́мывать) **1.** to break, smash. **2.** (*coll.*) to break (*in health*); (*impers.*) to have (crippling) rheumatism; всю спи́ну у неё ~ло she is crippled with rheumatism in her back. **3.** (*fig., coll.*) to warp, corrupt.

излома́|ться, юсь, *pf.* (*of* изла́мываться) **1.** to be broken, be smashed. **2.** (*fig., coll.*) to be affected; to resort to hypocrisy.

излуч|а́ть, а́ю, *impf.* (*of* ~и́ть) to radiate (*also fig.*); её глаза́ ~а́ли не́жность her eyes radiated tenderness.

излуч|а́ться, а́ется *impf.* (*of* ~и́ться) **1.** (из) to emanate (from). **2.** *pass. of* ~а́ть.

излуче́ни|е, я, *n.* radiation; emanation.

излу́чин|а, ы, *f.* bend, wind.

излу́чист|ый (~, ~а), *adj.* winding, meandering.

излуч|и́ть(ся), у́(сь), и́шь(ся), *pf. of* ~а́ть(ся).

излюбленный, *adj.* favourite.

изма́|зать, жу, жешь, *pf.* (*of* ма́зать 3 *and* ~зывать) (*coll.*) **1.** to make dirty, smear; и. пальто́ кра́ской to get paint all over one's coat. **2.** to use up (*paint, grease, etc.*).

изма́|заться, жусь, жешься, *pf.* (*of* ма́заться 1 *and* ~зываться) (*coll.*) **1.** to get dirty; он ~зался в кра́ске he has got paint all over himself. **2.** *pass of* ~зать.

изма́зыва|ть(ся), ю(сь), *impf. of* изма́зать(ся).

измар|а́ть, а́ю, *pf.* (*of* ~ывать) to make dirty, soil.

изма́рыва|ть, ю, *impf. of* измара́ть.

изма́тыва|ть(ся), ю(сь), *impf. of* измота́ть(ся).

изма́чива|ть(ся), ю(сь), *impf. of* измочи́ть(ся).

изма́|ять, ю, *pf.* (*coll.*) to exhaust, tire out.

изма́|яться, юсь, *pf.* (*coll.*) to be exhausted, tired out.

измельча́ни|е, я, *n.* growing small; growing shallow; (*fig.*) becoming shallow, becoming superficial.

измельча́|ть, ю, *pf. of* мельча́ть.

измельч|и́ть, у́, и́шь, *pf. of* мельчи́ть.

изме́н|а, ы, *f.* betrayal; treachery; госуда́рственная и. high treason; супру́жеская и. unfaithfulness, (conjugal) infidelity.

измене́ни|е, я, *n.* change, alteration; (*gram.*) inflexion.

измен|и́ть[1], ю́, ~ишь, *pf.* (*of* ~я́ть) to change, alter; (*polit.*) и. законопрое́кт to amend a bill.

измен|и́ть[2], ю́, ~ишь, *pf.* (*of* ~я́ть) (+*d.*) to betray; to be unfaithful (to); (*fig.*) зре́ние ~и́ло ему́ his eyesight had failed him; сча́стье нам ~и́ло our luck is out.

измен|и́ться, ю́сь, ~и́шься, *pf.* (*of* ~я́ться) **1.** to change, alter (*intrans.*); to vary (*intrans.*); и. к лу́чшему, к ху́дшему to change for the better, for the worse; и. в лице́ to change countenance.

изме́нник, а, *m.* traitor.

изме́ннический, *adj.* treacherous, traitorous.

изме́нчивост|ь, и, *f.* **1.** changeableness; mutability; inconstancy, fickleness. **2.** (*biol.*) variability.

изме́нчив|ый (~, ~а), *adj.* changeable; inconstant, fickle; ~ая пого́да changeable weather.

изменя́ем|ый, *pres. part. pass. of* изменя́ть *and adj.* variable; ~ые величи́ны (*math.*) variables.

измен|я́ть(ся), я́ю(сь), *impf. of* ~и́ть(ся).

измере́ни|е, я, *n.* **1.** measurement, measuring; sounding, fathoming (*of sea bottom*); taking (*of temperature*). **2.** (*math.*) dimension; двух, трёх ~й two-, three-dimensional.

измери́м|ый (~, ~а), *adj.* measurable.

измери́тел|ь, я, *m.* 1. measuring instrument, gauge. 2. (*econ.*) index.

измери́тельный, *adj.* (for) measuring.

изме́р|ить, ю, ишь, *pf.* (*of* ~я́ть) to measure; и. кому́-н. температу́ру to take someone's temperature.

измер|я́ть, я́ю, *impf. of* ~ить.

изможде́н|ный (~, ~а́), *adj.* emaciated; worn out.

измок|а́ть, а́ю, *impf. of* ~нуть.

измо́к|нуть, ну, нешь, *past* ~, ~ла, *pf.* (*of* ~а́ть) (*coll.*) to get soaked, get drenched.

измо́р, а, *no pl.*, *m.*; взять ~ом to reduce by starvation, starve out; (*fig.*, *coll.*) взять кого́-н. ~ом to nag, worry someone into doing something.

измор|и́ть, ю́, и́шь, *pf.* (*coll.*) to wear out, exhaust.

и́змороз|ь, и, *f.* hoar-frost; rime.

и́зморос|ь, и, *f.* drizzle.

измота́|ть, ю, *pf.* (*of* изма́тывать) (*coll.*) to exhaust, wear out.

измота́|ться, юсь, *pf.* (*of* изма́тываться) (*coll.*) to be exhausted, worn out.

измоча́лива|ть(ся), ю(сь), *impf. of* измоча́лить(ся).

измоча́л|ить, ю, ишь, *pf.* (*of* ~ивать) to shred; to reduce to shreds (*also fig.*, *coll.*).

измоча́л|иться, юсь, ишься, *pf.* (*of* ~иваться) to become frayed, be in shreds; (*fig.*, *coll.*) to be worn to a shred, go to pieces.

измоч|и́ть, у́, ~ишь, *pf.* (*of* изма́чивать) (*coll.*) to soak through.

измоч|и́ться, у́сь, ~ишься, *pf.* (*of* изма́чиваться) (*coll.*) to be soaked through.

изму́ч|ать, аю, *pf.* = ~ить.

изму́ч|аться, аюсь, *pf.* = ~иться.

изму́ченный, *p.p.p. of* изму́чить *and adj.* worn out, tired out; у вас и. вид you look worn out.

изму́чива|ть(ся), ю(сь), *impf. of* изму́чить(ся).

изму́ч|ить, у, ишь, *pf.* 1. (*pf. of* ~ивать) to torment; to tire out, exhaust. 2. *pf. of* му́чить.

изму́ч|иться, усь, ишься, *pf.* 1. (*pf. of* ~иваться) to be tired out, be exhausted. 2. *pf. of* му́читься.

измыва́тельств|о, а, *n.* (*coll.*) mocking, scoffing.

измыва́|ться, юсь, *impf.* (над; *coll.*) to mock (at), scoff (at).

измы́зг|ать, аю, *pf.* (*of* ~ивать) (*coll.*) 1. to make dirty all over. 2. to wear threadbare.

измы́зг|аться, аюсь, *pf.* (*of* ~иваться) (*coll.*) 1. to get dirty all over. 2. to become threadbare.

измы́згива|ть(ся), ю(сь), *impf. of* измы́згать(ся).

измы́лива|ть, ю, *impf. of* измы́лить.

измы́л|ить, ю, ишь, *pf.* (*of* ~ивать) to use up (*soap*).

измы́сл|ить, ю, ишь, *pf.* (*of* измышля́ть) 1. to fabricate, invent. 2. to contrive.

измыта́р|ить, ю, ишь, *pf.* (*coll.*) to wear out; to try.

измыта́р|иться, юсь, ишься, *pf.* (*coll.*) to be worn out; to be sorely tried.

измышле́ни|е, я, *n.* fabrication, invention (*action and product*).

измышля́|ть, ю, *impf. of* измы́слить.

измя́т|ый, *p.p.p. of* ~ь *and adj.* 1. crumpled, creased. 2. (*fig.*) haggard, jaded.

из|мя́ть(ся), омну́, омнёт(ся), *pf. of* мять(ся)[1].

изна́нк|а, и, *f.* the wrong side (*of material, clothing*); с ~и on the inner side; вы́вернуть на ~у to turn inside out; и. жи́зни the seamy side of life.

изнаси́ловани|е, я, *n.* rape, assault, violation.

изнаси́л|овать, ую, *pf.* (*of* наси́ловать 2) to rape, assault, violate.

изнача́льный, *adj.* primordial.

изна́шивани|е, я, *n.* wear; wear and tear.

изна́шива|ть(ся), ю(сь), *impf. of* износи́ть(ся).

изне́женност|ь, и, *f.* delicacy; softness; effeminacy.

изне́женный, *p.p.p. of* изне́жить *and adj.* 1. pampered; delicate. 2. soft, effete; effeminate.

изне́жива|ть(ся), ю(сь), *impf. of* изне́жить(ся).

изне́ж|ить, у, ишь, *pf.* (*of* ~ивать) to pamper, coddle; to render effeminate.

изне́ж|иться, усь, ишься, *pf.* (*of* ~иваться) to go soft, become effete; to become effeminate.

изнемога́|ть, ю, *impf. of* изнемо́чь.

изнеможе́ни|е, я, *n.* exhaustion; быть в ~и to be utterly exhausted; рабо́тать до ~я to work to the point of exhaustion.

изнеможё́н|ный (~, ~а́), *adj.* exhausted.

изнемо́|чь, гу́, ~жешь, ~гут, *past* ~г, ~гла́, *pf.* (*of* ~га́ть) (от) to be exhausted (from), grow faint (from).

изне́рвнича|ться, юсь, *pf.* (*coll.*) to get into a state of nerves.

изничтож|а́ть, а́ю, *impf. of* ~и́ть.

изничто́ж|ить, у, ишь, *pf.* (*of* ~а́ть) (*coll.*) to destroy, wipe out.

изно́с, а (у), *m.* (*coll.*) wear; wear and tear, deterioration; не знать ~у (а) to wear well; носи́ть что-н. до ~у (а) to wear something until quite worn out; (+*d.*) э́тим боти́нкам нет ~у (а) these boots will stand any amount of hard wear.

изно|си́ть, шу́, ~сишь, *pf.* (*of* изна́шивать) to wear out.

изно|си́ться, шу́сь, ~си́шься, *pf.* (*of* изна́-шиваться) to wear out (*intrans.*); (*fig., coll.*) to be used up, be played out; to age (prematurely).

изно́шенный, *p.p.p.* of износи́ть *and adj.* worn out; и. костю́м threadbare suit; (*fig., coll.*) worn; (prematurely) aged.

изнуре́ни|е, я, *n.* (*physical*) exhaustion.

изнурённый, *p.p.p.* of изнури́ть *and adj.* (*physically*) exhausted, worn out; jaded; у него́ был и. вид he looked worn out; и. го́лодом faint with hunger.

изнури́тель|ный (~ен, ~ьна), *adj.* exhausting; ~ьная боле́знь wasting disease.

изнур|и́ть, ю́, и́шь, *pf.* (*of* ~я́ть) to exhaust, wear out.

изнур|я́ть, я́ю, *impf. of* ~и́ть.

изнутри́, *adv.* from within; дверь запира́ется и. the door fastens on the inside.

изнывá|ть, ю, *impf. of* изны́ть.

изн|ы́ть, о́ю, о́ешь, *pf.* (*of* ~ыва́ть) to languish, be exhausted; и. от жа́жды to be tormented by thirst; и. от тоски́ (по+*d.*; *poet.*) to pine (for).

изо, *prep.* = из.

изо-[1], *prefix* = из-.

изо-[2], iso-.

изоба́р|а, ы, *f.* (*meteor.*) isobar.

изоба́т|а, ы, *f.* (*geogr.*) isobath, depth curve, submarine contour.

изоби́|деть, жу, дишь, *pf.* (*coll.*) to hurt, insult.

изоби́ли|е, я, *n.* abundance, plenty, profusion; рог ~я cornucopia.

изоби́л|овать, ую, *impf.* (+*i.*) to abound (in), be rich (in).

изоби́л|ьный (~ен, ~ьна), *adj.* 1. abundant. 2. (+*i.*) abounding in.

изоблич|а́ть, а́ю, *impf. of* ~и́ть. 2. (*no pf.*) (+*a.* в+*p.*) to show (to be), point to (as being); все его́ посту́пки ~а́ли в нём моше́нника his every action pointed to his being a swindler; его́ похо́дка ~а́ет в нём моряка́ one can tell by his gait that he is a sailor.

изобличе́ни|е, я, *n.* exposure; conviction.

изобличи́тельный, *adj.* damning.

изоблич|и́ть, у́, и́шь, *pf.* (*of* ~а́ть) (+*a.* в+*p.*) to expose (as), convict (of); to unmask; его́ ~и́ли во лжи he stands convicted as a liar.

изобража́|ть(ся), ю(сь), *impf. of* изобрази́ть(ся).

изображе́ни|е, я, *n.* 1. (*artistic*) representation. 2. representation, portrayal; image; imprint; и. в зе́ркале reflection.

изобрази́тель|ый, *adj.* graphic; decorative; ~ые иску́сства fine arts.

изобра|зи́ть, жу́, зи́шь, *pf.* (*of* ~жа́ть) 1. (+*i.*) to depict, portray, represent (as);

и. из себя́ (+*a.*; *coll.*) to make oneself out (to be), represent oneself (as); и. Га́млета сла́бым челове́ком to portray Hamlet as a weak character (*of actor or producer*); и. из себя́ хоро́шего певца́ to make oneself out a good singer. 2. to imitate, take off.

изобра|зи́ться, зи́тся, *pf.* (*of* ~жа́ться) 1. to appear, show itself. 2. *pass. of* ~жа́ться.

изобре|сти́, ту́, тёшь, *past* ~л, ~ла́, *pf.* (*of* ~та́ть) to invent; to devise, contrive.

изобрета́тел|ь, я, *m.* inventor.

изобрета́тельность, и, *f.* inventiveness.

изобрета́тел|ьный (~ен, ~ьна), *adj.* inventive; resourceful.

изобрета́тель|ский, *adj.* of ~.

изобрета́тель|ство, ства, *n.* = ~ность.

изобрета́|ть, ю, *impf. of* изобрести́.

изобрете́ни|е, я, *n.* invention (*process and product*).

изо́гнутый, *p.p.p.* of ~ь *and adj.* bent, curved, winding.

изогн|у́ть, у́, ёшь, *pf.* (*of* изгиба́ть) to bend, curve.

изогн|у́ться, у́сь, ёшься, *pf.* (*of* изгиба́ться) to bend, curve (*intrans.*).

изогра́ф, а, *m.* (*obs.*) icon-painter.

изогра́фи|я, и, *f.* (*obs.*) icon-painting.

изо́дранный, *p.p.p.* of изодра́ть *and adj.* tattered.

из|одра́ть, деру́, дерёшь, *past* ~одра́л, ~одрала́, ~одра́ло, *pf.* (*of* ~дира́ть) (*coll.*) 1. to tear to pieces; to tear in several places. 2. to scratch all over.

изо|йти́, йду́, йдёшь, *past* ~шёл, ~шла́, *pf. of* исходи́ть[2].

изол|га́ться, гу́сь, жёшься, гу́тся, *past* ~га́лся, ~гала́сь, ~га́лось, *pf.* to become an inveterate, hardened liar.

изоли́рованный, *p.p.p.* of изоли́ровать *and adj.* 1. isolated; separate. 2. (*tech.*) insulated.

изоли́р|овать, ую, *impf. and pf.* 1. to isolate; to quarantine. 2. (*tech.*) to insulate.

изолиро́вк|а, и, *f.* (*tech.*) 1. insulation. 2. (*coll.*) insulating tape.

изолиро́вочный, *adj.* (*tech.*) insulating.

изоля́тор[1], а, *m.* (*tech.*) insulator.

изоля́тор[2], а, *m.* 1. (*med.*) isolation ward. 2. solitary confinement cell. 3. (*polit.* 'isolator' (*special prison in U.S.S.R. for political detainees and espionage suspects*).

изоляциони́зм, а, *m.* (*polit.*) isolationism.

изоляциони́ст, а, *m.* (*polit.*) isolationist.

изоля|цио́нный, *adj.* of ~ция; ~цио́нная ле́нта (*tech.*) insulating tape.

изоля́ци|я, и, *f.* 1. isolation; (*med.*) quarantine. 2. (*tech.*) insulation.

изома́слян|ый, *adj.* ~ая кислота́ (*chem.*) isobutyric acid.

изомéрный, *adj.* (*chem.*) isomeric.
изомóрфный, *adj.* (*min.*) isomorphous.
изóрванный, *p.p.p. of* изорвáть *and adj.* tattered, torn.
изорв|áть, ý, ёшь, *past* ~áл, ~алá, ~áло, *pf.* (*of* изрывáть¹) to tear (to pieces).
изорв|áться, ётся, *past* ~áлся, ~алáсь, ~áлось, *pf.* (*coll.*) to be in tatters.
изотéрм|а, ы, *f.* (*geogr.*) isotherm.
изотермúческий, *adj.* 1. (*phys.*) isothermal. 2. having regulated temperature.
изотóп, а, *m.* (*chem.*) isotope.
изохрóнный, *adj.* isochronous.
изошýтк|а, и, *f.* (*coll.*) cartoon, humorous drawing.
изощрéни|е, я, *n.* sharpening (*fig.*); refinement.
изощрённый, *p.p.p. of* изощрúть *and adj.* refined; keen.
изощр|úть, ю, úшь, *pf.* (*of* ~я́ть) to sharpen (*fig.*); to cultivate, refine; и. слух to train one's ear; и. ум to cultivate one's mind.
изощр|úться, ю́сь, úшься, *pf.* (*of* ~я́ться) 1. to acquire refinement. 2. (в+*p.*) to excel (in); и. в придýмывании каламбýров to excel in punning.
изощр|я́ть(ся), я́ю(сь), *impf. of* ~úть(ся).
из-под, *prep.*+*g.* 1. from under; сдéлать что-н. из-под пáлки to do something under the lash; у негó укрáли бумáжник из-под нóсу he had his wallet stolen from under his nose; из-под полы́ on the sly; under the counter. 2. from near; мы приéхали из-под Москвы́ we have come from near Moscow 3. (for) (*indicates purpose of object*); бáнка из-под варéнья jam-jar.
израз|éц, цá, *m.* tile.
израз|цóвый, *adj. of* ~éц.
изрáильский, *adj.* 1. (*hist.*) Israelitish. 2. Israeli.
израильтя́н|ин, ина, *pl.* ~е, ~, *m.* 1. (*hist.*) Israelite. 2. Israeli.
израильтя́н|ка, ки, *f. of* ~ин.
изрáн|ить, ю, ишь, *pf.* to cover with wounds.
израсхóд|овать(ся), ую(сь), *pf. of* расхóдовать(ся).
йзредка, *adv.* now and then; from time to time.
изрéзанный, *p.p.p. of* изрéзать *and adj.*; и. бéрег indented coastline.
изрé|зать, жу, жешь, *pf.* (*of* ~зывать *and* ~зáть) 1. to cut to pieces; to cut up. 2. (*geogr.*) to indent.
изрез|áть, áю, *impf.* (*coll.*) *of* ~áть.
изрéзыва|ть, ю, *impf. of* изрéзать.
изрека́|ть, ю, *impf. of* изрéчь.
изречéни|е, я, *n.* apophthegm, dictum, saying.
изрé|чь, кý, чёшь, кýт, *past* ~к, ~клá, *pf.*

(*of* ~кáть) (*obs. or iron.*) to speak (solemnly); to utter; так ~к thus he spake; и. мýдрое слóво to utter a word of wisdom.
изреше|тúть, чý, тúшь, *pf.* (*of* ~чивать) to pierce with holes; и. пýлями to riddle with bullets.
изрешéчива|ть, ю, *impf. of* изрешетúть.
изрис|овáть, ýю, *pf.* (*of* ~óвывать) 1. to cover with drawings. 2. (*coll.*) to use up (*pencil, paper, etc.*).
изрисóвыва|ть, ю, *impf. of* изрисовáть.
изруб|áть, áю, *impf. of* ~úть.
изруб|úть, лю́, ~úшь, *pf.* (*of* ~áть) to chop up; to hack to pieces; to mince (*meat*).
изругá|ть, ю, *pf.* to abuse, curse violently.
изрывá|ть¹, ю, *impf. of* изорвáть.
изрывá|ть², ю, *impf. of* изры́ть.
изры́г|ать, áю, *impf.* (*of* ~нýть) to vomit, throw up; пýшки ~áли дым и плáмень the cannon were belching forth smoke and flames; (*fig.*) и. ругáтельства to let forth a stream of oaths.
изры́г|нуть, ну, нёшь, *pf. of* ~áть.
изры́тый, *p.p.p. of* ~ь pitted; и. óспой pock-marked.
изр|ы́ть, óю, óешь, *pf.* (*of* ~ывáть²) to dig up; to dig through.
изря́дно, *adv.* (*coll.*) fairly, pretty; tolerably; я и. устáл I am pretty tired; онú вчерá вéчером и. вы́пили they had a fair amount to drink last night.
изря́д|ный (~ен, ~на), *adj.* (*coll.*) fair, handsome; fairly large, tolerable; ~ое колúчество a fair amount; и. пья́ница a pretty heavy drinker.
изувéр, а, *m.* bigot, fanatic.
изувéрский, *adj.* bigoted, fanatical.
изувéрств|о, а, *n.* bigotry, fanaticism; (fanatical) cruelty.
изувéчива|ть, ю, *impf. of* изувéчить.
изувéч|ить, у, ишь, *pf.* (*of* ~ивать) to maim, mutilate.
изувéч|иться, усь, ишься, *pf.* (*coll.*) 1. to maim oneself, mutilate oneself. 2. *pass. of* ~ить.
изукрá|сить, шу, сишь, *pf.* (*of* ~шивать) to decorate (lavishly); и. дом флáгами to bedeck a house with flags; (*coll., iron.*) и. синякáми to 'adorn' with bruises.
изукрáшива|ть, ю, *impf. of* изукрáсить.
изумúтел|ьный (~ен, ~ьна), *adj.* amazing, astounding.
изум|úть, лю́, úшь, *pf.* (*of* ~ля́ть) to amaze, astound.
изум|úться, лю́сь, úшься, *pf.* (*of* ~ля́ться) to be amazed, astounded.
изумлéни|е, я, *n.* amazement.
изумлённый, *p.p.p. of* изумúть *and adj.* amazed, astounded; dumbfounded.

изумля́|ть(ся), ю(сь), *impf. of* изуми́ть(ся).

изумру́д, а, *m.* emerald.

изумру́дный, *adj.* **1.** emerald. **2.** emerald (-green).

изуро́дованный, *p.p.p. of* изуро́довать *and adj.* maimed, mutilated; disfigured.

изуро́д|овать, ую, *pf. of* уро́довать.

изу́стно, *adv.* (*obs.*) orally, by word of mouth.

изу́стный, *adj.* (*obs.*) oral.

изуч|а́ть, а́ю, *impf.* (*of* ~и́ть) to learn; (*impf. only*) to study; он два го́да ~а́ет гре́ческий язы́к he has been studying Greek for two years.

изуч|и́ть, у́, ~ишь, *pf.* (*of* ~а́ть) **1.** to learn; за шесть ме́сяцев она ~и́ла и испа́нский и италья́нский языки́ in six months she had learned both Spanish and Italian. **2.** to come to know (very well), come to understand; он кра́йне за́мкнут, но я всё-таки ~и́л его́ he is extremely reserved, but I came to understand him in the end.

изъеда́|ть, ю, *impf. of* изъе́сть.

изъе́денный, *p.p.p. of* изъе́сть *and adj.*; и. мо́лью moth-eaten.

изъе́з|дить, жу, дишь, *pf.* (*of* ~жива́ть) **1.** to travel all over, traverse; мы ~дили весь свет we have been all round the world. **2.** (*coll.*) to wear out (*vehicle or road surface*).

изъе́зженный, *p.p.p. of* изъе́здить *and adj.* well-worn, rutted.

изъе́зжива|ть, ю, *impf. of* изъе́здить.

изъе́|сть, ст, дя́т, *past* ~л, ~ла, *pf.* (*of* ~да́ть) **1.** to eat away. **2.** to corrode.

изъяви́тельн|ый, *adj., only used in phrase* ~ое наклоне́ние (*gram.*) indicative mood.

изъяв|и́ть, лю́, ~ишь, *pf.* (*of* ~ля́ть) to indicate, express; и. своё согла́сие to give one's consent.

изъявле́ни|е, я, *n.* expression.

изъявля́|ть, ю, *impf. of* изъяви́ть.

изъязв|и́ть, лю́, и́шь, *pf.* (*of* ~ля́ть) (*med.*) to ulcerate.

изъязвле́ни|е, я, *n.* (*med.*) ulceration.

изъязвлённый, *p.p.p. of* изъязви́ть *and adj.* ulcered, ulcerous.

изъязвля́|ть, ю, *impf. of* изъязви́ть.

изъя́н, а, *m.* **1.** defect, flaw; това́р с ~ом defective goods; у него́ мно́го ~ов he has many defects. **2.** damage, loss.

изъясне́ни|е, я, *n.* (*obs.*) explanation; declaration.

изъясни́тельный, *adj.* (*obs.*) explanatory.

изъясн|и́ть, ю́, и́шь, *pf.* (*of* ~я́ть) (*obs.*) to explain, expound.

изъясн|и́ться, ю́сь, и́шься, *pf.* (*of* ~я́ться) (*obs.*) to express oneself; и. в любви́ to declare one's love.

изъясн|я́ть(ся), я́ю(сь), *impf. of* ~и́ть(ся).

изъя́ти|е, я, *n.* **1.** withdrawal; removal; и.

из обраще́ния (моне́ты) (*fin.*) immobilization (of currency). **2.** exception; без вся́кого ~я without exception; в и. из пра́вил as an exception to the rule.

изъ|я́ть, иму́, и́мешь, *pf.* (*of* ~ыма́ть) to withdraw; to remove; и. из обраще́ния to withdraw from circulation; to immobilize (*currency*); и. в по́льзу госуда́рства to confiscate.

изыма́|ть, ю, *impf. of* изъя́ть.

из|ыму́, ы́мешь, *see* ~ъя́ть.

изыска́ни|е, я, *n.* (*usually pl.*) investigation, research; prospecting; survey.

изы́сканност|ь, и, *f.* refinement.

изы́сканный 1. (~, ~a), *p.p.p. of* изыска́ть. **2. (~, ~на),** *adj.* refined; recherché.

изыска́тел|ь, я, *m.* prospector.

изыска́тельский, *adj.* prospecting.

изы|ска́ть, щу́, ~щешь, *pf.* (*of* ~скивать) to find (*after search or investigation*); to search out; и. сре́дства на постро́йку домо́в to find funds for house-building.

изы́скива|ть, ю, *impf.* (*of* изыска́ть) to search out; to try to find.

изю́бр, а, *m.* (*zool.*) Manchurian deer.

изю́м, а (у), *no pl., m.* raisins; sultanas; э́то не фунт ~у! (*joc.*) it is no light matter, it is no joke.

изю́мин|а, ы, *f.* raisin.

изю́мин|ка, ки, *f., dim. of* ~a; (*fig.*) pep, go, spirit; с ~кой spirited; в ней нет ~ки she has no go in her.

изя́ществ|о, а, *n.* elegance, grace.

изя́щ|ный (~ен, ~на), *adj.* elegant, graceful; (*obs.*) ~ные иску́сства fine arts; ~ная литерату́ра belles-lettres.

ика́ни|е, я, *n.* hiccupping.

ик|а́ть, а́ю, *impf.* (*of* ~ну́ть) to hiccup.

ик|ну́ть, ну́, нёшь, *pf. of* ~а́ть.

ико́н|а, ы, *f.* icon.

ико́н|ный, *adj. of* ~a.

иконобо́р|ец, ца, *m.* (*hist.*) iconoclast.

иконобо́рческий, *adj.* (*hist.*) iconoclastic.

иконобо́рчеств|о, а, *n.* (*hist.*) iconoclasm.

иконогра́фи|я, и, *f.* **1.** iconography. **2.** (*collect.*) portraits.

иконопи́с|ец, ца, *m.* icon-painter.

иконопи́сный, *adj.* **1.** *adj. of* и́конопись. **2.** (*fig.*) icon-like (*severe, severely beautiful*).

и́конопис|ь, и, *f.* icon-painting.

иконоста́с, а, *m.* (*eccl.*) iconostasis.

ико́рный, *adj. of* икра́[1].

ико́т|а, ы, *f.* hiccups.

икр|а́[1], ы́, *no pl. f.* **1.** (hard) roe; spawn; мета́ть ~у́ to spawn; (*fig., coll.*) to rage. **2.** caviar(e); pâté; зерни́стая и. soft caviar(e); па́юсная и. pressed caviar(e); баклажа́нная и. aubergine pâté.

икр|а́[2], ы́, *pl.* ~ы, *f.* (*anat.*) calf.

икри́нк|а, и, *f.* (*coll.*) grain of roe.

икри́ст|ый (~, ~а), *adj.* containing much roe.

икр|и́ться, ю́сь, и́шься, *impf.* to spawn.

икроме́та́ни|е, я, *n.* spawning.

икряно́й, *adj.* **1.** hard-roed. **2.** (made from) roe.

икс, а, *m.* (*the letter*) x; (*math.*) x (*unknown quantity*).

икс-луч|и́, е́й, *no sing.* (*obs.*) X-rays.

ил, а, *m.* silt.

и́ли, *conj.* or; и.... и. either ... or; и. вы меня́ не понима́ете? don't you understand me?

и́лист|ый (~, ~а), *adj.* covered with silt; containing silt.

иллю́зи|я, и, *f.* illusion.

иллюзо́р|ный (~ен, ~на), *adj.* illusory.

иллюмина́тор, а, *m.* (*naut.*) porthole.

иллюмина́ци|я, и, *f.* illumination.

иллюмин|ова́ть, у́ю, *impf. and pf.* to illuminate.

иллюстрати́в|ный (~ен, ~на), *adj.* illustrative; и. материа́л illustration(s).

иллюстра́тор, а, *m.* illustrator.

иллюстра́ци|я, и, *f.* illustration (*in various senses*).

иллюстри́р|ованный, *p.p.p. of* ~ова́ть *and adj.* illustrated.

иллюстри́р|ова́ть, ую, *impf. and pf.* (*pf. also* про~) to illustrate (*also fig.*).

ило́т, а, *m.* (*hist. or fig.*) helot.

и́л|овый, *adj.* = ~и́стый.

иль = и́ли.

и́льк|а, и, *f.* (*zool.*) **1.** (North American) mink. **2.** mink (*fur*).

и́льк|овый, *adj. of* ~а.

ильм, а, *m.* (*bot.*) elm (*Ulmus scabra*).

и́льм|овый, *adj. of* ~.

им 1. *i. of pron.* он, оно́. **2.** *d. of pron.* они́.

имажини́зм, а, *m.* (*lit.*) imagism.

имажини́ст, а, *m.* (*lit.*) imagist.

има́м, а, *m.* imam (*Mohammedan priest or leader*).

има́ть (*inf. and past not used*), **е́млю, е́млешь,** *impf.* (*arch., now only iron.*) to take.

имби́р|ный, *adj. of* ~ь.

имби́р|ь, я, *m.* ginger.

и́м|ени, енем, *see* ~я.

име́ни|е, я, *n.* **1.** estate, landed property. **2.** (*sing. only; obs.*) property, possessions.

имени́нник, а, *m.* one whose name-day it is; сиде́ть, смотре́ть ~ом (*joc.*) to look cheery, look on top of the world.

имени́н|ный, *adj. of* ~ы; и. пиро́г name-day cake.

имени́н|ы, ~, *no sing.* **1.** name-day (*day of saint after whom person is named*); спра́вить и. to celebrate one's name-day. **2.** name-day celebration; пойти́ на и. к кому́-н. to go to someone's name-day party.

имени́тельный, *adj.* (*gram.*) nominative.

имени́т|ый (~, ~а), *adj.* (*obs.*) distinguished.

и́менно, *adv.* **1.** (a) и. namely; to wit, videlicet (viz.); нас там бы́ло тро́е, а и.: Петро́в, Ивано́в и я there were three of us there, namely Petrov, Ivanov, and myself. **2.** just, exactly; to be exact; где и. она́ живёт? where exactly does she live?; в то вре́мя я был в Росси́и, а и. в Оде́ссе I was in Russia then, in Odessa to be exact; вот и. э́то я и говори́л that's just what I was saying; вот и.! exactly!, precisely!

именн|о́й, *adj.* **1.** nominal; ~ы́е а́кции (*fin.*) inscribed stock; ~о́е кольцо́ ring engraved with owner's name; и. спи́сок nominal roll; и. ука́з edict signed by tsar; и. чек cheque payable to person named; и. экземпля́р autographed copy. **2.** *adj. of* и́мя 3.

имено́ван|ный, *p.p.p. of* именова́ть *and adj.*; (*math.*) ~ное число́ concrete number.

имен|ова́ть, у́ю, *impf.* (*of* на~) to name.

имен|ова́ться, у́юсь, *impf.* **1.** (+*i.*) to be called; to be termed. **2.** *pass. of* ~ова́ть.

именосло́в, а, *m.* **1.** (*arch.*) list of names, roll. **2.** (*eccl.*) litany (*of saints*).

имену́емый, *pres. part. pass. of* именова́ть; царь Ива́н, и. Гро́зным Tsar Ivan, called the Terrible.

име́|ть, ю, ешь, *impf.* **1.** to have (*of abstract possession*); и. возмо́жность (+*inf.*) to have an opportunity (to), be in a position (to); и. де́ло (с+*i.*) to have dealings (with), have to do (with); и. значе́ние (для) to matter (to), be important (to); и. ме́сто to take place; и. на́глость, несча́стье, *etc.* (+*inf.*) to have the effrontery, the misfortune, *etc.* (to); и. стыд to be ashamed; и. в виду́ to bear in mind, think of, mean; ничего́ не и. про́тив (+*g.*) to have no objection(s) (to); и. сто ме́тров в высоту́ to be 100 metres high. **2.** (+*inf. forms future tense in formal utterance; obs.*) за́втра ~ет быть банке́т there is to be a banquet tomorrow.

име́|ться, ется, *impf.* to be; to be present, be available (~ется у, ~ются у *are equivalent to* есть у); в на́шем го́роде ~ется два кино́ there are two cinemas in our town, we have two cinemas in our town; бана́нов у нас не ~ется we have no bananas, bananas are not to be had here; и. налицо́ to be available, be on hand.

име́|ющийся, *pres. part. of* ~ться *and adj.* available; present.

и́ми, *i. of pron.* они́.

имита́тор, а, *m.* mimic.

имита́ци|я, и, *f.* **1.** mimicry; mimicking. **2.** imitation (*artefact*); и. же́мчуга imitation pearl. **3.** (*mus.*) imitation.

имити́р|ова́ть, ую, *impf.* **1.** to mimic. **2.** to make imitation goods. **3.** (*mus.*) to imitate.

иммане́нт|ный (~ен, ~на), *adj.* (*philos., theol.*) immanent.

иммигра́нт, а, *m.* immigrant.

иммигра|цио́нный, *adj. of* ~ция; ~цио́нные зако́ны immigration laws.

иммиграци|я, и, *f.* **1.** immigration. **2.** (*collect.*) immigrants.

иммигри́р|овать, ую, *impf. and pf.* to immigrate.

иммора́л|ьный (~ен, ~ьна), *adj.* immoral.

иммунизаци|я, и, *f.* (*med.*) immunization.

иммунизи́р|овать, ую, *impf. and pf.* (*med.*) to immunize.

иммуните́т, а, *m.* (*med., leg.*) immunity.

имму́н|ный (~ен, ~на), *adj.* (к) immune (to).

императи́в, а, *m.* (*philos., gram.*) imperative.

императи́в|ный (~ен, ~на), *adj.* imperative.

импера́тор, а, *m.* emperor.

импера́торский, *adj.* imperial.

императри́ц|а, ы, *f.* empress.

империа́л[1], а, *m.* (*obs.*) imperial (*Russian gold coin of 10 or, after 1897, 15 roubles*).

империа́л[2], а, *m.* (*obs.*) imperial, outside (*of omnibus or tram*).

империали́зм, а, *m.* imperialism.

империали́ст, а, *m.* imperialist.

империалисти́ческий, *adj.* imperialist(ic).

импе́ри|я, и, *f.* empire.

импе́рский, *adj.* imperial.

импоза́нт|ный (~ен, ~на), *adj.* imposing, striking.

импони́р|овать, ую, *impf.* (+*d.*) to impress, strike (*fig.*); его́ зна́ния ~овали всем знако́мым everyone he knew was impressed by his learning.

и́мпорт, а, *m.* import.

импортёр, а, *m.* importer.

импорти́р|овать, ую, *impf. and pf.* (*econ.*) to import.

и́мпорт|ный, *adj. of* ~; ~ные по́шлины import duties.

импоте́нт, а, *m.* impotent man.

импоте́нт|ный (~ен, ~на), *adj.* (*med.*) impotent.

импоте́нци|я, и, *f.* (*med.*) impotence.

импреса́рио, *indecl.*, *m.* impresario.

импрессиони́зм, а, *m.* (*art*) impressionism.

импрессиони́ст, а, *m.* (*art*) impressionist.

импрессионисти́ческий, *adj.* (*art*) impressionistic.

импрессиони́ст|ский, *adj.* = ~и́ческий.

импровиза́тор, а, *m.* improvisator.

импровиза́торский, *adj.* improvisatory.

импровизаци|я, и, *f.* improvisation.

импровизи́рова|нный, *p.p.p. of* ~ть *and adj.* improvised; impromptu, extempore.

импровизи́р|овать, ую, *impf.* (*of* сымпровизи́ровать) to improvize; to extemporize.

и́мпульс, а, *m.* impulse, impetus.

импульси́в|ный (~ен, ~на), *adj.* impulsive.

и́мут, *3rd pl. of arch. verb* я́ти: мёртвые сра́му не и. (*rhet.*) 'de mortuis nil nisi bonum'.

иму́ществ|енный, *adj. of* ~о; и. ценз property qualification; и. иск (*leg.*) real action.

иму́ществ|о, а, *n.* property, belongings; stock; дви́жимое и. (*leg.*) personalty, personal estate; недви́жимое и. realty, real estate.

иму́щий, *adj.* propertied; well-off; власть иму́щие the powers that be.

им|я, *g., d., and p.* ~ени, *i.* ~енем, *pl.* ~ена́, ~ён, ~ена́м, *n.* **1.** first, Christian name; name; по ~ени О́льга Olga by name; во и. (+*g.*) in the name of; посла́ть на и. (+*g.*) to address to; запиши́те счёт на моё и. put it down to my account; от ~ени (+*g.*) on behalf of; то́лько по ~ени only in name, only nominally; он тепе́рь изве́стен под други́м ~енем he now goes by, under another name; ~енем зако́на in the name of the law; ~ени (+*g.*) named in honour of (*usually not translated*); Теа́тр ~ени Го́рького the Gorki Theatre; Вое́нная акаде́мия ~ени Фру́нзе the Frunze Military Academy; называ́ть ве́щи свои́ми ~ена́ми to call a spade a spade. **2.** (*fig.*) name, reputation; челове́к с больши́м ~енем a man with a great name; у него́ европе́йское и. he has a European reputation; приобрести́ и. to acquire, make a name; замара́ть своё и. to ruin one's good name; кру́пные ~ена́ в о́бласти фи́зики great names in the field of physics. **3.** (*gram.*) noun, nomen (*any part of speech declined as opp. to conjugated*); и. прилага́тельное (noun) adjective; и. существи́тельное noun (substantive); и. числи́тельное numeral.

имяре́к, а, *m.* **1.** (*obs. or joc.*) so-and-so. **2.** (*in official forms, etc.*) *indicates space for signatory's name.*

ин- (*abbr. of* иностра́нный) foreign.

инакомы́слящ|ий, *adj.* differently minded; heterodox; *as noun* и., ~его, *m.* dissident.

и́наче 1. (*adv.*) differently, otherwise; так и́ли и. in either event, at all events; не ина́че (как) (*coll.*) precisely, of course; не ина́че как полко́вник none other than the colonel. **2.** (*conj.*) otherwise, or (else); спеши́те, и. вы опозда́ете hurry up, or you will be late.

инвали́д, а, *m.* invalid; и. войны́ disabled soldier; и. труда́ industrial invalid.

инвали́дност|ь, и, *f.* disablement; посо́бие по ~и disablement relief; перейти́ на и. to be registered as a disabled person; по ~и перейти́ на пе́нсию (*mil.*) to be invalided out on pension; уво́литься по ~и (*mil.*) be invalided out.

инвали́д|ный, *adj. of* ~; и. дом home for invalids.

инвекти́в|а, ы, *f.* invective.

инвентариза́ци|я, и, *f.* inventory making, inventorying, stock-taking.

инвентариз|ова́ть, у́ю, *impf. and pf.* to inventory.

инвента́р|ный, *adj. of* ~ь; ~ная о́пись inventory.

инвента́р|ь, я́, *m.* **1.** stock; equipment, appliances; живо́й и. live stock; сельско-хозя́йственный и. agricultural implements; торго́вый и. stock-in-trade. **2.** inventory.

инве́рси|я, и, *f.* (*lit.*) inversion.

инвести́р|овать, ую, *impf. and pf.* to invest.

инвести́тор, а, *m.* investor.

инвеститу́р|а, ы, *f.* investiture.

инвести́ци|я, и, *f.* investment.

инволю́ци|я, и, *f.* (*physiol.*) involution.

ингаля́тор, а, *m.* (*med.*) inhaler.

ингаля|цио́нный, *adj. of* ~ция.

ингаля́ци|я, и, *f.* (*med.*) inhaling.

ингредие́нт, а, *m.* ingredient.

ингу́ш, а́, *g. pl.* ~е́й, *m.* Ingush.

ингу́ш|ка, ки, *f. of* ~.

ингу́шский, *adj.* Ingush.

и́ндеве|ть, ет, *impf.* (*of* за~) to become covered with hoar-frost.

инде́|ец, йца, *pl.* ~йцы, ~йцев, *m.* (American) Indian.

инде́йк|а, и, *f.* turkey(-hen).

инде́|йский, *adj. of* ~ец; и. пету́х turkey--cock.

и́ндекс, а, *m.* index; и. цен (*econ.*) price index.

индиа́нк|а, и, *f.* (*of* инде́ец *and* инди́ец) Indian (woman).

индиви́д, а, *m.* individual.

индивидуализа́ци|я, и, *f.* individualization.

индивидуализи́р|овать, ую, *impf. and pf.* to individualize.

индивидуали́зм, а, *m.* individualism.

индивидуали́ст, а, *m.* individualist.

индивидуалисти́ческий, *adj.* individualistic.

индивидуалисти́ч|ный (~ен, ~на), *adj.* individualistic.

индивидуа́льность|ь, и, *f.* individuality.

индивидуа́л|ьный (~ен, ~ьна), *adj.* individual; ~ьные осо́бенности individual peculiarities; ~ьное хозя́йство individual holding; в ~ьном поря́дке individually; и. слу́чай individual case, single case.

индиви́дуум, а, *m.* individual.

инди́го, *indecl., n.* **1.** indigo (*colour*). **2.** (*bot.*) indigo plant.

инди́|ец, йца, *pl.* ~йцы, ~йцев, *m.* Indian.

и́нди|й, я, *m.* (*chem.*) indium.

инди́йский, *adj.* Indian.

индикати́в, а, *m.* (*gram.*) indicative.

индика́тор, а, *m.* **1.** (*tech.*) indicator. **2.** (*chem.*) reagent.

индика́тор|ный, *adj. of* ~; ~ная диагра́мма indicator diagram; ~ная мо́щность indicated horse-power (*abbr.* I.H.P.).

инди́кт, а, *m.* (*hist.*) indiction (*period of 15 years*).

индифере́нтност|ь, и, *f.* indifference.

индиффере́нт|ный (~ен, ~на), *adj.* (к) indifferent (to).

индоевропе́йский, *adj.* Indo-European.

индокита́йский, *adj.* Indo-Chinese.

индонези́|ец, йца, *pl.* ~йцы, ~йцев, *m.* Indonesian.

индонези́|йка, йки, *f. of* ~ец.

индонези́йский, *adj.* Indonesian.

индоссаме́нт, а, *m.* (*fin.*) endorsement, indorsation.

индосса́нт, а, *m.* (*fin.*) endorser.

индосса́т, а, *m.* (*fin.*) endorsee.

индосси́р|овать, ую, *impf. and pf.* (*fin.*) to endorse.

индуи́зм, а, *m.* Hinduism.

индукти́вный, *adj.* (*philos., phys.*) inductive.

инду́ктор, а, *m.* (*electr.*) inductor, field magnet.

инду́ктор|ный, *adj. of* ~; и. вы́зов induction call; и. телефо́нный аппара́т magneto telephone, sound power telephone.

индукци|о́нный, *adj. of* ~я; ~о́нная кату́шка induction coil.

инду́кци|я, и, *f.* (*philos., phys.*) induction.

индульге́нци|я, и, *f.* (*eccl.*) indulgence.

инду́с, а, *m.* Hindu; (*obs.*) Indian.

инду́с|ка, ки, *f. of* ~.

инду́сский, *adj.* Hindu; (*obs.*) Indian.

индустриализа́ци|я, и, *f.* industrialization.

индустриализи́р|овать, ую, *impf. and pf.* to industrialize.

индустриа́льный, *adj.* industrial.

инду́стри|я, и, *f.* industry.

индю́к, а́, *m.* turkey(-cock); наду́лся как и. (*coll.*) he got on his high horse.

индю́ш|ачий, *adj.* = ~ечий.

индю́ш|ечий, *adj. of* ~ка.

индю́шк|а, и, *f.* turkey(-hen).

индю́ш|о́нок, о́нка, *pl.* ~а́та, ~а́т, *m.* turkey-poult.

и́не|й, я, *no pl., m.* hoar-frost, rime.

ине́ртност|ь, и, *f.* inertness, sluggishness, inaction.

ине́рт|ный (~ен, ~на), *adj.* inert (*phys. and fig.*); sluggish, inactive.

ине́рци|я, и, *f.* (*phys. and fig.*) inertia; momentum; дви́гаться по ~и to move under its own momentum; (*fig.*) де́лать что-н. по ~и to do something from force of inertia, mechanically.

инженер, а, *m.* person with higher technical education; engineer; гражданский и., и. путей сообщения, и.-строитель civil engineer.

инженерн|ый, *adj.* engineering; ~ые войска (*mil.*) Engineers; ~ое дело engineering.

инженю, *indecl., f.* (*theatr.*) ingénue.

инжир, а, *m.* fig.

инжирный, *adj.* fig.

инист|ый (~, ~а), *adj.* rimy, covered with hoar-frost.

инициал|ы, ов, *sing.* ~, ~а, *m.* initials.

инициатив|а, ы, *f.* initiative; по собственной ~е on one's own initiative.

инициатив|ный, *adj.* **1.** initiating, originating; ~ная группа organizing body, action committee. **2. (~ен, ~на)** full of initiative, enterprising.

инициатор, *m.* **а,** initiator, organizer.

инкассатор, а, *m.* (*fin.*) collector, receiver (*of bill, cheque, etc.*).

инкассаци|я, и, *f.* encashment, collection, receipt (*of money or bills*).

инкасси́р|овать, ую, *impf. and pf.* (*fin.*) to encash, collect, receive (*money, bill*).

инкассо, *indecl., n.* (*fin.*) encashment.

ин-кварто, *adv.* (*also as adj. and noun, indecl.*) (*typ.*) quarto.

инквизитор, а, *m.* inquisitor.

инквизиторский, *adj.* inquisitorial.

инквизици|я, и, *f.* inquisition.

инкогнито, *adv.* (*also as indecl. noun, m. and n.*) incognito.

инкорпораци|я, и, *f.* incorporation.

инкорпори́р|овать, ую, *impf. and pf.* to incorporate.

инкримини́р|овать, ую, *impf. and pf.* (+*a.* and *d.*) to charge (with); ему ~уют поджог he is being charged with arson.

инкрустаци|я, и, *f.* inlaid work, inlay.

инкрусти́р|овать, ую, *impf. and pf.* to inlay.

инкубатор, а, *m.* incubator.

инкубационный, *adj.* incubative, incubatory; и. период (*med.*) incubation.

инкубаци|я, и, *f.* incubation (*of chickens and med.*).

инкунабул|ы, ~, *sing.* ~а, ~ы, *f.* (*lit.*) incunabula.

иновер|ец, ца, *m.* (*rel.*) adherent of different faith, creed.

иновери|е, я, *n.* (*rel.*) adherence to different faith, creed.

иноверный, *adj.* (*rel.*) belonging to different faith, creed.

иногда, *adv.* sometimes.

иногородн|ий, *adj.* **1.** of, from another town; ~яя почта mail for, from other towns. **2.** *as noun* и., ~его, *m.* (*hist.*) non--Cossack peasant living in Cossack community.

инозем|ец, ца, *m.* (*obs.*) foreigner.

иноземный, *adj.* (*obs.*) foreign.

ин|ой, *adj.* **1.** different; other; ~ыми словами in other words; не кто и., как; не что ~ое, как none other than; тот или и. one or other, this or that. **2.** some; и. раз sometimes; и. (человек) мог и согласиться some might agree.

инок, а, *m.* monk.

инокин|я, и, *f.* nun.

ин-октаво, *adv.* (*also as adj. and noun, indecl.*) (*typ.*) octavo.

инокули́р|овать, ую, *impf. and pf.* to inoculate.

инокуляци|я, и, *f.* inoculation.

иномысли|е, я, *n.* (*obs.*) dissent, difference of opinion.

иноплеменник, а, *m.* (*obs.*) member of different tribe, nationality.

иноплеменный, *adj.* (*obs.*) of another tribe, nationality; foreign.

инород|ец, ца, *m.* (*hist.*) non-Russian (*member of national minority in tsarist Russia*).

инородн|ый, *adj.* heterogeneous; ~ое тело (*med. or fig.*) foreign body.

инород|ческий, *adj.* of ~ец.

иносказани|е, я, *n.* allegory.

иносказа́тел|ьный (~ен, ~ьна), *adj.* allegorical.

инославный, *adj.* (*rel.*) non-Orthodox.

иностран|ец, ца, *m.* foreigner.

иностранный, *adj.* foreign.

инотдел, а, *m.* foreign department (*of Soviet institutions*).

иноход|ец, ца, *m.* ambler (*horse*).

иноход|ь, и, *f.* amble.

иноческий, *adj.* monastic.

иночеств|о, а, *n.* monasticism; monastic life.

иноязы́чн|ый, *adj.* **1.** speaking another language. **2.** belonging to another language; ~ое слово loan-word.

инсинуаци|я, и, *f.* insinuation.

инсинуи́р|овать, ую, *impf. and pf.* to insinuate.

инсоляци|я, и, *f.* (*phys., med.*) insolation.

инспекти́р|овать, ую, *impf.* to inspect.

инспектор, а, *pl.* ~а, ~ов, *m.* inspector; (*mil.*) inspecting officer.

инспектор|ский, *adj.* of ~.

инспекци|я, и, *f.* **1.** inspection. **2.** inspectorate.

инспиратор, а, *m.* inciter.

инспири́р|овать, ую, *impf. and pf.* to incite; to inspire; кто ~овал эту статью? who inspired this article?; и. слухи to start rumours.

инстанци|я, и, *f.* (*leg.*) instance; суд первой ~и court of first instance; по ~ям from instance to instance, through all stages; (*mil.*) кома́ндная и. chain of command.

инсти́нкт, а, *m.* instinct.

инстинкти́в|ный (~ен, ~на), *adj.* instinctive.

институ́т, а, *m.* **1.** institution; и. бра́ка, и. ча́стной со́бственности the institution of marriage, of private property. **2.** (*educational or scientific*) institute, institution; педагоги́ческий и. teacher training college. **3.** girls' private boarding school (*in tsarist Russia*).

институ́тк|а, и, *f.* boarding schoolgirl (*in tsarist Russia*); (*fig., coll.*) innocent, unsophisticated girl.

институ́т|ский, *adj. of* ~ 2, 3.

инструкта́ж, а, *m.* instructing; (*mil., aeron.*) briefing.

инструкти́в|ный (~ен, ~на), *adj.* instructional.

инструкти́р|овать, ую, *impf. and pf.* (*pf. also* про~) to instruct, give instructions to.

инстру́ктор, а, *m.* instructor.

инстру́ктор|ский, *adj. of* ~.

инстру́кци|я, и, *f.* instructions, directions.

инструме́нт, а, *m.* instrument; tool, implement; (*sing.; collect.*) tools.

инструментали́ст, а, *m.* (*mus.*) instrumentalist.

инструмента́льн|ая, ой, *f.* tool-shop.

инструмента́льн|ый, *adj.* **1.** (*mus.*) instrumental. **2.** (*tech.*) tool-making; ~ая сталь tool steel.

инструмента́льщик, а, *m.* tool-maker, instrument-maker.

инструмента́ри|й, я, *m.* (*collect.*) instruments, tools.

инструмент|ова́ть, у́ю, *impf. and pf.* (*mus.*) to arrange for instruments.

инструменто́вк|а, и, *f.* (*mus.*) instrumentation.

инсули́н, а, *m.* (*med.*) insulin.

инсу́льт, а, *m.* (*med.*) cerebral thrombosis; (apoplectic) stroke.

инсурге́нт, а, *m.* (*obs.*) insurgent.

инсурре́кци|я, и, *f.* (*obs.*) insurrection.

инсцени́р|овать, ую, *impf. and pf.* **1.** to dramatize, adapt for stage *or* screen (*a novel, etc.*). **2.** (*fig.*) to feign, stage; и. о́бморок to stage a faint.

инсцениро́вк|а, и, *f.* **1.** dramatization, adaptation for stage *or* screen. **2.** (*fig.*) pretence; act.

интегра́л, а, *m.* (*math.*) integral.

интегра́льн|ый, *adj.* (*math.*) integral; ~ое исчисле́ние integral calculus.

интегра́ци|я, и, *f.* (*math.*) integration.

интегри́р|овать, ую, *impf. and pf.* (*math.*) to integrate.

интелле́кт, а, *m.* intellect.

интеллектуа́л|ьный (~ен, ~ьна), *adj.* intellectual.

интеллиге́нт, а, *m.* member of the intelligentsia, intellectual.

интеллиге́нт|ный (~ен, ~на), *adj.* cultured, educated.

интеллиге́нт|ский, *adj.* (*pejor.*) of ~; dilettante.

интеллиге́нци|я, и, *f.* intelligentsia.

интенда́нт, а, *m.* (*mil.*) quartermaster.

интенда́нтств|о, а, *n.* (*mil.*) quartermaster service, commissariat.

интенси́в|ный (~ен, ~на), *adj.* intensive.

интенсифици́р|овать, ую, *impf. and pf.* to intensify.

интерва́л, а, *m.* (*in var. senses*) interval.

интерве́нт, а, *m.* (*polit.*) interventionist.

интерве́нци|я, и, *f.* (*polit.*) intervention.

интервью́, *indecl.*, *n.* (*press*) interview.

интервьюе́р, а, *m.* (*press*) interviewer.

интервьюи́р|овать, ую, *impf. and pf.* to interview.

интере́с, а, *m.* interest **1.** (*attention*) предста́вить и. to be of interest; прояви́ть и. (к) to show interest (in). **2.** (*advantage*); (*pl.*) interests; како́й мне и.? how do I stand to gain?; в ва́ших ~ах пое́хать it is in your interest to go; игра́ть на и. (*coll., obs.*) to play for money.

интере́снича|ть, ю, *impf.* (*coll.*) to show off.

интере́сно, *as pred.* it is, would be interesting; и. знать, кто э́тот высо́кий иностра́нец it would be interesting to know who the tall foreigner is; и., что из него́ вы́йдет I wonder how he will turn out.

интере́с|ный (~ен, ~на), *adj.* **1.** interesting; в ~ном положе́нии (*euph.*) in an interesting condition. **2.** striking, attractive.

интерес|ова́ть, у́ю, *impf.* to interest.

интерес|ова́ться, у́юсь, *impf.* (+*i.*) to be interested (in).

интерлю́ди|я, и, *f.* (*mus.*) interlude.

интерме́ди|я, и, *f.* (*theatr.*) interlude.

интерме́ццо, *indecl.*, *n.* (*mus.*) intermezzo.

инте́рн, а, *m.* intern(e) (*in hospital*).

интерна́т, а, *m.* **1.** boarding school. **2.** boarding house (*at private school*).

интернациона́л, а, *m.* **1.** international (organization); Пе́рвый И. (*hist.*) the First International. **2.** И. the 'Internationale'.

интернационализа́ци|я, и, *f.* internationalization.

интернационализи́р|овать, ую, *impf. and pf.* to internationalize.

интернационали́зм, а, *m.* internationalism.

интернационали́ст, а, *m.* internationalist.

интернациона́льный, *adj.* international.

интерни́рова|нный, *p.p.p. of* ~ть; *as noun* и., ~нного, *m.* internee.

интерни́р|овать, ую, *impf. and pf.* to intern.

интерпелли́р|овать, ую, *impf. and pf.* (*polit.*) to interpellate.

интерпелля́ци|я, и, *f.* (*polit.*) interpellation; question in Parliament.

интерполи́р|овать, ую, *impf. and pf.* to interpolate.

интерполя́ци|я, и, *f.* interpolation.

интерпрета́тор, а, *m.* interpreter (*expounder*).

интерпрета́ци|я, и, *f.* interpretation; но́вая и. ро́ли Га́млета a new interpretation of the part of Hamlet.

интерпрети́р|овать, ую, *impf. and pf.* to interpret (*expound*).

интерфере́нци|я, и, *f.* (*phys.*) interference.

интерье́р, а, *m.* (*art*) interior.

инти́мност|ь, и, *f.* intimacy.

инти́м|ный (~ен, ~на), *adj.* intimate.

интоксика́ци|я, и, *f.* (*med.*) intoxication; алкого́льная и. alcoholic poisoning.

интона́ци|я, и, *f.* intonation.

интони́р|овать, ую, *impf.* to intone.

интри́г|а, и, *f.* 1. intrigue. 2. (*obs.*) (love-) affair. 3. plot of story *or* play.

интрига́н, а, *m.* intriguer, schemer.

интриг|ова́ть, у́ю, *impf.* 1. (*no pf.*) to intrigue, carry on an intrigue. 2. (*pf.* за~) to intrigue (*excite curiosity of*).

интроду́кци|я, и, *f.* (*mus.*) introduction.

интроспе́кци|я, и, *f.* introspection.

интуитиви́зм, а, *m.* (*philos.*) intuitionism.

интуити́в|ный (~ен, ~на), *adj.* intuitive.

интуи́ци|я, и, *f.* intuition; по ~и by intuition, intuitively.

инфанте́ри|я, и, *f.* (*obs.*) infantry.

инфантили́зм, а, *m.* infantilism.

инфанти́льный, *adj.* infantile.

инфа́ркт, а, *m.* (*med.*) infarct; infarction; coronary thrombosis; heart attack.

инфекцио́нный, *adj.* infectious.

инфе́кци|я, и, *f.* infection.

инферна́льный, *adj.* infernal, of hell.

инфильтра́ци|я, и, *f.* infiltration.

инфинити́в, а, *m.* (*gram.*) infinitive.

инфици́р|овать, ую, *impf. and pf.* to infect.

инфлюэ́нц|а, ы, *f.* influenza.

инфля́ци|я, и, *f.* (*econ.*) inflation.

ин-фо́лио, *adv.* (*also as adj. and noun, indecl.*) (*typ.*) folio.

информа́тор, а, *m.* informant; полити́ческий и. political information officer.

информ|ацио́нный, *adj. of* ~а́ция.

информа́ци|я, и, *f.* information.

информи́р|овать, ую, *impf. and pf.* to inform.

инфракра́сный, *adj.* infra-red.

инфузо́ри|я, и, *f.* (*zool.*) infusoria.

инциде́нт, а, *m.* incident (*quarrel, clash*); пограни́чный и. frontier incident.

инъе́кци|я, и, *f.* injection.

ио́д, ~истый, ~ный, ~офо́рм, *see* йод, *etc.*

ио́н, а, *m.* (*phys.*) ion.

иониза́ци|я, и, *f.* (*phys., med.*) ionization.

иони́|йский, *adj.* = ~ческий.

иони́ческ|ий, *adj.* Ionian, Ionic; ~ая коло́нна Ionic column.

ио́нный, *adj.* (*phys.*) ionic.

ио́та = йо́та.

иподья́кон, а, *m.* (*eccl.*) subdeacon.

ипоме́|я, и, *f.* (*bot.*) morning glory.

ипоста́с|ь, и, *f.* (*theol.*) hypostasis.

ипоте́к|а, и, *f.* mortgage.

ипоте́|чный, *adj. of* ~ка.

ипохо́ндрик, а, *m.* hypochondriac.

ипохо́ндри|я, и, *f.* hypochondria.

ипподро́м, а, *m.* hippodrome; racecourse.

иприт, а, *m.* mustard gas, yperite.

ира́к|ец, ца, *m.* Iraqi.

ира́кский, *adj.* Iraqi.

ира́н|ец, ца, *m.* Iranian.

ира́н|ка, ки, *f. of* ~ец.

ира́нский, *adj.* Iranian.

ира́чк|а, и, *f.* Iraqi (woman).

и́рбис, а, *m.* (*zool.*) ounce.

ири́ди|й, я, *m.* (*chem.*) iridium.

и́рис, а, *m.* (*bot.*) iris.

ири́с, а, *m.* toffee.

ири́ск|а, и, (*coll.*) *f.* (a) toffee.

ирла́нд|ец, ца, *m.* Irishman.

ира́н|ка, ки, *f. of* ~ец.

ирла́ндский, *adj.* Irish.

и́род, а, *m.* (*coll.*) tyrant, monster.

иронизи́р|овать, ую, *impf.* (над) to speak ironically (about).

ирони́ческий, *adj.* ironic(al).

иро́ни|я, и, *f.* irony.

иррациона́л|ьный (~ен, ~ьна), *adj.* irrational; ~ьное число́ (*math.*) irrational number, surd.

иррегуля́р|ный, *adj.* irregular; ~ые войска́ (*mil.*) irregulars.

иррига́тор, а, *m.* 1. (*agric.*) irrigation expert. 2. (*med.*) irrigator.

иррига́ци|я, и, *f.* (*agric. and med.*) irrigation.

иск, а, *m.* (*leg.*) suit, action; предъяви́ть и. (к) кому́-н. to sue, prosecute someone, bring an action against someone; отказа́ть в ~е to reject a suit; и. за клевету́ libel action; и. за оскорбле́ние де́йствием action for assault and battery.

искажа́|ть, ю, *impf. of* исказить.

искаже́ни|е, я, *n.* distortion, perversion; ~я в те́ксте corruptions of a text.

искажённый, *p.p.p. of* исказить *and adj.* distorted, perverted.

иска|зи́ть, жу́, зи́шь, *pf.* (*of* ~жа́ть) to distort, pervert, twist; to misrepresent; боль ~зи́ла черты́ её лица́ pain has distorted her features; и. чьи-н. слова́ to twist someone's words; и. фа́кты to misrepresent the facts.

искале́ч|енный, *p.p.p.* of ~ить *and adj.* crippled, maimed.

искале́чива|ть, ю, *impf. of* искале́чить.

искале́ч|ить, у, ишь, *pf. (of* ~ивать *and* кале́чить) 1. to cripple, maim. 2. (*coll.*) to break.

иска́лыва|ть, ю, *impf. of* исколо́ть.

иска́ни|е, я, *n.* 1. (+*g.*) search (for), quest (of). 2. (*pl.*) strivings.

иска́п|ать, аю, *pf. (of* ~ывать[1]) (*coll.*) to sprinkle all over, spill all over; и. свои́ брю́ки черни́лами to spill ink all over one's trousers.

иска́пыва|ть[1], ю, *impf. of* иска́пать.

иска́пыва|ть[2], ю, *impf. of* ископа́ть.

иска́тел|ь, я, m. 1. seeker, searcher; и. жемчуга́ pearl-diver. 2. (*tech.*) (view-)finder.

иска́тел|ьный (~ен, ~ьна), *adj.* ingratiating.

иска́тельств|о, а, *n.* ingratiating oneself.

иска́ть, ищу́, и́щешь, *impf.* 1. (+*a.*) to look for, search for; to seek (*something concr.*); и. иго́лку, кварти́ру to be looking for a needle, for a flat. 2. (+*g.*) to seek, look for (*something abstr.*); и. ме́ста to look for a job; и. слу́чая, сове́та to seek an opportunity, seek advice. 3. (с+*g.* or на+*p.*; *leg.*) to claim (from). 4. (+*inf.*; *obs.*) to seek (to).

исключа́ть, а́ю, *impf. of* ~и́ть.

исключа́|я, *pres. gerund of* ~ть *and prep.*+*g.* excepting, with the exception of; и. прису́тствующих the present company excepted.

исключе́ни|е, я, *n.* 1. exception; за ~ем (+*g.*) with the exception (of). 2. exclusion; expulsion; по ме́тоду ~я by process of elimination.

исключи́тельно, *adv.* 1. exceptionally. 2. exclusively, solely. 3. exclusive; до страни́цы семь и. to page seven exclusive.

исключи́тел|ьный (~ен, ~ьна), *adj.* 1. exceptional; и. слу́чай exceptional case; ~ьной ва́жности of exceptional importance. 2. exclusive; ~ьное пра́во exclusive right, sole right. 3. (*coll.*) excellent.

исключ|и́ть, у́, и́шь, *pf. (of* ~а́ть) 1. to exclude; to eliminate; и. из спи́ска to strike off a list. 2. to expel; to dismiss. 3. to rule out; не ~ено́, что на́ши проигра́ют the possibility of our side losing cannot be ruled out.

искове́рка|нный, *p.p.p. of* ~ть *and adj.* (*coll.*) corrupt(ed); ~нное сло́во corrupted word, corruption.

искове́рка|ть, ю, *pf. of* кове́ркать.

иск|ово́й, *adj. of* ~; ~ово́е заявле́ние (*leg.*) statement of claim.

искола́чива|ть, ю, *impf. of* исколоти́ть.

исколе|си́ть, шу́, си́шь, *pf.* (*coll.*) to travel all over.

исколо|ти́ть, чу́, ~ти́шь, *pf.* (*of* искола́чивать) (*coll.*) 1. to beat; и. кого́-н. до полусме́рти to beat someone within an inch of his life. 2. to spoil, damage by knocking in nails, *etc.*

искол|о́ть, ю́, ~ешь, *pf.* (*of* иска́лывать) to prick all over, cover with pricks.

иско́мка|ть, ю, *pf. of* ко́мкать.

иско́м|ый, *adj.* sought for; *as noun* ~ое, ~ого, *n.* (*math.*) unknown quantity.

искони́, *adv.* (*rhet.*) from time immemorial.

иско́нный, *adj.* primordial; immemorial.

ископа́ем|ое, ого, *n.* 1. mineral. 2. fossil (*also fig., iron.*).

ископа́емый, *adj.* fossilized.

ископа́|ть, ю, *pf. (of* иска́пывать[2]) to dig up.

искорёж|ить(ся), у(сь), ишь(ся), *pf. of* корёжить(ся).

искорене́ни|е, я, *n.* eradication.

искорен|и́ть, ю́, и́шь, *pf. (of* ~я́ть) to eradicate.

искорен|я́ть, я́ю, *impf. of* ~и́ть.

и́скорк|а, и, f. *dim. of* и́скра.

и́скоса, *adv.* (*coll.*) aslant, sideways; взгляд и. sidelong glance.

и́скр|а, ы, f. spark; (*fig.*) flash; промелькну́ть, как и. to flash by; и. наде́жды glimmer of hope; у меня́ ~ы из глаз посы́пались (*coll.*) I saw stars.

искре́ни|е, я, *n.* (*tech.*) sparking.

и́скренн|е = ~о.

и́скрен|ний (~ен, ~на), *adj.* sincere, candid.

и́скренно, *adv.* sincerely, candidly; и. ваш, и. пре́данный вам (*epistolary formula*) Yours sincerely; Yours faithfully.

и́скренност|ь, и, f. sincerity, candour.

искрив|и́ть, лю́, и́шь, *pf. (of* ~ля́ть) to bend; (*fig.*) to distort.

искривле́ни|е, я, *n.* bend; (*fig.*) distortion; и. позвоно́чника curvature of the spine.

искривля́|ть, ю, *impf. of* искриви́ть.

искри́ст|ый (~, ~а), *adj.* sparkling.

искр|и́ть, и́т, *impf.* (*tech.*) to spark.

и́скр|и́ться, ~и́тся, *impf.* to sparkle; to scintillate (*also fig.*).

искровен|ённый, *p.p.p. of* ~и́ть *and adj.* blood-stained.

искровен|и́ть, ю́, и́шь, *pf.* (*coll.*) 1. to wound so as to draw blood. 2. to stain with blood.

искр|ово́й, *adj. of* ~а; и. зазо́р, и. промежу́ток (*electr.*) spark-gap; и. разря́дник (*radio*) spark discharger; и. телегра́ф (*obs.*) wireless telegraph.

искрогаси́тел|ь, я, m. (*tech.*) spark-extinguisher.

искромётный, *adj.* sparkling; (*fig.*) и. взгляд flashing glance.

искромса|ть, ю, *pf. of* кромсáть.

искроудержáтел|ь, я, *m.* (*tech.*) spark-arrester.

искрош|и́ть, у́, ~ишь, *pf.* (*of* кроши́ть) to crumble; to mince; (*fig.*) to cut to pieces (*with sabres*).

искрош|и́ться, ~ится, *pf.* (*of* кроши́ться) to crumble (*intrans.*).

искупá|ть¹, ю, *pf.* (*coll.*) to bath.

искуп|áть², áю, *impf. of* ~и́ть.

искупá|ться¹, юсь, *pf.* (*coll.*) to bathe; to take a bath.

искупá|ться², юсь, *impf., pass. of* ~ть².

искупи́тел|ь, я, *m.* (*theol.*) redeemer.

искупи́тел|ьный (~ен, ~ьна), *adj.* expiatory, redemptive; ~ьная жéртва sin offering.

искуп|и́ть, лю́, ~ишь, *pf.* (*of* ~áть²) 1. (*theol. and fig.*) to redeem; to expiate, atone for. 2. to make up for, compensate for.

искуплéни|е, я, *n.* redemption, expiation, atonement.

иску́с, а, *m.* novitiate, probation (*in religious orders*); test, ordeal.

искус|áть, áю, *pf.* (*of* ~ывать) to bite badly, all over; to sting badly, all over.

искуси́тел|ь, я, *m.* tempter.

иску|си́ть, шу́, си́шь, *pf. of* ~шáть.

иску|си́ться, шу́сь, си́шься, *pf.* 1. (в+*p.*) to become expert (at), become a past master (in, of). 2. *pass. of* ~си́ть.

иску́сник, а, *m.* (*coll.*) expert, past master.

иску́с|ный (~ен, ~на), *adj.* skilful; expert.

иску́сственност|ь, и, *f.* artificiality.

иску́сствен|ный, *adj.* 1. artificial, synthetic; ~ное питáние (младéнца) bottle feeding; ~ная цепь (*tech.*) phantom circuit. 2. (~, ~на) (*fig.*) artificial, feigned.

иску́сств|о, а, *n.* 1. art; изобрази́тельные, изя́щные ~а fine arts. 2. craftsmanship, skill; и. верховóй езды́ horsemanship; дéлать что-н. из любви́ к ~у to do something for its own sake.

искусствовéд, а, *m.* art critic.

искусствовéдени|е, я, *n.* art criticism.

иску́сыва|ть, ю, *impf. of* искусáть.

искушá|ть, ю, *impf.* (*of* искуси́ть) to tempt; to seduce; и. судьбу́ to tempt fate, tempt Providence.

искушéни|е, я, *n.* temptation; seduction; ввести́ в и. to lead into temptation; поддáться ~ю, впасть в и. to yield to temptation.

искушённый, *p.p.p. of* искуси́ть *and adj.* experienced; tested.

ислáм, а, *m.* Islam.

ислáнд|ец, ца, *m.* Icelander.

ислáнд|ка, ки, *f. of* ~ец.

ислáндский, *adj.* Icelandic.

испáко|стить, щу, стишь, *pf. of* пáкостить.

испáн|ец, ца, *m.* Spaniard.

испáнк|а¹, и, *f.* Spanish woman.

испáнк|а², и, *f.* (*coll.*) Spanish 'flu.

испáнский, *adj.* Spanish.

испарéни|е, я, *n.* 1. evaporation. 2. exhalation; fumes.

испáрин|а, ы, *f.* perspiration.

испар|и́ть, ю́, и́шь, *pf.* (*of* ~я́ть) to evaporate (*trans.*); to exhale.

испар|и́ться, ю́сь, и́шься, *pf.* (*of* ~я́ться) to evaporate; (*fig., joc.*) to vanish into thin air.

испар|я́ть(ся), я́ю(сь), *impf. of* ~и́ть(ся).

испа|хáть, шу́, ~шешь, *pf.* (*of* ~хивать) (*coll.*) to plough all over.

испáхива|ть, ю, *impf. of* испахáть.

испáчка|ть, ю, *pf. of* пáчкать.

испепел|и́ть, ю́, и́шь, *pf.* (*of* ~я́ть) to reduce to ashes, incinerate.

испепел|я́ть, я́ю, *impf. of* ~и́ть.

испестр|ённый, *p.p.p. of* ~и́ть *and adj.* speckled, mottled; variegated.

испестр|и́ть, ю́, и́шь, *pf.* (*of* ~я́ть) to speckle; to mottle; to make variegated.

испестр|я́ть, я́ю, *impf. of* ~и́ть.

испечённый, *p.p.p. of* испéчь; вновь и. (*coll.*) new-fledged.

испе́|чь, ку́, чёшь, ку́т, *past* ~к, ~клá, *pf. of* печь.

испещр|и́ть, ю́, и́шь, *pf.* (*of* ~я́ть) (+*a. and i.*) to spot (with); to mark all over (with); и. стéну нáдписями to cover a wall with inscriptions.

испещр|я́ть, я́ю, *impf. of* ~и́ть.

испи|сáть, шу́, ~шешь, *pf.* (*of* ~сывать) 1. to cover with writing; он ужé ~сáл двáдцать тетрáдей he has already filled up twenty exercise books. 2. to use up (in writing) (*pencil, paper, etc.*).

испи|сáться, шу́сь, ~шешься, *pf.* (*of* ~сываться) (*coll.*) 1. to be used up (*of writing instrument*). 2. to write oneself out; to be used up (*of a writer*).

испи́сыва|ть(ся), ю(сь), *impf. of* исписáть(ся).

испитóй, *adj.* (*coll.*) haggard, gaunt; hollow-cheeked.

испи́|ть, изопью́, изопьёшь, *past* ~л, ~лá, ~ло, *pf.* 1. (*dial.*) to have a drink of, sup. 2. (*fig., rhet.*) to drain.

исповéдал|ьня, ьни, *g. pl.* ~ен, *f.* (*eccl.*) confessional.

исповéдани|е, я, *n.* creed, confession (*of faith*).

исповéд|ать, аю, *pf.* (*coll.*) = ~овать¹.

исповéд|аться, аюсь, *pf.* (*coll.*) = ~овать-ся¹.

исповéд|овать¹, ую, *impf. and pf.* 1. (*eccl.*)

to confess (*trans.*), hear confession (of). **2.** (*coll.*) to draw out. **3.** to confess.

исповед|овать², ую, *impf.* to profess (*a faith*).

исповед|оваться¹, уюсь, *impf. and pf.* **1.** (+*d. or* у; *eccl.*) to confess, make one's confession (to). **2.** (+*d. or* перед; *fig., coll.*) to confess; to unburden oneself of, acknowledge; он мне ∼овался в свои́х сомне́ниях he confessed his doubts to me.

исповед|оваться², уюсь, *impf. and pf., pass. of* ∼овать².

испове́дыва|ть(ся), ю(сь), *impf.* (*obs.*) = испове́довать(ся).

и́сповед|ь, и, *f.* (*eccl.*) confession; быть на ∼и to be at confession.

испога́нива|ть, ю, *impf. of* испога́нить.

испога́н|ить, ю, ишь, *pf.* (*of* ∼ивать) (*coll.*) to foul, defile.

испо́д, а, *m.* (*dial.*) underside, bottom; wrong side (*of garment*).

и́сподволь, *adv.* (*coll.*) in leisurely fashion; by degrees.

исподло́бья, *adv.* from under the brows (*distrustfully, sullenly*).

исподни́зу, *adv.* (*coll.*) from underneath.

испо́дн|ий, *adj.* (*obs.*) under; *as noun* ∼ее, ∼его, *n.* undergarment.

исподтишка́, *adv.* (*coll., pejor.*) in an underhand way; on the quiet, on the sly; смея́ться и. to laugh in one's sleeve.

испоко́н, *adv.*; *only in phrases* и. ве́ку, и. веко́в from time immemorial.

испола́ть, *interj.* (*rhet.*) hail!

испо́лза|ть, ю, *pf.* (*coll.*) to crawl all over.

исполи́н, а, *m.* giant.

исполи́нский, *adj.* gigantic.

исполко́м, а, *m.* (*abbr. of* исполни́тельный комите́т) executive committee.

исполне́ни|е, я, *n.* **1.** fulfilment (*of wish*); execution (*of order*); discharge (*of duties*); привести́ в и. to carry out, execute. **2.** performance (*of play, etc.*); execution (*of music*); (*theatr., mus.*) в ∼и (+*g.*) (as) played (by), (as) performed (by).

испо́лненный, *p.p.p. of* испо́лнить *and adj.* (+*g.*) full (of).

исполни́м|ый (∼, ∼а), *adj.* feasible, practicable, realizable.

исполни́тел|ь, я, *m.* **1.** executor; суде́бный и. bailiff. **2.** (*theatr., mus., etc.*) performer; соста́в ∼ей cast.

исполни́тельност|ь, и, *f.* assiduity; expedition.

исполни́тел|ьный, *adj.* **1.** executive; и. лист (*leg.*) writ, court order. **2.** (∼ен, ∼ьна) efficient and dependable.

исполн|ить¹, ю, ишь, *pf.* (*of* ∼я́ть) **1.** to carry out, execute (*orders, etc.*); to fulfil (*a wish*); и. обеща́ние to keep a promise; и.

про́сьбу to grant a request. **2.** to perform; и. роль (+*g.*) to take the part (of).

исполн|ить², ю, ишь, *pf.* (*of* ∼я́ть) (+*a. and i. or g.*; *obs.*) to fill (with); сообще́ние о побе́де ∼ило всех ра́достью (ра́дости) the report of the victory delighted everyone.

исполн|иться, юсь, ишься, *pf.* (*of* ∼я́ться) **1.** to be fulfilled. **2.** (+*i. or g.*; *obs.*) to become filled (with). **3.** (*impers.* +*d. expresses passage of time*) ему́ ∼илось семь лет he is seven, he was seven last birthday; ∼илось пять лет с тех пор, как он уе́хал в Аме́рику five years have passed (it is five years) since he went to America.

исполн|я́ть(ся), я́ю(сь), *impf. of* ∼и́ть(ся); ∼я́ющий обя́занности (+*g.*) acting.

исполос|ова́ть, у́ю, *pf. of* полосова́ть.

и́сполу, *adv.* half and half; де́лать что-н. и. to go halves; обрабо́тать зе́млю и. to farm land on the métayage system.

использовани|е, я, *n.* utilization.

испо́льз|овать, ую, *impf. and pf.* to make (good) use of, utilize; to turn to account.

испо́льщик, а, *m.* métayer; sharecropper (*under half-and-half system*).

испо́льщин|а, ы, *f.* métayage.

испо́р|тить(ся), чу(сь), тишь(ся), *pf. of* по́ртить(ся).

испо́рченност|ь, и, *f.* depravity.

испо́рчен|ный, *p.p.p. of* испо́ртить *and adj.* **1.** depraved; corrupted. **2.** (*of perishable goods, etc.*) spoiled; bad, rotten; ∼ные зу́бы rotten teeth; ∼ное мя́со tainted meat. **3.** (*coll.*) spoiled (*child*).

испоха́б|ить, лю, ишь, *pf.* (*coll.*) to corrupt.

испо́шл|ить, ю, ишь, *pf.* (*coll.*) to vulgarize.

исправи́лк|а, и, *f.* (*coll.*) reformatory.

исправи́м|ый (∼, ∼а), *adj.* corrigible.

исправи́тельно-трудово́й, *adj.* corrective labour; и.-т. ко́декс corrective labour code.

исправи́тельный, *adj.* correctional; corrective; и. дом reformatory.

испра́в|ить, лю, ишь, *pf.* (*of* ∼ля́ть) **1.** to rectify, correct, emend. **2.** to repair, mend. **3.** to reform, improve, amend.

испра́в|иться, люсь, ишься, *pf.* (*of* ∼ля́ться) **1.** to improve (*intrans.*); to reform (*intrans.*), turn over a new leaf. **2.** *pass. of* ∼ить.

исправле́ни|е, я, *n.* **1.** correcting; repairing. **2.** improvement; correction; и. те́кста emendation of a text.

испра́влен|ный, *p.p.p. of* испра́вить *and adj.* improved, corrected; ∼ное изда́ние revised edition; и. хара́ктер reformed character.

исправля́|ть, ю, *impf.* **1.** *impf. of* испра́вить. **2.** (*obs.*) и. обя́занности (+*g.*) to carry out the duties (of), act as.

исправля́|ться, юсь, *impf. of* испра́виться.

испра́вник, а, *m.* (*hist.*) (police) superintendent (*head of uyezd constabulary during period 1862–1917*).

испра́вност|ь, и, *f.* **1.** good condition; в (по́лной) ~и in good working order, in good repair. **2.** punctuality; preciseness; meticulousness.

испра́в|ный (~ен, ~на), *adj.* **1.** in good order. **2.** punctual; precise; meticulous.

испражне́ни|е, я, *n.* **1.** defecation. **2.** faeces.

испражн|и́ться, ю́сь, и́шься, *pf. of* ~я́ться.

испражн|я́ться, я́юсь, *impf.* (*of* ~и́ться) to defecate.

испра́шива|ть, ю, *impf.* (*of* испроси́ть) to beg, solicit; и. ми́лость to ask a favour.

испро́б|овать, ую, *pf.* **1.** to test. **2.** to make trial of, try out; и. все возмо́жности to try everything, leave no stone unturned.

испро|си́ть, шу́, ~сишь, *pf.* (*of* испра́шивать) to obtain (by asking).

испрям|и́ть, лю́, и́шь, *pf.* (*of* ~ля́ть) (*coll.*) to straighten (out).

испрямля́|ть, ю, *impf. of* испрями́ть.

испу́г, а (у), *m.* fright; alarm; с ~у from fright.

испу́ганный, *p.p.p. of* испуга́ть *and adj.* frightened, scared, startled.

испуга́|ть(ся), ю(сь), *pf. of* пуга́ть(ся).

испуска́|ть, ю, *impf. of* испусти́ть.

испу|сти́ть, щу́, ~стишь, *pf.* (*of* ~ска́ть) to emit, let out; и. вздох to heave a sigh; и. дух to breathe one's last; и. крик to utter a cry.

испыта́ни|е, я, *n.* **1.** test, trial; (*fig.*) ordeal; быть на ~и to be on trial, be on probation. **2.** examination; вступи́тельные ~я, приёмные ~я entrance examination.

испыт|анный, *p.p.p. of* ~а́ть *and adj.* tried, well-tried.

испыта́тел|ь, я, *m.* tester; лётчик-и. test pilot.

испыта́тельн|ый, *adj.* test, trial; probationary; ~ая коми́ссия examining board; и. полёт test-flight; и. полиго́н (*mil.*) testing ground; и. пробе́г trial run; и. срок, и. стаж period of probation; ~ая ста́нция experimental station.

испыт|а́ть, а́ю, *pf.* (*of* ~ывать) **1.** to test, put to the test; и. чьё-н. терпе́ние to try someone's patience. **2.** to feel, experience.

испыту́ющий, *adj.*; и. взгляд searching look.

испы́тыва|ть, ю, *impf. of* испыта́ть.

иссека́|ть, ю, *impf. of* иссе́чь.

и́ссера-, *adv.* grey-; и.-голубо́й grey-blue.

иссече́ни|е, я, *n.* (*med.*) excision, removal (*by means of operation*).

иссе́|чь[1], ку́, чёшь, ку́т, *past* ~к, ~кла́, *pf.* (*of* ~ка́ть) **1.** (*obs.*) to carve (*in stone, etc.*). **2.** (*med.*) to excise, remove (*by means of operation*).

иссе́|чь[2], ку́, чёшь, ку́т, *past* ~к, ~кла́, *pf.* (*of* ~ка́ть) **1.** to cut up, cleave. **2.** (*obs.*) to cut (*with a whip, etc.*), lash, cover with lashes.

и́ссиня-, *adv.* bluish-.

иссле|ди́ть, жу́, ди́шь, *pf.* (*of* ~жива́ть) (*coll.*) to cover with dirty footprints.

иссле́довани|е, я, *n.* **1.** investigation; research; exploration; и. больно́го examination of a patient; и. кро́ви blood analysis, test; он занима́ется ~ями по ру́сской исто́рии he is engaged in research on Russian history. **2.** (*scientific*) paper; study.

иссле́довател|ь, я, *m.* researcher; investigator; explorer.

иссле́довательский, *adj.* research.

иссле́д|овать, ую, *impf. and pf.* to investigate, examine; to research into; to explore; to analyse.

иссле́жива|ть, ю, *impf. of* исследи́ть.

иссо́х|нуть, ну, нешь, *past* ~, ~ла, *pf.* (*of* иссыха́ть) **1.** to dry up. **2.** to wither; (*fig., coll.*) to decline, fade away.

и́сстари, *adv.* from of old, of yore; так и. ведётся it is an old custom.

исстрада́|ться, юсь, *pf.* to become worn out, wretched (with suffering).

исстре́лива|ть, ю, *impf. of* исстреля́ть.

исстрел|я́ть, я́ю, *pf.* (*of* ~ивать) **1.** to use up (*ammunition*). **2.** (*coll.*) to riddle (*with shot*).

исступле́ни|е, я, *n.* frenzy; и. восто́рга ecstasy, transport; гне́вное и. rage.

исступлённост|ь, и, *f.* state of frenzy.

исступлённый, *adj.* frenzied; ecstatic.

иссуш|а́ть, а́ю, *impf. of* ~и́ть.

иссуш|и́ть, у́, ~ишь, *pf.* (*of* ~а́ть) to dry up; (*fig.*) to consume, waste.

иссыха́|ть, ю, *impf. of* иссо́хнуть.

иссяк|а́ть, а́ю, *impf. of* ~нуть.

иссяк|нуть, ну, нешь, *past* ~, ~ла, *pf.* (*of* ~а́ть) to run dry, dry up; (*fig.*) to run low, fail.

иста́плива|ть, ю, *impf. of* истопи́ть.

иста́ск|анный, *p.p.p. of* ~а́ть *and adj.* **1.** worn out; threadbare. **2.** (*fig., coll.*) worn; haggard.

истаск|а́ть, а́ю, *pf.* (*of* ~ивать) to wear out.

истаск|а́ться, а́юсь, *pf.* (*of* ~иваться) to wear out (*intrans.*); (*fig., coll.*) to be worn out.

иста́скива|ть(ся), ю(сь), *impf. of* истаска́ть(ся).

иста́чива|ть, ю, *impf. of* источи́ть[1].

иста́|ять, ю, ешь, *pf.* to melt (completely); и. от тоски́ to pine, languish.

истека́|ть, ю, *impf. of* исте́чь.

исте́|кший, *past part. of* ~чь *and adj.* past, preceding; в тече́ние ~кшего го́да during the past year; 15-го числа́ ~кшего ме́сяца on the 15th ult(imo).

истер|е́ть, изотру́, изотрёшь, *past* ~, ~ла, *pf.* (*of* истира́ть) 1. to grate. 2. to wear out, use up (*by rubbing*); и. в порошо́к to reduce to powder.

истер|е́ться, изотрётся, *past* ~ся, ~лась, *pf.* (*of* истира́ться) to wear out (*intrans.*), be worn out (*by rubbing*).

исте́рз|анный, *p.p.p.* of ~а́ть *and adj.* tattered, lacerated; (*fig.*) tormented.

истерза́|ть, ю, *pf.* 1. to tear in pieces; to mutilate. 2. to torment, worry the life out of.

исте́рик, а, *m.* hysterical subject.

исте́рик|а, и, *f.* hysterics.

истери́ческий, *adj.* hysterical; и. припа́док fit of hysterics.

истери́чк|а, и, *f.* hysterical woman.

истери́ч|ный (~ен, ~на), *adj.* hysterical.

истери́|я, и, *f.* (*med.*) hysteria; (*fig.*) вое́нная и. war hysteria.

истёртый, *p.p.p.* of истере́ть *and adj.* worn, old.

ист|е́ц, ца́, *m.* (*leg.*) plaintiff; petitioner (*in divorce case*).

истече́ни|е, я, *n.* 1. outflow; и. кро́ви haemorrhage. 2. expiry, expiration; по ~и сро́ка каранти́на on the expiry of the quarantine period.

исте́|чь, ку́, чёшь, ку́т, *past* ~к, ~кла́, *pf.* (*of* ~ка́ть) 1. (*obs.*) to flow out. 2. и. кро́вью to bleed profusely; (*fig., rhet.*) to pour out one's life-blood. 3. to expire, elapse; вре́мя ~кло́ time is up.

и́стин|а, ы, *f.* truth; изби́тая и. truism; свята́я и. God's truth, gospel truth; во ~у (*obs.*) in truth, verily.

и́стин|ный (~ен, ~на), *adj.* true, veritable; ~ная высота́ true altitude; ~ное со́лнечное вре́мя apparent solar time.

истира́ни|е, я, *n.* abrasion.

истира́|ть(ся), ю(сь), *impf.* of истере́ть(ся).

истле|ва́ть, ва́ю, *impf.* of ~ть.

истле́|ть, ю, *pf.* (*of* ~ва́ть) 1. to rot, decay. 2. to smoulder to ashes.

истма́т, а, *m.* (*abbr. of* истори́ческий материали́зм) historical materialism.

и́стово, *adv.* (*obs.*) properly, religiously, devoutly; assiduously, punctiliously; и. крести́ться to cross oneself religiously.

и́стов|ый (~, ~а), *adj.* (*obs.*) proper; devout; assiduous, punctilious.

исто́к, а, *m.* source.

истолкова́ни|е, я, *n.* interpretation, commentary.

истолкова́тел|ь, я, *m.* interpreter, commentator, expounder.

истолк|ова́ть, у́ю, *pf.* (*of* ~о́вывать) to interpret, expound; to comment upon; и. замеча́ние в дурну́ю сто́рону to put a nasty construction on a remark.

истолко́outлыва|ть, ю, *impf.* of истолкова́ть.

истол|о́чь, ку́, чёшь, ку́т, *past* ~о́к, ~кла́, *pf.* to pound, crush.

исто́м|а, ы, *f.* lassitude; (*pleasurable*) languor.

истом|и́ть, лю́, и́шь, *pf.* (*of* томи́ть *and* ~ля́ть) to exhaust, weary.

истом|и́ться, лю́сь, и́шься, *pf.* (*of* ~ля́ться) (от) to be exhausted, worn out (with, from); to be weary (of); и. от жа́жды to be faint with thirst.

истом|лённый, *p.p.p.* of ~и́ть *and adj.* exhausted, worn out.

истомля́|ть(ся), ю(сь), *impf.* of истоми́ть(ся).

истоп|и́ть, лю́, ~ишь, *pf.* (*of* иста́пливать) 1. to heat up. 2. (*coll.*) to spend, use up (*fuel*). 3. to melt down.

истопни́к, а́, *m.* stoker, boiler-man.

истоп|та́ть, чу́, ~чешь, *pf.* 1. to trample (down, over). 2. (*coll.*) to wear out (*footwear*).

исторг|а́ть, а́ю, *impf.* of ~нуть.

исто́рг|нуть, ну, нешь, *past* ~, ~ла, *pf.* (*of* ~а́ть) 1. (*rhet.*) to throw out, expel; и. из свое́й среды́ to ostracize. 2. (*y or* из; *obs.*) to wrest, wrench (from); (*fig.*) to force (from), extort; и. обеща́ние to extort a promise.

истори́зм, а, *m.* historical method.

исто́рийк|а, и, *f.* (*coll.*) 1. anecdote, story 2. episode, incident.

исто́рик, а, *m.* historian.

историо́граф, а, *m.* historiographer.

историогра́фи|я, и, *f.* historiography.

истори́ческий, *adj.* 1. historical. 2. historic.

истори́чност|ь, и, *f.* historicity.

истори́ч|ный (~ен, ~на), *adj.* historical.

исто́ри|я, и, *f.* 1. history; войти́ в ~ю to go down in history. 2. (*coll.*) story. 3. (*coll.*) incident, event; вчера́ случи́лась со мной заба́вная и. a funny thing happened to me yesterday; вот так и.! here's a pretty kettle of fish!; ве́чная (*or* обы́чная) и.! the (same) old story!

истоск|ова́ться, у́юсь, *pf.* (по+*d.*) to yearn (for); to be wearied with longing (for).

источ|а́ть, а́ю, *impf.* (*of* ~и́ть²) (*obs.*) to shed; to give off, impart.

источ|и́ть¹, у́, ~ишь, *pf.* (*of* иста́чивать) 1. to grind down. 2. to eat away, gnaw through.

источ|и́ть², у́, ~ишь, *pf.* of ~а́ть.

исто́чник, а, *m.* 1. spring. 2. (*fig.*) source; и. информа́ции source of information; ве́рный и. reliable source; и. све́та source of light; и. боле́зни (*med.*) nidus; служи́ть ~ом (+*g.*) to be a source (of).

источникове́дени|е, я, *n.* source study.

истóшный, *adj.* (*coll.*) heart-rending.

истощ|áть(ся), áю(сь), *impf. of* ∼и́ть(ся).

истощéни|е, я, *n.* emaciation; exhaustion; войнá на и. war of attrition.

истощ|ённый, *p.p.p. of* ∼и́ть *and adj.* emaciated; exhausted.

истощ|и́ть, у́, и́шь, *pf.* (*of* ∼áть) to emaciate; to exhaust; to drain, sap; и. кóпи to work out mines.

истощ|и́ться, у́сь, и́шься, *pf.* (*of* ∼áться) to become emaciated; to become exhausted (*also fig.*); все нáши запáсы ∼и́лись all our supplies had run out.

истрá|тить, чу, тишь, *pf. of* трáтить.

истрá|титься, чусь, тишься, *pf.* 1. *pass of* ∼тить. 2. (*coll.*) to overspend.

истреби́тел|ь, я, *m.* 1. destroyer. 2. fighter (*aircraft*).

истреби́тель|ный, *adj.* 1. destructive. 2. *adj. of* ∼ 2; ∼ная авиáция fighters (*collect.*), Fighter Command.

истреб|и́ть, лю́, и́шь, *pf.* (*of* ∼ля́ть) to destroy; to exterminate, extirpate.

истреблéни|е, я, *n.* destruction; extermination, extirpation.

истребля́|ть, ю, *impf. of* истреби́ть.

истрéбовани|е, я, *n.* demand, order.

истрéб|овать, ую, *pf.* to obtain on demand.

истрёп|анный, *p.p.p. of* ∼áть *and adj.* torn, frayed; worn.

истреп|áть, лю́, ∼лешь, *pf.* (*of* ∼ывать) to tear, fray; to wear to rags; и. нéрвы (*coll.*) to fray one's nerves.

истрёпыва|ть, ю, *impf. of* истрепáть.

истрéска|ться, ется, *pf.* (*coll.*) to crack, become cracked.

истукáн, а, *m.* idol, statue (*fig., coll.*; *of a person devoid of feeling or understanding*).

и́стый, *adj.* true, genuine; keen; и. учёный a true scholar; и. люби́тель живóтных a genuine animal-lover.

исты́к|ать, аю, *pf.* (*of* ∼ивать) (*coll.*) to riddle, pierce all over.

исты́кива|ть, ю, *impf. of* исты́кать.

истязáни|е, я, *n.* torture.

истязáтел|ь, я, *m.* torturer.

истязá|ть, ю, *impf.* to torture.

исхле|стáть, щу́, ∼щешь, *pf.* (*of* ∼сты́вать) (*coll.*) 1. to lash, flog. 2. to wear out (*a whip*).

исхлёстыва|ть, ю, *impf. of* исхлестáть.

исхлопáтыва|ть, ю, *impf. of* исхлопотáть.

исхлопо|тáть, чу́, ∼чешь, *pf.* (*of* исхлопáтывать) (*coll.*) to obtain (*by dint of application in the right quarters*).

исхóд, а, *m.* 1. outcome, issue; end; быть на ∼е to be nearing the end, be coming to an end; на ∼е дня towards evening; день был на ∼е the day was drawing to a close. 2. (*eccl.*) И. (the Book of) Exodus.

исходáтайств|овать, ую, *pf.* to obtain (*by petition, after official application*).

исхо|ди́ть¹, жу́, ∼дишь, *pf.* (*coll.*) to go, walk all over.

исхо|ди́ть², жу́, ∼дишь, *impf.* (*of* изойти́) 1. (*impf. only*) (из) to issue (from), come (from); to emanate (from); откýда ∼ди́л э́тот слух? where did this rumour come from? 2. (*impf. only*) (из) to proceed (from), base oneself (on); и. из необоснóванных предположéний to proceed from unfounded assumptions. 3. и. крóвью to become weak through loss of blood; и. слезáми to cry one's heart out.

исхóдн|ый, *adj.* initial; ∼ая тóчка, ∼ое положéние point of departure; и. пункт маршрýта (*aeron.*) flight departure point; ∼ая стáдия initial phase.

исходя́щ|ая, ей, *f.* outgoing paper.

исхудáлый, *adj.* emaciated, wasted.

исхудáни|е, я, *n.* emaciation.

исхудá|ть, ю, *pf.* to become emaciated, become wasted.

исцарáп|ать, аю, *pf.* (*of* ∼ывать) to scratch badly; to scratch all over.

исцарáпыва|ть, ю, *impf. of* исцарáпать.

исцелéни|е, я, *n.* 1. healing, cure. 2. recovery.

исцел|и́мый, *pres. part. pass. of* ∼и́ть *and adj.* curable.

исцели́тел|ь, я, *m.* healer.

исцел|и́ть, ю́, и́шь, *pf.* (*of* ∼я́ть) to heal, cure.

исцел|я́ть, я́ю, *impf. of* ∼и́ть.

исчáди|е, я, *n.* (*rhet.*) offspring, progeny; *esp. in phrase* и. áда fiend, devil incarnate.

исчáх|нуть, ну, нешь, *past* ∼, ∼ла, *pf.* to waste away.

исчез|áть, áю, *impf.* (*of* ∼нуть) to disappear, vanish.

исчезновéни|е, я, *n.* disappearance.

исчéз|нуть, ну, нешь, *past* ∼, ∼ла, *pf. of* ∼áть.

исчéрк|ать, аю (*and* ∼áть, ∼áю), *pf.* 1. to cover with crossings-out. 2. to scribble all over.

и́счерна- blackish-.

исчéрп|ать, аю, *pf.* (*of* ∼ывать) 1. to exhaust, drain; и. все свои́ срéдства to exhaust all one's resources; (*fig.*) и. терпéние to exhaust someone's patience. 2. to settle, conclude; и. вопрóс to settle a question; и. повéстку дня to conclude the agenda.

исчéрпыва|ть, ю, *impf. of* исчéрпать.

исчéрпыва|ющий, *pres. part. act. of* ∼ть *and adj.* exhaustive.

исчер|ти́ть, чу́, ∼тишь, *pf.* (*of* ∼чивать) 1. to cover with lines. 2. to use up (*pencil, chalk, etc.*).

исчёрчива|**ть, ю,** *impf. of* исчерти́ть.

исчи́рка|**ть, ю,** *pf.* (*coll.*) to use up (*matches*).

исчисле́ни|**е, я,** *n.* calculation; (*math.*) calculus.

исчисл|**ить, ю, ишь,** *pf.* (*of* ~я́ть) to calculate, compute; to estimate.

исчисл|**я́ть, я́ю,** *impf. of* ~и́ть.

исчисля́|**ться, ется,** *impf.* (+*i. or* в+*a.*) to amount to, come to; to be estimated (at); убы́тки ~лись в сто рубле́й the damages came to one hundred roubles; поте́ри ~ются ты́сячами the casualties are estimated at thousands.

ита́к, *conj.* thus; so then.

италья́н|**ец, ца,** *n.* Italian.

италья́н|**ка, ки,** *f. of* ~ец.

италья́нск|**ий,** *adj.* Italian; ~ая забасто́вка sit-down strike, working to rule.

и т. д. (*abbr. of* и так да́лее) et cetera; and so on, and so forth.

итерати́вный, *adj.* (*ling.*) iterative.

ито́г, а, *m.* **1.** sum, total; о́бщий и. grand total. **2.** (*fig.*) result; подвести́ и. to sum up; в ~е as a result, in the upshot; в коне́чном ~е in the end.

итого́, *adv.* in all, altogether.

ито́говый, *adj.* total, final.

итож|**ить, у, ишь,** *impf.* to sum up, add up.

и т. п. (*abbr. of* и тому́ подо́бное) and the like; et cetera.

итте́рби|**й, я,** *m.* (*chem.*) ytterbium.

итти́ = идти́.

и́ттри|**й, я,** *m.* (*chem.*) yttrium.

иудаи́зм, а, *m.* Judaism.

иуде́|**й, я,** *m.* Jew (*by religion*).

иуде́й|**ка, ки,** *f. of* ~.

иуде́йский, *adj.* (*hist. and rel.*) Judaic.

их¹, *a. and g. of* они́.

их², *possessive adj.* **1.** their(s); их маши́на ме́ньше, чем на́ша their car is smaller than ours. **2.** (*obs.*; *in formal speech*) his; her; э́то их пальто́ this is her coat.

ихневмо́н, а, *m.* (*zool.*) ichneumon.

и́хний, *possessive adj.* (*coll.*) their(s).

ихтиоза́вр, а, *m.* ichthyosaurus.

ихтио́л, а, *m.* (*med.*) ichthyol.

ихтио́лог, а, *m.* ichthyologist.

ихтиологи́ческий, *adj.* ichthyological.

ихтиоло́ги|**я, и,** *f.* ichthyology.

иша́к, á, *m.* **1.** donkey, ass (*also fig.*). **2.** hinny.

иша́|**чий,** *adj. of* ~к.

и́шиас, а, *m.* (*med.*) sciatica.

ишь, *interj.* (*coll.*) *expressing surprise or disgust:* look!; и. ты! = и.! *or expresses disagreement or objection.*

ище́йк|**а, и,** *f.* bloodhound, sleuth-hound (*also fig., pejor.*).

и́щущий, *pres. part. act. of* иска́ть *and adj.*; и. взгляд searching, wistful look.

июл|**ь, я,** *m.* July.

июль|**ский,** *adj. of* ~.

июн|**ь, я,** *m.* June.

июнь|**ский,** *adj. of* ~.

Й

йог, а, *m.* yogi.

йод, а, *m.* iodine.

йодист|**ый,** *adj.* (*chem.*) containing iodine; й. ка́лий potassium iodide; ~ая соль iodized salt.

йод|**ный,** *adj. of* ~; и. раство́р tincture of iodine.

йодофо́рм, а, *m.* iodoform.

йот, а, *m.* (*ling.*) letter J; yod (*name of sound* [j]).

йо́т|**а, ы,** *f.* iota; ни на ~у not a jot, not an iota.

йота́ци|**я, и,** *f.* (*ling.*) appearance of yod before vowel; vowel softening.

йоти́р|**овать, ую,** *impf. and pf.* (*ling.*) to pronounce (vowels) with yod; to give soft pronunciation.

К

к, ко, *prep.*+*d.* **1.** (*of space and fig.*) to, towards; мы приближа́лись к Берли́ну we were nearing Berlin; прислони́те его́ к стене́ place it against the wall; лицо́м к лицу́ face to face; к лу́чшему for the better; моли́тва к Бо́гу prayer to God; любо́вь к де́тям love of children; к о́бщему удивле́нию to everyone's surprise; к (не)сча́стью (un)fortunately; к чёрту его́! to hell with him!; шля́па ей к лицу́ her hat becomes her; к ва́шим услу́гам at your service; (*in addition to*) приба́вить три к пяти́ to add three and five; к тому́ же besides, moreover. **2.** (*of time*) to, towards; by; зима́ подходи́ла к концу́ winter was drawing to a close; к утру́ towards morning, by morning; к пе́рвому января́ by the first of January; я приду́ к восьми́ (часа́м) I will be there by eight (o'clock); к тому́ вре́мени by then, by that time; к сро́ку on time. **3.** for; к чему́? what for?; э́то ни к чему́ it is no good, no use; к обе́ду, к у́жину, etc., for dinner, for supper, etc. **4.** (*in titles of pamphlets, articles in newspapers and periodicals, etc.*) on; on the occasion of; к столе́тию со дня рожде́ния Льва Толсто́го (on the occasion of) the centenary of the birth of Lev Tolstoy; к вопро́су о... *often requires no translation.*

-ка, *particle* (*coll.*) **1.** *modifying force of imp.*: скажи́-ка мне do tell me; да́й-ка мне посмотре́ть just let me see; ну́-ка well; ну́-ка, спо́йте что-н.! come on, sing us something! **2.** *with 1st sing. of future tense, expressing decision or intention*: напишу́-ка ей письмо́ I think I'll write to her; куплю́-ка тот га́лстук perhaps I'll buy that tie, how would it be to buy that tie.

каба́к, а́, *m.* tavern, low bar; (*coll. fig.*) pigsty.

кабал|а́, ы́, *f.* **1.** (*hist.*) kabala (*agreement exacting obligation of labour for creditor in case of non-payment of debt*). **2.** (*hist.*) debt-slavery kabala slavery. **3.** (*fig.*) servitude, bondage.

кабал|и́ть, ю́, и́шь, *impf.* to enslave.

каба́л|ьный (~ен, ~ьна), *adj.* **1.** relating to, bound by kabala; к. холо́п kabala serf. **2.** (*fig.*) imposing bondage, enslaving; ~ьные усло́вия crushing terms. **3.** (*fig.*) in bondage.

каба́н¹, а́, *m.* **1.** wild boar. **2.** boar (*male domestic pig*).

каба́н², а́, *m.* block (*of unprocessed mineral ore, etc.*).

кабан|ий, *adj. of* ~¹.

кабар|га́, ги́, *g. pl.* ~о́г, *f.* (*zool.*) musk-deer.

кабаре́, *indecl.*, *n.* cabaret.

каба́тчик, а, *m.* (*obs.*) publican, tavern-keeper.

каба́тчи|ца, цы, *f. of* ~к.

каба́|цкий, *adj.* **1.** *adj. of* ~к. **2.** (*fig., coll.*) coarse, vulgar; ~цкие нра́вы public bar manners; голь ~цкая (*folk poet.*) tavern riff-raff.

кабач|о́к¹, ка́, *m.* **1.** *dim. of* каба́к. **2.** (*coll.*) small restaurant.

кабач|о́к², ка́, *m.* vegetable marrow.

каббал|а́, ы́, *f.* (*rel. and fig.*) cab(b)ala.

каббали́стик|а, и, *f.* (*rel. and fig.*) cab(b)al-ism.

каббалисти́ческий, *adj.* (*rel. and fig.*) cab-(b)alistic.

ка́бел|ь, я, *m.* (*electr. and naut.*) cable; воз-

ду́шный к. overhead cable; к. абоне́нта service cable.

ка́бель|ный, *adj. of* ~; к. кана́т cable-laid rope.

ка́бельтов, а, *pl.* ~ы, ~ых, ~ым, ~ыми, *m.* (*naut.*) **1.** cable('s length) (*measure = 185·2 metres*). **2.** cable, hawser.

ка́бельтовый, *adj.* (*naut.*) of one cable's length.

кабеста́н, а, *m.* (*tech.*) capstan.

каби́н|а, ы, *f.* cabin; cockpit; cab (*of a lorry*); (для купа́льщиков) bathing-hut.

кабине́т¹, а, *m.* **1.** study; consulting-room, surgery; физи́ческий к. physics laboratory; отде́льный к. private room (*in restaurant*); к. заду́мчивости (*euph., joc.*) lavatory. **2.** suite (*of furniture*).

кабине́т², а, *m.* (*polit.*) cabinet.

кабине́т|ный, *adj.* **1.** *adj. of* ~¹. **2.** к. портре́т cabinet photograph. **3.** (*fig.*) theoretical; к. учёный, страте́г armchair scientist, strategist.

кабине́т|ский, *adj. of* ~².

каби́н|ка, ки, *f. dim. of* ~а.

каблогра́мм|а, ы, *f.* cable(gram).

каблу́к, а́, *m.* heel (*of footwear*); ту́фли на рези́новых ~а́х rubber-heeled shoes; быть под ~о́м у кого́-н. (*fig., coll.*) to be under someone's thumb.

каблуч|о́к, ка́, *m.* **1.** *dim. of* каблу́к. **2.** (*archit.*) ogee.

кабота́ж, а, *m.* **1.** cabotage; coasting-trade. **2.** coastal shipping.

кабота́жник, а, *m.* coaster, coasting vessel.

кабота́жнича|ть, ю, *impf.* to coast; to ply coastwise.

кабота́ж|ный, *adj. of* ~; ~ное пла́вание coastwise navigation.

кабриоле́т, а, *m.* cabriolet.

кабы, *conj.* (*coll. and folk poet.*) if; е́сли бы да к., *see* е́сли.

кавале́р¹, а, *m.* **1.** partner (*at dances*); (*in mixed company on social occasions*) (gentle-)man; была́ весёлая вечери́нка, но ~ов не хвата́ло it was a gay party but there were not enough men. **2.** (*coll.*) admirer, cavalier; да́мский к. carpet-knight.

кавале́р², а, *m.* (о́рдена) knight, holder (of an order); гео́ргиевский к. holder of the St. George Cross.

кавалерга́рд, а, *m.* horse-guardsman.

кавалерга́рд|ский, *adj. of* ~.

кавалер|и́йский, *adj.* **1.** *adj. of* ~ия. **2.** of a cavalryman, of a horseman.

кавалери́ст, а, *m.* **1.** cavalryman. **2.** (*coll.*) horseman.

кавале́ри|я, и, *f.* cavalry; лёгкая к. light horse.

кавале́рственн|ый, *adj.*, *only in phrase* ~ая да́ма Dame of the Order of St. Catherine.

кавалька́д|а, ы, *f.* cavalcade.

кавардá|к, á, *m.* (*coll.*) mess, muddle.

ка́верз|а, ы, *f.* (*coll.*) **1.** chicanery. **2.** mean trick, dirty trick; устро́ить ∼у кому́-н. to play someone a mean trick.

ка́вер|зить, жу, зишь, *impf.* (*of* на∼) (*coll., pejor.*) to play mean, dirty tricks.

ка́верзник, а, *m.* (*coll.*) one who plays (enjoys playing) mean, dirty tricks.

ка́верзный, *adj.* (*coll.*) **1.** (*pejor.*) given to playing mean, dirty tricks. **2.** tricky, ticklish.

каве́рн|а, ы, *f.* (*med. and geol.*) cavity.

кавка́з|ец, ца, *m.* Caucasian.

кавка́зк|а, и, *f.* Caucasian (woman).

кавка́зский, *adj.* Caucasian.

каву́н, á, *m.* (*dial.*) water-melon.

ка́выч|ки, ек, *no sing.* inverted commas, quotation marks; откры́ть к. to quote; закры́ть к. to unquote; в ∼ках in inverted commas, in quotes; (*fig., coll.*) so-called, would-be; демокра́тия в ∼ках a so-called 'democracy'; знато́к в ∼ках would-be expert.

кагáл, а, *m.* **1.** (*hist.*) kahal (*assembly of elders of Jewish communes*). **2.** (*fig., coll.*) bedlam, uproar.

кадáстр, а, *m.* (*leg.*) land-survey.

кадáстровый, *adj.* (*leg.*) cadastral.

каде́нци|я, и, *f.* **1.** (*mus. and lit.*) cadence. **2.** (*mus.*) cadenza.

каде́т[1], а, *m.* cadet.

каде́т[2], а, *m.* (*abbr. of* конституцио́нный демокра́т) (*polit., hist.*) Constitutional Democrat (Cadet).

каде́т|ский[1], *adj. of* ∼[1]; к. ко́рпус (*hist.*) military school.

каде́т|ский[2], *adj. of* ∼[2].

кади́л|о, а, *n.* (*eccl.*) thurible, censer.

кади́л|ьный, *adj.* **1.** *adj. of* ∼о. **2.** of incense; к. за́пах smell of incense.

ка|ди́ть, жу́, ди́шь, *impf.* (*eccl.*) to burn incense; (+*d.*; *fig., coll.*) to burn incense to, flatter.

ка́дк|а, и, *f.* tub, vat.

ка́дми|й, я, *m.* (*chem.*) cadmium.

ка́дочник, а, *m.* cooper.

ка́д|очный, *adj. of* ∼ка.

кадр[1], а, *m.* **1.** (*mil.*) cadre; (*pl.*; *collect.*) (regular, peace-time) establishment; он слу́жит в ∼ах he is a regular (soldier). **2.** (*pl. only*) personnel; отде́л ∼ов personnel department (*of institution, factory, etc.*). **3.** (*pl. only*) specialists; skilled workers (*esp. of trained functionaries of a political party*); руководя́щие ∼ы парти́йной организа́ции моско́вской о́бласти the leadership of the Party organization in Moscow oblast.

кадр[2], а, *m.* (*cinema*) **1.** frame, still. **2.** close-up.

кадри́л|ь, и, *f.* quadrille (*dance*).

кадрови́к, á, *m.* **1.** (*mil.*) regular (soldier). **2.** member of permanent staff; experienced, skilled man.

ка́дровый, *adj.* **1.** (*mil.*) regular. **2.** experienced, skilled; trained.

кады́к, á, *m.* (*coll.*) Adam's apple.

каёмк|а, и, *f.* (*coll.*) *dim. of* кайма́.

каёмчатый, *adj.* with edge(s), with border(s).

кажде́ни|е, я, *n.* (*eccl.*) censing.

каждого́дный, *adj.* (*obs.*) annual.

каждодне́вный, *adj.* daily; diurnal.

ка́жд|ый, *adj.* **1.** every, each; к. день every day; ∼ые два дня every two days; ∼ую весну́ every spring; к. из них получи́л по пять фу́нтов they received five pounds each; на ∼ом шагу́ at every step. **2.** *as noun* everyone; всех и ∼ого (*coll.*) all and everyone, all and sundry.

кажи́сь (*coll., dial.*) it seems, it would seem.

ка|жу́[1], ди́шь, *see* ∼ди́ть.

ка|жу́[2], ∼жешь, *see* ∼зáть.

казáк, á, *pl.* ∼и́, *m.* Cossack.

казаки́н, а, *m.* kazakin (*man's knee-length coat with pleated skirt*).

казáн, а, *m.* (*dial.*) copper (*vessel*).

казáрм|а, ы, *f.* barracks (*also fig.*; *coll. of ugly, clumsy buildings*).

казáрм|енный, *adj. of* ∼а; (*fig., pejor.*) к. вид barrack-like appearance; ∼енная острота́ barrack-room humour.

ка|зáть, жу́, ∼жешь, *impf.* (*coll.*) to show; не к. глаз, но́су not to show up.

ка|зáться, жу́сь, ∼жешься, *impf.* (*of* показáться) **1.** to seem, appear; он ∼жется у́мным he appears clever; она́ ∼жется стáрше свои́х лет she looks older than she is. **2.** (*impers.*) (мне, *etc.*) ∼жется, ∼зáлось it seems, seemed (to me, *etc.*); apparently; мне ∼жется, что он был прав I think he was right; всё, ∼зáлось, шло хорошо́ everything seemed to be going well; за́втра, ∼жется, начина́ются его́ кани́кулы apparently his holidays begin tomorrow; вы, ∼жется, из Москвы́? you are from Moscow, I believe?; ∼зáлось бы it would seem, one would think.

казáх, а, *m.* Kazakh.

казáхский, *adj.* Kazakh.

казáцкий, *adj.* Cossack.

казáчеств|о, а, *n.* (*collect.*) the Cossacks.

казáчий, *adj.* Cossack.

казáчк|а, и, *f.* Cossack (woman).

казач|о́к[1], ка́, *m.* **1.** (*coll.*) *affect. dim. of* казáк. **2.** (*hist.*) page, boy-servant.

казач|о́к[2], ка́, *m.* kazachok (*Ukrainian dance*).

казáшк|а, и, *f.* Kazakh (woman).

казеи́н, а, *m.* (*chem.*) casein.

казеин|овый, *adj. of* ~.

каземат, а, *m.* casemate.

казёнк|а, и, *f.* (*coll., obs.*) **1.** state liquor store, wine-shop. **2.** (state-retailed) vodka.

казённик, а, *m.* breech ring (*of fire-arm*).

казённокоштный, *adj.* (*obs.*); к. студе́нт state-aided student, student receiving education and maintenance at state expense.

казённ|ый, *adj.* **1.** fiscal; of State, of Treasury; ~ое иму́щество State property; на к. счёт at public cost; (*joc., coll.*) free, gratis; ~ое вино́ (*obs.*) vodka (*sold under State monopoly*); ~ая пала́та (*hist.*) (provincial) revenue department. **2.** (*fig.*) bureaucratic formal; к. язы́к language of officialdom, official jargon. **3.** (*fig.*) banal, undistinguished, conventional. **4.** ~ая часть (*mil.*) breech, breech end.

казёнщин|а, ы, *f.* (*coll.*) **1.** conventionalism. **2.** red tape.

казими́р, а, *m.* (*text.*) kerseymere.

казими́р|овый, *adj. of* ~.

казино́, *indecl., n.* casino.

казн|а́, ы́, *no pl., f.* **1.** Exchequer, Treasury; public purse, public coffers. **2.** the State (*as a legal person*); перейти́ из ча́стных рук в ~у́ to pass from private ownership to the State. **3.** (*folk poet.*) money; property. **4.** (= казённая часть) breech, breech end.

казначе́|й, я, *m.* **1.** treasurer, bursar. **2.** (*mil.*) paymaster; (*naut.*) purser.

казначе́й|ский, *adj.* **1.** *of* ~. **2.** *of* ~ство; к. биле́т treasury note.

казначе́йств|о, а, *n.* Treasury, Exchequer.

казначе́йш|а, и, *f.* (*obs., coll.*) wife of treasurer.

казначе́|я, и, *f.* (*eccl.*) treasurer (*in a nunnery*).

казн|и́ть, ю, и́шь, *impf. and pf.* **1.** to execute, put to death. **2.** (*impf. only; fig.*) to punish, chastise; to castigate.

казн|и́ться, ю́сь, и́шься, *impf.* **1.** *pass. of* ~и́ть. **2.** (*coll.*) to blame oneself; to torment oneself (*with remorse*).

казнокра́д, а, *m.* embezzler of public funds.

казнокра́дств|о, а, *n.* embezzlement of public funds.

казн|ь, и, *f.* execution, capital punishment; сме́ртная к. death penalty; (*fig.*) torture, punishment.

ка́зов|ый, *adj.* (*obs.*) for show; к. това́р shop-window goods; ~ая сторона́ де́ла the bright side of the affair.

казуа́льный, *adj.* random; accidental.

казуа́р, а, *m.* (*orn.*) cassowary.

казуи́ст, а, *m.* casuist (*also fig.*).

казуи́стик|а, и, *f.* casuistry (*also fig.*).

казуисти́ческий, *adj.* casuistic(al).

ка́зус, а, *m.* **1.** (*leg.*) exceptional case, special case; (*med.*) isolated case. **2.** (*coll.*) extra-

ordinary occurrence; вот так к.! here's an amazing thing, here's a rum start! **3.** к. бе́лли casus belli.

ка́зусный, *adj.* (*obs.*) involved.

Ка́ин, а, *m.* (*coll.*) Cain (*fratricide, murderer*).

ка́ин|ов, *adj. of* ~; ~ова печа́ть the mark of Cain.

кайл|а́, ы́, *f.* (miner's) hack.

кайл|о́, а́, *n.* = ~а́.

ка|йма́, ймы́, *pl.* ~ймы́, ~ём, ~йма́м, *f.* edging, border; hem, selvedge.

кайма́к, а́, *no pl., m.* (*dial.*) kaymak (*cream off heated milk*).

кайма́н, а, *m.* (*zool.*) cayman.

кайнозо́йский, *adj.* (*geol.*) cainozoic.

ка́йр|а, ы, *f.* (*orn.*) guillemot.

как¹, *adv. and particle* **1.** how; к. вам нра́вится Москва́? how do you like Moscow?; к. чу́дно! how wonderful!; к. вы пожива́ете? how do you do?; к. (ва́ши) дела́? how are you getting on?; забы́л, к. э́то де́лается I have forgotten how to do this; к. вам не сты́дно! you ought to be ashamed!; к. его́ фами́лия, к. его́ зову́т? what is his name?, what is he called?; к. называ́ется э́тот цвето́к? what is this flower called?; к. вы ду́маете? what do you think?; к. его́ жена́ отно́сится к э́тому вопро́су? what does his wife think about the question?; *expressing surprise and/or displeasure*: к.! ты опя́ть здесь what! are you here again?; к. же так? how is that?; (*coll.*) к. знать? who knows?; (*coll.*) к. сказа́ть it all depends; ку́пишь ли э́то для меня́? ну, э́то ещё к. сказа́ть will you buy it for me? well, that all depends; (*coll.*) к. есть completely, utterly; он к. есть дура́к he is a complete fool; (*coll.*) расскажи́ нам к. и что tell us all about it, tell us how it's going; (*coll.*) к.-ника́к nevertheless, for all that; к.-ника́к, но мы попа́ли во́ время nevertheless, we managed to arrive in time; к. же (*coll. or iron.*) naturally, of course. **2.** *with fut. tense of pf. verbs expresses suddenness of action*: (*coll.*) мы споко́йно слу́шали ра́дио, а — он к. вско́чит! we were listening quietly to the wireless when all of a sudden he jumped up; она́ к. закричи́т! she suddenly cried out. **3.** к. ни, к.··· ни however; к. ни по́здно however late it is; к. он ни умён clever as he is; к. ни стара́йтесь however hard you may try, try as you may. **4.** (*following* беда́, пре́лесть, страх, ужа́сно, *etc., in elliptical construction; coll.*) terribly, awfully, wonderfully, *etc.*; мне страх к. хо́чется пить! I have a terrible thirst!; она́ пре́лесть к. оде́та she is beautifully dressed.

как², *conj.* **1.** as; like; бе́лый к. снег white as snow; сове́тую тебе́ э́то к. друг I give you this advice as a friend; он говори́т по-ру́сски к. настоя́щий ру́сский he speaks Russian like a native; бу́дьте к. до́ма make yourself at home; к. наприме́р as, for instance; к. наро́чно as luck would have it; к. попа́ло anyhow, at sixes and sevens; (*with comp.*) к. мо́жно, к. нельзя́ as . . . as possible; к. мо́жно, скоре́е as soon as possible; к. нельзя́ лу́чше as well as possible. **2.** к. . . ., так и both . . . and; к. ма́льчики, так и де́вочки both the boys and the girls. **3.** *following verbs of perceiving not translated*: я ви́дел, к. она́ ушла́ I saw her go out; ты слы́шал, к. часы́ би́ли по́лночь? did you hear the clock strike midnight? **4.** (*coll.*) when; since; к. пойдёшь, зайди́ за мной when you go, call for me; прошло́ два го́да, к. мы встре́тились it is two years since we met; к. ско́ро (*obs.*), к. то́лько as soon as, when; к. вдруг when suddenly. **5.** (+*neg.*) but, except, than; что ему́ остава́лось де́лать, к. не созна́ться? what could he do but confess? **6.** в то вре́мя к.; до того́ к.; ме́жду тем к.; тогда́ к., *see* вре́мя, до, ме́жду, тогда́. **7.** к. бу́дто, к. бы, к.-ли́бо, к.-нибудь, к. ра́з, к.-то, *see separate entries.*

какаду́, *indecl.*, *m.* (*orn.*) cockatoo.
кака́о, *indecl.*, *n.* **1.** cocoa. **2.** cacao(-tree).
кака́о|вый, *adj. of* ~; ~вые бобы́ cocoa-beans.

как бу́дто 1. *conj.* as if, as though; она́ побледне́ла, к. б. уви́дела при́зрак she turned pale as if she had seen a ghost; к. б. вы не зна́ете! as if you didn't know! **2.** *particle* (*coll.*) apparently, it would seem; они́ к. б. за́втра прие́дут apparently, they are coming tomorrow.

как бы 1. (+*inf.*) how; к. б. э́то сде́лать? how is it to be done, I wonder. **2.** к. б. ни however; к. б. то ни́ было however that may be, be that as it may. **3.** as if, as though; к. б. в шу́тку as if in jest. **4.** к. б. не (*expressing anxious expectation*) what if, supposing; (*following verb*) (that, lest); к. б. он не был в дурно́м настрое́нии! what if he is in a bad temper!; бою́сь, к. б. он не был в дурно́м настрое́нии I am afraid (that) he may be in a bad temper. **5.** (*coll.*) к. б. не так! not likely, certainly not.

ка́к-либо, *adv.* somehow.
ка́к-нибудь, *adv.* **1.** somehow (or other). **2.** (*coll.*) anyhow; он всё де́лает к.-н. he does things all anyhow. **3.** (*coll.*) some time; загляни́те ко мне к.-н. look in some time.

како́в (~á, ~ó, ~ы́), *pron.* (*interrog., and in exclamations expressing strong feeling*) what; of what sort; к. результа́т? what is the result?; к. он? what is he like?; к. он собо́й? what does he look like?; а пого́да-

-то ~á! what (splendid, filthy) weather!; вот он к.! (*coll.*) what a chap!
каково́, *adv.* (*coll.*) how; к. ему́ живётся? how is he getting on?; к. мне э́то слы́шать! I am extremely sorry to hear it.
каково́й, *relat. pron.* (*obs.*) which.
как|о́й, *pron.* **1.** (*interrog. and relat.; and in exclamations*) what; ~ие у вас впечатле́ния о Ло́ндоне? what are your impressions of London?; ~о́е сего́дня число́? what is today's date?; ~и́м о́бразом? how?; не зна́ю, ~у́ю кни́гу ему́ дать I don't know what book to give him; ~áя беда́! what a misfortune, how unfortunate!; ~áя на́глость! what impudence!; ~áя хоро́шень-кая де́вушка! what a pretty girl! **2.** (тако́й) к. such as; он (тако́й) плут, ~и́х никогда́ не быва́ло he is a rogue such as never was, there has never been such a rogue; гнев, ~о́го он никогда́ не испы́тывал anger such as he had never felt. **3.** к. ни whatever, whichever; к. есть, к. ни на есть (*coll.*) whatever you please, any you please; дай мне ~у́ю ни на есть кни́гу give me any book you please. **4.** *expressing negation*: (*in rhet. questions*) к. он учёный? what kind of scholar is that?, how can you call him a scholar?; (*coll.*) понра́вился ли тебе́ э́тот фильм? ~о́е! я не вы́терпел и получа́са! did you like the film? what! I stuck it less than half an hour; ~о́е там nothing of the kind, quite the contrary; ты хорошо́ спал? ~о́е там! did you sleep well? I most certainly did not! **5.** к. тако́й? which (exactly)?; пришёл Ивано́в. — К. тако́й Ивано́в? Ivanov is here. Which Ivanov? **6.** (*coll.*) any; нет ли у вас ~о́го вопро́са? have you any questions?; ни в ~у́ю in no circumstances, not for anything.
како́й-либо, *pron.* = како́й-нибудь 1.
как|о́й-нибудь, *pron.* **1.** some; any; мы э́то сде́лаем ~и́м-н. спо́собом we shall do it somehow; да́йте мне кни́гу хоть ~у́ю-н. give me a book, any one at all. **2.** (*with numerals*) some (*and not more*), only; за́мок нахо́дится в ~и́х-н. трёх киломе́трах отсю́да the castle is some three kilo-metres from here; ~и́е-н. пять рубле́й some five roubles.
как|о́й-то, *pron.* **1.** some, a. **2.** a kind of; э́то ~áя-то боле́знь it is a kind of disease.
какофони́ческий, *adj.* cacophonous.
какофо́ни|я, и, *f.* cacophony.
как ра́з, *adv.* just, exactly; к. р. то, что мне ну́жно just what I need; к. р. вас я иска́л you are the very person I was looking for; *as pred.* э́ти ту́фли мне к. р. these shoes are just right.
ка́к-то, *adv.* **1.** somehow; он к.-то ухитри́лся сде́лать э́то he managed to do it

somehow; в э́том до́ме к.-то всегда́ хо́лодно somehow it is always cold in this house. 2. how; посмотрю́, к.-то он вы́вернется из э́того положе́ния I wonder how he will get himself out of this situation. 3. (coll.) к.-то (раз) once. 4. namely, as for example.

ка́ктус, а, m. (bot.) cactus.

кал, а, m. faeces, excrement.

каламбу́р, а, m. pun.

каламбури́ст, а, m. punster.

каламбу́р|ить, ю, ишь, impf. (of c~) to pun.

каламбу́рный, adj. punning.

каламя́нк|а, и, f. (text.) stout linen cloth; calamanco.

кала́ндр, а, m. (tech.) calender.

каланч|а́, и́, g. pl. ~е́й, f. watch-tower; пожа́рная к. fire observation tower; (fig., coll.) bean-pole.

кала́ч, а́, m. kalach (kind of white, wheatmeal loaf); меня́ ~о́м туда́ не зама́нишь (coll.) nothing will induce me to go there; (fig., coll.) тёртый к. person who has knocked about the world.

кала́чиком, adv. (coll.) in the shape of a kalach; лежа́ть к. to lie curled up.

кала́ч|ный, adj. of ~.

калейдоско́п, а, m. kaleidoscope.

калейдоскопи́ческий, adj. kaleidoscopic.

кале́к|а, и, m. and f. cripple.

календа́р|ный, adj. of ~ь; к. ме́сяц calendar month; ~ное и́мя name derived from that of a saint.

календа́р|ь, я́, m. calendar.

кале́нд|ы, ~, no sing. (hist.) calends.

кале́ни|е, я, n. incandescence; бе́лое к. white heat; довести́ до бе́лого ~я (fig., coll.) to rouse to fury.

кале́н|ый, adj. 1. red-hot. 2. ~ые оре́хи roasted nuts.

кале́ч|ить, у, ишь, impf. (of искале́чить) to cripple, maim, mutilate; (fig.) to twist, pervert.

кале́ч|иться, усь, ишься, impf. (of искале́читься) 1. to become a cripple. 2. pass. of ~ить.

ка́ли, indecl., n. (chem.; obs.) potash; only used now in phrase е́дкое к. caustic potash.

кали́бр, а, m. 1. calibre. 2. (tech.) gauge.

калибр|ова́ть, у́ю, impf. (tech.) to calibrate.

калибро́вк|а, и, f. (tech.) calibration.

ка́лиевый, adj. (chem.) potassic, potassium.

ка́ли|й, я, m. (chem.) potassium.

ка́лийн|ый, adj. (chem.) potassium; ~ое удобре́ние potash fertilizer.

кали́к|а, и, m. 1. (hist.) pilgrim. 2. (folk poet.) ~и перехо́жие wandering minstrels.

кали́льн|ый, adj. (tech.) к. жар temperature of incandescence; ~ая печь temper furnace; ~ая се́тка (incandescent) mantle.

кали́н|а, ы, no pl., f. (bot.) guelder rose, snowball-tree.

кали́н|овый, adj. of ~a.

кали́тк|а, и, f. (wicket-)gate.

кал|и́ть, ю́, и́шь, impf. 1. (tech.) to heat. 2. to roast (chestnuts, etc.).

кали́ф, а, m. caliph; к. на час (iron.) king for a day.

каллиграфи́ческий, adj. calligraphic.

каллигра́фи|я, и, f. calligraphy.

калмы́к, а́, m. Kalmuck, Kalmyk.

калмы́цкий, adj. Kalmuck, Kalmyk.

калмы́чк|а, и, f. Kalmuck, Kalmyk (woman).

ка́л|овый, adj. of ~.

каломе́л|ь, и, f. calomel.

калори́йност|ь, и, f. calorie content.

калори́метр, а, m. (phys.) calorimeter.

калориме́три|я, и, f. (phys.) calorimetry.

калори́фер, а, m. (tech.) heater, radiator.

кало́ри|я, и, f. calorie; больша́я к. large (kilogram-)calorie; ма́лая к. small (gram-)calorie; брита́нская к. British thermal unit.

кало́ш|а, и, f. = гало́ша.

калу́жниц|а, ы, f. (bot.) king-cup, marsh marigold.

калы́м, а, no pl., m. (ethnol.) bride-money.

кальвини́зм, а, m. Calvinism.

кальвини́ст, а, m. Calvinist.

кальвинисти́ческий, adj. Calvinistic(al).

ка́л|ька, ьки, g. pl. ~ек, f. 1. tracing-paper. 2. (tracing-paper) copy. 3. (ling.) loan translation, calque.

кальки́р|овать, ую, impf. (of c~) 1. to trace. 2. (ling.) to make a loan translation of.

калькули́р|овать, ую, impf. (of c~) (comm.) to calculate.

калькуля́тор, а, m. (comm.) calculator.

калькуля|цио́нный, adj. of ~ция; ~цио́нная ве́домость cost sheet; cost record.

калькуля́ци|я, и, f. (comm.) calculation.

кальсо́н|ы, ~, no sing. pants, drawers.

ка́льциевый, adj. (chem.) calcium, calcic.

ка́льци|й, я, m. (chem.) calcium.

кальцина́ци|я, и, f. (chem.) calcination.

кальци́т, а, m. (min.) calcite.

кальа́н, а, m. hookah.

каля́ка|ть, ю, impf. (of по~) (coll.) to talk, chat.

камари́л|я, и, f. camarilla, clique.

кама́ринск|ая, ой, f. Kamarinskaya (Russian folk-dance).

ка́мбал|а, ы, f. 1. flat-fish (generic term). 2. plaice; flounder.

ка́мби|й, я, m. (bot.) cambium.

ка́мбуз, а, m. (naut.) galley, caboose.

камво́льный, adj. (text.) worsted.

каме́дистый, adj. gummy.

каме́д|ь, и, f. gum.

камел|ёк, ька́, m. fire-place.

каме́ли|я, и, f. (bot.) camellia.

камене́|ть, ю, *impf.* (*of* о~) to become petrified, turn to stone; (*fig.*) to⁴ harden (*intrans.*).

камени́ст|ый (~, ~а), *adj.* stony.

ка́менк|а¹, и, *f.* stove (*in bath-house in rural Russia*).

ка́менк|а², и, *f.* (*orn.*) wheat-ear.

каменноуго́льн|ый, *adj.* coal; к. бассе́йн coal-field; ~ые ко́пи coal-mine.

ка́менн|ый, *adj.* 1. stone-; stony; к. век the Stone Age; ~ая кла́дка masonry, stone--work; ~ая соль rock-salt; к. у́голь coal; ~ая боле́знь (*med.*) gravel; к. мешо́к (*hist.*; *rhet.*) prison cell. 2.(*fig.*) stony; hard, immovable; ~ое се́рдце stony heart.

каменобо́|ец, йца, *m.* stone-crusher.

каменоло́м|ня, ни, *g. pl.* ~ен, *f.* quarry.

каменотёс, а, *m.* (stone)mason.

ка́менщик, а, *m.* (stone)mason, bricklayer; (*hist.*) во́льные ~и Freemasons.

ка́м|ень, ня, *pl.* ~ни, ~не́й *and* (*coll.*) ~е́нья, ~е́ньев, *m.* stone; па́дать ~нем to fall like a stone; ~ня на ~не не оста́вить to raze to the ground; (*fig.*) броса́ть ~нем (в+*a.*) to cast stones (at); у него́ к. на се́рдце лежи́т a weight sits heavy on his heart; держа́ть к. за па́зухой (на+*a.*, про́тив) to harbour a grudge (against); к. с души́ мое́й свали́лся a load has been taken off my mind.

ка́мер|а, ы, *f.* 1. chamber (*in var. senses*); тюре́мная к. prison cell; к. хране́ния (багажа́) cloak-room. 2. (фотографи́ческая) к. camera. 3. inner tube (*of tire*); bladder (*of football*).

камерге́р, а, *m.* chamberlain.

камерди́нер, а, *m.* valet.

камери́стк|а, и, *f.* lady's maid.

ка́мер|ный¹, *adj. of* ~а.

ка́мерн|ый², *adj.* (*mus.*) к. конце́рт chamber concert; ~ая му́зыка chamber music.

камерто́н, а, *m.* tuning-fork.

ка́мер-ю́нкер, а, *m.* gentleman of the bed-chamber.

ка́меш|ек, ка, *m.* *dim. of* ка́мень; pebble; (*fig.*, *coll.*) бро́сить к. в чей-н. огоро́д to make digs at someone.

каме́|я, и, *f.* cameo.

камзо́л, а, *m.* camisole.

камила́вк|а, и, *f.* (*eccl.*) kamelaukion (*Orthodox priest's headgear*).

ками́н, а, *m.* fire-place; (open) fire.

ками́н|ный, *adj. of* ~; ~ная по́лка mantelpiece; ~ная решётка fender, fireguard.

камк|а́, и́, *f.* (*text.*) damask.

камло́т, а, *m.* (*text.*) camlet.

камло́т|овый, *adj. of* ~.

камнедроби́лк|а, и, *f.* stone-breaker, stone--crusher.

камнело́мк|а, и, *f.* (*bot.*) saxifrage.

камо́рк|а, и, *f.* (*coll.*) closet, very small room; box room.

кампане́йск|ий, *adj.* (*pejor.*) ~ая рабо́та work done by spurts.

кампане́йщин|а, ы, *f.* (*pejor.*) system of working by spurts (*as opp. to* working according to plan, methodically).

кампа́ни|я, и, *f.* 1. (*mil. and fig.*) campaign. 2. (*naut.*) cruise.

кампе́шев|ый, *adj.* (*bot.*) ~ое де́рево campeachy wood, logwood.

камуфле́т, а, *m.* (*mil.*) camouflet; (*fig.*, *coll.*, *joc.*) dirty trick.

камуфля́ж, а, *no pl.*, *m.* camouflage.

камфар|а́, ы́, *f.* camphor.

камфа́р|ный, *adj. of* ~а́.

камф|ора́ = ~ара́.

камфо́рк|а, и, *f.* = конфо́рка.

камча́тк|а, и, *f.* (*text.*) damask linen.

камча́т(н)ый, *adj.* 1. (*folk poet.*) damask. 2. damasked, figured (*of linen*).

камы́ш, а́, *m.* reed, rush (*also collect.*).

камы́ш|евый, *adj. of* ~.

камыш|о́вый, *adj. of* ~; ~о́вое кре́сло cane chair; ~о́вая жа́ба natterjack.

кана́в|а, ы, *f.* ditch; сто́чная к. gutter.

канавокопа́тел|ь, я, *m.* (*tech.*) trench digger, trench excavator.

кана́д|ец, ца, *g. pl.* ~цев, *m.* Canadian.

кана́дк|а, и, *f.* Canadian (woman).

кана́дск|ий, *adj.* Canadian; ~ая пи́хта balsam fir.

кана́л, а, *m.* 1. canal. 2. channel; (*fig.*) дипломати́ческие ~ы diplomatic channels. 3. (*anat.*) duct, canal; мочеиспуска́тельный к. urethra. 4. bore (*of barrel of gun*).

канализа|цио́нный, *adj. of* ~ция; ~цио́нная труба́ sewer(-pipe).

канализа́ци|я, и, *f.* 1. sewerage. 2. sewer (system).

канализи́р|овать, ую, *impf. and pf.* to provide with sewerage-system.

кана́льский, *adj.* (*coll.*, *obs.*) rascally, roguish.

кана́льств|о, а, *n.* (*coll.*, *obs.*) trickery, knavery.

кана́л|ья, ьи, *g. pl.* ~ий, *m. and f.* (*coll.*) rascal, scoundrel.

канаре́|ечный, *adj.* 1. *adj. of* ~йка. 2. canary(-coloured).

канаре́йк|а, и, *f.* canary.

кана́т, а, *m.* rope; cable, hawser.

кана́т|ный, *adj. of* ~; к. заво́д rope-yard; ~ная желе́зная доро́га funicular railway; к. плясу́н rope-dancer.

канатохо́д|ец, ца, *m.* rope-walker.

кана́ус, а, *m.* coarse silken fabric.

канв|а́, ы́, *no pl.*, *f.* canvas; (*fig.*) groundwork; outline, design; к. рома́на the outline of a novel.

канв|óвый, *adj. of* ~á.

кандал|ы́, óв, *no sing.* shackles, fetters; ручны́е к. manacles, handcuffs; закова́ть в к. to put into irons.

канда́л|ьный, *adj. of* ~ы́.

канделя́бр, а, *m.* candelabrum.

кандида́т, а, *m.* 1. candidate; к. в чле́ны коммунисти́ческой па́ртии candidate--member of the Communist Party. 2. kandididat (*holder of first higher degree, awarded on dissertation, in Soviet Union*).

кандида́т|ский, *adj. of* ~; к. ми́нимум qualifying examinations for admission to the course leading to the degree of kandidat; к. стаж (*polit.*) probation period (*period as candidate-member of the Soviet Communist Party*).

кандидату́р|а, ы, *f.* candidature; вы́ставить чью-н. ~у to nominate someone for election.

кани́кул|ы, ~, *no sing.* (*school*) holidays; (*university, etc.*) vacation.

кани|куля́рный, *adj. of* ~кулы.

кани́стр|а, ы, *f.* jerrican.

канител|ить, ю, ишь, *impf.* (*of* про~) (*coll., pejor.*) to drag out; к. кого́-н. to waste someone's time.

канител|иться, юсь, ишься, *impf.* (*of* про~) (*coll., pejor.*) to waste time; to mess about; to maunder.

канител|ь, и, *f.* 1. gold thread, silver thread; wire-ribbon. 2. (*fig., coll.*) long--drawn-out proceedings; тяну́ть, разводи́ть к. to spin out, drag out proceedings, procrastinate; дово́льно ~и! this has gone on, dragged on long enough!

канител|ьный (~ен, ~ьна), *adj.* (*coll.*) 1. long-drawn-out; tedious. 2. к. челове́к procrastinating person. 3. *adj. of* ~ь 1.

канитель|щик, а, *m.* 1. wire-ribbon spinner. 2. (*fig., coll.*) time-waster.

канифа́с, а, *m.* (*obs.*) 1. sail-cloth. 2. dimity.

канифо́л|ить, ю, ишь, *impf.* (*of* на~) to rosin.

канифо́л|ь, и, *f.* rosin, colophony.

канка́н, а, *m.* cancan.

канкани́р|овать, ую, *impf.* (*coll.*) to dance the cancan.

каннелю́р|а, ы, *f.* (*archit.*) flute.

каннибáл, а, *m.* cannibal.

каннибали́зм, а, *m.* cannibalism.

кано́н, а, *m.* (*in var. senses*) canon.

канона́д|а, ы, *f.* cannonade.

канонéрк|а, и, *f.* gunboat.

канонéрск|ий, *adj.*; ~ая ло́дка gunboat.

канониза́ци|я, и, *f.* (*eccl.*) canonization.

канонизи́р|овать, ую, *impf. and pf.* (*eccl. and fig.*) to canonize.

канониз|ова́ть, у́ю, *impf. and pf.* = ~и́ровать.

кано́ник, а, *m.* (*eccl.*) canon.

канони́р, а, *m.* gunner.

канони́ческ|ий, *adj.* 1. (*eccl.*) canonical; (*lit.*) definitive. 2. (*eccl.*) ~ое пра́во canon law.

канони́чност|ь, и, *f.* (*eccl. and lit.*) canonicity.

кант, а, *m.* 1. edging, piping. 2. mount (*for picture, etc.*).

канталу́п|а, ы, *f.* (*bot.*) cantaloup.

канта́т|а, ы, *f.* (*mus.*) cantata.

кантиа́н|ец, ца, *m.* (*philos.*) Kantian.

кантиа́нский, *adj.* (*philos.*) Kantian.

кантиа́нств|о, а, *n.* (*philos.*) Kantianism.

кантилéн|а, ы, *f.* (*mus.*) cantilena.

кант|ова́ть[1], у́ю, *impf.* (*of* о~) to border; to mount (*picture, etc.*).

кант|ова́ть[2], у́ю, *impf.* (*tech.*) to cant.

канто́н, а, *m.* (*administrative unit*) canton.

кантона́льный, *adj.* cantonal.

кану́н, а, *m.* eve; (*eccl.*) vigil; к. Но́вого го́да New Year's eve.

ка́н|уть, у, ешь, *pf.* (*obs.*) to drop, sink; к. в ве́чность, к. в Ле́ту (*fig.*) to sink into oblivion; как в во́ду к. to disappear without a trace, vanish into thin air.

канцеляри́ст, а, *m.* clerk.

канцеля́ри|я, и, *f.* office.

канцеля́р|ский, *adj. of* ~; ~ские принадле́жности stationery; ~ская рабо́та clerical work; к. стол office desk; ~ская кры́са (*fig., pejor.*) office drudge; к. по́черк clerkly hand; к. слог officialese.

канцеля́рщин|а, ы, *f.* (*coll.*) red tape.

ка́нцлер, а, *m.* chancellor.

канцо́н|а, ы, *f.* (*mus.*) canzonet.

каньо́н, а, *m.* (*geogr.*) canyon.

каню́к, а́, *m.* 1. (*orn.*) buzzard. 2. (*fig., dial.*) moaner, grumbler.

каню́ч|ить, у, ишь, *impf.* (*coll., pejor.*) to moan, grumble; to pester.

каоли́н, а, *m.* china clay, kaolin.

ка́п|ать, лю, лешь, (*coll.* ~аю, ~аешь), *impf.* (*of* ~нуть) 1. (*3rd person only*) to drip, drop; to trickle; to dribble; to fall (in drops); из глаз у неё ~али слёзы tear--drops were falling from her eyes; дождь ~лет it is spotting with rain; с потолка́ ~ало there was a drip from the ceiling; над на́ми не ~лет (*fig., coll.*) we can take our time, there is no hurry. 2. to pour out (*in drops*); к. лека́рство в рю́мку to pour medicine into a glass. 3. (+*i.*; *coll.*) to spill; ты ~лешь водо́й на ска́терть you are spilling water on the cloth.

капéлл|а, ы, *f.* 1. choir. 2. chapel; к. Богома́тери Lady chapel.

капелла́н, а, *m.* chaplain.

капéл|ь, и, *f.* 1. drip (*of thawing snow*). 2. thaw.

капельди́нер, а, *m.* (*obs.*) usher, box-keeper (*in theatre*).

ка́пельк|а, и, *f.* 1. small drop; к. росы́ dew-
-drop; вы́пить всё до ∼и to drink to the
last drop. 2. (*sing. only*; *fig.*) grain, minute
quantity; в нём нет ни ∼и здра́вого
смы́сла he has not a grain of common sense;
она́ ни ∼и не смути́лась she was not a
whit put out; *as adv.* ∼у (*coll.*) a little;
подожди́ ∼у! wait a moment!

капельме́йстер, а, *m.* (*mus.*) conductor,
bandmaster.

капельме́йстер|ский, *adj. of* ∼; ∼ская
па́лочка conductor's baton.

ка́пельниц|а, ы, *f.* (medicine) dropper.

ка́пельный, *adj.* (*coll.*) tiny.

ка́пер, а, *m.* (*naut.*) privateer.

ка́перс, а, *m.* 1. (*bot.*) caper. 2. (*pl. only*;
cul.) capers.

ка́перств|о, а, *n.* (*naut.*) privateering.

капилля́р, а, *m.* (*phys., anat.*) capillary.

капилля́рный, *adj.* (*phys., anat.*) capillary.

капита́л, а, *m.* (*fin.*) capital; к. и проце́нты,
к. с проце́нтами principal and interest.

капита́л|ец, ьца, *m. dim. of* ∼; *coll.* a tidy sum.

капитализа́ци|я, и, *f.* (*fin.*) capitalization.

капитализи́р|овать, ую, *impf. and pf.* (*fin.*)
to capitalize.

капитали́зм, а, *m.* capitalism.

капитали́ст, а, *m.* capitalist.

капиталисти́ческий, *adj.* capitalist(ic).

капиталовложе́ни|е, я, *n.* capital invest-
ment.

капита́льн|ый, *adj.* capital; main, funda-
mental; most important; к. вопро́с funda-
mental question; к. ремо́нт major repairs;
∼ая стена́ main wall.

капита́н, а, *m.* captain.

капита́н|ский, *adj. of* ∼; к. мо́стик captain's
bridge.

капите́л|ь, и, *f.* 1. (*archit.*) capital. 2. (*typ.*)
small capitals.

капиту́л, а, *m.* (*eccl., hist.*) chapter (*of canons
or of members of an order*).

капитули́р|овать, ую, *impf. and pf.* (пе́ред)
to capitulate (to).

капитуля́нт, а, *m.* (*pejor.*) faint-heart;
truckler.

капитуля́нтств|о, а, *n.* truckling.

капитуля́ци|я, и, *f.* capitulation.

ка́пищ|е, а, *n.* (*heathen*) temple.

капка́н, а, *m.* trap; попа́сться в к. to fall
into a trap (*also fig.*).

капка́н|ный, *adj. of* ∼; к. про́мысел trap-
ping.

капли́ц|а, ы, *f.* (*Roman Catholic*) chapel.

каплу́н, а́, *m.* capon.

ка́п|ля, ли, *g. pl.* ∼ель, *f.* 1. drop; по ∼ле,
к. за ∼лей drop by drop; до ∼ли to the
last drop; похо́жи как две ∼ли воды́ as
like as two peas; ∼ли в рот не беру́ (*euph.*)
I never touch a drop (*sc. of alcoholic liquor*);

(*fig.*) к. в мо́ре a drop in the ocean; по-
сле́дняя к. the last straw; би́ться до после́д-
ней ∼ли кро́ви to fight to the last. 2. (*pl.*;
med.) drops. 3. (*fig., coll.*) drop, bit; у него́
(нет) ни ∼ли благоразу́мия he hasn't a
drop of sense; ни ∼ли (*as adv.*) not a bit,
not a whit.

ка́п|нуть, ну, нешь, *pf.* (*of* ∼ать) to drop,
let fall a drop.

ка́п|о́к, ка́, *no pl.*, *m.* (*text.*) kapok.

ка́пор, а, *m.* hood; bonnet.

капо́т, а, *m.* 1. house-coat (*woman's informal
indoor attire*). 2. capote (*French soldier's*)
greatcoat. 3. (*tech.*) hood, bonnet, cowl;
к. мото́ра (*aeron.*) engine cowling.

капра́л, а, *m.* (*mil.*) corporal.

капра́л|ьский, *adj. of* ∼.

капра́льств|о, а, *n.* (*mil.*) rank of corporal.

капри́з, а, *m.* caprice, whim; vagary.

капри́зник, а, *m.* capricious person, capricious child.

капри́знича|ть, ю, *impf.* to behave capri-
ciously; (*of a child*) to play up.

капри́з|ный (∼ен, ∼на), *adj.* 1. capricious;
(*of a child*) wilful. 2. freakish.

капризу́л|я, и, *m. and f.* (*coll.*) capricious,
self-willed child.

каприфо́л|ь, и, *f.* (*bot.*) honeysuckle.

капри́ччио, *indecl.*, *n.* (*mus.*) capriccio.

капро́н, а, *m.* kapron (*artificial fibre, similar to
nylon, produced in Soviet Union*).

капро́н|овый, *adj. of* ∼.

ка́псул|а, ы, *f.* capsule.

ка́псюл|ь, я, *m.* (percussion) cap (*in explo-
sives*).

ка́псюль|ный, *adj. of* ∼; ∼ное ружьё per-
cussion musket.

каптена́рмус, а, *m.* (*mil.*) quartermaster-
-sergeant.

капу́ст|а, ы, *f.* cabbage.

капу́стник, а, *m.* 1. cabbage field. 2. cabbage worm. 3. actors', artists', *or* students'
party.

капу́стниц|а, ы, *f.* cabbage butterfly.

капу́ст|ный, *adj. of* ∼а.

капу́т, *indecl.*, *m.* (*coll.*) end, destruction;
used as adj. or adv. done for, kaput; тут
ему́ и к. he's done for, it's all up with him.

капуци́н, а, *m.* 1. Capuchin (friar). 2. (*zool.*)
Capuchin monkey. 3. (*bot.*) nasturtium.

капюшо́н, а, *m.* hood, cowl.

ка́р|а, ы, *f.* (*rhet.*) punishment, retribution.

караби́н, а, *m.* carbine.

карабине́р, а, *m.* car(a)bineer.

кара́бка|ться, юсь, *impf.* (*of* вс∼) (*coll.*) to
clamber.

карава́|й, я, *m.* cottage loaf.

карава́н, а, *m.* 1. caravan. 2. convoy (*of
ships, etc.*).

карава́н-сара́|й, я, *m.* caravanserai.

карага́ч, а́, *m.* (*bot.*) elm.

кара́емый, *adj.* (*leg.*) punishable.

карай́м, а, *m.* Karaite (*member of Jewish sect who reject the Talmud*).

каракалпа́к, а, *m.* (*ethnol.*) Karakalpak.

карака́тиц|а, ы, *f.* 1. (*zool.*) cuttlefish. 2. (*fig., joc.*) short-legged, clumsy person.

кара́ковый, *adj.* dark-bay.

кара́кул|евый, *adj. of* ~ь.

кара́кул|ь, я, *no pl., m.* astrakhan (fur).

каракульч|а́, й, *f.* astrakhan (fur).

кара́кул|я, и, *f.* scrawl, scribble.

карамбо́л|ь, я, *m.* (*in billiards*) cannon.

караме́л|ь, и, *no pl., f.* 1. (*collect.*) caramels. 2. caramel.

караме́льк|а, и, *f.* (*coll.*) caramel.

караме́ль|ный, *adj. of* ~.

каранда́ш, а́, *m.* pencil.

каранда́ш|ный, *adj. of* ~; к. рису́нок pencil drawing.

каранти́н, а, *m.* 1. quarantine; сня́тие ~а (*naut.*) pratique; подве́ргнуть ~у to place in quarantine. 2. quarantine station.

каранти́н|ный, *adj. of* ~; ~ное свиде́тель-ство (*naut.*) bill of health.

карапу́з, а, *m.* (*coll.*) chubby lad.

кара́с|ь, я́, *m.* (*fish*) crucian; сере́бряный к. Prussian carp.

кара́т, а, *m.* carat.

кара́тел|ь, я, *m.* 1. (*obs.*) punisher, chas-tiser. 2. member of punitive expedition.

кара́тельный, *adj.* punitive.

кара́|ть, ю, *impf.* (*of* по~) to punish, chastise.

карау́л, а, *m.* 1. guard; watch; вступи́ть в к. to mount guard; нести́ к., стоя́ть в ~е to be on guard; смени́ть к. to relieve the guard. 2. *word of command:* на к.! present arms!; взять на к. to present arms. 3. *as interj.* help!; крича́ть к. to shout for help.

карау́л|ить, ю, ишь, *impf.* 1. to guard. 2. (*coll.*) to lie in wait for, watch out for.

карау́лк|а, и, *f.* (*coll.*) guardroom.

карау́л|ьный, *adj. of* ~; ~ьная бу́дка sentry-box; *as noun* к., ~ьного, *m.* sentry, sentinel, guard.

карау́л|ьня, ьни, *g. pl.* ~ен, *f.* guardroom.

карау́льщик, а, *m.* (*coll.*) sentry, guard.

кара́ч|ки, ек, *no sing.* (*coll.*); на к., на ~ках on all fours; стать на к. to get on all fours.

карби́д, а, *m.* (*chem.*) carbide.

карбо́ван|ец, ца, *m.* 1. karbovanets (*Ukrai-nian name of the Russian rouble*). 2. (*pl.*) money.

карбо́лк|а, и, *f.* (*coll.*) carbolic acid.

карбо́ловый, *adj.* (*chem.*) carbolic.

карбона́т, а, *m.* (*chem.*) carbonate.

карбору́нд, а, *m.* carborundum.

карбу́нкул, а, *m.* (*min., med.*) carbuncle.

карбюра́тор, а, *m.* (*tech., chem.*) carburet-tor.

карбюри́р|овать, ую, *impf. and pf.* (*chem.*) to carburettor.

карг|а́, и́, *pl.* ~и́, ~, ~а́м, *f.* 1. (*dial.*) crow. 2. (*coll.*) ста́рая к. hag, harridan, crone.

ка́рд|а, ы, *f.* (*tech.*) card.

кардамо́н, а, *m.* (*bot.*) cardamom.

кардина́л, а, *m.* (*eccl.*) cardinal.

кардина́льный, *adj.* cardinal.

кардина́л|ьский, *adj. of* ~.

кардиогра́мм|а, ы, *f.* cardiogram.

каре́, *indecl., n.* (*mil.*) square.

каре́л, а, *m.* Karelian.

каре́лк|а, и, *f.* Karelian (woman).

каре́льск|ий, *adj.* Karelian; ~ая берёза Karelian birch.

каре́т|а, ы, *f.* carriage, coach; к. запряжён-ная па́рой, четвёркой carriage and pair, coach and four; почто́вая к. stage-coach; к. ско́рой по́мощи (*obs.*) ambulance.

каре́тк|а, и, *f.* (*tech.*) carriage, frame.

каре́тник, а, *m.* 1. coach-house. 2. coach--builder.

кариати́д|а, ы, *f.* (*archit.*) caryatid.

ка́рий, *adj.* (*of colour of eyes*) brown, dark--brown; (*of colour of horses*) chestnut, dark-chestnut.

карикату́р|а, ы, *f.* 1. caricature. 2. car-toon.

карикатури́ст, а, *m.* 1. caricaturist. 2. car-toonist.

карикату́р|ить, ю, ишь, *impf.* (*coll., obs.*) to caricature.

карикату́р|ный, *adj. of* ~а; ~ная фигу́ра ludicrous figure.

карио́з, а, *m.* (*med.*) caries, decay.

карио́зный, *adj.* (*med.*) carious.

карка́с, а, *m.* (*tech.*) frame; (*fig.*) framework.

карка́с|ный, *adj. of* ~; к. дом framehouse.

ка́рк|ать, аю, *impf.* (*of* ~нуть) 1. to caw, croak. 2. (*fig.*) to croak, prophesy ill.

ка́рк|нуть, ну, нешь, *pf. of* ~ать 1.

ка́рлик, а, *m.* dwarf; pygmy.

ка́рликов|ый, *adj.* (*anthrop., bot., and fig.*) dwarf; pygmean; ~ые племена́ the Pyg-mies.

ка́рли|ца, цы, *f. of* ~к.

кармази́н, а, *m.* (*obs.*) cramoisy, crimson (*cloth*).

кармази́н|ный, *adj. of* ~; к. цвет crimson.

карма́н, а, *m.* pocket; (*fig., coll.*) э́то мне не по ~у I can't afford it; бить по ~у to cost a pretty penny; наби́ть себе́ к. to fill one's pockets; то́щий к. empty pocket; держи́ к. ши́ре! you'll get nothing by waiting!; не лезть за сло́вом в к. to have a ready tongue.

карма́нник, а, *m.* pickpocket.

карма́н|ный, *adj. of* ~; к. вор pickpocket; ~ные де́ньги pocket money.

карми́н, а, *m.* carmine.

кармѝнный, *adj.* carmine.

карнавáл, а, *m.* carnival.

карнѝз, а, *m.* (*archit.*) 1. cornice. 2. ledge.

каротéл|ь, и, *f.* carrot (*variety having short roots*).

карп, а, *m.* (*fish*) carp.

кáрт|а, ы, *f.* 1. (*geogr.*) map. 2. (playing-) card; игрáть в ~ы to play cards; имѐть хорóшие ~ы to have a good hand; егó кáрта бѝта (*fig.*) his game is up; постáвить на ~у to stake, risk; раскрѝть свой ~ы to show one's hand.

картáв|ить, лю, ишь, *impf.* to burr.

картáвост|ь, и, *f.* (*ling.*) burr.

картáвый, *adj.* 1. pronounced gutturally. 2. having a burr.

картвéл, а, *m.* (*ethnol.*) Georgian.

картёж, á, *no pl., m.* (*coll.*) card-playing; gambling school.

картёжник, а, *m.* (*coll.*) card-player; gambler (*at cards*).

картёжный, *adj.* (*coll.*) card-playing; gambling.

картезиáнский, *adj.* (*philos.*) Cartesian.

картéл|ь, я, *m.* (*fin.*) cartel.

кáртер, а, *m.* (*tech.*) crank case.

картéч|ный, *adj. of* ~ь.

картéч|ь, и, *f.* 1. (*mil.*) case-shot; grape-shot. 2. buck-shot.

картѝн|а, ы, *f.* 1. (*in var. senses*) picture. 2. (*theatr.*) scene.

картѝнк|а, и, *f.* picture; illustration; лубóчные ~и crude, coloured woodcuts; (*pejor.*) crude pictures; мóдная к. fashion-plate; переводнѝе ~и transfers.

картѝн|ный (~ен, ~на), *adj.* 1. *adj. of* ~a; ~ная галерѐя picture-gallery. 2. picturesque.

картóграф, а, *m.* cartographer.

картографѝр|овать, ую, *impf.* to map, draw a map of.

картографѝческий, *adj.* cartographic.

картографѝ|я, и, *f.* cartography.

картóн, а, *m.* 1. cardboard, pasteboard. 2. (*artists' sl.*) sketch, cartoon.

картонáж, а, *m.* cardboard article; cardboard box.

картонáж|ный, *adj. of* ~; ~ная фáбрика cardboard box factory.

картóнк|а, и, *f.* cardboard box; к. для шлѝпы hat-box, bandbox.

картóн|ный, *adj. of* ~; (*fig.*) к. дóмик house of cards.

картотéк|а, и, *f.* card-index.

картофелекопáлк|а, и, *f.* (*agric.*) potato-digger.

картофелесажáлк|а, и, *f.* (*agric.*) potato planter.

картóфелин|а, ы, *f.* (*coll.*) potato.

картóфел|ь, я, *no pl., m.* 1. (*collect.*) potatoes;

к. в мундѝре potatoes boiled in their jackets; жáреный к. fried potatoes; молодóй к. new potatoes. 2. potato plant.

картóфель|ный, *adj. of* ~; ~ное пюрѐ mashed potatoes.

кáрточк|а, и, *f.* 1. card; визѝтная к. visiting card; к. вин wine-list; катáложная к. index card; к. кýшаний bill of fare; продовóльственная к. food-card, ration card. 2. season ticket. 3. (*coll.*) photo.

кáрточ|ный, *adj.* 1. *adj. of* кáрта; к. долг gambling-debt; к. стол card-table; (*coll.*) к. дóмик house of cards (*also fig.*); к. фóкус card trick. 2. *adj. of* ~ка; к. катáлог card index; ~ная систѐма rationing system.

картóшк|а, и, *f.* (*coll.*) 1. (*collect.*) potatoes. 2. potato; нос ~ой bulbous nose.

картýз, á, *m.* 1. (peaked) cap. 2. (*mil.*) powder bag. 3. (*obs.*) paper-bag.

карусéл|ь, и, *f.* roundabout, merry-go-round.

карусéль|ный, *adj. of* ~; (*tech.*) к. станóк vertical lathe.

кáрцер, а, *m.* cell, lock-up.

карьéр[1], а, *m.* career, full gallop; во весь к. at full speed, in full career; пустѝть лóшадь в к., ~ом to put a horse into full gallop; (*fig., coll.*) с мѐста в к. straight away, without more ado.

карьéр[2], а, *m.* quarry; sand-pit.

карьéр|а, ы, *f.* career; сдѐлать ~у to make good, get on.

карьерѝзм, а, *m.* careerism.

карьерѝст, а, *m.* careerist.

карьéр|ный, *adj. of* 1. ~[1,2]. 2. ~a.

касáни|е, я, *n.* contact; (*math.*) тóчка ~я point of contact.

касáтельн|ая, ой, *f.* (*math.*) tangent.

касáтельно, *prep.+g.* touching, concerning.

касáтельств|о, а, *n.* (к) connexion (with); я не имѐл никакóго ~а к э́тому заявлѐнию I had nothing to do with this statement.

касáтик, а, *m.* (*folk poet.*) darling (*addressed to man*).

касáт|ка, ки, *f.* 1. (*orn.*) swallow. 2. (*zool.*) killer whale. 3. (*folk poet.*) *f. of* ~ик.

касá|ться, юсь, *impf.* (*of* коснýться) 1. (+*g.*) to touch. 2. (+*g.; fig.*) to touch (on, upon); к. больнóго вопрóса to touch on a sore subject. 3. (+*g. or* до; *fig.*) to concern, relate (to); э́то тебя́ не ~ется it is no concern of yours; что ~ется as to, as regards, with regard to.

кáск|а, и, *f.* helmet.

каскáд, а, *m.* 1. cascade; к. красnorѐчия (*fig.*) flood of eloquence. 2. leaping from horseback (*as circus turn*).

каскáд|ный, *adj.* 1. *adj. of* ~. 2. (*theatr.*) music-hall.

каспѝйский, *adj.* (*geogr.*) Caspian.

ка́сс|а, ы, *f*. 1. till; cash-box; несгора́емая к. safe. 2. cash. 3. booking-office; box--office; к. взаимопо́мощи benefit fund, mutual aid fund; сберега́тельная к. savings bank. 4. (*typ.*) case.

ка́сса|цио́нный, *adj.* of ~ция; ~цио́нная жа́лоба appeal; к. суд Court of Appeal, Court of Cassation.

кассаци|я, и, *f*. (*leg.*) 1. cassation. 2. (*coll.*) пода́ть ~ю to appeal.

кассе́т|а, ы, *f*. (*phot.*) cassette; plate-holder.

касси́р, а, *m*. cashier.

касси́р|овать, ую, *impf. and pf.* (*leg.*) to annul, quash.

касси́р|ша, ши, *f.* of ~.

ка́сс|овый, *adj.* of ~а; ~овая кни́га cash--book; к. счёт cash-account.

ка́ст|а, ы, *f*. caste.

кастанье́т|ы, ~, *sing.* ~а, ~ы, *f*. castanets.

кастеля́нш|а, и, *f*. linen-keeper (*in institution*).

кастет, а, *m*. knuckleduster.

ка́стовост|ь, и, *f*. (*polit.*; *pejor.*) cliquishness, exclusiveness.

кастор, а, *m*. (*text.*) castor.

касто́рк|а, и, *f*. (*coll.*) castor oil.

касто́ров|ый[1], *adj.*; ~ое ма́сло castor oil.

касто́р|овый[2], *adj.* of ~; ~овая шля́па beaver (hat).

кастра́т, а, *m*. eunuch.

кастра́ци|я, и, *f*. castration.

кастри́р|овать, ую, *impf. and pf.* to castrate; to geld.

кастрю́л|я, и, *f*. saucepan.

кат[1], а, *m*. (*dial. or obs.*) executioner.

кат[2], а, *m*. (*naut.*) cat; к.-ба́лка cathead.

катава́си|я, и, *f*. (*coll.*) confusion, muddle.

катакли́зм, а, *m*. cataclysm.

катако́мб|а, ы, *f*. catacomb.

катала́жк|а, и, *f*. (*coll.*) lock-up.

катале́ктик|а, и, *f*. (*lit.*) catalectic verse.

катале́пси|я, и, *f*. (*med.*) catalepsy.

ката́лиз, а, *m*. (*chem.*) catalysis.

катализа́тор, а, *m*. (*chem.*) catalyst.

катало́г, а, *m*. catalogue.

каталогиза́тор, а, *m*. cataloguer.

каталогизи́р|овать, ую, *impf. and pf.* to catalogue.

катало́жн|ая, ой, *f*. catalogue room.

катало́|жный, *adj.* of ~г.

ка́тал|ь, я, *m*. porter, barrow man.

ката́ни|е, я, *n*. 1. rolling. 2. к. в экипа́же driving; к. верхо́м riding; к. на ло́дке boating; к. на конька́х skating; фигу́рное к. figure skating; к. с гор tobogganing.

ка́тань|е, я, *n.*, *only in phrase* не мытьём, так ~ем (*coll.*) by hook or by crook.

катапу́льт|а, ы, *f*. (*hist. and aeron.*) catapult.

ката́р, а, *m*. catarrh.

катара́кт|а, ы, *f*. (*med.*) cataract.

катара́льный, *adj.* catarrhal.

катастро́ф|а, ы, *f*. catastrophe, disaster; accident.

катастрофи́ческий, *adj.* catastrophic.

катастрофи́ч|ный (~ен, ~на), *adj.* catastrophic.

кат|а́ть, а́ю, *impf.* 1. (*indet. of* ~и́ть) to roll; to wheel, trundle. 2. to drive, take for a drive. 3. to roll (*from clay, dough, etc.*). 4. (*pf.* вы́~) к. бельё to mangle linen.

кат|а́ться, а́юсь, *impf.* 1. (*indet. of* ~и́ться) to roll (*intrans.*); (*coll.*) к. от бо́ли to roll in pain; к. со́ смеху to split one's sides with laughter. 2. to go for a drive; к. верхо́м to ride, go riding; к. на велосипе́де to cycle, go cycling; к. на конька́х to skate, go skating; к. на ло́дке to go boating.

катафа́лк, а, *m*. 1. catafalque. 2. hearse.

категори́чески, *adv.* categorically; к. отказа́ться to refuse flatly.

категори́ческий, *adj.* categorical.

категори́ч|ный (~ен, ~на), *adj.* categorical.

катего́ри|я, и, *f*. category.

ка́тер, а, *pl.* ~а́, *m*. (*naut.*) cutter; мото́рный к. motor-launch; сторожево́й к. patrol boat; торпе́дный к. motor torpedo-boat.

ка́тер|ный, *adj.* of ~.

ка́тет, а, *m*. (*math.*) cathetus.

катете́р, а, *m*. (*med.*) catheter.

катехи́зис, а, *m*. catechism.

ка|ти́ть, чу́, ~тишь, *impf.* (*of* по~) 1. *det. of* ~та́ть. 2. (*coll.*) to bowl along, rip, tear.

ка|ти́ться, чу́сь, ~тишься, *impf.* (*of* по~) 1. *det. of* ~та́ться; к. с горы́ to slide downhill; к. под гору (*fig.*) to go downhill. 2. (*coll.*) to rush, tear. 3. to flow, stream; (*fig.*) to roll; слёзы ~ти́лись по её щека́м tears were rolling down her cheeks; день ~тится за днём day after day rolls by. 4. (*coll.*) ~ти́сь, ~ти́тесь отсю́да! get out!

ка́т|кий (~ок, ~ка́), *adj.* (*coll.*) 1. that can be rolled easily. 2. slippery.

като́д, а, *m*. (*phys.*) cathode.

като́дн|ый, *adj.* (*phys.*) cathodic; ~ые лучи́ cathode rays; ~ая тру́бка cathode-ray tube.

кат|о́к[1], ка́, *m*. skating-rink.

кат|о́к[2], ка́, *m*. 1. (*in var. senses*) roller. 2. к. (для белья́) mangle.

като́лик, а, *m*. (Roman) Catholic.

католико́с, а, *m*. Catholicos (*head of the Armenian Church*).

католици́зм, а, *m*. (Roman) Catholicism.

католи́ческий, *adj.* (Roman) Catholic.

католи́честв|о, а, *n*. (Roman) Catholicism.

католи́чк|а, и, *f.* of като́лик.

ка́торг|а, и, *no pl.*, *f*. penal servitude, hard labour (*in a place of exile*).

каторжа́н|ин, ина, *pl.* ~е, ~, *m.* convict; ex-convict.

ка́торжник, а, *m.* convict.

ка́тор|жный, *adj. of* ~га; ~жные рабо́ты hard labour; (*fig.*) drudgery; ~жная тюрьма́ convict prison.

кату́шк|а, и, *f.* 1. reel, bobbin; (*text.*) spool. 2. (*electr.*) coil, bobbin.

ка́тыш, а, *m.* 1. pellet, ball. 2. block of wood.

ка́тыш|ек, ка, *m.* (*coll.*) pellet.

катю́ш|а, и, *f.* (*mil.*; *coll.*) Katyusha (*lorry-mounted multiple rocket launcher*).

кауза́льный, *adj.* (*philos.*) causal.

кау́рый, *adj.* (*of colour of horses*) light-chestnut.

каусти́ческий, *adj.* (*chem.*) caustic.

каучу́к, а, *m.* (india-)rubber, caoutchouc.

каучу́к|овый, *adj. of* ~; rubber.

каучуконо́с, а, *m.* (*bot.*) rubber-bearing plant.

кафе́, *indecl.*, *n.* café.

ка́федр|а, ы, *f.* 1. pulpit; rostrum, platform; говори́ть с ~ы to speak from the platform. 2. (*fig.*; *at a university*) chair; получи́ть ~у to obtain a chair. 3. (*fig.*; *at a university*) department, sub-faculty; заседа́ние ~ы sub-faculty meeting.

кафедра́льный, *adj.*; к. собо́р cathedral.

ка́фел|ь, я, *m.* Dutch tile.

ка́фел|ьный, *adj. of* ~; ~ная печь tiled stove.

кафете́ри|й, я, *m.* cafeteria.

кафешанта́н, а, *m.* café chantant.

кафоли́ческий, *adj.* (*epithet of the Orthodox Church*) ecumenical, universal.

кафта́н, а, *m.* caftan.

каца́п, а, *m.* 'butcher' (*term of abuse used by Ukrainians of Russians*).

кача́лк|а, и, *f.* rocking-chair; конь-к. rocking-horse.

кача́ни|е, я, *n.* 1. rocking, swinging; к. ма́ятника swing of pendulum. 2. pumping.

кач|а́ть, а́ю, *impf.* (*of* ~ну́ть) 1. (+*a. or i.*) to rock, swing; to shake; к. колыбе́ль to rock a cradle; к. голово́й to nod, shake one's head; (*impers.*) его́ ~а́ло из стороны́ в сто́рону he was reeling; ло́дку ~а́ет the boat is rolling. 2. to lift up, chair (*as mark of esteem or congratulation*). 3. to pump.

кач|а́ться, а́юсь, *impf.* (*of* ~ну́ться) 1. to rock, swing (*intrans.*); (*of vessel*) to roll, pitch. 2. to reel, stagger.

качел|и, ей, *no sing.* (*child's*) swing.

ка́чественный, *adj.* 1. qualitative. 2. high-quality.

ка́честв|о, а, *n.* 1. quality; ни́зкого ~a of inferior quality; в ~е (+*g.*) in the character (of), in the capacity (of); в ~е преподава́тельницы она́ отли́чна (in her capacity as a teacher she is excellent. 2. (*chess*)

вы́играть, проигра́ть к. to gain, lose an exchange.

ка́чк|а, и, *f.* rocking; tossing; (*naut.*) бортова́я к. rolling; килева́я к. pitching.

ка́чкий, *adj.* (*coll.*) unstable, wobbly.

кач|ну́ть(ся), ну́(сь), нёшь(ся), *pf. of* ~а́ть(ся).

ка|чу́, ~тишь, *see* ~ти́ть.

кашал́|а, и, *f.* 1. kasha (*dish of cooked grain or groats*); ма́нная к. semolina; ри́совая к. boiled rice. 2. (*fig.*, *coll.*) берёзовая к. the birch; с ним ~и не сва́ришь one can't get on with him; у него́ к. во рту he mumbles; ма́ло ~и ел (*of someone young and/or inexperienced*); сапоги́ у тебя́ ~и про́сят your boots are agape; завари́ть ~у to start something, stir up trouble; расхлеба́ть ~у to put things right.

кашало́т, а, *m.* (*zool.*) cachalot, sperm-whale.

кашева́р, а, *m.* (*obs.*) cook (*in mil. unit or workmen's canteen*).

ка́ш|ель, ля, *m.* cough.

кашеми́р, а, *m.* (*text.*) cashmere.

ка́шиц|а, ы, *f.* (*coll.*) thin gruel; бума́жная к. paper pulp.

ка́ш|ка[1], ки, *f. dim. of* ~a; pap.

ка́шк|а[2], и, *f.* (*bot.*; *coll.*) clover.

ка́шлян|уть, у, ешь, *pf.* to give a cough.

ка́шля|ть, ю, *impf.* 1. to cough. 2. to have a cough.

кашне́, *indecl.*, *n.* scarf, muffler.

кашта́н, а, *m.* 1. chestnut; таска́ть ~ы из огня́ (*fig.*) to pull the chestnuts out of the fire. 2. chestnut-tree; ко́нский к. horse-chestnut.

кашта́н|овый, *adj.* 1. *adj. of* ~. 2. chestnut(-coloured).

каю́к[1], а, *m.* caique.

каю́к[2] (*coll.*) *only in phrase* к. (пришёл) (+*d.*) it's the end (of); тут ему́ и к. that's the end of him, he's done for.

каю́р, а, *m.* dog-team (*or* reindeer-team) driver.

каю́т|а, ы, *f.* cabin, stateroom.

каю́т-компа́ни|я, и, *f.* 1. (*on warships*) wardroom. 2. (*on passenger vessels*) passengers' lounge.

ка́|ющийся, *pres. part. of* ~яться *and adj.* repentant, contrite, penitent.

ка́|яться, юсь, ешься, *impf.* 1. (*pf.* рас~) (в+*p.*) to repent (of); он сам тепе́рь ~ется he is sorry himself now. 2. (*pf.* по~) (в+*p.*) to confess. 3. (*coll.*) ~юсь I am sorry to say, I (must) confess; я, ~юсь, совсе́м об э́том забы́л I am sorry to say I had forgotten all about it.

квадра́нт, а, *m.* 1. (*math.*) quadrant. 2. (*mil.*) quadrant, gunner's clinometer.

квадра́т, а, *m.* (*math.*) square; возвести́ в к. to square; в ∼е squared; (*fig., joc.*) дура́к в ∼е doubly a fool.

квадра́тн|ый, *adj.* square; (*anat.*) ∼ая мы́шца quadrate muscle; (*math.*) к. ко́рень square root; ∼ое уравне́ние quadratic equation.

квадрату́р|а, ы, *f.* (*math.*) quadrature; (*fig.*) к. кру́га squaring the circle.

квадрильо́н, а, *m.* (*math.*) quadrillion.

ква́зи- quasi-.

ква́кань|е, я, *n.* croaking.

ква́ка|ть, ю, *impf.* to croak.

квакн|уть, у, ешь, *pf.* to give a croak.

квакушк|а, и, *f.* (*coll.*) frog.

квалификац|ио́нный, *adj. of* ∼ия; ∼ио́нная коми́ссия board of experts.

квалифика́ци|я, и, *f.* qualification.

квалифици́рова|нный (∼н, ∼на), *p.p.p. of* ∼ть *and adj.* 1. qualified, skilled. 2. к. труд skilled work, specialist work.

квалифици́р|овать, ую, *impf. and pf.* 1. to check, test. 2. to qualify (as); как к. тако́е поведе́ние? how should one qualify such conduct?

квант, а, *m. and* ∼а, ∼ы, *f.* (*phys.*) quantum.

ква́нт|овый, *adj. of* ∼; ∼овая тео́рия quantum theory.

ква́рт|а, ы, *f.* 1. (*liquid measure*) quart. 2. (*mus.*) fourth. 3. (*fencing and cards*) quart.

кварта́л, а, *m.* 1. block (*of buildings*); (*obs.*) quarter, ward. 2. quarter (*of year*).

кварта́льн|ый, *adj.* 1. quarterly; к. отчёт quarterly account. 2. of quarter of city; (*as noun*) к., ∼ого, *m.* (*hist.; coll.*) non-commissioned police officer.

кварте́т, а, *m.* (*mus.*) quartet(te).

кварти́р|а, ы, *f.* 1. flat; lodging; apartment(s); к. и стол board and lodging; сдаётся к. flat, apartment(s) to let; гла́вная к. (*mil.*) general headquarters. 2. *pl.* (*mil.*) quarters, billets; зи́мние ∼ы winter quarters.

квартира́нт, а, *m.* lodger, tenant.

квартира́нт|ка, ки, *f. of* ∼.

квартирме́йстер, а, *m.* (*mil. and naut.*) quartermaster.

кварти́рник, а, *m.* (*obs.*) craftsman working at home.

кварти́р|ный, *adj. of* ∼а; ∼ная пла́та rent; ∼ное расположе́ние (*mil.*) billeting.

квартир|ова́ть, у́ю, *impf.* 1. (*coll.*) to lodge. 2. (*mil.*) to be billeted, be quartered.

квартиронанима́тел|ь, я, *m.* tenant.

квартирохозя́ин, а, *m.* landlord.

квартирохозя́йк|а, и, *f.* landlady.

квартирье́р, а, *m.* (*mil.*) billeting officer.

квартпла́т|а, ы, *f.* (*abbr. of* кварти́рная пла́та) rent.

кварц, а, *m.* (*min.*) quartz.

ква́рц|евый, *adj. of* ∼.

кварци́т, а, *m.* (*min.*) quartzite.

квас, а, *pl.* ∼ы́, *m.* kvass.

ква́|сить, шу, сишь, *impf.* to pickle; to make sour.

квас|но́й, *adj. of* ∼; к. патриоти́зм (*fig.*) jingoism.

квас|о́к, ка́, *m.* 1. *dim. of* ∼. 2. (*coll.*) sour tang.

квасцо́вый, *adj.* (*chem.*) aluminous.

квасц|ы́, о́в, *no sing.* (*chem.*) alum.

квашени́н|а, ы, *f.* 1. (*coll.*) sauerkraut. 2. (*agric.*) fermented vegetable leaves.

ква́шен|ый, *adj.* sour, fermented; ∼ая капу́ста sauerkraut.

квашн|я́, и́, *g. pl.* ∼е́й, *f.* 1. kneading trough. 2. (*dial.*) leavened dough.

квёл|ый (∼, ∼а́, ∼о), *adj.* (*dial. or fig.*) weakly, poorly.

кве́рху, *adv.* up, upwards.

квиети́зм, а, *m.* quietism.

кви́нт|а, ы, *f.* (*mus.*) fifth; (*coll.*) пове́сить нос на ∼у to look dejected.

квинте́т, а, *m.* (*mus.*) quintet(te).

квинтэссе́нци|я, и, *f.* quintessence.

квит, ∼ы, *as pred.* (*coll.*) quits; мы с тобо́й ∼ы we are quits.

квитанц|ио́нный, *adj. of* ∼ия.

квита́нци|я, и, *f.* receipt; бага́жная к. luggage-ticket.

квит|о́к, ка́, *m.* (*coll.*) ticket, check.

кво́рум, а, *m.* quorum.

кво́т|а, ы, *f.* quota.

кеб, а, *m.* cab.

ке́гель = кегль.

кегельба́н, а, *m.* skittle-alley.

ке́гл|и, ей, *sing.* ∼я, ∼и, *f.* skittles.

кегл|ь, я, *m.* (*typ.*) point; к. 8 8 point.

кедр, а, *m.* cedar; гимала́йский к. deodar; лива́нский к. cedar of Lebanon; сиби́рский к. Siberian pine; европе́йский к. Cembran (Arolla) pine.

кедро́вк|а, и, *f.* (*orn.*) nutcracker.

кедр|о́вый, *adj. of* ∼; к. стла́ник dwarf Siberian pine (*Pinus pumila*).

ке́д|ы, ∼, *no sing.* baseball boots.

кекс, а, *m.* fruit-cake.

ке́лар|ь, я, *m.* (*eccl.*) cellarer.

келе́йник, а, *m.* (*eccl.*) lay brother.

келе́йно, *adv.* in secret, privately; они́ к. реши́ли де́ло they decided the matter in camera.

келе́йный, *adj.* 1. *adj. of* ке́лья. 2. (*fig., pejor.*) secret, private.

ке́льнер, а, *m.* waiter.

кельт, а, *m.* Celt.

ке́льтский, *adj.* Celtic.

ке́л|ья, ьи, *g. pl.* ∼ий, *f.* (*eccl.*) cell.

кем, *i. of* кто.

ке́мпинг, а, *m.* camping-site.

кенгуру́, *indecl.*, *m.* kangaroo.

кента́вр, а, *m.* (*myth.*) centaur.

ке́пк|а, и, *f.* (*coll.*) cloth cap.

кера́мик|а, и, *f.* ceramics.

керами́ческий, *adj.* ceramic.

ке́рбел|ь, я, *m.* (*bot.*) chervil; ди́кий к. cow-parsley.

керога́з, а, *m.* kerosene stove.

кероси́н, а, *m.* kerosene.

кероси́нк|а, и, *f.* (*coll.*) oil-stove.

ке́сарев, *adj.* (*med.*) ~о сече́ние Caesarean section.

ке́сар|ь, я, *m.* monarch, lord.

кессо́н, а, *m.* (*tech.*) 1. caisson, coffer-dam. 2. lacunar.

кессо́н|ный, *adj.* of ~; ~ная боле́знь caisson disease.

кёт|а, ы, *f.* Siberian salmon.

кетме́н|ь, я, *m.* (*agric.*) ketmen (*kind of hoe used in Central Asia*).

кёт|овый, *adj.* of ~a.

кефа́л|ь, и, *f.* grey mullet.

кефи́р, а, *m.* kefir.

киберне́тик|а, и, *f.* cybernetics.

кибернети́ческий, *adj.* cybernetic.

киби́тк|а, и, *f.* 1. kibitka, covered wagon. 2. nomad tent.

кив|а́ть, а́ю, *impf.* (*of* ~ну́ть) 1. (голово́й) to nod (one's head); to nod assent. 2. (на+*a.*) to motion (to); (*fig.*) refer (to), put the blame (on to).

ки́вер, а, *pl.* ~а́, *m.* shako.

кив|ну́ть, ну́, нёшь, *pf.* of ~а́ть.

кив|о́к, ка́, *m.* nod.

ки|да́ть, да́ю, *impf.* (*of* ~ну́ть) to throw, fling, cast (*usage as for* броса́ть).

ки|да́ться, да́юсь, *impf.* (*of* ~ну́ться) 1. to throw oneself, fling oneself; to rush. 2. (+*i.*) to throw, fling, shy. 3. *pass.* of ~да́ть.

кизи́л, а, *m.* (*bot.*) cornel.

кизя́к, а́, *m.* pressed dung (*used as fuel*).

ки|й, я́, *pl.* ~й, ~ёв, *m.* (billiard) cue.

кики́мор|а, ы, *f.* 1. (*folklore*) kikimora (*hobgoblin in female form*). 2. (*fig., coll.*) вы́глядеть ~ой to look a fright.

кикс, а, *m.* (*sl.*) miss (*at billiards*).

кил|а́, ы́, *f.* (*dial.*) rupture, hernia.

килева́ни|е, я, *n.* (*naut.*) careening, careenage.

кил|ева́ть, у́ю, *impf.* (*naut.*) to careen.

кил|ево́й, *adj.* of ~ь; ~ева́я ка́чка pitching.

кило́, *indecl.*, *n.* kilogram(me).

килова́тт, а, *m.* (*electr.*) kilowatt.

килогра́мм, а, *m.* kilogram(me).

килокало́ри|я, и, *f.* large calorie.

киломе́тр, а, *m.* kilometre.

кил|ь, я, *m.* 1. (*naut.*) keel. 2. (*aeron.*) fin.

кильва́тер, а, *m.* (*naut.*) wake; идти́ в к. (+*d.*) to follow in the wake (of).

кильва́тер|ный, *adj.* of ~; ~ная коло́нна line ahead.

ки́льк|а, и, *f.* sprat.

кимва́л, а, *m.* cymbal.

кимо́граф, а, *m.* (*tech.*) kymograph.

кимоно́, *indecl.*, *n.* kimono.

кингсто́н, а, *m.* (*naut.*) Kingston valve; откры́ть ~ы to scuttle (a ship).

кинемато́граф, а, *m.* (*obs.*) cinematograph.

кинематографи́ческий, *adj.* cinematographic.

кинематогра́фи|я, и, *f.* cinematography.

кинеско́п, а, *m.* television tube.

кине́тик|а, и, *f.* (*phys.*) kinetics.

кинети́ческий, *adj.* (*phys.*) kinetic.

кинжа́л, а, *m.* dagger.

кинжа́л|ьный, *adj.* 1. *adj.* of ~. 2. (*mil.*) close-range, hand-to-hand.

кино́, *indecl.*, *n.* (*abstr. and concr.*) cinema.

кино- film-, cine-.

киноаппара́т, а, *m.* cinecamera.

киноаппарату́р|а, ы, *f.* cinematographic equipment.

киноарти́ст, а, *m.* film actor.

киноарти́стк|а, и, *f.* film actress.

киноателье́, *indecl.*, *n.* film studio.

ки́новар|ь, и, *f.* cinnabar, vermilion.

киноведени|е, я, *n.* study of the film (*as an art*).

кинокарти́н|а, ы, *f.* (*non-documentary*) film.

кинолент|а, ы, *f.* reel (of film).

киномеха́ник, а, *m.* cinema operator.

кинооперáтор, а, *m.* camera-man.

кинопередви́жк|а, и, *f.* portable (motion picture) projector.

киноплёнк|а, и, *f.* (ciné) film.

кинорежиссёр, а, *m.* film director.

киносеа́нс, а, *m.* (cinema) performance, showing.

киносту́ди|я, и, *f.* film studio.

киносъёмк|а, и, *f.* filming, shooting.

кинотеа́тр, а, *m.* cinema.

киноустано́вк|а, и, *f.* projecting machine.

кинофика́ци|я, и, *f.* 1. inclusion in cinema circuit. 2. adaptation for the cinema, for the screen.

кинофици́р|овать, ую, *impf. and pf.* 1. to include in cinema circuit, bring cinema to. 2. to adapt for the cinema, for the screen.

кинохро́ник|а, и, *f.* news-reel.

ки́|нуть(ся), ну(сь), нешь(ся), *pf.* of ~да́ть(ся).

кио́ск, а, *m.* kiosk, stall; газе́тный к. news-stand.

киоскёр, а, *m.* stall-holder.

кио́т, а, *m.* icon-case.

ки́п|а, ы, *f.* 1. pile, stack. 2. (*measure*) pack, bale; к. хло́пка bale of cotton.

кипари́с, а, *m.* (*bot.*) cypress.

кипе́ни|е, я, *n.* boiling; то́чка ~я boiling point.

кип|е́ть, лю́, йшь, *impf.* (*of* вс~) to boil, seethe; к. ключо́м to gush up; к. негодова́нием (*fig.*) to seethe with indignation; рабо́та ~е́ла work was in full swing; как в котле́ к. to be hard pressed.

кипре́|й, я, *m.* (*bot.*) willow-herb.

кипу́чест|ь, и, *f.* ebullience, turbulence.

кипу́ч|ий (~, ~а), *adj.* 1. boiling, seething. 2. (*fig.*) ebullient, turbulent; ~ая де́ятельность feverish activity.

кипяти́льник, а, *m.* kettle, boiler, boiling-tank.

кипяти́льный, *adj.* for boiling; к. бак copper.

кипя|ти́ть, чу́, ти́шь, *impf.* (*of* вс~) to boil.

кипя|ти́ться, чу́сь, ти́шься, *impf.* 1. to boil (*intrans.*) 2. (*fig., coll.*) to get excited. 3. *pass. of* ~ти́ть.

кипят|о́к, ка́, *m.* 1. boiling water. 2. (*fig., coll.*) testy person, irritable person.

кипячёный, *adj.* boiled.

кира́с|а, ы, *f.* (*mil., hist.*) cuirass.

кираси́р, а, *m.* (*mil., hist.*) cuirassier.

кирги́з, а, *m.* Kirghiz.

кирги́зк|а, и, *f.* Kirghiz (woman).

кирги́зский, *adj.* Kirghiz.

кири́ллиц|а, ы, *f.* Cyrillic alphabet.

ки́рк|а, и, *f.* (Protestant) church.

кирк|а́, и́, *f.* pick(axe).

кирк|о́вый, *adj. of* ~а́.

киркомоты́г|а, и, *f.* pickaxe.

кирпи́ч, а́, *m.* 1. brick. 2. (*collect.*) bricks; необожжённый, сама́нный к. adobe. 3. (*coll.*) no-entry sign.

кирпи́ч|ик, а, *m.* 1. *dim. of* ~. 2. (*pl.*) bricks (*as child's plaything*).

кирпи́ч|ный, *adj. of* ~; к. заво́д brickworks; к. чай brick-tea.

ки́с|а, ы, *f.* = ~ка.

кисе́|йный, *adj. of* ~я; (*coll., obs.*) ~йная ба́рышня prim young lady.

кисе́л|ь, я́, *m.* kissel (*kind of blancmange*); (*fig., coll.*) деся́тая (*or* седьма́я) вода́ на ~é distant connexion, distant relative; за семь вёрст ~я́ хлеба́ть to go a long way for nothing, to go on a fool's errand.

кисе́ль|ный, *adj. of* ~; моло́чные ре́ки, ~ные берега́ land flowing with milk and honey.

кисе́т, а, *m.* tobacco pouch.

кисе|я́, и́, *f.* muslin.

ки́ск|а, и, *f.* (*coll.*) puss, pussy-cat.

кис-ки́с, *interj.* puss-puss! (*when calling cat*).

ки́сленький, *adj.* (*coll.*) slightly sour.

кисле́|ть, ю, *impf.* (*coll.*) to become sour.

кисли́нк|а, *f.*, only in phrase с ~ой (*coll.*) slightly sour, sourish.

кислова́т|ый (~, ~а), *adj.* sourish; acidulous.

кислоро́д, а, *m.* oxygen.

кислоро́дно-ацетиле́новый, *adj.* oxy-acety-

lene.

кислоро́дный, *adj.* (*chem.*) oxygen.

ки́сло-сла́дкий, *adj.* sour-sweet.

кислот|а́, ы́, *pl.* ~ы, *f.* 1. sourness; acidity. 2. (*chem.*) acid.

кислотност|ь, и, *f.* (*chem.*) acidity.

кисло́тный, *adj.* (*chem.*) acid.

кислотоупо́рный, *adj.* (*tech.*) acid-proof; acid resistant.

ки́с|лый (~ел, ~ла́, ~ло), *adj.* 1. sour; (*fig.*) ~лое настрое́ние sour mood; ~лая улы́бка sour smile. 2. fermented; ~лая капу́ста sauerkraut; ~лые щи sauerkraut soup. 3. (*chem.*) acid.

кисля́тин|а, ы, *f.* (*coll.*) 1. sour(-tasting) stuff. 2. (*fig., pejor.*) sour puss, misery.

ки́с|нуть, ну, нешь, *past* ~, ~ла, *impf.* 1. to turn sour. 2. (*fig., coll.*) to mope; to look sour.

кист|а́, ы́, *f.* (*med.*) cyst.

кистеви́дный, *adj.* (*bot.*) racemose.

кисте́н|ь, я́, *m.* bludgeon, flail.

ки́сточк|а, и, *f.* 1. brush; к. для бритья́ shaving-brush. 2. tassel.

кист|ь¹, и, *pl.* ~и, ~е́й, *f.* 1. (*bot.*) cluster, bunch; к. виногра́да bunch of grapes. 2. brush; маля́рная к. paintbrush. 3. tassel.

кист|ь², и, *pl.* ~и, ~е́й, *f.* hand.

кит, а, *m.* whale.

китаеве́д, а, *m.* sinologist, sinologue.

китаеве́дени|е, я, *n.* sinology.

кита́|ец, йца, *pl.* ~йцы, ~йцев, *m.* Chinese, Chinaman.

китаизи́р|овать, ую, *impf.* to sinify, adapt to Chinese conditions.

китаи́ст, а, *m.* sinologist, sinologue.

кита́йк|а, и, *f.* (*text.*) nankeen.

кита́йск|ий, *adj.* Chinese; ~ая гра́мота double-dutch; к. и́дол joss; к. храм joss-house; ~ая тушь India(n) ink.

китайч|о́нок, о́нка, *pl.* ~а́та, ~а́т, *m.* Chinese child.

китая́нк|а, и, *f.* Chinese woman.

ки́тел|ь, я, *pl.* ~я́, ~е́й, *m.* (*single-breasted, military or naval*) jacket with high collar.

китобо́|й, я, *m.* whaler, whaling ship.

китобо́йн|ый, *adj.* whaling; к. про́мысел whaling; ~ое су́дно whaler.

кит|о́вый, *adj. of* ~; к. жир blubber; к. ус whalebone, baleen.

китоло́в, а, *m.* whaleman.

кито|ло́вный, *adj.* = ~бо́йный.

китообра́зный, *adj.* (*zool.*) cetacean.

кич|и́ться, у́сь, и́шься, *impf.* (+*i.*) to plume oneself (on); to strut.

ки́чк|а, и, *f.* (*dial.*) 1. kichka (*married woman's head-dress*). 2. (*fig.*) front (*of boat*).

кичли́вост|ь, и, *f.* conceit; arrogance.

кичли́в|ый (~, ~а), *adj.* conceited, arrogant, haughty, strutting.

киш|éть, ý, и́шь, *impf.* (+*i.*) to swarm (with), teem (with).

кишéчник, а, *m.* (*anat.*) bowels, intestines; очи́стить к. to open the bowels.

киш|éчный, *adj. of* ~éчник *and* ~ка́; intestinal.

киш|ка́, ки́, *g. pl.* ~о́к, *f.* 1. (*anat.*) gut, intestine; двенадцатипéрстная к. duodenum; прямáя к. rectum; слепáя к. caecum; тóнкая, тóлстая к. small, large intestine; (*fig.*, *coll.*) к. тонка́! he, *etc.*, isn't up to that!; вы́пустить ~ки́ to disembowel; лезть из ~о́к to put one's guts into; надорвáть ~ки́ (со́ смеху) to laugh oneself sick; тянýться ~кóй to go in file. 2. hose; поли́ть ~кóй to hose.

кишла́к, á, *m.* kishlak (*village in Central Asia*).

кишла́|чный, *adj. of* ~к.

кишми́ш, á, *no pl.*, *m.* raisins, sultanas.

кишмя́, *adv.*, *only in phrase* к. кишéть to swarm.

клавеси́н, а, *m.* (*mus.*) harpsichord.

клавиатýр|а, ы, *f.* keyboard.

клавикóрд|ы, ов, *no sing.* (*mus.*) clavichord.

кла́виш, а, *m.* key (*of piano, typewriter, etc.*).

кла́виш|а, и, *f.* = ~.

кла́виш|ный, *adj. of* ~; ~ные инструмéнты keyboard instruments.

клад, а, *m.* treasure; (*fig.*, *coll.*) treasure (-house); моя́ секретáрша — настоя́щий к. my secretary is a real treasure.

кла́дбищ|е, а, *n.* cemetery, graveyard; churchyard.

кладби́щенский, *adj. of* кла́дбище; к. стóрож sexton.

кла́дез|ь, я, *m.*, *arch.*, *now only in joc. phrase* к. премýдрости mine of information.

кла́дк|а, и, *f.* laying; кáменная к. masonry; кирпи́чная к. brickwork.

кладов|áя, óй, *f.* pantry, larder; storeroom.

кладóвк|а, и, *f.* (*coll.*) pantry, larder.

кладовщи́к, á, *m.* storeman.

кла|дý, дёшь, *see* ~сть.

кла́дчик, а, *m.* bricklayer.

клад|ь, и, *f.* 1. (*sing. only*) load; ручнáя к. hand luggage. 2. haycock.

кла́к|а, и, *no pl.*, *f.* (*collect.*) claque.

клакёр, а, *m.* (*theatr.*) claqueur.

клан, а, *m.* clan.

кла́ня|ться, юсь, *impf.* (*of* поклони́ться) 1. (+*d.* or с+*i.*) to bow (to); to greet; к. в пóяс to bow from the waist; (*fig.*) мы с ним не ~емся I am not on speaking terms with him; честь имéю к. *obs. leave-taking formula.* 2. to send, convey greetings; ~йтесь емý от меня́ give him my regards. 3. (+*d.* or пéред; *coll.*) to cringe (before); to humiliate oneself (before). 4. (+*d.* and *i.*; *obs.*) lay before, offer; к. комý-н. хлéбом-сóлью to offer someone hospitality.

кла́пан, а, *m.* 1. (*tech.*) valve; предохрани́тельный к. safety valve. 2. (*mus.*) vent. 3. (*anat.*) сердéчный к. mitral valve. 4. (*on clothing, etc.*) flap.

кларнéт, а, *m.* clarinet.

кларнети́ст, а, *m.* clarinettist.

класс, а, *m.* 1. (*in various senses*) class; роспóдствующий, прáвящий к. ruling class; к. млекопитáющих (class of) mammalia; игрá высóкого ~a high class play. 2. class-room.

кла́ссик, а, *m.* 1. (*in various senses* (classic; classic(al) author. 2. classical scholar.

кла́ссик|а, и, *f.* the classics.

классификáтор, а, *m.* classifier.

классификáци|я, и, *f.* classification.

классифици́р|овать, ую, *impf. and pf.* to classify.

классици́зм, а, *m.* 1. (*lit.*, *art*) classicism. 2. classical education.

класси́ческий, *adj.* (*in var. senses*) classic(al).

класс|ный, *adj.* (*of* ~) 1. ~ная доскá blackboard; ~ная кóмната classroom; ~ная рабóта class work. 2. к. вагóн passenger coach. 3. (*sport*) first-class. 4. (*sl.*) classy.

кла́ссовост|ь, и, *f.* class character.

кла́ссов|ый, *adj.* (*polit.*) class; ~ая борьбá class struggle; к. враг class enemy; ~ые разли́чия class distinctions; ~ое сознáние class-consciousness.

класс|ы, ов (*children's game*) hopscotch.

кла|сть, дý, дёшь, *past* ~л, ~ла, *impf.* (*of* положи́ть) 1. to lay; to put (*into prone position or fig.*); to place; к. больнóго на носи́лки to lay a patient on a stretcher; к. сáхар в чай to put sugar in one's tea; к. на мéсто to replace; к. не на мéсто to mislay; к. на мýзыку to set to music; к. в лýзу, к. шарá (*billiards*) to pocket a ball; к. я́йца to lay eggs (*of birds and insects*); к. руль (*naut.*) to put the wheel over; к. начáло, к. конéц чемý-н. to start something, put an end to something; (*fig.*) к. под сукнó to shelve. 2. (*pf.* сложи́ть) to build. 3. to assign, set aside (*time, money*); мы ~дём пятьдеся́т рублéй на э́ту поéздку we are setting aside fifty roubles for this trip.

кла́узул|а, ы, *f.* (*leg.*) clause, proviso, stipulation.

клёв, а, *m.* biting, bite; сегóдня хорóший к. the fish are biting well today.

кл|евáть, юю́, юёшь, *impf.* (*of* ~ю́нуть) 1. to peck. 2. (*of fish*) to bite; вчерá ры́ба не ~евáла the fish were not biting yesterday. 3. (*coll.*) к. нóсом to nod (*from drowsiness*). 4. (*fig.*, *impers.*, *coll.*) ~ю́ёт things are going well, better.

кл|евáться, ~ю́ётся, *impf.* (*of birds*) to peck (one another).

клéвер, а, *m.* (*bot.*) clover.
клéвер|ный, *adj.* of ~.
клевет|á, ы́, *f.* slander; calumny, aspersion; libel; возвести́ на кого́-н. ~у́ to slander someone, cast aspersions on someone.
клеве|та́ть, щу́, ~щешь, *impf.* (*of* на~) (на+*a.*) to slander, calumniate; to libel.
клеветни́к, á, *m.* slanderer.
клеветн|и́ца, и́цы, *f.* of ~и́к.
клеветни́ческий, *adj.* slanderous; libellous, defamatory.
клеве|щу́, ~щешь, *see* ~та́ть.
клев|о́к, ка́, *m.* (*coll.*) 1. peck. 2. (*mil.*) burst (of shrapnel) on impact.
клевре́т, а, *m.* (*obs.*) minion, creature.
клеева́р, а, *m.* glue-boiler.
кле|ево́й, *adj.* of ~й; ~ева́я кра́ска size paint.
клеёнк|а, и, *f.* oil-cloth.
клеёнчатый, *adj.* oilskin.
клеёный, *adj.* gummed, glued.
кле|и́ть, ю, ишь, *impf.* (*of* с~) to glue; to gum; to paste; к. де́вушку (*vulg.*) to pick up a girl.
кле|и́ться, ится, *impf.* (*coll.*) 1. to become sticky. 2. (*fig.*; *usually with neg.*) to get on, go well; моя́ рабо́та что́-то пло́хо ~ится my work is not going too well somehow; разгово́р не ~и́лся the conversation was sticky. 3. *pass. of* ~и́ть.
кле|й, я, о ~е, на ~ю́, *m.* glue; мучно́й к. paste; пти́чий к. bird-lime; ры́бий к. isinglass; fish-glue; к. и но́жницы (*iron.*) scissors and paste.
клéйк|а, и, *f.* glueing.
клéйк|ий, *adj.* sticky; ~ая бума́га (для мух) fly-paper.
клейкови́н|а, ы, *f.* gluten.
клéйкост|ь, и, *f.* stickiness.
клеймёный, *adj.* branded.
клейм|и́ть, лю́, и́шь, *impf.* (*of* за~) to brand, stamp; (*fig.*) to brand, stigmatize; к. позо́ром to hold up to shame.
клеймлéни|е, я, *n.* branding, stamping.
клейм|о́, á, *pl.* ~а, *n.* brand, stamp; проби́рное к. hall-mark, mark of assay; фабри́чное к. trade-mark; к. позо́ра (*fig.*) stigma.
клéйстер, а, *m.* paste.
клёкот, а, *m.* (*of birds*) scream.
клеко|та́ть, чу́, ~чешь, *impf.* (*of birds*) to scream.
клéмм|а, ы, *f.* (*electr.*) terminal.
клён, а, *m.* maple.
клено́вый, *adj.* of клён.
клепáл|о, а, *n.* (*tech.*; *obs.*) riveting hammer.
клепáльн|ый, *adj.* riveting; ~ая маши́на riveter, riveting machine.
клепáльщик, а, *m.* riveter (*operator*).
клёпаный, *adj.* (*tech.*) riveted.
клепá|ть¹, ю, *impf.* (*tech.*) to rivet.

клеп|áть², лю, ~лешь, *impf.* (*of* наклепáть) (на+*a.*; *coll.*) to slander, cast aspersions (on).
клёпк|а¹, и, *f.* riveting.
клёпк|а², и, *f.* stave, lag; (*fig.*, *coll.*) у него́ како́й-то ~и не хвата́ет he has got a screw loose.
клептомáн, а, *m.* kleptomaniac.
клептомáни|я, и, *f.* kleptomania.
клерикали́зм, а, *m.* (*polit.*) clericalism.
клерк, а, *m.* clerk.
клер|овáть, у́ю, *impf.* (*tech.*) to refine, clarify.
клёст, á, *m.* (*orn.*) crossbill.
клéтк|а, и, *f.* 1. cage; coop; hutch. 2. (*on paper*) square; (*on material*) check. 3. (*anat.*) грудна́я к. thorax. 4. (*biol.*) cell.
клетн|евáть, ю́ю, ю́ешь, *impf.* (*naut.*) to serve (*a rope*).
клетýшк|а, и, *f.* (*coll.*) closet, tiny room.
клетчáтк|а, и, *f.* 1. (*bot.*, *tech.*) cellulose. 2. (*anat.*) cellular tissue.
клéтчатый, *adj.* 1. checked; к. плато́к checked head-scarf. 2. (*biol.*) cellular.
клет|ь, и, *pl.* ~и, ~éй, *f.* 1. (*dial.*) store-room; shed. 2. (*in mines*) cage.
клёцк|а, и, *f.* (*cul.*) dumpling.
клёш, а, *m.* (*and indecl. adj.*) flare; брю́ки-к. bell-bottomed trousers; ю́бка-к. flared skirt.
клешн|я́, и́, *g. pl.* ~éй, *f.* claw (*of a crustacean*).
клещ, á, *m.* (*zool.*) tick.
клещеви́н|а, ы, *f.* (*bot.*) Palma Christi (*castor-oil plant*).
клещ|и́, éй, *no sing.* 1. pincers, tongs; (*fig. coll.*) э́того из меня́ ~а́ми не вы́тянешь wild horses shall not drag it from me. 2. (*mil.*; *fig.*) pincers, pincer-movement.
кли́вер, а, *m.* (*naut.*) jib.
клиéнт, а, *m.* client.
клиентýр|а, ы, *f.* (*collect.*) clientèle.
кли́зм|а, ы, *f.* (*med.*) enema, clyster; ста́вить ~у (+*d.*) to give an enema.
клик, а, *m.* (*poet.*) cry, call.
кли́к|а, и, *f.* clique.
кли́|кать, чу, чешь, *impf.* (*of* ~кнуть) 1. (*coll.*) to call, hail. 2. (+*a. and i.*; *dial.*) to call (*name*); его́ ~чут Ива́ном he is called Ivan. 3. (*of geese and swans*) to honk.
кли́к|нуть, ну, нешь, *pf. of* ~ать.
клику́ш|а, и, *f.* hysterical woman.
клику́шеский, *adj.* hysterical.
клику́шеств|о, а, *n.* hysterics.
кли́|макс, а, *m.* = климакте́рий.
климакте́ри|й, я, *m.* (*physiol.*) climacteric.
климактери́ческий, *adj.* (*physiol.*) climacteric.
кли́мат, а, *m.* climate.
климати́ческий, *adj.* climatic.
клин, а, *pl.* ~ья, ~ьев, *m.* 1. wedge; загна́ть к. (в+*a.*) to drive a wedge (into); борода́

~ом wedge-shaped beard; (*fig.*) вбить к. (между) to drive a wedge (between); к. ~ом вышибается (*prov.*) like cures like; свет не ~ом сошёлся the world is large enough. 2. (*archit.*) quoin. 3. gore (*in skirt*); gusset (*in underwear*). 4. (*agric.*) field; озимый к. winter field; посевной к. sown area.

клиник|а, и, *f.* clinic.

клиницист, а, *m.* clinical physician, clinical surgeon.

клинический, *adj.* clinical.

клинкер, а, *m.* (*tech.*) clinker.

клиновидный, *adj.* wedge-shaped.

клин|овой, *adj.* of ~; к. затвор (*mil.*) breech mechanism.

клин|ок, ка, *m.* blade.

клинообраз|ный (~ен, ~на), *adj.* wedge--shaped; ~ные письмена cuneiform characters.

клинописный, *adj.* cuneiform.

клинопис|ь, и, *f.* cuneiform (characters, text).

клипер, а, *m.* (*naut.*) clipper.

клир, а, *m.* (*collect.*; *eccl.*) the clergy (*of a parish*).

клиренс, а, *m.* (*tech.*) clearance.

клиринг, а, *m.* (*fin.*) clearing, clearance.

клиринг|овый, *adj.* of ~.

клирос, а, *m.* choir (*part of church*).

клистир, а, *m.* (*med.*; *obs.*) enema, clyster.

клитор, а, *m.* (*anat.*) clitoris.

клич, а, *m.* (*rhet.*) call; боевой к. war-cry; кликнуть к. to issue a call.

кличк|а, и, *f.* 1. name (*of domestic animal, pet*). 2. nickname. 3. conspiratorial name.

кли|чу, чешь, *see* ~кать.

клише, *indecl.*, *n.* (*typ. and fig.*) cliché.

клоак|а, и, *f.* 1. cesspit, sink, sewer (*also fig., concr. and abstr.*). 2. (*zool.*) cloaca.

клобук, а, *m.* (*eccl.*) klobuk (*headgear of Orthodox monk*).

клозет, а, *m.* (*coll.*, *obs.*) water closet, W.C.

клозет|ный, *adj.* of ~; ~ная бумага toilet paper.

клок, а, *pl.* **клочья, клочьев** *and* ~й, ~ов, *m.* 1. rag, shred; разорвать в клочья to tear to shreds, tatters. 2. tuft; к. сена wisp of hay; к. шерсти flock.

клокот, а, *no pl.*, *m.* bubbling; gurgling.

клоко|тать, чу, ~чешь, *impf.* to bubble; to gurgle; to boil up (*also fig.*); в нём всё ~тало от гнева he was seething with rage.

клон|ить, ю, ~ишь, *impf.* 1. to bend; to incline; (*impers.*) лодку ~ило на бок the boat was heeling; старика уже ~ило ко сну the old man was already nodding. 2. (*fig.*, *coll.*) to lead (*conversation*); куда ты ~ишь? what are you driving at?

клон|иться, юсь, ~ишься, *impf.* 1. to bow, bend (*intrans.*). 2. (к; *fig.*) to be nearing;

to be leading up (to), be heading (for); день ~ился к вечеру the day was declining; дело ~ится к развязке the affair is coming to a head; к чему это ~ится? what is it leading up to?

клоп, а, *m.* 1. bug. 2. (*fig.*, *coll.*; *in addressing a child*) kid.

клоповник, а, *m.* (*coll.*) bug-infested place.

клоп|овый, *adj.* of ~.

клопомор, а, *m.* insecticide.

клоун, а, *m.* clown.

клоунад|а, ы, *f.* clownery, clowning.

клоун|ский, *adj.* of ~; к. колпак fool's cap.

клох|тать, чу, ~чешь, *impf.* (*coll.*) to cluck.

клочковат|ый (~, ~а), *adj.* 1. tufted, shaggy. 2. patchy, scrappy.

клоч|ок, ка, *m. dim.* of клок; разорвать в ~ки to tear to shreds, tatters; к. бумаги scrap of paper; к. земли plot of land; к. лазури среди облаков a patch of blue sky between the clouds.

клуб¹, а, *m.* 1. club. 2. club-house; офицерский к. officers' mess.

клуб², а, *pl.* ~ы, ~ов, *m.* puff; ~ы пыли clouds of dust.

клуб|ень, ня, *m.* (*bot.*) tuber.

клуб|ить, ит, *impf.* to blow up, puff out; к. пыль to raise clouds of dust.

клуб|иться, ится, *impf.* to swirl; to curl, wreathe.

клубневой, *adj.* (*bot.*) tuberose.

клубнеплод|ы, ов, *sing.* ~, ~а, *m.* (*bot.*, *agric.*) root crops, tuber crops.

клубник|а, и, *f.* 1. (cultivated) strawberry. 2. (*collect.*) (cultivated) strawberries.

клубни|чный, *adj.* of ~ка; ~чное варенье strawberry preserve.

клуб|ный, *adj.* of ~¹.

клуб|ок, ка, *m.* 1. ball; свернуться ~ком, в к. to roll oneself up into a ball. 2. (*fig.*) tangle, mass; к. интриг network of intrigue; к. противоречий mass of contradictions. 3. (*fig.*) lump (in the throat); слёзы у неё подступили ~ком к горлу a lump rose in her throat.

клумб|а, ы, *f.* (flower-)bed.

клупп, а, *m.* (*tech.*) die-stock, screw-stock.

клуш|а, и, *f.* 1. (*dial.*) broody hen. 2. lesser black-backed gull.

клык, а, *m.* 1. canine (tooth). 2. fang; tusk.

клюв, а, *m.* beak; bill.

клюз, а, *m.* (*naut.*) hawse-hole.

клюк|а, и, *f.* walking-stick.

клюк|ать, аю, *impf.* of ~нуть.

клюкв|а, ы, *f.* cranberry (*Oxycoccus palustris*); (*coll.*) вот так к.! here's a pretty kettle of fish!; развесистая к. myth, fable (*of credulous travellers' fabrications*).

клюкв|енный, *adj.* of ~а; к. кисель cranberry jelly; к. морс cranberry water.

клю́к|нуть, ну, нешь, *pf.* (*of* ~ать) (*coll.*) to take a drop.

клю́н|уть, у, ешь, *pf. of* клева́ть.

ключ¹, á, *m.* 1. (*in var. senses*) key; clue; запере́ть на к. to lock; ráечный к. spanner, wrench; францу́зский к. monkey-wrench; к. к ши́фру key to a cipher; (*mil.*) к. ме́стности key point. 2. (*archit.*) keystone. 3. (*mus.*) key, clef; басо́вый к. bass clef; скрипи́чный к. treble clef.

ключ², á, *m.* spring; source; кипе́ть ~о́м to bubble over; бить ~о́м to spout, jet; (*fig.*) to be in full swing.

ключа́р|ь, я́, *m.* (*eccl.*) sacrist.

ключ|ево́й¹, *adj. of* ~¹; ~евы́е о́трасли промы́шленности key industries; (*mil.*) ~евы́е пози́ции key positions; (*mus.*) к. знак clef.

ключ|ево́й², *adj. of* ~²; ~ева́я вода́ spring water.

ключи́ц|а, ы, *f.* (*anat.*) clavicle, collar-bone.

клю́чник, а, *m.* (*obs.*) steward.

клю́чниц|а, ы, *f.* (*obs.*) housekeeper.

клю́шк|а, и, *f.* (*sport*) (golf-)club; (hockey) stick; (*coll.*) walking-stick.

кл|юю, юёшь, *see* ~ева́ть.

кля́кс|а, ы, *f.* blot, smudge.

кля́|ну́, нёшь, *see* ~сть.

кля́нч|ить, у, ишь, *impf.* (у) (*coll.*) to beg (of).

кляп, а, *m.* gag; засу́нуть к. в рот (+*d.*) to gag.

кля́|сть, ну́, нёшь, *past* ~л, ~ла́, ~ло, *impf.* to curse.

кля́|сться, ну́сь, нёшься, *past* ~лся, ~ла́сь, *impf.* (*of* по~) (в+*p.*, +*inf. or* +что) to swear, vow; к. в ве́рности to vow fidelity; к. отомсти́ть to vow vengeance; к. че́стью to swear on one's honour.

кля́тв|а, ы, *f.* oath, vow; ло́жная к. perjury; дать ~у to take an oath.

кля́тв|енный, *adj. of* ~а; дать ~енное обеща́ние to promise on oath.

клятвопреступле́ни|е, я, *n.* perjury.

клятвопресту́пник, а, *m.* perjurer.

кля́уз|а, ы, *f.* 1. (*coll.*) slander, scandal; tale-bearing. 2. (*leg.*; *obs.*) barratry; затева́ть ~у to institute vexatious litigation.

кля́узник, а, *m.* (*coll.*) scandalmonger; tale-bearer.

кля́узнича|ть, ю, *impf.* (*of* на~) (*coll.*) to spread slander; to bear tales.

кля́узн|ый, *adj.* (*coll.*) captious, pettifogging; случи́лось ~ое де́ло a tiresome thing happened.

кля́ч|а, и, *f.* (*pejor.*; *of horse*) jade.

кнел|ь, и, *f.* (*collect.*; *cul.*) quenelles.

кнехт, а, *m.* (*naut.*) bollard, bitts.

кни́г|а, и, *f.* 1. book; тебе́ и ~и в ру́ки (*coll.*) you know best. 2. number (*of a journal, magazine*).

книгове́дени|е, я, *n.* bibliography.

книговеде́ни|е, я, *n.* book-keeping.

книгое́д, а, *m.* (*zool. and fig.*) bookworm.

книгоизда́тел|ь, я, *m.* publisher.

книгоизда́тельский, *adj.* publishing.

книгоизда́тельств|о, а, *n.* 1. publishing-house. 2. publishing.

книголю́б, а, *m.* bibliophile.

книгоно́ш|а, и, *m. and f.* book-pedlar, colporteur.

книгопеча́тани|е, я, *n.* (book-)printing.

книгопеча́т|ный, *adj. of* ~ание; к. стано́к printing-press.

книготорго́в|ец, ца, *m.* bookseller.

книготорго́вл|я, и, *f.* 1. book trade. 2. bookshop.

книгохрани́лищ|е, а, *n.* 1. library. 2. book-stack.

кни́жечк|а, и, *f.* booklet.

кни́жк|а¹, и, *f.* 1. *dim. of* кни́га; записна́я к. notebook. 2. (*document*) book, card; забо́рная к. ration book; расчётная к. pay-book; че́ковая к. cheque-book. 3. (сберега́тельная) к. savings-bank book; положи́ть де́ньги на ~у to deposit money at a savings-bank; на кни́жку on credit.

кни́жк|а², и, *f.* (*zool.*) third stomach (*of ruminants*).

кни́жник, а, *m.* 1. (*bibl.*) scribe. 2. bibliophile. 3. bookseller.

кни́жн|ый, *adj.* 1. *adj. of* кни́га; к. знак book-plate; ~ая по́лка bookshelf; к. шкаф bookcase. 2. bookish, abstract; pedantic; к. стиль pedantic style; ~ая учёность book-learning; к. червь bookworm.

кни́зу, *adv.* downwards.

кни́ксен, а, *m.* curts(e)y.

кни́ц|а, ы, *f.* (*tech.*, *naut.*) knee, gusset.

кно́пк|а, и, *f.* 1. drawing-pin; прикрепи́ть ~ой to pin. 2. press-button (*fastener*). 3. (*electr.*) button; knob; нажа́ть все ~и (*fig.*, *coll.*) to pull wires, do all in one's power.

кно́п|очный, *adj. of* ~ка.

кнут, á, *m.* whip; (*hist.*) knout; щёлкать ~о́м to crack a whip.

кнутови́щ|е, а, *n.* whip-handle.

княги́н|я, и, *f.* princess (*wife of prince*).

княже́ни|е, я, *n.* (*hist.*) reign.

кня́жеств|о, а, *n.* principality.

кня́ж|ить, у, ишь, *impf.* (*hist.*) to reign.

кня́жич, а, *m.* prince (*prince's unmarried son*).

княж|на́, ны́, *g. pl.* ~о́н, *f.* princess (*prince's unmarried daughter*).

княз|ёк, ька́, *m.* 1. (*coll.*) princeling. 2. (*tech.*) roof-ridge.

княз|ь, я, *pl.* ~ья́, ~е́й, *m.* prince; вели́кий к. (*in medieval Russia*) grand prince; (*in tsarist Russia*) grand duke.

ко, *see* к.

коагуля́ци|я, и, *f.* coagulation.

коалиц|ио́нный, *adj. of* ~ия.

коали́ци|я, и, *f.* (*polit.*) coalition.

ко́бальт, а, *m.* (*chem.*) cobalt.

ко́бальт|овый, *adj. of* ~; ~овая кра́ска cobalt; ~овое стекло́ smalt.

кобе́л|ь, я́, *m.* (male) dog.

кобе́н|иться, юсь, ишься, *impf.* (*coll.*) to be capricious; to make faces.

ко́бз|а́, ~ы́, *f.* kobza (*Ukrainian mus. instrument similar to guitar*).

кобза́р|ь, я́, *m.* kobza-player.

ко́бр|а, ы, *f.* cobra.

кобур|а́, ы́, *f.* holster.

ко́бчик, а, *m.* (*orn.*) merlin.

кобы́л|а¹, ы, *f.* mare.

кобы́л|а², ы, *f.* 1. (*hist.*) punishment-bench. 2. vaulting-horse.

кобы́л|ий, *adj. of* ~а¹.

кобы́лк|а¹, и, *f.* filly.

кобы́лк|а², и, *f.* bridge (*of stringed instruments*).

ко́ваный, *adj.* 1. forged; hammered. 2. (*fig.*) terse.

кова́р|ный (~ен, ~на), *adj.* insidious, crafty; perfidious.

кова́рств|о, а, *n.* insidiousness, craftiness; perfidy.

кова́ть, кую́, куёшь, *impf.* 1. (*pf.* вы́~) to forge (*also fig.*); to hammer (*iron*); к. побе́ду to forge victory; куй желе́зо, пока́ горячо́ (*prov.*) strike while the iron is hot. 2. (*pf.* под~) to shoe (*horses*).

ковбо́|й, я, *m.* cowboy.

ковбо́йк|а, и, *f.* (*coll.*) 1. cowboy hat. 2. cowboy shirt.

ков|ёр, ра́, *m.* carpet; rug; к.-самолёт the magic carpet.

кове́рка|ть, ю, *impf.* (*of* ис~) 1. to spoil, ruin (*concr. and abstr.*). 2. (*fig.*) to distort; to mangle, mispronounce; к. чужу́ю мысль to distort someone else's ideas; к. слова́ to mangle words; он ~ет францу́зский язы́к he murders the French language.

коверко́т, а, *m.* covert coat.

ко́вк|а, и, *f.* 1. forging. 2. shoeing.

ко́в|кий (~ок, ~ка́, ~ко), *adj.* malleable, ductile.

ко́вкост|ь, и, *f.* malleability, ductility.

коври́г|а, и, *f.* loaf.

коври́жк|а, и, *f.* gingerbread; ни за каки́е ~и (*coll.*) not for the world.

ко́врик, а, *m.* rug.

ковче́г, а, *m.* 1. ark; Но́ев к. Noah's ark. 2. (*eccl.*) shrine.

ковш, а́, *m.* 1. scoop, ladle, dipper. 2. (*tech.*) bucket.

ко́в|ы, ~, *no sing.* (*obs.*) snare, trap; toils; стро́ить к. кому́-н. to lay a trap for someone.

ковы́л|ь, я́, *m.* (*bot.*) feather-grass.

ковыля́|ть, ю, *impf.* (*coll.*) to hobble; to stump; (*of child*) to toddle.

ковырн|у́ть, у́, нёшь, *pf. of* ~я́ть.

ковыр|я́ть, я́ю, *impf.* (*of* ~ну́ть) (*coll.*) 1. to dig into; (в+*p.*) to pick (at); к. в зуба́х to pick one's teeth. 2. to tinker (up), potter.

ковыря́|ться, юсь, *impf.* (*coll.*) 1. (в+*p.*) to rummage (in). 2. to tinker.

когда́¹, *adv.* 1. (*interrog. and relat.*) when; (*coll.*) есть к.! there's no time for it!; есть к. мне болта́ть! I've no time for talk! 2. к. (бы) ни whenever; к. бы вы ни пришли́, к. (вы) ни придёте whenever you come. 3. (*coll.*) к...., к. sometimes . . ., sometimes; я занима́юсь к. у́тром, к. ве́чером sometimes I work in the morning, sometimes in the evening. 4. (*coll.*) к. как it depends. 5. (*coll.*) = к.-н.

когда́², *conj.* 1. when; while, as; я её встре́тил, к. шёл домо́й I met her as I was going home. 2. (*coll.*) if; к. так, согла́сен с тобо́й if that is the case, I agree.

когда́-либо, *adv.* = когда́-нибудь.

когда́-нибудь, *adv.* 1. (*in future*) some time, some day. 2. ever; вы бы́ли к.-н. в Кита́е? have you ever been in China?

когда́-то, *adv.* 1. (*in past*) once; some time; formerly. 2. (*in future*) some day (*indefinitely distant*); к.-то ещё бу́дет тако́й прия́тный ве́чер it will be a long time before we have such a pleasant evening again.

кого́, *a. and g. of* кто.

кого́рт|а, ы, *f.* cohort.

ко́г|оть, тя, *pl.* ~ти, ~те́й, *m.* claw; talon; показа́ть свои́ ~ти (*fig.*) to show one's teeth; попа́сть в ~ти (к кому́-н.) to fall into the clutches (of someone).

когти́ст|ый (~, ~а), *adj.* sharp-clawed.

когти́т|ь, ~, *impf.* (*dial.*) to claw to pieces, tear with claws.

код, а, *m.* code; телегра́фный к. cable code; по ~у in code.

ко́д|а, ы, *f.* (*mus.*) coda.

коде́ин, а, *m.* (*pharm.*) codeine.

ко́декс, а, *m.* 1. (*leg. and fig.*) code; мора́льный к. moral code; уголо́вный к. criminal code. 2. (*lit.*) codex.

кодифика́ци|я, и, *f.* codification.

кодифици́р|овать, ую, *impf. and pf.* (*leg.*) to codify.

ко́е-где́ (*and* кой-где́), *adv.* here and there, in places.

ко́е-ка́к (*and* кой-ка́к), *adv.* (*coll.*) 1. anyhow (*badly, carelessly*). 2. somehow (or other), just (*with great difficulty*); к.-к. мы доплы́ли до того́ бе́рега somehow we managed to swim to the other side.

ко́е-како́й (*and* кой-како́й), *pron.* some.

ко́е-кто́ (*and* кой-кто́), ко́е-кого́, *pron.* somebody; some people.

ко́ечный, *adj. of* ко́йка; к. больно́й in--patient.

ко́е-что́ (*and* кой-что́), ко́е-чего́, *pron.* something; a little.

ко́ж|а, и, *f.* 1. skin; hide; (*anat.*) cutis; гуси́ная к. goose-flesh; (*fig., coll.*) из ~и (вон) ле́зть to go all out, do one's utmost; к. да ко́сти skin and bone. 2. leather; свина́я к. pig-skin; теля́чья к. calf. 3. peel, rind; (*bot.*) epidermis.

кожа́н¹, á, *m.* (*obs.*) leather coat.

кожа́н², á, *m.* large bat.

ко́жанк|а, и, *f.* (*coll.*) leather jacket, jerkin.

ко́жаный, *adj.* leather(n).

кожеве́нный, *adj.* leather; leather-dressing, tanning; к. заво́д tannery; к. това́р leather goods.

коже́вник, а, *m.* currier, leather-dresser, tanner.

кожими́т, а, *m.* imitation leather, leatherette.

ко́жиц|а, ы, *f.* 1. thin skin, film, pellicle; к. колбасы́ sausage-skin. 2. peel, skin (*of fruit*).

ко́жник, а, *m.* (*coll.*) dermatologist.

ко́жный, *adj.* skin; (*med.*) cutaneous.

кожур|а́, ы́, *f.* rind, peel, skin (*of fruit*).

кожу́х, á, *m.* 1. leather jacket, sheepskin jacket. 2. (*tech.*) housing, casing, jacket; к. гребно́го колеса́ paddle-box.

коз|а́, ы́, *pl.* ~ы, *f.* 1. goat. 2. she-goat. 3. (*coll.*) tomboy.

коз|ёл, лá, *m.* he-goat; к. отпуще́ния scapegoat; от него́ как от ~лá молока́ he is good for nothing.

козеро́г, а, *m.* 1. (*zool.*) wild (mountain) goat, ibex. 2. К. (*astron.*) Capricorn.

козётк|а, и, *f.* (*coll.*) settee.

ко́з|ий, *adj. of* ~á; к. пасту́х goatherd; ~ья но́жка (*med.*) molar forceps; (*coll.*) *denotes home-made cigarette.*

козл|ёнок, ёнка, *pl.* ~я́та, ~я́т, *m.* kid.

коз|ли́ный, *adj. of* ~ёл; ~ли́ная боро́дка goatee; к. го́лос reedy voice.

козло́вый, *adj.* goatskin.

ко́з|лы, ел, лам, *no sing.* 1. (coach-)box. 2. trestle(s); saw-horse. 3. (*mil.*) соста́вить винто́вки в к. to pile arms.

козл|я́та, я́т, *pl. of* ~ёнок.

ко́зн|и, ей, *sing.* (*rare*) ~ь, ~и, *f.* (*obs.*) machinations, intrigues; snare.

козово́д, а, *m.* goat breeder.

козово́дств|о, а, *n.* goat-breeding.

козодо́|й, я, *m.* (*orn.*) nightjar, goatsucker.

козу́л|я, и, *f.* roe(buck).

козыр|ёк, ька́, *m.* 1. (cap) peak; взять под к. (+*d.*) to salute. 2. (*mil.*) head cover (*in trenches*).

козыр|но́й, *adj. of* ко́зырь.

козыр|ну́ть, ну́, нёшь, *pf. of* ~я́ть.

ко́зыр|ь, я, *pl.* ~и, ~е́й, *m.* 1. (*cards and fig.*) trump; объяви́ть ~я to call one's hand; откры́ть свои́ ~и (*fig.*) to lay one's cards on the table; покры́ть ~ем to trump; ходи́ть с ~я to lead trumps; (*fig.*) to play a trump card; гла́вный к. (one's) trump card. 2. (*coll.*) card, swell; ходи́ть ~ем to swagger.

козыр|я́ть¹, я́ю, *impf.* (*of* ~ну́ть) (*coll.*) 1. (*cards*) to lead trumps, play a trump; (*fig.*) to play one's trump card. 2. (+*i.*) to show off.

козыр|я́ть², я́ю, *impf.* (*of* ~ну́ть) (+*d.*; *coll.*) to salute.

козя́вк|а, и, *f.* (*coll.*) small insect.

кой, *interrog. and relat. pron.* (*obs.*) which; до ко́их пор? how long?; ни в ко́ем слу́чае on no account; (*coll.*) на к. чорт? why in the world, what the devil for?

ко́йк|а, и, *f.* 1. berth, bunk (*on board ship*). 2. bed (*in hospital*).

кок, а, *m.* 1. (ship's) cook. 2. quiff.

ко́к|а, и, *f.* (*bot.*) coca.

кока́ин, а, *m.* cocaine.

кокаини́зм, а, *m.* cocainism.

кокаини́ст, а, *m.* cocaine addict.

кока́рд|а, ы, *f.* cockade.

ко́к|ать, аю, *impf.* (*of* ~нуть) (*coll.*) to crack, break.

коке́тк|а, и, *f.* coquette.

коке́тлив|ый (~, ~а), *adj.* coquettish.

коке́тнича|ть, ю, *impf.* 1. (с+*i.*) to coquet(te), flirt (with). 2. (+*i.*) to show off, flaunt.

коке́тств|о, а, *n.* coquetry.

коки́л|ь, я, *m.* (*tech.*) chill mould.

коки́льн|ый, *adj.*; ~ое литьё (*tech.*) chill casting.

кокк, а, *m.* (*med.*) coccus.

коклю́ш, а, *m.* whooping-cough.

коклю́шк|а, и, *f.* bobbin.

ко́к|нуть, ну, нешь, *pf. of* ~ать.

ко́кон, а, *m.* cocoon.

коко́с, а, *m.* 1. coco(-tree). 2. coco-nut.

коко́с|овый, *adj. of* ~; ~овое волокно́ coir; ~овое ма́сло coco-nut oil; к. оре́х coco--nut; ~овая па́льма coco(-tree), coco-nut tree.

коко́тк|а, и, *f.* courtesan, cocotte.

коко́шник, а, *m.* kokoshnik (*Russian peasant woman's head-dress*).

кокс, а, *m.* coke; вы́жиг ~а (*tech.*) coke firing.

коксова́льн|ый, *adj.* (*tech.*) coking; ~ая печь coke oven.

кокс|ова́ть, у́ю, *impf.* (*tech.*) to coke.

кокс|ова́ться, у́юсь, *impf.* (*tech.*) to coke (*intrans.*).

ко́кс|овый, *adj. of* ~; ~овая печь coke oven; ~овое число́ coking value.

кокс|у́ющийся, *pres. part. act. of* ~ова́ться *and adj.*; к. у́голь coking coal.

кокте́йл|ь, я, *m.* cocktail; cocktail party.

кол, á, *m.* **1.** (*pl.* ~ья́, ~ье́в) stake, picket; посади́ть на́ к. to impale; (*coll.*) стоя́ть ~о́м в го́рле to stick in one's throat; ему́ хоть к. на голове́ теши́ he is very pig-headed; у него́ нет ни ~á ни двора́ he has neither house nor home. **2.** (*pl.* ~ы́, ~о́в) (*lowest mark in school*) one.

ко́лб|а, ы, *f.* (*chem.*) retort.

колбас|á, ы́, *pl.* ~ы́, *f.* sausage.

колба́сник, а, *m.* sausage-maker; pork butcher.

колба́с|ный, *adj. of* ~á; к. яд ptomaine.

колго́т|ки, ок, *no sing.* tights.

колдо́бин|а, ы, *f.* (*dial.*) **1.** rut, pothole (*in road*). **2.** deep place (*in lake, river, etc.*).

колд|ова́ть, у́ю, *impf.* to practise witchcraft.

колдовско́й, *adj.* magical; (*fig.*) magical, bewitching.

колдовств|о́, á, *n.* witchcraft, sorcery, magic.

колдо́говор, а, *m.* (*abbr. of* коллекти́вный догово́р) collective agreement.

колду́н, á, *m.* sorcerer, magician, wizard.

колду́н|ья, ьи, *g. pl.* ~ий, *f.* witch, sorceress.

колеба́ни|е, я, *n.* **1.** (*phys.*) oscillation, vibration; к. ма́ятника swing of the pendulum. **2.** fluctuation, variation; к. ку́рса (*fin.*) stock exchange fluctuations, fluctuations in the rate of exchange. **3.** (*fig.*) hesitation; wavering, vacillation.

колеба́тельный, *adj.* (*tech.*) oscillatory, vibratory.

колеб|а́ть, ~лю, ~лешь, *impf.* (*of* по~) to shake; (*fig.*) к. обще́ственные усто́и to shake the foundations of society.

колеб|а́ться, ~лю́сь, ~лешься, *impf.* (*of* по~) **1.** to shake to and fro, sway; (*phys.*) to oscillate. **2.** to fluctuate, vary. **3.** (*fig.*) to hesitate; to waver, vacillate.

коле́нк|а, и, f. (*coll.*) knee.

коленко́р, а, *m.* (*text.*) calico; (*coll.*) э́то совсе́м друго́й к. that's quite another matter.

коленко́р|овый, *adj. of* ~.

коле́н|ный, *adj. of* ~o; (*anat.*) к. суста́в knee-joint; ~ная ча́шка patella, knee-cap.

коле́н|о, а, *n.* **1.** (*pl.* ~и, ~ей, ~ям) knee; преклони́ть ~и to genuflect; стать на ~и (пе́ред) to kneel (to); стоя́ть на ~ях to be kneeling, be on one's knees; по к., по ~и knee-deep, up to one's knees; (*coll.*) ему́ мо́ре по к. he doesn't care a damn for anything; поста́вить кого́-н. на ~и to bring someone to his knees. **2.** (*pl. only*; ~и, ~ей, ~ям) lap; сиде́ть у кого́-н. на ~ях to sit

on someone's lap. **3.** (*pl.* ~ья, ~ьев) (*tech.*) knee, joint; (*bot.*) joint, node; к. трубы́ knee pipe, elbow pipe. **4.** (*pl.* ~а, ~, ~ам) bend (*of river, etc.*). **5.** (*pl.* ~а, ~, ~ам) (*obs.*) generation; ро́дственники до пя́того ~а cousins five times removed; двена́дцать ~ израи́левых the twelve tribes of Israel. **6.** (*pl.* ~а, ~, ~ам) (*coll.*) figure (*in dance, song, etc.*); выде́лывать к. to execute a figure; (*pejor.*) вы́кинуть к. to play a trick.

коленопреклоне́ни|е, я, *n.* genuflection.

коле́н|це, ца, g. pl. ~ец, *n.* (*coll.*) вы́кинуть к. to play a trick.

коле́нчат|ый, *adj.* (*tech.*) elbow-shaped, cranked; к. вал crankshaft; к. рыча́г toggle lever, bell crank; ~ая труба́ knee pipe.

ко́лер¹, а, *m.* (*art*) colour, shade.

ко́лер², а, *m.* staggers (*disease of horses*).

колёсик|о, а, *n.* **1.** *dim. of* колесо́. **2.** castor.

коле|си́ть, шу́, си́шь, *impf.* (*coll.*) **1.** to go in a roundabout way. **2.** to go all over, travel about.

коле́сник, а, *m.* wheelwright.

колесни́ц|а, ы, *f.* chariot; погреба́льная к. hearse; триумфа́льная к. triumphal car.

колёс|ный, *adj.* **1.** *adj. of* ~о́. **2.** wheeled, on wheels.

колес|о́, á, *pl.* ~а, *n.* wheel; гребно́е к. paddle-wheel; запасно́е к. spare wheel; зубча́тое к. cog-wheel; махово́е к. fly-wheel; рулево́е к. driving wheel; цепно́е к. sprocket; грудь ~о́м (*fig.*) well-developed chest; *as adv.* with chest well out; вста́вить кому́-н. па́лки в ~а to put a spoke in someone's wheel; кружи́ться, как бе́лка в ~е́ to run round in small circles; но́ги ~о́м bandy legs; ходи́ть ~о́м to turn somersaults.

колесова́ни|е, я, *n.* breaking on the wheel.

колес|ова́ть, у́ю, *impf. and pf.* to break on the wheel.

коле́ч|ко, ка, *pl.* ~ки, ~ек, ~кам, *n.* (*coll.*) ringlet.

коле|я́, и́, f. **1.** rut; (*fig.*) войти́ в ~ю́ to settle down (again); вы́битый из ~й unsettled. **2.** (*railways*) track; gauge.

ко́ли (and коль) (*obs. or dial.*) if; (*coll.*) к. на то пошло́ while we are about it; коль ско́ро if, as soon as.

коли́бри, *indecl.*, *m. and f.* (*orn.*) humming-bird.

ко́лик|и, ~, *no sing.* (*med.*) colic; смея́ться до ~ (*coll.*) to make oneself ill with laughing.

колир|ова́ть, у́ю, *impf.* (*hort.*) to graft.

колиро́вк|а, и, f. (*hort.*) grafting.

коли́т, а, *m.* (*med.*) colitis.

коли́чественн|ый, *adj.* quantitative; ~ое числи́тельное cardinal number.

коли́честв|о, а, *n.* quantity, amount; number.

ко́лк|а, и, *f.* chopping.

кол|кий[1] (~ок, ~ка́, ~ко), *adj.* easily split.

кол|кий[2] (~ок, ~ка́, ~ко), *adj.* prickly; (*fig.*) sharp, biting, caustic.

ко́лкост|ь, и, *f.* 1. (*fig.*) sharpness. 2. sharp, caustic remark; говори́ть ~и to make sharp remarks.

коллаборациони́ст, а, *m.* (*polit.*; *pejor.*) colborator.

коллаборациони́ст|ский, *adj.* of ~.

колле́г|а, и, *m.* colleague.

коллегиа́л|ьный (~ен, ~ьна), *adj.* joint, collective; corporate; ~ьное реше́ние collective decision.

колле́ги|я, и, *f.* 1. board, collegium. 2. college; к. адвока́тов, к. правозасту́пников the Bar.

колле́дж, а, *m.* college.

колле́жский, *adj.* (*in titles of officials in tsarist Russia*) collegiate; к. сове́тник collegiate councillor.

коллекти́в, а, *m.* group, body; (*in many phrases does not require separate translation*) к. машини́стов engine-drivers; нау́чный к. (the) scientists; парти́йный к. Party members.

коллективиза́ци|я, и, *f.* collectivization.

коллективизи́р|овать, ую, *impf. and pf.* to collectivize.

коллективи́зм, а, *m.* collectivism.

коллективи́ст, а, *m.* collectivist.

коллекти́вн|ый, *adj.* collective; joint; ~ое владе́ние joint ownership; ~ое хозя́йство collective farm; ~ое руково́дство (*polit.*) collective leadership (*as opp. to one-man rule*).

колле́ктор, а, *m.* 1. (*electr.*) commutator. 2. (*in sewage system*) manifold. 3. библиоте́чный к. central library.

коллекционе́р, а, *m.* collector.

коллекциони́р|овать, ую, *impf.* to collect.

колле́кци|я, и, *f.* collection.

колли́зи|я, и, *f.* clash, conflict.

коллю́ди|й, я, *m.* (*chem.*) collodion.

коллю́ид, а, *m.* (*chem.*) colloid.

коллоида́льный, *adj.* (*chem.*) colloidal.

колло́идный, *adj.* (*chem.*) colloidal.

колло́квиум, а, *m.* oral examination.

колоб|о́к, ка́, *m.* small round loaf.

колобро́|дить, жу, дишь, *impf.* (*coll.*) 1. to roam, wander; to loaf. 2. to make a noise; to get up to mischief.

коловоро́т, а, *m.* (*tech.*) brace.

коловра́тност|ь, и, *f.* (*obs.*) mutability, inconstancy.

коловра́т|ный (~ен, ~на), *adj.* 1. rotary. 2. (*fig., obs.*) inconstant, changeable.

коловраще́ни|е, я, *n.* (*obs.*) rotation.

коло́д|а[1], ы, *f.* 1. block, log. 2. (water-) trough.

коло́д|а[2], ы, *f.* pack (*of cards*).

коло́де|зный, *adj.* of ~ц.

коло́де|зь, зя, *m.* (*obs.*) = ~ц.

коло́д|ец, ца, *m.* 1. well. 2. (*tech.*) shaft.

коло́дк|а, и, *f.* 1. boot-tree; last. 2. (*tech.*) shoe. 3. (*pl.*; *hist.*) stocks; наби́ть ~и на́ ноги кому́-н. to put someone in stocks.

коло́дник, а, *m.* convict (*in stocks*).

кол|о́к, ка́, *m.* (*mus.*) peg.

ко́локол, а, *pl.* ~а́, ~о́в, *m.* bell.

колоко́льный, *adj.* of ко́локол; к. звон peal, chime.

колоко́л|ьня, ьни, *g. pl.* ~ен, *f.* steeple, bell-tower, church-tower; (*coll.*) смотре́ть со свое́й ~ьни на что-н. to take a narrow, parochial view of something.

колоко́льчик, а, *m.* 1. small bell; handbell. 2. (*bot.*) bluebell.

ко́ломаз|ь, и, *f.* wheel grease.

колониа́льный, *adj.* colonial; к. магази́н (*obs.*) grocer's shop.

колониза́тор, а, *m.* colonizer.

колониза́ци|я, и, *f.* colonization.

колониз|ова́ть, у́ю, *impf. and pf.* to colonize.

колони́ст, а, *m.* colonist.

коло́ни|я, и, *f.* (*in various senses*) colony; settlement.

коло́нк|а, и, *f.* 1. geyser. 2. (*street*) water fountain. 3. бензи́новая к. petrol pump. 4. (*typ.*) column; газе́тная полоса́ в шесть коло́нок newspaper page with six columns.

коло́нн|а, ы, *f.* column; к. цифр column of figures; (*mil.*) та́нковая к. tank column; похо́дная к. column of route; со́мкнутая к. close column; к. по три column of threes.

колонна́д|а, ы, *f.* colonnade.

коло́нн|ый, *adj.* columned.

колон|о́к, ка́, *m.* (*zool.*) Siberian polecat.

колонти́тул, а, *m.* (*typ.*) running title.

колонци́фр|а, ы, *f.* (*typ.*) page number.

колора́дский, *adj.*; к. жук Colorado beetle.

колорату́р|а, ы, *f.* (*mus.*) coloratura.

колорату́р|ный, *adj.* of ~а.

колори́ст, а, *m.* (*art*) colourist.

колори́т, а, *m.* colouring, colour; (*fig.*) ме́стный к. local colour; он прида́л расска́зу о встре́че я́ркий к. he painted a glowing picture of the encounter.

колори́т|ный (~ен, ~на), *adj.* colourful, picturesque, graphic (*also fig.*); язы́к у него́ о́чень к. his language is highly coloured.

ко́лос, а, *pl.* ~ья, ~ьев, *m.* (*agric.*) ear, spike.

колоси́ст|ый (~, ~а), *adj.* (*agric.*) full of ears.

коло|си́ться, си́тся, *impf.* (*agric.*) to form ears.

колосни́к, а́, *m.* 1. furnace-bar, grate-bar; (*pl.*) fire-bars. 2. (*pl.*; *theatr.*) flies; grid-iron.

коло́сс, а, *m.* colossus.

колосса́льный, *adj.* colossal.

коло|ти́ть, чу́, ~ти́шь, *impf.* (*of* поколо-
ти́ть) **1.** (по+*d.*, в+*a.*) to strike (on); to
batter (on), pound (on); к. в дверь to bang
on the door. **2.** (*coll.*) to thrash, drub.
3. (*impf. only*) к. лён to scutch flax. **4.** (*impf.
only*) (*coll.*) to break, smash. **5.** (*impf. only*)
(*coll.*) to shake; (*impers.*) его́ ~ти́ла лихо-
ра́дка he was shaking with fever.

коло|ти́ться, чу́сь, ~ти́шься, *impf.* (*of* по-
коло́ти́ться) **1.** (о+*a.*) to beat (against);
to strike (against); к. голово́й об сте́ну to
beat one's head against a wall. **2.** (*impf.
only*) (*coll.*) to pound; to shake; се́рдце у неё
~ти́лось her heart was pounding. **3.** *pass.
of* ~ти́ть.

колоту́шк|а, и, *f.* **1.** (*coll.*) punch. **2.** beetle
(*tech.*) **3.** (*wooden*) rattle (*used by night
watchman*).

ко́лот|ый¹ (~, ~а), *p.p.p. of* ~ь¹ *and adj.* к.
са́хар chipped sugar.

ко́лот|ый² (~, ~а), *p.p.p. of* ~ь² *and adj.* ~ая
ра́на stab.

кол|о́ть¹, ю́, ~ешь, *impf.* (*of* расколо́ть) to
break, chop, split; к. дрова́ to chop wood;
к. оре́хи to crack nuts.

кол|о́ть², ю́, ~ешь, *impf.* (*of* заколо́ть) **1.** to
prick; (*impers.*) у меня́ ~ет в боку́ I have a
stitch in my side. **2.** to stab. **3.** to slaughter
(*cattle*). **4.** (*fig.*) to sting, taunt; к. глаза́
кому́-н. (+*i.*) to cast a thing in someone's
teeth; пра́вда глаза́ ~ет (*prov.*) home
truths are unpalatable.

ко́лоть|е, я (*and* коло́ть|ё, я), *n.* (*coll.*) stitch.

кол|о́ться¹, ю́сь, ~ешься, *impf., pass. of
~*о́ть¹.

кол|о́ться², ю́сь, ~ешься, *impf.* to prick
(*intrans.*).

ко́лош|а, и, *f.* (*tech.*) blast furnace charge.

колошма́|тить, чу, тишь, *impf.* (*of* отколош-
ма́тить) (*coll.*) to beat, thrash.

колошни́к, а́, *m.* (*tech.*) furnace throat.

колошник|о́вый, *adj. of* ~; к. газ blast fur-
nace gas.

колпа́к, а́, *m.* **1.** cap; ночно́й к. nightcap;
шутовско́й к. fool's cap. **2.** lamp-shade;
(*tech.*) cowl; бронево́й к. armoured hood;
стекля́нный к. bell-glass; (*fig., coll.*) жить
под стекля́нным ~о́м to live in the public
view, have no privacy; держа́ть под стек-
ля́нным ~о́м to keep in cotton-wool (= *to
treat as a child*). **3.** (*fig., coll.*) simpleton.

колпач|о́к, ка́, *m.* **1.** *dim. of* колпа́к. **2.** (gas)
mantle.

колту́н, а́, *m.* (*med.*) plica (polonica).

колумба́ри|й, я, *m.* columbarium.

колу́н, а́, *m.* (wood-)chopper, hatchet.

колупа́|ть, ю, *impf.* (*coll.*) to pick, scratch.

колхо́з, а, *m.* (*abbr. of* коллекти́вное хозя́й-
ство) collective farm.

колхо́зник, а, *m.* member of collective farm.

колхо́зн|ица, ицы, *f. of* ~ик.

колхо́з|ный, *adj. of* ~; ~ное строи́тельство
organization of collective farms; к. строй
collective farm system.

колча́н, а, *m.* quiver.

колчеда́н, а, *m.* (*min.*) pyrites.

колчено́гий, *adj.* (*coll.*) **1.** lame. **2.** rickety,
wobbly (*of furniture*).

колыбе́л|ь, и, *f.* cradle; (*fig.*) к. нау́ки the
cradle of learning; с ~и from the cradle; от
~и до моги́лы from the cradle to the grave.

колыбе́ль|ный, *adj. of* ~; ~ная пе́сня
lullaby.

колыма́г|а, и, *f.* (*obs.*) heavy, unwieldy
carriage; (*iron.*) wagon, 'bus.

колы|ха́ть, ~шу, ~шешь, *impf.* (*of* ~хну́ть)
to sway, rock.

колы|ха́ться, ~шется, *impf.* (*of* ~хну́ться)
to sway, heave; to flutter; to flicker.

колых|ну́ть(ся), ну́(сь), нёшь(ся), *pf. of*
~а́ть(ся).

ко́лыш|ек, ка, *m.* peg.

колы́|шу, шешь, *see* ~ха́ть.

коль, *see* ко́ли.

кольдкре́м, а, *m.* cold cream.

колье́, *indecl., n.* necklace.

кол|ьну́ть, ьну́, ьнёшь, *inst. pf. of* ~о́ть².

кольра́би, *indecl., f.* (*bot.*) kohlrabi.

кольт, а, *m.* colt (*pistol*).

кольц|ева́ть, у́ю, *impf.* **1.** (*of* закольцева́ть)
to girdle, ring-bark (*a tree*). **2.** (*of* окольце-
ва́ть) to ring (*bird's leg., etc.*).

кольцево́й, *adj.* annular; circular.

кольцеобра́з|ный (~ен, ~на), *adj.* ring-
-shaped.

кол|ьцо́, ьца́, *pl.* ~ьца, ~е́ц, ~ьцам, *n.* **1.**
ring; сверну́ться ~ьцо́м to coil up; годи́ч-
ное к. (*bot.*) ring; обруча́льное к. wedding
ring; трамва́йное к. circle, terminus (on
tram-route). **2.** (*tech.*) ring; collar; hoop.

ко́льчат|ый, *adj.* annulate(d); ~ые че́рви
(*zool.*) Annelida.

кольчу́г|а, и, *f.* shirt of mail, hauberk.

колю́ч|ий (~, ~а), *adj.* prickly; thorny;
(*fig.*) sharp, biting; ~ая и́згородь prickly
hedge; ~ая про́волока barbed wire; к.
язы́к sharp tongue.

колю́чк|а, и, *f.* (*coll.*) **1.** prickle; thorn; quill
(*of porcupine*). **2.** burr.

ко́люшк|а, и, *f.* (*fish*) stickleback.

ко́л|ющий, *pres. part. act. of* ~о́ть² *and adj.*
~ющая боль shooting pain.

коля́д|а, ы́, *f.* kolyada (*custom of house-to-
house Christmas carol-singing*).

коляд|ова́ть, у́ю, *impf.* to go round carol-
-singing.

коля́ск|а, и, *f.* **1.** carriage, barouche. **2.**
perambulator. **3.** (motor-cycle) side-car.

ком¹, а, *pl.* ~ья, ~ьев, *m.* lump; ball; clod;
сне́жный к. snow-ball; (*fig.*) к. в го́рле

lump in the throat; пе́рвый блин ∼ом (*prov.*) practice makes perfect.

ком², *p. of* кто.

ком-, *abbr. of* **1.** коммунисти́ческий. **2.** команди́р. **3.** кома́ндный.

-ком, *abbr. of* **1.** комите́т. **2.** комисса́р. **3.** комиссариа́т.

ко́м|а, ы, *f.* (*med.*) coma.

кома́нд|а, ы, *f.* **1.** (word of) command, order; пода́ть ∼у to give a command. **2.** command; приня́ть ∼у (над) to take command (of). **3.** (*mil.*) party, detachment, crew; (*naut.*) crew, ship's company; пожа́рная к. fire-brigade. **4.** (*sport*) team.

команди́р, а, *m.* (*mil.*) commander, commanding officer; (*naut.*) captain.

командир|ова́ть, у́ю, *impf. and pf.* to post; to dispatch, send on a mission.

командиро́вк|а, и, *f.* **1.** posting, dispatching (*on official business*). **2.** mission; (official business) trip; е́хать в ∼у to go on a mission; он в ∼е he is away on business, on a commission; я получи́л ∼у в Казахста́н I have been given a commission to execute in Kazakhstan; нау́чная к. scientific mission. **3.** (*coll.*) warrant, authority (*for travelling on official business, on commission*).

командиро́в|очный, *adj. of* ∼ка; ∼очные де́ньги travelling allowance; ∼очное удостовере́ние warrant, authority (*for travelling on official business, on commission*); *as noun* ∼очные, ∼очных, travelling allowance, travelling expenses.

команди́тн|ый, *adj.* (*comm.*) ∼ое това́рищество sleeping partnership.

кома́нд|ный, *adj.* **1.** *adj. of* ∼а; ∼ная до́лжность duties of a commander; к. пункт command post; к. соста́в the officers (*of a military unit*). **2.** (*fig.*) commanding; ∼ные высо́ты commanding heights, key points.

кома́ндовани|е, я, *n.* **1.** commanding, command; приня́ть к. (над) to take command (of, over). **2.** (*collect.*) command.

кома́нд|овать, ую, *impf.* (*of* с∼) **1.** to give orders. **2.** (+*i.*) to command, be in command (of). **3.** (*fig., coll.*) (+*i or* над) to order about. **4.** (*fig.*) (над) to command (*terrain*).

командо́р, а, *m.* **1.** (*hist.*) knight commander. **2.** commodore (*of yacht club*).

кома́ндующ|ий, его, *m.* commander.

комар, а́, *m.* gnat, mosquito; (*coll.*) к. но́са не подто́чит not a thing can be said against it.

комар|и́ный, *adj. of* ∼; к. уку́с mosquito bite; (*fig., coll.*) minute, midget.

комато́зный, *adj.* (*med.*) comatose.

комба́йн, а, *m.* (*tech.*) combine, multi-purpose machine; зерново́й к. combine harvester.

комба́йнер, а, *m.* (*agric.*) combine operator.

комба́т, а, *m.* (*abbr. of* команди́р батальо́на) battalion commander.

комбико́рм, а, *pl.* ∼а́, *m.* (*agric.*) mixed fodder.

комбико́рм|овый, *adj. of* ∼.

комбина́т, а, *m.* **1.** industrial complex; combine; к. бытово́го обслу́живания, *see* бытово́й. **2.** comprehensive school.

комбина́тор, а, *m.* (*pejor.*) schemer, contriver.

комбинато́рный, *adj.* (*math.*) combinative.

комбинац|ио́нный, *adj. of* ∼ия.

комбина́ци|я¹, и, *f.* **1.** combination; (*econ.*) merger. **2.** (*fig.*) scheme, system; (*polit., sport*) manœuvre.

комбина́ци|я², и, *f.* (*underwear*) **1.** slip. **2.** combinations.

комбинезо́н, а, *m.* overalls.

комбини́рованный, *adj.* combined.

комбини́р|овать, ую, *impf.* (*of* скомбини́ровать) **1.** to combine, arrange. **2.** (*coll., pejor.*) to scheme, contrive; to devise a scheme, a system.

комди́в, а, *m.* (*abbr. of* команди́р диви́зии) divisional commander.

комедиа́нт, а, *m.* **1.** (*obs.*) actor. **2.** (*pejor.*) play-actor; hypocrite.

комеди́йный, *adj.* (*lit., theatr.*) comic; comedy; к. актёр comedy actor.

коме́ди|я, и, *f.* comedy. **2.** (*fig., pejor.*) play-acting; farce; лома́ть ∼ю, разы́грывать ∼ю to put on an act, enact a farce.

ко́м|ель, ля, *m.* butt, butt-end (*of tree, etc.*).

коменда́нт, а, *m.* **1.** (*mil.*) commandant; к. го́рода town major; к. (ста́нции) R.T.O. **2.** manager; warden; к. теа́тра theatre manager; к. общежи́тия warden of a hostel.

комендáнт|ский, *adj. of* ∼; к. час (*mil.*) curfew.

комендату́р|а, ы, *f.* commandant's office.

комендо́р, а, *m.* (*naut.*) seaman gunner.

коме́т|а, ы, *f.* comet.

коми́зм, а, *m.* **1.** comedy, the comic element; к. положе́ния the funny side of a situation. **2.** comicality; с ∼ом передразни́ть кого́-н. to give a comical imitation of someone.

ко́мик, а, *m.* **1.** comic actor. **2.** (*fig.*) comedian, comical fellow.

Коминте́рн, а, *m.* (*hist.*) (*abbr. of* Коммунисти́ческий Интернациона́л) Comintern.

коминте́рн|овский, *adj. of* ∼.

комисса́р, а, *m.* commissar; верхо́вный к. high commissioner.

комиссариа́т, а, *m.* commissariat.

комисса́р|ский, *adj. of* ∼.

комиссионе́р, а, *m.* (commission-)agent, factor, broker.

комисс|ио́нный, *adj. of* ∼ия 2; к. магази́н

commission shop (*where second-hand goods are sold on commission*); *as noun* ~ио́нные, ~ио́нных, (*comm.*) commission; получи́ть ~ио́нные to receive a commission.

комѝсси|я, и, *f.* 1. commission, committee; к. по разоруже́нию disarmament commission; сле́дственная к. committee of investigation. 2. (*comm.*) commission; брать на ~ю to take on commission.

комите́т, а, *m.* committee.

комѝческ|ий, *adj.* 1. comic; ~ая о́пера comic opera. 2. comical, funny.

комѝч|ный (~ен, ~на), *adj.* comical, funny.

ко́мка|ть, ю, *impf.* (*of* скомкать) 1. (*pf. also* искомкать) to crumple. 2. (*fig., coll.*) to make a hash of, muff.

коммента́ри|й, я, *m.* 1. commentary. 2. (*pl.*) comment; ~и изли́шни comment is superfluous.

коммента́тор, а, *m.* commentator.

комменти́р|овать, ую, *impf. and pf.* to comment (upon).

коммерса́нт, а, *m.* merchant; business man.

комме́рци|я, и, *f.* commerce, trade.

комме́рческ|ий, *adj.* 1. commercial, mercantile; к. флот mercantile marine. 2. of trade off the ration, on free market; к. магази́н shop retailing goods officially controlled at prices above those fixed; ~ие це́ны free market prices.

коммивояжёр, а, *m.* commercial traveller.

комму́н|а, ы, *f.* (*in var. senses*) commune.

коммуна́льник, а, *m.* municipal employee.

коммуна́льн|ый, *adj.* 1. communal; municipal; ~ая кварти́ра 'communal' flat (*in which kitchen and toilet facilities are shared by a number of tenants*); ~ые услу́ги public utilities; ~ое хозя́йство municipal economy. 2. *adj. of* комму́на.

коммуни́зм, а, *m.* communism.

коммуникацио́нн|ый, *adj.* ~ая ли́ния line of communication.

коммуника́ци|я, и, *f.* (*in var. senses*) communication; (*mil.*) line of communication.

коммуни́ст, а, *m.* communist.

коммунисти́ческ|ий, *adj.* communist; ~ое строи́тельство the building of communism.

коммута́тор, а, *m.* (*electr.*) 1. commutator. 2. switchboard.

коммюнике́, *indecl., n.* communiqué.

ко́мнат|а, ы, *f.* room.

ко́мнатн|ый, *adj.* 1. of a room. 2. indoor; ~ые и́гры indoor games; ~ые расте́ния indoor plants; ~ая соба́чка lap-dog; ~ая температу́ра room temperature.

комо́д, а, *m.* chest of drawers.

ком|о́к, ка́, *dim. of* ~; сверну́ться в к. to roll oneself up into a ball; (*fig.*) к. в го́рле lump in the throat; к. не́рвов bundle of nerves.

комо́лый, *adj.* (*dial.*) polled.

компа́кт|ный (~ен, ~на), *adj.* compact, solid.

компане́йск|ий, *adj.* (*coll.*) 1. sociable, companionable. 2. equally shared; расхо́ды на ~их нача́лах expenses equally shared; устро́ить ве́чер на к. счёт to go shares in giving a party.

компа́ни|я, и, *f.* (*in var. senses*) company; води́ть ~ю с кем-н. (*coll.*) to associate with someone; расстро́ить ~ю to break up a party; соста́вить кому́-н. ~ю to keep someone company; я провёл ве́чер в ~и с Воло́дей I spent the evening in Volodya's company; он тебе́ не к. he is no company for you; пойти́ це́лой ~ей to go all together; гуля́ть ~ей to go about in a group; (*coll.*) за ~ю for company; ну, ещё стака́нчик с тобо́й за ~ю! well, just one more to keep you company!

компаньо́н, а, *m.* 1. (*comm.*) partner. 2. companion.

компаньо́н|ка, ки, *f.* 1. *f. of* ~. 2. (lady's) companion.

компа́рти|я, и, *f.* (*abbr. of* Коммунисти́ческая па́ртия) Communist Party.

ко́мпас, а, *m.* compass; гла́вный к. standard compass; морско́й к. mariner's compass.

ко́мпас|ный, *adj. of* ~; ~ная стре́лка compass needle; к. я́щик binnacle.

компатрио́т, а, *m.* compatriot.

компа́унд, а, *m.* (*tech.*) compound.

компе́ндиум, а, *m.* compendium, digest.

компенсацио́нный, *adj.* compensatory, compensating; (*tech.*) к. ма́ятник compensation-pendulum.

компенса́ци|я, и, *f.* compensation.

компенси́р|овать, ую, *impf. and pf.* 1. to compensate, indemnify (for). 2. (*tech.*) to compensate, equilibrate.

компете́нт|ный (~ен, ~на), *adj.* competent.

компете́нци|я, и, *f.* competence; э́то не в мое́й ~и it is outside my competence, it is beyond my scope.

компили́р|овать, ую, *impf.* (*of* скомпили́ровать) (*pejor.*) to compile.

компиляти́в|ный (~ен, ~на), *adj. of* компиля́ция; к. труд compilation.

компиля́тор, а, *m.* (*pejor.*) compiler.

компиля́ци|я, и, *f.* (*pejor.*) compilation.

ко́мплекс, а, *m.* (*in var. senses*) complex; set; к. неполноце́нности inferiority complex.

ко́мплексн|ый, *adj.* 1. (*math.*) complex; ~ое число́ complex number. 2. over-all, all-embracing, all-in; к. обе́д table d'hôte dinner.

компле́кт, а, *m.* 1. complete set; к. белья́

bedding, bed-clothes; к. вы́пусков «Коммуни́ста» за 1955 г. a complete set of 'Communist' for 1955. **2.** complement; specified number; сверх ~а above the specified number; у нас ещё не хвата́ет двух челове́к до по́лного ~а we are still two short of the full complement.

компле́ктный, *adj.* complete.

комплект|ова́ть, у́ю, *impf.* (*of* у~) **1.** to complete; to replenish; к. журна́л to acquire a complete set of a periodical. **2.** (*mil.*) to bring up to strength; to (re)man.

компле́кци|я, и, *f.* build; (*bodily*) constitution.

комплеме́нт, а, *m.* complement.

комплиме́нт, а, *m.* compliment; сде́лать к. (+*d.*) to pay a compliment (to).

компло́т, а, *m.* (*obs.*) plot, conspiracy.

компози́тор, а, *m.* (*mus.*) composer.

компози́ци|я, и, *f.* (*in various senses*) composition; класс ~и (*mus.*) composition class.

компоне́нт, а, *m.* component.

компон|ова́ть, у́ю, *impf.* (*of* скомпонова́ть) to put together, arrange; to group; к. статью́ to put together an article.

компоно́вк|а, и, *f.* putting together, arrangement; grouping.

компо́ст, а, *m.* (*hort.*) compost.

компо́стер, а, *m.* punch (*for 'bus tickets, etc.*).

компости́р|овать, ую, *impf.* (*of* прокомпости́ровать) to punch ('*bus tickets, etc.*).

компо́ст|ный, *adj.* of ~; ~ная я́ма compost pit.

компо́т, а, *m.* compote, stewed fruit.

компре́сс, а, *m.* (*med.*) compress; согрева́ющий к. hot compress; поста́вить к. to apply a compress.

компре́ссор, а, *m.* (*tech., med.*) compressor.

компромети́р|овать, ую, *impf.* (*of* скомпромети́ровать) to compromise.

компроми́сс, а, *m.* compromise; идти́ на к. to make a compromise, meet half-way.

компроми́сс|ный, *adj.* of ~; ~ное реше́ние compromise settlement.

комсомо́л, а, *m.* (*abbr. of* Коммунисти́ческий Сою́з Молодёжи) Komsomol (Young Communist League).

комсомо́л|ец, ьца, *m.* member of Komsomol. ⇨

комсомо́л|ка, ки, *f.* of ~ец.

комсомо́л|ьский, *adj.* of ~.

комсо́рг, а, *m.* (*abbr. of* комсомо́льский организа́тор) Komsomol organizer.

кому́, *d. of* кто.

комфо́рт, а, *m.* comfort.

комфорта́бельный, *adj.* comfortable.

кон, а, о ~е, на ~у́, *m.* **1.** (*in games of chance*) kitty; поста́вить де́ньги на́ к. to place one's stake, put one's money in (the kitty); быть,

стоя́ть на ~у́ (*fig.*) to be at stake. **2.** (*games*) game; round.

кона́|ться, юсь, *impf.* (*dial.*) to draw lots (*for first turn at a game*).

конве́йер, а, *m.* (*tech.*) conveyor (belt); сбо́рочный к., к. сбо́рки assembly line.

конве́йер|ный, *adj.* of ~; ~ная систе́ма conveyor (belt) system.

конве́кци|я, и, *f.* (*phys.*) convection.

конве́нт, а, *m.* (*polit.*) convention.

конвенциона́льный, *adj.* conventional.

конвенц|ио́нный, *adj.* of ~ия; к. тари́ф agreed tariff.

конве́нци|я, и, *f.* (*leg.*) convention, agreement.

конверге́нци|я, и, *f.* convergence.

конве́рси|я, и, *f.* (*econ.*) conversion.

конве́рт, а, *m.* **1.** envelope. **2.** (*gramophone record*) sleeve. **3.** sleeping bag (*for infants*).

конверти́р|овать, ую, *impf. and pf.* (*econ.*) to convert.

конве́ртор, а, *m.* (*tech.*) converter.

конво́ир, а, *m.* escort.

конвои́р|овать, ую, *impf.* to escort, convoy.

конво́|й, я, *m.* escort, convoy; вести́ под ~ем to convoy, conduct under escort.

конво́й|ный, *adj.* of ~; ~ное су́дно escort vessel; *as noun* к., ~ного, *m.* escort.

конвульси́в|ный (~ен, ~на), *adj.* (*med.*) convulsive.

конву́льси|я, и, *f.* (*med.*) convulsion.

конгениа́л|ьный (~ен, ~ьна), *adj.* congenial; (+*d.*) well suited (to), in harmony (with); перево́д, к. оригина́лу a translation in the spirit of the original.

конгломера́т, а, *m.* **1.** conglomeration. **2.** (*geol.*) conglomerate.

конгре́сс, а, *m.* congress.

конда́ч|о́к, *only in coll. phrase* с ~ка́ off-hand, perfunctorily.

конденса́тор, а, *m.* condenser.

конденсацио́нн|ый, *adj.* condensing, obtained by condensation; ~ая вода́ condensation water; к. горшо́к condensing vessel.

конденса́ци|я, и, *f.* condensation.

конденси́р|овать, ую, *impf. and pf.* to condense.

конди́тер, а, *m.* confectioner, pastry-cook.

конди́терск|ая, ой, *f.* confectioner's, sweet-shop; pastry-cook's.

конди́терск|ий, *adj.* ~ие изде́лия confectionery; к. магази́н = ~ая.

кондициони́рование, я, *n.* conditioning; к. во́здуха air conditioning.

кондициони́р|овать, ую, *impf.* to condition.

конди́ци|я, и, *f.* **1.** (*comm.*) standard. **2.** (*hist.*) жить на ~ях to be a resident tutor.

ко́ндо́вый, *adj.* **1.** having solid, close-grained timber (*also fig. as epithet of old Russia*). **2.** (*fig.*) of the good old-fashioned sort.

ко́ндор, а, *m.* (*orn.*) condor.

кондотье́р, а, *m.* (*hist.*) condottiere; soldier of fortune.

кондуи́т, а, *m.* conduct-book.

кондýктор¹, а, *pl.* ~а́, ~о́в, *m.* (*'bus, tram*) conductor; (*railway*) guard.

кондýктор², а, *pl.* ~ы, ~ов, *m.* (*electr.*) conductor.

кондýкторш|а, и, *f.* (*coll.*) conductress.

конево́д, а, *m.* horse-breeder.

конево́дств|о, а, *n.* horse-breeding.

конево́д|ческий, *adj. of* ~ство.

кон|ёк, ька́, *m.* 1. *dim. of* ~ь; морско́й к. (*zool.*) hippocampus, sea-horse. 2. ornament on peak of gable. 3. (*fig., coll.*) hobby-horse; hobby; сесть на своего́ ~ька́ to mount one's hobby-horse. 4. (*orn.*) pipit. 5. *see* ~ьки́.

кон|е́ц, ца́, *m.* 1. (*in var. senses*) end; о́стрый к. point; то́лстый к. butt(-end); то́нкий к. tip; в к. (*coll.*) completely; в ~це́ ~цо́в in the end, after all; и де́ло с ~цо́м and there's an end to it; из ~ца́ в к. from end to end, all over; ~цы́ с ~ца́ми своди́ть (*coll.*) to make both ends meet; на э́тот (тот) к. to this (that) end; на худо́й к. (*coll.*) at the worst, if the worst comes to the worst; оди́н к. (*coll.*) it comes to the same thing in the end; со всех ~цо́в from all quarters; хорони́ть ~цы́ (*coll.*) to bury, remove traces; и ~цы́ в во́ду and none will be the wiser; пришёл ему́ к. that's the end of him. 2. (*coll.*) distance, way (*from one place to another*); в оди́н к. one way; в о́ба ~ца́ there and back. 3. (*naut.*) rope's end.

коне́чно, *adv.* of course, certainly; no doubt; он, к., прав no doubt he is right; к. да! rather!; к. нет! certainly not!

коне́чност|ь¹, и, *f.* finiteness.

коне́чност|ь², и, *f.* (*anat.*) extremity.

коне́ч|ный (~ен, ~на), *adj.* 1. final, last; ultimate; ~ная ста́нция terminus; ~ная цель ultimate aim; в ~ном ито́ге, счёте in the end, in the last analysis. 2. finite.

кони́н|а, ы, *no pl., f.* horse-flesh.

кони́ческ|ий, *adj.* conic(al); ~ое сече́ние conic section.

ко́нк|а, и, *f.* horse-tramway; horse-drawn tram.

конкла́в, а, *m.* conclave.

конкорда́т, а, *m.* concordat.

конкретизи́р|овать, ую, *impf. and pf.* to render concrete, give concrete expression to.

конкре́т|ный (~ен, ~на), *adj.* concrete; specific.

конкубина́т, а, *m.* concubinage.

конкуре́нт, а, *m.* competitor; rival.

конкуре́нци|я, и, *f.* competition; вне ~и hors-concours.

конкури́р|овать, ую, *impf.* (с+*i.*) to compete (with).

ко́нкурс, а, *m.* 1. competition; объяви́ть к. (на+*a.*) to announce a vacancy (for); вне ~а hors-concours; (*fig.*) in a class by itself.

ко́нкурс|ный, *adj. of* ~; к. экза́мен competitive examination.

ко́нник, а, *m.* cavalryman.

ко́нниц|а, ы, *f.* cavalry; horse (*collect.; mil.*).

конногварде́|ец, йца, *m.* (*mil.*) 1. horse-guardsman. 2. (*in tsarist Russian army*) life-guard.

коннозаво́дств|о, а, *n.* 1. horse-breeding. 2. stud(-farm).

коннозаво́дчик, а, *m.* owner of stud(-farm).

ко́н|ный, *adj. of* ~ь; horse; mounted; equestrian; ~ная а́рмия cavalry army; ~ная артилле́рия horse artillery; к. двор stables; к. приво́д horse-drive; ~ная ста́туя equestrian statue; на ~ной тя́ге horse-drawn; ~ная я́рмарка horse-market.

конова́л, а, *m.* 1. horse-doctor, farrier. 2. (*coll.*) quack(-doctor).

конво́д¹, а, *m.* (*mil.*) horse-holder.

конво́д², а, *m.* (*coll.*) ringleader.

конво́|дить, жу, дишь, *impf.* (+*i.*; *coll.*) to be ringleader (of).

коновя́з|ь, и, *f.* tether; tethering-post.

конокра́д, а, *m.* horse-thief.

конокра́дств|о, а, *n.* horse-stealing.

конопа́|тить, чу, тишь, *impf.* (*of* законопа́тить) to caulk.

конопа́тк|а, и, *f.* 1. caulking. 2. caulking-iron.

конопа́тчик, а, *m.* caulker.

конопа́тый, *adj.* (*dial.*) freckled; pock-marked.

конопа́|чу, тишь, *see* ~тить.

конопл|я́, и́, *f.* (*bot.*) hemp.

конопля́ник, а, *m.* hemp-field.

конопля́нк|а, и, *f.* (*orn.*) linnet.

конопля́|ный, *adj. of* ~; ~ное ма́сло hemp-seed oil.

коносаме́нт, а, *m.* (*comm.*) bill of lading.

консервати́в|ный (~ен, ~на), *adj.* conservative.

консервати́зм, а, *m.* conservatism.

консерва́тор, а, *m.* (*esp. polit.*) conservative.

консервато́ри|я, и, *f.* conservatoire, academy of music.

консерва́торский, *adj.* conservative.

консерва́тор|ский, *adj. of* ~ия.

консерва́ци|я, и, *f.* 1. conservation. 2. temporary closing-down.

консерви́рован|ный (~, ~а), *p.p.p. of* консерви́ровать *and adj.*; ~ные фру́кты bottled fruit, tinned fruit.

консерви́р|овать, ую, *impf. and pf.* (*pf. also* законсерви́ровать) 1. to preserve (*to tin, bottle, etc.*). **2.** к. предприя́тие to close down an enterprise temporarily.

консе́рв|ный, *adj. of* ~ы; ~ная ба́нка tin; ~ная фа́брика cannery.

консе́рв|ы, ов, *no sing.* **1.** tinned goods. **2.** goggles.

конси́лиум, а, *m. (med.)* consultation.

конси́стенци|я, и, *f. (phys., med.)* consistence.

консисто́ри|я, и, *f. (eccl.)* consistory.

ко́н|ский, *adj. of* ~ь; к. во́лос horse-hair; к. заво́д stud(-farm); ~ские состяза́ния horse-races.

консолида́ци|я, и, *f.* consolidation.

консолиди́р|овать, ую, *impf. and pf.* **1.** to consolidate. **2.** (*fin.*) to fund.

консо́л|ь, и, *f. (archit.)* **1.** console, cantilever. **2.** pedestal.

консоме́, *indecl., n. (cul.)* consommé.

консона́нс, а, *m. (mus.)* consonance.

консонанти́зм, а, *m. (ling.)* system of consonants.

консо́рциум, а, *m. (fin.)* consortium.

конспе́кт, а, *m.* synopsis, summary, abstract.

конспекти́в|ный (~ен, ~на), *adj.* concise, summary.

конспекти́р|овать, ую, *impf. (of* за~ *and* проконспекти́ровать) to make an abstract of.

конспирати́в|ный (~ен, ~на), *adj.* secret, clandestine.

конспира́тор, а, *m.* conspirator.

конспира́ци|я, и, *f.* security, secrecy (*of an illegal organization*).

конспири́р|овать, ую, *impf. (of* законспири́ровать) to observe the rules of security (*in an illegal organization*).

конста́нт|а, ы, *f. (math., phys.)* constant.

конста́нтный, *adj.* constant.

констата́ци|я, и, *f.* ascertaining; verification, establishment.

констати́р|овать, ую, *impf. and pf.* to ascertain; to verify, establish; к. смерть to certify death; к. факт to establish a fact.

констелля́ци|я, и, *f. (astron.)* constellation.

конститу́ир|овать, ую, *impf. and pf.* to constitute, set up.

конституционали́зм, а, *m. (polit.)* constitutionalism.

конституцио́нальный, *adj. (med., physiol.)* constitutional.

конституцио́нный, *adj. (polit.)* constitutional.

конститу́ци|я, и, *f. (polit., med.)* constitution.

конструи́р|овать, ую, *impf. and pf. (pf. also* сконструи́ровать) **1.** to construct; to design. **2.** to form (*a government, etc.*).

конструктиви́зм, а, *m. (art)* constructivism.

конструкти́вный, *adj* **1.** structural; constructional; к. фа́ктор (*tech.*) efficiency factor, construction factor. **2.** constructive.

констру́ктор, а, *m.* designer, constructor.

констру́ктор|ский, *adj. of* ~; ~ское бюро́ design office.

констру́кци|я, и, *f.* **1.** construction, structure; design. **2.** (*gram.*) construction.

ко́нсул, а, *m.* consul.

ко́нсульский, *adj.* consular.

ко́нсульств|о, а, *n.* consulate.

консульта́нт, а, *m.* consultant, adviser; tutor (*in higher education institution*).

консультати́вный, *adj.* consultative, advisory.

консультац|ио́нный, *adj. of* ~ия; ~ио́нное бюро́ advice bureau; ~ио́нная пла́та consultation fee.

консульта́ци|я, и, *f.* **1.** consultation; specialist advice. **2.** advice bureau; де́тская к. children's clinic; же́нская к. ante-natal clinic; юриди́ческая к. legal advice office. **3.** tutorial; supervision (*in higher education institution*).

консульти́р|овать, ую, *impf.* **1.** (c+*i.*) to consult. **2.** (*pf.* проконсульти́ровать) to advise; to act as tutor (to).

консульти́р|оваться, уюсь, *impf. (of* проконсульти́роваться) **1.** (c+*i.*) to consult. **2.** to have a consultation; to obtain advice; to be a pupil of.

конта́кт, а, *m.* **1.** contact; вступи́ть в к. с кем-н. to come into contact, get in touch with someone; быть в ~е (c+*i.*) to be in touch (with). **2.** (*electr.*) к. приёмный socket; к. штыково́й plug.

конта́ктн|ый, *adj. (tech.)* contact; к. рельс contact rail, live rail; ~ая сва́рка point welding; ~ые ли́нзы (*med.*) contact lenses.

контамина́ци|я, и, *f. (ling.)* contamination.

конте́кст, а, *m.* context.

континге́нт, а, *m.* **1.** (*econ.*) quota. **2.** contingent; batch; к. новобра́нцев batch, squad of recruits.

контине́нт, а, *m.* continent.

континента́льный, *adj.* continental.

контокорре́нт, а, *m.* account current (a/c).

конто́р|а, ы, *f.* office, bureau; почто́вая к. post office.

конто́рк|а, и, *f.* (writing-)desk, bureau.

конто́р|ский, *adj. of* ~а; ~ская кни́га (account-)book; ledger.

конто́рщик, а, *m.* clerk.

ко́нтр|а¹, ы, *f. (coll.) (pl.)* disagreement, dispute; быть в ~ах (c+*i.*) to be at odds (with); у них вы́шли ~ы they have fallen out.

ко́нтр|а², ы, *m. and f. (sl.)* counter-revolutionary.

контраба́нд|а, ы, *f.* **1.** contraband, smuggling; занима́ться ~ой to smuggle. **2.** contraband (*goods*).

контрабанди́ст, а, *m.* smuggler, contra-bandist.

контраба́ндный, *adj.* contraband.

контраба́с, а, *m.* (*mus.*) double-bass.

контраге́нт, а, *m.* contractor.

контр-адмира́л, а, *m.* rear-admiral.

контра́кт, а, *m.* contract.

контракта́ци|я, и, *f.* contracting (for).

контракт|ова́ть, у́ю, *impf.* (*of* законтракто-ва́ть) to contract for (*supply of, performance of work by*); к. рабо́тников to engage work-men.

контракт|ова́ться, у́юсь, *impf.* (*of* закон-трактова́ться) 1. to contract, undertake (*to supply goods, perform work*). 2. *pass of* ~ова́ть.

контра́кт|овый, *adj. of* ~; ~овая я́рмарка trade fair, industrial fair.

контра́льто, *indecl.*, *n.* (*mus.*) contralto.

контра́льто|вый, *adj. of* ~.

контрама́рк|а, и, *f.* complimentary ticket.

контрапу́нкт, а, *m.* (*mus.*) counterpoint.

контрапункти́ческий, *adj.* (*mus.*) contra-puntal.

контрапу́нкт|ный, *adj.* = ~и́ческий.

контрассигна́ци|я, и, *f.* countersign.

контрассигни́р|овать, ую, *impf. and pf.* to countersign.

контрассигно́вк|а, и, *f.* countersign.

контра́ст, а, *m.* contrast; по ~у (с+*i.*) by contrast (with).

контрасти́р|овать, ую, *impf.* (с+*i.*) to con-trast (with).

контра́стный, *adj.* contrasting.

контрата́к|а, и, *f.* (*mil.*) counter-attack.

контратак|ова́ть, у́ю, *impf. and pf.* to coun-ter-attack.

контргайк|а, и, *f.* (*tech.*) lock-nut, check-nut.

контрибу́ци|я, и, *f.* (war) indemnity; con-tribution; наложи́ть ~ю (на+*a.*) to impose an indemnity (on); to lay under contribu-tion.

ко́нтрик, а, *m.* (*sl.*) = ко́нтра.²

контр-манёвр, а, *m.* (*mil.*) counter-ma-nœuvre.

контрма́рш, а, *m.* (*mil.*) countermarch.

контрнаступле́ни|е, я, *n.* counter-offensive.

контрове́рз|а, ы, *f.* controversy.

контролёр, а, *m.* inspector; ticket-collector.

контроли́р|овать, ую, *impf.* (*of* про~) to check; к. биле́ты to inspect tickets.

контро́ллер, а, *m.* (*electr.*) controller.

контро́л|ь, я, *m.* 1. control. 2. check(ing); inspection; (*tech.*) monitoring; предста́вить ци́фры ~ю to check one's figures. 3. (*collect.*) inspectors.

контро́ль|ный, *adj. of* ~; ~ная вы́шка (*naut.*) conning tower; ~ная коми́ссия control commission; ~ная систе́ма (*radio*) monitor-ing system; ~ные ци́фры (*econ.*) scheduled figures; к. плённый (*mil.*) prisoner for iden-tification.

контрпа́р, а, *m.* (*tech.*) counter-steam, back--steam.

контрпрете́нзи|я, и, *f.* counter-claim.

контрприка́з, а, *m.* countermand.

контрразве́дк|а, и, *f.* counter-espionage.

контрразве́дчик, а, *m.* member of counter--espionage.

контрреволюционе́р, а, *m.* counter-revolu-tionary.

контрреволюцио́нный, *adj.* counter-revo-lutionary.

контрреволю́ци|я, и, *f.* counter-revolution.

контруда́р, а, *m.* (*mil.*) counter-blow.

контрфо́рс, а, *m.* (*archit.*) buttress, counter-fort.

контрэска́рп, а, *m.* (*mil.*) counterscarp.

конту́жен|ный (~, ~а), *p.p.p. of* конту́зить and *adj.*; ~ные (*mil.*) shell-shock cases.

конту́|зить, жу, зишь, *pf.* to contuse; to shell-shock.

конту́зи|я, и, *f.* contusion; shell-shock.

ко́нтур, а, *m.* 1. contour, outline. 2. (*electr.*) circuit.

ко́нтур|ный, *adj. of* ~; ~ная ка́рта contour map.

конур|а́, ы́, *f.* kennel (*also fig.*, *coll.*).

ко́нус, а, *m.* cone.

конусообра́з|ный (~ен, ~на), *adj.* conical.

конфедера́т, а, *m.* (*hist.*) confederate.

конфедерати́вный, *adj.* confederative.

конфедера́тк|а, и, *f.* (*hist.*) konfederatka (*Polish national or military headgear—rectan-gular cap with no peak*).

конфедера́ци|я, и, *f.* confederation.

конфекцио́н, а, *m.* ready-made clothes shop.

конфера́нс, а, *m.* (*theatr.*) compèring.

конферансье́, *indecl.*, *m.* (*theatr.*) compère, master of ceremonies.

конфере́нц-за́л, а, *m.* conference chamber.

конфере́нци|я, и, *f.* conference.

конфе́т|а, ы, *f.* sweet.

конфе́т|ный, *adj.* 1. *adj. of* ~а; ~ная бума́жка sweet wrapper. 2. (*coll.*, *pejor.*) sugary, treacly.

конфетти́, *indecl.*, *n.* confetti.

конфигура́ци|я, и, *f.* configuration, con-formation.

конфиденциа́л|ьный (~ен, ~ьна), *adj.* con-fidential.

конфирма́нт, а, *m.* (*eccl.*) confirmation can-didate.

конфирма́ци|я, и, *f.* 1. (*eccl.*) confirmation. 2. (*obs.*) ratification.

конфирм|ова́ть, у́ю, *impf. and pf.* 1. (*eccl.*) to confirm. 2. (*obs.*) to ratify.

конфиска́ци|я, и, *f.* confiscation, seizure.

конфиск|ова́ть, у́ю, *impf. and pf.* to confiscate.

конфли́кт, а, *m.* 1. clash, conflict. 2. (*polit.*) dispute.

конфли́кт|ный, *adj. of* ~; ~ная коми́ссия arbitration tribunal.

конфликт|ова́ть, у́ю, *impf.* (c+*i.*) (*coll.*) to to clash (with), come up (against).

конфо́рк|а, и, *f.* ring (*on cooking stove*); crown, top ring (*on samovar*).

конфу́з, а, *m.* discomfiture, embarrassment; како́й к. (получи́лся)! how awkward, how embarrassing!; привести́ в к. to place in an embarrassing position.

конфу́|зить, жу, зишь, *impf.* (*of* c~) to confuse, embarrass; to place in an embarrassing position.

конфу́|зиться, жусь, зишься, *impf.* (*of* c~) 1. to feel embarrassed; to be shy. 2. (+*g.*) to feel ashamed (of); to be shy (in front of).

конфу́злив|ый (~, ~а), *adj.* bashful; shy.

конфу́зный, *adj.* (*coll.*) awkward, embarrassing.

концев|о́й, *adj.* final; ~а́я строка́ end-line.

концентра́т, а, *m.* 1. concentrated product. 2. (*geol.*) concentrate.

концентрацио́нный, *adj.* к. ла́герь concentration camp.

концентра́ци|я, и, *f.* (*in var. senses*) concentration.

концентри́рова|нный, *p.p.p. of* ~ть *and adj.* concentrated.

концентри́р|овать, ую, *impf.* (*of* c~) (*in var. senses*) to concentrate; (*mil.*) to mass; (*fig.*) к. внима́ние на вопро́се to concentrate one's attention on a question.

концентри́р|оваться, уюсь, *impf.* (*of* c~) 1. to mass, collect (*intrans.*). 2.(*fig.*; на+*p.*) to concentrate.

концентри́ческий, *adj.* concentric.

концентри́чность|ь, и, *f.* concentricity.

концентр|ы, ов, *sing.* ~, ~а, *m.* concentric circles.

конце́пт, а, *m.* (*philos.*) concept.

концептуали́зм, а, *m.* (*philos.*) conceptualism.

конце́пци|я, и, *f.* conception, idea.

конце́рн, а, *m.* (*econ.*) concern.

конце́рт, а, *m.* (*mus.*) 1. concert; recital; симфони́ческий к. symphony concert; быть на ~e to be at a concert; (*coll.*) коша́чий к. caterwauling; (*fig.*) hooting, barracking. 2. concerto.

концерта́нт, а, *m.* performer (*in a concert*).

концерти́р|овать, ую, *impf.* to give concerts.

концертме́йстер, а, *m.* (*mus.*) 1. leader (*of orchestra*). 2. solo performer.

конце́рт|ный, *adj. of* ~; к. роя́ль concert grand (piano).

концессионе́р, а, *m.* concessionaire.

конце́сси|я, и, *f.* (*econ.*) concession.

концла́гер|ь, я, *m.* (*abbr. of* концентрацио́нный ла́герь) concentration camp.

концо́вк|а, и, *f.* 1. (*typ.*) tail-piece; colophon. 2. (*fig.*) ending (*of lit. work*).

конч|а́ть(ся), а́ю(сь), *impf. of* ~и́ть(ся).

ко́нч|енный, *p.p.p. of* ~ить; *as interj.* ~ено! enough!; всё ~ено! it's all over!; с ним всё ~ено it's all up with him.

ко́нчен|ый, *adj.* (*coll.*) decided, settled; э́то де́ло ~ое the matter is settled; к. челове́к (*coll.*) goner.

ко́нчик, а, *m.* tip; point; на ~е языка́ on the tip of one's tongue.

кончи́н|а, ы, *f.* (*rhet.*) decease, demise; end.

ко́нч|ить, у, ишь, *pf.* (*of* ~а́ть) 1. to finish, end; к. речь выраже́нием благода́рности to end a speech with thanks; на э́том он ~ил here he stopped; я ~ил that is all (I have to say); к. шко́лу to finish school course; к. университе́т to graduate, go down (*from university*); к. самоуби́йством to commit suicide; к. пло́хо, ду́рно, скве́рно to come to a bad end. 2. (c+*i.*) to be finished (with), give up. 3. (+*inf.*) to stop.

ко́нч|иться, усь, ишься, *pf.* (*of* ~а́ться) 1. (+*i.*) to end (in), finish (by); to come to an end; э́тим де́ло не ~илось that was not the end of it; де́ло ~илось ниче́м it came to nothing. 2. (*obs.*) to die, expire.

конъекту́р|а, ы, *f.* (*philol.*) conjecture.

конъекту́рный, *adj.* (*philol.*) conjectural.

конъюнктиви́т, а, *m.* (*med.*) conjunctivitis.

конъюнкту́р|а, ы, *f.* 1. state of affairs, juncture; междунаро́дная к. international situation. 2. (*econ.*) state of the market.

конъюнкту́р|ный, *adj. of* ~а 2; ~ные це́ны (free) market prices.

конъюнкту́рщик, а, *m.* (*coll., pejor.*) opportunist, time-server.

кон|ь, я́, *pl.* ~и, ~е́й, *m.* 1. horse; боево́й к. war-horse, charger; на́ к., по ~ям! (*mil. command*) mount!; (*prov.*) дарёному ~ю́ в зу́бы не смо́трят never look a gift horse in the mouth; не в ~я́ корм pearls before swine. 2. (vaulting-)horse. 3. (*chess*) knight.

кон|ьки́, ько́в, *sing.* ~ёк, ~ька́, *m.* skates; к. на ро́ликах roller skates; ката́ться на ~ька́х to skate.

конькобе́ж|ец, ца, *m.* skater.

конькобе́жный, *adj.* skating.

коньяк, а́, *m.* brandy.

конья́|чный, *adj. of* ~к.

ко́нюх, а, *m.* groom, stable-man.

коню́ш|ня, ни, *g. pl.* ~ен, *f.* stable; А́вгиевы ~ни (*myth. or fig.*) Augean stables.

кооперати́в, а, *m.* **1.** co-operative society. **2.** (*coll.*) co-operative store.

кооперати́вн|ый, *adj.* co-operative; ∼ое движе́ние (*econ., polit.*) the co-operative movement; ∼ое това́рищество co-operative society.

коопера́тор, а, *m.* co-operator, member of co-operative society.

коопера́ци|я, и, *f.* **1.** co-operation. **2.** (*collect.*) co-operative societies; потреби́тельская, сельскохозя́йственная к. consumers', agricultural co-operative societies.

коопери́р|овать, ую, *impf. and pf.* (*econ.*) **1.** to organize on co-operative lines. **2.** to recruit to a co-operative organization.

коопери́р|оваться, уюсь, *impf. and pf.* (*econ.*) **1.** to co-operate. **2.** *pass. of* ∼овать.

коопта́ци|я, и, *f.* co-optation.

коопти́р|овать, ую, *impf. and pf.* to co-opt.

координа́т|а, ы, *f.* (*math.*) co-ordinate.

координа́тный, *adj.* (*math.*) co-ordinate.

координа́тор, а, *m.* co-ordinator.

координа́ци|я, и, *f.* co-ordination.

координи́р|овать, ую, *impf. and pf.* to co-ordinate.

копа́л, а, *m.* copal.

копа́ни|е, я, *n.* digging.

коп|а́ть, а́ю, *impf.* **1.** (*pf.* ∼ну́ть) to dig. **2.** (*pf.* вы́∼) to dig up, dig out.

копа́|ться, юсь, *impf.* **1.** (в+*p.*) to rummage (in); to root (in); (*fig.*) к. в душе́ to be given to soul-searching. **2.** (*coll.;* с+*i.*) to dawdle (over). **3.** *pass. of* ∼ть.

копе́ечк|а, и, *f. dim. of* копе́йка; (*coll.*) э́то влети́т тебе́ в ∼у it will cost you a pretty penny.

копе́ечн|ый, *adj.* ˙**1.** one-kopeck; worth one kopeck. **2.** (*in price*) minute, insignificant; ∼ые расхо́ды trifling expenses. **3.** (*fig., coll.*) petty; twopenny-halfpenny.

копе́йк|а, и, *g. pl.* копе́ек, *f.* kopeck; к. в ∼у exactly; до после́дней ∼и to the last farthing; зашиби́ть, сколоти́ть ∼у to turn an honest penny; к. рубль бережёт (*prov.*) take care of the pence, the pounds will take care of themselves.

коп|ёр, ра́, *m.* (*tech.*) **1.** pile-driver. **2.** mine headframe.

ко́п|и, ей, *sing.* ∼ь, ∼и, *f.* mines.

копи́лк|а, и, *f.* money-box.

копи́рк|а, и, *f.* (*coll.*) carbon paper, copying paper; писа́ть под ∼у to make a carbon copy.

копирова́льн|ый, *adj.* copying; ∼ая бума́га carbon paper.

копи́р|овать, ую, *impf.* (*of* с∼) to copy; to imitate, mimic.

копиро́вк|а, и, *f.* copying.

копиро́вщик, а, *m.* copyist.

коп|и́ть, лю́, ∼ишь, *impf.* (*of* на∼) to accu-

mulate, amass; to store up; к. де́ньги to save up; (*fig.*) к. си́лы to save one's strength.

коп|и́ться, лю́сь, ∼ишься, *impf.* (*of* на∼) to accumulate (*intrans.*).

ко́пи|я, и, *f.* copy; duplicate; replica; заве́ренная к. (*leg.*) attested copy; снять ∼ю (с+*g.*) to copy, make a copy (of); (*fig.*) он то́чная к. своего́ отца́ he is the very image of his father.

коп|на́, ны́, *pl.* ∼ны, ∼ён, ∼на́м, *f.* shock, stook (*of corn*); к. се́на haycock; (*fig., coll.*) heap, pile; к. воло́с shock of hair.

копн|и́ть, ю́, и́шь, *impf.* (*of* с∼) (*agric.*) to shock, stook; to cock (*hay*).

коп|ну́ть, ну́, нёшь, *pf. of* ∼а́ть.

копотли́в|ый (∼, ∼а), *adj.* (*coll.*) slow, sluggish; ∼ое де́ло slow, sticky job.

копотн|я́, и́, *f.* (*coll.*) dawdling.

копоту́н, а́, *m.* (*coll.*) dawdler.

ко́пот|ь, и, *f.* soot; lamp-black.

копош|и́ться, у́сь, и́шься, *impf.* **1.** to swarm. **2.** (*fig., coll.*) to stir, creep in; у меня́ в голове́ ∼и́лось сомне́ние a doubt was beginning to stir in my head. **3.** (*coll.*) to potter about.

ко́пр|а, ы́, *f.* copra.

коп|ро́вый, *adj. of* ∼ёр.

копт|е́ть¹, и́т, *impf.* (*of* за∼) (*coll.*) to be blackened (*from smoke, with soot*).

коп|те́ть², чу́, ти́шь, *impf.* (над∼) (*coll.*) **1.** to swot (at), plug away (at). **2.** to vegetate, rot away (*fig.*).

копти́лк|а, и, *f.* (*coll.*) oil-lamp (*of primitive design*).

копти́льный, *adj.* for smoking.

копти́л|ьня, ьни, *g. pl.* ∼ен, *f.* smoking-shed.

коп|ти́ть, чу́, ти́шь, *impf.* **1.** (*pf.* за∼) to smoke, cure in smoke. **2.** (*pf.* за∼) to blacken (*with smoke*); к. стекло́ to smoke glass; к. не́бо (*coll.*) to idle one's life away. **3.** (*pf.* на∼) to smoke (*intrans.*).

копту́н, а́, *m.* (*coll.*) dawdler.

копчёни|е, я, *n.* **1.** smoking, curing in smoke. **2.** (*collect.*) smoked products.

копчён|ый, *adj.* smoked, smoke-dried; ∼ая селёдка bloater.

ко́пчик, а, *m.* (*anat.*) coccyx.

коп|чу́¹, ти́шь, *see* ∼те́ть².

коп|чу́², ти́шь, *see* ∼ти́ть.

копы́тн|ый, *adj.* **1.** hoof. **2.** (*zool.*) hoofed, ungulate; *as noun* ∼ые, ∼ых, ungulate animals.

копы́т|о, а, *n.* hoof.

коп|ь, *see* ∼и.

коп|ьё¹, ья́, *pl.* ∼ья, ∼ий, ∼ьям, *n.* spear, lance; мета́ние ∼ья́ (*sport*) javelin throwing; би́ться на ∼ьях to tilt, joust; (*fig., iron.*) ∼ья лома́ть (из-за) to break a lance (over).

копь|ё², я́, n. у меня́ ни ~я́ нет (coll.) I haven't a penny.

копьеви́д|ный (~ен, ~на), adj. (bot.) lanceolate.

кор|а́, ы́, f. 1. (bot.) cortex; bark, rind. 2. (anat.) к. головно́го мо́зга cerebral cortex. 3. crust; земна́я к. (earth-)crust; (fig.) под ~о́й его́ суро́вости бы́ло до́брое се́рдце he had a kind heart beneath his hard exterior.

кораб|е́льный, adj. of ~ль; ~е́льная авиа́ция shipborne aircraft; к. лес ship timber; к. инжене́р naval architect; к. ма́стер shipwright.

корабе́льщик, а, m. 1. (obs.) sea-captain. 2. (coll.) shipwright.

кораблевожде́ни|е, я, n. navigation.

кораблекруше́ни|е, я, n. ship-wreck; потерпе́ть к. to be ship-wrecked.

кораблестрое́ни|е, я, n. ship-building.

кораблестрои́тел|ь, я, m. ship-builder, naval architect.

кора́бл|ик, а, m. 1. dim. of ~ь. 2. toy boat. 3. (zool.) nautilus; argonaut.

кора́бл|ь, я́, m. 1. ship, vessel; лине́йный к. battleship; флагма́нский к. flagship; сади́ться на к. to go on board (ship); сжечь свои́ ~и́ (fig.) to burn one's boats; большо́му ~ю́ большо́е пла́ванье (prov.) a great ship asks deep waters. 2. (archit.) nave.

кора́лл, а, m. coral.

кора́ллов|ый, adj. 1. coral. 2. coralline; coral-red; ~ые уста́ coral lips.

Кора́н, а, m. the Koran.

корве́т, а, m. (naut.) corvette.

корд|а́, ы́, f. lunge (longe); гоня́ть ло́шадь на ~е to lunge a horse.

кордебале́т, а, m. corps de ballet.

корди́т, а, m. cordite.

кордо́н, а, m. cordon.

кор|ево́й, adj. of ~ь.

коре́|ец, йца, m. Korean.

корёж|ить, у, ишь, impf. (of ис~) (coll.) 1. to bend, warp; (impers.) его́ ~ило от бо́ли he was writhing with pain. 2. (fig.) to make indignant.

корёж|иться, усь, ишься, impf. (of ис~) (coll.) 1. to bend, warp (intrans.) 2. к. от бо́ли to writhe with pain.

коре́йк|а, и, f. brisket (of pork or veal).

коре́йский, adj. Korean.

корена́ст|ый (~, ~а), adj. 1. thickset, stocky. 2. with strong roots.

корениза́ци|я, и, f. (polit.) indigenisation.

корени́зи́р|овать, ую, impf. and pf. (polit.) to place under local (indigenous) authority.

корени́т|ься, ся, impf. (в+p.) to be rooted (in).

коренни́к, а́, m. shaft-horse, thill-horse, wheeler.

коренн|о́й, adj. radical, fundamental; к. зуб molar (tooth); к. жи́тель native; ~о́е населе́ние indigenous population; ~а́я ло́шадь = ~и́к.

ко́р|ень, ня, pl. ~ни, ~не́й, m. 1. (in var. senses) root; в ~не radically; в ~ню́ between the shafts; вы́рвать с ~нем to uproot, tear up by the roots (also fig.); красне́ть до ~не́й воло́с to blush to the roots of one's hair; пусти́ть ~ни to take root (also fig.); смотре́ть в к. чего́-н. to get at the root of something; хлеб на ~ню́ standing crop. 2. (math.) root; radical; знак ~ня́ radical sign; куби́ческий к. cube root; показа́тель ~ня́ root index.

коре́нь|я, ев, no sing. roots (of vegetables, herbs, etc., for culinary and medicinal purposes).

кореш|о́к, ка́, m. 1. back (of book-binding). 2. counterfoil. 3. dim. of ко́рень. 4. (sl.) pal, mate.

коре́йнк|а, и, f. Korean (woman).

корзи́н|а, ы, f. basket.

корзи́нк|а, и, f. small basket, punnet; рабо́чая к. work-basket; (bot.) calathide.

корзи́н|ный, adj. of ~a; ~ное произво́дство basket-making.

корзи́нщик, а, m. basket-maker.

коридо́р, а, m. corridor, passage.

коридо́р|ный, adj. of ~; as noun к., ~ного, m. boots (in hotel).

кори́нк|а, и, no pl., f. currants.

кори́нфский, adj. (archit.) Corinthian.

кор|и́ть, ю́, и́шь, impf. (+a. за) to upbraid (for); (+a. and i.) to reproach (with), cast in someone's teeth.

корифе́|й, я, m. (rhet.) coryphaeus (fig.), leading light.

кори́ц|а, ы, f. cinnamon.

кори́чневый, adj. brown.

ко́рк|а, и, f. 1. crust. 2. peel, rind. 3. scab. 4. (fig.) прочита́ть от ~и до ~и to read from cover to cover; руга́ть, брани́ть кого́-н. на все ~и (coll.) to give it someone hot, tear someone off a strip.

корм, а, о ~е, на ~е and на ~у́, pl. ~а́, ~о́в, m. 1. fodder; forage; на подно́жном ~у́ at grass. 2. feeding.

корм|а́¹, ы́, f. (naut.) stern, poop.

корм|а́², n. pl. of ~.

корме́жк|а, и, f. (coll.) feeding.

корми́л|ец, ьца, m. 1. bread-winner. 2. (obs.) benefactor. 3. (dial. mode of address to man) old man.

корми́лиц|а, ы, f. 1. wet-nurse. 2. (obs.) benefactress.

корми́л|о, а, n. (naut. and fig.) helm; (fig., rhet.) быть у ~а правле́ния to be at the helm.

корм|и́ть, лю́, ~ишь, impf. 1. (pf. на~ and по~) to feed; к. с ло́жки to spoon-feed; к.

грудью to nurse, (breast-)feed; не ~я (éхать) (*obs.*) (to ride) non-stop; (*coll.*) его хлебом не ~й, только дай смотреть футбол he is mad about watching football. **2.** (*pf.* про~ keep, maintain.

корм|и́ться, лю́сь, ~ишься, *impf.* **1.** (*pf.* по~) to eat, feed (*intrans.*). **2.** (*pf.* про~) (+ *i.*) to live (on); к. уроками to make a living by giving tuition.

кормле́ни|е, я, *n.* **1.** feeding. **2.** (*hist.*) 'feeding' (*in Muscovite Russia, system by which boyars responsible for local administration retained revenues for their own use*).

корм|овой¹, *adj.* of ~á; ~овое весло scull; к. флаг ensign; ~овая часть after-part, stern-part.

корм|овой², *adj.* of ~; fodder, forage; ~овые культу́ры, расте́ния fodder crops; ~овая свёкла mangel-wurzel.

корму́шк|а, и, *f.* (*agric.*) (feeding-) trough, (feeding-) rack, manger.

ко́рмч|ий, его, *m.* (*arch. or fig., rhet.*) helmsman, pilot; ~ая кни́га (*hist., lit.*) Nomocanon.

корна́|ть, ю, *impf.* (*of* о~ *and* об~) (*coll.*) to crop, cut short.

корневи́щ|е, я, *n.* (*bot.*) rhizome.

кор|нево́й, *adj.* of ~ень; ~невы́е языки́ (*ling.*) isolating languages.

корнепло́д, а, *m.* root plant.

ко́рнер, а, *pl.* ~ы *or* ~á, *m.* (*sport*) corner; забить гол с ~a to score a goal from, off a corner.

корнере́зк|а, и, *f.* (*agric.*) root-cutting machine.

корне́т, а, *m.* (*mil. and mus.*) cornet.

корне́т-а-писто́н, а, *m.* (*mus.*) cornet-à-piston(s).

корнети́ст, а, *m.* (*mus.*) cornet-player, cornetist.

корнишо́н, а, *m.* (*cul.*) gherkin.

корноу́х|ий (~, ~а), *adj.* (*coll.*) crop-eared.

ко́роб, а, *pl.* ~á, *m.* **1.** box, basket (*of bast*). **2.** (*tech.*) box, chest. **3.** (*mil.*) body (*of machine-gun*). **4.** body (*of a carriage*). **5.** (*fig., coll.*) це́лый к. новосте́й heaps of news; наговори́ть с три ~a to spin a long yarn.

коробе́йник, а, *m.* (*obs.*) pedlar.

коро́б|ить, лю, ишь, *impf.* (*of* по~) **1.** to warp. **2.** (*fig.*) to jar upon, grate upon; (*impers.*) меня́ ~ит от его́ акце́нта his accent jars upon me.

коро́б|иться, лю́сь, ишься, *impf.* (*of* по~ *and* с~) to warp, buckle.

коро́бк|а, и, *f.* box, case; дверна́я к. door-frame; к. скоросте́й (*tech.*) gear-box; черепна́я к. (*anat.*) cranium.

короб|о́к, ка́, *m.* small box.

коро́бочк|а, и, f.* **1. *dim. of* коро́бка. **2.** (*bot.*) boll.

коро́бчат|ый, *adj.* box shaped; (*tech.*) ~ое желе́зо channel iron.

коро́в|а, ы, *f.* cow; морска́я к. sea-cow manatee.

корова́|й, я, *m.* = карава́й.

коро́в|ий, *adj.* of ~a; ~ье ма́сло butter.

коро́в|ка, ки, *f.* affect. *dim.* of ~a; бо́жья к. lady-bird.

коро́вник¹, а, *m.* cow-shed.

коро́вник², а, *m.* cow-man.

коро́вниц|а, ы, *f.* dairy-maid.

короле́в|а, ы, *f.* queen.

короле́вич, а, *m.* king's son.

короле́в|на, ны, *g. pl.* ~ен, *f.* king's daughter.

короле́вский, *adj.* royal; king's; regal, kingly; (*chess*) к. слон king's bishop.

короле́вств|о, а, *n.* kingdom.

корол|ёк, ька́, *m.* **1.** (*orn.*) желтоголо́вый к. goldcrest; красноголо́вый к. firecrest. **2.** blood-orange. **3.** (*min.*) regulus.

коро́л|ь, я́, *m.* king; (*fig.*) нефтяно́й к. oil king.

коромы́сл|о, а, *n.* **1.** yoke (*for carrying buckets*); beam (*of scales*). **2.** (*tech.*) rocking shaft, rocker arm. **3.** (*coll.*) там шёл дым ~ом all hell was let loose.

коро́н|а, ы, *f.* **1.** crown (*also fig.*); coronet. **2.** (*astron.*) corona.

корона|цио́нный, *adj.* of ~ция.

корона́ци|я, и, *f.* coronation.

коро́нк|а, и, *f.* crown (*of tooth*).

коро́нн|ый, *adj.* crown, of state; (*theatr.*) ~ая роль best part.

корон|ова́ть, у́ю, *impf. and pf.* to crown.

коро́ст|а, ы, *f.* scab.

коросте́л|ь, я́, *m.* (*orn.*) corncrake, landrail.

корота́|ть, ю, *impf.* (*of* с~) (*coll.*) to pass, while away (*time*).

коро́т|кий (ко́роток, ~á, ко́ротко́, *pl.* ~ки́), *adj.* **1.** short; brief; э́то пальто́ тебе́ ~ко́ this coat is too short for you; рассказа́ть в ~ких слова́х to tell in a few words; ~кая распра́ва short shrift; к. уда́р short and sharp blow; (*coll.*) ру́ки ко́ротки́! just try! you couldn't if you tried!; ум ~ок limited intelligence. **2.** (*fig.*) close, intimate; (*coll.*) быть на ~кой ноге́ с кем-н. to be on intimate terms with someone.

коро́тк|о¹, *see* ~ий.

коро́тко², *adv.* **1.** briefly; к. говоря́ in short. **2.** intimately.

коротковолно́вый, *adj.* (*radio*) short-wave.

коро́ткост|ь, и, *f.* (*coll.*) intimacy, familiarity.

короты́шк|а, и, *m. and f.* (*coll.*) dumpy, tubby person; squab.

кор|о́че, *comp. of* ~о́ткий *and* ~о́тко shorter; к. говоря́ in short, to cut a long story short.

коро́чк|а, и, *f.* *dim. of* ко́рка.

корп|е́ть, лю́, и́шь, *impf.* (над, за+*i.*) (*coll.*) to pore (over), sweat (over).

ко́рпи|я, и, *f.* (*obs.*) lint.

корпорати́вный, *adj.* corporative.

корпора́ци|я, и, *f.* corporation.

корпуле́нтный, *adj.* corpulent.

ко́рпус¹, а, *pl.* ~ы, *m.* **1.** body; trunk, torso. **2.** length (*of animal, as unit of measurement*); на́ша ло́шадь опереди́ла други́х на три ~a our horse won by three lengths. **3.** hull; (*tech.*) frame, body, case. **4.** (*typ.*) long primer.

ко́рпус², а, *pl.* ~а́, ~о́в, *m.* **1.** (*mil.*) corps; каде́тский, морско́й к. military school, naval college; дипломати́ческий к. diplomatic corps. **2.** building; block.

корректи́в, а, *m.* amendment, correction.

корректи́р|овать, ую, *impf.* (*of* про~) to correct.

корректиро́вщик, а, *m.* (*mil.*) **1.** spotter. **2.** spotter (aircraft).

корре́кт|ный (~ен, ~на), *adj.* correct, proper.

корре́ктор, а, *m.* proof-reader, corrector.

корректу́р|а, ы, *f.* **1.** proof-reading, correction. **2.** proof(-sheet); держа́ть ~у to read, correct proofs; к. в гра́нках galley proof(s); к. в листа́х page proof(s). **3.** (*mil.*) correction, adjustment (*of fire*).

корректу́р|ный, *adj. of* ~а; ~ные зна́ки proof symbols; к. о́ттиск proof(-sheet).

корре́кци|я, и, *f.* (*med.*) correction.

корреля́т, а, *m.* correlate.

коррелят́ивный, *adj.* correlative.

корреля́ци|я, и, *f.* correlation.

корреспонде́нт, а, *m.* correspondent.

корреспонде́нци|я, и, *f.* **1.** correspondence; заказна́я, проста́я к. registered, non-registered mail. **2.** newspaper contribution from a correspondent.

корреспонди́р|овать, ую, *impf.* (*in var. senses*) to correspond.

корро́зи|я, и, *f.* (*chem.*) corrosion.

корру́пци|я, и, *f.* (*polit.*) corruption.

корса́ж, а, *m.* bodice, corsage.

корса́р, а, *m.* corsair.

корсе́т, а, *m.* corset.

корсе́тниц|а, ы, *f.* corsetière.

корт, а, *m.* (tennis-)court.

кортёж, а, *m.* cortège; motorcade.

ко́ртик, а, *m.* dagger, dirk.

ко́рточ|ки, ек, *no sing.* сиде́ть на ~ках, сесть на к. to squat.

кору́нд, а, *m.* (*min.*) corundum.

корча́г|а, и, *f.* (*dial.*) earthenware pot, ewer.

корч|ева́ть, у́ю, *impf.* to stub, grub up, root out.

корчёвк|а, и, *f.* stubbing, grubbing up, rooting out.

корче́мств|о, а, *n.* (*obs.*) bootlegging.

ко́рч|и, ей, *sing.* ~а, ~и, *f.* (*coll.*) convulsions, spasm; му́читься в ~ах to writhe with pain; зла́я ~а (*med.*) ergotism.

ко́рч|ить, у, ишь, *impf.* (*of* с~) **1.** to contort; (*coll.*) к. грима́сы, ро́жи to make, pull faces. **2.** (*impf. only*) (*coll.*) к. из себя́ to pose (as); к. дурака́ to play the fool.

корч|ма́, мы́, *g. pl.* ~ём, *f.* (*obs.*) inn, tavern (*in Ukraine and Byelorussia*).

корчма́р|ь, я́, *m.* (*obs.*) innkeeper.

ко́ршун, а, *m.* (*orn.*) kite; (*fig.*) налете́ть, набро́ситься ~ом (на+*a.*) to pounce (on), swoop (onto).

коры́ст|ный (~ен, ~на), *adj.* mercenary, mercenary-minded.

корыстолю́б|ец, ца, *m.* profit-seeker, mercenary-minded person.

корыстолюби́в|ый (~, ~а), *adj.* self-interested, mercenary-minded.

корыстолю́би|е, я, *n.* self-interest, cupidity.

коры́ст|ь, и, *f.* (*coll.*) **1.** profit, gain; кака́я тебе́ в э́том к.? what are you getting out of it? **2.** cupidity.

коры́т|о, а, *n.* wash-tub; trough; оста́ться у разби́того ~а to be no better off than before, be back where one started.

кор|ь, и, *f.* measles.

кор|ьё, я́, *n.* (*collect., dial.*) bark (*stripped from the tree*).

корю́шк|а, и, *f.* smelt (*fish*).

коря́в|ый (~, ~а), *adj.* (*coll.*) **1.** rough, uneven; gnarled. **2.** (*fig.*) clumsy, uncouth. **3.** (*dial.*) pock-marked.

коря́г|а, и, *f.* snag (*tree or boughs impeding navigation*).

кос|а́¹, ы́, *a.* ~у́, *pl.* ~ы, *f.* plait, tress, braid.

кос|а́², ы́, *a.* ~у́, *pl.* ~ы, *f.* scythe; нашла́ к. на ка́мень he (has) met his match, he ran (has run) into a brick wall.

кос|а́³, ы́, *a.* ~у́, *pl.* ~ы, *f.* (*geogr.*) **1.** spit. **2.** (*dial.*) belt (*of trees*).

коса́р|ь¹, я́, *m.* mower (*agent*).

коса́р|ь², я́, *m.* chopper (*tool*).

ко́свенн|ый, *adj.* indirect, oblique; ~ые ули́ки circumstantial evidence; (*gram.*) к. паде́ж oblique case; ~ая речь indirect speech.

косе́канс, а, *m.* (*math.*) cosecant.

коси́лк|а, и, *f.* mowing-machine, mower.

ко́синус, а, *m.* (*math.*) cosine.

ко|си́ть¹, шу́, ~сишь, *impf.* (*of* с~) to mow; to cut; (*fig.*) to mow down; ~си́ ~са́ пока́ роса́ (*prov.*) make hay while the sun shines.

ко|си́ть², шу́, си́шь, *impf.* (*of* с~) **1.** to squint; к. на о́ба гла́за to have a squint in both eyes. **2.** (+*a. or i.*) to twist, slant (*mouth, eyes*). **3.** to be crooked.

ко|си́ться, шу́сь, си́шься, *impf.* (*of* по~) **1.** to slant. **2.** (*coll.*) (на+*a.*) to cast a sidelong look (at); (*fig.*) to look askance (at).

коси́ц|а, ы, *f.* **1.** lock (*of hair*). **2.** (*dim. of* коса́¹) pigtail.

косма́|тить, чу, тишь, *impf.* (*coll.*) to tousle.

космáт|ый (~, ~а), *adj.* shaggy.

косме́тик|а, и, *f.* cosmetics.

космети́ческий, *adj.* cosmetic; к. кабине́т beauty parlour; к. ремо́нт redecoration (*papering, painting of interior of house*).

косми́ческий, *adj.* cosmic, outer space; к. кора́бль space vehicle, space ship.

космого́ни|я, и, *f.* cosmogony.

космогра́фи|я, и, *f.* cosmography.

космодро́м, а, m. space-vehicle launching site.

космона́вт, а, m. astronaut, cosmonaut, space man.

космона́втик|а, и, *f.* astronautics, (outer) space exploration.

космополи́т, а, m. cosmopolite.

космополити́зм, а, m. cosmopolitanism.

космополити́ческий, *adj.* cosmopolitan.

ко́смос, а, m. cosmos; outer space.

ко́см|ы, ~, *no sing.* (*coll.*) locks, mane.

косне́|ть, ю, *impf.* (*of* за~) **1.** (в+*p.*) to stagnate (in). **2.** to stick.

косноязы́чи|е, я, *n.* confused articulation.

косноязы́ч|ный (~ен, ~на), *adj.* speaking thickly.

косн|у́ться, у́сь, ёшься, *pf. of* каса́ться.

ко́с|ный (~ен, ~на), *adj.* inert, sluggish; stagnant.

ко́со, *adv.* slantwise, aslant, askew; obliquely; смотре́ть к. to look askance, scowl.

кособо́к|ий (~, ~а), *adj.* (*coll.*) crooked, lop--sided.

косови́ц|а, ы, *f.* hay-making (*time*).

косоворо́тк|а, и, *f.* (Russian) shirt, blouse (*with collar fastening at side*).

косогла́зи|е, я, *n.* squint, cast in the eye.

косогла́з|ый (~, ~а), *adj.* cross-eyed, squint-eyed.

косого́р, а, m. slope, hill-side.

кос|о́й¹ (~, ~а́, ~о), *adj.* **1.** slanting; oblique; к. по́черк sloping handwriting; к. у́гол (*math.*) oblique angle; ~а́я черта́ oblique stroke; ~а́я са́жень в плеча́х (*coll.*) broad shoulders. **2.** squinting; cross-eyed. **3.** к. взгляд (*fig.*) sidelong glance.

кос|о́й², о́го, m. (*folk poet.*) hare.

косола́п|ый (~, ~а), *adj.* pigeon-toed; (*fig.*) clumsy.

косоуго́льный, *adj.* (*math.*) oblique-angled.

костёл, а, m. (Roman Catholic) church.

костене́|ть, ю, *impf.* (*of* о~) to grow stiff; to grow numb.

кост|ёр, ра́, m. bonfire; camp-fire.

кости́ст|ый (~, ~а), *adj.* bony.

ко|сти́ть, щу́, сти́шь, *impf.* (*coll.*) to abuse.

костля́в|ый (~, ~а), *adj.* bony.

ко́стный, *adj.* osseous; (*anat.*) к. мозг marrow.

костое́д|а, ы, *f.* (*med.*) caries.

костопра́в, а, m. bone-setter.

ко́сточк|а, и, *f.* **1.** *dim. of* кость; (*coll.*) вое́нная к. old soldier, military man; перемыва́ть ~и (+*d.*) to gossip about, pull to pieces; разбира́ть по ~ам to go through (a thing, matter) with a fine comb. **2.** stone (*of fruit*). **3.** ball (*of abacus*). **4.** bone (*of corset, etc.*).

костре́ц, а́, m. leg of meat.

костыл|ь, я́, m. **1.** crutch; ходи́ть на ~я́х to walk on crutches. **2.** (*tech.*) spike, drive. **3.** (*aeron.*) tail skid.

костыля́|ть, ю, *impf.* (*coll.*) **1.** to cudgel. **2.** to hobble.

кост|ь, и, *pl.* **~и, ~е́й,** *f.* **1.** bone; слоно́вая к. ivory; (*fig., coll.*) бе́лая к. blue blood; язы́к без ~е́й loose tongue; лечь ~ьми́ (*rhet.*) to fall in battle; пересчита́ть кому́-н. ~и to give someone a drubbing. **2.** die; игра́ть в ~и to dice.

костю́м, а, m. **1.** dress, clothes; в ~е Ада́ма, Е́вы (*joc.*) in one's birthday suit; маскара́дный к. fancy-dress. **2.** suit; costume; англи́йский к. tailor-made coat and skirt; вече́рний к. dress suit; пара́дный к. full dress.

костюме́р, а, m. (*theatr.*) costumier.

костюме́р|ный, *adj. of* ~; *as noun* ~**ная, ~ной,** *f.* (*theatr.*) wardrobe.

костюмиро́ва|нный, *p.p.p. of* ~ть *and adj.* **1.** in costume; in fancy-dress. **2.** к. бал, ве́чер fancy-dress ball.

костюмир|ова́ть, у́ю, *impf. and pf.* (*theatr.*) to dress.

костюмир|ова́ться, у́юсь, *impf. and pf.* to put on costume; to put on fancy-dress.

костю́м|ный, *adj. of* ~; ~**ная пье́са** period play.

костя́к, а́, m. skeleton; (*fig.*) backbone.

костян|о́й, *adj.* (made of) bone; ~**а́я мука́** bone-meal; к. но́жик ivory knife.

костя́шк|а, и, f. **1.** *dim. of* кость. **2.** knuckle. **3.** ball (*of abacus*).

косу́л|я, и, *f.* wild goat.

косу́шк|а, и, *f.* (*obs.*) half-bottle of vodka.

косы́нк|а, и, *f.* (triangular) kerchief, scarf.

косьб|а́, ы́, *f.* mowing.

костя́к|¹, а́, m. **1.** (door-)post; jamb; cheek. **2.** slope; sloping object.

кося́к², а́, m. **1.** herd (*of mares with only one stallion*). **2.** shoal, school; flock.

кот, а́, m. **1.** tom-cat; морско́й к. (*zool.*) sea--bear; (*coll.*) к. напла́кал nothing to speak of, practically nothing; купи́ть ~а́ в мешке́ to buy a pig in a poke; (*prov.*) не всё ~у́ ма́сленица, придёт и вели́кий пост after dinner comes the reckoning. **2.** (*sl.*) pimp.

котáнгенс, a, *m.* (*math.*) cotangent.

кот|ёл, лá, *m.* 1. copper, cauldron; (*fig.*) óбщий к. common stock. 2. (*tech.*) boiler. 3. (*pl.*) hopscotch.

котел|óк, кá, *m.* 1. pot. 2. mess-tin. 3. bowler (hat).

котéльн|ая, ой, *f.* boiler-house.

котéл|ьный, *adj.* of ~ 2; ~ьное желéзо boiler plate.

котéльщик, a, *m.* boiler-maker.

кот|ёнок, ёнка, *pl.* ~я́та, ~я́т, *m.* kitten.

кóтик, a, *m.* 1. fur-seal. 2. sealskin. 3. *affect. dim.* of кот. 4. (*affect. mode of address*) darling. 5. (*pl.*) *dim.* of коты́.

кóтик|овый, *adj.* of ~ 1, 2; к. прóмысел sealing; sealskin trade; ~овая шáпка sealskin cap.

котильóн, a, *m.* cotillion.

коти́р|овать, ую, *impf. and pf.* (*fin.*) to quote.

коти́р|оваться, уюсь, *impf. and pf.* 1. (*fin.*) (в+a.) to be quoted (at). 2. (*fig.*) to be rated.

котирóвк|а, и, *f.* (*fin.*) quotation.

ко|ти́ться, чýсь, ти́шься, *impf.* (*of* о~) to kitten, have kittens; to have young.

котлéт|а, ы, *f.* cutlet; отбивнáя к. chop.

котловáн, a, *m.* (*tech.*) foundation ditch, trench.

котлови́н|а, ы, *f.* (*geogr.*) hollow, basin.

кот|овáть, ýю, *impf.* (*sl.*) to be courting.

котóмк|а, и, *f.* wallet; knapsack.

котóр|ый, *pron.* 1. *interrog. and relat.* which; к. час? what time is it?; в ~ом часý он зашёл? what time did he call?; к. раз? how many times?; (*coll.*) к. раз я тебé э́то говорю́? how many times have I told you! 2. *relat.* who. 3. (*coll.*) к.... к. some ... some (others); ~ые бы́ли в чулкáх, ~ые с гóлыми ногáми some were wearing stockings and some were bare-legged.

котóрый-либо, *pron.* = к.-нибýдь.

котóрый-нибýдь, *pron.* some; one or other.

коттéдж, a, *m.* small (detached) house.

котýрн, a, *m.* (*theatr., hist.*) buskin; станови́ться на ~ы (*fig.*) to assume a tragic tone.

кот|ы́, óв, *no sing.* (*dial.*) (*woman's*) fur slippers.

кот|я́та, я́т, *see* ~ёнок.

кóуш, a, *m.* (*naut.*) thimble.

кóфе, *indecl., m.* coffee; к. в зёрнах coffee beans.

кофеи́н, a, *m.* caffeine.

кóфе|й, я, *m.* (*coll., obs.*) coffee.

кофéйник, a, *m.* coffee-pot.

кофéйниц|а, ы, *f.* 1. coffee-grinder. 2. coffee tin.

коф|éйный, *adj.* of ~е.

кофé|йня, йни, *g. pl.* ~ен, *f.* (*obs.*) coffee-house.

кóфт|а, ы, *f.* 1. (*woman's*) jacket. 2. (*coll.*) (*woman's*) short, warm overcoat.

кóфточк|а, и, *f.* blouse.

кочáн, á (*and dial.* кочнá), *m.* к. капýсты head of cabbage.

коч|евáть, ýю, *impf.* 1. to be a nomad, to roam from place to place, wander. 2. (*of birds and animals*) to migrate.

кочёвк|а, и, *f.* (*coll.*) 1. nomad camp. 2. wandering; nomadic existence.

кочéвник, a, *m.* nomad.

кочевóй, *adj.* 1. nomadic. 2. (*of birds and animals*) migratory.

кочевря́ж|иться, усь, *impf.* (*coll.*) 1. to be obstinate. 2. to pose, put on airs.

кочéв|ье, ья, *g. pl.* ~ий, *n.* 1. nomad encampment. 2. nomad territory.

кочегáр, a, *m.* stoker, fireman.

кочегáрк|а, и, *f.* stoke-hole, stoke-hold.

кочене́|ть, ю, *impf.* (*of* за~ *and* о~) to become numb; to stiffen.

кочер|гá, ги́, *g. pl.* ~ёг, *f.* poker.

кочеры́жк|а, и, *f.* cabbage-stalk, cabbage-stump.

кóчет, a, *m.* (*dial.*) cock.

кóчк|а, и, *f.* hummock; tussock.

кочковáт|ый (~, ~а), *adj.* hummocky, tussocky.

ко|чýсь, ти́шься, *see* ~ти́ться.

кош, a, *m.* 1. (*nomads'*) tent. 2. (*hist.*) camp (*of Zaporozhian Cossacks*).

кошáтник, a, *m.* 1. dealer in (stolen) cats. 2. (*coll.*) cat-lover.

кош|áчий, *adj.* of ~ка; feline; к. глаз (*min.*) cat's eye; к. концéрт caterwauling; (*fig.*) hooting, barracking; ~áчьи ухвáтки cat-like (cattish) ways; *as noun* (*zool.*) ~áчьи, ~áчьих, Felidae.

кош|евóй, *adj.* of ~; к. атамáн commander of Cossack camp.

кошел|ёк, ькá, *m.* purse; (*fig.*) тугóй к. tight-filled purse.

кошёл|ь, я́, *m.* 1. (*obs.*) purse. 2. (*dial.*) bag.

кошени́л|евый, *adj.* of ~ь.

кошени́л|ь, и, *f.* cochineal.

кóшк|а, и, *f.* 1. cat; (*fig., coll.*) игрáть в ~и-мы́шки to play cat-and-mouse; жить как к. с собáкой to lead a cat-and-dog life; чёрная к. пробежáла мéжду ни́ми they have fallen out; нóчью все ~и сéры when candles are out all cats are grey; у негó ~и скребýт на сéрдце he is heavy-hearted. 2. (*tech., naut.*) grapnel, drag. 3. mountaineering boot. 4. (*pl.*) cat-o'-nine-tails.

кошм|á, ы́, *pl.* ~ы, ~, *f.* large piece of felt.

кошмáр, a, *m.* nightmare (*also fig.*).

кошмáр|ный (~ен, ~на), *adj.* nightmarish; (*fig.*) horrible, awful.

кошт, a, *m.* (*obs.*) expense; на казённом ~е at Government expense.

ко|шу́, си́шь, *see* ~си́ть.

коще́|й, я, *m.* **1.** Koshchei (*an evil being in Russian folk-lore*); *fig. of a tall, thin old man.* **2.** (*fig., coll.*) miser.

кощу́нствен|ный (~, ~на), *adj.* blasphemous.

кощу́нств|о, а, *n.* blasphemy.

кощу́нств|овать, ую, *impf.* to blaspheme.

коэффицие́нт, а, *m.* (*math.*) coefficient, factor; (*tech.*) к. мо́щности power factor; к. поле́зного де́йствия efficiency; к. поте́рь loss factor.

краб, а, *m.* (*zool.*) crab.

кра́вч|ий, его, *m.* royal carver (*in Muscovite Russia*).

кра́г|и, ~, *sing.* ~а, ~и, *f.* **1.** leggings. **2.** cuffs (of gloves).

кра́ден|ый, *adj.* stolen; ~ое (*collect.*) stolen goods.

кра|ду́, дёшь, *see* ~сть.

кра́дучись, *adv.* stealthily; идти́ к. to creep, slink.

краеве́д, а, *m.* student of local lore, history and economy.

краеве́дени|е, я, *n.* study of local lore, history and economy.

краеве́д|ческий, *adj. of* ~ение; к. музе́й museum of local lore, history, and economy.

краево́й, *adj. of* край 4.

краеуго́льный, *adj.* (*rhet.*) basic; к. ка́мень corner-stone.

кра́ж|а, и, *f.* theft; larceny; к. со взло́мом burglary; квалифици́рованная к. (*leg.*) aggravated theft.

кра|й, я, о ~е, в ~ю́, *pl.* ~я́, ~ёв, *m.* **1.** edge; brim; brink (*also fig.*); пере́дний к. (*mil.*) first line, forward positions; быть на ~ю́ моги́лы to have one foot in the grave; конца́-~ю нет there is no end to it; ~ем у́ха слу́шать to overhear; на ~ю́ све́та at the world's end; че́рез к. overmuch, beyond measure; хлебну́ть че́рез к. (*coll.*) to have a drop too much. **2.** side (*of meat*); то́лстый к. rib-steak; то́нкий к. chine (of beef), upper cut. **3.** land, country; в на́ших ~я́х in our part of the world; в чужи́х ~я́х in foreign parts. **4.** (*administrative division of U.S.S.R.*) krai.

край- *abbr. of* краево́й.

кра́йне, *adv.* extremely.

кра́йн|ий, *adj.* **1.** (*in var. senses*) extreme; last; uttermost; в ~ем слу́чае in the last resort; по ~ей ме́ре at least; ~яя плоть (*anat.*) foreskin, prepuce. **2.** (*sport*) outside, wing; к. напада́ющий outside forward, wing forward.

кра́йност|ь, и, *f.* **1.** extreme; в ~и in the last resort; до ~и in the extreme, extremely. **2.** extremity; быть в ~и to be reduced to extremity.

кракови́к, а, *m.* (*dance*) Cracovienne.

крал, а, *see* красть.

кра́л|я, и, *f.* (*coll.*) beauty; (*cards*) queen.

крамо́л|а, ы, *f.* (*obs.*) sedition.

крамо́льник, а, *m.* (*obs.*) maker of, participant in sedition; plotter.

крамо́льный, *adj.* (*obs.*) seditious.

кран[1], а, *m.* tap, cock.

кран[2], а, *m.* crane; к.-двуно́га (*naut.*) sheer-legs.

кра́н|ец, ца, *m.* (*naut.*) fender.

краниоло́ги|я, и, *f.* craniology.

крановщи́к, а́, *m.* crane operator.

кра́н|овый, *adj. of* ~[1], [2].

крап, а, *no pl.*, *m.* **1.** specks. **2.** pattern on the backs of playing cards.

кра́п|ать, ает *and* лет *impf.* to spatter; дождь ~лет it is spitting with rain.

крапи́в|а, ы, *f.* (stinging-)nettle; глуха́я к. dead nettle.

крапи́вник, а, *m.* (*orn.*) wren.

крапи́вниц|а, ы, *f.* nettle-rash.

крапи́в|ный, *adj. of* ~а; ~ная лихора́дка nettle-rash; ~ное се́мя (*obs., joc., of civil servants*) tribe of quill-drivers, pen-pushers.

кра́пин|а, ы, *f.* speck; spot.

кра́пин|ка, ки, *f.* = ~а.

краплёный, *adj.* (*of cards*) marked.

крас|а́, ы́, *f.* **1.** (*obs.*) beauty; (*iron.*) во всей свое́й ~е́ in all one's glory. **2.** (*rhet.*) ornament.

краса́в|ец, ца, *m.* handsome man; Adonis.

краса́виц|а, ы, *f.* beauty (*beautiful woman*).

краса́вчик, а, *m.* (*coll.*) **1.** = краса́вец. **2.** (*iron.*) dandy.

краси́вост|ь, и, *f.* (mere) prettiness.

краси́в|ый (~, ~а), *adj.* beautiful; handsome; fine.

краси́льный, *adj.* appertaining to dyes.

краси́|льня, ьни, *g. pl.* ~ен, *f.* dye-house, dye-works.

краси́льщик, а, *m.* dyer.

краси́тел|ь, я, *m.* dye(-stuff).

кра́|сить, шу, сишь, *impf.* (*of* по~) **1.** to paint; to colour; он кра́сит ло́дку в бе́лое с голубы́м he is painting the boat white and blue. **2.** to dye; to stain (*wood, glass*). **3.** (*impf. only*) to adorn.

кра́|ситься, шусь, сишься, *impf.* **1.** (*pf.* на~) to make up. **2.** (*of newly dyed or newly-painted objects*) to stain. **3.** *pass. of* ~сить.

кра́ск|а, и, *f.* **1.** painting; colouring; dyeing. **2.** paint; dye; акваре́льная к. water-colour; ма́сляная к. oil-colour; типогра́фская к. printer's ink; писа́ть ~ами to paint. **3.** (*pl., fig.*) colours; сгуща́ть ~и (*coll.*) to lay it on thick. **4.** blush; вогна́ть кого́-н. в ~у (*coll.*) to make someone blush.

красне́|ть, ю, *impf.* (*of* по~) **1.** to redden, become red. **2.** to blush, colour; (*fig.*) к. за+*a.* to blush for. **3.** (*impf. only*) to show red.

краснé|ться, юсь, *impf.* to show red.

красноармé|ец, йца, *m.* Red Army man.

красноармé|йский, *adj.* *of* ~ец *and* Крáсная Áрмия.

краснобá|й, я, *m.* (*coll.*) phrase-monger, rhetorician.

краснобáйств|о, а, *n.* (*coll.*) eloquence, fair--sounding speech.

краснобýрый, *adj.* reddish-brown.

красновáт|ый (~, ~а), *adj.* reddish.

красногвардé|ец, йца, *m.* (*hist.*) Red Guard.

красногвардé|йский, *adj.* *of* ~ец.

краснодерéв|ец, ца, *m.* cabinet-maker.

краснодерéв|щик, щика, *m.* = ~ец.

краснозвёздный, *adj.* having the red star (*emblem of the Soviet Army*).

краснознамённый, *adj.* holding the order of the Red Banner.

краснокóж|ий (~, ~а), *adj.* red-skinned; *as noun* к., ~его, *m.* red-skin.

краснолéсь|е, я, *n.* pine forest.

краснолúцый, *adj.* red-faced, rubicund.

красноречúв|ый (~, ~а), *adj.* eloquent; expressive; (*fig.*) telltale, significant.

красноречú|е, я, *n.* eloquence; oratory.

краснот|á, ы́, *f.* 1. redness. 2. red spot.

краснофлóт|ец, ца, *m.* Red Navy man.

краснофлóт|ский, *adj.* *of* ~ец *and* Крáсный Флот.

краснощёкий, *adj.* red-checked.

краснýх|а, и, *f.* (*med.*) German measles.

крáс|ный (~ен, ~нá, ~но), *adj.* 1. red (*also fig., polit.*); ~ное дéрево mahogany; ~ная шáпочка Little Red Riding Hood; к. уголóк 'Red Corner' (*room in factories, etc., providing recreational and educational facilities*); (*fig.*) ~ная строкá (first line of) new para-graph; сказáть для ~ного словцá to say as a joke, for effect; ~ная ценá (*coll.*) out-side figure, the most which one is willing to рау; проходúть ~ной нúтью to stand out, run through (*of theme, motif*); пустúть ~ного петухá (*coll.*) to set fire, commit act of arson; попáсть под ~ную шáпку (*coll., obs.*) to become a soldier. 2. (*obs., folk poet. or coll.*) beautiful; (*fig.*) fine; ~ная дéвица bonny lass; лéто ~ное glorious summer; (*prov.*) долг платежóм ~ен one good turn deserves another; к. ýгол place of honour (*in peasant hut*). 3. *signifies that object qualified is of high quality or value:* ~ная ры́ба cartila-ginous fish; (*obs.*) к. товáр textiles; к. зверь superior types of game (*such as bear, elk*); к. лес conifer forest.

крас|овáться, ýюсь, *impf.* 1. to impress by one's beauty, stand out vividly. 2. (+*i.*) (*coll.*) to flaunt, show off.

красот|á, ы́, *pl.* ~ы, *f.* beauty; (*coll.*) к.! splendid!

красóтк|а, и, *f.* (*coll.*) 1. good-looking girl. 2. (*obs.*) sweetheart.

крáс|очный, *adj.* 1. *adj. of* ~ка. 2. (~очен, ~очна) colourful, highly coloured.

кра|сть, дý, дёшь, *past* ~л, ~ла, *impf.* (*of у*~) to steal.

крá|сться, дýсь, дёшься, *past* ~лся, ~лась, *impf.* to steal, creep, sneak.

крат, *only in phrase* вó сто к. a hundredfold.

крáт|кий (~ок, ~á, ~ко), *adj.* short; brief; concise; в ~ких словáх in short, briefly; *as noun* ~кая, ~кой, *f.* only in и с ~кой *old name of Russian letter* й (*now* и ~кое).

крáтко, *adv.* briefly.

кратковрéменный, *adj.* of short duration, brief; transitory.

краткосрóч|ный (~ен, ~на), *adj.* short--term.

крáтн|ое, ого, *n.* (*math.*) multiple; óбщее наимéньшее к. least common multiple.

крáт|ный (~ен, ~на), *adj.* (+*i.*) divisible without remainder (by); дéвять — числó ~ное трём nine is a multiple of three.

крат|чáйший, *superl. of* ~кий.

крáт|че, *comp. of* ~кий *and* ~ко.

крах, а, *m.* (*fin. and fig.*) crash; failure.

крахмáл, а, *m.* starch.

крахмáлист|ый (~, ~а), *adj.* containing starch.

крахмáл|ить, ю, ишь, *impf.* (*of* на~) to starch.

крахмáл|ьный, *adj. of* ~; starched; к. ворот-ничóк stiff collar.

крáше (*coll.*) *comp. of* красúв|ый *and* ~о; к. в гроб клáдут pale as a ghost.

крáшени|е, я, *n.* dyeing.

крашенúн|а, ы, *f.* (*obs.*) coarse, thick linen.

крáшеный, *adj.* 1. painted; coloured. 2. dyed. 3. made-up, wearing make-up; (*pejor.*) painted.

краюх|а, и, *f.* (*coll.*) thick slice of bread.

креатýр|а, ы, *f.* creature, minion.

кревéтк|а, и, *f.* (*zool.*) shrimp.

крéдит, а, *m.* (*book-keeping*) credit.

кредúт, а, *m.* credit; откры́ть, предостáвить к. to give credit; отпустúть в к. to supply on credit; (*fig.*) пóльзоваться ~ом (у) to have credit (with).

кредúтк|а, и, *f.* (*obs.*) bank-note.

кредúт|ный, *adj. of* ~; к. билéт (*obs.*) bank--note.

кредит|овáть, ýю, *impf. and pf.* (*fin.*) to credit, give credit (to).

кредит|овáться, ýюсь, *impf. and pf.* (*fin.*) 1. to obtain funds on credit. 2. *pass. of* ~овáть.

кредитóр, а, *m.* creditor; к. по закладнóй mortgagee.

кредитоспосóбност|ь, и, *f.* solvency.

кредитоспосо́б|ный (~ен, ~на), *adj.* solvent.

кре́до, *indecl., n.* credo.

крез, а, *m.* Crœsus.

кре́йсер, а, *pl.* ~ы *and* ~а́, *m.* (*naut.*) cruiser; лине́йный к. battle cruiser.

кре́йсер|ский, *adj. of* ~; кре́йсерская ско́рость cruising speed.

кре́йсиров|о, а, *n.* (*naut.*) cruise, cruising.

крейси́р|овать, ую, *impf.* (*naut.*) to cruise.

кре́кинг, а, *m.* (*tech.*) **1.** cracking (*oil refining*). **2.** oil refinery.

кре́кинг-проце́сс, а, *m.* (*tech.*) cracking (*oil refining*).

креки́р|овать, ую, *impf. and pf.* (*tech.*) to crack.

крем, а, *m.* (*in var. senses*) cream; (сапо́жный) к. shoe-polish.

кремалье́р|а, ы, *f.* (*tech.*) rack and pinion gear.

кремато́ри|й, я, *m.* crematorium.

кремац|ио́нный, *adj. of* ~ия; ~ио́нная печь incinerator.

крема́ци|я, и, *f.* cremation.

крем|е́нь, ня́, *m.* flint; (*fig.*) hard-hearted person; skinflint.

кремеш|о́к, ка́, *m.* piece of flint.

кремл|ёвский, *adj. of* ~ь.

кремл|ь, я́, *m.* citadel; (моско́вский) к. the Kremlin.

кремнёв|ый, *adj.* made of flint; ~ое ружьё flint-lock.

кремнезём, а, *m.* (*min., chem.*) silica.

кремнеки́слый, *adj.* (*chem.*) silicic; к. на́трий sodium silicate.

кре́мниевый, *adj.* (*chem.*) silicic.

кре́мни|й, я, *m.* (*chem.*) silicon.

кремни́стый, *adj.* **1.** (*min.*) siliceous. **2.** (*obs.*) stony.

кре́м|овый, *adj.* **1.** *adj. of* ~. **2.** cream (-coloured).

крен, а, *m.* (*naut.*) list, heel; (*aeron.*) bank; дать к. (*naut.*) to list, heel (over); (*aeron.*) to bank.

кренде́л|ь, я, *pl.* ~и *and* ~я́, *m.* (*cul.*) pretzel; ни за каки́е ~я́ (*coll.*) not for anything; вы́писывать ~я́ to stagger, lurch; сверну́ться ~ем to curl up.

крен|и́ть, ю́, и́шь, *impf.* (*of* на~) to cause to heel, list.

крен|и́ться, ю́сь, и́шься, *impf.* (*of* на~) (*naut.*) to list, heel (over); (*aeron.*) to bank.

креозо́т, а, *m.* creosote.

креол, а, *m.* creole.

креол|ьский, *adj. of* ~.

креп, а, *m.* crêpe; тра́урный к. mourning crape.

крепдеши́н, а, *m.* crêpe de chine.

крепёжный, *adj.* к. лес pit-props.

крепи́льщик, а, m. (*tech.*) timberer (*in mines*).

крепи́тельный, *adj.* **1.** (*tech.*) strengthening. **2.** (*med.*) astringent.

креп|и́ть, лю́, и́шь, *impf.* **1.** (*tech. and fig.*) to strengthen; (*mining*) to timber. **2.** (*naut.*) to make fast, hitch, lash; к. паруса́ to furl sails. **3.** (*med.*) to constipate, render costive.

креп|и́ться, лю́сь, и́шься, *impf.* **1.** to hold out. **2.** *pass. of* ~и́ть.

креп|кий (~ок, ~ка́, ~ко), *adj.* strong; sound; sturdy, robust; (*fig.*) firm; к. моро́з hard frost; ~кие напи́тки spirits; ~кое словцо́ (*coll.*) swear-word, strong language; к. сон sound sleep; к. чай strong tea.

кре́пко, *adv.* strongly; firmly; soundly; (*coll.*) к.-на́крепко very firmly; к.-на́крепко завяза́ть to tie really tight.

крепкоголо́в|ый (~, ~а), *adj.* (*coll.*) pig-headed.

крепколо́б|ый (~, ~а), *adj.* (*coll.*) pig-headed.

крепле́ни|е, я, *n.* **1.** strengthening; fastening. **2.** (*mining*) timbering. **3.** (*naut.*) lashing; furling. **4.** (ski) binding.

креплёный, *adj.* (*of wines*) fortified.

кре́пн|уть, у, ешь, *impf.* (*of* о~) to get stronger.

крепостни́к, а́, *m.* advocate of serfdom.

крепостни́|ческий, *adj. of* ~к *and* ~чество.

крепостни́честв|о, а, *n.* serfdom.

крепостн|о́й¹, *adj.* serf; к. крестья́нин (*peasant*) serf; ~о́е пра́во serfdom; *as noun* к., ~о́го, *m.* serf.

**крепостно́й,² ** *adj.* of кре́пость².

кре́пост|ь¹, и, *f.* (*in var. senses*) strength.

кре́пост|ь², и, *f.* fortress.

кре́пост|ь³, и, f. (*hist., leg.*) ку́пчая к. deed of purchase.

крепча́|ть, ет, *impf.* to grow stronger, get up (*of wind*); to get harder (*of frost*).

кре́п|че, *comp. of* ~кий *and* ~ко.

крепы́ш, а́, *m.* (*coll.*) brawny fellow; sturdy child.

креп|ь, и, *f.* (*mining*) timbering.

кре́с|ло, ла, *g. pl.* ~ел, *n.* arm-chair, easy-chair; (*theatr.*) stall.

кресс-сала́т, а, *m.* cress, watercress.

крест, а́, *m.* **1.** cross; поста́вить к. (на+*p.*) to give up for lost; целова́ть к. (+*d.*) (*obs.*) to take an oath (to). **2.** the sign of the cross; осени́ть себя́ ~о́м to cross oneself, make the sign of the cross.

крест|е́ц, ца́, *m.* (*anat.*) sacrum.

крести́льный, *adj.* baptismal.

крести́н|ы, ~, (*no sing.*) **1.** christening. **2.** christening-party.

кре|сти́ть, щу́, ~стишь, *impf.* **1.** (*pf.* к. *or* о~) to baptize, christen. **2.** (*no pf.*) (+*a.* y) to be godfather, godmother (*to the child of*); (*obs., coll.*) не дете́й к. мне с ни́ми I have no connection with them. **3.** (*of* пере~) to make the sign of the cross over.

кре|сти́ться, щу́сь, ∼сти́шься, *impf.* **1.** (*pf.* к. *or* о∼) to be baptized, be christened. **2.** (*pf.* пере∼) to cross oneself.

крест-на́крест, *adv.* crosswise.

кре́стник, а, *m.* god-son, god-child.

кре́стниц|а, ы, *f.* god-daughter, god-child.

крёст|ный, *adj. of* ∼; ∼ное зна́мение sign of the cross; ∼ ход (religious) procession; ∼ное целова́ние oath-taking; (*coll.*) с на́ми ∼ная си́ла! good heavens!

крёстн|ый, *adj.* к. оте́ц (*also as noun* к., ∼ого, *m.*) god-father; ∼ая мать (*also as noun* ∼ая, ∼ой, *f.*) god-mother; ∼ые де́ти god-children.

крестови́к, а́, *m.* garden-spider.

крестови́н|а, ы, *f.* (*railways*) frog.

кресто́вник, а, *m.* (*bot.*) ragwort, groundsel.

крест|о́вый, *adj. of* ∼; к. похо́д crusade.

крестоно́с|ец, ца, *m.* crusader.

крестообра́з|ный (∼ен, ∼на), *adj.* cruciform; (*bot.*, *zool.*) cruciate.

крестоцве́тн|ые, ых (*bot.*) cruciferae.

крестцо́вый, *adj.* (*anat.*) sacral.

крестья́н|ин, ина, *pl.* ∼е, ∼, *m.* peasant.

крестья́нк|а, и, *f.* peasant woman.

крестья́нский, *adj.* peasant.

крестья́нств|о, а, *n.* **1.** (*collect.*) the peasants, peasantry. **2.** (*obs.*) the life of a peasant, farm-labouring.

крестья́нств|овать, ую, *impf.* (*obs.*) to till the soil.

крети́н, а, *m.* cretin; (*fig.*, *coll.*) idiot, imbecile.

кретини́зм, а, *m.* cretinism; (*fig.*, *coll.*) idiocy, imbecility.

крето́н, а, *m.* (*text.*) cretonne.

кре́чет, а, *m.* (*orn.*) gerfalcon.

креще́ндо, *adv.* (*mus.*) crescendo.

креще́ни|е, я, *n.* **1.** baptism, christening; боево́е к. baptism of fire. **2.** Epiphany.

креще́н|ский, *adj. of* ∼ие 2; к. моро́з, хо́лод *of severe frost, cold;* (*fig.*, *coll.*) coldness, severity.

крещён|ый, *adj.* baptized; *as noun* к., ∼ого, *m.* (*coll.*) Christian.

кре|щу́, ∼сти́шь, *see* ∼сти́ть.

крив|а́я, о́й, *f.* (*math.*, *econ.*, *etc.*) curve; (*coll.*) к. вы́везет something will turn up; его́ на ∼о́й не объе́дешь you won't catch him napping.

кри́вд|а, ы, *f.* (*arch. and folk poet.*) falsehood; injustice.

криве́|ть, ю, *impf.* (*of* о∼) to lose one eye.

кривизн|а́, ы́, *f.* crookedness; curvature.

крив|и́ть, лю́, и́шь, *impf.* (*of* с∼) to bend, distort; (*coll.*) к. гу́бы, рот to twist one's mouth, curl one's lip; к. (*pf.* по∼) душо́й to act against one's conscience.

крив|и́ться, лю́сь, и́шься, *impf.* **1.** (*pf.* по∼) to become crooked, bent. **2.** (*pf.* с∼) (*coll.*) to make a wry face.

кривля́к|а, и, *m. and f.* (*coll.*) poseur; affected person.

кривля́нь|е, я, *n.* affectation.

кривля́|ться, юсь, *impf.* (*coll.*) to be affected, behave in an affected manner.

кривобо́к|ий (∼, ∼а), *adj.* lop-sided.

кривогла́з|ый (∼, ∼а), *adj.* blind in one eye.

кридуши́|е, я, *n.* (*obs.*) duplicity, crookedness.

криводу́ш|ный (∼ен, ∼на), *adj.* (*obs.*) dishonest, crooked.

крив|о́й (∼, ∼а́, ∼о), *adj.* **1.** crooked; ∼о́е зе́ркало distorting mirror; ∼а́я улы́бка wry smile; (*fig.*) ∼ы́е пути́ crooked ways. **2.** (*coll.*) one-eyed.

криволине́йный, *adj.* (*math.*) curvilinear; (*tech.*) к. паз cam slot, cam groove.

кривоно́г|ий (∼, ∼а), *adj.* bandy-legged, bow-legged.

кривото́лк|и, ов, *no sing.* false rumours.

кривоши́п, а, *m.* (*tech.*) crank; crankshaft.

кри́зис, а, *m.* crisis.

крик, а, *m.* cry, shout; ∼и clamour, outcry; после́дний к. мо́ды the last word in fashion.

кри́кет, а, *m.* (*sport*) cricket.

крикли́в|ый (∼, ∼а), *adj.* **1.** clamorous, bawling. **2.** loud, penetrating. **3.** (*fig.*, *coll.*) loud; blatant.

кри́кн|уть, у, ешь, *inst. pf. of* крича́ть.

крику́н, а́, *m.* (*coll.*) **1.** shouter, bawler. **2.** babbler.

кримина́л, а, *m.* (*coll.*) **1.** foul play. **2.** crime.

криминали́ст, а, *m.* (*leg.*) specialist in crime detection.

криминали́стик|а, и, *f.* (science of) crime detection.

кримина́льный, *adj.* criminal.

кримино́лог, а, *m.* criminologist.

криминоло́ги|я, и, *f.* criminology.

кри́нка = кры́нка.

криноли́н, а, *m.* crinoline.

криптогра́мм|а, ы, *f.* cryptogram.

криптогра́фи|я, и, *f.* cryptography.

криста́лл, а, *m.* crystal.

кристаллиза́ци|я, и, *f.* crystallization.

кристаллиз|ова́ть, у́ю, *impf. and pf.* (*pf. also* за∼) to crystallize (*trans.*).

кристаллиз|ова́ться, у́юсь, *impf. and pf.* (*pf. also* за∼) to crystallize (*intrans.*; *also fig.*).

кристаллографи́ческий, *adj.* crystallographic.

кристаллогра́фи|я, и, *f.* crystallography.

криста́л|ьный, *adj.* **1.** crystalline. **2.** (∼ен, ∼ьна) (*fig.*) crystal-clear.

крите́ри|й, я, *m.* criterion.

кри́тик, а, *m.* critic.

кри́тик|а, и, *f.* **1.** criticism. **2.** critique.

критика́н, а, *m.* (*coll.*, *pejor.*) fault-finder, carper.

критика́нств|овать, ую, *impf.* (*coll., pejor.*) to engage in fault-finding; to carp.

критик|ова́ть, у́ю, *impf.* to criticize.

критици́зм, а, *m.* **1.** critical attitude. **2.** (*philos.*) criticism.

крити́ческий, *adj.* (*in var. senses*) critical; к. моме́нт (*fig.*) crucial moment.

кри́ц|а, ы, *f.* (*tech.*) bloom.

кри|ча́ть, чу́, чи́шь, *impf.* (*of* ~кнуть) **1.** to cry, shout; to yell, scream; к. (на+*a.*) to shout (at); к. о по́мощи to call for help. **2.** (о+*p.*) (*coll., pejor.*) to make a song (about), cry out (against).

крича́|щий, *pres. part. act. of* ~ть *and adj.* (*fig., coll.*) loud; blatant.

кри́|чный, *adj. of* ~ца (*tech.*); к. горн finery, bloomery; ~чное произво́дство finery process.

кроа́т, а, *m.* = хорва́т.

кроа́тский, *adj.* = хорва́тский.

кров, а, *m.* roof; shelter; оста́ться без ~а to be left without a roof over one's head.

крова́в|ый, *adj.* **1.** bloody; (*fig.*) ~ая ба́ня blood-bath. **2.** blood-stained.

крова́т|ь, и, *f.* bed; bedstead.

кро́в|ельный, *adj. of* ~ля.

кро́вельщик, а, *m.* roof-maker.

кровено́сн|ый, *adj.* appertaining to the circulation of the blood; ~ая систе́ма circulatory system; к. сосу́д blood-vessel.

крови́нк|а, и, *f.* (*coll.*) drop of blood; у него́ ни ~и в лице́ he is deathly pale.

кро́в|ля, ли, *g. pl.* ~ель, *f.* roof.

кро́вн|ый, *adj.* **1.** blood; ~ое родство́ blood relationship, consanguinity; ~ая месть blood feud. **2.** (*of animals*) thorough-bred. **3.** (*fig.*) vital, deep, intimate; моё ~ое де́ло an affair which concerns me closely; ~ые интере́сы vital interests; ~ые де́ньги money earned by the sweat of one's brow. **4.** (*fig.*) deadly; ~ая оби́да deadly insult.

кровожа́д|ный (~ен, ~на), *adj.* blood-thirsty.

кровоизлия́ни|е, я, *n.* (*med.*) haemorrhage.

кровообраще́ни|е, я, *n.* circulation of the blood.

кровооста́навливающ|ий, *adj.* ~ее сре́дство styptic.

кровопи́йц|а, ы, *g. pl.* ~, *m. and f.* (*fig., rhet.*) blood-sucker.

кровоподтёк, а, *m.* bruise.

кровопроли́ти|е, я, *n.* bloodshed.

кровопроли́тный, *adj.* bloody; sanguinary.

кровопуска́ни|е, я, *n.* (*med.*) blood-letting, phlebotomy.

кровосмеше́ни|е, я, *n.* incest.

кровосо́с, а, *m.* **1.** vampire bat. **2.** (*dial.*) vampire. **3.** (*coll.*) blood-sucker.

кровосо́сн|ый, *adj.* ~ая ба́нка cupping-glass.

кровотече́ни|е, я, *n.* haemorrhage; bleeding.

кровоточи́вост|ь, и, *f.* (*med.*) haemophilia.

кровоточи́в|ый (~, ~а), *adj.* **1.** bleeding. **2.** (*med.; obs.*) haemophiliac.

кровоточи́т|ь, ~, *impf.* to bleed.

кровоха́ркани|е, я, *n.* blood-spitting; (*med.*) haemoptysis.

кров|ь, и, о ~и, в ~и, *g. pl.* ~е́й, *f.* blood (*also fig.*); в к., до ~и till it bleeds, till blood flows; изби́ть, разби́ть в к. to draw blood; пусти́ть к. (+*d.*) to bleed (*trans.*); (*fig.*) по ~и by birth; к. с молоко́м (*coll.*) the very picture of health, blooming; у него́ к. кипи́т his blood is up; страсть к игре́ у него́ в ~й gambling is in his blood; войти́ в плоть и к. to become ingrained; по́ртить кому́-н. к. to put someone out, annoy someone; се́рдце у меня́ облива́ется ~ью my heart bleeds; пить чью-н. к. (*rhet.*) to suck someone's blood, batten on someone.

кровяни́ст|ый (~, ~а), *adj.* containing some blood.

кров|яно́й, *adj. of* ~ь.

кро|и́ть, ю́, и́шь, *impf.* (*of* с~) to cut (out).

кро́йк|а, и, *f.* cutting (out).

кроке́т, а, *m.* croquet.

кроке́т|ный, *adj. of* ~.

кроки́, *indecl., n.* sketch-map; rough sketch.

кроки́р|овать, ую, *impf.* to sketch.

крокир|ова́ть, у́ю, *impf. and pf.* (*at croquet*) to roquet.

крокоди́л, а, *m.* crocodile.

крокоди́л|ов *and* ~**овый,** *adj. of* ~.

кро́лик, а, *m.* rabbit.

кроликово́д, а, *m.* rabbit-breeder.

кроликово́дств|о, а, *n.* rabbit-breeding.

кро́ли|ковый *and* ~**чий,** *adj. of* ~к; ~чий мех rabbit-skin.

крол|ь, я, *m.* (*sport*) crawl (stroke).

крольча́тник, а, *m.* rabbit-hutch.

крольчи́х|а, и, *f.* doe-rabbit.

кро́ме, *prep.*+*g.* **1.** except. **2.** besides, in addition to; к. того́ besides, moreover, furthermore; (*coll.*) к. шу́ток joking apart.

кроме́шн|ый, *adj.* ад к. inferno; тьма ~ая (*New Testament*) outer darkness; (*fig.*) pitch darkness.

кро́мк|а, и, *f.* edge; (*of material*) selvage; пере́дняя, за́дняя к. leading (*aeron.*) edge, trailing edge; к. на ~у with edges overlapping, (*naut.*) clinker-built; к. тротуа́ра kerb.

кромса́|ть, ю, *impf.* (*of* ис~) (*coll.*) to cut up carelessly.

крон, а, *m.* chrome yellow.

кро́н|а¹, ы, *f.* crown (*of a tree*).

кро́н|а², ы, *f.* (*unit of currency*) crown.

кронци́ркул|ь, я, *m.* (*tech.*) calipers.

кро́ншнеп, а, *m.* (*orn.*) curlew.

кронштейн, а, *m.* (*tech.*) bracket; corbel.

кропа́|ть, ю, *impf.* (*coll.*) **1.** (*obs.*) to mend, patch. **2.** to potter away at. **3.** to scribble.

кропи́л|о, а, *n.* (*eccl.*) aspergillum.

кроп|и́ть, лю, и́шь, *impf.* (*of* о~) **1.** to besprinkle; to asperse. **2.** (*intrans.*; *of rain*) to trickle, spot.

кропотли́в|ый (~, ~а), *adj.* **1.** laborious; ~ая рабо́та minute, laborious work. **2.** painstaking, precise; minute.

кропоту́н, а́, *m.* (*coll.*) precisian.

кросс, а, *m.* (*sport*) cross-country (race).

кроссво́рд, а, *m.* crossword.

крот, а́, *m.* **1.** mole. **2.** moleskin.

крот|кий (~ок, ~ка́, ~ко), *adj.* gentle; mild, meek.

кротови́н|а, ы, *f.* mole-hill.

крот|о́вый, *adj.* **1.** *of* ~; ~о́вая нора́ mole--hill. **2.** moleskin.

кро́тост|ь, и, *f.* gentleness; mildness, meekness.

крох|а́, и́, а. ~у, *pl.* ~и, ~а́м, *f.* crumb (*pl. also fig.*).

крохобо́р, а, *m.* (*coll.*) narrow pedant.

крохобо́рств|о, а, *n.* (*coll.*) narrow pedantry.

крохобо́рств|овать, ую, *impf.* (*coll.*) to behave pedantically.

кро́хотный, *adj.* (*coll.*) tiny, minute.

кро́шев|о, а, *n.* (*coll.*) **1.** (*cul.*) hash. **2.** medley.

кро́шечк|а, и, *f.* *dim. of* кро́шка.

кро́шечный, *adj.* (*coll.*) tiny, minute.

крош|и́ть, у́, ~ишь, *impf.* **1.** (*pf.* ис~, на~ *or* рас~) to crumb, crumble; to chop, hack; (*fig.*) to hack to pieces. **2.** (*pf.* на~) (+*i.*) to drop, spill crumbs (of); к. хле́бом на́ пол to drop crumbs on to the floor.

крош|и́ться, ~ится, *impf.* (*of* ис~ *and* рас~) to crumble, break into small pieces.

кро́шк|а, и, *f.* **1.** crumb. **2.** (*fig.*) a tiny bit; ни ~и not a bit. **3.** (*coll., affect. of a child*) little one.

круг, а, *pl.* ~и́, *m.* **1.** (*p. sing.* в, на ~у́ = *circular area*; в, на ~е = *circumference*) circle; движе́ние по ~у movement in a circle; на к. on average, taking it all round; к. сы́ра a cheese; ~и́ (на воде́) ripples (on water); стать в к. to form a circle. **2.** (*sport*; *p. sing.* на ~у́) бегово́й к. race-course, ring. **3.** (*fig.*; *p. sing.* в ~у́) sphere, range; compass; вне ~а свои́х обя́занностей outside one's province. **4.** (*fig.*; *p. sing.* в ~у́) circle (*of persons*); официа́льные ~и́ official quarters; в семе́йном ~у́ in the family circle.

кру́гленьк|ий, *adj.* (*coll.*) **1.** *dim. of* кру́глый; ~ая су́мма a round sum. **2.** rotund, portly.

кругле́|ть, ю, *impf.* (*of* по~) to become round.

кругло ва́т|ый (~, ~а), *adj.* roundish.

круглогодово́й, *adj.* all-the-year-round.

круглогу́бц|ы, ев, *no sing.* (*tech.*) round pliers.

круглоли́ц|ый (~, ~а), *adj.* round-faced, chubby.

круглоро́т|ые, ых (*zool.*) Cyclostomata.

круглосу́точный, *adj.* round-the-clock, twenty-four-hour.

кру́гл|ый (~, ~а́, ~о), *adj.* **1.** (*in var. senses*) round; к. год all the year round; ~ые су́тки day and night; к. по́черк round hand; ~ая су́мма round sum; в ~ых ци́фрах, для ~ого счёта in round figures. **2.** (*coll.*) complete, utter, perfect; к. дура́к perfect fool; ~ое неве́жество crass ignorance; к., ~ая сирота́ orphan (having *neither* father *nor* mother).

круглы́ш, а́, *m.* (*dial.*) rounded stone.

кругов|о́й, *adj.* circular; ~а́я пору́ка mutual responsibility, guarantee; ~а́я ча́ша loving-cup; ~а́я доро́га roundabout route; ~а́я оборо́на all-round defence.

круговоро́т, а, *m.* rotation, circulation.

кругозо́р, а, *m.* **1.** prospect. **1.** (*fig.*) horizon, range of interests; с широ́ким (у́зким) ~ом with a wide (narrow) range of interests.

круго́м¹, *adv.* **1.** round, around; он обошёл маши́ну к. he walked around the car. **2.** (all) around, round about; к. всё бы́ло ти́хо all around was still. **3.** (*coll.*) completely, entirely; он был к. в долга́х he was head over heels in debt; вы к. винова́ты you are entirely to blame, you haven't a leg to stand on.

круго́м², *prep.*+*g.* round, around.

кругооборо́т, а, *m.* circuit, circulation.

кругообра́з|ный (~ен, ~на), *adj.* circular.

кругосве́тный, *adj.* round-the-world.

кружа́л|о¹, а, *n.* (*archit.*) bow member, curve piece.

кружа́л|о², а, *n.* (*hist.*) tavern, pothouse.

кру́ж|ева́, ~ев, ~ева́м = ~ево.

кружевни́ц|а, ы, *f.* lace-maker.

кру́жев|о, а, *n.* lace.

круж|и́ть, у́, ~ишь, *impf.* **1.** to whirl, spin round; (*fig.*) к. кому́-н. го́лову to turn someone's head. **2.** to circle. **3.** (*coll.*) to wander.

круж|и́ться, у́сь, ~ишься, *impf.* (*of* за~) to whirl, spin round; to circle; у меня́ ~ится голова́ my head is going round, I feel giddy.

кру́жк|а, и, *f.* **1.** mug; tankard; (*measure*) к. пи́ва glass of beer. **2.** collecting-box. **3.** (*med.*) douche.

кружковщи́н|а, ы, *f.* clannishness, cliquishness.

круж|ко́вый, *adj. of* ~о́к 2.

кру́жный, *adj.* roundabout, circuitous.

кру́ж|о́к, ка́, *m.* **1.** *dim. o,* круг; стри́чься в к. to have one's hair bobbed. **2.** (*lit., polit., etc.*) circle, study group.

круп¹, а, *m.* (*med.*) croup.

круп², а, *m.* croup, crupper (*of horse*).

круп|а́, ы́, *pl.* ~ы, *f.* **1.** (*collect.*) groats; гре́чневая к. buckwheat; ма́нная к. semolina; овся́ная к. oatmeal; перло́вая к. pearl-barley. **2.** (*fig.*) sleet.

крупени́к, а́, *m.* buckwheat pudding with curd.

крупи́нк|а, и, *f.* grain.

крупи́ц|а, ы, *f.* grain, fragment, atom; у него́ нет ни ~ы здра́вого смы́сла he hasn't a grain of common sense.

крупи́чатый, *adj.* (*coll.*) fine-ground.

крупне́|ть, ю, *impf.* (*of* по~) to grow larger.

кру́пн|о, *adv. of* ~ый; к. наре́зать to cut into large pieces; к. писа́ть to write large; к. поспо́рить (c+*i.*) to have high words (with), have a slanging-match (with).

крупнозерни́стый, *adj.* coarse-grained, large-grained.

крупнокали́берный, *adj.* large-calibre.

кру́п|ный (~ен, ~на́, ~но), *adj.* **1.** large, big; large-scale; (*fig.*) prominent, outstanding; ~ные де́ньги money in large denominations; ~ные поме́щики big landowners; ~ная промы́шленность large-scale industry; к. рога́тый скот (horned) cattle; ~ным ша́гом at a round pace; засня́ть ~ным пла́ном (*cinema*) to take a close-up (*of*). **2.** coarse; к. песо́к coarse sand; к. шаг (*tech., aeron.*) coarse pitch. **3.** important; serious; ~ная неприя́тность serious trouble; к. разгово́р (*fig.*) high words.

круп|о́зный, *adj. of* ~¹; ~о́зное воспале́ние лёгких lobar pneumonia.

крупору́шк|а, и, *f.* (*agric.*) hulling mill, peeling mill.

крупча́тк|а, и, *f.* finest wheaten flour.

крупча́тый, *adj.* granular.

крупье́, *indecl., m.* croupier.

крутизн|а́, ы́, *f.* **1.** steepness. **2.** steep slope.

крути́льн|ый, *adj.* (*tech.*) torsion(al); (*text.*) doubling; ~ая маши́на twisting machine, (*text.*) twiner.

кру|ти́ть, чу́, ~тишь, *impf.* (*of* за~ *and* c~) **1.** to twist; to twirl; к. верёвку to twist a rope; к. папиро́су to roll a cigarette; к. усы́ to twirl one's moustache; к. шёлк to twist, throw silk; (*coll.;* +*i.*) она́ ~тит им, как хо́чет she twists him round her little finger. **2.** to turn, wind (*tap, handle, etc.*). **3.** to whirl (*trans.*). **4.** (*coll.;* c+*i*) to go out (with), have an affair (with).

кру|ти́ться, чу́сь, ~тишься, *impf.* **1.** to turn, spin, revolve. **2.** to whirl. **3.** (*fig., coll.*) to be in a whirl.

кру́то, *adv.* **1.** steeply. **2.** suddenly; abruptly;

sharply; к. поверну́ть to turn round sharply. **3.** (*coll.*) sternly, severely; drastically; к. распра́виться с кем-н. to give someone short shrift. **4.** thoroughly; к. замеси́ть те́сто to make a thick dough; к. отжа́ть to squeeze dry, wring out thoroughly; к. посоли́ть to put (too) much salt (into).

крут|о́й (~, ~а́, ~о), *adj.* **1.** steep; к. вира́ж (*aeron.*) steep turn. **2.** sudden; abrupt, sharp. **3.** (*coll.*) stern, severe; drastic; к. нрав stern temper; ~ые ме́ры drastic measures. **4.** (*cul.*) thick; well-done; к. кипято́к fiercely boiling water; ~о́е яйцо́ hard-boiled egg.

кру́ч|а, и, *f.* steep slope, cliff.

кру́|че, *comp. of* ~то́й *and* ~то.

круче́ни|е, я, *n.* **1.** (*text.*) twisting, spinning. **2.** (*tech.*) torsion.

кручён|ый, *adj.* **1.** twisted; ~ые ни́тки lisle thread. **2.** (*sport*) spinning, turning; with spin on.

кручи́н|а, ы, *f.* (*folk poet.*) sorrow, woe.

кручи́н|иться, юсь, ишься, *impf.* (*folk poet.*) to sorrow, grieve.

кру́|чу́, ~тишь, see ~ти́ть.

круше́ни|е, я, *n.* **1.** wreck; ruin; к. по́езда derailment. **2.** (*fig.*) ruin; collapse; downfall.

круши́н|а, ы, *f.* (*bot.*) buckthorn.

круш|и́ть, у́, и́шь, *impf.* to shatter, destroy (*also fig.*).

круш|и́ться, у́сь, и́шься, *impf.* (*obs. or poet.*) to sorrow, be afflicted.

крыжо́венный, *adj.* gooseberry.

крыжо́вник, а, *m.* **1.** gooseberry bush(es). **2.** (*collect.*) gooseberries.

крыла́тк|а¹, и, *f.* (*obs.*) (man's) loose cloak with cape.

крыла́тк|а², и, *f.* (*tech.*) wing nut; vane.

крыла́т|ый, *adj.* winged (*also fig.*); ~ые слова́ pithy saying(s); (*tech.*) к. болт butterfly bolt; ~ая га́йка wing nut.

крыл|е́чко, е́чка, *n. dim. of* ~ьцо́.

крыл|о́, а́, *pl.* ~ья, ~ьев, *n.* (*in var. senses*) wing; sail, vane (*of windmill*); splash-board, mud-guard, wing (*of car, carriage*).

крылоно́г|ие, их, (*zool.*) Pteropoda.

кры́лыш|ко, ка, *pl.* ~ки, ~ек, ~кам, *n. dim. of* крыло́; (*fig.*) под ~ком under the wing (of).

крыл|ьцо́, ьца́, *pl.* ~ьца, ~е́ц, ~ьца́м, *n.* porch; perron; front (*or* back) steps.

кры́мский, *adj.* Crimean.

крымча́к, а́, *m.* inhabitant of the Crimea.

кры́нк|а, и, *f.* earthenware pot.

кры́с|а, ы, *f.* **1.** rat; су́мчатая к. opossum; канцеля́рская к. (*fig., coll.*) quill-driver.

крыс|ёнок, ёнка, *pl.* ~я́та, ~я́т, *m.* young rat.

крыс|и́ный, *adj. of* ~а; к. яд rat poison.

крысолóв, а, *m.* rat-catcher.

крысолóвк|а, и, *f.* **1.** rat-trap. **2.** (*dog*) rat--catcher.

кры́т|ый, *p.p.p. of* ~ь *and adj.* covered; sheltered, with an awning; к. ры́нок covered market.

крыть, крóю, крóешь, *impf.* (*of* по~) **1.** to cover; to roof; to coat (*with paint*); (*cards*) to cover, trump. **2.** (*coll.*) to swear (at); ему́ нéчем к. he hasn't a leg to stand on.

кры́ться, крóюсь, крóешься, *impf.* **1.** (в+*p.*) to be, lie (in). **2.** to be concealed.

кры́ш|а, и, *f.* roof.

кры́шк|а, и, *f.* **1.** lid; cover. **2.** (*sl.*) death, end; ему́ к. he's done for, he's finished.

крю́|к, ка́, *m.* **1.** (*pl.* ~ки́, ~кóв) hook; (*pl.* ~чья, ~чьев) hook (*for supporting load*). **2.** detour; (*coll.*) дать ~ку, сдéлать к. to make a detour. **3.** (*mus.*) (*pl.* ~ки́, ~кóв) kryuk (*old Russian neum*).

крюч|ить, ит, *impf.* (*of* с~) (*impers., coll.*) егó ~ит (от бóли) he is writhing (in pain).

крючковáт|ый (~, ~а), *adj.* hooked.

крючкотвóр, а, *m.* (*obs., coll.*) pettifogger.

крючкотвóрств|о, а, *n.* (*obs., coll.*) chicanery.

крю́чник, а, *m.* carrier, stevedore.

крюч|óк, ка́, *m.* **1.** hook; спусковóй к. trigger. **2.** (*fig.; obs., pejor.*) hitch, catch. **3.** (*fig., obs.*) pettifogger.

крюшóн, а, *m.* cup (*beverage*).

кря́ду, *adv.* (*coll.*) running; три дня к. онá опáздывала на слу́жбу three days running she was late for work.

кряж, а, *m.* **1.** (mountain-)ridge. **2.** block, log.

кря́жист|ый (~, ~а), *adj.* thick; (*fig.*) thick--set.

кря́к|ать, аю, *impf.* (*of* ~нуть) **1.** to quack. **2.** (*coll.*) to wheeze.

кря́кв|а, ы, *f.* wild duck, mallard.

кря́к|нуть, ну, нешь, *inst. pf. of* ~ать.

кряхтéть, чу́, ти́шь, *impf.* to groan; to wheeze, grunt.

ксёндз, á, *m.* Roman Catholic (*esp. Polish*) priest.

ксилогрáфи|я, и, *f.* **1.** wood-engraving. **2.** woodcut.

ксилофóн, а, *m.* (*mus.*) xylophone.

кстáти, *adv.* **1.** to the point, apropos. **2.** opportunely; вы пришли́ как раз к. you came just at the right moment; э́тот подáрок оказáлся óчень к. the present has proved most welcome. **3.** (*coll.*) at the same time, incidentally; к. зайди́те пожáлуйста в аптéку will you please call at the chemist's at the same time. **4.** к. (сказáть) by the way; к., где вы купи́ли э́тот гáлстук? by the way, where did you buy that tie?

кти́тор, а, *m.* churchwarden.

кто, когó, комý, кем, ком, *pron.* **1.** (*interrog.*) who; к. э́то такóй? who is that?; к. из вас э́то сдéлал? which of you did it?; к. идёт? (*mil.*) who goes there?; к. когó (*sc.* побьёт)? who will win? **2.** (*relat.*) who (*normally after pronoun antecedent*); тот, к. he who; те, к. those who; блажéн, к.... blessed is he who . . .; спасáйся к. мóжет! every man for himself! **3.** (*indef.*) к. (бы) ни who(so)-ever; к. ни придёт whoever comes; к. бы то ни́ был whoever it may be. **4.** (*indef.*) some . . . others; к. что лю́бит, комý что нрáвится tastes differ; разбежáлись к. кудá they scattered in all directions; к. в лес, к. по дровá (*coll.*) to be (*etc.*) at sixes and sevens. **5.** (*coll.; indef.*) anyone; к. позвони́т, дай мне знать if anyone rings, let me know. **6.** к.-к., а... (когó-когó, а..., комý-комý, а...) *contrasts action, attitude, etc., of one or more members of a group with that of remainder* (*coll.*): когó-когó, а меня́ э́то вполнé устрáивает I don't know about anyone else, but it suits me fine.

кто́-либо, когó-либо, *pron.* = кто́-нибудь.

кто́-нибудь, когó-нибудь, *pron.* anyone, anybody; someone, somebody.

кто́-то, когó-то, *pron.* someone, somebody.

куафёр, а, *m.* (*obs.*) coiffeur.

куафю́р|а, ы, *f.* (*obs.*) coiffure.

куб¹, а, *pl.* ~ы́, *m.* **1.** (*math.*) cube; два в ~е two cubed. **2.** (*coll.*) cubic metre.

куб², а, *pl.* ~ы́, *m.* boiler, water-heater, (tea)-urn; still.

кубáн|ец, ца, *m.* Kuban Cossack.

кубáнк|а, и, *f.* flat, round fur hat.

кубáнский, *adj.* (*geogr.*) (of the) Kuban.

ку́барем, *adv.* (*coll.*) head over heels, head-long; скати́ться к. to roll head over heels.

кубáр|ь, я́, *m.* peg-top.

кубату́р|а, ы, *f.* cubic content.

куби́зм, а, *m.* (*art*) cubism.

ку́бик, а, *m.* **1.** *dim. of* куб. **2.** (*pl.*) blocks, bricks (*as children's toy*). **3.** (*coll.*) cubic centimetre.

куби́н|ец, ца, *m.* Cuban.

куби́н|ка, ки, *f. of* ~ец.

куби́нский, *adj.* Cuban.

куби́ческий, *adj.* cubic; к. кóрень (*math.*) cube root.

кубови́д|ный (~ен, ~на), *adj.* cube-shaped, cuboid.

куб|овóй, *adj. of* ~².

ку́бовый, *adj.* indigo.

куб|óк, ка, *m.* goblet, bowl, beaker; перехóдящий к. (*sport, etc.*) cup; встрéча на к. cup-tie.

кубомéтр, а, *m.* cubic metre.

ку́брик, а, *m.* (*naut.*) crew's quarters; orlop (-deck).

кубы́шк|а и, *f.* (*coll.*) **1.** (*obs.*) money-box.

2. (*joc.*) dumpy woman. 3. yellow water-
-lily.

кува́лд|а, ы, *f.* sledge-hammer (*also fig.,
coll., of a clumsy woman*).

куве́рт, а, *m.* (*obs.*) place (*at table*); стол на
два́дцать ~ов table laid for twenty persons.

кувши́н, а, *m.* jug; pitcher.

кувши́нк|а, и, *f.* (*bot.*) water-lily.

кувырк|а́ться, а́юсь, *impf.* (*of* ~ну́ться) to
turn somersaults, go head over heels.

кувырк|ну́ться, ну́сь, нёшься, *inst. pf. of*
~а́ться.

кувырко́м, *adv.* (*coll.*) head over heels;
topsy-turvy; полете́ть к. to go head over
heels; всё пошло́ к. everything went haywire.

кугуа́р, а, *m.* (*zool.*) puma, cougar.

куда́, *adv.* 1. (*interrog. and relat.*) where (*expressing motion*), whither; к. ты идёшь?
where are you going?; к. он положи́л мою́
кни́гу? where did he put my book? 2. к.
(бы) ни wherever; к. бы то ни́ бы́ло anywhere; (*coll.*) к. ни кинь wherever one looks,
on all sides; к. ни шло come what may. 3.
(*coll.*) what for; к. вам сто́лько багажа́?
what do you want so much luggage for? 4.
(+*comp.*; *coll.*) much, far; сего́дня мне к.
лу́чше I am much better today. 5. (*coll.*)
хоть к. fine, excellent. 6. (*expressing doubt,
indredulity*; *coll.*) how (could that be; could
you, he, etc.); к ча́су я наме́рен дочита́ть
до страни́цы 200 — к. тебе́! I intend to
reach page 200 by one o'clock—you'll
never do it!; узна́ли ли тебя́ они́? к. им
did they recognize you? how could they?
7. (*coll., iron.*) к. как very; к. как прия́тно
слу́шать его́ го́лос it is *so* nice to listen to
his voice.

куда́-либо, *adv.* = куда́-нибудь.

куда́-нибудь, *adv.* anywhere; somewhere.

куда́-то, *adv.* somewhere.

куда́хтань|е, я, *n.* cackling, clucking.

куда́х|тать, чу, чешь, *impf.* to cackle,
cluck.

куде́л|ь, и, *f.* (*text.*) tow.

куде́сник, а, *m.* magician, sorcerer.

кудла́тый, *adj.* (*coll.*) shaggy.

кудрева́т|ый (~, ~a), *adj.* rather curly;
(*fig.*) florid, ornate.

ку́др|и, ей, *no sing.* curls.

кудря́в|иться, люсь, ишься, *impf.* to curl.

кудря́в|ый (~, ~a), *adj.* 1. curly; curly-
-headed. 2. leafy, bushy; ~ая капу́ста
curly kale. 3. (*fig.*) florid, ornate.

кудря́ш|ки, ек, *no sing.* (*coll.*) ringlets.

кузе́н, а, *m.* cousin.

кузи́н|а, ы, *f.* cousin.

кузне́ц, а́, *m.* (black)smith; farrier.

кузне́чик, а, *m.* grasshopper.

кузне́чный, *adj.* blacksmith's; к. mex bellows.

ку́зниц|а, ы, *f.* forge, smithy.

ку́зов, а, *pl.* ~ы *and* ~а́, *m.* 1. basket. 2.
body (*of carriage, etc.*).

кукаре́ка|ть, ю, *impf.* to crow.

кукареку́ cock-a-doodle-doo.

ку́киш, а, *m.* (*coll.*) fig (*gesture of derision or
contempt, generally accompanying refusal to
comply with a request, and consisting of extending
clenched fist with thumb placed between index
and middle fingers*); показа́ть кому́-н. к. *to
make this gesture* (*cf.* to cock a snook, give
the V-sign); к. в карма́не *of defiance expressed in the absence of the person defied*;
получи́ть к. с ма́слом to come away
empty-handed, receive a snub.

ку́к|ла, лы, *g. pl.* ~ол, *f.* doll; теа́тр ~ол
puppet-theatre.

кук|ова́ть, у́ю, *impf.* to (cry) cuckoo.

ку́колк|а, и, *f.* 1. (*affect. dim. of* ку́кла) dolly.
2. (*zool.*) chrysalis, pupa.

ку́кол|ь¹, я, *m.* (*bot.*) cockle.

ку́кол|ь², я, *m.* (*eccl.*) cowl.

ку́кольник, а, *m.* (*coll.*) puppeteer.

ку́кольн|ый, *adj.* 1. doll's; к. теа́тр puppet-
-theatre; ~ая коме́дия (*fig., coll.*) farce;
play-acting. 2. doll-like.

ку́к|ситься, шусь, сишься, *impf.* (*coll.*) to
sulk; to be in the dumps.

кукуру́з|а, ы, *f.* maize, Indian corn.

кукуру́з|ный, *adj. of* ~а.

куку́шк|а¹, и, *f.* cuckoo; часы́ с ~ой cuckoo-
-clock.

куку́шк|а², и, *f.* small steam locomotive.

кула́к¹, а́, *m.* 1. fist; брониро́ванный к. the
mailed fist; дойти́ до ~о́в to come to blows;
смея́ться в ~ to laugh in one's sleeve.
2. (*mil.*) striking force.

кула́к², а́, *m.* kulak.

кула́к³, а́, *m.* (*tech.*) cam.

кула́|цкий, *adj. of* ~к².

кула́честв|о, а, *n.* (*collect.*) the kulaks.

кула́чк|а, и, *f. of* кула́к².

кула́чк|и, *only in phrases* идти́ на к. to come
to blows; би́ться на ~ах to engage in fisti-
cuffs.

кула́ч|ко́вый, *adj. of* ~о́к²; к. вал camshaft.

кула́|чный, *adj. of* ~к¹, ³; к. бой fisticuffs;
~чное пра́во fist-law.

кула|чо́к¹, чка́, *m. dim. of* ~к¹.

кулач|о́к², ка́, *m.* (*tech.*) cam.

кулебя́к|а, и, *f.* kulebyaka (*pie containing
meat, fish, or vegetables, etc.*).

кул|ёк, ька́, *m.* bag (*made from bast or paper*);
из ~ька́ в рого́жку (*coll.*) out of the frying-
-pan into the fire.

куле́ш, а́, *m.* (*coll.*) thin gruel.

ку́ли, *indecl.,* *m.* coolie.

кули́к, а́, *m.* (*orn.*) stint; sandpiper (*Calidris*).

кулина́р, а, *m.* cookery specialist.

кулина́ри|я, и, *f.* cookery.

кулина́рный, *adj.* culinary.

кули́с|а, ы, *f.* (*tech.*) link.

кули́с|ный, *adj. of* ~а; к. ка́мень sliding block, link block, guiding shoe; ~ное распределе́ние link gear, link motion, slide block mechanism.

кули́с|ы, ~, *sing.* ~а, ~ы, *f.* (*theatr.*) wings, side-scenes, slips; за ~ами behind the scenes (*also fig.*).

кули́ч, а́, *m.* Easter cake.

кули́чк|и, *only in phrases.* (*coll.*) у чёрта на ~ах, к чёрту на к. at (to) the world's end.

куло́н¹, а, *m.* pendant.

куло́н², а, *m.* (*electr.*) coulomb.

кулуа́р|ный, *adj. of* ~ы.

кулуа́р|ы, ов, *sing. not used,* lobby (*in Parliament; also fig.*).

кул|ь, я́, *m.* sack (*formerly also dry measure* = 275–300 lb. approx.).

кульминацио́нный, *adj.* к. пункт culmination (point).

кульмина́ци|я, и, *f.* culmination.

кульмини́р|овать, ую, *impf. and pf.* to culminate.

культ, а, *m.* (*in var. senses*) cult; служи́тели ~a ministers of religion; к. ли́чности (*hist.*) cult of personality (*esp. of J. Stalin*).

культ- (*abbr. of* ~у́рный) cultural, educational, recreational.

культива́тор, а, *m.* (*agric.*) cultivator (*machine*).

культива́ци|я, и, *f.* (*agric.*) treatment of the ground with a cultivator (*machine*).

культиви́ровани|е, я, *n.* cultivation (*also fig.*).

культиви́р|овать, ую, *impf.* to cultivate (*also fig.*).

культма́ссов|ый, *adj.* ~ая рабо́та education of the masses.

ку́льт|овый, *adj. of* ~; ~овая му́зыка religious music.

культпохо́д, а, *m.* 1. cultural crusade. 2. cultural outing (*visit by group to museum, theatre, etc.*).

культрабо́тник, а, *m.* 'culture secretary', 'culture officer' (*person in charge of cultural, and/or educational activities in an organization or establishment*).

культтова́р|ы, ов, *no sing.* 'cultural supplies' (*office equipment, musical instruments, etc., used in the organization of cultural and/or educational activities*).

культу́р|а, ы, *f.* 1. (*in var. senses*) culture. 2. standard, level; к. ре́чи standard of speech; повы́сить ~у земледе́лия to raise the standard of farming. 3. (*agric.*) зерновы́е ~ы cereals; кормовы́е ~ы forage crops. 4. (*agric.*) cultivation, growing; к. карто́феля potato-growing.

культу́рничеств|о, а, *n.* (*pejor.*) culture-mongering (*promotion of cultural and/or educational activities to exclusion of political questions*).

культу́рно, *adv.* in a civilized manner.

культу́рно-бытов|о́й, *adj.* ~ое обслу́живание culture and welfare service.

культу́рно-просвети́тельный, *adj.* cultural and educational.

культу́рност|ь, и, *f.* (level of) culture; cultivation; (*fig.*) он отлича́лся ~ью he was exceptionally cultivated.

культу́р|ный (~ен, ~на), *adj.* 1. cultured, cultivated. 2. (*in var. senses*) cultural. 3. (*agric., hort.*) cultured; cultivated.

культуртре́гер, а, *m.* (*iron.*) 'Kulturträger', person with civilizing mission.

культ|я́, и́, *f.* stump (*of maimed or amputated limb*).

культя́|пка, пки, *f.* (*coll.*) = ~.

кум, а, *pl.* ~овья́, ~овьёв, *m.* god-father of one's child; fellow-sponsor; father of one's god-child; gossip (*in arch. sense*).

кум|а́, ы́, *f.* 1. god-mother of one's child; fellow-sponsor; mother of one's god-child; gossip (*in arch. sense*), cummer (*dial.*). 2. *in folklore, conventional epithet of fox.*

куман|ёк, ька́, *m.* (*coll.*) *affect. of* кум; *as form of address* my friend.

кума́ч, а́, *m.* red calico.

куми́р, а, *m.* idol (*also fig.*).

куми́р|ня, ни, *g. pl.* ~ен, *f.* heathen temple.

кум|и́ться, лю́сь, и́шься, *impf.* (*of* по~) (с+*i.; coll.*) to become god-parent to someone's child; (*fig.*) to become acquainted (with).

кумовств|о́, а́, *n.* 1. relationship of god-parent to parent, *or of god-parents.* 2. (*fig.*) favouritism, nepotism.

кумуляти́вн|ый, *adj.* cumulative; (*mil.*) к. заря́д hollow charge; снаря́д ~ого де́йствия hollow-charge projectile.

ку́мушк|а, и, *f.* 1. *affect. of* кума́; *as form of address* my good woman. 2. (*coll.*) gossip, scandal-monger.

кумы́с, а, *m.* koumiss (*fermented mare's milk*).

кумысолече́бниц|а, ы, *f.* koumiss-cure institution.

кумысолече́ни|е, я, *n.* koumiss cure, treatment.

куна́к, а́, *m.* friend (*among the mountaineers of the Caucasus*).

кунжу́т, а, *m.* (*bot.*) sesame.

кунжу́т|ный, *adj. of* ~.

ку́н|ий, *adj. of* ~и́ца.

куни́ц|а, ы, *f.* (*zool.*) marten.

кунстка́мер|а, ы, *f.* cabinet of curiosities.

кунту́ш, а́, *m.* (*hist.*) kuntush (*kind of coat worn by Polish noblemen*).

кунштю́к, а, *m.* (*coll.*) trick, dodge.

ку́п|а, ы, *f.* group, clump (*of trees*).

купа́ла, *see* Ива́н.

купа́льник, а, *m.* bathing costume.

купа́льный, *adj.* bathing, swimming; к. костю́м swimming costume.

купа́л|ьня, ьни, *g. pl.* ~ен, *f.* (enclosed) bathing-place; dressing-shed.

купа́льщик, а, *m.* bather.

купа́|ть, ю, *impf.* (*of* вы́~) to bathe; to bath.

купа́|ться, юсь, *impf.* (*of* вы́~) to bathe; to have, take a bath; (*coll.*) к. в зо́лоте to roll in money.

купе́, *indecl.*, *n.* compartment (*of railway carriage*).

купе́л|ь, и, *f.* (*eccl.*) font.

куп|е́ц, ца́, *m.* merchant.

купе́ческ|ий, *adj.* merchant, mercantile; ~ое сосло́вие the merchant class.

купе́честв|о, а, *n.* (*collect.*) the merchants.

купин|а́, ы́, *f.* (*arch.*) bush; неопали́мая к. (*bibl.*) the burning bush.

куп|и́ть, лю́, ~ишь, *pf.* (*of* покупа́ть) to buy, purchase.

купле́т, а, *m.* 1. couplet, verse. 2. (*pl.*) satirical ballad(s), song(s) (*containing topical allusions*).

куплети́ст, а, *m.* singer of satirical songs, ballads.

ку́пл|я, и, *f.* buying, purchase.

ку́пол, а, *pl.* ~а́, *m.* cupola, dome.

куполообра́з|ный (~ен, ~на), *adj.* dome-shaped.

ку́пол|ьный, *adj.* of ~.

купо́н, а, *m.* 1. coupon; (*theatr.*) ticket. 2. suit-length.

купоро́с, а, *m.* (*chem.*) vitriol.

ку́пч|ая, ей, *f.* (*also* к. кре́пость) (*hist., leg.*) deed of purchase.

купчи́х|а, и, *f.* 1. *f. of* купе́ц. 2. merchant's wife.

купю́р|а, ы, *f.* 1. cut (*in lit., mus., etc., work*). 2. (*fin.*) denomination (*of paper money, bonds, etc.*).

кур, а, *m.* (*arch.*) cock; *now only in phrase* (*coll.*) как к. во́ щи (попа́сть) (to get oneself) into the soup.

ку́р|а, ы, *f.* (*obs.*) = ~ица.

кураг|а́, и́, *f.* (*collect.*) dried apricots.

кура́ж, а́, *m.* (*obs.*) boldness, spirit; вы́пить для ~а́ to summon up Dutch courage; быть в ~е́ to be lit up.

кура́ж|иться, усь, ишься, *impf.* (*coll.*) to swagger, boast; (над) to bully.

кура́нт|ы, ов, *no sing.* 1. chiming clock.; chimes. 2. (*hist.*) gazette.

кура́тор, а, *m.* (*obs.*) curator.

куре́т, а, *m.* (*sport and fig.*) curvet.

ку́рв|а, ы, *f.* (*vulg.*) whore, tart.

курга́н, а, *m.* barrow, burial mound; tumulus.

кургу́з|ый (~, ~а), *adj.* (*coll.*) 1. too short

and/or tight. 2. bob-tailed. 3. short, stumpy.

курд, а, *m.* Kurd.

ку́рдский, *adj.* Kurd.

курдю́к, а́, *m.* fat(ty) tail (*of certain breeds of sheep*).

курдя́нк|а, и, *f.* Kurdish woman.

ку́рев|о, а, *n.* (*coll.*) tobacco, baccy; something to smoke; у меня́ нет ~а I haven't got a smoke.

куре́ни|е, я, *n.* 1. smoking. 2. incense.

кур|ёнок, ёнка, *pl.* ~я́та, ~я́т, *m.* (*dial.*) chicken.

куре́н|ь, я́, *m.* 1. (*dial.*) hut, shanty. 2. (*hist.*) kuren (*unit of Zaporozhian Cossack troop*).

курза́л, а, *m.* kursaal.

куриа́льный, *adj.* (*leg., eccl.*) curial.

кури́лк|а[1], и, *f.* (*coll.*) smoking-room.

кури́лка[2], *only in phrase* жив к.! there's life in the old dog yet.

кури́льниц|а, ы, *f.* (*obs.*) censer; incense-burner.

кури́л|ьня, ьни, *g. pl.* ~ен, *f.* к. о́пиума opium-den.

кури́льщик, а, *m.* smoker.

кури́н|ые, ых (*orn.*) Gallinaceae.

кури́н|ый, *adj.* hen's; chicken's; ~ая грудь pigeon-chest; ~ая слепота́ (*med.*) night-blindness; (*bot.*) buttercup.

кури́тельн|ый, *adj.* smoking; ~ая бума́га cigarette paper; ~ая (ко́мната) smoking-room.

кур|и́ть, ю́, ~ишь, *impf.* (*of* по~) 1. to smoke; к. тру́бку to smoke a pipe. 2. (+а. *or* i.) to burn; to fumigate (with); к. ла́даном to burn incense; к. фимиа́м кому́-н. (*fig.*) to burn incense to someone. 3. to distil.

кур|и́ться, ~ится, *impf.* 1. to smoke (*intrans.*). 2. (+i.) to emit (smoke, steam). 3. *pass. of* ~и́ть.

ку́р|ица, ицы, *pl.* ~ы, ~, *f.* `hen; (*fig., coll.*) мо́края к. milksop, wet hen; ~ам на́ смех it would make a cat laugh; де́нег у него́ ~ы не клюю́т he is rolling in money.

ку́ри|я, и, *f.* (*leg., eccl.*) curia.

курн|о́й, *adj.* ~а́я изба́ hut having stove but without chimney.

курно́с|ый (~, ~а) (*coll.*) snub-nosed.

куроводств|о, а, *n.* poultry-breeding.

кур|о́к, ка́, *m.* cocking-piece; взвести́ к. to cock; спусти́ть к. to pull the trigger.

куроле́|сить, шу, сишь, *impf.* (*of* на~) (*coll.*) to play tricks, get up to mischief.

куропа́тк|а, и, *f.* (*orn.*) (се́рая) partridge; бе́лая к. willow grouse; тундряна́я к. ptarmigan.

куро́рт, а, *m.* health resort.

куро́ртник, а, *m.* health resort visitor.

куро́рт|ный, *adj.* of ~; ~ное лече́ние spa treatment.

куросле́п, а, *m.* (*bot.*) buttercup.

ку́рочк|а, и, *f.* **1.** pullet. **2.** moor-hen.

курс, а, *m.* **1.** (*in var. senses*) course; но́вый к. (*polit.*) new policy; быть на тре́тьем ~e to be in the third year (*of course of studies*); держа́ть к. (на+*a.*) to head (for); быть в ~e дела́ to be au courant, be in the know. **2.** (*fin.*) rate (of exchange).

курса́нт, а, *m.* **1.** member of a course. **2.** student (*of mil. school or academy*).

курси́в, а, *m.* italic type, italics; ~ом in italics.

курси́вный, *adj.* (*typ.*) italic.

курси́р|овать, ую, *impf.* (ме́жду) to ply, run (between).

курси́стк|а, и, *f.* (*obs.*) girl-student.

курсо́вк|а, и, *f.* board and treatment authorization (*at health resort*).

курта́ж, а, *m.* (*comm.*) brokerage.

куртиза́нк|а, и, *f.* courtesan.

курти́н|а, ы, *f.* **1.** (*mil.*; *obs.*) curtain. **2.** flower-bed.

ку́ртк|а, и, *f.* (*man's*) jacket.

курфю́рст, а, *m.* (*hist.*) elector.

курча́в|иться, ится, *impf.* to curl.

курча́в|ый (~, ~а), *adj.* (*coll.*) curly; curly-headed.

курч|о́нок, о́нка, *pl.* ~а́та, ~а́т, *m.* (*coll.*) chicken.

ку́р|ы¹, *see* ~ица.

ку́ры², *only in phrase* стро́ить к. (+*d.*) (*joc.*) to flirt (with), pay court (to).

курьёз, а, *m.* curious, amusing incident; для, ра́ди ~a for fun.

курьёз|ный (~ен, ~на), *adj.* curious; funny.

курье́р, а, *m.* messenger; courier.

курье́р|ский, *adj.* **1.** *adj. of* ~. **2.** fast; к. по́езд express; на ~ских (*coll.*) post-haste.

кур|я́та, *see* ~ёнок.

куря́тин|а, ы, *f.* chicken, fowl (*as meat*).

куря́тник, а, *m.* hen-house, hen-coop.

кус, а, *pl.* ~ы́, *m.* (*coll.*) morsel.

куса́|ть, ю, *impf.* to bite; to sting; к. себе́ ло́кти (*fig.*) to be whipping the cat.

куса́|ться, юсь, *impf.* **1.** to bite (= *to be given to biting*). **2.** to bite one another. **3.** (*coll.*) to be exorbitant; э́то — хоро́шая вещь, но ~ется it's good, but they sting you for it.

куса́ч|ки, ек, *no sing.* pliers; wire-cutters.

кусково́й, *adj.* broken in lumps; к. са́хар lump sugar.

кус|о́к, ка́, *m.* lump; piece, bit; slice; cake (*of soap*); зарабо́тать к. хле́ба to earn one's bread and butter.

куст¹, а́, *m.* bush, shrub; спря́таться в ~ы́ (*fig.*) to rat, make oneself scarce.

куст², а́, *m.* (*econ.*) group.

куста́рник, а, *m.* (*collect.*) bush(es), shrub(s); shrubbery.

куста́рник|овый, *adj. of* ~; ~овое расте́ние shrub.

кустарнича|ть, ю, *impf.* **1.** to be a handicraftsman; to exercise a craft at home. **2.** (*coll.*, *pejor.*) to use primitive methods; to work in an amateurish manner.

куста́рничеств|о, а, *n.* (*pejor.*) work done by primitive methods; amateurish, inefficient work.

куста́рн|ый, *adj.* **1.** handicraft; ~ые изде́лия hand-made goods; ~ая промы́шленность cottage industry. **2.** (*fig.*, *pejor.*) amateurish, primitive.

куста́рщин|а, ы, *f.* = куста́рничество.

куста́р|ь, я́, *m.* handicraftsman.

кусти́ст|ый (~, ~а), *adj.* bushy.

куст|и́ться, и́тся, *impf.* to put out side-shoots.

кустова́ни|е, я, *n.* (*electr.*) interconnexion.

кустов|о́й, *adj. of* куст²; ~о́е совеща́ние group conference.

ку́та|ть, ю, *impf.* (*of* за~) (в+*a.*) to muffle up (in).

ку́та|ться, юсь, *impf.* (*of* за~) (в+*a.*) to muffle oneself up (in).

кутёж, а́, *m.* drinking-bout; riot, binge.

кутерьм|а́, ы́, *f.* (*coll.*) commotion, stir, bustle, hubbub.

кути́л|а, ы, *m.* fast liver; hard drinker.

ку|ти́ть, чу́, ~тишь, *impf.* (*of* ~тну́ть) to booze; to go on the booze.

кут|ну́ть, ну́, нёшь, *inst. pf.* (*of* ~и́ть) to go on the booze, go on a binge.

куту́зк|а, и, *f.* (*coll.*) jail, lock-up.

куха́рк|а, и, *f.* cook.

кухми́стерск|ая, ой, *f.* (*obs.*) eating-house, cook-shop.

ку́х|ня, ни, *g. pl.* ~онь, *f.* **1.** kitchen; cook-house. **2.** cooking, cuisine. **3.** (*fig.*, *coll.*; *sing. only*) intrigues, machinations.

ку́хонн|ый, *adj.* kitchen; ~ая плита́ kitchen-range; к. шкаф dresser; (*joc.*) ~ая латы́нь low Latin.

ку́ц|ый (~, ~а), *adj.* **1.** tailless; bob-tailed. **2.** (*of clothing*) short; (*fig.*) limited, abbreviated.

ку́ч|а, и, *f.* **1.** heap, pile; (*coll.*) вали́ть всё в одну́ ~y to lump everything together. **2.** (*coll.*; +*g.*) heaps (of), piles (of); у него́ к. де́нег he has heaps of money; ку́ча мала́ sacks on the mill (*children's game*).

кучево́й, *adj.* (*meteor.*) cumulus.

ку́чер, а, *m.* coachman, driver.

кучерско́й, *adj.* coachman's.

кучеря́в|ый (~, ~а), *adj.* (*dial.*) curly; curly-haired.

ку́ч|ка, ки, *f.* *dim. of* ~a; к. люде́й small group of people.

ку́чный, *adj.* (*of shots*) closely-grouped.

ку|чу́, ~тишь, *see* ~ти́ть.

куш[1], **а**, *m.* (*coll.*) large sum (*of money*).

куш[2], *interj.* (*coll.*; *to a dog*) lie down!

куша́к, **а́**, *m.* sash, girdle.

ку́шань|е, **я**, *n.* food; dish.

ку́ша|ть, **ю**, *impf.* (*of* по~ *and* с~) (*in polite invitation to eat*) to eat, have, take.

куше́тк|а, **и**, *f.* couch.

ку́щ|а, **и**, *g. pl.* ~ *and* ~**ей**, *f.* **1.** (*obs.*, *poet.*) tent, hut; пра́здник ~**ей** (Jewish) Feast of Tabernacles. **2.** foliage; crest (*of tree*).

ку|ю́, **ёшь**, *see* кова́ть.

кэб, **а**, *m.* cab.

кюве́т, **а**, *m.* **1.** (*mil.*) cuvette, cunette. **2.** ditch (*at side of road*).

кюве́тк|а, **и**, *f.* (*phot.*) cuvette, bath.

кюрасо́, *indecl.*, *n.* curaçao (*liqueur*).

кюре́, *indecl.*, *m.* (*eccl.*) curé.

Л

лаба́з, **а**, *m.* (*obs.*) corn-chandler's shop, ware-house; grain merchant's shop, ware-house.

лаба́зник, **а**, *m.* (*obs.*) corn-chandler, grain merchant.

лабиализа́ци|я, **и**, *f.* (*ling.*) labialization.

лабиализ|ова́ть, **у́ю**, *impf. and pf.* (*ling.*) to labialize.

лабиа́льный, *adj.* (*ling.*) labial.

лабио-дента́льный, *adj.* (*ling.*) labio-dental.

лабири́нт, **а**, *m.* (*in var. senses*) labyrinth, maze.

лабора́нт, **а**, *m.* laboratory assistant.

лаборато́ри|я, **и**, *f.* laboratory.

лаборато́р|ный, *adj. of* ~**ия**.

лабрадо́р, **а**, *m.* (*min.*) labradorite.

ла́в|а[1], **ы**, *f.* lava.

ла́в|а[2], **ы**, *f.* (*mining*) drift.

ла́в|а[3], **ы**, *f.* (Cossack) cavalry charge.

лава́нд|а, **ы**, *f.* (*bot.*) lavender.

лави́н|а, **ы**, *f.* avalanche (*also fig.*).

лави́р|овать, **ую**, *impf.* **1.** (*naut.*) to tack; л. про́тив ве́тра to beat up against the wind. **2.** (*fig.*) to manœuvre, avoid taking sides.

ла́вк|а[1], **и**, *f.* bench.

ла́вк|а[2], **и**, *f.* shop; store.

ла́вочк|а[1], **и**, *f.* *dim. of* ла́вка[1].

ла́вочк|а[2], **и**, *f.* *dim. of* ла́вка[2]; (*fig.*, *coll.*) shady concern; gang; на́до закры́ть э́ту ла́вочку a stop must be put to this business.

ла́вочник, **а**, *m.* shop-keeper, retailer.

лавр, **а**, *m.* **1.** (*bot.*) laurel; bay(-tree). **2.** (*pl.*; *fig.*) laurels; пожина́ть ~ы to win laurels; почи́ть на ~ах to rest on one's laurels.

ла́вр|а, **ы**, *f.* monastery (*of highest rank*).

лаврови́шн|евый, *adj. of* ~я; ~евые ка́пли laurel water.

лаврови́шн|я, **и**, *f.* (*bot.*) cherry-laurel.

ла́вр|о́вый, *adj. of* ~; ~о́вый вено́к laurel wreath, (*fig.*) laurels; ~о́вый лист bay leaf; ~о́вая ро́ща laurel grove; *as noun* ~о́вые, ~о́вых (*bot.*) Lauraceae.

ла́вр|ский, *adj. of* ~а.

лавса́н, **а**, *m.* lavsan (*synthetic fibre similar to terylene*).

лаг, **а**, *m.* (*naut.*) **1.** log. **2.** broadside; пали́ть всем ~ом to fire a broadside.

ла́герник, **а**, *m.* (*coll.*) inmate of camp.

ла́гер|ный, *adj. of* ~ь; ~ная жизнь nomad existence; л. сбор (*mil.*) annual camp; ~ная те́ма (*lit.*) 'the (concentration) camp theme' (*as genre of anti-Stalinist Soviet writing*).

ла́гер|ь, **я**, *m.* **1.** (*pl.* ~я́, ~е́й) camp; жить в ~я́х to camp out; (*mil.*) располага́ться, стоя́ть ~ем to camp, be encamped; снять л. to break up, strike camp. **2.** (*pl.* ~и, ~ей) (*fig.*) camp; де́йствовать на два ~я to have a foot in both camps.

лагли́н|ь, **я**, *m.* (*naut.*) log-line.

лагу́н|а, **ы**, *f.* lagoon.

лад, **а**, **о** ~**е**, **в** ~**у́**, *pl.* ~**ы́**, ~**о́в**, *m.* **1.** (*mus. and fig.*) harmony, concord; петь в л., не в л. to sing in, out of tune; запе́ть на друго́й л. (*fig.*) to sing a different tune; жить в ~у́ (c+i.) to live in harmony (with); быть не в ~а́х (c+i.) to be at odds (with), at variance (with); (*coll.*) идти́, пойти́ на л. to go well, be successful; де́ло не идёт на л. things are not going well. **2.** manner, way; на ра́зные ~ы́ in various ways; на свой л. in one's own way, after one's own fashion; на ста́рый л. in the old style. **3.** (*mus.*) stop; fret (*of stringed instrument*).

ла́д|а, **ы**, *m. and f.* (*folk poet.*) beloved.

ла́дан, **а**, *m.* incense, frankincense; л. ро́сный (*pharm.*) benzoin; дыша́ть на л. (*fig.*, *coll.*) to have one foot in the grave.

ла́данк|а, **и**, *f.* amulet.

ла́|дить, **жу**, **дишь**, *impf.* **1.** (c+i.) to get on (with), be on good terms (with); они́ не ~дят they don't get on. **2.** (*coll.*) to prepare, make ready; to tune (*mus. instrument*). **3.** (*coll.*) л. одно́ и то же to harp on the same string.

ла́д|иться, **ится**, *impf.* (*coll.*) to go well, succeed.

ла́дно, *adv.* (*coll.*) **1.** harmoniously. **2.** well;

all right; всё ко́нчилось л. everything ended happily. **3.** *particle* л.! all right!, very well!

ла́д|ный (~ен, ~на́, ~но), *adj.* (*coll.*) **1.** fine, excellent. **2.** harmonious.

ладо́нный, *adj.* (*anat.*) palmar.

ладо́н|ь, и, *f.* palm (*of hand*); быть (ви́дным) как на ~и to be clearly visible.

ладо́ши, *only in phrases* бить, ударя́ть, хло́пать в л. to clap one's hands.

лад|ья́, ьи́, *g. pl.* ~е́й, *f.* **1.** (*poet.*) boat. **2.** (*chess*) castle, rook.

лаж, а, *m.* (*comm.*) agio.

ла́|жу¹, дишь, *see* ~дить.

ла́|жу², зишь, *see* ~зить.

лаз, а, *m.* **1.** (*tech.*) manhole. **2.** (*hunting*) track; стать на л. (+*g.*) to get on the track (of).

лазаре́т, а, *m.* **1.** (*mil.*) field hospital; sick quarters; (*naut.*) sick-bay. **2.** (*obs.*) infirmary.

лазе́йк|а, и, *f.* hole, gap; (*fig., coll.*) loophole; оста́вить себе́ ~y to leave oneself a loophole.

ла́зер, а, *m.* (*phys., tech.*) laser.

ла́|зить, жу, зишь, *impf.* (*indet. of* ле́зть) **1.** (на+*a.*, по+*d.*) to climb, clamber (on to, up); л. на сте́ну to climb a wall; л. по дере́вьям to climb trees; л. по кана́ту to swarm up a rope. **2.** (в+*a.*) to climb (into), get (into); л. в окно́ to get in through the window.

лазо́ревк|а, и, *f.* (*orn.*) blue tit.

лазо́ревый, *adj.* (*poet.*) sky-blue, azure; л. ка́мень (*min.*) lapis lazuli.

лазу́ревый, *adj.* = лазо́ревый, лазу́рный.

лазу́р|ный (~ен, ~на), *adj.* sky-blue, azure.

лазу́р|ь, и, *f.* azure; берли́нская л. Prussian blue.

лазу́тчик, а, *m.* (*mil., obs.*) spy, scout.

ла́|й, я, *m.* bark(ing).

ла́йб|а, ы, *f.* (*one- or two-masted*) sailing boat (*used formerly in Baltic Sea and on rivers Dnieper and Dniester*).

ла́йк|а¹, и, *f.* Eskimo dog.

ла́йк|а², и, *f.* kid-skin.

ла́йк|овый, *adj.* of ~a²; ~овые перча́тки kid gloves.

ла́йнер, а, *m.* (*naut., aeron.*) liner.

лак, а, *m.* varnish, lacquer; япо́нский л. black japan.

лака́|ть, ю, *impf.* (*of* вы́~) to lap (up).

лаке́|й, я, *m.* footman, man-servant; lackey, flunkey (*also fig., pejor.*).

лаке́й|ский, *adj.* of ~; (*fig.*) servile.

лаке́йств|о, а, *n.* servility; dancing attendance.

лаке́йств|овать, ую, *impf.* (пе́ред) to dance attendance (on), kow-tow (to).

лакиро́в|анный, *p.p.p.* of ~а́ть *and adj.* var-

nished, lacquered; ~анная ко́жа patent leather; ~анные ту́фли patent-leather shoes.

лакир|ова́ть, у́ю, *impf.* (*of* от~) to varnish, lacquer; (*fig., pejor.*) to varnish.

лакиро́вк|а, и, *f.* **1.** varnishing, lacquering (*also fig., pejor.*). **2.** varnish. **3.** (*fig.*) gloss, polish.

лакиро́вщик, а, *m.* varnisher (*also fig., pejor.*).

ла́кмус, а, *m.* (*chem.*) litmus.

ла́кмус|овый, *adj.* of ~; ~овая бума́га litmus paper.

ла́ков|ый, *adj.* varnished, lacquered; ~ые ту́фли patent-leather shoes; (*bot.*) ~ое де́рево varnish-tree.

ла́ком|ить, лю, ишь, *impf.* (*of* по~) (*coll.*) to regale (with), treat (to).

ла́ком|иться, люсь, ишься, *impf.* (*of* по~) (+*i.*) to treat oneself (to).

ла́комк|а, и, *m. and f.* gourmand; быть ~ой to have a sweet tooth.

ла́комств|о, а, *n.* dainty, delicacy.

ла́ком|ый (~, ~a), *adj.* **1.** dainty, tasty; л. кусо́к titbit, tasty morsel (*also fig.*). **2.** (*coll.*) (до) fond (of), partial (to).

лакони́зм, а, *m.* laconic brevity.

лакони́ческий, *adj.* laconic.

лакони́ч|ный (~ен, ~на), *adj.* = ~еский.

лакрима́тор, а, *m.* tear gas.

лакри́ц|а, ы, *f.* (*bot.*) liquorice.

лакри́чник, а, *m.* = лакри́ца.

лакта́ци|я, и, *f.* lactation.

лактобацилли́н, а, *m.* yoghurt.

лакто́з|а, ы, *f.* (*chem.*) lactose.

ла́м|а¹, ы, *f.* (*zool.*) llama.

ла́м|а², ы, *m.* (*rel.*) lama.

ламаи́зм, а, *m.* (*rel.*) lamaism.

ла́мп|а, ы, *f.* **1.** lamp; предохрани́тельная л. safety-lamp; рудни́чная л. Davy lamp; л. дневно́го све́та fluorescent lamp. **2.** (*radio*) valve; tube; односе́точная л. onegrid valve; двухсе́точная л. space charge tetrode; смеси́тельная л. frequency changer valve.

лампа́д|а, ы, *f.* icon-lamp.

лампа́дн|ый, *adj.* ~ое ма́сло lamp-oil.

лампа́с, а, *m.* stripe (*on side of trousers*).

ла́мп|овый, *adj.* of ~a; ~овое стекло́ lamp-chimney; (*tech.*) л. выпрями́тель tube rectifier; л. генера́тор valve oscillator, vacuum tube generator; л. усили́тель valve amplifier, vacuum tube amplifier.

ла́мпочк|а, и, *f.* **1.** *dim. of* ла́мпа. **2.** (*electric light*) bulb; (*tech.*) л. нака́ливания incandescent lamp.

лангу́ст, а, *m.* (*also* лангу́ст|а, ~ы, *f.*) spiny lobster; rock lobster.

ландо́, *indecl., n.* landau.

ландскне́хт, а, *m.* **1.** (*hist.*) lansquenet, landsknecht. **2.** (*card game*) lansquenet.

ландша́фт, а, *m.* landscape.

ла́ндыш, а, *m.* lily of the valley.

лани́т|а, ы, *f.* (*arch.*) cheek.

ланоли́н, а, *m.* (*pharm.*) lanolin.

ланце́т, а, *m.* (*med.*) lancet; вскры́ть ∼ом to lance.

ланце́т|ный, *adj.* **1.** *adj. of* ∼. **2.** (*bot.*) lanceolate.

ланцетови́д|ный (∼ен, ∼на), *adj.* (*bot.*) lanceolate.

лан|ь, и, *f.* fallow deer; doe (*of fallow deer*).

ла́п|а, ы, *f.* **1.** paw; pad (*joc. of human hand*); (*fig., coll.*) попа́сть в ∼ы к кому́-н. to fall into someone's clutches; в ∼ах у кого́-н. in someone's clutches. **2.** (*tech.*) tenon, dovetail. **3.** (*naut.*) fluke (*of anchor*). **4.** (*fig.*) bough (*of coniferous tree*).

лапида́р|ный (∼ен, ∼на), *adj.* lapidary, terse.

ла́п|ка, ки, *f. dim. of* ∼а; (*fig., coll.*) стоя́ть, ходи́ть на за́дних ∼ках (перед) to dance attendance (upon).

лапла́нд|ец, ца, *m.* Lapp, Laplander.

лапла́нд|ка, ки, *f. of* ∼ец.

лапла́ндский, *adj.* Lappish.

ла́потник, а, *m.* **1.** bast-shoe maker. **2.** (*obs., coll.*) peasant.

ла́пот|ный, *adj. of* ∼ь; ∼ная Росси́я (*rhet.*) the old (*as opp. to post-1917*) Russia.

ла́п|оть, тя, *pl.* ∼ти, ∼те́й, *m.* bast shoe, bast sandal; ходи́ть в ∼тя́х to wear bast shoes, sandals.

лапсерда́к, а, *m.* lapserdak (*long overcoat worn by Jews*).

лапт|а́, ы́, *f.* **1.** (*Russian ball game*) lapta. **2.** lapta bat.

ла́пчатый, *adj.* **1.** (*bot.*) palmate. **2.** web-footed; гусь л. (*fig., coll.*) cunning fellow, sly one.

лапш|а́, и́, *f.* **1.** noodles. **2.** noodle soup.

лар|ёк, ька́, *m.* stall.

лар|е́ц, ца́, *m.* casket, small chest.

ларёчник, а, *m.* (*coll.*) stall-holder.

ларинги́т, а, *m.* laryngitis.

ларингоско́п, а, *m.* laryngoscope.

ларинготоми́|я, и, *f.* laryngotomy.

ла́рчик, а, *m.* small box; (*coll.*) а л. про́сто открыва́лся the explanation was quite simple.

ла́р|ы, ов, *sing.* ∼, ∼а, *m.* л. и пена́ты lares and penates.

лар|ь, я́, *m.* **1.** chest, coffer; bin; л. с муко́й bin containing flour. **2.** stall.

ла́ск|а¹, и, *f.* **1.** caress, endearment. **2.** kindness.

ла́с|ка², ки, *g. pl.* ∼ок, *f.* (*zool.*) weasel.

ласка́тельн|ый, *adj.* **1.** caressing; ∼ое и́мя pet name. **2.** (*obs.*) cajoling, unctuous. **3.** (*gram.*) affectionate, expressing endearment.

ласка́|ть, ю, *impf.* **1.** to caress, fondle, pet. **2.** (*obs.*) to comfort, console.

ласка́|ться, юсь, *impf.* **1.** (к) to make up to; to snuggle up to; to coax; (*of a dog*) to fawn (upon). **2.** (*coll.*) to exchange caresses.

ла́сковый, *adj.* affectionate, tender; (*fig.*) л. ве́тер soft wind.

лассо́, *indecl., n.* lasso.

ласт, а, *m.* flipper.

ла́стик¹, а, *m.* (*material*) lasting.

ла́стик², а, *m.* (*coll.*) india-rubber.

ла́|ститься, щусь, сти́шься, *impf.* (к, о́коло) (*coll.*) to make up (to), fawn (upon).

ла́стовиц|а, ы, *f.* gusset (*in shirt*).

ластоно́г|ое, ого, *n.* (*zool.*) Pinniped.

ла́сточк|а, и, *f.* swallow; берегова́я л. sand-martin; городска́я л. (*house*) martin; прыжо́к в во́ду ∼ой swallow-dive; пе́рвая л. (*fig.*) the first signs; одна́ л. весны́ не де́лает (*prov.*) one swallow does not make a summer.

ла́т|анный, *p.p.p. of* ∼а́ть *and adj.* worn, patched.

лататы́, *only in coll. phrase* зада́ть л. to take to one's heels.

лата́|ть, ю, *impf.* (*of* за∼) (*coll.*) to patch.

латви́|ец, йца, *m.* Latvian.

латви́|йка, йки, *f. of* ∼ец.

латви́йский, *adj.* Latvian.

латиниза́ци|я, и, *f.* latinization.

латини́зи́р|овать, ую, *impf. and pf.* to latinize.

латини́зм, а, *m.* **1.** Latin construction (*borrowed by another language*). **2.** Latin loan-word.

латини́ст, а, *m.* Latin scholar.

лати́ниц|а, ы, *f.* Roman alphabet, Roman letters.

лати́нский, *adj.* Latin.

лати́нств|о, а, *n.* (*obs.*) **1.** the Roman Catholic faith. **2.** (*collect.*) Roman Catholics.

лати́нщин|а, ы, *f.* Latin culture; Latinity.

лати́нян|ин, ина, *pl.* ∼е, ∼, *m.* **1.** (*hist.*) inhabitant of Latium. **2.** (*obs.*) Roman Catholic.

латифу́нди|и, й, *sing.* ∼я, ∼и, *f.* latifundia.

латифунди́ст, а, *m.* **1.** 'latifundista' (*large land-owner in South America*). **2.** *pejor.* = *feudal-type, exploiting land-owner*.

ла́тк|а, и, *f.* (*coll.*) patch.

ла́тник, а, *m.* armour-clad warrior.

лату́к, а, *m.* (*bot.*) lettuce.

лату́нный, *adj.* brass.

лату́н|ь, и, *f.* brass.

ла́т|ы, ∼, *no sing.* (*hist.*) armour.

латы́н|ь, и, *f.* (*coll.*) Latin.

латы́ш, а́, *pl.* ∼и́, ∼е́й, *m.* Lett.

латы́ш|ка, ки, *f. of* ∼.

латы́шский, *adj.* Lettish, Latvian.

лауреа́т, а, *m.* prize-winner.

лафа́, *as pred.*; *impers.* (*coll.*) тебе́, ему́, *etc.* л. you are, he is, *etc.*, in clover, having a wonderful time.

лафе́т, а, *m.* (*mil.*) gun-carriage.

ла́цкан, а, *pl.* ~ы, ~ов, *m.* lapel.

лачу́г|а, и, *f.* hovel, shack.

ла́|щусь, сти́шься, *see* ~сти́ться.

ла́|ять, ю, ешь, *impf.* to bark; to bay.

ла́|яться, юсь, ешься, *impf.* (*coll.*) (на+*a.*) to rail, snarl (at).

лба, лбу, *etc.*, *see* лоб.

лга́нь|ё, я́, *n.* (*coll.*) lying.

лгать, лгу, лжёшь, лгут, *past* лгал, лгала́, лга́ло, *impf.* 1. (*pf.* со~) to lie; tell lies. 2. (*pf.* на~) (на+*a.*) to slander.

лгун, а́, *m.* liar.

лгуни́шк|а, и, *m.* (*coll.*) paltry liar.

лгу́н|ья, ьи, *g. pl.* ~ий, *f. of* ~.

ле́бед|а́, ы́, *f.* (*bot.*) goose-foot, orach.

лебед|ёнок, ёнка, *pl.* ~я́та, ~я́т, *m.* cygnet.

лебеди́н|ый, *adj. of* ле́бедь; ~ая по́ступь graceful gait; (*fig.*) ~ая пе́сня swan-song; ~ая ше́я swan-neck; (*tech.*) S-bend pipe.

лебёдк|а¹, и, *f.* (female) swan, pen(-swan).

лебёдк|а², и, *f.* (*tech.*) winch, windlass.

ле́бед|ь, я, *pl.* ~и, ~е́й, *m.* swan, cob(-swan).

лебе|зи́ть, жу́, зи́шь, *impf.* (*coll.*) (пе́ред) to fawn (upon), cringe (to).

леб|я́жий, *adj. of* ~едь; л. пух swan's down.

лев¹, льва, *m.* lion; морско́й л. sea-lion; муравьи́ный л. ant-lion.

лев², а, *m.* (*Bulgarian monetary unit*) lev.

лева́д|а, ы, *f.* (*dial.*) 1. meadow. 2. riparian woodlands (*flooded at season of thaw; in S. Russia*).

лева́цкий, *adj.* (*polit.*; *pejor.*) ultra-left.

лева́честв|о, а, *n.* (*polit.*) leftism.

леве́|ть, ю, *impf.* (*of* по~) (*polit.*) to become more left, move to the left.

левиафа́н, а, *m.* leviathan.

левизн|а́, ы́, *f.* (*polit.*) leftishness.

левко́|й, я, *m.* (*bot.*) stock, gilly-flower.

ле́во, *adv.* (*naut.*) to port; л. руля́! port helm!; л. на борт! hard-a-port!

левобере́жный, *adj.* left-bank.

левре́тк|а, и, *f.* Italian greyhound.

левш|а́, и́, *i.* ~о́й, *g. pl.* ~е́й, *m. and f.* left-hander.

ле́в|ый, *adj.* 1. left; left-hand; (*naut.*) port; л. борт port side, port hand; ~ая сторона́ left-hand side, (*of horse, carriage, etc.*) near side; (*of material*) wrong side; (*fig.*) встать с ~ой ноги́ to get out of bed on the wrong side. 2. (*pl.*) left-wing; *as noun* л., ~ого, *m.* left-winger; (*pl.*; *collect.*) the left.

лега́в|ая, ой, *f.* (длинношёрстая) setter; (короткошёрстая) pointer.

лега́в|ый, ого, *m.* (*coll.*) police spy, informer.

легализа́ци|я, и, *f.* legalization.

легализи́|ровать(ся), и́рую(сь), = ~ова́ть(ся).

легализ|ова́ть, у́ю, *impf. and pf.* to legalize.

легализ|ова́ться, у́юсь, *impf. and pf.* to become legalized.

лега́л|ьный (~ен, ~ьна), *adj.* legal.

лега́т, а, *m.* legate.

лега́то, *mus.* 1. *adv.* legato. 2. *indecl. noun* slur.

леге́нд|а, ы, *f.* legend.

легенда́р|ный (~ен, ~на), *adj.* legendary (*also fig.*).

легио́н, а, *m.* (*in var. senses*) legion; иностра́нный л. the Foreign Legion; о́рден почётного ~а Legion of Honour; и́мя им л. their name is Legion.

легионе́р, а, *m.* legionary.

леги́рова|нный, *p.p.p. of* ~ть *and adj.* alloy(ed).

леги́р|овать, ую, *impf.* to alloy.

легислату́р|а, ы, *f.* (*leg.*) legislature.

лёг|кий (~ок, ~ка́, ~ко́, *pl.* ~ки́ *or* ~ки́), *adj.* 1. light (*in weight*). 2. easy; л. слог simple style; у него́ л. хара́ктер he is easy to get on with; ~ко́ сказа́ть! easier said than done! 3. (*in var. senses*) light; slight; ~кая атле́тика (*sport*) field and track athletics; ~кая просту́да slight cold; л. слу́чай (заболева́ния) mild case; ~кие фигу́ры (*chess*) minor pieces; ~кое чте́ние light reading(-matter); (*coll.*) ~ок на поми́не, вы ~ки́ на поми́не! talk of the devil!; (*coll.*) у него́ ~кая рука́ he is lucky, he has luck; с ва́шей ~ой руки́ once you start(ed) the ball rolling; же́нщина лёгкого поведе́ния woman of easy virtue.

легко́, *adv.* easily, lightly, slightly; э́то ему́ л. даётся it comes easily to him; л. косну́ться to touch lightly.

легкоатле́т, а, *m.* (field and track) athlete.

легкове́ри|е, я, *n.* credulity, gullibility.

легкове́р|ный (~ен, ~на), *adj.* credulous, gullible.

легкове́с, а, *m.* (*sport*) light-weight.

легкове́с|ный (~ен, ~на), *adj.* 1. light-weight; light. 2. (*fig.*, *pejor.*) superficial.

легково́й, *adj.* passenger (*conveyance*); л. автомоби́ль (motor) car; л. изво́зчик cab, cabman.

лёгк|ое, ого, *n.* 1. (*anat.*) lung; воспале́ние одного́ ~ого, обо́их ~их single, double pneumonia. 2. (*sing. only*; *cul.*) lights.

легкомы́слен|ный (~, ~на), *adj.* light (-minded), thoughtless; flippant, frivolous, superficial; л. посту́пок thoughtless action; ~ные слова́ flippant words.

легкомы́сли|е, я, *n.* light-mindedness, thoughtlessness; flippancy, levity.

легкопла́в|кий (~ок, ~ка), *adj.* fusible, easily melted.

лёгкост|ь, и, *f.* 1. lightness. 2. easiness.

легóнько, *adv.* (*coll.*) **1.** slightly. **2.** gently.

лёгочный, *adj.* (*med.*) pulmonary.

легчá|ть, ет, *impf.* (*of* по~) **1.** to lessen, abate. **2.** (*impers.* +*d.*); to get better; to feel better.

лéг|че, *comp. of* ~кий *and* ~кó; больнóму л. the invalid is feeling better; мне от э́того не л. I am none the better for it; (*coll.*) час óт часу не л. worse and worse; л. на поворóтах! mind what you say!

лёд, льда, о льдé, на льду́, *m.* ice; л. разби́т, л. слóман (*fig.*) the ice is broken.

ледáщий, *adj.* (*coll.*) puny; feeble.

леденé|ть, ю, *impf.* (*of* за~ *and* о~) (*intrans.*) **1.** to freeze. **2.** to become numb with cold; (*fig.*) кровь ~ет (one's) blood runs cold.

леден|éц, цá, *m.* fruit-drop.

ледени́ст|ый (~, ~а), *adj.* frozen; icy.

леден|и́ть, и́т, *impf.* (*of* о~) (*trans.*) to freeze; (*fig.*) to chill.

леден|я́щий, *pres. part. of* ~и́ть *and adj.* chilling, icy.

лéди, *indecl., f.* lady.

лéдник, а, *m.* **1.** ice-house. **2.** ice-box; вагóн-л. refrigerator van.

ледни́к, á, *m.* glacier.

леднико́вый, *adj.* glacial; л. перио́д ice age.

ледови́тый, *adj.* Céверный Л. океáн the Arctic Ocean.

ледóв|ый, *adj.* ice; ~ые плáвания Arctic voyages; ~ое побóище the Battle on the Ice (*fought on 15 April 1242 between the army of Alexander Nevsky and the Teutonic Knights*).

ледокóл, а, *m.* ice-breaker.

ледокóл|ьный, *adj. of* ~.

ледорéз, а, *m.* **1.** (*naut.*) ice-cutter. **2.** (*tech.*) starling.

ледору́б, а, *m.* ice-axe.

ледостáв, а, *m.* freezing-over (*of river*).

ледохóд, а, *m.* drifting of ice, floating of ice (*at time of freeze-up and thaw*).

ледь́шк|а, и, *f.* (*coll.*) **1.** piece of ice. **2.** (*fig., joc.*) iceberg.

лед|яно́й, *adj.* **1.** *adj. of* ~; ~янáя горá ice slope (*for tobogganing*); iceberg. **2.** icy (*also fig.*); ice-cold.

лéер, а, *m.* (*naut.*) taut rope, yard.

лёжа, *adv.* lying down, in lying position.

лежáк, á, *m.* chaise-longue, deck chair.

лежáлый, *adj.* stale, old.

лежáнк|а, и, *f.* stove-bench (*a shelf on which it is possible to sleep, running along the side of a Russian stove*).

леж|áть, у́, и́шь, *impf.* (*in var. senses*) to lie; to be (situated); л. в больни́це to be in hospital; л. больны́м to be laid up; врач велéл мне л. the doctor told me to stay in bed; л. на боку́, на печи́ (*fig., coll.*) to idle away one's time; л. у когó-н. на душé to be on one's mind; э́то ~и́т у меня́ на со́вести it

lies heavy on my conscience; э́то ~и́т на вáшей отвéтственности this is your responsibility; у меня́ душá не ~и́т (к) I have a distaste (for), an aversion (to, from, for).

леж|áться, и́тся, *impf.* (+*d.*) ему́ не ~áлось в постéли he would, could not stay in bed.

лежáч|ий, *adj.* lying, recumbent; л. больнóй bed-patient; ~его не бьют never hit a man when he is down.

лéжбищ|е, а, *n.* breeding-ground (*of certain aquatic mammals*); л. тюлéней seal-rookery.

лежебóк|а, и, *m. and f.* (*coll.*) lazy-bones, lie-abed.

лéж|ень, ня, *m.* (*tech.*) **1.** ledger; foundation beam; mud sill. **2.** (*railways*) sleeper.

лёжк|а, и, *f.* **1.** (*coll.*) lying. **2.** (*coll.*) lying position; лежáть в ~у to be on one's back (*of sick person*); напи́ться в ~у to become dead drunk. **3.** lair (*of wild animal*).

лежмя́, *adv.* (*coll.*) лежáть л. to lie without getting up; to lie helpless.

лéзви|е, я, *n.* **1.** edge (*of cutting instrument*). **2.** safety-razor blade.

лезги́нк|а, и, *f.* lezghinka (*Caucasian dance*).

лез|ть, у, ешь, *past* ~, ~ла, *impf.* (*of* по~) **1.** (на+*a.*, по+*d.*) to climb (up, on to). **2.** (в+*a.*, под+*a.*) to clamber, crawl (through, into, under). **3.** to make one's way stealthily; куда́ ~ешь? (*coll.*) where do you think you're going? **4.** (в+*a.*) to thrust the hand (into). **5.** (в+*a.*) to fit (into). **6.** to stick out (*intrans.*). **7.** to slip out of position. **8.** to come on (*in spite of obstacles*). **9.** (в+*a.*) to try to climb (*into a higher station in life*). **10.** to fall out (*of hair, fur*). **11.** to come to pieces (*of fabrics, leather, etc.*); л. нá стену (*fig., coll.*) to climb up the wall; не л. в кармáн за слóвом not to be at a loss for a word; л. в петлю́ (*coll.*) to stick one's neck out.

лé|й, я, *m.* lei (*Romanian monetary unit*).

лейб-гвáрди|я, и, *f.* (*hist.*) Life-Guards.

лейб-мéдик, а, *m.* (*hist.*) physician in ordinary.

лейбори́ст, а, *m.* (*polit.*) Labourite.

лейбори́стск|ий, *adj.* (*polit.*) Labour; ~ая пáртия Labour Party.

лéйденск|ий, *adj.* ~ая бáнка (*phys.*) Leyden jar.

лéйк|а¹, и, *f.* **1.** watering-can. **2.** (*naut.*) bail. **3.** funnel (*for pouring liquids*).

лéйк|а², и, *f.* Leica (*camera*).

лейкеми́|я, и, *f.* (*med.*) leucaemia.

лейкóм|а, ы, *f.* (*med.*) leucoma.

лейкоци́т, а, *m.* (*physiol.*) leucocyte.

лейтенáнт, а, *m.* lieutenant; млáдший л. second lieutenant (*but there are three ranks in the Soviet Army, viz.* млáдший л., л., *and* стáрший л., *corresponding to the two ranks of second lieutenant and lieutenant in the British Army*).

лейтмотив, а, *m.* (*mus. and fig.*) leit-motiv.

лекал|о, а, *n.* 1. (*tech.*) template, gauge, pattern. 2. instrument for drawing curves.

лекарственный, *adj.* medicinal; officinal.

лекарств|о, а, *n.* medicine; drug.

лекар|ь, я, *pl.* ~и, ~ей, *m.* (*obs. or pejor.*) physician.

лексик|а, и, *f.* vocabulary.

лексикограф, а, *m.* lexicographer.

лексикографический, *adj.* lexicographical.

лексикографи|я, и, *f.* lexicography.

лексиколог, а, *m.* lexicologist.

лексикологи|я, и, *f.* lexicology.

лексикон, а, *m.* 1. lexicon, dictionary. 2. vocabulary.

лексический, *adj.* lexical.

лектор, а, *m.* lecturer.

лектори|й, я, *m.* 1. centre organizing public lectures. 2. lecture-hall.

лектори|я, и, *f.* (*obs.*) reading-room (*in university library*).

лектор|ский, *adj.* of ~; *as noun* ~ская, ~ской, *f.* lecturers' common room.

лекторств|о, а, *n.* lecturing; lectureship.

лектрис|а, ы, *f.* lecturer, lectrice.

лекционный, *adj.* of **лекция**; л. зал lecture--room; л. метод преподавания teaching method based on lectures.

лекци|я, и, *f.* lecture; читать ~ю to lecture, deliver a lecture; (*fig., coll.*) to read a lecture.

леле|ять, ю, *impf.* 1. to coddle, pamper. 2. (*fig.*) to cherish, foster; л. мечту to cherish a hope.

лемех, а (*and* **лемех**, а), *m.* ploughshare.

лем|ешный, *adj.* of ~ех.

лемм|а, ы, *f.* (*math.; lit.*) lemma.

лемминг, а, *m.* (*zool.*) lemming.

лемур, а, *m.* (*zool.*) lemur.

лен, а, *m.* (*hist.*) fief, fee; отдать в л. to give in fee.

лён, льна, *m.* (*bot.*) flax; л.-долгунец long--fibred flax; горный л. (*min.*) asbestos.

лендлорд, а, *m.* landlord, land-owner (*in Great Britain and Ireland*).

ленив|ец, ца, *m.* 1. lazy-bones; sluggard. 2. (*zool.*) sloth. 3. (*tech.*) idler, idling sprocket.

ленив|ый (~, ~а), *adj.* 1. lazy, idle; sluggish. 2. (*cul.*) prepared in accordance with a hasty recipe.

ленин|ец, ца, *m.* Leninist.

ленинизм, а, *m.* Leninism.

ленинский, *adj.* of Lenin; Leninist; л. призыв (*hist.*) 'The Lenin enrolment' (*mass enrolment of new members of Communist Party following Lenin's death*).

лен|иться, юсь, ишься, *impf.* 1. to be lazy, idle. 2. (+*inf.*) to be too lazy (to); он признался, что он ~ился им писать he

admitted that he had been too lazy to write to them.

ленник, а, *m.* (*hist.*) vassal, feudatory.

ленный, *adj.* (*hist.*) feudatory; feudal.

леност|ь, и, *f.* laziness, idleness; sloth.

лент|а, ы, *f.* ribbon, band; tape; аннинская л. ribbon of Order of St. Anne; гусеничная л. caterpillar track; изоляционная л. insulating tape; кинематографическая л. (reel of) film; патронная л. cartridge belt; виться ~ой to twist, meander.

лент|очный, *adj.* of ~а; л. глист, л. червь tape-worm; ~очная пила band-saw; л. тормоз band brake; л. транспортёр conveyor belt.

лентя|й, я, *m.* lazy-bones; sluggard.

лентяйнича|ть, ю, *impf.* (*coll.*) to be lazy, idle; to loaf.

ленц|а, ы, *f.* (*coll.*) disposition to laziness; он с ~ой he is inclined to be lazy.

ленчик, а, *m.* saddle-tree.

лен|ь, и, *f.* 1. laziness, idleness; indolence. 2. (*as pred.*+*d. and inf.; coll.*) to feel too lazy (to), not to feel like; ему было л. выключить радио he was too lazy to turn the wireless off; надо бы пойти, да л. I ought to go, but I don't feel like it; все, кому не л. anyone who feels like it.

леопард, а, *m.* leopard.

лепестковый, *adj.* (*bot.*) petalled.

лепест|ок, ка, *m.* petal.

лепет, а, *m.* babble (*also fig.*); prattle.

лепе|тать, чу, ~чешь, *impf.* to babble; to prattle.

лепёшк|а, и, *f.* 1. flat cake; (*fig., coll.*) разбиться, расшибиться в ~у to strain every nerve, go through fire and water. 2. (*medicinal*) tablet, pastille.

леп|ить, лю, ~ишь, *impf.* 1. (*pf.* вы~ *and* с~) to model, fashion; to mould; л. гнездо to build a nest. 2. (*pf.* на~) (*coll.*) to stick (on). 3. (*sl.*) to lie, tell lies.

леп|иться, люсь, ~ишься, *impf.* 1. (по+*d.*) to cling (to) (*of things adhering to a steep or precipitous surface*). 2. (*coll.*) to crawl.

лепк|а, и, *f.* modelling.

леп|ой, *adj.* modelled, moulded; ~ое украшение stucco moulding.

лепрозори|й, я, *m.* hospital for lepers.

лепт|а, ы, *f.* mite; внести свою ~у to contribute one's mite.

лепщик, а, *m.* modeller, sculptor.

лес, а(у), *pl.* ~а, *m.* 1. (в ~у) forest, wood(s); выйти из ~а (из ~у) to come out of the wood; купить л. to buy woodlands; красный, чёрный л. coniferous, deciduous forest; быть как в ~у (*fig., coll.*) to be all at sea; л. рубят — щепки летят (*prov.*) you can't make omelettes without breaking eggs; кто в л., к. по дрова (to be, *etc.*) at sixes and sevens. **2.** (в ~е) (*sing. only*; *collect.*) timber; л. на корню́ standing timber.

лес|а́¹, *pl. of* ~.

лес|а́², **о́в** scaffolding.

леса́³, лёсы, *pl.* **лёсы, лёс,** *f.* fishing-line.

лесби́йск|ий, *adj.* of Lesbos; ~ая любо́вь Lesbianism.

лесбия́нк|а, и, *f.* Lesbian (*female homosexual*).

лесе́нк|а, и, *f.* (*coll.*) *dim. of* ле́стница; short flight of stairs; short ladder.

леси́н|а, ы, *f.* (*dial.*) trunk (*of a timber tree*).

леси́ст|ый (~, ~а), *adj.* wooded, woody.

лесни́к, а́, *m.* forester.

лесни́честв|о, а, *n.* forest area.

лесни́ч|ий, его, *m.* forestry officer; forest warden.

лес|но́й, *adj. of* ~; л. двор, склад timber-yard; ~ное де́ло timber industry; л. институ́т forestry institute, school of forestry; ~ны́е насажде́ния afforestation; л. пито́мник nursery forest.

лесово́д, а, *m.* forestry specialist; graduate of forestry institute.

лесово́дств|о, а, *n.* forestry.

лесово́з, а, *m.* timber ship; timber lorry.

лесозаво́д, а, *m.* timber mill.

лесозагото́вк|а, и, *f.* **1.** timber cutting. **2.** logging; wooding. **3.** (*pl.*) (State) timber purchasing.

лесозащи́тный, *adj.* appertaining to the protection of the forests.

лес|о́к, ка́, *m.* small wood, copse, grove.

лесоматериа́л, а, *m.* timber.

лесонасажде́ни|е, я, *n.* **1.** afforestation. **2.** (forest) plantation.

лесоохране́ни|е, я, *n.* forest preservation.

лесопа́рк, а, *m.* forest park.

лесопи́лк|а, и, *f.* saw-mill.

лесопи́льн|ый, *adj.* sawing; л. заво́д saw-mill; ~ая ра́ма log frame; gang saw.

лесопи́льня, ьни, *g. pl.* ~ен, *f.* = ~ка.

лесополос|а́, ы́, *f.* woodland belt, forest belt.

лесопоса́д|ки, ок forest plantations.

лесопромы́шленник, а, *m.* timber merchant.

лесопромы́шленност|ь, и, *f.* timber industry.

лесору́б, а, *m.* lumber-man.

лесосе́к|а, и, *f.* (wood-)cutting area.

лесоспла́в, а, *m.* timber rafting.

лесосте́п|ь, и, *f.* (*geogr.*) forest-steppe.

лесота́ск|а, и, *f.* (*tech.*) log conveyer.

лесоту́ндр|а, ы, *f.* (*geogr.*) forest-tundra.

леспромхо́з, а, *m.* (*abbr. of* лесно́е промы́шленное хозя́йство) (State) timber industry enterprise.

лёсс, а, *m.* (*geol.*) loess.

ле́стниц|а, ы, *f.* stairs, staircase; ladder; верёвочная л. rope-ladder; пара́дная л.

front staircase; пожа́рная л. fire-escape; складна́я л. steps, step-ladder; чёрная л. backstairs.

ле́стни|чный, *adj. of* ~ца; ~чная кле́тка well (*of stairs*).

ле́ст|ный (~ен, ~на), *adj.* **1.** complimentary. **2.** flattering; ему́ бы́ло ~но, что... he felt flattered that . . . .

лест|ь, и, *f.* flattery; adulation.

лёт, а, на ~у́, о ~е, *m.* flight, flying; стреля́ть в пти́цу в л. to shoot at a bird in flight; на ~у́ in the air, on the wing; (*fig.*, *coll.*) hurriedly, in passing; хвата́ть на ~у́ to be quick to grasp (*an idea, etc.*); to be quick on the uptake.

Ле́т|а, ы, *f.* (*myth.*) Lethe; ка́нуть в ~у to sink into oblivion.

лет|а́, ~, *pl.* 1. years; age; ско́лько вам ~? how old are you?; ему́ бо́льше, ме́ньше сорока́ ~ he is over, under forty; с де́тских лет from childhood; мы одни́х лет we are of the same age; сре́дних лет middle-aged; быть в ~а́х to be elderly, getting on (in years); на ста́рости ~ in one's old age. **2.** *g. pl.* (*as g. pl. of* год) years; прошло́ мно́го ~ many years (have) passed, elapsed.

лета́льный, *adj.* lethal, fatal.

летарги́ческий, *adj.* lethargic.

летарги́|я, и, *f.* lethargy.

лета́тельн|ый, *adj.* flying; л. аппара́т aircraft; (*zool.*) ~ая перепо́нка wing membrane (*in bats*).

лет|а́ть, а́ю, *indet. of* ~е́ть.

лета́|ющий, *pres. part. of* ~ть *and adj.*; ~ющая лягу́шка (*zool.*) tree-frog.

ле|те́ть, чу́, ти́шь, *impf.* (*of* по~) **1.** to fly. **2.** (*fig.*) (*in var. senses*) to rush, tear; л. на всех пара́х to run at full tilt; л. стрело́й to go like an arrow. **3.** (*fig.*, *coll.*) to fall, drop (*intrans.*); ли́стья ~тя́т the leaves are falling; а́кции ~тя́т вниз shares are dropping (sharply).

лётк|а, и, *f.* (*tech.*) tap hole; slag notch.

ле́тний, *adj.* summer.

ле́тник, а, *m.* (*bot.*) annual.

лётн|ый, *adj.* (suitable for, appertaining to) flying; ~ое де́ло flying; ~ое по́ле airfield; л. соста́в aircrew.

ле́т|о, а, *pl.* ~а́, *n.* summer; ба́бье л. Indian summer; (*coll.*) ско́лько ~, ско́лько зим it's ages since we met!

лет|о́к, ка́, *m.* (bee-keeping) entrance (*in hive*).

ле́том, *adv.* in summer.

летопи́с|ец, ца, *m.* chronicler, annalist.

летопи́сный, *adj.* annalistic.

ле́топис|ь, и, *f.* chronicle, annals.

летосчисле́ни|е, я, *n.* chronology.

лету́н, а́, *m.* **1.** flyer, flier. **2.** (*fig.*, *coll.*) rolling-stone, drifter.

лету́чест|ь, и, *f.* (*chem.*) volatility.
лету́ч|ий, *adj.* **1.** flying; ~ая мышь bat; ~ая ры́ба flying-fish. **2.** (*fig.*) passing, ephemeral; brief; л. листо́к leaflet; л. ми́тинг emergency, extraordinary meeting. **3.** (*med.*) shifting. **4.** (*chem.*) volatile.
лету́чк|а, и, *f.* (*coll.*) **1.** leaflet. **2.** emergency meeting, extraordinary meeting. **3.** mobile detachment; (*med.*) mobile dressing station; ремо́нтная л. emergency repairs team; хирурги́ческая л. mobile surgical unit.
лётчик, а, *m.* pilot; aviator, flyer; л.-испыта́тель test-pilot; л.-истреби́тель fighter pilot.
лече́бник, а, *m.* book of home cures.
лече́бниц|а, ы, *f.* clinic.
лече́бный, *adj.* **1.** medical. **2.** medicinal.
лече́ни|е, я, *n.* (medical) treatment; амбулато́рное л. out-patient treatment.
леч|и́ть, у́, ~ишь, *impf.* to treat (*medically*); его́~ат от шо́ка he is being treated for shock.
леч|и́ться, у́сь, ~ишься, *impf.* **1.** (от) to receive, undergo (medical) treatment (for); л. впры́скиваниями to take a course of injections. **2.** *pass. of* ~и́ть.
ле|чу́¹, ти́шь, *see* ~те́ть.
леч|у́², ~ишь, *see* ~и́ть.
лечь, ля́гу, ля́жешь, ля́гут, *past* лёг, легла́, *imp.* ляг, ля́гте, *pf.* (*of* ложи́ться) **1.** to lie (down); л. в больни́цу to go (in) to hospital; л. в посте́ль, л. спать to go to bed; (*coll.*) неуже́ли де́ти ещё не легли́? aren't the children in bed yet?; л. в осно́ву (+*g.*) to underlie; (*naut.*) л. в дрейф to lie to, heave to. **2.** (на+*a.*) to fall (on); (*rhet.*) л. костьми́ to fall in battle; (*fig.*) отве́тственность ля́жет на вас it will be your duty, it will be incumbent upon you; подозре́ние легло́ на иностра́нцев suspicion fell upon the foreigners; л. на со́весть to weigh on one's conscience.
ле́ш|ий, его, *m.* (*in Russ. myth.*) wood-goblin; к ~ему! (*coll. expletive*) go to the devil!; како́го ~его... what the devil, why the devil. . . .
лещ, а́, *m.* (*fish*) bream.
лещи́н|а, ы, *f.* (*bot.*) hazel.
лже- pseudo-, false-, mock-.
лжеприся́г|а, и, *f.* (*leg.*) perjury.
лжесвиде́тел|ь, я, *m.* false witness.
лжесвиде́тельств|о, а, *n.* false evidence.
лжесвиде́тельств|овать, ую, *impf.* to give false evidence.
лжеуче́ни|е, я, *n.* false doctrine.
лжец, а́, *m.* liar.
лжёшь, *see* лгать.
лжи́вост|ь, и, *f.* falsity, mendacity.
лжи́в|ый (~, ~а), *adj.* **1.** lying; mendacious. **2.** false, deceitful.

ли (ль) 1. *interrog. particle* возмо́жно ли? is it possible?; придёт ли он? is he coming? **2.** *conj.* whether, if; не зна́ю, придёт ли он I don't know whether he is coming; посмотри́, идёт ли по́езд go and see if the train is coming. **3.** ли... ли whether ... or; сего́дня ли, за́втра ли whether today or tomorrow; ра́но ли, по́здно ли, но приду́ I shall come sooner or later.
лиа́н|а, ы, *f.* (*bot.*) liana.
либера́л, а, *m.* liberal.
либерали́зм, а, *m.* **1.** liberalism. **2.** (*pejor.*) tolerance.
либера́льнича|ть, ю, *impf.* (*of* с~) (с+*i.*; *coll., pejor.*) to act the liberal; to show (excessive) tolerance (towards).
либера́л|ьный (~ен, ~ьна), *adj.* **1.** liberal. **2.** (excessively) tolerant.
ли́бо, *conj.* or; л.... л. (either) . . . or; л. пан, л. пропа́л all or nothing.
либретти́ст, а, *m.* librettist.
либре́тто, *indecl., n.* libretto.
лив|ень, ня, *m.* heavy shower, downpour; cloud-burst; (*fig.*) л. свинца́ hail of bullets.
ли́вер¹, а, *m.* (*cul.*) pluck.
ли́вер², а, *m.* (*tech.*) pipette.
ли́вер|ный, *adj. of* ~¹; ~ная колбаса́ liver sausage.
ливмя́, *adv.* (*coll.*) л. лить (*of rain*) to pour, come down in torrents.
ли́в|невый, *adj. of* ~ень; (*meteor.*) cumulo-nimbus.
ливре́|йный, *adj. of* ~я; л. слуга́ livery servant.
ливре́|я, и, *f.* livery.
ли́г|а, и, *f.* league; Л. на́ций (*hist.*) League of Nations.
лигату́р|а¹, ы, *f.* (*chem.*) base metal (*added to precious metals to harden them*).
лигату́р|а², ы, *f.* (*ling. and med.*) ligature.
лигни́н, а, *m.* (*chem.*) lignin(e).
лигни́т, а, *m.* (*min.*) lignite.
ли́дер, а, *m.* **1.** leader (*of political party or organisation*). **2.** (*sport*) leader (*in tournament, etc.*). **3.** (*naut.*) flotilla leader.
ли́дерств|о, а, *n.* **1.** leadership (*of political party or public organization*). **2.** (*sport*) first place, lead; занима́ть л. to be in the lead.
лиди́р|овать, ую, *impf.* (*sport*) to take first place, be in the lead.
ли|за́ть, жу́, ~жешь, *impf.* (*of* ~зну́ть) to lick; (*fig., coll.*) л. ру́ки (но́ги, пя́тки) кому́-н. to lick someone's boots.
ли|за́ться, жу́сь, ~жешься, *impf.* (*coll.*) to neck, smooch.
ли́зис, а, *m.* (*med.*) lysis.
лиз|ну́ть, ну́, нёшь, *inst. pf. of* ~а́ть.
лизоблю́д, а, *m.* (*coll., pejor.*) lickspittle.
лизо́л, а, *m.* (*chem.*) lysol.
лик¹, а, *m.* **1.** (*obs.*) face. **2.** representation

of face (*on icon*). **3.** л. луны́ face of the moon.

лик², а, *m.* (*eccl., arch.*) assembly; причи́слить к ~у святы́х to canonize.

ликбе́з, а, *m.* (*abbr. of* ликвида́ция безгра́мотности) campaign against illiteracy.

ликвида́тор, а, *m.* (*comm., etc.*) liquidator.

ликвида́ци|я, и, *f.* **1.** (*comm.*) liquidation; л. долго́в settlement of debts. **2.** (*polit., etc.*) liquidation; elimination, abolition.

ликвиди́р|овать, ую, *impf. and pf.* **1.** (*comm.*) to liquidate, wind up. **2.** to liquidate; to eliminate, abolish.

ликвиди́р|оваться, уюсь, *impf. and pf.* **1.** to wind up (one's activities). **2.** *pass. of* ~ова́ть.

ликви́дн|ый, adj. (*fin.*) liquid; ~ые сре́дства ready money.

ликёр, а, *m.* liqueur.

ликова́ни|е, я, *n.* rejoicing, exultation.

лик|ова́ть, у́ю, *impf.* to rejoice, exult.

ликопо́ди|й, я, *m.* (*bot., pharm.*) lycopodium.

ли́ктор, а, *m.* (*hist.*) lictor.

лик-трос, а, *m.* (*naut.*) bolt-rope.

лик|у́ющий, *pres. part. of* ~ова́ть *and adj.* exultant, triumphant.

лиле́йный, adj. **1.** (*poet.*) lily-white. **2.** (*bot.*) liliaceous.

лилипу́т, а, *m.* Lilliputian.

ли́ли|я, и, *f.* lily.

лилове́|ть, ю, *impf.* (*of* по~) to turn violet.

лило́вый, adj. lilac, violet.

лима́н, а, *m.* estuary.

лима́н|ный, adj. of ~.

лимб, а, *m.* (*astron., tech.*) limb.

лими́т, а, *m.* quota; limit.

лимити́р|овать, ую, *impf. and pf.* to establish a quota (or maximum) in respect of.

лимитро́ф, а, *m.* border state (*esp. of the Baltic states in relation to the U.S.S.R.*).

лимитро́ф|ный, adj. of ~.

лимо́н, а, *m.* lemon; вы́жатый л. (*fig., coll.*) has-been.

лимона́д, а, *m.* **1.** lemonade; lemon squash. **2.** squash (*of fruit or berries, not necessarily lemon, as beverage*).

лимо́н|ить, ю, ишь, *impf.* (*of* с~) (*thieves' sl.*) to knock off, pinch.

лимоннокислый, adj. (*chem.*) citric acid.

лимо́нн|ый, adj. lemon; ~ая кислота́ (*chem.*) citric acid.

лимузи́н, а, *m.* limousine.

ли́мф|а, ы, *f.* (*physiol.*) lymph.

лимфати́ческий, adj. (*physiol.*) lymphatic (*also fig., obs.*).

лингви́ст, а, *m.* linguist.

лингви́стик|а, и, *f.* linguistics.

лингвисти́ческий, adj. linguistic.

лине́йк|а¹, и, *f.* **1.** line (*on paper, blackboard, etc.*); писа́ть по ~ам to write on the lines;

нотные ~и (*mus.*) staves. **2.** ruler; логарифми́ческая л. slide-rule. **3.** (*typ.*) набо́рная л. setting-rule. **4.** ла́герная л. camp line(s).

лине́йк|а², и, *f.* (*obs.*) break, wagonette.

лине́йн|ый, adj. **1.** (*math.*) linear; ~ые ме́ры long measures. **2.** (*mil., naut.*) of the line; л. кора́бль battleship.

лин|ёк, ька́, *m.* (*naut.*) rope's end, colt.

ли́нз|а, ы, *f.* lens.

ли́ни|я, и, *f.* (*in var. senses*) line; (*fig.*) л. поведе́ния line of conduct, policy; провести́ ~ю в поли́тике to pursue a policy; вести́ (*coll. also* гнуть) свою́ ~ю to have one's own way; вести́ ~ю на что-н. to direct one's efforts towards something; по ~и наиме́ньшего сопротивле́ния on the line of least resistance.

линко́р, а, *m.* (*abbr. of* лине́йный кора́бль) battleship.

лино-бати́ст, а, *m.* lawn, cambric.

лино́ваный, adj. lined, ruled.

лин|ова́ть, у́ю, *impf.* (*of* на~) to rule.

лино́леум, а, *m.* linoleum.

линоти́п, а, *m.* linotype.

линоти́п|ный, adj. of ~.

линч, а, *m.* зако́н ~а, суд ~а lynch law.

линч|ева́ть, у́ю, *impf. and pf.* to lynch.

лин|ь¹, я́, *m.* (*fish*) tench.

лин|ь², я́, *m.* (*naut.*) line.

ли́ньк|а, и, *f.* moult(ing).

линю́ч|ий (~, ~а), adj. (*coll.*) liable to fade.

линя́лый, adj. (*coll.*) **1.** faded, discoloured., **2.** having moulted.

линя́|ть, ет, *impf.* **1.** (*pf.* по~) to fade, lose colour; (*of paint*) to run. **2.** (*pf.* вы́~) (*of animals*) to shed hair; to cast the coat; (*of birds*) to moult, shed feathers; (*of snakes*) to slough.

ли́п|а¹, ы, *f.* lime(-tree).

ли́п|а², ы, *f.* (*sl.*) forgery.

ли́п|ка, ки, *f.* dim. of ~а¹; (*coll.*) ободра́ть как ~ку to fleece.

ли́п|кий (~ок, ~ка́, ~ко), adj. sticky, adhesive; л. пла́стырь sticking plaster.

ли́п|нуть, ну, нешь; *past* ~, ~ла, *impf.* (к) to stick (to), adhere (to).

липня́к, а́, *m.* (*coll.*) lime-grove.

ли́п|овый¹, adj. of ~а¹; л. мёд white honey; л. цвет lime-blossom; л. чай limeleaf tea.

ли́повый², adj. (*sl.*) sham, fake, forged.

ли́р|а¹, ы, *f.* lyre.

ли́р|а², ы, *f.* (*monetary unit*) lira.

лири́зм, а, *m.* lyricism.

ли́рик, а, *m.* lyric poet.

ли́рик|а, и, *f.* **1.** lyric poetry; lyrics. **2.** (*fig., pejor.*) lyricism.

лири́ческ|ий, adj. **1.** lyric; (*lit.*) л. беспоря́док poetic disorder; ~ое отступле́ние lyrical digression. **2.** (*of disposition, etc.*) lyrical.

лири́ч|ный (~ен, ~на), *adj.* lyrical.

ли́р|ный, *adj.* (*obs. or poet.*) of ~а¹.

лирохво́ст, а, *m.* lyre-bird.

лис, а, *m.* (*obs.*) (dog-)fox.

лис|а́, ы́, *pl.* ~ы, *f.* fox; чернобу́рая л. silver fox; Л. Патрике́евна (*in Russ. folk--tales*) Reynard; прики́дываться ~о́й (*fig., coll.*) to fawn, toady.

лисе́л|ь, я, *pl.* ~я́, *m.* (*naut.*) studding-sail.

лис|ёнок, ёнка, *pl.* ~я́та, ~я́т, *m.* fox-cub.

ли́с|ий, *adj.* of ~а́; л. мех fox fur; л. хвост (fox-)brush.

лис|и́ть, и́шь, *impf.* (*coll.*) to fawn, flatter.

лиси́ц|а, ы, *f.* fox; vixen.

лиси́чк|а, и, *f.* 1. *dim.* of лиси́ца. 2. (*mushroom*) chanterelle. 3. paper-chase.

лист¹, а́, *pl.* ~ья, ~ьев, *m.* leaf (*of plant*); blade (*of cereal*).

лист², а́, *pl.* ~ы́, ~о́в, *m.* 1. leaf, sheet (*of paper, etc.*); (*metal*) plate; в л. in folio; корректу́ра в ~а́х page-proofs; печа́тный л. printer's sheet, quire; игра́ть с ~а́ (*mus.*) to play at sight. 2. исполни́тельный л. (*leg.*) writ of execution; опро́сный л. questionnaire; охра́нный л. safe-conduct; похва́льный л. (*obs.*) certificate of progress and good conduct (*in schools*).

листа́ж, а́, *m.* number of sheets (*in a book*).

листа́|ть, ю, *impf.* (*coll.*) to turn over the pages of.

листв|а́, ы́, *f.* (*collect.*) leaves, foliage.

ли́ственниц|а, ы, *f.* (*bot.*) larch.

ли́ственный, *adj.* (*bot.*) deciduous.

листо́вк|а, и, *f.* leaflet.

лист|ово́й, *adj.* of ~; ~ово́е желе́зо sheet iron; ~ова́я peccópa laminated spring.

лист|о́к, ка́, *m.* 1. *dim.* of ~¹. 2. leaflet. 3. form, pro-forma. 4. (*sl.*) rag (*newspaper.*)

листопа́д, а, *m.* (autumn) fall of the leaves.

лит- *abbr.* of литерату́рный.

лита́врщик, а, *m.* (kettle)drummer.

лита́вр|ы, ~, *sing.* ~а, ~ы, *f.* kettledrum.

литви́н, а, *m.* (*obs.*) Lithuanian.

литви́нк|а, и, *f.* (*obs.*) Lithuanian (woman).

лите́йн|ая, ой, *f.* foundry, smelting-house.

лите́йный, *adj.* founding, casting.

лите́йщик, а, *m.* founder, caster, smelter.

ли́тер, а, *m.* (*coll.*) travel warrant.

ли́тер|а, ы, *f.* 1. (*typ.*) type. 2. (*obs.*) letter (*of the alphabet*).

литера́тор, а, *m.* literary man, man of letters.

литерату́р|а, ы, *f.* literature; худо́жественная л. belles-lettres, literature.

литерату́р|ный (~ен, ~на), *adj.* literary; ~ная со́бственность copyright.

литературове́д, а, *m.* specialist in study of literature; literary critic.

литературове́дени|е, я, *n.* study of literature; literary criticism.

литерату́рщин|а, ы, *f.* (*coll.*) striving after literary effect; selfconscious writing.

ли́терный, *adj.* 1. marked with a letter. 2. (*sl.*) hush-hush (*of factories, etc., designated only by a letter of the alphabet for security reasons*).

литер|ова́ть, у́ю, *impf. and pf.* to rate by system of letters.

ли́ти|й, я, *m.* (*chem.*) lithium.

ли́тник, а, *m.* (*tech.*) pouring gate, pouring channel, flow gate.

лито́в|ец, ца, *m.* Lithuanian.

лито́вк|а, и, *f.* Lithuanian (woman).

лито́вский, *adj.* Lithuanian.

литóгра́ф, а, *m.* lithographer.

литографи́р|овать, ую, *impf. and pf.* to lithograph.

литогра́фи|я, и, *f.* 1. lithograph. 2. lithography.

литогра́фск|ий, *adj.* lithographic; ~ая печа́ть lithograph.

лит|о́й, *adj.* cast; ~а́я сталь cast steel, ingot steel.

литр, а, *m.* litre.

литра́ж, а́, *m.* capacity (*in litres*).

литро́вый, *adj.* litre (*of one litre capacity*).

литурги́ческий, *adj.* liturgical.

литурги́|я, и, *f.* liturgy.

лить, лью, льёшь, *past* лил, лила́, ли́ло, *imp.* лей, *impf.* 1. to pour (*trans. and intrans.*); to shed, spill; л. слёзы to shed tears; дождь льёт как из ведра́ it is raining cats and dogs; л. во́ду на чью-н. ме́льницу to play into someone's hands. 2. (*tech.*) to found, cast, mould.

лить|ё, я́, *no pl., n.* (*tech.*) 1. founding, casting, moulding. 2. (*collect.*) castings, mouldings.

ли́|ться, льётся, *past* ~лся, ~ла́сь, ~ло́сь, *impf.* 1. to flow; to stream, pour. 2. *pass.* of ~ть.

лиф, а, *m.* bodice.

лифт, а, *m.* lift, elevator.

лифтёр, а, *m.* lift operator, lift-boy.

ли́фчик, а, *m.* 1. brassière. 2. (child's) bodice.

лиха́ч, а́, *m.* 1. (*obs.*) driver of smart cab. 2. (*pejor.*) road-hog. 3. bold, daring fellow.

лиха́честв|о, а, *n.* foolhardiness.

лихв|а́, ы́, *f.* (*obs.*) interest; отплати́ть с ~о́й to repay with interest.

ли́х|о¹, а, *n.* (*poet.*) evil, ill; не помина́йте ~ом (*coll.*) remember me (us) kindly; узна́ть, почём фунт ~а (*coll.*) to fall on hard times, plumb the depths of misfortune.

ли́х|о², *adv.* of ~о́й²; л. заломи́ть ша́пку to cock one's hat at a jaunty angle.

лиходе́|й, я, *m.* (*obs.*) evil-doer.

лиходейств|о, а, *n.* (*obs.*) evil-doing.

лихойм|ец, ца, *m.* (*obs.*) usurer; extortioner.

лихоймств|о, а, *n.* (*obs.*) extortion; bribe-taking; bribery and corruption.

лих|ой¹ (~, ~á, ~о), *adj.* (*dial. and folk poet.*) evil; ~á бедá начáло (*or* начáть) (*coll.*) the first step is the hardest.

лих|ой² (~, ~á, ~о), *adj.* (*coll.*) dashing, spirited; jaunty.

лихорá|дить, жу, дишь, *impf.* **1.** to be in a fever. **2.** *impers.* меня ~дит I feel feverish.

лихорáдк|а, и, *f.* **1.** fever (*also fig.*); перемежáющаяся (болóтная) л. malaria. **2.** rash.

лихорáдоч|ный (~ен, ~на), *adj.* feverish (*also fig.*).

лúхост|ь, и, *f.* (*coll.*) spirit, mettle; swagger.

лúхтер, а, *m.* (*naut.*) lighter.

лиц|евáть, ýю, *impf.* (*of* пере~) to turn (*clothing*).

лицев|óй, *adj.* **1.** (*anat.*) facial. **2.** exterior; ~áя сторонá (*of building*) façade, front; (*of material*) right side; (*of coin, etc.*) obverse. **3.** ~áя рýкопись illuminated manuscript. **4.** (*book-keeping*) л. счёт personal account.

лицедé|й, я, *m.* (*obs.*) **1.** actor. **2.** (*fig.*) hypocrite, dissembler.

лицедéйств|о, а, *n.* (*obs.*) **1.** acting. **2.** theatrical performance. **3.** (*fig.*) play-acting, dissembling.

лицезр|éть, ю, ишь, *impf.* (*obs. and iron.*) to behold with one's own eyes.

лицéйст, а, *m.* pupil of Lyceum, lycée.

лицé|й, я, *m.* **1.** Lyceum (*high school or law school in pre-revolutionary Russia*). **2.** lycée (*in France*).

лицéй|ский, *adj. of* ~.

лицемéр, а, *m.* hypocrite, dissembler.

лицемéри|е, я, *n.* hypocrisy, dissimulation.

лицемéр|ить, ю, ишь, *impf.* to play the hypocrite, dissemble.

лицемéр|ный (~ен, ~на), *adj.* hypocritical.

лицéнзи|я, и, *f.* (*econ.*) licence.

лицеприя́ти|е, я, *n.* (*obs.*) partiality.

лицеприя́т|ный (~ен, ~на), *adj.* (*obs.*) partial, based on partiality.

лицеприя́тств|овать, ую, *impf.* (*obs.*) to be partial; to show bias.

лиц|ó, á, *pl.* ~а, *n.* **1.** face; черты́ ~á features; измениться, перемениться ~óм, в ~é to change countenance; сказáть в л. комý-н. to say to someone's face; знáть когó-н. в л. to know someone by sight; на нём ~á нет he looks awful; ~óм в грязь не удáрить not to disgrace oneself; быть к ~ý (+*d.*) to suit, become; (*fig.*) to become, befit; нам не к ~ý такие постýпки such actions do not become us; ~óм к ~ý face to face; постáвить ~óм к ~ý to confront; они́ на однó л. (*coll.*) they are as like as two

peas; рáдость былá напи́сана у неё на ~é joy was written all over her face; показáть своё (настоя́щее) л. to show one's true worth; перед (пред) ~óм (+*g.*) in the face (of); с ~á некраси́в (*coll.*) ugly; (исчéзнуть) с ~á земли́ (to vanish) from the face of the earth. **2.** exterior; (*of material*) right side; (*fig.*) показáть товáр ~óм to show something to advantage; to make the best of something. **3.** person; действующее л. (*theatr., lit.*) character; действующие ~а dramatis personae; должностнóе л. official, functionary; перемещённые ~а displaced persons; подставнóе л. dummy, man of straw; физи́ческое л. (*leg.*) natural person; юриди́ческое л. (*leg.*) juridical person; в ~é (+*g.*) in the person (of); невзирáя на ~а without respect of persons; от ~á (+*g.*) in the name (of), on behalf (of).

личи́н|а¹, ы, *f.* mask; (*fig.*) guise; под ~ой (+*g.*) in the guise (of), under cover (of); сорвáть ~у с когó-н. to unmask someone.

личи́н|а², ы, *f.* (*tech.*) scutcheon, key-plate.

личи́нк|а¹, и, *f.* larva, grub; maggot.

личи́нк|а², и, *f.* (*mil.*) боевáя л. bolt head (*of rifle*); elevator (*in machine-gun*).

ли́чно, *adv.* personally, in person.

личн|óй, *adj.* **1.** face; ~óй крем face cream. **2.** (*anat.*) facial.

ли́чност|ь, и, *f.* **1.** personality. **2.** person, individual; тёмная л. shady character; удостоверéние ~и identity card; установи́ть чью-н. л. to establish someone's identity. **3.** (*pl.*) personal remarks, personalities; переходи́ть на ~и to become personal.

ли́чн|ый, *adj.* personal, individual; private; ~ое местоимéние (*gram.*) personal pronoun; ~ая охрáна body-guard; л. секретáрь private secretary; ~ая собственность personal property; л. состáв staff.

лиша́|й, я, *m.* **1.** (*bot.*) lichen. **2.** (*med.*) herpes; опоя́сывающий л. shingles; стригýщий л. ringworm; чешуйчатый л. psoriasis.

лиша́йник, а, *m.* (*bot.*) lichen.

лиш|áть(ся), áю(сь), *impf. of* ~и́ть(ся).

ли́ш|ек, ка, *m.* (*coll.*) surplus; с ~ком odd, and more, just over; дéсять миль с ~ком ten odd miles, ten miles and a bit.

лишён|ец, ца, *m.* disfranchised person (*in U.S.S.R. up to 1936*).

лишéни|е, я, *n.* **1.** deprivation; л. граждáнских прав (*leg.*) disfranchisement. **2.** privation, hardship.

лишён|ный (~, ~á, ~ó), *p.p.p. of* лиши́ть *and adj.* (+*g.*) lacking (in), devoid (of); он не лишён остроýмия he is not without wit.

лиш|и́ть, у́, и́шь, *pf.* (*of* ~а́ть) (+*g.*) to deprive (of); л. кого́-н. насле́дства to disinherit someone; л. себя́ жи́зни to take one's life.

лиш|и́ться, у́сь, и́шься. *pf.* (*of* ~а́ться) (+*g.*) to lose, be deprived (of); л. зре́ния to lose one's sight; л. чувств to faint away.

ли́шн|ий, *adj.* **1.** superfluous; unnecessary; бы́ло бы не ~е (+*inf.*) it would not be out of place; он здесь л. he is one too many here. **2.** left over; spare, odd; л. раз once more; с ~им (*coll.*) and more, odd; со́рок фу́нтов с ~им forty pounds odd.

лишь, *adv. and conj.* only; не хвата́ет л. одного́ one thing only is lacking; л. вошёл, соба́ка зала́яла no sooner had he entered than the dog began to bark; л. то́лько as soon as; л. бы if only, provided that; л. бы он мог прие́хать provided that he can come.

лоб, лба, о лбе́, во (на) лбу́; *pl.* **лбы, лбов,** *m.* forehead, brow; пока́тый л. receding forehead; стреля́ть в л. to fire point-blank; ата́ка в л. frontal attack; пусти́ть себе́ пу́лю в л. to blow out one's brains; (*coll.*) на лбу́ напи́сано writ large on one's face; что в л., что по́ лбу it is all one, it comes to the same thing; будь он семи́ пяде́й во лбу be he a Solomon.

лоба́ст|ый (~, ~а), *adj.* having a large forehead.

лобби́ст, а, *m.* (*polit.*) lobbyist.

лобза́ни|е, я, *n.* (*obs.*) kiss.

лобза́|ть, ю, *impf.* (*obs.*) to kiss.

ло́бзик, а, *m.* fret-saw.

лобко́в|ый, *adj.* ~ая кость (*anat.*) pubis.

ло́бн|ый, *adj.* (*anat.*) frontal; ~ое ме́сто (*hist.*) place of execution.

лобов|о́й, *adj.* frontal, front; ~а́я ата́ка (*mil.*) frontal attack; л. фона́рь headlight; ~ое сопротивле́ние (*aeron.*) drag.

лобогре́йк|а, и, *f.* (*agric.*) harvester, reaping machine (*of simple design*).

лоб|о́к, ка́, *m.* (*anat.*) pubis.

лоботря́с, а, *m.* (*coll.*) lazy-bones, idler.

лобыза́|ть, ю, *impf.* (*obs.*) to kiss.

лов, а, *m.* **1.** = ~ля. **2.** = уло́в.

ловела́с, а, *m.* (*coll.*) Lovelace, lady-killer.

лов|е́ц, ца́, *m.* fisherman; hunter.

лов|и́ть, лю́, ~ишь, *impf.* (*of* пойма́ть) to (try to) catch; (*fig.*) л. ры́бу в му́тной воде́ to fish in troubled waters; л. чей-н. взгляд to try to catch someone's eye; л. (удо́бный) моме́нт, слу́чай to seize an opportunity; л. ка́ждое сло́во to devour every word; л. себя́ на чём-н. to catch oneself at something; л. кого́-н. на сло́ве to take someone at his word; л. ста́нцию (*radio*) to try to pick up a station.

ловка́ч, а́, *m.* (*coll.*) dodger.

ло́в|кий (~ок, ~ка́, ~ко), *adj.* **1.** adroit, dexterous, deft; л. ход master stroke. **2.** cunning, smart. **3.** (*coll.*) comfortable.

ло́вк|о, *adv. of* ~ий; л. ли вам здесь сиде́ть? (*coll.*) are you comfortable sitting here?

ло́вкост|ь, и, *f.* **1.** adroitness, dexterity, deftness; л. рук sleight of hand. **2.** cunning, smartness.

ло́в|ля, ли, *g. pl.* ~ель, *f.* **1.** catching, hunting; ры́бная л. fishing; л. силка́ми snaring. **2.** fishing-ground.

лову́шк|а, и, *f.* snare, trap (*also fig.*); пойма́ть в ~у to ensnare, entrap.

ло́в|че (and ~чее), *comp. of* ~кий *and* ~ко.

ло́вчий¹, *adj.* **1.** hunting. **2.** serving as snare, trap.

ло́вч|ий², его, *m.* (*hist.*) huntsman, master of hounds.

лог, а, в ~е *or* **в ~у́,** *pl.* **~а́, ~о́в,** *m.* broad gully.

логари́фм, а, *m.* (*math.*) logarithm.

логарифми́р|овать, ую, *impf. and pf.* (*math.*) to find the logarithm of.

логарифми́ческ|ий, *adj.* (*math.*) logarithmic; ~ая лине́йка slide-rule.

ло́гик|а, и, *f.* logic.

логи́ческий, *adj.* logical.

логи́чност|ь, и, *f.* logicality.

логи́ч|ный (~ен, ~на), *adj.* = ~еский.

ло́говищ|е, а, *n.* den, lair.

ло́гов|о, а, *n.* = ~ище.

логопа́ти|я, и, *f.* speech defect.

логопе́д, а, *m.* speech therapist.

логопеди́|ческий, *adj. of* ~ия.

логопеди́|я, и, *f.* speech therapy.

ло́дк|а, и, *f.* boat; двухвесе́льная л. pair-oar; го́ночная л. gig, yawl; подво́дная л. submarine; спаса́тельная л. life-boat; лета́ющая л. flying-boat; ката́ться на ~е to go boating.

ло́дочк|а, и, *f.* dim. of ло́дка.

ло́дочник, а, *m.* boatman.

ло́д|очный, *adj. of* ~ка.

лоды́жк|а, и, *f.* **1.** (*anat.*) ankle-bone. **2.** (*mil.*) tumbler (*part of the lock of a machine-gun*).

ло́дырнича|ть, ю, *impf.* (*coll.*) to loaf, idle.

ло́дыр|ь, я, *m.* (*coll.*) loafer, idler; гоня́ть ~я to loaf, idle.

ло́ж|а¹, и, *f.* **1.** (*theatr.*) box. **2.** (*masonic*) lodge.

ло́ж|а², и, *f.* (gun-)stock.

ложби́н|а, ы, *f.* (*geogr.*) narrow, shallow gully.

ло́ж|е, а, *n.* **1.** (*obs.*) bed, couch. **2.** bed, channel (*of river*). **3.** gun-stock.

ло́жечк|а¹, и, *f.* dim. of ло́жка.

ло́жечк|а², и, *f.* под ~ой in the pit of the stomach.

лож|и́ться, у́сь, и́шься, *impf. of* лечь.

ло́жк|а, и, *f.* 1. spoon; десе́ртная л. dessert-spoon; столо́вая л. table-spoon; ча́йная л. tea-spoon; че́рез час по ча́йной ~е (*fig.*, *coll.*) in minute doses. 2. spoonful; л. дёгтя в бо́чке мёда a fly in the ointment.

ло́жно- pseudo-.

ло́жност|ь, и, *f.* falsity, error.

ло́ж|ный (~ен, ~на), *adj.* false, erroneous; sham, dummy; ~ная скро́мность false modesty; ~ная трево́га false alarm.

ложь, лжи, *f.* lie, falsehood.

лоз|а́, ы́, *pl.* **~ы,** *f.* 1. rod. 2. withe. 3. vine.

лозня́к, а́, *m.* willow-bush.

ло́зунг, а, *m.* 1. slogan, catchword; watch-word. 2. (*mil.*; *obs.*) pass-word.

лойя́льн|ость, ~ый = лоя́льн|ость, ~ый.

локализа́ци|я, и, *f.* localization.

локализ|ова́ть, у́ю, *impf. and pf.* to localize.

лока́льный, *adj.* local.

лока́ут, а, *m.* (*polit.*) lock-out.

локаути́р|овать, ую, *impf. and pf.* (*polit.*) to lock-out.

локомоби́л|ь, я, *m.* traction-engine, portable engine.

локомоти́в, а, *m.* locomotive.

ло́кон, а, *m.* lock, curl, ringlet.

локотни́к, а́, *m.* arm (*of a chair*); elbow-rest.

ло́к|оть, тя, *pl.* **~ти, ~те́й,** *m.* 1. elbow; с про́дранными ~тя́ми out at elbow(s); рабо́тать ~тя́ми (*coll.*) to elbow one's way; чу́вство ~тя (*fig.*) feeling of comradeship; бли́зок л., да не уку́сишь (*prov.*) so near and yet so far. 2. (*measure*) (*obs.*) cubit, ell.

локтев|о́й, *adj.* (*anat.*) ~а́я кость ulna; funny-bone.

лом, а, *pl.* **~ы, ~о́в,** *m.* 1. crow-bar. 2. (*sing. only*; *collect.*) scrap, waste; желе́зный л. scrap-iron.

лома́к|а, и, *m. and f.* (*coll.*) poser, affected person.

ло́ман|ый, *adj.* broken; л. англи́йский язы́к broken English; ~ого гроша́ не сто́ит (*coll.*) it is not worth a brass farthing.

лома́нь|е, я, *n.* (*coll.*) affectation; mincing, simpering.

лома́|ть, ю, *impf.* (*of* с~) 1. to break; to fracture. 2. (*no pf.*) (*fig.*) л. себе́ го́лову (над) to rack one's brains (over); л. дурака́ to play the fool; л. ру́ки to wring one's hands; л. ша́пку (пе́ред) to bow obsequiously (to). 3. (*no pf.*) л. ка́мень to quarry stone. 4. (*no pf.*; *of pain, sickness*) (*coll.*) to rack; to cause to ache; (*impers.*) меня́ всего́ ~ло I was aching all over.

лома́|ться, юсь, *impf.* 1. (*pf.* с~) to break (*intrans.*). 2. (*no pf.*) (*of voice*) to crack, break. 3. (*pf.* по~) (*coll.*) to pose, put on airs. 4. (*pf.* по~) (*coll.*) to make difficulties, be obstinate.

ломба́рд, а, *m.* pawn-shop; заложи́ть в л. to pawn.

ломба́рд|ный, *adj.* of ~; ~ная квита́нция pawn ticket.

ло́мберный, *adj.* л. стол card-table.

лом|и́ть, лю́, ~ишь, *impf.* (*coll.*) 1. to break. 2. to break through, rush. 3. (*impers.*) to cause to ache; у меня́ ~ит спи́ну my back aches. 4. (*coll.*) л. це́ну to demand an extortionate price.

лом|и́ться, лю́сь, ~ишься, *impf.* 1. to be (near to) breaking; (от) to burst (with), be crammed (with); ве́тви ~ятся от плодо́в the boughs are groaning with fruit. 2. (*coll.*) to force one's way; л. в откры́тую дверь (*fig.*) to force an open door.

ло́мк|а, и, *f.* 1. breaking (*also fig.*). 2. (*usually pl.*, *obs.*) quarry.

ло́м|кий (~ок, ~ка́, ~ко), *adj.* fragile, brittle.

ломови́к, а́, *m.* = ломово́й изво́зчик.

ломов|о́й, *adj.* dray, draught; л. изво́зчик drayman, carter; ~а́я ло́шадь cart-horse, draught-horse; ~а́я подво́да dray; *as noun* л., ~о́го, *m.* = л. изво́зчик.

ломоно́с, а, *m.* (*bot.*) clematis.

ломо́т|а, ы, *f.* (*coll.*) rheumatic pain, ache.

ломо́т|ный, *adj.* of ~а.

лом|о́ть, тя́, *pl.* **~ти́, ~те́й,** *m.* large flat slice; round (*of bread*); отре́занный л. *fig.*, *of person no longer dependent, standing on his own feet.*

ло́мтик, а, *m.* slice; ре́зать ~ами to slice.

лонжеро́н, а, *m.* (*tech.*) longeron; (*aeron.*) (wing) spar.

ло́н|о, а, *no pl.*, *n.* (*obs.*) bosom, lap; л. семьи́ the bosom of the family; на ~е приро́ды in the open air.

лопа́р|ка, ки, *f.* of ~ь¹.

лопа́рский, *adj.* Lapp(ish).

лопа́р|ь¹, я́, *m.* Lapp, Laplander.

лопа́р|ь², я́, *m.* (*naut.*) fall.

ло́паст|ный, *adj.* of ~ь; (*bot.*) laciniate.

ло́паст|ь, и, *pl.* **~и, ~е́й,** *f.* 1. blade; fan, vane (*of propeller, etc.*); (*wheel*) paddle; л. о́си axle tree. 2. (*bot.*) lamina.

лопа́т|а, ы, *f.* spade, shovel; грести́ де́ньги ~ой (*fig.*, *coll.*) to rake it (*sc.* money) in.

лопа́тк|а, и, *f.* 1. shovel; trowel, scoop; blade (*of turbine*). 2. (*anat.*) shoulder-blade, scapula; (*part of joint of meat*) shoulder; положи́ть на о́бе лопа́тки to throw (*in wrestling*); бежа́ть во все ~и (*coll.*) to run as fast as one's legs can carry one.

лопа́|ть, ю, *impf.* (*of* с~) (*coll.*) to devour, gobble up.

ло́п|аться, аюсь, *impf.* of ~нуть.

лоп|нуть, ну, нешь, *pf.* (*of* ~аться) 1. to break, burst; to split, crack; чуть не л. от сме́ха to split one's sides with laughter, burst with laughter; (*fig.*) у меня́ терпе́ние ~нуло my patience is exhausted. **2.** (*fig.*, *coll.*) to fail, be a failure; (*fin.*) to go bankrupt, crash.

лопо|та́ть, чу́, ~чешь, *impf.* (*coll.*) to mutter, mumble.

лопоу́х|ий (~, ~a), *adj.* lop-eared.

лопу́х, á, *m.* **1.** (*bot.*) burdock. **2.** (*sl.*) fool.

лорд, a, *m.* lord; пала́та ~ов House of Lords.

лорд-ка́нцлер, a, *m.* Lord Chancellor.

лорд-мэ́р, a, *m.* Lord Mayor.

лоре́тк|а, и, *f.* (*obs.*) courtesan, cocotte.

лорне́т, a, *m.* lorgnette.

лорни́р|овать, ую, *impf. and pf.* to quiz(z).

лоси́н|а, ы, *f.* **1.** elk-skin, chamois leather. **2.** (*pl.*; *hist.*) buckskin breeches. **3.** (*meat*) elk.

лос|и́ный, *adj. of* ~ь.

лоск, a, *m.* lustre, gloss, shine (*also fig.*); в л. (*coll.*) completely, entirely; пья́ный в л. blind drunk.

ло́скут, a, *no pl.*, *m.* (*collect.*) rags, pieces.

лоску́т, á, *pl.* ~ы́, ~о́в *and* ~ья́, ~ьев, *m.* rag, shred, scrap.

лоску́тник, a, *m.* rag merchant, rag dealer.

лоску́тн|ый, *adj.* **1.** scrappy. **2.** made of scraps; ~ая мона́рхия *iron. of Austro-Hungarian Empire.*

лосн|и́ться, ю́сь, и́шься, *impf.* to be glossy, shine.

лососи́н|а, ы, *f.* salmon (flesh).

ло́сос|ь, я, *pl.* ло́соси, лосо́сей, *m.* salmon; каспи́йский и. Caspian sea-trout.

лос|ь, я, *pl.* ~и, ~е́й, *m.* elk.

лосьо́н, a, *m.* lotion.

лот¹, a, *m.* (*naut.*) (sounding-)lead, plummet.

лот², a, *m.* (*obs.*) lot (*unit of measurement equivalent to half an ounce or 12·8 gr.*).

лотере́|йный, *adj. of* ~я; л. биле́т lottery-ticket.

лотере́|я, и, *f.* lottery, raffle; разы́грывать в ~ю to raffle, dispose of by lottery.

ло́тлин|ь, я, *m.* (*naut.*) leadline.

лото́, *indecl.*, *n.* lotto.

лот|о́к, ка́, *m.* **1.** hawker's stand; hawker's tray. **2.** chute; gutter; (*tech.*) trough; ме́льничный л. mill-race.

ло́тос, a, *m.* (*bot.*) lotus.

лото́чник, a, *m.* hawker.

лото́шник, a, *m.* (*coll.*) lotto player, bingo player.

лоха́нк|а, и, *f.* (wash-)tub; по́чечная л. (*anat.*) calix (of the kidney).

лоха́н|ь, и, *f.* (wash-)tub.

лохма́|тить, чу, тишь, *impf.* (*coll.*) to tousle.

лохма́|титься, чусь, тишься, *impf.* (*coll.*) to become tousled, dishevelled.

лохма́т|ый (~, ~a), *adj.* **1.** shaggy(-haired). **2.** dishevelled, tousled.

лохмо́ть|я, ев, *no sing.* rags; в ~ях in rags, ragged.

ло́ци|я, и, *f.* (*naut.*) sailing directions.

ло́цман, a, *m.* **1.** (*naut.*) pilot. **2.** pilot-fish.

лошадёнк|а, и, *f.* (*pejor.*) jade.

лошади́н|ый, *adj.* of horses; equine; ~ая до́за (*joc.*) very large dose; ~ая си́ла horse-power.

лоша́дк|а, и, *f.* **1.** *dim. of* ло́шадь; (*in child's speech*) gee-gee. **2.** hobby-horse; rocking-horse.

лоша́дник, a, *m.* (*coll.*) horse-lover.

ло́шад|ь, и, *pl.* ~и, ~е́й, ~я́м, ~ьми́, ~я́х, *f.* horse; беговая́, скаковая́ л. race-horse; верховая́ л. saddle-horse; вьючная л. pack-horse; заводна́я л. (*mil.*) led horse; заво́дская л. stud-horse; кавалери́йская л. troop-horse, cavalry horse; коренна́я л. shaft-horse; ломовая́ л. dray-horse; пристяжна́я л. outrunner; упряжна́я л. draught horse; чистокро́вная л. thoroughbred; сади́ться на л. to mount; ходи́ть за ~ью to groom a horse.

лоша́к, á, *m.* hinny.

лощён|ый, *adj.* glossy, polished; ~ая пря́жа glazed yarn; (*fig.*) ~ые мане́ры polished manners; л. молодо́й челове́к (*coll.*) swell, masher.

лощи́н|а, ы, *f.* (*geogr.*) hollow, depression.

лощ|и́ть, у́, и́шь, *impf.* (*of* на~) **1.** to polish. **2.** to gloss, glaze.

лоя́льност|ь, и, *f.* fairness; honesty; loyalty.

лоя́л|ьный (~ен, ~ьна), *adj.* fair; honest; loyal (*to State authorities*).

луб, a, *pl.* ~ья, ~ьев, *m.* (*bot.*) (lime) bast.

луб|о́к¹, ка́, *m.* **1.** (*med.*) splint. **2.** strip of bast.

луб|о́к², ка́, *m.* **1.** cheap popular print. **2.** (*fig.*) popular literature.

луб|о́чный¹, *adj. of* ~о́к¹.

луб|о́чный², *adj. of* ~о́к²; ~о́чная карти́нка cheap popular print.

луб|яно́й, *adj. of* ~.

луг, a, *o* ~е, *на* ~у́, *pl.* ~á, ~о́в, *m.* meadow; заливно́й л. water-meadow.

луговодств|о, a, *n.* grass farming, meadow cultivation.

луг|ово́й, *adj. of* ~; л. бе́рег lower bank (*= right bank of most rivers in European Russia*); ~овая соба́чка (*zool.*) prairie-dog.

луди́льщик, a, *m.* tinsmith, tinman.

лу|ди́ть, жу́, ~дишь, *impf.* (*of* вы~ *and* по~) (*tech.*) to tin.

лу́ж|а, и, *f.* puddle, pool; сесть в ~у (*fig.*, *coll.*) to get into a mess; to slip up.

лужа́йк|а, и, *f.* grass-plot, (forest)glade.

луже́ни|е, я, *n.* (*tech.*) tinning.

лужён|ый, *adj.* tinned, tin-plate; ~ая гло́тка (*fig.*, *coll.*) throat of cast iron, iron palate.

луж|о́к, ка́, *m. dim. of* луг.

лу́з|а, ы, *f.* (billiard-)pocket.

лузг|а́, и́, *f.* (*collect.*) husks.

лук¹, а, *m.* (*collect.*) onions; зелёный л. spring onions; л.-поре́й leek; голо́вка ~а onion.

лук², а, *m.* bow; натяну́ть л. to bend, draw a bow.

лук|а́, и́, *pl.* ~и, *f.* 1. bend (*of river, road, etc.*). 2. pommel (*of saddle*); за́дняя л. rear arch; пере́дняя л. front arch.

лука́в|ец, ца, *m.* (*coll.*) crafty, sly person; (*joc.*) slyboots.

лука́в|ить, лю, ишь, *impf.* (*of* с~) to be cunning.

лука́вств|о, а, *n.* craftiness, slyness.

лука́в|ый (~, ~а), *adj.* 1. crafty, sly, cunning; *as noun* л., ~ого, *m.* the Evil One. 2. arch.

лу́ковиц|а, ы, *f.* 1. an onion. 2. (*bot., anat.*) bulb. 3. 'onion' cupola (*of Russian churches*).

лу́кови|чный, чный, *adj. of* ~ца; bulbous.

лукомо́рь|е, я, *n.* (*poet.*) cove, creek.

луко́ш|ко, ка, *pl.* ~ки, ~ек, *n.* bast basket; punnet.

лун|а́, ы́, *pl.* ~ы, *f.* moon.

лунати́зм, а, *m.* sleep-walking, somnambulism.

луна́тик, а, *m.* sleep-walker, somnambulist.

лунати́ческий, *adj.* somnambulistic.

лу́нк|а, и, *f.* hole; (*anat.*) alveolus, socket.

лу́нник¹, а, *m.* (*bot.*) honesty.

лу́нник², а, *m.* lunik, Moon rocket.

лу́н|ный, *adj. of* ~а́; (*astron.*) lunar; л. год lunar year; ~ное затме́ние lunar eclipse; ~ная ночь moonlit night; л. свет moonlight; л. ка́мень (*min.*) moonstone.

луноxо́д, а, *m.* Moon research vehicle.

лун|ь, я́, *m.* (*orn.*) harrier; полево́й л. hen-harrier; седо́й, бе́лый, как л. white as snow (*of hair*).

лу́п|а, ы, *f.* magnifying glass.

лупи́н, а, *m.* (*bot.*) lupin(e).

луп|и́ть¹, лю, ~ишь, *impf.* 1. (*pf.* об~) to peel; to bark. 2. (*pf.* с~) (*coll.*) to fleece; л. с кого́-н. втри́дорога to make someone pay through the nose.

луп|и́ть², лю, ~ишь, *impf.* (*of* от~) (*coll.*) to thrash, flog.

луп|и́ться, ~ится, *impf.* (*of* об~) to peel (off), scale; (*coll.*) to come off, chip (*of paint, plaster, etc.*).

лупогла́зый, *adj.* (*coll.*) pop-eyed, goggle--eyed.

лупц|ева́ть, у́ю, *impf.* (*of* от~) (*coll.*) to beat, flog.

луч, а́, *m.* ray; beam; рентге́новские, рентге́новы ~й X-rays; л. наде́жды (*fig.*) ray, gleam of hope.

луч|ево́й, *adj.* 1. *adj. of* ~. 2. radial. 3.

(*anat.*) ~ева́я кость radius. 4. (*med.*) ~ева́я боле́знь radiation sickness.

лучеза́р|ный (~ен, ~на), *adj.* (*poet.*) radiant, resplendent.

лучеиспуска́ни|е, я, *n.* (*phys.*) radiation.

лучепреломле́ни|е, я, *n.* (*phys.*) refraction.

лучи́н|а, ы, *f.* 1. splinter, chip (*of kindling wood*; *also collect.*). 2. torch (*for lighting peasant hut*).

лучи́ст|ый (~, ~а), *adj.* 1. radiant (*also fig. and phys.*); л. грибо́к (*med.*) Actinomyces. 2. radial.

луч|и́ть, у́, и́шь, *impf.* л. ры́бу to spear fish (*at night, with the aid of torch-light*).

луч|и́ться, и́тся, *impf.* (*poet.*) to shine brightly, sparkle.

лучко́в|ый, *adj.* bow-shaped; ~ая пила́ frame-saw.

лу́чник, а, *m.* (*hist.*) archer.

лу́чше, *adj. and adv.* (*comp. of* хоро́ший *and* хорошо́) better; тем л. so much the better; л. всего́, л. всех best of all; как мо́жно л. as well as possible, to the best of one's abilities; (*pred.*) it is better; л. ли вам сего́дня? are you better today?; л. не спра́шивай better not ask; нам л. верну́ться we had better go back.

лу́чш|ий, *adj.* (*comp. and superl. of* хоро́ший) better; best; к ~ему for the better; в ~ем слу́чае at best; всего́ ~его! all the (very) best!

лущёный, *adj.* (*agric.*) hulled.

лущ|и́ть, у́, и́шь, *impf.* 1. (*pf.* об~) to shell, hull, pod (*peas, etc.*); to crack (*nuts*). 2. (*pf.* вз~) to remove stubble (from).

лы́ж|а, и, *f.* ski; snow-shoe; бе́гать, ходи́ть на ~ах to ski; навостри́ть ~и (*fig.*) to take to one's heels, show a clean pair of heels; напра́вить ~и (*fig.*) to head (for).

лы́жник, а, *m.* skier.

лы́жн|я, и́, *f.* ski-track.

лы́к|о, а, *pl.* ~и, *n.* bast; драть л. to bark lime-trees; не вся́кое л. в стро́ку (*prov.*) an inch breaks no square, one must make allowances; я не ~ом шит I was not born yesterday; ~а не вя́жет *of the incoherent speech of a drunk person*.

лысе́|ть, ю, *impf.* (*of* об ~ *and* по~) to grow bald.

лы́син|а, ы, *f.* bald spot, bald patch; star (*on horse's forehead*).

лысу́х|а, и, *f.* (*orn.*) coot.

лы́с|ый (~, ~а́, ~о), *adj.* bald.

ль = ли.

льв|ёнок, ёнка, *pl.* ~я́та, ~я́т, *m.* young lion, lion cub.

льви́н|ый, *adj. of* лев¹; ~ая до́ля (*fig.*) the lion's share; (*bot.*) л. зев, ~ая пасть snap--dragon; л. зуб dandelion.

льви́ц|а, ы, *f.* lioness.

льв|я́та, *pl. of* ~ёнок.

льго́т|а, ы, *f.* privilege; advantage,

льго́тник, а, *m.* (*coll.*) privileged person.

льго́тн|ый, *adj.* privileged; favourable; л. биле́т privilege ticket, free ticket; ~ые дни (*comm.*) days of grace; на ~ых усло́виях on preferential terms.

льда, *g. sing. of* лёд.

льди́н|а, ы, *f.* block of ice, ice-floe.

льди́нк|а, и, *f.* piece of ice.

льди́стый, *adj.* icy; ice-covered.

льна, льну, *see* лён.

льново́д, а, *m.* flax grower.

льново́дств|о, а, *n.* flax growing.

льнопряде́ни|е, я, *n.* flax spinning.

льнопряди́льн|ый, *adj.* flax-spinning; ~ая фа́брика flax-mill.

льнопряди́л|ьня, ьни, *g. pl.* ~ен, *f.* flax-mill.

льнотереби́лк|а, и, *f.* (*agric.*) flax puller.

льнотрепа́лк|а, и, *f.* (*agric.*) scutching--sword; swingling machine.

льнуть, льну, льнёшь, *impf.* (*of* при~) (к) 1. to cling (to), stick (to). 2. (*fig., coll.*) to have a weakness (for). 3. (*fig., coll.*) to make up (to), (*sl.*) try to get in (with).

льня́н|о́й, *adj.* 1. of flax; ~о́е ма́сло linseed--oil; ~о́е се́мя linseed, flax-seed; ~о́го цве́та flaxen. 2. linen; ~а́я промы́шленность linen industry.

льсте́ц, а́, *m.* flatterer.

льсти́в|ый (~, ~а), *adj.* flattering; (*of a person*) smooth-tongued.

льсти́ть, льщу, льсти́шь, *impf.* (*of* по~) 1. (+*dat.*) to flatter; to gratify; э́то льстит его́ самолю́бию it flatters his self-esteem; 2. (+*a.*, *with reflexive pron. only*) to delude; л. себя́ наде́ждой to flatter oneself with the hope.

льсти́ться, льщу́сь, льсти́шься, *impf.* (*of* по~) (на+*a.*, *obs.*+*i.*) to be tempted (by).

лью, льёшь, *see* лить.

люб, ~а́, ~о, *adj.* (*pred. only*; *coll.*) dear; pleasant; ~о (+*inf.*) it is pleasant (to); ~о-до́рого it is a real pleasure.

любвеоби́л|ьный (~ен, ~ьна), *adj.* loving; full of love.

любе́знича|ть, ю, *impf.* (с+*i.*) (*coll.*) 1. to pay compliments (to); to pay court (to). 2. to stand on ceremony (with).

любе́зност|ь, и, *f.* 1. courtesy; politeness, civility. 2. kindness; оказа́ть, сде́лать кому́-н. л. to do someone a kindness. 3. compliment; говори́ть ~и кому́-н. to pay someone compliments.

любе́з|ный (~ен, ~на), *adj.* 1. courteous; polite; obliging. 2. kind, amiable; л. чита́тель gentle reader; бу́дьте ~ны... (*polite form of request*) be so kind as . . . . 3. (*obs.*) dear; (*as mode of address to inferior*)

my (good) man. 4. *as noun* л., ~ного, *m.*, ~ная, ~ной, *f.* (*coll. and folk poet.*) beloved.

люби́м|ец, ца, *m.* pet, favourite.

люби́мчик, а, *m.* (*coll., pejor.*) favourite.

люби́м|ый (~, ~а), *adj.* 1. beloved, loved. 2. favourite.

люби́тел|ь, я, *m.* 1. (+*g. or* +*inf.*) lover; л. му́зыки music-lover; л. соба́к dog--fancier; он л. спле́тничать he loves gossiping. 2. amateur.

люби́тельский, *adj.* 1. amateur; л. спекта́кль amateur performance. 2. amateurish. 3. choice.

люби́тельств|о, а, *n.* amateurishness.

люб|и́ть, лю́, ~ишь, *impf.* 1. to love. 2. to like, be fond (of). 3. (*of plants, etc.*) (*coll.*) to need, require, like; фиа́лки ~ят тень violets like shade.

люб|ова́ться, у́юсь, *impf.* (*of* по~) (+*i.*, на+*a.*) to admire; to feast one's eyes (upon); л. на себя́ в зе́ркало to admire oneself in the looking-glass.

любо́вник, а, *m.* 1. lover. 2. (*theatr.*) jeune premier.

любо́вниц|а, ы, *f.* mistress.

любо́вн|ый, *adj.* 1. love-; ~ая исто́рия love-affair; л. напи́ток love-potion; ~ое письмо́ love-letter. 2. loving.

люб|о́вь, ви́, *i.* ~о́вью, *f.* (к) love (for, of); де́лать что-н. с ~о́вью to do something with enthusiasm, con amore.

любозна́тел|ьный (~ен, ~ьна), *adj.* inquisitive.

любо́й 1. *adj.* any; either (*of two*); л. цено́й at any price. 2. *as noun* anyone.

любопы́т|ный (~ен, ~на), *adj.* (*in var. senses*) curious; interesting; *as noun* л., ~ного, *m.* curious, inquisitive person; (*impers.*; +*d. and inf.*) ~но знать, что с ним ста́ло it would be interesting to know what happened to him; мне ~но слу́шать, о чём они́ спо́рят I am curious to hear what they are arguing about; ~но, придёт ли она́ I wonder if she will come.

любопы́тств|о, а, *n.* curiosity; пра́здное л. idle curiosity.

любопы́тств|овать, ую, *impf.* (*of* по~) to be curious.

любостяжа́ни|е, я, *n.* (*obs.*) cupidity.

люб|я́щий, *pres. part. act. of* ~и́ть *and adj.* loving, affectionate; л. вас (*in letters*) yours affectionately.

лю́гер, а, *m.* (*naut.*) lugger.

люд, а, *m.* (*collect.*; *coll.*) people; рабо́чий л. working-people.

лю́д|и, е́й, ~ям, ~ьми́, о ~ях, *no sing.* 1. (*pl. of* челове́к) people; вы́биться, вы́йти в л. to rise in the world, get on in life; вы́вести кого́-н. в л. to put someone on his feet, set someone up; уйти́ в л. to go away from home (*to work*); на ~я́х in the presence of others, in company; на ~я́х и смерть красна́ (*prov.*) two in distress make sorrow less. 2. (*mil.*) men. 3. (*obs.*) servants.

лю́д|ный (~ен, ~на́), *adj.* 1. populous, thickly-populated. 2. crowded.

людое́д, а, *m.* 1. cannibal. 2. ogre.

людое́дств|о, а, *n.* cannibalism.

людск|а́я, о́й, *f.* (*obs.*) servants' hall.

людск|о́й, *adj.* 1. human; ~и́е пересу́ды talk of the town. 2. (*mil.*) л. соста́в personnel, effectives. 3. (*obs.*) servants'.

люизи́т, а, *m.* (*chem.*) lewisite.

люк, а, *m.* 1. (*naut.*) hatch hatchway. 2. (*theatr.*) trap. 3. световой л. sky-light.

люкс[1], а, *m.* (*phys.*) lux (*unit of light*).

люкс[2], *indecl. adj.* de luxe, luxury.

лю́льк|а[1], и, *f.* cradle.

лю́льк|а[2], и, *f.* (*dial.*) pipe.

люмба́го, *indecl., n.* lumbago.

люмина́л, а, *m.* (*pharm.*) luminal.

люминесце́нтн|ый, *adj.* luminescent; ~ые ла́мпы fluorescent lighting.

люминесце́нци|я, и, *f.* (*phys.*) luminescence.

лю́мпен-пролетариа́т, а, *m.* Lumpenproletariat.

люне́т, а, *m.* 1. (*mil.*) lunette. 2. (*tech.*) rest, support, collar plate.

лю́рик, а, *m.* (*orn.*) little auk.

лю́стр|а, ы, *f.* chandelier.

люстри́н, а, *m.* lustrine, lutestring.

люстри́н|овый, *adj. of* ~.

лютера́н|ин, ина, *pl.* ~е, ~, *m.* (*rel.*) Lutheran.

лютера́нский, *adj.* (*rel.*) Lutheran.

лютера́нств|о, а, *n.* (*rel.*) Lutheranism.

лю́тик, а, *m.* (*bot.*) buttercup.

лю́тиков|ые, ых, (*bot.*) ranunculi.

лю́тн|евый, *adj. of* ~я.

лю́т|ня, ни, *g. pl.* ~ен, *f.* (*mus.*) lute.

лю́т|ый (~, ~а́, ~о), *adj.* ferocious, fierce, cruel (*also fig.*).

люф|а́, ы́, *f.* (*bot.*) loofah.

люце́рн|а, ы, *f.* (*bot.*) lucerne.

люэс, а, *m.* (*med.*) syphilis.

люэти́ческий, *adj.* (*med.*) syphilitic.

ля, *indecl., n.* (*mus.*) A; ля дие́з A sharp; ля бемо́ль A flat.

ляг(те), *imp. of* лечь.

ляга́вая = лега́вая.

ляг|а́ть, а́ю, *impf.* (*of* ~ну́ть) to kick.

ляга́|ться, юсь, *impf.* to kick (*intrans.*); to kick one another.

ляг|ну́ть, ну́, нёшь, *inst. pf. of* ~а́ть.

ля́|гу, жешь, гут, *see* лечь.

лягу́ш|ачий (*and* ~ечий), *adj. of* ~ка.

лягу́шк|а, и, *f.* frog.

лягу́ш|о́нок, о́нка, *pl.* ~а́та, ~а́т, *m.* young frog.

ляд, а, *m.* (*coll.*) на кой л.? what the devil, why the devil?; ну его́ к ~у! to hell with him!

ляду́нк|а, и, *f.* cartridge-pouch.

ля́жк|а, и, *f.* thigh, haunch.

лязг, а, *no pl., m.* clank, clang; clack (*of teeth*).

ля́зга|ть, ю, *impf.* (+*i.*) to clank, clang; он ~л зуба́ми his teeth were chattering; л. це́пью to rattle a chain.

ля́мз|ить, ю, ишь, *impf.* (*sl.*) to pinch (= to steal).

ля́мк|а, и, *f.* strap; тяну́ть ~ами, на ~ах to tow, take in tow; тяну́ть ~у (*fig., coll.*) to toil, sweat, be engaged in drudgery.

ля́п|ать, аю, *impf.* (*coll.*) 1. (*pf.* на~) to make hastily *or* any old how. 2. *impf. of* ~нуть.

ля́пис, а, *m.* (*chem.*) lunar caustic, silver nitrate.

ля́пис-лазу́р|ь, и, *f.* lapis lazuli.

ля́п|нуть, ну, нешь, *pf.* (*of* ~ать) (*coll.*) 1. to blurt out, blunder out. 2. to strike, slap; л. кого́-н. по́ уху to box someone's ears.

ля́псус, а, *m.* blunder, lapsus; slip (of tongue, pen).

ля́сы, *only in phrase* (*coll.*) точи́ть л. to chatter, talk idly.

лях, а, *m.* (*hist.*) Pole.

М

мавзоле́|й, я, *m.* mausoleum.

мавр, а, *m.* Moor.

маврита́нский, *adj.* 1. Moorish; (*archit., etc.*) Moresque. 2. Mauritanian.

ма́врский, *adj.* (*obs.*) Moorish.

маг, а, *m.* 1. (*hist.*) magus; Magian. 2. magician, wizard.

магази́н, а, *m.* 1. shop; универса́льный м. department store. 2. (*obs.*) store, depot; (*mil.*) magazine. 3. (*in fire-arm*) magazine.

магази́н|ный, *adj. of* ~; ~ная коро́бка magazine (*of fire-arm*)

магази́нщик, а, *m.* 1. (*coll., obs.*) shop-keeper. 2. (*sl.*) shop-lifter.

магара́дж|а, и, *f.* Maharaja(h).

магары́ч, а́, *m.* (*coll.*) entertainment (*provided by person on. making a good bargain*); wetting a bargain; поста́вить м. to stand a round (of drinks); с вас м.! you owe us a drink!

маги́ст|ерский, *adj. of* ~р 3.

магист|е́рский, *adj. of* ~р 1, 2.

маги́стр, а, *m.* **1.** holder of a master's degree. **2.** master's degree. **3.** head of a knightly *or* monastic order.

магистра́л|ь, и, *f.* main; main line; га́зовая м. gas main; доро́жная м. arterial road; железнодоро́жная м. main railway line.

магистра́ль|ный, *adj. of* ~; м. локомоти́в long-haul locomotive.

магистра́т, а, *m.* city, town council.

магистрату́р|а, ы, *f.* magistracy.

маги́ческий, *adj.* magic(al).

ма́ги|я, и, *f.* magic.

магна́т, а, *m.* **1.** (*hist.*) member of Upper House of Diet in Poland *or* Hungary. **2.** magnate.

магнези́т, а, *m.* (*min.*) magnesite.

магне́зи|я, и, *f.* (*chem.*) magnesia.

магнетизёр, а, *m.* (*obs.*) mesmerist.

магнетизи́р|овать, ую, *impf.* (*obs.*) to mesmerize.

магнети́зм, а, *m.* **1.** magnetism. **2.** (*phys.*) magnetics.

магнети́т, а, *m.* (*min.*) magnetite.

магнети́ческий, *adj.* magnetic.

магне́то, *indecl.*, *n.* (*tech.*) magneto.

магнетро́н, а, *m.* (*radio*) magnetron.

ма́гниевый, *adj.* magnesium.

ма́гни|й, я, *m.* (*chem.*) magnesium.

магни́т, а, *m.* magnet.

магни́тный, *adj.* magnetic; м. железня́к magnetite, loadstone.

магнитофо́н, а, *m.* tape-recorder, tape-recording machine.

магнитофо́н|ный, *adj. of* ~; ~ная за́пись tape-recording.

магни́то-электри́ческий, *adj.* electro-magnetic.

магно́ли|я, и, *f.* (*bot.*) magnolia.

магомета́н|ин, ина, *pl.* ~е, ~, *m.* Mohammedan.

магомета́нств|о, а, *n.* Mohammedanism.

мада́м, *indecl.*, *f.* **1.** madam(e). **2.** (*obs.*, *coll.*) governess. **3.** (*obs.*) dressmaker.

мадемуазе́л|ь, и, *f.* **1.** mademoiselle. **2.** (*obs.*, *coll.*) governess.

маде́р|а, ы, *f.* Madeira (*wine*).

мадо́нн|а, ы, *f.* madonna.

мадрига́л, а, *m.* madrigal.

мадья́р, а, *pl.* ~ы, ~, *m.* Magyar.

мадья́рский, *adj.* Magyar.

мае́вк|а, и, *f.* **1.** May-Day meeting (*workers' gathering on 1 May, illegal before the 1917 Russian revolution*). **2.** spring-time outing, picnic.

мает|а́, ы́, *f.* (*coll.*) trouble, bother.

мажо́р, а, *m.* **1.** (*mus.*) major key. **2.** (*fig.*) a cheerful mood; быть в ~е to be in high spirits.

мажордо́м, а, *m.* major-domo.

мажо́рный, *adj.* **1.** (*mus.*) major. **2.** (*fig.*) cheerful.

ма́|жу, жешь, *see* ~зать.

ма́занк|а, и, *f.* (*dial.*) cottage of daubed brick *or* wood (*esp. in S. Russia*).

ма́заный, *adj.* **1.** (*coll.*) dirty, stained, soiled. **2.** adobe.

ма́|зать, жу, жешь, *impf.* **1.** (*pf.* на~, по~) to oil, grease, lubricate. **2.** (*pf.* вы́~, на~, по~) to smear (with), anoint (with); м. хлеб ма́слом to spread butter on bread, butter bread; м. по губа́м (*fig.*, *coll.*) to excite false expectations. **3.** (*pf.* за~, из~; *coll.*) to soil, stain. **4.** (*pf.* на~; *coll.*) to daub. **5.** (*pf.* про~²; *coll.*) to miss (*in shooting, football, etc.*).

ма́|заться, жусь, жешься, *impf.* **1.** (*pf.* вы́~, за~, из~) to soil oneself, stain oneself. **2.** (*coll.*) to soil, stain (*of objects*; *intrans.*). **3.** (*pf.* на~, по~) to make up; она́ си́льно ~жется (*coll.*) she makes up heavily.

мази́лк|а¹, и, *f.* paint-brush.

мази́лк|а², и, *m. and f.* (*coll.*, *pejor.*) dauber.

ма́з|кий (~ок, ~ка́, ~ко), *adj.* (*coll.*) liable to stain, soil (*of newly-painted wall, etc.*).

мазн|у́ть, у́, ёшь, *pf.* **1.** to dab. **2.** (*coll.*) to hit.

мазн|я́, и́, *f.* (*coll.*) **1.** daub. **2.** poor play.

маз|о́к, ка́, *m.* **1.** dab; stroke (*of paint-brush*). **2.** (*med.*) smear (*for microscopic examination*). **3.** (*coll.*) miss (*in shooting, football, etc.*).

мазохи́зм, а, *m.* (*med.*) masochism.

мазохи́ст, а, *m.* masochist.

мазу́рик, а, *m.* (*sl.*) rogue, swindler.

мазу́рк|а, и, *f.* mazurka.

мазу́т, а, *m.* (*tech.*) fuel oil.

маз|ь, и, *f.* **1.** ointment. **2.** grease; де́ло на ~й (*fig.*, *coll.*) things are going swimmingly.

ма́ис, а, *m.* maize.

ма́ис|овый, *adj. of* ~; ~овая ка́ша polenta.

ма́|й, я, *m.* May.

майда́н, а, *m.* **1.** public square. **2.** (*sl.*) gambling-den (*in bazaar or prison*).

ма́йк|а, и, *f.* T-shirt, sports-jersey; vest.

ма́йна, *interj.* (*naut.*) heave ho!

майо́лик|а, и, *f.* majolica.

майоне́з, а, *m.* (*cul.*) mayonnaise.

майо́р, а, *m.* major (*mil. rank*).

майора́н, а, *m.* (*bot.*) marjoram.

майора́т, а, *m.* (*leg.*) **1.** (right of) primogeniture. **2.** entailed estate.

майо́р|ский, *adj. of* ~.

ма́й|ский, *adj. of* ~; м. жук may-bug, cockchafer.

мак, а, *m.* **1.** poppy. **2.** (*collect.*) poppy-seed.

мака́к|а, и, *f.* (*zool.*) macaque.

мака́о, *indecl.* **1.** *m.* (*orn.*) macaw. **2.** *n.* macao (*gambling game*).

макарони́зм, а, *m.* (*lit.*) macaronism.

макарони́ческий, *adj.* (*lit.*) macaronic.

макаро́нник, а, *m.* baked macaroni pudding.

макаро́н|ный, *adj. of* ~ы.

макаро́н|ы, ~, *sing.* ~а, ~ы, *f.* macaroni.

мак|а́ть, а́ю, *impf.* (*of* ~ну́ть) to dip.

македо́н|ец, ца, *m.* Macedonian.

македо́нский, *adj.* Macedonian; Александр ~ Alexander the Great.

маке́т, а, *m.* 1. model. 2. (*mil.*) dummy.

макиавелли́зм, а, *m.* Machiavellianism.

макиавеллисти́ческий, *adj.* Machiavellian.

макинто́ш, а, *m.* mackintosh.

макла́к, а́, *m.* (*obs.*) 1. second-hand dealer. 2. jobber, middleman.

макла́честв|о, а, *n.* (*obs.*) 1. second-hand dealing. 2. jobbing.

ма́клер, а, *m.* (*comm.*) broker.

ма́клерств|о, а, *n.* (*comm.*) brokerage.

мак|ну́ть, ну́, нёшь, *pf. of* ~а́ть.

ма́ковк|а, и, *f.* 1. poppy-head. 2. (*coll.*) crown (*of head*). 3. (*coll.*) cupola.

ма́к|овый, *adj. of* ~; *as noun* ~овые, ~овых (*bot.*) Papaveraceae; (*fig., coll.*) как ~ов цвет blooming, ruddy (*of complexion*).

макре́л|ь, и, *f.* mackerel.

макроко́см, а, *m.* macrocosm.

макроскопи́ческий, *adj.* macroscopic.

макроцефа́ли|я, и, *f.* (*anthrop.*) macrocephalism.

макси́м, а, *m.* Maxim gun.

ма́ксим|а, ы, *f.* maxim.

максимали́зм, а, *m.* (*hist.*) maximalism.

максимали́ст, а, *m.* (*hist.*) maximalist.

максима́льный, *adj.* maximum.

макси́мк|а, и, *f.* (*coll.*) slow train.

ма́ксимум, а, *m.* 1. maximum. 2. *as adv.* at most; м. сто рубле́й a hundred roubles at most.

макулату́р|а, ы, *f.* 1. (*typ.*) spoiled sheet(s), spoilage. 2. (*fig.*) pulp literature.

маку́шк|а, и, *f.* 1. top, summit. 2. crown (*of head*); у нас у́шки на ~е (*fig.*) we are on the qui vive, on our guard.

мала́г|а, и, *f.* Malaga (wine).

мала́|ец, йца, *m.* Malay.

мала́йский, *adj.* Malay, Malayan.

малаха́|й, я, *m.* (*dial.*) malakhai (= 1. *fur cap with large ear-flaps.* 2. *beltless caftan*).

малахи́т, а, *m.* (*min.*) malachite.

мал|ева́ть, ю́ю, ю́ешь, *impf.* (*of* на~) 1. (*coll.*) to paint; не так стра́шен чёрт, как его́ ~ю́ют (*prov.*) the devil is not so black as he is painted.

мале́йший, *adj.* (*superl. of* ма́лый) least, slightest.

мал|ёк, ька́, *m.* young fish; (*collect.*) fry.

ма́леньк|ий, *adj.* 1. little, small; ~ие лю́ди humble folk. 2. slight; diminutive; игра́ть по ~ой to play for small stakes. 3. young; *as noun* м., ~ого, *m.*; ~ая, ~ой, *f.* the baby, the child; ~ие the young.

мале́нько, *adv.* (*coll.*) a little, a bit.

ма́л|ец, ьца-ьца́, *m.* (*coll.*) lad, boy.

мали́н|а, ы, *no pl., f.* 1. (*collect.*) raspberries. 2. raspberry-bush; raspberry-cane. 3. raspberry juice. 4. *fig., coll. of something pleasurable* (*cf.* a piece of cake); у нас житьё — м. we are in clover.

мали́нник, а, *no pl., m.* raspberry-canes.

мали́н|ный, *adj. of* ~а.

мали́новк|а¹, и, *f.* (*orn.*) robin (redbreast).

мали́новк|а², и, *f.* (*coll.*) raspberry-flavoured vodka.

мали́новый¹, *adj.* 1. raspberry. 2. crimson.

мали́новый², *adj. only in phrase* м. звон mellow chime.

ма́лк|а, и, *f.* (*tech.*) bevel.

ма́ло, *adv.* little, few; not enough; у нас м. вре́мени we have little time; э́того ма́ло this is not enough; об э́том м. кто зна́ет few (people) know about it; я м. где быва́л I have been in few places; м. ли что! what does it matter!; м. ли что мо́жет случи́ться who knows what may happen, anything may happen; м. того́ moreover; м. того́, что... not only...., it is not enough that...; м. того́, что он сам прие́хал, он привёз всех това́рищей it was not enough that he came himself, but he had to bring all his friends.

малоазиа́тский, *adj.* of Asia Minor.

малоблагоприя́т|ный (~ен, ~на), *adj.* unfavourable.

малова́ж|ный (~ен, ~на), *adj.* of little importance, insignificant.

малова́т (~а, ~о), *adj.* (*coll.*) on the small side; м. ро́стом undersized.

малова́то, *adv.* (*coll.*) not quite enough; not very much.

малове́р, а, *m.* sceptic.

малове́ри|е, я, *n.* lack of faith, scepticism.

малове́р|ный (~ен, ~на), *adj.* lacking faith, lacking conviction, sceptical.

малове́роя́т|ный (~ен, ~на), *adj.* unlikely, improbable.

малове́с|ный (~ен, ~на), *adj.* light-weight; (*comm.*) light, short-weight.

малово́дный, *adj.* containing little water; shallow; dry (*of land*).

малово́дь|е, я, *n.* 1. shortage of water. 2. low water-level, shallowness.

малов́ыгод|ный (~ен, ~на), *adj.* unprofitable, unrewarding.

малоговоря́щий, *adj.* not enlightening, not illuminating.

малогра́мот|ный (~ен, ~на), *adj.* 1. semi-literate. 2. crude, ignorant.

малодействи́тел|ьный (~ен, ~ьна), *adj.* ineffective.

малодоказа́тел|ьный (~ен, ~ьна), *adj.* not persuasive, unconvincing.

малодостове́р|ный (~ен, ~на), *adj.* improbable; not well-founded.

малодохо́д|ный (~ен, ~на), *adj.* unprofitable.

малоду́шеств|овать, ую, *impf.* to lose heart; to be faint-hearted.

малоду́ши|е, я, *n.* faint-heartedness, pusillanimity.

малоду́ш|ный (~ен, ~на), *adj.* faint-hearted, pusillanimous.

малое́зжен(н)ый, *adj.* **1.** (*of horse, etc.*) little ridden; (*of carriage*) little used. **2.** (*of road*) little used, unfrequented.

малое́зж|ий, *adj.* = ~ен(н)ый 2.

малозаме́т|ный (~ен, ~на), *adj.* **1.** barely visible, barely noticeable. **2.** ordinary, undistinguished.

малоземе́ль|е, я, *n.* shortage of (arable) land.

малоземе́льный, *adj.* having insufficient (arable) land.

малознако́м|ый (~, ~а), *adj.* little known, unfamiliar.

малозначи́тел|ьный (~ен, ~ьна), *adj.* of little significance, of little importance.

малоиму́щ|ий (~, ~а), *adj.* needy, indigent.

малокали́берный, *adj.* small-calibre; (*of fire-arm*) small-bore.

малокро́ви|е, я, *n.* anaemia.

малокро́в|ный (~ен, ~на), *adj.* anaemic.

малоле́тн|ий, *adj.* **1.** young; juvenile. **2.** *as noun* м., ~его, *m.* infant; juvenile, minor.

малоле́тств|о, а, *n.* infancy; nonage, minority.

малолитра́жк|а, и, *f.* (*coll.*) car with small cylinder capacity, mini-car.

малолитра́жный, *adj.* of small (cylinder) capacity.

малолю́дност|ь, и, *f.* scarcity of people; poor attendance (*at meeting, etc.*).

малолю́д|ный (~ен, ~на), *adj.* **1.** not crowded, unfrequented; ~ное собра́ние poorly attended meeting. **2.** thinly populated.

малолю́д|ье, ья, *n.* = ~ность.

мало-ма́льски, *adv.* (*coll.*) in the slightest degree, at all.

малома́льский, *adj.* (*coll.*) slightest, most insignificant.

маломо́ч|ный (~ен, ~на), *adj.* (*econ.*) having small resources; ~ные крестья́не poor peasants.

маломо́щ|ный (~ен, ~на), *adj.* lacking power; ~ное предприя́тие small concern.

малонадёжный, *adj.* unreliable, undependable.

малонаселённый, *adj.* thinly, sparsely populated.

малообщи́тел|ьный (~ен, ~ьна), *adj.* unsociable, uncommunicative.

малооснова́тел|ьный (~ен, ~ьна), *adj.* **1.** unfounded. **2.** (*of person*) undependable.

малоподви́ж|ный (~ен, ~на), *adj.* not mobile, slow-moving.

малоподе́ржанный, *adj.* little used, almost unused.

мало-пома́лу, *adv.* (*coll.*) little by little, bit by bit.

малопоня́тлив|ый (~, ~а), *adj.* (*coll.*) not very bright, slow in the uptake.

малопоня́т|ный (~ен, ~на), *adj.* hard to understand; obscure.

малоприбы́л|ьный (~ен, ~ьна), *adj.* bringing little profit, of little profit.

малоприго́д|ный (~ен, ~на), *adj.* of little use.

малоразви́т|ый (~, ~а), *adj.* **1.** undeveloped. **2.** underdeveloped. **3.** uneducated.

малоразгово́рчив|ый (~, ~а), *adj.* taciturn.

малоро́сл|ый (~, ~а), *adj.* undersized, stunted.

малоро́сс, а, *m.* (*obs.*) Little Russian (*Ukrainian*).

малоросси́йский, *adj.* (*obs.*) Little Russian (*Ukrainian*).

малоросси́я|н|ин, ина, *pl.* ~е, *m.* = малоро́сс.

мало|ру́сский, *adj.* = ~росси́йский.

малосве́дущ|ий (~, ~а), *adj.* ill-informed.

малосеме́йный, *adj.* having a small family.

малоси́л|ьный (~ен, ~ьна), *adj.* **1.** weak, feeble. **2.** (*tech.*) low-powered.

малосодержа́тел|ьный (~ен, ~ьна), *adj.* uninteresting; (*fig.*) empty, shallow.

малосо́л|ьный (~ен, ~ьна), *adj.* slightly, inadequately salted.

малосостоя́тел|ьный¹ (~ен, ~ьна), *adj.* poor, poorer.

малосостоя́тел|ьный² (~ен, ~ьна), *adj.* unconvincing.

ма́лост|ь, и, *f.* (*coll.*) **1.** a bit; trifle, bagatelle. **2.** *as adv.* a little, a bit; м. поспа́ть to take a nap.

малосуще́ствен|ный (~, ~на), *adj.* of small importance, immaterial.

малотира́жный, *adj.* of small circulation, published in a small number of copies.

малоубеди́тел|ьный (~ен, ~ьна), *adj.* unconvincing.

малоупотреби́тел|ьный (~ен, ~ьна), *adj.* infrequent, rarely used.

малоуспе́ш|ный (~ен, ~на), *adj.* unsuccessful.

малоце́н|ный (~ен, ~на), *adj.* of little value.

малочи́сленност|ь, и, *f.* small number; paucity.

малочи́слен|ный (~, ~на), *adj.* small (in numbers); scanty.

ма́л|ый[1] (~, ~á, ~ó), *adj.* little, (too) small; м. ро́стом short, of small stature; м. ход! (*naut.*) slow speed (ahead)!; э́ти сапоги́ мне ~ы́ these boots are too small for me; ~ ~á ме́ньше (*coll.*) *of children of one family, viewed in descending order of size*; от ~а до вели́ка young and old (*i.e. all, regardless of age*); с ~ых лет from childhood; *as noun* ~ое, ~ого, *n.* little; са́мое ~ое (*coll.*) at the least; без ~ого almost, all but; за ~ым де́ло ста́ло (*frequently iron.*) one small thing is lacking.

ма́л|ый[2], ого, *m.* (*coll.*) fellow, chap; lad, boy.

малы́ш, á, *m.* (*coll.*) child, kid; little boy.

ма́льв|а, ы, *f.* (*bot.*) mallow, hollyhock.

мальва́зи|я, и, *f.* malmsey (*wine*).

мальти́|ец, йца, *m.* Maltese.

мальти́йский, *adj.* Maltese.

мальто́з|а, ы, *f.* (*chem.*) maltose.

мальтузиа́нский, *adj.* Malthusian.

мальтузиа́нств|о, а, *n.* Malthusianism.

ма́льчик, а, *m.* 1. boy, lad; (male) child; м. с па́льчик Tom Thumb. 2. (*obs.*) apprentice.

мальчико́вый, *adj.* boy's, boys'.

мальчи́шеский, *adj.* 1. boyish. 2. (*pejor.*) childish, puerile.

мальчи́шеств|о, а, *n.* boyishness; (*pejor.*) childishness.

мальчи́шк|а, и, *m.* (*coll.*) urchin, boy; в сравне́нии с однокла́ссниками он м. by comparison with his class-mates he is a child.

мальчи́шник, а, *m.* stag-party.

мальчуга́н, а, *m.* (*coll., affect.*) little boy.

малю́сенький, *adj.* (*coll.*) tiny, wee.

малю́тк|а, и, *m. and f.* baby, little one.

маля́р, á, *m.* (house-)painter, decorator.

маляри́йный, *adj.* malarial.

маляри́|я, и, *f.* (*med.*) malaria.

маля́р|ный, *adj. of* ~.

ма́м|а, ы, *f.* mummy, mamma.

мамалы́г|а, и, *f.* (*dial.*) polenta.

мама́ш|а, и, *f.* (*coll.*) mummy, mamma.

мамелю́к, а, *m.* (*hist.*) Mameluke.

ма́меньк|а, и, *f.* = мама́ша.

ма́менькин, *adj.* mother's; м. сыно́к (*coll., iron.*) mother's darling.

ма́мин, *adj.* mother's.

ма́мк|а, и, *f.* (*obs.*) (wet-)nurse.

мамо́н|а, ы, *f.* mammon.

ма́монт, а, *m.* mammoth.

ма́монт|овый, *adj. of* ~; ~овое де́рево (*bot.*) sequoia, Wellingtonia.

ма́мочк|а, и, *f.* (*coll.*) mummy.

мана́т|ки, ок, *no sing.* (*sl.*) possessions, goods, and chattels.

манат|ья́, ьи́, *g. pl.* ~е́й, *f.* monk's habit.

мангани́т, а, *m.* (*min.*) manganite.

ма́нго, *indecl., n.* (*bot.*) mango.

ма́нго|вый, *adj. of* ~.

ма́нгровый, *adj.* (*bot.*) mangrove.

мангу́ст|а, ы, *f.* (*zool.*) mongoose.

мандари́н[1]**, а,** *m.* mandarin (*Chinese official*).

мандари́н[2]**, а,** *m.* mandarin(e), tangerine.

мандари́н|ный, *adj. of* ~[2].

мандари́н|овый, *adj.* = ~ный.

мандари́н|ский, *adj. of* ~[1].

манда́т, а, *m.* 1. warrant. 2. (*polit.*) mandate; credentials.

манда́т|ный, *adj. of* ~; ~ная коми́ссия credentials committee; ~ная систе́ма голосова́ния card vote system; ~ная террито́рия mandated territory.

мандоли́н|а, ы, *f.* (*mus.*) mandolin(e).

мандолини́ст, а, *m.* mandolin(e)-player.

мандраго́р|а, ы, *f.* (*bot.*) mandragora.

мандри́л, а, *m.* (*zool.*) mandrill.

мане́вр, а, *m.* 1. (*in var. senses*) manœuvre; (*pl.; mil.*) manœuvres. 2. (*pl.*) shunting.

манёвренност|ь, и, *f.* manœuvrability.

манёвр|енный, *adj. of* ~; ~енная война́ war of movement; ~енный самолёт manœuvrable aircraft; м. парово́з shunting engine.

маневри́р|овать, ую, *impf.* (*of* с~) 1. to manœuvre. 2. (+*i.*) to make good use (of), use to advantage. 3. (*railways*) to shunt.

маневро́вый, *adj.* (*railways*) shunting.

мане́ж, а, *m.* riding-school, manège.

мане́жик, а, *m.* play-pen.

мане́ж|ить, у, ишь, *impf.* 1. to break in (*a horse*). 2. (*fig., coll.*) to tire out (*with waiting*).

манеке́н, а, *m.* lay figure, dummy.

манеке́нщиц|а, ы, *f.* mannequin.

мане́р, а, *m.* (*coll.*) manner; таки́м ~ом in this manner, in this way; на англи́йский м. in the English manner.

мане́р|а, ы, *f.* 1. manner, style; м. вести́ себя́ way of behaving; м. держа́ть себя́ bearing, carriage; у него́ неприя́тная м. опа́здывать на свида́ния he has an unpleasant way of being late for appointments; петь в ~е Кару́зо to sing in the style of Caruso. 2. (*pl.*) manners; у него́ плохи́е ~ы he has no manners.

мане́рк|а, и, *f.* (*mil.*) mess tin.

мане́рнича|ть, ю, *impf.* (*coll.*) to behave affectedly.

мане́рност|ь, и, *f.* affectation; preciosity.

мане́р|ный (~ен, ~на), *adj.* affected; precious.

манже́т|а, ы, *f.* cuff.

маниака́льный, *adj.* maniacal.

ма́ни|е, я, *n.* (*arch.*) *now only in phrases* ~ем, по ~ю (руки́, жезла́, *etc.*) with a motion (of the hand, the baton, *etc.*); (*fig.*) по ~ю (бого́в, царя́, *etc.*) by the will (of the gods, the Tsar, *etc.*).

маникю́р, а, *m.* manicure.

маникюрш|а, и, *f.* manicurist.

манипули́р|овать, ую, *impf.* to manipulate.

манипуля́ци|я, и, *f.* 1. manipulation. 2. (*fig.*) machination, intrigue.

ман|и́ть, ю́, ~и́шь, *impf.* (*of* по~) 1. to beckon. 2. (*fig.*) to attract; to lure, allure.

манифе́ст, а, *m.* manifesto.

манифеста́нт, а, *m.* (*polit.*, *etc.*) demonstrator.

манифеста́ци|я, и, *f.* (street) demonstration.

манифести́р|овать, ую, *impf. and pf.* to demonstrate, take part in a demonstration.

мани́шк|а, и, *f.* (false) shirt-front, dicky.

ма́ни|я, и, *f.* 1. mania; м. вели́чия megalomania. 2. (*fig.*) passion, craze; у неё м. противоре́чить she has a passion for contradicting.

манки́р|овать, ую, *impf. and pf.* 1. (+*i.*) to neglect. 2. to be absent; (+*a.*; *obs.*) to miss, be absent from. 3. (+*d.*; *obs.*) to be impolite to.

ма́нн|а, ы, *f.* manna; ждать (+*g.*) как ~ы небе́сной to await with impatience; пита́ться ~ой небе́сной (*joc.*) to be half-starved.

ма́нн|ый, *adj.* ~ая крупа́ semolina.

манове́ни|е, я, *n.* (*obs.*) beck, nod; ~ем руки́ with a wave of one's hand.

мано́метр, а, *m.* (*tech.*) pressure-gauge, manometer.

манометри́ческий, *adj.* (*tech.*) manometric.

манса́рд|а, ы, *f.* attic, garret.

манти́ль|я, и, *f.* mantilla.

манти́сс|а, ы, *f.* (*math.*) mantissa.

ма́нти|я, и, *f.* cloak, mantle; robe, gown.

манто́, *indecl.*, *n.* (lady's) coat.

манускри́пт, а, *m.* manuscript.

мануфакту́р|а, ы, *f.* 1. manufactory. 2. (*obs.*) textile mill. 3. (*sing. only*; *collect.*) cotton textiles.

мануфакту́р|ный, *adj. of* ~а.

манче́стер, а, *m.* (*text.*) velveteen.

маньчжу́р, а, *m.* Manchurian.

маньчжу́рский, *adj.* Manchurian.

манья́к, а, *m.* maniac, person in the grip of an obsession.

марабу́, *indecl.*, *n.* (*orn.*) marabou.

мара́зм, а, *m.* (*med.*) marasmus; ста́рческий м. senility, dotage; (*fig.*) decay.

марак|овать, у́ю, *impf.* (*coll.*) to have some notion (about), be not completely at sea.

мара́л, а, *m.* (*zool.*) Siberian deer.

мараски́н, а, *m.* maraschino (*liqueur*).

мара́тел|ь, я, *m.* (*coll.*) dauber; scribbler.

мара́|ть, ю, *impf.* (*coll.*) 1. (*pf.* за~) to soil, dirty; (*fig.*) to sully, stain; м. ру́ки (о+*a.*) to soil one's hands (on). 2. (*pf.* на~) to

daub; to scribble. 3. (*pf.* вы~) to cross out, strike out.

мара́|ться, юсь, *impf.* (*coll.*) 1. (*pf.* за~) to soil oneself, get dirty. 2. (*no pf.*) to be dirty; to stain (*intrans.*). 3. (*no pf.*; *fig.*) to soil one's hands. 4. (*of infants*; *euph.*) to soil oneself, make a mess. 5. *pass. of* ~ть.

марафо́нский, *adj.* м. бег (*sport*) Marathon race.

мара́шк|а, и, *f.* (*typ.*) turn.

ма́рган|ец, ца, *m.* (*chem.*) manganese.

ма́рган|цевый, *adj. of* ~ец.

марганцо́вистый, *adj.* (*chem.*) manganous, manganic.

марганцо́вый, *adj.* = ма́рганцевый.

маргари́н, а, *m.* margarine.

маргари́н|овый, *adj. of* ~; (*fig.*) bogus, ersatz.

маргари́тк|а, и, *f.* (*bot.*) daisy.

маргина́ли|и, ев *and* ий, *no sing.* marginalia.

ма́рев|о, а, *n.* 1. mirage. 2. heat haze.

маре́н|а, ы, *f.* (*bot.*) madder.

маре́нго, *indecl. adj.* black flecked with grey.

ма́ри, *indecl.* (*collect.*) the Mari (*inhabitants of Mari Autonomous Republic in U.S.S.R.*, *formerly the Cheremis*).

мари́|ец, йца, *m.* Mari.

мари́йский, *adj.* Mari.

мари́н|а, ы, *f.* (*art*) sea-scape.

марина́д, а, *m.* marinade; pickles.

марини́ст, а, *m.* painter of sea-scapes.

марино́в|анный, *p.p.p. of* ~а́ть *and adj.* (*cul.*) pickled.

марин|ова́ть, у́ю, *impf.* 1. (*pf.* за~) to pickle. 2. (*pf.* про~) (*fig.*, *coll.*) to put off, shelve.

марионе́т|ка, ки, *f.* marionette; puppet (*also fig.*); теа́тр ~ок puppet-theatre.

марионе́т|очный, *adj. of* ~ка; ~очное госуда́рство puppet state.

ма́рк|а¹, и, *f.* 1. (postage-)stamp. 2. (*monetary unit in Germany and Finland*) mark. 3. mark; brand; фабри́чная м. trade-mark; како́й ма́рки? what make? 4. counter. 5. grade, sort, brand; това́р вы́сшей ~и goods of the highest grade. 6. (*fig.*) name, reputation; держа́ть ~у to maintain one's reputation.

ма́рк|а², и, *f.* (*hist.*) mark (*medieval German territorial unit or rural commune*).

маркгра́ф, а, *m.* (*hist.*) margrave.

марке́р, а, *m.* (*in var. senses*) marker.

маркетри́, *indecl.*, *n. and adj.* marquetry.

марки́з, а, *m.* marquis, marquess.

марки́з|а¹, ы, *f.* marchioness.

марки́з|а², ы, *f.* sun-blind; awning; marquee.

маркизе́т, а, *m.* (*text.*) voile.

маркизе́т|овый, *adj. of* ~.

ма́рк|ий (~ок, ~ка), *adj.* easily soiled.

маркир|ова́ть, у́ю, *impf. and pf.* (*in var. senses*) to mark.

маркита́нт, а, *m.* (*hist.*) sutler.

маркси́зм, а, *m.* Marxism.

маркси́зм-ленини́зм, а-а, *m.* Marxism-Leninism.

маркси́ст, а, *m.* Marxist.

маркси́стский, *adj.* Marxist, Marxian.

маркси́стско-ле́нинский, *adj.* Marxist-Leninist.

маркше́йдер, а, *m.* mine-surveyor.

маркше́йдер|ский, *adj. of* ~; ~ская съёмка mine surveying.

ма́рл|евый, *adj. of* ~я; м. бинт gauze bandage.

ма́рл|я, и, *f.* gauze; cheesecloth.

мармела́д, а, *m.* fruit jelly (*sweets*).

мармори́р|овать, ую, *impf. and pf.* (*tech.*) to marble.

мароде́р, а, *m.* marauder, pillager.

мароде́рск|ий, *adj.* marauding; ~ие це́ны (*fig., coll.*) exorbitant prices.

мароде́рств|о, а, *n.* pillage, looting.

мароде́рств|овать, ую, *impf.* to maraud, pillage, loot.

мароке́н, а, *m.* 1. morocco(-leather). 2. (*text.*) marocain.

мароке́н|овый, *adj. of* ~.

ма́р|очный, *adj. of* ~ка¹; ~очное вино́ fine wine.

марс¹, а, *m.* (*naut.*) top.

Марс², а, *m.* (*astron., myth.*) Mars (*in myth. sense, a.* ~а).

марсал|а́, ы́, *f.* Marsala (*wine*).

ма́рсел|ь, я, *m.* (*naut.*) topsail.

марселье́з|а, ы, *f.* Marseillaise.

марсиа́н|ин, ина, *pl.* ~е, ~, *m.* Martian.

ма́рс|овый, *adj. of* ~¹.

март, а, *m.* March.

марте́н, а, *m.* (*tech.*) 1. open-hearth furnace. 2. open-hearth steel.

марте́новский, *adj.* (*tech.*) open-hearth.

мартенси́т, а, *m.* (*tech.*) martensite.

мартинга́л, а, *m.* martingale.

мартироло́г, а, *m.* martyrology.

ма́рт|овский, *adj. of* ~.

мартышк|а, и, *f.* marmoset; (*fig., coll.*) monkey.

марципа́н, а, *m.* marzipan.

марш¹, а, *m.* (*in var. senses*) march.

марш², *interj.* (*as word of command*) forward!; ша́гом м.! quick march!; (*coll.*) off you go!

марш³, а, *m.* flight of stairs.

ма́ршал, а, *m.* marshal.

ма́ршал|ьский, *adj. of* ~.

ма́ршальств|о, а, *n.* rank of marshal.

ма́рш|евый, *adj. of* ~¹; м. поря́док marching order; ~евые ча́сти drafts, reinforcements.

маршир|ова́ть, у́ю, *impf.* to march; м. на ме́сте to mark time.

марширо́вк|а, и, *f.* marching.

марш-марш, а, *m.* quick march.

маршру́т, а, *m.* 1. route, itinerary. 2. through goods-train.

маршрутиза́ци|я, и, *f.* conveyance by through goods-train.

маршру́т|ный, *adj. of* ~; м. по́езд through goods-train; ~ное такси́ fixed-route taxi.

маседуа́н, а, *m.* (*cul.*) macedoine.

ма́ск|а, и, *f.* mask; противога́зовая м. gas-mask; (*fig.*) сбро́сить с себя́ ~у to throw off the mask.

маскара́д, а, *m.* masked ball, masquerade.

маскара́д|ный, *adj. of* ~; м. костю́м fancy dress.

маскир|ова́ть, у́ю, *impf.* (*of* за~) to mask, disguise; (*mil.*) to camouflage; м. свой наме́рения (*fig.*) to disguise one's intentions.

маскиро́вк|а, и, *f.* masking, disguise; (*mil.*) camouflage.

маскиро́вщик, а, *m.* (*mil.*) camouflage expert.

ма́слениц|а, ы, *f.* Shrove-tide; carnival; не всё ко́ту м., *see* кот.

ма́слени|чный, *adj. of* ~ца.

маслёнк|а, и, *f.* 1. butter-dish. 2. oil-can.

масл|ёнок, ёнка, *pl.* ~я́та, ~я́т, *m.* *Boletus lutens* (*edible mushroom*).

ма́слен|ый, *adj.* 1. buttered; oiled, oily, ~ая неде́ля = ~ица; ~ые кра́ски = ма́сло 3. 2. (*fig., coll.*) oily, unctuous. 3. (*fig., coll.*) voluptuous, sensual.

масли́н|а, ы, *f.* 1. olive-tree. 2. olive.

ма́сл|ить, ю, ишь, *impf.* (*of* на~ *and* по~) 1. to butter. 2. to oil; to grease.

ма́сл|иться, ится, *impf.* 1. to leave greasy marks. 2. (*coll.*) to shine; to glisten. 3. *pass. of* ~ить.

ма́сличный, *adj.* (*of plants*) oil-yielding.

масли́|чный, *adj. of* ~на; ~чная гора́ Mount of Olives.

ма́с|ло, ла, *pl.* ~ла́, ~ел, ~ла́м, *n.* 1. (сли́вочное) butter. 2. oil; как по ~лу (*fig., coll.*) swimmingly. 3. oil (paints); писа́ть ~лом to paint in oils.

маслобо́йк|а, и, *f.* 1. churn. 2. oil press.

маслобо́йн|ый, *adj.* м. заво́д = ~я.

маслобо́|йня, йни, *g. pl.* ~ен, *f.* 1. creamery. 2. oil-mill.

масло́дел, а, *m.* 1. butter manufacturer. 2. oil manufacturer.

масло́дели|е, я, *n.* 1. butter manufacturing. 2. oil manufacturing.

маслозаво́д, а, *m.* 1. creamery, butter-dairy. 2. oil-mill.

масломе́р, а, *m.* oil gauge; dipstick.

маслопрово́д, а, *m.* oil pipe, oil pipe-line.

маслоро́дный, *adj.* м. газ (*chem.*) ethylene.

маслосисте́м|а, ы, *f.* lubrication system.

ма́сл|яный, *adj. of* ~о; ~яная кислота́ (*chem.*) butyric acid.

масо́н, а, *m.* freemason, mason.

масо́нский, *adj.* masonic.

масо́нств|о, а, *n.* freemasonry.

ма́сс|а, ы, *f.* **1.** (*in var. senses*) mass; ~ы (*polit.*) the masses; в ~е on the whole, in the mass. **2.** (*ceramics*) paste. **3.** древе́сная м. wood-pulp. **4.** (*coll.*) a lot, lots.

масса́ж, а, *m.* massage.

массажи́ст, а, *m.* masseur.

массажи́стк|а, и, *f.* masseuse.

масси́в, а, *m.* (*geogr.*) massif, mountain--mass; (*fig.*) expanse; жили́щный м. housing unit; лесно́й м. forest tract.

масси́в|ный (~ен, ~на), *adj.* massive.

масси́ровани|е, я, *n.* massing, concentration.

масси́рова|нный, *p.p.p. of* ~ть[1] *and adj.* (*mil.*) massed, concentrated.

масси́р|овать[1], ую, *impf. and pf.* (*mil.*) to mass, concentrate.

масси́р|овать[2], ую, *impf. and pf.* to massage.

массови́к, а́, *m.* organizer of popular cultural and recreational activities.

массо́вк|а, и, *f.* (*coll.*) **1.** mass meeting. **2.** group excursion. **3.** crowd scene (*in play, film*).

ма́ссов|ый, *adj.* (*in var. senses*) mass; popular; ~ые аре́сты mass arrests; ~ое произво́дство mass production.

маста́к, а́, *m.* (*coll.*) expert, past master.

ма́стер, а, *pl.* ~а́, *m.* **1.** foreman. **2.** master craftsman, skilled workman; золоты́х дел м. goldsmith. **3.** (на+*a.*, *or* +*inf.*) expert, master (at, of); м. на все ру́ки all-round expert; быть ~ом своего́ де́ла to be an expert at one's job; он м. танцева́ть вальс he is an expert at the waltz.

ма́стер|ить, ю, и́шь, *impf.* (*of* с~) (*coll.*) to make, build; мы ~и́м себе́ са́ни we are making ourselves a sledge.

мастеро́в|о́й, о́го, *m.* (*obs.*) workman, (factory-)hand.

мастерск|а́я, о́й, *f.* workshop; studio; (*in factory*) shop.

мастерски́, *adv.* skilfully; in masterly fashion.

мастерско́й, *adj.* masterly.

мастерств|о́, а́, *n.* **1.** trade, craft. **2.** skill, craftsmanship.

масти́к|а, и, f. **1.** mastic. **2.** putty. **3.** floor--polish.

масти́к|овый, *adj. of* ~а; ~овое де́рево mastic (tree).

масти́т, а, *m.* (*med.*) mastitis.

масти́т|ый (~, ~а), *adj.* venerable; м. учёный old and eminent scholar.

мастодо́нт, а, *m.* mastodon.

мастурба́ци|я, и, f. masturbation.

мастурби́р|овать, ую, *impf.* to masturbate.

маст|ь, и, *pl.* ~и, ~е́й, *f.* **1.** colour (*of animal's hair or coat*). **2.** (*cards*) suit; ходи́ть в м. to follow suit.

масшта́б, а, *m.* scale; м.—две ми́ли в дю́йме the scale is two miles to the inch; (*fig.*) в большо́м, ма́леньком ~е on a large, small scale; конфли́кт большо́го ~а large-scale conflict.

масшта́бност|ь, и, f. (*fig.*) (large) scale, range, dimensions.

масшта́б|ный (~ен, ~на), *adj.* (*fig.*) mathematical.

мат[1], а, *m.* (*chess*) checkmate, mate; объяви́ть м. (+*d.*) to mate.

мат[2], а, *m.* (floor-, door-)mat.

мат[3], а, *m.* mat (*roughened or frosted ground-work*); нанести́ м. (на+*a.*) to mat, frost.

мат[4], а, *m.* (*coll.*) *only in phrase* благи́м ~ом at the top of one's voice.

мат[5], а, *m.* foul language, abuse; руга́ться ~ом to use foul language.

матадо́р, а, *m.* matador.

матема́тик, а, *m.* mathematician.

матема́тик|а, и, f. mathematics.

математи́ческий, *adj.* mathematical.

матере́|ть, ю, *impf.* (*coll.*) **1.** to grow to full size. **2.** (*fig.*) to become hardened.

матереуби́йств|о, а, *n.* matricide (*act*).

матереуби́йц|а, ы, *m. and f.* matricide (*agent*).

материа́л, а, *m.* (*in var. senses*) material; stuff.

материали́зм, а, *m.* materialism.

материализ|ова́ть(ся), у́ю(сь), *impf. and pf.* to materialize (*trans. and intrans.*).

материали́ст, а, *m.* materialist.

материалисти́ческий, *adj.* (*philos.*) materialist.

материалисти́ч|ный (~ен, ~на), *adj.* (*pejor.*) materialistic.

материа́льност|ь, и, f. materiality.

материа́л|ьный (~ен, ~ьна), *adj.* (*in var. senses*) material; ~ьная заинтересо́ванность material incentive(s); ~ьные затрудне́ния financial difficulties; ~ьное положе́ние economic conditions; ~ьная часть (*tech., mil.*) equipment, matériel.

матери́к, а́, *m.* **1.** continent, mainland. **2.** subsoil.

материко́вый, *adj.* continental.

матери́нский, *adj.* maternal, motherly.

матери́нств|о, а, *n.* maternity, motherhood.

матер|и́ться, ю́сь, и́шься, *impf.* (*coll.*) to use foul language.

матери|я́[1], и, f. **1.** (*philos.*) matter. **2.** (*med.*) matter, pus. **3.** (*fig., coll.*) subject, topic (*of conversation*).

матери|я́[2], и, f. (*text.*) material, cloth.

ма́терный, *adj.* (*coll.*) obscene, abusive.

матеро́й, *adj.* (*coll.*) full-grown, grown-up; м. волк (*fig.*) an old hand.

матéрчатый, *adj.* (*coll.*) made of cloth.

матерщи́н|а, ы, *f.* (*coll.*) foul language.

матёрый, *adj.* (*coll.*) **1.** experienced, practised. **2.** inveterate, out-and-out.

матинé, *indecl., n.* **1.** matinée coat. **2.** (*obs.*) matinée.

ма́тиц|а, ы, *f.* (*tech.*) tie-beam, joist.

ма́тк|а, и, *f.* **1.** (*anat.*) uterus, womb. **2.** female (*of animals*); queen (bee). **3.** (*coll.*) mother. **4.** (*naut.*) (submarine) tender.

ма́тов|ый, *adj.* mat(t); dull; suffused (*of light*); ~ое стекло́ frosted glass.

ма́точник, а, *m.* **1.** queen bee's cell. **2.** (*bot.*) style, ovary.

ма́точн|ый, *adj.* **1.** (*anat.*) uterine. **2.** (*min.*) ~ая поро́да matrix.

матра́с, а, *m.* mattress.

матра́|ц = ~с.

матриарха́льный, *adj.* matriarchal.

матриарха́т, а, *m.* matriarchy.

матри́кул, а, *m.* student's record card.

матримониа́льный, *adj.* matrimonial.

ма́триц|а, ы, *f.* **1.** (*typ.*) matrix. **2.** (*tech.*) die, mould.

матрици́р|овать, ую, *impf. and pf.* (*typ.*) to make matrix-moulds (of).

матро́н|а, ы, *f.* matron.

матро́с, а, *m.* sailor, seaman.

матро́ск|а¹, и, *f.* sailor's jacket.

матро́ск|а², и, *f.* (*coll.*) sailor's wife.

ма́тушк|а, и, *f.* (*coll.*) **1.** mother; ~и (мой)! *exclamation of surprise or fright.* **2.** priest's wife. **3.** *familiar term of address to a woman.*

матч, а, *m.* (*sport*) match; выездно́й м. away match.

мат|ь, *g., d., p.* ~ери, ~ерью, *pl.* ~ери, ~ере́й, *f.* **1.** mother. **2.** (*coll.*) *term of address to a woman.*

ма́ть-и-ма́чех|а, и, *f.* (*bot.*) coltsfoot.

ма́узер, а, *m.* Mauser (*automatic pistol or rifle*).

мах, а (у), *m.* swing, stroke; (*coll.*) дать ~у to let a chance slip; to make a blunder; одни́м ~ом, с одного́ ~у at one stroke, in a trice; с ~у rashly, without thinking.

маха́льн|ый, ого, *m.* (*mil., sport*) signaller.

ма|ха́ть, шу́, ~шешь, *impf.* (*of* ~хну́ть) (+*i.*) to wave; to brandish; to wag; to flap.

махи́н|а, ы, *f.* (*coll.*) bulky and cumbersome object.

махина́ци|я, и, *f.* machination, intrigue.

мах|ну́ть, ну́, нёшь, *pf.* **1.** *pf. of* ~а́ть; м. руко́й (на+*a.*) (*fig., coll.*) to give up as a bad job. **2.** (*coll.*) to go, travel. **3.** (*coll.*) to rush; to leap.

махови́к, а́, *m.* fly-wheel.

махов|о́й, *adj.* **1.** (*tech.*) ~о́е колесо́ fly-wheel. **2.** (*orn.*) ~ы́е пе́рья wing-feathers.

ма́хонький, *adj.* (*coll.*) wee.

махо́рк|а, и, *f.* makhorka (*inferior kind of tobacco*).

махро́вый, *adj.* **1.** (*bot.*) double. **2.** (*fig., coll.*) double-dyed, arrant. **3.** (*text.*) terry.

махр|ы́, о́в, *no sing.* (*coll.*) frayed edges (*of garment*).

мац|а́, ы́, *no pl., f.* matzoth (*Jewish biscuits of unleavened wheatmeal*).

ма́чех|а, и, *f.* stepmother.

ма́чт|а, ы, *f.* mast.

ма́чт|овый, *adj. of* ~а.

маши́н|а, ы, *f.* **1.** machine, mechanism (*also fig.*). **2.** car. **3.** (*obs., coll.*) train.

машина́л|ьный (~ен, ~ьна), *adj.* mechanical (*fig.*); м. отве́т an automatic response.

машиниза́ци|я, и, *f.* mechanization.

машинизи́р|овать, ую, *impf. and pf.* to mechanize.

машини́ст, а, *m.* **1.** machinist, engineer (*workman in charge of machinery*). **2.** (*railways*) engine-driver. **3.** (*theatr.*) scene-shifter.

машини́стк|а, и, *f.* (girl-)typist.

маши́н|ка, ки, *f. dim. of* ~а; (пи́шущая) м. typewriter.

маши́нно-тра́кторн|ый, *adj.* ~ая ста́нция machine and tractor station.

маши́н|ный, *adj. of* ~а.

машинопи́сный, *adj.* typewritten; м. текст typescript.

маши́нопис|ь, и, *f.* **1.** typewriting. **2.** typescript.

машинострое́ни|е, я, *n.* mechanical engineering, machinery construction.

маэ́стро, *indecl., m.* maestro; master.

мая́к, а́, *m.* **1.** lighthouse; beacon (*also fig.*). **2.** (*fig.*) leading light.

ма́ятник, а, *m.* pendulum.

ма́|яться, юсь, ешься, *impf.* (*coll.*) **1.** (с+*i.*) to toil (with, over). **2.** to pine, suffer.

мая́ч|ить, у, ишь, *impf.* (*coll.*) **1.** to loom (up), appear indistinctly. **2.** to lead a wretched life.

мгл|а, ы, *f.* **1.** haze; mist. **2.** gloom, darkness.

мгли́ст|ый (~, ~а), *adj.* hazy.

мгнове́ни|е, я, *n.* instant, moment; в м. о́ка in the twinkling of an eye.

мгнове́н|ный (~ен, ~на), *adj.* instantaneous.

ме́бел|ь, и, *f.* furniture; (*fig.*) для ~и a figurehead, fifth wheel (*said of a useless person*).

ме́бельщик, а, *m.* upholsterer; furniture-dealer.

меблиро́|ванный, *p.p.p. of* ~ва́ть *and adj.* furnished.

меблир|ова́ть, у́ю, *impf. and pf.* to furnish.

меблиро́вк|а, и, *f.* **1.** furnishing. **2.** furniture, furnishings.

мегаге́рц, а, *m.* (*radio*) megahertz.

мегаломáни|я, и, *f.* megalomania.
мегафóн, а, *m.* megaphone.
мегéр|а, ы, *f.* (*coll.*) shrew, termagant.
мегóм, а, *m.* (*electr.*) megohm.
мёд, а, о ~e, в ~ý, *pl.* ~ы, ~óв, *m.* 1. honey.
2. mead.
мед- *abbr. of* медицúнский.
медалúст, а, *m.* medallist; medal winner.
медáл|ь, и, *f.* medal.
медальóн, а, *m.* medallion, locket.
медвéдиц|а, ы, *f.* she-bear; (*astron.*) Боль-
шáя М. the Great Bear (Ursa Major);
Мáлая М. the Little Bear (Ursa Minor).
медвéдк|а, и, *f.* 1. (*zool.*) mole-cricket. 2.
handcart. 3. (*tech.*) punch press.
медвéд|ь, я, *m.* 1. bear; бéлый м. polar bear.
2. (*obs., coll.*) bearskin.
медвеж|áта, *pl. of* ~óнок.
медвежáтин|а, ы, *f.* bear's flesh.
медвéд|ь, я, *m.* 1. bear (*also fig.*); бéлый м.
polar bear. 2. (*obs., coll.*) bearskin.
медвé|жий, *adj. of* ~дь; м. ýгол (*coll.*) god-
-forsaken place; ~жья услýга well-meant
action having opposite effect; ~жья болéзнь (*euph.*) diarrhoea induced by fear.
медвеж|óнок, óнка, *pl.* ~áта, ~áт, *m.* bear-
-cub.
медвя́н|ый, *adj.* 1.(*poet.*) honeyed. 2. smell-
ing of honey. 3. ~ая росá honey-dew.
меделя́нск|ий, *adj.* ~ая собáка mastiff.
медеплавúльный, *adj.* copper-smelting.
медж|илúс = ~лúс.
меджлúс, а, *m.* Majlis (*Persian parliament*).
медиáн|а, ы, *f.* (*math.*) median.
мéдик, а, *m.* 1. physician, doctor. 2. medical
student.
медикамéнт, а, *m.* medicine.
медицúн|а, ы, *f.* medicine.
медицúнский, *adj.* medical.
медúчк|а, и, *f.* (*coll.*) (woman) medical
student.
мéдленно, *adv.* slowly.
мéдленный, *adj.* slow.
медлúтел|ьный (~ен, ~ьна), *adj.* sluggish;
slow, tardy.
мéдл|ить, ю, ишь, *impf.* to linger; to tarry;
(с+*i.*) to be slow (in); он ~ит с отвéтом
he is a long time replying.
мéдник, а, *m.* copper-smith; tinker.
мéдно-крáсный, *adj.* copper-coloured.
меднолитéйный, *adj.* copper-smelting.
мéдн|ый, *adj.* 1. copper; brazen (*also fig.*);
м. лоб (*fig., coll.*) blockhead; учúться на
~ые гроши, на ~ые дéньги to receive a
poor boy's schooling. 2. (*chem.*) cupric,
cuprous; м. колчедáн copper pyrites; м.
купорóс copper sulphate, bluestone.
медóвый, *adj. of* мёд; м. мéсяц honeymoon.
мед|óк[1], кá, *m. dim. of* мёд.
медóк[2], а, *m.* Médoc (*wine*).

медонóсный, *adj.* melliferous, nectariferous.
медосмóтр, а, *m.* (*abbr. of* медицúнский
осмóтр) medical examination.
медоточúв|ый (~, ~a), *adj.* (*obs.*) melli-
fluous, honeyed.
медпýнкт, а, *m.* (*abbr. of* медицúнский
пункт) first aid post.
медсестр|á, ы́, *f.* (*abbr. of* медицúнская
сестрá) (hospital) nurse.
медýз|а, ы, *f.* 1. (*zool.*) jellyfish, medusa.
2. М. (*myth.*) Medusa.
медунúц|а, ы, *f.* (*bot.*) lungwort.
мед|ь, и, *f.* 1. copper; жёлтая м. brass.
медя́к, á, *m.* (*coll.*) copper (coin).
медянúц|а, ы, *f.* slow-worm, blind-worm.
медя́нк|а[1], и, *f.* grass-snake.
медя́нк|а[2], и, *f.* (*chem.*) verdigris.
меж = мéжду.
меж- inter-.
меж|á, ú, *pl.* ~и, ~, ~áм, *f.* boundary;
boundary-strip.
междомéти|е, я, *n.* (*gram.*) interjection.
междоусóби|е, я, *n.* civil strife; intestine
strife (*especially in mediaeval Russia*).
междоусóб|ица, ицы, *f.* (*obs.*) = ~ие.
междоусóбный, *adj.* intestine.
мéжду, *prep.*+*i.* (+*g. pl., obs.*) 1. between;
м. дéлом at odd moments; м. нáми (говоря́)
between ourselves; between you and me;
м. прóчим incidentally; м. тем meanwhile; м. тем, как while, whereas; м.
двух огнéй between two fires. 2. among,
amongst.
междувéдомственный, *adj.* inter-depart-
mental.
междугорóдный, *adj.* inter-town, inter-
urban.
междунарóдник, а, *m.* specialist on international law *or* affairs.
междунарóдный, *adj.* international.
междупýть|е, я, *n.* (*railways*) track spacing.
междуря́дь|е, я, *n.* (*agric.*) space between
rows.
междуцáрстви|е, я, *n.* interregnum.
межевáни|е, я, *n.* land surveying, survey.
меж|евáть, ýю, *impf.* to survey; to establish
the boundaries (of).
межевúк, á, *m.* surveyor.
меж|евóй, *adj. of* ~á; м. знак landmark,
boundary-mark.
межéн|ь, и, *f.* 1. lowest water-level (*in river
or lake*). 2. (*dial.*) midsummer.
межеýм|ок, ка, *m.* (*coll.*) 1. person of limited
intelligence; a mediocrity. 2. person *or*
thing lacking definite qualities.
межеýмочный, *adj.* (*coll.*) mediocre; ill-
-defined; neither one thing nor another.
межзýбный, *adj.* (*ling.*) interdental.
межклéточный, *adj.* (*biol.*) intercellular.
межконтинентáльный, *adj.* inter-conti-

nental; м. баллисти́ческий снаря́д intercontinental ballistic missile.

межплане́тн|ый, adj. interplanetary; ~ая автомати́ческая ста́нция 'interplanetary automatic station' (unmanned space research vehicle).

межрёберный, adj. (anat.) intercostal.

мездр|а́, ы́, f. inner side (of hide).

мезозо́йский, adj. (geol.) mesozoic.

мезолити́ческий, adj. (archaeol.) mesolithic.

мезони́н, а, m. 1. attic story. 2. mezzanine (floor).

мексика́н|ец, ца, m. Mexican.

мексика́нк|а, и, f. Mexican (woman)

мексика́нский, adj. Mexican.

мел, а, о ~е, в ~у́, m. chalk; whiting; whitewash.

меланези́йский, adj. Melanesian.

мела́нжев|ый, adj. (text.) ~ая ни́тка blended yarn; ~ое произво́дство blended yarn fabric production.

меланхо́лик, а, m. melancholic (person).

меланхоли́ческий, adj. melancholy.

меланхоли́ч|ный (~ен, ~на), adj. = ~еский.

меланхо́ли|я, и, f. melancholy; (med.) melancholia.

мела́сс|а, ы, f. molasses.

меле́|ть, ет, impf. (of об~) to grow shallow.

мелиор|ати́вный, adj. of ~а́ция.

мелиора́тор, а, m. (agric.) specialist in melioration, land improvement.

мелиора́ци|я, и, f. (agric.) melioration, land improvement (either by drainage or by irrigation).

мел|и́ть, ю́, и́шь, impf. (of на~) to chalk; to polish with whiting.

ме́л|кий (~ок, ~ка́, ~ко), adj. 1. small, petty. 2. shallow; shallow-draught. 3. (of rain, sand, etc.) fine; м. шаг (tech.) fine pitch. 4. (fig.) petty, small-minded; ~кая душо́нка petty person; ~кая со́шка small fry.

ме́лко, adv. 1. fine, into small particles. 2. not deep; м. пла́вать (fig., coll.) to lack depth.

мелкобуржуа́з|ный (~ен, ~на), adj. petty--bourgeois.

мелково́д|ный (~ен, ~на), adj. shallow.

мелково́дь|е, я, n. shallow water.

мелкозерни́ст|ый (~, ~а), adj. fine-grained, small-grained.

мелколесь|е, я, n. young forest.

мелкопоме́стный, adj. (hist.) small (of landowners).

мелкособ ственнический, adj. relating to small property holders.

мелкот|а́, ы́, f. 1. smallness; (fig.) pettiness, meanness. 2. (collect.; coll.) small fry.

мелкотова́рный, adj. (econ.) small-scale.

меловой, adj. 1. consisting of chalk. 2. white as chalk. 3. cretaceous.

мелодеклама́ци|я, и, f. recitation of poetry to musical accompaniment.

мело́дик|а, и, f. melodics.

мелоди́ческий, adj. melodious, tuneful.

мелоди́ч|ный (~ен, ~на), adj. = ~еский.

мело́ди|я, и, f. melody, tune.

мелодра́м|а, ы, f. melodrama.

мелодрамати́ческий, adj. melodramatic.

мел|о́к, ка́, m. piece of chalk; игра́ть на м. (cards, billiards, etc.) to play on credit.

мелома́н, а, m. music-lover.

мелочно́й[1], adj. (obs.) retail.

мелочно́й[2] = ме́лочный.

ме́лочност|ь, и, f. pettiness, small-mindedness, meanness.

ме́лоч|ный (~ен, ~на), adj. 1. petty, trifling. 2. (pejor.) petty, paltry, small-minded.

ме́лоч|ь, и, pl. ~и, ~е́й, f. 1. (collect.) small items; small fry; кру́пные я́блоки мы съе́ли, оста́лась м. we had eaten the big apples, only the small ones were left. 2. (collect.) small coin; (small) change. 3. (pl.) trifles, trivialities; разме́ниваться на ~и, по ~а́м to fritter away one's energies.

мел|ь, и, о ~и, на ~й, f. shoal; bank; песча́ная м. sandbank; на ~й aground; (fig.) on the rocks, in low water; сесть на м. to run aground; сиде́ть (как рак) на ~й (fig., coll.) to be on the rocks, be in low water.

мельк|а́ть, а́ю, impf. (of ~ну́ть) to be glimpsed fleetingly.

мельк|ну́ть, ну́, нёшь, inst. pf. of ~а́ть; у меня́ ~ну́ла мысль I had a sudden idea.

ме́льком, adv. in passing, cursorily.

ме́льник, а, m. miller.

ме́льниц|а, ы, f. mill; э́то вода́ на на́шу ~у (fig., coll.) it is grist to our mill.

ме́льничих|а, и, f. (coll.) miller's wife.

ме́льни|чный, adj. of ~ца.

мельхио́р, а, m. cupro-nickel, German silver.

мельхио́р|овый, adj. of ~.

мельча́йший, superl. of ме́лкий.

мельча́|ть, ю, impf. (of из~) 1. to grow shallow. 2. to become small; to grow smaller. 3. (fig.) to become petty.

ме́л|ьче, comp. of ~кий and ~ко.

мельч|и́ть, у́, и́шь, impf. (of из~ and раз~) 1. to crush, crumble. 2. to reduce in size. 3. to reduce the significance of.

мелю́, ме́лешь, see моло́ть.

мелюзг|а́, и́, f. (collect.; coll.) small fry.

мембра́н|а, ы, f. (phys.) membrane; (tech.) diaphragm.

мемора́ндум, а, m. (dipl.) memorandum.

мемориа́л, а, m. 1. (comm.) day-book. 2. (obs.) note-book.

мемориа́льный, adj. memorial.

мемуари́ст, а, *m.* author of memoirs.

мемуа́р|ы, ов, *no sing.* memoirs.

мен|а, ы, *f.* exchange, barter.

менажёр, а, *m.* (*sport*) manager.

менажи́р|овать, ую, *impf.* (*sport*) to manage, be manager (of).

ме́нее, *adv.* (*comp. of* ма́ло) less; тем не м. none the less.

менестре́л|ь, я, *m.* (*hist.*) minstrel.

мензу́л|а, ы, *f.* (*tech.*) plane-table.

мензу́рк|а, и, *f.* (*pharm.*) measuring-glass.

менинги́т, а, *m.* (*med.*) meningitis.

мени́ск, а, *m.* (*math., phys.*) meniscus.

менов|о́й, *adj.* (*econ.*) exchange; ~а́я торго́вля barter.

менструа́льный, *adj.* (*physiol.*) menstrual.

менструа́ци|я, и, *f.* (*physiol.*) menstruation.

менструи́р|овать, ую, *impf.* (*physiol.*) to menstruate.

ме́нтик, а, *m.* (*obs.*) hussar's pelisse.

менто́л, а, *m.* (*chem.*) menthol.

ме́нтор, а, *m.* (*obs.*) mentor.

менуэ́т, а, *m.* minuet.

ме́ньше, *comp. of* ма́ленький *and* ма́ло, smaller, less.

меньшеви́зм, а, *m.* (*polit.*) Menshevism.

меньшеви́к, а́, *m.* (*polit.*) Menshevik.

меньшеви́стский, *adj.* (*polit.*) Menshevist.

ме́ньш|ий, *adj.* (*comp. of* ма́ленький, ма́лый) lesser, smaller; younger; по ~ей ме́ре at least; са́мое ~ее at the least.

меньшинств|о́, а́, *n.* minority.

меньшо́й, *adj.* (*coll.*) youngest.

меню́, *indecl., n.* menu, bill of fare.

меня́, *a. and g. of* я.

меня́л|а, ы, *m.* (*coll.*) money-changer.

меня́льный, *adj.* (*comm.*) money-changing.

меня́|ть, ю, *impf.* **1.** (*no pf.*) to change. **2.** (+*a.* на+*a.*; *pf.* об~, по~) to exchange (for).

меня́|ться, юсь, *impf.* **1.** (*no pf.*) to change; м. в лице́ to change countenance. **2.** (+*i.*; *pf.* об~, по~) to exchange; м. с кем-н. ко́мнатами to exchange rooms with someone.

мер|а, ы, *f.* (*in var. senses*) measure; вы́сшая м. наказа́ния capital punishment; в ~у (+*g.*) to the extent (of); по ~е возмо́жности, по ~е сил as far as possible; по ~е того́, как аs, (in proportion) as; по кра́йней ~е, по ме́ньшей ~е at least; в ~у fairly; сверх ~ы, чрез ~у, не в ~у excessively, immoderately.

ме́ргел|ь, я, *m.* (*geol.*) marl.

мере́жк|а, и, *f.* hem-stitch, open work.

мере́нг|а, и, *f.* meringue.

мере́ть, мру, мрёшь, *past* мёр, мёрла, *impf.* (*coll.*) **1.** to die (*in large numbers*); мрут, как му́хи they are dying like flies. **2.** (*of the heart*) to stop beating.

мере́щ|иться, усь, ишься, *impf.* (*of* по~) (*coll.;* +*d.*) **1.** to seem (to), appear (to); она́ мне ~ится her image haunts me; э́то тебе́ ~ится you only imagine you see it. **2.** (*obs.*) to appear dimly.

мерза́в|ец, ца, *m.* (*coll.*) blackguard, scoundrel.

ме́рз|кий (~ок, ~ка́, ~ко), *adj.* disgusting, loathsome; abominable, foul.

мерзлот|а́, ы́, *f.* frozen condition of ground; ве́чная м. permafrost.

мерзлотове́дени|е, я, *n.* study of frozen soil conditions.

мёрзлый, *adj.* frozen, congealed.

мёрз|нуть, ну, нешь, *past* ~, ~ла, *impf.* (*of* за~) to freeze.

мерзост|ь, и, *f.* **1.** vileness, loathsomeness. **2.** loathsome thing, nasty thing; abomination; м. запусте́ния (*bibl. or iron.*) abomination of desolation.

меридиа́н, а, *m.* meridian.

мери́л|о, а, *n.* standard, criterion.

мери́льный, *adj.* measuring.

ме́рин, а, *m.* gelding; врёт как си́вый м. (*coll.*) he's an out-and-out liar.

мерино́с, а, *m.* **1.** merino (sheep). **2.** merino (wool).

мерино́совый, *adj.* merino.

ме́р|ить, ю, ишь, *impf.* **1.** (*pf.* с~) to measure; м. взгля́дом to look up and down. **2.** (*pf.* по~, при~) to try on (*clothing, footwear*).

ме́р|иться, юсь, ишься, *impf.* (*of* по~) (+*i.*) to measure (against); м. ро́стом с кем-н. to compare heights with someone.

ме́рк|а, и, *f.* measure; подходи́ть ко всему́ с одно́й ~ой (*fig.*) to apply the same standard to all alike.

меркантили́зм, а, *m.* **1.** (*econ.*) mercantilism. **2.** (*fig.*) mercenary spirit.

мерканти́л|ьный, *adj.* **1.** mercantile. **2.** (~ен, ~ьна) (*fig., pejor.*) mercenary.

ме́рк|нуть, нет, *past* ~нул *and* ~, ~ла, *impf.* (*of* по~) to grow dark, grow dim; (*fig.*) to fade.

Мерку́ри|й, я, *m.* (*myth., astron.*) Mercury.

мерла́н, а, *m.* (*fish*) whiting.

мерлу́шк|а, и, *f.* lambskin.

ме́рный, *adj.* **1.** measured; rhythmical. **2.** (*tech.*) measuring.

мероприя́ти|е, я, *n.* measure.

мерсериза́ци|я, и, *f.* (*tech.*) mercerization.

мерсеризо́в|анный, *p.p.p. of* ~а́ть *and adj.* (*tech.*) mercerized.

мерсериз|ова́ть, у́ю, *impf. and pf.* (*tech.*) to mercerize.

мёртвенный, *adj.* deathly, ghastly.

мертве́|ть, ю, *impf.* **1.** (*pf.* о~) to grow numb; (*med.*) to mortify. **2.** (*pf.* по~) to be benumbed (*with fright, grief, etc.*).

мертве́ц, á, *m.* corpse, dead man.

мертве́цк|ая, ой, *f.* (*coll.*) mortuary, morgue.

мертве́цки, *adv.* (*coll.*) *only in phrases* м. пьян dead drunk; напи́ться м. to become dead drunk.

мертвечи́н|а, ы, *f.* 1. (*collect.*) carrion. 2. (*fig., coll.*) spiritual stagnation.

мертв|и́ть, лю́, и́шь, *impf.* to deaden.

мертворождённый, *adj.* still-born.

мёртв|ый (~, ~á, ~о, *pl.* **~ы;** *in fig. senses* **~б, ~ы́),** *adj.* dead; ни жив ни ~ more dead than alive; ~ая зыбь (*naut.*) swell; м. инвента́рь (*agric.*) dead stock; м. капита́л (*fin.*) dead stock, unemployed capital; ~ая пе́тля (*aeron.*) loop; пить ~ую (*coll.*) to drink hard; ~ое простра́нство (*geogr., mil.*) dead ground; спать ~ым сном (*coll.*) to sleep like the dead; быть на ~ой то́чке to be at a standstill; ~ая хва́тка mortal grip; м. час quiet time (*in sanatoria, etc.*).

мерца́|ть, ю, *impf.* to twinkle, glimmer, flicker.

меси́в|о, а, *n.* 1. mash. 2. (*fig., coll.*) medley; jumble.

ме|си́ть, шу́, ~сишь, *impf.* (*of* с~) to knead; м. грязь (*coll., joc.*) to wade through mud.

месмери́зм, а, *m.* mesmerism.

ме́сс|а, ы, *f.* (*rel., mus.*) mass.

мессиа́нский, *adj.* Messianic.

мессиа́нств|о, а, *n.* Messianism.

месси́|я, и, *m.* Messiah.

места́ми, *adv.* (*coll.*) here and there, in places.

месте́ч|ко¹, ка, *pl.* **~ки, ~ек, ~кам,** *n.* small town (*in Ukraine and Byelorussia*).

месте́ч|ко², ка, *pl.* **~ки, ~ек, ~кам,** *n. dim.* of ме́сто; тёплое м. (*coll.*) cushy job.

ме|сти́, ту́, тёшь, *past* мёл, ~ла́, *impf.* 1. to sweep. 2, to whirl; *impers.* ~тёт there is a snow-storm.

местко́м, а, *m.* (*abbr. of* ме́стный комите́т) local (trade union) committee.

ме́стничес|кий, *adj. of* ~тво.

ме́стничеств|о, а, *n.* 1. (*hist.*) order of precedence (*based on birth and service*). 2. (*pejor.*) regionalism, giving priority to local interests.

ме́стност|ь, и, *f.* 1. locality, district; area. 2. (*mil.*) ground, country, terrain.

ме́стный, *adj.* (*in var. senses*) local; м. колори́т local colour. 2. (*gram.*) locative.

-ме́стный -seated, -seater.

ме́ст|о, а, *pl.* **~á, ~, ~áм,** *n.* 1. place; site; больно́е м. (*fig.*) tender spot, sensitive point; де́тское м. (*anat.*) after-birth, placenta; о́бщее м. platitude; отхо́жее м. latrine; пусто́е м. blank (space), (*fig.*) a nobody, a nonentity; сла́бое м. (*fig.*) weakness, weak spot; у́зкое м. bottleneck; м. дейст-

вия, м. происше́ствия scene (of action); на ~е преступле́ния in the act, red-handed; знать своё м. (*fig.*) to know one's place; име́ть м. to take place; поста́вить на своё м., указа́ть кому́-н. его́ м. (*fig.*) to put someone in his place; не находи́ть себе́ ~а (*fig.*) to fret, worry; не к ~у (*fig.*) out of place; по ~áм! to your places!; ни с ~а! don't move!, stay put!; честь и м.! (*obs., now joc.*) kindly be seated! 2. (*in theatre, etc.*) seat; (*on ship or train*) berth, seat. 3. space; room; нет ~а there is no room. 4. post, situation; job; быть без ~а to be out of work. 5. passage (*of book or mus. work*). 6. piece (*of luggage*). 7. (*pl.*) the provinces, the country; на ~áх in the provinces; делега́ты с~ provincial delegates, delegates from the country.

местоблюсти́тел|ь, я, *m.* (*eccl.*) locum tenens.

местожи́тельств|о, а, *n.* (place of) residence; без определённого ~а of no fixed abode.

местоиме́ни|е, я, *n.* (*gram.*) pronoun.

местоиме́нный, *adj.* (*gram.*) pronominal.

местонахожде́ни|е, я, *n.* location, the whereabouts.

местоположе́ни|е, я, *n.* site, situation, position.

местопребыва́ни|е, я, *n.* abode, residence.

месторожде́ни|е, я, *n.* 1. (*geol.*) deposit; layer. 2. (*obs*). birth-place.

мест|ь, и, *f.* vengeance, revenge.

ме́сяц, а, *m.* 1. month; медо́вый м. honeymoon. 2. moon; молодо́й м. new moon.

месяцесло́в, а, *m.* (*obs.*) calendar.

ме́сячник, а, *m.* month (*marked by special observances or devoted to some special cause*).

ме́сячн|ый, *adj.* monthly; *as noun* ~ые, ~ых, *no sing.* (*coll.*) (menstrual) period.

мета́лл, а, *m.* metal; презре́нный м. filthy lucre.

металлиза́ци|я, и, *f.* (*tech.*) metallization.

металлизи́р|овать, ую, *impf. and pf.* to metallize.

металли́ст, а, *m.* metal-worker.

металли́ческ|ий, *adj.* metal; metallic (*also fig.*); ~ая болва́нка pig-metal; ~ая отли́вка cast metal.

металло́ид, а, *m.* (*chem.*) metalloid.

металлоно́с|ный (~ен, ~на), *adj.* metalliferous.

металлообраба́тывающий, *adj.* metal-working.

металлоплави́льный, *adj.* smelting.

металлопрока́тный, *adj.* (*tech.*) rolling.

металлопромы́шленност|ь, и, *f.* metal industry.

металлу́рг, а, *m.* metallurgist.

металлурги́ческий, *adj.* metallurgical.

металлу́рги|я, и, *f.* metallurgy.

метаморфо́з, а, *m.* = ~а.

метаморфо́з|а, ы, *f.* metamorphosis.

мета́н, а, *m.* (*chem.*) methane, marsh gas.

мета́ни|е, я, *n.* 1. throwing, casting, flinging. 2. м. икры́ spawning.

метано́л, а, *m.* (*chem.*) methanol, methyl alcohol.

метаста́з, а, *m.* (*med.*) metastasis.

метате́з|а, ы, *f.* (*ling.*) metathesis.

мета́тел|ь, я, *m.* (*sport*) thrower; м. ди́ска discus thrower.

мета́тельный, *adj.* missile; м. снаря́д projectile.

ме|та́ть¹, чу́, ~чешь, *impf.* (*of* ~ну́ть) 1. to throw, cast, fling; м. гром и мо́лнии (*fig., coll.*) to rage, fulminate; рвать и м. (*coll.*) to be in a rage; м. жре́бий to cast lots; м. се́но to stack hay. 2. м. икру́ to spawn. 3. (*cards*) м. банк to keep the bank.

мета́|ть², ю, *impf.* (*of* на~, с~) to baste, tack; м. пе́тли to edge buttonholes.

ме|та́ться, чу́сь, ~чешься, *impf.* to rush about; to toss (*in bed*).

метафи́зик, а, *m.* metaphysician.

метафи́зик|а, и, *f.* metaphysics.

метафизи́ческий, *adj.* metaphysical.

мета́фор|а, ы, *f.* metaphor.

метафори́ческий, *adj.* metaphorical.

метаце́нтр, а, *m.* (*phys.*) metacentre.

мете́л|ица, ицы, *f.* (*poet.*) = ~ь.

метёлк|а, и, *f.* 1. *dim. of* метла́; под ~у (*fig., coll.*) entirely, to the last particle. 2. (*bot.*) panicle.

мете́л|ь, и, *f.* snow-storm; blizzard.

мете́льчатый, *adj.* (*bot.*) panicular, paniculate.

мете́льщик, а, *m.* sweeper.

метемпсихо́з, а, *m.* metempsychosis.

метео́р, а, *m.* meteor.

метеори́зм, а, *m.* (*med.*) flatulence.

метеори́т, а, *m.* (*astron.*) meteorite.

метеори́ческий, *adj.* meteoric.

метео́р|ный, *adj. of* ~.

метеоро́лог, а, *m.* meteorologist.

метеорологи́ческий, *adj.* meteorological.

метеороло́ги|я, и, *f.* meteorology.

метеосво́дк|а, и, *f.* (*abbr. of* метеорологи́ческая сво́дка) weather report.

метеоста́нци|я, и, *f.* (*abbr. of* метеорологи́ческая ста́нция) meteorological station.

метиза́ци|я, и, *f.* (*biol.*) cross-breeding.

мети́зный, *adj.* metal-ware, hardware.

мети́з|ы, ов, *no sing.* (*abbr. of* металли́ческие изде́лия) metal wares, hardware.

мети́л, а, *m.* (*chem.*) methyl.

мети́с, а, *m.* 1. (*biol.*) mongrel, half-breed. 2. (*anthrop.*) metis, mestizo.

ме́|тить¹, чу, тишь, *impf.* (*of* на~ *and* по~) to mark.

ме́|тить², чу, тишь, `*impf.* (*of* на~) 1. (в+*a.*) to aim(at); (*fig., coll*; в+*n.-a. pl.*) to aim(at), aspire (to); он всегда́ ~тил в профессора́ it had always been his aim (ambition) to become a professor. 2. (*fig.*; в+*a.*, на+*a.*) to drive (at), mean.

ме́тк|а, и, *f.* 1. marking. 2. mark.

ме́т|кий (~ок, ~ка́, ~ко), *adj.* well-aimed, accurate; м. стрело́к a good shot; (*fig.*) ~кое замеча́ние apt remark; ~ко выра́зиться to be very much to the point.

ме́ткост|ь, и, *f.* marksmanship; accuracy; (*fig.*) neatness, pointedness.

мет|ла́, лы́, *pl.* ~лы, ~ел, ~лам, *f.* broom.

мет|ну́ть, ну́, нёшь, *inst. pf. of* ~а́ть¹.

ме́тод, а, *m.* method.

мето́д|а, ы, *f.* (*obs.*) method.

методи́зм, а, *m.* (*rel.*) Methodism.

мето́дик|а, и, *f.* 1. method(s), system; principles; м. ру́сского языка́ methods of teaching Russian; м. пожа́рного де́ла principles of fire-fighting. 2. methodology.

методи́ст¹, а, *m.* methodologist; specialist (*on principles of, methods of teaching, etc.*).

методи́ст², а, *m.* (*rel.*) Methodist.

методи́ст|ский, *adj. of* ~².

метод|и́ческий, *adj.* 1. methodical, systematic. 2. *adj. of* ~ика; м. приём a procedure; ~и́ческое совеща́ние conference on (*teaching, etc.*) methods.

методи́ч|ный (~ен, ~на), *adj.* methodical, orderly.

методо́лог, а, *m.* methodologist.

методологи́ческий, *adj.* methodological.

методоло́ги|я, и, *f.* methodology.

метони́ми|я, и, *f.* (*lit.*) metonymy.

мето́п, а, *m.* (*archit.*) metope.

метр¹, а, *m.* (*unit of measurement and lit.*) metre.

метр², а, *m.* (*obs. or joc.*) master.

метра́ж, а, *m.* 1. metric area. 2. length in metres.

метранпа́ж, а, *m.* (*typ.*) maker-up.

метрдоте́л|ь, я, *m.* head waiter.

ме́трик|а¹, и, *f.* (*lit.*) metrics.

ме́трик|а², и, *f.* birth-certificate.

метри́ческий¹, *adj.* metric.

метри́ческ|ий², *adj.* (*lit.*) metrical; ~ое ударе́ние ictus, metrical stress.

метри́ческ|ий³, *adj.* ~ая кни́га register of births; ~ое свиде́тельство birth-certificate.

метро́, *indecl., n., abbr. of* ~полите́н.

метрологи́ческий, *adj.* metrological.

метроло́ги|я, и, *f.* metrology.

метроно́м, а, *m.* (*phys., mus.*) metronome.

метрополите́н, а, *m.* underground (railway), metro(politan railway).

метропо́ли|я, и, *f.* mother country, centre (*of empire*).

ме|ту́, тёшь, *see* ~сти́.

мёт|че, *comp. of* ~кий *and* ~ко.

ме́тчик, а, *m.* (*tech.*) 1. punch, stamp. 2. marker.

метчи́к, а́, *m.* (*tech.*) tap-borer, screw-tap.

мех¹, а, о ~е, в ~у́ (~е), на ~у́, *pl.* ~а́, ~о́в, *m.* fur; на ~у́ fur-lined.

мех², а, *pl.* ~и́, ~о́в, *m.* 1. (*pl.*) bellows. 2. wine-skin, water-skin.

механиза́тор, а, *m.* 1. specialist on mechanization. 2. (*agric.*) machine operator, machine servicer.

механиза́ци|я, и, *f.* mechanization.

механизи́рова|нный, *p.p.p. of* ~ть *and adj.* mechanized.

механизи́р|овать, ую, *impf. and pf.* to mechanize.

механи́зм, а, *m.* mechanism, gear(ing); (*pl., collect.*) machinery (*also fig.*).

меха́ник, а, *m.* 1. mechanic. 2. student of, specialist in mechanics.

меха́ник|а, и, *f.* 1. mechanics. 2. (*fig., coll.*) trick; knack; подвести́ (подстро́ить) ~у кому́-н. to play a trick on someone.

механи́ст, а, *m.* (*philos.*) mechanist.

механисти́ческий, *adj.* (*philos.*) mechanistic.

механи́ческий, *adj.* 1. (*in var. senses*) mechanical; power-driven; м. моме́нт momentum; м. пресс power press; м. тка́цкий стано́к power loom; м. цех machine shop. 2. of mechanics. 3. (*philos.*) mechanistic.

механи́ч|ный (~ен, ~на), *adj.* (*fig.*) mechanical, automatic.

мехово́й, *adj. of* мех¹.

меховщи́к, а́, *m.* furrier.

мецена́т, а, *m.* Maecenas, patron.

мецена́тств|о, а, *n.* patronage of literature, of arts.

ме́ццо-сопра́но, *indecl., f. and n.* (*mus.*) mezzo-soprano.

ме́ццо-ти́нто, *indecl., n.* (*art*) mezzotint.

меч, а́, *m.* sword; дамо́клов м. sword of Damocles; преда́ть огню́ и ~у́ to put to the sword; скрести́ть ~и́ (*fig., rhet.*) to cross swords.

мечено́с|ец, ца, *m.* 1. sword-bearer. 2. member of German order of Knights of the Sword.

ме́чен|ый, *adj.* marked; ~ые а́томы (*phys.*) labelled, tagged atoms.

мече́т|ь, и, *f.* mosque.

меч-ры́б|а, ы, *f.* sword-fish.

мечт|а́ (*g. pl. not used*) *f.* dream, day-dream.

мечта́ни|е, я, *n.* day-dreaming, reverie.

мечта́тел|ь, я, *m.* dreamer; day-dreamer.

мечта́тел|ьный (~ен, ~ьна), *adj.* dreamy.

мечта́|ть, ю, *impf.* (о+*p.*) to dream (of, about); м. мно́го, высоко́, *etc.*, о себе́ (*coll.*) to think much of oneself.

ме́|чу, тишь, *see* ~тить.

ме|чу́, ~чешь, *see* ~та́ть¹.

меша́лк|а, и, *f.* mixer, stirrer.

мешани́н|а, ы, *f.* (*coll.*) medley, jumble.

меша́|ть¹, ю, *impf.* (*of* по~) 1. (+*d.*+*inf.*) to prevent (from); to hinder, impede, hamper; что ~ет вам прие́хать в Москву́? what prevents you from coming to Moscow? 2. (+*d.*) to disturb; вам не ~ет, что я игра́ю на пиани́но? does it disturb you when I play the piano? не ~ло бы (+*inf.*) (*coll.*) it would be advisable (to), would not be a bad thing (to).

меша́|ть², ю, *impf.* 1. (*pf.* по~) to stir, agitate; м. у́голь в пе́чке to poke the fire; м. в котле́ to stir the cauldron. 2. (*pf.* с~) (с+*i.*) to mix (with), blend (with). 3. (*pf.* с~) to confuse, mix up.

меша́|ться, юсь, *impf.* 1. (*coll.*; в+*a.*) to interfere (in), meddle (with); не ~йтесь не в своё де́ло! mind your own business! 2. (*pf.* с~) *pass. of* ~ть².

ме́шка|ть, ю, *impf.* (*coll.*; с+*i.*) to linger, tarry (over); to loiter.

мешкова́т|ый (~, ~а), *adj.* 1. (*of clothing*) baggy. 2. awkward, clumsy.

мешкови́н|а, ы, *f.* sacking, hessian.

ме́шкот|ный (~ен, ~на), *adj.* (*coll.*) 1. sluggish, slow. 2. long (*of a job*).

меш|о́к, ка́, *m.* 1. bag; sack; вещево́й м. haversack, knapsack; kit-bag; ка́менный м. (*hist.; rhet.*) prison cell; огнево́й м. (*mil.*) fire pocket. 2. (*dry measure*) bag (= 3 *poods*). 3. (*fig., coll.*) clumsy fellow.

мешо́ч|ек, ка, *m.* *dim. of* мешо́к; sac, follicle, utricle.

меща́н|и́н, и́на, *pl.* ~е, ~, *m.* 1. (*hist.*) petty bourgeois (*member of urban lower middle class comprising small traders, craftsmen, junior officials, etc.*). 2. (*fig.*) Philistine.

меща́н|ский, *adj. of* ~и́н; (*fig.*) Philistine; bourgeois, vulgar, narrow-minded.

меща́нств|о, а, *n.* 1. (*collect.*) petty bourgeoisie, lower middle class. 2. (*fig.*) philistinism, vulgarity, narrow-mindedness.

мзд|а, ы, *no pl., f.* (*arch., now joc.*) recompense, payment (*iron.* = bribe).

мздо́им|ец, ца, *m.* (*obs.*) bribe-taker.

мздо́имств|о, а, *n.* (*obs.*) bribery.

ми, *indecl., n.* (*mus.*) mi; E.

миа́зм|ы, ~, *sing.* (*rare*) ~а, ~ы, *f.* miasma.

миг¹, а, *m.* moment, instant.

миг², а, *m.* (*abbr. of* Микоя́н и Гуре́вич, *designers' names*) Mig (*Soviet fighter aircraft*).

мига́тель|ный, *adj.* ~ая перепо́нка nict(i-t)ating membrane.

мига́ни|е, я, *n.* 1. winking; twinkling. 2. blinking.

миг|а́ть, а́ю, *impf.* (*of* ~ну́ть) 1. to blink. 2. (+*d.*) to wink (at); (*fig.*) to wink, twinkle.

миг|ну́ть, ну́, нёшь, *inst. pf. of* ~а́ть.

ми́гом, *adv.* (*coll.*) in a flash; in a jiffy.

миграцио́нный, *adj. of* мигра́ция.

мигра́ци|я, и, *f.* migration.

мигре́н|ь, и, *f.* migraine.

мигри́р|овать, ую, *impf.* to migrate.

мид, а, *m.* (*abbr. of* Министе́рство ино-
стра́нных дел) Ministry of Foreign Affairs,
Foreign Office.

ми́дел|ь, я, *m.* (*naut.*) midship section.

мизансце́н|а, ы, *f.* (*theatr.*) mise en scène.

мизантро́п, а, *m.* misanthrope.

мизантропи́ческий, *adj.* misanthropic.

мизантро́пи|я, и, *f.* misanthropy.

мизги́р|ь, я́, *m.* (*dial.*) spider.

мизере́ре, *indecl., n.* (*eccl.*) miserere.

мизе́р|ный (~ен, ~на), *adj.* scanty,
wretched.

мизи́н|ец, ца, *m.* little finger; little toe; он
не сто́ит ва́шего ~ца (*fig.*) he is not a patch
on you.

мизи́н|цевый, *adj. of* ~ец.

мика́до, *indecl., m.* mikado.

миколо́ги|я, и, *f.* mycology.

микроавто́бус, а, *m.* minibus.

микроампе́р, а, *m.* (*electr.*) microampere.

микро́б, а, *m.* microbe.

микробио́лог, а, *m.* microbiologist.

микробиоло́ги|я, и, *f.* microbiology.

микроко́кк, а, *m.* (*biol., med.*) micrococcus.

микроко́см, а, *m.* microcosm.

микро́метр, а, *m.* micrometer.

микрометри́ческий, *adj.* micrometrical.

микроме́три|я, и, *f.* micrometry.

микро́н, а, *m.* (*phys.*) micron.

микроорганизм, а, *m.* (*biol.*) micro-organism.

микрорайо́н, а, *m.* 1. mikroraion (*administrative subdivision of urban raion in U.S.S.R.*).
2. (*town planning*) neighbourhood unit; м.
шко́лы school catchment area.

микроско́п, а, *m.* microscope.

микроскопи́ческий, *adj.* microscopic.

микроскопи́ч|ный (~ен, ~на), *adj.* =
~еский.

микроскопи́|я, и, *f.* microscopy.

микроспо́р|а, ы, *f.* (*bot.*) microspore.

микрострукту́р|а, ы, *f.* microstructure.

микрофо́н, а, *m.* microphone.

микроцефа́л, а, *m.* (*med.*) microcephalic.

микроцефа́ли|я, и, *f.* (*med.*) microcephaly.

миксту́р|а, ы, *f.* (liquid) medicine, mixture.

мила́ш|а, и, *f.* (*coll.*) darling.

мила́шк|а, и, *f.* 1. (*coll.*) pretty girl; nice
girl. 2. (*vulg.*) sweetheart, tart.

ми́ленький, *adj.* 1. pretty; nice; sweet;
dear. 2. (*as form of address*) darling.

милитариза́ци|я, и, *f.* militarization.

милитари́зм, а, *m.* militarism.

милитариз|ова́ть, у́ю, *impf. and pf.* to
militarize.

милитари́ст, а, *m.* militarist.

милитаристи́ческий, *adj.* militaristic.

милиционе́р, а, *m.* 1. militia-man. 2.
policeman (*in the U.S.S.R.*).

мили́ци|я, и, *f.* militia (*in U.S.S.R.*, civil
force, corresponding to police force in other countries, responsible for maintaining public order*).

миллиампе́р, а, *m.* (*electr.*) milliampere.

миллиа́рд, а, *m.* milliard; (*in U.S. usage*)
billion.

миллиарде́р, а, *m.* multi-millionaire.

миллиа́рдный, *adj.* 1. milliardth; (*in U.S.
usage*) billionth. 2. worth a milliard.

миллиба́р, а, *m.* (*meteor.*) millibar.

милливо́льт, а, *m.* (*electr.*) millivolt.

миллигра́мм, а, *m.* milligramme.

миллиме́тр, а, *m.* millimetre.

миллио́н, а, *m.* million.

миллионе́р, а, *m.* 1. millionaire. 2. (*fig.*)
one who has accomplished something
which can be estimated in millions of units;
лётчик-м. pilot who has flown over a
million kilometres.

миллио́нный, *adj.* 1. millionth. 2. worth
millions. 3. million strong.

ми́л|овать, ую, *impf.* (*of* по~) (*obs.*) to par-
don, spare.

мил|ова́ть, у́ю, *impf.* (*folk poet.*) to caress,
fondle.

мил|ова́ться, у́юсь, *impf.* (*folk poet.*) to ex-
change caresses.

милови́д|ный (~ен, ~на), *adj.* pretty, nice-
-looking.

мило́рд, а, *m.* (mi)lord.

милосе́рди|е, я, *n.* mercy, charity; сестра́
~я (*obs.*) nurse.

милосе́рд|ный (~ен, ~на), *adj.* merciful,
charitable.

ми́лостив|ый (~, ~а), *adj.* (*obs.*) gracious,
kind; м. госуда́рь (*form of address*) sir; (*in
letters*) (Dear) Sir; ~ая госуда́рыня madam;
(*in letters*) (Dear) Madam.

ми́лостын|я, и, *no pl., f.* alms.

ми́лост|ь, и, *f.* 1. favour, grace; *pl.* favours;
~и про́сим! (*coll.*) welcome!; you are
always welcome!; сде́лай(те) м. (*obs.*) be
so kind, be so good; скажи́(те) на м.! (*coll.,
iron.*) you don't say (so)! 2. mercy; charity;
сда́ться на м. победи́теля to surrender at
discretion; из ~и out of charity. 3. (*form
of address to superior*) ва́ша м. your worship.

ми́лочк|а, и, *f.* (*coll.*) dear, darling.

ми́л|ый (~, ~а́, ~о), *adj.* 1. nice, sweet;
lovable; э́то о́чень ~о с ва́шей стороны́ it
is very nice of you. 2. dear; *as noun* м.,
~ого, *m.*; ~ая, ~ой, *f.* dear, darling.

мильдью, *indecl., n.* (*agric.*) mildew.

ми́л|я, и, *f.* mile.

мим, а, *m.* (*theatr.*) mime.

ми́мик|а, и, *f.* mimicry.

мимикри́|я, и, *f.* (*biol.*) mimicry, mimesis.
мими́ст, а, *m.* mimic.
мими́ческий, *adj.* mimic.
ми́мо, *adv. and prep.*+*g.* by, past; пройти́, прое́хать м. to pass by, go past; м.! miss(ed)!;
мимое́здом, *adv.* (*coll.*) in passing.
мимо́з|а, ы, *f.* (*bot.*) mimosa.
мимолёт|ный (~ен, ~на), *adj.* fleeting, transient.
мимохо́дом, *adv.* in passing; м. упомяну́ть (*fig., coll.*) to mention in passing.
ми́н|а¹, ы, *f.* 1. (*mil., naut.*) mine. 2. (*mil.*) mortar shell, bomb.
ми́н|а², ы, *f.* mien, expression; сде́лать весёлую (хоро́шую) ~у при плохо́й игре́ to put a brave face on a sorry business.
минаре́т, а, *m.* minaret.
миндалеви́дн|ый, *adj.* almond-shaped; ~ая железа́ (*anat.*) tonsil.
минда́лин|а, ы, *f.* 1. almond. 2. (*anat.*) tonsil.
минда́л|ь, я́, *m.* 1. almond-tree. 2. (*collect.*) almonds.
минда́льнича|ть, ю, *impf.* (c+*i.*; *coll.*) to sentimentalize (over), be excessively soft (towards).
минда́ль|ный, *adj. of* ~.
минёр, а, *m.* (*mil.*) mine-layer.
минера́л, а, *m.* mineral.
минерализа́ци|я, и, *f.* mineralization.
минералоги́ческий, *adj.* mineralogical.
минерало́ги|я, и, *f.* mineralogy.
минера́льный, *adj.* mineral.
минздра́в, а, *m.* (*abbr. of* Министе́рство здравоохране́ния) Ministry of Health.
миниатю́р|а, ы, *f.* (*art*) miniature.
миниатюри́ст, а, *m.* miniature-painter, miniaturist.
миниатю́р|ный (~ен, ~на), *adj.* 1. *adj. of* ~а. 2. (*fig.*) diminutive, tiny, dainty.
минима́л|ьный (~ен, ~ьна), *adj.* minimum.
ми́нимум, а, *m.* 1. minimum; м. за́работной пла́ты minimum wage; прожи́точный м. living wage; техни́ческий м. essential technical qualifications. 2. (*as adv.*) at the least, at the minimum.
мини́р|овать, ую, *impf. and pf.* (*mil., naut.*) to mine.
министе́рский, *adj.* ministerial.
министе́рств|о, а, *n.* (*polit.*) ministry.
мини́стр, а, *m.* (*polit.*) minister; м.-президе́нт, пре́мьер-м. Prime Minister, premier.
миннези́нгер, а, *m.* (*hist., lit.*) minnesinger.
ми́нн|ый, *adj.* (*mil.*) mine; ~ое загражде́ние minefield.
мин|ова́ть, у́ю, *impf. and pf.* 1. to pass (by); ~у́я подро́бности omitting details. 2. (*pf. only*) to be over, be past; опа́сность ~ова́ла the danger is past. 3. (*only with* не+*g.*) to

escape; не м. тебе́ тюрьмы́ you cannot escape being sent to prison.
мино́г|а, и, *f.* (*zool.*) lamprey.
миноиска́тел|ь¹, я, *m.* (*mil.*) mine-detector (*apparatus*).
миноиска́тел|ь², я, *m.* (*mil.*) sapper.
миномёт, а, *m.* (*mil.*) mortar; гварде́йский м. multi-rail rocket launcher.
миномёт|ный, *adj. of* ~.
миномётчик, а, *m.* (*mil.*) mortar man.
миноно́с|ец, ца, *m.* (*naut.*) torpedo-boat; эска́дренный м. destroyer.
мино́р, а, *m.* 1. (*mus.*) minor key. 2. (*fig.*) blues; быть в ~е to have the blues, be in the dumps.
мино́рн|ый, *adj.* 1. (*mus.*) minor. 2. (*fig.*) gloomy, depressed; быть в ~ом настрое́нии to have the blues, be in the dumps.
мину́вш|ий, *adj.* past; *as noun* ~ее, ~его, *n.* the past.
ми́нус, а, *m.* 1. (*math.*) minus. 2. (*fig., coll.*) defect, shortcoming.
ми́нусовый, *adj.* (*electr.*) negative.
мину́т|а, ы, *f.* (*in var. senses*) minute.
мину́т|ный, *adj.* 1. *adj. of* ~а; ~ная стре́лка minute-hand. 2. momentary; transient, ephemeral; ~ная встре́ча brief encounter.
мин|у́ть, ~ешь, *pf.* 1. (*past* ~у́л, ~у́ла) = минова́ть. 2. (*past* ~ул, ~ула) (+*d.*) to pass (*only in expressions of age*); ему́ ~у́ло два́дцать лет he has turned twenty.
миньо́н, а, *m.* (*typ.*) minion (7-point type).
миокарди́т, а, *m.* (*med.*) myocarditis.
миоло́г, а, *m.* myologist.
миоло́ги|я, и, *f.* myology.
миопи́|я, и, *f.* (*med.*) myopia.
миоце́н, а, *m.* miocene.
мир¹, а, *m.* peace; почётный м. peace with honour; заключи́ть м. to make peace; м. вам! peace be with you!; иди́те с ~ом go in peace.
мир², а, *pl.* ~ы́, *m.* world (*also fig.*); universe; не от ~а сего́ (*coll.*) other-worldly, not of this world; в ~у́ in the world (*as opp. to in a monastery*); ходи́ть по ~у to beg, live by begging; пусти́ть по ~у to ruin utterly; на ~у́ и смерть красна́ (*prov.*) company in distress makes trouble less.
мир³, а, *m.* (*hist.*) mir (*Russian village community*); всем ~ом all together; с ~у по ни́тке го́лому руба́шка (*prov.*) every little helps.
мирабе́л|ь, и, *f.* mirabelle plum.
мира́ж, а, *m.* mirage (*also fig.*); optical illusion.
мира́кл|ь, я, *m.* (*lit., theatr.*) miracle-play.
мирво́л|ить, ю, ишь, *impf.* (+*d.*; *coll.*) to connive (at); to be over-indulgent (towards).
мир|и́ть, ю, и́шь, *impf.* 1. (*pf.* по~) to reconcile. 2. (*pf.* при~) (c+*i.*) to reconcile

(to); больша́я зарпла́та ~и́ла его́ с неприя́тными усло́виями рабо́ты high wages reconciled him to unpleasant working conditions.

мир|и́ться, ю́сь, и́шься, *impf.* (c+*i*.) **1.** (*pf.* по~) to be reconciled (with), make it up (with). **2.** (*pf.* при~) to reconcile oneself (to); м. со свои́м положе́нием to accept the situation.

ми́р|ный (~ен, ~на), *adj.* **1.** *adj. of* ~¹; **2.** peaceful; peaceable; ~ное сосуществова́ние (*polit.*) peaceful co-existence.

мир|о, а, *n.* (*eccl.*) chrism; одни́м ~ом ма́заны (*fig., joc.*) tarred with the same brush.

миров|а́я, о́й, *f.* peaceful settlement; amicable agreement.

мировоззре́ни|е, я, *n.* (world-)outlook, Weltanschauung; (one's) philosophy.

мир|ово́й¹, *adj. of* ~²; (*coll., joc.*) first-rate, first-class.

мирово́й², *adj.* (*obs.*) conciliatory; (*hist.*) м. посре́дник arbitrator; м. судья́ Justice of the Peace.

мирое́д, а, *m.* (*obs., coll.*) extortioner, bloodsucker (*among peasants*).

мироздани́|е, я, *n.* the universe.

миролюби́вост|ь, и, *f.* peaceable disposition.

миролюби́в|ый (~, ~а), *adj.* peaceable, pacific.

миролюби|е, я, *n.* peaceableness.

мироощуще́ни|е, я, *n.* attitude, disposition.

миропома́зани|е, я, *n.* (*eccl.*) anointing.

миропонима́ни|е, я, *n.* = мировоззре́ние.

миросозерца́ни|е, я, *n.* = мировоззре́ние.

миротво́р|ец, ца, *m.* peace-maker.

ми́рр|а, ы, *f.* (*bot.*) myrrh.

мирско́й¹, *adj.* secular, lay; mundane, worldly.

мир|ско́й², *adj. of* ~³; ~ска́я схо́дка peasants' meeting.

мирт, а, *m.* (*bot.*) myrtle.

ми́рт|овый, *adj. of* ~.

миря́н|ин, ина, *pl.* ~е, ~, *m.* (*obs.*) layman (*as opp. to clergy*).

ми́ск|а, и, *f.* basin, bowl.

мисс, *indecl., f.* Miss.

миссионе́р, а, *m.* missionary.

миссионе́р|ский, *adj. of* ~.

миссионе́рств|о, а, *n.* missionary work.

ми́ссис, *indecl., n.* missis, Mrs.

ми́сси|я, и, *f.* **1.** (*in var. senses*) mission. **2.** legation.

ми́стер, а, *m.* mister, Mr.

мисте́ри|я, и, *f.* **1.** (*rel.*) mystery; элевси́нские ~и the Eleusinian mysteries. **2.** (*hist., theatr.*) mystery, miracle-play.

ми́стик, а, *m.* mystic.

ми́стик|а, и, *f.* mysticism.

мистифика́тор, а, *m.* hoaxer.

мистифика́ци|я, и, *f.* hoax, leg-pull.

мистифици́р|овать, ую, *impf. and pf.* to hoax, mystify.

мистици́зм, а, *m.* mysticism.

мисти́ческий, *adj.* mystic(al).

мистра́л|ь, я, *m.* mistral (*wind*).

мите́н|ки, ок, *sing.* ~ка, ~ки, *f.* mittens.

ми́тинг, а, *m.* (political) mass-meeting.

митинг|ова́ть, у́ю, *impf.* (*coll.*) **1.** to hold a mass-meeting (about). **2.** (*pejor.*) to discuss endlessly.

митинго́вый, *adj. of* ми́тинг.

митка́л|евый, *adj. of* ~ь.

митка́л|ь, я́, *m.* (*text.*) calico.

ми́тр|а, ы, *f.* (*eccl.*) mitre.

митрале́з|а, ы, *f.* (*mil.*) mitrailleuse.

митрополи́т, а, *m.* (*eccl.*) metropolitan.

митрополи́|чий, *adj. of* ~т.

митрополи́|я, и, *f.* (*eccl.*) metropolitan see.

ми́ттел|ь, я, *m.* (*typ.*) English (*14-point type*).

миф, а, *m.* myth (*also fig.*).

мифи́ческий, *adj.* mythic(al).

мифологи́ческий, *adj.* mythological.

мифоло́ги|я, и, *f.* mythology.

мице́ли|й, я, *m.* (*bot.*) mycelium.

ми́чман, а, *pl.* (*in naval usage*) ~а́, ~о́в, *m.* (*naut.*) **1.** (*in Soviet Navy*) warrant officer. **2.** (*in Imperial Russian Navy*) midshipman.

ми́чман|ский, *adj. of* ~.

мише́н|ь, и, *f.* target (*also fig.*).

ми́шк|а, и, *m.* (*dim. of* Михаи́л) **1.** (*pet-name for*) bear. **2.** Teddy bear.

мишур|а́, ы́, *f.* **1.** tinsel. **2.** (*fig.*) trumpery.

мишу́рный, *adj.* tinsel, trumpery, tawdry; (*also fig.*).

миэли́т, а, *m.* (*med.*) myelitis.

младе́н|ец, ца, *m.* baby, infant.

младе́нческий, *adj.* infantile.

младе́нчеств|о, а, *n.* infancy, babyhood.

млад|о́й (~, ~а́, ~о), *adj.* (*arch. or poet.*) young; стар и ~ one and all (*without respect of age*).

младопи́сьменный, *adj.* м. язы́к language having newly acquired a written form.

младост|ь, и, *f.* (*arch. or poet.*) youth.

мла́дший, *adj.* (*comp. and superl. of* молодо́й) **1.** younger. **2.** the youngest. **3.** junior; м. кома́ндный соста́в non-commissioned officers; м. офице́рский соста́в junior officers, subaltern officers; м. лейтена́нт second lieutenant (*see also* лейтена́нт).

млекопита́ющ|ее, его, *n.* (*zool.*) mammal.

мле|ть, ю, *impf.* **1.** (*obs.*) to grow numb. **2.** (от) to be overcome (*with delight, with fright, etc.*).

мле́чный, *adj.* milk; lactic; м. сок (*bot.*) latex; (*physiol.*) chyle; М. путь (*astron.*) the Milky Way, the Galaxy.

мне, *d. and p. of* я.

мнемони́ческий, *adj.* mnemonic.

мне́ни|е, я, *n.* opinion.

мнимоуме́рший, *adj.* apparently dead.

мни́м|ый, *adj.* 1. imaginary (*also math.*); ~ая величина́ imaginary quantity. 2. sham, pretended; м. больно́й hypochondriac.

мни́тельност|ь, и, *f.* 1. hypochondria. 2. mistrustfulness, suspiciousness.

мни́тел|ьный (~ен, ~ьна), *adj.* 1. hypochondriac; valetudinarian. 2. mistrustful, suspicious.

мн|и́ть, ю, ишь, *impf.* 1. (*obs.*) to think, imagine. 2. м. мно́го о себе́ to think much of oneself.

мни́т|ься, ~ся, *impf.* (*impers.*; *obs. or poet.*) ~ся it seems, methinks.

мно́г|ие, их, *adj. and noun* many; во ~их отноше́ниях in many respects.

мно́го, *adv.* (+*g.*) much; many; a lot (of); м. вре́мени much time; м. лет many years; о́чень м. знать to know a great deal; м. лу́чше much better; ни м., ни ма́ло (*coll.*) neither more nor less.

много- many-, poly-, multi-.

многоа́томный, *adj.* (*phys.*) polyatomic.

многобо́жи|е, я, *n.* polytheism.

многобра́чи|е, я, *n.* polygamy.

многобра́ч|ный (~ен, ~на), *adj.* polygamous.

многова́то, *adv.* (*coll.*) a bit too much, rather much (many).

многовеково́й, *adj.* centuries-old.

многовла́сти|е, я, *n.* = многонача́лие.

многово́д|ный (~ен, ~на), *adj.* (*of rivers, etc.*) full, having high water-level.

многово́дь|е, я, *n.* 1. fulness, high water-level. 2. time of high water-levels.

многоговоря́щий, *adj.* revealing, suggestive.

многогра́нник, а, *m.* (*math.*) polyhedron.

многогра́нный, *adj.* (*math.*) polyhedral; (*fig.*) many-sided.

многоде́тност|ь, и, *f.* possession of many children.

многоде́т|ный (~ен, ~на), *adj.* having many children.

мно́г|ое, ого, *n.* much, a great deal; во ~ом in many respects.

многожён|ец, ца, *m.* polygamist.

многожёнств|о, а, *n.* polygamy.

многожи́льный, *adj.* (*tech.*) multiple.

многоземе́л|ьный (~ен, ~ьна), *adj.* possessing, owning much land; ~ьное хозя́йство large-scale cultivation.

многозначи́тельност|ь, и, *f.* significance.

многозначи́тел|ьный (~ен, ~ьна), *adj.* significant.

многозна́ч|ный (~ен, ~на), *adj.* 1. (*math.*)

expressed by several figures. 2. (*ling.*) polysemantic; ~ое сло́во polyseme.

многокаска́дный, *adj.* (*radio*) multistage.

многокле́точный, *adj.* (*biol.*) multi-cellular.

многокра́сочный, *adj.* polychromatic, many-coloured.

многокра́т|ный, *adj.* 1. repeated, re-iterated; multiple. 2. (*gram.*) frequentative, iterative.

многола́мповый, *adj.* multi-valve.

многоле́ти|е, я, *n.* expression of wishes for long life.

многоле́тний, *adj.* 1. lasting *or* living many years; of many years' standing. 2. (*bot.*) perennial.

многоле́тник, а, *m.* (*bot.*) perennial.

многоли́кий, *adj.* many-sided.

многолю́дност|ь, и, *f.* populousness; size (*of meeting, etc.*).

многолю́д|ный (~ен, ~на), *adj.* populous; crowded.

многолю́дств|о, а, *n.* throng.

многомиллио́нн|ый, *adj.* of many millions.

многому́жи|е, я, *n.* polyandry.

многонациона́л|ьный (~ен, ~ьна), *adj.* multi-national.

многонача́ли|е, я, *n.* multiple authority (*absence of clearly-defined spheres of authority*).

многоно́жк|а, и, *f.* (*zool.*) myriapod.

многообеща́ющий, *adj.* 1. promising, hopeful. 2. significant.

многообра́зи|е, я, *n.* variety, diversity.

многообра́з|ный (~ен, ~на), *adj.* varied, diverse.

многопо́ль|е, я, *n.* (*agric.*) crop-rotation system involving seven or eight fields.

многопо́ль|ный, *adj.* of ~е.

многоречи́в|ый (~, ~а), *adj.* loquacious, verbose, prolix.

многосеме́|йный (~ен, ~йна), *adj.* having a large family.

многосло́в|ный (~ен, ~на), *adj.* verbose, prolix.

многосло́жный, *adj.* 1. complex, complicated. 2. polysyllabic.

многосло́йн|ый, *adj.* multi-layer; multi-ply; ~ая фане́ра plywood.

многостано́чник, а, *m.* workman operating a number of machines simultaneously.

многостепе́нн|ый, *adj.* many-stage; ~ые вы́боры election by several stages.

многосторо́н|ний (~ен, ~ня), *adj.* 1. (*math.*) polygonal; multilateral (*also fig.*). 2. (*fig.*) many-sided, versatile.

многострада́л|ьный (~ен, ~ьна), *adj.* suffering, unfortunate.

многоступе́нчатый, *adj.* (*tech.*) multi-stage.

многотира́жк|а, и, *f.* (*coll.*) factory newspaper; house organ.

многотира́жный, *adj.* published in large editions.

многотóмный, *adj.* in many volumes.

многотóчи|е, я, *n.* dots (...); (*typ.*) marks of omission; omission points.

многоуважáемый, *adj.* respected; (*in letters*) dear.

многоугóльник, а, *m.* (*math.*) polygon.

многоугóльный, *adj.* (*math.*) polygonal.

многофáзный, *adj.* (*electr.*) polyphase.

многоцвéтный, *adj.* 1. many-coloured, multi-coloured. 2. (*typ.*) polychromatic. 3. (*bot.*) multiflorous.

многочи́сленный, *adj.* numerous.

многочлéн, а, *m.* (*math.*) multinomial.

мнóжественност|ь, и, *f.* plurality.

мнóжественн|ый, *adj.* plural; ~ое число́ (*gram.*) plural (number).

мнóжеств|о, а, *n.* a great number, a quantity; multitude; (*math.*) set.

мнóжим|ое, ого, *n.* (*math.*) multiplicand.

мнóжитель|ь, я, *m.* multiplier, factor.

мнóж|ить, у, ишь, *impf.* 1. (*pf.* по~, у~) (*math.*) to multiply. 2. (*pf.* у~) to increase, augment.

мнóж|иться, усь, ишься, *impf.* (*of* у~) 1. to multiply, increase (*intrans.*). 2. *pass. of* ~ить.

мной, мнóю, *i. of* я.

мобилиза|цио́нный, *adj. of* ~ция.

мобилизáци|я, и, *f.* mobilization.

мобилизóванност|ь, и, *f.* complete readiness for action.

мобилизóв|анный, *p.p.p. of* ~áть; *as noun* mobilized soldier.

мобилиз|овáть, ýю, *impf. and pf.* (на+*a.*) to mobilize (for).

моби́льный *adj.* mobile.

могикáн|е, ~, *pl. only,* the Mohicans; после́дний из ~ the last of the Mohicans.

моги́л|а, ы, *f.* grave; свести́ в ~у to bring to one's grave.

моги́льник, а, *m.* (*archaeol.*) burial ground.

моги́льный, *adj.* 1. *adj. of* моги́ла. 2. sepulchral.

моги́льщик, а, *m.* grave-digger.

мо|гý, ~гут, *see* мочь.

могýч|ий (~, ~а), *adj.* mighty, powerful.

могýществен|ный (~, ~на), *adj.* powerful; potent.

могýществ|о, а, *n.* power, might.

мóд|а, ы, *f.* fashion, vogue; выходи́ть из ~ы to go out of fashion; по после́дней ~е in the latest fashion.

модáльност|ь, и, *f.* (*philos.*) modality.

модáльный, *adj.* modal.

модели́зм, а, *m.* modelling.

модели́р|овать, ую, *impf. and pf.* to model, fashion.

модéл|ь, и, *f.* (*in var. senses*) model, pattern.

модельéр, а, *m.* modeller.

модéль|ный, *adj.* 1. *adj. of* ~. 2. fashionable.

модéльщик, а, *m.* (*tech.*) modeller, pattern maker.

модерáтор, а, *m.* (*tech.*) governor.

модéрн, а, *m.* modernist style (*in art, furnishing, etc.*); *as indecl. adj.* modern.

модернизáци|я, и, *f.* modernization.

модернизи́р|овать, ую, *impf. and pf.* to modernize.

модерни́зм, а, *m.* (*art*) modernism.

модерниз|овáть, ýю, *impf. and pf.* = ~и́ровать.

модерни́ст, а, *m.* (*art*) modernist.

моди́стк|а, и, *f.* milliner, modiste.

модификáци|я, и, *f.* modification.

модифици́р|овать, ую, *impf. and pf.* to modify.

мóдник, а, *m.* (*coll.*) dandy.

мóднича|ть, ю, *impf.* (*coll.*) 1. to dress in the latest fashion, follow the fashion. 2. (*coll.*) to behave affectedly.

мóд|ный (~ен, ~нá, ~но), *adj.* 1. fashionable, stylish. 2. *adj. of* ~а; м. журнáл fashion magazine.

модули́р|овать, ую, *impf.* (*mus. and tech.*) to modulate.

мóдул|ь, я, *m.* (*math.*) modulus.

модуля́ци|я, и, *f.* (*mus. and tech.*) modulation.

мóдус, а, *m.* modus.

мóжет, *see* мочь.

можжевéловый, *adj.* juniper.

можжевéльник, а, *m.* (*bot.*) juniper.

мóжно, *pred.* (*impers.*+*inf.*) 1. it is possible; м. бы́ло э́то предви́деть it was possible to foresee it, it could have been foreseen; как м.+*comp.* as ... as possible; как м. скоре́е as soon as possible. 2. it is permissible, one may; м. идти́? may I (we) go?; м.! (*sc.* войти́) come in!

мозáик|а, и, *f.* mosaic; inlay.

мозáичный, *adj.* inlaid, mosaic, tesselated.

мозг, а, в ~ý, *pl.* ~и́, ~óв, *m.* 1. brain (*also fig.*), nerve tissue; головнóй м. brain, cerebrum; спиннóй м. spinal cord; шевели́ть ~áми (*coll.*) to use one's head. 2. (*anat.*) marrow; до ~а косте́й (*fig., coll.*) to the core.

мóзглый, *adj.* dank.

мозгля́вый, *adj.* (*coll.*) weakly, puny.

мозгови́т|ый (~, ~а), *adj.* (*coll.*) brainy.

мозговóй, *adj.* (*anat.*) cerebral; (*fig.*) brain.

мозжеч|óк, кá, *m.* (*anat.*) cerebellum.

мозж|и́ть, и́т, *impf.* (*coll.*) to ache; мозжи́т ногá my leg is aching; (*impers.*) мозжи́т нóгу my leg is aching; мозжи́т в ноге́ I've an ache in my leg.

мозоли́ст|ый (~, ~а), *adj.* callous(ed); (*fig.*) toil-hardened; ~ые рýки horny hands.

мозóл|ить, ю, ишь, *impf.* (*of* на~) to make callous; м. глазá (+*d.*; *fig., coll.*) to plague (with one's presence).

мозо́л|ь, и, *f.* corn; callus, callosity; ру́ки в ~я́х callus(ed) hands; наступи́ть кому́-н. на люби́мую м. (*fig.*, *coll.*) to tread on someone's pet corn.

мозо́ль|ный, *adj. of* ~; м. пла́стырь corn--plaster.

мой, *possessive adj.* my; mine; ты зна́ешь лу́чше моего́ (*coll.*) you know better than I; *as noun* мой, мои́х my people; по-мо́ему in my opinion; as I think right.

мо́йк|а, и, *f.* **1.** washing. **2.** (*tech.*) washer.

мо́кко, *indecl.,* *m.* mocha (*coffee*).

мо́к|нуть, ну, нешь, *past* ~, ~ла, *impf.* **1.** (*pf.* вы́~) to become wet, become soaked. **2.** to soak (*intrans.*).

мокри́ц|а, ы, *f.* wood-louse.

мокрова́тый, *adj.* moist, damp.

мокро́т|а, ы, *f.* (*med.*) phlegm.

мокрот|а́, ы́, *f.* humidity, moistness.

мо́кр|ый (~, ~а́, ~о) *adj.* wet, damp; soggy; ~о (*impers.*, *pred.*) it is wet; ~ая ку́рица (*coll.*) milksop; у неё глаза́ на ~ом ме́сте (*coll.*) she is easily moved to tears.

мол¹, а, *m.* mole, pier.

мол², (*contraction of* мо́лвил) he says (said), they say (said), *etc.* (*indicating reported speech*); он, м., никогда́ там не́ был he said he had never been there.

молв|а́, ы́, *f.* (*obs.*) rumour, talk; идёт м. it is rumoured, rumour has it; дурна́я м. ill repute.

мо́лв|ить, лю, ишь, *pf.* (*obs.*) to say.

молдава́н|ин, ина, *pl.* ~e, ~, *m.* Moldavian.

молдава́нк|а, и, *f.* Moldavian (woman).

молдав|а́нский = ~ский.

молда́вский, *adj.* Moldavian.

моле́б|ен, на, *m.* (*eccl.*) service; public prayer.

моле́бстви|е, я, *n.* = моле́бен.

моле́кул|а, ы, *f.* (*phys.*) molecule.

молекуля́рный, *adj.* molecular.

моле́л|ьня, ьни, *g. pl.* ~ен, *f.* chapel, meeting-house (*of rel. sects*).

моле́ни|е, я, *n.* **1.** praying. **2.** entreaty, supplication.

молески́н, а, *m.* (*text.*) moleskin.

молибде́н, а, *m.* (*chem.*) molybdenum.

молибде́н|овый, *adj. of* ~.

моли́тв|а, ы, *f.* prayer.

моли́твенник, а, *m.* prayer-book.

моли́тв|енный, *adj. of* ~a.

мол|и́ть, ю́, ~ишь, *impf.* (*a. and* о+*p.*) to pray (for), entreat (for), supplicate (for), beseech; ~ю́ вас о по́мощи I beg you to help me.

мол|и́ться, ю́сь, ~ишься, *impf.* **1.** (*pf.* по~; о+*p.*) to pray (for), offer prayers (for); он ~ится Бо́гу he is saying his prayers. **2.** (*fig.*; на+*a.*) to idolize.

мо́лкн|уть, у, ешь, *impf.* (*poet.*) to fall silent.

моллю́ск, а, *m.* mollusc; shell-fish.

молниено́сно, *adv.* with lightning speed, like lightning.

молниено́с|ный (~ен, ~на), *adj.* (quick as) lightning; ~ная война́ blitzkrieg.

молниеотво́д, а, *m.* lightning-conductor.

молни́р|овать, ую, *impf. and pf.* to inform by express telegram.

мо́лни|я, и, *f.* **1.** lightning. **2.** (телегра́м-ма-)м. express telegram. **3.** (застёжка-)м. zip-fastener.

молодёж|ный, *adj. of* ~ь.

молодёж|ь, и, *f.* (*collect.*) youth; young people.

молоде́|ть, ю, ешь, *impf.* (*of* по~) to grow young again.

молод|е́ц, ца́, *m.* fine fellow; вести́ себя́ ~цо́м (*coll.*) to put up a good show; *as interj.* м.! (*coll.*) well done!

молоде́цкий, *adj.* (*coll.*) dashing, spirited.

молоде́честв|о, а, *n.* spirit, mettle, dash.

моло|ди́ть, жу́, ди́шь, *impf.* to make look younger.

моло|ди́ться, жу́сь, ди́шься, *impf.* to try to look younger than one's age.

молоди́ц|а, ы, *f.* (*dial.*) young married (peasant) woman.

молод|ка, ки, *f.* **1.** = ~и́ца. **2.** pullet.

молодня́к, а́, *m.* (*collect.*) **1.** saplings. **2.** young animals; cubs. **3.** (*coll.*) the younger generation.

молодожён|ы, ов, *sing.* ~, ~а, *m.* **1.** newly--married couple, newly-weds. **2.** (*sing.*) newly-married man.

молод|о́й (мо́лод, ~а́, мо́лодо), *adj.* **1.** young; youthful (*also of inanimate objects*); м. задо́р youthful hotheadedness; м. карто́фель new potatoes; м. ме́сяц new moon; мо́лодо-зе́лено! (*iron.*, *of young or inexperienced person*) he has a lot to learn! **2.** *as noun* (*coll.*) м., ~о́го, *m.* bridegroom; ~а́я, ~о́й, *f.* bride; ~ы́е, ~ы́х newly-married couple, newly-weds.

мо́лодост|ь, и, *f.* youth; youthfulness.

молоду́х|а, и, *f.* (*dial.*) = молоди́ца.

молодцева́т|ый (~, ~а), *adj.* dashing, sprightly.

моло́дчик, а, *m.* (*coll.*) **1.** rogue, rascal. **2.** (*pejor.*) lackey, myrmidon.

молодчи́н|а, ы, *m.* (*coll.*) fine fellow; *as interj.* м.! well done!

моложа́вост|ь, и, *f.* youthful appearance (*for one's years*).

моложа́в|ый (~, ~а), *adj.* young-looking; име́ть м. вид to look young for one's age.

моло́|же, *comp. of* ~до́й.

моло́зив|о, а, *no pl.,* *n.* colostrum; (*of cow*) beestings.

моло́к|и, ~, *no sing.* soft roe, milt.

молок|о́, а́, *no pl.,* *n.* milk.

молокосо́с, а, *m.* (*coll.*) greenhorn, raw youth.

мо́лот, а, *m.* hammer; кузне́чный м. sledge-hammer.

молоти́лк|а, и, *f.* threshing-machine.

молоти́л|о, а, *n.* (*agric.*) swingle.

моло́тильщик, а, *m.* thresher.

моло|ти́ть, чу́, ~ти́шь, *impf.* (*of* с~) to thresh.

молотобо́|ец, йца, *m.* (*tech.*) hammerer; blacksmith's striker.

молот|о́к, ка́, *m.* hammer; прода́ть с ~ка́ to sell by auction.

молото́ч|ек, ка, *m.* **1.** *dim. of* молото́к. **2.** (*anat.*) malleus.

мо́лот-ры́б|а, ы, *f.* (*zool.*) hammer-head shark.

мо́лот|ый (~, ~а), *p.p.p. of* моло́ть *and adj.* ground.

моло́ть, мелю́, ме́лешь, *impf.* (*of* с~) to grind, mill; м. вздор (*fig., coll.*) to talk nonsense, talk rot.

молотьб|а́, ы́, *f.* threshing.

молоча́|й, я, *m.* (*bot.*) spurge, euphorbia.

моло́чн|ая, ой, *f.* dairy; creamery.

моло́чник¹, а, *m.* milk-jug; milk-can.

моло́чник², а, *m.* milkman.

моло́чниц|а¹, ы, *f.* milk-seller; dairy-maid.

моло́чниц|а², ы, *f.* (*med.*) thrush.

моло́чность|, и, *f.* (*agric.*) yield (*of cow*).

моло́чн|ый, *adj.* **1.** *adj. of* молоко́; м. брат foster-brother; ~ое стекло́ frosted glass; opal glass; ~ое хозя́йство dairy-farm(ing). **2.** milky; lactic; ~ая кислота́ (*chem.*) lactic acid.

мо́лча, *adv.* silently, in silence.

молчали́в|ый (~, ~а), *adj.* **1.** taciturn, silent. **2.** tacit, unspoken.

молча́льник, а, *m.* (*eccl.*) one who has taken a vow of silence.

молча́ни|е, я, *n.* silence.

молч|а́ть, у́, и́шь, *impf.* to be silent, keep silence.

молч|ко́м, *adv.* (*coll.*) = ~а.

молчо́к, *indecl.*, *m.* (*coll.*) silence; об э́том — м.! not a word of (about) this!

мол|ь¹, и, *f.* (clothes-)moth.

мол|ь², и, *f.* (*chem.*) mole (*gram molecule*).

мольб|а́, ы́, *f.* entreaty, supplication.

мольбе́рт, а, *m.* easel.

моме́нт, а, *m.* **1.** moment; instant. **2.** feature, element, factor (*of process, situation, etc.*). **3.** (*phys.*) moment; м. ине́рции moment of inertia.

момента́льно, *adv.* in a moment, instantly.

момента́льный, *adj.* instantaneous; м. сни́мок snapshot.

моме́нтами, *adv.* (*coll.*) now and then.

мона́д|а ы, *f.* (*philos.*) monad.

мона́рх, а, *m.* monarch.

монархи́зм, а, *m.* monarchism.

монархи́ст, а, *m.* monarchist.

монархи́ческ|ий, *adj.* monarchic(al).

мона́рхи|я, и, *f.* monarchy.

мона́рший, *adj. of* мона́рх.

монасты́рский, *adj.* monastic, conventual, cloistral.

монасты́р|ь, я́, *m.* monastery; (же́нский) convent; в чужо́й м. со свои́м уста́вом не су́йся (*prov.*) when in Rome do as the Romans do.

мона́х, а, *m.* monk; friar; постри́чься в ~и to take the monastic vows; жить ~ом (*fig., iron.*) to have a monkish existence.

мона́хин|я, и, *f.* nun; постри́чься в ~и to take the veil. `

мона́шенк|а, и, *f.* **1.** (*coll.*) nun. **2.** (*zool.*) praying mantis.

мона́шеский, *adj.* monastic; (*fig., joc.*) monkish.

мона́шеств|о, а, *n.* **1.** monasticism. **2.** (*collect.*) monks, regular clergy.

монго́л, а, *m.* Mongol, Mongolian.

монголове́дени|е, я, *n.* Mongolian studies.

монго́льский, *adj.* Mongolian.

моне́т|а, ы, *f.* coin; зво́нкая м. specie, hard cash; разме́нная м. change; ходя́чая м. currency; плати́ть кому́-н. той же ~ой (*fig.*) to pay someone in his own coin; приня́ть за чи́стую ~у (*fig., coll.*) to take at face value, take in good faith.

моне́тный, *adj.* monetary; м. двор mint.

моне́тчик, а, *m.* coiner.

мони́зм, а, *m.* (*philos.*) monism.

монисти́ческий, *adj.* (*philos.*) monistic.

монист|о, а, *n.* necklace.

монито́р, а, *m.* (*naut.*) monitor.

моногами|я, и, *f.* monogamy.

моногра́мм|а, ы, *f.* monogram.

монографи|я, и, *f.* monograph.

монокл|ь, я, *m.* (*single*) eye-glass, monocle.

моноко́к, а, *m.* (*aeron.*) monocoque.

монокульту́р|а, ы, *f.* (*agric.*) one-crop system, monoculture.

моноли́т, а, *m.* monolith.

моноли́тность|, и, *f.* monolithic character, solidity.

моноли́т|ный (~ен, ~на), *adj.* monolithic (*also fig.; polit.*); (*fig.*) solid.

моноло́г, а, *m.* monologue, soliloquy.

моно́м, а, *m.* (*math.*) monomial.

мономан, а, *m.* (*med.*) monomaniac.

мономани|я, и, *f.* (*med.*) monomania.

монометалли́зм, а, *m.* (*econ.*) monometallism.

монопла́н, а, *m.* monoplane.

монополиза́ци|я, и, *f.* monopolization.

монополизи́р|овать, ую, *impf. and pf.* to monopolize.

монополи́ст, а, *m.* monopolist.

монополисти́ческий, *adj.* monopolistic.

монопо́ли|я, и, *f.* (*econ. and fig.*) monopoly.

монопо́л|ьный, *adj. of* ~ия; ~ьное пра́во exclusive rights.

моноре́льсовый, *adj.* monorail.

монотеи́зм, a, *m.* monotheism.

монотеисти́ческий, *adj.* monotheistic.

моноти́п, a, *m.* (*typ.*) monotype.

моното́нный, *adj.* monotonous.

монофто́нг, a, *m.* (*ling.*) monophthong.

монохо́рд, a, *m.* (*mus.*) monochord.

монпансье́, *indecl., n.* fruit drops.

монстр, a, *m.* monster.

монта́ж, a, *m.* **1.** (*tech.*) assembling, mounting, installation. **2.** (*cinema*) montage; (*art, mus., lit.*) arrangement; м. о́перы по ра́дио arrangement of an opera for radio.

монтажёр, a, *m.* (*cinema, phot.*) montage specialist.

монта́жник, a, *m.* rigger, erector, fitter.

монта́ж|ный, *adj. of* ~; *as noun* ~ная, ~ной, *f.* (*tech.*) assembly shop; (*cinema*) clipping room.

монтёр, a, *m.* **1.** fitter. **2.** electrician.

монти́р|овать, ую, *impf.* (*of* с~) **1.** (*tech.*) to assemble, mount, fit. **2.** (*art, cinema, etc.*) to mount; to arrange.

монуме́нт, a, *m.* monument.

монумента́льный, *adj.* monumental (*also fig.*).

мопс, a, *m.* pug(-dog).

мор, a, *m.* (*obs. and coll.*) wholesale deaths, high mortality.

морализи́р|овать, ую, *impf.* to moralize.

морали́ст, a, *m.* moralist.

мора́л|ь, и, *f.* **1.** (code of) morals, ethics. **2.** (*coll.*) moralizing; чита́ть м. to moralize. **3.** moral (*of a story, etc.*).

мора́льный, *adj.* (*in var. senses*) moral; ethical.

морато́ри|й, я, *m.* (*leg., comm.*) moratorium.

морг¹, a, *m.* morgue, mortuary.

морг², a, *m.* (*obs.*) *land measure* = *approx.* 1¼ *acres* (*in Poland and Lithuania*).

морганати́ческий, *adj.* morganatic.

морг|а́ть, а́ю, *impf.* (*of* ~ну́ть) to blink; to wink.

морг|ну́ть, ну́, нёшь, *pf. of* ~а́ть; гла́зом не ~ну́в (*coll.*) without batting an eyelid.

мо́рд|а, ы, *f.* **1.** snout, muzzle. **2.** (*coll.; of human face*) mug.

морда́ст|ый (~, ~a), *adj.* (*coll.*) **1.** with a large muzzle. **2.** (*of people*) with a big, fat face.

мордв|а́, ы́, *f.* (*collect.*) the Mordva, the Mordvinians.

мордви́н, a, *m.* Mordvinian.

мордви́н|ка, ки, *f. of* ~.

мордо́вский, *adj.* Mordvinian.

мо́р|е, я, *pl.* ~я́, ~е́й, *n.* sea; за́ ~ем oversea(s); из-за ~я from overseas; на́ м. at sea; у ~я by the sea; ему́ м. по коле́но (*coll.*) he doesn't care a damn.

море́н|а, ы, *f.* (*geol.*) moraine.

море́н|ный, *adj. of* ~a.

морёный, *adj.* (*of wood*) water-seasoned.

морепла́вани|е, я, *n.* navigation, seafaring.

морепла́вател|ь, я, *m.* navigator, seafarer.

морепла́вательный, *adj.* nautical, navigational.

морехо́д, a, *m.* sea-farer.

морехо́дност|ь, и, *f.* seaworthiness.

морехо́дный, *adj.* nautical.

морехо́дств|о, a, *n.* (*obs.*) navigation.

морж, а́, *m.* walrus.

моржи́х|а, и, *f. of* морж.

морж|о́вый, *adj. of* ~.

Мо́рзе, *indecl.* morse; а́збука М. Morse code.

морзи́ст, a, *m.* Morse code signaller.

морзя́нк|а, и, *f.* (*coll.*) Morse code.

мори́лк|а, и, *f.* (*tech.*) mordant.

мор|и́ть¹, ю́, и́шь, *impf.* **1.** (*pf.* вы́~ *and* по~) to exterminate. **2.** (*pf.* у~) to exhaust wear out; м. го́лодом to starve. **3.** (*dial.*) to quench.

мор|и́ть², ю́, и́шь, *impf.* to stain (*wood*); м. дуб to fume oak.

морко́вк|а, и, *f.* (*coll.*) a carrot.

морко́в|ный, *adj. of* ~ь.

морко́в|ь, и, *f.* carrots.

мормо́н, a, *m.* (*rel.*) Mormon.

моров|о́й, *adj.* ~о́е пове́трие, ~а́я я́зва plague, pestilence.

моро́жен|ое, ого, *n.* ice(-cream).

моро́женщик, a, *m.* ice-cream vendor.

моро́женщи|ца, ы, *f. of* ~к.

моро́жен|ый, *adj.* frozen, chilled; ~ое мя́со chilled meat.

моро́з, a, *m.* **1.** frost; у меня́ м. по ко́же подира́ет (пошёл) it makes (made) my flesh creep. **2.** (*usually in pl.*) intensely cold weather.

морози́льник, a, *m.* deep-freezer.

морози́льщик, a, *m.* (*coll.*) refrigerator ship.

моро́|зить, жу, зишь, *impf.* (*of* по~) **1.** to freeze, congeal. **2.** *impers.* ~зит it is freezing.

моро́зн|ый, *adj.* frosty; ~о (*impers., pred.*) it is freezing.

морозосто́йкий, *adj.* (*bot.*) frost-resisting.

морозоусто́йчив|ый (~, ~a), *adj.* = морозосто́йкий.

моро́к|а, и, *f.* (*coll., fig.*) darkness, confusion; с ним одна́ м. you can get no sense out of him.

морос|и́ть, и́т, *impf.* to drizzle.

моро́ч|ить, у, ишь, *impf.* (*of* об~) (*coll.*) to fool, pull the wool over the eyes of; м. го́лову кому́-н. to take someone in.

моро́шк|а, и, *f.* cloudberry (*Rubus chamaimorus*).

морс, а, *m.* fruit drink.

морск|о́й, *adj.* **1.** sea; maritime; marine, nautical; м. волк (*coll.*) old salt, sea-dog; ~а́я звезда́ starfish; м. ёж (*zool.*) sea-urchin, echinus; ~а́я игла́ needle-fish, pipe-fish; ~а́я капу́ста (*bot.*) sea-kale; м. конёк (*zool.*) sea-horse, hippocamp; ~а́я пе́нка (*min.*) meerschaum; м. разбо́йник pirate; ~а́я сви́нка guinea-pig; ~а́я свинья́ porpoise. **2.** naval; ~а́я пехо́та marines; м. флот navy, fleet.

морти́р|а, ы, *f.* (*mil.*) mortar.

морти́р|ный, *adj. of* ~а.

морфе́м|а, ы, *f.* (*ling.*) morpheme.

мо́рфи|й, я, *m.* (*pharm.*) morphia, morphine.

морфини́зм, а, *m.* addiction to morphine.

морфини́ст, а, *m.* morphine addict.

морфологи́ческий, *adj.* morphological.

морфоло́ги|я, и, *f.* morphology.

морщи́н|а, ы, *f.* wrinkle; crease.

морщи́нист|ый (~, ~а), *adj.* wrinkled, lined; creased.

мо́рщ|ить, у, ишь, *impf.* **1.** (*pf.* на~) м. лоб to knit one's brow. **2.** (*pf.* с~) to wrinkle, pucker; м. гу́бы to purse one's lips.

морщ|и́ть, и́т, *impf.* to crease, ruck up (*intrans.*).

мо́рщ|иться, усь, ишься, *impf.* **1.** (*pf.* на~) to knit one's brow. **2.** (*pf.* по~ *and* с~) to make a wry face, wince. **3.** (*pf.* с~) to crease, wrinkle.

моря́к, а́, *m.* sailor.

москáл|ь, я́, *m.* (*obs., pejor.*) Muscovite.

москатéл|ь, и, *f.* (*collect.*) dry-salter's wares (*paints, oil, gum, etc.*).

москатéль|ный, *adj. of* ~; ~ная торго́вля dry-saltery.

москатéльщик, а, *m.* dry-salter.

москвитя́н|ин, ина, *pl.* ~е, *m.* (*obs.*) Muscovite.

москви́ч, á, *m.* **1.** Muscovite, inhabitant of Moscow. **2.** Moskvich (*trade name of a Soviet-made motor-car*).

моски́т, а, *m.* mosquito.

моски́т|ный, *adj. of* ~; ~ная сéтка mosquito net.

москóвк|а, и, *f.* (*orn.*) coal tit.

москóвск|ий, *adj.* (of) Moscow; ~ая Русь (*hist.*) Muscovy.

мост, ~á, о ~е, на ~ý, *pl.* ~ы́, *m.* **1.** bridge. **2.** (*tech.*) shaft.

мóстик, а, *m.* **1.** *dim. of* мост. **2.** капита́нский м. (*naut.*) (*captain's*) bridge.

мости́льщик, а, *m.* paviour.

мо|сти́ть, щу́, сти́шь, *impf.* **1.** (*pf.* вы́~, за~) to pave. **2.** (*pf.* на~) to lay (*a floor*).

мостк|и́, óв, *no sing.* **1.** planked footway. **2.** wooden platform (*at edge of stream, on scaffolding*).

мостов|áя, óй, *f.* road(way), carriage way.

мостови́к, á, *m.* bridge-building specialist.

мост|ово́й, *adj. of* ~.

мóськ|а, и, *f.* (*coll.*) pug-dog.

мот, а, *m.* prodigal, spendthrift.

мотáльный, *adj.* (*tech.*) winding.

мот|áть[1], áю, *impf.* **1.** (*pf.* за~, на~) to wind, reel; м. себé что-н. на ус (*fig., coll.*) to make a mental note of something. **2.** (*pf.* ~ну́ть) (+*i.*; *coll.*) to shake (*head, etc.*).

мотá|ть[2], ю, *impf.* (*of* про~) (*coll.*) to squander.

мотá|ться[1], ется, *impf.* (*coll.*) to dangle.

мотá|ться[2], юсь, *impf.* (*coll.*) to rush about; м. пó свету to knock about the world.

моти́в[1], а, *m.* **1.** motive. **2.** reason; привести́ ~ы в пóльзу предложéния to adduce reasons in support of an assertion.

моти́в[2], а, *m.* **1.** (*mus.*) tune. **2.** (*mus. and fig.*) motif.

мотиви́р|овать, ую, *impf. and pf.* to give reasons (for), justify.

мотивирóвк|а, и, *f.* reason(s), justification.

мот|ну́ть, ну́, нёшь, *pf. of* ~áть[1].

мото- 1. (*abbr. of* мото́рный) motor-. **2.** (*abbr. of* моторизóванный) motorized.

мотобóт, а, *m.* motor-boat.

мотови́л|о, а, *n.* (*tech.*) reel.

мотóвк|а, и, *f.* (*coll.*) *of* мот.

мотовóз, а, *m.* petrol engine (*on railways for shunting, etc.*).

мотовскóй, *adj.* wasteful, extravagant.

мотовств|ó, á, *n.* wastefulness, extravagance, prodigality.

мотогóн|ки, ок, *no sing.* motor-cycle races.

мотодрези́н|а, ы, *f.* motor trolley (*on rails*).

мотодрóм, а, *m.* motor-cycle racing track.

мот|óк, ка́, *m.* skein, hank.

мотоколя́ск|а, и, *f.* motorized wheel-chair.

мотокрóсс, а, *m.* motocross, scramble.

мотолопáт|а, ы, *f.* motor shovel.

мотомеханизи́рованный, *adj.* (*mil.*) mechanized.

мотопéд, а, *m.* moped.

мотопехóт|а, ы, *f.* motorized infantry.

мотóр, а, *m.* motor, engine; подвеснóй м. outboard engine.

моторесýрс, а, *m.* (*tech.*) life (*of an engine, etc.*).

моторизáци|я, и, *f.* motorization.

моторизóв|анный, *p.p.p. of* ~áть *and adj.* (*mil.*) motorized.

моториз|овáть, ýю, *impf. and pf.* to motorize.

мотори́ст, а, *m.* motor-mechanic.

мотóрк|а, и, *f.* (*coll.*) motor-boat.

мотóр|ный[1], *adj. of* ~; м. ваго́н front car (*of set, on electric railway or tramway, and containing power unit*); ~ная устанóвка power plant, power unit.

мотóрный[2], *adj.* (*physiol., psych.*) motor.

моторо́ллер, а, *m.* (motor-)scooter.

мотоци́кл, а, *m.* motor-cycle.

мотоцикле́т, а, *m.* = мотоци́кл.

мотоцикли́ст, а, *m.* motor-cyclist.

моты́г|а, и, *f.* hoe, mattock.

моты́ж|ить, у, ишь, *impf.* to hoe.

моты́л|ёк, ька́, *m.* butterfly, moth.

моты́л|ь¹, я́, *m.* mosquito grub (*used to feed fish in aquaria*).

моты́л|ь², я́, *m.* (*tech.*) crank.

мотылько́в|ые, ых (*bot.*) Papilionaceae.

мох, мха *and* мо́ха, о мхе *and* о мо́хе, во (на) мху́, *pl.* мхи, мхов, *m.* moss.

мохна́т|ый (~, ~а), *adj.* hairy, shaggy; ~ое полоте́нце Turkish towel.

моцио́н, а, *m.* exercise; де́лать, соверша́ть м. to take exercise.

моч|а́, и́, *f.* urine, water.

моча́л|ить, ю, ишь, *impf.* 1. to strip into fibres. 2. (*coll.*) to torment, vex.

моча́лк|а, и, *f.* loofah.

моча́л|о, а, *n.* bast.

мочеви́н|а, ы, *f.* (*chem.*) urea.

мочево́й, *adj.* urinary, uric; м. пузы́рь (*anat.*) bladder.

мочего́нный, *adj.* (*med.*) diuretic.

мочеиспуска́ни|е, я, *n.* urination.

мочеиспуска́тельный, *adj.* м. кана́л (*anat.*) urethra.

мо́ч|енный, *p.p.p. of* ~и́ть.

мо́ченый, *adj.* soaked.

мочеотделе́ни|е, я, *n.* urination.

мочеполово́й, *adj.* (*anat.*) urino-genital.

мочето́чник, а, *m.* (*anat.*) ureter.

моч|и́ть, у́, ~ишь, *impf.* (*of* на~) 1. to wet, moisten. 2. to soak; to steep, macerate; м. селёдку to souse herring.

моч|и́ться, ~ишься, *impf.* (*of* по~) (*coll.*) to urinate, make water.

мо́чк|а¹, и, *f.* soaking, macerating; retting.

мо́чк|а², и, *f.* 1. (*anat.*) lobe of the ear. 2. (*bot.*) fibril.

мочь¹, могу́, мо́жешь, мо́гут, *past* мог, могла́, *impf.* (*of* с~) to be able; мо́жет быть, быть мо́жет perhaps, maybe; мо́жет (*coll.*) = мо́жет быть; не мо́жет быть! impossible!; как живёте-мо́жете? (*coll.*) how are you? how are things with you?; не могу́ знать (*obs.*) I don't know.

моч|ь², и, *f.* (*coll.*) power, might; во всю м., изо всей ~и, что есть ~и with all one's might, with might and main; ~и нет (как) it is unendurable, unbearable; ~и нет, как хо́лодно it's so cold, I can stand it no longer.

моше́нник, а, *m.* rogue, scoundrel; swindler.

моше́ннича|ть, ю, *impf.* (*of* с~) to play the swindler.

моше́ннический, *adj.* rascally, swindling.

моше́нничеств|о, а, *n.* swindling; cheating (*at games*).

мо́шк|а, и, *f.* midge.

мошкар|а́, ы́, *f.* (*collect.*) (swarm of) midges.

мош|на́, ны́, *pl.* ~ны́, ~о́н, *f.* purse, pouch; больша́я, туга́я м. (*fig.*, *coll.*) well-filled purse; наби́ть ~ну́ (*fig.*, *coll.*) to fill one's purse.

мошо́нк|а, и, *f.* (*anat.*) scrotum.

мошо́ночный, *adj.* scrotal.

мощёни|е, я, *n.* paving.

мощённый, *p.p.p.* of мости́ть.

мощёный, *adj.* paved.

мо́щ|и, е́й, *no sing.* (*rel.*) relics; живы́е м. (*coll.*, *joc.*, *of a very thin person*) walking skeleton.

мо́щност|ь, и, *f.* power; (*tech.*) capacity, rating; output; номина́льная м. rated power, rated capacity; дви́гатель ~ью в сто лошади́ных сил a hundred horsepower engine.

мо́щ|ный (~ен, ~на́, ~но), *adj.* powerful, mighty; vigorous.

мо|щу́, сти́шь, *see* ~сти́ть.

мощ|ь, и, *f.* power, might.

мо́|ю, ешь, *see* мыть.

мо́ющ|ий, *pres. part. act. of* мыть *and adj.* detergent; ~ие сре́дства detergents.

мраз|ь, и, *no pl.*, *f.* (*coll.*) rubbish; (*pejor.*, *of human beings*) dregs, scum.

мрак, а, *m.* darkness, gloom (*also fig.*, *rhet.*); покры́то ~ом неизве́стности shrouded in mystery; у него́ м. на душе́ he is in the dumps, in a black mood.

мракобе́с, а, *m.* obscurantist.

мракобе́си|е, я, *n.* obscurantism.

мра́мор, а, *m.* marble.

мра́морный, *adj.* marble; (*fig.*) (white as) marble; marmoreal.

мра́морщик, а, *m.* marble-cutter.

мрачне́|ть, ю, *impf.* (*of* по~) to grow dark; to grow gloomy.

мра́ч|ный (~ен, ~на́, ~но), *adj.* 1. dark, sombre. 2. (*fig.*) gloomy, dismal.

мре|ть, ешь, *impf.* (*coll.*) to be dimly visible.

мсти́тел|ь, я, *m.* avenger.

мсти́тел|ьный (~ен, ~ьна), *adj.* vindictive.

мсти́ть, мщу, мсти́шь, *impf.* (*of* ото~) (+*d.* за+*a.*) to take vengeance (on for), revenge oneself (upon for); (за+*a.*) to avenge; м. врагу́ to take vengeance on one's enemy; м. за дру́га to avenge one's friend.

муа́р, а, *m.* moire, watered silk.

муа́ровый, *adj.* moiré.

мудрен|е́е, *comp. of* ~ый, *only in phrase* (*coll.*) у́тро ве́чера м. sleep on it.

мудрён|ый (~, ~а́), *adj.* (*coll.*) 1. strange, queer, odd; не ~о́, что... it is no wonder that... 2. difficult, abstruse, complicated.

мудре́ц, а́, *m.* (*rhet.*) sage, wise man; на вся́кого ~а́ дово́льно простоты́ (*prov.*) Homer sometimes nods.

мудр|и́ть, ю́, и́шь, *impf.* (*of* на~) (*coll.*) to

subtilize; to complicate matters unnecessarily; не ~и́те! don't try to be clever!

му́дрост|ь, и, *f.* wisdom; в э́том нет никако́й ~и (*coll.*) there is nothing mysterious about it.

му́дрств|овать, ую, *impf.* (*coll.*) to philosophize; to bandy sophistries.

му́др|ый (~, ~á, ~о), *adj.* wise, sage.

муж, а, *m.* 1. (*pl.* ~ья́, ~éй, ~ья́м) husband. 2. (*pl.* ~и́, ~éй, ~áм) (*obs. or rhet.*) man; госуда́рственный м. statesman; м. нау́ки man of science.

мужá|ть, ю, *impf.* (*obs.*) to grow up, reach manhood.

мужá|ться, юсь, *impf.* to take heart, take courage; ~йтесь! courage!

мужелóж|ец, ца, *m.* bugger, sodomite.

мужелóжств|о, а, *n.* buggery, sodomy.

мужен|ёк, ька́, *m.* (*coll.*) hubby.

мужеподóб|ный (~ен, ~на), *adj.* mannish; masculine.

му́ж|еский, *adj.* (*obs.*) = ~ско́й; м. род (*gram.*) masculine gender.

му́жествен|ный (~, ~на), *adj.* manly, steadfast.

му́жеств|о, а, *n.* courage, fortitude.

мужи́к, á, *m.* 1. muzhik, moujik (*Russian peasant*). 2. (*fig.*) lout, clod, bumpkin. 3. (*coll.*) man, fellow. 4. (*dial.*) husband.

мужиковáт|ый (~, ~а), *adj.* (*coll.*) loutish, boorish.

мужи́цкий, *adj. of* мужи́к 1.

му́жний, *adj.* (*coll.*) husband's.

му́жн|ин, *adj.* = ~ий.

мужск|óй, *adj.* masculine; male; м. портнóй gentlemen's tailor; м. род (*gram.*) masculine gender; ~áя шкóла boys' school.

мужчи́н|а, ы, *m.* man.

му́з|а, ы, *f.* muse.

музеевéдени|е, я, *n.* museum management studies.

музé|й, я, *m.* museum.

музéй|ный, *adj. of* ~.

му́зык|а, и, *f.* 1. music. 2. instrumental music. 3. (*coll.*) band; воéнная м. military band. 4. (*fig., coll.*) (*complicated, protracted*) business, affair; он испóртил всю ~y he upset the apple-cart.

музыкáльност|ь, и, *f.* 1. melodiousness. 2. musical talent.

музыкáл|ьный (~ен, ~ьна), *adj.* (*in var. senses*) musical.

музыкáнт, а, *m.* musician.

музыковéд, а, *m.* musicologist.

музыковéдени|е, я, *n.* musicology.

му́к|а, и, *f.* torment; torture; (*pl.*) pangs, throes; родовы́е ~и birth-pangs; хождéние по ~ам (*rel.*) Purgatory; (*fig.*) (*series of*) trials and tribulations, purgatory.

мук|á, и́, *f.* meal; flour; перемéлется —

м. бу́дет (*coll.*) it will all come right in the end.

мукомóл, а, *m.* miller.

мукомóльный, *adj.* flour-grinding.

мул, а, *m.* mule.

мулáт, а, *m.* mulatto.

мулл|á, ы́, *m.* mullah.

му́льд|а, ы, *f.* 1. (*geol.*) flexure. 2. (*tech.*) charging box, charging trough.

мультипликáтор, а, *m.* (*in var. tech. senses*) multiplier.

мультипликáци|я, и, *f.* (animated) cartoon (*film*).

мультфи́льм, а, *m.* = мультипликáция.

муля́ж, á, *m.* (*art*) plaster cast.

мумификáци|я, и, *f.* mummification.

мумифици́р|оваться, уется, *impf. and pf.* to be (become) mummified.

му́ми|я¹, и, *f.* mummy (*embalmed corpse*).

му́ми|я², и, *f.* mummy (*brown pigment*).

мунди́р, а, *m.* full-dress uniform; полковóй м. regimentals; картóфель в ~е potatoes cooked in their jackets.

мундшту́к, á, *m.* 1. mouth-piece (*of Russian cigarette*); cigarette-holder. 2. mouth-piece (*of musical instrument, pipe*). 3. curb, curb-bit.

муниципализи́р|овать, ую, *impf. and pf.* to municipalize.

муниципалитéт, а, *m.* municipality.

муниципáльный, *adj.* municipal.

мур|á, ы́, *f.* (*coll.*) mess; nonsense.

мурав|á¹, ы́, *f.* (*poet.*) grass, sward.

мурав|á², ы́, *f.* (*tech.*) glaze.

мурав|éй, ья́, *m.* ant.

муравéйник, а, *m.* 1. ant-hill. 2. ant-bear.

мурáв|ить, лю, ишь, *impf.* to glaze (*pottery*).

мурáвленый, *adj.* (*tech.*) glazed.

муравьéд, а, *m.* (*zool.*) ant-eater.

мурав|ьи́ный, *adj.* 1. *adj. of* ~éй. 2. (*chem.*) formic.

мурáш, á, *m.* = ~ка.

мурáшк|а, и, *f.* 1. (*dial.*) small ant. 2. (*coll.*) small insect; ~и по спинé бéгают it gives one the creeps.

мурл|ó, á, *n.* (*coll.*) (ugly) mug.

мурлы́|кать, чу, чешь, *impf.* 1. to purr. 2. (*coll.*) to hum.

мускáт, а, *m.* 1. nutmeg. 2. (*kind of grape*) muscadine, muscat. 3. muscatel, muscat (*wine*).

мускáт|ный, *adj. of* ~; м. орéх nutmeg; м. цвет mace.

му́скул, а, *m.* muscle; у негó ни оди́н м. не дрóгнул (*fig.*) he didn't move a muscle.

мускулату́р|а, ы, *f.* (*collect.*) muscular system.

му́скулист|ый (~, ~а), *adj.* muscular, sinewy, brawny.

му́скульный, *adj.* muscular.

му́скус, а, *m.* musk.

му́скусн|ый, *adj.* musky; м. бык musk-ox; ~ая кры́са musk-rat, musquash; ~ая у́тка musk-duck, Muscovy duck.

мусли́н, а, *m.* muslin.

мусли́н|овый, *adj. of* ~.

му́сл|ить, ю, ишь, *impf.* (*of* на~) (*coll.*) 1. to wet moisten (*with saliva*); м. ни́тку to moisten a thread (*when threading a needle*). 2. to beslobber; to soil (*with wet or sticky hands*); м. кни́гу to dog-ear, soil a book.

му́сл|иться, юсь, ишься, *impf.* (*of* на~) to slobber over oneself; to dirty oneself.

мусо́л|ить, ю, ишь, *impf.* (*of* за~, на~) 1. = му́слить. 2. (*fig.*) to spend much time (over); м. вопро́с to drag out a question.

му́сор, а, *m.* 1. sweepings, dust; rubbish, refuse, garbage. 2. débris.

му́сор|ить, ю, ишь, *impf.* (*of* на~) (*coll.*) to litter, leave litter about.

му́сор|ный, *adj. of* ~; ~ная пово́зка dust cart; м. я́щик dustbin.

мусоропрово́д, а, *m.* refuse chute.

мусоросжига́тельн|ый, *adj.* ~ая печь incinerator.

мусороубо́рочный, *adj.* refuse collection.

му́сорщик, а, *m.* 1. dustman. 2. scavenger.

мусс, а, *m.* (*cul.*) mousse.

мусси́р|овать, ую, *impf.* 1. to whip up, make to foam. 2. (*fig.*) to puff up (*reports*), inflate (*significance of something*).

муссо́н, а, *m.* (*geogr.*) monsoon.

муст, а, *n.* must.

муста́нг, а, *m.* (*zool.*) mustang.

мусульма́н|ин, ина, *pl.* ~е, ~, *m.* Moslem.

мусульма́нский, *adj.* Moslem.

мусульма́нств|о, а, *n.* Mohammedanism, Islam.

мута́ци|я, и, *f.* (*biol.*) mutation.

му|ти́ть, чу́, ти́шь, *impf.* 1. (*pf.* вз~, за~) (*pres. also* ~ти́шь, *etc.*) to trouble, make muddy (*liquids*). 2. (*pf.* по~) (*fig.*) to stir up, upset. 3. (*pf.* по~) (*fig.*) to dull, make dull. 4. (*impers.*) меня́, *etc.*, ~ти́т I *etc.*, feel sick.

му|ти́ться, чу́сь, ти́шься, *impf.* 1. (*pf.* за~) (*pres. also* ~ти́шься, *etc.*) to grow turbid (*of liquids*). 2. (*pf.* по~) (*fig.*) to grow dull, dim. 3. (*impers.*; *coll.*) у меня́ ~ти́тся в голове́ my head is going round.

мутне́|ть, ет, *impf.* (*of* по~) to grow turbid, grow muddy; (*fig.*) to grow dull.

му́тност|ь, и, *f.* 1. turbidity. 2. dullness.

му́т|ный (~ен, ~на́, ~но), *adj.* 1. turbid; в ~ной воде́ ры́бу лови́ть (*fig.*) to fish in troubled waters. 2. (*fig.*) dull(ed); confused; ~ные глаза́ lacklustre eyes; ~ное созна́ние dulled consciousness.

муто́вк|а[1], и, *f.* whisk.

муто́вк|а[2], и, *f.* (*bot.*) whorl.

му́тор|ный (~ен, ~на), *adj.* (*coll.*) disagree-

able; dreary, sombre; ему́ бы́ло ~но на душе́ he was in a sombre mood.

мут|ь, и, *f.* 1. lees, sediment. 2. murk.

му́фел|ь, я, *m.* (*tech.*) muffle.

муфло́н, а, *m.* (*zool.*) moufflon.

му́фт|а, ы, *f.* 1. muff. 2. (*tech.*) sleeve joint, coupling; соедини́тельная м. coupling sleeve, clutch sleeve; (*electr.*) connecting box; м. сцепле́ния clutch.

му́фти|й, я, *m.* (*rel.*) mufti.

му́х|а, и, *f.* fly; кака́я м. его́ укуси́ла? (*fig., coll.*) what's bitten him?; де́лать из ~и слона́ (*fig.*) to make a mountain out of a mole-hill; быть под ~ой, с ~ой (*coll.*) to be three sheets in the wind; зашиби́ть ~у to hit the bottle.

мухоло́вк|а, и, *f.* 1. fly-paper. 2. (*bot.*) Venus's fly-trap, sundew. 3. (*orn.*) fly-catcher.

мухомо́р, а, *m.* 1. fly-agaric (*mushroom*). 2. (*coll.*) decrepit old person.

мухо́ртый, *adj.* (*colour of horse*) bay with yellowish markings.

муче́ни|е, я, *n.* torment, torture.

му́ченик, а, *m.* martyr.

му́чени|ца, цы, *f. of* ~к.

му́чени|ческий, *adj. of* ~к; му́ка ~ческая (*coll.*) excruciating torment.

му́ченичеств|о, а, *n.* martyrdom.

му́ченск|ий, *adj. only in phrase* му́ка ~ая (*coll.*) excruciating torment.

мучи́тел|ь, я, *m.* torturer; tormentor.

мучи́тел|ьный (~ен, ~ьна), *adj.* excruciating; agonizing.

му́ч|ить, у, ишь, *impf.* (*of* за~, из~) to torment; to worry, harass.

му́ч|иться, усь, ишься, *impf.* (*of* за~, из~) 1. (+*i.*, от) *pass. of* ~ить; м. от бо́ли to be racked with pain. 2. (из-за) to worry (about), feel unhappy (about). 3. (над) to torment oneself (over, about).

мучни́к, а́, *m.* dealer in flour and meal.

мучни́ст|ый (~, ~а), *adj.* farinaceous.

мучн|о́е, о́го, *n.* farinaceous foods.

мучно́й, *adj. of* мука́.

му́шк|а[1], и, *f.* 1. *dim. of* му́ха; шпа́нская м. (*med.*) Spanish fly, cantharides. 2. (*artificial*) beauty-spot (*on face*).

му́шк|а[2], и, *f.* foresight (*of fire-arm*); взять на ~у to take aim (at).

мушке́т, а, *m.* musket.

мушкетёр, а, *m.* musketeer.

мушта́бел|ь, я, *m.* maulstick.

муштр|а́, ы́, *f.* 1. drill. 2. regimentation.

муштр|ова́ть, у́ю, *impf.* (*of* вы́~) to drill.

муэдзи́н, а, *m.* muezzin.

мха, мху, *see* мох.

мчать, мчу, мчишь, *impf.* to rush, whirl along (*trans.*; *coll. also intrans.*).

мч|а́ться, усь, и́шься, *impf.* to rush, race,

tear along; м. во весь опóр to go at full speed; врéмя ~ится time flies.

мши́ст|ый (~, ~а), adj. mossy.

мщéни|е, я, n. vengeance, revenge.

мы, a., g., p. нас, d. нам, i. нáми, pron. we; мы с вáми you and I.

мы́з|а, ы, f. farm-stead, country house (in Estonia and other regions bordering on Gulf of Finland).

мы́зга|ть, ю, impf. (coll.) to soil, crumple.

мы́ка|ть, ю, impf. (tech.) to ripple, hackle (flax); гóре м. (fig., coll.) to lead a dog's life.

мы́ка|ться, юсь, impf. (coll.) to roam, wander.

мы́л|ить, ю, ишь, impf. (of на~) to soap; to lather; м. комý-н. гóлову (fig., coll.) to give someone a dressing down.

мы́л|иться, юсь, ишься, impf. (of на~) 1. to soap oneself. 2. to lather, form a lather.

мы́л|кий (~ок, ~кá, ~ко), adj. freely lathering.

мы́л|о, а, pl. ~á, ~, ~áм, n. 1. soap. 2. (of horse) foam, lather.

мылова́р, а, m. soap-boiler.

мылова́рени|е, я, n. soap-boiling.

мылова́р|енный, adj. of ~éние; м. завóд soap works, soap factory.

мы́льниц|а, ы, f. soap-dish; soap-box.

мы́л|ьный, adj. of ~о; м. кáмень soapstone, steatite; ~ьные хлóпья soap-flakes.

мыс, а, m. (geog.) cape, promontory.

мы́сик, а, m. (coll.) protuberance; jutting out part.

мы́сленн|ый, adj. mental; м. óбраз mental image; ~ое пожелáние unspoken wish.

мы́слим|ый (~, ~а), adj. conceivable, thinkable.

мысли́тел|ь, я, m. thinker.

мысли́тельный, adj. intellectual, of thought; м. процéсс thought process.

мы́сл|ить, ю, ишь, impf. 1. to think; to reason. 2. to conceive.

мысл|ь, и, f. (o+p.) thought (of, about); idea; зáдняя м. ulterior motive, arrière pensée; óбраз ~ей way of thinking, views; у негó э́того и в ~ях нé было it never even crossed his mind; быть с кем-н. одни́х ~ей to be of the same opinion as someone; подáть м. to suggest an idea; собирáться с ~ями to collect one's thoughts.

мыта́р|ить, ю, ишь, impf. (of за~) (coll.) to harass, torment, try.

мыта́р|иться, юсь, ишься, impf. (of за~) (coll.) to be harassed; to suffer afflictions, undergo trials.

мыта́рств|о, а, n. ordeal, affliction, hardship.

мы́тар|ь, я, m. 1. (in Bible) publican. 2. (hist.) collector of transit dues.

мыть, мóю, мóешь, impf. (of вы́~, по~) to wash.

мыть|ё, я́, n. wash, washing; не ~ём, так кáтаньем by hook or by crook.

мы́ть|ся, мóюсь, мóешься, impf. (of вы́~, по~) 1. to wash (oneself). 2. pass. of ~.

мыч|áть, ý, и́шь, impf. 1. to low, moo; to bellow. 2. (fig., coll.) to mumble.

мыша́ст|ый (~, ~а), adj. mouse-coloured, mousey.

мышелóвк|а, и, f. mouse-trap.

мы́шечный, adj. muscular.

мыш|и́ный, adj. of ~ь; ~и́ная возня́ (суетá) pointless fussing over trifles; м. жеребчик (obs.) old lecher.

мы́шк|а[1], и, f. dim. of мышь.

мы́шк|а[2], и, f. oxter; под ~у, под ~и, под ~ой, под ~ами under one's arm; in one's armpit(s); взять под ~у to put under one's arm; нести́ под ~ой to carry under one's arm.

мышлéни|е, я, n. thinking, thought.

мыш|óнок, óнка, pl. ~áта, ~áт, m. young mouse.

мы́шц|а, ы, f. muscle.

мыш|ь, и, pl. ~и, ~éй, f. 1. mouse. 2. летý-чая м. bat.

мышья́к, á, m. (chem., pharm.) arsenic.

мышьякóвистый, adj. (chem.) arsenious.

мышьякóвый, adj. (chem.) arsenic.

мэр, а, m. mayor.

мю́зик-хóлл, а, m. music-hall.

мя́г|кий (~ок, ~кá, ~ко), adj. soft; (fig.) mild, gentle; м. вагóн (railways) soft-(seated) carriage, sleeping car; м. знак (ling.) soft sign (name of Russian letter 'ь'); ~кое крéсло easy chair; ~кая посáдка soft landing (of space vehicle); м. хлеб new bread.

мя́гко, adv. softly; (fig.) mildly, gently; м. выража́ясь (iron.) to put it mildly, to say the least.

мягкосердéчи|е, я, n. soft-heartedness.

мягкосердéч|ный (~ен, ~на), adj. soft-hearted.

мягкотéлый, adj. soft; (fig.) spineless.

мягкошёрстный, adj. soft-haired.

мя́г|че, comp. of ~кий and ~ко.

мягчи́тельный, adj. (med.) emollient.

мягч|и́ть, ý, и́шь, impf. (of c~) to soften.

мяки́н|а, ы, f. chaff; стáрого воробья́ на ~е не проведёшь (prov.) an old bird is not caught with chaff.

мя́киш, а, m. inside, soft part (of loaf).

мя́к|нуть, ну, нешь, past ~, ~ла, impf. (of раз~) to soften; to become soft (also fig.).

мя́кот|ь, и, f. 1. fleshy part of body. 2. pulp (of fruit).

мя́лк|а, и, f. (tech.) brake (for flax or hemp).

мя́мл|ить, ю, ишь, impf. (coll.) 1. (pf. про~)

to mumble. **2.** (*no pf.*) to vacillate; to procrastinate.

мя́мл|я, и, *g. pl.* **∼ей,** *m. and f.* (*coll.*) **1.** mumbler. **2.** irresolute person.

мяси́ст|ый (∼, ∼а), *adj.* fleshy; meaty; pulpy.

мясн|а́я, о́й, *f.* butcher's (shop).

мясни́к, а́, *m.* butcher.

мяс|но́й, *adj.* of ∼о; ∼ны́е консе́рвы tinned meat.

мя́с|о, а, *n.* **1.** flesh; сла́дкое м. (*anat.*) sweetbread; вы́рвать пу́говицу с ∼ом to rip out a button with a bit of cloth. **2.** meat; пу́шечное м. (*fig.*) cannon fodder. **3.** (*coll.*) beef.

мясое́д, а, *m.* (*eccl.*) season during which it is allowed to eat meat (*esp. from Christmas to Shrovetide*).

мясокомбина́т, а, *m.* meat processing and packing factory.

мясопу́ст, а, *m.* (*eccl.*) **1.** season during which it is forbidden to eat meat. **2.** Shrovetide.

мясору́бк|а, и, *f.* mincing-machine.

мясохладобо́|йня, йни, *g. pl.* **∼ен,** *f.* combined slaughter-house and meat store.

мя|сти́сь, ту́сь, тёшься, *impf.* (*obs.*) to be disturbed.

мя́т|а, ы, *f.* (*bot.*) mint; пе́речная м. peppermint.

мятёж, а́, *m.* mutiny, revolt.

мяте́жник, а, *m.* mutineer, rebel.

мяте́жный, *adj.* **1.** rebellious, mutinous. **2.** (*fig.*) restless; stormy.

мяте́ль = **мете́ль.**

мя́тн|ый, *adj.* mint; ∼ые леденцы́ peppermints.

мя|ту́сь, тёшься, *see* ∼сти́сь.

мя́т|ый, *p.p.p.* of ∼ь and *adj.*; м. пар (*tech.*) waste steam, exhaust steam.

мять, мну, мнёшь, *impf.* **1.** (*pf.* раз∼) to work up, knead; м. гли́ну to pug clay; м. лён to brake flax. **2.** (*pf.* из∼, с∼) to crumple; to rumple (*a dress, etc.*); м. траву́ to trample grass.

мя́ться¹, мнётся, *impf.* (*of* из∼, по∼, *and* с∼) to become crumpled; to rumple easily.

мя́ться², мнусь, мнёшься, *impf.* (*coll.*) to vacillate, hum and ha.

мя́ука|ть, ю, *impf.* to mew, miaow.

мяч, а́, *m.* ball.

мя́чик, а, *m.* *dim. of* мяч.

Н

на¹, *interj.* (*coll.*) here; here you are; here, take it; на́ кни́гу! here, take the book!; вот тебе́ на́! well, I never! well, how d'you like that?

на², *prep.* **I.** +*a.* **1.** on (to); to; into; положи́те кни́гу на стол put the book on the table; сесть на авто́бус, по́езд to board a 'bus, a train; сесть на парохо́д to go on board; на Украи́ну to the Ukraine; на Се́вер to the North; на се́вер от (to the) north of; на заво́д to the factory; на конце́рт to a concert; слепо́й на оди́н глаз blind in one eye; перевести́ на англи́йский to translate into English; положи́ть на му́зыку to set to music. **2.** (*of time*) at; on; until, to (*or untranslated*); на друго́й день, на сле́дующий день (the) next day; на Но́вый год on New Year's day; на Рождество́ at Christmas; на Па́сху at Easter; отложи́ть на бу́дущую неде́лю to put off until the following week. **3.** for; на два дня for two days; на́ зиму for the winter; на э́тот раз this time, for this once; на чёрный день (*fig.*) for a rainy day; собра́ние назна́чено на понеде́льник the meeting is fixed for Monday; на что э́то тебе́ ну́жно? what do you want it for?; ко́мната на двои́х a room for two; уро́к на за́втра the lesson for tomorrow; лес на постро́йку building timber; учи́ться на инжене́ра

(*coll.*) to study engineering; на беду́ unfortunately. **4.** by (*or untranslated*); коро́че на дюйм shorter by an inch; купи́ть на вес to buy by weight; опозда́ть на час to be an hour late; четы́ре ме́тра (в длину́) на два (в ширину́) four metres (long) by two (broad); помно́жить пять на три to multiply five by three; дели́ть на два to divide into two. **5.** worth (*of something*); на рубль ма́рок a rouble's worth of stamps.

II. +*p.* **1.** on, upon; in; at; на столе́ on the table; на бума́ге on paper (*also fig.*); на Украи́не in the Ukraine; на Се́вере in the North; на заво́де at the factory; на конце́рте at a concert; на со́лнце in the sun; на чи́стом, во́льном во́здухе in the open air; на дворе́, на у́лице out of doors; на рабо́те at work; на излече́нии undergoing medical treatment; на вёслах under oars; на мо́ре at sea; идти́ на паруса́х to go sailing; игра́ть на роя́ле to play the piano; висе́ть на потолке́ to hang from the ceiling; жа́рить на ма́сле to fry; на свои́х глаза́х before one's eyes; на его́ па́мяти within his recollection; писа́ть на неме́цком языке́ to write in German; оши́бка на оши́бке blunder upon blunder. **2.** (*of time*) in (*or untranslated*); during; на э́той неде́ле this week; на лету́ in flight, during (the) flight; на кани́кулах during the holidays. **3.**

(*made, prepared with, of*); on (= *operated by means of*); на вáте padded; матрáц на рессóрах sprung mattress; э́тот дви́гатель рабóтает на не́фти this engine runs on oil.

на- *as verbal prefix* **I.** *forms pf. aspect.*
  II. *indicates* **1.** action continued to sufficiency, to point of satisfaction or exhaustion. **2.** action relating to determinate quantity or number of objects.

набáв|ить, лю, ишь, *pf.* (*of* ~ля́ть) to add (to), increase; н. шáгу to quicken one's pace.

набáвк|а, и, *f.* addition, increase; extra charge; н. к зарплáте rise (in wages).

набавля́|ть, ю, *impf. of* набáвить.

набáвочный, *adj.* (*coll.*) extra, additional.

набаламý|тить, чу, тишь, *pf.* (*coll.*) to make trouble; to upset.

набалдáшник, а, *m.* knob; walking-stick handle.

набалóв|анный, *p.p.p. of* ~áть *and adj.* spoiled.

набал|овáть, ýю, *pf.* (*coll.*) **1.** to spoil. **2.** to get up to mischief.

набальзами́р|овать, ую, *pf. of* бальзами́ровать.

набáт, а, *m.* alarm bell, tocsin; бить (ударя́ть) (в) н. to sound the alarm (*also fig.*).

набáт|ный, *adj. of* ~.

набéг, а, *m.* raid; foray, inroad, incursion.

набéга|ть, ю, *pf.* (*coll.*) to cause oneself (*heart trouble, etc.*) by running.

набегá|ть, ю, *impf.* **1.** *impf. of* набежáть. **2.** *impers.* (*coll.*) to ruck up.

набéга|ться, юсь, *pf.* to be tired out with running about; to have one's fill of running.

набе|гý, жи́шь, гýт, *see* ~жáть.

набедокýр|ить, ю, ишь, *pf. of* бедокýрить.

набе|жáть, гý, жи́шь, гýт, *pf.* (*of* ~гáть) **1.** (на+*a.*) to run against, run into. **2.** (*coll.*) to come running (together). **3.** (*of liquids*) to run into; to fill up; (*fig.*; *of money, etc.*) to accumulate. **4.** (*of wind*) to spring up.

набекрéнь, *adv.* (*coll.*) (*of hats*) aslant, tilted; с шля́пой н. with one's hat on one side; у негó мозги́ н. (*joc.*) he is crack-brained.

набел|и́ть(ся), ю́(сь), ~и́шь(ся), *pf. of* бели́ть(ся) 2.

нáбело, *adv.* clean, without corrections and erasures; переписáть н. to make a fair copy of.

нáбережн|ая, ой, *f.* embankment, quay.

набивá|ть(ся), ю(сь), *impf. of* набить(ся).

набивк|а, и, *f.* **1.** (*action and substance*) stuffing, padding, packing. **2.** (*text.*) printing.

набивнóй, *adj.* (*text.*) printed.

набирá|ть(ся), ю(сь), *impf. of* набрáть(ся).

наби́т|ый (~, ~а), *p.p.p. of* ~ь *and adj.* packed, crowded; зал ~ биткóм the hall is crowded out; н. дурáк arrant fool.

наб|и́ть[1], ью, ьёшь, *pf.* (*of* ~ивáть) **1.** (+*a. and i.*) to stuff (with), pack (with), fill (with); н. трýбку to fill one's pipe; н. цéны to knock up the prices; to bid up; н. оскóмину to set one's teeth on edge (*also fig.*); н. рýку на чём-н. (*fig., coll.*) to become a practised hand at something, become a dab hand. **2.** (*text.*) to print.

наб|и́ть[2], ью, ьёшь, *pf.* н. гвоздéй в стéну to drive (*a number of*) nails into a wall; н. ýток to bag (*a number of*) duck; н. посýды to smash (*a lot of*) crockery.

наб|и́ться, ью́сь, ьёшься, *pf.* (*of* ~ивáться) **1.** to crowd (*into a place*); биткóм н. to be crowded out. **2.** (*coll.*; +*d.*) to impose oneself (upon), inflict oneself (upon); н. к комý-н. в гóсти to invite oneself to someone's house (*etc.*).

наблюдáтел|ь, я, *m.* observer, spectator.

наблюдáтельност|ь, и, *f.* power of observation, observation.

наблюдáтел|ьный, *adj.* **1.** (~ен, ~ьна) observant. **2.** observation; н. пункт (*mil.*) observation post.

наблюдá|ть, ю, *impf.* **1.** to observe; to watch. **2.** (за+*i.*) to take care (of), look after. **3.** (за+*i.*) to supervise, superintend; н. за ýличным движéнием to control traffic; н. за поря́дком to be responsible for keeping order.

наблюдéни|е, я, *n.* **1.** observation. **2.** supervision, superintendence.

наблю|сти́, дý, дёшь, *past* ~л, ~лá, *pf.* (*obs.*) to make an observation.

набóб, а, *m.* nabob.

нáбожност|ь, и, *f.* piety.

нáбож|ный (~ен, ~на), *adj.* devout, pious.

набóйк|а, и, *f.* **1.** (*text.*) printed cloth. **2.** printed pattern on cloth. **3.** heel (*of foot-wear*).

набóйщик, а, *m.* **1.** (*text.*) (linen-)printer. **2.** filler, stuffer.

нáбок, *adv.* on one side, awry.

наболé|вший, *past part. of* ~ть *and adj.* sore, painful (*also fig.*).

наболé|ть, éет, *pf.* to become painful.

наболтá|ть[1], ю, *pf.* (*coll.*) to mix in (*a quantity of*).

наболтá|ть[2], ю, *pf.* (*coll.*) **1.** (+*a. or g.*) to talk a lot (*of nonsense, etc.*). **2.** (на+*a.*) to gossip (about), talk (about); на неё ~ли they told a lot of lies about her.

нáбольш|ий, его, *m.* (*dial.*) **1.** boss. **2.** head of family.

набóр, а, *m.* **1.** recruitment. **2.** levy. **3.** (*typ.*) composition, type-setting. **4.** (*typ.*)

composed matter. **5.** set, collection; н. слов mere verbiage. **6.** decorative plate (*on harness, belt, etc.*).

набо́рн|ая, ой, *f.* type-setting office.

набо́рн|ый,| **adj. type-setting; ~ая доска́ galley.

набо́рщик, а, *m.* compositor, type-setter.

набра́сыва|ть(ся), ю(сь), *impf. of* набро-са́ть(ся) *and* набро́сить(ся).

набра́|ть, наберу́, наберёшь, *past* ~л, ~ла́, ~ло, *pf.* (*of* набира́ть) **1.** (+*g. or a.*) to gather; to collect, assemble; н. у́гля to take on coal; н. но́мер to dial a (telephone) number; н. ско́рость to pick up, gather speed; н. высоту́ (*aeron.*) to climb; н. воды́ в рот (*fig.*) to keep mum. **2.** to re-cruit, enrol, engage. **3.** (*typ.*) to compose, set up.

набра́|ться, наберу́сь, наберёшься, *past* ~лся, ~ла́сь, ~ло́сь, *pf.* (*of* набира́ться) **1.** (*usually impers.*) to assemble, collect; to accumulate; ~ло́сь мно́го наро́ду a large crowd collected. **2.** (+*g.*; *coll.*) to find, collect; to acquire; (*pejor.*) to pick up; н. хра́брости to take courage; н. блох to pick up fleas.

набре|сти́, ду, дёшь, *past* ~л, ~ла́, *pf.* **1.** (на+*a.*) to come across; to happen upon; я ~л на интере́сную мысль I have hit on an interesting idea. **2.** to collect, gather; ~ло́ мно́го наро́ду a large crowd gathered.

наброса́|ть[1], ю, *pf.* (*of* набра́сывать) **1.** to sketch, outline, adumbrate; н. план to out-line a plan. **2.** to jot down.

наброса́|ть[2], ю, *pf.* to throw about; to throw (*in successive instalments*).

набро́|сить, шу, сишь, *pf.* (*of* набра́сывать) to throw (on, over); н. шаль на пле́чи to throw a shawl over one's shoulders.

набро́|ситься, шусь, сишься, *pf.* (*of* набра́сываться) (*in var. senses*) to fall upon; to go for; соба́ка ~силась на меня́ the dog went for me; н. на кого́-н. с вопро́сами to deluge someone with questions.

набро́с|ок, ка, *m.* sketch, draft.

набры́зга|ть, ю, *pf.* (+*i. or g.*) to splash.

набрю́шник, а, *m.* abdominal band.

набрю́шный, adj. abdominal.

набуха́|ть, а́ю, *impf. of* ~нуть.

набу́х|нуть, ну, нешь, *past* ~, ~ла, *pf.* (*of* ~а́ть) to swell.

наб|ью́, ьёшь, *see* ~и́ть.

нава́г|а, и, *f.* (*zool.*) navaga (*a small fish of the cod family*).

наважде́ни|е, я, *n.* delusion; hallucination.

нава́к|сить, шу, сишь, *pf. of* ва́ксить.

нава́лива|ть(ся), ю(сь), *impf. of* навали́ть-(ся).

навал|и́ть, ю, ~ишь, *pf.* (*of* ~ивать) to heap, pile; to load (*also fig.*); *impers.* сне́гу

~и́ло по коле́но the snow had piled up knee deep.

навал|и́ться, ю́сь, ~ишься, *pf.* (*of* ~ивать-ся) (на+*a.*) **1.** (*coll.*) to fall (upon). **2.** to lean (on, upon); to bring all one's weight to bear (on).

нава́лк|а, и, *f.* loading, lading; в ~y loose, unpacked.

нава́лом, *adv.* piled up.

наваля́|ть[1], ю, *pf. of* валя́ть 5.

наваля́|ть[2], ю, *pf.* н. во́йлока, ва́ленок to make (*a quantity of*) felt, felt boots.

нава́р, а, *m.* grease (*on the surface of soup*).

нава́рива|ть, ю, *impf. of* навари́ть[1].

нава́рист|ый (~, ~а), *adj.* with large fat content (*of soup*).

навар|и́ть[1], ю́, ~ишь, *pf.* (*of* ~ивать) to weld on.

навар|и́ть[2], ю́, ~ишь, *pf.* to cook, boil (*a quantity of*).

наварно́й, *adj.* (*tech.*) welded.

навева́|ть, ю, *impf. of* наве́ять.

наве́д|аться, аюсь, *pf.* (*of* ~ываться) (к; *coll.*) to call (on).

наведе́ни|е, я, *n.* **1.** laying; placing. **2.** (*philos.; obs.*) induction.

наве|ду́, дёшь, *see* ~сти́.

наве́дыва|ться, юсь, *impf. of* наве́даться.

навез|ти́[1], у́, ёшь, *past* ~, ~ла́, *pf.* (*of* наво-зи́ть[1]) (на+*a.*; *coll.*) to drive (on, against).

навез|ти́[2], у́, ёшь, *past* ~, ~ла́, *pf.* (*of* наво-зи́ть[2]) to bring (*a quantity of*).

наве́к, *adv.* for ever.

наве́к|и = ~.

наверб|ова́ть, у́ю, *pf. of* вербова́ть.

наве́рно, *adv.* **1.** probably, most likely. **2.** (*obs.*) for sure; certainly, exactly.

наве́рно|е, *adv.* = ~ 1.

наверн|у́ть, у́, ёшь, *pf.* (*of* навёртывать) **1.** to screw (on). **2.** to wind (round). **3.** (*sl.*) to scoff up (= eat).

наверн|у́ться, у́сь, ёшься, *pf.* (*of* навёрты-ваться) **1.** (*coll.*) to turn up; (*of tears*) to well up. **2.** *pass. of* ~у́ть.

наверняка́, *adv.* (*coll.*) **1.** for sure, certainly. **2.** safely, without taking risks; бить н. to take no chances; держа́ть пари́ н. to bet on a certainty.

наверста́|ть, ю, *pf.* (*of* навёрстывать) to make up (for), catch up (with); н. поте́рян-ное вре́мя to make up for lost time; н. упу́щенное to repair an omission.

навёрстыва|ть, ю, *impf. of* наверста́ть.

навер|те́ть[1], чу́, ~тишь, *pf.* (*of* ~тывать) to wind (round), twist (round).

навер|те́ть[2], чу́, ~тишь, *pf.* (*of* ~чивать) to drill (*a number of*) (*holes, etc.*).

навёртыва|ть, ю, *impf. of* наверну́ть *and* навертеть[1].

навёртыва|ться, юсь, *impf. of* наверну́ться.

наве́рх, *adv.* up, upward; upstairs; to the top.

наверху́, *adv.* above; upstairs.

наве́рчива|ть, ю, *impf. of* наверте́ть².

наве́с, а, *m.* penthouse; awning.

навеселе́, *adv.* (*coll.*) tipsy.

наве́сист|ый (~, ~а), *adj.* overhanging, jutting.

наве́|сить, шу, сишь, *pf.* (*of* ~шивать¹) (+*a. or g.*) to hang (up), suspend; н. карти́н to hang (*a number of*) pictures.

навеск|а¹, и, *f.* hinge-plate.

навеск|а², и, *f.* (*chem.*) dose by weight.

навесн|о́й, *adj.* ~а́я дверь door on hinges; ~а́я пе́тля hinge.

наве́сный, *adj.* (*mil.*) н. ого́нь plunging fire.

наве|сти́¹, ду́, дёшь, *past* ~л, ~ла́, *pf.* (*of* наводи́ть) (на+*a.*) 1. to direct (at); to aim (at); н. кого́-н. на мысль to suggest an idea to someone; н. на след to put on the track. 2. to cover (with); н. лоск, гля́нец to polish, gloss, glaze. 3. to lay, put, make; н. поря́док to introduce order, establish order; н. спра́вку to make an inquiry; н. ску́ку to bore; н. страх to inspire fear.

наве|сти́², ду́, дёшь, *past* ~л, ~ла́, *pf.* (*of* наводи́ть) to bring (*a quantity of*).

наве|сти́ть, щу́, сти́шь, *pf.* (*of* ~ща́ть) to visit, call on.

наве́т, а, *m.* (*obs.*) slander, calumny.

наве́тренный, *adj.* windward.

наве́тчик, а, *m.* (*obs.*) slanderer.

наве́чно, *adv.* for ever; in perpetuity.

наве́ш|ать¹, аю, *pf.* (*of* ~ивать¹) (+*a. or g.*) to hang (up), suspend.

наве́ш|ать², аю, *pf.* (*of* ~ивать²) to weigh out (*a quantity of*).

наве́шива|ть¹, ю, *impf. of* наве́сить *and* наве́шать¹.

наве́шива|ть², ю, *impf. of* наве́шать².

навеща́|ть, ю, *impf. of* навести́ть.

наве́|ять¹, ю, ешь, *pf.* (*of* ~ва́ть) to blow; (*fig.*;+ *a.* на+*a.*) to cast (on, over), plunge (into); его́ расска́з ~ял грусть на слу́шателей his story cast a gloom over the audience, plunged the audience into gloom.

наве́|ять², ю, ешь, *pf.* (*of* ~ва́ть) to winnow (*a quantity of*).

на́взничь, *adv.* backwards, on one's back.

навзры́д, *adv.* пла́кать н. to sob.

навива́|ть, ю, *impf. of* нави́ть.

навига́тор, а, *m.* navigator.

навигаци|о́нный, *adj. of* ~ия.

навига́ци|я, и, *f.* (*in var. senses*) navigation.

навин|ти́ть, чу́, ти́шь, *pf.* (*of* ~чивать) (на+*a.*) to screw (on).

нави́нчива|ть, ю, *impf. of* навинти́ть.

навис|а́ть, а́ю, *impf.* (*of* ~нуть) (на+*a.*, над) to hang (over), overhang; (*of cliffs,*

etc.) to beetle; (*fig.*) to impend, threaten; над на́ми ~а́ет опа́сность danger threatens us, is imminent; н. над фла́нгами врага́ to hang on the enemy's flanks.

нави́слый, *adj.* (*coll.*) overhanging, beetling.

нави́с|нуть, ну, нешь, *past* ~, ~ла, *pf. of* ~а́ть.

нави́с|ший, *past part. act. of* ~нуть *and adj.* ~шие бро́ви beetling brows.

нав|и́ть, ью, ьёшь, *past* ~и́л, ~ила́, ~и́ло, *pf.* (*of* ~ива́ть) (+*a. or g.*) 1. to wind (on). 2. to load, stack (*straw, hay*).

навлека́|ть, ю, *impf. of* навле́чь.

навле|ку́, чёшь, ку́т, *see* ~чь.

навле́|чь, ку́, чёшь, ку́т, *past* ~к, ~кла́, *pf.* (*of* ~ка́ть) (на+*a.*) to bring (on); to draw (on); н. на себя́ гнев to incur anger.

наво|ди́ть, жу́, ~дишь, *impf. of* навести́; наводя́щие вопро́сы leading questions; наводя́щий, наводи́вший 'he' (*in children's games*).

наво́дк|а, и, *f.* (*mil.*) laying, training; прямо́й ~ой over open sights.

наводне́ни|е, я, *n.* flood, inundation.

наводн|и́ть, ю́, и́шь, *pf.* (*of* ~я́ть) (+*a. and i.*) to flood (with), inundate (with), deluge (with); (*fig.*) н. ры́нок дешёвыми това́рами to flood the market with cheap goods.

наводн|я́ть, я́ю, *impf. of* ~и́ть.

наво́дчик, а, *m.* 1. gun-layer. 2. (*sl.*) tipper-off (*thieves' informant*).

наво|жу́, зишь, *see* ~зить.

наво|жу́¹, ~дишь, *see* ~ди́ть.

наво|жу́², ~зишь, *see* ~зи́ть.

наво́з, а, *m.* manure, dung.

наво́|зить, жу, зишь, *impf.* (*of* у~) to manure.

наво|зи́ть¹, ², жу́, ~зишь, *impf. of* навезти́¹, ².

наво|зи́ть³, жу́, ~зишь, *pf.* (*coll.*) to get in (*a supply of*).

наво́зник, а, *m.* dung-beetle.

наво́з|ный, *adj. of* ~; н. жук dung-beetle; гром не из ту́чи, а из ~ной ку́чи (*coll.*) his bark is worse than his bite.

наво́|й, я, *m.* (*text.*) weaver's beam.

на́волок|а, и, *f.* pillow-case, pillow-slip.

на́воло|чка = ~ка.

навоня́|ть, ю, *pf.* (*coll.*; +*i.*) to stink (of).

навора́жива|ть, ю, *impf. of* наворожи́ть.

навора́чива|ть, ю, *impf. of* навороти́ть.

навор|ова́ть, у́ю, *pf.* (*coll.*) to steal (*a quantity of*).

наворож|и́ть, у́, и́шь, *pf.* (*of* навора́живать) (*coll.*) 1. to foretell, prophesy; она́ ~и́ла мне до́лгий век she prophesied me a long life. 2. to make, earn by fortune-telling. 3. to endow with magical properties.

наворо|ти́ть, чу́, ~ти́шь, *pf.* (*of* навора́чивать) (*coll.*; +*a. or g.*) to heap up, pile up.

наворо|чу́, ~ти́шь, *see* ~ти́ть.

наворс|ова́ть, у́ю, *pf. of* ворсова́ть.

наворч|а́ть, у́, и́шь, *pf.* (*coll.*; на+*a.*) to grumble (at).

навостр|и́ть, ю́, и́шь, *pf.* (*coll.*) to sharpen; н. у́ши to prick up one's ears; н. лы́жи to take to one's heels.

навостр|и́ться, ю́сь, и́шься, *pf.* (в+*p. or* +*inf.*; *coll.*) to become good (at), become adept (at); он ~и́лся пляса́ть he has become a good dancer.

навощ|и́ть, у́, и́шь, *pf. of* вощи́ть.

навр|а́ть¹, у́, ёшь, *past* ~а́л, ~ала́, ~а́ло, *pf.* (*coll.*) 1. (*pf. of* врать) to romance, tell yarns. 2. (в+*p.*) to make mistakes (in); н. в расска́зе to get the story wrong. 3. (на+*a.*) to slander.

навр|а́ть², у́, ёшь, *pf.* (*coll.*; +*a. or g.*) to tell (*a lot of*) (*sc.* lies); н. вся́ких небылиц to tell all manner of tales.

навре|ди́ть, жу́, ди́шь, *pf.* (+*d.*) to do much harm (to).

навря́д (ли), *adv.* scarcely, hardly.

навсегда́, *adv.* for ever, for good; раз н. once (and) for all.

навстре́чу, *adv.* to meet; towards; пойти́ н. кому́-н. to go to meet someone; (*fig.*) to meet someone half-way.

навы́ворот, *adv.* (*coll.*) 1. inside out, wrong side out. 2. (*fig.*) wrong way round.

на́вык, а, *m.* experience, skill (*in practical or manual work*).

навы́кат(е), *adv.* глаза́ н. bulging eyes.

навык|а́ть, а́ю, *impf. of* ~нуть.

навы́к|нуть, ну, нешь, *past* ~, ~ла, *pf.* (*of* ~а́ть) (*coll.*; к *or* +*inf.*) to acquire the habit (of), skill (in).

навы́лет, *adv.* (right) through; он был ра́нен н. в ру́ку he was wounded by a bullet passing right through his arm.

навы́нос, *adv.* for consumption off the premises.

навы́пуск, *adv.* worn outside; брю́ки н. trousers worn over boots; руба́ха н. shirt worn outside trousers.

навы́рез, *adv.* купи́ть арбу́з н. to buy a water-melon with the right to sample a section.

навы́тяжку, *adv.* стоя́ть н. to stand at attention.

нав|ь, и, *f.* (*in Russian myth.*) ghost, spirit.

нав|ью, ьёшь, *see* ~и́ть.

навьючива|ть, ю, *impf. of* навью́чить.

навью́ч|ить, у, ишь, *pf.* (*of* вью́чить *and* ~ивать) to load (up).

навя|за́ть¹, жу́, ~жешь, *pf.* (*of* ~зывать) 1. (на+*a.*) to tie on (to), fasten (to). 2. (*fig.*; +*d. and a.*) to thrust (on); to foist (on); н. кому́-н. сове́т to thrust advice on someone.

навя|за́ть², жу́, ~жешь, *pf.* (*of* ~зывать) (+*a. or g.*) to knit (*a number of*).

навяз|а́ть³, а́ет, *impf. of* ~нуть.

навя|за́ться, жу́сь, ~жешься, *pf.* (*of* ~зываться) (*coll.*; +*d.*) 1. to thrust oneself (upon), intrude oneself (upon). 2. *pass. of* ~за́ть¹.

навя́з|нуть, нет, *past* ~, ~ла, *pf.* (*of* ~а́ть) to stick; э́то ~ло у нас в зуба́х (*fig.*) we are sick and tired of it.

навя́зчив|ый (~, ~а), *adj.* 1. importunate; obtrusive. 2. persistent; ~ая иде́я idée fixe, obsession.

навя́зыва|ть(ся), ю(сь), *impf. of* навяза́ть(ся).

нагада́|ть, ю, *pf.* (*coll.*; +*a. or g.*) to foretell, predict.

нага́|дить, жу, дишь, *pf. of* га́дить.

нага́йк|а, и, *f.* whip.

нага́н, а, *m.* revolver.

нага́р, а, *m.* deposit formed as result of combustion; (candle-)snuff.

на́гел|ь, я, *m.* (*tech.*) wooden pin.

нагиба́|ть(ся), ю(сь), *impf. of* нагну́ть(ся).

нагишо́м, *adv.* (*coll.*) stark naked.

нагла́|дить¹, жу, дишь, *pf.* (*of* ~живать) to smooth (out).

нагла́|дить², жу, дишь, *pf.* (*of* ~живать) to iron (*a quantity of*).

нагла́жива|ть, ю, *impf. of* нагла́дить.

нагла́зник, а, *m.* 1. eye-shade. 2. blinker.

нагле́|ть, ю, *impf.* (*of* об~) to become impudent, become insolent.

наглец́, а́, *m.* impudent fellow, insolent fellow.

на́глост|ь, и, *f.* impudence, insolence, effrontery, impertinence.

наглота́|ться, юсь, *pf.* (+*g.*) to swallow (*a large quantity of*).

на́глухо, *adv.* tightly, hermetically; застегну́ться н. to do up all one's buttons.

на́гл|ый (~, ~а́, ~о), *adj.* impudent, insolent, impertinent.

нагля|де́ться, жу́сь, ди́шься, *pf.* (на+*a.*) to see enough (of); на э́тот вид гляжу́ — не ~жу́сь I never tire of looking at this view.

нагля́дно, *adv.* clearly, graphically; by visual demonstration.

нагля́дност|ь, и, *f.* 1. clearness. 2. use of visual methods, use of visual aids.

нагля́д|ный (~ен, ~на), *adj.* 1. clear; graphic, obvious; ~ное доказа́тельство ocular demonstration. 2. visual; ~ные посо́бия visual aids; н. уро́к object-lesson.

наг|на́ть¹, оню́, о́нишь, *past* ~на́л, ~нала́, ~на́ло, *pf.* (*of* ~оня́ть) 1. to overtake, catch up (with). **2.** to make up (for). **3.** (*fig.*, *coll.*) to inspire, arouse, occasion.

наг|нáть², оню́, óнишь, *pf.* (+*a. or g.*) **1.** to herd together (*a number of*). **2.** to distil (*a quantity of*).

нагне|стú, тý, тёшь, *pf.* (*of* ~тáть) to compress, force; (*tech.*) to supercharge.

нагнетáтел|ь, я, *m.* (*tech.*) supercharger.

нагнетáтельн|ый, *adj.* (*tech.*) н. клáпан pressure valve; ~ая трубá force pipe.

нагнетá|ть, ю, *impf. of* нагнестú.

нагне|тý, тёшь, *see* ~стú.

нагноéни|е, я, *n.* (*med.*) **1.** fester. **2.** suppuration.

нагнойт|ься, úтся, *pf.* (*med.*) to fester, suppurate.

нагн|ýть, ý, ёшь, *pf.* (*of* нагибáть) to bend.

нагн|ýться, ýсь, ёшься, *pf.* (*of* нагибáться) to bend (down), stoop.

нагова́рива|ть, ю, *impf. of* наговорúть¹.

наговóр, а, *m.* **1.** slander, calumny. **2.** incantation.

наговор|úть¹, ю́, úшь, *pf.* (*of* нагова́ривать) **1.** (*coll.*; на+*a.*) to slander, calumniate. **2.** н. пласти́нку to have a recording made (of one's voice), record (one's voice). **3.** to pronounce incantations over.

наговор|úть², ю́, úшь, *pf.* (+*a. or g.*) to talk, say a lot (of); н. чепухú to talk a lot of nonsense.

наговор|úться, ю́сь, úшься, *pf.* to talk oneself out; онú не мóгут н. they cannot talk enough.

наг|óй (~, ~á, ~o), *adj.* naked, nude, bare.

наголéнный, *adj.* worn, *etc.*, on shin(s); н. щитóк shin-pad.

нáголó, *adv.* bare; остри́чь нáголо to cut close to the skin, crop close; с шáшками наголó with drawn swords.

нáголову, *adv.* разби́ть н. to rout, smash.

наголодá|ться, ю́сь, *pf.* to be half-starved.

нагóльный, *adj.* н. тулýп uncovered sheepskin coat.

нагоня́|й, я, *m.* (*coll.*) scolding, rating.

нагоня́|ть, ю, *impf. of* нагнáть.

на-горá, *adv.* (*mining*) to the surface, to the top.

нагорáжива|ть, ю, *impf. of* нагородúть.

нагор|áть, áю, *impf. of* ~éть.

нагор|éть¹, úт, *pf.* (*of* ~áть) **1.** to need snuffing (*of a candle*). **2.** (+*g.*) to be used up (*of fuel*).

нагор|éть², úт, *pf.* (*of* ~áть) (*impers.*; +*d.*) (*coll.*) тебé за э́то ~úт you'll get it hot for this.

нагóрн|ый, *adj.* **1.** mountainous, hilly. **2.** (*of river bank*) high. **3.** ~ая пропóведь (*bibl.*) Sermon on the Mount.

нагоро|дúть, жý, ~дишь, *pf.* (*of* нагорáжи-

вать) **1.** to build, erect (*in large quantity*). **2.** (*coll.*) to pile up, heap up. **3.** (*fig.*) to talk, write (*a lot of nonsense*); н. вздóра, чепухú to talk a lot of nonsense.

нагóрь|е, я, *n.* table-land, plateau.

нагот|á, ы́, *f.* nakedness, nudity.

наготóве, *adv.* in readiness; ready to hand; быть н. to hold oneself in readiness, be on call.

наготóв|ить, лю, ишь, *pf.* (+*a. or g.*) **1.** to lay in (*a supply of*). **2.** to cook (*a large quantity of*).

наготóв|иться, люсь, ишься, *pf.* (*coll.*; +*g.* на+*a.*) to have enough (for), provide enough (for); на них не ~ишься еды́ one cannot provide enough food for them; он так бы́стро растёт, на негó не ~ишься одéжды he is growing so fast, it is impossible to keep him in clothes.

награ́б|ить, лю, ишь, *pf.* (+*a. or g.*) to amass by robbery.

нагрáд|а, ы, f. **1.** reward, recompense. **2.** award; decoration; (*in schools*) prize.

награ|дúть, жý, дúшь, *pf.* (*of* ~ждáть) (+*a. and i.*) **1.** to reward (with). **2.** to decorate (with); to award, confer; (*fig.*) to endow (with); н. когó-н. óрденом to confer a decoration upon someone, award someone a decoration; приро́да ~дúла егó вели́кими талáнтами nature has endowed him with great talents.

наград|нóй, *adj. of* ~a.

наградн|ы́е, ы́х, *pl. only* bonus.

награжда́|ть, ю, *impf. of* наградúть.

награждённ|ый, *p.p.p. of* наградúть; *as noun* н., ~ого, *m.* recipient (of an award).

нагрéв, а, *m.* (*tech.*) heat, heating; повéрхность ~a heating surface.

нагревáтел|ь, я, *m.* (*tech.*) heater.

нагревáтельн|ый, *adj.* (*tech.*) heating.

нагревá|ть(ся), ю(сь), *impf. of* нагрéть(ся).

нагрé|ть, ю, *pf.* (*of* ~вáть) **1.** to warm, heat; н. рýки (*fig.*) to feather one's nest. **2.** (*coll.*) to swindle; онú ~ли меня́ на пять рублéй they swindled me out of five roubles.

нагрé|ться¹, юсь, *pf.* (*of* нагревáться) to become warm, become hot; to warm up, heat up.

нагрé|ться², юсь, *pf.* (*of* ~вáться) (*coll.*) to be swindled.

нагримир|овáть, ýю, *pf. of* гримировáть.

нагромождá|ть, ю, *impf. of* нагромоздúть.

нагромоз|дúть, жý, дúшь, *pf.* (*of* громоздúть *and* нагромождáть) to pile up, heap up.

нагруб|úть, лю́, úшь, *pf. of* грубúть.

нагрубия́н|ить, ю, ишь, *pf. of* грубия́нить.

нагрýдник, а, *m.* **1.** bib. **2.** breastplate.

нагрýдный, *adj.* breast.

нагружá|ть(ся), ю(сь), *impf. of* нагрузúть(ся).

нагру|зи́ть, жу́, ∠зи́шь, *pf.* (*of* грузи́ть *and* ∼жа́ть) (+*a. and i.*) **1.** to load (with). **2.** (*fig.*) to burden (with).

нагру|зи́ться, жу́сь, ∠зи́шься, *pf.* (*of* ∼жа́ться) (+*i.*) to load oneself (with), burden oneself (with).

нагру́зк|а, и, *f.* **1.** loading. **2.** load; поле́зная н. (*tech.*) paying load, working load. **3.** (*fig.*) work; commitments, obligation(s); парти́йная н. party work, party obligations; преподава́тельская н. teaching load.

нагрязн|и́ть, ю́, и́шь, *pf. of* грязни́ть.

нагря́н|уть, у, ешь, *pf.* (*coll.*) to appear unexpectedly; (на+*a.*) to descend (on).

нагу́л, а, *m.* (*agric.*) fattening.

нагу́лива|ть, ю, *impf. of* нагуля́ть.

нагул|я́ть, я́ю, *pf.* (*of* ∼ивать) to acquire, develop (*as result of feeding, exercise, etc.*); н. жи́ру (*agric.*) to fatten, put on weight; н. брюшко́ (*fig., joc.*) to develop a paunch; н. аппети́т to work up an appetite.

нагуля́|ться, юсь, *pf.* to have had a long walk.

над, *prep.*+*i.* **1.** over, above. **2.** on; at; рабо́тать над диссерта́цией to be working on a dissertation; смея́ться над to laugh at.

над- super-, over-.

нада|ва́ть, ю́, ёшь, *pf.* (*coll.*; +*d. and a. or g.*) to give (*a large quantity of*).

надав|и́ть¹, лю́, ∠ишь, *pf.* (*of* ∼ливать) (на+*a.*) to press (on).

надав|и́ть², лю́, ∠ишь, *pf.* (+*a. or g.*) **1.** to press, squeeze (*a number of*). **2.** (*coll.*) to swat (*a quantity of*).

нада́влива|ть, ю, *impf. of* надави́ть¹.

нада́ива|ть, ю, *impf. of* надои́ть.

нада́рива|ть, ю, *impf. of* надари́ть.

надар|и́ть, ю́, и́шь, *pf.* (*of* ∼ивать) (*coll.*; +*a. or g. and d.*) to present (*a large quantity of*).

надба́в|ить, лю, ишь, *pf.* = наба́вить.

надба́вк|а, и, *f.* = наба́вка.

надбавля́|ть, ю, *impf. of* надба́вить.

надбива́|ть, ю, *impf. of* надби́ть.

надби́т|ый, *p.p.p. of* ∼ь *and adj.* cracked; chipped.

над|би́ть, обью́, обьёшь, *pf.* (*of* ∼бива́ть) to crack; to chip.

надбро́вный, *adj.* (*anat.*) superciliary.

надвига́|ть(ся), ю(сь), *impf. of* надви́нуть(ся).

надви́н|уть, у, ешь, *pf.* (*of* надвига́ть) to move, pull (up to, over).

надви́н|уться, усь, ешься, *pf.* (*of* надвига́ться) to approach, draw near.

надво́дный, *adj.* above-water; н. борт free-board; н. кора́бль surface ship.

на́двое, *adv.* **1.** in two. **2.** ambiguously; ба́бушка н. сказа́ла (*coll.*) I wouldn't be too sure about that.

надво́рный, *adj.* situated in the yard; н.

сове́тник (*obs.*) court counsellor (*civil servant of seventh class, equivalent in rank to lieutenant-colonel*).

надвя|за́ть, жу́, ∼жешь, *pf.* (*of* ∼зывать) to add (*in knitting*); to add a length (*of string, thread, etc.*).

надвя́зыва|ть, ю, *impf. of* надвяза́ть.

надгорта́нник, а, *m.* (*anat.*) epiglottis.

надгро́би|е, я, *n.* **1.** (*obs.*) epitaph. **2.** gravestone.

надгро́бн|ый, *adj.* (placed on, over, a) grave; funeral, graveside; ∼ое сло́во graveside oration.

надгрыз|а́ть, а́ю, *impf. of* ∼ть.

надгры́з|ть, у́, ёшь, *past* ∼, ∼ла, *pf.* (*of* ∼а́ть) to nibble (at).

надда|ва́ть, ю́, ёшь, *impf. of* ∼ть.

надда́|ть, м, шь, ст, ди́м, ди́те, ду́т, *past* ∼л, ∼ла́, ∼ло, *pf.* (*of* ∼ва́ть) (*coll.*; +*a. or g.*) to add, increase, enhance; н. хо́ду to increase the pace; ∼й! get a move on!

надду́в, а, *m.* (*tech., aeron.*) supercharge.

наде́в|анный, *p.p.p. of* ∼а́ть *and adj.* worn, used (*of clothing*).

надева́|ть, ю, *impf. of* наде́ть.

наде́жд|а, ы, *f.* hope, prospect; подава́ть ∼у to hold out hope; подава́ть ∼ы to promise well, shape well.

надёж|ный (∼ен, ∼на), *adj.* reliable, trustworthy; safe.

наде́л, а, *m.* allotment.

наде́ла|ть, ю, *pf.* (+*a. or g.*) **1.** to make (*a quantity of*). **2.** (*coll.*; +*g.*) to cause (*a lot of*), make (*a lot of*). **3.** (*coll.*) to do (*something wrong*); что ты ∼л? what have you done?

надел|ённый, *p.p.p. of* ∼и́ть; он ∼ён больши́ми спосо́бностями he is richly talented.

надел|и́ть, ю́, и́шь, *pf.* (*of* ∼я́ть) (+*a. and i.*) to invest (with), to provide (with); (*fig.*) to endow (with).

наде́|ну, нешь, *see* ∼ть.

надёрг|ать, аю, *pf.* (*of* ∼ивать) (+*a. or g.*) to pull, pluck (*a quantity of*).

надёргива|ть, ю, *impf. of* надёргать *and* надёрнуть.

надёр|нуть, ну, нешь, *pf.* (*of* ∼гивать) (на+*a.*) to pull (on, over).

над|еру́, ерёшь, *see* ∼ра́ть.

наде́|ть, ну, нешь, *pf.* (*of* ∼ва́ть) to put on (*clothes, etc.*).

наде́|яться, юсь, ешься, *impf.* (*of* по∼) **1.** (на+*a.*) to hope (for). **2.** (на+*a.*) to rely (on). **3.** to expect.

надзе́мный, *adj.* overground.

надзира́тел|ь, я, *m.* overseer, supervisor; кла́ссный н. (*obs.*) form-master.

надзира́тельниц|а, ы, *f. of* надзира́тель.

надзира́|ть, ю, *impf.* (за+*i.*) to oversee, supervise.

надзо́р, а, *m.* **1.** supervision, surveillance. **2.** (*collect.*) inspectorate; прокуро́рский н. Directorate of Public Prosecutions.

надив|и́ться, лю́сь, и́шься, *pf.* (*coll.*; +*d.* or на+*a.*) to admire sufficiently; не мо́жешь н. на его́ му́жество one cannot sufficiently admire his courage.

нади́р, а, *m.* (*astron.*) nadir.

надира́|ть, ю, *impf. of* надра́ть.

надира́|ться, юсь, *impf. of* надра́ться.

надка́лыва|ть, ю, *impf. of* надколо́ть.

надкла́ссовый, *adj.* (*polit.*) transcending class.

надко́жиц|а, ы, *f.* (*bot.*) cuticle.

надколе́нн|ый, *adj.* ~ая ча́шка knee-cap; (*anat.*) patella.

надкол|о́ть, ю́, ⌐ешь, *pf.* (*of* надка́лывать) **1.** to crack. **2.** to score.

надко́стниц|а, ы, *f.* (*anat.*) periosteum; воспале́ние ~ы (*med.*) periostitis.

надкры́ль|е, я, n. (*zool.*) shard, elytron; wing-case.

надку|си́ть, шу́, ⌐сишь, *pf.* (*of* ⌐сывать) to take a bite (of).

надку́сыва|ть, ю, *impf. of* надкуси́ть.

надла́мыва|ть(ся), ю(сь), *impf. of* надломи́ть(ся).

надлежа́щий, *adj.* fitting, proper; appropriate.

надлеж|и́т, *past* ~а́ло, (*impers.*; +*d. and inf.*) it is necessary, it is required; н. вам яви́ться в де́сять часо́в you are required to present yourself at ten o'clock.

надло́м, а, *m.* **1.** crack. **2.** (*fig.*) sharp deterioration of psychological state; crack-up. **3.** violent expression of emotion.

надлом|и́ть, лю́, ⌐ишь, *pf.* (*of* надла́мывать) to break partly; to crack; (*fig.*) to overtax, break down.

надлом|и́ться, лю́сь, ⌐ишься, *pf.* (*of* надла́мываться) **1.** to crack (*also fig.*); здоро́вье у него́ ~и́лось he has had a breakdown. **2.** *pass. of* ~и́ть.

надло́м|ленный, p.p.p. *of* ~и́ть *and adj.* broken (*also fig.*).

надме́нност|ь, и, *f.* haughtiness, arrogance.

надме́н|ный (~ен, ~на), *adj.* haughty, arrogant.

надня́х, *adv.* **1.** in a few days' time; one of these days. **2.** the other day.

на́до¹ = над.

на́до², +*d. and inf.* it is necessary; one must, one ought (+*a. or g.*) there is need of; мне н. идти́ I must go, I ought to go; мне н. вина́ I need some wine; так ему́ и н. serves him right!; н. быть (*coll.*) probably; что н. (*as pred.*; *coll.*) the best there is.

на́до|бно (*obs.*) = ~.

на́добност|ь, и, *f.* necessity, need; име́ть

н. в чём-н. to require something.

на́доб|ный (~ен, ~на), *adj.* (*obs.*) necessary, needful.

надоеда́|ть, ю, *impf. of* надое́сть.

надое́длив|ый (~, ~а), *adj.* boring, tiresome.

надое́|сть, м, шь, ст, ди́м, ди́те, дя́т, *pf.* (*of* ~да́ть) **1.** (+*d. and i.*) to get on the nerves (of), to pester (with), plague (with); to bore (with); он мне до чёртиков ~л I'm sick to death of him. **2.** (*impers.*; +*d. and inf.*) мне, *etc.*, ~ло I, *etc.*, am tired (of), sick (of); нам ~ло игра́ть в чехарду́ we are tired of playing leapfrog.

надо|и́ть, ю́, и́шь, *pf.* (*of* нада́ивать) (+*a. or g.*) to obtain (*a quantity of* milk).

надо́|й, я, *m.* (*agric.*) yield (of milk).

на́долб|а, ы, *f.* stake; противота́нковые ~ы anti-tank obstacles.

надо́лго, *adv.* for a long time.

надо́мник, а, *m.* craftsman working at home.

надорв|а́ть, у́, ёшь, *past* ~а́л, ~ала́, ~а́ло, *pf.* (*of* надрыва́ть) to tear slightly; (*fig.*) to (over)strain, overtax; н. живо́тики (со́ смеху) (*coll.*) to split one's sides (with laughter).

надорв|а́ться, у́сь, ёшься, *past* ~а́лся, ~ала́сь, ~а́лось, *pf.* (*of* надрыва́ться) tear slightly (*intrans.*); to (over)strain oneself.

надоу́м|ить, лю, ишь, *pf.* (*of* ~ливать) (*coll.*) to advise, to give the (*required*) idea.

надоу́млива|ть, ю, *impf. of* надоу́мить.

надпа́рыва|ть, ю, *impf. of* надпоро́ть.

надпи́лива|ть, ю, *impf. of* надпили́ть.

надпил|и́ть, ю́, ⌐ишь, *pf.* (*of* ⌐ивать) to make an incision in (*by sawing*).

надпи|са́ть, шу́, ⌐шешь, *pf.* (*of* ⌐сывать) **1.** to inscribe; to superscribe. **2.** (*obs.*) to address (*an envelope, etc.*).

надпи́сыва|ть, ю, *impf. of* надписа́ть.

на́дпис|ь, и, *f.* inscription; superscription; (*on medal, coin, etc.*) legend; переда́точная н. (*comm.*) endorsement.

надпор|о́ть, ю́, ⌐ешь, *pf.* (*of* надпа́рывать) (*coll.*) to unstitch, unpick (*a few stitches*).

надпо́чечный, *adj.* (*anat.*) adrenal.

над|ра́ть, еру́, ерёшь, *past* ~ра́л, ~рала́, ~ра́ло, *pf.* (*of* ~ира́ть) (+*a. or g.*) to tear off, strip (*a quantity of*); н. у́ши кому́-н. to pull someone's ears.

над|ра́ться, еру́сь, ерёшься, *past* ~ра́лся, ~рала́сь, ~ра́лось, *pf.* (*of* ~ира́ться) (*coll.*) to become sozzled.

надре́з, а, *m.* cut, incision; notch.

надре́|зать, жу, жешь, *pf.* (*of* ~за́ть *and* ~зывать) to make an incision (in).

надрез|а́ть, а́ю, *impf. of* ~а́ть.

надре́зыва|ть, ю, *impf.* = надреза́ть.

надруга́тельств|о, а, *n.* (над) outrage (upon).

надруга́|ться, юсь, *pf.* (над) to outrage, do violence to.

надры́в, а, *m.* 1. slight tear, rent. 2. strain. 3. (*fig.*) sharp deterioration of psychological state; crack-up. 4. violent expression of emotion.

надрыва́|ть(ся), ю(сь), *impf. of* надорва́ть(ся).

надры́в|ный (~ен, ~на), *adj.* 1. hysterical. 2. heart-rending.

надса́д|а, ы, *f.* (*coll.*) strain; effort.

надса|ди́ть, жу́, ~дишь, *pf.* (*of* ~жива́ть) (*coll.*) 1. to (over)strain. 2. (+*d.*) to vex, distress.

надса|ди́ться, жу́сь, ~дишься, *pf.* (*of* ~жива́ться) (*coll.*) to (over)strain oneself.

надса́д|ный (~ен, ~на), *adj.* (*coll.*) back-breaking; heavy; н. ка́шель hacking cough.

надса́жива|ть(ся), ю(сь), *impf. of* надсади́ть(ся).

надсма́трива|ть, ю, *impf.* (за+*i. or* над) to oversee, supervise; to inspect.

надсмо́тр, а, *m.* supervision; surveillance.

надсмо́трщик, а, *m.* overseer, supervisor; jailer.

надста́в|ить, лю, ишь, *pf.* (*of* ~ля́ть) to lengthen (*garment or part of garment*).

надста́вк|а, и, *f.* added piece, extension.

надставля́|ть, ю, *impf. of* надста́вить.

надстра́ива|ть, ю, *impf. of* надстро́ить.

надстро́|ить, ю, ишь, *pf.* (*of* надстра́ивать) 1. to build on. 2. to raise the height (of).

надстро́йк|а, и, *f.* 1. building on; raising. 2. superstructure (*also philos.*).

надстро́чн|ый, *adj.* superlinear.

надтре́снут|ый (~, ~а), *adj.* cracked (*also fig.*).

надува́л|а, ы, *m. and f.* (*coll.*) swindler, cheat.

надува́тельский, *adj.* (*coll.*) swindling, underhand.

надува́тельств|о, а, *n.* (*coll.*) swindling, cheating.

надува́|ть(ся), ю(сь), *impf. of* наду́ть(ся).

надувн|о́й, *adj.* pneumatic; ~а́я рези́новая ло́дка inflatable rubber dinghy.

наду́манный, *adj.* far-fetched, forced.

наду́м|ать, аю, *pf.* (*coll.*) 1. (+*inf.*) to decide (to). 2. (*impf.* ~ывать) to think up, make up.

наду́мыва|ть, ю, *impf. of* наду́мать.

наду́т|ый (~, ~а), *p.p.p. of* ~ь *and adj.* (*coll.*) 1. swollen. 2. haughty; puffed up. 3. sulky. 4. (*lit.*) inflated, turgid.

наду́|ть, ю, ешь, *pf.* (*of* ~ва́ть) 1. to inflate, blow up; to puff out; н. велосипе́дную ка́меру to inflate, blow up a bicycle tire; *impers.* (*pf. only*) ве́тром ~ло пы́ли the wind

blew the dust up; мне ~ло в у́хо I have ear-ache from the draught; н. гу́бы (*coll.*) to pout one's lips. 2. (*coll.*) to dupe; to swindle.

наду́|ться[1], юсь, ешься, *pf.* (*of* ~ва́ться) 1. to fill out, swell out; паруса́ ~лись the sails filled out. 2. (*fig.*, *coll.*) to be puffed up. 3. (*fig.*, *coll.*) to pout; to sulk.

наду́|ться[2], юсь, ешься, *pf.* (*coll.*; +*g.*) to swig (*a quantity of*).

надуш|енный, *p.p.p. of* ~и́ть *and adj.* scented, perfumed.

надуш|и́ть(ся), у́(сь), ~ишь(ся), *pf. of* души́ть(ся).

надшива́|ть, ю, *impf. of* надши́ть.

над|ши́ть, ошью́, ошьёшь, *pf.* (*of* ~шива́ть) 1. to lengthen (*a garment*). 2. to stitch on (to).

надым|и́ть, лю́, и́шь, *pf. of* дыми́ть.

надыш|а́ть, у́, ~ишь, *pf.* 1. to make the air (*in a room, etc.*) warm with one's breathing. 2. (*coll.*; на+*a.*) to breathe (on).

надыш|а́ться, у́сь, ~ишься, *pf.* 1. (+*i.*) to breathe in, inhale. 2. не н. (на+*a.*) to dote (on, upon).

наеда́|ться, юсь, *impf. of* нае́сться.

наедине́, *adv.* privately, in private; н. с (+*i.*) alone (with).

нае́|ду, дешь, *see* ~хать.

нае́зд, а, *m.* 1. flying visit; быва́ть ~ом to pay short, infrequent visits. 2. (*cavalry*) raid.

нае́з|дить, жу, дишь, *pf.* (*of* ~жа́ть) 1. to cover (*driving or riding*); мы ~дили сто миль за два часа́ we covered a hundred miles in two hours. 2. (*coll.*) to make (= gain, acquire) (*by conveying*); н. де́сять рубле́й to make ten roubles. 3. (доро́гу, *etc.*) to use (a road, *etc.*) a good deal. 4. to break in (*a horse*).

нае́здник, а, *m.* 1. horseman, rider; jockey; (*mil.*; *obs.*) raider. 2. (*zool.*) ichneumon-fly.

нае́здничеств|о, а, *n.* 1. horsemanship. 2. (*obs.*) (cavalry) raiding.

наезжа́|ть, ю, *impf.* 1. (*coll.*) to pay occasional visits. 2. *impf. of* нае́хать.

нае́з|женный, *p.p.p. of* ~дить *and adj.* well-trodden, beaten.

нае́зжива|ть, ю, *impf. of* нае́здить.

нае́зж|ий, *adj.* (*coll.*) newly-arrived; ~ие лю́ди new-comers.

нае́з|жу, дишь, *see* ~дить.

на|ём, ~йма, *m.* hire; renting; взять в н. to rent; сдать в н. to let.

наёмник, а, *m.* 1. (*hist.*) mercenary. 2. hireling (*also fig.*).

наёмный, *adj.* hired; rented.

наёмщик, а, *m.* tenant, lessee.

нае́|сться, мся, шься, стся, ди́мся, ди́тесь, дя́тся, *past* ~лся, ~лась, *pf.* (*of* ~да́ться)

1. to eat one's fill. **2.** (+*g. or i.*) to eat (a large quantity of), stuff oneself (with).

нае|хать, ду, дешь, *pf.* (*of* ~зжáть) **1.** (на+*a.*) to run (into, over), collide (with); на нас ~хал автóбус a 'bus ran into us (over us). **2.** (*coll.*) to come, arrive (*unexpectedly or in numbers*).

нажáл|оваться, уюсь, *pf.* (*coll.*; на+*a.*) to complain (of).

нажáрива|ть(ся), ю(сь), *impf. of* нажáрить-(ся).

нажáр|ить[1], ю, ишь, *pf.* (*of* ~ивать) (*coll.*) to overheat.

нажáр|ить[2], ю, ишь, *pf.* to roast, fry (*a quantity of*).

нажáр|иться, юсь, ишься, *pf.* (*of* ~иваться) (*coll.*) to bask, warm oneself (*for a long time*).

наж|áть[1], му́, мёшь, *pf.* (*of* ~имáть) **1.** (+*a. or* на+*a.*) to press (on); н. (на) кнóпку to press the button. **2.** (*fig., coll.*; на+*a.*) to put pressure (upon). **3.** (*fig., coll.*) to press on, press ahead; ~мём и вы́полним э́ту рабóту! let us press on and finish this job!

наж|áть[2], ну́, нёшь, *pf.* (*of* ~инáть) (+*a. or g.*) to reap, harvest (*a quantity of*).

наждáк, á, *m.* emery.

наждá|чный, *adj. of* ~к; ~чная бумáга emery paper.

наж|éчь, гу́, жёшь, гу́т, *past* ~ёг, ~глá, *pf.* (*of* ~игáть) (+*a. or g.*) to burn (*a quantity of*).

нажи́в|а[1], ы, *f.* gain, profit.

нажи́в|а[2], ы, *f.* = ~ка.

наживá|ть(ся), ю(сь), *impf. of* нажи́ть(ся).

нажив|и́ть, лю́, и́шь, *pf.* (*of* ~ля́ть) to bait.

нажи́вк|а, и, *f.* bait.

наживля́|ть, ю, *impf. of* наживи́ть.

наживн|óй[1], *adj., only in phrase* э́то дéло ~óе (*coll.*) it'll come (with time).

наживнóй[2], *adj.* usable as bait.

нажи|ву́, вёшь, *see* ~ть.

нажигá|ть, ю, *impf. of* нажéчь.

нажи́м, а, *m.* **1.** pressure (*also fig.*). **2.** (*tech.*) clamp.

нажимá|ть, ю, *impf. of* нажáть[1].

нажи́мист|ый (~, ~а), *adj.* (*coll.*) exacting; stubborn, insistent.

нажимн|óй, *adj.* (*tech.*) pressure; н. винт stop screw; ~óе приспособлéние pressure mechanism.

нажинá|ть, ю, *impf. of* нажáть[2].

нажирá|ться, юсь, *impf. of* нажрáться.

наж|и́ть, иву́, ивёшь, *past* ~ил, ~илá, ~ило, *pf.* (*of* ~ивáть) to acquire, gain; (*fig.*) to contract (*disease*), incur.

наж|и́ться[1], иву́сь, ивёшься, *past* ~и́лся, ~илáсь, *pf.* (*of* ~ивáться) to become rich, make a fortune.

нажи́|ться[2], ву́сь, вёшься, *pf.* (*coll.*) to live (*somewhere*) long enough.

наж|му́, мёшь, *see* ~áть[1].

наж|ну́, нёшь, *see* ~áть[2].

нажр|áться, у́сь, ёшься, *pf.* (*of* нажирáть-ся) (*coll.*; +*g. or i.*) to gorge oneself (with).

назáвтра, *adv.* (*coll.*) on *or* for the next day.

назáд, *adv.* **1.** back, backwards; н.! back!, stand back! **2.** (томý) н. ago.

назади́, *adv.* (*coll.*) behind.

назализáци|я, и, *f.* (*ling.*) nasalization.

назализи́р|овать, ую, *impf. and pf.* (*ling.*) to nasalize.

назáльный, *adj.* (*ling.*) nasal.

назвáнива|ть, ю, *impf.* (*coll.*) to keep ringing (*on telephone, etc.*).

назвáни|е, я, *n.* name, appellation; title (*book*).

назвáный, *adj.* sworn; adopted; (*fig.*) он мой н. брат he is my sworn brother.

наз|вáть[1], ову́, овёшь, *past* ~вáл, ~валá, ~вáло, *pf.* (*of* ~ывáть) (+*i.*) to call; to name, designate; они́ ~вáли дочь Татья́ной they have called their daughter Tatyana; он ~вáл себя́ Николáем he gave his name as Nicholas.

наз|вáть[2], ову́, овёшь, *past* ~вáл, ~валá, ~вáло, *pf.* (*coll.*; +*g.*) to invite (*a number of*).

наз|вáться[1], ову́сь, овёшься, *past* ~вáлся, ~валáсь, *pf. of* ~ывáться.

наз|вáться[2], ову́сь, овёшься, *past* ~вáлся, ~валáсь, *pf.* (*coll.*) to invite oneself.

наздрáвств|оваться, уюсь, *pf.* на вся́кое чихáнье не ~уешься (*coll.*) one cannot please everyone.

назём, а, *m.* (*dial.*) manure, dung.

назéмн|ый, *adj.* ground, surface; terrestrial; ~ые войскá (*mil.*) ground troops; ~ая (пóчта) surface mail.

нáземь, *adv.* (down) to the ground.

назидáни|е, я, *n.* (*obs., now iron.*) edification; сказáть что-н. в н. комý-н. to say something for someone's edification.

назидáтел|ьный (ен, ~ьна), *adj.* edifying.

нáзло́ **1.** *adv.* out of spite. **2.** *prep.* (+*d.*) to spite.

назнач|áть, áю, *impf. of* ~и́ть.

назначéни|е, я, *n.* **1.** fixing, setting. **2.** appointment. **3.** (*med.*) prescription. **4.** purpose.

назнáч|ить, у, ишь, *pf.* (*of* ~áть) **1.** to fix, set, appoint; н. день встрéчи to fix, appoint a day for a meeting; н. оплáту to fix a rate of pay. **2.** (+*i.*) to appoint, nominate; егó ~или командúром рóты he has been appointed company commander. **3.** (*med.*) to prescribe.

назóйливост|ь, и, *f.* importunity.

назóйлив|ый (~, ~а), *adj.* importunate.

назревá|ть, ю, *impf.* (*of* назрéть) **1.** to ripen, mature; to gather head. **2.** (*fig.*) to become imminent; кри́зис ~л a crisis was brewing.

назре́|ть, ю, ешь, *pf. of* ~ва́ть.

назубо́к, *adv.* (*coll.*) знать н. to know by heart.

называ́|емый, *pres. part. pass. of* ~ть; так н. so-called.

называ́|ть, ю, *impf. of* назва́ть[1].

называ́|ться[1], юсь, *impf.* (*of* назва́ться[1]) (+*i.*) **1.** to call oneself. **2.** to be called; как ~ется э́то село́? what is this village called? what is the name of this village?; что ~ется (*coll.*) as they say. **3.** (*obs.*) to give one's name.

наибо́лее, *adv.* (the) most.

наибо́льший, *adj.* the greatest; the largest; о́бщий н. дели́тель (*math.*) highest common factor.

наивнича́|ть, ю, *impf.* (*coll.*) to affect naïveté.

наи́вност|ь, и, *f.* naïveté (naivety).

наи́в|ный (~ен, ~на), *adj.* naïve.

наивы́сш|ий, *adj.* the highest; в ~ей сте́пени to the utmost.

наи́гранн|ый 1. *p.p.p. of* наигра́ть. **2.** *adj.* (*fig.*) put on, assumed; forced; ~ая весё́лость assumed gaiety.

наигра́|ть, ю, *pf.* (*of* наи́грывать) **1.** (*coll.*) to make, acquire (*by playing*). **2.** (*coll.*) to strum. **3.** н. пласти́нку to make a recording.

наигра́|ться, юсь, *pf.* (*coll.*) to play for a long time, for long enough.

наи́грыва|ть, ю, *impf. of* наигра́ть.

на́игрыш, а, *m.* **1.** folk-tune. **2.** (*theatr. sl.*) artificiality.

наизна́нку, *adv.* inside out; вы́вернуть н. to turn inside out.

наизу́сть, *adv.* by heart; from memory.

наилу́чший, *adj.* (the) best.

наиме́нее, *adv.* (the) least.

наименова́ни|е, я, *n.* appellation, designation.

наимен|ова́ть, у́ю, *pf. of* именова́ть.

наиме́ньш|ий, *adj.* (the) least; о́бщее ~ее кра́тное (*math.*) lowest common multiple.

наипа́че, *adv.* (*obs.*) still more; in particular.

наискосо́к, *adv.* = на́искось.

на́искось, *adv.* obliquely, slantwise.

наи́ти|е, я, *n.* inspiration; по ~ю instinctively, intuitively.

наиху́дший, *adj.* (the) worst.

найдё́ныш, а, *m.* foundling.

найми́т, а, *m.* hireling.

на|йти́[1], йду́, йдёшь, *past* ~шё́л, ~шла́, *pf.* (*of* ~ходи́ть) (*in var. senses*) to find; to discover; н. себе́ моги́лу, смерть (*rhet.*) to meet one's death.

на|йти́[2], йду́, йдёшь, *past* ~шё́л, ~шла́, *pf.* (*of* ~ходи́ть) **1.** (на+*a.*) to come (across, over, upon); to come (up against); что э́то на неё ~шло́? what has come over her?

2. (*impers.; coll.*) to gather, collect; ~шло́ мно́го наро́ду a large crowd collected.

на|йти́сь, йду́сь, йдёшься, *past* ~шё́лся, ~шла́сь, *pf.* (*of* ~ходи́ться[1]) **1.** to be found; to turn up. **2.** (*pf. only*) not to be at a loss; я не ~шё́лся, что сказа́ть I was at a loss for what to say.

найто́в, а, *m.* (*naut.*) lashing, seizing.

найто́в|ить, лю, ишь, *impf.* (*of* об~) (*naut.*) to lash, seize.

нака́вер|зить, жу, зишь, *pf. of* ка́верзить.

нака́з, а, *m.* **1.** (*obs.*) order; instructions. **2.** mandate (*in Soviet governmental system, list of desiderata presented by electors to deputy*).

наказа́ни|е, я, *n.* **1.** punishment. **2.** (*fig., coll.*) nuisance; мне с ним (су́щее, пря́мо, про́сто) н. he is a (perfect) nuisance to me.

нака|за́ть[1], жу́, ~жешь, *pf.* (*of* ~зывать) to punish.

нака|за́ть[2], жу́, ~жешь, *pf.* (*of* ~зывать) (*obs. or dial.; +d.*) to instruct, bid.

наказу́емый, *adj.* (*leg.*) punishable.

нака́л, а, *m.* **1.** incandescence. **2.** (*radio*) heating.

нака́л|ённый, *p.p.p. of* ~и́ть *and adj.* **1.** incandescent; white-hot. **2.** (*fig.*) strained, tense; ~ённая междунаро́дная обстано́вка tense international situation.

нака́ливани|е, я, *n.* (*tech.*) incandescing.

нака́лива|ть(ся), ю(сь), *impf. of* накали́ть(ся).

накал|и́ть, ю́, и́шь, *pf.* (*of* ~ивать) to heat, incandesce.

накал|и́ться, ю́сь, и́шься, *pf.* (*of* ~иваться) to glow, incandesce.

нака́лыва|ть(ся), ю(сь), *impf. of* наколо́ть(ся).

наканифо́л|ить, ю, ишь, *pf. of* канифо́лить.

накану́не 1. (*adv.*) the day before. **2.** (*prep.+g.*) on the eve (of); н. Рождества́ Христо́ва on Christmas Eve.

нака́п|ать, аю, *pf.* (*of* ~ывать[1]) **1.** (+*a. or g.*) to pour by drops; н. лека́рства to pour out some medicine. **2.** (+*g. or i.*) to spill; он ~ал на столе́ черни́лами (черни́л) he has spilled ink on the table.

нака́пливать(ся) = накопля́ть(ся).

нака́пыва|ть[1], ю, *impf. of* нака́пать.

нака́пыва|ть[2], ю, *impf. of* накопа́ть.

нака́рка|ть, ю, *pf.* (*coll.*) to bring down (evil) by one's own prophecies.

нака́т, а, *m.* layer (*of beams or planks*).

накат|а́ть[1], а́ю, *pf.* (*of* ~ывать) **1.** to roll out; to roll smooth. **2.** (*coll.*) to write hurriedly; н. письмо́ to dash off a letter.

накат|а́ть[2], а́ю, *pf.* (*of* ~ывать) (+*a. or g.*) to roll (*a quantity of*).

наката́|ться, юсь, *pf.* (*coll.*) to have had enough (*of driving, riding*).

нака|ти́ть, чу́, ~тишь, *pf.* (*of* ~тывать)

(на+*a*.) to roll up (onto); (*impers.*; *coll.*) на негó ~тѝло he is out of his senses, he has taken leave of his senses.

накáтыва|ть, ю, *impf. of* накатáть *and* накатѝть.

накач|áть¹, áю, *pf.* (*of* ~ивать) to pump up, pump full.

накачá|ть², ю, *pf.* to pump (*a quantity of*).

накачá|ться¹, юсь, *pf.* (*coll.*) to have been swinging long enough.

накач|áться², áюсь, *pf.* (*of* ~иваться) **1.** (*coll.*) to become sozzled. **2.** *pass. of* ~áть.

накáчива|ть(ся), ю(сь), *impf. of* накачáть(ся).

накид|áть, áю, *pf.* (*of* ~ывать) = набросáть².

накѝдк|а, и, *f.* **1.** cloak, mantle; wrap. **2.** pillow-cover. **3.** increase; extra charge.

накѝдыва|ть(ся), ю(сь), *impf. of* накидáть *and* накѝнуть(ся).

накѝ|нуть, ну, нешь, *pf.* (*of* ~дывать) **1.** to throw on, throw over. **2.** (на+*a*.) to add (*to the price of*).

накѝ|нуться, нусь, нешься, *pf.* (*of* ~дываться) (на+*a*.) to fall (on, upon).

накип|áть, áет, *impf. of* ~éть.

накип|éть, ѝт, *pf.* (*of* ~áть) to form a scum; to form a scale; (*fig.*; *impers.*) to swell, boil; в нём ~éла злóба he is boiling with resentment.

нáкип|ь, и, *f*. **1.** scum. **2.** scale, fur, coating, deposit.

наклáд, а, *m*. быть, остáться в ~е (*coll.*) to be down, come off loser.

наклáдк|а, и, *f*. **1.** (*tech.*) bracket. **2.** false hair, hair-piece.

накладн|áя, óй, *f*. invoice, way-bill.

наклáдно, *adv.* (*coll.*) to one's disadvantage, to one's cost.

накладн|óй, *adj.* **1.** laid on, super-imposed; ~óе зóлото rolled gold; ~ые расхóды overhead expenses, overheads. **2.** false; ~áя борóда false beard.

наклáдыва|ть, ю, *impf. of* наложѝть.

наклеве|тáть, щý, ~щешь, *pf. of* клеветáть.

наклёвыва|ться, юсь, *impf. of* наклюнуться.

наклéива|ть, ю, *impf. of* наклéить.

наклé|ить, ю, ешь, *pf.* (*of* ~ивать) to stick on, paste on.

наклéйк|а, и, *f*. **1.** sticking on, pasting on. **2.** label.

наклепá|ть¹, ю, *pf.* (*of* наклёпывать) to rivet.

наклеп|áть², лю, ~лешь, *pf. of* клепáть².

наклёпыва|ть, ю, *impf. of* наклепáть¹.

наклик|áть, áю, *impf. of* ~áть.

наклѝ|кать, чу, чешь, *pf.* (*of* ~кáть) н. на себя́ to bring upon oneself; н. бедý (на+*a*.) to bring disaster (upon).

наклóн, а, *m*. slope, incline; declivity.

наклонéни|е¹, я, *n*. inclination.

наклонéни|е², я, *n*. (*gram.*) mood.

наклон|ѝть, ю, ~ишь, *pf.* (*of* ~я́ть) to incline, bend; to bow.

наклон|ѝться, юсь, ~ишься, *pf.* (*of* ~я́ться) to stoop, bend.

наклóнност|ь, и, *f*. **1.** (к) leaning (towards), penchant (for). **2.** inclination, propensity, proclivity; дурны́е ~и evil propensities.

наклóнн|ый, *adj.* inclined, sloping; ~ая плóскость inclined plane; катѝться по ~ой плóскости (*fig.*) to go downhill, go to the dogs (*morally*).

наклон|я́ть(ся), я́ю(сь), *impf. of* ~ѝть(ся).

наклюн|уться, усь, ешься, *pf.* (*of* наклёвываться) **1.** to peck its way out of the shell. **2.** (*coll.*) to turn up; случáй ~ется an occasion will present itself.

накля́узнича|ть, ю, *pf. of* кля́узничать.

наковáл|ьня, ьни, *g. pl.* ~ен, *f*. **1.** anvil. **2.** (*anat.*) incus.

накóжный, *adj.* (*med.*) cutaneous.

наколáчива|ть, ю, *impf. of* наколотѝть¹, ².

наколéнник, а, *m*. knee-guard.

наколéнный, *adj.* worn on the knee.

наколк|а, и, *f*. head-dress (*fastened with pins*).

наколо|тѝть¹, чý, ~тишь, *pf.* (*of* наколáчивать) (*coll.*) **1.** to knock on. **2.** to knock up (*money*).

наколо|тѝть², чý, ~тишь, *pf.* (*of* наколáчивать) (+*a. or g.*) н. гвоздéй to drive in (*a number of*) nails; н. посýды to smash (*a quantity of*) crockery.

накол|óть¹, ю, ~ешь, *pf.* (*of* накáлывать) (+*a. or g.*) to split (*a quantity of*); н. дров to chop (*a quantity of*) wood.

накол|óть², ю, ~ешь, *pf.* (*of* накáлывать) **1.** to prick; н. узóр to prick out a pattern. **2.** to pin down; н. бáбочку на булáвку to pin down a butterfly. **3.** to slaughter, stick (*a number of*).

накол|óться, юсь, ~ешься, *pf.* (*of* накáлываться) to prick oneself.

наконéц, *adv.* **1.** at last. **2.** finally, in the end.

наконéчник, а, *m*. tip, point; ferrule; н. стрелы́ arrow-head.

наконéчн|ый, *adj.* final; ~ое ударéние (*gram.*) end-stress.

накопá|ть, ю, *pf.* (*of* накáпывать) (+*a. or g.*) to dig up (*a number of*).

накоп|ѝть, лю́, ~ишь, *pf.* (*of* копѝть; ~ля́ть *and* накáпливать) (+*a. or g.*) to accumulate, amass.

накоп|ѝться, лю́сь, ~ишься, *pf.* (*of* ~ля́ться *and* накáпливаться) to accumulate.

накоплéни|е, я, *n*. accumulation.

накопля́|ть(ся), ю(сь), *impf. of* накопѝть(ся).

накоп|ти́ть[1], **чу́, ти́шь**, *pf. of* копти́ть 3.

накоп|ти́ть[2], **чу́, ти́шь**, *pf.* (+*a. or g.*) to smoke (= cure) (*a quantity of*).

накорм|и́ть, лю́, ~ишь, *pf. of* корми́ть.

накоротке́, *adv.* произвести́ ата́ку н. to carry out a rapid attack at close range.

нако|си́ть, шу́, ~сишь, *pf.* (+*a. or g.*) to mow (down) (*a quantity of*).

нако́стн|ый, *adj.* (situated on) bone; ~ая о́пухоль bone tumour.

накра́пыва|ть, ет, *impf.* (*impers. or* +*дождь*) to trickle, drizzle; ста́ло н. it began to spit (*with rain*).

накра́|сить, шу, сишь, *pf.* (*of* ~шивать) 1. to paint. 2. to make up.

накра́|сится, шусь, сишься, *pf. of* кра́сить-ся.

накра́|сть, ду́, дёшь, *past* ~л, *pf.* (*of* ~ды-вать) (+*a. or g.*) to steal (*a number of*).

накрахма́л|ить, ю, ишь, *pf. of* крахма́лить.

накра́шива|ть, ю, *impf. of* накра́сить.

накрен|и́ть, ю́, и́шь, *pf.* 1. *pf. of* крени́ть. 2. (*impf.* ~я́ть) to tilt to one side, tilt.

накрен|и́ться, ю́сь, и́шься, *pf.* 1. *pf. of* крени́ться. 2. (*impf.* ~я́ться) to tilt, list.

накрен|я́ть(ся), я́ю(сь), *impf. of* ~и́ть(ся).

на́крепко, *adv.* 1. fast, tight; закры́ть н. to shut fast. 2. (*coll.*) categorically; strictly; приказа́ть н. to give a strict injunction.

на́крест, *adv.* crosswise; сложи́ть ру́ки крест-н. to cross one's arms.

накрич|а́ть, у́, и́шь, *pf.* (на+*a.*) to shout (at).

накрич|а́ться, у́сь, и́шься, *pf.* (*coll.*) to have shouted to one's heart's content.

накро|и́ть, ю́, и́шь, *pf.* (+*a. or g.*) to cut out (*a quantity of*).

накрош|и́ть, у́, ~ишь, *pf.* (*of* кроши́ть) 1. to crumble, shred (*a quantity of*). 2. to spill crumbs.

накр|о́ю, о́ешь, *see* ~ы́ть.

накро|ю́, и́шь, *see* ~и́ть.

накру|ти́ть[1], **чу́, ~тишь**, *pf.* (*of* ~чивать) to wind, turn.

накру|ти́ть[2], **чу́, ~тишь**, *pf.* 1. to twist (*a quantity of*). 2. (*coll.*) to do, say (*something complicated or unusual*).

накру́чива|ть, ю, *impf. of* накрути́ть[1].

накрыва́|ть(ся), ю(сь), *impf. of* накры́ть(ся).

накр|ы́ть, о́ю, о́ешь, *pf.* (*of* ~ыва́ть) 1. to cover; н. (на) стол to lay the table; н. к у́жину to lay supper. 2. (*fig., coll.*) to catch; н. на ме́сте преступле́ния to catch red--handed.

накр|ы́ться, о́юсь, о́ешься, *pf.* (*of* ~ыва́ть-ся) (+*i.*) to cover oneself (with).

накто́уз, а, *m.* (*naut.*) binnacle.

накуп|а́ть, а́ю, *impf. of* ~и́ть.

накуп|и́ть, лю́, ~ишь, *pf.* (*of* ~а́ть) (+*a. or g.*) to buy up (*a number or quantity of*).

наку́р|енный, *p.p.p. of* ~и́ть *and adj.* smoky,

smoke-filled; в ко́мнате ~ено the room is full of (tobacco) smoke.

накур|и́ть[1], **ю́, ~ишь**, *pf.* (+*i.*) to fill with smoke, with fumes.

накур|и́ть[2], **ю́, ~ишь**, *pf.* (+*a. or g.*) to distil (*a quantity of*).

накур|и́ться, ю́сь, ~ишься, *pf.* (*coll.*) to smoke to one's heart's content.

наку́т|ать, аю, *pf.* (*of* ~ывать) (+*a. or g.* на+*a.*) to put on (*clothing, etc.*); мно́го ~али на ребёнка the child was well wrapped up.

наку́тыва|ть, ю, *impf. of* накутать.

нала́влива|ть, ю, *impf. of* налови́ть.

налага́|ть, ю, *impf. of* наложи́ть.

нала́|дить, жу, дишь, *pf.* (*of* ~живать) 1. to regulate, adjust; to repair, put right. 2. to set going, arrange; н. дела́ to get things going.

нала́|диться, жусь, дишься, *pf.* (*of* ~жи-ваться) 1. to go right, get going; рабо́та ~дилась the work is well in hand. 2. *pass. of* ~дить.

нала́дчик, а, *m.* (*tech.*) adjuster.

нала́жива|ть(ся), ю(сь), *impf. of* нала́-дить(ся).

налака́|ться, юсь, *pf.* 1. н. молока́ to lap up one's fill of milk. 2. (*coll.*) to get drunk.

налакир|ова́ть, у́ю, *pf.* to varnish.

нала́ком|иться, люсь, ишься, *pf.* (*coll.*; +*i.*) to have one's fill (of dainties).

на|лга́ть, лгу́, лжёшь, лгу́т, *past* ~лга́л, ~лгала́, ~лга́ло, *pf.* 1. to lie, tell lies. 2. (*impf.* лгать 2) (на+*a.*) to slander.

нале́во, *adv.* 1. (от) to the left (of); н.! (*mil.*) left turn! 2. (*coll.*) on the side (= *illicitly*)

налега́|ть, ю, *impf. of* нале́чь.

налегке́, *adv.* (*coll.*) 1. without luggage; путеше́ствовать н. to travel light. 2. lightly clad.

належ|а́ть, у́, и́шь, *pf.* (*coll.*) to acquire as result of lying a long time; н. про́лежни to develop bed-sores.

налеза́|ть[1, 2], **а́ю**, *impf. of* ~ть[1, 2].

нале́з|ть[1], **у, ешь**, *past* ~, ~ла, *pf.* (*of* ~а́ть[1]) to get in, get on (*in large numbers, in quantities*).

нале́з|ть[2], **ет**, *pf.* (*of* ~а́ть[2]) (*of clothing or footwear*) (на+*a.*) to fit, go on.

налеп|и́ть[1], **лю́, ~ишь**, *pf.* (*of* лепи́ть 2 *and* ~ля́ть) to stick on.

налеп|и́ть[2], **лю́, ~ишь**, *pf.* (+*a. or g.*) to model (*a number of*).

налеп|ля́ть, ля́ю, *impf. of* ~и́ть.

налёт[1], **а**, *m.* (*in var. senses*) raid; кавалери́й-ский н. cavalry raid; возду́шный н. air--raid; с ~а (*fig.*) suddenly, without warning, without preparation; бить с ~а to swoop down on; он ду́мает, что он смо́жет по-би́ть реко́рд с ~а he thinks he will be able to beat the record just like that.

налёт², а, m. deposit; thin coating; (on bronze) patina; (fig.) touch, soupçon; н. в го́рле (med.) patch, spot; с ~ом иро́нии with a touch of irony.

налет|а́ть¹, а́ю, impf. of ~е́ть.

налет|а́ть², а́ю, pf. to have flown (so many hours or miles).

нале|те́ть¹, чу́, ти́шь, pf. (of ~та́ть¹) 1. (на+a.) to fall (upon); to swoop down (on); to fly (upon, against); to run (into) (of vehicles). 2.(of wind, storm) to spring up.

нале|те́ть², чу́, ти́шь, pf. (of ~та́ть¹) to fly in, drift in (in quantities, in large numbers).

налётчик, а, m. burglar, robber; raider.

на|ле́чь, ля́гу, ля́жешь, ля́гут, imp. ~ля́г, past ~лёг, ~легла́, pf. (of ~лега́ть) (на+a.) 1. to lean (on); to weigh down (on); to lie (upon); н. плечо́м на дверь to try to force the door with one's shoulder; н. на подчинённых (fig.) to come down upon one's subordinates. 2. to apply oneself (to), throw oneself (into); н. на вёсла to ply one's oars.

нали́в, а, m. 1. pouring in. 2. swelling, ripening; «бе́лый н.» name of kind of apple.

налива́|ть(ся), ю(сь), impf. of нали́ть(ся).

нали́вк|а, и, f. fruit liqueur; вишнёвая н. cherry brandy.

наливн|о́й, adj. 1. (tech.) worked by water; for conveying liquids; ~о́е колесо́ overshot wheel; ~о́е су́дно (naut.) tanker. 2. ripe, juicy.

нали́м, а, m. (fish) burbot, eel-pout.

налин|ова́ть, у́ю, pf. of линова́ть.

налип|а́ть, а́ет, impf. of ~нуть.

нали́п|нуть, нет, past ~, ~ла, pf. (of ~а́ть) (на+a.) to stick (to).

налито́й, adj. 1. juicy, ripe. 2. fleshy, wellfleshed.

нал|и́ть, ью́, ьёшь, past ~и́л, ~ила́, ~и́ло, pf. (of ~ива́ть) to pour out; (+i.) to fill (with); н. бо́чку водо́й to fill a barrel with water.

нал|и́ться, ью́сь, ьёшься, past ~и́лся, ~ила́сь, ~и́ло́сь, pf. (of ~ива́ться) 1. (+i.) to fill (with); н. кро́вью to become bloodshot. 2. to ripen, become juicy. 3. pass. of ~и́ть.

налицо́, adv. present, available, on hand.

нали́честв|овать, ую, impf. to be present, be on hand.

нали́чи|е, я, n. presence; быть, оказа́ться в ~и to be present, be available; при ~и (+g.) in the presence (of), given.

нали́чник, а, m. 1. casing, jambs and lintel of a door or window. 2. lock-plate.

нали́чност|ь, и, f. 1. amount on hand; cash-in-hand; н. това́ров в магази́не stock-in-trade. 2. = нали́чие.

нали́чн|ый, adj. on hand, available; ~ые (де́ньги) ready money, cash; плати́ть ~ыми to pay in cash, pay down; за н. расчёт for cash; н. соста́в (mil.) available personnel, effectives.

нало́бник, а, m. (part of harness) frontlet.

налов|и́ть, лю́, ~ишь, pf. (+a. or g.) to catch (a number of).

наловч|и́ться, у́сь, и́шься, pf. (+inf.) to become proficient (in), become good (at).

нало́г, а, m. tax.

нало́г|овый, adj. of ~.

налогоплате́льщик, а, m. tax-payer.

наложе́ни|е, я, n. 1. imposition; н. аре́ста (leg.) seizure; н. швов (med.) suture, stitching. 2. (math.) superposition.

нало́ж|енный, p.p.p. of ~и́ть; ~енным платежо́м cash on delivery (C.O.D.).

налож|и́ть¹, у́, ~ишь, pf. 1. (impf. накла́дывать) to lay in, on; to put in, on; to superimpose; to apply; н.·повя́зку to apply a bandage; н. на себя́ ру́ки to lay hands on oneself. 2. (impf. накла́дывать) to load, pack; н. корзи́ну бельём, н. белья́ в корзи́ну to load a basket with linen. 3. (impf. налага́ть) (на+a.) to lay (on), impose; н. на себя́ бре́мя to undertake a burden; н. штраф to impose a fine; н. аре́ст на чьё-н. иму́щество (leg.) to seize someone's property.

налож|и́ть², у́, ~ишь, pf. (of накла́дывать) to put, lay (a quantity of).

нало́жниц|а, ы, f. (obs.) concubine.

нало́|й, я, m. = анало́й.

налома́|ть, ю, pf. (+a. or g.) to break (a quantity of); н. бока́ кому-н. (coll.) to give someone a sound thrashing; н. дров (coll., joc.) to commit follies.

налопа́|ться, юсь, pf. (coll.) to gorge oneself.

налощ|и́ть, у́, и́шь, pf. of лощи́ть.

нал|ью́, ьёшь, see ~и́ть.

налюб|ова́ться, у́юсь, pf. (+i. or на+a.) to gaze to one's heart's content (at) (usually with neg.).

нал|я́гу, я́жешь, я́гут, see ~е́чь.

наля́па|ть, ю, pf. of ля́пать.

нам, d. of мы.

намагни́|тить, чу, тишь, pf. (of ~чивать) to magnetize.

намагни́чива|ть, ю, impf. of намагни́тить.

нама́з, а, m. (Mohammedan) prayer.

нама́|зать, жу, жешь, pf. of ма́зать and ~зывать.

нама́|заться, жусь, жешься, pf. 1. (impf. ~зываться) (+i.) to rub oneself (with). 2. pf. of ма́заться.

нама́зыва|ть(ся), ю(сь), impf. of нама́зать(ся).

намал|ева́ть, юю, юешь, pf. of малева́ть.

намара́|ть, ю, pf. of мара́ть 2.

намарин|ова́ть, у́ю, *pf.* (+*a. or g.*) to pickle (*a quantity of*).

нама́слива|ть, ю, *impf.* = ма́слить.

нама́сл|ить, ю, ишь, *pf. of* ~ивать *and* ма́слить.

нама́тывани|е, я, *n.* winding, reeling.

нама́тыва|ть, ю, *impf. of* намота́ть².

нама́чива|ть, ю, *impf. of* намочи́ть.

нама́|яться, юсь, ешься, *pf.* (*coll.*) **1.** to be tired out. **2.** to have had a lot of trouble.

наме́дни, *adv.* (*dial.*) the other day, lately.

намёк, а, *m.* **1.** hint, allusion; то́нкий н. gentle hint; сде́лать н. to drop a hint; с ~ом (на+*a.*) with a suggestion (of). **2.** (*fig.*) faint resemblance.

намек|а́ть, а́ю, *impf.* (*of* ~ну́ть) (на+*a.*, о+*p.*) to hint (at), allude (to).

намек|ну́ть, ну́, нёшь, *pf. of* ~а́ть.

намел|и́ть, ю, и́шь, *pf. of* мели́ть.

наменя́|ть, ю, *pf.* (+*a. or g.*) to obtain (*a quantity of*) by exchange.

намерева́|ться, юсь, *impf.* (+*inf.*) to intend (to), mean (to).

наме́рен (~а, ~о), *adj.* used as *pred.* быть н. (+*inf.*) to intend; я н. за́втра е́хать I intend to go tomorrow; что вы ~ы сде́лать? what do you intend to do?

наме́рени|е, я, *n.* intention; purpose.

наме́ренный, *adj.* intentional, deliberate.

намерз|а́ть, а́ю, *impf. of* ~ну́ть.

намёрз|нуть, ну, нешь, *past* ~, ~ла, *pf.* (*of* ~а́ть) to freeze (on); на ступе́ньках ~ло мно́го льда a lot of ice had formed on the steps.

намёрз|нуться, нусь, нешься, *past* ~ся, ~лась, *pf.* (*coll.*) to get frozen.

наме́р|ить, ю, ишь, *pf.* **1.** (+*a. or g.*) to measure out (*a quantity of*). **2.** to measure (*a certain quantity* or *distance*).

на́мертво, *adv.* tightly, fast.

наме|си́ть, шу́, ~сишь, *pf.* (+*a. or g.*) to knead (*a quantity of*).

наме|сти́, ту́, тёшь, *past* ~л, ~ла́, *pf.* (*of* ~та́ть¹) (+*a. or g.*) **1.** to sweep together (*a quantity of*). **2.** to cause to drift; ~ло́ мно́го сне́гу big snow-drifts have formed.

наме́стник, а, *m.* **1.** deputy. **2.** (*hist.*) governor-general.

наме́стни|ческий, *adj. of* ~к.

наме́стничеств|о, а, *n.* (*hist.*) region ruled by governor-general.

намёт¹, а, *m.* casting-net.

намёт², а, *m.* (*dial.*) gallop.

намета́|ть¹, ю, *impf. of* намести́.

намета́|ть², ю, *pf. of* мета́ть².

наме|та́ть³, чу́, ~чешь, *pf.* (+*a. or g.*) to throw together (*a quantity of*).

наме|та́ть⁴, чу́, ~чешь, *pf.* (*of* ~тывать) (*coll.*) to train; н. глаз to acquire a (good)

eye; н. ру́ку (на+*a.*) to become proficient (in).

наме́|тить¹, чу, тишь, *pf. of* ме́тить¹ *and* ~ча́ть¹.

наме́|тить², чу, тишь, *pf.* **1.** (*impf.* ~ча́ть²) to plan, project; to have in view; н. пое́здку в Росси́ю to plan a visit to Russia. **2.** (*impf.* ~ча́ть²) to nominate; to select; его́ ~тили кандида́том в председа́тели he has been nominated for chairman; н. зда́ние к разруше́нию to designate a building for demolition. **3.** *pf. of* ме́тить².

наме́|титься, чусь, тишься, *pf.* (*of* ~ча́ться) to be outlined; to take shape.

намётк|а¹, и, *f.* **1.** basting, tacking. **2.** basting thread, tacking thread.

намётк|а², и, *f.* rough draft, preliminary outline.

намётыва|ть, ю, *impf. of* намета́ть⁴.

намеча́|ть, ю, *impf.* = ме́тить.

намеча́|ть², ю, *impf. of* наме́тить².

намеча́|ться¹, юсь, *impf. of* наме́титься.

наме́|чу, тишь, *see* ~тить.

наме|чу́, чешь, *see* ~та́ть.

намеш|а́ть, а́ю, *pf.* (*of* ~ивать) (+*a. or g.* в+*a.*) to add (to), mix in(to).

наме́шива|ть, ю, *impf. of* намеша́ть.

на́ми, *i. of* мы.

намина́|ть, ю, *impf. of* намя́ть.

намно́го, *adv.* much, far (*with comparatives*); н. лу́чше much better.

нам|ну́, нёшь, *see* ~я́ть.

намозо́л|ить, ю, ишь, *pf. of* мозо́лить.

намок|а́ть, а́ю, *impf.* (*of* ~нуть) to become wet, get wet.

намо́к|нуть, ну, нешь, *past* ~, ~ла, *pf. of* ~а́ть.

намоло|ти́ть, чу́, ~тишь, *pf.* (+*a. or g.*) to thresh (*a quantity of*).

нам|оло́ть, елю́, е́лешь, *pf.* (+*a. or g.*) to grind, mill (*a quantity of*); н. вздо́ру, чепухи́ (*coll.*) to talk a lot of nonsense.

намо́рдник, а, *m.* muzzle.

намо́рщ|ить(ся), у(сь), ишь(ся), *pf. of* мо́рщить(ся).

намо|сти́ть, щу́, сти́шь, *pf. of* мости́ть 2.

намота́|ть¹, ю, *pf. of* мота́ть¹.

намота́|ть², ю, *pf.* (*of* нама́тывать) (+*a. or g.*) to wind (*a quantity of*).

намоч|и́ть, у́, ~ишь, *pf.* (*of* нама́чивать) **1.** to wet, moisten. **2.** to soak, steep. **3.** (*intrans.; coll.*) to spill water (on the floor, etc.).

намудр|и́ть, ю́, и́шь, *pf. of* мудри́ть.

намусл|ить, ю, ишь, *pf. of* му́слить.

наму́с|олить = ~лить.

наму́сор|ить, ю, ишь, *pf. of* му́сорить.

наму|ти́ть, чу́, ~ти́шь, *pf.* **1.** to stir up mud; to make muddy. **2.** (*intrans.; fig., coll.*) to make a mess; to create chaos.

наму́ч|иться, усь, ишься, *pf.* (*coll.*) to be worn out; to have had a hard time.

намы́в, а, *m.* (*geol.*) alluvium.

намывно́й, *adj.* (*geol.*) alluvial.

намы́ливать(ся) = мы́лить(ся).

намы́л|ить(ся), ю(сь), ишь(ся), *pf. of* ~ива́ть(ся) *and* мы́лить(ся).

нам|ы́ть, о́ю, о́ешь, *pf.* (+*a. or g.*) 1. to wash (*a quantity of*). 2. (*of a river*) to deposit.

нам|я́ть¹, ну́, нёшь, *pf.* (*of* ~ина́ть) to hurt (*by pressure or friction*); to crush; н. кому́-н. бока́, шею to give someone a sound thrashing.

нам|я́ть², ну́, нёшь, *pf.* (+*a. or g.*) 1. to mash (*a quantity of*). 2. to trample down (*a certain area of*).

нанесе́ни|е, я, *n.* 1. drawing, plotting (*on a map*). 2. infliction; н. уда́ров assault and battery.

нанес|ти́¹, у́, ёшь, *past* ~, ~ла́, *pf.* (*of* наноси́ть) 1. (на ка́рту) to draw, plot (on a map). 2. to cause; to inflict; н. оскорбле́ние to insult; н. визи́т to pay a visit. 3. (+*a.* на+*a.*) to dash (against); (*impers.*) ло́дку ~ло́ на мель the boat struck a shoal.

нанес|ти́², у́, ёшь, *past* ~, ~ла́, *pf.* (+*a. or g.*) 1. to bring (*a quantity of*). 2. to pile up (*a quantity of*); (*of sand, snow, etc.*) to drift.

нанес|ти́³, ёт, *past* ~ла́, *pf.* н. яи́ц to lay (*a number of*) eggs.

нани|за́ть, жу́, ~жешь, *pf. of* низа́ть *and* ~зывать.

нани́зыва|ть, ю, *impf.* = низа́ть.

нанима́тел|ь, я, *m.* 1. tenant. 2. (*obs.*) employer.

нанима́|ть(ся), ю(сь), *impf. of* наня́ть(ся).

на́нк|а, и, *f.* (*text.*) nankeen.

на́нк|овый, *adj. of* ~а.

на́ново, *adv.* (*coll.*) anew, afresh.

нано́с, а, *m.* (*geol.*) alluvium; drift.

нано|си́ть¹, шу́, ~сишь, *impf. of* нанести́.

нано|си́ть², шу́, ~сишь, *pf.* (+*a. or g.*) to bring (*a quantity of*).

нано́сный, *adj.* 1. (*geol.*) alluvial. 2. (*fig., coll.*) alien; borrowed. 3. (*obs.*) slanderous.

на́нсук, а, *m.* (*text.*) nainsook.

наню́х|аться, аюсь, *pf.* (*of* ~иваться) (+*g.*) 1. to smell to one's heart's content; to take snuff to one's heart's content. 2. to be intoxicated (with).

наню́хива|ться, юсь, *impf. of* наню́хаться.

**на́н|ятый, p.p.p. of* ~я́ть.

на|ня́ть, найму́, наймёшь, *past* ~нял, ~няла́, ~няло, *pf.* (*of* ~нима́ть) to rent; to hire; н. на рабо́ту to engage, take on.

на|ня́ться, найму́сь, наймёшься, *past* ~ня́лся, ~няла́сь, *pf.* (*of* ~нима́ться) (*coll.*) to become employed, get a job.

наобеща́|ть, ю, *pf.* (+*a. or g.*) to promise (much); н. с три ко́роба to promise the world.

наоборо́т, *adv.* 1. back to front; проче́сть сло́во н. to read a word backwards. 2. the other way round; the wrong way (round); он всё понима́ет н. he takes everything the wrong way. 3. on the contrary; как раз н. quite the contrary; и н. and vice versa; я не сержу́сь, а, н., рад был, что вы пришли́ I am not angry; on the contrary, I was glad that you came.

наобу́м, *adv.* without thinking; at random.

наор|а́ть, у́, ёшь, *pf.* (на+*a.*; *coll.*) to shout (at).

наотма́шь, *adv.* 1. with the back of the hand; уда́рить н. to strike a swinging blow. 2. out from the body.

наотре́з, *adv.* flatly, point-blank.

напада́|ть, ет, *pf.* to fall (*in a certain quantity*); в тече́ние но́чи ~ло мно́го сне́га there was a heavy fall of snow during the night.

напада́|ть, ю, *impf. of* напа́сть.

нападаю́щ|ий, его, *m.* (*sport*) forward.

нападе́ни|е, я, *n.* 1. attack, assault. 2. (*sport*) forwards, forward-line.

напа́д|ки, ок, кам, *no sing.* attacks.

напа|ду́, дёшь, *see* ~сть.

напа́ива|ть¹, ю, *impf. of* напои́ть.

напа́ива|ть², ю, *impf. of* напая́ть.

напа́ко|стить, щу, стишь, *pf. of* па́костить.

напа́лм, а, *m.* (*chem.; mil.*) napalm.

напа́лм|овый, *adj. of* ~.

напа́р|ить, ю, ишь, *pf.* (+*a. or g.*) to steam (*a quantity of*).

напа́рник, а, *m.* fellow worker, mate.

напа́рыва|ть(ся), ю(сь), *impf. of* напоро́ть(ся).

напас|ти́сь, у́сь, ёшься, *past* ~ся, ~ла́сь, *pf.* (*coll.*; *usually* +*neg.*) to lay in, save up enough.

напа́|сть¹, ду́, дёшь, *past* ~л, *pf.* (*of* ~да́ть) (на+*a.*) 1. to attack; to descend (on). 2. to come (over); to grip, seize; на нас всех ~л страх fear seized us all. 3. to come (upon, across); я ~л на мысль the thought occurred to me.

напа́ст|ь², и, *f.* (*coll.*) misfortune, disaster.

напа́чка|ть, ю, *pf. of* па́чкать.

напая́|ть, ю, ешь, *pf.* (*of* напа́ивать²) to solder (onto).

напе́в, а, *m.* tune, melody.

напева́|ть, ю, *impf.* 1. *impf. of* напе́ть. 2. to croon; to hum; to croon.

напе́в|ный (~ен, ~на), *adj.* melodious.

напека́|ть, ю, *impf. of* напе́чь¹.

на́перво, *adv.* (*coll.*) at first.

напербо́й, *adv.* vying with one another.

наперве́с, *adv.* in a horizontal position.

наперегонки́, *adv.* racing one another; бе́гать н. to race (with) one another.

наперёд, *adv.* (*coll.*) 1. in front. 2. in advance.

наперекор, *adv. and prep.* (+*d.*) in defiance (of), counter (to).

наперерез, *adv.* (*and prep.*+*d.*) so as to cross one's path; бежа́ть кому́-н. н. to run to head someone off.

наперерыв, *adv.* = наперебой.

на|переть, пру́, прёшь, *past* ~пёр, ~пёрла, *pf.* (*of* ~пира́ть) (*coll.*; на+*a.*) to press; to put pressure (upon).

напере|хва́т, *adv.* (*dial.*) 1. = ~ре́з. 2. = ~бой.

наперечёт, *adv.* 1. through and through; every single one. 2. (*pred. only*) very few, not many.

наперсник, а, *m.* (*obs.*) confidant.

наперсниц|а, ы, *f.* (*obs.*) 1. confidante. 2. mistress.

наперсный, *adj.* (*eccl.*) pectoral.

наперст|ок, ка, *m.* thimble.

наперстянк|а, и, *f.* (*bot.*) foxglove.

наперч|ить, у, ишь, *pf. of* перчить.

нап|еть, ою́, оёшь, *pf.* (*of* ~ева́ть) 1. to sing (*air, melody*). 2. н. пласти́нку to make a recording of one's voice. 3. (*coll.*; +*d. or* в у́ши +*d.*) to give someone a piece of one's mind.

напеча́та|ть(ся), ю(сь), *pf. of* печа́тать(ся).

напе́|чь¹, чёт, *past* ~кло́, *pf.* (*of* ~ка́ть) (*impers.*; *coll.*) to burn, scorch (*with the sun*); го́лову у меня́ ~кло́ my head got scorched.

напе́|чь², ку́, чёшь, ку́т, *past* ~к, ~кла́, *pf.* (+*a. or g.*) to bake (*a number of*); н. расска́зов (*fig., coll.*) to concoct stories.

напива́|ться, юсь, *impf. of* напи́ться.

напи́лива|ть, ю, *impf. of* напили́ть.

напил|и́ть, ю́, ~ишь, *pf.* (*of* ~ивать) (+*a. or g.*) to saw (*a quantity of*).

напи́л|ок, ка, *m.* (*coll.*) = ~ьник.

напи́льник, а, *m.* (*tech.*) file.

напира́|ть, ю, *impf.* (*coll.*; на+*a.*) 1. *impf. of* наперёть. 2. to emphasize, stress.

написа́ни|е, я, *n.* 1. way of writing (*a letter of the alphabet*). 2. spelling.

напи|са́ть, шу́, ~шешь, *pf. of* писа́ть.

напит|а́ть, а́ю, *pf.* 1. (*impf.* пита́ть) to sate, satiate. 2. (*impf.* ~ывать) (+*i.*) to impregnate (with).

напит|а́ться, а́юсь, *pf.* 1. (*coll.*) to sate oneself; to take one's fill. 2. (*impf.* ~ываться) (+*i.*) to be impregnated (with).

напи́т|ок, ка, *m.* drink, beverage; прохлади́тельные ~ки soft drinks.

напи́тыва|ть(ся), ю(сь), *impf. of* напита́ть(ся).

нап|и́ться, ью́сь, ьёшься, *past* ~и́лся, ~ила́сь, ~и́лось, *pf.* (*of* ~ива́ться) 1. (+*g.*) to slake one's thirst (with, on); to have a drink (of). 2. to get drunk.

напих|а́ть, а́ю, *pf.* (*of* ~ивать) (в+*a.*) to cram (into), stuff (into).

напи́хива|ть, ю, *impf. of* напиха́ть.

напи́чка|ть, ю, *pf. of* пи́чкать.

напи|шу́, ~шешь, *see* ~са́ть.

наплав|ить, лю, ишь, *pf.* (+*a. or g.*) to melt, smelt (*a quantity of*).

напла́канный, *adj.* tear-stained, red (with crying).

напла́|каться, чусь, чешься, *pf.* 1. to have one's cry out, have a good cry. 2. (*coll.*) to have trouble; он ещё ~чется there is trouble in store for him yet.

напла́ст|анный, *p.p.p. of* ~а́ть *and adj.* sliced.

напласта́|ть, ю, *pf.* (*coll.*; +*g.*) to slice, cut in slices.

напластова́ни|е, я, *n.* (*geol.*) bedding, stratification.

напла́|чу, чешь, *see* ~кать.

наплева́тельский, *adj.* (*coll.*) devil-may-care.

напл|ева́ть, юю́, юёшь, *pf.* 1. (+*g.*) to spit (out). 2. (*fig., coll.*; на+*a.*) to wash one's hands (of); н.! to hell with it! who cares!; н. на него́! damn him! to hell with him!; мне н.! I don't give a damn!

напле|сти́¹, ту́, тёшь, *past* ~л, ~ла́, *pf.* (+*a. or g.*) to make by weaving (*a number of*); н. вздо́ру (*fig., coll.*) to talk a lot of nonsense.

напле|сти́², ту́, тёшь, *past* ~л, ~ла́, *pf.* (на+*a.*; *coll.*) to slander.

наплечник, а, *m.* shoulder strap.

наплечный, *adj.* (worn on the) shoulder.

напло|ди́ть, жу́, ди́шь, *pf.* (*coll.*) to bring forth, produce (*in great numbers*); (*joc.*) to breed.

напло|ди́ться, жу́сь, ди́шься, *pf.* (*coll.*) to multiply.

напло|и́ть, ю́, и́шь, *pf. of* плои́ть.

наплы́в, а, *m.* 1. influx (*of people, etc.*). 2. (*med., bot.*) canker; excrescence.

наплыва́|ть, ю, *impf. of* наплы́ть.

наплы́|ть, ву́, вёшь, *past* ~л, ~ла́, ~ло, *pf.* (*of* ~ва́ть) 1. (на+*a.*) to run (against), dash (against). 2. (*of incrustation, etc.*) to form.

наповал, *adv.* outright, on the spot.

наподо́бие, *prep.* (+*g.*) like, resembling, in the likeness of.

напо́|енный, *p.p.p. of* ~и́ть 1, 2.

напо|ённый, *p.p.p. of* ~и́ть 3.

напо|и́ть, ю́, и́шь, *pf.* (*of* пои́ть *and* напа́ивать¹) 1. to give to drink; to water (*an animal*). 2. to make drunk. 3. (*poet.*) to impregnate; to fill.

напока́з, *adv.* for show; вы́ставить н. to show off (*also fig.*).

наполз|а́ть, а́ю, *impf. of* ~ти́.

наполз|ти́, у́, ёшь, *past* ~, ~ла́, *pf.* (*of* ~а́ть) (на+*a.*) to crawl (over, against).

наполз|ти́², у́, ёшь, *past* ⌣, ~ла́, *pf.* to crawl in (*in great numbers*).

наполне́ни|е, я, *n.* filling; пульс хоро́шего ~я (*med.*) normal pulse.

наполни́тел|ь, я, *m.* (*tech.*) filler.

наполн|и́ть, ю́, и́шь, *pf.* (*of* ~я́ть) to fill.

наполн|и́ться, ю́сь, и́шься, *pf.* (*of* ~я́ться) (+*i.*) to fill (with) (*intrans.*).

наполн|я́ть(ся), я́ю(сь), *impf. of* ~и́ть(ся).

наполови́ну, *adv.* half; зал ещё н. пуст the hall is still half empty; де́лать де́ло н. to do a thing by halves.

напома́|дить, жу, дишь, *pf. of* пома́дить.

напомина́ни|е, я, *n.* 1. reminding. 2. reminder.

напомина́|ть, ю, *impf. of* напо́мнить.

напо́мн|ить, ю, ишь, *pf.* (+*d.* о+*p. or* +*d. and a.*) to remind (of); портре́т ~ил мне о про́шлом *or* ~ил мне про́шлое the portrait reminded me of the past. 2. to remind (of), recall (= *to resemble*); он ~ил мне моего́ де́да he reminded me of my grandfather.

напо́р, а, *m.* pressure (*also fig.*); (*of water, steam, etc.*) head; он подде́рживал меня́ с ~ом (*coll.*) he supported me vigorously.

напо́ристост|ь, и, *f.* (*coll.*) energy; push, go.

напо́рист|ый (~, ~а), *adj.* (*coll.*) energetic; pushing.

напо́р|ный, *adj. of* ~ (*tech.*); н. бак pressure tank; н. кла́пан pressure valve; н. насо́с force pump; ~ная труба́ rising pipe, rising main.

напор|о́ть¹, ю́, ~ешь, *pf.* (*of* напа́рывать) (*coll.*) to tear, cut; н. ру́ку на гвоздь to cut one's hand on a nail.

напор|о́ть², ю́, ~ешь, *pf.* to rip (*a quantity of*); (*coll.*) н. вздо́ру, чепухи́ to talk a lot of nonsense.

напор|о́ться, ю́сь, ~ешься, *pf.* (*of* напа́рываться) (на+*a.*) 1. to cut oneself (on). 2. to run (upon, against); (*fig.*) to run (into, up against).

напор|оти́ть¹, чу, тишь, *pf.* (+*a. or g.*) to spoil (*a quantity of*).

напор|оти́ть², чу, тишь, *pf.* (+*d.*) to injure, harm.

напосле́док, *adv.* (*coll.*) in the end, finally, after all.

нап|ою́¹, оёшь, *see* ~е́ть.

нап|ою́², и́шь, *see* ~и́ть.

напра́в|ить, лю, ишь, *pf.* (*of* ~ля́ть) 1. (на+*a.*) to direct (to, at); н. внима́ние to direct one's attention (to); н. свой путь to bend one's steps (towards); н. уда́р to aim a blow (at). 2. to send; н. заявле́ние to send in an application. 3. to sharpen; н. бри́тву to set a razor. 4. (*coll.*) н. рабо́ту to organize work.

напра́в|иться, люсь, ишься, *pf.* (*of* ~ля́ть-ся) 1. (к, в+*a.*, на+*a.*) to make (for). 2. (*coll.*) to get going, get under way (*fig.*). 3. *pass. of* ~ить.

напра́вк|а, и, *f.* setting (*of razor, etc.*).

направле́ни|е, я, *n.* 1. (*in var. senses*) direction; по ~ю (к) in the direction (of), towards; взять н. на се́вер to make for, head for the north. 2. (*mil.*) sector. 3. (*fig.*) trend, tendency; н. ума́ turn of mind; либера́льное н. liberal tendency. 4. (*official*) order, warrant; directive; н. в санато́рий warrant for stay at, certificate approving treatment at a sanatorium. 5. (*official*) action; effect; дать н. де́лу to take action on a matter.

напра́вленност|ь, и, *f.* 1. direction, tendency, trend. 2. purposefulness.

напра́в|ленный, *p.p.p. of* ~ить *and adj.* 1. (*radio*) directional. 2. purposeful; unswerving.

направля́|ть, ю, *impf. of* напра́вить.

направля́|ться, ю́сь, *impf. of* напра́виться; ~емся в Му́рманск we are bound for Murmansk.

направля́ющ|ая, ей, *f.* (*tech.*) guide.

направля́|ющий, *pres. part. act. of* ~ть *and adj.* (*tech.*) guiding, guide; leading; н. ва́лик, н. ро́лик guide roller; ~ющая лине́йка, н. шабло́н former bar; н. сте́ржень, н. штифт guide pin, guide bolt.

напра́во, *adv.* to the right; on the right.

напракти́к|оваться, у́юсь, *pf.* (в+*p.*; *coll.*) to acquire skill (in).

напра́слин|а, ы, *f.* (*coll.*) wrongful accusation, slander.

напра́сно, *adv.* 1. vainly, in vain; to no purpose. 2. wrong, unjustly, mistakenly; н. вы пришли́ без де́нег it was a mistake for you to come without money.

напра́с|ный (~ен, ~на), *adj.* 1. vain, idle; ~ная наде́жда vain hope. 2. unfounded, wrongful.

напра́шива|ться, юсь, *impf. of* напроси́ть-ся; (*impf. only*) to arise, suggest itself; ~ется вопро́с the question inevitably arises.

наприме́р for example, for instance.

напрока́|зить, жу, зишь, *pf. of* прока́зить.

напрока́знича|ть, ю, *pf. of* прока́зничать.

напрока́т, *adv.* for hire, on hire; взять н. to hire; дать н. to hire out, let.

напролёт, *adv.* (*coll.*) through, without a break; рабо́тать всю ночь н. to work the whole night through.

напроло́м, *adv.* straight, regardless of obstacles (*also fig.*).

напропалу́ю, *adv.* (*coll.*) regardless of the consequences; all out.

напроро́ч|ить, у, ишь, *pf. of* проро́чить.

напро|си́ться, шу́сь, ~си́шься, *pf.* (*of* на-пра́шиваться) (*coll.*) to thrust oneself upon;

н. на комплиме́нты to fish for compliments.

напро́тив, *adv. and prep.*+*g.* **1.** opposite; он живёт н. (на́шего до́ма) he lives opposite (our house). **2.** (+*d.*) in defiance (of); to contradict; она́ всё де́лает мне н. she does everything to spite me. **3.** on the contrary.

на́прочь, *adv.* (*coll.*) completely.

нап|ру́, рёшь, *see* ∼ере́ть.

напру́жива|ть(ся), ю(сь), *impf. of* напру́житься.

напру́ж|ить, у, ишь, *pf.* (*of* ∼ива́ть) (*coll.*) to strain; to tense, tauten.

напру́ж|иться, усь, ишься, *pf.* (*of* ∼иваться) (*coll.*) to become tense, become taut.

напряга́|ть(ся), ю(сь), *impf. of* напря́чь(ся).

напря|гу́, жёшь, *see* ∼чь.

напряже́ни|е, я, *n.* **1.** tension; effort, exertion. **2.** (*phys., tech.*) strain; stress; (*electr.*) tension; voltage; н. на зажи́мах terminal voltage, electrode potential; н. смеще́ния grid bias.

напряжённост|ь, и, *f.* tenseness; intensity; tension.

напряжён|ный (∼, ∼на), *adj.* tense, strained; intense; intensive; ∼ные отноше́ния strained relations; ∼ная рабо́та intensive work.

напрями́к, *adv.* (*coll.*) **1.** straight. **2.** (*fig.*) straight out, bluntly.

напря́|чь, гу́, жёшь, гу́т, *past* ∼г, ∼гла́, *pf.* (*of* ∼га́ть) to tense, strain (*also fig.*); н. все си́лы to strain every nerve.

напря́|чься, гу́сь, жёшься, гу́тся, *past* ∼гся, ∼гла́сь, *pf.* **1.** to become tense. **2.** to exert oneself, strain oneself.

напуга́|ть(ся), ю(сь), *pf. of* пуга́ть(ся).

напу́др|ить(ся), ю(сь), ишь(ся), *pf. of* пу́дрить(ся).

напу́льсник, а, *m.* wrist-band.

на́пуск, а, *m.* **1.** letting in. **2.** (*hunting*) letting loose, slipping (*from leash*). **3.** (*in dress, blouse, etc.*) full front. **4.** (*tech.*) lap joint.

напуска́|ть(ся), ю(сь), *impf. of* напусти́ть(ся).

напускно́й, *adj.* assumed, put on.

напу́|стить, щу́, ∼стишь, *pf.* (*of* ∼ска́ть) **1.** (+*g.*) to let in; н. воды́ в ва́нну to fill a bath. **2.** to let loose, slip, set on (*hounds, etc.*). **3.** (на себя́+*a.*) to affect, put on; н. на себя́ ва́жность to assume an air of importance. **4.** н. стра́ху на кого́-н. (*coll.*) to strike fear into someone.

напу́|ститься, щу́сь, ∼стишься, *pf.* (*of* ∼ска́ться) (*coll.*; на+*a.*) to fly at, go for.

напу́та|ть, ю, *pf.* (*coll.*; в+*p.*) to make a mess (of), make a hash (of); to confuse, get wrong; вы ∼ли в а́дресе you got the address wrong.

напу́тственн|ый, *adj.* parting, farewell; ∼ое сло́во parting words.

напу́тстви|е, я, *n.* parting words, farewell speech.

напу́тств|овать, ую, *impf. and pf.* to address, counsel (at parting); н. до́брыми пожела́ниями to bid farewell, wish bon voyage.

напух|а́ть, а́ет, *impf. of* ∼нуть.

напу́х|нуть, нет, *past* ∼, ∼ла, *pf.* (*of* ∼а́ть) to swell.

напу|щу́, ∼стишь, *see* ∼сти́ть.

напы́ж|иться, усь, ишься, *pf. of* пы́житься.

напыл|и́ть, ю́, и́шь, *pf. of* пыли́ть.

напы́щенност|ь, и, *f.* **1.** pomposity. **2.** bombast.

напы́щен|ный (∼, ∼на), *adj.* **1.** pompous. **2.** bombastic, high-flown.

напя́лива|ть, ю, *impf. of* напя́лить.

напя́л|ить, ю, ишь, *pf.* (*of* ∼ива́ть) **1.** to stretch on. **2.** (*coll.*) to pull on, struggle into (*a tight garment*).

нар- (*abbr. of* наро́дный) people's; national.

нараба́тыва|ть, ю, *impf. of* нарабо́тать².

нарабо́та|ть¹, ю, *pf.* (+*a. or g.*) to make, turn out (*a quantity of*).

нарабо́та|ть², ю, *pf.* (*of* нараба́тывать) to make, earn.

нарабо́та|ться, юсь, *pf.* (*coll.*) to have worked enough; to have tired oneself with work.

наравне́, *adv.* (с+*i.*) **1.** on a level (with); ма́льчик шёл н. с солда́тами the small boy kept pace with the soldiers. **2.** equally (with); on an equal footing (with).

нара́д|оваться, уюсь, *pf.* (+*d. or* на+*a.*; *usually*+*neg.*) to rejoice, delight sufficiently (in); она́ на сы́на не ∼уется she dotes on her son.

нараспа́шку, *adv.* (*coll.*) unbuttoned; у него́ душа́ н. (*fig.*) he wears his heart upon his sleeve.

нараспе́в, *adv.* in a sing-song voice; drawlingly.

нараста́ни|е, я, *n.* growth, accumulation.

нараст|а́ть, а́ю, *impf. of* ∼и́.

нарас|ти́, ту́, тёшь, *past* наро́с, наросла́, *pf.* (*of* ∼та́ть) **1.** (на+*p.*) to grow (on), form (on); мох наро́с на камня́х moss has grown on the stones. **2.** to increase; (*of sound*) to swell. **3.** to accumulate.

нара|сти́ть, щу́, сти́шь, *pf.* (*of* ∼щива́ть) **1.** to graft (on). **2.** to lengthen; (*fig.*) to increase, augment.

нарасхва́т, *adv.* продава́ться н. to sell like hot cakes; э́ту кни́гу покупа́ют н. there is a great demand for this book.

нара́щива|ть, ю, *impf. of* нарасти́ть.

нарва́л, а, *m.* (*zool.*) narwhal.

нарв|а́ть¹, у́, ёшь, *past* ∼а́л, ∼ала́, ∼а́ло

pf. (+*a.* or *g.*) **1.** to pick (*a quantity of*). **2.** to tear (*a quantity of*).

нарв|а́ть², **ёт**, *past* ~а́л, ~ала́, ~а́ло, *pf.* (*of* нарыва́ть) to gather, come to a head (*of a boil or abscess*); у меня́ па́лец ~а́л or (*impers.*) па́лец ~а́ло I have a gathering on my finger.

нарв|а́ться, **у́сь**, **ёшься**, *past* ~а́лся, ~ала́сь, ~а́лось, *pf.* (*of* нарыва́ться) (*coll.*; на+*a.*) to run into, run up (against).

нард, **а**, *m.* spikenard, nard.

наре́|жу, **жешь**, *see* ~зать.

наре́з, **а**, *m.* **1.** (*tech.*) thread; groove (*in rifling*). **2.** (*hist., econ.*) lot, plot (*of land*).

наре́|зать¹, **жу**, **жешь**, *pf.* (*of* ~за́ть) **1.** to cut into pieces; to slice; to carve. **2.** (*tech.*) to thread; to rifle. **3.** (*hist., econ.*) to allot, parcel out (*land*).

наре́|зать², **жу**, **жешь**, *pf.* (+*a.* or *g.*) to cut, slice (*a quantity of*).

нареза́|ть, **а́ю**, *impf. of* ~а́ть¹.

наре́|заться, **жусь**, **жешься**, *pf.* (*of* ~за́ться) **1.** (*coll.*) to get drunk. **2.** *pass. of* ~зать¹.

нареза́|ться, **а́юсь**, *impf. of* ~а́ться.

наре́зк|а, **и**, *f.* **1.** cutting (into pieces), slicing. **2.** (*tech.*) thread; rifling.

нарезно́й, *adj.* (*tech.*) threaded; rifled.

нарека́ни|е, **я**, *n.* censure; reprimand.

нарека́|ть, **ю**, *impf. of* наре́чь.

нареч|ённый, *p.p.p. of* ~ь and *adj.* (*obs.*) betrothed; *as noun* **н.**, ~ённого, *m.* fiancé; ~ённая, ~ённой, *f.* fiancée.

наре́чи|е¹, **я**, *n.* dialect.

наре́чи|е², **я**, *n.* adverb.

наре́чный, *adj.* adverbial.

наре́|чь, **ку́**, **чёшь**, **ку́т**, *past* ~к, ~кла́, *pf.* (*of* ~ка́ть) (+*a.* and *i.* or *d.* and *a.*) to name; ма́льчика ~кли́ Серге́ем, ма́льчику ~кли́ и́мя Серге́й they named the boy Sergei.

нарза́н, **а**, *m.* Narzan (*kind of mineral water*).

нарза́н|ный, *adj. of* ~.

нарис|ова́ть, **у́ю**, *pf. of* рисова́ть.

нарица́тельн|ый, *adj.* **1.** (*econ.*) nominal; ~ая сто́имость nominal cost. **2.** (*gram.*) и́мя ~ое common noun.

нарко́з, **а**, *m.* **1.** narcosis, anaesthesia. **2.** anaesthetic, drug; ме́стный н. local anaesthetic.

нарко́м, **а**, *m.* (*abbr. of* наро́дный комисса́р) (*hist.*) people's commissar.

наркома́н, **а**, *m.* drug addict.

наркома́ни|я, **и**, *f.* drug addiction, narcotism.

наркома́т, **а**, *m.* (*abbr. of* наро́дный комиссариа́т) (*hist.*) people's commissariat.

наркотизи́р|овать, **ую**, *impf. and pf.* (*med.*) to narcotize, anaesthetize.

нарко́тик, **а**, *m.* narcotic.

наркоти́ческ|ий, *adj.* narcotic; ~ие сре́дства narcotics, drugs.

наро́д, **а** (**у**), *m.* (*in var. senses*) people; англи́йский н. the English people, the people of England; челове́к из ~а a man of the people; ма́ло бы́ло ~у на ми́тинге there were not many people at the meeting.

наро́д|ец, **ца**, *m. dim.* (*affect. or pejor.*) of ~.

наро|ди́ть, **жу́**, **ди́шь**, *pf.* (+*a.* or *g.*) to give birth to (*a number of*).

наро|ди́ться, **жу́сь**, **ди́шься**, *pf.* (*of* ~жда́ться) **1.** (*coll.*) to be born. **2.** (*fig.*) to come into being, arise.

наро́дник, **а**, *m.* (*hist.*) narodnik, populist.

наро́дничес|кий, *adj. of* ~тво.

наро́дничеств|о, **а**, *n.* (*hist.*) narodnik movement, populism.

наро́дност|ь, **и**, *f.* **1.** nationality. **2.** (*sing. only*) national character; national traits.

народнохозя́йственный, *adj.* pertaining to the national economy.

наро́дн|ый, *adj.* **1.** national; ~ое хозя́йство national economy; н. поэ́т national poet; н. арти́ст СССР (*designation of recipient of official honour*) national artist of the U.S.S.R. **2.** folk; ~ое иску́сство folk art. **3.** (*polit.*) of the (*sc. common, working*) people, popular; ~ая во́ля (*hist.*) Narodnaya volya ('The People's Will'); Н. фронт Popular Front. **4.** *forms part of the official designation of certain Communist states, also of certain organs of power and offices in the U.S.S.R.*: стра́ны ~ой демокра́тии 'the People's Democracies'; Венге́рская ~ая Респу́блика the Hungarian People's Republic; н. заседа́тель assessor (*in courts*); н. сле́дователь examining magistrate; н. суд 'People's Court' (*court of first instance*); н. судья́ judge in 'Peoples' Court' (*elected presiding magistrate*).

народове́дени|е, **я**, *n.* ethnology.

народовла́сти|е, **я**, *n.* (*obs.*) democracy, sovereignty of the people.

народово́л|ец, **ьца**, *m.* (*hist.*) member of 'Narodnaya volya'.

народово́л|ьческий, *adj. of* ~ец.

народонаселе́ни|е, **я**, *n.* population.

нарожда́|ться, **юсь**, *impf. of* народи́ться.

нарожде́ни|е, **я**, *n.* birth, springing up; н. ме́сяца appearance of new moon.

наро́ст, **а**, *m.* **1.** outgrowth, excrescence; burr, tumour (*in animals and plants*). **2.** (*tech.*) incrustation, scale.

наро́чито, *adv.* deliberately, intentionally.

наро́чит|ый (~, ~а), *adj.* deliberate, intentional.

наро́чно, *adv.* **1.** on purpose, purposely. **2.** for fun, pretending.

наро́чн|ый (*obs.* **наро́чный**), **ого**, *m.* courier; express messenger, special messenger.

наро́ч|ный, *adj.* = ~итый.

на́рт|енный, *adj. of* ~ы.

на́рт|ы, ~, *sing.* ~a, ~ы, *f.* sledge (*drawn by reindeer or dogs*).

наруб|и́ть, лю́, ~ишь, *pf.* (+*a. or g.*) to chop (*a quantity of*); to cut (*a quantity of*).

нару́бк|а, и, *f.* notch.

нару́жно, *adv.* outwardly.

нару́жн|ое, ого, *n.* = н. лека́рство.

нару́жност|ь, и, *f.* exterior; (outward) appearance; н. обма́нчива appearances are deceptive.

нару́жн|ый, *adj.* (*in var. senses*) external, exterior, outward; ~ое (лека́рство) medicine for outward application, 'not to be taken'; ~ое споко́йствие outward calm.

нару́жу, *adv.* outside, on the outside; вы́йти н. to come out; (*fig.*) to come to light, transpire.

нарука́вник, а, *m.* oversleeve; armlet.

нарука́вн|ый, *adj.* (worn on the) sleeve; ~ая повя́зка arm-band, brassard.

нарумя́н|ить(ся), ю(сь), ишь(ся), *pf. of* румя́нить(ся).

нару́чник, а, *m.* handcuff, manacle.

нару́чн|ый, *adj.* worn on the arm; ~ые часы́ wrist-watch.

наруш|а́ть, а́ю, *impf. of* ~ить.

наруше́ни|е, я, *n.* breach; infringement, violation; offence (*against the law*).

наруши́тел|ь, я, *m.* transgressor, infringer.

нару́ш|ить, у, ишь, *pf.* (*of* ~а́ть) 1. to break, disturb (*sleep, quiet, etc.*). 2. to break, infringe (upon), violate, transgress.

нарци́сс, а, *m.* narcissus, daffodil.

на́р|ы, ~, *no sing.* plank-bed; bunk.

нары́в, а, *m.* abscess; boil.

нарыва́|ть(ся), ю(сь), *impf. of* нарва́ть²(ся).

нарывно́й, *adj.* vesicatory; н. пла́стырь poultice.

нар|ы́ть, о́ю, о́ешь, *pf.* (+*a. or g.*) to dig (*a quantity of*).

наря́д¹, а, *m.* attire, apparel, costume.

наря́д², а, *m.* 1. order, warrant. 2. (*mil.*) detail (*group of soldiers*). 3. (*mil.*) duty; расписа́ние ~ов roster; duty detail, orders.

наря|ди́ть¹, жу́, ~ди́шь, *pf.* (*of* ~жа́ть) 1. (в+*a.*) to dress (in), array (in). 2. (+*i.*) to dress up (as).

наря|ди́ть², жу́, ~ди́шь, *pf.* (*of* ~жа́ть) to detail, appoint; н. в карау́л to put on guard; н. сле́дствие to set up, order an inquiry.

наря|ди́ться¹, жу́сь, ~ди́шься, *pf.* (*of* ~жа́ться) 1. (в+*a.*) to array oneself (in). 2. to dress up. 3. *pass. of* ~ди́ть¹.

наря|ди́ться², жу́сь, ~ди́шься, *pf.* (*of* ~жа́ться) *pass. of* ~ди́ть².

наря́дност|ь, и, *f.* elegance, smartness.

наря́д|ный¹ (~ен, ~на**),** *adj.* well-dressed; elegant; smart (*also of items of dress*).

наря́д|ный², adj. of ~²; *as noun* ~ная, ~ной, *f.* (*coll.*) office (*where work is assigned*).

наряду́, *adv.* (c+*i.*) side by side (with), equally (with); де́ти н. со взро́слыми grown-ups and children alike; н. с э́тим at the same time.

наряжа́|ть(ся), ю(сь), *impf. of* наряди́ть(ся).

нас, *a., g., and p. of* мы.

наса|ди́ть¹, жу́, ~дишь, *pf.* (*of* ~жива́ть) (+*a. or g.*) 1. to plant (*a quantity of*). 2. to sit (*a number of*).

наса|ди́ть², жу́, ~дишь, *pf.* (*of* ~жива́ть) to stick, pin; to haft; н. на ве́ртел to spit; н. червяка́ на крючо́к to fix a worm on to a hook.

наса|ди́ть³, жу́, ~дишь, *pf.* (*of* ~жда́ть) (*fig.*) to implant, inculcate; to propagate.

наса́дк|а, и, *f.* 1. setting, fixing, putting on. 2. (*tech.*) nozzle, mouthpiece. 3. bait.

насажа́|ть, ю, *pf.* = насади́ть¹.

насажда́|ть, ю, *impf. of* насади́ть³.

насажде́ни|е, я, *n.* 1. planting, plantation; (*fig.*) spreading, propagation, dissemination. 2. (*forest*) stand; wood.

наса|ждённый, р.р.р. of ~ди́ть³.

наса́|женный, р.р.р. of ~ди́ть¹,².

наса́жива|ть, ю, *impf. of* насади́ть¹,².

наса́жива|ться, юсь, *impf. of* насе́сть¹.

наса́лива|ть, ю, *impf. of* насоли́ть.

наса́харива|ть, ю, *impf. of* наса́харить.

наса́хар|ить, ю, ишь, *pf.* (*of* ~ивать) to sugar, sweeten (*with sugar*).

насви́стыва|ть, ю, *impf.* (*coll.*) to whistle (*a tune*); (*of birds*) to pipe, twitter.

наседа́|ть, ю, *impf.* (*of* насе́сть²) (на+*a.*) 1. to press (*of mil. forces, crowds, etc.*). 2. (*of dust, etc.*) to settle, collect.

насе́дк|а, и, *f.* brood-hen, sitting hen.

насека́|ть, ю, *impf. of* насе́чь.

насеко́м|ое, ого, *n.* insect.

насекомоя́дный, *adj.* insectivorous.

населе́ни|е, я, n. 1. population; inhabitants. 2. peopling, settling.

населённост|ь, и, *f.* density of population.

насел|ённый, р.р.р. of ~и́ть *and adj.* 1. populated; н. пункт (*official designation*) locality, place; built-up area. 2. populous, densely populated.

насел|и́ть, ю́, и́шь, *pf.* (*of* ~я́ть) to people, settle.

насе́льник, а, *m.* inhabitant.

насел|я́ть, я́ю, *impf.* 1. to inhabit. 2. *impf. of* ~и́ть.

насе́ст, а, *m.* roost, perch.

нас|е́сть¹, я́дет, *past* ~е́л, *pf.* (*of* ~а́живаться) to sit down (*in numbers*).

нас|е́сть², я́ду, я́дешь, *past* ~е́л, *pf. of* ~еда́ть.

насе́чк|а, и, *f.* 1. notching; making incisions; embossing; (*med.*) scarification. 2. cut, incision; notch. 3. inlay.

насе́|чь, ку́, чёшь, ку́т, past ∼к, ∼кла́, pf. (of ∼ка́ть) 1. to make incisions (in, on); to notch. 2. to emboss; to damascene.

насе́|ять, ю, ешь, pf. (+a. or g.) to sow (a quantity of).

наси|де́ть, жу́, ди́шь, pf. (of ∼жива́ть) 1. to hatch. 2. to warm (by sitting).

наси|де́ться, жу́сь, ди́шься, pf. (coll.) to sit long enough.

наси́|женный, p.p.p. of ∼де́ть; ∼женное яйцо́ fertilized egg; ∼женное ме́сто (fig.) familiar spot, old haunt.

насижива|ть, ю, impf. of насиде́ть.

наси|жу́, ди́шь, see ∼де́ть.

наси́ли|е, я, n. violence, force.

наси́л|овать, ую, impf. 1. to coerce, constrain. 2. (pf. из∼) to rape, violate.

наси́лу, adv. (coll.) with difficulty, hardly.

наси́льник, а, m. 1. user of force; aggressor. 2. violator.

наси́льнича|ть, ю, impf. (coll.) 1. to commit acts of violence. 2. to rape.

наси́льнический, adj. forcible, violent.

наси́льно, adv. by force, forcibly; н. мил не бу́дешь (prov.) love cannot be compelled.

наси́льственный, adj. violent; forcible.

наска|за́ть, жу́, ∼жешь, pf. (coll.; +a. or g.) to say, talk a lot (of); н. новосте́й to have a lot of news to tell.

наска|ка́ть, чу́, ∼чешь, pf. (of ∼кива́ть) 1. (на+a.) to ride (into); to run (against), collide (with). 2. to ride up, gallop up.

наска́кива|ть, ю, impf. of наскака́ть and наскочи́ть.

наскандал|ить, ю, ишь, pf. of сканда́лить.

насквозь, adv. through (and through); throughout; промо́кнуть н. to get wet through; ви́деть (знать) кого́-н. н. (fig.) to see through someone.

наско́к, а, m. 1. swoop; sudden attack, descent; де́йствовать ∼ом to act on impulse; с ∼а (fig., coll.) hurriedly, just like that. 2. (fig., coll.) attack.

наско́лько, adv. 1. (interrog.) how much?; how far? 2. (relat.) as far as, so far as; н. мне изве́стно as far as I know, to the best of my knowledge.

на́скоро, adv. (coll.) hastily, hurriedly.

наскоч|и́ть, у́, ∼ишь, pf. (of наска́кивать) 1. to run (against), collide (with); н. на неприя́тность (fig.) to get into trouble. 2. (fig., coll.) to fly (at).

наскреба́|ть, ю, impf. of наскрести́.

наскре|сти́, бу́, бёшь, past ∼б, ∼бла́, pf. (of ∼ба́ть) to scrape up, scrape together; (fig.) н. де́нег на пое́здку to scrape up some money for an outing.

наску́ч|ить, у, ишь, pf. (coll.) 1. (+d.) to bore; мне э́то ∼ило I am sick of it. 2. (obs.; +i.) to be bored (by), grow tired (of).

насла|ди́ть, жу́, ди́шь, pf. (of ∼жда́ть) to delight, please.

насла|ди́ться, жу́сь, ди́шься, pf. (of ∼жда́ться) (+i.) to enjoy; to take pleasure (in), delight (in).

наслажда́|ть(ся), ю(сь), impf. of наслади́ть(ся).

наслажде́ни|е, я, n. enjoyment, delight.

насла́ива|ться, юсь, impf. of насло́иться.

насла|сти́ть, щу́, сти́шь, pf. (coll.) to make very (too) sweet.

на|сла́ть[1], шлю́, шлёшь, pf. (of ∼ сыла́ть) (obs.) to send down (calamities, etc.).

на|сла́ть[2], шлю́, шлёшь, pf. (+a. or g.) to send (a quantity of).

насле́ди|е, я, n. legacy; heritage.

насле|ди́ть, жу́, ди́шь, pf. (of следи́ть[2]) to leave (dirty) marks, traces.

насле́дник, а, m. heir; legatee; (fig.) successor.

насле́дниц|а, ы, f. heiress.

насле́дный, adj. first in the line of succession; н. принц Crown prince.

насле́довани|е, я, n. inheritance.

насле́д|овать, ую, impf. and pf. 1. (pf. also у∼) to inherit. 2. (+d.) to succeed (to).

насле́дственност|ь, и, f. heredity.

насле́дственный, adj. hereditary, inherited.

насле́дств|о, а, n. 1. inheritance, legacy; получи́ть в н., по ∼у to inherit. 2. (fig.) heritage.

наслое́ни|е, я, n. 1. (geol.) stratification. 2. layer, deposit. 3. (fig.) later development, extraneous feature (of culture or individual personality).

насло|и́ться, ю́сь, и́шься, pf. (of насла́иваться) (на+a.) to be deposited (on), accumulate (on).

наслуж|и́ться, у́сь, ∼ишься, pf. (coll.) to have served for long enough.

наслу́ша|ться, юсь, pf. (+g.) 1. to hear (a lot of). 2. to hear enough, listen to long enough; я не ∼юсь э́тих пе́сен I cannot hear enough of these songs.

наслы́шан, adj. used as pred. (obs.; о+p.) familiar (with) by hearsay; мы о вас мно́го ∼ы we have heard a lot about you.

наслы́ш|аться, усь, ишься, pf. (о+p.) to have heard a lot (about).

наслы́шк|а, и, f. по ∼е (coll.) by hearsay.

насма́рку, adv. (coll.) пойти́ н. to come to nothing.

на́смерть, adv. to death; стоя́ть н. to fight to the last ditch; испуга́ть н. to frighten to death.

насмеха́тельств|о, а, n. (obs.) mockery.

насмеха́|ться, impf. (над) to jeer (at), gibe (at), ridicule.

насмеш|и́ть, у́, и́шь, pf. (of смеши́ть) (кого́-н.) to make (someone) laugh.

насме́шк|а, и, *f.* mockery, ridicule; gibe.

насме́шлив|ый (∼, ∼а), *adj.* **1.** mocking, derisive. **2.** sarcastic.

насме́шник, а, *m.* (*coll.*) scoffer.

насме|я́ться, ю́сь, ёшься, *pf.* **1.** (*coll.*) to have a good laugh. **2.** (над) to laugh (at); н. над чьи́ми-н. чу́вствами to insult someone's feelings.

на́сморк, а, *m.* cold (in the head); схвати́ть, получи́ть н. to catch a cold; у меня́ сде́лался на́сморк I have caught a cold.

насмотр|е́ться, ю́сь, ∼ишься, *pf.* **1.** (+*g.*) to see a lot (of). **2.** (на+*a.*) to have looked enough (at), to see enough (of); не н. not to tire of looking (at).

насобач|иться, усь, ишься, *pf.* (*coll.*; +*inf.*) to become adept (at), become a good hand (at).

нас|ова́ть, ую́, уёшь, *pf.* (*of* ∼о́вывать) (*coll.*; +*g. or a.*) to shove in, stuff in (*a quantity of*); н. конфе́т в карма́ны to stuff sweets into one's pockets.

насо́выва|ть, ю, *impf. of* насова́ть.

насол|и́ть¹, ю́, ∼и́шь, *pf.* (*of* наса́ливать) **1.** to salt; to put much salt (into). **2.** (*fig.*; +*d.*) to spite, injure; to do a bad turn (to).

насол|и́ть², ю́, ∼и́шь, *pf.* (+*a. or g.*) to salt, pickle (*a quantity of*).

насоло|ди́ть, жу́, ди́шь, *pf. of* солоди́ть.

насор|и́ть, ю́, и́шь, *pf. of* сори́ть.

насо́с¹, а, *m.* pump.

насо́с², а, *m.* (*disease of horses*) lampas.

насос|а́ть, у́, ёшь, *pf.* (+*a. or g.*) **1.** to suck (*a quantity of*). **2.** to pump.

насос|а́ться, у́сь, ёшься, *pf.* **1.** (+*g.*) to have sucked one's fill. **2.** (*coll.*) to get drunk.

насо́с|ный, *adj. of* ∼¹; н. агрега́т pumping unit; ∼ная ста́нция pumping station.

насочин|и́ть, ю́, и́шь, *pf.* (*coll.*) (+*a. or g.*) to talk a lot of nonsense; to make up (a lot of falsehoods).

на́спех, *adv.* hastily; carelessly.

насплётнича|ть, ю, *pf. of* спле́тничать.

наст, а, *m.* thin crust of ice over snow.

наста|ва́ть, ю́, ёшь, *impf. of* ∼ть.

настави́тел|ьный (∼ен, ∼ьна), *adj.* edifying, instructive; н. тон didactic tone.

наста́в|ить¹, лю, ишь, *pf.* (*of* ∼ля́ть) **1.** to lengthen; to put on, add on; н. нос кому́-н. to fool, dupe someone; н. рога́ кому́-н. to cuckold someone. **2.** (на+*a.*) to aim (at), point (at); н. револьве́р на кого́-н. to point a revolver at someone.

наста́в|ить², лю, ишь, *pf.* (*of* ∼ля́ть) to edify; to exhort, admonish; н. на путь и́стинный to set on the right path.

наста́в|ить³, лю, ишь, *pf.* (+*a. or g.*) to set up, place (*a quantity of*).

наста́вк|а, и, *f.* addition.

наставле́ни|е, я, *n.* **1.** exhortation, admoni-

tion. **2.** directions, instructions; (*mil.*) manual.

наставля́|ть, ю, *impf. of* наста́вить.

наста́вник, а, *m.* **1.** (*obs.*) mentor, preceptor; кла́ссный н. form-master. **2.** instructor (*of apprentices*).

наста́вни|ческий, *adj. of* ∼к; н. тон edifying tone.

наста́вничеств|о, а, *n.* (*obs.*) tutorship.

наставно́й, *adj.* lengthened; added.

наста́ива|ть¹,², ю, *impf. of* настоя́ть¹,²

наста́ива|ться, юсь, *impf. of* настоя́ться².

наста́|ть, ну, нешь, *pf.* (*of* ∼ва́ть) (*of times or seasons*) to come, begin.

наста́|ю, ёшь, *see* ∼ва́ть.

на́стежь, *adv.* wide open; откры́ть н. to open wide.

настели́ть = настла́ть.

наст|елю́, е́лешь, *see* ∼ла́ть.

насте́нный, *adj.* wall.

настиг|а́ть, а́ю, *impf. of* ∼нуть *and* насти́чь.

настигн|уть, у, ешь, *pf.* = насти́чь.

насти́л, а, *m.* flooring; planking.

настила́|ть, ю, *impf. of* настла́ть.

насти́лк|а, и, *f.* **1.** laying, spreading. **2.** = насти́л.

насти́льн|ый, *adj.* (*mil.*) grazing; н. ого́нь grazing fire; ∼ая бо́мба anti-personnel bomb.

настира́|ть, ю, *pf.* (+*a. or g.*) to wash, launder (*a quantity of*).

насти́|чь, гну, гнёшь, *past* ∼г, ∼гла, *pf.* (*of* ∼га́ть) to overtake (*also fig.*).

наст|ла́ть, елю́, ∼е́лешь, *pf.* (*of* ∼ила́ть) to lay, spread; н. пол to lay a floor; н. соло́му to spread straw.

насто́|й, я, *m.* infusion.

насто́йк|а, и, *f.* **1.** liqueur (*prepared by maceration, not distilled*). **2.** (*pharm.*) tincture.

насто́йчив|ый (∼, ∼а), *adj.* **1.** persistent. **2.** urgent, insistent.

насто́лько, *adv.* so; so much; н., наско́лько as much as.

насто́льн|ый, *adj.* **1.** table, desk; н. те́ннис table tennis. **2.** (*fig.*) for constant reference, in constant use; ∼ая кни́га, ∼ое руково́дство reference book; handbook, manual.

настора́жива|ть(ся), ю(сь), *impf. of* насторожи́ть(ся).

насторо́же, *adv.* быть н. to be on one's guard; to be on the qui vive.

насторо|жённый (*and* ∼женный), *p.p.p. of* ∼жи́ть *and adj.* guarded, suspicious.

насторож|и́ть, у́, и́шь, *pf.* (*of* настора́живать) to set (a trap); н. слух, у́ши (н. внима́ние *fig. only*) to prick up one's ears (*also fig.*).

насторож|и́ться, у́сь, и́шься, *pf.* (*of* настора́живаться) to prick up one's ears.

настоя́ни|е, я, *n.* insistence.

настоя́тел|ь, я, *m.* (*eccl.*) **1.** prior, superior. **2.** senior priest (*of a church*).

настоя́тельниц|а, ы, *f.* (*eccl.*) prioress, mother superior.

настоя́тел|ьный (~ен, ~ьна), *adj.* **1.** persistent; insistent. **2.** urgent, pressing.

насто|я́ть¹, ю́, и́шь, *pf.* (*of* наста́ивать) (на+*p.*) to insist (on); н. на своём to insist on having it one's own way; он ~я́л на том, что́бы пойти́ самому́ he insisted on going himself.

насто|я́ть², ю́, и́шь, *pf.* (*of* наста́ивать) to draw, infuse; н. чай to let tea draw; н. во́дку на ви́шнях to prepare a liqueur from cherries.

насто|я́ться¹, ю́сь, и́шься, *pf.* (*coll.*) to stand a long time.

насто|я́ться², ю́сь, и́шься, *pf.* (*of* наста́иваться) **1.** to draw, brew (*of tea, etc.*). **2.** *pass. of* ~я́ть².

настоя́щ|ий, *adj.* **1.** present; this; в ~ее вре́мя at present, now; ~ее вре́мя (*gram.*) the present tense; *as noun* ~ее, ~его, *n.* the present (time). **2.** real, genuine; ~ая цена́ fair price. **3.** (*coll., pejor.*) complete, utter, absolute; он н. дура́к he is an absolute fool.

настрада́|ться, юсь, *pf.* to suffer much.

настра́ива|ть(ся), ю(сь), *impf. of* настро́ить(ся).

настра́чива|ть, ю, *impf. of* настрочи́ть².

настреля́|ть, ю, *pf.* (+*a. or g.*) to shoot (*a quantity of*).

настри́г, а, *m.* (*agric.*) **1.** shearing, clipping. **2.** clip.

настри́|чь, гу́, жёшь, гу́т, *past* ~г, ~гла, *pf.* (+*a. or g.*) (*agric.*) to shear, clip (*a number of*).

на́строго, *adv.* (*coll.*) strictly.

настрое́ни|е, я, *n.* **1.** (*also* н. ду́ха) mood, temper, humour; челове́к ~я a man of moods; быть в плохо́м, *etc.*, ~и to be in a bad, *etc.*, mood; н. умо́в state of opinion, public mood. **2.** (+*inf.*) mood (for); у меня́ нет ~я танцева́ть, я не в ~и танцева́ть I am not in a mood for dancing, I don't feel like dancing.

настро́енност|ь, и, *f.* mood, humour.

настро́|ить¹, ю, ишь, *pf.* (*of* настра́ивать) **1.** (*mus.*) to tune; to tune up, attune; н. приёмник на сре́днюю волну́ to tune in to medium wave. **2.** (*fig.*; на+*a.*) to dispose (to), incline (to); to incite; н. кого́-н. на весёлый лад to make someone happy, cheer someone up; н. кого́-н. (про́тив) to incite someone (against).

настро́|ить², ю, ишь, *pf.* (+*a. or g.*) to build (*a quantity of*).

настро́|иться, юсь, ишься, *pf.* (*of* настра́иваться) **1.** (на+*a.*) to dispose oneself (to);

(+*inf.*) to make up one's mind (to); он ~и́лся на мра́чный лад he has made himself gloomy, he has got into a gloomy mood; я ~и́лся е́хать в Москву́ I made up my mind to go to Moscow. **2.** *pass. of* ~и́ть¹.

настро́йк|а, и, *f.* **1.** (*mus., radio*) tuning. **2.** (*radio, aeron.*) tuning call. **3.** (*tech.*) н. станка́ tooling.

настро́йщик, а, *m.* tuner.

настропал|и́ть, ю́, и́шь, *pf.* (*coll.*) to incite, set on.

настроч|и́ть¹, у́, и́шь, *pf.* of строчи́ть.

настроч|и́ть², у́, и́шь, *pf.* (*of* настра́чивать) (*coll.*) to incite, set on.

настря́па|ть, ю, *pf.* **1.** (+*a. or g.*) to cook (*a quantity of*). **2.** (*fig., coll.*) to cook up.

насту|ди́ть, жу́, ~дишь, *pf.* (*of* ~жива́ть) (*coll.*) to cool, make cold.

настуж|а́ть = ~ива́ть.

насту́жива|ть, ю, *impf. of* настуди́ть.

насту́к|ать, аю, *pf.* (*of* ~ивать) (*coll.*) **1.** to discover by tapping. **2.** to knock out, bash out (*on typewriter*).

насту́кива|ть, ю, *impf. of* насту́кать.

наступа́тельный, *adj.* (*mil.*) offensive; (*fig.*) aggressive.

наступа́|ть¹, а́ю, *impf. of* ~и́ть.

наступа́|ть², ю, *impf.* (*mil.*) to advance, be on the offensive.

наступа́|ющий¹, *pres. part. act. of* ~ть¹ *and adj.* coming.

наступа́|ющий², *pres. part. act. of* ~ть² *and noun* н., ~ющего, *m.* attacker.

наступ|и́ть¹, лю́, ~ишь, *pf.* (*of* ~а́ть¹) (на+*a.*) to tread (on); медве́дь (*or* слон) наступи́л ему́ на у́хо he has absolutely no ear for music.

наступ|и́ть², ~ит, *pf.* (*of* ~а́ть¹) (*of times or seasons*) to come, begin; to ensue; to set in (*also fig.*); ~ит вре́мя, когда́... there will come a time, when . . . .

наступле́ни|е¹, я, *n.* (*mil.*) offensive; attack; перейти́ в н. to assume the offensive.

наступле́ни|е², я, *n.* coming, approach.

насту́рци|я, и, *f.* (*bot.*) nasturtium.

настыва́|ть, ю, *impf. of* насты́ть.

насты́|ть, ну, нешь, *pf.* (*of* ~ва́ть) (*coll.*) to become cold.

насул|и́ть, ю́, и́шь, *pf.* (+*a. or g.*) (*coll.*) to promise (much).

насу́п|ить(ся), лю(сь), ишь(ся), *pf. of* су́пить(ся) *and* ~ливать(ся).

насу́пливать(ся) = су́пить(ся).

насупро́тив, *adv. and prep.*+*g.* (*dial.*) opposite.

насурьм|и́ть(ся), лю́(сь), и́шь(ся), *pf. of* сурьми́ть(ся).

на́сухо, *adv.* dry; вы́тереть н. to wipe dry.

насуш|и́ть, у́, ~ишь, *pf.* (+*a. or g.*) to dry (*a quantity of*).

насу́щност|ь, и, *f.* urgency.

насу́щ|ный (ен, ~на), *adj.* vital, urgent; хлеб н. daily bread (*also fig.*).

нас|у́ю, уёшь, *see* ~ова́ть.

насчёт, *prep.*+*g.* about; as regards, concerning.

насчита́ть, а́ю, *pf.* (*of* ~ывать) to count, number.

насчи́тыва|ть, ю, *impf.* 1. *impf. of* насчита́ть. 2. (*no pf.*) to number (= *to contain*); э́тот го́род ~ет свы́ше ста ты́сяч жи́телей this city has over one hundred thousand inhabitants.

насчи́тыва|ться, ется, *impf.* (*impers.*) to number (= *to be, be contained*); в на́шем селе́ ~ется не бо́лее двухсо́т жи́телей the population of our village numbers no more than two hundred.

насыла́|ть, ю, *impf. of* насла́ть[1].

насы́п|ать, лю, лешь, *pf.* (*of* ~а́ть) 1. (+*a. or g.*) to pour (in, into); to fill (with); н. муки́ в мешо́к to pour flour into a bag; н. мешо́к муко́й to fill up a bag with flour. 2. (+*a. or g.* на+*a.*) to spread (on); н. песку́ на доро́жку to spread sand on the path. 3. to raise (*a heap or pile of sand, etc.*).

насып|а́ть, а́ю, *impf. of* ~а́ть.

насы́пк|а, и, *f.* pouring (in), filling.

насыпно́й, *adj.* poured; piled (up); н. холм artificial mound.

на́сып|ь, и, *f.* embankment (*of railway or road*).

насы́|тить, щу, тишь, *pf.* (*of* ~ща́ть) 1. to sate, satiate. 2. (*chem.*) to saturate, impregnate.

насы́|титься, щусь, тишься, *pf.* (*of* ~ща́ться) 1. to be full; to be sated. 2. (*chem.*) to become saturated.

насыща́|ть(ся), ю(сь), *impf. of* насы́тить(ся).

насыще́ни|е, я, *n.* 1. satiety, satiation. 2. (*chem.*) saturation.

насы́щенност|ь, и, *f.* 1. saturation. 2. (*fig.*) richness.

насы́|щенный, *p.p.p. of* ~тить *and adj.* 1. saturated. 2. (*fig.*) rich.

ната́лкива|ть(ся), ю(сь), *impf. of* натолкну́ть(ся).

ната́плива|ть, ю, *impf. of* натопи́ть[1].

ната́птыва|ть, ю, *impf. of* натопта́ть.

ната́ск|анный, *p.p.p. of* ~а́ть.

натаск|а́ть[1], а́ю, *pf.* (*of* ~ивать) to train (*hounds*); (*fig., coll.*) to coach, cram.

натаск|а́ть[2], а́ю, *pf.* (+*a. or g.*) 1. to bring, lay (*a quantity of*). 2. (*coll.*) to fish out, hook (*a quantity of*); н. из устаре́вших сочине́ний (*fig., pejor.*) to fish up outdated authorities.

ната́скива|ть, ю, *impf. of* натаска́ть[1] *and* натащи́ть[1].

ната́счик, а, *m.* trainer (of hounds).

натащ|и́ть[1], у́, ~ишь, *pf.* (*of* ната́скивать) to pull (on, over).

натащ|и́ть[2], у́, ~ишь, *pf.* (+*a. or g.*) to bring (*a quantity of*); to pile up (*a quantity of*).

ната́|ять, ю, ешь, *pf.* (+*a. or g.*) to melt (*a quantity of snow or ice*) (*also intrans.*).

натвор|и́ть, ю́, и́шь, *pf.* (+*g.*; *coll., pejor.*) to do, get up to; н. вся́ких глу́постей to get up to every sort of stupid trick; что ты ~и́л! what ever have you done?

на́те, *interj.* (*coll., addressed to more than one person or, politely, to one*) here (you are)!, there (you are)! (= take it!); тепе́рь н. вам and now see what's happened.

натёк, а, *m.* 1. (*geol.*) deposit. 2. (*coll.*) pool (*of some liquid*).

натека́|ть, ет, *impf. of* нате́чь.

нате́льн|ый, *adj.* worn next the skin; ~ое бельё (*collect.*) underclothes, body linen; ~ая фуфа́йка vest.

на|тере́ть[1], тру́, трёшь, *past* ~тёр, ~тёрла, *pf.* (*of* ~тира́ть) 1. to rub (in, on); н. ру́ки вазели́ном to rub vaseline into one's hands. 2. to polish (*floors, etc.*). 3. to rub sore; to chafe; н. себе́ мозо́ль to get a corn.

на|тере́ть[2], тру́, трёшь, *past* ~тёр, ~тёрла, *pf.* (+*a. or g.*) to grate, rasp (*a quantity of*).

на|тере́ться, тру́сь, трёшься, *past* ~тёрся, ~тёрлась, *pf.* (*of* ~тира́ться) 1. (+*i.*) to rub oneself (with). 2. *pass. of* ~тере́ть.

натерп|е́ться, лю́сь, ~ишься, *pf.* (+*g.*; *coll.*) to have endured much; to have gone through much.

натёр|тый, *p.p.p. of* ~е́ть.

нате́|чь, чёт, ку́т, *past* ~к, ~кла́, *pf.* (*of* ~ка́ть) (*of liquids*) to accumulate.

нате́ш|иться, усь, ишься, *pf.* (*coll.*) 1. to enjoy oneself, have a good time. 2. (над) to have a good laugh (at).

натира́ни|е, я, *n.* 1. rubbing in. 2. polishing (*of floors, etc.*). 3. (*coll.*) embrocation, ointment.

натира́|ть(ся), ю(сь), *impf. of* натере́ть(ся).

на́тиск, а, *m.* 1. onslaught, charge, onset. 2. pressure. 3. (*typ.*) impress.

нати́ска|ть, ю, *pf.* (+*a. or g.*) 1. (*coll.*) to cram in, stuff in (*a quantity of*). 2. (*coll.*) to shove (someone) about. 3. (*typ.*) to impress (*a quantity of*).

на́-тка = на́те (*but addressed familiarly to one person*).

натк|а́ть, у́, ёшь, *past* ~а́л, ~ала́, ~а́ло, *pf.* (+*a. or g.*) to weave (*a quantity of*).

наткн|у́ть, у́, ёшь, *pf.* (*of* натыка́ть) 1. to stick, pin. 2. to stick, pin (*a quantity of*).

наткн|у́ться, у́сь, ёшься, *pf.* (*of* натыка́ться) (на+*a.*) 1. to run (against), strike; to stumble (upon); н. на гвоздь to run against a nail; н. на неожи́данное сопротивле́ние (*fig.*) to meet with unexpected resistance. **2.** (*fig.*) to stumble (upon, across), come (across); н. на интере́сную мысль to stumble across an interesting idea.

натолкн|у́ть, у́, ёшь, *pf.* (*of* ната́лкивать) (+*a.* на+*a.*) **1.** to push (against), shove (against). **2.** (*fig.*) to direct, lead (into, onto); он меня́ ~у́л на мысль he suggested the idea to me; н. на грех to lead into sin.

натолкн|у́ться, у́сь, ёшься, *pf.* (*of* ната́лкиваться) (на+*a.*) to run (against); (*fig.*) to run across.

натол|о́чь, ку́, чёшь, ку́т, *past* ~о́к, ~кла́, *pf.* (+*a. or g.*) to pound, crush (*a quantity of*).

натоп|и́ть[1], лю́, ~ишь, *pf.* (*of* ната́пливать) to heat well, heat up.

натоп|и́ть[2], лю́, ~ишь, *pf.* (+*a. or g.*) **1.** to melt (*a quantity of*). **2.** to heat (*a quantity of*).

натоп|та́ть, чу́, ~чешь, *pf.* (*of* ната́птывать) (*coll.*; в, на+*p.*) to make dirty footmarks (in, on).

наторг|ова́ть, у́ю, *pf.* (*coll.*) **1.** (+*a. or g.*) to make, gain (*by commerce*). **2.** (на+*a.*) to sell (for).

натаре́лый, *adj.* (*coll.*) skilled, expert.

наторе́|ть, ю, *pf.* (в+*p.*; *coll.*) to become skilled (at, in), become expert (at, in).

наточ|и́ть, у́, ~ишь, *pf. of* точи́ть[1].

натоща́к, *adv.* on an empty stomach.

натр, а, *m.* (*chem.*) natron; е́дкий н. caustic soda.

натрав|и́ть[1], лю́, ~ишь, *pf.* (*of* ~ливать) (на+*a.*) to set (*dog*) (on); (*fig.*) to stir up (against).

натрав|и́ть[2], лю́, ~ишь, *pf.* (*of* ~ливать) to etch.

натрав|и́ть[3], лю́, ~ишь, *pf.* (+*a. or g.*) to exterminate (*a quantity of*).

натра́влива|ть, ю, *impf. of* натрави́ть[1, 2].

натравл|я́ть = ~ивать.

натрениро́ванный, *adj.* trained.

натренир|ова́ть(ся), у́ю(сь), *pf. of* трениро́ва́ть(ся).

на́три|евый, *adj. of* ~й.

на́три|й, я, *m.* (*chem.*) sodium.

на́трое, *adv.* in three.

натро́нн|ый, *adj.* (*chem.*) sodium; ~ая и́звесть sodium carbonate.

нат|ру́, рёшь, *see* ~ере́ть.

натруб|и́ть, лю́, и́шь, *pf.* (*coll.*) to trumpet a good deal; н. в у́ши кому́-н. to din into someone's ears.

натру|ди́ть, жу́, ~ди́шь, *pf.* (*of* ~жива́ть) to tire out, overwork.

натру|ди́ться, жу́сь, ~ди́шься, *pf.* (*coll.*) **1.** to become tired out. **2.** to have worked long enough; to have overworked.

натру́жива|ть, ю, *impf. of* натруди́ть.

натряс|ти́, у́, ёшь, *past* ~, ~ла́, *pf.* (+*a. or g.*) to scatter, let fall (*a quantity of*).

натряс|ти́сь, у́сь, ёшься, *past* ~ся, ~ла́сь, *pf.* (*coll.*) **1.** to be shaken much; (*fig.*) to shake, quake much. **2.** to be scattered; to spill.

нату́г|а, и, *f.* effort, strain.

на́туго, *adv.* (*coll.*) tightly; ту́го-на́туго very tightly.

нату́жива|ть(ся), ю(сь), *impf. of* нату́жить(ся).

нату́ж|ить, у, ишь, *pf.* (*of* ~ивать) (*coll.*) to tense, tighten.

нату́ж|иться, усь, ишься, *pf.* (*of* ~иваться) (*coll.*) to exert all one's strength; to strain.

нату́жный, *adj.* (*coll.*) strained, forced.

нату́р|а, ы, *f.* **1.** (*in var. senses*) nature. **2.** (artist's) model, sitter; рисова́ть с ~ы to paint from life. **3.** (*econ.*) kind; плати́ть ~ой to pay in kind. **4.** на ~е (*cinema*) on location.

натурализа́ци|я, и, *f.* naturalization.

натурали́зм, а, *m.* naturalism.

натурализ|ова́ть, у́ю, *impf. and pf.* to naturalize.

натурали́ст, а, *m.* (*in var. senses*) naturalist.

натуралисти́ческий, *adj.* naturalistic.

натура́льно, *adv.* (*obs.*) naturally, of course.

натура́льност|ь, и, *f.* genuineness; naturalness.

натура́л|ьный (~ен, ~ьна), *adj.* **1.** (*in var. senses*) natural; в ~ьную величину́ life-size. **2.** real; genuine; н. смех unforced laughter. **3.** (*econ.*) in kind; н. обме́н barter.

нату́рн|ый, *adj.* (*art*) from life; н. класс life class; ~ая съёмка (*cinema*) shooting on location, take made on location.

натуропла́т|а, ы, *f.* payment in kind.

нату́рщик, а, *m.* (artist's) model, sitter.

нату́рщи|ца, цы, *f. of* ~к.

натыка́|ть(ся), ю(сь), *impf. of* наткну́ть(ся).

натюрмо́рт, а, *m.* (*art*) still life.

натюрмо́рт|ный, *adj. of* ~.

натя́гива|ть(ся), ю(сь), *impf. of* натяну́ть(ся).

натяже́ни|е, я, *n.* pull, tension.

натя́жк|а, и, *f.* (*coll.*) **1.** strained interpretation; допусти́ть ~у to stretch a point; с ~ой (*fig.*) at a stretch. **2.** = натяже́ние.

натяжн|о́й, *adj.* (*tech.*) tension; ~о́е приспособле́ние tension device, stretcher; н. ро́лик tension pulley; н. рыча́г tension lever.

натя́нутост|ь, и, *f.* tension (*also fig.*).

натя́н|утый, *p.p.p. of* ~уть *and adj.* **1.** tight. **2.** (*fig.*) strained; forced; ~утые отноше́ния strained relations; ~утое сравне́ние far--fetched simile.

натя|ну́ть, ну́, ~нешь, *pf.* (*of* ~гивать) **1.** to stretch; to draw (tight); н. лук to draw a bow; н. верёвку (*naut.*) to haul a rope taut. **2.** to pull on; н. ша́пку на́ уши to pull a cap over one's ears.

натя|ну́ться, ну́сь, ~нешься, *pf.* (*of* ~гиваться) to stretch (*intrans.*).

науга́д, *adv.* at random, by guess-work.

науго́льник, а, *m.* (*tech.*) (try-)square, back square; bevel, bevel square.

наудалу́ю, *adv.* (*coll.*) at a venture.

науда́чу, *adv.* at random; by guesswork.

нау|ди́ть, жу́, ~дишь, *pf.* (+*a. or g.*) to hook (*a number of*).

нау́к|а, и, *f.* **1.** science; learning; study; scholarship; обще́ственные ~и social sciences, social studies; прикладны́е ~и applied science; то́чные ~и exact science. **2.** (*coll.*) lesson; э́то тебе́ н.! let this be a lesson to you!

нау|сти́ть, щу́, сти́шь, *pf.* (*of* ~ща́ть) (*obs.*) to incite, egg on.

нау́ськ|ать, аю, *pf.* (*of* ~ивать) (на+*a.*) to set (*dogs on*).

нау́ськива|ть, ю, *impf. of* нау́ськать.

наутёк, *adv.* пусти́ться н. (*coll.*) to take to one's heels.

нау́тро, *adv.* next morning.

науч|и́ть, у́, ~ишь, *pf.* (*of* учи́ть) (+*a. and d. or* +*inf.*) to teach; н. кого́-н. ру́сскому языку́ to teach someone Russian; н. кого́-н. пра́вить маши́ной to teach someone to drive (a car).

науч|и́ться, у́сь, ~ишься, *pf.* (*of* учи́ться) (+*d. or inf.*) to learn.

нау́чно-иссле́довательск|ий, *adj.* scientific research; ~ая рабо́та (scientific) research work.

нау́чно-фантасти́ческий, *adj.* science fiction.

нау́ч|ный (~ен, ~на), *adj.* scientific; н. рабо́тник member of staff of scientific or other learned body; ~ная фанта́стика science fiction.

нау́шник¹, а, *m.* **1.** ear-flap; ear-muff. **2.** ear-phone, head-phone.

нау́шник², а, *m.* (*pejor.*) informer, slanderer.

нау́шнича|ть, ю, *impf.* (+*d.* на+*a.*) to tell tales (about), inform (on, about).

нау́шничеств|о, а, *n.* tale-bearing, informing.

науща́|ть, ю, *impf. of* наусти́ть.

нау|щу́, сти́шь, *see* ~сти́ть.

нафа́бр|ить, ю, ишь, *pf. of* фа́брить.

нафтали́н, а, *m.* (*chem.*) naphthalene, naphthaline.

нафтали́н|ный, *adj. of* ~.

нафтали́н|овый = ~ный; н. ша́рик camphor ball, moth-ball.

наха́л, а, *m.* impudent, insolent fellow, cheeky fellow; smart aleck.

наха́лк|а, и, *f.* impudent, insolent woman.

наха́льнича|ть, ю, *impf.* to be impudent, insolent.

наха́л|ьный (~ен, ~ьна), *adj.* impudent, impertinent; cheeky, brazen.

наха́льств|о, а, *n.* impudence, impertinence, effrontery; име́ть н. (+*inf.*) to have the cheek (to), have the face (to).

нахам|и́ть, лю́, и́шь, *pf.* (*coll.*; +*d.*) to play someone a caddish trick, to speak offensively.

нахва́лива|ть, ю, *impf. of* нахвали́ть.

нахвал|и́ть, ю́, ~ишь, *pf.* (*of* ~ивать) (*coll.*) to praise (highly).

нахвал|и́ться, ю́сь, ~ишься, *pf.* (*coll.*) **1.** to boast much. **2.** (+*i.*; *usually* +*neg.*) to praise sufficiently; я не могу́ им н. I cannot speak too highly of him.

нахват|а́ть, а́ю, *pf.* (*of* ~ывать) (*coll.*; +*a. or g.*) to pick up, get hold (of), come by.

нахват|а́ться, а́юсь, *pf.* (*of* ~ываться) (*coll.*, *fig.*; +*g.*) to pick up, come by; в солда́тах он нахвата́лся ара́бских слов in the army he picked up a few words of Arabic.

нахле́бник, а, *m.* **1.** (*obs.*) boarder, paying guest. **2.** parasite, hanger-on.

нахле|ста́ть, щу́, ~щешь, *pf.* (*of* ~стывать) (*coll.*) to whip.

нахле|ста́ться, щу́сь, ~щешься, *pf.* (*of* ~стываться) (*sl.*) to get sloshed (*drunk*).

нахлёстыва|ть(ся), ю(сь), *impf. of* нахлеста́ть(ся).

нахлобу́чива|ть, ю, *impf. of* нахлобу́чить.

нахлобу́ч|ить, у, ишь, *pf.* (*of* ~ивать) (*coll.*) **1.** to pull down (over one's head *or* eyes). **2.** н. кому́-н. (*fig.*) to rate someone, give someone a dressing down.

нахлобу́чк|а, и, *f.* **1.** (*coll.*) rating, dressing down. **2.** (*obs.*) blow on the head.

нахлы́н|уть, ет, *pf.* (на+*a.*) to flow, gush (over, into); (*fig.*) to surge, crowd; ~ули слёзы tears welled (in my, her, *etc.*, eyes); на меня́ ~ули мы́сли thoughts crowded into my mind.

нахму́р|енный, *p.p.p. of* ~ить *and adj.* frowning, scowling.

нахму́р|ить(ся), ю(сь), ишь(ся), *pf. of* хму́рить(ся).

нахо|ди́ть, жу́, ~дишь, *impf. of* найти́.

нахо|ди́ться¹, жу́сь, ~дишься, *impf. of* найти́сь.

нахо|ди́ться², жу́сь, ~дишься, *impf.* to be (situated); где ~дится ста́нция? where is the station?

нахо|ди́ться³, жу́сь, ~дишься, *pf.* (*coll.*) to tire oneself by walking; to have walked long enough.

нахо́дк|а, и, *f.* **1.** find. **2.** (*fig.*, *coll.*) godsend.

нахо́дчивост|ь, и, *f.* 1. resource, resource-fulness. 2. readiness, quick-wittedness.

нахо́дчив|ый (~, ~а), *adj.* 1. resourceful. 2. ready, quick-witted.

нахожде́ни|е, я, *n.* 1. finding. 2. ме́сто ~я the whereabouts.

нахоло|ди́ть, жу́, ди́шь, *pf. of* холоди́ть 1.

нахо́хл|ить(ся), ю(сь), ишь(ся), *pf. of* хо́хлить(ся).

нахоxо|та́ться, чу́сь, ~чешься, *pf.* (*coll.*) to have had a good laugh.

нахра́пист|ый (~, ~а), *adj.* (*coll.*, *pejor.*) high-handed.

нахра́пом, *adv.* (*coll.*) unceremoniously, insolently, with a high hand.

нацара́п|ать, аю, *pf.* (*of* ~ывать) 1. to scratch. 2. (*fig.*, *coll.*) to scrawl, scribble.

нацара́пыва|ть, ю, *impf. of* нацара́пать.

наце|ди́ть, жу́, ~дишь, *pf.* (+*a. or g.*) 1. to fill (*a vessel*) through a strainer. 2. to pour through a strainer (*a quantity of*).

наце́лива|ть(ся), ю(сь), *impf. of* наце́лить(ся).

наце́л|ить, ю, ишь, *pf.* 1. (*impf.* це́лить *and* ~ивать) to aim, level. 2. (*impf.* ~ивать) (*fig.*) to aim, direct.

наце́л|иться, юсь, ишься, *pf.* (*of* ~иваться) 1. (в+*a.*) to aim (at), take aim (at). 2. (*fig.*, *coll.*; на+*a.*) to aim (at, for).

на́цело, *adv.* (*coll.*) entirely, without remainder.

наце́нива|ть, ю, *impf. of* нацени́ть.

нацен|и́ть, ю́, ~ишь, *pf.* (*of* ~ивать) (*comm.*) to raise the price of.

наце́нк|а, и, *f.* addition (to price).

нацеп|и́ть, лю́, ~ишь, *pf.* (*of* ~ля́ть) to fasten on; to attach (*by means of hook or pin*).

нацеп|ля́ть, ля́ю, *impf. of* ~и́ть.

наци́зм, а, *m.* Nazism.

национализа́ци|я, и, *f.* nationalization.

национализи́р|овать, ую, *impf. and pf.* to nationalize.

национали́зм, а, *m.* nationalism.

национали́ст, а, *m.* nationalist.

националисти́ческий, *adj.* nationalist(ic).

национа́льност|ь, и, *f.* 1. nationality (*in var. senses: the words* н. *and* национа́льный *in Soviet parlance refer not to the State but to the particular national groups which compose it;* e.g. гражда́нство — сове́тское, национа́льность — ру́сская (*or* евре́йская, армя́нская, *etc.*) citizenship—Soviet, nationality Russian (*or* Jewish, Armenian, *etc.*)); ethnic group. 2. national character, national idiosyncrasy.

национа́льн|ый, *adj.* national (*see also* ~ость); ~ые словари́ dictionaries of languages of peoples of the Soviet Union.

наци́ст, а, *m.* Nazi.

наци́стский, *adj.* Nazi.

на́ци|я, и, *f.* nation.

нацме́н, а, *m.* (*coll.*) member of a national minority.

нацме́н|ка, ки, *f. of* ~.

нача|ди́ть, жу́, ди́шь, *pf. of* чади́ть.

нача́л|о, а, *n.* beginning; commencement; в ~е четвёртого soon after three (o'clock); для ~а to start with, for a start; по ~у at first; положи́ть н. (+*d.*) to begin, commence. 2. origin, source; вести́ н. (от), взять н. (в+*p.*) to originate (from, in). 3. principle, basis; рабо́тать на но́вых ~ах to work on a new basis; ~а матема́тики the elements of mathematics. 4. (*obs.*) command, authority; быть под ~ом у кого́-н. to be under someone; отда́ть под н., под ~а (+*d.*) to put under, place in the charge (of).

нача́льник, а, *m.* head, chief; superior; н. свя́зи chief signal officer; н. отде́ла head of a department.

нача́льнический, *adj.* overbearing, imperious.

нача́льн|ый, *adj.* 1. initial, first; ~ая ско́рость initial speed; (*artillery*) muzzle velocity. 2. elementary; ~ая шко́ла primary school.

нача́льственный, *adj.* overbearing, domineering.

нача́льств|о, а, *n.* 1. (*collect.*) (the) authorities. 2. command, direction. 3. (*coll.*) head, boss.

нача́льствовани|е, я, *n.* command.

нача́льств|овать, ую, *impf.* (над) to command, be in command (of).

нача́тк|и, ов, *no sing.* rudiments, elements.

нач|а́ть, ну́, нёшь, *past* ~ал, ~ала́, ~ало, *pf.* (*of* ~ина́ть) to begin, start, commence; н. с ~а́ла to begin at the beginning; н. всё снача́ла to start all over again, start afresh; н. с того́, что он ни одного́ сло́ва не по́нял to begin with, he did not understand a single word; он на́чал моли́твой (*or* с моли́твы) he began with a prayer.

нач|а́ться, ну́сь, нёшься, *past* ~ался́, ~ала́сь, *pf.* (*of* ~ина́ться) to begin, start; to break out.

начека́н|ить, ю, ишь, *pf.* (+*a. or g.*) to mint (*a quantity of*).

начеку́, *adv.* on the alert, on the qui vive.

начерн|и́ть, ю́, и́шь, *pf. of* черни́ть 1.

на́черно, *adv.* roughly; написа́ть н. to make a rough copy.

наче́рпа|ть, ю, *pf.* (+*a. or g.*) to scoop up (*a quantity of*).

начерта́ни|е, я, *n.* tracing; outline.

начерта́тельн|ый, *adj.* only in phrase ~ая геоме́трия descriptive geometry.

начерта́|ть, ю, *pf.* to trace (*also fig.*); to inscribe.

начер|ти́ть, чу́, ∠тишь, *pf. of* черти́ть[1].

начёс, а, *m.* **1.** nap (*of material*). **2.** (hair dressed in) fringe.

наче|са́ть[1]**, шу́, ∠шешь,** *pf.* (+*a. or g.*) to comb, card (*a quantity of*).

наче|са́ть[2]**, шу́, ∠шешь,** *pf.* (*of* ∠сывать) (*coll.*) to injure by scratching.

нач|е́сть, ту́, тёшь, *pf.* (*of* ∠и́тывать) (*bookkeeping*) to recover.

начёсыва|ть, ю, *impf. of* начеса́ть[2].

начёт, а, *m.* (*book-keeping*) recovery of unauthorized expenditure; recovery of deficit in account; сде́лать н. на кого́-н. to recover unauthorized expenditure from someone.

начётист|ый (∼, ∼а), *adj.* (*coll.*) disadvantageous, unprofitable.

начётничеств|о, а, *n.* (*pejor.*) dogmatism (*based on uncritical, mechanical reading*).

начётчик, а, *m.* **1.** person well-read in Scriptures. **2.** (*fig., pejor.*) dogmatist (*person basing opinions uncritically on wide but mechanical reading*).

начина́ни|е, я, *n.* undertaking.

начина́тел|ь, я, *m.* originator, initiator.

начина́тельный, *adj.* (*gram.*) н. глаго́л inceptive verb.

начина́|ть(ся), ю(сь), *impf. of* нача́ть(ся).

начина́|ющий, *pres. part. act. of* ∼ть; *as noun* **н., ∼ющего,** *m.* beginner.

начина́я, *as prep.* (с+*g.*) as (from), starting (with).

начин|и́ть[1]**, ю́, и́шь,** *pf.* (*of* ∼я́ть) (+*i.*) to fill (with), stuff (with).

начин|и́ть[2]**, ю́, ∠ишь,** *pf.* (+*a. or g.*) **1.** to mend (*a quantity of*). **2.** карандаше́й to sharpen (*a number of*) pencils.

начи́нк|а, и, *f.* (*cul.*) stuffing, filling.

начин|я́ть, я́ю, *impf. of* ∼и́ть[1].

начисле́ни|е, я, *n.* additional sum; extra.

начи́сл|ить, ю, ишь, *pf.* (*of* ∼я́ть) (*book-keeping*) to add (to someone's account); to charge extra.

начисл|я́ть, я́ю, *impf. of* ∼ить.

начи́|стить[1]**, щу, стишь,** *pf.* (*of* ∼ща́ть) to polish, shine (*trans.*).

начи́|стить[2]**, щу, стишь,** *pf.* (+*a. or g.*) to peel (*a quantity of*); to clean (*a quantity of*) (*vegetables, etc.*).

на́чисто, *adv.* **1.** clean, fair; переписа́ть н. to make a fair copy (of). **2.** (*coll.*) completely, thoroughly; н. отказа́ться to refuse flatly. **3.** (*coll.*) openly, without equivocation.

начистоту́, *adv.* openly, without equivocation.

начист|у́ю, *adv.* (*coll.*) **1.** = ∼оту́. **2.** utterly, altogether.

начи́танност|ь, и, *f.* (wide) reading; erudition.

начи́тан|ный (∼, ∼на), *adj.* well-read, widely-read.

начита́|ть, ю, *pf.* (+*a. or g.*) to read (*a number of*).

начита́|ться, юсь, *pf.* **1.** (+*g.*) to have read (*much of*). **2.** to have read one's fill.

начи́тыва|ть, ю, *impf. of* наче́сть.

начища́|ть, ю, *impf. of* начи́стить.

нач|ну́, нёшь, *see* ∼а́ть.

начу|ди́ть, жу́, ди́шь, *pf.* (*coll.*) to behave oddly; что ты там начуди́л? what have you been up to?

наш, ∠его, f. ∠а, ∠ей; *n.* **∠е, ∠его;** *pl.* **∠и, ∠их,** *possessive pronoun* our(s); ∠его (*after comp.*) we; у них де́нег бо́льше ∠его they have more money than we; ∠а взяла́! (*coll.*) we've won!; знай ∠их! (*coll.*) that's the sort we are! we'll show you!; ∠е вам! (*coll.*) hello there! (служи́ть) и ∠им и ва́шим (*coll.*) to run with the hare and hunt with the hounds; *as noun* ∠и, ∠их, our people, people on our side; его́ счита́ют одни́м из ∠их they regard him as one of us.

нашал|и́ть, ю́, и́шь, *pf.* to be naughty.

нашаты́р|ный, *adj. of* ∼ь; н. спирт liquid ammonia.

нашаты́р|ь, я́, *m.* (*chem.*) sal ammoniac, ammonium chloride.

нашеп|та́ть, чу́, ∠чешь, *pf.* (*of* ∼тывать) **1.** (+*a. or g.*) to whisper (*a number of*) (*also fig.*). **2.** (на+*a.*) to put a spell (upon).

нашёптыва|ть, ю, *impf. of* нашепта́ть.

наше́стви|е, я, *n.* invasion, descent.

на́шивать, *freq. of* носи́ть.

нашива́|ть, ю, *impf. of* наши́ть[1].

наши́вк|а, и, *f.* (*mil.*) stripe, chevron (*on sleeve*); tab.

нашивно́й, *adj.* sewed (sewn) on.

наш|и́ть[1]**, ью, ьёшь,** *pf.* (*of* ∼ива́ть) to sew on.

наш|и́ть[2]**, ью, ьёшь,** *pf.* (+*a. or g.*) to sew (*a quantity of*).

нашлёпа|ть, ю, *pf.* (*coll.*) to slap; to spank.

на|шлю́, шлёшь, *see* ∼сла́ть.

нашпиг|ова́ть, у́ю, *pf. of* шпигова́ть.

нашпи́лива|ть, ю, *impf. of* нашпи́лить.

нашпи́л|ить, ю, ишь, *pf.* (*of* ∼ивать) (*coll.*) to pin on.

нашум|е́ть, лю́, и́шь, *pf.* to make much noise; (*fig.*) to cause a sensation.

нащёлка|ть, ю, *pf.* (+*a. or g.*) to crack (*a quantity of*) (*nuts, etc.*).

нащип|а́ть, лю́, ∠лешь, *pf.* (+*a. or g.*) to pluck, pick (*a quantity of*).

нащу́п|ать, аю, *pf.* (*of* ∼ывать) to find, discover (*by groping*).

нащу́пыва|ть, ю, *impf.* (*of* нащу́пать) to grope (for, after); to fumble (for, after); to feel about (for) (*also fig.*); н. по́чву (*fig.*) to feel one's way, see how the land lies.

наэлектриз|ова́ть, у́ю, *pf.* (*of* ~о́вывать) to electrify (*also fig.*).

наэлектризо́выва|ть, ю, *impf. of* наэлектризова́ть.

найбе́днича|ть, ю, *pf. of* я́бедничать.

наяву́, *adv.* waking; in reality; гре́зить н. to day-dream.

на́йд|а, ы, *f.* (*myth.*) naiad.

найрива|ть, ю, *impf.* (*coll.*) to bash out (*a tune, etc., on a mus. instrument*).

не¹, not; не..., не neither . . . nor.

не², *separable component of pronouns* не́кого *and* не́чего; мне не́ с кем разгова́ривать I have no one to talk to; не́ о чём бы́ло говори́ть there was nothing to talk about.

не- un-, in-, non-, mis-, dis-.

неаккура́тност|ь, и, *f.* 1. carelessness; inaccuracy. 2. unpunctuality. 3. untidiness.

неаккура́т|ный (~ен, ~на), *adj.* 1. careless; inaccurate. 2. unpunctual. 3. untidy.

неандерта́л|ец, ьца, *m.* (*anthrop.*) Neanderthal man.

неандерта́льский, *adj.* (*anthrop.*) Neanderthal.

неаполита́н|ец, ца, *m.* Neapolitan.

неаполита́нский, *adj.* Neapolitan.

неаппети́т|ный (~ен, ~на), *adj.* unappetizing (*also fig.*).

небезопа́с|ный (~ен, ~на), *adj.* unsafe, insecure.

небезоснова́тел|ьный (~ен, ~ьна), *adj.* not unfounded.

небезразли́ч|ный (~ен, ~на), *adj.* not indifferent.

небезрезульта́т|ный (~ен, ~на), *adj.* not fruitless, not futile.

небезупре́ч|ный (~ен, ~на), *adj.* not irreproachable.

небезуспе́ш|ный (~ен, ~на), *adj.* not unsuccessful.

небезызве́ст|ный (~ен, ~на), *adj.* not unknown; ~но, что... it is no secret that....

небезынтере́с|ный (~ен, ~на), *adj.* not without interest.

небелёный, *adj.* unbleached.

небережли́в|ый (~, ~а), *adj.* thriftless, improvident.

неб|еса́, *pl. of* ~о.

небескоры́ст|ный (~ен, ~на), *adj.* not disinterested.

небе́сн|ый, *adj.* heavenly, celestial; ~ая импе́рия (*hist.*) the Celestial Empire (*China*); ~ая меха́ника (*astron.*) celestial mechanics; ~ые свети́ла heavenly bodies; н. свод firmament; Ца́рство ~ое the Kingdom of Heaven; ~ого цве́та sky-blue.

небесполе́з|ный (~ен, ~на), *adj.* of some use.

небеспристра́ст|ный (~ен, ~на), *adj.* not impartial.

неблагови́д|ный (~ен, ~на), *adj.* 1. unseemly, improper. 2. (*obs.*) unsightly.

неблагода́рност|ь, и, *f.* ingratitude.

неблагода́р|ный (~ен, ~на), *adj.* 1. ungrateful. 2. thankless.

неблагожела́т|ельный (~ен, ~ьна), *adj.* malevolent, ill-disposed.

неблагозву́чи|е, я, *n.* disharmony, dissonance.

неблагозву́ч|ный (~ен, ~на), *adj.* inharmonious, disharmonious.

неблагонадёж|ный (~ен, ~на), *adj.* unreliable (*esp. politically*).

неблагополу́чи|е, я, *n.* trouble.

неблагополу́чно, *adv.* not successfully, not favourably; дела́ у них обстоя́т н. their affairs are in a bad way, things are not turning out happily for them.

неблагополу́ч|ный (~ен, ~на), *adj.* unfavourable, bad; де́ло име́ло н. исхо́д the affair had a bad ending; (*impers.*) у нас ~но things are going badly, we are in a bad way.

неблагопристо́йност|ь, и, *f.* obscenity, indecency, impropriety.

неблагопристо́|йный (~ен, ~йна), *adj.* obscene, indecent, improper.

неблагоприя́т|ный (~ен, ~на), *adj.* unfavourable, inauspicious.

неблагоразу́м|ный (~ен, ~на), *adj.* imprudent, ill-advised, unwise.

неблагоро́д|ный (~ен, ~на), *adj.* ignoble, base; н. мета́лл base metal.

неблагоро́дств|о, а, *n.* baseness.

неблагоскло́н|ный (~ен, ~на), *adj.* unfavourable; (к) ill-disposed (towards).

неблагоустро́ен|ный (~, ~на), *adj.* uncomfortable; badly planned.

нёбн|ый, *adj.* 1. (*anat.*) palatine; ~ая занаве́ска uvula. 2. (*ling.*) palatal.

нёб|о, а, *pl.* ~еса́, ~е́с, ~еса́м, *n.* sky; heaven; попа́сть па́льцем в н. (*coll.*) to miss the point, be wide of the mark; как н. от земли́ (as far removed) as heaven from earth, worlds apart; жить ме́жду ~ом и землёй not to have a roof above one's head; под откры́тым ~ом in the open (air); с ~а свали́ться (*fig., coll.*) to fall from the moon; упа́сть с ~а на зе́млю (*fig.*) to come down to earth; нам н. с овчи́нку показа́лось (*coll.*) we were frightened out of our wits.

нёб|о, а, *n.* (*anat.*) palate.

небога́т|ый (~, ~а), *adj.* 1. of modest means. 2. (*fig.*) modest.

небожи́тел|ь, я, *m.* (*myth.*) celestial being, god.

небольш|о́й, *adj.* small; not great; о́чень ~ое расстоя́ние a very short distance; ты́сяча с ~им a thousand odd; де́ло ста́ло за ~им one small thing is lacking.

небосво́д, **а**, *m.* firmament; the vault of heaven.

небоскло́н, **а**, *m.* horizon (*strictly*, sky immediately over horizon).

небоскрёб, **а**, *m.* (*obs.*) skyscraper.

небо́сь, *adv.* (*coll.*) 1. probably, most likely, I dare say; ты, н., мно́го книг чита́л I suppose you've read lots of books. 2. (*obs.*) don't be afraid (= не бо́йся).

небре́жнича|ть, **ю**, *impf.* (*coll.*) to be careless.

небре́жност|ь, **и**, *f.* carelessness, negligence.

небре́ж|ный (~ен, ~на), *adj.* careless, negligent; slipshod; offhand.

небри́т|ый (~, ~а), *adj.* unshaven.

небыва́лый, *adj.* 1. unprecedented. 2. fantastic, imaginary. 3. (*coll.*) inexperienced.

небыва́льщин|а, **ы**, *f.* 1. (*obs.*) fable. 2. fantastic story.

небыли́ц|а, **ы**, *f.* fable; cock-and-bull story.

небыти́|е́, **я́**, *n.* non-existence.

небью́щийся, *adj.* unbreakable.

неважне́цкий, *adj.* (*coll.*) indifferent, so-so.

нева́жно, *adv.* not too well, indifferently; дела́ иду́т н. things are not going too well.

нева́ж|ный (~ен, ~на́, ~но), *adj.* 1. unimportant, insignificant. 2. poor, indifferent.

невдалеке́, *adv.* not far away, not far off.

невдо|га́д (*dial.*) = ~мёк.

невдомёк, *adv.* (+*d.*) (*coll.*) мне бы́ло н. it never occurred to me, I never thought of it.

неве́дени|е, **я**, *n.* ignorance; пребыва́ть в блаже́нном ~и (*iron.*) to be in a state of blissful ignorance.

неве́домо, *adv.* (*coll.*; +что, как, когда́, куда́, *etc.*) God knows, no one knows; он так и появи́лся, н. отку́да he just turned up, God knows where from.

неве́дом|ый (~, ~а), *adj.* 1. unknown. 2. (*fig.*) mysterious.

неве́ж|а, **и**, *m. and f.* boor, lout.

неве́жд|а, **ы**, *m. and f.* ignoramus.

неве́жествен|ный (~, ~на), *adj.* ignorant.

неве́жеств|о, **а**, *n.* 1. ignorance. 2. (*coll.*) rudeness, bad manners.

неве́жливост|ь, **и**, *f.* rudeness, impoliteness, bad manners.

неве́жлив|ый (~, ~а), *adj.* rude, impolite.

невезе́ни|е, **я**, *n.* (*coll.*) bad luck.

невели́к|ий (~, ~а́, ~о́), *adj.* 1. small, short. 2. slight, insignificant.

неве́ри|е, **я**, *n.* unbelief; lack of faith.

неве́рност|ь, **и**, *f.* 1. incorrectness. 2. disloyalty; infidelity, unfaithfulness.

неве́р|ный (~ен, ~на́, ~но), *adj.* 1. incorrect; ~ная но́та false note. 2. unsteady,

uncertain; ~ная похо́дка unsteady gait; н. слух (*mus.*) unsure ear; Фома́ н. (*coll.*) a doubting Thomas. 3. faithless, disloyal; unfaithful; н. друг false friend. 4. dim, flickering (*of light*). 5. *as noun* н., ~ного, *m.* (*rel.*) infidel.

невероя́ти|е, **я**, *n.* *now only in phrase* до ~я incredibly.

невероя́тно, *adv.* incredibly, unbelievably.

невероя́тност|ь, **и**, *f.* 1. improbability. 2. incredibility; до ~и incredibly, to an unbelievable extent.

невероя́т|ный (~ен, ~на), *adj.* 1. improbable, unlikely. 2. incredible, unbelievable (*also fig.*); ~но (*impers., as pred.*) it is incredible, it is unbelievable, it is beyond belief.

неве́рующ|ий, *adj.* (*rel.*) unbelieving; *as noun* н., ~его, *m.*; ~ая, ~ей, *f.* unbeliever.

невес|ёлый (~ел, ~ела́, ~ело), *adj.* joyless, mirthless; melancholy, sombre.

невесо́мост|ь, **и**, *f.* weightlessness.

невесо́мый, *adj.* 1. (*phys.*) imponderable. 2. weightless (*also fig.*).

невест|а, **ы**, *f.* 1. fiancée; bride. 2. (*coll.*) marriageable girl.

неве́стк|а, **и**, *f.* 1. daughter-in-law (*son's wife*). 2. sister-in-law (*brother's wife*).

неве́сть, *adv.* (*coll.*; +кто, что, ско́лько, *etc.*) God knows, goodness knows, heaven knows.

невеще́ственный, *adj.* immaterial.

невзачёт, *adv.* (*coll.*) э́то н. it does not count.

невзго́д|а, **ы**, *f.* adversity, misfortune.

невзира́я, *prep.* (на+*a.*) in spite of, regardless of; н. на ли́ца without respect of persons.

невзнача́й, *adv.* (*coll.*) by chance; unexpectedly.

невзно́с, **а**, *m.* non-payment (*of fees, etc.*).

невзра́ч|ный (~ен, ~на), *adj.* unprepossessing, unattractive; insignificant.

невзыска́тел|ьный (~ен, ~ьна), *adj.* modest, undemanding.

неви́дал|ь, **и**, *f.* (*coll.*) wonder, prodigy; вот н.!, эка(я) н.! (*iron.*) that's nothing.

невида́н|ный (~, ~а), *adj.* unprecedented.

невиди́мк|а, **и** 1. *m. and f.* invisible being; сде́латься ~ой to become invisible; челове́к-н. invisible man; ша́пка-н. cap of darkness. 2. invisible hairpin.

невиди́мост|ь, **и**, *f.* invisibility.

неви́дим|ый (~, ~а), *adj.* invisible.

неви́д|ный (~ен, ~на), *adj.* 1. invisible. 2. (*coll.*) insignificant.

неви́дящ|ий, *adj.* unseeing; смотре́ть ~им взгля́дом to look vacantly.

неви́нност|ь, **и**, *f.* (*in var. senses*) innocence.

неви́н|ный (~ен, ~на), *adj.* (*in var. senses*)

innocent; ~ная же́ртва innocent victim; ~ные удово́льствия innocent pleasures.

невино́в|ный (~ен, ~на), *adj.* (в+*p.*) innocent (of); (*leg.*) not guilty; призна́ть ~ным to acquit.

невку́с|ный (~ен, ~на), *adj.* unpalatable.

невменя́емост|ь, и, *f.* (*leg.*) irresponsibility.

невменя́ем|ый (~, ~а), *adj.* 1. (*leg.*) irresponsible. 2. (*coll.*) beside oneself.

невмеша́тельств|о, а, *n.* (*polit.*) non-intervention, non-interference.

невмоготу́, *adv.* (*coll.*; +*d.*) unbearable (to, for), unendurable (to, for); э́то мне н. I can't stand it, this is more than I can stand; ста́ло н. it became unbearable, it became too much.

невмо́чь = невмоготу́.

невнима́ни|е, я, *n.* 1. inattention; carelessness. 2. (к) lack of consideration (for).

невнима́тельност|ь, и, *f.* inattention, thoughtlessness.

невнима́тел|ьный (~ен, ~ьна), *adj.* (*in var. senses*) inattentive, thoughtless.

невня́т|ный (~ен, ~на), *adj.* indistinct, incomprehensible.

не́вод, а, *pl.* ~а́, ~о́в, *m.* seine, sweep-net.

невозбра́н|ный (~ен, ~на), *adj.* (*obs.*) free, unrestricted.

невозвра́т|ный (~ен, ~на), *adj.* irrevocable, irretrievable.

невозвраще́н|ец, ца, *m.* (*polit.*) defector.

невозвраще́ни|е, я, *n.* failure to return.

невозде́ланн|ый, *adj.* uncultivated, untilled; ~ая земля́ waste land.

невозде́ржанност|ь, и, *f.* intemperance; incontinence; (*fig.*) lack of self-control, lack of self-restraint.

невозде́ржан|ный (~, ~на), *adj.* intemperate; incontinent; (*fig.*) uncontrolled, unrestrained; он ~ на язы́к he has a loose tongue.

невозде́ржност|ь, и, *f.* = невозде́ржанность.

невозде́рж|ный (~ен, ~на), *adj.* = невозде́ржанный.

невозмо́жност|ь, и, *f.* impossibility; до ~и (*coll.*) to the last degree; за ~ью (+*g. or inf.*) owing to the impossibility (of).

невозмо́ж|ный (~ен, ~на), *adj.* 1. impossible; ~но (*impers., as pred.*) it is impossible; *as noun* ~ное, ~ного, *n.* the impossible. 2. insufferable.

невозмути́м|ый (~, ~а), *adj.* 1. imperturbable. 2. calm, unruffled.

невознагради́м|ый (~, ~а), *adj.* 1. irreparable. 2. that can never be repaid.

нево́лей, *adv.* (*obs.*) against one's will, forcibly.

нево́л|ить, ю, ишь, *impf.* (*of* при~) (*coll.*) to force, compel.

нево́льник, а, *m.* (*obs.*) slave.

нево́льн|ица, ицы, *f. of* ~ик.

нево́льничеств|о, а, *n.* (*obs.*) slavery.

нево́льн|ичий, *adj. of* ~ик; н. ры́нок slave market; н. труд slave labour.

нево́льно, *adv.* involuntarily; unintentionally, unwittingly.

нево́льн|ый, *adj.* 1. involuntary; unintentional. 2. forced; ~ая поса́дка forced landing.

нево́л|я, и, *f.* 1. bondage; captivity. 2. (*coll.*) necessity.

невообрази́м|ый (~, ~а), *adj.* unimaginable, inconceivable; н. шум (*fig.*) unimaginable din.

невооружённ|ый, *adj.* unarmed; ~ым гла́зом with the naked eye.

невоспи́танност|ь, и, *f.* ill breeding; bad manners.

невоспи́танный, *adj.* ill-bred.

невоспламеня́ем|ый (~, ~а), *adj.* uninflammable, non-inflammable.

невосполни́м|ый (~, ~а), *adj.* irreplaceable.

невосприи́мчивост|ь, и, *f.* 1. lack of receptivity. 2. (*med.*) immunity.

невосприи́мчив|ый (~, ~а), *adj.* 1. unreceptive. 2. (*med.*) (к) immune (to).

невостре́бованный, *adj.* not called for, unclaimed.

невпопа́д, *adv.* (*coll.*) out of place, inopportunely; отвеча́ть н. to answer irrelevantly.

невповоро́т, *adv.* (*coll.*) 1. a lot, a great deal. 2. too much; э́то нам н. it's too hard for us.

невразуми́тел|ьный (~ен, ~ьна), *adj.* unintelligible, incomprehensible.

невралги́ческий, *adj.* neuralgic.

невралги́|я, и, *f.* neuralgia; н. седа́лищного не́рва sciatica.

неврасте́ник, а, *m.* neurasthenic.

неврастени́|ческий, *adj. of* ~я.

неврастени́ч|ный (~ен, ~на), *adj.* neurasthenic (*of person*).

неврастени́|я, и, *f.* neurasthenia.

невреди́м|ый (~, ~а), *adj.* unharmed, intact; цел и ~ safe and sound.

неври́т, а, *m.* neuritis.

невро́з, а, *m.* neurosis.

неврологи́ческий, *adj.* neurological.

невроло́ги|я, и, *f.* neurology.

невропато́лог, а, *m.* neuro-pathologist.

невропатоло́ги|я, и, *f.* neuro-pathology.

невроти́ческий, *adj.* neurotic.

невруче́ни|е, я, *n.* non-delivery.

невтерпёж, *adv.* (+*d.*; *coll.*) unbearable; мне, им, etc., ста́ло н. I, etc., cannot stand it any longer.

невы́год|а, ы, *f.* 1. disadvantage. 2. loss.

невы́год|ный (~ен, ~на), *adj.* 1. disadvantageous, unfavourable; показа́ть себя́ с ~ной стороны́ to place oneself in an unfavourable light, show oneself at a disadvantage; ста́вить в ~ное положе́ние to place at a disadvantage. 2. unprofitable, unremunerative; ~но (*impers.*, *pred.*) it does not pay.

невы́держанност|ь, и, *f.* 1. lack of self-control. 2. inconsistency.

невы́держанный, *adj.* 1. lacking self-control. 2. inconsistent; н. стиль uneven style. 3. (*of cheese, wine, etc.*) unmatured.

невы́езд, а, *m.* constant residence in one place; дать подпи́ску о ~е to give a written undertaking not to leave a place.

невыла́з|ный (~ен, ~на), *adj.* such that one cannot emerge from it; ~ная грязь a veritable quagmire; быть ~ных долга́х (*fig.*) to be up to the eyes in debt.

невыноси́м|ый (~, ~а), *adj.* unbearable, insufferable, intolerable.

невыполне́ни|е, я, *n.* non-fulfilment; (+*g.*) failure to carry out.

невыполни́м|ый (~, ~а), *adj.* impracticable; unrealizable.

невырази́м|ый (~, ~а), *adj.* inexpressible, beyond expression; as noun ~ые, ~ых (*joc.*, *euph.*) inexpressibles (= pants).

невырази́тел|ьный (~ен, ~ьна), *adj.* inexpressive, expressionless.

невы́сказанный, *adj.* unexpressed, unsaid.

невысо́к|ий (~, ~а́, ~о), *adj.* rather low; rather short; ~ого ка́чества of poor quality; быть ~ого мне́ния (о+*p.*) to have a low opinion (of).

невы́ход, а, *m.* failure to appear; н. на рабо́ту absence (from work).

невя́зк|а, и, *f.* (*coll.*) discrepancy.

не́г|а, и, f. 1. comfort; abundance. 2. voluptuousness, languor.

негаси́м|ый (~, ~а), *adj.* (*rhet.*) ever-burning, eternal (*of flame, etc.*); unquenchable (*also fig.*).

негати́в, а, *m.* (*phot.*) negative.

негати́вный, *adj.* (*in var: senses*) negative.

негашён|ый, *adj.* ~ая и́звесть quick-lime.

не́где, *adv.* (+*inf.*) there is nowhere; н. доста́ть э́ту кни́гу this book is nowhere to be had; я́блоку н. упа́сть there's not an inch of room.

неги́бкий, *adj.* inflexible.

негла́сный, *adj.* secret.

неглиже́, *indecl.*, *n.* négligé.

неглижи́р|овать, ую, *impf.* (*coll.*, *obs.*; +*i.*) to neglect, disregard.

неглубо́кий, *adj.* rather shallow; (*fig.*) superficial.

неглу́п|ый (~, ~а́, ~о), *adj.* quite intelligent; он о́чень ~ he is no fool.

него́, *a.* and *g.* of он *when governed by preps.*

него́дник, а, *m.* reprobate, scoundrel; ne'er-do-well.

него́дност|ь, и, f. worthlessness; привести́ в н. to put out of commission.

него́д|ный (~ен, ~на), *adj.* 1. unfit, unsuitable. 2. worthless, good-for-nothing; н. чек dud cheque.

негодова́ни|е, я, *n.* indignation.

негод|ова́ть, у́ю, *impf.* (на+*a.*, про́тив) to be indignant (with).

негод|у́ющий, *pres. part. act. of* ~ова́ть *and* *adj.* indignant.

негодя́|й, я, *m.* scoundrel, rascal.

негостеприи́мный, *adj.* inhospitable.

негоциа́нт, а, *m.* (*obs.*) merchant.

негр, а, *m.* Negro.

негра́мотност|ь, и, f. illiteracy (*also fig.*).

негра́мот|ный (~ен, ~на), *adj.* 1. illiterate (*also fig.*); as noun н., ~ного, *m.*; ~ная, ~ной, *f.* illiterate person. 2. (*fig.*) crude, inexpert.

негрит|ёнок, ёнка, pl. ~я́та, ~я́т, *m.* Negro child, piccaninny.

негрито́с, а, *m.* Negrito.

негритя́нк|а, и, f. Negress.

негритя́нский, *adj.* Negro.

негро́мкий, *adj.* low.

не́гр|ский = ~итя́нский.

не́гус, а, *m.* Negus.

неда́вний, *adj.* recent.

неда́вно, *adv.* recently.

недалёк|ий (~, ~а́, ~о *or* ~о́**),** *adj.* 1. not far off, near; short; на ~ом расстоя́нии at a short distance. 2. (*fig.*) not bright, dull-witted.

недалеко́ (and недалёко), *adv.* not far, near; за приме́ром идти́ н. one does not have to search far for an example.

недальнови́дност|ь, и, f. lack of foresight, short-sightedness (*fig.*).

недальнови́д|ный (~ен, ~на), *adj.* short-sighted (*fig.*).

неда́ром, *adv.* not for nothing, not without reason; not without purpose.

недви́жимост|ь, и, f. (*leg.*) immovable property, real estate.

недви́жим|ый¹, immovable; ~ое иму́щество = ~ость.

недви́жим|ый² (~, ~а), *adj.* motionless.

недвусмы́сленный, *adj.* unequivocal, unambiguous.

недееспосо́б|ный (~ен, ~на), *adj.* 1. (*leg.*) incapable. 2. unable to function.

недействи́тельност|ь, и, f. 1. ineffectiveness; inefficacity. 2. (*leg.*) invalidity; nullity.

недействи́тел|ьный (~ен, ~ьна), *adj.* 1. (*obs.*) ineffective, ineffectual. 2. (*leg.*) invalid; null, null and void.

неделика́т|ный (~ен, ~на), *adj.* 1. indelicate, indiscreet. 2. rude, coarse.

недели́мост|ь, и, *f.* indivisibility.

недели́м|ый (~, ~а), *adj.* indivisible; н. фонд (*fig.*, *leg.*) indivisible fund (*of a collective farm*).

неде́льный, *adj.* of a week's duration; я вы́полню э́ту рабо́ту в н. срок I will finish this work in a week's time; н. о́тпуск a week's leave.

неде́л|я, и, *f.* week; ~ями for weeks (at a time); на э́той ~е this week.

недержа́ни|е, я, *n.* only in phrase н. мочи́ (*med.*) irretention of urine.

недёшево, *adv.* (*coll.*) at a considerable price, rather dear (*also fig.*).

недисциплини́рованност|ь, и, *f.* indiscipline.

недисциплини́рованный, *adj.* undisciplined.

недобо́р, а, *m.* arrears; shortage.

недоброжела́тел|ь, я, *m.* ill-wisher.

недоброжела́тельност|ь, и, *f.* malevolence, ill-will.

недоброжела́тел|ьный (~ен, ~ьна), *adj.* malevolent, ill-disposed.

недоброжела́тель|ство = ~ность.

недоброка́чественност|ь, и, *f.* poor quality, bad quality.

недоброка́чествен|ный (~, ~на), *adj.* of poor quality, low-grade, bad.

недобросо́вестност|ь, и, *f.* 1. bad faith; unscrupulousness, lack of scruple. 2. carelessness.

недобросо́вест|ный (~ен, ~на), *adj.* 1. unscrupulous. 2. lacking in conscientiousness; careless.

недо́бр|ый, *adj.* 1. unkind; unfriendly. 2. bad, evil; ~ая весть bad news; ~ые лю́ди (*obs.*) wicked men (*euph.* = brigands).

недове́ри|е, я, *n.* distrust; mistrust; во́тум ~я vote of no confidence.

недове́рчив|ый (~, ~а), *adj.* distrustful; mistrustful.

недове́с, а, *m.* short weight.

недове́|сить, шу, сишь, *pf.* (*of* ~шивать) 1. (+*g.*) to give short weight (of). 2. to prove to be short-weight.

недове́шива|ть, ю, *impf. of* недове́сить.

недово́л|ьный (~ен, ~ьна), *adj.* (+*i.*) dissatisfied, discontented, displeased (with); as noun н., ~ьного, *m.* malcontent.

недово́льств|о, а, *n.* dissatisfaction, discontent, displeasure.

недовы́работк|а, и, *f.* underproduction.

недога́длив|ый (~, ~а), *adj.* slow(-witted).

недогля|де́ть, жу́, ди́шь, *pf.* 1. (+*g.*) to overlook, miss. 2. (за+*i.*) not to take sufficient care (of), not to look after properly.

недоговорённост|ь, и, *f.* 1. reticence. 2. lack of agreement.

недогру́зк|а, и, *f.* underloading; (*fig.*) short time (*in factory or works*).

недода|ва́ть, ю́, ёшь, *impf. of* ~ть.

недо|да́ть, да́м, да́шь, да́ст, дади́м, дади́те, даду́т, *past* ~дал, ~дала́, ~дало, *pf.* (*of* ~дава́ть) to give short; to deliver short; он мне ~дал три рубля́ he gave me three roubles short.

недода́ч|а, и, *f.* deficiency in payment *or* supply.

недоде́ланный, *adj.* unfinished.

недоде́лк|а, и, *f.* incompleteness.

недодержа́ть, у́, ~ишь, *pf.* 1. (*phot.*) to under-expose; to under-develop. 2. to keep for too short a time in the necessary place.

недоде́ржк|а, и, *f.* 1. (*phot.*) under-exposure; under-development. 2. keeping for too short a time in the necessary place.

недоеда́ни|е, я, *n.* under-nourishment, malnutrition.

недоеда́|ть, ю, *impf.* to be undernourished, be underfed.

недозво́лен|ный (~, ~а), *adj.* illicit, unlawful.

недозре́лый, *adj.* unripe, immature (*also fig.*).

недои́мк|а, и, *f.* arrears.

недои́м|очный, *adj.* of ~ка.

недои́мщик, а, *m.* person in arrears (*in paying taxes, etc.*).

недока́зан|ный (~, ~а), *adj.* not proved, not proven.

недоказа́тельный, *adj.* unconvincing, inadequate.

недоказу́емый, *adj.* indemonstrable.

недоко́нчен|ный (~, ~а), *adj.* unfinished, incomplete.

недолга́, only in phrase (вот) и вся н. (*coll.*) and that is all there is to it.

недо́л|гий (~ог, ~га́, ~го), *adj.* short, brief.

недо́лго, *adv.* 1. not long; н. ду́мая without hesitation. 2. (*coll.*) н. и (+*inf.*) one can easily; it is easy (to), it is a simple matter (to); тут и потону́ть н. one could easily drown here; недо́лго и до греха́ serious trouble could easily happen.

недолгове́ч|ный (~ен, ~на), *adj.* short-lived, ephemeral.

недолёт, а, *m.* (*mil.*) falling short (*of bullets, shells*).

недолю́блива|ть, ю, *impf.* (+*a.* or *g.*; *coll.*) not to be overfond of; они́ ~ли друг дру́га there was no love lost between them.

недоме́рива|ть, ю, *impf. of* недоме́рить.

недоме́р|ить, ю, ишь, *pf.* (*of* ~ивать) to give short measure.

недоме́р|ок, ка, *m.* undersize object.

недомога́ни|е, я, *n.* indisposition.

недомога́|ть, ю, *impf.* to be indisposed, be unwell.

недомо́лвк|а, и, *f.* innuendo; reservation, omission.

недомы́сли|е, я, *n.* thoughtlessness, inability to think things out.

недонесéни|е, я, *n.* failure to give information (*concerning crime committed or meditated*); н. о преступлéнии (*leg.*) misprision of felony.

недонóс|ок, ка, *m.* **1.** prematurely born child. **2.** (*fig.*, *coll.*, *pejor.*) retarded person, immature person.

недонóшен|ный (∼, ∼а), *adj.* prematurely born.

недооцéнива|ть, ю, *impf. of* недооцени́ть.

недооцен|и́ть, ю́, ∼ишь, *pf.* (*of* ∼ивать) to underestimate, underrate.

недооцéнк|а, и, *f.* underestimation, underestimate.

недопечённый, *adj.* half-baked.

недополуч|а́ть, а́ю, *impf. of* ∼и́ть.

недополуч|и́ть, ý, ∼ишь, *pf.* (*of* ∼а́ть) to receive less (than one's due).

недопроизвóдств|о, а, *n.* underproduction.

недопусти́м|ый (∼, ∼а), *adj.* inadmissible, intolerable.

недора́звитост|ь, и, *f.* under-development, backwardness.

недора́звит|ый, *adj.* under-developed, backward; ∼ые стра́ны (*polit.*, *econ.*) under-developed countries.

недоразумéни|е, я, *n.* misunderstanding.

недóрого, *adv.* not dear, cheaply.

недор|огóй (∼ог, ∼огá, ∼огó), *adj.* inexpensive; reasonable (*of price*).

недорóд, а, *m.* harvest failure.

нéдоросл|ь, я, *m.* **1.** (*hist.*) minor. **2.** (*fig.*, *coll.*) young ignoramus, young oaf.

недослы́ш|ать, у, ишь, *pf.* **1.** (+*a. or g.*) to fail to hear all of. **2.** (*intrans.*; *coll.*) to be hard of hearing.

недосмóтр, а, *m.* oversight.

недосмотр|éть, ю́, ∼ишь, *pf.* **1.** (+*g.*) to overlook, miss. **2.** (за+*i.*) not to take sufficient care (of), not to look after properly.

недосóл, а, *m.* insufficient salting; н. на столé, *see* пересóл.

недос|па́ть, плю́, пи́шь, *pf.* (*of* ∼ыпа́ть) not to have one's sleep out.

недоста|ва́ть, ёт, *impf.* (*of* ∼ть) (*impers.*; +*g.*) to be missing, be lacking, be wanting; емý ∼ёт óпыта he lacks experience; мне óчень ∼ва́ло вас I missed you very much; э́того ещё ∼ва́ло! that would be (*or* is) the limit!, that would be (*or* is) the last straw!

недоста́т|ок, ка, *m.* **1.** (+*g. or* в+*p.*) shortage (of), lack (of), deficiency (in); за ∼ком (+*g.*) for want (of); имéть н. в рабóчей си́ле to be short-handed. **2.** shortcoming, imperfection; defect; н. зрéния defective eyesight.

недоста́точно, *adv.* **1.** insufficiently. **2.** not enough.

недоста́точност|ь, и, *f.* insufficiency; inadequacy.

недоста́точ|ный (∼ен, ∼на), *adj.* insufficient; inadequate; н. глагóл (*gram.*) defective verb.

недоста́|ть, нет, *pf. of* ∼ва́ть.

недоста́ч|а, и, *f.* (*coll.*) lack, shortage.

недостаю́щий, *adj.* missing.

недостижи́м|ый (∼, ∼а), *adj.* unattainable.

недостовéр|ный (∼ен, ∼на), *adj.* not authentic, apocryphal.

недостó|йный (∼ин, ∼йна), *adj.* unworthy.

недостýпност|ь, и, *f.* inaccessibility.

недостýп|ный (∼ен, ∼на), *adj.* inaccessible (*also fig.*); э́то ∼но моемý понима́нию it is beyond my comprehension.

недосýг, а, *m.* (*coll.*) lack of time, lack of leisure; придёт он на концéрт? нет, емý, мол, н. is he coming to the concert? No, he says he is busy.

недосчит|а́ться, а́юсь, *pf.* (*of* ∼ываться) (+*g.*) to find missing, miss; to be out (in one's accounts); он ∼а́лся десяти́ рублéй he found he was ten roubles short; пócлe налёта мы ∼а́лись трёх бомбарди́ровщиков after the raid we found three of our bombers were missing.

недосчи́тыва|ться, юсь, *impf. of* недосчита́ться.

недосыпа́|ть, ю, *impf. of* недоспа́ть.

недосяга́ем|ый (∼, ∼а), *adj.* unattainable.

недотёп|а, ы, *m. and f.* (*coll.*) duffer.

недотрóг|а, и, *m. and f.* (*coll.*) touchy person.

недоумева́|ть, ю, *impf.* to be perplexed, be at a loss; to wonder.

недоумéни|е, я, *n.* perplexity, bewilderment; быть в ∼и to be in a quandary.

недоумённый, *adj.* puzzled, perplexed.

недоýчк|а, и, *m. and f.* (*coll.*) half-educated person.

недохва́тк|а, и, *f.* (*coll.*) shortage.

недочёт, а, *m.* **1.** deficit; shortage. **2.** defect, shortcoming.

нéдр|а, ∼, *no sing.* **1.** depths (*of the earth*); н. земли́ bowels of the earth; развéдка ∼ prospecting of mineral wealth. **2.** (*fig.*) depths, heart.

недрема́нн|ый, *adj.* (*obs.*) unwinking, unslumbering; ∼ое óко (*fig.*, *iron.*) the unwinking eye (*sc. of authority*).

недрéмлющий, *adj.* unwinking, unslumbering; vigilant, watchful.

нéдруг, а, *m.* enemy, foe.

недружелю́б|ный (∼ен, ∼на), *adj.* unfriendly.

недрýжный, *adj.* disunited; disjointed.

недýг, а, *m.* ailment, disease.

недýжит|ься, ∼ся, *impf.* (*impers.*; +*d.*; *coll.*) to be unwell, to be poorly.

недурно, *adv.* not badly, well enough; н.! not bad!

недур|ной (~ён, ~на́, ~но), *adj.* 1. not bad. 2. (собой) not bad-looking.

недю́жинный, *adj.* out of the ordinary, outstanding, exceptional.

неё, *a. and g.* of она́ when governed by preps.

неесте́ствен|ный (~, ~на), *adj.* (*in var. senses*) unnatural.

нежда́нно, *adv.* (*coll.*) unexpectedly; н.-негада́нно quite unexpectedly.

нежда́нный, *adj.* (*coll.*) unexpected.

нежела́ни|е, я, *n.* unwillingness, disinclination.

нежела́тел|ьный (~ен, ~ьна), *adj.* 1. undesirable. 2. unwanted; (+d.) contrary to the wishes (of); н. посети́тель unwanted visitor; э́то бы́ло мне ~ьно it was not what I wanted.

не́жели, *conj.* (*obs.*) than.

не́женк|а, и, *m. and f.* (*coll.*) molly-coddle.

нежив|ой, *adj.* 1. lifeless; роди́ться ~ы́м to be still-born. 2. inanimate, inorganic. 3. (*fig.*) dull, lifeless.

нежизнен|ный (~, ~на), *adj.* 1. impracticable; inapplicable. 2. weird.

нежилой, *adj.* 1. uninhabited. 2. not fit for habitation; uninhabitable.

не́жит|ь¹, и, *f.* (*collect.*) (*in Russian folklore*) the spirits (*gnomes, goblins, etc.*).

не́ж|ить², у, ишь, *impf.* to pamper, coddle; caress.

не́ж|иться, усь, ишься, *impf.* to luxuriate; н. на со́лнце to bask in the sun.

не́жнича|ть, ю, *impf.* (*coll.*) 1. to bill and coo, canoodle. 2. (*fig.*) to be over-indulgent.

не́жност|ь, и, *f.* 1. tenderness. 2. delicacy. 3. (*pl. only*) display of affection, endearments; compliments, flattery.

не́ж|ный (~ен, ~на́, ~но), *adj.* 1. tender; affectionate; ~ные взгля́ды tender glances. 2. delicate (= soft, fine, *of colours, taste, skin, etc.*). 3. tender, delicate; н. пол the weaker sex.

незабвен|ный (~, ~на), *adj.* unforgettable.

незабу́дк|а, и, *f.* (*bot.*) forget-me-not.

незабыва́ем|ый (~, ~а), *adj.* unforgettable.

незаве́ренный, *adj.* uncertified.

незави́д|ный (~ен, ~на), *adj.* unenviable; poor.

незави́симо, *adv.* independently; н. от irrespective of.

незави́симост|ь, и, *f.* independence.

незави́сим|ый (~, ~а), *adj.* independent.

незави́сящ|ий, *only in phrase* по ~им от нас, *etc.,* обстоя́тельствам (*or* причи́нам) owing to circumstances beyond our, *etc.,* control.

незада́ч|а, и, *f.* (*coll.*) ill-luck.

незада́члив|ый (~, ~а), *adj.* (*coll.*) unlucky, luckless.

незадо́лго, *adv.* (до, пе́ред) shortly (before), not long (before).

незаконнорождённост|ь, и, *f.* illegitimacy.

незаконнорождённый, *adj.* illegitimate.

незако́нност|ь, и, *f.* illegality, unlawfulness.

незако́нный, *adj.* illegal, illicit, unlawful; illegitimate.

незакономе́рност|ь, и, *f.* exceptionality, exceptional character.

незакономе́р|ный (~ен, ~на), *adj.* exceptional.

незако́нченност|ь, и, *f.* incompleteness, unfinished state.

незако́нчен|ный (~, ~а), *adj.* incomplete, unfinished.

незамедли́тельно, *adv.* without delay.

незамедли́тел|ьный (~ен, ~ьна), *adj.* immediate.

незамени́м|ый (~, ~а), *adj.* 1. irreplaceable. 2. indispensable.

незамерза́ющий, *adj.* non-freezing; ice-free; (*tech.*) anti-freeze.

незаме́тно, *adv.* imperceptibly, insensibly.

незаме́т|ный (~ен, ~на), *adj.* 1. imperceptible. 2. inconspicuous, insignificant.

незаму́жняя, *adj.* unmarried, single, maiden.

незамыслова́т|ый (~, ~а), *adj.* simple, uncomplicated.

незапа́мятн|ый, *adj.* immemorial; с ~ых времён from time immemorial.

незапя́тнанный, *adj.* unsullied, stainless.

незарабо́танный, *adj.* unearned.

незара́зный, *adj.* non-contagious.

незаслу́жен|ный (~, ~на), *adj.* undeserved, unmerited.

незастро́енный, *adj.* undeveloped, not built over.

незате́йлив|ый (~, ~а), *adj.* simple, plain; modest.

незатуха́ющий, *adj.* (*radio*) undamped; continuous.

незауря́д|ный (~ен, ~на), *adj.* outstanding, exceptional.

неза́чем, *adv.* (+inf.) there is no point (in), it is pointless; there is no need (to); it is no use, it is useless; н. бо́льше ждать there is no point in waiting any longer.

незашифро́ванный, *adj.* not in cipher, not in code; en clair.

незва́ный, *adj.* uninvited.

незде́шний, *adj.* 1. (*coll.*) not of these parts; я н. I am a stranger here. 2. unearthly, supernatural, mysterious; н. мир the other world.

нездоро́вит|ься, ~ся, *impf.* (*impers.*; +d.) to feel unwell.

нездоро́в|ый (~, ~а), *adj.* 1. unhealthy, morbid (*also fig.*); sickly; unwholesome;

~ая обстано́вка unhealthy environment.
2. (*pred.*) unwell, poorly.

нездоро́вь|е, я, *n.* indisposition; ill-health.

неземно́й, *adj.* **1.** (*obs.*) supernatural, unearthly. **2.** not belonging *or* pertaining to the earth.

незло́бив|ый (~, ~**a**), *adj.* mild, forgiving.

незлопа́мят|ный (~**ен**, ~**на**), *adj.* forgiving.

незнако́м|ец, ца, *m.* stranger.

незнако́м|ка, ки, *f. of* ~**ец.**

незнако́м|ый (~, ~**a**), *adj.* **1.** unknown, unfamiliar. **2.** (c+*i.*) unacquainted (with).

незна́ни|е, я, *n.* ignorance.

незна́чащий, *adj.* insignificant, of no significance.

незначи́тел|ьный (~**ен**, ~**ьна**), *adj.* insignificant, negligible; unimportant.

незна́ющ|ий, *adj.* (+*g.*) ignorant (of); н. уста́ли indefatigable; ~ая грани́ц любо́вь love that knows no bounds.

незре́лост|ь, и, *f.* unripeness; (*fig.*) immaturity.

незре́л|ый (~, ~**a**), *adj.* unripe (*also fig.*); (*fig.*) immature.

незри́м|ый (~, ~**a**), *adj.* invisible.

незы́блем|ый (~, ~**a**), *adj.* unshakeable, stable.

неизбе́жност|ь, и, *f.* inevitability.

неизбе́ж|ный (~**ен**, ~**на**), *adj.* inevitable, unavoidable; inescapable.

неизбы́в|ный (~**ен**, ~**на**), *adj.* unescapable, permanent.

неизве́дан|ный (~, ~**на**), *adj.* unexplored, unknown; not experienced before.

неизве́стност|ь, и, *f.* **1.** uncertainty; быть в ~и (о+*p.*) to be uncertain (about), be in the dark (about). **2.** obscurity; жить в ~и to live in obscurity.

неизве́ст|ный (~**ен**, ~**на**), *adj.* (*in var. senses*) unknown; uncertain; ~но где, когда́, *etc.*, no one knows where, when, *etc.* (= somewhere, at some time, *etc.*); *as noun* н., ~ного, *m.*, ~ная, ~ной, *f.* unknown person; ~ное, ~ного, *n.* (*math.*) unknown (quantity).

неизвини́тел|ьный (~**ен**, ~**ьна**), *adj.* inexcusable, unpardonable.

неизглади́м|ый (~, ~**a**), *adj.* indelible, ineffaceable.

неи́зданный, *adj.* unpublished.

неизлечи́м|ый (~, ~**a**), *adj.* incurable.

неизме́н|ный (~**ен**, ~**на**), *adj.* **1.** invariable, immutable. **2.** (*rhet.*) devoted, true.

неизменя́ем|ый (~, ~**a**), *adj.* unalterable.

неизмери́мо, *adv.* immeasurably.

неизмери́мост|ь, и, *f.* immeasurability; immensity.

неизмери́м|ый (~, ~**a**), *adj.* immeasurable; immense.

неизрече́нный, *adj.* (*obs.*) ineffable.

неизъясни́м|ый (~, ~**a**), *adj.* inexplicable; ineffable, indescribable.

неиме́ни|е, я, *n.* absence; lack, want; за ~ем лу́чшего for want of something better.

неимове́р|ный (~**ен**, ~**на**), *adj.* incredible, unbelievable.

неиму́щий, *adj.* indigent, poor.

неискорени́м|ый (~, ~**a**), *adj.* ineradicable.

неи́скрен|ний (~**ен**, ~**на**), *adj.* insincere.

неи́скренност|ь, и, *f.* insincerity.

неиску́с|ный (~**ен**, ~**на**), *adj.* unskilful, inexpert.

неискушённост|ь, и, *f.* inexperience, innocence.

неискушён|ный (~, ~**á**), *adj.* inexperienced, innocent, unsophisticated.

неисповеди́м|ый (~, ~**a**), *adj.* inscrutable.

неисполне́ни|е, я, *n.* non-execution, non-performance; н. зако́на failure to observe a law.

неисполни́м|ый (~, ~**a**), *adj.* impracticable; unrealizable.

неиспо́рчен|ный (~, ~**a**), *adj.* (*fig.*) unspoiled, innocent.

неиспо́рченност|ь, и, *f.* (*fig.*) innocence.

неисправи́м|ый (~, ~**a**), *adj.* **1.** incorrigible. **2.** irremediable, irreparable.

неиспра́вност|ь, и, *f.* **1.** disrepair. **2.** carelessness.

неиспра́в|ный (~**ен**, ~**на**), *adj.* **1.** out of order; faulty, defective. **2.** careless.

неиспы́танный, *adj.* untried, untested.

неиссяка́ем|ый (~, ~**a**), *adj.* inexhaustible.

не́йстовств|о, а, *n.* **1.** fury, frenzy. **2.** brutality, savagery.

не́йстовств|овать, ую, *impf.* **1.** to rage, rave. **2.** to commit brutalities.

не́йстов|ый (~, ~**a**), *adj.* furious, frenzied; ~ые аплодисме́нты tempestuous applause.

неистощи́м|ый (~, ~**a**), *adj.* inexhaustible.

неистреби́м|ый (~, ~**a**), *adj.* ineradicable; undying.

неисчерпа́ем|ый (~, ~**a**), *adj.* inexhaustible.

неисчисли́м|ый (~, ~**a**), *adj.* innumerable; incalculable.

ней, *d., i., and p. of* она́ *when governed by preps.*

нейзи́льбер, а, *m.* German silver.

нейло́н, а, *m.* nylon.

нейло́новый, *adj.* nylon, made of nylon.

неймёт (*no other form in use*), *impf., only in prov.* (хоть) ви́дит о́ко, да зуб н. there's many a slip 'twixt cup and lip.

неймётся, *impf.* (*impers.*; +*d.*; *coll.*) ему́ н. he is set on it, there is no holding him; ей н. she will not sit still.

нейро́н, а, *m.* (*physiol.*) neuron.

нейтрализа́ци|я, и, *f.* (*in var. senses*) neutralization.

нейтрали́зм, а, *m.* (*polit.*) neutralism.

нейтрализ|ова́ть, у́ю, *impf. and pf.* (*in var. senses*) to neutralize.

нейтралите́т, а, *m.* (*polit.*) neutrality.

нейтра́льност|ь, и, *f.* (*in var. senses*) neutrality.

нейтра́л|ьный (~ен, ~ьна), *adj.* (*in var. senses*) neutral.

нейтро́н, а, *m.* (*phys.*) neutron.

неказ́ист|ый (~, ~а), *adj.* (*coll.*) not much to look at; unprepossessing.

неквалифици́рованный, *adj.* unqualified; **н. рабо́чий** unskilled labourer.

не́кий, *pron.* a certain; a kind of; **вас спра́шивал н. господи́н Па́влов** a (certain) Mr. Pavlov was asking for you.

некле́точный, *adj.* (*biol.*) non-cellular.

не́когда¹, *adv.* once, formerly; in the old days.

не́когда², *adv.* there is no time; **мне сего́дня н. разгова́ривать с ва́ми** I have no time to chat today.

не́кого, не́кому, не́кем, не́ о ком, *pron.* (+*inf.*) there is nobody (to); **н. вини́ть** nobody is to blame; **ей не́ с кем пойти́** she has nobody to go with (her).

неколеби́мый = **непоколеби́мый.**

некомпете́нт|ный (~ен, ~на), *adj.* not competent, unqualified.

некомпле́кт|ный (~ен, ~на), *adj.* incomplete; not up to strength.

некороно́ванный, *adj.* uncrowned.

некорре́ктност|ь, и, *f.* discourtesy, impoliteness.

некорре́кт|ный (~ен, ~на), *adj.* discourteous, impolite.

не́котор|ый, *pron.* some; **он ~ое вре́мя не дви́гался с ме́ста** for a time he did not budge; **мы с ~ых пор живём здесь** we have been living here for some time; **~ым о́бразом** somehow, in some way; **в, до ~ой сте́пени** to some extent, to a certain extent; *as noun* **~ые, ~ых,** some; some people.

некраси́в|ый (~, ~а), *adj.* **1.** ugly, not good-looking; unsightly. **2.** (*coll.*; *of conduct, actions, etc.*) ugly, dirty.

некредитоспосо́бност|ь, и, *f.* insolvency.

некредитоспосо́б|ный (~ен, ~на), *adj.* insolvent.

некре́п|кий (~ок, ~ка́), *adj.* rather weak.

некро́з, а, *m.* (*med.*) necrosis.

некроло́г, а, *m.* obituary (notice).

некрома́нти|я, и, *f.* necromancy.

некро́пол|ь, я, *m.* necropolis.

некру́п|ный (~ен, ~на́, ~но), *adj.* medium-sized, not large.

некры́т|ый (~, ~а), *adj.* roofless.

некста́ти, *adv.* inopportunely; mal à propos. **вот н.!** what a nuisance!

некта́р, а, *m.* nectar.

не́кто, *pron.* someone; **н. Петро́в** one Petrov, a certain Petrov.

не́куда, *adv.* (+*inf.*) there is nowhere (to); **мне н. пойти́** I have nowhere to go.

некульту́рност|ь, и, *f.* **1.** low level of civilization; uncivilized ways. **2.** bad manners, boorishness.

некульту́р|ный (~ен, ~на), *adj.* **1.** uncivilized; backward. **2.** rough(-mannered), boorish. **3.** (*bot.*) uncultivated.

некуря́щ|ий, *adj.* non-smoking; *as noun* **н., ~его,** *m.* non-smoker; **ваго́н для ~их** non-smoking carriage.

нела́д|ный (~ен, ~на), *adj.* (*coll.*) wrong, bad; **у него́ ~но с гру́дью** there is something the matter with his chest; **будь он ~ен!** blast him!

нела́д|ы, ов, *no sing.* (*coll.*) **1.** discord, disagreement; **у них н.** they don't hit it off. **2.** trouble, something wrong.

нела́сковый, *adj.* reserved, unfriendly.

нелега́льност|ь, и, *f.* illegality.

нелега́л|ьный (~ен, ~ьна), *adj.* illegal; **перейти́ на ~ьное положе́ние** (*of resistance movements, etc.*) to go underground.

нелега́льщин|а, ы, *f.* (*coll.*) illegal activities; illegal literature.

нелёгкая (*coll.*) **н. его́ сюда́ несёт!** what the deuce brings him here?; **куда́ их н. понесла́?** where the deuce have they gone?

нелёг|кий (~ок, ~ка́), *adj.* **1.** difficult, not easy. **2.** heavy, not light (*also fig.*).

неле́пост|ь, и, *f.* absurdity, nonsense.

неле́п|ый (~, ~а), *adj.* absurd, ridiculous.

неле́ст|ный (~ен, ~на), *adj.* unflattering, uncomplimentary.

нелету́чий, *adj.* (*chem.*) non-volatile.

нелицеприя́т|ный (~ен, ~на), *adj.* (*obs.*) impartial.

нели́шний, *adj.* not superfluous; not out of place.

нело́в|кий (~ок, ~ка́, ~ко), *adj.* **1.** awkward; gauche; clumsy. **2.** uncomfortable. **3.** (*fig.*) awkward; embarrassing; **~кое молча́ние** awkward silence; **~ко при нём ссыла́ться на э́то** it is awkward to refer to it in his presence; **ему́ ~ко приглаша́ть ı бал незнако́мую да́му** he feels awkward about inviting a lady he does not know to the dance.

нело́вко, *adv.* awkwardly; uncomfortably; **чу́вствовать себя́ н.** to feel ill at ease, feel awkward, feel uncomfortable.

нело́вкост|ь, и, *f.* **1.** awkwardness, gaucherie, clumsiness (*also fig.*); **чу́вствовать н.** to feel awkward, feel uncomfortable. **2.** blunder, gaffe.

нелоги́чност|ь, и, *f.* illogicality.

нелоги́ч|ный (~ен, ~на), *adj.* illogical.

нельзя́, *adv.* (+*inf.*) **1.** it is impossible; **н**

не призна́ть it is impossible not to admit, one cannot but admit. **2.** it is not allowed; здесь н. кури́ть smoking is not allowed here. **3.** one ought not, one should not; н. ложи́ться (спать) так по́здно you ought not to go to bed so late. **4.** как н. (+*comp. adv.*) as . . . as possible; как н. лу́чше in the best possible way.

нéльм|а, ы, *f.* white salmon.

нелюбéзност|ь, и, *f.* ungraciousness; discourtesy.

нелюбéз|ный (~ен, ~на), *adj.* ungracious, unobliging; discourteous.

нелюби́м|ый (~, ~а), *adj.* unloved.

нелюб|о́вь, ви́, *f.* (к) dislike (for).

нелюбопы́т|ный (~ен, ~на), *adj.* **1.** incurious. **2.** uninteresting.

нелюди́м, а, *m.* unsociable person.

нелюди́м|ый (~, ~а), *adj.* unsociable.

нём, *p. of* он, оно́.

немáло, *adv.* **1.** not a little; not a few. **2.** a good deal; considerably.

немаловáж|ный (~ен, ~на), *adj.* of no small importance.

немáлый, *adj.* no small; considerable.

немéдленно, *adv.* immediately, forthwith.

немéдленный, *adj.* immediate.

немéркнущий, *adj.* (*fig., rhet.*) unfading.

немéтчин|а, ы, *f.* (*obs.*) **1.** Germany; foreign parts. **2.** (*pejor.*) German (*or* foreign) way of life.

немé|ть, ю, *impf.* (*of* о~) **1.** to become dumb, grow dumb. **2.** (*pf. also* за~) to become numb, grow numb.

нéм|ец, ца, *m.* **1.** German. **2.** (*obs.*) foreigner.

немéцк|ий, *adj.* **1.** German; ~ая овчáрка Alsatian (dog). **2.** (*obs.*) foreign.

немигáющий, *adj.* unwinking.

немилосéрд|ный (~ен, ~на), *adj.* merciless, unmerciful (*also fig.*).

немúлостив|ый (~, ~а), *adj.* ungracious; harsh.

немúлост|ь, и, *f.* disgrace, disfavour; впасть в н. to fall into disgrace.

немúл|ый (~, ~á, ~o), *adj.* (*folk poet.*) unloved; hated.

неминýем|ый (~, ~а), *adj.* inevitable, unavoidable.

нéмк|а, и, *f.* German (woman).

немнóг|ие, *adj.* few, a few; *as noun* н., ~их few.

немнóго, *adv.* **1.** (+*g.*) a little, some, not much; a few, not many; врéмени остáлось н. little time is left, time is short. **2.** a little, somewhat, slightly; я н. устáл I am a little tired; н. спустя́ not long after.

немнóг|ое, ого, *n.* few things, little.

немногослóв|ный (~ен, ~на), *adj.* laconic, brief, terse.

немнóжко, *adv.* (*coll.*) a little; a trifle, a bit.

немнýщийся, *adj.* (*text.*) non-creasing crease-resistant; 'non-iron'.

немóжется, *impers.*; +*d.* (*coll.*) мне, *etc.* н. I, *etc.*, am unwell, poorly.

нем|óй (~, ~á, ~o), *adj.* **1.** dumb; ~áя áзбука deaf-and-dumb alphabet; *as noun* н., ~óго, *m.* dumb man, mute; ~ы́е (*collect.*) the dumb. **2.** (*fig.*) dead, silent; ~áя тишинá deathly hush. **3.** (*fig.*) mute; н. соглáсный (*ling.*) mute consonant; н. фильм silent film.

немóлчный, *adj.* (*poet.*) incessant, unceasing.

немот|á, ы́, *f.* dumbness; muteness.

нéмоч|ь, и, *f.* (*coll.*) illness, sickness; блéдная н. (*med.*) chlorosis, green sickness; чёрная н. (*coll., obs.*) falling sickness (*epilepsy*).

нéмощ|ный (~ен, ~на), *adj.* sick; feeble, sickly.

нéмощ|ь, и, *f.* (*coll.*) sickness; feebleness.

немý, *d. of* он, оно́ *after preps.*

немудрён|ый (~, ~á), *adj.* (*coll.*) simple, easy; э́то дéло ~oe it is a simple matter; ~ó (*impers.*; *as pred.*) it is no wonder.

немы́слим|ый (~, ~а), *adj.* (*coll.*) unthinkable, inconceivable.

ненави́|деть, жу, дишь, *impf.* to hate, detest, loathe.

ненави́стник, а, *m.* hater.

ненави́ст|ный (~ен, ~на), *adj.* hated; hateful.

нéнавист|ь, и, *f.* hatred, detestation.

ненагля́дный, *adj.* (*coll.*) **1.** beloved. **2.** (*folk poet.*) wondrously beautiful.

ненадéванный, *adj.* (*coll.*) new, not yet worn.

ненадёж|ный (~ен, ~на), *adj.* unreliable, untrustworthy; insecure.

ненáдобност|ь, и, *f.* uselessness; за ~ью as not wanted.

ненадóлго, *adv.* for a short while, not for long.

ненамéренно, *adv.* unintentionally, unwittingly, accidentally.

ненамéрен|ный (~, ~а), *adj.* unintentional, accidental.

ненападéни|е, я, *n.* non-aggression; пакт о ~и non-aggression pact.

ненарóком, *adv.* (*coll.*) unintentionally, accidentally.

ненаруши́м|ый (~, ~а), *adj.* inviolable.

ненáст|ный (~ен, ~на), *adj.* (*of weather*) bad, foul.

ненастоя́щий, *adj.* artificial; counterfeit.

ненáст|ье, я, *n.* bad, foul weather.

ненасы́т|ный (~ен, ~на), *adj.* insatiable (*also fig.*).

ненатурáл|ьный (~ен, ~ьна), *adj.* **1.** affected; not natural. **2.** artificial, imitation.

ненаýч|ный (~ен, ~на), *adj.* unscientific.

ненорма́льност|ь, и, *f.* abnormality.
ненорма́л|ьный (~ен, ~ьна), *adj.* 1. (*in var. senses*) abnormal. 2. mad.
нену́ж|ный (~ен, ~на́, ~но), *adj.* unnecessary; superfluous.
необду́ман|ный (~, ~на), *adj.* thoughtless, precipitate.
необспе́ченн|ый, *adj.* 1. without means; unprovided for; ~ая жизнь precarious existence. 2. (+*i.*) not provided (with).
необита́ем|ый (~, ~а), *adj.* uninhabited; н. о́стров desert island.
необозри́м|ый (~, ~а), *adj.* boundless, immense.
необосно́ванност|ь, и, *f.* groundlessness.
необосно́ван|ный (~, ~на), *adj.* unfounded, groundless.
необрабо́тан|ный (~, ~а), *adj.* 1. (*of land*) uncultivated, untilled. 2. (*of materials*) raw, crude. 3. (*fig.*) unpolished; untrained.
необразо́ванность|ь, и, *f.* lack of education.
необразо́ван|ный (~, ~на), *adj.* uneducated.
необрати́м|ый (~, ~а), *adj.* irreversible.
необу́здан|ный (~, ~на), *adj.* unbridled; ungovernable.
необходи́мост|ь, и, *f.* necessity; по ~и perforce, necessarily.
необходи́м|ый (~, ~а), *adj.* necessary, essential; ~о (*impers.*; *as pred.*) it is necessary, it is imperative.
необщи́тел|ьный (~ен, ~ьна), *adj.* unsociable.
необъясни́м|ый (~, ~а), *adj.* inexplicable, unaccountable.
необъя́т|ный (~ен, ~на), *adj.* immense, unbounded.
необыкнове́н|ный (~ен, ~на), *adj.* unusual, uncommon.
необыча́|йный (~ен, ~йна), *adj.* extraordinary, exceptional.
необы́ч|ный (~ен, ~на), *adj.* unusual.
необяза́тел|ьный (~ен, ~ьна), *adj.* 1. not obligatory, optional. 2. unobliging.
неограни́чен|ный (~, ~на), *adj.* unlimited, unbounded; ~ная мона́рхия absolute monarchy; ~ные полномо́чия plenary powers.
неоднокра́тно, *adv.* repeatedly.
неоднокра́тный, *adj.* repeated.
неоднородност|ь, и, *f.* heterogeneity; н. строе́ния (*tech.*) non-uniformity of structure.
неодноро́д|ный (~ен, ~на), *adj.* heterogeneous; dissimilar, not uniform.
неодобре́ни|е, я, *n.* disapproval, disapprobation.
неодобри́тел|ьный (~ен, ~ьна), *adj.* disapproving.

неодоли́м|ый (~, ~а), *adj.* invincible, insuperable.
неодушевлён|ный (~, ~на), *adj.* inanimate.
неожи́данност|ь, и, *f.* 1. unexpectedness, suddenness. 2. surprise.
неожи́дан|ный (~, ~на), *adj.* unexpected, sudden.
неозо́йский, *adj.* (*geol.*) neozoic.
неоклассици́зм, а, *m.* neo-classicism.
неоконча́тел|ьный (~ен, ~ьна), *adj.* inconclusive.
неоко́нченный, *adj.* unfinished.
неоли́т, а, *m.* (*archaeol.*) New Stone Age.
неолити́ческий, *adj.* (*archaeol.*) neolithic.
неологи́зм, а, *m.* neologism.
нео́н, а, *m.* (*chem.*) neon.
нео́н|овый, *adj.* of ~; ~овая ла́мпа neon lamp.
неопа́с|ный (~ен, ~на), *adj.* harmless, not dangerous.
неопери́вшийся, *adj.* unfledged; (*fig.*) callow.
неопису́ем|ый (~, ~а), *adj.* indescribable.
неопла́тн|ый, *adj.* that cannot be repaid; н. должни́к insolvent debtor; я у вас в ~ом долгу́ (*fig.*) I am eternally indebted to you.
неопо́знан|ный (~, ~а), *adj.* unidentified.
неопра́вданный, *adj.* unjustified, unwarranted.
неопределённост|ь, и, *f.* vagueness, uncertainty.
неопределён|ный (~ен, ~на), *adj.* 1. indefinite; ~ное наклоне́ние, ~ная фо́рма глаго́ла (*gram.*) infinitive; н. член (*gram.*) indefinite article. 2. indeterminate; vague, uncertain; ~ное уравне́ние (*math.*) indeterminate equation.
неопредели́м|ый (~, ~а), *adj.* indefinable.
неопровержи́м|ый (~, ~а), *adj.* irrefutable.
неопря́тност|ь, и, *f.* slovenliness; untidiness, sloppiness.
неопря́т|ный (~ен, ~на), *adj.* slovenly; untidy, sloppy; dirty.
нео́пытност|ь, и, *f.* inexperience.
нео́пыт|ный (~ен, ~на), *adj.* inexperienced.
неорганизо́ванност|ь, и, *f.* lack of organization; disorganization; lack of co-ordination.
неорганизо́ван|ный (~, ~на), *adj.* unorganized; disorganized; uncoordinated.
неоргани́ческий, *adj.* inorganic.
неосведомлённый, *adj.* ill-informed.
неосе́длый, *adj.* nomadic.
неосла́б|ный (~ен, ~на), *adj.* unremitting, unabated.
неосмотри́тельност|ь, и, *f.* imprudence; indiscretion.
неосмотри́тел|ьный (~ен, ~ьна), *adj.* imprudent, incautious; indiscreet.

неоснова́тел|ьный (~ен, ~ьна), *adj.* **1.** unfounded, lacking foundation. **2.** (*coll.*) frivolous.

неоспори́мост|ь, и, *f.* incontestability, indisputability.

неоспори́м|ый (~, ~а), *adj.* unquestionable, incontestable, indisputable.

неосторо́жност|ь, и, *f.* carelessness; imprudence.

неосторо́ж|ный (~ен, ~на), *adj.* careless; imprudent, indiscreet, incautious.

неосуществи́м|ый (~, ~а), *adj.* impracticable, unrealizable.

неосяза́ем|ый (~, ~а), *adj.* impalpable, intangible.

неотврати́мост|ь, и, *f.* inevitability.

неотврати́м|ый (~, ~а), *adj.* inevitable.

неотвя́з|ный (~ен, ~на), *adj.* importunate; obsessive.

неотвя́зчив|ый (~, ~а), *adj.* importunate; obsessive.

неотдели́м|ый (~, ~а), *adj.* inseparable.

неотёсан|ный (~, ~на), *adj.* **1.** unpolished. **2.** (*fig.*) uncouth.

не́откуда, *adv.* there is nowhere; мне н. э́то получи́ть there is nowhere I can get it from.

неотло́жност|ь, и, *f.* urgency.

неотло́ж|ный (~ен, ~на), *adj.* urgent, pressing; ~ная по́мощь first aid.

неотлу́чно, *adv.* constantly, permanently.

неотлу́ч|ный (~ен, ~на), *adj.* ever-present; permanent.

неотрази́м|ый (~, ~а), *adj.* irresistible (*also fig.*); ~ые до́воды incontrovertible arguments.

неотсту́пност|ь, и, *f.* persistence; importunity.

неотсту́п|ный (~ен, ~на), *adj.* persistent; importunate.

неотчётлив|ый (~, ~а), *adj.* vague, indistinct.

неотчужда́емост|ь, и, *f.* (*leg.*) inalienability.

неотчужда́ем|ый (~, ~а), *adj.* (*leg.*) inalienable.

неотъе́млем|ый (~, ~а), *adj.* inalienable; ~ое пра́во inalienable right, imprescriptible right; ~ая часть integral part.

неофи́т, а, *m.* neophyte.

неофициа́л|ьный (~ен, ~ьна), *adj.* unofficial.

неохо́т|а, ы, *f.* **1.** reluctance. **2.** (+*d.,* as *pred.*) мне, *etc.,* н. идти́ I, *etc.,* have no wish to go, am not keen to go.

неохо́тно, *adv.* reluctantly; unwillingly.

неоцени́м|ый (~, ~а), *adj.* inestimable, priceless, invaluable.

неощути́м|ый (~, ~а), *adj.* imperceptible.

неощути́тел|ьный (~ен, ~ьна), *adj.* imperceptible, insensible.

непа́рный, *adj.* odd (*not forming a pair*).

непарти́йный, *adj.* **1.** non-Party; н. большеви́к non-Party Bolshevik (*one, not a member of the Soviet Communist Party, but acting in its spirit*). **2.** unbefitting a member of the Communist Party.

непереводи́м|ый (~, ~а), *adj.* untranslatable.

непередава́ем|ый (~, ~а), *adj.* inexpressible, indescribable.

непереходный, *adj.* (*gram.*) intransitive.

непеча́тный, *adj.* (*coll.*) unprintable.

непи́сан|ый, *adj.* unwritten; ~ые пра́вила unwritten rules.

неплатёж, á, *m.* non-payment.

неплатёжеспосо́бност|ь, и, *f.* (*fin.*) insolvency.

неплатёжеспосо́б|ный (~ен, ~на), *adj.* (*fin.*) insolvent.

неплате́льщик, а, *m.* defaulter; person in arrears with payment (*of taxes, etc.*).

неплодоро́д|ный (~ен, ~на), *adj.* barren, sterile; infertile.

неплодотво́р|ный (~ен, ~на), *adj.* unproductive.

непло́хо, *adv.* not badly, quite well.

неплох|о́й (~, ~á, ~о), *adj.* not bad, quite good.

непобеди́м|ый (~, ~а), *adj.* invincible.

непова́дно, as *pred.* (*impers.*; +*d.* and *inf.*) (*coll.*) чтобы н. бы́ло to teach (someone) not (to do something again); мальчи́шку вы́пороли, чтобы ему́ н. бы́ло кра́сть я́блоки they gave the boy a thrashing to teach him not to steal apples again.

непови́н|ный (~ен, ~на), *adj.* innocent.

неповинове́ни|е, я, *n.* insubordination, disobedience.

неповоро́тлив|ый (~, ~а), *adj.* clumsy, awkward; sluggish, slow.

неповтори́м|ый (~, ~а), *adj.* unique.

непого́д|а, ы, *f.* bad weather.

непогреши́мост|ь, и, *f.* infallibility.

непогреши́м|ый (~, ~а), *adj.* infallible.

неподалёку, *adv.* not far off.

непода́тлив|ый (~, ~а), *adj.* stubborn, intractable; unyielding, tenacious.

неподатно́й, *adj.* exempt from capitation.

неподве́домствен|ный (~, ~на), *adj.* (+*d.*) not subject to the authority (of), beyond the jurisdiction (of).

неподви́жно, *adv.* motionless(ly).

неподви́жност|ь, и, *f.* immobility.

неподви́ж|ный (~ен, ~на), *adj.* motionless, immobile, immovable (*also fig.*); fixed, stationary; ~ное лицо́ immobile countenance; н. загради́тельный ого́нь (*mil.*) standing barrage.

неподде́льност|ь, и, *f.* genuineness; sincerity.

неподде́л|ьный (~ен, ~ьна), *adj.* genuine; unfeigned, sincere.

неподку́пност|ь, и, *f.* incorruptibility, integrity.

неподку́п|ный (~ен, ~на), *adj.* incorruptible.

неподоба́ющий, *adj.* unseemly, improper.

неподража́ем|ый (~, ~а), *adj.* inimitable.

неподсу́д|ный (~ен, ~на), *adj.* (+*d.*) not under the jurisdiction (of).

неподходя́щий, *adj.* unsuitable, inappropriate.

неподчине́ни|е, я, *n.* insubordination; н. суде́бному постановле́нию (*leg.*) contempt of court.

непозволи́тел|ьный (~ен, ~ьна), *adj.* inadmissible, impermissible.

непознава́ем|ый (~, ~а), *adj.* (*philos.*) unknowable.

непокла́дист|ый (~, ~а), *adj.* 1. obstinate, uncompromising. 2. (*coll.*, *obs.*) clumsy.

непоко́|йный (~ен, ~йна), *adj.* (*coll.*) troubled; restless, disturbed.

непоколеби́м|ый (~, ~а), *adj.* steadfast, unshakeable, inflexible.

непоко́рност|ь, и, *f.* recalcitrance; unruliness.

непоко́р|ный (~ен, ~на), *adj.* refractory, recalcitrant; unruly.

непокры́т|ый (~, ~а), *adj.* uncovered, bare.

непола́дк|а, и, *f.* (*coll.*) 1. defect, fault. 2. (*in pl.*) disagreement, quarrel.

неполнопра́вный, *adj.* not possessing full rights.

неполнот|а́, ы́, *f.* incompleteness.

неполноце́нност|ь, и, *f.* ко́мплекс ~и inferiority complex.

непо́л|ный (~он, ~на́, ~но), *adj.* not fully; incomplete; defective; с тех пор прошло́ непо́лных два́дцать лет since then not quite twenty years had passed; ~ное сре́днее образова́ние incomplete secondary education (*comprising seven years' schooling*).

непоме́р|ный (~ен, ~на), *adj.* excessive, inordinate.

непонима́ни|е, я, *n.* misunderstanding; incomprehension.

непоня́тливост|ь, и, *f.* slowness, dulness.

непоня́тлив|ый (~, ~а), *adj.* slow-witted, stupid, dull.

непоня́т|ный (~ен, ~на), *adj.* unintelligible, incomprehensible; ~но (*impers.*, *as pred.*) it is incomprehensible; мне ~но, как он мог э́то сде́лать I cannot understand how he could do it.

непопада́ни|е, я, *n.* miss (*in shooting*).

непоправи́м|ый (~, ~а), *adj.* irreparable, irremediable; irretrievable.

непоро́ч|ный (~ен, ~на), *adj.* pure, chaste;

~ное зача́тие (*rel.*) the Immaculate Conception (*of the Virgin*).

непоря́д|ок, ка, *m.* disorder; violation of order.

непоря́доч|ный (~ен, ~на), *adj.* dishonourable.

непосвящён|ный (~, ~á), *adj.* uninitiated.

непосе́д|а, ы, *m. and f.* (*coll.*) fidget; rolling stone.

непосе́дливост|ь, и, *f.* restlessness.

непосе́длив|ый (~, ~а), *adj.* fidgety, restless.

непосеще́ни|е, я, *n.* (+*g.*) non-attendance (at).

непоси́л|ьный (~ен, ~ьна), *adj.* beyond one's strength, excessive.

непосле́довательност|ь, и, *f.* inconsistency; inconsequence.

непосле́довател|ьный (~ен, ~ьна), *adj.* inconsistent; inconsequent.

непослуша́ни|е, я, *n.* disobedience.

непослу́ш|ный (~ен, ~на), *adj.* disobedient, naughty.

непосре́дственност|ь, и, *f.* spontaneity; ingenuousness.

непосре́дствен|ный (~, ~на), *adj.* 1. immediate, direct. 2. (*fig.*) direct; spontaneous, ingenuous.

непостижи́м|ый (~, ~а), *adj.* incomprehensible, inscrutable; уму́ ~о it passes understanding.

непостоя́н|ный (~ен, ~на), *adj.* inconstant, changeable.

непостоя́нств|о, а, *n.* inconstancy.

непоти́зм, а, *m.* nepotism.

непотопля́ем|ый (~, ~а), *adj.* unsinkable.

непотре́б|ный (~ен, ~на), *adj.* (*obs.*) obscene, indecent; ~ные слова́ obscenities.

непотре́бств|о, а, *n.* (*obs.*) obscenity; indecent conduct.

непоча́тый, *adj.* (*coll.*) untouched, not begun, entire; н. край (*or* у́гол) (+*g.*) a wealth (of), a whole host (of).

непочте́ни|е, я, *n.* disrespect.

непочти́тел|ьный (~ен, ~ьна), *adj.* disrespectful.

непра́вд|а, ы, *f.* untruth, falsehood, lie; все́ми пра́вдами и ~ами by fair means or foul; by hook or by crook.

неправдоподо́бби|е, я, *n.* improbability, unlikelihood.

неправдоподо́б|ный (~ен, ~на), *adj.* improbable, unlikely; implausible.

непра́вед|ный (~ен, ~на), *adj.* (*obs.*) iniquitous, unjust.

непра́вильно, *adv.* 1. irregularly. 2. incorrectly, erroneously; *in conjunction with verbs frequently* = mis-; *e.g.*, н. истолкова́ть to misinterpret.

непра́вильност|ь, и, *f.* **1.** irregularity; anomaly. **2.** incorrectness.

непра́вил|ьный (~ен, ~ьна), *adj.* **1.** irregular; anomalous; **н.** глаго́л irregular verb; ~ьная дробь (*math.*) improper fraction; ~ьные черты́ лица́ irregular features. **2.** incorrect, erroneous, wrong, mistaken; **н.** подхо́д (к де́лу) wrong approach, wrong attitude.

неправоме́рност|ь, и, *f.* illegality.

неправоме́р|ный (~ен, ~на), *adj.* illegal.

неправомо́чност|ь, и, *f.* (*leg.*) incompetence.

неправомо́ч|ный (~ен, ~на), *adj.* (*leg.*) not competent; not entitled.

неправоспосо́бност|ь, и, *f.* (*leg.*) disability, disqualification; incapacity.

неправоспосо́б|ный (~ен, ~на), *adj.* (*leg.*) disqualified.

непра́вот|а́, ы́, *f.* **1.** error. **2.** wrongness; injustice.

непра́в|ый (~, ~а́, ~о), *adj.* **1.** wrong, mistaken. **2.** unjust.

непревзойдённый, *adj.* unsurpassed; matchless.

непредви́денный, *adj.* unforeseen.

непреднаме́рен|ный (~, ~на), *adj.* unpremeditated.

непредубеждённый, *adj.* unprejudiced, unbiased.

непредумы́шленный. *adj.* unpremeditated.

непредусмотри́тельност|ь, и, *f.* improvidence, short-sightedness

непредусмотри́тел|ьный (~ен, ~ьна), *adj.* improvident, short-sighted.

непрекло́нност|ь, и, *f.* inflexibility; inexorability.

непрекло́н|ный (~ен, ~на), *adj.* inflexible, unbending; inexorable, adamant.

непрело́ж|ный•(~ен, ~на), *adj.* **1.** immutable, unalterable. **2.** indisputable.

непреме́нно, *adv.* **1.** without fail; certainly; они́ н. приду́т за́втра they are sure to come tomorrow. **2.** absolutely; мне н. ну́жно поговори́ть с ним it is absolutely essential that I speak to him.

непреме́н|ный (~ен, ~на), *adj.* indispensable; **н.** секрета́рь permanent secretary.

непреобори́м|ый (~, ~а), *adj.* insuperable; irresistible.

непреодоли́м|ый (~, ~а), *adj.* insuperable, insurmountable; irresistible; ~ая си́ла (*leg.*) force majeure.

непререка́ем|ый (~, ~а), *adj.* unquestionable, indisputable; **н.** тон peremptory tone.

непреры́вно, *adv.* uninterruptedly, continuously.

непреры́вност|ь, и, *f.* continuity.

непреры́в|ный (~ен, ~на), *adj.* uninterrupted, unbroken; continuous; ~ная дробь (*math.*) continued fraction; **н.** лист through

plate (*in ship-building*); ~ная па́луба (*naut.*) flush deck; **н.** сварно́й шов (*tech.*) line welding, continuous weld.

непреста́нно, *adv.* incessantly, continually.

непреста́н|ный (~ен, ~на), *adj.* incessant, continual.

непривет́лив|ый (~, ~а), *adj.* unfriendly, ungracious; bleak.

непривы́чк|а, и, *f.* want of habit; с ~и он бы́стро захмеле́л being unaccustomed to strong drink, he quickly became drunk.

непривы́ч|ный (~ен, ~на), *adj.* unaccustomed, unwonted; unusual.

непригля́д|ный (~ен, ~на), *adj.* unattractive, unsightly.

неприго́д|ный (~ен, ~на), *adj.* unfit, useless; unserviceable; ineligible.

неприе́млем|ый (~, ~а), *adj.* unacceptable.

непри́знанный, *adj.* unrecognized, unacknowledged.

неприка́янный, *adj.* (*coll.*) restless, unable to find anything to do; ходи́ть, броди́ть, *etc.,* как н. to go about, wander about, *etc.,* like a lost soul.

неприкоснове́нност|ь, и, *f.* inviolability; дипломати́ческая н. diplomatic immunity.

неприкоснове́н|ный (~ен, ~на), *adj.* inviolable; **н.** запа́с (*mil.*) emergency ration, iron ration; **н.** капита́л reserve capital.

неприкра́шенный, *adj.* plain, unvarnished.

неприкры́т|ый (~, ~а), *adj.* undisguised; ~ая ложь barefaced lie.

неприли́чи|е, я, *n.* indecency, impropriety, unseemliness.

неприли́ч|ный (~ен, ~на), *adj.* indecent, improper; unseemly, unbecoming.

неприменим́|ый (~, ~а), *adj.* inapplicable.

неприме́т|ный (~ен, ~на), *adj.* **1.** imperceptible. **2.** (*fig.*) unremarkable, undistinguished.

непримири́мост|ь, и, *f.* irreconcilability; intransigence.

непримири́м|ый (~, ~а), *adj.* irreconcilable; intransigent, uncompromising.

непринуждённост|ь, и, *f.* unconstraint; naturalness, ease.

непринуждён|ный (~, ~на), *adj.* unconstrained; natural, relaxed, easy; spontaneous.

неприспосо́блен|ный (~, ~на), *adj.* (к) unadapted (to); maladjusted.

непристо́йност|ь, и, *f.* obscenity; indecency.

непристо́|йный (~ен, ~йна), *adj.* obscene; indecent.

непристу́п|ный (~ен, ~на), *adj.* **1.** inaccessible; unassailable, impregnable. **2.** (*fig.*) inaccessible, unapproachable.

непрису́тственный, *adj.* (*obs.*) **н.** день public holiday.

непритво́р|ный (∼ен, ∼на), *adj.* unfeigned, genuine.

неприхотли́вост|ь, и, *f.* **1.** unpretentiousness; modesty. **2.** simplicity, plainness.

неприхотли́в|ый (∼, ∼а), *adj.* **1.** unpretentious; modest, undemanding. **2.** simple, plain; ∼ая пи́ща frugal meal.

непричáст|ный (∼ен, ∼на), *adj.* (к) not implicated (in), not privy (to).

неприя́знен|ный (∼, ∼на), *adj.* hostile, inimical.

неприя́зн|ь, и, *f.* hostility, enmity.

неприя́тел|ь, я, *m.* enemy; (*mil.*) the enemy.

неприя́тельский, *adj.* hostile; (*mil.*) enemy.

неприя́тност|ь, и, *f.* unpleasantness; nuisance, annoyance, trouble.

неприя́т|ный (∼ен, ∼на), *adj.* unpleasant, disagreeable; annoying, troublesome.

непробу́дный, *adj.* from which there is no waking; н. сон deep sleep; н. пья́ница inveterate drunkard.

непроводни́к, á, *m.* (*phys.*) non-conductor, dielectric.

непрогля́д|ный (∼ен, ∼на), *adj.* (*of darkness, fog, etc.*) impenetrable; pitch-dark.

непродолжи́тел|ьный (∼ен, ∼ьна), *adj.* of short duration, short-lived; в ∼ьном вре́мени shortly, in a short time.

непродукти́в|ный (∼ен, ∼на), *adj.* unproductive.

непроéзжий, *adj.* impassable.

непрозра́чност|ь, и, *f.* opacity.

непрозра́ч|ный (∼ен, ∼на), *adj.* opaque.

непроизводи́тел|ьный (∼ен, ∼ьна), *adj.* unproductive; wasteful.

непроизво́л|ьный (∼ен, ∼ьна), *adj.* involuntary.

непрола́з|ный (∼ен, ∼на), *adj.* (*coll.*) impassable.

непромока́ем|ый (∼, ∼а), *adj.* waterproof; н. плащ mackintosh, waterproof (coat), raincoat.

непроница́емост|ь, и, *f.* impenetrability; impermeability.

непроница́ем|ый (∼, ∼а), *adj.* **1.** impenetrable, impermeable; (для) impervious (to); н. для зву́ка sound-proof. **2.** inscrutable, impassive.

непропорциона́льност|ь, и, *f.* disproportion.

непропорциона́л|ьный (∼ен, ∼ьна), *adj.* disproportionate.

непрости́тел|ьный (∼ен, ∼ьна), *adj.* unforgivable, unpardonable, inexcusable.

непротивле́ни|е, я, *n.* non-resistance.

непроходи́мо, *adv.* (*coll.*) utterly, hopelessly.

непроходи́м|ый (∼, ∼а), *adj.* **1.** impassable. **2.** (*fig., coll.*) complete, utter; н. дура́к utter fool.

непро́ч|ный (∼ен, ∼на), *adj.* fragile, flimsy; (*fig.*) precarious, unstable.

непро́шеный, *adj.* (*coll.*) unbidden, uninvited; непро́шеное одолже́ние an un-solicited service.

непрям|о́й (∼, ∼á, ∼о), *adj.* **1.** indirect; circuitous. **2.** (*fig., coll.*) evasive.

непутёвый, *adj.* (*coll.*) good-for-nothing, useless.

непутём, *adv.* (*coll.*) badly; де́лать всё н. to make a mess of everything.

непью́щий, *adj.* non-drinking; temperate, abstemious (*in relation to alcoholic liquor*).

неработоспосо́б|ный (∼ен, ∼на), *adj.* unable to work, disabled.

нерабо́ч|ий, *adj.* non-working; ∼ее вре́мя time off, free time.

нера́венств|о, а, *n.* inequality, disparity.

неравно́, *particle expressing anticipation of disagreeable eventuality* (*coll.*); н. опозда́ем suppose we are late; н. он зайдёт, а нас до́ма не бу́дет what if he comes while we are out.

неравноду́ш|ный (∼ен, ∼на), *adj.* (к) not indifferent (to).

неравноме́р|ный (∼ен, ∼на), *adj.* uneven, irregular.

неравнопра́в|ный (∼ен, ∼на), *adj.* not enjoying equal rights.

нера́в|ный (∼ен, ∼на́, ∼но), *adj.* unequal.

нераде́ни|е, я, *n.* (*obs.*) = неради́вость.

неради́вост|ь, и, *f.* negligence, carelessness, remissness.

неради́в|ый (∼, ∼а), *adj.* negligent, careless, remiss.

неразбери́х|а, и, *f.* (*coll.*) muddle, confusion.

неразбо́рчив|ый (∼, ∼а), *adj.* **1.** illegible, indecipherable. **2.** (*fig.*) undiscriminating; not fastidious; н. в сре́дствах unscrupulous.

неразвит|о́й (нера́звит, ∼á, ∼о), *adj.* undeveloped; (intellectually) backward.

нера́звитост|ь, и, *f.* lack of development; у́мственная н. backwardness.

неразга́данн|ый, *adj.* unsolved; ∼ая та́йна unresolved mystery.

неразгово́рчив|ый (∼, ∼а), *adj.* taciturn, not talkative.

нераздели́м|ый (∼, ∼а), *adj.* indivisible, inseparable.

неразде́л|ьный (∼ен, ∼ьна), *adj.* indivisible, inseparable; ∼ьное иму́щество (*leg.*) common estate.

неразличи́м|ый (∼, ∼а), *adj.* indistinguishable; indiscernible.

неразлу́ч|ный (∼ен, ∼на), *adj.* inseparable.

неразрешённый, *adj.* **1.** unsolved. **2.** prohibited, banned.

неразреши́м|ый (∼, ∼а), *adj.* insoluble.

неразры́в|ный (~ен, ~на), *adj.* indissoluble.

неразу́ми|е, я, *n.* (*obs.*) folly, foolishness.

неразу́м|ный (~ен, ~на), *adj.* unreasonable; unwise; foolish.

нераска́янный, *adj.* unrepentant.

нерасположе́ни|е, я, *n.* (к) dislike (for), disinclination (for, to).

нерасполо́женный, *adj.* (к) ill-disposed (towards); unwilling (to), disinclined (to).

нераспоряди́тел|ьный (~ен, ~ьна), *adj.* inefficient, unauthoritative.

нерассуди́тельност|ь, и, *f.* lack of common sense, want of sense.

нерассуди́тел|ьный (~ен, ~ьна), *adj.* unreasoning; lacking common sense.

нераствори́м|ый (~, ~а), *adj.* insoluble.

нерасторжи́м|ый (~, ~а), *adj.* indissoluble.

нерасторо́п|ный (~ен, ~на), *adj.* sluggish, slow.

нерасчётливост|ь, и, *f.* 1. extravagance, wastefulness. 2. improvidence.

нерасчётлив|ый (~, ~а), *adj.* 1. extravagant, wasteful. 2. improvident.

нерациона́л|ьный (~ен, ~ьна), *adj.* irrational.

нерв, а, *m.* (*anat. and fig.*) nerve; гла́вный н. (*fig.*) nerve-centre; де́йствовать кому́-н. на ~ы to get on someone's nerves.

нерва́ци|я, и, *f.* (*bot.*) nervation.

нерви́р|овать, ую, *impf.* to get on someone's nerves, irritate.

нерви́ческий, *adj.* (*obs.*) nervous.

не́рвнича|ть, ю, *impf.* to be *or* become fidgety, fret, be *or* become irritable.

нервнобольн|о́й, о́го, *m.* nervous patient, person suffering from nervous disorder.

не́рвност|ь, и, *f.* irritability, edginess.

не́рв|ный (~ен, ~на́, ~но), *adj.* 1. (*in var. senses*) nervous; neural; ~ное волокно́ nerve-fibre; н. припа́док fit of nerves; ~ная систе́ма the nervous system; н. у́зел (*anat.*) ganglion; н. центр nerve-centre. 2. irritable, highly strung.

нервоз|ный (~ен, ~на), *adj.* nervy, irritable.

нервю́р|а, ы, *f.* (*aeron.*) rib; н. крыла́ wing-rib.

нереа́л|ьный (~ен, ~ьна), *adj.* 1. unreal. 2. impracticable.

нерегуля́р|ный (~ен, ~ьна), *adj.* irregular (*also mil.*).

нере́д|кий (~ок, ~ка́, ~ко), *adj.* not infrequent; not uncommon.

нере́дко, *adv.* not infrequently, quite often.

нерента́бельный, *adj.* (*econ.*) unprofitable, uneconomic.

не́рест, а, *m.* (*zool.*) spawning.

нерести́лищ|е, а, *n.* spawning-ground.

нереши́мост|ь, и, *f.* indecision.

нереши́тельност|ь, и, *f.* indecision; indecisiveness; быть в ~и to be undecided.

нереши́тел|ьный (~ен, ~ьна), *adj.* indecisive, irresolute.

нержаве́йк|а, и, *f.* (*coll.*) stainless steel.

нержаве́ющ|ий, *adj.* non-rusting; ~ая сталь stainless steel.

неро́б|кий (~ок, ~ка́, ~ко), *adj.* not timid; он челове́к ~кого деся́тка he is no coward.

неро́вност|ь, и, *f.* 1. unevenness, roughness. 2. inequality; irregularity.

неро́в|ный (~ен, ~на́, но), *adj.* 1. uneven, rough; н. грунт rough country. 2. unequal; irregular; н. пульс irregular pulse; ~ён час (*coll.*) who knows what may happen; one never knows.

неро́вн|я, и, (*and* неровн|я́, й), *m. and f.* (*coll.*) он ей н. he is not her equal.

не́рп|а, ы, *f.* (*zool.*) nerpa (*species of freshwater seal*).

неру́дный, *adj.* (*tech.*) non-metallic.

нерукотво́рный, *adj.* (*rel. and poet.*) not made by hands.

неруши́м|ый (~, ~а), *adj.* inviolable, indissoluble.

неря́х|а, и, *m. and f.* sloven; (*f.*) slattern, slut.

неря́шеств|о, а, *n.* = неря́шливость.

неря́шливост|ь, и, *f.* slovenliness, slatternliness; untidiness.

неря́шлив|ый (~, ~а), *adj.* 1. slovenly, untidy. 2. careless, slipshod.

несваре́ни|е, я, *n.* only in phrase н. желу́дка indigestion.

несве́дущ|ий (~, ~а), *adj.* (в+*p.*) ignorant (about), not well-informed (about).

несве́ж|ий (~, ~а́, ~е), *adj.* 1. not fresh, stale; tainted. 2. (*fig.*) weary, wan.

несвобо́дн|ый, *adj.* ~ое сочета́ние (*ling.*) set phrase.

несвоевре́мен|ный (~ен, ~на), *adj.* inopportune, untimely, unseasonable.

несво́йствен|ный (~ен, ~на), *adj.* not characteristic; э́то ему́ ~но it is not like him.

несвя́з|ный (~ен, ~на), *adj.* disconnected, incoherent.

несгиба́емый, *adj.* unbending, inflexible.

несгово́рчив|ый (~, ~а), *adj.* intractable.

несгора́емый, *adj.* fire-proof, incombustible; н. шкаф safe.

несде́ржанный, *adj.* unrestrained.

несе́ни|е, я, *n.* performance, execution.

несесе́р, а, *m.* toilet-case.

несжима́ем|ый (~, ~а), *adj.* incompressible.

несказа́нный, *adj.* unspeakable, ineffable.

нескла́диц|а, ы, *f.* (*coll.*) nonsense.

нескла́д|ный (~ен, ~на), *adj.* 1. incoherent. 2. ungainly, awkward. 3. absurd.

несклоня́ем|ый (~, ~а), *adj.* (*gram.*) indeclinable.

не́скольк|о[1], **их,** *adv.* some, several; a few; в ~их слова́х in a few words; н. челове́к several people.

не́сколько[2], *adv.* somewhat, rather, slightly; они́ ста́ли н. разочаро́ванными they have become rather disillusioned.

несконча́ем|ый (~, ~а), *adj.* interminable, never-ending.

нескро́мност|ь, и, *f.* 1. immodesty, lack of modesty. 2. indelicacy; indiscretion. 3. indiscreetness.

нескро́м|ный (~ен, ~на́, ~но), *adj.* 1. immodest; vain. 2. indiscreet.

несло́ж|ный (~ен, ~на́, ~но), *adj.* simple, not complicated.

неслы́хан|ный (~, ~на), *adj.* unheard of, unprecedented.

неслы́ш|ный (~ен, ~на), *adj.* inaudible.

несменя́емост|ь, и, *f.* irremovability (from office).

несменя́ем|ый (~, ~а), *adj.* irremovable.

несме́т|ный (~ен, ~на), *adj.* countless, incalculable, innumerable.

несмолка́ем|ый (~, ~а), *adj.* ceaseless, unremitting, never-abating.

несмотря́, *prep.* (на+*a.*) in spite of, despite; notwithstanding; н. ни на что in spite of everything.

несмыва́ем|ый (~, ~а), *adj.* indelible, ineffaceable.

несно́с|ный (~ен, ~на), *adj.* intolerable, insupportable.

несоблюде́ни|е, я, *n.* non-observance.

несовершенноле́ти|е, я, *n.* minority.

несовершенноле́тн|ий, *adj.* under age; *as noun* н., ~его, *m.* minor.

несоверше́н|ный (~ен, ~на), *adj.* 1. imperfect, incomplete. 2. (*gram.*) imperfective.

несовмести́м|ый (~, ~а), *adj.* incompatible.

несогла́си|е, я, *n.* 1. disagreement; н. в мне́ниях difference of opinion; н. ме́жду двумя́ ве́рсиями discrepancy between two versions. 2. discord, variance. 3. (*sing. only*) refusal.

несогла́с|ный (~ен, ~на), *adj.* 1. (с+*i.*) not agreeing (with). 2. (с+*i.*) inconsistent (with), incompatible (with). 3. (на+*a.* or +*inf.*) not consenting (to), not agreeing (to); я на э́то ~ен I cannot agree to this. 4. discordant.

несогласова́ни|е, я, *n.* (*gram.*) non-agreement.

несогласо́ванност|ь, и, *f.* lack of co-ordination, non-coordination.

несогласо́ванный, *adj.* uncoordinated, not concerted.

несозву́ч|ный (~ен, ~на), *adj.* (+*d.*) dissonant; inconsonant (with).

несозна́тельност|ь, и, *f.* thoughtlessness; irresponsibility; (*political*) backwardness.

несозна́тел|ьный (~ен, ~ьна), *adj.* 1. irresponsible. 2. unconscious of social obligations.

несоизмери́мост|ь, и, *f.* incommensurability.

несоизмери́м|ый (~, ~а), *adj.* incommensurable, incommensurate.

несократи́мый, *adj.* (*math.*) irreducible.

несокруши́м|ый (~, ~а), *adj.* indestructible; unconquerable.

несоли́д|ный (~ен, ~на), *adj.* not impressive, unimpressive, light-weight.

несо́лоно, *adv.* (*coll.*) *only in phrase* уйти́ н. хлеба́вши to get nothing for one's pains, go away empty-handed.

несомне́нно, *adv.* undoubtedly, doubtless, beyond all question.

несомне́н|ный (~ен, ~на), *adj.* undoubted, indubitable, unquestionable.

несообрази́тел|ьный (~ен, ~ьна), *adj.* slow(-witted).

несообра́зност|ь, и, *f.* 1. incongruity, incompatibility. 2. absurdity.

несообра́з|ный (~ен, ~на), *adj.* 1. (с+*i.*) incongruous (with), incompatible (with). 2. absurd.

несоотве́тствен|ный (~, ~на), *adj.* (+*d.*) incongruous (with), not corresponding (to).

несоотве́тстви|е, я, *n.* lack of correspondence, disparity.

несоразме́рност|ь, и, *f.* disproportion.

несоразме́р|ный (~ен, ~на), *adj.* disproportionate.

несосве́тимый, *adj.* = несусве́тный.

несостоя́тельност|ь, и, *f.* 1. insolvency, bankruptcy. 2. modest means. 3. groundlessness.

несостоя́тел|ьный (~ен, ~ьна), *adj.* 1. insolvent, bankrupt. 2. not wealthy, of modest means. 3. groundless, unsupported.

неспе́л|ый (~, ~а́, ~о), *adj.* unripe.

неспе́ш|ный (~ен, ~на), *adj.* unhurried.

несподру́ч|ный (~ен, ~на), *adj.* (*coll.*) inconvenient, awkward.

неспоко́|йный (~ен, ~йна), *adj.* restless, uneasy.

неспосо́бност|ь, и, *f.* incapacity, inability.

неспосо́б|ный (~ен, ~на), *adj.* dull, not able; (к+*d.*, на+*a.*) incapable (of); она́ ~на к му́зыке she has no aptitude for music; н. на ложь incapable of a lie.

несправедли́вост|ь, и, *f.* injustice, unfairness.

несправедли́в|ый (~, ~а), *adj.* 1. unjust, unfair. 2. incorrect, unfounded.

неспроста́, *adv.* (*coll.*) not without purpose; with an ulterior motive.

несравне́нно, *adv.* 1. incomparably, matchlessly. 2. far, by far; н. лу́чше far better.

несравнён|ный (~ен, ~на), *adj.* incomparable, matchless.

несравним|ый (~, ~а), *adj.* **1.** incomparable; unmatched. **2.** not comparable.

нестерпим|ый (~, ~а), *adj.* unbearable, unendurable.

нес|ти́[1], у́, ёшь, *past* ~, ~ла́, *impf.* (*of* по~), *det.* **1.** to carry. **2.** to bear; to support. **3.** (*fig.*) to bear; to suffer; to incur; н. убы́тки (*fin.*) to incur losses. **4.** to perform; н. дежу́рство to be on duty. **5.** (*fig.*) to bear, bring; н. ги́бель to bring destruction. **6.** (*impers.*; *coll.*) куда́ вас ~ёт? wherever are you going? **7.** (*impers.*; *coll.*; +*i.*) to stink (of), reek (of); от него́ ~ёт чесноко́м he reeks of garlic. **8.** (*impers.*; *coll.*) его́, *etc.*, ~ёт he has, *etc.*, diarrhoea. **9.** (*coll.*) (вздор, чепуху́, *etc.*) to talk (nonsense).

нес|ти́[2], ёт, *past* ~, ~ла́, *impf.* (*of* с~) to lay (eggs).

нес|ти́сь[1], у́сь, ёшься, *past* ~ся, ~ла́сь, *impf.* (*of* по~), *det.* **1.** to rush, tear, fly; (*on water, in the air*) to float, drift; (по+*d.*, вдоль; над) to skim (along; over). **2.** (*of sounds, smells, etc.*) to spread, be diffused.

нес|ти́сь[2], ётся, *past* ~ся, ~ла́сь, *impf.* (*of* с~) to lay (eggs) (*intrans.*).

нестойкий, *adj.* (*chem.*) unstable, non-persistent.

нестоя́щий, *adj.* (*coll.*) worthless, good-for-nothing.

нестроеви́к, а́, *m.* (*mil.*) non-combatant.

нестроево́й[1], *adj.* unfit for building purposes.

нестроево́й[2], *adj.* (*mil.*) non-combatant, administrative.

нестро́|йный (~ен, ~йна́, ~йно), *adj.* **1.** clumsily built. **2.** discordant, dissonant. **3.** disorderly.

несть (*obs.*) there is not.

несура́зност|ь, и, *f.* **1.** absurdity, senselessness. **2.** awkwardness.

несура́з|ный (~ен, ~на), *adj.* **1.** absurd, senseless. **2.** awkward.

несусве́т|ный (~ен, ~на), *adj.* (*coll.*) extreme, utter; unimaginable; ~ная чепуха́ utter nonsense.

несу́шк|а, и, *f.* (*coll.*) laying hen, hen in lay.

несуще́ствен|ный (~, ~на), *adj.* inessential, immaterial.

несу́щ|ий, *pres. part. act. of* нести́ *and adj.* (*tech.*) carrying; supporting; н. винт rotor (*of helicopter*); ~ая пове́рхность lifting surface; (*aeron.*) airfoil.

несхо́д|ный (~ен, ~на), *adj.* **1.** unlike, dissimilar. **2.** (*coll.*; *of price*) unreasonable.

несчастли́в|ец, ца, *m.* unlucky person, an unfortunate.

несчастли́в|ый (~, ~а), *adj.* **1.** unfortunate, luckless. **2.** unhappy.

несча́ст|ный (~ен, ~на), *adj.* **1.** unhappy; unfortunate, unlucky; н. слу́чай accident. **2.** *as noun* н., ~ного, *m.* wretch; an unfortunate.

несча́сть|е, я, *n.* **1.** misfortune; к ~ю unfortunately. **2.** accident.

несчёт|ный (~ен, ~на), *adj.* innumerable, countless.

несъедо́бный, *adj.* **1.** uneatable. **2.** inedible; н. гриб toadstool.

нет[1] **1.** no; not; вы его́ ви́дели? н. you saw him?—No; вы не ви́дели его́? н., ви́дел you didn't see him? Yes, I did; н. да н., н. как н. (*coll.*; *emphatic*) absolutely not, absolutely nothing; н.-н. да и взгля́нет на меня́ he glanced at me from time to time. **2.** nothing, naught; свести́ на н. to bring to naught; свести́сь (сойти́) на н. to come to naught; *as noun* н., ~а, *m.*; на н. и суда́ н. (*prov.*) what cannot be cured must be endured; пироги́ с ~ом (*joc.*) pie without filling; быть в ~ях (в ~ех) (*obs. or joc.*) to be missing, be adrift.

нет[2], (+*g.*) (there) is not, (there) are not; здесь н. собо́ра there is not a cathedral here; у меня́ н. вре́мени I have no time.

нетакти́ч|ный (~ен, ~на), *adj.* tactless.

нетвёрдо, *adv.* **1.** unsteadily, not firmly. **2.** not definitely; знать н. to have a shaky knowledge of; я н. уве́рен I am not quite sure.

нетвёрд|ый (~, ~а́, ~о), *adj.* unsteady; shaky (*also fig.*).

нетерпёж, а́, *m.* (*coll.*) impatience.

нетерпели́в|ый (~, ~а), *adj.* impatient.

нетерпе́ни|е, я, *n.* impatience.

нетерпи́мост|ь, и, *f.* intolerance.

нетерпи́м|ый (~, ~а), *adj.* **1.** intolerable. **2.** intolerant.

нетле́н|ный (~ен, ~на), *adj.* imperishable.

нетопы́р|ь, я́, *m.* (*zool.*) bat.

неторопли́в|ый (~, ~а), *adj.* leisurely, unhurried.

нето́чност|ь, и, *f.* **1.** inaccuracy, inexactitude. **2.** error, slip.

нето́ч|ный (~ен, ~на́, ~но), *adj.* inaccurate, inexact.

нетре́бовател|ьный (~ен, ~ьна), *adj.* not exacting, undemanding; unpretentious.

нетре́зв|ый (~, ~а́, ~о), *adj.* not sober, drunk; в ~ом ви́де in a state of intoxication.

нетро́нут|ый (~, ~а), *adj.* untouched; (*fig.*) chaste, virginal.

нетрудово́й, *adj.* **1.** not derived from labour; н. дохо́д unearned income. **2.** not engaged in labour.

нетрудоспосо́бност|ь, и, *f.* disablement, disability; incapacity for work.

нетрудоспосо́б|ный (~ен, ~на), *adj.* disabled; invalid.

нéтто, *indecl. adj.* (*comm.*) net.

нéту (*coll.*) = нет².

нéтях, *see* нет¹.

неубеди́тел|ьный (~ен, ~ьна), *adj.* unconvincing.

неу́бранный, *adj.* 1. untidy. 2. unharvested.

неуважéни|е, я, *n.* disrespect, lack of respect.

неуважи́тел|ьный (~ен, ~ьна), *adj.* 1. (*of cause, ground, etc.*) inadequate; not acceptable. 2. (*obs.*) disrespectful.

неувéренност|ь, и, *f.* uncertainty; н. в себé diffidence.

неувéрен|ный, *adj.* 1. (~, ~a) uncertain; н. в себé diffident. 2. (~, ~на) hesitating; vacillating.

неувядá|емый (~ем, ~ема), *adj.* = ~ющий.

неувядáющий, *adj.* (*rhet.*) unfading, everlasting.

неувя́зк|а, и, *f.* (*coll.*) lack of co-ordination; misunderstanding.

неугаси́м|ый (~, ~a), *adj.* inextinguishable, unquenchable (*also fig.*).

неугомóн|ный (~ен, ~на), *adj.* (*coll.*) indefatigable, irrepressible.

неудáч|а, и, *f.* failure.

неудáчлив|ый (~, ~a), *adj.* unlucky.

неудáчник, а, *m.* unlucky person, failure.

неудáч|ный (~ен, ~на), *adj.* unsuccessful; unfortunate; ~ное выражéние unfortunate expression; ~ное начáло bad start.

неудержи́м|ый (~, ~a), *adj.* irrepressible.

неудóб|ный (~ен, ~на), *adj.* 1. uncomfortable. 2. (*fig.*) inconvenient; awkward; embarrassing.

неудобовари́м|ый (~, ~a), *adj.* indigestible (*also fig.*).

неудобопоня́т|ный (~ен, ~на), *adj.* unintelligible, obscure.

неудобопроизноси́м|ый (~, ~a), *adj.* 1. unpronounceable. 2. (*joc.*) unrepeatable (= obscene), risqué.

неудобочитáемый, *adj.* difficult to read, obscure.

неудóбств|о, а, *n.* 1. discomfort; inconvenience. 2. embarrassment.

неудóбь, *adv. now only in joc. phrase* н. скáзуемый risqué.

неудовлетворéни|е, я, *n.* 1. non-compliance; н. жáлобы rejection of a complaint, failure to act on a complaint. 2. dissatisfaction.

неудовлетворённост|ь, и, *f.* dissatisfaction, discontent.

неудовлетворён|ный, *adj.* 1. (~, ~на) dissatisfied, discontented. 2. (~, ~á) unsatisfied.

неудовлетвори́тел|ьный (~ен, ~ьна), *adj.* unsatisfactory.

неудовóльстви|е, я, *n.* displeasure.

неуём|ный (~ен, ~на), *adj.* (*coll.*) irrepressible; ~ная печáль uncontrollable grief.

неужéли, *interrog. particle* really? is it possible?; н. он так дýмает? does he really think that?; н. ты не знал, что мы здесь? did you really not know that we were here? surely you knew that we were here?

неужи́вчивост|ь, и, *f.* unaccommodating nature; quarrelsome disposition.

неужи́вчив|ый (~, ~a), *adj.* unaccommodating, difficult (to get on with); quarrelsome.

неýжто, *interrog. particle* (*coll.*) = неужéли.

неузнавáемост|ь, и, *f.* unrecognizability; он похудéл до ~и he has become so thin that you would not recognize him.

неузнавáем|ый (~, ~a), *adj.* unrecognizable.

неуклóн|ный (~ен, ~на), *adj.* steady, steadfast; undeviating.

неуклю́жест|ь, и, *f.* clumsiness, awkwardness.

неуклю́ж|ий (~, ~a, ~e), *adj.* clumsy; awkward.

неукосни́тел|ьный (~ен, ~ьна), *adj.* (*obs.*) strict, rigorous.

неукроти́м|ый (~, ~a), *adj.* indomitable.

неулови́м|ый (~, ~a), *adj.* 1. elusive, difficult to catch. 2. (*fig.*) imperceptible.

неумéл|ый (~, ~a), *adj.* clumsy; unskilful.

неумéни|е, я, *n.* inability; lack of skill.

неумéренност|ь, и, *f.* 1. immoderation. 2. intemperance.

неумéрен|ный (~, ~на), *adj.* 1. immoderate; excessive. 2. intemperate.

неумéст|ный (~ен, ~на), *adj.* 1. inappropriate; misplaced, out of place. 2. irrelevant.

неýм|ный (~ён, ~нá, ~нó), *adj.* foolish, silly.

неумоли́м|ый (~, ~a), *adj.* implacable; inexorable.

неумолкáем|ый (~, ~a), *adj.* (*of sounds*) incessant, unceasing.

неумóл|чный (~чен, ~чна), *adj.* = ~кáемый.

неумы́шлен|ный (~, ~на), *adj.* unpremeditated; unintentional, inadvertent.

неуплáт|а, ы, *f.* non-payment.

неупотреби́тел|ьный (~ен, ~ьна), *adj.* not in use, not current.

неуравновéшен|ный (~, ~на), *adj.* (*psych.*) unbalanced.

неурожá|й, я, *m.* bad harvest, failure of crops.

неурожáй|ный, *adj. of* ~; н. год lean year, bad harvest year.

неурóчный, *adj.* untimely.

неуря́диц|а, ы, *f.* (*coll.*) 1. disorder, mess. 2. (*pl.*) squabbling.

неуси́дчив|ый (~, ~a), *adj.* restless, not persevering.

неуспева́емост|ь, и, *f.* poor progress (*in studies*).

неуспева́ющий, *adj.* backward, not making satisfactory progress.

неуста́н|ный (~ен, ~на), *adj.* tireless, unwearying.

неусто́йк|а, и, *f.* 1. (*leg.*) forfeit (*for breach of contract*). 2. (*coll.*) failure.

неусто́йчивост|ь, и, *f.* instability, unsteadiness.

неусто́йчив|ый (~, ~a), *adj.* unstable, unsteady; ~ое равнове́сие unstable equilibrium.

неустрани́м|ый (~, ~a), *adj.* unremovable; ~ое препя́тствие insurmountable obstacle.

неустраши́м|ый (~, ~a), *adj.* fearless, intrepid, undaunted.

неустро́ен|ный (~, ~на), *adj.* unsettled, not put in order, badly organized.

неустро́йств|о, а, *n.* disorder.

неусту́пчив|ый (~, ~a), *adj.* unyielding, uncompromising.

неусы́п|ный (~ен, ~на), *adj.* vigilant; indefatigable.

неутеши́тел|ьный (~ен, ~ьна), *adj.* not comforting, depressing; ~ьные ве́сти distressing news.

неуте́ш|ный (~ен, ~на), *adj.* inconsolable; disconsolate.

неутоли́м|ый (~, ~a), *adj.* unquenchable; unappeasable; (*fig.*) insatiable.

неутоми́м|ый (~, ~a), *adj.* tireless, indefatigable.

нéуч, а, *m.* (*coll.*) ignoramus.

неучти́вост|ь, и, *f.* discourtesy, impoliteness, incivility.

неучти́в|ый (~, ~a), *adj.* discourteous, impolite, uncivil.

неую́т|ный (~ен, ~на), *adj.* bleak, comfortless.

неуязви́м|ый (~, ~a), *adj.* 1. invulnerable. 2. unassailable.

неф, а, *m.* (*archit.*) nave.

нефри́т[1], а, *m.* (*med.*) nephritis.

нефри́т[2], а, *m.* (*min.*) nephrite, jade.

нефте- oil-.

нефтеналивн|о́й, *adj.* equipped for carrying oil in bulk; ~о́е су́дно oil-tanker.

нефтено́с|ный (~ен, ~на), *adj.* oil-bearing.

нефтеперего́нный, *adj.* oil-refining; н. заво́д oil refinery.

нефтеперераба́тывающий, *adj.* oil-refining.

нефтепрово́д, а, *m.* oil pipe-line.

нефтехрани́лищ|е, а, *n.* oil-tank, oil reservoir.

нефт|ь, и, *f.* oil, petroleum; н.-сыре́ц crude oil.

нефтя́ник, а, *m.* oil(-industry) worker.

нефтя́нк|а, и, *f.* (*coll.*) 1. oil-engine. 2. oil-barge.

нефтян|о́й, *adj.* oil; ~áя вы́шка derrick; н. фонта́н oil-gusher.

нехва́тк|а, и, *f.* (*coll.*) shortage.

нехи́т|рый (~ёр, ~pá, ~pó), *adj.* 1. artless, guileless. 2. (*coll.*) simple; uncomplicated.

нехоро́ш|ий (~, ~á, ~ó), *adj.* bad.

нехорошо́, *adv.* badly; чу́вствовать себя́ н. to feel unwell.

не́хотя, *adv.* 1. reluctantly, unwillingly. 2. inadvertently, unintentionally.

не́христ|ь, я, *m.* 1. (*obs.*) unbeliever. 2. (*coll.*) brute, hard-hearted person.

нецелесообра́з|ный (~ен, ~на), *adj.* inexpedient; pointless.

нецензу́р|ный (~ен, ~на), *adj.* unprintable.

неча́янност|ь, и, *f.* 1. unexpectedness. 2. surprise. 3. unexpected event.

неча́янный, *adj.* 1. unexpected. 2. accidental; unintentional.

не́чего, не́чему, не́чем, не о чём 1. *pron.* (+*inf.*) there is nothing (to); мне н. чита́ть I have nothing to read; не о чём бы́ло говори́ть there was nothing to talk about; от н. де́лать for want of something better to do, to while away the time; н. сказа́ть! (*coll., iron.*) indeed!; well, I declare! 2. *as pred.* (*impers.*; +*inf.*) it's no good, it's no use; there is no need; н. жа́ловаться it's no use complaining; н. и говори́ть, что... it goes without saying that . . . .

нечелове́ческий, *adj.* 1. superhuman. 2. inhuman.

нечести́в|ый (~, ~a), *adj.* impious, profane.

нече́стност|ь, и, *f.* dishonesty.

нече́ст|ный (~ен, ~на́), *adj.* 1. dishonest. 2. dishonourable.

не́чет, а, *m.* (*coll.*) odd number.

нечёт|кий (~ок, ~ка́), *adj.* illegible; indistinct; inaccurate, slipshod.

нечётный, *adj.* odd.

нечистопло́т|ный (~ен, ~на), *adj.* 1. dirty; untidy, slovenly. 2. (*fig.*) unscrupulous.

нечистот|а́, ы́, *pl.* ~ы, ~, *f.* 1. dirtiness. 2. *pl. only* sewage, garbage.

нечи́ст|ый (~, ~á, ~o), *adj.* 1. unclean, dirty (*also fig.*); ~ое де́ло suspicious affair; ~ая пи́ща (*rel.*) unclean food. 2. impure, adulterated; ~ая поро́да impure breed; ~ое произноше́ние defective pronunciation. 3. careless, inaccurate. 4. dishonourable; dishonest; быть ~ым на́ руку to be light-fingered. 5. ~ая си́ла; *also as noun* н., ~ого, *m.* the Evil one, the Evil Spirit.

нечи́ст|ь, и, *f.* (*collect.*; *coll.*) 1. evil spirits. 2. (*fig., pejor.*) scum, vermin.

нечленоразде́л|ьный (∼ен, ∼ьна), *adj.* in-articulate.

не́что, *pron.* (*nom. and a. cases only*) something.

нечувстви́тел|ьный (∼ен, ∼ьна), *adj.* **1.** (к) insensitive (to). **2.** imperceptible.

нешу́точ|ный (∼ен, ∼на), *adj.* grave, serious; де́ло ∼ное it is no joke, it is no laughing matter.

неща́д|ный (∼ен, ∼на), *adj.* merciless.

неэвкли́дов, *adj.* ∼а геоме́трия non-Euclidean geometry.

нея́вк|а, и, *f.* non-appearance, failure to appear.

неядови́тый, *adj.* non-poisonous; (*chem.*) non-toxic.

нея́сност|ь, и, *f.* vagueness, obscurity.

нея́с|ный (∼ен, ∼на́, ∼но), *adj.* vague, obscure.

нея́сыт|ь, и, *f.* tawny owl.

ни 1. *correlative conj.* ни… ни neither … nor; ни тот ни друго́й neither (the one nor the other); ни то ни сё neither one thing nor the other; ни ры́ба, ни мя́со neither fish, flesh nor good red herring; ни с того́, ни с сего́ all of a sudden; for no apparent reason; ни за что, ни про что for no reason at all. **2.** *particle* not a; ни оди́н, ни одна́, ни одно́ not a, not one, not a single; на у́лице не́ было ни (одно́й) души́ there was not a soul about; ни ша́гу да́льше! not a step further!; ни гу-гу́! (*coll.*) not a word! mum's the word! **3.** *separable component of prons.* никако́й, никто́, ничто́, *following preps.*; ни в како́м (ни в ко́ем) слу́чае on no account; ни за что на све́те! not for the world! **4.** (*particle, in combination with* как, кто, куда́, *etc.*) = -ever; как бы мы ни стара́лись however hard we tried; что бы он ни говори́л whatever he might say.

ни́в|а, ы, *f.* (corn-)field; на ∼е просвеще́ния (*fig.*) in the field of education.

нивели́р, а, *m.* (*tech.*) level.

нивели́р|овать, ую, *impf. and pf.* (*tech. and fig.*) **1.** to level. **2.** to survey, contour.

нивелиро́вк|а, и, *f.* **1.** levelling. **2.** surveying, contouring.

нивелиро́вщик, а, *m.* **1.** leveller. **2.** surveyor.

нигде́, *adv.* nowhere.

нигили́зм, а, *m.* nihilism.

нигили́ст, а, *m.* nihilist.

нигилисти́ческий, *adj.* nihilistic.

нидерла́нд|ец, ца, *m.* Dutchman.

нидерла́ндский, *adj.* Netherlands.

нижа́йший, *superl. of* ни́зкий; ваш н. слуга́ your very humble servant.

ни́же, 1. *comp. of* ни́зкий *and* ни́зко. **2.** *prep.* (+*g.*) *and adv.* below, beneath.

нижеподписа́вшийся, *adj.* (the) undersigned.

нижеследу́ющий, *adj.* following.

нижеупомя́нутый, *adj.* undermentioned.

ни́жн|ий, *adj.* (*in var. senses*) lower; ∼ее бельё underclothes, underwear; ∼яя пала́та Lower Chamber, Lower House; н. чин (*mil., obs.*) other rank, ranker; н. эта́ж ground floor.

ни|жу́, ∼жешь, *see* ∼за́ть.

низ, а, *pl.* ∼ы́, *m.* **1.** bottom; ground floor. **2.** (*pl.*) lower classes. **3.** (*pl.*; *mus.*) low notes.

ни|за́ть, жу́, ∼жешь, *impf.* (*of* на∼) to string, thread; н. слова́ to speak very smoothly.

низачто́, *adv.* in no circumstances.

низведе́ни|е, я, *n.* bringing down.

низверг|а́ть, а́ю, *impf.* (*of* ∼нуть) to precipitate; (*fig.*) to overthrow.

низверг|а́ться, а́юсь, *impf.* (*of* ∼нуться) **1.** to crash down. **2.** *pass. of* ∼а́ть.

низве́рг|нуть(ся), ну(сь), нешь(ся), *past* ∼(ся), ∼ла(сь), *pf. of* ∼а́ть(ся).

низверже́ни|е, я, *n.* overthrow.

низве|сти́, ду́, дёшь, *past* ∼л, ∼ла́, *pf.* (*of* низводи́ть) to bring down; (*fig.*) to bring low; to reduce.

низво|ди́ть, жу́, ∼дишь, *impf. of* низвести́.

низи́н|а, ы, *f.* low place, depression.

ни́з|кий (∼ок, ∼ка́, ∼ко), *adj.* **1.** (*in var. senses*); low; ∼кого происхожде́ния of humble origin. **2.** base, mean; н. посту́пок shabby act.

низколо́б|ый (∼, ∼а), *adj.* with a low forehead.

низкоопла́чиваемый, *adj.* poorly-paid.

низкопокло́нник, а, *m.* toady, crawler.

низкопокло́ннича|ть, ю, *impf.* (пе́ред) to cringe (to), grovel (before).

низкопокло́нств|о, а, *n.* cringing, servility.

низкопро́б|ный (∼ен, ∼на), *adj.* **1.** base, low-grade (*of precious metals*). **2.** (*fig.*) base; inferior.

низкоро́сл|ый (∼, ∼а), *adj.* undersized, stunted.

низкосо́рт|ный (∼ен, ∼на), *adj.* low-grade; of inferior quality.

низлага́|ть, ю, *impf. of* низложи́ть.

низложе́ни|е, я, *n.* deposition, dethronement.

низлож|и́ть, у́, ∼ишь, *pf.* (*of* низлага́ть) to depose, dethrone.

ни́зменност|ь, и, *f.* **1.** (*geogr.*) lowland (*not exceeding 600 ft. above sea-level*). **2.** baseness.

ни́змен|ный (∼, ∼на), *adj.* **1.** low-lying. **2.** low; base, vile.

низово́й[1], *adj.* (*geogr.*) lower; situated down stream; н. ве́тер wind blowing from downstream (*esp. from mouth of Volga*).

низово́й[2], *adj.* local; (*polit.*) grass-roots; н. аппара́т basic organization; н. рабо́тник worker in basic organization.

низо́в|ье, ья, g. pl. ~ьев, n. the lower reaches (of a river).

низо|йти́, йду́, йдёшь, past нисшёл, ~шла́, pf. (of нисходи́ть) (obs.) to descend.

ни́зом, adv. (coll.) along the bottom; е́хать н. to take the lower road.

ни́зост|ь, и, f. lowness; baseness, meanness.

низри́н|уть, у, ешь, pf. (rhet.) to throw down, overthrow.

низри́н|уться, усь, ешься, pf. (rhet.) to crash down.

ни́зш|ий, superl. of ни́зкий, lowest; ~ee образова́ние primary education; ~ие слу́жащие the most junior employees.

никáк¹, adv. by no means, in no way, nowise; он н. не мог узна́ть её а́дрес in no way could he discover her address; н. нельзя́ it is quite impossible; н. нет respectful reply in negative to question.

никáк², adv. (coll.) it seems, it would appear; они́, н., уже́ пришли́ they are here already, it seems.

никак|о́й, pron. no; не... ~о́го, ~о́й, ~и́х no . . . whatever; я не име́ю ~о́го представле́ния (поня́тия) I have no idea, no conception; ~и́х возраже́ний! no objections!; учёный он н. (coll.) he is no scholar; и ~и́х (гвозде́й)! (coll.) and that's all there is to it, and that's that.

ни́келевый, adj. nickel.

никелиро́в|анный, p.p.p. of ~а́ть and adj. nickel-plated.

никелир|ова́ть, у́ю, impf. and pf. to plate with nickel, nickel.

никелиро́вк|а, и, f. nickel-plating.

ни́кел|ь, я, m. nickel.

ни́к|нуть, ну, нешь, past. ~, ~ла, impf. (of по~ and с~) to droop, flag (also fig.).

никогда́, adv. never; как н. as never before.

нико́|й, pron. (obs.) no; now only in phrases ~им о́бразом by no means, in no way; ни в ко́ем слу́чае on no account, in no circumstances.

никоти́н, а, m. nicotine.

никоти́н|ный, adj. of ~.

никоти́н|овый, adj. = ~ный.

никто́, никого́, никому́, нике́м, ни о ком, pron. nobody, no one; там никого́ не́ было there was nobody there; н. друго́й nobody else; ни у кого́ нет э́того no one has it.

никуда́, adv. nowhere; э́то н. не годи́тся (fig.) this won't do, it is no good at all; н. не го́дный good-for-nothing, worthless, useless.

никуд|ы́шный, adj. (coll.) = ~а́ не го́дный.

никчёмный, adj. (coll.) useless, good-for-nothing; needless.

ним, i. of он, оно́; d. of они́ after preps.

нима́ло, adv. not in the least, not at all.

нимб, а, m. halo, nimbus.

ни́ми, i. of они́ after preps.

ни́мф|а, ы, f. 1. nymph. 2. (pl., anat.) labia minora. 3. (zool.) pupa.

нимфома́ни|я, и, f. nymphomania.

нимфома́нк|а, и, f. nymphomaniac.

нио́би|й, я, m. (chem.) niobium.

ниотку́да, adv. from nowhere; н. не сле́дует, что... it in no way follows that . . .

нипочём, adv. (coll.) 1. (+d.) it is nothing (to); э́то ему́ н. it is child's play to him; ему́ н. провести́ це́лую ночь на заня́тиях he thinks nothing of spending a whole night working. 2. for nothing, dirt-cheap; прода́ть н. to sell for a song. 3. never, in no circumstances.

ни́ппел|ь, я, pl. ~я́, ~е́й, m. (tech.) nipple.

нирва́н|а, ы, f. nirvana.

ниско́лько 1. adv. not at all, not in the least; no whit; ей от э́того бы́ло н. не лу́чше she was none the better for it. 2. pron. (coll.) none at all; ско́лько вам э́то сто́ило? — н. how much did it cost you? It cost me nothing.

ниспада́|ть, ет, impf. of ниспа́сть.

ниспа́|сть, ду́, дёшь, past ~л, ~ла, pf. (of ~да́ть) (obs.) to fall, drop.

ниспо|сла́ть, шлю́, шлёшь, pf. (of ~сыла́ть) (rel.) to send down (sc. from heaven).

ниспосыла́|ть, ю, impf. of ниспосла́ть.

ниспроверг|а́ть, а́ю, impf. (of ~нуть) to overthrow, overturn (also fig.).

ниспрове́рг|нуть, ну, нешь, past ~, ~ла, pf. of ~а́ть.

ниспроверже́ни|е, я, n. overthrow.

ниста́гм, а, m. (med.) nystagmus.

нисхо|ди́ть, жу́, ~дишь, impf. of низойти́.

нисход|я́щий, pres. part. act. of ~и́ть and adj. 1. descending; по ~я́щей ли́нии in the line of descent, in a descending line. 2. (ling.) falling.

нисше́стви|е, я, n. descending, descent.

нитеви́д|ный (~ен, ~на), adj. thread-like, filiform; н. пульс (med.) thready pulse.

нитево́д, а, m. (text.) thread guide; ро́лик ~a yarn tension bowl.

нитело́вк|а, и, f. (text) thread picker.

нитере́зк|а, и, f. (text.) thread cutter.

ни́тк|а, и, f. thread; н. же́мчуга string of pearls; на живу́ю ~у (fig., coll.) hastily, anyhow; ши́то бе́лыми ~ами (fig., coll.) transparent, patent, obvious; до (после́дней) ~и обобра́ть (fig., coll.) to fleece, leave without a shirt to one's back; промо́кнуть до ~и (fig.) to get soaked to the skin; вы́тянуться в ~у (fig., coll.) (i) to stand in line, (ii) to become worn to a shadow.

нито́н, а, m. (chem.) niton.

ни́точк|а, и, f. dim. of ни́тка; по ~е разобра́ть (fig.) to analyse minutely, subject to minute scrutiny; ходи́ть по ~е (*fig.*) to toe the line, sing small.

ни́т|очный, *adj. of* ~ка; ~очное произво́дство spinning.

нитра́т, а, *m.* (*chem.*) nitrate.

нитри́ровани|е, я, *n.* (*chem.*) nitriding.

нитри́р|овать, ую, *impf. and pf.* (*chem.*) 1. to nitride. 2. to nitrate.

нитри́т, а, *m.* (*chem.*) nitrite.

нитрифика́ци|я, и, *f.* (*chem.*) nitrification.

нитрифици́р|овать, ую, *impf. and pf.* (*chem., bot.*) to nitrify.

нитробензо́л, а, *m.* (*chem.*) nitrobenzene.

нитрова́ни|е, я, *n.* (*chem.*) nitration.

нитроглицери́н, а, *m.* (*chem.*) nitroglycerine.

нитроипри́т, а, *m.* (*chem., mil.*) nitrogen mustard (gas).

нитроклетча́тк|а, и, *f.* (*chem.*) nitrocellulose.

нитросоедине́ни|е, я, *n.* nitro-compound.

нитча́тк|а, и, *f.* 1. tape-worm. 2. (*bot.*) hair-weed, crow-silk.

ни́тчатый, *adj.* filiform.

нит|ь, и, *f.* 1. (*in var. senses*) thread; путево́дная н. clue; ~и дру́жбы bonds of friendship; проходи́ть кра́сной ~ью (*fig.*) to stand out, run through (*of theme, motif*). 2. (*bot., electr.*) filament; н. нака́ла (*electr.*) glow-lamp filament; (*radio*) heated filament. 3. (*med.*) suture.

ни́тянк|а, и, *f.* (*coll.*) knitted cotton glove.

ни́тяный, *adj.* cotton.

ниц, *adv.* (*obs.*) face downwards; пасть н. to prostrate oneself, kiss the ground.

ничего́¹, *g. of* ничто́.

ничего́², *adv.* 1. (*also* н. себе́) so-so; passably, not (too) badly; all right; ко́рмят здесь н. the food here is not too bad; как вы чу́вствуете себя́? — н. how do you feel? all right. 2. *as indecl. adj.* not (too) bad, passable, tolerable; на́ша кварти́ра н. our flat is not too bad; па́рень он н. he is not a bad chap.

ничегонеде́лани|е, я, *n.* (*coll.*) idleness.

нич|е́й (~ья́, ~ьё), *pron.* nobody's, no one's; ~ья́ земля́ no man's land; *as noun* ~ья́, ~ье́й, *f.* (*sport*) draw, drawn game; сыгра́ть в ~ью́ to play a drawn game, draw.

ниче́йный, *adj.* (*coll.*) 1. no man's. 2. (*sport*) drawn.

ничко́м, *adv.* prone, face downwards.

ничто́, ничего́, ничему́, ниче́м, ни о чём, *pron.* 1. nothing; э́то ничего́ не зна́чит it means nothing; ниче́м не ко́нчилось it came to nothing; ничего́ подо́бного! nothing of the kind!; э́то ничего́! it's nothing! it doesn't matter!; ничего́! (*coll.*) that's all right! never mind! 2. nought; nil.

ничто́же, *pron.* н. сумня́ся, н. сумня́шеся (*iron.*) without a second's hesitation.

ничто́жеств|о, а, *n.* 1. nothingness. 2. a nonentity, a nobody.

ничто́жност|ь, и, *f.* 1. insignificance. 2. a nonentity, a nobody.

ничто́ж|ный (~ен, ~на), *adj.* insignificant; paltry, worthless.

ничу́ть, *adv.* (*coll.*) not at all, not in the least, not a bit; н. не быва́ло not at all.

ничь|я́, е́й, *f.* *see* ниче́й.

ни́ш|а, и, *f.* niche, recess; (*archit.*) bay.

нища́|ть, ю, *impf.* (*of* об~) to grow poor, be reduced to beggary.

ни́щенк|а, и, *f.* beggar-woman.

ни́щенский, *adj.* beggarly.

ни́щенств|о, а, *n.* 1. begging. 2. beggary.

ни́щенств|овать, ую, *impf.* 1. to beg, go begging. 2. to be destitute.

нищет|а́, ы́, *f.* 1. destitution; indigence, poverty (*also fig.*). 2. (*collect.*) beggars; the poor.

ни́щ|ий, *adj.* 1. destitute; indigent, poverty-stricken; ~ая бра́тия (*folk poet.*) the poor; н. ду́хом poor in spirit. 2. *as noun* н., ~его, *m.* beggar, mendicant; pauper.

но¹, *conj.* 1. but; *after concessive clause not translated or* still, nevertheless; хотя́ он и бо́лен, но наме́рен прийти́ although he is ill, he (still) intends to come. 2. (*coll.*) *as noun* a 'but'; snag, difficulty; тут есть одно́ «но» there is just one snag in it.

но², *interj.* gee up!

нова́тор, а, *m.* innovator.

нова́тор|ский, *adj. of* ~ *and* ~ство.

нова́торств|о, а, *n.* innovation.

нове́йший, *superl. of* но́вый; newest; latest.

нове́лл|а, ы, *f.* 1. short story. 2. (*in Roman law*) novel.

новелли́ст, а, *m.* short story-writer.

но́веньк|ий, *adj.* 1. brand-new. 2. *as noun* н., ~ого, *m.* new boy; ~ая, ~ой, *f.* new girl.

новизн|а́, ы́, *f.* novelty; newness.

нови́к, а́, *m.* 1. (*hist.*) young courtier. 2. (*obs.*) novice.

новин|а́, ы́, *f.* (*dial.*) 1. virgin soil. 2. freshly-reaped corn. 3. piece of unbleached linen.

нови́нк|а, и, *f.* novelty; мне в ~у е́хать самолётом it is a new experience for me to travel by 'plane.

новичо́к, ка́, *m.* 1. (в+*p.*) novice (at), beginner (at), tiro; (*sport*) colt. 2. (*in school*) new boy; new girl.

новобра́н|ец, ца, *m.* recruit.

новобра́чн|ая, ой, *f.* bride.

новобра́чн|ые, ых, *pl.* newly-married couple, newly-weds.

новобра́чн|ый, ого, *m.* bridegroom.

нововведе́ни|е, я, *n.* innovation.

нового́дний, *adj.* new year's.

новогре́ческий, *adj.* н. язы́к modern Greek.

новозавéтный, *adj.* of the New Testament.

новозелáнд|ец, ца, *m.* New Zealander.

новозелáнд|ка, ки, *f. of* ~ец.

новозелáндский, *adj.* New Zealand.

новоиспечённый, *adj.* (*coll., joc.*) newly made; newly fledged.

новокаúн, а, *m.* (*pharm.*) novocaine.

новолýни|е, я, *n.* new moon.

новомóд|ный (~ен, ~на), *adj.* in the latest fashion, up-to-date; (*fig., pejor.*) new-fangled.

новообразовáни|е, я, *n.* new growth; new formation; (*med.*) neoplasm.

нóжик, а, *m.* knife.

новообращённый, *adj.* (*rel. and fig.*) newly converted.

новопрестáвленный, *adj.* (*rel.*) the late, the late-lamented.

новоприбы́вш|ий, *adj.* newly-arrived; *as noun* н., ~его, *m.* new-comer.

новорождённ|ый, *adj.* **1.** new-born; *as noun* н., ~ого, *m.* the baby. **2.** *as noun* one celebrating his birthday; поздрáвить ~ого to wish many happy returns (of a birthday).

новосёл, а, *m.* new settler.

новосéль|е, я, *n.* **1.** new home; new abode. **2.** house-warming; справля́ть н. to give a house-warming party.

новострóйк|а, и, *f.* **1.** erection of new buildings. **2.** newly-erected building; шкóла-н. new school.

нóвост|ь, и, *g. pl.* ~éй, *f.* **1.** news; tidings; э́то что ещё за ~и!, вот ещё ~и! (*coll.*) that is something new! that's news! **2.** novelty.

новотéльный, *adj.* newly-calved.

новоя́вленный, *adj.* (*rel. or iron.*) newly brought to light.

нóвшеств|о, а, *n.* innovation, novelty.

нóв|ый (~, ~á, ~о), *adj.* **1.** new; novel; fresh; Н. год new year's day; Н. завéт the New Testament; Н. свет the New World; что ~ого? what's the news?, what's new? **2.** modern; recent; ~ая истóрия modern history; ~ые языки́ modern languages.

нóв|ь, и, *f.* virgin soil.

ног|á, и́, a. ~у, *pl.* ~и, ног, ~áм, *f.* foot; leg; вверх ~áми head over heels; без (зáдних) ног (*coll.*) dead-beat; в ~áх постéли at the foot of the bed; валя́ться в ~áх у кого́-н. to prostrate oneself before someone; идти́ в ~у (c+*i.*) to keep step (with), keep pace (with) (*also fig.*); идти́ н. зá ~у (*coll.*) to plod along; к ~é! (*mil.*) order arms!; положи́ть ~у нá ~у to cross one's legs; сидéть н. нá ~у to sit with legs crossed; он не стоя́л на ~áх he could barely stand upright (*sc. from weakness, intoxication, etc.*); постáвить кого́-н. нá ~и (*fig.*) to set someone on his feet; стать нá ~и (*fig.*) to stand on one's own feet; под-

ня́ть кого́-н. нá ~и to goad someone into action; жить на широ́кую (большу́ю, бáрскую) ~у to live in (grand) style, live like a lord; быть на коро́ткой ~é (c+*i.*) to be on a good footing (with), be intimate (with); хромáть на óбе ~й to be lame in both legs; (*fig., coll.*) to go badly, creak; вертéться у кого́-н. под ~áми to get under someone's feet; сбить с ног to knock down; сби́ться с ~й to lose the step, get out of step; дать ~у to keep in step, get in step; встать с лéвой ~й to get out of bed on the wrong side; со всех ног (*coll.*) as fast as one's legs will carry one; éле ~и унести́ to escape by the skin of one's teeth; он давáй Бог ~и (*coll.*) he took to his heels; ног под собóй не слы́шать (от рáдости) (*coll.*) to be beside oneself (with joy); ног под собóй не чýвствовать (от устáлости, *etc.*) to be barely able to stand (from tiredness, *etc.*); моéй ~й у вас не бýдет (*coll.*) I shall not set foot in your house again; мы — ни ~óй тудá (*coll.*) we never go near the place; стоя́ть одно́й ~ой в моги́ле to have one foot in the grave; протяну́ть ~и (*coll.*) to turn up one's toes.

ногтоéд|а, ы, *f.* (*med.*) whitlow.

нóг|оть, тя, *pl.* ~ти, ~тéй, *m.* (finger-, toe-) nail.

ноготк|и́, óв (*bot.*) marigold.

ногот|óк, кá, *m. dim. of* нóготь; мужичóк с н. Tom Thumb.

ног|тевóй, *adj. of* ~оть.

нож, á, *m.* knife; перочи́нный н. penknife; разрезнóй . н. paper-knife; садóвый н. pruning-knife; н. в спи́ну (*fig.*) stab in the back; э́то мне н. óстрый (*fig.*) for me this is sheer hell; без ~á зарéзать to do for; быть на ~áх (c+*i.*) to be at daggers drawn (with); под ~óм under the knife (= *during a surgical operation*); пристават́ь к кому́-н. с ~óм к гóрлу to pester someone, importune someone.

нож|евóй, *adj. of* ~; н. мáстер cutler; ~евы́е товáры cutlery.

нóжк|а, и, *f.* **1.** *dim. of* ногá; подстáвить ~у (+*d.*) to trip up. **2.** leg (*of furniture, utensils, etc.*); stem (*of wine-glass*). **3.** (*bot.*) stalk; stem (*of mushroom*).

нóжниц|ы, ~, *pl.* **1.** scissors, pair of scissors; shears. **2.** (*econ.*) discrepancy.

ножн|óй, *adj. of* ногá; н. привóд foot drive, pedal operation, treadle drive; н. тóрмоз foot brake, pedal brake; ~áя швéйная маши́на treadle sewing-machine.

нóж|ны, ~ен, ~нам (*and* нож|ны́, ~óн, ~нáм) sheath; scabbard.

ножóвк|а, и, *f.* hacksaw.

ножóвщик, а, *m.* cutler.

ножóвый, *adj.* = ножевóй.

ноздрева́тост|ь, и, *f.* porosity, sponginess.

ноздрева́т|ый (~, ~а), *adj.* porous, spongy.

ноздр|я́, и́, *pl.* ~и, ~е́й, *f.* nostril.

нока́ут, а, *m.* (*sport*) knock-out.

нокаути́р|овать, ую, *impf. and pf.* (*sport*) to knock out.

нока́ун, а, *m.* (*sport*) knock-down.

ноктю́рн, а, *m.* (*mus.*) nocturne.

нолево́й, *adj.* = нулево́й.

нол|ь, я́, *m.* = нуль; ноль-ноль *indicates timing of event at the hour exactly*; экспре́сс в Берли́н отхо́дит в пять н.-н., в двена́дцать н.-н., в семна́дцать н.-н. the express for Berlin departs at five o'clock (0500), at twelve noon (1200), at seventeen hundred (1700).

нома́д, а, *m.* nomad.

номенклату́р|а, ы, *f.* 1. nomenclature. 2. list, schedule, catalogue. 3. nomenklatura (*system by which in the U.S.S.R. appointments to specified posts in government or economic administration are made by organs of the Communist Party*).

номенклату́р|ный, *adj. of* ~а.

но́мер, а, *pl.* ~а́, *m.* 1. number; number, issue (*of newspaper, magazine, etc.*). 2. size; како́й н. боти́нок вы но́сите? what size do you take in shoes? 3. room (*in hotel*). 4. item on the programme, number, turn; со́льный н. solo (number); эстра́дный н. music-hall turn. 5. (*coll.*) trick; вы́кинуть н. to play a trick; вот так н.! (*coll.*) what a funny thing! 6. (*mil.*) н. оруди́йного расчёта member of a gun crew, gun number.

номерн|о́й 1. *adj. of* но́мер; numbered. 2. *as noun* н,. ~о́го, *m.* boots (*in a hotel*).

номер|о́к, ка́, *m.* 1. tally; label, ticket (*in cloakroom, etc.*). 2. small room (*in a hotel*).

номина́л, а, *m.* (*econ.*) face-value; по ~у at face-value.

номина́льн|ый, *adj.* 1. nominal; ~ая цена́ face value. 2. (*tech.*) rated, indicated, nominal.

номогра́мм|а, ы, *f.* (*math.*) nomogram, nomograph.

но́н|а, ы, *f.* (*mus.*) ninth.

но́не, *adv.* (*dial.*) = ны́не.

нонпаре́л|ь, и, *f.* (*typ.*) nonpareil.

но́нче, *adv.* (*dial.*) = ны́нче.

но́н|ы, ~ (*in Roman calendar*) nones.

нор|а́, ы́, *pl.* ~ы, ~, ~а́м, *f.* burrow, hole; lair; (*of hare*) form.

норве́ж|ец, ца, *m.* Norwegian.

норве́жк|а, и, *f.* Norwegian (woman).

норве́жский, *adj.* Norwegian.

норд, а, *m.* (*naut.*) 1. north. 2. north wind.

норд-ве́ст, а, *m.* (*naut.*) 1. north-west. 2. north-wester(-ly wind).

норд-о́ст, а, *m.* (*naut.*) 1. north-east. 2. north-easter(-ly wind).

но́ри|я, и, *f.* (*tech.*) noria, bucket chain.

но́рк|а¹, и, *f.* *dim. of* нора́.

но́рк|а², и, *f.* (америка́нская) н. mink (*mustela vison*); (европе́йская) н. marsh-otter (*mustela lutreola*).

но́рк|овый, *adj. of* ~а².

но́рм|а, ы, *f.* 1. standard, norm. 2. rate; н. вы́работки rate of output; сверх ~ы in excess of planned rate.

нормализа́ци|я, и, *f.* standardization.

нормализ|ова́ть, у́ю, *impf. and pf.* to standardize.

норма́л|ь, и, *f.* (*math., phys.*) normal.

норма́льно, *as pred.* (*coll.*) it is all right, O.K.

норма́льност|ь, и, *f.* normality.

норма́л|ьный (~ен, ~ьна), *adj.* (*in var. senses*) normal; н. уста́в model regulations; ~ьная коле́я (*railways*) standard gauge.

норма́нд|ец, ца, *m.* Norman (*inhabitant of Normandy*).

норма́ндски|й, *adj.* Norman; ~е острова́ Channel Islands.

норма́нн, а, *m.* (*hist.*) Northman, Norseman.

норма́нский, *adj.* (*hist.*) Norse.

норматив, а, *m.* (*econ.*) norm.

нормати́в|ный (~ен, ~на), *adj.* 1. *adj. of* ~; corresponding to norm. 2. normative.

нормирова́ни|е, я, *n.* 1. regulation, normalization; н. труда́ norm-fixing, norm-setting (*in production*). 2. rationing.

нормиро́в|анный, *p.p.p. of* ~а́ть; н. рабо́чий день fixed working hours; ~анное снабже́ние rationing.

нормир|ова́ть, у́ю, *impf. and pf.* 1. to regulate, normalize; н. за́работную пла́ту to fix wages. 2. to ration, place on the ration.

нормиро́в|ка, ки, *f.* (*coll.*) = ~а́ние.

нормиро́вщик, а, *m.* regulator; н. труда́ norm-setter.

но́ров, а, *m.* 1. (*obs.*) custom. 2. (*coll.*) obstinacy, capriciousness; челове́к с ~ом difficult person. 3. (*of horses*) restiveness.

норови́ст|ый (~, ~а), *adj.* (*coll.*) restive; jibbing.

нoров|и́ть, лю́, и́шь, *impf.* (*coll.*) 1. (+*inf.*) to strive (to), aim (at). 2. (в+*n.-a.*) to strive to become; он ~и́т в писа́тели he has literary aspirations.

нос, а, о ~е, на ~у́, *pl.* ~ы́, *m.* 1. nose; у меня́ идёт кровь ~ом (из ~у) my nose is bleeding; говори́ть в н. to speak through one's nose; ~ом к ~у (*coll.*) face to face; на ~у́ (*coll.*) near at hand, imminent; заруби́ э́то себе́ на ~у́! put that in your pipe and smoke it!; э́то мне не по́ ~у (*coll.*) it's not to my liking; оста́вить с ~ом (*coll.*) to dupe, make a fool of; оста́ться с ~ом (*coll.*) to be duped, be left looking a fool; задра́ть н., подня́ть н. (*coll.*) to cock one's nose, put on airs; клева́ть ⌣ом (*coll.*) to nod; натяну́ть н. кому́-н. (*coll.*) to make a fool of someone; н. вороти́ть (от) (*coll.*) to turn up one's nose (at); пове́сить ⌣ом (на кви́нту) (*coll.*) to be crestfallen, be discouraged; показа́ть н. (*coll.*) to cock a snook; сова́ть н. не в своё де́ло (*coll.*) to poke one's nose into other people's affairs; ткнуть кого́-н. ⌣ом во что-н. (*coll.*) to thrust something under someone's nose; уткну́ться ⌣ом во что-н. (*coll.*) to bury one's face (oneself) in something. **2.** beak. **3.** (*naut.*) bow, head; prow.

носа́ст|ый (~, ~а), *adj.* big-nosed.

носа́т|ый (~, ~а), *adj.* = носа́стый.

но́сик, а, *m.* **1.** *dim. of* нос. **2.** toe (*of a shoe*). **3.** spout.

носи́л|ки, ок, *no sing.* **1.** stretcher. **2.** sedan(-chair); litter. **3.** (hand-)barrow.

носи́льн|ый, *adj.* for personal wear; ~ое бельё personal linen.

носи́льщик, а, *m.* porter.

носи́тел|ь, я, *m.* **1.** (*fig.*) bearer; repository. **2.** н. зара́зы (*biol., med.*) carrier. **3.** (*chem.*) vehicle.

но|си́ть, шу́, ⌣сишь, *impf.* **1.** *indet. of* нести́. **2.** (*indet. only*) to carry; to bear (*also fig.*); н. свою́ де́вичью фами́лию to use one's maiden name; н. кого́-н. на рука́х (*indet. only*) to make a fuss of someone, make much of someone. **3.** (*indet. only*) to wear; to carry.

но|си́ться, шу́сь, ⌣сишься, *impf.* **1.** *indet. of* нести́сь; э́то ⌣сится в во́здухе (*fig.*) it is in the air, it is rumoured. **2.** (c+*i.*) to fuss (over), make much (of); н. с мы́слью to nurse an idea, be obsessed with an idea. **3.** (*intr.*) to wear; э́та мате́рия хорошо́ ⌣сится this stuff wears well.

но́ск|а¹, и, *f.* **1.** carrying; bearing. **2.** wearing.

но́ск|а², и, *f.* laying.

но́ск|ий¹ (~ок, ~ка), *adj.* (*of clothing, footwear, etc.*) hard-wearing, durable.

но́ск|ий², *adj.* ~ая ку́рица a good layer.

носов|о́й, *adj.* **1.** *adj. of* нос; н. плато́к (pocket) handkerchief. **2.** (*ling.*) nasal. **3.** (*naut.*) bow, fore; ~а́я часть (су́дна) ship's bows, fore part; ~а́я ча́шка (*aeron.*) bow cap.

носогло́тк|а, и, *f.* (*anat.*) nasopharynx.

носогло́точный, *adj.* (*anat.*) nasopharyngeal.

**носогре́йк|а, и, ** *f.* (*coll.*) nose-warmer (*short pipe*).

нос|о́к¹, ка́, *m.* **1.** toe (*of boot or stocking*). **2.** *dim. of* ~.

нос|о́к², ка́, *pl.* ~ки́, ~ко́в, *m.* sock.

носоло́ги|я, и, *f.* (*med.*) nosology.

носоро́г, а, *m.* rhinoceros.

носо́|чный, *adj. of* ~к².

ностальги́|я, и, *f.* nostalgia.

носу́х|а, и, *f.* (*zool.*) coati.

но́счик, а, *m.* carrier, porter.

но́т|а¹, ы, *f.* **1.** (*mus.*) note. **2.** (*pl.*) (sheet) music; игра́ть по ~ам (без нот) to play from music (without music); как по ~ам (*fig.*) without a hitch, according to plan.

но́т|а², ы, *f.* (diplomatic) note.

нотабе́н|а, ы, *f.* *and* **нотабе́н|е** *indecl.* nota bene (N.B.); поста́вить ~у to mark.

нотариа́льный, *adj.* notarial.

нота́риус, а, *m.* notary.

нота́ци|я¹, и, *f.* (*coll.*) lecture, reprimand; прочита́ть кому́-н. ~ю to read someone a lecture.

нота́ци|я², и, *f.* notation.

нотифика́ци|я, и, *f.* notification.

нотифици́р|овать, ую, *impf. and pf.* to notify, inform officially.

но́т|ка, ки, *f. dim. of* ~а¹.

но́тный, *adj. of* но́ты.

ноу́мен, а, *m.* (*philos.*) noumenon.

ноумена́льный, *adj.* (*philos.*) noumenal.

ноч|ева́ть, у́ю, *impf.* (*of* пере~) to pass the night.

ночёвк|а, и, *f.* spending the night, passing the night.

но́ч|ка, ки, *f.* (*coll.*) *dim. of* ~ь.

ночле́г, а, *m.* **1.** lodging for the night. **2.** = ночёвка.

ночле́жк|а, и, *f.* (*coll.*) doss-house.

ночле́жник, а, *m.* **1.** (*coll.*) (overnight) visitor, guest. **2.** dosser.

ночле́|жный, *adj. of* ~г; н. дом doss-house.

ночни́к¹, а́, *m.* night-light.

ночни́к², а́, *m.* (*coll.*) night-driver; night-flier; night-flying ace.

ночн|о́е, о́го, *n.* pasturing of horses for the night.

ночн|о́й, *adj.* night; nocturnal; ~а́я ба́бочка moth; н. горшо́к chamber-pot; н. сто́лик bedside table; ~ые ту́фли bedroom slippers; ~а́я фиа́лка wild orchid.

ноч|ь, и, о ~и, в ~й, *pl.* ~и, ~е́й, *f.* night; глуха́я н. the dead of night; споко́йной ~и! good-night!; по ~а́м (*of recurring events*) by night, at night.

но́чью, *adv.* by night.

но́ш|а, и, *f.* burden.

ноше́ни|е, я, *n.* **1.** carrying. **2.** wearing.

но́шеный, *adj.* worn; second-hand.

но́щно, *adv. only in phrase.* де́нно и н. (*coll.*) day and night.

но́|ю, ешь, *see* ныть.

но́ющ|ий, *pres. part. act. of* ныть; ~ая боль ache.

ноя́бр|ь, я́, *m.* November.

ноя́брь|ский, *adj. of* ~.

нрав, а, *m.* **1.** disposition, temper; быть (+*d.*) по ~у to please. **2.** (*pl.*) manners, customs, ways.

нра́в|иться, люсь, ишься, *impf.* (*of* по~) (+*d.*) to please; мне, емý, *etc.*, ~ится I like, he likes, *etc.*; мне óчень ~ится э́та пье́са I like this play very much; онá мне ка́к-то ~ится I rather like her; мы стара́емся н. вам we try to please you; (*impers.*) ей не ~ится катáться на лóдке she does not like going in boats.

нра́в|ный (~ен, ~на), *adj.* (*coll.*) testy, peppery.

нравоописа́тельный, *adj.* descriptive of manners; н. ромáн novel of manners.

нравоуче́ни|е, я, *n.* **1.** moralizing; moral admonition. **2.** (*lit.*) moral.

нравоучи́тельный, *adj.* edifying.

нра́вственност|ь, и, *f.* morality; morals.

нра́вствен|ный (~, ~на), *adj.* moral.

ну, *interj. and particle* **1.** well!; well . . . then!; come on!; ну, ну! come, come!, come now! **2.** (да) ну? not really?, you don't mean to say so! **3.** *expressing surprise and pleasure or displeasure* well; what; why; ну и... what (a) . . .!, here's . . . (for you)!, there's . . . (for you)!; ну вот и...! there you are, you see . . .!; ну, неуже́ли?! what! really?; no? really?; ну, прáво!, ну, однáко же! well, to be sure!; ну и денёк! what a day!; ну и молодéц! (*also iron.*) there's a good boy!, there's a clever chap! **4.** *indicating resumption of talk; expressing concession, resignation, relief, qualified recognition of point* well, well then; ну вот (*in narration*) well, well then; ну что ж, нý так well then; ну хорошó all right then, very well then; ведь вы сказáли, что вы их увидели, не прáвда ли? — ну да, но тóлько сзáди but you did say you saw them, didn't you? Yes, I know, but only from behind. **5.** нý как (+*fut.*) suppose, what if; нý как они́ не придýт вó-время? suppose they don't come in time? **6.** (*as pred.*; +*inf.*) to start; он ну кричáть he started yelling. **6.** а нý (+*g.*) to hell (with)!, to the deuce (with)!; а нý тебя́! to hell with you!

нуби́йский, *adj.* Nubian.

нуг|á, и́, *f.* nougat.

нý|дить, жу, дишь, *impf.* (*obs.*) **1.** to force, compel. **2.** to wear out.

ну|ди́ть, жý, ди́шь, *impf.* (*coll.*) to wear out (*with complaints, questions, etc.*).

нýдност|ь, и, *f.* tediousness.

нýд|ный (~ен, ~на), *adj.* (*coll.*) tedious, boring.

нужд|á, ы́, *pl.* ~ы, *f.* **1.** want, straits; indigence. **2.** need; necessity; в слýчае ~ы́ if necessary, if need be; н. всемý научит necessity is the mother of invention; ~ы́ нет, нет ~ы́ (*coll.*) no matter!, never mind; ~ы́ нет, что здесь те́сно, затó нам ве́село it doesn't matter if it's a bit crowded here

so long as we enjoy ourselves. **3.** (*coll., euph.*) call of nature.

нужда́емост|ь, и, *no pl.,f.* (в+*p.*) needs (in), requirements (in).

нужда́|ться, юсь, *impf.* **1.** to be in want; to be needy, hard-up. **2.** (в+*p.*) to need, require; to be in need (of).

нýжник, а, *m.* (*coll.*) latrine.

нýжно (+*d.*) **1.** (*impers.*; +*inf. or* +чтóбы) it is necessary; (one) ought, (one) should, (one) must, (one) need(s); н. бы́ло (бы) взять такси́ you should have taken a taxi; н., чтóбы онá реши́лась she ought to make up her mind. **2.** (*impers.*, +*a. or g.*; *coll.*) I, *etc.*, need; мне н. пять рублéй I need five roubles. **3.** *see* нýжный.

нýж|ный (~ен, ~нá, ~но, ~ны́), *adj.* necessary; requisite; (*predic. forms* +*d.*) I, *etc.*, need; что вам ~но? what do you want? óчень (мне) ~но! (*coll., iron.*) won't that be nice! a fat lot of good that is!

нý-ка, *interj.* now!, now then!; come!, come on!

нýка|ть, ю, *impf.* (*coll.*) to urge; to say 'come on'.

нуклеи́н, а, *m.* (*chem.*) nuclein.

нул|евóй, *adj. of* ~ь; (*math.*) zero.

нул|ь, я́, *m.* **1.** nought; zero; nil; cipher; своди́ться к ~ю́ (*fig.*) to come to nothing, come to nought. **2.** (*fig.*) nonentity, cipher.

нумера́тор, а, *m.* **1.** numerator. **2.** (*electr.*) annunciator.

нумера́ци|я, и, *f.* **1.** numeration. **2.** numbering.

нумер|овáть, ýю, *impf.* (*of* за~ *and* пере~) to number; н. страни́цы to paginate.

нумизма́т, а, *m.* numismatist.

нумизма́тик|а, и, *f.* numismatics.

нумизмати́ческий, *adj.* numismatic.

нýнци|й, я, *m.* nuncio.

нýте(-ка), *interj.* well then!, come on!

нутромéр, а, *m.* (*tech.*) internal calipers.

нутр|ó, á, *n.* (*coll.*) **1.** inside, interior. **2.** (*fig.*) core, kernel. **3.** (*fig.*) instinct(s), intuition; ~óм понимáть to understand intuitively; всем ~óм with one's whole being; э́то мне не по ~ý it goes against the grain with me; игрáть ~óм (*theatr. sl.*) to play by inspiration.

нутряно́й, *adj.* internal.

нýтри|я, и, *f.* (*zool.*) coypu; (*fur of coypu*) nutria.

ны́не, *adv.* (*obs.*) **1.** now. **2.** today.

ны́нешн|ий, *adj.* present; present-day; в ~ие временá nowadays.

ны́нче, *adv.* (*coll.*) **1.** today; не н.-зáвтра any day now. **2.** now.

ныр|нýть, нý, нёшь, *pf. of* ~я́ть.

ныр|óк¹, кá, *m.* (*coll.*) **1.** dive. **2.** diver.

ныр|о́к², **ка́**, *m.* (*orn.*) pochard.

ныря́л|о, **а**, *n.* (*tech.*) plunger, plunger piston.

ныр|я́ть, **я́ю**, *impf.* (*of* ~ну́ть) to dive.

ны́тик, **а**, *m.* (*coll*). grumbler, moaner, whiner.

ныть, **но́ю**, **но́ешь**, *impf.* 1. to ache. 2. (*coll., pejor.*) to moan, whine; to make a fuss.

ныть|ё, **я́**, *n.* (*coll., pejor.*) moaning, whining.

нэп, **а**, *m.* (*abbr. of* но́вая экономи́ческая поли́тика) (*polit., econ., hist.*) NEP (New Economic Policy).

нэ́пман, **а**, *m.* (*pejor.*) 'Nepman', profiteer (*during period of New Economic Policy*).

нэ́п|овский, *adj. of* ~.

нюа́нс, **а**, *m.* nuance, shade.

нюанси́р|овать **ую**, *impf. and pf.* (*mus.*) to bring out fine shades of feeling, observe nuances.

нюни, *only in phrase* распусти́ть н. (*coll.*) to snivel, whimper.

нюн|я, **и**, *m. and f.* (*coll.*) sniveller, cry-baby.

нюх, **а**, *m.* scent; (*fig.*) flair.

ню́хальщик, **а**, *m.* (*coll.*) snuff-taker.

ню́хательный, *adj.* н. таба́к snuff.

нюха|ть, **ю**, *impf.* (*of* по~) to smell (at); н. таба́к to take snuff; не ~л (+*g.*) to have no experience (of); по́роха не ~л (*fig.*) he's still wet behind the ears; он матема́тики и не ~л he doesn't know the first thing about mathematics.

нюхн|у́ть, **у́**, **ёшь**, *inst. pf.* (*coll.*) to take a sniff of.

ня́нч|ить, **у**, **ишь**, *impf.* to nurse.

ня́нч|иться, **усь**, **ишься**, *impf.* (с+*i.*) 1. to (dry-)nurse. 2. (*fig.*) to fuss (over).

ня́ньк|а, **и**, *f.* (*coll.*) = ня́ня; у семи́ ня́нек дитя́ без гла́зу (*prov.*) too many cooks spoil the broth (*lit.* where there are seven nurses the child is without supervision).

ня́н|я, **и**, *f.* 1. (dry-) nurse. 2. (*coll.*) (hospital) nurse.

О

о¹ (**об, о́бо**), *prep.* 1. (+*p.*) of, about, concerning; on; о чём вы ду́маете? what are you thinking about?; ле́кция бу́дет о Пу́шкине the lecture will be on Pushkin. 2. (+*p.*) with, having; стол о трёх но́жках a table with three legs, three-legged table; па́лка о двух конца́х a two-edged weapon. 3. (+*a.*) against; on, upon; опере́ться о сте́ну to lean against the wall; споткну́ться о ка́мень to stumble against a stone; бок о́ бок side by side; рука́ о́б руку hand in hand. 4. (+*a. or p.*; *obs. or coll.*) (*of time*) on, at, about; об э́ту по́ру about this time; о Рождестве́ about Christmas-time.

о², *interj.* oh!

о- (**об-, обо-, объ-**) *verbal prefix indicating* 1. transformation; process of becoming something. 2. action applied to entire surface of object *or* to series of objects.

оа́зис, **а**, *m.* oasis (*also fig.*).

об, *prep. see* о¹.

об- (**обо-, объ-**) *verbal prefix* 1. = о-. 2. indicating action *or* motion about an object.

о́ба, **обо́их**, *m. and n.*; **о́бе, обе́их**, *f. num.* both; гляде́ть в о., смотре́ть в о. (*coll.*) to keep one's eyes open, be on one's guard; обе́ими рука́ми with both hands (*fig., coll.*); very willingly, readily.

обаб|и́ться, **люсь**, **ишься**, *pf.* 1. (*of a man*) to become effeminate. 2. (*of a woman*) to become sluttish; to become coarse.

обагр|и́ть, **ю́**, **и́шь**, *pf.* (*of* ~я́ть) to crimson,

incarnadine; о. кро́вью to stain with blood; о. ру́ки в крови́ (кро́вью) to steep one's hands in blood.

обагр|и́ться, **ю́сь**, **и́шься**, *pf.* (*of* ~я́ться) to be crimsoned; о. (кро́вью) to be stained with blood.

обагр|я́ть(ся), **я́ю(сь)**, *impf. of* ~и́ть(ся).

обалдева́|ть, **ю**, *impf. of* обалде́ть.

обалде́лый, *adj.* (*coll.*) crazed; stunned.

обалде́|ть, **ю**, *pf.* (*of* ~ва́ть) (*coll.*) to become dulled, become crazed; to be stunned (*by surprise, etc.*).

обанкро́|титься, **чусь**, **тишься**, *pf. of* банкро́титься.

обая́ни|е, **я**, *n.* fascination, charm.

обая́тел|ьный (~ен, ~ьна), *adj.* fascinating, charming.

обва́л, **а**, *m.* 1. fall(ing), crumbling; collapse; caving-in. 2. landslip; сне́жный о. snow-slip, avalanche.

обва́лива|ть¹**(ся)**, **ю(сь)**, *impf. of* обвали́ть(ся).

обва́лива|ть², **ю**, *impf. of* обваля́ть.

обва́листый (~, ~а), *adj.* (*coll.*) liable to fall, liable to cave in.

обвал|и́ть, **ю́**, ~**ишь**, *pf.* (*of* ~ива́ть¹) 1. to cause to fall, cause to collapse; to crumble (*trans.*). 2. to heap round; о. избу́ камня́ми to heap stones round a hut.

обвал|и́ться, **ю́сь**, ~**ишься**, *pf.* (*of* ~ива́ться) to fall, collapse, cave in; to crumble.

обвал|я́ть, **я́ю**, *pf.* (*of* ~ива́ть²) (+*a.*, в+*p.*) to roll (in).

обва́рива|ть(ся), ю(сь), *impf. of* обвари́ть-(ся).

обвар|и́ть, ю́, ∼ишь, *pf.* (*of* ∼ивать) **1.** to pour boiling water over. **2.** to scald.

обвар|и́ться, ю́сь, ∼ишься, *pf.* (*of* ∼иваться) **1.** to scald oneself. **2.** *pass. of* ∼и́ть.

обвева́|ть, ю, *impf. of* обве́ять.

обве|ду́, дёшь, *see* ∼сти́.

обвез|ти́, у́, ёшь, *past* ∼, ∼ла́, *pf.* (*of* обвози́ть) **1.** to convey round. **2.** (*coll.*) to go the round of.

обвенча́|ть(ся), ю(сь), *pf. of* венча́ть(ся)¹.

обверн|у́ть, у́, ёшь, *pf.* (*of* обвёртывать) (+*i.*) to wrap up (in).

обвер|те́ть, чу́, ∼тишь, *pf.* (*of* ∼тывать) (+*i.*) to wrap up (in); о. ше́ю ша́рфом to wrap a scarf about one's neck.

обвёртыва|ть, ю, *impf. of* обверну́ть *and* обвертеть.

обве́с¹, а, *m.* false weight, short weight.

обве́с², а, *m.* о. мо́стика (*naut.*) bridge cloth, dodger.

обве́|сить, шу, сишь, *pf.* (*of* ∼шивать¹) to give short weight to; to cheat (*in weighing goods*).

обве|сти́, ду́, дёшь, *past* ∼л, ∼ла́, *pf.* (*of* обводи́ть) **1.** to lead round, take round; о. вокру́г па́льца (*fig., coll.*) to twist round one's little finger. **2.** (+*i.*) to encircle (with); to surround (with); о. рвом to surround with a ditch; о. взо́ром, глаза́ми to look round (at), take in (with one's eyes). **3.** to outline; о. чертёж ту́шью to outline a sketch in ink. **4.** (*sport*) to dodge; to get past.

обве́тр|енный, *p.p.p. of* ∼ить *and adj.* weather-beaten; chapped.

обве́тре|ть, ет, *pf.* to become weather--beaten.

обве́трива|ть(ся), ю(сь), *impf. of* обве́трить-(ся).

обве́тр|ить, ю, ишь, *pf.* (*of* ∼ивать) to expose to the wind; (*impers.*) мне ∼ило гу́бы my lips are chapped.

обве́тр|иться, юсь, ишься, *pf.* (*of* ∼иваться) to become weather-beaten.

обветша́лый, *adj.* decrepit, decayed; dilapidated.

обветша́|ть, ю, *pf. of* ветша́ть.

обве́ш|ать, аю, *pf.* (*of* ∼ивать²) (*coll.*; +*i.*) to hang round (with), cover (with).

обве́шива|ть¹, ю, *impf. of* обве́сить.

обве́шива|ть², ю, *impf. of* обве́шать.

обве́|ять, ю, ешь, *pf.* (*of* ∼вать) **1.** (+*i.*) to fan (with). **2.** (*agric.*) to winnow.

обвива́|ть(ся), ю(сь), *impf. of* обви́ть(ся).

обвине́ни|е, я, *n.* **1.** charge, accusation; пу́нкты ∼я (*leg.*) counts of an indictment; по ∼ю (в+*p.*) on a charge (of); возвести́ на кого́-н. о. (в+*p.*) to charge someone

(with); вы́нести о. to find guilty. **2.** (*leg.*) the prosecution (*as party in lawsuit*).

обвини́тел|ь, я, *m.* accuser; (*leg.*) prosecutor; госуда́рственный о. public prosecutor.

обвини́тельн|ый, *adj.* accusatory; о. акт (bill of) indictment; о. пригово́р verdict of 'guilty'; ∼ая речь speech for the prosecution, indictment.

обвин|и́ть, ю́, и́шь, *pf.* (*of* ∼я́ть) **1.** (в+*p.*) to accuse (of), charge (with). **2.** (*leg.*) to prosecute, indict.

обвиня́ем|ый, ого, *m.* (*leg.*) the accused; defendant.

обвин|я́ть, я́ю, *impf. of* ∼и́ть.

обвис|а́ть, а́ет, *impf.* (*of* ∼нуть) to hang, droop; to sag; to grow flabby.

обви́сл|ый, *adj.* (*coll.*) flabby; hanging; ∼ые усы́ drooping moustache.

обви́с|нуть, нет, *past* ∼, ∼ла, *pf. of* ∼а́ть.

обви́|ть, обовью́, обовьёшь, *past* ∼л, ∼ла́, ∼ло, *pf.* (*of* ∼ва́ть) to wind (round), entwine; о. ше́ю рука́ми to throw one's arms round someone's neck.

обви́|ться, обовью́сь, обовьёшься, *past* ∼лся, ∼ла́сь, *pf.* (*of* ∼ва́ться) to wind round, twine oneself round.

обво́д, а, *m.* **1.** enclosing, surrounding. **2.** outlining; о. су́дна (*naut., tech.*) line.

обводне́ни|е, я, *n.* **1.** irrigation. **2.** filling up (with water).

обводни́тельный, *adj.* irrigation.

обводн|и́ть, ю́, и́шь, *pf.* (*of* ∼я́ть) **1.** to irrigate. **2.** to fill up (with water).

обво́дный, *adj.* о. кана́л (*tech.*) by-pass.

обводн|я́ть, я́ю, *impf. of* ∼и́ть.

обвола́кива|ть(ся), ю(сь), *impf. of* обволо́чь(ся).

обволо́|чь, ку́, чёшь, ку́т, *past* ∼к, ∼кла́, *pf.* (*of* обвола́кивать) to cover; to envelope (*also fig.*).

обволо́|чься, ку́сь, чёшься, ку́тся, *past* ∼кся, ∼кла́сь, *pf.* (*of* обвола́киваться) (+*i.*; *coll.*) to become covered (with), enveloped (by, in).

обвора́жива|ть, ю, *impf. of* обворожи́ть.

обвор|ова́ть, у́ю, *pf.* (*of* ∼о́вывать) (*coll.*) to rob.

обворо́выва|ть, ю, *impf. of* обворова́ть.

обворожи́тел|ьный (∼ен, ∼ьна), *adj.* fascinating, charming, enchanting.

обворож|и́ть, у́, и́шь, *pf.* (*of* обвора́живать) to fascinate, charm, enchant.

обвя|за́ть¹, жу́, ∼жешь, *pf.* (*of* ∼зывать) to tie round; о. верёвкой to cord, rope; о. го́лову платко́м to tie a head-scarf round one's head.

обвя|за́ть², жу́, ∼жешь, *pf.* (*of* ∼зывать) to edge in chain-stitch.

обвя|за́ться, жу́сь, ∼жешься, *pf.* (*of*

~зыва́ться) **1.** (+*i.*) to tie round oneself; о. верёвкой to tie a rope round oneself. **2.** *pass. of* ~за́ть.

обвя́зыва|ть(ся), ю(сь), *impf. of* обвяза́ть(ся).

обга́|дить, жу, дишь, *pf.* (*of* ~живать) (*vulg.*) to shit on, shit up.

обга́жива|ть, ю, *impf. of* обга́дить.

обгла́дыва|ть, ю, *impf. of* обглода́ть.

обгло́д|анный, *p.p.p. of* ~а́ть; ~анная кость picked bone, bare bone.

обгло|да́ть, жу́, ~жешь, *pf.* (*of* обгла́дывать) to pick, gnaw round.

обгло́д|ок, ка, *m.* (*coll.*) bare bone.

обго́н, а, *m.* passing.

обгон|ю́, ~ишь, *see* обогна́ть.

обгоня́|ть, ю, *impf. of* обогна́ть.

обгоре́лый, *adj.* burnt; charred; scorched.

обгор|е́ть, ю́, и́шь, *pf.* to be scorched; to be burnt on the surface, receive surface burns.

обгрыз|а́ть, а́ю, *impf. of* ~ть.

обгрыз|ть, у́, ёшь, *past* ~, ~ла, *pf.* (*of* ~а́ть) to gnaw round.

обда|ва́ть(ся), ю́(сь), ёшь(ся), *impf. of* обда́ть(ся).

обд|а́ть, а́м, а́шь, а́ст, ади́м, ади́те, аду́т, *past* ~а́л, ~ала́, ~а́ло, *pf.* (*of* ~ава́ть) (+*i.*) **1.** to pour over; о. кого́-н. кипятко́м to pour boiling water over someone. **2.** (*fig.*) to seize, cover; о. взгля́дом презре́ния to fix with a look of scorn; меня́ ~а́ло хо́лодом (*impers.*) I came over cold.

обд|а́ться, а́мся, а́шься, а́стся, ади́мся, ади́тесь, аду́тся, *past* ~а́лся, ~ала́сь, *pf.* (*of* ~ава́ться) (+*i.*) to pour over oneself; о. кипятко́м to scald oneself.

обде́л|ать, аю, *pf.* (*of* ~ывать) **1.** to finish; to dress (*leather, stone, etc.*); о. драгоце́нные ка́мни to set precious stones. **2.** (*fig.*) to manage, arrange; о. те́му (*coll.*) to treat, handle a subject; о. свои́ дели́шки (*coll.*) to manage one's affairs with profit; он ма́стер о. свои́ дели́шки he is expert at taking care of number one. **3.** *euph.* = обга́дить.

обдел|и́ть, ю́, ~ишь, *pf.* (*of* ~я́ть) (+*a. and i.*) to do out of one's (fair) share (of); он ~и́л сестёр насле́дством he did his sisters out of their share of the legacy.

обде́лыва|ть, ю, *impf. of* обде́лать.

обдел|я́ть, я́ю, *impf. of* ~и́ть.

обдёрга|нный, *p.p.p. of* ~ть *and adj.* (*coll.*) shabby; ragged, in rags.

обдёрг|ать, аю, *pf.* (*of* ~ивать) (*coll.*) to tear down, pull down; to trim, even up.

обдёргива|ть, ю, *impf. of* обдёргать *and* обдёрнуть.

обдёргива|ться, юсь, *impf. of* обдёрнуться.

обдерн|и́ть, ю́, и́шь, *pf.* (*of* ~я́ть) to turf.

обдёр|нуть, ну, нешь, *pf.* (*of* ~гивать) to adjust, pull down (*dress, skirt, etc.*).

обдёр|нуться, нусь, нешься, *pf.* (*of* ~гиваться) (*coll.*) **1.** to adjust one's dress. **2.** (*cards*) to pull out the wrong card.

обдерн|я́ть, я́ю, *impf. of* ~и́ть.

обдер|у́, ёшь, *see* ободра́ть.

обдира́л|а, ы, *m.* (*coll.*) fleecer.

обдира́|ть, ю, *impf. of* ободра́ть.

обди́р|ка, и, *f.* **1.** peeling; hulling; skinning, flaying. **2.** (*dial.*) groats.

обди́рный, *adj.* peeled; hulled.

обдува́л|а, ы, *m.* (*coll.*) cheat, trickster.

обдува́|ть, ю, *impf. of* обду́ть.

обду́манно, *adv.* after careful consideration; deliberately (= after deliberation).

обду́манност|ь, и, *f.* deliberation; deliberateness; careful planning.

обду́ман|ный **1.** (~, ~а), *p.p.p. of* обду́мать. **2.** (~, ~на), *adj.* well-considered, well-weighed, carefully thought out; с зара́нее ~ным наме́рением deliberately; (*leg.*) of malice prepense.

обду́м|ать, аю, *pf.* (*of* ~ывать) to consider, think over, weigh.

обду́мыва|ть, ю, *impf. of* обду́мать.

обду́|ть¹, ю, ешь, *pf.* (*of* ~ва́ть) to blow (on, round).

обду́|ть², ю, ешь, *pf.* (*of* ~ва́ть) (*coll.*) to cheat; to fool, dupe.

о́бе, *see* о́ба.

обега́|ть, ю, *pf.* (*of* обега́ть) **1.** to run (all over, all round). **2.** to run round (to see); за неде́лю до отъе́зда нам удало́сь о. всех знако́мых in the week before our departure we managed to look in on all our acquaintances.

обега́|ть, ю, *impf. of* обе́гать *and* обежа́ть.

обе́д, а, *m.* **1.** dinner; зва́ный о. dinner-party; сесть за о. to sit down to dinner; звать к ~у to ask to dinner. **2.** dinner-time (= mid-day); пе́ред ~ом before dinner; in the morning; по́сле ~а after dinner; in the afternoon.

обе́да|ть, ю, *impf.* (*of* по~) to have dinner, dine.

обе́д|енный¹, *adj. of* ~; ~енное вре́мя dinner time; о. переры́в lunch hour, lunch break; о. стол dinner table.

обе́д|енный², *adj. of* ~ня.

обедне́|вший, *past part. act. of* ~ть *and adj.* impoverished.

обедне́|лый, *adj.* (*coll.*) = ~вший.

обедне́ни|е, я, *n.* impoverishment.

обедне́|ть, ю, *pf. of* бедне́ть.

обедн|и́ть, ю́, и́шь, *pf.* (*of* ~я́ть) to impoverish.

обе́д|ня, ни, *g. pl.* ~ен, *f.* (*eccl.*) mass; испо́ртить ~ню кому́-н. (*fig., coll.*) to spoil someone's game, put a spoke in someone's wheel.

обедн|я́ть, я́ю, *impf. of* ~и́ть.

обе|жа́ть, гу́, жи́шь, гу́т, *pf.* (*of* ~га́ть) 1. to run (over, round). 2. to run (past). 3. (*sport*) to outrun, pass.

обезбо́ливани|е, я, *n.* anaesthetization.

обезбо́лива|ть, ю, *impf. of* обезбо́лить.

обезбо́лива|ющий, *pres. part. act. of* ~ть; ~ющее сре́дство anaesthetic.

обезбо́л|ить, ю, ишь, *pf.* (*of* ~ивать) to anaesthetize.

обезво́|дить, жу, дишь, *pf.* (*of* ~живать) to dehydrate.

обезво́|женный, *p.p.p. of* ~дить *and adj.* dehydrated.

обезво́жива|ть, ю, *impf. of* обезво́дить.

обезвре́|дить, жу, дишь, *pf.* (*of* ~живать) to render harmless; to neutralize.

обезвре́жива|ть, ю, *impf. of* обезвре́дить.

обезгла́в|ить, лю, ишь, *pf.* (*of* ~ливать) 1. to behead, decapitate. 2. (*fig.*) to deprive of a head, of a leader.

обезгла́влива|ть, ю, *impf. of* обезгла́вить.

обезде́неже|ть, ю, *pf.* (*coll.*) to run short of money.

обездо́л|енный, *p.p.p. of* ~ить *and adj.* unfortunate, hapless.

обездо́лива|ть, ю, *impf. of* обездо́лить.

обездо́л|ить, ю, ишь, *pf.* (*of* ~ивать) to deprive of one's share.

обезжи́р|енный, *p.p.p. of* ~ить *and adj.* fatless; skimmed.

обезжи́рива|ть, ю, *impf. of* обезжи́рить.

обезжи́р|ить, ю, ишь, *pf.* (*of* ~ивать) to deprive of fat, remove fat (from); to skim.

обеззара́жива|ть, ю, *impf. of* обеззара́зить.

обеззара́жива|ющий, *p.p.p. of* ~ть *and adj.* disinfectant.

обеззара́|зить, жу, зишь, *pf.* (*of* ~живать) to disinfect.

обеззема́л|енный, *p.p.p. of* ~ить *and adj.* landless, deprived of land.

обеззема́лива|ть, ю, *impf. of* обеззема́лить.

обеззема́л|ить, ю, ишь, *pf.* (*of* ~ивать) to dispossess of land.

обеззу́бе|ть, ю, *pf.* (*coll.*) to lose one's teeth.

обезле́си|ть, шь, *pf.* to deforest.

обезли́чени|е, я, *n.* 1. depersonalization. 2. depriving of personal responsibility; removal of personal responsibility (from).

обезли́ч|енный, *p.p.p. of* ~ить *and adj.* 1. pooled (*of workshop tools, etc.: assigned to and made the responsibility of no one individual user*). 2. impersonal, multiple, group (*in which no one individual bears responsibility*); ~енное руково́дство group management. 3. (*econ., fin.*) not owned by a specified person; ~енная облига́ция (*fin.*) bearer bond.

обезли́чива|ть, ю, *impf. of* обезли́чить.

обезли́ч|ить, у, ишь, *pf.* (*of* ~ивать) 1. to deprive of individuality, depersonalize. 2. to deprive of personal responsibility; to do away with personal responsibility (for). 3. (*econ., fin.*) to remove from ownership by a specified person; to make available to bearer unspecified.

обезли́чк|а, и, *f.* lack of personal responsibility; (*railways*) multiple manning.

обезлю́де|ть, ю, *pf.* to become depopulated.

обезобра́жива|ть, ю, *impf. of* обезобра́зить.

обезобра́|зить, жу, зишь, *pf.* (*of* ~живать *and* безобра́зить) to disfigure.

обезопа́|сить, шу, сишь, *pf.* (от) to secure (against).

обезопа́|ситься, шусь, сишься, *pf.* (от) secure oneself, make oneself secure (against).

обезору́жива|ть, ю, *impf. of* обезору́жить.

обезору́ж|ить, у, ишь, *pf.* (*of* ~ивать) to disarm (*also fig.*).

обезу́ме|ть, ю, *pf.* to lose one's senses, lose one's head; о. от испу́га to become panic-stricken.

обезья́н|а, ы, *f.* monkey; ape.

обезья́н|ий, *adj. of* ~a; (*zool.*) simian; (*fig.*) ape-like.

обезья́нник, а, *m.* monkey-house.

обезья́нничань|е, я, *n.* (*coll.*) aping.

обезья́ннича|ть, ю, *impf.* (*of* с~) (*coll.*) to ape.

обел|и́ть, ю́, и́шь, *pf.* (*of* ~я́ть) (*fig.*) to whitewash; to vindicate; to prove the innocence (of).

обел|и́ться, ю́сь, и́шься, *pf.* (*of* ~я́ться) vindicate oneself, obtain recognition of one's innocence.

обел|я́ть(ся), я́ю(сь), *impf. of* ~и́ть(ся).

обер- 1. (*in designations of holders of rank or office*) chief-. 2. (*coll., pejor.*) arch-.

оберега́|ть(ся), ю(сь), *impf. of* обере́чь(ся).

обере́|чь, гу́, жёшь, гу́т, *past* ~г, ~гла́, *pf.* (*of* ~га́ть) (от) to guard (against), protect (from).

обере́|чься, гу́сь, жёшься, гу́тся, *past* ~гся, ~гла́сь, *pf.* (*of* ~га́ться) 1. (от) to guard oneself (from, against), protect oneself (from). 2. *pass. of* ~чь.

обер-конду́ктор, а, *m.* chief guard (*of a train*).

оберн|у́ть, у́, ёшь, *pf.* (*of* обора́чивать) 1. (*impf. also* обёртывать) to wind (round), twist (round); о. вокру́г па́льца (*coll.*) to twist round one's little finger. 2. (*impf. also* обёртывать) to wrap up. 3. (*impf. also* обёртывать) to turn; о. лицо́ (к) to turn one's face (towards); о. в свою́ по́льзу (*fig.*) to turn to account, turn to advantage. 4. (*coll.*) to overturn, upturn. 5. (*comm.*) to turn over. 6. (*coll.*) to work through, go through.

оберн|у́ться, у́сь, ёшься, *pf.* (*of* обора́чиваться) **1.** (*impf. also* обёртываться) to turn; о. лицо́м to turn one's head. **2.** (*impf. also* обёртываться) to turn out; собы́тия ~у́лись ина́че, чем мы ожида́ли events turned out otherwise than we expected. **3.** (*coll.*) to (go and) come back; я ~у́сь за два часа́ I shall be back in two hours. **4.** (*coll.*) to manage, get by. **5.** (*impf. also* обёртываться) (+*i. or* в+*a.*) to turn into, become (*also fig.*); о. вампи́ром to turn into a vampire.

о́бер-прокуро́р, а, *m.* (*hist.*) chief procurator (*title of official in charge of Holy Synod set up in 1721*).

обёртк|а, и, *f.* wrapper; envelope; (*of book*) (*obs.*) dust-jacket, cover.

оберто́н, а, *m.* (*mus.*) overtone.

обёрт|очный, *adj. of* ~ка; ~очная бума́га wrapping paper.

обёртыва|ть(ся), ю(сь), *impf. of* оберну́ть(ся).

обескро́в|ить, лю, ишь, *pf.* (*of* ~ливать) to drain of blood; to bleed white; (*fig.*) to render lifeless.

обескро́в|ленный, *p.p.p. of* ~ить *and adj.* bloodless; (*fig.*) anaemic, lifeless.

обескро́влива|ть, ю, *impf. of* обескро́вить.

обескура́жива|ть, ю, *impf. of* обескура́жить.

обескура́ж|ить, у, ишь, *pf.* (*coll.*) to discourage, dishearten; to dismay.

обеспа́мяте|ть, ю, *pf.* **1.** to lose one's memory. **2.** to lose consciousness, become unconscious, faint.

обеспе́чени|е, я, *n.* **1.** securing, guaranteeing; ensuring. **2.** (+*i.*) providing (with), provision (of, with). **3.** guarantee; security (= pledge). **4.** security (= material maintenance); safeguard(s); социа́льное о. social security. **5.** (*mil.*) security; protection.

обеспе́ченност|ь, и, *f.* **1.** (+*i.*) being provided (with), provision (of, with); о. школ уче́бниками the provision of schools with text-books. **2.** (material) security.

обеспе́ч|енный, *p.p.p. of* ~ить *and adj.* well--to-do; well provided for.

обеспе́чива|ть, ю, *impf. of* обеспе́чить.

обеспе́ч|ить, у, ишь, *pf.* (*of* ~ивать) **1.** to provide for. **2.** (+*i.*) to provide (with), guarantee supply (of); о. экспеди́цию оборудованием to provide an expedition with equipment. **3.** to secure, guarantee; to ensure, assure. **4.** (от) to safeguard (from), protect (from).

обеспло́|дить, жу, дишь, *pf.* (*of* ~живать) to sterilize; to render barren.

обеспло́жива|ть, ю, *impf. of* обеспло́дить.

обеспоко́|ить(ся), ю(сь), *pf. of* беспоко́ить(ся) 1.

обесси́ле|ть, ю, *pf.* to grow weak, lose one's

strength; to collapse, break down.

обесси́лива|ть, ю, *impf. of* обесси́лить.

обесси́л|ить, ю, ишь, *pf.* (*of* ~ивать) to weaken.

обессла́в|ить, лю, ишь, *pf.* (*of* бессла́вить) to defame.

обессме́р|тить, чу, тишь, *pf.* to immortalize.

обессу́д|ить, *pf. now only used in imp.* не ~ь(те) (please) don't take it amiss, (please) don't be angry.

обесто́чива|ть, ю, *impf. of* обесто́чить.

обесто́ч|ить, у ишь, *pf.* (*of* ~ивать) (*electr.*) to de-energise.

обесцве́|тить, чу, тишь, *pf.* (*of* ~чивать) to decolo(u)rize, deprive of colour; (*fig.*) to render colourless, tone down.

обесцве́|титься, чусь, тишься, *pf.* (*of* ~чиваться) to become colourless (*also fig.*).

обесцве́чива|ть(ся), ю(сь), *impf. of* обесцве́тить(ся).

обесце́нени|е, я, *n.* depreciation; loss of value.

обесце́н|енный, *p.p.p. of* ~ить *and adj.* depreciated.

обесце́нива|ть(ся), ю(сь), *impf. of* обесце́нить(ся).

обесце́н|ить, ю, ишь, *pf.* (*of* ~ивать) to depreciate, cheapen.

обесце́н|иться, юсь, ишься, *pf.* (*of* ~ивать ся) **1.** (*intrans.*) to depreciate, cheapen. **2** *pass. of* ~ить.

обесче́|стить, щу, стишь, *pf. of* бесче́стить.

обе́т, а, *m.* (*rhet.*) vow, promise.

обето́ванн|ый, *adj.* ~ая земля́, о. край the Promised Land.

обеща́ни|е, я, *n.* promise; дать, сдержа́ть о. to give, keep a promise (one's word).

обеща́|ть, ю, *impf. and pf.* to promise.

обеща́|ться, юсь, *impf. and pf.* (*coll.*) **1.** to promise. **2.** to give (exchange) a promise (*sc.* to marry).

обжа́ловани|е, я, *n.* appeal; о. пригово́ра (*leg.*) appealing against a sentence.

обжа́л|овать, ую, *pf.* (*leg.*) to lodge a complaint (against); to appeal (against).

обжа́рива|ть, ю, *impf. of* обжа́рить.

обжа́р|ить, ю, ишь, *pf.* (*of* ~ивать) (*cul.*) to fry on both sides, all over.

обжа́ть[1], обожму́, обожмёшь, *pf. of* (обжима́ть) to press out; to wring out.

обжа́ть[2], обожну́, обожнёшь, *pf. of* обжина́ть (*dial.*) to reap (*the whole of*).

обже́чь, обожгу́, обожжёшь, обожгу́т, *past* обжёг, обожгла́, *pf.* (*of* обжига́ть) **1.** to burn, scorch; о. себе́ па́льцы to burn one's fingers (*also fig.*). **2.** to bake (*bricks, etc.*); to calcine (*lime*).

обже́чься, обожгу́сь, обожжёшься, обожгу́тся, *past* обжёгся, обожгла́сь, *pf.* **1.** (+*i. or* на+*p.*) to burn oneself (on, with); о.

горя́чим ча́ем to scald oneself with hot tea; о. крапи́вой to be stung by a nettle; обжёгшись на молоке́, ста́нешь дуть и на́ во́ду (*prov.*) a burnt child dreads the fire. **2.** (*fig.*, *coll.*) to burn one's fingers.

обжива́|ть(ся), ю(сь), *impf. of* обжи́ть(ся).

обжи́г, а, *m.* (*tech.*) kilning, glazing; (*of clay*) baking; (*of ores*) roasting; (*of lime*) calcining.

обжига́л|а, ы, *m.* (*tech.*) kiln-worker.

обжига́тельн|ый, *adj.* (*tech.*) glazing; baking; roasting; ~ая печь kiln.

обжига́|ть(ся), ю(сь), *impf. of* обже́чь(ся).

обжи́м, а, *m.* (*tech.*) **1.** pressing out. **2.** cap tool, snap tool, riveting set.

обжима́|ть, ю, *impf. of* обжа́ть¹.

обжи́м|ка, ки, *f.* (*tech.*) = ~; пла́тье в ~ку (*coll.*) tight-fitting dress.

обжи́мный, *adj.* (*tech.*) pressing, blooming; о. стан blooming mill, roughing mill.

обжина́|ть, ю, *impf. of* обжа́ть².

обжира́|ться, юсь, *impf. of* обожра́ться.

обжит|о́й (*and* ~ый), *p.p.p. of* ~ь.

обж|и́ть, иву́, иве́шь, *past* ~и́л, ~ила́, ~и́ло, *pf.* (*of* ~ива́ть) (*coll.*) to render habitable.

обж|и́ться, иву́сь, иве́шься, *past* ~и́лся, ~ила́сь, *pf.* (*of* ~ива́ться) (*coll.*) to make oneself at home, feel at home.

обжо́р|а, ы, *m. and f.* (*coll.*) glutton, gormandizer.

обжо́рлив|ый (~, ~а), *adj.* gluttonous.

обжо́рный, *adj.* о. ряд (*obs.*) refreshment stall (*in market*).

обжо́рств|о, а, *n.* gluttony.

обжу́лива|ть, ю, *impf. of* обжу́лить.

обжу́л|ить, ю, ишь, *pf.* (*coll.*) to cheat, swindle.

обзаведе́ни|е, я, *n.* **1.** (+*i.*) providing (with), fitting out. **2.** (*coll.*) establishment; (*collect.*) fittings, appointments, paraphernalia.

обзаве|сти́сь, ду́сь, дёшься, *past* ~лся, ~ла́сь, *pf.* (*of* обзаводи́ться) (+*i.*; *coll.*) to provide oneself (with); to set up; о. семьёй to settle down to married life; о. хозя́йством to start a home of one's own, set up house.

обзаво|ди́ться, жу́сь, ~дишься, *impf. of* обзавести́сь.

обзо́р, а, *m.* **1.** survey, review. **2.** (*mil.*) field of view.

обзо́р|ный, *adj. of* ~; ~ная ле́кция, ~ная статья́ survey.

обзыва́|ть, ю, *impf. of* обозва́ть.

обива́|ть, ю, *impf. of* оби́ть; о. (все) поро́ги (*fig.*) to leave no stone unturned.

оби́вк|а, и, *f.* **1.** upholstering. **2.** upholstery.

обивно́й, *adj.* for upholstery.

оби́д|а, ы, *f.* **1.** offence, injury, insult; быть на кого́-н. в оби́де to bear a grudge

against someone; затаи́ть ~у to bear a grudge, nurse a grievance; проглоти́ть ~у to swallow an insult; не дава́ть себя́ в ~у to (be able to) stick up for oneself; не в ~у будь ска́зано no offence meant. **2.** (*coll.*) annoying thing, nuisance; кака́я о.! what a nuisance!

оби́|деть, жу, дишь, *pf.* (*of* ~жа́ть) **1.** to offend; to hurt (the feelings of), wound. **2.** to hurt; to do damage (to); му́хи не ~дит (*fig.*) he would not harm a fly. **3.** (+*i.*; *following* Бог, приро́да, *etc.*) to stint, begrudge; приро́да не ~дела его́ тала́нтом he has plenty of natural ability.

оби́|деться, жусь, дишься, *pf.* (*of* ~жа́ться) (на+*a.*) to take offence (at), take umbrage (at); to feel hurt (by), resent.

оби́д|ный (~ен, ~на), *adj.* **1.** offensive; мне ~но I feel hurt, it pains me. **2.** (*coll.*) annoying, tiresome; ~но (*impers.*) it is a pity, it is a nuisance; ~но, что мы опозда́ли it is a pity that we were late.

оби́дчивост|ь, и, *f.* touchiness, susceptibility (*to offence*), sensitivity.

оби́дчив|ый (~, ~а), *adj.* touchy, susceptible (*to offence*), sensitive.

оби́дчик, а, *m.* (*coll.*) offender.

обижа́|ть, ю, *impf. of* оби́деть.

обижа́|ться, юсь, *impf. of* оби́деться; не ~йтесь don't be offended.

оби́|женный, *p.p.p. of* ~деть *and adj.* offended, hurt, aggrieved; быть ~жен (на+*a.*) to have a grudge (against); у него́ был о. вид he had an aggrieved air, he looked offended; о. Бо́гом, о. приро́дой (*joc.*) not over-blessed (with talents); ill-starred.

оби́ли|е, я, *n.* abundance, plenty; жить в ~и to live in comfort.

оби́л|овать, ую, *impf.* (+*i.*; *obs.*) to abound (in).

оби́л|ьный (~ен, ~ьна), *adj.* abundant, plentiful; (+*i.*) rich (in); ~ьное угоще́ние lavish entertainment; о. урожа́й bumper crop; день, о. происше́ствиями an eventful day.

обину́ясь, *only in phrase* не о. without a moment's hesitation.

обиня́к, а́, *m. only in phrases* говори́ть ~о́м, ~а́ми to beat about the bush; говори́ть без ~о́в to speak plainly, speak in plain terms.

обира́|ть, ю, *impf. of* обобра́ть.

обита́ем|ый (~, ~а), *adj.* inhabited.

обита́тел|ь, я, *m.* inhabitant; resident; (*of a house*) inmate.

обита́|ть, ю, *impf.* (в+*p.*) to live (in), dwell (in), reside (in).

оби́тел|ь, и, *f.* **1.** cloister. **2.** (*fig.*; *obs.*) abode, dwelling-place.

обѝтель|скій, *adj. of* ~.

обѝ|ть, обобью, обобьёшь, *pf.* (*of* ~ва́ть)
1. (с+*g.*) to knock (off, down from); о.
плоды́ с я́блони to knock down fruit from
an apple-tree. **2.** (+*i.*) to upholster (with),
cover (with); о. гвоздя́ми to stud; о. желе́-
зом to bind with iron. **3.** to wear out (*the
surface of, at the edges*); о. подо́л ю́бки to
wear the hem of a skirt; о. штукату́рку to
chip off plaster.

обихо́д, а, *m.* **1.** custom, use, practice;
повседне́вный о. everyday practice; предме́-
ты дома́шнего ~a household articles;
пусти́ть в о. to bring into (general) use;
вы́йти из ~a to be no longer in use, fall
into disuse. **2.** (*eccl.*) ordinary; rules of
church singing.

обихо́д|ный (~ен, ~на), *adj.* everyday;
~ное выраже́ние colloquial expression.

обка́лыва|ть, ю, *impf. of* обколо́ть.

обка́п|ать, аю, *pf.* (*of* ~ывать¹) (+*i.*) to let
drops (of) fall on; to cover with drops (of).

обка́пыва|ть¹, ю, *impf. of* обка́пать.

обка́пыва|ть², ю, *impf. of* обкопа́ть.

обка́рмлива|ть, ю, *impf. of* обкорми́ть.

обкат|а́ть, а́ю, *pf.* (*of* ~ывать) **1.** to roll.
2. to roll smooth (*a road surface, etc.*). **3.**
(*tech.*) to run in (*a new vehicle, etc.*).

обка́тк|а, и, *f.* (*tech.*) running in.

обка́тыва|ть, ю, *impf. of* обката́ть.

обкла́дк|а, и, *f.* (*in var. senses*) facing; о.
дёрном turfing.

обкла́дыва|ть, ю, *impf. of* обложи́ть.

обкол|о́ть, ю́, ~ешь, *pf.* (*of* обка́лывать)
1. to cut away (ice, etc.). **2.** to prick all
over.

обко́м, а, *m.* (*abbr. of* областно́й комите́т)
oblast committee.

обкопа́|ть, ю, *pf.* (*of* обка́пывать²) (*coll.*)
to dig round.

обкорм|и́ть, лю́, ~ишь, *pf.* (*of* обка́рмли-
вать) to overfeed.

обкорна́|ть, ю, *pf. of* корна́ть.

обкра́дыва|ть, ю, *impf. of* обокра́сть.

обку́р|енный, *p.p.p. of* ~ить *and adj.* ~енная
тру́бка seasoned pipe; ~енные па́льцы
tobacco-stained fingers.

обку́рива|ть, ю, *impf. of* обкури́ть.

обкур|и́ть, ю́, ~ишь, *pf.* (*of* ~ивать) **1.** о.
тру́бку to season a pipe. **2.** to fumigate.
3. (*coll.*) to envelope with (tobacco) smoke;
to stain with tobacco.

обкус|а́ть, а́ю, *pf.* (*of* ~ывать) to bite
round; to nibble.

обку́сыва|ть, ю, *impf. of* обкуса́ть.

обла́в|а, ы, *f.* **1.** (*hunting*) battue; beating
up. **2.** (*fig.*) (*police*) raid, swoop; cordon;
cordoning off; round-up.

облага́емый, *adj.* taxable.

облага́|ть, ю, *impf. of* обложи́ть.

облага́|ться, юсь, *impf.* (*of* обложи́ться) о.
нало́гом to be liable to tax, be taxable.

облагоде́тельств|овать, ую, *pf.* (*obs. or
iron.*) to do a great favour.

облагора́жива|ть, ю, *impf. of* облагоро́дить.

облагоро́|дить, жу, дишь, *pf.* (*of* облаго-
ра́живать) to ennoble.

облада́ни|е, я, *n.* possession.

облада́тел|ь, я, *m.* possessor.

облада́|ть, ю, *impf.* (+*i.*) to possess, be
possessed (of); о. хоро́шим здоро́вьем to
enjoy good health; о. пра́вом to have the
right; о. больши́м тала́нтом to have great
talents, be very talented.

обла́|зить, жу, зишь, *pf.* (*coll.*) to climb
round, climb all over.

о́блак|о, а, *pl.* ~а́, ~о́в, *n.* cloud; кучевы́е
~а́ cumuli; пери́стые ~а́ cirri; сло́истые
~а́ strati; быть, носи́ться в ~а́х (*fig.*) to
live in the clouds; свали́ться с ~о́в (*fig.*) to
appear from nowhere.

обла́мыва|ть(ся), ю(сь), *impf. of* облома́ть-
(ся).

обла́п|ить, лю, ишь, *pf.* (*of* ~ливать) (*coll.*)
to hug.

обла́плива|ть, ю, *impf. of* обла́пить.

облапо́шива|ть, ю, *impf. of* облапо́шить.

облапо́ш|ить, у, ишь, *pf.* (*of* ~ивать) (*coll.*)
to cheat, swindle.

обласка́|ть, ю, *pf.* to treat with affection,
display much kindness towards.

областно́й, *adj.* **1.** oblast; provincial;
regional. **2.** (*ling.*) dialectal; regional.

о́бласт|ь, и, *g. pl.* ~е́й, *f.* **1.** (*designation of
administrative division of U.S.S.R.*) oblast;
province; прие́хать из ~и to come from
oblast (*fig., coll.* = from administrative
centre of oblast). **2.** region, district; belt;
о. вечнозелёных расте́ний evergreen belt;
озёрная о. lake district. **3.** (*anat., med.*)
tract; region. **4.** (*fig.*) province, field,
sphere, realm, domain; о. микробиоло́гии
the field of microbiology; о. мифоло́гии
the realm of mythology.

обла́тк|а, и, *f.* **1.** (*eccl.*) wafer, host. **2.**
(*pharm.*) capsule. **3.** paper seal.

обла́т|очный, *adj. of* ~ка.

облач|а́ть(ся), а́ю(сь), *impf. of* ~и́ть(ся).

облаче́ни|е, я, *n.* **1.** (в+*a.*) robing (in).
2. (*eccl.*) vestments, robes.

облач|и́ть, у́, и́шь, *pf.* (*of* ~а́ть) (в+*a.*)
1. (*eccl.*) to robe (in). **2.** (*rhet. or coll., joc.*)
to array (in), get up (in).

облач|и́ться, у́сь, и́шься, *pf.* (*of* ~а́ться)
1. (*eccl.*) to robe, put on robes. **2.** (*rhet. or
coll., joc.*) to array oneself.

облачк|о́, а́, *pl.* ~а́, ~о́в, *n. dim. of* о́блако.

о́блачност|ь, и, *f.* **1.** cloudiness. **2.** (*meteor.*)
cloud conditions; о. в де́сять ба́ллов ten
tenths cloud.

о́блач|ный (~ен, ~на), *adj.* cloudy.

обла́|ять, ю, ешь, *pf.* (*coll.*) 1. to bark at. 2. (*fig.*) to swear at.

облега́|ть, ю, *impf.* 1. *impf. of* обле́чь¹. 2. (*of clothes*) to fit tightly; о. фигу́ру to outline the figure.

облега́|ющий, *pres. part. act. of* ~ть *and adj.* tight-fitting.

облегч|а́ть(ся), а́ю(сь), *impf. of* ~и́ть(ся).

облегче́ни|е, я, *n.* 1. facilitation. 2. relief; вздохну́ть с ~ем to heave a sigh of relief.

облегч|и́ть, у́, и́шь, *pf.* (*of* ~а́ть) 1. to facilitate. 2. to lighten. 3. to relieve; to alleviate; to mitigate; (*leg.*) to commute; о. ду́шу to relieve one's mind.

облегч|и́ться, у́сь, и́шься, *pf.* (*of* ~а́ться) 1. to be relieved, find relief. 2. to become easier; to become lighter. 3. (*coll., euph.*) to relieve oneself.

обледене́лый, *adj.* ice-covered.

обледене́ни|е, я, *n.* icing(-over); перио́д ~я Ice Age.

обледене́|ть, ю, *pf.* to ice over, become covered with ice.

облез|а́ть, а́ет, *impf. of* ~ть.

обле́зл|ый, *adj.* (*coll.*) shabby, bare; ~ая ко́шка mangy cat.

обле́з|ть, ет, *past* ~, ~ла, *pf.* (*of* ~а́ть) (*coll.*) 1. (*of fur, etc.*) to come out, come off. 2. to grow bare (*of fur, feathers, etc.*); to grow mangy. 3. (*of paintwork, etc.*) to peel off.

облека́|ть(ся), ю(сь), *impf. of* обле́чь²(ся).

обле́нива|ться, юсь, *impf. of* облени́ться.

облен|и́ться, ю́сь, ~ишься, *pf.* (*of* ~ива́ться) to grow lazy.

облеп|и́ть, лю́, ~ишь, *pf.* (*of* ~ля́ть) 1. to stick (to); (*fig.*) to cling (to); to surround, throng; нас ~и́ла ку́ча мальчи́шек we were surrounded by a swarm of small boys. 2. (+*a. and i.*) to paste all over (with), plaster (with); о. сте́ну объявле́ниями to plaster a wall with notices.

облепля́|ть, ю, *impf. of* облепи́ть.

облесе́ни|е, я, *n.* afforestation.

обле|си́ть, шу́, си́шь, *pf.* to afforest.

облёт, а, *m.* buzzing (*by aircraft*).

облет|а́ть¹, а́ю, *impf. of* ~е́ть.

облет|а́ть², а́ю, *pf.* (*of* ~ывать) 1. to fly (all round, all over); мы ~а́ли всю Евро́пу we have flown all over Europe; она́ ~а́ла всех подру́г (*fig., coll.*) she flew round to all her girl-friends. 2. to test (*an aircraft*).

обле|те́ть, чу́, ти́шь, *pf.* (*of* ~та́ть¹) 1. (+*a. or* вокру́г) to fly (round). 2. (*of news, rumours, etc.*) to spread (round, all over); за полчаса́ весть о побе́де ~те́ла го́род in half an hour the news of the victory had spread round the town. 3. (*of leaves*) to fall.

облётыва|ть, ю, *impf. of* облета́ть².

облеч|ённый, *p.p.p. of* ~ь² *and adj.* 1. о.

вла́стью invested with power. 2. (*ling.*) ~ённое ударе́ние circumflex accent (*as mark of perispomenon or properispomenon stress in ancient Greek*).

обл|е́чь¹, я́гу, я́жешь, я́гут, *past* ~ёг, ~егла́, *pf.* (*of* ~ега́ть) to cover, surround, envelop (*also fig.*); ту́чи ~егли́ го́ру rain-clouds enveloped the mountain.

обле́|чь², ку́, чёшь, ку́т, *past* ~к, ~кла́, *pf.* (*of* ~ка́ть) (+*a.* в+*a. or* +*a. and i.*) to clothe (in); to invest (with), vest (in); (*fig.*) to wrap (in), shroud (in); о. полномо́чиями to invest with authority, commission; о. та́йной to shroud in mystery; о. свою́ мысль непоня́тными слова́ми to wrap one's idea in unintelligible words; о. кого́-н. дове́рием to express confidence in someone.

обле́|чься, ку́сь, чёшься, ку́тся, *past* ~кся, ~кла́сь, *pf.* (*of* ~ка́ться) (в+*a.*) to clothe oneself (in), dress oneself (in); (*fig.*) to take the form (of), assume the shape (of).

облива́ни|е, я, *n.* 1. spilling (over), pouring (over). 2. shower-bath; sponge-down.

облива́|ть, ю, *impf. of* обли́ть.

облива́|ться, юсь, *impf. of* обли́ться; се́рдце у меня́ кро́вью ~ется my heart bleeds.

обли́вк|а, и, *f.* 1. glazing. 2. glaze.

обливно́й, *adj.* glazed.

облигац|ио́нный, *adj. of* ~ия.

облига́ци|я, и, *f.* (*fin.*) bond, debenture.

обли́з|анный, *p.p.p. of* ~а́ть *and adj.* (*fig.*) smooth.

обли|за́ть, жу́, ~жешь, *pf.* (*of* ~зывать) to lick (all over); to lick clean; па́льчики ~жешь (*fig., coll.*) (*sc.* it is, it will be) a real treat.

обли|за́ться, жу́сь, ~жешься, *pf.* (*of* ~зываться) 1. to smack one's lips (*also fig.*). 2. (*of an animal*) to lick itself.

обли́зыва|ть, ю, *impf. of* облиза́ть; о. гу́бы (*fig., coll.*) to smack one's lips.

обли́зыва|ться, юсь, *impf. of* облиза́ться.

о́блик, а, *m.* 1. look, aspect, appearance. 2. (*fig.*) cast of mind, temper.

облиня́|ть, ю, *pf.* (*coll.*) 1. to fade, lose colour (*also fig.*). 2. to moult, lose hair *or* feathers.

облип|а́ть, а́ю, *impf. of* ~нуть.

обли́п|нуть, ну, нешь, *past* ~, ~ла, *pf.* (*of* ~а́ть) (+*i.*) to become stuck (in, with).

облисполко́м, а, *m.* (*abbr. of* областно́й исполни́тельный комите́т) oblast executive committee.

о́блит|ый (~, ~а́, ~о), *and* обли́тый (~, ~а́, ~о), *p.p.p. of* обли́ть; (*fig.*; +*i.*) covered (by), enveloped (in); о. све́том луны́ bathed in moonlight.

обл|и́ть, оболью́, обольёшь, *past* ~и́л, ~ила́, ~и́ло *and* ~и́л, ~ила́, ~и́ло, *pf.* (*of* ~ива́ть) 1. (*p.p.p.* ~и́тый) to pour (over), sluice (over); to spill (over); о. ска́терть вино́м to spill wine over the table-cloth; о. презре́нием (*fig.*) to pour contempt (on); о. гря́зью, о. помо́ями (*fig.*, *coll.*) to fling mud (at). **2.** (*p.p.p.* ∼и́тый) to glaze.

обли́|ться, оболью́сь, обольёшься, *past* ∼лся, ∼ла́сь, ∼ло́сь *and* ∼ло́сь, *pf.* (*of* ∼ва́ться) **1.** to have a shower-bath, douche oneself; to sponge down; о. холо́дной водо́й to have a cold shower. **2.** to pour over oneself, spill over oneself; о. по́том to be bathed in sweat; о. слеза́ми to melt into tears. **3.** *pass. of* ∼ть.

облиц|ева́ть, у́ю, у́ешь, *pf.* (*of* ∼о́вывать) (+*a. and i.*) to face (with), revet (with).

облицо́вк|а, и, *f.* facing, revetment; lining, coating.

облицо́в|очный, *adj. of* ∼ка; о. кирпи́ч facing brick, decorative tile.

облицо́выва|ть, ю, *impf. of* облицева́ть.

облич|а́ть, а́ю, *impf.* (*of* ∼и́ть) **1.** to expose, unmask, denounce. **2.** (*impf. only*) to reveal, display, manifest; to point (to).

обличе́ни|е, я, *n.* exposure, unmasking, denunciation.

обличи́тел|ь, я, *m.* exposer, unmasker, denouncer.

обличи́тельн|ый, *adj.* denunciatory; ∼ая речь, ∼ая статья́ diatribe, tirade.

облич|и́ть, у́, и́шь, *pf. of* ∼а́ть.

обли́чь|е, я, *n.* **1.** (*coll.*) face; **2.** aspect, appearance (*also fig.*).

облобыза́|ть, ю, *pf.* (*obs., joc.*) to kiss.

обложе́ни|е, я, *n.* **1.** taxation; assessment, rating. **2.** (*mil.; obs.*) investment.

обло́ж|енный, *p.p.p. of* ∼и́ть; о. язы́к (*med.*) furred tongue.

облож|и́ть, у́, ∼ишь, *pf.* **1.** (*impf.* обкла́дывать) to put (round); to edge; о. больно́го поду́шками to surround a patient with pillows; о. сте́ну мра́мором to face a wall with marble. **2.** (*impf.* обкла́дывать) to cover; (*impers.*) круго́м ∼и́ло (не́бо) the sky is completely overcast; го́рло у него́ ∼и́ло (*med.*) his throat is furred. **3.** (*impf.* обкла́дывать) to surround; о. кре́пость (*mil.; obs.*) to invest a fortress; (*hunting*) to close round, corner. **4.** (*impf.* облага́ть) to assess; о. нало́гом to tax; о. ме́стным нало́гом to rate. **5.** (*impf.* обкла́дывать) (*coll.*) to swear (at), berate.

облож|и́ться, у́сь, ∼ишься, *pf.* **1.** (*impf.* обкла́дываться) (+*i.*) to put round oneself, surround oneself (with). **2.** *pass. of* ∼и́ть.

обло́жк|а, и, *f.* (dust-)cover; folder.

обложно́й, *adj.* о. дождь (*coll.*) incessant rain.

облока́чива|ться, юсь, *impf. of* облоко-ти́ться.

облоко|ти́ться, чу́сь, ∼ти́шься, *pf.* (*of*

облока́чиваться) (на+*a.*) to lean one's elbow(s) (on, against).

обло́м, а, *m.* **1.** breaking off. **2.** break. **3.** (*archit.*) profile. **4.** (*coll.*) clodhopper, bumpkin.

облома́|ть, ю, *pf.* (*of* обла́мывать) **1.** to break off; о. зу́бы (обо что-н.) (*coll.*) to come a cropper. **2.** to break (*horses*). **3.** (*fig., coll.*) to talk into, cajole.

облома́|ться, юсь, *pf.* (*of* обла́мываться) to break off, snap.

облом|и́ть, лю́, ∼ишь, *pf.* to break off.

облом|и́ться, лю́сь, ∼ишься, *pf.* = ∼а́ться.

обло́мовщин|а, ы, *f.* 'oblomovism' (*sluggishness and indecision, as typified by the hero of Goncharov's novel 'Oblomov'*).

обло́м|ок, ка, *m.* **1.** fragment. **2.** (*pl.*) débris, wreckage.

обло́мо|чный, *adj. of* ∼к; ∼чные го́рные поро́ды (*geol.*) disintegrated rock formations; detritus.

облоно́, *n. indecl.* (*abbr. of* областно́й отде́л наро́дного образова́ния) oblast education department.

облуп|и́ть, лю́, ∼ишь, *pf. of* лупи́ть[1] 1 *and* ∼ливать.

облуп|и́ться, лю́сь, ∼ишься, *pf. of* лупи́ться *and* ∼ливаться.

облу́п|ленный, *p.p.p. of* ∼и́ть *and adj.* chipped; знать как ∼ленного (*coll.*) to know inside out.

облу́плива|ть, ю, *impf.* (*of* облупи́ть) **1.** to peel; to shell (*eggs*). **2.** (*fig., coll.*) to fleece.

облу́плива|ться, юсь, *impf.* (*of* облупи́ться) to peel (off), scale; to come off, chip (*of paint, plaster, etc.*).

облупл|я́ть(ся), я́ю(сь), *impf.* = ∼ивать-(ся).

облуч|а́ть, а́ю, *impf. of* ∼и́ть.

облуче́ни|е, я, *n.* (*med.*) irradiation.

облуч|и́ть, у́, и́шь, *pf.* (*of* ∼а́ть) to irradiate.

облуч|о́к, ка́, *m.* coachman's seat.

облущ|и́ть, у́, и́шь, *pf. of* лущи́ть.

облы́ж|ный (∼ен, ∼на), *adj.* (*coll.*) false.

облысе́|ть, ю, ешь, *pf. of* лысе́ть.

облюб|ова́ть, у́ю, *pf.* (*of* ∼о́вывать) to pick, choose, select.

облюбо́выва|ть, ю, *impf. of* облюбова́ть.

обл|я́гу, я́жешь, я́гут, *see* ∼е́чь[1].

обма́|зать, жу, жешь, *pf.* (*of* ∼зывать) **1.** to coat (with); to putty (with). **2.** to soil (with), besmear (with); о. себе́ ру́ки ма́слом to cover one's hands with oil.

обма́|заться, жусь, жешься, *pf.* (*of* ∼зываться) **1.** (+*i.*) to besmear oneself (with), get oneself covered (with). **2.** *pass. of* ∼зать.

обма́зк|а, и, *f.* **1.** coating; puttying.

обма́зыва|ть(ся), ю(сь), *impf. of* обма́-зать(ся).

обма́кива|ть, ю, *impf. of* обмакну́ть.

обма́к|ну́ть, ну́, нёшь, *past* ~ну́л, *pf.* (*of* ~ива́ть) to dip; о. блин в смета́ну to dip a pancake into sour cream.

обма́н, а, *m.* fraud, deception; о. зре́ния optical illusion; ввести́ в о. to deceive; не да́ться кому́-н. в о. not to be taken in by someone.

обма́нк|а, и, *f.* (*min.*) blende; рогова́я о. hornblende; смоляна́я о. pitchblende.

обма́нны|й, *adj.* fraudulent; ~м путём fraudulently, by fraud.

обман|у́ть, у́, ~ешь, *pf.* (*of* ~ывать) to deceive; to cheat, swindle; о. чьё-н. дове́рие to betray someone's trust; о. чьи-н. наде́жды to disappoint someone's hopes.

обман|у́ться, у́сь, ~ешься, *pf.* (*of* ~ыва́ться) to be deceived; о. в свои́х ожида́ниях to be disappointed in one's expectations.

обма́нчив|ый (~, ~а), *adj.* deceptive, delusive; нару́жность ~а appearances are deceptive.

обма́нщик, а, *m.* deceiver; cheat, fraud.

обма́ныва|ть(ся), ю(сь), *impf. of* обману́ть(ся).

обмар|а́ть, а́ю, *pf.* (*of* ~ывать) (*coll.*) to soil, dirty.

обма́рыва|ть, ю, *impf. of* обмара́ть.

обма́тыва|ть(ся), ю(сь), *impf. of* обмота́ть(ся).

обма́хива|ть(ся), ю(сь), *impf. of* обмахну́ть(ся).

обмах|ну́ть, ну́, нёшь, *pf.* (*of* ~ивать) **1.** to fan. **2.** to dust (off); to brush (off); о. сор со ска́терти to brush crumbs off the cloth.

обмах|ну́ться, ну́сь, нёшься, *pf.* (*of* ~ива́ться) **1.** to fan oneself. **2.** *pass. of* ~ну́ть.

обма́чива|ть(ся), ю(сь), *impf. of* обмочи́ть(ся).

обмеле́ни|е, я, *n.* shallowing, shoaling.

обмеле́|ть, ет, *pf.* (*of* меле́ть) **1.** to become shallow. **2.** (*naut.*) to run aground.

обме́н, а, *m.* (+*i.*) exchange (of), interchange (of); barter; о. мне́ниями exchange of opinions; о. веще́ств (*biol.*) metabolism; в о. (за+*a.*) in exchange (for).

обме́нива|ть(ся), ю(сь), *impf. of* обмени́ть(ся) *and* обменя́ть(ся).

обмен|и́ть, ю́, ~ишь, *pf.* (*of* ~ивать) (*coll.*) to exchange (*accidentally*); to barter; to swop.

обмен|и́ться, ю́сь, ~ишься, *pf.* (*of* ~ива́ться) (+*i.*) (*coll.*) to exchange (*accidentally*).

обме́н|ный, *adj. of* ~.

обмен|я́ть, я́ю, *pf.* (*of* меня́ть 2 *and* ~ивать) (+*a.* на+*a.*) to exchange (for).

обмен|я́ться, я́юсь, *pf.* (*of* меня́ться 2 *and* ~иваться) (+*i.*) to exchange; to swop; о. взгля́дами to exchange looks; о. впечатле́ниями to compare notes.

обме́р[1], а, *m.* measurement.

обме́р[2], а, *m.* false measure.

об|мере́ть, омру́, омрёшь, *past* ~мер, ~мерла́, ~мерло, *pf.* (*of* ~мира́ть) (*coll.*) to faint; о. от у́жаса to be horror-struck; я ~мер my heart stood still.

обме́рива|ть(ся), ю(сь), *impf. of* обме́рить(ся).

обме́р|ить[1], ю, ишь, *pf.* (*of* ~ивать) to measure.

обме́р|ить[2], ю, ишь, *pf.* (*of* ~ивать) to cheat in measuring; to give short measure (to).

обме́р|иться, юсь, ишься, *pf.* (*of* ~иваться) (*coll.*) to make a mistake in measuring.

обме|сти́, ту́, тёшь, *past* ~л, ~ла́, *pf.* (*of* ~та́ть[1]) to sweep off; to dust.

обмета́|ть[1], ю, *impf. of* обмести́.

обме|та́ть[2], чу́, ~чешь, *pf.* (*of* ~тывать) **1.** to overstitch, oversew; to whipstitch; to hem. **2.** (*impers.*; *coll.*) у меня́ ~та́ло гу́бы my lips are cracked (with cold sores).

обмётыва|ть, ю, *impf. of* обмета́ть[2].

обмина́|ть, ю, *impf. of* обмя́ть.

обмира́|ть, ю, *impf. of* обмере́ть.

обмозг|ова́ть, у́ю, *pf.* (*of* ~о́вывать) (*coll.* to think over, turn over (in one's mind).

обмозго́выва|ть, ю, *impf. of* обмозгова́ть.

обмок|а́ть, а́ю, *impf. of* ~нуть.

обмо́к|нуть, ну, нешь, *past* ~, ~ла, *pf.* (*of* ~а́ть) (*coll.*) to get wet all over.

обмола́чива|ть, ю, *impf. of* обмолоти́ть.

обмо́лв|иться, люсь, ишься, *pf.* (*coll.*) **1.** to make a slip in speaking. **2.** (+*i.*) to say; to utter; не о. ни сло́вом (о+*p.*) to say not a word (about).

обмо́лвк|а, и, *f.* slip of the tongue.

обмоло́т, а, *m.* (*agric.*) threshing.

обмоло|ти́ть, чу́, ~тишь, *pf.* (*of* обмола́чивать) (*agric.*) to thresh.

обмора́жива|ть(ся), ю(сь), *impf. of* обморо́зить(ся).

обморо́жени|е, я, *n.* frost-bite.

обморо́|женный, *p.p.p. of* ~зить *and adj.* frost-bitten.

обморо́|зить, жу, зишь, *pf.* (*of* обмора́живать); я ~зил себе́ нос, ру́ки, *etc.* my nose is, hands, *etc.*, are frost-bitten.

обморо́|зиться, жусь, зишься, *pf.* (*of* обмора́живаться) to suffer frost-bite, be frost-bitten.

о́бморок, а, *m.* fainting-fit; swoon; (*med.*) syncope; в глубо́ком ~e in a dead faint; упа́сть в о. to faint (away); to swoon.

обморо́ч|ить, у, ишь, *pf. of* моро́чить.

о́бморо́|чный, *adj. of* ~к; ~чное состоя́ние (*med.*) syncope.

обмота́|ть, ю, *pf.* (*of* обма́тывать) (+*a. and i. or a.* вокру́г) to wind (round); о. ше́ю ша́рфом, о. шарф вокру́г ше́и to wind a scarf round one's neck.

обмота́|ться, юсь, *pf.* (*of* обма́тываться)
1. (+*i.*) to wrap oneself (in). **2.** *pass. of* ~ть.

обмо́тк|а, и, *f.* (*electr.*) winding.

обмо́т|ки, ок, *no sing.* puttees, leg-wrap-pings.

обмо́т|очный, *adj. of* **1.** ~ка. **2.** ~ки.

обмоч|и́ть, у́, ~ишь, *pf.* (*of* обма́чивать) to wet; о. посте́ль (*coll.*) to wet the bed.

обмоч|и́ться, у́сь, ~ишься, *pf.* (*of* обма́чиваться) to wet oneself (*also coll.*).

обм|о́ю, о́ешь, *see* ~ы́ть.

обмундирова́ни|е, я, *n.* **1.** fitting out (with uniform). **2.** uniform.

обмундир|ова́ть, у́ю, *pf.* (*of* ~о́вывать) to fit out (with uniform).

обмундир|ова́ться, у́юсь, *pf.* (*of* ~о́вывать-ся) to fit oneself out (with uniform); to draw uniform.

обмундиро́в|ка, ки, *f.* = ~а́ние.

обмундиро́в|очный, *adj. of* ~ка; ~очные де́ньги uniform allowance.

обмундиро́выва|ть(ся), ю(сь), *impf. of* обмундирова́ть(ся).

обмуро́вк|а, и, *f.* brick-work.

обмыва́ни|е, я, *n.* bathing, washing.

обмыва́|ть(ся), ю(сь), *impf. of* обмы́ть(ся).

обмы́л|ок, ка, *m.* (*coll.*) remnant of a cake of soap.

обм|ы́ть, о́ю, о́ешь, *pf.* (*of* ~ыва́ть) to bathe, wash; о. ра́ну to bathe a wound.

обм|ы́ться, о́юсь, о́ешься, *pf.* (*of* ~ыва́ться) **1.** to bathe, wash. **2.** *pass. of* ~ы́ть.

обмяк|а́ть, а́ю, *impf.* (*of* ~нуть) (*coll.*) to become soft; (*fig.*) to become flabby.

обмя́к|нуть, ну, нешь, *past* ~, ~ла, *pf. of* ~а́ть.

об|мя́ть, омну́, омнёшь, *pf.* (*of* ~мина́ть) to press down; to trample down.

обнагле́|ть, ю, ешь, *pf. of* нагле́ть.

обнадёжива|ть, ю, *impf. of* обнадёжить.

обнадёж|ить, у, ишь, *pf.* (*of* ~ивать) to give hope (to), reassure.

обнаж|а́ть(ся), а́ю(сь), *impf. of* ~и́ть(ся).

обнаже́ни|е, я, *n.* **1.** baring, uncovering. **2.** (*fig.*) revealing. **3.** (*geol.*) о. го́рной поро́ды outcrop.

обнаж|ённый, *p.p.p. of* ~и́ть *and adj.* naked, bare; nude.

обнаж|и́ть, у́, и́шь, *pf.* (*of* ~а́ть) **1.** to bare, uncover; о. го́лову to bare one's head; о. шпа́гу to draw the sword. **2.** (*fig.*) to lay bare, reveal.

обнаж|и́ться, у́сь, и́шься, *pf.* (*of* ~а́ться) **1.** to bare oneself, uncover oneself. **2.** *pass. of* ~и́ть.

обнайто́в|ить, лю, ишь, *pf. of* найто́вить.

обнаро́довани|е, я, *n.* publication, promul-gation.

обнаро́д|овать, ую, *pf. and impf.* (*lit.*) to publish, promulgate.

обнаруже́ни|е, я, *n.* **1.** disclosure; display-ing, revealing. **2.** discovery; detection.

обнару́жива|ть(ся), ю(сь), *impf. of* обнару́жить(ся).

обнару́ж|ить, у, ишь, *pf.* (*of* ~ивать) **1.** to disclose; to display, reveal; о. свою́ ра́дость to betray one's joy. **2.** to discover, bring to light; to detect.

обнару́ж|иться, усь, ишься, *pf.* (*of* ~ивать-ся) **1.** to be revealed; to come to light. **2.** *pass. of* ~иваться.

обна́шива|ть, ю, *impf. of* обноси́ть¹.

обнес|ти́¹, у́, ёшь, *past* ~, ~ла́, *pf.* (*of* обноси́ть²) (+*i.*) to enclose (with); о. и́зго-родью to fence (in); о. пери́лами to rail in, off.

обнес|ти́², у́, ёшь, *past* ~, ~ла́, *pf.* (*of* обноси́ть³) (+*i.*) to serve round; ~ли ли вы всех госте́й шампа́нским? have you passed round the champagne to all the guests? have all the guests had cham-pagne?

обнес|ти́³, у́, ёшь, *past* ~, ~ла́, *pf.* (*of* обноси́ть⁴) (+*a. and i.*) to pass over, leave out (*in serving something*); меня́ ~ли вино́м I have not had (been offered) wine.

обнима́|ть(ся), ю(сь), *impf. of* обня́ть(ся).

обни́мк|а, и, *f. only in phrase* в ~у (*coll.*) in an embrace, embracing one another.

обним|у́, ~ешь, *see* обня́ть.

обнища́лый, *adj.* impoverished; beggarly.

обнища́ни|е, я, *n.* impoverishment, pauper-ization.

обнища́|ть, ю, *pf. of* нища́ть.

обно́в|а, ы, *f.* = ~ка.

обнов|и́ть, лю́, и́шь, *pf.* (*of* ~ля́ть) **1.** to renovate; to renew; to reform. **2.** to repair, restore; о. свои́ зна́ния (*fig.*) to refresh one's knowledge; о. свои́ си́лы (*fig.*) to recruit (one's forces). **3.** (*coll.*) to use for the first time, inaugurate; to wear for the first time.

обнов|и́ться, лю́сь, и́шься, *pf.* (*of* ~ля́ться) **1.** to revive, be restored. **2.** *pass. of* ~и́ть.

обно́вк|а, и, *f.* (*coll.*) new acquisition, 'new toy'; new dress.

обновле́ни|е, я, *n.* renovation, renewal.

обновля́|ть(ся), ю(сь), *impf. of* обнови́ть-(ся).

обно|си́ть¹, шу́, ~сишь, *pf.* (*of* обна́шивать) (*coll.*) to wear in (*new clothing or foot-wear*).

обно|си́ть², ³, ⁴, шу́, ~сишь, *impf. of* об-нести́¹, ², ³.

обно|си́ться, шу́сь, ~сишься, *pf.* (*coll.*) **1.** to have worn out all one's clothes; to be out at elbow. **2.** to become worn in, be-come comfortable (*of new clothes*).

обно́с|ки, ков, *sing.* ~ок, ~ка, *m.* (*coll.*) old clothes.

обню́х|ать, аю, *pf.* (*of* ~ивать) to sniff (around).

обню́хива|ть, ю, *impf. of* обнюхать.

обн|я́ть, иму́, и́мешь, *past* ~я́л, ~яла́, ~я́ло, *pf.* (*of* ~има́ть) (*in var. senses*) to embrace; to clasp in one's arms; (*fig.*) to envelop; он шёл, ~я́в её за та́лию he was walking with his arm round her waist; о. взгля́дом to survey; о. умо́м (*fig.*) to comprehend, take in.

обн|я́ться, иму́сь, и́мешься, *past* ~я́лся, ~яла́сь, ~яло́сь, *pf.* (*of* ~има́ться) to embrace; to hug one another.

обо, *prep.* = о.

обобра́|ть, оберу́, оберёшь, *past* ~л, ~ла́, ~ло, *pf.* (*of* обира́ть) (*coll.*) 1. to pick, gather; о. кусты́ мали́ны to pick raspberries. 2. to rob; (*sl.*) to clean out.

обобра́ться, оберу́сь, оберёшься, *pf.* (*coll.*) +*g.*) не оберёшься beyond count, innumerable.

обобщ|а́ть, а́ю, *impf. of* ~и́ть.

обобще́ни|е, я, *n.* generalization.

обобществ|и́ть, лю́, и́шь, *pf.* (*of* ~ля́ть) to socialize; to collectivize.

обобществле́ни|е, я, *n.* socialization; collectivization.

обобществля́|ть, ю, *impf. of* обобществи́ть.

обобщ|и́ть, у́, и́шь, *pf.* (*of* ~а́ть) to generalize.

обобь|ю́, ёшь, *see* обби́ть.

обовши́ве|ть, ю, ешь, *pf. of* вши́веть.

обогати́тел|ь, я, *m.* (*mining tech.*) 1. concentrator; enriching agent. 2. ore concentration specialist.

обогати́тельный, *adj.* (*mining tech.*) concentrating; о. аппара́т ore separator.

обога|ти́ть, щу́, ти́шь, *pf.* (*of* ~ща́ть) 1. (*in var. senses*) to enrich. 2. (*mining tech.*) to concentrate; о. руду́ to concentrate ore, dress ore.

обога|ти́ться, щу́сь, ти́шься, *pf.* (*of* ~ща́ться) 1. to become rich; (+*i.*) to enrich oneself (with). 2. *pass. of* ~ти́ть.

обогаща́|ть(ся), ю(сь), *impf. of* обогати́ть(ся).

обогаще́ни|е, я, *n.* 1. (*in var. senses*) enrichment. 2. (*mining tech.*) concentration; о. руды́ ore concentration, ore dressing.

обогна́|ть, обгоню́, обго́нишь, *past* ~л, ~ла́, ~ло, *pf.* (*of* обгоня́ть) to pass, leave behind; to outstrip, outdistance (*also fig.*).

обогн|у́ть, у́, ёшь, *pf.* (*of* огиба́ть) 1. to round; to skirt; (*naut.*) to double. 2. to bend round; о. о́бруч вокру́г бо́чки to hoop a barrel.

обоготворе́ни|е, я, *n.* deification, idolization.

обоготвор|и́ть, ю́, и́шь, *pf.* (*of* ~я́ть) to deify, idolize.

обоготвор|я́ть, я́ю, *impf. of* ~и́ть.

обогре́в, а, *m.* (*tech.*) heating.

обогрева́ни|е, я, *n.* heating, warming.

обогрева́тел|ь, я, *m.* (*tech.*) heater.

обогрева́|ть(ся), ю(сь), *impf. of* обогре́ть(ся).

обогре́|ть, ю, ешь, *pf.* (*of* ~ва́ть) to heat, warm.

обогре́|ться, юсь, ешься, *pf.* (*of* ~ва́ться) 1. to warm oneself; to warm up. 2. *pass. of* ~ть.

о́бод, а, *pl.* ~ья, ~ев, *m.* rim; felloe.

обод|о́к, ка́, *m.* thin rim, thin border, fillet.

ободо́|чный, *adj. of* ~к; ~чная кишка́ (*anat.*) colon.

ободра́н|ец, ца, *m.* (*coll.*) ragamuffin, ragged fellow.

обо́др|анный, *p.p.p. of* ~а́ть *and adj.* ragged.

ободра́ть, обдеру́, обдерёшь, *pf.* (*of* обдира́ть) 1. to strip; to skin, flay; to peel; о. кору́ с де́рева to bark a tree. 2. (*fig., coll.*) to fleece.

ободре́ни|е, я, *n.* encouragement, reassurance.

ободри́тел|ьный (~ен, ~ьна), *adj.* encouraging, reassuring.

ободр|и́ть, ю́, и́шь, *pf.* (*of* ~я́ть) to cheer up; to encourage, reassure.

ободр|и́ться, ю́сь, и́шься, *pf.* (*of* ~я́ться) 1. to cheer up, take heart. 2. *pass. of* ~и́ть.

ободр|я́ть(ся), я́ю(сь), *impf. of* ~и́ть(ся).

обо́его, обо́ему (*no nom. or a.*), *m. and n. num.* both; обо́его по́ла of both sexes.

обоепо́л|ый (~, ~а), *adj.* (*biol.*) bisexual; (*bot.*) monoecious.

обожа́ни|е, я, *n.* adoration.

обожа́тел|ь, я, *m.* (*coll.*) admirer.

обожа́|ть, ю, *impf.* to adore, worship.

обож|гу́, жёшь, гу́т, *see* обжёчь.

обожд|а́ть, у́, ёшь, *past* ~а́л, ~ала́, ~а́ло, *pf.* (*coll.*) to wait (for a while).

обожеств|и́ть, лю́, и́шь, *pf.* (*of* ~ля́ть) to deify, worship.

обожествле́ни|е, я, *n.* deification, worshipping.

обожествля́|ть, ю, *impf. of* обожестви́ть.

обожжённый, *p.p.p. of* обжёчь.

обожм|у́, ёшь, *see* обжа́ть¹.

обожн|у́, ёшь, *see* обжа́ть².

обожр|а́ться, у́сь, ёшься, *past* ~а́лся, ~ала́сь, *pf.* (*of* обжира́ться) (*coll.*) to guzzle, stuff oneself.

обо́з, а, *m.* 1. string of carts; string of sledges; пожа́рный о. (*collect.*) fire-fighting vehicles, fire brigade. 2. (*mil.*) (*unit*) transport; быть в ~е (*fig.*) to bring up the rear, be left behind.

обозва́|ть, обзову́, обзовёшь, *past* ~л, ~ла́, ~ло, *pf.* (*of* обзыва́ть) (+*a. and i.*) to call; о. кого́-н. дурако́м to call someone a fool.

обозл|ённый, *p.p.p.* of ~и́ть *and adj.* embittered.

обозл|и́ть, ю́, и́шь, *pf.* 1. *pf.* of зли́ть. 2. to embitter.

обозл|и́ться, ю́сь, и́шься, *pf.* of зли́ться.

обознава́|ться, ю́сь, ёшься, *impf.* of ~ться.

обозна́|ться, ю́сь, ешься, *pf.* (*of* ~ва́ться) (*coll.*) to take someone for someone else; to be mistaken.

обознач|а́ть, а́ю, *impf.* 1. (*no pf.*) to mean. 2. (*pf.* ~ить) to mark, designate; о. на ка́рте грани́цу to mark a frontier on a map. 3. (*pf.* ~ить) to reveal; to emphasize.

обознач|а́ться, а́юсь, *impf.* (*of* ~иться) 1. to appear; to reveal oneself. 2. *pass.* of ~а́ть 2, 3.

обозначе́ни|е, я, *n.* 1. marking, designation. 2. sign, symbol; усло́вные ~я conventional signs (*on maps, etc.*).

обозна́ч|ить, у, ишь, *pf.* of ~а́ть 2, 3.

обозна́ч|иться, усь, ишься, *pf.* of ~а́ться.

обо́зник, а, *m.* driver.

обо́з|ный, *adj.* of ~; *as noun* о., ~ного, *m.* (*mil.*) driver.

обозрева́тел|ь, я, *m.* author of survey, author of review; columnist (*see* обозре́ние 2); полити́ческий о. political correspondent (*of newspaper*).

обозрева́|ть, ю, *impf.* of обозре́ть.

обозре́ни|е, я, *n.* 1. surveying, viewing; looking round. 2. survey; review (*exposé, not critical notice*). 3. review (*periodical journal*). 4. (*theatr.*) revue.

обозр|е́ть, ю́, и́шь, *pf.* (*of* ~ева́ть) 1. to survey, view; to look round. 2. (*fig.*) to survey, (pass in) review (*in print*).

обозри́м|ый (~, ~а), *adj.* visible.

обо́|и, ев, *no sing.* wall-paper; окле́ить ~ями to paper.

обой|дённый, *p.p.p.* of ~ти́.

обо́йм|а, ы, *g. pl.* ~, *f.* 1. (*mil.*) cartridge clip, charger. 2. (*tech.*) iron ring; о. шарикоподши́пника ball race.

обо́|йный, *adj.* of ~и.

обо|йти́, йду́, йдёшь, *past* ~шёл, ~шла́, *pf.* (*of* обходи́ть[1]) 1. to go round, pass; о. фланг проти́вника (*mil.*) to turn the enemy's flank. 2. to make the round (of), go (all) round; (*of doctor, sentry, etc.*) to make (go) one's round(s); слух ~шёл весь го́род the rumour spread all over the town. 3. to avoid; to leave out; to pass over; о. молча́нием to pass over in silence; о. зако́н to get round (evade) a law; о. затрудне́ние to get round a difficulty. 4. (*coll., pejor.*) to take in, get round.

обо|йти́сь, йду́сь, йдёшься, *past* ~шёлся, ~шла́сь, *pf.* (*of* обходи́ться) 1. (с+*i.*) to treat; пло́хо о. с кем-н. to treat someone badly. 2. (*coll.*) to cost, come to; во ско́лько

~шёлся ваш костю́м? how much did your suit come to? 3. (+*i.*) to manage (with, on), make do (with, on); о. ста рубля́ми to make do with one hundred roubles; без ва́шей по́мощи мы бы не ~шли́сь without your aid we could not have managed. 4. to turn out, end; всё ~шло́сь благополу́чно everything turned out all right; как-н. ~йдётся! things will turn out all right somehow! things will sort themselves out!

обо́йщик, а, *m.* paper-hanger; interior decorator, upholsterer.

обо́к, *adv. and prep.* +*g. or d.* (*coll.*) close by; near.

обокра́|сть, обкраду́, обкрадёшь, *past* ~л, ~ла, *pf.* (*of* обкра́дывать) to rob.

оболва́нива|ть, ю, *impf.* of оболва́нить.

оболва́н|ить, ю, ишь, *pf.* (*of* ~ивать) (*coll.*) 1. to rough-hew. 2. (*fig.*) to make a fool of.

обо|лга́ть, лгу́, лжёшь, *past* ~лга́л, ~лгала́, ~лга́ло, *pf.* to slander, calumniate.

оболо́чк|а, и, *f.* 1. cover, envelope, jacket; shell; (*tech.*) casing. 2. (*anat.*) membrane; ра́дужная о. iris; рогова́я о. cornea; сли́зистая о. mucous membrane. 3. (*bot.*) coat.

обо́лтус, а, *m.* (*coll.*) blockhead, booby.

обольсти́тел|ь, я, *m.* (*obs.*) seducer.

обольсти́тел|ьный (~ен, ~ьна), *adj.* seductive, captivating.

оболь|сти́ть, щу́, сти́шь, *pf.* (*of* ~ща́ть) 1. to captivate. 2. to seduce.

оболь|сти́ться, щу́сь, сти́шься, *pf.* (*of* ~ща́ться) to be (labour) under a delusion; (+*i.*) to flatter oneself (with).

обольща́|ть(ся), ю(сь), *impf.* of обольсти́ть(ся).

обольще́ни|е, я, *n.* 1. seduction. 2. delusion.

оболь|ю́, ёшь, *see* обли́ть.

обомле́|ть, ю, ешь, *pf.* (*coll.*) to be stupefied.

обомн|у́, ёшь, *see* обмя́ть.

обомр|у́, ёшь, *see* обмере́ть.

обомше́лый, *adj.* moss-grown.

обоня́ни|е, я, *n.* (sense of) smell; име́ть то́нкое о. to have a fine sense of smell.

обоня́тельный, *adj.* (*anat.*) olfactory.

обоня́|ть, ю, *impf.* to smell.

обора́чиваемост|ь, и, *f.* (*fin., econ.*) turnover.

обора́чива|ть(ся), ю(сь), *impf.* of оберну́ть(ся) *and* обороти́ть(ся).

оборва́н|ец, ца, *m.* ragamuffin, ragged fellow.

оборв|анный, *p.p.p.* of ~а́ть *and adj.* torn, ragged.

оборв|а́ть, у́, ёшь, *past* ~а́л, ~ала́, ~а́ло, *pf.* (*of* обрыва́ть) 1. to tear off, pluck

(*petals, etc.*); to strip (*a shrub of blossom, etc.*).
2. to break; to snap. 3. (*fig.*) to cut short,
interrupt; (*coll.*) to snub.

оборв|а́ться, у́сь, ёшься, *past* ~а́лся,
~ала́сь, ~а́ло́сь, *pf.* (*of* обрыва́ться) 1. to
break; to snap. 2. to (*lose one's hold of something and*) fall; (*of objects*) to come away. 3.
to stop suddenly, stop short, come abruptly
to an end.

обо́рвыш, а, *m.* (*coll.*) ragamuffin.

обо́рк|а, ы, *f.* frill, flounce.

оборо́н|а, ы, *no pl., f.* 1. defence. 2. (*mil.*)
defences, defensive positions.

оборони́тельный, *adj.* defensive.

оборон|и́ть, ю́, и́шь, *pf.* (*of* ~я́ть) to de-
fend; ~и́ Бог (~и́ Бо́же, ~и́ Го́споди)!
(*obs.*) God forbid!

оборон|и́ться, ю́сь, и́шься, *pf.* (*of* ~я́ться)
(от) to defend oneself (from).

оборо́н|ный, *adj. of* ~а; ~ная промы́шлен-
ность war industry.

обороноспосо́бност|ь, и, *f.* defence ca-
pacity.

обороноспосо́б|ный (~ен, ~на), *adj.* pre-
pared for defence.

оборон|я́ть(ся), я́ю(сь), *impf. of* ~и́ть(ся).

оборо́т, а, *m.* 1. turn; (*tech.*) revolution,
rotation; приня́ть дурно́й о. (*fig.*) to take
a bad turn. 2. circulation; (*fin., comm., railways*) turnover; ввести́, пусти́ть в о. to put
into circulation. 3. back (= *reverse side*);
смотри́ на ~е please turn over; взять
кого́-н. в о. (*fig., coll.*) to get at someone.
4. turn (of speech); о. ре́чи phrase, locution.
5. (*tech.*) knee, bend (*in a pipe*).

обо́рот|ень, ня, *m.* werewolf.

оборо́тист|ый (~, ~а), *adj.* (*coll.*) resource-
ful.

оборо|ти́ть, чу́, ~тишь, *pf.* (*of* обора́чивать)
(*coll.*) to turn.

оборо|ти́ться, чу́сь, ~тишься, *pf.* (*of* обо-
ра́чиваться) (*coll.*) 1. to turn (round).
2. (в+*a.* or +*i.*) to turn (into).

оборо́тлив|ый (~, ~а), *adj.* (*coll.*) resource-
ful.

оборо́т|ный, *adj. of* ~; о. капита́л (*fin.,
comm.*) working capital; ~ная сторона́
verso; reverse side (*also fig.*); э ~ное *name
of letter* 'э'.

обору́довани|е, я, *n.* 1. equipping. 2. equip-
ment.

обору́д|овать, ую, *impf. and pf.* to equip,
fit out; (*fig., coll.*) to manage, arrange.

обо́рыш, а, *m.* (*coll.*) left-over, remnant.

обоснова́ни|е, я, *n.* 1. basing. 2. basis,
ground.

обосно́в|анный, *p.p.p. of* ~а́ть *and adj.* well-
-founded, well-grounded.

обосн|ова́ть, у́ю, у́ёшь, *pf.* (*of* ~о́вывать)
to ground, base; to substantiate.

обосн|ова́ться, у́сь, у́ёшься, *pf.* (*of* ~о́вы-
ваться) 1. to settle down. 2. *pass. of*
~ова́ть.

обосно́выва|ть(ся), ю(сь), *impf. of* обосно-
ва́ть(ся).

обосо́б|ить, лю, ишь, *pf.* (*of* ~ля́ть) to iso-
late.

обосо́б|иться, люсь, ишься, *pf.* (*of* ~ля́ться)
to stand apart, keep aloof.

обособле́ни|е, я, *n.* isolation.

обосо́бленно, *adv.* apart; aloof; жить о. to
live by oneself.

обосо́б|ленный, *p.p.p. of* ~ить *and adj.* iso-
lated, solitary.

обособля́|ть(ся), ю(сь), *impf. of* обосо́бить-
(ся).

обостре́ни|е, я, *n.* aggravation, exacerba-
tion; о. боле́зни (*med.*) acute condition.

обостр|ённый, *p.p.p. of* ~и́ть *and adj.* 1.
sharp, pointed. 2. of heightened sensitivity;
о. слух a keen ear. 3. strained, tense.

обостр|и́ть, ю́, и́шь, *pf.* (*of* ~я́ть) 1. to
sharpen, intensify. 2. to strain; to aggra-
vate, exacerbate.

обостр|и́ться, ю́сь, и́шься, *pf.* (*of* ~я́ться)
1. to become sharp, become pointed. 2. (*of
the senses, etc.*) to become more sensitive,
become keener. 3. to become strained; to
become aggravated, become exacerbated;
боле́знь ~и́лась (*med.*) the condition has
become acute. 4. *pass. of* ~и́ть.

обостр|я́ть(ся), я́ю(сь), *impf. of* ~и́ть(ся).

оботр|у́, ёшь, *see* обтере́ть.

обо́чин|а, ы, *f.* edge; side (*of road, etc.*).

обою́дност|ь, и, *f.* mutuality, reciprocity.

обою́д|ный (~ен, ~на), *adj.* mutual, reci-
procal; по ~ному согла́сию by mutual
consent.

обоюдоо́стрый, *adj.* double-edged, two-
-edged (*also fig.*).

обраба́тыва|ть, ю, *impf. of* обрабо́тать.

обраба́тыва|ющий, *pres. part. act. of* ~ть *and
adj.* ~ющая промы́шленность manufac-
turing industry.

обрабо́та|ть, ю, *pf.* (*of* обраба́тывать) 1.
to work (up); to treat, process; (*tech.*) to
machine; о. зе́млю to work the land; о.
ра́ну to dress a wound. 2. to polish, perfect
(*a lit. production, etc.*). 3. (*fig., coll.*) to work
upon, win round.

обрабо́тк|а, и, *f.* working (up); treatment,
processing; (*tech.*) machining; о. земли́ cul-
tivation of the land.

обра́д|овать(ся), ую(сь), *pf. of* ра́довать-
(ся).

о́браз[1], а, *m.* 1. shape, form; appearance;
по ~у своему́ и подо́бию (*rhet. or joc.*) in
one's own image. 2. (*lit.*) image; мы́слить
~ами to think in images. 3. (*lit.*) type;
figure; о. Га́млета the Hamlet type. 4.

mode, manner; way; о. действий line of action, policy; о. жизни way of life, mode of life; о. правления form of government; по ~у пешего хождения (*joc.*) on foot, on Shank's mare; обстоятельство ~а действия (*gram.*) adverbial modifier of manner; каким ~ом? how?; таким ~ом thus: главным ~ом mainly, chiefly, largely; равным ~ом equally.

образ², а, *pl.* ~а, *m.* icon.

образ|ец, ца, *m.* **1.** model, pattern (*also fig.*); ставить в о. to set up as a model. **2.** specimen, sample; (*of material*) pattern.

образин|а, ы, *f.* (*coll., pejor.*) ugly mug; (*as term of abuse*) scum.

образн|ой, *adj.* of образ²; *as noun* ~ая, ~ой, *f.* **1.** icon-room. **2.** icon-maker's workshop.

образность, и, *f.* picturesqueness; (*lit.*) figurativeness; imagery.

образ|ный (~ен, ~на), *adj.* picturesque, graphic; (*lit.*) figurative; employing images.

образовани|е¹, я, *n.* formation; о. слов word-formation; о. пара (*tech.*) production of steam.

образовани|е², я, *n.* education.

образов|анный¹, *p.p.p.* of ~ать¹.

образов|анный², *p.p.p.* of ~ать² and *adj.*; о. человек an educated person.

образовател|ьный (~ен, ~ьна), *adj.* educational; о. ценз educational qualification.

образ|овать¹, ую, *impf.* (*in pres. tense*) *and pf.* (*of* ~овывать) to form; to make up.

образ|овать², ую, *pf.* (*of* ~овывать) (*obs.*) to educate.

образ|оваться, уется, *pf.* (*of* ~овываться) **1.** to form; to arise. **2.** (*coll.*) to turn out well; не беспокойтесь, всё ~уется! don't worry, everything will be all right! **3.** *pass.* *of* ~овать.

образовыва|ть(ся), ю(сь), *impf. of* образовать(ся).

образум|ить, лю, ишь, *pf.* (*coll.*) to bring to reason, make listen to reason.

образум|иться, люсь, ишься, *pf.* (*coll.*) to come to one's senses, see reason.

образующ|ая, ей, *f.* (*math.*) generatrix.

образцов|ый, *adj.* model; exemplary; ~ое поведение exemplary conduct; ~ое произведение masterpiece; ~ое хозяйство model farm.

образчик, а, *m.* specimen, sample; (*of material*) pattern.

обрам|ить, лю, ишь, *pf.* (*of* ~лять) to frame.

обрамлени|е, я, *n.* **1.** framing. **2.** frame; (*fig.*) setting.

обрамля|ть, ю, *impf. of* обрамить.

обрастани|е, я, *n.* **1.** overgrowing. **2.** (*fig.*) accumulation, acquisition.

браст|ать, аю, *impf. of* ~й.

обраст|и, у, ёшь, *past* **оброс**, **обросла**, *pf.*

(*of* ~ать) (+*i.*) **1.** to become (be) overgrown (with); о. грязью (*coll.*) to be coated with mud. **2.** (*fig.*) to become (be) surrounded (by), become (be) cluttered (with); to acquire, accumulate; он оброс ненужной мебелью he has surrounded himself with superfluous items of furniture.

обрат, а, *m.* (*agric.*) skim milk.

обратимост|ь, и, *f.* reversibility.

обратим|ый (~, ~а), *adj.* reversible.

обра|тить, щу, тишь, *pf.* (*of* ~щать) (*in var. senses*) to turn; (в+*a.*) to turn (into); о. внимание (на+*a.*) to pay attention (to), take notice (of), notice; о. чьё-н. внимание (на+*a.*) to call, draw someone's attention (to); о. на себя внимание to attract attention (to oneself); о. имущество в капитал to realize property; о. в бегство to put to flight; о. в свою веру to convert (to one's faith); о. в шутку to turn into a joke.

обра|титься, щусь, тишься, *pf.* (*of* ~щаться) **1.** to turn; to revert; о. лицом к стене to turn (one's face) towards the wall; о. в бегство to take to flight. **2.** (к) to turn (to), appeal (to); to apply (to); to accost; она не знала, к кому о. за помощью she did not know to whom to turn for help; о. с призывом к кому-н. to appeal to someone; о. к юристу to take legal advice; о. к славяноведению to take up Slavonic studies. **3.** (в+*a.*) to turn (into), become; о. в циника to become a cynic; о. в слух (*fig.*) to be all ears; to prick up one's ears. **4.** (в+*a.*) to be converted (to).

обратно, *adv.* **1.** back; backwards; туда и о. there and back; поездка туда и о. round trip; взять о. to take back; идти о., ехать о. to go back; to return, retrace one's steps. **2.** conversely; inversely; о. пропорциональный inversely proportional. **3.** (*vulg.*) again.

обратн|ый, *adj.* **1.** reverse; о. адрес sender's address; о. билет return ticket; ~ая вспышка back-firing; о. клапан (*tech.*) return valve; о. путь return journey; ~ые растяжки (*aeron.*) landing wires; имеющий ~ую силу (*leg.*) retroactive, retrospective; о. удар backfire; о. ход (*tech.*) reverse motion, back stroke; ~ая связь (*electr.*) feed-back circuit. **2.** opposite; в ~ую сторону in the opposite direction. **3.** (*math.*) inverse; ~ое отношение inverse ratio.

обраща|ть, ю, *impf. of* обратить.

обраща|ться, юсь, *impf.* **1.** *impf. of* обратиться. **2.** (*physiol., econ., etc.*) to circulate. **3.** (с+*i.*) to treat; плохо о. с кем-н. to treat someone badly, maltreat someone. **4.** (с+*i.*) to handle, manage (*an inanimate object*); он, по-видимому, не умеет о. с автоматом apparently he does not know how to handle a sub-machine-gun.

обращёни|е, я, *n.* **1.** (к) appeal (to), address (to). **2.** (в+*a.*) conversion (to, into); о. в вёру conversion to faith. **3.** circulation; изъя́ть из ∼я to withdraw from circulation; пусти́ть в о. to put in circulation. **4.** (с+*i.*) treatment (of); плохо́е о. ill-treatment. **5.** (с+*i.*) handling (of), use (of). **6.** manner.

обревиз|ова́ть, у́ю, *pf. of* ревизова́ть.

обрёз[1], а, *m.* edge; о. доро́ги road-side; в о. (*coll.*; +*g.*) only just enough; дёнег у меня́ в о. I have not a penny to spare.

обрёз[2], а, *m.* sawn-off gun.

обрёзани|е, я, *n.* circumcision.

обреза́ни|е, я, *n.* **1.** cutting. **2.** trimming; paring; pruning; bevelling.

обрё|зать, жу, жешь, *pf.* (*of* ∼зывать *and* ∼за́ть) **1.** to clip, trim; to pare; to prune; to bevel; о. кому́-н. кры́лья (*fig.*) to clip someone's wings. **2.** to cut; о. себё па́лец to cut one's finger. **3.** to circumcise. **4.** (*coll.*) to cut short; to snub.

обрез|а́ть, а́ю, *impf. of* ∼ать.

обрё|заться, жусь, жешься, *pf.* (*of* ∼за́ться *and* ∼зыва́ться) **1.** to cut oneself. **2.** *pass. of* ∼зать.

обрез|а́ться, а́юсь, *impf. of* ∼аться.

обрезно́й, *adj.* (*tech.*) trimming.

обрё́з|ок, ка, *m.* scrap; (*pl.*) ends; clippings.

обрё́зыва|ть(ся), ю(сь), *impf. of* обрё́зать(ся).

обрека́|ть, ю, *impf. of* обрё́чь.

обре|ку́, чёшь, ку́т, *see* ∼чь.

обремени́тел|ьный (∼ен, ∼ьна), *adj.* burdensome, onerous.

обремен|и́ть, ю́, и́шь, *pf.* (*of* ∼я́ть) to burden.

обремен|я́ть, я́ю, *impf. of* ∼и́ть.

обреми́|зиться, жусь, зишься, *pf.* (*obs.,* *coll.*) to get into a mess, into difficulties.

обре|сти́, ту́, тёшь (*arch.* **обря́щу, обря́щешь**), *past* ∼л, ∼ла́, *pf.* (*of* ∼та́ть) (*rhet.*) to find; ищи́те да обря́щете seek and ye shall find.

обре|сти́сь, ту́сь, тёшься, *past* ∼лся, ∼ла́сь, *pf.* (*obs.*) to be found; to turn up.

обрета́|ть, ю, *impf. of* обрести́.

обрета́|ться, юсь, *impf.* (*obs. or coll.*) to be; to pass one's time.

обречёни|е, я, *n.* doom.

обречённост|ь, и, *f.* being doomed; чу́вство ∼и feeling of doom.

обречё́нный, *p.p.p. of* ∼ь *and adj.* doomed.

обрё́|чь, ку́, чёшь, ку́т, *past* ∼к, ∼кла́, *pf.* (*of* ∼ка́ть) to condemn, doom.

обреше́|тить, чу, тишь, *pf.* (*of* ∼чивать) to lath.

обреше́чива|ть, ю, *impf. of* обреше́тить.

обрис|ова́ть, у́ю, *pf.* (*of* ∼о́вывать) to outline, delineate, depict (*also fig.*).

обрис|ова́ться, у́юсь, *pf.* (*of* ∼о́вываться)

1. to appear (in outline); to take shape. **2.** *pass of* ∼ова́ть.

обрисо́вк|а, и, *f.* outlining, delineation, depicting.

обрисо́выва|ть(ся), ю(сь), *impf. of* обрисова́ть(ся).

обри́т|ый, *p.p.p. of* ∼ь *and adj.* shaven.

обр|и́ть, ёю, ёешь, *pf.* to shave (off).

обр|и́ться, ёюсь, ёешься, *pf.* to shave one's head.

обро́к, а, *m.* (*hist.*) quit-rent; быть на ∼е, ходи́ть по ∼у to be liable for quit-rent.

оброн|и́ть, ю́, ∼ишь, *pf.* **1.** to drop (*sc. and lose*). **2.** to let drop, let fall (*a remark, etc.*).

обро́|чный, *adj. of* ∼к; о. крестья́нин peasant on quit-rent.

обруб|а́ть, а́ю, *impf. of* ∼и́ть.

обруб|и́ть[1], лю́, ∼ишь, *pf.* (*of* ∼а́ть) to chop off; to lop off; to dock.

обруб|и́ть[2], лю́, ∼ишь, *pf.* (*of* ∼а́ть) to hem.

обру́б|ок, ка, *m.* stump.

обруга́|ть, ю, *pf.* to curse; to call names; (*coll.*; *of book reviews, etc.*) to tear to pieces.

обрусё́лый, *adj.* russified, russianized.

обрусё́ни|е, я, *n.* russification, russianization.

обрусё́|ть, ю, *pf.* to become russified, become russianized.

обруси́|ть, шь, *pf.* to russify, russianize.

о́бруч, а, *pl.* ∼и, ∼ёй, *m.* hoop.

обруча́льн|ый, *adj.* ∼ое кольцо́ engagement ring; о. обря́д betrothal.

обруч|а́ть(ся), а́ю(сь), *impf. of* ∼и́ть(ся).

обручё́ни|е, я, *n.* betrothal.

обруч|и́ть, у́, и́шь, *pf.* (*of* ∼а́ть) to betrothe.

обруч|и́ться, у́сь, и́шься, *pf.* (*of* ∼а́ться) (с+*i.*) to become engaged (to).

обру́шива|ть(ся), ю(сь), *impf. of* обру́шить(ся).

обру́ш|ить, у, ишь, *pf.* (*of* ∼ивать) to bring down, rain down.

обру́ш|иться, усь, ишься, *pf.* (*of* ∼иваться) **1.** to come down, collapse, cave in. **2.** (*fig.*) to come down (upon), fall (upon).

обры́в, а, *m.* **1.** precipice. **2.** (*tech.*) break, rupture.

обрыва́|ть(ся), ю(сь), *impf. of* оборва́ть(ся).

обры́вист|ый (∼, ∼а), *adj.* steep, precipitous; (*fig.*) abrupt.

обры́в|ок, ка, *m.* scrap; snatch (*of tune, song, etc.*); ∼ки мы́слей desultory thoughts; ∼ки разгово́ра scraps of conversation.

обры́зг|ать, аю, *pf.* (*of* ∼ивать) (+*i.*) to besprinkle (with); to splash; to bespatter (with).

обры́згива|ть, ю, *impf. of* обры́згать.

обры́ска|ть, ю, *pf.* (*coll.*) to go through, hunt through.

обрю́зглый, *adj.* flabby, flaccid.

обрю́зг|нуть, ну, нешь, *past* ~, ~ла, *pf.* to become flabby, become flaccid.

обрю́зг|ший = ~лый.

обря́д, а, *m.* rite, ceremony.

обря|ди́ть, жу́, ~ди́шь, *pf.* (*of* ~жа́ть) (*coll., joc.*) (+*i.*) to get up (in), trick out (in).

обря|ди́ться, жу́сь, ~ди́шься, *pf.* (*of* ~жа́ться) (*coll., joc.*) (+*i.*) to get oneself up (in).

обря́дност|ь, и, *f.* (*collect.*) rites, ritual, ceremonial.

обря́д|ный, *adj.* (*obs.*) = ~овый.

обря́довый, *adj.* ritual, ceremonial.

обряжа́|ть(ся), ю(сь), *impf. of* обряди́ть(ся).

обса|ди́ть, жу́, ~дишь, *pf.* (*of* ~живать) to plant round; о. кла́дбище ти́сами to surround a cemetery with yew-trees.

обса́жива|ть, ю, *impf. of* обсади́ть.

обса́ли|ть, ю, *impf. of* обса́лить *and* обсоли́ть.

обса́л|ить, ю, ишь, *pf.* (*of* ~ивать) (*coll.*) to smear with grease, spill grease on.

обса́сыва|ть, ю, *impf. of* обсоса́ть.

обса́харива|ть, ю, *impf. of* обса́харить.

обса́хар|ить, ю, ишь, *pf.* (*of* ~ивать) (*coll.*) to sugar.

обсемене́ни|е, я, *n.* 1. (*agric.*) sowing. 2. (*bot.*) going to seed.

обсемен|и́ть, ю́, и́шь, *pf.* (*of* ~я́ть) (*agric.*) to sow (*a field*).

обсемен|и́ться, ю́сь, и́шься, *pf.* (*of* ~я́ться) 1. (*bot.*) to go to seed. 2. *pass. of* ~и́ть.

обсемен|я́ть(ся), я́ю(сь), *impf. of* ~и́ть(ся).

обсерва́тори|я, и, *f.* observatory.

обсерва|цио́нный, *adj. of* ~ция.

обсерва́ци|я, и, *f.* observation.

обсидиа́н, а, *m.* (*min.*) obsidian.

обска|ка́ть, чу́, ~чешь, *pf.* (*of* ~кивать) 1. to gallop round. 2. (*pf. only*) to outgallop.

обска́кива|ть, ю, *impf. of* обскака́ть 1.

обскура́нт, а, *m.* obscurant, obscurantist.

обскуранти́зм, а, *m.* obscurantism.

обскуранти́стский, *adj.* obscurantist.

обсле́довани|е, я, *n.* (+*g.*) inspection (of), inquiry (into); investigation (of).

обсле́довател|ь, я, *m.* inspector, investigator.

обсле́д|овать, ую, *impf. and pf.* to inspect; to investigate; о. больно́го to examine a patient.

обслу́живани|е, я, *n.* service; (*tech.*) servicing, maintenance; бытово́е о. consumer service (*including such facilities as hairdressing, dry-cleaning, domestic utensil repairs, etc.*) медици́нское о. health service.

обслу́жива|ть, ю, *impf. of* обслужи́ть; о. стано́к to mind a machine; (*naut.*) о. ору́дия to man the guns; ~ющий персона́л (serving) staff; (*collect.*) assistants, attendants.

обслуж|и́ть, у́, ~ишь, *pf.* (*of* ~ивать) to attend (to), serve; (*tech.*) to service; to mind, operate; о. потреби́теля to serve a customer.

обслюн|и́ть, ю, и́шь, *pf.* (*coll.*) to slobber all over.

обсол|и́ть, ю, *pf.* (*of* обса́ливать) to salt all over.

обсос|а́ть, у́, ёшь, *pf.* (*of* обса́сывать) 1. to suck round (*a sweet, etc.*). 2. (*fig., coll.*) to chew over.

обсо́х|нуть, ну, нешь, *past* ~, ~ла, *pf.* (*о* обсыха́ть) to dry, become dry; у него́ молоко́ на губа́х не ~ло (*fig.*) he is still green.

обста́в|ить, лю, ишь, *pf.* (*of* ~ля́ть) 1. (+*i.*) to surround (with), encircle (with). 2. (+*i.*) to furnish (with). 3. (*fig.*) to arrange; to organize. 4. (*coll.*) to get the better (of); to get round, cheat.

обста́в|иться, люсь, ишься, *pf.* (*of* ~ля́ться) 1. (+*i.*) to surround oneself (with). 2. to establish oneself, set oneself up (*in lodgings, etc.*). 3. *pass. of* ~ить.

обставля́|ть(ся), ю(сь), *impf. of* обста́вить(ся).

обстано́вк|а, и, *f.* 1. furniture; décor (*also theatr.*). 2. situation, conditions; environment; set-up; боева́я о. (*mil.*) tactical situation.

обстано́в|очный, *adj. of* ~ка; ~очная пье́са (*theatr.*) spectacular.

обстир|а́ть, а́ю, *pf.* (*of* ~ывать) (*coll.*) to do the washing (*for a number of*).

обсти́рыва|ть, ю, *impf. of* обстира́ть.

обстоя́тел|ьный (~ен, ~ьна), *adj.* 1. circumstantial, detailed. 2. (*coll.; of a person*) thorough, reliable.

обстоя́тельственный, *adj.* (*gram.*) adverbial.

обстоя́тельств|о¹, а, *n.* circumstance; смягча́ющие ~а ˉextenuating circumstances; по незави́сящим от меня́ ~ам for reasons beyond my control; по семе́йным ~ам due to family circumstances; ни при каки́х ~ax in no circumstances; смотря́ по ~ам depending on circumstances.

обстоя́тельств|о², а, *n.* (*gram.*) adverbial modifier.

обсто|я́ть, и́т, *impf.* to be; to get on; как ~и́т де́ло? how is it going? how are things going?; как ~я́т ва́ши дела́? how are you getting on?; всё ~и́т благополу́чно all is well, everything is going all right; вот как ~и́т де́ло that is the way it is, that's how matters stand.

обстра́гива|ть, ю, *impf. of* обстрога́ть.

обстра́ива|ть(ся), ю(сь), *impf. of* обстро́ить(ся).

обстрека́|ть, ю, *pf. of* стрека́ть.

обстрéл, а, *m.* firing, fire; артилле́рийский о. bombardment, shelling; быть под ~ом to be under fire; попáсть под о. to come under fire.

обстрéлива|ть(ся), ю(сь), *impf. of* обстре-ля́ть(ся).

обстрéл|янный, *p.p.p. of* ~я́ть *and adj.* seasoned, experienced (of *soldiers, also fig.*); ~янная пти́ца (*coll.*) old hand, person who has knocked around.

обстрел|я́ть, я́ю, *pf.* (*of* ~ивать) to fire (at, on); to bombard.

обстрел|я́ться, я́юсь, *pf.* (*of* ~ивáться) (*coll.*) to become seasoned (by being in battle); to receive a baptism of fire.

обстрогá|ть, ю, *pf.* (*of* обстрáгивать) to plane; to whittle.

обстрó|ить, ю, ишь, *pf.* (*of* обстрáивать) to build (up).

обстрó|иться, юсь, ишься, *pf.* (*of* обстрáиваться) 1. to be built (up); (*coll.*) to spring up. 2. to build for oneself.

обстругá|ть, ю, *pf.* = обстрогáть.

обструкциони́зм, а, *m.* (*polit.*) obstructionism.

обструкциони́ст, а, *m.* (*polit.*) obstructionist.

обстру́кци|я, и, *f.* (*polit.*) obstruction; filibuster.

обступ|а́ть, а́ю, *impf. of* ~и́ть.

обступ|и́ть, лю́, ~ишь, *pf.* (*of* ~а́ть) to surround; to cluster (round).

обсу|ди́ть, жу́, ~дишь, *pf.* (*of* ~ждáть) to discuss; to consider.

обсуждá|ть, ю, *impf. of* обсуди́ть.

обсуждéни|е, я, *n.* discussion.

обсу́шива|ть(ся), ю(сь), *impf. of* обсуши́ть-(ся).

обсуш|и́ть, у́, ~ишь, *pf.* (*of* ~ивать) to dry (out).

обсуш|и́ться, у́сь, ~ишься, *pf.* (*of* ~ивáть-ся) to dry oneself, get dry.

обсчит|а́ть, а́ю, *pf.* (*of* ~ывать) to cheat (*in counting out money*).

обсчит|а́ться, а́юсь, *pf.* (*of* ~ывáться) to make a mistake (*in counting*); вы ~а́лись на шесть копéек you were six kopecks out.

обсчи́тыва|ть(ся), ю(сь), *impf. of* обсчи-тáть(ся).

обсы́п|ать, лю, лешь, *pf.* (*of* ~áть) (+*i.*) to strew; to sprinkle.

обсып|а́ть, а́ю, *impf. of* ~áть.

обсып|а́ться, лю́сь, лешься, *pf.* = осы́-паться.

обсыхá|ть, ю, *impf. of* обсóхнуть.

обтáива|ть, ю, *impf. of* обтáять.

обтáчива|ть, ю, *impf. of* обточи́ть.

обтá|ять, ю, *pf.* (*of* ~ивать) 1. to melt away (around). 2. to become clear (*of ice*).

обтекáем|ый, *adj.* (*tech.*) streamlined; ~ая фóрма streamline form.

обтекáтел|ь, я, *m.* (*aeron. tech.*) fairing.

обтекá|ть, ю, *impf. of* обтéчь.

обтер|éть, оботру́, оботрёшь, *past* ~, ~лá, *pf.* (*of* обтирáть) 1. to wipe; to wipe dry. 2. (+*i.*) to rub (with).

обтер|éться, оботру́сь, оботрёшься, *past* ~ся, ~лась, *pf.* (*of* обтирáться) 1. to wipe oneself dry, dry oneself. 2. to sponge down. 3. (*coll.*) to wear thin, rub (*as result of friction*). 4. (*fig., coll.*) to adapt oneself, become acclimatized.

обтерп|éться, лю́сь, ~ишься, *pf.* (*coll.*) to become acclimatized, become accustomed.

обтёс|анный, *p.p.p. of* ~áть; грýбо о. rough--finished.

обте|сáть, шу́, ~шешь, *pf.* (*of* ~сывать) 1. to square; to rough-hew; to dress, trim. 2. (*fig., coll.*) to teach manners (to), lick into shape.

обте|сáться, шу́сь, ~шешься, *pf.* (*of* ~сы-вáться) (*coll.*) to acquire (*polite*) manners, acquire polish.

обтёсыва|ть(ся), ю(сь), *impf. of* обтесáть(ся).

обтé|чь, ку́, чёшь, ку́т, *past* ~к, ~клá, *pf.* (*of* ~кáть) 1. to flow round. 2. (*mil.*) to by-pass.

обтирáни|е, я, *n.* 1. sponge-down. 2. (*coll.*) lotion.

обтирá|ть(ся), ю(сь), *impf. of* обтерéть(ся).

обточ|и́ть, у́, ~ишь, *pf.* (*of* обтáчивать) to grind; (*tech.*) to turn, machine, round off.

обтóчк|а, и, f. (*tech.*) turning, machining, rounding off.

обтрёп|анный, *p.p.p. of* ~áть *and adj.* 1. frayed. 2. shabby.

обтреп|áть, лю́, ~лешь, *pf.* to fray.

обтреп|áться, лю́сь, ~лешься, *pf.* 1. to become frayed, fray. 2. to become shabby.

обтюрáтор, а, *m.* 1. (*anat. and tech.*) obturator. 2. (*phot.*) shutter. 3. (*mil.*) gas-check (*in breech of gun*).

обтюрáци|я, и, f. (*tech.*) obturation; stopping-up.

обтя́гива|ть, ю, *impf. of* обтяну́ть.

обтя́жк|а, и, f. 1. cover (*for furniture*). 2. (*aeron.*) skin. 3. плáтье в ~у close-fitting dress.

обтя|ну́ть, ну́, ~нешь, *pf.* (*of* ~гивать) 1. (+*i.*) to cover (*furniture*) (with). 2. to fit close (to).

обувá|ть(ся), ю(сь), *impf. of* обу́ть(ся).

обу́вк|а, и, f. (*coll.*) boots.

обувн|óй, *adj. of* óбувь; о. магази́н shoe shop; ~áя промы́шленность boot and shoe industry.

обувщи́к, á, *m.* boot and shoe operative.

óбув|ь, и, *no pl., f.* footwear; boots, shoes.

обу́гливани|е, я, *n.* carbonization.

обу́глива|ть(ся), ю(сь), *impf. of* обу́глить-(ся).

обу́гл|ить, ю, ишь, *pf.* (*of* ~ивать) to char; to carbonize.

обу́гл|иться, юсь, ишься, *pf.* (*of* ~иваться) to become charred, char.

обу́жива|ть, ю, *impf. of* обу́зить.

обу́з|а, ы, *f.* burden; быть ~ой для кого-н. to be a burden to someone.

обузда́|ть, а́ю, *pf.* (*of* ~ывать) to bridle, curb (*also fig.*); (*fig.*) to restrain, control; о. свой хара́ктер to restrain oneself; о. свои стра́сти to curb one's passions.

обузды́ва|ть, ю, *impf. of* обузда́ть.

обу́|зить, жу, зишь, *pf.* (*of* ~живать) to make too tight.

обурева́|ть, ет, *impf.* to shake; to grip; его́ ~ют сомне́ния he is a prey to doubts.

обуржуа́зивани|е, я, *n.* embourgeoisement.

обуржуа́|зиться, жусь, зишься, *pf.* to become bourgeois, undergo embourgeoisement.

обусло́в|ить, лю, ишь, *pf.* (*of* ~ливать) 1. to condition; (+*i.*) to make conditional (upon), stipulate (for); он ~ил своё согла́сие предоставле́нием маши́ны he made his consent conditional upon the provision of a car. 2. to cause, bring about; to be the condition of.

обусло́в|иться, люсь, ишься, *pf. of* ~ливаться.

обусло́влива|ть, ю, *impf. of* обусло́вить.

обусло́влива|ться, юсь, *impf.* (*of* обусло́виться) (+*i.*) to be conditioned (by), be conditional (upon); to depend (on); разме́р ~ется тре́бованиями the size is conditioned by the requirements.

обу́т|ый, *p.p.p. of* ~ь; оде́тый и о. clothed and shod.

обу́|ть, ю, ешь, *pf.* (*of* ~ва́ть) 1. о. кого́-н. to put on someone's boots (shoes) for him. 2. to provide with boots, shoes.

обу́|ться, юсь, ешься, *pf.* (*of* ~ва́ться) 1. to put on one's boots, shoes. 2. to provide oneself with boots, shoes.

о́бух, а (*and* обу́х, а́), *m.* butt, back; head (*of an axe*); (*naut.*) eye-bolt; меня́ то́чно ~ом по голове́ (*coll.*) you could have knocked me down with a feather; пле́тью ~а не перешибёшь (*prov.*) the weakest goes to the wall.

обуч|а́ть(ся), а́ю(сь), *impf. of* ~и́ть(ся).

обуче́ни|е, я, *n.* teaching; instruction, training; совме́стное о. (лиц обо́его по́ла) co-education.

обуч|и́ть, у́, ~ишь, *pf.* (*of* учи́ть *and* ~а́ть) (кого́-н. чему́-н.) to teach (someone something); to instruct, train (in).

обуч|и́ться, у́сь, ~ишься, *pf.* (*of* учи́ться *and* ~а́ться) (+*d.* or +*inf.*) to learn.

о́бу́шный, *adj. of* о́бух.

обуш|о́к, ка́, *m.* pick (with detachable point); (*naut.*) eye-bolt.

обуя́|ть, ет, *pf.* (*obs.*) to seize; to grip; его́ ~л страх fear had seized him.

обха́жива|ть, ю, *impf.* (*coll.*) to cajole, try to get round.

обхва́т, а, *m.* (*measurement of circumference*) girth; в ~е in circumference; ме́рить в ~е to girth.

обхва|ти́ть, чу́, ~тишь, *pf.* (*of* ~тывать) to encompass (with outstretched arms); to clasp.

обхва́тыва|ть, ю, *impf. of* обхвати́ть.

обхо́д, а, *m.* 1. (*doctor's, postman's, etc.*) round; (*guard's, policeman's*) beat; пойти́ в о. to go round, make (go) one's round(s). 2. roundabout way; by-pass. 3. (*mil.*) turning movement, wide enveloping movement. 4. evasion, circumvention (*of law, etc.*).

обходи́тел|ьный (~ен, ~ьна), *adj.* pleasant; courteous; well-mannered.

обхо|ди́ть[1], жу́, ~дишь, *impf. of* обойти́.

обхо|ди́ть[2], жу́, ~дишь, *pf.* to go all round.

обхо|ди́ться, жу́сь, ~дишься, *impf. of* обойти́сь.

обхо́дн|ый, *adj.* roundabout, circuitous; о. путь detour; ~ым путём in a roundabout way; ~ое движе́ние (*mil.*) turning movement.

обхо́дчик, а, *m.* (*railway*) trackman.

обхожде́ни|е, я, *n.* manners; (с+*i.*) treatment (of); behaviour (towards).

обче́сться, обочту́сь, обочтёшься, *past* обчёлся, обочла́сь, *pf.* (*coll.*) = обсчита́ться; (их) раз, два и обчёлся (they) can be counted on the fingers of one hand.

обчи́|стить, щу, стишь, *pf.* (*of* ~ща́ть) 1. to clean; to brush. 2. (*fig., coll.*) to clean out (= to rob).

обчи́|ститься, щусь, стишься, *pf.* (*of* ~ща́ться) 1. to clean oneself; to brush oneself. 2. *pass. of* ~стить.

обчища́|ть(ся), ю(сь), *impf. of* обчи́стить(ся).

обша́рива|ть, ю, *impf. of* обша́рить.

обша́р|ить, ю, ишь, *pf.* (*of* ~ивать) to rummage; to ransack.

обша́рка|ть, ю, *pf.* (*coll.*) to wear out (*by much walking*).

обша́рпа|нный, *p.p.p. of* ~ть; ~нное зда́ние dilapidated building.

обша́рпа|ть, ю, *pf.* (*coll.*) to wear (away).

обшива́|ть, ю, *impf. of* обши́ть[1, 2].

обши́вк|а, и, *f.* 1. edging, bordering. 2. trimming, facing. 3. boarding, panelling; о. фане́рой veneering; (*tech.*) sheathing; (*naut.*) planking; стальна́я о. plating; нару́жная о. skin-plating.

обши́в|очный, *adj. of* ~ка.

обши́р|ный (~ен, ~на), *adj.* extensive (*also*

fig.); spacious; vast; у него́ ~ное знако́мство he has a very wide circle of acquaintance.

об|ши́ть[1], ошью́, ошьёшь, *pf.* (*of* ~шива́ть) **1.** to edge, border. **2.** to trim, face. **3.** to sew round (*a package*). **4.** to plank; to revet; (*tech.*) to sheathe.

об|ши́ть[2], ошью́, ошьёшь, *pf.* (*of* ~шива́ть) to sew for; to make clothes for; она́ сама́ ~ши́ла всю семью́ she has made all the family's clothes herself.

обшла́г, а́, *pl.* ~а́, *m.* cuff.

обща́|ться, юсь, *impf.* (с+*i.*) to associate (with), mix (with).

общевойсково́|й, *adj.* (*mil.*) common to all arms; ~е кома́ндование combined command.

общедосту́п|ный (~ен, ~на), *adj.* **1.** of moderate price. **2.** (*of book, etc.*) popular.

общежите́йский, *adj.* everyday, ordinary.

общежи́ти|е, я, *n.* **1.** hostel. **2.** society, community; communal life.

общеизве́ст|ный (~ен, ~на), *adj.* well--known, generally known; notorious.

общенаро́дный, *adj.* common to whole people; national, public; о. пра́здник public holiday.

обще́ни|е, я, *n.* intercourse; relations, links; ли́чное о. personal contact.

общеобразова́тельны|й, *adj.* of general education; ~е предме́ты general subjects.

общепоня́т|ный (~ен, ~на), *adj.* comprehensible to all, within the grasp of all.

общепри́знан|ный (~, ~а), *adj.* universally recognized.

общепри́нят|ый (~, ~а), *adj.* generally accepted.

общераспространённый, *adj.* in general use, generally used, generally found.

общесою́зн|ый, *adj.* All-Union (*common to or valid for the entire U.S.S.R.*); ~ого значе́ния of importance for the entire U.S.S.R.

обще́ственник, а, *m.* public man; person actively engaging in public life.

обще́ственност|ь, и, *f.* **1.** (*collect.*) (the) public, the community; public opinion; англи́йская о. the English public. **2.** (*collect.*) community; communal organizations; о. заво́да factory organizations; нау́чная о. the scientific community, scientific circles. **3.** disposition to public work, disposition to serve the community; дух ~и public spirit, public-spiritedness.

обще́ственн|ый, *adj.* **1.** social, public; ~ая жизнь public life; ~ое мне́ние public opinion; ~ые нау́ки social sciences; ~ое пита́ние public catering; ~ое порица́ние public censure; ~ая рабо́та public work, social work; ~ые рабо́ты public works; ~ая со́бственность public property, public

ownership. **2.** voluntary, unpaid, amateur; на ~ых нача́лах on a voluntary basis; ~ые организа́ции voluntary organizations.

обществ|о, а, *n.* **1.** (*in var. senses*) society; association; первобы́тное о. primitive society; нау́ка об ~е social science; быва́ть в ~е to frequent society, be a socialite. **2.** (*econ.*) company; акционе́рное о. joint-stock company. **3.** company, society; в ~е кого́-н. in someone's company; попа́сть в дурно́е о. to fall into bad company.

обществове́дени|е, я, *n.* social science, civics.

обществове́д|ческий, *adj. of* ~ение.

общеупотреби́тел|ьный (~ен, ~ьна), *adj.* in general use.

общечелове́ческий, *adj.* common to all mankind.

о́бщ|ий, *adj.* general; common; о. враг common enemy; ~ее де́ло common cause; о. знако́мый mutual acquaintance; ~ее ме́сто commonplace; ~ее собра́ние general meeting; ~ее согла́сие common consent; ~ая су́мма sum total; о. наибо́льший дели́тель (*math.*) the greatest common divisor; ~ее наиме́ньшее кра́тное (*math.*) the least common multiple; в ~ем on the whole, in general, in sum; в ~их черта́х in general outline; не име́ть ничего́ ~его (с+*i.*) to have nothing in common (with).

о́бщин|а, ы, *f.* community; commune.

о́бщи́нн|ый, *adj.* communal; ~ая земля́ common (land).

общип|а́ть, лю́, ~лешь, *pf.* (*of* щипа́ть 4 *and* ~ывать) to pluck.

общи́пыва|ть, ю, *impf. of* общипа́ть.

общи́тельност|ь, и, *f.* sociability.

общи́тел|ьный (~ен, ~ьна), *adj.* sociable.

о́бщност|ь, и, *f.* community; о. интере́сов community of interests.

общо́, *adv.* (*coll.*) generally; он изложи́л свои́ взгля́ды сли́шком о. he expounded his views in too general terms.

объего́рива|ть, ю, *impf. of* объего́рить.

объего́р|ить, ю, ишь, *pf.* (*of* ~ивать) (*coll.*) to cheat, swindle.

объеда́|ть(ся), ю(сь), *impf. of* объе́сть(ся).

объедине́ни|е, я, *n.* **1.** unification. **2.** union, association.

объедин|ённый, *p.p.p. of* ~и́ть *and adj.* united; Организа́ция Объединённых На́ций United Nations Organization.

объедини́тельный, *adj.* unifying, uniting.

объедин|и́ть, ю́, и́шь, *pf.* (*of* ~я́ть) to unite; to join; о. ресу́рсы to pool resources; о. уси́лия to combine efforts.

объедин|и́ться, ю́сь, и́шься, *pf.* (*of* ~я́ться) (с+*i.*) to unite (with).

объедин|я́ть(ся), я́ю(сь), *impf. of* ~и́ть(ся).

объе́д|ки, ко́в, *sing.* **~ок, ~ка,** *m.* *(coll.)* leavings (*of food*), leftovers, scraps.

объе́зд, а, *m.* **1.** riding round, going round. **2.** circuit, detour. **3.** *(obs.)* mounted posse.

объе́з|дить¹, жу, дишь, *pf.* (*of* ~жа́ть¹) to travel over.

объе́з|дить², жу, дишь, *pf.* (*of* ~жа́ть²) to break in (*horses*).

объе́здк|а, и, *f.* breaking in (*of horses*).

объе́здчик¹, а, *m.* mounted patrol; лесно́й о. forest warden.

объе́здчик², а, *m.* horse-breaker.

объезжа́|ть¹, ю, *impf.* *of* объе́здить¹ *and* объе́хать.

объезжа́|ть², ю, *impf.* *of* объе́здить².

объе́зжий, *adj.* roundabout, circuitous; о. путь detour.

объе́кт, а, *m.* **1.** (*in var. senses*) object. **2.** (*mil.*) objective. **3.** establishment; works; строи́тельный о. building site.

объекти́в, а, *m.* (*opt.*) objective, object-glass, lens.

объектива́ци|я, и, *f.* = объективиза́ция.

объективиза́ци|я, и, *f.* objectification.

объективи́зм, а, *m.* **1.** (*term of Marxist philosophy*) objectivism. **2.** objectivity.

объективи́р|овать, ую, *impf. and pf.* to objectify.

объекти́вность|ь, и, *f.* objectivity.

объекти́в|ный (~ен, ~на), *adj.* **1.** objective. **2.** unbiassed.

объе́кт|ный, *adj. of* ~ 1.

объе́кт|овый, *adj. of* ~ 3.

объе́м, а, *m.* volume (*also fig.*); bulk, size, capacity.

объёмист|ый (~, ~а), *adj.* (*coll.*) voluminous, bulky.

объём|ный, ый, *adj.* by volume, volumetric; о. вес weight by volume; о. заря́д space charge; ~ое отноше́ние volume ratio.

объе́|сть, м, шь, ст, ди́м, ди́те, дя́т, *past* ~**л,** *pf.* (*of* ~да́ть) **1.** to eat round; to nibble. **2.** (*coll.*) о. кого́-н. to eat someone out of house and home.

объе́|сться, мся, шься, стся, ди́мся, ди́тесь, дя́тся, *past* ~**лся,** *pf.* (*of* ~да́ться) to overeat.

объе́|хать, ду, дешь, *pf.* (*of* ~зжа́ть¹) **1.** to go round, skirt. **2.** to overtake, pass. **3.** to travel over.

объяв|и́ть, лю́, ~ишь, *pf.* (*of* ~ля́ть) to declare, announce; to publish, proclaim; to advertise; о. войну́ to declare war; о. ко́нкурс to announce a competition; о. собра́ние откры́тым to declare a meeting open; о. вне зако́на to outlaw.

объяв|и́ться, лю́сь, ~ишься, *pf.* (*of* ~ля́ться) **1.** (*coll.*) to turn up, appear. **2.** (+*i.*) to announce oneself (to be), declare oneself (to be). **3.** *pass. of* ~и́ть.

объявле́ни|е, я, *n.* **1.** declaration, announcement; notice; о. войны́ declaration of war. **2.** advertisement; дать о. в газе́ту, помести́ть о. в газе́те to put an advertisement in a paper.

объявля́|ть(ся), ю(сь), *impf. of* объяви́ть(ся).

объяде́ни|е, я, *n.* **1.** (*obs.*) overeating. **2.** (*as pred.*; *coll.*) something delicious; то́рты э́ти — пря́мо о. these cakes are simply delicious.

объясне́ни|е, я, *n.* (*in var. senses*) explanation; о. в любви́ declaration of love.

объясни́м|ый (~, ~а), *adj.* explicable, explainable.

объясни́тельный, *adj.* explanatory.

объясн|и́ть, ю́, и́шь, *pf.* (*of* ~я́ть) to explain.

объясн|и́ться, ю́сь, и́шься, *pf.* (*of* ~я́ться) **1.** to explain oneself; (c+*i.*) to have a talk (with); to have it out (with); о. в любви́ (+*d.*) to make a declaration of love (to). **2.** to become clear, be explained; тепе́рь всё ~и́лось everything is now clear.

объясн|я́ть, я́ю, *impf. of* ~и́ть.

объясн|я́ться, я́юсь, *impf.* **1.** *impf. o,* ~и́ться. **2.** to speak; to make oneself understood; уме́ете ли вы о. по-францу́зски? can you make yourself understood in French?; о. же́стами и зна́ками to use sign language. **3.** (+*i.*) to be explained (by), be accounted for (by); э́тим ~я́ется его́ стра́нное поведе́ние that accounts for his strange behaviour.

объя́ти|е, я, *n.* embrace; с распростёртыми ~ями with open arms; бро́ситься кому́-н. в ~я to fall into someone's arms; заключи́ть в ~я to embrace, fold in one's arms.

объя́т|ый, p.p.p. of ~ь; о. пла́менем enveloped in flames; о. стра́хом terror-stricken; о. ду́мой wrapped in thought.

объя́|ть, обойму́, обоймёшь (*and coll.* обыму́, обы́мешь**),** *pf.* (*obs.*) **1.** to comprehend, grasp. **2.** to seize, grip, come over; у́жас ~л его́ terror seized him.

обыва́тел|ь, я, *m.* **1.** (*obs.*) inhabitant, resident. **2.** (*fig.*) philistine.

обыва́тельский, *adj.* **1.** (*obs.*) belonging to the local inhabitants. **2.** (*fig.*) philistine; narrow-minded.

обыва́тельщин|а, ы, *f.* philistinism; narrow-mindedness.

обыгр|а́ть, а́ю, *pf.* (*of* ~ывать) **1.** to beat (*at a game*); to win; о. кого́-н. на что́-н. to win something of someone. **2.** (*theatr.*) to use with (good) effect, play up; (*fig.*) to turn to advantage, turn to account. **3.** (*mus.*) to mellow (*an instrument by playing*).

обы́грыва|ть, ю, *impf. of* обыгра́ть.

обыдёнкой, *adv.* (*dial.*) in one day.

обы́денност|ь, и, *f.* **1.** ordinariness. **2.** everyday occurrence.

обы́денн|ый, *adj.* ordinary; commonplace; everyday; ~ое происше́ствие everyday occurrence.

обыдёнщин|а, ы, *f.* uneventfulness; commonplaceness.

обыкнове́ни|е, я, *n.* habit, wont; по ~ю as usual; име́ть о. (+*inf.*) to be in the habit (of).

обыкнове́нно, *adv.* usually, as a rule.

обыкнове́н|ный (~ен, ~на), *adj.* usual; ordinary; commonplace; ~ная исто́рия everyday occurrence; бо́льше ~ного more than usual.

о́быск, а, *m.* search; о́рдер на пра́во ~а search warrant.

обы|ска́ть, щу́, ~щешь, *pf.* (*of* ~скивать) to search.

обы|ска́ться, щу́сь, ~щешься, *pf.* (*coll.*) to carry out a search (in vain).

обы́скива|ть, ю, *impf. of* обыска́ть.

обы́ча|й, я, *m.* custom; (*leg.*) usage; по ~ю in accordance with custom; э́то у нас в ~е it is our custom.

обы́чно, *adv.* usually; as a rule.

обы́чн|ый, *adj.* usual; ordinary; ~ое пра́во (*leg.*) customary law.

обюрокра́|тить, чу, тишь, *pf.* (*of* ~чивать) (*coll.*) to make bureaucratic.

обюрокра́|титься, чусь, тишься, *pf.* (*of* ~чиваться) (*coll.*) to become a bureaucrat, become bureaucratic.

обюрокра́чива|ть(ся), ю(сь), *impf. of* обюрокра́тить(ся).

обя́занност|ь, и, *f.* duty; responsibility; во́инская о. military service; по ~и as in duty bound; in the line of duty; исполня́ть ~и дире́ктора to act as director; исполня́ющий ~и дире́ктора acting director.

обя́зан|ный (~, ~a), *adj.* **1.** (+*inf.*) obliged, bound; он ~ верну́ться he is obliged to go back, it is his duty to go back. **2.** (+*d.*) obliged, indebted (to); я вам о́чень ~ I am very much obliged to you; она́ вам ~a свое́й жи́знью she owes you her life; мы э́тим ~ы Петро́ву we have Petrov to thank for this.

обяза́тельно, *adv.* without fail; я о. приду́ I shall come without fail; он о. там бу́дет he is sure to be there, he is bound to be there.

обяза́тельност|ь, и, *f.* **1.** obligatoriness; binding force. **2.** (*obs.*) obligingness.

обяза́тел|ьный (~ен, ~ьна), *adj.* **1.** obligatory; compulsory; binding; ~ьное обуче́ние compulsory education; ~ьное постановле́ние binding decree. **2.** (*obs.*) obliging.

обяза́тельственн|ый, *adj.* (*leg.*) ~ое пра́во liability law.

обяза́тельств|о, а, *n.* **1.** obligation; engagement; долгово́е о. promissory note; взять на себя́ о. (+*inf.*) to pledge oneself (to), undertake (to). **2.** (*pl.*; *leg.*) liabilities.

обя|за́ть, жу́, ~жешь, *pf.* (*of* ~зывать) **1.** to bind, oblige, commit; о. кого́-н. яви́ться в определённое вре́мя to bind someone to appear at a stated time. **2.** to oblige; вы меня́ о́чень ~жете you will oblige me greatly, you will do me a great favour, I shall be greatly indebted to you.

обя|за́ться, жу́сь, ~жешься, *pf.* (*of* ~зываться) to bind oneself, pledge oneself, undertake.

обя́зыва|ть, ю, *impf. of* обяза́ть; ни к чему́ не ~ющий non-committal.

обя́зыва|ться, юсь, *impf. of* обяза́ться; не хочу́ ни пе́ред кем о. I wish to be beholden to no one.

ова́л, а, *m.* oval.

ова́льный, *adj.* oval.

ова́ци|я, и, *f.* ovation.

овдове́|вший, *past part. of* ~ть *and adj.* widowed.

овдове́|ть, ю, *pf.* to become a widow(er).

овева́|ть, ю, *impf. of* ове́ять.

ов|е́н, на́, *m.* **1.** (*obs.*) ram. **2.** (*astron.*) Aries, the Ram (*first sign on the Zodiac*).

ов|ёс, са́, *m.* oats.

ов|е́чий, *adj. of* ~ца́; волк в ~е́чьей шку́ре a wolf in sheep's clothing.

ове́чк|а, и, *f.* *dim. of* овца́; (*fig.*) harmless creature.

овеществ|и́ть, лю́, и́шь, *pf.* (*of* ~ля́ть) to substantiate.

овеществля́|ть, ю, *impf. of* овеществи́ть.

**ове́я|нный, *p.p.p. of* ~ть; о. сла́вой covered with glory.

ове́|ять, ю, ешь, *pf.* (*of* ~вать) (+*i.*) **1.** to fan. **2.** (*fig.*) to surround (with), cover (with).

ови́н, а, *m.* barn (*for drying crops*).

овладева́|ть, ю, *impf. of* овладе́ть.

овладе́ни|е, я, *n.* (+*i.*) mastery; mastering.

овладе́|ть, ю, *pf.* (*of* ~ва́ть) (+*i.*) **1.** to seize; to take possession (of); о. собо́й to get control of oneself, regain self-control; мно́ю ~ла ра́дость I was overcome with joy. **2.** (*fig.*) to master.

о́вод, а, *pl.* ~ы, ~ов (*and* ~á, ~óв), gadfly.

овощево́дств|о, а, *n.* vegetable-growing.

овощехрани́лищ|е, а, *n.* vegetable store.

о́вощ|и, е́й, *sing.* ~, ~a, *m.* vegetables; вся́кому ~у своё вре́мя (*prov.*) there is a time for everything, everything in good season.

овощно́й, *adj.* vegetable; о. магази́н greengrocery, greengrocer's (shop); о. стол vegetarian cooking.

овра́г, а, *m.* ravine, gully.

овра́ж|ек¹, ка, *m. dim. of* овра́г.

овра́ж|ек², ка, *m.* (*zool.*) gopher.

овра́жист|ый (~, ~а), *adj.* abounding in ravines.

овра́|жный, *adj. of* ~г; о. песо́к pit sand.

овсе́ц, á, *no pl., m.* (*coll.*) *dim. of* овёс; дать ло́шади ~á to give a horse his oats.

овсю́г, á, *m.* (*bot.*) wild oats.

овся́ниц|а, ы, *f.* (*bot.*) fescue.

овся́нк|а¹, и, *f.* 1. oatmeal. 2. oatmeal porridge.

овся́нк|а², и, *f.* (*orn.*) (yellow) bunting, yellow-hammer.

овсян|о́й, *adj. of* овёс; о. ко́лос ear of oats; ~о́е по́ле field of oats.

овся́н|ый, *adj.* made of oats; oatmeal; ~ая ка́ша oatmeal porridge; ~ая крупа́ oatmeal.

овуля́ци|я, и, *f.* (*biol.*) ovulation.

овц|á, ы́, *pl.* ~ы, ове́ц, ~ам, *f.* sheep; ewe; заблу́дшая о. (*fig.*) lost sheep.

овцебы́к, а, *m.* musk-ox.

овцево́д, а, *m.* sheep-breeder.

овцево́дств|о, а, *n.* sheep-breeding.

овча́р, а, *m.* shepherd.

овча́рк|а, и, *f.* sheep-dog; неме́цкая о. Alsatian (*dog*).

овча́р|ня, ни, *g. pl.* ~ен, *f.* sheep-fold.

овчи́н|а, ы, *f.* sheepskin.

овчи́н|ка, ки, *f. dim. of* ~а; ей не́бо с ~ку показа́лось she was frightened out of her wits; о. вы́делки не сто́ит (*fig.*) the game is not worth the candle.

овчи́нный, *adj.* sheepskin.

ога́р|ок, ка, *m.* candle-end; *pl.* cinders; (*tech.*) skimmings, scoria.

огиба́|ть, ю, *impf. of* обогну́ть.

оглавле́ни|е, я, *n.* table of contents.

огла|си́ть, шу́, си́шь, *pf.* (*of* ~ша́ть) 1. to proclaim, announce; о. резолю́цию to read out a resolution; о. жениха́ и неве́сту to publish banns of marriage. 2. to divulge, make public. 3. to fill (*with loud cries, etc.*).

огла|си́ться, шу́сь, си́шься, *pf.* (*of* ~ша́ть-ся) 1. (+*i.*) to resound (with). 2. *pass. of* ~си́ть.

огла́ск|а, и, *f.* publicity; избега́ть ~и to shun publicity; получи́ть ~у to be made known, receive publicity; преда́ть ~е to make known, make known.

оглаша́|ть(ся), ю(сь), *impf. of* огласи́ть(ся).

оглаше́ни|е, я, *n.* proclaiming, publication; не подлежи́т ~ю confidential (*classification of document*).

оглашённый, *adj.* как о. (*coll.*) like one possessed.

оглоб|ля, ли, *g. pl.* ~ель, *f.* shaft; поверну́ть ~ли (*fig., coll.*) to turn back, retrace one's steps.

огло́х|нуть, ну, нешь, *past* ~, ~ла, *pf. of* гло́хнуть 1.

оглуп|и́ть, лю́, ~и́шь, *pf.* (*of* ~ля́ть) 1. to fool, make a fool of; to deceive. 2. to distort; to misrepresent.

оглупля́|ть, ю, *impf.* 1. *impf. of* оглупи́ть. 2. to try to fool, try to deceive.

оглуш|а́ть, а́ю, *impf. of* ~и́ть.

оглуши́тел|ьный (~ен, ~ьна), *adj.* deafening.

оглуш|и́ть, у́, и́шь, *pf.* 1. *pf. of* глуши́ть 1. 2. (*impf.* ~а́ть) to deafen; to stun (*also fig.*).

огля|де́ть, жу́, ди́шь, *pf.* (*of* ~дывать) to look round; to examine, inspect.

огля|де́ться, жу́сь, ди́шься, *pf.* (*of* ~дываться) 1. to look round. 2. to get used to things around one; (*fig.*) to adapt oneself, become acclimatized; о. в темноте́ to become accustomed to the darkness.

огля́дк|а, и, *f.* 1. looking back; бежа́ть без ~и to run without turning one's head. 2. care, caution; без ~и carelessly; де́йствовать с ~ой to act circumspectly.

огля́дыва|ть(ся), ю(сь), *impf. of* огляде́ть-(ся) *and* огляну́ть(ся).

огля|ну́ть, ну́, ~нешь, *inst. pf.* (*of* ~дывать) to take a look over.

огля|ну́ться, ну́сь, ~нешься, *pf.* (*of* ~дываться) to turn (back) to look at something; to glance back.

огневи́дный, *adj.* (*geol.*) igneous, plutonic.

огневи́к, á, *m.* 1. fire-stone. 2. (*med.*) anthrax. 3. (*coll.*) gunner.

огневи́ц|а, ы, *f.* (*dial.*) fever.

огнев|о́й, *adj. of* ого́нь; (*fig.*) fiery; (*geol.*) igneous, pyrogenous; о. бой (*mil.*) firing; о. вал (*mil.*) barrage; ~ая коро́бка fire-box; ~о́е окаймле́ние box barrage; ~ы́е сре́дства weapons; ~а́я то́чка (*mil.*) weapon emplacement.

огнегаси́тельный, *adj.* fire-extinguishing; о. прибо́р fire-extinguisher.

огнеды́шащ|ий, *adj.* fire-spitting; ~ая гора́ (*obs.*) volcano.

огнемёт, а, *m.* (*mil.*) flame-thrower.

о́гненный, *adj.* fiery (*also fig.*).

огнеопа́с|ный (~ен, ~на), *adj.* inflammable.

огнепокло́нник, а, *m.* fire-worshipper.

огнепокло́нни|ческий, *adj. of* ~к.

огнепокло́нничеств|о, а, *n.* fire-worship.

огнеприпа́с|ы, ов, *no sing.* ammunition.

огнесто́|йкий (~ек, ~йка), *adj.* fire-proof, fire-resistant.

огнестре́льн|ый, *adj.* ~ое ору́жие fire-arm(s); ~ая ра́на bullet wound.

огнетуши́тел|ь, я, *m.* fire-extinguisher.

огнеупо́р|ный (~ен, ~на), *adj.* fire-resistant, fire-proof; refractory; ~ная гли́на fire-clay; о. кирпи́ч fire-brick.

огнеупо́ры, ов, *no sing.* (*tech.*) refractory materials.

огни́в|о, а, *n.* steel (*used formerly for striking fire from a flint*).

ого́, *interj.* oho!

огова́рива|ть(ся), ю(сь), *impf. of* оговори́ть(ся).

огово́р, а, *m.* slander.

оговор|и́ть¹, ю́, и́шь, *pf.* (*of* огова́ривать) to slander.

оговор|и́ть², ю́, и́шь, *pf.* (*of* огова́ривать) 1. to stipulate (for); to fix, agree (on); мы ~и́ли усло́вия рабо́ты we have fixed the conditions of work. 2. to make a reservation, make a proviso (concerning); to specify; он ~и́л своё несогла́сие he specified his disagreement.

оговор|и́ться, ю́сь, и́шься, *pf.* (*of* огова́риваться) 1. to make a reservation, make a proviso. 2. to make a slip in speaking. 3. *pass. of* ~и́ть.

огово́р|ка, ки, *f.* 1. reservation, proviso; без ~ок without reserve; он согласи́лся, но с не́которыми ~ками he agreed but made certain reservations. 2. slip of the tongue.

огово́рщик, а, *m.* (*coll.*) slanderer.

оголе́ни|е, я, *n.* denudation.

огол|ённый, *p.p.p. of* ~и́ть *and adj.* bare, nude; uncovered, exposed.

огол|е́ц, ьца́, *m.* (*coll.*) lad, (young) fellow.

огол|и́ть, ю́, и́шь, *pf.* (*of* ~я́ть) to bare; to strip, uncover; о. фланг (*mil.*) to expose one's flank.

огол|и́ться, ю́сь, и́шься, *pf.* (*of* ~я́ться) 1. to strip (oneself). 2. to become exposed. 3. *pass. of* ~и́ть.

оголте́лый, *adj.* (*coll.*) unbridled; frenzied.

огол|я́ть(ся), я́ю(сь), *impf. of* ~и́ть(ся).

огон|ёк, ька́, *m.* 1. (small) light; блужда́ющий о. will o' the wisp; весёлый о. merry twinkle; зайти́ к кому́-н. на о. (*coll.*) to drop in on someone (*seeing a light in the window*). 2. (*fig.*) zest, spirit.

ог|о́нь, ня́, *m.* 1. fire (*also fig.*); говори́ть с ~нём to speak with fervour; анто́нов о. gangrene; ~нём и мечо́м with fire and sword; меж двух ~не́й between two fires, between the devil and the deep blue sea; пройти́ о. и во́ду to go through fire and water; из ~ня́ да в по́лымя (*fig.*) out of the frying-pan into the fire. 2. (*mil.*) fire; firing; управле́ние ~нём fire control; закреплённый о. в то́чку fire on fixed lines; отвеча́ть ~нём to fire back. 3. light; хвостово́й о. (*aeron.*) tail light; опозна́тельный о. recognition lights; тако́го челове́ка днём с ~нём не найдёшь (*coll.*) you will not find another such in a month of Sundays.

огора́жива|ть(ся), ю(сь), *impf. of* огороди́ть(ся).

огоро́д, а, *m.* kitchen-garden; бро́сить ка́мешек в чей-н. о. (*fig., coll.*) to throw stones at someone; to make hints about someone.

огоро|ди́ть, жу́, ~ди́шь, *pf.* (*of* огора́живать) to fence in, enclose.

огоро|ди́ться, жу́сь, ~ди́шься, *pf.* (*of* огора́живаться) 1. to fence oneself in. 2. *pass. of* ~ди́ть.

огоро́дник, а, *m.* market-gardener.

огоро́днича|ть, ю, *impf.* (*coll.*) to go in for market-gardening, be a market-gardener.

огоро́дничеств|о, а, *n.* market-gardening.

огоро́д|ный, *adj. of* ~; ~ное хозя́йство market-gardening, market-garden.

огоро́ш|ить, у, ишь, *pf.* (*coll.*) to take aback, disconcert.

огорч|а́ть(ся), а́ю(сь), *impf. of* ~и́ть(ся).

огорче́ни|е, я, *n.* grief, affliction; chagrin; быть в ~и to be in distress.

огорчи́тел|ьный (~ен, ~ьна), *adj.* distressing.

огорч|и́ть, у́, и́шь, *pf.* (*of* ~а́ть) to grieve, distress, pain.

огорч|и́ться, у́сь, и́шься, *pf.* (*of* ~а́ться) to grieve; to be distressed, be pained; не ~а́йтесь! cheer up!

огра́б|ить, лю, ишь, *pf. of* гра́бить¹.

ограбле́ни|е, я, *n.* robbery; burglary.

огра́д|а, ы, *f.* fence.

огра|ди́ть, жу́, ди́шь, *pf.* (*of* ~жда́ть) 1. (*obs.*) to enclose, fence in. 2. (от) to guard (against, from), protect (against).

огра|ди́ться, жу́сь, ди́шься, *pf.* (*of* ~жда́ться) (от) to defend oneself (against); to protect oneself (against), guard oneself (against, from).

огражда́|ть(ся), ю(сь), *impf. of* огради́ть(ся).

ограниче́ни|е, я, *n.* limitation, restriction.

ограни́ченност|ь, и, *f.* limitedness, scantiness; (*fig.*) narrowness, narrow-mindedness.

ограни́ч|енный, *p.p.p. of* ~ить *and adj.* limited; о. челове́к (*fig.*) narrow(-minded) person, hidebound person.

ограни́чива|ть(ся), ю(сь), *impf. of* ограничить(ся).

ограничи́тел|ь, я, *m.* (*tech.*) о. хо́да catch, stop, stop piece, arresting device.

ограничи́тельный, *adj.* restrictive, limiting.

ограни́ч|ить, у, ишь, *pf.* (*of* ~ивать) to limit, restrict, cut down; о. себя́ в расхо́дах to cut down one's expenditure; о. ора́тора вре́менем to set a speaker a time limit.

ограни́ч|иться, усь, ишься, *pf.* (*of* ~иваться) (+*i.*) 1. to limit oneself (to), confine oneself (to); он ~и́лся кра́ткой ре́чью he confined himself to a short speech. 2. to be limited (to), be confined (to).

огребá|ть, ю, *impf. of* **огрестú; о. дéньги** (*coll.*) to rake in money.

огре|стú, бý, бёшь, *past* ⌣б, ∼блá, *pf.* (*of* ∼бáть) to rake round.

огрé|ть, ю, *pf.* (*coll.*) to catch a blow, fetch a blow.

огрéх, а, *m.* **1.** (*agric.*) gap (*in sowing, ploughing, etc.*). **2.** (*coll.*) fault, imperfection (*in work*).

огрóм|ный (∼ен, ∼на), *adj.* huge; vast; enormous.

огрубéлый, *adj.* coarse, hardened.

огрубé|ть, ю, *pf. of* **грубéть.**

огрýз|нуть, ну, нешь, *past* ∼, ∼ла, *pf.* (*coll.*) to grow stout.

огрыз|áться, áюсь, *impf.* (*of* ∼нýться) (на+*a.*) to snap (at) (*of a dog; also fig.*).

огрыз|нýться, нýсь, нёшься, *pf. of* ∼áться.

огрýз|ок, ка, *m.* bit, end; **о. карандашá** (*coll.*) pencil stub, stump.

огýз|ок, ка, *m.* rump.

огýлом, *adv.* (*coll.*) wholesale, indiscriminately.

огýльно, *adv.* without grounds; **о. обвинять** to make a groundless accusation.

огýль|ный (∼ен, ∼ьна), *adj.* **1.** wholesale, indiscriminate; ∼ьное охáивание wholesale disparagement. **2.** unfounded, groundless. **3.** (*obs.*) wholesale (*comm.*).

огур|éц, цá, *m.* cucumber.

огурé|чный, *adj. of* ∼ц; ∼чная трава́ (*bot.*) borage.

огýрчик, а, *m. affect. dim. of* **огурéц; как о.** (*coll.*) *of person of ruddy, healthy appearance.*

óд|а, ы, *f.* ode.

одáлжива|ть, ю, *impf. of* **одолжúть.**

одалúск|а, и, *f.* odalisque.

одарённост|ь, и, *f.* endowments, (natural) gifts, talent.

одар|ённый, *p.p.p. of* ∼úть *and adj.* gifted, talented.

одáрива|ть, ю, *impf. of* **одарúть.**

одар|úть, ю, úшь, *pf.* **1.** (*impf.* ∼ивать) to give presents (to); онá ∼úла всех детéй игрýшками she has given all the children toys. **2.** (*impf.* ∼я́ть) (+*i.*) to endow (with); прирóда ∼úла егó разнообрáзными спо-сóбностями nature has endowed him with a variety of talents.

одар|я́ть, я́ю, *impf. of* ∼úть.

одевá|ть(ся), ю(сь), *impf. of* **одéть(ся).**

одёж|а, и, *f.* (*coll.*) clothes.

одéжд|а, ы, *f.* **1.** clothes; garments; clothing; вéрхняя о. outer clothing, overcoat; произвóдственная о. industrial clothing, overalls; фóрменная о. uniform. **2.** (*tech.*) surfacing, top dressing (*of road*).

одёжк|а, и, *f. dim. of* **одéжда; по ∼е протя́-гивай нóжки** (*prov.*) cut your coat according to the cloth.

одеколóн, а, *m.* eau-de-Cologne; цветóч-ный о. flower-scented eau-de-Cologne.

одеколóн|ный, *adj. of* ∼.

одел|úть, ю, úшь, *pf.* (*of* ∼я́ть) (+*i.*) **1.** to present (with). **2.** (*obs.*) to endow (with).

одел|я́ть, я́ю, *impf. of* ∼úть.

од|ёр, рá, *m.* (*coll.*) old hack (*horse*).

одёргива|ть, ю, *impf. of* **одёрнуть.**

одеревенéлый, *adj.* numb; (*fig.*) lifeless.

одеревенé|ть, ю, *pf. of* **деревенéть.**

одерж|áть, ý, ∼ишь, *pf.* (*of* ∼ивать) to gain; о. верх (над) to gain the upper hand (over), prevail (over); о. побéду to gain a (the) victory, carry the day.

одéржива|ть, ю, *impf. of* **одержáть.**

одержúм|ый (∼, ∼а), *adj.* **1.** (+*i.*) possessed (by); afflicted (by); о. стрáхом ridden by fear; о. навя́зчивой идéей obsessed by an idée fixe. **2.** *as noun* **о., ∼ого,** *m.* one possessed, madman.

одёр|нуть, ну, нешь, *pf.* (*of* ∼гивать) **1.** to pull down, straighten (*article of clothing*). **2.** (*fig., coll.*) to call to order; to silence; to snub.

одеснýю, *adv.* (*obs.*) to the right; on the right hand.

одессúт, а, *m.* inhabitant of Odessa.

одéт|ый, *p.p.p. of* ∼ь *and adj.* (+*i. or* в+*a.*) dressed (in), clothed (in); with one's clothes on; о. снéгом snow-clad; хорошó о. well-dressed.

одé|ть, ну, нешь, *pf.* (*of* ∼вáть) (+*i. or* в+*a.*) to dress (in), clothe (in).

одé|ться, нусь, нешься, *pf.* (*of* ∼вáться) **1.** to dress (oneself); to clothe oneself; о. в вечéрнее плáтье to put on an evening dress. **2.** *pass. of* ∼ть.

одея́л|о, а, *n.* blanket; coverlet; стёганое о. counterpane, quilt; лоскýтное о. patch-work quilt.

одея́ни|е, я, *n.* garb, attire.

одúн, одногó, *m.*; **однá, однóй,** *f.*; **однó, одногó,** *n.*; *pl.* **однú, однúх,** *num. and pron.* **1.** one; о. стол one table; однú нóжницы one pair of scissors; однó онó one thing; однó дéло..., другóе дéло... it is one thing . . ., another thing . . .; о. за другúм one after the other; однú... другúе some . . . others; с однóй стороны́... с другóй (стороны́) on the one hand . . . on the other hand; однó врéмя at one time; о. раз once; однúм рóсчерком перá with a stroke of the pen; однúм слóвом in a word; о.-двá one or two; о.-едúнственный one and only; о. из ты́сячи one in a thousand; в о. гóлос with one voice, with one accord; в о. пре-крáсный день one fine day, once upon a time; все до одногó all to a man; однó к одномý (*coll.*) moreover; one way and another; все, как о. one and all; о. на о.

in private, tête-à-tête; face to face; по
одному́ one by one, one at a time; in single
file. **2.** a, an; a certain; я встре́тил одного́
моего́ бы́вшего колле́гу I met an old colleague of mine. **3.** alone; by oneself; да́йте
ей сде́лать э́то одно́й let her do it by herself; я живу́ о. I live alone; о.-одинёхонек,
о.-одинёшенек all by oneself. **4.** only;
alone; nothing but; он о. зна́ет доро́гу he
alone knows the way; она́ чита́ет одни́
детекти́вные рома́ны she reads nothing
but detective stories. **5.** о., о. и тот же the
same, one and the same; мы с ней одного́
во́зраста she and I are the same age; э́то
одно́ и то же it is the same thing; мне э́то
всё одно́ it is all one to me.

одина́кий, *adj.* (*obs. or coll.*) identical.

одина́ково, *adv.* equally.

одина́ковост|ь, и, *f.* identity (*of views, etc.*).

одина́ков|ый (~, ~а), *adj.* (c+*i.*) identical
(with), the same (as).

одина́рный, *adj.* single.

одинё|хонек, ~шенек, *see* **оди́н** 3.

одиннадцатиле́тний, *adj.* eleven-year-old.

оди́ннадцат|ь, и, *num.* eleven.

оди́ннадцатый, *adj.* eleventh.

одино́к|ий (~, ~а), *adj.* **1.** solitary; lonely;
lone. **2.** *as noun* о., ~ого, *m.* single man,
bachelor; ~ая, ~ой, *f.* single woman.

одино́ко, *adv.* lonely; чу́вствовать себя́ о.
to feel lonely.

одино́честв|о, а, *n.* solitude; loneliness.

одино́чк|а, и **1.** *m. and f.* lone person;
куста́рь-о. craftsman working alone; мать-
-о. unmarried mother; жить ~ой to live
alone; в ~у alone, on one's own; по ~е one
by one. **2.** (*coll.*) one-man cell, solitary
confinement. **3.** single-oar (*rowing-boat*).

одино́чн|ый, *adj.* **1.** individual; one-man;
~ое заключе́ние solitary confinement. **2.**
single; о. вы́стрел single shot; о. ого́нь
(*mil.*) single-round firing.

одио́з|ный (~ен, ~на), *adj.* odious, offensive.

одиссе́|я, и, *f.* (*fig.*) Odyssey.

одича́лый, *adj.* (having gone) wild.

одича́ни|е, я, *n.* running wild.

одича́|ть, ю, *pf. of* **дича́ть.**

одна́жды, *adv.* once; one day; о. у́тром
(ве́чером, но́чью) one morning (evening,
night).

одна́ко **1.** *adv. and conj.* however; but;
though. **2.** *interj.* you don't say so!; not
really!

одноа́ктный, *adj.* (*theatr.*) one-act.

одноа́то́мный, *adj.* monoatomic.

однобо́к|ий (~, ~а), *adj.* one-sided (*also
fig.*).

однобо́ртный, *adj.* single-breasted.

одновале́нтный, *adj.* (*chem.*) univalent,
monovalent.

одновесе́льный, *adj.* one-oared.

одновреме́нно, *adv.* simultaneously, at the
same time.

одновреме́нность|ь, и, *f.* simultaneity; syn-
chronism.

одновреме́нный, *adj.* simultaneous; synchronous.

одногла́зк|а, и, *f.* (*zool.*) cyclops.

одногла́зый, *adj.* one-eyed.

одногоди́чный, *adj.* one-year, of one year's
duration.

одного́д|ок, ка, *m.* (c+*i.*; *coll.*) of the same
age (as).

одного́рбый, *adj.* о. верблю́д dromedary,
Arabian camel.

однодво́р|ец, ца, *m.* (*hist.*) smallholder (*mem-
ber of special group of State peasantry, intermediate between peasants and small landowning
gentry*).

однодне́вный, *adj.* one-day.

однодо́льный, *adj.* (*bot.*) monocotyledonous.

однодо́мный, *adj.* (*bot.*) monoecious.

однаду́м, а, *m.* person with idée fixe, obses-
sional.

одножи́льный, *adj.* (*electr.*) single-core.

однозву́чный, *adj.* monotonous.

однозна́чащий, *adj.* **1.** synonymous. **2.**
monosemantic.

однозна́ч|ный (~ен, ~на), *adj.* **1.** synony-
mous. **2.** (*ling.*) monosemantic. **3.** (*math.*)
simple; ~ное число́ simple number, digit.

одноимён|ный (~ен, ~на), *adj.* of the same
name.

однокали́берный, *adj.* of the same calibre.

однока́мерный, *adj.* (*zool.*) monothalamous.

однока́шник, а, *m.* (*obs., coll.*) school-fellow.

однокла́ссник, а, *m.* classmate.

однокле́точный, *adj.* (*biol.*) unicellular.

одноклу́бник, а, *m.* (*coll.*) fellow-member of
club.

одноколе́йный, *adj.* single-track.

одноколе́нчатый, *adj.* (*tech.*) single-jointed.

одноко́лк|а, и, *f.* (*coll.*) gig.

одноко́нный, *adj.* one-horse.

однокопы́тный, *adj.* (*zool.*) solidungular,
solid-hoofed.

одноко́нтурный, *adj.* (*electr.*) single-circuit.

однокорпусный, *adj.* (*naut.*) single-hull.

однокра́тный, *adj.* single; о. глаго́л (*gram.*)
instantaneous verb.

однокурсник, а, *m.* fellow-member of
course.

однола́мповый, *adj.* (*radio*) single-valve.

одноле́тний, *adj.* **1.** one-year. **2.** (*bot.*)
annual.

одноле́тник, а, *m.* (*bot.*) annual.

одноле́т|ок, ка, *m.* (c+*i.*) (*coll.*) of the same
age (as).

однома́стный, *adj.* of one colour.

одномá́чтовый, *adj.* single-masted.

одноме́стный, *adj.* single-seated, single-seater.

одномото́рный, *adj.* single-engine.

однonóгий, *adj.* one-legged.

однообра́зи|е, я, *n.* monotony.

однообра́зность|ь, и, *f.* = однообра́зие.

однообра́з|ный (~ен, ~на), *adj.* monotonous.

одноо́кис|ь, и, *f.* (*chem.*) monoxide.

одноо́сный, *adj.* uniaxial, monoaxial.

однопала́тный, *adj.* (*polit.*) unicameral, single-chamber.

однопалубный, *adj.* one-decked.

одноплеме́нный, *adj.* of the same tribe.

однополча́н|ин, ина, *pl.* ~е, ~, *m.* comrade-in-arms (*one serving in same regiment*).

однопо́лый, *adj.* (*bot.*) unisexual.

однопо́люсный, *adj.* (*phys.*) unipolar.

однопу́тк|а, и, *f.* (*coll.*) single-track railway.

однопу́тный, *adj.* one-way.

одноро́гий, *adj.* one-horned, unicornous.

одноро́дность|ь, и, *f.* homogeneity, uniformity.

одноро́д|ный (~ен, ~на), *adj.* 1. homogeneous, uniform. 2. similar.

однору́кий, *adj.* one-handed, one-armed.

одноря́дк|а, и, *f.* (*hist.*) single-breasted caftan.

односельча́н|ин, ина, *pl.* ~е, ~, *m.* fellow-villager.

односло́жно, *adv.* говори́ть о. to speak in monosyllables.

односло́жность|ь, и, *f.* 1. monosyllabism. 2. (*fig.*) terseness, abruptness.

односло́ж|ный, *adj.* 1. monosyllabic. 2. (~ен, ~на) (*fig.*) terse, abrupt.

однослойный, *adj.* single-layer; one-ply, single-ply.

односпа́льн|ый, *adj.* ~ая крова́ть single bed.

одноство́льн|ый, *adj.* ~ое ружьё single-barrelled gun.

одностворчат|ый, *adj.* 1. (*zool.*) univalve. 2. ~ая дверь single door.

односторо́нн|ий, *adj.* 1. one-sided (*also fig.*); unilateral. 2. one-way; ~ее движе́ние one-way traffic; о. ум (*fig.*) one-track mind.

однота́ктный, *adj.* (*tech.*) one-stroke, single-cycle.

однотёс, а, *m.* plank nail.

одноти́п|ный (~ен, ~на), *adj.* of the same type, of the same kind; о. кора́бль sister-ship.

одното́мник, а, *m.* one-volume edition.

одното́мный, *adj.* one-volume.

одноу́хий, *adj.* one-eared.

однофа́зный, *adj.* (*electr.*) single-phase, monophase.

однофами́л|ец, ьца, *m.* (c+*i.*) person bearing the same surname (as), namesake.

одноцве́тный, *adj.* one-colour; (*typ.*) monochrome.

одноцили́ндровый, *adj.* one-cylinder.

одночле́н, а, *m.* (*math.*) monomial.

одночле́нный, *adj.* (*math.*) monomial.

одношёрстный, *adj.* (*of animals*) of one colour.

одноэта́жный, *adj.* 1. single-stage. 2. one-storeyed.

однoя́дерный, *adj.* mononuclear.

однoя́корный, *adj.* (*electr.*) single-armature.

однoя́русный, *adj.* single-stage.

одобре́ни|е, я, *n.* approval.

одобри́тел|ьный (~ен, ~ьна), *adj.* approving.

одо́бр|ить, ю, ишь, *pf.* (*of* ~я́ть) to approve (of); не о. to disapprove (of).

одобр|я́ть, я́ю, *impf. of* ~ить.

одолева́|ть, ю, *impf. of* одоле́ть.

одоле́|ть, ю, *pf.* (*of* ~ва́ть) 1. to overcome, conquer; его́ ~л сон he was overcome by sleepiness; нас ~ло злово́ние the stench overpowered us. 2. (*fig.*) to master; to cope (with); to get through; о. всю прему́дрость to master all the ins and outs.

одолжа́|ться, юсь, *impf.* (+*d. or* у) to be obliged (to), be beholden (to); ~йтесь! (*obs., coll.*) have some!

одолже́ни|е, я, *n.* favour, service; сде́лайте мне о. do me a favour; я сочту́ э́то за о. I shall esteem it, regard it as a favour.

одолж|и́ть, у́, и́шь, *pf.* (*of* ода́лживать) 1. (+*d.*) to lend. 2. (*coll.*; у) to borrow (from).

одома́шнени|е, я, *n.* domestication, taming.

одома́шн|енный, *p.p.p. of* ~ить *and adj.* domesticated.

одома́шнива|ть, ю, *impf. of* одома́шнить.

одома́шн|ить, ю, ишь, *pf.* (*of* ~ивать) to domesticate, tame.

одонто́лог, а, *m.* odontologist.

одонтоло́ги|я, и, *f.* (*med.*) odontology.

одр, а́, *m.* (*arch.*; *now only in certain phrases*) bed, couch; на сме́ртном ~е́ on one's death-bed.

одревесне́ни|е, я, *n.* lignification.

одряхле́|ть, ю, *pf. of* дряхле́ть.

одува́нчик, а, *m.* (*bot.*) dandelion.

оду́м|аться, аюсь, *pf.* (*of* ~ываться) to change one's mind; to think better of it; to bethink oneself.

оду́мыва|ться, юсь, *impf. of* оду́маться.

одура́чива|ть, ю, *impf. of* одура́чить.

одура́ч|ить, у, ишь, *pf.* (*of* дура́чить *and* ~ивать) (*coll.*) to make a fool (of), fool.

одуре́лый, *adj.* (*coll.*) dulled, besotted.

одуре́ни|е, я, *n.* stupefaction, torpor.

одуре́|ть, ю, *pf. of* дуре́ть.

одурма́нива|ть, ю, *impf. of* одурма́нить.

одурма́н|ить, ю, ишь, *pf.* (*of* дурма́нить *and* ~ива́ть) to stupefy.

о́дур|ь, и, *f.* (*coll.*) stupefaction, torpor; со́нная о. (*bot.*) deadly nightshade.

одуря́|ть, ю, *impf.* (*coll.*) to stupefy; ~ющий за́пах heavy scent.

одутлова́т|ый (~, ~a), *adj.* puffy.

одухотворённост|ь, и, *f.* spirituality.

одухотворённый, *p.p.p. of* одухотвори́ть *and adj.* inspired.

одухотвор|и́ть, ю́, и́шь, *pf.* (*of* ~я́ть) 1. to inspire; to animate. 2. to attribute soul (to) (*natural phenomena, animals, etc.*).

одухотвор|я́ть, я́ю, *impf. of* ~и́ть.

одушев|и́ть, лю́, и́шь, *pf.* (*of* ~ля́ть) to animate.

одушев|и́ться, лю́сь, и́шься, *pf.* (*of* ~ля́ть-ся) to be animated.

одушевле́ни|е, я, *n.* animation.

одушевлённый, *p.p.p. of* одушеви́ть *and adj.* animated.

одушевля́|ть(ся), ю(сь), *impf. of* одушеви́ть(ся).

оды́шк|а, и, *f.* short breath; страда́ть ~ой to be short-winded.

ожереб|и́ться, лю́сь, и́шься, *pf. of* жереби́ться.

ожере́ль|е, я, *n.* necklace.

ожесточа́|ть(ся), а́ю(сь), *impf. of* ~и́ть(ся).

ожесточе́ни|е, я, *n.* bitterness.

ожесточённост|ь, и, *f.* = ожесточе́ние.

ожесточённый, *p.p.p. of* ожесточи́ть *and adj.* bitter; embittered; hardened.

ожесточ|и́ть, у́, и́шь, *pf.* (*of* ~а́ть) to embitter; to harden.

ожесточ|и́ться, у́сь, и́шься, *pf.* (*of* ~а́ться) to become embittered; to become hardened.

оже́чь(ся) = обже́чь(ся).

ожива́льный, *adj.* (*archit.*) ogival.

ожива́|ть, ю, *impf. of* ожи́ть.

ожив|и́ть, лю́, и́шь, *pf.* (*of* ~ля́ть) 1. to revive. 2. (*fig.*) to enliven, vivify, animate.

ожив|и́ться, лю́сь, и́шься, *pf.* (*of* ~ля́ться) 1. to become animated, liven (up). 2. *pass. of* ~и́ть.

оживле́ни|е, я, *n.* 1. animation, gusto. 2. reviving; enlivening.

оживлённый, *p.p.p. of* оживи́ть *and adj.* animated; lively.

оживля́|ть(ся), ю(сь), *impf. of* оживи́ть(ся).

оживотвор|и́ть, ю́, и́шь, *pf. of* животвори́ть.

ожида́ни|е, я, *n.* expectation; waiting; обману́ть ~я to disappoint; в ~и (+*g.*) pending; быть в ~и (*of a woman*; *euph.*) to be expecting; сверх ~я beyond expectation.

ожида́|ть, ю, *impf.* (+*g.*) to wait (for); to expect, anticipate; о. ребёнка (*of a woman*)

to be expecting a baby; мы э́того не ~ли we were not expecting that; как я и ~л just as I expected.

ожижа́тел|ь, я, *m.* (*tech.*) liquefier.

ожижа́|ть, ю, *impf.* (*tech.*) to liquefy.

ожиже́ни|е, я, *n.* (*chem.*) liquefaction (*of gas*); (*meteor.*) thinning; liquation.

ожире́ни|е, я, *n.* obesity; о. се́рдца adipose heart.

ожире́|ть, ю, *pf. of* жире́ть.

ож|и́ть, иву́, ивёшь, *past* ~и́л, ~ила́, ~и́ло, *pf.* (*of* ~ива́ть) to come to life, revive (*also fig.*).

ожо́г, а, *m.* burn; scald.

озабо́|тить, чу, тишь, *pf.* (*of* ~чивать) to trouble, worry, cause anxiety.

озабо́|титься, чусь, тишься, *pf.* (*of* ~чиваться) (+*i.*) to attend (to); о. загото́вкой то́плива to see to the laying in of fuel.

озабо́ченност|ь, и, *f.* preoccupation; anxiety.

озабо́|ченный, *p.p.p. of* ~тить *and adj.* preoccupied; anxious, worried.

озабо́чива|ть(ся), ю(сь), *impf. of* озабо́тить(ся).

озагла́в|ить, лю, ишь, *pf.* (*of* ~ливать) to entitle; to head (*a chapter, etc.*).

озагла́влива|ть, ю, *impf. of* озагла́вить.

озада́ченност|ь, и, *f.* perplexity, puzzlement.

озада́ч|енный, *p.p.p. of* ~ить *and adj.* perplexed, puzzled.

озада́чива|ть, ю, *impf. of* озада́чить.

озада́ч|ить, у, ишь, *pf.* (*of* ~ивать) to perplex, puzzle, take aback.

озар|и́ть, ю́, и́шь, *pf.* (*of* ~я́ть) to light up, illuminate, illumine; улы́бка ~и́ла её лицо́ a smile lit up her face; их ~и́ло (*fig.*) it dawned upon them.

озар|и́ться, ю́сь, и́шься, *pf.* (*of* ~я́ться) 1. (+*i.*) to light up (with); её лицо́ ~и́лось ра́достью her face lit up with joy. 2. *pass. of* ~и́ть.

озар|я́ть(ся), я́ю(сь), *impf. of* ~и́ть(ся).

озвере́лый, *adj.* brutal; brutalized.

озвере́|ть, ю, *pf. of* звере́ть.

озву́ч|енный, *p.p.p. of* ~ить; о. фильм sound film.

озву́чива|ть, ю, *impf. of* озву́чить.

озву́ч|ить, у, ишь, *pf.* (*of* ~ивать) (*cinema*) to wire for sound.

оздорови́тел|ьный (~ен, ~ьна), *adj.* sanitary.

оздоров|и́ть, лю́, и́шь, *pf.* (*of* ~ля́ть) to render (more) healthy, bring into a healthy state (*also fig.*); о. ме́стность to improve the sanitary conditions of a locality.

оздоровля́|ть, ю, *impf. of* оздорови́ть.

озелене́ни|е, я, *n.* planting with trees and gardens.

озелен|и́ть, ю́, и́шь, *pf.* (*of* ~я́ть) to plant with trees and gardens.

озелен|я́ть, я́ю, *impf. of* ~и́ть.

о́земь, *adv.* (*coll.*) to the ground, down.

озерк|о́, а́, *pl.* ~и́, ~о́в, *n. dim. of* о́зеро.

озёрный, *adj. of* о́зеро; о. райо́н lake district.

о́зер|о, а, *pl.* озёра, озёр, *n.* lake.

ози́м|ый, *adj.* winter; ~ая культу́ра winter crop; ~ое по́ле winter-field; *as noun* ~ые, ~ых winter crops.

о́зим|ь, и, *f.* winter crop.

озира́|ть, ю, *impf.* (*obs.*) to view.

озира́|ться, ю́сь, *impf.* to look round; to look back.

озлоб|и́ть, лю́, и́шь, *pf.* (*of* ~ля́ть) to embitter.

озлоб|и́ться, лю́сь, и́шься, *pf.* (*of* ~ля́ться) to become embittered.

озлобле́ни|е, я, *n.* bitterness, animosity.

озлоб|ленный, *p.p.p. of* ~и́ть *and adj.* embittered.

озлобля́|ть(ся), ю(сь), *impf. of* озло́бить(ся).

ознако́м|ить, лю́, и́шь, *pf.* (*of* ~ля́ть) (с+*i.*) to acquaint (with).

ознако́м|иться, лю́сь, и́шься, *pf.* (*of* ~ля́ться) (с+*i.*) to familiarize oneself with.

ознакомля́|ть(ся), ю(сь), *impf. of* ознако́мить(ся).

ознаменова́ни|е, я, *n.* marking, commemoration; в о. (+*g.*) to mark, to commemorate, in commemoration (of).

ознамен|ова́ть, у́ю, *pf.* (*of* ~о́вывать) to mark, commemorate; to celebrate.

означа́|ть, ю, *impf.* to mean, signify, stand for; что ~ют э́ти бу́квы? what do these letters stand for?

озна́ченный, *adj.* (*obs.*) the aforesaid.

озно́б, а, *m.* shivering; chill; почу́вствовать о. to feel shivery.

озноб|и́ть, лю́, и́шь, *pf.* (*of* ~ля́ть) (*coll.*) я ~и́л себе́ у́ши, *etc.*, my ears, *etc.*, are frozen.

озно́бля́|ть, ю, *impf. of* озноби́ть.

озокери́т, а, *m.* (*min.*) ozocerite.

озоло|ти́ть, чу́, ти́шь, *pf.* **1.** to gild. **2.** (*coll.*) to load with money.

озо́н, а, *m.* ozone.

озона́тор, а, *m.* (*phys.*) ozonizer.

озони́рова́ни|е, я, *n.* ozonization.

озони́рова|нный, *p.p.p. of* ~ть *and adj.* ozonized.

озони́р|овать, ую, *impf. and pf.* to ozonize.

озорни́к, а́, *m.* (*coll.*) **1.** naughty child, mischievous child. **2.** mischief-maker.

озорнича́|ть, ю, *impf.* (*of* с~) (*coll.*) **1.** (*of a child*) to be naughty, get up to mischief. **2.** (*of an adult*) to make mischief, play dirty tricks.

озорно́й, *adj.* (*coll.*) mischievous, naughty.

озорств|о́, а́, *n.* (*coll.*) mischief, naughtiness.

озя́б|нуть, ну, нешь, *past* ~, ~ла, *pf.* to be cold, be chilly; я ~ ! I am frozen!

ой (*or* **ой-ой-ой), ***interj. expressing surprise, fright or pain* o; oh.

ой-ли, *interj.* (*coll.*) *expressing doubt* really?; is it possible?

ока|за́ть, жу́, ~жешь, *pf.* (*of* ~зывать) to render, show; о. влия́ние (на+*a.*) to influence, exert influence (upon); о. внима́ние (+*d.*) to pay attention (to); о. давле́ние (на+*a.*) to exert pressure (upon), bring pressure to bear (upon); о. де́йствие (на+*a.*) to have an effect (upon); to take effect; о. му́жество (*obs.*) to display bravery; о. по́мощь (+*d.*) to help, give help; о. предпочте́ние (+*d.*) to show preference (for), prefer; о. соде́йствие (+*d.*) to render assistance; о. сопротивле́ние (+*d.*) to offer, put up resistance (to); о. услу́гу (+*d.*) to do, render a service; to do a good turn; о. честь (+*d.*) to do an honour.

ока|за́ться, жу́сь, ~жешься, *pf.* (*of* ~зываться) **1.** to turn out (to be), prove (to be); to be found (to be); он ~за́лся отли́чным расска́зчиком he proved to be a first-rate story-teller; ~за́лось, что она́ всё вре́мя лгала́ it turned out that she had been telling lies all the time. **2.** to find oneself; to be found; я ~за́лся в больни́це I found myself in hospital; трёх экземпля́ров не ~за́лось three copies were missing.

ока́зи|я, и, *f.* **1.** opportunity; посла́ть письмо́ с ~ей to profit by an opportunity to send a letter. **2.** unexpected happening; что за о.! what an odd thing! how odd!

ока́зыва|ть(ся), ю(сь), *impf. of* оказа́ть(ся).

окайм|и́ть, лю́, и́шь, *pf.* (*of* ~ля́ть) (+*i.*) to border (with), edge (with).

окаймля́|ть, ю, *impf. of* окайми́ть.

ока́лин|а, ы, *f.* cinder; (*tech.*) scale; slag, dross.

окамене́лост|ь, и, *f.* fossil.

окамене́лый, *adj.* fossilized; petrified.

окамене́|ть, ю, *pf. of* камене́ть.

окант|ова́ть, у́ю, *pf. of* кантова́ть¹.

окантовк|а, и, *f.* mount (*for picture, etc.*).

ока́нчива|ть(ся), ю(сь), *impf. of* око́нчить(ся).

о́кань|е, я, *n.* okanie (*pronunciation of unstressed 'o' as 'o'*).

ока́пыва|ть(ся), ю(сь), *impf. of* окопа́ть(ся).

ока́рмлива|ть, ю, *impf. of* окорми́ть.

ока|ти́ть, чу́, ~ти́шь, *pf.* (*of* ~чивать) to pour (over); о. холо́дной водо́й to pour cold water (over) (*also fig.*).

ока|ти́ться, чу́сь, ~ти́шься, *pf.* (*of* ~чиваться) to pour over oneself.

о́ка|ть, ю, *impf.* to pronounce unstressed 'o' as 'o' in Russian words.

окáчива|ть(ся), ю(сь), *impf. of* **окатúть(ся).**

окаáнный, *adj.* damned, cursed.

окаáнств|о, а, *n.* (*eccl.*) sinfulness.

окаáнств|овать, ую, *pf.* (*eccl.*) to live a life of sin.

океáн, а, *m.* ocean.

океанográфи|я, и, *f.* oceanography.

океанográфический, *adj.* oceanographic.

океáнский, *adj.* ocean; oceanic; о. парохóд ocean(-going) liner.

окúдыва|ть, ю, *impf. of* **окúнуть.**

окú|нуть, ну, нешь, *pf.* (*of* ~**дывать**) to cast round; о. взглáдом, о. взóром to take in at a glance; to glance over.

óкис|ел, ла, *m.* (*chem.*) oxide.

окислéни|е, я, *n.* (*chem.*) oxidation.

окислúтел|ь, я, *m.* (*chem.*) oxidizer, acidifier.

окислúтельный, *adj.* (*chem.*) oxidizing.

окисл|úть, ю, úшь, *pf.* (*of* ~**ять**) (*chem.*) to oxidize.

окисл|úться, юсь, úшься, *pf.* (*of* ~**яться**) (*chem.*) 1. to oxidize. 2. *pass. of* ~**úть.**

окисл|ять(ся), яю(сь), *impf. of* ~**úть(ся).**

óкис|ь, и, *f.* (*chem.*) oxide; безвóдная о. anhydride; воднáя о. hydroxide; о. желéза ferric oxide; о. мéди cupric oxide; о. углерóда carbon monoxide.

окклюдúр|овать, ую, *impf. and pf.* (*chem.*) to occlude.

окклюзи|я, и, *f.* (*chem.*) occlusion.

оккультúзм, а, *m.* occultism.

оккýльтный, *adj.* occult.

оккупáнт, а, *m.* invader, occupier.

оккупа|цióнный, *adj. of* ~**ция;** ~**цióнная áрмия** army of occupation.

оккупáци|я, и, *f.* (*mil.*) occupation.

оккупúр|овать, ую, *impf. and pf.* (*mil.*) to occupy.

оклáд¹, а, *m.* 1. salary scale; salary; основнóй о. (*mil.*) basic pay. 2. tax, assessment.

оклáд², а, *m.* setting, framework (*of icon*).

оклáдист|ый (~, ~а), *adj.* (*of beard*) broad and thick.

окладнóй, *adj. of* **оклáд¹;** о. лист tax sheet.

оклеве|тáть, щý, ~щешь, *pf.* to slander, calumniate, defame.

оклéива|ть, ю, *impf. of* **оклéить.**

оклé|ить, ю, ишь, *pf.* (*of* ~**ивать**) (+*i.*) to cover (with); to glue over (with), paste over (with); о. кóмнату обóями to paper a room.

оклéйк|а, и, *f.* glueing, pasting; о. обóями papering.

óклик, а, *m.* hail, call.

оклик|áть, áю, *impf. of* ~**нуть.**

оклúк|нуть, ну, нешь, *pf.* (*of* ~**áть**) to hail, call (to).

окн|ó, á, *pl.* ~**а, óкон,** ~**ам,** *n.* 1. window; опускнóе о. sash window; слуховóе о. dormer-window; кóмната в три ~á room with three windows; о. выдачи serving-

hatch. 2. (*fig.*) gap; aperture. 3. (*school sl.*) free period.

óк|о, а, *pl.* **óчи, очéй,** *n.* (*arch. or poet.*) eye; в мгновéние ~а in the twinkling of an eye; о. за о. an eye for an eye.

ок|овáть, ую, уёшь, *pf.* (*of* ~**óвывать**) to bind (*with metal*); (*fig.*) to fetter, shackle.

окóвк|а, и, *f.* binding (*with metal*); nailing (*of boots*).

окóв|ы, ~, *no sing.* fetters (*also fig.*); сбрóсить с себя о. to cast off one's chains.

окóвыва|ть, ю, *impf. of* **оковáть.**

околáчива|ться, юсь, *impf.* (*coll.*) to lounge about, kick one's heels.

околд|овáть, ýю, *pf.* (*of* ~**óвывать**) to bewitch, entrance, enchant (*also fig.*).

околдóвыва|ть, ю, *impf. of* **околдовáть.**

околевá|ть, ю, *impf. of* **околéть.**

околéлый, *adj.* (*coll.*; *of animals*) dead.

околéсиц|а, ы, *f.* (*coll.*) nonsense, rubbish; нестú ~у to talk stuff and nonsense.

околéс|ная, ной, *f.* = ~**ица.**

околé|ть, ю, *pf.* (*of* ~**вáть**) (*of animals and pejor. of persons*) to die.

окóлиц|а, ы, *f.* 1. outskirts (of a village); выехать за ~у to leave the confines of a village; на ~е on the outskirts. 2. (*dial.*) neighbourhood. 3. (*dial.*) roundabout route.

околúчност|ь, и, *f.* (*obs.*) circumlocution; innuendo; говорúть без ~ей to speak plainly.

óколо, *prep.*+*g. and adv.* 1. by; close (to), near; around, about; он сидéл о. меня he was sitting by me; никогó нет о. there is nobody about; гдé-н. о. (этого мéста) hereabouts, somewhere here; (что́-н.) о. этого, о. тогó thereabouts. 2. about; о. полýночи about midnight; о. шестú мéтров about six metres.

околодо́|к, ~чный = **околотóк, околотóчный.**

околоплóдник, а, *m.* (*bot.*) pericarp, seed vessel.

околосердéчн|ый, *adj.* ~**ая сýмка** (*anat.*) pericardium.

околóт|ок, ка, *m.* 1. neighbourhood. 2. (*obs.*) ward, town district, precinct; area, sector (*of public transport*). 3. (*obs.*) police-station. 4. (*mil.*; *obs.*) aid post, dressing-station.

околóто|чный, *adj. of* ~**к;** о. надзирáтель *or as noun* **о., ~чного,** *m.* (*obs.*) police-officer.

околоýшный, *adj.* (*anat.*) parotid.

околоцвéтник, а, *m.* (*bot.*) perianth.

околпáчива|ть, ю, *impf. of* **околпáчить.**

околпáч|ить, у, ишь, *pf.* (*of* ~**ивать**) (*coll.*) to fool, dupe.

окóлыш, а, *m.* cap-band.

окóльнич|ий, его, *m.* (*hist.*) okolnichy (*in Muscovite period, member of social group with status second to that of boyars*).

окóльны|й, *adj.* roundabout; ~е пути́ devious ways; вы́ведать ~м путём (*fig.*) to find out in a roundabout way.

окольц|евáть, у́ю, *pf. of* кольцевáть 2.

оконéчност|ь, и, *f.* extremity.

окóнн|ый, *adj. of* окнó; ~ая рáма window-frame, sash; ~ое стеклó window-pane; window-glass.

оконфу́|зить, жу, зишь, *pf.* (*coll.*) to embarrass, confuse.

окончáни|е, я, *n.* **1.** end; conclusion, termination; о. срóка expiration; по ~и университéта on graduating; о. слéдует (*note to serial article, story, etc.*) to be concluded. **2.** (*gram.*) ending.

окончáтельно, *adv.* finally, definitively; completely.

окончáтельный, *adj.* final, definitive.

оконч|и́ть, у, ишь, *pf.* (*of* окáнчивать) to finish, end; о. шкóлу to leave school; о. университéт to graduate, go down (from university).

окóнч|иться, ится, *pf.* (*of* окáнчиваться) **1.** to finish, end, terminate; to be over. **2.** *pass. of* ~и́ть.

окóп, а, *m.* (*mil.*) trench; entrenchment.

окопá|ть, ю, *pf.* (*of* окáпывать) to dig round.

окопá|ться, юсь, *pf.* (*of* окáпываться) **1.** (*mil.*) to entrench (oneself), dig in. **2.** (*fig., iron.*) to find oneself a soft spot, comfortable hide-out. **3.** *pass. of* ~ть.

окóп|ный, *adj. of* ~; ~ная войнá trench warfare.

окорáчива|ть, ю, *impf. of* окороти́ть.

окóрк|а, и, *f.* barking, bark stripping.

окорм|и́ть, лю́, ~ишь, *pf.* (*of* окáрмливать) **1.** to overfeed, cram (stuff) with food. **2.** to poison with bad food.

окорнá|ть, ю, *pf. of* корнáть.

óкоро|к, ка, *pl.* ~кá, *m.* ham, gammon; (*of mutton, veal*) leg.

окоро|ти́ть, чу́, ти́шь, *pf.* (*of* окорáчивать) (*coll.*) to make too short; to crop.

окостеневá|ть, ю, *impf. of* окостенéть.

окостенéлый, *adj.* ossified (*also fig.*).

окостенé|ть, ю, *pf.* (*of* костенéть *and* ~вáть) to ossify (*also fig.*).

окóт, а, *m.* (time of) having kittens (*also of time of bringing forth young of certain other animals*).

око|ти́ться, чу́сь, ти́шься, *pf. of* коти́ться.

окоченéлый, *adj.* stiff with cold.

окоченé|ть, ю, *pf. of* коченéть.

окóш|ко, ка, *pl.* ~ки, ~ек, ~кам, *n. dim. of* окнó.

окрáин|а, ы, *f.* **1.** outskirts; outlying districts. **2.** (*obs.*) ~ы borders, marches (*of a country*).

окрá|сить, шу, сишь, *pf.* (*of* ~шивать) to paint, colour; to dye; to stain; слегкá о. to tinge, tint.

окрáск|а, и, *f.* **1.** painting, colouring; dyeing; staining. **2.** colouring, coloration; colour; защи́тная о. (*zool.*) protective coloration. **3.** (*fig.*) tinge, tint; (*polit.*) slant; ирони́ческая о. ironic tinge, touch of irony; стилисти́ческая о. stylistic nuance; придáть чему́-н. другу́ю ~y to put a different complexion on something.

окрáшива|ть, ю, *impf. of* окрáсить.

окрéп|нуть, ну, нешь, *past* ~, ~ла, *pf. of* крéпнуть.

окрéст, *prep.+g. and adv.* (*obs.*) around, about.

окре|сти́ть, щу́, ~сти́шь, *pf.* **1.** (*impf.* крести́ть) to baptize, christen. **2.** (*coll.* +*a. and i.*) to nickname; егó ~сти́ли медвéдем he was nicknamed 'the bear'.

окре|сти́ться, щу́сь, ~сти́шься, *pf. of* крести́ться 1.

окрéстност|ь, и, *f.* **1.** environs. **2.** neighbourhood, vicinity.

окрéстный, *adj.* **1.** neighbouring. **2.** surrounding.

окриве́|ть, ю, *pf. of* криве́ть.

óкрик, а, *m.* hail; shout, cry; грýбый о. harsh bellow.

окри́кива|ть, ю, *impf. of* окри́кнуть.

окри́к|нуть, ну, нешь, *pf.* (*of* ~ивать) to hail, shout (to).

окровáв|ить, лю, ишь, *pf.* (*of* ~ливать) to stain with blood.

окровáв|иться, люсь, ишься, *pf.* (*of* ~ливаться) to spill blood on oneself.

окровáв|ленный, *p.p.p. of* ~ить *and adj.* blood-stained; bloody.

окровáвлива|ть(ся), ю(сь), *impf. of* окровáвить(ся).

окровенé|ть, ю, *pf.* (*coll.*) to become covered with blood; to become soaked in blood.

окровен|и́ть, ю́, и́шь, *pf.* (*coll.*) to stain with blood.

окроп|и́ть, лю́, и́шь, *pf.* (*of* кропи́ть *and* ~ля́ть) to (be)sprinkle.

окропля́|ть, ю, *impf. of* окропи́ть.

окрóшк|а, и, *f.* **1.** okroshka (*cold kvass soup with chopped vegetables and meat or fish*). **2.** (*fig., coll.*) hodge-podge, jumble.

óкруг, а, *pl.* ~á, *m.* (*territorial division of U.S.S.R. for administrative, legal, military, etc., purposes*) okrug; region, district; circuit; воéнный о. military district, command; избирáтельный о. electoral district.

окру́г|а, и, *f.* (*coll.*) neighbourhood.

округл|ённый, *p.p.p. of* ~и́ть *and adj.* rounded (*also fig.*).

округле́|ть, ю, *pf. of* кругле́ть.

округл|и́ть, ю́, и́шь, *pf.* (*of* ~я́ть) **1.** to round (off) (*also fig.*). **2.** to express in round numbers.

округл|и́ться, ю́сь, и́шься, *pf.* (*of* ~я́ться) **1.** to become rounded. **2.** to be expressed in round numbers.

окру́глост|ь, и, *f.* **1.** roundedness. **2.** protuberance, bulge.

окру́гл|ый (~, ~а), *adj.* rounded, roundish.

округл|я́ть(ся), я́ю(сь), *impf. of* ~и́ть(ся).

окруж|а́ть, а́ю, *impf. of* ~и́ть.

окружа́|ющий, *pres. part. act. of* ~ть *and adj.* surrounding; ~ющая обстано́вка surroundings; *as noun* ~ющее, ~ющего, *n.* environment; ~ющие, ~ющих one's associates; entourage.

окруже́ни|е, я, *n.* **1.** encirclement; попа́сть в о. (*mil.*) to be encircled, be surrounded. **2.** surroundings; environment; milieu; в ~и (+*g.*) accompanied (by); surrounded (by), in the midst (of); он появи́лся в ~и боле́льщиков he appeared surrounded by fans.

окруж|и́ть, у́, и́шь, *pf.* (*of* ~а́ть) (*in var. senses*) to surround; to encircle; о. кого́-н. забо́тами to lavish attentions on someone.

окружко́м, а, *m.* (*abbr. of* окружно́й комите́т), *see* окружно́й.

окружн|о́й, *adj.* **1.** *adj. of* о́круг; о. комите́т district committee; о. суд circuit court. **2.** operating (situated) about a circle; ~а́я желе́зная доро́га circle line; ~а́я ско́рость (*tech.*) peripheral speed.

окру́жност|ь, и, *f.* **1.** circumference; circle; име́ть де́сять ме́тров в ~и to be ten metres in circumference; на три ми́ли в ~и within a radius of three miles, for three miles round. **2.** (*obs.*) neighbourhood.

окру́жн|ый, *adj.* (*obs.*) **1.** = ~о́й. **2.** neighbouring.

окру|ти́ть, чу́, ~тишь, *pf.* (*of* ~чивать) **1.** (+*i.*) to wind round. **2.** (*coll.*) to marry (*see* ~ти́ться).

окру|ти́ться, чу́сь, ~тишься, *pf.* (*of* ~чиваться) **1.** (+*i.*) to wind round oneself. **2.** (*coll.*) to get spliced (= to get married).

окру́чива|ть(ся), ю(сь), *impf. of* окрути́ть(ся).

окрыл|и́ть, ю́, и́шь, *pf.* (*of* ~я́ть) to inspire, encourage.

окрыл|я́ть, я́ю, *impf. of* ~и́ть.

окры́с|иться, ишься, *pf.* (на+*a.*; *coll.*) to snap (at).

оксиацетиле́нов|ый, *adj.* ~ая сва́рка oxy-acetylene welding.

оксиди́р|овать, ую, *impf. and pf.* (*chem.*) to oxidize.

оксидиро́вк|а, и, *f.* (*chem.*) oxidation.

оксю́морон, а, *m.* (*lit.*) oxymoron.

окта́в|а, ы, *f.* **1.** (*mus. and lit.*) octave. **2.** (*mus.*) low bass.

окта́н, а, *m.* (*chem.*) octane.

окта́нов|ый, *adj.* (*chem.*) octane; ~ое то́пливо (high-)octane fuel; ~ое число́ octane number, octane rating.

окта́эдр, а, *m.* (*math.*) octahedron.

окте́т, а, *m.* (*mus.*) octet.

октрои́р|овать, ую, *impf. and pf.* to grant; to concede.

октябр|ёнок, ёнка, *pl.* ~я́та, ~я́т, *m.* oktyabryonok ('pre-Pioneer': *Soviet child of seven years or upward preparing for entry into Pioneers*).

октя́бр|ь, я́, *m.* October (*fig.* = *Russian revolution of October 1917*).

октя́брь|ский, *adj. of* ~.

оку́кливани|е, я, *n.* (*zool.*) pupation.

оку́клива|ться, ется, *impf. of* оку́клиться.

оку́кл|иться, ится, *pf.* (*of* ~иваться) (*zool.*) to pupate.

окули́р|овать, ую, *impf. and pf.* (*hort.*) to inoculate, engraft.

окулиро́вк|а, и, *f.* (*hort.*) inoculation, grafting.

окули́ст, а, *m.* oculist.

окуля́р, а, *m.* eye-piece, ocular.

окун|а́ть(ся), а́ю(сь), *impf. of* ~у́ть(ся).

о́кун|евый, *adj. of* ~ь.

окун|у́ть, у́, ёшь, *pf.* (*of* ~а́ть) to dip; о. ло́жку в па́току to dip a spoon into the treacle.

окун|у́ться, у́сь, ёшься, *pf.* (*of* ~а́ться) **1.** to dip (oneself). **2.** (*fig.*; в+*a.*) to plunge (into), become (utterly) absorbed (in), engrossed (in); о. в спор to plunge into an argument; он ~у́лся в сочине́ния Плато́на he has become utterly absorbed in the works of Plato.

о́кун|ь, я, *pl.* ~и, ~е́й, *m.* perch (*fish*).

окуп|а́ть(ся), а́ю(сь), *impf. of* ~и́ть(ся).

окуп|и́ть, лю́, ~ишь, *pf.* (*of* ~а́ть) to compensate, repay, make up (for); о. расхо́ды to cover one's outlay.

окуп|и́ться, лю́сь, ~ишься, *pf.* (*of* ~а́ться) to be compensated, be repaid; (*fig.*) to pay; to be justified, be requited, be rewarded; затра́ченные на́ми уси́лия ~и́лись our efforts were rewarded.

окургу́|зить, жу, зишь, *pf.* (*coll.*) to cut too short.

оку́ривани|е, я, *n.* fumigation.

оку́рива|ть, ю, *impf. of* окури́ть.

окур|и́ть, ю́, ~ишь, *pf.* (*of* ~ивать) to fumigate; о. се́рой to sulphurate.

оку́р|ок, ка, *m.* cigarette-end, cigarette stub; cigar-butt.

оку́т|ать, аю, *pf.* (*of* ~ывать) **1.** (+*i.*) to wrap up (in). **2.** (*fig.*) to shroud, cloak; о. та́йной to shroud in mystery.

оку́т|аться, аюсь, *pf.* (*of* ~ываться) **1.** (+*i.*) wrap up (in). **2.** (*fig.*) to shroud, cloak; о. та́йной to shroud in mystery.

оку́тыва|ть(ся), ю(сь), *impf. of* оку́тать(ся).

оку́чива|ть, ю, *impf. of* окучить.

оку́ч|ить, у, ишь, *pf.* (*of* ~ивать) (*agric.*) to earth up.

ола́д|ья, ьи, *g. pl.* ~ий, *f.* fritter; карто́фельная о. potato cake.

олеа́ндр, а, *m.* oleander.

оледене́лый, *adj.* frozen.

оледене́|ть, ю, *pf. of* леденѣть.

оледен|и́ть, ю́, и́шь, *pf. of* ледени́ть.

олеи́н, а, *m.* (*chem.*) olein.

олеи́нов|ый, *adj.* (*chem.*) olein, oleic; ~ая кислота́ oleic acid.

оленево́д, а, *m.* reindeer-breeder.

оленево́дств|о, а, *n.* reindeer-breeding.

олён|ий, *adj. of* ~ь; ~ьи рога́ antlers; о. лиша́й, о мох (*bot.*) reindeer moss; о. рог (*chem.*) hartshorn; о. язы́к (*bot.*) hart's tongue.

олѣ́нин|а, ы, *f.* venison.

олѣ́н|ь, я, *m.* deer; безро́гий о. pollard; благоро́дный о. stag, red deer; се́верный о. reindeer; кана́дский о. wapiti.

олеогра́фи|я, и, *f.* oleograph(y).

оли́в|а, ы, *f.* olive; olive-tree.

оливи́н, а, *m.* (*min.*) olivine, chrysolite.

оли́вк|а, и, *f.* olive; olive-tree.

оли́вков|ый, *adj.* **1.** olive; ~ая ветвь olive branch (*fig.*; *as symbol of peace*); ~ое ма́сло olive oil. **2.** olive-coloured.

олига́рх, а, *m.* oligarch.

олигархи́ческий, *adj.* oligarchical.

олига́рхи|я, и, *f.* oligarchy.

олигоце́н, а, *m.* (*geol.*) oligocene (epoch).

олимпиа́д|а, ы, *f.* olympiad, competition.

олимпи́|ец, йца, *m.* (*myth. and fig.*) Olympian.

олимпи́йски|й¹, *adj.* Olympic; ~е и́гры Olympic games, Olympics.

олимпи́йск|ий², *adj.* of Olympus; ~ое споко́йствие (*fig.*) Olympian calm.

оли́ф|а, ы, *f.* drying oil.

олицетворе́ни|е, я, *n.* personification; embodiment.

олицетвор|ённый, *p.p.p. of* ~и́ть; он — ~ённая хи́трость he is cunning personified.

олицетвор|и́ть, ю́, и́шь, *pf.* (*of* ~я́ть) to personify; to embody.

олицетвор|я́ть, я́ю, *impf. of* ~и́ть.

о́лов|о, а, *n.* tin; за́кись ~a stannous oxide; о́кись ~a stannic oxide.

оловоно́сный, *adj.* tin-bearing, stanniferous.

оловя́нистый, *adj.* stannous.

оловя́нн|ый, *adj.* tin; stannic; о. ка́мень (*min.*) tin spar, tin ore, cassiterite; ~ая кислота́ stannic acid; о. колчеда́н (*min.*) tin pyrites, stannite; ~ое ма́сло (*chem.*) stannic

chloride; ~ая посу́да tinware; pewter; ~ая соль stannic salt; ~ая фо́льга tin foil.

о́лух, а, *m.* (*coll.*) blockhead, dolt, oaf; о. царя́ небе́сного perfect fool, complete idiot.

олу́ш|а, и, *f.* се́верная о. (*orn.*) gannet.

ольх|а́, и́, *pl.* ~и, *f.* alder(-tree).

ольх|о́вый, *adj. of* ~а́.

ольша́ник, а, *m.* alder thicket.

оля́пк|а, и, *f.* (*orn.*) dipper.

ом, а, *m.* (*electr.*) ohm.

ома́р, а, *m.* lobster.

оме́г|а, и, *f.* omega; от а́льфы до ~и (*fig.*) from A to Z, from beginning to end.

омѣ́л|а, ы, *f.* mistletoe.

омерзе́ни|е, я, *n.* loathing; внуши́ть о. (+*d.*) to inspire loathing (in).

омерзе́|ть, ю, *pf.* to become loathsome; мне э́тот пейза́ж ~л I have come to loathe this view.

омерзи́тел|ьный (~ен, ~ьна), *adj.* loathsome, sickening; быть в ~ьном настрое́нии (*coll.*) to be in a foul mood.

омертве́лост|ь, и, *f.* stiffness, numbness; (*med.*) necrosis, mortification.

омертве́л|ый, *adj.* stiff, numb; (*med.*) necrotic; ~ая ткань dead tissue.

омертве́ни|е, я, *n.* = омертве́лость.

омертве́|ть, ю, *pf. of* мертве́ть 1.

омертв|и́ть, лю́, и́шь, *pf.* (*of* ~ля́ть) **1.** to deaden. **2.** (*econ.*) to withdraw from circulation.

омёт, а, *m.* stack of straw.

омеща́нива|ться, юсь, *impf. of* омеща́ниться.

омеща́н|иться, юсь, ишься, *pf.* (*of* ~иваться) (*coll., pejor.*) to become a philistine.

оми́ческий, *adj.* (*electr.*) ohmic.

омле́т, а, *m.* omelette.

омме́тр, а, *m.* (*electr.*) ohmmeter.

о́мнибус, а, *m.* (horse-drawn) omnibus.

омове́ни|е, я, *n.* ablution(s); (*eccl.*) lavabo.

омола́жива|ть(ся), ю(сь), *impf. of* омолоди́ть(ся).

омоло|ди́ть, жу́, ди́шь, *pf.* (*of* омола́живать) to rejuvenate.

омоло|ди́ться, жу́сь, ди́шься, *pf.* (*of* омола́живаться) to rejuvenate, rejuvenesce.

омоложе́ни|е, я, *n.* rejuvenation.

омо́ним, а, *m.* (*ling.*) homonym.

омони́мик|а, и, *f.* **1.** study of homonyms. **2.** (*collect.*) homonyms.

омоними́ческий, *adj.* (*ling.*) homonymous.

омони́ми|я, и, *f.* (*ling.*) homonymy.

омоч|и́ть, у́, ~ишь, *pf.* (*obs.*) to wet; to moisten.

омоч|и́ться, у́сь, ~ишься, *pf.* (*obs.*) to become wet; to become moist.

омрач|а́ть(ся), а́ю(сь), *impf. of* ~и́ть(ся).

омрач|и́ть, у́, и́шь, *pf.* (*of* ~а́ть) to darken, cloud.

омрач|и́ться, у́сь, и́шься, *pf.* (*of* ~а́ться) to become darkened, become clouded (*also fig.*).

омулёвый, *adj. of* о́муль.

о́мул|ь, я, *g. pl.* ~ей, *m.* omul (*sea fish of salmon family, found also in Lake Baikal*).

о́мут, а, *m.* 1. whirlpool; (*fig.*) whirl, maelstrom. 2. deep place (*in river or lake*); в ти́хом ~е че́рти во́дятся (*prov.*) still waters run deep.

омша́ник, а, *m.* heated structure (*for housing bees in winter, etc.*).

омыва́|ть, ю, 1. *impf. of* омы́ть. 2. *impf.* (*geogr.*) to wash (*of seas*).

омыва́|ться, юсь, *impf.* (*geogr.*) to be washed; за́падный бе́рег Ирла́ндии ~ется Атланти́ческим океа́ном the west coast of Ireland is washed by the Atlantic.

омыле́ни|е, я, *n.* (*chem.*) saponification.

ом|ы́ть, о́ю, о́ешь, *pf.* (*of* ~ыва́ть) (*rhet., obs.*) to wash, lave; о. кро́вью to steep in blood.

он, его́, ему́, им, о нём, *pron.* he.

она́, её, ей, ей (е́ю), о ней, *pron.* she.

она́гр, а, *m.* (*zool.*) onager.

онани́зм, а, *m.* onanism, masturbation.

онани́р|овать, ую, *impf.* to masturbate.

онани́ст, а, *m.* masturbator.

онда́тр|а, ы, *f.* (*animal*) musk-rat, musquash; (*fur*) musquash.

онда́тр|овый, *adj. of* ~а.

ондуля́тор, а, *m.* (*electr.*) undulator.

онеме́лый, *adj.* 1. dumb. 2. numb.

онеме́|ть, ю, *pf. of* неме́ть.

онеме́чива|ть, ю, *impf. of* онеме́чить.

онеме́ч|ить, у, ишь, *pf.* (*of* ~ивать) to Germanize.

онёр, а, *m.* (*cards*) honour; со всеми́ ~ами (*fig., joc.*) with everything it takes, with everything one could want.

они́, их, им, и́ми, о них, *pron.* they.

о́никс, а, *m.* onyx.

онколо́ги|я, и, *f.* (*med.*) oncology.

онко́л|ь, я, *m.* (*fin., comm.*) call-account.

оно́, его́, ему́, им, о нём, *pron.* 1. it. 2. (= э́то) this, that; о. и ви́дно that is evident. 2. *as emphatic particle* о. коне́чно well, of course; вот о. что! oh, I see!

онома́стик|а, и, *f.* (*ling.*) onomastics.

онтогене́з, а, *m.* (*biol.*) ontogenesis.

онтологи́ческий, *adj.* (*philos.*) ontological.

онтоло́ги|я, и, *f.* (*philos.*) ontology.

ону́ч|а, и, *f.* onucha (*sock or cloth puttee worn in boot or bast-shoe*).

о́ный, *pron.* (*obs.*) that; the above-mentioned; во вре́мя о́но in those days; (*joc.*) in days of old.

ооли́т, а, *m.* (*min.*) oolite.

опада́|ть, ю, *impf. of* опа́сть.

опада́|ющий, *pres. part. act. of* ~ть *and adj.* (*bot.*) deciduous.

опа́здыва|ть, ю, *impf.* 1. *impf. of* опозда́ть. 2. (*impf. only*) (*coll.*) to be slow (*of clocks and watches*).

опа́ива|ть, ю, *impf. of* опои́ть.

опа́л, а, *m.* opal.

опа́л|а, ы, *f.* disgrace, disfavour; быть в ~е to be in disgrace, be out of favour.

опалесце́нци|я, и, *f.* (*phys.*) opalescence.

опалесци́р|овать, ую, *impf. and pf.* (*phys.*) to opalesce.

опа́лива|ть(ся), ю(сь), *impf. of* опали́ть(ся).

опал|и́ть, ю́, и́шь, *pf.* (*of* пали́ть[1] *and* ~ивать) to singe.

опал|и́ться, ю́сь, и́шься, *pf.* (*of* ~иваться) to singe oneself.

опа́ловый, *adj.* opal; opaline.

опа́луб|ить, лю, ишь, *pf.* (*tech.*) to case, sheathe, tub.

опа́лубк|а, и, *f.* (*tech.*) 1. casing, lining, sheathing, tubbing; о. кры́ши roof-boarding. 2. concrete mould, form.

опа́лый, *adj.* (*coll.*) sunken; emaciated.

опа́льный[1], *adj.* disgraced; in disgrace, out of favour.

опа́льн|ый[2], *adj.* ~ая маши́на (*tech.*) cloth singeing machine.

опа́мят|оваться, уюсь, *pf.* (*obs.*) to come to one's senses, collect oneself.

опа́р|а, ы, *f.* 1. leavened dough. 2. leaven.

опарши́ве|ть, ю, *pf. of* парши́веть.

опаса́|ться, юсь, *impf.* 1. (+*g.*) to fear, be afraid (of). 2. (+*g. or inf.*) to beware (of); to avoid, keep off; он ~ется алкого́ля he does not touch alcohol; о. сли́шком мно́го пить to beware of drinking to excess.

опасе́ни|е, я, *n.* fear; apprehension; misgiving(s).

опа́ск|а, и, *f.* с ~ой (*coll.*) with caution, cautiously; warily.

опа́слив|ый (~, ~а), *adj.* (*coll.*) cautious; wary.

опа́сност|ь, и, *f.* danger; peril; вне ~и out of danger; смотре́ть ~и в глаза́ to look dangers in the face.

опа́с|ный (~ен, ~на), *adj.* dangerous, perilous.

опа́|сть, ду́, дёшь, *pf.* (*of* ~да́ть) 1. (*of leaves*) to fall (off). 2. to subside; (*of a swelling, etc.*) to go down.

опаха́л|о, а, *n.* fan.

опа|ха́ть, шу́, ~шешь, *pf.* (*of* ~хива́ть[1]) to plough round.

опа́хива|ть[1], ю, *impf. of* опаха́ть.

опа́хива|ть[2], ю, *impf. of* опахну́ть.

опах|ну́ть, ну́, нёшь, *pf.* (*of* ~ивать[2]) to fan.

опе́к|а, и, *f.* 1. guardianship, wardship, tutelage (*also fig.*); trusteeship; быть под ~ой кого́-н. to be under someone's guardianship; взять под ~y to take as ward; (*fig.*) to take charge (of), take under one's wing; учреди́ть ~y над кем-н. to place someone in ward. **2.** (*collect.*) guardians, board of guardians; Междунаро́дная о. International Trusteeship. **3.** (*fig.*) care; surveillance; вы́йти из-под ~и to become one's own master.

опека́|емый, *pres. part. pass. of* ~ть; *as noun* **о., ~емого,** *m.* ward.

опека́|ть, ю, *impf.* **1.** to be guardian (to), have the wardship (of). **2.** (*fig.*) to take care (of), watch (over).

опеку́н, а́, *m.* (*leg.*) guardian, tutor; trustee.

опеку́н|ский, *adj. of* ~; о. сове́т (*obs.*) board of guardians.

опеку́нств|о, а, *n.* guardianship, tutorship.

опён|ок, ка, *pl.* ~ки, ~ков, *m.* honey agaric (*mushroom*).

о́пер|а, ы, *f.* opera; из друго́й ~ы, не из той ~ы (*coll.*) quite another thing, quite a different matter.

операти́вност|ь, и, *f.* drive; energy (*in getting things done*).

операти́в|ный, *adj.* **1.** (~ен, ~на) energetic; efficient; ~ное руково́дство efficient and flexible leadership. **2.** executive. **3.** (*med.*) operative; surgical; ~ное вмеша́тельство surgical interference. **4.** (*mil.*) operation(s), operational; strategical; ~ное иску́сство campaign tactics; ~ная сво́дка summary of operations.

опера́тор, а, *m.* operator; (*med.*) surgeon.

опера|цио́нный, *adj. of* ~ция; ~цио́нное отделе́ние (*in hospital*) surgical wing; о. стол operating-table; *as noun* ~цио́нная, ~цио́нной, *f.* theatre, operating-room.

опера́ци|я, и, f. (*med., mil., etc.*) operation; перенести́ ~ю to have, undergo an operation; to be operated (upon); сде́лать ~ю to perform an operation.

опере|ди́ть, жу́, ди́шь, *pf.* (*of* ~жа́ть) **1.** to outstrip, leave behind. **2.** to forestall.

опережа́|ть, ю, *impf. of* опереди́ть.

опере́ни|е, я, *n.* feathering, plumage; хвостово́е о. (*aeron.*) tail unit.

опере́нный, *adj.* feathered.

опере́т|ка, ки, f. = ~та.

опере́т|очный, *adj. of* ~ка *and* ~та.

опере́тт|а, ы, f. musical comedy, operetta.

опере́ть, обопру́, обопрёшь, *past* опёр, оперла́, *pf.* (*of* опира́ть) (о+a.) to lean (against).

опере́ться, обопру́сь, обопрёшься, *past* опёрся, оперла́сь, *pf.* (*of* опира́ться) (на+a.; о+a.) to lean (on; against); о. о подоко́нник to lean against the window-sill; о. на подде́ржку жены́ (*fig.*) to lean for support on one's wife.

опери́р|овать, ую, *impf. and pf.* **1.** (*med.*) to

operate (upon). **2.** (*mil.*) to operate, act. **3.** (+*i.; fin., etc.*) to operate (with), execute operations (with); (*fig.*) to use, handle; о. недоста́точными да́нными to operate with inadequate data.

опер|и́ть, ю́, и́шь, *pf.* (*of* ~я́ть) to feather (*an arrow*); to adorn with feathers.

опер|и́ться, ю́сь, и́шься, *pf.* (*of* ~я́ться) **1.** (*of birds*) to be fledged. **2.** (*fig.*) to stand on one's own feet.

о́перн|ый, *adj.* opera; operatic; о. певе́ц, ~ая певи́ца opera singer; о. теа́тр opera-house.

опёрт|ый (~, ~а́, ~о), *p.p.p. of* опере́ть.

опер|ши́сь, *past gerund of* ~е́ться; о. (на+a.) leaning (on).

опер|я́ть(ся), я́ю(сь), *impf. of* ~и́ть(ся).

опеча́л|ить(ся), ю(сь), ишь(ся), *pf. of* печа́лить(ся).

опеча́т|ать, аю, *pf.* (*of* ~ывать) to seal up.

опеча́т|ка, ки, f. misprint; спи́сок ~ок (list of) errata.

опе́ш|ить, у, ишь, *pf.* (*coll.*) to be taken aback.

опива́|ться, юсь, *impf. of* опи́ться.

опи́вк|и, ов, *no sing.* (*coll.*) dregs.

о́пи|й, я, *m.* opium.

о́пий|ный, *adj. of* ~.

опи́лива|ть, ю, *impf. of* опили́ть.

опил|и́ть, ю́, ~ишь, *pf.* (*of* ~ивать) to saw; to file.

опи́л|ки, ок, *no sing.* sawdust; (metal) filings.

опира́|ть(ся), ю(сь), *impf. of* опере́ть(ся).

описа́ни|е, я, *n.* description; account; э́то не поддаётся ~ю it is beyond description, it beggars description.

опи́с|анный, *p.p.p. of* ~а́ть *and adj.* (*math.*) circumscribed.

описа́тельный, *adj.* descriptive.

описа́тельств|о, а, *n.* (*pejor.*) (bare) description.

опи|са́ть, шу́, ~шешь, *pf.* (*of* ~сывать) **1.** to describe. **2.** to iist, inventory; о. иму́щество (*leg.*) to distrain property. **3.** (*math.*) to describe, circumscribe.

опи|са́ться, шу́сь, ~шешься, *pf.* to make a slip of the pen.

опи́ск|а, и, f. slip of the pen.

опи́сыва|ть, ю, *impf. of* описа́ть.

о́пис|ь, и, f. list, schedule; inventory; о. иму́щества (*leg.*) distraint.

опи́|ться, обопью́сь, обопьёшься, *past* ~лся, ~ла́сь, ~ло́сь, *pf.* (*of* ~ва́ться) (*coll.*) to drink to excess, drink oneself stupid.

о́пиум, а, *m.* opium.

о́пиум|ный, *adj. of* ~.

опла́|кать, чу, чешь, *pf.* (*of* ~кивать) to mourn (over); to bewail, bemoan.

опла́кива|ть, ю, *impf. of* опла́кать.

опла́т|а, ы, f. pay, payment; remuneration;

поча́сная о. payment by the hour; сде́льная о. piece work payment.

опла|ти́ть, чу́, ~тишь, *pf.* to pay (for); о. расхо́ды to meet the expenses, foot the bill; о. счёт to settle the account, pay the bill; о. убы́тки to pay damages.

опла́|ченный, *p.p.p.* of ~ти́ть; с ~ченным отве́том reply-paid.

опла́чива|ть, ю, *impf.* of оплати́ть.

опла́|чу, чешь, *see* ~кать.

опла|чу́, ~тишь, *see* ~ти́ть.

оплёв|анный, *p.p.p.* of ~а́ть; как о. as if in disgrace.

опл|ева́ть, юю́, юёшь, *pf.* (*of* ~ёвывать) **1.** (*coll.*) to cover with spittle. **2.** (*fig.*) to spit upon, humiliate.

оплёвыва|ть, ю, *impf.* of оплева́ть.

опле|сти́, ту́, тёшь, *past* ~л, ~ла́, *pf.* (*of* ~та́ть) **1.** to twine (round); to braid; о. буты́ль соло́мой to wicker a bottle. **2.** (*fig., coll.*) to twist, get round.

оплета́|ть, ю, *impf.* of оплести́.

оплеу́х|а, и, *f.* (*coll.*) slap in the face.

опле́ч|ье, ья, *g. pl.* ~ий, *n.* (*obs.*) shoulder(s) (*of garment*).

оплешиве|ть, ю, *pf.* of плеши́веть.

оплодотворе́ни|е, я, *n.* impregnation, fecundation; fertilization.

оплодотвори́тел|ь, я, *m.* (*bot.*) fertilizer.

оплодотвор|и́ть, ю́, и́шь, *pf.* (*of* ~я́ть) to impregnate (*also fig.*), fecundate; to fertilize.

оплодотвор|я́ть, я́ю, *impf.* of ~и́ть.

опломбир|ова́ть, у́ю, *pf.* of пломбирова́ть.

опло́т, а, *m.* (*rhet.*) stronghold, bulwark.

оплоша́|ть, ю, *pf.* (*coll.*) to take a false step, blunder.

опло́шност|ь, и, *f.* false step, blunder.

опло́ш|ный (~ен, ~на), *adj.* (*obs.*) **1.** mistaken; о. посту́пок false step. **2.** blundering.

оплыва́|ть, ю, *impf.* of оплы́ть.

оплы́|ть¹, ву́, вёшь, *pf.* (*of* ~ва́ть) **1.** to become swollen, swell up. **2.** (*of a candle*) to gutter. **3.** to fall (*as result of a landslide*).

оплы́|ть², ву́, вёшь, *pf.* (*of* ~ва́ть) to sail round; to swim round; о. о́стров to sail round an island; о. о́зеро to sail round (the edge of) a lake.

опове|сти́ть, щу́, сти́шь, *pf.* (*of* ~ща́ть) to notify, inform.

оповеща́|ть, ю, *impf.* of оповести́ть.

оповеще́ни|е, я, *n.* notification; радиосе́тка ~я (*mil.*) (early) warning system.

опога́н|ить, ю, ишь, *pf.* of пога́нить.

оподельдо́к, а, *m.* (*med., hist.*) opodeldoc.

оподле́|ть, ю, *pf.* of подле́ть.

опо́|ек, йка, *m.* calf(-leather).

опо́ечный, *adj.* calf(-skin).

опозда́|вший, *past part. act.* of ~ть; *as noun* о., ~вшего, *m.* late-comer.

опозда́ни|е, я, *n.* being late; lateness; delay; по́езд при́был без ~я the train arrived on time; с ~ем на де́сять мину́т ten minutes late.

опозда́|ть, ю, *pf.* (*of* опа́здывать) to be late; to be overdue; о. на ле́кцию to be late for the lecture; о. на полчаса́ to be half an hour late; о. с упла́той нало́гов to be late in paying taxes.

опознава́ни|е, я, *n.* identification; о. самолётов aircraft recognition.

опознава́тельный, *adj.* distinguishing; о. знак landmark, (*naut.*) beacon; (*on wings of aircraft*) marking.

опозна|ва́ть, ю́, ёшь, *impf.* of ~ть.

опознава́ни|е, я, *n.* (*leg.*) identification.

опозна́|ть, ю, *pf.* (*of* ~ва́ть) to identify.

опозо́рени|е, я, *n.* (*leg.*) defamation.

опозо́р|ить(ся), ю(сь), ишь(ся), *pf.* of позо́рить(ся).

опо|и́ть, ю́, и́шь, *pf.* (*of* опа́ивать) **1.** to injure by giving too much to drink. **2.** (*obs.*) to poison (*by means of a potion*).

опо́йковый, *adj.* calf(-skin).

опо́к|а¹, и, *f.* (*tech.*) flask, mould box, casting box, box form; литьё в ~ax flask casting.

опо́к|а², и, *f.* (*geol.*) silica clay.

ополо́скива|ть, ю, *impf.* of ополоска́ть and ополосну́ть.

ополз|а́ть, а́ю, *impf.* of ~ти́¹,².

о́ползень, ня, *m.* landslide, landslip.

о́ползневый, *adj.* of ~ень.

ополз|ти́¹, у́, ёшь, *past* ~, ~ла́, *pf.* (*of* ~а́ть) to crawl round.

ополз|ти́², ёт, *past* ~, ~ла́, *pf.* (*of* ~а́ть) to slip.

ополо|ска́ть, щу́, ~щешь, *pf.* (*of* ополо́скивать) = ~сну́ть.

ополосн|у́ть, у́, ёшь, *pf.* (*of* ополо́скивать) to rinse; to swill.

ополоу́ме|ть, ю, *pf.* (*coll.*) to go crazy, be beside oneself.

ополч|а́ть(ся), а́ю(сь), *impf.* of ~и́ть(ся).

ополче́н|ец, ца, *m.* militiaman; home guard.

ополче́ни|е, я, *n.* **1.** militia; home guard. **2.** (*collect.; hist.*) irregulars; levies.

ополче́н|ский, *adj.* of ~ец and ~ие.

ополч|и́ть, у́, и́шь, *pf.* (*of* ~а́ть) (на+*a.* or про́тив; *obs.*) to arm (against); (*fig.*) to enlist the support of (against).

ополч|и́ться, у́сь, и́шься, *pf.* (*of* ~а́ться) (на+*a.* or про́тив) to take up arms (against); (*fig.*) to be up in arms (against); to turn (against).

ополя́ч|ить, у, ишь, *pf.* to polonize.

опо́мн|иться, юсь, ишься, *pf.* to come to one's senses, collect oneself.

опо́р, а, *m.* only in phrase во весь о. at full speed, at top speed, full tilt.

опо́р|а, ы, *f.* support (*also fig.*); (*tech.*) bearing; pier (*of a bridge*); (*fig.*) buttress; то́чка

~ы (*phys.*, *tech.*) fulcrum, bearing, point of rest.

опора́жнива|ть, ю, *impf. of* опоро́жнить.

опо́р|ки, ков, *sing.* ~ок, ~ка, *m.* down-at--heel shoes.

опо́р|ный, *adj. of* ~a; (*tech.*) bearing, supporting; о. ка́мень abutment stone; ~ная при́зма fulcrum; о. пункт (*mil.*) strong point; ~ная сва́я bridge pile; о. столб chock (block).

опоро́жн|ить, ю, ишь, *pf.* (*of* опора́жнивать) to empty; to drain (at a draught); о. кише́чник to evacuate one's bowels.

опорожня́|ть, ю, *impf.* = опора́жнивать.

опоро́с, а, *m.* farrow (*of sow*).

опороси́|ться, шься, *pf. of* пороси́ться.

опоро́ч|ить, у, ишь, *pf. of* поро́чить.

опосля́, *adv.* (*coll. or dial.*) afterwards.

опосре́дств|овать, ую, *impf. and pf.* (*philos.*) to mediate.

опо́ссум, а, *m.* (*zool.*) opossum.

опосты́ле|ть, ю, *pf.* (*coll.*; +*d.*) to grow hateful (to), grow wearisome (to).

опохмел|и́ться, ю́сь, и́шься, *pf.* (*of* ~я́ться) (*coll.*) to take a hair of the dog that bit you.

опохмел|я́ться, я́юсь, *impf. of* ~и́ться.

опочива́л|ьня, ьни, *g. pl.* ~ен, *f.* (*obs.*) bedchamber.

опочива́|ть, ю, *impf. of* опочи́ть.

опочи́|ть, ю, ешь, *pf.* (*of* ~ва́ть) (*obs.*) 1. to go to sleep. 2. (*fig., poet.*) to pass to one's rest.

опошле́|ть, ю, *pf. of* пошле́ть.

опо́шл|ить, ю, ишь, *pf.* (*of* ~я́ть) to vulgarize, debase.

опоя́|сать, шу, шешь, *pf.* (*of* ~сывать) 1. to gird, engird(le). 2. (*fig.*) to girdle.

опоя́|саться, шусь, шешься, *pf.* (*of* ~сываться) 1. (+*i.*) to gird oneself (with), gird on. 2. *pass. of* ~сать.

опоя́сыва|ть(ся), ю(сь), *impf. of* опоя́сать(ся).

оппозиционе́р, а, *m.* member of the opposition.

оппози|цио́нный, *adj. of* ~ция.

оппози́ци|я, и, *f.* opposition.

оппоне́нт, а, *m.* opponent; официа́льный о. official opponent (*at defence of dissertation, etc.*).

оппони́р|овать, ую, *impf.* (+*d.*) to oppose, act as opponent (to).

оппортуни́зм, а, *m.* opportunism.

оппортуни́ст, а, *m.* opportunist.

оппортунисти́ческий, *adj.* opportunist.

оппортунисти́ч|ный (~ен, ~на), *adj.* = ~еский.

оппортуни́ст|ский, *adj. of* ~.

опра́в|а, ы, *f.* setting, mounting; case; очки́ без ~ы rimless spectacles.

оправда́ни|е, я, *n.* 1. justification. 2. excuse. 3. (*leg.*) acquittal, discharge.

оправда́тельный, *adj.* о. пригово́р verdict of 'not guilty'; о. докуме́нт voucher.

оправд|а́ть, а́ю, *pf.* (*of* ~ывать) 1. to justify, warrant; to vindicate; to authorize; о. ожида́ния to come up to expectations; о. себя́ to justify oneself; о. расхо́ды to authorize expenses. 2. to excuse; о. посту́пок боле́знью to excuse an action by reason of sickness. 3. (*leg.*) to acquit, discharge.

оправд|а́ться, а́юсь, *pf.* (*of* ~ываться) 1. to justify oneself; to vindicate oneself; о. незна́нием (*leg.*) to plead ignorance. 2. to be justified; моё предсказа́ние ~а́лось my prediction has come true; расхо́ды ~а́лись the expense was worth it.

опра́вдыва|ть, ю, *impf. of* оправда́ть.

опра́вдыва|ться, юсь, *impf.* 1. *impf. of* оправда́ться. 2. to try to justify oneself, try to vindicate oneself.

опра́в|ить, лю, ишь, *pf.* (*of* ~ля́ть) 1. to put in order, set right, adjust (*dress, coiffure, etc.*). 2. to set, mount.

опра́в|иться, люсь, ишься, *pf.* (*of* ~ля́ться) 1. to put (one's dress, *etc.*) in order. 2. (от) to recover (from). 3. (*coll.*) to urinate.

опра́вк|а, и, *f.* 1. (*tech.*) mandrel, chuck; (riveting) drift. 2. setting, mounting.

оправля́|ть(ся), ю(сь), *impf. of* опра́вить(ся).

опра́стыва|ть(ся), ю(сь), *impf. of* опроста́ть(ся).

опра́шива|ть, ю, *impf. of* опроси́ть.

определе́ни|е, я, *n.* 1. definition; (*chem., phys., etc.*) determination. 2. (*leg.*) decision. 3. (*gram.*) attribute.

определё́н|ный (~ен, ~на), *adj.* 1. definite; determinate; fixed; о. за́работок fixed wage; о. член (*gram.*) definite article. 2. certain; в ~ных слу́чаях in certain cases.

определи́м|ый (~, ~а), *adj.* definable.

определи́тел|ь, я, *m.* (*math.*) determinant.

определ|и́ть, ю́, и́шь, *pf.* (*of* ~я́ть) 1. to define; to determine; to fix, appoint; о. боле́знь to diagnose a disease; о. ме́ру наказа́ния to fix a punishment; о. расстоя́ние to judge a distance. 2. (*obs.*) to appoint; to allot, assign; о. на слу́жбу to appoint to a post; о. пай to assign a share.

определ|и́ться, ю́сь, и́шься, *pf.* (*of* ~я́ться) 1. to be formed; to take shape; to be determined. 2. (*obs.*) to find a place; о. на слу́жбу to take service. 3. (*aeron.*) to obtain a fix, find one's position. 4. *pass. of* ~и́ть.

определ|я́ть(ся), я́ю(сь), *impf. of* ~и́ть(ся).

опресне́ни|е, я, *n.* desalination.

опресн|ё́нный, *p.p.p. of* ~и́ть; ~ё́нная вода́ distilled water.

опресни́тел|ь, я, *m.* (water-)distiller.

опресн|и́ть, ю́, и́шь, *pf.* (*of* ~я́ть) to distil (*salt water*); to desalinate.

опрéснок|и, ов, *sing.* ~, ~а, *m.* unleavened bread.

опресн|я́ть, я́ю, *impf. of* ~и́ть.

опри́чник, а, *m.* (*hist.*) oprichnik (*member of oprichnina*).

опри́чнин|а, ы, *f.* (*hist.*) oprichnina (*special administrative élite established in Russia by Ivan IV, also the territory assigned to this élite*).

опри́чн|ый, *adj. of* ~ина.

опри́чь, *prep.+g.* (*obs.*) except, save.

опро́б|овать, ую, *pf.* 1. (*tech.*) to test. 2. to sample, try.

опроверг|а́ть, а́ю, *impf. of* ~нуть.

опрове́рг|нуть, ну, нешь, *past* ~, ~ла, *pf.* (*of* ~а́ть) to refute, disprove.

опроверже́ни|е, я, *n.* refutation; disproof; denial.

опрокидн|о́й, *adj.* грузови́к с ~ым я́щиком tip-up lorry.

опроки́дывател|ь, я, *m.* (*tech.*) tipper, tipple, dumper.

опроки́дыва|ть(ся), ю(сь), *impf. of* опроки́нуть(ся).

опроки́|нуть, ну, нешь, *pf.* (*of* ~дывать) 1. to overturn; to topple over. 2. (*mil.*) to overthrow; to overrun. 3. (*sl.*) to knock back (= *drink off*). 4. (*fig.*) to upset; to refute.

опроки́|нуться, нусь, нешься, *pf.* (*of* ~дываться) 1. to overturn; to topple over, tip over; to capsize. 2. *pass. of* ~нуть.

опроме́тчив|ый (~, ~а), *adj.* precipitate, rash, hasty, unconsidered.

о́прометью, *adv.* headlong.

опро́с, а, *m.* (*mil., etc.*) interrogation; (*leg., etc.*) (cross-)examination; referendum.

опро́|си́ть, шу́, ~сишь, *pf.* (*of* опра́шивать) to interrogate; to (cross-)examine.

опро́с|ный, *adj. of* ~; о. лист questionnaire; (*leg.*) interrogatory.

опроста́|ть, ю, *pf.* (*of* опра́стывать) (*coll.*) to empty; to remove the contents (of).

опроста́|ться, юсь, *pf.* (*of* опра́стываться) (*coll.*) 1. to become empty. 2. *pass. of* ~ть. 3. to defecate.

опро|сти́ться, щу́сь, сти́шься, *pf.* (*of* ~ща́ться) to adopt the 'simple life'.

опростоволо́|ситься, шусь, сишься, *pf.* (*coll.*) to make a fool of oneself.

опротест|ова́ть, у́ю, *pf.* (*of* ~о́вывать) 1. о. ве́ксель (*fin.*) to protest a bill. 2. (*leg.*) to appeal (against).

опротесто́выва|ть, ю, *impf. of* опротестова́ть.

опроти́ве|ть, ю, *pf.* to become loathsome, become repulsive.

опроща́|ться, юсь, *impf. of* опрости́ться.

опроще́ни|е, я, *n.* adoption of the 'simple life'.

опры́ск|ать, аю, *pf.* (*of* ~ивать) to sprinkle; to spray.

опры́ск|аться, аюсь, *pf.* (*of* ~иваться) 1. to sprinkle oneself; to spray oneself. 2. *pass. of* ~ать.

опры́скиватель|ь, я, *m.* (*agric.*) sprinkler; sprayer.

опры́скива|ть(ся), ю(сь), *impf. of* опры́скать(ся).

опрыща́ве|ть, ю, *pf. of* прыща́веть.

опря́тность|ь, и, *f.* neatness, tidiness.

опря́т|ный (~ен, ~на), *adj.* neat, tidy.

опта́нт, а, *m.* (*leg.*) person having right of option (*of citizenship*).

оптати́вный, *adj.* (*gram.*) optative.

опта́ци|я, и, *f.* (*leg.*) option (*of citizenship*); пра́во ~и right of option (*of citizenship of one or other of two states*).

о́птик, а, *m.* optician.

о́птик|а, и, *f.* 1. optics. 2. (*collect.*) optical instruments.

оптима́льный, *adj.* optimum, optimal.

оптими́зм, а, *m.* optimism.

оптими́ст, а, *m.* optimist.

оптимисти́ческий, *adj.* optimistic.

о́птимум, а, *m.* (*biol., etc.*) optimum.

опти́р|овать, ую, *impf. and pf.* (*leg.*) to opt (for).

опти́ческ|ий, *adj.* optic, optical; о. обма́н optical illusion; ~ая ось optic axis; ~ое стекло́ optical glass, lens.

оптови́к, а́, *m.* wholesale dealer, wholesaler.

опто́вый, *adj.* wholesale.

о́птом, *adv.* wholesale; о. и в ро́зницу wholesale and retail.

опубликова́ни|е, я, *n.* publication; о. зако́на promulgation of a law.

опублик|ова́ть, у́ю, *pf.* (*of* публикова́ть *and* ~о́вывать) to publish; о. закон to promulgate a law.

опублико́выва|ть, ю, *impf. of* опубликова́ть.

о́пус, а, *m.* (*mus.*) opus.

опуска́|ть(ся), ю(сь), *impf. of* опусти́ть(ся).

опускн|о́й, *adj.* movable; ~а́я дверь trapdoor.

опусте́лый, *adj.* deserted.

опусте́|ть, ю, *pf. of* пусте́ть.

опу|сти́ть, щу́, ~стишь, *pf.* (*of* ~ска́ть) 1. to lower; to let down; о. што́ры to draw the blinds; о. глаза́ to look down; о. го́лову (*fig.*) to hang one's head; о. ру́ки (*fig.*) to lose heart. 2. to turn down (*collar, etc.*). 3. to omit.

опу|сти́ться, щу́сь, ~стишься, *pf.* (*of* ~ска́ться) 1. to lower oneself. 2. to sink; to fall; to go down; о. в кре́сло to sink into a chair; о. на коле́ни to go down on one's knees; у него́ ру́ки ~сти́лись (*fig.*) he has lost heart. 3. (*fig.*) to sink; to let oneself go, go to pieces.

опустош|а́ть, а́ю, *impf. of* ~и́ть.

опустоше́ни|е, я, *n.* devastation, ruin.

опустоши́тел|ьный (~ен, ~ьна), *adj.* devastating.

опустош|и́ть, у́, и́шь, *pf. (of* ~а́ть) to devastate, lay waste, ravage.

опу́т|ать, аю, *pf. (of* ~ывать) to enmesh, entangle (*also fig.*); (*fig.*) to ensnare.

опу́тыва|ть, ю, *impf. of* опу́тать.

опух|а́ть, а́ю, *impf. of* ~нуть.

опу́хлый, *adj.* (*coll.*) swollen.

опу́х|нуть, ну, нешь, *past* ~, ~ла, *pf. (of* ~а́ть) to swell (up).

о́пухол|ь, и, *f.* swelling; (*med.*) tumour.

опуш|а́ть, а́ю, *impf. of* ~и́ть.

опуш|и́ть, у́, и́шь, *pf. (of* ~а́ть) **1.** (ме́хом) to edge, trim (with fur). **2.** (*of hoar-frost or snow*) to powder; to cover; бо́роду у него́ ~и́ло сне́гом his beard was powdered with snow.

опу́шк|а¹, и, *f.* edging, trimming.

опу́шк|а², и, *f.* edge (*of a forest, of a wood*).

опуще́ни|е, я, *n.* **1.** lowering; letting down; о. ма́тки (*med.*) prolapsus (prolapse) of the uterus. **2.** omission.

опу́|щенный, *p.p.p. of* ~сти́ть; как в во́ду о. (*fig.*) crestfallen, downcast.

опыле́ни|е, я, *n.* (*bot.*) pollination; перекрёстное о. cross-pollination.

опы́ливател|ь, я, *m.* (*agric.*) insecticide dust sprayer.

опы́лива|ть, ю, *impf. of* опыли́ть 2.

опыли́тел|ь, я, *m.* **1.** (*bot.*) pollinator. **2.** (*agric.*) = опы́ливатель.

опыл|и́ть, ю́, и́шь, *pf.* **1.** (*impf.* ~я́ть) (*bot.*) to pollinate. **2.** (*impf.* ~ивать) (*agric.*) to spray with insecticide dust.

опыл|я́ть, я́ю, *impf. of* ~и́ть 1.

о́пыт, а, *m.* **1.** experience; на ~е, по ~у by experience. **2.** experiment; test, trial; attempt.

о́пытник, а, *m.* experimenter.

о́пытност|ь, и, *f.* experience.

о́пыт|ный, *adj.* **1.** (~ен, ~на) experienced. **2.** experimental; узна́ть ~ным путём to learn by means of experiment; ~ная ста́нция experimental station.

опьяне́лый, *adj.* intoxicated.

опьяне́ни|е, я, *n.* intoxication.

опьяне́|ть, ю, *pf. of* пьяне́ть.

опьян|и́ть, ю́, и́шь, *pf. (of* пьяни́ть *and* ~я́ть) to intoxicate, make drunk; успе́х ~и́л его́ success has gone to his head.

опьян|я́ть, я́ю, *impf. of* ~и́ть.

опьяня́|ющий, *pres. part. act. of* ~ть *and adj.* intoxicating.

опя́ть, *adv.* again.

опя́ть-таки, *adv.* (*coll.*) **1.** (and) what is more; он холостя́к, о.-т. бога́тый челове́к he is a bachelor, and what is more is a

rich man. **2.** but again; however; я постуча́л ещё раз, о.-т. ничего́ не послы́шалось I knocked again, but again there was nothing to be heard.

ора́в|а, ы, *f.* (*coll.*) crowd, horde.

ора́кул, а, *m.* oracle.

ора́л|о, а, *n.* (*obs. and dial.*) plough.

орангута́нг, а, *m.* orang-outang.

ора́нжевый, *adj.* orange (*colour*).

оранжере́|йный, *adj. of* ~я; ~йное расте́ние hothouse plant (*also fig.*).

оранжере́|я, и, *f.* hothouse, greenhouse, conservatory.

ора́тор, а, *m.* orator, (public) speaker.

орато́ри|я, и, *f.* **1.** (*mus.*) oratorio. **2.** (*eccl.*) oratory.

ора́тор|ский, *adj. of* ~; oratorical; ~ское иску́сство oratory.

ора́торств|овать, ую, *impf.* to orate, harangue, speechify.

ор|а́ть¹, у́, ёшь, *impf.* (*coll.*) to bawl, yell.

ор|а́ть², у́, ёшь, *impf.* (*dial.*) to plough.

орби́т|а, ы, *f.* **1.** (*astron. and fig.*) orbit; вы́вести на ~у to put into orbit; о. влия́ния sphere of influence. **2.** (*anat.*) eye-socket; глаза́ у него́ вы́шли из ~ (*fig.*) his eyes leaped from their sockets.

орг-, *abbr. of* организацио́нный.

орга́зм, а, *m.* (*physiol.*) orgasm.

о́рган, а, *m.* (*biol., polit., etc.*) organ; исполни́тельный о. agency; ~ы вла́сти organs of government; ~ы печа́ти organs of the press; ~ы ре́чи speech organs.

орга́н, а, *m.* (*mus.*) organ.

организа́тор, а, *m.* organizer.

организа́тор|ский, *adj. of* ~; о. тала́нт talent for organization.

организа|цио́нный, *adj. of* ~ция.

организа́ци|я, и, *f.* (*in var. senses*) organization; О. Объединённых На́ций United Nations' Organization.

органи́зм, а, *m.* organism.

организо́ванност|ь, и, *f.* (good) organization; orderliness.

организо́ванный, *p.p.p. of* организова́ть *and adj.* organized; orderly, disciplined.

организ|ова́ть, у́ю, *impf. and pf. (pf. also* с~) to organize.

организ|ова́ться, у́юсь, *impf. and pf.* **1.** to be organized. **2.** to organize (*intrans.*).

орга́ник, а, *m.* specialist in organic chemistry.

орга́ник|а, и, *f.* (*coll.*) organic chemistry.

органи́ст, а, *m.* organist.

органи́ческ|ий, *adj.* organic; ~ая хи́мия organic chemistry; ~ое це́лое integral whole.

органи́ч|ный (~ен, ~на), *adj.* organic.

орга́н|ный, *adj. of* ~; о. конце́рт concerto for organ.

органогра́фи|я, и, *f.* (*biol.*) organography.

органотерапи|я, и, *f.* organotherapy.

орга́нчик, а, *m.* **1.** *dim. of* орга́н. **2.** musical--box.

о́рги|я, и, *f.* orgy.

орд|а́, ы́, *pl.* ~ы, ~, ~а́м, *f.* (*hist. and fig.*) horde; Золота́я о. the Golden Horde.

орда́ли|я, и, *f.* (*hist.*) ordeal.

о́рден¹, а, *pl.* ~а́, ~о́в, *m.* order; decoration; о. Подвя́зки Order of the Garter; о. Почётного Легио́на Legion of Honour; о. Трудово́го Кра́сного Зна́мени Order of the Red Banner of Labour.

о́рден², а, *pl.* ~ы, ~ов, *m.* **1.** order; иезуи́тский о. Society of Jesus; о. тамплие́ров Order of Knights Templars. **2.** = о́рдер².

орденоно́с|ец, ца, *m.* holder of an order *or* decoration.

орденоно́сный, *adj.* decorated with an order.

о́рден|ский, *adj. of* ~; ~ская ле́нта ribbon.

о́рдер¹, а, *pl.* ~а́, ~о́в, *m.* order, warrant; (*leg.*) writ; о. на о́быск search warrant; о. на поку́пку coupon; о. на кварти́ру authorization to an apartment.

о́рдер², а, *pl.* ~ы, ~ов, *m.* (*archit.*) order; кори́нфский о. Corinthian order.

ордина́р, а, *m.* normal level (*of water in reservoir, etc.*).

ордина́р|ец, ца, *m.* (*mil.*) orderly; batman.

ордина́р|ный (~ен, ~на), *adj.* **1.** ordinary. **2.** (*obs.*) on the staff, permanent.

ордина́т|а, ы, *f.* (*math.*) ordinate.

ордина́тор, а, *m.* house-surgeon.

ординату́р|а, ы, *f.* **1.** appointment as house--surgeon; permanent appointment (*of professor*). **2.** clinical studies (*in medical school*).

орд|ы́нский, *adj. of* ~а́.

ор|ёл, ла́, *m.* eagle; о. и́ли ре́шка heads or tails.

орео́л, а, *m.* halo, aureole.

оре́х, а, *m.* **1.** nut; америка́нский о. Brazil nut; гре́цкий о. walnut; коко́совый о. coco-nut; лесно́й о., обыкнове́нный о. hazel-nut; муска́тный о. nutmeg; бу́дет тебе́ на ~и!; ему́ доста́лось (попа́ло) на ~и! (*fig.*) you'll catch it!; he's caught it!; разде́лать (отде́лать) кого́-н. под о. (*coll.*) to give it someone hot. **2.** nut-tree. **3.** (*wood*) walnut; шкаф из ~а walnut cupboard.

оре́ховк|а, и, *f.* (*orn.*) nutcracker.

оре́х|овый, *adj. of* ~; ~овое де́рево nut-tree; (*wood*) walnut; ~овая скорлупа́ nutshell; ~ового цве́та nut-brown; о. шокола́д nut chocolate.

орехотво́рк|а, и, *f.* (*zool.*) gall-fly.

оре́ш|ек, ка, *m.* *dim. of* оре́х; черни́льный о. nut-gall.

оре́шник, а, *m.* **1.** (hazel) nut-tree. **2.** hazel--grove.

оригина́л, а, *m.* **1.** original. **2.** eccentric (person).

оригина́льнича|ть, ю, *impf.* (*of* с~) (*coll.*) to put on an act, try to be clever.

оригина́л|ьный (~ен, ~ьна), *adj.* (*in var. senses*) original.

ориентали́ст, а, *m.* orientalist.

ориента́льный, *adj.* oriental.

ориента́ци|я, и, *f.* **1.** (на+*a.*) orientation (toward); direction of attention (toward). **2.** (*fig.*) (в+*p.*) understanding (of), grasp (of); у него́ хоро́шая о. в ю́жно-америка́нских дела́х he has a firm grasp of South American affairs; у меня́ нет ~и в торго́вом де́ле I have no head for business.

ориенти́р, а, *m.* (*mil.*) reference point; guiding line; (есте́ственный) о. landmark.

ориенти́рова|нный, *p.p.p. of* ~ть *and adj.* knowledgeable.

ориенти́р|овать, у́ю, *impf. and pf.* **1.** orient, orientate; (в+*p.*) to enlighten (concerning); он не ~овал меня́ в экономи́ческом положе́нии he did not put me in the picture about the economic position. **2.** (на+*a.*) to direct (toward).

ориенти́р|оваться, у́юсь, *impf. and pf.* **1.** to orient oneself; to find one's bearings (*also fig.*); я пло́хо ~уюсь I have a poor sense of direction; она́ ско́ро ~ова́лась в но́вой обстано́вке (*fig.*) she soon found her feet in her new surroundings. **2.** (на+*a.*) to head (for), make (for); (*fig.*) to direct one's attention (to, toward); о. на рабо́чих слу́шателей to cater for a working-class audience.

ориентиро́вк|а, и, *f.* = ориента́ция.

ориентиро́вочно, *adv.* tentatively; approximately; гру́бо о. as a rough guide.

ориентиро́воч|ный, *adj.* **1.** position-finding. **2.** (~ен, ~на) tentative; rough, approximate.

орке́стр, а, *m.* **1.** orchestra; band. **2.** orchestra-pit.

оркестра́нт, а, *m.* member of an orchestra *or* band.

оркестрио́н, а, *m.* (*obs.*) orchestrina, orchestrion.

оркестр|ова́ть, у́ю, *impf. and pf.* to orchestrate.

оркестро́вк|а, и, *f.* orchestration.

оркестро́вый, *adj.* **1.** *adj. of* орке́стр. **2.** orchestral.

орла́н, а, *m.* sea eagle.

орл|ёнок, ёнка, *pl.* ~я́та, ~я́т, *m.* eaglet.

орле́ц, а́, *m.* **1.** (*min.*) rhodonite. **2.** (*eccl.*) round hassock (*with woven design of eagle; placed under feet of officiating bishop*).

орли́|ный, *adj. of* орёл; aquiline; о. взгляд eagle eye; о. нос aquiline nose.

орли́ц|а, ы, *f.* female eagle.

орля́нк|а, и, *f.* pitch-and-toss.

орна́мент, а, *m.* ornament; ornamental design.

орнамента́льный, *adj.* ornamental.

орнамента́ци|я, и, *f.* ornamentation.

орнаменти́р|овать, ую, *impf. and pf.* to ornament.

орнито́лог, а, *m.* ornithologist.

орнитологи́ческий, *adj.* ornithological.

орнитоло́ги|я, и, *f.* ornithology.

орнитопте́р, а, *m. (aeron.)* ornithopter.

оробе́лый, *adj.* timid; frightened.

оробе́|ть, ю, *pf. of* робе́ть.

орогове́|ть, ет, *pf.* to become horny.

орографи́ческий, *adj.* orographic(al).

орогра́фи|я, и, *f.* orography.

ороси́тельный, *adj.* irrigation; irrigating; о. кана́л irrigation canal.

оро|си́ть, шу́, си́шь, *pf. (of ~ша́ть)* to irrigate; to water; о. слеза́ми to wash with tears.

оро|ша́ть, ша́ю, *impf. of ~си́ть.*

ороше́ни|е, я, *n.* irrigation; поля́ ~я sewage-farm.

ортодо́кс, а, *m.* orthodox person, conformist.

ортодокса́л|ьный (~ен, ~ьна), *adj.* orthodox.

ортодокси|я, и, *f.* orthodoxy.

ортопеди́ст, а, *m.* orthopaedic specialist.

ортопеди́ческий, *adj.* orthopaedic.

ортопе́ди|я, и, *f.* orthopaedy.

ору́ди|е, я, *n.* 1. instrument; implement; tool *(also fig.)*; сельскохозя́йственные ~я agricultural implements. 2. piece of ordnance; gun; зени́тное о. anti-aircraft gun; полево́е о. field-gun; самохо́дное о. self-propelled gun.

оруд|и́йный, *adj. of* ~ие 2; о. ого́нь gun-fire; о. око́п gun-entrenchment; ~и́йная па́льба́ cannonade; о. расчёт gun crew.

ору́д|овать, ую, *impf. (coll.; +i.)* 1. to handle. 2. *(fig., pejor.)* to be active; он там всем ~ует he bosses the whole show.

оруже́йник, а, *m.* gunsmith, armourer.

оруж|е́йный, *adj. of* ~ие; ~е́йная пала́та armoury; о. ма́стер armourer.

оружено́с|ец, ца, *m.* armour-bearer, sword-bearer; *(fig.)* henchman.

ору́жи|е, я, *n.* arm(s); weapons; огнестре́льное о. fire-arm(s); стрелко́вое о. small arms; холо́дное о. cold steel; род ~я arm of the service; к ~ю! to arms!; бра́ться за о. to take up arms; подня́ть о. (на+а.) to take up arms (against); положи́ть о., сложи́ть о. to lay down one's arms; бить кого́-н. его́ же ~ем *(fig.)* to beat someone at his own game.

орфографи́ческ|ий, *adj.* orthographic(al); ~ая оши́бка spelling mistake.

орфогра́фи|я, и, *f.* orthography, spelling.

орфоэпи́ческий, *adj.* о. слова́рь pronouncing dictionary.

орфоэ́пи|я, и, *f.* (rules of) correct pronunciation.

орхиде́|я, и, *f. (bot.)* orchid.

оря́син|а, ы, *f. (coll.)* rod, pole.

ос|а́, ы́, *pl.* ~ы, *f.* wasp.

оса́д|а, ы, *f.* siege; снять ~у to raise a siege.

оса|ди́ть¹, жу́, ди́шь, *pf. (of ~жда́ть)* to besiege, lay siege to; to beleaguer; о. вопро́сами to ply with questions; о. про́сьбами to bombard with requests.

оса|ди́ть², жу́, ~ди́шь, *pf. (of ~жда́ть) (chem.)* to precipitate.

оса|ди́ть³, жу́, ~ди́шь, *pf. (of ~жива́ть)* 1. to check, halt; to force back; о. ло́шадь to rein in a horse. 2. *(fig.)* о. кого́-н. to put someone in his place, take someone down a peg.

оса́дк|а, и, *f.* 1. set, settling *(of soil, etc.)*. 2. *(naut.)* draught; су́дно с небольшо́й ~ой vessel of shallow draught.

оса́д|ный, *adj. of* ~а; ~ная артилле́рия siege artillery; ~ная война́ siege war(fare); ~ное положе́ние state of siege.

оса́д|ок, ка, *m.* 1. *(pl.)* precipitation. 2. sediment, deposition. 3. *(fig.)* after-taste; у меня́ от э́того разгово́ра был неприя́тный о. the conversation left an unpleasant taste in my mouth.

оса́д|очный, *adj. of* ~ок; ~очные поро́ды *(geol.)* sedimentary rocks; о. чан *(chem.)* precipitation tank; ~очная маши́на *(tech.)* upsetting machine.

осажда́|ть, ю, *impf. of* осади́ть¹,².

осажда́|ться, юсь, *impf.* 1. *(of atmospheric precipitations)* to fall. 2. *(chem.)* to be precipitated; to fall out.

осаждённый, *p.p.p. of* осади́ть¹,².

оса́женный, *p.p.p. of* осади́ть³.

оса́жива|ть, ю, *impf. of* осади́ть³.

оса́нист|ый (~, ~а), *adj.* portly.

оса́нк|а, и, *f.* carriage, bearing.

оса́нн|а, ы, *f.* hosanna; восклица́ть, петь ~у кому́-н. *(fig.)* to sing someone's praises.

осатане́лый, *adj. (coll.)* possessed; diabolical, demoniacal.

осва́ива|ть(ся), ю(сь), *impf. of* осво́ить(ся).

осведоми́тел|ь, я, *m.* informant.

осведоми́тельн|ый, *adj.* 1. informative. 2. *(giving, conveying)* information; ~ая рабо́та information work, publicity work.

осве́дом|ить, лю, ишь, *pf. (of ~ля́ть)* to inform.

осве́дом|иться, люсь, ишься, *pf. (of ~ля́ться) (o+p.)* to inquire (about).

осведомле́ни|е, я, *n.* informing, notification.

осведомлённост|ь, и, *f.* knowledge, (possession of) information; у него́ хоро́шая о. в исла́ндских са́гах he is very knowledgeable about the Icelandic sagas.

осведомлённый, *p.p.p.* of осве́домить *and* *adj.* (в+*p.*) well-informed (about), knowledgeable (about); versed (in), conversant (with).

осведом|ля́ть(ся), ля́ю(сь), *impf.* of ~ить(ся).

освеж|а́ть, а́ю, *impf.* of ~и́ть.

освеж|ева́ть, у́ю, *pf.* of свежева́ть.

освежи́тельный, *adj.* refreshing.

освеж|и́ть, у́, и́шь, *pf.* (*of* ~а́ть) 1. to refresh; to freshen; о. ко́мнату to give a room an airing. 2. (*fig.*) to refresh, revive; о. свои́ зна́ния to refresh one's knowledge; о. соста́в предприя́тия (*coll.*) to introduce fresh blood into the staff of an enterprise.

освети́тел|ь, я, *m.* 1. person in charge of lighting effects. 2. condenser (*of microscope*).

освети́тельн|ый, *adj.* lighting, illuminating; ~ая бо́мба candle bomb; ~ая раке́та (*aeron.*) flare; ~ая сеть lighting system; о. снаря́д star shell.

осве|ти́ть, щу́, ти́шь, *pf.* (*of* ~ща́ть) to light up; to illuminate, illumine; (*fig.*) to throw light on.

осве|ти́ться, щу́сь, ти́шься, *pf.* (*of* ~ща́ться) 1. to light up; to brighten; её лицо́ ~ти́лось улы́бкой (*fig.*) a smile lit up her face. 2. *pass.* of ~ти́ть.

осветли́тел|ь, я, *m.* (*chem.*) clarifying agent.

осветл|и́ть, ю́, и́шь, *pf.* (*of* ~я́ть) (*chem.*) to clarify.

осветл|я́ть, я́ю, *impf.* of ~и́ть.

освеща́|ть(ся), ю(сь), *impf.* of освети́ть(ся).

освеще́ни|е, я, *n.* light, lighting, illumination; иску́сственное о. artificial light(ing); электри́ческое о. electric light.

освещённост|ь, и, *f.* (*degree of, area of*) illumination.

осве|щённый, *p.p.p.* of ~ти́ть; о. звёздами star-lit; о. луно́й moonlit; о. свеча́ми candle-lit.

освиде́тельств|овать, ую, *pf.* of свиде́тельствовать 3.

освинц|ева́ть, у́ю, *pf.* to lead, lead-plate.

осви|ста́ть, щу́, ~щешь, *pf.* (*of* ~сты́вать) to hiss (off), catcall; о. актёра to hiss an actor off the stage.

освисты́ва|ть, ю, *impf.* of освиста́ть.

освободи́тел|ь, я, *m.* liberator.

освободи́тельн|ый, *adj.* liberation, emancipation; ~ая война́ war of liberation.

освобо|ди́ть, жу́, ди́шь, *pf.* (*of* ~жда́ть) 1. to free, liberate; to release, set free; to emancipate; о. аресто́ванного to discharge a prisoner; о. от вое́нной слу́жбы to exempt from military service. 2. to dismiss; о. от до́лжности to relieve of one's post. 3. to vacate; to clear, empty.

освобо|ди́ться, жу́сь, ди́шься, *pf.* (*of*

~жда́ться) 1. (от) to free oneself (of, from); to become free. 2. *pass.* of ~ди́ть.

освобожда́|ть(ся), ю(сь), *impf.* of освободи́ть(ся).

освобожде́ни|е, я, *n.* 1. liberation; release; emancipation; discharge. 2. dismissal. 3. vacation (*of premises, etc.*).

освобо|ждённый, *p.p.p.* of ~ди́ть; о. от нало́га tax-free, exempt from tax.

освое́ни|е, я, *n.* assimilation, mastery, familiarization; о. но́вой те́хники learning to handle new machinery; о. кра́йнего се́вера the opening up of the Far North.

осво́|ить, ю, ишь, *pf.* (*of* осва́ивать) 1. to assimilate, master; to cope (with); to become familiar (with). 2. (*bot.*) to acclimatize.

осво́|иться, юсь, ишься, *pf.* (*of* осва́иваться) 1. (с+*i.*) to familiarize oneself (with). 2. to feel at home; о. в но́вой среде́ to get the feel of new surroundings.

освя|ти́ть, щу́, ти́шь, *pf.* 1. (*impf.* святи́ть) (*eccl.*) to consecrate; to bless, sanctify. 2. (*impf.* ~ща́ть) (*fig.*) to sanctify, hallow.

освяща́|ть, ю, *impf.* of освяти́ть.

освя|щённый, *p.p.p.* of ~ти́ть; обы́чай, о. века́ми time-honoured custom.

ос|ево́й, *adj.* of ~ь; axial; о. кана́л (*electr.*) axial duct; ~ева́я ша́йба axle tree.

оседа́ни|е, я, *n.* 1. settling, subsidence. 2. settlement.

оседа́|ть, ю, *impf.* of осе́сть.

осёдл|анный, *p.p.p.* of ~а́ть.

оседла́|ть, ю, *pf.* 1. (*impf.* седла́ть) to saddle. 2. (*mil.*; *fig.*) to establish a grip (upon); о. доро́гу to get astride a road.

осе́длост|ь, и, *f.* settled (way of) life; черта́ ~и (*hist.*) the Pale of Settlement (*area to which Jews were confined in tsarist Russia*).

осе́длый, *adj.* settled (*as opp. to nomadic*).

осека́|ться, юсь, *impf.* of осе́чься.

ос|ёл, ла́, *m.* donkey; ass (*also fig. of a human being*).

оселе́д|ец, ца, *m.* top-knot (*hist.*; *long forelock left by Ukrainians on shaven head*).

осел|о́к, ка́, *m.* 1. touchstone (*also fig.*). 2. whetstone; oil-stone; hone.

осемене́ни|е, я, *n.* (*artificial*) insemination.

осемен|и́ть, ю́, и́шь, *pf.* (*of* ~я́ть) to inseminate (*by artificial means*).

осемен|я́ть, я́ю, *impf.* of ~и́ть.

осен|и́ть, ю́, и́шь, *pf.* (*of* ~я́ть) 1. to overshadow; (*fig.*) to shield; о. кресто́м to make the sign of the cross (over). 2. (*fig.*) to dawn upon, strike; его́ ~и́ла мысль it dawned upon him; меня́ внеза́пно ~и́ло (*impers.*) it suddenly occurred to me.

осен|и́ться, ю́сь, и́шься, *pf.* (*of* ~я́ться) *pass.* of ~и́ть; о. кресто́м to cross oneself.

осе́нний, *adj.* of о́сень; autumnal.

о́сен|ь, и, *f.* autumn.

о́сенью, *adv.* in autumn.

осен|я́ть(ся), я́ю(сь), *impf. of* ~и́ть(ся).

осер|ди́ться, жу́сь, ~ди́шься, *pf.* (на+*a.*; *coll.*) to become angry (with).

осеребр|и́ть, ю́, и́шь, *pf.* (*of* ~я́ть) (*poet.*) to silver (over).

осерча́|ть, ю, *pf. of* серча́ть.

ос|е́сть, я́ду, я́дешь, *past* ~е́л, ~е́ла, *pf.* (*of* ~еда́ть) 1. to settle, subside; to sink; to form a sediment. 2. (*of human beings*) to settle.

осётр, а́, *m.* sturgeon.

осетри́н|а, ы, *f.* (flesh of) sturgeon.

осетро́вый, *adj. of* осётр.

осе́чк|а, и, *f.* misfire; дать ~y to misfire (*also fig.*).

осе́|чься, ку́сь, чёшься, ку́тся, *past* ~кся, ~кла́сь, *pf.* (*of* ~ка́ться) (*coll.*) 1. to misfire (*also fig.*). 2. to stop short (*in speaking*).

оси́лива|ть, ю, *impf. of* оси́лить.

оси́л|ить, ю, ишь, *pf.* (*of* ~ивать) 1. to overpower. 2. (*coll.*) to master; to manage; о. гре́ческий алфави́т to master the Greek alphabet; я е́ле ~ил ещё оди́н стака́н I was hardly able to manage another glass.

оси́н|а, ы, *f.* asp(en).

оси́нник, а, *m.* aspen wood.

оси́н|овый, *adj. of* ~а; дрожа́ть как о. лист to tremble like an aspen leaf.

ос|и́ный, *adj. of* ~а́; ~и́ное гнездо́ (*fig.*) hornets' nest; потрево́жить ~и́ное гнездо́ to bring a hornets' nest about one's ears; ~и́ная та́лия wasp waist.

оси́плый, *adj.* hoarse, husky.

оси́п|нуть, ну, нешь, *past* ~, ~ла, *pf.* to go hoarse.

осироте́лый, *adj.* orphaned.

осироте́|ть, ю, *pf.* to become an orphan, be orphaned.

оска́блива|ть, ю, *impf. of* оскобли́ть.

оска́л, а, *m.* bared teeth; grin.

оска́лива|ть(ся), ю(сь), *impf. of* оска́лить-(ся).

оска́л|ить, ю, ишь, *pf.* (*of* ска́лить *and* ~ивать) о. зу́бы to bare one's teeth.

оска́л|иться, юсь, ишься, *pf.* (*of* ска́литься *and* ~иваться) to bare one's teeth.

оскальпи́р|овать, ую, *pf. of* скальпи́ровать.

осканда́л|ить(ся), ю(сь), ишь(ся), *pf. of* сканда́лить(ся).

осокверне́ни|е, я, *n.* defilement; profanation.

оскверни́тел|ь, я, *m.* defiler; profaner.

осокверн|и́ть, ю́, и́шь, *pf.* (*of* ~я́ть) to defile; to profane.

оскверн|и́ться, ю́сь, и́шься, *pf.* (*of* ~я́ться) 1. to defile oneself. 2. *pass. of* ~и́ть.

оскверн|я́ть(ся), я́ю(сь), *impf. of* ~и́ть(ся).

оскла́б|иться, люсь, ишься, *pf.* to grin.

оскобл|и́ть, ю́, ~и́шь, *pf.* (*of* оска́бливать) to scrape (off).

оско́л|ок, ка, *m.* splinter, shiver; fragment.

оско́ло|чный, *adj. of* ~к; ~чная бо́мба fragmentation bomb, anti-personnel bomb.

оско́мин|а, ы, *f.* bitter taste (in the mouth); наби́ть ~y to set the teeth on edge (*also fig.*).

оско́мист|ый (~, ~а), *adj.* (*coll.*) sour, bitter.

оскоп|и́ть, лю́, и́шь, *pf.* (*of* ~ля́ть) to castrate.

оскопля́|ть, ю, *impf. of* оскопи́ть.

оскорби́тельност|ь, и, *f.* abusiveness.

оскорби́тел|ьный (~ен, ~ьна), *adj.* insulting, abusive.

оскорб|и́ть, лю́, и́шь, *pf.* (*of* ~ля́ть) to insult, offend.

оскорб|и́ться, лю́сь, и́шься, *pf.* (*of* ~ля́ться) to take offence; to be offended, be hurt.

оскорбле́ни|е, я, *n.* insult; (*leg.*) assault and battery; о. де́йствием (*leg.*) assault and battery; о. сло́вом contumely; переноси́ть ~я to bear insults.

оскорб|лённый, *p.p.p. of* ~и́ть; ~лённая неви́нность outraged innocence.

оскорбля́|ть, ю, *impf. of* оскорби́ть.

оскоро́м|иться, люсь, ишься, *pf. of* скоро́миться.

оскрёб|ки, ков, *sing.* ~ок, ~ка, *m.* (*coll.*) scrapings.

оскудева́|ть, ю, *impf. of* оскуде́ть.

оскуде́лый, *adj.* scarce, scanty.

оскуде́ни|е, я, *n.* scarcity; impoverishment.

оскуде́|ть, ю, *pf.* (*of* скуде́ть *and* ~ва́ть) to grow scarce.

ослабева́|ть, ю, *impf. of* ослабе́ть.

ослабе́лый, *adj.* weakened, enfeebled.

ослабе́|ть, ю, *pf.* (*of* слабе́ть *and* ~ва́ть) to weaken, become weak; to slacken; to abate.

ослаби́тел|ь, я, *m.* (*phot.*) clearing agent.

осла́б|ить, лю, ишь, *pf.* (*of* ~ля́ть) 1. to weaken. 2. to slacken, relax; to relax; о. внима́ние to relax one's attention; о. нажи́м to slacken pressure; о. по́яс to loosen a belt.

ослабле́ни|е, я, *n.* weakening; slackening, relaxation; о. напряже́ния slackening of tension.

ослабля́|ть, ю, *impf. of* осла́бить.

ослаб|нуть, ну, нешь, *past* ~, ~ла, *pf.* = ~е́ть.

осла́в|ить, лю, ишь, *pf.* (*of* ~ля́ть) (*coll.*) to defame, decry; to give a bad name.

осла́в|иться, люсь, ишься, *pf.* (*of* ~ля́ться) (*coll.*) to get a bad name.

ославля́|ть(ся), ю(сь), *impf. of* осла́вить-(ся).

осл|ёнок, ёнка, *pl.* ~я́та, *m.* foal (*of ass*).

ослепи́тел|ьный (~ен, ~ьна), *adj.* blinding, dazzling.

ослеп|и́ть, лю́, и́шь, *pf.* (*of* ~ля́ть) to blind, dazzle (*also fig.*).

ослепле́ни|е, я, *n.* **1.** blinding, dazzling. **2.** (*fig.*) blindness; де́йствовать в ~и to act blindly.

ослепля́|ть, ю, *impf. of* ослепи́ть.

осле́п|нуть, ну, нешь, *past* ~, ~ла, *pf. of* сле́пнуть.

ослизлый, *adj.* slimy.

ослиз|нуть, нет, *past* ~, ~ла, *pf.* to become slimy.

осли́ный, *adj. of* осёл ass's; (*fig.*) asinine.

ослиц|а, ы, *f.* she-ass.

осложне́ни|е, я, *n.* complication.

осложн|и́ть, ю, и́шь, *pf.* (*of* ~я́ть) to complicate.

осложн|и́ться, ю́сь, и́шься, *pf.* (*of* ~я́ться) to become complicated.

осложн|я́ть(ся), я́ю(сь), *impf. of* ~и́ть(ся).

ослуша́ни|е, я, *n.* disobedience.

ослу́ш|аться, аюсь, *pf.* (*of* ~иваться) to disobey.

ослу́шива|ться, юсь, *impf. of* ослу́шаться.

ослу́шник, а, *m.* (*obs.*) disobedient person.

ослы́ш|аться, усь, ишься, *pf.* to mishear, not hear aright.

ослы́шк|а, и, *f.* mishearing, mistake of hearing.

осма́н, а, *m.* Osmanli Turk, Ottoman.

осма́нский, *adj.* Osmanli, Ottoman.

осма́трива|ть(ся), ю(сь), *impf. of* осмотре́ть(ся).

осме́ива|ть, ю, *impf. of* осмея́ть.

осмеле́|ть, ю, *pf. of* смеле́ть.

осме́лива|ться, юсь, *impf. of* осме́литься.

осме́л|иться, юсь, ишься, *pf.* (*of* ~иваться) (+*inf.*) to dare; to take the liberty (of); ~юсь доложи́ть... (*obs. polite formula*) I beg to report . . . .

осме|я́ть, ю́, ёшь, *pf.* (*of* ~ивать) to mock, ridicule.

о́сми|й, я, *m.* (*chem.*) osmium.

осмо́л, а, *m.* tar-impregnated wood.

осмол|и́ть, ю́, и́шь, *pf. of* смоли́ть.

о́смос, а, *m.* (*phys.*) osmosis.

осмоти́ческий, *adj.* (*phys.*) osmotic.

осмо́тр, а, *m.* examination, inspection; медици́нский о. medical (examination).

осмотр|е́ть, ю́, ~ишь, *pf.* (*of* осма́тривать) to examine, inspect; to look round, look over.

осмотр|е́ться, ю́сь, ~ишься, *pf.* (*of* осма́триваться) **1.** to look round. **2.** (*fig.*) to take one's bearings, see how the land lies. **3.** *pass. of* ~е́ть.

осмотри́тельност|ь, и, *f.* circumspection.

осмотри́тел|ьный (~ен, ~ьна), *adj.* circumspect.

осмо́трщик, а, *m.* inspector.

осмы́сл|енный, *p.p.p. of* ~ить *and adj.* intelligent, sensible.

осмы́слива|ть, ю, *impf. of* осмы́слить.

осмы́сл|ить, ю, ишь, *pf.* (*of* ~ивать *and* ~я́ть) to interpret, give a meaning to; to comprehend.

осмысл|я́ть, я́ю, *impf.* = ~ивать.

осна|сти́ть, щу́, сти́шь, *pf.* (*of* ~ща́ть) (*naut.*) to rig; (*fig.*) to fit out, equip.

осна́стк|а, и, *f.* (*naut.*) rigging.

оснаща́|ть, ю, *impf. of* оснасти́ть.

оснаще́ни|е, я, *n.* **1.** rigging; fitting out. **2.** equipment.

онеж|ённый, *p.p.p. of* ~и́ть *and adj.* snow-covered.

онеж|и́ть, у́, и́шь, *pf.* (*poet.*) to cover with snow.

осно́в|а, ы, *f.* **1.** base, basis, foundation; ~ы fundamentals; лежа́ть в ~е (+*g.*) to be the basis (of). **2.** (*gram.*) stem. **3.** (*text.*) warp.

основа́ни|е, я, *n.* **1.** founding, foundation. **2.** (*chem., math., etc.*) base; foundation (*of building*); о. горы́ foot of a mountain; о. коло́нны (*archit.*) column socle; разру́шить до ~я to raze to the ground; изучи́ть до ~я (*fig.*) to study from A to Z. **3.** (*fig.*) foundation, basis; ground, reason; на како́м ~и вы э́то утвержда́ете? on what grounds do you assert this?; на ра́вных ~ях with equal reason; не без ~я not without reason; име́ть о. предполага́ть to have reason to suppose.

основа́тел|ь, я, *m.* founder.

основа́тел|ьный (~ен, ~ьна), *adj.* **1.** well-founded; just; ~ьная жа́лоба reasonable complaint. **2.** solid, sound (*also fig.*); thorough; ~ьные до́воды sound arguments. **3.** (*coll.*) bulky.

осн|ова́ть, ую́, уёшь, *pf.* (*of* ~о́вывать) **1.** to found. **2.** (на+*p.*) to base (on).

осн|ова́ться, ую́сь, уёшься, *pf.* (*of* ~о́вываться) **1.** to settle. **2.** *pass. of* ~ова́ть.

основн|о́й, *adj.* fundamental, basic; principal; ~о́е значе́ние primary meaning; о. капита́л (*fin.*) fixed capital; ~а́я мысль keynote; ~ы́е цвета́ primary colours; в ~о́м on the whole.

осно́в|ный¹, *adj. of* ~а 3; ~ные ни́ти warp threads.

осно́в|ный², *adj. of* ~а́ние 2 (*chem.*); ~ные со́ли basic salts.

основополо́жник, а, *m.* founder, initiator.

осно́выва|ть, ю, *impf. of* основа́ть.

осно́выва|ться, юсь, *impf.* **1.** *impf. of* основа́ться. **2.** *impf. only* (на+*p.*) to base oneself (on); to be based (on), be founded (on); о. на дога́дках to base oneself on conjecture.

осо́б|а, ы, *f.* person, individual, personage; ва́жная о. (*iron.*) big noise, big-wig.

осо́бенно, *adv.* especially; particularly; unusually; не о. not very, not particularly; она́ сего́дня ве́чером о. болтли́ва

she is unusually talkative this evening; вы
лю́бите соба́к? — не о. do you like dogs?
Not very much.

осо́бенност|ь, и, *f.* peculiarity; в ~и
especially, in particular, (more) particularly.

осо́бенн|ый, *adj.* (e)special, particular,
peculiar; ничего ~ого nothing in particular; nothing much.

особня́|к, á, *m.* private residence; detached
house.

особняко́м, *adv.* by oneself; держа́ться о.
to keep aloof.

осо́б|ый, *adj.* special; particular; peculiar;
оста́ться при ~ом мне́нии to reserve one's
own opinion; (*leg.*) to dissent; удели́ть ~ое
внима́ние (+*d.*) to give special attention
(to).

о́соб|ь, и, *f.* individual.

осо́бь, *indecl. adj. only in phrase* о. статья́ (*coll.*)
quite another matter.

осове́лый, *adj.* (*coll.*) dazed, dreamy.

осове́|ть, ю, *pf.* (*coll.*) to fall into a dazed,
dreamy state.

осовреме́нива|ть, ю, *impf. of* осовреме́нить.

осовреме́н|ить, ю, ишь, *pf.* (*of* ~ивать) to
bring up to date; to modernize.

осое́д, а, *m.* (*orn.*) honey-buzzard.

осозна|ва́ть, ю, ёшь, *impf. of* ~ть.

осозна́|ть, ю, *pf.* (*of* ~ва́ть) to realize.

осо́к|а, и, *f.* (*bot.*) sedge.

осоко́р|ь, я, *m.* (*bot.*) black poplar.

осолове́лый, *adj.* (*coll.*) = осове́лый.

осолове́|ть, ю, ешь, *pf. of* солове́ть.

о́сп|а, ы, *f.* **1.** smallpox; ветряна́я о.
chicken-pox; коро́вья о. cow-pox; чёрная
о. smallpox. **2.** (*coll.*) pock-marks; vac-
cination marks; лицо́ в ~е pock-marked
face.

оспа́рива|ть, ю, *impf.* **1.** *impf. of* оспо́рить.
2. *impf. only* to contend (for); он ~ет
зва́ние чемпио́на ми́ра he is contending
for the title of world champion.

о́сп|енный, *adj. of* ~a; variolar, variolic,
variolous; о. знак pock-mark.

о́спин|а, ы, *f.* pock-mark.

оспопривива́ни|е, я, *n.* vaccination.

оспо́р|ить, ю, ишь, *pf.* (*of* оспа́ривать) to
dispute, question; о. завеща́ние to dispute
a will.

осрам|и́ть(ся), лю́(сь), и́шь(ся), *pf. of*
срами́ть(ся).

ост¹, а, *m.* (*naut.*) east.

ОСТ², а, *m. abbr. of* общесою́зный станда́рт.

оста|ва́ться, ю́сь, ёшься, *impf. of* оста́ться.

оста́в|ить, лю, ишь, *pf.* (*of* ~ля́ть) **1.** to
leave; to abandon, give up; о. в поко́е to
leave alone, let alone; о. на второ́й год
(*in schools*) to keep in the same form, not
move up; ~ь(те)! stop that!, lay off! **2.** to

reserve; to keep; о. за собо́й пра́во to reserve the right.

оставля́|ть, ю, *impf. of* оста́вить; ~ет жела́ть
мно́гого (*or* лу́чшего) it leaves much to be
desired.

остальн|о́й, *adj.* the rest (of); в ~о́м in other
respects; *as noun* ~ы́е the others; ~о́е the
rest; всё ~о́е everything else.

остана́влива|ть(ся), ю(сь), *impf. of* остa-
нови́ть(ся).

оста́нк|и, ов, *no sing.* remains.

остано́в, а, *m.* (*tech.*) stop, stopper, ratchet-
-gear.

останов|и́ть, лю́, ~ишь, *pf.* (*of* остана́вли-
вать) **1.** to stop. **2.** to stop short, restrain.
3. (на+*p.*) to direct (to), concentrate (on);
о. взгляд to rest one's gaze (on); о. вни-
ма́ние to concentrate one's attention (on).

останов|и́ться, лю́сь, ~ишься, *pf.* (*of*
остана́вливаться) **1.** to stop; to come to a
stop, come to a halt; ни пе́ред чем не о.
(*fig.*) to stop at nothing. **2.** to stay, put up,
(*coll.*) stop; о. у знако́мых to stay with
friends. **3.** (на+*p.*) (*fig.*) to dwell (on) (*in
a speech, lecture, etc.*); to settle (on), rest (on);
взор ма́льчика ~и́лся на но́вой игру́шке
the boy's gaze rested on the new toy.

остано́вк|а, и, *f.* **1.** stop; stoppage; о. за
ва́ми you are holding us up; о. за ви́зами
there is a hold-up over the visas. **2.** ('bus,
tram) stop; коне́чная о. terminus; мне на́до
прое́хать ещё одну́ ~у I have to go one
stop further.

остано́в|очный, *adj. of* ~ка; о. пункт stop,
stopping place.

оста́т|ок, ка, *m.* **1.** (*in var. senses*) remainder;
rest; residue; remnant (*of material*); *pl.* remains; leavings, leftovers; распрода́жа
~ков clearance sale. **2.** (*chem.*) residuum.
3. (*fin., comm.*) rest, balance.

оста́то|чный, *adj. of* ~к; (*chem., tech.*) re-
sidual.

оста́|ться, нусь, нешься, *pf.* (*of* ~ва́ться)
to remain; to stay; to be left (over); о. в
бары́ша́х to gain, be up; о. в долгу́ to be
in debt; о. в живы́х to survive, come
through; о. на́ ночь to stay the night; о.
при своём мне́нии to remain of the same
opinion; о. на второ́й год (в том же
кла́ссе) to remain in the same form a
second year; за ним ~лось пять фу́нтов he
owes five pounds; по́сле него́ ~лись жена́
и тро́е дете́й he left a wife and three children; от обе́да ничего́ не ~лось there is
nothing left over from dinner; *impers.* ~ётся,
~лось (+*d.*) it remains (remained), it is
(was) necessary; нам не ~лось ничего́
друго́го, как согласи́ться we had no choice
but to consent; ~лось то́лько заплати́ть it
remained only to pay.

остеклене|ть, ю, *pf. of* стекленеть.

остекл|ить, ю, ишь, *pf.* (*of* ~ять) to glaze.

остекл|ять, яю, *impf. of* ~ить.

остеоблог, а, *m.* osteologist.

остеологический, *adj.* osteological.

остеологи|я, и, *f.* osteology.

остеомиэлит, а, *m.* (*med.*) osteomyelitis.

остепен|ить, ю, ишь, *pf.* (*of* ~ять) to make staid; to calm, mellow.

остепен|иться, юсь, ишься, *pf.* (*of* ~яться) to settle down; to become staid, become respectable; to mellow.

остервенелый, *adj.* frenzied.

остервене́ни|е, я, *n.* frenzy; работать с ~ем to work like a maniac.

остервене|ть, ю, *pf. of* стервенеть.

остервен|иться, юсь, ишься, *pf.* to be frenzied.

остерега|ть, ю, *impf. of* остеречь.

остерега|ться, юсь, *impf.* (*of* остеречься) (+*g. or inf.*) to beware (of); to be careful (of); ~йтесь собаки! beware of the dog!; ~йся, чтобы не упасть! mind you don't fall!

остере|чь, гу, жёшь, гут, *past* ~г, ~гла, *pf.* (*of* ~гать) to warn, caution.

остере|чься, гусь, жёшься, гутся, *past* ~гся, ~глась, *pf. of* ~гаться.

остери|я, и, *f.* inn, hostelry (*in Italy*).

остзе́|ец, йца, *m.* (*obs.*) Baltic German.

остзейский, *adj.* (*obs.*) Baltic (German); о. барон (*hist.*) 'Baltic baron'.

остист|ый (~, ~а), *adj.* (*bot.*) awned, bearded, aristate.

остит, а, *m.* (*med.*) osteitis.

о́стов, а, *m.* 1. frame, framework (*also fig.*); shell; hull. 2. (*anat.*) skeleton.

остойчивост|ь, и, *f.* (*naut.*) stability.

остойчив|ый (~, ~а), *adj.* (*naut.*) stable.

остолбенелый, *adj.* (*coll.*) dumbfounded.

остолбене|ть, ю, *pf. of* столбенеть.

остолоп, а, *m.* (*coll.*) blockhead.

осторо́жно, *adv.* carefully; cautiously; guardedly; gingerly; о.! look out! mind out!; (*on package*) with care.

осторо́жност|ь, и, *f.* care; caution.

осторо́ж|ный (~ен, ~на), *adj.* careful; cautious; будьте ~ны! take care! be careful!

осточерте|ть, ю, *pf.* (+*d.*; *coll.*) to bore; to repel; мне э́то ~ло I am fed up with it.

остраки́зм, а, *m.* ostracism; подве́ргнуть ~у to ostracize.

остра́стк|а, и, *f.* (*coll.*) warning, caution; в ~у, для ~и as a warning.

острека́в|ить, лю, ишь, *pf. of* стрека́вить.

острига|ть(ся), ю(сь), *impf. of* остричь(ся).

остри|ё, я́, *n.* 1. point; spike; о. кли́на (*mil.*) spearhead of the attack. 2. (cutting) edge; о. кри́тики (*fig.*) the edge of a criticism.

остр|ить[1], ю, ишь, *impf.* to sharpen, whet.

остр|ить[2], ю, ишь, *impf.* (*of* с~) to be witty; to make witticisms, crack jokes; о. на чужо́й счёт to be witty at others' expense, score off others.

остри́|чь, гу, жёшь, гут, *past* ~г, ~гла, *pf.* (*of* стричь *and* ~гать) to cut; to clip.

остри́|чься, гусь, жёшься, гутся, *past* ~гся, ~глась, *pf.* (*of* стри́чься *and* ~га́ться) to cut one's hair; to have one's hair cut.

о́стров, а, *pl.* ~а́, *m.* island; isle.

островитя́н|ин, ина, *pl.* ~е, ~, *m.* islander.

островно́й, *adj.* island; insular.

остров|о́к, ка́, *m.* islet; о. безопа́сности island (*in road, for pedestrians crossing*).

остро́г, а, *m.* 1. (*obs.*) gaol. 2. (*hist.*) stockaded town. 3. (*hist.*) stockade, palisade.

острог|а́, и́, *f.* fish-spear, harpoon.

острогла́з|ый (~, ~а), *adj.* (*coll.*) sharp-sighted, keen-eyed.

острогу́бц|ы, ев (*tech.*) cutting nippers.

остро́жник, а, *m.* (*obs.*) imprisoned criminal, convict.

остро́|жный, *adj. of* ~г.

остроконе́чный, *adj.* pointed.

остроли́ст, а, *m.* (*bot.*) holly.

остроно́с|ый (~, ~а), *adj.* sharp-nosed; (*fig.*) pointed, tapered.

остросло́в, а, *m.* wit.

остро́т|а, ы, *f.* witticism, joke; зла́я о. sarcasm; пло́ская о. stupid joke; то́нкая о. subtle crack.

острот|а́, ы́, *f.* sharpness; keenness; acuteness; pungency, poignancy.

остроуго́льник, а, *m.* (*math.*) acute-angled figure.

остроуго́л|ьный (~ен, ~ьна), *adj.* (*math.*) acute-angled.

остроу́ми|е, я, *n.* 1. wit; wittiness. 2. ingenuity.

остроу́м|ный (~ен, ~на), *adj.* witty.

о́стр|ый (~ *and* остёр, ~а́, ~о), *adj.* sharp (*also fig.*); pointed (*also fig.*); acute; keen; ~ое воспале́ние (*med.*) acute inflammation; ~ое замеча́ние pointed remark; о. за́пах acrid smell; ~ое зре́ние keen eyesight; о. интере́с (к) keen interest (in); о. недоста́ток acute shortage; ~ое положе́ние critical situation; о. со́ус piquant sauce; о. сыр strong cheese; о. у́гол (*math.*) acute angle; он остёр на язы́к (*coll.*) he has a sharp tongue.

остря́к, а́, *m.* wit.

осту|ди́ть, жу́, ~дишь, *pf.* (*of* студи́ть *and* ~жа́ть) to cool.

остужа́|ть, ю, *impf. of* остуди́ть.

оступа́|ться, а́юсь, *impf. of* ~и́ться.

оступ|и́ться, люсь, ~ишься, *pf.* (*of* ~а́ться) to stumble.

остыва́|ть, ю, *impf. of* остыть.

осты́|ть, ну, нешь, *pf.* (*of* ~ва́ть) to get

cold; (*fig.*) to cool (down); у вас чай ~л your tea is cold.

ост|**ь, и,** *pl.* ~**и, ~éй,** *f.* (*bot.*) awn, beard.

осу|**дить, жý, ~дишь,** *pf.* (*of* ~**ждáть**) **1.** to censure, condemn. **2.** (*leg.*) to condemn, sentence; to convict.

осуждá|**ть, ю,** *impf. of* осудить.

осуждéни|**е, я,** *n.* **1.** censure, condemnation. **2.** (*leg.*) conviction.

осуждённ|**ый,** *p.p.p. of* осудить *and adj.* condemned; convicted; *as noun* **о., ~ого,** *m.* convict, convicted person.

осýн|**уться, усь, ешься,** *pf.* (*coll.*) (*of the face*) to grow thin, get pinched(-looking).

осуш|**áть, áю,** *impf. of* ~**ить.**

осушéни|**е, я,** *n.* drainage.

осуш|**ительный,** *adj. of* ~**éние;** **о. канáл** drainage canal.

осуш|**ить, ý, ~ишь,** *pf.* (*of* ~**áть**) to drain; to dry; **о. глазá** to dry one's eyes; **о. лугá** to drain meadows; **о. слёзы комý-н.** to console someone; **о. стакáн пива** to drain a glass of beer.

осуществим|**ый (~, ~a),** *adj.* practicable, realizable, feasible.

осуществ|**ить, лю, ишь,** *pf.* (*of* ~**лять**) to realize, bring about; to accomplish, carry out; to implement.

осуществ|**иться, ится,** *pf.* (*of* ~**ляться**) **1.** to be fulfilled, come true; **её дéтская мечтá ~илась** her childhood dream has come true. **2.** *pass. of* ~**ить.**

осуществлéни|**е, я,** *n.* realization; accomplishment; implementation.

осуществля|**ть(ся), ю(сь),** *impf. of* осуществить.

осциллóграф, а, *m.* (*phys.*) oscillograph.

осциллятор, а, *m.* (*phys.*) oscillator.

осчастлив|**ить, лю, ишь,** *pf.* (*of* ~**ливать**) to make happy.

осчастливлива|**ть, ю,** *impf. of* осчастливить.

осы|**нный,** *p.p.p. of* ~**ть; о. звёздами** star--studded, star-spangled.

осып|**ать, лю, лешь,** *pf.* (*of* ~**áть**) **1.** (+*a. and i.*) to strew (with); to shower (on); (*fig.*) to heap (on); **о. когó-н. брáнью** to heap abuse on someone; **о. поцелýями** to smother with kisses; **о. когó-н. удáрами** to rain blows on someone. **2.** to pull down, knock down (*a heap of sand, etc.*). **3.** to shed (*foliage, etc.*).

осып|**аться, люсь, лешься,** *pf.* (*of* ~**áться**) to crumble; (*of leaves, etc.*) to fall.

осып|**áть(ся), áю(сь),** *impf. of* ~**ать(ся).**

óсыпь, и, *f.* scree.

ос|**ь, и,** *pl.* ~**и, ~éй,** *f.* **1.** axis; **земнáя о.** axis of the equator; **имéющий óбщую о.** coaxial. **2.** axle; (*tech.*) spindle; pin.

осьминóг, а, *m.* (*zool.*) octopus.

осязáем|**ый (~, ~a),** *adj.* tangible; palpable.

осязáни|**е, я,** *n.* touch; **чýвство ~я** sense of touch.

осязáтел|**ьный (~ен, ~ьна),** *adj.* **1.** tactile, tactual; **~ьные óрганы** tactile organs. **2.** (*fig.*) tangible, palpable, sensible; **~ьные результáты** tangible results.

осязá|**ть, ю,** *impf.* to feel.

от (ото) *prep.+g.* from; of; for; **1.** (*indicates initial point, point of origin of action, prior of pair of termini, source, etc.*) **от цéнтра гóрода** from the centre of the town; **отплыть от бéрега** to put out from the shore; **от начáла до концá** from beginning to end; **от Пýшкина до Маякóвского** from Pushkin to Mayakovsky; **от девяти (часóв) до пяти (часóв)** from nine (o'clock) to five (o'clock); **дéти в вóзрасте от пяти до десяти лет** children from five to ten (years); **цéны от рубля и выше** prices from a rouble upward; **близко от гóрода** near the town; **на сéвер от Ленингрáда** to the north of Leningrad; **врéмя от врéмени** from time to time; **день ото дня** from day to day; **от всей души** with all one's heart; **от имени (+g.)** on behalf (of); **слóво, произведённое от латинского** a word derived from the Latin; **узнáть от дрýга** to learn from a friend; **я получил письмó от дóчери** I have received a letter from my daughter; **сын от прéжнего брáка** a son by a previous marriage; **жеребёнок от А. и Б.** a foal by A. out of B. **2.** (*indicates cause or instrumentality*) **вскрикнуть от рáдости** to cry out for joy; **дрожáть от стрáха** to tremble with fear; **умерéть от гóлода** to die of hunger; **глазá, крáсные от слёз** eyes red with weeping. **3.** (*indicates date of document*) **вáше письмó от пéрвого áвгуста** your letter of the first of August. **4.** (*indicates use, purpose, or assignment*) **ключ от двéри** door key; **пýговица от пиджакá** coat button; **цепóчка от часóв** watch--chain; **рабóчий от станкá** machine operative. **5.** for; against; **срéдство от сеннóй лихорáдки** remedy for hay-fever; **микстýра от кáшля** cough mixture; **защищáть глазá от сóлнца** to shield one's eyes from the sun; **застраховáть от огня** to insure against fire.

от- (*also* **ото-** *and* **отъ-**) *verbal prefix indicating* **1.** completion of action *or* task assigned. **2.** action *or* motion away from given point. **3.** (*verbs in form reflexive*) action of negative character.

отáв|**а, ы,** *f.* (*agric.*) after-grass, aftermath.

отáплива|**ть, ю,** *impf. of* отопить.

отáр|**а, ы,** *f.* large flock (*of sheep*).

отбáв|**ить, лю, ишь,** *pf.* (*of* ~**лять**) to pour off.

отбавля́|ть, ю, *impf. of* **отба́вить;** хоть ~й (*coll.*) more than enough.

отбараба́н|ить, ю, ишь, *pf.* (*coll.*) to rattle off.

отбега́|ть, ю, *impf. of* **отбежа́ть.**

отбе|жа́ть, гу́, жи́шь, гу́т, *pf.* (*of* ~га́ть) to run off.

отбел|ённый, *p.p.p. of* ~и́ть; о. чугу́н chilled cast iron.

отбе́лива|ть, ю, *impf. of* **отбели́ть.**

отбел|и́ть, ю́, ~ишь, *pf.* (*of* ~ива́ть) to bleach; (*tech.*) to blanch; to chill, refine.

отбе́лк|а, и, *f.* bleaching; (*tech.*) blanching; chilling, refining.

отбе́льный, *adj.* (*tech.*) blanching; chilling, refining.

отбива́|ть(ся), ю(сь), *impf. of* **отби́ть(ся).**

отби́вк|а, и, *f.* **1.** marking out, delineation. **2.** whetting, sharpening.

отбивн|о́й, *adj.* ~а́я котле́та (*cul.*) chop.

отбира́|ть, ю, *impf. of* **отобра́ть.**

отби́ти|е, я, *n.* repulse; repelling.

отби́|ть, отобью́, отобьёшь, *pf.* (*of* ~ва́ть) **1.** to beat off, repulse, repel; о. ата́ку to beat off an attack; о. мяч (*sport*) to return a ball; о. уда́р to parry a blow. **2.** to take (*by force*); to win over; (*coll.*) о. у кого́-н. to take off someone, do someone out of; о. пле́нных to liberate prisoners; о. покупа́телей (*fig.*) to win customers; он ~л у това́рища его́ де́вушку he has taken his friend's girl. **3.** to remove, dispel; о. у кого́-н. охо́ту к чему́-н. to discourage someone from something, take away someone's inclination for something. **4.** to break off, knock off; о. но́сик у ча́йника to knock the spout off a tea-pot. **5.** to whet, sharpen. **6.** о. такт to beat (out) time. **7.** to knock up; to damage by blows, by knocks; о. ру́ку нело́вким уда́ром to hurt one's hand with a clumsy blow. **8.** to mark out.

отби́|ться, отобью́сь, отобьёшься, *pf.* (*of* ~ва́ться) **1.** (от) to defend oneself (against); to repulse, beat off. **2.** to drop behind, straggle; о. от ста́да to stray from the herd; о. от рук (*coll.*) to get out of hand. **3.** to break off. **4.** *pass. of* ~ть.

отблагове́|стить, щу, стишь, *pf. of* **бла́говестить 1.**

отблагодар|и́ть, ю́, и́шь, *pf.* to show one's gratitude (to).

о́тблеск, а, *m.* reflection.

отбо́|й, я, *m.* **1.** repulse; repelling; о. мяча́ (*sport*) return; ~ю нет (от; *coll.*) there is no getting rid (of). **2.** (*mil.*) retreat; о. возду́шной трево́ги all-clear signal; бить о. to beat a retreat (*also fig.*); труби́ть о. to sound off. **3.** ringing off (*on telephone*); дать о. to ring off.

отбо́йк|а, и, *f.* (*tech.*) breaking, cutting.

отбо́й|ный, *adj.* **1.** *adj. of* ~ка; о. молото́к miner's pick; пневмати́ческий о. молото́к pneumatic drill (*for coal-cutting*). **2.** *adj. of* ~ 3.

отбомб|и́ться, лю́сь, и́шься, *pf.* (*coll.*) to have dropped one's load (of bombs).

отбо́р, а, *m.* selection; есте́ственный о. (*biol.*) natural selection.

отбо́рн|ый, *adj.* choice, select(ed); picked; ~ые войска́ crack troops; ~ые выраже́ния refined language; ~ая ру́гань choice swear-words.

отбо́рочн|ый, *adj.* ~ая коми́ссия selection board; ~ое соревнова́ние (*sport*) knock-out competition.

отбо́рщик, а, *m.* **1.** grader, sorter. **2.** selector.

отбоя́рива|ться, юсь, *impf.* (*of* **отбоя́риться**) (*coll.*) to try to escape, get out of.

отбоя́р|иться, юсь, ишься, *pf.* (*of* ~ива-ся) (*coll.*; от) to escape (from), get rid (of), give the slip (to).

отбра́сыва|ть, ю, *impf. of* **отбро́сить.**

отбрива́|ть, ю, *impf. of* **отбрить.**

отбр|и́ть, е́ю, е́ешь, *pf.* (*of* ~ива́ть) (*coll.*) to rebuff, rebuke.

отбро́с|ы, ов, *sing.* ~, ~а, *m.·* garbage, refuse; offal; ведро́ для ~ов dust-bin; о. произво́дства industrial waste; о. о́бщест-ва (*fig.*) dregs of society.

отбро́|сить, шу, сишь, *pf.* (*of* **отбра́сывать**) **1.** to throw off; to cast away; о. тень to cast a shadow. **2.** (*mil.*) to throw back, thrust back, hurl back. **3.** to give up, reject, discard; о. мысль to give up an idea.

отбукси́р|овать, ую, *pf.* to tow off.

отбыва́ни|е, я, *n.* serving; о. сро́ка наказа́ния serving of a sentence.

отбыва́|ть, ю, *impf. of* **отбы́ть.**

отбы́ти|е, я, *n.* departure.

от|бы́ть¹, бу́ду, бу́дешь, *past* ~был, ~была́, ~было,** *pf.* (*of* ~быва́ть) to depart, leave.

от|бы́ть², бу́ду, бу́дешь, *past* ~был, ~была́, ~было,** *pf.* (*of* ~быва́ть) to serve (a period of); о. наказа́ние to serve one's sentence, do time (*in prison*); о. во́инскую пови́нность to serve one's time in the army, do (one's) military service.

отва́г|а, и, *f.* courage, bravery.

отва́|дить, жу, дишь, *pf.* (*of* ~жива́ть) **1.** (+а. от) to break (of), make to stop; о. кого́-н. от пья́нства to break someone of drunkenness. **2.** to scare away, drive off.

отва́жива|ть, ю, *impf. of* **отва́дить.**

отва́ж|иться, усь, ишься, *pf.* (+*inf.*) to dare, venture; to have the courage (to).

отва́ж|ный (~ен, ~на), *adj.* courageous, brave.

отва́л¹, а, *m.* до ~а (*coll.*) to satiety; нае́сть-ся до ~а to stuff oneself.

отва́л², а, *m.* **1.** mould-board (*of a plough*). **2.** (*mining*) dump; slag-heap; bank, terrace (*of open-cast mine*).

отва́л³, а, *m.* (*naut.*) putting off, pushing off, casting off.

отва́лива|ть(ся), ю(сь), *impf. of* отвали́ть(ся).

отвал|и́ть, ю́, ∼ишь, *pf.* (*of* ∼ивать) **1.** to heave off; to push aside. **2.** (*naut.*) to put off, push off, cast off. **3.** (*coll.*) to fork out, stump up (*a sum of money*).

отвал|и́ться, ю́сь, ∼ишься, *pf.* (*of* ∼ивать-ся) **1.** to fall off, slip. **2.** *pass. of* ∼и́ть.

отва́л|ьный, *adj. of* ∼², ³; *as noun* ∼ьная, ∼ьной, *f.* (*coll., obs.*) farewell party.

отва́р, а, *m.* broth; decoction; ячме́нный о. barley-water.

отва́рива|ть, ю, *impf. of* отвари́ть.

отвар|и́ть, ю́, ∼ишь, *pf.* (*of* ∼ивать) **1.** to boil (*cabbage, etc.*). **2.** (*tech.*) to unweld.

отварно́й, *adj.* (*cul.*) boiled.

отве́д|ать, аю, *pf.* (*of* ∼ывать) (+*a. or g.*) to taste; to try.

отве|дённый, *p.p.p. of* ∼сти́.

отве́дыва|ть, ю, *impf. of* отве́дать.

отвез|ти́, у́, ёшь, *past* ∼, ∼ла́, *pf.* (*of* отво-зи́ть) to take (away); to cart away.

отверг|а́ть, а́ю, *impf. of* ∼нуть.

отве́рг|нуть, ну, нешь, *past* ∼, ∼ла, *pf.* (*of* ∼а́ть) to reject, turn down; to repudiate; to spurn.

отвердева́|ть, ю, *impf. of* отверде́ть.

отверде́лост|ь, и, *f.* hardening, callus.

отверде́лый, *adj.* hardened.

отверде́|ть, ю, *pf.* (*of* ∼ва́ть) to harden.

отве́ржен|ец, ца, *m.* outcast.

отве́р|женный, *p.p.p.* (*obs.*) *of* ∼гнуть *and adj.* outcast.

отверз|а́ть, а́ю, *impf.* (*of* ∼ть) (*obs., poet.*) to open.

отве́рз|ть, у, ешь, *past* ∼, ∼ла, *pf. of* ∼а́ть.

отвер|ну́ть, ну́, нёшь, *pf.* (*of* ∼тывать) **1.** (*impf. also* отвора́чивать) to turn away, turn aside; о. лицо́ to turn one's face away; о. одея́ло to turn down a blanket. **2.** to turn on (*a tap, etc.*). **3.** to unscrew. **4.** (*coll.*) to screw off, twist off; он едва́ не ∼ну́л мне ру́ку he almost twisted my arm off.

отвер|ну́ться, ну́сь, нёшься, *pf.* (*of* ∼ты-ваться) **1.** (*impf. also* отвора́чиваться) to turn away, turn aside; о. от кого́-н. (*fig.*) to turn one's back upon someone; to send someone to Coventry. **2.** (*of a tap, etc.*) to come on. **3.** to come unscrewed.

отве́рсти|е, я, *n.* **1.** opening, aperture, ori-fice; hole; входно́е о. inlet; выходно́е о. outlet; о. для опуска́ния моне́ты slot; о. решета́, о. си́та mesh. **2.** (*zool.*) foramen; заднепрохо́дное о. (*anat.*) anus.

отве́рст|ый (∼, ∼a), *adj.* (*obs., poet.*) open.

отвер|те́ть, чу́, ∼тишь, *pf.* (*of* ∼тывать) **1.** to unscrew. **2.** to screw off, twist off.

отверт|е́ться¹, ∼ится, *pf.* (*of* ∼ываться) to come unscrewed.

отвер|те́ться², чу́сь, ∼тишься, *pf.* (*coll.*; от) to get off; to get out (of), wriggle out (of); нам удало́сь о. we managed to get out of it.

отвёртк|а, и, *f.* screwdriver.

отвёртыва|ть(ся), ю(сь), *impf. of* отвер-ну́ть(ся) *and* отверте́ть(ся).

отве́с, а, *m.* **1.** (*tech.*) plumb, plummet; груз ∼а bob. **2.** slope; по ∼у plumb, per-pendicularly.

отве́|сить, шу, сишь, *pf.* (*of* ∼шивать) to weigh out; о. фунт са́хару to weigh out a pound of sugar; о. покло́н (+*d.*) to make a low bow (to); о. пощёчину (+*d.*) (*fig., coll.*) to deal someone a slap in the face.

отве́сно, *adv.* plumb; sheer.

отве́с|ный (∼ен, ∼на), *adj.* perpendicular; steep.

отве|сти́, ду́, дёшь, *past* ∼л, ∼ла́, *pf.* (*of* отводи́ть) **1.** to lead, take, conduct; о. ло́шадь в коню́шню to lead a horse to the stable. **2.** to draw aside, take aside; о. от собла́зна to lead out of temptation's way. **3.** to deflect; to draw off; о. войска́ (*mil.*) to draw off one's troops; о. во́ду (из) to drain; о. ду́шу to unburden one's heart; о. обвине́ние to justify oneself; о. уда́р to parry a blow; он не мог о. глаз от неё he could not take his eyes off her; о. глаза́ кому́-н. (*fig.*) to distract someone's atten-tion, pull the wool over someone's eyes. **4.** to reject; (*leg.*) to challenge (*jurors, etc.*). **5.** to allot, assign.

отве́т, а, *m.* **1.** answer, reply, response; держа́ть о. to answer; в о. (на+*a.*) in reply (to), in response (to). **2.** (*obs.*) respon-sibility; быть в ∼е (за+*a.*) to be answer-able (for); призва́ть к ∼у to call to account.

ответв|и́ть, лю́, и́шь, *pf.* (*of* ∼ля́ть) (*tech.*) to take off, tap, shunt.

ответв|и́ться, лю́сь, и́шься, *pf.* (*of* ∼ля́ться) to branch off.

ответвле́ни|е, я, *n.* branch, offshoot (*also fig.*); branch pipe; (*electr.*) tap, shunt.

ответв|лённый, *p.p.p. of* ∼и́ть; ∼лённая цепь (*electr.*) branch circuit, derived cir-cuit.

ответвля́|ть(ся), ю(сь), *impf. of* ответви́ть-(ся).

отве́|тить, чу, тишь, *pf.* (*of* ∼ча́ть) **1.** (на+*a.*) to answer, reply (to); о. на письмо́ to answer a letter; о. уро́к to repeat one's lesson. **2.** (на+*a.* +*i.*) to answer (with), return; о. на чьё-н. чу́вство to return someone's feelings. **3.** (за+*a.*) to answer (for), pay (for); вы ~ти́те за э́ти слова́! you will pay for these words!

отве́тн|ый, *adj.* given in answer, answering о. вы́стрел reply (to shots fired); ~ое чу́вство response, reciprocation of feelings.

отве́тственност|ь, и, *f.* responsibility; (*leg.*) amenability; снять о. с кого́-н. to relieve someone of responsibility; привле́чь к ~и (за+*a.*) to call to account, bring to book.

отве́тствен|ный (~, ~на), *adj.* **1.** responsible; о. реда́ктор editor-in-chief; о. рабо́тник executive. **2.** crucial; о. моме́нт crucial point.

отве́тств|овать, ую, *impf. and pf.* (*obs.*) to answer, reply.

отве́тчик, а, m. 1. (*leg.*) defendant, respondent. **2.** (*coll.*) bearer of responsibility.

отвеча́|ть, ю, *impf.* **1.** *impf. of* отве́тить. **2.** (за+*a.*) to answer (for), be answerable (for). **3.** (+*d.*) to answer (to), meet, be up (to); о. своему́ назначе́нию to answer the purpose, be up to the mark; о. тре́бованиям to meet requirements.

отве́шива|ть, ю, *impf. of* отве́сить.

отви́лива|ть, ю, *impf. of* отвильну́ть.

отвильн|у́ть, у́, ёшь, *pf.* (*of* отви́ливать) (*coll., pejor.*; от) to dodge.

отвин|ти́ть, чу́, ти́шь, *pf.* (*of* ~чивать) to unscrew.

отвин|ти́ться, чу́сь, ти́шься, *pf.* (*of* ~чиваться) to unscrew, come unscrewed.

отви́нчива|ть(ся), ю(сь), *impf. of* отвинти́ть(ся).

отвис|а́ть, а́ю, *impf.* (*of* ~нуть) to hang down, sag.

отви|се́ться, шу́сь, си́шься, *pf.* (*coll.*) дать пла́тью о. to hang out a dress so as to remove the creases.

отви́слы|й, *adj.* loose-hanging, baggy; с ~ми уша́ми lop-eared.

отви́с|нуть, ну, нешь, *past* ~, ~ла, *pf. of* ~а́ть.

отвлека́|ть(ся), ю(сь), *impf. of* отвле́чь(ся).

отвлека́|ющий, *pres. part. act. of* ~ть; ~ющее сре́дство (*med.*) counter-attraction.

отвлече́ни|е, я, n. 1. abstraction. **2.** distraction; для ~я внима́ния to distract attention. **3.** (*med.*) counter-attraction.

отвлечён|ный (~, ~на), *adj.* abstract; ~ная величина́ abstract quantity; ~ное и́мя существи́тельное abstract noun.

отвле́|чь, ку́, чёшь, ку́т, *past* ~к, ~кла́, *pf.* (*of* ~ка́ть) **1.** to distract, divert; о. чьё-н. внима́ние to divert someone's attention. **2.** to abstract.

отвле́|чься, ку́сь, чёшься, ку́тся, *past* ~кся, ~кла́сь, *pf.* (*of* ~ка́ться) **1.** to be distracted; о. от те́мы to digress; его́ мы́сли ~кли́сь далеко́ his thoughts were far away. **2.** (от) to abstract oneself (from).

отво́д, а, m. 1. leading, taking, conducting. **2.** taking aside; deflection; diversion; о. воды́ draining off of water; о. войск withdrawal of troops; для ~а глаз (*coll.*) as a blind. **3.** rejection; (*leg.*) challenge; дать о. кандида́ту to reject a candidate. **4.** allotment, allocation; полоса́ ~а designated strip of land (*for building of railway, highway, etc.*). **5.** (*tech.*) pipe-bend, elbow. **6.** (*electr.*) tap, tapping; о. тепла́ heat elimination.

отво|ди́ть, жу́, ~дишь, *impf. of* отвести́.

отво́дк|а, и, *f.* (*tech.*) **1.** branch pipe. **2.** belt shifter.

отво́дн|ый, *adj.* (*tech.*) branch; drain, outlet; о. кана́л drain; о. кран drain cock; ~ая труба́ branch pipe; outlet pipe, discharge pipe.

отво́д|ок, ка, m. (*hort.*) cutting, layer.

отво́д|ящий, *pres. part. act. of* ~и́ть *and adj.* о. (му́скул) (*anat.*) abductor; ~ящая труба́ (*tech.*) exhaust (pipe).

отво|ева́ть[1], ю́ю, ю́ешь, *pf.* (*of* ~ёвывать) (у) to win back (from), reconquer (from).

отво|ева́ть[2], ю́ю, ю́ешь, *pf.* (*coll.*) **1.** to fight, spend in fighting; мы де́сять лет ~ева́ли we have fought for ten years. **2.** to finish fighting, finish the war.

отвоёвыва|ть, ю, *impf. of* отвоева́ть.

отво|зи́ть, жу́, ~зишь, *impf. of* отвезти́.

отвола́кива|ть, ю, *impf. of* отволо́чь.

отволо́|чь, ку́, чёшь, ку́т, *past* ~к, ~кла́, *pf.* (*of* отвола́кивать) to drag away, drag aside.

отвора́чива|ть(ся), ю(сь), *impf. of* отверну́ть(ся) *and* отвороти́ть(ся).

отвор|и́ть, ю́, ~ишь, *pf.* (*of* ~я́ть) to open; о. кровь (*med.; obs.*) to let blood.

отвор|и́ться, ю́сь, ~ишься, *pf.* (*of* ~я́ться) to open.

отворо́т, а, m. lapel, flap; top (*of boot*).

отворо|ти́ть, чу́, ~тишь, *pf.* (*of* отвора́чивать) to turn away, turn aside; о. взгляд to avert one's gaze.

отворо|ти́ться, чу́сь, ~тишься, *pf.* (*of* отвора́чиваться) to turn away, turn aside; о. от кого́-н. to look away from someone; (*fig.*) to turn one's back on someone, cut someone.

отвор|я́ть(ся), я́ю(сь), *impf. of* ~и́ть(ся).

отврати́тел|ьный (~ен, ~ьна), *adj.* repulsive, disgusting, loathsome; abominable.

отвра|ти́ть, щу́, ти́шь, *pf.* (*of* ~ща́ть) **1.** to avert, stave off. **2.** (*obs.*) (+*a.* от) to deter (from), stay (from); о. кого́-н. от преда́тельства to deter someone from committing an act of treachery.

отвра́т|ный (~ен, ~на), *adj.* (*coll.*) = ~и́тельный.

отвраще́ни|е, я, n. aversion, disgust, repugnance; loathing; внуши́ть о. (+*d.*) to disgust, fill with disgust, repel; пита́ть о. (к) to have an aversion (for), be repelled (by), loathe.

отвыка́|ть, а́ю, *impf. of* ~нуть.

отвы́к|нуть, ну, нешь, *past* ~, ~ла, *pf.* (*of* ~а́ть) (от *or* +*inf.*) to break oneself (of the habit of), give up; to get out of the habit of; to grow out (of); о. от куре́ния, о. кури́ть to give up smoking; о. от дурно́й привы́чки to break oneself of a bad habit.

отвя|за́ть, жу́, ~жешь, *pf.* (*of* ~зыва́ть) to untie, unfasten; to untether; (*naut.*) to unbend.

отвя|за́ться, жу́сь, ~жешься, *pf.* (*of* ~зыва́ться) 1. to come untied, come loose. 2. (*fig., coll.*; от) to get rid (of), shake off, get shut (of). 3. (*fig., coll.*; от) to leave alone, leave in peace; stop nagging; ~жи́сь от меня́! leave me alone!

отвя́зыва|ть(ся), ю(сь), *impf. of* отвяза́ть(ся).

отгад|а́ть, а́ю, *pf.* (*of* ~ывать) to guess.

отга́дк|а, и, *f.* answer (*to a riddle*).

отга́дчик, а, *m.* (*coll.*) guesser, diviner.

отга́дыва|ть, ю, *impf. of* отгада́ть.

отгиба́|ть(ся), ю(сь), *impf. of* отогну́ть(ся).

отглаго́льный, *adj.* (*gram.*) verbal.

отгла́|дить, жу, дишь, *pf.* (*of* ~живать) to iron (out).

отгла́жива|ть, ю, *impf. of* отгла́дить.

отглода́|ть, ю, *pf.* (*coll.*) to bite off.

отгова́рива|ть(ся), ю(сь), *impf. of* отговори́ть(ся).

отговор|и́ть, ю́, и́шь, *pf.* (*of* отгова́ривать) (от *or* +*inf.*) to dissuade (from); я ~и́л его́ е́хать I have talked him out of going.

отговор|и́ться, ю́сь, и́шься, *pf.* (*of* отгова́риваться) (+*i.*) to excuse oneself (on the ground of); to plead; о. нездоро́вьем to plead ill-health.

отгово́рк|а, и, *f.* excuse; pretext; пуста́я о. lame excuse, hollow pretence.

отголо́с|ок, ка, *m.* echo (*also fig.*).

отго́н[1], а, *m.* 1. driving off. 2. pasturing (*of cattle*).

отго́н[2], а, *m.* (*tech.*) distillation products.

отго́нк|а[1], *f.* driving off.

отго́нк|а[2], и, *f.* distillation.

отгоня́|ть, ю, *impf. of* отогна́ть.

отгора́жива|ть(ся), ю(сь), *impf. of* отгороди́ть(ся).

отгоро|ди́ть, жу́, ~ди́шь, *pf.* (*of* отгора́живать) to fence off, partition off; о. ши́рмой to screen off.

отгоро|ди́ться, жу́сь, ~ди́шься, *pf.* (*of* отгора́живаться) to fence oneself off; (*fig., coll.*; от) to shut oneself off (from), cut oneself off (from).

отго|сти́ть, щу́, сти́шь, *pf.* (*coll.*; у) to have been a guest (of), have stayed (with).

отграни́чива|ть, ю, *impf. of* отграни́чить.

отграни́ч|ить, у, ишь, *pf.* (*of* ~ивать) to delimit.

отгреба́|ть, ю, *impf. of* отрести́.

отгре|сти́[1], бу́, бёшь, *past* ~б, ~бла́, *pf.* (*of* ~ба́ть) to rake away.

отгре|сти́[2], бу́, бёшь, *past* ~б, ~бла́, *pf.* (*of* ~ба́ть) to row off.

отгружа́|ть, ю, *impf. of* отгрузи́ть.

отгру|зи́ть, жу́, ~зи́шь, *pf.* (*of* ~жа́ть) to ship, dispatch.

отгру́зк|а[1], и, *f.* shipment, dispatching.

отгру́зк|а[2], и, *f.* unloading.

отгрыза́|ть, а́ю, *impf. of* ~ть.

отгры́з|ть, у́, ёшь, *past* ~, ~ла, *pf.* (*of* ~а́ть) to bite off, gnaw off.

отгу́лива|ть, ю, *impf. of* отгуля́ть 2.

отгул|я́ть, я́ю, *pf.* (*coll.*) 1. to have spent, to have finished (*holidays, leave, etc.*); мы ~я́ли о́тпуск our holidays are over. 2. (*impf.* ~ивать) to take (time) off; о. день to take a day off.

отда|ва́ть[1](ся), ю́(сь), ёшь(ся), *impf. of* отда́ть(ся).

отда|ва́ть[2], ёт, *impf.* (*coll.*; *impers.*+*i.*) to taste (of); to smell (of); (*fig.*) to smack (of) от него́ ~ёт во́дкой he reeks of vodka; э́то ~ёт суеве́рием this smacks of superstition.

отдав|и́ть, лю́, ~ишь, *pf.* to crush; о. кому́-н. но́гу to tread on someone's foot.

отдале́ни|е, я, *n.* 1. removal; (*fig.*) estrangement. 2. distance; держа́ть в ~и to keep at a distance.

отдалённост|ь, и, *f.* remoteness.

отдалён|ный (~, ~на), *adj.* distant, remote; о. ро́дственник distant relative; ~ное схо́дство remote likeness.

отдал|и́ть, ю́, и́шь, *pf.* (*of* ~я́ть) 1. to remove; (*fig.*) to estrange, alienate. 2. to postpone, put off.

отдал|и́ться, ю́сь, и́шься, *pf.* (*of* ~я́ться) 1. (от) to move away (from) (*also fig.*). 2. (*fig.*) to digress; о. от те́мы to stray from the subject. 3. *pass. of* ~и́ть.

отдал|я́ть(ся), я́ю(сь), *impf. of* ~и́ть(ся).

отда́ни|е, я, *n.* 1. giving back, returning; о. че́сти (*mil.*) saluting. 2. (*eccl.*) keeping, observing (*of a festival*).

отда́рива|ть(ся), ю(сь), *impf. of* отдари́ть(ся).

отдар|и́ть, ю́, и́шь, *pf.* (*of* ~ивать) (*coll.*) to give in return.

отдар|и́ться, ю́сь, и́шься, *pf.* (*of* ~иваться) (*coll.*) to make a present in return, repay a gift.

отд|а́ть, а́м, а́шь, а́ст, ади́м, ади́те, аду́т, *past* ~ал, ~ала́, ~ало, *pf.* (*of* ~ава́ть) 1. to give back, return; о. до́лжное кому́-н. to

render someone his due; о. после́дний долг
(+d.) to pay the last honours; о. себе́ отчёт
(в+p.) to be aware (of), realize; не о. себе́
отчёта (в+p.) to fail to realize. **2.** to give
(up), devote; о. жизнь нау́ке to devote
one's life to learning. **3.** +a. and d. or +a.
за+a.) to give in marriage (to), give away.
4. (в+a., под+a.) to give, put, place
(= *hand over for certain purpose*); о. кни́гу в
переплёт to have a book bound, send a
book to be bound; о. ма́льчика в шко́лу to
send (put) a small boy to school; о. под
стра́жу to give into custody; о. под суд to
prosecute. **5.** (*in combination with certain
nouns*) to give; to make (*or not requiring
separate translation*); о. покло́н (*obs.*) to bow,
make a bow; о. прика́з (+d.) to issue an
order, give orders (to); о. распоряже́ние to
give instructions; о. честь (+d.) to salute.
6. (*coll.*) to sell, let have; он мне э́то ⌐ал за
бесце́нок he let me have it for a song.
7. (*of a fire-arm*) to kick. **8.** мне ⌐ало в спи́ну
(*fig.*; *impers.*) I felt a twinge in my back.
9. (*naut.*) to unbend; to let go; to cast off;
о. я́корь to cast anchor, let go the anchor;
о. концы́! let go!

**отд|а́ться, а́мся, а́шься, а́стся, ади́мся,
ади́тесь, аду́тся,** *past* **⌐а́лся, ⌐ала́сь,** *pf.*
(*of* ⌐ава́ться) **1.** (+d.) to give oneself up
(to); to devote oneself (to); (*of a woman*) to
give oneself (to). **2.** to resound; to rever-
berate; to ring (*in one's ears*).

отда́ч|а, и, *f.* **1.** return; payment, reimburse-
ment. **2.** о. внаём letting. **3.** (*naut.*) letting
go; casting off. **4.** (*tech.*) efficiency, performance; output. **5.** (*mil.*) recoil, kick.

отдежу́р|ить, ю, ишь, *pf.* **1.** to come off
duty. **2.** to spend on duty; о. во́семь часо́в
to have had eight hours on (duty).

отде́л, а, *m.* **1.** department; о. ка́дров personnel department. **2.** section, part (*of
book, periodical, etc.*).

отде́л|ать, аю, *pf.* (*of* ⌐ывать) **1.** to finish,
put the finishing touches (to); о. пла́тье
кружева́ми to trim a dress with lace. **2.**
(*coll.*) to give a dressing down.

отде́л|аться, аюсь, *pf.* (*of* ⌐ываться) **1.** (от)
to get rid (of), get shut (of). **2.** (+i.) to
escape (with), get off (with); сча́стливо
о. to have a lucky escape; о. цара́пиной to
get off with a scratch.

отделе́ни|е, я, *n.* **1.** separation. **2.** depart-
ment, branch; о. мили́ции local police-
station; о. свя́зи local post office. **3.** compartment, section; part (*of concert programme,
etc.*); о. шка́фа pigeon-hole; маши́нное о.
(*naut.*) engine-room. **4.** (*mil.*) section.

отделён|ный², *adj. of* ⌐ие 3; о. команди́р
section commander.

отделе́н|ский, *adj.* = ⌐ческий.

отделе́нческий, *adj.* department(al), branch.

отдели́м|ый (⌐, ⌐а), *adj.* separable.

отдели́тел|ь, я, *m.* (*tech.*, *chem.*) separator.

отдел|и́ть, ю́, ⌐ишь, *pf.* (*of* ⌐я́ть) **1.** to
separate, part; to detach. **2.** to separate
off; о. перегоро́дкой to partition off. **3.**
(*obs.*) to cut off (*with portion of estate, property,
etc.*).

отдел|и́ться, ю́сь, ⌐ишься, *pf.* (*of* ⌐я́ться)
1. to separate, part; to get detached; to
come apart; to come off. **2.** (*obs.*) to set up
on one's own.

отде́лк|а, и, *f.* **1.** finishing; trimming. **2.**
finish, decoration.

отде́лыва|ть(ся), ю(сь), *impf. of* отде́лать-
(ся).

отде́льно, *adv.* separately.

отде́льност|ь, и, *f.* в ⌐и taken separately,
individually.

отде́льный, *adj.* **1.** separate, individual.
2. (*mil.*) independent.

отдел|я́ть(ся), я́ю(сь), *impf. of* ⌐и́ть(ся).

отдёргива|ть, ю, *impf. of* отдёрнуть.

отдёр|нуть, ну, нешь, *pf.* (*of* ⌐гивать) **1.** to
draw aside, pull aside; о. занаве́ску to
draw back the curtain. **2.** to jerk back,
withdraw.

отдира́|ть, ю, *impf. of* отодра́ть.

отдохнове́ни|е, я, *n.* (*obs.*) repose.

отдохн|у́ть, у́, ёшь, *pf.* (*of* отдыха́ть) to
rest; to have (take) a rest.

отдуба́|сить, шу, сишь, *pf. of* дуба́сить.

отдува́|ть, ю, *impf. of* отду́ть.

отдува́|ться, юсь, *impf.* **1.** to pant, blow,
puff. **2.** (*fig.*, *coll.*; за+a.) to be answerable
(for), take the rap (for).

отду́м|ать, аю, *pf.* (*of* ⌐ывать) (*coll.*) to
change one's mind; мы ⌐али перее́хать
we have changed our mind about
moving.

отду́мыва|ть, ю, *impf. of* отду́мать.

отду́|ть, ю, ешь, *pf.* (*of* ⌐ва́ть). (**1.** *coll.*)
to blow away. **2.** to thrash soundly.

отду́шин|а, ы, *f.* air-hole, (air) vent; (*fig.*)
safety-valve.

отду́шник, а, *m.* air-hole, (air) vent.

о́тдых, а, *m.* rest; relaxation; holiday; день
⌐а a day of rest, rest day.

отдыха́|ть, ю, *impf.* (*of* отдохну́ть) to be
resting; to be on holiday.

отдыха́|ющий, *pres. part. of* ⌐ть; *as noun* о.,
⌐ющего, *m. and* ⌐ющая, ⌐ющей, *f.* holiday-maker.

отдыш|а́ться, у́сь, ⌐ишься, *pf.* to recover
one's breath.

отёк, а, *m.* (*med.*) oedema; о. лёгких emphy-
sema.

отека́|ть, ю, *impf. of* оте́чь.

отёл, а, *m.* calving.

отел|и́ться, ю́сь, ⌐ишься, *pf. of* тели́ться.

отéл|**ь, я,** *m.* hotel.

отéль|**ный,** *adj. of* ~.

отепл|**и́ть, ю́, и́шь,** *pf. (of* ~**я́ть)** to protect against cold, make (*house, room, etc.*) proof against cold.

отепл|**я́ть, я́ю,** *impf. of* ~**и́ть.**

от|**éц, цá,** *m.* father (*also fig. in var. senses*); нáши ~цы́ (*fig.*) our (fore)fathers; О. небéсный (*rel.*) the heavenly Father; о. семéйства (*coll.*) paterfamilias; ~цы́ цéркви (*eccl., hist.*) the Fathers of the Church.

отéческий, *adj.* fatherly, paternal.

отéчеств|**енный,** *adj. of* ~о; ~енная промы́шленность home industry; ~енная войнá (*hist.*) the Patriotic War (*designation of Russian operations against Napoleon in 1812*); Вели́кая ~енная войнá the Great Patriotic War (*official Soviet designation of war of 1941–1945 against Germany and her allies*).

отéчеств|**о, а,** *n.* native land, fatherland, home (country).

отé|**чь, кý, чёшь, кýт,** *past* ~**к,** ~**клá,** *pf. (of* ~**кáть)** 1. to swell, become swollen. 2. (*of a candle*) to gutter.

от|**жáть¹, отожмý, отожмёшь,** *pf. (of* ~**жимáть)** 1. to wring out. 2. (*coll.*) to press back.

от|**жáть², отожнý, отожнёшь,** *pf. (of* ~**жинáть)** to finish harvesting.

от|**жéчь, отожгý, отожжёшь,** *past* ~**жёг,** ~**ожглá,** *pf. (of* ~**жигáть)** (*tech.*) to anneal.

отживá|**ть, ю,** *impf. of* отжи́ть.

отживá|**ющий,** *pres. part. act. of* ~**ть** *and adj.* moribund.

отжи́|**вший,** *past part. act. of* ~**ть** *and adj.* obsolete; outmoded.

отжи́г, а, *m.* (*tech.*) 1. annealing. 2. (glass) fritting.

отжигá|**ть, ю,** *impf. of* отжéчь.

отжимá|**ть, ю,** *impf. of* отжáть¹.

отжинá|**ть, ю,** *impf. of* отжáть².

от|**жи́ть, живý, живёшь,** *past* ~**жил,** ~**жилá,** ~**жило,** *pf. (of* ~**живáть)** to become obsolete, become outmoded; о. свой век to have had one's day; to go out of fashion.

отзáвтрака|**ть, ю,** *pf.* (*coll.*) to have had breakfast.

отзвон|**и́ть, ю́, и́шь,** *pf.* 1. to stop ringing; to stop striking (*of a clock*); ~и́л и с колокóльни долóй (*coll.*) finished and done with. 2. (*fig., coll.*) to rattle off.

óтзвук, а, *m.* echo (*also fig.*).

отзвуч|**áть, и́т,** *pf.* to be heard no more.

óтзыв, а, *m.* 1. opinion, judgement; похвáльный о. honourable mention. 2. reference; testimonial; дать хорóший о. о кóм-н. to give someone a good reference. 3. review. 4. (*mil.*) reply (*to password*).

отзы́в, а, *m.* recall (*of diplomatic representative*).

отзывá|**ть, ю,** *impf.* 1. *impf. of* отозвáть. 2. (+*i.*) to taste (of); о. гóречью to have a bitter taste.

отзывá|**ться, юсь,** *impf.* 1. *impf. of* отозвáться. 2. (+*i.*) = ~**ть.**

отзывн|**óй,** *adj.* ~ые грáмоты letters of recall.

отзы́вчив|**ый (~, ~а),** *adj.* responsive.

оти́т, а, *m.* (*med.*) otitis.

откáз, а, *m.* 1. refusal; denial; repudiation; (*leg.*) rejection, nonsuit; получи́ть о. to be refused, be turned down; не принимáть ~а to take no denial; до ~а to overflowing, to satiety; пóлный до ~а cram-full, full to capacity. 2. (от) renunciation (of), giving up (of). 3. (*tech.*) failure; дéйствовать без ~а to run smoothly. 4. (*mus.*) natural.

отка|**зáть, жý,** ~**жешь,** *pf. (of* ~**зывать)** 1. (+*d.* в+*p.*) to refuse, deny; онá ~зáла емý в прóсьбе she refused his request; емý нельзя́ о. в талáнте there is no denying that he has talent; не ~жи́те в любéзности… be so kind as .... 2. (+*d.* от) to dismiss, discharge; о. от дóма to forbid the house. 3. (*obs.*) to leave, bequeath. 4. (*tech.*) to fail, break down; (*coll.*) to conk out.

отка|**зáться, жýсь,** ~**жешься,** *pf. (of* ~**зываться)** 1. (от *or* +*inf.*) to refuse, decline; to turn down; о. от предложéния to turn down a proposal; о. от своéй пóдписи to deny one's signature; о. от свои́х слов to retract one's words; о. от уплáты дóлга to repudiate a debt; о. служи́ть (*fig.*, *coll.*) to be out of order; мои́ часы́ ~зáлись служи́ть my watch would not go; не ~жýсь (*coll.*) I don't mind if I do; не ~зáлся бы (*coll.*) I wouldn't say no. 2. to renounce, give up; to relinquish, abdicate; о. от борьбы́ to give up the struggle.

откáзыва|**ть(ся), ю(сь),** *impf. (of* отказáть(ся)) ни в чём себé не о. to deny oneself nothing.

откáлыва|**ть(ся), ю(сь),** *impf. of* отколóть(ся).

откáпыва|**ть, ю,** *impf. of* откопáть.

откáрмлива|**ть, ю,** *impf. of* откорми́ть.

откáт, а, *m.* (*mil.*) recoil.

отка|**ти́ть, чý,** ~**тишь,** *pf. (of* ~**тывать)** 1. to roll away. 2. (*in coalmines, etc.*) to haul; to tram, truck.

отка|**ти́ться, чýсь,** ~**тишься,** *pf. (of* ~**тываться)** 1. to roll away. 2. (*mil.; fig., coll.*) to roll back, be forced back.

откáтк|**а, и,** *f.* (*in coal-mines, etc.*) haulage; trucking.

откáтчик, а, *m.* haulage-man.

откач|**áть, áю,** *pf. (of* ~**ивать)** 1. to pump out. 2. to resuscitate (*a person saved from drowning*).

откáчива|**ть, ю,** *impf. of* откачáть.

откачн|у́ть, у́, ёшь, *pf.* **1.** to swing to one side. **2.** (*fig.*, *coll.*; *impers.*) его́ ∼у́ло от бы́вших его́ собуты́льников he has drifted away from his former boon-companions.

откачн|у́ться, у́сь, ёшься, *pf.* (*coll.*) **1.** to swing to one side. **2.** (*of a person*) to reel back; to slump back. **3.** (*fig.*; от) to swing away (from), turn away (from).

отка́шл|ивать, иваю, *impf. of* ∼януть.

отка́шл|иваться, иваюсь, *impf. of* ∼яться.

отка́шл|януть, яну, янешь, *pf.* (*of* ∼ивать) to hawk up.

отка́шл|яться, яюсь, *pf.* (*of* ∼иваться) to clear one's throat.

отквит|а́ть, а́ю, *pf.* (*of* ∼ывать) (*coll.*; +d.) to settle accounts (with), give as good as one gets.

откв*и́*тыва|ть, ю, *impf. of* отквита́ть.

откидно́й, *adj.* folding, collapsible.

отки́дыва|ть(ся), ю(сь), *impf. of* отки́нуть-(ся).

отки́|нуть, ну, нешь, *pf.* (*of* ∼дывать) **1.** to throw away; to cast away (*also fig.*). **2.** to turn back, fold back.

отки́|нуться, нусь, нешься, *pf.* (*of* ∼дываться) **1.** to lean back; to recline, settle back. **2.** *pass. of* ∼нуть.

откла́дыва|ть, ю, *impf. of* отложи́ть.

откла́нива|ться, юсь, *impf. of* откла́няться.

откла́н|яться, яюсь, *pf.* (*of* ∼иваться) (*obs.*) to take one's leave.

откле́ива|ть(ся), ю(сь), *impf. of* откле́ить-(ся).

откле́|ить, ю, ишь, *pf.* (*of* ∼ивать) to un-stick.

откле́|иться, ится, *pf.* (*of* ∼иваться) **1.** to come unstuck. **2.** *pass. of* ∼ить.

о́тклик, а, *m.* **1.** response; (*fig.*) comment. **2.** (*fig.*) echo; repercussion; ∼и неда́вних собы́тий echoes of recent happenings.

отклик|а́ться, а́юсь, *impf.* (*of* ∼нуться) (на+a.) to answer, respond (to) (*also fig.*).

откли́к|нуться, нусь, нешься, *pf. of* ∼а́ться.

отклоне́ни|е, я, *n.* **1.** deviation; divergence; о. от те́мы digression. **2.** declining, refusal. **3.** (*phys.*) deflection, declination; error; diffraction; вероя́тное о. probable error; магни́тное о. deflection of the needle; у́гол ∼я angle of deviation.

отклон|и́ть, ю́, ∼ишь, *pf.* (*of* ∼я́ть) **1.** to deflect. **2.** to decline; о. попра́вку to vote down an amendment; о. предложе́ние to decline an offer.

отклон|и́ться, ю́сь, ∼и́шься, *pf.* (*of* ∼я́ться) **1.** to deviate; to diverge; to swerve; о. от те́мы to digress. **2.** *pass. of* ∼и́ть.

отключ|а́ть, а́ю, *impf. of* ∼и́ть.

отключ|ённый, *p.p.p. of* ∼и́ть *and adj.* (*electr.*) dead.

отключ|и́ть, у́, и́шь, *pf.* (*of* ∼а́ть) (*electr.*) to cut off, disconnect; о. телефо́нный аппара́т to cut off a telephone.

отковы́рива|ть, ю, *impf. of* отковыря́ть.

отковыр|я́ть, я́ю, *pf.* (*of* ∼ивать) to pick off.

откозыря́|ть[1], ю, *pf.* (*coll.*; +d.) to salute.

откозыря́|ть[2], ю, *pf.* (*coll.*; *cards*) to play a trump in reply.

отко́л, а, *m.* (*fig.*; *polit.*, *etc.*) split; splitting, splintering, breaking away.

отко́л|е, *adv.* = ∼ь.

отколо|ти́ть, чу́, ∼тишь, *pf.* **1.** to knock off. **2.** to beat up.

откол|о́ть, ю́, ∼ешь, *pf.* (*of* отка́лывать) **1.** to break off; to chop off. **2.** to unpin. **3.** (*coll.*, *pejor.*) о. глу́пость to get up to a stupid trick; о. словцо́ to make a wise-crack.

откол|о́ться, ю́сь, ∼ешься, *pf.* (*of* отка́лы-ваться) **1.** to break off. **2.** to come un-pinned, come undone. **3.** (*fig.*) to break away, cut oneself off.

отколуп|а́ть, а́ю, *pf.* (*of* ∼ывать) to pick off.

отколу́пыва|ть, ю, *impf. of* отколупа́ть.

отко́ль, *adv.* (*obs.*) whence, where from.

откомандир|ова́ть, у́ю, *pf.* (*of* ∼о́вывать) **1.** to detach; to post (*to new duties or establish-ment*). **2.** (за+i.) (*coll.*) to send (*to fetch*).

откомандиро́выва|ть, ю, *impf. of* откоман-дирова́ть.

откопа́|ть, ю, ю, *pf.* (*of* отка́пывать) **1.** to dig out; to exhume, disinter. **2.** (*fig.*, *coll.*) to dig up, unearth.

отко́рм, а, *m.* fattening (up).

откорм|и́ть, лю́, ∼ишь, *pf.* (*of* отка́рмли-вать) to fatten (up).

откорм|ленный, *p.p.p. of* ∼и́ть *and adj.* fat, fatted, fattened; о. скот fat stock.

отко́с, а, *m.* slope (*esp. of railway embankment*); о. холма́ hillside; пусти́ть по́езд под о. to derail a train; у́гол есте́ственного ∼а (*phys.*) angle of rest.

откреп|и́ть, лю́, и́шь, *pf.* (*of* ∼ля́ть) **1.** to unfasten, untie. **2.** to strike off the re-gister.

откреп|и́ться, лю́сь, и́шься, *pf.* (*of* ∼ля́ться) **1.** to become unfastened. **2.** to remove one's name (*from a register, etc.*).

открепля́|ть(ся), ю(сь), *impf. of* откре-пи́ть(ся).

откре́щива|ться, юсь, *impf.* (*coll.*; от) to disown; to refuse to have anything to do (with).

открове́ни|е, я, *n.* revelation.

открове́ннича|ть, ю, *impf.* (*coll.*; с+i.) to be candid (with), be frank (with).

открове́нност|ь, и, *f.* candour, frankness; bluntness, outspokenness; *pl.* (*coll.*) candid revelations.

открове́н|ный (~ен, ~на), *adj.* **1.** candid, frank; blunt, outspoken. **2.** open, unconcealed; ~ная неприя́знь unconcealed hostility. **3.** (*coll.*; *of dress*) revealing.

откру|ти́ть, чу́, ~тишь, *pf.* (*of* ~чивать) to untwist; о. кран to turn off a tap.

откру|ти́ться, чу́сь, ~тишься, *pf.* (*of* ~чиваться) **1.** to come untwisted. **2.** (*coll.*; от) to get out (of).

откру́чива|ть(ся), ю(сь), *impf. of* открути́ть(ся).

открыва́|ть(ся), ю(сь), *impf. of* откры́ть(ся).

откры́л|ок, ка, *m.* (*aeron.*) stub-wing.

откры́ти|е, я, *n.* **1.** opening. **2.** discovery.

откры́тк|а, и, *f.* post-card; о. с ви́дом picture post-card.

откры́то, *adv.* (*in var. senses*) openly; жить о. (*obs.*) to keep open house.

откры́т|ый, *p.p.p. of* ~ь and *adj.* (*in var. senses*) open; в ~ую (*cards and fig.*) showing one's hand; на ~ом во́здухе, под ~ым не́бом out of doors, in the open air; с ~ыми глаза́ми (*fig.*) with open eyes; при ~ых дверя́х open to the public; о. дом (*fig.*) open house; ~ое заседа́ние public sitting; ~ое мо́ре the open sea; ~ое письмо́ (*i*) post-card, (*ii*) open letter; ~ое пла́тье low-necked dress; ~ые го́рные рабо́ты open-cast mining; ~ая сце́на open-air stage.

откр|ы́ть, о́ю, о́ешь, *pf.* (*of* ~ыва́ть) **1.** (*in var. senses*) to open; о. кому́-н. глаза́ на что-н. (*fig.*) to open someone's eyes to something; о. кровь (*med.*; *obs.*) to let blood; о. ми́тинг to open a meeting; о. ого́нь (*mil.*) to open fire; о. па́мятник to unveil a monument; о. счёт to open an account. **2.** to uncover, reveal (*also fig.*); о. грудь to bare one's breast; о. ду́шу to lay bare one's heart; о. ка́рты (*fig.*) to show one's hand; о. секре́т to reveal a secret. **3.** to discover; о. Аме́рику (*fig., iron.*) to retail stale news. **4.** to turn on (*gas, water, etc.*).

откр|ы́ться, о́юсь, о́ешься, *pf.* (*of* ~ыва́ться) **1.** to open. **2.** to come to light, be revealed; пе́ред на́ми ~ылся великоле́пный вид a magnificent view unfolded before us. **3.** (+*d.*) to confide (in, to). **4.** *pass. of* ~ы́ть.

отку́да, *adv.* (*interrog.*) whence, where from; (*relat.*) whence, from which; о. вы? where do you come from? where are you from?; о. вы об э́том зна́ете? how do you come to know about it?; о. ни возьми́сь (*coll.*) quite unexpectedly, suddenly.

отку́да-либо, *adv.* from somewhere or other.

отку́да-нибудь, *adv.* = о.-либо.

отку́да-то, *adv.* from somewhere.

о́ткуп, а, *pl.* ~а́, *m.* farming (*of revenues, etc.*); взять на о. to farm; отда́ть на о. to farm out (*also fig.*).

откуп|а́ть(ся), а́ю(сь), *impf. of* ~и́ть(ся).

откуп|и́ть, лю́, ~ишь, *pf.* (*of* ~а́ть) to lay up.

откуп|и́ться, лю́сь, ~ишься, *pf.* (*of* ~а́ться) (от) to pay off.

откупо́рива|ть, ю, *impf. of* откупо́рить.

отку́пор|ить, ю, ишь, *pf.* (*of* ~ивать) to uncork; to open (*a bottle*).

отку́порк|а, и, *f.* opening, uncorking.

откупщи́к, а́, *m.* tax-farmer.

отку|си́ть, шу́, ~сишь, *pf.* (*of* ~сывать) to bite off; to snap off (*with pincers, etc.*).

отку́сыва|ть, ю, *impf. of* откуси́ть.

отку́ша|ть, ю, *pf.* (*obs.*) **1.** to have finished eating. **2.** to eat; to try (*food*); позва́ть о. to invite to a meal.

отлага́тельств|о, а, *n.* delay; procrastination; де́ло не те́рпит ~а the matter is urgent.

отлага́|ть(ся), ю(сь), *impf. of* отложи́ть(ся).

отлакир|ова́ть, у́ю, *pf. of* лакирова́ть.

отла́мыва|ть(ся), ю(сь), *impf. of* отлома́ть(ся) *and* отломи́ть(ся).

отлега́|ть, ю, *impf. of* отле́чь.

отлеж|а́ть, у́, и́шь, *pf.* (*of* ~ивать) я ~а́л но́гу my foot has gone to sleep.

отлеж|а́ться, у́сь, и́шься, *pf.* **1.** to lie up; to rest (*in bed*). **2.** to lie, be stored (*in order to season, ripen, etc.*).

отлёжива|ть(ся), ю(сь), *impf. of* отлежа́ть(ся).

отлеп|и́ть, лю́, ~ишь, *pf.* (*of* ~ля́ть) (*coll.*) to unstick, take off (*something adhesive*).

отлеп|и́ться, ~ится, *pf.* (*of* ~ля́ться) (*coll.*) to come unstuck, come off.

отлепля́|ть(ся), ю(сь), *impf. of* отлепи́ть(ся).

отлёт, а, *m.* flying away; departure (*of aircraft*); быть на ~е to be about to leave, be on the point of departure; держа́ть на ~е to hold in one's outstretched hand; держа́ться на ~е (*coll.*) to hold oneself aloof, be stand-offish; дом на ~е house standing by itself.

отлета́|ть[1], ю, *pf.* **1.** to have completed a flight. **2.** (*coll.*) to have been flying (*for a given period*); он ~л два́дцать лет he has done twenty years' flying.

отлет|а́ть[2], а́ю, *impf. of* ~е́ть.

отле|те́ть, чу́, ти́шь, *pf.* (*of* ~та́ть) **1.** to fly (away, off); (*fig.*) to fly, vanish. **2.** to rebound, bounce back. **3.** (*coll.*; *of buttons, etc.*) to come off.

отл|е́чь, я́гу, я́жешь, я́гут, *past* ~ёг, ~егла́, *pf.* (*of* ~ега́ть) **1.** (*obs.*; от) to move away (from). **2.** (*coll.*; *impers.*) у неё ~егло́ от се́рдца she felt relieved, she felt as if a weight had been lifted from her.

отли́в[1], а, *m.* ebb, ebb-tide.

отли́в[2], а, *m.* tint; play of colours; с золоты́м ~ом shot with gold.

отлива́|ть¹, ю, *impf. of* отли́ть.

отлива́|ть², ет, *impf.* (+*i*.) to be shot (*with a colour*).

отли́вк|а, и, *f.* (*tech.*) 1. casting, founding. 2. cast, ingot, moulding.

отливн|о́й, *adj.* (*tech.*) cast, founded, moulded; ~а́я печь founding furnace.

отлип|а́ть, а́ет, *impf. of* ~нуть.

отли́п|нуть, нет, *past* ~, ~ла, *pf.* (*of* ~а́ть) to come off, come unstuck.

отли́т|ый (о́тлит, ~а́, о́тлито *and* ~, ~а́, ~о), *p.p.p. of* ~ь; в ~ом ви́де (*tech.*) as cast.

отли́ть, отолью́, отольёшь, *past* о́тли́л, отлила́, о́тли́ло, *pf.* (*of* отлива́ть¹) 1. (+*a.* or *g.*) to pour off; to pump out. 2. (*tech.*) to cast, found. 3. (*vulg.*) to urinate.

отлич|а́ть, а́ю, *impf. of* ~и́ть.

отлич|а́ться, а́юсь, *impf.* 1. (*pf.* ~и́ться) to distinguish oneself, excel (*also joc., iron.*). 2. (*impf. only*) (от) to differ (from). 3. (*impf. only*) (+*i.*) to be notable (for).

отли́чи|е, я, *n.* 1. difference, distinction; знак ~я distinguishing feature; (*mil.*) order, decoration; в о. от in contradistinction to. 2. distinction (*as grade of merit*); distinguished services; получи́ть дипло́м с ~ем to obtain a distinction (*in university examination, etc.*).

отличи́тельный, *adj.* distinctive; distinguishing; о. при́знак distinguishing feature.

отлич|и́ть, у́, и́шь, *pf.* (*of* ~а́ть) 1. to distinguish; о. одно́ от друго́го to tell one thing from another. 2. to single out.

отлич|и́ться, у́сь, и́шься, *pf. of* ~а́ться.

отли́чник, а, *m.* 1. pupil obtaining 'excellent' marks. 2. о. произво́дства exemplary worker.

отли́чно 1. *adv.* excellently; perfectly; extremely well; о. знать to know perfectly well; он о. понима́ет по-ру́сски he understands Russian perfectly. 2. *as indecl. noun* 'excellent' mark (*in school, etc.*).

отли́ч|ный (~ен, ~на), *adj.* 1. (*obs.*) (от) different (from). 2. excellent; perfect; extremely good; ~но! excellent!

отло́г|ий (~, ~а), *adj.* sloping.

отло́гост|ь, и, *f.* slope.

отло́|же, *comp. of* ~гий.

отложе́ни|е, я, *n.* 1. secession. 2. sediment, precipitation; (*geol.*) deposit.

отлож|и́ть, у́, и́шь, *pf.* 1. (*impf.* откла́дывать) to put aside, set aside; to put away, put by; о. на чёрный день to put by for a rainy day. 2. (*impf.* откла́дывать *and* отлага́ть) to put off, postpone; о. па́ртию to adjourn a game; о. реше́ние to suspend judgement; о. в до́лгий я́щик to shelve. 3. (*impf.* откла́дывать) (*of insects*) to lay. 4. (*impf.* откла́дывать) (*obs.*) to turn back, turn down. 5. (*impf.* откла́дывать) to un-

harness. 6. (*impf.* отлага́ть) (*geol.*) to deposit.

отлож|и́ться, у́сь, ~и́шься, *pf.* (*of* отлага́ться) 1. (*obs.*; от) to detach oneself (from), separate (from); (*polit.*) to secede. 2. (*geol.*) to deposit; be deposited.

отложн|о́й, *adj.* о. воротни́к turn-down collar.

отлома́|ть, ю, *pf.* (*of* отла́мывать) to break off.

отлома́|ться, юсь, *pf.* (*of* отла́мываться) to break off.

отлом|и́ть(ся), лю́(сь), ~ишь(ся), *pf.* = ~а́ть(ся).

отлуп|и́ть, лю́, ~ишь, *pf. of* лупи́ть².

отлупц|ева́ть, у́ю, *pf. of* лупцева́ть.

отлуч|а́ть(ся), а́ю(сь), *impf. of* отлучи́ть(ся).

отлуче́ни|е, я, *n.* (*eccl. and fig.*) excommunication.

отлуч|и́ть, у́, и́шь, *pf.* (*of* ~а́ть) (*obs.*; от) to separate (from), remove (from); о. (от це́ркви) (*eccl.*) to excommunicate.

отлуч|и́ться, у́сь, и́шься, *pf.* (*of* ~а́ться) 1. to absent oneself. 2. *pass. of* ~и́ть.

отлу́чк|а, и, *f.* absence; самово́льная о. (*mil.*) absence without leave; быть в ~е to be absent, be away.

отлы́нива|ть, ю, *impf.* (*coll.*; от) to shirk.

отма́лчива|ться, юсь, *impf. of* отмолча́ться.

отма́тыва|ть, ю, *impf. of* отмота́ть.

отма́|хать¹, шу́, ~шешь, *pf.* (*of* ~хивать) 1. to stop waving. 2. о. ру́ки to tire one's arms by waving.

отмаха́|ть², ю, *pf.* (*coll.*) to cover (*a distance*); за день мы ~ли свы́ше тридцати́ миль in the day we covered more than thirty miles.

отма́хива|ть(ся), ю(сь), *impf. of* отмаха́ть¹ *and* отмахну́ть(ся).

отмах|ну́ть, ну́, нёшь, *pf.* (*of* ~ивать) (*coll.*) to wave away, brush off (*with one's hand*).

отмах|ну́ться, ну́сь, нёшься, *pf.* (*of* ~иваться) (от) 1. = ~ну́ть; о. от комаро́в to brush mosquitoes off. 2. (*fig.*) to brush aside.

отма́чива|ть, ю, *impf. of* отмочи́ть.

отмеж|ева́ть, у́ю, *pf.* (*of* ~ёвывать) to mark off, draw a boundary line (between).

отмеж|ева́ться, у́юсь, *pf.* (*of* ~ёвываться) 1. (от) to dissociate oneself (from); to refuse to acknowledge. 2. *pass. of* ~ева́ть.

отмежёвыва|ть(ся), ю(сь), *impf. of* отмежева́ть(ся).

о́тмел|ь, и, *f.* (sand-)bar, (sand-)bank.

отме́н|а, ы, *f.* abolition; abrogation, repeal, revocation; cancellation, countermand; о. крепостно́го пра́ва abolition of serfdom; о. зако́на repeal of a law; о. спекта́кля cancellation of a show.

отмен|и́ть, ю́, ~ишь, *pf.* (*of* ~я́ть) to abolish; to abrogate, repeal, revoke, rescind; to cancel, countermand; (*leg.*) to disaffirm.

отме́н|ный (~ен, ~на), *adj.* excellent.

отмен|я́ть, я́ю, *impf. of* ~и́ть.

отмер|е́ть, отомрёт, *past* о́тмер, ~ла́, о́тмерло, *pf.* (*of* отмира́ть) to die off; (*fig.*) to die out, die away.

отмерз|а́ть, а́ет, *impf. of* ~нуть.

отмёрз|нуть, нет, *past* ~, ~ла, *pf.* (*of* ~а́ть) to freeze; ру́ки у меня́ ~ли my hands are frozen.

отме́рива|ть, ю, *impf. of* отме́рить.

отме́р|ить, ю, ишь, *pf.* (*of* ~ивать *and* ~я́ть) to measure off.

отмер|я́ть, я́ю, *impf. =* ~ивать.

отме|сти́, ту́, тёшь, *past* ~л, ~ла́, *pf.* (*of* ~та́ть) to sweep aside (*also fig.*).

отмёстк|а, и, *f.* (*coll.*) revenge; в ~у in revenge.

отмета́|ть, ю, *impf. of* отмести́.

отме́тин|а, ы, *f.* mark; (*on forehead of horse, etc.*) star.

отме́|тить, чу, тишь, *pf.* (*of* ~ча́ть) **1.** to mark, note; to make a note (of); о. пти́чкой to tick off. **2.** to point to, mention, record; о. чьи-н. по́двиги to point to someone's feats. **3.** to register (out), sign out (*departing tenant, etc.*). **4.** to celebrate, mark by celebration.

отме́|титься, чусь, тишься, *pf.* (*of* ~ча́ться) **1.** to sign one's name (*on a list*). **2.** to register (out), sign out (*on departure*).

отме́тк|а, и, *f.* **1.** note. **2.** (*in school or examinations*) mark.

отме́тчик, а, *m.* marker.

отмеча́|ть(ся), ю(сь), *impf. of* отме́тить(ся).

отмира́ни|е, я, *n.* dying off; dying away, fading away, withering away.

отмобилиз|ова́ть, у́ю, *pf.* (*coll.*) to mobilize totally.

отмок|а́ть, а́ет, *impf. of* ~нуть.

отмо́к|нуть, нет, *past* ~, ~ла, *pf.* (*of* ~а́ть) **1.** to grow wet. **2.** to soak off.

отмолч|а́ться, у́сь, и́шься, *pf.* (*of* отма́лчиваться) (*coll.*) to keep silent, say nothing.

отмора́жива|ть, ю, *impf. of* отморо́зить.

отморо́жени|е, я, *n.* frost-bite.

отморо́|женный, *p.p.p. of* ~зить *and adj.* frost-bitten.

отморо́|зить, жу, зишь, *pf.* (*of* отмора́живать) to injure by frost-bite; я ~зил себе́ у́ши my ears are frost-bitten.

отмота́|ть, ю, *pf.* (*of* отма́тывать) to unwind.

отмоч|и́ть, у́, ~ишь, *pf.* (*of* отма́чивать) **1.** to unstick by wetting. **2.** to soak, steep. **3.** (*coll.*) to do, say (*something ludicrous or outrageous*).

отмсти́ть = отомсти́ть.

отмще́ни|е, я, *n.* (*obs.*) vengeance.

отмыва́|ть(ся), ю(сь), *impf. of* отмы́ть(ся).

отмыка́|ть(ся), ю(сь), *impf. of* отомкну́ть-(ся).

отм|ы́ть, о́ю, о́ешь, *pf.* (*of* ~ыва́ть) **1.** to wash clean. **2.** to wash off, wash away.

отм|ы́ться, о́юсь, о́ешься, *pf.* (*of* ~ыва́ться) **1.** to wash oneself clean. **2.** (*of dirt, etc.*) to come out, come off.

отмы́чк|а, и, *f.* lock-pick.

отмяк|а́ть, а́ет, *impf. of* ~нуть.

отмя́к|нуть, нет, *past* ~, ~ла, *pf.* (*of* ~ать) to grow soft.

отне́кива|ться, юсь, *impf.* (*coll.*) to refuse.

отнес|ти́, у́, ёшь, *past* ~, ~ла́, *pf.* (*of* относи́ть) **1.** (в+*a.*, к) to take (to). **2.** to carry away, carry off; (*impers.*) ло́дку ~ло́ тече́нием the boat was carried away by the current. **3.** (*coll.*) to cut off. **4.** (к) to ascribe (to), attribute (to), refer (to); ру́копись ~ли́ к пя́тому ве́ку the manuscript was believed to date from the fifth century; мы ~ли́ его́ раздражи́тельность на счёт глухоты́ we put his irritability down to his deafness.

отнес|ти́сь, у́сь, ёшься, *past* ~ся, ~ла́сь, *pf.* (*of* относи́ться) (к) **1.** to treat; to regard; хорошо́ о. к кому́-н. to treat someone well, be nice to someone; скепти́чески о. к предположе́нию to be sceptical about an hypothesis; как вы ~ли́сь к э́той ле́кции? what did you think of the lecture? **2.** (*obs.*) to apply (to).

отникелир|ова́ть, у́ю, *pf. of* никелирова́ть.

отнима́|ть(ся), ю(сь), *impf. of* отня́ть(ся).

относи́тельно 1. *adv.* relatively. **2.** *prep.* (+*g.*) concerning, about, with regard to.

относи́тельност|ь, и, *f.* relativity; тео́рия ~и Эйнште́йна Einstein's Theory of Relativity.

относи́тел|ьный (~ен, ~ьна), *adj.* relative; ~ьное местоиме́ние (*gram.*) relative pronoun.

отно|си́ть, шу́, ~сишь, *impf. of* отнести́.

отно|си́ться, шу́сь, ~сишься, *impf.* **1.** *impf. of* отнести́сь. **2.** *impf. only* (к) to concern, have to do (with), relate (to); э́то к де́лу не ~сится that's beside the point, that is irrelevant; два ~сится к трём как шесть к девяти́ (*math.*) two is to three as six is to nine. **3.** *impf. only* (к) to date (from); монасты́рь э́тот ~сится к двена́дцатому ве́ку this monastery dates from the twelfth century.

отноше́ни|е, я, *n.* **1.** (к) attitude (to); treatment (of); внима́тельное о. к ста́рым consideration for the old; у него́ стра́нное о. к же́нщинам he has a strange attitude to women. **2.** relation; respect; име́ть о. к чему́-н. to bear a relation to something, have a bearing on something; не име́ть ~я (к) to bear no relation (to), have nothing to do (with); в ~и (+*g*.), по ~ю (к) with respect (to), with regard (to); в не́которых ~ях in some respects. **3.** (*pl*.) relations; terms; дипломати́ческие ~я diplomatic relations; быть в дру́жеских ~ях (с+*i*.) to be on friendly terms (with). **4.** (*math*.) ratio; в прямо́м (обра́тном) ~и in direct (inverse) ratio. **5.** (*official*) letter, memorandum.

отны́не, *adv*. (*obs*.) henceforth, henceforward.

отню́дь, *adv*. by no means, not at all.

отня́ти|е, я, *n*. taking away; о. руки́ amputation of an arm; о. от груди́ weaning.

от|ня́ть, ниму́, ни́мешь, *past* ~ня́л, ~няла́, ~ня́ло, *pf*. (*of* ~нима́ть) **1.** to take (away); о. от груди́ to wean; о. жизнь у кого́-н. to take someone's life; от шести́ о. три то take away three from six; э́то ~ня́ло у меня́ три часа́ it took me three hours. **2.** to amputate.

от|ня́ться, ни́мется, *past* ~ня́лся, ~няла́сь, *pf*. (*of* ~нима́ться) to be paralyzed; у него́ ~няла́сь пра́вая рука́ he has lost the use of his right arm; у неё ~ня́лся язы́к she has lost the power of speech.

ото, *prep*. = от.

отобе́да|ть, ю, *pf*. **1.** to have finished dinner. **2.** (*obs*.) to dine, have dinner.

отобража́|ть, ю, *impf*. *of* отобрази́ть.

отображе́ни|е, я, *n*. reflection; representation.

отобра|зи́ть, жу́, зи́шь, *pf*. (*of* ~жа́ть) to reflect; to represent.

от|обра́ть, беру́, берёшь, *past* ~обра́л, ~обрала́, ~обра́ло, *pf*. (*of* отбира́ть) **1.** to take (away); to seize; о. биле́ты to collect tickets; о. показа́ние у свиде́теля (*leg*.) to take a deposition from a witness. **2.** to select, pick out.

отова́рива|ть, ю, *impf*. *of* отова́рить.

отова́р|ить, ю, ишь, *pf*. (*of* ~ивать) to pledge goods in support of; о. чек to issue goods against a sale receipt.

отовсю́ду, *adv*. from everywhere, from every quarter.

от|огна́ть[1], гоню́, го́нишь, *past* ~огна́л, ~огнала́, ~огна́ло, *pf*. (*of* ~гоня́ть) to drive off; to keep off; (*fig*.) to suppress.

от|огна́ть[2], гоню́, го́нишь, *past* ~огна́л, ~огнала́, ~огна́ло, *pf*. (*of* ~гоня́ть) (*chem*.) to distill (off).

отогн|у́ть, у́, ёшь, *pf*. (*of* отгиба́ть) to bend back; to flange.

отогн|у́ться, у́сь, ёшься, *pf*. (*of* отгиба́ться) to bend back.

отогрева́|ть(ся), ю(сь), *impf*. *of* отогре́ть(ся).

отогре́|ть, ю, *pf*. (*of* ~ва́ть) to warm.

отогре́|ться, юсь, *pf*. (*of* ~ва́ться) to warm oneself.

отодвига́|ть(ся), ю(сь), *impf*. *of* отодви́нуть(ся).

отодви́|нуть, ну, нешь, *pf*. (*of* ~га́ть) **1.** to move aside. **2.** (*fig*.) to put off, put back.

отодви́|нуться, нусь, нешься, *pf*. (*of* ~га́ться) **1.** to move aside. **2.** *pass. of* ~нуть.

от|одра́ть, деру́, дерёшь, *past* ~одра́л, ~одрала́, ~одра́ло, *pf*. (*of* ~дира́ть) **1.** to tear off, rip off. **2.** (*coll*.) to flog; о. кого́-н. за́ уши to pull someone's ears.

отож(д)еств|и́ть, лю́, и́шь, *pf*. (*of* ~ля́ть) to identify.

отож(д)ествля́|ть, ю, *impf*. *of* отож(д)естви́ть.

отожжённый, *p.p.p. of* отжёчь *and adj*. (*tech*.) annealed.

от|озва́ть, зову́, зовёшь, *past* ~озва́л, ~озвала́, ~озва́ло, *pf*. (*of* ~зыва́ть) **1.** to take aside. **2.** to recall (*a diplomatic representative*).

от|озва́ться, зову́сь, зовёшься, *past* ~озва́лся, ~озвала́сь, ~озва́ло́сь, *pf*. (*of* ~зыва́ться) **1.** (на+*a*.) to answer; to respond (to). **2.** (о+*p*.) to speak (of); реце́нзенты хорошо́ ~озва́лись о его́ второ́й кни́ге his second book was well received by (received good notices from) the reviewers. **3.** (на+ *a*.) to tell (on, upon); деторожде́ние ~озвало́сь на её здоро́вье child-bearing has told on her health.

ото|йти́, йду́, йдёшь, *past* ~шёл, ~шла́, *pf*. (*of* отходи́ть[1]) **1.** to move away; to move off; (*of trains, etc*.) to leave, depart. **2.** to withdraw; to recede; (*mil*.) to withdraw, fall back; (*fig*.) от) to move away (from); to digress (from), diverge (from); он далеко́ ~шёл от пре́жних взгля́дов he has moved a long way from his earlier views. **3.** (*of stains, etc*.) to come out; (от) to come away (from), come off; обо́и ~шли́ от стены́ the paper has come off (the wall). **4.** to recover (normal state); to come to oneself, come round; у меня́ ~шло́ от се́рдца (*impers*.; *coll*.) I felt better, I felt relieved. **5.** (к) to pass (to), go (to) (= *pass into the possession of, by inheritance, etc*.). **6.** to be lost (*in processing*). **7.** (*obs*.) to pass; ле́то ~шло́ summer was over; о. в ве́чность (*rhet*.) to pass away, pass to one's eternal rest.

отол|га́ться, гу́сь, жёшься, *past* ~га́лся, ~гала́сь, *pf*. (*coll*.) to lie one's way out (*of a difficult situation*).

отологи́ческий, *adj*. otological.

отоло́ги|я, и, *f*. otology.

отомкн|у́ть, у́, ёшь, *pf*. (*of* отмыка́ть) to unlock, unbolt.

отомкн|у́ться, у́сь, ёшься, *pf*. (*of* отмыка́ться) **1.** to unlock. **2.** *pass. of* ~у́ть.

отом|сти́ть, щу́, сти́шь, *pf*. *of* мсти́ть.

отопи́тельный, *adj*. heating; о. сезо́н cold season, season for fires.

отоп|и́ть, лю́, ~шь, *pf.* (*of* ота́пливать *and* отопля́ть) to heat.

отоплён|ец, ца, *m.* heating appliances expert.

отоплéни|е, я, *n.* heating.

отопля́|ть, ю, *impf. of* отопи́ть.

ора́чива|ть, ю, *impf. of* ороочи́ть.

ото́рванност|ь, и, *f.* isolation; loneliness; чу́вствовать о. от цивилиза́ции to feel cut off from civilization.

оторв|а́ть, у́, ёшь, *past* ~а́л, ~ала́, ~а́ло, *pf.* (*of* отрыва́ть¹) to tear off; to tear away (*also fig.*); о. кого́-н. от рабо́ты to tear someone away from his work; с рука́ми о. (*coll.*) to seize with both hands.

оторв|а́ться, у́сь, ёшься, *past* ~а́лся, ~ала́сь, ~а́ло́сь, *pf.* (*of* отрыва́ться) 1. to come off, be torn off. 2. (*aeron.*) о. от земли́ to take off. 3. (*fig.*; от) to be cut off (from), lose touch (with); to break away (from); о. от проти́вника to lose contact with the enemy. 4. (*fig.*; от) to tear oneself away (from); от э́той кни́ги я не мог о. I could not tear myself away from this book.

оторопéл|ый, *adj.* (*coll.*) dumb-founded.

оторопé|ть, ю, *pf.* (*coll.*) to be struck dumb.

о́тороп|ь, и, *f.* (*coll.*) confusion, fright; меня́ о. взяла́ I was dumb-founded.

ороч|и́ть, у́, и́шь, *pf.* (*of* ороа́чивать) to edge, trim.

ороо́чк|а, и, *f.* edging, trimming.

ото|сла́ть, шлю́, шлёшь, *pf.* (*of* отсыла́ть) 1. to send off, dispatch; о. де́ньги to send a remittance. 2. (к) to refer (to); о. чита́теля к предыду́щему то́му to refer the reader to the preceding volume; его́ ~сла́ли к заве́дующему he was referred to the manager.

отосп|а́ться, лю́сь, и́шься, *past* ~а́лся, ~ала́сь, *pf.* (*of* отсыпа́ться²) to have a long sleep, have one's sleep out; о. по́сле доро́ги to sleep off a journey.

отоше́дший, *past part. of* отойти́.

ото|шёл, шла́, *see* ~йти́.

ото|шлю́, шлёшь, *see* ~сла́ть.

отоща́лый, *adj.* (*coll.*) emaciated.

отоща́|ть, ю, *pf. of* тоща́ть.

отпада́|ть, ю, *impf. of* отпа́сть.

отпадéни|е, я, *n.* falling away; (*fig.*; от) defection (from).

отпа́ива|ть¹, ю, *impf. of* отпая́ть.

отпа́ива|ть², ю, *impf. of* отпои́ть.

отпа́рива|ть, ю, *impf. of* отпа́рить.

отпари́р|овать, ую, *pf. of* пари́ровать.

отпа́р|ить, ю, ишь, *pf.* (*of* ~ивать) 1. to steam; о. брю́ки to press trousers through a damp cloth. 2. to steam off.

отпа́рыва|ть, ю, *impf. of* отпоро́ть¹.

отпа́|сть, ду́, дёшь, *past* ~л, *pf.* (*of* ~да́ть) 1. to fall off, drop off; to fall away. 2. (*fig.*;

от) to fall away (from), defect (from), drop away (from); мно́гие чле́ны ~ли от па́ртии many members have fallen away from the party. 3. (*fig.*) to pass, fade; у него́ ~ла охо́та к путеше́ствию по Африке his desire to travel in Africa has passed; вопро́с об э́том ~л the question no longer arises.

отпа|я́ть, я́ю, *pf.* (*of* ~ивать¹) to unsolder.

отпева́ни|е, я, *n.* burial service.

отпева́|ть, ю, *impf. of* отпе́ть.

от|пере́ть, опру́, опрёшь, *past* ~пер, ~перла́, ~перло, *pf.* (*of* ~пира́ть) to unlock; to open.

от|пере́ться¹, опрётся, *past* ~пёрся, ~перла́сь, *pf.* (*of* ~пира́ться) to open.

от|пере́ться², опру́сь, опрёшься, *past* ~пёрся, ~перла́сь, *pf.* (*of* ~пира́ться) (*coll.*; от) to deny; to disown.

отпёр|тый *p.p.p. of* ~ь. *and adj.* (*coll.*) arrant, inveterate.

отп|е́ть, ою́, оёшь, *pf.* (*of* ~ева́ть) to read the burial service (for, over).

отпеча́т|ать, аю, *pf.* 1. (*impf.* печа́тать) to print (off). 2. (*impf.* ~ывать) to imprint; о. па́льцы на стекле́ to leave finger-prints on glass. 3. (*impf.* ~ывать) to open (up).

отпеча́т|аться, ается, *pf.* 1. to leave an imprint. 2. *pass. of* ~ать.

отпечатле́|ться, ется, *pf.* (*obs.*) to leave its mark.

отпеча́т|ок, ка, *m.* imprint, impress (*also fig.*); о. па́льца finger-print.

отпеча́тыва|ть(ся), ю(сь), *impf. of* отпеча́тать(ся).

отпива́|ть, ю, *impf. of* отпи́ть.

отпи́лива|ть, ю, *impf. of* отпили́ть.

отпил|и́ть, ю́, ~ишь, *pf.* (*of* ~ивать) to saw off.

отпира́тельств|о, а, *n.* denial, disavowal.

отпира́|ть(ся), ю(сь), *impf. of* отпере́ть(ся).

отпи|са́ть, шу́, ~шешь, *pf.* (*of* ~сывать) 1. (*obs.*) to bequeath, leave. 2. (*obs.*) to confiscate. 3. (*dial.*) to notify (in writing).

отпи|са́ться, шу́сь, ~шешься, *pf.* (*of* ~сываться) to make a (purely) formal reply.

отпи́ск|а, и, *f.* (*pejor.*) formal reply.

отпи́сыва|ть(ся), ю(сь), *impf. of* отписа́ть(ся).

от|пи́ть, опью́, опьёшь, *past* ~пил, ~пила́, ~пило, *pf.* (*of* ~пива́ть) (+*a. or g.*) to take a sip (of).

отпи́хива|ть(ся), ю(сь), *impf. of* отпихну́ть(ся).

отпих|ну́ть, ну́, нёшь, *pf.* (*of* ~ивать) (*coll.*) to push off; to shove aside.

отпих|ну́ться, ну́сь, нёшься, *pf.* (*of* ~иваться) (*coll.*) to push off (*esp. in a boat*).

отпла́т|а, ы, *f.* repayment.

отпла|ти́ть, чу́, ~тишь, *pf.* (*of* ~чивать) (+*d.*) to pay back (to), repay, requite; о, кому́-н. той же моне́той to pay someone in his own coin.

отпла́чива|ть, ю, *impf. of* отплати́ть.

отплёвыва|ть, ю, *impf. of* отплю́нуть.

отплёвыва|ться, юсь, *impf.* to spit (*also fig.*, to express disgust).

отплыва́|ть, ю, *impf. of* отплы́ть.

отплы́ти|е, я, *n.* sailing, departure.

отплы́|ть, ву́, вёшь, *past* ~л, ~ла́, ~ло, *pf.* (*of* ~ва́ть) to sail, set sail; to swim off.

отплю́н|уть, у, ешь, *pf.* (*of* отплёвывать) to spit (out), expectorate.

отпля|са́ть, шу́, ~шешь, *pf.* **1.** to dance (*trans.*). **2.** to finish dancing.

отпля́сыва|ть, ю, *impf.* (*coll.*) to dance with zest.

о́тповед|ь, и, *f.* reproof, rebuke.

отпо|и́ть, ю́, и́шь, *pf.* (*of* отпа́ивать[2]) **1.** to finish watering. **2.** to fatten (on liquids). **3.** (*coll.*; +*i.*) to cure by giving to drink; о. отра́вленного молоко́м to give milk to someone suffering from poisoning.

отполз|а́ть, а́ю, *impf. of* ~ти́.

отполз|ти́, у́, ёшь, *past* ~, ~ла́, *pf.* (*of* ~а́ть) to crawl away.

отполир|ова́ть, у́ю, *pf. of* полирова́ть.

отпо́р, а, *m.* repulse; rebuff; дать о. (+*d.*) to repulse; встре́тить о. to be repulsed; to meet with a rebuff.

отпор|о́ть[1], ю, ~ешь, *pf.* (*of* отпа́рывать) to rip off.

отпор|о́ть[2], ю, ~ешь, *pf.* (*of* поро́ть) (*coll.*) to flog, thrash.

отпотева́|ть, ю, *impf. of* отпоте́ть.

отпоте́|ть, ю, *pf.* (*of* потеть *and* ~ва́ть) to moisten, be covered with moisture.

отпочк|ова́ться, у́ется, *pf.* (*of* ~о́вываться) (*biol.*) to gemmate, propagate by gemmation; (*fig.*) to detach oneself.

отпочко́выва|ться, юсь, *impf. of* отпочкова́ться.

отправи́тел|ь, я, *m.* sender.

отпра́в|ить, лю, ишь, *pf.* (*of* ~ля́ть) to send, forward, dispatch; о. на тот свет to send to kingdom come; о. есте́ственные потре́бности to relieve nature.

отпра́в|иться, люсь, ишься, *pf.* (*of* ~ля́ться) to set out, set off, start; to leave, depart; о. на боковую (*coll.*) to turn in, go to bed.

отпра́вк|а, и, *f.* sending off, forwarding, dispatch.

отправле́ни|е, я, *n.* **1.** sending. **2.** departure (*of trains, ships*). **3.** function (*of the organism*). **4.** exercise, performance; о. обя́занностей exercise of one's duties.

отправля́|ть, ю, *impf.* **1.** *impf. of* отпра́вить. **2.** (*impf. only*) to exercise, perform (*duties, functions*).

отправля́|ться, юсь, *impf.* **1.** *impf. of* отпра́виться. **2.** (*fig.*; от) to proceed (from).

отправн|о́й, *adj.* о. пункт, ~а́я то́чка starting-point.

отпра́здн|овать, ую, *pf. of* пра́здновать.

отпра́шива|ться, юсь, *impf.* (*of* отпроси́ться) to ask (for) leave.

отпресс|ова́ть, у́ю, *pf. of* прессова́ть.

отпро|си́ться, шу́сь, ~сишься, *pf.* (*of* отпра́шиваться) **1.** to ask (for) leave. **2.** to obtain leave.

отпры́гива|ть, ю, *impf. of* отпры́гнуть.

отпры́г|нуть, ну, нешь, *pf.* (*of* ~ивать) to jump back, spring back; to jump aside, spring aside; to bounce back.

о́тпрыск, а, *m.* (*bot. and fig.*) offshoot, scion.

отпряга́|ть, ю, *impf. of* отпря́чь.

отпря́дыва|ть, ю, *impf. of* отпря́нуть.

отпря́|нуть, ну, нешь, *pf.* (*of* ~дывать) to recoil, start back.

отпря́|чь, гу́, жёшь, гу́т, *past* ~г, ~гла́, *pf.* (*of* ~га́ть) to unharness.

отпу́гива|ть, ю, *impf. of* отпугну́ть.

отпуг|ну́ть, ну́, нёшь, *pf.* (*of* ~ивать) to frighten off, scare away.

о́тпуск, а, в ~е *or* **в ~у́,** *pl.* ~а́, ~о́в, *m.* **1.** leave, holiday(s); (*mil.*) leave, furlough; в ~е, в ~у́ on leave; о. по боле́зни sick-leave. **2.** issue, delivery, distribution. **3.** (*tech.*) tempering, drawing.

отпуска́|ть, ю, *impf. of* отпусти́ть.

отпускни́к, а́, *m.* person on leave, holiday-maker; soldier on leave.

отпускн|о́й, *adj.* **1.** *adj. of* о́тпуск 1; ~ы́е де́ньги holiday pay; ~о́е свиде́тельство authorization of leave (*of absence*); (*mil.*) leave pass. **2.** (*econ.*) ~а́я цена́ selling price.

отпу|сти́ть, щу́, ~стишь, *pf.* (*of* ~ска́ть) **1.** to let go, let off; to let out; to set free; to release; give leave (of absence); ~сти́ мою́ ру́ку! let go (of) my arm!; о. на пра́здник to release for the holiday; о. комплиме́нт (*coll.*) to make a compliment; о. шу́тку (*coll.*) to crack a joke. **2.** to relax, slacken; о. по́вод ло́шади to give a horse its head; боль ~сти́ло (*impers.*; *coll.*) the pain has eased. **3.** to (let) grow; о. (себе́) бо́роду to grow a beard. **4.** to issue, give out; (*in a shop, etc.*) to serve. **5.** to assign, allot. **6.** to remit; to forgive; о. кому́-н. грехи́ (*eccl.*) to give someone absolution. **7.** (*tech.*) to temper, draw (the temper of).

отпуще́ни|е, я, *n.* remission; о. грехо́в (*eccl.*) absolution; козёл ~я (*coll.*) scapegoat.

отпу́щенник, а, *m.* (*hist.*) freedman.

отраба́тыва|ть, ю, *impf. of* отрабо́тать.

отрабо́та|нный, p.p.p. of ~ть *and adj.* (*tech.*) worked out; waste, spent, exhaust; о. газ waste gas, exhaust gas.

отрабо́та|ть[1], ю, *pf.* (*of* отраба́тывать) **1.** to work off (*a debt, etc.*). **2.** (*coll.*) to work (a given *length of time*). **3.** to work through, give a work-out to.

отрабо́та|ть², ю, *pf.* to finish one's work.

отрабо́тк|а, и, *f.* working off, paying by work.

отрабо́точн|ый, *adj.* ~ая систе́ма statute labour, corvée.

отра́в|а, ы, *f.* poison; (*fig.*) bane.

отрави́тел|ь, я, *m.* poisoner.

отрав|и́ть, лю́, ~ишь, *pf.* (*of* ~ля́ть) to poison (*also fig.*).

отрав|и́ться, лю́сь, ~ишься, *pf.* (*of* ~ля́ться) **1.** to poison oneself. **2.** *pass. of* ~и́ть.

отравля́|ть(ся), ю(сь), *impf. of* отрави́ться.

отра́д|а, ы, *f.* joy, delight; comfort.

отра́дный, *adj.* gratifying, pleasing; comforting.

отража́тел|ь, я, *m.* **1.** (*phys.*) reflector; (*radar*) scanner. **2.** (*in fire-arm*) ejector.

отража́тельн|ый, *adj.* (*tech.*) reflecting, deflecting; ~ая засло́нка, о. лист, ~ая плита́ deflector (plate), baffle (plate); ~ая печь reverberatory furnace.

отража́|ть(ся), ю(сь), *impf. of* отрази́ть(ся).

отраже́ни|е, я, *n.* **1.** reflection; reverberation. **2.** repulse, parry; warding off.

отра|зи́ть, жу́, зи́шь, *pf.* (*of* ~жа́ть) **1.** to reflect (*also fig.*). **2.** to repulse, repel, parry; to ward off.

отра|зи́ться, жу́сь, зи́шься, *pf.* (*of* ~жа́ться) **1.** to be reflected; to reverberate. **2.** (*fig.*; на+*p.*) to affect; to tell (on); пое́здка в го́ры благоприя́тно ~зи́лась на его́ рабо́те the mountain trip had a beneficial effect on his work.

отрапорт|ова́ть, у́ю, *pf.* to report.

отраслев|о́й, *adj.* of о́трасль; ~о́е объедине́ние trade association of a branch of industry.

о́трасл|ь, и, *f.* (*obs. and fig.*) branch; о. дре́внего ро́да scion of an ancient line; о. промы́шленности branch of industry.

отраст|а́ть, а́ю, *impf. of* ~и́.

отраст|и́, у́, ёшь, *past* отро́с, отросла́, *pf.* (*of* ~а́ть) to grow.

отра|сти́ть, щу́, сти́шь, *pf.* (*of* ~щивать) to (let) grow; о. во́лосы to grow one's hair long; о. брю́хо (*coll.*) to develop a paunch.

отра́щива|ть, ю, *impf. of* отрасти́ть.

отре́бь|е, я, *n.* (*collect.*) **1.** (*obs.*) waste, refuse. **2.** (*fig.*) rabble.

отрегули́р|овать, ую, *pf.* (*tech.*) to regulate, adjust.

отредакти́р|овать, ую, *pf. of* редакти́ровать.

отре́з, а, *m.* **1.** cut; ли́ния ~а line of the cut; perforated line; (*on document, ticket, etc.*) 'tear off here'. **2.** length (*of material*); о. на пла́тье dress length.

отре́занность, и, *f.* (от) lack of communication (with), being cut off (from).

отрез|а́ть, а́ю, *impf. of* ~ать.

отре́|зать, жу, жешь, *pf.* (*of* ~за́ть) **1.** to cut off (*also fig.*); to divide, apportion (*land*); проти́вник ~зал нам отступле́ние the enemy had cut off our retreat. **2.** (*coll.*) to snap out.

отрезве́|ть, ю, *pf. of* трезве́ть.

отрезви́тельный, *adj.* sobering (*also fig.*).

отрезв|и́ть, лю́, и́шь, *pf.* (*of* ~ля́ть) to sober (*also fig.*).

отрезв|и́ться, лю́сь, и́шься, *pf.* (*of* ~ля́ться) to become sober, sober up.

отрезвле́ни|е, я, *n.* sobering (up).

отрезвля́|ть(ся), ю(сь), *impf. of* отрезви́ть(ся).

отрезно́й, *adj.* perforated; о. тало́н tear-off coupon.

отре́з|ок, ка, *m.* piece, cut; section; (*hist.*) portion (*of land*); (*math.*) segment; о. вре́мени space (*of time*).

отрека́|ться, юсь, *impf. of* отре́чься.

отрекоменд|ова́ть, у́ю, *pf.* to introduce.

отрекоменд|ова́ться, у́юсь, *pf.* to introduce oneself.

отремонти́р|овать, ую, *pf. of* ремонти́ровать.

отре́пь|е, я, (*pl.* ~я, ~ев), *n.* (*collect.*) rags; ходи́ть в о., в ~ях to be in rags.

отрече́ни|е, я, *n.* (от) renunciation (of); о. от престо́ла abdication.

отре́|чься, ку́сь, чёшься, ку́тся, *past* ~кся, ~кла́сь, *pf.* (*of* ~ка́ться) (от) to renounce, disavow, give up; о. от престо́ла to abdicate.

отреш|а́ть(ся), а́ю(сь), *impf. of* ~и́ть(ся).

отрешённост|ь, и, *f.* estrangement, aloofness.

отреш|и́ть, у́, и́шь, *pf.* (*of* ~а́ть) (от) to release (from); о. от до́лжности to dismiss, suspend.

отреш|и́ться, у́сь, и́шься, *pf.* (*of* ~а́ться) (от) to renounce, give up; я не мог о. от мы́сли I could not get rid of the idea.

отри́н|уть, у, ешь, *pf.* (*obs.*) to reject.

отрица́ни|е, я, *n.* denial; negation.

отрица́тел|ьный (~ен, ~ьна), *adj.* (*in var. senses*) negative; (*fig.*) bad, unfavourable; ~ьное электри́чество negative electricity; ~ьная сторона́ bad side, drawback.

отрица́|ть, ю, *impf.* to deny; to disclaim; о. вино́вность (*leg.*) to plead not guilty.

отро́г, а, *m.* (*geogr.*) spur.

о́троду, *adv.* (*coll.*) **1.** in age; ему́ пять лет о. he is five years old. **2.** не... о. never in one's life, never in one's born days; я о. не вида́л ничего́ подо́бного I have never seen the like

отро́дь|е, я, *n.* (*coll., pejor.*) race, breed; Ха́мово о. (*obs.*) hoi polloi.

отродя́сь, *adv.* (*coll.*) не… о. never in one's life, never in one's born days.

о́трок, а, *m.* boy, lad; adolescent.

отрокови́ц|а, ы, *f.* (*obs.*) girl, lass, maiden.

отро́ст|ок, ка, *m.* 1. (*bot.*) shoot, sprout. 2. (*tech.*) branch, extension. 3. (*anat.*) appendix.

о́трочеcкий, *adj.* adolescent.

о́трочеств|о, а, *n.* adolescence.

о́труб, а, *pl.* ~á, ~óв, *m.* (*hist.*) holding (*consolidated peasant small-holding, 1906–17*).

отру́б, а, *pl.* ~ы, ~ов, *m.* butt (*of tree*).

о́труб|и, éй, *no sing.* bran.

отруб|áть, áю, *impf. of* ~и́ть.

отруб|и́ть, лю́, ~ишь, *pf.* (*of* ~áть) 1. to chop off. 2. (*fig., coll.*) to snap back.

отрубнóй, *adj. of* о́труб.

о́труб|ный, *adj. of* ~и.

отруги́ва|ться, юсь, *impf.* (*coll.*) to return abuse.

отры́в, а, *m.* 1. tearing off. 2. (*fig.*) alienation, isolation; loss of contact, loss of communication; в ~е (от) out of touch (with); учи́ться без ~а от произвóдства to study while continuing (normal) work; о. от земли́ (*aeron.*) take-off; о. от проти́вника (*mil.*) disengagement.

отрывá|ть¹, ю, *impf. of* оторвáть.

отрывá|ть², ю, *impf. of* отры́ть.

отрывá|ться, юсь, *impf. of* оторвáться.

отры́вист|ый (~, ~а), *adj.* jerky, abrupt; curt.

отрывнóй, *adj.* perforated; о. календáрь tear-off calendar.

отры́в|ок, ка, *m.* fragment, excerpt; passage (*of book, etc.*).

отры́воч|ный (~ен, ~на), *adj.* fragmentary, scrappy.

отрыги́ва|ть, ю, *impf. of* отрыгнýть.

отры́г|нуть, нý, нёшь, *pf.* (*of* ~ивать) (+*a.* or *g.*) to belch.

отры́жк|а, и, *f.* 1. belch; belching, eructation. 2. (*fig.*) survival, throw-back.

отр|ы́ть, óю, óешь, *pf.* (*of* ~ывáть²) to dig out; to unearth (*also fig.*).

отря́д, а, *m.* 1. detachment; передовóй о. (*fig.*) vanguard. 2. (*biol.*) order.

отря|ди́ть, жý, ди́шь, *pf.* (*of* ~жáть) to detach, detail, tell off.

отряжá|ть, ю, *impf. of* отряди́ть.

отряс|áть, áю, *impf. of* ~ти́.

отряс|ти́, ý, ёшь, *past* ~, ~лá, *pf.* (*of* ~áть) (*obs.*) to shake off; о. прах от свои́х ног (*fig.*) to shake off the dust from one's feet.

отря́хива|ть(ся), ю(сь), *impf. of* отряхнýть(ся).

отрях|нýть, нý, нёшь, *pf.* (*of* ~ивать) to shake down, shake off; о. снег с воротникá to shake snow off one's collar.

отрях|нýться, нýсь, нёшься, *pf.* (*of* ~ивáться) to shake oneself down.

отса|ди́ть, жý, ~дишь, *pf.* (*of* ~живать) 1. (*hort.*) to transplant, plant out. 2. to seat apart. 3. (*tech.*) to jig.

отсáдк|а, и, *f.* 1. (*hort.*) transplanting, planting out. 2. (*tech.*) jigging.

отсáжива|ть, ю, *impf. of* отсади́ть.

отсáжива|ться, юсь, *impf. of* отсéсть.

отсалют|овáть, ýю, *pf. of* салютовáть.

отсáсывани|е, я, *n.* suction.

отсáсыватель, я, *m.* suction pump.

отсáсыва|ть, ю, *impf. of* отсосáть.

отсвéт, а, *m.* reflection; reflected light.

отсвéчива|ть, ю, *impf.* 1. to be reflected; (+*i.*) to shine (with); в кóмнате ~л с ýлицы фонáрь the light of the street-lamp was reflected in the room. 2. (*coll.*) to stand (be) in the light.

отсебя́тин|а, ы, *f.* (*coll.*) words of one's own; something of one's own devising; (*theatr.*) ad-libbing.

отсéв, а, *m.* 1. sifting, selection. 2. siftings, residue.

отсевá|ть, ю = отсéивать.

отсéива|ть(ся), ю(сь), *impf. of* отсéять(ся).

отсéк, а, *m.* 1. (*naut., etc.*) compartment. 2. (*astronautics*) module.

отсекá|ть, ю, *impf. of* отсéчь.

отсéле, *adv.* (*obs.*) hence, from here.

отсел|и́ть, ю́, и́шь, *pf.* (*of* ~я́ть) to settle out, move further out.

отсел|и́ться, ю́сь, и́шься, *pf.* (*of* ~я́ться) to settle out, move further out.

отсéл|ь = ~е.

отсел|я́ть(ся), я́ю(сь), *impf. of* ~и́ть(ся).

отс|éсть, я́ду, я́дешь, *past* ~éл, *pf.* (*of* ~áживаться) to seat oneself apart; (от) to move away (from).

отсечéни|е, я, *n.* cutting off, severance; дать гóлову на о. (*coll.*) to stake one's life.

отсéчк|а, и, *f.* (*tech.*) cut-off.

отсé|чь, кý, чёшь, кýт, *past* ~к, ~клá, *pf.* (*of* ~кáть) to cut off, chop off, sever.

отсé|ять, ю, ешь, *pf.* (*of* ~ивать) 1. to sift, screen. 2. (*fig.*) to eliminate.

отсé|яться, юсь, ешься, *pf.* (*of* ~иваться) 1. *pass. of* ~ять. 2. (*fig.*) to fall off, fall away; бóльшая часть слýшателей ~ялась the greater part of the audience had fallen away.

отси|дéть, жý, ди́шь, *pf.* (*of* ~живать) 1. to stay (for); to sit out; он ~дéл дéсять лет в тюрьмé he has done ten years (in prison). 2. to make numb by sitting; я ~дéл себé нóгу I have pins and needles in my leg.

отси|дéться, жýсь, ди́шься, *pf.* (*of* ~живаться) (*coll.*) to sit out (a siege); (*fig., pejor.*) to sit on the fence.

отси́жива|ть(ся), ю(сь), *impf. of* отсиде́ть-
(ся).

отска́блива|ть, ю, *impf. of* отскобли́ть.

отска|ка́ть, чу́, ~чешь, *pf.* (*coll.*) to gallop,
cover by galloping.

отска́кива|ть, ю, *impf. of* отскочи́ть.

отскобл|и́ть, ю́, ~ишь, *pf.* (*of* отска́бли-
вать) to scratch off.

отскоч|и́ть, у́, ~ишь, *pf.* (*of* отска́кивать)
1. to jump aside, jump away; to rebound,
bounce back. **2.** (*coll.*) to come off, break
off.

отскреба́|ть, ю, *impf. of* отскрести́.

отскре|сти́, бу́, бёшь, *past* ~б, ~бла́, *pf.* (*of*
~ба́ть) to scrape off, scratch off.

отсла́ива|ться, ется, *impf. of* отслои́ться.

отслое́ни|е, я, *n.* (*geol.*) exfoliation.

отсло|и́ться, и́тся, *pf.* (*of* отсла́иваться)
(*geol.*) to exfoliate, to scale off.

отслу́жива|ть, ю, *impf.* отслужи́ть.

отслуж|и́ть, у́, ~ишь, *pf.* (*of* ~ивать) **1.** to
serve; to serve one's time. **2.** (*coll.*) (*of implements, etc.*) to have served its turn, be
worn out. **3.** (*eccl.*) to finish (*a service*).

отсове́т|овать, ую, *pf.* (+*d. and inf.*) to dis-
suade (from).

отсортир|ова́ть, у́ю, *pf.* (*of* ~о́вывать) to
sort (out).

отсортиро́выва|ть, ю, *impf. of* отсортиро-
ва́ть.

отсос|а́ть, у́, ёшь, *pf.* (*of* отса́сывать) (+*a.
or g.*) to suck off, draw off; to filter by suction.

отсо́х|нуть, нет, *past* ~, ~ла, *pf.* (*of* отсы-
ха́ть) to dry up; to wither.

отсро́чива|ть, ю, *impf. of* отсро́чить.

отсро́ч|ить, у, ишь, *pf.* (*of* ~ивать) **1.** to
postpone, delay, defer; (*leg.*) to adjourn.
2. (*coll.*) to extend (*period of validity of a document*).

отсро́чк|а, и, *f.* **1.** postponement, delay, de-
ferment; (*leg.*) adjournment; о. наказа́ния
respite; дать ме́сячную ~у to grant a
month's grace. **2.** (*coll.*) extension (*of period
of validity of document*).

отстава́ни|е, я, *n.* lag.

отста|ва́ть, ю́, ёшь, *impf. of* ~ть.

отста́в|ить, лю, ишь, *pf.* (*of* ~ля́ть) **1.** to set
aside, put aside. **2.** (*obs.*) to dismiss, discharge. **3.** (*coll.*) to rescind; о.! (*mil. word
of command*) as you were!

отста́вк|а, и, *f.* **1.** dismissal, discharge;
получи́ть ~у у кого́-н. to be dismissed by
someone, get the sack from someone. **2.**
resignation; retirement; вы́йти в ~у to
resign, retire; пода́ть в ~у to send in
one's resignation; в ~е retired, in retirement.

отставля́|ть, ю, *impf. of* отста́вить.

отставно́й, *adj.* retired.

отста́ива|ть, ю, *impf.* **1.** *impf. of* отстоя́ть¹.
2. to fight, dispute; to try to vindicate;
мы бу́дем о. на́шу то́чку зре́ния we shall
dispute our point of view.

отста́ива|ться, юсь, *impf. of* отстоя́ться.

отста́лост|ь, и, *f.* (*fig.*) backwardness.

отста́лый, *adj.* (*fig.*) backward.

отста́|ть, ну, нешь, *pf.* (*of* ~ва́ть) **1.** (от)
to fall behind, drop behind; to lag behind;
(*fig.*) to be backward, be retarded; to be
behind, be behindhand; о. в рабо́те to be
behind in (with) one's work; о. от кла́сса
to be behind (the rest of) one's class; ещё
в нача́льной шко́ле он о́чень ~л even in
primary school he was very backward; о.
от ве́ка, о. от совреме́нности to be behind
the times. **2.** (от) to be left behind (by),
become detached (from); о. от гру́ппы to
become detached from a group; о. от
по́езда to be left behind by the train (*sc. at
a station en route*). **3.** (от) to lose touch (with);
to break (with); я ~л от всех свои́х знако́-
мых вое́нного вре́мени I have lost touch
with all my war-time acquaintances. **4.**
(*coll.*; от) to give up; о. от привы́чки to
break oneself of a habit. **5.** (*of a clock or
watch*) to be slow; о. на полчаса́ to be half
an hour slow. **6.** (*of plaster, wall-paper, etc.*)
to come off. **7.** (*coll.*; от) to leave alone;
~нь от меня́! leave me alone!

отстега́|ть, ю, *pf.* (*of* стега́ть¹) to beat, lash.

отстёгива|ть(ся), ю(сь), *impf. of* отстег-
ну́ть(ся).

отстег|ну́ть, ну́, нёшь, *pf.* (*of* ~ивать) to
unfasten, undo; to unbutton.

отстег|ну́ться, нётся, *pf.* (*of* ~иваться) to
come unfastened, come undone.

отстир|а́ть, а́ю, *pf.* (*of* ~ывать) to wash off.

отстир|а́ться, а́юсь, *pf.* (*of* ~ываться) to
wash off, come out in the wash.

отсти́рыва|ть(ся), ю(сь), *impf. of* отсти-
ра́ть(ся).

отсто́|й, я, *m.* sediment, deposit.

отсто́йник, а, *m.* settling tank; sedimenta-
tion tank; cesspool.

отсто|я́ть¹, ю́, и́шь, *pf.* (*of* отста́ивать) to
defend, save; to stand up for; о. свои́
права́ to assert one's rights.

отсто|я́ть², ю́, и́шь, *pf.* to stand through,
stand out; мы ~я́ли весь спекта́кль we
stood through the entire show.

отсто|я́ть³, ю́, и́шь, *impf.* (от) to be ... dis-
tant (from); ста́нция ~и́т от це́нтра го́рода
на два киломе́тра the station is two kilometres (away) from the centre of the town;
э́ти дере́вни ~я́т друг от дру́га на пять
вёрст these villages are five versts apart.

отсто|я́ться, и́тся, *pf.* (*of* отста́иваться)
1. (*chem.*) to settle, precipitate. **2.** (*fig.*) to
settle, become stabilized, become fixed.

отстра́ива|ть(ся), ю(сь), *impf. of* отстро́ить-(ся).

отстране́ни|е, я, *n.* **1.** pushing aside. **2.** dismissal, discharge.

отстран|и́ть, ю́, и́шь, *pf.* (*of* ~я́ть) **1.** to push aside; о. от себя́ все забо́ты to lay aside all one's cares. **2.** to dismiss, discharge.

отстран|и́ться, ю́сь, и́шься, *pf.* (*of* ~я́ться) **1.** (от) to move away (from); (*fig.*) to keep out of the way (of), keep aloof (from); о. от уда́ра to dodge a blow; о. от до́лжности to relinquish a post. **2.** *pass. of* ~и́ть.

отстран|я́ть(ся), я́ю(сь), *impf. of* ~и́ть(ся).

отстре́лива|ть[1], ю, *impf. of* отстрели́ть.

отстре́лива|ть[2], ю, *impf. of* отстреля́ть.

отстре́лива|ться, юсь, *impf. of* отстреля́ть-ся[1].

отстрел|и́ть, ю́, ~ишь, *pf.* (*of* ~ивать[1]) to shoot off.

отстрел|я́ть, я́ю, *pf.* (*of* ~ивать[2]) to shoot (*for commercial purposes, etc.*).

отстрел|я́ться[1], я́юсь, *pf.* (*of* ~иваться) **1.** to defend oneself (by shooting). **2.** to return fire, fire back.

отстрел|я́ться[2], я́юсь, *pf.* to have finished firing; to have completed a practice (shoot).

отстрига́|ть, ю, *impf. of* отстри́чь.

отстри́|женный, *p.p.p. of* ~чь.

отстри́|чь, гу́, жёшь, гу́т, *past* ~г, ~гла, *pf.* (*of* ~га́ть) to cut off, clip.

отстр|о́ить[1], о́ю, о́ишь, *pf.* (*of* ~а́ивать) to complete construction (of), finish building; to build up.

отстр|о́ить[2], о́ю, о́ишь, *pf.* (*of* ~а́ивать) (*radio*) to tune out, reject (*interfering wavelength*).

отстр|о́иться[1], о́юсь, о́ишься, *pf.* (*of* ~а́иваться) (*coll.*) **1.** to finish building. **2.** *pass. of* ~о́ить[1].

отстр|о́иться[2], о́юсь, о́ишься, *pf.* (*of* ~а́иваться) (*radio*) to tune out (*adjust receiver so as to avoid interference*).

отстро́йк|а, и, *f.* (*radio*) tuning out.

отстук|ать, аю, *pf.* (*of* ~ивать) (*coll.*) to tap out; о. мело́дию to strum a tune; о. на маши́нке to bash out on a typewriter.

отсту́кива|ть, ю, *impf. of* отсту́кать.

о́тступ, а, *m.* (*typ.*) break off, indention.

отступа́тельный, *adj.* (*mil.*) retreat, withdrawal.

отступ|а́ть(ся), а́ю(сь), *impf. of* ~и́ть(ся).

отступ|и́ть, лю́, ~ишь, *pf.* (*of* ~а́ть) **1.** to step back; to recede. **2.** (*mil.*) to retreat, fall back. **3.** (*fig.*) to back down; (от) to go back (on); to give up; о. от реше́ния to go back on a decision. **4.** (*fig.*; от) to swerve (from), deviate (from); о. от обы́чая to depart from custom; о. от те́мы to digress. **5.** (*typ.*) to indent.

отступ|и́ться, лю́сь, ~ишься, *pf.* (*of* ~а́ть-ся) (*coll.*; от) to give up, renounce; о. от своего́ сло́ва to go back on one's word; они́ все ~и́лись от него́ they have all given him up.

отступле́ни|е, я, *n.* **1.** (*mil. and fig.*) retreat. **2.** deviation; digression.

отсту́пник, а, *m.* apostate; recreant.

отсту́пничеств|о, а, *n.* apostasy.

отступн|о́й, *adj.* ~ые де́ньги (*or as noun* ~о́е, ~о́го, *n.*) smart-money; indemnity, compensation.

отступ|я́, *ger. of* ~и́ть; *as adv.* (от) off, away (from); о. два-три ме́тра two or three metres off; немно́го о. от до́ма a little way away from the house.

отсу́тстви|е, я, *n.* absence; (+*g.*) lack (of); в его́ о. in his absence; за ~ем (+*g.*) in the absence (of); for lack (of), for want (of); находи́ться в ~и to be absent; блиста́ть свои́м ~ем to be conspicuous by one's absence.

отсу́тств|овать, ую, *impf.* to be absent; (*leg.*) to default.

отсу́тств|ующий, *pres. part. of* ~овать *and adj.* absent (*also fig.*); о. вид blank expression; *as noun* о., ~ующего, *m.* absentee; ~ующие those absent.

отсу́чива|ть, ю, *impf. of* отсучи́ть.

отсуч|и́ть, у́, ~ишь, *pf.* (*of* ~ивать) (*coll.*; рукава́, *etc.*) to unroll, roll down (sleeves, *etc.*).

отсчёт, а, *m.* reading (*on an instrument*).

отсчит|а́ть, а́ю, *pf.* (*of* ~ывать) **1.** to count out, count off; о. пять шаго́в от до́ма to count five paces from the house; о. кому́-н. де́сять рубле́й to count out ten roubles to someone. **2.** to read off, take a reading.

отсчи́тыва|ть, ю, *impf. of* отсчита́ть.

отсыла́|ть, ю, *impf. of* отосла́ть.

отсы́лк|а, и, *f.* 1. dispatch; о. де́нег remittance. **2.** reference.

отсы́п|ать, лю, лешь, *pf.* (*of* ~а́ть) (+*a. or g.*) to pour off; to measure off.

отсып|а́ть, а́ю, *impf. of* ~ать.

отсы́п|аться, люсь, лешься, *pf.* (*of* ~а́ться[1]) **1.** to pour out. **2.** *pass. of* ~ать.

отсып|а́ться[1], а́юсь, *impf. of* ~аться.

отсып|а́ться[2], а́юсь, *impf. of* отоспа́ться.

отсыре́лый, *adj.* damp.

отсыре́|ть, ю, *pf. of* сыре́ть.

отсыха́|ть, ю, *impf. of* отсо́хнуть.

отсю́да, *adv.* from here; hence (*also fig.*); (*fig.*) from this; о. сле́дует, что... from this it follows that . . . .

отта́ива|ть, ю, *impf. of* отта́ять.

отта́лкивани|е, я, *n.* (*phys.*) repulsion.

отта́лкива|ть, ю, *impf. of* оттолкну́ть.

отта́лкива|ющий, *pres. part. act. of* ~ть *and adj.* repulsive, repellent.

отта́птыва|ть, ю, *impf. of* оттопта́ть.

оттаска́|ть, ю, *pf.* (*of* таска́ть 2.) to pull; о. кого́-н. за́ во́лосы to pull someone's hair.

отта́скива|ть, ю, *impf. of* оттащи́ть.

отта́чива|ть, ю, *impf. of* отточи́ть.

оттащ|и́ть, у́, ~ишь, *pf.* (*of* отта́скивать) to drag aside (away), pull aside (away).

отта́|ять, ю, ешь, *pf.* (*of* ~ивать) (*trans. and intrans.*) to thaw out.

оттен|и́ть, ю́, и́шь, *pf.* (*of* ~я́ть) 1. to shade (in). 2. (*fig.*) to set off, make more prominent.

оттён|ок, ка, *m.* shade, nuance (*also fig.*); tint, hue; о. значе́ния shade of meaning; он говори́л с ~ком иро́нии there was a note of irony in his voice.

оттен|я́ть, я́ю, *impf. of* ~и́ть.

о́ттепел|ь, и, *f.* thaw.

оттер|е́ть, ототру́, ототрёшь, *past* ~, ~ла, *pf.* (*of* оттира́ть) 1. to rub off, rub out. 2. to restore sensation (*to parts of the body*) by rubbing. 3. (*coll.*) to press back, push aside.

оттер|е́ться, ототру́сь, ототрёшься, *past* ~ся, ~лась, *pf.* (*of* оттира́ться) to rub out; to come out (*by rubbing*).

оттесн|и́ть, ю́, и́шь, *pf.* (*of* ~я́ть) to drive back, press back; to push aside, shove aside (*also fig.*); о. проти́вника (*mil.*) to force the enemy back; о. конкуре́нта (*fig.*) to edge a competitor out.

оттесн|я́ть, я́ю, *impf. of* ~и́ть.

о́ттиск, а, *m.* 1. impression. 2. off-print, separate.

отти́скива|ть, ю, *impf. of* отти́снуть.

отти́с|нуть, ну, нешь, *pf.* (*of* ~кивать) 1. (*coll.*) to push aside. 2. (*coll.*) to crush. 3. to print.

оттого́, *adv.* that is why; о. мы и не могли́ прие́хать that's why we couldn't come; о... что because; я о. опозда́л, что мото́р не заводи́лся I was late because the engine would not start.

отто́ле, *adv.* (*obs.*) thence, from there.

оттолкн|у́ть, у́, ёшь, *pf.* (*of* отта́лкивать) 1. to push away, push aside. 2. (*fig.*) to antagonize, alienate.

оттолкн|у́ться, у́сь, ёшься, *pf.* (*of* отта́лкиваться) 1. (от) to push off (from). 2. (*fig.*; от) to dispense (with), discard.

отто́л|ь = ~е.

оттома́нк|а, и, *f.* ottoman.

оттоп|та́ть, чу́, ~чешь, *pf.* (*of* отта́птывать) (*coll.*) 1. to hurt, damage (*by much walking*). 2. о. кому́-н. но́гу to tread (heavily) on someone's foot.

оттопы́р|енный, *p.p.p. of* ~ить *and adj.* protruding, sticking out.

оттопы́рива|ть(ся), ю(сь), *impf. of* оттопы́рить(ся).

оттопы́р|ить, ю, ишь, *pf.* (*of* ~ивать) (*coll.*) to stick out; о. ло́кти to stick out one's elbows.

оттопы́р|иться, ится, *pf.* (*of* ~иваться) to protrude, stick out; to bulge.

отторг|а́ть, а́ю, *impf. of* ~нуть.

отто́рг|нуть, ну, нешь, *past* ~, ~ла, *pf.* (*of* ~а́ть) to tear away, seize.

отторже́ни|е, я, *n.* tearing away; (*med.*) rejection (*of a transplanted organ*).

отточ|и́ть, у́, ~ишь, *pf.* (*of* отта́чивать) to sharpen, whet.

отту́да, *adv.* from there.

оттуш|ева́ть, у́ю, у́ешь, *pf.* (*of* ~ёвывать) to shade (off).

оттушёвыва|ть, ю, *impf. of* оттушева́ть.

оттяга́|ть, ю, *pf.* (*coll.*) to gain by a lawsuit.

оття́гива|ть, ю, *impf. of* оттяну́ть.

оття́жк|а, и, *f.* 1. delay, procrastination. 2. (*naut.*) guy(-rope); strut, brace, stay.

оття|ну́ть, ну́, ~нешь, *pf.* (*of* ~гивать) 1. to draw out, pull away. 2. (*mil.*) to draw off. 3. (*coll.*) to delay; что́бы о. вре́мя to gain time. 4. (*tech.*) to forge out.

оття́п|ать, аю, *pf.* (*of* ~ывать) (*coll.*) to chop off.

оття́пыва|ть, ю, *impf. of* оття́пать.

оту́жина|ть, ю, *pf.* 1. to have had supper. 2. (*obs.*) to have supper.

отума́нива|ть, ю, *impf. of* отума́нить.

отума́н|ить, ю, ишь, *pf.* (*of* ~ивать) 1. to blur; to dim; её глаза́ ~ило слеза́ми her eyes were dimmed with tears. 2. (*fig.*) to (be)cloud, obscure; моё созна́ние ~ило вино́м wine had clouded my reason.

отупе́лый, *adj.* (*coll.*) stupefied, dulled.

отупе́ни|е, я, *n.* stupefaction, dullness, torpor.

отупе́|ть, ю, *pf.* (*coll.*) to grow dull, sink into torpor.

отутю́жива|ть, ю, *impf. of* отутю́жить.

отутю́ж|ить, у, ишь, *pf.* (*of* ~ивать) 1. to iron (out). 2. (*fig., coll.*) to beat up.

отуч|а́ть(ся), а́ю(сь), *impf. of* ~и́ть(ся).

оту́чива|ться, юсь, *impf. of* отучи́ться[2].

отуч|и́ть, у́, ~ишь, *pf.* (*of* ~а́ть) (от *or* +*inf.*) to break (of); о. от груди́ to wean.

отуч|и́ться[1], у́сь, ~ишься, *pf.* (*of* ~а́ться) (от *or* +*inf.*) to break oneself (of).

отуч|и́ться[2], у́сь, ~ишься, *pf.* (*of* ~ива́ться) to have finished one's lessons; to finish learning.

отха́жива|ть, ю, *impf. of* отходи́ть[2, 3].

отха́рк|ать, аю, *pf.* (*of* ~ивать) to expectorate.

отха́ркива|ть, ю, *impf. of* отха́ркать.

отха́ркива|ться, юсь, *impf. of* отха́ркнуться.

отха́ркива|ющий, *pres. part. act. of* ~ть; ~ющее (сре́дство) (*med.*) expectorant.

отха́ркн|уть, у, ешь, *pf.* to hawk up.

отха́рк|нуться, нусь, нешься, *pf.* (*of* ~и-
ваться) **1.** (*coll.*) to clear one's throat. **2.** to
come up (*as result of expectoration*).

отхва|ти́ть, чу́, ~тишь, *pf.* (*of* ~тывать)
(*coll.*) **1.** to snip off; to chop off; он ~ти́л
себе́ па́лец топоро́м he chopped his finger
off with an axe. **2.** to perform, execute in
lively fashion.

отхва́тыва|ть, ю, *impf. of* отхвати́ть.

отхлеб|ну́ть, ну́, нёшь, *pf.* (*of* ~ывать)
(*coll.*; +*a. or g.*) to take a sip (of); to take a
mouthful (of).

отхлёбыва|ть, ю, *impf. of* отхлебну́ть.

отхле|ста́ть, щу́, ~щешь, *pf.* (*coll.*) to give
a lashing.

отхлы́н|уть, у, ешь, *pf.* to rush back, flood
back (*also fig.*).

отхо́д, а, *m.* **1.** departure; sailing. **2.** (*mil.*)
withdrawal, retirement, falling back. **3.**
(от) deviation (from); break (with). **4.** *see*
~ы.

отхо|ди́ть¹, жу́, ~ди́шь, *impf. of* отойти́.

отхо|ди́ть², жу́, ~ди́шь, *pf.* (*of* отха́живать)
(*coll.*) to cure, heal, nurse back to health.

отхо|ди́ть³, жу́, ~ди́шь, *pf.* (*of* отха́живать)
(*coll.*) to tire, hurt (*by walking*).

отхо́дн|ая, ой, *f.* prayer for the dying;
справля́ть ~ую кому́-н. (*fig.*) to write someone off.

отхо́дник, а, *m.* (*obs.*) seasonal worker (*esp.
of peasants going to cities*).

отхо́дничеств|о, а, *n.* (*obs.*) seasonal work.

отхо́дчив|ый (~, ~а), *adj.* not bearing
grudges.

отхо́д|ы, ов (*tech.*) waste (products); siftings,
screenings; tailings.

отхо́|женный, *p.p.p. of* ~ди́ть³; но́ги у меня́
~жены I have been walked off my feet.

отхо́ж|ий, *adj.* о. про́мысел seasonal work;
~ее ме́сто (*coll.*) latrine, earth closet.

отцве|сти́, ту́, тёшь, *past* ~л, ~ла́, *pf.* (*of*
~та́ть) to finish·blossoming, fade (*also fig.*);
она́ ~ла́ she has lost her bloom.

отцве|та́ть, та́ю, *impf. of* ~сти́.

отце|ди́ть, жу́, ~ди́шь, *pf.* (*of* ~живать) to
strain off, filter.

отце́жива|ть, ю, *impf. of* отцеди́ть.

отцеп|и́ть, лю́, ~ишь, *pf.* (*of* ~ля́ть) to un-
hook; to uncouple.

отцеп|и́ться, лю́сь, ~ишься, *pf.* (*of* ~ля́ть-
ся) **1.** to come unhooked; to come uncoupled. **2.** (*fig., coll.*) to leave alone; ~и́сь
ты от меня́! leave me alone!

отце́пк|а, и, *f.* (*railways*) uncoupling.

отцепля́|ть(ся), ю(сь), *impf. of* отцепи́ть-
(ся).

отцеуби́йств|о, а, *n.* parricide, patricide
(*act*).

отцеуби́йц|а, ы, *m. and f.* parricide, patri-
cide (*agent*).

отцо́в, *adj.* one's father's.

отцо́вск|ий, *adj.* one's father's; paternal;
~ое насле́дие patrimony.

отцо́вств|о, а, *n.* paternity.

отча́ива|ться, юсь, *impf. of* отча́яться.

отча́лива|ть, ю, *impf. of* отча́лить; ~й!
(*coll.*) be off!

отча́л|ить, ю, ишь, *pf.* (*of* ~ивать) (*naut.*)
1. to cast off. **2.** (*intrans.*) to push off, cast off.

отча́сти, *adv.* partly.

отча́яни|е, я, *n.* despair.

отча́ян|ный (~, ~на), *adj.* despairing; (*fig.,
coll.; in var. senses*) desperate; о. взор despair-
ing look; о. дура́к (*coll.*) awful fool; о. игро́к
desperate gambler; ~ное положе́ние desperate plight.

отча́|яться, юсь, ешься, *pf.* (*of* ~иваться)
(+*inf. or* в+*p.*) to despair (of).

о́тче (*obs.*) *voc. of* оте́ц; О. наш our Father
(*the Lord's prayer*).

отчего́, *adv.* why; вот о. that's why.

отчего́-либо, *adv.* for some reason or other.

отчего́-то, *adv.* for some reason.

отчека́нива|ть, ю, *impf. of* отчека́нить.

отчека́н|ить, ю, ишь, *pf.* (*of* чека́нить *and*
~ивать) **1.** to coin, mint. **2.** (*fig.*) to execute clearly and distinctly; о. слова́ to rap
out (one's words).

отчёркива|ть, ю, *impf. of* отчеркну́ть.

отчерк|ну́ть, ну́, нёшь, *pf.* (*of* ~ивать) to
mark off.

отчерп|ну́ть, ну́, нёшь, *pf.* (*of* ~ывать)
(+*a. or g.*) to ladle out.

отче́рпыва|ть, ю, *impf. of* отчерпну́ть.

о́тчеств|о, а, *n.* patronymic; как его́ по ~у?
what is his patronymic?

отчёт, а, *m.* account; дать о. (в+*p.*) to give
an account (of), report (on); взять де́ньги
под о. to take money on account; отда́ть
себе́ о. (в+*p.*) to be aware (of), realize.

отчётливост|ь, и, *f.* **1.** distinctness; preci-
sion. **2.** intelligibility, clarity.

отчётлив|ый (~, ~а), *adj.* **1.** distinct; pre-
cise. **2.** intelligible, clear.

отчётно-вы́борн|ый, *adj.* ~ое собра́ние
meeting held to hear reports and elect new
officials.

отчётност|ь, и, *f.* **1.** book-keeping. **2.** ac-
counts.

отчёт|ный, *adj. of* ~; о. бланк report card;
о. год financial year, current year; о. док-
ла́д report.

отчи́зн|а, ы, *f.* (*poet.*) one's country, native
land; mother country, fatherland.

о́тчий, *adj.* (*obs., poet.*) paternal.

о́тчим, а, *m.* step-father.

о́тчин|а, ы, *f.* = во́тчина.

отчисле́ни|е, я, *n.* **1.** deduction. **2.** assign-
ment. **3.** dismissal.

отчи́сл|ить, ю, ишь, *pf.* (*of* ~я́ть) **1.** to de-

duct; o. часть зарпла́ты в упла́ту подохо́д-
ного нало́га to deduct part of wages for
income-tax payment. **2.** to assign. **3.** to
dismiss; o. в запа́с (*mil.*) to transfer to the
reserve.

отчисл|я́ть, я́ю, *impf. of* ~и́ть.

отчи́|стить, щу, стишь, *pf.* (*of* ~ща́ть) **1.** to
clean off; to brush off. **2.** to clean up.

отчи́|ститься, щусь, стишься, *pf.* (*of*
~ща́ться) **1.** to come off, come out. **2.** to
become clean.

отчит|а́ть, а́ю, *pf.* (*of* ~ывать) (*coll.*) to read
a lecture (to), tell off.

отчит|а́ться, а́юсь, *pf.* (*of* ~ываться) (в+*p.*)
to give an account (of), report (on); o.
пе́ред избира́телями to report back to the
electors.

отчи́тыва|ть(ся), ю(сь), *impf. of* отчита́ть-
(ся).

отчища́|ть(ся), ю(сь), *impf. of* отчи́стить-
(ся).

отчу|ди́ть, жу́, ди́шь, *pf.* (*of* ~жда́ть) (*leg.*)
to alienate, estrange.

отчужда́|емый, *pres. part. pass. of* ~ть *and*
adj. (*leg.*) alienable.

отчужда́|ть, ю, *impf. of* отчуди́ть.

отчужде́ни|е, я, *n.* **1.** (*leg.*) alienation. **2.**
estrangement.

отчуждённост|ь, и, *f.* estrangement.

отшага́|ть, ю, *pf.* (*coll.*) to walk; to tramp;
to trudge.

отшагн|у́ть, у́, ёшь, *pf.* (*coll.*) to step aside,
step back.

отшатн|у́ться, у́сь, ёшься, *pf.* (от) **1.** to
start back (from); to recoil (from). **2.** (*fig.*)
to give up; to forsake; to break (with); o.
от дру́га to give up a friend.

отшвы́рива|ть, ю, *impf. of* отшвырну́ть.

отшвыр|ну́ть, ну́, нёшь, *pf.* (*of* ~ивать) to
fling away; to throw off.

отше́льник, а, *m.* hermit, anchorite; (*fig.*)
recluse.

отше́льни|ческий, *adj. of* ~к.

отше́льничеств|о, а, *n.* a hermit's life, a
recluse's life (*also fig., iron.*).

отши́б, а, *m. only in phrase* на ~е at a distance (*from a settlement*); жить на ~е (*fig.*)
to live in seclusion, live a recluse's life.

отшиб|а́ть, а́ю, *impf. of* ~и́ть.

отшиб|и́ть, у́, ёшь, *past* ~, ~ла, *pf.* (*of* ~а́ть)
(*coll.*) **1.** to break off; to knock off; o. ру́чку
у ча́йника to knock the handle off a tea-
pot; у меня́ ~ло па́мять my memory has
failed me. **2.** to hurt; o. себе́ ру́ку to
hurt one's arm. **3.** to throw back.

отши́ть, отошью́, отошьёшь, *pf.* (*coll.*) to
snub, rebuff.

отшлёп|ать, аю, *pf.* (*of* ~ывать) (*coll.*) to
spank.

отшлёпыва|ть, ю, *impf. of* отшлёпать.

отшлиф|ова́ть, у́ю, *pf.* (*of* ~о́вывать) to
grind; to polish (*also fig.*).

отшпи́лива|ть(ся), ю(сь), *impf. of* отшпи́-
лить(ся).

отшпи́л|ить, ю, ишь, *pf.* (*of* ~ивать) to un-
pin, unfasten.

отшпи́л|иться, юсь, ишься, *pf.* (*of* ~ивать-
ся) to come unpinned, come unfastened.

отштукату́р|ить, ю, ишь, *pf. of* штукату́-
рить.

отшу|ти́ться, чу́сь, ~тишься, *pf.* (*of* ~чи-
ваться) to laugh off; to make a joke in reply.

отшу́чива|ться, юсь, *impf. of* отшути́ться.

отщелка́|ть, ю, *pf.* (*coll.*) to slang.

отщепе́н|ец, ца, *m.* renegade.

отщеп|и́ть, лю́, и́шь, *pf.* (*of* ~ля́ть) to chip
off.

отщепля́|ть, ю, *impf. of* отщепи́ть.

отщип|а́ть, лю́, ~лешь, *pf.* (*of* ~ывать) to
pinch off, nip off.

отщи́пыва|ть, ю, *impf. of* отщипа́ть.

отъеда́|ть(ся), ю(сь), *impf. of* отъе́сть(ся).

отъе́зд, а, *m.* departure.

отъе́з|дить, жу, дишь, *pf.* (*coll.*) to have
driven; to have covered (*driving, riding*).

отъезжа́|ть, ю, *impf. of* отъе́хать.

отъезжа́|ющий, *pres. part. of* ~ть; *as noun* **o.,**
~ющего, *m.* departing person.

отъе́зжий, *adj.* (*obs.*) distant.

отъёмный, *adj.* removable, detachable.

отъе́|сть, м, шь, ст, ди́м, ди́те, дя́т, *past*
~л, ~ла, *pf.* (*of* ~да́ть) to eat off.

**отъе́|сться, мся, шься, стся, ди́мся, ди-
тесь, дя́тся,** *past* ~лся, ~лась, *pf.* (*of*
~да́ться) to put on weight; to feed well.

отъе́|хать, ду, дешь, *pf.* (*of* ~зжа́ть) to
drive off.

отъя́вленный, *adj.* (*coll. pejor.*) thorough,
inveterate, out-and-out.

от|ъя́ть, иму́, и́мешь, *pf.* (*obs.*) = ~ня́ть.

отыгр|а́ть, а́ю, *pf.* (*of* ~ывать) to win back.

отыгр|а́ться, а́юсь, *pf.* (*of* ~ываться) **1.** to
win back, get back what one has lost. **2.**
(*fig., coll.*) to get out (*of an awkward situation*).

оты́грыва|ть(ся), ю(сь), *impf. of* отыгра́ть-
(ся).

о́тыгрыш, а, *m.* sum won back.

отымённый, *adj.* (*ling.*) denominative.

оты|ска́ть, щу́, ~щешь, *pf.* (*of* ~скивать)
to find; to track down, run to earth.

оты|ска́ться, щу́сь, ~щешься, *pf.* (*of* ~ски-
ваться) to turn up, appear.

оты́скива|ть, ю, *impf.* **1.** *impf. of* отыска́ть.
2. (*impf. only*) to look for, try to find.

оты́скива|ться, юсь, *impf. of* отыска́ться.

отэкзамен|ова́ть, у́ю, *pf.* to finish examining.

отяго|ти́ть, щу́, ти́шь, *pf.* (*of* ~ща́ть) to
burden.

отягоща́|ть, ю, *impf. of* отяготи́ть.

отягч|а́ть, а́ю, *impf. of* ~и́ть; ~а́ющие (вину́) обстоя́тельства aggravating circumstances.

отягч|и́ть, у́, и́шь, *pf.* (*of* ~а́ть) to aggravate.

отяжеле́лый, *adj.* heavy.

отяжеле́|ть, ю, *pf.* to become heavy.

офе́н|ский, *adj. of* ~я.

офе́н|я, и, *m.* (*hist.*) pedlar, huckster.

офи́т, а, *m.* (*min.*) ophite.

офице́р, а, *m.* officer.

офице́р|ский, *adj. of* ~; ~ское собра́ние officers' mess.

офице́рств|о, а, *n.* 1. (*collect.*) the officers. 2. commissioned rank.

официа́льн|ый, *adj.* official; ~ое лицо́ an official.

официа́нт, а, *m.* waiter.

официа́нтк|а, и, *f.* waitress.

официо́з, а, *m.* semi-official organ (*of press*).

официо́з|ный (~ен, ~на), *adj.* semi-official.

оформи́тел|ь, я, *m.* decorator, stage-painter.

офо́рм|ить, лю, ишь, *pf.* (*of* ~ля́ть) 1. to get up, mount, put into shape; о. пье́су to stage a play. 2. to register officially, legalize; о. вступле́ние в брак to register a marriage; о. докуме́нт to draw up a paper. 3. to enrol, take on the staff.

офо́рм|иться, люсь, ишься, *pf.* (*of* ~ля́ться) 1. to take shape. 2. to be registered; to legalize one's position. 3. to be taken on the staff, join the staff.

оформле́ни|е, я, *n.* 1. get-up; mounting; сцени́ческое о. staging. 2. registration, legalization.

оформля́|ть(ся), ю(сь), *impf. of* офо́рмить-(ся).

офо́рт, а, *m.* etching.

офранцу́|зить, жу, зишь, *pf.* to frenchify.

офранцу́|зиться, жусь, зишься, *pf.* to become frenchified.

офсе́т, а, *m.* (*typ.*) offset process.

офтальми́|я, и, *f.* (*med.*) ophthalmia.

офтальмо́лог, а, *m.* ophthalmologist.

офтальмологи́ческий, *adj.* ophthalmological.

офтальмоло́ги|я, и, *f.* ophthalmology.

ох, *interj.* oh! ah!

оха́ива|ть, ю, *impf. of* оха́ять.

оха́льник, а, *m.* (*coll.*) mischief-maker.

оха́льнича|ть, ю, *impf.* (*coll.*) to get up to mischief.

оха́льный, *adj.* mischievous.

о́хань|е, я, *n.* (*coll.*) moaning, groaning.

оха́пк|а, и, *f.* armful; взять в ~у (*coll.*) to take in one's arms.

охарактериз|ова́ть, у́ю, *pf.* to characterize, describe.

о́х|ать, аю, *impf.* (*of* ~нуть) to moan, groan; to sigh.

оха́|ять, ю, *pf.* (*of* ха́ять *and* ~ивать) (*coll.*) to criticize, censure.

охва́т, а, *m.* 1. scope, range. 2. inclusion. 3. (*mil.*) outflanking, envelopment.

охва|ти́ть, чу́, ~тишь, *pf.* (*of* ~тывать) 1. to envelop; to enclose; дом ~ти́ло пла́менем the house was enveloped in flames; о. бо́чку обруча́ми to hoop a cask. 2. to grip, seize; их ~ти́л у́жас they were seized with panic. 3. (+*i.*) (*coll.*) to draw (in), involve (in); о. молодёжь обще́ственной рабо́той to draw young people into social work. 4. (*fig.*) to comprehend, take in. 5. (*mil.*) to outflank, envelop.

охва́тн|ый, *adj.* ~ое движе́ние (*mil.*) flanking movement, enveloping movement.

охва́тыва|ть, ю, *impf. of* охвати́ть.

охва́|ченный, *p.p.p. of* ~ти́ть; о. у́жасом terror-stricken.

охво́сть|е, я, *n.* (*collect.*) 1. chaff, husks. 2. (*fig.*) rabble.

охладева́|ть, ю, *impf. of* охладе́ть.

охладе́лый, *adj.* (*obs.*) cold; grown cold.

охладе́|ть, ю, *pf.* (*of* ~ва́ть) to grow cold; (*fig.*; к) to grow cool (towards), lose interest (in).

охлади́тел|ь, я, *m.* (*tech.*) cooler, refrigerator; condenser.

охлади́тельный, *adj.* cooling.

охла|ди́ть, жу́, ди́шь, *pf.* (*of* ~жда́ть) to cool, cool off (*also fig.*); о. чей-н. пыл to damp someone's ardour.

охла|ди́ться, жу́сь, ди́шься, *pf.* (*of* ~жда́ться) to become cool, cool down (*also fig.*).

охлажда́|ть(ся), ю(сь), *impf. of* охлади́ть-(ся).

охлажда́|ющий, *pres. part. act. of* ~ть *and adj.* cooling, refrigerating; ~ющая жи́дкость coolant; ~ющее простра́нство condensation chamber.

охлажде́ни|е, я, *n.* 1. cooling (off); пове́рхность ~я cooling surface; с возду́шным ~ем air-cooled. 2. (*fig.*) coolness.

охло́п|ок, ка, *pl.* ~ки, ~ков (*and* ~ья, ~ьев), *m.* tuft; (*sing. only.*; *collect.*) waste (*of fibrous substances*).

охмеле́|ть, ю, *pf.* (*of* хмеле́ть) (*coll.*) to become tight.

охмел|и́ть, ю́, и́шь, (*pf. of* ~я́ть) to make intoxicated (*also fig.*).

охмел|я́ть, я́ю, *impf. of* ~и́ть.

о́х|нуть, ну, нешь, *pf. of* ~ать.

охоло|сти́ть, щу́, сти́шь, *pf.* to castrate, geld.

охора́шива|ться, юсь, *impf.* (*coll.*) to smarten oneself up.

охо́т|а¹, ы, *f.* hunt, hunting; chase; о. с ружьём shooting; псо́вая о. riding to hounds; соколи́ная о. falconry.

охо́т|а², ы, *f.* 1. (к *or* +*inf.*) desire, wish,

inclination; у него́ бо́льше нет ~ы писа́ть he no longer has any desire to write; по свое́й ~е of one's own accord; что ему́ за о.! what makes him do it!; о. тебе́ спо́рить с ним! (*coll.*) what makes you argue with him! 2. heat (*in female animals*).

охо́|титься, чусь, тишься, *impf.* (на+*a.* or за+*i.*) to hunt; (*fig.*; за+*i.*) to hunt for.

охо́тк|а, и, *f.* в ~у (*coll.*) with pleasure, eagerly.

охо́тник¹, а, *m.* hunter; sportsman.

охо́тник², а, *m.* 1. (до or +*inf.*) lover (of); enthusiast (for); он большо́й о. до грибо́в he is a great mushroom lover. 2. volunteer; есть ли ~и пойти́? are there any volunteers? will anyone volunteer to go?

охо́тнич|ий, *adj.* hunting; sporting, shooting; о. биле́т hunting permit; о. до́мик shooting-box; ~ье ружьё fowling-piece, sporting gun; ~ья соба́ка hound, gun-dog; о. расска́з (*joc.*) traveller's tale, tall story.

охо́тно, *adv.* willingly, gladly, readily.

охо́ч|ий (~, ~а), *adj.* (+*inf.*; *coll.*) inclined (to), keen (to), having an urge (to).

о́хр|а, ы, *f.* ochre; кра́сная о. raddle, ruddle.

охра́н|а, ы, *f.* 1. guarding; protection; о. труда́ measures for protection of labour. 2. guard; ли́чная о. body-guard; пограни́чная о. frontier guard; в сопровожде́нии ~ы under escort, in custody.

охране́ни|е, я, *n.* safeguarding; (*mil.*) protection; сторожево́е о. outposts.

охрани́тел|ь, я, *m.* 1. (*rhet.*) protector, guardian. 2. (*obs.*) conservative.

охрани́тельный, *adj.* 1. (*leg.*) protective. 2. (*obs.*) conservative.

охран|и́ть, ю́, и́шь, *pf.* (*of* ~я́ть) to guard, protect.

охра́нк|а, и, *f.* (*coll.*) Okhranka (*Secret Police Department in tsarist Russia*).

охра́нник, а, *m.* (*coll.*) 1. guard. 2. secret police agent; member of Okhranka.

охра́н|ный, *adj. of* ~а; ~ная гра́мота, о. лист safe-conduct, pass; ~ная зо́на (*mil.*) restricted area; ~ное отделе́ние (*hist.*) Secret Police Department (*in tsarist Russia*).

охран|я́ть, я́ю, *impf. of* ~и́ть.

охри́плый, *adj.* (*coll.*) hoarse.

охри́п|нуть, ну, нешь, *past* ~, ~ла, *pf.* (*of* хри́пнуть) to become hoarse.

о́хр|ить, ю, ишь, *impf.* to colour with ochre.

охроме́|ть, ю, *pf.* (*of* хроме́ть) (*coll.*) to go lame.

оху́лк|а, и, *only in phrases* ~и на́ руку не класть (положи́ть); он ~и на́ руку не поло́жит (*coll.*) he is no fool.

оцара́па|ть, ю, *pf.* (*of* цара́пать) to scratch.

оцара́па|ться, юсь, *pf.* to scratch oneself.

оце́жива|ть, ю, *impf.* о. комара́ (*fig.*) to

strain at a gnat.

оцело́т, а, *m.* (*zool.*) ocelot.

оце́нива|ть, ю, *impf. of* оцени́ть.

оцен|и́ть, ю́, ~ишь, *pf.* (*of* ~ивать) 1. to estimate, evaluate; to appraise; о. в де́сять рубле́й to estimate at ten roubles. 2. to appreciate; о. что-н. по досто́инству to appreciate something at its true value.

оце́нк|а, и, *f.* 1. estimation, evaluation; appraisal; estimate; о. иму́щества valuation of property; о. обстано́вки (*mil.*) estimate of the situation. 2. appreciation; дать настоя́щую ~у чему́-н. to give something a proper appreciation.

оце́н|очный, *adj. of* ~ка.

оце́нщик, а, *m.* valuer.

оцепене́лый, *adj.* torpid; benumbed.

оцепене́|ть, ю, *pf. of* цепене́ть.

оцеп|и́ть, лю́, ~ишь, *pf.* (*of* ~ля́ть) to surround; to cordon off.

оцепле́ни|е, я, *n.* 1. surrounding; cordoning off. 2. cordon.

оцепл|я́ть, ю, *impf. of* оцепи́ть.

оцинко́в|анный, *p.p.p. of* ~а́ть *and adj.* zinc-coated, galvanized.

оцинк|ова́ть, у́ю, *pf.* (*of* ~о́вывать) to (coat with) zinc, galvanize.

оцинко́выва|ть, ю, *impf. of* оцинкова́ть.

оча́г, а́, *m.* 1. hearth (*also fig.*); ку́хонный о. kitchen range; дома́шний о. (*fig.*) hearth, home. 2. (*fig.*) centre, seat; nidus; о. войны́ seat of war; о. зара́зы nidus of infection; о. землетрясе́ния earthquake centre.

оча́нк|а, и, *f.* (*bot.*) euphrasy, eyebright.

очарова́ни|е, я, *n.* charm, fascination.

очарова́тел|ьный (~ен, ~ьна), *adj.* charming, fascinating.

очар|ова́ть, у́ю, *pf.* (*of* ~о́вывать) to charm, fascinate.

очаро́выва|ть, ю, *impf. of* очарова́ть.

очеви́д|ец, ца, *m.* eye-witness.

очеви́дно, *adv.* obviously, evidently; вы, о., не согла́сны you obviously do not agree.

очеви́д|ный (~ен, ~на), *adj.* obvious, evident, manifest, patent.

очелове́чива|ть(ся), ю(сь), *impf. of* очелове́чить(ся).

очелове́ч|ить, у, ишь, *pf.* (*of* ~ивать) to make human, humanize.

очелове́ч|иться, усь, ишься, *pf.* (*of* ~ивать-ся) to become human.

о́чень, *adv.* very; very much.

очерви́ве|ть, ю, *pf. of* черви́веть.

очередн|о́й, *adj.* 1. next; next in turn; о. вопро́с the next question; о. вы́пуск latest issue (*of a journal, etc.*); ~а́я зада́ча the immediate task; ~о́е зва́ние the next higher rank. 2. periodic(al); recurrent; usual, regular; (*pejor.*) routine; ~ые неприя́тности the usual trouble; о. о́тпуск regular holidays; ~áя эпиде́мия гри́ппа periodical epidemic of influenza.

очерёдност|ь, и, *f.* periodicity; regular succession; order of priority.

о́черед|ь, и, *pl.* **~и, ~éй,** *f.* **1.** turn; пропусти́ть свою́ о. to miss one's turn; о. за ва́ми it is your turn; в свою́ о. in one's turn; на ~и next (in turn); по ~и in turn, in order, in rotation; в пе́рвую о. in the first place, in the first instance. **2.** queue, line; стоя́ть в ~и (за+i.) to queue (for), stand in line (for). **3.** (*mil.*) (пулемётная) о. burst; батаре́йная о. (battery) salvo.

очерёт, а, *m.* (*bot.*) bog-rush.

о́черк, а, *m.* essay, sketch, study; outline; ~и ру́сской исто́рии studies in Russian history.

очёркива|ть, ю, *impf. of* очеркну́ть.

очерки́ст, а, *m.* essayist.

очерк|ну́ть, ну́, нёшь, *pf.* (*of* ~ивать) to place a circle round.

очерк|о́вый, *adj. of* ~; ~о́вая тема́тика subject-matter for an essay.

очерн|и́ть, ю́, и́шь, *pf. of* черни́ть 2.

очерстве́лый, *adj.* hardened, callous.

очерстве́|ть, ю, *pf. of* черстве́ть 2.

очерта́ни|е, я, *n.* outline.

очер|ти́ть, чу́, ~тишь, *pf.* (*of* ~чивать) to outline; ~тя́ го́лову (*coll.*) without thinking, headlong.

очёрчива|ть, ю, *impf. of* очерти́ть.

очёс, а, *m.* (*collect.*) = ~ки.

оче|са́ть, шу́, ~шешь, *pf.* (*of* ~сывать) to comb out.

очёс|ки, ков, *sing.* **~ок, ~ка,** *m.* combings; flocks; льняны́е о. flax tow.

очёсыва|ть, ю, *impf. of* очеса́ть.

оче́чник, а, *m.* spectacle case.

о́чи, *pl. of* о́ко.

очи́нива|ть, ю, *impf. of* очини́ть.

очин|и́ть, ю́, ~ишь, *pf.* (*of* ~ивать *and* чини́ть[2]) to sharpen, point.

очи́н|ка, и, *f.* sharpening; маши́нка для ~и карандаше́й pencil-sharpener.

очисти́тельн|ый, *adj.* purifying, cleansing; о. аппара́т (*tech.*) purifier; rectifier; о. бак (sugar) clarifier, clearing pan; о. заво́д refinery; ~ое сре́дство cleanser, detergent.

очи́|стить, щу, стишь, *pf.* (*of* ~ща́ть) **1.** to clean; to cleanse, purify; (*tech.*) to refine; to rectify. **2.** (от) to clear (of); to fee; о. почто́вый я́щик to clear a letter-box; о. кише́чник to open the bowels. **3.** to peel.

очи́|ститься, щусь, стишься, *pf.* (*of* ~ща́ться) **1.** to clear oneself. **2.** (от) to become clear (of). **3.** *pass. of* ~стить.

очи́ст|ка, и, *f.* **1.** cleaning; cleansing, purification; (*tech.*) refinement; rectification; мо́края о. га́за gas scrubbing; о. сто́чных вод sewage disposal; для ~и со́вести (*coll.*)

for conscience' sake. **2.** clearance; freeing; (*mil.*) mopping-up; о. кише́чника evacuation of the bowels.

очи́стк|и, ов, *no sing.* peelings.

очи́т|ок, ка, *m.* (*bot.*) stonecrop.

очища́|ть(ся), ю(сь), *impf. of* очи́стить(ся).

очище́ни|е, я, *n.* cleansing; purification; ме́сячное о. (*obs.*) menstruation.

очи́|щенный, *p.p.p. of* ~стить; *as noun* ~щенная, ~щенной, *f.* (*coll.*) vodka.

очк|и́, о́в, *no sing.* spectacles.

очк|о́[1], а́, *pl.* **~и́, ~о́в,** *n.* **1.** (*on cards or dice*) pip. **2.** (*in scoring*) point; дать ~о́в вперёд to give points. **3.** hole; смотрово́е о. peephole.

очк|о́[2], а́, *n.* втере́ть кому́-н. ~и́ (*coll.*) to throw dust in someone's eyes.

очковтира́тельств|о, а, *n.* (*coll.*) eye-wash.

очко́|вый[1], *adj. of* ~[1]; ~вая систе́ма points system (*of scoring*).

очко́в|ый[2], *adj.* ~ая змея́ cobra.

очн|у́ться, у́сь, ёшься, *pf.* **1.** to wake. **2.** to come to (oneself), regain consciousness.

о́чн|ый, *adj.* **1.** (*as opp. to* зао́чный) internal (*instruction, student, etc., as opp. to* external, extra-mural). **2.** ~ая ста́вка (*leg.*) confrontation.

очу́вств|оваться, уюсь, *pf.* **1.** to come to (oneself), regain consciousness. **2.** (*coll.*) to have a change of heart; to repent.

очуме́лый, *adj.* (*coll.*) mad, off one's head; бежа́ть, как о. to run like a mad thing.

очуме́|ть, ю, *pf.* (*coll.*) to go mad, go off one's head.

очут|и́ться, ~ишься, *pf.* to find oneself, come to be; о. в нело́вком положе́нии to find oneself in an awkward position; как вы здесь ~и́лись? how did you come to be here?

очу́|ться, юсь, *pf.* (*coll.*) to come to oneself.

ошале́лый, *adj.* (*coll.*) crazy, crazed.

ошале́|ть, ю, *pf. of* шале́ть.

ошара́шива|ть, ю, *impf. of* ошара́шить.

ошара́ш|ить, у, ишь, *pf.* (*of* ~ивать) (*coll.*) **1.** to beat, bang. **2.** (*fig.*) to strike dumb, flabbergast.

ошварт|ова́ть, у́ю, *pf.* (*naut.*) to make fast.

оше́йник, а, *m.* (*animal's*) collar; соба́чий о. dog-collar.

ошеломи́тельный, *adj.* stunning.

ошеломи́|ть, лю́, и́шь, *pf.* (*of* ~ля́ть) to stun.

ошеломле́ни|е, я, *n.* stupefaction.

ошеломля́|ть, ю, *impf. of* ошеломи́ть; ~ющий stunning.

ошельм|ова́ть, у́ю, *pf. of* шельмова́ть.

ошиба́|ться, а́юсь, *impf. of* ~и́ться.

ошиб|и́ться, у́сь, ёшься, *past* ~ся, ~лась,

pf. (*of* ~а́ться) to be mistaken, make a mistake, make mistakes; to be wrong; to err, be at fault.

оши́бк|а, и, *f.* mistake; error; blunder; по ~е by mistake.

оши́боч|ный (~ен, ~на), *adj.* erroneous, mistaken.

оши́ка|ть, ю, *pf.* (*of* ши́кать 2) (*coll.*) to hiss off the stage.

ошлак|ова́ть, у́ю, *pf.* (*no impf.*) (*tech.*) to form slack, form clinker.

ошмёт|ки, ков, *sing.* ~ок, ~ка, *m.* (*coll.*) worn out shoes; rags.

ошпа́рива|ть, ю, *impf. of* ошпа́рить.

ошпа́р|ить, ю, ишь, *pf.* (*of* ~ивать) to scald.

оштраф|ова́ть, у́ю, *pf. of* штрафова́ть.

оштукату́р|ить, ю, ишь, *pf. of* штукату́рить.

ошу́юю, *adv.* (*arch.*) to the left, on the left hand.

ощен|и́ться, и́тся, *pf. of* щени́ться.

ощёрива|ть(ся), ю(сь), *impf. of* ощёрить(ся).

ощёр|ить, ю, ишь, *pf.* (*of* ~ивать) (*coll.*) to gnash.

ощёр|иться, юсь, ишься, *pf.* (*of* ~иваться) (*coll.*) to gnash one's teeth.

ощети́нива|ться, юсь, *impf. of* ощети́ниться.

ощети́н|иться, юсь, ишься, *pf.* (*of* ~иваться *and* щети́ниться) to bristle up (*also fig.*).

ощи́п|анный, *p.p.p. of* ~а́ть *and adj.* (*fig., coll.*) wretched, piteous.

ощип|а́ть, лю́, ~лешь, *pf.* (*of* щипа́ть 4 *and* ~ывать) to pluck.

ощи́пыва|ть, ю, *impf. of* ощипа́ть.

ощу́п|ать, аю, *pf.* (*of* ~ывать) to feel; to grope about (in).

ощу́пыва|ть, ю, *impf. of* ощу́пать.

о́щуп|ь, и, *f.* на о. to the touch; by touch; идти́ на о. to grope one's way.

о́щупью, *adv.* 1. gropingly, fumblingly; by touch; иска́ть о. to grope for; пробра́ться о. to grope one's way. 2. (*fig.*) blindly.

ощут|и́мый (~и́м, ~и́ма), *adj.* = ~и́тельный.

ощути́тел|ьный (~ен, ~ьна), *adj.* 1. perceptible, tangible, palpable. 2. (*fig.*) appreciable.

ощу|ти́ть, щу́, ти́шь, *pf.* (*of* ~ща́ть) to feel, sense, experience; о. го́лод to feel hunger; он ~ти́л её отсу́тствие he felt her absence.

ощуща́|ть, ю, *impf. of* ощути́ть.

ощуще́ни|е, я, *n.* 1. (*physiol.*) sensation. 2. feeling, sense.

оягн|и́ться, и́тся, *pf. of* ягни́ться.

П

па, *indecl., n.* (*dance*) step.

па́в|а, ы, *f.* peahen.

павиа́н, а, *m.* baboon.

павильо́н, а, *m.* 1. pavilion. 2. film studio.

павли́н, а, *m.* peacock.

павли́н|ий, *adj. of* ~.

па́вод|ок, ка, *m.* flood (*esp. resulting from melting of snow*); freshet.

па́волок|а, и, *f.* (*hist.*) pavoloka (*in Kievan Russia, heavy ornamented brocade, imported as a luxury item*).

пагина́ци|я, и, *f.* pagination.

па́год|а, ы, *f.* pagoda.

па́голен|ок, ка, *m.* (*dial.*) leg (*of boot or stocking*).

па́губ|а, ы, *f.* ruin, destruction; bane.

па́губ|ный (~ен, ~на), *adj.* pernicious, ruinous; baneful; fatal.

па́дал|ь, и, *f.* (*usu. collect.*) carrion.

па́дан|ец, ца, *m.* faller (*fallen fruit*).

па́да|ть, ю, *impf.* 1. (*pf.* пасть *and* упа́сть) (*in var. senses*) to fall; to sink; to drop; to decline; баро́метр ~л the barometer was falling; ~ет снег it is snowing; це́ны ~ют prices are dropping; се́рдце у них ~ло their spirits were sinking; п. ду́хом to lose heart, lose courage; п. в о́бморок to faint; п. от уста́лости to be ready to drop. 2. (*pf.* пасть) (*fig.*; на+*a.*) to fall (on, to); отве́тственность ~ет на вас the responsibility falls on you. 3. (*impf. only*) (*ling.*; *of stress or accent*) to fall, be; ударе́ние ~ет на пе́рвый слог the stress is on the first syllable. 4. (*impf. only*) (*of hair, teeth, etc.*) to fall out, drop out. 5. (*pf.* пасть) (*of cattle*) to die.

па́да|ющий, *pres. part. of* ~ть *and adj.* (*phys.*) incident; ~ющие звёзды shooting stars.

паде́ж, а́, *m.* (*gram.*) case.

падёж, а́, *m.* murrain, cattle plague.

паде́ж|ный, *adj. of* ~; ~ное оконча́ние case ending.

падёж|ный, *adj. of* ~.

**паде́ни|е, я, n.* 1. fall; drop, sinking; мора́льное п. degradation; п. цен slump in prices. 2. (*phys.*) incidence; у́гол ~я angle of incidence. 3. (*geol.*) dip. 4. п. ударе́ния (*ling.*) incidence of stress.

падиша́х, а, *m.* padishah.

па́д|кий (~ок, ~ка), *adj.* (на+*a. or* до) having a weakness (for), having a penchant (for); susceptible (to); п. на де́ньги mercenary; он ∼ок до сла́дкого he has a sweet tooth.

па́дуб, а, *m.* holly.

паду́ч|ий, *adj.* (*obs.*) falling; ∼ая звезда́ shooting star; ∼ая (боле́знь) falling sickness, epilepsy.

па́дчериц|а, ы, *f.* step-daughter.

паево́й, *adj. of* пай¹; п. взнос share.

па|ёк, йка́, *m.* ration.

паенакопле́ни|е, я, *n.* (*econ.*) share-accumulation.

паж, а́, *m.* (*hist.*) page.

па́ж|еский, *adj. of* ∼; П. Ко́рпус Corps of Pages (*hist.*; *name of mil. school in St. Petersburg*).

па́жит|ь, и, *f.* (*obs.*, *poet.*) pasture.

паз, а, о ∼е, в ∼у́, *pl.* ∼ы́, ∼о́в, *m.* (*tech.*) groove, slot, mortise, rabbet.

па|зи́ть, жу́, зи́шь, *impf.* (*tech.*) to groove, mortise.

па́зух|а, и, *f.* 1. bosom; за ∼ой in one's bosom; держа́ть ка́мень за ∼ой (*fig.*) to nurse a grievance, harbour a grudge; жить как у Христа́ за ∼ой to live in clover. 2. (*anat.*) sinus; ло́бные ∼и frontal sinuses. 3. (*bot.*) axil.

па́ин|ька, ьки, *g. pl.* ∼ек, *m. and f.* (*coll.*) good child; будь п.! be a good boy (girl)!; п.-ма́льчик good (little) boy.

па|й¹, я, *pl.* ∼й, ∼ёв, *m.* share; вступи́тельный п. initial shares; това́рищество на ∼я́х joint-stock company; на ∼я́х (*fig.*, *coll.*) on an equal footing, going shares.

пай², *indecl.*, *m. and f.* (*coll.*) good child; п.-ма́льчик good (little) boy.

па́йк|а, и, *f.* solder(ing).

пайко́вый, *adj. of* паёк; rationed.

па́йщик¹, а, *m.* shareholder.

па́йщик², а, *m.* solderer.

пак, а, *no pl.*, *m.* pack-ice.

пакга́уз, а, *m.* warehouse, storehouse; тамо́женный п. bonded warehouse.

паке́т, а, *m.* 1. parcel, package; packet; индивидуа́льный п. (*mil.*) individual field dressing, first-aid packet. 2. (official) letter. 3. paper bag.

пакиста́н|ец, ца, *m.* Pakistani.

пакиста́нк|а, и, *f.* Pakistani (woman).

пакиста́нский, *adj.* Pakistani.

па́кл|я, и, *f.* tow; oakum.

пак|ова́ть, у́ю, *impf.* (*of* у∼) to pack.

па́ко|стить, щу, стишь, *impf.* (*coll.*) 1. (*pf.* за∼ *and* на∼) to soil, dirty. 2. (*pf.* ис∼) to spoil, mess up. 3. (*pf.* на∼) (+*d.*) to play dirty tricks (on).

па́костник, а, *m.* (*coll.*) 1. dirty dog, wretch. 2. debauchee.

па́кост|ный (∼ен, ∼на), *adj.* dirty, mean, foul; nasty.

па́кост|ь, и, *f.* 1. dirty trick; де́лать ∼и (+*d.*) to play dirty tricks (on). 2. filth. 3. obscenity, filthy word.

пакт, а, *m.* pact; п. о ненападе́нии non-aggression pact.

пал¹, а, *m.* (*naut.*) bollard; pawl.

пал², а, *m.* (*dial.*) fire.

паланти́н, а, *m.* fur tippet.

пала́т|а, ы, *f.* 1. (*pl. only*; *obs.*) palace. 2. (*obs.*) chamber, hall; Оруже́йная п. Armoury Museum (*in Moscow*); у него́ ума́ п. (*coll.*) he is as wise as Solomon. 3. (*hospital*) ward. 4. (*polit.*) chamber, house; ве́рхняя, ни́жняя п. Upper, Lower Chamber; П. ло́рдов House of Lords; П. о́бщин House of Commons. 5. *as name of State institutions*; Всесою́зная кни́жная п. All-Union Book Chamber (*national bibliographical centre in Moscow*); П. мер и весо́в Weights and Measures Office; Торго́вая п. Chamber of Commerce.

палатализа́ци|я, и, *f.* (*ling.*) palatalization.

палатализ|ова́ть, у́ю, *impf. and pf.* (*ling.*) to palatalize.

палата́льный, *adj.* (*ling.*) palatal.

пала́тк|а, и, *f.* 1. tent; marquee; в ∼ах under canvas. 2. stall, booth.

пала́т|ный, *adj. of* ∼а; ∼ная сестра́ ward sister.

пала́ццо, *indecl.*, *n.* palace (*esp. of Venetian doges*).

пала́ч, а́, *m.* hangman; executioner; (*fig.*) butcher.

пала́ш, а́, *m.* broadsword.

па́левый, *adj.* straw-coloured, pale yellow.

палёны|й, *adj.* singed, scorched; па́хнет ∼м there is a smell of burning.

палео́граф, а, *m.* palaeographer.

палеографи́ческий, *adj.* palaeographic.

палеогра́фи|я, и, *f.* palaeography.

палеоза́вр, а, *m.* palaeosaurus.

палеозо́йский, *adj.* (*geol.*) palaeozoic.

палеоли́т, а, *m.* (*geol.*) palaeolithic period.

палеолити́ческий, *adj.* (*geol.*) palaeolithic.

палеонто́лог, а, *m.* palaeontologist.

палеонтологи́ческий, *adj.* palaeontologic(al).

палеонтоло́ги|я, и, *f.* palaeontology.

па́лехский, *adj.* (made in) Palekh (*place famed for its lacquer-work*).

па́л|ец, ьца, *m.* 1. finger; п. ноги́ toe; большо́й п. thumb; указа́тельный п. forefinger, index (finger); сре́дний п. middle finger, third finger; безымя́нный п. fourth finger, ring-finger; предохрани́тельный п. finger-stall; (*fig.*) п. о п. не уда́рить, ∼ьцем не шевельну́ть (*coll.*) not to raise a finger, not to stir oneself; ему́ ∼ьца в рот не клади́ (*coll.*) he is not to be trusted, he needs to be watched; ~ьцы лома́ть to tear one's hair; смотре́ть сквозь ~ьцы на что-н. (*coll.*) to shut one's eyes to something; знать что-н., как свои́ пять ~ьцев (*coll.*) to have something at one's finger-tips; обвести́ кого́-н. вокру́г ~ьца (*coll.*) to twist someone round one's (little) finger; вы́сосать из ~ьца (*coll.*) to fabricate, concoct; он ~ьцем никого́ не тро́нет he wouldn't hurt a fly; попа́сть ~ьцем в не́бо (*coll.*) to be wide of the mark; как по ~ьцам рассказа́ть to recount in detail, recount circumstantially. **2.** (*tech.*) pin, peg; cam, cog, tooth.

пале|я́, й, *f.* (*hist. lit.*) Palaea (*early Russian lit. form, borrowed from Byzantium, comprising exposition of Old Testament texts*).

палимпсе́ст, а, *m.* palimpsest.

палингене́з, а, *m.* (*biol.*) palingenesis.

палингене́з|ис, иса, *m.* = ~.

палиндро́м, а, *m.* palindrome.

палиса́д, а, *m.* **1.** paling. **2.** (*mil.*) palisade, stockade.

палиса́дник, а, *m.* front garden.

палиса́ндр, а, *m.* rosewood.

палиса́ндр|овый, *adj. of* ~.

пали́тр|а, ы, *f.* palette.

пал|и́ть¹, ю́, и́шь, *impf.* **1.** (*pf.* с~) to burn, scorch. **2.** (*pf.* о~) to singe.

пал|и́ть², ю́, и́шь, *impf.* (*coll.*) to fire (*from gun*); ~и́! (*word of command*) fire!

па́лиц|а, ы, *f.* club, cudgel.

па́лк|а, и, *f.* stick; cane, staff; п. метлы́ broom-stick; поста́вить в ~и (*obs.*) to cane, give a caning; вста́вить кому́-н. ~и в колёса to put a spoke in someone's wheel; из-под ~и under the lash; п. о двух конца́х two-edged weapon; э́то п. о двух конца́х it cuts both ways.

палла́ди|й, я, *m.* (*chem.*) palladium.

паллиати́в, а, *m.* palliative.

паллиати́вный, *adj.* palliative.

пало́мник, а, *m.* **1.** pilgrim (*also fig.*). **2.** (*hist. lit.*) pilgrim's tale.

пало́мнича|ть, ю, *impf.* to go on (a) pilgrimage.

пало́мничеств|о, а, *n.* pilgrimage (*also fig.*).

па́лочк|а, и, *f.* **1.** *dim. of* па́лка; бараба́нная п. drumstick; волше́бная п. magic wand; дирижёрская п. conductor's baton; п.-вы́руча́лочка (*children's game*) 'I spy'. **2.** (*med.*) bacillus.

па́лочковый, *adj.* (*med.*) bacillary.

па́л|очный, *adj. of* ~ка; ~очные уда́ры strokes of the cane; ~очная дисципли́на discipline of the rod.

па́лтус, а, *m.* halibut, turbot.

па́луб|а, ы, *f.* deck; полётная п. flight deck; жила́я п. messdeck; шлю́почная п. boat deck.

па́луб|ный *adj. of* ~a; п. груз deck cargo.

па́лый, *adj.* (*dial.*; *of cattle*) dead.

пальб|а́, ы́, *f.* firing; пу́шечная п. cannonade.

па́льм|а, ы, *f.* palm(-tree); коко́совая п. coco-nut(-tree); фи́никовая п. date(-palm); получи́ть ~у пе́рвенства to bear the palm.

па́льм|овый, *adj. of* ~a; ~овое де́рево boxwood; *as noun* ~овые, ~овых Palmaceae.

па́льник, а, *m.* (*mil.*; *obs.*) linstock.

пал|ьну́ть, ьну́, ьнёшь, *inst. pf.* (*of* ~и́ть²) to fire a shot; to discharge a volley.

пальте́ц|о́, а́, *n.* (*coll.*) *dim. of* пальто́.

пальти́ш|ко, ка, *pl.* ~ки, ~ек, *n.* (*coll.*, *pejor.*) *dim. of* пальто́.

пальто́, *indecl.* *n.* (over)coat; topcoat.

пальто́|вый, *adj. of* ~.

пальцеви́д|ный (~ен, ~на), *adj.* finger-shaped.

пальцево́й, *adj. of* па́лец.

пальцеобра́з|ный (~ен, ~на), *adj.* (*bot.*) digitate.

па́ль|чатый, *adj.* = ~цеобра́зный.

па́льчик, а, *m.* *dim. of* па́лец; *see* ма́льчик.

па́льщик, а, *m.* (*tech.*) shot-firer, blaster.

пал|я́щий, *pres. part. act. of* ~и́ть¹ *and adj.* burning, scorching.

пампа́с|овый, *adj. of* ~ы; ~овая трава́ pampas grass.

пампа́с|ы, ов, *no sing.* (*geogr.*) pampas.

пампу́шк|а, и, *f.* (*dial.*) pampushka (*kind of fritter*).

памфле́т, а, *m.* lampoon.

памфлети́ст, а, *m.* lampoonist.

па́мятк|а, и, *f.* **1.** (commemorative) booklet. **2.** instruction, written rules. **3.** (*coll.*, *obs.*) memento.

па́мятлив|ый (~, ~а), *adj.* (*coll.*) having a retentive memory, retentive.

па́мятник, а, *m.* monument; memorial; tombstone; statue; ~и пи́сьменности literary texts.

па́мят|ный (~ен, ~на), *adj.* **1.** memorable. **2.** serving to assist the memory; ~ная доска́ memorial plate, plaque; ~ная кни́жка notebook, memorandum book.

па́мят|овать, ую, *impf.* (*obs.*; о+*p.*) to remember.

па́мят|ь, и, *f.* **1.** memory; у него́ кури́ная п. he has a memory like a sieve; на мое́й ~и within my memory; говори́ть на п. to speak from memory; вдруг мне пришло́ на п., что... suddenly I remembered that...; по ~и from memory; по ста́рой ~и from force of habit. **2.** memory, recollection, remembrance; ве́чная п. ему́! may his memory live for ever!; оста́вить по себе́ до́брую п. to leave fond memories of oneself; в п. (+*g.*) in memory (of); подари́ть на п. to give as a keepsake. **3.** mind, consciousness; быть без ~и to be unconscious; быть от кого-н. без ~и (coll.) to be head over heels in love with someone, be crazy about someone. **4.** (eccl.; +g.) commemoration of death (of), feast (of).

пан, а, pl. ~ы́, m. **1.** (hist.) Polish land-owner. **2.** gentleman; либо п., либо про-па́л (prov.) all or nothing.

панаги́|я, и, f. (eccl.) panagia (image worn round neck by Orthodox bishops).

пана́м|а, ы, f. Panama (hat).

панаце́|я, и, f. panacea; п. от всех зол (fig.) universal panacea.

панба́рхат, а, m. panne (dress material).

панда́н, а, m. (obs.) complement; в п. (к) to complement.

панда́н|ус, уса, m. (bot.) screw-pine.

панде́кт|ы, ов, no sing. (leg., hist.) pandects.

пандеми́|я, и, f. (med.) pandemia.

па́ндус, а, m. (tech.) ramp.

панеги́рик, а, m. panegyric, eulogy.

панегири́ст, а, m. panegyrist, eulogist.

панегири́ческий, adj. panegyrical, eulogistic.

пане́л|ь, и, f. **1.** pavement, footpath. **2.** panel(ling), wainscot(ing).

пане́ль|ный, adj. of ~; ~ная обши́вка panelling, wainscotting.

па́н|и, indecl., f. of ~.

панибра́тский, adj. (coll.) familiar.

панибра́тств|о, а, n. (coll.) familiarity.

па́ник|а, и, f. panic; впасть в ~у to become panic-stricken, panic.

паникади́л|о, а, n. (eccl.) chandelier.

паникёр, а, m. panic-monger, scaremonger, alarmist.

паникёр|ский, adj. of ~.

паникёрств|о, а, n. alarmism.

паникёрств|овать, ую, impf. (no pf.) (coll.) to be panic-stricken, panic.

паник|ова́ть, у́ю, impf. (no pf.) (coll.) to panic.

панихи́д|а, ы, f. office for the dead; requiem; гражда́нская п. civil funeral.

панихи́д|ный, adj. of ~a; (fig.) funereal.

пани́ческий, adj. **1.** panic. **2.** (coll.) panicky.

па́нкреас, а, m. (anat.) pancreas.

панкреати́ческий, adj. (anat.) pancreatic.

па́нн|а, ы, f. (Polish) young lady.

панно́, indecl., n. panel.

панора́м|а, ы, f. **1.** (in var. senses) panorama. **2.** (mil.) panoramic sight.

панора́мный, adj. panoramic; п. фильм cinerama film.

пансио́н, а, m. **1.** boarding school. **2.** boarding-house. **3.** (full) board and lodging; ко́мната с ~ом room and board; жить на ~e to have full board and lodging, live en pension.

пансионе́р, а, m. **1.** boarder (in school). **2.** guest (in boarding-house).

па́н|ский, adj. of ~.

панслави́зм, а, m. (hist.) Pan-Slavism.

па́нств|о, а, n. (obs.) **1.** (collect.) Polish land-owners. **2.** superciliousness.

пантало́н|ы, ~, no sing. **1.** (obs.) trousers. **2.** (woman's) drawers, knickers.

пантал|ы́к, а (у), m. (coll.) only in phrases сбить с ~у to drive demented; сбиться с ~у to be driven demented, be at one's wit's end.

пантеи́зм, а, m. pantheism.

пантеи́ст, а, m. pantheist.

пантеисти́ческий, adj. pantheistic(al).

пантео́н, а, m. pantheon.

панте́р|а, ы, f. panther.

панто́граф, а, m. (tech.) pantograph.

пантоми́м|а, ы, f. pantomime, mime; dumb show.

пантомими́ческий, adj. pantomimic.

пантоми́м|ный, adj. = ~и́ческий.

панту́ф|ли, ель, no sing. (obs.) slippers.

па́нт|овый, adj. of ~ы.

пантокри́н, а, m. Pantocrin (medicament prepared from antlers of young Siberian stag).

па́нт|ы, ов, no sing. antlers of young Siberian stag (as used in preparation of medicament).

па́нцирн|ый, adj. **1.** armour-clad, iron--clad. **2.** (zool.) testaceous; as noun ~ые, ~ых Testacea.

па́нцир|ь, я, m. **1.** (hist.) coat of mail, armour. **2.** (zool.) test. **3.** (obs.) diving suit.

па́п|а¹, ы, m. (coll.) papa, daddy.

па́п|а², ы, m. п. ри́мский (the) Pope.

папа́х|а, и, f. papakha (Caucasian fur cap).

папа́ш|а, и, m. (coll.) = па́па.

па́перт|ь, и, f. church-porch, parvis.

папи́зм, а, m. papism.

папиль́отк|а, и, f. curling-paper.

папироло́ги|я, и, f. papyrology.

папиро́с|а, ы, f. cigarette (of Russian type with cardboard mouthpiece).

папиро́сник, а, m. (coll.) cigarette vendor.

папиро́сниц|а¹, ы, f. cigarette girl.

папиро́сниц|а², ы, f. cigarette-case.

папиро́с|ный, adj. of ~a; ~ная бума́га rice--paper.

папи́рус, а, m. papyrus.

папи́рус|ный, adj. of ~.

папи́ст, а, m. papist.

па́пк|а, и, f. **1.** file; document case, paper--case. **2.** cardboard, pasteboard; перепле-тённый в ~у in boards.

па́поротник, а, m. fern.

па́поротник|овый, adj. of ~; ferny; as noun ~овые, ~овых (bot.) Filicinae.

па́прик|а, и, f. paprika.

па́пский, adj. papal; п. престо́л St. Peter's chair.

па́пств|о, а, n. papacy; papal authority.

папуа́с, а, m. Papuan.

папуа́сский, *adj.* Papuan.

папье́-маше́, *indecl.*, *n.* papier-mâché.

пар[1], а, о ~е, в ~у́, *pl.* ~ы́, *m.* **1.** steam; быть под ~а́ми to be under steam, have steam up; на всех ~а́х (*fig.*) full steam ahead, at full speed; очи́стить ~а́ми to fumigate. **2.** exhalation.

пар[2], а, *pl.* ~ы́, *m.* (*agric.*) fallow; находи́ться под ~ом to lie fallow.

па́р|а, ы, *f.* **1.** (*in var. senses*) pair; couple; супру́жеская п. married couple; п. сил (*tech.*) couple; ходи́ть ~ами to walk in couples; е́хать на ~е to drive a pair (*of horses*); на ~у мину́т for a couple of minutes; п. пустяко́в! it's child's play! it's a mere bagatelle!; на ~у слов for a few words; под ~у to match, to make up a pair; она́ ему́ не п. she is no match for him; два сапога́ п. (*coll.*, *pejor.*) they make a pair. **2.** suit (*of clothes*). **3.** (*school sl.*) a 'two'.

пара́бол|а[1], ы, *f.* (*math.*) parabola.

пара́бол|а[2], ы, *f.* parable.

параболи́ческий[1], *adj.* (*math.*) parabolic.

параболи́ческий[2], *adj.* parabolical.

парава́н, а, *m.* (*naut.*) paravane.

пара́граф, а, *m.* paragraph.

пара́д, а, *m.* **1.** parade (*mil.*) review; возду́шный п. air display; морско́й п. naval review; приня́ть п. to inspect a parade. **2.** (*coll.*, *joc.*) ceremonial get-up; быть в по́лном ~е to be all tricked out, be in one's best bib and tucker; что э́то за п. у вас? what's the big show?

паради́гм|а, ы, *f.* (*gram.*) paradigm.

пара́дно-выходн|о́й, *adj.* ~а́я фо́рма вне стро́я (*mil.*) ceremonial walking-out dress.

пара́дност|ь, и, *f.* magnificence; ostentation.

пара́д|ный (~ен, ~на), *adj.* **1.** *adj. of* ~ **1**; п. костю́м ceremonial dress; ~ная фо́рма full dress (uniform). **2.** gala; п. спекта́кль gala night. **3.** main, front; ~ная дверь front door; п. подъе́зд main entrance; *as noun* ~ное, ~ного, *n. and* ~ная, ~ной, *f.* front door.

парадо́кс, а, *m.* paradox.

парадокса́л|ьный (~ен, ~ьна), *adj.* paradoxical.

парази́т, а, *m.* (*biol. and fig.*) parasite.

паразита́р|ный (~ен, ~на), *adj.* parasitic(al).

паразити́зм, а, *m.* (*biol. and fig.*) parasitism.

паразити́р|овать, ую, *impf.* to parasitize.

паразити́ческий, *adj.* (*biol. and fig.*) parasitic(al).

парази́тный, *adj.* (*biol.*) parasitic.

паразитоло́ги|я, и, *f.* parasitology.

парализо́ванност|ь, и, *f.* paralysis.

парализо́в|анный, *p.p.p. of* ~а́ть *and adj.* paralysed.

парализ|ова́ть, у́ю, *impf. and pf.* to paralyse (*also fig.*).

парали́тик, а, *m.* paralytic.

паралити́ческий, *adj.* paralytic.

парали́ч, а́, *m.* paralysis; palsy.

парали́чный, *adj.* paralytic; п. больно́й paralytic.

паралла́кс, а, *m.* (*astron.*) parallax.

параллелепи́пед, а, *m.* (*math.*) parallelepiped.

параллели́зм, а, *m.* parallelism.

параллелогра́мм, а, *m.* (*math.*) parallelogram.

параллел|ь, и, *f.* (*in var. senses*) parallel; провести́ п. (ме́жду) to draw a parallel (between).

паралле́льно, *adv.* (с+*i.*) **1.** parallel (with). **2.** simultaneously (with), at the same time (as).

паралле́льност|ь, и, *f.* parallelism.

паралле́л|ьный (~ен, ~ьна), *adj.* (*in var. senses*) parallel; ~ьные бру́сья (*sport*) parallel bars.

паралоги́зм, а, *m.* paralogism.

парамагнети́зм, а, *m.* (*phys.*) paramagnetism.

парамагни́тный, *adj.* (*phys.*) paramagnetic.

пара́метр, а, *m.* (*math.*) parameter.

парандж|а́, и́, *f.* yashmak.

парано́ик, а, *m.* (*med.*) paranoiac.

паранои́ческий, *adj.* (*med.*) paranoid; paranoiac.

парано́|я, и, *f.* (*med.*) paranoia.

парапе́т, а, *m.* parapet.

парасо́л|ь, я, *m.* (*aeron.*) parasol.

парати́ф, а, *m.* paratyphoid.

пара́ф, а, *m.* **1.** paraph. **2.** initials.

парафи́н, а, *m.* paraffin (wax).

парафи́н|овый, *adj. of* ~.

парафи́р|овать, ую, *impf. and pf.* (*dipl.*) to initial.

парафра́з, а, *m.* paraphrase.

парафра́з|а, ы, *f.* = ~.

парафрази́р|овать, ую, *impf. and pf.* to paraphrase.

пара́ш|а, и, *f.* (*prison sl.*) close-stool.

парашю́т, а, *m.* parachute; на ~е by parachute; прыжо́к с ~ом parachute jump.

парашюти́зм, а, *m.* parachute-jumping (*as sport*).

парашюти́ровани|е, я, *n.* (*aeron.*) pancaking.

парашюти́р|овать, ую, *impf.* (*of* с~) (*aeron.*) to pancake.

парашюти́ст, а, *m.* parachute jumper; (*mil.*) parachutist, paratrooper.

парвеню́, *indecl.*, *m.* parvenu, upstart.

пардо́н **1.** *interj.* (I beg your) pardon. **2.** *as noun, in phrase* проси́ть ~y to ask forgiveness.

паренхи́м|а, ы, *f.* (*anat.*, *bot.*) parenchyma.

па́рен|ый, *adj.* stewed; дешéвле ~ой рéпы dirt-cheap.

па́р|ень, ня, *pl.* ~ни, ~нéй, *m.* **1.** boy, lad. **2.** (*coll.*) chap, fellow.

пари́, *indecl., n.* bet; держáть п., идти́ на п. to bet, lay a bet; п. держу́, что... I bet that . . . .

парижа́н|ин, ина, *pl.* ~e, ~, *m.* Parisian.

парижа́н|ка, ки, *f.* Parisian (woman), Parisienne.

пари́жск|ий, *adj.* Parisian; ~ая лазу́рь, ~ая синь Paris blue, ferric ferrocyanide.

пари́к, á, *m.* wig.

парикмáхер, а, *m.* barber; hairdresser.

парикмáхерск|ая, ой, *f.* barber's (shop), hairdresser's; hair-dressing saloon.

пари́|льня, ьни, *g. pl.* ~ен, *f.* **1.** sweating--room (*in baths*). **2.** (*tech.*) steam-shop.

па́рильщик, а, *m.* sweating-room attendant.

пари́р|овать, ую, *impf. and pf.* (*pf. also* от~) to parry, counter.

парите́т, а, *m.* parity.

парите́т|ный, *adj. of* ~; на ~ных начáлах (c+*i.*) on a par (with), on an equal footing (with).

па́р|ить, ю, ишь, *impf.* (*no pf.*) **1.** to steam. **2.** to steam out, sweat out (*in baths, to beat about the body with a heated besom to induce perspiration*). **3.** (*cul.*) to stew. **4.** (*impers.*) ~ит it is sultry.

пар|и́ть, ю́, и́шь, *impf.* (*no pf.*) to soar, swoop, hover; п. в облакáх (*fig.*) to live in the clouds.

па́р|иться, юсь, ишься, *impf.* **1.** (*pf.* по~) to steam, sweat (*in baths*). **2.** (*cul.*) to stew.

па́ри|я, и, *g. pl.* ~й, *m. and f.* pariah, outcast.

парк, а, *m.* **1.** park; разби́ть п. to lay out a park. **2.** yard, depot; (*mil.*) park, depot; артиллери́йский п. ordnance depot; трамвáйный п. tram depot. **3.** fleet; stock; pool; автомоби́льный п. fleet of motor vehicles; вагóнный п. rolling-stock.

па́рк|а[1], и, *f.* **1.** steaming. **2.** (*cul.*) stewing.

па́рк|а,[2] и, *f.* parka (*skin jacket worn by Eskimos, etc.*).

парке́т, а, *m.* parquet; parquetry; настлáть п. to parquet, lay a parquet floor.

парке́тин|а, ы, *f.* parquet block.

парке́т|ный, *adj. of* ~; п. пол parquet floor; п. шаркýн (*fig., coll., pejor.*) socialite.

парке́тчик, а, *m.* parquet floor layer.

па́р|кий (~ок, ~ка), *adj.* (*coll.*) steamy.

па́рк|овый, *adj. of* ~; ~овые культу́ры park plants.

парлáмент, а, *m.* parliament.

парламентари́зм, а, *m.* parliamentarism.

парламентáри|й, я, *m.* parliamentarian.

парламентáрный, *adj.* parliamentarian.

парламентёр, а, *m.* (*mil.*) envoy; bearer of a flag of truce.

парламентёр|ский, *adj. of* ~; п. флаг flag of truce.

парлáментский, *adj.* parliamentary; п. закóн Act of Parliament; п. запрóс interpellation.

пармезáн, а, *m.* Parmesan (cheese).

парнáс|ец, ца, *m.* (*lit.*) Parnassian.

парнáсский, *adj.* (*lit.*) Parnassian.

парни́к, á, *m.* hotbed, seed-bed; forcing bed; в ~é under glass.

парник|óвый, *adj. of* ~; ~óвые растéния hothouse plants.

парни́шк|а, и, *m.* (*coll.*) boy, lad.

парн|óй, *adj.* **1.** fresh; ~óe молокó milk fresh from the cow; ~óe мя́со fresh meat. **2.** (*coll.*) steamy.

парнокопы́тн|ые, ых, *sing.* ~ое, ~ого, *n.* (*zool.*) Artiodactyla.

па́рн|ый[1], *adj.* **1.** pair; forming a pair; twin; п. носóк, п. сапóг, *etc.*, pair, fellow (*other one of pair of socks, boots, etc.*); ~ая грéбля sculling. **2.** pair-horse. **3.** ~ые ли́стья (*bot.*) conjugate leaves.

па́рный[2], *adj.* (*coll.*) steamy.

парови́к, á, *m.* **1.** (*tech.*) boiler. **2.** (*coll., obs.*) steam-engine. **3.** local steam-train.

парово́з, а, *m.* (steam-)engine, locomotive.

парово́зник, а, *m.* loco man (*engine-driver or fireman*).

парово́з|ный, *adj. of* ~; ~ная бригáда engine crew; ~ное депó engine-shed.

паровозоремóнтный, *adj.* engine-repair, locomotive-repair.

паровозострое́ни|е, я, *n.* engine building, locomotive building.

паровозостро|и́тельный, *adj. of* ~éние; п. завóд engine-building works.

паров|óй[1], *adj.* **1.** *adj. of* пар[1]; ~áя маши́на steam-engine; ~óe отоплéние steam heating; central heating; ~áя прáчечная steam laundry. **2.** (*cul.*) steamed.

паров|óй[2], *adj.* lying fallow.

паровпускн|óй, *adj.* (*tech.*) п. клáпан inlet valve; ~áя трубá steam supply pipe.

паровыпускнóй, *adj.* (*tech.*) exhaust.

парогенерáтор, а, *m.* (*tech.*) steam-generator.

парод|и́йный, *adj. of* ~ия.

пароди́р|овать, ую, *impf. and pf.* to parody.

паро́ди|я, и, *f.* parody.

парокóнный, *adj.* two-horse.

парокси́зм, а, *m.* paroxysm.

паро́л|ь, я, *m.* password, countersign.

парóм, а, *m.* ferry(-boat); п.-самолёт flying bridge, air ferry; перепрáвить на ~e to ferry.

парóмщик, а, *m.* ferryman.

паронепроницáемый, *adj.* steam-tight, steam-proof.

парообрáзный, *adj.* vaporous.

парообразова́ни|е, я, *n.* (*phys., tech.*) steam-
-generation, vaporization.

пароотво́дн|ый, *adj.* ~ая труба́ (*tech.*)
steam exhaust pipe, steam-escape pipe.

пароотсека́тел|ь, я, *m.* steam cut-off valve.

пароперегрева́тел|ь, я, *m.* (*tech.*) steam
superheater.

паро-пескостру́йный, *adj.* п. аппара́т
(*tech.*) steam sand blaster.

паропрово́д, а, *m.* (*tech.*) steam pipe.

парораспредели́тел|ь, я, *m.* (*tech.*) steam
distributor, steam header.

парораспредели́тельн|ый, *adj.* ~ая коро́б-
ка (*tech.*) steam-box.

парораспыли́тел|ь, я, *m.* (*tech.*) steam
atomizer.

паросбо́рник, а, *m.* (*tech.*) steam collector;
dome (*of boiler*).

паросилов|о́й, *adj.* ~а́я устано́вка (*tech.*)
steam power plant.

паро́сский, *adj.* Parian; п. мра́мор Parian
marble.

паростру́йный, *adj.* steam-jet.

парохо́д, а, *m.* steamer; steamship; бук-
си́рный п. steam tug; океа́нский п. ocean
liner.

парохо́дик, а, *m.* (*coll.*) 1. *dim. of* парохо́д.
2. toy boat.

парохо́д|ный, *adj. of* ~; ~ное о́бщество
steamship company.

парохо́дств|о, а, *n.* 1. steam-navigation.
2. steamship-line.

парт- *abbr. of* парти́йный Party-.

па́рт|а, ы, *f.* (school) desk; сесть за ~у to
begin to learn.

партакти́в, а, *m.* (*polit.*) Party activists.

партбиле́т, а, *m.* (*polit.*) party-membership
card.

партеногене́з, а, *m.* (*zool.*) parthenogenesis.

парте́р, а, *m.* (*theatr.*) the pit; the stalls.

партесн|ый, *adj.* ~ое пе́ние (*eccl.*) part-
-singing.

парти́|ец, йца, *m.* (*Soviet Communist*) Party-
member.

партиза́н, а, *pl.* ~ы, ~, *m.* partisan; guerilla.

партиза́н|ить, ю, ишь, *impf.* (*coll.*) to be a
partisan, fight with the partisans.

партиза́н|ский, *adj.* 1. *adj. of* ~; ~ская
война́ guerilla warfare; ~ское движе́ние
the Resistance (movement) (*e.g. against
Germany during Second World War*); п.
отря́д partisan detachment. 2. (*fig., pejor.*)
unplanned, haphazard.

партиза́нств|о, а, *n.* 1. guerilla warfare;
resistance movement. 2. (*collect.*) partisans,
guerillas.

партиза́нщин|а, ы, *f.* 1. guerilla warfare.
2. (*fig., pejor.*) unplanned work, haphazard
work.

па́ртийк|а, и, *f.* (*coll.*) *dim. of* па́ртия.

парти́йк|а, и, *f. of* парти́ец.

парти́йност|ь, и, *f.* 1. Party spirit. 2. party
membership.

парти́йн|ый, *adj.* (*polit.*) 1. party; (Commun-
ist) Party; п. биле́т party-(Party-)member-
ship card; п. стаж length of party (Party)
membership; ~ая яче́йка Party cell.
2. Party (*in accordance with the spirit of the
Soviet Communist Party*); п. дух Party spirit.
3. *as noun* п., ~ого, *m.* (*Communist*) Party
member.

партикуляри́зм, а, *m.* (*polit.*) particularism.

партикуля́р|ный (~ен, ~на), *adj.* (*obs.*)
1. private; unofficial. 2. civil; ~ное пла́тье
civilian clothes, mufti.

партиту́р|а, ы, *f.* (*mus.*) score.

па́рти|я¹, и, *f.* (*polit.*) party; the Party.

па́рти|я², и, *f.* 1. party, group. 2. batch;
lot; consignment (*of goods*). 3. (*sport*) game;
set. 4. (*mus.*) part. 5. (*obs.*) (good) match
(*marriage*); сде́лать хоро́шую ~ю to make a
good match.

парткабине́т, а, *m.* Party educational
centre.

партко́м, а, *m.* (*abbr. of* парти́йный коми-
те́т) Party committee.

партнёр, а, *m.* partner.

парто́рг, а, *m.* (*abbr. of* парти́йный орга-
низа́тор) Party organizer.

парторганиза́ци|я, и, *f.* Party organiza-
tion.

партсъе́зд, а, *m.* Party congress.

па́руб|ок, ка, *m.* (*Ukrainian*) boy, lad, youth.

па́рус, а, *pl.* ~а́, *m.* sail; идти́ под ~а́ми to
sail, be under sail; подня́ть ~а́, поста́вить
~а́ to make sail, set sail; на всех ~а́х in full
sail (*also fig.*).

паруси́н|а, ы, *f.* canvas, sail-cloth; duck.

па́русник, а, *m.* sailing vessel, sailer.

па́рус|ный, *adj. of* ~; п. спорт sailing.

парфо́рсн|ый, *adj.* ~ая езда́ circus riding.

парфюме́р, а, *m.* perfumer.

парфюме́ри|я, и, *f.* (*collect.*) perfumery.

парфюме́р|ный, *adj. of* ~ия; п. магази́н per-
fumer's shop; ~ная фа́брика perfumery.

парце́лл|а, ы, *f.* (*agric.*) parcel (of land).

парцелли́р|овать, ую, *impf. and pf.* (*agric.*)
to parcel (out).

парцелля́ци|я, и, *f.* (*agric.*) parcelling (out).

парч|а́, и́, *g. pl.* ~е́й, *f.* brocade.

парч|о́вый, *adj. of* ~а́.

парш|а́, и́, *f.* tetter ·mange; scab.

парши́ве|ть, ю, *impf.* (*of* за~ *and* о~) to be-
come mangy; to be covered with scabs.

парши́в|ец, ца, *m.* (*coll.*) lousy fellow.

парши́в|ый (~, ~а), *adj.* 1. mangy, scabby;
~ая овца́ (*fig.*) black sheep. 2. (*coll.*) nasty,
rotten, lousy.

пас¹, а, *m.* (*cards*) pass; объяви́ть п. to pass;
as interj. я п. (I) pass; в э́том де́ле я п.

(*fig.*, *coll.*) I'm no good at this, this is not in my line.

пас², **а**, *m.* (*sport*) pass; *as interj.* п. сюда́! pass!

па́сек|а, **и**, *f.* apiary, bee-garden.

па́се|чный, *adj. of* ~ка.

па́сквил|ь, **я**, *m.* libel, lampoon, pasquinade; squib.

па́сквильный, *adj.* libellous.

пасквиля́нт, **а**, *m.* lampoonist, slanderer.

паску́д|ный (~ен, ~на), *adj.* (*coll.*) foul, filthy.

паслён, **а**, *m.* (*bot.*) solanum; morel; сла́дко--го́рький п. bitter-sweet; чёрный п. deadly nightshade.

паслён|овый, *adj. of* ~; *as noun* ~овые, ~овых Solanaceae.

па́см|о, **а**, *n.* (*text.*) lea.

па́смур|ный (~ен, ~на), *adj.* 1. dull, cloudy; overcast. 2. (*fig.*) gloomy, sullen.

пас|ова́ть¹, **у́ю**, *impf.* (*of* с~) 1. (*also pf. in past tense*) (*cards*) to pass. 2. (*fig.*, *coll.*) to give up, give in; п. пе́ред тру́дностями to give in to difficulties.

пас|ова́ть², **у́ю**, *impf. and pf.* (*sport*) to pass.

па́сок|а, **и**, *f.* (*anat.*; *obs.*) lymph.

па́сочниц|а, **ы**, *f.* (*cul.*) mould for paskha.

па́с|очный, *adj. of* ~ха з.

паспарту́, *indecl.*, *n.* passe-partout.

па́спорт, **а**, *pl.* ~а́, *m.* 1. passport. 2. registration certificate (*of motor vehicle, piece of machinery, etc.*).

паспортиза́ци|я, **и**, *f.* 1. passport system. 2. (*tech.*) certification.

паспорти́ст, **а**, *m.* passport officer.

па́спорт|ный, *adj. of* ~; п. стол passport office.

пасс, **а**, *m.* (*in hypnotism*) pass.

пасса́ж, **а**, *m.* 1. passage; arcade. 2. (*mus.*) passage. 3. (*obs.*, *coll.*) unexpected turn (of events); како́й п.! a pretty pass!

пассажи́р, **а**, *m.* passenger.

пассажи́р|ский, *adj. of* ~; ~ское движе́ние passenger services.

пасса́т, **а**, *m.* (*geogr.*) trade wind.

пасса́т|ный, *adj. of* ~; п. ве́тер trade wind.

пасси́в, **а**, *m.* 1. (*comm.*) liabilities. 2. (*gram.*) passive voice.

пасси́вност|ь, **и**, *f.* passiveness, passivity.

пасси́в|ный (~ен, ~на), *adj.* 1. passive; ~ное избира́тельное пра́во (*polit.*) eligibility. 2. (*econ.*) п. бала́нс unfavourable balance.

пасси|я, **и**, *f.* (*obs.*, *coll.*) passion; бы́вшая п. old flame.

па́ст|а, **ы**, *f.* paste; зубна́я п. toothpaste.

па́стбищ|е, **а**, *n.* pasture.

па́стбищ|ный, *adj.* pasturable.

па́ств|а, **ы**, *f.* (*eccl.*) flock, congregation.

пасте́л|ь, **и**, *f.* 1. pastel, crayon. 2. pastel (drawing).

пасте́льный, *adj.* (drawn in) pastel.

пастериза́ци|я, **и**, *f.* pasteurization.

пастеризо́в|анный, *p.p.p. of* ~а́ть *and adj.* pasteurized.

пастериз|ова́ть, **у́ю**, *impf. and pf.* to pasteurize.

пастерна́к, **а**, *m.* parsnip.

пас|ти́, **у́**, **ёшь**, *past* ~, ~ла́, *impf.* (*no pf.*) to graze, pasture; to shepherd, tend.

пастил|а́, **ы́**, *pl.* ~ы, *f.* pastila (*sort of fruit fudge*).

пас|ти́сь, **ётся**, *past* ~ся, ~ла́сь, *impf.* (*no pf.*) to graze, pasture; to browse.

па́стор, **а**, *m.* (*Protestant*) minister, pastor.

пастора́л|ь, **и**, *f.* 1. (*lit.*) pastoral. 2. (*mus.*) pastorale.

пастора́льный, *adj.* pastoral, bucolic.

пасту́х, **а́**, *m.* herdsman; shepherd; cowboy.

пасту́|шеский, *adj. of* ~х; п. по́сох shepherd's crook.

пасту́|ший, *adj. of* ~х; ~шья су́мка (*bot.*) shepherd's purse.

пасту́шк|а, **и**, *f.* shepherdess.

пастуш|о́к, **ка́**, *m.* 1. *affect. dim. of* пасту́х. 2. (*poet.*) swain. 3. водяно́й п. (*orn.*) water--rail.

па́стыр|ский, *adj. of* ~ь; (*eccl.*) pastoral.

па́стыр|ь, **я**, *m.* 1. (*obs.*) shepherd. 2. (*eccl.*) pastor.

па|сть¹, **ду́**, **дёшь**, *past* ~л, ~ла, *pf. of* ~да́ть.

паст|ь², **и**, *f.* mouth (*of animal*); jaws.

паст|ь³, **и**, *f.* (*dial.*) trap.

пастьб|а́, **ы́**, *f.* pasturage.

Па́сх|а, **и**, *f.* 1. Passover. 2. Easter. 3. п. (*cul.*) paskha (*sweet cream-cheese dish eaten at Easter*).

пасха́ли|я, **и**, *f.* (*eccl.*) paschal cycle, paschal tables.

па́сын|ок, **ка**, *m.* 1. stepson, stepchild. 2. (*fig.*) outcast.

пасья́нс, **а**, *m.* (*card-game*) patience; раскла́дывать п. to play patience.

пат¹, **а**, *m.* (*in chess*) stalemate.

пат², **а**, *m.* (*cul.*) paste.

пате́нт, **а**, *m.* (на+*a.*) patent (for); licence (for); владе́лец ~а, держа́тель ~а patentee.

пате́нт|ный, *adj. of* ~.

патенто́в|анный, *p.p.p. of* ~а́ть *and adj.* patent; ~анное лека́рство patent medicine.

патент|ова́ть, **у́ю**, *impf.* to patent, take out a patent (for).

па́тер, **а**, *m.* Father (*in designation of Catholic priest*).

патери́к, **а́**, *m.* (*eccl.*; *lit.*) Lives of the Fathers.

патети́к|а, **и**, *f.* (the) pathetic element.

патети́ческий, *adj.* 1. enthusiastic; passionate. 2. emotional. 3. bombastic.

патети́ч|ный (~ен, ~на), *adj.* = ~еский.

патефо́н, а, *m.* (*small, portable*) gramophone.

патефо́н|ный, *adj. of* ~.

па́тин|а, ы, *f.* (*archaeol., tech.*) patina.

па́тл|ы, ~, *sing.* ~а, ~ы, *f.* (*coll.*) locks (*of hair*).

пат|ова́ть, у́ю, *impf.* (*of* за~) (*in chess*) to stalemate.

па́ток|а, и, *f.* treacle; syrup; све́тлая п. golden syrup; чёрная п. molasses.

пато́лог, а, *m.* pathologist.

патологи́ческий, *adj.* pathological.

патологи|я, и, *f.* pathology.

па́то|чный, *adj. of* ~ка; treacly.

патриа́рх, а, *m.* (*ethnol. and eccl.*) patriarch.

патриарха́льност|ь, и, *f.* patriarchal character.

патриарха́л|ьный (~ен, ~ьна), *adj.* (*ethnol. and fig.*) patriarchal.

патриарха́т, а, *m.* (*ethnol.*) patriarchy.

патриа́рхи|я, и, *f.* (*eccl.*) patriarchate.

патриа́ршеств|о, а, *n.* (*eccl.*) patriarchate.

патриа́р|ший, *adj. of* ~х (*eccl.*).

патрио́т, а, *m.* patriot.

патриоти́зм, а, *m.* patriotism.

патриоти́ческий, *adj.* patriotic.

патриоти́ч|ный (~ен, ~на), *adj.* = ~еский.

патри́стик|а, и, *f.* (*eccl., lit.*) patristic studies.

па́триц|а, ы, *f.* (*typ.*) punch.

патрициа́нский, *adj. of* патри́ций.

патрициа́т, а, *m.* (*hist.*) patriciate, patrician order.

патри́ци|й, я, *m.* (*hist.*) patrician.

патро́н¹, а, *m.* 1. (*in var. senses*) patron; (*eccl.*) patron saint. 2. boss.

патро́н², а, *m.* 1. cartridge. 2. (*tech.*) chuck (*of drill, lathe*), holder. 3. lamp socket, lamp holder. 4. (tailor's) pattern.

патрона́т, а, *m.* patronage.

патрони́р|овать, ую, *impf.* to patronize.

патро́нник, а, *m.* (*mil.*) (cartridge-)chamber.

патро́н|ный, *adj. of* ~²; ~ная ги́льза cartridge case; п. заво́д cartridge factory; ~ная обо́йма charger; cartridge clip; ~ная су́мка cartridge pouch; п. ключ socket wrench; п. стано́к chucking lathe.

патронта́ш, а, *m.* bandolier, ammunition belt.

па́труб|ок, ка, *m.* (*tech.*) 1. nipple, nozzle. 2. socket, sleeve, connexion; branch pipe. 3. boss (*of thermometer*).

патрули́р|овать, ую, *impf.* (*no pf.*) (*mil.*) to patrol.

патру́л|ь, я, *m.* patrol.

патру́ль|ный, *adj. of* ~; *as noun* п., ~ного, *m.* patrol.

па́уз|а, ы, *f.* pause; interval; (*mus.*) rest.

па́уз|ок, ка, *m.* (*river*) lighter.

пауќ, а́, *m.* spider.

паукообра́зн|ые, ых, *sing.* ~ое, ~ого, *n.* (*zool.*) Arachnida.

па́упер, а, *m.* pauper.

паупериза́ци|я, и, *f.* pauperization.

паупери́зм, а, *m.* pauperism.

паути́н|а, ы, *f.* cobweb, spider's web; gossamer; (*fig.*) web.

паути́н|ка, ки, *f. dim. of* ~а; чулки́-п. very fine stockings.

пау́|чий, *adj. of* ~к.

па́фос, а, *m.* 1. pathos. 2. (+g.) enthusiasm (for), zeal (for); п. коммунисти́ческого строи́тельства enthusiasm for the building of Communism. 3. spirit; emotional content; п. рома́на the spirit of a novel. 4. (*pejor.*) (*affected*) pathos, bombast.

пах, а, о ~е, в ~у́, *m.* (*anat.*) groin.

па́ханы|й, *adj.* ploughed (up); ~е зе́мли ploughland.

па́хар|ь, я, *m.* ploughman.

па|ха́ть, шу́, ~шешь, *impf.* to plough, till.

па́хн|уть, у, ешь, *impf.* (*no pf.*) (+i.) to smell (of); to reek (of); ~ет лу́ком there is a smell of onions; (*fig.*) to savour (of), smack (of); ~ет бедо́й this means trouble; ~уло ссо́рой a quarrel was in the air.

пахн|у́ть, ёт, *pf.* (*no impf.*) (+i.; *coll.*) to puff, blow; ~ул ве́тер there was a gust of wind; ~уло хо́лодом (*impers.*) there came a cold blast.

паховой, *adj.* (*anat.*) inguinal.

па́хот|а, ы, *f.* ploughing, tillage.

па́хотный, *adj.* arable.

па́хтань|е, я, *n.* 1. churning. 2. butter-milk.

па́хта|ть, ю, *impf.* to churn.

паху́ч|ий (~, ~а), *adj.* odorous, strong-smelling.

паца́н, а́, *m.* (*coll.*) boy, lad.

пацие́нт, а, *m.* patient.

пацифи́зм, а, *m.* pacifism.

пацифи́ст, а, *m.* pacifist.

па́че, *adv.* (*arch.*) more; *now only in phrases* тем п. the more so, the more reason; п. ча́яния contrary to expectation; beyond expectation.

па́чк|а, и, *f.* 1. bundle; batch; packet, pack; п. пи́сем bundle of letters; п. папиро́с packet of cigarettes; п. книг parcel of books. 2. (*mil.*) (*cartridge*) clip; стреля́ть ~ами (*obs.*) to fire bursts. 3. 'tutu' (*ballet dancer's fluffy skirt, with layers of underskirts*).

па́чка|ть, ю, *impf.* 1. (*pf.* за ~ *and* ис ~) to dirty, soil, stain, sully (*also fig.*); п. ру́ки (*fig.*) to soil one's hands; п. чье́-н. до́брое и́мя to sully someone's good name. 2. (*pf.* на~) (*coll.*) to daub.

па́чка|ться, юсь, *impf.* (*of* за~, ис~, *and* на~) 1. to make oneself dirty, soil oneself. 2. to become dirty.

пачкотн|я́, и́, *f.* (*coll.*) daub.

пачку́н, а́, *m.* (*coll.*) **1.** sloven. **2.** dauber.

паш|а́, и́, *g. pl.* ~е́й, *m.* pasha.

па́ш|ня, ни, *g. pl.* ~ен, *f.* ploughed field.

паште́т, а, *m.* pâté, pie.

па́юсн|ый, *adj.* ~ая икра́ pressed caviar(e).

пая́льник, а, *m.* soldering iron.

пая́льн|ый, *adj.* soldering; ~ая ла́мпа blow lamp; ~ая тру́бка blowpipe, blow torch.

пая́льщик, а, *m.* tinman, tinsmith.

па́яный, *adj.* soldered.

пая́снича|ть, ю, *impf.* (*no pf.*) (*coll.*) to clown, play the fool.

пая́|ть, ю, *impf.* (*no pf.*) to solder.

пая́ц, а, *m.* **1.** (*circus*) clown. **2.** (*fig., pejor.*) clown.

пеа́н¹, а, *m.* paean.

пеа́н², а, *m.* (*med.*) Pean's forceps, clamp forceps.

пев|е́ц, ца́, *m.* singer.

певи́ц|а, ы, *f. of* певе́ц.

певу́н, а́, *m.* (*coll.*) songster.

певу́ч|ий (~, ~а), *adj.* melodious.

пе́вч|ий **1.** *adj.* singing; ~ая пти́ца song--bird. **2.** *as noun* п., ~его, *m.* chorister, choirboy.

пега́нк|а, и, *f.* (*orn.*) shelduck.

пе́г|ий (~, ~а), *adj.* skewbald.

педаго́г, а, *m.* teacher; pedagogue.

педаго́гик|а, и, *f.* pedagogy, pedagogics.

педагоги́ческий, *adj.* pedagogic(al); educational; п. институ́т teachers' training college; п. факульте́т education department (*for training educationalists*).

педагоги́ч|ный (~ен, ~на), *adj.* sensible, wise (*in sphere of education*).

педализа́ци|я, и, *f.* (*mus.*) pedalling.

педализи́р|овать, ую, *impf. and pf.* **1.** (*mus.*) to pedal. **2.** (*fig.*) to harp upon.

педа́л|ь, и, *f.* pedal; treadle; брать п., нажа́ть п. to pedal; рабо́тать ~ью, to treadle; нажа́ть на все ~и (*fig., coll.*) to go flat out.

педа́ль|ный, *adj. of* ~; п. нажи́м pedalling; п. автомоби́ль pedal car (*child's motor-car operated by pedal*).

педа́нт, а, *m.* pedant.

педанти́зм, а, *m.* pedantry.

педанти́ческий, *adj.* pedantic.

педанти́чност|ь, и, *f.* pedantry.

педанти́ч|ный (~ен, ~на), *adj.* = ~еский.

пе́дел|ь, я, *m.* bedel.

педера́ст, а, *m.* p(a)ederast, sodomite.

педера́сти|я, и, *f.* p(a)ederasty, sodomy.

педиа́тр, а, *m.* p(a)ediatrician.

педиатри́|я, и, *f.* p(a)ediatrics.

педикю́р, а, *m.* chiropody.

педикю́рш|а, и, *f.* chiropodist.

педо́метр, а, *m.* pedometer.

пе́жин|а, ы, *f.* **1.** skewbaldness. **2.** patch (*on skewbald horse*).

пезе́т|а, ы, *f.* (*Spanish currency unit*) peseta.

пейза́ж, а, *m.* **1.** landscape; scenery. **2.** (*art*) landscape.

пейзажи́ст, а, *m.* landscape painter.

пейза́ж|ный, *adj. of* ~; ~ная жи́вопись landscape painting.

пек, а, *m.* (*tech.*) pitch.

пёк, пекла́, *see* печь¹.

пека́рн|ый, *adj.* baking; ~ая печь bakehouse oven; ~ое ремесло́ bakery trade.

пека́р|ня, ни, *g. pl.* ~ен, *f.* bakery, bakehouse.

пе́кар|ский, *adj. of* ~ь; ~ские дро́жжи baker's yeast.

пе́кар|ь, я, *pl.* ~я́, ~е́й *and* ~и, ~ей, *m.* baker.

пеклева́нник, а, *m.* fine rye bread.

пеклева́нн|ый, *adj.* finely ground; ~ая мука́ rye flour (of the best quality); п. хлеб fine rye bread.

пеклев|а́ть, ю́ю, ю́ешь, *impf.* to grind fine.

пе́кл|о, а, *n.* **1.** scorching heat; попа́сть в са́мое п. (*fig., coll.*) to get into the thick of it. **2.** (*coll.*) hell.

пекти́н, а, *m.* (*chem.*) pectin.

пекти́новы|й, *adj.* (*chem.*) pectic; ~е вещества́ pectins.

пеку́, пеку́т, *see* печь¹.

пелен|а́, ы́, *pl.* ~ы́, ~, ~а́м, *f.* shroud; с ~ (*obs., fig.*) from the cradle; у него́ (сло́вно) п. (с глаз) упа́ла the scales fell from his eyes.

пелена́|ть, ю, *impf.* (*of* за~ *and* с~) to swaddle.

пе́ленг, а, *m.* (*naut., aeron.*) bearing.

пеленга́тор, а, *m.* (*naut., aeron.*) direction finder.

пеленг|и́ровать, и́рую, *impf. and pf.* = ~ова́ть.

пеленг|ова́ть, у́ю, *impf. and pf.* (*naut., aeron.*) to take the bearings (of), set.

пелён|ка, ки, *f.* nappy; (*pl.*) swaddling clothes; с пелёнок (*fig.*) from the cradle.

пелери́н|а, ы, *f.* cape, pelerine.

челика́н, а, *m.* pelican.

пельме́н|и, ей, *sing.* ~ь, ~я, *m.* (*cul.*) pelmeni (*kind of ravioli*).

пемз|а, ы, *f.* pumice(-stone).

пе́мз|овый, *adj. of* ~а.

пе́н|а, ы, *f.* **1.** foam, spume; scum; froth, head (*on liquids*); мы́льная п. soapsuds; говори́ть с ~ой у рта, с ~ой на уста́х (*fig.*) to foam at the mouth. **2.** lather (*on horses*).

пена́л, а, *m.* pencil-box.

пена́т|ы, ов, *no sing.* (*myth. and fig.*) penates; верну́ться к (свои́м, родны́м) ~ам to return to one's hearth and home.

пе́ни|е, я, *n.* singing; п. (птиц) (birds') song; п. петуха́ cock's crow.

пе́нист|ый (~, ~а), *adj.* foamy; frothy; ~ое вино́ sparkling wine.

пенитенциа́рный, *adj.* (*leg.*) penitentiary.

пе́н|ить, ю, ишь, *impf.* to froth.

пе́н|иться, ится, *impf.* to foam; to froth (*intrans.*).

пеницилли́н, а, *m.* penicillin.

пе́нк|а¹, и, *f.* (*on milk, etc.*) skin; снять ~и (с+*g.*) to skim; (*fig.*) to take the pickings (of).

пе́нк|а², и, *f.* (*min.*) морска́я п. meerschaum.

пе́нк|овый, *adj.* of ~а²; ~овая тру́бка meerschaum (pipe).

пе́нни, *indecl.*, *n.* penny.

пе́н|ный, *adj.* (*obs.*) = ~истый.

пенопла́ст, а, *m.* foam rubber.

пенопласт|и́ческий, *adj.* of ~.

пеностекл|о́, а́, *n.* glass fibre.

пеностек|о́льный, *adj.* of ~ло́.

пе́ночк|а, и, *f.* (*orn.*) warbler (*Phylloscopus*).

пенс, а, *m.* penny.

пенсионе́р, а, *m.* pensioner.

пенсио́нн|ый, *adj.* of пе́нсия; ~ая кни́жка pension book.

пе́нси|я, и, *f.* pension.

пенсне́, *indecl.*, *n.* pince-nez.

пента́метр, а, *m.* (*lit.*) pentameter.

пе́нтюх, а, *m.* (*coll.*) lout, bumpkin.

пень, пня, *m.* stump, stub; стоя́ть как п. (*coll.*) to be rooted to the ground; вали́ть че́рез п. коло́ду (*coll.*) to do a thing anyhow.

пенык|а́, и́, *f.* hemp.

пенько́вый, *adj.* hempen.

пеньюа́р, а, *m.* peignoir.

пе́н|я, и, *f.* fine.

пеня́|ть, ю, *impf.* (*of* по~) (+*d. or* на+*a.*; *coll.*) to blame, reproach; ~й на себя́! you have only yourself to blame!

пео́н¹, а, *m.* (*lit.*) paeon.

пео́н², а, *m.* peon.

пе́п|ел, ла, *m.* ash(es).

пепели́щ|е, а, *n.* 1. site of fire. 2. (hearth and) home; верну́ться на ста́рое п. to return to one's old home.

пе́пельниц|а, ы, *f.* ash-tray.

пе́пельно-се́рый, *adj.* ash-grey.

пе́пельн|ый, *adj.* ashy; ~ого цве́та ash-grey.

пепси́н, а, *m.* (*physiol.*) pepsin.

пепси́новый, *adj.* peptic.

пепто́н, а, *m.* (*physiol.*) peptone.

перва́ч, а́, *m.* (*coll.*) first-quality goods.

перве́йший, *adj.* (*coll.*) the first; first-class.

пе́рвен|ец, ца, *m.* first-born; (*fig.*) firstling.

пе́рвенств|о, а, *n.* first place; (*sport*) championship; завоева́ть п. ми́ра по футбо́лу to win the world championship at football.

пе́рвенств|овать, ую and ~ова́ть, ~у́ю, *impf.* (*no pf.*) to take first place; (над) to take precedence (of), take priority (over).

пе́рвенств|у́ющий, *pres. part. act. of* ~ова́ть *and adj.* pre-eminent; primary.

перви́нк|а, и, *f.* в ~у (*coll.*) for the first time; мне не в ~у предупрежда́ть её this is not the first time I have warned her.

перви́чность|ь, и, *f.* primacy; priority.

перви́чн|ый, *adj.* primary; initial; ~ая парторганиза́ция primary Party organization; п. пери́од боле́зни initial period of illness; ~ые поро́ды (*geol.*) primary rocks.

первобы́тность|ь, и, *f.* primitive state.

первобы́тный, *adj.* (*ethnol. and fig.*) primitive; primordial; primeval.

первого́д|ок, ка, *m.* (*coll.*) young of animal less than one year old.

пе́рв|ое, ого, *n.* first course (*of a meal*).

первозда́нный, *adj.* primordial; (*geol.*) primitive, primary; п. хао́с primordial chaos (*also fig., iron.*).

первоисто́чник, а, *m.* primary source; origin.

первокатего́рник, а, *m.* first-rank (first-flight) player (*esp. of chess-players*).

первокла́ссник, а, *m.* pupil of the first class, first-former.

первокла́ссный, *adj.* first-class, first-rate.

первоку́рсник, а, *m.* first-year student, freshman.

Первома́|й, я, *m.* (*coll.*) May Day.

первома́й|ский, *adj.* of ~.

пе́рво-на́перво, *adv.* (*coll.*) first of all.

первонача́льно, *adv.* originally.

первонача́льн|ый, *adj.* 1. original. 2. primary; initial; ~ое накопле́ние (*econ.*) primary accumulation; ~ая причи́на (*philos.*) first cause. 3. elementary. 4. ~ые чи́сла (*math.*) prime numbers.

первообра́з, а, *m.* prototype, original; protoplast.

первообра́зный, *adj.* prototypal; protoplastic.

первоосно́в|а, ы, *f.* (*philos.*) first principle.

первооткрыва́тель|ь, я, *m.* discoverer.

первоочередн|о́й, *adj.* first and foremost, immediate; ~а́я зада́ча immediate task.

первоочередн|о́й, *adj.* = ~о́й.

первопеча́тник, а, *m.* printing pioneer.

первопеча́тн|ый, *adj.* 1. printed early, belonging to the first years of printing; ~ые кни́ги incunabula. 2. first printed.

первопресто́льн|ый, *adj.* (*rhet.*) being the oldest (first) capital; *as noun* Первопресто́льная, ~ой, *f.* Moscow (*by contrast with St. Petersburg*).

первопричи́н|а, ы, *f.* (*philos.*) first cause.

первопу́т|ок, ка, *m.* (*coll.*) the first sledging (*of the winter*); е́хать по ~ку to traverse a road after the first snowfall.

перворазря́дник, а, *m.* (*sport*) first-rank player.

перворазря́дный, *adj.* first-class, first-rank.

первородный, *adj.* (*obs.*) **1.** first-born. **2.** primal; п. грех (*eccl.*) original sin.

первородств|о, а, *n.* **1.** (*leg.*) primogeniture. **2.** (*fig.*) primacy.

перворождённый, *adj.* first-born.

первосвященник, а, *m.* high priest, chief priest; pontiff.

первосортный, *adj.* **1.** of the best quality. **2.** (*coll.*) first-class, first-rate.

первостатейный, *adj.* **1.** (*obs.*) of the first order; of consequence. **2.** (*coll.*) first-rate, first-class.

первостепенный, *adj.* paramount, of the first order.

первоцвет, а, *m.* (*bot.*) primrose.

перв|ый, *adj.* (*in var. senses*) first; former; earliest; ~ое (число месяца) the first (of the month); ~ого января on the first of January; половина ~ого half past twelve; в ~ом часу after twelve, past twelve, between twelve and one; он п. вошёл he was the first to enter; быть ~ым, идти ~ым to come first, lead; ~ое время at first; п. встречный the first comer; ~ое дело, ~ым делом (*coll.*) first of all, first thing; не ~ой молодости not in one's first youth; ~ая помощь first aid; п. рейс maiden voyage; не ~ой свежести not quite fresh, stale; ~ая скрипка first violin; (*fig.*) first fiddle; п. этаж ground floor; в ~ую голову (*coll.*) first and foremost; в ~ую очередь in the first place; из ~ых рук first-hand; на п. взгляд, с ~ого взгляда at first sight; при ~ой возможности at one's earliest convenience, as soon as possible; с ~ого раза from the first; п. блин комом (*prov.*) you must spoil before you spin.

перг|а, и, *f.* bee-bread.

пергамен, а, *m.* = ~т.

пергамент, а, *m.* parchment.

пергамент|ный, *adj.* of ~; ~ная бумага oil-paper.

перд|еть, ит, *impf.* (*vulg.*) to fart.

пере- *verbal prefix indicating* **1.** action across *or* through something (trans-). **2.** repetition of action (re-). **3.** superiority, excess, *etc.* (over-, out-). **4.** extension of action to encompass many *or* all objects *or* cases of a given kind. **5.** division into two *or* more parts. **6.** (*reflexives*) reciprocity of action.

переадрес|овать, ую, *pf.* (*of* ~овывать) to re-address.

переадресовыва|ть, ю, *impf. of* переадресовать.

перебази́р|овать, ую, *pf.* (*no impf.*) to shift.

перебаллоти́р|овать, ую, *pf.* (*of* ~овывать) to submit to second ballot.

перебаллотиро́вк|а, и, *f.* second ballot.

перебаллотиро́выва|ть, ю, *impf. of* перебаллоти́ровать.

перебарщива|ть, ю, *impf. of* переборщи́ть.

перебега́|ть, ю, *impf. of* перебежать.

перебе|жа́ть, гу́, жи́шь, гу́т, *pf.* (*of* ~га́ть) **1.** (через) to cross (running); п. (через) улицу to run across the street; п. кому-н. дорогу to cross someone's path. **2.** (*fig.*, *coll.*; к) to go over (to), desert (to).

перебе́жк|а, и, *f.* (*mil.*) bound, rush.

перебе́жчик, а, *m.* deserter; (*fig.*) turncoat.

перебе́лива|ть, ю, *impf. of* перебели́ть.

перебел|и́ть, ю́, и́шь, *pf.* (*of* ~ивать) **1.** to whitewash again. **2.** to make a fair copy (of).

перебе|си́ться, шу́сь, ~си́шься, *pf.* **1.** to go mad, run mad. **2.** (*coll.*) to have sown one's wild oats.

перебива́|ть(ся), ю(сь), *impf. of* переби́ть(ся)[1,2].

переби́вк|а, и, *f.* re-upholstering.

перебинт|ова́ть[1], у́ю, *pf.* (*of* ~о́вывать) to change the dressing (on), put a new dressing (on).

перебинт|ова́ть[2], у́ю, *pf.* (*of* ~о́вывать) to dress, bandage (*all, a quantity of*).

перебинто́выва|ть, ю, *impf. of* перебинтова́ть.

перебира́|ть(ся), ю(сь), *impf. of* перебра́ть(ся).

перебира́|ть[2], ю, *impf.* **1.** to finger; п. стру́ны to run one's fingers over the strings; п. чётки to tell one's beads. **2.** (+*i.*) to move, advance (*in turn or in a regular manner*).

переб|и́ть[1], ью, ьёшь, *pf.* (*of* ~ива́ть) **1.** to re-upholster. **2.** to beat up again (*pillow, feather-bed, etc.*).

переб|и́ть[2], ью, ьёшь, *pf.* (*of* ~ива́ть) **1.** to interrupt. **2.** to intercept; п. кому-н. дорогу to cross someone's path; п. поку́пку (*coll.*) to outbid for something.

переб|и́ть[3], ью, ьёшь, *pf.* **1.** to kill, slay, slaughter. **2.** to beat. **3.** to break.

переб|и́ться[1], ью́сь, ьёшься, *pf.* (*of* ~ива́ться) to break.

переб|и́ться[2], ью́сь, ьёшься, *pf.* (*of* ~ива́ться) (*coll.*) to make ends meet; п. с хле́ба на квас to live from hand to mouth.

перебо́|й, я, *m.* interruption, intermission; stoppage, hold-up; misfire (*of engine*); пульс с ~ями intermittent pulse.

перебо́йный, *adj.* interrupted, intermittent.

переболе́|ть[1], ю, *pf.* (+*i.*) to have had, have been down (*with an illness*); де́ти все ~ли коклю́шем the children have all been down with whooping-cough.

перебол|е́ть[2], и́т, *pf.* to recover, become well again.

перебо́рк|а[1], и, *f.* **1.** sorting out. **2.** (*tech.*) re-assembly.

перебо́рк|а[2], и, *f.* partition; (*naut.*) bulk-head.

перебор|о́ть, ю́, ~ешь, *pf.* (*no impf.*) to master.

переборщ|и́ть, у́, и́шь, pf. (of перебáрщивать) (в+p.; coll.) to go too far; to overdo it.

перебрáнива|ться, юсь, impf. (c+i.; coll.) to bandy angry words (with), have words (with).

перебран|и́ться, ю́сь, и́шься, pf. (c+i.; coll.) to quarrel (with), fall out (with).

перебрáнк|а, и, f. (coll.) wrangle, squabble.

перебрáсыва|ть(ся), ю(сь), impf. of перебрóсить(ся).

пере|брáть¹, беру́, берёшь, past ~брáл, ~бралá, ~брáло, pf. (of ~бирáть) **1.** to sort out (also fig.); to look through. **2.** (fig.) to turn over (in one's mind). **3.** to take in excess; п. пять очкóв to score five extra points.

пере|брáть², беру́, берёшь, past ~брáл, ~бралá, ~брáло, pf. (of ~бирáть) **1.** (typ.) to reset. **2.** (tech.) to (dismantle and) re-assemble.

пере|брáться, беру́сь, берёшься, past ~брáлся, ~бралáсь, ~брáлóсь, pf. (coll.) **1.** to get over, cross. **2.** to move; п. на нóвую кварти́ру to change one's lodgings.

перебр|оди́ть, óдит, pf. to have fermented; to have risen.

переброса́|ть, ю, pf. to throw one after another.

перебро́|сить, шу, сишь, pf. (of перебрáсывать) **1.** to throw over; п. мост чéрез рéку to throw a bridge across a river. **2.** to transfer (troops, etc.).

перебро́|ситься, шусь, сишься, pf. (of перебрáсываться) **1.** (+i.) to throw one to another; п. нéсколькими словáми (fig.) to exchange a few words. **2.** (of fire, disease, etc.) to spread.

перебрóск|а, и, f. transfer.

перебывá|ть, ю, pf. to have called, have been; он вездé ~л he has been all over the world.

перевáл, а, m. **1.** passing, crossing. **2.** (geogr.) pass.

перевáл|ец, ьца, m. ходи́ть с ~ьцем (coll.) to waddle.

перевáлива|ть, ю, impf. of перевали́ть.

перевáлива|ться¹, юсь, impf. of перевали́ться.

перевáлива|ться², юсь, impf. (no pf.) to waddle.

перевал|и́ть, ю́, ~ишь, pf. (of ~ивать) **1.** to transfer, shift. **2.** to cross; (impers.; coll.) ~и́ло за пóлночь it is past midnight; ей ~и́ло зá сорок (лет) she has turned forty, she is past forty.

перевал|и́ться, ю́сь, ~ишься, pf. (of ~ивáться¹) to roll over; to fall over; п. на прáвый бок to roll over on to one's right side.

перевáлк|а, и, f. **1.** trans-shipment, conveyance. **2.** trans-shipping point.

перевáл|очный, adj. of ~ка; п. пункт (in var. senses) staging post.

перевáрива|ть, ю, impf. of переварúть.

перевари́м|ый (~, ~a), adj. digestible.

перевар|и́ть¹, ю́, ~ишь, pf. (of ~ивать) **1.** to cook again; to boil again. **2.** (in cooking) to overdo.

перевар|и́ть², ю́, ~ишь, pf. (of ~ивать) **1.** to digest; п. прочи́танное (fig.) to digest what one has read. **2.** (fig.) to swallow; to bear, stand.

перевéд|аться, аюсь, pf. (of ~ываться) (obs.; c+i.) to demand satisfaction (from).

перевéдыва|ться, юсь, impf. of перевéдаться.

перевез|ти́, у́, ёшь, past ~, ~лá, pf. (of перевози́ть) **1.** to take across, put across. **2.** to transport, convey (from A to B); to (re)move (furniture, etc.).

переверн|у́ть, у́, ёшь, pf. (of перевёртывать and перевора́чивать) to turn over; to invert; п. страни́цу to turn over the page; п. наизна́нку to turn inside out.

переверн|у́ться, у́сь, ёшься, pf. (of перевёртываться and перевора́чиваться) to turn over; ~ётся в гробу́ (joc.) he would turn in his grave.

перевер|тéть, чу́, ~тишь, pf. (of ~тывать and ~чивать) (coll.) to overwind.

перевёртыва|ть(ся), ю(сь), impf. of перевернýть(ся) and перевертéть.

переверчива|ть, ю, impf. of перевертéть.

перевéс, а, m. preponderance; advantage; чи́сленный п. numerical superiority; взять п. to gain the upper hand; п. на нáшей сторонé, в нáшу пóльзу the odds are in our favour.

перевé|сить¹, шу, сишь, pf. (of ~шивать) to hang somewhere else; п. карти́ну с однóй стены́ на другýю to move a picture from one wall to another.

перевé|сить², шу, сишь, pf. (of ~шивать) **1.** to weigh again. **2.** to outweigh, outbalance (also fig.); (fig.) to tip the scales

перевé|ситься, шусь, сишься, pf. (of ~шиваться) to lean over.

переве|сти́¹, ду́, дёшь, past ~л, ~лá, pf. (of переводи́ть) **1.** to take across; п. детéй чéрез ýлицу to escort children across the road. **2.** to transfer, move, switch, shift; п. на другýю рабóту to transfer to another post; п. в слéдующий класс to move up into the next form; п. валю́ту to transfer currency; п. дéньги по телегрáфу to wire money; п. стрéлку to shunt, switch; п. стрéлку часóв вперёд (назáд) to put a clock on (back). **3.** (c+g. нa+a.) to translate (from into); (в, на+*a*.) to convert (to), express (as, in); п. с русского языка на английский to translate from Russian into English; п. в метрические меры to convert to the metric system, express according to the metric system. **4.** п. дух to take breath. **5.** (*art*) to transfer, copy.

переве|сти[2], **ду, дёшь**, *past* ~л, ~ла, *pf.* (*of* переводить) (*coll.*) **1.** to destroy, exterminate. **2.** to spend, use up.

переве|стись[1], **дусь, дёшься**, *past* ~лся, ~лась, *pf.* (*of* переводиться) **1.** to move, be transferred. **2.** *pass. of* ~сти[1,2].

переве|стись[2], **дусь, дёшься**, *past* ~лся, ~лась, *pf.* (*of* переводиться) (*coll.*) to come to an end; to become extinct; к концу недели деньги у меня ~лись by the end of the week I was spent up.

перевеш|ать[1], **аю**, *pf.* (*of* ~ивать) to weigh (*all or a quantity of*).

перевеш|ать[2], **аю**, *pf.* to hang (*a number of*).

перевешива|ть, ю, *impf. of* перевесить *and* перевешать[1].

перевешива|ться, юсь, *impf. of* перевеситься.

перевива|ть, ю, *impf. of* перевить.

перевида|ть, ю, *pf.* (*coll.*) to have seen (*also fig.* = to have experienced).

перевира|ть, ю, *impf. of* переврать.

перев|ить[1], **ью, ьёшь**, *past* ~ил, ~ила, ~ило, *pf.* (*of* ~ивать) to weave again.

перев|ить[2], **ью, ьёшь**, *past* ~ил, ~ила, ~ило, *pf.* (*of* ~ивать) (+*i.*) to interweave (with), intertwine (with).

перевод[1], **а, *m*. 1.** transfer, move, switch, shift; п. денег remittance; почтовый п. postal order; п. стрелки shunting, switching; п. стрелки часов вперёд (назад) putting a clock on (back). **2.** translation; version; п. мер conversion of measures.

перевод[2], **а, *m*.** (*coll.*) spending, using up; пустой п. денег (деньгам) squandering; нет ~у (+*d.*) there is no shortage (of), there is an inexhaustible supply (of).

перево|дить(ся), жу(сь), ~дишь(ся), *impf. of* перевести(сь).

переводн|ой, *adj. of* перевод[1]; ~ая бумага carbon paper; transfer paper; ~ая картинка transfer.

перевод|ный, *adj. of* ~[1]; п. роман novel in translation; п. бланк postal order form.

переводчик, а, *m*. translator; interpreter.

перевоз, а, *m*. 1. transportation. **2.** ferry.

перево|зить, жу, ~зишь, *impf. of* перевезти.

перевозк|а, и, *f*. conveyance, transportation.

перевоз|очный, *adj. of* ~ка; ~очные средства means of conveyance.

перевозчик, а, *m*. 1. ferryman; boatman. **2.** (*orn.*) common sandpiper.

переволн|овать, ую, *pf.* (*coll.*) to alarm.

переволн|оваться, уюсь, *pf.* (*coll.*) to be alarmed; to suffer prolonged anxiety.

перевооруж|ать(ся), аю(сь), *impf. of* ~ить(ся).

перевооружени|е, я, *n*. re-armament.

перевооруж|ить, у, ишь, *pf.* (*of* ~ать) to re-arm.

перевооруж|иться, усь, ишься, *pf.* (*of* ~аться) to re-arm (*intrans.*).

перевопло|тить, щу, тишь, *pf.* (*of* ~щать) to reincarnate; to transform.

перевопло|титься, щусь, тишься, *pf.* (*of* ~щаться) to be reincarnated; to undergo a transformation.

перевоплоща|ть(ся), ю(сь), *impf. of* перевоплотить(ся).

переворачива|ть(ся), ю(сь), *impf. of* перевернуть(ся).

переворот, а, *m*. 1. revolution; overturn; государственный п. coup d'état. **2.** (*geol.*) cataclysm.

переворош|ить, у, ишь, *pf.* (*coll.*) **1.** to turn (over) (*also fig.*); п. сено to turn hay; п. свою память to search through one's memories. **2.** (*fig.*) to turn upside down.

перевоспитани|е, я, *n*. re-education.

перевоспит|ать, аю, *pf.* (*of* ~ывать) to re-educate.

перевоспит|аться, аюсь, *pf.* (*of* ~ываться) to re-educate oneself, be re-educated.

перевоспитыва|ть(ся), ю(сь), *impf. of* перевоспитать(ся).

перевр|ать, у, ёшь, *past* ~ал, ~ала, ~ало, *pf.* (*of* перевирать) (*coll.*) to garble, confuse; to misinterpret; п. цитату to misquote.

перевыбира|ть, ю, *impf. of* перевыбрать.

перевыбор|ы, ов, *no sing.* re-election.

перевыб|рать, еру, ерешь, *pf.* (*of* ~ирать) to re-elect.

перевыполнени|е, я, *n*. over-fulfilment.

перевыполн|ить, ю, ишь, *pf.* (*of* ~ять) to over-fulfil.

перевыполн|ять, яю, *impf. of* ~ить.

перевя|зать[2], **жу**, ~жешь, *pf.* (*of* ~зывать) **1.** to dress, bandage. **2.** to tie up, cord.

перевя|зать[3], **жу**, ~жешь, *pf.* (*of* ~зывать) to knit again.

перевязк|а, и, *f*. dressing, bandage.

перевяз|очный, *adj. of* ~ка; п. материал dressing; п. пункт dressing station.

перевязыва|ть, ю, *impf. of* перевязать.

перевяз|ь, и, *f*. 1. (*mil.*, *hist.*) cross-belt, shoulder-belt, baldric. **2.** (*med.*) sling; рука у него была на ~и he had his arm in a sling.

перегар, а, *m*. (*coll.*) (*unpleasant*) residual taste of alcohol in the mouth; smell of alcohol; от него несло́ ~ом he reeked of alcohol.

переги́б, а, *m.* **1.** bend, twist; fold. **2.** (*fig.*) exaggeration; допусти́ть п. в чём-н. to carry something too far.

перегиба́|ть(ся), ю(сь), *impf. of* перегну́ть(ся).

перегласо́вк|а, и, *f.* (*ling.*) mutation.

перегля́дыва|ться, юсь, *impf. of* перегляну́ться.

перегля|ну́ться, ну́сь, ~нешься, *pf.* (*of* ~дываться) (c+*i.*) to exchange glances (with).

перегн|а́ть, перегоню́, перего́нишь, *past* ~а́л, ~ала́, ~а́ло, *pf.* (*of* перегоня́ть) **1.** to outdistance, leave behind; (*fig.*) to overtake, surpass. **2.** to drive (*somewhere else*; *from A to B*); п. самолёты to ferry planes. **3.** (*chem.*, *tech.*) to distil, sublimate.

перегнива́|ть, ю, *impf. of* перегни́ть.

перегн|и́ть, иёт, *past* ~и́л, ~ила́, ~и́ло, *pf.* (*of* ~ива́ть) to rot through.

перегно́|й, я, *m.* humus.

перегно́й|ный, *adj. of* ~; ~ная по́чва humus.

перег|ну́ть, ну́, нёшь, *pf.* (*of* ~иба́ть) to bend; п. па́лку (*fig.*, *coll.*) to go too far.

перег|ну́ться, ну́сь, нёшься, *pf.* (*of* ~иба́ться) **1.** to bend. **2.** to lean over.

перегова́рива|ть, ю, *impf. of* переговори́ть².

перегова́рива|ться, юсь, *impf.* (c+*i.*) to exchange remarks (with).

переговор|и́ть, ю́, и́шь, *pf.* (о+*p.*) to talk (about); to talk over, discuss; п. по телефо́ну to speak over the telephone.

переговор|и́ть², ю́, и́шь, *pf.* (*of* перегова́ривать) to silence; to out-talk.

переговóрн|ый, *adj.* ~ая бу́дка telephone booth; п. телефо́нный пункт trunk-call office.

переговóр|ы, ов, *no sing.* negotiations; (*mil.*) parley; вести́ п. (c+*i.*) to negotiate (with), carry on negotiations (with); (*mil.*) to parley (with); иду́т п. negotiations are in progress.

перегóн¹, а, *m.* driving.

перегóн², а, *m.* stage (*between two railway stations*).

перегóнк|а, и, *f.* (*tech.*, *chem.*) distillation; суха́я п. sublimation.

перегóн|ный, *adj. of* ~ка; п. заво́д distillery; п. куб still.

перегоня́|ть, ю, *impf. of* перегна́ть.

перегора́жива|ть, ю, *impf. of* перегороди́ть.

перегор|а́ть, а́ю, *impf. of* ~е́ть.

перегоре́лый, *adj.* (*coll.*) burnt out.

перегор|е́ть, и́т, *pf.* (*of* ~а́ть) **1.** to burn out, fuse. **2.** to burn through. **3.** to rot through.

перегоро|ди́ть, жу́, ~ди́шь, *pf.* (*of* перегора́живать) to partition off.

перегоро́дк|а, и, *f.* **1.** partition. **2.** (*tech.*) baffle (plate). **3.** (*fig.*) barrier.

перегоро́д|очный, *adj. of* ~ка.

перегре́в, а, *m.* overheating; (*tech.*) super-heating.

перегрева́тел|ь, я, *m.* (*tech.*) superheater.

перегрева́|ть(ся), ю(сь), *impf. of* перегре́ть(ся).

перегре́|ть, ю, *pf.* (*of* ~ва́ть) **1.** to overheat. **2.** (*tech.*) to superheat.

перегре́|ться, юсь, *pf.* (*of* ~ва́ться) to burn (out), get burned.

перегружа́|ть, ю, *impf. of* перегрузи́ть.

перегру|зи́ть¹, жу́, ~зи́шь, *pf.* (*of* ~жа́ть) to overload, surcharge; п. рабо́той to over-work.

перегру|зи́ть², жу́, ~зи́шь, *pf.* (*of* ~жа́ть) to load (*somewhere else*; *from A to B*); to trans-ship; п. с по́езда на парохо́д to load from a train on to a ship.

перегру́зк|а¹, и, *f.* overload, surcharge; overloading; п. рабо́той overwork.

перегру́зк|а², и, *f.* reloading; shifting; transfer, trans-shipping.

перегру́з|очный, *adj. of* ~ка².

перегруппир|ова́ть, у́ю, *pf.* (*of* ~о́вывать) to re-group.

перегруппиро́вк|а, и, *f.* re-grouping.

перегруппир|о́вывать, о́вываю, *impf. of* ~ова́ть.

перегры́з|ть, у́, ёшь, *past* ~, ~ла, *pf.* (*of* ~а́ть) to gnaw through, bite through.

перегры́з|ться, у́сь, ёшься, *past* ~ся, ~лась, *pf.* (*no impf.*) (из-за; *coll.*; *of dogs*) to fight (over); (*fig.*) to quarrel (over), wrangle (about).

пéред *and* **пéредо**, *prep.* +*i.* **1.** (*of place*; *also fig.*) before; in front of; in the face of; п. дворцо́м in front of the palace; при́зрак стоя́л пéредо мно́й the apparition stood before me; п. опа́сностью in the face of danger. **2.** (*in relation to, as compared with*) to; извини́ться п. кем-н. to apologize to someone; ва́ша исто́рия ничто́ п. на́шей your story is nothing to ours. **3.** (*of time*) before; п. обéдом before dinner; п. тем, как (*conj.*) before.

пéред, пéреда, *pl.* ~а́, ~о́в, *m.* front, fore-part.

переда|ва́ть(ся), ю́(сь), ёшь(ся), *impf. of* переда́ть(ся).

переда́|точный, *adj. of* ~ча; п. вал (*tech.*) countershaft; п. механи́зм driving gear, drive; ~точная на́дпись (*fin.*) endorse-ment; ~точное число́ (*tech.*) gear ratio.

переда́тчик, а, *m.* (*radio*) transmitter; п. тепла́ (*phys.*) heat conductor.

переда́|ть¹, м, шь, ст, ди́м, ди́те, ду́т, *past* пéредал, ~ла́, пéредало, *pf.* (*of* ~ва́ть) **1.** to pass; to hand; to hand over; п. по наслéдству, to hand down; п. свой правá to make over one's rights; п. дéло в суд to bring a matter into court, take a matter to law, sue. **2.** to tell; to communicate; to transmit, convey; п. по рáдио to broadcast; п. благодáрность to convey thanks; п. зарáзу to communicate infection; п. поручéние to deliver a message; п. приказáние to transmit an order; п. привéт to convey greetings, send one's regards; ~й(те) им (мой) привéт give them my regards, remember me to them. **3.** to reproduce (a *sound, a thought, etc.*).

передá|ть², м, шь, ст, дим, дите, дут, *past* пéредал, ~лá, пéредало, *pf.* (*of* ~вáть) to pay too much, give too much; вы пéредали три рубля́ you have paid three roubles too many.

передá|ться, стся, дутся, *past* ~лся, ~лáсь, *pf.* (*of* ~вáться) **1.** to pass; to be transmitted, be communicated; to be inherited; корь ~лáсь ему́ от живу́щих ря́дом детéй he picked up measles from the children next door. **2.** (+*d.*; *coll.*) to go over, (to).

передáч|а, и, *f.* **1.** passing; transmission; communication; п. иму́щества (*leg.*) assignation; без прáва ~и not transferable; Петрóву для ~и Ивáновой (*form of address on letter*) (Mrs., Miss) Ivanova, c/o (Mr.) Petrov. **2.** parcel (*delivered to person in hospital or prison*). **3.** broadcast. **4.** (*tech.*) drive; gear(ing); transmission; балансѝрная п. transmission by rocking lever; большáя п. high gear ratio; зубчáтая п. train of gears, toothed gearing; конéчная п. end drive; пéрвая п. low gear; реверсѝвная п. reversing gear; ремённая п. belt drive; червя́чная п. worm-gear.

передвигá|ть(ся), ю(сь), *impf. of* передвѝнуть(ся).

передвижéни|е, я, *n.* movement; (*tech.*) travel; срéдства ~я means of conveyance.

передвижж|ка, ки, *f.* **1.** = ~éние. **2.** *as adj.* travelling, itinerant; библиотéка-п. travelling library; теáтр-п. strolling players.

передвѝжник, а, *m.* (*art*) Peredvizhnik (*member of Russian school of realist painters of second half of nineteenth century*).

передвижн|óй, *adj.* **1.** movable, mobile; п. кран travelling crane. **2.** travelling, itinerant; ~áя вы́ставка travelling exhibition.

передвѝ|нуть, ну, нешь, *pf.* (*of* ~гáть) to move, shift (*also fig.*); п. стрéлки часóв вперёд (назáд) to put the clock on (back); п. срóки экзáменов to alter the date of examinations.

передвѝ|нуться, нусь, нешься, *pf.* (*of* ~гáться) to move, shift; (*tech.*) to travel.

передéл, а, *m.* re-partition; re-division, re-

-distribution; п. земли́ re-allotment of land.

передéл|ать¹, аю, *pf.* (*of* ~ывать) to do anew; to alter; (*fig.*) to re-fashion, recast; п. плáтье to alter a dress.

передéл|ать², аю, *pf.* (*coll.*) to do; я ~ал все делá I have done all I had to do.

передел|ѝть, ю, ~ишь, *pf.* (*of* ~я́ть) to re--divide.

передéлк|а, и, *f.* **1.** alteration; отдáть что-н. в ~у to have something altered; попáсть в ~у (*coll.*) to get into a pretty mess. **2.** adaptation (*of lit. work, etc.*).

передéлыва|ть, ю, *impf. of* передéлать¹.

передел|я́ть, я́ю, *impf. of* ~ѝть.

передёргива|ть(ся), ю(сь), *impf. of* передёрнуть(ся).

передерж|áть¹, у́, ~ишь, *pf.* (*of* ~ивать) **1.** to overdo; to overcook. **2.** (*phot.*) to over--expose.

передерж|áть², у́, ~ишь, *pf.* (*of* ~ивать) (*coll.*) п. экзáмен to take an examination again.

передéржива|ть, ю, *impf. of* передержáть.

передéржк|а¹, и, *f.* (*phot.*) over-exposure.

передéржк|а², и, *f.* (*coll.*) re-examination.

передéржк|а³, и, *f.* (*coll.*) cheating (*at cards*), juggling (*with facts*).

передёр|нуть, ну, нешь, *pf.* (*of* ~гивать) **1.** to pull aside. **2.** (*impers.*) егó ~нуло от бóли he was convulsed with pain. **3.** to cheat (*at cards*). **4.** (*fig.*) to distort, mis-represent; п. фáкты to juggle with facts.

передёр|нуться, нусь, нешься, *pf.* (*of* ~гиваться) (*coll.*) to flinch, wince.

перед|кóвый, *adj. of* ~óк; *as noun* п., ~кóвого, *m.* (*mil.*) limber number.

передненёбный, *adj.* (*ling.*) front palatal.

передн|ий, *adj.* front; anterior; first; ~ие конéчности fore-legs; п. край оборóны (*mil.*) main line of resistance; ~яя крóмка (крылá) (*aeron.*) leading edge (of wing); ~яя лóшадь leader; п. план foreground; ~яя часть fore-part.

передник, а, *m.* apron; pinafore.

передн|яя, ей, *f.* ante-room; (entrance) hall, lobby.

пéредо = пéред.

передовéр|ить, ю, ишь, *pf.* (*of* ~я́ть) (+*d.*) to transfer trust (to); (*leg.*) to transfer power of attorney (to); п. договóр to sub-contract (to).

передовер|я́ть, я́ю, *impf. of* ~ить.

передовѝк, á, *m.* **1.** peredovik (*factory worker, etc., winning distinction for display of initiative and/or exemplary work*). **2.** (*coll.*) leader-writer.

передовѝц|а, ы, *f.* (*coll.*) leading article, leader; editorial.

передов|óй, *adj.* forward, headmost; foremost, advanced (*also fig.*); ~ые взгля́ды advanced views; п. отря́д (*mil.*) advanced detachment; (*fig.*) vanguard; ~áя статья́ leading article, leader; editorial; *as noun* ~áя, ~óй, *f.* = ~áя статья́.

перед|óк, ка́, *m.* 1. front (*of carriage, etc.*). 2. (*mil.*; *usu. pl.*) limber.

передóм, *adv.* (*coll.*) in front.

передóх|нуть, нет, *past* ~, ~ла, *pf.* (*no impf.*) to die off (*usually of animals*).

передохн|у́ть, у́, ёшь, *pf.* (*of* передыха́ть) (*coll.*) to pause for breath, take a short rest.

передрáзнива|ть, ю, *impf. of* передразни́ть.

передразн|и́ть, ю́, ~ишь, *pf.* (*of* ~ивать) to take off, mimic.

пере|дра́ться, деру́сь, дерёшься, *past* ~дра́лся, ~драла́сь, ~дра́лóсь, *pf.* (*no impf.*) (*coll.*) to fight, exchange blows (*of many people, etc.*).

передрóг|нуть, ну, нешь, *past* ~, ~ла, *pf.* (*no impf.*) (*coll.*) to get chilled through.

передря́г|а, и, *f.* (*coll.*) row, scrape.

переду́м|ать, аю, *pf.* (*of* ~ывать) 1. to (think it over and) change one's mind; to think better of it. 2. to do a great deal of thinking.

переду́мыва|ть, ю, *impf. of* переду́мать.

передыха́|ть, ю, *impf. of* передохну́ть.

переды́шк|а, и, *f.* respite, breathing-space; не дава́я ни мину́ты ~и without a moment's respite.

переедáни|е, я, *n.* overeating; surfeit.

переедá|ть, ю, *impf. of* перее́сть.

перее́зд¹, а, *m.* (*in var. senses*) crossing.

перее́зд², а, *m.* removal.

переезжá|ть, ю, *impf. of* перее́хать.

перее́|сть¹, м, шь, ст, ди́м, ди́те, дя́т, *past* ~л, *pf.* (*of* ~да́ть) 1. to overeat, surfeit. 2. (*coll.*) to out-eat, surpass in eating.

перее́|сть², м, шь, ст, ди́м, ди́те, дя́т *past* ~л, *pf.* (*of* ~да́ть) to corrode, eat away.

перее́|хать¹, ду, дешь, *pf.* (*of* ~зжа́ть) 1. to cross. 2. to run over, knock down.

перее́|хать², ду, дешь, *pf.* (*of* ~зжа́ть) to move (*to a new place of residence*).

пережа́рива|ть, ю, *impf. of* пережа́рить¹.

пережа́р|ить¹, ю, ишь, *pf.* (*of* ~ивать) to overdo, overroast.

пережа́р|ить², ю, ишь, *pf.* to roast (*all or a number of*).

пережд|а́ть, у́, ёшь, *past* ~а́л, ~ала́, ~а́ло, *pf.* (*of* пережида́ть) to wait through; мы ~а́ли грозу́ we waited till the storm was over.

переж|ева́ть, ую́, уёшь, *pf.* (*of* ~ёвывать) to masticate, chew.

пережёвыва|ть, ю, *impf.* 1. *impf. of* пережева́ть. 2. (*fig.*) to repeat over and over again.

пережен|и́ться, ~ится, *pf.* (*coll.*) to marry; все её бра́тья ~и́лись all her brothers have married.

переж|е́чь, гу́, жёшь, гу́т, *past* ~ёг, ~гла́, *pf.* (*of* ~ига́ть) 1. to burn more than one's quota (*of fuel, etc.*). 2. to burn through. 3. (*tech.*) to calcine.

пережива́ни|е, я, *n.* experience; feeling.

пережива́|ть, ю, *impf.* 1. *impf. of* пережи́ть. 2. (*impf. only*) (*coll.*) to be upset, worry.

пережида́|ть, ю, *impf. of* переждáть.

пережит|о́е, о́го, *n.* one's past.

пережи́т|ок, ка, *m.* survival.

пережи́|ть, ву́, вёшь, *past* пе́режил, ~ла́, пе́режило, *pf.* (*of* ~ва́ть) 1. to live through; п. жизнь to live one's life through. 2. to experience; to go through; to endure, suffer; тяжело́ п. что-н. to feel something keenly, take something hard; она́ ещё не совсе́м ~ла́ потрясе́ния she has still not completely got over the shock. 3. to outlive, outlast, survive.

перезаб|ы́ть, у́ду, у́дешь, *pf.* (*no impf.*) (*coll.*) to forget.

перезакла́дыва|ть, ю, *impf. of* перезаложи́ть.

перезаключ|а́ть, а́ю, *impf. of* ~и́ть.

перезаключ|и́ть, у́, и́шь, *pf.* (*of* ~а́ть) to renew; п. догово́р to renew a contract.

перезалож|и́ть, у́, ~ишь, *pf.* (*of* перезакла́дывать) to pawn again, re-pawn; to mortgage again.

перезаря|ди́ть, жу́, ~ди́шь, *pf.* (*of* ~жа́ть) 1. to re-charge; to re-load. 2. (*electr.*) to overcharge.

перезаря́дк|а, и, *f.* 1. re-charging; re-loading. 2. (*electr.*) overcharging.

перезаряжа́|ть, ю, *impf. of* перезаряди́ть.

перезвóн, а, *m.* ringing, chime.

перезим|ова́ть, у́ю, *pf.* (*of* зимова́ть) to winter, pass the winter.

перезнако́м|ить, лю, ишь, *pf.* (*coll.*; c+*i.*) to acquaint (with), introduce (to).

перезнако́м|иться, люсь, ишься, *pf.* (*no impf.*) (*coll.*) to become acquainted (with).

перезрева́|ть, ю, *impf. of* перезре́ть.

перезре́лый, *adj.* overripe; (*fig.*) passé, past one's prime.

перезре́|ть, ю, *pf.* (*of* ~ва́ть) 1. to become overripe. 2. (*fig.*) to be past one's prime; to have lost the bloom of youth.

переигр|а́ть¹, а́ю, *pf.* (*of* ~ывать) to play again.

переигр|а́ть², а́ю, *pf.* (*of* ~ывать) (*theatr.*; *coll.*) to overact, overdo.

переигр|а́ть³, а́ю, *pf.* to play, act, perform (*all or a number of*).

переигрыва|ть, ю, *impf. of* переигра́ть¹, ².

переизбира́|ть, ю, *impf. of* переизбра́ть.

переизбра́ни|е, я, *n.* re-election.

переиз|бра́ть, беру́, берёшь, *past* ~бра́л, ~брала́, ~бра́ло, *pf.* (*of* ~бира́ть) to re--elect.

переизда|ва́ть, ю́, ёшь, *impf. of* ~ть.

переизда́ни|е, я, *n.* 1. re-publication. 2. new edition; reprint.

переизда́|ть, м, шь, ст, ди́м, ди́те, ду́т, *past* ~л, ~ла́, ~ло, *pf.* (*of* ~ва́ть) to re-publish, reprint.

переимен|ова́ть, у́ю, *pf.* (*of* ~о́вывать) to rename.

переимено́выва|ть, ю, *impf. of* переименова́ть.

переи́мчив|ый (~, ~а), *adj.* (*coll.*) imitative.

переина́чива|ть, ю, *impf. of* переина́чить.

переина́ч|ить, у, ишь, *pf.* (*of* ~ивать) to alter; to modify.

пере|йти́, йду́, йдёшь, *past* ~шёл, ~шла́, *pf.* (*of* ~ходи́ть) 1. (+*a. or* че́рез) to cross; to get across, get over, go over; п. грани́цу to cross the frontier; п. че́рез мо́ст to go across a bridge. 2. (в, на+*a. or* к) to pass (to); to turn (to); п. в наступле́ние to pass to the offensive, assume the offensive; п. в ру́ки (+*g.*) to pass into the hands (of); п. из рук в ру́ки to change hands; п. в сле́дующий класс (*in school*) to move up; п. в сосе́днюю ко́мнату to go into the next room; п. к друго́му владе́льцу to change hands; п. на другу́ю рабо́ту to change one's job; п. на произво́дство тра́кторов to go over to making tractors; п. на сто́рону проти́вника to go over to the enemy. 3. (в+*a.*) to turn (into); их ссо́ра ~шла́ в дра́ку from words they came to blows.

перека́л, а, *m.* (*tech.*) overheating; over-tempering.

перекале́чива|ть, ю, *impf. of* перекале́чить.

перекале́ч|ить, у, ишь, *pf.* (*of* ~ивать) to cripple, main, mutilate.

перека́лива|ть, ю, *impf. of* перекали́ть.

перекал|и́ть, ю́, и́шь, *pf.* (*of* ~ивать) (*tech.*) to overtemper; (*coll.*) to overheat.

перека́лыва|ть, ю, *impf. of* переколо́ть.

перека́пыва|ть, ю, *impf. of* перекопа́ть.

перека́рмлива|ть, ю, *impf. of* перекорми́ть.

перека́т¹, а, *m.* shoal.

перека́т², а, *m.* roll, peal (*of thunder*).

перекати́-по́л|е, я, *n.* 1. (*bot.*) baby's breath (*Gypsophila paniculata*). 2. (*fig.*; *of person*) rolling stone.

перека|ти́ть, чу́, ~ти́шь, *pf.* (*of* ~тывать) to roll (*somewhere else*).

перека|ти́ться, чу́сь, ~ти́шься, *pf.* (*of* ~тываться) to roll (*somewhere else*).

перека́тн|ый, *adj.* 1. rolling; голь ~ая (*collect.*) the down-and-outs. 2. (*geol.*) erratic.

перекач|а́ть, а́ю, *pf.* (*of* ~ивать) to pump over, pump across.

перека́чива|ть, ю, *impf. of* перекача́ть.

перека́шива|ть(ся), ю(сь), *impf. of* перекоси́ть(ся).

переквалифика́ци|я, и, *f.* re-qualification; changing one's profession.

переквалифици́р|овать, ую, *impf. and pf.* to re-qualify.

переквалифици́р|оваться, уюсь, *impf. and pf.* to re-qualify; to change one's profession.

перекид|а́ть, а́ю, *pf.* (*of* ~ывать) to throw (one after another).

перекидно́й, *adj.* п. мо́стик footbridge, gangway.

переки́дыва|ть(ся), ю(сь), *impf. of* перекида́ть *and* переки́нуть(ся).

переки́|нуть, ну, нешь, *pf.* (*of* ~дывать) to throw (over).

переки́|нуться, нусь, нешься, *pf.* (*of* ~дываться) 1. to leap (over). 2. (*of fire, disease, etc.*) to spread. 3. (+*i.*) to throw (one to another). 4. (*obs., coll.*) (к) to go over (to), defect (to).

перекипя|ти́ть, чу́, ти́шь, *pf.* to boil again.

перекис|а́ть, а́ет, *impf. of* ~нуть.

переки́с|нуть, нет, *past* ~, ~ла, *pf.* (*of* ~а́ть) to turn sour.

пе́рекис|ь, и, *f.* (*chem.*) peroxide.

перекла́дин|а, ы, *f.* 1. cross-beam, cross--piece, transom; joist. 2. (*sport*) horizontal bar.

перекладн|ы́е, ы́х, *sing.* ~а́я, ~о́й, *f.* (*hist.*) post-horses, relay-horses; е́хать на ~ы́х to travel by post-chaise.

перекла́дыва|ть, ю, *impf. of* переложи́ть.

переклёива|ть, ю, *impf. of* переклёить.

переклё|ить¹, ю, ишь, *pf.* (*of* ~ивать) to re-stick; to glue again, paste again.

переклё|ить², ю, ишь, *pf.* (*of* ~ивать) to stick (*a number of*).

переклёйк|а¹, и, *f.* re-sticking.

переклёйк|а², и, *f.* ply-wood.

перекли|ка́ться, а́юсь, *impf.* (с+*i.*) 1. (*pf.* ~нуться) to call to one another. 2. (*fig.*) to have something in common (with); to call up, have a ring (of).

перекли́чк|а, и, *f.* 1. roll-call, call-over. 2. interchange, exchange (*of views, etc., on radio or in press*).

переключа́тел|ь, я, *m.* (*tech.*) switch; commutator; конта́ктный п. stud switch, tap switch.

переключ|а́ть(ся), а́ю(сь), *impf. of* ~и́ть(ся).

переключ|и́ть, у́, и́шь, *pf.* (*of* ~а́ть) (*tech. and fig.*; на+*a.*) to switch (over to); п. своё внима́ние на друго́й вопро́с to switch one's attention to another question.

переключ|и́ться, у́сь, и́шься, *pf.* (*of* ~а́ться) (*tech. and fig.*; на+*a.*) to switch (over to); заня́вшись бы́ло дре́вними языка́ми, он вдруг ~и́лся на изуче́ние совреме́нных having started to study ancient languages, he suddenly switched (over) to studying modern.

перек|ова́ть, ую́, уёшь, *pf.* (*of* ~о́вывать) **1.** to re-forge; to hammer again; п. коня́ to re-shoe a horse. **2.** to hammer out, beat out; п. мечи́ на ора́ла to beat swords into ploughshares (*also fig.*).

переко́выва|ть, ю, *impf. of* перекова́ть.

переколо|ти́ть, чу́, ~тишь, *pf.* (*coll.*) to break, smash.

переко́л|оть¹, ю, ~ешь, *pf.* (*of* перека́лывать) to pin (*somewhere else*).

переко́л|оть², ю, ~ешь, *pf.* (*of* перека́лывать) to prick all over.

переко́л|оть³, ю, ~ешь, *pf.* (*of* перека́лывать) to chop, hew.

перекопа́|ть, ю, *pf.* (*of* перека́пывать) **1.** to dig over again. **2.** to dig (*all of*). **3.** to dig across.

перекорм|и́ть, лю́, ~ишь, *pf.* (*of* перека́рмливать) **1.** to overfeed, surfeit. **2.** (*pf. only*) to feed (*all of, many*).

переко́р|ы, ов, *no sing.* (*coll.*) squabble.

перекоря́|ться, юсь, *impf.* (*no pf.*) (*coll.*) to squabble.

переко|си́ть¹, шу́, ~сишь, *pf.* (*of* перека́шивать) to warp; (*fig.*) to distort; (*impers.*) ~си́ло око́нную ра́му the window-frame has warped; от зло́бы его́ ~си́ло his face was distorted with malice.

переко|си́ть², шу́, ~сишь, *pf.* to mow (*all of, a large area of*).

переко|си́ться, шу́сь, ~сишься, *pf.* (*of* перека́шиваться) to warp, be warped; (*fig.*) to become distorted.

перекоч|ева́ть, у́ю, *pf.* (*of* ~ёвывать) to migrate; to move on (*of nomads, also coll.*).

перекочёвыва|ть, ю, *impf. of* перекочевать.

переко́|шенный, p.p.p. of ~си́ть *and adj.* distorted, twisted.

перекра́ива|ть, ю, *impf. of* перекройть.

перекра́|сить¹, шу, сишь, *pf.* (*of* ~шивать) to re-colour, re-paint; to re-dye.

перекра́|сить², шу, сишь, *pf.* (*of* ~шивать) to colour, paint; to dye.

перекра́|ситься, шусь, сишься, *pf.* (*of* ~шиваться) **1.** to change colour. **2.** (*fig.*) to become a turn-coat.

перекра́шива|ть(ся), ю(сь), *impf. of* перекра́сить(ся).

перекре|сти́ть¹, щу́, ~стишь, *pf.* (*of* крести́ть 3) to make the sign of the cross over.

перекре|сти́ть², щу́, ~стишь, *pf.* (*of* ~щивать) to cross.

перекре|сти́ть³, щу́, ~стишь, *pf.* (*of* ~щивать) to baptize (*all of, a large number of*).

перекре|сти́ться¹, щу́сь, ~стишься, *pf.* (*of* крести́ться 2) to cross oneself.

перекре|сти́ться², щу́сь, ~стишься, *pf.* (*of* ~щиваться) to cross, intersect.

перекрёстн|ый, *adj.* cross; п. допро́с cross--examination; п. ого́нь (*mil.*) cross-fire; ~ое опыле́ние (*bot.*) cross-pollination; ~ая ссы́лка cross-reference.

перекрёст|ок, ка, *m.* cross-roads, crossing; крича́ть на всех ~ках (*coll.*) to shout from the house-tops.

перекре́щива|ть(ся), ю(сь), *impf. of* перекрести́ть², ³(ся)².

перекри́кива|ть, ю, *impf. of* перекрича́ть.

перекри|ча́ть, чу́, чи́шь, *pf.* (*of* ~кивать) to out-voice, drown; to shout down.

перекро|и́ть, ю́, и́шь, *pf.* (*of* перекра́ивать) to cut out again; (*fig.*) to rehash; to re--shape; п. ка́рту ми́ра to re-draw the map of the world.

перекру|ти́ть, чу́, ~тишь, *pf.* (*of* ~чивать) to overwind.

перекру́чива|ть, ю, *impf. of* перекрути́ть.

перекрыва́|ть, ю, *impf. of* перекры́ть.

перекры́ти|е, я, n. **1.** (*archit.*) ceiling, overhead cover. **2.** (*tech.*) overlap(ping); damming (*of a river*).

перекр|ы́ть¹, о́ю, о́ешь, *pf.* (*of* ~ыва́ть) to re-cover.

перекр|ы́ть², о́ю, о́ешь, *pf.* (*of* ~ыва́ть) **1.** (*coll.*) to exceed; п. реко́рд to break a record. **2.** (*cards*) to beat; to trump. **3.** to close, cut off; to dam (*a river*).

перекувы́ркива|ть(ся), ю(сь), *impf. of* перекувырну́ть(ся).

перекувыр|ну́ть, ну́, нёшь, *pf.* (*of* ~кивать) (*coll.*) to upset, overturn.

перекувыр|ну́ться, ну́сь, нёшься, *pf.* (*of* ~киваться) (*coll.*) **1.** to topple over. **2.** to turn a somersault.

перекуп|а́ть¹, а́ю, *impf. of* ~и́ть.

перекупа́|ть², ю, *pf.* to bath.

перекупа́|ть³, ю, *pf.* (*coll.*) to bathe too long.

перекупа́|ться, юсь, *pf.* (*coll.*) to bathe too long, stay in (the water) too long.

перекуп|и́ть, лю́, ~ишь, *pf.* (*of* ~а́ть) to buy up (*something sought by others*); to outbid for.

переку́пщик, а, *m.* second-hand dealer.

перекуса́|ть, ю, *pf.* to bite.

переку|си́ть, шу́, ~сишь, *pf.* (*of* ~сывать) **1.** to bite through. **2.** (*coll.*) to have a bite, have a snack.

переку́сыва|ть, ю, *impf. of* перекуси́ть.

перелага́|ть, ю, *impf. of* переложи́ть.

перела́мыва|ть(ся), ю(сь), *impf. of* переломи́ть(ся).

перележ|а́ть, у́, и́шь, *pf.* to lie too long.

перелез|а́ть, а́ю, *impf. of* ~ть.

перелез|ть, у, ешь, *past* ~, ~ла, *pf.* (*of* ~а́ть) to climb over, get over.

перелесо́к, ка, *m.* copse, coppice.

перелéсь|е, я, *n.* (*dial.*) glade.

перелёт, а, *m.* **1.** flight (*of aircraft*). **2.** migration (*of birds*). **3.** shot over the target, plus round.

перелет|áть, áю, *impf. of* ~éть.

переле|тéть, чу́, ти́шь, *pf.* (*of* ~тáть) **1.** (+*a. or* чéрез) to fly over. **2.** to fly too far; to overshoot (the mark).

перелётн|ый, *adj.* ~ая пти́ца bird of passage (*also fig.*); migratory bird.

пере|лéчь, ля́гу, ля́жешь, ля́гут, *past* ~лёг, ~леглá, *pf.* (*no impf.*) to lie somewhere else; п. с одногó бóка на другóй to turn from one side to another.

перели́в, а, *m.* tint, tinge; play (*of colours*); modulation (*of voice*).

переливáни|е, я, *n.* **1.** decantation. **2.** (*med.*) transfusion.

перелива́|ть[1], ю, *impf. of* перели́ть; п. из пустóго в порóжнее (*fig.*) to mill the wind, beat the air.

перелива́|ть[2], ет, *impf.* (*of colours*) to play; п. всéми цветáми рáдуги to be iridescent.

перелива́|ться[1], юсь, *impf. of* перели́ться.

перелива́|ться[2], ется, *impf.* (*of colours*) to play; (*of voices*) to modulate; п. всéми цветáми рáдуги to be iridescent.

перели́вк|а, и, *f.* (*tech.*) re-casting.

перели́вчат|ый (~, ~а), *adj.* iridescent; (*of voice*) modulating; (*of silk*) shot.

перелист|áть, áю, *pf.* (*of* ~ывать) **1.** to turn over, leaf. **2.** to look through, glance at.

перели́стыва|ть, ю, *impf. of* перелистáть.

перел|и́ть[1], ью, ьёшь, *past* ~и́л, ~илá, ~и́ло, *pf.* (*of* ~ивáть) **1.** to pour (*somewhere else; from A into B*); to decant; п. молокó из кастрю́ли в кувши́н to pour milk from a saucepan into a jug. **2.** (*med.*) to transfuse; п. кровь (+*d.*) to administer a blood transfusion (to). **3.** to let overflow.

перел|и́ть[2], ью, ьёшь, *past* ~и́л, ~илá, ~и́ло, *pf.* (*of* ~ивáть) **1.** to re-cast. **2.** to melt down; п. колоколá на пу́шки to melt down bells for guns.

перел|и́ться, ью́сь, ьёшься, *past* ~и́лся, ~илáсь, ~и́лóсь, *pf.* (*of* ~ивáться) **1.** to flow (*somewhere else; from A to B*). **2.** to overflow, run over.

перелиц|евáть, у́ю, *pf.* (*of* ~óвывать) to turn (*an article of clothing*); to have turned.

перелицóвыва|ть, ю, *impf. of* перелицевáть.

перелов|и́ть, лю́, ~ишь, *pf.* to catch (*all or a number of*).

перелóг, а, *m.* (*agric.*) fallow.

переложéни|е, я, *n.* (*mus.*) arrangement; transposition; п. в стихи́ versification.

перелож|и́ть, у́, ~ишь, *pf.* **1.** (*impf.* перекла́дывать *and* перелагáть) to put some-

---

where else; to shift, move; (*fig.*) to shift off, transfer; п. руль (*naut.*) to put the helm over; п. отвéтственность на когó-н. to shift off the responsibility on to someone. **2.** (*impf.* перекла́дывать) (+*a. and i.*) to interlay (with); п. посу́ду солóмой to interlay crockery with straw. **3.** (*impf.* перекла́дывать) to re-set, re-lay. **4.** (*impf.* перелагáть) (в, на+*a.*) to set (to), arrange (for); to transpose; to put (into); п. на му́зыку to set to music; п. в стихи́ to put into verse. **5.** (*impf.* перекла́дывать) (+*g.*) to put in too much; вы ~и́ли сóли в суп you have put too much salt in the soup.

перелóжный, *adj.* of перелóг.

перелó|й, я, *m.* (*obs.*) gonorrhoea.

перелóм, а, *m.* **1.** break, breaking; fracture. **2.** (*fig.*) turning point, crisis; sudden change.

переломá|ть, ю, *pf.* to break (*all or a number of*).

переломá|ться, юсь, *pf.* (*coll.*) to break, be broken.

перелом|и́ть, лю́, ~ишь, *pf.* (*of* перелáмывать) **1.** to break in two; to break, fracture. **2.** (*fig.*) to break, master; п. себя́ to master oneself, restrain one's feelings; п. комý-н. вóлю to break someone's will.

перелом|и́ться, ~ится, *pf.* (*of* перелáмываться) to break in two; to be fractured.

перелóм|ный, *adj.* of ~; п. момéнт critical moment, crucial moment.

перемá|зать[1], жу, жешь, *pf.* (*of* ~зывать) (*coll.*; +*i.*) to soil (with), make dirty (with).

перемá|зать[2], жу, жешь, *pf.* (*of* ~зывать) to re-coat (*with paint, etc.*).

перемá|заться, жусь, жешься, *pf.* (*of* ~зываться) (*coll.*) to soil oneself, besmear oneself.

перемáзыва|ть(ся), ю(сь), *impf. of* перемáзать(ся).

перемáлыва|ть, ю, *impf. of* перемолóть.

перемáнива|ть, ю, *impf. of* переманúть.

переман|и́ть, ю́, ~ишь, *pf.* (*of* ~ивать) to entice; п. на свою́ стóрону to win over.

перемáтыва|ть, ю, *impf. of* перемотáть.

перемáхива|ть, ю, *impf. of* перемахну́ть.

перемах|ну́ть, ну́, нёшь, *pf.* (*of* ~ивать) (*coll.*) to jump over, leap over.

перемежá|ть, ю, *impf.* (*no pf.*) (+*a. and i. or* с+*i.*) to alternate; он ~л угрóзы (с) лéстью he alternated threats and blandishments.

перемежá|ться, ется, *impf.* (*no pf.*) (с+*i.*) to alternate; снег ~лся с грáдом snow alternated with hail, it snowed and hailed by turns; ~ющаяся лихорáдка (*med.*) intermittent fever, remittent (fever).

перемеж|евáть, у́ю, *pf.* (*of* ~ёвывать) to re--survey.

перемежёвыва|ть, ю, *impf. of* перемежевать.

перемен|а, ы, *f.* **1.** change, alteration; без ~ (there is) no change. **2.** change (of clothes). **3.** (*school*) interval, break; большая п. long (*sc.* midday) break.

перемен|и́ть, ю́, ~ишь, *pf.* (*of* ~я́ть) to change; п. пози́цию to shift one's ground (*also fig.*); п. тон (*fig.*) to change one's tune.

перемен|и́ться, ю́сь, ~ишься, *pf.* (*of* ~я́ться) to change; п. места́ми to change places; п. в лице́ to change countenance; п. к кому́-н. to change (one's attitude) towards someone.

переме́нн|ый, *adj.* variable; ~ая величина́ (*math.*) variable (quantity); ~ая пого́да changeable weather; п. ток (*electr.*) alternating current.

переме́нчив|ый (~, ~а), *adj.* (*coll.*) changeable.

перемен|я́ть(ся), я́ю(сь), *impf. of* ~и́ть(ся).

пере|мере́ть, мрёт, *past* пе́ремер, ~мерла́, пе́ремерло, *pf.* (*coll.*) to die (off).

перемерз|а́ть, а́ю, *impf. of* ~нуть.

перемёрз|нуть, ну, нешь, *pf.* (*of* ~а́ть) (*coll.*) **1.** to get chilled, freeze. **2.** (*of plants*) to be nipped by the frost.

переме́рива|ть, ю, *impf. of* перемерить.

переме́р|ить[1], ю, ишь, *pf.* (*of* ~ивать) to re-measure.

переме́р|ить[2], ю, ишь, *pf.* to try on.

переме|сти́ть, щу́, сти́шь, *pf.* (*of* ~ща́ть) to move (*somewhere else*); to transfer.

переме|сти́ться, щу́сь, сти́шься, *pf.* (*of* ~ща́ться) **1.** to move. **2.** *pass. of* ~сти́ть.

перемёт, а, *m.* seine (*net*).

переме́|тить[1], чу, тишь, *pf.* (*of* ~ча́ть) to mark again.

переме́|тить[2], чу, тишь, *pf.* (*no impf.*) to mark (*a quantity of*).

переметн|у́ться, у́сь, ёшься, *pf.* (*no impf.*) (*coll.*) to go over, desert.

перемётн|ый, *adj.* ~ая сума́ saddle bag; сума́ ~ая (*fig., obs.*) weathercock.

перемеш|а́ть, а́ю, *pf.* (*of* ~ивать) **1.** to (inter)mix, intermingle; п. ка́рты to shuffle cards; п. у́гли в пе́чке to poke the fire. **2.** (*coll.*) to mix up; (*fig.*) to confuse; он, по-ви́димому, ~а́л на́ши фами́лии he evidently got our names mixed up.

перемеш|а́ться, а́юсь, *pf.* (*of* ~иваться) **1.** to get mixed (up); всё у него́ в голове́ ~а́лось he has got everything mixed up. **2.** *pass. of* ~а́ть.

перемешива|ть(ся), ю(сь), *impf. of* перемеша́ть(ся).

перемеща́|ть(ся), ю(сь), *impf. of* перемести́ть(ся).

перемеще́ни|е, я, *n.* **1.** transference, shift;

displacement. **2.** (*geol.*) dislocation, displacement. **3.** (*tech.*) travel.

переме|щённый, *p.p.p. of* ~сти́ть; ~щённые ли́ца (*polit.*) displaced persons.

переми́гива|ться, юсь, *impf. of* перемигну́ться.

перемиг|ну́ться, ну́сь, нёшься, *pf.* (*of* ~иваться) (*coll.*; c+*i.*) to wink (at); п. между собо́й to wink at each other.

перемина́|ться, юсь, *impf.* (*no pf.*) п. с ноги́ на́ ногу (*coll.*) to shift from one foot to the other.

переми́ри|е, я, *n.* armistice, truce.

перемнож|а́ть, а́ю, *impf. of* ~ить.

перемно́ж|ить, у, ишь, *pf.* (*of* ~а́ть) to multiply.

перемога́|ть, ю, *impf.* (*coll.*) **1.** (*pf.* перемо́чь) to overcome (*an illness, etc.*). **2.** to try to overcome (*an illness, etc.*).

перемога́|ться, юсь, *impf.* (*coll.*) to try to overcome an illness; три дня он ~лся, но наконе́ц ему́ пришло́сь позва́ть врача́ he held out for three days, but in the end he had to call in the doctor.

перемок|а́ть, а́ю, *impf. of* ~нуть.

перемо́к|нуть, ну, нешь, ~, ~ла, *pf.* (*of* ~а́ть) (*coll.*) to get drenched.

перемо́лв|ить, лю, ишь, *pf.* (*no impf.*) п. сло́во (c+*i.*; *coll.*) to exchange a word (with).

перемо́лв|иться, люсь, ишься, *pf.* (*no impf.*) (+*i.*; c+*i.*; *coll.*) to exchange words (with); п. не́сколькими слова́ми с сосе́дом to exchange a few words with a neighbour.

перем|оло́ть, елю́, е́лешь, *pf.* (*of* ~а́лывать) to grind, mill; (*fig.*) to pulverize.

перем|оло́ться, е́лется, *pf.* (*of* ~а́лываться) *pass. of* ~оло́ть; ~е́лется — мука́ бу́дет (*prov.*) it will all come right in the end, time is a great healer.

перемота́|ть, ю, *pf.* (*of* перема́тывать) **1.** to wind; to reel. **2.** to re-wind.

перемо́|чь, гу́, ~жешь, *pf. of* ~га́ть.

перемудр|и́ть, ю́, и́шь, *pf.* (*no impf.*) (*coll.*) to be too clever by half.

перему́ч|иться, усь, ишься, *pf.* (*no impf.*) (*coll.*) to have suffered very much.

перемыва́|ть, ю, *impf. of* перемы́ть.

перемы́ть[1], ю́ю, о́ешь, *pf.* (*of* ~ыва́ть) to wash up again.

перем|ы́ть[2], о́ю, о́ешь, *pf.* to wash (up) (*all or a quantity of*).

перемы́чк|а, и, *f.* (*tech.*) **1.** straight arch. **2.** cross piece; tie plate. **3.** bulkhead; dam.

перенапряга́|ть(ся), ю(сь), *impf. of* перенапря́чь(ся).

перенапря́|чь, гу́, жёшь, *past* ~г, ~гла́, *pf.* (*of* ~га́ть) to overstrain.

перенапря́|чься, гу́сь, жёшься, *past* ~гся, ~гла́сь, *pf.* (*of* ~га́ться) to overstrain oneself.

перенаселе́ни|е, я, *n.* overpopulation.

перенаселённост|ь, и, *f.* overpopulation; overcrowding (*in a dwelling*).

перенасел|ённый, *p.p.p.* of ~и́ть and *adj.* overpopulated; overcrowded.

перенасел|и́ть, ю́, и́шь, *pf.* (*of* ~я́ть) to overpopulate.

перенасел|я́ть, я́ю, *impf.* of ~и́ть.

перенасы́|тить, щу, тишь, *pf.* (*of* ~ща́ть) (*chem.*) to over-saturate.

перенасыща́|ть, ю, *impf.* of перенасы́тить.

перенасы́|щенный, *p.p.p.* of ~тить and *adj.* (*chem.*) over-saturated.

перенесе́ни|е, я, *n.* transference, transportation.

перенес|ти́[1], у́, ёшь, *past* ~, ~ла́, *pf.* (*of* переноси́ть) 1. to carry (*somewhere else*); to transport; to transfer; п. ого́нь (*mil.*) to switch fire; п. де́ло в областно́й суд to take the matter to the oblast court; п. столи́цу в Москву́ to move the capital to Moscow. 2. п. сло́во (*typ.*) to carry over (*part of word*) to the next line. 3. to put off, postpone; to carry over.

перенес|ти́[2], у́, ёшь, *past* ~, ~ла́, *pf.* (*of* переноси́ть) to endure, bear, stand; п. боле́знь to have an illness; я э́того не мог п. I couldn't stand that.

перенес|ти́сь, у́сь, ёшься, *past* ~ся, ~ла́сь, *pf.* (*of* переноси́ться) 1. to be carried, be borne; (*fig.*) to be carried away (*in thought*). 2. *pass.* of ~ти́[1].

перенима́|ть, ю, *impf.* of переня́ть.

перено́с, а, *m.* 1. transfer; transportation. 2. (*typ.*) division of words; знак ~а hyphen.

переноси́м|ый (~, ~а), *pres. part. pass.* of переноси́ть and *adj.* bearable, endurable.

перено|си́ть(ся), шу́(сь), ~сишь(ся), *impf.* of перенести́(сь).

перено́сиц|а, ы, *f.* bridge of the nose.

перено́ск|а, и, *f.* carrying over, transporting; carriage.

перено́сный, *adj.* 1. portable. 2. (*ling.*) figurative; metaphorical.

перено́счик, а, *m.* carrier; п. слу́хов talebearer, rumour-monger.

переноч|ева́ть, у́ю, *pf.* (*of* ночева́ть) to spend the night.

перенумер|ова́ть, у́ю, *pf.* (*of* нумерова́ть) to number; п. страни́цы to page.

пере|ня́ть, йму́, ймёшь, *past* пе́ренял, ~няла́, пе́реняло, *pf.* (*of* ~нима́ть) (*coll.*) 1. to imitate, copy; п. привы́чку to acquire a habit; п. чей-н. приём to take a leaf out of someone's book. 2. to intercept, bar the way (to).

переобору́д|овать, ую, *impf. and pf.* to re-equip.

переобремен|и́ть, ю́, и́шь, *pf.* (*of* ~я́ть) to overburden.

переобремен|я́ть, я́ю, *impf. of* ~и́ть.

переобува́|ть(ся), ю(сь), *impf. of* переобу́ть(ся).

переобу́|ть, ю, ешь, *pf.* (*of* ~ва́ть) to change someone's shoes; п. боти́нки to change one's shoes.

переобу́|ться, юсь, ешься, *pf.* (*of* ~ва́ться) to change one's shoes, boots, *etc.*

переодева́|ть(ся), ю(сь), *impf. of* переоде́ть(ся).

переоде́|ть, ну, нешь, *pf.* (*of* ~ва́ть) 1. to change someone's clothes; они́ ~ли де́вочку в наря́дное пла́тье they changed the little girl into a party frock; п. бельё ребёнку (*coll.*) to change a baby; п. пла́тье to change one's dress. 2. (+*i.*; в+*a.*) to dress up, disguise (as, in); п. де́вочку ма́льчиком to dress up a little girl as a boy.

переоде́|ться, нусь, нешься, *pf.* (*of* ~ва́ться) 1. to change (one's clothes). 2. (+*i.*, в+*a.*) to dress up, disguise oneself (as, in); она́ ~лась в ма́льчика she disguised herself as a boy.

переосвиде́тельств|овать, ую, *impf. and pf.* (*med.*) to re-examine.

переоце́нива|ть, ю, *impf. of* переоцени́ть.

переоцен|и́ть, ю́, ~ишь, *pf.* (*of* ~ивать) 1. to overestimate, overrate; п. свои́ си́лы to overestimate one's strength, bite off more than one can chew. 2. to revalue, reappraise.

переоце́нк|а, и, *f.* 1. overestimation. 2. revaluation, reappraisal.

перепа́д, а, *m.* (*tech.*) overfall.

перепа́да|ть, ет, *pf.* (*coll.*) to fall (one after another).

перепада́|ть, ю, *impf. of* перепа́сть.

перепа́ива|ть, ю, *impf. of* перепои́ть.

перепа́лк|а, и, *f.* (*coll.*) exchange of fire, skirmish (also *fig.*).

перепа́рхива|ть, ю, *impf. of* перепорхну́ть.

перепа́|сть, дёт, *past* ~л, *pf.* (*of* ~да́ть) (*coll.*) 1. to fall intermittently; дождь ~дёт there will be rain at intervals, it will be showery. 2. (*impers.*; +*d.*) to fall to one's lot.

перепа́|ха́ть, шу́, ~шешь, *pf.* (*of* ~хивать) to plough (up) again; to plough over.

перепа́хива|ть, ю, *impf. of* перепаха́ть.

перепа́чка|ть, ю, *pf.* to soil, make dirty (all over).

перепа́чка|ться, юсь, *pf.* to make oneself dirty (all over).

перепе́в, а, *m.* repetition, rehash.

перепека́|ть, ю, *impf. of* перепе́чь.

пе́репел, а, *pl.* ~а́, *m.* (*orn.*) quail.

перепелен|а́ть, а́ю, *pf.* (*of* ~ывать) п. ребёнка to change a baby, change a baby's nappy.

перепелёныва|ть, ю, *impf. of* перепелена́ть.

перепели́ный, *adj. of* пе́репел.

перепёлк|а, и, *f.* female quail.

перепеля́тник, а, *m.* 1. quail-shooter. 2. (sparrow-)hawk.

перепе́рчива|ть, ю, *impf. of* переперчить.

перепе́рч|ить, у, ишь, *pf.* (*of* ~ивать) to put too much pepper into.

перепеча́т|ать, аю, *pf.* (*of* ~ывать) 1. to reprint. 2. to type (out).

перепеча́тк|а, и, *f.* 1. reprinting; п. воспреща́ется copyright reserved. 2. reprint.

перепеча́тыва|ть, ю, *impf. of* перепеча́тать.

перепе́|чь[1], ку́, чёшь, *pf.* (*of* ~ка́ть) to overbake.

перепе́|чь[2], ку́, чёшь, *pf.* to bake (*all or a number of*).

перепива́|ть(ся), ю(сь), *impf. of* перепи́ть(ся).

перепи́лива|ть, ю, *impf. of* перепили́ть.

перепил|и́ть[1], ю́, ~ишь, *pf.* (*of* ~ивать) to saw in two.

перепил|и́ть[2], ю́, ~ишь, *pf.* to saw (*all or a number of*).

перепи|са́ть[1], шу́, ~шешь, *pf.* (*of* ~сывать) 1. to re-write; to re-type; п. на́бело to make a fair copy (of). 2. to re-copy.

перепи|са́ть[2], шу́, ~шешь, *pf.* (*of* ~сывать) to make a list (of), list; п. всех прису́тствующих to take the names of all those present.

перепи́ск|а, и, *f.* 1. copying; typing. 2. correspondence; быть в ~e (c+*i.*) to be in correspondence (with). 3. (*collect.*) correspondence, letters.

перепи́счик, а, *m.* copyist; typist.

перепи́сыва|ть, ю, *impf. of* переписа́ть.

перепи́сыва|ться, юсь, *impf.* (c+*i.*) to correspond (with).

пе́репис|ь, и, *f.* 1. census. 2. inventory.

переп|и́ть, ью́, ьёшь, *past* ~и́л, ~ила́, ~и́ло, *pf.* (*of* ~ива́ть) (*coll.*) 1. to drink excessively. 2. to out-drink; к утру́ он ~и́л всех това́рищей by morning he had drunk all his companions·under the table.

переп|и́ться, ью́сь, ьёшься, *past* ~и́лся, ~ила́сь, ~и́ло́сь, *pf.* (*of* ~ива́ться) (*coll.*) to get completely drunk.

перепла́в|ить[1], лю, ишь, *pf.* (*of* ~ля́ть) to smelt.

перепла́в|ить[2], лю, ишь, *pf.* (*of* ~ля́ть) 1. to float; to raft. 2. (*fig., coll.*) to convey surreptitiously.

переплавля́|ть, ю, *impf. of* перепла́вить.

переплани́р|овать, ую, у́ю, *pf.* (*of* ~о́вывать) 1. to re-plan, make new plans (for), alter plan (of). 2. to re-plan (*streets, districts, etc.*).

переплани́ро́вк|а, и, *f.* re-planning (*of streets, districts, etc.*).

переплани́ро́выва|ть, ю, *impf. of* переплани́рова́ть.

перепла́т|а, ы, *f.* surplus payment.

перепла|ти́ть, чу́, ~тишь, *pf.* (*of* ~чивать) to overpay; to pay excessively.

перепла́чива|ть, ю, *impf. of* переплати́ть.

переплёвыва|ть, ю, *impf. of* переплю́нуть.

перепле|сти́[1], ту́, тёшь, *past* ~л, ~ла́, *pf.* (*of* ~та́ть) 1. to bind (*books*). 2. (+*i.*) to interlace (with), interknit (with).

перепле|сти́[2], ту́, тёшь, *past* ~л, ~ла́, *pf.* (*of* ~та́ть) to braid again, plait again.

перепле|сти́сь, тётся, *past* ~лся, ~ла́сь, *pf.* (*of* ~та́ться) 1. to interlace, interweave. 2. (*fig.*) to get mixed up.

переплёт, а, *m.* 1. binding; отда́ть кни́гу в п. to have a book bound. 2. binding, book-cover. 3. transom (*of door or window*); око́нный п. window-sash. 4. caning (*of a chair*). 5. (*coll.*) mess, scrape; попа́сть в п. to get into a mess, get into trouble.

переплета́|ть(ся), ю(сь), *impf. of* переплести́(сь).

переплётн|ая, ой, *f.* bindery, bookbinder's shop.

переплётчик, а, *m.* bookbinder.

переплыва́|ть, ю, *impf. of* переплы́ть.

переплы́|ть, ву́, вёшь, *past* ~л, ~ла́, ~ло, *pf.* (*of* ~ва́ть) to swim (across); to sail (across).

переплю́н|уть, у, ешь, *pf.* (*of* переплёвывать) (*coll.*) to spit further than; (*fig.*) to do better than, surpass.

переподгота́влива|ть, ю, *impf. of* переподгото́вить.

переподгото́в|ить, лю, ишь, *pf.* (*of* переподгота́вливать) to train anew.

переподгото́вк|а, и, *f.* further training; training anew; ку́рсы по ~e refresher courses.

перепо|и́ть, ю́, ~и́шь, *pf.* (*of* перепа́ивать) 1. to give too much to drink (*to an animal*). 2. (*coll.*) to make drunk.

перепо́|й, я, *m.* excessive drinking; у меня́ разболе́лась голова́ с ~я (с ~ю) I had a hangover.

переполз|а́ть, а́ю, *impf. of* ~ти́.

переполз|ти́, у́, ёшь, *past* ~, ~ла́, *pf.* (*of* ~а́ть) to crawl across; to creep across.

переполне́ни|е, я, *n.* overfilling; overcrowding; п. желу́дка repletion.

перепо́лн|ить, ю, ишь, *pf.* (*of* ~я́ть) to overfill; to overcrowd.

перепо́лн|иться, ится, *pf.* (*of* ~я́ться) to overfill; to be overcrowded; её се́рдце ~илось ра́достью her heart overflowed with joy.

переполн|я́ть(ся), я́ю(сь), *impf. of* ~и́ть(ся).

переполо́х, а, *m.* alarm; commotion, rumpus.

переполош|и́ть, у́, и́шь, *pf.* (*coll.*) to alarm; to rouse.

перепо́нк|а, и, *f.* membrane; web (*of bat or water-fowl*); бараба́нная п. (*anat.*) ear--drum, tympanum.

перепо́нчатокры́лы|й, *adj.* (*zool.*) hymen-opterous; *as noun* ~е, ~х Hymenoptera.

перепо́нчатый, *adj.* membraneous, mem-branous; webbed; web-footed.

перепоруч|а́ть, а́ю, *impf. of* ~и́ть.

перепоруч|и́ть, у́, ~и́шь, *pf.* (*of* ~а́ть) (+*d.*) to turn over (to), reassign (to); п. веде́ние де́ла друго́му защи́тнику to turn over one's case to another lawyer.

перепорхн|у́ть, у́, ёшь, *pf.* (*of* перепа́рхи-вать) to flutter, flit (*somewhere else*; *from A to B*).

перепра́в|а, ы, *f.* passage, crossing; ford.

перепра́в|ить[1], лю, ишь, *pf.* (*of* ~ля́ть) 1. to convey, transport to; take across. 2. to for-ward (*mail*).

перепра́в|ить[2], лю, ишь, *pf.* (*of* ~ля́ть) (*coll.*) to correct.

перепра́в|иться, люсь, ишься, *pf.* (*of* ~ля́ть-ся) to cross, get across; to swim across; to sail across.

переправля́|ть(ся), ю(сь), *impf. of* пере-пра́вить(ся).

перепрева́|ть, ю, *impf. of* перепре́ть.

перепре́|ть, ю, *pf.* (*of* ~ва́ть) 1. to rot. 2. (*coll.*) to be overdone.

перепро́б|овать, ую, *pf.* to taste (*all or a quantity of*); (*fig.*) to try.

перепрода|ва́ть, ю́, ёшь, *impf. of* ~ть.

перепрода́в|е́ц, ца́, *m.* re-seller.

перепрода́ж|а, и, *f.* re-sale.

перепрода́|ть, м, шь, ст, ди́м, ди́те, ду́т, *past* перепро́дал, ~ла́, перепро́дало, *pf.* (*of* ~ва́ть) to re-sell.

перепроизво́дств|о, а, *n.* overproduction.

перепры́гива|ть, ю, *impf. of* перепры́гнуть.

перепры́г|нуть, ну, нешь, *pf.* (*of* ~ивать) to jump (over).

перепря|га́ть, га́ю, *impf. of* ~чь.

перепря́жк|а, и, *f.* 1. changing of horses. 2. (*hist.*) stage (*on post-chaise route*).

перепря́|чь, гу́, жёшь, гу́т, *past* ~г, ~гла́, *pf.* (*of* ~га́ть) 1. to re-harness. 2. to change (*horses*).

перепу́г, а (у), *m.* (*coll.*) с ~у, от ~у in one's fright.

перепуга́|ть, ю, *pf.* (*no impf.*) to frighten, give a fright, give a turn.

перепуга́|ться, юсь, *pf.* (*no impf.*) to get a fright.

перепуска́|ть, ю, *impf. of* перепусти́ть.

перепу|сти́ть, щу́, ~сти́шь, *pf.* (*of* ~ска́ть) 1. to let flow (*from A to B*). 2. to let go; to slacken.

перепу́т|ать, аю, *pf.* (*of* ~ывать) 1. to en-tangle. 2. (*fig.*) to confuse, mix up, muddle up.

перепу́т|аться, аюсь, *pf.* (*of* ~ываться) 1. to get entangled. 2. (*fig.*) to get confused, get mixed up.

перепу́тыва|ть(ся), ю(сь), *impf. of* пере-пу́тать(ся).

перепу́ть|е, я, *n.* cross-roads; быть на п. (*fig.*) to be at the cross-roads.

перерабо́тыва|ть(ся), ю(сь), *impf. of* пере-рабо́тать(ся).

перерабо́та|ть[1], ю, *pf.* (*of* перераба́тывать) 1. (в, на+*a.*) to work (into), make (into); to convert (to); to treat; п. свёклу в са́хар to convert beet to sugar; п. пи́щу to digest food. 2. to re-make; (*fig.*) to re-cast, re--shape; п. статью́ to re-cast an article.

перерабо́та|ть[2], ю, *pf.* (*of* перераба́тывать) (*coll.*) to exceed fixed hours of work, work overtime; мы вчера́ ~ли три часа́ we did three hours overtime yesterday.

перерабо́та|ться[1], юсь, *pf.* (*of* перераба́ты-ваться) *pass. of* ~ть.

перерабо́та|ться[2], юсь, *pf.* (*of* перераба́ты-ваться) (*coll.*) to overwork.

перерабо́тк|а[1], и, *f.* 1. working over, treat-ment. 2. re-making; (*fig.*) re-casting, re--shaping.

перерабо́тк|а[2], и, *f.* overtime work.

перераспределе́ни|е, я, *n.* re-distribution.

перераспредел|и́ть, ю́, и́шь, *pf.* (*of* ~я́ть) to re-distribute.

перераспредел|я́ть, я́ю, *impf. of* ~и́ть.

перераста́ни|е, я, *n.* 1. outgrowing. 2. (в+ *a.*) growing (into), development (into). 3. (*mil.*) escalation.

перераст|а́ть, а́ю, *impf. of* ~и́.

перераст|и́, у́, ёшь, *past* переро́с, переросла́, *pf.* (*of* ~а́ть) 1. to outgrow, (over)top; to outstrip (*in height, also fig.*); трина́дцати лет она́ уже́ переросла́ отца́ at thirteen she had already topped her father; п. своего́ учи́теля to outstrip one's teacher. 2. (*fig.*; в+*a.*) to grow (into), develop (into), turn (into). 3. to be too old (for); для де́тского са́да он переро́с he is too old for kindergarten.

перерасхо́д, а, *m.* 1. over-expenditure. 2. (*fin.*) overdraft.

перерасхо́д|овать, ую, *pf.* (*no impf.*) 1. to spend to excess. 2. (*fin.*) to overdraw.

перерасчёт, а, *m.* re-computation.

перерв|а́ть, у́, ёшь, *past* ~а́л, ~ала́, ~а́ло, *pf.* (*of* перерыва́ть[1]) to break, tear as-under.

перерв|а́ться, у́сь, ёшься, *past* ~а́лся, ~ала́сь, ~а́лось, *pf.* (*of* перерыва́ться[1]) to break, come apart.

перерегистра́ци|я, и, *f.* re-registration.

перерегистри́р|овать, ую, *pf.* to re-register.

перерегистри́р|оваться, уюсь, *pf.* 1. to re-register. 2. *pass. of* ~овать.

перере́|зать¹, жу, жешь, *pf.* (*of* ~за́ть *and* ~зыва́ть) **1.** to cut. **2.** (*fig.*) to cut off; п. путь неприя́телю to bar the enemy's way. **3.** (*geogr.*) to break.

перере́|зать², жу, жешь, *pf.* to kill, slaughter (*all or a number of*).

перере́з|а́ть, а́ю, *impf. of* ~а́ть¹.

перере́зыва|ть, ю, *impf.* = перере́зать.

перереш|а́ть¹, а́ю, *impf. of* ~и́ть.

перереш|а́ть², а́ю, *pf.* to solve (*all or a number of problems*).

перереш|и́ть, у́, и́шь, *pf.* (*of* ~а́ть¹) **1.** to re-solve; to decide, settle in a different way. **2.** to change one's mind, reconsider one's decision.

переро|ди́ть, жу́, ди́шь, *pf.* (*of* ~жда́ть) to regenerate.

переро|ди́ться, жу́сь, ди́шься, *pf.* (*of* ~жда́ться) **1.** (*coll.*) to be re-born. **2.** (*fig.*) to regenerate, be regenerated. **3.** (*biol. and fig.*) to degenerate.

перерожде́ни|е, я, *n.* **1.** regeneration. **2.** degeneration.

переро́ст|ок, ка, *m.* (*coll.*) backward child (*pupil older than his class-mates*).

переруб|а́ть, а́ю, *impf. of* ~и́ть.

переруб|и́ть, лю́, ~ишь, *pf.* (*of* ~а́ть) to chop in two; to hew asunder.

переруга́|ться, юсь, *pf.* (*coll.*; c+*i.*) to fall out (with), fall foul (of), break (with).

переру́гива|ться, юсь, *impf.* (*coll.*; c+*i.*) to quarrel (with), squabble (with).

переры́в, а, *m.* interruption; interval, break, intermission; обе́денный п. dinner *or* lunch break; п. на пять мину́т five minutes' interval; без ~а without a break; с ~ами off and on.

перерыва́|ть¹, ю, *impf. of* перерва́ть.

перерыва́|ть², ю, *impf. of* переры́ть.

перерыва́|ться, юсь, *impf. of* перерва́ться.

перер|ы́ть, о́ю, о́ешь, *pf.* (*of* ~ыва́ть²) **1.** to dig up. **2.** (*fig., coll.*) to rummage (in).

переря|ди́ть, жу́, ~ди́шь, *pf.* (*of* ~жива́ть) (+*i.*; *coll.*) to disguise (as), dress up (as).

переря|ди́ться, жу́сь, ~ди́шься, *pf.* (*of* ~жива́ться) (+*i.*; *coll.*) to disguise oneself (as), dress up (as).

переря́жива|ть(ся), ю(сь), *impf. of* переряди́ть(ся).

переса|ди́ть, жу́, ~дишь, *pf.* (*of* ~жива́ть) **1.** to make someone change his seat. **2.** п. кого́-н. че́рез что-н. to help someone across something. **3.** (*bot.*) to transplant. **4.** (*med.*) to graft.

переса́дк|а, и, *f.* **1.** (*bot.*) transplantation. **2.** (*med.*) grafting; опера́ция по~е се́рдца heart transplant operation. **3.** (*on railway*) change; changing; в Ленингра́д без ~и по change for Leningrad; through train to Leningrad.

переса́жива|ть, ю, *impf. of* пересади́ть.

переса́жива|ться, юсь, *impf. of* пересе́сть.

переса́лива|ть, ю, *impf. of* пересоли́ть.

пересда|ва́ть, ю́, ёшь, *impf. of* ~ть.

пересда́|ть, м, шь, ст, ди́м, ди́те, ду́т, *past* ~л, ~ла́, ~ло, *pf.* (*of* ~ва́ть) **1.** to re-let; to sub-let. **2.** (*cards*) to re-deal. **3.** (*coll.*) to re-sit (*an examination*).

пересека́|ть(ся), ю(сь), *impf. of* пересе́чь-(ся).

переселе́н|ец, ца, *m.* **1.** migrant, emigrant; immigrant. **2.** settler.

переселе́ни|е, я, *n.* **1.** migration, emigration; immigration, re-settlement. **2.** move (*to new place of residence*).

переселе́н|ческий, *adj. of* ~ец; ~ческая организа́ция emigration, re-settlement organization.

пересел|и́ть, ю́, и́шь, *pf.* (*of* ~я́ть) to move; to transplant; to resettle.

пересел|и́ться, ю́сь, и́шься, *pf.* (*of* ~я́ться) to move; to migrate.

пересел|я́ть(ся), я́ю(сь), *impf. of* ~и́ть(ся).

пересе́|сть, я́ду, я́дешь, *pf.* (*of* ~а́живаться) **1.** to change one's seat. **2.** to change (*trains*, *etc.*).

пересече́ни|е, я, *n.* crossing, intersection; то́чка ~я point of intersection.

пересе́|чённый, *p.p.p. of* ~чь¹; ~ечённая ме́стность (*geogr.*) broken terrain.

пересе́|чь¹, ку́, чёшь, ку́т, *past* ~к, ~кла́, *pf.* (*of* ~ка́ть) **1.** to cross; to traverse; п. у́лицу to cross the road; п. путь неприя́телю (*fig.*) to cut the enemy off, bar the enemy's way. **2.** to cross, intersect.

пересе́|чь², ку́, чёшь, ку́т, *past* ~к, ~кла́, *pf.* (*of* ~ка́ть) (*coll.*) to flog.

пересе́|чься, чётся, ку́тся, *past* ~кся, ~кла́сь, *pf.* (*of* ~ка́ться) to cross, intersect.

переси|де́ть, жу́, ди́шь, *pf.* (*of* ~живать) **1.** (*coll.*) to out-sit; он ~де́л всех други́х госте́й he outstayed all the other guests. **2.** to sit too long.

переси́жива|ть, ю, *impf. of* пересиде́ть.

переси́лива|ть, ю, *impf. of* пересили́ть.

переси́л|ить, ю, ишь, *pf.* (*of* ~ивать) to overpower; (*fig.*) to overcome, master.

переска́з, а, *m.* **1.** re-telling, narration. **2.** exposition.

переска|за́ть, жу́, ~жешь, *pf.* (*of* ~зывать) **1.** to re-tell, narrate; ~жи́(те) мне содержа́ние э́того рома́на tell me the story of this novel (in your own words). **2.** to retail, relate; п. слу́хи to retail rumours.

переска́зыва|ть, ю, *impf. of* пересказа́ть.

переска́кива|ть, ю, *impf. of* перескочи́ть.

перескоч|и́ть, у́, ~ишь, *pf.* (*of* переска́кивать) **1.** (+*a. or* че́рез) to jump (over); to vault (over); (*fig.*; *in reading*) to skip (over).

2. (*fig.*) to skip; п. с одно́й те́мы на другу́ю to skip from one topic to another.

пересла|сти́ть, щу́, сти́шь, *pf.* (*of* ~щивать) to make too sweet, put too much sugar (into).

пере|сла́ть, шлю́, шлёшь, *pf.* (*of* ~сыла́ть) to send; to remit; to forward.

пересла́щива|ть, ю, *impf. of* пересласти́ть.

пересма́трива|ть, ю, *impf. of* пересмотре́ть.

пересме́ива|ть, ю, *impf.* (*coll.*) to mock, make fun of.

пересме́ива|ться, юсь, *impf.* (*coll.*; с+*i.*) to exchange smiles (with).

пересме́шк|а, и, *f.* (*coll.*) mockery, banter.

пересме́шник, а, *m.* **1.** (*coll.*) mocker, banterer. **2.** (*orn.*) mocking-bird.

пересмо́тр, а, *m.* **1.** revision. **2.** reconsideration; (*leg.*) review (*of a sentence*); re-trial.

пересмотр|е́ть¹, ю́, ~ишь, *pf.* (*of* пересма́тривать) **1.** to revise; to go over again. **2.** to re-consider; (*leg.*) to review. **3.** to go through (*in search of something*).

пересмотр|е́ть², ю́, ~ишь, *pf.* to have seen (*all or a quantity of*); to have gone all through.

пересснима́|ть, ю, *impf. of* пересня́ть.

пересн|я́ть, иму́, и́мешь, *past* ~я́л, ~яла́, ~я́ло, *pf.* (*of* ~има́ть) **1.** to photograph again, take another photo (of). **2.** to make a copy.

пересозда|ва́ть, ю́, ёшь, *impf. of* ~ть.

пересозда́|ть, м, шь, ст, ди́м, ди́те, ду́т, *past* ~л, ~ла́, ~ло, *pf.* (*of* ~ва́ть) to re-create.

пересо́л, а, *m.* excess of salt; недосо́л на столе́, п. на спине́ (*coll.*) better too little than too much.

пересол|и́ть, ю́, ~и́шь, *pf.* (*of* переса́ливать) **1.** to put too much salt (into). **2.** (*fig., coll.*) to go too far.

пересо́х|нуть, нет, *past* ~, ~ла, *pf.* (*of* пересыха́ть, to dry out; to dry up, become parched.

пересп|а́ть, лю́, и́шь, *past* ~а́л, ~ала́, ~а́ло, *pf.* (*coll.*) **1.** to oversleep. **2.** to spend the night. **3.** (с+*i.*; *euph.*) to sleep (with).

переспе́лый, *adj.* overripe.

переспо́р|ить, ю, ишь, *pf.* to out-argue, defeat in argument; его́ не ~ишь he must have the last word.

переспра́шива|ть, ю, *impf. of* переспроси́ть.

переспро|си́ть¹, шу́, ~сишь, *pf.* (*of* переспра́шивать) to ask again; to ask to re-peat.

переспро|си́ть², шу́, ~сишь, *pf.* to question (*all or a number of*).

пересо́р|ить, ю, ишь, *pf.* (*coll.*) to set at variance.

пересо́р|иться, юсь, ишься, *pf.* (*coll.*; с+*i.*) to quarrel (with), fall out (with).

переста|ва́ть, ю́, ёшь, *impf. of* ~ть.

переста́в|ить, лю, ишь, *pf.* (*of* ~ля́ть) to move, shift; п. ме́бель to re-arrange the furniture; п. слова́ во фра́зе to transpose the words in a sentence; п. часы́ вперёд (наза́д) to put the clock on (back).

переставля́|ть, ю, *impf. of* переста́вить.

переста́ива|ть, ю, *impf. of* перестоя́ть.

перестано́вк|а, и, *f.* **1.** re-arrangement, transposition. **2.** (*math.*) permutation.

перестара́|ться, юсь, *pf.* (*coll.*) to overdo it, put too much into it.

перестар|ок, ка, *m.* (*coll.*) person over age (*for given purpose*); он мог бы ещё воева́ть —не п. he could still fight, he is not too old.

переста́|ть, ну, нешь, *pf.* (*of* ~ва́ть) (+*inf.*) to stop, cease.

перестел|и́ть, ю́, ~ешь, *pf.* (*coll.*) = перестла́ть.

перестел|ю́, ~ешь, *see* перестла́ть.

перестила́|ть, ю, *impf. of* перестели́ть *and* перестла́ть.

перестир|а́ть¹, а́ю, *pf.* (*of* ~ывать) to wash again.

перестир|а́ть², а́ю, *pf.* (*no impf.*) to wash (*all or a number of*).

перести́рыва|ть, ю, *impf. of* перестира́ть¹.

перест|ла́ть, елю́, е́лешь, *pf.* (*of* ~ила́ть) to re-lay; п. пол в ко́мнате to re-floor a room; п. посте́ль to re-make a bed.

пересто|я́ть, ю́, и́шь, *pf.* (*of* перестаивать) to stand too long.

перестрада́|ть, ю, *pf.* (*no impf.*) to have suffered, have gone through.

перестра́ива|ть(ся), ю(сь), *impf. of* перестро́ить(ся).

перестрах|ова́ть, у́ю, *pf.* (*of* ~о́вывать) to re-insure.

перестрах|ова́ться, у́юсь, *pf.* (*of* ~о́вываться) **1.** to re-insure oneself. **2.** (*fig., pejor.*) to play safe (*by seeking to transfer or share responsibility*).

перестрахо́вк|а, и, *f.* **1.** re-insurance. **2.** (*pejor.*) playing safe, 'double insurance' (*esp. of editors of magazines unwilling to risk publishing controversial material*).

перестрахо́вщик, а, *m.* (*pejor.*) adherent of policy of 'playing safe'.

перестрахо́выва|ть(ся), ю(сь), *impf. of* перестрахова́ть(ся).

перестре́лива|ть, ю, *impf. of* перестреля́ть.

перестре́лива|ться, юсь, *impf.* to fire (at each other).

перестре́лк|а, и, *f.* firing; skirmish; exchange of fire; артиллери́йская п. artillery duel.

перестрел|я́ть, я́ю, *pf.* (*of* ~ивать) **1.** to shoot (down). **2.** to use up, expend (*in shooting*).

перестро́|ить, ю, ишь, *pf.* (*of* перестра́ивать) **1.** to rebuild, reconstruct. **2.** to re-design, re-fashion, re-shape; to re-organize; п. фра́зу to reshape a sentence; п. на вое́нный лад to put on a war footing. 3. (*mil.*) to re-form. 4. (*mus., radio*) to re-tune.

перестро́|иться, юсь, ишься, *pf.* (*of* перестра́иваться) 1. to re-form; to re-organize oneself; to improve one's methods of work. 2. (*mil.*) to re-form. 3. (*radio*) (на+*a.*) to switch over (to), tune (on to); п. на коро́ткую волну́ to switch over to short wave.

перестро́йк|а, и, *f.* 1. rebuilding, reconstruction. 2. re-organization. 3. (*mil.*) re-formation. 4. (*mus., radio*) re-tuning.

пересту́кивани|е, я, *n.* (*in prison, etc.*) communication by tapping.

пересту́кива|ться, юсь, *impf.* (c+*i.*) (*in prison, etc.*) to communicate (with) by tapping.

переступ|а́ть, а́ю, *impf.* 1. *impf. of* ~и́ть. 2. (*impf. only*) to move slowly; он е́ле ~а́л (нога́ми) his feet would hardly carry him; п. с ноги́ на́ ногу to shift from one foot to the other.

переступ|и́ть, лю́, ~ишь, *pf.* (*of* ~а́ть) (+*a.* *or* че́рез) to step over; (*fig.*) to overstep; п. поро́г to cross the threshold; п. зако́н to break the law; п. грани́цы прили́чия to overstep the bounds of decency.

пересу́д, а, *m.* (*coll.*) re-trial.

пересу́д|ы, ов, *no sing.* (*coll.*) gossip.

пересуши́|ть, ю, *impf. of* пересуши́ть[1].

пересуш|и́ть[1], у́, ~ишь, *pf.* (*of* ~ивать) to overdry.

пересуш|и́ть[2], у́, ~ишь, *pf.* (*no impf.*) to dry (*all or a quantity of*).

пересчит|а́ть[1], а́ю, *pf.* (*of* ~ывать) 1. to re-count; п. ко́сти (рёбра) кому́-н. (*fig., coll.*) to give someone a drubbing. 2. (на+*a.*) to convert (to), express (in terms of).

пересчит|а́ть[2], а́ю, *pf.* (*no impf.*) to count.

пересчи́тыва|ть, ю, *impf. of* пересчита́ть[1].

пересыла́|ть, ю, *impf. of* пересла́ть.

пересы́лк|а, и, *f.* sending; forwarding; п. де́нег remittance; сто́имость ~и postage; п. беспла́тно post free; carriage paid.

пересы́л|очный, *adj. of* ~ка.

пересы́льн|ый, *adj.* transit; ~ая тюрьма́ transit prison.

пересы́п|ать[1], лю, лешь, *pf.* (*of* ~а́ть) to pour (*dry substance*) into another container; п. зерно́ в мешки́ to pour off grain into bags.

пересы́п|ать[2], лю, лешь, *pf.* (*of* ~а́ть) (+*i.*) 1. to powder (with). 2. (*fig.*) to intersperse (with); п. речь руга́тельствами to intersperse one's speech with swear-words.

пересып|а́ть, а́ю, *impf. of* ~а́ть.

пересыха́|ть, ет, *impf. of* пересо́хнуть.

перетя́плива|ть, ю, *impf. of* перетопи́ть[1].

перетаск|а́ть, а́ю, *pf.* (*of* ~ивать) 1. to carry away. 2. (*fig., coll.*) to pinch, lift.

перета́скива|ть, ю, *impf. of* перетаска́ть *and* перетащи́ть.

перетас|ова́ть, у́ю, *pf.* (*of* ~о́вывать) to re-shuffle (*cards, also fig.*).

перетасо́выва|ть, ю, *impf. of* перетасова́ть.

перетащ|и́ть, у́, ~ишь, *pf.* (*of* перета́скивать) 1. to drag over; to carry over; to move, shift; п. сунду́к на черда́к to move a trunk into the attic. 2. (*fig., coll.*) to win over, gain over.

перетека́|ть, ю, *impf. of* перете́чь.

пере|тере́ть, тру́, трёшь, *past* ~тёр, ~тёрла, *pf.* (*of* ~тира́ть) 1. to wear out, wear down; терпе́ние и труд всё ~тру́т (*coll.*) it's dogged does it. 2. (в+*a.*) to grind (into).

пере|тере́ться, трётся, *past* ~тёрся, ~тёрлась, *pf.* (*of* ~тира́ться) 1. to wear out, wear through. 2. *pass. of* ~тере́ть.

перетерп|е́ть, лю, ~ишь, *pf.* (*coll.*) to suffer, endure.

перете́|чь, ку́, чёшь, ку́т, *past* ~к, ~кла́, *pf.* (*of* ~ка́ть) to overflow.

перетира́|ть(ся), ю(сь), *impf. of* перетере́ть(ся).

перето́лк|и, ов, *no sing.* (*coll.*) tittle-tattle.

перетолк|ова́ть[1], у́ю, *pf.* (*no impf.*) (*coll.*) to talk over, discuss; на́до нам с тобо́й об э́том п. we must talk it over.

перетолк|ова́ть[2], у́ю, *pf.* (*of* ~о́вывать) (*coll.*) to misinterpret.

перетолко́выва|ть, ю, *impf. of* перетолкова́ть[2].

перетоп|и́ть[1], лю, ~ишь, *pf.* (*of* перета́пливать) to melt.

перетоп|и́ть[2], лю, ~ишь, *pf.* (*coll.*) to heat; to kindle.

перето́ржк|а, и, *f.* re-auctioning.

перетрево́ж|ить, у, ишь, *pf.* (*no impf.*) (*coll.*) to disturb, alarm.

перетрево́ж|иться, усь, ишься, *pf.* (*no impf.*) (*coll.*) to be alarmed, become anxious.

пере|тру́, трёшь, тёр, тёрла, *see* ~тере́ть.

перетру́|сить, шу, шу, *pf.* (*no impf.*) (*coll.*) to have a fright; to take fright.

перетряс|а́ть, а́ю, *impf. of* ~ти́.

перетряс|ти́, у́, ёшь, *past* ~, ~ла́, *pf.* (*of* ~а́ть) to shake up.

пере́ть, пру, прёшь, *past* пёр, пёрла, *impf.* (*coll.*) 1. to go, make one's way; п. сквозь толпу́ to barge through the crowd. 2. to push, press. 3. to drag. 4. to come out; to appear, show; ре́вность так и прёт из него́ his jealousy will out. 5. (*pf.* c~) to steal, pinch.

перетя́гивани|е, я, *n.* п. кана́та (*sport*) tug-of-war.

перетя́гива|ть(ся), ю(сь), *impf. of* перетяну́ть(ся).

перетя|ну́ть[1], **ну́, ⌣нешь,** *pf.* (*of* ⌣гива́ть) **1.** to pull, draw (*somewhere else; from A to B*); п. ло́дку к бе́регу to pull the boat to the shore. **2.** (*fig., coll.*) to pull over, attract; п. на свою́ сто́рону to win over, gain support of. **3.** to pull in too tight. **4.** to outbalance, outweigh.

перетя|ну́ть[2], **ну́, ⌣нешь,** *pf.* (*of* ⌣гива́ть) to stretch again.

перетя|ну́ться, ну́сь, ⌣нешься, *pf.* (*of* ⌣гива́ться) to lace oneself too tight.

переубе|ди́ть, ди́шь, *pf.* (*of* ⌣жда́ть) to make change one's mind, over-persuade.

переубе|ди́ться, дишься, *pf.* (*of* ⌣жда́ться) to change one's mind, be over-persuaded.

переубежда́|ть(ся), ю(сь), *impf. of* переубеди́ть(ся).

переу́л|ок, ка, *m.* lane, narrow street.

переупря́м|ить, лю, ишь, *pf.* (*no impf.*) (*coll.*) to prove more stubborn than.

переусе́рдств|овать, ую, *pf.* (*no impf.*) (*coll.*) to be over-diligent, show excess of zeal.

переустро́йств|о, а, *n.* reconstruction.

переутом|и́ть, лю, и́шь, *pf.* (*of* ⌣ля́ть) to overtire, overstrain; to overwork.

переутом|и́ться, лю́сь, и́шься, *pf.* (*of* ⌣ля́ться) to overtire oneself, overstrain oneself; to overwork; (*pf. only*) to be run down.

переутомле́ни|е, я, *n.* overstrain; overwork.

переутомля́|ть(ся), ю(сь), *impf. of* переутоми́ть(ся).

переуч|е́сть, ту́, тёшь, *past* ёл, ла́, *pf.* (*of* ⌣и́тывать) to take stock.

переучёт, а, *m.* stock-taking.

переу́чива|ть(ся), ю(сь), *impf. of* переучи́ть(ся).

переуч|и́ть, у́, ⌣ишь, *pf.* (*of* ⌣ива́ть) to teach again.

переуч|и́ться, у́сь, ⌣ишься, *pf.* (*of* ⌣ива́ться) **1.** to re-learn. **2.** (*coll.*) to study too much.

переформир|ова́ть, у́ю, *pf.* (*of* ⌣о́вывать) (*mil.*) to re-form.

переформиро́выва|ть, ю, *impf. of* переформирова́ть.

перефрази́р|овать, ую, *impf. and pf.* to paraphrase.

перефразиро́вк|а, и, f. paraphrase.

перехва́лива|ть, ю, *impf. of* перехвали́ть.

перехвал|и́ть, ю́, ⌣ишь, *pf.* (*of* ⌣ивать) to over-praise.

перехва́т, а, *m.* **1.** interception. **2.** intake, taking in (*of article of clothing*).

перехва|ти́ть, чу́, ⌣тишь, *pf.* (*of* ⌣тывать) **1.** to intercept, catch; я ⌣ти́л его́ по доро́ге на слу́жбу I caught him on the way to work. **2.** to take in; п. верёвкой to lash. **3.** (*coll.*) to take a snack; to catch up (*some-*

thing to eat). **4.** (*coll.*) to borrow (*for a short time*). **5.** (*coll.*) to overshoot the mark.

перехва́тчик, а, *m.* (*aeron.*) interceptor.

перехва́тыва|ть, ю, *impf. of* перехвати́ть.

перехвора́|ть, ю, *pf.* (*no impf.*) (+*i.*) to have had; to have been down (with) (*sc.* an illness).

перехитр|и́ть, ю́, и́шь, *pf.* to outwit, overreach.

перехо́д, а, *m.* **1.** (*in var. senses*) passage, transition; crossing. **2.** (*mil.*) (day's) march. **3.** (*rel.*) going over, conversion.

перехо|ди́ть[1], **жу́, ⌣дишь,** *impf. of* перейти́.

перехо|ди́ть[2], **жу́, ⌣дишь,** *pf.* (*no impf.*) (*coll.*) to go all over.

перехо|ди́ть[3], **жу, ⌣дишь,** *pf.* (*no impf.*) (*coll.; at games*) to have one's turn again, make one's move again.

перехо́дный, adj. **1.** transitional. **2.** (*gram.*) transitive. **3.** (*tech.*) transient.

перехо́д|я́щий, *pres. part.* of ⌣и́ть *and adj.* **1.** transient, transitory; п. ку́бок (*sport*) challenge cup. **2.** intermittent. **3.** (*fin.*) brought forward, carried over.

перехо́жий, adj., see кали́ка.

пе́р|ец, ца, *m.* pepper; стручко́вый п. capsicum; зада́ть кому́-н. ⌣цу (*coll.*) to give it someone hot.

перецара́па|ться, юсь, *pf.* **1.** to scratch oneself. **2.** to scratch each other.

перецел|ова́ть, у́ю, *pf.* (*no impf.*) to kiss (*all or a number of*).

перецел|ова́ться, у́юсь, *pf.* (*no impf.*) to kiss one another.

переце́нива|ть, ю, *impf. of* перецени́ть.

перецен|и́ть, ю, ⌣ишь, *pf.* (*of* ⌣ивать) **1.** to price too high. **2.** = переоцени́ть.

пе́реч|ень, ня, *m.* list; enumeration.

перечёркива|ть, ю, *impf. of* перечеркну́ть.

перечерк|ну́ть, ну́, нёшь, *pf.* (*of* ⌣ивать) to cross (out), cancel.

перечер|ти́ть, чу́, ⌣тишь, *pf.* (*of* ⌣чивать) **1.** to draw again. **2.** to copy, trace.

перечёрчива|ть, ю, *impf. of* перечерти́ть.

перече|са́ться, ⌣шешься, *pf.* (*no impf.*) (*coll.*) **1.** to do one's hair again. **2.** to do one's hair differently.

пере|че́сть[1], **чту́, чтёшь,** *past* ⌣чёл, ⌣чла́, *pf.* = ⌣счита́ть[2]; их мо́жно по па́льцам п. you could count them on the fingers of one hand.

пере|че́сть[2], **чту́, чтёшь,** *past* ⌣чёл, ⌣чла́, *pf.* = ⌣чита́ть.

перечи́нива|ть, ю, *impf. of* перечини́ть[1].

перечин|и́ть[1], **ю́, ⌣ишь,** *pf.* (*of* ⌣ивать) to mend again, repair again; п. каранда́ш to re-sharpen a pencil.

перечин|и́ть[2], **ю́, ⌣ишь,** *pf.* to mend, repair (*all or a number of*).

перечисле́ни|е, я, *n.* **1.** enumeration. **2.** (*fin.*) transferring.

перечи́сл|ить, ю, ишь, *pf.* (*of* ~я́ть) **1.** to enumerate. **2.** to transfer; его́ ~или в запа́с he has been transferred to the reserve; п. на теку́щий счёт (*fin.*) to transfer to one's current account.

перечисл|я́ть, я́ю, *impf. of* ~и́ть.

перечит|а́ть¹, а́ю, *pf.* (*of* ~ывать) to re-read.

перечит|а́ть², а́ю, *pf.* to read (*all or a quantity of*); он ~а́л все кни́ги в библиоте́ке he has read all the books in the library.

переч|и́ть, у, ишь, *impf.* (*no pf.*) (+*d.*; *coll.*) to contradict; п. go against.

пе́речниц|а, ы, *f.* pepper-pot; чёртова п. (*vulg.*; *of cantankerous old woman*) old hag.

пе́ре|чный, *adj. of* ~ц.

перечу́вств|овать, ую, *pf.* (*no impf.*) to feel, experience.

переша́гива|ть, ю, *impf. of* перешагну́ть.

перешаг|ну́ть, ну́, нёшь, *pf.* (*of* ~ивать) to step over; п. (че́рез) поро́г to cross the threshold.

переше́|ек, йка, *m.* isthmus, neck (of land).

перешёптыва|ться, юсь, *impf.* to whisper to one another.

перешиб|а́ть, а́ю, *impf. of* ~и́ть.

перешиб|и́ть, у́, ёшь, *past* ~, ~ла, *pf.* (*of* ~а́ть) (*coll.*) to break, fracture.

перешива́|ть, ю, *impf. of* переши́ть.

переши́вк|а, и, *f.* altering, alteration (*of clothes*).

переш|и́ть, ью́, ьёшь, *pf.* (*of* ~ива́ть) **1.** to alter; to have altered. **2.** (*tech.*) to alter (*gauge of railway, etc.*).

перешто́п|ать¹, аю, *pf.* (*of* ~ывать) to darn over, darn again.

перешто́п|ать², аю, *pf.* (*no impf.*) to darn (*all or a number of*).

перешто́пыва|ть, ю, *impf. of* перешто́пать.

перещеголя́|ть, ю, *pf.* (*no impf.*) (*coll.*) to beat, outdo, surpass.

переэкзамен|ова́ть, у́ю, *pf.* (*of* ~о́вывать) to re-examine.

переэкзамен|ова́ться, у́юсь, *pf.* (*of* ~о́вываться) to take an examination again.

переэкзамено́вк|а, и, *f.* re-examination (of *those failing at first attempt*).

переэкзамено́выва|ть(ся), ю(сь), *impf. of* переэкзаменова́ть(ся).

пе́ри, *indecl., f.* (*myth.*) peri.

периге́|й, я, *m.* (*astron.*) perigee.

периге́ли|й, я, *m.* (*astron.*) perihelium.

перика́рд, а, *m.* (*anat.*) pericardium.

перика́рд|ий, *m.* = ~.

перикарди́т, а, *m.* (*med.*) pericarditis.

пери́л|а, ~, *no sing.* rail(ing); handrail; banisters.

пери́метр, а, *m.* (*math.*) perimeter.

пери́н|а, ы, *f.* feather-bed.

пери́од, а, *m.* (*in var. senses*) period; леднико́вый п. (*geol.*) glacial period, ice age.

периодиза́ци|я, и, *f.* division into periods.

перио́дик|а, и, *f.* (*collect.*) periodicals.

периоди́ческ|ий, *adj.* periodic(al); recurring; ~ая дробь recurring decimal; п. журна́л periodical, magazine; ~ая печа́ть the periodical press; (*collect.*) periodicals; ~ое явле́ние recurrent phenomenon.

периоди́чност|ь, и, *f.* periodicity.

периоди́ч|ный (~ен, ~на), *adj.* periodic(al).

перипате́тик, а, *m.* (*hist. philos.*) peripatetic.

перипат|ети́ческий, *adj. of* ~е́тик.

перипети́|я, и, *f.* (*lit.*) peripeteia; (*fig.*) reversal of fortune, upheaval.

периско́п, а, *m.* periscope.

перископи́ческий, *adj.* periscopic.

периста́льтик|а, и, *f.* (*physiol.*) peristalsis.

пери́сти|л, я, *m.* (*archit.*) peristyle.

пе́ристо-кучево́й, *adj.* (*meteor.*) cirro--cumulus.

пе́ристы|й, *adj.* **1.** (*zool., bot.*) pinnate. **2.** feather-like, plumose; ~е облака́ fleecy clouds; cirri.

перитони́т, а, *m.* (*med.*) peritonitis.

перифери́йный, *adj.* provincial.

перифери́ческий, *adj.* peripheral.

перифери́|я, и, *f.* **1.** periphery. **2.** (*collect.*) the provinces; the outlying districts.

перифра́з|а, ы, *f.* periphrasis.

перифрази́р|овать, ую, *impf. and pf.* to use a periphrasis (for).

перифрасти́ческий, *adj.* periphrastic.

пёрк|а, и, *f.* (*tech.*) bit, flat bit, cutter, drill point; drill; flat drill; ло́жечная п. shell auger.

перка́л|ь, и, *f.* (*and* ~я, *m.*) (*text.*) percale.

перку́сси|я, и, *f.* (*med.*) percussion.

перкути́р|овать, ую, *impf. and pf.* (*med.*) to percuss.

перл, а, *m.* (*obs. in literal sense*; *fig., rhet. and typ.*) pearl.

перламу́тр, а, *m.* mother-of-pearl, nacre.

перламу́тр|овый, *adj. of* ~; ~овая пу́говица pearl button.

перли́н|ь, я, *m.* (*naut.*) hawser.

перло́в|ый, *adj.* ~ая крупа́ pearl barley.

перлюстра́ци|я, и, *f.* opening and inspection of correspondence.

перлюстри́р|овать, ую, *impf. and pf.* to open and inspect (*correspondence*).

пермане́нт, а, *m.* permanent wave.

пермане́нтный, *adj.* permanent.

пе́рм|ский, *adj.* Permian (*branch of Finno--Ugric ethnic and linguistic group*); ~ская систе́ма (*geol.*) Permian formation (*from Perm, a town in the Urals*).

перна́т|ый (~, ~а), *adj.* feathered, feathery; ~ое ца́рство 'feathered world' (*birds*).

пёр|нуть, нет (*inst. pf. of* ~де́ть) (*vulg.*) to give a fart.

пер|о́, а́, *pl.* ~ья, ~ьев, *n.* **1.** feather; ни пу́ха, ни ~а́! good luck! **2.** pen; ве́чное п. fountain-pen; взя́ться за п. (*fig.*) to take up the pen; владе́ть ~о́м to wield a skilful pen; про́ба ~а́ (*fig.*) first attempt at writing. **3.** leaf (*of onion or garlic*). **4.** fin. **5.** blade (*of an oar*); paddle (*of wheel*).

перочи́нный, *adj.* п. нож pen-knife.

перпендикуля́р, а, *m.* (*math.*) perpendicular; опусти́ть п. to drop a perpendicular.

перпендикуля́р|ный (~ен, ~на), *adj.* perpendicular.

перро́н, а, *m.* platform (*on railway station*).

перро́н|ный, *adj.* of ~; п. биле́т platform ticket.

перс, а, *m.* Persian.

перс|и, ей, *no sing.* (*arch. or poet.*) breast, bosom.

перси́дский, *adj.* Persian; п. порошо́к insect-powder.

пе́рсик, а, *m.* **1.** peach. **2.** peach-tree.

пе́рсик|овый, *adj.* of ~; peachy; ~овое де́рево peach-tree.

перси|я́нин, я́нина, *pl.* я́не, я́н, *m.* (*obs.*) = перс.

персия́нк|а, и, *f.* Persian (woman).

персо́н|а, ы, *f.* person; ва́жная п. (*coll.*) big wig; со́бственная п. one's own self; яви́ться со́бственной ~ой (*obs. or iron.*) to appear in person; п. гра́та persona grata; обе́д на́ шесть ~ dinner for six.

персона́ж, а, *m.* (*lit.*) character; (*fig.*) personage.

персона́л, а, *m.* personnel, staff.

персона́льный, *adj.* personal; individual; п. пенсионе́р person in receipt of special pension.

персонифика́ци|я, и, *f.* personification.

персонифици́р|овать, ую, *impf. and pf.* to personify.

перспекти́в|а, ы, *f.* **1.** (*art*) perspective. **2.** vista, prospect. **3.** (*fig.*) prospect, outlook; что в ~е? what is in prospect?, what are the prospects?; име́ть ~у to have prospects, have a future (before one).

перспекти́в|ный, *adj.* **1.** (*art*) perspective. **2.** forward-looking; envisaging future development; ~ное плани́рование (*econ.*) long-term planning. **3.** (~ен, ~на) having prospects; promising; ~ная молода́я балери́на a promising young ballerina.

перст, а́, *m.* (*obs.*) finger; оди́н, как п. all alone.

пе́рст|ень, ня, *m.* (finger-)ring; (с печа́тью) signet-ring.

перстневи́дный, *adj.* п. хрящ (*anat.*) cricoid.

перст|ь, и, *f.* (*arch. or rhet.*) dust, earth.

перуа́н|ец, ца, *m.* Peruvian.

перуа́нк|а, и, *f.* Peruvian (woman).

перуа́нский, *adj.* Peruvian; п. бальза́м Peru balsam.

перу́н|ы, ов, *no sing.* (*obs.*,*poet.*) thunderbolts; (*fig.*) fulminations; мета́ть п. to fulminate.

перфе́кт, а, *m.* (*gram.*) perfect (tense).

перфока́рт|а, ы, *f.* punched card (*in computer programming, etc.*).

перфора́тор, а, *m.* (*tech.*) **1.** perforator; punch. **2.** drill, boring machine.

перфора́ци|я, и, *f.* (*tech.*) **1.** perforation, punching. **2.** drilling, boring.

перфори́р|овать, ую, *impf. and pf.* (*tech.*) **1.** to perforate, punch. **2.** to drill, bore.

перха́|ть, ю, *impf.* (*no pf.*) (*coll.*) to cough (*in trying to remove an irritation of the throat*).

перхлора́т, а, *m.* (*chem.*) perchlorate.

перхо́т|а, ы, *f.* (*coll.*) tickling in the throat.

пе́рхот|ь, и, *f.* dandruff, scurf.

перце́пци|я, и, *f.* (*philos.*) perception.

перцо́вк|а, и, *f.* pepper-brandy.

перцо́вый, *adj.* of пе́рец.

перча́тк|а, и, *f.* glove; gauntlet; бро́сить ~у (*fig.*) to throw down the gauntlet.

перча́точник, а, *m.* glover.

перчи́нк|а, и, *f.* peppercorn.

перч|и́ть, у, ишь, *impf.* (*of* на~ *and* по~) (*coll.*) to pepper.

першеро́н, а, *m.* percheron (*breed of horse*).

перш|и́ть, и́т, *impf.* (*coll.*; *impers.*) у меня́ в го́рле ~и́т I have a tickle in my throat.

пёрыш|ко, ка, *pl.* ~ки, ~ек, ~кам, *n.* (*coll.*) *dim. of* перо́; лёгкий, как п. light as a feather.

пёс, пса, *m.* (*coll.*) dog; (*astron.*) созве́здие Большо́го Пса Canis Major; созве́здие Ма́лого Пса Canis Minor; (*coll.*) п. знает the devil only knows.

пе́сельник, а, *m.* (*coll.*) singer.

пе́сенк|а, и, *f.* song; его́ п. спе́та (*coll.*) his song is ended, he has had it.

пе́сенник, а, *m.* **1.** song-book. **2.** (*chorus*) singer. **3.** song-writer.

пе́с|енный, *adj.* of ~ня.

песе́т|а, ы, *f.* (*Spanish currency unit*) peseta.

пес|е́ц, ца́, *m.* polar fox; бе́лый, голубо́й п. white, blue fox (fur).

пё́с|ий *and* пе́сий, *adj.* of ~; пе́сья звезда́ (*astron.*) Sirius, the Dog Star.

пё́сик, а, *m.* (*coll.*) *dim. of* пёс; doggie.

песка́р|ь, я́, *m.* gudgeon (*fish*).

пескостру́йный, *adj.* (*tech.*) sand-blast.

песнопе́в|ец, ца, *m.* **1.** (*obs. rhet.*) singer; psalmist. **2.** (*poet.*) poet, bard.

песнопе́ни|е, я, *n.* **1.** (*eccl.*) psalm; canticle. **2.** (*poet.*) poetry, poesy.

песн|ь, и, *g. pl.* ~ей, *f.* **1.** (*obs.*) song; П. ~ей the Song of Songs, Song of Solomon. **2.** (*lit.*) canto, book.

пе́с|ня, ни, *g. pl.* ~ен, *f.* song; air; до́лгая п. (*fig., coll.*) a long story; э́то стара́ (ста́-

рая) п. (*coll.*) it's the same old story; тяну́ть всё ту же ∼ню (*coll.*) to harp on one string; п. спе́та = пе́сенка спе́та.

пес|о́к, ка́, *m.* 1. sand; золото́й п. gold dust; са́харный п. granulated sugar; стро́ить на ∼ке́ (*fig.*) to build on sand; как п. морско́й, как ∼ку́ морско́го (numerous) as the sands of the sea. 2. (*pl.*) sands; зыбу́чие ∼ки́ quicksands. 3. (*med.*) gravel.

песо́чник, а, *m.* (*orn.*) sand-piper.

песо́чниц|а, ы, *f.* 1. sand-box. 2. sanding apparatus.

песо́чн|ый, *adj.* 1. *adj. of* песо́к; sandy; ∼ые часы́ sand-glass, hour-glass. 2. (*cul.*) short; ∼ое пече́нье shortbread, shortcake.

пессими́зм, а, *m.* pessimism.

пессими́ст, а, *m.* pessimist.

пессимисти́ческий, *adj.* pessimistic.

пессимисти́ч|ный (∼ен, ∼на), *adj.* = ∼еский.

пест, а́, *m.* pestle; п., знай свою́ сту́пу (*prov.*) cobbler, stick to your last; как п. в ло́жках a square peg in a round hole.

пе́стик[1], а, *m.* (*bot.*) pistil.

пе́стик[2], а, *m. dim. of* пест.

пест|ова́ть, у́ю, *impf.* (*of* вы́∼) 1. (*obs.*) to nurse. 2. (*fig.*) to cherish, foster.

пестр|е́ть[1], е́ет, *impf.* (*no pf.*) 1. to become many-coloured. 2. (+*i.*) to be gay (with); корабли́ ∼е́ли фла́гами the ships were gay with bunting. 3. to show colourfully, make a brave show (*of objects of different colours*).

пестр|е́ть[2], и́т, *impf.* (*no pf.*) 1. (*of many-coloured objects*) to strike the eye (*also fig.*); его́ и́мя ∼и́т в газе́тах (*coll.*) he is always getting his name in the papers. 2. (*coll.*) to be too gaudy, be flashy. 3. (+*i.*) to abound (in), be rich (in); письмо́ ∼и́т оши́бками the letter bristles with mistakes.

пестр|и́ть, ю́, и́шь, *impf.* (*no pf.*) 1. to make gaudy; to make colourful. 2. (*impers.*) у меня́ ∼и́ло в глаза́х I was dazzled (*sc.* by the colours).

пестрот|а́, ы́, *no pl., f.* diversity of colours; (*fig.*) mixed character.

пестру́шк|а, и, *f.* 1. speckled trout. 2. (*zool.*) lemming.

пёстр|ый (∼, ∼а́, ∼о *and* ∼о́), *adj.* 1. motley, variegated, many-coloured, particoloured. 2. (*fig., coll.*) mixed; п. соста́в населе́ния mixed population. 3. (*fig.*) florid; pretentious, mannered; п. слог florid style.

пестрядёвый, *adj. of* пестря́дь.

пестря́д|ь, и, *f.* a coarse, coloured, cotton fabric.

песту́н, а́, *m.* (*obs.*) mentor.

пес|цо́вый, *adj. of* ∼е́ц.

песча́ник, а, *m.* (*geol.*) sandstone.

песча́нк|а, и, *f.* (*orn.*) sanderling.

песча́н|ый, *adj.* sandy; ∼ая коса́ sandbar; п. холм dune.

песчи́нк|а, и, *f.* grain of sand.

пета́рд|а, ы, *f.* 1. (*hist. mil.*) petard. 2. detonating cartridge (*as alarm signal on railways*). 3. fire-cracker.

пети́т, а, *m.* (*typ.*) brevier.

пети́ци|я, и, *f.* petition.

петли́ц|а, ы, *f.* 1. buttonhole. 2. tab (*on uniform collar*).

пе́т|ля, ли, *g. pl.* ∼ель, *f.* 1. loop; мёртвая п. (*aeron.*) loop; сде́лать мёртвую ∼лю to loop the loop. 2. (*fig.*) noose; он досто́ин ∼ли he deserves to hang; лезть в ∼лю to put one's neck into the noose, take risks needlessly; наде́ть ∼лю на ше́ю to hang a millstone about one's neck. 3. buttonhole; мета́ть ∼ли to work buttonholes, buttonhole; (*fig., joc.*) (i) to conceal one's tracks, (ii) to confuse the issue. 4. stitch; спусти́ть ∼лю to drop a stitch; to ladder one's stocking. 5. hinge; дверь соскочи́ла с ∼ель the door has come off its hinges.

петля́|ть, ю, *impf.* (*coll.*) to dodge.

петрифика́ци|я, и, *f.* petrification; fossilization.

петро́граф, а, *m.* petrographer.

петрогра́фи|я, и, *f.* petrography.

петроле́йный, *adj.* (*chem.*) petroleum.

петру́шк|а[1], и, *f.* parsley.

петру́шк|а[2], и, *m. and f.* 1. (*m.*) Punch. 2. (*f.*) Punch-and-Judy show. 3. (*f.*) (*fig., coll.*) foolishness, absurdity; кака́я-то п. получи́лась an absurd thing happened; брось валя́ть ∼у! stop being a fool!

пету́н|ия, ии, *f.* (*bot.*) petunia.

пету́н|ья, ьи, *g. pl.* ∼ий, *f.* = ∼ия.

пету́х, а́, *m.* 1. cock; инде́йский п. turkey-cock; фаза́н-п. cock-pheasant; до ∼о́в before cock-crow; встать с ∼а́ми to rise with the lark; пусти́ть ∼а́ (*mus. sl.*) to let out a squeak (*on a high note*); пусти́ть кра́сного ∼а́ to set fire, commit act of arson. 2. *fig., of an irascible person.*

пету́|ший, *adj. of* ∼х; п. гре́бень cockscomb.

петуши́ный, *adj. of* пету́х; п. бой cock-fight(-ing); п. го́лос squeaky voice.

петуш|и́ться, у́сь, и́шься, *impf.* (*of* вс∼) (*coll.*) to ride the high horse; to take umbrage.

петуш|о́к, ка́, *m.* 1. cockerel; идти́ ∼ко́м (*coll., joc.*) to mince, walk mincingly. 2. (*electr.*) commutator lug, commutator riser.

пе́т|ый, *p.p.p. of* ∼ь; (*coll.*) п. дура́к perfect fool.

петь, пою́, поёшь, *impf.* (*of* про∼ *and* с∼) to sing (*also of birds and, fig., of inanimate objects*); to chant, intone; п. ба́сом to have a bass voice; п. ве́рно, фальши́во to sing in tune, out of tune; п. вполго́лоса to hum; п. другу́ю пе́сню to sing another tune; п. Ла́заря (coll., pejor.) to bemoan one's fate, grumble, complain; п. сла́ву (+d.) to sing the praises (of).

пехо́т|а, ы, f. infantry, foot; морска́я п.(the) marines.

пехоти́н|ец, ца, m. infantryman.

пехо́тный, adj. infantry.

печа́л|ить, ю, ишь, impf. (of o~) to grieve, sadden.

печа́л|иться, юсь, ишься, impf. (of o~) to grieve, be sad.

печа́л|ь, и, f. grief, sorrow; кака́я п.! how sad!; не твоя́ п. it's no concern of yours; тебе́ что за п.? what has that to do with you?

печа́льник, а, m. (obs., now iron.) one who feels for others, sympathizer.

печа́л|ьный (~ен, ~ьна), adj. 1. sad, mournful, doleful; wistful. 2. grievous; п. коне́ц dismal end, bad end; ~ьные результа́ты unfortunate results; оста́вить по себе́ ~ьную па́мять to leave a bad reputation.

печа́тани|е, я, n. printing.

печа́та|ть, ю, impf. (of на~) to print; to type.

печа́та|ться, юсь, impf. (of на~) 1. to write (for a journal, etc.); to have (literary compositions, etc.) published; тридцати́ лет он ещё нигде́ не ~лся at thirty he had not yet had anything published. 2. to be at the printer's, be in the press.

печа́тк|а, и, f. signet.

печа́тник, а, m. printer.

печа́тн|ый, adj. 1. printing; ~ое де́ло printing; п. лист quire, printer's sheet; п. стано́к printing-press. 2. printed; in the press; ~ая кни́га printed book (as opp. to manuscript); п. о́тзыв о но́вом рома́не press comment on a new novel. 3. писа́ть по ~ому, ~ыми бу́квами to (write in) print; to write in block capitals.

печа́т|ь¹, и, f. seal, stamp (also fig.); госуда́рственная п. State Seal, Great Seal; наложи́ть п. (на+a.) to affix a seal (to); носи́ть п. (+g.) to have the seal (of), bear the stamp (of); п. го́ря the stamp of grief; на мои́х уста́х п. молча́ния my lips are sealed.

печа́т|ь², и, f. 1. print(ing); быть в ~и to be in print, be at the printer's; вы́йти из ~и to appear, come out, be published; подписа́ть к ~и to send to press; «подписано к ~и» 'passed for printing'. 2. print, type; ме́лкая п. small print; кру́пная п. large print; убо́ристая п. close print. 3. (the) press; свобо́да ~и freedom of the press; име́ть благоприя́тные о́тзывы в ~и to have a good press.

печени|е, я, n. baking.

печёнк|а, и, f. 1. liver (of animal, as food). 2. (coll.) liver; сиде́ть (у кого́-н.) в ~ах to plague (someone).

печёночник, а, m. (bot.) liverwort.

печён|очный, adj. of ~ка and пе́чень; hepatic.

печёный, adj. (cul.) baked.

пе́чен|ь, и, f. liver; воспале́ние ~и (med.) hepatitis, inflammation of the liver.

пече́нь|е, я, n. pastry; biscuit; минда́льное п. macaroon.

пе́чк|а, и, f. stove; танцева́ть от ~и (coll., iron.) to begin again from the beginning.

печни́к, а́, m. stove-setter; stove-repairer.

печ|но́й, adj. of ~ь²; п. агрега́т furnace unit; п. газ furnace gas; п. ка́мень oven-stone; ~но́е отопле́ние stove heating; ~на́я труба́ chimney, flue.

печь¹, пеку́, печёшь, пеку́т, past пёк, пекла́, impf. (of ис~) to bake; со́лнце пекло́ there was a scorching sun.

печ|ь², и, о ~и, в ~и́, pl. ~и, ~е́й, f. 1. stove; oven. 2. (tech.) furnace, kiln, oven; до́менная п. blast-furnace; кремацио́нная п. incinerator.

пе́чься¹, печётся, пеку́тся, past пёкся, пекла́сь, impf. (of ис~) to bake; to broil (in the sun).

пе́чься², пеку́сь, печёшься, пеку́тся, past пёкся, пекла́сь, impf. (no pf.) (о+p.) to take care (of), care (for), look after.

пешедра́лом, adv. (coll.) = пешко́м.

пешехо́д, а, m. pedestrian.

пешехо́дн|ый, adj. pedestrian; п. мост foot--bridge; ~ая тропа́ footpath.

пе́ш|ечный, adj. of ~ка.

пе́ш|ий, adj. 1. pedestrian; по о́бразу ~его хожде́ния on Shanks' mare. 2. (mil.) unmounted, foot.

пе́шк|а, и, f. (in chess, also fig.) pawn.

пешко́м, adv. on foot.

пеще́р|а, ы, f. cave, cavern; grotto.

пеще́рист|ый (~, ~а), adj. 1. with many caves. 2. (anat.) cavernous.

пеще́р|ный, adj. of ~а; п. челове́к (archaeol.) cave-dweller, cave-man, troglodyte.

пи, indecl., n. (math.) pi (π).

пиани́но, indecl., n. (upright) piano.

пиани́ссимо, adv. (mus.) pianissimo.

пиани́ст, а, m. pianist.

пиа́но, adv. (mus.) piano.

пианол|а, ы, f. (mus.) pianola.

пиа́стр, а, m. piastre.

пива́|ть, ю, impf. (coll.) freq. of пить.

пивн|а́я, о́й, f. alehouse; pub.

пив|но́й, adj. of ~о; ~ны́е дро́жжи brewer's yeast; ~на́я кру́жка beer mug.

пи́в|о, а, n. beer; све́тлое п. pale ale; тёмное п. brown ale; ~а не сва́ришь с ним (fig., coll.) he's an awkward customer.

пивова́р, а, *m.* brewer.

пивова́рени|е, я, *n.* brewing.

пивова́ренн|ый, *adj.* п. заво́д brewery; ~ая промы́шленность brewing.

пига́лиц|а, ы, *f.* (*orn.*) lapwing, peewit; (*fig., coll.*) puny person.

пигме́|й, я, *m.* pygmy (*also fig.*).

пигме́нт, а, *m.* pigment.

пигмента́ци|я, и, *f.* pigmentation.

пигме́нтный, *adj.* pigmental, pigmentary.

пиджа́к, а́, *m.* jacket, coat.

пиджа́|чный, *adj.* of ~к; п. костю́м, ~чная па́ра (lounge-)suit.

пиете́т, а, *m.* piety.

пижа́м|а, ы, *f.* pyjamas.

пижо́н, а, *m.* (*coll.*) fop.

пизд|а́, ы́, *f.* (*vulg.*) cunt.

пии́т, а, *m.* (*arch.*) poet.

пик[1], а, *m.* (*geogr.*) peak; spire; pinnacle.

пик[2], а, *m.* peak (*of work, traffic, etc.*); п. нагру́зки (*electr.*) peak load; (*as indecl. adj.*) часы́ пик rush-hour.

пи́к|а[1], и, *f.* pike, lance.

пи́к|а[2], и, *f.* (*cards*) spade; да́ма ~ the queen of spades; пойти́ ~ой to play a spade.

пи́к|а[3], и, *f.* only in phrase сде́лать что-н. в ~у кому́-н. to do a thing to spite someone.

пика́нтност|ь, и, *f.* piquancy, savour, zest.

пика́нт|ный (~ен, ~на), *adj.* piquant (*also fig.*), savoury; (*fig.*) poignant; п. анекдо́т risqué story.

пика́п, а, *m.* pick-up (van).

пике́[1], *indecl., n.* (*text.*) piqué.

пике́[2], *indecl., n.* (*aeron.*) dive; перейти́ в п. to go into a dive.

пике́|йный, *adj.* of ~[1].

пике́т[1], а, *m.* picket (picquet, piquet).

пике́т[2], а, *m.* (*card-game*) piquet.

пикети́р|овать, ую, *impf.* to picket.

пике́тчик, а, *m.* picket.

пики́ровани|е, я, *n.* (*aeron.*) dive, diving.

пики́рованный, *adj.* (*obs.*) piqued, in pique.

пики́р|овать, ую, *impf. and pf.* (*pf. also* с~) (*aeron.*) to dive, swoop.

пикир|ова́ть, у́ю, *impf. and pf.* (*agric.*) to thin out.

пики́р|оваться, уюсь, *impf.* (*no pf.*) (с+*i.*) to exchange caustic remarks, cross swords.

пикиро́вк|а[1], и, *f.* (*agric.*) thinning.

пикиро́вк|а[2], и, *f.* (*coll.*) altercation, slanging-match.

пикиро́вщик, а, *m.* dive-bomber.

пики́р|ующий, *pres. part of* ~овать *and adj.*; п. бомбардиро́вщик dive-bomber.

пи́кколо, *indecl., n.* piccolo.

пи́кник, а, *m.* (*anthrop.*) pyknic person.

пикни́к, а́, *m.* picnic.

пи́кн|уть, у, ешь, *pf.* (*coll.*) to let out a squeak; (*fig.*) to make a sound (of protest);

попро́буй то́лько п. (*with implied threat*) one sound out of you!; п. не сметь not to dare utter a word; он п. не успе́л before he could say knife.

пи́к|овый, *adj.* **1.** *adj. of* ~а[2]; ~овая да́ма queen of spades; ~овая масть spades. **2.** (*fig., coll.*) awkward; unfavourable; попа́сть в ~овое положе́ние to get into a pretty mess; оста́ться при ~овом интере́се to get nothing for one's pains.

пикра́т, а, *m.* (*chem.*) picrate.

пикри́новый, *adj.* (*chem.*) picric.

пиксафо́н, а, *m.* liquid tar soap.

пиктографи́ческий, *adj.* pictographic.

пиктогра́фи|я, и, *f.* pictography.

пи́кул|и, ей, *no sing.* pickles.

пил|а́, ы́, *pl.* ~ы, ~, *f.* **1.** saw; ле́нточная п. band-saw; лучко́вая п. sash saw, bow saw; механи́ческая п. поперечная п. cross-cut saw; столя́рная п. buck-saw. **2.** (*fig.*) nagger.

пила́в, а, *m.* (*cul.*) pilaff (pilau, pilaw).

пила́-ры́ба, пилы́-ры́бы, *f.* saw-fish.

пилёный, *adj.* sawn; п. лес timber; п. са́хар lump sugar.

пилигри́м, а, *m.* pilgrim.

пили́ка|ть, ю, *impf.* (*coll.*) to scrape, strum (*on a fiddle, etc.*).

пил|и́ть, ю́, ~ишь, *impf.* **1.** to saw. **2.** (*fig., coll.*) to nag (at).

пи́лк|а, и, *f.* **1.** sawing. **2.** fret-saw. **3.** nail-file.

пи́ллерс, а, *m.* (*naut.*) deck stanchion.

пиломатериа́л|ы, ов, *no sing.* saw-timber.

пило́н, а, *m.* (*archit.*) pylon.

пилообра́зный, *adj.* serrated, notched.

пилора́м|а, ы, *f.* power-saw bench.

пило́т, а, *m.* pilot.

пилота́ж, а, *m.* pilotage; вы́сший п. aerobatics.

пилоти́р|овать, ую, *impf.* to pilot.

пило́тк|а, и, *f.* (*mil.*) forage cap.

пиль, *interj.* (*command to hounds*) take!

пи́льщик, а, *m.* sawyer, wood-cutter.

пилю́л|я, и, *f.* pill (*also fig.*); проглоти́ть ~ю (*fig.*) to swallow the pill; позолоти́ть ~ю to gild the pill.

пиля́стр|а, ы, *f.* (*archit.*) pilaster.

пим|ы́, о́в, *sing.* ~, ~а́, *m.* pimy (**1.** *deer-skin boots worn in N. regions of U.S.S.R.* **2.** *dial. name for valenki*).

пинакоте́к|а, и, *f.* picture gallery.

пина́|ть, ю, *impf. of* пнуть.

пингви́н, а, *m.* penguin.

пинг-по́нг, а, *m.* ping-pong.

пине́тк|а, и, *f.* (baby's) bootee.

пи́ни|я, и, *f.* Italian pine.

пин|о́к, ка́, *m.* (*coll.*) kick.

пи́нт|а, ы, *f.* pint.

пинце́т, а, *m.* pincers, tweezers.

пи́нчер, а, *m.* (*breed of dog*) Dandie Dinmont, pincher.

пио́н, а, *m.* (*bot.*) peony.

пионе́р, а, *m.* (*in var. senses*) pioneer; (ю́ный) пионе́р Pioneer (*member of Communist children's organization in U.S.S.R.*).

пионервожа́т|ый, ого, *m.* (*and* ~ая, ~ой, *f.*) Pioneer leader.

пионе́ри|я, и, *f.* (*collect.; coll.*), Pioneers.

пионе́р|ский, *adj. of* ~.

пиоре́|я, и, *f.* (*med.*) pyorrhoea.

пипе́тк|а, и, *f.* pipette; medicine dropper.

пи-пи́, *indecl.* (*in children's speech*) wee-wee.

пир, а, о ~е, в ~у́, *pl.* ~ы́, *m.* feast, banquet; п. горо́й, п. на весь мир sumptuous feast; в чужо́м ~у́ похме́лье carrying the can (for others).

пирами́д|а, ы, *f.* pyramid.

пирамида́льный, *adj.* pyramidal; п. то́поль Lombardy poplar.

пирамидо́н, а, *m.* (*pharm.*) pyramidon, amidopyrine; headache tablets.

пира́т, а, *m.* pirate.

пира́тский, *adj.* piratic(al).

пира́тств|о, а, *n.* piracy.

пирене́йский, *adj.* Pyrenean.

пириди́н, а, *m.* (*chem.*) pyridine.

пири́т, а, *m.* (*min.*) pyrites.

пир|ова́ть, у́ю, *impf.* to feast, banquet; to celebrate with feasting.

пирови́нн|ый, ~ая кислота́ (*chem.*) pyrotartaric acid.

пиро́г, а́, *m.* pie; tart; п. с мя́сом meat pie; возду́шный п. soufflé; сва́дебный п. wedding cake; ешь п. с гриба́ми, держи́ язы́к за зуба́ми (*prov.*) keep your breath to cool your porridge.

пиро́г|а, и, *f.* pirogue.

пирогравю́р|а, ы, *f.* pyrogravure, poker-work.

пиро́жник, а, *m.* pastry-cook.

пиро́жн|ое, ого, *n.* 1. (*collect.*) pastries; (fancy) cake, pastry. 2. (*obs.*) sweet.

пирож|о́к, ка́, *m.* pasty, patty, pie.

пироксили́н, а, *m.* pyroxylin, gun-cotton.

пироксили́н|овый, *adj. of* ~; ~овая ша́шка slab of gun-cotton.

пиро́метр, а, *m.* (*phys., tech.*) pyrometer.

пиросе́рн|ый, ~ая кислота́ (*chem.*) pyrosulphuric acid.

пироте́хник, а, *m.* pyrotechnics.

пиротехни́ческий, *adj.* pyrotechnic.

пирри́хи|й, я, *m.* (*lit.*) pyrrhic (foot).

пи́рров, *adj.* ~а побе́да Pyrrhic victory.

пиру́шк|а, и, *f.* (*coll.*) carousal; binge.

пируэ́т, а, *m.* pirouette.

пи́ршеств|о, а, *n.* feast, banquet.

пи́ршеств|овать, ую, *impf.* to feast, banquet.

писа́к|а, и, *m.* (*coll.*) scribbler, quill-driver.

писа́ни|е, я, *n.* 1. writing. 2. writing, screed; (свяще́нное) п. Holy Scripture, Holy Writ.

пи́сан|ый, *adj.* written, manuscript; ~ая краса́вица a picture (of beauty); говори́ть как по-~ому to speak as from the book; носи́ться с чем-н. как (дура́к) с ~ой то́рбой to fuss over something like a child with a new toy.

писарско́й, *adj. of* пи́сарь.

пи́сар|ь, я, *pl.* ~я́, *m.* (*obs.*) clerk.

писа́тел|ь, я, *m.* writer, author.

писа́тель|ский, *adj. of* ~; п. труд writing, literary work.

пи́са|ть, ю, *impf.* (*vulg.*) to piss.

пи|са́ть, шу́, ~шешь, *impf.* (*of* на~) 1. to write; п. на маши́нке to type; п. про́зой, стиха́ми to write prose, verse; п. дневни́к to keep a diary; п. под дикто́вку to take dictation; не про нас ~сано (*coll.*) (i) it is Greek to us, (ii) it is not (intended, meant) for us; дурака́м зако́н не ~сан (*coll.*) fools rush in where angels fear to tread; ~ши́ пропа́ло it is as good as lost. 2. (+*i.*) to paint (in); п. портре́ты ма́слом to paint portraits in oils.

пи|са́ться, шу́сь, ~шешься, *impf.* 1. to spell, be spelled; как ~шется э́то сло́во? how do you spell this word? 2. (*impers.*; +*d.*) to feel an inclination for writing; мне сего́дня не ~шется I don't feel like writing today. 3. (+*i.*; *obs.*) to style oneself; to sign oneself; он ~шется торго́вцем he styles himself a merchant. 4. *pass. of* ~са́ть.

пис|е́ц, ца́, *m.* 1. (*obs.*) clerk. 2. (*hist.*) scribe.

писк, а, *m.* peep; chirp; squeak; (*of chicks*) cheep.

пискли́в|ый (~, ~а), *adj.* squeaky.

пискля́в|ый (~, ~а), *adj.* (*coll.*) = пискли́вый.

пи́скн|уть, у, ешь, *inst. pf.* (*of* пища́ть) (*coll.*) to give a squeak; то́лько ~и у меня́! (*with implied threat*) one squeak out of you!

пискотн|я́, и́, *f.* (*coll.*) squeaking; chirruping.

писку́н, а́, *m.* (*coll.*) 1. squeaker. 2. whiner.

писсуа́р, а, *m.* urinal.

пистоле́т, а, *m.* pistol; п.-пулемёт sub-machine-gun.

писто́н, а, *m.* 1. (percussion) cap. 2. (*mus.*) piston.

писто́н|ный, *adj. of* ~; ~ное ружьё percussion musket.

писцо́вы|й, *adj. of* писе́ц; ~е кни́ги (*hist.*) cadastres.

писчебума́жны|й, *adj.* п. магази́н stationer's (shop); ~е принадле́жности stationery.

пи́сч|ий, *adj.* ~ая бума́га writing paper; п. материа́л writing materials.

письмена́, письмён, ~м, *no sing.* characters, letters; дре́вние еги́петские п. ancient Egyptian characters.

пи́сьменно, *adv.* in writing, in written form; изложи́ть п. to set down in writing, put down on paper.

пи́сьменност|ь, и, *f.* 1. literature; (*collect.*) literary texts. 2. the written language.

пи́сьменн|ый, *adj.* 1. writing; п. прибо́р desk set; п. стол writing-table, bureau. 2. written; в ~ом ви́де, в ~ой фо́рме in writing, in written form; п. знак letter; п. о́тзыв written testimonial; п. экза́мен written examination.

письм|о́, а́, *pl.* ~а, пи́сем, ~ам, *n.* 1. letter; заказно́е п. registered letter; це́нное п. registered letter (with statement of value); поздрави́тельное п. letter of congratulation. 2. writing; иску́сство ~а́ art of writing. 3. script; hand(-writing); ара́бское п. Arabic script; ме́лкое п. small hand.

письмо́вник, а, *m.* (*hist.*) manual of letter-writing (*containing specimen letters*).

письмоводи́тел|ь, я, *m.* (*obs.*) clerk.

письмоно́с|ец, ца, *m.* postman.

пита́ни|е, я, *n.* 1. nourishment, nutrition; feeding; недоста́точное п. malnutrition; обще́ственное п. public catering; уси́ленное п. high-calorie diet, nourishing diet. 2. (*tech.*) feed, feeding; резервуа́р ~я feed tank.

пита́тел|ь, я, *m.* (*tech.*) feeder.

пита́тельност|ь, и, *f.* nutritiousness, food value.

пита́тел|ьный (~ен, ~ьна), *adj.* 1. nourishing, nutritious; supplying nutriment; п. пункт refreshment place (*kiosk, etc.*); ~ьная среда́ (*biol.*) culture medium; (*fig.*) breeding-ground; ~ьное сре́дство nutriment. 2. (*anat.*) alimentary. 3. (*tech.*) feed, feeding; ~ьная труба́ feed pipe, supply pipe.

пита́|ть, ю, *impf.* (*of* на~) 1. to feed; to nourish (*also fig.*); to sustain; п. больно́го to feed a patient; п. наде́жду to nourish the hope; п. отвраще́ние (к) to have an aversion (for); п. привя́занность (к) to be attached (to), cultivate an attachment (to). 2. (*tech.*) to feed, supply; п. го́род электро-эне́ргией to supply a city with electricity.

пита́|ться, юсь, *impf.* (+*i.*) to feed (on), live (on); хорошо́ п. to be well fed, eat well; п. наде́ждами to live on hope.

пите́йн|ый, *adj.* (*obs.*) п. дом, ~ое заведе́ние public house.

питека́нтроп, а, *m.* (*anthrop.*) pithecanthropus.

пи́терский, *adj.* (*coll.*) of St. Petersburg.

пито́м|ец, ца, *m.* 1. foster-child, nursling; charge. 2. pupil; alumnus.

пито́мник, а, *m.* nursery (*for plants or*

animals; *also fig.*); дре́весный п. arboretum.

пито́н, а, *m.* python.

питу́х, а́, *m.* (*obs. or coll.*) (big) drinker.

пить, пью, пьёшь, *past* пил, пила́, пи́ло, *impf.* (*of* вы́~) to drink; to have, take (*liquids*); мне п. хо́чется I am thirsty; п. за (+*a.*), за здоро́вье (+*g.*) to drink to, to the health (of); п. го́рькую, п. мёртвую (*coll.*) to drink hard; как п. дать (*coll.*) for sure, as sure as eggs is eggs; как п. дать придёт he will come for sure.

пить|ё, я́, *n.* 1. drinking. 2. drink, beverage.

питьев|о́й, *adj.* drinkable; ~а́я вода́ drinking water; ~а́я со́да household soda.

пифагоре́|ец, йца, *m.* Pythagorean.

пифагоре́йский, *adj.* Pythagorean.

пифаго́ров, *adj.* ~а теоре́ма Pythagoras' theorem.

пифи|я, и, *f.* (*hist.*) the Pythian, Pythoness.

пих|а́ть, а́ю, *impf.* (*of* ~ну́ть) (*coll.*) 1. to push; to elbow, jostle. 2. to shove, cram; п. ве́щи в чемода́н to cram things into a suitcase.

пиха́|ться, юсь, *impf.* (*coll.*) to push; to elbow, shove; to jostle one another.

пих|ну́ть, ну́, нёшь, *pf. of* ~а́ть.

пи́хт|а, ы, *f.* fir(-tree) (*Abies*); европе́йская п. silver fir (*Abies alba, Abies pectinata*).

пи́хт|овый, *adj. of* ~а.

пиццика́то = пиччика́то.

пичка́|ть, ю, *impf.* (*of* на~) (*coll.*) to stuff, cram (*also fig.*).

пичу́г|а, и, *f.* (*coll.*) bird.

пичу́жк|а, и, *f.* (*coll.*) = пичу́га.

пиччика́то, *indecl., n., and adv.* (*mus.*) pizzicato.

пи́шущ|ий, *pres. part. act. of* писа́ть *and adj.*; п. э́ти стро́ки the present writer; ~ая бра́тия (*coll.*) the literary fraternity; ~ая маши́нка typewriter.

пи́щ|а, и, *no pl., f.* food; п. для ума́ food for thought; mental pabulum; дава́ть ~у слу́хам to feed rumours.

пища́л|ь, и, *f.* (*hist.*) (h)arquebus.

пищ|а́ть, у́, и́шь, *impf.* (*of* пи́скнуть) 1. to squeak; (*of chicks, etc.*) to cheep, peep. 2. (*fig., coll.*) to whine; to sing (*of kettle, etc.*).

пищеваре́ни|е, я, *n.* digestion; расстро́йство ~я indigestion, dyspepsia.

пищевари́тельный, *adj.* digestive; п. кана́л alimentary canal.

пищеви́к, а́, *m.* worker in food industry.

пищево́д, а, *m.* (*anat.*) oesophagus, gullet.

пищ|ево́й, *adj. of* ~а; ~евы́е проду́кты foodstuffs; eatables; ~ева́я промы́шленность food industry.

пи́щик, а, *m.* 1. (*hunting*) pipe for luring birds. 2. (*mus.*) reed. 3. buzzer.

пия́вк|а, и, *f.* leech; ста́вить ~и (*med.*) to apply leeches; приставать как п. (*fig., coll.*) to stick like a leech.

плав, а, *m.* на ~ý afloat.

пла́вани|е, я, *n.* **1.** swimming. **2.** sailing; navigation; су́дно да́льнего ~я ocean-going ship; отпра́виться в п., пусти́ться в п. to put out to sea.

пла́вательн|ый, *adj.* swimming; natatorial, natatory; п. бассе́йн swimming pool; ~ая перепо́нка (*of birds, bats*) web; (*of tortoise*) flipper; п. пузы́рь (fish-)sound, swimming-bladder.

пла́ва|ть, ю, *impf.* **1.** *indet. of* плыть; ме́лко п. (*fig., coll.*) to be a shallow person. **2.** to float (*have the property of floating*).

пла́в|ень, ня, *m.* (*tech.*) flux, fusing agent.

плави́к, а́, *m.* (*min.*) fluorspar.

плавико́в|ый, *adj. of* плави́к; ~ая кислота́ (*chem.*) hydrofluoric acid; п. шпат (*min.*) fluorspar.

плави́льник, а, *m.* (*tech.*) crucible.

плави́льн|ый, *adj.* (*tech.*) melting, smelting; п. горн smelting hearth; п. жар fusion temperature; ~ая печь smelting furnace; п. ти́гель crucible, melting pot.

плави́л|ьня, ьни, *g. pl.* ~ен, *f.* foundry, smeltery.

плави́льщик, а, *m.* founder, smelter.

пла́в|ить, лю, ишь, *impf.* to melt, smelt; to fuse.

пла́в|иться, ится, *impf.* to melt; to fuse (*intrans.*).

пла́вк|а, и, *f.* fusing; fusion.

пла́в|ки, ок, *no sing.* swimming trunks.

пла́вк|ий, *adj.* fusible; п. предохрани́тель, п. штепсель, ~ая про́бка (*electr.*) fuse; ~ая про́волока fuse wire.

пла́вкост|ь, и, *f,* fusibility.

плавле́ни|е, я, *n.* melting, fusion; то́чка ~я melting point.

пла́вленый, *adj.* п. сыр processed cheese.

пла́вн|и, ей, *no sing.* (*reed-covered*) flats (*on lower reaches of rivers Dnieper, Kuban, etc.*).

плавни́к, а́, *m.* fin; flipper; брюшно́й п. abdominal fin; грудно́й п. thoracic fin; спинно́й п. dorsal fin; хвостово́й п. caudal fin.

плавн|о́й, *adj.* ~а́я сеть drift net.

пла́вност|ь, и, *f.* smoothness; facility.

пла́вн|ый (~ен, ~на), *adj.* **1.** smooth; ~ная речь flowing speech; п. стих rhythmical verse. **2.** (*ling.*) liquid.

плаву́н, а́, *m.* (*geol.*) quick ground.

плаву́н|е́ц, ца́, *m.* жук-п. (*zool.*) water-tiger.

плаву́нчик, а, *m.* (*orn.*) phalarope.

плаву́чест|ь, и, *f.* buoyancy.

плаву́ч|ий, *adj.* **1.** floating; ~ая льди́на ice-floe; п. маяк lightship, light-vessel; ~ая бурова́я устано́вка sea drilling rig. **2.** buoyant.

плагиа́т, а, *m.* plagiarism.

плагиа́тор, а, *m.* plagiarist.

плаз, а, *m.* (*shipbuilding*) loft.

пла́зм|а, ы, *f.* (*biol. and phys.*) plasma.

пла́кальщик, а, *m.* (*hired*) mourner, mute.

плака́т, а, *m.* placard; poster, bill.

плакати́ст, а, *m.* poster artist.

плака́т|ный, *adj. of* ~; ~ные кра́ски poster paints.

пла́|кать, чу, чешь, *impf.* **1.** to weep, cry; п. навзры́д to sob; хоть ~чь! it is enough to make you weep!; ~кали де́нежки! (*coll.*) the money has simply vanished (*sc.* has been spent)! **2.** to weep (for), cry (for); to mourn.

пла́|каться, чусь, чешься, *impf.* (*of* по~) (на+*a.*) to complain (of), lament; п. на свою судьбу́ to bemoan one's fate.

плаки́р|ова́ть, у́ю, *impf. and pf.* (*tech.*) to plate.

плакиро́вк|а, и, *f.* (*tech.*) plating.

пла́кс|а, ы, *m. and f.* (*coll.*) cry-baby.

плакси́в|ый (~, ~а), *adj.* (*coll.*) whining; (*fig.*) piteous, pathetic; п. ребёнок cry-baby; п. тон pathetic tone.

плаку́н-трав|а́, ы́, *f.* (*bot.*) purple loosestrife (*Lythrum salicaria*).

плаку́ч|ий, *adj.* weeping; ~ая и́ва weeping willow.

пламегаси́тел|ь, я, *m.* (*mil.*) **1.** flash eliminator, flash-hider. **2.** flash extinguisher, anti-flash charge.

пламене́|ть, ю, *impf.* (*poet.*) to flame, blaze; п. стра́стью to burn with passion.

пла́менник, а, *m.* **1.** (*poet.*) torch, flambeau. **2.** (*bot.*) phlox.

пла́менност|ь, и, *f.* ardour.

пла́менн|ый, *adj.* **1.** flaming, fiery; (*fig.*) ardent, burning. **2.** (*tech.*) ~ая труба́ flue; ~ая печь flame furnace, reverbatory furnace; п. у́голь bituminous coal.

пла́мен|ь, и, *m.* (*obs., poet.*) = пла́мя.

пла́м|я, ени, *n.* flame; fire, blaze; вспы́хнуть ~енем to burst into flame.

план, а, *m.* **1.** (*in var. senses*) plan; scheme; учéбный п. curriculum; по ~у according to plan. **2.** plane (*also fig.*); пере́дний п. foreground; за́дний п. background; кру́пный п. close-up (*in filming*); вы́двинуть на пе́рвый п. (*fig.*) to bring to the forefront.

плане́р, а, *m.* (*aeron.*) glider; п. самолёта airframe.

планери́зм, а, *m.* gliding.

планери́ст, а, *m.* glider-pilot.

планёр|ный, *adj. of* ~; п. спорт gliding.

плане́т|а, ы, *f.* **1.** planet; больши́е ~ы major planets; ма́лые ~ы minor planets. **2.** (the) planet (= Earth). **3.** (*obs., coll.*) (bad) fortune.

планета́ри|й, я, *m.* planetarium.

плане́т|ный, *adj. of* ~а; planetary.
планиме́тр, а, *m.* (*surveying*) planimeter.
планиметр|и́ческий, *adj.* 1. *of* ~. 2. *of* ~ия.
планиме́три|я, и, *f.* (*math.*) plane geometry.
плани́ровани|е¹, я, *n.* planning; п. городо́в town-planning.
плани́ровани|е², я, *n.* (*aeron.*) gliding; glide.
плани́р|овать¹, ую, *impf.* (*of* за~) to plan.
плани́р|овать², ую, *impf.* (*of* с~) (*aeron.*) to glide (down).
планир|ова́ть, у́ю, *impf.* (*of* рас~) to lay out (*a park, etc.*).
планиро́вк|а, и, *f.* laying out; lay-out.
планиро́вщик, а, *m.* workman engaged in laying out (*park, etc.*).
планисфе́р|а, ы, *f.* (*astron.*) planisphere.
пла́нк|а, и, *f.* lath, slat.
планкто́н, а, *m.* (*biol.*) plankton.
планкто́н|ный, *adj. of* ~.
планови́к, а́, *m.* planner.
пла́новост|ь, и, *f.* planned character; development according to plan.
пла́нов|ый, *adj.* 1. planned, systematic; ~ое хозя́йство planned economy. 2. planning; ~ая коми́ссия planning commission.
планоме́рност|ь, и, *f.* systematic character, planned character.
планоме́р|ный (~ен, ~на), *adj.* systematic, planned, regular.
планта́ж, а, *m.* deep ploughing.
планта́тор, а, *m.* planter.
планта́ци|я, и, *f.* plantation.
планша́йб|а, ы, *f.* (*tech.*) face plate.
планше́т, а, *m.* 1. (*surveying*) plane-table; огнево́й п. (*mil.*) artillery board. 2. map-case. 3. busk (*of corset*).
планши́р, а, *m.* (*naut.*) gunwale, top strake.
планши́р|ь, я, *m.* = ~.
пласт, а́, *m.* layer; sheet; (*archit.*) course; (*geol.*) stratum, bed; лежа́ть ~о́м to lie motionless; to be on one's back.
пласта́|ть, ю, *impf.* to cut in layers.
пла́стик, а, *m.* plastic (*material*).
пла́стик|а, и, *f.* 1. (*collect.*) the plastic arts. 2. eurhythmics.
пластили́н, а, *m.* plasticine.
пласти́н|а, ы, *f.* plate.
пласти́нк|а, и, *f.* 1. (*in var. senses*) plate; граммофо́нная п. gramophone record; чувстви́тельная п. (*phot.*) sensitive plate. 2. (*bot.*) blade, lamina.
пласти́нчатый, *adj.* lamellar, lamellate.
пласти́ческ|ий, *adj.* plastic; ~ая ма́сса plastic; ~ая хирурги́я plastic surgery.
пласти́чност|ь, и, *f.* plasticity.
пласти́ч|ный, *adj.* 1. plastic; supple, pliant. 2. (~ен, ~на) rhythmical; fluent, flowing; ~ное движе́ние те́ла rhythmical movement of the body; п. жест flowing gesture.

пластма́сс|а, ы, *f.* (*abbr. of* пласти́ческая ма́сса) plastic.
пластма́сс|овый, *adj. of* ~а.
пласт|ова́ть, у́ю, *impf.* 1. to lay in layers. 2. to cut in layers.
пласту́н, а́, *m.* (*hist.*) dismounted Cossack.
пласту́н|ский, *adj. of* ~; переполза́ние по-~ски (*mil.*) the leopard crawl.
пла́стыр|ь, я, *m.* 1. (*med.*) plaster; вытяжно́й п. drawing plaster; ли́пкий п. sticking plaster. 2. (*naut.*) collision mat.
плат, а, *m.* (*obs.*) = ~о́к.
пла́т|а, ы, *f.* 1. pay; salary; за́работная п. wages. 2. payment, charge; fee; входна́я п. entrance fee; п. за прое́зд fare.
плата́н, а, *m.* plane(-tree), platan.
плата́|ть, ю, *impf.* (*of* за~) (*coll.*) to patch.
платёж, а́, *m.* payment; нало́женным ~о́м cash on delivery; прекрати́ть ~й suspend payment(s).
платёжеспосо́бност|ь, и, *f.* solvency.
платёжеспосо́б|ный (~ен, ~на), *adj.* solvent.
платёж|ный, *adj. of* ~; п. бала́нс balance of payments; ~ная ве́домость pay-sheet; pay-roll; п. день pay-day.
плате́льщик, а, *m.* payer.
пла́тин|а, ы, *f.* (*min.*) platinum.
пла́тин|овый, *adj. of* ~а.
пла|ти́ть, чу́, ~тишь, *impf.* 1. to pay; п. дань (+*d.*) to pay tribute (to); п. нали́чными to pay in cash, pay in ready money; п. нату́рой to pay in kind. 2. (*fig.*; +*i.* за+*a.*) to pay back, return; п. кому́-н. услу́гой за услу́гу to make it up to someone, return a favour; п. кому́-н. взаи́мностью to reciprocate someone's love.
пла|ти́ться, чусь, ~тишься, *impf.* (*of* по~) (+*i.* за+*a.*) to pay (with for); п. жи́знью за свои́ оши́бки to pay for one's mistakes with one's life.
пла́т|ный, *adj.* 1. paid; requiring payment, chargeable; ~ое ме́сто paid seat. 2. paying; п. посети́тель paying guest.
**плато́, **indecl., *n.* plateau.
плат|о́к, ка́, *m.* shawl; kerchief; носово́й п. (pocket) handkerchief.
платони́зм, а, *m.* Platonism.
плато́ник, а, *m.* Platonist.
платони́ческий, *adj.* (*philos.*) Platonic; (*fig.*) platonic.
платфо́рм|а, ы, *f.* 1. platform (*of railway station*). 2. (open) goods truck. 3. (*fig., polit.*) platform.
пла́ть|е, я, *g. pl.* ~ев, *n.* 1. clothes, clothing; ве́рхнее п. outer garments. 2. dress, gown, frock; вече́рнее п. evening dress.
плат|яно́й, *adj. of* ~ье; п. шкаф wardrobe; ~яна́я щётка clothes-brush.
плау́н, а́, *m.* (*bot.*) lycopodium, wolf's-claw, club-moss.

плафо́н, а, *m.* **1.** (*archit.*) plafond. **2.** shade (*for lamp suspended from ceiling*).

пла́х|а, и, *f.* block; (*hist.*) executioner's block; взойти́ на ~у to mount the scaffold.

плац, а, о ~е, на ~у́, *m.* (*mil.*) parade--ground; уче́бный п. drill square.

плацда́рм, а, *m.* **1.** (*mil.*) bridgehead; beach-head. **2.** (*polit.*; *fig.*) base.

плаце́нт|а, ы, *f.* (*anat.*) placenta.

плацка́рт|а, ы, *f.* reserved seat *or* berth ticket.

плацка́рт|ный, *adj. of* ~а; п. ваго́н carriage with numbered reserved seats; ~ное ме́сто reserved seat.

плац-пара́д, а, *m.* (*mil.*) parade ground.

плач, а, *m.* **1.** weeping, crying. **2.** (*cere-monial*) wailing; keening. **3.** lament.

плаче́в|ный (~ен, ~на), *adj.* **1.** mournful, sad; име́ть п. вид to be a sorry sight. **2.** (*fig.*) lamentable, deplorable, sorry; в ~ном состоя́нии in a sad state, in a sorry plight.

плашко́ут, а, *m.* (*naut.*) lighter.

плашко́утный, *adj.* п. мост pontoon bridge.

плашмя́, *adv.* flat; flatways; prone; упа́сть п. to fall flat; уда́рить са́блей п. to strike with the flat of the sword.

плащ, а́, *m.* **1.** cloak. **2.** mackintosh, rain-coat; waterproof cape.

плащани́ц|а, ы, *f.* (*eccl.*) shroud of Christ.

плащ-пала́тк|а, и, *f.* ground sheet.

плебе́|й, я, *m.* (*hist.*) plebeian.

плебе́йский, *adj.* plebeian.

плебисци́т, а, *m.* plebiscite.

плебс, а, *m.* (*collect.*; *hist.*) plebs.

плев|а́, ы́, *f.* (*anat.*) membrane, film, coat; де́вственная п. hymen; лёгочная п. pleura.

плева́тельниц|а, ы, *f.* spittoon.

плева́ть, плюю́, плюёшь, *impf.* (*of* плю́нуть) **1.** to spit; to expectorate; п. в потоло́к (*fig.*, *joc.*) to idle, fritter away the time. **2.** (на+*a.*; *coll.*) to spit (upon); not to care a rap about; им п. на всё they don't give a damn about anything.

плева́ться, плюю́сь, плюёшься, *impf.* (*coll.*) to spit.

пле́вел, а, *m.* (*bot.*) darnel, cockle; weed.

плев|о́к, ка́, *m.* **1.** spit(tle). **2.** (*med.*) sputum.

плевр|а, ы, *f.* (*anat.*) pleura.

плеври́т, а, *m.* (*med.*) pleurisy.

плёв|ый, *adj.* (*coll.*) **1.** worthless; rubbishy; п. челове́к good-for-nothing. **2.** trifling, trivial; де́ло ~ое trifling matter.

плед, а, *m.* rug; plaid.

плейстоце́н, а, *m.* (*geol.*) pleistocene.

плейстоце́н|овый, *adj. of* ~.

племенно́й, *adj.* **1.** tribal. **2.** pedigree; п. скот pedigree cattle, bloodstock.

пле́м|я, ени, *pl.* ~ена́, ~ён, ~ена́м, *n.* **1.**

tribe. **2.** breed; на п. for breeding. **3.** (*fig.*) tribe; breed, stock; пти́чье п. (*joc.*) the feathered tribe.

племя́нник, а, *m.* nephew.

племя́нниц|а, ы, *f.* niece.

плен, а, о ~е, в ~у́, *m.* captivity; быть в ~у́ to be in captivity; взять в п. to take prisoner; попа́сть в п. (к) to be taken prisoner (by).

плена́рный, *adj.* plenary.

плене́ни|е, я, *n.* (*obs.*) capture; captivity.

плени́тельност|ь, и, *f.* fascination.

плени́тел|ьный (~ен, ~ьна), *adj.* captivat-ing, fascinating, charming.

плен|и́ть, и́шь, *pf.* (*of* ~я́ть) **1.** (*obs.*) to take prisoner, take captive. **2.** (*fig.*) to cap-tivate, fascinate, charm.

плен|и́ться, ю́сь, и́шься, *pf.* (*of* ~я́ться) (+*i.*) to be captivated (by), be fascinated (by).

плёнк|а, и, *f.* (*in var. senses*) film; pellicle.

пле́нник, а, *m.* (*obs. or fig.*) prisoner, captive.

пле́нн|ый, *adj.* captive; *as noun* п., ~ого, *m.* captive, prisoner.

плён|очный, *adj. of* ~ка; filmy.

пле́нум, а, *m.* plenum, plenary session.

плен|я́ть(ся), я́ю(сь), *impf. of* ~и́ть(ся).

плеона́зм, а, *m.* (*lit.*) pleonasm.

плеонасти́ческий, *adj.* (*lit.*) pleonastic.

плёс, а, *m.* reach (*of river*); stretch (*of river or lake*).

пле́сенный, *adj.* mouldy, musty.

пле́сен|ь, и, *f.* mould.

плеск, а, *m.* splash; п. вёсел plash of oars; п. волн lapping of waves.

пле|ска́ть, щу́, ~щешь, *impf.* (*of* ~сну́ть) to splash; to plash; to lap; п. о бе́рег to lap against the shore; п. на кого́-н. водо́й to splash someone (with water).

пле|ска́ться, щу́сь, ~щешься, *impf.* to splash; to lap.

пле́снев|еть, еет, *impf.* (*of* за~) to grow mouldy, grow musty.

плес|ну́ть, ну́, нёшь, *pf. of* ~ка́ть.

пле|сти́, ту́, тёшь, *past* ~л, ~ла́, *impf.* (*of* с~) to braid, plait; to weave, tat; п. вено́к to make a wreath; п. корзи́ну to make a basket; п. небыли́цы (*coll.*, *pejor.*) to spin yarns; п. паути́ну to spin a web; п. се́ти to net; п. вздор, п. чепуху́ (*coll.*, *pejor.*) to talk rubbish.

пле|сти́сь, ту́сь, тёшься, *past* ~лся, ~ла́сь, *impf.* (*coll.*) to drag oneself along, trudge; п. в хвосте́ (*fig.*) to lag behind.

плете́ни|е, я, *n.* **1.** braiding, plaiting; п. слове́с (*iron.*) verbiage. **2.** wicker-work.

плетёнк|а, и, *f.* **1.** (wicker) basket. **2.** hurdle.

плетён|ый, *adj.* wattled, wicker; ~ая кор-зи́нка wicker basket.

плет|е́нь, ня́, *m.* hurdle; wattle fencing.

плётк|а, и, *f.* lash.

плет|ь, и, *pl.* ~и, ~éй, *f.* lash.

плечев|óй, *adj.* (*anat.*) humeral; ~ая кость humerus.

плéчик|и, ов, *no sing.* (*coll.*) (coat-)hanger.

плéчик|о, а, *pl.* ~и, ~ов, *n.* **1.** shoulder--strap. **2.** *dim. of* плечó.

плечúст|ый (~, ~а), *adj.* broad-shouldered.

плеч|ó, á, *pl.* ~и, ~, ~áм, *n.* **1.** shoulder; лéвое, прáвое п. вперёд! (*mil.*) right wheel, left wheel!; всё э́то у меня́ ~áми (*fig.*) all that is behind me; ~óм к ~ý shoulder to shoulder; взять нá ~и to shoulder; на п.! (*mil.*) slope arms!; на ~áх проти́вника on top of, on the heels of the enemy; имéть гóлову на ~áх to have a good head on one's shoulders; вы́нести на свои́х ~áх to bear (the full brunt of); э́то ему́ не по ~ý he is not up to it; с ~á straight from the shoulder; (слóвно) горá с мои́х ~ свали́-лась that's a weight off my mind; с ~ долóй! that's done, thank goodness; с чужóго ~á (*of clothing*) worn, second-hand; пожáть ~áми to shrug one's shoulders. **2.** (*anat.*) upper arm, humerus. **3.** (*tech.*) arm.

плешúве|ть, ю, *impf.* (*of* о~) to grow bald.

плешúв|ый (~, ~а), *adj.* bald.

плешúн|а, ы, *f.* bald patch.

плеш|ь, и, *f.* bald patch; bare patch.

плея́д|ы, ~, *sing.* ~а, ~ы, *f.* **1.** П. (*astron.*) Pleiades. **2.** (*sing.; fig.*) Pleiad; galaxy.

пли, *interj.* (= палú) (*mil.; obs.*) fire!

плúнтус, а, *m.* **1.** plinth. **2.** skirting board.

плиоцéн, а, *m.* (*geol.*) pl(e)iocene.

плис, а, *m.* velveteen.

плúс|овый, *adj. of* ~.

плиссé, *indecl., n.* pleat(s); *as adj.* pleated; юбка п. pleated skirt.

плиссир|овáть, ýю, *impf.* (*no pf.*) to pleat.

плиссирóвк|а, и, *f.* pleating.

плит|á, ы́, *pl.* ~ы, *f.* **1.** plate, slab; flag-(stone); моги́льная п. gravestone, tomb-stone; мрáморная п. marble slab. **2.** stove; cooker.

плúтк|а, и, *f.* **1.** *dim. of* плитá; tile, (thin) slab; крáски в ~ах solid water-colours; п. шоколáда bar of chocolate. **2.** stove; cooker.

плитня́к, á, *m.* flagstone.

плúт|очный, *adj. of* ~ка; п. пол tiled floor.

плúц|а, ы, *f.* **1.** bailer. **2.** (*obs.*) blade (*of paddle-wheel*).

плов, а, *m.* (*cul.*) = пилáв.

плов|éц, цá, *m.* swimmer.

пловýчий, *adj.* = плавýчий.

плод, á, *m.* **1.** fruit (*also fig.*); приноси́ть п. to bear fruit; запрéтный п. (*fig.*) forbidden fruit. **2.** (*biol.*) foetus.

пло|ди́ться, жý, ди́шь, *impf.* (*of* рас~) to produce, procreate; to engender (*also fig.*).

пло|ди́ться, жýсь, ди́шься, *impf.* (*of* рас~) to multiply; to propagate.

плóдный, *adj.* **1.** (*biol.*) fertile. **2.** fertilized.

плодови́тост|ь, и, *f.* fruitfulness, fertility, fecundity.

плодови́т|ый (~, ~а), *adj.* fruitful, prolific (*also fig.*); fertile, fecund; п. писáтель prolific writer.

плодовóдств|о, а, *n.* fruit-growing.

плодовóд|ческий, *adj. of* ~ство.

плодóв|ый, *adj. of* плод; ~ое дéрево fruit--tree; п. сад orchard.

плодоли́стик, а, *m.* (*bot.*) carpel.

плодонóжк|а, и, *f.* (*bot.*) fruit stem.

плодоно|си́ть, ~си́т, *impf.* (*no pf.*) to bear fruit.

плодонóс|ный (~ен, ~на), *adj.* fruit-bear-ing, fruitful.

плодоóвощ|и, éй, *no sing.* fruit and vegetables.

плодоовощнóй, *adj.* fruit and vegetable.

плодорóди|е, я, *n.* fertility, fecundity.

плодорóд|ный (~ен, ~на), *adj.* fertile, fecund.

плодосмéнн|ый, *adj.* ~ая систéма (*agric.*) rotation of crops.

плодотвóр|ный (~ен, ~на), *adj.* fruitful.

плоён|ый, *adj.* (*obs.*) pleated; ~ые вóлосы waved hair.

пло|и́ть, ю́, и́шь, *impf.* (*of* на~) (*obs.*) to pleat; to wave (*hair*).

плóмб|а, ы, *f.* **1.** (*lead*) stamp, seal. **2.** stop-ping, filling (*for tooth*); стáвить ~у в зуб to stop, fill a tooth.

пломби́р, а, *m.* 'plombières' (*ice-cream with candied fruit*).

пломбир|овáть, ýю, *impf.* **1.** (*pf.* о~) to seal. **2.** (*pf.* за~) to stop, fill (*a tooth*).

плóс|кий (~ок, ~ка́, ~ко), *adj.* **1.** flat; plane; ~кая грудь flat chest; ~кая повéрх-ность plane surface; ~кая стопá (*med.*) flat-foot. **2.** (*fig.*) trivial, tame; ~кая шýтка feeble joke.

плоскогóрь|е, я, *n.* plateau; tableland.

плоскогрýд|ый (~, ~а), *adj.* flat-chested.

плоскогýбц|ы, ев, *no sing.* pliers.

плоскодóнк|а, и, *f.* flat-bottomed boat; punt.

плоскодóнный, *adj.* flat-bottomed.

плоскостнóй, *adj.* plane.

плоскостóпи|е, я, *n.* (*med.*) flat-foot, flat feet.

плóскост|ь, и, *pl.* ~и, ~éй, *f.* **1.** flatness. **2.** plane (*also fig.*); наклóнная п. inclined plane; кати́ться по наклóнной ~и (*fig.*) to go downhill. **3.** platitude, triviality.

плот, á, *m.* raft.

плотв|á, ы́, *f.* (*fish*) roach.

плоти́н|а, ы, *f.* dam; weir; dike, dyke.

плотнé|ть, ю, *impf.* (*of* по~) to grow stout.

плóтник, а, *m.* carpenter.

плóтнича|ть, ю, *impf.* to work as a carpenter.

плóтничеств|о, а, *n.* carpentry.

плóтничный, *adj.* carpentering.

плóтно, *adv.* 1. close(ly), tightly; п. заколотить дверь to board up, nail up a door. 2. п. поéсть to have a square meal, eat heartily.

плóтност|ь, и, *f.* 1. thickness; compactness; solidity, strength; п. населéния density of population. 2. (*phys.*) density.

плóт|ный (~ен, ~нá, ~но), *adj.* 1. thick; compact; dense (*also phys.*); п. огóнь (*mil.*) heavy fire. 2. solid, strong; (*of a person*; *coll.*) thick-set, solidly built. 3. tightly-filled. 4. (*coll.*; *of a meal*) square, hearty.

плотовóд, а, *m.* rafter, raftsman (*floating timber on rafts*).

плотовщи́к, á, *m.* rafter, raftsman (*floating timber or ferrying passengers on rafts*).

плотоя́д|ный (~ен, ~на), *adj.* 1. carnivorous. 2. lustful; voluptuous.

плóтский, *adj.* (*arch.*) carnal, fleshly.

плот|ь, и, *f.* flesh; во ~й in the flesh; п. от ~и flesh of one's flesh; п. и кровь (one's) flesh and blood; облéчь в п. и кровь to embody; крáйняя п. (*anat.*) foreskin, prepuce.

плóхо, 1. *adv.* bad(ly); ill; п. вести́ себя́ to behave badly; п. обращáться (с+*i.*) to ill-treat, ill-use; чýвствовать себя́ п. to feel unwell, feel bad; п. пáхнуть to smell bad; п. кóнчить (*coll.*) to come to a bad end; п. лежáть (*coll.*) to lie in temptation's way; п.-п. (*coll.*) at (the very) least. 2. *as indecl. noun, n.* bad mark; я опя́ть получи́л п. по áлгебре I have got a bad mark in algebra again.

плоховáто, *adv.* (*coll.*) rather badly, not too well.

плоховáт|ый (~, ~а), *adj.* (*coll.*) rather bad, not too good.

плох|óй (~, ~á, ~о), *adj.* (*in var. senses*) bad; poor; ~áя погóда bad weather; ~óе настроéние bad mood, low spirits; п. рабóтник a poor workman; ~óе пищеварéние poor digestion; ~óе утешéние poor consolation; с ним шýтки ~и he is not one to be trifled with; (*as pred.*) емý óчень ~о he is very bad, he is in a very bad way.

плошá|ть, ю, *impf.* (*of* с~) (*coll.*) to make a mistake, slip up.

плóшк|а, и, *f.* 1. (*coll.*) flat dish, saucer. 2. lampion.

площáдк|а, и, *f.* 1. ground, area; дéтская п. children's playground; спорти́вная п. sports ground; строи́тельная п. building site; тéнннисная п. tennis court. 2. landing (*on staircase*). 3. platform; пусковáя п. launching pad (*of rocket*).

площадн|óй, *adj.* vulgar, coarse; ~áя брань Billingsgate language.

плóщад|ь, и, *pl.* ~и, ~éй, *f.* 1. (*math.*) area. 2. area; space; жилáя п. living space, floor-space; посевнáя п. sown area, area under crops. 3. square; базáрная п. market-place.

плó|ще, *comp. of* ~ский *and* ~ско.

плуг, а, *pl.* ~и́, *m.* plough.

плугáр|ь, я́, *m.* ploughman.

плуговóй, *adj. of* плуг.

плýнжер, а, *m.* (*tech.*) plunger.

плут, á, *m.* 1. cheat, swindler, knave. 2. (*joc.*) rogue.

плутá|ть, ю, *impf.* (*coll.*) to stray.

плути́шк|а, и, *m.* (*coll.*) little rogue, mischievous imp.

плýтн|и, ей, *sing.* ~я, ~и, *f.* (*coll.*) cheating, swindling; tricks.

плутовáт|ый (~, ~а), *adj.* cunning.

плут|овáть, ýю, *impf.* (*of* на~ *and* с~) (*coll.*) to cheat, swindle.

плутóвк|а, и, *f. of* плут, плути́шка.

плутовск|óй, *adj.* 1. knavish; ~и́е приёмы knavish tricks. 2. (*coll.*) roguish, mischievous. 3. (*lit.*) picaresque.

плутовств|ó, á, *n.* cheating; trickery, knavery.

плутокрáт, а, *m.* plutocrat.

плутократи́ческий, *adj.* plutocratic.

плутокрáти|я, и, *f.* plutocracy.

плывýн, á, *m.* = плавýн.

плывýчий, *adj.* flowing, deliquescent.

плы|ть, вý, вёшь, *past* ~л, ~лá, ~ло, *impf.* (*det. of* плáвать) 1. to swim; to float; п. стóя to tread water; п. комý-н. в рýки (*fig.*, *coll.*) to drop into someone's lap; всё ~ло пéред мои́ми глазáми everything was swimming before my eyes. 2. to sail; п. на вёслах to row; п. под парусáми to sail, go under sail; п. по течéнию to go down stream; (*fig.*) to go with the stream; п. прóтив течéния to go up stream; (*fig.*) to go against the stream; п. по вóле волн to drift.

плювиóметр, а, *m.* pluviometer.

плюгáв|ый (~, ~а), *adj.* (*coll.*) shabby, mean; despicable.

плюмáж, а, *m.* plume (*on hat*).

плюн|уть, у, ешь, *pf. of* плевáть; п. нéкуда no room to swing a cat.

плюрали́зм, а, *m.* (*philos.*) pluralism.

плюралисти́ческий, *adj.* (*philos.*) pluralistic.

плюрáльный, *adj.* п. вóтум (*leg.*) plural vote.

плюс, а, *m.* 1. plus; *as connective in math. expressions* два п. два равнó четырём two plus two equals four. 2. (*fig.*, *coll.*) advantage; э́тот проéкт не без ~ов this scheme has some advantages.

плюс|нá, ны́, *pl.* ~ны, ~ен, ~нам, *f.* (*anat.*) metatarsus.

плюс|ова́ть, у́ю, *impf.* (*tech.*) to dip, immerse.

плюс|овый, *adj. of* ~; п. гандика́п (*sport*) plus handicap.

плюх|ать(ся), аю(сь), *impf. of* ~нуть(ся).

плюх|нуть, ну, нешь, *pf.* (*of* ~ать) (*coll.*) to flop (down), plump (down); п. в кре́сло to flop into an arm-chair.

плюх|нуться, нусь, нешься, *pf.* (*of* ~аться) = ~нуть.

плюш, а, *m.* plush.

плюш|евый, *adj. of* ~.

плюшк|а, и, *f.* (*coll.*) bun.

плющ, а́, *m.* ivy; вью́щийся п. tree ivy.

плющи́льн|ый, *adj.* (*tech.*) flattening, laminating; п. мо́лот planing hammer, flatter; п. стано́к flatting mill, rolling mill; ~ая маши́на upsetting machine.

плющ|ить, у, ишь, *impf.* (*of* c~) (*tech.*) to flatten, laminate.

пляж, а, *m.* beach.

пляс, а, *no pl.*, *m.* (*coll.*) dance; пусти́ться в п. to break into a dance.

пляск|а, и, *f.* dance; dancing (*esp. folk-dancing*); п. свято́го Ви́та (*med.*) St. Vitus's dance, chorea.

пля|са́ть, шу́, ~шешь, *impf.* (*of* c~) to dance.

плясов|о́й, *adj.* dancing; *as noun* ~а́я, ~о́й, *f.* dance tune.

плясу́н, а́, *m.* (*coll.*) dancer; кана́тный п. rope-dancer.

пневма́тик, а, *m.* pneumatic tire.

пневма́тик|а, и, *f.* pneumatics.

пневмати́ческий, *adj.* pneumatic.

пневмоко́кк, а, *m.* (*med.*) pneumococcus.

пневмони́|я, и, *f.* pneumonia.

пневмото́ракс, а, *m.* (*med.*) pneumothorax.

пни́ст|ый (~, ~а), *adj. of* пень.

пнуть, пну, пнёшь, *pf.* (*of* пина́ть) (*coll.*) to kick.

по, *prep.* I. +*d.* **1.** on; along; идти́ по траве́ to walk on the grass; спусти́ться по верёвке to come down on a rope; е́хать по у́лице to go along the street; идти́ по следа́м (+*g.*) to follow in the tracks (of); хло́пнуть по спине́ to slap on the back; по всему́, по всей all over. **2.** round, about (*or not translated*); ходи́ть по магази́нам to go round the shops; ходи́ть по ко́мнате to pace the room; размести́ть войска́ по го́роду to quarter troops about the town. **3.** by, on, over (*sc. some means of communication*); по во́здуху by air; по желе́зной доро́ге by rail, by train; по по́чте by post; по ра́дио on the wireless, over the radio; по телефо́ну on, over the telephone; переда́ть по ра́дио to broadcast. **4.** according to; by; in accordance with; по пра́ву by right(s); по расписа́нию according to schedule; по статье́ зако́на according to the letter of the law; жени́ться по любви́ to marry for love; звать по и́мени to call by first name; рабо́тать по пла́ну to work according to plan; су́дя по результа́там judging by results; по мне in my opinion, in my view, as far as I am concerned; жить по сре́дствам to live within one's means; по Плато́ну according to Plato. **5.** by, in (= *in respect of*); по профе́ссии by profession; по положе́нию by one's position; ex officio; по происхожде́нию он армяни́н he is an Armenian by descent, he is of Armenian origin; лу́чший по ка́честву better in quality; това́рищ по ору́жию comrade in arms; това́рищ по шко́ле school-mate; ро́дственник по ма́тери a relative on one's mother's side. **6.** at, on, in (= *in the field of*); чемпио́н по ша́хматам champion at chess, chess champion; ле́кции по европе́йской исто́рии lectures on European history; специали́ст по я́дерной фи́зике specialist in (on) nuclear physics. **7.** by (reason of); on account of; from; по боле́зни on account of sickness; по рассе́янности from absentmindedness; его́ прости́ли по мо́лодости лет he was pardoned by reason of his youth; по счастли́вому стече́нию обстоя́тельств by a happy conjunction of circumstances. **8.** (*indicating the object of an action or feeling*), at, for (*or not translated*); стреля́ть по проти́внику to fire at the enemy; охо́та по кру́пному зве́рю big game hunting; скуча́ть по де́тям to miss one's children; тоска́ по до́му, по ро́дине homesickness; по а́дресу (+*g.*) to the address (of); э́то по его́ а́дресу (*fig.*) this is meant for him. **9.** (*in temporal phrases*) on; in; по понеде́льникам on Mondays; по пра́здникам on holidays; она́ рабо́тает по утра́м she works (in the) mornings; я не вида́л её по це́лым неде́лям I did not see her for weeks at a time; он прие́дет по весне́ he will come in the spring.

II. +*d. or a. of cardinal num. forms distributive num.* (+*d.*, *but also* +*a.*, *esp. in coll. usage*) по одному́ (одно́й); по пяти́, по шести́, *etc.*; по оди́ннадцати, *etc.*; по двадцати́, *etc.*; по ста; по пятисо́т, *etc.*; по полтора́ (полторы́); (+*a.*) по́ два (две), по́ три, по четы́ре; по две́сти, по три́ста, по четы́реста; да́йте им по (*sc.* одному́) я́блоку give them an apple each; мы получи́ли по три фу́нта we received three pounds each; по рублю́ шту́ка one rouble each; по де́сять (десяти́) рубле́й шту́ка ten roubles each; по́ два, по́ двое in twos, two by two.

III. +*a.* **1.** to, up to; по по́яс в воде́ up to the waist in water; за́нят по го́рло up to one's eyes in work; по́ уши в долгáх up to one's ears in debt; пó уши влюблён head over heels in love; по сегóдня up to today; по пéрвое мáя up to (and including) the first of May; по сю (ту) стóрону on this (that) side. 2. (*following verbs of motion*; coll.) for (= *to fetch*, *to get*); идти́ пó воду to go for water.

IV. +p. 1. on, after; по истечéнии срóка on expiry of the term set; по окончáнии рабóты after work; по прибы́тии on arrival; по рассмотрéнии on examination. 2. (*after verbs of grieving, mourning, etc.*) for; плáкать по мýже to mourn (for) one's husband; носи́ть трáур по ком-н. to be in mourning for someone. 3. по нём, *etc.*, as he, *etc.*, likes, is used.

по-¹ as *verbal prefix*. 1. *forms perfective aspect*. 2. *indicates action of short duration or of incomplete character, as* поработáть to do a little work; поспáть to have a sleep. 3. (+*suffixes* -ыва-, -ива-) *indicates action repeated at intervals or of indet. duration, as* позвáнивать to keep ringing; покри́кивать to keep shouting.

по-² +d. *of adj. or ending* -ски *forms adv. indicating* 1. *manner of action, conduct, etc., as* жить по-стáрому to live in the old style; рабóтать по-товáрищески to work in a comradely fashion. 2. *use of given language, as* говори́ть по-рýсски to speak Russian. 3. *accordance with opinion or wish, as* по-мóему in my opinion; пусть бýдет по-вáшему (let it be) as you wish.

поаккóрдн|ый, adj. ~ая плáта piece-work rate.

побагровé|ть, ю, pf. of багровéть.

побáива|ться, юсь, impf. (+g. *or inf.*; coll.) to be rather afraid.

побáлива|ть, ю, impf. (coll.) to ache a little; to ache on and off.

по-бáрски, adv. like a lord.

побасёнк|а, и, f. (coll.) tale, story.

побéг¹, а, m. flight; escape.

побéг², а, m. (bot.) sprout, shoot; sucker; set; graft.

побéга|ть, ю, pf. to run a little, have a run.

побегýшк|и: быть у когó-н. на ~ах (coll.) to run errands for someone; (fig.) to be at someone's beck and call.

побéд|а, ы, f. victory; войнá до пóлной ~ы total war; одержáть ~y to gain a victory.

победи́тел|ь, я, m. victor, conqueror; (sport) winner.

побед|и́ть, и́шь, pf. (of побеждáть) to conquer, vanquish; to defeat, win a victory (over); (fig.) to master, overcome.

побéдный, adj. victorious, triumphant.

победонóс|ный (~ен, ~на), adj. victorious, triumphant; говори́ть с ~ным ви́дом (fig.) to speak with a triumphant air.

побежá|лост|ь, и, f. (chem., tech.) iridescence; цвет ~и oxide tint.

побе|жáть, гý, жи́шь, гýт, pf. 1. pf. of бежáть. 2. to break into a run.

побеждá|ть, ю, impf. of победи́ть.

побéжк|а, и, f. pace, gait.

побелé|ть, ю, pf. of белéть.

побел|и́ть, ю́, ~и́шь, pf. of бели́ть 2.

побéлк|а, и, f. whitewashing.

поберéжный, adj. coastal.

побéрежь|е, я, n. coast, seaboard, littoral.

побере́|чь, гý, жёшь, гýт, past ~г, ~глá, pf. (coll.) to look after, take care (of); п. здорóвье to take care of one's health; ~ги́ мои́ вéщи до моегó возвращéния look after my things until I come back.

побере́|чься, гýсь, жёшься, гýтся, past ~гся, ~глáсь, pf. to take care of oneself; ~ги́сь! mind out!

побесéд|овать, ую, pf. to have a (little) talk, have a chat.

побеспокó|ить, ю, ишь, pf. of беспокóить 2; позвóльте вас п. may I trouble you?

побеспокó|иться, юсь, ишься, pf. 1. pf. of беспокóиться 2. 2. to be rather worried.

побирá|ться, юсь, impf. (coll.) to beg, live by begging.

побирýшк|а, и, m. and f. (coll.) beggar.

поб|и́ть, ью, ьёшь, pf. 1. pf. of бить 1, 2; п. рекóрд to break a record. 2. (of rain, hail, etc.) to beat down; (of frost) to nip. 3. to break, smash (a number of). 4. to kill (a number of).

поб|и́ться, ьётся, pf. 1. pf. of би́ться. 2. to break.

поблагодар|и́ть, ю́, и́шь, pf. of благодари́ть.

поблáжк|а, и, f. indulgence; allowance(s); дéлать ~y (+d.) to indulge, make allowance(s) (for).

поблéдне|ть, ю, pf. of бледнéть.

поблёклый, adj. faded; withered.

поблёк|нуть, ну, нешь, past ~, ~ла, pf. of блёкнуть.

поблёскива|ть, ю, impf. to gleam.

поблúзости, adv. near at hand, hereabout(s); п. (от) near (to).

побож|и́ться, ýсь, и́шься, pf. of божи́ться.

побó|и, ев, no sing. beating, blows; терпéть п. to take a beating.

побóищ|е, а, n. slaughter, carnage; bloody battle; ледóвое п. see ледóвый.

поболтá|ть, ю, pf. (coll.) to have a chat.

побóрник, а, m. champion, upholder.

побор|óть, ю́, ~ешь, pf. to overcome; to fight down; to beat (in wrestling).

побóр|ы, ов, sing. ~, ~а, m. requisitions; extortion.

побóчн|ый, adj. side; secondary; collateral; п. эффéкт side effect; п. наслéдник collateral heir; п. проду́кт by-product; ~ая рабо́та side-line; п. сын natural son.

побо|я́ться, ю́сь, и́шься, *pf.* (+*g. or inf.*) to be afraid; он хоте́л возрази́ть, да ~я́лся he wanted to raise an objection but did not venture to.

побран|и́ть, ю́, и́шь, *pf.* to give a scolding, tick off.

побран|и́ться, ю́сь, и́шься, *pf.* (c+*i.*; *coll.*) to have a quarrel (with), have words (with).

побрата́|ться, юсь, *pf. of* брата́ться.

побрати́м, а, *m.* (*obs.*) sworn brother.

побрати́мств|о, а, *n.* (*obs.*) sworn brother-hood.

по-бра́тски, *adv.* like a brother; fraternally.

по|бра́ть, беру́, берёшь, *past* ~бра́л, ~брала́, ~бра́ло, *pf.* (*coll.*) to take (*a quantity of*); чёрт тебя́ ~бери́, чёрт бы тебя́ ~бра́л! the devil take you!

побре́зга|ть, ю, *pf. of* бре́згать; не ~йте! (*coll.; polite form of invitation*) make yourself free!

побре|сти́, ду́, дёшь, *past* ~л, ~ла́, *pf.* to plod.

побр|и́ть(ся), е́ю(сь), *pf. of* бри́ть(ся).

побро|ди́ть¹, жу́, ~дишь, *pf.* to wander for some time.

побро|ди́ть², жу́, ~дишь, *pf.* to ferment for some time.

поброса́|ть, ю, *pf.* 1. to throw up; to throw about. 2. to desert, abandon.

побря́к|ать, аю, *pf.* (*of* ~ивать) (+*i.*; *coll.*) to rattle.

побря́кива|ть, ю, *impf. of* побря́кать.

побряку́шк|а, и, *f.* (*coll.*) trinket.

побуди́тельн|ый, *adj.* stimulating; ~ая причи́на motive, incentive; ~ые сре́дства stimulants.

побу|ди́ть¹, жу́, ~дишь, *pf.* 1. to try to wake. 2. to wake, rouse.

побу|ди́ть², жу́, ~ди́шь, *pf.* (*of* ~жда́ть) (к or +*inf.*) to induce (to), impel (to), prompt (to), spur (to); что ~ди́ло вас уйти́? what made you go?

побу́дк|а, и, *f.* (*mil.*) reveille.

побужда́|ть, ю, *impf. of* побуди́ть.

побужде́ни|е, я, *n.* motive; inducement; incentive; по со́бственному ~ю of one's own accord.

побуре́|ть, ю, *pf. of* буре́ть.

побыва́льщин|а, ы, *f.* (*obs.*) narration; true story.

побыва́|ть, ю, *pf.* 1. to have been, have visited; он ~л всю́ду he has been every-where; в про́шлом году́ мы ~ли в Нор-ве́гии и в Шве́ции last year we were in Norway and Sweden. 2. (*coll.*) to look in, visit; мне на́до п. в конто́ре I have to look in at the office.

побы́вк|а, и, *f.* leave, furlough; прие́хать домо́й на ~у to come home on leave.

по|бы́ть, бу́ду, бу́дешь, *past* ~бы́л, ~была́, ~бы́ло, *pf.* to stay (*for a short time*); мы ~бы́ли в Ло́ндоне два дня we stayed in London for two days.

пова́|дить, жу, дишь, *pf.* (*of* ~жива́ть¹) (*coll.*) to accustom; to train.

пова́|диться, жусь, дишься, *pf.* (+*inf.*; *coll., pejor.*) to get into the habit (of); to take to going (somewhere).

пова́дк|а, и, *f.* (*coll.*) habit.

пова́дливост|ь, и, *f.* (*coll.*) susceptibility; amenableness.

пова́длив|ый (~, ~a), *adj.* (*coll.*) susceptible; amenable.

пова́дно, *only in phrase* чтобы не́ было п. (+*d.*) (in order) to teach not to do so (again).

пова́жива|ть¹, ю, *impf. of* пова́дить.

пова́жива|ть², ю, *impf.* (*coll.*) to take from time to time.

повал|и́ть¹, ю́, ~ишь, *pf. of* вали́ть¹.

повал|и́ть², ю́, ~ишь, *pf.* to begin to throng, begin to pour; дым ~и́л из трубы́ smoke began to belch from the chimney; снег ~и́л хло́пьями snow began to fall in flakes.

пова́льно, *adv.* without exception.

пова́льн|ый, *adj.* general, mass; п. о́быск general search; ~ая боле́знь epidemic.

пова́нива|ть, ет, *impf.* (*coll.*) to smell slightly.

пова́пленный, *adj. only in phrase* гроб п. (*fig.*) whited sepulchre.

по́вар, а, *pl.* ~á, *m.* cook.

пова́ренн|ый, *adj.* culinary; ~ая кни́га cookery-book; ~ая соль common salt, table salt (*sodium chloride*).

повар|ёнок, ёнка, *pl.* ~я́та, ~я́т, *m.* (*coll.*) kitchen-boy.

поварёшк|а, и, *f.* (*coll.*) ladle, strainer.

повари́х|а, и, *f. of* по́вар.

поварнича|ть, ю, *impf.* (*coll.*) to cook, be a cook.

повар|ня, ни, *g. pl.* ~ен, *f.* (*obs.*) kitchen.

поварско́й, *adj. of* по́вар.

по-ва́шему, *adv.* 1. in your opinion. 2. as you wish.

пове́д|ать, аю, *pf.* (*of* ~ывать) to relate, communicate; п. та́йну to disclose a secret.

поведе́ни|е, я, *n.* conduct, behaviour.

пове́дыва|ть, ю, *impf. of* пове́дать.

повез|ти́, у́, ёшь, *past* ~, ~ла́, *pf. of* везти́.

повелева́|ть, ю, *impf.* 1. (+*i.*; *obs.*) to command, rule. 2. (+*d. and inf.*) to enjoin; так ~ет мне со́весть thus my conscience enjoins.

повеле́ни|е, я, *n.* (*obs.*) command, injunc-tion.

повел|е́ть, ю́, и́шь, *pf.* to order, command.

повели́тел|ь, я, *m.* (*obs., rhet.*) sovereign, master.

повели́тельниц|а, ы, *f.* (*obs., rhet.*) sovereign, mistress, lady.

повели́тел|ьный (~ен, ~ьна), *adj.* imperious, peremptory; authoritative; п. жест imperious gesture; п. тон peremptory tone; ~ьное наклоне́ние (*gram.*) imperative mood.

повенча́|ть(ся), ю(сь), *pf. of* венча́ть(ся)[1].

поверг|а́ть, а́ю, *impf. of* ~ну́ть.

пове́рг|нуть, ну, нешь, *past* ~, ~ла, *pf.* (*of* ~а́ть) 1. (*obs.*) to throw down, lay low; боле́знь ~ла его́ в посте́ль the illness has prostrated him. 2. (в+*a.*) to plunge (into); п. в отча́яние, уны́ние to plunge into despair, depression.

пове́ре|нный, *p.p.p. of* ~ить[2]; *as noun* п., ~енного, *m.* 1. (*also* ~енная, ~енной, *f.*) confidant(e). 2. attorney; прися́жный п. (*obs.*) barrister; п. в дела́х chargé d'affaires.

пове́р|ить[1], ю, ишь, *pf. of* ве́рить.

пове́р|ить[2], ю, ишь, *pf.* (*of* ~я́ть) 1. to check (up); to verify. 2. (+*d.*) to confide (to), entrust (to); п. кому́-н. та́йну to confide a secret to someone.

пове́рк|а, и, f. 1. check, check-up; checking up, verification; (*math.*) proof. 2. (*mil.*) roll-call; п. карау́лов turning-out of the guard.

повер|ну́ть, ну́, нёшь, *pf.* (*of* ~тывать) to turn; (*fig.*) to change; п. разгово́р to change the subject (*of a conversation*).

повер|ну́ться, ну́сь, нёшься, *pf.* (*of* ~тываться) to turn; п. круго́м to turn round, turn about; п. спино́й (к) to turn one's back (upon); п. на я́коре to swing at anchor; п. к лу́чшему to take a turn for the better.

пове́р|очный, *adj. of* ~ка; ~очные испыта́ния tests.

поверстн|ый, *adj.* (*measured*) by versts; ~ая пла́та payment by the verst.

повёртыва|ть(ся), ю(сь), *impf. of* поверну́ть(ся).

пове́рх, *prep.*+*g.* over, above; on top of; смотре́ть п. очко́в to look over the top of one's spectacles.

пове́рхностност|ь, и, f. superficiality.

пове́рхност|ный, *adj.* 1. surface, superficial; ~ная зака́лка (*tech.*) case hardening; ~ное натяже́ние (*tech.*) surface tension; п. разря́д (*electr.*) surface discharge; ~ная ра́на superficial injury; ~ное унаво́живание (*agric.*) top dressing. 2. (~ен, ~на) (*fig.*) superficial; shallow; perfunctory.

пове́рхност|ь, и, f. surface.

по́верху, *adv.* on the surface, on top.

пове́р|ье, ья, g.pl. ~ий, n. popular belief, superstition.

повер|я́ть, я́ю, *impf. of* ~ить.

пове́с|а, ы, m. (*coll.*) rake, scapegrace.

повесел́е|ть, ю, pf. to cheer up, become cheerful.

повесел|и́ть(ся), ю́(сь), и́шь(ся), pf. of весели́ть(ся).

по-весе́ннему, *adv.* as in spring.

пове́|сить(ся), шу(сь), сишь(ся), pf. of ве́шать(ся)[1].

повесни́ча|ть, ю, impf. (*coll.*) to lead a wild life.

повествова́ни|е, я, n. narrative, narration.

повествова́тельный, *adj.* narrative.

повеств|ова́ть, у́ю, impf. (о+*p.*) to narrate, recount, relate.

пове|сти́[1], ду́, дёшь, *past* ~л, ~ла́, *pf. of* вести́ 1.

пове|сти́[2], ду́, дёшь, *past* ~л, ~ла́, *pf.* (*of* поводи́ть[1]) (+*i.*) to move; п. бровя́ми to raise one's eye-brows; он и бро́вью не ~л he did not turn a hair.

пове|сти́сь, ду́сь, дёшься, *past* ~лся, ~ла́сь, *pf. of* вести́сь; уж так ~ло́сь (*coll.*) such is the custom.

пове́стк|а, и, f. 1. notice, notification; п. на заседа́ние notice of meeting; п. в суд summons, writ, sub-poena; п. дня agenda, order of the day; на ~е дня on the agenda (*also fig.*). 2. signal; bugle call.

по́вест|ь, и, pl. ~и, ~е́й, f. story, tale.

пове́три|е, я, n. (*coll.*) epidemic, infection (*also fig.*); п. на дифтери́т diphtheria epidemic.

пове́шени|е, я, n. hanging.

пове́|шенный, *p.p.p. of* ~сить; *as noun* п., ~шенного, *m.* hanged man.

пове́|ять, ет, pf. 1. to begin to blow; to blow softly. 2. (*impers.*, +*i.*) to breathe (of); (*fig.*) to begin to be felt; ~яло прохла́дой there came a breath of fresh air.

повзво́дно, *adv.* in, by platoons.

повздо́р|ить, ю, ишь, pf. of вздо́рить.

повзросле́|ть, ю, pf. (*coll.*) to grow up.

повива́льн|ый, *adj.* (*obs.*) obstetric; ~ая ба́бка midwife; ~ое иску́сство midwifery.

повида́|ть, ю, pf. (*coll.*) to see.

повида́|ться, юсь, pf. of вида́ться.

по-ви́димому, *adv.* apparently, to all appearance, seemingly.

пови́дл|о, а, n. jam.

повили́к|а, и, f. (*bot.*) dodder.

повин|и́ться, ю́сь, и́шься, pf. of вини́ться.

пови́нн|ая, ой, f. confession, acknowledgement of guilt; принести́ ~ую, яви́ться с ~ой to give oneself up; to plead guilty; to acknowledge one's guilt, own up.

пови́нност|ь, и, f. duty, obligation; доро́жная п. compulsory road maintenance; во́инская п. compulsory military service, conscription.

пови́н|ный (~ен, ~на), *adj.* **1.** guilty. **2.** (*obs.*) obliged, bound.

повин|ова́ться, у́юсь, *impf.* (*in past tense also pf.*) (+*d.*) to obey.

повинове́ни|е, я, *n.* obedience.

повис|а́ть, а́ю, *impf. of* ~нуть.

пови|се́ть, шу́, си́шь, *pf.* to hang for a time.

пови́с|нуть, ну, нешь, *past* ~, ~ла, *pf.* (*of* ~а́ть) **1.** (на+*p.*) to hang (by). **2.** to hang down, droop; п. в во́здухе (*fig.*) to hang in mid-air.

повиту́х|а, и, *f.* (*coll.*) midwife.

повлажне́|ть, ю, *pf. of* влажне́ть.

повле́|чь, ку́, чёшь, ку́т, *past* ~к, ~кла́, *pf.* (за собо́й) to entail, bring in one's train; п. за собо́й неприя́тные после́дствия to have unpleasant consequences.

повлия́|ть, ю, *pf. of* влия́ть.

по́вод[1], а, *pl.* ~ы, *m.* (к) occasion, cause, ground (for, of); п. к войне́ casus belli; дать п. (+*d.*) to give occasion (to), give cause (for); дать п. к напа́дкам to lay oneself open; без вся́кого ~а without cause; по ~у (+*g.*) apropos (of), as regards, concerning; по како́му ~у? in what connection? why?

по́вод[2], а, о ~е, на ~у́, *pl.* ~а́, ~ов, *or* ~ья, ~ьев, *m.* rein; быть у кого́-н. на ~у́ (*fig.*) to be under someone's thumb.

пово|ди́ть[1], жу́, ~ди́шь, *impf. of* повести́[2].

пово|ди́ть[2], жу́, ~ди́шь, *pf.* to make go; п. ло́шадь to walk a horse.

повод|о́к, ка́, *m.* (dog's) lead.

поводы́р|ь, я́, *m.* (*coll.*) leader, guide.

пово́зк|а, и, *f.* **1.** vehicle, conveyance. **2.** (*unsprung*) carriage.

пово́йник, а, *m.* (*obs.*) povoynik (*kind of kerchief worn on the head by married Russian peasant woman*).

пово́лжский, *adj.* situated on the Volga.

поволо́к|а, и, *f.* глаза́ с ~ой languishing eyes.

повора́чива|ть(ся), ю(сь), *impf. of* поворо-ти́ть(ся); ~йся!, ~йтесь! (*coll.*) get a move on! look sharp!

поворож|и́ть, у́, и́шь, *pf. of* ворожи́ть.

поворо́т, а, *m.* turn(ing); (*fig.*) turning-point; п. реки́ bend; пе́рвый п. напра́во the first turning to the right; на ~е доро́ги at the turn of the road; п. к лу́чшему turn for the better.

поворо|ти́ть(ся), чу́(сь), ~ти́шь(ся), *pf. of* повора́чивать(ся) to turn.

поворо́тливост|ь, и, *f.* **1.** nimbleness, agility, quickness. **2.** (*tech., naut.*) manœuvrability, handiness.

поворо́тлив|ый (~, ~а), *adj.* **1.** nimble, agile, quick. **2.** (*tech., naut.*) manœuvrable, handy.

поворо́тн|ый, *adj.* rotary, rotating, revolv-

ing; (*fig.*) turning; п. кран slewing crane, swing crane; п. круг turn-table; п. крюк shackle hook; п. мост swing bridge; п. резе́ц swing tool; ~ое сиде́нье swivel seat; ~ые сала́зки swivel carriage; п. моме́нт, п. пункт turning-point.

повре|ди́ть, жу́, ди́шь, *pf.* **1.** *pf. of* вреди́ть. **2.** (*pf. of* ~жда́ть) to damage; to injure, hurt; п. себе́ но́гу to hurt one's leg.

повре|ди́ться, жу́сь, ди́шься, *pf.* (*of* ~жда́ться) to be damaged; to be injured; п. в уме́ (*coll.*) to become mentally deranged.

поврежда́|ть(ся), ю(сь), *impf. of* повре-ди́ть(ся).

поврежде́ни|е, я, *n.* damage, injury.

повре|ждённый, *p.p.p. of* ~ди́ть; п. в уме́ (*coll.*) mentally deranged.

повремен|и́ть, ю́, и́шь, *pf.* (*coll.*) to wait a little; (с+*i.*) to delay (over).

повреме́нн|ый, *adj.* **1.** periodical. **2.** reckoned on time basis; ~ая опла́та payment by time (*by the hour, etc.*); ~ая рабо́та time-work (*work paid by the hour, etc.*).

повседне́вно, *adv.* daily, every day.

повседне́вност|ь, и, *f.* daily occurrence.

повседне́вн|ый, *adj.* daily; everyday; ~ая рабо́та daily task; п. слу́чай everyday occurrence.

повсеме́стно, *adv.* everywhere, in all parts.

повсеме́ст|ный (~ен, ~на), *adj.* universal, general.

повска|ка́ть, ~чет, *pf.* to jump up one after another.

повска́кива|ть, ет, *pf.* = повскака́ть.

повста́н|ец, ца, *m.* insurrectionist, insurgent, rebel.

повста́нческий, *adj.* insurgent, rebel.

повстреча́|ть, ю, *pf.* (*coll.*) to meet, run into.

повстреча́|ться, юсь, *pf.* (+*d. or* с+*i.*) to meet, run into; мне ~лся знако́мый, я ~лся с знако́мым I met an acquaintance.

повсю́ду, *adv.* everywhere.

повторе́ни|е, я, *n.* **1.** repetition; reiteration; кра́ткое п. recapitulation. **2.** recurrence.

повтори́тельный, *adj.* recapitulatory; п. курс refresher course.

повтор|и́ть, ю́, и́шь, *pf.* (*of* ~я́ть) to repeat; to reiterate.

повтор|и́ться, ю́сь, и́шься, *pf.* (*of* ~я́ться) **1.** to repeat oneself. **2.** to recur. **3.** *pass. of* ~и́ть.

повто́рный, *adj.* repeated; recurring.

повтор|я́ть(ся), я́ю(сь), *impf. of* ~и́ть(ся).

повыси́тельный, *adj.* (*electr.*) step-up.

повы́|сить, шу, сишь, *pf.* (*of* ~ша́ть) **1.** to raise, heighten; п. вдво́е, втро́е to double, treble; п. в пять раз, *etc.*, to raise five-fold, *etc.*; п. давле́ние to increase pressure; п. го́лос to raise one's voice (*also fig., in anger*).

2. to promote, prefer, advance; п. кого́-н. по слу́жбе to give someone promotion.

повы́|ситься, шусь, сишься, *pf.* (*of* ~ша́ться) **1.** to rise; to improve; п. в чьём-н. мне́нии to rise in someone's estimation; на́ши а́кции ~сились our shares have gone up; (*fig.*) our stock has risen. **2.** to be promoted, receive advancement.

повыша́|ть(ся), ю(сь), *impf. of* повы́сить-(ся).

повы́ше, *comp. adj. and adv.* a little higher (up); a little taller.

повыше́ни|е, я, *n.* rise, increase; п. по слу́жбе advancement, promotion, preferment.

повы́|шенный, *p.p.p. of* ~сить *and adj.* heightened; increased; ~шенное настрое́ние state of excitement; ~шенная температу́ра high temperature; ~шенная чувстви́тельность heightened sensibility.

повя|за́ть¹, жу́, ~жешь, *pf.* (*of* ~зывать) to tie; п. га́лстук to tie a tie; п. го́лову платко́м to tie a scarf on one's head.

повя|за́ть², жу́, ~жешь, *pf.* to do a little knitting, knit for a while.

повя|за́ться, жу́сь, ~жешься, *pf.* (*of* ~зываться) (+*i.*) to tie oneself (with); п. (платко́м) to tie a scarf on one's head.

повя́зк|а, и, f. 1. band; fillet. **2.** bandage.

повя́зыва|ть(ся), ю(сь), *impf. of* повяза́ть(ся).

погада́|ть, ю, *pf. of* гада́ть.

пога́н|ец, ца, m. (*coll.*) rascal.

пога́н|ить, ю, ишь, *impf.* (*of* о~) (*coll.*) to pollute, defile.

пога́н|ка, ки, f. 1. = ~ый гриб. **2.** shelldrake. **3.** *f. of* ~ец.

пога́н|ый (~, ~а), adj. 1. foul, unclean; п. гриб non-edible mushroom, toadstool; ~ая пи́ща (*rel.*) unclean food; ~ое ведро́ garbage can, refuse pail. **2.** (*coll.*) foul, filthy, vile; ~ое настрое́ние foul mood. **3.** (*obs.*) non-Christian.

по́ган|ь, и, f. (*collect.; pejor.*) filth; dregs.

погаса́|ть, ю, *impf.* to go out, be extinguished.

пога|си́ть, шу́, ~сишь, *pf.* (*of* гаси́ть *and* ~ша́ть) to liquidate, cancel; п. долг to clear off a debt; п. ма́рку to cancel a stamp.

пога́с|нуть, ну, нешь, *past* ~, ~ла, *pf. of* га́снуть.

погаша́|ть, ю, *impf. of* погаси́ть.

пога́|шенный, *p.p.p. of* ~си́ть *and adj.* used (*of postage stamps, etc.*); cashed.

погиб|а́ть, а́ю, *impf. of* ~нуть.

поги́бел|ь, и, f. (*obs.*) ruin, perdition; согну́ться в три ~и to be hunched up; (*fig.*) to be reduced to submission, be cowed.

поги́бельный, adj. (*obs.*) ruinous, fatal.

поги́б|нуть, ну, нешь, *past* ~, ~ла, *pf. (of* ги́бнуть *and* ~а́ть) to perish; (*naut. and fig.*) to be lost; кора́бль ~ со всей кома́ндой the ship was lost with all hands.

поги́б|ший, *past part. of* ~нуть *and adj.* (*obs.*) lost, ruined.

погла́|дить¹, жу, дишь, *pf. of* гла́дить.

погла́|дить², жу, дишь, *pf.* to do a little ironing.

погла́жива|ть, ю, *impf.* to stroke (*every so often, from time to time*).

поглазе́|ть, ю, *pf. of* глазе́ть.

погло|ти́ть, щу́, ~тишь, *pf.* (*of* ~ща́ть) to swallow up, take up, absorb (*also fig.*); п. во́ду to absorb water; п. чьё-н. внима́ние to engross someone; п. рома́н to devour a novel.

поглоща́емост|ь, и, f. absorbability.

поглоща́|ть, ю, *impf. of* поглоти́ть.

поглупе́|ть, ю, *pf. of* глупе́ть.

погля|де́ть, жу́, ди́шь, *pf.* **1.** *pf. of* гляде́ть. **2.** to have a look. **3.** to look for a while.

погля|де́ться, жу́сь, ди́шься, *pf. of* гляде́ться.

погля́дыва|ть, ю, *impf.* **1.** (на+*a.*) to cast looks, glance (at, upon); to look from time to time (at). **2.** (за+*i.; coll.*) to keep an eye (on).

по|гна́ть, гоню́, го́нишь, *past* ~гна́л, ~гнала́, ~гна́ло, *pf.* to drive; to begin to drive.

по|гна́ться, гоню́сь, го́нишься, *past* ~гна́лся, ~гнала́сь, ~гна́лось, *pf.* (за+*i.*) to run (after); to start in pursuit (of), give chase; (*fig.*) to strive (after, for); п. за эффе́ктами to strive for effect.

погни́|ть, ю, ёшь, *past* ~л, ~ла́, ~ло, *pf.* to rot, decay, moulder.

погн|у́ть, у́, ёшь, *pf.* to bend.

погн|у́ться, ётся, *pf.* to bend (*intrans.*).

погнуша́|ться, юсь, *pf. of* гнуша́ться.

погова́рива|ть, ю, *impf.* (о+*p.*) to talk (of); ~ют there is talk (of), it is rumoured; ~ют о его́ жени́тьбе there is talk of his marrying, it is rumoured that he is getting married.

поговор|и́ть, ю, и́шь, *pf.* to have a talk.

погово́рк|а, и, f. (*proverbial*) saying, by-word; войти́ в ~у to become a by-word, become proverbial.

пого́д|а, ы, f. weather; кака́я бы ни была́ п. rain or shine, wet or fine; э́то не де́лает ~ы that is not what counts, this does not affect the matter; ждать у мо́ря (*or* у моря) ~ы to wait for something to turn up.

пого|ди́ть, жу́, ди́шь, *pf.* (*coll.*) to wait a little; ~ди́те! wait a moment! one moment!; немно́го ~дя́ a little later.

пого́д|ки, ков, sing. ~ок, ~ка, *m.* brothers *or* sisters born at a year's interval; мы с ней п. there is a year's difference between us.

пого́дный¹, adj. annual, yearly.

погóд|ный², *adj. of* ~а.

погóжий, *adj.* fine, lovely (*of weather*).

поголóвно, *adv.* one and all; (all) to a man.

поголóвн|ый, *adj.* general, universal; п. налóг poll-tax, capitation(-tax); ~ое ополчéние levy in mass; ~ая перепись universal census.

поголóвь|е, я, *n.* (number of) live-stock.

поголубé|ть, ю, *pf. of* голубéть.

погóн¹, а, *m.* (*mil.*) 1. shoulder-strap. 2. (rifle-)sling.

погóн², а, *m.* distillate, fraction.

погóнный, *adj.* linear.

погóнщик, а, *m.* driver, teamster; п. мýлов muleteer.

погóн|я, и, *f.* pursuit, chase.

погоня́|ть¹, ю, *impf.* to urge on, drive (*also fig.*).

погоня́|ть², ю, *pf.* to drive (*for a certain time*).

погор|áть, áю, *impf. of* ~éть¹.

погорéл|ец, ьца, *m.* one who has lost all his possessions in a fire.

погор|éть¹, ю, ишь, *pf.* (*of* ~áть) 1. to lose all one's possessions in a fire. 2. to burn down; to be burnt out.

погор|éть², ю, ишь, *pf.* to burn for a while.

погоряч|и́ться, ýсь, и́шься, *pf.* to get heated (*fig.*), get worked up.

погóст, а, *m.* (*obs.*) 1. country churchyard. 2. pogost (*country church together with cemetery and clergy house and adjacent buildings*).

пого|сти́ть, щý, сти́шь, *pf.* (у) to stay for a while (at, with).

погран- frontier(-).

пограни́чник, а, *m.* frontier-guard.

пограни́чн|ый, *adj.* frontier; boundary; п. столб boundary post; ~ая стрáжа frontier guards.

пóгреб, а, *pl.* ~á, *m.* cellar (*also fig.*); ви́нный п. wine-cellar; пороховóй п. powder-magazine (*also fig.*).

погребáльн|ый, *adj.* funeral; п. звон knell; ~ое пéние dirge.

погребá|ть, ю, *impf. of* погрести́¹.

погребéни|е, я, *n.* burial, interment.

погреб|éц, цá, *m.* (*obs.*) provisions hamper.

погремýшк|а, и, *f.* rattle.

погре|сти́¹, бý, бёшь, *past* ~б, ~блá, *pf.* (*of* ~бáть) to bury.

погре|сти́², бý, бёшь, *past* ~б, ~блá, *pf.* to row a little.

погрé|ть, ю, *pf.* to warm.

погрé|ться, юсь, *pf.* to warm oneself.

погреш|áть, áю, *impf. of* ~и́ть.

погреш|и́ть, ý, и́шь, *pf.* (*of* ~áть) (прóтив) to sin (against); to err.

погрéшност|ь, и, *f.* error, mistake, inaccuracy; треугóльник ~и (*naut.*) cocked hat.

погро|зи́ть, жý, зи́шь, *pf. of* грози́ть 2.

погро|зи́ться, жýсь, зи́шься, *pf. of* грози́ться.

погрóм, а, *m.* pogrom, massacre.

погрóм|ный, *adj. of* ~.

погрóмщик, а, *m.* person organizing *or* taking part in a pogrom.

погромых|áть, áю, *pf.* (*of* ~ивать) (*of thunder*) to rumble intermittently.

погромы́хива|ть, ю, *impf. of* погромыхáть.

погружá|ть(ся), ю(сь), *impf. of* погрузи́ть(ся).

погружéни|е, я, *n.* sinking, submergence; immersion; (*of a submarine*) dive, diving.

погрý|женный *and* ~жённый, *p.p.p. of* ~зи́ть; п. в вóду immersed (in water); п. в размышлéния deep in thought; п. в себя́ wrapped up in oneself.

погру|зи́ть, жý, ~зи́шь, *pf.* (*of* ~жáть) 1. (в+а.) to dip (into), plunge (into), immerse; to submerge; to duck. 2. *pf. of* грузи́ть 2.

погру|зи́ться, жýсь, ~зи́шься, *pf.* 1. (в+а.) to sink (into), plunge (into); (*of a submarine*) to submerge, dive; (*fig.*) to be plunged (in); to be absorbed (in), be buried (in), be lost (in); п. в темнотý to be plunged into darkness; п. в чтéние to be absorbed in reading; п. в размышлéния to be deep in thought. 2. *pf. of* грузи́ться.

погрýзк|а, и, *f.* loading; lading, shipment.

погрýзочно-разгрýзочный, *adj.* loading-and-unloading.

погрýзочный, *adj.* loading; п. жёлоб loading chute.

погряз|áть, áю, *impf. of* ~нуть.

погря́з|нуть, ну, нешь, *past* ~, ~ла, *pf.* (*of* ~áть) (в+*p.*) to be stuck (in); to be bogged down (in); to wallow (in) (*also fig.*); п. в долгáх to be up to one's eyes in debt.

погуб|и́ть, лю, ~ишь, *pf. of* губи́ть.

погýдк|а, и, *f.* (*coll.*) tune, melody; стáрая п. на нóвый лад (*fig.*) the same tune in a new setting, the (same) old story.

погýлива|ть, ю, *impf.* (*coll.*) 1. to walk up and down. 2. to go on the spree from time to time.

погуля́|ть, ю, *pf. of* гуля́ть.

погустé|ть, ет, *pf. of* густéть.

под¹, а, о ~е, на ~ý, *m.* hearth(-stone); sole (*of furnace*).

под² *and* подо, *prep.* 1. (+*a. and i.*) under; постáвить п. стол to put under the table; находи́ться п. столóм to be under the table; п. арéстом under arrest; п. ви́дом (+*g.*) under, in the guise (of); п. влия́нием (+*g.*) under the influence (of); п. вопрóсом open to question; пóд гору downhill; п. замкóм under lock and key; п. землёй underground; быть п. ружьём to be under arms; взять когó-н. пóд руку to take

someone's arm; п. рукóй (close) at hand, to
hand; отдáть п. суд to prosecute; п.
услóвием on condition. 2. (+*a. and i.*) in
the environs of; near; жить п. Москвóй to
live in the environs of Moscow; поéхать
на дáчу п. Ленингрáд to go to a dacha
near Leningrad; бúтва п. Бородинóм the
battle of Borodino. 3. (+*i.*) occupied by,
used as; (+*a.*) for; (to serve) as; помещéние
под шкóлой premises occupied by a school;
отвестú помещéние п. шкóлу to earmark
premises for a school; бáнка п. варéнье
jam-jar; пóле п. пшенúцей wheat-field.
4. (+*a.*) towards (*of time*); on the eve of; п.
вéчер towards evening; п. Нóвый год on
New Year's Eve; емý п. пятьдесят (лет) he is
getting on for fifty. 5. (+*a.*) to (the accompaniment of); танцевáть п. граммофóн-
ные пластúнки to dance to gramophone
records; писáть п. диктóвку to write from
dictation. 6. (+*a.*) in imitation of; это
сдéлано п. орéх it is imitation walnut; он
пúшет п. Тургéнева he writes in imitation
of (*the style of*) Turgenev. 7. (+*a.*) on
(= *in exchange for*); п. залóг on security; п.
распúску on receipt. 8. (+*i.*) (*meant, etc.*)
by; что нáдо понимáть п. этим выраже-
нием? what is meant by this expression?;
что п. этим подразумевáется? what is
implied by this? 9. (+*i.; cul.*) in, with;
рыба п. бешамéлью fish cooked in white
sauce; говядина п. хрéном beef with horse-
-radish.

под- (подо-, подъ-)[1] *as verbal prefix indicates*
1. *action from beneath or affecting lower part of
something, as* подчеркнýть *to underline.* 2.
motion upwards, as поднять *to raise.* 3. *motion
towards, as* подъéхать *to approach.* 4. *action
carried out or event occurring in slight degree, as*
подкрáсить *to touch up;* поджúть *to begin
to heal up.* 5. *supplementary action, as* под-
рабóтать *to earn additionally.* 6. *underhand
action, as* подкупúть *to bribe.*

под- (подо-, подъ-)[2] *as prefix of nouns and adjs.*
under-, sub-.

подавáльщик, а, *m.* 1. waiter. 2. supplier.
3. (*sport; in game of lapta*) pitcher.

подавáльщиц|а, ы, *f.* waitress.

пода|вáть(ся), ю(сь), ёшь(ся), *impf. of*
подáть(ся).

подав|úть[1]**, лю, ~ишь,** *pf. (of ~лять)* 1. to
suppress, put down; to repress; п. вос-
стáние to put down a rising; п. стон to
stifle a groan. 2. (*fig.*) to depress; to crush,
overwhelm. 3. (*mil.*) to neutralize.

подав|úть[2]**, лю, ~ишь,** *pf. (no impf.)* 1. (*coll.*)
to press, trample (*a quantity of*). 2. to press,
squeeze for a time.

подав|úться, люсь, ~ишься, *pf. of* да-
вúться.

подавлéни|е, я, *n.* 1. suppression; repres-
sion. 2. (*mil.*) neutralization.

подáвленност|ь, и, *f.* depression; blues.

подáв|ленный, p.p.p. of ~úть and adj. 1.
suppressed; п. стон muffled groan. 2. depressed, dispirited.

подáвлива|ть, ю, *impf.* to exert slight pres-
sure.

подавля|ть, ю, *impf. of* подавúть[1].

подавля|ющий, pres. part. act. of ~ть and adj.
overwhelming; overpowering; ~ющее
большинствó overwhelming majority.

подáвно, *adv.* so much the more, all the
more.

подáгр|а, ы, *f.* gout, podagra.

подáгрик, а, *m.* gouty person, sufferer from
gout.

подагрúческий, adj. gouty.

подáльше, *adv.* (*coll.*) a little farther.

подар|úть, ю, ~ишь, *pf. of* дарúть.

подáр|ок, ка, *m.* present, gift; получúть в
п. to receive as a present.

подáтел|ь, я, *m.* bearer (*of a letter, etc.*); п.
прошéния petitioner.

подáтливост|ь, и, *f.* 1. pliancy, pliability.
2. (*fig.*) complaisance.

подáтлив|ый (~, ~а), adj. 1. pliant, pliable.
2. (*fig.*) complaisant.

податн|óй, adj. (*hist.*) tax, duty; п. инспéк-
тор assessor of taxes; ~áя систéма taxation;
as noun п., ~óго, *m.* = п. инспéктор.

подáт|ь, и, *pl.* ~и, ~éй, *f.* (*hist.*) tax, duty,
assessment.

**по|дáть, дáм, дáшь, дáст, дадúм, дадúте,
дадýт,** *past* ~дáл, ~далá, ~дáло, *pf.* (*of
~давáть*) 1. (*in var. senses*) to give; to
proffer; п. гóлос to vote; п. знак to give a
sign; п. пóмощь to lend a hand, proffer
aid; п. примéр to set an example; п.
рýку (+*d.*) to offer one's hand; п. сигнáл
to give the signal; ~дáйте ей пальтó help
her on with her coat. 2. to serve (*food*); п.
на стол to serve up; обéд ~дан dinner is
served. 3. to bring up (*train or other conveyance*); слéдующий пóезд ~дадýт на эту
платфóрму the next train will come in at
this platform. 4. to put, move, turn; п.
лóшадь в галóп to put a horse into a gallop.
5. (*sport*) п. мяч to serve. 6. to serve, forward, present, hand in (*application, complaint, etc.*); п. апелляцию to appeal; п.
жáлобу to lodge a complaint; п. заявлéние
to hand in an application; п. телегрáмму
to send a telegram; п. в отстáвку to send
in one's resignation; п. в суд (на+*a.*) to
bring an action (against). 7. (*lit., theatr.*)
to present, display. 8. (*tech.*) to feed.

**по|дáться, дáмся, дáшься, дáстся, дадúм-
ся, дадúтесь, дадýтся,** *past* ~дáлся, ~да-
лáсь, ~далóсь, *pf.* (*of ~давáться*) 1. to

move; п. назад to draw back; п. в сторону to move aside. **2.** (*coll.*) to give way, yield (*also fig.*); to cave in, collapse. **3.** (на+*a.*; *coll.*) to make (for), set out (for).

пода́ч|а, и, *f.* **1.** giving, presenting; п. го́лоса voting; п. заявле́ния sending in of application. **2.** (*sport*) service, serve. **3.** (*tech.*) feed, feeding, supply; (*chem.*) introduction; высота́ ~и lift (*of pump*); коро́бка ~ gear box, feed unit.

пода́чк|а, и, *f.* (*coll.*) **1.** sop; crumb. **2.** (*fig.*) tip.

подая́ни|е, я, *n.* charity, alms; dole.

подба́в|ить, лю, ишь, *pf.* (*of* ~ля́ть) (+*a. or g.*) to add; п. са́хару в ко́фе to put (more) sugar in coffee; п. ро́му в чай to lace tea with rum.

подба́вк|а, и, *f.* addition.

подбавля́|ть, ю, *impf. of* подба́вить.

подба́лтыва|ть, ю, *impf. of* подболта́ть.

подбега́|ть, ю, *impf. of* подбежа́ть.

подбе|жа́ть, гу́, жи́шь, гу́т, *pf.* (*of* ~га́ть) (к) to run up (to), come running up (to).

подберёзовик, а, *m.* brown mushroom (*Boletus scaber*).

подбива́|ть, ю, *impf. of* подби́ть.

подби́вк|а, и, *f.* **1.** lining. **2.** re-soling.

подбира́|ть(ся), ю(сь), *impf. of* подобра́ть(ся).

подби́т|ый, *p.p.p. of* ~ь; п. ва́той wadded; п. ме́хом fur-lined; п. глаз black eye.

под|би́ть, обью́, обьёшь, *pf.* (*of* ~бива́ть) **1.** (+*i.*) to live (with). **2.** to re-sole. **3.** to injure; to bruise; п. кому́-н. глаз to give someone a black eye. **4.** (*mil.*) to put out of action, knock out; п. самолёт to shoot down a plane. **5.** (+*inf. or* на+*a.*; *coll.*) to incite (to), instigate (to).

подбодр|и́ть, ю́, и́шь, *pf.* (*of* ~я́ть) (*coll.*) to cheer up, encourage.

подбодр|и́ться, ю́сь, и́шься, *pf.* (*of* ~я́ться) to cheer up, take heart. ˙

подбодр|я́ть(ся), я́ю(сь), *impf. of* ~и́ть(ся).

подбо́йк|а, и, *f.* **1.** lining. **2.** re-soling. **3.** (*tech.*) swage.

подболта́|ть, ю, *pf.* (*of* подба́лтывать) (+*a. or g.*) to mix in, stir in; п. молока́ в суп to stir milk into soup.

подбо́р, а, *m.* **1.** selection, assortment; (как) на п. choice, well-matched. **2.** в п. (*typ.*) run on.

подбо́рк|а, и, *f.* set, selection (*esp. a section of related news items under a single heading in a newspaper*).

подборо́д|ок, ка, *m.* chin.

подбоче́нива|ться, юсь, *impf. of* подбоче́ниться.

подбоче́нившись, *adv.* with one's arms akimbo, with one's hands on one's hips.

подбоче́н|иться, юсь, ишься, *pf.* (*of* ~иваться) to place one's arms akimbo.

подбра́сыва|ть, ю, *impf. of* подбро́сить.

подбро́|сить, шу, сишь, *pf.* (*of* подбра́сывать) **1.** to throw up, toss up; (под) to throw (under); п. моне́ту to toss up. **2.** (+*a. or g.*) to throw in, throw on; п. резе́рвы (*mil.*) to throw in one's reserves; п. дров в печь to throw more wood on the fire. **3.** to place surreptitiously; п. младе́нца to abandon a baby.

подбрю́шник, а, *m.* belly-band (*of horse*).

подва́л, а, *m.* **1.** cellar; basement. **2.** (*in newspaper*) feuilleton.

подва́лива|ть, ю, *impf. of* подвали́ть.

подвал|и́ть, ю́, ~ишь, *pf.* (*of* ~ивать) **1.** (*coll.*) (+*a. or g.*) to heap up. **2.** (+*a. or g.*) (*coll.*) to add; наро́ду ~и́ло (*impers.*) still more people came. **3.** (*naut.*; к) to come in (to), steam in (to).

подва́л|ьный, *adj. of* ~; п. эта́ж basement.

подва́рива|ть, ю, *impf. of* подвари́ть.

подвар|и́ть, ю́, ~ишь, *pf.* (*of* ~ивать) (*coll.*) **1.** (+*g.*) to boil in addition. **2.** to heat up again.

подва́хтенны|й, *adj.* ~е матро́сы (*naut.*) watch below.

подве́домствен|ный (~, ~на), *adj.* (+*d.*) dependent (on), within the jurisdiction (of).

подвез|ти́, у́, ёшь, *past* ~, ~ла́, *pf.* (*of* подвози́ть) **1.** to bring, take (with one); to give a lift (*on the road*). **2.** (+*a. or g.*) to bring up, transport. **3.** (*coll.*) мне, *etc.*, ~ло́ I, *etc.*, have had a stroke of luck.

подвене́чн|ый, *adj.* ~ое пла́тье wedding dress.

подверг|а́ть(ся), а́ю(сь), *impf. of* ~нуть(ся).

подверг|нуть, ну, нешь, *past* ~, ~ла, *pf.* (*of* ~а́ть) (+*d.*) to subject (to); to expose (to); п. испыта́нию to put to the test; п. наказа́нию to impose a penalty (upon); п. опа́сности to expose to danger, endanger; п. сомне́нию to call in question; п. штра́фу to fine.

подверг|нуться, нусь, нешься, *past* ~ся, ~лась, *pf.* (*of* ~а́ться) **1.** (+*d.*) to undergo. **2.** *pass. of* ~нуть.

подве́рженност|ь, и, *f.* (+*d.*) liability (to), susceptibility (to).

подве́ржен|ный (~, ~а), *adj.* (+*d.*) subject (to), liable (to); susceptible (to).

подвер|ну́ть, ну́, нёшь, *pf.* (*of* ~тывать) **1.** to screw up a little; п. винт to tighten a screw. **2.** to tuck in, tuck up; п. одея́ло to tuck in a blanket; п. брю́ки to tuck up one's trousers. **3.** to twist, sprain; п. но́гу to sprain one's ankle.

подвер|ну́ться, ну́сь, нёшься, *pf.* (*of* ~тываться) **1.** to be twisted, sprained; нога́ у

меня́ ~ну́лась I have sprained my ankle.
2. (*fig.*, *coll.*) to turn up, crop up; он кста́ти
~ну́лся he turned up just at the right
moment. **3.** *pass. of* ~ну́ть.

подвёртыва|ть(ся), ю(сь), *impf. of* подвер-
ну́ть(ся).

подве́с, а, *m.* (*tech.*) suspension; hanger.

подвесе́льный, *adj.* at the oars.

подве́|сить, шу, сишь, *pf.* (*of* ~шивать) to
hang up, suspend.

подве́|ситься, шусь, сишься, *pf.* (*of* ~ши-
ваться) (на+*p.*) to hang (on to, on by), be
suspended (from).

подве́ск|а, и, *f.* **1.** hanging up, suspension.
2. pendant; се́рьги с ~ами drop ear-rings.
3. (*tech.*) hanger; suspension bracket, suspension clip.

подвесно́й, *adj.* hanging, suspended, pendant; overhead; п. конве́йер overhead
conveyer; п. мост suspension bridge; п.
мото́р outboard motor.

подве́с|ок, ка, *m.* pendant.

подве|сти́, ду́, дёшь, *past* ~л, ~ла́, *pf.* (*of*
подводи́ть) **1.** to lead up, bring up; to extend; п. резе́рвы to bring up reserves. **2.**
(под+*a.*) to place (under); п. фунда́мент
to under-pin; п. дом под кры́шу to roof a
house; п. ми́ну под мост to mine a bridge;
п. про́чную ба́зу под свои́ до́воды to place
one's arguments on a sound footing; п.
бро́ви to pencil one's eyebrows. **3.** to sub-
sume; to put together; п. бала́нс (+*g.*) to
balance; п. ито́ги to reckon up; to sum up
(*also fig.*); он ~л ва́ши гру́бые слова́ под
оскорбле́ние he took your rude words as an
insult. **4.** (*coll.*) to let down; to put in a spot.
5. (*impers.*; *coll.*) у меня́ живо́т ~ло́ I feel
pinched (with hunger).

подве́тренн|ый, *adj.* leeward; п. борт (*naut.*)
lee side; бе́рег с ~ой стороны́ lee shore.

подве́шива|ть(ся), ю(сь), *impf. of* под-
ве́сить(ся).

подвздо́шный, *adj.* (*anat.*) iliac.

подвива́|ть(ся), ю(сь), *impf. of* подви́ть(ся).

по́двиг, а, *m.* exploit, feat; heroic deed;
боево́й п. feat of arms; геро́ический п.
epic of heroism.

подви́га|ть, ю, *pf.* (+*i.*) to move a little.

подвига́|ть(ся), ю(сь), *impf. of* подви́нуть-
(ся).

подви́гн|уть, у, ешь, *pf.* (на+*a.*) (*rhet.*, *obs.*)
to rouse (to).

подви́д, а, *m.* (*biol.*) subspecies.

подви́жник, а, *m.* **1.** (*rel.*) ascetic; zealot.
2. (*fig.*) zealot, devotee; hero; п. нау́ки
person utterly devoted to (*the cause of*)
learning.

подви́жничеств|о, а, *n.* **1.** (*rel.*) asceticism.
2. selfless devotion (*to a cause*); heroic conduct; endeavour.

подвижн|о́й, *adj.* **1.** (*in var. senses*) mobile;
movable; (*tech.*) travelling; п. блок travelling block; п. го́спиталь mobile hospital;
~ые и́гры outdoor games; п. кран travelling crane; п. масшта́б sliding scale; п.
пра́здник (*eccl.*) movable feast; ~ое равно-
ве́сие (*chem.*) mobile equilibrium; п.
соста́в (*railway*) rolling stock. **2.** lively;
agile; ~ое лицо́ mobile features.

подви́жност|ь, и, *f.* **1.** mobility. **2.** liveli-
ness; agility.

подви́жный, *adj.* mobile; lively; agile.

подвиза́|ться, юсь, *impf.* (*rhet. or iron.*) to
work, act; to pursue an occupation; п. на
юриди́ческом по́прище to follow the law;
п. на сце́не to tread the boards.

подвин|ти́ть, чу́, ти́шь, *pf.* (*of* ~чивать)
1. to screw up, tighten. **2.** (*fig.*, *coll.*) to
urge, goad.

подви́|нуть, ну, нешь, *pf.* (*of* ~га́ть) **1.** to
move; to push. **2.** (*fig.*) to advance, push
forward.

подви́|нуться, нусь, нешься, *pf.* (*of* ~га́ть-
ся) **1.** to move. **2.** (*fig.*) to advance, progress.

подви́нчива|ть, ю, *impf. of* подвинти́ть.

под|ви́ть, овью́, овьёшь, *past* ~ви́л, ~вила́,
~ви́ло, *pf.* (*of* ~вива́ть) to curl slightly,
friz(z).

под|ви́ться, овью́сь, овьёшься, *past* ~ви́л-
ся, ~вила́сь, ~ви́лось, *pf.* (*of* ~вива́ться)
to curl one's hair slightly, friz(z) one's hair.

подвла́ст|ный (~ен, ~на), *adj.* (+*d.*) sub-
ject to, dependent on.

подво́д, а, *m.* (*tech.*) supply, feed, admission;
(*electr.*) lead, feeder.

подво́д|а, ы, *f.* cart.

подво|ди́ть, жу́, ~дишь, *impf. of* подвести́.

подво́дник, а, *m.* (*naut.*) submariner.

подводн|о́й, *adj.* ~а́я труба́ (*tech.*) feed pipe.

подво́дн|ый[1], *adj.* submarine; under-water;
п. загради́тель mine-layer; п. ка́бель submarine cable; п. ка́мень reef, rock; ~ая
ло́дка submarine; ~ое тече́ние under-
current.

подво́дн|ый[2], *adj. of* ~а; ~ная пови́нность
(*hist.*) obligation to provide transport.

подво́дчик, а, *m.* carter.

подво́з, а, *m.* transport; supply.

подво|зи́ть, жу́, ~зишь, *impf. of* подвезти́.

подво́|й, я, *m.* (*bot.*) wilding.

подво́рн|ый, *adj.* household; ~ая пе́репись
census of (*peasant*) households; ~ая по́дать
(*hist.*) hearth-money, chimney-money; п.
спи́сок list of homesteads.

подворотнич|о́к, ка́, *m.* undercollar (*of sol-
dier's tunic*).

подворо́т|ня, ни, *g. pl.* ~ен, *f.* **1.** space be-
tween gate and ground. **2.** board attached
to bottom of gate.

подво́р|ье, ья, g. pl. ~ий, n. (obs.) 1. town house (daughter church in town, usu. with hostel attached, belonging to monastery). 2. town residence, town house (belonging to person normally residing elsewhere).

подво́х, а, m. (coll.) dirty trick; устро́ить п. кому́-н. to play someone a dirty trick.

подвы́пи|вший, past part. of ~ть and adj. (coll.) slightly tight.

подвы́п|ить, ью, ьешь, pf. (coll.) to become slightly tight.

подвя|за́ть, жу́, ~жешь, pf. (of ~зывать) to tie up; to keep up.

подвя́зк|а, и, f. garter; (stocking) suspender.

подвя́зыва|ть, ю, impf. of подвяза́ть.

подга́|дить, жу, дишь, pf. (coll.) 1. to spoil the effect (of), make a mess (of). 2. (+d.) to play a dirty trick (on).

подгиба́|ть(ся), ю(сь), impf. of подогну́ть(ся).

подгла́зь|е, я, n. bag under the eyes.

подгля|де́ть, жу́, ди́шь, pf. (of ~дывать) (в+a.; coll.) to peep (at); to spy (on), watch furtively.

подгля́дыва|ть, ю, impf. of подгляде́ть.

подгнива́|ть, ю, impf. of подгни́ть.

подгни́|ть, ю, ёшь, past ~л, ~ла́, ~ло, pf. (of ~ва́ть) to begin to rot, rot slightly.

подгова́рива|ть, ю, impf. of подговори́ть.

подговор|и́ть, ю́, и́шь, pf. (of подгова́ривать) (на+a. or +inf.) to put up (to), incite (to), instigate (to).

подголо́вник, а, m. head-rest.

подголо́с|ок, ка, m. 1. (mus.) second part, supporting voice. 2. (coll., pejor.) yes-man.

подгоня́|ть, ю, impf. of подогна́ть.

подгор|а́ть, а́ю, impf. of ~е́ть.

подгоре́лый, adj. slightly burnt.

подгор|е́ть, и́т, pf. (of ~а́ть) to burn slightly.

подго́рный, adj. lowland.

подгоро́дный, adj. situated in the outskirts of a town.

подгота́влива|ть(ся), ю(сь), impf. of подгото́вить(ся).

подгото́в|ить, лю, ишь, pf. (of подгота́вливать and ~ля́ть) (для, к) to prepare (for); п. по́чву (fig.) to pave the way.

подгото́в|иться, люсь, ишься, pf. (of подгота́вливаться and ~ля́ться) (к) to prepare (for), get ready (for).

подгото́вк|а, и, f. 1. (к) preparation (for), training (for); артилле́рийская п. artillery preparation, preparatory bombardment. 2. (в+p. or по+d.) grounding (in), schooling (in).

подгото́вленност|ь, и, f. preparedness.

подготовля́|ть(ся), ю(сь), impf. of подгото́вить(ся).

подгреба́|ть, ю, impf. of подгрести́.

подгре|сти́¹, бу́, бёшь, past ~б, ~бла́, pf. (of ~ба́ть) to rake up.

подгре|сти́², бу́, бёшь, past ~б, ~бла́, pf. (of ~ба́ть) (к) to row up (to).

подгру́д|ок, ка, m. dewlap.

подгру́пп|а, ы, f. sub-group.

подгу́зник, а, m. nappy, diaper, pilch.

подгуля́|ть, ю, pf. (coll.) 1. to take a drop too much, be slightly under the weather. 2. (joc.) to be rather bad, be rather poor, be pretty poor; обе́д немно́го ~л the dinner was pretty poor.

подда|ва́ть(ся), ю́(сь), ёшь(ся), impf. of подда́ть(ся).

поддавк|и́, о́в, no sing. игра́ть в п. to play at give-away (to play draughts according to convention that winner is the first player to lose all his pieces).

подда́кива|ть, ю, impf. (of подда́кнуть) (+d.; coll.) to say yes (to), assent (to); (also pejor.).

подда́к|нуть, ну, нешь, pf. of ~ивать.

по́дданн|ый, p.p.p. of подда́ть; as noun п., ~ого, m., and ~ая, ~ой, f. subject, national.

по́дданств|о, а, n. citizenship, nationality.

под|да́ть, да́м, да́шь, да́ст, дади́м, дади́те, даду́т, past ~да́л, ~дала́, ~да́ло, pf. (of ~дава́ть) 1. to strike; to kick. 2. (at draughts, etc.) to give away. 3. (+g.; coll.) to add, increase; п. жа́ру to add fuel to the fire; п. па́ру to increase steam; п. га́зу to get a move on.

под|да́ться, да́мся, да́шься, да́стся, дади́мся, дади́тесь, даду́тся, past ~да́лся, ~дала́сь, pf. (of ~дава́ться) 1. (+d.) to yield (to), give way (to), give in (to); дверь не ~дала́сь the door would not give; п. искуше́нию to yield to temptation; не п. описа́нию to beggar description; п. отча́янию to give way to despair; п. угро́зам to give in to threats. 2. (coll.) to give oneself up.

поддева́|ть, ю, impf. of подде́ть.

поддёвк|а, и, f. poddyovka (man's light tight-fitting coat).

подде́л|ать, аю, pf. (of ~ывать) to counterfeit, falsify, fake; to forge; to fabricate; п. по́дпись to forge a signature.

подде́л|аться, аюсь, pf. (of ~ываться) 1. (под+a.) to imitate, put on. 2. (к; coll.) to ingratiate oneself (with).

подде́лк|а, и, f. falsification; forgery; counterfeit; imitation, fake; п. под же́мчуг imitation pearls.

подде́лывател|ь, я, m. forger; counterfeiter, falsifier.

подде́лыва|ть(ся), ю(сь), impf. of подде́лать(ся).

подде́льн|ый, adj. false, counterfeit; forged;

sham, spurious; ~ые драгоце́нности artificial jewelry; ~ая моне́та counterfeit
coin; п. па́спорт forged passport.

поддёргива|ть, ю, *impf. of* поддёрнуть.

поддержа́ни|е, я, *n.* maintenance.

поддерж|а́ть, у́, ~ишь, *pf.* (*of* ~ивать) **1.** to
support (*also fig.*); to back (up), second;
мора́льно п. to give moral support; п.
резолю́цию to second a resolution. **2.** to
keep up, maintain; п. ого́нь to keep up the
fire; п. разгово́р to keep up a conversation;
п. регуля́рное сообще́ние to maintain a
regular service; п. отноше́ния (с+*i.*) to
keep in touch (with).

подде́ржива|ть, ю, *impf.* **1.** *impf. of* поддер-
жа́ть. **2.** (*impf. only*) to bear, support.

подде́ржк|а, и, *f.* **1.** (*in var. senses*) support;
backing; seconding; огневая п. (*mil.*) fire
support; covering fire. **2.** support, prop,
stay.

поддёр|нуть, ну, нешь, *pf.* (*of* ~гивать) to
pull up.

подде́|ть, ну, нешь, *pf.* (*of* ~ва́ть) **1.** (под
+*a.*; *coll.*) to put on under, wear under;
~нь(те) сви́тер под ку́ртку put a sweater on
under your jacket. **2.** to hook; to catch up.
3. (*fig., coll.*) to catch out.

поддо́нник, а, *m,* saucer (*placed under flower-
pot*).

поддра́знива|ть, ю, *impf. of* поддразни́ть.

поддразн|и́ть, ю́, ~ишь, *pf.* (*of* ~ивать)
(*coll.*) to tease.

поддува́л|о, а, *n.* ash-pit (*of stove, furnace*).

поддува́|ть, ю, *impf.* **1.** to blow (*from under-
neath*). **2.** to blow slightly.

по-де́довски, *adv.* (*coll.*) as of old.

поде́йств|овать, ую, *pf. of* де́йствовать 2.

подека́дно, *adv.* every ten days.

подела́|ть, ю, *pf.* (*no impf.*) (*coll.*) **1.** to do;
ничего́ не ~ешь there is nothing to be
done, it can't be helped; ничего́ не могу́ с
ни́ми п.! I can't do anything with them. **2.**
to make, build.

подел|и́ть(ся), ю́(сь), ~ишь(ся), *pf. of*
дели́ть(ся).

поде́лк|а, и, *f.* **1.** odd job. **2.** article; ~и из
де́рева wood articles.

подело́м, *adv.*; (*coll.*) п. ему́, *etc.*, it serves him,
etc., right.

поде́лыва|ть, *impf.* (*coll.*) *only used in question*
что ~ешь?, что ~ете? how are you getting
on?

подёнк|а, и, *f.* (*insect*) ephemeron, ephe-
mera.

подённо, *adv.* by the day.

подённ|ый, *adj.* by the day; ~ая опла́та
pay by the day; ~ая рабо́та day-labour,
time-work.

подёнщик, а, *m.* day-labourer, time-
-worker.

подёнщин|а, ы, *f.* work paid by the day,
day-labour.

подёнщиц|а, ы, *f.* woman hired by the day.

подёрг|ать, аю, *pf. of* ~ивать.

подёргивани|е, я, *n.* twitch(ing), jerk.

подёргива|ть, ю, *impf.* **1.** (*impf. of* подёр-
гать) (+*a.* or за+*a.*) to pull (at), tug (at).
2. (*impf. only*) (+*i.*) to twitch.

подёргива|ться, юсь, *impf.* to twitch.

подержа́ни|е, я, *n.* на п. for temporary use;
взять на п. to borrow; дать на п. to lend.

поде́ржанный, *adj.* second-hand.

подерж|а́ть, у́, ~ишь, *pf.* to hold for some
time; to keep for some time.

подерж|а́ться, у́сь, ~ишься, *pf.* **1.** (за+*a.*)
to hold (on to) for some time. **2.** to hold
(out), last, stand.

подёрн|уть, ет, *pf.* to cover, coat; реку́
~уло льдом (*impers.*) the river was coated
with ice.

подёрн|уться, ется, *pf.* (+*i.*) to be covered
(with).

подешеве́|ть, ет, *pf. of* дешеве́ть.

поджа́рива|ть(ся), ю(сь), *impf. of* поджа́-
рить(ся).

поджа́рист|ый (~, ~а), *adj.* brown,
browned; crisp.

поджа́р|ить, ю, ишь, *pf.* (*of* ~ивать) to fry,
roast, grill (slightly); п. хлеб to toast bread.

поджа́р|иться, юсь, ишься, *pf.* (*of* ~ивать-
ся) **1.** to fry, roast (slightly). **2.** *pass. of* ~ить.

поджа́рк|а, и, *f.* (*cul.*; *coll.*) grilled or fried
piece of beef.

поджа́р|ый (~, ~а), *adj.* (*coll.*) lean, wiry,
sinewy.

под|жа́ть, ожму́, ожмёшь, *pf.* (*of* ~жима́ть)
to draw in; п. гу́бы to purse one's lips; п.
хвост to have one's tail between one's legs
(*also fig.*); сиде́ть ~жа́в но́ги to sit cross-
-legged.

поджелу́дочн|ый, *adj.* ~ая железа́ (*anat.*)
pancreas.

под|же́чь, ожгу́, ожжёшь, ожгу́т, *past* ~жёг,
~ожгла́, *pf.* (*of* ~жига́ть) **1.** to set fire (to),
set on fire (*with criminal intent or otherwise*).
2. (*coll.*) to burn slightly.

поджига́|ть, ю, *impf. of* поджи́ть.

поджига́тел|ь, я, *m.* **1.** incendiary. **2.** (*fig.*)
instigator; п. войны́ warmonger.

поджига́тельский, *adj.* inflammatory.

поджига́тельств|о, а, *n.* **1.** incendiarism. **2.**
(*fig.*) instigation; п. войны́ warmongering.

поджига́|ть, ю, *impf. of* подже́чь.

поджида́|ть, ю, *impf.* to wait (for); to lie
in wait (for).

поджи́л|ки, ок, *no sing.* knee tendons; у меня́
от стра́ха п. затрясли́сь (*fig., coll.*) I was
shaking in my shoes, I was quaking with
fear.

поджима́|ть, ю, *impf. of* поджа́ть.

поджи́|ть, ивёт, *past* ~и́л, ~ила́, ~и́ло, *pf.* (*of* ~ива́ть) to heal (up); (*of a cut*) to close (up).

поджо́г, а, *m.* arson.

подзаб|ы́ть, у́ду, у́дешь, *pf.* (*coll.*) to forget partially; я ~ы́л ру́сский язы́к my Russian is a little rusty.

подзаголо́в|ок, ка, *m.* sub-title, sub-heading.

подзадо́рива|ть, ю, *impf. of* подзадо́рить.

подзадо́р|ить, ю, ишь, *pf.* (*of* ~ивать) (*coll.*) to egg on, set on.

подзаты́льник, а, *m.* (*coll.*) clip (on the back of the head).

подзащи́тн|ый, ого, *m.* (*leg.*) client.

подземе́л|ье, ья, *g.pl.* ~ий, *n.* cave; dungeon.

подзе́мк|а, и, *f.* (*coll.*) underground (railway), tube.

подзе́мн|ый, *adj.* underground, subterranean; ~ая (городска́я) желе́зная доро́га underground (railway), tube; ~ые рабо́ты underground workings; п. толчо́к earthquake shock; tremor.

подзерка́льник, а, *m.* looking-glass table, dressing-table with looking-glass.

подзо́л, а, *m.* (*agric.*) podzol (*sterile greyish--white soil, deficient in salts*).

подзо́лист|ый (~, ~а), *adj.* (*agric.*) containing podzol.

подзо́р, а, *m.* 1. cornice (*of Russian wood building*). 2. edging, trimming.

подзо́рн|ый, *adj.*; ~ая труба́ spy-glass, telescope.

подзу|ди́ть, жу́, ~ди́шь, *pf.* (*of* ~жива́ть) (*coll.*) to egg on, set on.

подзу́жива|ть, ю, *impf. of* подзуди́ть.

подзыва́|ть, ю, *impf. of* подозва́ть.

поди́¹ (*coll.*) = пойди́ (*imp. of* пойти́); п. сюда́! come here!

поди́² (*coll.*) 1. probably, I dare say, I shouldn't wonder; *or translated* must (be), is sure (to be); ты, п., уста́ла you must be tired; он, п., забы́л he has probably forgotten; они́, п., прие́дут I dare say they'll be there. 2. *particle expressing amazement, incredulity, etc.* (*also* на́ п.); п. ты, ра́зве он э́то сказа́л? go on, he never said that?; impossible! he couldn't have said that!; он на́чал так руга́ться, что на́ п. he began to swear so, you can't imagine; вот п. ж ты just imagine; well, who would have thought it possible. 3. *particle + imp.* just try; п. удержи́ его́ just try to stop him.

подив|и́ть, лю́, и́шь, *pf.* (*no impf.*) (*coll., obs.*) to cause to marvel, astonish.

подив|и́ться, лю́сь, и́шься, *pf. of* диви́ться.

подира́|ть, ет, *impf.* моро́з по ко́же ~ет (*coll.*) it makes one's flesh creep, it gives one the creeps.

подка́лыва|ть, ю, *impf. of* подколо́ть.

подка́пыва|ть(ся), ю(сь), *impf. of* подкопа́ть(ся).

подкара́улива|ть, ю, *impf.* (*of* подкарау́лить) 1. to catch. 2. (*impf. only*) to be on the watch (for), lie in wait (for).

подкарау́л|ить, ю, ишь, *pf. of* подкарау́ливать.

подка́рмлива|ть, ю, *impf. of* подкорми́ть.

подка|ти́ть, чу́, ~ти́шь, *pf.* (*of* ~тывать) 1. to roll. 2. (*coll.; of a carriage, etc.*) to roll up, drive up. 3. (*coll.*) у меня́ ком ~ти́л к го́рлу I felt a lump rise in my throat.

подка|ти́ться, чу́сь, ~ти́шься, *pf.* (*of* ~тываться) (под+*a.*) to roll (under).

подка́тыва|ть(ся), ю(сь), *impf. of* подкати́ть(ся).

подкач|а́ть, а́ю, *pf.* (*of* ~ивать) (*coll.*) to make a mess (of things); to let one down.

подка́чива|ть, ю, *impf. of* подкача́ть.

подка́чк|а, и, *f.* (*phys.*) pump.

подка́шива|ть(ся), ю(сь), *impf. of* подкоси́ть(ся).

подка́шлива|ть, ю, *impf.* (*coll.*) to cough (*intentionally, to draw attention, etc.*).

подка́шлян|уть, у, ешь, *pf.* to give a cough.

подки́дыва|ть, ю, *impf. of* подки́нуть.

подки́дыш, а, *m.* foundling.

подки́|нуть, ну, нешь, *pf.* (*of* ~дывать) = подбро́сить.

подки́сл|енный, *p.p.p. of* ~и́ть *and adj.* (*chem.*) acidified, acidulous.

подкисл|и́ть, ю́, и́шь, *pf.* (*of* ~я́ть) (*chem.*) to acidify.

подкисл|я́ть, я́ю, *impf. of* ~и́ть.

подкла́дк|а, и, f. 1. lining; на шёлковой ~е silk-lined. 2. (*fig., coll.*) the inside, the secret (of); мы обнару́жили ~у э́того собы́тия we have discovered what lay behind this event.

подкладно́|й, *adj.* put under; ~е су́дно bed-pan.

подкла́д|очный, *adj. of* ~ка; п. материа́л lining (material).

подкла́дыва|ть, ю, *impf. of* подложи́ть.

подкла́сс, а, *m.* (*biol.*) sub-class.

подкле́ива|ть, ю, *impf. of* подкле́ить.

подкле́|ить, ю, ишь, *pf.* (*of* ~ивать) 1. (под+*a.*) to glue (under), paste (under). 2. to glue up, paste up.

подкле́йк|а, и, f. glueing, pasting.

подключ|а́ть(ся), а́ю(сь), *impf. of* ~и́ть(ся).

подключ|и́ть, у́, и́шь, *pf.* (*of* ~а́ть) (*coll.*) 1. (*tech.*) to link up, connect up. 2. (*fig.*) to attach; его́ ~и́ли ко второ́му ку́рсу he has been attached to the second year.

подключ|и́ться, у́сь, и́шься, *pf.* (*of* ~а́ться) (*coll.*) 1. (*tech. and fig.*) pass. of ~и́ть. 2. (*fig.*) to settle down; to get the hang of things.

подключи́чный, *adj.* (*anat.*) subclavian, sub-clavicular.

подкóв|а, ы, f. (horse-)shoe.

подк|овáть, ую́, уёшь, pf. (of ковáть and ~óвывать) 1. to shoe. 2. (в+p.; fig., coll.) to ground (in), give a grounding (in).

подкóвыва|ть, ю, impf. of подковáть.

подковы́рива|ть, ю, impf. of подковырну́ть.

подковы́рк|а, и, f. (coll.) catch; attempt to catch out.

подковы́р|ну́ть, ну́, нёшь, pf. (of ~ивать) 1. to pick (a sore, etc.). 2. (fig., coll.) to catch out.

подкóжный, adj. subcutaneous, hypodermic.

подколéнный, adj. (anat.) popliteal.

подколóдн|ый, adj. змея́ ~ая (fig., coll.) snake in the grass.

подкол|óть, ю́, ~ешь, pf. (of подкáлывать) 1. to pin up. 2. to chop up. 3. to attach, append (to a document or file).

подкоми́сси|я, и, f. sub-committee.

подкомитéт, а, m. sub-committee.

подконтрóльный, adj. under control.

подкóп, а, m. 1. undermining. 2. underground passage. 3. (fig., coll.) intrigue(s), underhand plotting.

подкопá|ть, ю, pf. (of подкáпывать) to undermine, sap.

подкопá|ться, юсь, pf. (of подкáпываться) (под+a.) 1. to undermine, sap; (of animals) to burrow (under). 2. (fig., coll.) to intrigue (against).

подкорм|и́ть, лю́, ~ишь, pf. (of подкáрмливать) 1. to feed up; to fatten (livestock). 2. (agric.) to add fertilizer to.

подкóрмк|а, и, f. 1. feeding; fattening. 2. additional fertilization.

подкóс, а, m. (tech.) strut, brace, angle brace.

подко|си́ть, шу́, ~сишь, pf. (of подкáшивать) 1. to cut down. 2. to fell, lay low (also fig.); э́то окончáтельно ~си́ло (меня́, егó, etc.) that was the last straw.

подкос|и́ться, ~ится, pf. (of подкáшиваться) to give way, fail one.

подкрáдыва|ться, юсь, impf. of подкрáсться.

подкрá|сить, шу, сишь, pf. (of ~шивать) to tint, colour; to touch up (make-up, etc.).

подкрá|ситься, шусь, сишься, pf. (of ~шиваться) to touch up one's make-up.

подкрá|сться, ду́сь, дёшься, pf. (of ~дываться) (к) to steal up (to), sneak up (to).

подкрáшива|ть(ся), ю(сь), impf. of подкрáсить(ся).

подкреп|и́ть, лю́, и́шь, pf. (of ~ля́ть) 1. to support. 2. (fig.) to support, back; to confirm, corroborate; п. пригово́р ссы́лкой на прецедéнты to support a judgement by reference to precedent. 3. to fortify, recruit (with food and/or drink); п. себя́ пéред

дорóгой to fortify oneself for a journey. 4. (mil.) to reinforce.

подкреп|и́ться, лю́сь, и́шься, pf. (of ~ля́ться) 1. to fortify oneself (with food and/or drink). 2. pass. of ~и́ть.

подкреплéни|е, я, n. 1. confirmation, corroboration. 2. sustenance. 3. (mil.) reinforcement.

подкрепля́|ть(ся), ю(сь), impf. of подкрепи́ть(ся).

подкузьм|и́ть, лю́, и́шь, pf. (coll.) to do a bad turn; to do (down).

подкулáчник, а, m. (pejor.) kulak's henchman, kulak's man.

пóдкуп, а, m. bribery; graft.

подкуп|áть, áю, impf. of ~и́ть.

подкуп|и́ть, лю́, ~ишь, pf. (of ~áть) 1. to bribe; to suborn. 2. (fig.) to win over; всех нас ~и́ла её доброта́ her kindness won all our hearts.

подлá|диться, жусь, дишься, pf. (of ~живаться) (к; coll.) 1. to adapt oneself (to), fit in (with). 2. to humour; to make up (to).

подлáжива|ться, юсь, impf. of подлáдиться.

подлáмыва|ться, ется, impf. of подломи́ться.

пóдле, prep.+g. by the side of, beside.

подлёдный, adj. under the ice.

подлеж|áть, у́, и́шь, impf. (+d.) to be liable (to), be subject (to); п. вéдению когó -н. to be within someone's competence; э́тот дом ~и́т снóсу this house is to be pulled down; п. суду́ to be indictable; «не ~и́т оглашéнию» (classification of document) 'Confidential'; не ~и́т сомнéнию it is beyond doubt, it is not open to question.

подлежáщ|ее, его, n. (gram.) subject.

подлежá|щий, pres. part. act. of ~ть and adj. (+d.) liable (to), subject (to); п. обложéнию сбóром dutiable; не п. обложéнию сбóром exempt from duty, duty-free; не п. оглашéнию confidential, private; off--the-record.

подлез|áть, áю, impf. of ~ть.

подлéз|ть, у, ешь, pf. (of ~áть) (под+a.) to crawl (under), creep (under).

подлéкар|ь, я, m. (obs.) doctor's assistant.

подлéс|ок, ка, m. undergrowth.

подлет|áть, áю, impf. of ~éть.

подле|тéть, чу́, ти́шь, pf. (of ~тáть) (к) to fly up (to); (fig.) to run up (to), rush up (to).

подлé|ть, ю, ешь, impf. (of о~) (coll.) to grow mean; to become a scoundrel.

подлéц, á, m. scoundrel, villain, rascal.

подлéчива|ть(ся), ю(сь), impf. of подлечи́ть(ся).

подлеч|и́ть, у́, ~ишь, pf. (of ~ивать) (coll.) to treat.

подлеч|и́ться, у́сь, ~ишься, pf. (of ~иваться) (*coll.*) to take medical treatment (*for a while*).

подлива́|ть, ю, *impf. of* подли́ть.

подли́вк|а, и, *f.* sauce, dressing; gravy.

подливн|о́й, *adj.* ~о́е колесо́ (*tech.*) undershot wheel.

подли́з|а, ы, *m. and f.* (*coll.*) lickspittle, toady.

подли|за́ть, жу́, ~жешь, *pf.* (*of* ~зыва́ть) to lick up.

подли|за́ться, жу́сь, ~жешься, *pf.* (*of* ~зыва́ться) (к; *coll.*) to lick someone's boots; to suck up (to).

подли́зыва|ть(ся), ю(сь), *impf. of* подлиза́ть(ся).

по́длинник, а, *m.* original (*as opp. to* copy).

по́длинно, *adv.* really; genuinely; п. хоро́ший фильм a really good film.

по́длинност|ь, и, *f.* authenticity.

по́длин|ный (~ен, ~на), *adj.* 1. genuine; authentic; original; его́ ~ные слова́ his very words, his own words; «с ~ным ве́рно» 'certified true copy'. 2. true, real; п. учёный a true scholar.

под|ли́ть, олью́, ольёшь, *past* ~ли́л, ~лила́, ~ли́ло, *pf.* (*of* ~лива́ть) (+*a. or g.* в+*a.*) to add (to); п. ма́сла в ого́нь (*fig.*) to add fuel to the fire.

по́длича|ть, ю, *impf.* to act meanly; to behave like a scoundrel, cad.

подлог, а, *m.* forgery.

подлож|и́ть, у́, ~ишь, *pf.* (*of* подкла́дывать) 1. (под+*a.*) to lay under; to line; п. ва́ту to wad. 2. (+*a. or g.*) to add; ~и́те дрова́ *or* дров put some more wood on. 3. to put furtively; п. свинью́ кому́-н. to play a dirty trick on someone.

подло́ж|ный (~ен,~на), *adj.* false, spurious; counterfeit, forged.

подлоко́тник, а, *m.* elbow-rest.

подлом|и́ться, ~ится, *pf.* (*of* подла́мываться) (под+*i.*) to break (under).

по́длост|ь, и, *f.* 1. meanness, baseness. 2. mean trick, low-down trick.

подлу́нный, *adj.* sublunar.

по́дл|ый (~, ~а́, ~о), *adj.* mean, base, ignoble.

подма́|зать, жу, жешь, *pf.* (*of* ~зывать) to grease, oil; (*fig., coll.*) to grease someone's palm.

подма́|заться, жусь, жешься, *pf.* (*of* ~зываться) 1. to touch up one's make-up. 2. (к) to curry favour (with), make up (to).

подма́зыва|ть(ся), ю(сь), *impf. of* подма́зать(ся).

подмал|ева́ть, юю, юешь, *pf.* (*of* ~ёвывать) to tint, colour; to touch up.

подмалёвыва|ть, ю, *impf. of* подмалева́ть.

подманда́тн|ый, *adj.* (*polit.*) mandated; ~ая террито́рия mandated territory.

подма́нива|ть, ю, *impf. of* подмани́ть.

подман|и́ть, ю́, ~ишь, *pf.* (*of* ~ивать) to call (to); to beckon.

подмасте́рь|е, я, *g. pl.* ~ев, *m.* apprentice.

подма́хива|ть, ю, *impf. of* подмахну́ть.

подмах|ну́ть, ну́, нёшь, *pf.* (*of* ~ивать) (*coll.*) to scribble a signature to; to sign (hastily and negligently).

подма́чива|ть, ю, *impf. of* подмочи́ть.

подме́н, а, *m.* substitution (*of something false for something real*).

подме́н|а, ы, *f.* = ~.

подме́нива|ть, ю, *impf. of* подмени́ть.

подмен|и́ть, ю́, ~ишь, *pf.* (*of* ~ивать *and* ~я́ть) (+*a. and i.*) to substitute (for) (*intentionally*); кто́-то на вечери́нке ~и́л мне шля́пу someone at the party took my hat (and left his instead).

подмен|я́ть, я́ю, *impf. of* ~и́ть.

подмерз|а́ть, а́ет, *impf. of* ~нуть.

подмёрз|нуть, нет, *past* ~, ~ла, *pf.* (*of* ~а́ть) to freeze slightly.

подме|си́ть, шу́, ~сишь, *pf.* (*of* ~шивать¹) to add, mix in.

подме|сти́, ту́, тёшь, *past* ~л, ~ла́, *pf.* (*of* ~та́ть¹) to sweep.

подмета́|ть¹, ю, *impf. of* подмести́.

подме|та́ть², чу́, ~чешь, *pf.* (*of* ~тывать) to baste, tack.

подме́|тить, чу, тишь, *pf.* (*of* ~ча́ть) to notice.

подмётк|а, и, *f.* sole; в ~и кому́-н. не годи́ться (*coll.*) not to be fit to hold a candle to someone.

подмётн|ый, *adj.* ~ое письмо́ (*obs.*) anonymous letter.

подмётыва|ть, ю, *impf. of* подмета́ть².

подмеча́|ть, ю, *impf. of* подме́тить.

подмеш|а́ть, а́ю, *pf.* (*of* ~ивать²) to stir in.

подме́шива|ть¹, ю, *impf. of* подмеси́ть.

подме́шива|ть², ю, *impf. of* подмеша́ть.

подми́гива|ть, ю, *impf. of* подмигну́ть.

подмиг|ну́ть, ну́, нёшь, *pf.* (*of* ~ивать) (+*d.*) to wink (at).

подмина́|ть, ю, *impf. of* подмя́ть.

подмо́г|а, и, *f.* (*coll.*) help, assistance; идти́ на ~у (+*d.*) to come to the aid (of), lend a hand.

подмок|а́ть, а́ю, *impf. of* ~нуть.

подмо́к|нуть, ну, нешь, *past* ~, ~ла, *pf.* (*of* ~а́ть) to get slightly wet.

подмора́жива|ть, ет, *impf. of* подморо́зить.

подморо́женный, *adj.* frost-bitten, frozen (slightly).

подморо́з|ить, ит, *pf.* (*of* подмора́живать) to freeze; к ве́черу ~ило towards evening it began to freeze.

подмоско́вн|ый, *adj.* (situated) near Moscow; *as noun* ~ая, ~ой, *f.* (*obs.*) estate near Moscow.

подмо́стк|и, ов, *no sing.* 1. scaffolding, staging. 2. (*theatr.*) stage; boards.

подмо́ч|енный, *p.p.p. of* ~и́ть *and adj.* 1. slightly wet, damp. 2. damaged (*also fig.*); ~енная репута́ция tarnished reputation.

подмоч|и́ть, у́, ~ишь, *pf.* (*of* подма́чивать) 1. to wet slightly, damp. 2. to damage by exposing to damp.

подмы́в, а, *m.* washing away, undermining.

подмыва́|ть, ю, *impf.* 1. *impf. of* подмы́ть. 2. (*impers.*) to urge; меня́ так и ~ет (+*inf.*) I feel an urge (to), I can hardly keep (from).

подм|ы́ть, о́ю, о́ешь, *pf.* (*of* ~ыва́ть) 1. to wash. 2. to wash away, undermine.

подмы́ш|ечный, *adj. of* ~ки.

подмы́шк|а, и, *f.* arm-pit (*of article of cloth-ing*).

подмы́ш|ки, ек, *no sing.* arm-pits (*see also* мы́шка²).

подмы́шник, а, *m.* dress protector.

под|мя́ть, омну́, омнёшь, *pf.* (*of* ~мина́ть) to crush; to trample down.

поднадзо́р|ный (~ен, ~на), *adj.* under sur-veillance, under supervision.

поднаж|а́ть, му́, мёшь, *pf.* (на+*a.*; *coll.*) to press, put pressure (on); to chivvy.

поднача́льный, *adj.* (*obs., now joc. only*) subordinate.

подна́чива|ть, ю, *impf. of* подна́чить.

подна́ч|ить, у, ишь, *pf.* (*of* ~ивать) (*coll.*) to egg on.

поднебе́сн|ая, ой, *f.* (*folk poet.*) the earth.

поднебе́сь|е, я, *n.* (*folk poet.*) the heavens.

поднево́л|ьный (~ен, ~ьна), *adj.* 1. depen-dent; subordinate. 2. forced; п. труд forced labour.

поднес|ти́, у́, ёшь, *past* ~, ~ла́, *pf.* (*of* под-носи́ть) 1. (к) to take (to), bring (to). 2. (+*d. and a.*) to present (with); to take (as a present); to treat (to); п. кому́-н. буке́т цвето́в to present someone with a bouquet; ~и́ ему́ рю́мку конья́ку take him, treat him to a (glass of) brandy.

подне́сь, *adv.* (*obs.*) to this day, up to now.

по́дниз|ь, и, *f.* (*obs.*) string (*of beads, etc.*).

поднима́|ть(ся), ю(сь), *impf. of* подня́ть(ся); ~й вы́ше! (*coll.*) try again!

поднов|и́ть, лю́, и́шь, *pf.* (*of* ~ля́ть) to re-new, renovate.

подновля́|ть, ю, *impf. of* поднови́ть.

подного́тн|ая, ой, *f.* (*coll.*) the whole truth, all there is to know; the ins and outs, the tricks of the trade; он зна́ет про них всю ~ую he knows all (there is to know) about them.

подно́жи|е, я, *n.* 1. foot (*of an inanimate object, mountain, etc.*). 2. pedestal.

подно́жк|а¹, и, *f.* step, footboard.

подно́жк|а², и, *f.* (*in wrestling*) backheel;

дать кому́-н. ~у to trip someone up.

подно́жн|ый, *adj.* п. корм pasture, pastur-age; быть на ~ом корму́ to be at grass; пусти́ть на п. корм to put to grass.

подно́с, а, *m.* tray; salver; ча́йный п. tea-tray.

подноси́тел|ь, я, *m.* giver, donor.

подно|си́ть, шу́, ~сишь, *impf. of* поднести́.

подно́ск|а, и, *f.* transporting, bringing up.

подно́счик, а, *m.* 1. carrier; п. патро́нов ammunition carrier. 2. innkeeper's assis-tant, drinks server.

подноше́ни|е, я, *n.* 1. presenting, giving. 2. present, gift; цвето́чные ~я floral tri-butes.

подня́ти|е, я, *n.* raising; rise; rising; п. за́навеса curtain-rise; голосова́ть ~ем рук to vote by show of hands.

под|ня́ть, ниму́, ни́мешь, *past* ~ня́л, ~няла́, ~ня́ло, *pf.* (*of* ~нима́ть) 1. (*in var. senses*) to raise; to lift; to hoist; п. ка́рту to colour a map; п. настрое́ние (+*g.*) to cheer up, raise the spirits (of); п. ору́жие to take up arms; п. паруса́ to raise sail, set sail; п. ру́ку (на+*a.*) to lift up one's hand (against); п. флаг to hoist a flag; (*naut.*) to make the colours; п. целину́ to open up virgin lands, break fresh ground; п. шерсть to bristle up; п. я́корь to weigh anchor; п. на во́здух to blow up; п. на́ смех to make a laughing-stock (of). 2. to pick up; п. пе́тли to pick up stitches. 3. to rouse, stir up; п. восста́-ние to stir up rebellion; п. ссо́ру to pick a quarrel; п. на́ ноги to rouse, get up. 4. (*fig.*) to improve; to enhance; п. де́ло (*coll.*) to cope with an affair, manage an affair successfully.

под|ня́ться, ниму́сь, ни́мешься, *past* ~ня́л-ся́, ~няла́сь, *pf.* (*of* ~нима́ться) 1. (*in var. senses*) to rise; to go up; to get up; п. на́ ноги to rise to one's feet; п. в ата́ку to go in to the attack; п. в гало́п to break into a gallop. 2. (на+*a.*) to climb, ascend, go up. 3. to arise; to break out, develop; ~няла́сь ссо́ра a quarrel arose; ~няла́сь дра́ка a fight started. 4. (*econ.; fig.*) to improve; to recover.

подо, *prep.* = под.

подоба́|ть, ет, *impf.* (*impers.; +d. and inf.*) to become, befit; как ~ет as befits one; не ~ет it does not do.

подоба́|ющий, *pres. part. act. of* ~ть *and adj.* proper, fitting.

подо́би|е, я, *n.* 1. likeness; по своему́ о́бразу и ~ю in one's own image. 2. (*math.*) simi-larity.

подо́блачный, *adj.* under the clouds.

подо́бно, *adv.* (+*d.*) like; п. верблю́ду like a camel; п. тому́, как just as.

подо́б|ный (~ен, ~на), *adj.* like; similar;

~ное поведéние such behaviour; ~ные треугóльники (*math.*) similar triangles; я никогдá не встречáл ~ного дуракá I have never met such a fool; ничегó ~ного! (*coll.*) nothing of the kind!; и томý ~ное (*abbr.* и т. п.) and so on, and such like.

подобострáсти|е, я, *n.* servility.

подобострáст|ный (~ен, ~на), *adj.* servile.

подóбранность|ь, и, *f.* neatness, tidiness.

подóбр|анный, *p.p.p.* of ~áть and *adj.* neat, tidy.

под|обрáть, берý, берёшь, *past* ~обрáл, ~обралá, ~обрáло, *pf.* (*of* ~бирáть) 1. to pick up; п. колóсья to glean. 2. to tuck up; to take up; п. вóлосы to put up one's hair. 3. to select, pick; п. десятников to pick foremen; п. ключ к замкý to fit a key to a lock; п. джéмпер под цвет костюма to choose a jumper to match a suit.

под|обрáться, берýсь, берёшься, *past* ~обрáлся, ~обралáсь, ~обрáлось, *pf.* (*of* ~бирáться) 1. (к) to steal up (to), approach stealthily. 2. to make oneself tidy. 3. *pass.* *of* ~обрáть.

подобрé|ть, ю, *pf. of* добрéть¹.

подобрý-поздорóву, *adv.* (*coll.*) in good time, while the going is good.

подóбвый, *adj.* baked in the hearth.

подóг, á, *m.* (*dial.*) stick.

под|огнáть, гоню, гóнишь, *past* ~огнáл, ~огналá, ~огнáло, *pf.* (*of* ~гонять) 1. (к) to drive (to). 2. (*coll.*) to drive on, urge on, hurry. 3. (к) to adjust (to), fit (to).

под|огнýть, огнý, огнёшь, *pf.* (*of* ~гибáть) to tuck in; to bend under.

под|огнýться, огнýсь, огнёшься, *pf.* (*of* ~гибáться) to bend; нóги, колéни у негó ~огнýлись he was bent, doubled up (*from fatigue, etc.*).

подогрéв, а, *m.* (*tech.*) heating; предвари́тельный п. pre-heating.

подогревáтел|ь, я, *m.* (*tech.*) heater.

подогревáтельный, *adj.* (*tech.*) heating.

подогревá|ть, ю, *impf. of* подогрéть.

подогрé|ть, ю, *pf.* (*of* ~вáть) to warm up, heat up; (*fig.*) to rouse.

пододвигá|ть, ю, *impf. of* пододвинуть.

пододви́|нуть, ну, нешь, *pf.* (*of* ~гáть) (к) to move up (to), push up (to).

подожд|áть, ý, ёшь, *past* ~áл, ~алá, ~áло, *pf.* (+*a. or g.*) to wait (for).

под|озвáть, зовý, зовёшь, *past* ~озвáл, ~озвалá, ~озвáло, *pf.* (*of* ~зывáть) to call up; to beckon.

подозревá|емый, *pres. part. pass. of* ~ть and *adj.* suspected; suspect.

подозревá|ть, ю, *impf.* (*no pf.*) to suspect (*someone or that something is the case*); я ~ю егó

в преступлéнии I suspect him of a crime; я ~ю, что он совершил преступлéние I suspect that he has committed a crime.

подозрéни|е, я, *n.* suspicion; остáться вне ~й to remain above suspicion; по ~ю (в+*p.*) on suspicion (of); быть под ~ем, на ~и to be under suspicion.

подозри́тельно, *adv.* suspiciously; вести́ себя п. to behave suspiciously; смотрéть п. (на+*a.*) to regard with suspicion.

подозри́тельност|ь, и, *f.* suspiciousness.

подозри́тел|ьный (~ен, ~ьна), *adj.* 1. suspicious; suspect; shady, fishy; ~ьного ви́да suspicious-looking; п. субъéкт shady character. 2. suspicious (= mistrustful).

подо́|ить, ю, ~́ишь, *pf. of* дои́ть.

подо́йник, а, *m.* milk-pail.

подо́|йти́, йдý, йдёшь, *past* ~шёл, ~шла, *pf.* (*of* подходи́ть) 1. (к) to approach (*also fig.*); to come up (to), go up (to); пóезд ~шёл к стáнции the train pulled in to the station; джунгли ~шли к сáмому поселéнию the jungle came right up to the settlement; крити́чески п. к вопрóсу to approach a question critically, adopt a critical approach to a question. 2. (+*d.*) to do (for); to suit; to fit; этот пиджáк óчень мне ~йдёт this coat will suit me very well; это слóво не ~йдёт в дáнном контéксте this word will not do in the context under consideration; вáше крéсло едвá ли ~йдёт к сти́лю кóмнаты your chair will hardly go with the room.

подокóнник, а, *m.* window-sill.

подóл, а, *m.* 1. hem (*of skirt*); держáться за чей-н. п. to cling to someone's skirts. 2. (*dial.*) lower part, lower slopes; foot (*of hill*).

подóлгу, *adv.* for long; for hours, days, weeks, months, *etc.*; мы с ним п. болтáли he and I used to chat by the hour; они́ п. к нам не заходи́ли they have not been in to see us for ages.

подоль|сти́ться, щýсь, сти́шься, *pf.* (к; *coll.*) to worm oneself into someone's favour, into someone's good graces.

подольщá|ться, юсь, *impf. of* подольсти́ться.

по-домáшнему, *adv.* simply; without ceremony; одéт п. (dressed) in clothes worn about the house.

подóнк|и, ов, *no sing.* dregs (*also fig.*); (*fig.*) scum; riff-raff.

подопéчн|ый, *adj.* under wardship; ~ая террито́рия (*polit.*) trust territory.

подоплёк|а, и, *f.* (*coll.*) the real (*as opp. to the ostensible, apparent*) state of affairs; the real cause, the underlying cause; знать ~у перемéны отношéний to know the real cause of a volte-face.

подо́пытный, *adj.* experimental; п. кро́лик (*fig.*) guinea-pig.

подорв|а́ть, у́, ёшь, *past* ~а́л, ~ала́, ~а́ло, *pf.* (*of* подрыва́ть[1]) **1.** to blow up; to blast. **2.** (*fig.*) to undermine; to sap; to damage severely; п. чей-н. авторите́т to undermine someone's authority; п. здоро́вье to sap one's health.

подо́рлик, а, *m.* (*orn.*) spotted eagle.

подорожа́|ть, ю, *pf. of* дорожа́ть.

подоро́жн|ая, ой, *f.* (*hist.*) order for (fresh) post-horses.

подоро́жник, а, *m.* **1.** (*bot.*) plantain. **2.** (*coll.*) provisions taken on a journey. **3.** (*obs.*) highwayman. **4.** лапла́ндский п. (*orn.*) Lapland bunting.

подоро́жный, *adj.* on the road, along the road; п. столб milestone.

подоси́новик, а, *m.* orange-cap boletus (*mushroom*) (*Boletus versipellis*).

подо|сла́ть, шлю́, шлёшь, *pf.* (*of* подсыла́ть) to send, dispatch (*secretly, on a secret mission*).

подосно́в|а, ы, *f.* real cause, underlying cause.

подоспева́|ть, ю, *impf. of* подоспе́ть.

подоспе́|ть, ю, *pf.* (*of* ~ва́ть) (*coll.*) to arrive, appear (*in time*).

под|остла́ть, стелю́, сте́лешь, *pf.* (*of* ~стила́ть) (под+*a.*) to lay (under), stretch (under).

подотде́л, а, *m.* section, subdivision.

подоткн|у́ть, у́, ёшь, *pf.* (*of* подтыка́ть) to tuck in, tuck up; п. простыню́ to tuck in a sheet; п. ю́бку to tuck up one's skirt.

подотря́д, а, *m.* (*biol.*) sub-order.

подотчёт|ный (~ен, ~на), *adj.* **1.** (+*d.*) accountable (to). **2.** (*fin.*) on account; ~ная су́мма sum paid out on account; imprest.

подо́хн|уть, у, ешь, *pf.* (*of* до́хнуть *and* подыха́ть) **1.** (*of animals*) to die. **2.** (*coll.*; *of human beings*) to peg out, kick the bucket.

подохо́дный, *adj.* п. нало́г income tax.

подо́шв|а, ы, *f.* **1.** sole (*of foot or boot*). **2.** foot (*of slope*). **3.** (*tech.*) base.

подо́шв|енный, *adj. of* ~а.

подпада́|ть, ю, *impf. of* подпа́сть.

подпа́ива|ть, ю, *impf. of* подпои́ть.

подпа́лин|а, ы, *f.* burnt place, scorch-mark; ло́шадь с ~ой dappled horse.

подпал|и́ть, ю́, и́шь, *pf.* (*of* ~ивать) (*coll.*) **1.** to singe, scorch. **2.** to set on fire.

подпа́рыва|ть(ся), ю(сь), *impf. of* подпоро́ть(ся).

подпа́с|ок, ка, *m.* herdsboy.

подпа́|сть, ду́, дёшь, *past* ~л, *pf.* (*of* ~да́ть) (под+*a.*) to fall (under); п. под чьё-н. влия́ние to fall under someone's influence.

подпа|ха́ть, шу́, ~шешь, *pf.* (*of* ~хивать) to plough a little.

подпа́хива|ть[1], ю, *impf. of* подпаха́ть.

подпа́хива|ть[2], ет, *impf.* (*coll.*) to stink a little.

подпева́л|а, ы, *m. and f.* (*coll.*) yes-man.

подпева́|ть, ю, *impf.* (+*d.*) to join (in singing); to take up a song; (*fig.*) to echo.

под|пере́ть, опру́, опрёшь, *past* ~пёр, ~пёрла, *pf.* (*of* ~пира́ть) to prop up.

подпи́лива|ть, ю, *impf. of* подпили́ть.

подпил|и́ть, ю́, ~ишь, *pf.* (*of* ~ивать) **1.** to saw; to file. **2.** to saw a little off; to file down.

подпи́л|ок, ка, *m.* file.

подпира́|ть, ю, *impf. of* подпере́ть.

подписа́вш|ий, его, *m.* signatory.

подписа́ни|е, я, *n.* signing.

подпи|са́ть, шу́, ~шешь, *pf.* (*of* ~сывать) **1.** to sign. **2.** to add (*to something written*); п. ещё одно́ подстро́чное примеча́ние to add another footnote. **3.** to subscribe (= *include in list of subscribers*); п. кого́-н. на журна́л to take out a magazine subscription for someone.

подпи|са́ться, шу́сь, ~шешься, *pf.* (*of* ~сываться) **1.** (под+*i.*) to sign, put one's name (to); (*fig.*) to subscribe (to). **2.** (на+*a.*) to subscribe (to, for); п. на журна́л to subscribe to, take out a subscription for a magazine.

подпи́ск|а, и, *f.* **1.** subscription. **2.** engagement; written undertaking; signed statement; дать ~у о невы́езде to give a written undertaking not to leave a place.

подписн|о́й, *adj.* subscription; п. лист subscription list; ~а́я цена́ the price of subscription.

подпи́счик, а, *m.* (на+*a.*) subscriber (to).

по́дпис|ь, и, *f.* **1.** signature; поста́вить свою́ п. (под+*i.*) to put one's signature (to, beneath), affix one's signature (to); за ~ью (+*g.*) signed (by); за ~ью и печа́тью signed and sealed. **2.** caption; inscription.

подплыва́|ть, ю, *impf. of* подплы́ть.

подплы|ть, ву́, вёшь, *past* ~л, ~ла́, ~ло, *pf.* (*of* ~ва́ть) (к) to swim up (to); to sail up (to).

подпо|и́ть, ю́, ~и́шь, *pf.* (*of* подпа́ивать) (*coll.*) to make tipsy.

по́дпол, а, *m.* (*dial.*) cellar.

подполз|а́ть, а́ю, *impf. of* ~ти́.

подполз|ти́, у́, ёшь, *past* ~, ~ла́, *pf.* (*of* ~а́ть) (к) to creep up (to); (под+*a.*) to creep (under).

подполко́вник, а, *m.* lieutenant-colonel.

подпо́ль|е, я, *n.* **1.** cellar. **2.** (*fig.*) underground work; (the) underground (organization); уйти́ в п. to go underground.

подпо́льный, *adj.* **1.** under the floor. **2.** (*fig.*) underground; secret, clandestine.

подпо́льщик, а, *m.* member of an underground organization.

подпо́р, а, *m.* (*tech.*) head (*of water*).

подпо́р|а, ы, *f.* prop, support; brace, strut.

подпо́рк|а, и, *f.* = подпо́ра.

подпо́р|ный, *adj. of* ~а; ~ная сте́нка breast--wall; (*naut.*) bulkhead.

подпор|о́ть, ю́, ~ешь, *pf.* (*of* подпа́рывать) to rip; to unpick, unstitch.

подпор|о́ться, ~ется, *pf.* (*of* подпа́рывать-ся) to rip; to come unpicked, come unstitched.

подпору́чик, а, *m.* (*hist.*) second lieutenant.

подпо́чв|а, ы, *f.* subsoil, substratum.

подпо́чвенн|ый, *adj.* subsoil; subterranean; ~ая вода́ underground water; п. слой pan.

подпоя|са́ть, шу, шешь, *pf.* (*of* ~сывать) to belt; to gird (on).

подпоя|са́ться, шу́сь, шешься, *pf.* (*of* ~сываться) to belt oneself; to gird oneself; to put on a belt, girdle.

подпоя́сыва|ть(ся), ю(сь), *impf. of* подпоя́сать(ся).

подпра́в|ить, лю, ишь, *pf.* (*of* ~ля́ть) to rectify; to touch up, retouch.

подправля́|ть, ю, *impf. of* подпра́вить.

подпру́г|а, и, *f.* saddle-girth, belly-band.

подпры́гива|ть, ю, *impf. of* подпры́гнуть.

подпры́г|нуть, ну, нешь, *pf.* (*of* ~ивать) to leap up, jump up; to bob up and down.

подпуска́|ть, ю, *impf. of* подпусти́ть.

подпу|сти́ть, щу́, ~стишь, *pf.* (*of* ~ска́ть) **1.** to allow to approach; п. на расстоя́ние вы́стрела to allow to come within range. **2.** (+*a. or g.*; *coll.*) to add in. **3.** (*coll.*) to get in, put in (*a sarcasm, a witticism, etc.*).

подпя́тник, а, *m.* (*tech.*) step bearing.

подраба́тыва|ть, ю, *impf. of* подрабо́тать.

подрабо́та|ть, ю, *pf.* (*of* подраба́тывать) (*coll.*) **1.** (+*a. or g.*) to earn additionally. **2.** to work up.

подра́внива|ть, ю, *impf. of* подровня́ть.

подра́гива|ть, ю, *impf.* (*coll.*) to shake, tremble intermittently.

подража́ни|е, я, *n.* imitation.

подража́тел|ь, я, *m.* imitator.

подража́тел|ьный (~ен, ~ьна), *adj.* imitative.

подража́тельств|о, а, *n.* (*pejor.*) imitativeness.

подража́|ть, ю, *impf.* (*no pf.*) (+*d.*) to imitate.

подразде́л, а, *m.* subsection.

подразделе́ни|е, я, *n.* **1.** subdivision. **2.** (*mil.*) sub-unit, element.

подраздел|и́ть, ю́, и́шь, *pf.* (*of* ~я́ть) to subdivide.

подраздел|я́ть, я́ю, *impf. of* ~и́ть.

подразумева́|ть, ю, *impf.* to imply, entail, mean.

подразумева́|ться, ется, *impf.* to be implied, be entailed, be meant; что ~ется

под э́тим выраже́нием? what is meant by this expression?; (само́ собо́й) ~ется it is understood, it goes without saying.

подра́мник, а, *m.* stretcher (*frame for canvas*).

подра́м|ок, ка, *m.* = ~ник.

подра́н|ок, ка, *m.* (*hunting*) wounded game; winged bird.

подраст|а́ть, а́ю, *impf. of* ~и́; ~а́ющее поколе́ние the rising generation.

подраст|и́, у́, ёшь, *past* подро́с, подросла́, *pf.* to grow (a little).

подра|сти́ть, щу́, сти́шь, *pf.* (*of* ~щивать) to grow; to breed; п. цыпля́т to keep chickens.

по|дра́ться, деру́сь, дерёшься, *past* ~дра́л-ся, ~драла́сь, ~драло́сь, *pf.* (с+*i.*) to come to blows (with).

подра́щива|ть, ю, *impf. of* подрасти́ть.

подрёберный, *adj.* (*anat.*) sub-costal.

подре́|зать, жу, жешь, *pf.* (*of* ~за́ть) **1.** to cut; to clip, trim; to prune, lop; п. коло́ду (*cards*; *sl.*) to cut the pack; п. кому́-н. кры́лья (*fig.*) to clip someone's wings. **2.** (+*g.*) to cut off in addition; п. хле́ба to cut some more bread.

подреза́|ть, ю, *impf. of* подре́зать.

подрем|а́ть, лю́, ~лешь, *pf.* to have a nap; to doze.

подрешётник, а, *m.* counter-lathing.

подрис|ова́ть, у́ю, *pf.* (*of* ~о́вывать) **1.** to retouch, touch up. **2.** to add, put in (*on a painting, photograph, etc.*).

подрисо́выва|ть, ю, *impf. of* подрисова́ть.

подро́бно, *adv.* minutely, in detail; at (great) length.

подро́бност|ь, и, *f.* **1.** detail; вдава́ться в ~и to go into detail; рассказа́ть, не вдава́ясь в ~и to relate without going into detail; во всех ~ях in every detail; до мельча́йших ~ей to the minutest detail. **2.** minuteness.

подро́б|ный (~ен, ~на), *adj.* detailed, minute.

подровня́|ть, ю, *pf.* (*of* подра́внивать) to level, even; to trim.

подро́ст|ок, ка, *m.* juvenile; teenager; youth; young girl.

подруб|а́ть, а́ю, *impf. of* ~и́ть.

подруб|и́ть[1], лю́, ~ишь, *pf.* (*of* ~а́ть) to hew.

подруб|и́ть[2], лю́, ~ишь, *pf.* (*of* ~а́ть) to hem.

подру́г|а, и, *f.* (*female*) friend; п. по шко́ле school-friend; п. жи́зни helpmate (*sc.* one's wife).

по-дру́жески, *adv.* in a friendly way; as a friend.

подруж|и́ться, у́сь, и́шься, *pf. of* дружи́ться.

подру́жк|а, и, *f. affect. dim. of* подру́га.

подру́лива|ть, ю, *impf. of* подрули́ть.

подрул|и́ть, ю́, и́шь, *pf.* (*of* ~ивать) (к; *aeron.*) to taxi up (to).

подрумя́нива|ть(ся), ю(сь), *impf. of* подрумя́нить(ся).

подрумя́н|ить, ю, ишь, *pf.* (*of* ~ивать) 1. to rouge; to touch up with rouge. 2. to make ruddy, make rosy; моро́з ~ил им щёки the frost brought a flush to their cheeks. 3. (*cul.*) to brown.

подрумя́н|иться, юсь, ишься, *pf.* (*of* ~иваться) 1. to apply rouge, use rouge. 2. to become ruddy, become rosy; to flush, become flushed. 3. (*cul.*) to brown.

подру́чн|ый, *adj.* 1. at hand, to hand; improvised, makeshift; ~ые сре́дства improvised means. 2. *as noun* п., ~ого, *m.* assistant, mate; п. водопрово́дчика plumber's mate.

подры́в, а, *m.* undermining; (*fig.*) injury, detriment; п. самолю́бия a blow to one's pride; п. здоро́вья sapping of health; п. торго́вли injury to trade.

подрыва́|ть[1], ю, *impf. of* подорва́ть.

подрыва́|ть[2], ю, *impf. of* подры́ть.

подрывни́к, а́, *m.* (*mil.*) member of demolition squad.

подрывн|о́й, *adj.* blasting, demolition; (*fig.*) undermining, subversive; ~а́я рабо́та blasting, demolition work; ~а́я де́ятельность subversive activities.

подр|ы́ть, о́ю, о́ешь, *pf.* (*of* ~ыва́ть[2]) to undermine, sap.

подря́д[1], *adv.* in succession; running; on end; три го́да п. three years running; не́сколько дней п. шёл дождь it rained for days on end.

подря́д[2], а, *m.* contract; по ~у by contract; взять п. на постро́йку плоти́ны to contract for the building of a dam; сдать п. (на+а.), сдать с ~а to put out to contract.

подря|ди́ть, жу́, ди́шь, *pf.* (*of* ~жа́ть) (*coll.*) to hire.

подря|ди́ться, жу́сь, ди́шься, *pf.* (*of* ~жа́ться) (*coll.*) 1. to contract, undertake. 2. *pass. of* ~ди́ть.

подря́д|ный, *adj. of* ~[2]; ~ная рабо́та work done by contract.

подря́дчик, а, *m.* contractor.

подряжа́|ть(ся), ю(сь), *impf. of* подряди́ть(ся).

подря́сник, а, *m.* cassock.

подса́д, а, *m.* (*forestry*) plantation.

подса|ди́ть[1], жу́, ~ди́шь, *pf.* (*of* ~жива́ть) 1. to help (to) sit down; п. кого́-н. на ло́шадь to help someone mount a horse. 2. (к) to place next (to); меня́ ~ди́ли к глухо́й да́ме I was placed next to a deaf lady. 3. to fit in (*extra people in a compartment, etc.*).

подса|ди́ть[2], жу́, ~ди́шь, *pf.* (*of* ~жива́ть) (+*a. or g.*) to plant some more.

подсадн|о́й, *adj.* ~а́я у́тка decoy duck.

подса́жива|ть, ю, *impf. of* подсади́ть.

подса́жива|ться, юсь, *impf. of* подсе́сть.

подса́лива|ть, ю, *impf. of* подсоли́ть.

подса́чива|ть, ю, *impf. of* подсочи́ть.

подсве́чник, а, *m.* candlestick.

подсви́стыва|ть, ю, *impf.* (+*d.*) to whistle as accompaniment to.

подсева́|ть, ю, *impf. of* подсе́ять.

подсе́д, а, *m.* (*disease of horses*) malanders, mallenders.

подседе́льник, а, *m.* girth, belly-band.

подсе́к|а, и, *f.* (*hist., agric.*) slash-burn clearing.

подсека́|ть, ю, *impf. of* подсе́чь.

подсе́кци|я, и, *f.* sub-section.

под|се́сть, ся́ду, ся́дешь, *past* ~се́л, *pf.* (*of* ~са́живаться) (к) to sit down (near, next to), take a seat (near, next to).

подсе́|чь, ку́, чёшь, ку́т, *past* ~к, ~кла́, *pf.* (*of* ~ка́ть) 1. to hew; to hack (down). 2. hook, strike (*a fish*).

подсе́|ять, ю, ешь, *pf.* (*of* ~ва́ть) (+*a. or g.*) to sow (*in addition*).

подси|де́ть, жу́, ди́шь, *pf.* (*of* ~живать) lie in wait (for). 2. (*fig., coll.*) to scheme, intrigue (against).

подси́живани|е, я, *n.* (*coll.*) scheming, intriguing.

подси́жива|ть, ю, *impf. of* подсиде́ть.

подси́нива|ть, ю, *impf. of* подсини́ть.

подсин|и́ть, ю́, и́шь, *pf.* (*of* ~ивать) to blue, apply blueing to.

подска́блива|ть, ю, *impf. of* подскобли́ть.

подска|за́ть, жу́, ~жешь, *pf.* (*of* ~зывать) (+*d.*) to prompt (*also fig.*); to suggest.

подска́зк|а, и, *f.* prompting.

подска́зчик, а, *m.* prompter (*in verbal sense; in theatre* = суфлёр).

подска́зыва|ть, ю, *impf. of* подсказа́ть.

подска|ка́ть, чу́, ~чешь, *pf.* (*of* ~кивать[1]) (к) to come galloping up (to).

подска́кива|ть[1], ю, *impf. of* подскака́ть.

подска́кива|ть[2], ю, *impf. of* подскочи́ть.

подскобл|и́ть, ю́, ~и́шь, *pf.* (*of* подска́бливать) to scrape off.

подскоч|и́ть, у́, ~ишь, *pf.* (*of* подска́кивать[2]) 1. (к) to run up (to), come running (to). 2. to jump up, leap up; п. от ра́дости to jump with joy; це́ны ~и́ли prices soared.

подскреба́|ть, ю, *impf. of* подскрести́.

подскре|сти́, бу́, бёшь, *past* ~б, ~бла́, *pf.* (*of* ~ба́ть) to scrape; to scrape clean.

подсла|сти́ть, щу́, сти́шь, *pf.* (*of* ~щивать) to sweeten, sugar.

подсла́щива|ть, ю, *impf. of* подсласти́ть.

подсле́дственный, *adj.* (*leg.*) under investigation.

подслепова́т|ый (~, ~а), *adj.* weak-sighted.

подслу́жива|ться, юсь, *impf. of* подслужи́ться.

подслуж|и́ться, у́сь, ~ишься, *pf. (of ~и-ваться)* (к; *coll.*) to fawn (upon), cringe (before); to worm oneself into the favour (of).

подслу́ш|ать, аю, *pf. (of ~ивать)* to overhear.

подслу́шива|ть, ю, *impf.* 1. *impf. of* подслу́шать. 2. *impf. only* to eavesdrop.

подсма́трива|ть, ю, *impf. of* подсмотре́ть.

подсме́ива|ться, юсь, *impf.* (над) to laugh (at), make fun (of).

подсме́н|а, ы, f. next shift; relief.

подсмотр|е́ть, ю́, ~ишь, *pf. (of* подсма́тривать) to spy.

подсне́жник, а, m. (*bot.*) snowdrop.

подсне́жный, *adj.* under the snow.

подсо́бн|ый, *adj.* subsidiary, supplementary; secondary; auxiliary; accessory; ~ое предприя́тие subsidiary enterprise; п. проду́кт by-product.

подсо́выва|ть, ю, *impf. of* подсу́нуть.

подсозна́ни|е, я, n. the subconscious.

подсозна́тел|ьный (~ен, ~ьна), *adj.* subconscious.

подсол|и́ть, ю́, ~и́шь, *pf. (of* подса́ливать) to add more salt (to), put more salt (into).

подсо́лнечник, а, m. sunflower.

подсо́лнечн|ый[1], *adj. of* ~ик; ~ое ма́сло sunflower oil.

подсо́лнечн|ый[2], *adj.* in the sun; ~ая сторона́ the sunny side; *as noun* ~ая, ~ой, *f.* (*obs.*) the universe.

подсо́лнух, а, m. (*coll.*) 1. sunflower. 2. sunflower-seeds.

подсо́х|нуть, ну, нешь, *pf. (of* подсыха́ть) to get dry, dry out a little.

подсоч|и́ть, у́, и́шь, *pf. (of* подса́чивать) to tap (*trees, for resin or sap*).

подсо́чк|а, и, f. tapping.

подспо́рь|е, я, n. (*coll.*) help, support; служи́ть больши́м ~ем to be a great help.

подспу́дн|ый, *adj.* latent; unused; secret, hidden; ~ые си́лы latent strength; ~ые мы́сли secret thoughts.

подста́в|а, ы, f. (*obs.*) relay (*of horses*).

подста́в|ить, лю, ишь, *pf. (of* ~ля́ть) 1. (под+а.) to put (under), place (under); п. го́лову под струю́ воды́ из кра́на to put one's head under a tap; п. но́жку кому́-н. to trip someone up (*also fig.*). 2. (+d.) to bring up (to), put up (to); to hold up (to); п. кому́-н. стул to offer someone a seat. 3. (*fig.*) to expose, lay bare; п. ферзя́ под уда́р (*chess*) to expose one's queen. 4. (*math.*) to substitute.

подста́вк|а, и, f. stand; support, rest, prop.

подставн|о́й, *adj.* false; substitute; ~о́е

лицо́ dummy, figure-head, man of straw; ~ы́е свиде́тели suborned witnesses.

подстака́нник, а, m. glass-holder (*for use in drinking Russian tea*).

подстано́вк|а, и, f. (*math.*) substitution.

подста́нци|я, и, f. sub-station.

подстёгива|ть, ю, *impf. of* подстегну́ть.

подстег|ну́ть[1], ну́, нёшь, *pf. (of ~ивать)* to fasten underneath.

подстег|ну́ть[2], ну́, нёшь, *pf. (of ~ивать)* to whip up, urge forward, urge on (*also fig.*).

подстерега́|ть, ю, *impf. of* подстере́чь.

подстере́|чь, гу́, жёшь, гу́т, *past ~́г, ~гла́*, *pf. (of ~га́ть)* to be on the watch (for), lie in wait (for); п. моме́нт to seize an opportunity.

подстила́|ть, ю, *impf. of* подостла́ть.

подсти́лк|а, и, f. bedding; litter.

подстора́жива|ть, ю, *impf. (of* подсторожи́ть) to be on the watch for.

подсторож|и́ть, у́, и́шь, *pf. of* подстора́живать.

подстра́ива|ть, ю, *impf. of* подстро́ить.

подстрека́тел|ь, я, m. instigator; firebrand.

подстрека́тельств|о, а, n. instigation, incitement, setting-on.

подстрек|а́ть, а́ю, *impf. of* ~ну́ть.

подстрек|ну́ть, ну́, нёшь, *pf. (of ~а́ть)* 1. (к) instigate (to), incite (to), set on (to). 2. to excite; п. любопы́тство to excite one's curiosity.

подстре́лива|ть, ю, *impf. of* подстрели́ть.

подстрел|и́ть, ю́, ~ишь, *pf. (of ~ивать)* to wound (*by a shot*); to wing.

подстрига́|ть(ся), ю(сь), *impf. of* подстри́чь(ся).

подстри́|женный, p.p.p. of ~чь; ко́ротко ~женные во́лосы (closely) cropped hair.

подстри́|чь, гу́, жёшь, гу́т, *past ~г, ~гла*, *pf. (of ~га́ть)* to cut; to clip, trim; to prune; п. бо́роду to trim one's beard; п. но́гти to cut one's nails.

подстри́|чься, гу́сь, жёшься, гу́тся, *past ~гся, ~глась*, *pf. (of ~га́ться)* to trim one's hair; to have a hair-trim.

подстро́|ить, ю, ишь, *pf. (of* подстра́ивать) 1. (к) to build on (to); п. фли́гель к до́му to build on a wing to a house. 2. to tune (up). 3. (*fig., coll.*) to contrive; (*pejor.*) to arrange; п. шу́тку (+d.) to play a trick (on); э́то де́ло ~ено it's a put-up job.

подстро́чник, а, m. word for word translation.

подстро́чн|ый, *adj.* п. перево́д word for word translation; ~ое примеча́ние footnote.

по́дступ, а, m. (*geogr.; fig.*) approach; да́льние ~ы к го́роду the distant approaches to the city; к нему́ и ~а нет he is quite inaccessible.

подступ|а́ть(ся), а́ю(сь), *impf. of* ~и́ть(ся).

подступ|и́ть, лю́, ~ишь, *pf.* (*of* ~а́ть) (к) to approach, come up (to), come near; слёзы ~и́ли к её глаза́м tears came to her eyes.

подступ|и́ться, лю́сь, ~ишься, *pf.* (*of* ~а́ться) (к) to approach; к нему́ не ~ишься he is quite inaccessible; к э́тому мне не п. it is quite beyond my means.

подсуди́м|ый, ого, *m.* (*leg.*) defendant; the accused; prisoner at the bar; скамья́ ~ых the dock, the bar.

подсу́дност|ь, и, *f.* jurisdiction; cognizance.

подсу́д|ный (~ен, ~на), *adj.* (+*d.*) under, within the jurisdiction (of); within the competence (of); cognizable (to).

подсу́м|ок, ка, *m.* (*mil.*) cartridge pouch.

подсу́н|уть, у, ешь, *pf.* (*of* подсо́вывать) 1. (под+*a.*) to shove (under). 2. (+*d. and a.*; *coll.*) to slip (into); to palm off (on, upon); они́ мне ~ули не ту кни́гу they palmed off the wrong book on me.

подсу́шива|ть, ю, *impf. of* подсуши́ть.

подсуш|и́ть, у́, ~ишь, *pf.* (*of* ~ивать) to dry a little.

подсчёт, а, *m.* calculation; count.

подсчит|а́ть, а́ю, *pf.* (*of* ~ывать) to count up, reckon up; to calculate.

подсчи́тыва|ть, ю, *impf. of* подсчита́ть.

подсыла́|ть, ю, *impf. of* подосла́ть.

подсып|а́ть, лю, лешь, *pf.* (*of* ~а́ть) (+*a. or g.*) to add, pour in.

подсыха́|ть, ю, *impf. of* подсо́хнуть.

подта́ива|ть, ет, *impf. of* подта́ять.

подта́лкива|ть, ю, *impf. of* подтолкну́ть.

подта́плива|ть, ю, *impf. of* подтопи́ть.

подта́скива|ть, ю, *impf. of* подтащи́ть.

подтас|ова́ть, у́ю, *pf.* (*of* ~о́вывать) to shuffle unfairly; (*fig.*) to garble, juggle (with); п. фа́кты to juggle with facts.

подтасо́вк|а, и, *f.* unfair shuffling; (*fig.*) garbling, juggling.

подтасо́выва|ть, ю, *impf. of* подтасова́ть.

подта́чива|ть, ю, *impf. of* подточи́ть.

подтащ|и́ть, у́, ~ишь, *pf.* (*of* подта́скивать) (к) to drag up (to).

подта́|ять, ет, *pf.* (*of* ~ивать) to thaw a little, melt a little.

подтверди́тельн|ый, *adj.* confirmatory; посла́ть ~ое письмо́ to send a letter to confirm.

подтвер|ди́ть, жу́, ди́шь, *pf.* (*of* ~жда́ть) to confirm; to corroborate, bear out; п. получе́ние чего́-н. to acknowledge receipt of something.

подтвержда́|ть, ю, *impf. of* подтверди́ть.

подтвержде́ни|е, я, *n.* confirmation; corroboration.

подтёк, а, *m.* bruise.

подтека́|ть, ет, *impf.* 1. *impf. of* подте́чь. 2. (*impf. only*) to leak; to be leaking.

подте́кст, а, *m.* concealed meaning; угада́ть п. to read between the lines.

подтексто́вк|а, и, *f.* 1. words (*of song or other vocal music*). 2. composition of words (*for vocal music*).

под|тере́ть, отру́, отрёшь, *past* ~тёр, ~тёрла, *pf.* (*of* ~тира́ть) to wipe (up).

подте́|чь, чёт, ку́т, *past* ~к, ~кла́, *pf.* (*of* ~ка́ть) (под+*a.*) to flow (under), run (under).

подтира́|ть, ю, *impf. of* подтере́ть.

подтолкн|у́ть, у́, ёшь, *pf.* (*of* подта́лкивать) 1. to push slightly; п. ло́ктем to nudge. 2. (*fig.*) to urge on.

подтоп|и́ть, лю́, ~ишь, *pf.* (*of* подта́пливать) (*coll.*) to heat a little.

подточ|и́ть, у́, ~ишь, *pf.* (*of* подта́чивать) 1. to sharpen slightly, give an edge (to). 2. to eat away, gnaw; to undermine (*also fig.*); тюре́мное заключе́ние ~и́ло его́ здоро́вье imprisonment has undermined his health.

подтру́нива|ть, ю, *impf. of* подтруни́ть.

подтрун|и́ть, ю́, и́шь, *pf.* (*of* ~ивать) (над) to chaff, tease.

подтуш|ева́ть, у́ю, *pf.* (*of* ~ёвывать) to shade slightly.

подтушёвыва|ть, ю, *impf. of* подтушева́ть.

подтыка́|ть, ю, *impf. of* подоткну́ть.

подтя́гива|ть(ся), ю(сь), *impf. of* подтяну́ть(ся).

подтя́ж|ки, ек, *no sing.* braces, suspenders.

подтя́нутост|ь, и, *f.* smartness.

подтя́н|утый, *p.p.p. of* ~у́ть *and adj.* smart.

подтя|ну́ть, ну́, ~нешь, *pf.* (*of* ~гивать) 1. to tighten. 2. (к) to pull up (to), haul up (to); п. ло́дку к бе́регу to haul up a boat on shore. 3. (*mil.*) to bring up, move up. 4. (*fig., coll.*) to take in hand, pull up, chase up.

подтя|ну́ться, ну́сь, ~нешься, *pf.* (*of* ~гиваться) 1. to gird oneself more tightly; п. по́ясом to tighten one's belt. 2. to pull oneself up (*on gymnastic apparatus, etc.*). 3. (*mil.*) to move up, move in. 4. (*fig., coll.*) to pull oneself together, take oneself in hand.

поду́ма|ть, ю, *pf.* 1. *pf. of* ду́мать; п. (то́лько), ~й(те) (то́лько)! just think!; ~ешь (*as iron. interj.; coll.*) I say!; what do you know?; ~ешь, кака́я блестя́щая мысль! I say, what a brain-wave!; и не ~ю! I wouldn't think of it!, I wouldn't dream of it!; мо́жно п. one might think. 2. to think a little, for a while.

поду́мыва|ть, ю, *impf.* (о+*p. or* +*inf.; coll.*) to think (of, about); п. об отъе́зде, п. уе́хать to think of leaving.

по-дура́цки, *adv.* (*coll.*) foolishly, like a fool.

подура́ч|иться, усь, ишься, *pf.* (*coll.*) to fool about, play the fool.

подурне́|ть, ю, *pf. of* дурне́ть.

подуськ|ать, аю, *pf. (of* ~ивать) (*coll.*) to set on; (*fig.*) to egg on; п. соба́ку на кого́-н. to set a dog on someone.

поду́ськива|ть, ю, *impf. of* поду́ськать.

поду́|ть, ю, ешь, *pf.* 1. *pf. of* дуть 1. 2. to begin to blow.

поду́чива|ть(ся), ю(сь), *impf. of* подучи́ть-(ся).

подуч|и́ть, у́, ~ишь, *pf. (of* ~ивать) 1. (+*a. and d.*) to teach, instruct (in); п. кого́-н. стрельбе́ to give someone a few lessons in shooting. 2. to learn. 3. (*inf.; coll.*) to prompt (to), egg on (to), put up (to).

подуч|и́ться, у́сь, ~ишься, *pf.* to learn (a little more, a little better).

поду́шечк|а, и, *f.* 1. *dim. of* поду́шка; п. для була́вок pincushion. 2. sweet, bon--bon.

подуш|и́ть, у́, ~ишь, *pf.* to spray with perfume.

подуш|и́ться, у́сь, ~ишься, *pf.* to spray oneself with perfume, put some perfume on.

поду́шк|а, и, *f.* 1. pillow; cushion; п. для штемпеле́й ink-pad. 2. (*tech.*) cushion; bolster.

поду́шн|ый, *adj.* ~ая по́дать (*hist.*) poll-tax, capitation.

подфа́рник, а, *m.* (*tech.*) fender lamp, side--light.

подхали́м, а, *m.* toady, lickspittle.

подхалима́ж, а, *m.* (*coll.*) toadying, boot-licking, grovelling.

подхали́мнича|ть, ю, *impf.* (*coll.*) to toady.

подхали́мств|о, а, *n.* = подхалима́ж.

подхва|ти́ть, чу́, ~тишь, *pf. (of* ~тывать) (*in var. senses*) to catch (up); to pick up; to take up; п. су́мку to catch up one's bag; п. мяч to catch a ball; п. на́сморк to catch, pick up a cold; п. пе́сню to catch up a melody, join in a song.

подхва́тыва|ть, ю, *impf. of* подхвати́ть.

подхлест|ну́ть, ну́, нёшь, *pf. (of* ~ывать) to whip up (*also fig., coll.*).

подхлёстыва|ть, ю, *impf. of* подхлестну́ть.

подхо́д, а, *m.* (*in var. senses*) approach; у него́ непра́вильный п. к де́лу he has the wrong approach to the matter.

подхо́д|ец, ца, *m.* (*coll.*) approach; говори́ть с ~цем to make reservations, speak in a roundabout way.

подхо|ди́ть, жу́, ~дишь, *impf. of* подойти́.

подходя́щий, *pres. part. of* ~и́ть *and adj.* suitable, proper, appropriate; п. моме́нт the right moment.

подцеп|и́ть, лю́, ~ишь, *pf. (of* ~ля́ть) to hook on, couple on; (*fig., joc.*) to pick up; п. ваго́н-рестора́н к по́езду to attach a restaurant car to a train; п. на́сморк to pick up a cold.

подцепля́|ть, ю, *impf. of* подцепи́ть.

подча́с, *adv.* sometimes, at times.

подча́с|ок, ка, *m.* relief sentry.

подчелюстно́й, *adj.* (*anat.*) sub-maxillary.

подчёркива|ть, ю, *impf. of* подчеркну́ть.

подчерк|ну́ть, ну́, нёшь, *pf. (of* ~ивать) 1. to underline; to score under. 2. (*fig.*) to emphasize, stress, accentuate.

подчине́ни|е, я, *n.* 1. subordination; submission, subjection; быть в ~и (у) to be subordinate (to). 2. (*gram.*) subordination.

подчинённост|ь, и, *f.* subordination.

подчинённый 1. *p.p.p. of* ~и́ть; (+*d.*) under, under the command (of). 2. *adj.* subordinate; ~ённое госуда́рство tributary state; *as noun* п., ~ённого, *m.* subordinate.

подчини́тельный, *adj.* (*gram.*)subordinative.

подчин|и́ть, ю́, и́шь, *pf. (of* ~я́ть) (+*d.*) to subordinate (to), subject (to); to place (under), place under the command (of); п. свое́й во́ле to bend to one's will.

подчин|и́ться, ю́сь, и́шься, *pf. (of* ~я́ться) (+*d.*) to submit (to); п. прика́зу to obey an order.

подчин|я́ть(ся), я́ю(сь), *impf. of* ~и́ть(ся).

подчи́|стить, щу, стишь, *pf. (of* ~ща́ть) to rub out, erase.

подчи́стк|а, и, *f.* rubbing out, erasure.

подчисту́ю, *adv.* (*coll.*) completely, without remainder; мы съе́ли всё п. we left our plates clean.

подчи́тчик|а, *m.* (*typ.*) copy-holder.

подчища́|ть, ю, *impf. of* подчи́стить.

подше́фник, а, *m.* dependent (*person or institution*).

подше́фный, *adj.* aided, assisted; (+*d.*) under the patronage (of), sponsored by, supported (by).

подшиба́|ть, а́ю, *impf. of* ~и́ть.

подшиб|и́ть, у́, ёшь, *past* ~, ~ла, *pf.* (*o,* ~а́ть) to knock; п. кому́-н. глаз to give someone a black eye.

подши́б|ленный, *p.p.p. of* ~и́ть; п. глаз black eye.

подшива́|ть, ю, *impf. of* подши́ть.

подши́вк|а, и, *f.* 1. hemming; lining; soling. 2. hem. 3. filing (*of papers*); п. газе́ты newspaper file.

подши́пник, а, *m.* (*tech.*) bearing; bush; обыкнове́нный п. journal bearing; ро́ликовый п. roller bearing; ша́риковый п. ball bearing.

подши́пник|овый, *adj. of* ~; п. сплав babbit; п. щит bearing housing.

под|ши́ть, ошью́, ошьёшь, *pf. (of* ~шива́ть) 1. to sew underneath; to hem; to line; to sole. 2. to file (*papers*).

подшле́мник, а, *m.* cap comforter.

подшта́нник|и, ов, *no sing.* (*coll.*) drawers.

подштóп|ать, аю, *pf.* (*of* ~ывать) to darn.

подштóпыва|ть, ю, *impf. of* подштóпать.

подшу|ти́ть, чу́, ~тишь, *pf.* (*of* ~чивать) (над) to chaff, mock (at); to play a trick (on).

подшу́чива|ть, ю, *impf. of* подшути́ть.

подъеда́|ть, ю, *impf. of* подъéсть.

подъéзд, а, *m.* 1. porch, entrance, doorway. 2. approach(es).

подъéзд|нóй, *adj. of* ~ 2; ~на́я алле́я drive; ~на́я доро́га access road; п. путь spur track.

подъéзд|ный, *adj. of* ~ 1.

подъезжа́|ть, ю, *impf. of* подъéхать.

подъём, а, *m.* 1. lifting; raising; п. фла́га hoisting of colours; п. затону́вшего су́дна salvaging of a sunken vessel; п. паро́в ploughing up. 2. ascent. 3. (*aeron.*) climb. 4. rise, upgrade slope. 5. (*fig.*) raising, development; rise; промы́шленный п. boom, upsurge; круто́й п. произво́дства a sharp rise in production; на ~е on the up and up, on the upgrade. 6. (*fig.*) élan; enthusiasm, animation; говори́ть с больши́м ~ом to speak with great animation; лёгок на п. quick on one's toes, quick off the mark; тяжёл на п. sluggish, slow to start. 7. instep. 8. rising time; (*mil.*) reveille. 9. (*tech.*) lever, hand screw, jack.

подъёмник, а, *m.* lift, elevator, hoist.

подъёмн|ый, *adj.* 1. lifting; п. кран crane, jenny, derrick; ~ая маши́на lift; п. механи́зм, ~ое устро́йство lifting device, hoist. 2. п. мост drawbridge, bascule bridge. 3. ~ые (де́ньги) travelling expenses (*when moving house*).

подъ|éсть, éм, éшь, éст, еди́м, еди́те, едя́т, *past* ~éл, *pf.* (*of* ~еда́ть) (*coll.*) 1. to eat up, finish off. 2. to eat through, eat into.

подъé|хать, ду, дешь, *pf.* (*of* ~зжа́ть) (к) 1. to drive up (to), draw up (to). 2. (*coll.*) to call (on). 3. (*fig., coll.*) to get round.

подъязы́чный, *adj.* (*anat.*) sub-lingual.

подъярёмн|ый, *adj.* yoked; ~ое живо́тное beast of burden; ~ая жизнь (*fig.*) a life under the yoke, enslavement.

подыгр|а́ть, а́ю, *pf.* (*of* ~ывать) (+*d.*; *coll.*) 1. (*mus.*) to accompany; to vamp. 2. (*theatr.*) to play up (to). 3. (*cards*) to play into someone's hand.

подыгр|а́ться, а́юсь, *pf.* (*of* ~ываться) (к; *coll.*) to get round.

подьы́грыва|ть, ю, *impf. of* подыгра́ть.

поды́грыва|ться, юсь, *impf.* 1. *impf. of* подыгра́ться. 2. (*impf. only*) to try to get round.

подыма́|ть(ся), ю(сь), *impf.* (*coll.*) = поднима́ть(ся).

поды|ска́ть, щу́, ~щешь, *pf.* (*of* ~скивать) to seek out, find.

поды́скива|ть, ю, *impf.* 1. *impf. of* подыска́ть. 2. (*impf. only*) to seek, try to find.

подытóжива|ть, ю, *impf. of* подытóжить.

подытóж|ить, у, ишь, *pf.* (*of* ~ивать) to sum up.

подыха́|ть, ю, *impf. of* подóхнуть.

подыш|а́ть, у́, ~ишь, *pf.* to breathe; вы́йти п. све́жим во́здухом to go out for a breath of fresh air.

подья́ч|ий, его, *m.* (*hist.*) scrivener, clerk, government official (*in Muscovite Russia*).

поеда́|ть, ю, *impf. of* поéсть.

поеди́н|ок, ка, *m.* duel, single combat.

поедóм, *adv.* п. есть когó-н. (*coll.*) to make someone's life a misery (by nagging).

пóезд, а, *pl.* ~á, *m.* 1. train; ~ом by train; п. да́льнего сле́дования long-distance train; п. прямо́го сообще́ния through train. 2. (*obs.*) convoy, procession (*of vehicles*); сва́дебный п. wedding procession.

поéз|дить, жу, дишь, *pf.* to travel about.

поéздк|а, и, *f.* journey; trip, excursion, outing, tour.

пóездник, а, *m.* (*coll.*) commuter (*by rail*).

поезд|нóй, *adj. of* пóезд; ~на́я брига́да train crew.

поезжáй(те): *used as imp. of* éхать and поéхать.

поезжáн|ин, ина, *pl.* ~е, ~, *m.* (*obs.*) member of wedding procession.

поёмн|ый, *adj.* under water at flood times; ~ые луга́ water-meadows.

поёный, *adj.* (*agric.*) udder-fed.

по|éсть, éм, éшь, éст, еди́м, еди́те, едя́т, *past* ~éл, *pf.* (*of* ~еда́ть) 1. to eat (up). 2. to eat a little; to take some food, have a bite. 3. (*of rodents, insects, etc.*) to eat, devour.

поé|хать, ду, дешь, *pf.* (*of* éхать) to go (*in or on a vehicle or on an animal*); to set off, depart; ~хали! (*coll.*) come on!, come along!, let's go!; ну, ~хал! (*coll.*) now he's off!

пожале́|ть, ю, *pf. of* жале́ть.

пожáл|овать, ую, *pf. of* жáловать; добрó п.! welcome!; ~уйте *formula of polite request*; ~уйте сюдá! would you mind coming here?; this way, please!; ~уйте в столóвую! dinner (supper, *etc.*) is served!

пожáл|оваться, уюсь, *pf. of* жáловаться.

пожáлуй, *adv.* perhaps; very likely; it may be; мы, п., поéдем we shall very likely go; п., ты прав you may be right; по мне п. (*coll.*) it's all right by me.

пожáлуйста, *particle* 1. please; передáйте мне, п., карандáш will you please pass me a pencil; сади́тесь, п. please sit down. 2. (*polite expression of consent*) certainly!, by all means!, with pleasure! (*or not translated*); мóжно посмотре́ть э́ти сни́мки? — п. may I look at these photos? Certainly; переда́йте мне, п., кни́гу. — п. would you mind passing me the book? — There you are. **3.** (*polite acknowledgement of thanks*) don't mention it; not at all.

пожа́р, а, *m.* fire; conflagration; как на п. бежа́ть (*coll.*) to run like hell; не на п.! (*coll.*) hold your horses!, there's no hurry!

пожа́рищ|е¹, а, *m.* (*coll.*) big fire.

пожа́рищ|е², а, *n.* site of a fire.

пожа́рник, а, *m,* fireman.

пожа́р|ный, *adj.* of ~; ~ная кома́нда fire-brigade; п. кран fire-cock; ~ная маши́на fire-engine; п. насо́с fire-pump; в ~ном поря́дке (*coll.*, *joc.*) hastily, in slapdash fashion; на вся́кий п. слу́чай (*coll.*, *joc.*) in case of dire need; *as noun* **п., ~ного,** *m.* fireman.

пожа́ти|е, я, *n.* п. руки́ handshake.

по|жа́ть¹, жму́, жмёшь, *pf.* (*of* ~жима́ть) press, squeeze; п. ру́ку (+*d.*) to shake hands (with); п. плеча́ми to shrug one's shoulders.

по|жа́ть², жну, жнёшь, *pf.* (*of* ~жина́ть) to reap (*also fig.*); п. сла́ву to win renown; п. плоды́ чужо́го труда́ (*fig.*) to reap where one has not sown; что посе́ешь, то и ~жнёшь (*prov.*) one must reap as one has sown.

по|жа́ться, жму́сь, жмёшься, *pf.* (*of* ~жима́ться) to shrink up, huddle up.

пож|ева́ть, ую́, уёшь, *pf.* (*of* ~ёвывать) to chew, masticate.

пожёвыва|ть, ю, *impf.* of пожева́ть.

пожела́ни|е, я, *n.* wish, desire.

пожела́|ть, ю, *pf.* of жела́ть.

пожелте́лый, *adj.* yellowed; gone yellow.

пожелте́|ть, ю, *pf.* of желте́ть.

пожен|и́ть, ю́, ~ишь, *pf.* of жени́ть.

пожен|и́ться, ~имся, *pf.* (*pl. used only*; *of man and woman*) to get married.

пожéртвовани|е, я, *n.* donation, offering.

пожéртв|овать, ую, *pf.* of жéртвовать.

по|жéчь, жгу, жжёшь, жгут, *past* ~жёг, ~жгла́, *pf.* to burn up; to destroy by fire.

пожи́в|а, ы, *f.* (*coll.*) gain, profit.

пожива́|ть, ю, *impf.* to live; как (вы) ~ете? how are you (getting on)?; ста́ли они́ жить-п. да добра́ нажива́ть they lived happily ever after.

пожив|и́ться, лю́сь, и́шься, *pf.* (+*i.*; *coll.*) to live (off), profit (by); п. на счёт друго́го to make good at another's expense.

пожи́|вший, *past part. act.* of ~ть *and adj.* (*usu. pejor.*) experienced.

пожиде́|ть, ю, *pf.* (*coll.*) (*of liquids*) to become thinner, become more dilute.

пожи́зненн|ый, *adj.* life; for life; ~ое заключе́ние life imprisonment; ~ая ре́нта life annuity.

пожило́й, *adj.* middle-aged; elderly.

пожима́|ть(ся), ю(сь), *impf.* of пожа́ть¹(ся).

пожина́|ть, ю, *impf.* of пожа́ть².

пожира́|ть, ю, *impf.* of пожра́ть; п. глаза́ми to devour with one's eyes.

пожи́тк|и, ов, *no sing.* (*coll.*) belongings; (one's) things; goods and chattels; со все́ми ~ами bag and baggage.

по|жи́ть, живу́, живёшь, *past* ~жи́л, ~жила́, ~жи́ло, *pf.* **1.** to live (*for a time*); to stay; мы ~жи́ли три го́да в Ки́еве we lived for three years in Kiev; я там ~живу́ неде́ли две I shall stay there about a couple of weeks. **2.** (*coll.*) to lead a gay life, live it up, live fast; п. в своё удово́льствие to lead a gay life, live for pleasure; ~живём-уви́дим we shall see what we shall see.

пожм|у́, ёшь, *see* пожа́ть¹

пожн|у́, ёшь, *see* пожа́ть².

по́ж|ня, ни, *g. pl.* ~ен, *f.* (*dial.*) stubble (-field).

пожр|а́ть, у́, ёшь, *past* ~а́л, ~ала́, ~а́ло, *pf.* (*of* пожира́ть) to devour; (*coll.*) to gobble up.

по́з|а, ы, *f.* pose, attitude, posture; (*fig.*) pose; приня́ть каку́ю-н. ~у to strike an attitude, adopt a pose; приня́ть ~у вели́кого учёного to pose as a great scholar; э́то то́лько п. it is a mere pose.

позаба́в|ить, лю, ишь, *pf.* to amuse a little.

позаба́в|иться, люсь, ишься, *pf.* to amuse oneself a little.

позабо́|титься, чусь, тишься, *pf.* of забо́титься.

позабыва́|ть, ю, *impf.* of позабы́ть.

позаб|ы́ть, у́ду, у́дешь, *pf.* (*of* ~ыва́ть) (+*a.* or о+*p.*; *coll.*) to forget (about).

позави́д|овать, ую, *pf.* of зави́довать.

поза́втрака|ть, ю, *pf.* of за́втракать.

позавчера́, *adv.* the day before yesterday.

позавчера́|шний, *adj.* of ~.

позади́¹, *adv.* (*of place*; *fig. of time*) behind; оста́вить п. to leave behind; наиху́дшие времена́ оста́лись п. the worst times are behind, are past.

позади́², *prep.*+*g.* behind.

позаймств|овать, ую, *pf.* of заи́мствовать.

позапро́шлый, *adj.* before last; п. год the year before last.

поза́р|иться, юсь, ишься, *pf.* of за́риться.

по|зва́ть, зову́, зовёшь, *past* ~зва́л, ~звала́, ~зва́ло, *pf.* of звать.

по-зве́рски, *adv.* brutally, like a beast.

позволе́ни|е, я, *n.* permission, leave; с ва́шего ~я with your permission, by your leave; с ~я сказа́ть if one may say so; э́тот, с ~я сказа́ть, вождь (*iron.*) this apology for a leader; this, if one may so call him, leader.

позволи́тельный (~ен, ~ьна), *adj.* permissible.

позво́л|ить, ю, ишь, *pf.* (*of* ~я́ть) (+*d. of person and inf.*, +*a. of inanimate object*) to allow, permit; е́сли доктора́ ~ят мне пое́хать, я уви́жу вас в Москве́ if the doctors allow me to travel, I shall see you in Moscow; п. себе́ (+*inf.*) to permit oneself, venture, take the liberty (of); (+*a.*) to be able to afford; п. себе́ сде́лать замеча́ние to venture a remark; п. себе́ пое́здку в Пари́ж to be able to afford a trip to Paris; п. себе́ во́льность (c+*i.*) to take liberties (with); ~ьте (*i*) *polite form of request* ~ьте предста́вить до́ктора Х. allow me to introduce Doctor X., (*ii*) *expression of disagreement or objection* ~ьте, что э́то зна́чит? excuse me, what does that mean?

позвол|я́ть, я́ю, *impf. of* ~и́ть.

позвон|и́ть(ся), ю́(сь), и́шь(ся), *pf. of* звони́ть(ся).

позвон|о́к, ка́, *m.* (*anat.*) vertebra.

позвоно́чник, а, *m.* (*anat.*) spine, backbone, spinal column, vertebral column.

позвоно́чн|ый, *adj.* (*anat.*) vertebral; п. столб spinal column, vertebral column; *as noun* ~ые, ~ых (*zool.*) vertebrates.

поздн|е́е, *comp. of* ~ий *and* ~о later; приди́ не п. пяти́ часо́в come by five o'clock at latest.

поздне́йший, *adj.* later, latest.

по́здн|ий, *adj.* late; tardy; до ~ей но́чи until late at night, late into the night; ~о it is late.

по́здно, *adv.* late.

поздоро́ва|ться, юсь, *pf. of* здоро́ваться.

поздорове́|ть, ю, *pf. of* здорове́ть.

поздоро́в|иться, ится, *pf. only in phrase* (*coll.*) не ~ится ему́, *etc.*, (от) much good will it do him, *etc.*

поздрави́тел|ь, я, *m.* bearer of congratulations, well-wisher.

поздрави́тельный, *adj.* congratulatory.

поздра́в|ить, лю, ишь, *pf.* (*of* ~ля́ть) (c+*i.*) to congratulate (on, upon); п. кого́-н. с днём рожде́ния to wish someone many happy returns of the day; п. кого́-н. с Но́вым го́дом to wish someone a happy New Year.

поздравле́ни|е, я, *n.* congratulation.

поздравля́|ть, ю, *impf. of* поздра́вить.

позёвыва|ть, ю, *impf.* (*coll.*) to yawn (from time to time).

позелене́|ть, ю, *pf. of* зелене́ть 1.

позелен|и́ть, ю́, и́шь, *pf. of* зелени́ть.

позём, а, *m.* (*dial.*) manure.

поземе́льный, *adj.* land; п. нало́г land-tax.

позёмк|а, и, *f.* blizzard accompanied by ground wind.

позёр, а, *m.* poseur.

по́з|же, *comp. of* ~дний *and* ~дно; later (on).

по-зи́мнему, *adv.* as in winter, as for winter; оде́т п. (dressed) in winter clothes.

пози́р|овать, ую, *impf.* (+*d.*) to sit (to), pose (for); (*fig.*) to pose.

позити́в, а, *m.* (*phot.*) positive.

позитиви́зм, а, *m.* (*philos.*) positivism.

позитиви́ст, а, *m.* (*philos.*) positivist.

позити́в|ный (~ен, ~на), *adj.* (*in var. senses*) positive.

позитро́н, а, *m.* (*phys.*) positron, positive electron.

позицио́нн|ый, *adj. of* пози́ция; ~ая война́ trench warfare.

пози́ци|я, и, *f.* (*in var. senses*) position; stand; вы́годная п. advantage-ground; выжида́тельная п. wait-and-see attitude; заня́ть ~ю (*mil.*) to take up a position; (*fig.*) to take one's stand; с ~и си́лы from (a position of) strength.

позла|ти́ть, щу́, ти́шь, *pf.* (*of* ~ща́ть) (*obs. or fig.*) to gild.

позлаща́|ть, ю, *impf. of* позлати́ть.

позл|и́ть, ю́, и́шь, *pf.* to tease a little.

познава́емост|ь, и, *f.* (*philos.*) cognoscibility.

познава́ем|ый (~, ~а), *pres. part. pass. of* познава́ть *and adj.* cognizable, knowable.

познава́тельный, *adj.* cognitive; п. проце́сс cognition.

позна|ва́ть, ю́, ёшь, *impf. of* ~ть.

позна|ва́ться, ю́сь, ёшься, *impf.* (*no pf.*) to become known; друзья́ ~ю́тся в беде́ (*prov.*) a friend in need is a friend indeed.

познако́м|ить(ся), лю(сь), ишь(ся), *pf. of* знако́мить(ся).

познако́м|ленный, *p.p.p. of* ~ить.

позна́ни|е, я, *n.* 1. (*philos.*) cognition; тео́рия ~я theory of knowledge, epistemology. 2. (*pl.*) knowledge.

позна|ть, ю, *pf.* (*of* ~ва́ть) to get to know; to become acquainted with; (*philos.*) to cognize; п. го́ре to become acquainted with grief; п. же́нщину (*euph.*) to know a woman.

позоло́т|а, ы, *f.* gilding, gilt.

позоло|ти́ть, чу́, ти́шь, *pf. of* золоти́ть.

позо́р, а, *m.* shame, disgrace; infamy, ignominy; быть ~ом (для) to be a disgrace (to); вы́ставить на п. to put to shame; покры́ть себя́ ~ом to disgrace oneself, cover oneself with ignominy.

позо́р|ить, ю, ишь, *impf.* (*of* о~) to disgrace, defame, discredit.

позо́р|иться, юсь, ишься, *impf.* (*of* о~) to disgrace oneself.

позо́рищ|е, а, *n.* (*coll.*) shameful event, disgrace.

позо́р|ный (~ен, ~на), *adj.* shameful, disgraceful; infamous, ignominious; п. столб pillory; поста́вить к ~ному столбу́ (*fig.*) pillory.

позумéнт, а, *m.* galoon, braid; золотóй п. gold braid, gold lace.

позы́в, а, *m.* (*physiological*) urge, call; п. на рвóту urge to be sick, (feeling of) nausea.

позывá|ть, ет, *impf.* (*impers.*) to feel an urge, feel a need; меня́ ~ет на рвóту I feel an urge to be sick.

позывн|óй, *adj.* п. сигнáл (*radio*) call sign; *as noun* ~ы́е, ~ы́х call sign; (*naut.*) ship's number; подня́ть ~ы́е to make the ship's number.

поигрá|ть, ю, *pf.* to have a game, play a little.

поигрывá|ть, ю, *impf.* (*coll.*) to play now and then.

пойл|ец, ьцá, *m.* п. и кормúлец (*obs.*) bread--winner.

пойлк|а, и, *f.* **1.** feeding-trough; feeding--bowl. **2.** feeding-vessel (*for invalids*).

поимённо, *adv.* by name; вызывáть п. to call over (*the roll of*).

поимённый, *adj.* nominal; п. спúсок list of names, nominal roll.

поимен|овáть, ýю, *pf.* to name, call out by name.

поимк|а, и, *f.* catching, capture; п. на мéсте преступлéния catching in the act, catching red-handed.

поимýщественный, *adj.* п. налóг property tax.

по-инóму, *adv.* differently, in a different way.

поинтерес|овáться, ýюсь, *pf.* (+*i.*) to be curious (about); to display interest (in); он ~овáлся узнáть, кто вы he was curious to find out who you are.

пóиск, а, *m.* **1.** (*pl.*) search; в ~ax (+*g.*) in search (of), in quest (of). **2.** (*mil.*) (reconnaissance) raid.

пои|скáть, щý, ~щешь, *pf.* to look for, search for; ~щúте хорошéнько have a good look.

пойстине, *adv.* indeed, in truth.

по|úть, ю́, ~úшь, *impf.* (*of* на~) to give to drink; to water (*cattle*); п. ребёнка to feed a baby (*at the breast*); п. винóм to treat to wine; п. и кормúть семью́ to maintain the family, be the family bread-winner.

по|ищý, úщешь, *see* ~искáть.

пой|дý, дёшь, *see* ~тú.

пóйл|о, а, *n.* swill, mash; п. для свинéй hog--wash, pig-swill.

пойм|а, ы, *g. pl.* ~, *f.* flood-lands; water--meadow.

поймá|ть, ю, *pf. of* ловúть.

пойм|ý, ёшь, *see* поня́ть.

пóйнтер, а, *m.* (*dog*) pointer.

пой|тú, дý, дёшь, *past* пошёл, пошлá, *pf.* **1.** *pf. of* идтú *and* ходúть; пошёл! off you go!; пошёл вон! be off!, off with you!; уж

éсли на то пошлó if it comes to that, for that matter; (так) не ~дёт (*coll.*) that won't work, that won't wash. **2.** to begin to (be able to) walk. **3.** (+*inf.*; *coll.*) to begin (to). **4.** (в+*a.*) to take after; он пошёл в отцá he takes after his father.

покá¹, *adv.* for the present, for the time being; п. что (*coll.*) in the meanwhile; п. ещё, п.-то ещё (*coll.*) not for a while yet; э́то п. всё that is all for now; э́то п. остáвьте leave it for the time being; не беспокóйтесь, п.-то ещё он поя́вится don't worry, he won't turn up for a while yet; ну, п.! (*coll.*) cheerio!, bye-bye!

покá², *conj.* **1.** while; нам нáдо попросúть егó, п. он тут we must ask him while he is here. **2.** п. не until, till; не нáдо уходúть, п. онá не придёт we must not go until she comes.

покáз, а, *m.* showing, demonstration; (*fig.*) portrayal; п. нóвого фúльма showing of a new film.

показáни|е, я, *n.* **1.** testimony, evidence. **2.** (*leg.*) deposition; affidavit; давáть п. to testify, bear witness, make a deposition. **3.** reading (*on an instrument*).

покáз|анный, *p.p.p. of* ~áть *and adj.* **1.** (*obs. or coll.*) fixed, appointed; в ~анное врéмя at the time appointed. **2.** (*med.*) indicated.

показáтел|ь, я, *m.* **1.** (*math.*) exponent, index. **2.** index; (*fig.*) showing; кáчественные ~и qualitative indices; дать хорóшие ~и, добúться хорóших ~ей to make a good showing.

показáтел|ьный (~ен, ~ьна), *adj.* **1.** significant; instructive, revealing; óчень ~ьное заявлéние a very significant pronouncement. **2.** model; demonstration; п. суд show-trial; п. урóк demonstration lesson, object-lesson; ~ьное хозя́йство model farm. **3.** (*math.*) exponential.

пока|зáть, жý, ~жешь, *pf.* (*of* ~зывать) **1.** to show; to display, reveal; п. себя́ to prove oneself, prove one's worth; он ~зáл себя́ хорóшим орáтором he has shown himself to be a good speaker; п. свои знáния to display one's knowledge; онú ~зáли дéвочку врачý they took the little girl to the doctor; он ~зáл вид, что сéрдится he feigned anger; п. товáр лицóм (*fig., coll.*) to display oneself in a favourable light. **2.** (*of instruments*) to show, register, read. **3.** (на+*a.*) to point (at, to); п. комý-н. на дверь (*fig., coll.*) to show someone the door. **4.** (*leg.*) to testify, give evidence, bear witness.

пока|зáться, жýсь, ~жешься, *pf.* **1.** *pf. of* казáться. **2.** (*pf. of* ~зываться) to show oneself, appear; to come in sight; из-за облако́в ∼за́лась луна́ the moon appeared from behind the clouds; п. врачу́ to see a doctor. **3.** *pass. of* ∼за́ть.

показно́й, *adj.* for show; ostentatious.

показу́х|а, и, *f.* (*coll.*) show; э́то сплошна́я п. it's all put on, just for show.

пока́зыва|ть(ся), ю(сь), *impf. of* показа́ть(ся).

по-ка́ковски, *adv.* (*coll.*) in what language?

пока́лыва|ть, ю, *impf.* to prick occasionally; у меня́ ∼ет в боку́ (*impers.*) I have an occasional stitch in my side.

покаля́ка|ть, ю, *pf. of* каля́кать.

пока́мест, *adv. and conj.* (*coll.*) = пока́.

покара́|ть, ю, *pf. of* кара́ть.

поката́|ть¹, ю, *pf.* to roll.

поката́|ть², ю, *pf.* to take for a drive; п. дете́й to take children out.

поката́|ться, юсь, *pf.* to go for a drive; п. на ло́дке to go out boating.

пока|ти́ть, чу́, ∼тишь, *pf.* **1.** *pf. of* кати́ть. **2.** to start (rolling), set rolling.

пока|ти́ться, чу́сь, ∼тишься, *pf.* **1.** *pf. of* кати́ться; п. со́ смеху (*coll.*) to roar with laughter. **2.** to start rolling.

пока́тост|ь, и, *f.* slope, incline; declivity.

пока́т|ый (∼, ∼а), *adj.* sloping; slanting; п. лоб retreating forehead.

покача́|ть, ю, *pf.* to rock, swing (for a time); п. ребёнка на каче́лях to give a child a swing; п. голово́й to shake one's head.

покача́|ться, юсь, *pf.* to rock, swing (for a time); to have a swing.

пока́чива|ться, юсь, *impf.* to rock slightly; идти́ ∼ясь to walk unsteadily.

покачн|у́ть, у́, ёшь, *pf.* to shake.

покачн|у́ться, у́сь, ёшься, *pf.* **1.** to sway, totter, give a lurch. **2.** (*fig., coll.*) to totter, go downhill.

пока́шлива|ть, ю, *impf.* to have a slight cough; to cough intermittently.

пока́шля|ть, ю, *pf.* to cough.

покая́ни|е, я, *n.* **1.** (*eccl.*) confession. **2.** penitence, repentance; принести́ п. (в+*p.*) to repent (of); отпусти́ть ду́шу на п. (*obs. or coll.*) to let go in peace.

покая́нный, *adj.* penitential.

пока́|яться, юсь, ешься, *pf. of* ка́яться.

поквата́льно, *adv.* by the quarter, per quarter, every quarter.

поквита́|ться, юсь, *pf.* (с+*i.*; *coll.*) to be quits (with); to get even (with); тепе́рь мы с ва́ми ∼лись now we're quits; я ещё с ним ∼юсь I'll get even with him yet.

по́кер, а, *m.* (*card-game*) poker.

по́кер|ный, *adj. of* ∼.

покива́|ть, ю, *pf.* to nod (*several times*).

покида́|ть, ю, *impf. of* поки́нуть.

поки́нут|ый, *p.p.p. of* ∼ь *and adj.* deserted; abandoned.

поки́|нуть, ну, нешь, *pf.* (*of* ∼да́ть) to leave; to desert, abandon, forsake.

поклада́я, *only in phrase* не п. рук indefatigably.

покла́дист|ый (∼, ∼а), *adj.* complaisant, obliging.

покла́ж|а, и, *f.* (*coll.*) load; luggage.

поклёп, а, *m.* (*coll.*) slander, calumny; взвести́ п. (на+*a.*) to slander, cast aspersions (on).

поклй|кать, чу, чешь, *pf.* (*coll.*) to call (to).

покло́н, а, *m.* **1.** bow; сде́лать п. to bow (*in greeting*); класть ∼ы to bow (*in prayer*); идти́ на п., идти́ с ∼ом к кому́-н. to go cap in hand to someone. **2.** (*fig.*) greeting; посла́ть ∼ы to send one's compliments, send one's kind regards.

поклоне́ни|е, я, *n.* worship.

поклон|и́ться, ю́сь, ∼ишься, *pf. of* кла́няться.

покло́нник, а, *m.* admirer, worshipper.

поклоня́|ться, юсь, *impf.* (+*d.*) to worship.

покля́|сться, ну́сь, нёшься, *pf. of* кля́сться.

поко́вк|а, и, *f.* (*tech.*) forging; forged piece.

поко́ем, *adv.* (*obs.*) in the shape of the letter п.

поко́|ить, ю, ишь, *impf.* (*obs.*) to tend, cherish.

поко́|иться, юсь, ишься, *impf.* **1.** (на+*p.*) to rest (on, upon), repose (on, upon), be based (on, upon); п. на дога́дке to be based on conjecture. **2.** (*of the dead*) to lie; здесь ∼ится прах (+*g.*) here lies (the body of).

поко́|й¹, я, *m.* rest, peace; ве́чный п. (*fig., poet.*) eternal rest; оста́вить в ∼е to leave in peace; уйти́ на п., удали́ться на п. to retire; то́чка ∼я (*phys.*) point of rest, fulcrum; у́гол ∼я (*phys.*) angle of repose.

поко́|й², я, *m.* (*obs.*) room, chamber.

поко́йник, а, *m.* the deceased.

поко́йницк|ая, ой, *f.* mortuary.

поко́йницкий, *adj.* (*coll.*) corpse-like.

поко́|йный¹ (∼ен, ∼йна), *adj.* **1.** calm, quiet; бу́дьте ∼йны don't be alarmed, don't (you) worry. **2.** comfortable; restful; ∼йной но́чи! good night!

**поко́йн|ый², *adj.* (the) late; п. коро́ль the late king; *as noun* п., ∼ого, *m. and* ∼ая, ∼ой, *f.* the deceased.

поколеб|а́ть, ∼лю, ∼лешь, *pf. of* колеба́ть.

поколеб|а́ться, ∼люсь, ∼лешься, *pf.* **1.** *pf. of* колеба́ться. **2.** to waver for a time, hesitate for a time.

поколе́ни|е, я, *n.* generation; из ∼я в п. from generation to generation.

поколо|ти́ть(ся), чу́(сь), ∼тишь(ся), *pf. of* колоти́ть(ся).

поко́нч|ить, у, ишь, *pf.* (с+*i.*) **1.** to finish off; to finish (with), be through (with), have done (with); с э́тим ∼ено that's done with. **2.** to put an end (to), do away (with); п. с собо́ю to put an end to one's life, make away with oneself; п. жизнь самоуби́йством to commit suicide.

покоре́ни|е, я, *n.* subjugation, subdual; п. во́здуха conquest of the air.

покори́тел|ь, я, *m.* subjugator; п. серде́ц lady-killer.

покор|и́ть, ю́, и́шь, *pf.* (*of* ~я́ть) to subjugate, subdue; п. чьё-н. се́рдце to win someone's heart.

покор|и́ться, ю́сь, и́шься, *pf.* (*of* ~я́ться) (+*d.*) to submit (to); to resign oneself (to); п. свое́й у́части to resign oneself to one's lot.

покорм|и́ть(ся), лю́(сь), ~ишь(ся), *pf. of* корми́ть(ся).

покорн|е́йший, *superl. of* ~ый; ваш п. слуга́ (*polite formula in concluding letter*; *obs.*) your most humble servant; ~е́йшая про́сьба most humble petition.

поко́рно, *adv.* humbly; submissively, obediently; п. благодарю́ (*coll.*) thank you; благодарю́ п. (*iron.*; *expresses refusal and/or astonishment*) thank you (very much)!; благодарю́ п., я уж лу́чше пешко́м thank you, I would rather walk.

поко́рност|ь, и, *f.* submissiveness, obedience.

поко́р|ный (~ен, ~на), *adj.* **1.** (+*d.*) submissive (to), obedient; п. судьбе́ resigned to one's fate. **2.** (*in conventional expressions of politeness*; *obs.*) humble, obedient; ваш п. слуга́ your obedient servant; слуга́ п.! (*coll., iron.*) no, thank you!; I'm not having any!

покороб|ить(ся), лю(сь), ишь(ся), *pf. of* коро́бить(ся).

поко́рств|овать, ую, *impf.* (+*d.*; *obs.*) to submit (to); to be submissive (to), be obedient (to).

покор|я́ть(ся), я́ю(сь), *impf. of* ~и́ть(ся).

поко́с, а, *m.* **1.** mowing, haymaking; второ́й п. aftermath. **2.** meadow(-land).

покоси́|вшийся, *past part. of* ~ться *and adj.* rickety, crazy, ramshackle.

поко|си́ться, шу́сь, си́шься, *pf. of* коси́ться.

покра́ж|а, и, *f.* **1.** theft. **2.** stolen goods.

покра́п|ать, лет, *pf.* (*of rain*) to spit.

покра́пыва|ть, ет, *impf.* ~л дождь, ~ло (*impers.*) it was spitting with rain off and on.

покра́|сить, шу, сишь, *pf. of* кра́сить.

покра́ск|а, и, *f.* painting, colouring.

покрасне́|ть, ю, *pf. of* красне́ть I.

покрив|и́ть(ся), лю́(сь), и́шь(ся), *pf. of* криви́ть(ся).

покри́кива|ть, ю, *impf.* (на+*a.*; *coll.*) to shout (at).

покро́в¹, а, *m.* **1.** cover; covering; hearse--cloth, pall; (*fig.*) cloak, shroud, pall; ко́ж-

ный п. (*anat.*) integument; по́чвенный п. top-soil; сне́жный п. blanket of snow; твёрдый п. (*biol.*) crust, incrustation; под ~ом но́чи under cover of night. **2.** (*obs.*) coverlet; blanket. **3.** (*fig., obs.*) protection; взять под свой п. to take under one's protection.

Покро́в², а́, *m.* (*eccl.*) (festival of) the Protection (of the Virgin).

покрови́тел|ь, я, *m.* patron, protector.

покрови́тельниц|а, ы, *f.* patroness, protectress.

покрови́тельственн|ый, *adj.* **1.** (*in var. senses*) protective; ~ая систе́ма (*econ.*) protectionism; п. тари́ф (*econ.*) protective tariff; ~ая окра́ска (*zool.*) protective colouring. **2.** condescending, patronizing.

покрови́тельств|о, а, *n.* protection, patronage; О́бщество ~а живо́тным Society for the Prevention of Cruelty to Animals; под ~ом (+*g.*) under the patronage (of), under the auspices (of).

покрови́тельств|овать, ую, *impf.* (+*d.*) to protect, patronize.

покро́в|ный, *adj. of* ~; (*anat.*) integumentary; ~ные культу́ры, ~ные расте́ния (*agric.*) cover crops; ~ное стёклышко cover glass (*of microscope*).

покро́|й, я, *m.* cut (*of garment*); все на оди́н п. (*fig.*) all in the same style.

покро́мк|а, и, *f.* selvedge.

покрош|и́ть, у́, ~ишь, *pf.* (+*a. or g.*) to crumble; to crumb; to mince, chop.

покругле́|ть, ю, *pf. of* кругле́ть.

покруж|и́ть, у́, ~ишь, *pf.* (*coll.*) **1.** to circle several times. **2.** to roam, wander (*for some time*).

покрупне́|ть, ю, *pf. of* крупне́ть.

покрыва́л|о, а, *n.* **1.** coverlet, bedspread, counterpane. **2.** shawl; veil. **3.** cover; нефтяно́е п. oil-slick.

покрыва́|ть(ся), ю(сь), *impf. of* покры́ть(ся).

покры́ти|е, я, *n.* **1.** covering; п. доро́ги road surfacing; п. кры́ши roofing. **2.** covering, discharge, payment; п. расхо́дов defrayment of expenses.

покр|ы́ть, о́ю, о́ешь, *pf.* (*of* крыть *and* ~ыва́ть) **1.** to cover; п. кры́шей to roof; п. кра́ской to coat with paint; п. ла́ком to varnish, lacquer; п. позо́ром to cover with shame; п. себя́ сла́вой to cover oneself with glory; п. та́йной to shroud in mystery. **2.** to meet, pay off; п. расхо́ды to cover expenses, defray expenses. **3.** to drown (*sound*). **4.** to shield, cover up (for); to hush up. **5.** to cover (*distance*). **6.** (*cards*) to cover. **7.** (*coll.*) to curse, swear (at). **8.** (*zool.*; *of stallion, bull, etc.*) to cover.

покр|ы́ться, о́юсь, о́ешься, *pf.* (*of* ~ыва́ться) to cover oneself; to get covered.

покры́шк|а, и, *f.* 1. cover(ing); ни дна ни ~и, *see* дно. 2. tire-cover, (outer) tire.

покуда, *adv. and conj.* (*coll.*) = пока́.

покум|и́ться, лю́сь, и́шься, *pf. of* куми́ться.

покупа́тел|ь, я, *m.* buyer, purchaser; customer, client.

покупа́тельн|ый, *adj.* purchasing; ~ая спосо́бность (*econ.*) purchasing power.

покупа́тель|ский, *adj. of* ~.

покупа́|ть[1], ю, *impf. of* купи́ть.

покупа́|ть[2], ю, *pf.* to bathe; to bath.

покупа́|ться, юсь, *pf.* to bathe, have a bathe; to have, take a bath.

поку́пк|а, и, *f.* 1. buying; purchasing, purchase. 2. (*object purchased*) purchase; вы́годная п. bargain; де́лать ~и to go shopping.

покуп|но́й, *adj.* 1. bought, purchased (*as opp. to home-made or obtained as a gift*). 2. = ~а́тельный; ~на́я цена́ purchase price.

покупщи́к, а́, *m.* (*obs.*) buyer, purchaser.

поку́рива|ть, ю, *impf.* (*coll.*) to smoke (a little, from time to time).

покур|и́ть, ю́, ~ишь, *pf.* 1. *pf. of* кури́ть. 2. to have a smoke; дава́й ~им let's have a smoke.

покуса́|ть, ю, *pf.* to bite; to sting.

поку|си́ться, шу́сь, си́шься, *pf.* (*of* ~ша́ться) (на + *a.*) 1. to attempt, make an attempt (upon); п. на свою́ жизнь to make an attempt upon one's own life; п. на самоуби́йство to attempt suicide. 2. to encroach (on, upon); п. на чьи-н. права́ to encroach on someone's rights.

поку́ша|ть, ю, *pf. of* ку́шать.

покуша́|ться, юсь, *impf. of* покуси́ться.

покуше́ни|е, я, *n.* attempt; п. на жизнь (+ *g.*) (*or* на + *a.*) attempt upon the life (of).

пол[1], а, о ~е, на ~у́, *pl.* ~ы́, *m.* floor.

пол[2], а, *m.* sex; обо́его ~а of both sexes.

пол- half (*as in* получаса́ half an hour; полдеся́того half past nine; полдю́жины half a dozen, *etc.*).

пол|а́, ы́, *pl.* ~ы, *f.* skirt, flap, lap; из-под ~ы on the sly, under cover; торгова́ть из--под ~ы́ to sell under the counter.

полага́|ть[1], ю, *impf.* (*obs.*) to lay, place.

полага́|ть[2], ю, *impf.* to suppose, think; ~ют, что он умира́ет he is believed to be dying; на́до п. it is to be supposed, one must suppose.

полага́|ться, юсь, *impf.* 1. *impf. of* положи́ться. 2. ~ется (*impers.*) one is supposed (to); так ~ется it is the custom; не ~ется it is not done; здесь ~ется снима́ть шля́пу one is supposed to take off one's hat here. 3. ~ется (+ *d.*) to be due (to); нам э́то ~ется it is our due, we have a right to it.

пола́|дить, жу, дишь, *pf.* (с + *i.*) to come to an understanding (with); to get on (with).

пола́ком|ить(ся), лю(сь), ишь(ся), *pf. of* ла́комить(ся).

пола́т|и, ей, *no sing.* sleeping-bench (*on high raised platform in Russian peasant hut*).

по́лб|а, ы, *f.* (*bot.*) spelt, German wheat.

полбеды́, *f.* (*coll.*) a small loss, a minor misfortune; э́то ещё п. it is not so very serious.

по́лб|енный, *adj. of* ~а.

полве́ка, полуве́ка, *m.* half a century.

полго́да, полуго́да, *m.* half a year, six months; с п., о́коло полуго́да for about six months.

полго́ря = полбеды́.

по́лдень, полу́дня, *and* по́лдня, *m.* 1. noon, midday; за п. (*or* за́ полдень) past noon; к полу́дню towards noon; вре́мя до полу́дня forenoon; вре́мя по́сле полу́дня afternoon. 2. (*obs.*) south.

полдне́вный, *adj. of* по́лдень.

по́лдник, а, *m.* (afternoon) snack *light meal between dinner and supper*).

по́лднича|ть, *impf.* (*coll.*) to have an (afternoon) snack.

полдоро́г|и, *f.* half-way; встре́титься на ~е to meet half-way; останови́ться на ~е to stop half-way (*also fig.*).

по́л|е, я, *pl.* ~я́, ~е́й, *n.* (1. (*in var. senses*) field; спорти́вное п. playing field, sports ground; п. би́твы, п. бра́ни (*obs.*), п. сраже́ния battle-field; п. де́ятельности sphere of action; п. зре́ния field of vision; оди́н в п. не во́ин (*prov.*) the voice of one man is the voice of no one. 2. (*art*) ground; (*heraldry*) field. 3. (*pl.*) margin; заме́тки на ~я́х notes in the margin. 4. (*pl.*) brim (*of hat*).

полеве́ни|е, я, *n.* (*polit.*) leftward movement.

полеве́|ть, ю, *pf. of* леве́ть.

полёвк|а, и, *f.* field-vole.

полево́дств|о, а, *n.* field-crop cultivation.

полев|о́й, *adj.* (*in var. senses*) field; ~а́я артилле́рия field artillery; п. бино́кль field glasses; п. го́спиталь field hospital; ~а́я мышь field-mouse; ~а́я су́мка (*mil.*) map case; ~ые цветы́ wild flowers; п. шпат (*min.*) feldspar.

полега́ни|е, я, *n.* (*agric.*) lodging (*of crops*).

полега́|ть, ю, *impf. of* полечь 3.

полего́ньку, *adv.* (*coll.*) by easy stages.

полегча́|ть, ет, *pf. of* легча́ть; больно́му ~ло the patient is feeling better; у меня́ на душе́ ~ло I feel a load off my mind.

поле́гче, *comp. of* лёгкий *and* легко́ 1. (*somewhat, a little*) lighter. 2. a little easier, a little less difficult; п! take it easy!, ease up a bit!, not so fast!

полеж|а́ть, у́, и́шь, *pf.* to lie down (*for a while*).

полёжива|ть, ю, *impf.* (*coll.*) to lie down (*off and on*).

полѐз|ный (~ен, ~на), *adj.* useful; helpful; wholesome, health-giving; ~ное дѐйствие efficiency, duty (*of a machine*); ~ная жилáя плóщадь actual living space; ~ная лошадúная сúла effective horsepower, working horsepower; ~ная нагрýзка (*tech.*) working load, pay-load; ѐто лекáрство óчень ~но от кáшля this medicine is very good for coughs; чем могý быть ~ен? can I help you?

полѐз|ть, у, ешь, *past* ~, ~ла, *pf.* 1. *pf. of* лезть. 2. to start to climb.

полемизúр|овать, ую, *impf.* (c+*i.*) to carry on polemics (with).

полѐмик|а, и, *f.* polemic(s); dispute, controversy; вступúть в ~у (c+*i.*) to enter into polemics (with).

полемúст, а, *m.* polemicist, controversialist.

полемúческий, *adj.* polemic(al), controversial.

полемúч|ный (~ен, ~на), *adj.* polemical.

полѐнива|ться, юсь, *impf.* (*coll.*) to be rather lazy.

полен|úться, юсь, ~ишься, *pf.* (+*inf.*) to be too lazy to.

полѐниц|а, ы, *m. and f.* (*folk poet.*) hero, heroine.

полѐнниц|а, ы, *f.* pile (*of logs*); stack (*of firewood*).

полѐн|о, а, *pl.* ~ья, ~ьев, *n.* log, billet.

полѐсь|е, я, *n,* wooded locality; woodlands.

полёт, а, *m.* flight; flying; брѐющий п. hedge-hopping; высóтный п. altitude flying; пикúрующий п. diving; слепóй п. blind flying; фигýрный п. aerobatics; вид с птúчьего ~a bird's-eye view; п. фантáзии flight of fancy; высóкого ~a (птúца) (*fig., often iron.*) person of exalted rank, member of the upper ten.

полетá|ть, ю, *pf.* to fly (*for a while*), do some flying.

поле|тѐть, чý, тúшь, *pf.* 1. *pf. of* летѐть. 2. to start to fly; to fly off. 3. (*fig., coll.*) to fall, go headlong.

по-лѐтнему, *adv.* as in summer, as for summer; одѐт п. (dressed) in summer clothes.

полеч|úть, ý, ~ишь, *pf.* to treat (*for a while*).

полеч|úться, ýсь, ~ишься, *pf.* to undergo treatment (*for a while*).

пол|ѐчь, ягу, яжешь, ягут, *past* ~ёг, ~еглá, *pf.* 1. to lie down (*in numbers*). 2. (*fig.*) to fall, be killed (*in numbers*). 3. (*impf.* ~егáть) (*agric.*) to be lodged (*of standing crops*).

пóлз|ать, аю, *impf., indet. of* ~тú; п. в ногáх у когó-н. (*fig.*) to grovel at someone's feet.

ползкóм, *adv.* crawling, on all fours.

полз|тú, ý, ~лá, *impf.* 1. to crawl, creep (along); пóезд ~ the train was

crawling. 2. to ooze (out). 3. (*fig., coll.; of rumour, etc.*) to spread. 4. (*coll.; of fabric*) to fray, ravel out. 5. (*of soil*) to slip, collapse.

ползýн, á, *m.* (*tech.*) slide-block, slider, runner.

ползун|óк, кá, *m.* 1. (*coll.*) toddler. 2. *pl.* (*coll.*) (child's) romper suit.

ползýч|ий, *adj.* creeping; ~ие растѐния (*bot.*) creepers.

поли- poly-.

полиáндри|я, и, *f.* polyandry.

полиартрúт, а, *m.* (*med.*) polyarthritis.

полúв|а, ы, *f.* glaze.

поливá|ть(ся), ю(сь), *impf. of* полúть(ся).

полúвк|а¹, и, *f.* watering.

полúвк|а², и, *f.* gravy.

поливн|óй, *adj.* requiring irrigation; requiring watering; ~ые зѐмли irrigation area.

полúв|очный, *adj. of* ~ка¹; ~очная жúдкость cooling mixture, coolant; ~очная машúна watering machine.

полигáми|я, и, *f.* polygamy.

полиглóт, а, *m.* polyglot.

полигóн, а, *m.* (*mil.*) (artillery *or* bombing) range; испытáтельный п. proving ground, testing area; учѐбный п. training ground.

полигрáф, а, *m.* (*tech.*) polygraph.

полиграфúст, а, *m.* printing trades worker.

полиграфúческ|ий, *adj.* 1. polygraphic; ~ое произвóдство printing. 2. п. отдѐл non-specialist section (*of library*).

полиграфú|я, и, *f.* 1. (*tech.*) polygraphy; printing trades. 2. non-specialist section (*of library, in which books are classified by authors' names only, without regard to subject-matter*).

поликлúник|а, и, *f.* 1. polyclinic, clinic. 2. outpatients' department (*of hospital*).

полиловѐ|ть, ю, *pf. of* лиловѐть.

полимѐр, а, *m.* (*chem.*) polymer.

полимеризáци|я, и, *f.* (*chem.*) polymerization.

полиморфúзм, а, *m.* polymorphism.

полиморфúческий, *adj.* polymorphic, polymorphous.

полимóрфный, *adj.* polymorphous.

полинезú|ец, йца, *m.* Polynesian.

полинезúйский, *adj.* Polynesian.

полинóм, а, *m.* (*math.*) polynomial.

полинялый, *adj.* faded, discoloured.

полиня|ть, ет, *pf. of* линять.

полиомиелúт, а, *m.* (*med.*) poliomyelitis, infantile paralysis.

полúп, а, *m.* 1. (*zool.*) polyp. 2. (*med.*) polypus.

полúп|ный, *adj. of* ~.

полировáл|ьный, *adj.* polishing; ~ая бумáга sandpaper; п. станóк buffing machine.

полир|овáть, ýю, *impf.* (*of* от~) to polish.

полирóвк|а, и, *f.* polish(ing); buffing.

полиро́вочный, *adj.* polishing; buffing.

полиро́вщик, **а**, *m.* polisher.

по́лис, **а**, *m.* policy; страхово́й п. insurance policy.

полисеманти́зм, **а**, *m.* (*ling.*) polysemy.

полисемати́ческий, *adj.* (*ling.*) polysemantic.

полисеми́|я, **и**, *f.* (*ling.*) polysemy.

полисинтети́ческий, *adj.* (*ling.*) polysynthetic.

полисме́н, **а**, *m.* policeman; constable.

полиспа́ст, **а**, *m.* block and tackle; pulley block; tackle block.

поли́стный, *adj.* per sheet.

полит- *abbr.*, *used to form compounds, of* полити́ческий.

политбюро́, *indecl.*, *n.* the Politbureau (*Political Bureau of the Central Committee of the Soviet Communist Party*).

политгра́мот|а, **ы**, *f.* elementary course of political education.

политеи́зм, **а**, *m.* polytheism.

полите́ст, **а**, *m.* polytheist.

политеисти́ческий, *adj.* polytheistic.

политехниза́ци|я, **и**,*f.* introduction of polytechnic education.

политехни́зм, **а**, *m.* system of polytechnic education.

полите́хник, **а**, *m.* student of polytechnic.

полите́хникум, **а**, *m.* polytechnic (school).

политехни́ческий, *adj.* polytechnic(al).

политзаключённ|ый, **ого**, *m.* political prisoner.

поли́тик, **а**, *m.* 1. politician. 2. student of politics; expert on political questions. 3. (*fig.*, *coll.*) politician, politic person.

поли́тик|а, **и**, *f.* 1. policy; п. на гра́ни войны́ 'brinkmanship'; провести́ ~у to carry out a policy. 2. politics; п. си́лы power politics; говори́ть о ~е to talk politics.

политика́н, **а**, *m.* (*pejor.*) politician, intriguer.

политика́нств|о, **а**, *n.* intrigue.

политика́нств|овать, **ую**, *impf.* to intrigue, be an intriguer.

политинформа́тор, **а**, *m.* political information officer.

политипа́ж, **а**, *m.* (*typ.*) polytype.

полити́ческ|ий, *adj.* political; п. де́ятель political figure, politician; ~ая эконо́мия political economy; по ~им соображе́ниям for political reasons.

полити́ч|ный (~ен, ~на), *adj.* (*coll.*) politic.

политкаторжа́н|ин, **ина**, *pl.* ~е, ~, *m.* political convict (*in Russia before 1917*).

политкруж|о́к, **ка́**, *m.* political study circle.

политпросве́т, **а**, *m.* (*formed from abbr. of* полити́ческий *and* просвети́тельный) political education.

политрабо́тник, **а**, *m.* political worker.

политру́к, **а**, *m.* (*abbr. of* полити́ческий руководи́тель) political instructor (*in units of the Soviet armed forces*).

политуправле́ни|е, **я**, *n.* Political Administration.

политу́р|а, **ы**, *f.* polish, varnish.

политучёб|а, **ы**, *f.* political education; study of current affairs.

политшко́л|а, **ы**, *f.* political school.

пол|и́ть, **ью**, **ьёшь**, *past* ~и́л, ~ила́, ~и́ло, *pf.* (*of* ~ива́ть) 1. (+*a. and i.*) to pour (on, upon); п. что-н. водо́й to pour water on something; п. цветы́ to water the flowers. 2. to begin to pour.

пол|и́ться, **ью́сь**, **ьёшься**, *past* ~и́лся, ~ила́сь, ~и́ло́сь, *pf.* (*of* ~ива́ться) 1. (+*i.*) to pour over oneself. 2. to begin to flow.

политэконо́ми|я, **и**, *f.* political economy.

политэмигра́нт, **а**, *m.* political emigrant.

полифони́ческий, *adj.* polyphonic.

полифони́|я, **и**, *f.* (*mus.*) polyphony.

полицейме́йстер, **а**, *m.* (*hist.*) chief of police.

полице́йск|ий, *adj.* police; п. уча́сток police-station; *as noun* п., ~ого, *m.* policeman, police-officer.

полици́|я, **и**,*f.* police; сыскна́я п. criminal investigation department.

полицме́йстер, **а**, *m.* = полицейме́йстер.

поли́чн|ое, **ого**, *n.* пойма́ть с ~ым to catch red-handed.

полишине́л|ь, **я**, *m.* Punch(inello); секре́т ~я open secret.

полиэ́др, **а**, *m.* (*math.*) polyhedron.

полк, **а́**, **о** ~é, **в** ~у́, *m.* regiment; авиацио́нный п. group (*in air force*); на́шего ~у́ при́было our numbers have grown.

по́лк|а¹, **и**, *f.* 1. shelf; кни́жная п. bookshelf. 2. (*in railway sleeping-car*) berth.

по́лк|а², **и**, *f.* weeding.

полко́вник, **а**, *m.* colonel.

полково́д|ец, **ца**, *m.* (*not denoting specific mil. rank*) captain, commander; military leader.

полково́й, *adj.* regimental.

поллю́ци|я, **и**, *f.* (*physiol.*) spermatorrhoea, nocturnal emission.

полмиллио́на, *m.* half a million.

полмину́ты, *f.* half a minute.

полне́йший, *adj.* sheer, uttermost.

полне́|ть, **ю**, *impf.* (*of* по~) to grow stout, put on weight.

полнёхон|ький (~ек, ~ька), *adj.* (*coll.*) brim-full, crammed, packed.

полн|и́ть, **ю**, **и́шь**, *impf.* (*coll.*) to overfill; э́то пла́тье её ~и́т this dress makes her look fat.

по́лно¹, *adv.* brim-full, full to the brim; сли́шком п. too full.

по́лно², *adv.* (*coll.*) 1. enough (of that)!; that

will do!; п. ворча́ть! stop grumbling! **2.** you don't mean that, you don't mean to say so.

полно́, *adv.* (+*g.*) (*coll.*) lots; в ко́мнате полно́ наро́ду the room is packed with people.

полнове́сност|ь, и, *f.* **1.** full weight. **2.** (*fig.*) soundness.

полнове́с|ный (~ен, ~на), *adj.* **1.** of full weight, full-weight. **2.** (*fig.*) sound.

полновла́сти|е, я, *n.* sovereignty.

полновла́ст|ный (~ен, ~на), *adj.* sovereign; п. хозя́ин sole master.

полново́д|ный (~ен, ~на), *adj.* deep.

полново́дь|е, я, *n.* high water.

полногла́си|е, я, *n.* (*ling.*) full vocalism, pleophony.

полнозву́ч|ный (~ен, ~на), *adj.* sonorous.

полнокро́ви|е, я, *n.* (*med.*) plethora.

полнокро́в|ный (~ен, ~на), *adj.* **1.** (*med.*) plethoric. **2.** (*fig.*) full-blooded, sanguineous.

полнолу́ни|е, я, *n.* full moon.

полнометра́жный, *adj.* п. фильм full-length film.

полномо́чи|е, я, *n.* authority, power, plenary powers; commission; (*leg.*) proxy; чрезвыча́йные ~я emergency powers; срок ~й term of office; превыше́ние ~й exceeding one's commission; дать ~я (+*d.*) to empower; име́ть ~я вы́ступить от и́мени (+*g.*) to have authority to speak (for); предъяви́ть свои́ ~я (на+*a.*) to show one's authority (to, for).

полномо́ч|ный (~ен, ~на), *adj.* plenipotentiary; п. представи́тель plenipotentiary.

полнопра́ви|е, я, *n.* full rights; competency.

полнопра́в|ный (~ен, ~на), *adj.* enjoying full rights; competent; п. член full member.

полноро́дный, *adj.* (*leg.*) full (*brother or sister, as opp. to half-brother, half-sister*).

по́лностью, *adv.* fully, in full; completely, utterly; п. верну́ть долг to pay a debt in full; п. утверди́ть ме́ру to approve a measure in its entirety.

полнот|а́, ы́, *no pl., f.* **1.** fullness, completeness; plentitude; от ~ы́ се́рдца, души́ in the fullness of one's heart; п. вла́сти absolute power. **2.** stoutness, corpulence; plumpness.

по́лноте, *interj.* (*coll.*) enough! come come!

полноце́нност|ь, и, *f.* full value.

полноце́н|ный (~ен, ~на), *adj.* **1.** of full value. **2.** (*fig.*) of value; ~ная рабо́та work done in accordance with requirements.

полно́чи, *indecl., f.* half the (a) night.

полно́чный, *adj.* **1.** midnight. **2.** (*obs.*) northern.

по́лночь, по́лночи, *and* полу́ночи, *f.* **1.** midnight; за́ п. after midnight. **2.** (*obs.*) north.

пол|ный (~он, ~на́, ~но́), *adj.* **1.** (+*g. or i.*) full (of); complete, entire, total; absolute; в состоя́нии ~ного безу́мия stark mad; п. биле́т whole ticket (*as opp. to child's ticket of half fare*); ~ным го́лосом at the top of one's voice; сказа́ть ~ным го́лосом (*fig.*) to say outright; жить ~ной жи́знью to live a full life; ~ное затме́ние total eclipse; п. карма́н (+*g.*) a pocketful (of); ~ная незави́симость complete independence, full sovereignty; ~ное ничто́жество a complete nonentity; п. пансио́н full board and lodging; п. поко́й absolute rest; ~ное собра́ние сочине́ний complete works; п. ход вперёд! full speed ahead!; идти́ ~ным хо́дом to be in full swing; ~ная ча́ша (*fig.*) plenty; в ~ной ме́ре fully, in full measure; в ~ном расцве́те сил in one's prime; они́ пришли́ в ~ном соста́ве they came in full force; на ~ном ходу́ at full speed; он пи́шет с ~ным зна́нием де́ла he writes with a complete grasp of his subject. **2.** stout, portly; plump.

полны́м-полно́, *adv.* chock-full, chock-a-block; в авто́бусе бы́ло п.-п. наро́ду the 'bus was chock-a-block with people.

по́ло, *indecl., n.* (*sport*) polo; во́дное п. water polo.

пол-оборо́та, *indecl., m.* half-turn; п. нале́во, напра́во (*mil.*) left, right incline.

поло́в|а, ы, *f.* chaff.

полови́к, а́, *m.* mat, matting floor-covering; door-mat.

полови́н|а, ы, *f.* **1.** half; middle; два с ~ой two and a half; п. шесто́го half past five; в ~е девятна́дцатого ве́ка in the middle of the nineteenth century; на ~е доро́ги halfway; п. две́ри leaf of a door. **2.** (*obs.*) apartment, rooms, wing.

полови́нк|а, и, *f.* **1.** half. **2.** leaf (*of door*).

полови́н|ный, *adj.* half; п. окла́д half-pay; заплати́ть за что́-н. в ~ом разме́ре to pay half-price for something.

полови́нчатост|ь, и, *f.* half-heartedness; indeterminateness.

полови́нчат|ый (~, ~а), *adj.* **1.** halved; half-and-half; п. кирпи́ч half-brick; п. чугу́н mottled iron. **2.** (*fig.*) half-hearted; undecided; indeterminate; ~ое реше́ние compromise decision.

полови́ц|а, ы, *f.* floor board.

поло́вник[1], а, *m.* (*hist.*) share-cropper.

поло́вник[2], а, *m.* (*dial.*) ladle.

полово́дь|е, я, *n.* flood, high water (*at time of spring thaw*).

полов|о́й[1], *adj.* floor; ~а́я тря́пка floor cloth; ~а́я щётка broom.

полов|о́й[2], *adj.* sexual; ~о́е бесси́лие impotence; ~о́е влече́ние sexual attraction;

~а́я зре́лость puberty; ~ы́е о́рганы genitals, sexual organs; ~а́я связь sexual intercourse.

полов|о́й³, о́го, *m.* (*obs.*) waiter.

поло́вый, *adj.* pale yellow, sandy.

по́лог, а, *m.* bed-curtain; под ~ом но́чи (*poet.*) under cover of night.

поло́гий, *adj.* gently sloping.

поло́гост|ь, и, *f.* slope, declivity.

положе́ни|е, я, *n.* **1.** position; whereabouts. **2.** position; posture; attitude; в сидя́чем ~и in a sitting position. **3.** (*in var. senses*) position; condition, state; situation; status, standing; circumstances; семе́йное п. marital status; социа́льное п. social status; вое́нное п. martial law; перевести́ на ми́рное п. to transfer to a peace-time footing; оса́дное п. state of siege; чрезвыча́йное п. state of emergency; п. веще́й state of affairs; при тако́м ~и дел as things stand, things being as they are; хозя́ин ~я master of the situation; быть на высоте́ ~я to be up to the mark, be on top of the situation; выходи́ть из ~я to find a way out; войти́ в чье-н. п. to understand someone's position; челове́к с ~ем a man of high position; быть в стеснённом ~и to be in straightened, reduced circumstances; быть на нелега́льном ~и to be in hiding; быть в (интере́сном) ~и (*coll., euph.*) to be in the family way, be expecting. **4.** regulations, statute; по ~ю according to the regulations. **5.** thesis; tenet; clause, provisions (*of an agreement, etc.*).

поло́ж|енный, *p.p.p. of* ~и́ть *and adj.* agreed, determined; в п. час at a time agreed.

поло́жим let us assume; он, п., всё ви́дел he saw everything, let us assume; п., что он всё ви́дел assuming that he saw everything. (*Also in expressions indicating doubt or dissent.*)

положи́тельно, *adv.* **1.** positively; favourably; п. отве́тить (*i*) to answer in the affirmative, (*ii*) to give a favourable answer; to agree, consent; отнести́сь п. (к) to take a favourable view (of), look favourably (upon). **2.** (*coll.*) positively, completely, absolutely; она́ п. ничего́ не понима́ет she understands absolutely nothing.

положи́тель|ный (~ен, ~ьна), *adj.* **1.** (*in var. senses*) positive; ~ьная сте́пень сравне́ния (*gram.*) positive degree; ~ьная филосо́фия positive philosophy, positivism; п. электри́ческий заря́д positive electric charge. **2.** affirmative; п. отве́т affirmative reply. **3.** favourable; possessing good qualities; п. геро́й (*lit.*) positive hero; ~ьная оце́нка favourable reception. **4.** (*coll.*) complete, absolute; п. дура́к complete fool.

полож|и́ть, у́, ~ишь, *pf.* **1.** *pf. of* класть; п. жизнь to lay down one's life; п. ору́жие to lay down one's arms. **2.** (+*inf.*; *obs.*) to decide; to agree. **3.** (*coll., obs.*) to propose, offer; to fix; они́ ~и́ли ему́ хоро́шее жа́лованье they have offered him a good salary.

полож|и́ться, у́сь, ~ишься, *pf.* (*of* полага́ться) (на+*a.*) to rely (upon), count (upon); to pin one's hopes (upon).

по́лоз¹, а, *pl.* поло́зья, поло́зьев, *m.* (sledge) runner.

по́лоз², а, *m.* grass-snake.

пол|о́к¹, ка́, *m.* (*in Russian steam bath*) sweating shelf.

пол|о́к², ка́, *m.* dray.

поло́льник, а, *m.* hoe.

поло́льщик, а, *m.* weeder.

полома́|ть, ю, *pf.* to break.

полома́|ться, юсь, *pf. of* лома́ться.

поло́мк|а, и, *f.* breakage.

поломо́йк|а, и, *f.* (*coll.*) charwoman.

поло́н, а, *m.* (*arch.*) captivity.

полоне́з, а, *m.* polonaise.

полониза́ци|я, и, *f.* polonization.

полонизи́р|овать, ую, *impf. and pf.* to polonize.

полони́зм, а, *m.* (*ling.*) polonism.

поло́ни|й, я, *m.* (*chem.*) polonium.

полон|и́ть, ю́, и́шь, *pf.* (*arch.*) to take captive.

полоро́ги|й, *adj.* horned; *pl. as noun* ~е, ~х horned ruminant mammals.

полос|а́, ы́, *a.* по́лосу, *pl.* по́лосы, поло́с, ~а́м, *f.* **1.** stripe; streak; мате́рия (с) бе́лыми и голубы́ми ~а́ми material in blue and white stripes. **2.** (*in var. senses*) strip; (*of iron, etc.*) band, flat bar. **3.** wale, weal. **4.** region, zone, belt; strip; оборони́тельная п. defence zone; песча́ная п. sandy strip; чернозёмная п. black-earth belt. **5.** (*agric.; obs.*) patch, strip. **6.** period; phase; ~о́й, ~а́ми (*as adv. of time*) in patches; п. хоро́шей пого́ды spell of fine weather; п. неуда́ч run of bad luck; мра́чная п. нашла́ на него́ he is going through a gloomy patch. **7.** (*typ.*) type page.

полоса́тик, а, *m.* (*zool.*) rorqual.

полоса́т|ый (~, ~а), *adj.* striped, stripy.

поло́ск|а, и, *f. dim. of* полоса́; в ~у striped.

полоска́ни|е, я, *n.* **1.** rinse, rinsing; gargling. **2.** gargle.

полоска́тельниц|а, ы, *f.* slop-basin.

полоска́тельн|ый, *adj.* ~ая ча́шка slop-basin.

поло|ска́ть, щу́, ~щешь, *impf.* (*of* вы~) to rinse; п. го́рло to gargle.

поло|ска́ться, щу́сь, ~щешься, *impf.* **1.** to paddle. **2.** (*of a flag, sail, etc.*) to flap.

полосн|у́ть, у́, ёшь, *pf.* (*no impf.*) (*coll.*) to slash.

полосный, *adj.* (*typ.*) full page.

полос|овать, *ую*, *impf.* 1. (*pf.* рас~) (*tech.*) to make into bars. 2. (*pf.* ис~) (*coll.*) to flog, scourge, welt.

полосов|ой, *adj.* (*tech.*) band, strip, bar; ~ое железо bar-iron.

полост|ь¹, *и*, *g. pl.* ~ей, *f.* (*anat.*) cavity; брюшная п. abdominal cavity.

полост|ь², *и*, *g. pl.* ~ей, *f.* travelling rug.

полотен|це, *ца*, *g. pl.* ~ец, *n.* towel; мохнатое п. Turkish towel; посудное п. tea-towel; п. на валике roller towel.

полотёр, *а*, *m.* floor-polisher.

полотёрн|ый, *adj.* floor-polishing; ~ая щётка brush, broom.

полотнищ|е, *а*, *n.* 1. (*of material*) width; panel; п. палатки tent section, ground sheet; парус в пять ~ sail of five panels. 2. flat (part), blade.

полот|но, *на*, *pl.* ~на, ~ен, ~нам, *n.* 1. linen; бледный как п. white as a sheet. 2. (*art*) canvas (*fig.* = *painting*). 3. железнодорожное п. permanent way. 4. (*tech.*) web; blade; п. пилы saw blade, saw web.

полотняный, *adj.* linen.

полот|ок, *ка*, *m.* (*obs.*) half of a (smoked, dried, *or* salted) bird or other game.

пол|оть, *ю*, ~ешь, *impf.* (*of* вы~) to weed.

полоуми|е, *я*, *n.* craziness.

полоум|ный (~ен, ~на), *adj.* (*coll.*) half-witted, crazy.

полпив|о, *а*, *n.* (*obs.*, *coll.*) light beer.

полпред, *а*, *m.* (*abbr. of* полномочный представитель) (ambassador) plenipotentiary.

полпути, *indecl.*, *m.* на п. half-way; вернуться с п. to turn back half-way; остановиться на п. (*fig.*) to stop half-way.

полслов|а, на ~е, *n.* п. от него не услышишь you cannot get a word out of him; можно вас на п.? may I have a word with you?, may I speak to you for a minute?

полтин|а, *ы*, *f.* (*coll.*) = ~ник; два с ~ой two roubles fifty kopecks.

полтинник, *а*, *m.* 1. fifty kopecks. 2. fifty-kopeck piece.

полтора, **полутора**, *m. and n.* one and a half; в п. раза больше half as much again; ни два ни п. neither one thing nor the other.

полтораста, **полутораста**, *num.* a hundred and fifty.

полтор|ы, *f.* = ~а; п. тысячи one and a half thousand.

полу- half-, semi-, demi-.

полубак, *а*, *m.* (*naut.*) forecastle; top-gallant forecastle.

полубессознательный, *adj.* semi-unconscious.

полубог, *а*, *m.* demigod.

полуботин|ки, ок, *sing.* ~ок, ~ка, *m.* shoes.

полуваттный, *adj.* (*electr.*) half-watt.

полугласн|ый, ого, *m.* (*ling.*) semivowel.

полугоди|е, *я*, *n.* half-year, six months.

полугодичны|й, *adj.* half-yearly; of six months' duration; ~е курсы six-months courses.

полугодовалый, *adj.* six-month(s)-old.

полугодовой, *adj.* half-yearly, six-monthly; п. отчёт half-yearly report.

полуграмотный, *adj.* semi-literate.

полуд|а, *ы*, *f.* tinning; tin plate.

полуденный, *adj.* 1. midday. 2. (*obs.*, *poet.*) southern.

полудикий, *adj.* semi-barbarian, half savage.

полу|дить, жу, ~дишь, *pf. of* лудить.

полужёсткий, *adj.* (*tech.*) semi-rigid.

полужив|ой (~, ~а, ~о), *adj.* half dead; more dead than alive.

полузащит|а, ы, *f.* (*collect.*; *sport*) half-backs; центр ~ы centre half.

полузащитник, *а*, *m.* (*sport*) half-back.

полуим|я, ени, *pl.* ~ена, ~ён, ~енам, *n.* (*obs.*, *coll.*) diminutive (*of personal name*), affectionate form of name (*e.g.* Volodya *for* Vladimir, Nadya *for* Nadezhda).

полукафтан, *а*, *m.* short caftan.

полукровк|а, *и*, *f.* half-breed, first-hybrid.

полукруг, *а*, *m.* semicircle.

полукруглый, *adj.* semicircular.

полукружны|й, *adj.* ~е каналы (*anat.*) semicircular canals.

полулеж|ать, у, ишь, *impf.* to recline.

полумгл|а, ы, *f.* mist, half-light (*before sunrise or sunset*); gloaming.

полумер|а, ы, *f.* half-measure.

полумёртв|ый (~, ~а), *adj.* half-dead.

полумесяц, *а*, *m.* half moon; crescent.

полумесячный, *adj.* fortnightly; of a fortnight's duration.

полумрак, *а*, *m.* semi-darkness, shade.

полунагой, *adj.* half-naked.

полундра, *interj.* (*naut.*) stand from under!

полуночник, *а*, *m.* (*coll.*) night-bird.

полуночнича|ть, ю, *impf.* (*coll.*) to burn the midnight oil.

полуночный, *adj.* 1. midnight. 2. (*obs.*, *poet.*) northern.

полуоборот, *а*, *m.* half-turn.

полуодет|ый (~, ~а), *adj.* half-dressed, half-clothed.

полуосвещённый, *adj.* half-lit.

полуостров, *а*, *m.* peninsula.

полуостровной, *adj.* peninsular.

полуотворен|ный (~, ~а), *adj.* half-open; ajar.

полуоткрыт|ый (~, ~а), *adj.* half-open; ajar.

полуофициальный, *adj.* semi-official.

полупальто, *indecl.*, *n.* short coat.

полуперехо́д, а, m. (mil.) half day's march.

полуподва́льный, adj. п. эта́ж semi-basement.

полупокло́н, а, m. slight bow.

полупроводни́к, а́, m. (phys.) semi-conductor, transistor.

полупроводнико́вый, adj. transistor(ized).

полупья́н|ый (~, ~а́, ~о), adj. half tight, tipsy.

полуразру́шен|ный (~, ~а), adj. tumbledown, dilapidated.

полуро́т|а, ы, f. (mil.) half-company.

полусве́т¹, а, m. twilight.

полусве́т², а, m. demi-monde.

полусерьёзный, adj. half-serious; half in joke.

полусло́в|о, а, n. оборва́ть кого́-н. на ~е to cut someone short; останови́ться на ~е to stop short, stop in the middle of a sentence; поня́ть с ~а to take the hint, be quick in the uptake.

полусме́рт|ь, и,f. до ~и (fig., coll.) to death; изби́ть кого́-н. до ~и to beat someone within an inch of his life; испуга́ться до ~и to be frightened to death.

полусо́н, на́, m. half sleep; somnolence, drowsiness.

полусо́нный, adj. half asleep; dozing.

полуспу́щенный, adj. п. флаг flag at half-mast.

полуста́н|ок, ка, m. (railway) halt.

полусти́ши|е, я, n. hemistich.

полуте́н|ь, и, о ~и, в ~й, f. penumbra.

полуто́н, а, pl. ~ы and ~а́, m. 1. (mus.) semitone. 2. (art) half-tint.

полуто́нк|а, и, f. (coll.) ten-hundredweight lorry.

полуторато́нк|а, и, f. (coll.) thirty-hundredweight lorry.

полу́торн|ый, adj. of one and a half; в ~ом разме́ре half as much again.

полутьм|а́, ы́, f. semi-darkness; twilight.

полууста́в, а, m. (philol.) semi-uncial.

полуфабрика́т, а, m. half-finished product; prepared raw material (esp. of foodstuffs).

полуфина́л, а, m. (sport) semi-final.

полуфина́л|ьный, adj. of ~; ~ьные встре́чи semi-finals.

получасово́й, adj. of half an hour's duration; half-hourly.

получа́тел|ь, я, m. recipient.

получ|а́ть(ся), а́ю(сь), impf. of ~и́ть(ся).

получе́ни|е, я, n. receipt; распи́ска в ~и receipt; по ~и on receipt, on receiving.

получ|и́ть, у́, ~ишь, pf. (of ~а́ть) to get, receive, obtain; п. замеча́ние to receive a reprimand; п. на́сморк to catch a cold; п. обра́тно to recover, get back; п. огла́ску to become known, receive publicity; п. паёк to draw rations; п. призна́ние to ob-

tain recognition; п. прика́з to receive an order; п. примене́ние to come into use, effect; п. удово́льствие to derive pleasure.

получ|и́ться, ~ится, pf. (of ~а́ться) 1. to come, arrive, turn up; ~и́лась посы́лка a parcel has come. 2. to turn out, prove, be; результа́ты ~и́лись нева́жные the results are poor; ~и́лось, что он был прав it turned out that he was right, he proved right. 3. pass. of ~и́ть.

полу́чк|а, и, f. (coll.) 1. receipt. 2. pay (packet), sum paid.

полу́чше, adv. rather better, a little better.

полуша́ри|е, я, n. hemisphere; ~я головно́го мо́зга cerebral hemispheres.

полушёпот, а, m. говори́ть ~ом to speak in undertones.

полуше́рст|ь, и, f. wool mixture.

полу́шк|а, и, f. (obs.) quarter-kopeck piece; не име́ть ни ~и to be penniless.

полушто́ф, а, m. (obs.) half-shtof (see што́ф¹).

полушу́б|ок, ка, m. sheepskin coat.

полушутя́, adv. half in joke.

полцены́, indecl., f. за п. at half price; for half its value.

полчаса́, получа́са, m. half an hour.

по́лчищ|е, а, n. horde; (fig.) mass, flock.

полшага́, indecl., m. half-pace.

по́л|ый, adj. 1. hollow. 2. ~ая вода́ flood-water.

по́лымя, n. (dial.) flame; из огня́ да в п. (prov.) out of the frying-pan into the fire.

полы́н|ный, adj. of ~ь; ~ная во́дка absinth.

полы́н|ь, и, f. wormwood.

полы́н|ья́, ьи́, g. pl. ~е́й, f. polynia (unfrozen patch of water in the midst of ice).

полысе́|ть, ю, pf. of лысе́ть.

полыха́|ть, ет, impf. to blaze.

по́льз|а, ы, f. use; advantage, benefit, profit; кака́я от э́того п.? what good will it do?, what use is it?; что ~ы говори́ть об э́том? what's the use of talking about it?; извлека́ть из чего́-н. ~у to benefit from something, profit by something; принести́ ~у (+d.) to be of benefit (to); для ~ы (+g.) for the benefit (of); в ~у (+g.) in favour (of), on behalf (of); до́воды в ~у чего́-н. arguments in favour; э́то говори́т не в ва́шу ~у it does not speak well for you, it is not to your credit; два-ноль в ~у Дина́мо (sport) 2-о to Dynamo.

по́льзовани|е, я, n. use; о́бщего ~я in general use; пра́во ~я (leg.) right of user, usufruct; находи́ться в чьём-н. ~и (leg.) to be in someone's use.

по́льз|овать, ую, impf. (obs.) to treat.

по́льз|оваться, уюсь, impf. (+i.) 1. to make use (of), utilize. 2. (pf. вос~) to profit (by); п. слу́чаем to take an opportunity. 3. to enjoy; п. дове́рием (+g.) to enjoy the confidence (of); п. креди́том to possess credit; п. права́ми to enjoy rights; п. уваже́нием to be held in respect; п. успе́хом to have success, be a success.

пóльк|а[1], **и,** Pole, Polish woman.

пóльк|а[2], **и,** *f.* polka.

пóльск|ий, *adj.* Polish; *as noun* (*obs.*) п., ∼ого, *m.* polonaise.

поль|сти́ть(ся), щу́(сь), сти́шь(ся), *pf. of* льсти́ть(ся).

полюб|и́ть, лю́, ∼ишь, *pf.* to come to like, grow fond (of); to fall in love (with).

полюб|и́ться, лю́сь, ∼ишься, *pf.* (*coll.*) (+*d.*) to catch the fancy (of); to become attractive (to); она́ мне сра́зу же ∼и́лась I was immediately attracted by her, I took an immediate liking to her.

полюб|ова́ться, у́юсь, *pf. of* любова́ться; ∼у́йся, ∼у́йтесь (на+*a.*; *coll., iron.*) just look; ∼у́йся на э́того дурака́! just look at that fool!

полюбóвно, *adv.* amicably; реши́ть, кóнчить де́ло п. to come to an amicable agreement.

полюбóвный, *adj.* amicable.

полюбы́тств|овать, ую, *pf. of* любопы́тствовать.

по-людски́, *adv.* (*coll.*) as others do, in the accepted manner; жить п. to live as other people do; to live like a (normal) human being.

пóлюс, а, *m.* (*geogr., phys., and fig.*) pole; Се́верный п. North Pole; они́ — два ∼а they are poles apart.

пóлюсный, *adj.* (*phys.*) polar; п. зажи́м (*electr.*) pole terminal.

поля́к, а, *m.* Pole.

поля́н|а, ы, *f.* glade, clearing.

поляриза́тор, а, *m.* (*phys.*) polarizer.

поляризациóнный, *adj.* (*phys.*) polarizing.

поляриза́ци|я, и, *f.* (*phys.*) polarization.

поляриз|ова́ть, у́ю, *impf. and pf.* (*phys.*) to polarize.

поля́рник, а, *m.* polar explorer, member of polar expedition.

поля́рност|ь, и, *f.* (*phys.*) polarity.

поля́рн|ый, *adj.* **1.** polar, arctic; ∼ая звезда́ Pole-star, North star; се́верный п. круг arctic circle. **2.** (*fig.*) polar, diametrically opposed.

поля́чк|а, и, *f.* (*obs.*) = пóлька[1].

пом- *in compound words, abbr. of* помóщник.

помава́|ть, ю, *impf.* (*obs.*) (+*i.*) to wave, brandish.

помáд|а, ы, *f.* pomade; губна́я п. lipstick.

помá|дить, жу, дишь, *impf.* (*of* на∼) (*obs.*) to pomade; п. вóлосы to grease one's hair; п. гу́бы to put lipstick on.

помáдк|а, и, *f.* (*collect.*) fruit candy.

помáд|ный, *adj. of* ∼а; п. каранда́ш lipstick.

помáзани|е, я, *n.* (*eccl.*) anointing (*of monarch at coronation*).

помáзанник, а, *m.* (*eccl.*) anointed sovereign.

помá|зать, жу, жешь, *pf.* **1.** *pf. of* мáзать[1]. **2.** (*eccl.*) to anoint.

помá|заться, жусь, жешься, *pf. of* мáзаться.

помаз|óк, кá, *m.* small brush (*shaving brush, brush for painting throat, etc.*).

помале́ньку, *adv.* (*coll.*) **1.** gradually, gently; рабóтать п. to take one's time over one's work, take things easily. **2.** in a small way, modestly; жить п. to live modestly. **3.** tolerably, so-so.

помáлкива|ть, ю, *impf.* (*coll.*) to hold one's tongue, keep mum.

по-мальчи́шески, *adv.* in a boyish way, like a boy.

поман|и́ть, ю́, ∼ишь, *pf. of* мани́ть.

помáрк|а, и, *f.* blot; pencil mark; correction.

помá|хать, шу́, ∼шешь, *pf.* (+*i.*) to wave (*for a while, a few times*).

помáхива|ть, ю, *impf.* (+*i.*) to wave, brandish, swing (*from time to time*); собáка ∼ла хвостóм the dog would wag his tail.

помбу́х, а, *m.* (*abbr. of* помóщник бухгáлтера) assistant book-keeper.

помéдл|ить, ю, ишь, *pf.* (с+*i.; coll.*) to linger (over).

помел|ó, á, *pl.* ∼ья, ∼ьев, *n.* mop.

помéньше, *comp. of* мáленький *and* мáло somewhat smaller, a little smaller; somewhat less, a little less.

поменя́|ть(ся), ю(сь), *pf. of* меня́ть(ся) 2.

померáн|ец, ца, *m.* bitter orange, wild orange.

померáн|цевый, *adj. of* ∼ец; ∼цевые цветы́ orange-blossom.

по|мерéть, мру́, мрёшь, *past* ∼мер, ∼мерлá, ∼мерло, *pf.* (*of* ∼мирáть) (*coll.*) to die; п. сó смеху to split one's sides (with laughing).

померéщ|иться, усь, ишься, *pf. of* мерéщиться.

помёрз|нуть, ну, нешь, *past* ∼, ∼ла, *pf.* to be frost-bitten; (*of flowers, etc.*) to be killed by frost.

помéр|ить(ся), ю(сь), ишь(ся), *pf. of* мéрить(ся).

помéрк|нуть, ну, нешь, *past* ∼, ∼ла, *pf. of* мéркнуть.

помертвéлый, *adj.* deadly pale; (*fig.*) lifeless, deathly; gloomy.

помертвé|ть, ю, *pf. of* мертвéть.

помести́тельност|ь, и, *f.* spaciousness; capaciousness.

помести́тел|ьный (∼ен, ∼ьна), *adj.* spacious, roomy; capacious.

поме|сти́ть, щу́, сти́шь, *pf.* (*of* ∼щáть) **1.** to lodge, accommodate; to put up; мы могли́ бы их п. в свобóдную кóмнату we could put them into the spare room. 2. to place, locate; (*fin.*) to invest; п. объявле́ние в газе́те to put an advertisement in a paper; п. на пе́рвой страни́це to carry on the front page; п. ребёнка в де́тский сад to place a child in a kindergarten; п. сбереже́ния в сберка́ссу to put one's savings in a savings bank.

помести́|ться, щу́сь, сти́шься, *pf.* (*of* ~ща́ться) 1. to find room; to put up; (*of things*) to go in; в э́тот я́щик мои́ ве́щи не ~стя́тся my things will not go into this drawer. 2. *pass. of* ~сти́ть.

поместн|ый[1], *adj.*; ~ое дворя́нство landed gentry; п. строй (*hist.*) estate system of land tenure.

поме́стный[2], *adj.* (*obs.*) local; п. собо́р (*hist., eccl.*) local council.

помест|ье, ья, *g. pl.* ий, *n.* estate.

по́мес|ь, и, *f.* 1. cross-breed, hybrid; cross; mongrel; п. терье́ра и овча́рки, п. терье́ра с овча́ркой a cross between a terrier and a sheepdog. 2. (*fig.*) mixture, hotch-potch.

помеся́чно, *adv.* by the month; monthly, per month.

помеся́чный, *adj.* monthly.

помёт, а, *m.* 1. dung, excrement; droppings. 2. litter, brood; (*of piglets*) farrow.

помет|а, ы, *f.* mark, note; сде́лать ~ы на поля́х to make notes in the margin.

поме́|тить, чу, тишь, *pf.* (*of* ~ча́ть) to mark; to date; п. га́лочкой to tick; я ~тил письмо́ 2-м января́ I dated my letter the 2nd of January.

помех|а, и, *f.* 1. hindrance; obstacle; encumbrance; быть ~ой (+*d.*) to hinder, impede, stand in the way (of). 2. (*pl. only*) (*radio*) interference.

помеча́|ть, ю, *impf. of* поме́тить.

поме́шан|ный (~, ~a), *adj.* 1. mad, crazy; insane; *as noun* п., ~ного, *m.* madman; ~ная, ~ной, *f.* madwoman. 2. (на+*p.*; *fig., coll.*) mad (on, about), crazy (about); они́ ~ы на бри́дже they are mad about bridge.

помеша́тельств|о, а, *n.* 1. madness, craziness; lunacy, insanity. 2. (на+*p.*; *fig., coll.*) craze (for).

помеша́|ть[1, 2], ю, *pf. of* меша́ть[1, 2].

помеша́|ться, юсь, *pf.* 1. to go mad, go crazy. 2. (на+*p.*; *fig., coll.*) to become mad (on, about), become crazy (about).

помеща́|ть, ю, *impf. of* помести́ть.

помеща́|ться, юсь, *impf.* 1. (*impf. only*) to be; to be located, be situated; to be housed; где ~ется ваш кабине́т? where is your office? 2. (*impf. only*) в э́том стадио́не ~ется се́мьдесят ты́сяч челове́к this stadium holds seventy thousand people. 3. *impf. of* помести́ться.

помеще́ни|е, я, *n.* 1. placing, location; investment. 2. room, lodging, apartment; premises; жило́е п. housing, accommodation.

поме́щик, а, *m.* landowner, landlord.

поме́щи|чий, *adj. of* ~к; п. дом manor-house.

помидо́р, а, *g. pl.* ~ов, *m.* tomato.

помидо́р|ный, *adj. of* ~.

поми́ловани|е, я, *n.* (*leg.*) pardon, forgiveness; про́сьба о ~и appeal (for pardon).

поми́л|овать, ую, *pf.* to pardon, forgive; ~уй!, ~уйте! *as interj. expressing disagreement or protest* (*coll.*) pardon me!, excuse me!, for pity's sake!; Го́споди, ~уй! (*petition in liturgy*) Lord, have mercy (upon us)!

поми́мо, *prep.*+*g.* 1. apart from; besides; п. всего́ про́чего apart from anything else; п. други́х соображе́ний other considerations apart. 2. without the knowledge (of), unbeknown (to); всё э́то реши́лось п. меня́ all this was decided without my knowledge.

поми́н, а, *m.* 1. (*coll.*) mention; лёгок на ~е talk of the devil (and he is sure to appear); его́ и в ~е нет there is no trace of him; об э́том и ~у не́ было there was not so much as a mention of it. 2. (*eccl.*) prayer (*for the dead or for sick persons*).

помина́льн|ый, *adj.* п. обе́д funeral repast; ~е обря́ды funeral rites, last rites.

помина́ни|е, я, *n.* (*eccl.*) 1. prayer (for the dead *or* for sick persons). 2. list of names of dead and sick persons.

помина́|ть, ю, *impf. of* помяну́ть; не ~й(те) меня́ ли́хом! remember me kindly!; а его́ ~й, как зва́ли! (*coll.*) he just vanished into thin air.

поми́н|ки, ок, *no sing.* funeral repast, funeral banquet, wake.

поминове́ни|е, я, *n.* (*eccl.*) prayer for the dead *and/or* for the sick; remembrance (of the dead *and/or* the sick) in prayer.

помину́тно, *adv.* every minute; (*fig., coll.*) continually, constantly.

помину́тн|ый, *adj.* 1. occurring every minute; (*fig., coll.*) continual, constant. 2. by the minute; ~ая пла́та payment by the minute.

помира́|ть, ю, *impf. of* помере́ть.

помир|и́ть(ся), ю́(сь), и́шь(ся), *pf. of* мири́ть(ся).

по́мн|ить, ю, ишь, *impf.* (+*a.* or о+*p.*) to remember; не п. себя́ (от) to be beside oneself (with).

по́мн|иться, ится, *impf.* (*impers.*+*d.*) I, *etc.*, remember; мне ещё ~ится день пожа́ра I still remember the day of the fire; насколько мне ~ится as far as I can remember; ~ится, э́то произошло́ в декабре́ as I remember, it happened in December.

помнóгу, *adv.* (*coll.*) in plenty, in large quantities; in large numbers.

помнож|áть, áю, *impf. of* ~ить.

помнóж|ить, у, ишь, *pf.* (*of* мнóжить *and* ~áть) to multiply; п. два нá три to multiply two by three.

помогá|ть, ю, *impf. of* помóчь.

пом|огý, óжешь, óгут, *see* ~óчь.

по-мóему, *adv.* 1. in my opinion; to my mind, to my way of thinking. 2. in conformity with my wishes, as I would have it.

помó|и, ев, *no sing.* slops; облúть когó-н. ~ями (*fig.*, *coll.*) to fling mud at someone.

помóй|ка, ки, *g. pl.* **помóек,** *f.* rubbish heap, rubbish dump; cesspit.

помóй|ный, *adj. of* ~и; ~йное ведрó slop--pail; ~йная яма refuse pit; cesspit.

помóл, а, *m.* grinding; мукá крýпного, мéлкого ~a coarse-ground, fine-ground flour.

помóлвв|ить, лю, ишь, *pf.* (+*a.* c+*i., or* +*a.* за+*a.*; *obs.*) to betroth (to); to announce the engagement (of); её ~или с Ивáном *or* за Ивáна she is engaged to Ivan, her engagement to Ivan is announced.

помóлвк|а, и, *f.* betrothal, engagement; объявúть ~у to announce an engagement.

помóлвв|ленный, *p.p.p. of* ~ить; быть ~ленным с кем-н. to be engaged to someone.

помол|úться, юсь, ~ишься, *pf.* 1. *pf. of* молúться. 2. to spend some time in prayer.

помолóги|я, и, *f.* pomology.

помолодé|ть, ю, *pf. of* молодéть.

помолч|áть, ý, úшь, *pf.* to be silent for a while.

помóр, а, *m.* coast-dweller (*esp. of Russian inhabitants of coasts of White Sea*).

помор|úть, ю, úшь, *pf. of* морúть¹.

помóр|ка, ки, *f. of* ~.

помóрник, а, *m.* (*orn.*) skua.

поморó|зить, жу, зишь, *pf. of* морóзить.

помóр|ский, *adj. of* ~ *and* ~ье.

помóрщ|иться, усь, ишься, *pf. of* мóрщиться.

помóрь|е, я, *n.* seaboard, coastal region; балтúйское п. Pomorze, Pomerania (*S. coast of Baltic Sea*); сéверное п. White Sea Coast.

поморя́н|ин, ина, *pl.* ~е, ~, *m.* (*ethnol.*) Pomeranian (*member of W. Slav tribes inhabiting Baltic seaboard*).

помóст, а, *m.* dais; platform, stage, rostrum; scaffold.

помóч|и, éй, *no sing.* 1. leading strings; быть, ходúть на ~áх (*fig.*) to be in leading strings. 2. braces.

помоч|úться, ýсь, ~ишься, *pf. of* мочúться.

пóмоч|ь, и, f. 1. (*obs.*) = пóмощь. 2. (*obs.*) mutual aid (*afforded one another by villagers*).

помó|чь, гý, жешь, гут, *past* ~г, ~глá, *pf.*

(*of* ~гáть) 1. (+*d.*) to help, aid, assist; to succour; ~гú(те) ей надéть пальтó help her on with her coat. 2. to relieve, bring relief; инъéкции ~глú от бóли the injections relieved the pain.

помóщник, а, *m.* 1. help, helper; helpmate, helpmeet. 2. assistant; mate; п. дирéктора assistant director; п. капитáна (*naut.*) mate; п. машинúста engine-driver's mate.

пóмощ|ь, и, f. help, aid, assistance; succour; relief; оказáть п. to help, render assistance; отказáть в ~и to refuse aid; подáть рýку ~и (+*d.*) to lend a hand, lend a helping hand; позвáть на п. to call for help; прийтú на п. (+*d.*) to come to the aid (of); на п.! help!; с ~ью (+*g.*), при ~и (+*g.*) with the help (of), by means (of); без посторóнней ~и unaided, single-handed; скóрая п. ambulance; карéта скóрой ~и (*obs.*) ambulance; п. на домý home visiting (*by doctors to patients*); пéрвая п. first aid.

пóмп|а¹, ы, f. pomp, state.

пóмп|а², ы, f. pump.

помпéзност|ь, и, f. pomposity.

помпéзный, *adj.* pompous.

помпóн, а, *m.* pompon.

помрач|áть(ся), áет(ся), *impf. of* ~úть(ся).

помрачéни|е, я, *n.* darkening, obscuring; п. зрéния loss of sight; умý п. (*of unusual event or object*) it takes one's breath away.

помрач|úть, úт, *pf.* (*of* ~áть) (*obs.*) to darken, obscure, cloud.

помрач|úться, úтся, *pf.* (*of* ~áться) to grow dark, become obscured, become clouded.

помрачнé|ть, ю, *pf. of* мрачнéть.

пому|тúть(ся), чý, тúшь, тúт(ся), *pf. of* мутúть(ся).

помýч|ить, у, ишь, *pf.* to make suffer, torment.

помýч|иться, усь, ишься, *pf.* to suffer (*for a while*); п. с задáчей to torment oneself over a problem.

помч|áть, ý, úшь, *pf.* 1. to begin to whirl, rush. 2. (*coll.*) = ~áться.

помч|áться, ýсь, úшься, *pf.* to begin to rush, begin to tear along.

помыкá|ть, ю, *impf.* (+*i.*; *coll.*) to order about.

пóмыс|ел, ла, *m.* thought; intention, design; благúе ~лы good intentions.

помы́сл|ить, ю, ишь, *pf.* (*of* помышля́ть) (о+*p.*) to think (of, about), contemplate; об э́том и п. мы не смéли we dared not even dream of it.

пом|ы́ть(ся), ó́ю(сь), ó́ешь(ся), *pf. of* мы́ть(ся).

помышлéни|е, я, *n.* (*obs.*) thought; intention, design; он остáвил вся́кое п. о женúтьбе he has put aside any idea of marriage.

помышля|ть, ю, *impf. of* помы́слить.

помя́н|утый, *p.p.p. of* ~у́ть; не тем будь ~у́т (~у́та, ~у́ты) (*expression of regret at speaking ill of a person*) God forgive him (her, them)!; may it not be remembered against him (her, them)!

помян|у́ть, у́, ~ешь, *pf.* (*of* помина́ть) **1.** to mention, make mention (of); п. добро́м кого́-н. to speak well of someon**e;** ~и́ моё сло́во (*coll.*) mark my words. **2.** to pray (for), remember in one's prayers (*pray for repose of the dead or recovery of the sick*). **3.** to give a funeral banquet (for, in memory of).

помя́т|ый, *p.p.p. of* ~ь *and adj.* (*coll.*) flabby, baggy.

пом|я́ть, ну́, нёшь, *pf.* to rumple slightly; to crumple slightly.

пом|я́ться¹, ну́сь, нёшься, *pf. of* мя́ться¹.

пом|я́ться², ну́сь, нёшься, *pf.* (*coll.*) to vacillate, hum and ha (*for a while*).

пона- *verbal prefix indicating action performed gradually or by instalments.*

по-над, *prep.+i.* (*dial.*) along, by.

понаде́|яться, юсь, ешься, *pf.* (на+*a.*; *coll.*) to count (upon), rely (on); нельзя́ на него́ п. you cannot rely on him.

понадоб|иться, люсь, ишься, *pf.* to be, become necessary; е́сли ~ится if necessary.

понапра́сну, *adv.* (*coll.*) in vain.

понаслы́шке, *adv.* (*coll.*) by hearsay.

по-настоя́щему, *adv.* in the right way, properly.

понача́лу, *adv.* (*coll.*) at first, in the beginning.

по-на́шему, *adv.* **1.** in our opinion. **2.** as we would wish.

понёв|а, ы, (*dial.*) homespun skirt (*of checked or striped pattern*).

понево́ле, *adv.* willy-nilly; against one's will.

понеде́льник, а, *m.* Monday.

понеде́льно, *adv.* by the week, per week; weekly.

понеде́льный, *adj.* weekly.

понёже, *conj.* (*arch.*) because, since.

понемно́гу, *adv.* **1.** little, a little at a time. **2.** little by little.

понемно́жку, *adv.* = понемно́гу; (*in answer to question* как пожива́ете?) (doing) all right.

понес|ти́, у́, ёшь, *past* ~, ~ла́, *pf.* **1.** *pf. of* нести́. **2.** (*of horses*) to bolt.

понес|ти́сь, у́сь, ёшься, *past* ~ся, ~ла́сь, *pf.* **1.** *pf. of* нести́сь. **2.** to rush off, tear off, dash off.

по́ни, *indecl.*, *m.* pony.

понижа́|ть(ся), ю(сь), *impf. of* пони́зить-(ся).

пони́же, *adv.* rather lower; rather shorter.

пониже́ни|е, я, *n.* fall, drop; lowering; re-

duction; п. давле́ния drop in pressure; п. зарпла́ты wage-cut; п. цен reduction, fall in prices; п. по слу́жбе demotion; игра́ть на п. (*fin.*) to speculate for a fall, sell short, bear.

понизи́тельный, *adj.* (*electr.*) step-down.

пони|зить, жу, зишь, *pf.* (*of* ~жа́ть) to lower; to reduce; п. го́лос to lower one's voice; п. по слу́жбе to demote.

пони|зиться, жусь, зишься, *pf.* (*of* ~жа́ть-ся) to fall, drop, sink, go down.

понизо́вь|е, я, *n.* lower reaches.

по́низу, *adv.* low; along the ground.

понижа́|ть, ю, *impf. of* пони́кнуть.

пони́к|нуть, ну, нешь, *past* ~, ~ла, *pf.* (*of* ни́кнуть *and* ~а́ть) to droop, flag, wilt; п. голово́й to hang one's head.

понима́ни|е, я, *n.* **1.** understanding, comprehension; э́то вы́ше моего́ ~я it is past my comprehension, it is beyond me. **2.** interpretation, conception; но́вое п. исто́рии a new interpretation of history; в моём ~и as I see it.

понима́|ть, ю, *impf.* (*of* поня́ть) **1.** to understand; to comprehend; to realize; ~ю! I see! **2.** to interpret; непра́вильно п. to misunderstand; как вы ~ете э́тот посту́пок? what do you make of this action? **3.** (*impf. only*) (+*a.* or в+*p.*) to be a (good) judge (of), know (about); я ничего́ не ~ю в му́зыке I know nothing about music.

по-но́вому, *adv.* in a new fashion; нача́ть жить п. to start life afresh, turn over a new leaf.

поножо́вщин|а, ы, *f.* (*coll.*) knife-fight; knifing.

пономар|ь, я́, *m.* sexton, sacristan.

поно́с, а, *m.* diarrhoea; крова́вый п. bloody flux.

поно|си́ть¹, шу́, ~сишь, *impf.* to abuse, revile.

поно|си́ть², шу́, ~сишь, *pf.* **1.** to carry (*for a while*). **2.** to wear (*for a while*).

поно́ск|а, и, *f.* **1.** object carried by a dog between its teeth. **2.** carrying; обучи́ть соба́ку ~е to train a dog to carry things.

поно́сный, *adj.* (*obs.*) abusive, defamatory.

поно|шенный, *p.p.p. of* ~си́ть² *and adj.* worn, shabby, threadbare; п. вид (*fig.*) haggard appearance, worn look.

понра́в|иться, люсь, ишься, *pf. of* нра́вить-ся.

понтёр, а, *m.* (*cards*) punter.

понти́р|овать, ую, *impf.* (*of* с~) (*cards*) to punt.

понто́н, а, *m.* **1.** pontoon. **2.** pontoon bridge.

понтонёр, а, *m.* pontoneer, pontonier.

понто́н|ный, *adj. of* ~; ~ный мост pontoon bridge.

понуди́тельный, *adj.* impelling, pressing; coercive.

пону́|дить, жу, дишь, *pf.* (*of* ~жда́ть) to force, compel, coerce; to impel; его́ ~ди́ли к реше́нию he was forced into a decision.

понужда́|ть, ю, *impf. of* понуди́ть.

понука́|ть, ю, *impf.* (*coll.*) to urge on, goad.

пону́р|ить, ю, ишь, *pf.* п. го́лову to hang one's head.

пону́р|иться, юсь, ишься, *pf.* to hang one's head.

пону́рый, *adj.* downcast, depressed.

по́нчик, а, *m.* doughnut.

поны́не, *adv.* (*obs.*) up to the present, until now.

поню́ха|ть, ю, *pf. of* ню́хать.

поню́шк|а, и, *f.* п. табаку́ pinch of snuff; ни за ~у табаку́ (*fig., coll.*) for nothing, to no purpose.

поня́ти|е, я, *n.* **1.** concept. **2.** notion, idea; у него́ о́чень сму́тное п. о геогра́фии he has very confused notions about geography; име́ть п. (о+*p.*) to have an idea (about, of); ~я не име́ю! (*coll.*) I've no idea!; где нахо́дится центр го́рода? — не име́ю ни мале́йшего ~я! where is the city centre? I haven't the faintest idea! **3.** (*usu. pl.*) notions; level (of understanding); счита́ться с ~ями слу́шателей to take into account one's audience level.

поня́тливост|ь, и, *f.* comprehension, understanding.

поня́тлив|ый (~, ~а), *adj.* quick (in the uptake).

поня́тност|ь, и, *f.* clearness, intelligibility; perspicuity.

поня́т|ный (~ен, ~на), *adj.* **1.** understandable; ~но, что... it is understandable that...; it is natural that...; ~но (*coll.*) of course, naturally; я, ~но, не мог согласи́ться of course, I could not consent; ~ное де́ло (*coll.*) of course, naturally. **2.** clear, intelligible; perspicuous; ~но? (*coll.*) (do you) see?; is that clear?; ~но! (*coll.*) I see!; I understand!; quite!

поня́т|ой, о́го, *m.* witness (*at an official search, etc.*).

пон|я́ть, пойму́, поймёшь, *past* ~я́л, ~яла́, ~я́ло, *pf.* (*of* ~има́ть) to understand; to comprehend; to realize; п. намёк to take a hint; дать п. to give to understand.

пообе́да|ть, ю, *pf. of* обе́дать.

пообеща́|ть, ю, (*of* обеща́ть) to promise.

пообжи́|ться, ву́сь, вёшься, *pf.* (*coll.*) to get accustomed to one's new surroundings.

поо́даль, *adv.* at some distance, a little way away.

поодино́чке, *adv.* one at a time, one by one.

по-осе́ннему, *adv.* as in autumn.

поосмотр|е́ться, ю́сь, ~ишься, *pf.* (*coll.*) to take a look round; (*fig.*) to feel one's feet.

поочерёдно, *adv.* in turn, by turns.

поочерёдный, *adj.* taken in turn, proceeding by turns.

поощре́ни|е, я, *n.* encouragement; incentive, spur.

поощри́тел|ьный (~ен, ~ьна), *adj.* encouraging.

поощр|и́ть, ю́, и́шь, *pf.* (*of* ~я́ть) to encourage; to give an incentive (to), give a spur (to).

поощр|я́ть, я́ю, *impf. of* ~и́ть.

поп[1], а́, *m.* (*coll.*) priest; како́в п., тако́в и прихо́д (*prov.*) like master, like man.

поп[2], а́, *m.* pin (*in game of gorodki*); поста́вить на ~а́ (*coll.*) to place upright.

попада́ни|е, я, *n.* hit (*on target*); прямо́е п. direct hit.

попа́да|ть, ет, *pf.* to fall (*of a number of objects*).

попада́|ть(ся), ю(сь), *impf. of* попа́сть(ся).

попадь|я́, и́, *f.* (*coll.*) priest's wife.

попа́|ло, как п., etc., see ~сть.

попа́рно, *adv.* in pairs, two by two.

попа́|сть, ду́, дёшь, *past* ~л, *pf.* (*of* ~да́ть) **1.** (в+*a.*) to hit; п. в цель to hit the target; не п. в цель to miss; пу́ля ~ла ему́ в лоб the bullet hit him in the forehead; п. ни́ткой в ушко́ иглы́ to get a thread through a needle; п. па́льцем в не́бо (*coll.*) to be wide of the mark. **2.** (в+*a.*) to get (to), find oneself (in); (на+*a.*) to hit (upon), come (upon); п. в Ло́ндон to get to London; п. на по́езд to catch a train; п. домо́й to get home; п. в плен to be taken prisoner; п. кому́-н. в ру́ки to fall into someone's hands; п. под суд to be brought to trial; не туда́ п. to get the wrong number (*on telephone*); п. на рабо́ту to land a job; п. впроса́к to put one's foot into it; п. в беду́ to get into trouble, come to grief; п. в са́мую то́чку to hit the nail on the head; (*impers.; coll.*) ему́ ~ло he caught it (hot); ему́ ~дёт! he'll catch it! **3.** (*coll.*) ~ло *gives indefinite force to certain pronouns and adverbs*: как ~ло anyhow; helter-skelter; что ~ло any old thing; где ~ло anywhere; он э́то сде́лал чем ~ло he made it with whatever came to hand.

попа́|сться, ду́сь, дёшься, *past* ~лся *pf.* (*of* ~да́ться) **1.** to find oneself; он мне ~лся навстре́чу на у́лице I ran into him in the street; э́то письмо́ мне ~лось соверше́нно случа́йно I came across the letter quite by chance; п. кому́-н. на глаза́ to catch someone's eye; что ~дётся anything; пе́рвый ~вшийся the first comer, the first person one happens to meet. **2.** to be caught; (в+*a.*) to get (into); п. в кра́же to be caught stealing; п. с поли́чным to be taken red-handed; п. на у́дочку to swallow the bait, fall for the bait (*also fig.*); п. в беду́ to get into trouble; смотри́, бо́льше не ~ди́сь! don't let me catch you again!

попа́хива|ть, ет, *impf.* (*coll.*) (+*i.*) to smell slightly (of).

попённ|ый, *adj.* ~ая опла́та payment by number of trees cut down.

попеня́|ть, ю, *pf. of* пеня́ть.

поперёк, *adv. and prep.*+*g.* across; разре́зать п. to cut across; положи́те их п. lay them crosswise; де́рево упа́ло п. доро́ги the tree fell across the road; стоя́ть у кого́-н. п. доро́ги to be in someone's way; стать кому́-н. п. го́рла to stick in someone's throat; вдоль и п. far and wide; знать что-н. вдоль и п. to know something inside out, know all the ins and outs of something.

попереме́нно, *adv.* in turn, by turns.

попере́чин|а, ы, *f.* cross-beam, cross-piece, cross-bar; boom jib (*of crane*).

попере́чник, а, *m.* diameter; шесть ме́тров в ~е six metres in diameter, six metres across.

попере́чн|ый, *adj.* transverse, diametrical, cross; (*aeron.*) dihedral; ~ая ба́лка cross--beam, cross-tie; ~ая пила́ cross-cut saw; ~ая си́ла transverse force; п. разре́з, ~ое сече́ние cross-section; (ка́ждый) встре́чный и п. anybody and everybody, (every) Tom, Dick, and Harry.

поперхн|у́ться, у́сь, ёшься, *pf.* (+*i.*) to choke (over).

попе́рч|ить, у, ишь, *pf. of* пе́рчить.

попече́ни|е, я, *n.* care; charge; быть на ~и (+*g.*) to be in the charge (of); оста́вить дете́й на п. отца́ to leave children in care of their father; отложи́ть п. о чём-н. to cease caring about something.

попечи́тел|ь, я, *m.* 1. guardian, trustee. 2. (*hist.*) warden, administrator (*of educational or similar institution or district*).

попечи́тель|ный, *adj.* 1. (*obs.*) solicitous. 2. *adj. of* ~ство; п. сове́т board of guardians.

попечи́тельств|о, а, *n.* 1. guardianship, trusteeship. 2. (*hist.*) board of guardians.

попива́|ть, ю, *impf.* (*coll.*) to have a little drink (of); стать п. to take to drink.

попира́|ть, ю, *impf. of* попра́ть.

попи́скива|ть, ю, *impf.* to cheep, give a cheep.

попи́сыва|ть, ю, *impf.* (*coll.*) to write (*from time to time*); (*of a literary man; iron.*) to do a bit of writing.

по́пито, *p.p.p. of* попи́ть (*coll.*); нема́ло бы́ло п. a fair quantity was drunk.

по|пи́ть, пью, пьёшь, *past* ~пи́л, ~пила́, ~пи́ло, *pf.* to have a drink.

по́пк|а, и, *m.* (*coll.*) parrot; Polly.

попла́ва|ть, ю, *pf.* to have, take a swim.

поплав|ко́вый, *adj. of* ~о́к; ~ко́вая ка́мера float chamber (*of carburettor*); п. кран ball-cock.

поплав|о́к, ка́, *m.* 1. float. 2. (*coll.*) floating restaurant.

попла́|кать, чу, чешь, *pf.* to cry (*a little, for a while*); to shed a few tears.

попла|ти́ться, чу́сь, ~ти́шься, *pf. of* плати́ться.

попл|ева́ть, юю́, юёшь, *pf.* (*coll.*) to spit (*a few times*).

поплёвыва|ть, ю, *impf.* (*coll.*) to spit (at *intervals*).

попле|сти́сь, ту́сь, тёшься, *past* ~лся, ~ла́сь, *pf.* (*coll.*) to push off; to drag oneself along; я тепе́рь ~ту́сь домо́й I shall push off home now.

попли́н, а, *m.* (*text.*) poplin.

попли́н|овый, *adj. of* ~.

поплотне́|ть, ю, *pf. of* плотне́ть.

поплы́|ть, ву́, вёшь, *past* ~л, ~ла́, ~ло, *pf.* to strike out, start swimming.

попля|са́ть, шу́, ~шешь, *pf.* (*coll.*) to have a bit of dancing; ты у меня́ ~шешь! (*coll.*) you'll pay for this!, you'll catch it!

попо́вич, а, *m.* (*coll.*) son of a priest.

попо́в|на, ны, *g. pl.* ~ен, *f.* (*coll.*) daughter of a priest.

попо́вник, а, *m.* (*bot.*) marguerite, white ox-eye.

попо́вский, *adj. of* поп¹.

попо́вщин|а, ы, *f.* 1. (*coll., pejor.*) religious superstition. 2. popovshchina (*movement in part of the Russian Old Believer sect, retaining role of priests*).

попо́йк|а, и, *f.* (*coll.*) drinking-bout.

попола́м, *adv.* in two, in half; half-and-half; раздели́ть п. to divide in two, divide in half, halve; дава́йте запла́тим п. let's go halves; ви́ски п. с водо́й whisky and water half-and-half.

по́полз|ень, ня, *m.* (*orn.*) nuthatch.

поползнове́ни|е, я, *n.* 1. feeble impulse; half-formed intention; я име́л п. вы́сказать своё мне́ние, но в конце́ концо́в сдержа́лся I had half a mind to say what I thought but in the end I restrained myself. 2. (на+*a.*) pretension(s) (to).

попол|зти́, у́, ёшь, *past* попо́лз, ~ла́, *pf.* to begin to crawl.

пополне́ни|е, я, *n.* 1. replenishment; re--stocking; п. горю́чим re-fuelling. 2. (*mil.*) reinforcement; п. поте́рь replacement of casualties.

пополне́|ть, ю, *pf. of* полне́ть.

попо́лн|ить, ю, ишь, *pf.* (*of* ~я́ть) to replenish, supplement, fill up; to re-stock; (*mil.*) to reinforce; п. горю́чим to re-fuel; п. свои́ зна́ния to supplement one's knowledge.

попо́лн|иться, ится, *pf.* (*of* ~я́ться) 1. to increase. 2. *pass. of* ~ить.

пополн|я́ть(ся), я́ю, я́ет(ся), *impf. of* ~и́ть(ся).

пополу́дни, *adv.* in the afternoon, post meridiem; в два часа́ п. at 2 p.m.

пополу́ночи, *adv.* after midnight, ante meridiem; в два часа́ п. at 2 a.m.

попо́мн|ить, ю, ишь, *pf.* (coll.) 1. to remember; ~и (те) моё сло́во mark my words. 2. (+*d.*) to remind; я тебе́ э́то ~ю! I'll get even with you!

попо́н|а, ы, *f.* horse-cloth.

попо́тч|евать, ую, *pf. of* по́тчевать.

поправе́|ть, ю, *pf. of* праве́ть.

поправи́м|ый (~, ~а), *adj.* reparable, remediable.

попра́в|ить, лю, ишь, *pf.* (*of* ~ля́ть) 1. to mend, repair. 2. to correct, set right, put right. 3. to adjust, set straight; п. причёску to tidy one's hair. 4. to improve, better; п. своё здоро́вье to restore one's health; де́ла п. нельзя́ the matter cannot be mended.

попра́в|иться, люсь, ишься, *pf.* (*of* ~ля́ться) 1. to correct oneself. 2. to get better, recover; я совсе́м ~и́лся I am completely recovered. 3. to put on weight; to look better; он о́чень ~и́лся he has put on a lot of weight; he looks much better. 4. to improve.

попра́вк|а, и, *f.* 1. mending, repairing. 2. correction; amendment; п. к резолю́ции amendment to a resolution; внести́ ~и в законопрое́кт to amend a bill. 3. adjustment. 4. recovery; де́ло идёт на ~у things are improving, things are on the mend.

поправле́ни|е, я, *n.* 1. correction, correcting. 2. recovery; improvement; он вы́ехал на Кавка́з для ~я здоро́вья he has gone to the Caucasus for his health.

поправля́|ть(ся), ю(сь), *impf. of* попра́вить(ся).

попра́вочный, *adj.* correction; п. коэффицие́нт (*phys.*) correction factor.

попр|а́ть, у́, ёшь, *pf.* (*of* попира́ть) to trample (upon); (*fig.*) to flout.

по-пре́жнему, *adv.* as before; as usual.

попрёк, а, *m.* reproach.

попрек|а́ть, а́ю, *impf.* (*of* ~ну́ть) (+*a. and i. or* +*a.* за+*a.*) to reproach (with); п. кого́-н. гру́бостью *or* за гру́бость to reproach someone with rudeness.

попрек|ну́ть, ну́, нёшь, *pf. of* ~а́ть.

по́прищ|е, а, *n.* field; walk of life, profession; вое́нное п. soldiering; литерату́рное п. the world of letters; вступи́ть на но́вое п. to embark on a new career.

по-прия́тельски, *adv.* as a friend; in a friendly manner.

попро́б|овать, ую, *pf. of* про́бовать.

попро|си́ть(ся), шу́(сь), ~си́шь(ся), *pf. of* проси́ть(ся).

по́просту, *adv.* (coll.) simply; without ceremony; п. говоря́ to put it bluntly.

попроша́йк|а, и, *m. and f.* 1. (obs.) beggar. 2. (coll., pejor.) cadger.

попроша́йнича|ть, ю, *impf.* 1. (obs.) to beg. 2. (coll., pejor.) to cadge.

попроша́йничеств|о, а, *n.* 1. (obs.) begging. 2. (coll., pejor.) cadging.

попроща́|ться, юсь, *pf.* (с+*i.*) to take leave (of), say good-bye (to).

попру́[1], *see* попра́ть.

попру́[2], *see* попере́ть.

попры́гива|ть, ю, *impf.* (coll.) to hop about.

попрыгу́н (*oblique cases not used*) *m.* (coll., joc.) fidget.

попрыгу́н|ья, ьи, *f. of* ~.

попры́ска|ть, ю, *pf.* (+*i.*) to sprinkle (with).

попря́|тать, чу, чешь, *pf.* (coll.) to hide.

попря́|таться, чусь, чешься, *pf.* (coll.) to hide (oneself); п. от дождя́ to take cover from the rain.

попуга́|й, я, *m.* parrot.

попуга́йнича|ть, ю, *impf.* (coll.) to parrot.

попуга́|ть, ю, *pf.* (coll.) to scare, put the wind up a little.

попу́гива|ть, ю, *impf.* (coll.) to give a scare (*from time to time*).

попу́дно, *adv.* (obs.) by the pood (*see* пуд).

попу́др|ить, ю, ишь, *pf.* to powder.

попу́др|иться, юсь, ишься, *pf.* to powder one's face.

популяриза́тор, а, *m.* popularizer.

популяриза́ци|я, и, *f.* popularization.

популяризи́р|овать, ую, *impf. and pf.* to popularize.

популяриз|ова́ть, у́ю, *impf. and pf.* = ~и́ровать.

популя́рност|ь, и, *f.* popularity.

популя́р|ный (~ен, ~на), *adj.* popular.

попурри́, *indecl., n.* (mus.) pot-pourri.

попусти́тел|ь, я, *m.* (pejor.) one who tolerates (*dishonest practices, etc.*).

попусти́тельств|о, а, *n.* (pejor.) tolerance, toleration; permissiveness; connivance; при ~е (+*g.*) with the connivance (of).

попусти́тельств|овать, ую, *impf.* (+*d.*) (pejor.) to tolerate, put up (with); to connive (at); почему́ она́ ~ует его́ пья́нству? why does she put up with his drunkenness?

по-пусто́му, *adv.* (coll.) in vain, to no purpose.

по́пусту, *adv.* (coll.) = по-пусто́му.

попу́та|ть, ет, *pf.* (coll., joc.) to beguile; чёрт ~л it's the devil's work.

попу́тно, *adv.* on one's way; at the same time; (*fig.*) in passing; incidentally; мо́жно п. заме́тить, что... it may be observed in passing that . . .

попу́тн|ый, *adj.* **1.** accompanying; following; passing; п. ве́тер fair wind, favourable wind; идти́ ~ым ве́тром (*naut.*) to sail free; ~ая струя́ back-eddy, backwash. **2.** (*fig.*) passing, incidental; п. вопро́с incidental question; ~ое замеча́ние passing remark.

попу́тчик, а, *m.* fellow-traveller (*also fig., polit.*).

попуще́ни|е, я, *n.* (*obs.*) **1.** (*pejor.*) tolerance; connivance. **2.** calamity.

попыта́|ть, ю, *pf.* (+*a.* or *g.*; *coll.*) to try (out); п. сча́стья to try one's luck.

попыта́|ться, юсь, *pf. of* пыта́ться.

попы́тк|а, и, *f.* attempt, endeavour; предприня́ть ~у to make an attempt; ~и сближе́ния (*polit.*) approaches.

попы́хива|ть, ю, *impf.* (*coll.*) to let out puffs; п. тру́бкой, п. из тру́бки to puff away at a pipe.

попя́|титься, чусь, тишься, *pf. of* пя́титься.

попя́тн|ый, *adj.* (*obs.*) backward; идти́ на п. *or* на ~ую (*coll.*) to go back on one's word.

по́р|а, ы, *f.* pore.

пор|а́, ы́, *a.* ~у, *f.* **1.** time, season; весе́нняя п. springtime; осе́нняя п. autumn; вече́рней ~о́й of an evening; в ~у opportunely, at the right time; не в ~у inopportunely, at the wrong time; вы прие́хали в са́мую ~у you came just at the right time; в ту ~у then, at that time; в ~е́ (*coll.*) in one's prime; до ~ы, до вре́мени for the time being; до каки́х ~? till when?, till what time?; до каки́х ~ вы оста́нетесь здесь? how long will you be here?; до сих ~ till now, up to now, hitherto; до сей ~ы to this day; на пе́рвых ~а́х at first; с да́вних ~ long, for a long time, for ages; с каки́х ~?, с кото́рых ~? since when?; с тех ~, как... (ever) since...; с э́тих ~ since then, since that time. **2.** *as pred.* it is time; давно́ п. it is high time; п. спать! (it is) bedtime!

порабо́та|ть, ю, *pf.* to do some work, put in some work.

работи́тел|ь, я, *m.* enslaver.

порабо|ти́ть, щу́, ти́шь, *pf.* (*of* ~ща́ть) to enslave; (*fig.*) to enthral(l).

порабоща́|ть, ю, *impf. of* поработи́ть.

порабоще́ни|е, я, *n.* enslavement; enthralment.

поравня́|ться, юсь, *pf.* (с+*i.*) to come up (to), come alongside.

пораде́|ть, ю, *pf. of* раде́ть.

пора́д|овать, ую, *pf.* **1.** *pf. of* ра́довать. **2.** to give pleasure for a while, make happy for a while.

пора́д|оваться, уюсь, *pf.* **1.** *pf. of* ра́доваться. **2.** to be happy for a while.

поража́|ть(ся), ю(сь), *impf. of* порази́ть(ся).

пораже́н|ец, ца, *m.* defeatist.

пораже́ни|е, я, *n.* **1.** defeat; не име́ть ~й (*sport*) to be unbeaten. **2.** (*mil.*) hitting (*the target, the objective*). **3.** (*med.*) affection; lesion. **4.** п. в права́х (*leg.*) disfranchisement.

пораже́нческий, *adj.* defeatist.

пораже́нчеств|о, а, *n.* defeatism.

порази́тел|ьный (~ен, ~ьна), *adj.* striking; staggering, startling.

пора|зи́ть, жу́, зи́шь, *pf.* (*of* ~жа́ть) **1.** to defeat; to rout. **2.** (*mil.*) to hit, strike; п. кинжа́лом to stab with a dagger. **3.** (*med.*) to affect, strike. **4.** (*fig.*) to strike; to stagger; to startle; меня́ ~зи́л её мра́чный вид I was struck by her gloomy appearance; нас ~зи́ли све́дения об их помо́лвке we were staggered by the news of their engagement.

пора|зи́ться, жу́сь, зи́шься, *pf.* (*of* ~жа́ться) **1.** to be staggered, be startled, be astounded. **2.** *pass. of* ~зи́ть.

по-ра́зному, *adv.* differently, in different ways.

порайо́нный, *adj.* (by) area.

пора́н|ить, ю, ишь, *pf.* to wound; to injure; to hurt.

пора́н|иться, юсь, ишься, *pf.* to injure oneself; to hurt oneself.

пораст|а́ть, а́ет, *impf. of* ~и́.

пораст|и́, ёт, *past* поро́с, поросла́, *pf.* (+*i.*) to become overgrown (with).

порв|а́ть, у́, ёшь, *past* ~а́л, ~ала́, ~а́ло, *pf.* **1.** to tear slightly. **2.** (*impf.* порыва́ть) (с+*i.*; *fig.*) to break (with); to break off (with); она́ давно́ ~ала́ с ним she broke with him long ago; п. дипломати́ческие сноше́ния to break off diplomatic relations.

порв|а́ться, ётся, *past* ~а́лся, ~ала́сь, ~а́ло́сь, *pf.* **1.** to break (off), snap. **2.** to tear slightly. **3.** (*impf.* порыва́ться[1]) (*fig.*) to be broken (off).

пореде́|ть, ет, *pf. of* реде́ть.

поре́з, а, *m.* cut.

поре́|зать, жу, жешь, *pf.* **1.** to cut; п. себе́ па́лец to cut one's finger. **2.** (+*a.* or *g.*) to cut (*a quantity of*); п. хле́ба to cut some bread. **3.** (+*a.* or *g.*) to kill, slaughter (*a number of*).

поре́|заться, жусь, жешься, *pf.* to cut oneself.

поре́|й, я, *m.* leek.

порекоменд|ова́ть, у́ю, *pf. of* рекомендова́ть.

пореш|и́ть, у́, и́шь, *pf.* **1.** (*coll.*) to make up one's mind. **2.** (*obs.*) to decide, finish, settle; вот мы ~и́ли де́ло now we have settled the matter. **3.** (*fig., coll.*) to finish off, do away (with), do for.

поржаве́|ть, ет, *pf. of* ржаве́ть.

по́ристост|ь, и, *f.* porosity.

по́рист|ый (~, ~a), *adj.* porous.

порица́ни|е, я, *n.* blame, censure; reproof, reprimand; досто́йный ~я reprehensible; вы́разить п. (+*d.*) to censure, pass a vote of censure (on); вы́нести обще́ственное п. (+*d.*) to reprimand publicly, administer a public reprimand.

порица́тел|ьный (~ен, ~ьна), *adj.* disapproving; reproving.

порица́|ть, ю, *impf.* to blame; to censure.

по́рк|а¹, и, *f.* unstitching, unpicking, undoing, ripping.

по́рк|а², и, *f.* (*coll.*) flogging, thrashing; whipping, lashing.

порно́граф, а, *m.* pornographer.

порнографи́ческий, *adj.* pornographic.

порногра́фи|я, и, *f.* pornography.

по́ровну, *adv.* equally, in equal parts; разде́лить п. to divide equally, into equal parts.

поро́г, а, *m.* 1. threshold (*also fig.*); переступи́ть п. to cross the threshold; обива́ть ~и у кого́-н. to haunt someone's threshold, pester someone; я их на п. не пущу́ they shall not set foot on my threshold, they shall not darken my door; стоя́ть на ~e сме́рти to be at death's door; светово́й п. (*physiol.*) visual threshold; слухово́й п., п. слы́шимости (*physiol.*) threshold of audibility. 2. (*geogr.*) rapids. 3. (*tech.*) baffle (plate), dam, altar (*of furnace*).

поро́д|а, ы, *f.* 1. breed, race, strain, species; (*fig.*) kind, sort, type; они́ как раз одно́й и той же ~ы they are of exactly the same type. 2. (*obs.*) breeding. 3. (*geol.*) rock; го́рная п. rock; layer, bed, stratum; материко́вая п. bed-rock; matrix, gauge; пуста́я п. barren rock, dead rock, waste rock.

поро́дистост|ь, и, *f.* (pure) breeding.

поро́дист|ый (~, ~a), *adj.* pure-breed; thoroughbred, pedigree.

поро|ди́ть, жу́, ди́шь, *pf.* (*of* ~жда́ть) (*obs.*) to give birth (to), beget; (*fig.*) to raise, generate, engender, give rise (to); его́ отсу́тствие ~ди́ло мно́го то́лков his absence produced a crop of rumours.

породн|ённый, *p.p.p. of* ~и́ть; ~ённые города́ linked cities, twinned cities.

породн|и́ть(ся), ю́(сь), и́шь(ся), *pf. of* родни́ть(ся).

поро́дность|, и, *f.* (*agric.*) race, breed.

поро́дный, *adj.* (*agric.*) pedigree.

порожда́|ть, ю, *impf. of* породи́ть.

порожде́ни|е, я, *n.* result, outcome; (*rhet.*) fruit, handiwork.

поро́жист|ый (~, ~a), *adj.* full of rapids.

поро́жний, *adj.* (*coll.*) empty; п. ход (*tech.*) idling.

порожня́|к, а́, *m.* empties (*empty wagons on railway*).

порожняко́вый, *adj.* п. соста́в = порожня́к.

порожняко́м, *adv.* (*coll.*) empty, without a load.

по́рознь, *adv.* separately, apart.

порозове́|ть, ю, *pf. of* розове́ть.

поро́й (*and* поро́ю), *adv.* at times, now and then.

поро́к, а, *m.* 1. vice. 2. defect; flaw, blemish; ~и ре́чи defects of speech; п. се́рдца heart disease, heart trouble.

порос|ёнок, ёнка, *pl.* ~я́та, ~я́т, *m.* piglet; (*cul.*) sucking-pig.

порос|и́ться, и́тся, *impf.* (*of* o~) to farrow.

по́росл|ь, и, *f.* verdure, shoots.

порося́тин|а, ы, *f.* sucking-pig (*meat*).

порос|я́чий, *adj. of* ~ёнок.

поро́тно, *adv.* (*mil.*) by companies.

пор|о́ть¹, ю́, ~ешь, *impf.* (*of* рас~) to unstitch, unpick, undo, rip; п. вздор, ерунду́, чушь (*coll.*) to talk nonsense; п. горя́чку (*coll.*) to be in a (tearing) hurry; не́чего п. горя́чку there's no hurry.

пор|о́ть², ю́, ~ешь, *impf.* (*of* вы́~) (*coll.*) to flog, thrash; to whip, lash; to give a flogging, thrashing, *etc.*

пор|о́ться, ~ется, *impf.* (*of* рас~) 1. to come unstitched, come undone; to rip. 2. *pass. of* ~о́ть¹.

по́рох, а (у), *pl.* ~а́, ~о́в, *m.* gun-powder; powder; он как п. he is hot-blooded; ему́ ~a не хвата́ет (*coll.*) he has not it in him, he is not up to it; п. да́ром тра́тить to spend one's wits to no purpose; держа́ть п. сухи́м (*fig.*) to keep one's powder dry; ни синь ~a (*coll.*) not a trace; ~ом па́хнет (*fig.*) there's a smell of gunpowder in the air, there is trouble brewing; он ~a не вы́думает (*coll.*) he will not set the Thames on fire.

пороховни́ц|а, ы, *f.* powder-flask.

пороховой, *adj. of* по́рох; п. заво́д powder-mill; п. по́греб powder-magazine.

пороч|ить, у, ишь, *impf.* (*of* o~) 1. to discredit; п. чьи-н. вы́воды to discredit someone's conclusions. 2. to cover with shame, bring into disrepute; to defame, denigrate, blacken, smear; п. чью-н. репута́цию to blacken someone's reputation.

поро́чность|, и, *f.* 1. viciousness, depravity. 2. fallaciousness.

по́р|очный, *adj. of* ~ка.

поро́ч|ный (~ен, ~на), *adj.* 1. vicious, depraved; wanton. 2. faulty, defective; fallacious; п. круг vicious circle.

поро́ш|а, и, *f.* newly-fallen snow.

пороши́нк|а, и, *f.* grain of powder.

пороши́ть, и́т, *impf.* (*of snow*) to fall in

powdery form; ~и́ло (*impers.*) it was snowing slightly, a light snow was falling.

порош|ко́вый, *adj. of* ~о́к.

порошкообра́з|ный (~ен, ~на), *adj.* powder-like, powdery.

порош|о́к, ка́, *m.* powder; зубно́й п. tooth-powder; стере́ть в п. to grind into dust; (*fig., coll.*) to make mincemeat (of).

по́рск|ать, аю, *impf. of* ~нуть.

порск|а́ть, а́ю, *impf.* (*of* ~ну́ть) to set on (*hounds*).

поро́ю = поро́й.

по́рск|нуть, ну, нешь, *pf.* (*of* ~ать) (*dial.*) 1. to snort (*with laughter*). 2. to flee, dash off.

порск|ну́ть, ну́, нёшь, *pf. of* ~а́ть.

порт¹, а, о ~е, в ~у́, *pl.* ~ы́, ~о́в, *m.* port; harbour; вое́нный п. naval port, naval dockyard; возду́шный п. airport; морско́й п. seaport.

порт², а, *m.* (*naut.*) port(hole).

По́рт|а, ы, *f.* (*hist.*) The (Sublime *or* Ottoman) Porte.

порта́л, а, *m.* 1. (*archit.*) portal. 2. (*tech.*) gantry (*of crane*).

порта́л|ьный, *adj. of* ~; п. кран gantry crane.

порта́тивност|ь, и, *f.* portability, portableness.

порта́тив|ный (~ен, ~на), *adj.* portable; ~ная радиоустано́вка, п. приёмник-переда́тчик portable radio set, walkie-talkie.

портве́йн, а, *m.* port (*wine*).

по́ртер, а, *m.* porter, stout.

по́ртерн|ая, ой, *f.* (*obs.*) pub, bar, ale-house.

по́ртик, а, *m.* portico.

по́р|тить, чу, тишь, *impf.* (*of* ис~) 1. to spoil, mar; to damage; п. своё зре́ние to ruin one's eyesight; п. кому́-н. удово́льствие to mar someone's pleasure; п. меха́низм to damage the works; не ~тите себе́ не́рвы don't take it to heart; don't worry. 2. to corrupt.

по́р|титься, чусь, тишься, *impf.* (*of* ис~) 1. to deteriorate; (*of foodstuffs*) to go bad; (*of teeth*) to decay; to rot; не п. от жары́ to be heatproof; отноше́ния ста́ли п. relations have begun to deteriorate. 2. to get out of order. 3. to become corrupt.

порт|ки́, ко́в *or* ~о́к, *no sing.* (*coll.*) = ~ы́.

портмоне́, *indecl., n.* (*obs.*) purse.

портни́х|а, и, *f.* dressmaker.

портно́вский, *adj.* tailor's, tailoring.

портн|о́й, о́го, *m.* tailor.

портня́ж|ить, у, ишь, *impf.* (*coll.*) to be a tailor.

портня́жнича|ть, ю, *impf.* (*coll.*) = портня́жить.

портня́жн|ый, *adj.* tailor's, sartorial; ~ое де́ло tailoring.

портови́к, а́, *m.* docker.

порто́вый, *adj. of* порт; п. го́род port; п. рабо́чий docker.

портомо́|йня, йни, *g. pl.* ~ен, *f.* (*obs.*) wash-house.

по́рто-фра́нко, *indecl., n.* (*econ.*) free port.

портпле́д, а, *m.* hold-all.

портре́т, а, *m.* portrait; likeness; п. во весь рост full-length portrait; поясно́й п. half-length portrait; он — живо́й п. своего́ отца́ he is the image of his father.

портрети́ст, а, *m.* portrait-painter, portraitist.

портре́т|ный, *adj. of* ~; ~ная галере́я portrait gallery.

портсига́р, а, *m.* cigarette-case; cigar-case.

португа́л|ец, ьца, *m.* Portuguese.

португа́лк|а, и, *f.* Portuguese (woman).

португа́льский, *adj.* Portuguese.

портула́к, а, *m.* (*bot.*) purslane.

портупе́й-ю́нкер, а, *m.* (*mil., hist.*) 1. senior cadet. 2. junior ensign (*in pre-Revolutionary Russian cavalry*).

портупе́|я, и, *f.* (*mil.*) sword-belt; waist-belt; shoulder-belt.

портфе́л|ь, я, *m.* 1. brief-case; portfolio. 2. (*fig.*) portfolio; мини́стр без ~я Minister without Portfolio; он получи́л п. мини́стра просвеще́ния he has been made Minister of Education.

портше́з, а, *m.* sedan(-chair).

порт|ы́, о́в, *no sing.* (*coll.*) trousers.

портье́, *indecl., m.* (*hotel*) porter, doorman.

портье́р|а, ы, *f.* portière, door-curtain.

портя́нк|а, и, *f.* foot binding (*worn instead of sock or stocking*); puttee.

поруб|и́ть, лю́, ~ишь, *pf.* 1. to chop down (*all or a large number of*). 2. to do a bit of chopping.

пору́бк|а, и, *f.* tree-felling, wood-chopping.

пору́бщик, а, *m.* wood-stealer.

поруга́ни|е, я, *n.* profanation, desecration; отда́ть на п. to profane, desecrate.

пору́ганн|ый, *adj.* profaned, desecrated; ~ая честь outraged honour.

поруга́|ть, ю, *pf.* (*coll.*) to scold, swear (at).

поруга́|ться, юсь, *pf.* 1. to swear, curse. 2. (с+*i.*; *coll.*) to fall out (with).

пору́к|а, и, *f.* bail; guarantee; surety; кругова́я п. collective guarantee; взять на ~и (*i*) to bail (out), go bail (for), (*ii*) to take on probation; отпусти́ть на ~и to accept bail (for), release on bail, put on probation.

по-ру́сски, *adv.* (in) Russian; говори́ть п. to speak Russian.

поруч|а́ть, а́ю, *impf. of* ~и́ть.

поруче́йник, а, *m.* (*orn.*) marsh sandpiper.

поруче́н|ец, ца, *m.* special messenger.

поруче́ни|е, я, *n.* commission, errand; message; mission; дать п. to give a commission, charge; по ~ю (+g.) on the instructions (of); on behalf (of); per procurationem (per pro., p.p.).

поруч|ень, ня, *m.* handrail.

поручик, а, *m.* (*obs.*) lieutenant.

поручитель|ь, я, *m.* 1. guarantee, guarantor. 2. warrantor, bail, surety.

поручительств|о, а, *n.* guarantee; bail.

поруч|ить, у́, ~ишь, *pf.* (*of* ~а́ть) to charge, commission; to entrust; to instruct; он ~и́л мне переда́ть вам де́ньги he charged me to hand you the money; ма́льчика ~и́ли тата́рской ня́не the little boy has been entrusted to the care of a Tatar nannie.

поруч|и́ться, у́сь, ~ишься, *pf.* *of* руча́ться.

порфи́р, а, *m.* (*min.*) porphyry.

порфи́р|а, ы, *f.* (the) purple (*as Roman emperor's or other monarch's robe*).

порфи́р|ный, *adj.* 1. *adj. of* ~. 2. (*obs.*) purple.

порх|а́ть, а́ю, *impf.* (*of* ~ну́ть) to flutter, flit, fly about.

порх|ну́ть, ну́, нёшь, *pf. of* ~а́ть.

порцио́н, а, *m.* ration; полево́й п. (*mil.*; *obs.*) field ration allowance.

порцио́н|ный, *adj.* 1. à la carte. 2. *adj. of* ~; ~ные де́ньги (*mil.*; *obs.*) ration allowance.

по́рци|я, и, *f.* portion; (*of food*) helping; две ~и ды́ни two portions of melon, melon for two, melon twice.

по́рч|а, и, *f.* 1. spoiling; damage; wear and tear; п. отноше́ний deterioration of relations. 2. corruption. 3. (*dial.*) wasting disease (*in popular belief caused by magic spells*); навести́ ~у на кого́-н. to put the evil eye on someone.

по́рченый, *adj.* (*coll.*) 1. spoiled; (*of foodstuffs*) bad; damaged, out of order, unserviceable. 2. (*dial.*) bewitched, under the evil eye.

по́рш|ень, ня, *m.* (*tech.*) piston; plunger, sucker (*of pump*).

порш|нево́й, *adj. of* ~ень; ~нево́е кольцо́ piston ring; ~нева́я маши́на reciprocating engine; п. приво́д piston drive; п. самолёт piston aircraft (*as opp. to jet aircraft*); п. сте́ржень piston rod.

поры́в¹, а, *m.* 1. gust; rush. 2. (*fig.*) fit, gust; uprush, upsurge; благоро́дный п. noble impulse; п. гне́ва fit of temper; под влия́нием ~а on an impulse, on the spur of the moment.

поры́в², а, *m.* breaking, snapping.

порыва́ть, ю, *impf. of* порва́ть.

порыва́|ться¹, юсь, *impf. of* порва́ться.

порыва́|ться², юсь, *impf.* 1. to make jerky movements. 2. (+*inf.*) to try, endeavour.

поры́висто, *adv.* fitfully, by fits and starts.

поры́вистост|ь, и, *f.* impetuosity, violence.

поры́вист|ый (~ , ~а), *adj.* 1. gusty. 2. jerky. 3. (*fig.*) impetuous, violent; fitful.

порыже́лый, *adj.* (*coll.*) reddish-brown (*as result of fading*).

порыже́|ть, ю, *pf. of* рыже́ть.

пор|ы́ться, ою́сь, о́ешься, *pf.* (в+*p.*; *coll.*) to rummage (in, among); п. в па́мяти to give one's memory a jog.

по-ры́царски, *adv.* in a chivalrous manner.

порябе́|ть, ю, *pf. of* рябе́ть.

поря|ди́ться, жу́сь, ди́шься, *pf. of* ряди́ться.

поря́дков|ый, *adj.* ordinal; ~ое числи́тельное ordinal numeral.

поря́дком, *adv.* (*coll.*) 1. pretty, rather; мне п. надое́л э́тот фильм I found it a rather boring film. 2. properly, thoroughly; он не объясни́л п., как туда́ попа́сть he did not explain properly how to get there.

поря́длив|ый (~, ~а), *adj.* neat, orderly.

поря́д|ок, ка, *m.* (*in var. senses*) order. 1. = *correct state or arrangement*; навести́ п. (в+*a.*) to introduce order (in); привести́ в п. to put in order; привести́ себя́ в п. to tidy oneself up, set oneself to rights; призва́ть к ~ку to call to order; следи́ть за ~ком to keep order; всё в ~ке! everything is all right!, it's quite all right!, all correct!, O.K.!; э́то в ~ке веще́й it is in the order of things, it is quite natural; не в ~ке out of order, not right; у него́ кише́чник ещё не в ~ке his bowels are not right yet, there is still something the matter with his bowels; для ~ка (*i*) to maintain order, (*ii*) to preserve the conventions; к ~ку! (*at a meeting*) order!; взять сло́во к ~ку веде́ния собра́ния to rise to a point of order. 2. = *sequence*; алфави́тный п. alphabetical order; после́довательный п. sequence; де́ло идёт свои́м ~ком things are taking their (regular, normal) course; по ~ку in order, in succession; п. дня agenda, order of business, order of the day; стоя́ть в ~ке дня to be on the agenda. 3. manner, way; procedure; в ~ке (+*g.*) by way (of), on the basis (of); в администрати́вном ~ке administratively; в обяза́тельном ~ке without fail; в спе́шном ~ке quickly; в устано́вленном ~ке in accordance with established procedure; зако́нным ~ком legally; пресле́довать суде́бным ~ком to prosecute; п. вы́боров election procedure; п. голосова́ния voting procedure, method of voting. 4. (*mil.*) = *formation*; боево́й п. battle order. 5. (*polit.*)' = *system, régime*; ста́рый п. the old order; устано́вленный п. the established order. 6. (*pl.*) customs, usages, observances.

поря́дочно, *adv.* 1. decently; honestly; respectably; они́ поступи́ли вполне́ п.

they acted perfectly decently. 2. (*coll.*) fairly, pretty; a fair amount; она́ п. уста́ла she was pretty tired; мы п. вы́пили we had a fair amount to drink. 3. (*coll.*) fairly well, quite decently; он поёт п. he sings quite decently, he has quite a decent voice.

поря́дочност|ь, и, *f.* decency; honesty, probity.

поря́доч|ный (~ен, ~на), *adj.* 1. decent; honest; respectable; ~ные лю́ди respectable people, decent folk. 2. (*coll.*) fair, considerable, decent; они́ живу́т на ~ном расстоя́нии отсю́да they live a fair distance from here; он уже́ накопи́л ~ную су́мму he has already saved up a decent sum; п. дохо́д a respectable income; он — п. плут he is pretty much of a rogue.

поса́д, а, *m.* 1. (*hist.*) trading quarter (*situated outside city wall*). 2. (*obs.*) suburb.

поса|ди́ть, жу́, ~ди́шь, *pf. of* сади́ть *and* сажа́ть.

поса́дк|а, и, *f.* 1. planting. 2. embarkation; boarding (*train, bus, etc.*); (*mil.*) entrainment; embussing. 3. (*aeron.*) landing; alighting (*on water*); вы́нужденная п. forced landing. 4. seat (*manner of sitting in saddle*).

поса́дник, а, *m.* (*hist.*) posadnik (*governor of medieval Russian city-state, appointed by prince or elected by citizens*).

поса́дничеств|о, а, *n.* (*hist.*) office of posadnik.

поса́дни|чий, *adj. of* ~к.

поса́дочн|ый, *adj.* 1. planting. 2. (*aeron.*) landing; ~ые огни́ flare path; ~ая пло́щадка landing ground; п. пробе́г landing run; ~ая фа́ра landing light.

поса́д|ский, *adj. of* ~; ~ские лю́ди (*hist.*) tradespeople; *as noun* п., ~ского, *m.* (*obs.*) inhabitant of suburb.

посажа́|ть, ю, *pf.* (*coll.*) 1. (+*a. or g.*) to seat (*a number of*). 2. (+*g.*) to do a bit of planting.

поса́|женный, *p.p.p. of* ~ди́ть.

посажёный, *adj.* by the sazhen (*see* са́жень); by the fathom.

посажёный, *adj.* proxy (*for parent of bride or bridegroom at wedding ceremony*), sponsor.

поса́пыва|ть, ю, *impf.* (*coll.*) to snuffle; to breathe heavily (*in sleep*).

поса́сыва|ть, ю, *impf.* (*coll.*) to suck (at).

поса́хар|ить, ю, ишь, *pf. of* са́харить.

посва́та|ть(ся), ю(сь), *pf. of* сва́тать(ся).

посвеже́|ть, ю, *pf. of* свеже́ть.

посве|ти́ть, чу́, ~тишь, *pf.* 1. to shine for a while. 2. (+*d.*) to hold a light (for); я тебе́ ~чу́ до угла́ переу́лка I will light you to the corner of the lane.

посветле́|ть, ю, *pf. of* светле́ть.

по́свист, а, *m.* whistle; whistling.

посви|ста́ть, щу́, ~щешь, *pf.* to whistle (to, up).

посви|сте́ть, щу́, сти́шь, *pf.* to whistle, give a whistle.

посви́стыва|ть, ю, *impf.* to whistle (*softly, from time to time*).

по-сво́ему, *adv.* in one's own way; де́лайте п., поступа́йте п. have it your own way.

по-сво́йски, *adv.* (*coll.*) 1. in one's own way; он всегда́ поступа́ет п. he always pleases himself. 2. in a familiar way, as between friends.

посвяти́тельный, *adj.* dedicatory.

посвя|ти́ть, щу́, ти́шь, *pf.* (*of* ~ща́ть) 1. (+*a.* в+*a.*) to let (into), initiate (into); мы вас ~ти́м в на́шу та́йну we will let you into our secret. 2. (+*a. and d.*) to devote (to), give up (to); to dedicate (to); п. себя́ нау́ке to devote oneself to (the cause of) learning; он ~ти́л пе́рвую кни́гу свое́й ма́тери he dedicated his first book to his mother. 3. (+*a.* в+*n.–a.*) to ordain, consecrate; п. в дья́коны to ordain deacon; п. в епи́скопы to consecrate bishop; п. в ры́цари to knight, confer a knighthood (upon).

посвяща́|ть, ю, *impf. of* посвяти́ть.

посвяще́ни|е, я, *n.* 1. initiation. 2. (*in lit. work*) dedication. 3. ordination; consecration; п. в ры́цари knighting.

посе́в, а, *m.* 1. sowing. 2. crops; пло́щадь ~ов sown area, area under crops.

посевн|о́й, *adj.* sowing; ~а́я пло́щадь sown area, area under crops; *as noun* ~а́я, ~о́й, *f.* sowing campaign.

поседе́лый, *adj.* grown grey, grizzled.

поседе́|ть, ю, *pf. of* седе́ть.

посейча́с, *adv.* (*coll.*) up to now, up to the present.

поселе́н|ец, ца, *m.* 1. settler. 2. deportee.

поселе́ни|е, я, *n.* 1. settling. 2. settlement. 3. deportation; отпра́вить на п. to deport.

посел|и́ть, ю, и́шь, *pf.* (*of* ~я́ть) 1. to settle; to lodge. 2. to inspire, arouse, engender; п. вражду́ ме́жду друзья́ми to engender enmity between friends.

посел|и́ться, ю́сь, и́шься, *pf.* (*of* ~я́ться) to settle, take up residence, make one's home.

посел|ко́вый, *adj. of* ~о́к.

посёл|ок, ка, *m.* 1. settlement (*of urban type*); (*new*) housing estate. 2. (*name of administrative unit in U.S.S.R.*) settlement.

поселя́н|ин, ина, *pl.* ~е, ~, *m.* (*obs.*) peasant.

посел|я́ть(ся), я́ю(сь), *impf. of* ~и́ть(ся).

посему́, *adv.* (*obs.*) therefore.

посеребр|ённый, *p.p.p. of* ~и́ть *and adj.* silver-plated.

посеребр|и́ть, ю́, и́шь, *pf. of* серебри́ть.

посереди́, *adv. and prep.* +*g.* (*coll.*) = ~не.

посереди́не, *adv. and prep.* +*g.* in the middle (of), half way along.

посерёд|ке, *adv.* (*coll.*) = ~и́не.

посере́|ть, ю, *pf. of* cepе́ть.

посессио́нный, *adj.* (*hist.*) possessional.

посе́ссия, и, *f.* (*hist., leg.*) leasehold landed property.

посети́тел|ь, я, *m.* visitor; caller; guest; ежедне́вный п. пивно́й habitué of a bar, regular.

посети́тель|ский, *adj. of* ~.

посе|ти́ть, щу́, ти́шь, *pf.* (*of* ~ща́ть) to visit, call on; п. ле́кции to attend lectures; п. музе́й to see a museum.

посе́т|овать, ую, *pf. of* се́товать.

посе́|чься, чётся, ку́тся, *pf. of* се́чься.

посеща́емост|ь, и, *f.* attendance; плоха́я п. poor attendance.

посеще́ни|е, я, *n.* visiting; visit.

посе́|ять, ю, *pf. of* се́ять.

посиве́|ть, ю, *pf. of* сиве́ть.

посиде́л|ки, ок, *no sing.* (*obs.*) young people's gathering (*for recreation on winter evenings*).

поси|де́ть, жу́, ди́шь, *pf.* to sit (*for a while*); п. вечеро́к в гостя́х to spend an evening at friends.

поси́л|ьный (~ен, ~ьна), *adj.* within one's powers, feasible; ~ьная зада́ча feasible task; оказа́ть ~ьную по́мощь to do what one can to help; э́то не была́ ~ьная для него́ рабо́та he was not up to the work.

посине́лый, *adj.* gone blue.

посине́|ть, ю, *pf. of* сине́ть.

поска|ка́ть¹, чу́, ~чешь, *pf. of* скака́ть.

поска|ка́ть², чу́, ~чешь, *pf.* to hop, jump.

поскользн|у́ться, у́сь, ёшься, *pf.* to slip.

поско́льку, *conj.* 1. so far as, as far as; никто́ не звони́л, п. мне изве́стно no one has rung as far as I know; мы путеше́ствуем посто́льку, п. позволя́ют сре́дства we travel (just) as much as we can afford. 2. in so far as, since; so long as; п. вы гото́вы подписа́ть, гото́в и я so long as you are ready to sign, I am too.

поско́нный, *adj.* hempen.

поско́н|ь, и, *f.* 1. (*bot.*) hemp-plant. 2. (*obs.*) home-spun hempen sacking.

поскоре́е, *adv.* somewhat quicker; ~! quick!, make haste!

поскрёбк|и, ов, *no sing.* scrapings, leftovers (*of food*).

поскуп|и́ться, лю́сь, и́шься, *pf. of* скупи́ться.

послабле́ни|е, я, *n.* indulgence.

посла́н|ец, ца, *m.* messenger, envoy.

посла́ни|е, я, *n.* 1. message. 2. (*lit.*) epistle; Посла́ния (*bibl.*) the Epistles.

посла́нник, а, *m.* envoy, minister; чрезвыча́йный п. и полномо́чный мини́стр envoy extraordinary and minister plenipotentiary.

по́сл|анный, *p.p.p. of* ~а́ть; *as noun* п., ~анного, *m.* messenger, envoy.

по|сла́ть, шлю́, шлёшь, *pf.* (*of* ~сыла́ть) 1. to send, dispatch; п. за до́ктором to send for the doctor; п. по по́чте to post; п. покло́н to send one's regards; п. кого́-н. к чёрту (*fig., coll.*) to send someone to the devil. 2. (*sport, etc.*) to move (*part of the body*).

по́сле, *adv. and prep.* +*g.* after; afterwards, later (on); (*after a neg.*) since; п. войны́ after the war; мы с ним не вида́лись п. войны́ he and I have not seen one another since the war; он пришёл п. всех he came last; п. всего́ after all, when all is said and done; п. чего́ whereupon.

после- post-.

послевое́нный, *adj.* post-war.

после́д, а, *m.* (*anat.*) placenta.

после|ди́ть, жу́, ди́шь, *pf.* (за+*i.*) to look (after), see (to).

после́дк|и, ов, *no sing.* (*coll.*) remnants, leftovers.

после́дн|ий, *adj.* 1. last; final; (в) ~ее вре́мя, за ~ее вре́мя lately, of late, latterly, recently; (в) п. раз for the last time; до ~его вре́мени until very recently; до ~ей кра́йности to the very uttermost. 2. (the) latest; ~ие изве́стия the latest news; ~яя мо́да the latest fashion. 3. the latter. 4. (*coll.*) worst, lowest; ~ие времена́ (*obs.*) bad times, hard times; ~ее де́ло the end; э́то уже́ ~ее де́ло! it's the end!, it's the very limit!; ~яя ка́пля the drop to fill the cup, the last straw; руга́ться ~ими слова́ми to use foul language. 5. *as noun* ~ее, ~его, *n.* the last; the uttermost.

после́дователь, я, *m.* follower.

после́довательност|ь, и, *f.* 1. succession, sequence; п. времён (*gram.*) sequence of tenses; в стро́гой ~и in strict sequence. 2. consistency.

после́довател|ьный (~ен, ~ьна), *adj.* 1. successive, consecutive. 2. consistent, logical.

после́д|овать, ую, *pf. of* сле́довать.

после́дстви|е, я, *n.* consequence, sequel; after-effect; чрева́тый ~ями fraught, pregnant with consequences; оста́вить жа́лобу без ~й to take no action on a complaint.

после́дующий, *adj.* subsequent, succeeding, following, ensuing; (*math.*) consequent.

после́дыш, а, *m.* 1. (*coll.*) last-born child, youngest child (*in a family*). 2. (*fig., pejor.*) belated follower.

послеза́втра, *adv.* the day after tomorrow.

послеза́втра|шний, *adj. of* ~.

послело́г, а, *m.* (*gram.*) postposition.

послеобе́денный, *adj.* after-dinner.

послеоктя́брьский, *adj.* post-October (*occurring or having occurred since the 1917 Russian Revolution*).

послереволюцио́нный, *adj.* post-revolutionary.

послеродово́й, *adj.* post-natal.

послесло́ви|е, я, *n.* postface; concluding remarks.

послеуда́рный, *adj.* (*ling.*) post-tonic.

посло́виц|а, ы, *f.* proverb, saying; войти́ в ~у to become proverbial.

посло́вичный, *adj.* proverbial.

послуж|и́ть¹, у́, ~ишь, *pf. of* служи́ть.

послуж|и́ть², у́, ~ишь, *pf.* to serve (*for a while*).

послужно́й, *adj.* п. спи́сок service record.

послуша́ни|е, я, *n.* **1.** obedience. **2.** (*eccl.*) work of penance; назна́чить кому́-н. п. to impose a penance on someone.

послу́ша|ть(ся), ю(сь), *pf. of* слу́шать(ся).

по́слушник, а, *m.* novice, lay brother.

по́слушниц|а, ы, *f.* novice, lay sister.

послу́ш|ный (~ен, ~на), *adj.* obedient, dutiful.

послы́ш|ать, у, ишь, *pf.* (*obs.*) to hear.

послы́ш|аться, усь, ишься, *pf. of* слы́шаться.

послюн|и́ть, ю́, и́шь, *pf. of* слюни́ть.

посма́трива|ть, ю, *impf.* (на+*a.*) to look (at) from time to time; п. на часы́ to consult one's watch from time to time; to watch the clock; ~й(те)! keep an eye out!

посме́ива|ться, юсь, *impf.* to chuckle, laugh softly; п. в кула́к to laugh up one's sleeve.

посме́нно, *adv.* in turns, by turns; by shifts.

посме́нн|ый, *adj.* by turns, in shifts; ~ая рабо́та shift work.

посме́ртный, *adj.* posthumous.

посме́|ть, ю, *pf. of* сметь.

посме́шищ|е, а, *n.* laughing-stock, butt.

посмея́ни|е, я, *n.* mockery, ridicule; отда́ть кого́-н. на п. to make a laughing-stock of someone.

посме|я́ться, ю́сь, ёшься, *pf. of* смея́ться.

посмотр|е́ть(ся), ю́(сь), ~ишь(ся), *pf. of* смотре́ть(ся).

посмугле́|ть, ю, *pf. of* смугле́ть.

поснима́|ть, ю, *pf.* (*coll.*) to take off, take away (all *or* a number of); пора́ нам п. все рожде́ственские украше́ния it is time we took down all the Christmas decorations.

по-соба́чьи, *adv.* like a dog.

посо́би|е, я, *n.* **1.** (*financial*) aid, help, relief, assistance; allowance, benefit; п. безрабо́тным unemployment benefit, the dole; ~я матеря́м family allowances; п. по боле́зни sick benefit, sick pay; п. по нетрудо-

спосо́бности disablement allowance. **2.** textbook; (educational) aid; нагля́дные ~я visual aids; уче́бные ~я educational supplies; school text-books.

пособ|и́ть, лю́, и́шь, *pf.* (*of* ~ля́ть) (*coll.*) to aid; to relieve; п. го́рю to assuage grief.

пособля́|ть, ю, *impf. of* пособи́ть.

пособник, а, *m.* accomplice; abettor.

пособничеств|о, а, *n.* (+*g.*) complicity (in); aiding and abetting.

посове́|ститься, щусь, стишься, *pf. of* сове́ститься.

посове́т|овать(ся), ую(сь), *pf. of* сове́товать(ся).

посоде́йств|овать, ую, *pf. of* соде́йствовать.

посо́л|¹, ла́, *m.* ambassador.

посо́л|², а, *m.* salting.

посол|и́ть, ю́, ~ишь, *pf. of* соли́ть.

посолове́лый, *adj.* bleary, bleared.

посолове́|ть, ю, *pf. of* солове́ть.

по́солонь, *adv.* (*obs.*) with the sun, clockwise.

посо́льс|кий, *adj.* **1.** ambassadorial, ambassador's. **2.** *adj. of* ~тво; п. автомоби́ль embassy car.

посо́льств|о, а, *n.* embassy.

по-сосе́дски, *adv.* in a neighbourly way.

посо́тенно, *adv.* by the hundred, by hundreds.

по́сох, а, *m.* **1.** staff, crook. **2.** (bishop's) crozier.

посо́х|нуть, ну, нешь, *past* ~, ~ла, *pf.* to wither, become withered.

посо́ш|о́к, ка́, *m.* **1.** *dim. of* по́сох. **2.** (*coll.*, *joc.*) one for the road (*final drink before departure*).

посп|а́ть, лю́, и́шь, *past* ~а́л, ~ала́, ~а́ло, *pf.* to have a sleep, have a nap, snooze.

поспева́|ть¹, ет, *impf. of* поспе́ть¹.

поспева́|ть², ю, *impf. of* поспе́ть².

поспекта́кльн|ый, *adj.* ~ая опла́та (*theatr.*) pay by the performance, pay per night.

поспе́|ть¹, ет, *pf.* (*of* ~ва́ть¹) (*coll.*) **1.** to ripen. **2.** (*of food in preparation*) to be done.

поспе́|ть², ю, *pf.* (*of* ~ва́ть²) (*coll.*) to have time; (к, на+*a.*) to be in time (for); (за+*i.*) to keep up (with), keep pace (with); ~ли ли вы? were you in time?, did you make it?; она́ е́ле-е́ле ~ла на по́езд she just caught the train; мы не могли́ п. за ни́ми we could not keep up with them.

поспеша́|ть, ю, *impf.* (*coll.*) to hurry.

поспе́шеств|овать, ую, *pf.* (+*d.*; *arch.*) to help, assist.

поспеш|и́ть, у́, и́шь, *pf. of* спеши́ть; ~и́шь, люде́й насмеши́шь (*prov.*) more haste, less speed.

поспе́шно, *adv.* in a hurry, hurriedly, hastily; п. отступи́ть to beat a hasty retreat; п. уйти́ to hurry off, hurry away.

поспе́шност|ь, и, *f.* haste.

поспе́ш|ный (~ен, ~на), *adj.* hasty, hurried.

посплётнича|ть, ю, *pf.* to have a gossip; to tattle, talk scandal.

поспо́р|ить¹, ю, ишь, *pf.* **1.** *pf. of* спо́рить. **2.** (c+*i.*) to contend (with). **3.** to bet, have a bet.

поспо́р|ить², ю, ишь, *pf.* to argue (*for a while*).

посрам|и́ть, лю́, и́шь, *pf.* (*of* ~ля́ть) to disgrace.

посрам|и́ться, лю́сь, и́шься, *pf.* (*of* ~ля́ться) to disgrace oneself, cover oneself with shame.

посрамле́ни|е, я, *n.* disgrace.

посрамля́|ть(ся), ю(сь), *impf. of* посрами́ть(ся).

посреди́, *adv. and prep.* +*g.* in the middle (of), in the midst (of); п. у́лицы in the middle of the street; п. толпы́ in the midst of the crowd.

посреди́не, *adv.* = посереди́не.

посре́дник, a, *m.* **1.** mediator, intermediary; go-between. **2.** (*comm.*) middle-man. **3.** (*mil.*) umpire (*on manœuvres*).

посре́днича|ть, ю, *impf.* to act as a go-between, mediate, come in between.

посре́днический, *adj.* intermediary, mediatory.

посре́дничеств|о, a, *n.* mediation.

посре́дственно, *adv.* **1.** so-so, not outstandingly well, not all that well; он п. игра́ет в те́ннис he is not particularly good at tennis. **2.** *as noun, indecl.* fair, satisfactory (*as examination mark*); я сдал экза́мен по фи́зике на п. I got a 'fair' in physics.

посре́дственност|ь, и, *f.* mediocrity (*also* = *mediocre person*).

посре́дствен|ный (~, ~на), *adj.* **1.** mediocre, middling. **2.** (*of school marks, etc.*) fair, satisfactory.

посре́дств|о, a, *n.* mediation; при ~е, че́рез п. (+*g.*) by means of, through the instrumentality of; thanks to.

посре́дством, *prep.*+*g.* by means of; by dint of; with the aid of.

посре́дствующий, *adj.* intermediate; connecting.

поссо́р|ить(ся), ю(сь), ишь(ся), *pf. of* ссо́рить(ся).

пост¹, á, o ~é, **на** ~ý, *pl.* ~ы́, *m.* (*in var. senses*) post; наблюда́тельный п. observation post; быть на своём ~ý to be at one's post; стоя́ть на ~ý to be at one's post; (*of policeman*) to be on one's beat; (*of traffic controller*) to be on point-duty; занима́ть высо́кий п. to hold a high post; расста́вить ~ы́ (*mil.*) to post sentries.

пост², á, o ~é, **в** ~ý, *m.* **1.** fasting; (*fig.,* *coll.*) abstinence. **2.** (*eccl.*) fast; вели́кий п. Lent.

поста́в, a, *pl.* ~á, ~о́в, *m.* **1.** pair of mill-stones. **2.** (*dial.*) loom; piece of canvas.

поста́в|е́ц, ца́, *m.* (*obs. or dial.*) **1.** provisions hamper. **2.** sideboard, dresser.

поста́в|ить¹, лю, ишь, *pf. of* ста́вить.

поста́в|ить², лю, ишь, *pf.* (*of* ~ля́ть) to supply, purvey.

поста́вк|а, и, *f.* supply; delivery; ма́ссовая п. bulk delivery.

поставщи́к, á, *m.* supplier, purveyor, provider; caterer; outfitter.

постаме́нт, a, *m.* pedestal, base.

постана́влива|ть, ю, *impf.* = постановля́ть.

постанов|и́ть, лю́, ~ишь, *pf.* (*of* постана́вливать *and* ~ля́ть) to decide, resolve; to decree, enact, ordain.

постано́вк|а, и, *f.* **1.** erection, raising. **2.** (*in var. senses*) putting, placing, setting; arrangement, organization; п. вопро́са formulation of a question; у неё хоро́шая п. головы́ she holds her head well; п. го́лоса (*mus.*) voice training; п. па́льцев (*mus.*) fingering; finger training; п. рабо́ты arrangement of work. **3.** (*theatr.*) staging, production; вчера́ мы ви́дели «Ча́йку» Че́хова в но́вой ~е yesterday we saw a new production of Chekhov's 'Seagull'.

постановле́ни|е, я, *n.* **1.** decision, resolution; вы́нести п. to pass a resolution. **2.** decree, enactment; изда́ть п. to issue a decree.

постано́в|очный, *adj. of* ~ка 3; ~очная пье́са play suitable for staging; play effective in stage production; ~очные эффе́кты (stage) effects.

постано́вщик, a, *m.* producer (*of play*), stage-manager; director (*of film*).

постара́|ться, юсь, *pf. of* стара́ться.

постаре́|ть, ю, *pf. of* старе́ть.

по-ста́рому, *adv.* **1.** as before. **2.** as of old.

постате́йный, *adj.* by paragraphs, paragraph-by-paragraph, clause-by-clause.

постел|и́ть, ю, ~ишь, *pf.* (*coll.*) = постла́ть.

посте́л|ь, и, *f.* **1.** bed; лечь в п. to get into bed; лежа́ть в ~и to be in bed; встать с ~и to get out of bed; постла́ть п. to make up a bed; прико́ванный к ~и bed-ridden. **2.** (*geol., tech.*) bed; bottom.

посте́ль|ный, *adj. of* ~; ~ное бельё bed-clothes; ~ные принадле́жности bedding; п. режи́м confinement to bed; коме́дия ~ного содержа́ния (*coll.*) bedroom comedy.

постепе́нно, *adv.* gradually, little by little.

постепе́нност|ь, и, *f.* gradualness; п. разви́тия gradual development.

постепе́н|ный (~ен, ~на), *adj.* **gradual.**

постепе́новщин|а, ы, *f.* (*polit.*; *pejor.*) gradualism.

постесня́|ться, юсь, *pf. of* стесня́ться.

постиг|а́ть, а́ю, *impf. of* ∼нуть *and* пости́чь.

пости́гнуть, = пости́чь.

постиже́ни|е, я, *n.* comprehension, grasp.

постижи́м|ый (∼, ∼a), *adj.* comprehensible.

постила́|ть, ю, *impf. of* постла́ть.

пости́лк|а, и, *f.* 1. spreading, laying. 2. bedding; litter.

пости́л|очный, *adj. of* ∼ка; ∼очная соло́ма bed-straw.

постира́|ть, ю, *pf.* 1. (*coll.*) to wash. 2. to do some washing.

по|сти́ться, щу́сь, сти́шься, *impf.* to fast, keep the fast.

пости́|чь, гну, гнешь, *past* ∼г *and* (*obs.*) ∼гнул, ∼гла, *pf.* (*of* ∼га́ть) 1. to comprehend, grasp. 2. to overtake, befall, strike; их ∼гло ещё одно́ несча́стье yet another misfortune has befallen them.

пост|ла́ть, елю́, е́лешь, *past* ∼ла́л, ∼лала́, ∼ла́ло, *pf.* (*of* стлать *and* ∼ила́ть) to spread, lay; п. ковёр to lay a carpet (down); п. посте́ль to make one's bed; как ∼е́лешь, так и поспи́шь (*prov.*) as you make your bed, so must you lie.

по́стник, а, *m.* faster, person observing fast.

по́стнича|ть, ю, *impf.* to fast.

по́стничеств|о, а, *n.* fasting.

пост|ный (∼ен, ∼на́, ∼но), *adj.* 1. lenten; п. день (*eccl.*) fast-day; ∼ная еда́ lenten fare; п. обе́д meatless dinner (*comprising fish and/or vegetables*); п. са́хар boiled sweets. 2. (*coll.*; *of meat*) lean. 3. (*fig., coll., joc.*) glum. 4. (*fig., coll., joc.*) pious, sanctimonious.

постов|о́й, *adj. of* пост[1]; ∼а́я бу́дка sentry--box; п. милиционе́р militia-man on point--duty; ∼а́я слу́жба sentry duty; *as noun* п., ∼о́го, *m.* = п. милиционе́р.

посто́й[1], ∼те (*coll.*) stop!, wait (a minute)!

посто́й[2], я, *m.* billeting, quartering; поста́вить на п. to billet, quarter; свобо́ден от ∼я exempt from billeting.

посто́льку, *conj.* (*in main clause, following* поско́льку *in subordinate clause*) to that extent (*or not translated*); поли́тика п. поско́льку (*fig.*) wait-and-see policy, policy of sitting on the fence.

посторон|и́ться, ю́сь, ∼и́шься, *pf. of* сторони́ться.

посторо́нн|ий, *adj.* 1. strange; extraneous, outside; ∼ие вопро́сы side issues; без ∼ей по́мощи unassisted, single-handed; ∼ие соображе́ния extraneous considerations; ∼ее те́ло foreign body. 2. *as noun* п., ∼его, *m.* stranger; outsider; ∼им вход запрещён 'unauthorized persons not admitted'.

постоя́л|ец, ьца, *m.* (*obs.*) lodger; (*in hotel, etc.*) guest.

постоя́лый, *adj.* п. двор (*obs.*) coaching inn.

постоя́нн|ая, ой, *f.* (*math.*) constant; п. вре́мени time constant.

постоя́нно, *adv.* constantly, continually, perpetually, always.

постоя́н|ный, *adj.* 1. constant, continual; п. ка́шель continual cough; п. посети́тель constant visitor. 2. constant; permanent, invariable; п. а́дрес permanent address; ∼ная а́рмия regular army; ∼ная величина́ (*math.*) constant; п. жи́тель permanent resident; п. капита́л (*econ.*) constant capital; ∼ное напряже́ние (*electr.*) direct-current voltage; п. ого́нь (*naut.*) fixed light; п. ток (*electr.*) direct current. 3. (∼ен, ∼на) (*of personal, moral qualities, etc.*) constant, steadfast, unchanging; она́ далеко́ не ∼на во вку́сах she is far from constant in her tastes.

постоя́нств|о, а, *n.* constancy; permanency.

посто|я́ть[1], ю́, и́шь, *pf.* to stand (*for a while*).

посто|я́ть[2], ю́, и́шь, *pf.* (за+*a.*) to stand up (for).

постпаке́т, а, *m.* mail packet.

пострада́|вший, *past part. of* ∼ть; *as noun* п., ∼вшего, *m.* victim.

пострада́|ть, ю, *pf. of* страда́ть.

пострани́чный, *adj.* paginal, by the page, per page.

постра́нств|овать, ую, *pf.* to do some travelling.

постраща́|ть, ю, *pf. of* страща́ть.

постре́л, а, *m.* (*coll.*) little imp, little rascal.

постре́лива|ть, ю, *impf.* to fire intermittently, at intervals.

постреля́|ть, ю, *pf.* 1. to spend some time shooting, do some shooting. 2. (+*a.* or *g.*; *coll.*) to shoot, bag (*a number of*).

по́стриг, а, *m.* taking of monastic vows; (*of a woman*) taking the veil.

пострига́|ть(ся), ю(сь), *impf. of* постри́чь(ся)[2].

постри́жен|ец, ца, *m.* one who has taken monastic vows.

пострижéни|е, я, *n.* admission to monastic vows, tonsure; taking of monastic vows.

постри́женик, а, *m.* = постри́женец.

постри́жен|ка, ки, *f. of* ∼ец *and* ∼ик.

постри́|чь[1], гу́, жёшь, гу́т, *past* ∼г, ∼гла, *pf.* to clip, trim.

постри́|чь[2], гу́, жёшь, гу́т, *past* ∼г, ∼гла, (*pf.* (*of* ∼га́ть) to make a monk (nun), admit to monastic vows.

постри́|чься[1], гу́сь, жёшься, гу́тся, *past* ∼гся, ∼гла́сь, *pf.* to have a (hair-)trim.

постри́|чься[2], гу́сь, жёшься, гу́тся, *past*

~гся, ~глась, *pf.* (*of* ~гаться) to take monastic vows; to take the veil (*of a woman*).

построе́ни|е, я, *n.* 1. (*in var. senses*) construction. 2. (*mil.*) formation.

постро́|ечный, *adj. of* ~йка.

постро́|ить(ся), ю(сь), ишь(ся), *pf. of* стро́ить(ся).

постро́йк|а, и, *f.* 1. (*action*) building, erection, construction. 2. (*edifice*) building. 3. building-site.

постро́мк|а, и, *f.* trace (*part of harness*).

постро́чный, *adj.* by the line, per line.

постскри́птум, а, *m.* postscript.

посту́ка|ть, ю, *pf.* to knock (*for a while*).

посту́кива|ть, ю, *impf.* to knock (*from time to time*), tap, patter; ходи́ть, ~я па́лочкой to walk tapping with one's stick.

постула́т, а, *m.* (*math., philos.*) postulate.

постули́р|овать, ую, *impf. and pf.* to postulate.

поступа́тельно-возвра́тный, *adj.* (*tech.*) reciprocating.

поступа́тельн|ый, *adj.* forward, advancing; ~ое движе́ние forward movement; (*tech.*) translation; п. ход step forward, onward march.

поступ|а́ть(ся), а́ю(сь), *impf. of* ~и́ть(ся).

поступ|и́ть, лю́, ~ишь, *pf.* (*of* ~а́ть) 1. to act; в да́нных обстоя́тельствах он пра́вильно ~и́л in the circumstances he acted rightly, did right; они́ с ним пло́хо ~и́ли they have treated him badly. 2. (в, на+а.) to enter, join; п. в шко́лу to go to school, enter school; п. в университе́т to enter the university; п. на рабо́ту to go to work; п. на вое́нную слу́жбу to join up, enlist. 3. (*of inanimate objects*) to come through, come in; to be forthcoming; to be received; ~и́ла жа́лоба a complaint has been received, has come in; ~и́ло ли его́ заявле́ние? has his application come through, been received?; де́ло ~и́ло в суд the matter was taken to court, came up before the court; ~и́ло 1/хii (*of an article submitted to a periodical, etc.*) Received 1 December; п. в прода́жу to be on sale, come on the market; п. в произво́дство to go into production.

поступ|и́ться, лю́сь, ~ишься, *pf.* (*of* ~а́ться) (+*i.*) to waive, forgo; to give up; п. свои́ми права́ми to waive one's rights.

поступле́ни|е, я, *n.* 1. entering, joining; п. на вое́нную слу́жбу enlisting, joining up. 2. receipt; (*book-keeping*) entry; п. изве́стий receipt of news; п. дохо́дов revenue return.

посту́п|ок, ка, *m.* action; act, deed; (*pl., collect.*) conduct, behaviour.

по́ступ|ь, и, *f.* gait; step, tread; ме́рная п. measured tread.

постуч|а́ть(ся), у́(сь), и́шь(ся), *pf. of* стуча́ть(ся).

постфа́ктум, *adv.* post factum, after the event.

посты|ди́ть, жу́, ди́шь, *pf.* (*coll.*) to reprimand slightly, pull up.

посты|ди́ться, жу́сь, ди́шься, *pf. of* стыди́ться; ~ди́тесь! you ought to be ashamed (*of yourself*)!

посты́д|ный (~ен, ~на), *adj.* shameful.

посты́л|ый (~, ~а), *adj.* (*coll.*) hateful, repellent.

посу́д|а, ы, . 1. (*collect.*) crockery; plates and dishes, service; гли́няная п., фая́нсовая п. earthenware; жестяна́я п. tinware; ку́хонная п. kitchen utensils; стекля́нная п. glassware; фарфо́ровая п. china; ча́йная п. tea-service; би́тая п. два ве́ка живёт (*prov.*) creaking doors hang the longest. 2. (*coll.*) vessel, crock.

посуда́ч|ить, у, ишь, *pf.* (*coll.*) to gossip.

посу́дин|а, ы, *f.* 1. vessel, crock. 2. (*coll.*) (*naut.*) old tub.

посу|ди́ть, жу́, ~дишь, *pf.* (*obs.*) to judge, consider; ~ди́ сам judge for yourself.

посу́дник, а, *m.* 1. dish-washer. 2. (*coll.*) dresser.

посу́д|ный, *adj. of* ~а; п. магази́н china-shop; ~ное полоте́нце dish-cloth, tea-towel; п. шкаф dresser, china cupboard.

посудомо́йк|а, и, *f.* dishwashing machine.

посу́л, а, *m.* 1. (*coll.*) promise. 2. (*obs.*) bribe.

посул|и́ть, ю́, и́шь, *pf. of* сули́ть.

посу́точно, *adv.* by the day, for every 24 hours.

посу́точн|ый, *adj.* 24-hour, round-the-clock; у них ~ое дежу́рство they have a 24-hour spell of duty, they have 24 hours on; ~ая опла́та pay by the day.

по́суху, *adv.* (*coll.*) on dry land.

посчастли́в|иться, ится, *pf.* (*impers.+d.*) to have the luck (to); to be lucky enough (to); ей ~илось побы́ть в Пари́же she had the luck to stay in Paris.

посчита́|ть, ю, *pf.* to count (up).

посчита́|ться, юсь, *pf.* 1. (с+*i.*; *coll.*) to get even (with). 2. *pf. of* счита́ться.

посыла́|ть, ю, *impf. of* посла́ть.

посы́лк|а¹, и, *f.* 1. sending. 2. parcel. 3. errand; быть на ~ах (у) to run errands (for).

посы́лк|а², и, *f.* (*philos.*) premise; больша́я, ма́лая п. major, minor premise.

посы́лочный, *adj.* parcel.

посы́льн|ый, *adj.* 1. dispatch; ~ое су́дно dispatch-boat. 2. *as noun* п., ~ого, *m.* messenger.

посып|а́ть, а́ю, *impf. of* ~ать.

посы́п|ать, лю, лешь, *pf.* (*of* ~а́ть) (+*i.*) to strew (with); to sprinkle (with); п. гра́вием to gravel; п. со́лью to sprinkle with salt, to salt.

посы́п|аться, лется, *pf.* to begin to fall; (*fig.*) to rain, pour down; ∼а́лись ли́стья the leaves had begun to fall; несча́стья ∼а́лись на них misfortunes came upon them thick and fast.

посяга́тельств|о, а, *n.* (на+*a.*) encroachment (on, upon), infringement (of); п. на свобо́ду infringement of liberty.

посяг|а́ть, а́ю, *impf. of* ∼ну́ть.

посяг|ну́ть, ну́, нёшь, *pf.* (*of* ∼а́ть) (на+*a.*) to encroach (on, upon), infringe (on, upon); п. на чью-н. жизнь to make an attempt on someone's life.

пот, а, о ∼**е, в** ∼**у́,** *pl.* ∼**ы́,** ∼**о́в,** *m.* sweat, perspiration; весь в ∼у́ all of a sweat, bathed in sweat; облива́ясь ∼ом dripping with sweat; в ∼е лица́ by the sweat of one's brow; ∼ом и кро́вью with blood and sweat; труди́ться до седьмо́го (четвёртого) ∼а (*coll.*) to sweat one's guts out; вогна́ть кого́-н. в п., согна́ть семь ∼о́в с кого́-н. (*coll.*) to work someone to the bone, make someone sweat blood.

потаённый, *adj.* = потайно́й.

потайно́й, *adj.* secret; (*tech.*) countersunk, flush; п. ход secret passage.

потака́|ть, ю, *impf.* (*no pf.*) (+*d.*; *coll.*) to indulge; п. же́нщине в капри́зах, п. капри́зам же́нщины to indulge a woman's whims.

пота́л|ь, и, *f.* Dutch gold, brass leaf.

пота́ль|ный, *adj. of* ∼.

потанц|ева́ть, у́ю, *pf.* to dance (*for a while*), do some dancing.

потаска́|ть, ю, *pf.* (*coll.*) to pinch, filch (*all or a number of*).

потаску́н, а, *m.* (*coll.*) lecher, rake.

потаску́х|а, и, *f.* (*coll.*) strumpet, trollop.

потаску́шк|а, и, *f.* = потаску́ха.

потасо́вк|а, и, *f.* (*coll.*) 1. brawl, fight. 2. beating, hiding; зада́ть кому́-н. ∼у to give someone a hiding. 3. *pl.* (*fig.*) tight spot(s).

пота́тчик, а, *m.* (*coll.*) indulger.

пота́чк|а, и, *f.* indulgence.

пота́ш, а́, *m.* potash.

потащ|и́ть, у́, ∼ишь, *pf.* to begin to drag.

потащ|и́ться, у́сь, ∼ишься, *pf.* to begin to drag oneself, begin slowly to make one's way.

по-тво́ему, *adv.* 1. in your opinion. 2. as you wish; as you advise; пусть бу́дет п. have it your own way; just as you think.

потво́рств|о, а, *n.* indulgence, pandering.

потво́рств|овать, ую, *impf.* (+*d.*) to show indulgence (towards), pander (to).

потво́рщик, а, *m.* panderer.

потёк, а, *m.* stain; damp patch.

потём|ки, ок, *no sing.* darkness.

потемне́ни|е, я, *n.* darkening; dimness.

потемне́|ть, ю, *pf. of* темне́ть.

потѣ́ни|е, я, *n.* sweating, perspiration.

потенциа́л, а, *m.* (*phys. and fig.*) potential; ра́зность ∼ов potential difference; вое́нный п. war potential.

потенциа́л|ьный (∼**ен,** ∼**ьна),** *adj.* potential.

потенцио́метр, а, *m.* (*electr.*) potentiometer.

потенци|я, и, *f.* potentiality.

потепле́ни|е, я, *n.* getting warmer; наступи́ло п. a warm spell set in.

потепле́|ть, ет, *pf. of* тепле́ть.

по|тере́ть, тру́, трёшь, *past* ∼тёр, ∼тёрла, *pf.* to rub.

по|тере́ться, тру́сь, трёшься, *past* ∼тёрся, ∼тёрлась, *pf. of* тере́ться.

потерпе́|вший, *past part. act. of* ∼ть; *as noun* п., ∼вшего, *m.* victim; survivor; п. от пожа́ра fire victim; п. кораблекруше́ние ship-wrecked person, shipwreck survivor.

потерп|е́ть, лю́, ∼ишь, *pf.* 1. to be patient (*for a while*). 2. to suffer, tolerate, stand (for); я не ∼лю́ никако́й на́глости I won't stand for any cheek. 3. to suffer, undergo; п. кораблекруше́ние to be shipwrecked; п. пораже́ние to sustain a defeat, be defeated; п. убы́тки to suffer losses.

потёртост|ь, и, *f.* place sore from rubbing.

потёр|тый, *p.p.p. of* ∼еть *and adj.* (*coll.*) 1. shabby, threadbare. 2. (*fig.*) washed-out.

потёр|я, и, *f.* loss; waste; *pl.*; (*mil.*) losses; п. вре́мени waste of time; спи́сок ∼ь (*mil.*) casualty list; ∼и уби́тыми и ра́неными losses in killed and wounded.

потёр|янный, *p.p.p. of* ∼я́ть *and adj.* (*fig.*) lost; у неё был п. вид she had a lost expression; он — челове́к п. he is done for.

потеря́|ть(ся), ю(сь), *pf. of* теря́ть(ся).

потесн|и́ть, ю́, и́шь, *pf. of* тесни́ть.

потесн|и́ться, ю́сь, и́шься, *pf.* to make room; to sit closer, stand closer, move up (*so as to make room for others*).

поте́|ть, ю, *impf.* 1. (*pf.* вс∼) to sweat, perspire. 2. (*pf.* за∼ *and* от∼) to mist over, become covered with steam. 3. (*impf. only*) (над; *fig.*) to sweat (over), toil (over).

поте́ха, и, *f.* (*coll.*) fun, amusement; устро́ить что-н. для ∼и to do something for fun; вот п.! what fun!; и пошла́ п.! now the fun has begun!

поте́|чь, ку́, чёшь, ку́т, *past* ∼к, ∼кла́, *pf.* to begin to flow.

потеша́|ть, ю, *impf.* to amuse.

потеша́|ться, юсь, *impf.* 1. to amuse oneself. 2. (над) to laugh (at), mock (at), make fun (of).

потѣ́ш|ить, у, ишь, *pf.* 1. *pf. of* тѣ́шить. 2. to amuse (for a while).

потѣ́ш|иться, усь, ишься, *pf.* 1. *pf. of* тѣ́-

шиться. 2. to amuse oneself (*for a while*), have a bit of fun.

потѐш|ный, *adj.* **1.** (~ен, ~на) (*coll.*) funny, amusing. **2.** (*obs.*) (done, contrived) for fun, for amusement; п. полк (*hist.*) 'poteshny' regiment, 'toy-soldiers' (*regiment of boy-soldiers formed by Peter the Great*). **3.** *as noun* (*pl.*) ~ные, ~ных = п. полк.

потѝр, а, *m.* (*eccl.*) chalice.

потира́|ть, ю, *impf.* to rub (*from time to time*); п. ру́ки от ра́дости to rub one's hands with joy.

потихóньку, *adv.* (*coll.*) **1.** slowly. **2.** softly, noiselessly. **3.** on the sly, secretly.

потлѝвост|ь, и, f. disposition to sweat, perspire.

потлѝв|ый (~, ~а), *adj.* sweaty; subject to sweating.

потнѝк, á, *m.* sweat-cloth, saddle-cloth.

пóт|ный (~ен, ~на́, ~но), *adj.* **1.** sweaty, damp with perspiration; ~ные ру́ки clammy hands. **2.** (*of glass, etc.*) misty, covered with steam.

потов|óй, *adj.* of пот; ~ые желе́зы sweat glands; п. жир wool yolk, suint.

потогóнн|ый, *adj.*; ~ое (сре́дство) (*med.*) sudorific, diaphoretic; ~ая систе́ма труда́ sweated labour system.

потóк, а, *m.* **1.** (*in var. senses*) stream; flow; гóрный п. mountain stream; людскóй п. stream of people; проходи́ть несконча́емым ~ом to file past in an endless stream; п. слов flow of words; скос ~а (*aeron.*) downwash; лить ~и слёз to weep in floods; отда́ть на п. и разграбле́ние (*hist.*) to give over to wholesale pillage. **2.** production line. **3.** (*in education*) stream, group.

потолка́|ться, юсь, *pf.* (*coll.*) to knock about.

потолк|ова́ть, у́ю, *pf.* (с+*i.*; *coll.*) to have a talk (with).

потол|óк, ка́, *m.* ceiling (*also aeron.*).; взять что-н. с ~ка́ (*joc.*) to make something up.

потолó|чный, *adj.* of ~к; (*fig., joc.*) chance, random; ~чные доказа́тельства unfounded arguments.

потолсте́|ть, ю, *pf.* of толсте́ть.

потóм, *adv.* afterwards; later (on); then, after that; мы п. придём we shall come later; ну, что вы сде́лали п.? well, what did you do then?

потóм|ок, ка, *m.* descendant; scion; *pl.* offspring, progeny.

потóмственный, *adj.* hereditary; он п. сере́бряных дел ма́стер he comes of a family of silversmiths.

потóмств|о, а, n. (*collect.*) posterity, descendants.

потому́ 1. *adv.* that is why; я был в отпу-ску́, п. я и не знал об э́том I was on leave,

that is why I did not know about it. **2.** *conj.* п. что; п... что because, as; я не знал об э́том, п. что был в отпуску́ I did not know about it because I was on leave; я п. не знал об э́том, что был в отпуску́ (*division of conj. alters emphasis*) the reason I did not know about it was that I was on leave.

потон|у́ть, у́, ~ешь, *pf.* of тону́ть.

потóп, а, *m.* flood, deluge; всеми́рный п. (*bibl.*) the Flood, the Deluge; до ~а (*fig., joc.*) before the Flood.

потопа́|ть, ю, *impf.* = тону́ть.

потоп|и́ть[1], лю, ~ишь, *pf.* to heat (*for a while*).

потоп|и́ть[2], лю, ~ишь, *pf.* (*of* ~ля́ть) to sink.

потопле́ни|е, я, n. sinking.

потоп|та́ть, чу́, ~чешь, *pf.* of топта́ть.

поторáплива|ть, ю, *impf.* (*coll.*) to hurry up, urge on.

поторáплива|ться, юсь, *impf.* (*coll.*) to hurry, make haste; ~йтесь! get a move on!

поторг|ова́ться, у́юсь, *pf.* (*coll.*) to bargain (*for a while*), haggle.

потороп|и́ть(ся), лю́(сь), ~ишь(ся), *pf.* of торопи́ть(ся).

потó|чный, *adj.* of ~к; ~чная ? ния production-line; ма́ссовое ~чное произвóдство mass production.

потра́в|а, ы, f. damage (*causea to crops by cattle*).

потрав|и́ть, лю, ~ишь, *pf.* of трави́ть[1] 4.

потра́|тить(ся), чу(сь), тишь(ся), *pf.* of тра́тить(ся).

потрáф|ить, лю, ишь, *pf.* (*of* ~ля́ть) (+*d.* or на+*a.*; *coll.*) to please, satisfy; им не ~ишь there's no pleasing them.

потрафля́|ть, ю, *impf.* of потра́фить.

потрéб|а, ы, f. (*obs.*) need, want.

потреби́тел|ь, я, m. consumer, user.

потреби́тельн|ый, *adj.* consumption; ~ая стóимость (*econ.*) use value.

потреби́тель|ский, *adj.* of ~; ~ская коопе-ра́ция (*collect.*) consumers' co-operatives.

потреб|и́ть, лю, и́шь, *pf.* of ~ля́ть.

потребле́ни|е, я, n. consumption, use; това́ры широ́кого ~я consumer goods.

потребля́|ть, ю, *impf.* (*of* потреби́ть) to consume, use.

потрéбност|ь, и, f. need, want, necessity, requirement; жи́зненные ~и the necessities of life; физи́ческая п. physical need; испы́тывать п. в чём-н. to feel a need for something; кака́я у вас п. в кни́гах? what are your requirements for books?

потрéб|ный (~ен, ~на), *adj.* necessary, required, requisite.

потрéб|овать(ся), ую(сь), *pf.* of тре́бовать-(ся).

потревóж|ить(ся), у(сь), ишь(ся), *pf.* of тревóжить(ся).

потрёп|анный, *p.p.p. of* ~а́ть *and adj.* **1.** shabby; ragged, tattered; ~анные брю́ки frayed trousers; ~анная кни́га a tattered book. **2.** battered. **3.** (*fig.*) worn, seedy.

потреп|а́ть(ся), лю́, ~лет(ся), *pf. of* трепа́ть(ся).

потре́ска|ться, ется, *pf. of* тре́скаться.

потре́скива|ть, ю, *impf.* to crackle.

потро́га|ть, ю, *pf.* to touch, run one's hand over (*to get the feel of something*); п. па́льцем to finger.

потрох|а́, о́в, *no sing.* pluck (*animal viscera*); жа́реные п. haslet(s); гуси́ные п. goose giblets; свины́е п. pig's fry; со все́ми ~а́ми (*fig., joc.*) lock, stock, and barrel.

потрош|и́ть, у́, и́шь, *impf.* (*of* вы~) to disembowel, clean; to draw (*fowl*).

потру|ди́ться, жу́сь, ~дишься, *pf.* **1.** to take some pains; to do some work. **2.** ~ди́сь, ~ди́тесь (+*inf.*) (*official or joc. injunction*) be so kind as (to); ~ди́тесь зайти́ ко мне за́втра be so kind as to call on me tomorrow; ~ди́сь, ~ди́тесь вы́йти! kindly leave the room!

потряса́|ющий, *pres. part. act. of* ~ть *and adj.* (*coll.*) staggering, stupendous, tremendous.

потряс|а́ть, а́ю, *impf. of* ~ти́.

потрясе́ни|е, я, *n.* shock.

потряс|ти́[1], у́, ёшь, *past* ~, ~ла́, *pf.* (*of* ~а́ть) **1.** to shake; to rock; п. во́здух кри́ками to rend the air with shouts; п. до основа́ния to rock to its foundations. **2.** (+*i.*) to brandish, shake; п. кулако́м to shake one's fist. **3.** (*fig.*) to shake; to stagger, stun.

потряс|ти́[2], у́, ёшь, *past* ~, ~ла́, *pf.* to shake (*a little, a few times*).

потря́хива|ть, ю, *impf.* (+*i.*) to shake (*a little, from time to time*); to jolt.

поту́г|а, и, *f.* **1.** muscular contraction; родовы́е ~и birth-pangs. **2.** (*fig.*) (*vain, unsuccessful*) attempt; ~и на остроу́мие attempts to be funny.

поту́п|ить, лю, ишь, *pf.* (*of* ~ля́ть) to lower, cast down; ~я взор with downcast eyes.

поту́п|и́ть, лю́, ~ишь, *pf.* to blunt.

поту́п|иться, люсь, ишься, *pf.* (*of* ~ля́ться) to look down, cast down one's eyes.

потупля́|ть(ся), ю(сь), *impf. of* поту́пить(ся).

по-туре́цки, *adv.* in Turkish; in the Turkish fashion; сиде́ть п. to sit cross-legged.

потускне́лый, *adj.* tarnished; (*fig.*) lacklustre.

потускне́|ть, ю, *pf. of* тускне́ть.

потусторо́нний, *adj.*; п. мир the other world.

потуха́ни|е, я, *n.* extinction.

поту́х|ать, а́ю, *impf. of* ~нуть.

поту́х|нуть, ну, нешь, *past* ~, ~ла, *pf.* (*of* ту́хнуть[1] *and* ~а́ть) to go out; (*fig.*) to die out.

поту́х|ший, *past part. act. of* ~нуть *and adj.* extinct; (*fig.*) lifeless, lack-lustre; п. вулка́н extinct volcano.

потучне́|ть, ю, *pf. of* тучне́ть.

потуш|и́ть[1], у́, ~ишь, *pf. of* туши́ть.

потуш|и́ть[2], у́, ~ишь, *pf.* to stew (*for a while*); to leave to stew.

по́тч|евать, ую, *impf.* (*of* по~) (+*i.*; *coll.*) to regale (with), treat (to), entertain (to).

потяга́|ться, юсь, *pf. of* тяга́ться.

потя́гивани|е, я, *n.* stretching oneself.

потя́гива|ть, ю, *impf.* (*coll.*) **1.** to pull (*a little*); to tug (at), give a tug; п. папиро́су to draw at a cigarette. **2.** to sip; to have a swig (of).

потя́гива|ться, юсь, *impf. of* потяну́ться.

потяго́т|а, ы, *f.* (*coll.*) = потя́гивание.

потя́н|уть, у́, ~ешь, *pf.* to begin to pull.

потя́н|у́ться, у́сь, ~ешься, *pf.* (*of* тяну́ться *and* потя́гиваться) to stretch oneself.

поу́жина|ть, ю, *pf. of* у́жинать.

поумне́|ть, ю, *pf. of* умне́ть.

поуро́чно, *adv.* **1.** by the piece. **2.** by the lesson.

поуро́чн|ый, *adj.* **1.** by the piece; ~ая опла́та piece-work payment. **2.** by the lesson.

поутру́, *adv.* in the morning.

поуча́|ть, ю, *impf.* **1.** (*obs.*) to teach, instruct. **2.** (*coll., iron.*) to preach (at), lecture.

поуче́ни|е, я, *n.* (*lit.*) exhortation, homily; (*coll., iron.*) preaching; sermon, sermonizing.

поучи́тел|ьный (~ен, ~ьна), *adj.* instructive.

поуч|и́ть, у́, ~ишь, *pf.* **1.** to do a bit of teaching. **2.** (+*a. and d.*) to give a bit of instruction (in); to give a few tips (on).

поуч|и́ться, у́сь, ~ишься, *pf.* to study (*for a while*); to do a bit of studying.

пофарт|и́ть, и́т, *pf.* (*impers.* +*d.*; *coll.*) be lucky, be in luck; нам ~и́ло we were in luck.

пофор|си́ть, шу́, си́шь, *pf.* (+*i.*; *coll.*) to show off, parade.

поха́бник, а, *m.* (*coll.*) foul-mouthed person.

поха́бнича|ть, ю, *impf.* (*of* с~) (*coll.*) to use foul language, use obscenities.

поха́б|ный (~ен, ~на), *adj.* (*coll.*) obscene, bawdy.

поха́бщин|а, ы, *f.* (*coll.*) obscenity, bawdiness.

поха́жива|ть, ю, *impf.* (*coll.*) **1.** to pace; to stroll. **2.** to come, go (*from time to time*).

похвал|а́, ы́, *f.* praise; отозва́ться с ~о́й (о+*p.*) to praise, speak favourably (of).

похва́лива|ть, ю, *impf.* (*coll.*) to praise; to pay repeated tributes to.

похвал|и́ть(ся), ю́(сь), ~ишь(ся), *pf. of* хвали́ть(ся).

похвальб|а́, ы́, *f.* (*coll.*) bragging, boasting.

похва́л|ьный (~ен, ~ьна), *adj.* 1. praiseworthy, laudable, commendable. 2. laudatory; ~ьная гра́мота, п. лист (*obs.*) certificate of merit; (school) certificate of good conduct and progress; ~ьное сло́во eulogy, encomium, panegyric.

похваля́|ться, юсь, *impf.* (+*i.*; *coll.*) to boast (of, about), brag (about).

похва́рыва|ть, ю, *impf.* (*coll.*) to be frequently unwell, be subject to indisposition.

похва́ста|ть(ся), ю(сь), *pf. of* хва́стать(ся).

похе́р|ить, ю, ишь, *pf.* (*coll.*) to cross out, cancel.

похити́тел|ь, я, *m.* thief; kidnapper; abductor; hijacker.

похи́|тить, щу, тишь, *pf.* (*of* ~ща́ть) to steal; to kidnap; to abduct, carry off; to hijack.

похища́|ть, ю, *impf. of* похи́тить.

похище́ни|е, я, *n.* theft; kidnapping; abduction; hijacking.

похлёбк|а, и, *f.* soup, broth, skilly.

похло́па|ть, ю, *pf.* to slap, clap (a few times).

похлопо|та́ть, чу́, ~чешь, *pf. of* хлопота́ть.

похме́ль|е, я, *n.* hangover; 'the morning after the night before'; быть с ~я to have a hangover; в чужо́м пиру́ п. unpleasantness suffered through no fault of one's own.

похо́д¹, а, *m.* 1. march; (*naut.*) cruise; вы́ступить в п. to take the field, get on the march; в ~е (*naut.*) cruising, on cruise; на ~е on the march. 2. (*mil.*; *fig.*) campaign; кресто́вый п. crusade. 3. walking tour, hike.

похо́д², а, *m.* (*coll.*) overweight.

похода́тайств|овать, ую, *pf. of* хода́тайствовать.

похо|ди́ть¹, жу́, ~дишь, *impf.* (на+*a.*) to resemble, bear a resemblance (to), be like.

похо|ди́ть², жу́, ~дишь, *pf.* to walk (*for a while*).

похо́дк|а, и, *f.* gait, walk, step.

похо́д|ный, *adj. of* ~¹; п. го́спиталь field hospital; ~ное движе́ние march; ~ная жизнь camp life; ~ная коло́нна column of route; ~ная крова́ть camp-bed; ~ная ку́хня mobile kitchen, field kitchen; ~ная пе́сня marching song; п. поря́док marching order; ~ная ра́ция walkie-talkie set; ~ное снаряже́ние field kit; п. строй march formation; ~ная фо́рма marching order, field dress.

похо́дя, *adv.* (*coll.*) 1. as one goes along; on the march; мы е́ли п. we ate as we went along. 2. (*fig.*) in passing; in an offhand manner.

похожде́ни|е, я, *n.* adventure, escapade.

похо́ж|ий (~, ~а), *adj.* resembling, alike; (на+*a.*) like; он ~ на де́да he is like his grandfather; они́ о́чень ~и друг на дру́га they are very much alike; э́то на неё не ~е (*fig.*) that's not like her; э́то на Пе́тю ~е! just like Petya!, that's Petya all over!; он не ~ на самого́ себя́ he is not himself; э́то ни на что́ не ~е (*fig.*, *pejor.*) it's like nothing on earth; it is unheard of. 2. (*coll.*) ~е it appears, it would appear; ~е на то, что... it looks as if . . .; он, ~е, бо́лен it would appear he is ill.

по-хозя́йски, *adv.* thriftily; израсхо́довать насле́дство п. to spend a legacy wisely.

похолода́ни|е, я, *n.* fall of temperature, cold spell, cold snap.

похолода́|ть, ет, *pf. of* холода́ть.

похолоде́|ть, ю, *pf. of* холоде́ть.

похолодне́|ть, ю, *pf. of* холодне́ть.

похорон|и́ть, ю́, ~ишь, *pf. of* хорони́ть.

похоро́нн|ый, *adj.* 1. funeral; ~ое бюро́ undertaker's, funeral parlour; п. звон (funeral) knell; п. марш dead march. 2. (*fig.*, *coll.*) funereal.

по́хор|оны, о́н, она́м, *no sing.* funeral; burial.

по-хоро́шему, *adv.* in an amicable way.

похороше́|ть, ю, *pf. of* хороше́ть.

похотли́вост|ь, и, *f.* lustfulness, lewdness, lasciviousness.

похотли́в|ый (~, ~а), *adj.* lustful, lewd, lascivious.

похотни́к, а́, *m.* (*anat.*) clitoris.

по́хот|ь, и, *f.* lust.

похохо|та́ть, чу́, ~чешь, *pf.* to laugh (*a little, for a while*); to have a laugh.

похрабре́|ть, ю, *pf. of* храбре́ть.

похра́пыва|ть, ю, *impf.* (*coll.*) to snore (softly, gently).

похристо́с|оваться, уюсь, *pf. of* христо́соваться.

поцара́па|ть, ю, *pf.* to scratch slightly.

похуде́|ть, ю, *pf. of* худе́ть.

похул|и́ть, ю́, и́шь, *pf.* (*obs.*) to curse, abuse.

поцара́па|ться, юсь, *pf.* to get slightly scratched.

поца́рств|овать, ую, *pf.* to reign (*for some time*).

поцел|ова́ть(ся), у́ю(сь), *pf. of* целова́ть(ся).

поцелу́|й, я, *m.* kiss.

поцеремо́н|иться, юсь, ишься, *pf. of* церемо́ниться.

почасово́й, *adj.* by the hour.

поча́т|ок, ка, *m.* 1. (*bot.*) ear; spadix; п. кукуру́зы corn-cob. 2. (*text.*) cop.

поч|а́ть, ну́, нёшь, *past* ~а́л, ~ала́, ~а́ло, *pf.* (*of* ~ина́ть) (*obs. or dial.*) to begin.

по́чв|а, ы, *f.* 1. soil, ground, earth. 2. (*fig.*) ground, basis, footing; на ~е (+*g.*) owing (to), because (of); вы́бить ~у из-под чьих-н. ног to cut the ground from under someone's feet, take the wind out of

someone's sails; зонди́ровать ~у to explore
the ground; подгото́вить ~у to prepare the
ground, pave the way; стоя́ть на твёрдой
~е, не теря́ть ~ы под нога́ми to be on
firm ground; его́ утвержде́ния не име́ют
под собо́й никако́й ~ы his assertions
are quite groundless, have no foundation.

по́чв|енный, *adj. of* ~а.

почвове́д, а, *m.* soil scientist.

почвове́дени|е, я, *n.* soil science.

почвове́д|ческий, *adj. of* ~ение.

почвоуглуби́тел|ь, я, *m.* (*agric.*) subsoil
plough.

почвоутомле́ни|е, я, *n.* (*agric.*) exhaustion
of soil, soil depletion.

почём¹, *interrog. and relat. adv.* (*coll.*) how
much; п. сего́дня я́блоки? how much are
apples today?; узна́ть, п. фунт ли́ха (*coll.*)
to fall upon hard times, plumb the depths
of misfortune.

почём², *interrog. adv.* (*only used with parts of
verb* знать; *coll.*) how?; п. знать? who
knows?, who can tell?, how is one to
know?; п. я зна́ю, кто ей э́то рассказа́л?
how should I know who told her about
it?

почему́ 1. *interrog. and relat. adv.* why; п. вы
так ду́маете? why do you think that?;
я зна́ю и́стинную причи́ну, п. он так
ду́мает I know the real reason why he
thinks that. 2. *as conj.* (and) so; (and) that's
why; она́ простуди́лась, п. и оста́лась
до́ма she has caught a cold, (and) so she
has stayed at home.

почему́-либо = почему́-нибудь.

почему́-нибудь, *adv.* for some reason or
other.

почему́-то, *adv.* for some reason.

по́черк, а, *m.* hand(writing).

почерне́лый, *adj.* darkened.

почерне́|ть, ю, *pf. of* черне́ть.

почерп|а́ть, а́ю, *impf. of* ~ну́ть.

почерп|ну́ть, ну́, нёшь, *pf.* (*of* ~а́ть) 1.
(+*a. or g.*) to draw. 2. (*fig.*) to get; п. све́-
дения to glean, pick up information.

почерстве́|ть, ю, *pf. of* черстве́ть.

поче|са́ть(ся), шу́(сь), ~шешь(ся), *pf. of*
чеса́ть(ся).

по́чест|ь, и, *f.* honour; возда́ть ~и, ока-
за́ть ~и (+*d.*) to do honour (to), render
homage (to).

по|че́сть, чту́, чтёшь, *past* ~чёл, ~чла́, *pf.*
(*of* ~чита́ть¹) (*obs.*) to consider, think; он
~чёл свои́м до́лгом вы́ступить he considered
it his duty to speak.

почёсыва|ть, ю, *impf.* (*coll.*) to scratch (*from
time to time*).

почёт, а, *m.* honour; respect, esteem; быть
в ~е у кого́-н., по́льзоваться ~ом у кого́-н.

to stand high in someone's esteem; to be
highly thought of by someone; п. и уваже́-
ние! (*coll.*) my compliments!

почёт|ный, *adj.* 1. honoured, respected,
esteemed; п. гость guest of honour. 2.
honorary; ~ное зва́ние honorary title; п.
член honorary member. 3. (~ен, ~на)
honourable; doing honour; п. карау́л
guard of honour; ~ное ме́сто place of
honour; п. мир honourable peace.

по́ч|ечный¹, *adj. of* ~ка¹.

по́чечн|ый², *adj.* (*anat.*, *med.*) nephritic;
renal; ~ые ка́мни gall-stones; ~ая лоха́нка
calix (of kidney).

почечу́|й, я, *m.* (*obs.*) piles.

почива́л|ьня, ьни, *g. pl.* ~ен, *f.* (*obs.*) bed-
-chamber.

почива́|ть, ю, *impf.* (*obs.*) 1. to sleep. 2.
impf. of почи́ть.

почи́|вший, *past part. of* ~ть; *as noun* п.,
~вшего, *m. and* ~вшая, ~вшей, *f.* the
deceased.

почи́н, а, *m.* 1. initiative; взять на себя́ п.
to take the initiative; по со́бственному ~у
on one's own initiative. 2. beginning,
start; (*comm.*) first sale of day.

почин|и́ть, ю́, ~ишь, *pf.* (*of* чини́ть¹ *and*
~я́ть) to repair, mend.

почи́нк|а, и, *f.* repairing, mending; отда́ть
что́-н. в ~у to have something repaired,
mended.

почи́н|ок, ка, *m.* (*dial.*) 1. forest clearing. 2.
small *or* new settlement.

почин|я́ть, я́ю, *impf. of* ~и́ть.

почи́|стить(ся), щу(сь), стишь(ся), *pf. of*
чи́стить(ся).

почита́й, *adv.* (*dial.*) 1. almost; nigh on. 2.
it seems; very likely.

почита́ни|е, я, *n.* 1. honouring; (+*g.*)
respect (for). 2. reverence, worship.

почита́тел|ь, я, *m.* admirer; worshipper.

почита́|ть¹, ю, *impf. of* почесть.

почита́|ть², ю, *impf.* 1. to honour, respect,
esteem. 2. to revere.

почита́|ть³, ю, *pf.* 1. to read (a little, for a
while). 2. (*coll.*) to read.

почи́тыва|ть, ю, *impf.* (*coll.*) to read (now
and then).

почи́|ть, ю, ешь, *pf.* (*of* ~ва́ть (*rhet.*) to
rest, take one's rest; (*fig.*) to pass away,
pass to one's rest; п. на ла́врах to rest on
one's laurels.

почи́ще, *adv.* 1. cleaner. 2. (*fig.*, *coll.*) better;
stronger, more vividly; он вы́разился п.
остальны́х he expressed himself more
vividly than the others.

по́чк|а¹, и, *f.* 1. (*bot.*) bud. 2. (*bot.*, *zool.*)
gemma.

по́ч|ка², ки, *f.* 1. (*anat.*) kidney; воспале́ние
~ек nephritis. 2. (*pl.*; *cul.*) kidneys.

почкова́ни|е, я, *n.* (*biol.*) budding; gemmation.

почк|ова́ться, у́ется, *impf.* (*biol.*) to bud; to gemmate.

по́чк|овый, *adj. of* ~а[1].

по́чт|а, ы, *f.* 1. post; возду́шная п. air mail; спе́шная п. special delivery, express delivery; посла́ть по ~е, ~ой to send by post, post; с у́тренней (с вече́рней) ~ой by the morning (evening) post; с обра́тной ~ой by return (of post). 2. (the) post, (the) mail; пришла́ ли п.? has the post come? 3. post office; рабо́тники ~ы postal workers.

почтальо́н, а, *m.* postman.

почта́мт, а, *m.* head post office (*of city or town*); гла́вный п. General Post Office.

почте́ни|е, я, *n.* respect, esteem; deference; относи́ться с ~ем (к) to treat with respect; с соверше́нным ~ем (*epistolary formula*) respectfully yours; моё п.! (*coll.*) my compliments!

почте́н|ный (~ен, ~на), *adj.* 1. honourable; respectable, estimable; venerable; ~ная рабо́та estimable work; п. во́зраст venerable age. 2. (*fig., coll.*) considerable, respectable; труд ~ных разме́ров a work of respectable dimensions.

почти́, *adv.* almost, nearly; п. ничего́ next to nothing; п. что = п.

почти́тельност|ь, и, *f.* respect, deference.

почти́тел|ьный (~ен, ~ьна), *adj.* 1. respectful, deferential. 2. (*fig., coll.*) considerable, respectable.

по|чти́ть, чту́, чти́шь, *pf.* to honour; п. чью-н. па́мять встава́нием to stand in someone's memory.

почтме́йстер, а, *m.* (*obs.*) postmaster.

почто́, *adv.* (*obs.*) why; what for.

почто́во-телегра́фн|ый, *adj.* post and telegraph; ~ое учрежде́ние postal and telecommunications establishment.

почт|о́вый, *adj. of* ~а; ~о́вая бума́га notepaper; п. ваго́н mail-van; п. го́лубь carrier-pigeon, homing pigeon; ~о́вая ка́рточка postcard; ~о́вая ма́рка (postage) stamp; ~о́вое отделе́ние post-office; п. перево́д postal order; п. по́езд mail train; ~о́вые расхо́ды postage; п. я́щик letter-box, pillar-box; е́хать на ~о́вых (*hist.*) to travel by post-chaise.

поч|ту́[1], тёшь, *see* ~е́сть.

поч|ту́[2], ти́шь, *see* ~ти́ть.

почу́вств|овать, ую, *pf. of* чу́вствовать.

почу́д|иться, ится, *pf. of* чу́диться.

почу́|ять, ю, *pf. of* чу́ять.

пошаба́ш|ить, у, ишь, *pf. of* шаба́шить.

поша́лива|ть, ю, *impf.* (*coll.*) 1. to be naughty; to play up (*from time to time*) (*also fig.*); се́рдце у меня́ ~ет my heart plays

me up, I have trouble with my heart (*from time to time*). 2. (*fig.*) to engage in robbery; в э́том райо́не ~ют your wallet isn't safe in these parts.

пошал|и́ть, ю́, и́шь, *pf.* to play pranks, get up to mischief (*for a while*).

поша́р|ить, ю, ишь, *pf. of* ша́рить.

пошатн|у́ть, у́, ёшь, *pf.* to shake (*also fig.*); п. чью-н. ве́ру to shake someone's faith; меня́ ~у́ло (*impers.*) I was shaken.

пошатн|у́ться, у́сь, ёшься, *pf.* 1. to shake; to totter, reel, stagger; он ~у́лся и упа́л he staggered and fell. 2. (*fig.*) to be shaken; её здоро́вье ~у́лось her health has cracked.

поша́тыва|ться, юсь, *impf.* to totter, reel, stagger.

пошеве́лива|ть, ю, *impf.* (*coll.*) to stir (*from time to time*).

пошеве́лива|ться, юсь, *impf.* (*coll.*) to stir, budge (*from time to time*); ну, ~йся! come on!, get a move on!

пошевел|и́ть(ся), ю́(сь), ~и́шь(ся), *pf. of* шевели́ть(ся).

пошевельн|у́ть(ся), у́(сь), ёшь(ся), *pf.* = пошевели́ть(ся).

по́шевн|и, ей, *no sing.* (*dial.*) (wide) sledge.

пош|ёл, ла́, *see* пойти́.

пошеп|та́ть, чу́, ~чешь, *pf.* to say in a whisper; to talk in whispers (*for a while*).

пошеп|та́ться, чу́сь, ~чешься, *pf.* (*coll.*) to converse in whispers.

пошехо́н|ец, ца, *m.* Gothamite; bumpkin (*from* Пошехо́нье, *place popularized by Saltykov-Shchedrin as symbol of backwardness*).

пошиб, а, *m.* (*coll.*) manners; ways.

поши́вк|а, и, *f.* sewing.

поши́вочн|ый, *adj.* sewing; ~ая мастерска́я (sewing) workshop.

пош|и́ть, ью́, ьёшь, *pf.* to sew (*for a while*); to do some sewing.

пошле́|ть, ю, *impf.* (*of* о~) (*coll.*) to become commonplace, become vulgar.

по́шлин|а, ы, *f.* duty; customs; ввозна́я п., и́мпортная п. import duty; э́кспортная п. export duty; ге́рбовая п. stamp-duty; суде́бная п. costs, legal expenses; тамо́женная п. customs; обложи́ть ~ой to impose duty (on).

по́шлин|ный, *adj. of* ~а.

по́шлост|ь, и, *f.* 1. vulgarity, commonness. 2. triviality; triteness, banality; говори́ть ~и to utter banalities, talk commonplaces.

по́шл|ый (~, ~а́, ~о), *adj.* 1. vulgar, common; у него́ о́чень ~ые вку́сы he has very vulgar tastes. 2. commonplace, trivial; trite, banal; ~ая по́весть banal story.

пошля́к, а́, *m.* (*coll.*) vulgar person, common person.

пошля́тин|а, ы, *f.* (*coll.*) 1. vulgarity; vulgar action. 2. triviality; triteness, banality.

пошту́чно, *adv.* by the piece.

пошту́чн|ый, *adj.* by the piece; ~ая опла́та piecework payment.

пошум|е́ть, лю́, и́шь, *pf.* to make a bit of a noise.

пошу|ти́ть, чу́, ~тишь, *pf. of* шути́ть.

поща́д|а, ы, *f.* mercy; без ~ы without mercy; не дать ~ы to give no quarter; проси́ть ~ы to ask for mercy, cry quarter.

поща|ди́ть, жу́, ди́шь, *pf. of* щади́ть.

пощеко|та́ть, чу́, ~чешь, *pf. of* щекота́ть.

пощёлкивани|е, я, *n.* clicking.

пощёлкива|ть, ю, *impf.* to click; п. па́льцами to snap one's fingers.

пощёчин|а, ы, *f.* box on the ear; slap in the face (*also fig.*); дать ~y (+*d.*) to slap in the face.

пощип|а́ть, лю́, ~лешь, *pf.* **1.** (+*a. or g.*) to nibble. **2.** (*coll.*) to pull out, pull up. **3.** (*fig., joc.*) to pinch (from), rob. **4.** (*fig., joc.*) to pick holes in; to tear a strip off.

пощи́пыва|ть, ю, *impf.* (*coll.*) to pinch (*from time to time*).

пощу́па|ть, ю, *pf. of* щу́пать.

поэ́зи|я, и, *f.* poetry.

поэ́м|а, ы, *f.* poem (*usu. of large proportions, as opp. to* стихотворе́ние).

поэ́т, а, *m.* poet.

поэте́сс|а, ы, *f.* poetess.

поэтизи́р|овать, ую, *impf. and pf.* to poeticize, wax poetic (about).

поэ́тик|а, и, *f.* **1.** poetics; theory of poetry. **2.** poetic manner, poetic style; п. Пу́шкина Pushkin's (poetic) manner.

поэти́ческ|ий, *adj.* (*in var. senses*) poetic(al); ~ая во́льность poetic licence.

поэти́ч|ный (~ен, ~на), *adj.* (*fig.*) poetic(al).

поэ́тому, *adv.* therefore, and so.

по|ю́[1], ёшь, *see* петь.

по|ю́[2], и́шь, *see* пои́ть.

появ|и́ться, лю́сь, ~ишься, *pf.* (*of* ~ля́ться) to appear, make one's appearance; to show up; to heave in sight; луна́ ~и́лась из-за облако́в the moon emerged from behind the clouds.

появле́ни|е, я, *n.* appearance.

появля́|ться, юсь, *impf. of* появи́ться.

пояркóвый, *adj.* felt.

поя́р|ок, ка, *no pl., m.* lamb's wool.

по́яс, а, *pl.* ~а́, ~о́в, *m.* **1.** belt, girdle; waistband; спаса́тельный п. lifebelt; заткну́ть за́ п. (*coll.*) to outdo. **2.** (*fig.*) waist; кла́няться в п. to bow from the waist; по п. up to the waist, waist-deep, waist-high. **3.** (*pl.* ~ы́) (*geogr., econ.*) zone, belt; поля́рный п. frigid zone; тропи́ческий п. torrid zone.

поясне́ни|е, я, *n.* explanation, elucidation.

поясни́тельный, *adj.* explanatory, elucidatory.

поясн|и́ть, ю́, и́шь, *pf.* (*of* ~я́ть) to explain, elucidate.

поясни́ц|а, ы, *f.* waist, loins; small of the back; боль, простре́л в ~е lumbago.

поясни́чный, *adj.* (*anat.*) lumbar.

поясн|о́й, *adj.* **1.** *adj. of* по́яс 1; п. реме́нь (waist-)belt. **2.** to the waist, waist-high; ~а́я ва́нна hip-bath; п. покло́н bow from the waist; п. портре́т half-length portrait. **3.** (*geogr., econ.*) zonal; ~о́е вре́мя zone time; п. тари́ф zonal tariff; ~о́е распределе́ние zoning.

поясн|я́ть, я́ю, *impf. of* ~и́ть.

праба́б|ка, ки, *f.* = ~ушка.

праба́бушк|а, и, *f.* great-grandmother.

пра́вд|а, ы, *f.* **1.** truth; the truth; э́то и́стинная п. (*coll.*) it's the simple truth; су́щая п. the honest truth; э́то п. it is true, it is the truth; по ~е сказа́ть, ~у говоря́ to tell the truth, truth to tell; ва́ша п. you are right; что п., то п. there's no denying the truth; все́ми ~ами и непра́вдами by fair means or foul; п. глаза́ ко́лет (*prov.*) home truths are hard to swallow. **2.** justice; иска́ть ~ы to seek justice. **3.** (*hist.*) law, code of laws; Сали́ческая п. the Salic Law. **4.** п.? is that so?, indeed?, really?; п. (ли)? is it so?, is it true?; п. ли, что он умира́ет? is it true that he is dying?; не п. ли? *in interrog. sentences indicates that affirmative answer is expected*; вы погаси́ли свет, не п. ли? you (did) put out the light, didn't you? **5.** (*as concessive conj.*) true; п., я ему́ не написа́л true, I had not written to him; п., я ему́ не написа́л, но я вот-во́т собира́лся позвони́ть true I had not written to him, but I was on the point of ringing.

правди́вост|ь, и, *f.* **1.** truth; veracity. **2.** truthfulness; uprightness.

правди́в|ый (~, ~а), *adj.* **1.** true; veracious; п. расска́з true story. **2.** truthful; upright; п. отве́т honest answer.

правди́ст, а, *m.* (*coll.*) person employed on production of newspaper 'Pravda'.

правдоподо́би|е, я, *n.* verisimilitude; probability, likelihood; plausibility.

правдоподо́б|ный (~ен, ~на), *adj.* probable, likely; plausible.

пра́ведник, а, *m.* righteous man; upright person, moral person; спать сном ~a to sleep the sleep of the just.

пра́ведн|ица, ицы, *f. of* ~ик.

пра́вед|ный (~ен, ~на), *adj.* **1.** righteous; upright. **2.** just.

правёж, а́, *m.* (*hist.*) flogging (*of insolvent debtor*); поста́вить кого́-н. на п. to have someone flogged.

правё|ть, ю, *impf.* (*of* по~) (*polit.*) to become more conservative, swing to the right.

пра́вил|о, а, *n.* **1.** rule; regulation; грамматические ~а grammatical rules; тройно́е п. (*math.*) the rule of three; ~а вну́треннего распоря́дка the regulations (*of an establishment*); ~а у́личного движе́ния traffic regulations, highway code; как п. as a rule; по всем ~ам according to all the rules. **2.** rule, principle; взять за п. to make it a rule; взять себе́ за п. (+*inf.*) to make a point (*of*).

прави́л|о, а, *n.* **1.** (*tech.*) reversing rod, guide-bar; (*mil.*) traversing handspike. **2.** boot-tree. **3.** (*hunting*) tail, brush. **4.** (*obs.*) helm, rudder.

пра́вильно, *adv.* **1.** rightly; correctly; п. ли иду́т ва́ши часы́? is your watch right? **2.** regularly.

пра́вильност|ь, и, *f.* **1.** rightness; correctness. **2.** regularity.

пра́вил|ьный (~ен, ~ьна), *adj.* **1.** right, correct; п. отве́т the right answer; ~ьное реше́ние sound decision; ~ьная дробь proper fraction; ~ьно (*as pred.*) it is correct; ~ьно! that's right!, exactly!, just so! **2.** (*in var. senses*) regular; ~ьное движе́ние поездо́в regular train service(s); ~ьное соотноше́ние just proportion; ~ьное спряже́ние (*gram.*) regular conjugation; ~ьные черты́ лица́ regular features. **3.** (*math.*) rectilineal, rectilinear.

прави́л|ьный, *adj.* **1.** *adj. of* ~о. **2.** (*tech.*) correcting, levelling, straightening; ~ьная маши́на levelling machine.

прави́тел|ь, я, *m.* **1.** ruler. **2.** (*obs.*) manager, head; п. дел head clerk, first secretary.

прави́тельственн|ый, *adj.* governmental; government; ~ое реше́ние governmental decision; ~ое учрежде́ние government establishment.

прави́тельств|о, а, *n.* government.

пра́в|ить¹, лю, ишь, *impf.* (*no pf.*) (+*i.*) **1.** to rule (over), govern. **2.** to drive; п. маши́ной to drive a car; п. руле́м to steer.

пра́в|ить², лю, ишь, *impf.* (*no pf.*) **1.** to correct; п. корректу́ру to read, correct proofs. **2.** to set (*metal tools*).

пра́вк|а, и, *f.* **1.** correcting; п. корректу́ры proof correcting, proof-reading. **2.** setting (*of metal tools*).

правле́ни|е, я, n. **1.** governing, government; о́браз ~я form of government. **2.** board (*of directors, of management, etc.*), governing body; быть чле́ном ~я to be on the board.

пра́вленый, *adj.* corrected; п. экземпля́р fair copy.

пра́внук, а, *m.* great-grandson.

пра́внучк|а, и, f. great-granddaughter.

пра́в|о¹, а, *pl.* **~а́,** *n.* **1.** law; гражда́нское п. civil law; обы́чное п. common law, customary law; уголо́вное п. criminal law; изучи́ть п. to study law, read for the law. **2.** right; (води́тельские) ~а́ driving licence; п. ве́то (right of) veto; п. го́лоса, избира́тельное п. the vote, suffrage; лиши́ть ~а го́лоса to disfranchise; ~а́ гражда́нства civic rights; п. да́вности (*leg.*) prescriptive right; п. убе́жища asylum, right of sanctuary; п. на насле́дство right of inheritance; по ~у by rights; с по́лным ~ом rightfully; быть в ~е (+*inf.*) to have the right (to), be entitled (to); воспо́льзоваться свои́м ~ом (на+*a.*) to exercise one's right (to); восстанови́ться в ~а́х to be rehabilitated; вступи́ть в свои́ ~а to come into one's own; име́ть п. (на+*a.*) to have the right (to), be entitled (to).

пра́во², *adv.* (*coll.*) really, truly, indeed; я, п., не зна́ю, куда́ де́лась I really do not know where she has got to.

правобере́жный, *adj.* situated on the right bank, right-bank.

правове́д, а, m. **1.** lawyer, jurist. **2.** (*obs.*) student, graduate of law school.

правове́дени|е, я, n. (*obs.*) jurisprudence, science of law.

правове́рност|ь, и, f. orthodoxy.

правове́р|ный (~ен, ~на), *adj.* (*rel.*) **1.** orthodox. **2.** *as noun* п., ~ного, *m.* true believer (*esp. of Moslems*); ~ные the faithful.

правови́к, а́, m. (*coll.*) jurist.

правово́й, *adj.* **1.** legal, of the law; п. контра́кт legal contract. **2.** lawful, rightful.

правоме́р|ный (~ен, ~на), *adj.* lawful, rightful.

правомо́чи|е, я, n. competence.

правомо́ч|ный (~ен, ~на), *adj.* competent.

правонаруше́ни|е, я, n. infringement of the law, offence.

правонаруши́тел|ь, я, m. infringer of the law, offender, delinquent; ю́ный п. juvenile delinquent.

правописа́ни|е, я, n. spelling, orthography.

правопоря́д|ок, ка, m. law and order.

правосла́ви|е, я, n. (*rel.*) orthodoxy.

правосла́вный, *adj.* (*rel.*) orthodox; ~ая це́рковь Orthodox Church; *as noun* п., ~ого, *m. and* ~ая, ~ой, *f.* member of the Orthodox Church.

правосозна́ни|е, я, n. feeling for law and order, sense of justice.

правоспосо́бност|ь, и, f. (*leg.*) (legal) capacity.

правоспосо́б|ный (~ен, ~на), *adj.* (*leg.*) capable.

правосторо́нний, *adj.* right-side.

правосу́ди|е, я, n. justice; отправля́ть п. to administer the law.

правот|а́, ы́, *f.* rightness; (*leg.*) innocence; доказа́ть свою́ ~у́ to prove one's case.

правофланго́вый, *adj.* right-flank, right--wing.

пра́в|ый[1], *adj.* **1.** right; right-hand; (*naut.*) starboard; п. борт starboard side; ~ая ло́шадь off(-side) horse; ~ая рука́ (*fig.*) right hand, right-hand man; ~ая сторона́ right side, off side. **2.** (*polit.*) right-wing, right; ~ая па́ртия party of the right.

пра́в|ый[2] (~, ~а́, ~о), *adj.* **1.** right, correct; вы не совсе́м ~ы you are not quite right. **2.** righteous, just; ~ое де́ло a just cause. **3.** (*leg.*) innocent, not guilty.

пра́в|ящий, *pres. part. act. of* ~ить *and adj.* ruling; ~ящая верху́шка ruling clique; ~ящие кла́ссы the ruling classes.

прагмати́зм, а, *m.* (*philos.*) pragmatism.

прагма́тик, а, *m.* (*philos.*) pragmatist.

прагмати́ческ|ий, *adj.* pragmatic; ~ая са́нкция (*hist.*) pragmatic sanction.

пра́дед, а, *m.* **1.** great-grandfather. **2.** (*pl.*) ancestors, forefathers.

праде́довск|ий, *adj. of* пра́дед; ~ие времена́ ancestral times.

праде́душк|а, и, *m. dim. of* пра́дед.

пра́зднеств|о, а, *n.* festival, solemnity; festivities.

пра́здник, а, *m.* **1.** (public) holiday; (religious) feast, festival; по ~ам on high days and holidays; с ~ом! compliments of the season; бу́дет и на на́шей у́лице п. (*fig.*) our day will come. **2.** festive occasion, occasion for celebration; по слу́чаю ~а to celebrate the occasion.

пра́здничн|ый, *adj.* holiday; festive; п. день red-letter day, holiday; п. наря́д holiday attire; ~ое настрое́ние festive mood.

пра́здновани|е, я, *n.* celebration.

пра́здн|овать, ую, *impf.* (*of* от~) to celebrate.

праздносло́ви|е, я, *n.* idle talk, empty talk.

пра́здност|ь, и, *f.* **1.** idleness, inactivity. **2.** emptiness.

праздношата́ни|е, я, *n.* (*coll.*) idling, lounging.

пра́зд|ный (~ен, ~на), *adj.* **1.** idle, inactive; ~ная жизнь a life of idleness. **2.** idle, empty; ~ное любопы́тство idle curiosity; п. разгово́р empty talk. **3.** idle, vain, useless; ~ные попы́тки idle attempts.

пра́ктик, а, *m.* **1.** practical worker; он хоро́ший п., но слаб в теорети́ческих зна́ниях he is a good practical worker but his theoretical knowledge is weak. **2.** practical person.

пра́ктик|а, и, *f.* **1.** (*in var. senses*) practice; на ~е in practice; вам нужна́ ещё разгово́рная п. you need more conversational practice; у на́шего врача́ больша́я п. our doctor has a large practice. **2.** practical work.

практика́нт, а, *m.* probationer; student engaged in practical work.

практик|ова́ть, у́ю, *impf.* **1.** to practise, apply in practice. **2.** (*intrans.; of a doctor or lawyer*) to practise.

практик|ова́ться, у́юсь, *impf.* **1.** (*pf.* на~) (в+*p.*) to practise, have practice (in); п. в игре́ на скри́пке to practise the violin; п. в ру́сском языке́ to practise speaking Russian. **2.** *pass. of* ~ова́ть; э́тот приём бо́льше не ~у́ется this method is no longer used.

пра́ктикум, а, *m.* practical work.

практици́зм, а, *m.* **1.** practicalness; (*slightly pejor.*) savoir-faire. **2.** (*in polit. philosophy of Lenin, etc.*) over-emphasis of practice (*as opp. to theory*).

практи́ческ|ий, *adj.* (*in var. senses*) practical; ~ие заня́тия practical training; ~ая медици́на applied medicine; ~ая рабо́та practical work.

практи́чност|ь, и, *f.* practicalness; efficiency.

практи́ч|ный (~ен, ~на), *adj.* practical; efficient; п. челове́к practical person; п. спо́соб efficient method.

прама́тер|ь, и, *f.* (*rhet.*) the first mother; mother of the human race.

пра́от|ец, ца, *m.* forefather; отпра́виться к ~цам (*joc.*) to be gathered to one's forefathers.

пра́порщик, а, *m.* (*in tsarist army*) ensign.

прапра́дед, а, *m.* great-great-grandfather.

прароди́тел|ь, я, *m.* primogenitor; forefather.

пра́сол, а, *m.* (*obs.*) cattle-dealer; fish- and meat-wholesaler.

прах, а, *no pl., m.* **1.** (*obs. or rhet.*) dust, earth; обрати́ть в п., поверну́ть в п. to reduce to dust, to ashes; отрясти́ п. с ног (*fig.*) to shake the dust from one's feet; пойти́ ~ом, рассы́паться ~ом to go to rack and ruin; п. и суета́ a hollow sham; разби́ть, разнести́ в пух и п., *see* пух. **2.** ashes, remains; здесь поко́ится п. (+*g.*) here lies; мир ~у его́ may he rest in peace. **3.** п. его́ возьми́! may he rot!

пра́чечн|ая, ой, *f.* laundry; wash-house.

пра́чк|а, и, *f.* laundress.

пращ|а́, и́, *g. pl.* ~е́й, *f.* sling (*weapon*).

пра́щур, а, *m.* ancestor, forefather.

праязы́к, а́, *m.* (*ling.*) parent language.

пре-[1] *adjectival prefix indicating superlative degree* very, most, exceedingly.

пре-[2] *verbal prefix indicating action in extreme degree or superior measure* sur-, over-, out- (*cf.* пере-).

преа́мбул|а, ы, *f.* preamble.

пребыва́ни|е, я, *n.* stay, sojourn; ме́сто постоя́нного ~я permanent residence, per-

manent address; п. в до́лжности, п. на
посту́ tenure of office, period of office.
пребыва́|ть, ю, *impf.* **1.** to be; to abide,
reside; п. в отсу́тствии to be absent. **2.** to
be (*in a state of*); п. в неве́дении to be in
the dark; п. в уны́нии to be in the dumps;
п. у вла́сти to be in power.
превали́р|овать, ую, *impf.* to prevail.
превенти́вн|ый, *adj.* preventive; ~ая война́
preventive war.
превзо|йти́, йду́, йдёшь, *past* ~шёл, ~шла́,
pf. (*of* превосходи́ть) (в+*p.* or +*i.*) to surpass (in); to excel (in); п. всех в мета́нии
ди́ска to excel in discus-throwing; п. все
ожида́ния to exceed expectations; п. само-
го́ себя́ to surpass oneself; п. чи́сленностью
to outnumber.
превозмога́|ть, ю, *impf. of* превозмо́чь.
превозмо́|чь, гу́, ~жешь, ~гут, *past* ~г,
~гла́, *pf.* (*of* ~га́ть) to overcome, surmount.
превознес|ти́, у́, ёшь, *past* ~, ~ла́, *pf.* (*of*
превозноси́ть) to extol.
превозно|си́ть, шу́, ~сишь, *impf. of* превоз-
нести́.
превозно|си́ться, шу́сь, ~сишься, *impf.* to
put on airs, have a high opinion of oneself.
превосходи́тельный, *adj.* having the title
of excellency.
превосходи́тельств|о, а, *n.* (*as title*) excel-
lency.
превосхо|ди́ть, жу́, ~дишь, *impf. of* пре-
взойти́.
превосхо́д|ный (~ен, ~на), *adj.* **1.** superla-
tive; superb, outstanding. **2.** (*obs.*) superior;
~ные си́лы superior forces. **3.** ~ная сте́-
пень (*gram.*) superlative degree.
превосхо́дств|о, а, *n.* superiority; чи́слен-
ное п. numerical superiority; я́вное п.
marked superiority; п. в во́здухе (*mil.*) air
superiority.
превосходя́щий, *pres. part. of* ~и́ть *and adj.*
superior.
превра|ти́ть, щу́, ти́шь, *pf.* (*of* ~ща́ть)
(в+*a.*) to convert (into), turn (to, into), reduce (to); to transmute; п. я́рды в ме́тры
to convert yards into metres; п. в ка́мень
to turn to stone; п. в у́голь to carbonize;
п. в шу́тку to turn into a joke.
превра|ти́ться, щу́сь, ти́шься, *pf.* (*of*
~ща́ться) (в+*a.*) to turn (into), change
(into); п. в слух to be all ears.
превра́тно, *adv.* wrongly; п. истолкова́ть
to misinterpret.
превра́тност|ь, и, *f.* **1.** wrongness, falsity.
2. vicissitude; ~и судьбы́ vicissitudes of
fate, reverses of fortune.
превра́т|ный (~ен, ~на), *adj.* **1.** wrong,
false; у него́ бы́ло ~ное поня́тие о том,
что произошло́ he had a false impression
of what happened. **2.** changeful, incon-

stant, perverse; ~ная судьба́ perverse
fate.
превраща́|ть(ся), ю(сь), *impf. of* превра-
ти́ть(ся).
превраще́ни|е, я, *n.* transformation, con-
version; transmutation; metamorphosis.
превы́|сить, шу, сишь, *pf.* (*of* ~ша́ть) to
exceed; п. власть, п. полномо́чия to exceed one's authority; п. свой креди́т в
ба́нке to overdraw (one's account).
превыша́|ть, ю, *impf. of* превы́сить.
превы́ше, *adv.* (*obs.*) far above; п. всего́
above all.
превыше́ни|е, я, *n.* exceeding, excess; п.
вла́сти exceeding one's authority; п. своего́
креди́та в ба́нке overdrawing; зада́ние
бы́ло вы́полнено с ~ем the task was accomplished and to spare.
прегра́д|а, ы, *f.* bar, barrier; obstacle.
прегра|ди́ть, жу́, ди́шь, *pf.* (*of* ~жда́ть)
to bar, obstruct, block; п. путь кому́-н. to
bar someone's way.
прегражда́|ть, ю, *impf. of* прегради́ть.
прегреш|а́ть, а́ю, *impf. of* ~и́ть.
прегреше́ни|е, я, *n.* sin, transgression.
прегреш|и́ть, у́, и́шь, *pf.* (*of* ~а́ть) (*obs.*) to
sin, transgress.
пред, *prep.* = пе́ред.
пред-[1] *prefix* pre-, fore-, ante-.
пред-[2] *abbr., in compound formations, of* пред-
седа́тель.
преда|ва́ть(ся), ю́(сь), ёшь(ся), *impf. of*
преда́ть(ся).
преда́ни|е[1], я, *n.* legend; tradition.
преда́ни|е[2], я, *n.* handing over, committing;
п. забве́нию burying in oblivion; п. земле́
committing to the earth; п. сме́рти putting
to death; п. суду́ bringing to trial.
пре́данност|ь, и, *f.* devotion.
пре́дан|ный (~, ~на), *p.p.p. of* преда́ть *and*
adj. (+*d.*) devoted (to); п. друг staunch
friend, faithful friend; п. Вам (*epistolary for-*
mula) yours faithfully, yours truly.
преда́тел|ь, я, *m.* traitor, betrayer; оказа́ть-
ся ~ем to turn traitor.
преда́тельниц|а, ы, *f.* traitress.
преда́тельск|ий, *adj.* traitorous, perfidious;
treacherous (*also fig.*); ~ая пого́да treacherous weather; п. румя́нец telltale blush.
преда́тельств|о, а, *n.* treachery, betrayal,
perfidy.
пре|да́ть, да́м, да́шь, да́ст, дади́м, дади́те,
даду́т, *past* ~дал, ~дала́, ~дало, *pf.* (*of*
~дава́ть) **1.** (+*d.*) to hand over (to), commit (to); п. гла́сности to make known,
make public; п. забве́нию to bury in
oblivion; п. земле́ to commit to the earth;
п. огню́ to commit to the flames; п. огню́
и мечу́ to give over to fire and sword; п.
суду́ to bring to trial. **2.** to betray.

пре|да́ться, да́мся, да́шься, да́стся, дади́мся, дади́тесь, даду́тся, *past* ~да́лся, ~дала́сь, *pf.* (*of* ~дава́ться) (+*d.*) **1.** to give oneself up (to); п. мечта́м to fall into a reverie, lapse into day-dreams; п. отча́янию to give way to despair; п. поро́кам to indulge in vices; п. страстя́м to abandon oneself to one's passions. **2.** (*obs.*) to entrust oneself (to), put oneself in the hands (of); п. врагу́ to go over to the enemy.

предба́нник, а, *m.* dressing-room (*in a bath-house*).

предваре́ни|е, я, *n.* **1.** (*obs.*) forewarning, telling beforehand. **2.** forestalling; п. равноде́нствия (*astron.*) precession (of the equinox); п. впу́ска па́ра (*tech.*) pre-admission of steam. **3.** (*tech.*) lead.

предвари́лк|а, и, *f.* (*coll.*) lock-up (*place of detention before trial*).

предвари́тельно, *adv.* beforehand; as a preliminary; п. нагре́ть to pre-heat.

предвари́тельн|ый, *adj.* preliminary; prior; ~ое заключе́ние (*leg.*) imprisonment before trial; ~ая кома́нда (*mil.*) preparatory command; п. нагре́в (*tech.*) pre-heating; ~ые перегово́ры preliminary talks, pourparlers; ~ая прода́жа биле́тов advance sale of tickets, advance booking; ~ое сле́дствие (*leg.*) preliminary investigation, inquest; по ~ому соглаше́нию by prior arrangement; ~ое усло́вие prior condition, pre-requisite; п. экза́мен preliminary examination.

предвар|и́ть, ю́, и́шь, *pf.* (*of* ~я́ть) **1.** (*obs.*) to forewarn, tell beforehand. **2.** to forestall, anticipate.

предвар|я́ть, я́ю, *impf. of* ~и́ть.

предве́сти|е, я, *n.* presage, portent.

предве́стник, а, *m.* forerunner, precursor; herald, harbinger; presage, portent.

предве́ч|ный (~ен), *adj.* (*theol.*; *epithet of God*) everlasting; existing from before time.

предвеща́|ть, ю, *impf.* (*no pf.*) to betoken, foretoken, ...adow, herald, presage, portend; ¬чи ~ли грозу́ the clouds betokened a storm; э́то ~ет хоро́шее this bodes well, this augurs well.

предвзя́тост|ь, и, *f.* preconception; prejudice, bias.

предвзя́т|ый (~, ~а), *adj.* preconceived; prejudiced, biassed.

предви́дени|е, я, *n.* foresight, prevision; foreseeing; foreknowledge.

предви́|деть, жу, дишь, *impf.* (*no pf.*) to foresee.

предви́д|еться, ится, *impf.* (*no pf.*) to be foreseen; to be expected.

предвку|си́ть, шу́, ~си́шь, *pf.* (*of* ~ша́ть) to look forward (to), anticipate (with pleasure).

предвкуша́|ть, ю, *impf. of* предвкуси́ть.

предвкуше́ни|е, я, *n.* (pleasurable) anticipation.

предводи́тел|ь, я, *m.* leader; п. дворя́нства (*hist.*) marshal of the nobility (*in tsarist Russia: representative of nobility of province or district, elected to manage their affairs and represent their interests in local government organs*).

предводи́тельств|о, а, *n.* **1.** leadership; под ~ом (+*g.*) under the leadership (of), under the command (of). **2.** (*hist.*) office of marshal of the nobility.

предводи́тельств|овать, ую, *impf.* (+*i.*) to lead, be the leader (of).

предводи́тельш|а, и, *f.* (*hist.*; *coll.*) wife of marshal of the nobility.

предвое́нный, *adj.* **1.** preceding the outbreak of war. **2.** pre-war.

предвозве|сти́ть, щу́, сти́шь, *pf.* (*of* ~ща́ть) to foretell.

предвозве́стник, а, *m.* herald; harbinger, precursor.

предвозвеща́|ть, ю, *impf. of* предвозвести́ть.

предвосхи́|тить, щу, тишь, *pf.* (*of* ~ща́ть) to anticipate; п. пригово́р to anticipate the verdict.

предвосхища́|ть, ю, *impf. of* предвосхити́ть.

предвосхище́ни|е, я, *n.* anticipation.

предвы́борн|ый, *adj.* (pre-)election; ~ая кампа́ния election campaign; ~ое собра́ние (pre-)election meeting.

предго́р|ье, ья, *g. pl.* ~ий, *n.* foothills.

предгрозов|о́й, *adj.*; ~а́я мо́лния lightning before a storm.

предгро́зь|е, я, *n.* time before a storm (*also fig.*).

преддве́ри|е, я, *n.* threshold (*also fig.*); в ~и (+*g.*) on the threshold (of).

преде́л, а, *m.* (*in var. senses*) limit; bound, boundary; end; (*pl.*) range; в ~ах (+*g.*) within, within the limits (of), within the bounds (of); за ~ами (+*g.*) outside, beyond the bounds (of); в ~ах го́рода, городско́й черты́ within the city, within the bounds of the city; в ~ах досяга́емости within striking distance; в ~ах го́да within the year; за ~ами страны́ outside the country; вы́йти за ~ы го́рода to go outside the city boundary; вы́йти за ~ы (+*g.*) to overstep the limits (of), exceed the bounds (of); э́то за ~ами мои́х сил it is beyond my power; родны́е ~ы (*arch. or poet.*) one's native borders; п. жела́ний summit, pinnacle ѡ (one's) desires; ~ы колеба́ния температу́ры temperature range; п. насыще́ния saturation point; п. про́чности (*tech.*) breaking point; положи́ть п. (+*d.*) to put an end (to), terminate.

преде́л|ьный, *adj.* **1.** *adj. of* ~; п. во́зраст

age-limit; ∼ьная ли́ния boundary line; п. сро́к time-limit, deadline; п. у́гол critical angle. **2.** maximum; utmost; ∼ьное напряже́ние (*tech*.) breaking point, pressure limit; ∼ьная ско́рость maximum speed; с ∼ьной я́сностью with the utmost clarity. **3.** (*chem*.) saturated.

предержа́щ|ий, *only in phrase* вла́сти ∼ие (*obs. or iron*.) the powers that be.

предзака́тный, *adj*. before sunset.

предзнаменова́ни|е, я, *n*. omen, augury.

предзнамен|ова́ть, у́ю, *impf*. to bode, augur, portend.

предика́т, а, *m*. (*philos. and gram*.) predicate.

предикати́вный, *adj*. (*gram*.) predicative; п. член predicate.

предика́ци|я, и, *f*. (*philos. and gram*.) predication.

предисло́ви|е, я, *n*. preface, foreword; без ∼й without more ado; про́сим без ∼й! don't beat about the bush!

предкры́л|ок, ка, *m*. (*aeron*.) stat.

предлага́|ть, ю, *impf. of* предложи́ть.

предло́г[1], а, *m*. pretext; под ∼ом (+*g*.) on the pretext (of), on a plea (of); под разли́чными ∼ами on various pretexts; п. для ссо́ры an excuse for a quarrel.

предло́г[2], а, *m*. (*gram*.) preposition.

предложе́ни|е[1], я, *n*. **1.** offer; proposition; proposal (of marriage); п. по́мощи offer of assistance; сде́лать п. кому́-н. to propose (marriage) to someone; приня́ть п. to accept an offer; to accept a proposal (of marriage). **2.** (*at meeting, etc*.) proposal, motion; suggestion; внести́ п. to introduce a motion; отклони́ть п. to turn down a proposal. **3.** (*econ*.) supply; зако́н спро́са и ∼я law of supply and demand.

предложе́ни|е[2], я, *n*. **1.** (*gram*.) sentence; гла́вное п. main clause; прида́точное п. subordinate clause; усло́вное п. conditional sentence; вво́дное п. parenthesis, parenthetic clause. **2.** (*philos*.) proposition.

предлож|и́ть, у́, ∼ишь, *pf*. (*of* предлага́ть) **1.** to offer; п. свои́ услу́ги to offer one's services, come forward; п. ру́ку (и се́рдце) кому́-н. (*obs*.) to make a proposal of marriage to someone. **2.** to propose; to suggest; п. резолю́цию to move a resolution; п. тост to propose a toast; п. чью-н. кандидату́ру to propose someone for election; п. кого́-н. в председа́тели to propose someone for chairman; п. внима́нию to call attention (to); мы ∼и́ли ей обрати́ться к врачу́ we suggested that she should see a doctor; они́ ∼и́ли нам вме́сте с ни́ми пое́хать на бе́рег мо́ря they have invited us to go with them to the sea-side *or* they have suggested that we might go with them to the sea-side. **3.** to put, set, propound; п. вопро́с to put

a question; п. зада́чу to set a problem; п. но́вую тео́рию to propound a new theory. **4.** to order, require; им ∼и́ли освободи́ть кварти́ру they have been ordered to vacate their apartment.

предло́жный, *adj*. (*gram*.) prepositional; п. паде́ж prepositional case.

предма́йский, *adj*. pre-May Day (*taking place in the period immediately preceding May Day*).

предме́ст|ье, ья, *g. pl*. ∼ий, *n*. suburb.

предме́т, а, *m*. **1.** object; article, item; (*pl*.) goods; ∼ы дома́шнего обихо́да household goods, domestic utensils; ∼ы пе́рвой необходи́мости necessities; ∼ы широ́кого потребле́ния consumer goods. **2.** subject, topic, theme; (+*g*.) object (of); п. насме́шек object of ridicule, butt; п. спо́ра point at issue; п. (любви́) (*obs*.) object of one's affections; како́й п. ва́шего иссле́дования? what is the subject of your research? **3.** (*school*) subject; она́ сдала́ экза́мен по пяти́ ∼ам she passed the examination in five subjects. **4.** ме́стный п. (*mil*.) (ground) feature. **5.** object (= *purpose*); на п. (+*g*.) with the object (of); на сей п. (*official or joc*.) to this end, with this object; име́ть в ∼е (*obs*.) to have in view.

предме́тник, а, *m*. (*teachers' sl*.) specialist.

предме́т|ный, *adj. of* ∼; п. уро́к object-lesson; п. катало́г subject catalogue; п. указа́тель subject index; п. сто́лик stage (*of microscope*).

предмо́стн|ый, *adj*.; п. плацда́рм, ∼ое укрепле́ние bridge-head.

предназнач|а́ть, а́ю, *impf. of* ∼ить.

предназначе́ни|е, я, *n*. **1.** earmarking. **2.** (*obs*.) destiny.

предназна́ч|ить, у, ишь, *pf*. (*of* ∼а́ть) (для, *or* на+*a*.) to destine (for), intend (for), mean (for); to earmark (for), set aside (for); бо́мбу ∼или для импера́тора the bomb was intended for the emperor; мы ∼или э́ти де́ньги на поку́пку автомоби́ля we set aside this money to buy a car.

преднаме́ренно, *adv*. by design, deliberately.

преднаме́ренност|ь, и, *f*. premeditation.

преднаме́рен|ный (∼, ∼на), *adj*. premeditated; aforethought; deliberate.

предначерта́ни|е, я, *n*. outline, plan, design; п. судьбы́ predestination.

предначерта́|нный, *p.p.p. of* ∼ть; п. судьбо́й predestined.

предначерта́|ть, ю, *pf*. to plan beforehand; to foreordain.

предо = пред.

предобе́денный, *adj*. before-dinner, preprandial.

пред|о́к, ка, *m*. forefather, ancestor; (*pl*.) forbears.

предоктя́брьский, *adj.* pre-October (*taking place during the period immediately preceding the Russian Revolution of October 1917 or its anniversary*).

предоперацио́нный, *adj.* (*med.*) pre-operative.

предопределе́ни|е, я, n. 1. pre-determining. **2.** predestination.

**предопредел|и́ть, ю́, и́шь, *pf.* (*of* ~я́ть) to pre-determine; to predestine, foreordain.

**предопредел|я́ть, я́ю, *impf. of* ~и́ть.

предоста́в|ить, лю, ишь, *pf.* (*of* ~ля́ть) **1. to let; to leave; нам ~или сами́м реши́ть де́ло the decision was left to us, we were left to decide the matter for ourselves; п. кого́-н. самому́ себе́ to leave someone to his own devices, to his own resources. **2.** to give, grant; п. креди́т to give credit; п. пра́во to concede a right; п. возмо́жность to afford an opportunity, give a chance; п. кому́-н. сло́во to let someone have the floor, call upon someone to speak; они́ ~или ко́мнату в на́ше распоряже́ние they have put a room at our disposal.

**предоставля́|ть, ю, *impf. of* предоста́вить; ~ю сло́во това́рищу X (*formula of chairman introducing speaker at meeting*) I call upon Comrade X to speak.

**предостерега́|ть, ю, *impf. of* предостере́чь.

**предостереже́ни|е, я, n. warning, caution.

**предостере́|чь, гу́, жёшь, гу́т, *past* ~г, ~гла́, *pf.* (*of* ~га́ть) (от) to warn (against), caution (against), put on one's guard (against).

предосторо́жност|ь, и, f. 1. (*no pl.*) caution; ме́ры ~и precautionary measures, precautions. **2.** precaution.

**предосуди́тельност|ь, и, f. reprehensibility, blameworthiness.

**предосуди́тел|ьный (~ен, ~ьна), *adj.* wrong, reprehensible, blameworthy.

**предотвра|ти́ть, щу́, ти́шь, *pf.* (*of* ~ща́ть) to prevent, avert; to stave off; п. войну́ to avert a war; п. опа́сность to stave off danger.

**предотвраща́|ть, ю, *impf. of* предотврати́ть.

**предотвраще́ни|е, я, n. prevention, averting; staving off.

**предохране́ни|е, я, n. (от) protection (against), preservation (from).

**предохрани́тел|ь, я, m. guard, safety device; safety catch; (пла́вкий) п. (*electr.*) safety fuse, cut-out; п. от обледене́ния (*aeron.*) de-icer.

предохрани́тельн|ый, *adj.* **1. preservative; preventive; ~ые ме́ры precautionary measures, precautions; ~ая приви́вка preventive inoculation. **2.** (*tech.*) safety; preventive; п. кла́пан safety-valve; ~ая коро́бка fuse box; ~ые очки́ safety goggles; ~ая

плита́ (*radio*) baffle plate; п. штепсель fuse; п. щит guard shield, fender.

**предохран|и́ть, ю́, и́шь, *pf.* (*of* ~я́ть) (от) to preserve, protect (from, against).

**предохран|я́ть, я́ю, *impf. of* ~и́ть.

**предписа́ни|е, я, n. order, injunction; (*pl.*) directions, instructions; (*med., etc.*) prescription; п. суда́ court order; согла́сно ~ю by order.

предпи|са́ть, шу́, ~шешь, *pf.* (*of* ~сывать) **1. (+*inf.*) to order, direct, instruct (to). **2.** to prescribe (*a cure, a diet, etc.*); врач ~са́л ей курс инъе́кций the doctor prescribed for her, put her on a course of injections.

**предпи́сыва|ть, ю, *impf. of* предписа́ть.

**предпле́ч|ье, ья, g. pl. ~ий, n. (*anat.*) forearm.

**предплу́жник, а, m. (*agric.*) coulter.

**предплюс|на́, ны́, pl. ~ны, ~ен, f. (*anat.*) tarsus.

**предполага́емый, *pres. part. pass. of* предполага́ть *and adj.* proposed.

предполага́|ть, ю, *impf.* **1. *impf. of* предположи́ть. **2.** (*impf. only*) to intend, propose; to contemplate; мы ~ем оста́вить дете́й у ба́бушки we propose to leave the children at their grandmother's; он как бу́дто ~ет жени́ться apparently he is contemplating marrying. **3.** (*impf. only*) to presuppose; успе́х в э́том де́ле ~ет хоро́шую пого́ду the success of this business presupposes good weather.

предполага́|ться, ется, *impf.* **1. *pass. of* ~ть. **2.** ~ется (*impers.*) it is proposed, it is intended; ~ется проложи́ть отсю́да автостра́ду it is proposed to build a motorway from here.

предположе́ни|е, я, n. **1. supposition, assumption. **2.** intention; у меня́ п. жени́ться I am thinking of marrying.

предположи́тельно, *adv.* **1. supposedly, presumably. **2.** (*in parenthesis*) probably; мы прие́дем в Ло́ндон, п., к десяти́ часа́м we shall be in London probably by ten o'clock.

**предположи́тельн|ый, *adj.* conjectural; hypothetical; э́то ещё лишь ~о this is still only hypothetical.

**предполож|и́ть, у́, ~ишь, *pf.* (*of* предполага́ть) to suppose, assume; to conjecture, surmise; ~им, что он опозда́л на по́езд (let us) suppose he missed the train.

**предпо́ль|е, я, n. (*mil.*) forward defensive positions.

**предполя́рный, *adj.* sub-arctic.

**предпо|сла́ть, шлю́, шлёшь, *pf.* (*of* ~сыла́ть) (+*d. and a.*) to preface (with); дире́ктор шко́лы ~сла́л вы́говору не́сколько о́бщих замеча́ний the headmaster prefaced the ticking-off with a few general remarks.

предпослéдн|ий, *adj.* penultimate, last but one, next to last; one from the bottom (*on list*); Вáше ~ee письмó your last letter but one; п. слог penultimate syllable.

предпосылá|ть, ю, *impf. of* предпослáть.

предпосы́лк|а, и, *f.* **1.** pre-requisite, pre--condition. **2.** (*philos.*) premise.

предпоч|éсть, тý, тёшь, *past* ~ёл, ~лá, *pf.* (*of* ~итáть) to prefer; п. говя́дину барáнине to prefer beef to mutton; я ~ёл бы идти́ пешкóм I would rather walk, go on foot.

предпочитá|ть, ю, *impf. of* предпочéсть.

предпочтéни|е, я, *n.* preference; predilection; оказáть п., отдáть п. (+*d.*) to show a preference (for), give preference.

предпочти́тельно, *adv.* **1.** rather, preferably. **2.** (пéред; *obs.*) by preference (to).

предпочти́тел|ьный (~ен, ~ьна), *adj.* preferable.

предпрáздничн|ый, *adj.* holiday (*taking place in the period immediately preceding a holiday*); ~ое настроéние holiday mood; ~ая суетá holiday rush.

предприи́мчивост|ь, и, *f.* enterprise.

предприи́мчив|ый (~, ~а), *adj.* enterprising.

предпринимáтел|ь, я, *m.* owner (of a firm *or* business); employer; entrepreneur.

предпринимáтель|ский, *adj. of* ~.

предпринимáтельств|о, а, *no pl., n.* (private) business undertakings; свобóдное п. free enterprise.

предпринимá|ть, ю, *impf. of* предприня́ть.

предпри|ня́ть, мý, ~мешь, *past* ~ня́л, ~няла́, ~ня́ло, *pf.* (*of* ~нимáть) to undertake; (*mil., etc.*) to launch; п. атáку to launch an attack; п. шаги́ to take steps.

предприя́ти|е, я, *n.* **1.** undertaking, enterprise; business; рискóванное п. risky undertaking, venture. **2.** (*econ.*) enterprise, concern, business; works; мéлкое п. small business; фабри́чно-завóдскóе п. (industrial) works.

предрасполагá|ть, ю, *impf. of* предрасполо́жить.

предрасположéни|е, я, *n.* (к) predisposition (to); (*med.*) diathesis.

предрасполóж|енный, *p.p.p. of* ~ить; (к) predisposed (to).

предрасполóж|и́ть, ý, ~ишь, *pf.* (*of* предрасполагáть) (к) to predispose (to).

предрассвéтн|ый, *adj.* occurring before dawn; ~ая мгла early morning mist; ~ые сýмерки false dawn; п. хóлод the chill of approaching dawn.

предрассýд|ок, ка, *m.* prejudice; закоснé-лый в ~ках steeped in prejudice.

предрекá|ть, ю, *impf. of* предрéчь.

предрé|чь, кý, чёшь, кýт, *past* ~к, ~кла́, *pf.* (*of* ~кáть) (*obs.*) to foretell.

предреш|áть, áю, *impf. of* ~и́ть.

предреш|и́ть, ý, и́шь, *pf.* (*of* ~áть) **1.** to decide beforehand. **2.** to pre-determine.

председáтел|ь, я, *m.* chairman; president.

председáтель|ский, *adj. of* ~; ~ское мéсто the chair (*at a meeting*); заня́ть ~ское мéсто to take the chair.

председáтельств|о, а, *n.* chairmanship; presidency.

председáтельств|овать, ую, *impf.* to be in the chair, preside.

председáтельств|ующий, *pres. part. act. of* ~овать; *as noun* п., ~ующего, *m.* chairman.

предсéрди|е, я, *n.* (*anat.*) auricle.

предсказáни|е, я, *n.* prediction; forecast, prophecy; prognostication.

предсказáтел|ь, я, *m.* foreteller, forecaster; soothsayer.

предска|зáть, жý, ~жешь, *pf.* (*of* ~зывать) to foretell, predict; to forecast, prophesy; to prognosticate.

предскáзыва|ть, ю, *impf. of* предсказáть.

предсмéртн|ый, *adj.* occurring before death; ~ое желáние dying wish; ~ые страдáния death-agony; п. час one's last hour.

предста|вáть, ю́, ёшь, *impf. of* ~ть.

представи́тел|ь, я, *m.* **1.** representative; (+*g.*) spokesman (for); полномóчный п. plenipotentiary. **2.** (*bot., etc.*) specimen.

представи́тельност|ь, и, *f.* imposingness; imposing appearance, presence.

представи́тельный[1], *adj.* (*polit., leg.*) representative.

представи́тел|ьный[2] **(~ен, ~ьна),** *adj.* imposing.

представи́тельств|о, а, *n.* 1. representation, representing. **2.** (*collect.*) representation, representatives; дипломати́ческое п. diplomatic representatives; торгóвое п. trade delegates. **3.** (*polit., leg.*) election of, sending of representatives (*to organs of government*).

предстáв|ить, лю, ишь, *pf.* (*of* ~ля́ть) **1.** to present; п. трýдности to offer difficulty; п. интерéс to be of interest, have interest. **2.** to produce, submit; п. доказáтельства to produce evidence; п. спи́сок члéнов ассоциáции to submit a list of members of an association. **3.** (+*a. and d.*) to introduce (to), present (to). **4.** (к) to recommend (for), put forward (for); п. когó-н. к óрдену to recommend someone for a decoration. **5.** п. себé to imagine, fancy, picture, conceive; ~ь(те) себé, какáя э́то былá досáда! (just) imagine what a nuisance that was! **6.** to represent, display; п. чтó-то в смешнóм ви́де to hold something up to ridicule. **7.** (*theatr.*) to perform; to play.

предстáв|иться, люсь, ишься, *pf.* (*of* ~ля́ть-ся) **1.** to present itself, occur, arise; нáшим глаза́м ~и́лась мра́чная карти́на a gloomy picture rose before our eyes; ~и́лся слу́чай пое́хать в Москву́ a chance arose to go to Moscow; я им сообщу́, как то́лько ~и́тся возмо́жность I will inform them as soon as an opportunity arises. 2. (*impers.* +*d.*) to seem (to); э́то тебе́ то́лько ~и́лось you only imagined it, it was just your imagination. 3. (+*d.*) to introduce oneself (to). 4. (+*i.*) to pretend (to be), pass oneself off (as); п. больны́м to feign sickness.

представле́ни|е, я, *n.* 1. presentation; п. но́вого сотру́дника introduction of a new colleague; п. про́пуска presentation of a permit. 2. (written) declaration, statement; representation; ~я бы́ли сде́ланы всем прави́тельствам representations have been made to all the governments. 3. (*theatr.*) performance. 4. (*psych.*) representation. 5. idea, notion, conception; дать п. (о+*p.*) to give an idea (of); я не име́ю ни мале́йшего ~я I have not the faintest idea, remotest conception.

представля́|ть, ю, *impf.* 1. *impf. of* предста́вить. 2. (*impf. only*) to represent; он ~ет США в ООН he represents the U.S.A. in UNO. 3. п. собо́й to represent, be; to constitute; э́то ~ет собо́й исключе́ние this constitutes an exception.

представля́|ться, юсь, *impf. of* предста́виться.

представа́тел|ь, я, *m.* (*obs.*) protector; champion.

предста́тельн|ый, *adj.* ~ая железа́ (*anat.*) prostate (gland).

предста́|ть, ну, нешь, *pf.* (*of* ~ва́ть) (пе́ред) to appear (before); п. пе́ред судо́м to appear in court.

предсто|я́ть, и́т, *impf.* to be in prospect, lie ahead, be at hand; to be in store; ~я́ла суро́вая зима́ a hard winter lay ahead; нам ~и́т мно́го неприя́тностей we are in for a lot of trouble, there is a lot of trouble in store for us; ему́ ~и́т предста́вить диссерта́цию к пе́рвому ию́ня he has to submit his dissertation by the first of June.

предстоя́|щий, *pres. part. of* ~ть *and adj.* coming, forthcoming; impending, imminent; ~щие вы́боры the forthcoming elections; она́ страши́лась ~щего медици́нского осмо́тра she was dreading the impending medical (examination).

предте́ч|а, и, *m. and f.* forerunner, precursor; Иоа́нн п. John the Baptist.

предубе|ди́ть, ди́шь, *pf.* (*of* ~жда́ть) (*obs.*) to prejudice, bias.

предубежда́|ть, ю, *impf. of* предубеди́ть.

предубежде́ни|е, я, *n.* prejudice, bias.

предубе|жде́нный, *p.p.p. of* ~ди́ть (*obs.*) *and adj.* prejudiced, biased.

предуве́дом|ить, лю, ишь, *pf.* (*of* ~ля́ть) to inform beforehand, give advance notice; to warn, forewarn; вам сле́довало п. их о ва́шем прие́зде you should have warned them that you were coming.

предуведомле́ни|е, я, *n.* warning, forewarning; notice in advance.

предуведомля́|ть, ю, *impf. of* предуве́домить.

предугад|а́ть, а́ю, *pf.* (*of* ~ывать) to guess (in advance).

предуга́дыва|ть, ю, *impf. of* предугада́ть.

предуда́рный, *adj.* (*ling.*) pre-tonic.

предумы́шленност|ь, и, *f.* premeditation.

предумы́шленный, *adj.* premeditated, aforethought.

предупреди́тельност|ь, и, *f.* courtesy; attentiveness.

предупреди́тел|ьный, *adj.* 1. preventive, precautionary. 2. (~ен, ~ьна) courteous; attentive; obliging.

предупре|ди́ть, жу́, ди́шь, *pf.* (*of* ~жда́ть) 1. (о+*p.*) to let know beforehand (about), notify in advance (about), warn (about); to give notice (of, about); надлежи́т п. экскурсово́да о жела́нии посети́ть за́мок notice is to be given to the guide if it is wished to visit the castle; п. за неде́лю об увольне́нии to give a week's notice (*of dismissal*). 2. to prevent, avert; п. ава́рию to prevent an accident. 3. to anticipate; to forestall; п. замеча́ние to anticipate a remark; я как раз э́то хоте́л сказа́ть, но вы ~ди́ли меня́ that is just what I was about to say, but you took the words out of my mouth.

предупрежда́|ть, ю, *impf. of* предупреди́ть.

предупрежде́ни|е, я, *n.* 1. notice; notification. 2. prevention. 3. anticipating; forestalling. 4. warning; получи́ть вы́говор с ~ем (*leg.*) to be dismissed with a caution.

предусма́трива|ть, ю, *impf. of* предусмотре́ть.

предусмотр|е́ть, ю́, ~ишь, *pf.* (*of* предусма́тривать) to envisage, foresee; to stipulate (for), provide (for), make provision (for); п. все возмо́жности to provide for every eventuality.

предусмотри́тельност|ь, и, *f.* foresight, prudence.

предусмотри́тел|ьный (~ен, ~ьна), *adj.* prudent; provident; far-sighted; ~ьная поли́тика far-sighted policy.

предустано́вленный, *adj.* (*obs.*) pre-established, pre-determined.

преду́тренний, *adj.* occurring immediately before morning; п. час the hour before dawn.

предчу́встви|е, я, *n.* presentiment; foreboding, misgiving, premonition.

предчу́вств|овать, ую, *impf.* to have a presentiment (of, about), have a premonition (of, about); я ~ова́л, что вы сего́дня поя́витесь I had a feeling that you would turn up today.

предше́ственник, а, *m.* predecessor; forerunner, precursor.

предше́ств|овать, ую, *impf.* (+*d.*) to go in front (of); to precede; её сме́рти ~ова́ла дли́тельная боле́знь her death was preceded by a long illness.

предше́ств|ующий, *pres. part. act. of* ~овать *and adj.* previous; foregoing; *as noun* ~ующее, ~ующего, *n.* the foregoing.

предъяви́тел|ь, я, *m.* bearer; п. и́ска plaintiff, claimant; чек на ~я cheque payable to bearer.

предъяв|и́ть, лю́, ~ишь, *pf.* (*of* ~ля́ть) 1. to show, produce, present; п. биле́т to show one's ticket; п. доказа́тельства to produce evidence, present proofs. 2. (*leg., etc.*) to bring (forward); п. иск (к) to bring a suit (against); п. обвине́ние (+*d.* в+*p.*) to charge (with), bring an accusation (against of); ему́ ~и́ли обвине́ние в поджо́ге he is charged with arson; п. пра́во (на+*a.*) to lay claim (to), raise a claim (to); п. тре́бование (к) to lay claim (to); п. высо́кие тре́бования (к) to make great, high demands (of, on).

предъявле́ни|е, я, *n.* 1. showing, producing, presentation; вход разреша́ется по ~и удостовере́ния ли́чности entry is permitted on presentation of identity card. 2. (*leg., etc.*) bringing; п. и́ска bringing of a suit; п. обвине́ния (в+*p.*) accusation (of), charge (of); п. пра́ва assertion of a claim.

предъявля́|ть, ю, *impf. of* предъяви́ть.

предыду́щ|ий, *adj.* previous, preceding; *as noun* ~ее, ~его, *n.* the foregoing; из ~его сле́дует from the foregoing it follows.

прее́мник, а, *m.* successor.

прее́мственност|ь, и, *f.* succession; continuity.

прее́мственный, *adj.* successive.

прее́мств|о, а, *n.* succession.

пре́жде 1. *adv.* (*opp. to* пото́м) before; first; п. чем *as conj.* before; на́до бы́ло ду́мать об э́том п. you should have thought about it before; ты до́лжен п. дое́сть ка́шу you must eat up your kasha first; ты до́лжен дое́сть ка́шу, п. чем взять ды́ню you must eat up your kasha before you have any melon. 2. *adv.* (*opp. to* тепе́рь) formerly, in former times; before; п. он учи́л в интерна́те he taught in a boarding-school before. 3. *prep.*+*g.* before; они́ пришли́ п. нас they arrived before us; п. всего́ first of all, to begin with; first and foremost.

преждевре́менно, *adv.* prematurely; before one's time.

преждевре́менност|ь, и, *f.* prematurity, untimeliness.

преждевре́мен|ный (~ен, ~на), *adj.* premature, untimely; ~ные ро́ды (*med.*) premature birth.

пре́жн|ий, *adj.* previous, former; в ~ее вре́мя in the old days, in former times.

презе́нт, а, *m.* (*obs. or joc.*) present.

презента́бел|ьный (~ен, ~ьна), *adj.* presentable.

презент|ова́ть, у́ю, *impf. and pf.* (*obs. or joc.*) to present.

презервати́в, а, *m.* 1. contraceptive. 2. (*med.; obs.*) prophylactic.

презервати́вный, *adj.* (*med.*) prophylactic, preventive.

презерва́ци|я, и, *f.* preservation.

президе́нт, а, *m.* president.

президе́нт|ский, *adj. of* ~; ~ские вы́боры presidential elections.

президе́нтств|о, а, *n.* presidency.

прези́диум, а, *m.* presidium.

презира́|ть, ю, *impf.* 1. (*impf. only*) to despise, hold in contempt. 2. (*pf.* презре́ть) to disdain; п. опа́сность to scorn danger.

презре́ни|е, я, *n.* disdain, contempt, scorn.

презре́н|ный (~, ~на), *adj.* contemptible, despicable; п. мета́лл (*coll.*) filthy lucre.

презр|е́ть, ю́, и́шь, *pf. of* презира́ть.

презри́тел|ьный (~ен, ~ьна), *adj.* contemptuous, scornful, disdainful.

презу́мпци|я, и, *f.* (*philos., leg.*) presumption.

преиму́щественно, *adv.* mainly, chiefly, principally.

преиму́щественн|ый, *adj.* 1. primary, prime, principal. 2. preferential, priority. 3. (*leg.*) preferential; ~ое пра́во preference; ~ое пра́во на поку́пку pre-emption.

преиму́ществ|о, а, *n.* 1. advantage; име́ть п. (пе́ред) to possess, have an advantage (over); получи́ть п. (пе́ред) to gain an advantage (over); они́ име́ют то п., что у них телефо́н they have the advantage of being on the telephone. 2. preference; по ~у for the most part, chiefly. 3. (*leg.*) privilege.

преиспо́дн|яя, ей, *f.* (*obs.*) the nether regions, the underworld, inferno.

преиспо́лн|енный, *p.p.p. of* ~ить *and adj.* (+*g. or i.*) filled (with), full (of); п. опа́сности fraught with danger; п. реши́мости firmly resolved.

преиспо́лн|ить, ю, ишь, *pf.* (*of* ~я́ть) (+*g. or i.*) to fill (with).

преиспо́лн|иться, юсь, ишься, *pf.* (*of* ~я́ться) (+*g. or i.*) to be filled (with), become full (of).

преисполн|я́ть(ся), я́ю(сь), *impf. of* ~и́ть(ся).

прейскура́нт, а, *m.* price-list; bill of fare.

пре|йти́, йду́, йдёшь, *past* ~шёл, ~шла́, *pf.* (*of* ~ходи́ть) (*obs.*) **1.** to cross. **2.** to pass, have passed.

преклоне́ни|е, я, *n.* (пе́ред) admiration (for), worship (for).

преклон|и́ть, ю́, и́шь, *pf.* (*of* ~я́ть) to incline, bend; to lower; п. го́лову to bow (one's head) (*in token of respect or worship*); п. коле́на to genuflect.

преклон|и́ться, ю́сь, и́шься, *pf.* (*of* ~я́ться) (пе́ред) **1.** to bow down (before), bend down (before). **2.** (*fig.*) to admire, worship.

прекло́нный, *adj.* п. во́зраст old age, declining years.

преклон|я́ть(ся), я́ю(сь), *impf. of* ~и́ть(ся).

прекосло́ви|е, я, *n.* (*obs.*) contradiction; без вся́кого ~я without contradiction.

прекосло́в|ить, лю, ишь, *impf.* (+*d.*) to contradict.

прекра́сно, *adv.* **1.** excellently; perfectly well; они́ п. зна́ют, что э́то воспрещено́ they know perfectly well that it is forbidden. **2.** *as interj.* excellent!, splendid!

прекрасноду́ши|е, я, *n.* (*iron.*) starry-eyed idealism.

прекрасноду́ш|ный (~ен, ~на), *adj.* (*iron.*) starry-eyed.

прекра́с|ный (~ен, ~на), *adj.* **1.** beautiful, fine; п. пол the fair sex; ра́ди ~ных глаз pour les beaux yeux; в оди́н п. день one fine day, once upon a time; *as noun* ~ное, ~ного, *n.* (*philos.*) the beautiful. **2.** excellent, capital, first-rate.

прекра|ти́ть, щу́, ти́шь, *pf.* (*of* ~ща́ть) to stop, cease, discontinue; to put a stop (to), put an end (to); to break off, sever, cut off; п. войну́ to end the war; п. вое́нные де́йствия to cease hostilities; п. знако́мство (с+*i.*) to break (it off) (with), give up; п. обсужде́ние вопро́са to drop the subject; п. ого́нь (*mil.*) to cease fire; п. платежи́ to suspend, stop payments; п. подпи́ску to discontinue a subscription, stop subscribing; п. пода́чу га́за to cut off the gas (supply); п. пре́ния to close a debate; п. рабо́ту to leave off work, down tools; п. рабо́тать to stop work(ing); п. сноше́ния (с+*i.*) to sever relations (with).

прекра|ти́ться, ти́тся, *pf.* (*of* ~ща́ться) **1.** to cease, end. **2.** *pass. of* ~ти́ть.

прекраща́|ть(ся), ю, ет(ся), *impf. of* прекрати́ть(ся).

прекраще́ни|е, я, *n.* stopping, ceasing, cessation, discontinuance; п. вое́нных де́йствий cessation of hostilities; п. огня́ cease-fire; п. платеже́й suspension of payments; п. пре́ний closure of a debate.

прела́т, а, *m.* prelate.

преле́ст|ный (~ен, ~на), *adj.* charming, delightful, lovely.

пре́лест|ь, и, *f.* charm, fascination; кака́я п.! how lovely!; ~и жи́зни в дере́вне the delights of living in the country; езда́ в автомоби́ле уже́ потеря́ла п. новизны́ the novelty of driving had already worn off.

прелимина́ри|и, ев, *no sing.* (*dipl.*) preliminaries.

прелимина́рный, *adj.* (*dipl.*) preliminary.

прелом|и́ть, лю́, ~ишь, *pf.* (*of* ~ля́ть) **1.** (*phys.*) to refract. **2.** (*fig.*) to interpret, put a construction (upon).

прелом|и́ться, ~ится, *pf.* (*of* ~ля́ться) **1.** (*phys.*) to be refracted. **2.** (*fig.*) to be interpreted; to take on a different aspect; в све́те но́вых све́дений исто́рия ~и́лась по-ино́му in the light of new information a different construction was put upon the affair.

преломле́ни|е, я, *n.* **1.** (*phys.*) refraction. **2.** (*fig.*) interpretation, construction.

преломля́емост|ь, и, f. (*phys.*) refrangibility.

преломля́|емый, *pres. part. pass. of* ~ть *and adj.* (*phys.*) refractable, refrangible.

преломля́|ть(ся), ю, ет(ся) *impf. of* преломи́ть(ся).

преломля́|ющий, *pres. part. act. of* ~ть *and adj.* (*phys.*) refractive, refracting.

пре́л|ый (~, ~а), *adj.* rotten, fusty.

прель, и, f. rot, mouldiness, mould.

прель|сти́ть, щу́, сти́шь, *pf.* (*of* ~ща́ть) **1.** to attract; его́ ~сти́ла перспекти́ва повы́шенной зарпла́ты he was attracted by the prospect of higher wages. **2.** to lure, entice; п. обеща́ниями to lure with promises.

прель|сти́ться, щу́сь, сти́шься, *pf.* (*of* ~ща́ться) (+*i.*) to be attracted (by); to be tempted (by), fall (for); мы ~сти́лись предложе́нием со́бственной кварти́ры we fell for the offer of having accommodation of our own.

прельща́|ть(ся), ю(сь), *impf. of* прельсти́ть(ся).

прелюбоде́|й, я, *m.* (*obs.*) adulterer.

прелюбоде́йств|овать, ую, *impf.* (*obs.*) to commit adultery.

прелюбодея́ни|е, я, *n.* (*obs.*) adultery.

прелю́ди|я, и, f. (*mus. and fig.*) prelude.

премиа́льн|ый, *adj. of* пре́мия; ~ая систе́ма bonus system; п. фонд bonus funds; *as noun* (*pl.*) ~ые, ~ых bonus.

премин|у́ть, у, ешь, *pf. only with neg.* (+*inf.*) not to fail (to); я не ~у зайти́ к вам I shall not fail to call in to see you.

премирова́ни|е, я, *n.* awarding of a prize; awarding of a bonus.

премиро́в|анный, *p.p.p. of* ~а́ть *and adj.*

prize-winning, prize; п. проéкт пáмятника prize-winning design for a monument; п. бык prize bull; *as noun* п., ~анного, *m.* prize-winner.

премир|овáть, ýю, *impf. and pf.* to award a prize (to); to give a bonus (to).

прéми|я, и, *f.* 1. prize; bonus; bounty, gratuity; нóбелевская п. Nobel Prize. 2. (*fin.*) premium; страховáя п. premium, insurance.

премнóго, *adv.* (*obs.*) very much, extremely.

премýдрост|ь, и, *f.* wisdom; ~и (*iron.*) subtleties.

премýдр|ый (~, ~a), *adj.* (very) wise, sage.

премьéр, а, *m.* 1. prime minister, premier. 2. (*theatr.*) leading actor, lead.

премьéр|а, ы, *f.* (*theatr.*) première, first night, opening night.

премьéр-минúстр, а, *m.* prime minister, premier.

премьéрш|а, и, *f.* (*theatr.*) leading lady, lead.

пренебрегá|ть, ю, *impf. of* пренебрéчь.

пренебрежéни|е, я, *n.* 1. scorn, contempt, disdain; обнарýжить, вы́казать своё п. (к) to show one's contempt (for); говори́ть с ~ем (o+*p.*) to disparage, speak slightingly (of). 2. neglect, disregard; п. свои́ми обя́занностями neglect of one's duties, dereliction of duty.

пренебрежи́тельност|ь, и, *f.* scorn.

пренебрежи́тел|ьный (~ен, ~ьна), *adj.* scornful, slighting, disdainful.

пренебрé|чь, гý, жёшь, гýт, *past* ~г, ~глá, *pf.* (*of* ~гáть) (+*i.*) 1. to scorn, despise; п. опáсностью to scorn danger; п. совéтом to scorn advice. 2. to neglect, disregard.

прéни|е, я, *n.* rotting.

прéни|я, й, *no sing.* debate; discussion; судéбные п. pleadings; откры́ть, прекрати́ть п. to open, close a debate.

преобладáни|е, я, *n.* predominance.

преобладá|ть, ет, *impf.* to predominate; to prevail.

преобладá|ющий, *pres. part. act. of* ~ть *and adj.* predominant; prevalent.

преображá|ть, ю, *impf. of* преобрази́ть.

преображéни|е, я, *n.* 1. transformation. 2. (*rel.*) the Transfiguration.

преобра|зи́ть, жý, зи́шь, *pf.* (*of* ~жáть) to transform, transfigure.

преобразовáни|е, я, *n.* 1. transformation. 2. reform; re-organization.

преобразовáтел|ь, я, *m.* 1. reformer; re-organizer. 2. (*phys., tech.*) transformer.

преобраз|овáть, ýю, *pf.* (*of* ~óвывать) 1. to transform (*also phys., tech.*). 2. to reform, re-organize.

преобразóвыва|ть, ю, *impf. of* преобразовáть.

преодолевá|ть, ю, *impf. of* преодолéть.

преодолé|ть, ю, *pf.* (*of* ~вáть) to overcome, get over; п. препя́тствия to surmount obstacles; п. трýдности to get over difficulties; п. отставáние to make up lee-way.

преодоли́м|ый (~, ~a), *adj.* surmountable; э́то затруднéние ~o this difficulty is not insuperable.

преосвящéнн|ый, *adj.* 1. (*title of bishop*) Right Reverend. 2. (*eccl.*) pre-consecrated; ~ые дары́ reserved sacrament.

преосвящéнств|о, а, *n.* егó п. (*title of bishop*) his Grace.

препарáт, а, *m.* (*chem., pharm.*) preparation.

препарáтор, а, *m.* laboratory assistant.

препари́р|овать, ую, *impf. and pf.* (*chem., pharm.*) to prepare, make a preparation (of).

препинáни|е, я, *n.*; знáки ~я (*gram.*) stops, punctuation marks.

препирáтельств|о, а, *n.* altercation, wrangling, squabbling.

препирá|ться, юсь, *impf.* (c+*i.*; *coll.*) to wrangle (with), squabble (with).

преподавáни|е, я, *n.* teaching, tuition, instruction.

преподавáтел|ь, я, *m.* teacher; (*in university or other higher education institution*) lecturer, instructor.

преподавáтель|ский, *adj. of* ~; п. состáв teaching staff.

препода|вáть, ю́, ёшь, *impf.* to teach; п. хи́мию to teach, be a lecturer in chemistry.

преподá|ть, м, шь, ст, ди́м, ди́те, дýт, *past* преподáл, ~лá, преподáло, *pf.* (*obs.*) to give (*advice, a lesson, etc.*).

преподнесéни|е, я, *n.* presentation.

преподнес|ти́, ý, ёшь, *past* ~, ~лá, *pf.* (*of* преподноси́ть) (+*a. and d.*) to present (with), make a present (of); он ~ нам неприя́тную нóвость he brought us a piece of bad news; п. что-н. комý-н. в готóвом ви́де (*fig.*) to hand something to someone on a plate.

преподно|си́ть, шý, ~сишь, *impf. of* преподнести́.

преподóби|е, я, *n.* егó п. (*title of priest*) his Reverence, the Reverend.

преподóбный, *adj.* (*title of canonized monks*) Saint; Venerable.

препóн|а, ы, *f.* (*obs.*) obstacle, impediment.

препорýч|ать, áю, *impf. of* ~и́ть.

препорýч|и́ть, ý, ~ишь, *pf.* (*of* ~áть) (*obs.*) to entrust, commit.

препоя́|сать, шу, шешь, *pf.* (*obs.*) to gird; п. свои́ чрéсла (*fig., rhet.*) to gird up one's loins.

препроводи́тельный, *adj.* accompanying (*document, etc.*).

препрово|ди́ть, жý, ди́шь, *pf.* (*of* ~ждáть) to send, forward, dispatch.

препровожда́|ть, ю, *impf. of* препроводи́ть.

препровожде́ни|е[1], я, *n.* forwarding, dispatching.

препровожде́ни|е[2], я, *n.* passing; для ∼я вре́мени to pass the time.

препя́тстви|е, я, *n.* **1.** obstacle, impediment, hindrance; чини́ть кому́-н. ∼я to put obstacles in someone's way. **2.** (*sport*) obstacle; бег с ∼ями, ска́чки с ∼ями steeple-chase; взять п. to clear an obstacle; (*fig.*) to clear a hurdle; сбить п. to bring down an obstacle.

препя́тств|овать, ую, *impf.* (*of* вос∼) (+*d.*) to hinder, impede, hamper; to stand in the way (of); непого́да ∼овала их свида́ниям bad weather interfered with their rendezvous.

прерв|а́ть, у́, ёшь, *past* ∼а́л, ∼ала́, ∼а́ло, *pf.* (*of* прерыва́ть) to break off, sever; to interrupt; to cut short; п. заня́тия to interrupt one's studies; п. молча́ние to break a silence; п. ора́тора to interrupt a speaker; п. дипломати́ческие отноше́ния to break off, sever diplomatic relations; п. перего́воры to break off negotiations, suspend talks; п. рабо́ту to take a break; п. рабо́ту на кани́кулы (*of parliament, etc.*) to go into recess; п. разгово́р to interrupt a conversation; нас ∼а́ли (*of telephone conversation*) we have been cut off.

прерв|а́ться, ётся, *past* ∼а́лся, ∼ала́сь, ∼а́лось, *pf.* (*of* прерыва́ться) **1.** to be interrupted; перегово́ры ∼а́лись conversations have been broken off, have broken down. **2.** (*of a voice, from emotion*) to break.

пререка́ни|е, я, *n.* altercation, wrangle, argument; вступи́ть в п. с кем-н. to start an argument with someone.

пререка́|ться, юсь, *impf.* (с+*i.*) to argue (with).

пре́ри|я, и, *f.* prairie.

прерогати́в|а, ы, *f.* prerogative.

прерыва́тел|ь, я, *m.* (*radio*) interrupter; (*electr.*) (circuit) breaker, cut-out.

прерыва́|ть(ся), ю(сь), *impf. of* прерва́ть(ся).

прерыва́|ющийся, *pres. part. of* ∼ться; ∼ющимся го́лосом with a catch in one's voice.

преры́висто, *adv.* in a broken way; говори́ть п. to speak in a staccato way; дыша́ть п. to gasp.

преры́вист|ый (∼, ∼а), *adj.* broken, interrupted, intermittent; п. ток (*tech.*) intermittent current.

пресви́тер, а, *m.* (*eccl.*) **1.** presbyter. **2.** (*in Presbyterian Church*) elder.

пресвитериа́нский, *adj.* (*rel.*) Presbyterian.

пресвитериа́нств|о, а, *n.* (*rel.*) Presbyterianism.

пресека́|ть(ся), ю, ет(ся), *impf. of* пресе́чь(ся).

пресече́ни|е, я, *n.* **1.** interruption, cutting off. **2.** (*lit.*; *obs.*) caesura.

пресе́|чь, ку́, чёшь, ку́т, *past* ∼к, ∼кла, *pf.* (*of* ∼ка́ть) to cut short, stop; п. в ко́рне to nip in the bud.

пресе́|чься, чётся, ку́тся, *past* ∼кся, ∼кла́сь, *pf.* (*of* ∼ка́ться) **1.** to stop. **2.** (*of a voice, from emotion*) to break. **3.** *pass. of* ∼чь.

пресле́довани|е, я, *n.* **1.** pursuit, chase. **2.** persecution, victimization; ма́ния ∼я persecution complex. **3.** (*leg.*) суде́бное п. prosecution.

пресле́дователь|ь, я, *m.* persecutor.

пресле́д|овать, ую, *impf.* **1.** to pursue, chase, be after; (*fig.*) to haunt; подозре́ние ∼ует меня́ a suspicion haunts me. **2.** (*fig.*) to strive (for, after), pursue; п. цель to pursue an end. **3.** to persecute, torment; to victimize. **4.** (*leg.*) to prosecute.

пресловут́ый, *adj.* notorious; (*iron.*) famous, celebrated.

пресмыка́тельств|о, а, *n.* grovelling, crawling.

пресмыка́|ться, юсь, *impf.* **1.** (*obs.*) to creep, crawl. **2.** (пе́ред; *fig.*) to grovel (before), cringe (before), lick the boots (of).

пресмыка́ющ|ееся, егося, *n.* reptile.

пресново́дный, *adj.* freshwater.

пре́с|ный (∼ен, ∼на́, ∼но), *adj.* **1.** (*of water*) fresh, sweet. **2.** unsalted; п. хлеб unleavened bread. **3.** (*of food*) flavourless, tasteless; (*fig.*) insipid, vapid, flat; ∼ные остро́ты feeble jokes.

преспоко́йно, *adv.* (*coll.*) **1.** very quietly. **2.** calmly, cooly.

преспоко́|йный (∼ен, ∼йна), *adj.* (*coll.*) very quiet; very peaceful.

пресс, а, *m.* press; punch.

пре́сс|а, ы, *f.* (*collect.*) the press.

пресс-атташе́, *indecl.*, *m.* press attaché.

пресс-бюро́, *indecl.*, *n.* press department.

пресс-конфере́нци|я, и, *f.* press conference.

пресс|ова́ть, у́ю, *impf.* (*of* с∼) to press, compress.

прессо́вк|а, и, *f.* pressing, compressing.

прессовщи́к, а́, *m.* presser, press operator.

пресс-папье́, *indecl.*, *n.* **1.** paper-weight. **2.** blotter.

преста́в|иться, люсь, ишься, *pf.* (*obs.*) to pass away.

преставле́ни|е, я, *n.* (*obs.*) passing (away).

престаре́лый, *adj.* aged; advanced in years.

престидижита́тор, а, *m.* juggler, prestidigitator.

прести́ж, а, *m.* prestige; поте́ря ∼а loss of face; охраня́ть свой п. to save one's face.

престо́л, а, *m.* **1.** throne; вступи́ть на п. to

come to the throne, mount the throne; отречься от ~a to abdicate; свергнуть с ~a to dethrone. **2.** (*eccl.*) altar, communion table.

престолонаследи|е, я, *n.* succession to the throne.

престолонаследник, а, *m.* successor to the throne.

престол|ьный, *adj. of* ~; п. город capital (city); п. праздник patron saint's day, patronal festival.

преступ|ать, аю, *impf. of* ~ить.

преступ|ить, лю, ~ишь, *pf.* (*of* ~ать) to transgress, trespass (against); п. закон to violate the law.

преступлени|е, я, *n.* crime, offence; (*leg.*) felony; transgression; государственное п. treason; уголовное п. criminal offence; п. по должности (*leg.*) malfeasance; состав ~я (*leg.*) corpus delicti.

преступник, а, *m.* criminal, offender; (*leg.*) felon; военный п. war criminal.

преступност|ь, и, *f.* **1.** criminality. **2.** (*collect.*) crime; рост ~и increase in crime.

преступ|ный (~ен, ~на), *adj.* criminal; (*leg.*) felonious.

пресуществлени|е, я, *n.* (*rel.*) transubstantiation.

пресы|тить, щу, тишь, *pf.* (*of* ~щать) (*obs.*) (+*i.*) to satiate (with); to surfeit (on), sate (with).

пресы|титься, щусь, тишься, *pf.* (*of* ~щаться) (+*i.*) to be satiated (with); be surfeited (with), have had a surfeit (of).

пресыща|ть(ся), ю(сь), *impf. of* пресытить(ся).

пресыщени|е, я, *n.* satiety; surfeit; до ~я to satiety.

пресыщенност|ь, и, *f.* satiety; surfeit.

пресы|щенный, *p.p.p. of* ~тить *and adj.* satiated; surfeited, sated, replete.

претворени|е, я, *n.* conversion; transubstantiation (*esp. rel.*); п. в жизнь realization, putting into practice.

претвор|ить, ю, ишь, *pf.* (*of* ~ять) **1.** (в+*a*.) to turn (into), change (into), convert (into); to transubstantiate (*esp. rel.*). **2.** п. в жизнь, п. в дело to realize, carry out, put into practice.

претвор|иться, ится, *pf.* (*of* ~яться) **1.** (в+*a.*) to turn (into), become; вода ~илась в вино the water was turned into wine. **2.** п. в жизнь to be realized, come true; моя мечта ~илась в жизнь my dream has come true.

претвор|ять(ся), яю, яет(ся), *impf. of* ~ить(ся).

претендент, а, *m.* (на+*a.*) **1.** claimant (to, upon), aspirant (to); candidate (for); он п. на руку принцессы he aspires to the

hand of the princess. **2.** pretender (to); п. на престол pretender to the throne.

претенд|овать, ую, *impf.* (на+*a.*) to pretend (to), have pretensions (to); to aspire (to); to lay claim (to); он ~ует на должность министра иностранных дел he aspires to the position of Minister of Foreign Affairs.

претензи|я, и, *f.* **1.** claim; иметь ~ю (на+*a.*) to claim, lay claim (to), make claims (on); заявить ~ю to lodge a claim; отклонить ~ю to reject a claim. **2.** pretension; человек с ~ями, без ~й a pretentious, an unpretentious person; у него нет никаких ~й на остроумие he has no pretensions to wit; быть в ~и на кого-н. to have a grudge against someone, bear someone a grudge, have a grievance against someone.

претенциозност|ь, и, *f.* pretentiousness, affectation.

претенциоз|ный (~ен, ~на), *adj.* pretentious, affected.

претерпева|ть, ю, *impf. of* претерпеть.

претерп|еть, лю, ~ишь, *pf.* (*of* ~евать) to undergo; to suffer, endure; план ~ел изменения the plan has undergone changes; п. лишения to endure privations.

прет|ить, ит, *impf.* (+*d.*) to sicken; от этой пищи мне ~ит I am sick of this food.

преткновени|е, я, *n.* камень ~я stumbling-block.

претор, а, *m.* (*hist.*) praetor.

претори́ан|ец, ца, *m.* (*hist.*) praetorian (guard).

преторианский, *adj.* (*hist.*) praetorian.

пре|ть, ю, *impf.* **1.** (*pf.* со~) to rot. **2.** (*impf. only*) to become damp (*of ground, in spring, from warmth of atmosphere*). **3.** (*pf* y~) to stew. **4.** (*pf.* взо~) (*coll.*) to sweat, perspire.

преувеличени|е, я, *n.* exaggeration; overstatement.

преувеличива|ть, ю, *impf. of* преувеличить.

преувелич|ить, у, ишь, *pf.* (*of* ~ивать) to exaggerate; to overstate.

преуменьш|ать, аю, *impf. of* ~ить.

преуменьшени|е, я, *n.* underestimation; understatement.

преуменьш|ить, ~у, ~ишь, *pf.* (*of* ~ать) to underestimate, minimize; to belittle; to understate; п. опасность to underestimate the danger; п. чью-н. помощь to belittle someone's assistance.

преуспева|ть, ю, *impf.* **1.** *impf. of* преуспеть. **2.** (*impf. only*) to thrive, prosper, flourish.

преуспева|ющий, *pres. part. act. of* ~ть *and adj.* successful, prosperous.

преуспе|ть, ю, *pf.* (*of* ~вать) (в+*p.*) to succeed (in), be successful (in); п. в жизни to get on in life.

преуспеяни|е, я, *n.* (*obs. or iron.*) success.

префект, а, *m.* prefect.

префекту́р|а, ы, *f.* prefecture.

преферáнс, а, *m.* preference (*card-game*).

пре́фикс, а, *m.* (*gram.*) prefix.

префи́кс, *indecl., adj.*; платёж п. (*comm.*) payment made before term appointed, prior payment.

префиксáльный, *adj.* (*gram.*) with a prefix.

префиксáци|я, и, *f.* (*gram.*) addition of prefix (*to a verb, etc.*).

прехо|ди́ть, жу́, ~ди́шь, *impf. of* прейти́.

преходя́щий, *adj.* transient.

прецеде́нт, а, *m.* precedent; установи́ть п. to establish a precedent.

прецесси|я, и, *f.* (*astron.*) precession.

прецизио́нный, *adj.* (*tech.*) precision; п. прибо́р precision instrument.

при, *prep.+p.* **1.** (*of local proximity*) by, at; in the presence of; при доро́ге by the road(-side); би́тва при Бородине́ the battle of Borodino; письмо́ бы́ло подпи́сано при мне the letter was signed in my presence; не нáдо так выражáться при де́тях you should not use such language in front of the children. **2.** attached to, affiliated to, under the auspices of (*usu. not translated*); он рабо́тает при университе́те he is attached to the university; военврáч при батальо́не battalion medical officer. **3.** (*indicating possession, presence of object(s) mentioned*) by, with; about, on; у него́ не́ было при себе́ де́нег he had no money on him; есть ли у вас при себе́ перочи́нный нож? do you have a pen-knife about you?; быть при ору́жии to have arms about one, be armed. **4.** with (= *taking into account the attribute, etc., referred to*); for, notwithstanding; при таки́х талáнтах он должно́ быть далеко́ пойдёт with such talent he ought to go far; при желáнии всего́ мо́жно доби́ться where there's a will there's a way; при всех его́ досто́инствах, он мне не нрáвится for all his virtues, I do not like him; при всём том (*i*) with it all, moreover, (*ii*) for all that. **5.** in the time of, in the days of; under (*sc.* the rule of); during; при Ивáне Гро́зном during the reign of, in the time of Ivan the Terrible; при Ромáновых under the Romanovs; при мне бы́ло не так in my day it was not like this. **6.** (*indicating accompanying circumstances*) by; при дневно́м све́те by daylight; при све́те лáмпы by lamplight. **7.** (*referring to action on occasion unspecified*) when; on; in case of; при перехо́де че́рез у́лицу when crossing the street; при случае when the occasion arises, at convenience; при анáлизе on analysis; при маляри́и in case of malaria; при усло́вии under the condition (that). **8.** with (= *by means of, thanks to*); при по́мощи рыбако́в нам удало́сь оттолкну́ть

ло́дку with the aid of the fishermen we succeeded in pushing the boat off.

при-[1] *verbal prefix indicating* **1.** *completion of action or motion up to given terminal point, as* прие́хать *to arrive.* **2.** *action of attaching, as* пристро́ить *to build on.* **3.** *direction of action towards speaker, as* пригласи́ть *to invite.* **4.** *direction of action from above downward, as* придави́ть *to press down.* **5.** *incompleteness or tentativeness of action, as* приоткры́ть *to open slightly.* **6.** *exhaustiveness of action, as* приучи́ть *to train.* **7.** (+*suffixes* -ыва-, -ива-) *accompaniment, as* припля́сывать *to dance (to a tune).*

при-[2] *as prefix of nouns and adjs.* (*esp. geogr.*) *indicates juxtaposition or proximity, as* приозе́рье lake-side; прибре́жный, приморский coastal.

прибáв|ить, лю, ишь, *pf.* (*of* ~ля́ть) **1.** (+*a. or g.*) to add; п. (в ве́се) to put on (weight); за три ме́сяца онá ~ила де́сять фу́нтов she put on ten pounds in three months. **2.** (+*g.*) to increase, augment; п. жáлованья to increase a salary, give a rise; п. шáгу to quicken, hasten one's steps; п. хо́ду (*coll.*) to put on speed. **3.** (в+*p.*) to lengthen, widen (*part of an item of clothing*); нáдо п. в рукавáх the sleeves need to be lengthened. **4.** (*fig., coll.*) to lay it on (= *exaggerate*).

прибáв|иться, ится, *pf.* (*of* ~ля́ться) **1.** to increase; (*of water*) to rise; (*of the moon*) to wax; п. в ве́се to put on weight; воды́ ~илось (*impers.*) the water has risen; нарóду ~илось (*impers.*) the crowd has grown; день ~ился the days are getting longer. **2.** *pass. of* ~ить.

прибáвк|а, и, *f.* **1.** addition, augmentation, **2.** increase, supplement; получи́ть ~у to get a rise.

прибавле́ни|е, я, *n.* **1.** addition, augmentation; п. семе́йства addition to the family; сказáть в п. to say in addition, add. **2.** supplement, appendix. **3.** (*fig., coll.*) embroidery (= *exaggeration*).

прибавля́|ть(ся), ю, ~ет(ся), *impf. of* прибáвить(ся).

прибáвочн|ый, *adj.* **1.** additional. **2.** (*econ.*) surplus; ~ая сто́имость surplus value.

прибалти́йский, *adj.* Baltic (= *adjacent to the Baltic Sea*).

прибáутк|а, и, *f.* humorous catchphrase, facetious saying.

прибегá|ть[1]**, ю,** *impf. of* прибе́гнуть.

прибегá|ть[2]**, ю,** *impf. of* прибежáть.

прибе́г|нуть, ну, нешь, *past* ~, ~ла, *pf.* (*о ~áть*[1]) (к) to resort (to), have resort (to); to fall back (on); п. к си́ле to resort to force.

прибедн|и́ться, ю́сь, и́шься, *pf.* (*of* ~я́ться)

(*coll.*) **1.** to pretend to be poorer than one is, feign poverty. **2.** to show false modesty.

прибедни|я́ться, я́юсь, *impf. of* ~и́ться.

прибе|жа́ть, гу́, жи́шь, гу́т, *pf.* (*of* ~га́ть[2]) to come running.

прибе́жищ|е, а, *n.* refuge; после́днее п. (*fig.*) last resort; найти́ п. (в+*p.*) to take refuge (in).

прибега́|ть, ю, *impf. of* прибере́чь.

прибере́|чь, гу́, жёшь, гу́т, *past* ~г, ~гла́, *pf.* (*of* ~га́ть) to save up.

прибива́|ть, ю, *impf. of* приби́ть[1].

прибира́|ть(ся), ю(сь), *impf. of* прибра́ть(ся).

приб|и́ть[1], ью́, ьёшь, *pf.* (*of* ~ива́ть) **1.** to nail, affix with nails; п. флаг к дре́вку to nail a flag to a pole. **2.** to lay, flatten; град ~и́л посе́вы the hail has laid the corn. **3.** (*usu. impers.*) to throw up; труп ~и́ло к бе́регу a body was washed ashore.

приб|и́ть[2], ью́, ьёшь, *pf. of* бить I.

приближа́|ть, ю, *impf. of* прибли́зить.

приближа́|ться, юсь, *impf.* **1.** *impf. of* прибли́зиться. **2.** (*impf. only*) to approximate; п. к и́стине to approximate to the truth.

приближе́ни|е, я, n. **1.** approach; approaching, drawing near. **2.** (*math.*) approximation.

приближённост|ь, и, f. proximity.

приближённый[1], adj. approximate, rough; п. ме́тод (*math.*) method of approximation.

приближённ|ый[2], ого, m. (*obs.*) retainer, person in attendance; (*pl.*) retinue.

приблизи́тельно, adv. approximately, roughly.

приблизи́тельност|ь, и, f. approximateness.

приблизи́тел|ьный (~ен, ~ьна), adj. approximate, rough.

прибли|зить, жу, зишь, *pf.* (*of* ~жа́ть) **1.** to bring nearer, move nearer; п. кни́гу к глаза́м to bring a book nearer one's eyes. **2.** to hasten, advance; я наме́рен п. мой отъе́зд I intend to hasten my departure; ~зили его́ призы́в в а́рмию the date of his call-up has been advanced.

прибли|зиться, жусь, зишься, *pf.* (*of* ~жа́ться) (к) to approach, draw near; to draw nearer (to), come nearer (to).

приблу́дный, adj. (*coll.*; *of animals*) stray.

прибо́|й, я, m. surf, breakers.

прибо́р, а, m. **1.** instrument, device, apparatus, appliance, gadget. **2.** set; бри́твенный п. shaving things; ками́нный п. set of fire-irons; пи́сьменный п. desk-set; столо́вый п. cover; накры́ть стол на шесть ~ов to lay (places) for six; туале́тный п. toilet set, washing things; ча́йный п. tea-service. **3.** fittings; печно́й п. stove fittings.

прибо́р|ный, adj. of ~; ~ная доска́ dashboard; (*aeron.*) instrument panel.

приборостро́ени|е, я, n. instrument-making.

при|бра́ть, беру́, берёшь, *past* ~бра́л, ~брала́, ~бра́ло, *pf.* (*of* ~бира́ть) **1.** to clear up, clean up, tidy (up); п. посте́ль to make a bed; п. ко́мнату, п. в ко́мнате to do a room; п. на столе́ to clear the table; п. кого́-н. к рука́м to take someone in hand; п. что-н. к рука́м to lay one's hands on something. **2.** to put away; ~бери́ игру́шки — пора́ спать! put your toys away, it's time for bed!

при|бра́ться, беру́сь, берёшься, *past* ~бра́лся, ~брала́сь, ~брало́сь, *pf.* (*of* ~бира́ться) to tidy oneself up; to have a clear-up of one's things.

прибре́жн|ый, adj. **1.** coastal, littoral; ~ые острова́ off-shore islands; ~ая полоса́ coastal strip. **2.** riverside; riverain, riparian.

прибре́жь|е, я, n. littoral; coastal strip.

прибре|сти́, ду́, дёшь, *past* ~л, ~ла́, *pf.* (*coll.*) to come trudging (along); п. домо́й to crawl home.

прибыва́|ть, ю, *impf. of* прибы́ть.

при́был|ь, и, f. **1.** profit, gain (*also fig.*); return; валова́я п. gross profit; чи́стая п. net profit; кака́я мне в э́том п.? (*coll.*) what do I get out of it? **2.** increase, rise; п. населе́ния increase of population; вода́ идёт на п. the water is rising. **3.** (*tech.*) riser; п. отли́вки head of casting, lost head.

при́быльност|ь, и, f. profitability, lucrativeness.

при́быль|ный, adj. **1.** profitable, lucrative. **2.** *adj. of* ~ 3; п. коне́ц deadhead.

прибы́ти|е, я, n. arrival.

при|бы́ть[1], бу́ду, бу́дешь, *past* ~был, ~была́, ~было, *pf.* (*of* ~быва́ть) to arrive; (*of a train, etc.*) to get in; по́езд ~был the train is in; по́чта ~была́ the post has come.

при|бы́ть[2], бу́дет, *past* ~был, ~была́, ~было, *pf.* (*of* ~быва́ть) (*coll.*) to increase, grow; (*of water*) to rise, swell; (*of the moon*) to wax; вода́ ~была́ the water has risen; на́шего полку́ ~было our numbers have grown.

прива́д|а, ы, f. lure, bait (*put out to catch birds or fish*).

прива́|дить, жу, дишь, *pf.* (*of* ~живать). **1.** to train (*a bird, etc., by putting out food*). **2.** (к) to attract (to), predispose (towards).

прива́жива|ть, ю, *impf. of* прива́дить.

прива́л, а, m. **1.** halt, stop. **2.** stopping-place.

прива́лива|ть, ю, *impf. of* привали́ть.

привал|и́ть, ю́, ~ишь, *pf.* (*of* ~ивать) **1.** to lean, rest; п. дрова́ к забо́ру to pile logs against the fence. **2.** (*of a vessel*) to come alongside. **3.** (*fig., coll.*) to turn up; на матч ~и́ло мно́го наро́ду people flocked to the match; сча́стье нам ~и́ло fortune smiled on us.

прива́рива|ть, ю, *impf. of* привари́ть.

привар|и́ть, ю́, ~ишь, *pf.* (*of* ~ивать) **1.** (к) to weld on (to). **2.** (+*a. or g.*) to boil some more, cook some more.

прива́рк|а, и, *f.* welding.

прива́р|ок, ка, *m.* (*mil. and coll.*) **1.** (*collect.*) victuals, rations. **2.** cooked food, hot meal.

прива́т-доце́нт, а, *m.* privat-docent (*unestablished university lecturer*).

прива́т-доцентур|а, ы, *f.* **1.** post of privat-docent. **2.** (*collect.*) the privat-docents.

прива́тный, *adj.* (*obs.*) private.

приведе́ни|е, я, *n.* **1.** bringing; п. к прися́ге administration of oath, swearing in. **2.** putting; п. в движе́ние setting in motion; п. в исполне́ние carrying out, putting into effect; п. в поря́док putting in order. **3.** (*math.*) reduction; п. к о́бщему знамена́телю reduction to a common denominator. **4.** adduction, adducing; п. приме́ров adducing of instances.

привез|ти́, у́, ёшь, *past* ~, ~ла́, *pf.* (*of* привози́ть) to bring (*not on foot*).

привере́длив|ый (~, ~a), *adj.* fastidious, pernickety; squeamish.

привере́дник, а, *m.* fastidious person; squeamish person.

привере́днича|ть, ю, *impf.* to be hard to please; to be fastidious; to be squeamish.

привержен|ец, ца, *m.* adherent; follower.

приве́рженност|ь, и, *f.* adherence; attachment, devotion.

привержен|ный (~, ~a), *adj.* (к) attached (to), devoted (to).

приверн|у́ть, у́, ёшь, *pf.* (*of* приве́ртывать) **1.** to screw tight, tighten, clamp. **2.** to turn down; п. фити́ль to turn a wick down.

привер|те́ть, чу́, ~тишь, *pf.* (*of* ~тывать) to screw tight, tighten, clamp.

приве́ртыва|ть, ю, *impf. of* приверну́ть *and* приверте́ть.

приве́с, а, *m.* additional weight.

приве́с|ить, шу, сишь, *pf.* (*of* ~шивать) to hang up, suspend.

приве́с|ок, ка, *m.* (*coll.*) **1.** makeweight. **2.** (*fig.*) appendage.

приве|сти́, ду́, дёшь, *past* ~л, ~ла́, *pf.* (*of* приводи́ть) **1.** to bring; to lead, take; он ~л с собо́й неве́сту he has brought his fiancée (with him); п. кого́-н. к прися́ге to administer the oath to someone, swear someone in; ~л Бог сви́деться! (*obs.*) we were meant to meet again! **2.** (к; *fig.*) to lead (to), bring (to), conduce (to), result (in); э́то к добру́ не ~дёт no good will

come of it; её поведе́ние ~ло меня́ к заключе́нию, что она́ душе́вно расстро́ена her behaviour led me to the conclusion that she is out of her mind. **3.** (в+*a.*) to put, set (*or translated by verb corresponding to noun governed by* в); п. в бе́шенство to throw into a rage, drive mad; п. в движе́ние, в де́йствие to set in motion, set going; п. в затрудне́ние to cause difficulties, put in a difficult position; п. в изумле́ние to astonish, astound; п. в исполне́ние to carry out, carry into effect, put into effect; п. пригово́р в исполне́ние to execute a sentence; п. в хоро́шее настрое́ние to put in a good mood; п. в него́дность to put out of commission; п. в отча́яние to reduce to despair; п. в поря́док to put in order, tidy (up); to arrange, fix; п. в у́жас to horrify; п. в чу́вство to bring to, bring round. **4.** (к; *math.*) to reduce (to). **5.** to adduce, cite; п. доказа́тельства to adduce proofs; п. приме́р to give an example, cite an instance; п. цита́ту (из) to make a quotation (from), quote.

приве|сти́сь, дётся, *past* ~ло́сь, *pf.* (*of* приводи́ться) (*impers.*+*d.*; *coll.*) to happen, chance; to be one's lot; мне ~ло́сь там быть тогда́, когда́ они́ проезжа́ли I happened to be there when they drove past; ему́ ~ло́сь быть свиде́телем преступле́ния it was his lot to be a witness of the crime.

приве́т, а, *m.* greeting(s); regards; горя́чий п. (one's) warmest regards; переда́ть п., слать п. to send one's regards; моя́ жена́ шлёт вам п. my wife sends her regards, asks to be remembered to you; переда́йте п. ва́шим колле́гам remember me to your colleagues, my regards to your colleagues; с серде́чным ~ом (*epistolary formula*) yours sincerely; п. из Москвы́! greetings from Moscow!

приве́тливост|ь, и, *f.* affability; cordiality.

приве́тлив|ый (~, ~a), *adj.* affable; cordial.

приве́тственн|ый, *adj.* salutatory; welcoming; ~ая речь speech of welcome.

приве́тстви|е, я, *n.* **1.** greeting, salutation. **2.** speech of welcome.

приве́тств|овать, ую, *impf.* **1.** (*in past tense also pf.*) to greet, salute, hail; to welcome. **2.** (*fig.*) to welcome; п. предложе́ние to welcome a suggestion. **3.** (*also pf.*) (*mil.*) to salute.

приве́|шенный, *p.p.p. of* ~сить; у него́ язы́к хорошо́ ~шен (*coll.*) he has a ready tongue.

приве́шива|ть, ю, *impf. of* приве́сить.

привива́|ть(ся), ю, ет(ся), *impf. of* приви́ть(ся).

приви́вк|а, и, *f.* **1.** (от, про́тив; *med.*) inoculation (against); vaccination. **2.** (*bot.*) inoculation, grafting, engrafting.

приви́в|очный, *adj. of* ~ка.

привиде́ни|е, я, *n.* ghost, spectre; apparition.

приви́|деться, дится, *pf. of* ви́деться 2.

привилегиро́ванност|ь, и, *f.* privilege(s).

привилегиро́ванн|ый, *adj.* privileged; ~ое положе́ние privileged position.

привиле́ги|я, и, *f.* privilege.

привин|ти́ть, чу́, ти́шь, *pf.* (*of* ~чивать) to screw on.

приви́нчива|ть, ю, *impf. of* привинти́ть.

привира́|ть, ю, *impf. of* привра́ть.

приви́ти|е, я, *n.* inculcation.

прив|и́ть, ью́, ьёшь, *past* ~и́л, ~ила́, ~и́ло, *pf.* (*of* ~ива́ть) (+*a. and d.*) **1.** (*med.*) to inoculate (with); п. кому́-н. о́спу to vaccinate someone against smallpox. **2.** (*bot.*) to graft, engraft (upon); to inoculate (with); (*fig.*) to implant (in). **3.** (*fig.*) to inculcate (in); to cultivate (in), foster (in); п. кому́-н. вкус к стиха́м to inculcate in someone a taste for poetry; п. но́вую мо́ду to set a new fashion.

прив|и́ться, ьётся, *past* ~и́лся, ~ила́сь, *pf.* (*of* ~ива́ться) **1.** (*of an inoculation or graft*) to take. **2.** (*fig.*) to become established, find acceptance, catch on; э́ти взгля́ды ~или́сь не всю́ду these views did not find universal acceptance; мо́да носи́ть цветны́е чулки́ не ~ила́сь у нас the fashion for coloured stockings did not catch on here.

при́вкус, а, *m.* after-taste; smack (*also fig.*); его́ слова́ име́ли п. на́глости his words smacked of insolence.

привлека́тельност|ь, и, *f.* attractiveness.

привлека́тел|ьный (~ен, ~ьна), *adj.* attractive; fetching; ~ьная улы́бка smile.

привлека́|ть, ю, *impf. of* привле́чь.

привлече́ни|е, я, *n.* attraction.

привле́|чь, ку́, чёшь, ку́т, *past* ~к, ~кла́, *pf.* (*of* ~ка́ть) **1.** to draw, attract; п. внима́ние to attract attention; кри́ки ~кли́ нас к ра́неному cries drew us to the wounded man. **2.** to draw in; п. на свою́ сто́рону to win over (*to one's side*); п. к рабо́те to recruit, enlist the services (of). **3.** (*leg.*) to have up; п. к суду́ to sue (in court), take to court; to bring to trial, put on trial; п. к отве́тственности (за+*a.*) to make answer (for), make answerable (for), call to account (for); п. к уголо́вной отве́тственности to institute criminal proceedings (against).

привнес|ти́, у́, ёшь, *past* ~, ~ла́, *pf.* (*of* привноси́ть) to introduce, insert; п. эле́мент коми́зма в де́ло to introduce an element of comedy into proceedings.

привно|си́ть, шу́, ~сишь, *impf. of* привнести́.

приво́д[1], а, *m.* (*leg.*) bringing to court (*of accused or witness for questioning*); taking into custody; постановле́ние о ~е warrant for arrest.

приво́д[2], а, *m.* (*tech.*) drive, driving gear; кулачко́вый п. cam drive; ремённый п. belt drive; ручно́й п. hand gear; червя́чный п. worm gear.

приво|ди́ть(ся), жу́(сь), ~дишь(ся), *impf. of* привести́(сь).

приво́дк|а, и, *f.* (*typ.*) registration.

приводне́ни|е, я, *n.* splash-down.

приводн|и́ться, ю́сь, и́шься, *pf.* (*of* ~я́ться) to land, come down on water.

приводн|о́й, *adj.* (*tech.*) driving; п. вал driving shaft; п. механи́зм driving gear; ~а́я радиоста́нция homing wireless set; ~а́я цепь sprocket chain, chain drive.

привод|я́ться, я́юсь, *impf. of* ~и́ться.

приво|жу́[1], ~дишь, *see* ~ди́ть.

приво|жу́[2], ~зишь, *see* ~зи́ть.

приво́з, а, *m.* **1.** bringing, supply; import, importation. **2.** (*coll.*) load.

приво|зи́ть, жу́, ~зишь, *impf. of* привезти́.

привозно́й, *adj.* imported.

привозн|ый = ~о́й.

приво́|й, я, *m.* (*agric.*) graft.

привола́кива|ть, ю, *impf. of* приволочи́ть *and* приволо́чь.

привола́кива|ться, юсь, *impf. of* **1.** приволочи́ться *and* приволо́чься. **2.** приволокну́ться.

приволокн|у́ться, у́сь, ёшься, *pf.* (*of* привола́киваться) (за+*i.*; *coll.*) to flirt (with).

приволоч|и́ть(ся), у́(сь), и́шь(ся), *pf. =* ~ь(ся).

приволо́|чь, ку́, чёшь, ку́т, *past* ~к, ~кла́, *pf.* (*of* привола́кивать) (*coll.*) to drag (over).

приволо́|чься, ку́сь, чёшься, ку́тся, *past* ~кся, ~кла́сь, *pf.* (*of* привола́киваться) (*coll.*) to drag oneself.

приво́ль|е, я, *n.* **1.** free space; степны́е ~я 'wide open spaces' of the steppe. **2.** freedom.

приво́льн|ый, *adj.* free; ~ая жизнь free and easy life.

привора́жива|ть, ю, *impf. of* приворожи́ть.

приворож|и́ть, у́, и́шь, *pf.* (*of* привора́живать) (*obs. or fig.*) to bewitch, charm.

приворо́тн|ый, *adj.*; ~ое зе́лье (*folk poet.*) love-philtre.

привра́тник, а, *m.* **1.** door-keeper, porter, janitor. **2.** (*anat.*) pylorus.

привр|а́ть, у́, ёшь, *past* ~а́л, ~ала́, ~а́ло. *pf.* (*of* привира́ть) (*coll.*) to make up; to exaggerate.

привска́кива|ть, ю, *impf. of* привскочи́ть.

привскоч|и́ть, у́, ~ишь, *pf.* (*of* привска́кивать) to start, jump up.

привста|ва́ть, ю́, ёшь, *impf. of* ~ть.

привста́|ть, ну, нешь, *pf.* (*of* ~ва́ть) to rise, stand up (*for a moment*); to half-rise; когда́ судья́ вошёл, все ~ли when the judge entered everyone stood up.

привходя́щ|ий, *adj.* ~ие обстоя́тельства attendant circumstances.

привыка́|ть, а́ю, *impf. of* ~нуть.

привы́к|нуть, ну, нешь, *past* ~, ~ла, *pf.* (*of* ~а́ть) (к *or*+*inf.*) **1.** to get accustomed (to), get used (to); она́ ско́ро ~ла к его́ храпе́нию she soon got used to his snoring. **2.** to get into the habit (of), get into the way (of); он ~ руга́ться he has got into the habit of swearing.

привы́чк|а, и, *f.* habit; войти́ в ~у to become a habit; вы́работать в себе́ ~у to form a habit; име́ть ~у (к) to be accustomed (to); to be in the habit (of), be given (to); приобрести́ ~у (+*inf.*) to get into the habit (of), fall into the habit (of); э́то не в на́ших ~ах it is not our habit, not our practice.

привы́чност|ь, и, *f.* habitualness.

привы́ч|ный (~ен, ~на), *adj.* **1.** habitual, usual, customary. **2.** (к) accustomed (to), used (to); он челове́к п. he is a man of habit, of set habits.

привя́занност|ь, и, *f.* **1.** (к) attachment (to); affection (for, towards). **2.** (*fig.*) (object of) attachment, object of affection; ста́рая п. old flame.

привя́з|анный, *p.p.p. of* ~а́ть *and adj.* (к) attached (to).

привя́|за́ть, жу́, ~жешь, *pf.* (*of* ~зыва́ть) (к) **1.** to tie (to), bind (to), fasten (to), attach (to), secure (to); п. козу́ to tether a goat. **2.** (к себе́; *fig.*) to attach (to oneself), get a hold (over the affections of).

привя́|за́ться, жу́сь, ~жешься, *pf.* (*of* ~зы-ва́ться) (к) **1.** to become attached (to); она́ о́чень к вам ~за́лась she has become very attached to you. **2.** to attach oneself (to); на доро́ге како́й-то ни́щий ~за́лся к нам a beggar attached himself to us on the road. **3.** (*coll.*) to pester, bother.

привязно́й, *adj.* fastened, secured; п. аэро-ста́т captive balloon, balloon on bearings; п. трос ground cable.

привя́зчивост|ь, и, *f.* **1.** capacity for giving affection; susceptibility to affection. **2.** disposition to annoy, pester, bother.

привя́зчив|ый (~, ~а), *adj.* **1.** affectionate; susceptible (*to affection*), given to forming attachments easily. **2.** importunate, annoying; given to pestering.

привя́з|ь, и, *f.* tie; lead, leash; tether; на ~и on a leash; посади́ть соба́ку на п. to put a dog on a leash.

пригар, а, *m.* (*coll.*) burnt place, burnt part (*of cooked food*).

при́гар|ь, и, *f.* taste of burning; молоко́ с ~ью milk tasting burned.

пригвожда́|ть, ю, *impf. of* пригвозди́ть.

пригвоз|ди́ть, жу́, ди́шь, *pf.* (*of* пригвож-да́ть) (к) to nail (to); (*fig.*) to pin (down); п. к ме́сту to root to the spot; п. к позо́р-ному столбу́ to pillory; п. взгля́дом to fix with a look.

пригиба́|ть(ся), ю(сь), *impf. of* пригну́ть(ся).

пригла́|дить, жу, дишь, *pf.* (*of* ~живать) to smooth.

пригла́|диться, жусь, дишься, *pf.* (*of* ~жи-ваться) to smooth one's hair.

пригла́жива|ть(ся), ю(сь), *impf. of* пригла́-дить(ся).

пригласи́тельный, *adj.* conveying an invi-tation; п. биле́т invitation card.

пригла|си́ть, шу́, си́шь, *pf.* (*of* ~ша́ть) **1.** to invite, ask; п. на обе́д to invite, ask to dinner; п. на та́нцы to ask to a dance; п. кого́-н. на та́нец to ask someone to dance, ask someone for a dance; п. в го́сти to invite, ask round. **2.** to call (*a doctor, etc.*). **3.** to offer; его́ ~си́ли на рабо́ту в но́вой шко́ле he has been offered a job in a new school.

приглаша́|ть, ю, *impf. of* пригласи́ть.

приглаше́ни|е, я, *n.* **1.** invitation; по ~ю by invitation; разосла́ть ~я to send out invitations. **2.** offer (*of employment*).

приглуш|а́ть, а́ю, *impf. of* ~и́ть.

приглуш|и́ть, у́, и́шь, *pf.* (*of* ~а́ть) to damp down; to muffle, deaden (*sound*); to choke, damp (*a fire*).

пригля|де́ть, жу́, ди́шь, *pf.* (*of* ~дывать) (*coll.*) **1.** to choose; to find, look out; п. себе́ удо́бную кварти́ру to look oneself out con-venient lodgings. **2.** (за+*i.*) to look after; п. за детьми́ to look after children.

пригля|де́ться, жу́сь, ди́шься, *pf.* (*of* ~ды-ваться) (*coll.*) **1.** (к) to look closely (at), scrutinize. **2.** (к) to get accustomed (to), get used (to); п. к темноте́ to get accus-tomed to darkness. **3.** (+*d.*) to tire, bore; мне ~де́лись кинофи́льмы о вое́нных де́йствиях I am tired of war-films.

пригля́дыва|ть(ся), ю(сь), *impf. of* пригля-де́ть(ся).

пригля́н|уться, усь, ~ешься, *pf.* (+*d.*; *coll.*) to take one's fancy, attract; она́ сра́зу ~у́лась ему́ he was attracted by her instantly.

при|гна́ть[1], гоню́, го́нишь, *past* ~гна́л, ~гнала́, ~гна́ло, *pf.* (*of* ~гоня́ть) to drive home, bring in (*cattle*).

при|гна́ть[2], гоню́, го́нишь, *past* ~гна́л, ~гнала́, ~гна́ло, *pf.* (*of* ~гоня́ть) to fit, adjust, joint.

пригн|у́ть, у́, ёшь, *pf.* (*of* пригиба́ть) to bend down, bow.

пригн|у́ться, у́сь, ёшься, *pf.* (*of* приги-ба́ться) to bend down, bow.

приговáрива|ть¹, ю, *impf.* (*coll.*) to keep saying, keep repeating (*as accompaniment to given action*).

приговáрива|ть², ю, *impf. of* приговори́ть.

пригово́р, а, *m.* sentence; verdict; вы́нести п. to pass sentence; to bring in a verdict.

приговор|и́ть, ю́, и́шь, *pf.* (*of* приговáри-вать²) (к) to sentence (to), condemn (to); п. к пожи́зненному заключе́нию to sentence to imprisonment for life.

приго|ди́ться, жу́сь, ди́шься, *pf.* (+*d.*) to prove useful (to); to come in useful, come in handy; to stand in good stead.

приго́дност|ь, и, *f.* fitness, suitableness.

приго́д|ный (∼ен, ∼на), *adj.* (к) fit (for), suitable (for), good (for); useful (for); ни к чему́ не п. good-for-nothing, worthless.

пригож|ий (∼, ∼а), *adj.* (*folk poet.*) **1.** comely. **2.** (*of weather*) fine.

приголу́б|ить, лю, ишь, *pf.* (*of* голу́бить *and* ∼ливать) (*folk poet.*) to caress, fondle.

приголу́блива|ть, ю, *impf. of* приголу́бить.

приго́н, а, *m.* **1.** driving home, bringing in. **2.** drove, herd.

приго́нк|а, и, *f.* fitting, adjusting, jointing; п. часте́й (*tech.*) assembling.

пригоня́|ть, ю, *impf. of* пригна́ть.

пригор|а́ть, а́ет, *impf. of* ∼е́ть.

пригоре́лый, *adj.* burnt.

пригор|е́ть, и́т, *pf.* (*of* ∼а́ть) to be burnt; молоко́ ∼е́ло the milk is burnt.

при́город, а, *m.* **1.** suburb. **2.** (*hist.*) subject town; small town.

при́городн|ый, *adj.* suburban; ∼ое движе́-ние (*railways*) local service(s); п. по́езд local train.

пригор|ок, ка, *m.* hillock, knoll.

при́горш|ня, ни, *g. pl.* ∼ен *and* ∼ней, *f.* handful; пить во́ду ∼нями to drink water from cupped hands; ме́рить по́лными ∼нями to give good measure; хвата́ть по́лными ∼нями to seize with both hands.

пригорю́нива|ться, юсь, *impf. of* пригорю́-ниться.

пригорю́н|иться, юсь, ишься, *pf.* (*of* ∼иваться) (*folk poet.*) to become sad.

приготáвлива|ть(ся), ю(сь), *impf.* = приго-товля́ть(ся).

приготови́тельный, *adj.* preparatory.

приготóв|ить, лю, ишь, *pf.* (*of* приготáвл∧и-вать *and* ∼ля́ть) to prepare; п. обе́д to cook, prepare a dinner; п. роль to learn (up) a part; п. ру́копись к набо́ру to pre-pare a manuscript for setting-up; п. кому́-н. сюрпри́з to prepare a surprise for someone.

приготóв|иться, люсь, ишься, *pf.* (*of* приго-тáвливаться *and* ∼ля́ться) (+*inf.*) to pre-pare (to); (к) to prepare (oneself) (for).

приготовле́ни|е, я, *n.* preparation; без ∼я off-hand, extempore.

приготовля́|ть(ся), ю(сь), *impf. of* приго-то́вить(ся).

пригребá|ть(ся), ю(сь), *impf. of* при-грести́(сь).

пригревá|ть, ю, *impf. of* пригре́ть.

пригре́|зиться, жусь, зишься, *pf. of* гре́-зиться.

пригре|сти́, бу́, бёшь, *past* ∼б, ∼бла́, *pf.* (*of* ∼ба́ть) (*coll.*) **1.** to rake up. **2.** (к) to row (towards).

пригре|сти́сь, бу́сь, бёшься, *past* ∼бся, ∼бла́сь, *pf.* (*of* ∼ба́ться) (*coll.*) = ∼сти́ 2.

пригре́|ть, ю, *pf.* (*of* ∼вáть) **1.** to warm. **2.** (*fig.*) to cherish; to give shelter (to), take to one's care; п. змею́ на груди́ to cherish a snake in one's bosom.

пригро|зи́ть, жу́, зи́шь, *pf. of* грози́ть 1.

пригу́б|ить, лю, ишь, *pf.* to take a sip (of), taste.

прида|вáть, ю́, ёшь, *impf. of* прида́ть.

придав|и́ть, лю́, ∼ишь, *pf.* (*of* ∼ли́вать) to press; to press down, weigh down (*also fig.*); to squeeze.

прида́влива|ть, ю, *impf. of* придави́ть.

прида́ни|е, я, *n.* adding, giving, imparting; для ∼я хра́брости to give courage; для ∼я зако́нной си́лы (+*d.*; *leg.*) for the enforc-ing (of).

прида́н|ое, ого, *n.* **1.** dowry; trousseau. **2.** layette.

прида́т|ок, ка, *m.* appendage, adjunct.

прида́точн|ый, *adj.* **1.** additional, supple-mentary. **2.** (*gram.*) subordinate; ∼ое предложе́ние subordinate clause. **3.** (*bot.*) adventitious.

прида́|ть, м, шь, ст, ди́м, ди́те, ду́т, *past* при́дал, ∼ла́, при́дало, *pf.* (*of* ∼вáть) **1.** to add; (*mil.*) to attach. **2.** to increase, strengthen; п. бо́дрости (+*d.*) to hearten, put heart (into); п. ду́ху (+*d.*) to inspire, encourage. **3.** (+*a. and d.*) to give (to), im-part (to); (*fig.*) attach (to); п. вкус to impart relish (to), give piquancy (to); п. лоск to give a polish, impart lustre (to); п. водо-непроница́емость to waterproof; п. зна-че́ние to attach importance (to).

прида́ч|а, и, *f.* **1.** adding; (*mil.*) attaching. **2.** addition, supplement; в ∼у into the bargain, in addition.

придвигá|ть(ся), ю(сь), *impf. of* придви́-нуть(ся).

придви́|нуть, ну, нешь, *pf.* (*of* ∼гáть) to move (up), draw (up); ∼нь(те) кре́сло к пе́чке draw your chair up to the stove.

придви́|нуться, нусь, нешься, *pf.* (*of* ∼гáться) to move up, draw near.

придво́рн|ый, *adj.* court; п. врач court phy-sician; п. поэ́т poet laureate; п. шут court jester; *as noun* п., ∼ого, *m.* courtier.

придѐл, а, *m.* (*eccl.*) side-altar; side-chapel.

придѐл|ать, аю, *pf.* (*of* ~ывать) (к) to fix (to), attach (to).

придѐлыва|ть, ю, *impf. of* приделать.

придерж|ать, у́, ~ишь, *pf.* (*of* ~ивать) to hold back (*also fig.*); п. товар to hold back goods; п. язык to hold one's tongue.

придержива|ть, ю, *impf. of* придержать.

придержива|ться, юсь, *impf.* 1. (за + *a.*) to hold on (to); п. за поручень to hold on to the rail. 2. (+ *g.*) to hold (to), keep (to) (*also fig.*); (*fig.*) to stick (to), adhere (to); п. правой стороны to keep to the right; п. договора to adhere to an agreement; п. мнения to hold the opinion, be of the opinion; п. темы to stick to the subject; он ~ется рюмочки (*coll.*) he is fond of the bottle.

приди́р|а, ы, *m. and f.* (*coll.*) caviller, captious fellow, fault-finder.

придира́|ться, юсь, *impf. of* придраться.

придирк|а, и, *f.* (*coll.*) cavil, captious objection; (*pl.*) fault-finding, nagging, carping.

придирчивост|ь, и, *f.* captiousness.

придирчив|ый (~, ~а), *adj.* captious, fault-finding, carping, nagging.

придорож|ный, *adj.* roadside, wayside.

при|дра́ться, деру́сь, дерёшься, *past* ~дра́лся, ~драла́сь, ~драло́сь, *pf.* (*of* ~дира́ться) (к) 1. to find fault (with), cavil (at), carp (at); to nag (at), pick (on); п. к кому́-н. из-за пустяко́в to find fault with someone over trifles. 2. (*coll.*) to seize (on, upon); п. к слу́чаю to seize (upon) an opportunity.

приду́м|ать, аю, *pf.* (*of* ~ывать) to think (of), think up, devise, invent; п. отгово́рку to think up an excuse; п. развлече́ние to devise an entertainment.

приду́мыва|ть, ю, *impf. of* приду́мать.

придуркова́тост|ь, и, *f.* (*coll.*) silliness, daftness, imbecility.

придуркова́т|ый (~, ~а), *adj.* (*coll.*) silly, daft, imbecile, half-baked.

приду́р|ь, и, *f.*; с ~ью (*coll.*) a bit crazy, a bit daft.

придуш|и́ть, у́, ~ишь, *pf.* (*coll.*) to strangle, smother.

придыха́ни|е, я, *n.* (*ling.*) aspiration.

придыха́тельн|ый, *adj.* (*ling.*) aspirate; *as noun* п., ~ого, *m.* aspirate.

при|ду́, *see* ~йти́.

приеда́|ться, юсь, *impf. of* приесться.

прие́зд, а, *m.* arrival, coming; с ~ом! welcome!

приезжа́|ть, ю, *impf. of* прие́хать.

приезжа́ющ|ий, *pres. part. of* приезжа́ть; *as noun* п., ~его, *m. and* ~ая, ~ей, *f.* newcomer, (new) arrival; гости́ница для ~их hotel.

прие́зж|ий, *adj.* newly arrived; passing through; ~ая тру́ппа troupe on tour; *as*

noun п., ~его, *m.*; ~ая, ~ей, *f.* newcomer; (*in hotel, etc.*) visitor; ~ие лю́ди strangers (*as opp. to local inhabitants*).

прие́м, а, *m.* 1. receiving; reception; часы́ ~а (reception) hours, calling hours; (*of a doctor*) surgery (hours). 2. reception, welcome; оказа́ть кому́-н. раду́шный п. to accord someone a hearty welcome. 3. admittance (*to membership of association, party, etc.*). 4. reception (= *formal party*); быть приглашённым на п. to be invited to a reception. 5. dose. 6. go; motion, movement; в оди́н п. at one go; вы́пить стака́н в два ~а to drain a glass in two draughts; исполнить команду в три ~а to execute a command in three movements. 7. method, way, mode; device, trick (*also pejor.*); (*sport*) hold, grip; лече́бный п. method of treatment; жу́льнический п. a rogue's trick, a cad's trick. 8. (*mil.*) position; (*pl.*; *collect.*) manual; п. «в ру́ку» 'trail arms' position; ружейные ~ы manual of the rifle; ~ы с ору́жием manual of arms.

прие́мк|а, и, *f.* formal acceptance (*of building, etc., on completion of construction*).

прие́млемост|ь, и, *f.* acceptability; admissibility.

прие́млем|ый (~, ~а), *adj.* acceptable; admissible.

прие́мн|ая, ой, *f.* 1. waiting-room. 2. drawing-room; reception room.

прие́мник¹, а, *m.* wireless (set), radio (set), receiver.

прие́мник², а, *m.* reception centre (*for orphaned children, etc.*).

прие́мн|ый, *adj.* 1. receiving; reception; п. день visiting day; 'at home' day; ~ые часы́ (reception) hours, calling hours; (*of a doctor*) surgery (hours); п. поко́й casualty ward; п. жёлоб hopper; ~ое отве́рстие intake, inlet. 2. relating to admittance, entrance; ~ая коми́ссия selection committee, selection board; п. экза́мен entrance examination. 3. foster, adoptive; п. оте́ц foster-father; ~ая мать foster-mother; п. сын adopted son, foster-son.

прие́мо-переда́точный, *adj.* (*radio*) two-way.

прие́мочн|ый, *adj.* reception; acceptance; п. пункт reception centre; п. акт acceptance certificate, inspection certificate; ~ое испыта́ние acceptance test, official test.

прие́мщик, а, *m.* examiner, inspector (*of goods at a factory*).

прие́мыш, а, *m.* adopted child, foster-child.

при|е́сться, е́стся, едя́тся, *past* ~е́лся, ~е́лась, *pf.* (*of* ~еда́ться) (+ *d.*; *coll.*) to pall (on), tire, bore; мне ~е́лась э́та рабо́та I am fed up with this work.

приѐ|хать, ду, дешь, *pf.* (*of* ~зжа́ть) to arrive, come (*not on foot*).

прижа́т|ый, *p.p.p. of* ~ь; быть ~ым к стенѐ (*fig.*) to have one's back to the wall.

приж|а́ть, му́, мёшь, *pf.* (*of* ~има́ть) 1. (к) to press (to), clasp (to); п. к землѐ (*mil.*) to pin down; п. к груди́ to clasp to one's bosom; п. к стенѐ (*fig.*) to drive into a corner; п. ýши (*of a horse*) to lay back its ears. 2. (*fig.*) to press, bring pressure to bear (upon); п. до́лжников to press one's debtors.

приж|а́ться, му́сь, мёшься, *pf.* (*of* ~има́ться) 1. (к) to press oneself (to, against); to cuddle up (to), snuggle up (to), nestle up (to); п. к стенѐ to flatten oneself against the wall. 2. *pass. of* ~а́ть.

при|жѐчь, жгу́, жжёшь, жгут, *past* ~жёг, ~жгла́, *pf.* (*of* ~жига́ть) to cauterize, sear.

прижива́л|ка, ки, *f. of* ~ьщик.

прижива́льщик, а, *m.* (1. (*hist.*) dependant. 2. (*fig.*) hanger-on, sponger, parasite.

прижива́|ть(ся), ю(сь), *impf. of* прижи́ть(ся).

прижига́ни|е, я, *n.* (*med.*) cauterization, searing.

прижига́|ть, ю, *impf. of* прижѐчь.

прижи́зненный, *adj.* occurring during one's lifetime.

прижима́|ть(ся), ю(сь), *impf. of* прижа́ть(ся).

прижи́мист|ый (~, ~а), *adj.* (*coll.*) close-fisted, tight-fisted, stingy.

прижи́мк|а, и, *f.* (*fig., coll.*) pressure; clamping down.

приж|и́ть, иву́, ивёшь, *past* ~и́л, ~ила́, ~и́ло, *pf.* (*of* ~ива́ть) (*coll.*) to beget (*usu. of extra-marital unions*).

приж|и́ться, иву́сь, ивёшься, *past* ~и́лся, ~ила́сь, *pf.* (*of* ~ива́ться) 1. to settle down, get acclimatized. 2. (*of plants*) to take root, strike root.

приз¹, а, *pl.* ~ы́, *m.* prize; переходя́щий п. challenge prize; получи́ть п. to win a prize; присуди́ть п. (+*d.*) to award a prize (to).

приз², а, *m.* (*naut., leg.*) prize.

призаду́м|аться, аюсь, *pf.* (*of* ~ываться) to become thoughtful, become pensive.

призаду́мыва|ться, юсь, *impf. of* призаду́маться.

приза|ня́ть, йму́, ймёшь, *past* ~ня́л, ~няла́, ~ня́ло, *pf.* (*coll.*) to borrow.

призва́ни|е, я, *n.* vocation, calling; слѐдовать своему́ ~ю to follow one's vocation; чу́вствовать п. к духо́вному са́ну to have a vocation to go into the church; хиру́рг по ~ю a surgeon by vocation.

при|зва́ть, зову́, зовёшь, *past* ~зва́л, ~звала́, ~зва́ло, *pf.* (*of* ~зыва́ть) to call, summon; to call upon, appeal; п. на по́-

мощь to call for help; п. на вое́нную слу́жбу to call up (*for military service*), call to the colours; п. к поря́дку to call to order; п. прокля́тия на чью-н. го́лову to call down curses on someone's head.

при|зва́ться, зову́сь, зовёшься, *past* ~звался, ~звала́сь, ~звало́сь, *pf.* (*of* ~зыва́ться) 1. to be called up. 2. *pass. of* ~зва́ть.

при́звук, а, *m.* additional sound.

призѐмист|ый (~, ~а), *adj.* stocky, squat; thickset.

приземлѐни|е, я, *n.* (*aeron.*) landing, touch-down.

приземл|и́ть, ю́, и́шь, *pf.* (*of* ~я́ть) (*aeron.*) to land, bring in to land.

приземл|и́ться, ю́сь, и́шься, *pf.* (of ~я́ться) (*aeron.*) to land, touch down.

приземля́|ть(ся), ю(сь), *impf. of* приземли́ть(ся).

призёр, а, *m.* prize-winner, prizeman.

при́зм|а, ы, *f.* prism; сквозь ~у (+*g.*; *fig.*) in the light (of).

призмати́ческий, *adj.* prismatic.

призна|ва́ть(ся), ю́(сь), ёшь(ся), *impf. of* призна́ть(ся).

при́знак, а, *m.* sign; indications; п. бол́ѐзни symptom; служи́ть ~ом (+*g.*) to be a sign (of); обнару́живать ~и (+*g.*) to show signs (of); имѐются все ~и того́, что there is every indication that; не подава́ть ~ов жи́зни to show no sign of life; по ~у (+*g.*) on the basis (of).

призна́ни|е, я, *n.* 1. confession, declaration; admission, acknowledgement; нево́льное п. involuntary admission; п. вины́ avowal of guilt; п. в любви́ declaration of love; по о́бщему ~ю by general admission. 2. recognition; п. де-фа́кто (*leg., polit.*) de facto recognition; получи́ть п. to obtain, win recognition; получи́ть всео́бщее п. to be generally recognized.

при́зн|анный, *p.p.p. of* ~а́ть *and adj.* acknowledged, recognized.

призна́тельност|ь, и, *f.* gratitude.

призна́тел|ьный (~ен, ~ьна), *adj.* grateful.

призна́|ть, ю, *pf.* (*of* ~ва́ть) 1. to recognize; to spot, identify; вы меня́ не ~ли? did you not recognize me?; я ~л в нём иностра́нца по одѐжде I spotted him as a foreigner by his dress. 2. (*leg., polit.*) to recognize; п. прави́тельство to recognize a government. 3. to admit, own, acknowledge; п. вину́, п. себя́ вино́вным (*leg.*) to plead guilty; п. свою́ оши́бку to admit one's mistake; п. себя́ побеждённым to acknowledge defeat. 4. to deem, vote; п. ну́жным to deem (it) necessary; п. недействи́тельным to declare invalid, nullify; п. (не)вино́вным to find (not) guilty; п. неуда́чным to vote a failure.

призна́|ться, юсь, *pf.* (*of* ~ва́ться) (в+*p.*) to confess (to), own (to); п. в любви́ to make a declaration of love; п. в преступле́нии to confess to a crime; на́до п., что it must be admitted that, the truth is that; п. (сказа́ть) to tell the truth; п., и фами́лии его́ не зна́ю to tell the truth I don't even know his name.

призов|о́й, *adj.* *of* приз; ~ы́е де́ньги prize-money; ~о́е су́дно (*naut.*, *leg.*) prize.

призо́р, а, *m.* без ~a (*coll.*) untended, neglected.

при́зрак, а, *m.* spectre, ghost, phantom, apparition; гоня́ться за ~ами to catch at shadows.

при́зрачност|ь, и, *f.* illusoriness.

при́зрач|ный (~ен, ~на), *adj.* 1. spectral, ghostly, phantasmal. 2. (*fig.*) illusory, imagined; ~ная опа́сность imagined danger.

призрева́|ть, ю, *impf.* *of* призре́ть.

призре́ни|е, я, *n.* care, charity; дом ~я бе́дных alms-house, poor people's home.

призр|е́ть, ю, ~и́шь, *pf.* (*of* ~ева́ть) to support by charity.

призы́в, а, *m.* 1. call, appeal; откли́кнуться на чей-н. п. to respond to someone's call. 2. slogan; первома́йские ~ы May-day slogans; 3. (*mil.*) call-up, conscription. 4. (*collect.*; *mil.*) levy; (group of) conscripts, draft; ле́нинский п. (*hist.*) the Lenin Enrolment (*large entry into Soviet Communist Party after death of Lenin*).

призыва́|ть(ся), ю(сь), *impf.* *of* призва́ть-(ся).

призывни́к, а́, *m.* man called up for military service; man due for call-up.

призывно́й, *adj.* call-up; п. во́зраст call-up age; п. уча́сток reception unit.

призы́вный, *adj.* invocatory; inviting; п. клич call.

при́иск, а, *m.* mine (*for precious metals*); золоты́е ~и gold-field(s).

приискáни|е, я, *n.* finding.

при́иск|ать, ищу́, и́щешь, *pf.* (*of* ~и́скивать) to find.

прии́скива|ть, ю, *impf.* (*coll.*) 1. *impf.* *of* приискáть. 2. (*impf.* *only*) to look for, hunt for; мы ~ем кварти́ру без ме́бели we are looking for unfurnished accommodation.

прииско́вый, *adj.* *of* при́иск.

при|йти́, ду́, дёшь, *past* ~шёл, ~шла́, *pf.* (of ~ходи́ть) (*in var. senses*) to come; to arrive; п. пе́рвым to come in first; п. в восто́рг (от) to go into raptures (over); п. в плохо́е настрое́ние to get into a bad mood; п. в у́жас to be horrified; п. в я́рость to fly into a rage; п. в го́лову кому́-н., на ум кому́-н. to occur to someone, strike someone, cross

one's mind; мысль ~шла́ мне в го́лову the idea occurred to me; п. в себя́, п. в чу́вство to come round, regain consciousness; (*fig.*) to come to one's senses; п. к концу́ to come to an end; п. к заключе́нию, п. к убежде́нию to come to the conclusion, arrive at a conclusion; п. к соглаше́нию to come to an agreement.

при|йти́сь, ду́сь, дёшься, *past* ~шёлся, ~шла́сь, *pf.* (*of* ~ходи́ться) 1. (по+*d.*) to fit; ковёр ~шёлся как раз по разме́рам спа́льни the carpet fitted the bedroom floor just right; п. кому́-н. по вку́су, по нра́ву to be to someone's taste, liking; га́лстук ~шёлся мне по вку́су the tie was just what I wanted. 2. (на+*a.*; *of dates, days or occasions*) to fall (on); Па́сха ~шла́сь на 28-ое ма́рта Easter fell on the 28th of March. 3. (*impers.*+*d.*) to have (to); нам ~шло́сь подожда́ть ещё два часа́ we had to wait another two hours; ей ~дётся неме́дленно верну́ться в Москву́ she will have to return to Moscow immediately. 4. (*impers.*+*d.*) to happen (to), fall to the lot (of); мне ~шло́сь быть ря́дом в тот моме́нт, когда́ он упа́л в о́бморок I happened to be standing by when he fainted; им ту́го ~шло́сь they had a rough time; как ~дётся (*coll.*) anyhow, at haphazard. 5. (*impers.*; на+*a.* or с+*g.*; *coll.*) to be owing (to, from); на ка́ждого ~шло́сь по фу́нту they got a pound each; с вас ~дётся де́сять рубле́й there is ten roubles to come from you.

прика́з, а, *m.* 1. order, command; по ~y by order; п. по войска́м order of the day; п. о выступле́нии (*mil.*) marching orders; отда́ть п. to give an order, issue an order. 2. (*hist.*) office, department.

приказа́ни|е, я, *n.* order, command, injunction.

прика|за́ть, жу́, ~жешь, *pf.* (*of* ~зывать) (+*d.*) to order, command; to give orders; to direct; п. до́лго жить (*coll.*) to pass on, depart this life; что ~жете? what do you wish?, what can I do for you?; как ~жете as you please, as you wish; как ~жете понима́ть э́то? how am I supposed to take this?; what do you mean by this?

прика́з|ный, *adj.* 1. *adj.* *of* ~ 1; в ~ном поря́дке in the form of an order. 2. (*hist.*) departmental; п. язы́к chancery language (*as opp. to literary language*); *as noun* п., ~ного, *m.* clerk, scribe. 3. *as noun* (*obs.*) petty official.

прика́зчик, а, *m.* (*obs.*) 1. shop-assistant, salesman. 2. steward, bailiff.

прика́зыва|ть, ю, *impf.* *of* приказа́ть.

прика́лыва|ть, ю, *impf.* *of* приколо́ть.

прика́нчива|ть, ю, *impf.* *of* прикончить.

прикармáнива|ть, ю, *impf. of* прикармá-
нить.

прикармá|нить, ю, ишь, *pf.* (*of* ~ивать)
(*coll.*) to pocket.

прикáрмлива|ть, ю, *impf.* 1. *impf. of* при-
корми́ть. 2. (*impf. only*) to give additional
food (*during the weaning period*).

прикасá|ться, юсь, *impf. of* прикосну́ться.

прика|ти́ть, чу́, ~тишь, *pf.* (*of* ~тывать)
1. (к) to roll up (to). 2. (*coll.*) to roll up,
turn up.

прикáтыва|ть, ю, *impf. of* прикати́ть.

прики́дыва|ть(ся), ю(сь), *impf. of* прики́-
нуть(ся).

прики́|нуть, ну, нешь, *pf.* (*of* ~дывать)
1. to throw in, add. 2. to estimate (approximately); п. на весáх to weigh; п. в
умé (*fig.*) to weigh (up), ponder.

прики́|нуться, нусь, нешься, *pf.* (*of* ~ды-
ваться) (+*i.*; *coll.*) to pretend (to be), feign;
п. больны́м to pretend to be ill, feign
illness; п. лисо́й to fawn, toady; п. раскáяв-
шимся to feign repentance; он ~нулся, что не
ви́дит меня́ he pretended that he could not
see me.

прикла́д[1], а, *m.* butt, butt-stock (*of firearm*).

прикла́д[2], а, *m.* trimmings (*used by tailor or
boot-maker*).

прикла́дк|а, и, *f.* levelling (*of rifle*); posi-
tion; п. лёжа, п. с колéна, п. стóя lying,
kneeling, standing position (*with rifle in
hand*).

прикладн|о́й, *adj.* applied; ~óе иску́сство
applied art(s); ~áя фи́зика applied physics.

прикла́дыва|ть(ся), ю(сь), *impf. of* прило-
жи́ть(ся).

прикле́ива|ть(ся), ю(сь), *impf. of* при-
кле́ить(ся).

прикле́|ить, ю, ишь, *pf.* (*of* ~ивать) to
stick; to glue; to paste; to affix; п. мáрку to
stick on a stamp; п. афи́шу к стенé to stick
(up) a bill on a wall.

прикле́|иться, ится, *pf.* (*of* ~иваться) (к)
to stick (to), adhere (to).

приклеп|áть, áю, *pf.* (*of* ~ывать) to rivet.

приклёпк|а, и, *f.* riveting.

приклёпыва|ть, ю, *impf. of* приклепáть.

приклон|и́ть, ю́, ~ишь, *pf.*; п. гóлову to lay
one's head; у негó нéгде п. гóлову he has
nowhere to lay his head; п. слух, п. у́хо
(*obs.*) to listen intently.

приключ|áть(ся), áю, áет(ся), *impf. of*
~и́ть(ся).

приключéни|е, я, *n.* adventure.

приключéнческий, *adj.* adventure; п. ромáн
adventure story.

приключéнчеств|о, а, *n.* adventure litera-
ture.

приключ|и́ть, у́, и́шь, *pf.* (*of* ~áть) (*tech.*) to
connect up.

приключ|и́ться, и́тся, *pf.* (*of* ~áться) (*coll.*)
to happen, occur.

прикноп|и́ть, лю́, ~ишь, *pf.* to pin up (*with
a drawing pin*).

прикóв|анный, *p.p.p. of* ~áть; п. к постéли
bed-ridden, confined to one's bed.

прик|овáть, у́ю, уёшь, *pf.* (*of* ~óвывать)
1. (к) to chain (to). 2. (*fig.*) to chain; to
rivet; нáше внимáние ~овáла к себé их
блестя́щая фóрма our attention was riveted
on their gorgeous uniforms; страх ~овáл
нас к мéсту fear rooted us to the spot.

прикóвыва|ть, ю, *impf. of* прикóвáть.

прикóл, а, *m.* stake; палáточный п. tent-
-peg; стоя́ть на ~е (*naut.*) to be laid up, be
idle.

приколáчива|ть, ю, *impf. of* приколоти́ть.

приколо|ти́ть, чу́, ~тишь, *pf.* (*of* приколá-
чивать) to nail, fasten with nails.

прикол|о́ть, ю́, ~ешь, *pf.* (*of* прикáлывать)
1. to pin, fasten with a pin. 2. (*coll.*) to stab,
transfix; п. штыкóм to bayonet.

прикомандир|овáть, у́ю, *pf.* (*of* ~óвывать)
(к) to attach (to), second (to).

прикомандирóвыва|ть, ю, *impf. of* прико-
мандировáть.

прикóнч|ить, у, ишь, *pf.* (*of* прикáнчивать)
(*coll.*) 1. to use up. 2. (*fig.*) to finish off.

прикоп|и́ть, лю́, ~ишь, *pf.* (+*a. or g.*; *coll.*)
to save (up), put by.

прикóрм, а, *m.* 1. lure, bait (*for birds or fish*).
2. additional food.

прикóрм|ить, лю́, ~ишь, *pf.* (*of* прикáрмли-
вать) to lure (*by putting out food*).

прикóрм|ка, ки, *f.* = ~.

прикорн|у́ть, у́, ёшь, *pf.* (*coll.*) (к) to lean
up (against), prop oneself up (against) (*with
a view to taking a nap*); п. на дивáне to curl
up on the sofa.

прикосновéни|е, я, *n.* 1. touch; тóчка ~я
point of contact. 2. (*sing. only*) concern; я не
имéю никакóго ~я к э́тому дéлу this affair
is no concern of mine, is nothing to do with
me.

прикосновéнност|ь, и, *f.* (к) concern (in),
involvement (in).

прикосновéн|ный (~, ~на), *adj.* (к) con-
cerned (in), involved (in), implicated (in);
он был ~ к уби́йству he was implicated in
a murder.

прикосн|у́ться, у́сь, ёшься, *pf.* (*of* прикá-
саться) (к) to touch (lightly).

прикрáс|а, ы, *f.* (*coll.*) embellishment; без
~ unvarnished, unadorned; рассказáть
без ~ to give a straightforward account.

прикрá|сить, шу, сишь, *pf.* (*of* ~шивать)
to embellish, embroider (*in speech*).

прикрáшива|ть, ю, *impf. of* прикрáсить.

прикрепи́тельный, *adj.* п. талóн registration card (*document certifying that customer is*

registered with stated retailer for supply of provisions, etc.).

прикреп|и́ть, лю́, и́шь, *pf.* (*of* ~ля́ть) (к) **1.** to fasten (to). **2.** (*fig.*) to attach (to); п. де́тский сад к больни́це to attach a kindergarten to a hospital.

прикреп|и́ться, лю́сь, и́шься, *pf.* (*of* ~ля́ться) (к) **1.** to register (at, with). **2.** *pass. of* ~и́ть.

прикрепле́ни|е, я, *n.* **1.** fastening. **2.** (*fig.*) attachment; п. к земле́ (*hist.*) attaching to the soil (*as serf*). **3.** registration.

прикрепля́|ть(ся), ю(сь), *impf. of* прикрепи́ть(ся).

прикри́кива|ть, ю, *impf. of* прикри́кнуть.

прикри́к|нуть, ну, нешь, *pf.* (*of* ~ивать) (на+*a.*) to shout (at), raise one's voice (at).

прикру|ти́ть, чу́, ~тишь, *pf.* (*of* ~чивать) **1.** (к) to tie (to), bind (to), fasten (to). **2.** (*coll.*) to turn down (*a wick*).

прикру́чива|ть, ю, *impf. of* прикрути́ть.

прикрыва́|ть(ся), ю(сь), *impf. of* прикры́ть(ся).

прикры́ти|е, я, *n.* cover; escort; (*fig.*) screen, cloak; под ~ем (+*g.*) under cover (of), screened (by); артилле́рийское п. artillery cover; п. истреби́телями fighter cover, fighter escort.

прикр|ы́ть, о́ю, о́ешь, *pf.* (*of* ~ыва́ть) **1.** (+*i.*) to cover (with); to screen; п. кастрю́лю кры́шкой to put the lid on a saucepan. **2.** to protect, shelter, shield; п. глаза́ руко́й to shade, shield one's eyes (with one's hand); п. наступле́ние артилле́рией to cover an attack with an artillery barrage. **3.** (*fig.*) to cover (up), conceal, screen; п. своё неве́жество to conceal one's ignorance. **4.** (*coll.*) to close down, wind up.

прикр|ы́ться, о́юсь, о́ешься, *pf.* (*of* ~ыва́ться) **1.** (+*i.*) to cover oneself (with); (*fig.*) to use as a cover, take refuge (in), shelter (behind); он ~ы́лся положе́нием иностра́нца he took refuge in the fact of being a foreigner. **2.** (*coll.*) to close down, go out of business. **3.** *pass. of* ~ы́ть.

прикуп|а́ть, а́ю, *impf. of* ~и́ть.

прикуп|и́ть, лю́, ~ишь, *pf.* (*of* ~а́ть) (+*a.* or *g.*) to buy (*some more*).

прикупк|а, и, *f.* additional purchase.

прикури́ва|ть, ю, *impf. of* прикури́ть.

прикур|и́ть, ю́, ~ишь, *pf.* (*of* ~ивать) (у кого́-н.) to get a light (*from someone's cigarette*).

прику́с, а, *m.* bite.

прику|си́ть, шу́, ~сишь, *pf.* (*of* ~сывать) to bite; п. (себе́) язы́к to bite one's tongue; (*fig., coll.*) to hold one's tongue, keep one's mouth shut.

прику́сыва|ть, ю, *impf. of* прикуси́ть.

прила́в|ок, ка, *m.* counter; рабо́тник ~ка counter hand, salesman, (shop) assistant.

прилага́|емый, *pres. part. pass. of* ~ть *and adj.* accompanying; enclosed; subjoined; п. почто́вый перево́д the enclosed postal order.

прилага́тельн|ый, *adj.* и́мя ~ое (*or as noun* ~ое, ~ого, *n.*) adjective.

прилага́|ть, ю, *impf. of* приложи́ть.

прила́|дить, жу, дишь, *pf.* (*of* ~живать) (к) to fit (to), adjust (to).

прила́жива|ть, ю, *impf. of* прила́дить.

приласка́|ть, ю, *pf.* to caress, fondle, pet.

приласка́|ться, юсь, *pf.* (к) to snuggle up (to).

прилгн|у́ть, у́, ёшь, *pf.* (*coll.*) to insert fabrications (*into a narrative*).

прилега́|ть, ет, *impf.* (к) **1.** (*pf.* приле́чь[1]) to fit. **2.** (*no pf.*) to adjoin, be adjacent (to), border (upon); сад ~ет к те́ннисному ко́рту the garden adjoins the tennis court.

прилега́|ющий, *pres. part. of* ~ть *and adj.* **1.** close-fitting, tight-fitting. **2.** (к) adjoining, adjacent (to), contiguous (to).

прилежа́ни|е, я, *n.* diligence, industry, assiduousness; application.

прилежа́щий, *adj.* (*math.*) adjacent, adjoining, contiguous.

приле́ж|ный (~ен, ~на), *adj.* diligent, industrious, assiduous.

прилеп|и́ть, лю́, ~ишь, *pf.* (*of* ~ля́ть) (к) to stick (to, on).

прилеп|и́ться, лю́сь, ~ишься, *pf.* (*of* ~ля́ться) **1.** (к) to stick (to, on). **2.** *pass. of* ~и́ть.

прилепля́|ть(ся), ю(сь), *impf. of* прилепи́ть(ся).

прилёт, а, *m.* arrival (*by air*).

прилет|а́ть, а́ю, *impf. of* ~е́ть.

приле|те́ть, чу́, ти́шь, *pf.* (*of* ~та́ть) **1.** to arrive (*by air*), fly in. **2.** (*fig., coll.*) to fly, come flying.

при|ле́чь[1], ля́жет, ля́гут, *past* ~лёг, ~легла́, *pf. of* ~лега́ть.

при|ле́чь[2], ля́гу, ля́жешь, ля́гут, *past* ~лёг, ~легла́, *pf.* **1.** to lie down (*for a short while*). **2.** (*of standing crops*) to be laid flat.

прили́в, а, *m.* **1.** flow, flood (*of tide*); rising tide; (*fig.*) surge, influx; волна́ ~a tidal wave; п. и отли́в ebb and flow; п. негодова́ния (up)surge of indignation. **2.** (*med.*) congestion; п. кро́ви rush of blood; (*fig.*) п. эне́ргии burst of energy. **3.** (*tech.*) boss, lug; (*naut.*) cleat.

прилива́|ть, ет, *impf. of* прили́ть.

прили́вный, *adj.* tidal.

прили́з|анный, *p.p.p. of* ~а́ть; ~анные во́лосы smarmed-down hair.

прили|за́ть, жу́, ~жешь, *pf.* (*of* ~зыва́ть) to lick smooth.

прили́зыва|ть, ю, *impf. of* прилиза́ть.

прилип|а́ть, а́ет, *impf. of* ~нуть.

прилип|нуть, нет, *past* ~, ~ла, *pf.* (*of* ~а́ть) (к) to stick (to), adhere (to).

прили́пчив|ый (~, ~а), *adj.* (*coll.*) 1. sticking, adhesive. 2. (*fig.*) boring, tiresome. 3. (*of diseases*) catching.

прили́стник, а, *m.* (*bot.*) stipule.

при|ли́ть, льёт, *past* ~ли́л, ~лила́, ~ли́ло, *pf.* (*of* ~лива́ть) (к) to flow (to); (*of blood*) to rush (to); кровь ~лила́ к её щека́м blood rushed to her cheeks.

прили́честв|овать, ует, *impf.* (+*d.*; *obs.*) to befit, become.

прили́чи|е, я, *n.* decency, propriety; decorum; соблюда́ть ~я to observe the decencies, the proprieties.

прили́ч|ный (~ен, ~на), *adj.* 1. decent, proper; decorous, seemly; п. анекдо́т a clean story. 2. (+*d.*; *obs.*) fitting; appropriate (to). 3. (*coll.*) decent, tolerable, fair; ~ная зарпла́та a decent wage.

приложе́ни|е, я, *n.* 1. application; п. я́дерной фи́зики к констру́кции подво́дных ло́док the application of nuclear physics to the design of submarines. 2. affixing; apposition; п. печа́ти affixing of a seal. 3. enclosure (*of document, etc., with letter*). 4. supplement (*to newspaper, periodical, etc.*). 5. appendix (*to a book*). 6. (*gram.*) apposition.

прилож|и́ть, у́, ~ишь, *pf.* 1. (*impf.* прикла́дывать) (к) to put (to), hold (to); п. ру́ку ко лбу to put one's hand to one's head; п. ру́ку to put one's hand (to), take a hand (in); to add one's signature (to). 2. (*impf.* прикла́дывать *and* прилага́ть) to add, join; to enclose; to affix; п. к заявле́нию характери́стику to enclose a testimonial with an application; п. печа́ть to affix a seal. 3. (*impf.* прилага́ть) to apply; п. си́лу to apply force; п. все уси́лия to strain every effort; п. всё стара́ние to do one's best, try one's hardest.

прилож|и́ться, у́сь, ~ишься, *pf.* (*of* прикла́дываться) 1. (+*i.*, к) to put (*one's ear, eye, or mouth*) (to); п. гла́зом к замо́чной сква́жине to put one's eye to the keyhole; п. (губа́ми) to kiss. 2. to take aim. 3. *pass. of* ~и́ть; остально́е ~ится the rest will come.

прилуне́ни|е, я, *n.* landing on the Moon.

прилун|и́ться, ю́сь, и́шься, *pf.* to land on the Moon.

прильн|у́ть, у́, ёшь, *pf. of* льнуть.

при́м|а, ы, *f.* (*mus.*) 1. tonic. 2. first string, top string. 3. first violin.

при́ма-балери́на, при́мы-балери́ны, *f.* prima ballerina.

примадо́нн|а, ы, *f.* prima donna.

прима́|заться, жусь, жешься, *pf.* (*of* ~зываться) (к; *coll.*, *pejor.*) to attach oneself (to), get in (with).

прима́зыва|ться, юсь, *impf. of* прима́заться.

прима́нива|ть, ю, *impf. of* примани́ть.

приман|и́ть, ю́, ~ишь, *pf.* (*of* ~ивать) (*coll.*) to lure; to decoy; to entice, allure.

прима́нк|а, и, *f.* bait, lure; (*fig.*) enticement, allurement.

прима́с, а, *m.* (*eccl.*) primate.

прима́т[1], а, *m.* (*philos.*) primacy; pre-eminence.

прима́т[2], а, *m.* (*zool.*) primate.

прима́чива|ть, ю, *impf. of* примочи́ть.

примелька́|ться, юсь, *pf.* (*coll.*) to become familiar; её лицо́ мне о́чень ~лось her face is very familiar to me.

примене́ни|е, я, *n.* application; use; п. к ме́стности (*mil.*) use of ground, adaptation to terrain; на́ши ме́тоды получи́ли широ́кое п. our methods have been widely adopted; в ~и (к) in application (to).

примени́мост|ь, и, *f.* applicability.

примени́м|ый (~, ~а), *adj.* applicable, suitable.

примени́тельно, *adv.* (к) conformably (to), in conformity (with); as applied (to).

примен|и́ть, ю́, ~ишь, *pf.* (*of* ~я́ть) to apply; to employ, use; п. свои́ зна́ния to apply one's knowledge; п. на пра́ктике to put into practice.

примен|и́ться, ю́сь, ~ишься, *pf.* (*of* ~я́ться) (к) to adapt oneself (to), conform (to).

приме́р, а, *m.* 1. example, instance; привести́ п. to give an example; привести́ в п. to cite as an example; поясни́ть ~ом to illustrate by means of an example; к ~у (*coll.*) by way of illustration, for example. 2. example; model; брать п. с кого́-н., сле́довать чьему́-н. ~у to follow someone's example; подава́ть п. to set an example; показа́ть п. to give an example, give the lead; для ~а as an example; по ~у (+*g.*) after the example (of), on the pattern (of); не в п. (+*d.*; *coll.*) unlike; (+*comp.*) far more, by far; не в п. про́чим unlike the others; она́ сего́дня игра́ет не в п. лу́чше, чем игра́ла на той неде́ле her playing today is better by far than it was last week.

примерз|а́ть, а́ю, *impf. of* ~нуть.

примёрз|нуть, ну, нешь, *past* ~, ~ла, *pf.* (*of* ~а́ть) (к) to freeze (to).

приме́р|ить, ю, ишь, *pf.* (*of* ме́рить 2 *and* ~я́ть) to try on; to fit.

приме́р|иться, юсь, ишься, *pf.* (*of* ~я́ться) (*coll.*) to contrive.

приме́рк|а, и, *f.* trying on; fitting.

приме́рно, *adv.* 1. in exemplary fashion;

п. вести́ себя́ to be an example. **2.** approximately, roughly.

приме́р|ный (~ен, ~на), *adj.* **1.** exemplary, model; п. перево́д a model version. **2.** approximate, rough.

пример|я́ть(ся), я́ю(сь), *impf. of* ~и́ть(ся).

при́мес|ь, и, *f.* admixture; dash; (*fig.*) touch; без ~ей unadulterated; молоко́ с ~ью ко́фе milk with a dash of coffee.

приме́т|а, ы, *f.* sign, token; mark; име́ть на ~e to have one's eye (on); быть на ~e to be before the eye, be the centre of attention.

примет|а́ть, а́ю, *pf.* (*of* ~ывать) to tack (on), stitch (on).

приме́|тить, чу, тишь, *pf.* (*of* ~ча́ть) to notice, perceive.

приме́тливост|ь, и, *f.* power(s) of observation.

приме́тлив|ый (~, ~а), *adj.* (*coll.*) observant.

приме́тно, *adv.* perceptibly, visibly, noticeably; он п. похуде́л he has grown perceptibly thinner.

приме́т|ный (~ен, ~на), *adj.* **1.** perceptible, visible, noticeable. **2.** conspicuous, prominent.

примётыва|ть, ю, *impf. of* примета́ть.

примеча́ни|е, я, *n.* **1.** note, footnote; снабди́ть ~ями to annotate. **2.** (*pl.*) comment(s), commentary.

примеча́тельност|ь, и, *f.* noteworthiness.

примеча́тел|ьный (~ен, ~ьна), *adj.* noteworthy, notable, remarkable.

примеча́|ть, ю, *impf.* **1.** *impf. of* приме́тить. **2.** (*impf. only*) (за+*i.*; *coll.*) to keep an eye (on), keep a watch out (on); ~й за ним, а то он дое́ст все конфе́ты keep a watch out on him, or else he'll finish off all the sweets.

примеш|а́ть, а́ю, *pf.* (*of* ~ивать) (+*a. or g.*) to add, admix; (*tech.*) to alloy.

примéшива|ть, ю, *impf. of* примеша́ть.

примина́|ть, ю, *impf. of* примя́ть.

примире́н|ец, ца, *m.* (*pejor.*) conciliator, compromiser.

примире́ни|е, я, *n.* reconciliation.

примире́нческий, *adj.* (*pejor.*) compromising.

примире́нчеств|о, а, *n.* (*pejor.*) conciliatoriness, spirit of compromise, appeasement.

примир|и́мый (~и́м, ~и́ма), *pres. part. pass. of* ~и́ть *and adj.* reconcilable.

примири́тел|ь, я, *m.* reconciler, conciliator, peace-maker.

примири́тел|ьный (~ен, ~ьна), *adj.* conciliatory.

примир|и́ть, ю́, и́шь, *pf.* (*of* ~я́ть) to reconcile; to conciliate; п. супру́гов to reconcile a husband and wife; п. кого́-н. с необхо-

ди́мостью больши́х жертв to reconcile someone to the necessity for great sacrifices.

примир|и́ться, ю́сь, и́шься, *pf.* (*of* ~я́ться) (c+*i.*) **1.** to be reconciled (to), make it up (with). **2.** to reconcile oneself (to); п. с неудо́бствами to reconcile oneself to, accept discomforts.

примир|я́ть(ся), я́ю(сь), *impf. of* ~и́ть(ся).

примити́в, а, *m.* **1.** (*art*) primitive. **2.** primitive artefact; specimen, *etc.*, in rude, undeveloped state. **3.** (*coll.*) primitive person.

примитиви́зм, а, *m.* (*art*) primitivism.

примити́в|ный (~ен, ~на), *adj.* primitive; rude, crude.

примкн|у́ть, у́, ёшь, *pf.* (*of* примыка́ть) (к) **1.** to fix (to), attach (to); п. штыки́! fix bayonets! **2.** (*fig.*) to join, attach oneself (to); to side (with).

примо́лкн|уть, у, ешь, *pf.* (*coll.*) to fall silent.

примо́рский, *adj.* seaside; maritime; п. куро́рт seaside resort.

примо́рь|е, я, *n.* littoral, seaside.

примо|сти́ть, щу́, сти́шь, *pf.* (*coll.*) to find room (for), stick (*in a crowded place or inconvenient surroundings*).

примо|сти́ться, щу́сь, сти́шься, *pf.* (*coll.*) to find room for oneself, perch oneself (*in a crowded place or inconvenient surroundings*).

примоч|и́ть, у́, ~ишь, *pf.* (*of* прима́чивать) to bathe, moisten; п. себе́ глаз to bathe one's eye.

примо́чк|а, и, *f.* wash, lotion; свинцо́вая п. Goulard (water); п. для глаз eye-lotion.

при́мул|а, ы, *f.* primula, primrose.

при́мус, а, *m.* primus(-stove).

при́мус|ный, *adj. of* ~; ~ная иго́лка primus pricker.

примч|а́ть, у́, и́шь, *pf.* (*coll.*) **1.** to bring in a hurry, hurry along with. **2.** = ~а́ться.

примч|а́ться, у́сь, и́шься, *pf.* to come tearing along.

примыка́ни|е, я, *n.* **1.** contiguity. **2.** (*gram.*) agglutination.

примыка́|ть, ю, *impf.* **1.** *impf. of* примкну́ть. **2.** (*impf. only*) (к) to adjoin, border (upon), abut (upon).

примыка́|ющий, *pres. part. act. of* ~ть *and adj.* affiliated.

при|мя́ть, мну́, мнёшь, *pf.* (*of* ~мина́ть) to crush, flatten; to trample down, tread down.

принадлеж|а́ть, у́, и́шь, *impf.* **1.** (+*d.*) belong (to); to appertain (to); п. по пра́ву to belong by right, belong rightfully; ему́ ~и́т честь э́того откры́тия to him belongs the credit for this discovery. **2.** (к) to belong (to), be a member (of); п. к аэроклу́бу to belong to a flying club.

принадлёжност|ь, и, *f.* **1.** (к) belonging (to), membership (of); п. к ассоциáции membership of an association. **2.** (*obs.*) property. **3.** по ~и to the proper quarter, through the proper channels. **4.** (*pl.*) accessories, appurtenances; equipment; outfit, tackle; брúтвенные ~и shaving tackle; канцелярские ~и office equipment; ~и костюма accessories (*gloves, handbag, etc.*).

прина|лéчь, лягу, ляжешь, лягут, *past* ~лёг, ~леглá, *pf.* (на+*a.*; *coll.*) **1.** to rest lightly (upon). **2.** to apply oneself (to), go (at, to) with a will; п. на вёсла to ply one's oars vigorously, pull vigorously.

принаря|дúть, жý, ~дúшь, *pf.* (*of* ~жáть) (*coll.*) to dress up, deck out.

принаря|дúться, жýсь, ~дúшься, *pf.* (*of* ~жáться) (*coll.*) to get oneself up, doll oneself up.

принаряжá|ть(ся), ю(сь), *impf. of* принарядúть(ся).

приневóлива|ть, ю, *impf. of* приневóлить.

приневóл|ить, ю, ишь, *pf.* (*of* ~ивать) (+ *inf.*; *coll.*) to force (to), make; онú ~или егó женúться they made him marry.

принес|тú, ý, ёшь, *past* ~, ~лá, *pf.* (*of* приносúть) **1.** to bring (*also fig.*); to fetch; п. обрáтно to bring back; ~лá тебя, *etc.*, нелёгкая! why the devil did you, *etc.*, have to turn up?; п. благодáрность to express gratitude, tender thanks; п. жáлобу (на+ *a.*) to bring, lodge a complaint (against); п. счáстье to bring luck; п. в жéртву to sacrifice. **2.** to bear, yield; to bring in; п. плоды́ to bear fruit, yield fruit; нáша кóшка ~лá шесть котя́т our cat had six kittens; п. большóй дохóд to bring in big revenue, show a large return; п. пóльзу to be of use, be of benefit.

принес|тúсь, ýсь, ёшься, *past* ~ся, ~лáсь, *pf.* (*of* приносúться) (*coll.*) **1.** to come tearing along. **2.** *pass. of* ~тú; (*of sounds, etc.*) to be borne along.

принижá|ть, ю, *impf. of* принúзить.

принижéни|е, я, *n.* disparagement, belittling, depreciation.

принú|женный, *p.p.p. of* ~зить *and adj.* humbled, submissive.

принú|зить, жу, зишь, *pf.* (*of* ~жáть) **1.** to humble, humiliate. **2.** to disparage, belittle, depreciate; п. значéние морскóго флóта to belittle the importance of the Navy.

приник|áть, áю, *impf. of* ~нуть.

принú|кнуть, ну, нешь, *past* ~, ~ла, *pf.* (*of* ~áть) (к) to press oneself (against), press oneself close (to); to nestle up (against); п. ýхом к замóчной скважине to put one's ear to the keyhole.

принимá|ть, ю, *impf.* **1.** *impf. of* приня́ть.

2. (*impf. only*) to be 'at home', entertain; to receive (*guests, visitors, patients*); онú ~ют по четвергáм they are 'at home' on Thursdays; онá чáсто ~ет she does a lot of entertaining; дóктор Петрóв сегóдня не ~ет Doctor Petrov does not see patients today. **3.** to deliver (*at birth of child*).

принимá|ться, юсь, *impf. of* приня́ться.

принорáвлива|ть(ся), ю(сь), *impf. of* приноровúть(ся).

приноров|úть, лю́, úшь, *pf.* (*of* принорáвливать) (*coll.*) to fit, adapt, adjust; п. переéзд на нóвую квартúру к лéтним канúкулам to arrange a move to new lodgings to fit in with the summer holidays.

приноров|úться, лю́сь, úшься, *pf.* (*of* принорáвливаться) (к; *coll.*) to adapt oneself (to), accommodate oneself (to).

прино|сúть(ся), шý(сь), ~сишь(ся), *impf. of* принестú(сь).

приношéни|е, я, *n.* gift, offering.

принудú|тельный (~ен, ~ьна), *adj.* **1.** compulsory, forced, coercive; ~ьные рабóты forced labour, hard labour; п. сбор levy. **2.** (*tech.*) forced; positive; ~ьное движéние positive motion; ~ьная перемéна хóда positive reversing; ~ьная подáча forced feed; positive feed.

прину́|дить, жу, дишь, *pf.* (*of* ~ждáть) to force, compel, coerce, constrain.

принуждá|ть, ю, *impf. of* прину́дить.

принуждéни|е, я, *n.* compulsion, coercion, constraint; по ~ю under compulsion, under duress.

принуждённост|ь, и, *f.* constraint; stiffness.

принуждённый, *p.p.p. of* прину́дить *and adj.* constrained, forced; п. смех forced laughter.

принц, а, *m.* prince (*other than a Russian* князь).

принцéсс|а, ы, *f.* princess.

прúнцип, а, *m.* principle; в ~е in principle, theoretically; из ~а on principle.

принципáл, а, *m.* (*obs.*) principal, head.

принципáт, а, *m.* (*hist.*) principate.

принципиáльно, *adv.* **1.** on principle; on a question of principle. **2.** in principle.

принципиáльност|ь, и, *f.* adherence to principle(s).

принципиáл|ьный (~ен, ~ьна), *adj.* **1.** of principle; based on, guided by principle; п. вопрóс question of principle; п. человéк man of principle; ~ьное разноглáсие disagreement on a question of principle; имéть ~ьное значéние to be a matter of principle; поднять вопрóс на ~ьную высотý to make a question a matter of principle. **2.** in principle; general; онú дáли ~ьное соглáсие they consented in principle.

принюх|аться, аюсь, *pf.* (*of* ~иваться) (к; *coll.*) to get used to the smell (of).

принюхива|ться, юсь, *impf. of* принюхаться.

приняти|е, я, *n.* **1.** taking; taking up, assumption; п. пищи taking of food; п. присяги taking of the oath; п. поста taking up a post. **2.** acceptance. **3.** admission, admittance; п. гражданства naturalization.

принят|ый, *p.p.p. of* принять; ~о it is accepted, it is usual; не ~о it is not done.

при|нять, му, ~мешь, *past* ~нял, ~няла, ~няло, *pf.* (*of* ~нимать) **1.** (*in var. senses*) to take; to accept; п. ванну to take, have a bath; п. гражданство to be naturalized; п. британское гражданство to take British citizenship, become a British citizen; п. крещение to be baptized; п. лекарство to take medicine; п. меры to take measures; п. меры предосторожности to take precautions; п. монашество to take monastic vows, become a monk; to take the veil; п. намерение to form the intention; п. подарок to accept a present; п. присягу to take the oath; п. решение to take, reach, come to a decision; п. товары to take receipt of goods; ~мите моё сочувствие accept my condolences; п. участие (в+*p.*) to take part (in); participate (in), partake (in, of); п. христианство to adopt, embrace Christianity; п. во внимание, п. в расчёт, п. к сведению to take into consideration, take into account, take cognizance (of); не п. во внимание, не п. к сведению to disregard; не п. в расчёт to discount, fail to take account of; п. в шутку to take as a joke; п. всерьёз to take seriously; п. за правило to make it a rule; п. (близко) к сердцу to take, lay to heart; п. что-н. на свой счёт to take something as referring to oneself; п. на себя to take upon oneself; п. на себя обязательство to assume an obligation, take on a commitment; п. на себя труд (+*inf.*) to undertake the labour (of); п. под расписку to sign for. **2.** to take up (*a post, a command, etc.*); to take over; п. новое назначение to take up a new appointment; п. командование (+*i.*) to take command (of), assume command (of, over); п. дивизию to take up command of a division; п. духовный сан to take holy orders; п. дела (от) to take over duties (from). **3.** to accept; п. бой to accept battle; п. закон to pass a law; п. законопроект to approve a bill; п. оправдания to accept excuses; п. предложение to accept an offer; to accept a proposal; п. резолюцию to pass, adopt, carry a resolution; п. совет to take advice; п. как должное to

accept as one's due, take as a matter of course. **4.** (в, на+*a.*) to admit (to); to accept (for); п. в партию to admit to a party; п. в школу to admit to, accept for a school; п. на службу to accept for a job; п. в гражданство to grant citizenship. **5.** (*see also* ~нимать) to receive; п. больных, гостей, делегацию to receive patients, guests, a delegation; они ~няли нас радушно they gave us a warm welcome, a cordial reception; п. в штыки (*coll.*) to meet with the point of the bayonet. **6.** to assume, take (on); п. весёлый вид to assume an air of gaiety; болезнь ~няла серьёзный характер the illness assumed a grave character; переговоры ~няли благоприятный оборот the talks took a favourable turn. **7.** (+*a.* за+*a.*) to take (for); по акценту я ~нял вас за шотландца I took you for a Scotsman by your accent. **8.** to move; п. в сторону (*mil.*) to execute a side step; ~ми к стороне! stand aside!, make way! **9.** (*coll.*) to remove, take away; ~мите руки прочь! take your hands off!

при|няться, мусь, ~мешься, *past* ~нялся, ~нялась, *pf.* (*of* ~ниматься) **1.** (+*inf.*) to begin; to start. **2.** (за+*a.*) to set (to), get down (to); п. за работу to set to work; п. за чтение to get down to reading. **3.** (за+*a.*; *coll.*) to take in hand. **4.** (*of plants*) to strike root, take root; (*of injections*) to take.

приободр|ить, ю, ишь, *pf.* (*of* ~ять) to cheer up, encourage, hearten.

приободр|иться, юсь, ишься, *pf.* (*of* ~яться) to cheer up, feel more cheerful, feel happier.

приободр|ять(ся), яю(сь), *impf. of* ~ить(ся).

приобре|сти, ту, тёшь, *past* ~л, ~ла, *pf.* (*of* ~тать) to acquire, gain; п. опыт to gain experience; п. меланхолический вид to acquire a melancholy look; п. новое значение to acquire a new significance.

приобрета|ть, ю, *impf. of* приобрести.

приобретени|е, я, *n.* **1.** acquisition, acquiring. **2.** acquisition, gain; (*fig., coll.*) bargain; 'a find'.

приобща|ть(ся), яю(сь), *impf. of* ~ить(ся).

приобщ|ить, у, ишь, *pf.* (*of* ~ать) **1.** (к) to introduce (to), associate (with); п. приёмного сына к семейной жизни to introduce an adopted son to family life. **2.** to join, attach; п. к делу to file. **3.** (*eccl.*) to administer the sacrament (to), communicate.

приобщ|иться, усь, ишься, *pf.* (*of* ~аться) **1.** (к) to join (in); п. к общественной жизни to join in social life. **2.** (*eccl.*) to communicate (*intrans.*).

приоде|ть, ну, нешь, *pf.* (*coll.*) to dress up, deck out.

приодé|ться, нусь, нешься, *pf.* (*coll.*) to dress up, get oneself up.

приозёрный, *adj.* lakeside, lakeland.

прио́р, а, *m.* (*eccl.*) prior.

приоритéт, а, *m.* priority.

приоса́нива|ться, юсь, *impf. of* приоса́ниться.

приоса́н|иться, юсь, ишься, *pf.* (*coll.*) to assume a dignified air.

приостана́влива|ть(ся), ю(сь), *impf. of* приостанови́ть(ся).

приостанов|и́ть, лю́, ⌐ишь, *pf.* (*of* приостана́вливать) to call a halt (to), suspend, check; п. исполнéние пригово́ра to suspend sentence.

приостанов|и́ться, лю́сь, ⌐и́шься, *pf.* (*of* приостана́вливаться) to halt, come to a halt; выступа́я с рéчью, п. to pause in making a speech.

приостано́вк|а, и, *f.* halt, suspension; п. исполнéния пригово́ра suspension of sentence; п. рабо́т stoppage (*of work*).

приотвор|и́ть, ю́, ⌐ишь, *pf.* (*of* ⌐я́ть) to open slightly, half-open; п. дверь to set a door ajar.

приотвор|и́ться, ⌐и́тся, *pf.* (*of* ⌐я́ться) to open slightly, half-open.

приотвор|я́ть(ся), я́ю(сь), *impf. of* ⌐и́ть(ся).

приоткрыва́|ть(ся), ю(сь), *impf. of* приоткры́ть(ся).

приоткр|ы́ть(ся), о́ю(сь), о́ешь(ся), *pf.* = приотвори́ть(ся).

приохо́|тить, чу, тишь, *pf.* (к; *coll.*) to give a taste (for).

приохо́|титься, чусь, тишься, *pf.* (к; *coll.*) to acquire a taste (for), take (to).

припада́|ть, ю, *impf.* 1. *impf. of* припа́сть[1]. 2. (*impf. only*) to be slightly lame; п. на лéвую но́гу to be lame in the left leg.

припа́д|ок, ка, *m.* fit; attack; paroxysm; нéрвный п. attack of nerves; сердéчный п. heart attack; эпилепти́ческий п. epileptic fit; п. бéшенства paroxysm of rage.

припа́дочн|ый, *adj.* subject to fits; ⌐ые явлéния fits; *as noun* п., ⌐ого, *m.* epileptic.

припа́ива|ть, ю, *impf. of* припая́ть.

припа́йк|а, и, *f.* soldering; brazing.

припа́рк|а, и, *f.* (*med.*) poultice; fomentation; приложи́ть ⌐у (+*d.*) to poultice, foment.

припас|а́ть, а́ю, *impf. of* ⌐ти́.

припас|ти́, у́, ёшь, *past* ⌐, ⌐ла́, *pf.* (*of* ⌐а́ть) (+*a. or g.*; *coll.*) to store, lay in, lay up; п. консéрвов to lay in tinned food.

припа́|сть[1], ду́, дёшь, *past* ⌐л, *pf.* (*of* ⌐да́ть) (к) to press oneself (to), fall down (before); п. к чьим-н. нога́м to prostrate oneself before someone; п. у́хом to press one's ear (to).

припа́|сть[2], дёт, *past* ⌐л, *pf.* (*coll., obs.*) to appear, show itself.

припа́с|ы, ов, *no sing.* stores, supplies; боевы́е п. ammunition; воéнные п. munitions; съестны́е п. provisions, victuals.

припа́хива|ть, ет, *impf.* (*coll.*) to stink.

припая́|ть, ю, *pf.* (*of* припа́ивать) (к) to solder (to); to braze (to); (*fig., coll.*) ему́ ⌐ли пять лет he was sentenced to five years.

припéв, а, *m.* refrain, burden.

припева́|ть, ю, *impf.* to hum; жить ⌐ючи (*coll.*) to live in clover.

припёк[1], а, *m.* surplus (*excess in weight of loaf when baked over that of flour used*).

припёк[2], а, *m.*; на ⌐e (*coll.*) right in the sun, exposed to the full heat of the sun.

припёк|а, и, *f.* сбо́ку п. (*coll.*) for no reason at all.

припека́|ть, ет, *impf.* (*coll.*) (*of the sun*) to be very hot.

при|перéть, пру́, прёшь, *past* ⌐пёр, ⌐пёрла, *pf.* (*of* ⌐пира́ть) 1. (к) to press (against); п. стул к двéри, п. дверь сту́лом to put a chair against the door; п. кого́-н. к стéнке (*fig., coll.*) to drive someone into a corner, put someone in a spot. 2. (*coll.*) to set ajar. 3. (*sl.*) to barge in, roll up.

припеча́т|ать, аю, *pf.* (*of* ⌐ывать) (*coll.*) to seal; п. сургучо́м to apply sealing-wax (to).

припеча́тыва|ть, ю, *impf. of* припеча́тать.

припира́|ть, ю, *impf. of* приперéть.

припи|са́ть, шу́, ⌐шешь, *pf.* (*of* ⌐сывать) 1. to add (*to something written*). 2. (к) to attach (to), register (at). 3. (+*d.*) to attribute (to); to ascribe (to); to put down (to), impute (to); п. стихотворéние Эсхи́лу to attribute a poem to Aeschylus; п. неуда́чу лéности to put a failure down to laziness.

припи́ск|а, и, *f.* 1. addition; postscript; п. к завеща́нию (*leg.*) codicil. 2. attaching, registration; порт ⌐и (*naut.*) port of registration.

приписно́й, *adj.* attached; on the establishment.

припи́сыва|ть, ю, *impf. of* приписа́ть.

припла́т|а, ы, *f.* additional payment.

припла|ти́ть, чу́, ⌐тишь, *pf.* (*of* ⌐чивать) to pay in addition.

припла́чива|ть, ю, *impf. of* приплати́ть.

припле|сти́, ту́, тёшь, *past* ⌐л, ⌐ла́, *pf.* (*of* ⌐та́ть) 1. to plait in. 2. (*fig., coll.*) to drag in; ра́зве бы́ло необходи́мо п. моё и́мя? was it really necessary to drag my name in?

припле|сти́сь, ту́сь, тёшься, *past* ⌐лся, ⌐ла́сь *pf.* to drag oneself along.

приплета́|ть, ю, *impf. of* приплести́.

припло́д, а, *m.* issue, increase (*of animals*).

приплыва́|ть, ю, *impf. of* приплы́ть.

приплы́|ть, ву́, вёшь, *past* ~л, ~ла́, ~ло, *pf.* (*of* ~ва́ть) to swim up; to sail up; п. к бе́регу to reach the shore.

приплю́снут|ый, *p.p.p. of* ~ь *and adj.* п. нос flat nose.

приплю́сн|уть, у, ешь, *pf.* (*of* приплю́щивать) to flatten.

приплюс|ова́ть, у́ю, *pf.* (*of* ~о́вывать) (*coll.*) to add on.

приплюсо́вывa|ть, ю, *impf. of* приплюсова́ть.

приплю́щивa|ть, ю, *impf. of* приплю́снуть.

припл773сывa|ть, ю, *impf.* to dance, hop, trip, skip; идти́ ~я по тротуа́ру to trip along the pavement.

приподнимá|ть(ся), ю(сь), *impf. of* приподня́ть(ся).

припо́днятост|ь, и, *f.* elation; animation.

припо́дн|ятый, *p.p.p. of* ~я́ть *and adj.* elated; animated; uplifted.

приподн|я́ть, иму́, и́мешь, *past* ~я́л, ~яла́, ~я́ло, *pf.* (*of* ~има́ть) to raise slightly; to lift slightly.

приподн|я́ться, иму́сь, и́мешься, *past* ~я́лся, ~яла́сь, *pf.* (*of* ~има́ться) to raise oneself (a little); п. на ло́кте to raise oneself on one's elbow; п. на цы́почках to stand on tiptoe; п. на носки́ to rise on one's toes.

припо́|й, я, *m.* solder; кре́пкий п. brazing solder.

приполз|а́ть, а́ю, *impf. of* ~ти́.

приполз|ти́, у́, ёшь, *past* ~, ~ла́, *pf.* (*of* ~а́ть) to creep up, crawl up.

приполя́рный, *adj.* polar.

припоминá|ть, ю, *impf. of* припо́мнить.

припо́м|нить, ню, нишь, *pf.* (*of* ~ина́ть) 1. to remember, recollect, recall; сму́тно п. to have a hazy recollection (of). 2. (+*d.*) to remind; я э́то тебе́ ~ню! (*coll.*) you won't forget this!; I'll get even with you for this!

припра́в|а, ы, *f.* relish, condiment, flavouring, seasoning, dressing; п. к сала́ту salad dressing.

припра́в|ить[1], лю, ишь, *pf.* (*of* ~ля́ть) (+*i.*) to season (with), flavour (with), dress (with).

припра́в|ить[2], лю, ишь, *pf.* (*of* ~ля́ть) (*typ.*) to make ready.

припра́вк|а, и, *f.* (*typ.*) making ready.

приправля́|ть, ю, *impf. of* приправить.

припры́гива|ть, ю, *impf.* (*coll.*) to hop, skip.

припря́|тать, чу, чешь, *pf.* (*of* ~тывать) (*coll.*) to secrete, put by (*for further use*).

припря́тыва|ть, ю, *impf. of* припря́тать.

припу́гива|ть, ю, *impf. of* припугну́ть.

припуг|ну́ть, ну́, нёшь, *pf.* (*of* ~ивать) (*coll.*) to intimidate, scare.

припу́дрива|ть(ся), ю(сь), *impf. of* припу́дрить(ся).

припу́др|ить, ю, ишь, *pf.* (*of* ~ивать) 1. to powder. 2. (*tech.*) to dust.

припу́др|иться, юсь, ишься, *pf.* (*of* ~иваться) to powder oneself.

при́пуск, а, *m.* (*tech.*) allowance, margin; п. на уса́дку shrinkage allowance; оста́вить п. (на+*a.*) to allow (for).

припуска́|ть, ю, *impf. of* припусти́ть.

припу|сти́ть, щу́, ~стишь, *pf.* (*of* ~ска́ть) 1. (к) to put (to) (*for coupling or feeding*); п. телёнка к коро́ве to put a calf to the cow. 2. (*tailoring*) to let out. 3. (*coll.*) to urge on. 4. (*coll.*) to quicken one's pace. 5. (*coll.*; *of rain*) to come down harder.

припу́т|ать, аю, *pf.* (*of* ~ывать) 1. to tie on, fasten. 2. (к; *fig., coll.*) to drag in (to), implicate (in).

припу́тыва|ть, ю, *impf. of* припу́тать.

припух|а́ть, а́ет, *impf. of* ~нуть.

припу́хлост|ь, и, *f.* (slight) swelling.

припу́хлый, *adj.* (slightly) swollen.

припу́х|нуть, нет, *past* ~, ~ла, *pf.* (*of* ~а́ть) to swell up a little.

прираба́тыва|ть, ю, *impf. of* прирабо́тать.

прирабо́та|ть, ю, *pf.* (*of* прираба́тывать) to earn extra, earn in addition.

при́работ|ок, ка, *m.* extra earnings, additional earnings.

прира́внива|ть, ю, *impf. of* приравня́ть.

приравн|я́ть, я́ю, *pf.* (*of* ~ивать) (к) to equate (with); to place on the same footing (as).

прираст|а́ть, а́ю, *impf. of* ~и́.

прираст|и́, у́, ёшь, *past* приро́с, приросла́, *pf.* (*of* ~а́ть) 1. (к) to adhere (to); (*of a graft*) to take; п. к ме́сту, п. к земле́ (*fig.*) to become rooted to the spot, to the ground. 2. to increase; to accrue.

прираще́ни|е, я, *n.* 1. increase, increment. 2. (*ling.*) augment.

приревн|ова́ть, у́ю, *pf.* (к) to be jealous (of); она́ ~ова́ла му́жа к свое́й прия́тельнице she was jealous of her husband's interest in her friend.

прирез|а́ть, а́ю, *impf. of* ~ать[2].

прире́|зать[1], жу, жешь, *pf.* (*of* ~зывать) (*coll.*) to kill; to cut the throat (of).

прире́|зать[2], жу, жешь, *pf.* (*of* ~зать *and* ~зывать) to add on; п. уча́сток к огоро́ду to add on a piece to a garden.

прире́з|ок, ка, *m.* additional piece.

приреза́зыва|ть, ю, *impf. of* приреза́ть.

прире́льсовый, *adj.* adjoining the (railway) line.

приречный, *adj.* riverside, riverain.

приро́д|а, ы, *f.* 1. nature; мёртвая п. the inorganic world; зако́н ~ы law of nature; отда́ть долг ~е (*i*) (*rhet.*) to pay the debt to nature, (*ii*) (*coll., euph.*) to answer a call of nature. 2. nature, character; от ~ы by nature, congenitally; по ~e by nature, naturally; э́то в ~е веще́й it is in the nature of things.

приро́дн|ый, *adj.* 1. natural; ~ые бога́тства natural resources; п. газ natural gas. 2. born; п. англича́нин an Englishman by birth. 3. inborn, innate; п. ум native wit.

природове́д, а, *m.* natural historian, naturalist.

природове́дени|е, я, *n.* natural history.

прирождённый, *adj.* 1. inborn, innate. 2. a born; п. лгун a born liar.

прирост, а, *m.* increase, growth.

прирост|ок, ка, *m.* (*bot.*; *coll.*) growth, excrescence.

прирубе́жный, *adj.* situated near the frontier, near the border.

прируч|а́ть, а́ю, *impf. of* ~и́ть.

приручéни|е, я, *n.* taming, domestication.

прируч|и́ть, у́, и́шь, *pf.* (*of* ~а́ть) to tame (*also fig.*); to domesticate.

приса́жива|ться, юсь, *impf. of* присе́сть.

приса́лива|ть, ю, *impf. of* присоли́ть.

приса́сыва|ться, юсь, *impf. of* присоса́ться.

присва́ива|ть, ю, *impf. of* присво́ить.

при́свист, а, *m.* 1. whistle. 2. sibilance, hissing in one's speech.

присви́стыва|ть, ю, *impf.* 1. to whistle. 2. to sibilate.

присвоéни|е, я, *n.* 1. appropriation; незако́нное п. misappropriation. 2. awarding, conferment.

присво́|ить, ю, ишь, *pf.* (*of* присва́ивать) 1. to appropriate; незако́нно п. сре́дства to misappropriate funds. 2. (+*a. and d.*) to give, award, confer; п. и́мя (+*d. and g.*) to name (after); ему́ ~или сте́пень до́ктора he has been given the degree of Doctor, a doctorate has been conferred upon him; моско́вскому метро́ ~ено и́мя Ле́нина the Moscow Underground (*railway*) was named after Lenin.

приседа́ни|е, я, *n.* 1. squatting. 2. (*obs.*) curts(e)y.

приседа́|ть, ю, *impf. of* присе́сть.

присе́ст, а, *m.* в оди́н п., за оди́н п. (*coll.*) at one sitting, at a stretch.

при|се́сть, ся́ду, ся́дешь, *past* ~се́л, *pf.* 1. (*impf.* ~са́живаться) to sit down, take a seat. 2. (*impf.* ~седа́ть) to squat; (*in fright*) to cower. 3. (*impf.* ~седа́ть) to curts(e)y, drop curts(e)ys.

при́сказк|а, и, *f.* (*story-teller's*) introduction; flourish, embellishment (*of a story*).

приска|ка́ть, чу́, ~чешь, *pf.* 1. to come galloping, arrive at a gallop; (*fig.*, *coll.*) to rush, tear. 2. to hop, come hopping.

прискорби|е, я, *n.* sorrow, regret; к моему́ ~ю to my regret; мы с глубо́ким ~ем извеща́ем о сме́рти (+*g.*) (*formula of*

obituary notices) we announce with deep regret the death (of).

прискорб|ный (~ен, ~на), *adj.* regrettable, lamentable, deplorable.

приску́ч|ить, у, ишь, *pf.* (+*d.*; *coll.*) to bore, tire, weary.

при|сла́ть, шлю́, шлёшь, *pf.* (*of* ~сыла́ть) to send, dispatch.

присло́вь|е, я, *n.* 1. (*coll.*) saying (*introduced into a speech, etc.*). 2. (*gram.*; *obs.*) inseparable particle (*e.g.* -то, -ка).

прислон|и́ть, ю́, ~и́шь, *pf.* (*of* ~я́ть) (к) to lean (against), rest (against).

прислон|и́ться, ю́сь, ~и́шься, *pf.* (*of* ~я́ться) (к) to lean (against), rest (against).

прислон|я́ть(ся), я́ю(сь), *impf. of* ~и́ть(ся).

прислу́г|а, и, *f.* 1. maid, servant. 2. (*collect.*; *obs.*) servants, domestics. 3. (*mil.*) crew; оруди́йная п. gun crew.

прислу́жива|ть, ю, *impf.* (+*d.*; *obs.*) to wait (upon), attend.

прислу́жива|ться, юсь, *impf. of* прислужи́ться.

прислуж|и́ться, у́сь, ~ишься, *pf.* (*of* ~иваться) (к; *obs.*) to worm oneself into the favour (of), fawn (upon), cringe (to).

прислу́жник, а, *m.* 1. (*obs.*) servant. 2. (*coll.*) lickspittle; underling.

прислу́жничеств|о, а, *n.* subservience, servility.

прислу́ш|аться, аюсь, *pf.* (*of* ~иваться) (к) 1. to listen (to). 2. (*fig.*) to listen (to), lend an ear (to); to heed, pay attention (to); п. к чьему́-н. сове́ту to listen to someone's advice. 3. (*coll.*) to accustom one's ear (to), become accustomed to the sound (of); мы уже́ ~ались к ночно́му у́личному движе́нию we are now accustomed to the (noise of) traffic at night.

прислу́шива|ться, юсь, *impf. of* прислу́шаться.

присма́трива|ть(ся), ю(сь), *impf. of* присмотре́ть(ся).

присмире́|ть, ю, *pf.* to grow quiet.

присмо́тр, а, *m.* care, looking after, tending; supervision, surveillance.

присмотр|е́ть, ю́, ~ишь, *pf.* (*of* присма́тривать) 1. (за+*i.*) to look after, keep an eye (on); to supervise, superintend; п. за ребёнком to mind the baby. 2. (*coll.*) to look for; п. себе́ рабо́ту to look for a job.. 3. *pf. only* to find.

присмотр|е́ться, ю́сь, ~ишься, *pf.* (*of* присма́триваться) (к) 1. to look closely (at); п. к кому́-н. to size someone up, take someone's measure. 2. to get accustomed (to), get used (to).

присн|и́ться, ю́сь, и́шься, *pf. of* сни́ться.

приснопа́мятный, *adj.* (*rhet.*) memorable, unforgettable.

при́сн|ый, *adj.* **1.** (*obs.*) eternal, everlasting. **2.** *as noun* ые, ~ых (*coll.*) associates; ты и твой ~ые you and your gang, you and your mates.

присове́т|овать, ую, *pf.* = посове́товать.

присовокуп|и́ть, лю́, и́шь, *pf.* (*of* ~ля́ть) to add; to say in addition; п. бума́гу к де́лу to file a paper.

присовокупля́|ть, ю, *impf. of* присовокупи́ть.

присоедине́ни|е, я, *n.* **1.** addition. **2.** (*polit.*) annexation, joining. **3.** (к) joining, associating oneself (with), adhesion (to). **4.** (*electr.*) connexion.

присоедини́тельный, *adj.* (*gram.*) connective.

присоедин|и́ть, ю́, и́шь, *pf.* (*of* ~я́ть) **1.** to add; to join. **2.** (*polit.*) to annex, join. **3.** (*electr.*) to connect.

присоедин|и́ться, ю́сь, и́шься, *pf.* (*of* ~я́ться) (к) **1.** to join; пора́ нам п. к остальны́м it is time we joined the others. **2.** (*fig.*) to join, associate oneself (with); п. к мне́нию to subscribe to an opinion.

присоедин|я́ть(ся), я́ю(сь), *impf. of* ~и́ть(ся).

присол|и́ть, ю́, ~и́шь, *pf.* (*of* приса́ливать) (*coll.*) to salt, add a pinch of salt (to).

присос|а́ться, у́сь, ёшься, *pf.* (*of* приса́сываться) (к) to stick (to), attach oneself (to) by suction; (*fig.*, *pejor.*) to fasten on (to).

присосе́|диться, жусь, ди́шься, *pf.* (к; *coll.*) to sit down next (to).

присо́ск|а, и, *f.* (*biol.*, *zool.*) sucker.

присо́х|нуть, нет, *past* ~, ~ла, *pf.* (*of* присыха́ть) (к) to adhere (in drying) (to); to stick (to), dry (on).

приспева́|ть, ю, *impf. of* приспе́ть.

приспе́|ть, ю, *pf.* (*of* ~ва́ть) (*coll.*; *of time*) to come, draw nigh, be ripe.

приспе́шник, а, *m.* stooge, myrmidon.

приспи́ч|ить, ит, *pf.* (*impers.*+*d. and inf.*; *coll.*) to feel, have an urge (to); to be impatient (to); им ~ило уходи́ть they were impatient to be off.

приспоса́блива|ть(ся), ю(сь), *impf.* = приспособля́ть(ся).

приспосо́б|ить, лю, ишь, *pf.* (*of* ~ля́ть) to fit, adjust, adapt, accommodate; п. шко́лу под больни́цу to adapt a school as a hospital.

приспосо́б|иться, люсь, ишься, *pf.* (*of* ~ля́ться) **1.** (к) to adapt oneself (to), accommodate oneself (to). **2.** *pass. of* ~ить.

приспособле́н|ец, ца, *m.* time-server.

приспособле́ни|е, я, *n.* **1.** adaptation, accommodation; п. к кли́мату acclimatization. **2.** device, contrivance, contraption; appliance, gadget.

приспосо́бленност|ь, и, *f.* fitness, suitability.

приспособле́нческий, *adj.* time-serving.

приспособле́нчеств|о, а, *n.* time-serving.

приспособля́емост|ь, и, *f.* adaptability.

приспособля́|ть(ся), ю(сь), *impf. of* приспосо́бить(ся).

приспуска́|ть, ю, *impf. of* приспусти́ть.

приспу|сти́ть, щу́, ~стишь, *pf.* (*of* ~ска́ть) to lower a little; п. флаг to lower a flag to half-mast; (*naut.*) to half-mast the colours.

приспу́|щенный, *p.p.p. of* ~сти́ть; ~щенные фла́ги flags at half-mast.

при́став, а, *pl.* ~а́, *m.* (*hist.*) police-officer; становой п. district superintendent of police; суде́бный п. bailiff.

пристава́ни|е, я, *n.* pestering, bothering.

приста|ва́ть, ю́, ёшь, *impf. of* приста́ть.

приста́в|ить, лю, ишь, *pf.* (*of* ~ля́ть) **1.** (к) to put (to, against), place (to, against), set (to, against), lean (against); п. ле́стницу к стене́ to put a ladder against the wall. **2.** to add (*a piece of material, etc.*). **3.** (к) to appoint to look after; п. проводника́ к иностра́нным тури́стам to appoint a guide to look after foreign tourists.

приста́вк|а, и, *f.* (*gram.*) prefix.

приставля́|ть, ю, *impf. of* приста́вить.

приставн|о́й, *adj.* added, attached; ~а́я ле́стница step ladder.

приста́вочный, *adj.* (*gram.*) **1.** of a prefix. **2.** having a prefix.

при́стально, *adv.* fixedly, intently; п. смотре́ть (на+*a.*) to look fixedly, intently (at); to stare (at), gaze (at).

при́стал|ьный (~ен, ~ьна), *adj.* fixed, intent; п. взгляд fixed, intent look; stare, gaze; с ~ьным внима́нием intently.

приста́нищ|е, а, *n.* refuge, shelter, asylum.

пристанцио́нный, *adj.* station.

при́стан|ь, и, *pl.* ~и, ~е́й, *f.* **1.** landing--stage, jetty; pier; wharf. **2.** (*obs.*) refuge, asylum. **3.** (*fig.*, *poet.*) haven.

приста́|ть, ну, нешь, *pf.* (*of* ~ва́ть) **1.** (к) to stick (to), adhere (to). **2.** (к) to join, attach oneself (to); п. к гру́ппе экскурса́н-тов to join a party of excursionists; ко мне ~ла чужа́я соба́ка someone's dog attached itself to me. **3.** (к; *fig.*, *coll.*; *of infectious disease*) to be passed on (to); к де́тям ~ла ветряна́я о́спа the children have picked up chickenpox. **4.** (к) to pester, bother, badger; п. с предложе́ниями to pester with suggestions. **5.** (к; *naut.*) to put in (to), come alongside. **6.** *pf. only* (*impers.*+*d.*; *coll.*) to befit; не ~ло тебе́ так говори́ть you ought not to speak like that. **7.** *pf. only* (+*d.*; *coll.*) to become, suit.

пристёгива|ть, ю, *impf. of* пристегну́ть.

пристег|ну́ть, ну́, нёшь, *pf.* (*of* ~ивать) **1.** to fasten; to button up. **2.** (*fig.*, *coll.*) to drag in.

пристежн|о́й, *adj.* fastening (*as opp. to sewn on*); руба́шка с ~ы́м воротничко́м shirt with separate collar.

присто́йност|ь, и, *f.* decency, propriety, decorum.

присто́|йный (~ен, ~йна), *adj.* decent, proper, decorous, becoming, seemly.

пристра́ива|ть(ся), ю(сь), *impf. of* пристро́ить(ся).

пристра́сти|е¹, я, *n.* (к) **1.** weakness (for), predilection (for); passion (for); у неё п. к верхово́й езде́ she has a passion for riding. **2.** partiality (for, towards), bias (towards); вы́казать п. to show partiality.

пристра́сти|е², я, *n.* допро́с с ~ем (*hist. and fig., joc.*) interrogation under torture.

пристра|сти́ть, щу́, сти́шь, *pf.* (к; *coll.*) to give one an impulse (to), make keen (on); его́ докла́д ~сти́л меня́ к заня́тиям по исто́рии Индии his talk made me keen on studying the history of India.

пристра|сти́ться, щу́сь, сти́шься, *pf.* (к) to take (to); to conceive a liking (for).

пристра́стност|ь, и, *f.* partiality, bias.

пристра́ст|ный (~ен, ~на), *adj.* partial, biassed.

пристра́чива|ть, ю, *impf. of* пристрочи́ть.

пристращ|а́ть, а́ю, *pf.* (*of* ~ивать) (*coll.*) to intimidate.

пристра́щива|ть, ю, *impf. of* пристраща́ть.

пристре́лива|ть, ю, *impf. of* пристрели́ть *and* пристреля́ть.

пристре́лива|ться, юсь, *impf. of* пристреля́ться.

пристрел|и́ть, ю́, ~ишь, *pf.* (*of* ~ивать) to shoot (down).

пристре́лк|а, и, *f.* (*mil.*) adjustment (of fire), ranging; fire for adjustment; п. ви́лки bracketing for range; п. репе́ра registration; вести́ ~у to find the range.

пристре́лочн|ый, *adj.* (*mil.*) ranging; registering; п. ориенти́р registration point; ~ое ору́дие registration gun; п. снаря́д projectile with spotting charge.

пристре́льный, *adj.* (*mil.*) п. ого́нь straddling fire.

пристре́л|янный, *p.p.p. of* ~я́ть *and adj.* (*mil.*) adjusted.

пристрел|я́ть, я́ю, *pf.* (*of* ~ивать) (*mil.*) to adjust.

пристрел|я́ться, я́юсь, *pf.* (*of* ~ива́ться) (*mil.*) to adjust fire; to find the range.

пристро́|ить, ю, ишь, *pf.* (*of* пристра́ивать) **1.** (к) to add (*to a building*), build on (to). **2.** (*coll.*) to place, settle, fix up; п. кого́-н. на слу́жбу to settle someone in a job. **3.** (к; *mil.*) to join up (with), form up (with).

пристро́|иться, юсь, ишься, *pf.* (*of* пристра́иваться) **1.** (*coll.*) to be placed, be settled, be fixed up, get a place; он ~и́лся

в конто́ру he has got a place in an office. **2.** (к; *mil.*) to join up (with), form up (with); (*aeron.*) to take up formation (with).

пристро́йк|а, и, *f.* annexe, extension; outhouse; lean-to.

пристроч|и́ть, у́, ~и́шь, *pf.* (*of* пристра́чивать) (к) to sew on (to).

приструни́ва|ть, ю, *impf. of* приструни́ть.

пристру́н|ить, ю, ишь, *pf.* (*of* ~ивать) (*coll.*) to have in hand.

присту́кива|ть, ю, *impf. of* присту́кнуть.

присту́к|нуть¹, ну, нешь, *pf.* (*of* ~ивать) (+*i.*; *coll.*) to tap; п. каблука́ми to tap one's heels.

присту́к|нуть², ну, нешь, *pf.* (*of* ~ивать) (*coll.*) to club to death; to kill (*with a blow*).

при́ступ, а, *m.* **1.** (*mil.*) assault, storm; пойти́ на п. to go in to the assault; взять ~ом to take by storm. **2.** fit, attack; bout, touch; п. бо́ли pang; paroxysm; п. гне́ва fit of temper; п. гри́ппа bout of influenza; п. ка́шля fit, bout of coughing. **3.** (*fig., coll.*) access; к нему́ ~у нет he is inaccessible, unapproachable; к э́той мате́рии ~у нет this material is out of the question (= *is too expensive*).

приступ|а́ть(ся), а́ю(сь), *impf. of* ~и́ть(ся).

приступ|и́ть, лю́, ~ишь, *pf.* (*of* ~а́ть) (к) **1.** (*obs.*) to approach; (*fig.*) to importune, pester. **2.** to set about, get down (to), start; п. к де́лу to set to work, get down to business.

приступ|и́ться, лю́сь, ~ишься, *pf.* (*of* ~а́ться) (к; *coll.*) to approach, accost, go up (to); к нему́ не ~ишься, нельзя́ п. he is inaccessible, unapproachable.

присту́п|ок, ка, *m.* (*coll.*) step.

присты|ди́ть, жу́, ди́шь, *pf. of* стыди́ть.

пристя́жк|а, и, *f.* **1.** в ~е (*of a horse*) in traces. **2.** trace-horse, outrunner.

пристяжн|а́я, о́й, *f.* trace-horse, outrunner.

прису|ди́ть, жу́, ~дишь, *pf.* (*of* ~жда́ть) **1.** (+*a.* к *or* +*a. and d.*) to sentence (to), condemn (to); п. кого́-н. к заключе́нию, п. заключе́ние кому́-н. to sentence someone to imprisonment; п. к штра́фу, п. штраф (+*d.*) to fine, impose a fine (on). **2.** (*leg.; coll.*) to award. **3.** (+*d.*) to award, adjudge (to); to confer (on); ему́ ~ди́ли сте́пень до́ктора a doctorate has been conferred on him.

присужда́|ть, ю, *impf. of* присуди́ть.

присужде́ни|е, я, *n.* awarding, adjudication; conferment.

прису́тственн|ый, *adj.* (*obs.*) п. день working-day; ~ое ме́сто office, work-place; ~ые часы́ office hours, business hours.

прису́тстви|е, я, *n.* **1.** presence; в ~и дете́й in the presence of the children, in front of the children; п. ду́ха presence of mind.

2. (*obs.*) business (of the day). **3.** (*obs.*) office.

присутств|овать, ую, *impf.* (на+*p.*) to be present (at), attend, assist (at).

присут́ств|ующий, *pres. part. act. of* ~овать *and adj.* present; *as noun* ~ующие, ~ующих those present; о ~ующих не говоря́т present company (always) excepted.

прису́щ|ий (~, ~а), *adj.* (+*d.*) inherent (in); characteristic, distinctive; ~ая ей ще́дрость the generosity characteristic of her; неприя́тные ~ие положе́нию после́дствия the disagreeable consequences inherent in the situation.

присчит|а́ть, а́ю, *pf.* (*of* ~ывать) to add on.

присчи́тыва|ть, ю, *impf. of* присчита́ть.

присыла́|ть, ю, *impf. of* присла́ть.

присы́п|ать, лю, лешь, *pf.* (*of* ~а́ть) **1.** (+*a.* or *g.*) to add some more, pour some more. **2.** (+*a.* and *i.*) to sprinkle (with), dust (with).

присып|а́ть, а́ю, *impf. of* ~ать.

присы́пк|а, и, *f.* **1.** sprinkling, dusting. **2.** powder.

присыха́|ть, ю, *impf. of* присо́хнуть.

прися́г|а, и, *f.* oath; oath of allegiance; ло́жная п. perjury; дать ~у to swear; приня́ть ~у to take the oath; привести́ к ~е to swear in, administer the oath (to); под ~ой on oath, under oath.

присяг|а́ть, а́ю, *impf.* (*of* ~ну́ть) (в+*p.*) to swear (to); to take one's oath, swear an oath; п. в ве́рности (+*d.*) to swear allegiance (to).

прися́г|нуть, ну́, нёшь, *pf. of* ~а́ть.

прися́жн|ый, *adj.* **1.** (*leg.*; *obs.*) sworn; п. пове́ренный barrister; п. заседа́тель juror, juryman; *as noun* п., ~ого, *m.* = п. заседа́тель; суд ~ых jury. **2.** (*coll.*) born, inveterate; п. ворчу́н born grumbler.

прита|и́ться, ю́сь, и́шься, *pf.* to hide, conceal oneself.

прита́птыва|ть, ю, *impf.* **1.** *impf. of* притопта́ть. **2.** *impf. only* (*coll.*) to tap (with) one's heels.

прита́скива|ть, ю, *impf. of* притащи́ть.

притач|а́ть, а́ю, *pf.* (*of* ~ивать) (к) to stitch (to), sew on (to).

прита́чива|ть, ю, *impf. of* притача́ть.

притащ|и́ть, у́, ~ишь, *pf.* (*of* прита́скивать) to bring, drag, haul.

притащ|и́ться, у́сь, ~ишься, *pf.* (*coll.*) to drag oneself.

притвор|и́ть, ю́, ~ишь, *pf.* (*of* ~я́ть) to set ajar; to leave not quite shut.

притвор|и́ться¹, ~и́тся, *pf.* (*of* ~я́ться) to be ajar; to be not quite shut.

притвор|и́ться², ю́сь, и́шься, *pf.* (*of* ~я́ться) (+*i.*) to pretend (to be); to feign, simulate; to sham; п. больны́м to pretend to be ill,

feign illness; п. безразли́чным to feign indifference.

притво́р|ный (~ен, ~на), *adj.* pretended, feigned, affected, sham; ~ное неве́жество feigned ignorance; ~ные слёзы crocodile tears.

притво́рств|о, а, *n.* pretence; sham; dissembling.

притво́рщик, а, *m.* **1.** pretender, sham. **2.** dissembler, hypocrite.

притвор|я́ть(ся), я́ю(сь), *impf. of* ~и́ть(ся).

притека́|ть, ю, *impf. of* прите́чь.

при|тере́ть, тру́, трёшь, *past* ~тёр, ~тёрла, *pf.* (*of* ~тира́ть) **1.** to rub in lightly. **2.** (*tech.*) to grind in, lap.

притерп|е́ться, лю́сь, ~ишься, *pf.* (к; *coll.*) to get accustomed (to), get used (to).

притёр|тый, *p.p.p. of* ~е́ть *and adj.*; ~тая про́бка ground-in stopper (*of bottle*); ~тое стекло́ ground glass.

притесне́ни|е, я, *n.* oppression.

притесни́тел|ь, я, *m.* oppressor.

притесни́тел|ьный (~ен, ~ьна), *adj.* oppressive.

притесн|и́ть, ю́, и́шь, *pf.* (*of* ~я́ть) to oppress, keep down.

притесн|я́ть, я́ю, *impf. of* ~и́ть.

прите́|чь, чёт, ку́т, *past* ~к, ~кла́, *pf.* (*of* ~ка́ть) to flow in, pour in (*also fig.*); выраже́ния соболезнова́ния ~кли́ со всех сторо́н messages of sympathy poured in from all sides.

притира́|ть, ю, *impf. of* притере́ть.

прити́скива|ть, ю, *impf. of* притисну́ть.

прити́с|нуть, ну, нешь, *pf.* (*of* ~кивать) (*coll.*) to press, squeeze; п. па́лец две́рью to pinch one's finger in the door.

притих|а́ть, а́ю, *impf. of* ~нуть.

прити́х|нуть, ну, нешь, *past* ~, ~ла, *pf.* (*of* ~а́ть) to quiet down, grow quiet, hush; (*fig.*) to pipe down, sing small.

приткн|у́ть, у́, ёшь, *pf.* (*of* притыка́ть) (*coll.*) to stick; ~й свои́ ве́щи куда́ хо́чешь stick your things anywhere you like.

приткн|у́ться, у́сь, ёшься, *pf.* (*coll.*) to perch oneself, find room for oneself; мне бы́ло не́где п. I could not find a spare inch.

прито́к, а, *m.* **1.** (*geogr.*) tributary. **2.** inflow, influx (*also fig.*); intake; п. све́жего во́здуха supply of fresh air; п. но́вых ка́дров (*fig.*) intake of fresh blood.

при́толок|а, и, *f.* lintel.

прито́м, *conj.* (and) besides; он был там не раз и п. прекра́сно зна́ет язы́к he has been there several times, (and) besides he knows the language extremely well.

притом|и́ть, лю́, и́шь, *pf.* (*coll.*) to tire.

притом|и́ться, лю́сь, и́шься, *pf.* (*coll.*) to get tired.

прито́н, а, *m.* den, haunt; воровско́й п. den

of thieves; игóрный п. gambling-den, gambling-hell.

притóп|нуть, ну, нешь, *pf.* (*of* ~ывáть) to stamp one's foot; п. каблукáми to tap one's heels.

притóп|тáть, чý, ~чешь, *pf.* (*of* притáпты- вать) to tread down.

притóпыва|ть, ю, *impf. of* притóпнуть.

приторáчива|ть, ю, *impf. of* приторочи́ть.

при́торност|ь, и, *f.* sickly sweetness, exces- sive sweetness.

при́тор|ный (~ен, ~на), *adj.* sickly sweet, luscious, cloying (*also fig.*); ~ная улы́бка unctuous smile.

приторóч|ить, ý, и́шь, *pf.* (*of* приторáчи- вать) to strap.

притрáгива|ться, юсь, *impf. of* притрóнуть- ся.

притрóн|уться, усь, ешься, *pf.* (*of* притрá- гиваться) (к) to touch; они́ не ~улись к у́жину they have not touched their supper.

притул|и́ться, ю́сь, и́шься, *pf.* (*coll.*) to find room for oneself; to find shelter.

притуп|и́ть, лю́, ~ишь, *pf.* (*of* ~ля́ть) to blunt, dull, take the edge of; (*fig.*) to dull, deaden.

притуп|и́ться, лю́сь, ~ишься, *pf.* (*of* ~ля́ть- ся) to become blunt; (*fig.*) to become dull.

притупля́|ть(ся), ю(сь), *impf. of* притупи́ть- (ся).

притуш|и́ть, ý, ~ишь, *pf.* (*coll.*) to damp (*a fire*); п. фáры to dip lights.

при́тч|а, и, *f.* parable; чтó за п.? (*coll.*) what is the meaning of all this?; what an extraordinary thing!; п. во язы́цех (*joc.*) the talk of the town.

притыкá|ть, ю, *impf. of* приткнýть.

притягáтельност|ь, и, *f.* attractiveness.

притягáтел|ьный (~ен, ~ьна), *adj.* attrac- tive, magnetic.

притя́гива|ть, ю, *impf. of* притянýть.

притяжáтельный, *adj.* (*gram.*) possessive.

притяжéни|е, я, *n.* (*phys.*) attraction; закóн земнóго ~я law of gravity.

притязáни|е, я, *n.* claim, pretension; имéть ~я (на+*a.*) to have claims (to, on).

притязáтел|ьный (~ен, ~ьна), *adj.* de- manding, exacting.

притязá|ть, ю, *impf.* (на+*a.*) to lay claim (to).

притя́н|утый, *p.p.p. of* ~ýть; п. зá уши, п. зá волосы (*fig.*) far-fetched.

притя́|нýть, нý, ~нешь, *pf.* (*of* ~гивать) **1.** to drag (up), pull (up); п. зá уши, зá волосы доказáтельства to adduce far- -fetched arguments. **2.** (*fig.*) to draw, attract; п. как магни́т to attract like a magnet. **3.** (*coll.*) to summon; п. к отвéту to call to account; п. к судý to have up, sue.

приуготóв|ить, лю, ишь, *pf.* (*of* ~ля́ть) (*obs.*) to prepare, have in store (*usu. fig.*).

приуготовля́|ть, ю, *impf. of* приуготóвить.

приудáр|ить, ю, ишь, (*of* ~я́ть) **1.** to deal a light blow. **2.** (*fig., coll.*) to get cracking. **3.** (зa+*i.*; *fig., coll.*) to go (after), pursue (= begin courting).

приудар|я́ть, я́ю, *impf. of* ~ить.

приукрá|сить, шу, сишь, *pf.* (*of* ~шивать) (*coll.*) to adorn; (*fig.*) to embellish, em- broider.

приукрáшива|ть, ю,, *impf. of* приукрáсить.

приуменьш|áть, áю, *impf. of* ~и́ть.

приумéньш|и́ть, ~ý, ~и́шь, *pf.* (*of* ~áть) to diminish, lessen, reduce.

приумнож|áть(ся), áю(сь), *impf. of* ~и́ть- (ся).

приумножéни|е, я, *n.* increase, augmenta- tion.

приумнóж|ить, у, ишь, *pf.* (*of* ~áть) to in- crease, augment, multiply.

приумнóж|иться, ится, *pf.* (*of* ~áться) to increase, multiply.

приумóлк|нуть, ну, нешь, *past* ~, ~ла, *pf.* (*coll.*) to fall silent (*for a while*).

приун|ы́ть, ó́ю, óешь, *pf.* (*coll.*) to become depressed, become gloomy.

приурóчива|ть, ю, *impf. of* приурóчить.

приурóч|ить, у, ишь, *pf.* (*of* ~ивать) (к) to time (for, to coincide with); ~или издáние кни́ги к прибы́тию áвтора publication of the book was timed to coincide with the author's arrival.

приусáдебный, *adj.* adjoining the farm (-house); п. учáсток (колхóзника) personal plot (belonging to collective farmer).

приути́х|нуть, ну, нешь, *past* ~, ~ла, *pf.* to quiet down; (*of a storm*) to abate; (*of wind*) to fall, drop.

приуч|áть(ся), áю(сь), *impf. of* ~и́ть(ся).

приуч|и́ть, ý, ~ишь, *pf.* (*of* ~áть) (к *or* +*inf.*) to train (to), school (to, in); to inure, accustom; п. когó-н. к дисципли́не to in- culcate discipline in someone; п. когó-н. купáться в холóдной водé to school some- one to taking cold baths.

приуч|и́ться, ýсь, ~ишься, *pf.* (*of* ~áться) (+*inf.*) to train oneself (to), school oneself (to), discipline oneself (to); to become inured (to), accustom oneself (to).

прифран|ти́ться, чýсь, ти́шься, *pf.* (*coll.*) to dress up, put on one's best bib and tucker.

прифронтовóй, *adj.* (*mil.*) front, front-line.

прихвáрыва|ть, ю, *impf.* (*coll.*) to be unwell off and on.

прихвастн|ýть, ý, ёшь, *pf.* (*coll.*) to boast a little, brag a little.

прихва|ти́ть, чý, ~тишь, *pf.* (*of* ~тывать) (*coll.*) **1.** to catch up, seize up (= take;

to get). **2.** to tie up, fasten. **3.** (*of frost*) to touch, nip.

прихва́тыва|ть, ю, *impf. of* прихвати́ть.

прихворн|у́ть, у́, ёшь, *pf.* (*coll.*) to be indisposed, be unwell.

при́хвост|ень, ня, *m.* (*coll.*) hanger-on, stooge.

прихлеба́тел|ь, я, *m.* (*coll.*) sponger, parasite.

прихлеба́тельств|о, а, *n.* (*coll.*) sponging.

прихлебн|у́ть, у́, ёшь, *pf.* to take a sip.

прихлёбыва|ть, ю, *impf.* (*coll.*) to sip.

прихло́п|нуть, ну, нешь, *pf.* (*of* ~ывать) (*coll.*) **1.** to slam. **2.** to squeeze, pinch; п. па́лец две́рью to pinch one's finger in the door. **3.** (*sl.*) to kill.

прихло́пыва|ть, ю, *impf.* **1.** *impf. of* прихло́пнуть. **2.** *impf. only* to clap.

прихлы́н|уть, у, ешь, *pf.* (к) to rush (towards), surge (towards).

прихо́д¹, а, *m.* coming, arrival; advent.

прихо́д², а, *m.* receipts; п. и расхо́д credit and debit.

**прихо́д³, а, *m.* (*eccl.*) parish; како́в поп, тако́в и п. (*prov.*) like master, like man.

прихо|ди́ть, жу́, ~дишь, *impf. of* прийти́.

прихо|ди́ться, жу́сь, ~дишься, *impf.* **1.** *impf. of* прийти́сь. **2.** *impf. only* (+*d. and i.*) to be (*in a given degree of relationship to*); я ей ~жу́сь дя́дей I am her uncle; они́ нам ~дятся ро́дственниками they are related to us.

прихо́д|ный, *adj. of* ~²; ~ная кни́га receipt-book.

прихо́д|овать, ую, *impf.* (*of* за~) (*book-keeping*) to enter (*of person receiving sum from client, customer, etc.*).

прихо́до-расхо́дн|ый, *adj.* credit and debit; ~ая кни́га account-book.

прихо́дский, *adj.* parochial; parish; п. свяще́нник parish priest; parson, vicar, rector.

прихо́д|ящий, *pres. part. act. of* ~и́ть *and adj.* non-resident; п. больно́й outpatient; ~я́щая домрабо́тница daily maid, charwoman; п. учени́к day-boy.

прихожа́н|ин, ина, *pl.* ~е, ~, *m.* parishioner.

прихо́ж|ая, ей, *f.* (entrance) hall, lobby; antechamber.

прихора́шива|ться, юсь, *impf.* (*coll.*) to doll oneself up, smarten oneself up.

прихотли́вост|ь, и, *f.* capriciousness, fastidiousness, whimsicality.

прихотли́в|ый (~, ~а), *adj.* **1.** capricious, fastidious, whimsical. **2.** fanciful, intricate (*of pattern, etc.*).

при́хот|ь, и, *f.* whim, caprice, whimsy, fancy.

прихра́мыва|ть, ю, *impf.* to limp, hobble.

прицве́тник, а, *m.* (*bot.*) bract.

прице́л, а, *m.* **1.** back-sight; опти́ческий п. telegraphic sight; п. для бомбомета́ния bomb sight; взять на п. to take aim (at), aim (at), point (at). **2.** aiming.

прице́лива|ться, юсь, *impf. of* прице́литься.

прице́л|иться, юсь, ишься, *pf.* (*of* ~иваться) to take aim, take sight.

прице́л|ьный, *adj. of* ~; ~ьная бомбарди́ровка precision bombing; ~ьная коло́дка back-sight bed; ~ьная ли́ния line of sight; п. ого́нь aimed fire; ~ьная пла́нка back-sight leaf; ~ьные приспособле́ния sighting device; back-sight; п. хому́тик back-sight slide.

прице́нива|ться, юсь, *impf. of* прицени́ться.

прицен|и́ться, ю́сь, ~ишься, *pf.* (*of* ~иваться) (к; *coll.*) to ask the price (of).

прице́п, а, *m.* trailer.

прицеп|и́ть, лю́, ~ишь, *pf.* (*of* ~ля́ть) (к) **1.** to hitch (to), hook on (to); to couple (to); п. ваго́ны к парово́зу to couple trucks to a locomotive. **2.** (*coll.*) to pin on (to), fasten (to), tack (to), tag on (to).

прицеп|и́ться, лю́сь, ~ишься, *pf.* (*of* ~ля́ть-ся) (к) **1.** to stick (to), cling (to). **2.** (*fig., coll.*) to pester; to nag (at).

прице́пк|а, и, *f.* **1.** hitching, hooking on; coupling. **2.** (*coll.*) pestering; nagging. **3.** (*coll.*) chaser.

прицепля́|ть(ся), ю(сь), *impf. of* прицепи́ть(ся).

прицепно́й, *adj.*; п. ваго́н trailer; п. инвента́рь (*agric.*) tractor-drawn implements.

прича́л, а, *m.* **1.** mooring, making fast. **2.** mooring line. **3.** berth, moorage; у ~ов at its, her moorings.

прича́лива|ть, ю, *impf. of* прича́лить.

прича́л|ить, ю, ишь, *pf.* (*of* ~ивать) **1.** (к) to moor (to). **2.** (*intrans.*) to moor.

прича́л|ьный, *adj. of* ~; п. кана́т mooring line.

прича́сти|е¹, я, *n.* (*gram.*) participle.

прича́сти|е², я, *n.* (*eccl.*) **1.** communion; the eucharist. **2.** making one's communion, communicating.

прича|сти́ть, щу́, сти́шь, *pf.* (*of* ~ща́ть) (*eccl.*) to give communion.

прича|сти́ться, щу́сь, сти́шься, *pf.* (*of* ~ща́ться) (*eccl.*) to receive communion, make one's communion, communicate.

прича́ст|ный¹ (~ен, ~на), *adj.* (к) participating (in), concerned (in), connected (with), involved (in); privy (to); быть ~ным (к) to participate (in), be concerned (in), connected (with), be involved (in); to be privy (to); быть ~ным к теа́тру to be connected with the theatre; быть ~ным к покуше́нию на жизнь короля́ to be privy to an attempt on the life of the king.

прича́стный², *adj.* (*gram.*) participial.

причаща́|ть(ся), ю(сь), *impf. of* прича-сти́ть(ся).

причаще́ни|е, я, *n.* (*eccl.*) receiving communion, making one's communion, communicating.

причём, *conj.* **1.** moreover, and (*or translated by means of participial clause*); бы́ло о́чень темно́, п. я пло́хо ориенти́руюсь в э́той ме́стности it was very dark and I don't know this area well. **2.** while (*+participial clause*); despite the fact that; он реши́л пое́хать, п. отдава́л себе́ отчёт в опа́сности he decided to go, while recognizing the danger.

приче|са́ть, шу́, ⌐шешь, *pf.* (*of* ⌐сывать) to comb; п. кого́-н. to do someone's hair; to brush, comb someone's hair.

приче|са́ться, шу́сь, ⌐шешься, *pf.* (*of* ⌐сываться) to do one's hair; to brush, comb one's hair; to have one's hair done.

причёск|а, и, *f.* haircut; hair style, hair-do, coiffure.

при|че́сть, чту́, чтёшь, *past* ⌐чёл, ⌐чла́, *pf.* (*of* ⌐чи́тывать) **1.** (*coll.*) to add on. **2.** (*obs.*) to number, reckon.

причёса́|ть(ся), ю(сь), *impf. of* приче-са́ть(ся).

приче́тник, а, *m.* (*eccl.*) junior deacon.

причи́н|а, ы, *f.* cause; reason; уважи́тельная п. good cause, good reason; по той и́ли ино́й ⌐е for some reason or other, for one reason or another; по той просто́й ⌐е, что for the simple reason that; по ⌐е (+*g.*) by reason (of), on account (of), owing (to) because (of).

причи́н|ить, ю́, и́шь, *pf.* (*of* ⌐я́ть) to cause; to occasion.

причи́нност|ь, и, *f.* causality.

причи́нн|ый, *adj.* causal, causative; ⌐ая связь causation; ⌐ое ме́сто (*coll.*) privy parts.

причин|я́ть, я́ю, *impf. of* ⌐и́ть.

причи́сл|ить, ю, ишь, *pf.* (*of* ⌐я́ть) (к) **1.** to add on (to). **2.** to reckon (among), number (among), rank (among); его́ ⌐или к са́мым выдаю́щимся матема́тикам he was ranked among the foremost mathematicians. **3.** to attach (to).

причисл|я́ть, я́ю, *impf. of* ⌐ить.

причита́ни|е, я, *n.* (ritual) lamentation; похоро́нные ⌐я keen, keening.

причита́|ть, ю, *impf.* (по+*p.*) to lament (for), keen (over); to bewail.

причита́|ться, ется, *impf.* (+*d.*; с+*g.*) to be due (to; from); вам ⌐ется два рубля́ there is two roubles due to you, you have two roubles to come; с вас ⌐ется два рубля́ you have two roubles to pay.

причи́тыва|ть, ю, *impf. of* приче́сть.

причмо́кива|ть, ю, *impf. of* причмо́кнуть.

причмо́к|нуть, ну, нешь, *pf.* (*of* ⌐ивать) to smack one's lips.

причт, а, *m.* (*collect.*) the clergy of a parish.

причу́д|а, ы, *f.* caprice, whim, whimsy, fancy; oddity, vagary; челове́к с ⌐ами crank, odd person, queer person.

причу́д|иться, ится, *pf. of* чу́диться.

причу́дливост|ь, и, *f.* **1.** oddity, queerness; quaintness, fantasticality. **2.** (*coll.*) capriciousness, whimsicality.

причу́длив|ый (⌐, ⌐а), *adj.* **1.** odd, queer; quaint, fantastical. **2.** (*coll.*) capricious, whimsical.

причу́дник, а, *m.* (*coll.*) crank, odd person, queer person.

пришварт|ова́ть, у́ю, *pf.* (*of* ⌐о́вывать) (к) to moor (to), make fast (to).

пришварт|ова́ться, у́юсь, *pf.* (*of* ⌐о́вываться) (к) to moor (to), tie up (at).

пришварто́выва|ть(ся), ю(сь), *impf. of* пришвартова́ть(ся).

пришёл|ец, ьца, *m.* newcomer, stranger.

пришепётыва|ть, ю, *impf.* (*coll.*) to lisp slightly.

прише́стви|е, я, *n.* (*obs.*) advent, coming; до второ́го ⌐я (*joc.*) till doomsday.

пришиб|и́ть, у́, ёшь, *past* ⌐, ⌐ла, *pf.* (*coll.*) **1.** to strike dead. **2.** (*fig.*) to knock out, break (= *to dispirit*).

пришиб|ленный, *p.p.p. of* ⌐и́ть *and adj.* (*coll.*) broken; crest-fallen.

пришива́|ть, ю, *impf. of* приши́ть.

пришивно́й, *adj.* sewn on; п. воротничо́к attached collar.

приш|и́ть, ью́, ьёшь, *pf.* (*of* ⌐ива́ть) **1.** to sew on. **2.** to nail on. **3.** (+*a.* к *or* +*a. and d.*; *fig.*, *coll.*) to pin (on), pin an accusation (of on).

пришко́льный, *adj.* (adjoining a) school.

при́шлый, *adj.* newly come, arrived; strange, alien.

пришпи́лива|ть, ю, *impf. of* пришпи́лить.

пришпи́л|ить, ю, ишь, *pf.* (*of* ⌐ивать) to pin.

пришпо́рива|ть, ю, *impf. of* пришпо́рить.

пришпо́р|ить, ю, ишь, *pf.* (*of* ⌐ивать) to spur; to put, set spurs (to).

прищёлкива|ть, ю, *impf. of* прищёлкнуть.

прищёлк|нуть, ну, нешь, *pf.* (*of* ⌐ивать) п. кнуто́м to crack the whip; п. па́льцами to snap one's fingers.

прищем|и́ть, лю́, и́шь, *pf.* (*of* ⌐ля́ть) to pinch, squeeze; п. себе́ па́лец две́рью to pinch one's finger in the door.

прищемля́|ть, ю, *impf. of* прищеми́ть.

прищеп|и́ть, лю́, и́шь, *pf.* (*of* ⌐ля́ть) (*bot.*) to graft.

прищепля́|ть, ю, *impf. of* прищепи́ть.

прищёпк|а, и, *f.* (clothes-) peg.

прищёп|ок, ка, *m.* = ⌐ка.

прищу́рива|ть(ся), ю(сь), *impf. of* прищу́рить(ся).

прищу́р|ить, ю, ишь, *pf.* (*of* ~ивать); п. глаза́ = ~иться.

прищу́р|иться, юсь, ишься, *pf.* (*of* ~иваться) to screw up one's eyes.

прию́т, а, *m.* 1. shelter, refuge. 2. (*obs.*) asylum; де́тский п. orphanage, orphan-asylum; роди́льный п. maternity home, lying-in hospital.

прию́|ти́ть, чу́, ти́шь, *pf.* to shelter, give refuge.

прию́|ти́ться, чу́сь, ти́шься, *pf.* to take shelter.

прия́знен|ный (~, ~на), *adj.* (*obs.*) friendly, amicable.

прия́зн|ь, и, *f.* (*obs.*) friendliness, good-will.

прия́тел|ь, я, *m.* friend.

прия́тельниц|а, ы, *f.* 1. (female) friend. 2. girl-friend, lady-friend.

прия́тельский, *adj.* friendly, amicable.

прия́т|ный (~ен, ~на), *adj.* nice, pleasant, agreeable, pleasing; п. на вид nice-looking, gratifying to the eye; п. на вкус palatable, tasty; ~но (*impers., pred.*) it is pleasant, it is nice.

при|я́ть, му́, ~мешь, *pf.* (*obs.*) = ~ня́ть.

про, *prep.*+*a.* 1. about; мы говори́ли про вас we were talking about you. 2. (*coll.*) for; э́то не про нас this is not for us. 3. про себя́ to oneself; я поду́мал про себя́ I thought to myself; прочти́ письмо́ вслух, а не про себя́! read the letter aloud, not to yourself!

про-¹ *verbal prefix indicating* 1. *action through, across or past object, as* простре́ли́ть to shoot through; прое́хать to pass (by). 2. *overall or exhaustive action, as* прогре́ть to warm thoroughly. 3. *duration of action throughout given period of time, as* просиде́ть всю ночь to sit up all night. 4. *loss or failure, as* проигра́ть to lose (*a game*).

про-² *as prefix of nouns and adjs.* pro-.

проанализи́р|овать, ую, *pf. of* анализи́ровать.

про́б|а, ы, *f.* 1. trial, test; try-out; assay; п. го́лоса voice test; п. сил trial of strength; взять на ~у to take on trial. 2. sample. 3. standard (*measure of purity of gold*); зо́лото 56-о́й ~ы 14 carat gold; зо́лото 96-о́й ~ы pure gold, 24 carat gold. 4. hallmark.

пробавля́|ться, юсь, *impf.* (*coll.*) to subsist (on), make do (on).

проба́лтыва|ть(ся), ю(сь), *impf. of* проболта́ть(ся).

проба|си́ть, шу́, си́шь, *pf.* (*coll.*) to speak in a bass, deep voice.

пробе́г, а, *m.* 1. (*sport*) run, race; лы́жный п. ski-run. 2. run, mileage, distance covered; су́точный п. парово́за 24 hours' run for a locomotive; находи́ться в ~e to be working, be operating.

пробе́га|ть, ю, *pf.* (*coll.*) to run about (*for a certain time*).

пробега́|ть, ю, *impf. of* пробежа́ть.

пробе|жа́ть, гу́, жи́шь, гу́т, *pf.* (*of* ~га́ть) 1. to pass (running), run past, run by; to run through; to run along; п. па́льцами по клавиату́ре to run one's fingers over the keyboard. 2. to run; to cover; по́езд ~жа́л шестьдеся́т миль ро́вно в час the train covered sixty miles in exactly one hour. 3. (*fig.*) to run, flit (over, down, across); хо́лод ~жа́л по её спине́ a chill ran down her spine. 4. (*fig., coll.*) to run through, look through, skim.

пробе|жа́ться, гу́сь, жи́шься, гу́тся, *pf.* to run, take a run.

пробе́л, а, *m.* 1. blank, gap; hiatus; lacuna; запо́лнить ~ы to fill in the blanks. 2. (*fig.*) deficiency, gap; ~ы в зна́ниях gaps in one's knowledge.

пробива́|ть(ся), ю(сь), *impf. of* проби́ть(ся).

проби́вк|а, и, *f.* 1. holing, piercing; punching. 2. caulking.

пробивн|о́й, *adj.* 1. piercing, punching; ~а́я си́ла penetrating power (*of missile*); п. стано́к (*tech.*) punch. 2. (*electr.*) disruptive. 3. (*coll.*) go-ahead, go-getting.

пробира́|ть(ся), ю(сь), *impf. of* пробра́ть(ся).

проби́рк|а, и, *f.* test-tube.

проби́рн|ый, *adj.* testing; assaying; п. ка́мень touchstone; ~ое клеймо́ hallmark; п. мета́лл test metal; ~ая пала́та assay office; ~ая скля́нка test-tube.

проби́р|овать, ую, *impf.* to test, assay.

проби́рщик, а, *m.* assayer, assay-master.

про|би́ть¹, бью, бьёшь, *past* ~би́л, ~би́ла, ~би́ло, *pf. of* бить 9.

про|би́ть², бью, бьёшь, *past* ~би́л, ~би́ла, *pf.* (*of* ~бива́ть) to make a hole (in); to hole, pierce; to punch; п. кора́бль to hole a ship; п. сте́ну to breach a wall; п. ши́ну to puncture a tyre; п. путь, доро́гу to open the way (*also fig.*); п. себе́ доро́гу (*fig.*) to carve one's way.

про|би́ться¹, бью́сь, бьёшься, *pf.* (*of* ~бива́ться) 1. to fight, force, make one's way through; to break, strike through; п. с трудо́м to struggle along; п. сквозь толпу́ to fight one's way through the crowd. 2. (*of plants*) to shoot, show, push up.

про|би́ться², бью́сь, бьёшься, *pf.* (над) to struggle (with) (*for a certain time*).

про́бк|а, и, *f.* 1. cork (*substance*). 2. cork; stopper; plug; глуп как п. daft as a brush. 3. (*electr.*) fuse. 4. (*fig.*) traffic jam; congestion.

про́бков|ый, *adj.* cork; subereous, suberic; п. дуб cork-oak; ~ая кислота́ suberic acid; п. по́яс cork jacket, life-jacket.

проблéм|а, ы, *f.* problem.

проблемáтик|а, и, *f.* (*collect.*) problems.

проблемати́ческий, *adj.* problematic(al).

проблемати́чност|ь, и, *f.* problematical character.

проблемати́ч|ный (~ен, ~на), *adj.* = ~еский.

про́блеск, а, *m.* flash; ray, gleam (*also fig.*); п. надéжды ray of hope.

проблéскива|ть, ю, *impf.* *of* проблеснýть.

проблес|нýть, нý, нёшь, *pf.* (*of* ~кивать) to flash, gleam.

проблуждá|ть, ю, *pf.* to wander, rove, roam (*for a certain time*).

про́бный, *adj.* 1. trial, test, experimental; п. кáмень touchstone; п. ковш assay spoon; п. полёт test flight; п. спирт proof spirit; п. шар ballon d'essai; п. экземпля́р specimen copy. 2. hallmarked.

про́б|овать, ую, *impf.* (*of* по~) 1. to test; п. пи́щу to taste, try food. 2. (+*inf.*) to try (to), attempt (to), endeavour (to).

прободá|ть[1], ет, *pf.* to gore.

прободá|ть[2], ет, *impf.* (*med.*) to perforate, puncture.

прободéни|е, я, *n.* (*med.*) perforation.

пробо́ин|а, ы, *f.* hole (*esp. caused by missile*); получи́ть ~у to be holed.

пробо́|й, я, *m.* 1. clamp, hasp, holdfast. 2. (*electr.*) spark-over.

пробо́йник, а, *m.* (*tech.*) punch.

проболé|ть[1], ю, *pf.* to be ill (*for a certain time*).

пробол|éть[2], и́т, *pf.* to hurt (*for a certain time*).

проболтá|ть, ю, *pf.* (*of* пробáлтывать) (*coll.*) 1. to play for time by talking. 2. to blab (out).

проболтá|ться[1], юсь, *pf.* (*of* пробáлтываться) (*coll.*) to blab, blurt out a secret, let the cat out of the bag.

проболтá|ться[2], юсь, *pf.* (*coll.*) to idle, loaf.

пробо́р, а, *m.* parting (*of the hair*); прямо́й п. parting in the middle; косо́й п. parting at one side; дéлать (себé) п. to part one's hair.

пробормо|тáть, чý, ~чешь, *pf.* *of* бормотáть.

про́бочник, а, *m.* (*coll.*) corkscrew.

пробрáсыва|ть, ю, *impf.* *of* пробро́сить.

про|брáть, берý, берёшь, *past* ~брáл, ~бралá, ~брáло, *pf.* (*of* ~бирáть) 1. to penetrate; моро́з ~брáл меня́ до костéй I was chilled to the marrow; их ~брáл страх fear had struck them; его́ ничéм не ~берёшь he cannot be got at. 2. (*coll.*) to scold, rate. 3. (*agric.*) to clear, weed.

про|брáться, берýсь, берёшься, *past* ~брáлся, ~бралáсь, ~брáлось, *pf.* (*of* ~бирáться). 1. to fight, force one's way. 2. to steal

(through, past); п. о́щупью to feel one's way; п. на цы́почках to tiptoe (through).

пробро|ди́ть, жý, ~дишь, *pf.* to wander (*for a certain time*).

пробро́|сить, шу, сишь, *pf.* (*of* пробрáсывать) (*coll.*) 1. to count up (*on an abacus*). 2. to overcount (by).

пробст, а, *m.* (*eccl.*) provost (*in Lutheran Church, clergyman in charge of principal church in town*).

пробу|ди́ть, жý, ~дишь, *pf.* (*of* буди́ть and ~ждáть) to wake; to awaken, rouse, arouse (*also fig.*).

пробу|ди́ться, жýсь, ~дишься, *pf.* (*of* ~ждáться) to wake up, awake (*also fig.*).

пробуждá|ть(ся), ю(сь), *impf.* *of* пробуди́ть(ся).

пробуждéни|е, я, *n.* waking up, awakening.

пробурáв|ить, лю, ишь, *pf.* (*of* ~ливать) to bore, drill, perforate.

пробурáвлива|ть, ю, *impf.* *of* пробурáвить.

пробурч|áть, ý, и́шь, *pf.* *of* бурчáть.

проб|ы́ть, ýду, ýдешь, *past* ~ыл, ~ылá, *pf.* to stay, remain; to be (*for a certain time*); он ~ыл у нас три недéли he stayed with us for three weeks.

провáл, а, *m.* 1. downfall. 2. (*geogr.*) gap; funnel. 3. failure; п. пáмяти failure of memory; како́й п.! what a flop!

провáлива|ть, ю, *impf.* 1. *impf.* *of* провали́ть. 2. ~й! (*coll.*) off with you!, get moving!, beat it!, hop it!

провáлива|ться, юсь, *impf.* *of* провали́ться.

провал|и́ть, ю́, ~ишь, *pf.* (*of* ~ивать) 1. to cause to collapse, knock down. 2. (*fig., coll.*) to ruin, make a mess (of); п. роль (*theatr.*) to ruin a part. 3. (*fig.*) to reject; п. кандидáта на экзáмене to fail a candidate in an examination; п. законопроéкт to kill a bill.

провал|и́ться, ю́сь, ~ишься, *pf.* (*of* ~ивáться) 1. to collapse, come down, fall through; потоло́к ~и́лся the ceiling has come down. 2. (*fig., coll.*) to fail, miscarry; (*in an examination*) to fail, be ploughed; по́лностью п. to be a complete, utter failure. 3. (*coll.*) to disappear, vanish; он как сквозь зéмлю ~и́лся he vanished into thin air; я гото́в был сквозь зéмлю ~и́ться I wished the earth could swallow me up; п. мне на э́том мéсте, éсли... I'll be damned if....

провансáл|ь, я, *m.* mayonnaise, salad dressing.

провансáльский, *adj.* Provençal.

провáнск|ий, *adj.* ~ое мáсло olive oil, salad-oil.

провáрива|ть, ю, *impf.* *of* провари́ть.

провар|и́ть, ю́, ~ишь, *pf.* (*of* ~ивать) to boil thoroughly.

провéд|ать, аю, *pf.* (*of* ~ывать) (*coll.*) 1. to

come to see, call on. **2.** (o+*p.*) to find out (about), learn (of, about).

проведéни|е, я, *n.* **1.** leading, taking; piloting. **2.** building; installation. **3.** carrying out, through; conducting; п. кампáнии (*mil. and fig.*) conduct of a campaign; п. в жизнь putting into effect.

провéдыва|ть, ю, *impf. of* провéдать.

провез|тú, ý, ёшь, *past* ~, ~лá, *pf.* (*of* провозúть) **1.** to convey, transport; п. контрабáндой to smuggle. **2.** to bring (with one).

провентилú|р|овать, ую, *pf. of* вентилúровать.

провéр|енный, *p.p.p. of* ~ить *and adj.* proved, of proved worth.

провéр|ить, ю, ишь, *pf.* (*of* ~ять) **1.** to check (up on); to verify; to audit; п. билéты to examine tickets; п. кáссу to check the till; п. чью-н. рабóту to check up on someone's work; п. тетрáди to correct exercise-books. **2.** to test; п. свои силы to try one's strength.

провéрк|а, и, *f.* **1.** checking; examination; verification; check-up; п. исполнéния work check-up; п. налúчия stock-taking, inventory-making; п. счетóв audit(ing); п. бóя оружия (*mil.*) checking the zero of a weapon; п. управлéния огнём (*mil.*) verification of fire. **2.** testing.

провер|нýть, нý, нёшь, *pf.* (*of* ~тывать) (*coll.*) **1.** to bore, perforate, pierce. **2.** to crank (*a motor*). **3.** (*fig.*) to rush through (*discussion of a question, etc.*).

провéрочн|ый, *adj.* checking, verifying; ~ая рабóта test paper.

провер|тéть, чý, ~тишь, *pf.* (*of* ~тывать) (*coll.*) to bore, perforate, pierce.

провёртыва|ть, ю, *impf. of* провернýть *and* провертéть.

провéрщик, а, *m.* checker, inspector.

провер|я́ть, я́ю, *impf. of* ~ить.

провéс¹, а, *m.* short weight.

провéс², а, *m.* sag; dip (*of wire*).

провé|сить¹, шу, сишь, *pf.* (*of* ~шивать) to give short weight.

провé|сить², шу, сишь, *pf.* (*of* ~шивать) to dry in the open, air.

провé|сить³, шу, сишь, *pf.* (*of* ~шивать) (*tech.*) to plumb.

прове|стú, дý, дёшь, *past* ~л, ~лá, *pf.* (*of* проводúть¹) **1.** to lead, take; п. сýдно (*naut.*) to pilot a vessel. **2.** to build; to install; п. железнодорóжную вéтку to build a branch line; п. водопровóд to lay on water; п. электрúчество to install electricity. **3.** to carry out, carry on; to conduct, hold; п. óпыты to carry out tests; п. заседáние to conduct a meeting; п. рефóрмы to carry out reforms; п. бесéду to give a talk. **4.** to carry through; to carry, pass,

get through (*a resolution, a bill, etc.*); to implement (*a decision, etc.*); им не удалóсь п. законопроéкт чéрез Палáту лóрдов they did not succeed in getting the bill through the House of Lords; п. идéю в жизнь to put an idea into effect, implement an idea. **5.** to advance, put forward (*an idea, etc.*). **6.** (*book-keeping*) to register; п. по книгам to book; п. по кáссе to register, ring up on the till. **7.** to draw (*a line, etc.*); п. граниïцу to draw a boundary-line. **8.** (+*i.*) to pass over, run over; она ~лá рукóй по лбу she passed her hand over her forehead. **9.** to spend, pass (*time*); чтóбы п. врéмя to pass the time; как вы ~ли врéмя? (*addressed to person on return from holiday, etc.*) did you have a good time?, what sort of time did you have? **10.** (*coll.*) to take in, trick, fool; меня не ~дёшь you can't fool me.

провéтрива|ть(ся), ю(сь), *impf. of* провéтрить(ся).

провéтр|ить, ю, ишь, *pf.* (*of* ~ивать) to air; to ventilate.

провéтр|иться, юсь, ишься, *pf.* (*of* ~иваться) **1.** to have an airing; (*fig., coll.*) to have a change of scene. **2.** *pass. of* ~ить.

провéшива|ть, ю, *impf. of* провéсить.

провиáнт, а, *m.* provisions, victuals.

провúдени|е, я, *n.* foresight, forecast.

провидéни|е, я, *n.* (*rel.*) Providence.

прови|дéть, жу, дишь, *impf.* to foresee.

провú|дец, ца, *m.* (*obs., rhet.*) seer, prophet.

провиз|иóнный, *adj. of* ~úя; п. магазúн provision shop.

провúзи|я, и, *no pl., f.* provisions; снабдúть ~ей to cater (for); to provision, victual.

провúзор, а, *m.* (*qualified*) pharmaceutical chemist.

провизóр|ный (~ен, ~на), *adj.* provisional; temporary.

провин|úться, юсь, úшься, *pf.* (в+*p.*) to be guilty (of); to commit an offence; п. пéред кем-н. to wrong someone, do someone an injury; в чём мы ~úлись? what have we done wrong?

провúнност|ь, и, *f.* (*coll.*) fault; offence.

провинциáл, а, *m.* provincial (*person*).

провинциалúзм, а, *m.* provincialism.

провинциáльност|ь, и, *f.* provinciality.

провинциáл|ьный (~ен, ~ьна), *adj.* provincial (*also fig.*).

провúнци|я, и, *f.* **1.** province. **2.** the provinces (*as opp. to capital or other centre*); жить в глухóй ~и to live in the depths of the country.

провирá|ться, юсь, *impf. of* проврáться.

провис|áть, áет, *impf. of* ~нуть.

провúс|нуть, нет, *pf.* (*of* ~áть) to sag.

прóвод, а, *pl.* ~á, *m.* wire, lead, conductor; воздýшный п. aerial conductor; заземля́ющий n. earth(-wire); п. с пу́щенным то́ком live wire.

проводи́мост|ь, и, *f.* (*electr.*) conductivity, conduction; акти́вная п., ва́ттная п. conductance; уде́льная п. specific conductivity.

прово|ди́ть¹, жу́, ~дишь, *impf.* **1.** *impf. of* провести́. **2.** *impf. only* (*phys., electr.*) to conduct, be a conductor.

прово|ди́ть², жу́, ~дишь, *pf.* (*of* ~жа́ть) to accompany; to see off; п. на по́езд to see off (on the train); п. кого́-н. домо́й to take, see someone home; п. кого́-н. до двере́й to see someone to the door; п. поко́йника to attend a funeral; п. глаза́ми to follow with one's eyes.

прово́дк|а, и, *f.* **1.** leading, taking. **2.** building; installation. **3.** (*collect.; electr.*) wiring, wires.

проводни́к¹, á, *m.* **1.** guide. **2.** (*of train*) conductor; guard.

проводни́к², á, *m.* **1.** (*phys., electr.*) conductor. **2.** (*fig.*) bearer; transmitter.

проводни́|ца, цы, *f. of* ~к¹.

проводн|о́й, *adj. of* про́вод; ~а́я связь telegraphic communication (*as opp. to radio*).

про́вод|ы, ов, *no sing.* seeing-off; send-off.

провожа́т|ый, ого, *m.* guide, escort.

провожа́|ть, ю, *impf. of* проводи́ть².

прово́з, а, *m.* carriage, conveyance, transport; пла́та за п. payment for carriage.

провозве|сти́ть, щу́, сти́шь, *pf.* (*of* ~ща́ть) (*obs.*) **1.** to prophesy. **2.** to proclaim.

провозвеща́|ть, ю, *impf. of* провозвести́ть.

провозгла|си́ть, шу́, си́шь, *pf.* (*of* ~ша́ть) to proclaim; п. ло́зунг to advance a slogan; п. тост to propose a toast; п. тост за кого́-н. to propose someone's health; его́ ~си́ли короле́м he was proclaimed king.

провозглаша́|ть, ю, *impf. of* провозгласи́ть.

провозглаше́ни|е, я, *n.* proclamation; declaration.

прово|зи́ть, жу́, ~зишь, *impf. of* провезти́.

прово|зи́ться¹, жу́сь, ~зишься, *pf.* **1.** (*coll.*) to play about (*for a certain time*). **2.** (с+*i.*) to spend (*a certain time*) (over, in seeing to); я~зи́лся це́лый ме́сяц с получе́нием ви́зы I spent a whole month over obtaining the visa.

прово|зи́ться², жу́сь, ~зишься, *impf. pass., of* ~зи́ть.

провозоспосо́бност|ь, и, *f.* carrying capacity (*of railways*).

провока́тор, а, *m.* **1.** agent provocateur. **2.** (*fig.*) instigator, provoker.

провокацио́нный, *adj.* provocative.

провока́ци|я, и, *f.* provocation.

про́волок|а, и, *f.* wire; колю́чая п. barbed wire.

про́волочк|а, и, *f. dim. of* про́волока; short wire, fine wire.

проволо́чк|а, и, *f.* (*coll.*) delay, procrastination.

про́воло|чный, *adj. of* ~ка; ~чное загражде́ние wire entanglement; ~чная сеть wire netting.

провоня́|ть, ет, *pf.* (+*i.; coll.*) to stink (of).

прово́рност|ь, и, *f.* = прово́рство.

прово́р|ный (~ен, ~на), *adj.* **1.** quick, swift, expeditious. **2.** agile, nimble, adroit, dexterous.

провор|ова́ться, у́юсь, *pf.* (*of* ~о́вываться) (*coll.*) to be caught stealing, embezzling.

провор́о́выва|ться, юсь, *impf. of* проворова́ться.

проворо́н|ить, ю, ишь, *pf.* (*coll.*) to miss, let slip, lose; п. свою́ о́чередь to miss one's turn; п. ме́сто to lose one's place.

прово́рств|о, а, *n.* **1.** quickness, swiftness. **2.** agility, nimbleness, adroitness, dexterity.

проворч|а́ть, у́, и́шь, *pf.* to mutter.

провоци́р|овать, ую, *impf. and pf.* (*pf. also* с~) to provoke.

провр|а́ться, у́сь, ёшься, *past* ~а́лся, ~ала́сь, ~ало́сь,* *pf.* (*of* провира́ться) (*coll.*) to give oneself away, slip up (*in lying*).

провя́л|ить, ю, ишь, *pf. of* вя́лить.

прогад|а́ть, а́ю, *pf.* (*of* ~ывать) (*coll.*) to miscalculate.

прога́дыва|ть, ю, *impf. of* прогада́ть.

прога́лин|а, ы, *f.* glade.

проги́б, а, *m.* (*tech.*) caving in, sagging, flexure, deflection; camber; стрела́ ~а sag, sagging; depth of camber.

прогиба́|ть(ся), ю(сь), *impf. of* прогну́ть(ся).

прогла́|дить¹, жу, дишь, *pf.* (*of* ~живать) to iron (out).

прогла́|дить², жу, дишь, *pf.* to iron (*for a certain time*).

прогла́жива|ть, ю, *impf. of* прогла́дить¹.

прогла́тыва|ть, ю, *impf. of* проглоти́ть; говори́ть, ~я слова́ to swallow one's words.

прогло|ти́ть, чу́, ~тишь, *pf.* (*of* прогла́тывать) to swallow (*also fig.*); п. оскорбле́ние to swallow, pocket an insult; п. язы́к to lose one's tongue; п. кни́гу to devour a book; язы́к ~тишь it makes your mouth water.

прогля|де́ть¹, жу́, ди́шь, *pf.* (*of* ~дывать) to look through, glance through; п. глаза́ (*coll.*) to wear one's eyes out.

прогля|де́ть², жу́, ди́шь, *pf.* to overlook.

прогля́дыва|ть, ю, *impf. of* прогляде́ть *and* проглянуть.

прогля|ну́ть, ~нет, *pf.* (*of* ~дывать) to show (up, through), peep (out, through); to be perceptible; со́лнце ~ну́ло из-за облако́в the sun peeped out from behind the clouds; в её взгля́де ~ну́ла тоска́ there was a touch of wistfulness in her look.

про|гна́ть, гоню́, го́нишь, *past* ~гна́л, ~гнала́, ~гна́ло, *pf.* (*of* ~гоня́ть) 1. to drive away (*also fig.*); (*fig.*) to banish; п. с глаз доло́й to banish from one's sight; п. забо́ты to banish care. 2. to drive (through); п. коро́в в по́ле to drive the cows into the field; п. кого́-н. сквозь строй (*hist.*) to make someone run the gauntlet. 3. (*coll.*) to sack, fire.

прогне́ва|ть, ю, *pf.* (*obs.*) to anger, incense.

прогне́ва|ться, юсь, *pf.* (*obs.*) (на+*a.*) to become angry (with).

прогневи́ть, лю́, и́шь, *pf. of* гневи́ть.

прогнива́|ть, ю, *impf. of* прогни́ть.

прогн|и́ть, ию́, иёшь, *past* ~и́л, ~ила́, ~и́ло, *pf.* (*of* ~ива́ть) to rot through.

прогно́з, а, *m.* prognosis; forecast; п. пого́ды weather forecast.

прогн|у́ть, у́, ёшь, *pf.* (*of* прогиба́ть) to cause to cave in, cause to sag.

прогн|у́ться, у́сь, ёшься, *pf.* (*of* прогиба́ться) to cave in, sag.

прогова́рива|ть(ся), ю(сь), *impf. of* проговори́ть(ся).

проговор|и́ть, ю́, и́шь, *pf.* (*of* прогова́ривать) 1. to say, pronounce, utter; п. сквозь зу́бы to mutter; он ни сло́ва не ~и́л he did not utter a word. 2. to speak, talk (*for a certain time*); они́ ~и́ли три часа́ подря́д they talked for three hours on end.

проговор|и́ться, ю́сь, и́шься, *pf.* (*of* прогова́риваться) to blab (out), talk; to let the cat out of the bag.

проголода́|ть, ю, *pf.* to starve, go hungry.

проголода́|ться, юсь, *pf.* to get hungry, grow hungry.

проголос|ова́ть, у́ю, *pf. of* голосова́ть.

прого́н¹, а, *m.* 1. (*archit.*) purlin; (*of a bridge*) bearer, baulk. 2. (*archit.*) well, well-shaft (*for a staircase*).

прого́н², а, *m.* (*dial.*) cattle track.

прого́н³, а, *m.* (*theatr. sl.*) run-through(= *first full rehearsal of play in order of scenes*).

прого́нк|а, и, *f.* (*tech.*) die, screw die.

прого́н|ный, *adj. of* ~ы; ~ные (де́ньги) (*obs.*) travelling allowance.

прого́н|ы, ов, *no sing.* (*obs.*) travelling allowance.

прогоня́|ть, ю, *impf. of* прогна́ть.

прогор|а́ть, а́ю, *impf. of* ~е́ть¹.

прогор|е́ть¹, ю́, и́шь, *pf.* (*of* ~а́ть) 1. to burn through; to burn to a cinder. 2. (*coll.*) to go bankrupt, go bust.

прогор|е́ть², ю́, и́шь, *pf.* to burn (*for a certain time*).

прого́рклост|ь, и, *f.* rancidity, rankness.

прого́рклый, *adj.* rancid, rank.

прого́рк|нуть, ну, нешь, *past* ~, ~ла, *pf. of* го́ркнуть.

прого|сти́ть, щу́, сти́шь, *pf.* to stay.

програ́мм|а, ы, *f.* programme; schedule; театра́льная п. play-bill; уче́бная п. syllabus; curriculum; п. ска́чек race-card; п. спорти́вных состяза́ний fixture list.

програ́мм|ный, *adj.* 1. *adj. of* ~а; ~ная му́зыка programme music. 2. (*tech.*) programmed, automatically operated.

прогрева́|ть(ся), ю(сь), *impf. of* прогре́ть(ся).

прогрем|е́ть, лю́, и́шь, *pf.* to thunder.

прогре́сс, а, *m.* progress.

прогресси́вк|а, и, *f.* (*abbr. of* прогресси́вная опла́та; *coll.*) payment on sliding scale (*for completion of piece-work in excess of plan*).

прогресси́в|ный (~ен, ~на), *adj.* (*in var. senses*) progressive.

прогресси́р|овать, ую, *impf.* to progress, make progress; (*of an illness*) to grow progressively worse.

прогре́сси|я, и, *f.* (*math.*) progression.

прогре́|ть, ю, *pf.* (*of* ~ва́ть) to heat, warm thoroughly; п. мото́р to warm up an engine.

прогре́|ться, юсь, *pf.* (*of* ~ва́ться) to get thoroughly warmed; (*of an engine, etc.*) to warm up.

прогрохо|ти́ть, чу́, ти́шь, *pf. of* грохоти́ть.

прогрыз|а́ть, а́ю, *impf. of* ~ть.

прогры́з|ть, у́, ёшь, *past* ~, ~ла, *pf.* (*of* ~а́ть) to gnaw through.

прогу́л, а, *m.* absence (from work); absenteeism; truancy.

прогу́лива|ть, ю, *impf.* 1. *impf. of* прогуля́ть¹. 2. *impf. only* to walk; п. ло́шадь to walk a horse.

прогу́лива|ться, юсь, *impf.* 1. *impf. of* прогуля́ться. 2. *impf. only* to stroll, saunter.

прогу́лк|а, и, *f.* 1. walk; stroll; ramble; п. для моцио́на constitutional. 2. outing; п. в экипа́же, п. в автомоби́ле drive; п. в ло́дке row; п. под паруса́ми sail; п. верхо́м ride.

прогу́л|очный, *adj. of* ~ка; ~очная ло́дка pleasure-boat (*as opp. to racing-craft*).

прогу́л|ьный, *adj. of* ~; ~ьное вре́мя time off work (*without good cause*).

прогу́льщик, а, *m.* absentee; truant.

прогуля́|ть¹, ю, *pf.* (*of* прогу́ливать) 1. to be absent from work (*without good cause*); to play truant. 2. to miss; п. обе́д to miss one's dinner (*as result of failing to appear at right time*); п. уро́ки to play truant.

прогуля́|ть², ю, *pf.* to walk; to stroll.

прогуля́|ться, юсь, *pf.* (*of* прогу́ливаться) to take a walk, stroll; пойти́ п. to go for a walk.

прода|ва́ть, ю́, ёшь, *impf. of* ~ть.

прода|ва́ться, ю́сь, ёшься, *impf.* 1. (*impf. only*) to be on sale, be for sale; дом ~ётся the house is for sale; ~ётся мотоци́кл (*for-*

mula of advertisement of sale) 'motor-cycle for sale'. **2.** (*impf. only*) to sell; дёшево п. to sell cheap, go cheap; его́ но́вый рома́н хорошо́ ~ётся his new novel is selling well, is having good sales. **3.** *impf. of* ~ться.

прода́в|е́ц, ца́, *m.* **1.** seller; vendor. **2.** salesman, shop-assistant.

прода́в|и́ть, лю́, ~ишь, *pf.* (*of* ~ливать) to break (through); to crush.

прода́влива|ть, ю, *impf. of* продави́ть.

прода́вщи́ц|а, ы, *f.* **1.** seller; vendor. **2.** saleswoman, shop-assistant, shop-girl.

прода́ж|а, и, *f.* sale, selling; опто́вая п. wholesale; п. в ро́зницу retail; п. с торго́в auction sale, public sale; пусти́ть в ~y to put on sale; пойти́ в ~y to be offered for sale, be on the market, be up for sale; поступи́ть в ~y to be on sale, be on the market; нет в ~e is not on sale, is not obtainable; (*of a book*) is out of print.

прода́жност|ь, и, *f.* mercenariness, venality.

прода́ж|ный, *adj.* **1.** to be sold, for sale; ~ная цена́ sale price. **2.** (~ен, ~на) (*fig.*) mercenary, venal; ~ная душа́ mercenary creature; ~ная же́нщина streetwalker.

прода́лблива|ть, ю, *impf. of* продолби́ть.

прода́|ть, м, шь, ст, ди́м, ди́те, ду́т, *past* про́дал, ~ла́, про́дало, *pf.* (*of* ~ва́ть) **1.** to sell; п. о́птом to sell wholesale; п. в ро́зницу to sell retail; п. с торго́в to auction; п. в креди́т to sell on credit, on tick; п. себе́ в убы́ток to sell at a loss. **2.** (*fig., pejor.*) to sell, sell out.

прода́|ться, мся, шься, стся, ди́мся, ди́тесь, ду́тся, *past* ~лся, ~ла́сь, *pf.* (*of* ~ва́ться) to sell oneself.

продвига́|ть(ся), ю(сь), *impf. of* продви́нуть(ся).

продвиже́ни|е, я, *n.* **1.** advancement. **2.** (*mil.; fig.*) progress, advance.

продви́|нуть, ну, нешь, *pf.* (*of* ~га́ть) **1.** to move forward, push forward. **2.** (*fig.*) to promote, further, advance; п. по слу́жбе to promote, give promotion; п. де́ло to expedite a matter.

продви́|нуться, нусь, нешься, *pf.* (*of* ~га́ться) **1.** to advance (*also fig.*); to move on, move forward; to push on, push forward; to forge ahead; п. вперёд (*mil. and fig.*) to gain ground, make headway, make an advance. **2.** to be promoted, receive promotion, receive advancement. **3.** *pass. of* ~нуть.

продева́|ть, ю, *impf. of* проде́ть.

продежу́р|ить, ю, ишь, *pf.* to be on duty (*for a certain time*).

продеклами́р|овать, ую, *pf. of* деклами́ровать.

проде́л|ать, аю, *pf.* (*of* ~ывать) **1.** to make (*an aperture, a way through, etc.*). **2.** to do,

perform, accomplish; п. большу́ю рабо́ту to accomplish a great work.

проде́лк|а, и, *f.* trick; prank, escapade; моше́нническая п. dirty trick, swindle, fraud.

проде́лыва|ть, ю, *impf. of* проде́лать.

продемонстри́р|овать, ую, *pf. of* демонстри́ровать.

проде́рг|ать, аю, *pf.* (*of* ~ивать) (*agric.*) to thin (out), weed (out).

продёргива|ть, ю, *impf. of* продёргать *and* продёрнуть.

продерж|а́ть, у́, ~ишь, *pf.* to hold (*for a certain time*); to keep (*for a certain time*); его́ ~а́ли два ме́сяца в больни́це he was kept in hospital for two months.

продерж|а́ться, у́сь, ~ишься, *pf.* to hold out.

продёр|нуть, ну, нешь, *pf.* (*of* ~гивать) (*coll.*) **1.** to pass, run; п. ни́тку в иго́лку to thread a needle. **2.** (*fig.*) to tear to shreds, pull to pieces (= *to criticize severely*).

проде́|ть, ну, нешь, *pf.* (*of* ~ва́ть) to pass, run; п. ни́тку в иго́лку to thread a needle.

продефили́р|овать, ую, *pf. of* дефили́ровать.

продешев|и́ть, лю́, и́шь, *pf.* (*coll.*) to sell too cheap.

продикт|ова́ть, у́ю, *pf. of* диктова́ть.

продира́|ть(ся), ю(сь), *impf. of* продра́ть(ся).

продлева́|ть, ю, *impf. of* продли́ть.

продле́ни|е, я, *n.* extension, prolongation.

продл|ённый, *p.p.p. of* ~и́ть; шко́ла с ~ённым днём extended-day school.

продл|и́ть, ю́, и́шь, *pf.* (*of* ~ева́ть) to extend, prolong; п. о́тпуск to extend leave; п. срок де́йствия ви́зы to extend a visa.

продл|и́ться, ю́сь, и́шься, *pf. of* дли́ться.

продна́лог, а, *m.* (*abbr. of* продово́льственный нало́г) (*hist.*) tax in kind.

продово́льств|енный, *adj. of* ~ие; ~енная ка́рточка ration book, ration card, food-card; п. магази́н grocery (store), provision store; ~енные райо́ны food-producing areas; п. склад food store; (*mil.*) ration store, ration dump; ~енное снабже́ние food supply; ~енные това́ры food-stuffs.

продово́льстви|е, я, *n.* food-stuffs, provisions; (*mil.*) rations; но́рма ~я ration scale.

продолб|и́ть, лю́, и́шь, *pf.* (*of* прода́лбливать) to make a hole (in), chisel through.

продолгова́тост|ь, и, *f.* oblong form.

продолгова́т|ый (~, ~а), *adj.* oblong; п. мозг (*anat.*) medulla oblongata.

продолжа́тел|ь, я, *m.* continuer, successor.

продолж|а́ть, а́ю, *impf.* **1.** to continue, go on, proceed; п. свою́ рабо́ту to continue, go on with one's work; п. рабо́тать to

continue to work, go on working. **2.** *impf.*
of ~ить.

продолж|а́ться, а́ется, *impf.* (*of* ~и́ться) to
continue, last, go on, be in progress;
восста́ние ~а́ется уже́ второ́й год the in-
surrection is now in its second year.

продолже́ни|е, я, *n.* **1.** continuation; se-
quel; п. сле́дует to be continued. **2.** extension, prolongation; continuation; п. ли́нии
extension of a line; забо́р слу́жит ~ем
стены́ the fence serves as a continuation of
the wall. **3.** в п. (+*g.*) in the course (of),
during, for, throughout; в п. го́да throughout the year; в п. почти́ двух лет я ни
ра́зу её не вида́л during almost two years
I did not see her once.

продолжи́тельност|ь, и, *f.* duration, length.
продолжи́тел|ьный (~ен, ~ьна), *adj.* long;
prolonged, protracted.

продо́лж|ить, у, ишь, *pf.* (*of* ~а́ть) **1.** to
extend, prolong. **2.** *pf. of* ~а́ть 1.

продо́лж|иться, усь, ишься, *pf. of* ~а́ться.

продо́льн|ый, *adj.* longitudinal, lengthwise,
linear; (*naut.*) ~ая ось longi-
tudinal axis; ~ая перебо́рка (*naut.*) fore-
-and-aft bulkhead; ~ая пила́ rip-saw; п.
разре́з longitudinal section.

продохн|у́ть, у́, ёшь, *pf.* (*coll.*) to breathe
freely.

продразвёрстк|а, и, *f.* (*abbr. of* продово́ль-
ственная развёрстка) (*hist.*) requisitioning
of farm produce.

про|дра́ть, деру́, дерёшь, *past* ~дра́л,
~драла́, ~дра́ло, *pf.* (*of* ~дира́ть) (*coll.*)
to tear; to wear holes (in); п. глаза́ to open
one's eyes.

про|дра́ться, деру́сь, дерёшься, *past* ~дра́л-
ся, ~драла́сь, ~дра́ло́сь, *pf.* (*of* ~дира́ть-
ся) (*coll.*) **1.** to tear; to wear into holes; у
меня́ ло́кти ~дра́лись my coat is out at the
elbows. **2.** to squeeze through, force one's
way through.

продрем|а́ть, лю́, ~лешь, *pf.* to doze (*for a
certain time*).

продро́г|нуть, ну, нешь, *past* ~, ~ла, *pf.* to
be chilled to the marrow.

продува́ни|е, я, *n.* = продувка.

продува́тельный, *adj.* = продувочный.

продува́|ть, ю, *impf.* **1.** *impf. of* проду́ть.
2. (*impf. only*) to blow (*from all sides*);
прия́тно ~л ветеро́к there was a pleasant
breeze.

продува́|ться, юсь, *impf. of* проду́ться.

проду́вк|а, и, *f.* (*tech.*) blowing through,
blowing off; scavenging.

продув|но́й¹, *adj.* (*tech.*) = ~о́чный.

продувн|о́й², *adj.* (*coll.*) crafty, sly, roguish;
~а́я бе́стия rogue.

проду́в|очный, *adj. of* ~ка; п. во́здух
scavenging air; п. кла́пан blow valve,

blow-off valve; п. насо́с scavenging pump;
~о́чная труба́ blow-off pipe, blast pipe.

проду́кт, а, *m.* **1.** product; побо́чный п.
by-product; ~ы сгора́ния (*chem.*) products
of combustion. **2.** *pl.* produce; provisions,
food-stuffs; моло́чные ~ы dairy produce;
~ы се́льского хозя́йства farm produce.

продукти́вно, *adv.* productively; with a
good result, to good effect.

продукти́вност|ь, и, *f.* productivity.

продукти́в|ный (~ен, ~на), *adj.* (*in var.
senses*) productive; (*fig.*) fruitful; п. скот
productive livestock; п. су́ффикс (*ling.*)
productive suffix.

продукто́вый, *adj.* food, provision; п. мага-
зи́н grocery (store), provision store.

проду́кци|я, и, *f.* production, output.

проду́ма|нный, *p.p.p. of* ~ть и and *adj.* well
thought-out, considered; ~нное реше́ние
a considered decision.

проду́м|ать, аю, *pf.* (*of* ~ывать) to think
over; to think out.

проду́мыва|ть, ю, *impf. of* проду́мать.

проду́|ть, ю, ешь, *pf.* (*of* ~ва́ть) **1.** to blow
through; (*tech.*) to blow through, blow off,
blow out; to scavenge. **2.** (*impers.+а.*) to
be in a draught; придви́ньте стул, а то
вас ~ет bring your chair up, or else you will
be in a draught. **3.** (*coll.*) to lose (*at games*).

проду́|ться, юсь, ешься, *pf.* (*of* ~ва́ться)
(*coll.*) to lose (*at games*).

проду́шин|а, ы, *f.* air-hole, vent.

продыря́в|ить, лю, ишь, *pf.* (*of* ~ливать)
to make a hole (in), pierce.

продыря́в|иться, люсь, ишься, *pf.* (*of*
~ливаться) to become full of holes.

продыря́влива|ть(ся), ю(сь), *impf. of* про-
дыря́вить(ся).

проеда́|ть(ся), ю(сь), *impf. of* прое́сть(ся).

прое́зд, а, *m.* **1.** passage, thoroughfare; ~а
нет! no thoroughfare! **2.** journey.

прое́з|дить¹, жу, дишь, *pf.* (*of* ~жа́ть) **1.** to
exercise (*a horse, etc.*). **2.** (*coll.*) to spend on
a journey, in travelling; мы ~дили сто
рубле́й we got through a hundred roubles
on the journey.

прое́з|дить², жу, дишь, *pf.* to spend (*a cer-
tain time*) driving, riding, travelling; они́
~дили тро́е су́ток they had travelled for
three days and nights.

прое́з|диться, жусь, дишься, *pf.* (*coll.*) to
have spent all one's money on a journey,
in travelling.

проездн|о́й, *adj.* travelling; п. биле́т
ticket; ~а́я пла́та fare; *as noun* ~ы́е, ~ы́х
travelling expenses.

прое́здом, *adv.* en route, in transit, while
passing through.

проезжа́|ть, ю, *impf. of* прое́здить *and* про-
е́хать.

проéзж|ий, *adj.*; ~ая дорóга thoroughfare, public road; ~ие лю́ди passers-by; *as noun* п., ~его, *m.* passer-by.

проéкт, **а**, *m.* **1.** project, scheme, design. **2.** draft; п. договóра draft treaty.

проекти́вн|ый, *adj.* ~ая геомéтрия descriptive geometry, projecting geometry.

проекти́ровани|е, **я**, *n.* projecting, planning, designing.

проекти́р|овать¹, **ую**, *impf.* **1.** (*pf.* за~ and с~) to project, plan, design; п. нóвый теáтр to design a new theatre. **2.** *impf. only* (*fig.*) to plan; мы ~уем уéхать веснóй we plan to go away in the spring.

проекти́р|овать², **ую**, *impf.* (*math.*) to project.

проектирóвк|а, **и**, *f.* = проекти́рование.

проектирóвщик, **а**, *m.* planner, designer.

проéктн|ый, *adj.* **1.** planning, designing; ~ое бюрó planning office. **2.** designed; ~ая мóщность (*tech.*) rated capacity; ~ая скóрость designed speed.

проекциóнный, *adj.* п. фонáрь projector, magic lantern.

проéкци|я, **и**, *f.* **1.** (*math.*) projection; вертикáльная п. vertical projection, front view; elevation; горизонтáльная п. horizontal projection, plan view. **2.** projection (*on to a screen*).

проём, **а**, *m.* (*archit.*) aperture; embrasure; двернóй п. doorway.

проé|сть, **м**, **шь**, **ст**, **ди́м**, **ди́те**, **дя́т**, *past* ~л, *pf.* (*of* ~дáть) **1.** to eat through; to corrode. **2.** (*coll.*) to spend on food.

проé|сться, **мся**, **шься**, **стся**, **ди́мся**, **ди́тесь**, **дя́тся**, *past* ~лся, *pf.* (*of* ~дáться) (*coll.*) to spend all one's money on food.

проé|хать, **ду**, **дешь**, *pf.* (*of* ~зжáть) **1.** to pass (by, through); to drive (by, through), ride (by, through). **2.** to pass, go past (*inadvertently or by mistake*). **3.** to go, do, make, cover (*a certain distance*).

проé|хаться, **дусь**, **дешься**, *pf.* (*coll.*) to go for an outing; п. на чей-н. счёт, п. по чьему-н. áдресу (*joc.*) to take it out of someone, have a laugh at someone's expense.

прожáр|енный, *p.p.p. of* ~ить *and adj.* (*cul.*) well-done.

прожáрива|ть(ся), **ю(сь)**, *impf. of* прожáрить(ся)

прожáр|ить, **ю**, **ишь**, *pf.* (*of* ~ивать) to fry, roast thoroughly.

прожáр|иться, **юсь**, **ишься**, *pf.* (*of* ~иваться) **1.** to fry, roast thoroughly. **2.** *pass. of* ~ить.

прожд|áть, **у́**, **ёшь**, *past* ~áл, ~алá, ~áло, *pf.* (+*a.* or *g.*) to wait (for), spend (*a certain time*) waiting (for).

прож|евáть, **ую**, **уёшь**, *pf.* (*of* ~ёвывать) to chew well, masticate well.

прожёвыва|ть, **ю**, *impf. of* прожевáть.

прожéкт, **а**, *m.* **1.** (*obs.*) = проéкт. **2.** (*coll., iron.*) (hare-brained, impracticable) project, scheme.

прожектёр, **а**, *m.* deviser of impracticable schemes.

прожектёрств|о, **а**, *n.* penchant for, indulging in, hare-brained schemes.

прожектёрств|овать, **ую**, *impf.* to devote oneself to devising hare-brained schemes.

прожéктор, **а**, *pl.* ~ы *and* ~á, *m.* searchlight; п. заливáющего свéта floodlight projector.

прожектори́ст, **а**, *m.* searchlight operator.

прожéктор|ный, *adj. of* ~.

прóжелт|ь, **и**, *f.* yellow tint.

про|жéчь, **жгу́**, **жжёшь**, **жгу́т**, *past* ~жёг, ~жглá *pf.* (*of* ~жигáть) **1.** to burn thorugh; п. дыру́ в чём-н. to burn a hole in something. **2.** to burn, leave alight (*for a certain time*).

про|жжённый, *p.p.p. of* ~жéчь. *and adj.* (*coll.*) arch, double-dyed; п. плут arch-scoundrel.

прожива́|ть, **ю**, *impf.* **1.** to live, reside. **2.** *impf. of* прожи́ть.

прожива́|ться, **юсь**, *impf. of* прожи́ться.

прожига́тел|ь, **я**, *m.* п. жи́зни fast liver.

прожига́|ть¹, **ю**, *impf. of* прожéчь.

прожига́|ть², **ю**, *impf.* п. жизнь to lead a fast life, live fast.

прожи́лк|а, **и**, *f.* (*in var. senses*) vein.

прожи́ти|е, **я**, *n.* living, livelihood; хватáет ли у них дéнег на п.? have they enough to live on?

прожи́точный, *adj.* necessary, sufficient to live on; п. ми́нимум living wage, subsistence wage.

про|жи́ть, **живу́**, **живёшь**, *past* ~жи́л, ~жилá, ~жи́ло, *pf.* (*of* ~живáть) **1.** to live; он ~жи́л сто лет he lived to be a hundred (*years of age*). **2.** to spend; мы ~жи́ли мéсяц áвгуст на берегу́ мóря we spent the month of August at the seaside. **3.** to spend, run through (*money*); в оди́н год я ~жи́л наслéдство in a year I had run through the legacy.

про|жи́ться, **живу́сь**, **живёшься**, *past* ~жи́лся, ~жилáсь, *pf.* (*of* ~живáться) (*coll.*) to have spent all one's money, be spent up.

прожóрливост|ь, **и**, *f.* voracity, voraciousness, gluttony.

прожóрлив|ый (~, ~а), *adj.* voracious, gluttonous.

прожужж|áть, **у́**, **и́шь**, *pf.* to buzz, drone, hum; п. у́ши кому́-н. (*coll.*) to keep dinning something into someone's ears, drone on at someone.

про́з|а, ы, *f.* prose; п. жи́зни the prosaic side of life.

прозаи́зм, а, *m.* prosaic expression (*in poetry*).

проза́ик, а, *m.* prose-writer, prosaist.

прозаи́ческий, *adj.* **1.** prose; п. перево́д prose translation. **2.** prosaic; matter-of--fact; prosy.

прозаи́чност|ь, и, *f.* **1.** matter-of-factness; prosiness. **2.** (*fig.*) dullness, flatness.

прозаи́ч|ный (~ен, ~на), *adj.* **1.** prosaic; matter-of-fact; prosy. **2.** (*fig.*) common-place, humdrum.

прозакла́дыва|ть, ю, *impf. and pf.* (*coll.*) **1.** to stake, wager. **2.** (*obs.*) to lose (*in betting*).

прозва́ни|е, я, *n.* nickname, sobriquet; по ~ю nicknamed, otherwise known as.

про|зва́ть, зову́, зовёшь, *past* ~зва́л, ~звала́, ~зва́ло, *pf.* (*of* ~зыва́ть) to nick-name, name.

про́звищ|е, а, *n.* nickname, sobriquet.

прозвон|и́ть, ю́, и́шь, *pf.* **1.** to ring out, peal. **2.** to ring for, announce by ringing; ~и́ли обе́д, ~и́ли обе́дать the bell (gong, *etc.*) went for dinner.

прозвуч|а́ть, и́т, *pf. of* звуча́ть.

прозева́|ть[1], ю, *pf. of* зева́ть 3.

прозева́|ть[2], ю, *pf.* to yawn (*for a certain time*).

прозе́ктор, а, *m.* prosector, dissector.

прозе́кторск|ая, ой, *f.* dissecting-room.

прозели́т, а, *m.* proselyte.

прозим|ова́ть, у́ю, *pf. of* зимова́ть.

прозна́|ть, ю, *pf.* (+*a.* or *o*+*p.*; *coll.*) to find out (about), hear (about).

прозоде́жд|а, ы, *f.* (*abbr. of* произво́дственная оде́жда) working clothes; overalls.

прозорли́вост|ь, и, *f.* sagacity, perspicacity, intuition.

прозорли́в|ый (~, ~а), *adj.* sagacious, per-spicacious.

прозра́чност|ь, и, *f.* transparence, trans-parency.

прозра́ч|ный (~ен, ~на), *adj.* transparent (*also fig.*); limpid, pellucid; п. намёк trans-parent hint.

прозрева́|ть, ю, *impf. of* прозре́ть.

прозре́ни|е, я, *n.* **1.** recovery of sight. **2.** (*fig.*) insight.

прозр|е́ть, ю́, и́шь, *pf.* (*of* ~ева́ть) **1.** to recover one's sight. **2.** (*fig.*) to begin to see clearly; тут-то я и ~е́л my eyes were opened, I saw the light.

прозыва́|ть, ю, *impf. of* прозва́ть.

прозыва́|ться, юсь, *impf.* to be nicknamed, have a nickname.

прозяба́ни|е, я, *n.* vegetation (*also fig.*).

прозяба́|ть, ю, *impf.* to vegetate (*also fig.*).

прозя́б|нуть, ну, нешь, *past* ~, ~ла, *pf.* (*coll.*) to be chilled.

проигр|а́ть[1], а́ю, *pf.* (*of* ~ывать) to lose (= *to be defeated, etc.*); п. фигу́ру to lose a piece (*at chess*); п. суде́бный проце́сс to lose a case; мы ничего́ не ~а́ли, прие́хав авто́бусом we lost nothing in coming by 'bus; п. в чьём-н. мне́нии to sink in some-one's estimation.

проигр|а́ть[2], а́ю, *pf.* (*of* ~ывать) to play (through, over); п. конце́рт на патефо́нных пласти́нках to play through a concerto on gramophone records; п. магнитофо́н-ную ле́нту to play over a tape (*on a tape recorder*).

проигр|а́ть[3], а́ю, *pf.* to play (*for a certain time*).

проигр|а́ться, а́юсь, *pf.* (*of* ~ываться) to lose all one's money (*at gambling*).

прои́грыватель, я, *m.* record-player.

прои́грыва|ть(ся), ю(сь), *impf. of* про-игра́ть(ся).

про́игрыш, а, *m.* loss; оста́ться в ~е to be the loser, come off loser.

произведе́ни|е, я, *n.* **1.** work, production; и́збранные ~я Л. Н. Толсто́го selected works of L. N. Tolstoy; ме́лкие ~я minor works. **2.** (*math.*) product.

произве|сти́, ду́, дёшь, *past* ~л, ~ла́, *pf.* (*of* производи́ть) **1.** to make; to carry out; to execute; п. вы́стрел to fire a shot; п. о́пыты to carry out experiments; п. пла-тёж to effect payment; п. сле́дствие to hold an inquest; п. смотр (+*d.*) to hold a review (of), review; п. съёмку кино-фи́льма to shoot a film; п. уче́ние (*mil.*) to drill, train. **2.** to give birth (to); п. на свет to bring into the world. **3.** (*fig.*) to cause, produce; п. впечатле́ние (на+*a.*) to make, create an impression (on, upon); п. сен-са́цию to cause, make a sensation. **4.** (в+ *n.-a.*) to promote (to, to the rank of); его́ ~ли́ в подполко́вники he has been promoted (to the rank of) lieutenant--colonel.

производи́тел|ь[1], я, *m.* **1.** producer; ме́л-кие ~и small producers. **2.** sire; жеребе́ц--п. stud-horse.

производи́тел|ь[2], я, *m.* п. рабо́т clerk of the works.

производи́тельност|ь, и, *f.* productivity, output; productiveness.

производи́тел|ьный (~ен, ~ьна), *adj.* pro-ductive; efficient.

произво|ди́ть, жу́, ~дишь, *impf.* **1.** *impf. of* произвести́. **2.** *impf. only* to produce. **3.** *impf. only* (*ling.*) to derive.

произво́дн|ый, *adj.* derivative, derived; ~ое сло́во derivative; *as noun* ~ая, ~ой, *f.* (*math.*) derivative.

произво́дственник, а, *m.* one (directly) en-gaged in production.

произво́дств|енный, *adj. of* ~о; ~енное зада́ние production target, production quota; ~енное обуче́ние industrial training; ~енная пра́ктика practical training; ~енное совеща́ние production conference; п. стаж industrial work record, industrial experience.

произво́дств|о, а, *n.* 1. production, manufacture; изде́ржки ~а production costs; сре́дства ~а means of production; изде́лия куста́рного, фабри́чного ~а hand-made, factory-made goods; сове́тского ~а Soviet--made, Soviet-produced; рабо́тать на ~е to work on production. 2. factory, works; пойти́ на п. to go to work at a factory. 3. carrying-out, execution. 4. (в+*n.–a.*) promotion (to, to the rank of).

производ|я́щий, *pres. part. act. of* ~и́ть *and adj.* (*econ.*) producing, producer.

произво́л, а, *m.* 1. arbitrariness; оста́вить на п. судьбы́ to leave to the mercy of fate. 2. arbitrary rule.

произво́льно, *adv.* 1. arbitrarily. 2. at will.

произво́льност|ь, и, *f.* arbitrariness.

произво́л|ьный (~ен, ~ьна), *adj.* arbitrary.

произнесе́ни|е, я, *n.* pronouncing; utterance, delivery.

произнес|ти́, у́, ёшь, *past* ~, ~ла́, *pf.* (*of* произноси́ть) 1. to pronounce; to articulate. 2. to pronounce, say, utter; п. пригово́р to pronounce sentence; п. речь to deliver a speech; он не ~ ни сло́ва he did not utter a word.

произноси́тельн|ый, *adj.* (*ling.*) articulatory; п. аппара́т articulatory apparatus; ~ые тру́дности англи́йского языка́ the difficulties of English pronunciation.

произно|си́ть, шу́, ~сишь, *impf. of* произнести́.

произноше́ни|е, я, *n.* pronunciation; articulation.

произо|йти́, йду́, йдёшь, *past* ~шёл, ~шла́, *pf.* (*of* происходи́ть) 1. to happen, occur, take place. 2. (от, из-за) to spring (from), arise (from), result (from); ава́рия ~шла́ от небре́жности the crash resulted from carelessness. 3. (из, от) to come (from, of), descend (from), be descended (from).

произраста́ни|е, я, *n.* growth, growing, sprouting.

произраст|а́ть, а́ет, *impf. of* ~и́.

произраст|и́, ёт, *past* произро́с, произросла́, *pf.* (*of* ~а́ть) to grow, sprout, spring up.

проиллюстри́р|овать, ую, *pf.* (*of* иллюстри́ровать) to illustrate.

проинструкти́р|овать, ую, *pf.* (*of* инструкти́ровать) to instruct, give instructions (to).

проинтервьюи́р|овать, ую, *pf.* (*of* интервью́ировать) to interview.

проинформи́р|овать, ую, *pf.* (*of* информи́ровать) to inform.

прои|ска́ть, щу́, ~щешь, *pf.* to look (for), search (for), spend (*a certain time*) in search (of).

про́иск|и, ов, *no sing.* intrigues; machinations, underhand plotting.

проистека́|ть, ю, *impf. of* происте́чь.

происте́|чь, ку́, чёшь, ку́т, *past* ~к, ~кла́, *pf.* (*of* ~ка́ть) (из, от) to spring (from), result (from).

происхо|ди́ть, жу́, ~дишь, *impf.* 1. *impf. of* произойти́. 2. *impf. only* to go on, be going on; что тут ~дит? what is going on here?

происхожде́ни|е, я, *n.* (*in var. senses*) origin; provenance; parentage, descent, extraction, birth; п. ви́дов (*biol.*) origin of species; он по ~ю армяни́н he is an Armenian by birth, he is of Armenian extraction.

происше́стви|е, я, *n.* event, incident, happening, occurrence; accident; отде́л ~й (*in newspaper*) local news.

пройдо́х|а, и, *m. and f.* (*coll.*) creeper; scoundrel, rascal.

про́йм|а, ы, *f.* armhole.

про|йти́, йду́, йдёшь, *past* ~шёл, ~шла́, *pf.* (*of* ~ходи́ть¹) 1. to pass (by, through); to go (by, through); п. ми́мо to pass by, go by, go past; (+*g.*; *fig.*) to overlook, disregard; п. по́лем to go by, through the field(s); п. торже́ственным ма́ршем to march past; п. молча́нием to pass over in silence; п. по мосту́ to cross a bridge; п. в жизнь to be put into effect. 2. to pass, go past (*inadvertently or by mistake*). 3. to go, do, make, cover (*a certain distance*); п. две ты́сячи миль за неде́лю to do two thousand miles in a week. 4. (*of news, rumours, etc.*) to travel, spread. 5. (*of rain, etc.*) to fall. 6. (*of time*) to pass, elapse, go, go by; ~шёл це́лый год a whole year had passed; не ~шло́ шести́ ме́сяцев, как он верну́лся not six months had passed before he returned. 7. to be over; to pass (off), abate, let up; ~шло́ ле́то summer was over; боль ~шла́ the pain passed (off); дождь ~шёл the rain abated. 8. (+*a. or* че́рез) to pass, go through, get through; де́ло ~шло́ мно́го инста́нций the case went through many instances; его́ пье́са снача́ла не ~шла́ че́рез цензу́ру his play at first did not pass the censorship; э́то не ~йдёт (*coll.*) it won't work. 9. to go, go off; как ~шёл ваш докла́д? how did your lecture go?; заседа́ние ~шло́ уда́чно the meeting went off successfully. 10. (в+*n.–a.*) to become, be made; to be placed (on), be taken (on); он ~шёл в доце́нты he has been made a reader, he has received a readership; она́

~шла́ в шта́т she has been taken on the staff. **11.** (*coll.*) to do, take; п. хи́мию to do chemistry; мы уже́ ~шли́ вое́нную слу́жбу we have already done military service; п. курс лече́ния to take a course of treatment.

про|йти́сь, йду́сь, йдёшься, *past* ~шёлся, ~шла́сь, *pf.* (*of* ~ха́живаться) **1.** to walk up and down, stroll; to take a stroll; п. по ко́мнате to pace up and down the room. **2.** (*coll.*) to dance. **3.** (по+*d.*; *coll.*) to run (over), go (over); п. по кла́вишам to run one's fingers over the keys. **4.** п. на чей-н. счёт, п. по чьему́-н. а́дресу (*coll.*) to have a fling at someone, give someone a bad write-up.

прок, а (у), *m.* (*coll.*) use, benefit; что в э́том ~у? what is the good of it?; из э́того не бу́дет ~у no good will come of this.

прокажённ|ый, *adj.* leprous; *as noun* п., ~ого, *m. and* ~ая, ~ой, *f.* leper.

прока́з|а¹, ы, *f.* leprosy.

прока́з|а², ы, *f.* mischief, prank, trick.

прока́|зить, жу, зишь, *impf.* (*of* на~) (*coll.*) to be up to mischief, play pranks.

прока́злив|ый (~, ~а), *adj.* mischievous.

прока́зник, а, *m.* mischievous person; mischievous child, bundle of mischief.

прока́знича|ть, ю, *impf.* (*of* на~) = прока́зить.

прока́лива|ть, ю, *impf. of* прокали́ть.

прокал|и́ть, ю́, и́шь, *pf.* (*of* ~ивать) (*tech.*) to temper, anneal; to calcine, fire.

прока́лк|а, и, *f.* (*tech.*) tempering.

прока́лыва|ть, ю, *impf. of* проколо́ть.

проканите́л|ить(ся), ю(сь), ишь(ся), *pf. of* каните́лить(ся).

прока́пыва|ть, ю, *impf. of* прокопти́ть.

прока́пыва|ть, ю, *impf. of* прокопа́ть.

прокарау́л|ить¹, ю, ишь, *pf.* (*coll.*) to let slip, let go (*by carelessness, inattention*) while on guard; он ~ил аресто́ванного he let the prisoner escape.

прокарау́л|ить², ю, ишь, *pf.* to be on guard (*for a certain time*); to guard, watch (*for a certain time*).

прока́т¹, а, *m.* (*tech.*) **1.** rolling. **2.** rolled iron.

прока́т², а, *m.* hire; отда́ть на п. to hire out.

прокат|а́ть¹, а́ю, *pf.* (*of* ~ывать) **1.** to spread flat with a roller. **2.** (*tech.*) to roll, laminate.

прокат|а́ть², а́ю, *pf.* to take out (for a drive, etc.) (*for a certain time*).

прокат|а́ться¹, а́юсь, *pf.* (*of* ~ываться) (*tech.*) to roll out.

прокат|а́ться², а́юсь, *pf.* to go out (for a drive, etc.) (*for a certain time*).

прока|ти́ть, чу́, ~тишь, *pf.* (*of* ~тывать) **1.** to take out; to take for a drive, ride. **2.** to roll. **3.** to roll by, past. **4.** (*coll.*) to

slate. **5.** п., (*obs.*) п. на вороны́х to blackball.

прока|ти́ться, чу́сь, ~тишься, *pf.* (*of* ~тываться) **1.** to roll (*also fig., of thunder, etc.*). **2.** to go for a drive, go for a spin.

прока́тк|а, и, *f.* (*tech.*) rolling, lamination.

прока́тн|ый¹, *adj.* (*tech.*) rolling; ~ое желе́зо rolled iron; п. стан rolling mill.

прока́тный², *adj.* hired, let out on hire.

прока́тчик, а, *m.* roller, rolling mill operative.

прока́тыва|ть(ся), ю(сь), *impf. of* проката́ть(ся)¹ *and* прокати́ть(ся).

прока́шлива|ть(ся), ю(сь), *impf. of* прока́шлять(ся).

прока́шл|ять, яю, *pf.* **1.** to cough. **2.** (*impf.* ~ивать) to cough up.

прока́шл|яться, яюсь, *pf.* (*of* ~иваться) to clear one's throat.

прокип|е́ть, и́т, *pf.* to boil thoroughly, sufficiently.

прокипя|ти́ть, чу́, ти́шь, *pf.* to boil thoroughly, sufficiently.

проки́с|ать, а́ет, *impf. of* ~нуть.

проки́с|нуть, нет, *pf.* (*of* ~а́ть) to turn (sour).

прокла́дк|а, и, *f.* **1.** laying; building, construction; п. доро́ги road building; breaking a road; п. трубопрово́да pipe laying. **2.** (*tech.*) washer, gasket; packing, padding, cushion.

прокладн|о́й, *adj.* packing; кни́га с ~ыми листа́ми book with blank sheets (*for notes*).

прокла́дыва|ть, ю, *impf. of* проложи́ть.

проклама́ци|я, и, *f.* (political) leaflet.

прокламм|и́ровать, ую, *impf. and pf.* to proclaim.

прокле́ива|ть, ю, *impf. of* прокле́ить.

прокле́|ить, ю, ишь, *pf.* (*of* ~ивать) to paste, glue; to size.

проклина́|ть, ю, *impf.* **1.** *impf. of* прокля́сть. **2.** (*coll.*) to curse, swear at.

прокл|я́сть, яну́, янёшь, *past* ~ял, ~яла́, ~яло, *pf.* (*of* ~ина́ть) to curse, damn.

прокля́ти|е, я, *n.* **1.** damnation; преда́ть ~ю to consign to perdition. **2.** curse; imprecation. **3.** *as interj.* п.! curse it!, damn it!, damnation!

про́кл|ятый, *p.p.p. of* ~я́сть; будь я ~ят, е́сли... I'm damned if, I'll be damned if...; будь он ~ят! damn him!, curse him!

прокля́тый, *adj.* accursed, damned; (*coll.*) damnable, confounded.

проковы́рива|ть, ю, *impf. of* проковыря́ть.

проковыр|я́ть, я́ю, *pf.* (*of* ~ивать) to pick a hole (in).

проко́л, а, *m.* **1.** puncture. **2.** pricking, piercing.

прокол|о́ть, ю́, ~ешь, *pf.* (*of* прока́лывать) **1.** to prick, pierce; to perforate. **2.** to run through (*with a bayonet, etc.*).

прокоммент́ир|овать, ую, *pf.* to comment (upon).

прокомпост́ир|овать, ую, *pf. of* компости́ровать.

проконоп́а|тить, чу, тишь, *pf. of* конопа́тить.

проконспект́ир|овать, ую, *pf. of* конспект́ировать.

проќонсул, а, *m.* (*hist.*) proconsul.

проконсульт́ир|овать(ся), ую(сь), *pf. of* консульти́ровать(ся).

проконтрол́ир|овать, ую, *pf. of* контроли́ровать.

прокоп́а|ть, ю, *pf.* (*of* прокапывать) 1. to dig. 2. to dig through.

прокоп́а|ться, юсь, *pf.* (*coll., pejor.*) to dawdle, mess about (*for a certain time*).

прокопт́елый, *adj.* (*coll.*) sooty, soot-caked.

прокопт́ить, чу́, ти́шь, *pf.* (*of* прокапчивать) 1. to smoke, cure in smoke. 2. (*coll.*) to foul with smoke, soot.

проќорм, а, *m.* nourishment, sustenance.

прокорм́|ить(ся), лю́(сь), ~ишь(ся), *pf. of* корми́ть(ся).

прокоррект́ир|овать, ую, *pf. of* корректи́ровать.

проќос, а, *m.* swath.

прокр́адыва|ться, юсь, *impf. of* прокра́сться.

прокр́а|сить, шу, сишь, *pf.* (*of* ~шивать) to paint over, cover with paint.

прокр́а|сться, ду́сь, дёшься, *pf.* (*of* ~дываться) to steal; п. ми́мо to steal by, past.

прокр́ашива|ть, ю, *impf. of* прокра́сить.

прокрич́|ать, у́, и́шь, *pf.* 1. to shout, cry; to give a shout, raise a cry. 2. (о+*p.*; *coll.*) to trumpet; п. у́ши кому́-н. о чём-н. to din something into someone's ears.

прокр́устов, *adj.* ~о ло́же (*myth. and fig.*) bed of Procrustes.

прокурат́ур|а, ы, *f.* office of public prosecutor.

проќурива|ть, ю, *impf. of* прокури́ть.

прокур́|ить, ю́, ~ишь, *pf.* (*of* ~ивать) (*coll.*) 1. to spend on smoking. 2. to fill with tobacco smoke.

прокур́ор, а, *m.* public prosecutor; procurator; investigating magistrate; counsel for the prosecution (*in criminal cases*); речь ~а speech for the prosecution.

прокур́ор|ский, *adj. of* ~; п. надзо́р powers of procurator; довести́ до све́дения ~ского надзо́ра to inform the procurator's office.

проќус, а, *m.* bite.

проку|си́ть, шу́, ~сишь, *pf.* (*of* ~сывать) to bite through.

проќусыва|ть, ю, *impf. of* прокуси́ть.

проку|ти́ть, чу́, ~тишь, *pf.* (*of* ~чивать) (*coll.*) 1. to squander, dissipate. 2. to go on the spree, go on the binge.

проку|ти́ться, чу́сь, ~тишься, *pf.* (*of* ~чиваться) (*coll.*) to dissipate one's money.

проќучива|ть(ся), ю(сь), *impf. of* прокути́ть(ся).

пролаѓа|ть, ю, *impf. of* проложи́ть.

прол́аз|а, ы, *m. and f.* (*coll.*) creeper; scoundrel, rascal.

прол́амыва|ть(ся), ю(сь), *impf. of* проломи́ть(ся) *and* проломи́ть(ся).

прилеѓа|ть, ет, *impf.* to lie, run; доро́га ~ла вдоль бе́рега кана́ла the path lay by the canal.

пролеж́|ать, у́, и́шь, *pf.* (*of* ~ивать) to lie; to spend (*a certain time*) lying; она́ всю зи́му ~а́ла в посте́ли she spent the whole winter in bed; посы́лка неде́лю ~а́ла на по́чте the parcel lay for a week in the post office.

прол́еж|ень, ня, *m.* (*med.*) bedsore.

прол́ёжива|ть, ю, *impf. of* пролежа́ть.

пролез|а́ть, а́ю, *impf. of* ~ть.

прол́ез|ть, у, ешь, *past* ~, ~ла, *pf.* (*of* ~а́ть) 1. to get through, climb through. 2. (в+*a.*; *fig., coll., pejor.*) to worm oneself (into, on to); он ~ в чле́ны комите́та he has wormed his way on to the committee.

прол́ёт[1], а, *m.* flight.

прол́ёт[2], а, *m.* 1. (*archit.*) bay; п. мо́ста span. 2. stair-well. 3. (*coll.*) stage (*distance between stations on railway*).

пролетари́ат, а, *m.* proletariat.

пролетариз́аци|я, и, *f.* proletarianization.

пролетар́из|овать, ую, *impf. and pf.* to proletarianize.

пролетар́и|й, я, *m.* proletarian; ~и всех стран, соединя́йтесь! workers of the world, unite!

пролет́арский, *adj.* proletarian.

пролет|а́ть[1], а́ю, *pf. of* ~е́ть.

пролет|а́ть[2], а́ю, *pf.* to fly (*for a certain time*).

проле|те́ть, чу́, ти́шь, *pf.* (*of* ~та́ть[1]) 1. to fly, cover (*a certain distance*). 2. to fly (by, through, past) (*also fig.*); кани́кулы ~те́ли the holidays flew (by). 3. (*fig.*) to flash, flit; у неё в голове́ ~те́ла мысль a thought flashed through her mind.

прол́ётк|а, и, *f.* droshky, (horse-)cab.

прол́ётн|ый, *adj.* ~ая пти́ца bird of passage.

прол́ив, а, *m.* (*geogr.*) strait, sound.

пролив́а|ть, ю, *impf. of* проли́ть.

проливн́ой, *adj.* п. дождь pouring rain, pelting rain; шёл п. дождь it was pouring.

прол́ити|е, я, *n.* shedding; п. кро́ви bloodshed.

прол́|ить, ью, ьёшь, *past* ~и́л, ~ила́, ~и́ло, *pf.* (*of* ~ива́ть) to spill, shed; п. чью-н. кровь to shed someone's blood; п. слёзы (по+*d. or p.*, о+*p.*) to shed tears (over); п. свет (на+*a.*; *fig.*) to shed light (on).

про́лог, а, *m.* (*lit.*) calendar (*collection of*

saints' lives, homilies, etc., arranged in order of the calendar).

проло́г, а, *m.* prologue.

проло́ж|и́ть, у́, ~ишь, *pf.* (*of* прокла́дывать) **1.** (*impf. also* пролага́ть) to lay; to build, construct; п. доро́гу to build, break a road; (*fig.*) to pave the way; п. себе́ доро́гу че́рез толпу́ to hack one's way through the crowd; п. курс (*naut., aeron.*) to lay a course; п. путь (*fig.*) to pave the way; п. но́вые пути́ (*fig.*) to pioneer, blaze new trails. **2.** (ме́жду *or* +*a. and i.*) to interlay; to insert (between); п. кни́гу бе́лыми листа́ми to interleave a book; п. соло́му ме́жду стекля́нными изде́лиями, п. стекля́нные изде́лия соло́мой to insert straw between items of glass-ware.

проло́м, а, *m.* **1.** breach, break; gap. **2.** (*med.*) fracture.

пролома́|ть, ю, *pf.* (*of* прола́мывать) to break (through); п. лёд to break the ice.

пролома́|ться, ется, *pf.* (*of* прола́мываться) to break.

пролом|и́ть, лю́, ~ишь, *pf.* (*of* прола́мывать) to break (through); п. ды́ру to make a hole; п. себе́ че́реп to fracture one's skull.

пролом|и́ться, ~ится, *pf.* (*of* прола́мываться) to break (down), give way; береги́тесь! по́ручень ~и́лся look out! the handrail has given way.

пролонга́ци|я, и, *f.* (*leg., fin.*) prolongation.

пролонги́р|овать, ую, *impf. and pf.* (*leg., fin.*) to prolong.

пром- *abbr. of* промы́шленный.

прома́|зать[1], жу, жешь, *pf.* (*of* ~зывать) to smear thoroughly; to oil thoroughly.

прома́|зать[2], жу, жешь, *pf. of* ма́зать 5.

прома́ргива|ть, ю, *impf. of* проморга́ть.

промарин|ова́ть, у́ю, *pf.* (*of* маринова́ть (*coll.*) to delay (intentionally), hold up, shelve (*for a certain time*).

прома́сл|енный, *p.p.p. of* ~ить *and adj.* oiled, greased; oily, greasy; ~енная бума́га oil-paper.

прома́слива|ть, ю, *impf. of* прома́слить.

прома́сл|ить, ю, ишь, *pf.* (*of* ~ивать) to oil, treat with oil, grease.

прома́тыва|ть(ся), ю(сь), *impf. of* промота́ть(ся).

про́мах, а, *m.* miss; (*fig.*) slip, blunder; дать п. to be unlucky; он ма́лый не п. (*coll.*) he's nobody's fool.

прома́хива|ться, юсь, *impf. of* промахну́ться.

промах|ну́ться, ну́сь, нёшься, *pf.* (*of* ~иваться) to miss, miss the mark; (*at billiards*) to miscue; (*fig., coll.*) to miss the mark, be wide of the mark; to make a mistake; to miss an opportunity.

прома́чива|ть, ю, *impf. of* промочи́ть.

промедле́ни|е, я, *n.* delay; procrastination.

проме́дл|ить, ю, ишь, *pf.* to delay, dally; to procrastinate.

проме́ж, *prep.* (+*g. or i.*) (*coll.*) between; among; п. нас between ourselves.

проме́жност|ь, и, *f.* (*anat.*) perineum.

промежу́т|ок, ка, *m.* interval; space; п. вре́мени period, space, stretch of time; interim.

промежу́точный, *adj.* intermediate (*also fig.*); intervening; interim.

промельк|ну́ть, у́, ёшь, *pf.* **1.** to flash; (*of time*) to fly by; п. в голове́ to flash through one's mind. **2.** to be faintly perceptible; в его́ слова́х ~у́ло разочарова́ние there was a shade of disappointment in his words.

проме́нива|ть, ю, *impf. of* променя́ть.

промен|я́ть, я́ю, *pf.* (*of* ~ивать) (на+*a.*) **1.** to exchange (for), trade (for), barter (for). **2.** to change (for).

проме́р, а, *m.* **1.** measurement; survey; sounding. **2.** error in measurement.

промерз|а́ть, а́ю, *impf. of* ~нуть.

промёрзлый, *adj.* frozen.

промёрз|нуть, ну, нешь, *past* ~, ~ла, *pf.* (*of* ~а́ть) to freeze through.

проме́рива|ть, ю, *impf. of* проме́рить.

проме́р|ить, ю, ишь, *pf.* (*of* ~ивать *and* ~я́ть) **1.** to measure; to survey; to sound. **2.** (*pf. only*) to make an error in measurement.

промер|я́ть, я́ю, *impf.* = ~ивать.

проме|си́ть, шу́, ~сишь, *pf.* (*of* ~шивать) to stir well, thoroughly; to knead well, thoroughly.

проме́шива|ть, ю, *impf. of* промеси́ть.

проме́шка|ть, ю, *pf.* (*coll.*) to linger, dawdle.

промина́|ть(ся), ю(сь), *impf. of* промя́ть(ся).

промо́зглый, *adj.* dank.

промо́ин|а, ы, *f.* pool, gully (*formed by flood, rain, etc.*).

промока́тельн|ый, *adj.*; ~ая бума́га blotting-paper.

промок|а́ть[1], а́ю, *impf.* **1.** *impf. of* ~нуть. **2.** *impf. only* to let water through, not be waterproof; э́ти боти́нки ~а́ют these boots are not waterproof. **3.** *impf. only* to absorb ink.

промок|а́ть[2], а́ю, *impf. of* ~нуть.

промока́шк|а, и, *f.* (*coll.*) blotting-paper.

промо́к|нуть, ну, нешь, *pf.* (*of* ~а́ть[1]) to get soaked, get drenched; п. до косте́й to get soaked to the skin.

промок|ну́ть, ну́, нёшь, *pf.* (*of* ~а́ть[2]) (*coll.*) to blot.

промо́лв|ить, лю, ишь, *pf.* to say, utter.

промолч|а́ть, у́, и́шь, *pf.* to keep silent, say nothing, hold one's peace.

проморга́|ть, ю, *pf.* (*of* прома́ргивать)

(*coll.*) to miss, overlook; п. удо́бный слу́чай to miss an opportunity, let a chance slip.

промо́р|и́ть, ю́, и́шь, *pf.* (*coll.*) **1.** (го́лодом) to starve (*for a certain time*). **2.** to impose privations (upon) (*for a certain time*).

промота́|ть, ю, *pf. (*of* мота́ть² *and* прома́тывать) to squander.

промота́|ться, ю́сь, *pf. (*of* прома́тываться) (*coll.*) to squander one's money, dissipate one's substance.

промоч|и́ть, у́, ∼ишь, *pf.* (*of* прома́чивать) to get wet (through); to soak, drench; п. но́ги to get one's feet wet; п. го́рло, п. гло́тку (*coll.*) to wet one's whistle.

промтова́р|ный, *adj.* *of* ∼ы; п. магази́н manufactured goods shop.

промтова́р|ы, ов, *no sing.* (*abbr. of* промы́шленные това́ры) manufactured goods (*collect. name of manufactured consumer goods other than foodstuffs*).

промфинпла́н, а, *m.* (*abbr. of* промы́шленно--фина́нсовый план) industrial and financial plan.

промч|а́ться, у́сь, и́шься, *pf.* **1.** to tear (by, past); п. стрело́й to dart (by, past), flash (by, past). **2.** (*fig.; of time*) to fly (by).

промыва́ни|е, я, *n.* washing (out); (*med.*) bathing, irrigation; (*tech.*) scrubbing.

промыва́|ть, ю, *impf. of* промы́ть.

промы́вк|а, и, *f.* washing, flushing.

про́мыс|ел, ла, *m.* **1.** hunting, catching; охо́тничий п. hunting; game-shooting; пушно́й п. trapping; ры́бный п. fishing. **2.** trade, business; го́рный п. mining; куста́рный п. handicraft industry, cottage industry; отхо́жий п. seasonal work; пушно́й п. fur trade. **3.** *pl.* works; го́рные ∼лы mines; золоты́е ∼лы gold-fields, gold--mines; нефтяны́е ∼лы oil-fields; соляны́е ∼лы salt-mines, salt-works.

про́мысл, а, *m.* (*rel.*) Providence.

промы́сл|ить, ю, ишь, *pf.* (*of* промышля́ть) (*coll.*) to get, come by.

промыслови́к, а́, *m.* **1.** hunter. **2.** miner.

промысло́в|ый, *adj.* **1.** *adj. of* про́мысел 1; ∼ая избу́шка shooting-box, hunter's (trapper's, *etc.*) hut; ∼ые пти́цы game-birds; ∼ое свиде́тельство licence. **2.** *adj. of* про́мысел 2, 3; ∼ая коопера́ция traders' co-operative (*organization*), producers' co--operative; п. нало́г business tax; ∼ая ры́ба marketable fish.

пром|ы́ть, о́ю, о́ешь, *pf.* (*of* ∼ыва́ть) **1.** to wash well, thoroughly; п. мозги́ (+*d.*) to brain-wash. **2.** (*med.*) to bathe; п. желу́док to irrigate the stomach. **3.** (*tech.*) to wash; to scrub (*gas*); п. зо́лото to pan out gold; п. руду́ to jig ore.

промы́шленник, а, *m.* manufacturer, industrialist.

промы́шленност|ь, и, *f.* industry.

промы́шленный, *adj.* industrial.

промышля́|ть, ю, *impf.* **1.** *impf. of* промы́слить. **2.** (+*i.*) to earn one's living (by). **3.** to hunt; to trade (in).

промя́мл|ить, ю, ишь, *pf. of* мя́млить 1.

про|мя́ть, мну, мнёшь, *pf.* (*of* ∼мина́ть) **1.** to break (through), crush. **2.** (*coll.*) to give a shaking-up; п. но́ги to stretch one's legs.

про|мя́ться, мну́сь, мнёшься, *pf.* (*of* ∼мина́ться) (*coll.*) to stretch one's legs.

прона́шива|ть(ся), ю(сь), *impf. of* проноси́ть(ся)¹.

пронес|ти́, у́, ёшь, *past* ∼, ∼ла́, *pf.* (*of* проноси́ть³) **1.** to carry (by, past, through). **2.** (*impers.; coll.*) to have a motion; to open one's bowels. **3.** ∼ло́! the danger is over!

пронес|ти́сь, у́сь, ёшься, *past* ∼ся, ∼ла́сь, *pf.* (*of* проноси́ться²) **1.** to rush (by, past, through); (*of clouds*) to scud (past). **2.** (*fig.*) to fly by. **3.** (*of rumours, etc.*) to spread.

пронз|и́ть, жу́, зи́шь, *pf. of* ∼а́ть.

пронзи́тел|ьный (∼ен, ∼ьна), *adj.* penetrating; piercing; (*of sounds*) shrill, strident; п. взгляд penetrating glance; ∼ьным го́лосом in a shrill voice; п. крик piercing shriek.

прон|зи́ть, жу́, зи́шь, *pf.* (*of* ∼за́ть) to pierce, run through, transfix; п. взгля́дом to pierce with a glance.

прони|за́ть, жу́, ∼жешь, *pf.* (*of* ∼зыва́ть) to pierce; to permeate, penetrate; (*fig.*) to run through; свет ∼за́л темноту́ the light pierced the darkness; одна́ иде́я ∼за́ла все его́ произведе́ния one idea ran through all his works.

прони́зыва|ть, ю, *impf. of* прониза́ть.

прони́зыва|ющий, *pres. part. act. of* ∼ть *and* *adj.* piercing, penetrating.

проник|а́ть, а́ю, *impf. of* ∼нуть.

проникнове́ни|е, я, *n.* **1.** penetration. **2.** = проникнове́нность.

проникнове́нност|ь, и, *f.* feeling; heartfelt conviction; говори́ть с ∼ью to speak with feeling.

проникнове́н|ный (∼ен, ∼на), *adj.* full of feeling; heartfelt.

прони́кнут|ый (∼, ∼а), *adj.* (+*i.*) imbued (with), instinct (with), full (of).

прони́к|нуть, ну, нешь, *past* ∼, ∼ла, *pf.* (*of* ∼а́ть) (в+*a.*) to penetrate (*also fig.*); (че́рез) to percolate (through); п. в чьи-н. наме́рения to fathom someone's designs; п. в суть де́ла to get to the bottom of the matter.

пронима́|ть, ю, *impf. of* проня́ть.

проница́емост|ь, и, *f.* penetrability, permeability, perviousness.

проница́ем|ый (~, ~a), *adj.* permeable, pervious; п. для све́та pellucid.

проница́тельност|ь, и, *f.* penetration; perspicacity; insight, acumen, shrewdness.

проница́тел|ьный (~ен, ~ьна), *adj.* perspicacious; acute, shrewd; penetrating; п. взор penetrating gaze.

проница́|ть, ю, *impf.* (*obs.*) to penetrate.

проно|си́ть[1], шу́, ~сишь, *pf.* (*of* прона́шивать) to wear out, wear to shreds.

проно|си́ть[2], шу́, ~сишь, *pf.* to wear (*for a certain time*).

проно|си́ть[3], шу́, ~сишь, *impf. of* пронести́.

проно|си́ться[1], ~сится, *pf.* (*of* прона́шиваться) to wear through, wear to shreds.

проно|си́ться[2], шу́сь, ~сишься, *impf. of* пронести́сь.

проны́р|а, ы, *m. and f.* (*coll.*) pushful person; sly-boots; intriguer.

проны́рлив|ый (~, ~a), *adj.* pushful, pushing.

проню́х|ать, аю, *pf.* (*of* ~ивать) (*coll.*) to smell out, nose out, get wind (of).

проню́хива|ть, ю, *impf. of* проню́хать.

про|ня́ть, йму́, ймёшь, *past* ~ня́л, ~няла́, ~ня́ло, *pf.* (*of* ~нима́ть) (*coll.*) 1. to penetrate, strike through. 2. (*fig.*) to get at; его́ ниче́м не ~ймёшь you can't get at him.

прообраз, а, *m.* prototype.

пропага́нд|а, ы, *f.* propaganda; propagation.

пропаганди́р|овать, ую, *impf.* to engage in propaganda (for); to propagandize.

пропаганди́ст, а, *m.* propagandist.

пропаганди́ст|ский, *adj. of* ~.

пропада́|ть, ю, *impf. of* пропа́сть.

пропа́ж|а, и, *f.* 1. loss. 2. lost object, missing object.

пропа́лыва|ть, ю, *impf. of* прополо́ть.

про́паст|ь, и, *f.* 1. precipice (*also fig.*); abyss; на краю́ ~и (*fig.*) on the brink of a precipice. 2. (*coll.*) a mass (of), masses (of); у него́ п. де́нег he has masses of money; наро́ду бы́ло п. there were swarms of people; бы́ло их до ~и there were scores of them.

пропа́|сть, ду́, дёшь, *past* ~л, *pf.* (*of* ~да́ть) 1. to be missing; to be lost; п. без вести (*mil.*) to be missing; пиши́ ~ло (*coll.*) it is as good as lost. 2. to disappear, vanish; куда́ вы ~ли? where did you vanish to?; очарова́ние ~ло the glamour faded away. 3. to be lost, be done for; (*of flowers, etc.*) to die; тепе́рь мы ~ли! now we're done for!; ~ди́ пропа́дом! (*coll.*) the devil take it! 4. to be wasted; п. да́ром to go for naught, go to waste; всё у́тро и без того́ ~ло the whole morning was wasted as it was.

пропа|ха́ть[1], шу́, ~шешь, *pf.* (*of* ~хивать) to plough thoroughly.

пропа|ха́ть[2], шу́, ~шешь, *pf.* to plough (*for a certain time*).

пропа́хива|ть, ю, *impf. of* пропаха́ть[1].

пропа́х|нуть, ну, нешь, *past* ~, ~ла, *pf.* to become permeated with the smell (of).

пропа́шк|а, и, *f.* (*agric.*) tilling between rows.

пропа́шник, а, *m.* (*agric.*) cultivator, furrow plough.

пропашн|о́й, *adj.*; ~ы́е культу́ры crops requiring tilling between rows; п. тра́ктор tractor-cultivator.

пропа́щ|ий, *adj.* (*coll.*) hopeless; good-for-nothing; он п. челове́к he's a hopeless case; это ~ее де́ло it's a bad job.

пропеде́втик|а, и, *f.* propaedeutics; preliminary study.

пропедевти́ческий, *adj.* propaedeutic; п. курс introductory course.

пропека́|ть(ся), ю(сь), *impf. of* пропе́чь(ся).

пропе́ллер, а, *m.* propeller.

проп|е́ть[1], ою́, оёшь, *pf.* 1. *pf. of* петь. 2. п. го́лос (*coll.*) to lose one's voice (*from singing*); п. to sing oneself hoarse.

проп|е́ть[2], ою́, оёшь, *pf.* to sing (*for a certain time*).

пропеча́т|ать, аю, *pf.* (*of* ~ывать) (*coll.*) to expose (*in the press*).

пропеча́тыва|ть, ю, *impf. of* пропеча́тать.

пропе́|чь, ку́, чёшь, ку́т, *past* ~к, ~кла́, *pf.* (*of* ~ка́ть) to bake well, thoroughly.

пропе́|чься, ку́сь, чёшься, ку́тся, *past* ~кся, ~кла́сь, *pf.* (*of* ~ка́ться) to bake well, get baked through.

пропива́|ть(ся), ю(сь), *impf. of* пропи́ть(ся).

пропи́л, а, *m.* (saw-)kerf, slit, notch.

пропи́лива|ть, ю, *impf. of* пропили́ть.

пропил|и́ть, ю́, ~ишь, *pf.* (*of* ~ивать) to saw through.

пропи|са́ть, шу́, ~шешь, *pf.* (*of* ~сывать) 1. to prescribe. 2. to register; п. па́спорт to stamp a passport. 3. (+*d.*; *coll.*) to give it hot, tear off a strip.

пропи|са́ться, шу́сь, ~шешься, *pf.* (*of* ~сываться) to register (*intrans.*).

пропи́ск|а, и, *f.* 1. registration; п. па́спорта stamping of a passport. 2. residence permit.

прописн|о́й, *adj.* 1. (*of letters of the alphabet*) capital; писа́ться с п. бу́квы to be written with a capital letter. 2. commonplace, trivial; ~а́я и́стина truism; ~а́я мора́ль copy-book ethics.

пропи́сыва|ть(ся), ю(сь), *impf. of* прописа́ть(ся).

про́пис|ь, и, *f.* 1. *usu. pl.* sample(s) of writing. 2. (*fig., pejor.*) copy-book maxim; жить по ~ям to live according to the copy-book.

про́писью, *adv.* in words, in full; написа́ть число́ п. to write out a number in words, in full.

пропита́ни|е, я, *n.* subsistence, sustenance; зарабо́тать себе́ на п. to earn one's living.

пропит|а́ть, а́ю, *pf.* (*of* ～ывать) 1. to keep, provide (for). 2. (+*i.*) to impregnate (with), saturate (with), soak (in), steep (in); п. ма́слом to oil.

пропит|а́ться, а́юсь, *pf.* (*of* ～ываться) 1. (+*i.*) to become saturated (with), become steeped (in). 2. *pass. of* ～а́ть.

пропи́тк|а, и, *f.* (*tech.*) impregnation.

пропи́тыва|ть(ся), ю(сь), *impf. of* пропита́ть(ся).

про|пи́ть, пью, пьёшь, *past* ～пи́л, ～пила́, ～пи́ло, *pf.* (*of* ～пива́ть) 1. to spend on drink, squander on drink. 2. (*coll.*) to ruin (*through excessive drinking*).

про|пи́ться, пью́сь, пьёшься, *past* ～пи́лся, ～пила́сь, ～пи́ло́сь, *pf.* (*of* ～пива́ться) (*coll.*) to ruin oneself (*through excessive drinking*).

пропих|а́ться, а́юсь, *pf.* = ～ну́ться.

пропи́хива|ть(ся), ю(сь), *impf. of* пропих-ну́ть(ся).

пропих|ну́ть, ну́, нёшь, *pf.* (*of* ～ивать) (*coll.*) to shove through, force through.

пропих|ну́ться, ну́сь, нёшься, *pf.* (*of* ～иваться) (*coll.*) to shove, force one's way through.

проплáва|ть, ю, *pf.* to swim (*for a certain time*); to sail (*for a certain time*).

проплá|кать, чу, чешь, *pf.* 1. to cry, weep (*for a certain time*). 2. п. глазá (*coll.*) to cry one's eyes out.

проплéсневе|ть, ет, *pf.* to go mouldy all through.

проплы́в, а, *m.* (*swimming*) race, heat.

проплывá|ть, ю, *impf. of* проплы́ть.

проплы́|ть, ву́, вёшь, *past* ～л, ～лá, ～ло, *pf.* (*of* ～вáть) 1. to swim (by, past, through); to sail (by, past, through); to float, drift (by, past, through); (*fig., joc.*) to sail (by, past). 2. to cover (*a certain distance*).

проповéдник, а, *m.* 1. preacher. 2. (+*g.*; *fig.*) advocate (of).

проповéд|овать, ую, *impf.* 1. to preach. 2. (*fig.*) to advocate, propagate.

пропо́вед|ь, и, *f.* 1. sermon; homily. 2. (+*g.*; *fig.*) advocacy (of), propagation (of).

пропо́йный, *adj.* (*coll.*) drunken, besotted.

пропо́йц|а, ы, *m.* (*coll.*) drunkard.

прополáскива|ть, ю, *impf. of* прополоскáть.

прополз|áть, áю, *impf. of* ～ти́.

прополз|ти́, у́, ёшь, *past* ～, ～лá, *pf.* (*of* ～áть) to creep, crawl (by, past, through).

прополк|а, и, *f.* weeding.

прополо|скáть, щу́, ～щешь, *pf.* (*of* про-

полáскивать) to rinse, swill; п. го́рло to gargle.

пропол|о́ть, ю́, ～ешь, *pf.* (*of* пропа́лывать) to weed.

пропорциона́льност|ь, и, *f.* proportionality; proportion; обра́тная п. inverse proportion.

пропорциона́л|ьный (～ен, ～ьна), *adj.* 1. proportional; proportionate; ～ьное представи́тельство proportional representation; сре́днее ～ьное (*math.*) the mean proportional. 2. well-proportioned.

пропо́рци|я, и, *f.* proportion; ratio.

пропоте́лый, *adj.* sweat-soaked.

пропоте́|ть, ю, *pf.* 1. to sweat thoroughly. 2. to be soaked in sweat.

про́пуск, а, *m.* 1. *no pl.* admission. 2. (*pl.* ～и *and* ～á) pass, permit. 3. (*pl.* ～á) (*mil.*) password. 4. (*pl.* ～и) (+*g.*) non-attendance (at), absence (from). 5. (*pl.* ～и) blank, gap.

пропускá|ть, ю, *impf.* 1. *impf. of* пропу-сти́ть. 2. *impf. only* to let pass; п. во́ду to leak; не п. воды́ to be waterproof; э́та бума́га ～ет черни́ла this paper absorbs ink.

пропускни́к, á, *m.* disinfection centre.

пропускн|о́й, *adj.* ～áя бума́га blotting--paper; ～áя спосо́бность capacity.

пропу|сти́ть, щу́, ～стишь, *pf.* (*of* ～скáть) 1. to let pass, let through; to make way (for); to let in, admit; to take, have a capacity (of); п. на перро́н to let on to the platform; вы́ставка ～сти́ла пять миллио́-нов посети́телей the exhibition had five million visitors; п. ми́мо уше́й to give no ear (to), pay no heed (to). 2. (че́рез) to run (through), pass (through); п. че́рез фильтр to filter. 3. to omit, leave out; (*in reading*) to skip. 4. to miss; to let slip; п. ле́кцию to miss a lecture, cut a lecture; п. удо́бный слу́чай to miss an opportunity. 5. (*coll.*) to drink.

пропых|те́ть, чу́, ти́шь, *pf. of* пыхте́ть.

прора́б, а, *m.* (*abbr. of* производи́тель рабо́т) clerk of the works.

прораба́тыва|ть, ю, *impf. of* проработать[1].

прорабо́та|ть[1], ю, *pf.* (*of* прораба́тывать) (*coll.*) 1. to work (at), study; to get up, mug up. 2. to slate, pick holes (in).

прорабо́та|ть[2], ю, *pf.* to work (*for a certain time*).

прорабо́тк|а, и, *f.* 1. study, studying, getting up. 2. slating.

прора́н, а, *m.* (*tech.*) passage (*through dam while under construction*).

прораста́ни|е, я, *n.* germination; sprouting.

прораст|а́ть, а́ет, *impf. of* ～и́.

прораст|и́, ёт, *past* проро́с, проросла́, *pf.* (*of* ～а́ть) to germinate, sprout, shoot (*of plant*).

про́рв|а, ы, *f.* (*coll.*) 1. (+*g.*) a mass (of); masses (of), heaps (of). 2. glutton.

прорв|а́ть, у́, ёшь, *past* ~а́л, ~ала́, ~а́ло, *pf.* (*of* прорыва́ть) **1.** to break through; to tear, make a rent (in), make a hole (in); п. блока́ду to run the blockade; п. ли́нию оборо́ны проти́вника to break through the enemy's defence line; ~а́ло плоти́ну (*impers.*) the dam has burst; я ~а́л носо́к I have a hole in my sock. **2.** (*impers.*; *coll.*) to lose patience.

прорв|а́ться, у́сь, ёшься, *past* ~а́лся, ~ала́сь, ~а́ло́сь, *pf.* (*of* прорыва́ться) **1.** to break, burst (open). **2.** to tear. **3.** to break (out, through); to force one's way (through).

проре|ди́ть, жу́, ди́шь, *pf.* (*of* ~жива́ть) (*agric.*) to thin out.

проре́жива|ть, ю, *impf. of* прореди́ть.

проре́з, а, *m.* cut; slit, notch, nick.

проре́|зать, жу, жешь, *pf.* (*of* ~зыва́ть *and* ~за́ть) to cut through (*also fig.*)

проре́|заться, жется, *pf.* (*of* ре́заться, ~зыва́ться *and* ~за́ться) (*of teeth*) to cut, come through; у неё уже́ ~зались зу́бы she has already cut her teeth.

прорез|а́ть(ся), а́ю(сь), *impf. of* ~ать(ся).

прорези́нива|ть, ю, *impf. of* прорези́нить.

прорези́н|ить, ю, ишь, *pf.* (*of* ~ивать) to rubberize.

прорезыва́ни|е, я, *n.* п. зубо́в teething, dentition.

проре́зыва|ть(ся), ю(сь), *impf. of* проре́зать(ся).

про́рез|ь, и, *f.* opening, aperture.

проре́ктор, а, *m.* pro-rector.

прорепети́р|овать, ую, *pf. of* репети́ровать.

проре́х|а, и, *f.* **1.** rent, tear. **2.** (*in garment*) slit; застегну́ть ~у (брюк) to do up one's flies. **3.** (*fig., coll.*) gap, deficiency.

прорецензи́р|овать, ую, *pf. of* рецензи́ровать.

проржа́ве|ть, ет, *pf.* to rust through.

прорис|ова́ть, у́ю, *pf.* (*of* ~о́вывать) to trace clearly.

прорисо́выва|ть, ю, *impf. of* прорисова́ть.

прорица́ни|е, я, *n.* (*obs.*) soothsaying, prophecy.

прорица́тел|ь, я, *m.* (*obs.*) soothsayer, prophet.

прорица́|ть, ю, *impf.* (*obs.*) to prophesy.

проро́к, а, *m.* prophet.

пророн|и́ть, ю́, ~ишь, *pf.* to utter, breathe, drop (*a word, a sound, etc.*); он не ~и́л ни зву́ка he did not utter a sound.

проро́ческий, *adj.* prophetic, oracular.

проро́честв|о, а, *n.* prophecy, oracle.

проро́честв|овать, ую, *impf.* (о+*p.*) to prophesy.

пророч|ить, у, ишь, *impf.* (*of* на~) to prophesy, predict.

проруб|а́ть, а́ю, *impf. of* ~и́ть.

проруб|и́ть, лю́, ~ишь, *pf.* (*of* ~а́ть) to hack through, cut through, hew through.

про́руб|ь, и, *f.* ice-hole.

прору́х|а, и, *f.* (*coll.*) blunder, mistake.

проры́в, а, *m.* **1.** break; (*mil.*) break-through, breach. **2.** (*fig.*) hitch, hold-up; по́лный п. breakdown.

прорыва́|ть[1], ю, *impf. of* прорва́ть.

прорыва́|ть[2], ю, *impf. of* проры́ть.

прорыва́|ться[1], юсь, *impf. of* прорва́ться.

прорыва́|ться[2], юсь, *impf. of* проры́ться.

прор|ы́ть, о́ю, о́ешь, *pf.* (*of* ~ыва́ть[2]) to dig through.

прор|ы́ться, о́юсь, о́ешься, *pf.* (*of* ~ыва́ться[2]) to dig one's way through, burrow through.

проса|ди́ть[1], жу́, ~дишь, *pf.* (*of* ~жива́ть) (+*i.*; *coll.*) to stick (into); п. но́гу гвоздём to get a nail into one's foot.

проса|ди́ть[2], жу́, ~дишь, *pf.* (*of* ~жива́ть) (*coll.*) to squander, lose.

проса́жива|ть, ю, *impf. of* просади́ть.

проса́лива|ть[1], ю, *impf. of* просали́ть.

проса́лива|ть[2], ю, *impf. of* просоли́ть.

проса́л|ить, ю, ишь, *pf.* (*of* ~ивать[1]) to grease.

проса́чивани|е, я, *n.* **1.** percolation; oozing, exudation. **2.** (*fig.*) leakage; infiltration.

проса́чива|ться, юсь, *impf. of* просочи́ться.

просва́та|ть, ю, *pf.* (*of bride-to-be's parents*) to promise in marriage.

просве́рлива|ть, ю, *impf. of* просверли́ть.

просверл|и́ть, ю́, и́шь, *pf.* (*of* ~ивать) to drill, bore; to perforate, pierce.

просве́т, а, *m.* **1.** shaft of light; (*fig.*) ray of hope. **2.** (*archit.*) light; aperture, opening.

просвети́тел|ь, я, *m.* **1.** educator, teacher. **2.** (*hist.*) representative of the Enlightenment.

просвети́тельн|ый, *adj.* educational; ~ая филосо́фия (*hist.*) philosophy of the Enlightenment.

просвети́тель|ский, *adj. of* ~.

просвети́тельств|о, а, *n.* educational activities, cultural activities.

просве|ти́ть[1], щу́, ти́шь, *pf.* (*of* ~ща́ть) to educate; to enlighten.

просве|ти́ть[2], чу́, ~тишь, *pf.* (*of* ~чивать[1]) (*med.*) to X-ray.

просветле́ни|е, я, *n.* **1.** (*of weather*) clearing up, brightening up. **2.** (*fig.*) lucid interval.

просветл|ённый, p.p.p. *of* ~и́ть *and adj.* (*fig.*) clear, lucid.

просветле́|ть, ю, *pf.* **1.** (*of weather*) to clear up, brighten up. **2.** (*fig.*) to brighten; п. от ра́дости to light up with joy. **3.** (*fig.*; *of consciousness, etc.*) to become lucid.

просветл|и́ть, ю́, и́шь, *pf.* (*of* ~я́ть) to clarify.

просветл|я́ть, я́ю, *impf. of* ~и́ть.

просвёчива|ть¹, ю, *impf. of* просветйть².

просвёчива|ть², ю, *impf.* **1.** to be translucent. **2.** (чёрез, сквозь) to be visible (through), show (through), appear (through); to shine (through); шрам ~л чёрез её чулок the scar showed through her stocking.

просвещá|ть, ю, *impf. of* просветйть¹.

просвещён|ец, ца, *m.* educationalist.

просвещёни|е, я, *n.* **1.** education, instruction; наро́дное п. public education. **2.** enlightenment; Эпоха ~я (*hist.*) the Age of the Enlightenment.

просвещённост|ь, и, *f.* enlightenment, culture.

просве|щённый, *p.p.p. of* ~тйть¹ *and adj.* enlightened; educated, cultured; ~щённое мнёние expert opinion; п. человёк educated person.

просвир|á, ы́, *pl.* **про́свиры, про́свир, про́свирáм,** *f.* (*eccl.*) (communion) bread; host.

просвйр|ня, ни, *g. pl.* ~ен, *f.* woman making communion bread.

просвирня́к, á, *m.* (*bot.*) marsh mallow.

просви|стёть, щу́, стйшь, *pf.* **1.** to whistle; п. мелодию to whistle a tune. **2.** to give a whistle; to whistle (by, past); ~стёла над головой пу́ля a bullet whistled overhead.

про́сед|ь, и, *f.* streak(s) of grey; волосы с ~ью greying hair, hair touched with grey.

просёива|ть, ю, *impf. of* просёять.

про́сек|а, и, *f.* cutting (*in a forest*).

просёл|ок, ка, *m.* country road, cart-track.

просеминáр, а, *m.* (*in higher educational institutions*) beginners' class, beginners' seminar.

просеминáри|й, я, *m.* (*obs.*) = просеминáр.

просё|ять, ю, ешь, *pf.* (*of* ~ивать) to sift, riddle, screen.

просигнализйр|овать, ую, *pf. of* сигнализйровать.

проси|дёть¹, жу́, дйшь, *pf.* (*of* ~́живать) to sit (*for a certain time*); п. ночь у постёли больного to sit up all night with a patient.

проси|дёть², жу́, дйшь, *pf.* (*of* ~́живать) to wear out the seat (of); to wear into holes (*by sitting*).

просй|жива|ть, ю, *impf. of* просидёть.

про́син|ь, и, *f.* (*coll.*) bluish tint.

просйтел|ь, я, *m.* applicant; suppliant; petitioner.

просйтельный, *adj.* pleading.

про|сйть, шу́, ~сишь, *impf.* (*of* по~) **1.** (+*a.* *of person asked*; +*a. or g. of thing sought, or* о+*p.*) to ask (for), beg; ~шу́ (вас) please; п. кого́-н. о помощи to ask someone for help, ask someone's assistance; п. врёмени на размышлёние to ask for time to think (something) over; п. разрешёния to ask

permission; п. совёта to ask (for) advice; п. извинёния у кого́-н. to beg someone's pardon, apologize to someone; п. мйлостыню to beg, go begging; ~шу́ покорнёйше (*coll.*, *obs.*; *as expression of surprise*) if you please. **2.** (за+*a.*) to intercede (for). **3.** to invite; вас ~́сят к столу́ please to take your places at the table; ~́сят не курйть no smoking.

про|сйться, шу́сь, ~сишься, *impf.* (*of* по~) **1.** (+*inf. or* в+*a.*, на+*a.*) to ask (for); to apply (for); п. в о́тпуск to apply for leave. **2.** (*of children and household pets*) to want to go (*sc.* to relieve oneself). **3.** (*fig.*, *coll.*) to ask (for); п. с языкá to be on the tip of one's tongue; закáт так и ~сйлся на картйну the sunset was just asking to be painted.

просия́|ть, ю, *pf.* **1.** (*of the sun*) to begin to shine. **2.** (от) to beam (with), light up (with); онá ~ла от счáстья she beamed with joy; лицо́ у него́ ~ло his face lit up.

проска|кáть, чу́, ~чешь, *pf.* to gallop (by, past, through).

проскáкива|ть, ю, *impf. of* проскочйть.

проскáльзыва|ть, ю, *impf. of* проскользнýть.

проскво́з|йть, йт, *pf.* (*impers.*; *coll.*) меня́, *etc.*, ~йло I, *etc.*, have caught cold from being in a draught.

проскло́ня|ть, ю, *pf. of* склоня́ть².

проскользн|ýть, ý, ёшь, *pf.* (*of* проскáльзывать) (*coll.*) to slip in, creep in (*also fig.*); ~ýло мно́го ошйбок many errors have crept in.

проскоч|йть, ý, ~ишь, *pf.* (*of* проскáкивать) **1.** to rush by, tear by. **2.** (чёрез) to slip (through). **3.** (сквозь, мёжду) to fall (through, between); п. мёжду пáльцами to fall through one's fingers. **4.** (*fig.*, *coll.*) to slip in, creep in; ~йло нёсколько ошйбок a few errors crept in.

проскрип|ёть, лю́, йшь, *pf.* **1.** *pf. of* скрипёть. **2.** (*coll.*) to creak along.

проскрипцио́нный, *adj.* п. спйсок (*hist.*) proscription list; black list.

проскрйпци|я, и, *f.* (*hist.*) proscription.

проскурня́к, á, *m.* (*bot.*) marsh mallow.

проскучá|ть, ю, *pf.* to have a dull, boring time; мы ~ли всю недёлю we had a dull week.

прослáб|ить, ит, *pf. of* слáбить.

прослáв|ить, лю, ишь, *pf.* (*of* ~ля́ть) to glorify; to bring glory (to), bring fame (to); to make famous, make illustrious.

прослáв|иться, люсь, ишься, *pf.* (*of* ~ля́ться) (+*i.*) to become fámous (for), become renowned (for); он ~ился острóтами he became famous for his witticisms.

прославлёни|е, я, *n.* glorification; apotheosis.

прослав|ленный, *p.p.p.* *of* ~ить *and adj.* famous, renowned, celebrated, illustrious.

прославля|ть(ся), ю(сь), *impf.* *of* просла́-вить(ся).

просла́ива|ть, ю, *impf.* *of* прослои́ть.

просле|ди́ть, жу́, ди́шь, *pf.* (*of* ~жива́ть) 1. to track (down). 2. to trace (through); to trace back, retrace; п. разви́тие па́пства to trace the development of the papacy.

просле́д|овать, ую, *pf.* to proceed, go in state.

прослёжива|ть, ю, *impf.* *of* проследи́ть.

просле|зи́ться, жу́сь, зи́шься, *pf.* to shed a few tears.

прасло|и́ть, ю́, и́шь, *pf.* (*of* просла́ивать) (+*i.*) to interlay (with), sandwich (with).

прослойк|а, и, *f.* 1. layer, stratum (*also fig.*). 2. (*geol.*) seam, streak.

прослуж|и́ть, у́, ~ишь, *pf.* 1. to work, serve (*for a certain time*); он ~и́л три го́да на Да́льнем Восто́ке he served for three years in the Far East. 2. to be in use, serve; э́то пальто́ ~ит мне ещё оди́н год this coat will last me another year.

прослу́ш|ать, аю, *pf.* 1. (*impf.* слу́шать) to hear (through); п. курс ле́кций to attend a course of lectures. 2. (*impf.* ~ивать) (*med.*) to listen to; п. чьё-н. се́рдце to listen to someone's heart. 3. (*impf.* ~ивать) (*coll.*) to miss, not to catch; прости́те, я ~ал, что вы сказа́ли I am sorry, I did not catch what you said.

прослу́шива|ть, ю, *impf.* *of* прослу́шать.

прослы́|ть, ву́, вёшь, *past* ~л, ~ла́, ~ло, *pf.* (+*i.*) to pass (for), be reputed.

прослы́ш|ать, у, ишь, *pf.* (*coll.*) to find out, hear; я то́лько что ~ал о ва́шем несча́стном слу́чае I have only just heard about your accident.

просма́лива|ть, ю, *impf.* *of* просмоли́ть.

просма́трива|ть, ю, *impf.* *of* просмотре́ть.

просмол|и́ть, ю́, и́шь, *pf.* (*of* просма́ливать) to tar; to coat, impregnate with tar; (*naut.*) to pay.

просмо́тр, а, *m.* survey; view, viewing; п. докуме́нтов examination of papers; закры́-тый п. private view; предвари́тельный п. preview.

просмотр|е́ть, ю́, ~ишь, *pf.* (*of* просма́тривать) 1. to survey; to view. 2. to look over, look through; to glance over, glance through; to run over; п. ру́копись to glance through a manuscript; п. партиту́ру to run over the score. 3. to overlook, miss.

прос|ну́ться, ну́сь, нёшься, *pf.* (*of* ~ыпа́ть-ся¹) to wake up, awake.

прос|о, а, *n.* millet.

просо́выва|ть(ся), ю(сь), *impf.* *of* просу́-нуть(ся).

просоди́ческий, *adj.* (*lit.*) prosodic, proso-dial.

просо́ди|я, и, *f.* (*lit.*) prosody.

просол|и́ть, ю́, ~и́шь, *pf.* (*of* проса́ливать²) to salt; п. мя́со to corn meat.

просо́х|нуть, ну, нешь, *past* ~, ~ла, *pf.* (*of* просыха́ть) to get dry, dry out.

просоч|и́ться, и́тся, *pf.* (*of* проса́чиваться) 1. to percolate; to filter; to leak, ooze; to seep out. 2. (*fig.*) to filter through; to leak out; ~и́лись све́дения о пораже́нии news of the defeat filtered through.

просп|а́ть¹, лю́, и́шь, *past* ~а́л, ~ала́, ~а́ло, *pf.* (*of* просыпа́ть²) 1. to oversleep. 2. to miss, pass (*due to being asleep*).

просп|а́ть², лю́, и́шь, *past* ~а́л, ~ала́, ~а́ло, *pf.* to sleep (*for a certain time*).

просп|а́ться, лю́сь, и́шься, *past* ~а́лся, ~ала́сь, ~а́лось, *pf.* (*coll.*) to sleep one-self sober, sleep off one's drunkenness.

проспе́кт¹, а, *m.* avenue.

проспе́кт², а, *m.* 1. prospectus. 2. summary, résumé.

проспирт|ова́ть, у́ю, *pf.* (*of* ~о́вывать) to alcoholize.

проспирто́выва|ть, ю, *impf.* *of* проспирто-ва́ть.

проспо́рива|ть, ю, *impf.* *of* проспо́рить¹.

проспо́р|ить¹, ю, ишь, *pf.* (*of* ~ивать) to lose (*in a wager*).

проспо́р|ить², ю, ишь, *pf.* to argue (*for a certain time*).

проспряга́|ть, ю, *pf.* *of* спряга́ть.

просро́ч|енный, *p.p.p.* *of* ~ить *and adj.* over-due.

просро́чива|ть, ю, *impf.* *of* просро́чить.

просро́ч|ить, у, ишь, *pf.* (*of* ~ивать) to exceed the time limit; п. о́тпуск to over-stay one's leave; п. платёж to fail to pay in time.

просро́чк|а, и, *f.* delay; expiration of a time limit; п. в предъявле́нии и́ска (*leg.*) non--claim.

проста́в|ить, лю, ишь, *pf.* (*of* ~ля́ть) 1. to put down (in writing), state, fill in; п. да́ту (в, на+*p.*) to date. 2. (*coll.*) to stake and lose (*at cards, etc.*).

проставля́|ть, ю, *impf.* *of* проста́вить.

проста́ива|ть, ю, *impf.* *of* простоя́ть.

проста́к, а́, *m.* simpleton.

проста́т|а, ы, *f.* (*anat.*) prostate, prostatic gland.

простег|а́ть, а́ю, *pf.* (*of* ~ивать) to quilt.

простёгива|ть, ю, *impf.* *of* простега́ть.

простейш|ий, *superl.* *of* просто́й; *pl.* *as noun* ~ие, ~их (*zool.*) protozoa.

простён|ок, ка, *m.* (*archit.*) pier.

про́стенький, *adj.* (*coll.*) quite simple; plain, unpretentious.

прос|тере́ть, тру́, трёшь, *past* ~тёр, ~тёрла,

pf. (*of* ～тира́ть¹). **1.** to extend, hold out, reach out; п. ру́ку to hold out one's hand. **2.** (*fig.*) to raise, stretch; они́ сли́шком далеко́～тёрли свои́ тре́бования they raised their demands too high.

прос|тере́ться, трётся, *past* ～тёрся, ～тёр-лась, *pf.* (*of* ～тира́ться¹) to stretch, extend; п. на со́тни миль to stretch for hundreds of miles.

простира́|ть¹, ю, *impf. of* простере́ть.

простира́|ть², ю, *pf.* to wash (*for a certain time*).

простир|а́ть³, а́ю, *pf.* (*of* ～ывать) (*coll.*) to wash well, thoroughly.

простира́|ться, юсь, *impf. of* простере́ться.

простирн|у́ть, у́, ёшь, *pf.* (*coll.*) to give a wash.

прости́рыва|ть, ю, *impf. of* простира́ть³.

прости́тел|ьный (～ен, ～ьна), *adj.* pardonable, excusable, justifiable.

проститу́и́р|овать, ую, *impf. and pf.* to prostitute.

проститу́тк|а, и, *f.* prostitute.

проституци|я, и, *f.* prostitution.

про|сти́ть, щу́, сти́шь, *pf.* (*of* ～ща́ть) **1.** to forgive, pardon; п. грехи́ to forgive sins; ～сти́те (меня́)! excuse me!, I beg your pardon! **2.** to remit; п. долг кому́-н. to remit someone's debt. **3.** ～сти́(те)! (*obs.*) good-bye!, farewell!; сказа́ть после́днее ～сти́ to say the last farewell.

про|сти́ться, щу́сь, сти́шься, *pf.* (*of* ～ща́ть-ся) (c+*i.*) to say good-bye (to), take one's leave (of), bid farewell.

про́сто, *adv.* simply; п. по привы́чке from mere habit, purely out of habit; п. так for no particular reason; э́то п. невероя́тно it is simply incredible; я п. не зна́ю I really don't know.

простова́тост|ь, и, *f.* simplicity, simple-mindedness.

простова́т|ый (～, ～а), *adj.* simple, simple-minded.

простоволо́с|ый (～, ～а), *adj.* bare-headed, with head uncovered.

простоду́ши|е, я, *n.* open-heartedness; simple-heartedness, simple-mindedness; ingenuousness, artlessness.

простоду́ш|ный (～ен, ～на), *adj.* open-hearted; simple-hearted, simple-minded; ingenuous, artless.

прост|о́й¹ (～, ～а́, ～о,), *adj.* **1.** simple; easy; вам ～о критикова́ть it is easy for you, all very well for you to criticize. **2.** simple (= *unitary*); ～о́е предложе́ние (*gram.*) simple sentence; ～о́е те́ло (*chem.*) simple substance, element; ～о́е число́ (*math.*) prime number. **3.** simple; ordinary; ～ым глазом with the naked eye; п. наро́д the common people; ～о́е письмо́ non-regis-

tered letter. **4.** simple, plain; unaffected, unpretentious; ～ые лю́ди ordinary people; homely people; ～ые мане́ры unaffected manners; п. о́браз жи́зни plain living. **5.** mere; ～ое любопы́тство mere curiosity; п. сме́ртный a mere mortal; по той ～ой причи́не, что for the simple reason that.

просто́|й², я, m. standing idle, enforced idle-ness; stoppage; пла́та за п. demurrage.

простокваш|а, и, f. sour milk, yoghurt.

простолюди́н, а, m. man of the common people.

про́сто-на́просто, *adv.* (*coll.*) simply.

простонаро́д|ный (～ен, ～на), *adj.* of the common people.

простонаро́дь|е, я, n. the common people.

простон|а́ть, у́, ～ешь, *pf.* **1.** to utter a groan, moan. **2.** to groan, moan (*for a certain time*).

просто́р, а, m. **1.** spaciousness; space, ex-panse; степны́е ～ы the expanses of the steppe(s). **2.** freedom, scope; elbow-room; дать п. (+*d.*) to give scope, give free range, give full play.

проторе́чи|е, я, n. popular speech; в ～и in common parlance.

проторе́ч|ный (～ен, ～на), *adj. of* ～ие.

просто́р|ный (～ен, ～на), *adj.* spacious, roomy; (*of clothing*) ample; здесь ～но there is plenty of room here, there is ample space here.

простосерде́чи|е, я, n. simple-heartedness; frankness; openness.

простосерде́ч|ный (～ен, ～на), *adj.* simple-hearted; frank; open.

простот|а́, ы́, f. (*in var. senses*) simplicity; по ～е́ серде́чной in one's innocence.

простофи́л|я, и, m. and f. (*coll.*) duffer, ninny.

просто|я́ть, ю́, и́шь, *pf.* (*of* проста́ивать) **1.** to stay, stand (*for a certain time*); по́езд ～я́л на запасно́м пути́ всю ночь the train stood in a siding all night. **2.** to stand idle, lie idle. **3.** to stand, last.

простра́нност|ь, и, f. **1.** extensiveness, ex-tent. **2.** diffuseness, prolixity; verbosity.

простра́н|ный (～ен, ～на), *adj.* **1.** extensive, vast. **2.** diffuse, prolix; verbose.

простра́нственный, *adj.* spatial.

простра́нств|о, а, n. space; expanse; воз-ду́шное п. air space; безвозду́шное п. (*phys.*) vacuum; вре́дное п. (*tech.*) clear-ance; мёртвое п. (*mil.*) dead ground; пусто́е п. void; боя́знь ～а (*med.*) agoraphobia.

простра́ци|я, и, f. prostration (*mental and physical exhaustion*).

простра́чива|ть, ю, *impf. of* прострочи́ть.

простре́л, а, m. (*coll.*) lumbago.

простре́лива|ть, ю, *impf.* **1.** *impf. of* простре-ли́ть. **2.** *impf. only* (*mil.*) to rake, sweep with fire. **3.** *impf. only* (*mil.*) to cover, have covered.

простре́лива|ться, юсь, *impf.* (*mil.*) **1.** to be exposed to fire. **2.** *pass. of* ~ть.

прострел|и́ть, ю́, ~ишь, *pf.* (*of* ~ивать) to shoot through.

простроч|и́ть, у́, ~ишь, *pf.* (*of* простра́чивать) to stitch; to back-stitch.

просту́д|а, ы, *f.* cold; chill; схвати́ть ~у (*coll.*) to catch (a) cold, catch a chill.

просту|ди́ть, жу́, ~дишь, *pf.* (*of* ~жа́ть) to let catch cold.

просту|ди́ться, жу́сь, ~дишься, *pf.* (*of* ~жа́ться) to catch (a) cold; to catch, take a chill.

просту́дный, *adj.* catarrhal.

простужа́|ть(ся), ю(сь), *impf. of* простуди́ть(ся).

просту́|женный, *p.p.p. of* ~ди́ть *and adj.*; я вновь ~жен I have caught another cold.

просту́к|ать, аю, *pf.* (*of* ~ивать) (*med.*) to tap.

просту́кива|ть, ю, *impf. of* просту́кать.

проступ|а́ть, а́ет, *impf. of* ~и́ть.

проступ|и́ть, ~ит, *pf.* (*of* ~а́ть) to appear, show through, come through; сыры́е пя́тна ~и́ли на стена́х damp patches have appeared on the walls; пот ~и́л у него́ на лбу perspiration stood out on his forehead.

просту́п|ок, ка, *m.* fault; breach of manners; (*leg.*) misdemeanour.

простыва́|ть, ю, *impf. of* просты́ть.

просты́н|ный, *adj. of* ~я́; ~ное полотно́ sheeting.

простын|я́, и́, *pl.* про́стыни, ~ь, ~я́м, *f.* sheet.

просты́|ть, ну, нешь, *pf.* (*of* ~ва́ть) **1.** to get cold; to cool; и след ~л (+*g.*; *coll.*) not a trace (of). **2.** (*coll.*) to catch cold.

просу́н|уть, у, ешь, *pf.* (*of* просо́вывать) (в+*a.*) to push (through, in), shove (through, in), thrust (through, in).

просу́н|уться, усь, ешься, *pf.* (*of* просо́вываться) to push through, force one's way through.

просу́шива|ть(ся), ю(сь), *impf. of* просуши́ть(ся).

просуш|и́ть, у́, ~ишь, *pf.* (*of* ~ивать) to dry thoroughly, properly.

просуш|и́ться, у́сь, ~ишься, *pf.* (*of* ~ивать-ся) to (get) dry.

просу́шк|а, и, *f.* drying.

просуществ|ова́ть, у́ю, *pf.* to exist (*for a certain time*); to last, endure.

просфор|а́, ы́, *f.* (*eccl.*) (communion) bread; host.

просце́ниум, а, *m.* (*theatr.*) proscenium.

просчёт, а, *m.* **1.** counting (up), reckoning (up). **2.** error (*in counting, reckoning*).

просчит|а́ть, а́ю, *pf.* (*of* ~ывать) **1.** to count (up), reckon (up). **2.** to count out, give in error; вы ~а́ли пятьдеся́т рубле́й you have given fifty roubles too much.

просчит|а́ться, а́юсь, *pf.* (*of* ~ываться) **1.** to make an error in counting; to be out in counting; to go wrong; мы ~а́лись на два́дцать рубле́й we are out by twenty roubles. **2.** (*fig.*) to miscalculate.

просчи́тыва|ть(ся), ю(сь), *impf. of* просчита́ть(ся).

про́сып, а, *m.*; без ~у (*coll.*) without waking, without stirring.

просы́п|ать, лю, лешь, *pf.* (*of* ~а́ть¹) to spill.

просып|а́ть¹, а́ю, *impf. of* ~ать.

просып|а́ть², а́ю, *impf. of* проспа́ть.

просы́п|аться, лется, *pf.* (*of* ~а́ться²) to spill, get spilled.

просып|а́ться¹, а́юсь, *impf. of* просну́ться.

просып|а́ться², а́юсь, *impf. of* ~аться.

просыха́|ть, ю, *impf. of* просо́хнуть.

про́сьб|а, ы, *f.* **1.** request; обраща́ться с ~ой to make a request; удовлетвори́ть ~у to comply with a request; у меня́ к вам п. I have a favour to ask you; по мое́й ~е at my request; п. не кури́ть! no smoking, please! **2.** (*obs.*) application, petition; пода́ть ~у об отста́вке to send in one's resignation.

прося́нк|а, и, *f.* овся́нка-п. (*orn.*) corn-bunting.

прося́ной, *adj.* millet.

прота́лин|а, ы, *f.* thawed patch (*of earth*).

прота́лкива|ть, ю, *impf. of* протолкну́ть.

прота́лкива|ться, юсь, *impf. of* протолка́ться *and* протолкну́ться.

протанц|ева́ть, у́ю, *pf.* **1.** to dance; п. вальс to dance a waltz, do a waltz. **2.** to dance (*for a certain time*).

прота́плива|ть, ю, *impf. of* протопи́ть.

прота́птыва|ть, ю, *impf. of* протопта́ть.

протара́н|ить, ю, ишь, *pf.* (*of* тара́нить) **1.** (*mil.*) to ram. **2.** (*fig.*) to break through, smash.

прота́скива|ть, ю, *impf. of* протащи́ть.

прота́чива|ть, ю, *impf. of* проточи́ть.

протащ|и́ть, у́, ~ишь, *pf.* (*of* прота́скивать) **1.** to pull (through, along), drag (through, along), trail. **2.** (*coll., pejor.*) to insinuate, work in.

прота́|ять, ю, ешь, *pf.* to thaw through.

протеже́, *indecl.*, *m. and f.* protégé(e).

протежи́р|овать, ую, *impf.* (+*d.*) to favour; to pull strings (for).

проте́з, а, *m.* prosthetic appliance; artificial limb; зубно́й п. false tooth, denture.

протези́р|овать, ую, *impf. and pf.* to equip with a prosthetic appliance; to make a prosthetic appliance.

протéзн|ый, *adj.* prosthetic; ~ая мастер-скáя orthopaedic workshop.

протеи́н, а, *m.* (*chem.*) protein.

протекá|ть, ю, *impf.* **1.** *impf. of* протéчь. **2.** *impf. only* (*of a river or stream*) to flow, run. **3.** *impf. only* to leak, be leaky.

протéктор, а, *m.* **1.** (*polit.*) power exercising protectorate. **2.** (*obs.*) protector, patron. **3.** (*tech.*) protector, protective device; двойнóй п. double tread (*of pneumatic tire*).

протекторáт, а, *m.* protectorate.

протекциони́зм, а, *m.* **1.** (*polit.*, *econ.*) protectionism. **2.** (*coll.*) favouritism.

протекциони́ст, а, *m.* protectionist.

протéкци|я, и, *f.* patronage, influence; оказáть комý-н. ~ю to use one's influence on someone's behalf, pull strings for someone.

протé|кший, *past part. act. of* ~чь *and adj.* past, last.

про|терéть, трý, трёшь, *past* ~тёр, ~тёрла, *pf.* (*of* ~тирáть) **1.** to rub a hole (in); to wear into holes. **2.** to rub through, grate; п. чéрез си́то to rub through a sieve. **3.** to rub over, wipe over. **4.** п. глазá (*coll.*) to rub one's eyes.

про|терéться, трётся, *past* ~тёрся, ~тёрлась, *pf.* (*of* ~тирáться) to wear through, wear into holes.

протерп|éть, лю́, ~ишь, *pf.* to wait, last out; to endure, stand.

протесн|и́ться, ю́сь, и́шься, *pf.* to push one's way (through), elbow one's way (through), barge (through).

протéст, а, *m.* **1.** protest; remonstrance; заяви́ть п. to make a protest; подáть п. to enter, register a protest. **2.** п. вéкселя (*fin.*, *comm.*) protest of a promissory note. **3.** (*leg.*) objection; принести́ п. to bring an objection.

протестáнт[1], а, *m.* protester, objector.

протестáнт[2], а, *m.* (*rel.*) Protestant.

протестанти́зм, а, *m.* = протестáнтство.

протестáнтский, *adj.* (*rel.*) Protestant.

протестáнтств|о, а, *n.* (*rel.*) Protestantism.

протест|овáть, ýю, *impf.* (прóтив) to protest (against), object (to).

протé|чь, чёт, кýт, *past* ~к, ~клá, *pf.* (*of* ~кáть) **1.** to ooze, seep. **2.** (*of time*) to elapse, pass; кани́кулы бы́стро ~кли́ the holidays flew by. **3.** (*of an illness, etc.*) to take its course.

прóтив, *prep.+g.* **1.** (*in var. senses*) against; п. течéния against the current; не найдётся ли у вас что-н. п. головнóй бóли? do you happen to have anything for a headache?; за и п. for and against, pro and con; имéть что-н. п. to have something against; to mind, object; вы ничегó не имéете п. тогó, что я курю́? do you mind my smok-

ing?; вы ничегó не бýдете имéть п., éсли я закурю́? will you mind if I smoke? **2.** opposite; facing; друг п. дрýга facing one another; остановитесь, пожáлуйста, п. цéркви please stop opposite the church. **3.** contrary to; п. нáших ожидáний contrary to our expectations. **4.** (*coll.*) as against; in proportion to; according to; в э́том годý п. прóшлого this year as against last (year); дéсять шáнсов п. одногó ten to one; кáждому п. потрéбностей егó to each according to his needs.

прóтив|ень, ня, *m.* griddle.

проти́вительный, *adj.* (*gram.*) adversative.

проти́в|иться, люсь, ишься, *impf.* (*of* вос~) (+*d.*) to oppose; to resist, stand up (against).

проти́вник, а, *m.* **1.** opponent, adversary, antagonist. **2.** (*collect.*; *mil.*) the enemy.

проти́вно[1], *adv.* in a disgusting way.

проти́вно[2], *prep.+d.* against; contrary to; поступáть п. своéй сóвести to go against one's conscience.

проти́вн|ый[1], *adj.* **1.** opposite; contrary; п. вéтер contrary wind, head wind; ~ое мнéние a contrary opinion; в ~ом слýчае otherwise; доказáтельство от ~ого the rule of contraries. **2.** opposing, opposed; ~ые стóроны opposing sides.

проти́в|ный[2] (~ен, ~на), *adj.* nasty, offensive, disgusting; unpleasant, disagreeable; п. зáпах nasty smell; он мне ~ен I find him offensive; мне ~но припоминáть э́то происшéствие I find it disagreeable to recollect the event.

проти́во- anti-, contra-, counter-.

противоалкогóльный, *adj.* temperance; п. закóн prohibition.

противобóрств|о, а, *n.* struggle; (*polit.*) confrontation.

противобóрств|овать, ую, *impf.* (+*d.*; *obs.*) to oppose; to fight (against).

противовéс, а, *m.* (*tech. and fig.*) counterbalance, counterpoise.

противовоздýшн|ый, *adj.* anti-aircraft; ~ая оборóна air defence.

противогáз, а, *m.* gas-mask, respirator.

противогáзов|ый, *adj.* anti-gas; ~ая сýмка gas-mask case.

противодéйстви|е, я, *n.* opposition, counteraction.

противодéйств|овать, ую, *impf.* (+*d.*) to oppose, counteract.

противодетони́рующий, *adj.* п. материáл (*tech.*) anti-knock compound.

противоестéствен|ный (~, ~на), *adj.* unnatural.

противозакóнност|ь, и, *f.* illegality.

противозакóн|ный (~ен, ~на), *adj.* unlawful; (*leg.*) illegal.

противозача́точн|ый, *adj.* contraceptive; ~ые сре́дства contraceptives.

противозени́тный, *adj.* п. манёвр (*aeron.*) evasive action.

противоипри́тный, *adj.* anti-mustard-gas.

противокисло́тный, *adj.* acid-proof.

противолежа́щий, *adj.* (*math.*) opposite; п. у́гол alternate angle.

противолихора́дочн|ый, *adj.* (*med.*) anti-febrile; ~ое сре́дство febrifuge.

противоло́дочный, *adj.* (*naut.*) anti-submarine.

противоми́нн|ый, *adj.* (*naut.*) anti-mine-and-torpedo; ~ая артилле́рия secondary armament.

противообще́ственный, *adj.* antisocial.

противоотка́тн|ый, *adj.* (*mil.*) anti-recoil; ~ые устро́йства recoil mechanism.

противоподло́дочный, *adj.* (*naut.*) anti-submarine.

противопожа́рн|ый, *adj.* anti-fire; ~ые ме́ры fire-prevention measures.

противопоказа́ни|е, я, *n.* 1. (*leg.*) contradictory evidence. 2. (*med.*) contra-indication.

противопока́занный, *adj.* (*med.*) contra-indicated.

противополага́|ть, ю, *impf. of* противоположи́ть.

противоположе́ни|е, я, *n.* opposition.

противополож|и́ть, у́, ~ишь, *pf.* (*of* противополага́ть) (+*d.*) to oppose (to).

противополо́жност|ь, и, *f.* 1. opposition; contrast; в п. (+*d.*) as opposed (to), by contrast (with). 2. opposite, antipode, antithesis; по́лная п. complete antithesis; пряма́я п. exact opposite.

противополо́ж|ный (~ен, ~на), *adj.* 1. opposite. 2. opposed, contrary; диаметра́льно п. diametrically opposed.

противопоста́в|ить, лю, ишь, *pf.* (*of* ~ля́ть) (+*d.*) 1. to oppose (to). 2. to contrast (with), set off (against).

противопоставле́ни|е, я, *n.* (+*d.*) 1. opposing (to), opposition (to). 2. contrasting (with), setting off (against).

противопоставля́|ть, ю, *impf. of* противопоста́вить.

противоправи́тельственный, *adj.* anti-government(al).

противораке́тн|ый, *adj.* (*mil.*) anti-missile; ~ая раке́та anti-missile missile.

противоречи́вост|ь, и, *f.* contradictoriness; discrepancy.

противоречи́в|ый (~, ~а), *adj.* contradictory; discrepant, conflicting; ~ые сообще́ния conflicting reports.

противоречи|е, я, *n.* 1. contradiction; inconsistency; ~я в показа́ниях contradictions in evidence. 2. contrariness; defiance;

дух ~я spirit of defiance, contrariness; вы э́то де́лаете про́сто из ду́ха ~я you are doing it simply out of contrariness. 3. conflict, clash; кла́ссовые ~я conflicts of class interests; находи́ться в ~и (c+*i.*) to be at variance (with), conflict (with).

противоре́ч|ить, у, ишь, *impf.* (+*d.*) 1. to contradict; п. самому́ себе́ to contradict oneself; он всё ~ил ма́тери he was always contradicting his mother. 2. to be at variance (with), conflict (with), run counter (to), be contrary (to); э́то ~ит действи́тельности it is contrary to the facts; их показа́ния ~ат одно́ друго́му their evidence is conflicting.

противосамолётный, *adj.* (*mil.*) anti-aircraft.

противоснаря́дный, *adj.* (*mil.*) shell-proof.

противостолбня́чный, *adj.* (*med.*) anti-tetanus.

противостоя́ни|е, я, *n.* 1. (*astron.*) opposition. 2. (*polit.*) confrontation.

противосто|я́ть, ю́, и́шь, *impf.* (+*d.*) 1. to resist, withstand. 2. to countervail. 3. (*astron.*) to be in opposition.

противота́нков|ый, *adj.* anti-tank; anti-mechanized; ~ая лову́шка tank trap; ~ое ружьё anti-tank rifle.

противото́к, а, *m.* (*tech.*) counter-current, counterflow.

противохими́ческий, *adj.* (*mil.*) anti-gas.

противоцинго́тный, *adj.* (*med.*) anti-scorbutic.

противочу́мный, *adj.* (*med.*) anti-plague.

противоя́ди|е, я, *n.* antidote.

протира́|ть(ся), ю(сь), *impf. of* протере́ть(ся).

проти́рк|а, и, *f.* cleaning rag.

проти́ск|аться, аюсь, *pf.* (*of* ~иваться) to push one's way through, elbow one's way through.

проти́скива|ть, ю, *impf. of* проти́снуть.

проти́скива|ться, юсь, *impf. of* проти́скаться.

проти́с|нуть, ну, нешь, *pf.* (*of* ~кивать) to push through, shove through.

проти́с|нуться, нусь, нешься, *pf. = ~*каться.

проткн|у́ть, у́, ёшь, *pf.* (*of* протыка́ть) to pierce; to transfix; to spit, skewer.

протодья́кон, а, *m.* (*eccl.*) archdeacon.

протозо́а, *indecl. pl.* (*zool.*) protozoa.

протоиере́|й, я, *m.* (*eccl.*) archpriest.

протоисто́ри|я, и, *f.* pre-history.

прото́к, а, *m.* 1. channel. 2. (*anat.*) duct.

протоко́л, а, *m.* 1. minutes, record of proceedings; report; вести́ п. to take the minutes, record the minutes; занести́ в п. to enter in the minutes. 2. (*leg.*) statement; charge-sheet; п. дозна́ния, п. допро́са examination record; соста́вить п. to draw up a report. 3. (*diplomatic*) protocol.

протоколи́зм, а, *m.* dry, factual exposition.

протоколи́р|овать, ую, *impf. and pf.* (*pf. also* за~) to minute; to record.

протоко́л|ьный, *adj. of* ~; п. отде́л protocol department; п. стиль (*fig.*) officialese (= *dry, factual style of exposition*, not *long-winded jargon*).

протолка́|ться, юсь, *pf.* (*of* прота́лкиваться) (*coll.*) 1. to force, jostle one's way (through). 2. to lounge about.

протолкн|у́ть, у́, ёшь, *pf.* (*of* прота́лкивать) to push through, press through; (*fig.*) п. де́ло to push a matter forward.

протолкн|у́ться, у́сь, ёшься, *pf.* = протолка́ться.

прото́н, а, *m.* (*phys.*) proton.

прото́н|ный, *adj. of* ~.

протоп|и́ть, лю́, ~ишь, *pf.* (*of* прота́пливать) to heat thoroughly.

протопла́зм|а, ы, *f.* (*biol.*) protoplasm.

протопо́п, а, *m.* (*obs.*) archpriest.

протоп|та́ть, чу́, ~чешь, *pf.* (*of* прота́птывать) 1. to beat, make (*by walking*); п. тропи́нку to make a path. 2. to wear out (*footwear*).

проторг|ова́ть, у́ю, *pf.* (*coll.*) to lose (*in trading*).

проторг|ова́ться, у́юсь, *pf.* (*coll.*) to have losses (*in trading*); to be ruined (*in trade, in business*).

протор|ённый, *p.p.p. of* ~и́ть *and adj.* beaten, well-trodden; ~ённая доро́жка beaten track.

про́тор|и, ей, *no sing.* (*obs.*) expenses.

протор|и́ть, ю́, и́шь, *pf.* (*of* ~я́ть) to beat; п. путь to blaze a trail.

протор|я́ть, я́ю, *impf. of* ~и́ть.

прототи́п, а, *m.* prototype.

прото́ч|енный, *p.p.p. of* ~и́ть; п. червя́ми worm-eaten.

проточ|и́ть, у́, ~ишь, *pf.* (*of* прота́чивать) 1. to gnaw through, eat through. 2. (*of running water*) to wash. 3. to turn (*on a lathe*).

прото́чн|ый, *adj.* flowing, running; ~ая вода́ running water; п. пруд pond fed by springs.

протра́в|а, ы, *f.* (*chem.*) mordant; pickle, dip.

протрави́тел|ь, я, *m.* 1. (*tech.*) mordanting machine, pickling machine. 2. (*chem.*) mordant.

протрав|и́ть[1], лю́, ~ишь, *pf.* (*of* ~ливать *and* ~ля́ть) (*tech.*) 1. to treat with a mordant; to pickle, dip. 2. to etch.

протрав|и́ть[2], лю́, ~ишь, *pf.* (*in hunting*) to fail to catch, let go.

протра́влива|ть, ю, *impf. of* протрави́ть[1].

протравл|я́ть, я́ю, *impf.* = ~ивать.

протра́л|ить, ю, ишь, *pf. of* тра́лить.

протрезв|и́ть, лю́, и́шь, *pf.* (*of* ~ля́ть) to sober.

протрезв|и́ться, лю́сь, и́шься, *pf.* (*of* ~ля́ться) to sober up, get sober.

протрезвля́|ть(ся), ю(сь), *impf. of* протрезви́ть(ся).

протубера́н|ец, ца, *m.* (*astron.*) solar prominence.

протур|и́ть, ю́, ~и́шь, *pf.* (*coll.*) to drive away, chuck out.

протух|а́ть, а́ю, *impf. of* ~нуть.

проту́х|нуть, ну, нешь, *past* ~, ~ла, *pf.* (*of* ~а́ть) to become foul, rotten; to go bad.

проту́х|ший, *past part. act. of* ~нуть *and adj.* foul, rotten; (*of food*) bad, tainted.

протыка́|ть, ю, *impf. of* проткну́ть.

протя́гива|ть(ся), ю(сь), *impf. of* протяну́ть(ся).

протяже́ни|е, я, *n.* 1. extent, stretch; distance, expanse, area; на большо́м ~и over a wide area; на всём ~и (+*g.*) along the whole length (of), all along. 2. space (*of time*); на ~и (+*g.*) during, for the space (of).

протяжённост|ь, и, *f.* extent, length.

протяжён|ный (~, ~на), *adj.* extensive.

протя́жност|ь, и, *f.* slowness; п. ре́чи drawl.

протя́ж|ный (~ен, ~на), *adj.* long drawn-out; ~ое произноше́ние drawl.

протя|ну́ть, ну́, ~нешь, *pf.* (*of* ~гивать) 1. to stretch; to extend. 2. to stretch out, extend, hold out, reach out; п. ру́ку to hold out one's hand; п. ру́ку по́мощи to extend a helping hand; п. табаке́рку to proffer a snuff-box; п. но́ги (*fig., coll.*) to turn up one's toes. 3. to protract. 4. to drawl out. 5. (*pf. only*) to last; больно́й недо́лго ~нет the patient won't last long. 6. (*hunting*) to fly over (*of birds*).

протя|ну́ться, ну́сь, ~нешься, *pf.* (*of* ~гиваться) 1. to stretch out; to reach out; п. на дива́не to stretch out on the sofa. 2. to extend, stretch, reach. 3. *pf. only* to last, go on.

проу́л|ок, ка, *m.* (*coll.*) lane.

проу́чива|ть, ю, *impf. of* проучи́ть[1].

проуч|и́ть[1], у́, ~ишь, *pf.* (*of* ~ивать) (*coll.*) to teach, give a good lesson; я его́ ~у́! I'll teach him!

проуч|и́ть[2], у́, ~ишь, *pf.* to study, learn up (*for a certain time*).

проуч|и́ться, у́сь, ~ишься, *pf.* to spend (*a certain time*) in study.

проу́шин|а, ы, *f.* lug; staple.

проф- *abbr. of* 1. профессиона́льный. 2. профсою́зный.

профа́н, а, *m.* 1. (*in relation to a given field of knowledge*) layman. 2. ignoramus.

профана́ци|я, и, *f.* profanation.

профани́р|овать, ую, *impf. and pf.* to profane.

профбиле́т, а, *m.* (*abbr. of* профсою́зный биле́т) trade-union card.

профершпи́л|иться, юсь, ишься, *pf.* (*coll.*) to lose all one's money, be completely ruined.

профессиона́л, а, *m.* professional.

профессионали́зм, а, *m.* professionalism.

профессиона́льн|ый, *adj.* 1. professional, occupational; ~ое заболева́ние occupational disease; ~ое образова́ние vocational training; п. сою́з trade union. 2. professional (*as opp. to* amateur).

профе́сси|я, и, *f.* profession, occupation, trade; по ~и by profession, by trade.

профе́ссор, а, *pl.* ~а́, *m.* professor.

профе́ссорск|ий, *adj.* 1. professorial. 2. *as noun* ~ая, ~ой, *f.* staff common room.

профе́ссорств|о, а, *n.* professorship, (university) chair.

профе́ссорств|овать, ую, *impf.* to be a professor, have a (university) chair.

профессу́р|а, ы, *f.* 1. professorship, (university) chair. 2. (*collect.*) the professors.

профила́ктик|а, и, *f.* 1. (*med.*) prophylaxis. 2. (*collect.*) preventive measures, precautions.

профилакти́ческий, *adj.* 1. (*med.*) prophylactic. 2. preventive, precautionary.

профилакто́ри|й, я, *m.* dispensary.

про́фил|ь, я, *m.* 1. profile; side-view; (*fig.*) outline; в п. in profile, half-faced. 2. section; попере́чный п. cross-section; п. крыла́ (*aeron.*) airfoil. 3. type; шко́лы ра́зного ~я schools of various types.

про́филь|ный, *adj. of* ~; ~ное желе́зо section iron; п. резе́ц, п. фре́зер (*tech.*) profile cutter, forming tool.

профильтр|ова́ть, у́ю, *pf. of* фильтрова́ть.

профин|ти́ть, чу́, ти́шь, *pf.* (*coll.*) to squander.

профко́м, а, *m.* (*abbr. of* профсою́зный комите́т) trade-union committee.

профо́рг, а, *m.* (*abbr. of* профсою́зный организа́тор) trade-union organizer.

профо́рм|а, ы, *f.* form, formality; чи́стая п. pure, mere formality; для ~ы, ра́ди ~ы for form's sake, as a matter of form.

профрабо́т|а, ы, *f.* (*abbr. of* профсою́зная рабо́та) trade-union work.

профрабо́тник, а, *m.* (*abbr. of* профсою́зный рабо́тник) trade-union official.

профсою́з, а, *m.* (*abbr. of* профессиона́льный сою́з) trade union.

профсою́зный, *adj.* trade-union.

профтехшко́л|а, ы, *f.* (*abbr. of* профессиона́льно-техни́ческая шко́ла) trade school.

профшко́л|а, ы, *f.* (*abbr. of* профсою́зная шко́ла) trade-union school.

проха́жива|ться, юсь, *impf. of* пройти́сь.

прохва|ти́ть, чу́, ~тишь, *pf.* (*of* ~тывать) (*coll.*) 1. (*of cold, draught, etc.*) to penetrate; меня́ ~ти́ло на сквозняке́ I caught a chill from being in a draught. 2. to bite through. 3. (*fig.*) to tear to pieces.

прохва́тыва|ть, ю, *impf. of* прохвати́ть.

прохвора́|ть, ю, *pf.* (*coll.*) to be ill (*for a certain time*); to be laid up (*for a certain time*).

прохво́ст, а, *m.* (*coll.*) scoundrel.

прохла́д|а, ы, *f.* coolness; вече́рняя п. the cool of the evening.

прохла́д|ец, ца, *m.* с ~цем (*coll.*) without making much effort; listlessly.

прохлади́тельн|ый, *adj.* refreshing, cooling; ~ые напи́тки soft drinks.

прохла|ди́ться, жу́сь, ди́шься, *pf.* (*coll.*) to cool off.

прохла́д|ный (~ен, ~на), *adj.* 1. cool; fresh; ~но (*impers., pred.*) it is cool, it is fresh. 2. (*fig.*) cool; отноше́ния у них ста́ли ~ными there has been a cooling-off between them.

прохла́д|ца, цы, *f.* = ~ец.

прохлажда́|ться, юсь, *impf.* (*coll.*) to take it easy.

прохо́д, а, *m.* 1. (*in var. senses*) passage; пра́во ~а right of way; не дава́ть ~а (+*d.*) to give no peace, pester; мне от него́ ~а нет I cannot get rid of him, shake him off. 2. passageway; gangway, aisle; кры́тый п. covered way. 3. (*anat.*) duct; за́дний п. anus; слухово́й п. acoustic duct.

проходи́м|ец, ца, *m.* rogue, rascal.

проходи́мост|ь, и, *f.* 1. (*of roads, etc.*) passability. 2. (*anat.*) permeability. 3. (*of motor, etc., transport*) cross-country ability.

проходи́м|ый (~, ~а), *adj.* passable.

прохо|ди́ть¹, жу́, ~дишь, *impf.* 1. *impf. of* пройти́. 2. *impf. only* (че́рез) to lie (through), go (through), pass (through); кана́л ~дит че́рез джу́нгли the canal passes through jungle.

прохо|ди́ть², жу́, ~дишь, *pf.* to walk (*for a certain time*); мы ~ди́ли весь день we have spent the whole day walking.

прохо́дк|а, и, *f.* (*mining*) working; sinking (*of shaft*); drift.

проходн|о́й, *adj.* of passage; ~а́я бу́дка entrance check-point, entrance lodge; ~а́я ко́мната inter-communicating room, room giving access into another; ~а́я конто́ра entrance-gate office; ~о́е свиде́тельство (*hist.*) travel permit, travel document (*issued by police to deportees*).

прохо́дчик, а, *m.* (*mining*) shaft sinker; drifter.

прохожде́ни|е, я, *n.* passing, passage; п. торже́ственным ма́ршем (*mil.*) march past.

прохо́ж|ий, *adj.* passing, in transit; *as noun* п., **∼его**, *m. and* **∼ая**, **∼ей**, *f.* passer--by.

процвета́ни|е, я, *n.* prosperity, well-being; flourishing, thriving.

процвета́|ть, ю, *impf.* to prosper, flourish, thrive.

проце|ди́ть, жу́, **∼дишь**, *pf.* (*of* **∼живать**) to filter, strain.

процеду́р|а, ы, *f.* 1. procedure. 2. (*usu. pl.*) treatment.

проце́жива|ть, ю, *impf. of* процеди́ть.

проце́нт, а, *m.* 1. percentage; rate (per cent); сто **∼ов** one hundred per cent; ба́нковский учётный п. bank rate; просты́е, сло́жные **∼ы** (*math.*) simple, compound interest; рабо́тать на **∼ах** to work on a percentage basis. 2. interest; разме́р **∼а** rate of interest.

проце́нт|ный, *adj. of* **∼** interest-bearing; **∼ное** отноше́ние percentage; **∼ные** бума́ги interest-bearing securities; **∼ные** облига́ции interest-bearing bonds.

проце́сс, а, *m.* 1. process. 2. (*leg.*) trial; legal action, legal proceedings; lawsuit; cause, case; вести́ п. (с+*i.*) to be at law (with). 3. (*med.*) active condition; п. в лёгких active pulmonary tuberculosis.

процесси|я, и, *f.* procession.

процессуа́льн|ый, *adj. of* проце́сс 2; **∼ые** но́рмы legal procedure.

процити́р|овать, ую, *pf. of* цити́ровать.

прочёркива|ть, ю, *impf. of* прочеркну́ть.

прочерк|ну́ть, ну́, нёшь, *pf.* (*of* **∼ивать**) to strike through, draw a line through.

прочер|ти́ть, чу́, **∼тишь**, *pf.* (*of* **∼чивать**) to draw.

прочёрчива|ть, ю, *impf. of* прочерти́ть.

проче|са́ть, шу́, **∼шешь**, *pf.* (*of* **∼сывать**) 1. to comb out thoroughly. 2. (*mil.; fig.*) to comb.

прочёск|а, и, *f.* screening (*as a security measure*).

про|че́сть, чту́, чтёшь, *past* **∼чёл**, **∼чла́**, *pf.* = **∼**чита́ть.

прочёсыва|ть, ю, *impf. of* прочеса́ть.

прочёт, а, *m.* (*coll.*) error (*in counting*).

проч|ий, *adj.* other; и **∼ее** (*abbr.* и пр., и проч.) etcetera, and so on; **∼ие** (the) others; ме́жду **∼им** by the way; поми́мо всего́ **∼его** in addition.

прочи|стить, щу, стишь, *pf.* (*of* **∼ща́ть**) clean; to cleanse thoroughly; п. тру́бку to clean a pipe.

прочита́|ть[1], ю, *pf. of* чита́ть.

прочита́|ть[2], ю, *pf.* to read (*for a certain time*).

прочи́тыва|ть, ю, *impf.* (*coll.*) to read through, peruse.

про́ч|ить, у, ишь, *impf.* (в+*a.*) to intend

(for), destine (for); его́ **∼или** в свяще́нники he was intended for the church.

прочища́|ть, ю, *impf. of* прочи́стить.

про́чно, *adv.* firmly, soundly, solidly, well.

про́чност|ь, и, *f.* firmness, soundness, stability, solidity; durability; endurance; п. на изги́б (*tech.*) bending strength; п. на изно́с (*tech.*) resistance to wear; п. на разры́в (*tech.*) tensile strength; п. на уда́р (*tech.*) resistance to shock, impact value; запа́с **∼и**, коэффицие́нт **∼и** safety factor, safety margin.

про́ч|ный (**∼ен**, **∼на́**, **∼но**), *adj.* firm, sound, stable, solid; durable, lasting; **∼ные** зна́ния sound knowledge; **∼ная** кра́ска fast dye; **∼ное** сча́стье lasting happiness; **∼ная** ткань durable fabric.

прочте́ни|е, я, *n.* reading; perusal; по **∼и** (+*g.*) on reading.

прочу́вствова|нный, *p.p.p. of* **∼ть** *and adj.* full of emotion; heart-felt.

прочу́вств|овать, ую, *pf.* 1. to feel deeply, acutely, keenly. 2. to experience, go through. 3. to feel, get the feel (of); п. свою́ роль to get the feel of one's part.

прочь, *adv.* 1. away, off; (поди́) п.! go away!, be off!; (пошёл) п. отсю́да! get out of here!; п. с глаз мои́х! get out of my sight!; п. с доро́ги! (get) out of the way!, make way!; ру́ки п.! hands off! 2. (*pred.*) averse (to); не п. (+ *inf.*; *coll.*) to have no objection (to), not to be averse (to); я не п. пойти́ туда́ I have no objection to going there, I am quite willing to go there; он не п. вы́пить стака́нчик he is not averse to taking a drop.

проше́дш|ий, *past part. act. of* пройти́ *and adj.* past; last; **∼им** ле́том last summer; **∼ее** вре́мя (*gram.*) past tense; *as noun* **∼ее**, **∼его**, *n.* the past.

проше́ни|е, я, *n.* application, petition; пода́ть п. to submit an application, forward a petition.

прошеп|та́ть, чу́, **∼чешь**, *pf. of* шепта́ть.

проше́стви|е, я, *n.* по **∼и** (+*g.*) after the lapse (of), after the expiration (of); по **∼и** сро́ка after the expiration of the term.

прошиб|а́ть, а́ю, *impf. of* **∼ить**.

прошиб|и́ть, у́, ёшь, *past* **∼**, **∼ла**, *pf.* (*of* **∼а́ть**) (*coll.*) 1. to break through. 2. его́ **∼** пот he broke into a sweat; её **∼ла** слеза́ she shed a tear.

прошива́|ть, ю, *impf. of* проши́ть.

проши́вк|а, и, *f.* 1. insertion (on linen, *etc.*). 2. (*tech.*) broach, broaching bit.

прош|и́ть, ью́, ьёшь, *pf.* (*of* **∼ива́ть**) 1. to sew, stitch. 2. (*tech.*) to broach.

прошлого́дний, *adj.* last year's; of last year.

про́шл|ый, *adj.* 1. past; bygone, former; э́то де́ло **∼ое** it's a thing of the past; *as noun*

~ое, ~ого, n. the past; далёкое ~ое the distant past; отойти́ в ~ое to become a thing of the past. 2. last; в ~ом году́ last year; на ~ой неде́ле last week.

прошля́п|ить, лю, ишь, pf. (coll.) to blunder, slip up.

прошмы́гива|ть, ю, impf. of прошмыгну́ть.

прошмыг|ну́ть, ну́, нёшь, pf. (of ~ивать) (coll.) to slip (by, past, through).

прошнур|ова́ть, у́ю, pf. of шнурова́ть 2.

прошпакл|ева́ть, юю, юешь, pf. (of ~ёвывать) to putty; (naut.) to caulk.

прошпаклёвыва|ть, ю, impf. of прошпаклева́ть.

проштра́ф|иться, люсь, ишься, pf. (coll.) to be at fault.

проштуди́р|овать, ую, pf. of штуди́ровать.

прошум|е́ть, лю́, и́шь, pf. 1. to roar past. 2. (fig.) to become famous.

проща́й(те) good-bye!; farewell!, adieu!

проща́льн|ый, adj. farewell, parting; valedictory; ~ая пиру́шка farewell party; ~ые слова́ parting words.

проща́ни|е, я, n. farewell; parting, leave-taking; на п. at parting.

проща́|ть(ся), ю(сь), impf. of прости́ть(ся).

про́ще, comp. of просто́й and про́сто; simpler; plainer; easier.

прощелы́г|а, и, m. and f. (coll.) knave, rogue.

проще́ни|е, я, n. forgiveness, pardon; absolution; проси́ть ~я у кого́-н. to ask someone's pardon; прошу́ ~я! I beg your pardon!, (I am) sorry!

прощу́п|ать, аю, pf. (of ~ывать) 1. to feel; to detect (by feeling). 2. (fig., coll.) to sound (out).

прощу́пыва|ть, ю, impf. of прощу́пать.

проэкзамен|ова́ть(ся), у́ю(сь), pf. of экзаменова́ть(ся).

прояви́тел|ь, я, m. (phot.) developer.

прояв|и́ть, лю́, ~ишь, pf. (of ~ля́ть) 1. to show, display, manifest, reveal; п. забо́ту (о+p.) to show concern (for, about), take trouble (about); п. интере́с (к) to show interest (in); п. себя́ to show one's worth; п. себя́ (+i.) to show oneself, prove (to be); он ~и́л себя́ пре́данным колле́гой he proved to be a loyal colleague. 2. (phot.) to develop.

прояв|и́ться, ~ится, pf. (of ~ля́ться) 1. to show (itself), reveal itself, manifest itself. 2. pass. of ~и́ть.

проявля́|ть(ся), ю(сь), impf. of прояви́ть(ся).

проясне́|ть, ет, pf. (of the sky) to clear; ~ло (impers.) it cleared up.

прояснё|ть, ет, pf. to brighten (up); лицо́ ма́льчика вдруг ~ло the boy's face suddenly brightened up.

прояс|ни́ться, и́тся, pf. (of ~я́ться) (of weather and fig.) to clear (up); днём ~и́лось in the afternoon it cleared up; мы́сли у меня́ тепе́рь ~и́лись my thoughts have sorted themselves out now.

прояс|ня́ться, я́ется, impf. of ~и́ться.

пруд, а́, в ~у́, pl. ~ы́, m. pond.

пру|ди́ть, жу́, ~ди́шь, impf. (of за~) to dam (up); хоть пруд ~ди́ (coll.) in abundance; де́нег у них — хоть пруд ~ди́ they are rolling in money.

прудово́й, adj. of пруд.

пружи́н|а, ы, f. spring; гла́вная п. mainspring (also fig.); боева́я п. (mil.) mainspring, firing pin spring; п.-волосо́к hairspring.

пружи́нистост|ь, и, f. springiness, elasticity.

пружи́нист|ый (~, ~а), adj. springy, elastic.

пружи́н|ить, ю, ишь, impf. 1. (trans.) to tense. 2. (intrans.) to be elastic, possess spring; хорошо́ п. to be well sprung.

пружи́нк|а, и, f. (of watch or clock) mainspring; hairspring.

пружи́н|ный, adj. of ~а; ~ные весы́ spring scales, spring balance; п. матра́ц spring mattress; ~ная рессо́ра coil spring.

пруса́к, а́, m. (coll.) cockroach.

прусса́к, а́, m. Prussian.

пру́сск|ий, adj. Prussian; ~ая си́няя (кра́ска) Prussian blue.

прут, а–а́, m. 1. (pl. ~ья, ~ьев) twig; switch; и́вовый п. withe, withy. 2. (pl. ~ы́, ~о́в) (tech.) bar.

пру́тик, а, m. dim. of прут.

пртко́в|ый, adj. rod-shaped; ~ое желе́зо (tech.) rod iron, wire rod.

пры́галк|а, и, f. (coll.) skipping-rope.

пры́гани|е, я, n. jumping, leaping; skipping.

пры́г|ать, аю, impf. (of ~нуть) 1. to jump, leap, spring; to bound; п. на одно́й ноге́ to hop on one leg; п. со скака́лкой to skip; п. с упо́ром to vault; п. с шесто́м (sport) to pole-vault; п. от ра́дости to jump with, for joy. 2. to bounce.

пры́г|нуть, ну, нешь, pf. of ~ать.

прыгу́н, а́, m. 1. (sport) jumper. 2. (coll.) fidget, restless person.

прыж|о́к, ка́, m. 1. jump, leap, spring; caper; де́лать ~ки́ to caper, cut capers. 2. (sport) jump; ~ки́ jumping; ~ки́ в во́ду diving; ~ки́ с парашю́том parachute jumping; п. в высоту́ high jump; п. в длину́ long jump; п. с упо́ром vault(ing); п. шесто́м pole-vault; п. с ме́ста standing jump; п. с разбе́га running jump.

пры́ска|ть, ю, impf. of пры́снуть.

пры́ска|ться, юсь, impf. (of по~) (+i.; coll.) to (be)sprinkle oneself (with), spray oneself (with).

пры́с|нуть, ну, нешь, *pf.* (*of* ~кать) (*coll.*) **1.** (+*i.*) to (be)sprinkle (with); to spray (with). **2.** to spurt, gush; (со́ смеху) (*fig.*) to burst out laughing.

пры́т|кий (~ок, ~ка́, ~ко), *adj.* quick, lively, sharp.

прыть, и, *f.* (*coll.*) **1.** speed; во всю п. at full speed, as fast as one's legs can carry one. **2.** quickness, liveliness, go; отку́да у него́ така́я п.? where does he get his energy from?

прыщ, а́, *m.* pimple; (*med.*) pustule; лицо́ в ~а́х pimply face.

прыща́ве|ть, ю, *impf.* (*of* о~) to become covered in pimples.

прыща́в|ый (~, ~а), *adj.* pimply, pimpled.

прыщева́т|ый (~, ~а), *adj.* somewhat pimply.

прюне́л|евый, *adj. of* ~ь.

прюне́л|ь, и, *f.* (*text.*) prunella.

пря́да|ть, ю, *impf.* (*obs. or dial.*) п. уша́ми (*of, or in the manner of,* a horse) to move its ears.

пряде́ни|е, я, *n.* spinning.

пря́деный, *adj.* spun.

пряди́льн|ый, *adj.* spinning; п. стано́к spinning loom; ~ая фа́брика spinning mill.

пряди́л|ьня, ьни, *g. pl.* ~ен, *f.* (*obs.*) spinning mill.

пряди́льщик, а, *m.* spinner.

пряд|ь, и, *f.* **1.** lock (*of hair*). **2.** strand.

пря́ж|а, и, *no pl., f.* yarn, thread; шерстяна́я п. woollen yarn, worsted.

пря́жк|а, и, *f.* buckle, clasp.

пря́лк|а, и, *f.* distaff; spinning-wheel.

прям|а́я, о́й, *f.* straight line; провести́ ~у́ю to draw a straight line; расстоя́ние по ~о́й distance as the crow flies.

прямёхонько, *adv.* (*coll.*) straight, directly.

прямизн|а́, ы́, *f.* straightness.

прямико́м, *adv.* (*coll.*) straight; across country.

пря́мо, *adv.* **1.** straight (on); п.! (*mil. word of command*) forward!; иди́те п.! (go) straight on!; держа́ться п. to hold oneself straight, erect. **2.** straight, directly; п. к де́лу to the point; попа́сть п. в цель to hit the bull's eye (*also fig.*); смотре́ть п. в глаза́ кому́-н. to look someone straight in the face; п. со шко́льной скамьи́ (*fig.*) straight from school. **3.** (*fig.*) straight; frankly, openly, bluntly; сказа́ть что-н. кому́-н. п. в лицо́ to say something to someone's face; мы ему́ п. сказа́ли, что э́то ему́ не уда́стся we told him straight that he would not succeed. **4.** (*coll.*) real; really; он п. идио́т he is a real idiot; я п. не зна́ю, что с ней ста́ло I really don't know what has become of her.

прямоду́ши|е, я, *n.* directness, straightforwardness.

прямоду́ш|ный (~ен, ~на), *adj.* direct, straightforward.

прямое́зжий, *adj.* (*folk poet.*) straight.

прям|о́й (~, ~а́, ~о), *adj.* **1.** straight; upright, erect; ~а́я кишка́ (*anat.*) rectum; п. пробо́р parting in the middle; п. у́гол (*math.*) right angle; п. у́зел reef knot; п. ход forward stroke (*of engine*). **2.** (*of means of communication, etc.*) through; direct; по́езд ~о́го сообще́ния through train; п. про́вод direct (*telephone*) line. **3.** (*in var. senses*) direct; ~ые вы́боры direct elections; ~ое дополне́ние (*gram.*) direct object; ~а́я наво́дка (*mil.*) direct laying; ~о́й наво́дкой over open sights; п. нало́г direct tax; п. насле́дник heir in a direct line, direct heir; п. нача́льник immediate superior; ~о́е попада́ние (*mil.*) direct hit; ~а́я противополо́жность direct opposite, exact opposite; ~а́я речь (*gram.*) direct speech, oratio recta; п. смысл сло́ва the literal sense of a word. **4.** (*of character*) straightforward. **5.** (*coll.*) real; п. убы́ток sheer loss; п. расчёт пойти́ самому́ it is really worth while going oneself.

прямокры́л|ые, ых, *pl.* (*zool.*) orthoptera.

прямолине́йност|ь, и, *f.* straightforwardness.

прямоли́не́|йный (~ен, ~йна), *adj.* **1.** rectilinear. **2.** (*fig.*) straightforward; direct.

прямот|а́, ы́, *f.* straightforwardness; plain dealing.

прямото́чный, *adj.* (*tech.*) uniflow, direct-flow; п. котёл continuously operating boiler; п. дви́гатель (*aeron.*) ram jet engine.

прямоуго́льник, а, *m.* (*math.*) rectangle.

прямоуго́льный, *adj.* right-angled; rectangular; п. треуго́льник right-angled triangle.

пря́ник, а, *m.* spice cake; gingerbread; медо́вый п. honey-cake.

пря́ни|чный, *adj. of* ~к.

пря́ност|ь, и, *f.* spice.

пря́|нуть, ну, нешь, *pf.* (*obs.*) to jump aside.

пря́ный, *adj.* spicy (*also fig.*; *of smells*) heady.

пря|сть¹, ду́, дёшь, *past* ~л, ~ла́, ~ло, *impf.* (*of* с~) to spin.

пря|сть², ду́, дёшь, *impf.* = ~дать.

пря́|тать, чу, чешь, *impf.* (*of* с~) to hide, conceal.

пря́|таться, чусь, чешься, *impf.* (*of* с~) to hide, conceal oneself.

пря́т|ки, ок, *no sing.* hide-and-seek; игра́ть в п. to play hide-and-seek.

пря́х|а, и, *f.* spinner.

псал|о́м, ма́, *m.* psalm.

псало́мщик, а, *m.* (*eccl.*) (psalm-)reader; sexton.

псалты́р|ь, и, *f.* and (*coll.*) **п., ~я,** *m.* (*eccl.*) Psalter.

псáр|ня, ни, *g. pl.* **~ен,** *f.* kennel.

псар|ь, я́, *m.* huntsman (*person in charge of hounds*).

псéвдо- pseudo-.

псевдогеройческий, *adj.* (*lit.*) mock-heroic.

псевдони́м, а, *m.* pseudonym; pen-name; alias.

пси́н|а, ы, *f.* (*coll.*) 1. dog's flesh. 2. dog's smell, doggy smell. 3. dog.

пси́ный, *adj.* dog's; doggy.

псих, а, *m.* (*abbr. of* психопáт) (*coll.*) madman, lunatic, crank.

психастéник, а, *m.* (*med.*) psychasthenic.

психастени́ческий, *adj.* (*med.*) psychasthenic.

психастени́|я, и, *f.* (*med.*) psychasthenia.

психиáтр, а, *m.* psychiatrist.

психиатри́ческ|ий, *adj.* psychiatric(al); ~ая лечéбница mental hospital.

психиатри́|я, и, *f.* psychiatry.

пси́хик|а, и, *f.* state of mind; psyche; psychology; нездорóвая п. unhealthy state of mind; врéдно дéйствовать на ~у to have a harmful effect on the psyche; п. лётчиков-истребителей the psychology of fighter-pilots.

психи́чески, *adv.* mentally, psychically, psychologically; п. больнóй mentally diseased; *as noun* п. больнóй, п. больнóго, *m.* mental patient, mental case.

психи́ческ|ий, *adj.* mental, psychical; ~ая болéзнь mental illness, mental disease; ~ая атáка (*mil.*) psychological attack.

психоанáлиз, а, *m.* psychoanalysis.

психоаналити́ческий, *adj.* psychoanalytic(al).

псих|овáть, у́ю, *impf.* (*coll.*) 1. to behave like a madman; to feign insanity. 2. to be upset, hysterical; to have a (nervous) breakdown.

психóз, а, *m.* mental illness; (*med.*) psychosis; воéнный п. war hysteria.

психóлог, а, *m.* psychologist.

психологи́зм, а, *m.* (*philos.*) psychologism.

психологи́ческий, *adj.* psychological.

психолóги|я, и, *f.* psychology.

психоневрóз, а, *m.* (*med.*) psychoneurosis.

психопáт, а, *m.* psychopath; (*coll.*) lunatic.

психопатологи́ческий, *adj.* psychopathological.

психопатолóги|я, и, *f.* psychopathology.

психотерапéвт, а, *m.* psychotherapist.

психотерапи́|я, и, *f.* psychotherapy.

психотéхник|а, и, *f.* vocational psychology.

психофи́зик|а, и, *f.* psychophysics.

психофизиолóги|я, и, *f.* psychophysiology.

психофизи́ческий, *adj.* psychophysical.

псóв|ый, *adj.* ~ая охóта the chase, hunting (*with hounds*).

птáшк|а, и, *f.* little bird; birdie; рáнняя п. (*fig.*) early bird.

птен|éц, ца́, *m.* nestling; fledg(e)ling (*also fig.*).

птеродáктил|ь, я, *m.* pterodactyl.

пти́ц|а, ы, *f.* bird; болóтная п. wader; водоплáвающие ~ы waterfowl; домáшняя п. (*collect.*) poultry; перелётная п. bird of passage; хи́щные ~ы birds of prey; вáжная п. (*fig., coll.*) big noise; обстрéлянная п., стрéляная п. (*fig.; coll.*) old hand.

птицевóд, а, *m.* poultry farmer, poultry breeder.

птицевóдств|о, а, *n.* poultry farming, poultry-keeping.

птицевóдческий, *adj.* poultry-farming, poultry-keeping.

птицелóв, а, *m.* fowler.

птицелóвств|о, а, *n.* fowling.

птицефéрм|а, ы, *f.* poultry farm.

пти́ч|ий, *adj. of* пти́ца; п. двор poultry-yard; ~ье молокó (*coll., joc.*) pigeon's milk; вид с ~ьего полёта bird's-eye view; жить на ~ьих правáх to live from hand to mouth.

пти́чк|а¹, и, *f. dim. of* пти́ца.

пти́чк|а², и, *f.* tick; стáвить ~y to tick.

пти́чник¹, а, *m.* poultry-yard, hen-run; hen-house.

пти́чник², а, *m.* poultryman.

птомáйн, а, *m.* (*chem.*) ptomaine.

пуáнт, а, *m.*; на ~ах (*theatr.*) on the tips of the toes (*also fig.*).

пýблик|а, и, *f.* (*collect.*) (the) public; (*in theatres, etc.*) (the) audience.

публикáци|я, и, *f.* 1. publication. 2. advertisement, notice; помести́ть ~ю в газéте to place an advertisement in a newspaper; п. о смéрти obituary notice.

публик|овáть, у́ю, *impf.* (*of* о~) to publish.

публици́ст, а, *m.* publicist; commentator on current affairs.

публици́стик|а, и, *f.* social and political journalism; writing on current affairs.

публицисти́ческий, *adj.* publicistic.

публи́чно, *adv.* publicly; in public; openly.

публи́чност|ь, и, *f.* publicity.

публи́чн|ый, *adj.* public; ~ая библиотéка public library; п. дом brothel; ~ая жéнщина prostitute; ~ое прáво public law; ~ые торги́ auction, public sale.

пýгал|о, а, *n.* scarecrow.

пýган|ый, *adj.* (*coll.*) scared; ~ая ворóна (и) кустá бои́тся (*prov.*) the burnt child dreads the fire; once bitten twice shy.

пугá|ть, ю, *impf.* (*of* ис~) 1. to frighten, scare. 2. to intimidate; (+*i.*) to threaten (with).

пугá|ться, юсь, *impf.* (*of* ис~) (+*g.*) to be frightened (of), be scared (of); to take fright (at); (*of a horse*) to shy (at).

пуга́ч, а́, *m.* **1.** toy-pistol. **2.** (*orn.*) screech owl.

пугли́вост|ь, и, *f.* fearfulness, timorousness, timidity.

пугли́в|ый (~, ~a), *adj.* fearful, timorous; timid.

пугн|у́ть, у́, ёшь, *pf.* to give a fright, give a scare.

пу́говиц|а, ы, *f.* button; застегну́ться на все ~ы to have all one's buttons done up; держа́ть за ~y (*coll.*) to buttonhole.

пу́гови|чный, *adj.* of ~ца; ~чное произво́дство button-making.

пу́говк|а, и, *f.* (*small*) button.

пуд, а, *pl.* ~ы́, ~о́в, *m.* pood (*Russian measure of weight = 16·38 kg or approx. 36 lb. avoirdupois*).

пу́дел|ь, я, *pl.* ~и, ~ей *or* ~я́, ~е́й, *m.* poodle.

пу́динг, а, *m.* pudding.

пудлингова́ни|е, я, *n.* (*tech.*) puddling.

пудлинг|ова́ть, у́ю, *impf. and pf.* (*tech.*) to puddle.

пу́длингов|ый, *adj.* (*tech.*) puddling, puddled; ~ое желе́зо puddle iron; ~ая печь puddling furnace.

пудови́к, а́, *m.* **1.** one-pood bag. **2.** one-pood weight.

пудово́й, *adj.* one pood in weight.

пу́др|а, ы, *f.* powder; са́харная п. castor sugar.

пу́дрениц|а, ы, *f.* powder-case, powder-compact.

пу́дреный, *adj.* powdered.

пу́др|ить, ю, ишь, *impf.* (*of* на~) to powder.

пу́др|иться, юсь, ишься, *impf.* (*of* на~) to use powder, powder one's face.

пуза́н, а́, *m.* (*coll.*) person with a paunch.

пуза́т|ый (~, ~a), *adj.* (*coll.*) big-bellied, pot-bellied.

пу́з|о, а, *n.* (*coll.*) belly, paunch.

пузыр|ёк, ька́, *m.* **1.** phial, vial. **2.** bubble; bleb.

пузы́р|иться, ится, *impf.* **1.** (*coll.*) to bubble; to effervesce. **2.** (*coll.*) to pout, sulk.

пузы́рник, а, *m.* (*bot.*) senna-pod.

пузы́рчат|ый (~, ~a), *adj.* (*coll.*) covered with bubbles; blebby.

пузы́р|ь, я́, *m.* **1.** bubble; мы́льный п. soap-bubble; пуска́ть мы́льные ~и to blow bubbles. **2.** blister. **3.** (*anat.*) bladder; жёлчный п. gall-bladder; мочево́й п. (urinary) bladder; пла́вательный п. (fish-) sound, swimming-bladder. **4.** air-bladder; п. со льдом ice-bag. **5.** (*coll.*) kid, kiddy.

пук, а, *pl.* ~и́, *m.* bunch, bundle; tuft; п. цвето́в bunch of flowers; п. соло́мы wisp of straw.

пул|ево́й, *adj.* of ~я́.

пулемёт, а, *m.* machine-gun; ручно́й п.

light machine-gun; станко́вый п. heavy machine-gun.

пулемёт|ный, *adj.* of ~; ~ная ле́нта (machine-gun) cartridge belt; ~ная огнева́я то́чка machine-gun emplacement.

пулемётчик, а, *m.* machine-gunner.

пулесто́йкий, *adj.* bullet-proof.

пуло́вер, а, *m.* pullover.

пульвериза́тор, а, *m.* pulverizer, atomizer, sprayer.

пульвериза́ци|я, и, *f.* pulverization, spraying.

пульверизи́р|овать, ую, *impf. and pf.* to pulverize, spray.

пу́льк|а[1], и, *f.* *dim.* of пу́ля.

пу́льк|а[2], и, *f.* (*cards*) pool.

пу́льп|а, ы, *f.* (*anat.*) pulp.

пульс, а, *m.* pulse; pulse rate; бие́ние ~а pulsation, beating of the pulse; счита́ть п. to take the pulse; щу́пать п. to feel the pulse.

пульса́ци|я, и, *f.* pulsation, pulse.

пульси́р|овать, ую, *impf.* **1.** to pulse, pulsate; to beat, throb. **2.** (*tech.*) to pulse, pulsate.

пульсо́метр, а, *m.* (*tech.*) pulsometer, vacuum pump.

пульт, а, *m.* **1.** desk, stand; дирижёрский п. conductor's stand. **2.** (*in power station, etc.*) control panel; (*on aerodrome, etc.*) (traffic) control panel.

пу́л|я, и, *f.* bullet; лить, отлива́ть ~и (*fig., coll.*) to tell lies.

пуля́рк|а, и, *f.* fatted fowl.

пу́м|а, ы, *f.* puma, cougar.

пуни́ческий, *adj.* (*hist.*) Punic.

пункт, а, *m.* **1.** point; spot; наблюда́тельный п. observation post; населённый п. inhabited locality; built-up area; опо́рный п. (*mil.*) strong point; исхо́дный п., нача́льный п. starting point; коне́чный п. terminus, terminal; кульминацио́нный п. culmination, climax. **2.** (*centre operating special services*) point; centre; медици́нский п. (*mil.*) dressing-station, aid post; перегово́рный п. (*collect.*) public (telephone) call-boxes; призывно́й п. recruiting centre; ссыпно́й п. grain-collecting centre. **3.** point; paragraph, item; plank (*of polit. programme*); по ~ам point by point; согла-ше́ние из трёх ~ов a three-point agreement. **4.** (*typ.*) full point.

пу́нктик, а, *m.* (*coll.*) **1.** *dim.* of пункт. **2.** (*fig.*) eccentricity, peculiarity; он — челове́к с ~ом he is a bit odd.

пункти́р, а, *m.* dotted line.

пункти́рн|ый, *adj.* ~ая ли́ния dotted line.

пунктуа́льност|ь, и, *f.* punctuality.

пунктуа́л|ьный (~ен, ~ьна), *adj.* punctual.

пунктуа́ци|я, и, *f.* punctuation.

пу́нкци|я, и, *f.* (*med.*) puncture.

пу́ночк|а, и, *f.* (*orn.*) snow-bunting.

пунсо́н, а, *m.* (*tech.*) punch, die, stamp.

пунцо́вый, *adj.* crimson.

пунш, а, *m.* punch (*drink*).

пу́нш|евый, *adj.* of ~.

пуп, а́, *m.* navel; (*anat.*) umbilicus; п. земли́ the hub of the universe.

пупови́н|а, ы, *f.* (*anat.*) umbilical cord; navel-string.

пуп|о́к, ка́, *m.* 1. navel. 2. (*of birds*) gizzard.

пупо́чн|ый, *adj.* (*anat.*) umbilical; ~ая гры́жа umbilical hernia.

пупы́рыш|ек, ка, *m.* (*coll.*) pimple.

пург|а́, и́, *no pl., f.* snow-storm, blizzard.

пури́зм, а, *m.* purism.

пури́ст, а, *m.* purist.

пурита́н|ин, ина, *pl.* ~е, ~, *m.* Puritan.

пурита́нский, *adj.* Puritan; (*fig.*) puritanical.

пурита́нств|о, а, *n.* Puritanism.

пу́рпур, а, *m.* purple.

пурпу́рный, *adj.* purple.

пурпу́р|овый, *adj.* = ~ный; ~овая кислота́ (*chem.*) purpuric acid.

пуск, а, *m.* starting (up); setting in motion.

пуска́й, *particle and conj.* (*coll.*) = пусть.

пуска́|ть(ся), ю(сь), *impf. of* пусти́ть(ся).

пусков|о́й, *adj.* starting; п. пери́од starting period, initial phase (*of working of factory, etc.*); ~а́я рукоя́тка starting crank; ~о́е устро́йство starter; ~а́я площа́дка (rocket) launching platform.

пустельг|а́, и́, *f.* 1. (*orn.*) kestrel; staniel, windhover. 2. *m. and f.* (*coll.*) worthless fellow.

пусте́|ть, ет, *impf.* (*of* о~) to (become) empty; to become deserted.

пу|сти́ть, щу́, ~стишь, *pf.* (*of* ~ска́ть) 1. to let go; п. на во́лю to set free; п. кровь кому́-н. to bleed someone. 2. to let; to allow, permit; п. кого́-н. в о́тпуск to let someone go on leave; нас не ~сти́ли в пала́ту they would not let us into the ward; ~сти́те соба́ку на двор let the dog out. 3. to let in, allow to enter; не п. to keep out; п. по предъявле́нии биле́та to allow to enter on showing a ticket; п. жильцо́в to take in lodgers; п. козла́ в огоро́д (*prov.*) to set a cat among the pigeons. 4. to start, set in motion, set going; to set working; п. во́ду to turn on water; п. волчо́к to spin a top; п. заво́д to start up a factory; п. змея́ to fly a kite; п. слух to start a rumour; п. фейерве́рк to let off fireworks; п. фонта́н to set a fountain playing; п. часы́ to start a clock. 5. to set, put; to send; п. себе́ пу́лю в лоб to blow out one's brains, put a bullet through one's head; п. в обраще́ние to put in circulation; п. ло́шадь во

весь опо́р to give a horse his head; п. в прода́жу to offer, put up for sale; п. в произво́дство to put in production; п. в ход to start, launch, set going, set in train; п. в ход все сре́дства to move heaven and earth; п. кора́бль ко дну to send a ship to the bottom; п. по́ миру to ruin utterly; п. по́езд под отко́с to derail a train; п. по́ле под пар to put a field to lie fallow. 6. (+*a. or i.*) to throw, shy; п. ка́мнем в окно́ to throw a stone at a window; п. пыль в глаза́ to cut a dash, show off. 7. (*bot.*) to put forth, put out; п. ко́рни to take root (*also fig.*); п. ростки́ to shoot, sprout. 8. (*coll.; in painting*) to put on; to touch up; п. каёмку лило́вым to put violet on the border.

пу|сти́ться, щу́сь, ~сти́шься, *pf.* (*of* ~ска́ться) (в+*a. or* +*inf.; coll.*) 1. to set out, start; п. в путь to set out, get on the way. 2. to begin, start; to set to; п. в оправда́ния to start making excuses; п. в пляс to break into a dance.

пустобре́х, а, *m.* (*coll.*) chatterbox, windbag.

пустова́т|ый (~, ~а), *adj.* 1. rather empty. 2. fatuous.

пуст|ова́ть, у́ю, *impf.* to be empty, stand empty; to be tenantless, be uninhabited; (*of land*) to lie fallow.

пустоголо́в|ый (~, ~а), *adj.* empty-headed.

пустозво́н, а, *m.* (*coll.*) idle talker, windbag.

пустозво́н|ить, ю, ишь, *impf.* (*coll.*) to engage in idle talk.

пустозво́нств|о, а, *n.* (*coll.*) idle talk.

пуст|о́й (~, ~а́, ~о), *adj.* 1. empty; void; hollow; tenantless, uninhabited; deserted; ~о́е ме́сто blank space; ~а́я поро́да (*geol.*) barren rock, waste rock, dead rock; на п. желу́док on an empty stomach; с ~ы́ми рука́ми empty-handed; чтоб тебе́ ~о бы́ло! (*coll.*) I wish you at the bottom of the sea!, the devil take you! 2. (*fig.*) idle; shallow; futile, frivolous; ~а́я болтовня́ idle talk; п. челове́к shallow person. 3. (*fig.*) vain, ungrounded; ~а́я зате́я vain enterprise; ~ы́е мечты́ castles in the air; ~а́я отгово́рка lame excuse; ~ы́е слова́ mere words; ~ы́е угро́зы empty threats, bluster.

пустоме́л|я, и, *m. and f.* (*coll.*) idle talker, windbag.

пустопоро́жний, *adj.* (*coll.*) empty, vacant.

пустосло́в, а, *m.* (*coll.*) idle talker, windbag.

пустосло́ви|е, я, *n.* (*coll.*) idle talk, verbiage.

пустосло́в|ить, лю, ишь, *impf.* (*coll.*) to engage in idle talk.

пустот|а́, ы́, *pl.* ~ы, *f.* 1. emptiness; void; (*phys.*) vacuum. 2. (*fig.*) shallowness; futility, frivolousness.

пустоте́лый, *adj.* hollow.

пустоцве́т, а, *m.* barren flower (*also fig.*).

пу́стош|ь, и, *f.* waste (plot of) land, waste ground.

пусты́нник, а, *m.* hermit, anchorite.

пусты́н|ный (~ен, ~на), *adj.* 1. uninhabited; п. о́стров desert island. 2. deserted.

пусты́н|ь, и, *f.* hermitage, monastery.

пусты́н|я, и, *f.* desert, wilderness.

пусты́р|ь, я́, *m.* waste land, vacant plot (of land).

пусты́шк|а, и, *f.* (*coll.*) 1. baby's dummy. 2. hollow object; (*fig.*) shallow person, hollow man.

пусть 1. *particle* let; п. бу́дет так! so be it!; п. она́ сама́ реши́т let her decide herself; п. *x* ра́вен 3 (*math.*) let *x* = 3. 2. *as conj.* though, even if: п. им бу́дет проти́вно, но я до́лжен вы́сказать своё мне́ние even if they don't like it, I must express my opinion. 3. *particle* (*coll.*) all right, very well.

пустя́к, а́, *m.* trifle; bagatelle; су́щий п. a mere bagatelle; спо́рить из-за ~о́в to split hairs; па́ра ~о́в! (*coll.*) child's play!; ~и́! (*i*) it's nothing!, never mind!, (*ii*) nonsense!, rubbish!

пустяко́вый, *adj.* trifling, trivial.

пустя́чный, *adj.* = пустяко́вый.

пу́таник, а, *m.* muddle-headed person.

пу́таниц|а, ы, *f.* muddle, confusion; mess, tangle.

пу́таный, *adj.* 1. muddle, confused; confusing. 2. (*coll.*) muddle-headed.

пу́та|ть, ю, *impf.* (*of* с~) 1. to tangle (*a thread, etc.*). 2. to confuse, muddle; он всё ~л слу́шателей примене́нием анало́гий he always muddled his audience by his use of analogy. 3. to confuse, mix up; ты ещё ~ешь на́ши имена́ you are still mixing our names up. 4. (*pf.* в~) (в+*a.*; *coll.*) to implicate (in), mix up (in).

пу́та|ться, юсь, *impf.* (*of* с~) 1. to get tangled. 2. (*of thoughts*) to get confused. 3. to get mixed up, get muddled; п. в расска́зе to give a muddled account; п. в показа́ниях to contradict oneself in one's evidence. 4. (*pf.* в~) (в+*a.*; *coll.*) to get mixed up (in); п. в тёмные дели́шки to get mixed up in shady business. 5. *impf. only* (*coll.*) to mooch about. 6. (c+*i.*; *coll.*) to get mixed up (with), get entangled (with); to carry on (with) (*a person of the opposite sex*).

путёвк|а, и, *f.* 1. pass, authorization; сде́лать зая́вку на ~у в санато́рий to apply for a place in a sanatorium; п. в жизнь a start in life. 2. place in a tourist group; я купи́л ~у в Чехослова́кию I have booked a place on a tour of Czechoslovakia. 3. schedule of duties (*of public transport workers*).

путеводи́тел|ь, я, *m.* guide, guide-book.

путево́дн|ый, *adj.* guiding; ~ая звезда́ guiding star; (*fig.*) lodestar.

путев|о́й, *adj.* travelling, itinerary; ~ы́е заме́тки travel notes; ~а́я ка́рта road-map; п. ко́мпас (*naut.*) steering compass; п. обхо́дчик, п. сто́рож (*railways*) permanent way man; ~а́я ско́рость (*aeron.*) absolute speed, ground speed.

путе́|ец, йца́, *m.* (*coll.*) 1. railway engineer. 2. permanent way man.

путём[1], *prep.* (+*g.*) by means of, by dint of.

путём[2], *adv.* (*coll.*) properly; coherently; он ничего́ п. не уме́ет объясни́ть he cannot explain anything coherently.

путеме́р, а, *m.* pedometer.

путеобхо́дчик, а, *m.* (*railways*) permanent way man.

путепрово́д, а, *m.* 1. (*on roads*) overpass, underpass. 2. (*railway*) overbridge.

путеше́ственник, а, *m.* traveller.

путеше́стви|е, я, *n.* 1. journey; trip; (*on the sea*) voyage; cruise. 2. *pl.* (*lit.*) travels.

путеше́ств|овать, ую, *impf.* to travel, go on travels; (*on the sea*) to voyage.

пути́н|а, ы, *f.* fishing season.

пу́тлищ|е, а, *n.* stirrup strap.

пу́тник, а, *m.* traveller, wayfarer.

пу́тн|ый, *adj.* (*coll.*) sensible; из него́ ничего́ ~ого не вы́йдет you'll never make a man of him.

путч, а, *m.* (*polit.*) putsch.

пу́ты, пут, *no sing.* 1. hobble. 2. (*fig.*) fetters, chains, trammels.

пут|ь, и́, *i.* ём, о ~и́, *pl.* ~и́, ~е́й, ~я́м, *m.* 1. way, track, path; (*aeron.*) track; (*astron.*) race; (*fig.*) road, course; во́дный п. water-way; морски́е ~и́ shipping-routes, sea-lanes; са́нный п. sledge-track; тылово́й п. (*mil.*) line of retreat; ~и́ сообще́ния communications; жи́зненный п. (*fig.*) life; на пра́вильном ~и́ on the right track; друго́го, ино́го ~и́ нет there are no two ways about it; сби́ться с (ве́рного) ~и́ to lose one's way; (*fig.*) to go astray; стоя́ть попёрек ~и́ кому́-н. (*fig.*) to stand in someone's path. 2. (railway) track; запа́сный п. siding. 3. journey; voyage; в ~и́ on one's way, en route; в четырёх дня́х ~и́ (от) four days' journey (from); на обра́тном ~и́ on the way back; по ~и́ on the way; нам с ва́ми по ~и́ we are going the same way; держа́ть п. (на+*a.*) to head (for), make (for); счастли́вого ~и́! bon voyage! 4. *pl.* (*anat.*) passage, duct; дыха́тельные ~и́ respiratory tract. 5. (*fig.*) way, means; каки́м ~ём? how?, in what way?; ми́рным ~ём amicably, peaceably; око́льным ~ём, око́льными ~я́ми in, by a roundabout way; найти́ ~и́ и сре́дства to find ways and means; пойти́ по ~и́ (+*g.*) to take the path (of). **6.** (*coll.*) use, benefit; без ~и́ in vain, uselessly.

пуф, а, *m.* **1.** pouf(fe). **2.** canard, hoax.

пух, а, о ~**е, в** ~**у́,** *m.* down; fluff; **в п. и прах** (*coll.*) completely, utterly; **разряди́ться в п. и прах** to put on all one's finery; **разби́ть в п. и прах** to put to complete rout; **ни** ~**а, ни пера́!** (*coll.*) good luck!

пу́хл|ый (~**,** ~**á,** ~**о),** *adj.* chubby, plump.

пухля́к, á, *m.* (*orn.*) willow tit.

пу́х|нуть, ну, нешь, *past* ~, ~**ла,** *impf.* to swell.

пухови́к, á, *m.* feather-bed.

пухо́вк|а, и, *f.* powder-puff.

пухо́вый, *adj.* downy.

пучегла́зи|е, я, *n.* (*med.*) exophthalmus.

пучегла́з|ый (~, ~**а),** *adj.* goggle-eyed, lobster-eyed.

пучи́н|а, ы, *f.* gulf, abyss; the deep; (*fig.*) abyss.

пу́ч|ить, у, ишь, *impf.* (*coll.*) **1.** (*pf.* вс~) to become swollen; **у него́ живо́т** ~**ит** (*impers.*) he is troubled with wind. **2.** (*pf.* вы́~) **п. глаза́** to goggle.

пу́чност|ь, и, *f.* (*radio*) antinode, loop.

пуч|о́к, ка́, *m.* **1.** bunch, bundle; (*bot.*) fascicle; **п. луче́й** (*phys.*) pencil (of rays); **п. се́на** wisp of hay; **п. цвето́в** bunch of flowers. **2.** (*coll.*) bun (*hair-do*).

пу́ш|ечный, *adj. of* ~**ка¹; п. ого́нь** gunfire, cannon fire; ~**ечное мя́со** cannon-fodder.

пуши́нк|а, и, *f.* bit of fluff; **п. сне́га** snow-flake.

пуши́ст|ый (~, ~**а),** *adj.* fluffy, downy.

пуш|и́ть, у́, и́шь, *impf.* (*of* рас~) **1.** to fluff up. **2.** (*coll.*) to swear at.

пу́шк|а¹, и, *f.* gun, cannon; **стреля́ть из пу́шек по воробья́м** (*prov.*) to swat a fly with a sledgehammer.

пу́шк|а², и, *f.* (*coll.*) lying, lies; **на** ~**у взять кого́-н.** to trick someone; **получи́ть на** ~**у** (*i*) to obtain by a trick, (*ii*) to get for nothing.

пушка́р|ь, я́, *m.* **1.** (*hist.*) cannon-founder. **2.** (*obs., coll.*) gunner.

пушкини́ст, а, *m.* Pushkin scholar.

пушкинове́дени|е, я, *n.* Pushkin studies.

пушни́н|а, ы, *f.* (*collect.*) furs, fur-skins, pelts.

пушно́й, *adj.* **1.** fur-bearing; **п. зверь** (*collect.*) fur-bearing animals. **2.** fur; **п. про́мысел** fur trade; **п. това́р** furs.

пуш|о́к, ка́, *m.* **1.** fluff. **2.** (*on fruit*) bloom.

пу́щ|а, и, *f.* dense forest, virgin forest.

пу́ще, *adv.* (*coll.*) more; **п. всего́** most of all.

пу́щий, *adj., only in phrase* **для** ~**ей ва́жности** for greater show.

пчел|а́, ы́, *pl.* ~**ы,** *f.* bee; **рабо́чая п.** worker bee.

пчел|и́ный, *adj. of* ~**á; п. воск** beeswax; ~**и́ная ма́тка** queen bee; **п. рой** swarm of bees; **п. у́лей** beehive.

пчелово́д, а, *m.* bee-keeper, bee-master, apiarist.

пчелово́дств|о, а, *n.* bee-keeping, apiculture.

пчелово́дческий, *adj.* bee-keeping.

пче́льник, а, *m.* bee-garden, apiary.

пшени́ц|а, ы, *f.* wheat; **ярова́я п.** spring wheat; **ози́мая п.** winter wheat.

пшени́чный, *adj.* wheaten.

пшённик, а, *m.* millet-pudding.

пшён|ный, *adj. of* ~**ó.**

пшен|о́, á, *n.* millet.

пшик, а, *m.* (*coll.*) nothing; **око́нчиться** ~**ом** (*fig.*) to fizzle out, come to nought; **оста́лся оди́н п.** nothing was left.

пыж, á, *m.* wad (*used in loading fire-arm from muzzle*).

пы́жик, а, *m.* young deer; fur of young deer.

пы́жиковый, *adj.* deerskin.

пы́ж|иться, усь, ишься, *impf.* (*of* на~) (*coll.*) **1.** to be puffed up, strut. **2.** to go all out.

пыл, а, о ~**е, в** ~**у́,** *m.* **1.** (*dial.*) heat; **пирожки́ с** ~**у** hot pasties. **2.** (*fig.*) heat, ardour; **ю́ный п.** youthful ardour; **в** ~**у́ сраже́ния** in the heat of the battle.

пыла́|ть, ю, *impf.* **1.** to blaze, flame. **2.** (*fig.; of the face*) to glow. **3.** (+*i.*; *fig.*) to burn (with); **п. стра́стью** to be afire with passion.

пылеви́дный, *adj.* powdered.

пыленепроница́емый. *adj.* dust-proof.

пылесо́с, а, *m.* vacuum cleaner.

пыли́нк|а, и, *f.* speck of dust.

пыл|и́ть, ю́, и́шь, *impf.* **1.** (*pf.* на~) to raise dust. **2.** (*pf.* за~) to cover with dust, make dusty.

пыл|и́ться, ю́сь, и́шься, *impf.* (*of* за~) to get dusty, get covered with dust.

пы́л|кий (~**ок,** ~**ка́,** ~**ко),** *adj.* ardent, passionate; fervent; fervid; ~**кое воображе́ние** fervid imagination; ~**кая речь** impassioned speech.

пы́лкост|ь, и, *f.* ardour, passion; fervency.

пыл|ь, и, о ~**и, в** ~**и́,** *f.* dust; **водяна́я п.** spray; **у́гольная п.** coal-dust; slack; **смести́ п.** (c+*g.*) to dust.

пы́льник¹, а, *m.* (*bot.*) anther.

пы́льник², а, *m.* dust-coat.

пы́л|ьный (~**ен,** ~**ьна́,** ~**ьно),** *adj.* **1.** dusty; ~**ная тря́пка** (*coll.*) duster. **2. п. котёл** (*agric.*) dust bowl.

пыльц|а́, ы́, *f.* (*bot.*) pollen.

пыре́|й, я, *m.* (*bot.*) couch-grass.

пырн|у́ть, у́, ёшь, *pf.* (*coll.*) to jab; **п. ножо́м** to thrust a knife (into); **п. рога́ми** to butt.

пыта́|ть, ю, *impf.* **1.** to torture (*also fig.*);

(*fig.*) to torment. **2.** (*coll.*) to try (for); п. сча́стье to try one's luck.

пыта́|ться, юсь, *impf.* (*of* по~) to try, attempt, endeavour.

пы́тк|а, и, *f.* torture, torment (*also fig.*); ору́дие ~и instrument of torture.

пытли́вост|ь, и, *f.* inquisitiveness.

пытли́в|ый (~, ~а), *adj.* inquisitive; п. взгляд a searching look.

пы́|хать, шу, шешь, *impf.* **1.** (жа́ром) to blaze. **2.** (*fig.*) п. гне́вом to blaze with anger; п. здоро́вьем to be a picture of health.

пых|те́ть, чу́, ти́шь, *impf.* to puff, pant.

пышк|а, и, *f.* **1.** bun; doughnut. **2.** (*fig., coll.*) chubby child; plump woman.

пы́шност|ь, и, *f.* splendour, magnificence.

пы́ш|ный (~ен, ~на́, ~но), *adj.* **1.** splendid, magnificent. **2.** fluffy; light; luxuriant; ~ные во́лосы fluffy hair; п. пиро́г light pie; ~ные рукава́ puffed sleeves.

пьедеста́л, а, *m.* pedestal (*also fig.*); вознести́ на п. (*fig.*) to place on a pedestal.

пьезо́метр, а, *m.* (*tech.*) piezometer.

пье́ксы, пьекс, *no sing.* ski boots.

пье́с|а, ы, *f.* **1.** (*theatr.*) play. **2.** (*mus.*) piece.

пьяне́|ть, ю, ешь, *impf.* (*of* о~) to get drunk, get intoxicated.

пьян|и́ть, ю́, и́шь, *impf.* (*of* о~) to make drunk, intoxicate (*also fig.*); (*fig.*) to go to one's head.

пья́ниц|а, ы, *m. and f.* drunkard; tippler; toper; го́рький п. hard drinker, sot.

пья́нк|а, и, *f.* (*coll.*) drinking-bout, binge, booze-up.

пья́нств|о, а, *n.* drunkenness; hard drinking.

пья́нств|овать, ую, *impf.* to drink hard, drink heavily.

пья́н|ый (~, ~а́, ~о), *adj.* **1.** drunk; drunken; tipsy, tight; intoxicated; по ~ой ла́вочке, с ~ых глаз (*coll.*) one over the eight; *as noun* п., ~ого, *m.* (a) drunk. **2.** heady, intoxicating.

пэр, а, *m.* peer.

пюпи́тр, а, *m.* desk, reading-desk; но́тный п. music-stand.

пюре́, *indecl., n.* (*cul.*) purée; карто́фельное п. mashed potatoes.

пяд|ь, и, *pl.* ~и, ~е́й, *f.* span; ни ~и не уступи́ть (*fig.*) not to yield an inch; будь он семи́ ~е́й во лбу (*fig.*) be he a Solomon.

пя́л|ить, ю, ишь, *impf.* п. глаза́ (на+*a.*; *coll.*) to stare (at).

пя́л|ьцы, ец, *no sing.* tambour; lace-frame.

пяст|ь, и, *f.* (*anat.*) metacarpus.

пят|а́, ы́, *pl.* ~ы, ~, ~а́м, *f.* **1.** heel; ахилле́сова п. Achilles' heel; ходи́ть за кем-н. по ~а́м to follow on someone's heels, tread on someone's heels; под ~о́й (+*g.*; *fig.*)

under the heel (of); с, от головы́ до ~ from top to toe, all over, altogether. **2.** (*tech.*) abutment; п. сво́да skewback.

пята́к, а́, *m.* (*coll.*) five-copeck piece.

пятач|о́к¹, ка́, *m.* (*coll.*) = пята́к; аэродро́м с п. pocket handkerchief aerodrome.

пятач|о́к², ка́, *m.* (*coll.*) snout.

пятери́чный, *adj.* fivefold, quintuple.

пятёрк|а, и, *f.* **1.** (*number*) five. **2.** five (*top mark in Russian school marking system*). **3.** (*coll.*) five-rouble note. **4.** (*cards*) five; козырна́я п. five of trumps.

пятерн|я́, и́, *g. pl.* ~е́й, *f.* (*coll.*) five fingers; palm with fingers extended.

пя́тер|о, ы́х, *num.* five.

пятиалты́нн|ый, ого, *m.* (*coll.*) fifteen-kopeck piece.

пятибо́рь|е, я, *n.* (*sport*) pentathlon; совреме́нное п. modern pentathlon.

пятигла́вый, *adj.* five-headed; five-domed.

пятигра́нник, а, *m.* (*math.*) pentahedron.

пятигра́нный, *adj.* (*math.*) pentahedral.

пятидесятиле́ти|е, я, *n.* **1.** fifty years. **2.** fiftieth anniversary; fiftieth birthday.

пятидесятиле́тний, *adj.* **1.** fifty-year, of fifty years. **2.** fifty-year-old.

пятидеся́тник, а, *m.* (*hist.*) man of the 'Fifties (*member of group of Russian intelligentsia active during the 1850s*).

Пятидеся́тниц|а, ы, *f.* (*eccl.*) Pentecost.

пятидеся́т|ый, *adj.* fiftieth; ~ые го́ды the fifties; п. но́мер number fifty; ~ая страни́ца page fifty.

пятидне́вк|а, и, *f.* five-day period; five-day week.

пятикла́ссник, а, *m.* fifth-form pupil, fifth-former.

Пятикни́жи|е, я, *n.* (*eccl., lit.*) Pentateuch.

пятиконе́чн|ый, *adj.*; ~ая звезда́ five-pointed star.

пятикра́тный, *adj.* fivefold, quintuple.

пятиле́ти|е, я, *n.* **1.** five years. **2.** fifth anniversary.

пятиле́тк|а, и, *f.* **1.** five years. **2.** (*econ.*) five-year plan. **3.** five-year-old; де́вочка-п. five-year-old girl.

пятиле́тний, *adj.* **1.** five-year; п. план (*econ.*) five-year plan. **2.** five-year-old.

пятимеся́чный, *adj.* **1.** five-month. **2.** five-months-old.

пятинеде́льный, *adj.* **1.** five-week. **2.** five-week-old.

пятио́кис|ь, и, *f.* (*chem.*) pentoxide.

пятипо́л|е, я, *n.* (*agric.*) five-field crop rotation.

пятисло́жный, *adj.* pentasyllabic.

пятисло́йный, *adj.* five-ply.

пятисо́тенный, *adj.* five-hundred-rouble.

пятисотле́ти|е, я, *n.* **1.** five centuries. **2.** quincentenary.

пятисо́тый, *adj.* five-hundredth.

пятисто́пный, *adj.* (*lit.*) pentameter; п. ямб iambic pentameter.

пятито́нк|а, и, *f.* (*coll.*) five-ton lorry.

пятиты́сячный, *adj.* five-thousandth.

пя́|тить, чу, тишь, *impf.* (*of* по~) to back, move back.

пя́|титься, чусь, тишься, *impf.* (*of* по~) to back, move backward(s); (*of a horse*) to jib.

пятиуго́льник, а, *m.* (*math.*) pentagon.

пятиуго́льный, *adj.* pentagonal.

пятиэта́жный, *adj.* five-storied.

пятк|а, и, *f.* heel (*also of sock or stocking*); лиза́ть кому́-н. ~и to lick someone's boots; показа́ть ~и to show a clean pair of heels; удира́ть так, что то́лько ~и сверка́ют to take to one's heels, show a clean pair of heels; у меня́ душа́ в ~и ушла́ my heart sank to my boots.

пятнадцатиле́тний, *adj.* **1.** fifteen-year. **2.** fifteen-year-old.

пятна́дцатый, *adj.* fifteenth.

пятна́дцат|ь, и, *num.* fifteen.

пятна́|ть, ю, *impf.* (*of* за~) **1.** to spot, stain, smirch (*also fig.*). **2.** (*coll.*) to catch (*at tag*).

пятна́ш|ки, ек, *no sing.* (*coll.*) (*children's game*) tag.

пятни́ст|ый (~, ~а), *adj.* spotted, dappled; п. оле́нь spotted deer.

пя́тниц|а, ы, *f.* Friday; по ~ам on Fridays, every Friday; у него́ семь ~ на неде́ле he keeps changing his mind.

пят|но́, на́, *pl.* ~на, ~ен, ~нам, *n.* **1.** (*in var. senses*) spot; patch; blot; stain; роди́мое п. birth-mark; со́лнечные ~на (*astron.*) sun-spots; тёмное п. (*astron.*) nebula; выводи́ть ~на to remove stains. **2.** (*fig.*) blot, stain; stigma, blemish.

пя́тныш|ко, ка, *pl.* ~ки, ~ек, ~кам, *n.* speck.

пят|о́к, ка́, *m.* (+*g.*; *coll.*) five (*similar objects*).

пя́т|ый, *adj.* fifth; глава́ ~ая chapter five; ~ая коло́нна fifth column; п. но́мер number five; size five; ~ое число́ (ме́сяца) the fifth (*day of the month*); в ~ом часу́ after four (o'clock), past four; рассказа́ть из ~ого деся́тое to tell a story in snatches.

пят|ь, и́, ью́, *num.* five.

пятьдеся́т, пяти́десяти, пятью́десятью, *num.* fifty.

пятьсо́т, пятисо́т, пятиста́м, *num.* five hundred.

пя́тью, *adv.* five times.

ρ

раб, а́, *m.* slave (*also fig.*); bondsman.

раб- *abbr. of* рабо́чий.

раб|а́, ы́, *f.* slave; bondwoman, bondmaid.

рабко́р, а, *m.* (*abbr. of* рабо́чий корреспонде́нт) worker correspondent.

рабовладе́л|ец, ьца, *m.* slave-owner.

рабовладе́льческий, *adj.* slave-holding, slave-owning.

раболе́пи|е, я, *n.* servility.

раболе́п|ный (~ен, ~на), *adj.* servile.

раболе́пств|о, а, *n.* servility.

раболе́пств|овать, ую, *impf.* (*перед*) to fawn (on), cringe (to).

рабо́т|а, ы, *f.* **1.** work, working; functioning, running; лёгкая, тяжёлая р. (*tech.*) light, heavy duty; едини́ца ~ы (*phys.*) unit of work; режи́м ~ы, усло́вия ~ы (*tech.*) operating conditions, working conditions; обеспе́чить норма́льную ~у (+*g.*) to ensure normal functioning (of). **2.** (*in var. senses*) work; labour; дома́шняя р. homework; ка́торжные ~ы (*obs.*) penal servitude; лепна́я р. stucco work, plaster work; mouldings; принуди́тельные ~ы forced labour; сельскохозя́йственные ~ы agricultural work; совме́стная р. collaboration; у́мственная р. mental work, brain-work; взять

в ~у (*coll.*) to take to task. **3.** work, job; постоя́нная р. regular work; случа́йная р. casual work, odd job(s); иска́ть ~у to look for a job; поступи́ть на ~у to go to work; снять с ~ы to lay off, dismiss; быть без ~ы, не име́ть ~ы to be out of work. **4.** work, workmanship.

рабо́та|ть, ю, *impf.* **1.** (на+*a.*; над) to work (for; on); р. сверхуро́чно to work overtime; р. сде́льно to do piece-work; вре́мя ~ет на нас time is on our side; он ~ет над но́вым рома́ном he is working on a new novel. **2.** to work, run, function; не р. not to work, be out of order; р. на не́фти to run on oil. **3.** (*of an institution, etc.*) to be open; галере́я не ~ет по воскресе́ньям the gallery is not open on Sundays. **4.** (+*i.*) to work, operate; р. вёслами to ply the oars; р. локтя́ми (*coll.*) to elbow; р. рычаго́м to operate a lever.

рабо́та|ться, ется, *impf.* (*impers.*; *coll.*) сего́дня хорошо́ ~ется work is going well today; вчера́ мне не ~лось I didn't feel like working yesterday; I couldn't get on with my work yesterday.

рабо́тник, а, *m.* worker; workman; hand, labourer; нау́чный р. member of staff of scientific *and/or* learned institution; р. иску́сства person working in the arts, in the artistic world; р. наро́дного образова́ния educationalist; р. у́мственного труда́ brain worker; р. физи́ческого труда́ manual worker.

рабо́тниц|а, ы, *f.* (woman-)worker; дома́шняя р. domestic servant, (house)maid; home help.

рабо́тн|ый, *adj.* р. дом (*obs.*) workhouse; ~ые лю́ди (*hist.*) workers, working men.

работода́тел|ь, я, *m.* employer.

работорго́в|ец, ца, *m.* slave-trader, slaver.

работорго́вл|я, и, *f.* slave-trade.

работоспосо́бност|ь, и, *f.* capacity for work, efficiency.

работоспосо́б|ный (~ен, ~на), *adj.* 1. able--bodied. 2. hardworking.

работя́г|а, и, *m. and f.* (*coll.*) hard worker; slogger.

работя́щий, *adj.* (*coll.*) hard-working, industrious.

рабо́ч|ий¹, его, *m.* worker; working man; workman; hand, labourer; ~ие (*collect.*; *as social class*) the workers; подённый р. day--labourer; сезо́нный р. seasonal worker; сельскохозя́йственный р. farm labourer, agricultural worker; р. от станка́ factory worker, bench-worker.

рабо́ч|ий², adj. 1. worker's, working-class; ~ее движе́ние working-class movement; р. класс the working class; ~ая молодёжь young workers; р. по́езд workmen's train. 2. work, working; ~ая кома́нда (*mil.*) fatigue party, work party; ~ая ло́шадь draught-horse; р. мураве́й worker ant; ~ая пчела́ worker bee; ~ие ру́ки hands; ~ая си́ла (*i*) (*collect.*) manpower, labour force, (*ii*) labour; р. скот draught animals. 3. working; ~ее вре́мя working time, working hours; р. день working day; р. костю́м, ~ее пла́тье working clothes; ~ее ме́сто operator's position; ~ая характери́стика (*tech.*) performance, performance curve. 4. (*tech.*) working, driving; ~ее давле́ние working pressure, effective pressure; ~ее колесо́ driving wheel; rotor wheel (*of turbine*); р. ход working stroke; р. чертёж working drawing.

рабселько́р, а, *m.* (*abbr. of* рабо́че-се́льский корреспонде́нт) worker-peasant correspondent.

ра́б|ский, *adj.* 1. *adj. of* ~; р. труд slave labour. 2. (*fig.*) servile.

ра́бств|о, а, *n.* slavery, servitude; отме́на ~а abolition of slavery.

рабфа́к, а, *m.* (*hist.*) (*abbr. of* рабо́чий факульте́т) 'rabfak'; workers' school (*educational establishment in existence during the first years after the Russian Revolution, set up to pre-*

pare workers and peasants for higher education).

рабфа́ков|ец, ца, *m.* 'rabfak' student.

рабфа́к|овский, *adj. of* ~.

рабы́н|я, и, *g. pl.* ~ь, *f.* slave, bondwoman, bondmaid.

равви́н, а, *m.* rabbi.

равели́н, а, *m.* (*mil., hist.*) ravelin.

равенду́к, а, *m.* (*text.*) duck.

ра́венств|о, а, *n.* equality; знак ~а (*math.*) sign of equality, equals sign.

равне́ни|е, я, *n.* 1. dressing, alignment; р. нале́во!, р. напра́во! (*mil. words of command*) left dress!, right dress! 2. (на+*a.*) emulation (of).

равни́н|а, ы, *f.* plain.

равни́н|ный, *adj. of* ~а; р. жи́тель plainsman; ~ная ме́стность flat country.

равно́¹, *adv.* 1. alike, in like manner. 2. (*as conj.*) р. как (и), а р. и as well as; and also, as also; (*after neg.*) nor; золото́й брасле́т, р. как и други́е её драгоце́нности, пропа́л a gold bracelet, as well as other jewellery of hers, had disappeared.

равно́², *n. pred. form of* ра́вный 1. (*math.*) make(s), equals, is; три плюс три р. шести́ three plus three equals six. 2. всё р. it is all the same, it makes no difference; *as adv.* all the same; всё р., что it is just the same as, it is equivalent to; мне всё р. I don't mind; it's all the same, all one to me; я всё р. вам позвоню́ I will ring you all the same; не всё ли р.? what difference does it make?, what's the difference?; what does it matter?

равно- equi-, iso-.

равнобе́дренный, *adj.* (*math.*) isosceles.

равновели́к|ий (~, ~а), *adj.* (*math.*) equivalent; (*phys.*) isometric, equigraphic; ~ие треуго́льники equivalent triangles.

равнове́си|е, я, *n.* equilibrium (*also fig.*); balance, equipoise; душе́вное р. mental equilibrium; полити́ческое р. balance of power; вы́вести из ~я to disturb the equilibrium (of), upset the balance (of); привести́ в р. to balance; сохраня́ть р. to keep one's balance.

равноде́йствующ|ая, ей, *f.* (*math., phys.*) resultant (force).

равноде́нственный, *adj.* equinoctial, equidiurnal.

равноде́нстви|е, я, *n.* equinox; весе́ннее, осе́ннее р. vernal, autumnal equinox; то́чка ~я equinoctial point.

равноду́ши|е, я, *n.* indifference.

равноду́ш|ный (~ен, ~на), *adj.* (к) indifferent (to).

равнозна́чащий, *adj.* equivalent, equipollent.

равнозна́ч|ный (~ен, ~на), *adj.* = ~ащий.

равноме́рност|ь, и, *f.* evenness; uniformity.

равноме́р|ный (~ен, ~на), *adj.* even; (*phys.*, *tech.*) uniform; ~ное распределе́ние even distribution.

равноо́сный, *adj.* (*math.*, *phys.*) equiaxial.

равноотстоя́щий, *adj.* (*math.*) equidistant.

равнопра́ви|е, я, *n.* equality (of rights), possession of equal rights.

равнопра́в|ный (~ен, ~на), *adj.* possessing, enjoying equal rights.

равноси́л|ьный (~ен, ~ьна), *adj.* 1. of equal strength; equally matched. 2. (+*d.*) equal (to), equivalent (to), tantamount (to); э́то ~ьно изме́не it is tantamount to treachery, it amounts to treachery.

равносторо́нний, *adj.* (*math.*) equilateral.

равноуго́льный, *adj.* (*math.*) equiangular.

равноуско́ренный, *adj.* (*phys.*, *tech.*) uniformly accelerated.

равноце́н|ный (~ен, ~на), *adj.* of equal value, of equal worth; equivalent.

ра́в|ный (~ен, ~на́, ~но́), *adj.* equal; ~ным о́бразом equally, likewise; при про́чих ~ных усло́виях other things being equal; ему́ нет ~ного he has no equal, there is no match for him.

равня́|ть, ю, *impf.* (*of* с~) 1. to make even; to treat equally; р. счёт (*sport*) to equalize. 2. (с+*i.*; *coll.*) to compare (with), treat as equal (to).

равня́|ться, юсь, *impf.* (*of* с~) 1. (по+*d.*) (*mil.*) to dress; ~йсь! (*word of command*) right dress!; р. в заты́лок to cover off. 2. (с+*i.*; *coll.*) to compete (with), compare (with), match; по пода́че никто́ не мог р. с ним (*sport*) in serving no one could compete with him. 3. *impf. only* (+*d.*) to equal, be equal (to); (*fig.*) to be equivalent (to), be tantamount (to), amount (to); два́жды пять ~ется десяти́ twice five is ten.

рагу́, *indecl.*, *n.* (*cul.*) ragout.

рад (~а, ~о), *pred. adj.* (+*d.*; +*inf.*; что) glad (of; to; that); я был о́чень р. слу́чаю поговори́ть с ни́ми I was very glad of the opportunity to talk to them; о́чень р. (познако́миться с ва́ми)! (*acknowledgement of introduction*) very pleased to meet you!; р. стара́ться! (*i*) (*coll.*) gladly!, with pleasure!; (*ii*) (*obs.*; *soldiers' acknowledgement of commendation*) very good, sir!; и не р., сам не р. (*coll.*) I, *etc.*, regret it; I, *etc.*, am sorry; и не р., что пошёл I'm sorry I went; р. не р. (*coll.*) willy-nilly, like it or not; р.-раде́шенек (*coll.*) pleased as Punch, chuffed.

ра́д|а, ы, *f.* council, soviet (*in Ukraine and Byelorussia*).

рада́р, а, *m.* radar.

рада́р|ный, *adj.* of ~.

раде́ни|е, я, *n.* (*obs.*) 1. zeal. 2. (*rel.*) rites (*of some Russian sects*).

раде́|ть, ю, ешь, *impf.* (*obs.*) 1. (*pf.* по~)

(+*d.*) to oblige; (о+*p.*) to take care (of). 2. *impf. only* (*rel.*; *of some Russian sects*) to carry out rites.

ра́дж|а, и, *m.* rajah.

ра́ди, *prep.*+*g.* for the sake of; чего́ р.? what for?; шу́тки р. for fun; р. Бо́га, р. всего́ свято́го (*coll.*) for God's sake, for goodness' sake.

радиа́льный, *adj.* (*math.*, *tech.*) radial.

радиа́тор, а, *m.* radiator.

радиацио́нный, *adj.* radiation.

радиа́ци|я, и, *f.* radiation.

ра́диев|ый, *adj.* radium; ~ая ка́псула radium seed.

ра́ди|й, я, *m.* (*chem.*) radium.

радика́л¹, а, *m.* (*math.*, *chem.*) radical.

радика́л², а, *m.* (*polit.*) radical.

радикали́зм, а, *m.* (*polit.*) radicalism.

радика́льност|ь, и, *f.* 1. (*polit.*) radicalism. 2. radical nature, drastic nature, sweeping character.

радика́л|ьный (~ен, ~ьна), *adj.* 1. (*polit.*) radical. 2. radical, drastic, sweeping; ~ьные измене́ния sweeping changes; ~ьные ме́ры drastic measures; ~ьное сре́дство drastic remedy.

ра́дио, *indecl.*, *n.* 1. radio, wireless; по р. by radio, over the air; переда́ть по р. to broadcast; слу́шать р. to listen in. 2. radio set, wireless; провести́ р. to install a radio set, wireless. 3. (*coll.*) public address system, tannoy (system).

радиоакти́вност|ь, и, *f.* (*chem.*, *phys.*) radio-activity.

радиоакти́в|ный (~ен, ~на), *adj.* (*chem.*, *phys.*) radio-active; ~ное загрязне́ние, ~ное зараже́ние radio-active contamination; р. изото́п radio-active isotope, radio-isotope; ~ные оса́дки radio-active fall-out; р. ряд radio-active family, radio-active series, disintegration series, decay chain; р. яд radio-active poison, radiation poison.

радиоаппара́т, а, *m.* radio set.

радиобиологи́ческий, *adj.* radio-biological.

радиобиоло́ги|я, и, *f.* radio-biology.

радиовеща́ни|е, я, *n.* broadcasting.

радиовеща́тельн|ый, *adj.* broadcasting; ~ая ста́нция broadcasting station, transmitter.

радиоволн|а́, ы́, *f.* radio-wave.

радиогра́мм|а, ы, *f.* radio-telegram, wireless message.

радио́граф, а, *m.* radiographer.

радиографи́ческий, *adj.* radiographic.

радиогра́фи|я, и, *f.* radiography.

радиозо́нд, а, *m.* radio-sounding apparatus.

радио́л|а, ы, *f.* radiogram.

радио́лог, а, *m.* radiologist.

радиологи́ческ|ий, *adj.* radiological; ~ая устано́вка radiological unit.

радиоло́ги|я, и, *f.* radiology.

радиолока́тор, а, *m.* radio-location set; radar set.

радиолок|аци́онный, *adj. of* ~а́ция.

радиолока́ци|я, и, *f.* radio-location, radar.

радиолюби́тел|ь, я, *m.* radio amateur, 'ham'; wireless enthusiast.

радиома́чт|а, ы, *f.* radio-mast, wireless mast.

радиома́йк, а́, *m.* radio-beacon.

радиопе́ленг, а, *m.* radio directional bearing.

радиопеленга́тор, а, *m.* radio direction finder.

радиопеленга́ци|я, и, *f.* radio homing.

радиопереда́тчик, а, *m.* (wireless) transmitter.

радиопереда́ча, и, *f.* transmission, broadcast.

радиоперекли́чк|а, и, *f.* radio link-up.

радиоперехва́т, а, *m.* radio interception; radio intercept.

радиополуко́мпас, а, *m.* radio compass.

радиопостано́вк|а, и, *f.* radio show.

радиоприбо́р, а, *m.* wireless (set), radio (set).

радиоприёмник, а, *m.* (wireless) receiver; wireless (set), radio (set).

радиору́бк|а, и, *f.* (*naut., aeron.*) radio room, radio cabin.

радиосвя́з|ь, и, *f.* wireless communication.

радиосе́т|ь, и, *f.* radio network.

радиослу́шател|ь, я, *m.* (radio) listener.

радиоста́нци|я, и, *f.* radio station, broadcasting station.

радиотелегра́ф, а, *m.* radio telegraph.

радиотелеграфи́|я, и, *f.* radio-telegraphy, wireless telegraphy.

радиотелефо́н, а, *m.* radio-telephone.

радиотерапи́|я, и, *f.* radio-therapy.

радиоте́хник, а, *m.* radio mechanic.

радиоте́хник|а, и, *f.* radio engineering.

радио|техни́ческий, *adj. of* ~те́хника.

радиотрансляцио́нный, *adj.* broadcasting.

радиоу́з|ел, ла́, *m.* radio relay centre.

радиофика́ци|я, и, *f.* installation of radio.

радиофици́р|овать, ую, *impf. and pf.* to instal radio (in), equip with radio.

радиохими́ческий, *adj.* radiochemical.

радиохи́ми|я, и, *f.* radiochemistry.

ради́р|овать, ую, *impf. and pf.* to radio.

ради́ст, а, *m.* wireless operator, radio operator; (*naut.*) telegraphist.

ра́диус, а, *m.* radius.

ра́д|овать, ую, *impf.* (*of* об~) to gladden, make glad, make happy; р. се́рдце to rejoice the heart.

ра́д|оваться, уюсь, *impf.* (*of* об~) (+*d.*) to be glad (at), be happy (at), rejoice (in).

ра́дост|ный (~ен, ~на), *adj.* glad, joyous, joyful; ~ное изве́стие glad tidings, good news.

ра́дост|ь, и, *f.* gladness, joy; р. жи́зни joie

de vivre; не чу́вствовать себя́ от ~и to be beside oneself with joy; на ~ях (+*g.*; *coll.*) in celebration (of), to celebrate; с ~ью with pleasure, gladly; моя́ р., р. моя́ my darling.

ра́дуг|а, и, *f.* rainbow.

ра́дужно, *adv.* cheerfully; р. смотре́ть (на+*a.*) to look on the bright side (of).

ра́дужн|ый, *adj.* **1.** iridescent, opalescent; ~ая оболо́чка (гла́за) (*anat.*) iris. **2.** cheerful; optimistic; ~ые наде́жды high hopes; ~ое настрое́ние high spirits.

раду́ши|е, я, *n.* cordiality.

раду́ш|ный (~ен, ~на), *adj.* cordial; р. приём hearty welcome; р. хозя́ин kind host.

ра|ёк, йка́, *m.* (*theatr.; obs.*) gallery; the gods.

раж, а, *m.* (*coll.*) rage, passion; войти́ в р., прийти́ в р. to fly into a rage.

раз¹, а, *pl.* ~ы́, ~, *m.* **1.** time; occasion; оди́н р., ка́к-то р. once; два ~а twice; мно́го р. many times; ещё р. once again, once more; не р. more than once; time and again; ни ~у not once, never; р. навсегда́ once (and) for all; р. в день once a day; вся́кий р. every time, each time; вся́кий р., когда́ whenever; ино́й р. sometimes, now and again; во второ́й р. for the second time; в друго́й р. another time, some other time; в са́мый р. (*coll.*) at the right moment; just right; до друго́го ~а till another time; р. за ~ом time after time; на э́тот р. this time, on this occasion, for (this) once; с пе́рвого ~а from the very first; вот тебе́ (и) р.! (*coll.*) well, I never!; как р. just, exactly; как р. то the very thing. **2.** (*num.*) one.

раз², *adv.* once, one day.

раз³, *conj.* if; since; р. вы бу́дете во Фра́нции, не смо́жете ли вы прие́хать и сюда́? if you are going to be in France, can't you come here, too?

раз- (разо-, разъ-, рас-) *verbal prefix indicating* **1.** division into parts (dis-, un-). **2.** distribution; direction of action in different directions; (dis-). **3.** action in reverse (un-). **4.** termination of action *or* state. **5.** intensification of action.

разба́в|ить, лю, ишь, *pf.* (*of* ~ля́ть) to dilute.

разбавля́|ть, ю, *impf. of* разба́вить.

разбаза́ривани|е, я, *n.* (*coll.*) squandering.

разбаза́рива|ть, ю, *impf. of* разбаза́рить.

разбаза́р|ить, ю, ишь, *pf.* (*of* ~ивать) (*coll.*) to squander.

разба́лива|ться, юсь, *impf. of* разболе́ться.

разба́лтыва|ть(ся), ю(сь), *impf. of* разболта́ть(ся).

разбе́г, а, *m.* run, running start; пры́гнуть с ~у to take a running jump; нырну́ть с ~у to take a running dive; прыжо́к с ~у

running jump; р. при взлёте (*aeron.*) take-
-off run.

разбега́|ться, юсь, *impf. of* разбежа́ться.

разбе|жа́ться, гу́сь, жи́шься, гу́тся, *pf.* (*of*
~**га́ться**) **1.** to take a run, run up. **2.** to
scatter, disperse; р. по места́м to run to
one's places, (*mil.*) to one's stations, posts.
3. (*of thoughts, etc.*) to be scattered; глаза́ у
меня́ ~жа́лись I was dazzled.

разбере|ди́ть, жу́, ди́шь, *pf. of* береди́ть.

разби́ва|ть(ся), ю(сь), *impf. of* разби́ть(ся).

разби́вк|а, и, *f.* **1.** laying out (*of a garden,
etc.*). **2.** (*typ.*) spacing (out).

разбинт|ова́ть, у́ю, *pf.* (*of* ~**о́вывать**) to
remove a bandage (from).

разбинт|ова́ться, у́юсь, *pf.* (*of* ~**о́вываться**)
1. to remove one's bandage(s). **2.** (*of a
bandage*) to come off, come undone. **3.** to
come unbandaged; нога́ у меня́ ~ова́лась
the bandage has come off my leg.

разбинто́выва|ть(ся), ю(сь), *impf. of* раз-
бинтова́ть(ся).

разбира́тельств|о, а, *n.* (*leg.*) examination,
investigation; суде́бное р. court examination.

разбира́|ть, ю, *impf.* **1.** *impf. of* разобра́ть.
2. (*impf. only*) to be fastidious; не ~я indis-
criminately.

разбира́|ться, юсь, *impf. of* разобра́ться.

разбитно́й, *adj.* (*coll.*) bright, sprightly; sharp.

разби́т|ый, *p.p.p. of* ~**ь** *and adj.* (*coll.*) jaded,
down.

раз|би́ть, обью́, обьёшь, *pf.* (*of* ~**бива́ть**)
1. (*impf. also* бить) to break, smash; р.
вдре́безги to smash to smithereens. **2.** to
divide (up); to break up, break down; р.
на гру́ппы to divide up into groups; р.
компле́кт to break a set. **3.** to lay out,
mark out; р. ко́лышками to peg out; р.
ла́герь to pitch a camp. **4.** to damage
severely, hurt badly; to fracture; р. кому́-н.
нос в кровь to make someone's nose bleed.
5. to beat, defeat, smash (*also fig.*); р. чьи-н.
до́воды to destroy someone's arguments.
6. (*typ.*) to space (out).

раз|би́ться, обью́сь, обьёшься, *pf.* (*of*
~**бива́ться**) **1.** to break, get broken, get
smashed. **2.** to divide, break up. **3.** to hurt
oneself badly; to smash oneself up.

разбла́гове|стить, щу, стишь, *pf. of* бла́го-
вестить.

разблоки́р|овать, ую, *pf.* (*mil.*) to lift the
blockade (of).

разбогате́|ть, ю, ешь, *pf. of* богате́ть.

разбо́|й, я, *m.* robbery, brigandage; мор-
ско́й р. piracy.

разбо́йник, а, *m.* **1.** robber, brigand; мор-
ско́й р. pirate; р. с большо́й доро́ги highwayman. **2.** (*joc.*; *affect. form of address to
child, etc.*) rogue!, wretch!

разбо́йнича|ть, ю, *impf.* to rob, plunder.

разбо́йни|чий, *adj. of* ~**к**; р. прито́н den of
thieves.

разболе́|ться¹, ю́сь, е́шься, *pf.* (*of* разба́ли-
ваться) (*coll.*) to become ill; он совсе́м ~лся
his health has completely cracked.

разбол|е́ться², и́тся, *pf.* (*of* разба́ливаться)
to begin to ache badly.

разбо́лт|анный, *p.p.p. of* ~**а́ть¹** *and adj.* (*fig.*)
disorderly.

разболта́|ть¹, ю, *pf.* (*of* разба́лтывать) **1.** to
shake up, stir up. **2.** to loosen.

разболта́|ть², ю, *pf.* (*of* разба́лтывать) (*coll.*)
to blab out, give away.

разболта́|ться, юсь, *pf.* (*of* разба́лтываться)
1. to mix (*as result of stirring*). **2.** to come
loose, work loose. **3.** (*fig.*) to get out of
hand; to come unstuck.

разбомб|и́ть, лю́, и́шь, *pf.* (*no impf.*) to
destroy by bombing.

разбо́р, а, *m.* **1.** stripping, dismantling.
2. buying up. **3.** sorting out. **4.** investigation; р. де́ла (*leg.*) trial, hearing (*of a case*).
5. (*gram.*) parsing; analysis. **6.** critique.
7. selectiveness; без ~у indiscriminately,
promiscuously; с ~ом discriminatingly,
fastidiously. **8.** sort, quality; пе́рвого, вто-
ро́го ~a first, second quality.

разбо́рк|а, и, *f.* **1.** sorting out. **2.** stripping,
dismantling, taking to pieces.

разбо́рный, *adj.* collapsible.

разбо́рчивост|ь, и, *f.* **1.** fastidiousness;
scrupulousness. **2.** legibility.

разбо́рчив|ый (~, ~а), *adj.* **1.** fastidious,
exacting; discriminating; scrupulous. **2.**
legible.

разбран|и́ть, ю́, и́шь, *pf.* (*coll.*) to berate;
to blow up.

разбран|и́ться, ю́сь, и́шься, *pf.* (с+*i.*; *coll.*)
to fall out (with); to quarrel (with),
squabble (with).

разбра́сыватель, я, *m.* (*agric.*) spreader.

разбра́сыва|ть, ю, *impf. of* разброса́ть.

разбра́сыва|ться, юсь, *impf.* **1.** *impf. of*
разброса́ться. **2.** (*fig.*) to dissipate one's
energies; to try to do too much at once.

разбреда́|ться, юсь, *impf. of* разбрести́сь.

разбре|сти́сь, ду́сь, дёшься, *past* ~**лся,**
~**ла́сь,** *pf.* (*of* ~**да́ться**) to disperse; to
straggle; р. по дома́м to disperse and go
home.

разбро́д, а, *m.* disorder.

разброни́р|овать, ую, *pf.* to cancel reser-
vation (of), de-reserve.

разбро́санност|ь, и, *f.* **1.** sparseness; scat-
tered nature. **2.** (*fig.*) disconnectedness, in-
coherence.

разбро́с|анный, *p.p.p. of* ~**а́ть** *and adj.*
1. sparse, scattered; straggling. **2.** (*fig.*) dis-
connected, incoherent.

разброса́|ть, ю, *pf.* (*of* разбра́сывать) to throw about; to scatter, spread, strew; р. наво́з to spread manure; р. де́ньги на ве́тер to squander one's money.

разбры́з|гать, жу, жешь, *pf.* (*of* ~гивать) to splash; to spray.

разбры́згива|ть, ю, *impf. of* разбры́згать.

разбу|ди́ть, жу́, ~ди́шь, *pf. of* буди́ть.

разбуха́ни|е, я, *n.* swelling; р. шта́та overstaffing.

разбух|а́ть, а́ет, *impf. of* ~ну́ть.

разбу́х|нуть, нет, *past* ~, ~ла, *pf.* (*of* ~а́ть) to swell (*also fig.*).

разбуш|ева́ться, у́юсь, *pf.* 1. (*of a storm*) to rage; to blow up; (*of the sea*) to run high. 2. (*coll.*) to fly into a rage.

разбуя́н|иться, юсь, ишься, *pf.* (*coll.*) to fly into a rage.

разва́жнича|ться, юсь, *pf.* (*coll.*) to put on airs.

разва́л, а, *m.* breakdown, disintegration, disruption; disorganization.

разва́л|ец, ьца, *m.* (*coll.*) ходи́ть с ~ьцем to shamble; рабо́тать с ~ьцем to go slow.

разва́лива|ть(ся), ю(сь), *impf. of* развали́ть(ся).

разва́лин|а, ы, *f.* 1. *pl.* ruins; гру́да ~ a heap of débris; лежа́ть в ~ах to be in ruins; преврати́ть в ~ы to reduce to ruins. 2. (*fig., coll.*; *of a person*) wreck, ruin.

развал|и́ть, ю́, ~ишь, *pf.* (*of* ~ивать) 1. to pull down (*a building, etc.*). 2. (*fig.*) to mess up.

развал|и́ться, ю́сь, ~ишься, *pf.* (*of* ~иваться) 1. to fall down, tumble down, collapse. 2. (*fig.*) to go to pieces, fall to pieces, break down. 3. (*coll.*) to lounge, sprawl.

разва́л|ьца, ьцы, *f.* = ~ец.

разва́рива|ть(ся), ю(сь), *impf. of* развари́ть(ся).

развар|и́ть, ю́, ~ишь, *pf.* (*of* ~ивать) to boil soft.

развар|и́ться, ю́сь, ~ишься, *pf.* (*of* ~иваться) to be boiled soft; р. в ка́шу to be boiled to a pulp.

разварно́й, *adj.* boiled.

ра́зве 1. *interrog. particle, neutral or indicating that neg. answer is expected;* +*neg. indicates that affirmative answer is expected* р. они́ все вмести́тся в э́ту маши́ну? will they (really) all get in this car?; р. ты не знал, что он ру́сский? didn't you know that he is Russian?, surely you knew that he is Russian? 2. *interrog. particle, expressing hesitation about course of action to be followed* (+*inf.*; *coll.*) р. отложи́ть нам пое́здку? perhaps we had better postpone the trip?; р. поговори́ть вам с её отцо́м? perhaps you should have, mightn't it be a good thing to have a talk with her father? 3. р. (что), р. (то́лько) *as*

adv. only; perhaps; *as conj.* except that, only; кро́ме р. (+*g.*) except perhaps, with the possible exception (of); он вы́глядит так же как всегда́, р. что похуде́л he looks the same as ever, except that he has lost weight. 4. *conj.* (*obs.*) unless.

развева́|ть, ю, *impf.* 1. *impf. of* разве́ять. 2. *impf. only* to blow about; ве́тер ~л зна́мя the banner was flapping, streaming in the wind.

развева́|ться, юсь, *impf.* 1. *impf. of* разве́яться. 2. *impf. only* to fly, flutter; с ~ющимися знамёнами with banners flying.

развед- *abbr. of* разве́дывательный.

разве́д|ать, аю, *pf.* (*of* ~ывать) 1. (о+*p.*; *coll.*) to find out (about), ascertain. 2. (*mil.*) to reconnoitre. 3. (на+*a.*; *geol.*) to prospect (for); *pf. only* to locate; р. на нефть to prospect for oil.

разведе́ни|е¹, я, *n.* breeding, rearing; cultivation.

разведе́ни|е², я, *n.* opening, swinging open (*of a bascule bridge or draw-bridge*).

разведённ|ый, *p.p.p. of* развести́ *and adj.* divorced; *as noun* р., ~ого, *m. and* ~ая, ~ой, *f.* divorcee.

разве́дк|а, и, *f.* 1. (*geol., etc.*) prospecting. 2. (*mil.*) reconnaissance; звукова́я р. sound ranging; опти́ческая р. flash ranging; р. бо́ем reconnaissance in force; р. в глубину́ reconnaissance in depth. 3. (*mil.*) reconnaissance party. 4. secret service, intelligence service.

разве́дочн|ый, *adj.* (*geol.*) prospecting, exploratory; ~ая сква́жина test well.

разве́дчик¹, а, *m.* 1. (*mil.*) scout. 2. secret service man; intelligence officer. 3. (*geol.*) prospector.

разве́дчик², а, *m.* reconnaissance aircraft.

разве́дывательн|ый, *adj.* (*mil.*) 1. reconnaissance; р. бой probing attack; reconnaissance in force; р. дозо́р reconnaissance patrol; р. отря́д reconnaissance detachment. 2. intelligence; р. отде́л intelligence section; ~ая рабо́та intelligence work, secret-service work; ~ая слу́жба Intelligence Service (*corresponding to Intelligence Corps in British Army*); Гла́вное ~ое управле́ние Main Intelligence Directorate (*in U.S.S.R. Ministry of Defence*).

разве́дыва|ть, ю, *impf. of* разве́дать.

развез|ти́¹, у́, ёшь, *past* ~, ~ла́, *pf.* (*of* развози́ть) to convey, deliver.

развез|ти́², у́, ёшь, *past* ~, ~ла́, *pf.* (*of* развози́ть) (*coll.*) 1. to exhaust, wear out; от жары́ нас ~ло́ (*impers.*) we were exhausted from the heat. 2. to make impassable, make unfit for traffic; доро́гу ~ло́ от дожде́й (*impers.*) the road was made impassable by rain.

развéива|ть(ся), ю(сь), *impf. of* развéять-(ся).

развенч|áть, áю, *pf.* (*of* ~ивать) **1.** to dethrone. **2.** (*fig.*) to debunk.

развéнчива|ть, ю, *impf. of* развенчáть.

разверз|áть(ся), áю(сь), *impf. of* ~нуть(ся).

развéрз|нуть, ну, нешь, *past* ~, ~ла, *pf.* (*of* ~áть) (*obs., poet.*) to open wide.

развéрз|нуться, нусь, нешься, *past* ~ся, ~лась, *pf.* (*of* ~áться) (*obs., poet.*) to open wide, yawn, gape.

развéрн|утый, *p.p.p. of* ~ýть *and adj.* **1.** extensive, large-scale, all-out. **2.** detailed; ~утая прогрáмма detailed programme, comprehensive programme. **3.** (*mil.*) deployed; р. строй extended line formation.

развер|нýть, нý, нёшь, *pf.* (*of* ~тывать *and* разворáчивать) **1.** to unfold; to unroll; to unwrap; to unfurl; р. ковёр to unroll a carpet; р. знáмя to unfurl a banner. **2.** (*mil.*) to deploy. **3.** (в+*a.*; *mil.*) to expand (into); р. батальóн в полк to expand a battalion into a regiment. **4.** (*fig.*) to show, display. **5.** (*fig.*) to develop; to expand; р. аргументáцию to develop a line of argument; р. торгóвлю to expand trade. **6.** to turn; to swing (about, around). **7.** (*tech.*) to **ream**, broach. **8.** (*radar*) to scan.

развер|нýться, нýсь, нёшься, *pf.* (*of* ~тываться *and* разворáчиваться) **1.** to unfold; to unroll; to come unwrapped. **2.** (*mil.*) to deploy. **3.** (в+*a.*; *mil.*) to expand (into), be expanded (into). **4.** (*fig.*) to show oneself, display oneself. **5.** (*fig.*) to develop; to spread; to expand. **6.** to turn, swing (about, around); (*naut.*) to slew (about).

разверст|áть, áю, *pf.* (*of* ~ывать) to distribute, allot, apportion.

развёрстк|а, и, *f.* allotment, apportionment.

развёрстыва|ть, ю, *impf. of* разверстáть.

развер|стый, *p.p.p. of* ~знуть *and adj.* (*obs., poet.*) open, yawning, gaping; ~стая пасть gaping maw.

развер|тéть, чý, ~тишь, *pf.* (*of* ~чивать) **1.** to unscrew. **2.** (*tech.*) to ream.

развёртк|а¹, и, *f.* **1.** (*math.*) development, evolvement. **2.** (*tech.*) reaming. **3.** (*radar*) scanning.

развёртк|а², и, *f.* (*tech.*) reamer, broach bit.

развёртывани|е, я, *n.* **1.** unfolding; unrolling; unwrapping. **2.** (*mil.*) deployment. **3.** (*fig.*) development; expansion.

развёртыва|ть(ся), ю(сь), *impf. of* развернýть(ся).

развéрчива|ть, ю, *impf. of* развертéть.

развéс, а, *m.* weighing out.

развесел|ить, ю, ишь, *pf.* to cheer up, amuse.

развесел|иться, юсь, ишься, *pf.* to cheer up.

развесёлый, *adj.* (*coll.*) merry, gay.

развéсист|ый (~, ~а), *adj.* branchy; р. каштáн spreading chestnut; ~ая клюква myth, fable (*of credulous travellers' tales*).

развé|сить¹, шу, сишь, *pf.* (*of* ~шивать) to weigh out.

развé|сить², шу, сишь, *pf.* (*of* ~шивать) **1.** to hang. **2.** to spread (*branches*); р. ýши (*fig., coll.*) to listen open-mouthed.

развé|сить³, шу, сишь, *pf.* (*of* ~шивать) to hang.

развеснóй, *adj.* sold by weight.

разве|стѝ¹, дý, дёшь, *past* ~л, ~лá, *pf.* (*of* разводѝть) **1.** to take, conduct; р. детéй по домáм to take the children to their homes; р. войскá по квартѝрам to disperse troops to their billets; р. часовы́х to post sentries. **2.** (*in var. senses*) to part, separate; р. мост to raise a bridge, swing a bridge open; р. пилý to set a saw; р. рукáми to spread one's hands (*in a gesture of helplessness*). **3.** to divorce. **4.** to dilute; to dissolve; р. порошóк водóю, в водé to dissolve powder in water.

разве|стѝ², дý, дёшь, *past* ~л, ~лá, *pf.* (*of* разводѝть) **1.** to breed, rear; to cultivate; р. сад to plant a garden; р. парк to lay out a park. **2.** to start (*a source of heat or power*); р. костёр to make a camp fire; р. огóнь to light a fire, kindle a fire; р. пáры to raise steam, get up steam. **3.** (*fig., coll.; pejor.*) to start; р. чепухý to start talking nonsense.

разве|стѝсь¹, дýсь, дёшься, *past* ~лся, ~лáсь, *pf.* (*of* разводѝться) (с+*i.*) to divorce, be divorced (from).

разве|стѝсь², дýсь, дёшься, *past* ~лся, ~лáсь, *pf.* (*of* разводѝться) to breed, multiply.

разветв|ѝться, ѝтся, *pf.* (*of* ~ляться) to branch; to fork; to ramify.

разветвлéни|е, я, *n.* **1.** branching; ramification; forking. **2.** branch; fork (*of road, etc.*); р. нéрва (*anat.*) radicle.

разветвля́|ться, юсь, *impf. of* разветвѝться.

развéш|ать, аю, *pf.* (*of* ~ивать) to hang.

развéшива|ть, ю, *impf. of* развéсить *and* развéшать.

развé|ять, ю, ешь, *pf.* **1.** (*impf.* ~ивать) to scatter, disperse; (*fig.*) to dispel; р. миф to shatter a myth. **2.** (*impf.* ~вáть) to cause to flutter.

развé|яться, юсь, ешься, *pf.* (*of* ~иваться *and* ~вáться) to disperse; (*fig.*) to be dispelled.

развивá|ть(ся), ю(сь), *impf. of* развѝть(ся).

развѝлин|а, ы, *f.* fork, bifurcation.

развѝлист|ый (~, ~а), *adj.* forked.

развин|ти́ть, чу́, ти́шь, *pf.* (*of* ∼чива́ть) to unscrew.

развин|ти́ться, чу́сь, ти́шься, *pf.* (*of* ∼чива́ться) 1. to come unscrewed. 2. (*fig.*) to come unstuck.

разви́нченност|ь, и, *f.* (*coll.*) unbalance.

разви́н|ченный, *p.p.p. of* ∼ти́ть *and adj.* (*coll.*) 1. unstrung, unstuck. 2. (*of gait*) unsteady, lurching.

разви́нчива|ть(ся), ю(сь), *impf. of* развинти́ть(ся).

разви́ти|е, я, *n.* 1. (*in var. senses*) development; evolution; р. бо́я (*mil.*) progress of battle. 2. (*intellectual*) maturity.

разви́т|о́й (ра́звит, ∼а́, ра́звито), *adj.* 1. developed. 2. (intellectually) mature; adult.

разви́т|ый (∼, ∼а́, ∼о), *p.p.p. of* ∼ь.

раз|ви́ть[1], овью́, овьёшь, *past* ∼ви́л, ∼вила́, ∼ви́ло, *pf.* (*of* ∼вива́ть) to unwind, untwist.

раз|ви́ть[2], овью́, овьёшь, *past* ∼ви́л, ∼вила́, ∼ви́ло, *pf.* (*of* ∼вива́ть) (*in var. senses*) to develop; р. мускулату́ру to develop one's muscles; р. мысль to develop an idea; р. ско́рость to gather, pick up speed.

раз|ви́ться[1], овью́сь, овьёшься, *past* ∼ви́лся, ∼вила́сь, *pf.* (*of* ∼вива́ться) to untwist; (*of hair*) to come uncurled, lose its curl.

раз|ви́ться[2], овью́сь, овьёшься, *past* ∼ви́лся, ∼вила́сь, *pf.* (*of* ∼вива́ться) (*in var. senses*) to develop.

развлека́тел|ьный (∼ен, ∼ьна), *adj.* entertaining; ∼ьное чте́ние light reading.

развлека́|ться, юсь, *impf. of* развле́чь(ся).

развлече́ни|е, я, *n.* entertainment; amusement; diversion.

развле́|чь, ку́, чёшь, ку́т, *past* ∼к, ∼кла́, *pf.* (*of* ∼ка́ть) to entertain, amuse; to divert.

развле́|чься, ку́сь, чёшься, ку́тся, *past* ∼кся, ∼кла́сь, *pf.* (*of* ∼ка́ться) 1. to have a good time; to amuse oneself. 2. to be diverted, be distracted.

развод[1], а, *m.* divorce; дать р. кому́-н. to give someone a divorce, agree to a divorce; проце́сс о ∼е divorce suit, divorce proceedings; они́ в ∼е they are divorced.

развод[2], а, *m.* (*mil.*) р. карау́лов guard mounting; р. часовы́х posting of sentries.

развод[3], а, *m.* breeding; оста́вить на р. to keep for breeding.

разво|ди́ть(ся), жу́(сь), ∼дишь(ся), *impf. of* развести́(сь).

разводк|а[1], и, *f.* separation; р. мо́ста raising of a bridge, swinging a bridge open; р. пилы́ saw setting.

разводк|а[2], и, *f.* (*tech.*) saw set.

разводно́й, *adj.* р. ключ adjustable spanner, monkey wrench; р. мост drawbridge.

развод|ы, ов, *no sing.* 1. design, pattern.

2. stains; черни́льные р. ink-stains.

разво́дь|е, я, *g. pl.* ∼ев, *n.* 1. (*dial.*) spring floods. 2. patch of ice-free water.

разводя́щ|ий, его, *m.* (*mil.*) corporal of the guard; guard commander.

разво|ева́ться, ою́сь, ою́ешься, *pf.* (*coll.*) to bluster.

разво́з, а, *m.* conveyance.

разво|зи́ть, жу́, ∼зишь, *impf. of* развезти́.

разво|зи́ться, жу́сь, ∼зишься, *pf.* (*coll.*) (*of children*) to kick up a din.

разво́зк|а, и, *f.* 1. conveying; delivery. 2. (*coll.*) delivery cart.

разволн|ова́ть, у́ю, *pf.* to excite, agitate.

разволн|ова́ться, у́юсь, *pf.* to get excited, get agitated.

развора́чива|ть, ю, *impf. of* разверну́ть *and* развороти́ть.

развора́чива|ться, юсь, *impf. of* разверну́ться.

развор|ова́ть, у́ю, *pf.* (*of* ∼о́вывать) to loot, clean out.

разворо́выва|ть, ю, *impf. of* разворова́ть.

разворо́т, а, *m.* 1. (*aeron.*, *etc.*) turn; (*of motor transport*) U-turn. 2. (*coll.*) development; р. торго́вли growth of trade.

разворо|ти́ть, чу́, ∼тишь, *pf.* (*of* развора́чивать) 1. to make havoc (of); to knock to pieces. 2. to smash up, break up.

разворош|и́ть, у́, и́шь, *pf.* to turn upside down, scatter.

развра́т, а, *m.* debauchery, depravity, dissipation.

разврати́тел|ь, я, *m.* debaucher, seducer, corrupter.

развра|ти́ть, щу́, ти́шь, *pf.* (*of* ∼ща́ть) 1. to debauch, corrupt. 2. (*fig.*) to deprave.

развра|ти́ться, щу́сь, ти́шься, *pf.* (*of* ∼ща́ться) to become corrupted, become depraved; to go to the bad.

развра́тник, а, *m.* debauchee, profligate, libertine.

развра́тнича|ть, ю, *impf.* to indulge in debauchery, lead a depraved life.

развра́тност|ь, и, *f.* depravity, profligacy; corruptness.

развра́т|ный (∼ен, ∼на), *adj.* debauched, depraved, profligate; corrupt.

развраща́|ть(ся), ю(сь), *impf. of* разврати́ть(ся).

развращённост|ь, и, *f.* corruptness.

развра|щённый, *p.p.p. of* ∼ти́ть *and adj.* corrupt.

разв|ы́ться, о́юсь, о́ешься, *pf.* (*coll.*) to begin to howl, set up a howl.

развью́чива|ть, ю, *impf. of* развью́чить.

развью́ч|ить, у, ишь, *pf.* (*of* ∼ивать) to unload, unburden.

развя|за́ть, жу́, ∼жешь, *pf.* (*of* ∼зывать) to untie, unbind, undo; to unleash; р.

кому́-н. ру́ки to untie someone's hands (*also fig.*); р. войну́ to unleash war.

развя́з|**а́ться, жу́сь,** ~**жешься,** *pf.* (*of* ~зыва́ться) **1.** to come untied, come undone; у него́ ~за́лся язы́к (*fig.*) his tongue has been loosened. **2.** (c+*i.*; *fig.*) to have done (with), be through (with).

развя́зк|**а, и,** *f.* **1.** (*lit.*) dénouement. **2.** outcome, issue, upshot; счастли́вая р. happy ending; де́ло идёт к ~e things are coming to a head.

развя́з|**ный** (~**ен,** ~**на**), *adj.* (unduly) familiar; free-and-easy.

развя́зыва|**ть(ся), ю(сь),** *impf. of* развяза́ть(ся).

разгад|**а́ть, а́ю,** *pf.* (*of* ~ывать) **1.** to guess the meaning (of); р. зага́дку to solve a riddle; р. сны to interpret dreams; р. шифр to break a cipher. **2.** to guess, divine; р. челове́ка to size a person up, get to the bottom of a person.

разга́дк|**а, и,** *f.* solution (*of a riddle, etc.*).

разга́дыва|**ть, ю,** *impf. of* разгада́ть.

разга́р[1]**, а,** *m.* в ~e (+*g.*) at the height (of); в по́лном ~e in full swing; в ~e бо́я in the heat of the battle.

разга́р[2]**, а,** *m.* erosion (*of firearm barrel*).

разгиба́|**ть(ся), ю(сь),** *impf. of* разогну́ть(ся); не ~я спины́ without a let-up; ~ющий му́скул (*anat.*) extensor.

разгильдя́|**й, я,** *m.* (*coll.*) sloven; sloppy individual.

разгильдя́йнича|**ть, ю,** *impf.* (*coll.*) to be slovenly, be sloppy; to be slipshod.

разгильдя́йств|**о, а,** *n.* (*coll.*) slovenliness, sloppiness; slipshodness.

разглаго́льствовани|**е, я,** *n.* (*coll.*) big talk, lofty phrases.

разглаго́льств|**овать, ую,** *impf.* (*coll.*) to hold forth, expatiate; to talk big, use lofty phrases.

разгла́|**дить, жу, дишь,** *pf.* (*of* ~живать) to smooth out; to iron out, press; (*tech.*) to planish.

разгла́|**диться, дится,** *pf.* (*of* ~живаться) **1.** to become smoothed out. **2.** *pass. of* ~дить.

разгла́жива|**ть(ся), ет(ся),** *impf. of* разгла́дить(ся).

разгла|**си́ть, шу́, си́шь,** *pf.* (*of* ~ша́ть) **1.** to divulge, give away, let out. **2.** (o+*p.*; *coll.*) to trumpet, broadcast.

разглаша́|**ть, ю,** *impf. of* разгласи́ть.

разглаше́ни|**е, я,** *n.* divulging, (unauthorized) disclosure; р. вое́нной та́йны divulging of military secrets.

разгля|**де́ть, жу́, ди́шь,** *pf.* to make out, discern, descry.

разгля́дыва|**ть, ю,** *impf.* to examine closely, scrutinize.

разгне́ва|**ть, ю,** *pf.* to anger, incense.

разгне́ва|**ться, юсь,** *pf. of* гне́ваться.

разгова́рива|**ть, ю,** *impf.* (c+*i.*) to talk (to, with), speak (to, with), converse (with); переста́ньте р.! stop talking!; они́ друг с дру́гом не ~ют they are not on speaking terms.

разгов|**е́ться, е́юсь, е́ешься,** *pf.* (*of* ~ля́ться) to break a (period of) fast.

разговля́|**ться, юсь,** *impf. of* разговеться.

разгово́р, а (у), *m.* talk, conversation; кру́пный р. high words; перемени́ть р. to change the subject; об э́том и ~у быть не мо́жет there can be no question about it; об э́том бы́ло мно́го ~ов there was a great deal of talk about it; без ~ов! and no argument!

разговор|**и́ть, ю́, и́шь,** *pf.* (*coll.*) to dissuade.

разговор|**и́ться, ю́сь, и́шься,** *pf.* **1.** (c+*i.*) to get into conversation (with). **2.** to warm to one's theme; заста́вить кого́-н. р. to get someone talking.

разгово́рник, а, *m.* phrase-book.

разгово́р|**ный,** *adj.* **1.** colloquial; р. язы́к spoken language. **2.** ~ная бу́дка telephone booth; р. уро́к conversation class.

разгово́рчивост|**ь, и,** *f.* talkativeness, loquacity.

разгово́рчив|**ый** (~, ~**a**), *adj.* talkative, loquacious.

разго́н, а, *m.* **1.** dispersal; р. собра́ния breaking up of a meeting. **2.** быть в ~e (*coll.*) to be out. **3.** (*sport*) run, running start; прыжо́к с ~a running jump. **4.** distance (*between similar objects*). **5.** (*typ.*) space.

разго́нист|**ый** (~, ~**a**), *adj.* (*coll.*; *of handwriting or type*) spaced-out.

разгоня́|**ть(ся), ю(сь),** *impf. of* разогна́ть(ся).

разгора́жива|**ть, ю,** *impf. of* разгороди́ть.

разгор|**а́ться, а́ется,** *impf. of* ~е́ться.

разгор|**е́ться, и́тся,** *pf.* (*of* ~а́ться) **1.** to flame up, flare up. **2.** (*fig.*) to flare up; ~е́лся спор a heated argument developed; стра́сти ~е́лись feeling ran high, passions rose; глаза́ у неё ~е́лись на бриллиа́нтовое кольцо́ (*coll.*) she hankered after, she set her heart on a diamond ring. **3.** (*fig.*) to flush.

разгоро|**ди́ть, жу́,** ~**ди́шь,** *pf.* (*of* разгора́живать) to partition off.

разгоряч|**и́ть, у́, и́шь,** *pf. of* горячи́ть.

разгоряч|**и́ться, у́сь, и́шься,** *pf.* (*of* горячи́ться) (от) to be flushed (with); р. от вина́ to be flushed with wine.

разгра́б|**ить, лю, ишь,** *pf.* to plunder, pillage, loot.

разграбле́ни|**е, я,** *n.* plunder, pillage.

разгра|**ди́ть, жу́, ди́шь,** *pf.* (*of* ~жда́ть)

(*mil.*) to remove obstacles (from); to clear (*of mines*).

разгражда́|ть, ю, *impf. of* разгради́ть.

разгражде́ни|е, я, *n.* (*mil.*) removal of obstacles.

разграниче́ни|е, я, *n.* 1. demarcation, delimitation. 2. differentiation.

разграни́чива|ть, ю, *impf. of* разграни́чить.

разграничи́тельн|ый, *adj.* ~ая ли́ния line of demarcation, dividing line.

разграни́ч|ить, у, ишь, *pf.* (*of* ~ивать) 1. to delimit, demarcate. 2. to differentiate, distinguish.

разграф|и́ть, лю́, и́шь, *pf.* (*of* графи́ть *and* ~ля́ть) to rule (*in squares, columns, etc.*).

разграфле́ни|е, я, *n.* ruling.

разграфля́|ть, ю, *impf. of* разграфи́ть.

разгреба́|ть, ю, *impf. of* разгрести́.

разгре|сти́, бу́, бёшь, *past* ~б, ~бла́, *pf.* (*of* ~ба́ть) to rake (aside, away); to shovel (aside, away).

разгро́м, а, *m.* 1. crushing defeat, utter defeat, rout; knock-out blow. 2. (*coll.*) havoc, devastation; карти́на ~а scene of devastation; в кварти́ре был по́лный р. there was complete chaos in the flat.

разгром|и́ть, лю́, и́шь, *pf. of* громи́ть.

разгружа́|ть(ся), ю(сь), *impf. of* разгрузи́ть(ся).

разгру|зи́ть, жу́, ~зи́шь, *pf.* (*of* ~жа́ть) 1. to unload. 2. (от; *fig., coll.*) to relieve (of); р. от доба́вочных обя́занностей to relieve of extra commitments.

разгру|зи́ться, жу́сь, ~зи́шься, *pf.* (*of* ~жа́ться) 1. to unload. 2. (от; *fig., coll.*) to be relieved (of).

разгру́зк|а, и, *f.* 1. unloading. 2. (*fig., coll.*) relieving, affording relief.

разгрузн|о́й, *adj.* ~о́е су́дно (*naut.*) lighter.

разгру́зочн|ый, *adj.* unloading; ~ые рабо́ты unloading operations; ~ое су́дно (*naut.*) lighter.

разгруппир|ова́ть, у́ю, *pf.* (*of* ~о́вывать) to divide into groups, group.

разгруппиро́выва|ть, ю, *impf. of* разгруппирова́ть.

разгрыза́|ть, ю, *impf. of* разгры́зть.

разгры́з|ть, у́, ёшь, *past* ~, ~ла, *pf.* (*of* ~а́ть) to crack (*with one's teeth*); р. оре́х to crack a nut.

разгу́л, а, *m.* 1. revelry, debauch. 2. (+*g.*; *fig.*) raging (of); wild outburst (of); р. антисемити́зма a wild outburst of anti-semitism.

разгу́лива|ть, ю, *impf.* 1. to stroll about, walk about. 2. *impf. of* разгуля́ть.

разгу́лива|ться, юсь, *impf. of* разгуля́ться.

разгу́ль|е, я, *n.* (*coll.*) merry-making.

разгу́л|ьный (~ен, ~ьна), *adj.* (*coll.*) loose,

wild, rakish; вести́ ~ьную жизнь to lead a wild life.

разгул|я́ть, я́ю, *pf.* (*of* ~ивать) (*coll.*) 1. to amuse so as to keep awake. 2. to dispel; р. чью-н. хандру́ to dispel someone's gloom.

разгул|я́ться, я́юсь, *pf.* (*of* ~иваться) (*coll.*) 1. to spread oneself; to have free scope. 2. (*of children*) to wake up, stop feeling sleepy. 3. (*of weather*) to clear up, improve; день ~я́лся it has turned out a fine day.

разда|ва́ть(ся), ю́(сь), ёшь(ся), *impf. of* разда́ть(ся).

раздав|и́ть, лю́, ~ишь, *pf.* (*of* ~ливать) 1. to crush; to squash. 2. (*fig.*) to crush, overwhelm. 3. (*coll.*) to down, sink (*alcoholic beverages*).

разда́влива|ть, ю, *impf. of* раздави́ть.

разда́рива|ть, ю, *impf. of* раздари́ть.

раздар|и́ть, ю́, ~ишь, *pf.* (*of* ~ивать) (+*d.*) to give away (to), make a present of.

разда́точн|ый, *adj.* distributing, distribution; ~ая ве́домость list of those due to receive (*gifts, money, etc.*); р. пункт distribution centre.

разда́тчик, а, *m.* distributor, dispenser.

разда́|ть¹, м, шь, ст, ди́м, ди́те, ду́т, *past* ро́здал, ~ла́, ро́здало, *pf.* (*of* ~ва́ть) to distribute, give out, serve out, dispense; р. ми́лостыню to dispense charity; р. кни́ги to give out books.

разда́|ть², м, шь, ст, ди́м, ди́те, ду́т, *past* ро́здал, ~ла́, ро́здало, *pf.* (*of* ~ва́ть) (*coll.*) to stretch (*footwear*); to enlarge, widen, let out (*clothing*).

разда́|ться¹, мся, шься, стся, ди́мся, ди́тесь, ду́тся, *past* ~лся, ~ла́сь, ~ло́сь, *pf.* (*of* ~ва́ться) to be heard; to resound; to ring (out); ~лся вы́стрел a shot rang out; ~лся стук (в дверь) a knock at the door was heard.

разда́|ться², мся, шься, стся, ди́мся, ди́тесь, ду́тся, *past* ~лся, ~ла́сь, ~ло́сь, *pf.* (*of* ~ва́ться) (*coll.*) 1. to make way. 2. to stretch, expand. 3. to put on weight.

разда́ч|а, и, *f.* distribution.

раздва́ива|ть(ся), ю(сь), *impf. of* раздво́ить(ся).

раздвига́|ть(ся), ю(сь), *impf. of* раздви́нуть(ся).

раздвижно́й, *adj.* expanding; sliding; р. за́навес (*theatr.*) draw curtain; р. стол leaf table, expanding table.

раздви́|нуть, ну, нешь, *pf.* (*of* ~га́ть) to move apart, slide apart; р. занаве́ски to draw back the curtains; р. стол to extend a table, insert a leaf into a table.

раздви́|нуться, нется, *pf.* (*of* ~га́ться) to move apart, slide apart; за́навес ~нулся the curtain was drawn back; (*in theatre*) the curtain rose; толпá ~нýлась the crowd made way.

раздвоéни|е, я, *n.* division into two; bifurcation; р. лѝчности (*med.*) split personality.

раздвó|енный (and раздвоённый), *p.p.p. of* ~ѝть *and adj.* 1. forked; bifurcated; ~енное копы́то cloven hoof; ~енное сознáние split mind. 2. (*bot.*) dichotomous, furcate.

раздво|ѝть, ю́, ѝшь, *pf.* (*of* раздвáивать) to divide into two; to bisect.

раздво|ѝться, ю́сь, ѝшься, *pf.* (*of* раздвáиваться) to bifurcate, fork, split, become double.

раздевáлк|а, и, *f.* (*coll.*) cloak-room.

раздевáльный, *adj.* (for) undressing.

раздевáл|ьня, ьни, *g. pl.* ~ен, *f.* =~ка.

раздевáни|е, я, *n.* undressing.

раздевá|ть(ся), ю(сь), *impf. of* раздéть(ся).

раздéл, а, *m.* 1. division; partition; allotment. 2. section, part (*of book, etc.*).

раздéл|ать, аю, *pf.* (*of* ~ывать) to dress, prepare; р. грѝдки to prepare (flower-) beds (*for sowing*); р. под дуб to grain in imitation of oak; р. когó-н. под орéх (*coll.*) to give it someone hot.

раздéл|аться, аюсь, *pf.* (*of* ~ываться) (с+*i.*) 1. to be through (with); to settle (accounts) (with); р. с долгáми to pay off debts. 2. (*fig.*) to settle accounts (with), get even (with).

разделéни|е, я, *n.* division; р. трудá division of labour.

раздели́м|ый (~, ~а), *adj.* divisible.

раздели́тельн|ый, *adj.* 1. dividing, separating; ~ая чертá dividing line. 2. (*philos., gram.*) disjunctive; (*gram.*) distributive; р. сою́з disjunctive conjunction; ~ое местоимéние distributive pronoun.

раздел|и́ть, ю́, ~ишь, *pf.* (*of* ~я́ть) 1. to divide. 2. to separate, part. 3. to share.

раздел|и́ться, ю́сь, ~ишься, *pf.* (*of* ~я́ться) 1. (на+*a.*) to divide (into); to be divided; нам придётся р. на две грýппы we shall have to divide into two groups; мнéния ~и́лись opinions were divided. 2. to separate, part company. 3. *pf. only* (на+*a.*) to be divisible (by); число́ сóрок дéвять ~ится на семь forty-nine is divisible by seven.

раздéльн|ый, *adj.* 1. separate; ~ое обучéние separate education for boys and girls. 2. (*of pronunciation*) clear, distinct.

раздел|я́ть, я́ю, *impf. of* ~и́ть; р. чьи-н. взгля́ды to share someone's views.

раздел|я́ться, я́юсь, *impf. of* ~и́ться.

раздёрг|ать, аю, *pf.* (*of* ~ивать) (*coll.*) to tear up.

раздёргива|ть, ю, *impf. of* раздёргать *and* раздёрнуть.

раздёр|нуть, ну, нешь, *pf.* (*of* ~гивать)

to draw apart, pull apart; р. занавéски to draw back the curtains.

раздéт|ый, *p.p.p. of* ~ь *and adj.* 1. unclothed. 2. poorly clothed, ill-clad.

раздé|ть, ну, нешь, *pf.* (*of* ~вáть) to undress.

раздé|ться, нусь, нешься, *pf.* (*of* ~вáться) to undress, strip; to take off one's things.

раздирá|ть, ю, *impf.* 1. *impf. of* разодрáть. 2. *impf. only* (*fig.*) to rend, tear, lacerate, harrow.

раздирá|ться, ю, ет(ся), *impf. of* разодрáться.

раздирá|ющий, *pres. part. act. of* ~ть *and adj.*; р. (дýшу) heart-rending, heart-breaking, harrowing.

раздобрé|ть, ю, *pf. of* добрéть².

раздобр|и́ться, ю́сь, и́шься, *pf.* (*coll.*) to become generous, become kind.

раздобывá|ть, ю, *impf. of* раздобы́ть.

раздо|бы́ть, бýду, бýдешь, *past* ~бы́л, *pf.* (*of* ~бывáть) (*coll.*) get, procure, come by, get hold of; р. дéнег to raise money, come by some money.

раздóль|е, я, *n.* 1. expanse. 2. (*fig.*) freedom, liberty; им р. they are quite free to do as they please.

раздóл|ьный (~ен, ~ьна), *adj.* free.

раздóр, а, *m.* discord, dissension; я́блоко ~а apple of discord, bone of contention; сéять р. to breed strife.

раздосáд|овать, ую, *pf.* to vex.

раздраж|áть(ся), áю(сь), *impf. of* ~и́ть(ся).

раздражá|ющий, *pres. part. act. of* ~ть *and adj.* irritating, annoying, exasperating; *as noun* ~ющее, ~ющего, *n.* irritant.

раздражéни|е, я, *n.* irritation.

раздражи́тел|ь, я, *m.* (*med.*) irritant.

раздражи́тельност|ь, и, *f.* irritability; shortness of temper.

раздражи́тел|ьный (~ен, ~ьна), *adj.* irritable; short of temper, short-tempered.

раздраж|и́ть, ý, и́шь, *pf.* (*of* ~áть) 1. to irritate, annoy, exasperate, put out. 2. (*med.*) to irritate.

раздраж|и́ться, ýсь, и́шься, *pf.* (*of* ~áться) 1. to get irritated, get annoyed. 2. (*med.*) to become inflamed.

раздразн|и́ть, ю́, ~ишь, *pf.* 1. to tease. 2. to stimulate; р. чей-н. аппети́т to whet someone's appetite.

раздроб|и́ть, лю́, и́шь, *pf.* 1. *pf. of* дроби́ть. 2. (*impf.* ~ля́ть) (в+*a.*; *math.*) to turn (into), reduce (to); р. грáммы в сантигрáммы to turn grams into centigrams.

раздроб|и́ться, и́тся, *pf. of* дроби́ться.

раздроблéни|е, я, *n.* 1. breaking, smashing to pieces. 2. (*math.*) reduction.

раздрóб|ленный (and раздроблённый), *p.p.p. of* ~и́ть *and adj.* 1. (*of a bone*) shattered. 2. (*fig.*) small-scale; fragmented,

раздробля́|ть, ю, *impf. of* раздроби́ть.

раздруж|и́ться, у́сь, и́шься, *pf.* (*coll.*) to break it off (with); to break off friendly relations (with).

раздува́льный, *adj.* р. мех (*tech.*) bellows.

раздува́|ть(ся), ю(сь), *impf. of* разду́ть(ся).

разду́м|ать, аю, *pf.* (*of* ~ывать) to change one's mind; (+*inf.*) to decide not (to); я ~ал подава́ть заявле́ние на э́то ме́сто I decided not to apply for that job, I changed my mind about applying for that job.

разду́м|аться, аюсь, *pf.* (о+*p.*; *coll.*) to be absorbed in thinking (about).

разду́мыва|ть, ю, *impf.* **1.** *impf. of* разду́мать. **2.** *impf. only* (о+*p.*) to ponder (on, over), consider; я давно́ ~ю, купи́ть ли маши́ну и́ли нет for a long time I have been considering whether or not to buy a car; не ~я without a moment's thought.

разду́мь|е, я, *n.* **1.** meditation; thought, thoughtful mood; в глубо́ком р. deep in thought. **2.** hesitation; меня́ взяло́ р. I can't make up my mind.

разду́т|ый, *p.p.p. of* ~ь and *adj.* (*fig.*, *coll.*) exaggerated; inflated; ~ые шта́ты inflated staffs.

разду́|ть, ю, ешь, *pf.* (*of* ~ва́ть) **1.** to blow; to fan; р. пла́мя (*fig.*) to fan the flames. **2.** to blow (out); р. щёки to blow out one's cheeks; у него́ ~ло щёку (*impers.*) his cheek is swollen. **3.** (*fig.*, *coll.*) to exaggerate; to inflate, swell; р. поте́ри to exaggerate losses. **4.** to blow about; ~ло бума́ги по́ полу (*impers.*) the papers had blown all over the floor.

разду́|ться, юсь, ешься, *pf.* (*of* ~ва́ться) to swell.

раздуш|и́ть, у́, ~ишь, *pf.* (*coll.*) to drench in perfume.

разева́|ть, ю, *impf. of* рази́нуть.

разжа́лоб|ить, лю, ишь, *pf.* to move (to pity).

разжа́лоб|иться, люсь, ишься, *pf.* to be moved to pity.

разжа́ловани|е, я, *n.* demotion, degrading.

разжа́лова|нный, *p.p.p. of* ~ть; *as noun* р., ~нного, *m.* (*mil.*) demoted, degraded officer.

разжа́л|овать, ую, *pf.* (*mil.*) to demote, degrade; р. в солда́ты to reduce to the ranks.

раз|жа́ть, ожму́, ожмёшь, *pf.* (*of* ~жима́ть) to unclasp; to release, unfasten, undo; р. кула́к to unclench one's fist; р. ру́ки to unclasp one's hands.

раз|жа́ться, ожмётся, *pf.* (*of* ~жима́ться) to come loose; to relax.

разж|ева́ть, ую́, уёшь, *pf.* (*of* ~ёвывать) to chew, masticate; (*fig.*, *coll.*) to chew over.

разжёвыва|ть, ю, *impf. of* разжева́ть.

раз|же́чь, ожгу́, ожжёшь, ожгу́т, *past* ~жёг, ~ожгла́,** *pf.* (*of* ~жига́ть) **1.** to kindle. **2.** (*fig.*) to kindle, rouse, stir up; р. стра́сти to arouse passion.

разжи́в|а, ы, *f.* (*coll.*) gain, profit.

разжива́|ться, юсь, *impf. of* разжи́ться.

разжига́ни|е, я, *n.* kindling (*also fig.*).

разжига́|ть, ю, *impf. of* разже́чь.

разжи|ди́ть, жу́, ди́шь, *pf.* (*of* ~жа́ть) to dilute, thin.

разжижа́|ть, ю, *impf. of* разжиди́ть.

разжиже́ни|е, я, *n.* dilution, thinning; rarefaction.

разжима́|ть(ся), ет(ся), *impf. of* разжа́ть (ся).

разжире́|ть, ю, *pf. of* жире́ть.

разж|и́ться, иву́сь, ивёшься, *past* ~и́лся, ~ила́сь,** *pf.* (*of* ~ива́ться) (*coll.*) **1.** to get rich, make a pile. **2.** (+*i.*) to come by, get hold of.

раззаво́д, а, *m.* на р. (*coll.*) for breeding.

раззадо́рива|ть(ся), ю(сь), *impf. of* раззадо́рить(ся).

раззадо́р|ить, ю, ишь, *pf.* (*of* ~ивать) (*coll.*) to stir up, excite.

раззадо́р|иться, юсь, ишься, *pf.* (*of* ~иваться) (*coll.*) to get excited, get worked up.

раззва́нива|ть, ю, *impf. of* раззвони́ть.

раззвон|и́ть, ю́, и́шь, *pf.* (*of* раззва́нивать) (о+*p.*; *coll.*) to trumpet, proclaim (from the housetops).

раззнако́м|ить, лю, ишь, *pf.* to alienate.

раззнако́м|иться, люсь, ишься, *pf.* (с+*i.*) to break off one's acquaintance (with), break (with).

раззуд|е́ться, и́тся, *pf.* (*coll.*) to begin to itch (*also fig.*).

раззя́в|а, ы, *m. and f.* = рази́ня.

рази́н|уть, у, ешь, *pf.* (*of* разева́ть) (*coll.*) to open wide (*the mouth*); to gape; слу́шать, ~ув рот to listen open-mouthed.

рази́н|я, и, *m. and f.* (*coll.*) scatter-brained person.

рази́тел|ьный (~ен, ~ьна), *adj.* striking; р. приме́р striking example.

ра|зи́ть[1], жу́, зи́шь, *impf.* to strike, smite, hit.

раз|и́ть[2], и́т, *impf.* (*impers.* +*i.*; *coll.*) to reek (of), stink (of); из ко́мнаты ~и́ло чесноко́м the room reeked of garlic.

разлага́|ть(ся), ю(сь), *impf. of* разложи́ть(ся).

разла́д, а, *m.* **1.** disorder. **2.** discord, dissension.

разла́|дить, жу, дишь, *pf.* (*of* ~живать) to derange; (*coll.*) to mess up.

разла́|диться, дится, *pf.* (*of* ~живаться) to get out of order; (*coll.*) to go wrong.

разла́ком|ить, лю, ишь, *pf.* (+*i.*; *coll.*) to give someone a taste (for).

разла́ком|иться, люсь, ишься, *pf.* (+*i.*; *coll.*) to get a taste (for).

разла́мыва|ть(ся), ю, ет(ся), *impf. of* разлома́ть(ся) *and* разломи́ть(ся).

разлёжива|ться, юсь, *impf.* (*coll.*, *pejor.*) to lie about.

разлеза́|ться, а́ется, *impf.. of* ~ться.

разле́з|ться, ется, *past* ~ся, ~лась, *pf.* (*of* ~а́ться) (*coll.*) to come to pieces; to come apart at the seams; to fall apart.

разле́нива|ться, юсь, *impf. of* разлени́ться.

разлен|и́ться, ю́сь, ~ишься, *pf.* (*of* ~ива́ться) (*coll.*) to become sunk in sloth.

разлеп|и́ть, лю́, ~ишь, *pf.* (*of* ~ля́ть) to unstick.

разлеп|и́ться, ~ится, *pf.* (*of* ~ля́ться) to come unstuck.

разлепля́|ть(ся), ю(сь), ет(ся), *impf. of* разлепи́ть(ся).

разлёт, а, *m.* (*of birds*) flying away, departure.

разлета́|ться, а́юсь, *impf. of* ~е́ться.

разле|те́ться, чу́сь, ти́шься, *pf.* (*of* ~та́ться) 1. to fly away; to scatter (*in the air*). 2. (*coll.*) to smash, shatter; ста́туя ~те́лась вдре́безги the statue smashed to smithereens. 3. (*fig.*, *coll.*) to vanish, be shattered; её мечта́ ~те́лась her dream was shattered; все на́ши наде́жды ~те́лись all our hopes were dashed. 4. (*coll.*) to rush.

разл|е́чься, я́гусь, я́жешься, *past* ~ёгся, ~егла́сь, *pf.* (*coll.*) to sprawl, stretch oneself out.

разли́в, а, *m.* 1. bottling. 2. flood; overflow.

разлива́ни|е, я, *n.* pouring out.

разлива́нн|ый, *adj. only used in phrase* ~ое мо́ре (*joc.*) oceans, lashings (*usu. of alcoholic beverages*).

разлива́тельн|ый, *adj.*; ~ая ло́жка ladle.

разлива́|ть(ся), ю, ет(ся), *impf. of* разли́ть(ся).

разли́вк|а, и, *f.* 1. bottling. 2. (*tech.*) teeming, casting.

разливн|о́й, *adj.* on tap, on draught; ~о́е вино́ wine from the wood.

разли́вочн|ый, *adj.* (*tech.*) teeming, casting; ~ая маши́на casting machine, liquid filling machine.

разлин|ова́ть, у́ю, *pf.* (*of* ~о́вывать) to rule (*paper, etc.*).

разлино́выва|ть, ю, *impf. of* разлинова́ть.

разли́ти|е, я, *n.* overflow; р. же́лчи (*med.*) bilious attack.

раз|ли́ть, олью́, ольёшь, *past* ~ли́л, ~лила́, ~ли́ло, *pf.* (*of* ~лива́ть) 1. to pour out; р. по буты́лкам to bottle; р. чай to pour out tea. 2. to spill; р. водо́й to pour

water (over), douse, drench; их водо́й не ~ольёшь (*coll.*) they are thick as thieves. 3. (*fig.*) to pour out, spread, broadcast.

раз|ли́ться, ольётся, *past* ~ли́лся, ~лила́сь, *pf.* (*of* ~лива́ться) 1. to spill; суп ~ли́лся по ска́терти the soup has spilled over the table-cloth. 2. to overflow; река́ ~лила́сь the river has overflowed, has burst its banks. 3. (*med.*) у него́ ~лила́сь жёлчь he had a bilious attack. 4. (*fig.*) to spread; по её лицу́ ~лила́сь улы́бка a smile spread across her face.

различа́|ть, а́ю, *impf. of* ~и́ть.

различа́|ться, юсь, *impf.* to differ.

разли́чи|е, я, *n.* distinction; difference; де́лать р. (ме́жду) to make distinctions (between); без ~я without distinction; зна́ки ~я (*mil.*) badges of rank.

различи́тельный, *adj.* distinctive; р. при́знак distinctive feature, distinguishing feature.

различ|и́ть, у́, и́шь, *pf.* (*of* ~а́ть) 1. to distinguish; to tell the difference (between). 2. to discern, make out.

разли́ч|ный (~ен, ~на), *adj.* 1. different; у нас бы́ли ~ные мне́ния our opinions differed. 2. various, diverse; ~ные лю́ди all manner of people; по ~ным соображе́ниям for various reasons.

разложе́ни|е, я, *n.* 1. breaking down; (*chem.*) decomposition; (*math.*) expansion; (*phys.*) resolution. 2. decomposition, decay; putrefaction. 3. (*fig.*) demoralization; disintegration.

разложи́|вшийся, *past part. act. of* ~ться *and adj.* 1. decomposed, decayed. 2. (*fig.*) demoralized.

разлож|и́ть¹, у́, ~ишь, *pf.* (*of* раскла́дывать) 1. to put away; р. свои́ ве́щи по я́щикам to put away one's things in their respective drawers. 2. to lay out; to spread (out); to (lay and) make (*a fire*); р. ого́нь to make a fire; р. ска́терть to spread a table-cloth; р. складну́ю крова́ть to put up a camp bed. 3. to distribute, apportion; р. при́быль to distribute, share out profits.

разлож|и́ть², у́, ~ишь, *pf.* (*of* разлага́ть) 1. to break down; (*chem.*) to decompose; (*math.*) to expand; (*phys.*) to resolve; р. вещество́ на составны́е ча́сти to break a substance down into its component parts; р. число́ на мно́жители to factorize a number.

разлож|и́ться¹, у́сь, ~ишься, *pf.* (*of* раскла́дываться) (*coll.*) to arrange one's things, put one's things out.

разлож|и́ться², у́сь, ~ишься, *pf.* (*of* разлага́ться) 1. (*chem.*) to decompose; (*math.*) to expand. 2. to decompose, rot, decay; труп уже́ ~и́лся the body has already

decomposed. **3.** (*fig.*) to become demoralized; to disintegrate, crack up, go to pieces.
разло́м, а, *m.* **1.** breaking. **2.** break.
разлома́|ть, ю, *pf.* (*of* разла́мывать) to break (in pieces); р. дом to pull down a house.
разлома́|ться, ется, *pf.* (*of* разла́мываться) to break (in pieces); to break up.
разлом|и́ть, лю́, ~ишь, *pf.* (*of* разла́мывать) **1.** to break (in pieces). **2.** (*impers.*; *coll.*) меня́ всего́ ~и́ло every bone in my body aches.
разлом|и́ться, ~ится, *pf.* (*of* разла́мываться) to break in pieces.
разлу́к|а, и, *f.* **1.** separation; жить в ~е (c+i.) to live apart (from), be separated (from). **2.** parting; час ~и hour of parting.
разлуч|а́ть(ся), а́ю(сь), *impf. of* ~и́ть(ся).
разлуч|и́ть, у́, и́шь, *pf.* (*of* ~а́ть) (+a. c+i.) to separate (from), part (from), sever (from).
разлуч|и́ться, у́сь, и́шься, *pf.* (*of* ~а́ться) (c+i.) to separate, part (from).
разлюб|и́ть, лю́, ~ишь, *pf.* to cease to love, stop loving; to cease to like, like no longer.
размагни́|тить, чу, тишь, *pf.* (*of* ~чивать) (*tech.*) to demagnetize.
размагни́|титься, чусь, тишься, *pf.* (*of* ~чиваться) **1.** (*tech.*) to become demagnetized. **2.** (*fig.*, *coll.*) to lose grip; to become unbalanced.
размагни́чива|ть(ся), ю(сь), *impf. of* размагни́тить(ся).
разма́|зать, жу, жешь, *pf.* (*of* ~зывать) **1.** to spread, smear; р. варе́нье по всему́ лицу́ to get jam all over one's face. **2.** (*coll.*) to pad out, amplify (*a narration*).
разма́|заться, жется, *pf.* (*of* ~зываться) to spread; to get smeared.
размазн|я́, и́, *g. pl.* ~е́й, *f.* (*coll.*) **1.** thin gruel, thin porridge; (*fig.*) slush. **2.** *m. and f.* (*fig.*) ninny, wishy-washy person.
разма́зыва|ть(ся), ю, ет(ся), *impf. of* разма́зать(ся).
разма́ива|ть(ся), ю(сь), *impf. of* разма́ять-(ся).
размал|ева́ть, ю́ю, ю́ешь, *pf.* (*of* ~ёвывать) (*coll.*) to daub.
размалёвыва|ть, ю, *impf. of* размалева́ть.
разма́лыва|ть, ю, *impf. of* размоло́ть.
разма́рива|ть(ся), ю(сь), *impf. of* размори́ть(ся).
разма́тыва|ть(ся), ю, ет(ся), *impf. of* размота́ть(ся).
разма́х, а, *m.* **1.** sweep; со всего́ ~у with all one's might; уда́рить с ~у to strike with all one's might. **2.** span; р. кры́льев (*aeron.*) wing-span, wing-spread. **3.** (*tech.*) swing, amplitude (*of pendulum*). **4.** (*fig.*) scope, range, sweep, scale; широ́кий р. wide range, grand scale; у них широ́кий

жи́зни they live in style, they do things in a big way.
разма́хива|ть, ю, *impf.* (+i.) to swing; to brandish; р. рука́ми to gesticulate.
разма́хива|ться, юсь, *impf. of* размах-ну́ться.
размах|ну́ться, ну́сь, нёшься, *pf.* (*of* ~иваться) **1.** to swing one's arm (*to strike or as if to strike*). **2.** (*fig.*, *coll.*) to do things in a big way; (*pejor.*) to bite off more than one can chew.
разма́чива|ть, ю, *impf. of* размочи́ть.
разма́шисто, *adv.* sweepingly, boldly; писа́ть р. to write a bold hand; р. грести́ to row with vigorous strokes.
разма́шист|ый (~, ~а), *adj.* sweeping; р. жест sweeping gesture; р. по́черк bold hand; р. стиль (*fig.*) happy-go-lucky style.
разма́|ять, ю, ешь, *pf.* (*of* ~ивать) (*coll.*) to keep awake, prevent from sleeping.
разма́|яться, юсь, ешься, *pf.* (*of* ~иваться) (*coll.*) to become wakeful, cease to feel sleepy.
размежева́ни|е, я, *n.* demarcation, delimitation.
размеж|ева́ть, у́ю, у́ешь, *pf.* (*of* ~ёвывать) to divide out, delimit (*also fig.*); р. сфе́ры влия́ния to delimit spheres of influence.
размеж|ева́ться, у́юсь, у́ешься, *pf.* (*of* ~ёвываться) **1.** to fix the boundaries; (*fig.*) to delimit the functions, spheres of action. **2.** (*fig.*) to break off relations.
размежёвыва|ть(ся), ю(сь), *impf. of* размежева́ть(ся).
размельч|а́ть, а́ю, *impf. of* ~и́ть.
размельч|и́ть, у́, и́шь, *pf.* (*of* ~а́ть) to divide into particles; to pulverize.
разме́н, а, *m.* exchange; р. де́нег changing of money.
разме́нива|ть(ся), ю(сь), *impf. of* разменя́ть(ся).
разме́нн|ый, *adj.* ~ая моне́та small change.
размен|я́ть, я́ю, *pf.* (*of* ~ивать) to change; р. сторублёвку to change a hundred--rouble note.
размен|я́ться, я́юсь, *pf.* (*of* ~иваться) (*coll.*) **1.** (+i.) to exchange; р. пе́шками (*in chess*) to exchange pawns. **2.** (*fig.*) to dissipate one's talents.
разме́р, а, *m.* **1.** dimensions; воро́нка ~ом в де́сять квадра́тных ме́тров a crater measuring ten square metres. **2.** size; (*pl.*) measurements; како́й ваш р.? what size do you take? **3.** rate, amount; получа́ть зарпла́ту в ~е десяти́ рубле́й в день to be paid at the rate of ten roubles per day. **4.** scale, extent; (*pl.*) proportions; в широ́ких ~ах on a large scale; увели́читься до огро́мных ~ов to assume enormous proportions. **5.** metre (*of verse*); (*mus.*) measure.

размер|енный, *p.p.p. of* ~ить *and adj.* measured; ~енная похо́дка measured tread.

размер|ить, ю, ишь, *pf.* (*of* ~я́ть) to measure off; р. свои́ си́лы (*fig.*) to measure one's strength.

размер|я́ть, я́ю, *impf. of* ~ить.

разме|си́ть, шу́, ~сишь, *pf.* (*of* ~шивать) to knead.

разме|сти́, ту́, тёшь, *past* ~л, ~ла́, *pf.* (*of* ~та́ть[1]) 1. to sweep clear; р. доро́жку to clear a path. 2. to shovel away, sweep away.

разме|сти́ть, щу́, сти́шь, *pf.* (*of* ~ща́ть) 1. to place, accommodate; to stow; р. делега́тов по гости́ницам to accommodate the delegates in hotels; р. войска́ по кварти́рам to quarter troops. 2. to distribute; р. заём to float a loan.

разме|сти́ться, щу́сь, сти́шься, *pf.* (*of* ~ща́ться) 1. to take one's seat. 2. *pass. of* ~сти́ть.

размета́|ть[1], ю, *impf. of* размести́.

разме|та́ть[2], чу́, ~чешь, *pf.* (*of* ~тыва́ть) to scatter, disperse.

разме|та́ться, чу́сь, ~чешься, *pf.* 1. (*coll.*) to toss (*in sleep or delirium*). 2. to sprawl.

разме́|тить, чу, тишь, *pf.* (*of* ~ча́ть) to mark; р. курси́вный шрифт to mark italics.

разме́точн|ый, *adj.* (*tech.*) ~ая плита́ layout block; ~о-сверли́льный стано́к jig borer.

разме́тчик, а, *m.* marker.

размётыва|ть, ю, *impf. of* размета́ть[2].

размеча́|ть, ю, *impf. of* разме́тить.

размеш|а́ть, а́ю, *pf.* (*of* ~ивать) to stir.

размешива|ть, ю, *impf. of* размеси́ть *and* размеша́ть.

размеща́|ть(ся), ю(сь), *impf. of* размести́ть(ся).

размеще́ни|е, я, *n.* 1. placing, accommodation; distribution, disposal, allocation; siting; р. гру́за stowage; р. войск по кварти́рам quartering, billeting of troops; р. вооружённых сил stationing of armed forces; р. промы́шленности location of industry. 2. (*fin.*) placing, investment; р. за́йма floating a loan.

размина́|ть(ся), ю(сь), *impf. of* размя́ть(ся).

размини́ровани|е, я, *n.* (*mil.*) mine clearing.

размини́р|овать, ую, *pf.* to clear of mines.

размина́|ть(ся)... размини́нк|а, и, *f.* (*sport*) limbering-up.

размин|у́ться, у́сь, ёшься, *pf.* (*coll.*) 1. (*c+i.*) to pass (*without meeting*); to miss; когда́ я вошёл, никого́ не́ было; мы должно́-быть ~у́лись с ним на доро́ге when I went in there was no one there; we must have passed one another on the road. 2. (*of letters*) to cross. 3. to (be able to) pass; на э́том уча́стке доро́ги маши́нам нельзя́ р. it is impossible for cars to pass on this part of the road.

размнож|а́ть(ся), а́ю, ает(ся), *impf. of* ~ить(ся).

размноже́ни|е, я, *n.* 1. reproduction in quantity; duplicating; mimeographing. 2. (*biol.*) reproduction, propagation.

размно́ж|ить, у, ишь, *pf.* (*of* ~а́ть) 1. to multiply (copies of), manifold, duplicate; to mimeograph. 2. to breed, rear.

размно́ж|иться, ится, *pf.* (*of* ~а́ться) 1. (*biol.*) to propagate itself; to breed; to spawn. 2. *pass. of* ~ить.

размозж|и́ть, у́, и́шь, *pf.* to smash.

размок|а́ть, а́ет, *impf. of* ~нуть.

размо́к|нуть, нет, *past* ~, ~ла, *pf.* (*of* ~а́ть) to get soaked; to get sodden.

размо́л, а, *m.* 1. grinding. 2. quality (*of ground grain*); мука́ кру́пного, ме́лкого ~а coarse, coarse-ground flour; fine, finely ground flour.

размо́лвк|а, и, *f.* tiff, disagreement.

раз|моло́ть, мелю́, ме́лешь, *pf.* (*of* размалывать) to grind.

размора́жива|ть(ся), ю(сь), *impf. of* разморозить(ся).

размор|и́ть, и́т, *pf.* (*of* разма́ривать) (*coll.*) to exhaust; её ~и́ло на со́лнце (*impers.*) the sun was too much for her.

размор|и́ться, ю́сь, и́шься, *pf.* (*of* разма́риваться) (*coll.*) to be worn out.

разморо́|зить, жу, зишь, *pf.* (*of* размора́живать) to unfreeze, de-freeze (*frozen foods*); to de-frost (*a refrigerator*).

разморо́|зиться, жусь, зишься, *pf.* (*of* размора́живаться) to become unfrozen, de-frozen; to become de-frosted.

размота́|ть, ю, *pf.* (*of* разма́тывать) to unwind, uncoil, unreel.

размота́|ться, ется, *pf.* (*of* разма́тываться) to unwind, uncoil, unreel; to come unwound.

размоч|и́ть, у́, ~ишь, *pf.* (*of* разма́чивать) to soak, steep.

размусо́лива|ть, ю, *impf. of* размусо́лить.

размусо́л|ить, ю, ишь, *pf.* (*of* ~ивать) (*coll.*) 1. to slobber all over. 2. (*fig.*) to relate in a drivelling fashion.

размы́в, а, *m.* wash-out, erosion.

размыва́|ть, ю, *impf. of* размы́ть.

размыка́ни|е, я, *n.* (*electr.*) breaking, break, disconnection.

размы́ка|ть, ю, *pf.* (*coll.*) to shake off; р. го́ре (*poet.*) to shake off one's grief.

размыка́|ть, ю, *impf. of* разомкну́ть.

размы́сл|ить, ю, ишь, *pf.* (*of* размышля́ть) (о+*p.*) to reflect (on, upon), meditate (on, upon), ponder (over), muse (on, upon), turn over in one's mind.

разм|ы́ть, о́ю, о́ешь, *pf.* (*of* ~ыва́ть) to wash away; (*geol.*) to erode.

размышле́ни|е, я, *n.* reflection, meditation, thought; тяжёлые ~я brooding; по зре́лом ~и on second thoughts, on reflection; быть погружённым в ~я to be lost in thought.

размышля́|ть, ю, *impf. of* размы́слить.

размягч|а́ть(ся), а́ю(сь), *impf. of* ~и́ть(ся).

размягче́ни|е, я, *n.* softening; р. мо́зга (*med.*) softening of the brain.

размягч|и́ть, у́, и́шь, *pf.* (*of* ~а́ть) to soften.

размягч|и́ться, у́сь, и́шься, *pf.* (*of* ~а́ться) to soften, grow soft.

размя́к|нуть, ну, нешь, *past* ~, ~ла, *pf. of* мя́кнуть.

раз|мя́ть, омну́, омнёшь, *pf.* (*of* мять *and* ~мина́ть) 1. to knead; to mash (*potatoes, etc.*). 2. р. но́ги (*coll.*) to stretch one's legs.

раз|мя́ться, омну́сь, омнёшься, *pf.* (*of* ~мина́ться) 1. to grow soft (*as result of kneading*). 2. (*coll.*) to stretch one's legs; (*sport*) to limber up, loosen up.

разна́шива|ть(ся), ю, ет(ся), *impf. of* разноси́ть(ся)[1].

разнёжива|ть(ся), ю(сь), *impf. of* разнё-жить(ся).

разнёж|ить, у, ишь, *pf.* (*of* ~ивать) (*coll.*) to appeal to the tender feelings (of).

разнёж|иться, усь, ишься, *pf.* (*of* ~иваться) (*coll., pejor.*) to grow soft, become too soft.

разнемо́|чься, гу́сь, ~жешься, ~гутся, *past* ~гся, ~гла́сь, *pf.* (*coll.*) to become ill, be taken ill.

разнес|ти́, у́, ёшь, *past* ~, ~ла́, *pf.* (*of* разноси́ть[2]) 1. to carry, convey; to take round; р. газе́ты to deliver newspapers; р. слух to spread a rumour. 2. to enter, note down; р. цита́ты на ка́рточки to note down quotations on cards. 3. to smash, break up. 4. to scatter, disperse. 5. (*coll.*) to cause to swell; его́ щёку ~ло́ (*impers.*) his cheek is swollen. 6. (*fig., coll.*) to blow up.

разнес|ти́сь, ётся, *past* ~ся, ~ла́сь, *pf.* (*of* разноси́ться[2]) 1. to spread. 2. to resound.

разнима́|ть, ю, *impf. of* разня́ть.

ра́зн|иться, юсь, ишься, *impf.* to differ.

ра́зниц|а, ы, *f.* difference; disparity; кака́я р.? (*coll.*) what difference does it make?

разнобо́|й, я, *m.* lack of co-ordination; difference, disagreement.

разнове́с, а, *m.* (*collect.*) set of weights.

разнови́дност|ь, и, *f.* variety.

разновре́менный, *adj.* taking place at different times.

разногла́си|е, я, *n.* 1. difference, disagreement; р. во взгля́дах difference of opinion. 2. discrepancy; р. в показа́ниях conflicting evidence.

разноголо́сиц|а, ы, *f.* discordance, dissonance (*also fig., coll.*); р. во мне́ниях dissent.

разноголо́сый, *adj.* discordant.

разнокали́берный, *adj.* 1. (*mil.*) of different calibres. 2. (*fig., coll.*) mixed, heterogeneous.

разнома́стный, *adj.* 1. of different colours. 2. (*cards*) of different suits.

разномы́сли|е, я, *n.* difference of opinion(s).

разнообра́зи|е, я, *n.* variety, diversity; для ~я for a change.

разнообра́|зить, жу, зишь, *impf.* to vary, diversify.

разнообра́зност|ь, и, *f.* = разнообра́зие.

разнообра́з|ный (~ен, ~на), *adj.* various, varied, diverse.

разноплемённый, *adj.* of different races, tribes.

разнорабо́ч|ий, его, *m.* unskilled labourer.

разноречи́в|ый (~, ~а), *adj.* contradictory, conflicting.

разноре́чи|е, я, *n.* (*obs.*) contradiction.

разноро́дност|ь, и, *f.* heterogeneity.

разноро́д|ный (~ен, ~на), *adj.* heterogeneous.

разно́с, а, *m.* 1. carrying; delivery (*of mail, etc.*). 2. (*fig., coll.*) blowing-up.

разно|си́ть[1], шу́, ~сишь, *pf.* (*of* разна́шивать) to wear in (*footwear*).

разно|си́ть[2], шу́, ~сишь, *impf. of* разнести́.

разно|си́ться[1], ~сится, *pf.* (*of* разна́шиваться) (*of footwear*) to become comfortable.

разно|си́ться[2], ~сится, *impf. of* разнести́(сь).

разно́ск|а, и, *f.* delivery.

разносклоня́емый, *adj.* (*gram.*) irregularly declined.

разно́сн|ый[1], *adj.* ~ая кни́га delivery book; ~ая торго́вля street-trading, street-hawking.

разно́сн|ый[2], *adj.* (*coll.*) abusive; ~ая реце́нзия slashing review; ~ые слова́ swear-words.

разносо́л, а, *m.* (*cul.*) 1. (*obs.*) pickle(s). 2. (*pl. only*) (*coll.*) dainties, delicacies.

разноспряга́емый, *adj.* (*gram.*) irregularly conjugated.

разносторо́н|ний, *adj.* 1. (*math.*) scalene. 2. (~ен, ~ня) (*fig.*) many-sided; versatile; ~нее образова́ние all-round education.

разносторо́нност|ь, и, *f.* versatility.

ра́зност|ь, и, *f.* 1. (*math.*) difference. 2. difference, diversity; ра́зные ~и (*coll.*) this and that.

разно́счик, а, *m.* pedlar, hawker; barrow boy.

разнохара́ктер|ный (~ен, ~на), *adj.* diverse, varied.

разноцве́тный, *adj.* of different colours; many-coloured, variegated, motley.

разночи́н|ец, ца, *m.* (*hist.*) raznochinets (*in 19th century, Russian intellectual not of gentle birth*).

разночи́н|ный, *adj. of* ~ец.

разночте́ни|е, я, *n.* (*philol.*) variant reading.

разношёрст|ный (~ен, ~на), *adj.* **1.** (*of animals*) with coats of different colour. **2.** (*fig., coll.*) mixed; ill-assorted.

разошёрст|ый, *adj.* = ~ный.

разноязы́чный, *adj.* polyglot.

разну́зд|анный, *p.p.p. of* ~а́ть *and adj.* unbridled, unruly.

разнузд|а́ть, а́ю, *pf.* (*of* ~ывать) to unbridle.

разну́здыва|ть, ю, *impf. of* разнузда́ть.

ра́зн|ый, *adj.* **1.** different, differing. **2.** various, diverse; ~ого ро́да of various kinds; *as noun* ~ое, ~ого, *n.* (*on agenda of meeting, etc.*) any other business.

разню́х|ать, аю, *pf.* (*of* ~ивать) (*coll.*) to smell out (*also fig.*); (*fig.*) to nose out, ferret out.

разню́хива|ть, ю, *impf. of* разню́хать.

раз|ня́ть, ниму́, ни́мешь, *past* ~ня́л (*and* ро́знял), ~няла́, ~ня́ло (*and* ро́зняло), *pf.* (*of* ~нима́ть) **1.** to take to pieces, dismantle, disjoint. **2.** to part, separate (*persons fighting*).

разоби́|деть, жу, дишь, *pf.* (*coll.*) to offend greatly; to put someone's back up properly.

разоби́|деться, жусь, дишься, *pf.* (*coll.*) to take offence.

разоблач|а́ть(ся), а́ю(сь), *impf. of* ~и́ть(ся).

разоблаче́ни|е, я, *n.* exposure, unmasking.

разоблачи́тел|ь, я, *m.* unmasker.

разоблач|и́ть, у́, и́шь, *pf.* (*of* ~а́ть) **1.** (*eccl. or joc.*) to disrobe, divest. **2.** (*fig.*) to expose, unmask.

разоблач|и́ться, у́сь, и́шься, *pf.* (*of* ~а́ться) **1.** (*eccl. or joc.*) to disrobe. **2.** (*fig.*) to be exposed, be unmasked.

раз|обра́ть, беру́, берёшь, *past* ~обра́л, ~обрала́, ~обра́ло, *pf.* (*of* ~бира́ть) **1.** to take to pieces, strip, dismantle; р. дом to pull down a house. **2.** to buy up, take. **3.** to sort out. **4.** to investigate, look into; р. де́ло (*leg.*) to hear a case. **5.** (*gram.*) to parse; to analyse. **6.** to make out, understand; я не могу́ р. его́ по́черк I cannot make out his handwriting; мы не мо́жем р., в чём де́ло we cannot understand what it is all about. **7.** (*fig., coll.*) to fill (with), seize (with); её ~обрала́ ре́вность she was filled with jealousy.

раз|обра́ться, беру́сь, берёшься, *past* ~обра́лся, ~обрала́сь, ~обра́лось, *pf.* (*of* ~бира́ться) **1.** (*coll.*) to unpack. **2.** (в+*p.*) to investigate, look into; to understand; р. в пчелово́дстве to know about bee-keeping; я в нём не ~обра́лся I could not make him out.

разобщ|а́ть(ся), а́ю(сь), *impf. of* ~и́ть(ся).

разобще́ни|е, я, *n.* disconnection, uncoupling.

разобщённо, *adv.* apart, separately; де́йствовать р. to act independently.

разобщи́тел|ь, я, *m.* (*tech.*) disconnector.

разобщ|и́ть, у́, и́шь, *pf.* (*of* ~а́ть) **1.** to separate; (*fig.*) to estrange, alienate. **2.** (*tech.*) to disconnect, uncouple, disengage.

разобщ|и́ться, у́сь, и́шься, *pf.* (*of* ~а́ться) **1.** (*tech.*) to become disconnected. **2.** *pass. of* ~и́ть.

ра́зовый, *adj.* valid for one occasion (only).

раз|огна́ть, гоню́, го́нишь, *past* ~огна́л, ~огна́ла, ~огна́ло, *pf.* (*of* ~гоня́ть) **1.** to drive away; to disperse; (*fig.*) to dispel; р. демонстра́цию to break up a demonstration; р. го́ре to dispel grief. **2.** (*coll.*) to drive at high speed, race. **3.** (*typ.*) to space.

раз|огна́ться, гоню́сь, го́нишься, *past* ~огна́лся, ~огнала́сь, ~огна́ло́сь, *pf.* (*of* ~гоня́ться) to gather speed; to gather momentum.

разогн|у́ть, у́, ёшь, *pf.* (*of* разгиба́ть) to unbend, straighten; р. спи́ну to straighten one's back.

разогн|у́ться, у́сь, ёшься, *pf.* (*of* разгиба́ться) to straighten oneself up.

разогре́в, а, *m.* (*tech.*) initial heating; firing (*of furnace*).

разогрева́ни|е, я, *n.* warming-up.

разогрева́|ть(ся), ю(сь), *impf. of* разогре́ть(ся).

разогре́|ть, ю, *pf.* (*of* ~ва́ть) to warm up.

разогре́|ться, юсь, *pf.* (*of* ~ва́ться) to warm up, grow warm.

разоде́т|ый, *p.p.p. of* ~ь *and adj.* dressed up; весь р. all dressed up, in one's best bib and tucker.

разоде́|ть, ну, нешь, *pf.* (*coll.*) to dress up.

разоде́|ться, нусь, нешься, *pf.* (*coll.*) to dress up; р. в пух и прах to be dressed to kill.

разодолж|а́ть, а́ю, *impf. of* ~и́ть.

разодолж|и́ть, у́, и́шь, *pf.* (*of* ~а́ть) (*coll.*) to give a nasty surprise.

раз|одра́ть, деру́, дерёшь, *past* ~одра́л, ~одрала́, ~одра́ло, *pf.* (*of* ~дира́ть) to tear up.

раз|одра́ться, дерётся, *past* ~одра́лся, ~одрала́сь, ~одра́ло́сь, *pf.* (*of* ~дира́ться) (*coll.*) to tear.

разозл|и́ть, ю, и́шь, *pf.* (*of* злить) to make angry, enrage.

разозл|и́ться, юсь, и́шься, *pf.* (*of* зли́ться) to get angry, get in a rage.

раз|ойти́сь, ойду́сь, ойдёшься, *past* ~ошёлся, ~ошла́сь, *pf.* (*of* расходи́ться) **1.** to go away; to disperse; толпа́ ~ошла́сь the crowd broke up; ту́чи ~ошли́сь the clouds dispersed. **2.** (с+*i.*) to part (from), separate (from), to get divorced (from); мы ~ошли́сь друзья́ми we parted friends; он ~ошёлся с жено́й he has separated from his wife. **3.** to branch off, diverge; to radiate. **4.** to pass (*without meeting*). **5.** (c+*i*.) to be at variance (with), conflict (with); р. во мне́нии с кем-н. to disagree with someone. **6.** to dissolve; to melt. **7.** to be sold out; to be spent; (*of a book*) to be out of print; все де́ньги ~ошли́сь all the money has been spent. **8.** (*coll.*) to gather speed. **9.** (*coll.*) to let oneself go, fly off the handle; бу́ря ~ошла́сь the storm raged.

раз|о́к, ка́, *m.* (*coll.*) *dim. of* ~; ещё р. once more; р. друго́й once or twice.

ра́зом, *adv.* (*coll.*) at once, at one go.

разо́мкн|утый, *p.p.p. of* ~у́ть *and adj.*; р. строй (*mil.*) open order.

разомкн|у́ть, у́, ёшь, *pf.* (*of* размыка́ть) to open, unfasten; (*tech.*) to break, disconnect.

разомле́|ть, ю, *pf.* (*coll.*) to languish, grow languid.

разонра́в|иться, люсь, ишься, *pf.* (*coll.*; +*d.*) to cease to please, lose its attraction (for).

разопрева́|ть, ю, *impf. of* разопре́ть.

разопре́|ть, ю, *pf.* (*of* ~ва́ть) **1.** to become soft (*in cooking*). **2.** (*coll.*) to be worn out, done in (*from heat*).

разо́р, а, *m.* (*coll.*) ruin, destruction.

разор|а́ться, у́сь, ёшься, *pf.* (*coll.*) to become uproarious, raise a hullabaloo.

разорв|а́ть, у́, ёшь, *past* ~а́л, ~ала́, ~а́ло, *pf.* (*of* разрыва́ть¹) **1.** to tear (to pieces); р. кого́-н. на ча́сти (*fig., coll.*) to wear someone out (*with requests, entreaties, etc.*). **2.** (*impers.*) to blow up, burst; котёл ~а́ло the boiler has burst. **3.** (*fig.*) to break (off), sever; р. дипломати́ческие сноше́ния to break off diplomatic relations.

разорв|а́ться, ётся, *past* ~а́лся, ~ала́сь, ~а́лось, *pf.* (*of* разрыва́ться) **1.** to break, snap; to tear, become torn. **2.** to blow up, burst; to explode, go off. **3.** (*coll.*; *usu.*+*neg.*) to be everywhere at once; я не могу́ р. I can't be everywhere at once, I can't do half a dozen things at once; хоть ~и́сь! hold hard!, give us a chance!

разоре́ни|е, я, *n.* destruction, ravage; ruin.

разори́тел|ьный (~ен, ~ьна), *adj.* ruinous; wasteful.

разор|и́ть, ю́, и́шь, *pf.* (*of* ~я́ть) **1.** to destroy, ravage. **2.** to ruin, bring to ruin.

разор|и́ться, ю́сь, и́шься, *pf.* (*of* ~я́ться) to ruin oneself; to be ruined.

разоруж|а́ть(ся), а́ю(сь), *impf. of* ~и́ть(ся).

разоруже́ни|е, я, *n.* disarmament.

разоруж|и́ть, у́, и́шь, *pf.* (*of* ~а́ть) to disarm; (*naut.*) to dismantle, unrig.

разоруж|и́ться, у́сь, и́шься, *pf.* (*of* ~а́ться) to disarm.

разор|я́ть(ся), я́ю(сь), *impf. of* ~и́ть(ся).

разо|сла́ть, шлю́, шлёшь, *pf.* (*of* рассыла́ть) **1.** to send round, distribute, circulate; р. листо́вки to distribute leaflets. **2.** to send out, despatch.

разосп|а́ться, лю́сь, и́шься, *past* ~а́лся, ~ала́сь, ~а́лось, *pf.* (*coll.*) to be fast asleep; to oversleep.

разостла́ть (and расстели́ть), расстелю́, рассте́лешь, *pf.* (*of* расстила́ть) to spread (out), lay.

разостла́|ться (and расстели́ться), рассте́лется, *pf.* (*of* расстила́ться) to spread; тума́н ~лся по всей сте́пи fog spread over the whole steppe.

разохо́|тить, чу, тишь, *pf.* (к, на+*a.*; *coll.*) to stimulate (to), arouse an inclination (to, for).

разохо́|титься, чусь, тишься, *pf.* (+*inf.*; *coll.*) to take a liking (to), feel an inclination (for); сперва́ он не хоте́л танцева́ть, а тепе́рь ~тился he did not want to go to the dance at first, but now he is keen to go.

разочаро́вани|е, я, *n.* disappointment.

разочаро́в|анный, *p.p.p. of* ~а́ть *and adj.* disappointed, disillusioned.

разочар|ова́ть, у́ю, *pf.* (*of* ~о́вывать) to disappoint.

разочар|ова́ться, у́юсь, *pf.* (*of* ~о́вываться) (в ком-н., в чём-н.) to be disappointed (in someone, with something).

разочаро́выва|ть(ся), ю(сь), *impf. of* разочарова́ть(ся).

разраба́тыва|ть, ю, *impf. of* разрабо́тать.

разрабо́та|ть, ю, *pf.* (*of* разраба́тывать) **1.** (*agric.*) to cultivate. **2.** (*mining*) to work, exploit. **3.** to work out, work up; to develop; to elaborate; р. вопро́с to work up a subject; р. го́лос to develop a voice; р. ме́тоды to devise methods; р. пла́ны to work out plans.

разрабо́тк|а, и, *f.* **1.** (*agric.*) cultivation. **2.** (*mining*) working, exploitation; откры́тая р. open-cast mining. **3.** field; pit, working; р. сла́нца slate quarry. **4.** working out, working up; elaboration.

разра́внива|ть, ю, *impf. of* разровня́ть.

разража́|ться, юсь, *impf. of* разрази́ться.

разра|зи́ться, жу́сь, зи́шься, *pf.* (*of* ~жа́ться) (*of a storm, etc.*) to break out, burst out; р. слеза́ми to burst into tears; р. сме́хом to burst out laughing.

разраст|а́ться, а́ется, *impf. of* ~и́сь.

разраст|и́сь, ётся, *past* разро́сся, разросла́сь, *pf.* (*of* ~а́ться) to grow (up) (*also fig.*); to spread; to grow thickly; де́ло разросло́сь the business has grown; но́вый посёлок разро́сся a new estate has grown up.

разрев|е́ться, у́сь, ёшься, *pf.* (*coll.*) to raise a howl, start howling.

разре|ди́ть, жу́, ди́шь, *pf.* (*of* ~жа́ть) **1.** to thin out, weed out. **2.** to rarefy.

разрежа́|ть, ю, *impf. of* разреди́ть.

разре|жённый, *p.p.p. of* ~ди́ть *and adj.* (*phys.*) rarefied, rare; ~жённый во́здух rarefied air.

разре́з, а, *m.* **1.** cut; slit. **2.** section; попере́чный р. cross-section; продо́льный р. longitudinal section; р. глаз shape of one's eyes. **3.** (*fig., coll.*) point of view; в ~е (+*g.*) from the point of view (of), in the context (of).

разре́|зать, жу, жешь, *pf.* (*of* ~за́ть) to cut; to slit.

разрез|а́ть, а́ю, *impf. of* ~ать.

разрезн|о́й, *adj.* **1.** cutting; р. нож paper--knife; ~а́я пила́ rip saw. **2.** slit, with slits; ~а́я ю́бка slit skirt.

разреш|а́ть, а́ю, *impf. of* ~и́ть.

разреш|а́ться, а́юсь, *impf.* **1.** *impf. of* ~и́ться. **2.** *impf. only* to be allowed; здесь кури́ть не ~а́ется no smoking (is allowed here).

разреше́ни|е, я, *n.* **1.** permission; с ва́шего ~я with your permission, by your leave. **2.** permit, authorization; р. на въезд entry permit. **3.** solution (*of a problem*). **4.** settlement (*of a dispute*). **5.** (*med.*) resolution; р. от бре́мени (*obs.*) delivery.

разреши́м|ый (~, ~а), *adj.* solvable.

разреш|и́ть, у́, и́шь, *pf.* (*of* ~а́ть) **1.** (+*d.*) to allow, permit; ~и́те пройти́ allow me to pass; do you mind letting me pass? **2.** to authorize; р. кни́гу к печа́ти to authorize the printing of a book. **3.** (от; *obs.*) to release (from); (*eccl.*) to absolve (from), give dispensation (from); р. кого́-н. от обяза́тельства to release someone from an obligation; р. от поста́ to give dispensation from a fast. **4.** to solve (*a problem*). **5.** to settle; р. сомне́ния to resolve doubts.

разреш|и́ться, у́сь, и́шься, *pf.* (*of* ~а́ться) **1.** to be solved. **2.** to be settled. **3.** (от бре́мени) (+*i.*; *obs.*) to be delivered (of); она́ ~и́лась де́вочкой she was delivered of a girl.

разрис|ова́ть, у́ю, *pf.* (*of* ~о́вывать) **1.** to cover with drawings. **2.** (*fig.*) to paint a picture (of).

разрисо́выва|ть, ю, *impf. of* разрисова́ть.

разровня́|ть, ю, *pf.* (*of* разра́внивать) to level.

разро́зн|енный, *p.p.p. of* ~ить *and adj.* **1.** unco-ordinated. **2.** odd; р. компле́кт broken set, set made up of odd parts; ~енные тома́ odd volumes.

разро́знива|ть, ю, *impf. of* разро́знить.

разро́зн|ить, ю, ишь, *pf.* (*of* ~ивать) to break a set (of).

разруб|а́ть, а́ю, *impf. of* ~и́ть.

разруб|и́ть, лю́, ~ишь, *pf.* (*of* ~а́ть) to cut, cleave; р. го́рдиев у́зел to cut the Gordian knot.

разруга́|ть, ю, *pf.* (*coll.*) to berate; to blow up.

разруга́|ться, юсь, *pf.* (с+*i.*; *coll.*) to quarrel (with).

разрумя́нива|ть(ся), ю(сь), *impf. of* разрумя́нить(ся).

разрумя́н|ить, ю, ишь, *pf.* (*of* ~ивать) **1.** to rouge. **2.** to flush, redden; моро́з ~ил её щёки the frost brought a flush to her cheeks.

разрумя́н|иться, юсь, ишься, *pf.* (*of* ~иваться) **1.** to put rouge on. **2.** to blush; to be flushed.

разру́х|а, и, *f.* ruin, collapse; привести́ хозя́йство к ~е to dislocate the economy.

разруш|а́ть(ся), а́ю, а́ет(ся), *impf. of* ~ить(ся).

разруше́ни|е, я, *n.* destruction; (*pl.*) havoc.

разруши́тел|ьный (~ен, ~ьна), *adj.* destructive.

разру́ш|ить, у, ишь, *pf.* (*of* ~а́ть) **1.** to destroy; to demolish, wreck; to ruin (*also fig.*). **2.** (*fig.*) to frustrate, blast, blight; р. чьи-н. наде́жды to blight someone's hopes.

разру́ш|иться, ится, *pf.* (*of* ~а́ться) **1.** to go to ruin, collapse; все их пла́ны ~ились all their plans have fallen to the ground. **2.** *pass. of* ~ить.

разры́в, а, *m.* **1.** (*in var. senses*) break; gap; rupture, severance; breach; р. ли́нии фро́нта (*mil.*) breach in the front line; р. дипломати́ческих отноше́ний rupture, severance of diplomatic relations; ме́жду ни́ми произошёл р. they have broken it off. **2.** (*shell*) burst, explosion.

разрыва́|ть¹, ю, *impf. of* разорва́ть.

разрыва́|ть², ю, *impf. of* разры́ть.

разрыва́|ться, юсь, *impf. of* разорва́ться.

разрывно́й, *adj.* explosive, bursting.

разр|ы́ть, о́ю, о́ешь, *pf.* (*of* ~ыва́ть²) **1.** to dig up. **2.** (*fig., coll.*) to turn upside-down, rummage through.

разрыхле́ни|е, я, *n.* loosening.

разрыхл|и́ть, ю, и́шь, *pf.* (*of* ~я́ть) to loosen; to hoe.

разрыхл|я́ть, я́ю, *impf. of* ~и́ть.

разря́д¹, а, *m.* discharge.

разря́д², а, *m.* category, rank; sort; (*sport*) class, rating; пе́рвого ~a first-class.

разря|ди́ть¹, жу́, ~ди́шь, *pf.* (*of* ~жа́ть) (*coll.*) to dress up.

разря|ди́ть², жу́, ди́шь, *pf.* (*of* ~жа́ть) **1.** (*electr.*) to discharge; р. атмосфе́ру (*fig.*) to relieve tension, clear the air. **2.** to unload (*a fire-arm*). **3.** (*typ.*) to space out.

разря|ди́ться¹, жу́сь, ~ди́шься, *pf.* (*of* ~жа́ться) to dress up, doll oneself up.

разря|ди́ться², ди́тся, *pf.* (*of* ~жа́ться) **1.** (*electr.*) to run down; (*fig.*) to clear, ease; атмосфе́ра ~ди́лась the atmosphere has become less tense. **2.** *pass. of* ~ди́ть².

разря́дк|а, и, *f.* **1.** discharging; unloading; р. напряжённости (*polit.*) lessening of tension, détente. **2.** (*typ.*) spacing (out).

разря́дник¹, а, *m.* (*electr.*) discharger; spark--gap.

разря́дник², а, *m.* (*sport*) player with official rating.

разря́д|ный, *adj. of* ~¹; ~ная ёмкость, ~ная мо́щность discharge capacity.

разряжа́|ть(ся), ю(сь), *impf. of* разряди́ть(ся).

разубе|ди́ть, жу́, ди́шь, *pf.* (*of* ~жда́ть) (в+*p.*) to dissuade (from), argue (out of); мы их ~ди́ли we have made them change their mind.

разубе|ди́ться, жу́сь, ди́шься, *pf.* (*of* ~жда́ться) (в+*p.*) to change one's mind (about), change one's opinion (about).

разубежда́|ть(ся), ю(сь), *impf. of* разубеди́ть(ся).

разува́|ть(ся), ю(сь), *impf. of* разу́ть(ся).

разуве́рени|е, я, *n.* dissuasion.

разуве́р|ить, ю, ишь, *pf.* (*of* ~ять) (в+*p.*) to undermine faith (in); to argue (out of).

разуве́р|иться, юсь, ишься, *pf.* (*of* ~яться) (в+*p.*) to lose faith (in).

разузна|ва́ть, ю́, ёшь, *impf.* **1.** *impf. of* разузна́ть, **2.** *impf. only* to make inquiries (about).

разузна́|ть, ю, *pf.* (*of* ~ва́ть) to find out.

разукра́|сить, шу, сишь, *pf.* (*of* ~шивать) to adorn, decorate, embellish.

разукра́|ситься, шусь, сишься, *pf.* (*of* ~шиваться) to adorn oneself, decorate oneself.

разукра́шива|ть(ся), ю|сь/, *impf. of* разукра́сить(ся).

разукрупн|и́ть, ю́, и́шь, *pf.* (*of* ~я́ть) to break up into smaller units.

разукрупн|и́ться, и́тся, *pf.* (*of* ~я́ться) to break up into smaller units.

разукрупн|я́ть(ся), я́ю, я́ет(ся), *impf. of* ~и́ть(ся).

ра́зум, а, *m.* reason; mind, intellect; у него́ ум за р. зашёл (*coll.*) he is, was at his wit's end.

разуме́ни|е, я, *n.* **1.** (*obs.*) understanding. **2.** opinion, viewpoint; по моему́ ~ю to my mind, as I see it.

разуме́|ть, ю, *impf.* **1.** (*obs.*) to understand. **2.** (под) to understand (by), mean (by).

разуме́|ться, ется, *impf.* to be understood, be meant; под э́тим ~ется... by this is meant . . .; (са́мо собо́й) ~ется it stands to reason; it goes without saying, of course; он, ~ется, не знал, что вы уже́ пришли́ he,

of course, did not know that you were already here.

разу́мник, а, *m.* (*coll.*) clever chap, clever boy.

разу́м|ный (~ен, ~на), *adj.* **1.** possessing reason. **2.** judicious, intelligent. **3.** reasonable; э́то (вполне́) ~но it is (perfectly) reasonable, that makes (good) sense.

разу́|ть, ю, ешь, *pf.* (*of* ~ва́ть); р. кого́-н. to take someone's shoes off.

разу́|ться, юсь, ешься, *pf.* (*of* ~ва́ться) to take one's shoes off.

разуха́бист|ый (~, ~а), *adj.* (*coll.*) **1.** rollicking. **2.** (*pejor.*) free-and-easy.

разучива|ть(ся), ю(сь), *impf. of* разучи́ть(ся).

разуч|и́ть, у́, ~ишь, *pf.* (*of* ~ивать) to learn (up); р. роль to learn, study one's part.

разуч|и́ться, у́сь, ~ишься, *pf.* (*of* ~иваться) (+*inf.*) to forget (how to), lose the art (of); я ~и́лся ходи́ть на лы́жах I have forgotten how to ski.

разъеда́|ть(ся), ю(сь), *impf. of* разъе́сть(ся).

разъедине́ни|е, я, *n.* **1.** separation. **2.** (*electr.*) disconnection, breaking.

разъедини́тел|ь, я, *m.* (*electr.*) disconnecting switch, cut-out switch.

разъедин|и́ть, ю́, и́шь, *pf.* (*of* ~я́ть) **1.** to separate. **2.** (*electr.*) to disconnect, break; нас ~и́ли we were cut off (*on telephone*).

разъедин|и́ться, ю́сь, и́шься, *pf.* (*of* ~я́ться) **1.** to separate, part. **2.** *pass. of* ~и́ть.

разъедин|я́ть(ся), я́ю(сь), *impf. of* ~и́ть(ся).

разъе́зд, а, *m.* **1.** departure; dispersal. **2.** (*pl.*) travel, journeyings. **3.** (*mil.*) mounted patrol. **4.** section of double track (*on single-line railway*); station, halt (*on single--line railway*).

разъездн|о́й, *adj.* р. аге́нт (*obs.*) traveller, travelling representative; ~ые де́ньги travelling expenses; р. путь (*railway*) siding.

разъезжа́|ть, ю, *impf.* to drive (about, around), ride (about, around); to travel; р. по дела́м слу́жбы to travel about on business.

разъезжа́|ться, юсь, *impf. of* разъе́хаться.

разъе́|сть, ст, дя́т, *past* ~л, *pf.* (*of* ~да́ть) to eat away; to corrode (*also fig.*); его́ ~ли сомне́ния he was consumed with doubts.

разъе́|сться, мся, шься, стся, ди́мся, ди́тесь, дя́тся, *past* ~лся, *pf.* (*of* ~да́ться) (*coll.*) to get fat (*from good living*).

разъе́|хаться, дусь, дешься, *pf.* (*of* ~зжа́ться) **1.** to depart; to disperse; прие́хавшие на по́хороны ~хались the mourners have departed. **2.** to separate, cease living together. **3.** to (be able to) pass; тут грузовика́м нельзя́ р. it is impossible for lorries to pass here. **4.** to pass one another (*without meeting*), miss one another. **5.** (*coll.*) to slide apart. **6.** (*coll.*) to fall to pieces, fall apart.

разъяр|и́ть, ю́, и́шь, *pf.* (*of* ~я́ть) to infuriate, rouse to fury.

разъяр|и́ться, ю́сь, и́шься, *pf.* (*of* ~я́ться) to become furious, get into a fury.

разъяр|я́ть(ся), я́ю(сь), *impf. of* ~и́ть(ся).

разъясне́ни|е, я, n. explanation, elucidation; interpretation.

разъясни́тельный, *adj.* explanatory, elucidatory.

разъясн|и́ть, и́т, *pf.* (*coll.*) (*impers.*) to clear up (*of the weather*).

разъясн|и́ть, ю́, и́шь, *pf.* (*of* ~я́ть) to explain, elucidate; to interpret.

разъясн|и́ться, и́тся, *pf.* = ~и́ть.

разъясн|и́ться, и́тся, *pf.* (*of* ~я́ться) to become clear, be cleared up.

разъясн|я́ть(ся), я́ю, я́ет(ся), *impf. of* ~и́ть(ся).

разыгр|а́ть, а́ю, *pf.* (*of* ~ывать) **1.** to play (through); to perform; р. дурака́ to play the fool. **2.** to draw (*a lottery, etc.*); to raffle. **3.** (*coll.*) to play a trick (on), play a practical joke (on).

разыгр|а́ться, а́юсь, *pf.* (*of* ~ываться) **1.** to be carried away by a game, by play. **2.** (*of a pianist, an actor, etc.*) to warm up. **3.** (*of wind or sea*) to rise; to get up; (*of a storm*) to break; (*fig.*; *of feelings*) to run high.

разы́грыва|ть(ся), ю(сь), *impf. of* разыгра́ть(ся) 2, 3.

разы|ска́ть, щу́, ~щешь, *pf.* to find (after searching).

разы|ска́ться, щу́сь, ~щешься, *pf.* **1.** (*impf.* ~скиваться) to be sought for. **2.** to turn up, be found.

разы́скива|ть, ю, *impf.* to look for, search for.

разы́скива|ться, юсь, *impf. of* разыска́ться; р. поли́цией to be wanted by the police.

ра|й, я, о ~е, в ~ю́, m. (*bibl.*) paradise; (Garden of) Eden; земно́й р., р. земно́й (*fig.*) earthly paradise.

рай- *abbr. of* райо́нный.

райко́м¹, a, m. (*abbr. of* райо́нный комите́т) raion committee, district committee.

райко́м², i. sing. of раёк.

райо́н, a, m. 1. region; area; zone. **2.** (*designation of administrative division of U.S.S.R.*) raion, district.

райони́ровани|е, я, n. 1. division into districts. **2.** earmarking for a given area; zoning.

райони́р|овать, ую, *impf. and pf.* **1.** to divide into districts. **2.** to earmark for a given area; to zone.

райо́н|ный, adj. of ~.

ра́й|ский, adj. of ~; (*fig.*) heavenly; ~ская пти́ца bird of paradise.

райсове́т, a, m. (*abbr. of* райо́нный сове́т) raion soviet, district soviet.

рак, a, m. 1. (*zool.*) crawfish, crayfish; кра́сный как р. red as a lobster; показа́ть, где ~и зиму́ют (*coll.*) to give it someone hot; знать, где ~и зиму́ют (*coll.*) to know a thing or two, know what's what. **2.** (*med.*) cancer; (*bot.*) canker. **3.** P. (*astron.*) Crab, Cancer; тро́пик ~a (*geogr.*) Tropic of Cancer.

ра́к|a, и, f. (*eccl.*) shrine (*of a saint*).

раке́т|a¹, ы, f. 1. (air-)rocket; flare; пусти́ть ~y to let off a rocket. **2.** (*mil.*) rocket, ballistic missile; межконтинента́льная р. inter-continental ballistic missile (ICBM). **3.** (*outer-space*) rocket. **4.** (*coll.*) hydrofoil (vessel).

раке́т|a², ы, f. = ~ка.

раке́т|ка, ки, f. (*sport*) racket.

раке́тниц|a, ы, f. rocket projector; Very pistol, signal pistol.

раке́тный¹, adj. rocket(-powered), jet; р. дви́гатель rocket engine, jet engine.

раке́т|ный², adj. of ~a².

раке́тчик, a, m. 1. rocket signaller. **2.** missile specialist.

раки́т|a, ы, f. (*bot.*) brittle willow.

раки́тник, a, m. broom (*bush*); broom plantation.

ра́ковин|a, ы, f. 1. shell; ушна́я р. (*anat.*) helix. **2.** sink; wash-basin. **3.** (*in metal*) blister, bubble; уса́дочная р. air hole, blow hole.

ра́к|овый, adj. of ~; (*med.*) cancerous; ~овая о́пухоль cancerous tumour.

ракообра́зн|ые, ых, sing. ~ое, ~ого, n. (*zool.*) Crustacea.

ракообра́зный, adj. (*zool.*) cancroid.

раку́рс, a, m. (*art*) foreshortening; в ~e foreshortened.

раку́шечник, a, m. (*geol.*) coquina, shell rock.

раку́шк|a, и, f. cockle-shell; mussel.

ра́м|a, ы, f. 1. frame; око́нная р. window-frame, sash; вста́вить в ~y to frame. **2.** chassis, carriage.

рам|ена́, е́н, ена́м, no sing. (*arch. or poet.*) shoulders.

ра́мен|ь, и, f. (*dial.*) coniferous forest.

ра́мен|ье, ья, n. = ~ь.

ра́мк|a, и, f. frame; в ~e framed; без ~и unframed; объявле́ние о сме́рти в тра́урной ~e black-bordered obituary announcement.

ра́м|ки, ок, (pl. only) framework; limits; в ~ках (+g.) within the framework (of), within the limits (of); вы́йти за р. (+g.) to exceed the limits (of).

ра́м|ный, *adj. of* ~а.

ра́м|очный, *adj. of* ~ка; ~очная анте́нна loop aerial, frame aerial.

ра́мп|а, ы, *f.* (*theatr.*) footlights.

ра́н|а, ы, *f.* wound.

ранг, а, *m.* class, rank.

ранго́ут, а, *m.* (*naut.*) masts and spars.

ранго́ут|ный, *adj. of* ~; ~ное де́рево (*naut.*) spar.

ранево́й, *adj. of* ра́на.

ра́нее, *adv.* = ра́ньше.

ране́ни|е, я, *n.* **1.** wounding. **2.** wound; injury.

ра́нен|ый, *adj.* wounded; injured; *as noun* р., ~ого, *m.* wounded man; injured man.

ране́т, а, *m.* rennet (*kind of apple*).

ра́н|ец, ца, *m.* knapsack, haversack; satchel; (*mil.*) pack.

ранжи́р, а, *m.* по ~у (*coll.*) in order of size.

ра́н|ить, ю, ишь, *impf. and pf.* to wound; to injure.

ра́нн|ий, *adj.* early; ~им у́тром early in the morning; ~яя пти́чка (*fig.*) early bird; с ~его де́тства from early childhood; с ~их лет from (one's) earliest years.

ра́но¹, *pred.* it is early; ещё р. ложи́ться спать it is too early for bed.

ра́но², *adv.* early; р. и́ли по́здно sooner or later.

рант, а, о ~е, на ~у́, *m.* welt; сапоги́ на ~у́ welted boots.

рантье́, *indecl.*, *m.* rentier.

ран|ь, и, *f.* (*coll.*) early hour; куда́ ты направля́ешься в таку́ю р.? where are you bound for at this ungodly hour?

ра́ньше, *adv.* **1.** earlier; как мо́жно р. as early as possible; as soon as possible. **2.** before; до Ло́ндона он не дое́дет р. ве́чера he will not reach London before evening. **3.** first (of all). **4.** before, formerly; р. мы жи́ли в дере́вне we used to live in the country.

рапи́р|а, ы, *f.* foil.

ра́порт, а, *m.* report.

рапорт|ова́ть, у́ю, *impf. and pf.* to report.

рапс, а, *m.* (*bot.*) rape.

рапсо́ди|я, и, *f.* (*mus.*) rhapsody.

рарите́т, а, *m.* rarity, curiosity.

ра́с|а, ы, *f.* race.

раси́зм, а, *m.* racialism.

раси́ст, а, *m.* racialist.

раска́ива|ться, юсь, *impf. of* раска́яться.

раскал|ённый, *p.p.p. of* ~и́ть *and adj.* scorching, burning hot; р. добела́ white-hot; р. докрасна́ red-hot.

раскал|и́ть, ю́, и́шь, *pf.* (*of* ~я́ть) to bring to a great heat; р. добела́ to make white-hot; р. докрасна́ to make red-hot.

раскал|и́ться, ю́сь, и́шься, *pf.* (*of* ~я́ться) to glow, become hot; р. добела́ to become

white-hot; р. докрасна́ to become red-hot.

раска́лыва|ть(ся), ю(сь), *impf. of* расколо́ть(ся).

раскал|я́ть(ся), я́ю(сь), *impf. of* ~и́ть(ся).

раска́пыва|ть, ю, *impf. of* раскопа́ть.

раска́рмлива|ть, ю, *impf. of* раскорми́ть.

раскасси́р|овать, ую, *pf.* (*mil.*) to disband; (*fig.*) to wind up, liquidate.

раска́т, а, *m.* roll, peal; р. гро́ма peal of thunder.

раскат|а́ть, а́ю, *pf.* (*of* ~ывать) **1.** to unroll. **2.** to roll (out); to smooth out; to level; р. те́сто to roll out dough.

раскат|а́ться, а́юсь, *pf.* (*of* ~ываться) **1.** to unroll. **2.** to roll out.

раска́тист|ый (~, ~а), *adj.* rolling, booming; р. смех peal(s) of laughter.

раска|ти́ть, чу́, ~тишь, *pf.* (*of* ~тывать) **1.** to set rolling. **2.** to roll away.

раска|ти́ться, чу́сь, ~тишься, *pf.* (*of* ~тываться) **1.** to gather momentum. **2.** to roll away.

раска́тыва|ть, ю, *impf.* **1.** *impf. of* раската́ть *and* раскати́ть. **2.** (*coll.*) to drive (about, around), ride (about, around).

раска́тыва|ться, юсь, *impf. of* раската́ть-(ся) *and* раскати́ть(ся).

раскач|а́ть, а́ю, *pf.* (*of* ~ивать) **1.** to swing; to rock. **2.** to loosen, shake loose. **3.** (*fig.*, *coll.*) to shake up, stir up.

раскач|а́ться, а́юсь, *pf.* (*of* ~иваться) **1.** to swing (oneself); to rock (oneself). **2.** to shake loose. **3.** (*fig.*, *coll.*) to bestir oneself, get into the swing of.

раска́шля|ться, юсь, *pf.* to have a fit of coughing.

раска́яни|е, я, *n.* repentance.

раска́|яться, юсь, *pf.* (*of* ка́яться *and* ~ива-ться) (в+*p.*) to repent (of).

расквартирова́ни|е, я, *n.* quartering, billeting.

расквартир|ова́ть, у́ю, *pf.* (*of* ~о́вывать) to quarter, billet.

расквартиро́выва|ть, ю, *impf. of* расквартирова́ть.

расква́|сить, шу, сишь, *pf.* (*of* ~шивать) (*coll.*) to punch (*and draw blood from*); р. кому́-н. нос to give someone a bloody nose.

расква́шива|ть, ю, *impf. of* расква́сить.

расквита́|ться, юсь, *pf.* (с+*i.*; *coll.*) to settle accounts (with) (*also fig.*); (*fig.*) to get even (with).

раскида́|ть, а́ю, *pf.* (*of* ~ывать) to scatter; to throw about.

раски́дист|ый (~, ~а), *adj.* branchy, spreading.

раскидно́й, *adj.* folding.

раски́дыва|ть, ю, *impf. of* раскида́ть *and* раски́нуть.

раски́дыва|ться, юсь, *impf. of* раски́нуться.

раски́|нуть, ну, нешь, *pf.* (*of* ~дывать) 1. to stretch (out); р. ру́ки to stretch one's arms. 2. to spread (out); to set up; р. шатёр to pitch a tent. 3. р. умо́м to consider, think over.

раски́|нуться, нусь, нешься, *pf.* (*of* ~дываться) 1. to spread out, stretch out; по всему́ скло́ну холма́ ~нулось вое́нное кла́дбище the entire side of the hill was occupied by a military cemetery. 2. (*coll.*) to sprawl.

раскис|а́ть, а́ю, *impf. of* ~нуть.

раскисле́ни|е, я, *n.* (*chem.*) deoxidization.

раскисл|и́ть, ю́, и́шь, *pf.* (*of* ~я́ть) (*chem.*) to deoxidize, reduce.

раскисл|я́ть, я́ю, *impf. of* ~и́ть.

раски́с|нуть, ну, нешь, *past* ~, ~ла, *pf.* (*of* ~а́ть) 1. to rise (*from fermentation*). 2. (*fig., coll.*) to become limp.

раскла́дк|а, и, *f.* apportionment; going shares.

расклада́ушк|а, и, *f.* (*coll.*) folding bed, divan bed.

раскладн|о́й, *adj.* folding; ~а́я крова́ть camp-bed.

раскла́дыва|ть(ся), ю(сь), *impf. of* разложи́ть(ся)[1].

раскла́нива|ться, юсь, *impf. of* раскла́няться.

раскла́н|яться, яюсь, *pf.* (*of* ~иваться) 1. to exchange bows (*on meeting or leave-taking*). 2. to take leave (of).

расклеи́ва|ть(ся), ю(сь), *impf. of* расклеи́ть(ся).

расклеи́|ть, ю, ишь, *pf.* (*of* ~ивать) 1. to unstick. 2. to stick, paste (*in various places*).

расклеи́|ться, юсь, ишься, *pf.* (*of* ~иваться) 1. to come unstuck. 2. (*fig., coll.*) to fall through, fail to come off; сде́лка ~илась the deal fell through. 3. (*fig., coll.*) to feel seedy, be off colour; он совсе́м ~и́лся he has gone to pieces.

расклеи́к|а, и, *f.* sticking, pasting.

расклеи́щик, а, *m.* bill-sticker.

расклеп|а́ть, а́ю, *pf.* (*of* ~ывать) to unrivet, unclench.

расклёпыва|ть, ю, *impf. of* расклепа́ть.

раск|ова́ть, ую́, уёшь, *pf.* (*of* ~о́вывать) 1. to unchain, unfetter; to unshoe (*a horse*). 2. to hammer out, flatten; (*tech.*) to upset, jump (up).

раск|ова́ться, ую́сь, уёшься, *pf.* (*of* ~о́вываться) 1. (*of a horse*) to cast a shoe. 2. to free oneself (*from fetters*).

раско́выва|ть(ся), ю(сь), *impf. of* расковáть(ся).

расковы́р|ять, я́ю, *pf.* (*of* ~ивать) to pick open; to scratch raw.

раско́ка|ть, ю, *pf.* (*coll.*) to drop and break.

раско́л, а, *m.* 1. (*rel., hist.*) schism, dissent. 2. (*polit., etc.*) split, division.

раскола́чива|ть, ю, *impf. of* расколоти́ть.

расколо|ти́ть, чу́, ~ти́шь, *pf.* (*of* раскола́чивать) 1. to unnail; to prise open. 2. to stretch (*footwear*). 3. (*coll.*) to break; to smash (*crockery, etc.; fig., the enemy*).

раскол|о́ть, ю́, ~ешь, *pf.* 1. *pf. of* коло́ть[1]. 2. (*impf.* раскáлывать) (*fig.*) to disrupt, break up.

раскол|о́ться, ю́сь, ~ешься, *pf.* (*of* раскáлываться) to split (*also fig.*).

раско́льник, а, *m.* 1. (*rel., hist.*) schismatic, dissenter. 2. (*polit.; fig.*) splitter.

раско́льническ|ий, *adj.* 1. (*rel., hist.*) schismatic, dissenting. 2. ~ая та́ктика (*polit.*) splitting tactics.

раскопа́|ть, ю, *pf.* (*of* раскáпывать) to dig up, unearth (*also fig.*); (*archaeol.*) to excavate.

раско́пк|а, и, *f.* digging up; *pl.* (*archaeol.*) excavations.

раскорм|и́ть, лю́, ~ишь, *pf.* (*of* раскáрмливать) to fatten.

раскоря́к|а, и, *m. and f.* (*coll.*) bow-legged person; ходи́ть ~ой to walk bow-legged.

раско́с, а, *m.* (*tech.*) cross stay, diagonal strut, angle brace.

раско́сый, *adj.* (*of eyes*) slanting.

раскоше́лива|ться, юсь, *impf. of* раскоше́литься.

раскоше́л|иться, юсь, ишься, *pf.* (*of* ~иваться) (*coll.*) to loosen one's purse-strings; to fork out.

раскра́дыва|ть, ю, *impf. of* раскра́сть.

раскра́ива|ть, ю, *impf. of* раскрои́ть.

раскра́|сить, шу, сишь, *pf.* (*of* ~шивать) to paint, colour.

раскра́ск|а, и, *f.* 1. painting, colouring. 2. colours, colour scheme.

раскрасне́|ться, юсь, *pf.* to flush, go red (in the face).

раскра́|сть, ду́, дёшь, *past* ~л, *pf.* (*of* ~дывать) to loot, clean out.

раскрепо|сти́ть, щу́, сти́шь, *pf.* (*of* ~ща́ть) to set free, liberate, emancipate.

раскрепо|сти́ться, щу́сь, сти́шься, *pf.* (*of* ~ща́ться) 1. to free oneself, liberate oneself. 2. *pass. of* ~сти́ть.

раскрепоща́|ть(ся), ю(сь), *impf. of* раскрепости́ть(ся).

раскрепоще́ни|е, я, *n.* liberation, emancipation; р. же́нщины emancipation of women.

раскритик|ова́ть, у́ю, *pf.* to criticize severely, slate.

раскрич|а́ться, у́сь, и́шься, *pf.* 1. to start shouting, start crying. 2. (на+*a.*) to shout (at), bellow (at).

раскро|и́ть, ю́, и́шь, *pf.* (*of* раскра́ивать)

1. to cut out (*material*). **2.** (*fig., coll.*) to cut open; р. кому́-н. че́реп to split someone's skull.

раскрош|и́ть(ся), у́(сь), ~ишь(ся), *pf. of* кроши́ть(ся).

раскру|ти́ть, чу́, ~тишь, *pf.* (*of* ~чивать) to untwist, untwine, undo.

раскру|ти́ться, ти́тся, *pf.* (*of* ~чиваться) to come untwisted, come undone.

раскру́чива|ть(ся), ю, ет(ся), *impf. of* раскрути́ть(ся).

раскрыва́|ть(ся), ю(сь), *impf. of* раскры́ть-(ся).

раскры́ти|е, я, *n.* **1.** opening. **2.** exposure, disclosing.

раскр|ы́ть, о́ю, о́ешь, *pf.* (*of* ~ыва́ть) **1.** to open (wide); р. зо́нтик to put up an umbrella; р. кни́гу to open a book; р. ско́бки to open brackets. **2.** to expose, bare. **3.** to reveal, disclose, lay bare; to discover; р. секре́т to disclose a secret; р. свои́ ка́рты (*fig.*) to show one's cards, show one's hand.

раскр|ы́ться, о́юсь, о́ешься, *pf.* (*of* ~ыва́ть-ся) **1.** to open; лепестки́ то́лько что ~ы́лись the petals have only just opened. **2.** to uncover oneself. **3.** to come out, come to light.

раскуда́х|таться, чусь, чешься, *pf.* (*coll.*) to set up a cackling.

раскула́чивани|е, я, *n.* dispossession of the kulaks.

раскула́чива|ть, ю, *impf. of* раскула́чить.

раскула́ч|ить, у, ишь, *pf.* (*of* ~ивать) to dispossess the kulaks.

раскуме́ка|ть, ю, *pf.* (*coll.*) to learn, find out.

раскуп|а́ть, а́ю, *impf. of* ~и́ть.

раскуп|и́ть, лю́, ~ишь, *pf.* (*of* ~а́ть) to buy up.

раску́порива|ть(ся), ю, ет(ся), *impf. of* раску́порить(ся).

раску́пор|ить, ю, ишь, *pf.* (*of* ~ивать) to uncork, open.

раску́пор|иться, ится, *pf.* (*of* ~иваться) to open, come uncorked.

раску́порк|а, и, *f.* uncorking, opening.

раску́рива|ть(ся), ю, ет(ся), *impf. of* раскури́ть(ся).

раскур|и́ть, ю́, ~ишь, *pf.* (*of* ~ивать) to puff at (*a pipe or cigarette*).

раскур|и́ться, ~ится, *pf.* (*of* ~иваться) (*of a pipe or cigarette*) to draw.

раску|си́ть, шу́, ~сишь, *pf.* (*of* ~сывать) **1.** to bite through. **2.** (*pf. only*) to get to the core, heart (of); р. кого́-н. to see through someone, rumble someone.

раску́сыва|ть, ю, *impf. of* раскуси́ть.

раску́т|ать, аю, *pf.* (*of* ~ывать) to unwrap.

раску́т|аться, аюсь, *pf.* (*of* ~ываться) to unwrap oneself.

раску|ти́ться, чу́сь, ~тишься, *pf.* (*coll.*) to take to going on drinking-bouts.

раску́тыва|ть(ся), ю(сь), *impf. of* раску́-тать(ся).

ра́совый, *adj.* racial.

распа́д, а, *m.* **1.** disintegration, break-up; (*fig.*) collapse. **2.** (*chem.*) decomposition, dissociation.

распада́|ться, ю, ет(ся), *impf. of* распа́сться.

распа́ива|ть(ся), ю(сь), ет(ся), *impf. of* распая́ть(ся).

распак|ова́ть, у́ю, *pf.* (*of* ~о́вывать) to unpack.

распак|ова́ться, у́юсь, *pf.* (*of* ~о́вываться) **1.** (*of a parcel, etc.*) to come undone. **2.** (*coll.*) to unpack (one's things).

распако́выва|ть(ся), ю(сь), *impf. of* распаковать(ся).

распал|и́ть, ю́, и́шь, *pf.* (*of* ~я́ть) **1.** to make burning hot. **2.** (*fig.*) to inflame; р. гне́вом to incense.

распал|и́ться, ю́сь, и́шься, *pf.* (*of* ~я́ться) **1.** to get burning hot. **2.** (+*i.*; *fig.*) to burn (with); р. гне́вом to be incensed.

распал|я́ть(ся), я́ю(сь), *impf. of* ~и́ть(ся).

распа́р, а, *m.* (*tech.*) bosh, body (*of blast furnace*).

распа́рива|ть(ся), ю(сь), *impf. of* распа́-рить(ся).

распа́р|ить, ю, ишь, *pf.* (*of* ~ивать) **1.** to steam out; to stew well. **2.** to cause to sweat.

распа́р|иться, юсь, ишься, *pf.* (*of* ~ивать-ся) **1.** to steam out; to be well stewed. **2.** to break into a sweat.

распа́рыва|ть(ся), ю, ет(ся), *impf. of* рас-поро́ть(ся).

распа́|сться, дётся, *past* ~лся, *pf.* (*of* ~да́ться) **1.** to disintegrate, fall to pieces; (*fig.*) to break up; to collapse; коали́ция ~ла́сь the coalition broke up. **2.** (*chem.*) to decompose, dissociate.

распа|ха́ть, шу́, ~шешь, *pf.* (*of* ~хивать) to plough up.

распа́хива|ть, ю, *impf. of* распаха́ть *and* распахну́ть.

распа́хива|ться, юсь, *impf. of* распахну́ться.

распах|ну́ть, ну́, нёшь, *pf.* (*of* ~ивать) to open wide; to fling open, throw open; широко́ р. две́ри (+*d.*) to open wide the doors (to) (*also fig.*).

распах|ну́ться, ну́сь, нёшься, *pf.* (*of* ~иваться) **1.** to open wide; to fly open, swing open. **2.** to throw open one's coat.

распа́шк|а, и, *f.* ploughing up.

распашно́й¹, *adj.* (*obs.*; *of clothing*) worn open, unfastened.

распашн|о́й², *adj.* ~о́е весло́ paddle; ~а́я гре́бля paddling.

распашн|óй³, *adj.* (*dial.*) for ploughing up; ~áя земля́ ploughland.

распашóнк|а, и, *f.* baby's loose jacket.

распа|я́ть, я́ю, *pf.* (*of* ~и́вать) to unsolder.

распа|я́ться, я́ется, *pf.* (*of* ~и́ваться) to come unsoldered.

распева́|ть, ю, *impf.* 1. *impf. of* распéть. 2. to sing for a certain time.

распека́|ть, ю, *impf. of* распéчь.

распелен|а́ть, а́ю, *pf.* (*of* ~ывать) to unswaddle.

распере́ть, разопру́, разопрёшь, *past* распёр, распёрла, *pf.* (*of* распира́ть) (*coll.*) to burst open, cause to burst.

распетуш|и́ться, у́сь, и́шься, *pf.* (*coll.*) to get into a paddy; to have one's hackles up.

расп|éть, ою́, оёшь, *pf.* (*of* ~ева́ть) 1. to sing through. 2. to practise (*one's voice*).

расп|éться, ою́сь, оёшься, *pf.* (*coll.*) 1. (*of a singer*) to warm up. 2. to sing away.

распеча́т|ать, аю, *pf.* (*of* ~ывать) to unseal; р. письмó to open a letter.

распеча́т|аться, ается, *pf.* (*of* ~ываться) to come unsealed; to come open.

распеча́тыва|ть(ся), ю, ет(ся), *impf. of* распеча́тать(ся).

распé|чь, ку́, чёшь, ку́т, *past* ~к, ~кла́, *pf.* (*of* ~ка́ть) (*coll.*) to blow up.

распива́|ть, ю, *impf. of* распи́ть.

распи́вочно, *adv.* прода́жа питéй р. sale of liquor for consumption on the premises.

распи́вочн|ый, *adj.* (*obs.*) for consumption on the premises; *as noun* ~ая, ~ой, *f.* (*obs.*) tavern, bar.

распи́л, а, *m.* saw cut.

распи́лива|ть, ю, *impf. of* распили́ть.

распил|и́ть, ю́, ~ишь, *pf.* (*of* ~ива́ть) to saw up.

распи́лк|а, и, *f.* sawing.

распилóвк|а, и, *f.* = распи́лка.

распина́|ть, ю, *impf. of* распя́ть.

распина́|ться, юсь, *impf.* (за когó-н.; *coll.*) to put oneself out (on someone's behalf).

распира́|ть, ю, *impf. of* распере́ть.

расписа́ни|е, я, *n.* time-table, schedule; боевóе р. (*mil.*) order of battle; (*naut.*) battle stations; по ~ю according to time-table, according to schedule.

распи|са́ть, шу́, ~шешь, *pf.* (*of* ~сывать) 1. to enter; to note down; р. счета́ по кни́гам to enter bills in the account-book. 2. to assign, allot. 3. to paint. 4. (*fig.*, *coll.*) to paint a picture (of).

распи|са́ться, шу́сь, ~шешься, *pf.* (*of* ~сываться) 1. to sign (one's name); (в+*p.*) to sign (for); прочти́те э́ту бума́гу и ~ши́тесь read this paper and sign your name; р. в получéнии заказнóго пакéта to sign for a registered letter. 2. (*coll.*) to register

one's marriage. 3. (в+*p.*; *fig.*) to acknowledge, testify (to); р. в собственном невéжестве to acknowledge one's own ignorance.

распи́ск|а¹, и, *f.* painting.

распи́ск|а², и, *f.* receipt; р. в получéнии (+*g.*) receipt (for); письмó с обра́тной ~ой letter with advice of delivery; сдать письмó под ~у to make someone sign for a letter.

расписнóй, *adj.* painted, decorated.

распи́сыва|ть(ся), ю(сь), *impf. of* расписа́ть(ся).

рас|пи́ть, разопью́, разопьёшь, *past* ~пи́л (*and* рóспил), ~пила́, ~пи́ло (*and* рóспило), *pf.* (*of* ~пива́ть) (*coll.*) to drink up; р. буты́лку (с кем-н.) to split a bottle (with someone).

распих|а́ть, а́ю, *pf.* (*of* ~ивать) (*coll.*) 1. to push aside. 2. to shove; р. я́блоки по карма́нам to stuff apples into one's pockets.

распи́хива|ть, ю, *impf. of* распиха́ть.

распла́в|ить, лю, ишь, *pf.* (*of* ~ля́ть) to melt, fuse.

распла́в|иться, ится, *pf.* (*of* ~ля́ться) to melt, fuse (*intrans.*).

расплавлéни|е, я, *n.* melting, fusion.

расплавля́|ть(ся), ю, ет(ся), *impf. of* распла́вить(ся).

распла́|каться, чусь, чешься, *pf.* to burst into tears.

распланир|ова́ть, у́ю, *pf. of* плани́ровать.

распласт|а́ть, а́ю, *pf.* (*of* ~ывать) 1. to split, divide into layers. 2. to spread; р. кры́лья to spread one's wings.

распласт|а́ться, а́юсь, *pf.* (*of* ~ываться) to sprawl.

распла́стыва|ть(ся), ю(сь), *impf. of* распласта́ть(ся).

распла́т|а, ы, *f.* payment; (*fig.*) retribution; час ~ы day of reckoning.

распла|ти́ться, чу́сь, ~ти́шься, *pf.* (*of* ~чиваться) 1. (с+*i.*) to pay off; to pay off accounts (with), get even (with) (*also fig.*); р. с долга́ми to pay off one's debts; р. по ста́рым счета́м to pay off old scores. 2. (за+*a.*; *fig.*) to pay (for).

распла́чива|ться, юсь, *impf. of* расплати́ться.

распле|ска́ть, щу́, ~щешь, *pf.* (*of* ~скивать) to spill.

распле|ска́ться, щу́сь, ~щешься, *pf.* (*of* ~скиваться) 1. to spill. 2. *pass. of* ~ска́ть.

расплёскива|ть(ся), ю(сь), *impf. of* расплеска́ть(ся).

распле|сти́, ту́, тёшь, *past* ~л, ~ла́, *pf.* (*of* ~та́ть) to untwine, untwist, unweave, undo; to unplait.

распле|сти́сь, тётся, *past* ~лся, ~ла́сь, *pf.*

(*of* ~та́ться) to untwine, untwist; to come undone; to come unplaited.

расплета́|ть(ся), ю, ет(ся), *impf. of* распле-сти́(сь).

распло|ди́ть(ся), жу́(сь), ди́шь(ся), *pf. of* плоди́ть(ся).

расплыва́|ться, ется, *impf. of* расплы́ться.

расплы́вчат|ый (~, ~а), *adj.* dim, indistinct; diffuse, vague; ~ые очерта́ния dim outlines; р. стиль woolly style.

расплы́|ться, вётся, *past* ~лся, ~ла́сь, *pf.* (*of* ~ва́ться) **1.** to run; черни́ла ~лись the ink has run. **2.** (*coll.*) to spread; to run to fat; р. в улы́бку to break into a smile.

расплю́щива|ть(ся), ю, ет(ся), *impf. of* расплю́щить(ся).

расплю́щ|ить, у, ишь, *pf.* (*of* ~ивать) to flatten out, hammer out.

расплю́щ|иться, ится, *pf.* (*of* ~иваться) to become flat.

распознава́|емый, *pres. part. pass. of* ~ть *and* *adj.* recognizable, identifiable.

распознава́ни|е, я, *n.* recognition, identification.

распозна|ва́ть, ю́, ёшь, *impf. of* ~ть.

распозна́|ть, ю, ешь, *pf.* (*of* ~ва́ть) to recognize, identify; р. боле́знь to diagnose an illness.

располага́|ть¹, ю, *impf.* **1.** (+*i.*) to dispose (of), have at one's disposal, have available; р. вре́менем to have time available; р. больши́ми сре́дствами to dispose of ample means. **2.** (+*inf.*; *obs.*) to intend, propose.

располага́|ть², ю, *impf. of* расположи́ть.

располага́|ться, юсь, *impf. of* расположи́ться¹.

располага́|ющий, *pres. part. act. of* ~ть *and* *adj.* prepossessing.

располз|а́ться, а́юсь, *impf. of* ~ти́сь.

располз|ти́сь, у́сь, ёшься, *past* ~ся, ~ла́сь, *pf.* (*of* ~а́ться) **1.** to crawl (away). **2.** (*of* clothing, etc.; *coll.*) to come unravelled; to tear, give at the seams.

расположе́ни|е, я, n. **1.** disposition, arrangement; р. по кварти́рам (*mil.*) billeting; р. не́рвов (*bot.*) nervation; р. слов word-order. **2.** situation, location; р. на ме́стности (*mil.*) location on the ground. **3.** favour, liking; sympathies; по́льзоваться чьим-н. ~ем to enjoy someone's favour, be liked by someone, be in someone's good books; чу́вствовать к кому́-н. р. to be favourably disposed towards someone. **4.** (к) disposition (to), inclination (to, for); tendency (to), propensity (to); bias (towards), penchant (for); у неё р. к бронхи́ту she has a tendency to bronchitis, she is inclined to be bronchial. **5.** р. (ду́ха) disposition, mood, humour; быть в плохо́м ~и ду́ха to be in a bad

mood; у меня́ нет ~я танцева́ть I am not in the mood for dancing.

располо́жен|ный (~, ~а), *p.p.p. of* расположи́ть *and* *pred. adj.* **1.** (к) well disposed (to, towards). **2.** (к *or* +*inf.*) disposed (to), inclined (to); in the mood (for); я не ~ к отвлечённому размышле́нию I am not disposed to, am not in the mood for abstract speculation; я не о́чень ~ сего́дня рабо́тать I don't feel much like working today.

располож|и́ть, у́, ~ишь, *pf.* (*of* располага́ть²) **1.** to dispose, arrange, set out; р. свои́ войска́ to dispose, station one's troops. **2.** to win over, gain; р. кого́-н. к себе́, в свою́ по́льзу to gain someone's favour.

располож|и́ться¹, у́сь, ~ишься, *pf.* (*of* располага́ться) to take up position; to settle oneself, compose oneself, make oneself comfortable; р. спать to settle oneself to sleep.

располож|и́ться², у́сь, ~ишься, *pf.* (+*inf.*; *obs.*) to resolve, make up one's mind.

распо́р, а, *m.* (*tech.*) thrust.

распо́рк|а, и, *f.* (*tech.*) cross-bar, strut, tie-beam, tie-rod, spreader bar.

распор|о́ть, ю́, ~ешь, *pf.* (*of* поро́ть¹ *and* распа́рывать) to unstitch, unpick, undo, rip.

распор|о́ться, ~ется, *pf.* (*of* поро́ться *and* распа́рываться) to come unstitched, come undone, rip.

распоряди́тел|ь, я, *m.* manager; master of ceremonies.

распоряди́тельност|ь, и, *f.* good management; efficiency; отсу́тствие ~и mismanagement.

распоряди́тел|ьный (~ен, ~ьна), *adj.* capable; efficient; р. челове́к a good organizer.

распоря|ди́ться, жу́сь, ди́шься, *pf.* (*of* ~жа́ться) **1.** (о+*p. or* +*inf.*) to order; to see (that); мы ~ди́мся о проведе́нии э́того реше́ния we will see that this decision is implemented; я ~жу́сь возмести́ть вам расхо́ды I will see that you are reimbursed for the expenses. **2.** (+*i.*) to manage; to deal (with); разреши́ть кому́-н. р. по своему́ усмотре́нию to give someone a free hand; как р. э́тими деньга́ми? what is to be done with this money?, how should this money be used?

распоря́д|ок, ка, *m.* order; routine; пра́вила вну́треннего ~ка (в учрежде́нии, на фа́брике, *etc.*) (office, factory, *etc.*) regulations; р. дня the daily routine.

распоряжа́|ться, юсь, *impf.* **1.** *impf. of* распоряди́ться. **2.** *impf. only* to give orders, be in charge; to be the boss; р. как у себя́ до́ма to behave as though the place belongs to one.

распоряже́ни|е, я, n. **1.** order; instruction,

direction; до осо́бого ～я until further notice. **2.** disposal, command; быть в ～и кого́-н. to be at someone's disposal; име́ть в своём ～и to have at one's disposal, command.

распоя́|сать, шу, шешь, *pf.* (*of* ～сывать) to ungird.

распоя́|саться, шусь, шешься, *pf.* (*of* ～сываться) **1.** to take off one's belt, ungird oneself. **2.** (*fig., coll., pejor.*) to throw aside all restraint, let oneself go.

распоя́сыва|ть(ся), ю(сь), *impf. of* распоя́сать(ся).

распра́в|а, ы, *f.* **1.** (*hist.*) punishment, execution; твори́ть суд и ～у to administer justice and mete out punishment. **2.** violence; reprisal; крова́вая р. massacre; кула́чная р. fist-law; коро́ткая р. short shrift; у нас с ни́ми р. коротка́ we'll give them short shrift, we'll make short work of them.

распра́в|ить, лю, ишь, *pf.* (*of* ～ля́ть) **1.** to straighten; to smooth out; р. морщи́ны to smooth out wrinkles. **2.** to spread, stretch; р. кры́лья to spread one's wings (*also fig.*).

распра́в|иться[1], ится, *pf.* (*of* ～ля́ться) to get smoothed out.

распра́в|иться[2], люсь, ишься, *pf.* (*of* ～ля́ться) (с+*i.*) to deal (with), make short work (of); give short shrift; р. без суда́ to take the law into one's own hands.

расправля́|ть(ся), ю(сь), *impf. of* распра́вить(ся).

распределе́ни|е, я, *n.* distribution; allocation, assignment; р. нало́гов assessment of taxes; р. войск (*mil.*) order of battle.

распредели́тел|ь, я, *m.* **1.** distributor; retailer; закры́тый р. retail establishment closed to persons not registered. **2.** (*electr.*) distributor; spreader.

распредели́тельн|ый, *adj.* distributive, distributing; ～ая доска́, р. щит (*tech.*) switchboard; р. вал (*tech.*) cam shaft; р. кла́пан (*tech.*) regulating valve; ～ая коро́бка (*electr.*) switch box, junction box, panel box.

распредел|и́ть, ю́, и́шь, *pf.* (*of* ～я́ть) to distribute; to allocate, allot, assign; р. своё вре́мя to allocate one's time.

распредел|и́ться, и́тся, *pf.* (*of* ～я́ться) **1.** to divide up, split up. **2.** *pass. of* ～и́ть.

распредел|я́ть(ся), я́ю(сь), *impf. of* ～и́ть(ся).

распрекра́с|ный (～ен, ～на), *adj.* (*coll.*) beautiful, fine, splendid.

распрода|ва́ть, ю́, ёшь, *impf. of* ～ть.

распрода́ж|а, и, *f.* sale; clearance sale, bargain sale.

распрода́|ть, м, шь, ст, ди́м, ди́те, ду́т, *past* **распро́дал, ～ла́, распро́дало,** *pf.* (*of* ～ва́ть)

to sell off; to sell out; биле́ты распро́даны all the tickets are sold.

распростер|е́ть, *fut. tense not used, past* ～, ～ла, *pf.* (*of* распростира́ть) to stretch out, extend.

распростер|е́ться, *fut. tense not used, past* ～ся, ～лась, *pf.* (*of* распростира́ться) **1.** to stretch oneself out, prostrate oneself. **2.** (*fig.*) to spread.

распростёр|тый, p.p.p. *of* ～е́ть *and adj.* **1.** outstretched; встре́тить с ～тыми объя́тиями to receive with outstretched arms. **2.** prostrate, prone.

распростира́|ть(ся), ю(сь), *impf. of* распростере́ть(ся).

распро|сти́ться, щу́сь, сти́шься, *pf.* (с+*i.*) to take final leave (of); р. с мечто́й to bid farewell to one's dream(s).

распростране́ни|е, я, *n.* spreading, diffusion; dissemination; р. зара́зы spreading of infection; име́ть большо́е р. to be widely practised.

распространённост|ь, и, *f.* prevalence; diffusion.

распростран|ённый, p.p.p. *of* ～и́ть *and adj.* **1.** widespread, prevalent; широко́ р. widely-distributed. **2.** ～ённое предложе́ние (*gram.*) extended sentence.

распространи́тел|ь, я, *m.* spreader.

распространи́тельн|ый, *adj.* extended; (excessively) wide; ～ое толкова́ние прика́за a wide interpretation of an injunction.

распростран|и́ть, ю́, и́шь, *pf.* (*of* ～я́ть) **1.** to spread, diffuse; to disseminate, propagate; to popularize; р. слух to spread a rumour; р. но́вое уче́ние to disseminate a new doctrine. **2.** to extend; р. де́йствие зако́на на всех to extend the application of a law to all. **3.** to give off, give out (*a smell*).

распростран|и́ться, ю́сь, и́шься, *pf.* (*of* ～я́ться) **1.** to spread; to extend; (*of a law, etc.*) to apply. **2.** (о+*p.*; *coll.*) to enlarge (on), expatiate (on), dilate (on).

распростран|я́ть(ся), я́ю(сь), *impf. of* ～и́ть(ся).

распроща́|ться, юсь, *pf.* (с+*i.*; *coll.*) = распрости́ться.

распры́ска|ть, ю, *pf.* (*coll.*) to spray about; to use up (in spraying).

ра́спр|я, и, *g. pl.* ～ей, *f.* quarrel, feud.

распряга́|ть(ся), ю(сь), *impf. of* распря́чь(ся).

распрям|и́ть, лю́, и́шь, *pf.* (*of* ～ля́ть) to straighten, unbend.

распрям|и́ться, лю́сь, и́шься, *pf.* (*of* ～ля́ться) to straighten oneself up.

распрямля́|ть(ся), ю(сь), *impf. of* распрями́ть(ся).

распря́|чь, гу́, жёшь, гу́т, *past* ～г, ～гла́, *pf.* (*of* ～га́ть) to unharness.

распря́|чься, жётся, гу́тся, *past* **~гся, ~гла́сь,** *pf.* (*of* ~га́ться) to get unharnessed.

распублик|ова́ть, у́ю, *pf.* (*of* ~о́вывать) to publish; to promulgate.

распублико́выва|ть, ю, *impf. of* распубликова́ть.

распуг|а́ть, а́ю, *pf.* (*of* ~ивать) to scare away, frighten away.

распуска́|ть(ся), ю(сь), *impf. of* распусти́ть(ся).

распу|сти́ть, щу́, ~стишь, *pf.* (*of* ~ска́ть) 1. to dismiss; to disband; р. парла́мент to dissolve parliament; р. кома́нду (*naut.*) to pay off a crew; р. на кани́кулы to dismiss for the holidays. 2. to let out; to relax; р. во́лосы to let one's hair down; р. знамёна to unfurl banners; р. паруса́ to set sail. 3. (*fig.*) to allow to become undisciplined, allow to get out of hand; to spoil. 4. to dissolve; to melt. 5. (*coll.*) to spread, put out (*rumours, etc.*).

распу|сти́ться, щу́сь, ~стишься, *pf.* (*of* ~ска́ться) 1. (*bot.*) to open, blossom out, come out. 2. to come loose; чуло́к у неё ~сти́лся her stocking had come down. 3. (*fig.*) to become undisciplined, get out of hand, let oneself go. 4. to dissolve; to melt.

распу́т|ать, аю, *pf.* (*of* ~ывать) 1. to untangle, disentangle; to unravel. 2. to untie, loose (*an animal*). 3. (*fig.*) to disentangle, unravel; to puzzle out.

распу́т|аться, аюсь, *pf.* (*of* ~ываться) 1. to get disentangled, come undone. 2. (*fig., coll.*) to get disentangled, be cleared up. 3. (с+*i*.; *coll.*) to rid oneself (of), shake off.

распу́тиц|а, ы, *f.* time (*during spring and autumn*) of bad roads.

распу́тник, а, *m.* profligate, libertine.

распу́тнича|ть, ю, *impf.* to lead a dissolute life.

распу́т|ный (~ен, ~на), *adj.* dissolute, dissipated, debauched.

распу́тств|о, а, *n.* dissipation, debauchery, profligacy, libertinism.

распу́тыва|ть(ся), ю(сь), *impf. of* распу́тать(ся).

распу́ть|е, я, *n.* crossroads; быть на р. (*fig.*) to be at the crossroads, be at the parting of the ways.

распуха́|ть, а́ю, *impf. of* ~нуть.

распу́х|нуть, ну, нешь, *past* ~, ~ла, *pf.* (*of* ~а́ть) 1. to swell up. 2. (*fig., coll.*) to swell, become inflated.

распуш|и́ть, у́, и́шь, *pf. of* пуши́ть.

распу́щенност|ь, и, *f.* 1. lack of discipline. 2. dissoluteness, dissipation.

распу́|щенный, *p.p.p. of* ~сти́ть *and adj.* 1. undisciplined; р. ребёнок spoiled child. 2. dissolute, dissipated.

распыле́ни|е, я, *n.* 1. spraying; atomiza-

tion. 2. dispersion, scattering; р. средств dissipation of resources.

распыли́тел|ь, я, *m.* spray(er), atomizer, pulverizer.

распыл|и́ть, ю́, и́шь, *pf.* (*of* ~я́ть) 1. to spray; to atomize; to pulverize. 2. (*fig.*) to disperse, scatter; р. си́лы to scatter one's forces.

распыл|и́ться, и́тся, *pf.* (*of* ~я́ться) 1. to disperse; to get scattered. 2. *pass. of* ~и́ть.

распыл|я́ть(ся), я́ю(сь), *impf. of* ~и́ть(ся).

распя́лива|ть, ю, *impf. of* распя́лить.

распя́л|ить, ю, ишь, *pf.* (*of* ~ивать) to stretch (*on a frame*).

распя́ти|е, я, *n.* 1. crucifixion. 2. cross, crucifix.

расп|я́ть, ну́, нёшь, *pf.* (*of* ~ина́ть) to crucify.

расса́д|а, ы, *no pl., f.* seedlings.

расса|ди́ть, жу́, ~дишь, *pf.* (*of* ~жива́ть) 1. to seat, offer seats. 2. to separate, seat separately. 3. to transplant, plant out.

расса́дк|а, и, *f.* transplanting, planting out.

расса́дник, а, *m.* 1. seed-plot. 2. (*fig.*) hot-bed, breeding-ground.

расса́жива|ть, ю, *impf. of* рассади́ть.

расса́жива|ться, юсь, *impf. of* рассе́сться[1].

расса́сывани|е, я, *n.* (*med.*) resolution, resorption.

расса́сыва|ться, юсь, *impf. of* рассоса́ться.

рассве|сти́, тёт, *past* ~ло́, *pf.* (*of* ~та́ть) to dawn; уже́ ~ло́ it was already light; соверше́нно ~ло́ it was broad daylight.

рассве́т, а, *m.* dawn, daybreak.

рассвета́|ть, ет, *impf. of* рассвести́; ~ет day is breaking.

рассвирепе́|ть, ю, *pf.* (*of* свирепе́ть) to become savage; to turn nasty.

рассе́да|ться, юсь, *impf. of* рассе́сться[2].

рассе́дл|а́ть, а́ю, *pf.* (*of* ~ывать) to un-saddle.

рассе́ивани|е, я, *n.* dispersion; dispersal, scattering, dissipation.

рассе́ива|ть(ся), ю(сь), *impf. of* рассе́ять(ся).

рассека́|ть, ю, *impf. of* рассе́чь.

рассекре́|тить, чу, ~тишь, *pf.* (*of* ~чивать) 1. to declassify, remove from secret list. 2. to deny access to secret documents; to take off secret work.

рассекре́чива|ть, ю, *impf. of* рассекре́тить.

рассе́лени|е, я, *n.* 1. settling (*in a new place*). 2. separation; settling apart.

рассе́лин|а, ы, *f.* cleft, fissure.

рассел|и́ть, ю́, и́шь, *pf.* (*of* ~я́ть) 1. to settle (*in a new place*). 2. to separate; to settle apart.

рассел|и́ться, ю́сь, и́шься, *pf.* (*of* ~я́ться) 1. to settle (*in a new place*). 2. to separate, settle separately.

рассел|я́ть(ся), я́ю(сь), *impf. of* ~и́ть(ся).

рассер|ди́ть, жу́, ~дишь, *pf.* to anger, make angry.

рассер|ди́ться, жу́сь, ~дишься, *pf.* (на+*a.*) to get, become angry (with).

рассе́р|женный, *p.p.p. of* ~ди́ть *and adj.* angry.

рассерча́|ть, ю, *pf.* (*coll.*) to get angry.

рас|се́сться[1], ся́дусь, ся́дешься, *past* ~се́лся, *pf.* (*of* ~са́живаться) **1.** to take one's seat. **2.** (*coll.*) to sprawl.

рас|се́сться[2], ся́дется, *past* ~се́лся, *pf.* (*of* ~седа́ться) to crack.

рассе́|чь, ку́, чёшь, ку́т, *past* ~к, ~кла́, *pf.* (*of* ~ка́ть) **1.** to cut through; to cleave (*also fig.*). **2.** to cut (badly); я ~к себе́ па́лец I have cut my finger badly.

рассея́ни|е, я, *n.* diffusion; dispersion; р. тепла́ (*phys.*) dissipation of heat, thermal dispersion; р. све́та (*phys.*) diffusion of light.

рассе́янност|ь, и, *f.* **1.** diffusion; dispersion; dissipation. **2.** absent-mindedness, distraction.

рассе́я|нный, *p.p.p. of* ~ть *and adj.* **1.** diffused; dissipated; р. свет (*phys.*) diffused light. **2.** scattered, dispersed; ~нное населе́ние scattered population. **3.** absent-minded; р. взгляд vacant look. **4.** (*fig.*) dissipated.

рассе́|ять, ю, ешь, *pf.* (*of* ~ивать) **1.** to sow broadcast, scatter. **2.** (*fig.*) to place (about), establish (about), dot (about). **3.** to disperse, scatter; (*fig.*) to dispel; р. чьи-н. сомне́ния to dispel someone's doubts.

рассе́|яться, юсь, ешься, *pf.* (*of* ~иваться) **1.** to disperse, scatter; толпа́ ~ялась the crowd dispersed; неприя́тельский отря́д ~ялся the enemy detachment scattered; тума́н ~ялся the fog cleared; её го́ре ~ялось her grief passed; р. как дым to vanish into thin air, into smoke. **2.** to divert oneself, distract oneself; ему́ на́до р. he needs a break.

расси|де́ться, жу́сь, ди́шься, *pf.* (*of* ~жива́ться) (*coll.*) to sit for a long time.

рассижива|ться, юсь, *impf. of* расси-де́ться.

расска́з, а, *m.* **1.** account, narrative. **2.** story, tale.

расска|за́ть, жу́, ~жешь, *pf.* (*of* ~зывать) to tell, narrate, recount.

расска́зчик, а, *m.* story-teller, narrator.

расска́зыва|ть, ю, *impf. of* рассказа́ть.

расслабева́|ть, ю, *impf. of* расслабе́ть.

расслабе́|ть, ю, *pf.* (*of* ~ва́ть) to weaken, grow weak; to tire; to grow limp.

рассла́б|ить, лю, ишь, *pf.* (*of* ~ля́ть) to weaken, enfeeble; to enervate.

рассла́б|ленный, *p.p.p. of* ~ить *and adj.* weak; limp.

расслабля́|ть, ю, *impf. of* рассла́бить.

рассла́б|нуть, ну, нешь, *past* ~, ~ла, *pf.* (*coll.*) = ~е́ть.

рассла́в|ить, лю, ишь, *pf.* (*of* ~ля́ть) (*coll.*) **1.** to praise to the skies. **2.** to shout from the house-tops.

расславля́|ть, ю, *impf. of* рассла́вить.

рассла́ива|ть(ся), ю, ет(ся), *impf. of* рас-слои́ть(ся).

расследовани|е, я, *n.* investigation, examination; (*leg.*) inquiry; назна́чить р. (+*g.*) to order an inquiry (into); произвести́ р. (+*g.*) to hold an inquiry (into).

рассле́д|овать, ую, *impf. and pf.* to investigate, look into, hold an inquiry (into).

расслоéни|е, я, *n.* stratification (*also fig.*); exfoliation.

рассло|и́ть, ю́, и́шь, *pf.* (*of* рассла́ивать) to divide into layers, stratify (*also fig.*).

рассло|и́ться, и́тся, *pf.* (*of* рассла́иваться) to become stratified (*also fig.*); to exfoliate, flake off.

рассло́йк|а, и, *f.* **1.** stratification. **2.** (*geol.*) stratum.

расслу́ша|ть, ю, *pf.* (*obs.*) to listen properly (to).

расслы́ш|ать, у, ишь, *pf.* to catch; я не ~ал вас I didn't catch what you said.

рассма́трива|ть, ю, *impf.* **1.** *impf. of* рас-смотре́ть. **2.** *impf. only* to regard (as), consider; мы ~ем э́то как обма́н we regard it as a fraud. **3.** *impf. only* to scrutinize, examine.

рассмеш|и́ть, у́, и́шь, *pf.* to make laugh, set laughing.

рассме|я́ться, ю́сь, ёшься, *pf.* to burst out laughing.

рассмотрéни|е, я, *n.* examination, scrutiny; consideration; предста́вить на р. to submit for consideration; быть на ~и to be under consideration; оста́вить жа́лобу без ~я to reject a complaint; переда́ть де́ло на но́вое р. to submit a case for re-consideration.

рассмотр|е́ть, ю́, ~ишь, *pf.* (*of* рассма́тривать) **1.** to descry, discern, make out; мы с трудо́м ~е́ли на́дпись на па́мятнике we had difficulty in making out the inscription on the monument. **2.** to examine, consider; р. заявле́ние to consider an application.

расс|ова́ть, ую́, уёшь, *pf.* (*of* ~о́вывать) (*coll.*) to shove (about), stuff (about); р. свои́ ве́щи по чемода́нам to stuff one's things into suitcases.

рассо́выва|ть, ю, *impf. of* рассова́ть.

рассо́л, а, *m.* **1.** brine. **2.** (*cul.*) pickle.

рассо́льник, а, *m.* rassolnik (*meat or fish soup with pickled cucumbers*).

рассо́р|ить, ю, ишь, *pf.* to set at variance, set at loggerheads.

рассор|и́ть, ю́, и́шь, *pf.* (*coll.*) to drop (over); р. оку́рки по́ полу to litter the floor with cigarette-butts.

рассо́р|иться, ю́сь, и́шься, *pf.* (*c*+*i.*) to fall out (with), fall foul (of).

рассортир|ова́ть, у́ю, *pf.* (*of* ∼о́вывать) to sort out.

рассортиро́вк|а, и, *f.* sorting out.

рассортиро́выва|ть, ю, *impf. of* рассортирова́ть.

рассос|а́ться, ётся, *pf.* (*of* расса́сываться) (*med.*) to resolve.

рассо́х|нуться, нется, *past* ∼ся, ∼лась, *pf.* (*of* рассыха́ться) to crack.

расспра́шива|ть, ю, *impf. of* расспроси́ть.

расспро́с, а, *m.* question, questioning; надое́сть ∼ами to pester with questions.

расспро|си́ть, шу́, ∼сишь, *pf.* (*of* расспра́шивать) to question; р. кого́-н. о доро́ге to ask someone the way.

рассредото́чени|е, я, n. (*mil.*) dispersion, dispersal.

рассредото́чива|ть, ю, *impf. of* рассредото́чить.

рассредото́ч|ить, у, ишь, *pf.* (*of* ∼ивать) (*mil.*) to disperse.

рассро́чива|ть, ю, *impf. of* рассро́чить.

рассро́ч|ить, у, ишь, *pf.* (*of* ∼ивать) to spread (*over a period*); р. вы́плату до́лга to allow payment of a debt by instalments; р. изда́ние энциклопе́дии на де́сять лет to spread the publication of an encyclopaedia over (a period of) ten years.

рассро́чк|а, и, *f.* instalment system; в ∼у by, in instalments; купи́ть с ∼ой платежа́ to purchase by instalments, on the hire--purchase system; предоста́вить ∼у to grant the right to pay by instalments.

расстава́ни|е, я, n. parting; при ∼и on parting.

расста|ва́ться, ю́сь, ёшься, *impf. of* расста́ться.

расста́в|ить, лю, ишь, *pf.* (*of* ∼ля́ть) 1. (*impf. also* расстана́вливать) to place, arrange; р. часовы́х to post sentries; р. ша́хматы to set out chess-men. 2. to move apart; р. но́ги to stand with one's legs apart. 3. (*tailoring*) to let out.

расста́вк|а, и, *f.* (*tailoring*) letting out.

расставля́|ть, ю, *impf. of* расста́вить.

расстана́влива|ть, ю, *impf. of* расста́вить.

расстано́вк|а, и, *f.* 1. placing, arrangement; р. зна́ков препина́ния punctuation. 2. pause; spacing; говори́ть с ∼ой to speak without haste, speak slowly and deliberately.

расста́|ться, нусь, нешься, *pf.* (*of* ∼ва́ться) (*c*+*i.*) 1. to part (with); to leave; ∼немся друзья́ми let us part friends. 2. to give up;

р. с мы́слью to put the thought out of one's head.

расстега́|й, я, m. open-topped pasty.

расстёгива|ть(ся), ю(сь), *impf. of* расстегну́ть(ся).

расстег|ну́ть, ну́, нёшь, *pf.* (*of* ∼ивать) to undo, unfasten; to unbutton; to unhook, unclasp, unbuckle.

расстег|ну́ться, ну́сь, нёшься, *pf.* (*of* ∼иваться) 1. to come undone, become unfastened; to become unbuttoned; to become unhooked. 2. to undo one's coat, unbutton one's coat; to undo one's buttons.

расстел|и́ть(ся), ю́(сь), ∼ишь(ся), *pf.* = разостла́ть(ся).

расстила́|ть, ю, *impf. of* разостла́ть.

расстила́|ться, юсь, *impf.* 1. *impf. of* разостла́ться. 2. *impf. only* to extend, unfold; пе́ред на́шими глаза́ми ∼лась велича́вая панора́ма гор before our eyes unfolded a magnificent mountain panorama.

расстоя́ни|е, я, n. distance, space, interval; на бли́зком ∼и (от) at a short distance (from), a short way away (from); на далё-ком ∼и in the far distance, a great way off; на ∼и пу́шечного вы́стрела within gun-shot; на ∼и челове́ческого го́лоса within hail; они́ живу́т на ∼и двух миль от бли-жа́йшего сосе́да they live two miles from their nearest neighbour; держа́ть кого́-н. на ∼и to keep someone at arm's length; держа́ться на ∼и to keep one's distance, hold aloof.

расстра́ива|ть(ся), ю(сь), *impf. of* рас-стро́ить(ся).

расстре́л, а, m. 1. (military) execution; приговори́ть к ∼у to sentence to be shot. 2. shooting up.

расстре́лива|ть, ю, *impf. of* расстреля́ть.

расстрел|я́ть, я́ю, *pf.* (*of* ∼ивать) 1. to shoot, execute by shooting. 2. to shoot up; to fire upon at close range. 3. to use up (*in firing*).

расстри́г|а, и, m. unfrocked priest, un-frocked monk.

расстрига́|ть, ю, *impf. of* расстри́чь.

расстри́|чь, гу́, жёшь, гу́т, *past* ∼г, ∼гла, *pf.* (*of* ∼га́ть) (*eccl.*) to unfrock.

расстро́|енный, p.p.p. of ∼ить *and adj.* dis-ordered, deranged; р. вид downcast appearance.

расстро́|ить, ю, ишь, *pf.* (*of* расстра́ивать) 1. to disorder, derange; to throw into con-fusion; to unsettle; to upset; р. желу́док to cause indigestion; р. за́мыслы to thwart schemes; р. своё здоро́вье to ruin one's health; р. чьи-н. пла́ны to upset someone's plans; р. ряды́ проти́вника to break the enemy's ranks; р. сва́дьбу to break an engagement; р. хозя́йство to shatter the economy. **2.** to upset, put out. **3.** (*mus.*) to put out of tune, untune.

расстро́|иться, юсь, ишься, *pf.* (*of* расстра́иваться) **1.** to fall into confusion, fall apart; (*fig.*) to fall to the ground, fall through; все на́ши пла́ны ~ились all our plans have fallen through. **2.** (от) to be upset (over, about), be put out (about). **3.** (*mus.*) to become out of tune.

расстро́йств|о, а, *n.* **1.** disorder; derangement; confusion; р. желу́дка stomach disorder, stomach upset; (*coll.*) diarrhoea; р. пищеваре́ния indigestion; р. ре́чи speech defect; внести́ р. (в+*a.*), привести́ в р. to throw into confusion, derange, disorganize; дела́ пришли́ в р. things are in a sad state. **2.** (*coll.*) upset, discomposure; привести́ в р. to upset, put out; быть в ~е to be upset, be put out.

расступ|а́ться, а́ется, *impf. of* ~и́ться

расступ|и́ться, ~ится, *pf.* (*of* ~а́ться) to part, make way; толпа́ ~и́лась the crowd parted; земля́ ~и́лась (*poet.*) the earth opened.

рассуди́тельност|ь, и, *f.* reasonableness; good sense.

рассуди́тел|ьный (~ен, ~ьна), *adj.* reasonable; sober-minded; sensible.

рассу|ди́ть, жу́, ~дишь, *pf.* **1.** to judge (between), arbitrate (between); ~ди́те нас settle our dispute, be an arbiter between us; р. спор to settle a dispute. **2.** to think, consider; to decide; нам на́до р., как сообщи́ть ей э́ти но́вости we have to think how to break this news to her; мы ~ди́ли, что пришло́ вре́мя верну́ться домо́й we decided that the time had come to return home.

рассу́д|ок, ка, *m.* **1.** reason; intellect; го́лос ~ка the voice of reason; в по́лном ~ке in full possession of one's faculties; лиши́ться ~ка to lose one's reason, go out of one's mind. **2.** common sense, good sense.

рассу́доч|ный (~ен, ~на), *adj.* **1.** rational, of the reason. **2.** governed by the reason (*to exclusion of feelings*); ~ная любо́вь intellectual love.

рассужда́|ть, ю, *impf.* **1.** to reason. **2.** (о+*p.*) to discuss, debate; to argue (about); to discourse (on); р. на каку́ю-н. те́му to discuss a topic.

рассужде́ни|е, я, *n.* **1.** reasoning. **2.** (*usu. pl.*) discussion, debate; argument; discourse; без ~й without argument, without arguing. **3.** (*obs.*) dissertation. **4.** в ~и (+*g.*; *obs.*) with regard to, as regards.

рассу́чива|ться, ю, ет(ся), *impf. of* рассучи́ть(ся).

рассуч|и́ть, у́, ~ишь, *pf.* (*of* ~ивать) to

untwist; to undo; р. рукава́ to roll one's sleeves down.

рассуч|и́ться, ~ится, *pf.* (*of* ~ива́ться) to untwist; to come undone.

рассчи́т|анный, *p.p.p. of* ~а́ть *and adj.* **1.** calculated, deliberate; ~анная гру́бость calculated rudeness. **2.** (на+*a.*) intended (for), meant (for), designed (for); кни́га, ~анная на широ́кого чита́теля a book intended for the general public; автостра́да, ~анная на бы́строе движе́ние motorway designed for fast traffic.

рассчит|а́ть, а́ю, *pf.* (*of* ~ывать) **1.** to calculate, compute; (*tech.*) to rate; не р. свои́х сил to overrate one's strength. **2.** to dismiss, sack. **3.** (*mil.*) to number off, order to number.

рассчит|а́ться, а́юсь, *pf.* (*of* ~ываться) **1.** (с+*i.*) to settle accounts (with), reckon (with). **2.** (*mil.*) to number; по поря́дку номеро́в ~а́йсь! (*word of command*) number!

рассчи́тыва|ть, ю, *impf.* **1.** *impf. of* рассчита́ть *and* расче́сть. **2.** *impf. only* (на+*a.*) to calculate (on, upon), count (on, upon), reckon (on, upon); (+*inf.*) to expect (to), hope (to); р. на многочи́сленную пу́блику to count on a large attendance; мы ~ли ко́нчить рабо́ту в э́том году́ we were hoping to finish the work this year. **3.** *impf. only* (на+*a.*) to count (on, upon), rely (on, upon), depend (upon).

рассчи́тыва|ться, юсь, *impf. of* рассчита́ться *and* расче́сться.

рассыла́|ть, ю, *impf. of* разосла́ть.

рассы́лк|а, и, *f.* distribution, delivery.

рассы́льн|ый, *adj.* ~ая кни́га delivery book; *as noun* р., ~ого, *m.* delivery man, errand-boy.

рассы́п|ать, лю, лешь, *pf.* (*of* ~а́ть) to spill; to strew, scatter; р. в цепь (*mil.*) to draw up in extended line.

рассы́п|аться, люсь, лешься, *pf.* (*of* ~а́ться) **1.** to spill, scatter. **2.** to spread out, deploy; р. в цепь (*mil.*) to extend. **3.** to crumble; to go to pieces, disintegrate (*also fig.*). **4.** (в+*p.*) to be profuse (in); р. в благода́рностях to be profuse in the expression of thanks; р. в похвала́х (+*d.*) to shower praises (upon).

рассып|а́ть(ся), а́ю(сь), *impf. of* ~а́ть(ся).

рассыпн|о́й, *adj.* **1.** (sold) loose, (sold) by the piece; ~ы́е папиро́сы cigarettes sold loose. **2.** р. строй (*mil.*) extended order.

рассы́пчат|ый (~, ~а), *adj.* friable; (*cul.*) short, crumbly; ~ое пече́нье shortbread.

рассыха́|ться, юсь, *impf. of* рассо́хнуться.

раста́лкива|ть, ю, *impf. of* растолка́ть.

раста́плива|ть(ся), ю, ет(ся), *impf. of* растопи́ть(ся).

раста́птыва|ть, ю, *impf. of* растопта́ть.

растаск|а́ть, а́ю, *pf.* (*of* ~ивать) **1.** to take away, remove (*little by little, bit by bit*). **2.** to pilfer, filch.

раста́скива|ть, ю, *impf. of* растаска́ть *and* растащи́ть.

растас|ова́ть, у́ю, *pf.* (*of* ~о́вывать) (*coll.*) to shuffle (*cards*).

растасо́выва|ть, ю, *impf. of* растасова́ть.

раста́чива|ть, ю, *impf. of* расточи́ть².

растащ|и́ть, у́, ~ишь, *pf.* (*of* раста́скивать) **1.** to part, separate, drag asunder. **2.** = растаска́ть.

раста́|ять, ю, ешь, *pf. of* та́ять.

раство́р¹, а, *m.* (extent of) opening, span; р. две́ри doorway; р. окна́ extent to which a window is opened; р. ци́ркуля spread of a pair of compasses.

раство́р², а, *m.* **1.** (*chem.*) solution. **2.** (*tech.*) mortar; строи́тельный р. grout.

растворе́ни|е, я, *n.* solution, dissolution.

раствори́мост|ь, и, *f.* (*chem.*) solubility.

раствори́м|ый (~, ~а), *adj.* (*chem.*) soluble; р. в воде́ water-soluble.

раствори́тел|ь, я, *m.* (*chem.*) solvent.

раствор|и́ть¹, ю́, ~ишь, *pf.* (*of* ~я́ть) to open.

раствор|и́ть², ю́, и́шь, *pf.* (*of* ~я́ть) to dissolve.

раствор|и́ться¹, ~ится, *pf.* (*of* ~я́ться) to open.

раствор|и́ться², и́тся, *pf.* (*of* ~я́ться) to dissolve.

раствор|я́ть(ся), я́ю(сь), *impf. of* ~и́ть(ся).

растека́|ться, юсь, *impf. of* расте́чься.

расте́ни|е, я, *n.* plant; однолетнее р. annual; многолетнее р. perennial; ползу́чее р. creeper.

растениево́д, а, *m.* plant-grower.

растениево́дств|о, а, *n.* plant-growing.

растере́ть, разотру́, разотрёшь, *past* растёр, растёрла, *pf.* (*of* растира́ть) **1.** to grind; р. в порошо́к to grind to powder; (*chem.*) to triturate. **2.** (по+*d.*) to rub (over), spread (over). **3.** to rub, massage.

растере́ться, разотру́сь, разотрёшься, *past* растёрся, растёрлась, *pf.* (*of* растира́ться) **1.** to become powdered, turn into powder; (*chem.*) to become triturated. **2.** (+*i.*) to rub oneself briskly (with).

растерз|а́ть, а́ю, *pf.* (*of* ~ывать) **1.** to tear to pieces. **2.** (*fig., poet.*) to lacerate; to harrow.

растерзыва|ть, ю, *impf. of* растерза́ть.

расте́рива|ть(ся), ю(сь), *impf. of* растеря́ть(ся).

расте́рянност|ь, и, *f.* confusion, perplexity, dismay.

расте́р|янный, *p.p.p. of* ~я́ть *and adj.* confused, perplexed, dismayed; р. взгляд look of dismay.

растер|я́ть, я́ю, *pf.* (*of* ~ивать) to lose (little by little).

растер|я́ться, я́юсь, *pf.* (*of* ~иваться) **1.** to get lost. **2.** to lose one's head.

расте́|чься, чётся, ку́тся, *past* ~кся, ~кла́сь, *pf.* (*of* ~ка́ться) **1.** to spill; to run. **2.** (*fig.*) to spread; по её лицу́ ~кла́сь улы́бка a smile spread over her face.

раст|и́, у́, ёшь, *past* рос, росла́, *impf.* **1.** (*biol., bot.*) to grow; (*of children*) to grow up; он рос на Украи́не he grew up in the Ukraine. **2.** (*fig.*) to grow, increase. **3.** (*fig.*) to advance, develop; to grow in stature.

растира́ни|е, я, *n.* **1.** grinding. **2.** (*med.*) massage.

растира́|ть(ся), ю(сь), *impf. of* растере́ть-(ся).

расти́ск|ать, аю, *pf.* (*of* ~ивать) (*coll.*) to shove (in).

расти́скива|ть, ю, *impf. of* расти́скать *and* расти́снуть.

расти́с|нуть, ну, нешь, *pf.* (*of* ~кивать) (*coll.*) to unclench.

расти́тельност|ь, и, *f.* **1.** vegetation; verdure; лишённый ~и barren. **2.** hair (*on face or body*).

расти́тельн|ый, *adj.* vegetable; ~ое ма́сло vegetable oil; р. мир, ~ое ца́рство the vegetable kingdom; ~ая пи́ща vegetable diet; жить ~ой жи́знью (*fig., iron.*) to vegetate.

ра|сти́ть, щу́, сти́шь, *impf.* **1.** to raise, bring up; to train; р. дете́й to raise children. **2.** to grow, cultivate; р. бо́роду to grow a beard.

растлева́|ть, ю, *impf. of* растли́ть.

растле́ни|е, я, *n.* **1.** seduction (*of minors*). **2.** (*fig.*) corruption; decay, decadence.

растле́нный, *adj.* corrupt; decadent.

растл|и́ть, ю́, и́шь, *pf.* (*of* ~ева́ть) **1.** to seduce (*minors*). **2.** (*fig.*) to corrupt.

расто́лк|а́ть, а́ю, *pf.* (*of* раста́лкивать) **1.** to push asunder, apart. **2.** to shake (*in order to awaken*).

растолкн|у́ть, у́, ёшь, *pf.* (*coll.*) to push asunder, part forcibly.

растолк|ова́ть, у́ю, *pf.* (*of* ~о́вывать) to explain.

растолко́выва|ть, ю, *impf. of* растолкова́ть.

растол|о́чь, ку́, чёшь, ку́т, *past* ~о́к, ~окла́, *pf. of* толо́чь.

растолсте́|ть, ю, *pf.* to grow stout, put on weight.

растоп|и́ть¹, лю́, ~ишь, *pf.* (*of* раста́пливать) to light, kindle.

растоп|и́ть², лю́, ~ишь, *pf.* (*of* раста́пливать) to melt; to (cause to) thaw.

растоп|и́ться¹, ~ится, *pf.* (*of* раста́пливаться) to begin to burn.

растоп|и́ться², ~ится, *pf.* (*of* раста́пливаться) to melt.

расто́пк|а, и, *f.* 1. lighting, kindling. 2. (*collect.*) kindling (wood).

растоп|та́ть, чу́, ~чешь, *pf.* (*of* раста́птывать) to trample, stamp (on), crush.

растопы́рива|ть, ю, *impf. of* растопы́рить.

растопы́р|ить, ю, ишь, *pf.* (*of* ~ивать) to spread wide, open wide.

расторг|а́ть, а́ю, *impf. of* ~нуть.

расторг|нуть, ну, нешь, *past* ~, ~ла, *pf.* (*of* ~а́ть) to cancel, dissolve, annul, abrogate (*a contract or agreement*); р. брак to dissolve a marriage.

расторг|ова́ть, у́ю, *pf.* (*of* ~о́вывать) (*coll.*) to sell out.

расторг|ова́ться, у́юсь, *pf.* (*of* ~о́вываться) (*coll.*). 1. to begin to do a brisk trade. 2. to have sold out.

расторже́ни|е, я, *n.* cancellation, dissolution, annulment, abrogation.

растормош|и́ть, у́, и́шь, *pf.* (*coll.*) 1. to tug (*in order to awaken*). 2. (*fig.*) to stir up, spur to activity.

расторо́п|ный (~ен, ~на), *adj.* (*coll.*) quick, prompt, smart; efficient.

расточ|а́ть, а́ю, *impf.* (*of* ~и́ть¹) 1. to waste, squander, dissipate. 2. (*fig.*) to lavish, shower; р. похвалы́ (+*d.*) to lavish praises (on, upon).

расточи́тел|ь, я, *m.* squanderer, waster, spendthrift.

расточи́тел|ьный (~ен, ~ьна), *adj.* extravagant, wasteful.

расточ|и́ть¹, у́, и́шь, *pf. of* ~а́ть.

расточ|и́ть², у́, ~и́шь, *pf.* (*of* раста́чивать) (*tech.*) to bore (out).

расто́чк|а, и, *f.* (*tech.*) boring.

растрав|и́ть, лю́, ~ишь, *pf.* (*of* ~ля́ть) to irritate; р. ра́ну (*fig.*) to rub salt on a wound; р. ста́рое го́ре (*fig.*) to re-open an old wound.

растравля́|ть, ю, *impf. of* растрави́ть.

растранжи́р|ить, ю, ишь, *pf. of* транжи́рить.

растра́т|а, ы, *f.* 1. spending; waste, squandering. 2. embezzlement, peculation.

растра́|тить, чу, тишь, *pf.* (*of* ~чивать) 1. to spend; to waste, squander, dissipate; р. си́лы to dissipate one's energies; р. своё вре́мя to fritter away one's time. 2. to embezzle, peculate.

растра́тчик, а, *m.* embezzler, peculator.

растра́чива|ть, ю, *impf. of* растра́тить.

растрево́ж|ить, у, ишь, *pf.* (*coll.*) to alarm, agitate; to put the wind up; р. мураве́йник to stir up an ant-hill.

растрево́ж|иться, усь, ишься, *pf.* (*coll.*) to get the wind up.

растрезво́н|ить, ю, ишь, *pf. of* трезво́нить.

растрёп|а, ы, *m. and f.* (*coll.*) sloven; tousle-head.

растрёп|анный, *p.p.p. of* ~а́ть *and adj.* tousled, dishevelled; tattered; быть в ~анных чу́вствах (*coll.*) to be confused, be mixed up.

растреп|а́ть, лю́, ~лешь, *pf.* 1. to disarrange; р. во́лосы кому́-н. to tousle someone's hair. 2. to tatter, tear (*a book, etc.*).

растреп|а́ться, ~лется, *pf.* 1. to get disarranged, get dishevelled. 2. to get tattered, get torn.

растре́ск|аться, ается, *pf.* (*of* ~ иваться) to crack; (*of skin*) to chap.

растре́скива|ться, ется, *impf. of* растре́скаться.

растро́га|ть, ю, *pf.* to move, touch; р. кого́-н. до слёз to move someone to tears.

растро́га|ться, юсь, *pf.* to be (deeply) moved, touched.

растру́б, а, *m.* funnel-shaped opening; bell, bell-mouth; socket (*of pipe*); с ~ом bell-shaped, bell-mouthed; брю́ки с ~ами bell-bottomed trousers; соедине́ние ~ом bell-and-spigot joint.

раструб|и́ть, лю́, и́шь, *pf.* (+*a.* or о+*p.*; *coll.*) to trumpet.

растряс|ти́, у́, ёшь, *past* ~, ~ла́, *pf.* 1. to strew (*hay, etc.*). 2. (*coll.*) to shake (*in order to awaken*). 3. (*impers.*) to jolt about. 4. (*coll.*) to squander.

растуш|ева́ть, у́ю, у́ешь, *pf.* (*of* ~ёвывать) to shade.

растушёвк|а, и, *f.* 1. shading. 2. stump (*for softening pencil-marks, etc., in drawing*).

растушёвыва|ть, ю, *impf. of* растушева́ть.

растя́гива|ть(ся), ю(сь), *impf. of* растяну́ть(ся).

растяже́ни|е, я, *n.* tension; stretch, stretching; (*med.*) strain, sprain.

растяжи́мост|ь, и, *f.* tensility, tensile strength; extensibility; expansibility.

растяжи́м|ый (~, ~а), *adj.* tensile; extensible; expansible; ~ое поня́тие loose concept.

растя́жк|а, и, *f.* 1. stretching, extension, lengthening out. 2. (*aeron.*) bracing wire, anti-drag wire.

растя́нутост|ь, и, *f.* 1. long-windedness, prolixity. 2. (*mil.*) extension, stretching out.

растя́н|утый, *p.p.p. of* ~у́ть *and adj.* 1. long-winded, prolix. 2. stretched; р. фронт (*mil.*) extended front.

растя|ну́ть, ну́, ~нешь, *pf.* (*of* ~ гивать) 1. to stretch (out). 2. (*med.*) to strain, sprain; р. себе́ му́скул to pull a muscle; р. себе́ свя́зку to strain a ligament. 3. to stretch too far; (*fig.*) to prolong, drag out; р. расска́з to drag out, spin out a story; р. слова́ to drawl.

растя|ну́ться, ну́сь, ⌐нешься, *pf.* (*of* ⌐ги-
ваться) **1.** to stretch (out), lengthen out.
2. to stretch too far; (*fig.*) to be prolonged,
drag out; обсужде́ние его́ докла́да ⌐ну́-
лось на полтора́ часа́ discussion of his lecture dragged out for an hour and a half.
3. to stretch oneself out, sprawl. **4.** *pf. only*
(*coll.*) to measure one's length, go head-
long.

растя́п|а, ы, *m. and f.* (*coll.*) muddler,
bungler.

расфас|ова́ть, у́ю, *pf.* (*of* ⌐о́вывать) to
pack up, parcel up.

расфасо́вк|а, и, *f.* packing, parcelling.

расфасо́выва|ть, ю, *impf. of* расфасо-
ва́ть.

расформирова́ни|е, я, *n.* breaking up;
(*mil.*) disbandment.

расформир|ова́ть, у́ю, *pf.* (*of* ⌐о́вывать) to
break up; (*mil.*) to disband.

расформиро́выва|ть, ю, *impf. of* расфор-
мирова́ть.

расфран|ти́ться, чу́сь, ти́шься, *pf.* (*coll.*)
to dress up.

расфранчённый, *adj.* (*coll.*) dressed up to
the nines; overdressed.

расфуфы́р|иться, юсь, ишься, *pf.* (*coll.,*
pejor.) to dress flashily.

расха́жива|ть, ю, *impf.* to walk, pace; р. по
ко́мнате to pace up and down a room.

расва́лива|ть, ю, *impf. of* расвали́ть.

расхвал|и́ть, ю́, ⌐ишь, *pf.* (*of* ⌐ивать) to
lavish, shower praise (on, upon).

расхва́рыва|ться, юсь, *impf. of* расхво-
ра́ться.

расхва́ста|ться, юсь, *pf.* (o+*p.*; *coll.*) to
boast extravagantly (of, about); to shoot
a line (about).

расхват|а́ть, а́ю, *pf.* (*of* ⌐ывать) to snatch,
seize (*with the object of purchasing, etc.*).

расхва́тыва|ть, ю, *impf. of* расхвата́ть.

расхвора́|ться, юсь, *pf.* (*of* расхва́рываться)
to fall ill; она́ не на шу́тку ⌐лась she is
seriously ill.

расхити́тел|ь, я, *m.* plunderer.

расхи́|тить, щу, тишь, *pf.* (*of* ⌐ща́ть) to
plunder, misappropriate.

расхища́|ть, ю, *impf. of* расхи́тить.

расхище́ни|е, я, *n.* plunder, plundering,
misappropriation.

расхлеб|а́ть, а́ю, *pf.* (*of* ⌐ывать) **1.** to eat
up (*without leaving anything*). **2.** (*fig.*) to
disentangle.

расхлёбыва|ть, ю, *impf. of* расхлеба́ть;
завари́л ка́шу, тепе́рь сам и ⌐й (*coll.*) you
got yourself into this mess, now get yourself
out of it.

расхля́банност|ь, и, *f.* **1.** looseness; insta-
bility. **2.** (*fig.*) slackness; laxity, lack of
discipline.

расхля́банн|ый, *adj.* (*coll.*) **1.** loose; un-
stable; ⌐ое здоро́вье tottering health; ⌐ая
похо́дка unstable gait, slouching. **2.** (*fig.*)
lax, undisciplined.

расхля́ба|ться, юсь, *pf.* (*coll.*) **1.** to come
loose, work loose. **2.** (*fig.*) to go to pieces.

расхо́д, а, *m.* **1.** expense; (*pl.*) expenses, outlay, cost; накладны́е ⌐ы overhead ex-
penses, overheads; де́ньги на карма́нные
⌐ы pocket-money; ввести́ в ⌐ы to put to
expense; взять на себя́ ⌐ы to bear the
expenses. **2.** (*in var. senses*) expenditure,
consumption; р. горю́чего fuel consumption. **3.** (*book-keeping*) expenditure, outlay;
прихо́д и р. income and expenditure; спи-
са́ть в р. to write off; (*fig., coll.*) to liquidate;
быть в ⌐е (*fig., coll.*) to be absent, be
missing. **4.** вы́вести в р. (*coll.*) to shoot.

расхо|ди́ться, жу́сь, ⌐дишься, *impf. of*
разойти́сь.

расхо́д|ный, *adj. of* ⌐; ⌐ная кни́га expenses
book, housekeeping book.

расхо́довани|е, я, *n.* expense, expenditure.

расхо́д|овать, ую, *impf.* (*of* из⌐) **1.** to spend,
expend. **2.** to use up, consume.

расхо́д|оваться, уюсь, *impf.* (*of* из⌐) **1.**
(*coll.*) to spend; to lay out money. **2.** *pass.*
of ⌐овать.

расхожде́ни|е, я, *n.* divergence; р. во
мне́ниях difference of opinion.

расхола́жива|ть, ю, *impf. of* расхолоди́ть.

расхоло|ди́ть, жу́, ди́шь, *pf.* (*of* расхола́жи-
вать) to damp the ardour (of).

расхо|те́ть, чу́, ⌐чешь, ти́м, ти́те, тя́т, *pf.*
(+*inf.*; *coll.*) to cease to want.

расхо|те́ться, ⌐чется, *pf.* (*impers.*+*d.*; *coll.*)
to cease to want; мне ⌐те́лось есть I no
longer want to eat.

расхохо|та́ться, чу́сь, ⌐чешься, *pf.* to
burst out laughing; to start roaring with
laughter.

расхрабр|и́ться, ю́сь, и́шься, *pf.* (*coll.*) to
screw up one's courage, pluck up courage.

расцара́п|ать, аю, *pf.* (*of* ⌐ывать) to scratch
(all over).

расцара́п|аться, аюсь, *pf.* (*of* ⌐ываться) to
scratch oneself.

расцара́пыва|ть(ся), ю(сь), *impf. of* рас-
цара́пать(ся).

расцве|сти́, ту́, тёшь, *past* ⌐л, ⌐ла́, *pf.* (*of*
⌐та́ть) to bloom; to blossom (out) (*also*
fig.); (*fig.*) to flourish; не дать чему́-н. р.
(*fig.*) to nip something in the bud; его́ лицо́
⌐ло́ улы́бкой his face was wreathed in
smiles.

расцве́т, а, *m.* bloom, blossoming (out);
(*fig.*) flourishing; flowering, heyday; в ⌐е
сил in the prime of life, in one's prime, in
one's heyday.

расцвета́|ть, ю, *impf. of* расцвести́.

расцве|ти́ть, чу́, ти́шь, *pf.* (*of* ⌐чивать)
1. to paint in bright colours. **2.** to deck,
adorn; р. фла́гами (*naut.*) to dress.

расцве́тк|а, и, *f.* colours; coloration,
colouring; нас порази́ла я́ркая р. обста-
но́вки в их кварти́ре we were struck by the
bright colours of the furnishings in their flat.

расцве́чивани|е, я, *n.* (*naut.*) dressing.

расцве́чива|ть, ю, *impf. of* расцвети́ть.

расцел|ова́ть, у́ю, *pf.* to kiss, smother with
kisses.

расцел|ова́ться, у́юсь, *pf.* to exchange kisses.

расце́нива|ть, ю, *impf. of* расцени́ть.

расцен|и́ть, ю́, ⌐ишь, *pf.* (*of* ⌐ивать) **1.** to
estimate, assess, value. **2.** (*fig.*) to rate,
assess; to regard, consider; как вы ⌐и́ли
его́ игру́? what did you think of his acting?

расце́нк|а, и, *f.* **1.** valuation. **2.** price.
3. (wage-)rate.

расце́н|очный, *adj. of* ⌐ка; ⌐очно-кон-
фли́ктная коми́ссия rates and disputes tribunal.

расцеп|и́ть, лю́, ⌐ишь, *pf.* (*of* ⌐ля́ть) to
uncouple, unhook; to disengage, release.

расцеп|и́ться, ⌐ится, *pf.* (*of* ⌐ля́ться) to
come uncoupled, come unhooked.

расцепле́ни|е, я, *n.* uncoupling, unhook-
ing; disengaging, release; механи́зм ⌐я
release gear.

расцепля́|ть(ся), ю, ет(ся), *impf. of* рас-
цепи́ть(ся).

расча́лк|а, и, *f.* (*tech., aeron.*) brace, bracing
wire.

расчер|ти́ть, чу́, ⌐тишь, *pf.* (*of* ⌐чивать)
to rule, line.

расчёрчива|ть, ю, *impf. of* расчерти́ть.

расче|са́ть, шу́, ⌐шешь, *pf.* (*of* ⌐сывать)
1. to comb; to card. **2.** to scratch.

расче|са́ться, шу́сь, ⌐шешься, *pf.* (*of*
⌐сываться) (*coll.*) **1.** to comb one's hair.
2. to scratch oneself.

расчёск|а, и, *f.* **1.** combing. **2.** comb.

расче́сть, разочту́, разочтёшь, *past* **расчёл,
разочла́,** *pf.* (*of* рассчи́тывать) **1.** to cal-
culate, compute. **2.** to dismiss, sack.

расче́сться, разочту́сь, разочтёшься, *past*
расчёлся, разочла́сь, *pf.* (*of* рассчи́ты-
вать(ся)) (c+*i.*) to settle accounts (with).

расчёсыва|ть(ся), ю(сь), *impf. of* рас-
чеса́ть(ся).

расчёт¹, а, *m.* **1.** calculation (*also tech.*);
computation; estimate, reckoning; из ⌐а
(+*g.*) on the basis (of), at a rate (of);
распредели́ть танте́му из ⌐а чи́стой
при́были to distribute a bonus on the basis
of net profits; из ⌐а трёх проце́нтов
годовы́х at three per cent per annum;
приня́ть в р. to take into account, consideration; не принима́ть в р. to leave out
of account; не принима́емый в р. negli-

gible; по мои́м ⌐ам by my reckoning; э́то
не входи́ло в мои́ ⌐ы I had not reckoned
with that, I had not bargained for that;
ошиби́ться в свои́х ⌐ах to be out in one's
reckoning, miscalculate. **2.** (*coll.*) gain,
advantage; нет ⌐а (+*inf.*) it is not worth
while, there is nothing to be gained. **3.**
(c+*i.*) settling (with); нали́чный р. cash
payment; безнали́чный р. payment by
written order, by cheque; быть в ⌐е (c+*i.*)
to be quits (with), be even (with). **4.** dismissal, discharge; дать р. (+*d.*) to dismiss,
sack; получи́ть р. to be dismissed, get the
sack; взять р. to leave one's work, hand in
notice.

расчёт², а, *m.* (*mil.*) crew, team, detachment; оруди́йный р. gun crew.

расчётливост|ь, и, *f.* economy, thrift.

расчётлив|ый (⌐, ⌐a), *adj.* economical,
thrifty; careful.

расчётн|ый, *adj.* **1.** calculation, computa-
tion; ⌐ое ме́сто (*navigation*) dead reckoning
position; ⌐ая оши́бка error in computation; ⌐ая табли́ца calculation table. **2.**
pay, accounts; р. бала́нс balance of pay-
ments; ⌐ая ве́домость pay-roll, pay-sheet;
р. день pay-day; ⌐ая кни́жка pay-book;
р. отде́л accounts department. **3.** (*tech.*)
rated, calculated, designed; ⌐ая величина́
rating; ⌐ая мо́щность rated capacity; ⌐ая
ско́рость rated speed.

расчётчик, а, *m.* estimator, designer.

расчи́сл|ить, ю, ишь, *pf.* (*of* ⌐я́ть) to cal-
culate, compute, reckon.

расчисл|я́ть, я́ю, *impf. of* ⌐ить.

расчи́|стить, щу, стишь, *pf.* (*of* ⌐ща́ть) to
clear.

расчи́|ститься, стится, *pf.* (*of* ⌐ща́ться)
1. (*of the sky*) to clear. **2.** *pass. of* ⌐стить.

расчи́стк|а, и, *f.* clearing.

расчиха́|ться, юсь, *pf.* to sneeze repeatedly.

расчища́|ть(ся), ю, ет(ся), *impf. of* рас-
чи́стить(ся).

расчлене́ни|е, я, *n.* **1.** dismemberment; par-
tition. **2.** (*mil.*) development; dispersal;
deployment; extension.

расчлен|ённый, *p.p.p. of* ⌐и́ть *and adj.*;
поря́док (*mil.*) dispersed formation; р.
строй (*mil.*) extended order, open order
formation.

расчлен|и́ть, ю́, и́шь, *pf.* (*of* ⌐я́ть) **1.** to dis-
member; to partition; to break up, divide.
2. (*mil.*) to develop; to disperse; to deploy;
to extend.

расчлен|я́ть, я́ю, *impf. of* ⌐и́ть.

расчу́вств|оваться, уюсь, *pf.* (*coll.*) to be
deeply emotional.

расчу́ха|ть, ю, *pf.* (*coll.*) to nose out; (*fig.*)
to scent, sense; он ⌐л, в чём де́ло he sensed
what was the matter.

расшал|и́ться, ю́сь, и́шься, *pf.* to get up to mischief, start playing about.

расша́рк|аться, аюсь, *pf.* (*of* ~иваться) (*obs.*) to bow, scraping one's feet; (*fig.*) to bow and scrape.

расша́ркива|ться, юсь, *impf. of* расша́ркаться.

расша́танност|ь, и, *f.* shakiness; shattered condition.

расша́т|анный, *p.p.p. of* ~а́ть *and adj.* shaky; rickety; tottering; ~анные не́рвы shattered nerves.

расшат|а́ть, а́ю, *pf.* (*of* ~ывать) 1. to shake loose; to make rickety. 2. (*fig.*) to shatter; to impair; э́тот уда́р ~а́л её здоро́вье the blow shattered her health; р. дисципли́ну to impair discipline.

расшат|а́ться, а́юсь, *pf.* (*of* ~ываться) 1. to get loose; to become rickety. 2. (*fig.*) to go to pieces, crack up.

расша́тыва|ть(ся), ю(сь), *impf. of* расшата́ть(ся).

расшвы́рива|ть, ю, *impf. of* расшвыря́ть.

расшвыр|я́ть, я́ю, *pf.* (*of* ~ивать) to throw about, throw left and right, send flying.

расшеве́лива|ть, ю, *impf. of* расшевели́ть.

расшевел|и́ть, ю́, и́шь, *pf.* (*of* ~ивать) to stir, shake; (*fig.*) to stir, rouse.

расшевел|и́ться, ю́сь, и́шься, *pf.* to begin to stir; (*fig.*) to rouse oneself.

расшиб|а́ть(ся), а́ю(сь), *impf. of* расшиби́ть(ся).

расшиб|и́ть, у́, ёшь, *past* ~, ~ла, *pf.* (*of* ~а́ть) (*coll.*) 1. to hurt; to knock, stub; р. па́лец ноги́ об ка́мень to stub one's toe on a rock. 2. to break up, smash to pieces.

расшиб|и́ться, у́сь, ёшься, *past* ~ся, ~лась, *pf.* (*of* ~а́ться) (*coll.*) to hurt oneself, knock oneself.

расши́в|а, ы, *f.* rasshiva (*large flat-bottomed sailing-boat in use on Volga and Caspian Sea*).

расшива́|ть, ю, *impf. of* расши́ть.

расшивно́й, *adj.* embroidered.

расшире́ни|е, я, *n.* 1. broadening, widening, expansion, extension. 2. (*phys.*) expansion. 3. (*med.*) dilation, dilatation; distension; р. се́рдца dilation of the heart; р. вен varicose veins.

расши́р|енный, *p.p.p. of* ~ить *and adj.* broadened, expanded; enlarged; dilated; more extensive, more comprehensive; ~енная програ́мма more extensive programme; ~енные зрачки́ dilated pupils; с ~енными глаза́ми wide-eyed; ~енное воспроизво́дство (*phys.*) breeding.

расшири́тел|ь, я, *m.* (*tech.*) dilator; reamer.

расшири́тельн|ый, *adj.* broad, extended; ~ое толкова́ние broad interpretation.

расши́р|ить, ю, ишь, *pf.* (*of* ~я́ть) to broaden, widen; to enlarge; to expand; to extend; р. чей-н. кругозо́р to broaden someone's outlook, mind; р. сфе́ру влия́ния to extend a sphere of influence.

расши́р|иться, юсь, ишься, *pf.* (*of* ~я́ться) 1. to broaden, widen, gain in breadth; to extend. 2. (*phys.*) to expand, dilate.

расшир|я́ть(ся), я́ю(сь), *impf. of* ~и́ть(ся).

расши́ть¹, разошью́, разошьёшь, *pf.* (*of* расшива́ть) to embroider.

расши́ть², разошью́, разошьёшь, *pf.* (*of* расшива́ть) to undo, unpick.

расшифр|ова́ть, у́ю, *pf.* (*of* ~о́вывать) to decipher, decode; (*fig.*) to interpret.

расшифро́вк|а, и, *f.* deciphering, decoding; р. аэрофотосни́мков (*mil.*) interpretation of aerial photographs.

расшифро́вщик, а, *m.* decoder.

расшифро́выва|ть, ю, *impf. of* расшифрова́ть.

расшнур|ова́ть, у́ю, *pf.* (*of* ~о́вывать) to unlace.

расшнур|ова́ться, у́юсь, *pf.* (*of* ~о́вываться) 1. to come unlaced, come undone. 2. to unlace oneself (*from a corset, etc.*).

расшнуро́выва|ть(ся), ю(сь), *impf. of* расшнурова́ть(ся).

расшум|е́ться, лю́сь, и́шься, *pf.* (*coll.*) to get noisy, kick up a din.

расще́др|иться, юсь, ишься, *pf.* (*coll., also iron.*) to have a fit of generosity.

расще́лин|а, ы, *f.* cleft, crevice.

расщёлкива|ть, ю, *impf. of* расщёлкнуть.

расщёлк|нуть, ну, нешь, *pf.* (*of* ~ивать) to crack open.

расще́п, а, *m.* split.

расщеп|и́ть, лю́, и́шь, *pf.* (*of* ~ля́ть) 1. to split, splinter. 2. (*phys.*) to split; (*chem.*) to break up.

расщеп|и́ться, и́тся, *pf.* (*of* ~ля́ться) to split, splinter.

расщепле́ни|е, я, *n.* 1. splitting, splintering. 2. (*phys.*) splitting, fission; (*chem.*) break-up, disintegration; р. ядра́ nuclear fission.

расщепля́|ть(ся), ю, ет(ся), *impf. of* расщепи́ть(ся).

расщепля́|ющийся, *pres. part. of* ~ться *and adj.* (*phys.*) fissile, fissionable.

ра́та|й, я, *m.* (*folk poet.*) ploughman.

ратификацио́нн|ый, *adj.* ~ые гра́моты (*dipl.*) instruments of ratification.

ратифика́ци|я, и, *f.* (*dipl.*) ratification.

ратифици́р|овать, ую, *impf. and pf.* (*dipl.*) to ratify.

ра́тник, а, *m.* 1. (*arch.*) warrior. 2. (*obs.*) militiaman.

ра́тн|ый, *adj.* (*obs. or poet.*) martial, warlike; р. по́двиг feat of arms.

ра́т|овать, ую, *impf.* (*obs.*) (за + *a.*) to fight (for), stand up (for); (про́тив) to declaim (against), inveigh (against).

ра́туш|а, и, *f.* **1.** (*esp. in Poland and the Baltic States*) town hall. **2.** (*hist.*) town council.

рат|ь, и, *f.* (*arch. or poet.*) **1.** host, army. **2.** war; battle; идти́ на р. to go into battle.

ра́унд, а, *m.* (*sport*) round.

ра́ут, а, *m.* rout; reception.

рафина́д, а, *m.* lump sugar.

рафина́д|ный, *adj.* of ~; р. заво́д sugar refinery.

рафинёр, а, *m.* (*tech.*; *of paper*) refiner.

рафини́рованност|ь, и, *f.* refinement.

рафини́рова|нный, *p.p.p.* of ~ть and *adj.* (*fig.*) refined.

рафини́р|овать, ую, *impf. and pf.* to refine.

раха́т-луку́м, а, *m.* Turkish delight.

рахи́т, а, *m.* (*med.*) rachitis, rickets.

рахи́тик, а, *m.* sufferer from rachitis, rickets.

рахити́чный, *adj.* (*med.*) rachitic, rickety.

раце́|я, и, *f.* (*coll., iron.*) sermon, lecture; чита́ть кому́-н. ~ю to read someone a lecture.

рацио́н, а, *m.* ration, food allowance.

рационализа́тор, а, *m.* rationalizer.

рационализа́тор|ский, *adj.* of ~; ~ское предложе́ние rationalization proposal, proposal for improving production methods.

рационализа́ци|я, и, *f.* rationalization, improvement.

рационализи́р|овать, ую, *impf. and pf.* to rationalize, improve.

рационали́зм, а, *m.* (*philos.*) rationalism.

рационали́ст, а, *m.* rationalist.

рационалисти́ческий, *adj.* rationalistic.

рационалисти́ч|ный (~ен, ~на), *adj.* rational.

рациона́льно, *adv.* rationally; efficiently; р. испо́льзовать to make efficient use (of), make good use (of).

рациона́л|ьный (~ен, ~ьна), *adj.* **1.** rational; efficient. **2.** (*math.*) rational.

ра́ци|я, и, *f.* portable radio transmitter, walkie-talkie set.

ра́чий, *adj.* of рак; ра́чьи глаза́ goggle eyes.

рачи́тельност|ь, и, *f.* (*obs.*) zealousness; assiduity.

рачи́тел|ьный (~ен, ~ьна), *adj.* (*obs.*) zealous; assiduous.

ра́шкул|ь, я, *m.* (*art*) charcoal-pencil.

ра́шпил|ь, я, *m.* (*tech.*) rasp, rasp file; grater.

рван|у́ть, у́, ёшь, *pf.* **1.** to jerk; to tug (at); р. кого́-н. за рука́в to tug someone by the sleeve. **2.** to start with a jerk, get off with a jerk; вдруг ~у́л ве́тер suddenly a wind got up.

рван|у́ться, у́сь, ёшься, *pf.* to rush, dash, dart.

рва́н|ый, *adj.* torn; lacerated; ~ые баш-

маки́ broken shoes; ~ая ра́на (*med.*) lacerated wound, laceration.

рван|ь, и, *no pl., f.* **1.** rags; broken footwear. **2.** (*coll.*) scoundrel, scamp; (*collect.*) riff-raff.

рвать¹, рву, рвёшь, *past* рвал, рвала́, рва́ло, *impf.* **1.** to tear; to rend; to rip; р. в клочки́ to tear to pieces; р. на себе́ во́лосы to tear one's hair; р. и мета́ть to rant and rave. **2.** to pull out, tear out; р. зу́бы to pull out teeth; р. из рук у кого́-н. to snatch out of someone's hands; р. с ко́рнем to uproot. **3.** to pick, pluck; р. цветы́ to pick flowers. **4.** to blow up. **5.** (*fig.*) to break off, sever; р. отноше́ния с кем-н. to break off relations with someone.

рвать², рвёт, *past* рва́ло, *impf.* (*of* вы́рвать²) (*impers.*; *coll.*) to vomit, throw up, be sick.

рва́|ться¹, рвётся, *past* ~лся, ~ла́сь, ~ло́сь, *impf.* **1.** to break; to tear. **2.** to burst, explode.

рва́|ться², рвусь, рвёшься, *past* ~лся, ~ла́сь, ~ло́сь, *impf.* to strain (to, at); to be bursting (to); р. в бой to be bursting to go into action; р. в дра́ку to be spoiling for a fight; р. на свобо́ду to be dying to be free; р. с при́вязи to strain at the leash.

рвач, а́, *m.* (*coll.*) self-seeker, grabber.

рва́ческий, *adj.* (*coll.*) self-seeking, grabbing.

рва́честв|о, а, *n.* (*coll.*) self-seeking, grabbing.

рве́ни|е, я, *n.* zeal, fervour, ardour.

рво́т|а, ы, *f.* **1.** vomiting, retching. **2.** vomit.

рво́тн|ый, *adj.* vomitive, emetic; р. ка́мень nux vomica; р. ко́рень ipecacuanha; ~ое сре́дство, *also as noun* ~ое, ~ого, *n.* emetic.

рде|ть, ю, *impf.* (*of something red*) to glow.

реабилита́ци|я, и, *f.* rehabilitation.

реабилити́р|овать, ую, *impf. and pf.* to rehabilitate.

реабилити́р|оваться, уюсь, *impf. and pf.* **1.** to vindicate oneself. **2.** *pass.* of ~овать.

реаге́нт, а, *m.* (*chem.*) reagent.

реаги́р|овать, ую, *impf.* (на+*a.*) to react (to) (*also fig.*); (*fig.*) to respond (to).

реакти́в, а, *m.* (*chem.*) reagent.

реакти́вност|ь, и, *f.* (*physiol.*) reactivity.

реакти́вн|ый, *adj.* **1.** (*chem., phys.*) reactive; ~ая бума́га (*chem.*) reagent paper, test-paper; ~ая кату́шка (*electr.*) reactive coil, choke coil, inductance coil. **2.** (*tech., aeron.*) jet propulsion; jet(-propelled); р. дви́гатель jet engine; р. самолёт jet-propelled aircraft.

реа́ктор, а, *m.* (*phys., tech.*) reactor, pile; р. для дви́гателей propulsion reactor; р. на бы́стрых нейтро́нах fast (neutron) reactor; р.-размножи́тель, р. с расши́ренным воспроизво́дством я́дерного горю́чего breeder reactor, breeder plant.

реакционе́р, а, *m.* (*polit.*) reactionary.

реакцио́н|ный (~ен, ~на), *adj.* (*polit.*) reactionary.

реа́кци|я, и, *f.* (*chem., phys., polit.; fig.*) reaction.

реа́л¹, а, *m.* (*hist.*) real (*Spanish coin*).

реа́л², а, *m.* (*typ.*) composing frame.

реализа́ци|я, и, *f.* realization (= (*i*) implementation. (*ii*) sale).

реали́зм, а, *m.* (*in var. senses*) realism.

реализ|ова́ть, у́ю, *impf. and pf.* to realize (= (*i*) to implement. (*ii*) to sell); р. це́нные бума́ги to realize securities.

реали́ст, а, *m.* (*in var. senses*) realist.

реалисти́ческий, *adj.* 1. (*art, lit., etc.*) realist. 2. realistic.

реалисти́ч|ный (~ен, ~на), *adj.* = ~еский 2.

реа́льност|ь, и, *f.* 1. reality. 2. practicability.

реа́л|ьный (~ен, ~ьна), *adj.* 1. real. 2. realizable, practicable, workable; р. план workable plan. 3. realistic; practical; вести́ ~ьную поли́тику to pursue a realistic policy; ~ьная за́работная пла́та real wages; ~ьное учи́лище (*obs.*) modern school (*non-classical secondary school*).

ребёнок, ка (*as pl.* **ребя́та, ребя́т** *and* **де́ти, дете́й**), *m.* child, infant; грудно́й р. child in arms.

рёберный, *adj.* (*anat.*) costal.

ребо́рд|а, ы, *f.* flange.

ребри́ст|ый (~, ~а), *adj.* 1. having prominent ribs. 2. (*tech.*) ribbed; costate; finned.

ребр|о́, а́, *pl.* ~а, рёбер, ~ам, *n.* 1. (*anat., tech.*) rib; (*tech.*) fin; ни́жние ~а short ribs; пересчита́ть кому́-н. ~а (*coll.*) to give someone a drubbing. 2. edge, verge; поста́вить ~о́м to place edgewise, place on its side; поста́вить вопро́с ~о́м to put a question point-blank.

ре́бус, а, *m.* rebus.

ребя́та, ребя́т (*coll.*) 1. (*sing.* ребёнок) children. 2. (*of adults*) boys, lads.

ребяти́ш|ки, ек, кам, *no sing.* (*coll.*) children, kids.

ребя́ческий, *adj.* 1. of a child, childish. 2. (*fig.*) childish, infantile, puerile.

ребя́честв|о, а, *n.* childishness, puerility.

ребя́чий, *adj.* (*coll.*) childish.

ребя́ч|иться, усь, ишься, *impf.* (*coll.*) to behave like a child, behave childishly.

рев- *abbr. of* революцио́нный.

рёв, а, *m.* 1. roar; bellow, howl; р. ве́тра the howling of the wind. 2. (*coll.*) howl (*of a child, etc.*); подня́ть р. to raise a howl.

рева́нш, а, *m.* revenge; (*sport*) return match.

реванши́зм, а, *m.* (*polit.*) revanchism.

реванши́ст, а, *m.* (*polit.*) revanchist, revenge-seeker.

реве́н|ный, *adj. of* ~ь; р. порошо́к gregory-powder.

реве́н|ь, я́, *m.* rhubarb.

револю́ция, и, *f.* (*obs.*) curts(e)y; сде́лать р. to curts(e)y, drop a curts(e)y.

— *[the above entry reads]* **реверанс, а,** *m.* (*obs.*) curts(e)y; сде́лать р. to curts(e)y, drop a curts(e)y.

реверберáци|я, и, *f.* (*tech.*) reverberation.

ре́верс, а, *m.* 1. reverse (*of coin, etc.*). 2. (*tech.*) reversing gear. 3. (*obs.*) caution-money (*deposit required to be paid by young officers on marrying*).

реверси́вный, *adj.* (*tech.*) reversing, reversible.

реве́рси|я, и, *f.* 1. (*leg.*) reversion. 2. (*biol.*) reversion (to type). 3. (*tech.*) reversing.

рев|е́ть, у́, ёшь, *impf.* 1. to roar; to bellow, howl. 2. (*coll.*) to howl; ревмя́ р. to set up a fearful howl.

ревизиони́зм, а, *m.* (*polit.*) revisionism.

ревизиони́ст, а, *m.* (*polit.*) revisionist.

ревизио́нн|ый, *adj.* ~ая коми́ссия inspection commission; auditing commission.

реви́зи|я, и, *f.* 1. inspection; audit. 2. revision. 3. (*hist.*) census.

ревиз|ова́ть, у́ю, *impf. and pf.* 1. (*pf. also* об~) to inspect. 2. to revise.

ревизо́р, а, *m.* inspector.

ревко́м, а, *m.* (*abbr. of* революцио́нный комите́т) revolutionary committee.

ревмати́зм, а, *m.* rheumatism; rheumatics; суставно́й р. rheumatic fever.

ревма́тик, а, *m.* rheumatic.

ревмати́ческий, *adj.* rheumatic.

рев|мя́, *see* ~е́ть.

ревни́в|ец, ца, *m.* jealous man.

ревни́в|ый (~, ~а), *adj.* jealous.

ревни́тел|ь, я, *m.* (+*g.*; *obs.*) adherent (of), enthusiastic supporter (of).

ревн|ова́ть, у́ю, *impf.* to be jealous; р. кого́-н. (к) to be jealous because of someone's attachment (to), begrudge someone's attachment (to); она́ ~ова́ла му́жа к его́ рабо́те she was jealous of her husband's work.

ре́вност|ный (~ен, ~на), *adj.* zealous, earnest, fervent.

ре́вност|ь, и, *f.* 1. jealousy. 2. (*obs.*) zeal, earnestness, fervour.

револьве́р, а, *m.* revolver, pistol; шести́-заря́дный р. six-shooter.

револьве́р|ный, *adj.* 1. *adj. of* ~. 2. (*tech.*) ~ная голо́вка capstan head; р. стано́к capstan lathe, turret lathe.

револьве́рщик, а, *m.* capstan, turret lathe operator.

революционе́р, а, *m.* revolutionary.

революционизи́р|овать, ую, *impf. and pf.* 1. to spread revolutionary ideas (among, in). 2. to revolutionize.

революционизи́р|оваться, уюсь, *impf. and pf.* 1. to become permeated with revolutionary ideas. 2. to be revolutionized.

революцио́нност|ь, и, *f.* revolutionary character.

революцио́н|ный (~ен, ~на), *adj.* revolutionary.

револю́ци|я, и, *f.* revolution.

реву́н, а́, *m.* (*zool.*; *coll.*) howler.

ревю́, *indecl., n.* revue.

рега́ли|я, и, *f.* (*hist.*) state monopoly.

рега́ли|и, й, *pl.* (*sing.* ~я, ~и), *f.* regalia.

регенерати́вный, *adj.* (*tech.*) regenerative.

регенера́ци|я, и, *f.* (*tech.*) regeneration.

ре́гент, а, *m.* 1. regent. 2. precentor.

ре́гентств|о, а, *n.* regency.

региона́льный, *adj.* regional.

реги́стр, а, *m.* (*in var. senses*) register.

регистра́тор, а, *m.* registrar.

регистрату́р|а, ы, *f.* registry.

регистра́ци|я, и, *f.* registration.

регистри́р|овать, ую, *impf. and pf.* (*pf. also* за~) to register, record.

регистри́р|оваться, уюсь, *impf. and pf.* (*pf. also* за~) 1. to register (oneself). 2. to register one's marriage. 3. *pass. of* ~овать.

регла́мент, а, *m.* 1. regulations; standing orders. 2. (*at a meeting*) time-limit; установи́ть р. to fix a time-limit.

регламента́ци|я, и, *f.* regulation.

регламенти́р|овать, ую, *impf. and pf.* to regulate.

регла́н, а, *m.* raglan (*coat*).

регресси́в|ный (~ен, ~на), *adj.* regressive.

регресси́р|овать, ую, *impf.* to regress.

регули́ровани|е, я, *n.* 1. regulation, control. 2. adjustment.

регули́р|овать, ую, *impf.* 1. (*pf.* у~) to regulate; to control; р. у́личное движе́ние to control traffic. 2. (*pf.* от~) to adjust; р. мото́р to tune an engine.

регулиро́вщик, а, *m.* traffic-controller.

ре́гул|ы, ~, *no sing.* (*obs.*) menses, menstruation.

регуля́рност|ь, и, *f.* regularity.

регуля́р|ный (~ен, ~на), *adj.* regular; ~ные войска́ regular troops, regulars.

регуля́тор, а, *m.* (*tech.*) regulator; governor.

редакти́ровани|е, я, *n.* editing.

редакти́р|овать, ую, *impf.* 1. (*pf.* от~) to edit (*a manuscript, etc.*). 2. *impf. only* to edit, be editor of (*a journal, etc.*). 3. (*pf.* с~) to word.

реда́ктор, а, *m.* editor; гла́вный р., отве́тственный р. editor-in-chief.

реда́кторский, *adj.* editorial.

реда́кторств|о, а, *n.* editorship.

реда́кторств|овать, ую, *impf.* (*coll.*) to be an editor.

редакцио́нн|ый, *adj.* editorial, editing; ~ая коми́ссия drafting committee.

реда́кци|я, и, *f.* 1. editorial staff. 2. editorial office. 3. editing; под ~ей (+*g.*) edited (by). 4. wording.

реде́|ть, ю, *impf.* (*of* по~) to thin, thin out; ~ющие во́лосы thinning hair.

реди́с, а, *no pl., m.* radish(es).

реди́ск|а, и, *f.* radish.

ре́д|кий (~ок, ~ка́, ~ко), *adj.* 1. thin, sparse; ~кие во́лосы thin hair; ~кие зу́бы widely spaced teeth; р. лес sparse wood; ~кая ткань flimsy fabric. 2. rare; uncommon; ~кая кни́га rare book; ~кая красота́ rare beauty; он — р. подража́тель he is a rare mimic.

ре́дко, *adv.* 1. sparsely; far apart. 2. rarely, seldom.

редколе́сь|е, я, *n.* sparse growth of trees.

редколле́ги|я, и, *f.* (*abbr. of* редакцио́нная колле́гия) editorial board.

ре́дкост|ный (~ен, ~на), *adj.* rare; uncommon.

ре́дкост|ь, и, *f.* 1. thinness, sparseness. 2. rarity; на р. uncommonly; на р. проница́тельный челове́к a person of rare discernment; не р., что not uncommonly; не р., что он просиживает ночь за кни́гой it is not unusual for him to sit up all night reading. 3. rarity, curiosity, curio.

реду́ктор, а, *m.* 1. (*tech.*) reducing gear. 2. (*chem.*) reducing agent.

реду́кци|я, и, *f.* (*in var. senses*) reduction.

реду́т, а, *m.* (*mil., hist.*) redoubt.

редуци́рова|нный, *p.p.p. of* ~ть *and adj.* (*ling.*) reduced.

редуци́р|овать, ую, *impf. and pf.* (*in var. senses*) to reduce.

ре́дьк|а, и, *f.* radish; надое́ло э́то мне ху́же го́рькой ~и I am sick and tired of it.

реду́йт, а, *m.* (*mil.*) reduit.

рее́стр, а, *m.* list, roll, register.

ре́|же, *comp. of* ~дкий *and* ~дко.

режи́м, а, *m.* 1. (*polit.*) régime. 2. routine; procedure; (*med.*) regimen; (*tech.*) mode of operation; шко́льный р. school routine; р. пита́ния diet; р. безопа́сности safety measures; р. эконо́мии policy of economy. 3. conditions; (*tech.*) working conditions, operating conditions; р. реки́ habits of a river. 4. (*tech.*) rate; р. набо́ра высоты́ (*aeron.*) rate of climb.

режи́мный, *adj.* secret, classified.

режиссёр, а, *m.* (*theatr.*) producer; (*cinema*) director.

режиссёр|ский, *adj. of* ~.

режисси́р|овать, ую, *impf.* (*theatr.*) to produce, stage; (*cinema*) to direct.

режиссу́р|а, ы, *f.* (*theatr.*) 1. producing; profession of producer. 2. production. 3. (*collect.*) producers.

ре́жущ|ий, *pres. part. act. of* ре́зать *and adj.* cutting, sharp; ~ая кро́мка cutting edge,

blade; р. уда́р slash; р. штык knife
bayonet.

реза́к, а́, *m.* **1.** chopping-knife, chopper;
pole-axe. **2.** slaughterhouse worker.

ре́зан|ый, *adj.* **1.** cut; р. хлеб cut loaf.
2. (*sport*) slice, sliced; ~ая пода́ча (*tennis*)
slice service; р. уда́р slice.

ре́|зать, жу, жешь, *impf.* **1.** *impf. only* to cut;
to slice. **2.** *impf. only* (*med.*) to operate,
open; (*coll., joc.*) to carve. **3.** *impf. only* to
cut (= *to have the power of cutting*); э́ти
но́жницы бо́льше не ~жут these scissors
do not cut any longer. **4.** (*pf.* за~) to kill;
to slaughter; to knife. **5.** *impf. only* (по+*d.*)
to carve (on), engrave (on). **6.** *impf. only* to
cut (into); to cause sharp pain; реме́нь
~зал его́ плечо́ the strap was cutting into
his shoulder; у меня́ ~зало в желу́дке I had
griping pains in the stomach; р. глаза́ to
irritate the eyes; р. слух to pain the ear,
grate upon the ears. **7.** (*coll.*) to speak
bluntly; р. пра́вду в глаза́ to speak the
truth boldly. **8.** *impf. only* to pass close (to),
shave; р. корму́ (*naut.*) to pass close astern.
9. (*pf.* с~) (*sport*) to slice, cut, chop.

ре́|заться, жусь, жешься, *impf.* **1.** (*pf.*
про~) (*of teeth*) to cut, come through; у
него́ уже́ ~жутся зу́бы he is already teeth-
ing, cutting teeth. **2.** *impf. only* to play
(*games of chance*).

резв|и́ться, лю́сь, и́шься, *impf.* to sport,
gambol.

ре́звост|ь, и, *f.* **1.** sportiveness, playfulness,
friskiness. **2.** (*sport*; *of a horse*) speed; пока-
за́ть хоро́шую р. to show a good time.

ре́зв|ый (~, ~а́, ~о), *adj.* **1.** sportive, play-
ful, frisky. **2.** (*sport*; *of a horse*) fast.

резед|а́, ы́, *f.* (*bot.*) mignonette.

резе́кци|я, и, *f.* (*med.*) resection.

резе́рв, а, *m.* (*mil., etc.*) reserve(s); име́ть в
~e to have in reserve; перевести́ в р. (*mil.*)
to transfer to the reserve.

резерва́ци|я, и, *f.* reservation.

резерви́р|овать, ую, *impf. and pf.* to re-
serve.

резерви́ст, а, *m.* (*mil.*) reservist.

резе́рвный, *adj.* (*mil. and fin.*) reserve.

резервуа́р, а, *m.* reservoir, vessel, tank.

рез|е́ц, ца́, *m.* **1.** (*tech.*) cutter; cutting tool;
chisel. **2.** (*tooth*) incisor.

резиде́нт, а, *m.* (*dipl., etc.*) resident (*esp.
of member of Intelligence Service operating in
foreign country*).

резиде́нци|я, и, *f.* residence.

рези́н|а, ы, *f.* (india-)rubber.

рези́нк|а, и, *f.* **1.** (india-)rubber, eraser.
2. (piece of) elastic.

рези́нов|ый, *adj.* **1.** rubber; ~ая промы́ш-
ленность rubber industry; ~ые сапоги́
gum boots. **2.** elastic.

рези́нщик, а, *m.* worker in rubber industry.

ре́зк|а, и, *f.* cutting.

ре́з|кий (~ок, ~ка́, ~ко), *adj.* sharp; harsh;
abrupt; р. ве́тер sharp wind, cutting wind;
р. го́лос shrill voice; р. за́пах strong smell;
~кое измене́ние abrupt change, sudden
switch; ~кие мане́ры abrupt manners; р.
свет strong light, harsh light; ~кие слова́
sharp words; ~кие черты́ лица́ sharp
features.

ре́зкост|ь, и, *f.* **1.** sharpness; harshness;
abruptness. **2.** sharp words, harsh words;
наговори́ть ~ей to use harsh words.

резн|о́й, *adj.* carved, fretted; ~а́я рабо́та
(*archit.*) carving, fretwork.

резн|я́, и́, *f.* slaughter, butchery, carnage.

резолюти́вн|ый, *adj.* containing conclu-
sions, containing a resolution; в ~ой
фо́рме in the form of a resolution.

резолю́ци|я, и, *f.* **1.** resolution; вы́нести,
приня́ть ~ю to pass, adopt, approve, carry
a resolution. **2.** instructions (*on a document*);
наложи́ть ~ю to append instructions.

резо́н, а, *m.* (*coll.*) **1.** reason, basis; в э́том
есть свой р. there is a reason for this. **2.**
reasoning, argument; они́ не хоте́ли
слу́шать никаки́х ~ов they would not
listen to any argument.

резона́нс, а, *m.* **1.** (*phys.*) resonance. **2.**
(*fig.*) echo, response; дать, име́ть р. to have
repercussions.

резона́тор, а, *m.* (*phys.*) resonator.

резонёр, а, *m.* arguer, philosophizer.

резонёрств|овать, ую, *impf.* to argue, philo-
sophize.

резони́р|овать, ую, *impf.* to resound.

резо́н|ный (~ен, ~на), *adj.* reasonable.

результа́т, а, *m.* result; outcome; ~ы
обсле́дования findings; дать ~ы to yield
results; в ~e (+*g.*) as a result (of).

результати́вный, *adj.* resulting.

ре́з|че, *comp. of* ~кий *and* ~ко.

ре́зчик, а, *m.* engraver, carver.

рез|ь, и, *f.* colic; gripe.

резьб|а́, ы́, *f.* **1.** carving, fretwork. **2.** (*tech.*)
thread(ing).

резюме́, *indecl., n.* summary, résumé.

резюми́р|овать, ую, *impf. and pf.* to sum up,
summarize, recapitulate.

рейд[1], а, *m.* (*naut.*) road(s), roadstead.

рейд[2], а, *m.* **1.** (*mil.*) raid. **2.** 'swoop' (*by
group of journalists, to investigate alleged mal-
practice, grievance, etc.*); special (*journalistic*)
assignment.

ре́йдер, а, *m.* (*naut.*) (*commerce*) raider.

ре́йк|а, и, *f.* **1.** lath. **2.** зубча́тая р. (*tech.*)
rack; переда́ча зубча́той ~ой rack and
pinion gear. **3.** (*surveyor's*) rod, pole.

рейнве́йн, а, *m.* hock.

ре́йнск|ий, *adj.* Rhine, Rhenish; ~ое (вино́) Rhine wine, hock.

рейс¹, a, *m.* trip, run (*of public transport vehicle*); voyage, passage; пе́рвый р. maiden voyage, maiden trip.

рейс², a, *m.* reis (*Portuguese or Brazilian coin*).

рейсфе́дер, a, *m.* 1. drawing-pen, mapping pen. 2. pencil-holder.

рейсши́н|а, ы, *f.* T-square.

ре́йтер, a, *m.* (*tech.*) rider.

рейту́з|ы, ~, *no sing.* 1. (riding-)breeches. 2. (*women's or children's*) pantaloons, knickers.

река́, реку́, реки́, *pl.* **ре́ки, рек, ре́кам, ре́ками, ре́ках,** *f.* river; ли́ться, *etc.*, реко́й (*fig.*) to pour, flood.

рекапитуля́ци|я, и, *f.* recapitulation.

ре́квием, a, *m.* (*eccl. and mus.*) requiem.

реквизи́р|овать, ую, *impf. and pf.* to requisition, commandeer.

реквизи́т, a, *m.* (*theatr.*) properties, props.

реквизи́ци|я, и, *f.* requisition, commandeering.

рекла́м|а, ы, *f.* 1. advertising, publicity. 2. advertisement.

реклама́ци|я, и, *f.* claim for replacement (*of defective goods, etc.*).

реклами́р|овать, ую, *impf. and pf.* to advertise, publicize; to boost, push.

реклами́ст, a, *m.* 1. composer of advertisements. 2. (*coll., pejor.*) one given to self-advertisement.

рекла́мный, *adj.* publicity.

рекламода́тел|ь, я, *m.* advertiser.

рекогносци́р|овать, ую, *impf. and pf.* (*mil.*) to reconnoitre.

рекогносциро́вк|а, и, *f.* (*mil.*) reconnaissance; reconnoitring.

рекогносциро́вочный, *adj.* reconnaissance.

рекоменда́тельн|ый, *adj.* р. о́тзыв recommendation, testimonial; ~ое письмо́ letter of recommendation; р. спи́сок книг list of recommended books.

рекоменда́ци|я, и, *f.* recommendation.

рекоменд|ова́ть, у́ю, *impf. and pf.* 1. (*pf. also* по~ *and* от~) to recommend; to speak well for; э́то его́ не о́чень ~ует this does not speak too well for him. 2. (*pf. also* по~) (+*inf.*) to recommend, advise; я вам ~у́ю посове́товаться с до́ктором I recommend you to see a doctor.

рекоменд|ова́ться, у́юсь, *impf. and pf.* 1. (*pf. also* от~) to introduce oneself. 2. *pass. of* ~ова́ть; не ~у́ется it is not recommended, it is not advisable.

реконве́рси|я, и, *f.* reconversion.

реконструи́р|овать, ую, *impf. and pf.* to reconstruct.

реконструкти́вный, *adj.* р. пери́од period of reconstruction.

реконстру́кци|я, и, *f.* reconstruction.

реко́рд, a, *m.* record; поби́ть р. to break a record; установи́ть р. to set up, establish a record.

рекорди́ст, a, *m.* (*agric.*) champion.

реко́рдный, *adj.* record, record-breaking.

рекордсме́н, a, *m.* record-holder; record-breaker.

рекордсме́н|ка, ки, *f. of* ~.

ре́крут, a, *m.* recruit.

рекрути́р|овать, ую, *impf. and pf.* to recruit.

рекру́т|ский, *adj. of* ~; р. набо́р recruiting, recruitment.

ректифика́т, a, *m.* rectified spirit.

ректифика́ци|я, и, *f.* (*tech.*) rectification.

ректифици́р|овать, ую, *impf. and pf.* (*tech.*) to rectify.

ре́ктор, a, *m.* rector (*head of a university*).

ре́кторств|о, a, *n.* rectorship (*of a university*).

реле́, *indecl., n.* (*tech.*) relay.

реле́|йный, *adj. of* ~.

религио́зност|ь, и, *f.* religiosity; piety, piousness.

религио́з|ный, *adj.* 1. of religion, religious; ~ные во́йны (*hist.*) Wars of Religion; р. обря́д religious ceremony. 2. (~ен, ~на) religious; pious.

рели́ги|я, и, *f.* religion.

рели́кви|я, и, *f.* relic.

рели́кт, a, *m.* relic; survival.

рели́кт|овый, *adj. of* ~; surviving.

релье́ф, a, *m.* (*art and geol.*) relief.

релье́фно, *adv.* in relief, boldly.

релье́ф|ный (~ен, ~на), *adj.* relief, raised, bold; ~ная рабо́та embossed work; ~ная ка́рта relief map.

рельс, a, *g. pl.* ~ов, *m.* rail; сойти́ с ~ов to be derailed, go off the rails; поста́вить на ~ы (*fig.*) to get going, launch.

ре́льс|овый, *adj. of* ~; р. путь railway, track.

рельсопрока́тный, *adj.* rail-rolling.

релятиви́зм, a, *m.* (*philos.*) relativity.

реля́ци|я, и, *f.* (*mil.*; *obs.*) communiqué, report.

рема́рк|а, и, *f.* (*theatr.*) stage direction.

реме́нн|ый, *adj.* belt; ~ая переда́ча (*tech.*) belt-drive.

рем|е́нь, ня́, *m.* strap; belt; thong; поясно́й р. (*mil.*) (waist-)belt; руже́йный р. rifle sling; р. для пра́вки бритв (razor) strop.

реме́сленник, a, *m.* 1. artisan, craftsman. 2. (*fig., pejor.*) hack. 3. pupil of trade school.

реме́сленнический, *adj.* (*pejor.*) hack-working, mechanical.

реме́сленничеств|о, a, *n.* 1. workmanship, craftsmanship. 2. (*pejor.*) hack-work.

реме́сленн|ый, *adj.* 1. handicraft; trade; ~ое учи́лище trade school, industrial school. 2. (*fig., pejor.*) mechanical; stereotyped.

ремес|ло́, ла́, *pl.* ~ла, ~ел, *n.* 1. handicraft; trade. 2. profession.

ремеш|о́к, ка́, *m.* small strap; wristlet.
реми́з, а, *m.* (*cards*) fine; поста́вить р. to pay a fine.
ремилитариза́ци|я, и, *f.* remilitarization.
ремилитаризи́р|овать, ую, *impf. and pf.* to remilitarize.
ремилитариз|ова́ть, у́ю, *impf. and pf.* to remilitarize.
реминисце́нци|я, и, *f.* reminiscence.
ремо́нт, а, *m.* 1. repair(s); maintenance; капита́льный р. overhaul, refit, major repairs; теку́щий р. maintenance, routine repairs; закры́т на р. closed for repairs; в ~e under repair. 2. (*mil.*) remount (service).
ремонтёр, а, *m.* (*mil.*; *obs.*) remount officer.
ремонти́р|овать, ую, *impf. and pf.* 1. (*pf. also* от~) to repair; to refit, recondition, overhaul. 2. (*mil.*) to remount.
ремо́нт|ный, *adj. of* ~; ~ная лету́чка mobile repair shop; ~ная мастерска́я repair shop; ~ная ло́шадь (*mil.*) remount.
ренега́т, а, *m.* renegade.
ренега́тств|о, а, *n.* desertion; apostasy.
рене́т, а, *m.* rennet (*apple*).
ренкло́д, а, *m.* greengage.
реноме́, *indecl.*, *n.* reputation.
рено́нс, а, *m.* (*cards*) revoke.
ре́нт|а, ы, *f.* 1. rent; земе́льная р. ground-rent. 2. income (*from investments, etc.*); ежего́дная р. annuity; госуда́рственная р. (income from) government securities.
рента́бел|ьный (~ен, ~ьна), *adj.* paying, profitable.
рентге́н, а, *m.* X-ray treatment, X-rays.
рентгениза́ци|я, и, *f.* X-raying.
рентгенизи́р|овать, ую, *impf. and pf.* to X-ray.
рентге́нов, *adj.* ~ы лучи́ X-rays.
рентге́новск|ий, *adj.* X-ray; р. кабине́т X-ray room; ~ие лучи́ X-rays; р. сни́мок X-ray photograph.
рентгеногра́мм|а, ы, *f.* X-ray photograph, radiograph, röntgenogram.
рентгеногра́фи|я, и, *f.* radiography.
рентгено́лог, а, *m.* radiologist.
рентгеноло́ги|я, и, *f.* radiology, röntgenology.
рентгенотерапи́|я, и, *f.* X-ray therapy.
Реомю́р, а, *m.* Réaumur; 10° по ~y 10° Réaumur.
реорганиза́ци|я, и, *f.* reorganization.
реорганиз|ова́ть, у́ю, *impf. and pf.* to reorganize.
реоста́т, а, *m.* (*electr.*) rheostat.
ре́п|а, ы, *f.* turnip; деше́вле па́реной ~ы (*coll.*) dirt-cheap.
репар|ацио́нный, *adj. of* ~а́ция.
репара́ци|я, и, *f.* reparation.
репатриа́нт, а, *m.* repatriate.

репатриа́ци|я, и, *f.* repatriation.
репатрии́р|овать, ую, *impf. and pf.* to repatriate.
репатрии́р|оваться, уюсь, *impf. and pf.* to repatriate oneself.
репе́йник, а, *m.* (*bot.*) burdock.
репе́р, а, *m.* 1. (*surveying*) bench-mark, datum mark. 2. (*mil.*) registration mark, registration point.
репертуа́р, а, *m.* (*theatr. and fig.*) repertoire.
репети́р|овать, ую, *impf.* 1. (*pf.* про~ *and* с~) (*theatr.*) to rehearse. 2. *impf. only* to coach.
репети́тор, а, *m.* coach (*tutor*).
репетицио́нный, *adj.* rehearsal.
репети́ци|я, и, *f.* 1. rehearsal; генера́льная р. dress rehearsal. 2. repeater mechanism (*in watch*); часы́ с ~ей repeater.
ре́плик|а, и, *f.* 1. rejoinder, retort; heckling comment; подава́ть ~и ора́тору to heckle a speaker. 2. (*theatr.*) cue; пода́ть ~y to give the cue.
реполо́в, а, *m.* (*orn.*) linnet.
репорта́ж, а, *m.* reporting; account, ·piece of reporting.
репортёр, а, *m.* reporter.
репортёрств|овать, ую, *impf.* to report, be a reporter.
репресса́л|ии, ий, *pl.* (*sing.* ~ия, ~ии *rare*) *f.* (*polit.*) reprisals.
репресси́в|ный (~ен, ~на), *adj.* repressive.
репресси́р|овать, ую, *impf. and pf.* to subject to repression.
репре́сси|я, и, *f.* repression.
репроду́ктор, а, *m.* loud-speaker.
репроду́кци|я, и, *f.* reproduction (*of a picture, etc.*).
репс, а, *m.* (*text.*) rep(p), reps.
репти́ли|я, и, *f.* 1. reptile. 2. (*pejor.*) mercenary person, mercenary newspaper, *etc.*
репти́л|ьный (~ен, ~ьна), *adj.* (*pejor.*) mercenary, venal.
репута́ци|я, и, *f.* reputation, name; по́льзоваться хоро́шей ~ей to have a good reputation, name; по́льзоваться ~ей (+*g.*) to have a reputation, name (for); спасти́ свою́ ~ю to save one's face.
ре́пчатый, *adj.* turnip-shaped; р. лук large onion.
рескри́пт, а, *m.* (*obs.*) rescript.
ресни́ц|а, ы, *f.* eyelash.
ресни́чк|а, и, *f.* 1. *dim. of* ресни́ца. 2. *pl.* (*biol.*) cilia.
ресни́чный, *adj.* (*biol.*) ciliary.
респекта́бельност|ь, и, *f.* respectability.
респекта́бел|ьный (ен, ~ьна), *adj.* respectable.
респира́тор, а, *m.* respirator.
респу́блик|а, и, *f.* republic.
республика́н|ец, ца, *m.* republican.

республика́нский, *adj.* **1.** republican. **2.** of (situated in, *etc.*) a constituent republic of the U.S.S.R.

рессо́р|а, ы, *f.* spring (*of vehicle*).

рессо́рный, *adj.* spring; sprung.

реставра́тор, а, *m.* restorer.

реставра́ци|я, и, *f.* restoration.

реставри́р|овать, ую, *impf. and pf.* to restore.

рестора́н, а, *m.* restaurant.

рестора́тор, а, *m.* (*obs.*) restaurateur, restaurant-keeper.

ресу́рс, а, *m.* resource; де́нежные ~ы у них ничто́жны their financial resources are negligible; после́дний р. the last resort.

ретив|о́е, о́го, *n.* (*folk poet.*) heart.

рети́вост|ь, и, *f.* zeal, ardour.

рети́в|ый (~, ~а), *adj.* (*coll.*) zealous, ardent.

рети́н|а, ы, *f.* (*anat.*) retina.

ретир|ова́ться, у́юсь, *impf. and pf.* **1.** (*obs.*) to retire, withdraw. **2.** (*iron.*) to make off.

рето́рси|я, и, *f.* (*polit.*) retortion.

рето́рт|а, ы, *f.* (*chem.*) retort.

ретрогра́д, а, *m.* retrograde person, reactionary.

ретрогра́д|ный (~ен, ~на), *adj.* retrograde, backward.

ретрораке́т|а, ы, *f.* retro-rocket (*on space craft*).

ретроспекти́в|ный (~ен, ~на), *adj.* retrospective; р. взгляд backward glance.

ретушёр, а, *m.* retoucher.

ретуши́р|овать, ую, *impf. and pf.* (*pf. also* от~) to retouch.

ре́туш|ь, и, *f.* retouching.

рефера́т, а, *m.* **1.** synopsis, abstract (*of a book, dissertation, etc.*). **2.** paper, essay.

референ́дум, а, *m.* referendum.

рефере́нт, а, *m.* **1.** reader of a paper; seminar leader, colloquium leader. **2.** assessor (*of thesis, book, etc.*).

рефери́р|овать, ую, *impf. and pf.* to abstract, make a synopsis of.

рефле́кс, а, *m.* reflex; усло́вный р., безусло́вный р. conditioned, unconditioned reflex.

рефле́кси|я, и, *f.* reflection; introspection.

рефлексоло́ги|я, и, *f.* (*physiol.*) study of reflexes.

рефлекти́в|ный (~ен, ~на), *adj.* (*physiol.*) reflex.

рефле́ктор, а, *m.* reflector.

рефлекто́рный, *adj.* (*physiol., astron.*) reflex.

рефо́рм|а, ы, *f.* reform.

реформа́тор, а, *m.* reformer.

реформа́торский, *adj.* reformative, reformatory.

реформа́|тский, *adj.* of ~ция; ~тская це́рковь Reformed Church.

реформа́ци|я, и, *f.* (*hist.*) Reformation.

реформи́зм, а, *m.* (*polit.*) reformism.

реформи́р|овать, ую, *impf. and pf.* to reform.

реформи́ст, а, *m.* (*polit.*) reformist.

рефра́ктор, а, *m.* (*phys., astron.*) refractor.

рефра́кци|я, и, *f.* (*phys., astron.*) refraction.

рефре́н, а, *m.* (*lit.*) refrain, burden.

рефрижера́тор, а, *m.* **1.** (*tech.*) refrigerator; condenser, cooler. **2.** refrigerator van, ship.

рехн|у́ться, у́сь, ёшься, *pf.* (*coll.*) to go mad, go off one's head.

рецензе́нт, а, *m.* reviewer.

рецензи́р|овать, ую, *impf.* (*of* про~) to review, criticize.

реце́нзи|я, и, *f.* **1.** review; (*theatr.*) notice; р. на кни́гу, р. о кни́ге book review; дать на ~ю to send for review. **2.** (*philol.*) recension.

реце́пт, а, *m.* **1.** (*med.*) prescription. **2.** (*cul.*) recipe; (*fig.*) method, way, practice; поступи́ть по ста́рому ~у to follow the old practice.

рецепту́р|а, ы, *f.* (*med.*) principles of prescription-writing.

рециди́в, а, *m.* **1.** (*med., etc.*) recurrence; relapse. **2.** (*leg.*) repeated commission (*of offence*).

рецидиви́зм, а, *m.* (*leg.*) recidivism.

рецидиви́ст, а, *m.* (*leg.*) recidivist.

речев|о́й, *adj.* speech; vocal; р. аппара́т organs of speech, vocal organs; ~ы́е на́выки speech habits.

рече́ни|е, я, *n.* (*obs.*) set phrase; saying; (*ling.*) locution.

речи́ст|ый (~, ~а), voluble, garrulous.

речитати́в, а, *m.* (*mus.*) recitative.

ре́чк|а, и, *f.* small river; rivulet.

речни́к, а́, *m.* river transport worker.

речн|о́й, *adj.* river; riverine, fluvial; р. вокза́л river (steamer and 'bus) station; ~о́е сообще́ние river communication; ~ы́е пути́ сообще́ния inland waterways; ~о́е судохо́дство river navigation; р. трамва́й river 'bus, water 'bus.

реч|ь, и, *f.* **1.** speech; дар ~и faculty of speech, gift of speech. **2.** enunciation, speech, way of speaking; горта́нная р. guttural speech; отчётливая р. distinct enunciation. **3.** style of speaking, language; делова́я р. business language. **4.** discourse; о чём была́ р.? what was the topic of discussion?, what was it all about?; р. идёт о том, где сле́дует назна́чить ме́сто встре́чи the question is where to fix the meeting-place; е́сли р. идёт о сре́дствах if it is a question of funds, with regard to funds; не об э́том р. that is not the point; о пое́здке за грани́цу не мо́жет быть в э́том году́ и ~и a trip abroad is out of the question this year; завести́ р. (о+*p.*) to lead, turn the conversation (towards); р. несомне́нно зайдёт о вопрóсах релѝгии the conversation will undoubtedly turn to religion. **5.** speech; oration; address; вступѝтельная р. opening address; застóльная р. after-dinner speech; защитѝтельная р. speech for the defence; торжéственная р. oration; вы́ступить с ~ью to make a speech. **6.** (*gram.*) speech; пряма́я р. direct speech, oratio recta; кóсвенная р. indirect speech, oratio obliqua; чáсти ~и parts of speech.

реш|áть(ся), áю(сь), *impf. of* ~ѝть(ся).

решá|ющий, *pres. part. act. of* ~ть *and adj.* decisive, deciding; key, conclusive; р. гóлос deciding vote, casting vote; р. фáктор decisive factor; (*tech.*) determinant.

решéни|е, я, *n.* **1.** decision; приня́ть р. to take a decision, make up one's mind. **2.** decree, judg(e)ment; decision, verdict; заóчное р. judg(e)ment by default; вы́нести р. to deliver a judg(e)ment; to pass a resolution; отменѝть р. to revoke a decision; (*leg.*) to quash a sentence. **3.** solution; answer(*to a problem*).

решéтк|а, и, *f.* lath.

решётк|а, и, *f.* grating; grille; railing; lattice; trellis; fender, fireguard; за ~ой (*fig., coll.*) behind bars (= *in prison*); посадѝть за ~у to put behind bars. **2.** (fire-) grate. **3.** (*coll.*) tail (*of coin*).

решéтник¹, а, *m.* (*collect.*) lathing.

решéтник², а, *m.* sieve-maker.

решет|ó, á, *pl.* ~а, *n.* sieve.

решётчат|ый (and решéтчатый), *adj.* lattice, latticed; trellised; ~ая бáлка, ~ая фéрма lattice girder; ~ая констру́кция lattice-work; р. люк grating.

решѝмост|ь, и, ****f. resolution, resoluteness.

решѝтельно, *adv.* **1.** resolutely. **2.** decidedly, definitely; р. отказáться to refuse flatly; я р. прóтив э́того проéкта I am definitely opposed to this scheme. **3.** absolutely; э́то мне р. всё равнó it makes absolutely no difference to me; мы р. не знáли, куда́ мы попáли we had had absolutely no idea where we had got to; егó ждáли на вокзáле р. все practically everyone was at the station to meet him.

решѝтельност|ь, и, ****f. resolution, resoluteness, determination.

решѝтел|ьный (~ен, ~ьна), *adj.* **1.** resolute, determined; decided; firm; р. вид resolute air; ~ьные мéры strong measures, drastic measures; р. тон firm tone. **2.** definite; р. отвéт definite reply. **3.** .decisive; crucial; р. момéнт crucial point; ~ьная побéда sweeping victory. **4.** (*coll.*) absolute, blatant; р. дурáк absolute fool.

реш|ѝть, у́, ѝшь, *pf.* (*of* ~áть) **1.** (+*inf. or* +*a.*) to decide, determine; to make up

one's mind; р. дéло в чью-н. пóльзу to decide a case in someone's favour; р. чью-н. у́часть to decide someone's fate. **2.** to solve; to settle; р. задáчу to solve a problem; to accomplish a task.

реш|ѝться, у́сь, ѝшься, *pf.* (*of* ~áться) **1.** (на+*a.* or +*inf.*) to make up one's mind (to), decide (to), determine (to), resolve (to); to bring oneself (to). **2.** (+*g.*; *coll.*) to lose, be deprived (of).

рéшк|а, и, ****f. (*coll.*) tail (*of coin*); орёл и́ли р.? heads or tails?

реэвакуáци|я, и, ****f. re-evacuation.

реэвакуѝр|овать, ую, *impf. and pf.* to re-evacuate.

рé|ять, ю, ешь, *impf.* **1.** to soar, hover. **2.** to flutter.

рж|а, и, ****f. (*obs.*) = ржáвчина.

ржáве|ть, ет, *impf.* (*of* за~ *and* по~) to rust.

ржáвост|ь, и, ****f. rustiness.

ржáвчин|а, ы, ****f. **1.** rust. **2.** (*bot.*) mildew.

ржáвый, *adj.* rusty.

ржáни|е, я, *n.* neighing.

ржáнк|а, и, ****f. (*orn.*) plover; р. глу́пая dotterel; золотѝстая р. golden plover.

ржанóй, *adj.* rye.

рж|ать, у, ёшь, *impf.* to neigh; (*coll.*) laugh loudly.

рѝг|а, и, ****f. threshing barn.

рѝгел|ь, я, *m.* (*tech.*) cross-bar, collar-beam.

ригорѝзм, а, *m.* rigorism.

ригористѝческий, *adj.* rigorist.

ридикю́л|ь, я, *m.* (*obs.*) handbag.

рѝз|а, ы, ****f. **1.** (*eccl.*) chasuble. **2.** (*on icons*) riza. **3.** (*obs., poet.*) raiment, garments; напѝться до положéния ~ to drink oneself insensible.

рѝзниц|а, ы, ****f. (*eccl.*) vestry, sacristy.

рикошéт, а, *m.* ricochet, rebound; ~ом at the rebound (*also fig.*).

рикошетѝр|овать, ую, *impf.* to ricochet.

рѝкш|а, и, ****f. rickshaw, jinricksha.

рѝмлян|ин, ина, *pl.* ~е, ~, *m.* Roman.

рѝмлянк|а, и, ****f. Roman (woman).

рѝмск|ий, *adj.* Roman; пáпа р. the Pope; р. нос roman nose; ~ое прáво Roman law; ~ая свечá roman candle; ~ие цѝфры roman numerals.

ринг, а, *m.* (*sport*) ring.

рин|у́ться, у́сь, ешься, *pf.* to rush, dash, dart.

рис, а, *m.* rice; paddy.

риск, а, *m.* risk; на свой (страх и) р. at one's own risk, at one's peril; с ~ом (для) at the risk (of); пойтѝ на р. to run risks, take chances; р.—благорóдное дéло (*prov.*) nothing venture, nothing gain.

рискн|у́ть, у́, ёшь, *pf.* (+*inf.*) to take the risk (of), venture (to).

рискóванност|ь, и, ****f. riskiness.

рискóван|ный (~, ~на), *adj.* **1.** risky; ~ная игрá gamble; ~ное предприя́тие risky business, venture. **2.** risqué.

риск|овáть, ýю, *impf.* **1.** to run risks, take chances. **2.** (+*i.*) to risk; (+*inf.*) to risk, take the risk (of); р. головóй to risk one's neck; ничéм не р. to run no risk; не хотéть ничéм р. to take no chances; р. опоздáть на пóезд to risk missing the train.

рисовáльн|ый, *adj.* drawing; ~ое перó lettering pen.

рисовáльщик, a, *m.* graphic artist; draughtsman; я óчень плохóй р. I am no good at drawing, no draughtsman.

рисовáни|е, я, *n.* drawing.

рис|овáть, ýю, *impf.* (*of* на~) **1.** to draw; р. акварéлью to paint in water-colours; р. с натýры to draw, paint from life. **2.** (*fig.*) to depict, paint, portray.

рис|овáться, ýюсь, *impf.* **1.** to be silhouetted; to appear, present oneself; воéнная жизнь ~овáлась емý чи́стым кошмáром he saw life in the army as a pure nightmare. **2.** (*pejor.*) to pose, act. **3.** *pass. of* ~овáть.

рисóвк|а, и, *f.* (*pejor.*) posing, acting.

рисовóдств|о, a, *n.* rice-growing.

ри́сов|ый, *adj.* rice; ~ая кáша boiled rice; ~ое пóле rice-field, paddy-field.

ристáлищ|е, a, *n.* (*obs.*) stadium; hippodrome.

рисýн|ок, ка, *m.* **1.** drawing; illustration; (*in scientific work, article, etc.*) figure; pattern; design; outline; акварéльный р. water-colour painting. **2.** drawing, draughtsmanship (*as opp. to use of colour*).

рисýнчатый, *adj.* patterned, ornamented.

ритм, a, *m.* rhythm.

ри́тмик|а, и, *f.* **1.** (*lit.*) rhythm system. **2.** eurhythmics.

ритми́ческий, *adj.* rhythmic(al).

ритми́чность|ь, и, *f.* rhythm.

ритми́ч|ный (~ен, ~на), *adj.* rhythmic(al); ~ная рабóта smooth functioning.

ри́тор, a, *m.* **1.** (*hist.*) teacher of rhetoric. **2.** (*obs.*) rhetorician, orator.

ритóрик|а, и, *f.* rhetoric.

ритори́ческий, *adj.* rhetorical; р. вопрóс rhetorical question.

ритуáл, a, *m.* ritual; ceremonial.

ритуáльный, *adj.* ritual.

риф[1], a, *m.* reef; корáлловый р. coral reef.

риф[2], a, *m.* (*naut.*) reef; брать ~ы to reef.

рифлéни|е, я, *n.* (*tech.*) channelling, grooving, fluting, corrugating.

рифлён|ый, *adj.* (*tech.*) chequered, channelled, grooved, fluted, corrugated; ~ое желéзо corrugated iron.

ри́фм|а, ы, *f.* rhyme.

рифм|овáть, ýю, *impf.* (*of* с~) **1.** to rhyme. **2.** to select in order to make rhyme.

рифм|овáться, ýюсь, *impf.* to rhyme.

рифмóвк|а, и, *f.* rhyming, rhyme system.

рифмоплёт, a, *m.* (*pejor.*) rhymer, rhymester.

рици́н, a, *m.* **1.** (*bot.*) castor plant. **2.** (*med.*) castor oil.

рици́н|овый, *adj.* of ~; ~овое мáсло castor oil.

рóббер, a, *m.* (*cards*) rubber.

робé|ть, ю, *impf.* (*of* о~) to be timid; to quail; не ~й(те)! don't be afraid!

роб|кий (~ок, ~кá, ~ко), *adj.* timid, shy.

рóбост|ь, и, *f.* timidity, shyness.

рóбот, a, *m.* robot.

рóбче, *comp. of* рóбкий.

ров, рва, о рве, во рву, *m.* ditch; крепостнóй р. moat, fosse; противотáнковый р. anti-tank ditch.

ровéсник, a, *m.* person of the same age; он — мой р., мы с ним ~и we are of the same age.

рóвно, *adv.* **1.** regularly, evenly. **2.** exactly; (*of time*) sharp; р. пять рублéй five roubles exactly; р. в час at one o'clock sharp, on the stroke of one. **3.** (*coll.*) absolutely; онá р. ничегó не знáет she knows absolutely nothing. **4.** (*coll.*) exactly like, just like.

рóвност|ь, и, *f.* regularity, evenness.

рóв|ный (~ен, ~нá, ~но), *adj.* **1.** flat, even, level; ~ная повéрхность plane surface. **2.** regular, even; equable; р. пульс regular pulse; р. харáктер even temper, equable temperament. **3.** exact, even; equal; р. счёт even account, exact money; для ~ного счёта to make it even; to bring to a round figure; ~ным счётом ничегó (*coll.*) precisely nothing.

рóвня, рóвни, *m. and f.* equal, match; он ей не р. he is not her equal, he is no match for her.

ровня́|ть, ю, *impf.* (*of* с~) to even, level; р. с землёй to raze to the ground.

ровня́|ться, юсь, *impf.* (*of* с~) **1.** to become even, become level. **2.** (по+*d.*) to attain to the level (of).

рог, a, *pl.* ~á, ~óв, *m.* **1.** horn; antler; р. изоби́лия horn of plenty, cornucopia; брать быкá за ~á (*coll.*) to take the bull by the horns; настáвить ~á (+*d.*; *coll.*) cuckold; согнýть в барáний р. (*coll.*) make knuckle under; сломи́ть ~á (+*d.*; *coll.*) to bring to one's knees. **2.** bugle, horn; охóтничий р. hunting-horn.

рогáст|ый (~, ~а), *adj.* (*coll.*) large-horned.

рогáтин|а, ы, *f.* bear-spear.

рогáтк|а, и, *f.* **1.** turnpike; *pl.* chevaux-de-frise. **2.** (*boy's*) catapult.

рогáт|ый (~, ~а), *adj.* **1.** horned; крýпный р. скот cattle; мéлкий р. скот small cattle, sheep and goats. **2.** (*coll.*) cuckolded.

рогáч, á, *m.* **1.** stag. **2.** stag-beetle.

роговиц|а, ы, *f.* (*anat.*) cornea.

рогов|óй, *adj.* horn; horny; corneous; ~ые очки horn-rimmed spectacles; ~áя оболóчка глáза (*anat.*) cornea; ~áя мýзыка music for horn; ~áя обмáнка (*min.*) hornblende.

рогóж|а, и, *f.* bast mat, matting.

рогóз, а, *m.* (*bot.*) reed mace.

рогонóс|ец, ца, *m.* (*coll.*, *joc.*) cuckold.

рогýльк|а, и, *f.* (*cul.*) croissant.

род, а, о ~**е, в** ~**ý,** *pl.* ~**ы́,** ~**óв,** *m.* 1. family, kin, clan; человéческий р. mankind, human race; без ~у, без плéмени without kith or kin. 2. birth, origin, stock; generation; он ~ом из Ирлáндии he is an Irishman by birth, a native of Ireland; из ~а в р. from generation to generation; емý на ~ý напи́сано (+*inf.*) he was pre-ordained (to); ей дéсять лет от ~у she is ten years of age. 3. (*biol.*) genus. 4. sort, kind; литератýрный р. literary genre; р. войск arm of the service; вся́кого ~а of all kinds, all kind of; такóго ~а of such a kind, such; в э́том ~е of this sort; что-то в э́том ~е something of the kind, something to that effect; в нéкотором ~е in some sort, to some extent; в своём ~е in one's own way; своегó ~а a kind of; in one's own way; он своегó ~а гéний he is a genius in his own way. 5. (*gram.*) gender.

родáнист|ый, *adj.* (*chem.*) thiocyanate (of), sulphocyanate (of); ~ая кислотá thiocyanic acid, sulphocyanic acid.

роддóм, а, *m.* (*abbr. of* роди́льный дом) maternity home.

рóди|й, я, *m.* (*chem.*) rhodium.

роди́льниц|а, ы, *f.* woman recently confined.

роди́льн|ый, *adj.* р. дом maternity home, lying-in hospital; ~ая горя́чка puerperal fever; ~ое отделéние delivery room.

роди́мчик, а, *m.* (*coll.*) convulsions (*of mother or child about time of birth*).

роди́м|ый, *adj.* 1. own; native. 2. ~ое пятнó birth-mark. 3. (*as form of address*) (my) dear.

рóдин|а, ы, *f.* native land, mother country; home, homeland; вернýться на ~у to return home; тоскá по ~е home-sickness, nostalgia.

рóдинк|а, и, *f.* birth-mark.

роди́н|ы, ~, *no sing.* (*obs.*) celebration of birth of child.

роди́тел|и, ей, *no sing.* parents.

роди́тел|ь, я, *m.* (*obs.*) father.

роди́тельниц|а, ы, *f.* (*obs.*) mother.

роди́тельный, *adj.* (*gram.*) genitive.

роди́тельский, *adj.* parental, parents'; paternal; р. комитéт parents' committee.

ро|ди́ть, жý, ди́шь, *past* ~ди́л, ~дила́, ~ди́ло, *impf. and pf.* 1. (*impf. also* рожáть) to bear, give birth (to); в чём мать ~дила́

(*joc.*) in one's birthday suit. 2. (*impf. also* рождáть) (*fig.*) to give birth, rise (to).

ро|ди́ться, жýсь, ди́шься, *past* ~ди́лся, ~дила́сь, ~ди́лóсь, *impf. and pf.* 1. (*impf. also* рождáться) to be born; р. преподавáтелем to be a born teacher. 2. (*impf. also* рождáться) (*fig.*) to arise, come into being. 3. to spring up, thrive; кукурýза у нас ~дила́сь хорошó we had a good maize--crop.

рóдич, а, *m.* (*coll.*) relation, relative.

родни́к, á, *m.* spring.

роднико́в|ый, *adj.* of родни́к; ~ая водá spring water.

родн|и́ть, ю́, и́шь, *impf.* to make related, link.

родн|и́ться, ю́сь, и́шься, *impf.* (*of* по~) (с+*i.*) to become related (with).

роднич|óк[1], ка́, *m.* *dim. of* родни́к.

роднич|óк[2], ка́, *m.* (*anat.*) fontanel(le).

родн|óй, *adj.* 1. own (*by blood relationship in direct line*); р. брат one's brother (*as opp. to cousin, etc.*); *as noun* ~ы́е, ~ы́х relations, relatives, one's people; в кругý ~ы́х in the family circle, with one's people. 2. native; home; intimate, familiar; ~ая странá, ~ая земля́ native land; р. гóрод home town; р. язы́к mother tongue. 3. (*as form of address*) (my) dear.

родн|я́, и́, *f.* 1. (*collect.*) relations, relatives, kinsfolk. 2. relation, relative.

родови́тост|ь, и, *f.* blood; high birth, good birth.

родови́т|ый (~, ~а), *adj.* high-born, well--born, of the blood.

родов|óй[1], *adj.* 1. (*ethnol.*) clan. 2. ancestral, patrimonial; ~óе имéние, ~óе имýщество patrimony. 3. (*biol.*) generic. 4. (*gram.*) gender.

родов|óй[2], *adj.* birth, labour; ~ы́е схвáтки birth throes, labour.

родовспомогáтельн|ый, *adj.* ~ое учреждéние maternity home.

рододéндрон, а, *m.* (*bot.*) rhododendron.

родоначáльник, а, *m.* ancestor, forefather; (*fig.*) father.

родослóвн|ая, ой, *f.* genealogy, pedigree.

родослóвн|ый, *adj.* genealogical; ~ое дéрево family tree; ~ая кни́га family register; stud-book; ~ая табли́ца genealogical table.

рóдственник, а, *m.* relation, relative; ближáйший р. next of kin.

рóдственност|ь, и, *f.* 1. connection, tie. 2. familiarity, intimacy.

рóдствен|ный (~, ~на), *adj.* 1. kindred, related; ~ные отношéния blood relations; ~ные свя́зи kinship ties. 2. kindred, related, allied; ~ные нарóды related peoples; ~ные языки́ cognate languages. 3. familiar, intimate.

родств|о́, а́, *n.* **1.** relationship, kinship (*also fig.*); кро́вное р. blood relationship, blood tie, consanguinity; быть в ~е́ (c+*i.*) to be related (to); не по́мнящий ~а́ (*in official documents*; *obs.*) ancestry unknown. **2.** (*collect.*, *coll.*) relations, relatives.

ро́д|ы, ов, *no sing.* birth; childbirth, delivery, lying-in; в ~ах in labour.

рое́ни|е, я, *n.* swarming (*of bees, etc.*).

рож|а¹, и, *f.* (*coll.*) mug (= *face*).

рож|а², и, *f.* (*med.*) erysipelas.

рожа́|ть, ю, *impf. of* роди́ть.

рожда́емост|ь, и, *f.* birth-rate.

рожда́|ть(ся), ю(сь), *impf. of* роди́ть(ся).

рожде́ни|е, я, *n.* **1.** birth; день ~я birthday; ме́сто ~я birth-place; глухо́й от ~я deaf from birth. **2.** birthday.

рождённый, *p.p.p. of* роди́ть; (+*inf.*) born (to), destined (to).

рожде́ственск|ий, *adj.* Christmas; р. дед Father Christmas, Santa Claus; ~ая ёлка Christmas-tree; р. сочѐльник Christmas Eve.

Рождеств|о́, а́, *n.* Christmas; на Р. at Christmas(-time).

роже́ниц|а, ы, *f.* woman in childbirth.

роже́чник, а, *m.* horn-player; bugler.

ро́жист|ый, *adj.* (*med.*) erysipelatous; ~ое воспале́ние erysipelas.

рож|о́к, ка́, *m.* **1.** small horn. **2.** (*mus.*) horn, clarion; bugle; францу́зский р. French horn. **3.** ear-trumpet. **4.** feeding-bottle; корми́ть с ~ка́ to bottle-feed. **5.** (га́зовый) (gas-)burner, (gas-)jet. **6.** shoe-horn.

рож|о́н, на́, *m.* лезть, идти́ на р. (*coll.*) to kick against the pricks; про́тив ~на́ пере́ть (*coll.*) to swim against the tide; како́го ещё ~на́ на́до? (*coll.*) what the hell more do you need?

рожь, ржи, *f.* rye.

ро́з|а, ы, *f.* **1.** rose; rose-tree, rose-bush. **2.** (*archit.*) rose-window, rosace.

ро́зан, а, *m.* (*coll.*) rose.

розари|й, я, *m.* rosarium, rose-garden.

розва́льн|и, ей, *no sing.* rozvalni (*low, wide sledge*).

ро́з|га, ги, *g. pl.* ~ог, *f.* **1.** birch (rod); наказа́ть ~гой to birch. **2.** *pl.* blows of the birch; дать ~ог to give the birch.

ро́зговень|е, я, *n.* (*eccl.*) first meal after fast.

ро́здых, а, *m.* (*coll.*) pause (*from work*), breather.

розео́л|а, ы, *f.* (*med.*) roseola.

розе́тк|а, и, *f.* **1.** rosette. **2.** (*electr.*) socket; wall-plug. **3.** jam-dish. **4.** candle-ring (*glass, metal, or china ring on candlestick to collect wax*). **5.** (*archit.*) rose-window.

розмари́н, а, *m.* (*bot.*) rosemary.

ро́зниц|а, ы, *f.* retail; торгова́ть в ~y to engage in retail trade.

ро́зничный, *adj.* retail; р. торго́вец retailer.

ро́зно, *adv.* (*coll.*) apart, separately.

розн|ь, и, *f.* **1.** difference; челове́к челове́ку р. there are no two people alike, there are people and people. **2.** disagreement, dissension.

розова́т|ый (~, ~а), *adj.* pinkish.

розове́|ть, ю, *impf.* (*of* по~) to turn pink.

розовощёкий, *adj.* pink-cheeked, rosy--cheeked.

ро́зов|ый (~, ~а), *adj.* **1.** *adj. of* ро́за; ~ое де́рево rosewood; р. куст rose-bush; ~ое ма́сло attar of roses. **2.** pink, rose-coloured. **3.** (*fig.*) rosy; смотре́ть сквозь ~ые очки́ to view through rose-coloured spectacles.

ро́зыгрыш, а, *m.* **1.** drawing (*of a lottery, etc.*). **2.** (*sport*) playing off (*of a cup-tie, etc.*). **3.** (*sport*) draw, drawn game. **4.** practical joke.

ро́зыск, а, *m.* **1.** search. **2.** (*leg.*) inquiry. Уголо́вный р. Criminal Investigation Department.

ро|и́ться, и́тся, *impf.* (*of bees, etc.*) to swarm; (*fig.*; *of thoughts*) to crowd.

рой, ро́я, *pl.* ро́й, *m.* swarm (*of bees, etc.*).

рок, а, *m.* fate.

рока́д|а, ы, *f.* (*mil.*) belt road, lateral road.

рока́дный, *adj.* (*mil.*) belt, lateral.

рокир|ова́ть(ся), у́ю(сь), *impf. and pf.* (*chess*) to castle.

рокиро́вк|а, и, *f.* (*chess*) castling; (*mil.*; *fig.*) lateral troop movement.

роков|о́й, *adj.* **1.** fateful; fated; ~а́я краса́вица femme fatale. **2.** fatal.

рококо́, *indecl.*, *n.* rococo.

ро́кот, а, *m.* roar, rumble.

роко|та́ть, чу́, ~чешь, *impf.* to roar, rumble.

ро́лик, а, *m.* **1.** roller, castor. **2.** (*electr.*) (*porcelain*) cleat. **3.** *pl.* roller skates.

ро́лик|овый, *adj. of* ~; р. подши́пник roller bearing.

ро́ллер, а, *m.* (*child's*) scooter.

рол|ь, и, *pl.* ~и, ~е́й, *f.* (*theatr.*) role (*also fig.*); part; в ~и (+*g.*) in the role (of); игра́ть р. (+*g.*) to take the part (of), play, act; (*fig.*) to matter, count, be of importance; э́то не игра́ет ~и it is of no importance, it does not count; вы́держать свою́ р. (*fig.*) to keep up one's part.

ром, а, *m.* rum.

рома́н, а, *m.* **1.** novel; romance. **2.** (*coll.*) love affair; romance.

романи́ст¹, а, *m.* novelist.

романи́ст², а, *m.* Romance philologist.

романи́ческий, *adj.* romantic.

рома́нс, а, *m.* (*mus.*) romance.

рома́нск|ий, *adj.* Romance, Romanic; р. стиль (*archit.*) Romanesque; ~ие языки́ Romance languages.

романти́зм, а, *m.* romanticism.

рома́нтик, а, *m.* (*in var. senses*) romantic; romanticist.

рома́нтик|а, и, *f.* romance; р. медици́нских иссле́дований the romance of medical research.

романти́ческий, *adj.* romantic.

романти́чност|ь, и, *f.* romantic quality.

романти́ч|ный (~ен, ~на), *adj.* = ~еский.

рома́шк|а, и, *f.* (*bot. and pharm.*) camomile.

рома́шк|овый, *adj.* of ~а; р. чай camomile tea.

ромб, а, *m.* (*math.*) rhomb(us); (*mil.*) diamond formation; (*aeron.*) box of four.

ромби́ческий, *adj.* (*math.*) rhombic.

ро́мовый, *adj.* of ром.

ро́ндо, *indecl., n.* (*mus.*) rondo.

рондо́, *indecl., n.* (*lit.*) rondeau, rondel.

роня́|ть, ю, *impf.* (*of* урони́ть) **1.** to drop, let fall; р. слёзы to shed tears; р. сло́во to let fall a word. **2.** *impf. only* to shed; р. ли́стья to shed its leaves; р. опере́ние to moult. **3.** (*fig.*) to injure, discredit; р. себя́ в обще́ственном мне́нии to drop in public estimation.

ро́пот, а, *m.* murmur, grumble.

роп|та́ть, щу́, ~щешь, *impf.* to murmur, grumble.

рос, ла́, *see* расти́.

рос|а́, ы́, *pl.* ~ы, *f.* dew; то́чка ~ы́ dew-point; медо́вая р. (*bot.*) honey dew; до ~ы́ first thing (in the morning); по ~е́ while the dew is still on the ground.

роси́нк|а, и, *f.* dewdrop; (ни) ма́ковой ~и во рту не́ было neither food nor drink has passed (my) lips.

роси́ст|ый (~, ~а), *adj.* dewy.

роско́шеств|о, а, *n.* **1.** extravagant taste, exotic taste. **2.** extravagance.

роско́шеств|овать, ую, *impf.* to luxuriate, live in luxury.

роско́шнича|ть, ю, *impf.* = роско́шествовать.

роско́ш|ный (~ен, ~на), *adj.* **1.** luxurious, sumptuous. **2.** (*coll.*) luxuriant; splendid.

ро́скош|ь, и, *f.* **1.** luxury. **2.** luxuriance; splendour.

ро́слый, *adj.* tall, strapping.

ро́сный¹, *adj.* р. ла́дан benzoin, benjamin.

ро́с|ный², *adj.* (*dial.*) of ~а́.

росома́х|а, и, *f.* (*zool.*) wolverene, glutton.

ро́спис|ь, и, *f.* **1.** list, inventory. **2.** painting; р. стен wall-painting(s), mural(s).

ро́спуск, а, *m.* dismissal; (*mil.*) disbandment; р. парла́мента dissolution of Parliament; р. на кани́кулы breaking up for the holidays.

росси́йский, *adj.* Russian.

ро́ссказн|и, ей, *no sing.* (*coll.*) old wive's tale, cock-and-bull story.

ро́ссып|ь, и, *f.* **1.** scattering; грузи́ть зерно́ ~ью to load grain loose. **2.** (*pl.; min.*) deposit, placer.

рост, а, *m.* **1.** growth (*also fig.*); (*fig.*) increase, rise. **2.** height, stature; ~ом in height; он ~ом с вас he is (of) your height; высо́кого ~а tall; во весь р. full length; (*fig.*) in all its magnitude; встать во весь р. to stand upright, stand up straight. **3.** (*obs.*) interest; дать де́ньги в р. to lend money on interest.

ро́стбиф, а, *m.* roast beef.

ростовщи́к, а́, *m.* usurer, money-lender.

ростовщи́ческий, *adj.* usurious.

ростовщи́честв|о, а, *n.* usury, money-lending.

рост|о́к, ка́, *m.* sprout, shoot; пусти́ть ~ки́ to sprout, put out shoots.

ростра, а, *m.* (*hist.*) beak (*of war-galley*), rostrum.

ро́стр|а, ы, *f.* (*hist.*) rostrum.

ростра́льный, *adj.* (*archit.*) rostral.

ро́стр|ы, ~, *no sing.* (*naut.*) booms.

ро́счерк, а, *m.* flourish; одни́м ~ом пера́ with a stroke of the pen.

рося́нк|а, и, *f.* (*bot.*) sundew.

рот, рта, о рте́, во рту́, *m.* mouth; дыша́ть ртом to breathe through one's mouth; у меня́ пять ртов в семье́ I have five mouths to feed in my family; не брать в р. (+*g.*) not to touch; она́ мя́са в р. не брала́ she would never touch meat; рази́нуть р. to stand agape, be open-mouthed; не сметь рта раскры́ть not to dare to open one's mouth; зажа́ть, заткну́ть р. кому́-н. to stop someone's mouth, shut someone up; смотре́ть в р. кому́-н. to hang on someone's words; хлопо́т по́лон р. (*coll.*) to have one's hands full.

ро́т|а, ы, *f.* (*mil.*) company.

рота́тор, а, *m.* duplicator, duplicating machine.

ротаци́зм, а, *m.* (*ling.*) rhotacism.

ротацио́нн|ый, *adj.* ~ая маши́на (*typ.*) rotary press.

рота́ци|я, и, *f.* **1.** = ~о́нная маши́на. **2.** (*agric.*) rotation.

ро́тмистр, а, *m.* (*mil.*) captain (*of cavalry in tsarist Russian army*).

ро́т|ный, *adj.* of ~а; *as noun* р., ~ного, *m.* company commander.

ротозе́|й, я, *m.* (*coll.*) scatter-brain, gaper.

ротозе́йнича|ть, ю, *impf.* (*coll.*) to be scatter-brained.

ротозе́йств|о, а, *n.* (*coll.*) scatter-brainedness.

рото́нд|а, ы, *f.* **1.** (*archit.*) rotunda. **2.** (*lady's*) cloak.

ротоно́г|ие, их (*sing.* ~ое, ~ого), *n.* (*zool.*) Stomatopoda.

ро́тор, а, *m.* (*tech.*) rotor.

ро́хл|я, и, *g. pl.* ~ей, *m. and f.* (*coll.*) dawdler.

ро́щ|а, и, *f.* small wood, grove.

ро́щиц|а, ы, *f. dim. of* ро́ща.

рояли́ст, а, *m.* royalist.

рояли́стский, *adj.* royalist.

роя́л|ь, я, *m.* piano; grand piano; игра́ть на ~е to play the piano; у ~я at the piano.

рту́тн|ый, *adj.* mercury, mercurial; р. вы-прями́тель (*electr.*) mercury arc rectifier, mercury vapour rectifier; ~ая ла́мпа (*electr.*) mercury vapour lamp, mercury arc lamp; ~ая мазь (*pharm.*) mercury ointment; ~ое отравле́ние (*med.*) mercurialism, mercury poisoning; р. столб mercury (column).

ртут|ь, и, *f.* mercury, quicksilver.

руба́к|а, и, *m.* (*coll.*) fine swordsman.

руба́н|ок, ка, *m.* (*tech.*) plane.

руба́х|а, и, *f.* shirt; р.-па́рень (*coll.*) straight-forward fellow.

руба́шк|а, и, *f.* 1. shirt; ни́жняя р., нате́ль-ная р. petticoat, vest, singlet; ночна́я р. night-shirt, night-dress; роди́ться в ~е to be born with a silver spoon in one's mouth; своя́ р. бли́же к те́лу (*prov.*) charity begins at home. 2. colour (*of animal's coat*). 3. back (*of playing cards*). 4. (*tech.*) jacket, casing, lining.

рубе́ж, а́, *m.* 1. boundary, border(line); за ~о́м abroad. 2. (*mil.*) line; р. ата́ки assault position.

руберо́йд, а, *m.* (*tech.*) ruberoid.

руб|е́ц¹, ца́, *m.* 1. scar, cicatrice; weal. 2. hem, seam.

руб|е́ц², ца́, *m.* 1. (*zool.*) paunch (*ruminant's first stomach*). 2. (*cul.*) tripe.

руби́ди|й, я, *m.* (*chem.*) rubidium.

руби́льник, а, *m.* (*electr.*) knife-switch.

руби́н, а, *m.* ruby.

руби́новый, *adj.* ruby; ruby(-coloured).

руб|и́ть, лю́, ~ишь, *impf.* 1. to fell (*trees*). 2. to hew, chop, hack. 3. (*cul.*) to mince, chop up. 4. to put up, erect (*of logs*).

руб|и́ться, лю́сь,, ~ишься, *impf.* to fight (with cold steel).

ру́бищ|е, а, *no pl., n.* rags, tatters.

ру́бк|а¹, и, *f.* 1. felling. 2. hewing, chopping, hacking. 3. mincing, chopping up.

ру́бк|а², и, *f.* (*naut.*) deck house, deck cabin; боева́я р. conning tower; рулева́я р. wheel-house; шту́рманская р. chart house.

рубле́вк|а, и, *f.* (*coll.*) one-rouble note.

рубл|ёвый, *adj.* 1. *adj. of* ~ь. 2. one rouble (in price).

ру́блен|ый, *adj.* 1. minced, chopped; ~ая капу́ста chopped cabbage; ~ое мя́со minced meat, hash; ~ые котле́ты rissoles. 2. of logs; ~ая изба́ log hut, log cabin.

рубл|ь, я́, *m.* rouble.

ру́брик|а, и, *f.* 1. rubric, heading. 2. column (*of figures*).

рубц|ева́ться, у́ется, *impf.* (*of* за~) to cicatrize.

ру́бчатый, *adj.* ribbed.

ру́бчик, а, *m.* 1. *dim. of* рубе́ц¹. 2. rib (*on material*).

ру́ган|ь, и, *f.* abuse, bad language, swear-ing.

руга́тел|ь, я, *m.* habitual user of bad lan-guage.

руга́тельн|ый, *adj.* abusive; ~ые слова́ bad language, swear-words.

руга́тельств|о, а, *n.* oath, swear-word.

руга́|ть, ю, *impf.* (*of* вы~ *and* из~) 1. to curse, swear (at), abuse. 2. to tear to pieces, lash (= *criticize severely*).

руга́|ться, юсь, *impf.* 1. to curse, swear, use bad language; р. как изво́зчик to swear like a trooper. 2. to swear at one another, abuse one another.

ругн|у́ть(ся), у́(сь), ёшь(ся), *pf.* to swear.

руд|а́, ы́, *pl.* ~ы, *f.* ore; желе́зная р. iron--ore, iron-stone.

рудиме́нт, а, *m.* rudiment.

рудимента́рный, *adj.* rudimentary.

рудни́к, а́, *m.* mine, pit.

руднико́вый, *adj. of* рудни́к.

рудни́|чный, *adj. of* ~к; р. газ fire-damp; ~чная сто́йка pit prop; ~чная ла́мпа miner's lamp, Davy lamp.

ру́д|ный, *adj. of* ~а́; ~ная жи́ла vein; ~ное месторожде́ние ore deposit.

рудоко́п, а, *m.* miner.

рудоно́с|ный (~ен, ~на), *adj.* ore-bearing.

рудоподъёмник, а, *m.* ore lift.

рудопромы́вочный, *adj.* ore-washing.

руже́йник, а, *m.* gunsmith.

руже́йн|ый, *adj. of* ружьё; р. вы́стрел rifle--shot; р. ма́стер armourer, gunsmith; ~ые приёмы manual of the rifle.

руж|ьё, ья́, *pl.* ~ья, ~ей, ~ьям, *n.* (hand-)gun, rifle; дробово́е р. shot-gun; охо́тничье р. fowling-piece, sporting gun; противо-та́нковое р. anti-tank rifle; стать в р. to fall in; в р.! (*mil. command*) to arms!; быть под ~ьём to be under arms; призва́ть под р. to call to arms, call to the colours.

руи́н|а, ы, *f.* ruin (*usu. pl.*).

рук|а́, и́, *a.* ~у, *pl.* ~и, ~, ~а́м, *f.*

I. 1. hand; arm; пода́ть ~у (+*d.*) to offer one's hand; пожа́ть ~у (+*d.*), здоро́ваться за ~у (с+*i.*) to shake hands (with); ~и вверх! hands up!; ~а́ми не тро́гать! please, do not touch!; вести́ за ~у to lead by the hand; взя́ться за ~у to join hands, link arms; из ~ в ~и from hand to hand; взять на́ ~и to take in one's arms; держа́ть на ~а́х to hold in one's arms; р. об ~у hand in hand; написа́ть от ~й to write out by hand; взять кого́-н. под ~у to take someone's arm; идти́ с кем-н. по́д ~у to walk arm in arm with someone, walk with someone on one's arm. **2.** hand, handwriting; signature; приложи́ть ~у to append one's signature. **3.** side, hand; на ле́вой ~é on the left; по пра́вую ~у at the right hand. **4.** *pl.* hands (*fig.* = power, possession); взять в свои́ ~и to take into one's own hands; взять (себя́) в ~и to take (oneself) in hand; держа́ть в свои́х ~áх to have in one's clutches, have under one's thumb; попа́сться в ~и кому́-н. to fall into someone's hands; прибра́ть к ~áм to appropriate; быть в хоро́ших ~áх to be in good hands; ско́лько у вас на ~áх сове́тской валю́ты? how much Soviet currency have you on you?; свобо́да ~ a free hand; в со́бственные ~и (*on cover of letter, etc.*) 'personal'. **5.** (*fig.*) hand (*of person giving or receiving proposal of marriage*); проси́ть ~й у кого́-н. to ask someone's hand in marriage. **6.** (*fig.*) hand; source, authority; из пе́рвых, вторы́х ~ at first, second hand; узна́ть из ве́рных ~ to have on good authority. **7.** (*g. sing.*; *coll.*, *obs.*) sort, kind, quality; сре́дней ~й of medium quality; большо́й ~й негодя́й a scoundrel of the first order.

II. (*fig.*; *in var. senses*) hand; отда́ть в ~и кому́-н. to hand over to someone in person; игра́ть (на роя́ле) в четы́ре ~й to play duets (on the piano); переда́ть де́ло в чьи-н. ~и to put a matter in someone's hands; перейти́ в други́е ~и, из ~ в ~и to change hands; сон в ~у the dream has come true; вали́ться из ~ *see* вали́ться; из ~ вон (пло́хо) (*coll.*) thoroughly bad, quite useless; вы́дать на́ ~и to hand out; име́ть на ~áх to have on one's hands; умере́ть на чьих-н. ~áх to die in someone's arms; ма́стер на все ~и Jack of all trades; э́то бу́дет им на́ ~у that will serve their purpose; it will be playing into their hands; на́ ~у нечи́ст (*coll.*) dishonest, underhand; на ско́рую ~у off-hand; быть свя́занным по ~áм и нога́м to be bound hand and foot; дать кому́-н. по ~áм (*coll.*) to give rap over the knuckles; уда́рить по ~áм to strike a bargain; по ~áм! it's a bargain!, done!; говори́ть кому́-н. под ~у to distract someone by talking; под ~ой at hand, to hand; под пья́ную ~у under the influence (of drink); с ~ доло́й off one's hands; сбыть с ~ to get off one's hands; э́то тебе́ не сойдёт с ~ (*coll.*) you won't get away with it; греть ~и (на+*p.*) to make a good thing (out of); дать во́лю ~áм (*coll.*) to bring one's fists into play; дать ~у на отсече́ние to swear; э́то де́ло чужи́х ~ this is someone else's doing; живо́й ~ой rapidly; как ~ой сня́ло it has vanished as if by magic; ло-

ма́ть ~и to wring one's hands; махну́ть ~ой (на+*a.*) to give up as lost; наби́ть ~у to get one's hand in; наложи́ть на себя́ ~и to lay hands on oneself; не поднима́ется р. (+*inf.*) one cannot bring oneself (to); мне не р. (+*inf.*) I have no call (to), it does not suit me (to); приложи́ть ~у (к) to put one's hand (to), take a hand (in) (*see also* I. 2); развяза́ть ~и (+*d.*) to give a free hand; р. у него́ не дро́гнет (+*inf.*) he will not scruple (to); ~и у меня́ не дохо́дят до э́того it is beyond me, I cannot undertake it; ~и прочь! hands off!; ~ой пода́ть a stone's throw away, but a step; умы́ть ~и (в+*p.*) to wash one's hands (of); у меня́ ~и че́шутся (+*inf.*) my fingers are itching (to), I itch (to).

рука́в, á, *pl.* **~á, m. 1.** sleeve; спустя́ ~á (*coll.*) in a slipshod manner. **2.** branch, arm (*of river*). **3.** (*tech.*) hose; пожа́рный р. fire-hose.

рукави́ц|а, ы, *f.* mitten; gauntlet; держа́ть в ежо́вых ~ax to rule with an iron rod.

рука́вчик, а, *m.* **1.** *dim. of* рука́в. **2.** cuff.

рукоби́ть|е, я, *n.* (*obs.*) shaking hands on a bargain.

рукоблу́ди|е, я, *n.* masturbation.

рукоблу́дник, а, *m.* masturbator.

рукоблу́днича|ть, ю, *impf.* to indulge in masturbation.

руководи́тел|ь, я, *m.* **1.** leader; manager; кла́ссный р. (*in school*) form monitor. **2.** instructor; guide; нау́чный руководи́тель supervisor of studies.

руково|ди́ть, жу́, ди́шь, *impf.* (+*i.*) to lead; to guide; to direct, manage.

руково|ди́ться, жу́сь, ди́шься, *impf.* (+*i.*) to follow; to be guided (by).

руково́дств|о, а, *n.* **1.** leadership; guidance; direction. **2.** guiding principle, guide; р. к де́йствию guide to action. **3.** handbook, guide, manual; р. по эксплуата́ции instructions for use. **4.** (*collect.*) (the) leadership, leaders; governing body.

руково́дств|оваться, уюсь, *impf.* (+*i.*) to follow; to be guided (by).

руковод|я́щий, *pres. part. act. of* ~и́ть *and adj.* leading; guiding; ~я́щая статья́ editorial, leader; р. комите́т steering committee.

рукоде́ли|е, я, *n.* **1.** needlework. **2.** (*pl.*) hand-made wares.

рукоде́льниц|а, ы, *f.* needlewoman.

рукоде́льнича|ть, ю, *impf.* to do needlework.

рукокры́л|ые, ых (*sing.* ~ое, ~ого), *n.* (*zool.*) Cheiroptera.

рукомо́йник, а, *m.* wash-stand, wash-hand-stand.

рукопа́шн|ая, ой, *f.* hand-to-hand fight(-ing).

рукопа́шный, *adj.* hand-to-hand.

рукопи́сный, *adj.* manuscript; р. шрифт cursive, italics.

ру́копис|ь, и, *f.* manuscript.

рукоплеска́ни|е, я, *n.* applause, clapping.

рукопле|ска́ть, щу́, ~щешь, *impf.* (+*d.*) to applaud, clap.

рукопожа́ти|е, я, *n.* handshake; обменя́ться ~ями (с+*i.*) to shake hands (with).

руко́ят|ка, и, *f.* 1. handle; hilt; haft, helve; shaft; по ~у up to the hilt. 2. crank, crank handle.

руко́ят|ь, и, *f.* = ~ка 1.

рула́д|а, ы, *f.* (*mus.*) roulade, run.

рулев|о́й, *adj. of* руль; ~о́е колесо́ steering wheel; р. механи́зм, ~о́е устро́йство steering gear; *as noun* р., ~о́го, *m.* helmsman, man at the wheel.

рулёжк|а, и, *f.* (*aeron.*) taxiing.

руле́т, а, *m.* (*cul.*) 1. roll; мясно́й р. meat loaf. 2. boned gammon.

руле́тк|а, и, *f.* 1. tape-measure. 2. roulette; игра́ть в ~у to play roulette.

рул|и́ть, ю́, и́шь, *impf.* (*aeron.*) to taxi.

руло́н, а, *m.* roll.

рул|ь, я́, *m.* rudder; helm (*also fig.*); (steering-)wheel; handle-bars; р. высоты́ (*aeron.*) elevator; р. поворо́та (*aeron.*) rudder; пра́вить ~ём, сиде́ть за ~ём, быть на ~é, стоя́ть на ~é to steer; стать за р. to take the helm; ле́во руля́ port the helm; стоя́ть на ~é (*fig.*) to be at the helm; без ~я́ и без ветри́л (*fig.*) without any sense of purpose.

румб, а, *m.* (*naut.*) (compass) point.

ру́мпел|ь, я, *m.* (*naut.*) tiller.

румы́н, а, *m.* Romanian.

румы́нк|а, и, *f.* Romanian (woman).

румы́нский, *adj.* Romanian.

румя́н|а, ~, *no sing.* rouge.

румя́н|ец, ца, *m.* (high) colour; flush; blush.

румя́н|ить, ю, ишь, *impf.* 1. (*pf.* за~) to redden (*also fig.*); to cause to glow. 2. (*pf.* на~) to rouge.

румя́н|иться, юсь, ишься, *impf.* 1. (*pf.* за~) to redden; to glow; to flush. 2. (*pf.* на~) to use rouge.

румя́н|ый (~, ~а), *adj.* rosy, ruddy, rubicund.

ру́н|а, ы, *f.* (*philol.*) rune.

рунду́к, а́, *m.* (*obs.*) locker, bin.

руни́ст|ый (~, ~а), *adj.* (*obs.*) fleecy.

руни́ческий, *adj.* (*philol.*) runic.

рун|о́[1], а́, *pl.* ~а, *n.* (*obs. or poet.*) fleece; золото́е р. (*myth.*) the Golden Fleece.

рун|о́[2], а́, *pl.* ~а and ~ья, *n.* (*dial.*) school (*of fish*).

ру́пи|я, и, *f.* rupee.

ру́пор, а, *m.* megaphone, speaking-trumpet; loud hailer; (*fig.*) mouthpiece.

руса́к[1], а́, *m.* (grey) hare.

руса́к[2], а́, *m.* (*coll.*) Russian.

руса́лк|а, и, *f.* mermaid.

руса́л|очий, *adj. of* ~ка.

руси́зм, а, *m.* (*ling.*) Russicism, borrowing from Russian.

руси́н, а, *m.* Ruthenian.

руси́нский, *adj.* Ruthenian.

руси́ст, а, *m.* specialist in Russian philology.

руси́стик|а, и, *f.* Russian philology.

русифика́тор, а, *m.* russifier, russianizer.

русифика́ци|я, и, *f.* russification, russianization.

русифици́р|овать, ую, *impf. and pf.* to russify, russianize.

ру́сл|о, а, *g. pl.* ~, *n.* 1. (river-)bed, channel; измени́ть р. реки́ to change the course of a river. 2. (*fig.*) channel, course; мои́ дела́ пошли́ по но́вому ~у my affairs have taken a new turn.

русоволо́с|ый (~, ~а), *adj.* having light -brown hair.

ру́сск|ая, ой, *f.* 1. Russian (woman). 2. russkaya (*Russian folk-dance*).

ру́сск|ий, *adj.* Russian (*also as noun* р., ~ого, *m.*).

ру́с|ый (~, ~а), *adj.* light brown.

руте́ни|й, я, *m.* (*chem.*) ruthenium.

рути́л, а, *m.* (*min.*) rutile.

рути́н|а, ы, *f.* (*pejor.*) routine; rut, groove.

рутинёр, а, *m.* slave to routine, person in a rut, in a groove.

рутинёр|ский, *adj. of* ~; ~ские взгля́ды rigid views.

рутинёрств|о, а, *n.* slavery to routine.

рути́н|ный, *adj. of* ~а.

ру́хляд|ь, и, *f.* (*collect.*; *coll.*) junk, lumber.

ру́хн|уть, у, ешь, *pf.* to crash down, tumble down, collapse; (*fig.*) to crash, fall to the ground.

руча́тельств|о, а, *n.* guaranty, warrant; guarantee; с ~ом guaranteed.

руча́|ться, юсь, *impf.* (*of* поручи́ться) (за+*a.*) to warrant, guarantee, certify; to answer (for), vouch (for); р. голово́й (за+*a.*) to stake one's life (on); я не могу́ за него́ р. I cannot vouch for him.

руче|ёк, йка́, *m.* *dim. of* руче́й.

руч|е́й, ья́, *m.* 1. brook, stream; ~ьи́ слёз floods of tears. 2. (*tech.*) groove, calibre, pass (*of roller*).

ру́чк|а, и, *f.* 1. *dim. of* рука́. 2. handle; arm (*of chair*); р. две́ри door-handle, door-knob; дойти́ до ~и (*fig.*, *coll.*) to reach an impasse. 3. penholder; pen; автомати́ческая р. fountain-pen.

ручни́к, а́, *m.* (*tech.*) bench hammer.

ручн|о́й, *adj.* 1. hand; arm; manual; ~а́я

грана́та hand grenade; ~áя кладь hand luggage; ~áя пила́ hand-saw; ~óe полоте́нце hand towel; ~áя прода́жа counter sale; ~áя прода́жа лека́рств sale of medicines without prescription; p. пулемёт light machine-gun; ~áя рабо́та handwork; ~áя теле́жка hand-cart; p. труд manual labour; ~ы́е часы́ wrist watch. 2. tame.

ру́ш|ить¹, у, ишь, impf. to pull down.

ру́ш|ить², у, ишь, impf. to husk.

ру́ш|иться, усь, ишься, impf. and pf. to fall in, collapse; (fig.) to fall to the ground.

ры́б|а, ы, f. fish; (pl., astron.) Pisces; ни p., ни мя́со neither fish, flesh nor fowl; чу́вствовать себя́ как p. в воде́ to feel in one's element; би́ться как p. об лёд to struggle desperately.

рыба́к, á, m. fisherman.

рыба́лк|а, и, f. 1. (coll.) fishing; fishing trip; идти́ на ~y to go fishing. 2. (dial.) fishing spot. 3. (dial.) seagull.

рыба́р|ь, я (~я́), m. (obs.) = рыба́к.

рыба́|цкий, adj. of ~к; p. посёлок fishing village.

рыба́|чий, adj. of ~к; ~чья ло́дка fishing-boat.

рыба́ч|ить, у, ишь, impf. to fish.

рыба́чк|а, и, f. 1. fisherwoman. 2. fisherman's wife.

рыбёшк|а, и, f. (coll.) small fry.

ры́бий, adj. 1. fish; piscine; p. жир cod-liver oil; p. клей isinglass, fish-glue. 2. fish-like, fishy.

ры́бник, а, m. 1. fishmonger, fish vendor. 2. fish marketer.

ры́бн|ый, adj. fish; ~ые консе́рвы tinned fish; ~ая ло́вля fishing; p. магази́н fish-shop, fishmonger's; p. про́мысел fishery; p. ры́нок fish market; p. садо́к fish-pond.

рыбово́д, а, m. fish-breeder.

рыбово́дств|о, а, n. fish-breeding.

рыбозаво́д, а, m. fish-factory; плаву́чий p. fish-factory ship.

рыбоконсе́рвный, adj.; p. заво́д fish cannery.

рыболо́в, а, m. fisherman; angler.

рыболове́цкий, adj. fishing.

рыболо́вн|ый, adj. fishing; ~ые принадле́жности, ~ая снасть fishing tackle; p. райо́н fishing-ground, fishery.

рыболо́вств|о, а, n. fishing, fishery (as branch of economy).

рыбопромы́шленност|ь, и, f. fishing industry.

рыботорго́в|ец, ца, m. fishmonger.

рыботорго́вк|а, и, f. fishwife.

рыбохо́д, а, m. fish-run (in dam).

рыв|о́к, ка́, m. 1. jerk. 2. (sport) dash, burst, spurt.

рыг|а́ть, а́ю, impf. (of ~ну́ть) to belch.

рыг|ну́ть, ну́, нёшь, pf. of ~а́ть.

рыда́|ть, ю, impf. to sob.

рыдва́н, а, m. (hist.) large coach.

рыжева́т|ый (~, ~а), adj. reddish; rust-coloured.

рыжеволо́с|ый (~, ~а), adj. red-haired.

рыже́|ть, ю, impf. (of по~) to turn reddish.

ры́ж|ий (~, ~á, ~е), adj. 1. red, red-haired, ginger; (of a horse) chestnut. 2. of faded red-brown colour. 3. as noun p., ~его, m. circus clown; я что, p.? (coll.) why leave me out?

ры́жик¹, а, m. saffron milk-cap (mushroom).

ры́жик², а, m. (coll.) 'Ginger', 'Sandy' (pet name for red-haired child, or for dog, etc., with red coat).

рыка́|ть, ю, impf. to roar.

ры́л|о, а, n. 1. snout (of pig, etc.). 2. (coll.) snout, mug.

ры́л|ьце, ьца, g. pl. ~ец, n. 1. dim. of ~о; (dial.) spout; у него́ p. в пуху́ he has been at the jam-pot. 2. (bot.) stigma.

рым, а, m. (naut.) (mooring-)ring, eyebolt.

ры́нд|а¹, ы, f. (hist.) rynda (bodyguard of tsars in Muscovite period).

ры́нд|а², ы, f. ship's bell.

ры́н|ок, ка, m. 1. market(-place). 2. (econ.) market.

ры́но|чный, adj. of ~к; p. день market-day; ~чная торго́вля marketing; по~чной цене́ at the market price.

рыса́к, á, m. trotter.

ры́с|ий, adj. lynx; ~ьи глаза́ (fig.) lynx eyes.

рыси́ст|ый, adj. ~ые испыта́ния trotting races; ~ая ло́шадь trotter.

рыс|и́ть, и́шь, impf. to trot.

ры́|скать, щу, щешь, impf. 1. to rove, roam. 2. (по+d.) to scour, ransack (in search of something); p. по ска́лам to scour the cliffs; p. по карма́нам to ransack one's pockets. 3. (naut.) to gripe, yaw.

рысц|а́, ы́, f. jog-trot; е́хать ~о́й to go at a jog-trot.

рыс|ь¹, и, о ~и, на ~й, f. trot; кру́пная p. round trot; на ~я́х at a trot.

рыс|ь², и, f. lynx.

ры́сью, adv. at a trot.

ры́твин|а, ы, f. rut, groove.

рыть, ро́ю, ро́ешь, impf. to dig; to burrow; to root up; p. око́пы to dig trenches; p. зе́млю копы́том to paw the ground (also fig.).

рыть|ё, я́, n. digging.

ры́ться, ро́юсь, ро́ешься, impf. (в+p.) to dig (in); (fig.) to rummage (in), ransack, burrow (in).

рыхле́|ть, ю, impf. (of по~) to become friable.

рыхл|и́ть, ю́, и́шь, impf. to loosen; to make friable.

рыхл|ый (~, ~á, ~о), adj. 1. friable; mellow (of soil); loose; porous. 2. (fig.) podgy.

рыцар|ский, *adj.* **1.** *adj. of* ~ь; р. поединок joust; р. роман tale of chivalry. **2.** (*fig.*) chivalrous.

рыцарств|о, а, *n.* **1.** (*collect.*; *hist.*) knights. **2.** knighthood; получить р. to receive a knighthood. **3.** (*fig.*) chivalry.

рыцар|ь, я, *m.* knight; странствующий р. knight errant.

рыча́г, а́, *m.* lever; (*fig.*) key factor, linchpin; переводной р. switch lever; р. управления control lever; действие ~а́ leverage.

рыча́|жный, *adj. of* ~г; ~жные весы beam balance; р. молот sledge hammer.

рыча́ни|е, я, *n.* growl, snarl.

рыч|а́ть, у́, и́шь, *impf.* to growl, snarl.

рья́ност|ь, и, *f.* zeal.

рья́н|ый (~, ~а), *adj.* zealous.

рюкза́к, а́, *m.* rucksack, knapsack.

рюмк|а, и, *f.* wine-glass.

рюмочк|а, и, *f.* *dim. of* рюмка; талия ~ой, в ~у (*coll.*) wasp waist.

ряби́н|а¹, ы, f.* **1. rowan-tree, mountain ash, service-tree. **2.** rowan-berry, ashberry.

ряби́н|а², ы, *f.* (*coll.*) pit, pock; лицо с ~ами pocked-marked face.

ряби́нник, а, *m.* (*orn.*) fieldfare.

ряби́новк|а, и, *f.* rowanberry vodka.

ряби́н|овый, *adj. of* ~а.

ряб|и́ть, и́т, *impf.* **1.** to ripple. **2.** (*impers.*) у меня ~и́т в глаза́х I am dazzled.

ряб|о́й (~, ~а́, ~о), *adj.* **1.** pitted, pock-marked. **2.** speckled.

ряб|о́к, ка́, *m.* (*orn.*) sandgrouse.

ря́бчик, а, *m.* (*orn.*) hazel-grouse, hazel-hen.

ряб|ь, и, f.* **1. ripple(s). **2.** dazzle.

ря́вк|ать, аю, *impf.* (*of* ~нуть) (на+*a.*; *coll.*) to bellow (at), roar (at).

ря́вк|нуть, ну, нешь, *pf. of* ~ать.

ряд, а, в ~е *and* **в ~у́,** *pl.* **~ы́, ~о́в,** *m.* **1.** (*in var. senses*) row; line; первый р., последний р. (*theatr.*) front row, back row; р. за ~ом row upon row; из ~а вон выходя́щий out-

standing, extraordinary, out of the common (run); стоя́ть в одно́м ~у́ (с+*i.*) to rank (with). **2.** (*mil.*) file, rank; непо́лный р. blank file; ~ы́ вздвой! (*command*) form fours!; в ~а́х а́рмии in the ranks of the army; в пе́рвых ~а́х in the first ranks; (*fig.*) in the forefront. **3.** series (*also math.*); number; в це́лом ~е слу́чаев in a number of cases.

ря|ди́ть¹, жу́, ~ди́шь, *impf.* (+*i.*) to dress up (as), get up (as).

ря|ди́ть², жу́, ~ди́шь, *impf.* (*obs.*) **1.** to ordain, lay down the law. **2.** to contract.

ря|ди́ться¹, жу́сь, ~ди́шься, *impf.* **1.** (*coll.*) to dress up. **2.** (+*i.*) to dress up (as), disguise oneself (as).

ря|ди́ться², жу́сь, ~ди́шься, *impf.* (*of* по~) (*obs.*) **1.** (с+*i.*) to bargain (with). **2.** (+*inf.*) to undertake (to), contract (to).

рядко́м, *adv.* = **ря́дом.**

рядов|о́й¹, *adj.* **1.** ordinary, common. **2.** (*mil.*) р. соста́в rank and file; men, other ranks; *as noun* **р., ~о́го,** *m.* private (soldier).

рядов|о́й², *adj.* (*agric.*) ~а́я се́ялка seed drill; р. посе́в sowing in drills.

ря́дом, *adv.* **1.** alongside, side by side; (с+*i.*) next to; он сиди́т р. с премье́р-мини́стром he is sitting next to the Prime Minister. **2.** near, close by, just by, next door; э́то совсе́м р. it is a stone's throw away; он жил р. с бо́йней he lived next door to the slaughter-house. **3.** сплошь и р. more often than not; pretty often.

ря́дышком, *adv.* (*coll.*) = **ря́дом.**

ряж, а, *m.* (*tech.*) crib(-work).

ряжев|о́й, *adj. of* ряж; ~а́я плоти́на crib-dam.

ря́жен|ый, *adj.* dressed up, disguised; *as noun* **р., ~ого,** *m.*; ~ая, ~ой, *f.* mummer.

ря́с|а, ы, *f.* cassock.

**ря́ск|а, и, f.* (*bot.*) duckweed.

**ря́шк|а, и, f.* (*coll.*) mug (= face).

C

с, *prep.*

I. +*g.* **1.** (*in var. senses*) from; off; с юго-восто́ка from the South-East; с Во́лги from the Volga; с Кавка́за from the Caucasus; с ты́ла from the rear; с головы́ до ног from head to foot; со сна half awake; с пе́рвого взгля́да at first sight; шум со спорти́вной площа́дки the noise from the playing-field; пошлина с табака́ duty on tobacco; перево́д с ру́сского translation from Russian; сда́ча с рубля́ change of a

rouble; верну́ться с рабо́ты to return from work; убра́ть посу́ду со стола́ to clear the things from the table; упа́сть с ками́нной по́лки to fall off the mantelpiece; уста́ть с доро́ги to be tired after a journey; ходи́ть с туза́ to lead with the ace; снять с кого́-н. фотогра́фию to take someone's photograph; взять приме́р с кого́-н. to follow someone's example; дово́льно с тебя́! that's enough for you!; ско́лько с меня́? how much do I owe? **2.** for, from, with;

с ра́дости for joy; со стыда́ for shame, with shame. **3.** (*of position*) on, from; с ле́вой стороны́ от желе́зной доро́ги on the left-hand side of the railway; с одно́й, с друго́й стороны́ on the one, on the other hand; с како́й то́чки зре́ния? from what point of view? **4.** with (= *on the basis of*); с разреше́ния дире́ктора шко́лы with the headmaster's permission; с ва́шего согла́сия with your consent. **5.** by, with (= *by means of*); взять с бо́ю to take by storm; писа́ть с большо́й бу́квы to write with a capital letter. **6.** (*of time*) from; since; as from; с девяти́ (часо́в) до пяти́ from nine (o'clock) till five; с де́тства from childhood; с утра́ since morning; мы с ней не ви́делись с января́ I have not seen her since January; они́ бу́дут в Москве́ с двадца́того числа́ they will be in Moscow from the twentieth; с 1850 по 1900 from 1850 to 1900.

.II. +*a.* **1.** about; я бу́ду там с год I shall be there about a year; мы прошли́ с ми́лю we walked about a mile. **2.** the size of; с дом the size of a house; на́ша до́чка ро́стом с ва́шу our daughter is about the same height as yours; ма́льчик с па́льчик Tom Thumb.

III. +*i.* **1.** (*in var. senses*) with; and; с удово́льствием with pleasure; мы с ва́ми you and I; он с сестро́й he and his sister. **2.** (*indicates possession*) хлеб с ма́слом bread and butter; челове́к со стра́нностями queer, peculiar person. **3.** by, on (= *by means of*); получи́ть с пе́рвой по́чтой to receive by first post; я прие́хал с экспре́ссом I came on the express. **4.** with (= *with the passage of*); с года́ми with the years; с ка́ждым днём every day. **5.** with (*or not translated*) (= *in regard to, as regards*); как обстои́т у вас с рабо́той? how is the work going?; что с ва́ми? what is the matter with you?, what's up?; у неё пло́хо с се́рдцем her heart is bad; как у вас с деньга́ми? how are you off for money?

с- (со-, съ-) *verbal prefix indicating* **1.** *unification, movement from various sides to a point, as* свари́ть to weld. **2.** *movement or action made in a downward direction, as* спусти́ться to descend. **3.** *removal of something from somewhere, as* сорва́ть to tear off.

саа́м, а, *m.* Lapp, Laplander.
саа́мк|а, и, *f.* Lapp (woman).
саа́мский, *adj.* Lappish.
са́бельный, *adj.* sabre.
са́б|ля, ли, *g. pl.* ~ель, *f.* sabre.
сабота́ж, а, *m.* sabotage.
сабота́жник, а, *m.* saboteur.
сабота́жнича|ть, ю, *impf.* (*coll.*) to engage in sabotage.

саботи́р|овать, ую, *impf. and pf.* to sabotage.
сабу́р, а, *m.* (*pharm.*) juice of aloe leaves.
са́ван, а, *m.* shroud, cerement; сне́жный с. blanket of snow.
сава́нн|а, ы, *f.* (*geogr.*) savannah.
savра́сый, *adj.* (*of horses*) light brown with black mane and tail.
са́г|а, и, *f.* saga.
сагити́р|овать, ую, *pf.* **1.** *pf. of* агити́ровать. **2.** (*pf. only*) to win over.
са́го, indecl., n. (*bot.*) sago.
са́го|вый, *adj. of* ~; ~вая ка́ша sago pudding.
сад, а, о ~**е, в** ~**у́,** *pl.* ~**ы́,** *m.* garden; фрукто́вый с. orchard; зоологи́ческий с. zoological gardens, zoo; де́тский с. kindergarten.
сади́зм, а, *m.* sadism.
сади́ст, а, *m.* sadist.
сади́стский, *adj.* sadistic.
са|ди́ть¹, жу́, ~**дишь,** *impf.* (*of* по~) to plant.
са|ди́ть², жу́, ~**дишь,** *impf.* (*coll.*) **1.** to slap. **2.** (*fig.*) to hurtle; to dash; to stream.
са|ди́ться, жу́сь, ~**дишься,** *impf.* (*of* сесть); ~ди́(те)сь! (*polite request*) sit down!, take a seat!
са́дн|ить, ит, *impf.* (*impers.; coll.*) to smart, burn.
садо́вник, а, *m.* gardener.
садово́д, а, *m.* gardener; horticulturist.
садово́дств|о, а, *n.* **1.** gardening; horticulture. **2.** horticultural establishment.
садово́дческий, *adj.* horticultural.
сад|о́вый, *adj.* **1.** *adj. of* ~. **2.** garden, cultivated (*as opp. to wild*).
сад|о́к, ка́, *m.* place for keeping live creatures; кро́личий с. rabbit-hutch; ры́бный с. fish-pond; живоры́бный с. fish-well (*in river vessel or barge*); с. для птиц bird-cage.
са́ж|а, и, *f.* soot, lamp-black.
сажа́|ть, ю, *impf.* (*of* посади́ть) **1.** to plant. **2.** to seat; to set, put; to offer a seat; с. пти́цу в кле́тку to cage a bird; с. хлеб в печь to put bread into the oven; с. в тюрьму́ to put into prison, imprison, jail; с. ку́рицу на я́йца to set a hen on eggs; с. на хлеб и на во́ду to put on bread and water; с. под аре́ст to put under arrest.
са́жен|ец, ца, *m.* seedling; sapling.
саже́н|ки, ок, *no sing.* overarm stroke (*in swimming*).
саже́нный (*and* **саже́нный),** *adj.* (*coll.*) huge, enormous.
са́женый, *adj.* planted.
са́же́н|ь, и, *pl.* ~**и, са́жен** *and* **саже́ней,** *f.* sazhen (*Russian measure of length, equivalent to* 2·13 *metres*); морска́я с. Russian fathom (1·83 *metres*).

сазáн, а, *m.* wild carp (*Cyprinus carpo*).

сайг|á, и́, *f.* (*zool.*) saiga.

сáйк|а, и, *f.* (bread) roll.

сак, а, *m.* (*obs.*) 1. bag. 2. (*woman's*) sack-coat.

саквоя́ж, а, *m.* travelling-bag, grip.

сáкл|я, и, *g. pl.* ~ей, *f.* saklya (*Caucasian mountain hut*).

сакраментáл|ьный (~ен, ~ьна), *adj.* sacramental; sacred.

саксáул, а, *m.* (*bot.*) haloxylon.

саксóн|ец, ца, *m.* Saxon.

саксóнский, *adj.* Saxon; с. фарфóр Dresden (*or* Meissen) china.

саксофóн, а, *m.* saxophone.

салáз|ки, ок, *no sing.* 1. hand sled, toboggan. 2. (*tech.*) slide, slide rails; с. станкá sliding carriage.

саламáндр|а, ы, *f.* salamander.

саламáт|а, ы, *f.* (*obs. or dial.*) (*cul.*) salamata (*kind of porridge*).

салáт, а, *m.* 1. lettuce. 2. salad.

салáтник, а, *m.* salad-dish, salad-bowl.

салáтниц|а, ы, *f.* = салáтник.

салáт|ный, *adj. of* ~; ~ного цвéта light green.

сáлинг, а, *m.* (*naut.*) cross-trees.

сáл|ить, ю, ишь, *impf.* to grease.

салици́л, а, *m.* (*chem.*) salicylate.

салици́лк|а, и, *f.* (*coll.*) salicylic acid.

салици́ловый, *adj.* (*chem.*) salicylic.

сáл|ки, ок, *sing.* ~ка, ~ки, *f.* 1. (*children's game*) tag, 'he'. 2. (*sing.*) 'he' (*in this game*); кто у нас ~ка? who is 'he'?

сáл|о, а, *n.* 1. fat, lard; suet. 2. tallow. 3. thin broken ice (*on surface of water*); slush.

салóн, а, *m.* 1. salon. 2. saloon.

салóн-вагóн, а, *m.* saloon car, saloon carriage.

салóн|ный, *adj. of* ~; ~ные бесéды small talk; ~ное воспитáние high society upbringing.

салóп, а, *m.* (*obs.*) (*woman's*) coat.

салопи́йский, *adj.* (*geol.*) Salopian.

салóпниц|а, ы, *f.* (*coll., obs.*) 1. slut. 2. scandalmonger.

салотóпенный, *adj.* tallow-melting.

салты́к, *only in phrase* (*coll., obs.*) на свой с. in one's own fashion, in one's own way.

салфéтк|а, и, *f.* serviette, (table-)napkin.

салфéт|очный, *adj. of* ~ка; ~очное полотнó diaper-cloth, damask.

сáльдо, *indecl.*, *n.* (*book-keeping*) balance.

сáльник, а, *m.* 1. (*anat.*) epiploon. 2. (*tech.*) stuffing box, (packing) gland.

сáльност|ь, и, *f.* obscenity, bawdiness.

сáльн|ый, *adj.* 1. tallow; ~ая свечá tallow candle. 2. (*anat.*) sebaceous; ~ая железá sebaceous gland. 3. greasy. 4. obscene, bawdy; с. анекдóт bawdy story, dirty joke.

сáльто-мортáле, *indecl.*, *n.* somersault.

салю́т, а, *m.* (*mil., naut.*) salute.

салют|овáть, у́ю, *impf. and pf.* (*pf. also* от~) (+*d.*) to salute.

сам[1], самогó; *f.* самá, самóй, *a.* самоё; *n.* ~ó; *pl.* сáми, сами́х, *reflexive pron.* myself, yourself, himself, *etc.*; с. по себé in itself, per se; by oneself, unassisted; с. собóй of itself, of its own accord; он с. не свой he is not himself; с. себé хозя́ин one's own master; онá — самá добротá she is kindness itself.

сам[2], самогó, *m.* (*coll.*) boss, chief.

самáн, а, *m.* adobe.

самáн|ный, *adj. of* ~; с. кирпи́ч adobe (brick).

сáмбо, *indecl.*, *n.* (*abbr. of* самооборóна без ору́жия) unarmed combat.

самбу́к, а, *m.* (*cul.*) fruit purée.

сам- (*see* сам-дру́г, *etc.*) 1. (*of harvest yield*) *x* fold. 2. (*not alone but*) accompanied by *x* other persons (*reckoning the speaker as one*).

сам-дру́г, *indecl. adj.* 1. with one other, accompanied by one other person. 2. (*of harvest*) double, twice as much.

сам|éц, ца́, *m.* male (*of species*).

самиздáт, а, *m.* (*coll.*) samizdat (*unofficial reproduction of unpublished MSS.*).

сáмк|а, и, *f.* female (*of species*).

само- *prefix* self-, auto-.

самоанáлиз, а, *m.* self-examination, introspection.

самобичевáни|е, я, *n.* 1. self-flagellation. 2. (*fig.*) self-reproach.

самобы́тност|ь, и, *f.* originality.

самобы́т|ный (~ен, ~на), *adj.* original.

самовáр, а, *m.* samovar; постáвить с. to set a samovar to boil.

самовлáсти|е, я, *n.* absolute power, despotism.

самовлáст|ный (~ен, ~на), *adj.* 1. absolute. 2. (*fig.*) despotic, autocratic.

самовлюблённост|ь, и, *f.* narcissism.

самовлюблённый, *adj.* narcissistic; (*fig.*) vain, conceited.

самовнушéни|е, я, *n.* auto-suggestion.

самовозгорáни|е, я, *n.* spontaneous combustion, spontaneous ignition.

самовозгорá|ться, ется, *impf.* to ignite spontaneously.

самоволи|е, я, *n.* licence.

самовóл|ьный (~ен, ~ьна), *adj.* 1. wilful, self-willed. 2. unauthorized; ~ьная отлу́чка (*mil.*) absence without leave.

самовоспитáни|е, я, *n.* self-education.

самовоспламенéни|е, я, *n.* spontaneous ignition.

самовосхвалéни|е, я, *n.* self-praise, self-glorification.

самовя́з, а, *m.* tying (*as opp. to made-up*) tie.

самогóн, а, *m.* home-distilled vodka, hooch.
самогóн|ка, ки, *f.* = ~.
самодвѝжущийся, *adj.* self-propelled.
самодéйствующий, *adj.* self-acting, automatic.
самодéлк|а, и, *f.* (*coll.*) home-made product.
самодéл|ьный (~ен, ~ьна), *adj.* 1. home-made. 2. self-made.
самодержáви|е, я, *n.* autocracy.
самодержáв|ный (~ен, ~на), *adj.* autocratic.
самодéрж|ец, ца, *m.* autocrat.
самодéятельност|ь, и, *f.* 1. initiative, spontaneous action. 2. amateur performance, amateur talent activities (*theatricals, music, etc.*); вéчер ~и amateurs' night.
самодéятельный, *adj.* 1. amateur. 2. (*econ.*) self-employed.
самодисциплѝн|а, ы, *f.* self-discipline.
самодовлéющий, *adj.* self-sufficing, self-sufficient.
самодовóл|ьный (~ен, ~ьна), *adj.* self-satisfied, smug, complacent.
самодовóльств|о, а, *n.* self-satisfaction, smugness, complacency.
самодýр, а, *m.* petty tyrant, wilful person.
самодýрств|о, а, *n.* petty tyranny, wilfulness.
самоéд, а, *m.* (*ethnol., obs.*) Samoyed.
самозабвéни|е, я, *n.* selflessness.
самозабвéнный, *adj.* selfless.
самозаводя́щийся, *adj.* self-winding.
самозаготóвк|а, и, *f.* laying-in of one's own supplies.
самозажигáющийся, *adj.* self-igniting.
самозакáлк|а, и, *f.* (*tech.*) air-hardened steel.
самозарождéни|е, я, *n.* (*biol.*) spontaneous generation.
самозаря́дный, *adj.* self-loading.
самозащѝт|а, ы, *f.* self-defence; я убѝл егó в ~е I killed him in self-defence.
самозвáн|ец, ца, *m.* impostor, pretender.
самозвáнный, *adj.* false, self-styled.
самозвáнств|о, а, *n.* imposture.
самоиндýкци|я, и, *f.* (*phys.*) self-induction.
самокáт, а, *m.* 1. (*mil., obs.*) bicycle. 2. (*child's*) scooter.
самокáтчик, а, *m.* (*mil., obs.*) bicyclist.
самокрѝтик|а, и, *f.* self-criticism.
самокритѝч|ный (~ен, ~на), *adj.* containing self-criticism.
самокрýтк|а¹, и, *f.* (*coll.*) home-made cigarette, cigarette rolled by smoker.
самокрýтк|а², и, *f.* (*obs., coll.*) secret marriage, elopement.
самолёт, а, *m.* aeroplane, aircraft.
самолёт|ный, *adj.* of ~; ~ная радиостáнция airborne radio set.
самолётовождéни|е, я, *n.* air navigation.
самолётовы́лет, а, *m.* sortie (*of aircraft*).

самолётостроéни|е, я, *n.* aircraft construction.
самолёт-снаря́д, самолёта-снаря́да, *m.* flying bomb.
самолѝчно, *adv.* (*coll.*) oneself; сдéлать что-н. с. to do something by oneself; я с. вѝдел э́то I saw it with my own eyes.
самолѝчн|ый, *adj.* (*coll.*) personal; ~ое присýтствие attendance in person.
самолюбѝв|ый (~, ~а), *adj.* proud; touchy.
самолюби|е, я, *n.* pride, self-esteem; лóжное с. false pride; щадѝть чьё-н. с. to spare, respect someone's pride.
самомнéни|е, я, *n.* conceit, self-importance; он с бóльшим ~ем he has a high opinion of himself.
самонаблюдéни|е, я, *n.* (*psych.*) introspection.
самонадéянност|ь, и, *f.* (*pejor.*) self-sufficiency, independence.
самонадéян|ный (~, ~на), *adj.* (*pejor.*) self-sufficient, independent.
самоназвáни|е, я, *n.* native name, own name; рóмэни — с. цыгáн 'Romany' is the gypsies' own name for themselves.
самообвинéни|е, я, *n.* self-accusation.
самообладáни|е, я, *n.* self-control, self-possession; composure.
самообложéни|е, я, *n.* voluntary rate-paying.
самообмáн, а, *m.* self-deception.
самообольщéни|е, я, *n.* self-deception; пребывáть в ~и to live in a fool's paradise.
самооборóн|а, ы, *f.* self-defence.
самообразовáни|е, я, *n.* self-education.
самообслýживани|е, я, *n.* self-service.
самоокупáемост|ь, и, *f.* ability to pay its way (*without subsidy*).
самоокупáющийся, *adj.* paying its way.
самооплодотворéни|е, я, *n.* (*biol.*) self-fertilization.
самоопределéни|е, я, *n.* (*polit.*) self-determination.
самоопредел|ѝться, юсь, ѝшься, *pf.* (*of* ~я́ться) (*polit.*) to define one's position.
самоопредел|я́ться, я́юсь, *impf. of* ~ѝться.
самопрокѝдывающийся, *adj.* self-tipping; с. грузовѝк tip-up lorry.
самопылéни|е, я, *n.* (*bot.*) self-fertilization.
самовержéни|е, я, *n.* = самоотвéрженность.
самоотвéрженност|ь, и, *f.* selflessness.
самоотвéржен|ный (~, ~на), *adj.* selfless, self-sacrificing.
самоотвóд, а, *m.* withdrawal (*of candidature*), refusal to accept (*nomination for an office, etc.*).
самоотречéни|е, я, *n.* self-denial, (self-)abnegation, renunciation.
самооцéнк|а, и, *f.* self-appraisal.

самоочеви́дный, *adj.* self-evident.

самопи́шущ|ий, *adj.* (self-)recording, (self-) registering; с. прибóр recording instrument; ~ее перó fountain-pen.

самопожéртвовани|е, я, *n.* self-sacrifice.

самопознáни|е, я, *n.* (*philos.*) self-knowledge.

самопóмощ|ь, и, *f.* self-help, mutual aid.

самопроизвóльност|ь, и, *f.* spontaneity.

самопроизвóл|ьный (~ен, ~ьна), *adj.* spontaneous.

самопря́лк|а, и, *f.* (treadle) spinning-wheel.

самопу́ск, а, *m.* (*tech.*) self-starter.

саморазгружá|ющийся, *adj.* self-unloading; ~аяся бáржа hopper(-barge).

саморазоблачéни|е, я, *n.* self-exposure.

саморегули́рующий, *adj.* self-regulating.

саморекла́м|а, ы, *f.* self-advertisement.

саморóдный, *adj.* (*min.*) native, virgin.

саморóд|ок, ка, *m.* (*min.*) native metal, native ore; nugget; (*fig.*) person without education but possessing natural talents; композитор-с. born composer, natural composer.

самосáд, а, *m.* home-grown tobacco.

самосáдочн|ый, *adj.* ~ая соль lake-salt; ~ое óзеро salt lake.

самосвáл, а, *m.* tip-up (lorry), dump truck.

самосмáзк|а, и, *f.* (*tech.*) self-lubrication, automatic lubrication.

самосожжéни|е, я, *n.* self-immolation.

самосознáни|е, я, *n.* (self-)consciousness.

самосохранéни|е, я, *n.* self-preservation.

самости́йник, а, *m.* Ukrainian separatist.

самостоя́тельно, *adv.* independently; on one's own.

самостоя́тельност|ь, и, *f.* independence.

самостоя́тел|ьный (~ен, ~ьна), *adj.* (*in var. senses*) independent; ~ьное госудáрство independent state; с. учёный труд work of original scholarship.

самострéл[1], а, *m.* (*hist.*) arbalest, cross-bow.

самострéл[2], а, *m.* person with self-inflicted wound (*designed to escape onerous military duty, etc.*).

самострéльный, *adj.* self-firing, automatic.

самосу́д, а, *m.* lynch law, mob law.

самотёк, а, *m.* drift (*also fig.*); (*tech.*) gravity feed.

самотёком, *adv.* **1.** (*tech.*) by gravity. **2.** (*fig.*) haphazard; of its own accord; идти́ с. to drift.

самотё|чный, *adj.* of ~к; ~чное орошéние natural irrigation.

самоторможéни|е, я, *n.* self-braking.

самоуби́йственный, *adj.* suicidal (*also fig.*).

самоуби́йств|о, а, *n.* suicide; кончáть ~ом, покóнчить жизнь ~ом to commit suicide.

самоуби́йц|а, ы, *m. and f.* suicide (*agent*).

самоуважéни|е, я, *n.* self-esteem.

самоувéренност|ь, и, *f.* self-confidence, self-assurance.

самоувéрен|ный (~, ~на), *adj.* self-confident, self-assured.

самоунижéни|е, я, *n.* self-abasement, self-disparagement.

самоуничижéни|е, я, *n.* = самоунижéние.

самоуплотнéни|е, я, *n.* **1.** voluntary giving up of part of one's dwelling space. **2.** (*tech.*) self-packing.

самоуплотн|и́ться, ю́сь, и́шься, *pf.* (*of* ~я́ться) to give up voluntarily part of one's dwelling space.

самоуплотн|я́ться, я́юсь, *impf. of* ~и́ться.

самоуправлéни|е, я, *n.* self-government; мéстное с. local government.

самоуправля́ющийся, *adj.* self-governing.

самоупрáвно, *adv.* arbitrarily; поступáть с. to take the law into one's own hands.

самоупрáвный, *adj.* arbitrary.

самоупрáвств|о, а, *n.* arbitrariness.

самоуспокоéни|е, я, *n.* complacency.

самоуспокóенност|ь, и, *f.* = самоуспокоéние.

самоустанáвливающийся, *adj.* (*tech.*) self-adjusting, self-aligning.

самоустран|и́ться, ю́сь, и́шься, *pf.* (*of* ~я́ться) (от) to get out (of), dodge.

самоустран|я́ться, я́юсь, *impf.* **1.** *impf. of* ~и́ться. **2.** *impf. only* (от) to try to get out (of), try to dodge.

самоучи́тел|ь, я, *m.* self-instructor, manual for self-tuition; с. англи́йского языкá English self-taught.

самоу́чк|а, и, *m. and f.* self-taught person.

самохвáльств|о, а, *n.* self-advertisement.

самохóд, а, *m.* (*tech.*) self-feed, self-act travel.

самохóдк|а, и, *f.* (*mil.*) self-propelled gun.

самохóдный, *adj.* self-propelled.

самоцвéт, а, *m.* semi-precious stone, gem.

самоцвéт|ный, *adj.* с. кáмень = ~.

самоцéл|ь, и, *f.* end in itself.

самочи́нный, *adj.* arbitrary, unauthorized.

самочу́встви|е, я, *n.* general state; у негó плохóе с. he feels bad, he is in a bad way; как вáше с.? how do you feel?; (*in general, not restricted to sick persons*) how are you?

сам-пя́т, *indecl., adj.* **1.** with four others. **2.** (*of harvest*) fivefold.

сам-сём, *indecl., adj.* **1.** with six others. **2.** (*of harvest*) sevenfold.

сам-трети́й, *indecl., adj.* **1.** with two others. **2.** (*of harvest*) threefold.

саму́м, а, *m.* simoom.

самурá|й, я, *m.* samurai.

сам-четвёрт, *indecl., adj.* **1.** with three others. **2.** (*of harvest*) fourfold.

самши́т, а, *m.* box(-tree).

сам-шóст, *indecl., adj.* **1.** with five others. **2.** (*of harvest*) sixfold.

са́м|ый, *pron.* **1.** (*in conjunction with nouns, esp. denoting points of time or place, and with* тот *and* э́тот) the very, right; в ~ое вре́мя at the right time; с ~ого нача́ла from the very outset, right from the start; с ~ого утра́ ever since the morning, since first thing; в ~ом углу́ right in the corner; до ~ого ве́рха to the very top, right to the top; до ~ого Владивосто́ка right to, all the way to Vladivostok; в с. раз (*coll.*) just right; в ~ом де́ле indeed; в ~ом де́ле? indeed?, really?; на ~ом де́ле actually, in (actual) fact; тот с. челове́к, кото́рый... the very man who . . .; на э́том ~ом ме́сте on this very spot (*but* э́тот с. *is often purely pleonastic, being roughly equivalent to coll. Eng.* this here). **2.** тот же с. (кото́рый, что); тако́й же с. (как) the same (as); э́тот же с. the same. **3.** *forms superl. of adjs.; also expresses superl. in conjunction with certain nouns denoting degree of quantity or quality*; с. глу́пый the stupidest, the most stupid; ~ые пустяки́ the merest trifles; погоди́те ~ую ма́лость! wait just one moment, just a fraction of a second!

сан, а, *m.* dignity, office; высо́кий с. high office; духо́вный с. holy orders, the cloth; быть посвящённым в духо́вный с. to be ordained; из уваже́ния к ва́шему ~у out of respect for your cloth.

сан- *abbr. of* санита́рный.

санато́ри|й, я, *m.* sanatorium.

санато́р|ный, *adj. of* ~ий; с. режи́м sanatorium regimen.

санато́р|ский, *adj. of* ~ий; с. слу́жащий sanatorium attendant.

сангви́н, а, *m.* (*art*) sanguine.

сангви́н|а, ы, *f.* = ~.

сангви́ник, а, *m.* sanguine person.

сангвини́ческий, *adj.* sanguine.

санда́л, а, *m.* sandal-wood tree.

сандале́т|ы, ~, *no sing.* (*woman's*) sandals.

санда́ли|я, и, *f.* sandal.

санда́ловый, *adj.* sandal-wood.

са́н|и, е́й, *no sing.* sledge, sleigh; е́хать в, на ~я́х to drive in a sledge.

санита́р, а, *m.* hospital attendant, hospital orderly; (*mil.*) medical orderly.

санитари́|я, и, *f.* sanitation.

санита́р|ный, *adj.* **1.** medical; hospital; ~ое дово́льствие medical supplies; ~ая каре́та, ~ая маши́на ambulance; ~ая кни́жка (*mil.*) health record; с. по́езд hospital train; ~ая полева́я су́мка (*mil.*) first-aid kit; с. самолёт ambulance plane, aerial ambulance; ~ая слу́жба health service, medical service; ~ое су́дно hospital ship; ~ая часть (*mil.*) medical unit; с. я́щик first-aid box. **2.** sanitary; sanitation; с. врач sanitary inspector; ~ые

пра́вила sanitary regulations; с. у́зел lavatory; sanitary arrangements.

са́н|ки, ок, *no sing.* **1.** = ~и. **2.** toboggan.

санкциони́р|овать, ую, *impf. and pf.* to sanction.

са́нкци|я, и, *f.* **1.** sanction, approval. **2.** *pl.* (*polit., econ.*) sanctions.

санкюло́т, а, *m.* (*hist.*) sansculotte.

са́н|ный, *adj. of* ~и; с. путь sleigh-road.

санови́т|ый (~, ~а), *adj.* **1.** of exalted rank. **2.** (*fig.*) imposing.

сано́вник, а, *m.* dignitary, high official.

сано́вный, *adj.* of exalted rank.

са́ноч|ки, ек, *no sing. affect. dim. of* са́нки; лю́бишь ката́ться, люби́ и с. вози́ть (*prov.*) you must take the rough with the smooth.

санскри́т, а, *m.* Sanscrit.

санскрито́лог, а, *m.* Sanscrit scholar.

санскри́тский, *adj.* Sanscrit.

сантигра́мм, а, *m.* centigramme.

санти́м, а, *m.* centime.

сантиме́нт|ы, ов, *no sing.* (*coll.*) sentimentality; развести́ с. to sentimentalize.

сантиме́тр, а, *m.* **1.** centimetre. **2.** tape-measure.

сантони́н, а, *m.* (*pharm.*) santonin.

сану́з|ел, ла́, *m. see* санита́рный.

сап[1], а, *m.* (*med.*) glanders.

сап[2], а, *m.* (*coll.*) stertorous breathing.

са́п|а, ы, *f.* (*mil.*) sap; ти́хой ~ой on the sly, on the quiet.

сапёр, а, *m.* (*mil.*) sapper; pioneer.

сапёр|ный, *adj. of* ~; ~ные рабо́ты field engineering; ~ная ро́та engineer company; pioneer company.

сапно́й, *adj.* (*med.*) glanderous.

сапо́г, а́, *g. pl.* сапо́г, *m.* (high) boot; top-boot, jackboot; два ~а́ па́ра they make a pair.

сапо́жник, а, *m.* shoemaker, bootmaker, cobbler.

сапо́жнича|ть, ю, *impf.* to be a shoemaker.

сапо́жн|ый, *adj.* boot, shoe; ~ая ва́кса, с. крем blacking, shoe-polish; ~ое ремесло́ shoemaking; ~ая щётка shoe-brush.

сапфи́р, а, *m.* sapphire.

сапфи́ческий, *adj.* (*lit.*) sapphic.

сараба́нд|а, ы, *f.* (*mus.*) saraband.

сара́|й, я, *m.* shed; (*fig.*; *of uncomfortable room or dwelling*) barn; каре́тный с. coach-house; сенно́й с. hay-loft; с. для дров wood-shed.

саранч|а́, и́, *no pl., f.* locust(s).

сарафа́н, а, *m.* sarafan (*Russian peasant women's dress, without sleeves and buttoning in front*); tunic dress.

сараци́н, а, *m.* (*hist.*) Saracen.

сарде́льк|а, и, *f.* polony, saveloy.

сарди́н|а, ы, *f.* sardine, pilchard; ~ы в ма́сле (tinned) sardines.

сарди́н|ка, ки, *f.* = ~а.

сардони́кс, а, *m.* sardonyx.

сардони́ческий, *adj.* sardonic.

са́рж|а, и, *f.* (*text.*) serge.

сарка́зм, а, *m.* sarcasm.

саркасти́ческий, *adj.* sarcastic.

сарко́м|а, ы, *f.* (*med.*) sarcoma.

саркофа́г, а, *m.* sarcophagus.

сарма́т, а, *m.* (*hist.*) Sarmatian.

сарма́тский, *adj.* (*hist.*) Sarmatian.

сарпи́нк|а, и, *f.* (*text.*) printed calico.

сары́ч, а́, *m.* (*orn.*) buzzard.

сатан|а́, ы́, *m.* Satan.

сатани́нский, *adj.* satanic.

сателли́т, а, *m.* **1.** (*astron.*; *fig.*) satellite. **2.** (*tech.*) planet pinion (*of gear*), planet wheel.

сати́н, а, *m.* (*text.*) sateen.

сатине́т, а, *m.* (*text.*) satinet(te).

сатини́р|овать, ую, *impf. and pf.* to satin.

сати́н|овый, *adj. of* ~.

сати́р, а, *m.* (*myth.*) satyr.

сати́р|а, ы, *f.* satire.

сати́рик, а, *m.* satirist.

сатири́ческий, *adj.* satiric(al).

сатра́п, а, *m.* satrap.

сатра́пи|я, и, *f.* satrapy.

сатура́ци|я, и, *f.* (*tech.*) saturation.

сатурна́л|ии, ий, *no sing.* (*hist.*) saturnalia.

сафья́н, а, *m.* morocco (*leather*).

сафья́новый, *adj.* morocco.

са́хар, а (у), *m.* sugar; свекло́вичный с. beet sugar; тростнико́вый с. cane-sugar; моло́чный с. (*chem.*) milk sugar, lactose.

сахари́н, а, *m.* saccharin(e).

са́харист|ый (~, ~а), *adj.* sugary; saccharine.

са́хар|ить, ю, ишь, *impf.* (*of* по~) to sugar, sweeten.

са́харниц|а, ы, *f.* sugar-basin.

са́хар|ный, *adj. of* ~; (*fig.*) sugary; ~ная боле́знь (*med.*) diabetes; ~ная глазу́рь icing; ~ная голова́ sugar-loaf; с. заво́д sugar-refinery; ~ная кислота́ (*chem.*) saccharic acid; с. песо́к granulated sugar; ~ная пу́дра icing sugar; ~ная свёкла sugar-beet; с. тростни́к sugar-cane.

сахароваре́ни|е, я, *n.* sugar refining.

сахарозаво́дчик, а, *m.* (*obs.*) sugar manufacturer, owner of a sugar-refinery.

сахаро́з|а, ы, *f.* (*chem.*) saccharose, sucrose.

сач|о́к, ка́, *m.* net; с. для ры́бы landing-net; с. для ба́бочек butterfly-net.

сба́в|ить, лю, ишь, *pf.* (*of* ~ля́ть) (с+*g.*) to take off (from), deduct (from); с. с цены́ to reduce the price; с. в ве́се to lose weight; с. газ (*tech.*) to throttle back; с. спе́си кому́-н. (*coll.*) to take someone down a peg; с. тон (*fig.*) to change one's tune.

сбавля́|ть, ю, *impf. of* сба́вить.

сбаланси́р|овать, ую, *pf. of* баланси́ровать.

сба́лтыва|ть, ю, *impf. of* сболта́ть.

сбе́га|ть, ю, *pf.* (за+*i.*; *coll.*) to run (for), run to fetch; ~й за до́ктором! run for a doctor!

сбега́|ть(ся), ю(сь), *impf. of* сбежа́ть(ся).

сбе|жа́ть, гу́, жи́шь, гу́т, *pf.* (*of* ~га́ть) **1.** (с+*g.*) to run down (from); с. с ле́стницы to run downstairs. **2.** to run away. **3.** (с+*g.*; *fig.*) to disappear, vanish; хму́рое выраже́ние ~жа́ло с его́ лица́ the frown vanished from his face.

сбе|жа́ться, жи́тся, гу́тся, *pf.* (*of* ~га́ться) to come running; to gather, collect; вокру́г неё ~жа́лась толпа́ наро́ду a crowd gathered round her.

сберега́тельн|ый, *adj.* ~ая ка́сса savings bank; ~ая кни́жка savings-bank book.

сберега́|ть, ю, *impf. of* сбере́чь.

сбереже́ни|е, я, *n.* **1.** economy; с. сил (*mil.*) economy of force. **2.** (*pl.*) savings.

сбере́|чь, гу́, жёшь, гу́т, *past* ~г, ~гла́, *pf.* (*of* ~га́ть) **1.** to save, preserve; to protect; с. шу́бу от мо́ли to protect a fur coat from moth. **2.** to save, save up, put aside.

сберка́сс|а, ы, *f.* (*abbr. of* сберега́тельная ка́сса) savings bank.

сбива́|ть, ю, *impf. of* сбить.

сбива́|ться, юсь, *impf.* **1.** *impf. of* сби́ться. **2.** *impf. only* (на+*a.*) to resemble; to remind one (of).

сбивчивост|ь, и, *f.* inconsistency, contradictoriness.

сби́вчив|ый (~, ~а), *adj.* inconsistent, contradictory.

сби́т|ый, *p.p.p. of* ~ь *and adj.;* ~ые сли́вки whipped cream.

сбить, собью́, собьёшь, *pf.* (*of* сбива́ть) **1.** to bring down, knock down; to knock off, dislodge; с. самолёт to bring down, shoot down an aircraft; с. проти́вника с пози́ций to dislodge the enemy from his positions; с. це́ну to beat down the price; с. спесь с кого́-н. to bring someone down a peg. **2.** to put out; to distract; to deflect; с. с та́кта to throw out of time; с. кого́-н. с то́лку to muddle someone, confuse someone; с. кого́-н. с доро́ги to misdirect someone; с. с пути́ и́стинного (*fig.*) to lead astray. **3.** to wear down, tread down; с. каблуки́ to wear one's shoes down at the heels. **4.** to knock together; с. я́щик из досо́к to knock together a box out of planks. **5.** (*impf. also* бить) to churn; to beat up, whip, whisk.

сби́ться, собью́сь, собьёшься, *pf.* (*of* сбива́ться) **1.** to be dislodged; to slip; твоя́ шля́па сби́лась на́бок your hat is crooked, skew-whiff; с. с ног (*coll.*) to be run off one's legs, off one's feet. **2.** to be deflected;

to go wrong; с. в вычисле́ниях to be out in one's calculations; с. в показа́ниях to be inconsistent in one's testimony, contradict oneself in one's evidence; с. с доро́ги, с. с пути́ to lose one's way; to go astray (*also fig.*); с. с ноги́ to lose the step; с. со счёта to lose count; с. с та́кта to get out of time. **3.** to become worn down; to become blunt. **4.** с. в ку́чу, с. толпо́й to bunch, huddle.

сближа́|ть(ся), ю(сь), *impf. of* сбли́зить(ся).

сближе́ни|е, я, *n.* **1.** rapprochement. **2.** (*mil.*) approach, closing in. **3.** intimacy.

сбли́|зить, жу, зишь, *pf.* (*of* ~жа́ть) to bring together, draw together.

сбли́|зиться, жусь, зишься, *pf.* (*of* ~жа́ться) **1.** to draw together, converge. **2.** (c+i.) to become good friends (with). **3.** (*mil.*) to approach, close in.

сбо́|й, я, *m.* (*collect.*) head, legs, and entrails (of animal; *as meat*).

сбо́ку, *adv.* from one side; on one side; вид с. side-view; смотре́ть на кого́-н. с. to look sideways at someone.

сболта́|ть, ю, *pf.* (*of* сба́лтывать) to stir up, shake up, mix up; с. лека́рство to shake (a bottle of) medicine.

сболтн|у́ть, у́, ёшь, *pf.* (*coll., pejor.*) to blurt out.

сбор, а, *m.* **1.** collection; с. урожа́я harvest (-carrying); с. нало́гов tax collection; с. по́дписей collection of signatures. **2.** dues; duty; takings, returns; ге́рбовый с. stamp-duty; порто́вый с. harbour dues; тамо́женный с. customs duty; по́лный с. (*theatr.*) full house; де́лать хоро́шие ~ы (*theatr.*) to play to full houses, get good box-office returns. **3.** assemblage, gathering; быть в ~e to be assembled, be in session. **4.** (*mil.*) assembly (= *signal to assemble*). **5.** (*mil.*) (periodical) training; ла́герный с. camp; уче́бный с. refresher course. **6.** (*pl.*) preparations.

сбо́рищ|е, а, *n.* assemblage, mob.

сбо́рк|а, и, *f.* **1.** (*tech.*) assembling, assembly, erection. **2.** (*in dress, etc.*) gather; в ~ax, со ~ами with gathers.

сбо́рник, а, *m.* **1.** collection (*of stories, articles, etc.*). **2.** (*tech.*) storage tank, receptacle.

сбо́рн|ый, *adj.* **1.** that can be taken to pieces, detachable; с. дом pre-fabricated house. **2.** mixed, combined; ~ая кома́нда (*sport*) combined team, representative team. **3.** (*mil.*) assembly; с. пункт assembly point, rallying point. **4.** с. лист (*typ.*) preliminary sheets ('prelims').

сбо́рочный, *adj.* (*tech.*) assembly; с. конве́йер assembly belt; с. цех assembly shop.

сбо́рчатый, *adj.* gathered, with gathers.

сбо́рщик, а, *m.* **1.** collector; с. нало́гов tax-

-collector. **2.** (*tech.*) assembler, fitter, mounter.

сбра́сыватель, я, *m.* (*aeron.*) bomb-release mechanism.

сбра́сыва|ть(ся), ю(сь), *impf. of* сбро́сить(ся).

сбрива́|ть, ю, *impf. of* сбрить.

сбрить, сбре́ю, сбре́ешь, *pf.* (*of* сбрива́ть) to shave off.

сброд, а, *no pl.,* *m.* (*collect.*) riff-raff, rabble.

сбро́дн|ый, *adj.* (*coll.*) assembled by chance; ~ая компа́ния motley assembly, chance collection of people.

сброс, а, *m.* **1.** (*tech.*) overflow disposal (system). **2.** (*geol.*) fault, break. **3.** dropping, shedding. **4.** (*cards*) discard.

сбро́|сить, шу, сишь, *pf.* (*of* сбра́сывать) **1.** to throw down; to drop; с. бо́мбы to drop bombs; с. на парашю́те to drop by parachute. **2.** to throw off (*also fig.*); to cast off, shed; с. с себя́ одея́ло to throw off a blanket; с. и́го to throw off the yoke. **3.** (*cards*) to throw away, discard.

сбро́|ситься, шусь, сишься, *pf.* (*of* сбра́сываться) (c+g.) to leap (off, from).

сброшюр|ова́ть, у́ю, *pf. of* брошюрова́ть.

сбру́|я, и, *f.* (*collect.*) harness.

сбыва́|ть(ся), ю(сь), *impf. of* сбыть(ся).

сбыт, а, *no pl.,* *m.* (*econ., comm.*) sale; ры́нок ~а (seller's) market; хоро́ший с. good sales; найти́ себе́ хоро́ший с. to sell well.

сбытово́й, *adj.* (*econ., comm.*) selling, marketing.

сбы́точный, *adj.* (*obs.*) possible, feasible.

сбыть[1], сбу́ду, сбу́дешь, *past* сбыл, сбыла́, сбы́ло, *pf.* (*of* сбыва́ть) **1.** to sell, market. **2.** (*coll.*) to get rid (of), rid oneself (of); (*comm.*) to dump, push off; с. с рук to get off one's hands.

сбыть[2], сбу́дет, *past* сбыл, сбыла́, сбы́ло, *pf.* (*of* сбыва́ть) (*of level of water*) to fall.

сбы́ться, сбу́дется, *past* сбы́лся, сбыла́сь, *pf.* (*of* сбыва́ться) **1.** to come true, be realized. **2.** (*obs.*) to happen; что сбу́дется с ней? what will become of her?

сва́дебный, *adj.* wedding; nuptial; с. пода́рок wedding present.

сва́д|ьба, ьбы, *g. pl.* ~еб, *f.* wedding; справля́ть ~ьбу to celebrate a wedding.

свайнобо́йный, *adj.* pile-driving.

сва́йн|ый, *adj.* pile; ~ые постро́йки pile-dwellings.

сва́лива|ть(ся), ю(сь), *impf. of* свали́ться.

свал|и́ть[1], ю́, ~ишь, *pf.* (*of* вали́ть[1] *and* ~ивать) **1.** to throw down, bring down; to overthrow; to lay low. **2.** to heap up, pile up; с. вину́ (на+a.) to lump the blame (on).

свал|и́ть[2], ~и́т, *pf.* (*coll.*) to sink, drop, fall, abate.

свал|и́ться, ю́сь, ~ишься, *pf.* (*of* вали́ться *and* ~ива́ться) to fall (down), collapse; с. как снег на́ го́лову to come like a bolt from the blue.

сва́лк|а, и, *f.* 1. dump; scrap heap. 2. (*coll.*) scuffle, fight; о́бщая с. free-for-all, mêlée.

сва́лочн|ый, *adj. of* сва́лка; ~ое ме́сто dump, scrap heap (*also fig.*).

сваля́|ть, ю, *pf. of* валя́ть 3, 4.

сваля́|ться, ется, *pf.* to get tangled.

сва́рива|ть(ся), ю(сь), *impf. of* свари́ть(ся).

свар|и́ть, ю́, ~ишь, *pf.* 1. *pf. of* вари́ть. 2. (*impf.* ~ива́ть) (*tech.*) to weld.

свар|и́ться, ю́сь, ~ишься, *pf.* 1. *pf. of* вари́ться. 2. (*impf.* ~ива́ться) (*tech.*) to weld (together).

сва́рк|а, и, *f.* (*tech.*) welding; с. в прити́к butt welding; с. в цепь chain welding; с. по шву, с. со швом seam welding; с. с то́чками spot welding.

сварли́в|ый (~, ~а), *adj.* peevish, shrewish; ~ая же́нщина shrew.

сварно́й, *adj.* (*tech.*) welded; с. шов welded joint.

сва́рочн|ый, *adj.* (*tech.*) welding; ~ая горе́лка welding torch, burner; ~ое желе́зо weld iron, wrought iron; ~ая сталь weld steel, puddled steel.

сва́рщик, а, *m.* welder.

сва́стик|а, и, *f.* swastika.

сват, а, *m.* 1. matchmaker. 2. son-in-law's father; daughter-in-law's father.

сва́та|ть, ю, *impf.* (*of* по~) 1. (*pf. also* со~) (+*a. and d.*) to propose as husband; (*also* +*a.* за+*a.*) to propose as wife; to (try to) marry off (to); to (try to) arrange a match (between); ему́, за него́ ~ют каку́ю-то неме́цкую ба́рышню they are trying to arrange a match for him with a German girl, they are trying to marry him off to a German girl. 2. to ask in marriage.

сва́та|ться, юсь, *impf.* (*of* по~) (к; за+*a.*) to woo, court; to ask, seek in marriage.

сва́ть|я, и, *f.* son-in-law's mother; daughter-in-law's mother.

сва́х|а, и, *f.* matchmaker.

сва́|я, и, *f.* pile.

све́дени|е, я, *n.* 1. piece of information; (*pl.*) information, intelligence; по полу́ченным ~ям according to information received. 2. knowledge; attention, consideration, notice; дойти́ до чьего́-н. ~я to come to someone's notice; довести́ до чьего́-н. ~я to bring to someone's notice, inform someone; приня́ть к ~ю to take into consideration, take cognizance (of). 3. (*pl.*) knowledge; у него́ больши́е ~я по исто́рии Росси́и he is very knowledgeable about the history of Russia. 4. report, minute; отчётные ~я returns; предста́вить с. to

present a report.

сведе́ни|е, я, *n.* 1. reduction; с. счётов settling of accounts. 2. (*med.*) contraction, cramp.

све́дущ|ий (~, ~а), *adj.* (в+*p.*) knowledgeable (about); versed (in), experienced (in); ~ие ли́ца experts, persons in the know.

свеж|ева́ть, у́ю, *impf.* (*of* о~) to skin, dress.

свежезаморо́женный, *adj.* fresh-frozen, chilled.

свежеиспечённый, *adj.* newly-baked; (*fig., coll.*) raw, newly-fledged.

свежепросо́льный, *adj.* fresh-salted.

све́жест|ь, и, *f.* freshness; coolness; не пе́рвой ~и (*coll.*) past its (*fig., joc.*; one's) best.

свеже́|ть, ю, *impf.* (*of* по~) 1. to become cooler; (*of the wind*) to freshen (up), blow up. 2. to freshen up, acquire a glow of health.

све́ж|ий (~, ~а́, ~о́, ~и́), *adj.* (*in var. senses*) fresh; ~ее бельё clean underclothes; с. ве́тер fresh wind, fresh breeze; на ~ем во́здухе in the fresh air; ~ие но́вости recent news; ~ая ры́ба fresh fish; со ~ими си́лами with renewed strength; с. цвет лица́ fresh complexion; ~о́ в па́мяти fresh in one's memory; (*as pred.*) ~о́ (*impers.*) it is fresh, it is blowing up.

свез|ти́, у́, ёшь, *past* ~, ~ла́, *pf.* (*of* свози́ть¹) 1. to take, convey; его́ ~ли́ в больни́цу he has been taken to hospital. 2. to take down. 3. to take away, clear away.

свёкл|а, ы, *f.* beet, beetroot; кормова́я с. mangel-wurzel; са́харная с. sugar-beet, white beet; столо́вая с. red beet.

свеклови́ц|а, ы, *f.* sugar-beet.

свекло́ви|чный, *adj. of* ~ца; с. са́хар beet--sugar.

свеклово́дств|о, а, *n.* (sugar-)beet raising.

свеклоса́харный, *adj.* sugar-beet; beet--sugar.

свеклосовхо́з, а, *m.* State (sugar-)beet farm.

свеко́льник, а, *m.* 1. beetroot soup. 2. beetroot leaves.

свеко́льный, *adj. of* свёкла.

свёк|ор, ра, *m.* father-in-law (*husband's father*).

свекро́в|ь, и, *f.* mother-in-law (*husband's mother*).

свербёж, а́, *m.* (*coll.*) itch, irritation.

сверб|е́ть, и́т, *impf.* (*coll.*) to itch, irritate.

сверг|а́ть, а́ю, *impf. of* ~нуть.

све́рг|нуть, ну, нешь, *past* ~, ~ла, *pf.* (*of* ~а́ть) to throw down, overthrow; с. с престо́ла to dethrone.

сверже́ни|е, я, *n.* overthrow; с. с престо́ла dethronement.

све́р|зиться, жусь, зишься, *pf.* (с+*g.*; *coll.*) to tumble (off, from).

свéр|ить, ю, ишь, *pf.* (*of* ~я́ть) (+*a.* c+*i.*) to collate (with); to check (against); с. часы́ to check one's watch; с. корректу́ру с ру́кописью to check proofs against a manuscript.

свéр|иться, юсь, ишься, *pf.* (*of* ~я́ться) (c+*i.*) to check (with).

свéрк|а, и, *f.* collation.

сверкáни|е, я, *n.* sparkling, twinkling; glitter; glare.

сверкá|ть, ю, *impf.* to sparkle, twinkle; to glitter; to gleam.

сверкн|у́ть, у́, ёшь, *pf.* to flash (*also fig.*); у меня́ в головé ~у́ла мысль a thought flashed through my mind.

сверли́льный, *adj.* (*tech.*) boring, drilling; с. стано́к boring machine, drilling machine, drill.

сверл|и́ть, ю́, и́шь, *impf.* 1. (*tech.*) to bore, drill; с. зуб to drill a tooth. 2. to bore through. 3. (*fig.; of mental or physical pain*) to nag (at), gnaw (at); егó ~и́ла мысль об уби́том the image of the murdered man nagged at him; у меня́ ~и́т в у́хе I have a nagging ear-ache.

сверл|о́, á, *pl.* ~а, *n.* (*tech.*) borer, drill, auger.

сверло́вщик, а, *m.* borer, driller.

сверл|я́щий, *pres. part. act. of* ~и́ть *and adj.*; ~я́щая боль nagging, gnawing pain.

сверн|у́ть, у́, ёшь, *pf.* (*of* свёртывать *and* свора́чивать) 1. to roll (up); с. ковёр to roll up the carpet; с. папиро́су to roll a cigarette; с. парусá to furl sails; с. шéю кому́-н. to wring someone's neck. 2. (*fig.*) to reduce, contract, curtail, cut down; с. штáты to axe the establishment. 3. to turn; с налéво to turn to the left; с. с доро́ги to turn off the road; с. на прéжнее (*fig.*) to revert (*to former topic of conversation, etc.*).

сверн|у́ться, у́сь, ёшься, *pf.* (*of* свёртываться *and* свора́чиваться) 1. to roll up, curl up; to coil up; (*of petals or leaves*) to fold; с. клубко́м to roll oneself up into a ball. 2. to curdle, coagulate, turn. 3.(*fig.*) to contract. 4. *pass. of* ~у́ть.

сверстá|ть, ю, *pf. of* верстáть¹.

свéрстник, а, *m.* person of the same age; мы с ним ~и he and I are the same age.

свёрт|ок, ка, *m.* package, parcel, bundle.

свёртывани|е, я, *n.* 1. rolling (up). 2. curdling, turning; coagulation. 3. (*fig.*) reduction, curtailment, cutting down; с. произво́дства production cutting, cuts.

свёртыва|ть(ся), ю(сь), *impf. of* сверну́ть(ся).

сверх, *prep.*+*g.* 1. over, above, on top of. 2. (*fig.*) above, beyond; over and above; in excess of; с. плáна in excess of the plan,

over and above the plan; с. сил beyond one's strength; с. (вся́кого) ожидáния beyond (all) expectation; с. всегó to crown all, on top of everything; с. того́ moreover, besides.

сверх- super-, supra-, extra-, over-, preter-.

сверхзвуковóй, *adj.* (*phys., aeron.*) supersonic.

сверхкомплéктный, *adj.* supernumerary.

сверхмóщный, *adj.* (*tech.*) super-power, extra-high-power.

сверхнационáльный, *adj.* supranational.

сверхплáновый, *adj.* over and above the plan.

сверхпри́был|ь, и, *f.* excess profit.

сверхпроводи́мост|ь, и, *f.* (*electr.*) super-conductivity.

сверхскоростнóй, *adj.* super-high-speed.

сверхсмéтный, *adj.* in excess of estimates, not budgeted for.

сверхсрóчник, а, *m.* = сверхсрочнослужа́щий.

сверхсрочнослужа́щ|ий, его, *m.* (*mil.*) man re-engaging after completion of statutory military service.

сверхсрóчн|ый, *adj.* (*mil.*); ~ая слу́жба additional service (*voluntarily undertaken after completion of statutory period*); с. военно-слу́жащий = ~ослу́жащий.

свéрху, *adv.* 1. from above (*also fig.*); from the top; с. до́низу from top to bottom; директи́ва с. a directive from above; смотрéть на когó-н. с. вниз (*fig.*) to look down on someone. 2. on the surface.

сверхурóчн|ый, *adj.* overtime; ~ая рабóта overtime; *as noun* ~ые, ~ых (*payment for*) overtime.

сверхчеловéк, а, *m.* superman, overman.

сверхчеловéческий, *adj.* superhuman.

сверхчувстви́тельный, *adj.* supersensitive.

сверхштáтный, *adj.* supernumerary.

сверхъестéственный, *adj.* supernatural, preternatural.

сверч|о́к, кá, *m.* (*zool.*) cricket; всяк с. знай свой шесто́к (*prov.*) the cobbler should stick to his last.

сверша́|ть(ся), ю(сь), *impf.* = соверша́ть(ся).

сверш|и́ть(ся), у́(сь), и́шь(ся), *pf.* = совер-ши́ть(ся); ~и́лось! it has come to pass! it has come off!

свéрщик, а, *m.* collator.

свер|я́ть(ся), я́ю(сь), *impf. of* ~и́ть(ся).

свес, а, *m.* overhang.

свé|сить, шу, сишь, *pf.* (*of* ~шивать) 1. to let down, lower; сидéть, ~сив нóги to sit with one's legs dangling. 2. to weigh.

свé|ситься, шусь, сишься, *pf.* (*of* ~ши-ваться) to lean over; to hang over, over-hang; с. чéрез перила to lean over the banisters.

све|сти́, ду́, дёшь, *past* ~л, ~ла́, *pf.* (*of* своди́ть[1]) **1.** to take; с. дете́й в шко́лу to take the children to school; с. в моги́лу to send to the grave, be the death (of). **2.** (с+*g.*) to take down (from, off); с. кого́-н. с пьедеста́ла to take someone off his pedestal; с. с ума́ to drive mad. **3.** to take away; to lead off; с. коро́ву с доро́ги to take a cow off the road; с. разгово́р на другу́ю те́му to lead the conversation onto a different subject. **4.** to remove; с. пятно́ to remove, get out a stain. **5.** to bring together; to put together; to unite; с. ста́рых друзе́й to bring old friends together; судьба́ ~ла́ их fate threw them together; с. да́нные в табли́цу to tabulate data; с. концы́ с конца́ми to make (both) ends meet. **6.** с. дру́жбу (с+*i.*), с. знако́мство (с+*i.*) to make friends (with). **7.** (к, на+*a.*) to reduce (to), bring (to); с. на нет to bring to naught; с. к са́мому необходи́мому to reduce to barest essentials; с. расска́з к немно́гим слова́м to condense a story to a few words. **8.** to trace, transfer. **9.** to cramp, convulse; у меня́ ~ло́ но́гу I have cramp in my foot.

све|сти́сь, дётся, *past* ~лся, ~ла́сь, *pf.* (*of* своди́ться) **1.** (к, на+*a.*) to come (to), reduce (to); с. на нет to come to naught. **2.** (*of a transfer*) to come off.

свет[1], а, *m.* **1.** light (*also fig.*); лу́нный с. moonlight; заже́чь с. to put, turn the light on; в два ~а with two rows of windows; в ~е (+*g.*) in the light (of); предста́вить в невы́годном ~е to represent in an unfavourable light; на с. when placed in the light; на ~у́ in the light; при ~е (+*g.*) by the light (of); при ~е свечи́ by candlelight; стоя́ть про́тив ~а to stand in the light. **2.** daybreak; чем с. first thing (in the morning); чуть с. at daybreak, at first light; ни с., ни заря́ before dawn; (*iron.*) at the crack of dawn. **3.** (*pl. only* ~а́; *art*) lights; ~а́ и те́ни lights and shades.

свет[2], а, *m.* **1.** world (*also fig.*); Ста́рый, Но́вый с. the Old, the New World; тот с. the next, the other world; коне́ц ~а doomsday, the end of the world; стра́ны ~а the cardinal points (*of the compass*); произвести́ на с. to bring into the world; (по)яви́ться на с. to come into the world; вы́пустить в с. to bring out (= to publish); его́ нет на ~е he has departed this life; ни за что на ~е not for the world; на чём с. стои́т like nothing on earth, like hell; for all one is, was worth. **2.** society, beau monde; вы́сший с. the upper ten; мо́дный с. the fashionable set, the smart set.

света́|ть, ет, *impf.*; ~ет (*impers.*) it is dawning, it is getting light, day is breaking.

светёлк|а, и, *f.* (*obs.*) attic.

свети́л|о, а, *n.* luminary (*also fig.*); небе́сные ~а heavenly bodies.

свети́льник, а, *m.* **1.** lamp. **2.** (*obs.*) lampion.

свети́льный, *adj.* illuminating.

свети́л|ьня, ьни, *g. pl.* ~ен, *f.* wick.

све|ти́ть, чу́, ~тишь, *impf.* **1.** to shine. **2.** (+*d.*) to give light; to shine a light (for); он ~ти́л нам в тунне́ле he lit us through the tunnel.

све|ти́ться, чу́сь, ~тишься, *impf.* to shine, gleam; в окне́ ~тится огонёк there is a light in the window; в его́ глаза́х ~ти́лась безжа́лостность there was a hard glint in his eye(s).

светле́йший, *adj.* (*obs.*) (his, her) Highness (*as title of princes, etc.*).

светле́|ть, ю, *impf.* (*of* по~) to brighten (*also fig.*); (*of weather*) to clear up, brighten up.

светли́ц|а, ы, *f.* (*obs.*) front room.

све́тло- light.

све́т|лый (~ел, ~ла́, ~ло), *adj.* **1.** (*in var. senses*) light; bright; light-coloured; ~лые во́лосы light hair; с. день bright day; с. шрифт (*typ.*) light-face; на дворе́ ~ло́ it is daylight; ~ло́ вам, и́ли хоти́те, что́бы я зажёг свет? can you see, or do you want me to put the light on? **2.** (*fig.*) bright, radiant, joyous; pure, unclouded; ~лое бу́дущее radiant future; ~лая ли́чность good person, good soul; ~лой па́мяти of blessed memory. **3.** (*fig.*) lucid, clear; он — ~лая голова́ he has a lucid mind, a good head; ~лые мину́ты lucid intervals. **4.** (*eccl.*) Easter; ~лая неде́ля Easter week.

светлы́н|ь, и, *f.* brightness (*of moonlight and/or starlight*).

светля́к, а́, *m.* glow-worm; fire-fly.

светобоя́зн|ь, и, *f.* (*med.*) photophobia.

свето́в|ой, *adj. of* свет[1]; с. ба́кан light buoy; ~а́я волна́ light wave; ~а́я рекла́ма illuminated signs; с. сигна́л light signal, flare; с. эффе́кт (*theatr.*) lighting effect; ~о́е явле́ние luminous phenomenon.

светоза́р|ный (~ен, ~на), *adj.* (*poet.*) shining, flashing; radiant.

светокопирова́льный, *adj.* photostating; blueprinting.

светоко́пи|я, и, *f.* photostat; blueprint.

светолече́ни|е, я, *n.* (*med.*) phototherapy.

светомаскиро́вк|а, и, *f.* black-out.

светоме́три|я, и, *f.* (*mil.*) flash ranging, flash spotting.

светонепроница́емый, *adj.* light-proof.

светопреставле́ни|е, я, *n.* **1.** the end of the world, doomsday. **2.** (*fig., coll.*) chaos.

светорассе́яни|е, я, *n.* (*phys.*) light diffusion.

светосигнализа́ци|я, и, *f.* (*mil.*) lamp signalling.

светосигнáльн|ый, *adj.* (*mil.*) signal-lamp; ~ая связь lamp communication.

светосил|а, ы, *f.* (*phys.*) illumination; candlepower.

светостó|йкий (~ек, ~йка), *adj.* (*chem.*) stable in light; fast to light.

светотéн|ь, и, *f.* (*art*) chiaroscuro.

светотéхник|а, и, *f.* lighting engineering.

светофи́льтр, а, *m.* light filter.

светофóр, а, *m.* traffic lights; light signal.

свéточ, а, *m.* 1. (*obs.*) torch, lamp. 2. (*fig.*) light, luminary; torch-bearer.

светочувстви́тельност|ь, и, *f.* photo-sensitivity; speed (*of film*).

светочувстви́тел|ьный (~ен, ~ьна), *adj.* sensitive to light; ~ьная бумáга sensitized paper.

свéтск|ий, *adj.* 1. society, fashionable; ~ая жизнь high life; с. человéк man of the world, man about town. 2. (*obs.*) genteel, refined; ~ие манéры genteel manners. 3. temporal, lay, secular; worldly; ~ая власть temporal power.

свéтскост|ь. и, *f.* good manners, good breeding.

свет|я́щийся, *pres. part. of* ~и́ться *and adj.* luminous, luminescent, fluorescent, phosphorescent.

свеч|á, и́, *i.* ~óй, *pl.* ~и, ~ *and* ~éй, ~áм, *f.* 1. candle; taper; жечь ~ý с двух концóв to burn the candle at both ends. 2. зажигáтельная с., запáльная с. sparking-plug. 3. lamp candle-power; лáмпочка в пятьдеся́т ~éй lamp of fifty candle-power.

свечéни|е, я, *n.* luminescence, fluorescence; phosphorescence.

свéчк|а, и, *f.* candle. 2. (*med.*) suppository.

свеч|нóй, *adj. of* ~á; с. огáрок candle-end.

свéша|ть, ю, *pf.* to weigh.

свéшива|ть(ся), ю(сь), *impf. of* свéсить(ся).

свивáльник, а, *m.* swaddling-bands, swaddling-clothes.

свивá|ть, ю, *impf.* 1. *impf. of* свить. 2. *impf. only* to swaddle.

свидáни|е, я, *n.* meeting; appointment; rendezvous; date; назнáчить с. (на+*a.*) to make an appointment (for), make a date (for); до ~я! good-bye!; до скóрого ~я! see you soon!

свидéтел|ь, я, *m.* witness; с. обвинéния, защи́ты witness for the prosecution, for the defence; призвáть когó-н. в ~и to call someone to witness; вы́звать когó-н. ~ем, в кáчестве ~я (*leg.*) to subpoena as a witness.

свидéтель|ский, *adj. of* ~.

свидéтельств|о, а, *n.* 1. evidence; testimony. 2. certificate; метри́ческое с. birth certificate; с. о брáке certificate of marriage, marriage lines; с. о продáже bill of sale.

свидéтельств|овать, ую, *impf.* 1. (о+*p.*, +*a.* *or* +что) (*leg.*) to give evidence (concerning); to testify (to) (*also fig.*); (*fig.*) to show, attest, be evidence (of); письмó э́то ~ует о егó бестáктности this letter is evidence of his tactlessness. 2. (*pf.* за~) to witness; to attest, certify; с. кóпию to certify a copy; с. пóдпись to witness a signature; с. почтéние (+*d.*) to pay one's respects (to), present one's compliments (to). 3. (*pf.* о~) to examine, inspect; с. больнóго to examine a patient.

свидéтельств|оваться, уюсь, *impf.* 1. *pass. of* ~овать. 2. (+*i. or d.*; *obs.*) to call to witness.

сви́|деться, жусь, дишься, *pf.* (с+*i.*; *coll.*) to meet; to see one another.

свилевá́т|ый (~, ~а), *adj.* knotty, gnarled.

свил|ь, и, *f.* 1. knot (*in wood*). 2. waviness (*flaw in glass*).

свинáрк|а, и, *f.* pig-tender.

свинáрник, а, *m.* pigsty.

свинáр|ня, ни, *g. pl.* ~ен, *f.* = ~ник.

свин|éц, цá, *m.* lead (*also fig.* = bullet); óкись ~цá lead oxide.

свини́н|а, ы, *f.* pork.

сви́н|ка¹, ки, *f.* *dim. of* ~ья; морскáя с. guinea-pig.

сви́нк|а², и, *f.* (*med.*) mumps.

сви́нк|а³, и, *f.* (*tech.*) pig, ingot, bar; чугýн в ~ах pig iron.

свиновóд, а, *m.* pig-breeder.

свиновóдств|о, а, *n.* pig-breeding.

свиновóд|ческий, *adj. of* ~ство.

свин|óй, *adj. of* ~ья; ~áя кóжа pigskin; ~óе ры́ло snout; ~áя котлéта pork chop; ~óе сáло lard.

свиномáтк|а, и, *f.* sow.

свинопáс, а, *m.* swineherd.

свинофéрм|а, ы, *f.* pig-farm.

сви́нский, *adj.* (*coll.*) swinish; с. постýпок swinish trick.

сви́нств|о, а, *n.* (*coll.*) swinishness; swinish trick.

свин|ти́ть, чý, ти́шь, *pf.* (*of* ~чивать) 1. to screw together. 2. to unscrew.

сви́нтус, а, *m.* (*coll., joc.*) swine, rogue.

свинц|евáть, ýю, *impf.* (*tech.*) to plate with lead.

свинцóв|ый, *adj.* lead; leaden; leaden--coloured; ~ые бели́ла white lead; с. блеск (*min.*) galena; ~ая дробь lead shot; ~ая кислотá plumbic acid; ~ое отравлéние lead-poisoning; ~ая примóчка Goulard water; ~ая рудá lead-ore; с. сýрик red lead, minium; с. ýксус vinegar of lead; с. шлак lead dross, lead scoria.

сви́нчива|ть, ю, *impf. of* свинти́ть.

свин|ья́, ьи́, *pl.* ~ьи, ~éй, *f.* 1. pig, swine; hog; sow; морскáя с. porpoise. 2. (*fig.*)

swine; cad; вести́ себя́ ~ьёй to behave caddishly; подложи́ть ~ью (+ d.; coll.) to play a dirty trick (on).

свире́л|ь, и, f. (reed-)pipe.

свирепе́|ть, ю, impf. to grow fierce, grow savage.

свире́пост|ь, и, f. fierceness, ferocity, savageness; truculence.

свире́пств|овать, ую, impf. to rage.

свире́п|ый, adj. fierce, ferocious, savage; truculent; ~ая эпиде́мия violent epidemic.

свиристе́л|ь, я, m. (orn.) waxwing.

свис|а́ть, а́ю, impf. (of ~нуть) to hang down, droop, dangle; to trail.

свис|нуть, ну, нешь, pf. of ~а́ть.

свист, а, m. whistle; whistling; (of birds) singing, piping, warbling; hiss, hissing; с. в карма́не (coll., joc.) empty pockets.

сви|ста́ть, щу́, ~щешь, impf. to whistle; (of birds) to sing, pipe, warble; с. в свисто́к to blow a whistle; с. всех наве́рх (naut.) to pipe all hands on deck.

сви|сте́ть, щу́, сти́шь, impf. to whistle; to hiss; ищи́ ~щи́ (coll.) you can whistle for it; с. в кула́к to whistle for it.

свистн|у́ть, у, ешь, pf. 1. to give a whistle. 2. (coll.) to slap, smack; с. по́ уху to clip on the ear. 3. (coll.) to sneak (off with).

свист|о́к, ка́, m. whistle.

свистопля́ск|а, и, f. (coll.) pandemonium, bedlam; подня́ть ~у to let all hell loose.

свисту́льк|а, и, f. penny whistle, tin whistle.

свисту́н, а́, m. whistler.

сви́т|а, ы, f. 1. suite, retinue. 2. (geol.) suit, series, set.

сви́тер, а, m. sweater.

сви́т|ок, ка, m. roll, scroll.

свить, совью́, совьёшь, past свил, свила́, сви́ло, pf. (of вить and свива́ть) to twist, wind.

сви́ться, совью́сь, совьёшься, past сви́лся, свила́сь, pf. (of ви́ться) to roll up, curl up, coil.

свихн|у́ть, у́, ёшь, pf. to dislocate, sprain; с. себе́ ше́ю (fig., coll.) to come a cropper; с. с ума́ to go off one's head.

свихн|у́ться, у́сь, ёшься, pf. (coll.) 1. to go off one's head. 2. to go astray, go off the rails.

свищ, а́, m. 1. (tech.) flaw; (in metals) honeycomb. 2. (in wood) knot hole. 3. (med.) fistula.

свия́з|ь, и, f. (orn.) wigeon.

свобо́д|а, ы, f. freedom, liberty; с. во́ли free will; с. рук a free hand; с. сло́ва freedom of speech; с. собра́ний freedom of assembly; с. со́вести liberty of conscience; с. торго́вли free trade; вы́пустить на ~у

to set free, set at liberty; предоста́вить по́лную ~у де́йствий (+ d.) to give a free hand, give carte blanche; на ~е (i) at leisure, (ii) at large.

свобо́дно, adv. 1. freely; easily, with ease; fluently; дыша́ть с. to breathe freely; она́ с. говори́т на пяти́ языка́х she speaks five languages fluently. 2. (of clothing) loose, loosely.

свобо́д|ный (~ен, ~на), adj. 1. free (= at liberty). 2. free (= unhampered, unrestrained); easy; с. до́ступ easy access; с. уда́р (sport) free kick; с. от недоста́тков free from defects; челове́к ~ной профе́ссии professional man. 3. free (= disengaged); vacant; spare; ~ное вре́мя free time, time off; spare time; ~ное ме́сто vacant place, vacant seat; вы ~ны сего́дня ве́чером? will you be free this evening? 4. free(-and-easy). 5. (of clothing) loose, loose-fitting; flowing. 6. (chem.) free, uncombined.

свободолюби́в|ый (~, ~а), adj. freedom-loving.

свободолю́би|е, я, n. love of freedom.

свободомы́сли|е, я, n. free-thinking.

свободомы́слящ|ий, adj. free-thinking; as noun с., ~его, m. free-thinker.

свод¹, а, m. code; collection (of documents, manuscripts, etc.); с. зако́нов code of laws.

свод², а, m. arch, vault; небе́сный с. the firmament, the vault of heaven.

сво|ди́ть¹, жу́, ~дишь, impf. of свести́.

сво|ди́ть², жу́, ~дишь, pf. to take (and bring back); вчера́ мы ~ди́ли дете́й в кино́ we took the children to the cinema yesterday.

сво|ди́ться, жу́сь, ~дишься, impf. of свести́сь.

сво́дк|а, и, f. summary, resumé; report; операти́вная с. (mil.) summary of operations; с. пого́ды weather forecast, weather report.

сво́дник, а, m. procurer, pander, pimp.

сво́дни|ть, ю, impf. to procure, pander.

сво́дничеств|о, а, n. procuring, pandering, pimping.

сво́дн|ый, adj. 1. composite, combined; collated; ~ая афи́ша теа́тров theatre guide (bill listing all current productions); с. отря́д (mil.) combined force; ~ая табли́ца summary table, index. 2. step-; с. брат step-brother.

сво́дн|я, и, f. (coll.) procuress.

сво́дчатый, adj. arched, vaulted.

своевла́ст|ный (~ен, ~на), adj. despotic.

своево́ли|е, я, n. self-will, wilfulness.

своево́льнича|ть, ю, impf. to be self-willed, be wilful.

своево́л|ьный (~ен, ~ьна), adj. self-willed, wilful.

своевре́менно, *adv.* in good time; opportunely.

своевре́мен|ный (~ен, ~на), *adj.* timely, opportune; well-timed.

своекоры́сти|е, я, *n.* self-interest.

своекоры́ст|ный (~ен, ~на), *adj.* self--interested, self-seeking.

своеко́штный, *adj.* (*obs.*) (fee-)paying.

своенра́ви|е, я, *n.* wilfulness, waywardness, capriciousness.

своенра́в|ный (~ен, ~на), *adj.* wilful, wayward, capricious.

своеобра́зи|е, я, *n.* originality; peculiarity.

своеобра́з|ный (~ен, ~на), *adj.* original; peculiar, distinctive.

сво|зи́ть¹, жу́, ~зишь, *impf. of* свезти́.

сво|зи́ть², жу́, ~зишь, *pf.* to take (*and bring back*); мы ~зи́ли дете́й в цирк we took the children to the circus.

свой, *possessive adj.* one's (my, your, his, *etc.*, *in accordance with subject of sentence or clause*), one's own; у них с. дом they have a house of their own; своё варе́нье one's own, home-made jam; свои́ войска́ friendly troops; кри́кнуть не свои́м го́лосом to give a frenzied scream; умере́ть свое́й сме́ртью to die a natural death; в своё вре́мя (*i*) at one time; in my, his, *etc.*, time, (*ii*) in due time, in due course; в своём ро́де in one's own way; он не в своём уме́ he is not right in the head; на свои́х на дво́их on Shanks' mare, pony; она́ сама́ не своя́ she is not herself; он у нас с. челове́к he's one of us, he's quite at home here; *as noun* **свой** one's (own) people; **своё** one's own; доби́ться своего́ to get one's own way; to hold one's own; получи́ть своё to get one's own back.

сво́йственник, а, *m.* relation, relative by marriage; он мне с. he is related to me by marriage.

сво́йствен|ный (~, ~на), *adj.* (+*d.*) characteristic (of).

сво́йств|о, а, *n.* property, quality, attribute, characteristic.

сво́йств|о́, а́, *n.* relationship by marriage, affinity; быть в ~е́ с кем-н. to be related to someone by marriage.

свола́кива|ть, ю, *impf. of* сволочь.

сволочно́й, *adj.* (*coll.*) worthless, rubbishy.

сво́лоч|ь, и, *g. pl.* ~е́й, *f.* (*coll.*) 1. (*as term of abuse*) scum, swine. 2. (*collect.*) riff-raff, dregs.

своло́|чь, ку́, чёшь, ку́т, *past* ~к, ~кла́, *pf.* (*of* свола́кивать) (*coll.*) 1. to drag off. 2. (*fig.*) to knock off.

сво́р|а, ы, *f.* 1. leash; (*fig.*) pair (*of* greyhounds). 2. (*collect.*) pack (*of* hounds); (*fig.*) gang.

свора́чива|ть, ю, *impf. of* сверну́ть *and* свороти́ть.

свор|ова́ть, у́ю, *pf. of* ворова́ть.

своро|ти́ть, чу́, ~тишь, *pf.* (*of* свора́чивать) (*coll.*) 1. to dislodge, displace, shift. 2. to turn, swing (*also trans.*); с. с доро́ги to turn off the road; с. с ума́ to go off one's head. 3. to twist, dislocate; to break.

своя́к, а́, *m.* brother-in-law (*husband of wife's sister*).

своя́чениц|а, ы, *f.* sister-in-law (*wife's sister*).

свык|а́ться, а́юсь, *impf. of* ~нуться.

свы́к|нуться, нусь, нешься, *past* ~ся, ~лась, *pf.* (*of* ~а́ться) (с+*i.*) to get used (to), accustom oneself (to).

свысока́, *adv.* (*pejor.*) in a haughty manner, condescendingly; обраща́ться с кем-н. с. to condescend to, patronize someone.

свы́ше 1. *adv.* from above; (*rel.*) from on high. 2. *prep.*+*g.* over, more than; beyond; с. ты́сячи самолётов уча́ствовало в налёте over a thousand planes took part in the raid; э́то с. мои́х сил it is beyond me.

свя́з|анный, *p.p.p. of* ~а́ть *and adj.* 1. constrained; ~анная речь halting utterance. 2. (*chem.*) combined, bound.

свя|за́ть, жу́, ~жешь, *pf.* (*of* вяза́ть *and* ~зывать) 1. to tie; to bind (*also fig.*); с. в у́зел to bundle (up); с. по рука́м и нога́м to tie, bind hand and foot (*also fig.*); с. обеща́нием to bind by promise; с. свою́ судьбу́ (с+*i.*) to throw in one's lot (with). 2. (*fig.*) to connect, link; быть (те́сно) ~занным, ~зано (с+*i.*) to be (closely) connected (with), be bound up (with), be tied up (with). 3. (быть) ~зано (с+*i.*; *fig.*) to involve, entail; э́то предприя́тие бу́дет ~зано с огро́мными расхо́дами this undertaking will involve huge expense. 4. to connect, associate; не́которые ~за́ли эпиде́мию с плохи́м водоснабже́нием some connected the epidemic with the bad water-supply.

свя|за́ться, жу́сь, ~жешься, *pf.* (*of* ~зываться) (с+*i.*) 1. to get in touch (with), communicate (with); с. по ра́дио to establish a radio link. 2. (*coll.*, *pejor.*) to get involved (with), get mixed up (with).

связи́ст, а, *m.* 1. (*mil.*) signaller; member of Signal Corps. 2. postal *and/or* telecommunications worker.

свя́зк|а, и, *f.* 1. sheaf, bunch; с. бума́г sheaf of papers; с. ключе́й bunch of keys. 2. (*anat.*) chord; ligament; copula; голосовы́е ~и vocal chords. 3. (*gram.*) copula.

связн|о́й, *adj.* (*mil.*) liaison, communication; с. самолёт liaison aircraft; ~а́я соба́ка messenger dog; *as noun* с., ~о́го, *m.* messenger, runner, orderly.

свя́зный, *adj.* connected, coherent.

свя́зочный, *adj.* (*anat.*) ligamentous.

связу́ющий, *adj.* connecting, linking.

свя́зыва|ть, ю, *impf. of* связа́ть.

свя́зыва|ться, юсь, *impf.* **1.** *impf. of* связа́ться. **2.** *impf. only* (c+*i.*) to have to do (with); не ~йся с ни́ми don't have anything to do with them.

связ|ь, и, о ~и, в ~й, *f.* **1.** connexion; причи́нная с. (*philos.*) causation; в ~й с э́тим in this connexion. **2.** link, tie, bond; дру́жеские ~и friendly relations, ties of friendship; с. Великобрита́нии с содру́жеством на́ций the link between Great Britain and the Commonwealth; потеря́ть с. (c+*i.*) to lose touch (with). **3.** (*sexual*) liaison, association; вступи́ть в с. (c+*i.*) to form an association (with). **4.** (*pl.*) connexions, contacts; у него́ мно́го влия́тельных ~ей в Москве́ he has many influential connexions in Moscow. **5.** communication; (*mil.*) intercommunication; signals; liaison; возду́шная с. aerial communication; с. по ра́дио radio communication; с. с во́здухом (*mil.*) ground–air communication; с. с землёй (*mil.*) air–ground communication. **6.** (*sing. only*) (postal and tele-)communications; Министе́рство ~и Ministry of Communications; отделе́ние ~и (branch) post office; рабо́тник ~и post office worker. **7.** (*tech.*) tie, stay, brace, strut; (*electr.*) coupling.

святе́йшеств|о, а, *n.* его́ с. (*title of Patriarchs and of the Pope*) His Holiness.

святе́йший, *adj.* most holy (*pertaining to the Patriarchs and synod of the Orthodox Church, also to the Pope*); с. патриа́рх His Holiness the Patriarch; с. престо́л the papal throne.

святи́лищ|е, а, *n.* sanctuary.

святи́тел|ь, я, *m.* prelate.

свя|ти́ть, чу́, ти́шь, *impf.* (*of* о~) to consecrate; to bless, sanctify.

свя́т|ки, ок, *no sing.* Christmas-tide.

свя́то, *adv.* piously; religiously; с. бере́чь to treasure; с. чтить to hold sacred.

свят|о́й (~, ~а́, ~o), *adj.* **1.** holy; sacred (*also fig.*); ~а́я вода́ holy water; с. долг sacred duty; с. дух the Holy Ghost, the Holy Spirit; ~а́я (неде́ля) Holy Week; ~а́я ~ы́х holy of holies, sanctum. **2.** saintly. **3.** (*fig.*) pious. **4.** *preceding name, or as noun* **с.,** ~о́го, *m.*; ~а́я, ~о́й, *f.* saint; причи́слить к ли́ку ~ы́х (*eccl.*) to canonize.

свя́тост|ь, и, *f.* holiness; sanctity.

святота́т|ец, ца, *m.* person committing sacrilege.

святота́тственный, *adj.* sacrilegious.

святота́тств|о, а, *n.* sacrilege.

святота́тств|овать, ую, *impf.* to commit sacrilege.

свя́т|очный, *adj. of* ~ки; с. расска́з Christmas tale.

свято́ш|а, и, *m. and f.* sanctimonious person.

свя́тц|ы, ев, *no sing.* (church) calendar.

святы́н|я, и, *f.* **1.** (*eccl.*) object of worship; sacred place. **2.** (*fig.*) sacred object, sacred thing.

свяще́нник, а, *m.* priest (*of Orthodox Church*); clergyman.

свяще́ннический, *adj.* priestly; sacerdotal.

священноде́йстви|е, я, *n.* **1.** religious rite. **2.** (*fig.*) solemn performance (of ceremony, duties, *etc.*).

священноде́йств|овать, ую, *impf.* **1.** to perform a religious rite. **2.** (*fig.*) to do something with solemnity, with pomp.

свяще́н|ный (~ен, ~на), *adj.* holy; sacred (*also fig.*); ~ное писа́ние Holy Writ, Scripture; С. сою́з (*hist.*) the Holy Alliance.

свяще́нств|о, а, *n.* priesthood (*also collect.*).

сгиб, а, *m.* **1.** bend. **2.** (*anat.*) flexion.

сгиба́ем|ый (~, ~а), *adj.* flexible, pliable.

сгиба́|ть(ся), ю(сь), *impf. of* согну́ть(ся).

сги́н|уть, у, ешь, *pf.* (*coll.*) to disappear, vanish; ~ь с глаз мои́х! out of my sight!

сгла́|дить, жу, дишь, *pf.* (*of* ~живать) **1.** to smooth out. **2.** (*fig.*) to smooth over, soften.

сгла́|диться, дится, *pf.* (*of* ~живаться) **1.** to smooth out, become smooth. **2.** (*fig.*) to be smoothed over, be softened; to diminish, abate.

сгла́жива|ть(ся), ю(сь), *impf. of* сгла́дить(ся).

сглаз, а (у), *m.* (*coll.*) the evil eye.

сгла́|зить, жу, зишь, *pf.* to put the evil eye (on, upon); (*fig., coll.*) to endanger the success (of) (*an undertaking, etc., by forecasting the outcome*); чтобы не с.! touch wood!

сглуп|и́ть, лю́, и́шь, *pf. of* глупи́ть.

сгнива́|ть, ю, *impf. of* сгнить.

сгни|ть, ю́, ёшь, *pf.* (*of* гнить *and* ~ва́ть) to rot, decay.

сгно|и́ть, ю́, и́шь, *pf. of* гнои́ть.

сгова́рива|ть(ся), ю(сь), *impf. of* сговори́ть(ся).

сго́вор, а, *m.* **1.** (*obs.*) betrothal. **2.** (*usu. pejor.*) agreement, compact, deal.

сговор|и́ть, ю́, и́шь, *pf.* (*of* сгова́ривать) (*obs.*) to give consent to the marriage (of); to betroth.

сговор|и́ться, ю́сь, и́шься, *pf.* (*of* сгова́риваться) (c+*i.*) **1.** to arrange (with), make an appointment (with); мы ~и́лись встре́титься с ни́ми при вхо́де в парк we arranged to meet them at the entrance to the park. **2.** to come to an arrangement (with), reach an understanding (with).

сгово́рчивост|ь, и, *f.* compliancy, tractability.

сгово́рчив|ый (~, ~а), *adj.* compliant, complaisant, tractable.

сгон, а, *m.* driving; herding, rounding-up.

сго́нк|а, и, *f.* rafting, floating.

сго́нн|ый, *adj.* **1.** rounding up; rounded up; ~ая рабо́та rounding up, herding. **2.** rafting, floating.

сго́нщик, а, *m.* **1.** herdsman, drover. **2.** (lumber-)rafter.

сгоня́|ть, ю, *impf. of* согна́ть.

сгора́ни|е, я, *n.* combustion; дви́гатель вну́треннего ~я internal-combustion engine.

сгор|а́ть, а́ю, *impf. of* ~е́ть.

сго́рб|ить(ся), лю(сь), ишь(ся), *pf. of* го́рбить(ся).

сго́рб|ленный, *p.p.p. of* ~ить *and adj.* crooked, bent; hunchbacked.

сгор|е́ть, ю́, и́шь, *pf. (of* ~а́ть*)* **1.** to burn down; to be burnt out, down; наш дом ~е́л our house was burnt down. **2.** *(of fuel)* to be consumed, be used up; за год у нас ~е́ло три це́нтнера у́гля in the year we burned three hundredweight of coal. **3.** *(fig., coll.)* to burn oneself out. **4.** *(от; fig.)* to burn (with); с. от стыда́ to burn with shame.

сгоряча́, *adv.* in the heat of the moment; in a fit of temper.

сгреба́|ть, ю, *impf. of* сгрести́.

сгре|сти́, бу́, бёшь, *past* ~б, ~бла́, *pf. (of* ~ба́ть*)* **1.** to rake up, rake together. **2.** *(с+g.)* to shovel (off, from); с. снег с кры́ши to shovel snow off the roof.

сгруд|и́ться, и́тся, *pf. (coll.)* to crowd, mill, bunch.

сгружа́|ть, ю, *impf. of* сгрузи́ть.

сгру|зи́ть, жу́, ~зи́шь, *pf. (of* ~жа́ть*)* to unload.

сгруппир|ова́ть(ся), у́ю(сь), *pf. of* группирова́ть(ся).

сгрыза́|ть, ю, *impf. of* сгрызть.

сгрыз|ть, у́, ёшь, *past* ~, ~ла, *pf. (of* ~а́ть*)* to chew (up).

сгуб|и́ть, лю́, ~ишь, *pf. (coll.)* to ruin.

сгу|сти́ть, щу́, сти́шь, *pf. (of* ~ща́ть*)* to thicken; to condense; с. кра́ски *(fig.)* to lay it on thick.

сгу|сти́ться, сти́тся, *pf. (of* ~ща́ться*)* to thicken; to condense; to clot.

сгу́ст|ок, ка, *m.* clot; с. кро́ви clot of blood.

сгуща́|ть(ся), ю, ет(ся), *impf. of* сгусти́ть(ся).

сгуще́ни|е, я, *n.* thickening, condensation; clotting.

сгу́|щённый, *p.p.p. of* ~сти́ть *and adj.*; ~щённое молоко́ condensed milk, evaporated milk.

сда́брива|ть, ю, *impf. of* сдо́брить.

сда|ва́ть, ю́, ёшь, *impf. of* сдать; с. экза́мен to take, sit an examination.

сда|ва́ться[1], ю́сь, ёшься, *impf. of* ~ться[1].

сда|ва́ться[2], ётся, *impf. (impers., coll.)* it seems; мне ~ётся it seems to me, I think.

сдав|и́ть, лю́, ~ишь, *pf. (of* ~ливать*)* to squeeze.

сда́влива|ть, ю, *impf. of* сдави́ть.

сда́точн|ый, *adj.* delivery; ~ая квита́нция receipt; с. пункт delivery point.

сда́тчик, а, *m.* deliverer.

сдать[1], сдам, сдашь, сдаст, сдади́м, сда-ди́те, сдаду́т, *past* сдал, сдала́, сда́ло, *pf. (of* сдава́ть*)* **1.** to hand over, pass; с. дела́ прее́мнику to hand over to one's successor; с. бага́ж на хране́ние to deposit, leave one's luggage; с. в архи́в *(fig., coll.)* to give up as a bad job, write off. **2.** to let, let out, hire out; с. в аре́нду to lease. **3.** to give change; с. пятьдеся́т копе́ек to give fifty kopecks change. **4.** to surrender, yield, give up; с. пе́рвенство *(sport)* to yield first place. **5.** to pass *(an examination, examination subject, etc.)*; он сдал то́лько латы́нь he only passed in Latin. **6.** to deal *(cards).*

сдать[2], сдам, сдашь, сдаст, сдади́м, сдади́те, сдаду́т, *pf. (of* сдава́ть*)* **1.** to give out, give way; мото́р сдал the engine gave out. **2.** to be weakened, be in a reduced state.

сда́|ться[1], мся, шься, стся, ди́мся, ди́тесь, ду́тся, *past* ~лся, ~ла́сь, *pf. (of* ~ва́ться[1]*)* to surrender, yield; *(chess)* to resign; с. на про́сьбы to yield to entreaties.

сда́|ться[2], *not used in fut.,* ~лся, ~ла́сь, *pf. (coll.)* to be necessary; на что нам ~ли́сь их сове́ты? what need had we of advice from them?

сда́ч|а, и, *f.* **1.** handing over. **2.** letting out, hiring out; с. в аре́нду leasing. **3.** surrender. **4.** change; три рубля́ ~и three roubles change; с. с рубля́ change from one rouble; дать ~и *(+d.; fig., coll.)* to give as good as one got. **5.** *(cards)* deal; ва́ша с. it is your deal.

сдва́ива|ть, ю, *impf. of* сдво́ить.

сдвиг, а, *m.* **1.** displacement; *(geol.)* fault, dislocation; *(tech.)* shear; с. фаз *(electr.)* phase shift. **2.** *(fig.)* change (for the better), improvement.

сдвига́|ть(ся), ю(сь), *impf. of* сдви́нуть(ся).

сдвижн|о́й, *adj.* movable; ~а́я ма́чта *(naut.)* telescopic mast.

сдви́нут|ый, *p.p.p. of* ~ь *and adj.*; с. по фа́зе *(electr.)* out of phase.

сдви́|нуть, ну, нешь, *pf. (of* ~га́ть*)* **1.** to shift, move, displace; его́ с ме́ста не ~нешь he won't budge; с. с ме́ста *(fig.)* to get moving, set in motion. **2.** to move together, bring together; с. бро́ви to knit one's brows.

сдви́|нуться, нусь, нешься, *pf. (of* ~га́ться*)* **1.** to move, budge; с. с ме́ста *(fig.)* to progress; де́ло не ~нулось с ме́ста no headway has been made. **2.** to come together.

сдво|и́ть, ю́, и́шь, *pf.* (*of* сдва́ивать) to double.

сде́ла|ть(ся), ю(сь), *pf. of* де́лать(ся).

сде́лк|а, и, *f.* transaction, deal, bargain; войти́ в ~у (c+*i.*) to strike a bargain (with); заключи́ть ~у to conclude a bargain, do a deal.

сде́льно, *adv.* by the job.

сде́льн|ый, *adj.* piecework; ~ая опла́та payment by the piece, by the job; ~ая рабо́та piecework.

сде́льщик, а, *m.* piece-worker.

сде́льщин|а, ы, *f.* piece-work.

сде́ргива|ть, ю, *impf. of* сдёрнуть.

сде́ржанно, *adv.* with restraint, with reserve.

сде́ржанност|ь, и, *f.* restraint, reserve.

сде́ржан|ный, *p.p.p. of* сдержа́ть *and* (~, ~на) *adj.* restrained, reserved.

сдерж|а́ть¹, у́, ~ишь, *pf.* (*of* ~ивать) **1.** to hold (back); to hold in check, contain; с. проти́вника to hold the enemy in check. **2.** (*fig.*) to keep back, restrain; с. слёзы to suppress tears.

сдерж|а́ть², у́, ~ишь, *pf.* (*of* ~ивать) to keep (*a promise, etc.*); с. сло́во to keep one's word.

сдерж|а́ться, у́сь, ~ишься, *pf.* (*of* ~ива́ться) to control oneself; to restrain oneself, contain oneself; to check oneself.

сде́ржива|ть(ся), ю(сь), *impf. of* сдержа́ть-(ся).

сдёр|нуть, ну, нешь, *pf.* (*of* ~гивать) to pull off.

сдира́|ть, ю, *impf. of* содра́ть.

сдо́б|а, ы, *f.* **1.** (*cul.*) shortening. **2.** (fancy) cake, bun (*also collect.*).

сдо́бн|ый, *adj.* (*cul.*) rich, short; ~ая бу́лка bun; ~ое те́сто fancy pastry.

сдо́бр|ить, ю, ишь, *pf.* (*of* сда́бривать) (+*i.*) to flavour (with), spice (with); to add to taste.

сдоброва́ть, *only in phrase* ему́, *etc.*, не с. (*coll.*) it will be a bad look out for him, *etc.*

сдо́хн|уть, у, ешь, *pf.* (*of* сдыха́ть) (*of cattle, also coll. of people*) to die.

сдре́йф|ить, лю, ишь, *pf. of* дре́йфить.

сдруж|и́ть, у́, и́шь, *pf.* to bring together, unite in friendship.

сдруж|и́ться, у́сь, и́шься, *pf.* (c+*i.*) to become friends (with).

сду́ру, *adv.* (*coll.*) stupidly, not thinking what one was doing; он с. забы́л ключ до́ма he stupidly left his key at home.

сду|ть, ~ю, ~ешь, *pf.* (*of* ~ва́ть) **1.** to blow away, blow off. **2.** (c+*g.*, у; *school sl.*) to crib (from).

сдыха́|ть, ю, *impf. of* сдо́хнуть.

се, *particle* (*arch.*) lo, behold.

сё, сего́, *pron.* this (*arch. except in certain set phrases; see* тот).

сеа́нс, а, *m.* **1.** (*in cinema, etc.*) performance, showing, house; после́дний с. the last showing, the last house. **2.** sitting; написа́ть чей-н. портре́т в двена́дцать ~ов to paint someone's portrait in twelve sittings.

себе́¹, *see* себя́.

себе́², *particle* (*coll.*) *emphasizing preceding verb or pron. and containing hint of reproach*; он с. идёт вперёд he just goes ahead; а они́ с. молча́ли and they just kept their mouths shut; он о́чень с. на уме́ he is very crafty, wily; ничего́ с. not bad; так с. so-so.

себесто́имост|ь, и, *f.* (*econ.*) cost (*of manufacture*); cost price; прода́ть по ~и to sell at cost price.

себя́, себе́, собо́й (собо́ю), о себе́, *reflexive pron.* oneself; myself, yourself, himself, *etc.*; собо́ю in appearance; хоро́ш собо́ю nicelooking; прийти́ в с. (от) to get over; come to one's senses; не в себе́ not oneself; от с. (*i*) away from oneself, outwards, (*ii*) for oneself, on one's own behalf; рабо́та не по себе́ work that is beyond one; как-то не по себе́ not quite oneself; чита́ть про с. to read to oneself; у с. at home, at one's (own) place.

себялю́б|ец, ца, *m.* egoist.

себялюби́в|ый (~, ~а), *adj.* egoistical, selfish.

себялю́би|е, я, *n.* self-love, egoism.

сев, а, *m.* sowing.

се́вер, а, *m.* north.

се́вернее, *adv.* (+*g.*) to the north (of).

се́верн|ый, *adj.* north, northern; northerly; с. оле́нь reindeer; ~ое сия́ние northern lights, Aurora Borealis.

се́веро-восто́к, а, *m.* north-east.

се́веро-восто́чный, *adj.* north-east, north--eastern.

се́веро-за́пад, а, *m.* north-west.

се́веро-за́падный, *adj.* north-west, north--western.

северя́н|ин, ина, *pl.* ~е, ~, *m.* northerner.

севооборо́т, а, *m.* rotation of crops.

севр, а, *m.* Sèvres (*porcelain*).

се́вр|ский, *adj. of* ~.

севрю́г|а, и, *f.* stellate sturgeon (*Acipenser stellatus*).

сегме́нт, а, *m.* segment.

сегмента́ци|я, и, *f.* segmentation.

сего́дня, *adv.* today; с. ве́чером this evening, tonight; не с.-за́втра any day now.

сего́дня|шний, *adj. of* ~; с. день today; ~шняя газе́та today's paper.

седа́лищ|е, а, *n.* (*anat.*) seat, buttocks.

седа́лищн|ый, *adj.* (*anat.*) sciatic; воспале́ние ~ого не́рва (*med.*) sciatica.

седе́льник, а, *m.* saddler.

седе́льн|ый, *adj. of* седло́; ~ая лука́ saddle--bow.

седе́|ть, ю, *impf.* (*of* по~) to go grey, turn grey.

седе́|ющий, *pres. part. act. of* ~ть *and adj.* grizzled, greying.

седин|а́, ы́, *pl.* ~ы, ~, *f.* **1.** grey hair(s). **2.** grey streak (*in fur*).

седла́|ть, ю, *impf.* (*of* о~) to saddle.

сед|ло́, ла́, *pl.* ~ла, ~ел, *n.* saddle.

седловин|а, ы, *f.* 1. arch, saddle (*of back of animal*). **2.** (*geogr.*) col, saddle.

седоборо́д|ый (~), *adj.* grey-bearded.

седовла́с|ый (~, ~а), *adj.* grey-haired.

седоволо́с|ый (~, ~а), *adj.* = седовла́сый.

сед|о́й (~, ~а́, ~о), *adj.* (*of hair*) grey, gray; hoary; grey-haired; flecked with white; ~а́я старина́ hoary antiquity.

седо́к, а́, *m.* **1.** fare (*passenger*). **2.** rider, horseman.

седьм|о́й, *adj.* seventh; быть на ~о́м не́бе to be in the seventh heaven; одна́ ~а́я one seventh.

сеза́м, а, *m.* (*bot.*) sesame; с., откро́йся! open sesame!

сезо́н, а, *m.* season.

сезо́нник, а, *m.* seasonal worker.

сезо́нн|ый, *adj.* seasonal; с. биле́т season ticket; ~ые рабо́ты seasonal work.

сей, *f.* сия́, *n.* сие́, *pl.* сии́, *pron.* this; сию́ мину́ту this (very) minute; at once, instantly; сего́ го́да of this year; сего́ ме́сяца (*abbr.* с. м.) of this month; ва́ше письмо́ от 16-го с. м. (*formula of official correspondence*) your letter of the 16th inst.; до сих пор up to now, till now, hitherto; (*obs.*) up to here, up to this point; на с. раз this time, for this once; о сю по́ру (*obs.*) at the present time; по сю по́ру (*obs.*) up to now, up to the present; под сим ка́мнем поко́ится here lies; при сём прилага́ется (there is) enclosed herewith, herewith please find.

сейм, а, *m.* *m.* (*hist., representative assembly*) diet; (*in Poland*) the Sejm.

се́йн|а, ы, *f.* seine.

се́йнер, а, *m.* seiner.

сейсми́ческий, *adj.* seismic.

сейсмо́граф, а, *m.* seismograph.

сейсмогра́фи|я, и, *f.* seismography.

сейсмологи́ческий, *adj.* seismological.

сейсмоло́ги|я, и, *f.* seismology.

сейсмо́метр, а, *m.* seismometer.

сейф, а, *m.* safe.

сейча́с, *adv.* **1.** now, at present, at the (present) moment; они́ с. в Аме́рике they are in America at present. **2.** just, just now (= *in the immediate past*); она́ с. вы́шла she has just gone out. **3.** presently, soon; с. же at once, immediately; с.! in a minute!, half a minute! **4.** (*coll.*) straight away, immediately; с. бы́ло ви́дно, что ему́ э́то не

нра́вилось it was immediately apparent that he did not like it.

се́канс, а, *m.* (*math.*) secant.

сека́тор, а, *m.* sécateur(s).

секве́стр, а, *m.* **1.** (*leg.*) sequestration; наложи́ть с. (на + *a.*) to sequestrate. **2.** (*med.*) sequestrum.

секвестр|ова́ть, у́ю, *impf. and pf.* (*leg.*) to sequestrate.

секи́р|а, ы, *f.* pole-axe; hatchet, axe.

секре́т[1], а, *m.* **1.** secret; по ~у secretly, confidentially, in confidence; под больши́м ~ом in strict confidence; с. полишине́ля open secret. **2.** hidden mechanism. **3.** (*mil.*) listening post.

секре́т[2], а, *m.* (*physiol.*) secretion.

секретариа́т, а, *m.* secretariat.

секрета́рский, *adj.* secretarial; secretary's.

секрета́рств|о, а, *n.* secretaryship; secretarial duties.

секрета́рств|овать, ую, *impf.* to be a secretary, act as secretary.

секрета́рш|а, и, *f.* (woman) secretary.

секрета́р|ь, я́, *m.* secretary; генера́льный с. secretary-general; ли́чный с. private secretary, personal secretary; непреме́нный с. permanent secretary.

секре́тнича|ть, ю, *impf.* (*coll.*) **1.** to be secretive; to keep things secret, keep things dark. **2.** to converse in confidential tones.

секре́тно, *adv.* secretly, in secret; сообщи́ть с. to tell in confidence; (*on documents, etc.*) 'secret', 'confidential'; соверше́нно с. 'top secret'.

секре́тност|ь, и, *f.* secrecy.

секре́т|ный (~ен, ~на), *adj.* secret; confidential; с. замо́к combination lock; с. прика́з secret order; с. сотру́дник secret agent, undercover agent.

секрето́рный, *adj.* (*physiol.*) secretory.

секре́ци|я, и, *f.* (*physiol.*) secretion.

сексо́т, а, *m.* (*abbr. of* секре́тный сотру́дник) secret agent, undercover agent.

секст|а, ы, *f.* (*mus.*) sixth.

секста́нт, а, *m.* sextant.

сексте́т, а, *m.* (*mus.*) sextet.

сексуа́льност|ь, и, *f.* sexuality.

сексуа́л|ьный (~ен, ~ьна), *adj.* sexual.

се́кт|а, ы, *f.* sect.

секта́нт, а, *m.* sectarian; member of a sect.

секта́нтский, *adj.* sectarian.

секта́нтств|о, а, *n.* sectarianism.

се́ктор, а, *m.* **1.** (*math., mil.*) sector; с. обстре́ла (*mil.*) sector of fire, zone of fire. **2.** (*fig.*) section, part, zone, sphere; (*econ.*) sector; с. ка́дров personnel section; госуда́рственный с. хозя́йства State(-owned) sector of economy.

се́ктор|ный, *adj. of* ~.

секуляриза́ци|я, и, *f.* secularization.

секуляриз|ова́ть, у́ю, *impf. and pf.* to secularize.

секу́нд|а, ы, *f.* (*of time*) second; сию́ ~у! just a moment!

секунда́нт, а, *m.* (*in a duel or in boxing*) second.

секу́нд|ный, *adj. of* ~а; ~ная стре́лка second hand.

секундоме́р, а, *m.* stop-watch.

секу́щ|ая, ей, *f.* (*math.*) secant.

секцио́нный, *adj.* sectional.

се́кци|я, и, *f.* section.

селадо́н, а, *m.* (*obs.*) ladies' man, womanizer.

селёдк|а, и, *f.* herring.

селёдочниц|а, ы, *f.* herring-dish.

селёд|очный, *adj. of* ~ка.

селезёнк|а, и, *f.* (*physiol.*) spleen; воспале́ние ~и (*med.*) splenitis.

се́лез|ень, ня, *m.* drake.

селекти́вност|ь, и, *f.* (*radio*) selectivity.

селекцио́нный, *adj.* (*agric.*) selection; selected.

селе́кци|я, и, *f.* (*agric.*) selection, breeding.

селе́н, а, *m.* (*chem.*) selenium.

селе́ни|е, я, *n.* settlement.

сели́нистый, *adj.* (*chem.*) selenious; selenide (*of*).

селени́т[1], а, *m.* (*min.*) selenite.

селени́т[2], а, *m.* Moon-man (*in science fiction*).

селе́новый, *adj.* (*chem.*) selenium, selenic.

сели́тебный, *adj.* built-up; (allocated for) building, development.

сели́тр|а, ы, *f.* (*chem.*) saltpetre, nitre; ка́лийная с. potassium nitrate.

сели́тр|яный, *adj. of* ~а; ~яная кислота́ nitric acid.

сел|и́ть, ю́, и́шь, *impf.* (*of* по~) to settle.

сели́тьб|а, ы, *f.* 1. developed land. 2. settlement.

сел|и́ться, ю́сь, и́шься, *impf.* (*of* по~) to settle.

сел|о́, а́, *pl.* ~а, *n.* village; на ~é (*collect.*) in the country; ни к ~у́, ни к го́роду (*coll.*) for no reason at all; neither here nor there.

сель- *abbr. of* се́льский.

сельдере́|й, я, *m.* celery.

сельд|ь, и, *pl.* ~и, ~éй, *f.* herring; как ~и в бо́чке (*coll.*) like sardines (*of a crowd*).

сельд|яно́й, *adj. of* ~ь.

селько́р, а, *m.* (*abbr. of* се́льский корреспонде́нт) rural correspondent.

сельпо́, *indecl.*, *n.* (*abbr. of* се́льское потреби́тельское о́бщество) village general stores.

се́льск|ий, *adj.* 1. country, rural; ~ая ме́стность rural area; countryside (*of*). 2. village.

сельскохозя́йственный, *adj.* agricultural, farming.

сельсове́т, а, *m.* (*abbr. of* се́льский сове́т) village soviet, rural area soviet.

се́льтерск|ий, *adj.* ~ая вода́ seltzer water.

селя́н|ин, и́на, *pl.* ~е, ~, *m.* (*obs.*) peasant, villager.

селя́н|ка[1], ки, *f. of* ~и́н.

селя́нк|а[2], и, *f.* (*cul.*) hot-pot; сбо́рная с. (*fig.*) hotchpotch, hodge-podge.

сема́нтик|а, и, *f.* 1. semantics. 2. meanings (*of a particular word*).

семанти́ческий, *adj.* semantic.

семасиологи́ческий, *adj.* semasiological.

семасиологи|я, и, *f.* semasiology.

семафо́р, а, *m.* (*railways and naut.*) semaphore, signal-post; с. откры́т the signal is down.

семафо́р|ить, ю, *impf.* to semaphore.

сёмг|а, и, *f.* salmon.

семе́йн|ый, *adj.* 1. family; domestic; с. ве́чер family party; с. круг family circle; по ~ым обстоя́тельствам for domestic reasons; о́тпуск по ~ым обстоя́тельствам (*mil.*) compassionate leave. 2. having a family; с. челове́к family man.

семе́йственност|ь, и, *f.* 1. attachment to family life. 2. (*pejor.*) nepotism; use of 'influence'.

семе́йственн|ый, *adj.* 1. attached to family life. 2. (*fig., pejor.*) conducted by 'arrangement', by 'influence'; ~ые отноше́ния 'old boy system'.

семе́йств|о, а, *n.* family.

семена́, *see* се́мя.

семен|и́ть, ю́, и́шь, *impf.* to mince (*of gait*).

семен|и́ться, и́тся, *impf.* (*agric.*) to seed.

семенни́к, а́, *m.* 1. (*biol.*) testicle. 2. (*bot.*) pericarp; ~й трав grass seeds.

семенн|о́й, *adj.* 1. seed; с. карто́фель seed potato. 2. (*biol.*) seminal, spermatic; ~а́я нить spermatozoon.

семеново́дств|о, а, *n.* seed-growing.

семеново́д|ческий, *adj. of* ~ство.

семери́чный, *adj.* septenary.

семёрк|а, и, *f.* 1. seven; number seven ('*bus, tram, etc.*). 2. с. треф, *etc.* (*cards*) the seven of clubs, *etc.* 3. group of seven persons.

семерно́й, *adj.* sevenfold, septuple.

се́мер|о, ы́х, *num.* (*collect.*) seven.

семе́стр, а, *m.* term, semester.

семестро́вый, *adj.* terminal.

се́меч|ко, ка, *pl.* ~ки, ~ек, *n.* 1. *dim. of* се́мя. 2. (*pl.*) sunflower seeds.

сёмжин|а, ы, *f.* salmon (*flesh*).

семиве́рстн|ый, *adj.* of seven versts; ~ые сапоги́ seven-league boots.

семидесятиле́ти|е, я, *n.* 1. seventy years. 2. seventieth anniversary; seventieth birthday.

семидесятиле́тний, *adj.* 1. seventy-year, of seventy years. 2. seventy-year-old.

семидеся́т|ый, *adj.* seventieth; ~ые го́ды the seventies; с. но́мер number seventy; страни́ца ~ая page seventy.

семи́к, а́, *m.* (*eccl.*) feast of seventh Thursday after Easter.

семикла́ссник, а, *m.* seventh form pupil.

семикра́тный, *adj.* sevenfold, septuple.

семиле́ти|е, я, *n.* 1. seven years; seven-year period. 2. seventh anniversary.

семиле́тк|а, и, *f.* 1. seven-year school. 2. (*econ.*) seven-year plan. 3. (*coll.*) child of seven.

семиле́тний, *adj.* 1. seven-year; septennial. 2. seven-year-old.

семиме́сячный, *adj.* 1. seven-month. 2. seven-month-old.

семими́льн|ый, *adj.* of seven miles, seven-mile; идти́ ~ыми шага́ми (*fig.*) to make gigantic strides.

семина́р, а, *m.* seminar.

семина́ри|й, я, *m.* seminar.

семинари́ст, а, *m.* seminarist.

семина́ри|я, и, *f.* seminary, training college; духо́вная с. theological college; учи́тельская с. (*obs.*) teachers' training college.

семина́р|ский, *adj.* of ~ and ~ия.

семинеде́льный, *adj.* 1. seven-week. 2. seven-week-old.

семисо́тый, *adj.* seven-hundredth.

семисто́пный, *adj.* с. ямб (*lit.*) iambic heptameter.

семи́т, а, *m.* Semite.

семити́ческий, *adj.* Semitic.

семи́т|ский = ~и́ческий.

семито́лог, а, *m.* Semitologist.

семитоло́ги|я, и, *f.* Semitology.

семиты́сячный, *adj.* seven-thousandth.

семиуго́льник, а, *m.* (*math.*) heptagon.

семиуго́льный, *adj.* heptagonal.

семичасово́й, *adj.* 1. seven-hour, of seven hours' duration. 2. seven o'clock.

семнадцатиле́тний, *adj.* 1. seventeen-year. 2. seventeen-year-old.

семна́дцатый, *adj.* seventeenth.

семна́дцат|ь, и, *f.*, *num.* seventeen.

сёмужий, *adj.* salmon.

сем|ь, й, *i.* ~ью́, *num.* seven.

се́мьдесят, семи́десяти, семью́десятью, *num.* seventy.

семьсо́т, семисо́т, семиста́м, семью́ста́ми, о семиста́х, *num.* seven hundred.

се́мью, *adv.* seven times.

сем|ья́, ьи́, *pl.* ~ьи, ~е́й, ~ьям, *f.* family.

семьяни́н, а, *pl.* ~ы, *m.* family man.

се́м|я, ени, *pl.* ~ена́, ~я́н, ~ена́м, *n.* 1. (*bot.* and *fig.*) seed; пойти́ в ~ена́ to go to seed, run to seed; ~ена́ раздо́ра seeds of discord. 2. semen, sperm.

семядо́л|я, и, *g. pl.* ~ей, *f.* (*bot.*) seed-lobe,

cotyledon.

семяизлия́ни|е, я, *n.* (*physiol.*) ejaculation.

семяпо́чк|а, и, *f.* (*bot.*) seed-bud.

сена́т, а, *m.* senate.

сена́тор, а, *m.* senator.

сена́торский, *adj.* senatorial.

сена́т|ский, *adj.* of ~.

сенберна́р, а, *m.* St. Bernard (*dog*).

се́н|и, ей, *no sing.* (entrance-)hall, vestibule.

сенни́к, а́, *m.* 1. hay-mattress. 2. (*dial.*) hay-loft.

сенн|о́й[1], *adj.* hay; ~а́я лихора́дка hay fever.

сен|но́й[2], *adj.* of ~и́; ~на́я де́вушка (*obs.*) maid.

се́н|о, а, *n.* hay.

сенова́л, а, *m.* hay-loft, mow.

сенозагото́в|ки, ок, *sing.* ~ка, ~ки, *f.* State hay purchases.

сеноко́с, а, *m.* 1. hay-mowing, haymaking. 2. haymaking (*time*). 3. hayfield.

сенокоси́лк|а, и, *f.* (hay-)mowing machine.

сеноко́сный, *adj.* haymaking.

сеноубо́рк|а, и, *f.* hay harvesting, hay-making.

сенсацио́н|ный (~ен, ~на), *adj.* sensational.

сенса́ци|я, и, *f.* sensation.

сенсибилиза́тор, а, *m.* (*phot.*) sensitizer.

сенсибилиза́ци|я, и, *f.* (*phot.*) sensitization.

сенсо́рный, *adj.* (*physiol.*) sensory.

сенсуали́зм, а, *m.* (*philos.*) sensationalism.

сенсуали́ст, а, *m.* (*philos.*) sensationalist.

сенсуа́льный, *adj.* (*philos.*) sensational.

сентенцио́зный, *adj.* sententious.

сенте́нци|я, и, *f.* maxim.

сентиментали́зм, а, *m.* sentimentalism.

сентимента́ли́ст, а, *m.* sentimentalist.

сентимента́льнича|ть, ю, *impf.* 1. to be sentimental, sentimentalize. 2. (c+*i.*) to be soft (with).

сентимента́льность, и, *f.* sentimentality.

сентимента́л|ьный (~ен, ~ьна), *adj.* senti-mental.

сентя́бр|ь, я́, *m.* September; смотре́ть ~ём (*coll.*) to look glum.

сентя́брь|ский, *adj.* of ~.

се́н|цы, цев, *no sing.*, *dim. of* ~и.

сен|ь, и, о ~и, в ~й, *f.* (*obs. or poet.*) canopy; под ~ью (+*g.*) under the protection (of).

сеньо́р, а, *m.* 1. (*hist.*) seigneur, seignior. 2. señor, senhor.

сепарати́вный, *adj.* (*polit.*) separatist.

сепарати́зм, а, *m.* (*polit.*) separatism.

сепарати́ст, а, *m.* (*polit.*) separatist.

сепарати́стский, *adj.* (*polit.*) separatist.

сепара́тный, *adj.* (*polit.*) separate; с. ми́р-ный догово́р separate peace treaty.

сепара́тор, а, *m.* (*agric.*) separator.

се́пи|я, и, *f.* 1. sepia. 2. sepia drawing; sepia photograph.

сепсис, а, *m.* (*med.*) sepsis, septicaemia.

септет, а, *m.* (*mus.*) septet(te).

септический, *adj.* (*med.*) septic.

сер|а, ы, *f.* **1.** (*chem.*) sulphur, brimstone; двуокись ∼ы sulphur dioxide. **2.** ear-wax.

серал|ь, я, *m.* seraglio.

серб, а, *m.* Serb, Serbian.

сербиянк|а, и, *f.* (*obs.*) = сербка.

серб|ка, ки, *f.* *of* ∼.

сербохорватский, *adj.* Serbo-Croatian; с. язык Serbo-Croat.

сербский, *adj.* Serbian.

сервант, а, *m.* sideboard; dumb-waiter.

сервиз, а, *m.* service, set; столовый с. dinner service.

сервир|овать, ую, *impf. and pf.* **1.** с. стол to lay a table. **2.** to serve; с. завтрак to serve breakfast.

сервировк|а, и, *f.* **1.** laying. **2.** (*collect.*) table appointments (*crockery and table linen*).

сервомотор, а, *m.* (*tech.*) servo-motor.

сердечник¹, а, *m.* (*tech.*) core; strand (*of cable*).

сердечник², а, *m.* (*coll.*) **1.** heart specialist. **2.** sufferer from heart disease.

сердечник³, а, *m.* (*bot.*) cuckoo-flower, ladies' smock (*Cardamine*).

сердечност|ь, и, *f.* cordiality; warmth.

сердеч|ный (∼ен, ∼на), *adj.* **1.** of the heart (*also fig.*); (*anat.*) cardiac; ∼ная болезнь heart disease; с. припадок heart attack; ∼ное средство, ∼ное лекарство cardiac; ∼ные дела love affairs. **2.** cordial, hearty; heartfelt, sincere; ∼ная благодарность heartfelt gratitude, hearty thanks; оказать с. приём (+*d.*) to extend a cordial welcome (to); ∼ное согласие (*hist.*) Entente cordiale. **3.** warm, warm-hearted.

сердит|ый, *adj.* **1.** (на+*a.*) angry (with, at, about), cross (with, about); irate. **2.** (*fig.*, *coll.*; *of tobacco, mustard, etc.*) strong. **3.** дёшево и ∼о (*coll.*) cheap but good; a good bargain.

сер|дить, жу, ∼дишь, *impf.* (*of* рас∼) to anger, make angry.

сер|диться, жусь, ∼дишься, *impf.* (*of* рас∼) (на+*a.*) to be angry (with, at, about), be cross (with, about).

сердоболи|е, я, *n.* tender-heartedness, soft--heartedness.

сердобольнича|ть, ю, *impf.* (*coll., iron.*) to be (too) soft-hearted.

сердобол|ьный (∼ен, ∼ьна), *adj.* (*coll.*) tender-hearted, soft-hearted.

сердолик, а, *m.* (*min.*) cornelian, sard.

сердолик|овый, *adj. of* ∼.

серд|це, ца, *pl.* ∼ца, ∼ец, *n.* (*in var. senses*) heart; золотое с. heart of gold; в ∼цах in (a fit of) temper; с глаз долой, из ∼ца вон (*prov.*) out of sight, out of mind; принять (близко) к ∼цу to take to heart; от всего ∼ца from the bottom of one's heart, whole--heartedly; у меня отлегло от ∼ца I felt relieved; по ∼цу (*coll.*) to one's liking; с ∼цем testily, crossly; с замиранием ∼ца with a sinking heart; иметь с. (на+*a.*; *coll.*) to be cross (with); с. болит (+*inf.*) it pains one, one's heart bleeds; у него ∼ца лежит. (к) he has no inclination (to, for).

сердцебиени|е, я, *n.* palpitation; (*med.*) tachycardia.

сердцевед, а, *m.* student of human nature, reader of the human heart.

сердцевид|ный (∼ен, ∼на), *adj.* heart--shaped; (*bot.*) cordate.

сердцевин|а, ы, *f.* core, pith, heart (*also fig.*).

сердцеед, а, *m.* (*coll.*) lady-killer.

серебреник, а, *m.* = сребреник.

серебрёный, *adj.* silver-plated.

серебрист|ый (∼, ∼а), *adj.* silvery; с. тополь silver poplar.

серебр|ить, ю, ишь, *impf.* (*of* по∼) to silver, silver-plate.

серебр|иться, ится, *impf.* **1.** to silver, become silvery. **2.** *pass. of* ∼ить.

серебр|о, а, *n.* **1.** silver. **2.** (*collect.*) silver; столовое с. silver, plate; сдача ∼ом change in silver.

серебронос|ный (∼ен, ∼на), *adj.* argentiferous.

серебряник, а, *m.* silversmith.

серебрян|ый, *adj.* silver; с. блеск (*min.*) silver glance; ∼ая свадьба silver wedding.

середин|а, ы, *f.* middle, midst; золотая с. the golden mean; держаться ∼ы, знать ∼у (*fig.*) to observe the mean.

середин|ный, *adj.* middle, mean, intermediate.

середк|а, и, *f.* (*coll.*) middle, centre; с. на половинку neither one thing nor another.

середняк, а, *m.* **1.** peasant of average means (*classified as intermediate between* кулак *and* бедняк). **2.** (*fig., coll.*) middling person, undistinguished person.

серёжк|а, и, *f.* **1.** ear-ring. **2.** (*bot.*) catkin, amentum.

серенад|а, ы, *f.* serenade.

серенький, *adj.* grey (*also fig.*); (*fig.*) dull, drab.

сере|ть, ю, *impf.* **1.** (*pf.* по∼) to turn grey, go grey. **2.** (*impf. only*) to show grey.

сержант, а, *m.* sergeant.

серийный, *adj.* (*tech., econ.*) serial.

серистый, *adj.* (*chem.*) sulphureous.

сери|я, и, *f.* series; (*of film*) part; кинофильм в нескольких ∼ях film in several parts; с. бомб (*mil.*) bomb train.

сермяг|а, и, *f.* sermyaga (*coarse, undyed cloth or caftan of this material*).

серн|а, ы, *f.* (*zool.*) chamois.

серни́ст|ый, *adj.* (*chem.*) sulphureous; sulphide (of); с. аммо́ний ammonium sulphide; ~ое желе́зо ferrous sulphide.

сернокисл|ый, *adj.* (*chem.*) sulphate (of); ~ая соль sulphate.

се́рн|ый, *adj.* sulphuric; ~ая кислота́ sulphuric acid; с. цвет flowers of sulphur.

серова́т|ый (~, ~а), *adj.* greyish.

сероводоро́д, а, *m.* (*chem.*) hydrogen sulphide, sulphuretted hydrogen.

сероглаз|ый (~, ~а), *adj.* grey-eyed.

серозём, а, *m.* (*agric.*) grey earth.

серо́зный, *adj.* (*physiol.*) serous.

сероуглеро́д, а, m. (*chem.*) carbon bisulphide.

серп, á, m. sickle, reaping-hook; с. луны́ crescent moon.

серпанти́н, а, m. paper streamer.

серпенти́н, а, m. (*min.*) serpentine.

серпови́дный, *adj.* crescent(-shaped).

серсо́, *indecl.,* *n.* hoopla.

сертифика́т, а, m. certificate.

се́рум, а, m. (*med.*) serum.

серча́|ть, ю, *impf.* (*of о~*) (*coll.*) to be angry, be cross.

се́р|ый (~, ~á, ~о), *adj.* 1. grey; с. в я́блоках dappled. 2. (*fig.*) grey, dull; drab; с. день grey day. 3. (*fig.*) dull, dim (= *uneducated*).

серьг|á, и, *pl.* ~и, серёг, ~ám, *f.* 1. ear-ring. 2. (*tech.*) link. 3. (*naut.*) slip rope.

серьёзно, *adv.* seriously; earnestly; in earnest; с.? seriously?, really?

серьёзност|ь, и, f. seriousness; earnestness; gravity.

серьёз|ный (~ен, ~на, ~но), *adj.* serious; earnest; grave.

сессио́нный, *adj.* sessional.

се́сси|я, и, f. session, sitting; (*leg.*) term.

сестр|á, ы́, *pl.* ~ы, сестёр, ~ám, *f.* 1. sister; двою́родная с. (first) cousin. 2. медици́нская с., с. милосе́рдия (*obs.*) nurse; ста́ршая с. (*nursing*) sister; с.-хозя́йка (*hospital*) matron.

сестрёнк|а, и, f. little sister.

се́стрин, *adj.* sister's.

се́стринский, *adj.* nurse's; nursing.

сестри́ц|а, ы, f. *affect.* *dim.* of сестра́.

сестри́чк|а, и, f. = сестри́ца.

сесть¹, ся́ду, ся́дешь, *past* сел, *pf.* (*of* сади́ться) 1. to sit down; с. за стол to sit down to table; с. обе́дать to sit down to dinner; с. в ва́нну to get into the bath; с. рабо́тать to get down to work; с. в кало́шу, с. в лу́жу (*coll.*) to get into a mess, into a fix. 2. (в, на+*a.*) to board, take; с. на по́езд to board a train; с. на ло́шадь to mount a horse. 3. to alight, settle, perch; (*of an aircraft*) to land. 4. (*of the heavenly bodies*) to set. 5. с. в тюрьму́ to go to prison, jail.

сесть², ся́дет, *past* сел, *pf.* (*of* сади́ться) to shrink.

сет, а, m. (*sport*) set.

сетево́й, *adj.* net, netting, mesh.

се́тк|а, и, f. 1. net, netting; (luggage) rack; с. для головы́ hair-net; игра́ть у ~и (*tennis*) to play at net. 2. (*coll.*) string-bag. 3. (*geogr.*) grid; (*collect.*) co-ordinates. 4. (*radio*) grid. 5. scale (*of charges, etc.*).

сет|ова́ть, ую, *impf.* (*of* по~) 1. (на+*a.*) to complain (of), cry out (upon). 2. (о+*p.*) to lament, mourn.

се́точный, *adj.* 1. net. 2. (*radio*) grid.

се́ттер, а, m. setter (*dog*).

сетча́тк|а, и, f. (*anat.*) retina.

сетчатокры́л|ые, ых, *sing.* ~ое, ~ого, *n.* (*zool.*) Neuroptera.

се́тчат|ый, *adj.* netted, network; reticular; ~ая оболо́чка гла́за (*anat.*) retina.

сет|ь, и, о ~и, в ~и *and* в ~й, *pl.* ~и, ~е́й, *f.* 1. net (*also fig.*); расста́вить ~и кому́-н. to set a trap for someone. 2. network; circuit, system.

се́ч|а, и, f. (*obs.*) battle.

сече́ни|е, я, n. 1. cutting; ке́сарево с. Caesarean birth, operation. 2. section; живо́е с. cross section.

се́чк|а, и, f. 1. chopper, vegetable-cutting knife. 2. chopped straw, chaff.

сечь¹, секу́, сече́шь, секу́т, *past* сек, секла́, *impf.* 1. (*impf. only*) to cut to pieces. 2. (*pf.* вы́~, *past* сек, се́кла) to beat, flog.

сеч|ь², и, f. (*hist.*) (Cossack) host.

се́|чься, чётся, ку́тся, *past* ~кся, ~кла́сь, *impf.* (*of* по~) (*of hairs*) to split; (*of fabric*) to cut.

се́ялк|а, и, f. (*agric.*) sowing-machine, seed drill.

се́яльщик, а, m. sower.

се́ян|ец, ца, m. seedling.

се́ятел|ь, я, m. sower (*also fig., rhet.*); disseminator.

се́|ять, ю, ешь, *impf.* (*of* по~) 1. to sow (*also fig.*); с. раздо́р to sow the seeds of dissension. 2. (*fig., coll.*) to throw about; с. де́ньги to throw one's money about.

сжа́л|иться, юсь, ишься, *pf.* (над) to take pity (on).

сжа́ти|е, я, n. 1. pressing, pressure; grasp, grip. 2. compression, condensation; ка́мера ~я compression chamber.

сжа́тост|ь, и, f. 1. compression. 2. conciseness.

сжа́т|ый, *p.p.p.* of ~ь¹ *and* ~ь² *and adj.* 1. compressed (*air, gas*). 2. (*fig.*) condensed, compact; concise; ~ое изложе́ние exposition in condensed form.

сжать¹, сожму́, сожмёшь, *pf.* (*of* сжима́ть) to squeeze; to compress (*also fig.*); to grip; с. гу́бы to compress one's lips; с. зу́бы to grit one's teeth; с. кулаки́ to clench one's fists; с. в объя́тиях to hug; с. изложе́ние to compress an exposition.

сжать², сожну́, сожнёшь, *pf. of* жать².

сжа́|ться, сожму́сь, сожмёшься, *pf. (of* сжима́ться) **1.** to tighten, clench. **2.** to shrink, contract; её душа́ ~лась her heart sank.

сж|ева́ть, ую́, уёшь, *pf.* to chew up.

сжечь, сожгу́, сожжёшь, сожгу́т, *past* сжёг, сожгла́, *pf. (of* жечь *and* сжига́ть) to burn (up, down); to cremate; с. свои́ корабли́ (*fig.*) to burn one's boats.

сжива́|ть(ся), ю(сь), *impf. of* сжи́ть(ся).

сжига́|ть, ю, *impf. of* сжечь.

сжи|ди́ть, жу́, ди́шь, *pf. (of* ~жа́ть) (*chem.*) to liquefy.

сжижа́|ть, ю, *impf. of* сжиди́ть.

сжиже́ни|е, я, *n.* (*chem.*) liquation, liquefaction.

сжи́женный, *adj.* (*chem.*) liquefied.

сжим, а, *m.* clip, grip, clamp.

сжима́емост|ь, и, *f.* compressibility, condensability.

сжима́|ть(ся), ю(сь), *impf. of* сжа́ть¹(ся).

сжи|ть, ву́, вёшь, *past* ~л, ~ла́, ~ло, *pf. (of* ~ва́ть) (*coll.*) to force out, edge out; с. со све́ту to be the death (of).

сжи́|ться, ву́сь, вёшься, *past* ~лся, ~ла́сь, *pf. (of* ~ва́ться) (с+*i.*) to get used (to), get accustomed (to); с. с ро́лью (*theatr.*) to identify oneself with a part.

сжу́льнича|ть, ю, *pf. of* жу́льничать.

сза́ди, *adv. and prep.* +*g.* **1.** *adv.* from behind; behind; from the end; from the rear; вид с. rear view; тре́тий ваго́н с. the third coach from the rear. **2.** *prep.* +*g.* behind.

сзыва́|ть, ю, *impf. of* созва́ть.

сиа́мский, *adj.* Siamese.

сибари́т, а, *m.* sybarite.

сибари́тский, *adj.* sybaritic.

сибари́тств|о, а, *n.* sybaritism.

сибари́тств|овать, ую, *impf.* to lead the life of a sybarite.

сибиля́нт, а, *m.* (*ling.*) sibilant.

сибирея́звенный, *adj.* (*med.*) anthrax.

сиби́рк|а, и, *f.* **1.** (*obs.*) sibirka (*waist-length caftan*). **2.** (*coll., obs.*) clink (= *prison*). **3.** (*hist.*) sibirka (*paper money issued in Siberia during the Civil War, 1918–20*). **4.** (*coll.*) = сиби́рская я́зва.

сиби́рный, *adj.* (*coll., obs.*) hard, severe.

сиби́рск|ий, *adj.* Siberian; ~ая ко́шка Persian cat; ~ая я́зва (*med.*) anthrax.

сибиря́к, а́, *m.* Siberian.

сибиря́чк|а, и, *f.* Siberian (woman).

сиве́|ть, ю, *impf. (of* по~) to turn grey.

си́вк|а, и, *f.* dark grey (horse).

сивк|о́, а́, *m.* = ~а.

сивола́пый, *adj.* (*coll.*) rough, clumsy.

сиву́х|а, и, *f.* raw vodka.

сиву́шн|ый, *adj.*; ~ое ма́сло fusel oil.

си́в|ый (~, ~а́, ~о), *adj.* **1.** (*of horses*) grey; бред ~ой кобы́лы (*coll.*) raving nonsense. **2.** (*of hair*) grey, greying.

сиг, а́, *m.* white fish (*freshwater fish of salmon family*).

сига́н|уть, у́, ёшь, *pf.* (*coll.*) to leap.

сига́р|а, ы, *f.* cigar.

сигаре́т|а, ы, *f.* **1.** cigarette (*without mouthpiece*). **2.** small cigar.

сигаре́т|ный, *adj. of* ~а.

сига́рк|а, и, *f.* (*coll.*) (home-made) cigarette (*of shag rolled in newspaper*).

сига́р|ный, *adj. of* ~а.

сига́рочниц|а, ы, *f.* cigar box.

сигна́л, а, *m.* signal; вызывно́й с. call signal; пожа́рный с. fire-alarm; с. бе́дствия distress signal; с. возду́шной трево́ги air-raid alarm; с. на трубе́ trumpet-call; с. на рожке́, с. на го́рне bugle-call.

сигнализа́тор, а, *m.* (*tech.*) signalling apparatus.

сигнализа́ци|я, и, *f.* signalling.

сигнализи́р|овать, ую, *impf. and pf.* **1.** (*pf. also* про~) to signal. **2.** (+*a. or* о+*p.*; *fig.*) to give warning (of).

сигна́л|ьный, *adj. of* ~; ~ьная бу́дка signal-box; ~ьная ла́мпа signal lamp; с. пистоле́т Very pistol, signal pistol, flare gun; ~ьное поло́тнище signal panel, marking panel; ~ьная тормозна́я верёвка communication cord.

сигна́льщик, а, *m.* signaller, signal-man.

сигнату́р|а, ы, *f.* **1.** (*pharm.*) label. **2.** (*typ.*) signature.

сиде́л|ец, ьца, *m.* **1.** (*obs.*) salesman; shop-walker.

сиде́лк|а, и, *f.* (sick-)nurse.

сиде́ни|е, я, *n.* sitting.

си́д|ень, ня, *m.* (*coll.*) stay-at-home; сиде́ть ~нем to be a stay-at-home.

сиде́нь|е, я, *n.* seat.

сидери́т, а, *m.* (*min.*) siderite.

си|де́ть, жу́, ди́шь, *impf.* **1.** to sit; с., поджа́в но́ги to sit cross-legged; с. верхо́м to be on horseback; с. на ко́рточках to squat; с. на насе́сте to roost, perch; с. на я́йцах to sit (on eggs), brood; с. у мо́ря, ждать пого́ды (*coll.*) to wait for something to turn up; вот где ~ди́т кто-н., что-н. (*coll.*) that's where all the trouble lies, that's the source of all the trouble. **2.** to be; с. (в тюрьме́) to be in prison, serve a term of imprisonment; с. под аре́стом to be under arrest; с. без де́ла to have nothing to do; с. за кни́гой to be (engaged in) reading. **3.** (*of a vessel*) to draw (*water*); с. глубоко́ to be deep in the water, draw much water. **4.** (на+*p.*; *of clothing*) to fit, sit (on).

сид|е́ться, и́тся, *impf.* (*impers.*+*d.*) ему́, *etc.*, не ~и́тся до́ма he, *etc.*, can't bear staying at home; ей не ~и́тся на ме́сте she can't keep still.

сидр, а, *m.* cider.

сидя́ч|ий, *adj.* 1. sitting; в ~ей по́зе in a sitting posture. 2. (*fig.*) sedentary; с. о́браз жи́зни sedentary life. 3. (*zool.*) sessile.

сие́, *see* сей.

сие́н|а, ы, *f.* sienna; жжёная с. burnt sienna.

сиени́т, а, *m.* (*min.*) syenite.

сизиги́йный, *adj.* с. прили́в spring tide.

сизиги́|я, и, *f.* (*astron.*) syzygy.

сизи́фов, *adj.*; ~ труд labour of Sisyphus.

сизоворо́нк|а, и, *f.* (*orn.*) roller.

си́з|ый (~, ~а́, ~о), *adj.* blue-grey, dove-coloured.

сиккати́в, а, *m.* (*tech.*) siccative.

сикомо́р, а, *m.* (*bot.*) sycamore.

си́л|а, ы, *f.* 1. strength, force; в ~у (+*g.*) on the strength (of), by virtue (of), because (of); быть в ~ах (+*inf.*) to have the strength (to), have the power (to); изо всех ~, что есть ~ы with all one's might; крича́ть изо всех ~ to shout at the top of one's voice; от ~ы (*coll.*) at most; сверх ~, свы́ше ~, не по ~ам beyond one's power(s); outside one's competence; че́рез ~у beyond one's powers; рабо́тать че́рез ~у to overwork; ~ой by force; с по́мощью грубо́й ~ы by brute force; свои́ми ~ами unaided; ~ою веще́й through force of circumstances; ~ою (+*g.* or в+*a.*) to the strength (of); с. во́ли will-power; с. ду́ха strength of mind; с. привы́чки force of habit; в ~у привы́чки by force of habit. 2. (*phys., tech.*) force, power; жива́я с. kinetic energy; лошади́ная с. horse-power; подъёмная с. (*aeron.*) lift; с. све́та в свеча́х candle-power; с. тя́ги tractive force; с. тя́жести, с. притяже́ния force of gravity. 3. (*leg. and fig.*) force; име́ющий ~у valid; в ~е in force, valid; войти́, вступи́ть в ~у to come into force; take effect; оста́ться в ~е to remain valid; (*fig.*) to hold good. 4. (*pl.; mil.*) forces; вооружённые ~ы armed forces; вое́нно-возду́шные ~ы air force(s); сухопу́тные ~ы land forces, ground forces. 5. (*coll.*) point, essence; с. в том, что the crux of the matter is that. 6. (*coll.*) quantity, multitude.

сила́ч, а́, *m.* strong man.

силика́т, а, *m.* (*min.*) silicate.

си́л|иться, юсь, ишься, *impf.* to try, make efforts.

сили́ци|й, я, *m.* (*chem.*) silicium.

силко́м, *adv.* (*coll.*) by (main) force.

силлаби́ческий, *adj.* (*lit.*) syllabic.

силлоги́зм, а, *m.* (*philos.*) syllogism.

салови́к, а́, *m.* power-plant worker.

силов|о́й, *adj.* power; ~а́я ли́ния (*phys.*) line of force; ~о́е по́ле (*phys.*) field of force; с. про́вод (*electr.*) power-line; ~а́я ста́нция power-station, power-house; ~а́я устано́вка power-plant.

си́лой, *adv.* (*coll.*) by (main) force.

сил|о́к, ка́, *m.* noose, snare.

силоме́р, а, *m.* dynamometer.

си́лос, а, *m.* (*agric.*) 1. silo. 2. silage.

силосова́ни|е, я, *n.* siloing.

силос|ова́ть, у́ю, *impf. and pf.* to silo, ensile.

силосоре́зк|а, и, *f.* silage cutter.

силури́йский, *adj.* (*geol.*) Silurian.

силуэ́т, а, *m.* silhouette.

си́льно, *adv.* 1. strongly; violently; с. ска́зано that's going too far, that's putting it too strongly. 2. very much, greatly; badly; с. нужда́ться в чём-н. to want something badly.

сильноде́йствующий, *adj.* virulent; drastic.

си́л|ьный (~ен *and* **~ён, ~ьна́, ~ьно, ~ьны́),** *adj.* (*in var. senses*) strong; powerful; ~ьная во́ля strong will; с. до́вод powerful argument; ~ьное жела́ние intense desire; с. за́пах strong smell; с. моро́з hard frost; ~ьная речь impressive speech; он не ~ён в языка́х he is not good at languages, languages are not his strong suit.

сильф, а, *m.* (*myth.*) sylph.

сильфи́д|а, ы, *f.* (*myth. and fig.*) sylph.

симбио́з, а, *m.* (*biol.*) symbiosis.

си́мвол, а, *m.* symbol; emblem; с. ве́ры (*rel.*) creed.

символиза́ци|я, и, *f.* symbolization.

символизи́р|овать, ую, *impf.* to symbolize.

символи́зм, а, *m.* symbolism.

симво́лик|а, и, *f.* symbolism.

символи́ст, а, *m.* symbolist.

символи́ст|ский, *adj.* of ~.

символи́ческий, *adj.* symbolic(al).

символи́чност|ь, и, *f.* symbolical character.

символи́ч|ный (~ен, ~на), *adj.* = ~еский.

симметри́ческий, *adj.* symmetrical.

симметри́чност|ь, и, *f.* symmetry.

симметри́ч|ный (~ен, ~на), *adj.* = ~еский.

симметри́|я, и, *f.* symmetry.

симони́|я, и, *f.* (*hist.*) simony.

симпатизи́р|овать, ую, *impf.* 1. (+*d.*) be in sympathy (with), sympathize (with). 2. (с+*i.*; *obs.*) to accord (with).

симпати́ческ|ий, *adj.* (*physiol., etc.*) sympathetic; ~ая не́рвная систе́ма sympathetic nervous system; ~ие черни́ла invisible ink.

симпати́ч|ный (~ен, ~на), *adj.* likeable, attractive, nice.

симпа́ти|я, и, *f.* 1. (к) liking (for); чу́вствовать ~ю к кому́-н. to take a liking to someone, be drawn to someone. 2. (*fig., coll.*) loved one, object of one's affections.

симпто́м, а, *m.* symptom.

симптома́тик|а, и, *f.* (*med.*) study of symptoms.

симптомати́ческий, *adj.* **1.** symptomatic. **2.** (*med.*) eliminating symptoms, palliative.

симптомати́ч|ный (**~ен, ~на**), *adj.* = **~еский.**

симули́р|овать, ую, *impf. and pf.* to simulate, feign, sham.

симуля́нт, а, *m.* simulator; malingerer.

симуля́ци|я, и, *f.* simulation.

симфони́ческий, *adj.* symphonic; с. орке́стр symphony orchestra.

симфо́ни|я, и, *f.* **1.** symphony. **2.** (*eccl., lit.*) concordance.

синаго́г|а, и, *f.* synagogue.

синагога́льный, *adj.* synagogical.

синдетико́н, а, *m.* seccotine.

синдикали́зм, а, *m.* (*polit.*) syndicalism.

синдикали́ст, а, *m.* (*polit.*) syndicalist.

синдикали́стский, *adj.* (*polit.*) syndicalist, syndicalistic.

синдика́т, а, *m.* (*econ.*) syndicate.

синдици́р|овать, ую, *impf. and pf.* (*econ.*) to syndicate.

синев|а́, ы́, *f.* blue colour; с. небе́с the blue of the sky; с. под глаза́ми dark patches under the eyes.

синева́т|ый (**~, ~а**), *adj.* bluish.

синегла́з|ый (**~, ~а**), *adj.* blue-eyed.

синедрио́н, а, *m.* (*hist.*) sanhedrin; (*joc.*) meeting.

сине́кдох|а, и, *f.* (*lit.*) synecdoche.

синеку́р|а, ы, *f.* sinecure.

сине́л|ь, и, *f.* chenille.

синеро́д, а, *m.* (*chem.*) cyanogen.

синеро́дист|ый, *adj.* (*chem.*) cyanous; cyanide (of); **~ая** кислота́ cyanic acid.

синеро́дный, *adj.* (*chem.*) cyanic; cyanide (of).

сине́|ть, ю, *impf.* **1.** (*pf.* по**~**) to turn blue, become blue. **2.** (*impf. only*) to show blue.

си́н|ий (**~ь, ~я́, ~е**), *adj.* (dark) blue; с. чуло́к (*fig.*) blue-stocking.

сини́льн|ый, *adj.* **~ая** кислота́ (*chem.*) prussic acid, hydrocyanic acid.

син|и́ть, ю́, и́шь, *impf.* (*of* по**~**) **1.** to paint blue. **2.** to rinse in blue, blue.

сини́ц|а, ы, *f.* tit, titmouse, tomtit.

синкли́т, а, *m.* (*joc.*) council, synod.

синко́п|а, ы, *f.* (*mus. and ling.*) syncope.

синкрети́зм, а, *m.* syncretism.

сино́д, а, *m.* synod.

синода́льный, *adj.* synodal.

синоди́ческий, *adj.* (*astron.*) synodic(al).

сино́д|ский, *adj.* = **~а́льный.**

сино́лог, а, *m.* sinologist.

синоло́ги|я, и, *f.* sinology.

сино́ним, а, *m.* synonym.

синони́мик|а, и, *f.* **1.** study of synonyms. **2.** (*collect.*) synonyms.

синони́ми|я, и, *f.* synonymy, synonymity.

синоптик, а, *m.* weather forecaster, weather-chart maker.

сино́птик|а, и, *f.* weather forecasting.

синопти́ческ|ий, *adj.* synoptical; **~ая** ка́рта weather-chart.

си́нтаксис, а, *m.* syntax.

синтакси́ческий, *adj.* syntactical.

си́нтез, а, *m.* synthesis.

синтези́р|овать, ую, *impf. and pf.* to synthesize.

синтети́ческий, *adj.* synthetic.

си́нус[1], а, *m.* (*math.*) sine.

си́нус[2], а, *m.* (*anat.*) sinus.

синусо́ид|а, ы, *f.* (*math.*) sinusoid.

синхрониза́тор, а, *m.* (*tech.*) synchronizer.

синхрониза́ци|я, и, *f.* synchronization.

синхронизи́р|овать, ую, *impf. and pf.* to synchronize.

синхрони́зм, а, *m.* synchronism.

синхрони́ческий, *adj.* synchronic.

синхрони́|я, и, *f.* synchronism.

синхро́нный, *adj.* synchronous.

син|ь[1], и, *f.* blue colour.

синь[2], *see* **си́ний.**

синьг|а́, и́, *f.* (*orn.*) common scoter.

си́ньк|а, и, *f.* **1.** blue, blueing. **2.** blueprint.

синьо́р, а, *m.* signor.

синьо́р|а, ы, *f.* signora.

синьори́н|а, ы, *f.* signorina.

синю́х|а, и, *f.* (*med.*) cyanosis.

синя́к, а́, *m.* bruise; с. под гла́зом black eye; **~и́** под глаза́ми shadows, dark patches under the eyes; изби́ть до **~о́в** to beat black and blue.

сиони́зм, а, *m.* Zionism.

сиони́ст, а, *m.* Zionist.

сиони́стский, *adj.* Zionist.

сипа́|й, я, *m.* sepoy.

сип|е́ть, лю́, и́шь, *impf.* **1.** to make hoarse sounds; to speak hoarsely. **2.** (*impers.*) to be hoarse; у него́ в го́рле **~и́т** he is hoarse.

си́плый, *adj.* hoarse, husky.

си́пн|уть, у, ешь, *impf.* (*coll.*) to become hoarse, become husky.

сипу́х|а, и, *f.* (*orn.*) barn owl.

сире́н|а, ы, *f.* (*in var. senses*) siren.

сире́невый, *adj.* lilac; lilac-coloured.

сире́н|ь, и, *f.* lilac.

си́речь, *particle* (*arch.*) that is to say.

сири́|ец, йца, *m.* Syrian.

сири́|йка, йки, *f. of* **~ец.**

сири́йский, *adj.* Syrian.

сиро́кко, *indecl., m.* sirocco.

сиро́п, а, *m.* syrup.

сирот|а́, ы́, *pl.* **~ы,** *m. and f.* orphan; каза́нская с. (*fig., coll.*) person with 'hard luck story'.

сироте́|ть, ю, *impf.* to be orphaned.

сиротли́в|ый (**~, ~а**), *adj.* lonely.

сиро́т|ский, *adj. of* ~á; с. дом orphanage; ~ская зима́ mild winter.

сиро́тств|о, а, *n.* orphanhood.

си́р|ый (~, ~á, ~о), *adj.* (*obs.*) 1. orphaned. 2. (*fig.*) lonely.

систе́м|а, ы, *f.* 1. (*in var. senses*) system; стать ~ой, войти́ в ~у to become the rule. 2. type; пулемёт но́вой ~ы machine-gun of a new type.

систематиза́ци|я, и, *f.* systematization.

системати́зи́р|овать, ую, *impf. and pf.* to systematize.

системати́к|а, и, *f.* 1. systematization. 2. (*biol.*) taxonomy.

системати́ческий, *adj.* systematic; methodical.

системати́чност|ь, и, *f.* systematic character; system.

системати́ч|ный (~ен, ~на), *adj.* systematic; methodical.

си́стол|а, ы, *f.* (*med.*) systole.

си́с|ька, ьки, *g. pl.* ~ек, *f.* (*coll.*) nipple; tit.

си́т|ец, ца, *m.* cotton (print); calico (print); chintz.

си́теч|ко, ка, *pl.* ~ки, ~ек, *n. dim. of* си́то; ча́йное с. tea-strainer.

си́тник¹, а, *m.* = си́тный хлеб.

си́тник², а, *m.* (*bot.*) rush.

си́тн|ый, *adj.* (*obs.*) sifted; с. хлеб loaf made of sifted flour; *as noun* с., ~ого, *m.* = с. хлеб.

си́т|о, а, *n.* sieve; bolter.

ситро́, *indecl. n.* fruit-flavoured mineral water.

ситуа́ци|я, и, *f.* situation.

си́т|цевый, *adj. of* ~ец.

ситценабивно́й, *adj.* (*text.*) printing.

ситцепеча́тани|е, я, *n.* (*text.*) printing.

си́филис, а, *m.* (*med.*) syphilis.

сифили́тик, а, *m.* syphilitic.

сифилити́ческий, *adj.* syphilitic.

сифо́н, а, *m.* siphon.

сия́ни|е, я, *n.* radiance; се́верное с. northern lights, Aurora Borealis.

сия́тельств|о, а, *n.* его́, *etc.*, с. (*title of princes and counts*) his, *etc.*, Excellency.

сия́|ть, ю, *impf.* to shine, beam; to be radiant.

скабио́з|а, ы, *f.* (*bot.*) scabious.

скабрёзност|ь, и, *f.* scabrousness; говори́ть ~и to use scabrous language.

скабрёз|ный (~ен, ~на), *adj.* scabrous.

сказ, а, *m.* 1. tale; вот тебе́ и весь с. (*coll.*) that's the long and the short of it. 2. narration in first person.

сказа́ни|е, я, *n.* story, tale, legend.

сказан|у́ть, у́, ёшь, *pf.* (*coll.*) to blurt (out); ну и ~у́л словцо́! that's a fine thing to say! ска|за́ть, жу́, ~жешь, *pf.* 1. *pf. of* говори́ть; ~жи́(те)! (*coll., iron.*) I say!; как с. how

shall I put it?; лу́чше с., верне́е с., точне́е с. or rather; не́чего с.! well, to be sure!; ~зано — сде́лано (*coll.*) no sooner said than done. 2. to interpose, object; ничего́ не ~жешь, он прав there is no gainsaying it, he is right.

ска|за́ться¹, жу́сь, ~жешься, *pf.* (*of* ~зы́ваться) (*coll.*) 1. (+*d.*) to inform; to give notice, give warning; они́ уе́хали не ~за́вшись they went away without (giving) warning. 2. (+*i.*) to proclaim oneself; с. больны́м to report sick.

ска|за́ться², жу́сь, ~жешься, *pf.* (*of* ~зы́ваться) (на+*p.*, в+*p.*) to tell (on); бомбёжка ~за́лась на её не́рвах the bombing told on her nerves; в э́том посту́пке я́вно ~за́лась его́ некульту́рность this act just showed his lack of manners.

сказа́тел|ь, я, *m.* folk-tale narrator, story-teller.

ска́зк|а, и, *f.* 1. tale, story; волше́бная с. fairy-tale; с. про бе́лого бычка́ (*coll.*) the same old story. 2. (*coll.*) (tall) story, fib.

ска́зочник, а, *m.* story-teller.

ска́зочн|ый, *adj.* fairytale; fabulous, fantastic; ~ая страна́ fairyland; ~ое бога́тство fabulous wealth.

сказу́ем|ое, ого, *n.* (*gram.*) predicate.

ска́зыва|ться, юсь, *impf. of* сказа́ться.

скак, *m. only found in p. sing.*; на всём ~у́ at full tilt.

скака́лк|а, и, *f.* skipping-rope.

ска|ка́ть, чу́, ~чешь, *impf.* 1. to skip, jump; с. на одно́й ноге́ to hop. 2. to gallop.

скаков|о́й, *adj.* race, racing; ~а́я доро́жка racecourse; ~а́я ло́шадь racehorse.

скаку́н, а́, *m.* fast horse, racer.

ска́л|а, ы, *f.* (*obs.*) scale.

скал|а́, ы́, *pl.* ~ы, *f.* rock face, crag; (отве́сная) с. cliff; подво́дная с. reef.

скаламбу́р|ить, ю, ишь, *pf. of* каламбу́рить.

скали́ст|ый (~, ~а), *adj.* rocky.

ска́л|ить, ю, ишь, *impf.* (*of* о~) с. зу́бы to show one's teeth, bare one's teeth; (*impf. only*) (*fig. pejor.*) to grin, laugh.

ска́лк|а, и, *f.* rolling-pin; beater.

скалола́з, а, *m.* rock-climber.

ска́лыва|ть, ю, *impf. of* сколо́ть.

скальд, а, *m.* (*hist., lit.*) scald, skald.

скалькир|овать, ую, *pf. of* кальки́ровать.

скалькули́р|овать, ую, *pf. of* калькули́ровать.

ска́льн|ый, *adj.* (*geol.*) rock, rocky; ~ые рабо́ты rock excavations.

скальп, а, *m.* scalp.

ска́льпел|ь, я, *m.* scalpel.

скальпи́р|овать, ую, *impf. and pf.* (*pf. also* о~) to scalp.

скаме́ечк|а, и, *f.* small bench; с. для ног footstool.

скаме́йк|а, и, *f.* bench.

скам|ья́, ьи́, *pl.* **~ьи́, ~е́й,** *f.* bench; с. подсуди́мых (*leg.*) the dock; на шко́льной ~ье́ during one's schooldays; со шко́льной ~ьи́ straight from school.

сканда́л, а, *m.* 1. scandal; disgrace; како́й с.! what a scandal!, how scandalous! 2. brawl; rowdy scene.

скандализи́р|овать, ую, *impf. and pf.* to scandalize.

сканда́лист, а, *m.* brawler; trouble-maker; rowdy.

сканда́л|ить, ю, ишь, *impf.* 1. (*pf.* на~) (*coll.*) to brawl; to start a row. 2. (*pf.* о~) to scandalize.

сканда́л|иться, юсь, ишься, *impf.* (*of* о~) to disgrace oneself.

сканда́л|ьный (~ен, ~ьна), *adj.* 1. scandalous. 2. (*coll.*) rowdy; с. челове́к = ~и́ст. 3. scandal; ~ьная хро́ника scandal column, page (*of newspaper*).

ска́нди|й, я, *m.* (*chem.*) scandium.

скандина́в, а, *m.* Scandinavian.

скандина́в|ка, ки, *f. of* ~.

скандина́вский, *adj.* Scandinavian.

сканди́ровани|е, я, *n.* (*lit.*) scansion.

сканди́р|овать, ую, *impf. and pf.* to declaim, recite (*stressing individual syllables of words*).

ска́плива|ть(ся), ю(сь), *impf. of* скопи́ть(ся).

скапу́|ститься, щусь, стишься, *pf.* (*sl.*) to fold up, pack up; to peg out.

ска́пыва|ть, ю, *impf.* (*of* скопа́ть) to shovel away, level with a spade.

скарабе́|й, я, *m.* scarab.

скарб, а, *m.* (*coll.*) goods and chattels; со всем ~ом bag and baggage.

ска́ред, а, *m.* (*coll.*) stingy person, miser.

ска́реднича|ть, ю, *impf.* (*coll.*) to be stingy.

ска́ред|ный (~ен, ~на), *adj.* (*coll.*) stingy, miserly, niggardly.

скарифика́тор, а, *m.* 1. (*agric.*) scarifier. 2. (*med.*) scarificator.

скарифици́р|овать, ую, *impf.* (*agric.*) to scarify.

скарлати́н|а, ы, *f.* (*med.*) scarlet fever, scarlatina.

скарлати́н|ный, *adj. of* ~а.

скарлатин|о́зный, *adj.* = ~ный.

ска́рмлива|ть, ю, *impf. of* скорми́ть.

скат¹, а, *m.* slope, incline; pitch (*of a roof*).

скат², а, *m.* (*tech.*) wheelbase.

скат³, а, *m.* (*zool.*) ray, skate; электри́ческий с. electric ray.

ска́т|ать, а́ю, *pf.* (*of* ~ывать) 1. to roll (up); с. па́рус to furl a sail. 2. (за+*i.*; *coll.*) to run to fetch. 3. (*school sl.*) to crib.

ска́терт|ь, и, *pl.* **~и, ~е́й,** *f.* table-cloth; ~ью доро́га! (*coll.*) good riddance!

ска|ти́ть, чу́, ~тишь, *pf.* (*of* ~тывать) to roll down.

ска|ти́ться, чу́сь, ~тишься, *pf.* (*of* ~тываться) to roll down; (*fig., pejor.*) to slip, slide.

ска́тк|а, и, *f.* 1. (*mil.*) greatcoat roll. 2. rolling.

ска́тный, *adj.* (*folk poet., of a pearl*) large, round, and even.

ска́тыва|ть, ю, *impf. of* ската́ть *and* скати́ть.

ска́тыва|ться, юсь, *impf. of* скати́ться.

ска́ут, а, *m.* (boy) scout.

скафа́ндр, а, *m.* protective suit (*of divers, astronauts, etc.*).

ска́чк|а, и, *f.* 1. gallop, galloping. 2. (*pl.*) horse-race; race meeting, the races; с. с препя́тствиями steeplechase.

скачкообра́з|ный (~ен, ~на), *adj.* spasmodic; uneven.

скач|о́к, ка́, *m.* 1. jump, leap, bound; ~ка́ми by leaps. 2. (*fig.*) a great advance, leap forward.

ска́шива|ть, ю, *impf. of* скоси́ть.

ска́щива|ть, ю, *impf. of* скости́ть.

сква́жин|а, ы, *f.* slit, chink; бурова́я с. (*tech.*) bore-hole; замо́чная с. key-hole.

сква́жистый, *adj.* porous.

сквалы́г|а, и, *m. and f.* (*coll.*) stingy person, miser.

сквер, а, *m.* public garden.

скве́рн|а, ы, *no pl.* (*collect.; obs.*) pollution; filth.

скве́рно, *adv.* badly; с. чу́вствовать себя́ to feel bad, feel poorly; с. поступи́ть с кем-н. to treat someone badly.

скверносло́в, а, *m.* foul-mouthed person.

скверносло́ви|е, я, *n.* foul language.

скверносло́в|ить, лю, ишь, *impf.* to use foul language.

скве́р|ный (~ен, ~на́, ~но), *adj.* nasty, foul; bad; ~ная пого́да foul weather; мне ~но (*impers.*) I feel bad.

сквита́|ться, юсь, *pf.* (с+*i.*; *coll.*) to be quits (with), be even (with).

сквоз|и́ть, и́т, *impf.* 1. (*impers.*) ~и́т there is a draught. 2. (*obs.*) to be transparent, show light through. 3. to show through, be seen through (*also fig.*); синева́ небе́с ~и́ла меж ветвя́ми the blue of the sky could be seen through the branches; в его́ слова́х ~и́ла жа́лость к себе́ there was a hint of self-pity in his words.

сквозн|о́й, *adj.* 1. through; с. ве́тер draught; ~о́е движе́ние through traffic; с. по́езд through train. 2. all-round. 3. transparent.

сквозня́к, а́, *m.* draught.

**сквозь, prep.+*a.* through.

сквор|е́ц, ца́, *m.* starling.

скворе́чник, а, *m.* starling-house (*wooden box affixed to pole or on tree adjoining house*).

скворе́ч|ница, ницы, *f.* = ~ник.

скворе́ч|ня, ни, *g. pl.* **~ен,** *f.* = ~ник.

скелéт, а, *m.* skeleton.

скéпсис, а, *m.* scepticism.

скéптик, а, *m.* sceptic.

скептици́зм, а, *m.* scepticism.

скепти́ческий, *adj.* sceptic.

скепти́ч|ный (~ен, ~на), *adj.* sceptical.

скéрцо, *indecl., n.* (*mus.*) scherzo.

скéтинг-ри́нг, а, *m.* roller-skating rink.

скетч, а, *m.* (*theatr.*) sketch.

скид|áть¹, áю, *impf.* (*coll.*) to throw off.

скид|áть², áю, *pf.* (*of* ~ывать²) (*coll.*) to throw off.

ски́дк|а, и, *f.* 1. rebate, reduction, discount; со ~ой (в+*a.*) with a reduction (of), at a discount (of). 2. (на+*a.*; *fig.*) allowance(s) (for); сдéлать ~у на вóзраст to make allowances for age.

ски́дыва|ть¹, ю, *impf. of* ски́нуть.

ски́дыва|ть², ю, *impf. of* скидáть².

ски́|нуть, ну, нешь, *pf.* (*of* ~дывать¹) 1. (*coll.*) to throw off, down; с. с себя́ одéжду to throw off one's clothes. 2. (*coll.*) to knock off (*from price*).

скип, а, *m.* (*tech.*) skip.

ски́петр, а, *m.* sceptre.

скипидáр, а, *m.* turpentine.

скипидáр|ный, *adj. of* ~.

скирд, á, *pl.* ~ы́, *m.* stack, rick.

скирд|á, ы́, *pl.* ~ы, ~, ~áм, *f.* = ~.

скирд|овáть, ýю, *impf.* (*of* за~) to stack.

скис|áть, áю, *impf. of* ~нуть.

ски́с|нуть, ну, нешь, *past* ~, ~ла, *pf.* (*of* ~áть) to go sour, turn sour.

скит, á, о ~é, в ~ý, *m.* (small and secluded) monastery.

скитáл|ец, ьца, *m.* wanderer.

скитáльческий, *adj.* wandering.

скитáльчеств|о, а, *n.* wandering.

скитá|ться, юсь, *impf.* to wander; с. по свéту to be a globe-trotter.

скиф¹, а, *m.* (*hist.*) Scythian.

скиф², а, *m.* skiff.

ски́фский, *adj.* (*hist.*) Scythian.

склад¹, а, *m.* 1. storehouse; (*mil.*) depot; тамóженный с. bonded warehouse; товáрный с. warehouse. 2. store; с. боеприпáсов (*mil.*) ammunition dump.

склад², а, *m.* 1. stamp, mould; с. умá cast of mind, mentality. 2. (*coll.*) logical connexion; ни ~у, ни лáду neither rhyme nor reason.

склад³, а, *pl.* ~ы́, *m.* syllable; читáть по ~áм to read haltingly, spell out.

склáд|ень, ня, *m.* 1. hinged icon. 2. (*obs.*) folding object.

складир|овать, ую, *impf. and pf.* to store.

склáдк|а, и, *f.* 1. fold; pleat, tuck; crease; юбка в ~у pleated skirt; с. на брюках trouser crease. 2. wrinkle. 3. (*geol.*) fold; с. мéстности natural feature, accident of terrain.

склáдно, *adv.* smoothly, coherently.

складн|óй, *adj.* folding, collapsible; ~áя кровáть camp bed.

склáд|ный (~ен, ~нá, ~но), *adj.* 1. (*coll.*; *of human beings or animals*) well-knit, well--built. 2. (*coll.*) well-made. 3. (*of speech*) well-rounded, smooth, coherent; с. расскáз well-put-together story.

склáдочн|ый, *adj.* storage, warehousing; ~ое мéсто store-room, lumber-room.

склад|скóй, *adj.* = ~очный.

склáдчатый, *adj.* (*geol.*) plicated, folded.

склáдчин|а, ы, *f.* clubbing, pooling; устрóить ~у to club together, pool one's resources; купи́ть автомоби́ль в ~у to club together to buy a car.

склáдыва|ть(ся), ю(сь), *impf. of* сложи́ть(ся).

склéива|ть(ся), ю(сь), ет(ся), *impf. of* склéить(ся).

склé|ить, ю, ишь, *pf.* (*of* ~ивать) to stick together; to glue together, paste together.

склé|иться, ится, *pf.* (*of* ~иваться) to stick together (*intrans.*)

склéйк|а, и, *f.* glueing together, pasting together.

склеп, а, *m.* burial vault, crypt.

склеп|áть, áю, *pf.* (*of* ~ывать) to rivet.

склéпк|а, и, *f.* riveting.

склéпыва|ть, ю, *impf. of* склепáть.

склерóз, а, *m.* (*med.*) sclerosis.

склероти́ческий, *adj.* (*med.*) sclerotic, sclerous.

скли́|кать, чу, чешь, *pf. of* ~кáть.

склик|áть, áю, *impf.* (*of* ~áть) (*coll.*) to call together.

склóк|а, и, *f.* squabble; row.

склон, а, *m.* slope; на ~е лет in one's declining years.

склонéни|е, я, *n.* 1. (*math.*) inclination; (*astron.*) declination; с. кóмпаса variation of the compass; ýгол ~я angle of declination; круг ~я свети́ла hour-circle of a celestial body. 2. (*gram.*) declension.

склон|и́ть, ю́, ~ишь, *pf.* (*of* ~я́ть¹) 1. to incline, bend, bow; с. гóлову (пéред) (*fig.*) to bow one's head (to, before). 2. (*fig.*) to incline; to win over, gain over.

склон|и́ться, ю́сь, ~ишься, *pf.* (*of* ~я́ться¹) 1. to bend, bow. 2. (к; *fig.*) to give in (to), yield (to).

склóнност|ь, и, *f.* (к) inclination (to, for); disposition (to); susceptibility (to); bent (for); penchant (for).

склóн|ный (~ен, ~нá, ~но), *adj.* (к) inclined (to), disposed (to), susceptible (to), given (to), prone (to).

склоня́|емый, *pres. part. pass. of* ~ть² *and adj.* (*gram.*) declinable.

склон|я́ть¹, я́ю, *impf. of* ~и́ть.

склон|Я́ть², Я́ю, *impf.* (*of* про∼) (*gram.*) to decline.

склон|Я́ться¹, Я́юсь, *impf. of* ∼И́ться.

склон|Я́ться², Я́ется, *impf.* (*gram.*) to be declined.

склО́чник, а, *m.* (*coll.*) squabbler, trouble-maker.

склО́чнича|ть, ю, *impf.* (*coll.*) to squabble; to cause rows.

склО́ч|ный (∼ен, ∼на), *adj.* (*coll.*) troublesome, trouble-making.

склЯ́нк|а, и, *f.* 1. phial; bottle. 2. (*naut.*; *obs.*) hour-glass. 3. (*naut.*) bell (= *one half-hour*); шесть склЯ́нок six bells.

скоб|А́, Ы́, *pl.* ∼Ы, ∼А́м, *f.* cramp(-iron), clamp; staple; catch, fastening; (*naut.*) shackle.

скО́бел|ь, я, *m.* adze, scraper(-knife), drawing-knife.

скО́бк|а¹, и, *f.* 1. *dim. of* скобА́. 2. (*mark of punctuation, also math.*) bracket; *pl. also* parentheses; фигУ́рные ∼и braces; заключИ́ть в ∼и to parenthesize; в ∼ах in brackets; (*fig.*) in parenthesis, by the way, incidentally.

скО́бк|а², и, *f.* стрИ́чься в ∼у to have one's hair cut in a fringe.

скобл|И́ть, ю, ∼И́шь, *impf.* to scrape, plane.

скО́бочн|ый, *adj. of* скобА́ *and* скО́бка; ∼ая машИ́на stapler, stapling machine.

скобЯ́н|Ой, *adj.* с. товА́р, ∼Ы́е издЕ́лия hardware.

скО́ванност|ь, и, *f.* constraint.

скО́в|анный 1. *p.p.p. of* ∼А́ть; с. льдА́ми ice-bound. 2. *adj.* constrained.

сковА́|ть, скуЮ́, скуЁшь, *pf.* (*of* скО́вывать) 1. to forge, hammer out. 2. to forge together. 3. to chain; to fetter, bind (*also fig.*). 4. (*mil.*; *fig.*) to pin down, hold, contain. 5. (*of frost or ice*) to lock; морО́з ∼л рЕ́ку the river was frozen over.

сковорОд|А́, Ы́, *pl.* скО́вороды, сковорО́д, ∼А́м, *f.* 1. frying-pan. 2. (*tech.*) pan.

сковорОд|ень, ня, *m.* (*tech.*) dovetail (joint); вЯ́зка ∼нем, соединЕ́ние ∼нем dove-tailing.

сковорО́дк|а, и, *f.* (*coll.*) frying-pan.

скО́выва|ть, ю, *impf. of* сковА́ть.

сковЫ́рива|ть, ю, *impf. of* сковырнУ́ть.

сковыр|нУ́ть, нУ́, нЁшь, *pf.* (*of* ∼ивать) 1. to pick off, scratch off. 2. (*coll.*) to knock over, push over.

скок, а, *m.* galloping; во весь с. at full gallop, at full tilt.

сколА́чива|ть, ю, *impf. of* сколотИ́ть.

скОл|ок, ка, *m.* 1. chip. 2. pricked pattern. 3. (*fig.*) copy.

сколо|тИ́ть, чУ́, ∼тишь, *pf.* (*of* сколА́чивать) 1. to knock together, knock up. 2. (*fig.*, *coll.*) to put together, knock up; с. состоЯ́ние to knock up a fortune.

скол|О́ть¹, ю, ∼ешь, *pf.* (*of* скА́лывать) to split off, chop off.

скол|О́ть², ю, ∼ешь, *pf.* (*of* скА́лывать) to pin together.

сколь, *adv.* (*obs.*) how.

скольжЕ́ни|е, я, *n.* sliding, slipping; с. звУ́ка (*mus.*, *ling.*) glide; с. на крылО́ (*aeron.*) side-slip.

кольз|И́ть, жУ́, зИ́шь, *impf.* to slide, slip; to glide; с. глазА́ми (по+*d.*) to cast one's eye (over).

скОльз|кий (∼ок, ∼кА́, ∼ко), *adj.* slippery (*also fig.*); ∼кое положЕ́ние tricky position; говорИ́ть на ∼кую тЕ́му to be on slippery ground.

скользн|У́ть, У́, Ёшь, *pf.* to slide, slip; с. в дверь to slip through the door.

скользЯ́щий, *pres. part. act. of* ∼И́ть *and adj.* sliding; ∼Я́щая шкалА́ sliding scale; с. У́зел slip-knot.

скО́лько, *interrog. and relat. adv.* 1. how much; how many; с. стО́ит? how much does it cost?; с. вам лет? how old are you?; с. врЕ́мени? what time is it?; с. душЕ́ угО́дно to one's heart's content; с. раз я тебЕ́ об Э́том напоминА́л! how many times have I reminded you about it!; с. лет, с. зим! (*coll.*) what ages it has been (since we met)! 2. = наскО́лько.

скО́лько-нибудь, *adv.* any; есть у вас при себЕ́ с.-н. дЕ́нег? have you any money on you?

скомА́нд|овать, ую, *pf. of* комА́ндовать.

скомбинИ́р|овать, ую, *pf. of* комбинИ́ровать.

скО́мка|ть, ю, *pf. of* кО́мкать.

скоморО́х, а, *m.* 1. (*hist.*) skomorokh (*wandering minstrel-cum-clown*). 2. (*fig.*) buffoon, clown.

скоморО́шеств|о, а, *n.* buffoonery.

скоморО́шнича|ть, ю, *impf.* to play the buffoon.

скомпилИ́р|овать, ую, *pf. of* компилИ́ровать.

скомпон|овА́ть, У́ю, *pf. of* компоновА́ть.

скомпрометИ́р|овать, ую, *pf. of* компрометИ́ровать.

сконструИ́р|овать, ую, *pf. of* конструИ́ровать.

сконфУ́|женный, *p.p.p. of* ∼зить *and adj.* confused, abashed, disconcerted.

сконфУ́|зить(ся), жу(сь), зишь(ся), *pf. of* конфУ́зить(ся).

сконцентрИ́р|овать, ую, *pf. of* концентрИ́ровать.

сконча́ни|е, я, *n.* 1. (*obs.*) end, termination. 2. end, decease, passing.

скончА́|ться, юсь, *pf.* to pass away (= to die).

скоп|А́, Ы́, *f.* (*orn.*) osprey.

скопА́|ть, ю, *pf. of* скА́пывать.

скоп|е́ц, ца́, *m.* eunuch.

скопидо́м, а, *m.* (*coll.*) hoarder, miser.

скопидо́мнича|ть, ю, *impf.* (*coll.*) to be a hoarder, miser.

скопидо́мств|о, а, *n.* (*coll.*) hoarding; miserliness.

скопи́р|овать, ую, *pf. of* копи́ровать.

скоп|и́ть[1], лю́, ~ишь, *pf.* (*of* ска́пливать) (+*a.* or *g.*) to save (up); to amass, pile up.

скоп|и́ть[2], лю́, и́шь, *impf.* to castrate.

скоп|и́ться, ~ится, *pf.* (*of* ска́пливаться) **1.** to accumulate, pile up. **2.** (*of people*) to gather, collect.

ско́пищ|е, а, *n.* (*pejor.*) crowd, assemblage, throng.

скопле́ни|е, я, *n.* **1.** accumulation. **2.** crowd; concentration, conglomeration.

скопн|и́ть, ю́, и́шь, *pf. of* копни́ть.

ско́пом, *adv.* (*coll.*) in a crowd, in a bunch, en masse.

ско́пческий, *adj.* of a eunuch.

скорб|е́ть, лю́, и́шь, *impf.* (о+*p.*) to grieve (for, over), mourn (for, over), lament.

скорб|ный (~ен, ~на), *adj.* sorrowful, mournful, doleful.

скорбу́т, а, *m.* (*med.*) scurvy.

скорбу́тный, *adj.* (*med.*) scorbutic.

скорб|ь, и, *pl.* **~и, ~е́й,** *f.* sorrow, grief.

скор|е́е (and ~е́й) 1. *comp. of* ~ый *and* ~о; как мо́жно с. as soon as possible. **2.** *adv.* rather, sooner; с. всего́ most likely, most probably.

скорлуп|а́, ы́, *pl.* **~ы, ~ы,** *f.* shell; с. оре́ха nutshell; замкну́ться в свою́ ~у́ to retire into one's shell.

скорм|и́ть, лю́ ~ишь, *pf.* (*of* ска́рмливать) (+*d.*) to feed (to).

скорня́жн|ый, *adj.* ~ое де́ло furriery; с. това́р furs.

скорня́к, а́, *m.* furrier, fur-dresser.

ско́ро, *adv.* **1.** quickly, fast. **2.** soon; с. весна́! spring will soon be here!; как с., коль с. (*conj.*) as soon as.

скороб|и́ться, люсь, ишься, *pf. of* коро́биться.

скороговорк|а, и, *f.* **1.** patter. **2.** tongue-twister.

скором|и́ться, люсь, ишься, *impf.* (*of* о~) to break a fast, eat meat during a fast.

скоро́мник, а, *m.* (*coll.*) **1.** person failing to observe fast. **2.** lewd person.

скоро́м|ный (~ен, ~на), *adj.* **1.** (*of food*) forbidden to be consumed during fast (*viz.* meat dishes or dishes containing milk products); ~ные дни meat days; ~ное ма́сло animal (*as opp. to vegetable*) fat; *as noun* ~ное, ~ного, *n.* dishes containing meat and/or milk products. **2.** (*obs.*) lewd.

скоропали́тел|ьный (~ен, ~ьна), *adj.* (*coll.*) hasty, rash.

скоропеча́тный, *adj.* с. стано́к (*typ.*) engine press.

скоропи́сный, *adj.* cursive.

скоропис|ь, и, *f.* **1.** cursive (hand). **2.** (*obs.*) shorthand.

скороподъёмност|ь, и, *f.* (*aeron.*) rate of climb.

скоропо́ртящийся, *adj.* perishable.

скоропости́жн|ый, *adj.* ~ая смерть sudden death.

скоропреходя́щий, *adj.* transient, transitory.

скороспе́л|ый (~, ~а), *adj.* **1.** early; fast-ripening. **2.** (*fig., coll.*) premature; hasty; с. вы́вод hasty conclusion.

скоростни́к, а́, *m.* high-speed worker; high-speed performer.

скоростно́й, *adj.* high-speed; с. авто́бус express bus.

скорострельный, *adj.* rapid-firing, quick-firing.

скорост|ь, и, *pl.* **~и, ~е́й,** *f.* **1.** speed; velocity; rate; дозво́ленная с. (езды́) speed-limit; со ~ью тридцати́ миль в час at thirty miles per hour; с. подъёма (*aeron.*) rate of climb; с. све́та velocity of light. **2.** коро́бка ~е́й (*tech.*) gear-box; перейти́ на другу́ю с. to change gear. **3.** (*on railways*) category of transit; ма́лой ~ью by (slow) goods train; большо́й ~ью by fast goods train; отпра́вить груз пассажи́рской ~ью to send a consignment by passenger train. **4.** в ~и (*coll.*) soon; in the near future.

скоросшива́тел|ь, я, *m.* loose-leaf binder.

скорота́|ть, ю, *pf. of* коротать.

скороте́ч|ный (~ен, ~на), *adj.* **1.** (*obs.*) transient, short-lived. **2.** (*med.*) fulminant; ~ная чахо́тка galloping consumption.

скорохо́д, а, *m.* **1.** (*obs.*) footman. **2.** fast runner; конькобе́жец-с. high-speed skater.

скорпио́н, а, *m.* scorpion; С. Scorpio (*sign of zodiac*).

скорч|ить, у, ишь, *pf. of* ко́рчить.

ско́р|ый (~, ~а́, ~о), *adj.* **1.** quick, fast; rapid; с. по́езд fast train; с. по́мощь ambulance (service); на ~ую ру́ку off-hand, in rough-and-ready fashion. **2.** near, forthcoming, impending; в ~ом бу́дущем in the near future; в ~ом вре́мени shortly, before long; до ~ого (свида́ния)! see you soon!

скос[1], а, *m.* (*agric.*) mowing.

скос[2], а, *m.* slant, splay, chamfer, taper; у́гол ~а angle of taper.

ско|си́ть[1], шу́, ~сишь, *pf.* (*of* коси́ть[1] *and* ска́шивать) to mow.

ско|си́ть[2], шу́, си́шь, *pf.* (*of* коси́ть[2] *and* ска́шивать) to squint.

ско|сти́ть, щу́, сти́шь, *pf.* (*of* ска́щивать) (*coll.*) to strike off, knock off; с. три рубля́ с цены́ to knock three roubles off the price.

скот, á, *m.* **1.** (*collect.*) cattle; livestock. **2.** (*fig.*, *coll.*) swine, beast.

скоти́н|а, ы, *f.* **1.** (*collect.*) cattle; livestock. **2.** (*also m.*) (*fig.*, *coll.*) swine, beast.

скоти́нк|а, и, *f. dim. of* скоти́на; се́рая с. (*coll.*) simple soldiery.

ско́тник, а, *m.* herd, herdsman; cowman.

ско́т|ный, *adj. of* ~; с. двор cattle-yard.

скотобо́|ец, йца, *m.* slaughterer.

скотобо́|йня, йни, *g. pl.* ~ен, *f.* slaughter-house.

скотово́д, а, *m.* cattle-breeder.

скотово́дств|о, а, *n.* cattle-breeding, cattle-raising.

скотово́дческий, *adj.* cattle-breeding.

скотокра́дств|о, а, *n.* cattle-stealing.

скотоло́жств|о, а, *n.* bestiality.

скотоприго́нный, *adj.* с. двор stock-yard.

скотопромы́шленник, а, *m.* cattle-dealer.

скотопромы́шленност|ь, и, *f.* cattle-dealing, cattle-trade.

скотопромы́шленн|ый, *adj. of* ~ость.

ско́тский, *adj.* brutal, brutish, bestial.

скотств|о́, á, *n.* brutality, brutishness, bestiality.

скра́дыва|ть, ю, *impf.* to conceal, make less evident.

скра́|сить, шу, сишь, *pf.* (*of* ~шивать) (*fig.*) to smooth over; to relieve, take the edge off; он мно́го чита́л, чтобы с. своё одино́чество he read a lot to relieve his loneliness.

скра́шива|ть, ю, *impf. of* скра́сить.

скребко́вый, *adj.* (*tech.*) scraping, scraper.

скребни́ц|а, ы, *f.* curry-comb, horse-comb.

скреб|о́к, ка́, *m.* scraper.

скре́жет, а, *m.* gnashing, gritting (*of teeth*).

скреже|та́ть, щу́, ~щешь, *impf.* (зуба́ми) to gnash, grit one's teeth.

скре́п|а, ы, *f.* **1.** (*tech.*) tie, clamp, brace. **2.** counter-signature, authentication; ко́пия за ~ой секретаря́ copy countersigned by the secretary.

скре́пер, а, *m.* (*tech.*) earth-moving machine.

скреп|и́ть, лю́, и́шь, *pf.* (*of* ~ля́ть) **1.** to fasten (together), make fast; to pin (together); to clamp, brace; ~я́ се́рдце reluctantly, grudgingly. **2.** to countersign, authenticate, ratify.

скре́пк|а, и, *f.* paper-clip.

скрепле́ни|е, я, *n.* **1.** fastening; clamping. **2.** (*tech.*) tie, clamp.

скрепля́|ть, ю, *impf. of* скрепи́ть.

скре|сти́, бу́, бёшь, *past* ~б, ~бла́, *impf.* **1.** to scrape; to scratch, claw. **2.** (*impers.*; *fig.*, *coll.*) to nag, goad; у неё ~бло́ на се́рдце she felt a nagging anxiety.

скре|сти́сь, бу́сь, бёшься, *past* ~бся, ~бла́сь, *impf.* to scratch, make a scratching noise.

скре|сти́ть, щу́, сти́шь, *pf.* (*of* ~щивать) **1.** to cross; с. мечи́, с. шпа́ги (с + *i.*) to cross swords (with) (*also fig.*). **2.** (*biol.*) to cross, interbreed.

скрест|и́ться, и́тся, *pf.* (*of* скре́щиваться) **1.** to cross; (*fig.*) to clash. **2.** (*biol.*) to cross, interbreed.

скреще́ни|е, я, *n.* crossing; intersection.

скре́щивани|е, я, *n.* **1.** crossing. **2.** (*biol.*) crossing, interbreeding.

скре́щива|ть(ся), ю, ет(ся), *impf. of* скрести́ть(ся).

скрив|и́ть(ся), лю́(сь), и́шь(ся), *pf. of* криви́ть(ся).

скрижа́л|ь, и, *f.* tablet, table (*with sacred text inscribed upon* it); ~и (*fig.*, *arch.*) annals, memorials, records.

скрип, а, *m.* squeak, creak; crunch.

скрипа́ч, á, *m.* violinist.

скрип|е́ть, лю́, и́шь, *impf.* **1.** to squeak, creak; to crunch. **2.** (*coll.*, *joc.*) to be just alive, just keep going.

скрипи́чный, *adj.* violin; с. ма́стер violin-maker; с. ключ treble clef, G clef; с. конце́рт violin concerto.

скри́пк|а, и, *f.* violin; пе́рвая с. first violin; (*fig.*, *coll.*) first fiddle.

скрипн|у́ть, у, ешь, *pf.* to squeak, creak.

скрипу́чий, *adj.* (*coll.*) squeaky, creaking; с. го́лос rasping voice; с. снег crunching snow.

скро|и́ть, ю́, и́шь, *pf. of* кро́ить.

скро́мник, а, *m.* modest man.

скро́мнича|ть, ю, *impf.* to be overmodest.

скро́мност|ь, и, *f.* modesty.

скро́м|ный (~ен, ~на́, ~но), *adj.* (*in var. senses*) modest; по моему́ ~ному мне́нию in my humble opinion.

скру́пул, а, *m.* (*measure of weight*) scruple.

скрупулёзност|ь, и, *f.* scrupulousness, scrupulosity.

скрупулёз|ный (~ен, ~на), *adj.* scrupulous.

скру|ти́ть, чу́, ~тишь, *pf.* (*of* крути́ть *and* ~чивать) **1.** to twist; to roll. **2.** to bind, tie up.

скру́чива|ть, ю, *impf. of* скрути́ть.

скрыва́|ть, ю, *impf. of* скрыть.

скрыва́|ться, юсь, *impf.* **1.** *impf. of* скры́ться. **2.** *impf. only* to lie in hiding; to lie low.

скры́тнича|ть, ю, *impf.* (*coll.*) to be secretive, be reticent.

скры́т|ный (~ен, ~на), *adj.* reticent, secretive.

скры́т|ый, *p.p.p. of* ~ь *and adj.* secret, concealed; latent (*also phys.*); с. смысл hidden meaning; ~ая теплота́ (*phys.*) latent heat.

скры́ть, о́ю, о́ешь, *pf.* (*of* ~ыва́ть) (от) to hide (from), conceal (from); не с. того́, что to make no secret of the fact that; с. от кого́-н. неприя́тные изве́стия to keep bad news from someone.

скр|ы́ться, о́юсь, о́ешься, *pf.* (*of* ~ыва́ться) (от) **1.** to hide (oneself) (from); to go into hiding. **2.** to steal away (from), escape, give the slip. **3.** to disappear, vanish.

скрю́ч|ить, у, ишь, *pf. of* крю́чить.

скрю́ч|иться, усь, ишься, *pf.* to bend (*intrans.*); to hunch oneself up.

скря́г|а, и, *m. and f.* miser, skinflint.

скря́жнича|ть, ю, *impf.* (*coll.*) to be a miser, be a skinflint.

скуде́л|ь, и, *f.* (*arch.*) **1.** potter's clay. **2.** pot, vessel.

скуде́ль|ный, *adj.* **1.** *adj. of* ~. **2.** (*fig.*) frail, fragile; сосу́д с. (*eccl. or rhet.*) weak vessel.

скуде́|ть, ю, *impf.* (*of* о~) to grow scanty, run short; (+*i.*) to be short (of).

ску́д|ный (~ен, ~на́, ~но), *adj.* **1.** scanty, poor; slender, meagre; scant; с. обе́д meagre repast; ~ные све́дения scant information; ~ные сре́дства slender means. **2.** (+*i.*) poor (in), short (of).

ску́дост|ь, и, *f.* scarcity; poverty.

скудоу́ми|е, я, *n.* feeble-mindedness.

скудоу́м|ный (~ен, ~на), *adj.* feeble--minded.

ску́к|а, и, *f.* boredom, tedium; кака́я с.! what a bore!

скул|а́, ы́, *pl.* ~ы, *f.* cheek-bone.

скула́ст|ый (~, ~а), *adj.* with high cheek--bones, with prominent cheek-bones.

скул|и́ть, ю́, и́шь, *impf.* (*of a dog*) to whine, whimper (*also fig.*).

скулово́й, *adj.* (*anat.*) malar.

ску́льптор, а, *m.* sculptor.

скульпту́р|а, ы, *f.* sculpture.

скульпту́рный, *adj.* sculptural; (*fig.*) statuesque.

ску́мбри|я, и, *f.* mackerel; scomber.

скунс, а, *m.* skunk.

скуп|а́ть, а́ю, *impf. of* ~и́ть.

скупердя́|й, я, *m.* (*coll.*) miser, skinflint.

скуп|е́ц, ца́, *m.* miser, skinflint.

скуп|и́ть, лю́, ~ишь, *pf.* (*of* ~а́ть) to buy up; to corner.

скуп|и́ться, лю́сь, и́шься, *impf.* (*of* по~) (+*inf. or* на+*a.*) to stint, grudge, skimp; to be sparing (of); с. на де́ньги to be close--fisted; не с. на похвалы́ not to stint one's praise.

скуп́к|а, и, *f.* buying up; cornering.

скуп|но́й, *adj. of* ~ка.

ску́по, *adv.* sparingly.

скуп|о́й (~, ~а́, ~о), *adj.* **1.** stingy, miserly, niggardly; с. на похвалы́ chary of praise; с. на слова́ sparing of words. **2.** (*fig.*) inadequate; с. свет inadequate illumination.

ску́пост|ь, и, *f.* stinginess, miserliness, niggardliness.

скуп|о́чный, *adj. of* ~ка.

скуп́щик, а, *m.* buyer-up; с. кра́деного fence.

ску́тер, а, *m.* outboard-motor boat.

скуфе́йк|а, и, *f. dim. of* скуфья́.

скуфь|я́, и́, *f.* (*clerical*) skull-cap, calotte.

скуча́|ть, ю, *impf.* **1.** to be bored. **2.** (по+*d. or p.*) to miss, yearn (for).

ску́ченност|ь, и, *f.* density, congestion; с. населе́ния overcrowding.

ску́ченный, *adj.* dense, congested.

ску́чива|ть(ся), ю(сь), *impf. of* ску́чить(ся).

ску́ч|ить, у, ишь, *pf.* (*of* ~ивать) to crowd (together).

ску́ч|иться, усь, ишься, *pf.* (*of* ~иваться) to flock, cluster; to crowd together, huddle together.

ску́ч|ный (~ен, ~на́, ~но), *adj.* **1.** boring, depressing, tedious, dull. **2.** bored; с. взгляд look of boredom; *as pred.* мне, *etc.*, ~но I, *etc.*, am bored, depressed.

ску́ша|ть, ю, *pf. of* ку́шать.

слабе́|ть, ю, *impf.* (*of* о~) to weaken, grow weak(er); (*of wind, etc.*) to slacken, drop.

слабин|а́, ы́, *no pl.*, *f.* **1.** (*in a rope, etc.*) slack; вы́брать ~у́ (*naut.*) to haul in the slack. **2.** (*coll.*) weak spot, weak point.

слаби́тельн|ый, *adj.* (*med.*) laxative, purgative; *as noun* ~ое, ~ого, *n.* laxative, purgative.

слаб|и́ть, ит, *impf.* (*of* про~) **1.** (*impers.*) его́ ~ит he has diarrhoea. **2.** to purge, act as a laxative.

слаб|нуть, ну, нешь, *past* ~, ~ла, *impf.* (*of* о~) (*coll.*) **1.** to weaken, grow weak(er). **2.** to become slack.

слабово́ли|е, я, *n.* weak will.

слабово́л|ьный (~ен, ~ьна), *adj.* weak--willed.

слабогру́д|ый (~, ~а), *adj.* weak-chested.

слабоду́ши|е, я, *n.* faint-heartedness.

слабоду́ш|ный (~ен, ~на), *adj.* faint--hearted.

слабора́звитый, *adj.* (*econ.*) under-developed.

слабоси́ли|е, я, *n.* weakness, feebleness, debility.

слабоси́л|ьный (~ен, ~ьна), *adj.* **1.** weak, feeble. **2.** (*tech.*) low-powered.

сла́бост|ь, и, *f.* **1.** weakness, feebleness; debility. **2.** (к) weakness (for); foible; чу́вствовать с. (к) to have a weakness (for).

слабото́чный, *adj.* (*tech.*) low-current.

слабоу́ми|е, я, *n.* feeble-mindedness, imbecility.

слабоу́м|ный (~ен, ~на), *adj.* feeble--minded, imbecile.

слабохара́ктер|ный (~ен, ~на), *adj.* characterless, of weak character.

сла́б|ый (~, ~а́, ~о), *adj.* (*in var. senses*)

weak; feeble; slack, loose; (*fig.*) poor; ∼ое здоро́вье delicate health; ∼ое ме́сто, ∼ая сторона́ weak point, weak place; ∼ая наде́жда faint hope, slender hope; ∼ое оправда́ние lame excuse; с. пол the weaker sex; с. результа́т poor result.

сла́в|а, ы, *f.* **1.** glory; fame; во ∼у (+*g.*) to the glory (of); на ∼у (*coll.*) wonderfully well, excellently; (*as interj.*, +*d.*) hurrah (for)!, с. Бо́гу thank God, thank goodness. **2.** fame, name, repute, reputation; до́брая с. good name; дурна́я с. ill fame. **3.** (*coll.*) rumour.

сла́вильщик, а, *m.* (*obs.*) wait, carol-singer.

слави́ст, а, *m.* Slavist; Slavonic scholar.

слави́стик|а, и, *f.* Slavonic studies; Slavonic philology.

сла́в|ить, лю, ишь, *impf.* **1.** to celebrate, hymn, sing the praises (of); с. Христа́ to go carol-singing. **2.** (*coll.*) to give a bad name.

сла́в|иться, люсь, ишься, *impf.* (+*i.*) to be famous (for), be famed (for), be renowned (for); to have a reputation (for).

сла́вк|а, и, *f.* (*orn.*) warbler.

сла́в|ный (∼ен, ∼на́, ∼но), *adj.* **1.** glorious; famous, renowned. **2.** (*coll.*) nice, splendid; с. ма́лый good chap, nice chap.

славосло́ви|е, я, *n.* **1.** (*eccl.*) doxology; gloria. **2.** glorification, eulogy.

славосло́в|ить, лю, ишь, *impf.* to eulogize, extol, overpraise.

славяни́зм, а, *m.* (*ling.*) **1.** Slavism (*in a non-Slavonic language*). **2.** Slavonicism (*in Russian*).

славян|и́н, и́на, *pl.* ∼е, ∼, *m.* Slav.

славянове́д, а, *m.* Slavist; Slavonic scholar.

славянове́дени|е, я, *n.* Slavonic studies.

славянофи́л, а, *m.* Slavophil.

славянофи́л|ьский, *adj.* of ∼ *and* ∼ьство.

славянофи́льств|о, а, *n.* Slavophilism.

славя́нский, *adj.* Slavonic.

славя́нств|о, а, *n.* (*collect.*) the Slavonic peoples.

слага́ем|ое, ого, *n.* **1.** (*math.*) item. **2.** (*fig.*) component.

слага́|ть(ся), ю(сь), *impf. of* сложи́ть(ся).

слад, а (у), *m.*, now only in phrase с ним, *etc.*, ∼у нет (*coll.*) he, *etc.*, is unmanageable, is out of hand.

сла́ден|ький (∼ек, ∼ька), *adj.* (*coll.*) sweetish; (*fig.*) sugary, honeyed; ∼ькая улы́бка sugary smile.

сла́|дить, жу, дишь, *pf.* (*of* ∼живать) **1.** (*coll.*) to arrange. **2.** (с+*i.*) to cope (with), manage, handle; он про́сто не уме́л с. с подчинёнными he simply did not know how to handle his subordinates.

сла́д|кий (∼ок, ∼ка́, ∼ко), *adj.* **1.** sweet (*also fig.*); ∼кое мя́со (*cul.*) sweetbread; для меня́ э́то не ∼ко (*of food*) it is not sweet

enough for me; *as noun* ∼кое, ∼кого, *n.* sweet (course), dessert. **2.** (*fig.*, *pejor.*) sugary, sugared, honeyed.

сладкое́жк|а, и, *m. and f.* (*coll.*) (person with) sweet tooth.

сладкозву́ч|ный (∼ен, ∼на), *adj.* (*obs.*) mellifluous.

сладкоречи́в|ый (∼, ∼а), *adj.* smooth-spoken, smooth-tongued.

сла́дост|ный (∼ен, ∼на), *adj.* (*obs.*) sweet, delightful.

сладостра́сти|е, я, *n.* voluptuousness.

сладостра́стник, а, *m.* voluptuary.

сладостра́ст|ный (∼ен, ∼на), *adj.* voluptuous.

сла́дост|ь, и, *f.* **1.** sweetness. **2.** (*coll.*) sweetening. **3.** (*pl.*) sweets, sweetmeats.

сла́женност|ь, и, *f.* co-ordination, harmony, order.

сла́|женный, *p.p.p. of* ∼дить *and adj.* (well) co-ordinated, harmonious, orderly.

сла́жива|ть, ю, *impf. of* сла́дить.

сла́|зить, жу, зишь, *pf.* (*coll.*) to go; с. в подва́л за дрова́ми to go down to the cellar for logs.

сла́лом, а, *m.* (*sport*) slalom.

сла́н|ец, ца, *m.* (*min.*) shale, schist; slate; гли́нистый с. argillaceous schist; горю́чий с., нефтено́сный с. oil shale, bituminous shale.

сла́нцев|ый, *adj.* schistose, schistous; slate, slaty; shale; ∼ое ма́сло shale oil; с. пласт schist.

сластён|а, ы, *m. and f.* (*coll.*) (person with) sweet tooth.

сла|сти́ть, щу́, сти́шь, *impf.* (*of* по∼) to sweeten.

сластолюб|ец, ца, *m.* voluptuary.

сластолюби́в|ый (∼, ∼а), *adj.* voluptuous.

сластолюби|е, я, *n.* voluptuousness.

класт|ь, и, *pl.* ∼и, ∼е́й, *f.* **1.** (*pl.*) sweets, sweetmeats. **2.** (*fig.*) delight, pleasure; что за с. гуля́ть одному́? what fun is there in going out alone?

слать, шлю, шлёшь, *impf.* to send; с. приве́т to send greetings.

класта́в|ый (∼, ∼а), *adj.* (*lit. and fig.*) sugary, sickly-sweet.

сла́ще, *comp. of* сла́дкий.

сле́ва, *adv.* (от) on the left (of), to the left (of); с. напра́во from left to right.

слег|а́, и́, *pl.* ∼и, ∼, ∼а́м, *f.* beam.

слегка́, *adv.* lightly, gently; slightly, somewhat; с. суту́литься to stoop slightly; с. гла́дить to stroke gently.

след¹, а(у), *pl.* ∼ы́, ∼о́в, *m.* **1.** track; trail, footprint, footstep; верну́ться по свои́м ∼а́м to retrace one's steps; замести́ свои́ ∼ы́ to cover up one's tracks; идти́ по чьим-н. ~áм (*fig.*) to follow in someone's footsteps. **2.** (*fig.*) trace, sign, vestige; ~а нет егó there is no trace of it; ~ы óспы pockmarks. **3.** sole (*of the foot*).

след², не с. (*coll.*) = не ~ует.

сле|ди́ть¹, жу́, ди́шь, *impf.* (за+*i.*) **1.** to watch; to track; to shadow; с. глазáми за полётом мячá to follow (with one's eyes) the flight of a ball. **2.** (*fig.*) to follow; to keep up (with); с. за международными собы́тиями to keep up with international affairs. **3.** to look after; to keep an eye (on); с. за детьми́ to look after children; с. за поря́дком to keep order; с. за тем, чтóбы to see to it that.

сле|ди́ть², жу́, ди́шь, *impf.* (*of* на~) (на+*p.*) to mark; to leave traces (on), leave foot-marks, footprints (on).

сле́довани|е, я, *n.* movement, proceeding; пóезд дáльнего ~я long-distance train; во врéмя ~я пóезда while the train is moving; на всём пути́ ~я all along the line, through-out the entire journey; по пути́ ~я войск (*mil.*) along the line of march.

сле́довател|ь, я, *m.* investigator.

сле́довательно, *conj.* consequently, there-fore, hence.

след|овать¹, ую, *impf.* (*of* по~) **1.** (за+*i.*) to follow, go after; с. за кем-н. по пятáм to follow hard on someone's heels. **2.** (+*d.*) to follow; с. отцу́ to follow in one's father's footsteps. **3.** (+*d.*) to follow; to comply (with); с. прáвилам to conform to the rules; с. при́хоти to follow a whim. **4.** (*impf. only*) (до, в+*a.*) to be bound (for); э́тот пóезд ~ует в Варшáву this train is (bound) for Warsaw. **5.** (*impf. only*) to follow; to result; из э́того ~ует, что мы оши́блись it follows from this that we were mistaken.

след|овать², ует, *impf.* (*impers.*) **1.** (+*d. and inf.*) ought, should; вам ~ует обрати́ться к рéктору you should approach the rector; не ~ует забывáть it should not be for-gotten; кудá ~ует to the proper quarter; как и ~овáло ожидáть as was to be expected; как ~ует as it should be, properly, well and truly, good and proper. **2.** (+*d.* с+*g.*) to be owed, be owing; скóлько вам ~ует с меня́? how much do I owe you?; с вас ~ует дéсять рублéй you have ten roubles to pay.

сле́дом, *adv.* (за+*i.*) immediately (after, behind); идти́ с. за кем-н. to follow some-one close(ly).

следопы́т, а, *m.* pathfinder, tracker.

сле́дств|енный, *adj. of* ~ие; ~енная коми́с-сия committee of inquiry; с. материáл evidence; ~енные óрганы investigation agencies.

сле́дстви|е¹, я, *n.* consequence, result; причи́на и с. cause and effect.

сле́дстви|е², я, *n.* (*leg.*) investigation; судéб-ное с. inquest.

сле́дуем|ый, *adj.* (+*d.*) due (to); отдáть кáждому ~ое to give each his due.

след|ующий, *pres. part. act. of* ~овáть *and adj.* following, next; на с. день next day; на ~ующей недéле next week; постанóвлено ~ующее it has been resolved as follows.

слеж|áться, и́тся, *pf.* (*of* ~ивáться) to be-come caked; to deteriorate in storage.

слёжива|ться, ется, *impf. of* слежáться.

слéжк|а, и, *f.* shadowing; установи́ть ~у за кем-н. to have someone shadowed.

слез|á, ы́, *pl.* ~ы, ~, ~áм, *f.* tear; крокоди́-ловы ~ы crocodile tears; довести́ до ~ to reduce to tears; э́то до ~ оби́дно it is enough to make one weep.

слезá|ть, ю, *impf. of* слезть.

слез|и́ться, и́тся, *impf.* to water; её глазá ~и́лись her eyes were watering.

слези́в|ый (~, ~а), *adj.* **1.** given to crying. **2.** tearful, lachrymose.

слёзно, *adv.* (*coll.*) tearfully, with tears in one's eyes; (*fig.*) humbly, plaintively.

слёзн|ый, *adj.* **1.** (*anat.*) lachrymal; ~ая железá lachrymal gland; с. протóк lachry-mal duct, tear duct. **2.** (*fig.*, *coll.*) humble, plaintive; ~ая прóсьба humble petition.

слезоотделéни|е, я, *n.* tear-shedding; (*med.*) epiphora.

слезотечéни|е, я, *n.* = слезоотделéние.

слезоточи́в|ый (~, ~а), *adj.* **1.** ~ые глазá running eyes. **2.** lachrymatory; с. газ tear-gas.

слез|ть, у, ешь, *past* ~, ~ла, *pf.* (*of* ~áть) (с+*g.*) **1.** to come down (from), get down (from); to dismount (from). **2.** to alight (from), get off; с. с трамвáя to get off a tram. **3.** (*of paint or skin*) to come off, peel.

слеп|éнь, ня́, *m.* gadfly, horse-fly.

слеп|éц, цá, *m.* blind man.

слеп|и́ть¹, лю́, и́шь, *impf.* to blind; to dazzle.

слеп|и́ть², лю́, ~ишь, *pf. of* лепи́ть.

слеп|и́ть³, лю́, ~ишь, *pf.* (*of* ~ля́ть) **1.** to stick together. **2.** to make by sticking to-gether.

слеп|и́ться, ~ится, *pf.* (*of* ~ля́ться) to stick together.

слепля́|ть(ся), ю(сь), *impf. of* слепи́ть³(ся).

слéп|нуть, ну, нешь, *past* ~, ~ла *and* ~нул, ~нула, *impf.* to become blind, go blind.

слéпо, *adv.* **1.** (*fig.*) blindly; с. повиновáться to obey blindly. **2.** indistinctly.

слеп|óй (~, ~á, ~о), *adj.* **1.** blind (*also fig.*); с. на оди́н глаз blind in one eye; ~áя киш-кá blind gut, caecum; с. мéтод маши́нописи touch-typing; с. полёт blind flying; ~óе пятно́ (anat.) blind spot; as noun c., ~о́го, m. blind person; (pl., collect.) the blind. 2. indistinct.

слеп|о́к, ка, m. mould, copy.

слепорождённый, adj. blind from birth.

слепот|а́, ы́, f. blindness (also fig.).

слепы́ш, á, m. mole-rat.

слеса́рн|ый, adj. metal-work, metal worker's; ~ое де́ло metal work; ~ая (мастерска́я) metal workshop.

слеса́р|ня, ни, g. pl. ~ен, f. metal workshop.

слесар|ь, я, pl. ~и, ~ей and ~я́, ~е́й, m. metal worker; locksmith.

слёт, а, m. 1. flying together. 2. gathering, meeting; rally.

слётанност|ь, и, f. (of aircrews) co-ordination.

слета́|ть¹, ю, pf. 1. to fly (there and back). 2. (fig., coll.) to fly, dash, nip.

слет|а́ть², áю, impf. of ~е́ть.

слета́|ться¹, юсь, pf. to achieve co-ordination in flying.

слет|а́ться², áюсь, impf. of ~е́ться.

сле|те́ть, чу́, ти́шь, pf. (of ~та́ть²) (c+g). 1. to fly down (from). 2. (coll.) to fall down, fall off; с. с ло́шади to fall from a horse. 3. to fly away.

слет|е́ться, и́тся, pf. (of ~а́ться²) to fly together; (of birds) to congregate.

слечь, сля́гу, сля́жешь, past слёг, слегла́, pf. to take to one's bed.

слив, а, m. 1. pouring away; discharge. 2. sink, drain.

слив|а, ы, f. 1. plum. 2. plum-tree.

слива́|ть(ся), ю(сь), impf. of сли́ть(ся).

сли́в|ки, ок, no sing. cream (also fig.); сни-ма́ть с. (c+g.) to skim the cream (off); с. о́бщества the cream of society.

сливн|о́й, adj. 1. poured together. 2. over-flow, waste; ~áя труба́ overflow pipe. 3. collection (of milk and other fluid products); сдать молоко́ на с. пункт to deliver milk to the collection point.

сли́в|овый, adj. of ~a; ~овое варе́нье plum jam.

сли́вочник, а, m. cream-jug.

сли́вочн|ый, adj. cream; creamy; ~ое ма́сло butter; ~ое моро́женое ice-cream.

сливя́нк|а, и, f. plum brandy.

сли|за́ть, жу́, ~жешь, pf. (of ~зывать) 1. to lick off. 2. (fig., coll.) to copy; он э́то с меня́ слиза́л he got that idea from me.

сли́зист|ый (~, ~а), adj. mucous; mucila-ginous, slimy; ~ая оболо́чка (anat.) mucous membrane.

слизня́к, á, m. 1. slug. 2. (pejor., coll.) pathetic, worthless, helpless person.

сли́зыва|ть, ю, impf. of слиза́ть.

слиз|ь, и, f. mucus; mucilage, slime.

слимо́н|ить, ю, ишь, pf. of лимо́нить.

слиня́|ть, ет, pf. 1. to moult; to slough (off). 2. (coll.) to fade (of colours).

слип|а́ться, а́ется, impf. of ~нуться.

слип|нуться, нется, past ~ся, ~лась, pf. (of ~а́ться) to stick together.

сли́тно, adv. together.

сли́тн|ый, adj. joint, united, continuous; ~ое написа́ние слов omission of hyphen from words.

сли́т|ок, ка, m. ingot, bar; зо́лото в ~ках gold bullion.

слить, солью́, сольёшь, past слил, слила́, сли́ло, pf. (of слива́ть) 1. to pour out, pour off. 2. to pour together; (fig.) to fuse, merge, amalgamate; с. два конце́рна to amalgamate two concerns.

сли́ться, солью́сь, сольёшься, past сли́лся, слила́сь, pf. (of слива́ться) 1. to flow together. 2. (fig.) to blend, mingle; to merge, amalgamate.

слич|а́ть, а́ю, impf. of ~и́ть.

сличе́ни|е, я, n. collation, checking.

сличи́тельн|ый, adj. checking; ~ая ве́до-мость check-list.

слич|и́ть, у́, и́шь, pf. (of ~а́ть) (c+i.) to collate (with), check (with, against).

сли́шком, adv. too; too much; э́то с.! this is too much!

слия́ни|е, я, n. 1. confluence. 2. (fig.) blend-ing, merging, amalgamation; merger.

слобод|á, ы́, pl. слобо́ды, слобо́д, ~а́м, f. 1. (hist.) sloboda (settlement exempted from normal State obligations). 2. (obs.) suburb.

слобожа́н|ин, ина, pl. ~е, ~, m. (hist.) in-habitant of sloboda.

слова́к, а, m. Slovak.

слова́рный, adj. 1. lexical; с. соста́в языка́ vocabulary; с. фонд word stock. 2. lexico-graphic, dictionary.

слова́р|ь, я́, m. 1. dictionary; glossary, vocabulary (to particular text). 2. (collect.) vocabulary.

слова́цкий, adj. Slovak, Slovakian.

слова́чк|а, и, f. Slovak (woman.)

словéн|е, ~, no sing. (obs.) the Slavs.

словéн|ец, ца, m. Slovene.

словéнк|а, и, f. Slovene (woman).

словéнский, adj. Slovene, Slovenian.

слове́сник, а, m. 1. philologist; student of philology. 2. language and literature teacher.

слове́сност|ь, и, f. 1. literature. 2. (obs.) philology.

слове́сн|ый, adj. 1. verbal, oral; с. прика́з verbal order. 2. literary. 3. (obs.) philolo-gical; ~ые нау́ки philology.

словéч|ко, ка, pl. ~ки, ~ек, n., dim. of сло́во (coll.); замо́лвить с. за кого́-н. to put in a word for someone.

слóвник, а, *m.* glossary; word-list, selection of words (*for inclusion in a dictionary*).

слóвно, *conj.* **1.** as if. **2.** like, as.

слóв|о, а, *pl.* ~á, *n.* **1.** (*in var. senses*) word; другими ~áми in other words; одним ~ом in a word; с. в с. word for word; с. зá с. little by little; к ~у (пришлóсь, сказáть) by the way, by the by; на ~áх (*i*) by word of mouth, (*ii*) in word; вéрить нá с. комý-н. в чём-н. to take someone's word for something; человéк ~а a man of his word; игрá ~ play on words; ~ нет (*coll.*) it goes without saying; ~ нет, как тут дýрно пáхнет there is an indescribably nasty smell. **2.** speech, speaking; дар ~а talent for speaking; свобóда ~а freedom of speech. **3.** speech, address; заключительное с. concluding remarks; надгрóбное с. funeral oration; дать, предостáвить с. (+*d.*) to give the floor; to ask, call upon to speak; пéрвое с. принадлежит товáрищу X I call upon Comrade X to open the discussion; вам принадлежит решáющее с. (*fig.*) the final say rests with you. **4.** (*lit.*; *hist.*) lay, tale.

словоблýди|е, я, *n.* (mere) verbiage, phrase-mongering.

словоизвержéни|е, я, *n.* (*iron.*) spate of words.

словоизменéни|е, я, *n.* (*ling.*) inflection, accidence.

словолитный, *adj.* type-founding.

словолит|ня, ни, *g. pl.* ~ен, *f.* type foundry.

слóвом, *adv.* in a word, in short.

словообразовáни|е, я, *n.* (*ling.*) word-formation.

словообразовáтельный, *adj.* word-forming.

словоохóтливост|ь, и, *f.* talkativeness, loquacity.

словоохóтлив|ый (~, ~а), *adj.* talkative, loquacious.

словопрéни|е, я, *n.* (*obs.*) logomachy.

словопроизвóдный, *adj.* (*ling.*) productive.

словопроизвóдств|о, а, *n.* (*ling.*) derivation.

словосочетáни|е, я, *n.* combination of words; устóйчивое с. set phrase.

словотвóрчеств|о, а, *n.* creation of words.

словоупотреблéни|е, я, *n.* use of words, usage.

словц|ó, á, *n.* (*coll.*) word; для крáсного ~á for effect, in order to be witty.

слог[1], а, *pl.* ~и, ~óв, *m.* syllable.

слог[2], а, *m.* style.

слогов|óй, *adj.* **1.** syllabic; ~áя áзбука syllabary. **2.** syllable-forming.

слогообразýющий, *adj.* syllable-forming.

слоéни|е, я, *n.* stratification.

слоёный, *adj.* с. пирóг puff-pastry; с. детéктор (*phys.*) sandwich detector.

сложéни|е, я, *n.* **1.** adding; composition; (*math.*) addition; с. сил (*phys.*) composition of forces. **2.** build, constitution; крéпкого ~я of strong build, sturdily-built.

слóж|енный, *p.p.p. of* ~ить.

сложён|ный (~, ~á), *adj.* formed, built; хорошó с. well built, of fine physique.

сложи|вшийся, *past part. of* ~ться; вполнé с. fully developed, fully formed.

слож|ить[1], ý, ~ишь, *pf.* **1.** (*impf.* склáдывать) to put (together), lay (together); to pile, heap, stack; с. свои вéщи в сундýк to pack one's things in a trunk. **2.** (*impf.* склáдывать) to add (up). **3.** (*impf.* склáдывать) to fold (up); с. вдвóе to fold in two; с. рýки to give up the struggle; (*fig.*) idle. **4.** (*impf.* слагáть) to make up, compose; с. пéсню to compose a song.

слож|ить[2], ý, ~ишь, *pf.* **1.** (*impf.* склáдывать) to take off, put down, set down; с. груз to set down a load. **2.** (*impf.* слагáть) (с+*g.*; *fig.*) to lay down; to relieve (of); с. гóлову (*rhet.*) to lay down one's life; с. орýжие to lay down one's arms; с. с себя обязанности to resign; с. наказáние to remit a punishment.

слож|иться[1], ýсь, ~ишься, *pf.* (*of* склáдываться) (с+*i.*) to club together (with); to pool one's resources.

слож|иться[2], ýсь, ~ишься, *pf.* (*of* склáдываться) to form, turn out; to take shape; to arise; обстоятельства ~ились не осóбенно благоприятно circumstances did not turn out particularly favourably; у меня ~илось убеждéние the conviction has grown up in me.

сложноподчинённ|ый, *adj.* ~ое предложéние gram.) complex sentence.

сложносокращённ|ый, *adj.* compounded of abbreviations; ~ое слóво acronym.

сложносочинённ|ый, *adj.* ~ое предложéние (*gram.*) compound sentence.

слóжност|ь, и, *f.* complication; complexity; в óбщей ~и all in all, in sum.

сложноцвéтн|ые, ых, *sing.* ~ое, ~ого, *n.* (*bot.*) Compositae.

слóж|ный (~ен, ~нá, ~но), *adj.* **1.** compound; complex, multiple; ~ное предложéние (*gram.*) compound or complex sentence; ~ные процéнты compound interest; ~ное слóво compound (word); ~ное числó complex number; с. эфир (*phys.*) ester. **2.** complicated, complex, intricate.

слойст|ый (~, ~а), *adj.* stratified; lamellar; flaky, foliated; (*min.*) schistose, schistous; ~ые облакá strati.

сло|ить, ю, ишь, *impf.* to stratify; to make in layers.

сло|й, я, *pl.* ~й, *m.* layer; stratum (*also fig.*); coat(ing) (*of paint*), film; все ~й населéния all sections of the population.

слóйк|а, и, *f.* puff-pastry.

слом, а, *m.* pulling down, demolition, breaking up; пойтú на с. to be scrapped.

сломá|ть(ся), ю(сь), *pf. of* ломáть(ся).

слом|úть, лю, ~ишь, *pf.* to break, smash; (*fig.*) to overcome; ~я гóлову (*coll.*) like mad, at breakneck speed.

слом|úться, люсь, ~ишься, *pf.* to break.

слон, á, *m.* 1. elephant; дéлать из мýхи ~á to make mountains out of mole-hills; ~á не примéтить to miss the point. 2. (*chess*) bishop.

слон|ёнок, ёнка, *pl.* ~я́та, ~я́т, *m.* elephant calf.

слонúх|а, и, *f.* she-elephant, cow-elephant.

слонóвост|ь, и, *f.* (*med.*) elephantiasis.

слонóв|ый, *adj. of* слон; elephantine; ~ая болéзнь = ~ость; ~ая бумáга ivory paper; ~ая кость ivory.

слоня́|ться, юсь, *impf.* (*coll.*) to loiter about, mooch about.

слуг|á, й, *pl.* ~и, ~, *m.* 1. servant. 2. man, manservant.

служáк|а, и, *m.* (*coll.*) campaigner; old hand, veteran.

служáнк|а, и, *f.* maid, maidservant, house-maid.

слýжащ|ий, его, *m.* employee; white-collar worker, office worker.

слýжб|а, ы, *f.* 1. (*in var. senses*) service; work; employment; действúтельная с. (*mil.*) active service, service with the colours; идтú на ~у to go to work; быть на ~е у когó-н. to be in someone's employ, work for someone; по делáм ~ы on official business; сослужúть комý-н. ~у to do someone a good turn, stand someone in good stead; не в ~у, а в дрýжбу (*coll.*) as a favour. 2. (special) service; с. движéния (*railways*) traffic management; с. путú (*railways*) track maintenance; с. свя́зи (*mil.*) signals service; ~ы ты́ла (*mil.*) supply services. 3. *pl.* (*obs.*) outbuildings.

службúст, а, *m.* (*coll.*) red-tape-monger; martinet.

служéбн|ый, *adj.* 1. *adj. of* слýжба; office; official; work; ~ое врéмя office hours, working hours; ~ое дéло official business; с. наря́д duty roster; ~ая поéздка business trip; в ~ом поря́дке in the line of duty; ~ое правúтельство (*polit.*) caretaker government; с. простýпок dereliction of duty; с. путь official channels; с. стаж seniority; ~ая характерúстика service record. 2. auxiliary; secondary; ~ ое слóво (*gram.*) connective word.

служéни|е, я, *n.* service, serving.

служúв|ый, ого, *m.* (*coll., obs.*) soldier.

служúл|ый, *adj.* (*hist.*) service; ~ые лю́ди, ~ое сослóвие service class (*persons bound by obligations of service, esp. military service, to the Muscovite Russian state*).

служúтел|ь, я, *m.* 1. (*obs.*) servant, attendant. 2. votary, devotee; с. кýльта priest, minister.

служ|úть, ý, ~ишь, *impf.* (*of* по~) 1. (+*d.*) to serve, devote oneself (to). 2. (+*i.*) to serve (as), to work (as), be employed (as), be; с. в áрмии to serve in the Army; он ~ит дипломатúческим курьéром he is (employed as) a diplomatic courier; с. доказáтельством (+*g.*) to serve as evidence (of). 3. *impf. only* (+*i. or* для) to serve (for), do (for), be used (for); гостúная ~ит нам и спáльней our sitting-room serves also for a bedroom. 4. to be in use, do duty, serve; мой стáрый пластмáссовый плащ ещё ~ит my old plastic mac(k)intosh is still in use. 5. (*eccl.*) to celebrate; to conduct, officiate (at); с. обéдню to celebrate mass. 6. *impf. only* (*of a dog*) to (sit up and) beg.

слýжк|а, и, *m.* (*eccl.*) lay brother.

слукáв|ить, лю, ишь, *pf. of* лукáвить.

слуп|úть, лю, ~ишь, *pf. of* лупúть.

слух, а, *m.* 1. hearing, ear; абсолю́тный с. absolute pitch; игрáть по ~у, на с. to play by ear; онá вся обратúлась в с. she was all ears. 2. rumour; hearsay; есть с., что it is rumoured that; ни ~у ни дýху (о+*p.*) (*coll.*) not a word has been heard (of).

слухáч, á, *m.* monitor.

слуховóй, *adj.* acoustic, auditory, aural; с. аппарáт hearing aid; с. нерв (*anat.*) auditory nerve; ~óе окнó dormer(-window); с. рожóк, ~áя трýбка ear-trumpet.

слýча|й, я, *m.* 1. case; во вся́ком ~е in any case, anyhow, anyway; ни в кóем ~е in no circumstances; в лýчшем, хýдшем ~е at best, at worst; в протúвном ~е otherwise; в такóм ~е in that case; в ~е чегó (*coll.*) if anything crops up; на вся́кий с. to be on the safe side, just in case; на крáйний с. in case of special emergency; по ~ю (+*g.*) by reason (of), on account (of); купúть по ~ю (*coll.*) to buy secondhand. 2. event, incident, occurrence; несчáстный с. accident. 3. opportunity, occasion, chance; упустúть удóбный с. to miss an opportunity; при ~е when an opportunity offers; при ~е я емý сообщý I will inform him when I have the chance; стихú на с. occasional verse; от ~я к ~ю occasionally. 4. chance.

случáйно, *adv.* 1. by chance, by accident, accidentally; не с. он приéхал как раз вчерá it was no accident that he came yesterday; я с. подслýшал их разговóр

I happened to overhear their conversation. **2.** by any chance; вы, с., не ви́дели моего́ зо́нтика? have you by any chance seen my umbrella?

случа́йност|ь, и, *f.* chance; по счастли́вой ~и by a lucky chance, by sheer luck.

случа́|йный (~ен, ~йна), adj. 1. accidental, fortuitous; ~йная встре́ча chance meeting; ~йное уби́йство (*leg.*) homicide by misadventure. **2.** chance, casual, incidental; с. за́работок casual earnings.

случ|а́ть, а́ю, *impf. of* ~и́ть.

случ|а́ться, а́ется, *impf. of* ~и́ться.

случ|и́ть, у́, и́шь, *pf.* (*of* ~а́ть) (с+*i.*) (*of animals*) to couple (with), pair (with), mate (with).

случ|и́ться¹, и́тся, *pf.* (*of* ~а́ться) (*of animals*) to couple, pair, mate.

случ|и́ться², и́тся, *pf.* (*of* ~а́ться) **1.** to happen, come about, come to pass, befall; что бы ни ~и́лось whatever happens, come what may. **2.** (*impers.*; +*d. and inf.*) to happen; мне ~и́лось попа́сть в Москву́ I happened to land up in Moscow. **3.** (*coll.*) to turn up, show up; ~и́лось у меня́ как раз пять рубле́й I happened to have just five roubles on me.

случк|а, и, *f.* coupling, pairing, mating.

случно́й, adj. pairing, mating.

слу́шани|е, я, *n.* **1.** audition; hearing; с. ле́кции attendance at a lecture. **2.** (*leg.*) hearing.

слу́шател|ь, я, *m.* **1.** hearer, listener; (*pl.*; *collect.*) audience. **2.** student.

слу́ша|ть, ю, *impf.* (*of* по~) **1.** to listen (to), hear; с. ле́кцию to attend a lecture; ~й(те)! (*coll.*) listen!, look here!; ~ю! at your service!, very good!; (*on telephone*) hullo! **2.** to attend lectures (on), go to lectures (on). **3.** to listen (to), obey. **4.** (*leg.*) to hear.

слу́ша|ться, юсь, *impf.* (*of* по~) (+*g.*) **1.** to listen (to), obey; с. руля́ (*naut.*) to answer the helm; ~юсь! (*mil.*) yes, sir! (*indicating readiness to carry out order*). **2.** *pass. of* ~ть.

слуш|о́к, ка́, *m.* (*coll.*) rumour.

слы|ть, ву́, вёшь, *past* ~л, ~ла́, ~ло, *impf.* (*of* про~) (+*i.* or за+*d.*) to have a reputation (for), be said (to); to pass (for); он ~вёт безде́льником, за безде́льника he has a reputation for being an idler.

слыха́ть, *no pres.*, *impf.* **1.** to hear; что у вас с.? (*coll.*) what news have you of yourself?, tell us what you have been up to!; ничего́ не с. nothing can be heard. **2.** *as adv.* (*coll.*) apparently, it seems; ты, с., пи́шешь но́вый рома́н we hear you are writing a new novel.

слы́ш|ать, у, ишь, *impf.* (*of* у~) **1.** to hear; ~ишь, ~ите (*coll.*) do you hear? (*empha-*

sizing command or direction). **2.** (*impf. only*) to have the sense of hearing; не с. to be hard of hearing. **3.** to notice; to feel, sense. **4.** (*coll.*) to smell.

слы́ш|аться, ится, *impf.* (*of* по~) to be heard; to be audible.

слы́шимост|ь, и, *f.* audibility.

слы́шим|ый (~, ~а), adj. audible.

слы́шно¹, *adv.* audibly.

слы́ш|но², *as pred.*, *impers.* **1.** one can hear; бы́ло с., как она́ рыда́ла one could hear her sobbing; нам никого́ не́ было с. we could not hear anyone. **2.** (*coll.*); что с.? what news?, any news?; о них ничего́ не c. nothing has been heard of them. **3.** *as adv.* (*coll.*) it is said, they say, it is rumoured; она́, с., бере́менна they say she is pregnant.

слы́ш|ный (~ен, ~на́, ~но) adj. audible.

слю́бится, *see* стерпе́ться.

слюд|а́, ы́, *f.* mica.

слюдяно́й, adj. mica, micaceous.

слюн|а́, ы́, *f.* saliva.

слюн|и, е́й, *no sing.* (*coll.*) slobber, spittle; пусти́ть с. to slobber, drivel; распусти́ть с. (*coll.*) to dither, become a ditherer.

слюн|и́ть, ю́, и́шь, *impf.* **1.** (*pf.* по~) to wet with saliva. **2.** (*pf.* за~) to slobber over.

слюн|ки, ок, *no sing.*, *dim. of* ~и; от э́того с. теку́т it makes one's mouth water.

слюноотделе́ни|е, я, *n.* salivation.

слюнотече́ни|е, я, *n.* (*med.*) excessive salivation; (*fig.*, *pejor.*) sentimentalism.

слюнтя́|й, я, *m.* (*coll.*) ditherer.

слюня́в|ить, лю, ишь, *impf.* (*coll.*) to slobber over.

слюня́вый, adj. (*coll.*) dribbling, drivelling.

сля́котный, adj. slushy.

сля́кот|ь, и, *f.* slush.

сма́|зать, жу, жешь, *pf.* (*of* ~зывать) **1.** to oil, lubricate; to grease; с. йо́дом to paint with iodine. **2.** (*fig.*, *coll.*) to grease the palm (of), grease the wheels (of). **3.** to smudge; to rub off. **4.** (*fig.*, *coll.*) to slur (over). **5.** (*fig.*, *coll.*) to bash, dot.

сма́|заться, жусь, жешься, *pf.* (*of* ~зывать-ся) **1.** to grease oneself. **2.** (*of paint, etc.*) to become smudged; to come off.

сма́зк|а, и, *f.* **1.** oiling, lubrication; greasing. **2.** oil, lubricant; grease.

смазли́в|ый (~, ~а), adj. (*coll.*) pretty.

смазн|о́й, adj. ~ы́е сапоги́ blacked boots.

сма́зочн|ый, adj. *of* сма́зка; ~ая кана́вка (*tech.*) lubricating groove, oil groove; ~ая коро́бка oil can; ~ое ма́сло lubricating oil; с. материа́л, ~ое сре́дство lubricant.

сма́зчик, а, *m.* greaser.

сма́зывани|е, я, *n.* **1.** oiling, lubrication; greasing. **2.** (*fig.*) slurring over.

сма́зыва|ть(ся), ю(сь), *impf. of* сма́зать(ся).

смак, а, *m.* (*coll.*) relish, savour (*also fig.*); со ~ом with relish, with gusto.

смак|овáть, ýю, *impf.* (*coll.*) to savour; to eat, drink with relish; to relish (*also fig.*).

смáл|ец, ьца, *m.* lard.

смáльт|а, ы, *f.* smalt.

смáнива|ть, ю, *impf. of* сманить.

сман|ить, ю, ~ишь, *pf.* (*of* ~ивать) to entice, lure.

смарáгд, а, *m.* (*obs.*) emerald.

смарáгд|овый, *adj. of* ~.

смастер|ить, ю, ишь, *pf. of* мастерить.

смáтыва|ть, ю, *impf. of* смотáть.

смáтыва|ться, юсь, *impf. of* смотáться.

смáхива|ть¹, ю, *impf. of* смахнýть.

смáхива|ть², ю, *impf.* (на+*a.*; *coll.*) to look like, resemble.

смах|нýть, нý, нёшь, *pf.* (*of* ~ивать¹) to brush (away, off), flick (away, off), whisk (away, off), flap (away, off); с. пыль (с+*g.*) to dust.

смáчива|ть, ю, *impf. of* смочить.

смáч|ный (~ен, ~á, ~но), *adj.* (*coll.*) 1. savoury, tasty. 2. (*fig., pejor.*) fruity; ~ная рýгань colourful language.

смеж|áть, áю, *impf. of* ~ить.

смеж|ить, ý, ишь, *pf.* (*of* ~áть) (*obs. or poet.*); с. глазá to close one's eyes.

смéжник, а, *m.* factory producing parts for use by another.

смéжность|ь, и, *f.* contiguity.

смéж|ный (~ен, ~на), *adj.* adjacent, contiguous, adjoining, neighbouring; ~ные понятия closely-related concepts; с. ýгол (*math.*) adjacent angle.

смекáлист|ый (~, ~а), *adj.* (*coll.*) sharp, keen-witted.

смекáлк|а, и, *f.* (*coll.*) native wit, mother wit; nous; sharpness.

смек|áть, áю, *impf.* (*of* ~нýть) (*coll.*) to see the point (of), grasp; ~аешь, в чём дéло? do you get it?, do you see the point?

смек|нýть, нý, нёшь, *pf. of* ~áть.

смеле|ть, ю, *impf.* (*of* о~) to grow bold(er).

смéло, *adv.* 1. boldly; я могý с. сказáть I can safely say; с.! don't be afraid!, have a try! 2. easily, with ease; в этом зáле с. поместятся пятьсóт человéк this hall will hold five hundred with ease.

смéлост|ь, и, *f.* boldness, audacity, courage; взять на себя с. (+*inf.*) to take the liberty (of), make bold (to).

смéл|ый (~, ~á, ~о), *adj.* bold, audacious, courageous, daring.

смельчáк, á, *m.* (*coll.*) bold spirit; dare-devil.

смéн|а, ы, *f.* 1. changing, change; replacement; с. карáула changing of the guard; идти на ~у (+*d.*) to come to take the place (of), come to relieve. 2. (*collect.*) replacements; successors; (*mil.*) relief; готóвить себé ~у to prepare successors (*to take one's place, to take over*). 3. shift; ýтренняя, дневнáя, вечéрняя с. morning, day, night shift; рабóтать в три ~ы to work in three shifts, work a three-shift system. 4. change (*of linen, etc.*).

смен|ить, ю, ~ишь, *pf.* (*of* ~ять¹) 1. to change; to replace; (*mil.*) to relieve; с. бельё to change linen; с. завéдующего to replace the manager; с. карáул to relieve the guard; с. шины to change tyres; с. гнев на милость to temper justice with mercy. 2. to replace, relieve, succeed (someone).

смен|иться, юсь, ~ишься, *pf.* (*of* ~яться) 1. to hand over; (*mil.*) to be relieved; с. с дежýрства to go off duty. 2. (+*i.*) to give place (to); дневнóй зной ~ился прохлáдой вéчера the day's heat gave way to the coolness of evening.

смéнност|ь, и, *f.* shift system, shiftwork.

смéнн|ый, *adj.* 1. shift; с. мáстер shift foreman; ~ая рабóта shift work. 2. (*tech.*) changeable; ~ое колесó spare wheel.

смéнщик, а, *m.* relief (worker); *pl.* (*collect.*) new shift.

сменя́|емый, *pres. part. pass. of* ~ть¹ *and adj.* removable, interchangeable.

смен|ять¹, яю, *impf. of* ~ить.

смен|ять², яю, *pf.* (на+*a.*; *coll.*) to exchange (for).

смен|я́ться, яюсь, *impf. of* смениться.

смерд, а, *m.* (*hist.*) peasant farmer.

смер|дéть, жý, дишь, *impf.* (*obs.*) to stink.

смерз|áться, áется, *impf. of* ~нýться.

смёрз|нуться, нется, *past* ~ся, ~лась, *pf.* (*of* ~áться) to freeze together.

смéр|ить, ю, ишь, *pf.* (*coll.*) to measure; с. взгля́дом to look (someone) up and down, measure at a glance.

смерк|áться, áется, *impf.* (*of* ~нýться) to get dark; ~áлось it was getting dark, twilight was falling.

смéрк|нуться, нется, *pf. of* ~áться.

смертéльно, *adv.* 1. mortally; с. рáненный mortally wounded. 2. (*coll.*) extremely, terribly; с. устáть to be dead tired, be dead-beat.

смертéл|ьный (~ен, ~ьна), *adj.* 1. mortal, deadly enemy; с. удáр mortal blow. 2. (*coll.*) extreme, terrible.

смéртник, а, *m.* prisoner sentenced to death.

смéртност|ь, и, *f.* mortality, death-rate.

смéрт|ный (~ен, ~на), *adj.* 1. mortal; *as noun* с., ~ного, *m.* mortal; простóй с. ordinary mortal. 2. death; с. бой fight to the death; с. грех (*eccl.*) mortal sin; семь ~ных грехóв (*lit.*) the Seven Deadly Sins; ~ная казнь capital punishment, death penalty; ∼ное ло́же deathbed; на ∼ном одре́ on one's deathbed; с. пригово́р death sentence; (*fig.*) death-warrant; с. час last hour(s). **3.** (*fig.*) deadly, extreme.

смертоно́с|ный (∼ен, ∼на), *adj.* death--dealing, mortal, fatal, lethal; с. уда́р mortal blow.

смертоуби́йств|о, а, *n.* (*obs.*) murder.

смерт|ь, и, *pl.* ∼и, ∼е́й, *f.* **1.** death, decease; ве́рная с. certain death; умере́ть голо́дной ∼ью to starve to death; умере́ть свое́й ∼ью to die a natural death; до ∼и (*fig.*, *coll.*) to death; я уста́л до сме́рти I'm dead tired; боро́ться не на жизнь, а на с. to fight to the death; разби́ть на́ с. (*coll.*) to smash to bits; свиде́тельство о ∼и death certificate; быть при ∼и to be dying; двум ∼я́м не быва́ть, одно́й не минова́ть you only die once. **2.** с. как *as adv.* (*coll.*) awfully, terribly; ему́, *etc.*, с. как хо́чется (+*inf.*) he, *etc.*, is dying (for); мне с. как хо́чется купа́ться I'm dying for a bathe.

смерч, а, *m.* **1.** waterspout. **2.** sand-storm, tornado.

смеси́тельный, *adj.* (*tech.*) mixing.

сме|си́ть, шу́, ∼си́шь, *pf. of* меси́ть.

сме|сти́, ту́, тёшь, *past* ∼л, ∼ла́, *pf.* (*of* ∼та́ть²) **1.** to sweep off, sweep away; с. кро́шки со стола́ to sweep crumbs off the table; с. с лица́ земли́ to wipe off the face of the earth. **2.** to sweep into, together.

сме|сти́ть, щу́, сти́шь, (*of* ∼ща́ть) **1.** to displace, remove, move. **2.** (*fig.*) to remove, dismiss (*from one's post*).

сме|сти́ться, щу́сь, сти́шься, *pf.* (*of* ∼ща́ть-ся) to change position, become displaced.

смес|ь, и, *f.* (*in var. senses*) mixture; blend, miscellany, medley.

смёт|а, ы, *f.* (*fin.*) estimate.

смета́н|а, ы, *f.* soured (cultured) cream.

смет|а́ть¹, а́ю, *pf.* (*of* мета́ть² *and* ∼ывать) to tack (together).

смета́|ть², ю, *pf. of* смести́.

смётк|а, и, *f.* (*coll.*) quickness (in the up-take); gumption.

смётлив|ый (∼, ∼a), *adj.* quick (in the uptake).

смёт|ный, *adj. of* ∼а; ∼ные ассигно́вки budget allowances.

смётыва|ть, ю, *impf. of* смета́ть¹.

сме|ть, ю, *impf.* (*of* по∼) to dare; to make bold; не ∼й(те)! don't you dare!

смех, а (у), *m.* laughter; laugh; разрази́ть-ся ∼ом to burst out laughing; меня́ раз-бира́л с. I couldn't help laughing; без ∼у joking apart, in earnest; в с., на́ с., ∼а ра́ди for a joke, for fun, in jest, jokingly; нам не до ∼у we are in no mood for laughter; с. да и то́лько (*coll.*) one can't but laugh.

смехот|а́, ы́, *f.* (*coll.*) matter for laughter; э́то пря́мо с.! this is simply ludicrous!

смехотво́р|ный (∼ен, ∼на), *adj.* laughable, ludicrous, ridiculous.

смеш|анный, *p.p.p. of* ∼а́ть *and adj.* mixed; combined; ∼анное акционе́рное о́бщест-во joint-stock company; ∼анная опера́ция (*mil.*) combined operation; телефо́н ∼ан-ного по́льзования party-line; ∼анная поро́да crossbreed; ∼анное число́ (*math.*) mixed number.

смеш|а́ть, а́ю, *pf.* (*of* меша́ть² *and* ∼ивать) **1.** (с+*i.*) to mix (with), blend (with). **2.** to lump together. **3.** to confuse, mix up.

смеш|а́ться, а́юсь, *pf.* (*of* ∼ивáться) **1.** to mix; to (inter)blend, blend in; to mingle; с. с толпо́й to mingle in the crowd. **2.** to become confused, get mixed up.

смеше́ни|е, я, *n.* **1.** mixture, blending, merging. **2.** confusion, mixing up; с. поня́тий confusion of ideas.

сме́шива|ть(ся), ю(сь), *impf. of* смеша́ть-(ся).

смеш|и́ть, у́, и́шь, *impf.* to make laugh.

смешли́вост|ь, и, *f.* risibility.

смешли́в|ый (∼, ∼a), *adj.* risible; easily amused.

смеш|но́й (∼о́н, ∼на́), *adj.* **1.** funny, droll; *as pred.* ∼но́ it is funny, it makes one laugh; вам ∼но́? do you find it funny? **2.** absurd, ridiculous, ludicrous; э́то — ∼но́е пред-ложе́ние this is an absurd suggestion; до ∼но́го to the point of absurdity.

смеш|о́к, ка́, *m.* (*coll.*) chuckle; giggle.

смеща́|ть(ся), ю(сь), *impf. of* смести́ть(ся).

смеще́ни|е, я, *n.* displacement, removal. **2.** (*geol.*) slip, heave, upheaval, dislocation. **3.** (*radio*) bias.

сме|я́ться, ю́сь, ёшься, *impf.* **1.** to laugh; с. шу́тке to laugh at a joke. **2.** (над) to laugh (at), mock (at), make fun (of). **3.** to joke, say in jest.

сми́л|оваться, уюсь, *pf.* to have mercy, take pity.

смире́ни|е, я, *n.* humbleness, humility, meekness.

смире́нник, а, *m.* humble person, meek person.

смире́нност|ь, и, *f.* humility.

смире́н|ный (∼, ∼на), *adj.* humble, meek.

смири́тельн|ый, *adj.* ∼ая руба́шка strait--jacket.

смир|и́ть, ю́, и́шь, *pf.* (*of* ∼я́ть) to restrain, subdue.

смир|и́ться, ю́сь, и́шься, *pf.* (*of* ∼я́ться) to submit; to resign oneself.

сми́рно, *adv.* quietly; с.! (*mil. word of com-mand*) attention!

сми́р|ный (∼ен, ∼на́, ∼но), *adj.* quiet; sub-missive.

смир|я́ть(ся), я́ю(сь), *impf. of* ~и́ть(ся).

смо́кв|а, ы, *f.* fig.

смо́кинг, а, *m.* dinner-jacket.

смоко́вниц|а, ы, *f.* fig-tree.

смол|а́, ы́, *pl.* ~ы, *f.* resin; pitch, tar; rosin; иску́сственная с. synthetic resin.

смолёный, *adj.* resined; tarred, pitched.

смоли́ст|ый (~, ~а), *adj.* resinous.

смол|и́ть, ю́, и́шь, *impf. (of* вы́~ *and* о~) to resin; to tar, pitch.

смолк|а́ть, а́ю, *impf. of* ~нуть.

смо́лк|нуть, ну, нешь, *past* ~, ~ла, *pf. (of* ~а́ть) to fall silent; *(of sound)* to cease.

смо́лоду, *adv.* from one's youth; in one's youth.

смолоку́р, а, *m.* tar-extractor.

смолокуре́ни|е, я, *n.* extraction of tar.

смолоку́р|ня, ни, *g. pl.* ~ен, *f.* tar-works.

смоло|ти́ть, чу́, ~тишь, *pf. of* молоти́ть.

смоло́ть, смелю́, сме́лешь, *pf. of* моло́ть.

смолч|а́ть, у́, и́шь, *pf.* to hold one's tongue.

смоль, *only in phrase* чёрный как с. jet-black.

смол|яно́й, *adj. of* ~а́; ~яна́я бо́чка tar barrel; с. ка́мень pitchstone; ~яна́я кислота́ resin acid; с. клей resin sizing; ~яно́е ма́сло resin oil; с. соста́в resinous compound.

смонти́р|овать, ую, *pf. of* монти́ровать.

сморгн|у́ть, у́, ёшь, *pf. (coll.)* гла́зом не с. not to turn a hair, not to bat an eyelid.

сморка́|ть, ю, *impf. (of* вы́~) с. нос to blow one's nose.

сморка́|ться, юсь, *impf. (of* вы́~) to blow one's nose.

сморо́дин|а, ы, *no pl., f.* 1. currant; currant bush. 2. *(collect.)* currants; кра́сная, чёрная с. red currants, black currants.

сморо́дин|ный, *adj. of* ~а.

сморч|о́к, ка́, *m.* 1. morel *(mushroom)*. 2. *(fig., coll.; of person)* shrimp.

смо́рщ|енный, *p.p.p. of* ~ить *and adj.* wrinkled.

смо́рщ|ить(ся), у(сь), ишь(ся), *pf. of* мо́рщить(ся).

смота́|ть, ю, *pf. (of* сма́тывать) to wind, reel; *(coll.)* с. у́дочки to take to one's heels, make off, clear out.

смота́|ться, юсь, *pf. (of* сма́тываться) *(coll.)* 1. to dash (there and back). 2. to take to one's heels, make off.

смотр, а, *m.* 1. (на ~у́, *pl.* ~ы́) review, inspection; произвести́ с. (+*d.*) to review, inspect. 2. (на ~е, *pl.* ~ы) public showing; с. худо́жественной самоде́ятельности amateur arts' festival.

смотр|е́ть, ю́, *impf. (of* по~) 1. (на+ *a.*, в+*a.*) to look (at); с. в окно́ to look out of the window; с. в глаза́, в лицо́ (+*d.*) to look in the face; с. в о́ба *(coll.)* to keep one's eyes open, be on one's guard; с. сквозь па́льцы (на+*a.*; *coll.*) to make light (of), wink (at). 2. to see; to watch; to look through; с. чемпиона́т по те́ннису to see a tennis championship; с. телеви́дение to watch television. 3. to examine; to review, inspect; с. больно́го to inspect a patient. 4. (за+*i.*) to look (after); to be in charge (of), supervise; с. за поря́дком to keep order. 5. (на+*a.*; *coll.*) to follow the example (of). 6. *impf. only* (в+*a.*, на+*a.*) to look (on to, over); о́кна в мое́й ко́мнате ~ят в сад my windows look on to the garden. 7. *impf. only* (+*i.*; *coll.*) to look (like); он ~ит простако́м he looks a simple fellow. 8. ~й(те)! mind!, take care!; ~йте не опозда́йте! mind you are not late!; ~йте, чтобы на́шим гостя́м бы́ло удо́бно see that our guests are comfortable. 9. ~я́ (где, как, *etc.*) it depends (where, how, *etc.*); ~я́ (по+*d.*) depending (on), in accordance (with).

смотр|е́ться, ю́сь, ~ишься, *impf. (of* по~) 1. to look at oneself; с. в зе́ркало to look at oneself in the looking-glass. 2. *pass. of* ~е́ть.

смотри́н|ы, ~, *no sing. (hist.)* smotriny *(Russian folk-rite of inspection of prospective bride).*

смотри́тел|ь, я, *m.* supervisor; *(in museum, etc.)* keeper, custodian; *(obs.)* станцио́нный с. postmaster; тюре́мный с. warder.

смотров|о́й, *adj.* 1. *(mil.)* review. 2. ~о́е окно́ inspection window; ~о́е отве́рстие sighting aperture *(of gun sight)*; ~а́я щель vision slit *(in tank).*

смоч|и́ть, у́, ~ишь, *pf. (of* сма́чивать) to damp, wet, moisten.

смо|чь, гу́, ~жешь, *past* ~г, ~гла́, *pf. of* мочь.[1]

смоше́нинча|ть, ю, *pf. of* моше́нничать.

смрад, а, *m.* stink, stench.

смра́д|ный (~ен, ~на), *adj.* stinking.

смугле́|ть, ю, *impf.* to become dark-complexioned.

смуглоли́ц|ый (~, ~а), *adj.* dark-complexioned.

сму́гл|ый (~, ~а́, ~о), *adj.* dark-complexioned.

смугля́нк|а, и, *f.* dark-complexioned woman, girl.

сму́т|а, ы, *f. (obs.)* disturbance, sedition; се́ять ~у to sow discord.

сму|ти́ть, щу́, ти́шь, *pf. (of* ~ща́ть) 1. to embarrass, confuse. 2. to disturb, trouble; с. чей-н. поко́й to disturb someone's peace and quiet.

сму|ти́ться, щу́сь, ти́шься, *pf. (of* ~ща́ться) to be embarrassed, confused; to be confused.

сму́т|ный (~ен, ~на́, ~но), *adj.* 1. vague; confused; dim; ~ные воспомина́ния dim recollections. 2. disturbed, troubled; ~ное вре́мя *(hist.)* Time of Troubles *(1605–13).*

смутья́н, а, *m.* (*coll.*) trouble-maker.

сму́шк|а, и, *f.* astrakhan.

сму́шковый, *adj.* astrakhan.

смуща́|ть(ся), ю(сь), *impf. of* смути́ть(ся).

смуще́ни|е, я, *n.* embarrassment, confusion.

сму|щённый, *p.p.p. of* ~ти́ть *and adj.* embarrassed, confused.

смыв, а, *m.* (*geol.*) wash-out.

смыва́|ть(ся), ю(сь), *impf. of* смыть(ся).

смыка́|ть(ся), ю(сь), *impf. of* сомкну́ть(ся).

смысл, а, *m.* 1. sense, meaning; purport; прямо́й, перено́сный с. literal, metaphorical sense; в изве́стном ~e in a sense; в по́лном ~e сло́ва in the true sense of the word; в ~e (+g.) as regards. 2. sense, point; име́ть с. to make sense; нет никако́го ~a (+*inf.*) there is no sense (in), there is no point (in). 3. (good) sense; здра́вый с. common sense.

смы́сл|ить, ю, ишь, *impf.* (в+*p.*; *coll.*) to understand.

смыслов|о́й, *adj. of* смысл; ~ы́е отте́нки shades of meaning.

смыть, смо́ю, смо́ешь, *pf.* (*of* смыва́ть) 1. to wash off; (*fig.*) to clear, wipe away; (*mil.*) to wipe out. 2. to wash away; с. волно́й с су́дна to wash overboard.

смы́ться, смо́юсь, смо́ешься, *pf.* (*of* смыва́ться) 1. to wash off, come off. 2. (*fig.*, *coll.*) to slip away.

смы́чк|а, и, *f.* union; linking.

смыч|ко́вый, *adj. of* ~о́к.

смы́чный, *adj.* (*ling.*) occlusive; stop.

смыч|о́к, ка́, *m.* (*mus.*) bow.

смышлён|ый (~,~а), *adj.*(*coll.*) clever, bright.

смягча́|ть(ся), а́ю(сь), *impf. of* ~и́ть(ся).

смягча́|ющий 1. *pres. part. act. of* ~ть; ~ющие вину́ обстоя́тельства extenuating circumstances. 2. *adj.* (*med.*) emollient.

смягче́ни|е, я, *n.* 1. softening. 2. mollification; mitigation; extenuation. 3. (*ling.*) palatalization.

смягч|и́ть, у́, и́шь, *pf.* (*of* ~а́ть) 1. (*impf. also* мягчи́ть) to soften. 2. to mollify; to ease, alleviate; to assuage; с. боль to alleviate pain; с. гнев to assuage anger; с. наказа́ние to mitigate a punishment; с. напряже́ние to ease tension. 3. (*ling.*) to palatalize.

смягч|и́ться, у́сь, и́шься, *pf.* (*of* ~а́ться) 1. to soften, become soft, grow softer. 2. to be mollified; to relent, relax; to grow mild; to ease (off). 3. *pass. of* ~и́ть.

смяте́ни|е, я, *n.* confusion, disarray; commotion.

смяте́н|ный (~, ~на), *adj.* (*obs.*) troubled, perturbed.

смять, сомну́, сомнёшь, *pf.* (*of* мять) 1. to crumple; to rumple; с. пла́тье to crush a dress. 2. (*mil.*) to crush.

смя́ться, сомнётся, *pf.* (*of* мя́ться[1]) to get creased; to get crumpled.

снаб|ди́ть, жу́, ди́шь, *pf.* (*of* ~жа́ть) (+*i.*) to supply (with), furnish (with), provide (with).

снабжа́|ть, ю, *impf. of* снабди́ть.

снабже́н|ец, ца, *m.* supplier, provider.

снабже́ни|е, я, *n.* supply, supplying, provision.

снабже́н|ческий, *adj. of* ~ие.

сна́доб|ье, ья, *g. pl.* ~ий, *n.* (*coll.*) drug.

сна́йпер, а, *m.* sniper; sharp-shooter.

снару́жи, *adv.* on the outside; from (the) outside.

снаря́д, а, *m.* 1. projectile, missile; shell; управля́емый с. guided missile. 2. contrivance, machine, gadget; гимнасти́ческие ~ы gymnastic apparatus. 3. (*collect.*) tackle, gear; рыболо́вный с. fishing tackle.

снаря|ди́ть, жу́, ди́шь, *pf.* (*of* ~жа́ть) to equip, fit out.

снаря|ди́ться, жу́сь, ди́шься, *pf.* (*of* ~жа́ться) to equip oneself, get ready.

снаря́дн|ый, *adj.* 1. shell, projectile; ammunition; с. по́греб shell-room, (ammunition) magazine. 2. ~ая гимна́стика (*sport*) apparatus work.

снаряжа́|ть(ся), ю(сь), *impf. of* снаряди́ть(ся).

снаряже́ни|е, я, *n.* equipment, outfit; ко́нское с. harness.

снаст|ь, и, *pl.* ~и, ~е́й, *f.* 1. (*collect.*) tackle, gear. 2. (*usu. pl.*) rigging.

снача́ла, *adv.* 1. at first, at the beginning. 2. all over again.

сна́шива|ть, ю, *impf. of* сноси́ть.

снег, а, *pl.* ~á, *m.* snow; как с. на́ голову like a bolt from the blue.

снеги́р|ь, я́, *m.* bullfinch.

снегов|о́й, *adj.* snow; ~а́я вода́ snow-water; ~а́я ли́ния snow-line.

снегозадержа́ни|е, я, *n.* (*agric.*) retention of snow on fields (*as protection against drought and frost*).

снегозащи́тн|ый, *adj.* ~ое огражде́ние, с. щит snow-fence.

снегоочисти́тел|ь, я, *m.* snow-plough.

снегопа́д, а, *m.* snow-fall.

снегосту́пы, ов, *m.* (*sport*) snow-shoes.

снегота́ялк|а, и, *f.* snow-melter.

снегоубо́рочн|ый, *adj.* snow-removal; ~ая маши́на snow-plough.

снегохо́д, а, *m.* snow-tractor (*tracked vehicle used by Antarctic expeditions*).

Снегу́рочк|а, и, *f.* (*folklore*) Snow-Maiden.

снеда́|ть, ю, *impf.* to consume, gnaw; ~емый за́вистью consumed with envy.

снед|ь, и, *f.* (*obs. or dial.*) food, eatables.

снежи́нк|а, и, *f.* snow-flake.

снѐжн|ый, *adj.* snow; snowy; ~ая ба́ба snow man; с. зано́с, с. сугро́б snow-drift; ~ая зима́ snowy winter; снѐжная белизна́ snow-whiteness.

снеж|о́к, ка́, *m.* 1. light snow. 2. snowball; игра́ть в ~ки́ to play snowballs, have a snowball fight.

снес|ти́¹, у́, ёшь, *past* ~, ~ла́, *pf.* (*of* сноси́ть) 1. to take; с. письмо́ на по́чту to take a letter to the post. 2. to fetch down, bring down; с. сунду́к с чердака́ to fetch down a trunk from the attic. 3. (*usu. impers.*) to carry away; to blow off, take off; урага́ном ~ло́ кры́шу a hurricane took the roof off. 4. to demolish, take down, pull down. 5. to cut off, chop off; с. го́лову кому́-н. to chop someone's head off. 6. (*cards*) to throw away.

снес|ти́², у́, ёшь, *pf.* (*of* сноси́ть) to bring together, pile up.

снес|ти́³, у́, ёшь, *pf.* (*of* сноси́ть) to bear, endure, suffer, stand, put up (with).

снес|ти́⁴, у́, ёшь, *pf.* (*of* нести́²) to lay (*eggs*).

снес|ти́сь¹, у́сь, ёшься, *past* ~ся, ~ла́сь, *pf.* (*of* сноси́ться) (с+*i.*) to communicate (with).

снес|ти́сь², ётся, *pf. of* нести́сь².

снет|о́к, ка́, *m.* (*fish*) smelt, sparling.

снижа́|ть(ся), ю(сь), *impf. of* сни́зить(ся).

снижѐни|е| я, *n.* 1. lowering, reduction; с. зарпла́ты wage cut. 2. (*aeron.*) loss of height; идти́ на с. to reduce height.

сни́|зить, жу, зишь, *pf.* (*of* ~жа́ть) 1. to bring down, lower. 2. (*fig.*) to bring down, lower, reduce; с. себесто́имость to cut production costs; с. стиль (*lit.*) to deflate one's style; с. тон to sing small; с. по до́лжности to reduce, demote.

сни́|зиться, жусь, зишься, *pf.* (*of* ~жа́ться) 1. to descend, come down; (*of an aircraft*) to lose height. 2. (*fig.*) to fall, sink, come down; це́ны ~зились prices have come down.

снизо|йти́, йду́, йдёшь, *past* ~шёл, ~шла́, *pf.* (*of* снисходи́ть) (к) to condescend (to); с. к чьей-н. про́сьбе to deign to grant someone's request.

сни́зу, *adv.* from below (*polit.*; *also fig.*); from the bottom; с. вверх upwards; с. до́верху from top to bottom.

сни́к|нуть, ну, нешь, *pf. of* ни́кнуть.

снима́|ть(ся), ю(сь), *impf. of* снять(ся).

сни́м|ок, ка, *m.* photograph, photo, print.

сни́|скать, щу́, ~щешь, *pf.* (*of* сни́скивать) (*obs.*) to gain, get, win; с. чьё-н. расположе́ние to win someone's approval.

сни́скива|ть, ю, *impf. of* сниска́ть.

снисходи́тельност|ь, и, *f.* 1. condescension. 2. indulgence, tolerance, leniency.

снисходи́тел|ьный (~ен, ~ьна), *adj.* 1.

condescending. 2. indulgent, tolerant, lenient.

снисхо|ди́ть, жу́, ~дишь, *impf. of* снизойти́.

снисхождѐни|е, я, *n.* indulgence, leniency; име́ть с. (к) to be lenient (towards); заслу́живает ~я (*leg. formula*) recommended for mercy.

сни́|ться, снюсь, сни́шься, *impf.* (*of* при~) (+*d.*) to dream; ей ~лось, что she dreamed that; мне ~лся лев I dreamed about a lion.

сноб, а, *m.* snob.

сноби́зм, а, *m.* snobbery.

сно́ва, *adv.* again, anew, afresh.

снова́льный, *adj.* (*text.*) warping.

снова́льщик, а, *m.* (*text.*) warper.

снова́|ть¹, сную́, снуёшь, *impf.* to scurry about, dash about.

снова́|ть², сную́, снуёшь, *impf.* (*text.*) to warp.

сновидѐни|е, я, *n.* dream.

сногсшиба́тел|ьный (~ен, ~ьна), *adj.* (*coll., joc.*) stunning.

сноп, а́, *m.* sheaf; с. луче́й shaft of light; с. траекто́рий (*mil.*) cone of fire.

сноповяза́лк|а, и, *f.* (*agric.*) binder.

сноповяза́льн|ый, *adj.* ~ая маши́на = сноповяза́лка.

снорови́ст|ый (~, ~а), *adj.* (*coll.*) quick, smart, clever.

сноро́вк|а, и, *f.* skill, knack.

снос¹, а, *m.* 1. demolition, pulling down; дом назна́чен на с. the house is to be pulled down. 2. drift; у́гол ~а (*aeron.*) angle of drift.

снос², а (у), *m.* wear; тако́й мате́рии ~у нет this material won't wear out; не знать ~у to wear well, be very hard-wearing.

снос³: быть на ~ях (*coll.*; *of a pregnant woman*) to be near her time.

сно|си́ть¹, шу́, ~сишь, *pf.* (*of* сна́шивать) to wear out.

сно|си́ть², шу́, ~сишь, *pf.* (*coll.*) to take (*and bring back*); ему́ не с. головы́ it will cost him dear, he will pay for it.

сно|си́ть³, шу́, ~сишь, *impf. of* снести́¹, ², ³.

сно|си́ться, шу́сь, ~сишься, *impf. of* снести́сь¹.

сно́ск|а, и, *f.* footnote.

сно́сно, *adv.* (*coll.*) tolerably, so-so.

сно́с|ный (~ен, ~на), *adj.* (*coll.*) tolerable; fair, reasonable.

снотво́р|ный (~ен, ~на), *adj.* soporific (*also fig.*); ~ное сре́дство soporific, sleeping draught, tablet.

снох|а́, и́, *pl.* ~и, *f.* (father's) daughter-in-law.

сношѐни|е, я, *n.* (*usu. pl.*) intercourse; relations, dealings; дипломати́ческие ~я diplomatic relations; име́ть ~я (с+*i.*) to have dealings (with); to have (sexual) intercourse (with).

сну|ю, ёшь, see **сновáть.**

снюха|ться, юсь, pf. (coll.) **1.** to get to know one another by scent. **2.** (pejor.) to come to terms, come to an understanding.

снятие, я, n. **1.** taking down; с. урожáя gathering in the harvest. **2.** removal; с. запрéта lifting of a ban; с. с рабóты dismissal, the sack. **3.** taking, making; с. кóпии copying.

снят|óй, adj. ~óе молокó skimmed milk.

сня|ть, снимý, снúмешь, past ~л, ~лá, ~ло, pf. (of **снимáть) 1.** to take off; to take down; с. шляпу to take one's hat off; с. картúну to take down a picture; с. корáбль с мéли to refloat a ship; с. слúвки с молокá to skim milk, take the cream off milk; с. пьéсу to take a play off; с. урожáй to gather in the harvest; с. осáду to raise a siege; с. с себя to divest oneself (of); с. с себя отвéтственность to decline responsibility. **2.** (fig.) to remove; to withdraw, cancel; с. взыскáние to remit a punishment; с. запрéт to lift a ban; с. предложéние to withdraw a motion; с. с рабóты to discharge, sack; с. с учёта to strike off the register; с. с фрóнта to withdraw from the front. **3.** (mil.) to pick off. **4.** to take, make; to photograph, make a photograph (of); с. кóпию (c+g.) to copy, make a copy (of); с. мéрку с когó-н. to take someone's measurements; с. план to make a plan; с. показáния to take (down) evidence; с. показáния гáзового счётчика to read a gas-meter; с. фильм to shoot a film. **5.** to take, rent (a house, etc.); с. в арéнду to take on lease. **6.** (cards) to cut.

сня|ться, снимýсь, снúмешься, past ~лся, ~лáсь, pf. (of **снимáться) 1.** to come off. **2.** to move off; с. с якоря to weigh anchor; to get under way (also fig.). **3.** to have one's photograph taken.

со = с.

соáвтор, а, m. co-author.

соáвторств|о, а, n. co-authorship, joint authorship.

собáк|а, и, f. dog; дворóвая с. watchdog; морскáя с. dogfish; охóтничья с. gun dog, hound; служéбная с. guard dog, patrol dog; с.-ищéйка bloodhound; устáть как с. to be dog-tired; вéшать ~ (на+a.; coll.) to call names, pull to pieces; вот где с. зарыта! so that's the crux of the matter!; so that's what's at the bottom of it!; как ~ нерéзаных (+g.; coll.) any amount (of); ~у съесть (на+p.; coll.) to have at one's fingertips, know inside out.

собаковóд, а, m. dog-breeder.

собаковóдств|о, а, n. dog-breeding.

собá|чий, adj. of ~ка; canine; ~чья жизнь dog's life; с. хóлод intense cold.

собáчк|а¹, и, f. little dog, doggie.

собáчк|а², и, f. **1.** trigger. **2.** (tech.) catch, trip, arresting device; pawl (of ratchet).

собáчник, а, m. (coll.) dog-lover.

собезьянничá|ть, ю, pf. of обезьянничать.

собéс, а, m. (abbr. of социáльное обеспéчение) social security department (of local soviet).

собесéдник, а, m. collocutor, interlocutor; он — забáвный с. he is amusing company.

собесéдовани|е, я, n. conversation, discussion, interlocution.

собирáтел|ь, я, m. collector.

собирáтельный, adj. (gram.) collective.

собирáтельств|о, а, n. collecting.

собирá|ться, юсь, impf. **1.** (impf. of собрáться) **2.** (+inf.) to intend (to), be about (to), be going (to); я ~лся позвонúть вам I was going to ring you up.

соблаговол|úть, ю, úшь, pf. (+inf.; obs.) to deign (to), condescend (to); наконéц онá ~úла отвéтить finally she deigned to reply.

соблáзн, а, m. temptation.

соблазнúтел|ь, я, m. **1.** tempter. **2.** seducer.

соблазнúтельниц|а, ы. f. temptress.

соблазнúтел|ьный (~ен, ~ьна), adj. **1.** tempting; alluring; seductive. **2.** suggestive, corrupting.

соблазн|úть, ю, úшь, pf. (of ~ять) **1.** to tempt. **2.** to seduce, entice.

соблазн|ять, яю, impf. of ~úть.

соблюдá|ть, ю, impf. of соблюсти.

соблюдéни|е, я, n. observance; maintenance; с. обычая observance of a custom; с. порядка maintenance of order.

соблю|стú, дý, дёшь, past ~л, ~лá, pf. (of ~дáть) to keep (to), stick to; to observe; с. закóн to observe a law; с. срóки to keep to schedule.

соболéзновани|е, я, n. sympathy, condolence.

соболéзн|овать, ую, impf. (+d.) to sympathize (with), condole (with).

собóлий, adj. of сóболь; с. мех sable.

собо|лúный, adj. sable; ~лúные брóви (poet.) sable brows.

сóбол|ь, я, pl. ~я, ~éй and ~и, ~ей, m. **1.** sable. **2.** (pl. ~я, ~éй) sable (fur).

собóр, а, m. **1.** (hist.) council, synod, assembly; вселéнский с. ecumenical council; зéмский с. Assembly of the Land (in Muscovite Russia). **2.** cathedral.

собóрност|ь, и, f. (eccl., philos.) conciliarism.

собóр|ный, adj. of ~.

собóровани|е, я, n. (eccl.) extreme unction.

собор|овать, ую, *impf. and pf.* *(eccl.)* to administer extreme unction (to), anoint.

собор|оваться, уюсь, *impf. and pf.* *(eccl.)* to receive extreme unction.

собою = собой, *see* себя.

собрáни|е, я, *n.* **1.** meeting, gathering; óбщее с. general meeting; с. правлéния board meeting. **2.** assembly; учредíтельное с. constituent assembly. **3.** collection; с. закóнов code (of laws); с. сочинéний collected works; пóлное с. сочинéний complete works.

сóбр|анный, *p.p.p. of* ~áть *and adj.*; с. человéк precise, accurate, self-disciplined person.

собрáт, а, *pl.* ~ья, ~ьев, *m.* colleague; с. по орýжию brother-in-arms; с. по ремеслý fellow-worker, colleague.

собр|áть, соберý, соберёшь, *past* ~áл, ~алá, ~áло, *pf.* *(of* собирáть) **1.** to gather, collect, pick; с. цветы́ to pick flowers; с. свéдения to collect information. **2.** to assemble, muster; to convoke, convene; с. войскá to muster troops; с. всё своё мýжество to muster up one's courage; с. послéдние сíлы to make a last effort. **3.** *(tech.)* to assemble, mount. **4.** to obtain, poll *(stated number or percentage of votes).* **5.** to prepare, make ready, equip; с. когó-н. в дорóгу to equip someone for a journey; с. нá стол to lay the table. **6.** *(dressmaking)* to gather, make gathers (in), take in.

собр|áться, соберýсь, соберёшься, *past* ~áлся, ~алáсь, ~áлóсь, *pf.* *(of* собирáться) **1.** to gather, assemble, muster; to be amassed. **2.** (в+*a.*) to prepare (for), make ready (for); с. в гóсти to get ready to go away *(to visit someone).* **3.** (+*inf.*) to intend (to), be about (to), be going (to). **4.** (с+*i.*; *fig.*) to collect; с. с дýхом (*i*) to get one's breath, (*ii*) to pluck up one's courage; to pull oneself together; с. с мы́слями to collect one's thoughts; с. с сíлами to summon up one's strength, brace oneself, nerve oneself. **5.** с. в комóк to hunch up.

сóбственник, а, *m.* owner, proprietor; земéльный с. landowner.

сóбственнический, *adj.* possessive, proprietary.

сóбственно 1. *adv.* strictly; с. говоря́ strictly speaking, properly speaking, as a matter of fact; он, с. (говоря́), был прав strictly speaking he was right. **2.** *particle* proper; егó не интересýет с. медицúна he is not interested in medicine proper.

сóбственнорýчно, *adv.* with one's own hand.

сóбственнорýчн|ый, *adj.* done, made, written with one's own hand(s); ~ая пóдпись autograph.

сóбственност|ь, и, *f.* **1.** property. **2.** possession, ownership; приобрестú в с. to become the owner (of).

сóбственн|ый, *adj.* **1.** (one's) own; proper; ~ыми глазáми with one's own eyes; в ~ые рýки *(inscription on envelope, etc.)* 'personal'; чýвство ~ого достóинства proper pride, self-respect; ~ой персóной in person; úмя ~ое *(gram.)* proper name. **2.** true, proper; в ~ом смы́сле in the true sense. **3.** *(tech.)* natural; internal; ~ое сопротивлéние internal resistance; ~ая скóрость actual speed; ~ая частотá *(radio)* natural frequency.

собуты́льник, а, *m.* *(coll.)* drinking companion, boon companion.

собы́ти|е, я, *n.* event; текýщие ~я current affairs.

сов-, *abbr. of* совéтский.

сов|á, ы́, *pl.* ~ы, *f.* owl.

совáть, сую́, суёшь, *impf.* *(of* сýнуть) to shove, thrust, poke; с. рýки в кармáны to stick one's hands in one's pockets; с. монéту комý-н. в рýку to slip a coin into someone's hand; с. нос, с. ры́ло (в+*a.*) *(coll.)* to poke one's nose (into), pry (into).

совáться, сую́сь, суёшься, *impf.* *(of* сýнуться) *(coll.)* **1.** to push, strain; не знáвши брóду, не сýйся в вóду *(prov.)* look before you leap. **2.** (в+*a.*; *fig.*) to butt (in), poke one's nose (into).

сов|ёнок, ёнка, *pl.* ~я́та, ~я́т, *m.* owlet.

соверш|áть(ся), áю, áет(ся), *impf. of* ~úть(ся).

совершéни|е, я, *n.* accomplishment, fulfilment; perpetration.

совершéнно, *adv.* **1.** perfectly. **2.** absolutely, utterly, completely, totally, perfectly; с. вéрно! quite right!, perfectly true!, quite so!

совершеннолéти|е, я, *n.* majority; достúгнуть ~я to come of age, attain one's majority.

совершеннолéтний, *adj.* of age.

совершён|ный¹ (~ен, ~на), *adj.* **1.** perfect. **2.** *(coll.)* absolute, utter, complete, total, perfect; с. идиóт absolute idiot.

совершённый², *adj.* *(gram.)* perfective.

совершéнств|о, а, *n.* perfection; в ~е perfectly, to perfection.

совершéнств|овать, ую, *impf.* *(of* у~) to perfect.

совершéнств|оваться, уюсь, *impf.* *(of* у~) (в+*p.*) to perfect oneself (in).

соверш|úть, ý, úшь, *pf.* *(of* ~áть) **1.** to accomplish, carry out; to perform; to commit, perpetrate; с. ошúбку to make a mistake; с. преступлéние to commit a crime. **2.** to complete, conclude; с. сдéлку to complete a transaction, make a deal.

соверш|иться, ится, *pf.* (*of* ~áться) (*lit.*) 1. to happen. 2. to be accomplished, be completed.

сóве|стить, щу, стишь, *impf.* to shame, put to shame.

сóве|ститься, щусь, стишься, *impf.* (*of* по~) (+*g. or inf.*; *obs.*) to be ashamed (of).

сóвестлив|ый (~, ~а), *adj.* conscientious.

сóвестно, *as pred.*+*d. and inf. or* что to be ashamed; ему́ бы́ло с. проси́ть де́нег he was ashamed to ask for money; как вам не с.! you ought to be ashamed of yourself!

сóвест|ь, и, *f.* conscience; чи́стая, нечи́стая с. clear, guilty conscience; со споко́йной ~ью with a clear conscience; для очи́стки ~и to clear one's conscience; по ~и (говоря́) to be honest; свобо́да ~и freedom of worship; угрызе́ния ~и pangs of conscience; рабо́тать на ~ to work conscientiously.

совéт¹, а, *m.* advice, counsel; (*leg.*) opinion.

совéт², а, *m.* 1. Soviet, soviet. 2. council; С. Безопа́сности Security Council. 3. council, conference; вое́нный с. council of war.

совéт³, а, *m.* (*arch.*) concord, harmony.

совéтник, а, *m.* 1. adviser. 2. (*title of office*) counsellor.

совéт|овать, ую, *impf.* (*of* по~) (+*d.*) to advise.

совéт|оваться, уюсь, *impf.* (*of* по~) (с+*i.*) to consult, ask advice (of), seek advice (from).

советовéд, а, *m.* Sovietologist.

советовéдени|е, я, *n.* Sovietology.

совéтск|ий, *adj.* 1. Soviet, of the Soviet Union; ~ая власть Soviet power, the Soviet régime; с. наро́д the Soviet people; С. Сою́з the Soviet Union. 2. soviet (= *of local soviets*); ~ие рабо́тники officials of the soviets; ~ое строи́тельство development of the soviets.

совéтчик, а, *m.* adviser, counsellor.

совещáни|е, *n.* conference, meeting; с. на верха́х summit conference.

совещáтельный, *adj.* consultative, deliberative.

совещá|ться, юсь, *impf.* 1. (о+*p.*) to deliberate (on, about), consult (on, about). 2. (с+*i.*) to confer (with), consult.

сов|и́ный, *adj. of* ~á; owlish.

совладá|ть, ю, *pf.* (с+*i.*; *coll.*) to control; с. с собо́й to control oneself.

совладé|ец, ьца, *m.* joint owner, joint proprietor.

совладéни|е, я, *n.* joint ownership.

совмести́мост|ь, и, *f.* compatibility.

совмести́м|ый (~, ~а), *adj.* compatible.

совмести́тел|ь, я, *m.* person holding more than one office, combining jobs; pluralist.

совмести́тельств|о, а, *n.* holding of more than one office; pluralism; рабо́тать по ~у to hold more than one office, combine jobs.

совмести́тельств|овать, ую, *impf.* to hold more than one office, combine jobs.

совме|сти́ть, щу́, сти́шь, *pf.* (*of* ~ща́ть²) to combine.

совме|сти́ться, сти́тся, *pf.* (*of* ~ща́ться) 1. to coincide. 2. to be combined, combine.

совмéстно, *adv.* in common, jointly.

совмéстн|ый, *adj.* joint, combined; ~ые де́йствия concerted action; (*mil.*) combined operations; ~ое заседа́ние joint sitting; ~ое обуче́ние co-education; ~ая рабо́та team-work.

совмещá|ть¹, ю, *impf.* to hold more than one office, combine jobs.

совмещá|ть²(ся), ю(сь), *impf. of* совмести́ть(ся).

совми́н, а, *m.* (*abbr. of* Сове́т Мини́стров) Council of Ministers.

совнарко́м, а, *m.* (*abbr. of* Сове́т Наро́дных Комисса́ров; *re-named, in 1946,* Сове́т Мини́стров) Council of People's Commissars.

совнархо́з, а, *m.* (*abbr. of* Сове́т наро́дного хозя́йства) (*hist.*) Council of National Economy (*central or regional economic management board in U.S.S.R.*).

сов|о́к, ка́, *m.* shovel, scoop; садо́вый с. trowel; с. для му́сора dustpan.

совокуп|и́ть, лю́, и́шь, *pf.* (*of* ~ля́ть) to combine, unite.

совокуп|и́ться, лю́сь, и́шься, *pf.* (*of* ~ля́ться) (с+*i.*) to copulate (with).

совокуплéни|е, я, *n.* copulation.

совокупля́|ть(ся), ю(сь), *impf. of* совокупи́ть(ся).

совокýпно, *adv.* in common, jointly.

совокýпност|ь, и, *f.* aggregate, sum total; totality; в ~и in the aggregate; по ~и (+*g.*) on the basis (of), on the strength (of).

совокýпн|ый, *adj.* joint, combined, aggregate; ~ые уси́лия combined efforts.

совою́ющий, *adj.* co-belligerent.

совпадá|ть, ю, *impf. of* совпа́сть.

совпадéни|е, я, *n.* coincidence.

совпá|сть, ду́, дёшь, *past* ~л, *pf.* (*of* ~да́ть) 1. (с+*i.*) to coincide (with); части́чно с. to overlap. 2. to agree, concur, tally; их показа́ния не ~ли their evidence did not agree.

соврати́тел|ь, я, *m.* perverter, seducer.

совра|ти́ть, щу́, ти́шь, *pf.* (*of* ~ща́ть) to pervert, seduce; с. с пути́ и́стинного to lead astray.

совра|ти́ться, щу́сь, ти́шься, *pf.* (*of* ~ща́ться) to go astray.

совр|а́ть, у́, ёшь, *past* ~а́л, ~ала́, ~а́ло, *pf. of* врать.

совращá|ть(ся), ю(сь), *impf. of* совратúть-
(ся).

совращéни|е, я, *n.* perverting, seducing,
seduction.

совремéнник, а, *m.* contemporary.

совремéнност|ь, и, *f.* 1. contemporaneity.
2. the present (time).

совремéн|ный (~ен, ~на), *adj.* 1. (+*d.*)
contemporaneous (with), of the time (of);
~ные Ивáну Грóзному понятия ideas of
the time of Ivan the Terrible. 2. contemporary, present-day; modern; up-to-date;
~ная англúйская литератýра modern
English literature.

совсéм, *adv.* quite, entirely, completely,
altogether; с. не not at all, not in the least;
с. не то nothing of the kind.

совхóз, а, *m.* sovkhoz, State farm.

совхóз|ный, *adj. of* ~.

согбéн|ный (~, ~на), *adj.* (*obs.*) bent, stoop-
ing.

соглáси|е, я, n. 1. consent; assent; с вáшего
~я with your consent; с óбщего ~я by
common consent; дать своё с. to give one's
consent. 2. agreement; в ~и (с+*i.*) in
accordance (with). 3. accord; concord,
harmony.

согласúтельн|ый, *adj.* conciliatory; ~ая
комúссия conciliation commission.

согла|сúть, шý, сúшь, *pf.* (*of* ~шáть) to
reconcile.

согла|сúться, шýсь, сúшься, *pf.* (*of* ~шáть-
ся) 1. (на+*a.* or +*inf.*) to consent (to),
agree (to). 2. (с+*i.*) to agree (with), concur
(with).

соглáсно, *adv.* 1. in accord, in harmony, in
concord; петь с. to sing in harmony. 2. *as
prep.* (+*d.* or с+*i.*) in accordance (with);
according (to); с. договóру in accordance
with the treaty, under the treaty.

соглáсност|ь, и, *f.* harmony, harmonious-
ness.

соглáс|ный¹ (~ен, ~на), *adj.* 1. (на+*a.*)
agreeable (to); онú нé были ~ны на нáши
услóвия they would not agree to our conditions. 2. (с+*i.*) in agreement (with),
concordant (with); быть ~ным to agree
(with); ~ен, ~на, ~ны? do you agree?
3. harmonious, concordant.

соглáс|ный², *adj.* (*gram.*) consonant(al); *as
noun* с., ~ого, *m.* consonant.

согласовáни|е, я, n. 1. co-ordination; con-
cordance, agreement. 2. (*gram.*) concord,
agreement; с. времён sequence of tenses.

согласóванност|ь, и, f. co-ordination; с. во
врéмени synchronization.

согласóв|анный, *p.p.p. of* ~áть *and adj.*
co-ordinated; ~анные дéйствия concerted
action; с. текст agreed text.

соглас|овáть, ýю, *pf.* (*of* ~óвывать) (с+*i.*)

1. to co-ordinate (with). 2. с. что-н. с
кем-н. to submit something to someone's
approval; to come to an agreement with
someone about something. 3. (*gram.*) to
make agree (with).

соглас|овáться, ýется, *impf.* (с+*i.*) 1. to
accord (with); to conform (to). 2. (*gram.*)
to agree (with).

согласóвыва|ть, ю, *impf. of* согласовáть.

соглашáтел|ь, я, *m.* (*polit.*; *pejor.*) com-
promiser; appeaser.

соглашáтель|ский, *adj. of* ~; ~ская полú-
тика policy of compromise, appeasement
policy.

соглашáтельств|о, а, n. (*polit.*; *pejor.*) com-
promise, appeasement.

соглашá|ть(ся), ю(сь), *impf. of* согласúть-
(ся).

соглашéни|е, я, n. 1. agreement, under-
standing. 2. agreement, covenant;
заключúть с. to conclude an agreement.

соглядáта|й, я, m. (*obs.*) spy.

согнá|ть¹, сгоню, сгóнишь, *past* ~л, ~лá,
~ло, *pf.* (*of* сгонять) to drive away.

согнá|ть², сгоню, сгóнишь, *past* ~л, ~лá,
~ло, *pf.* (*of* сгонять) to drive together,
round up.

согн|ýть, ý, ёшь, *pf.* (*of* гнуть *and* сгибáть)
to bend, curve, crook.

согн|ýться, ýсь, ёшься, *pf.* (*of* гнýться *and*
сгибáться) to bend, bow (down); to stoop.

согражданúн, а, *m.* fellow-citizen.

согревáтельный, *adj.* с. компрéсс (*med.*)
hot compress.

согревá|ть(ся), ю(сь), *impf. of* согрéть(ся).

согрé|ть, ю, *pf.* (*of* ~вáть) to warm, heat.

согрé|ться, юсь, *pf.* (*of* ~вáться) to get
warm; to warm oneself.

согреш|áть, áю, *impf. of* ~úть.

согрешéни|е, я, n. sin, trespass.

согреш|úть, ý, úшь, *pf.* (*of* ~áть) (прóтив)
to sin (against), trespass (against).

сóд|а, ы, f. soda, sodium carbonate;
питьевáя с. household soda.

содéйстви|е, я, n. assistance, help; good
offices.

содéйств|овать, ую, *impf. and pf.* (*pf. also*
по~) (+*d.*) to assist, help; to further, promote; to make (for), contribute (to); с.
успéху предприятия to contribute to the
success of an undertaking.

содержáни|е, я, n. 1. maintenance, upkeep,
keeping; allowance; дéнежное с. money
allowance, financial support; с. под
арéстом custody; быть на ~и у когó-н. to
be kept, supported by someone. 2. pay;
оклáд ~я rate of pay; óтпуск с сохранé-
нием ~я holiday(s) with pay. 3. content;
кубúческое с. volume; с бóльшим ~ем
(+*g.*) rich (in). 4. matter, substance; con-

tent; фо́рма и с. form and content. **5.** content(s); plot (*of a novel, etc.*). **6.** table of contents.

содержа́нк|а, и, *f.* (*obs.*) kept woman.

содержа́тел|ь, я, *m.* (*obs.*) landlord (*of an inn, etc.*).

содержа́тел|ьный (~ен, ~ьна), *adj.* rich in content; ~ьное письмо́ interesting letter.

содерж|а́ть, у́, ⌣ишь, *impf.* **1.** to keep, maintain, support; с. семью́ to keep a family. **2.** to keep, have (*a business, enterprise, etc.*); с. магази́н to keep a shop. **3.** (в+*p.*) to keep (*in a given state*); с. в испра́вности to keep going, in working order; с. в поря́дке to keep in order; с. в та́йне to keep (as a) secret; с. под аре́стом to keep under arrest. **4.** to contain; его́ перево́д ⌣ит мно́го оши́бок his translation contains many mistakes.

содерж|а́ться, у́сь, ⌣ишься, *impf.* **1.** to be kept, be maintained. **2.** to be kept, be; с. под аре́стом to be under arrest. **3.** (в+*p.*) to be contained (by); в э́той руде́ ⌣ится ура́н this ore contains uranium.

содержи́м|ое, ого, *n.* contents.

соде́|ять, ю, ешь, *pf.* (*obs. or rhet.*) to commit, carry out.

соде́|яться, ется, *pf.* (*obs. or joc.*) to happen.

со́дов|ый, *adj.* soda; ~ая вода́ soda (water).

содокла́д, а, *m.* supplementary report, supplementary paper.

содокла́дчик, а, *m.* reader of supplementary report *or* paper.

содо́м, а, *m.* (*coll.*) uproar, row; подня́ть с. to raise hell.

содра́|ть, сдеру́, сдерёшь, *past* ~л, ~ла́, ~ло, *pf.* (*of* сдира́ть) **1.** to tear off, strip off; с. ко́жу (c+*g.*) to skin, flay; с. кору́ (c+*g.*) to bark. **2.** *pf. only* (*fig., coll.*) to fleece; с. с кого́-н. втри́дорога to make someone pay through the nose.

содрога́ни|е, я, *n.* shudder.

содрог|а́ться, а́юсь, *impf. of* ~ну́ться.

содрог|ну́ться, ну́сь, нёшься, *pf.* (*of* ~а́ться) to shudder, shake, quake.

содру́жеств|о, а, *n.* **1.** concord; рабо́тать в те́сном ~е (c+*i.*) to work in close co-operation (with). **2.** community, commonwealth; Брита́нское с. на́ций the British Commonwealth.

со́евый, *adj.* soya.

соедине́ни|е, я, *n.* **1.** joining, conjunction, combination. **2.** (*tech.*) joint, join, junction. **3.** (*chem.*) compound. **4.** (*mil.*) formation.

соедин|ённый, *p.p.p. of* ~и́ть *and adj.* united, joint; Соединённое Короле́вство the United Kingdom (*of Great Britain and Northern Ireland*).

соедини́тельн|ый, *adj.* connective, con-

necting; с. брус draw bar; ~ое звено́ connecting link; ~ая коро́бка (*electr.*) junction box; ~ые ско́бки (*typ.*) brace; с. сою́з (*gram.*) copulative conjunction; ~ая ткань (*biol.*) connective tissue; ~ая тя́га coupling rod.

соедин|и́ть, ю́, и́шь, *pf.* (*of* ~я́ть) **1.** to join, unite. **2.** to connect, link; с. по телефо́ну to put through. **3.** (*chem.*) to combine.

соедин|и́ться, ю́сь, и́шься, *pf.* (*of* ~я́ться) **1.** to join, unite. **2.** (*chem.*) to combine. **3.** *pass. of* ~и́ть.

соедин|я́ть(ся), я́ю(сь), *impf. of* ~и́ть(ся).

сожале́ни|е, я, *n.* **1.** (о+*p.*) regret (for); к на́шему ~ю to our sorrow, regrettably; к ~ю unfortunately. **2.** (к) pity (for).

сожале́|ть, ю, *impf.* (о+*p. or* +что) to regret, deplore.

сожже́ни|е, я, *n.* burning; cremation; с. на костре́ burning at the stake; преда́ть ~ю to commit to the flames.

сожи́тел|ь, я, *m.* **1.** room-mate. **2.** lover.

сожи́тельниц|а, ы, *f.* **1.** room-mate. **2.** mistress.

сожи́тельств|о, а, *n.* **1.** living together, lodging together. **2.** (*fig.*) living together, cohabitation.

сожи́тельств|овать, ую, *impf.* (c+*i.*) **1.** to live (with), lodge (with); to live together. **2.** (*fig.*) to live (with); to live together, cohabit.

сожр|а́ть, у́, ёшь, *past* ~а́л, ~ала́, ~а́ло, *pf. of* жрать.

созва́нива|ться, юсь, *impf. of* созвони́ться.

созва́|ть, созову́, созовёшь, *past* ~л, ~ла́, ~ло, *pf.* **1.** (*impf.* сзыва́ть) to gather; to invite. **2.** (*impf.* созыва́ть) to call (together), summon; to convoke, convene; с. ми́тинг to call a meeting.

созве́зди|е, я, *n.* constellation.

созвон|и́ться, ю́сь, и́шься, *pf.* (*of* созва́ниваться) **1.** (c+*i.*; *coll.*) to speak on the telephone (to). **2.** (о+*p.*; *coll.*) to arrange (*something*) on the phone; мы с тобо́й созвони́мся об э́том we'll arrange that over the telephone.

созву́чи|е, я, *n.* **1.** (*mus.*) accord, consonance. **2.** (*lit.*) assonance.

созву́ч|ный (~ен, ~на), *adj.* **1.** harmonious. **2.** (+*d.*) consonant (with), in keeping (with); произведе́ние, созву́чное эпо́хе a work in keeping with the times.

созда|ва́ть(ся), ю, ёт(ся), *impf. of* ⌣ть(ся).

созда́ни|е, я, *n.* **1.** creation, making. **2.** creation, work. **3.** creature.

созда́тел|ь, я, *m.* **1.** creator; founder, originator. **2.** the Creator.

созда́|ть, м, шь, ст, ди́м, ди́те, ду́т, *past* со́здал, ~ла́, со́здало, *pf.* (*of* ~ва́ть) (*in var. senses*) to create; to found, originate; to set up, establish; с. впечатле́ние to create the impression, give the impression; с. иллю́зию to create an illusion.

созда́|ться, стся, ду́тся, *past* ~лся, ~ла́сь, *pf.* (*of* ~ва́ться) to be created; to arise, spring up; ~ло́сь неприя́тное положе́ние a disagreeable situation arose; у нас ~ло́сь впечатле́ние, что we gained the impression that.

созерца́ни|е, я, *n.* contemplation.

созерца́тел|ь, я, *m.* contemplative person; passive observer.

созерца́тел|ьный (~ен, ~ьна), *adj.* contemplative, meditative.

созерца́|ть, ю, *impf.* to contemplate.

созида́ни|е, я, *n.* creation.

созида́тел|ь, я, *m.* creator.

созида́тел|ьный (~ен, ~ьна), *adj.* creative, constructive.

созида́|ть, ю, *impf.* (*no pf.*) to build up.

созна|ва́ть, ю́, ёшь, *impf.* **1.** *impf. of* ~ть. **2.** to be conscious (of), realize; я́сно с. to be alive (to); он ещё не ~ёт, что он сде́лал he still does not realize what he has done.

созна|ва́ться, ю́сь, ёшься, *impf. of* ~ться.

созна́ни|е, я, *n.* **1.** (*in var. senses*) consciousness; кла́ссовое с. class-consciousness; потеря́ть с. to lose consciousness; прийти́ в с. to regain, recover consciousness. **2.** recognition, acknowledgement; с. до́лга sense of duty. **3.** confession.

созна́тельност|ь, и, f. **1.** awareness; intelligence, acumen; полити́ческая с. political awareness, political sense. **2.** deliberateness.

созна́тел|ьный (~ен, ~ьна), *adj.* **1.** conscious; politically conscious. **2.** intelligent; у него́ ~ьное отноше́ние к собы́тиям he has an intelligent attitude to events. **3.** deliberate.

созна́|ть, ю, *pf.* (*of* ~ва́ть) to recognize, acknowledge; с. свою́ оши́бку to recognize one's mistake.

созна́|ться, ю́сь, *pf.* (*of* ~ва́ться) (в+*p.*) to confess (to); (*leg.*) to plead guilty; нельзя́ не с. it must be confessed.

созорнича́|ть, ю, *pf. of* озорнича́ть.

созрева́|ть, ю, *impf. of* созре́ть.

созре́|ть, ю, *pf.* (*of* ~ва́ть) to ripen, mature.

созы́в, а, *m.* calling, summoning; convocation; с. заседа́ния calling of a meeting; Верхо́вный Сове́т СССР девя́того ~а ninth U.S.S.R. Supreme Soviet (*i.e. ninth four-year term since adoption of new Soviet Constitution in 1936*).

созыва́|ть, ю, *impf. of* созва́ть.

соизво́л|ить, ю, ишь, *pf.* (*of* ~я́ть) (+*inf.*; *obs.*) to deign (to), be pleased (to).

соизвол|я́ть, я́ю, *impf. of* ~ить.

соизмери́мост|ь, и, f. commensurability.

соизмери́м|ый (~, ~а), *adj.* commensurable.

соиска́ни|е, я, *n.* competition; диссерта́ция на с. до́кторской сте́пени doctoral dissertation.

соиска́тел|ь, я, m. (+*g.*) competitor (for).

со́йк|а, и, g, pl. со́ек, *f.* (*orn.*) jay.

со|йти́[1], йду́, йдёшь, *past* ~шёл, ~шла́, *pf.* (*of* сходи́ть) **1.** to go down, come down; to descend, get off, alight; с. с ле́стницы to go downstairs; с. с ло́шади to dismount; с. на нет to come to naught. **2.** to leave; с. с доро́ги to get out of the way, step aside; с. с ре́льсов to be derailed, come off the rails; снег ~шёл the snow has melted; с. со сце́ны to leave the stage; (*fig.*) to quit the stage; с. с ума́ to go mad, go off one's head. **3.** (*of paint, skin, etc.*) to come off.

со|йти́[2], йду́, йдёшь, *pf.* (*of* сходи́ть) **1.** (за+*a.*) to pass (for), be taken (for). **2.** (*coll.*) to pass, go off; ~шло́ благополу́чно it went off all right; ~йдёт и так it will do as it is; э́то ~шло́ ему́ с рук he got away with it.

со|йти́сь, йду́сь, йдёшься, *past* ~шёлся, ~шла́сь, *pf.* (*of* сходи́ться) **1.** to meet; to come together, gather. **2.** (с+*i.*) to meet, take up (with), become friends (with); to become (*sexually*) intimate (with). **3.** (+*i.*, в+*p. or* на+*p.*) to agree (about); с. в цене́ to agree about a price; с. хара́ктером to get on, hit it off; они́ не ~шли́сь хара́ктерами they could not get on. **4.** (*fig.*) to agree, tally; счета́ не ~шли́сь the figures did not tally.

сок, а (у), о ~е, в *and* на ~у́, *m.* juice; sap; желу́дочный с. (*physiol.*) gastric juice; (*coll.*) в (по́лном) ~у́ in the prime of life; вари́ться в со́бственном ~у́ to stew in one's own juice.

соквартира́нт, а, m. flat-sharer, lodgings-sharer.

со́кол[1], а, m. falcon (*also fig., rhet.; of Soviet air aces*); гол как соко́л (*coll.*) as poor as a church mouse.

со́кол[2], а, m. (*tech.*) poker, slice bar.

соко́лик, а, m. **1.** *affect. dim. of* со́кол[1]. **2.** (*coll.*) my dear.

соколи́н|ый, *adj. of* со́кол[1]; ~ая охо́та falconry; ~ые о́чи (*poet.*) hawk eyes.

соко́л|ок, ка́, m. (*builder's*) trowel.

соко́льник, а, m. (*hist.*) falconer.

соко́льнич|ий, его, m. (*hist.*) falconer (*boyar in charge of falconry*).

сократи́м|ый (~, ~а), *adj.* **1.** (*math.*) able to be cancelled. **2.** (*physiol.*) contractile.

сокра|ти́ть, щу́, ти́шь, *pf.* (*of* ~ща́ть) **1.** to shorten; to curtail; to abbreviate; to abridge. **2.** to reduce, cut down; с. расхо́ды to cut down expenses, retrench; с. шта́ты to reduce the establishment, cut down the staff. **3.** to dismiss, discharge, lay off. **4.** (*math.*) to cancel.

сокра|ти́ться, ти́тся, *pf.* (*of* ~ща́ться) **1.** grow shorter. **2.** to decrease, decline. **3.** (*coll.*) to cut down (*on expenses*). **4.** (на + *a*.; *math.*) to be cancelled (by). **5.** (*physiol.*) to contract.

сокраща́|ть(ся), ю(сь), *impf. of* сократи́ть-(ся).

сокраще́ни|е, я, *n.* **1.** shortening. **2.** abridgement; с ~ями abridged, in abridged form. **3.** abbreviation. **4.** reduction, cutting down; curtailment; с. шта́тов staff reduction; уво́лить по ~ю шта́тов to dismiss on grounds of redundancy. **5.** (*math.*) cancellation. **6.** (*physiol.*) contraction; с. се́рд-ца systole.

сокращённо, *adv.* briefly; in abbreviated form.

сокра|щённый, *p.p.p. of* ~ти́ть *and adj.* brief; ~щённое сло́во abbreviation, contraction.

сокрове́нност|ь, и, *f.* secrecy.

сокрове́н|ный (~, ~на), *adj.* secret, concealed; ~ные мы́сли innermost thoughts.

сокро́вищ|е, а, *n.* treasure; ни за каки́е ~а not for the world.

сокро́вищниц|а, ы, *f.* treasure-house, treasury, storehouse, depository (*also fig.*); с. иску́сства treasure-house of art.

сокруш|а́ть, а́ю, *impf. of* ~и́ть.

сокруша́|ться, ю́сь, *impf.* (o + *p*.) to grieve (for, over); to be distressed (about).

сокруше́ни|е, я, *n.* **1.** smashing, shattering. **2.** (*obs.*) grief, distress.

сокруш|ённый, *p.p.p. of* ~и́ть *and adj.* grief-stricken.

сокруши́тел|ьный (~ен, ~ьна), *adj.* shattering; нанести́ с. уда́р (+ *d*.) to deal, strike a crippling blow.

сокруш|и́ть, у́, и́шь, *pf.* (*of* ~а́ть) **1.** to shatter, smash. **2.** (*fig.*) to shatter; to distress.

сокры́ти|е, я, *n.* concealment; с. кра́деного receiving of stolen goods.

сокр|ы́ть, о́ю, о́ешь, *pf.* (*obs.*) to hide, conceal, cover up.

сокр|ы́ться, о́юсь, о́ешься, *pf.* (*obs.*) to hide, conceal oneself.

со|лга́ть, лгу́, лжёшь, лгу́т, *past* ~лга́л, ~лгала́, ~лга́ло, *pf. of* лгать.

солда́т, а, *g. pl.* ~, *m.* soldier; служи́ть в ~ах (*obs.*) to soldier, be a soldier.

солда́тик, а, *m.* **1.** *dim. of* солда́т. **2.** toy soldier; игра́ть в ~и to play soldiers.

солда́тк|а, и, *f.* soldier's wife.

солдатн|я́, и́, *f.* (*collect.*; *pejor.*) soldiery.

солда́т|ский, *adj. of* ~; ~ская кни́жка soldier's pay book; ~ская ла́вка canteen.

солда́тчин|а, ы, *f.* **1.** (*hist.*) levy. **2.** military service; soldiering.

солдафо́н, а, *m.* (*coll.*) crude, loud-mouthed soldier.

солева́р, а, *m.* salt-worker.

солеваре́ни|е, я, *n.* salt production.

солева́р|енный, *adj. of* ~е́ние; с. заво́д salt-works.

солева́р|ный, *adj.* = ~енный.

солева́р|ня, ни, *g. pl.* ~ен, *f.* salt-works, saltern.

соле́ни|е, я, *n.* salting; pickling.

солено́ид, а, *m.* (*electr.*) solenoid.

солён|ый, *adj.* **1.** salt; ~ое о́зеро salt lake. **2.** (со́лон, солона́, со́лоно) salty; у меня́ во рту́ со́лоно I have a salt taste in my mouth. **3.** salted; pickled; с. огуре́ц pickled cucumber; *as noun* ~ое, ~ого, *n.* pickles. **4.** (*fig., coll.*) salty, spicy; с. анекдо́т spicy story. **5.** (*short forms only*) (*fig.*) hot; ему́ со́лоно пришло́сь he got it hot; в Пари́же им со́лоно доста́лось Paris was their undoing; Paris became too hot for them; верну́ться не со́лоно хлеба́вши to come home empty-handed.

соле́нь|е, я, *n.* salted food(s); pickles.

солеци́зм, а, *m.* solecism.

соле|я́, и́, *f.* (*eccl.*) solium.

солидариза́ци|я, и, *f.* making common cause.

солидаризи́р|оваться, уюсь, *impf. and pf.* (c + *i*.) to express one's solidarity (with), make common cause (with), identify oneself (with); с. с чьим-н. мне́нием to express one's agreement with someone's opinion.

солида́рно, *adv.* (*leg.*) collectively, jointly.

солида́рност|ь, и, *f.* **1.** solidarity; из ~и (c + *i*.) in sympathy (with); ста́чка ~и sympathetic strike. **2.** (*leg.*) collective, joint responsibility.

солида́р|ный, *adj.* **1.** (~ен, ~на) (c + *i*.) at one (with), in sympathy (with). **2.** (*leg.*) solidary.

соли́д|ный (~ен, ~на), *adj.* **1.** solid, strong, sound; ~ные зна́ния sound knowledge. **2.** (*fig.*) solid, sound; reliable, respectable; с. челове́к a solid man; с. журна́л respectable magazine. **3.** (*coll.*) respectable, sizable; ~ная су́мма tidy sum. **4.** middle-aged; челове́к ~ных лет a middle-aged man.

солипси́зм, а, *m.* (*philos.*) solipsism.

соли́ст, а, *m.* soloist.

солите́р, а, *m.* (*min.*) solitaire (diamond).

солитёр, а, *m.* tapeworm.

сол|и́ть, ю́, ~и́шь, *impf.* (*of* по~) **1.** to salt. **2.** to pickle; с. мя́со to corn meat.

со́лк|а, и, *f.* salting; pickling.

со́лнечн|ый, *adj.* **1.** sun; solar; ~ая ва́нна sun-bath; ~ое затме́ние solar eclipse; с. луч sunbeam; ~ые пя́тна (*astron.*) sun-spots; с. свет sunlight, sunshine; ~ая систе́ма solar system; ~ое сплете́ние (*anat.*) solar plexus; с. уда́р (*med.*) sunstroke; ~ые часы́ sun-dial. **2.** sunny.

со́лнц|е, а, *n.* sun; го́рное с. artificial sunlight, sun-lamp; ло́жное с. (*astron.*) parhelion; на с. in the sun; гре́ться на с. to sun oneself, bask in the sun; по ~y by the sun; with the sun, clockwise; про́тив ~a against the sun, anti-clockwise.

солнцепёк, а, *m.* на ~e right in the sun, in the full blaze of the sun.

солнцестоя́ни|е, я, *n.* solstice.

со́ло, *indecl.,* *n.* solo (*also as adv.*).

солов|е́й, ья́, *m.* nightingale; восто́чный с. thrush-nightingale.

солове́|ть, ю, ешь, *impf.* (*of* o~) (*coll.*) to become drowsy.

соло́вый, *adj.* light bay.

солов|ьи́ный, *adj. of* ~е́й.

со́лод, а, *m.* malt.

солоди́л|ьня, ьни, *g. pl.* ~ен, *f.* malthouse.

соло|ди́ть, жу́, ди́шь, *impf.* (*of* на~) to malt.

солодк|а, и, *f.* liquorice.

солодко́вый, *adj. of* соло́дка; с. ко́рень (*pharm.*) liquorice.

солодо́венный, *adj.* с. заво́д malt-house.

соложе́ни|е, я, *n.* malting.

соло́м|а, ы, *f.* straw; thatch; крыть ~ой to thatch.

соло́менн|ый, *adj.* **1.** straw; ~ая вдова́ grass widow; ~ая кры́ша thatch, thatched roof; ~ая шля́па straw hat. **2.** straw-coloured; ~ые во́лосы straw-coloured hair.

соло́минк|а, и, *f.* straw; хвата́ться за ~y to catch, clutch at a straw.

соло́мк|а, и, *f.* **1.** *dim. of* соло́ма. **2.** matchstick; спи́чечная с. (*collect.*) matchwood. **3.** (*collect.*) straw packing. **4.** stick (of toffee). **5.** (*collect.*) stick-like biscuits.

соломоре́зк|а, и, *f.* (*agric.*) chaff-cutter.

солони́н|а, ы, *f.* salted beef, corned beef.

соло́нк|а, и, *f.* salt-cellar.

со́лоно, *see* солёный.

солонча́к, а́, *m.* (*geol.*) saline soil.

сол|ь¹, и, *pl.* ~и, ~е́й, *f.* **1.** salt; ка́менная с. rock-salt; ню́хательная с. smelling salts; пова́ренная с. common salt, sodium chloride; столо́вая с. table-salt. **2.** (*fig.*) salt, spice; point; с. земли́ the salt of the earth; вот в чём вся с. that's the whole point; мно́го ~и съесть (с кем-н.) to spend a long time together (with someone).

соль², *indecl.,* *n.* (*mus.*) sol, G; с.-дие́з G sharp; с.-бемо́ль G flat; ключ с. treble clef, G clef.

со́л|ьный 1. *adj. of* ~о; с. но́мер solo; ~ьная па́ртия solo part. **2.** *adj. of* ~ь²; с. ключ treble clef.

сольфе́джио, *indecl.,* *n.* (*mus.*) solfeggio, sol-fa, solmization; петь с. to sol-fa, solmizate.

соля́нк|а, ~и, *f.* solyanka (*a sharp-tasting Russian soup of vegetables and meat or fish*).

соля́н|о́й, *adj.* salt, saline; ~а́я кислота́ (*chem.*) hydrochloric acid; ~ы́е ко́пи salt-mines; с. раство́р saline solution, brine.

солянокислый, *adj.* (*chem.*) hydrochloric.

соля́ри|й, я, *m.* solarium.

сом, а́, *m.* sheat-fish.

сомати́ческий, *adj.* somatic.

со́мкн|утый, *p.p.p. of* ~у́ть *and adj.;* с. строй (*mil.*) close order.

сомкн|у́ть, у́, ёшь, *pf.* (*of* смыка́ть) to close; с. глаза́ to close one's eyes; с. ряды́ (*mil.*) to close the ranks; ~и́сь! (*mil. word of command*) close order, march!

сомкн|у́ться, ётся, *pf.* (*of* смыка́ться) to close (up).

сомна́мбул|а, ы, *m. and f.* sleep-walker, somnambulist.

сомнамбули́зм, а, *m.* sleep-walking, somnambulism.

сомнева́|ться, юсь, *impf.* **1.** (в+*p.*) to doubt; to question; я не ~юсь в его́ че́стности I do not question his integrity. **2.** to worry; мо́жете не с., всё бу́дет в поря́дке you need not worry, everything will be all right.

сомне́ни|е, я, *n.* doubt; uncertainty; без (вся́кого) ~я, вне ~я without (any) doubt, beyond doubt; не подлежи́т ни мале́йшему ~ю, что there cannot be the slightest doubt that.

сомни́тел|ьный (~ен, ~ьна), *adj.* **1.** doubtful, questionable; ~ьно it is doubtful, it is open to question. **2.** dubious; equivocal; с. комплиме́нт dubious compliment; ~ьные дела́ shady dealings.

сомножи́тел|ь, я, *m.* (*math.*) factor.

сон, сна, *m.* **1.** sleep; ве́чный с. (*fig.*) eternal rest; во сне, сквозь с. in one's sleep; на с. гряду́щий at bedtime, the last thing; со сна half awake; у меня́ сна ни в одно́м глазу́ нет (*coll.*) I am not in the least sleepy. **2.** dream; ви́деть во сне to dream, have a dream (about).

сонасле́дник, а, *m.* co-heir.

сона́т|а, ы, *f.* (*mus.*) sonata.

сонати́н|а, ы, *f.* (*mus.*) sonatina.

соне́т, а, *m.* sonnet.

сонли́в|ец, ца, *m.* (*obs., coll.*) sleepyhead.

сонли́вост|ь, и, *f.* sleepiness, drowsiness; somnolence.

сонли́в|ый (~, ~а), *adj.* sleepy, drowsy; somnolent.

сонм, а, *m.* (*arch. or joc.*) assembly, throng; (*fig.*) swarm.

со́нмищ|е, а, *n.* = сонм.

со́нник, а, *m.* book of dream interpretations.

со́нн|ый, *adj.* **1.** sleepy, drowsy (*also fig.*); somnolent; slumberous; ∼ая арте́рия (*anat.*) carotid artery; ∼ая боле́знь (*med.*) (*i*) sleeping sickness (*morbus dormitivus*), (*ii*) sleepy sickness (*encephalitis lethargica*); ∼ое ца́рство the land of Nod; у них сейча́с ∼ое ца́рство they are all asleep. **2.** sleeping, soporific; ∼ые ка́пли sleeping-draught.

соно́рный, *adj.* (*ling.*) sonorous.

со́н|я, и, *f.* **1.** dormouse. **2.** *m. and f.* (*coll.*) sleepy person, sleepyhead.

соображá|ть, ю, *impf.* **1.** *impf. of* сообраз́ить. **2.** *impf. only* хорошо́, пло́хо с. to be quick, slow in the uptake.

соображе́ни|е, я, *n.* **1.** consideration, thought; приня́ть в с. to take into consideration; поступа́ть без ∼я to act without thinking. **2.** understanding, grasp. **3.** consideration, reason; notion, idea; по фина́нсовым ∼ям for financial reasons; вы́сказать свои́ ∼я to express one's views.

сообрази́тельност|ь, и, f. quickness, quick-wittedness.

сообрази́тел|ьный (∼ен, ∼ьна), *adj.* quick-witted, quick, sharp, bright.

сообра|зи́ть, жу́, зи́шь, *pf.* (*of* ∼жáть) **1.** to consider, ponder, think out; to weigh (the pros and cons of). **2.** to understand, grasp. **3.** (*coll.*) to think up, arrange.

сообра́зно, *adv.* (c+*i.*) in conformity (with).

сообра́зност|ь, и, f. conformity.

сообра́з|ный (∼ен, ∼на), *adj.* (c+*i.*) conformable (to), in conformity (with); э́то ни с чем не ∼но it makes no sense at all.

сообраз|ова́ть, у́ю, *impf. and pf.* (c+*i.*) to conform (to), make conformable (to), adapt (to); с. расхо́ды с дохо́дами to adapt expenditure to income.

сообраз|ова́ться, у́юсь, *impf. and pf.* (c+*i.*) to conform (to), adapt oneself (to).

сообщá, *adv.* together, jointly.

сообщ|а́ть, а́ю, *impf. of* ∼и́ть.

сообщ|а́ться, а́юсь, *impf.* **1.** *impf. of* ∼и́ться. **2.** *impf. only* (c+*i.*) to communicate (with), be in communication (with).

сообще́ни|е, я, *n.* **1.** communication, report; по после́дним ∼ям according to latest reports; проче́сть с., сде́лать с. to read a communication (*at a meeting of a learned society, etc.*). **2.** communication; возду́шное с. aerial communication; прямо́е с. through connexion; пути́ ∼я communications (*rail, road, canal, etc.*).

сообще́ств|о, а, *n.* association, fellowship; в ∼е (c+*i.*) in association (with), together (with).

сообщ|и́ть, у́, и́шь, *pf.* (*of* ∼áть) **1.** (+*a. or*

о+*p.*) to communicate, report, inform, announce; с. после́дние изве́стия to communicate the latest news; по ра́дио ∼и́ли о заключе́нии ми́рного догово́ра the conclusion of a peace treaty has been announced on the radio; нам ∼и́ли, что вас призва́ли на вое́нную слу́жбу we were told that you had been called up. **2.** to impart; с. материа́лу огнеупо́рность to make a material fireproof.

сообщ|и́ться, и́тся, *pf.* (*of* ∼áться) to be communicated, communicate itself.

сообщник, а, *m.* accomplice, confederate; partner (*in crime*); (*leg.*) accessory.

сообщничеств|о, а, *n.* complicity.

соору|ди́ть, жу́, ди́шь, *pf.* (*of* ∼жáть) to build, erect.

сооруже́ни|е, я, *n.* **1.** building, erection. **2.** building, structure; вое́нные ∼я military installations; оборони́тельные ∼я (*mil.*) defensive works, defences.

соотве́тственно, *adv.* **1.** accordingly, correspondingly. **2.** (+*d.*) according (to), in accordance (with), in conformity (with), in compliance (with).

соотве́тствен|ный (∼, ∼на), *adj.* (+*d.*) corresponding (to).

соотве́тстви|е, я, *n.* accordance, conformity, correspondence; в ∼и (c+*i.*) in accordance (with); привести́ в с. (c+*i.*) to bring into line (with).

соотве́тств|овать, ую, *impf.* (+*d.*) to correspond (to, with), conform (to), be in keeping (with); с. действи́тельности to correspond to the facts; с. тре́бованиям to meet the requirements; с. це́ли to answer the purpose.

соотве́тств|ующий, *pres. part. act. of* ∼овать *and adj.* **1.** (+*d.*) corresponding (to). **2.** proper, appropriate, suitable; поступа́ть ∼ующим о́бразом to act accordingly.

соотéчественник, а, *m.* compatriot, fellow-countryman.

соотнес|ти́, у́, ёшь, *past* ∼, ∼ла́, *pf.* (*of* соотноси́ть) to correlate.

соотноси́тел|ьный (∼ен, ∼ьна), *adj.* correlative.

соотно|си́ть, шу́, ∼сишь, *impf. of* соотнести́.

соотно|си́ться, ∼сится, *impf.* to correspond.

соотноше́ни|е, я, *n.* correlation; ratio; с. сил correlation of forces, alignment of forces.

сопе́рник, а, *m.* rival.

сопе́рнича|ть, ю, *impf.* to be rivals; (c+*i.*) to compete (with), vie (with).

сопе́рничеств|о, а, *n.* rivalry.

соп|е́ть, лю́, и́шь, *impf.* to breathe heavily and noisily through the nose.

со́пк|а, и, f. **1.** knoll, hill, mound. **2.** (*in Far East*) volcano.

соплеме́нник, а, *m.* fellow-tribesman.

соплеме́нный, *adj.* related, of the same tribe.

соплив|ый (~, ~а), *adj.* (*coll.*) snotty.

соп|ло́, а́, *pl.* ~ла, ~ел, *n.* (*tech.*) nozzle.

сопл|я́, и́, *pl.* ~и, ~е́й, *f.* **1.** (nose-)drip; (*pl.*) snivel, snot. **2.** (*coll., pejor.*) = сопля́к.

сопля́к, а́, *m.* (*coll., pejor.*) **1.** whimperer, sniveller. **2.** spineless creature; milksop.

соподчине́ни|е, я, *n.* co-ordination.

соподчинён|ный (~, ~а́), *adj.* (*gram.*) co-ordinative.

сопостави́м|ый (~, ~а), *adj.* comparable.

сопоста́в|ить, лю, ишь, *pf.* (*of* ~ля́ть) (c+*i.*) to compare (with), confront (with).

сопоставле́ни|е, я, *n.* comparison, confrontation.

сопоставля́|ть, ю, *impf. of* сопоста́вить.

сопра́но, *indecl.* (*mus.*) **1.** *n.* soprano (*voice*). **2.** *f.* soprano (*singer*).

сопреде́л|ьный (~ен, ~ьна), *adj.* contiguous; (*fig.*) kindred, related.

сопре́|ть, ю, *pf. of* преть.

соприкаса́|ться, юсь, *impf.* (*of* соприкосну́ться) (c+*i.*) **1.** to adjoin, be contiguous (to). **2.** (*fig.*) to come into contact (with).

соприкоснове́ни|е, я, *n.* contiguity; (*mil. and fig.*) contact; име́ть с. (c+*i.*) to come into contact (with).

соприкосн|у́ться, у́сь, ёшься, *pf. of* соприкаса́ться.

соприч́стност|ь, и, *f.* complicity, participation.

соприча́ст|ный (~ен, ~на), *adj.* быть с. (к) to be implicated (in), be a participant (in).

сопроводи́тел|ь, я, *m.* escort.

сопроводи́тельн|ый, *adj.* accompanying; ~ое письмо́ covering letter.

сопрово|ди́ть, жу́, ди́шь, *pf. of* ~жда́ть.

сопровожда́|ть, ю, *impf.* (*of* сопроводи́ть) (*in var. senses*) to accompany; to escort; to convey.

сопровожде́ни|е, я, *n.* accompaniment; escort, convoy; в ~и (+*g.*) accompanied (by); escorted (by).

сопротивле́ни|е, я, *n.* resistance, opposition; (*phys., tech.*) strength; (*electr.*) resistance, impedance; оказа́ть с. to offer, put up resistance; с. материа́лов (study of) strength of materials; с. разры́ву tensile strength; идти́ по ли́нии наиме́ньшего ~я to take the line of least resistance.

сопротивля́емост|ь, и, *f.* capacity to resist; (*electr.*) resistivity.

сопротивля́|ться, юсь, *impf.* (+*d.*) to resist, oppose.

сопряжён|ный (~, ~а́), *adj.* **1.** (c+*i.*) linked (with), attended (by), entailing; ваш прое́кт ~ с больши́м ри́ском your scheme

entails great risk. **2.** (*math., chem., tech.*) conjugate; bilateral.

сопу́тств|овать, ую, *impf.* (+*d.*) to accompany; ~ующие обстоя́тельства attendant circumstances, concomitants.

сор, а, *m.* litter, dust; не выноси́ть ~а из избы́ not to wash one's dirty linen in public.

соразме́р|ить, ю, ишь, *pf.* (*of* ~я́ть) (c+*i.*) to make commensurate (with), balance (with), match (with).

соразме́рност|ь, и, *f.* proportionality.

соразме́р|ный (~ен, ~на), *adj.* proportionate, commensurate; balanced; of the same order.

соразмер|я́ть, я́ю, *impf. of* ~ить.

сора́тник, а, *m.* companion-in-arms, comrade-in-arms.

сорван|е́ц, ца́, *m.* (*coll.*; *of a child*) a terror; (*of a girl*) tomboy.

сорв|а́ть, у́, ёшь, *past* ~а́л, ~ала́, ~а́ло, *pf.* (*of* срыва́ть) **1.** to tear off, break off, tear away, tear down; to pick, pluck; с. ве́тку to break off a branch; ве́тер ~а́л с меня́ шля́пу the wind took my hat off; с. ма́ску с кого́-н. to unmask someone. **2.** (*coll.*) to get, extract; с. с кого́-н. де́сять рубле́й to get ten roubles out of someone. **3.** (на+*p.*) to vent (upon); с. гнев на ком-н. to vent one's anger upon someone. **4.** to smash, wreck, ruin, spoil; с. вра́жеские пла́ны to foil, frustrate the enemy's plans; с. рабо́ту to upset work; с. забасто́вку to break a strike; с. банк (*cards*) to break the bank.

сорв|а́ться, у́сь, ёшься, *past* ~а́лся, ~ала́сь, ~а́ло́сь, *pf.* (*of* срыва́ться) **1.** to break away, break loose; с. с пе́тель to come off its hinges, come unhinged; с. с ме́ста (*coll.*) to dart off; с. с це́пи (*fig., coll.*) to break out, break loose; с. с языка́ to escape one's lips. **2.** to fall, come down; с. с колоко́льни to fall from the belfry. **3.** (*coll.*) to fall through, fall to the ground, miscarry.

сорвиголов|а́, ы́, *pl.* сорвиго́ловы, сорвиголо́в, сорвиголова́м, *m. and f.* (*coll.*) daredevil; desperate character.

сorganиз|ова́ть, у́ю, *pf. of* организова́ть.

со́рго, *indecl.* *n.* (*bot.*) sorghum.

соревнова́ни|е, я, *n.* **1.** (*sport*) competition, contest; event; кома́ндное с. team event; отбо́рочные ~я elimination contests; с. на пе́рвенство ми́ра world championship. **2.** competition, emulation; социалисти́ческое с. socialist emulation.

соревн|ова́ться, у́юсь, *impf.* (c+*i.*) to compete (with, against), contend (with); to engage in competition.

соревн|у́ющийся, *pres. part. of* ~ова́ться; *as noun* с., ~у́ющегося, *m.* competitor, contender.

соригина́льнича|ть, ю, *pf. of* оригина́льничать.

со́ринк|а, и, *f.* mote; speck of dust.

сор|и́ть, ю, и́шь, *impf.* (*of* на~) (+*a. or i.*) to litter; to throw about (*also fig.*); to make a mess; с. в ко́мнате оку́рками to litter a room with cigarette butts; с. деньга́ми to throw one's money about.

со́рн|ый, *adj.* 1. *adj. of* сор; ~ое ведро́ refuse pail; с. я́щик dustbin. 2. ~ое расте́ние; ~ая трава́ weed; ~ая трава́ (*collect.*) weeds.

сорня́к, а́, *m.* weed.

соро́дич, а, *m.* 1. relative, kinsman. 2. fellow--countryman; person from same part of country.

со́рок, *all other cases* а́, *num.* forty; с. ~о́в (*obs.*) a multitude, a great number.

соро́к|а, и, *f.* magpie; с. на хвосте́ принесла́ (*joc.; of something learned from an unrevealed source*) a little bird told me, us, *etc.*

сорокале́ти|е, я, *n.* 1. forty years. 2. fortieth anniversary, fortieth birthday.

сорокале́тний, *adj.* 1. forty-year, of forty years. 2. forty-year-old.

сорокаме́стный, *adj.* forty-seater.

сороков|о́й, *adj.* fortieth; ~ы́е го́ды the forties; с. но́мер number forty; ~а́я страни́ца page forty.

сороконо́жк|а, и, *f.* centipede.

сорокопу́т, а, *m.* (*orn.*) shrike.

сорокоу́ст, а, *m.* (forty days') prayers for the dead.

соро́чк|а, и, *f.* 1. shirt; blouse; camisole; ночна́я с. night-shirt, night-dress. 2. reverse (*of playing-card*). 3. (*med.*) caul; роди́ться в ~е to be born with a silver spoon in one's mouth 4. jacket, cover.

сорт, а, *pl.* ~а́, *m.* 1. grade, quality; brand; вы́сший с. best quality; пе́рвого ~а first grade, first quality; first-rate. 2. sort, kind, variety.

сорта́мент, а, *m.* = сортиме́нт.

сортиме́нт, а, *m.* (*tech.*) assortment.

сортир|ова́ть, у́ю, *impf.* to sort, assort, grade; с. по разме́рам to size.

сортиро́вк|а, и, *f.* 1. sorting, grading, sizing. 2. (*agric.*) separator.

сортиро́вочн|ая, ой, *f.* marshalling yard.

сортиро́вочный, *adj.* sorting.

сортиро́вщик, а, *m.* sorter.

со́ртност|ь, и, *f.* grade, quality.

со́ртный, *adj.* of high quality.

сортов|о́й, *adj.* high-grade, of high quality; ~о́е желе́зо section iron, profile iron, shaped iron; с. стан jobbing mill, shape mill.

соса́ни|е, я, *n.* sucking, suction.

соса́тельный, *adj.* sucking.

сос|а́ть, у́, ёшь, *impf.* to suck.

сосва́та|ть, ю, *pf. of* сва́тать.

сосе́д, а, *pl.* ~и, ~е́й, *m.* neighbour.

сосе́д|ить, ишь, *impf.* (с+*i.*) to neighbour.

сосе́дн|ий, *adj.* neighbouring; adjacent, next; с. дом the house next door; ~яя ко́мната the next room.

сосе́д|ский, *adj. of* ~; ~ские де́ти the neighbours' children, the children next door.

сосе́дств|о, а, *n.* neighbourhood, vicinity; по ~у (+*g.*) in the neighbourhood (of), in the vicinity (of); мы с ни́ми живём по ~у we (and they) are neighbours.

соси́ск|а, и, *f.* sausage; frankfurter.

со́ск|а, и, *f.* baby's dummy.

соска́блива|ть, ю, *impf. of* соскобли́ть.

соска́кива|ть, ю, *impf. of* соскочи́ть.

соска́льзыва|ть, ю, *impf. of* соскользну́ть.

соскобл|и́ть, ю́, ~и́шь, *pf.* (*of* соска́бливать) to scrape off.

соскользн|у́ть, у́, ёшь, *pf.* (*of* соска́льзывать) to slip off, slide off; to slide down, glide down.

соскоч|и́ть, у́, ~ишь, *pf.* (*of* соска́кивать) 1. to jump off, leap off; to jump down, leap down; с. с крова́ти to jump out of bed; с. с трамва́я to jump off a tram. 2. to come off; с. с пе́тель to come off its hinges. 3. (с+*g.*; *coll.*) to disappear (from), leave; хмель ~и́л с него́ he sobered up.

соскреба́|ть, ю, *impf. of* соскрести́.

соскре|сти́, бу́, бёшь, *past* ~б, ~бла́, *pf.* (*of* ~ба́ть) to scrape away, off.

соску́ч|иться, усь, ишься, *pf.* 1. to become bored. 2. (по+*p., preceding sing. nouns*; по+*d., preceding pl. nouns*) to miss; с. по дере́вне to miss the country; с. по друзья́м to miss one's friends.

сослага́тельный, *adj.* (*gram.*) subjunctive.

со|сла́ть, шлю, шлёшь, *pf.* (*of* ссыла́ть) to exile, banish, deport.

со|сла́ться¹, шлю́сь, шлёшься, *pf.* (*of* ссыла́ться) (на+*a.*) 1. to refer (to), allude (to), cite, quote. 2. to plead, allege; с. на недомога́ние to plead indisposition.

со|сла́ться², шлю́сь, шлёшься, *pf.* (*of* ссыла́ться) *pass. of* ~сла́ть.

со́слепа, *adv.* (*coll.*) due to poor sight.

со́слеп|у, adv. = ~а.

сосло́ви|е, я, *n.* 1. estate; дворя́нское с. the nobility; the gentry; духо́вное с. the clergy; купе́ческое с. the merchants. 2. corporation, professional association.

сосло́в|ный, *adj. of* ~ие; ~ная мона́рхия limited monarchy; ~ное представи́тельство (*hist.*) representation of the estates; с. предрассу́док class prejudice.

сослужи́в|ец, ца, *m.* colleague, fellow-employee.

сослуж|и́ть, у́, ~ишь, *pf.* с. кому́-н. слу́жбу

to do someone a good turn, stand someone in good stead.

сосн|а́, ы́, *pl.* ~ы, со́сен, *f.* pine(-tree); заблуди́ться в трёх ~ах, *see* заблуди́ться.

сосно́в|ый, *adj.* pine; pinewood; deal; с. бор pine forest; ~ая ме́бель deal furniture; ~ая смола́ pine tar.

сосн|у́ть, у́, ёшь, *pf.* (*coll.*) to have, take a nap.

сосня́к, á, *m.* pine forest.

сос|о́к, ка́, *m.* nipple, teat.

сосо́ч|ек, ка, *m.* **1.** *dim. of* сосо́к. **2.** (*anat.*) papilla.

сосредото́чени|е, я, *n.* (*mil., etc.*) concentration.

сосредото́ченност|ь, и, *f.* (degree of) concentration.

сосредото́ч|енный, *p.p.p. of* ~ить *and adj.* concentrated; (*tech.*) lumped, centred; с. взгляд fixed stare; ~енное внима́ние rapt attention; ~енная нагру́зка (*tech.*) point load; с. ого́нь (*mil.*) concentrated fire, convergent fire.

сосредото́чива|ть(ся), ю(сь), *impf. of* сосредото́чить(ся).

сосредото́ч|ить, у, ишь, *pf.* (*of* ~ивать) to concentrate; to focus; с. внима́ние (на+*p.*) to concentrate one's attention (on, upon).

сосредото́ч|иться, усь, ишься, *pf.* (*of* ~иваться) **1.** (на+*p.*) to concentrate (on, upon). **2.** *pass. of* ~ить.

соста́в, а, *m.* **1.** composition, make-up; structure; социа́льный с. social structure; хими́ческий с. (*i*) chemical composition, (*ii*) chemical compound; входи́ть в с. (+*g.*) to form part (of); с. преступле́ния (*leg.*) corpus delicti. **2.** staff; membership, composition; strength; ли́чный с. personnel; нали́чный с. available personnel; (*mil.*) effectives; офице́рский с. the officers; в по́лном ~е with its full complement; in, at full strength; в ~е (+*g.*) numbering, consisting (of), amounting (to); делега́ция в ~е тридцати́ челове́к a delegation of thirty (persons); входи́ть в с. (+*g.*) to become a member (of). **3.** train; подвижно́й с. rolling-stock.

состави́тел|ь, я, *m.* compiler, author; с. поездо́в train maker-up.

соста́в|ить[1], лю, ишь, *pf.* (*of* ~ля́ть) **1.** to put together, make up; с. винто́вки в ко́злы (*mil.*) to pile arms, stack arms; с. по́езд to make up a train; с. посу́ду to stack crockery. **2.** to compose, make up, draw up; to compile; to form, construct; с. библиоте́ку to form a library; с. мне́ние to form an opinion; с. предложе́ние to construct a sentence; с. прое́кт to draw up a draft; с. слова́рь to compile a dictionary; с. спи́сок to make a list. **3.** to be, consti-

tute, make; э́то не ~ит исключе́ния из пра́вила this will not constitute an exception to the rule; с. чьё-н. сча́стье to make someone's happiness. **4.** to form, make, amount to, total; с. в сре́днем to average; расхо́ды ~или пятьсо́т фу́нтов expenditure amounted to five hundred pounds. **5.** с. себе́ to make (for oneself); с. себе́ и́мя to make a name for oneself.

соста́в|ить[2], лю, ишь, *pf.* (*of* ~ля́ть) to take down, put down; с. я́щик на пол to put a drawer down on the floor.

соста́в|иться, ится, *pf.* (*of* ~ля́ться) to form, be formed, come into being.

составля́|ть(ся), ю(сь), *impf. of* соста́вить(ся).

составн|о́й, *adj.* **1.** compound, composite; ~а́я кни́жная по́лка sectional book-shelf. **2.** component; ~а́я часть component, constituent.

соста́р|ить(ся), ю(сь), ишь(ся), *pf. of* ста́рить(ся).

состоя́ни|е, я, *n.* **1.** state, condition; position; в хоро́шем, плохо́м ~и in good, bad condition; прийти́ в него́дное с. to be past repair; с. войны́ state of war; быть в ~и войны́ (с+*i.*) to be at war (with); с. пого́ды state of the weather, weather conditions; быть в ~и (+*inf.*) to be able (to), be in a position (to). **2.** (*obs.*) status, condition; гражда́нское с. civil status. **3.** fortune; нажи́ть с. to make a fortune.

состоя́тельност|ь[1], и, *f.* **1.** solvency. **2.** wealth.

состоя́тельност|ь[2], и, *f.* justifiability, strength (*of an argument, etc.*).

состоя́тел|ьный[1] (~ен, ~ьна), *adj.* **1.** solvent. **2.** well-off, well-to-do.

состоя́тел|ьный[2] (~ен, ~ьна), *adj.* well-grounded; не вполне́ с. до́вод lame argument.

состо|я́ть, ю́, и́шь, *impf.* **1.** (из) to consist (of), comprise, be made up (of); кварти́ра ~и́т из трёх ко́мнат the flat consists of three rooms; име́ние ~и́т преиму́щественно из торфяно́го боло́та the estate is largely made up of a peatbog. **2.** (в+*p.*) to consist (in), lie (in), be; ра́зница ~и́т в том, что the difference is that; в чём ~я́т на́ши обя́занности? what are our duties? **3.** to be; с. чле́ном о́бщества to be a member of a society; с. в до́лжности заве́дующего to occupy the post of director; с. на вооруже́нии (*mil.*) to be part of standard equipment; с. на своём иждиве́нии to keep oneself; с. под судо́м to be awaiting trial; с. при посо́льстве to be attached to the embassy.

состо|я́ться, и́тся, *pf.* to take place; визи́т не ~я́лся the visit did not take place;

изда́ние не ~я́лось the edition was never printed.

состра́гива|ть, ю, *impf. of* сострога́ть.

сострада́ни|е, я, *n.* compassion, sympathy.

сострада́тел|ьный (~ен, ~ьна), *adj.* compassionate, sympathetic.

сострада́|ть, ю, *impf.* (+*d.*; *obs.*) to feel pity (for).

сострига́|ть, ю, *impf. of* состри́чь.

состр|и́ть, и́, и́шь, *pf. of* остри́ть.

состри́|чь, гу́, жёшь, гу́т, *past* ~г, ~гла, *pf.* (*of* ~га́ть) to shear, clip off.

сострога́|ть, ю, *pf.* (*of* состра́гивать) to plane off.

состро́|ить, ю, ишь, *pf. of* стро́ить 3.; с. грима́су, с. ро́жу (*coll.*) to make a face.

состру́га|ть, ю, *pf.* = сострога́ть.

состря́па|ть, ю, *pf. of* стря́пать.

состык|ова́ть(ся), у́ю(сь), *pf. of* стыкова́ть(ся).

состяза́ни|е, я, *n.* 1. competition, contest; match; с. в пла́вании swimming contest; с. по фехтова́нию fencing match; с. в остроу́мии battle of wits. 2. (*leg.*) controversy.

состяза́тельный, *adj.* (*leg.*) controversial.

состяза́|ться, юсь, *impf.* (с+*i.*) to compete (with), contend (with).

сосу́д, а, *m.* (*in var. senses*) vessel; кровено́сные ~ы blood vessels.

сосу́дистый, *adj.* (*anat., biol.*) vascular.

сосу́льк|а, и, *f.* icicle.

сосу́н, а́, *m.* suckling, sucker.

сосуществова́ни|е, я, *n.* co-existence; ми́рное с. (*polit.*) peaceful co-existence.

сосуществ|ова́ть, у́ю, *impf.* to co-exist.

сос|у́щий, *pres. part. act. of* ~а́ть *and adj.* (*zool.*) suctorial.

сосцеви́д|ный (~ен, ~на), *adj.* mammiform, mammilliform.

сосчита́|ть, ю, *pf. of* счита́ть.

сосчита́|ться, юсь, *pf.* (с+*i.*) to settle accounts (with), get even (with) (*also fig.*).

сотворе́ни|е, я, *n.* creation, making; с. ми́ра the creation of the world.

сотвор|и́ть, ю́, и́шь, *pf. of* твори́ть.

со́тенн|ая, ой, *f.* (*coll.*) hundred-rouble note.

со́тенный, *adj.* (*coll.*) worth a hundred roubles.

со́тк|а, и, *f.* hundredth part.

сотк|а́ть, у́, ёшь, *past* ~а́л, ~ала́, ~а́ло, *pf. of* ткать.

со́тник, а, *m.* (*hist.*) sotnik (*lieutenant of Cossack troops*).

со́т|ня, ни, *g. pl.* ~ен, *f.* 1. a hundred (*esp. a hundred roubles*). 2. (*hist.*) sotnya, company (*mil. unit, originally of a hundred men*); каза́чья с. Cossack squadron.

сотова́рищ, а, *m.* associate, partner.

сотови́д|ный (~ен, ~на), *adj.* honeycomb.

со́т|овый, *adj.* 1. *adj. of* ~ы; с. мёд comb-honey. 2. (*tech.*; *fig.*) honeycomb; ~овая кату́шка honeycomb coil.

сотрапе́зник, а, *m.* (*obs.*) table-companion.

сотру́дник, а, *m.* 1. collaborator. 2. employee, official; нау́чный с. research officer, research fellow, research assistant (*of a learned body or scientific institution*); с. посо́льства embassy official. 3. contributor (*to a newspaper, journal, etc.*).

сотру́днича|ть, ю, *impf.* 1. (с+*i.*) to collaborate (with). 2. (в+*p.*) to contribute (to); с. в газе́те to contribute to a newspaper; to work on a newspaper.

сотру́дничеств|о, а, *n.* collaboration, co-operation.

сотряс|а́ть(ся), а́ю(сь), *impf. of* ~ти́(сь).

сотрясе́ни|е, я, *n.* shaking; с. мо́зга (*med.*) concussion.

сотряс|ти́, у́, ёшь, *past* ~, ~ла́, (*of* ~а́ть) to shake.

сотряс|ти́сь, у́сь, ёшься, *past* ~ся, ~ла́сь, *pf.* (*of* ~а́ться) to shake, tremble.

со́т|ы, ов, *no sing.* honeycombs; мёд в ~ах honey in combs.

со́т|ый, *adj.* hundredth; с. год the year one hundred; с. но́мер number one hundred; *as noun* ~ая, ~ой, *f.* (a) hundredth.

соумы́шленник, а, *m.* accomplice.

со́ус, а, *m.* sauce; gravy; dressing.

со́усник, а, *m.* sauce-boat, gravy-boat.

соуча́ств|овать, ую, *impf.* (в+*p.*) to participate (in), take part (in).

соуча́сти|е, я, *n.* participation; complicity.

соуча́стник, а, *m.* participator; accomplice; с. преступле́ния (*leg.*) accessory to a crime.

соучени́к, а́, *m.* schoolmate, schoolfellow.

соф|а́, ы́, *pl.* ~ы, *f.* sofa.

софи́зм, а, *m.* sophism, sophistry.

софи́ст, а, *m.* sophist.

софи́стик|а, и, *f.* sophistry.

софисти́ческий, *adj.* sophistic(al).

сох|а́, и́, *pl.* ~и, *f.* (*wooden*) plough.

соха́т|ый (~, ~а), *adj.* (*dial.*) with branching antlers; *as noun* с., ~ого, *m.* elk.

со́х|нуть, ну, нешь, *past* ~, ~ла, *impf.* 1. to dry, get dry; to become parched. 2. to wither; (*fig.*) to pine.

сохране́ни|е, я, *n.* 1. preservation; conservation; care, custody, charge; зако́н ~я эне́ргии law of conservation of energy; отда́ть кому́-н. на с. to give into someone's charge. 2. retention; о́тпуск с ~ем содержа́ния holiday(s) with pay.

сохран|и́ть, ю́, и́шь, *pf.* (*of* ~я́ть) 1. to preserve, keep; to keep safe; с. ве́рность (+*d.*) to remain faithful, loyal (to), keep, stand by; с. на па́мять to keep as a souvenir.

2. to keep, retain, reserve; с. хладнокро́вие to keep cool, keep one's head; с. за собо́й пра́во to reserve the right.

сохран|и́ться, ю́сь, и́шься, *pf.* (*of* ~я́ться) 1. to remain (intact); to last out, hold out; здоро́вье у неё ~и́лось до девяно́ста лет her health lasted out right up to her nine-tieth year; он хорошо́ ~и́лся he is well preserved. 2. *pass. of* ~и́ть.

сохра́нно, *adv.* safely, intact.

сохра́нност|ь, и, *f.* 1. safety, undamaged state; радиоприёмник пришёл в по́лной ~и the radio arrived quite intact. 2. safe keeping.

сохра́н|ный (~ен, ~на), *adj.* safe; un-damaged.

сохран|я́ть(ся), я́ю(сь), *impf. of* ~и́ть(ся).

соц- *abbr. of* 1. социа́льный. 2. социали-сти́ческий.

соцве́ти|е, я, *n.* (*bot.*) inflorescence.

соцдогово́р, а, *m.* socialist emulation agree-ment.

социа́л-демокра́т, а, *m.* social democrat.

социа́л-демократи́ческий, *adj.* social demo-cratic.

социа́л-демокра́ти|я, и, *f.* social demo-cracy.

социализа́ци|я, и, *f.* socialization.

социализи́р|овать, ую, *impf. and pf.* to so-cialize.

социали́зм, а, *m.* socialism.

социали́ст, а, *m.* socialist.

социалисти́ческий, *adj.* socialist.

социали́ст-революционе́р, а, *m.* (*hist.*) so-cialist revolutionary.

социа́л-революцио́нный, *adj.* (*hist.*) socialist-revolutionary.

социа́льно-бытово́й, *adj.* social, welfare.

социа́льн|ый, *adj.* (*in var. senses*) social; ~ое обеспе́чение social security; ~ое поло-же́ние social status; ~ая психоло́гия social psychology.

социогра́фи|я, и, *f.* descriptive sociology.

социо́лог, а, *m.* sociologist.

социологи́ческий, *adj.* sociological.

социоло́ги|я, и, *f.* sociology.

соцреали́зм, а, *m.* (*abbr. of* социалисти́-ческий реали́зм) socialist realism.

соцсоревнова́ни|е, я, *n.* (*abbr. of* социали-сти́ческое соревнова́ние) socialist emula-tion.

соцстра́х, а, *m.* (*abbr. of* социа́льное стра-хова́ние) social insurance.

соче́льник, а, *m.* (*eccl.*) рожде́ственский с. Christmas Eve; креще́нский с. Twelfth--night, eve of the Epiphany.

сочета́ни|е, я, *n.* combination.

сочета́|ть, ю, *impf. and pf.* (с+*i.*) to com-bine (with); с. бра́ком (*obs.*) to marry (to), wed (to).

сочета́|ться, юсь, *impf. and pf.* 1. to com-bine; в ней ~лся ум с красото́й she com-bined intelligence and good looks. 2. (с+*i.*) to harmonize (with), go (with); to match. 3. с. бра́ком (с+*i.*; *obs.*) to contract matri-mony (with).

сочине́ни|е, я, *n.* 1. composing. 2. (*literary*) work; и́збранные ~я Го́голя selected works of Gogol. 3. (*school*) composition, essay. 4. (*gram.*) co-ordination.

сочини́тел|ь, я, *m.* 1. (*obs.*) writer, author. 2. (*coll.*) story-teller, fabricator.

сочини́тельный, *adj.* (*gram.*) co-ordinative.

сочини́тельств|о, а, *n.* 1. (*obs.*) writing. 2. (*pejor.*) scribbling, hack-writing. 3. (*coll.*) fabrication.

сочин|и́ть, ю́, и́шь, *pf.* (*of* ~я́ть) 1. to com-pose (*a lit. or mus. work*); to write. 2. to make up, fabricate.

сочин|я́ть, я́ю, *impf.* 1. *impf. of* ~и́ть. 2. (*obs.*) to write, be a writer.

соч|и́ть, у́, и́шь, *impf.* to ooze (out), exude.

соч|и́ться, и́тся, *impf.* to ooze (out), exude, trickle; с. кро́вью to bleed.

сочле́н, а, *m.* fellow member.

сочлене́ни|е, я, *n.* (*anat. and tech.*) articula-tion, joint, coupling.

сочлен|и́ть, ю́, и́шь, *pf.* (*of* ~я́ть) to join.

сочлен|я́ть, я́ю, *impf. of* ~и́ть.

со́чност|ь, и, *f.* juiciness, succulence.

со́ч|ный (~ен, ~на́, ~но), *adj.* 1. juicy (*also fig.*); succulent. 2. (*fig.*) rich; lush; с. го́лос fruity voice; ~ная расти́тельность lush vegetation.

сочу́вственност|ь, и, *f.* sympathy.

сочу́вствен|ный (~, ~на), *adj.* sympathetic.

сочу́встви|е, я, *n.* sympathy; вы́звать с. to gain sympathy.

сочу́вств|овать, ую, *impf.* (+*d.*) to sympa-thize (with), feel (for).

сочу́вств|ующий, *pres. part. act. of* ~овать *and adj.* sympathetic; *as noun* с., ~ующего, *m.* sympathizer.

со́шк|а, и, *f.* 1. *dim. of* соха́; ме́лкая с. (*coll.*) small fry. 2. (*mil.*) bipod.

сошни́к, а́, *m.* 1. ploughshare. 2. (*mil.*) trail spade (*of gun carriage*).

со́|шный, *adj. of* ~ха́.

сощу́рива|ть(ся), ю(сь), *impf. of* сощу́рить-(ся).

сощу́р|ить, ю, ишь, *pf.* (*of* щу́рить *and* ~ивать) с. глаза́ to screw up one's eyes.

сощу́р|иться, юсь, ишься, *pf.* (*of* щу́риться *and* ~иваться) to screw up one's eyes.

сою́з¹, а, *m.* 1. alliance, union; agreement; заключи́ть с. (с+*i.*) to conclude an alliance (with). 2. union; league; профессиона́ль-ный с. trade union; Сове́тский С. the Soviet Union.

сою́з², а, *m.* (*gram.*) conjunction.

сою́зк|а, и, *f.* vamp (*of footwear*).

сою́зник, а, *m.* ally.

сою́знический, *adj.* ally's.

сою́зно-республика́нский, *adj.* Union-Republic (*in administration of U.S.S.R.*).

сою́зн|ый¹, *adj.* 1. allied; ~ые держа́вы allied powers; (*hist.*) the Allies. 2. (*of the U.S.S.R.*) Union; ~ое гражда́нство citizenship of the (Soviet) Union.

сою́з|ный², *adj. of* ~².

со́|я, и, *f.* soya bean.

спад, а, *m.* 1. (*econ.*) slump, recession. 2. abatement.

спада́|ть, ю, *impf. of* спасть.

спазм, а, *m.* spasm.

спа́зм|а, ы, *f.* = ~.

спа́ива|ть¹, ю, *impf. of* спои́ть.

спа́ива|ть², ю, *impf. of* спая́ть.

спа́|й, я, *m.* (*tech.*) (soldered) joint.

спа́йк|а, и, *f.* 1. soldering; soldered joint. 2. (*anat.*) commissure. 3. (*fig.*) cohesion; union.

спал|и́ть, ю, и́шь, *pf. of* пали́ть¹.

спа́льник, а, *m.* (*coll.*) sleeping-bag.

спа́льн|ый, *adj.* sleeping; с. ваго́н sleeping--car; ~ое ме́сто berth, bunk; с. мешо́к sleeping-bag; ~ые принадле́жности bedding.

спа́ль|ня, ьни, *g. pl.* ~ен, *f.* 1. bedroom. 2. bedroom suite.

спань|ё, я́, *n.* sleep(ing).

спарашюти́р|овать, ую, *pf. of* парашюти́ровать.

спа́р|енный, *p.p.p. of* ~ить *and adj.* paired, coupled; ~енная езда́ (*railways*) double--manning; с. пулемёт coaxial machine--gun; ~енная устано́вка (*mil.*) combination gun mount.

спа́рж|а, и, *f.* asparagus.

спа́рива|ть(ся), ю(сь), *impf. of* спа́рить(ся).

спа́р|ить, ю, ишь, *pf.* (*of* ~ивать) 1. to couple, pair, mate (*animals*). 2. to pair off (*to work together*).

спа́р|иться, юсь, ишься, *pf.* (*of* ~иваться) 1. (*of animals*) to couple, pair, mate. 2. to pair off (*to work together*).

спартакиа́д|а, ы, *f.* sports and/or athletics meeting; sports day.

спарта́н|ец, ца, *m.* Spartan.

спарта́нский, *adj.* Spartan.

спа́рхива|ть, ю, *impf. of* спорхну́ть.

спа́рыва|ть, ю, *impf. of* спороть.

Спас, а, *m.* (*rel.*) the Saviour.

спаса́ни|е, я, *n.* rescuing, life-saving.

спаса́тельн|ый, *adj.* rescue, life-saving; с. круг, с. по́яс lifebelt; ~ая ло́дка lifeboat; ~ая экспеди́ция rescue party.

спаса́|ть(ся), ю(сь), *impf. of* спасти́(сь).

спасе́ни|е, я, *n.* 1. rescuing, saving. 2. rescue, escape; salvation.

спаси́бо, *particle* thanks; thank you; с. и на том that's something at least, we must be thankful for small mercies; *as noun* thanks; большо́е вам с. thank you very much, many thanks; сде́лать что-н. за (одно́) с. (*coll.*) to do something for love.

спаси́тел|ь, я, *m.* 1. rescuer, saver. 2. (*rel.*) the Saviour.

спаси́тел|ьный (~ен, ~ьна), *adj.* saving; salutary; с. вы́ход, ~ьное сре́дство means of escape.

спас|ова́ть, у́ю, *pf. of* пасова́ть¹.

спас|ти́, у́, ёшь, *past* ~, ~ла́, *pf.* (*of* ~а́ть) to save; to rescue; с. положе́ние to save the situation.

спас|ти́сь, у́сь, ёшься, *past* ~ся, ~ла́сь, *pf.* (*of* ~а́ться) 1. to save oneself, escape. 2. (*rel.*) to be saved, save one's soul.

спа|сть, ду́, дёшь, *past* ~л, *pf.* (*of* ~да́ть) 1. (с+*g.*) to fall down (from); с. с го́лоса (*coll.*) to lose one's voice; с. с лица́ (*coll.*) to become thin in the face; с. с те́ла (*coll.*) to lose weight. 2. to abate; (*of water*) to fall.

спа|ть, сплю, спишь, *past* ~л, ~ла́, ~ло, *impf.* to sleep, be asleep; с. мёртвым сном to be fast asleep; лечь с. to go to bed; пора́ с. it is bedtime; с. и ви́деть (*fig.*) to dream (of); с. с(+*i.*) to sleep with (*euph.*).

спа́|ться, спится, *past* ~ло́сь, *impf.* (*impers.* +*d.*) мне не спится (*i*) I cannot sleep, I cannot get to sleep, (*ii*) I am not sleepy; ей пло́хо ~ло́сь she did not sleep well.

спа́янност|ь, и, *f.* cohesion, unity.

спа|я́ть, я́ю, *pf.* (*of* ~ивать²) 1. to solder together, weld. 2. (*fig.*) to weld, unite, knit together.

спева́|ться, юсь, *impf. of* спе́ться.

спе́вк|а, и, *f.* (choir) practice, rehearsal.

спека́|ться, юсь, *impf. of* спе́чься.

спекта́кл|ь, я, *m.* (*theatr.*) performance.

спектр, а, *m.* (*phys.*) spectrum.

спектра́льный, *adj.* (*phys.*) spectral, spectrum.

спектроско́п, а, *m.* (*phys.*) spectroscope.

спектроскопи́|я, и, *f.* (*phys.*) spectroscopy.

спекули́р|овать, ую, *impf.* 1. (+*i. or* на+*p.*) to speculate (in); to profiteer (in); to gamble (on). 2. (на+*p.*; *fig.*) to gamble (on), reckon (on); to profit (by).

спекуля́нт, а, *m.* speculator, profiteer.

спекуляти́вн|ый, *adj.* speculative; по ~ым це́нам at speculative prices.

спекуля́ци|я¹, и, *f.* 1. (+*i.*, с+*i.*, *or* на+*p.*) speculation (in); profiteering; с. на иностра́нной валю́те speculation in foreign currency. 2. (на+*p.*; *fig.*) gamble (on).

спекуля́ци|я², и, *f.* (*philos.*) speculation.

спелена́|ть, ю, *pf. of* пелена́ть.

спе́л|ый (~, ~á, ~о), *adj.* ripe.

спе́нсер, а, *m.* (*obs.*) spencer (*short woollen jacket*).

сперва́, *adv.* (*coll.*) at first; first.

спе́реди, *adv. and prep.*+*g.* in front (of); at the front, from the front.

спер|е́ть¹, сопрёт, *past* ~, ~ла, *pf.* (*of* спира́ть) (*coll.*) to press; у меня́ дыха́нье ~ло it took my breath away.

спер|е́ть², сопру́, сопрёшь, *past* ~, ~ла, *pf.* (*of* переть 5) (*coll.*) to filch, pinch.

спе́рм|а, ы, *f.* sperm.

сперматозо́ид, а, *m.* (*biol.*) spermatozoon.

спермаце́т, а, *m.* (*pharm.*) spermaceti.

спёр|тый, *p.p.p. of* ~е́ть¹ *and adj.* close, stuffy.

спеси́в|ец, ца, *m.* arrogant, conceited person.

спеси́вост|ь, и, *f.* arrogance, conceit, haughtiness, loftiness.

спеси́в|ый (~, ~а), *adj.* arrogant, conceited, haughty, lofty, stuck-up.

спес|ь, и, *f.* arrogance, conceit, haughtiness, loftiness; сбить с. с кого́-н. to take someone down a peg.

спе́|ть¹, ет, *impf.* to ripen.

спе́ть², спою́, споёшь, *pf. of* петь.

спе́ться, спою́сь, споёшься, *pf.* 1. (*impf.* спева́ться) (*of a choir*) to practise, rehearse. 2. *pf. only* (*coll.*) to get on, agree, see eye to eye.

спех, а (у), *m.* (*coll.*) hurry; что за с.? what's the hurry?; мне не к ~у I'm in no hurry.

спец, а, *m.* = специали́ст.

специализа́ци|я, и, *f.* specialization.

специализи́рова|нный, *p.p.p. of* ~ть *and adj.* specialized.

специализи́р|овать, ую, *impf. and pf.* to assign a specialization (to); to earmark for a special role.

специализи́р|оваться, уюсь, *impf. and pf.* (в+*p. or* по+*d.*) to specialize (in).

специали́ст, а, *m.* (в+*p. or* по+*d.*) specialist (in), expert (in).

специа́льно, *adv.* specially, especially.

специа́льност|ь, и, *f.* 1. speciality, special interest. 2. profession; trade.

специа́л|ьный, *adj.* 1. special, especial; с. корреспонде́нт special correspondent; по́езд ~ьного назначе́ния special (train); со ~ьной це́лью with the express purpose. 2. (~ен, ~ьна) specialist; ~ьное образова́ние specialist education; с. те́рмин technical term.

специ́фик|а, и, *f.* specific character.

специфика́ци|я, и, *f.* specification.

специфици́р|овать, ую, *impf. and pf.* to specify.

специфи́ческий, *adj.* specific.

спе́ци|я, и, *f.* spice.

спецко́р, а, *m.* (*abbr. of* специа́льный корреспонде́нт) special correspondent.

спецо́вк|а, и, *f.* (*coll.*) = спецоде́жда.

спецоде́жд|а, ы, *f.* working clothes, overalls.

спе́|чься, чётся, ку́тся, *past* ~кся, ~кла́сь, *pf.* (*of* ~ка́ться) 1. (*of blood*) to coagulate, curdle. 2. (*of coal*) to cake, clinker.

спе́шива|ть(ся), ю(сь), *impf. of* спе́шить(ся).

спе́ш|ить, у, ишь, *pf.* (*of* ~ивать) to dismount.

спеш|и́ть, у́, и́шь, *impf.* (*of* по~) 1. to hurry, be in a hurry; to make haste, hasten; (c+*i.*) to hurry up (with), get a move on (with); с. домо́й to be in a hurry to get home; де́лать не ~á to do in leisurely style, take one's time over. 2. (*of a timepiece*) to be fast; ва́ши часы́ ~а́т на че́тверть часа́ your watch is a quarter of an hour fast.

спеш|и́ться, усь, ишься, *pf.* (*of* ~ива́ться) to dismount.

спе́шк|а, и, *f.* hurry, haste, rush.

спе́шност|ь, и, *f.* hurry, haste.

спе́ш|ный (~ен, ~на), *adj.* urgent, pressing; с. зака́з rush order; ~ное письмо́ express letter; ~ная по́чта express delivery; в ~ном поря́дке quickly.

спива́|ться, юсь, *impf. of* спи́ться.

спидо́метр, а, *m.* speedometer.

спики́р|овать, ую, *pf. of* пики́ровать.

спи́лива|ть, ю, *impf. of* спили́ть.

спил|и́ть, ю́, ~ишь, *pf.* (*of* ~ивать) to saw down; to saw off.

спин|а́, ы́, *a.* ~у, *pl.* ~ы, *f.* back; за ~о́й кого́-н. (*fig.*) behind someone's back; гнуть ~у (пе́ред) to cringe (to), kowtow (to); нож в ~у, уда́р в ~у (*fig.*) stab in the back; узна́ть на со́бственной ~е́ to learn from (one's own) bitter experience.

спи́нк|а, и, *f.* 1. *dim. of* спина́. 2. back (*of article of furniture or clothing*).

спи́ннинг, а, *m.* (*sport*) 1. spinning (*fishing technique*). 2. spoon-bait.

спиннинги́ст, а, *m.* fisherman employing spinning technique.

спинно́й, *adj.* spinal; с. мозг spinal cord; с. хребе́т spinal column.

спинномозгов|о́й, *adj.* ~а́я жи́дкость (*anat.*) spinal fluid.

спира́л|ь, и, *f.* spiral.

спира́льный, *adj.* spiral, helical.

спира́нт, а, *m.* (*ling.*) spirant.

спира́|ть, ет, *impf. of* спере́ть¹.

спири́т, а, *m.* spiritualist, spiritist.

спирити́зм, а, *m.* spiritualism, spiritism.

спирити́ческий, *adj.* spiritualistic, spiritistic; с. сеа́нс (spiritualistic) seance.

спиритуали́зм, а, *m.* (*philos.*) spiritualism.

спиритуали́ст, а, *m.* (*philos.*) spiritualist.

спиро́метр, а, *m.* (*med.*) spirometer.

спирохе́т|а, ы, *f.* (*biol.*) spirochaete.

спирт, а, *m.* alcohol, spirit(s); безво́дный с.

absolute alcohol; дре́весный с. wood alcohol.

спиртн|о́й, *adj.* alcoholic, spirituous; ~ы́е напи́тки alcoholic drinks, spirits; *as noun* ~о́е, ~о́го, *n.* = ~ы́е напи́тки.

спиртовк|а, и, *f.* spirit-lamp.

спиртов|о́й, *adj.* alcoholic, spirituous; ~ы́е кра́ски (*text.*) spirit colours.

спиртоме́р, а, *m.* alcoholometer.

спи|са́ть, шу́, ~шешь, *pf.* (*of* ~сывать) **1.** (с+*g.*) to copy from. **2.** (y) to copy (off), crib (off). **3.** to write off. **4.** с. с корабля́ (*naut.*) to transfer, post (from a ship).

спи|са́ться, шу́сь, ~шешься, *pf.* (*of* ~сываться) (с+*i.*) **1.** to settle by letter, arrange by letter. **2.** to exchange letters. **3.** с. с корабля́ (*naut.*) to leave ship.

спис|ок, ка, *m.* **1.** manuscript copy. **2.** list; roll; именно́й с. nominal roll; с. избира́телей voters' list, electoral roll; с. опеча́ток errata; с. уби́тых и ра́неных casualty list; с. ли́чного соста́ва (*mil.*) muster-roll. **3.** record; послужно́й с., трудово́й с. service record.

спи́сыва|ть(ся), ю(сь), *impf. of* списа́ть(ся).

спито́й, *adj.* (*coll.*; *of hot beverages*) weak, watered down to excess; с. чай weak tea.

спи|ться, сопью́сь, сопьёшься, *past* ~лся́, ~ла́сь, ~ло́сь, *pf.* (*of* ~ва́ться) to become a drunkard, take to drink; с. с кру́гу (*coll.*) to go to seed through drink.

спи́хива|ть, ю, *impf. of* спихну́ть.

спих|ну́ть, ну́, нёшь, *pf.* (*of* ~ивать) to push aside, shove aside; to push down.

спи́ц|а, ы, *f.* **1.** knitting needle. **2.** spoke; после́дняя с. в колесни́це mere cog in the machine; пя́тая с. в колесни́це minor character.

спич, а, *m.* speech, address.

спи́чечниц|а, ы, *f.* **1.** match-box. **2.** match-box stand.

спи́ч|ечный, *adj. of* ~ка; ~ечная коро́бка match-box.

спи́чк|а, и, *f.* match.

сплав¹, а, *m.* (*tech.*) alloy; fusion.

сплав², а, *m.* (timber) floating.

спла́в|ить¹, лю, ишь, *pf.* (*of* ~ля́ть) (*tech.*) to alloy, melt, fuse.

спла́в|ить², лю, ишь, *pf.* (*of* ~ля́ть) **1.** to float (*timber*); to raft. **2.** (*coll.*) to send packing, shake off.

спла́в|иться, ится, *pf.* (*of* ~ля́ться) to fuse together, coalesce.

сплавля́|ть(ся), ю, ет(ся), *impf. of* спла́вить(ся).

спла́вщик¹, а, *m.* (*tech.*) melter.

спла́вщик², а, *m.* (timber-)floater, rafter.

сплани́р|овать, ую, *pf. of* плани́ровать².

спла́чива|ть(ся), ю(сь), *impf. of* сплоти́ть(ся).

сплёвыва|ть, ю, *impf. of* сплю́нуть.

сплёскива|ть, ю, *impf. of* сплесну́ть.

сплес|ну́ть, ну́, нёшь, *pf.* (*of* ~кивать) to splash (down).

спле|сти́, ту́, тёшь, *past* ~л, ла́, *pf.* (*of* плести́ *and* ~та́ть) to weave, plait, interlace.

сплета́|ть, ю, *impf. of* сплести́.

сплете́ни|е, я, *n.* **1.** interlacing; с. лжи tissue of lies; с. обстоя́тельств combination of circumstances. **2.** (*anat.*) plexus.

спле́тник, а, *m.* gossip, scandalmonger.

спле́тниц|а, ы, *f. of* спле́тник.

спле́тнича|ть, ю, *impf.* (*of* на~) to gossip, tittle-tattle; to talk scandal.

сплет|ня, ни, *g. pl.* ~ен, *f.* gossip, tittle-tattle; piece of scandal.

сплеча́, *adv.* **1.** straight from the shoulder (*also fig.*). **2.** (*fig., coll.*) on the spot, on the spur of the moment.

спло|ти́ть, чу́, ти́шь, *pf.* (*of* спла́чивать) **1.** to join. **2.** (*fig.*) to unite, rally; с. ряды́ to close the ranks.

спло|ти́ться, чу́сь, ти́шься, *pf.* (*of* спла́чиваться) to unite, rally; to close the ranks.

сплох|ова́ть, у́ю, *pf.* (*coll.*) to make a blunder, slip up.

сплочённост|ь, и, *f.* cohesion, unity.

спло|чённый, *p.p.p. of* ~ти́ть *and adj.* **1.** unbroken. **2.** united, firm; ~чённые ряды́ serried ranks.

сплоша́|ть, ю, *pf. of* плоша́ть.

сплошн|о́й, *adj.* **1.** unbroken, continuous; с. лёд solid mass of ice, ice-field; с. лес dense forest; ~а́я ма́сса solid mass. **2.** all-round, complete; ~а́я гра́мотность universal literacy. **3.** (*fig., coll.*) sheer, solid, complete and utter, unreserved; с. восто́рг sheer joy; ~а́я чепуха́ utter rubbish.

сплошь, *adv.* **1.** all over, throughout; without a break; её но́ги бы́ли с. покры́ты комари́ными уку́сами her legs were covered all over with gnat bites; с. и (да) ря́дом (*coll.*) nearly always; pretty often. **2.** (*coll.*) completely, utterly; without exception.

сплут|ова́ть, у́ю, *pf. of* плутова́ть.

сплыва́|ть(ся), ет(ся), *impf. of* сплы́ть(ся).

сплы|ть, вёт, *past* ~л, ~ла́, ~ло, *pf.* (*of* ~ва́ть) (*coll.*) **1.** to be carried away (*by a current of water, by a flood*); бы́ло да ~ло it was a short-lived joy; it's all over. **2.** to overflow, run over.

сплы́|ться, вётся, *past* ~лся, ~ла́сь, *pf.* (*of* ~ва́ться) (*coll.*) to run (together), merge, blend.

сплю́н|уть, у, ешь, *pf.* (*of* сплёвывать) **1.** to spit. **2.** (*coll.*) to spit out.

сплюсн|у́ть, у, ешь, *pf.* = сплю́щить.

сплю́шк|а, и, *f.* (*orn.*) scops owl.

сплю́щива|ть(ся), ю(сь), *impf. of* сплю́щить(ся).

сплю́щ|ить, у, ишь, *pf.* (*of* плю́щить *and* ~ивать) to flatten, laminate.

сплю́щ|иться, ится, *pf.* (*of* ~иваться) to become flat.

спля|са́ть, шу́, ~шешь, *pf.* to dance.

сподви́жник, а, *m.* (*rhet.*) associate; comrade-in-arms.

сподо́б|ить, ит, *pf.* (*impers.*+*inf.*; *obs. or joc.*) to manage (to), come (to), contrive (to); как э́то тебя́ ~ило упа́сть в ре́ку? how did you manage to fall in the river?

сподо́б|иться, люсь, ишься, *pf.* (+*g. or* +*inf.*; *obs. or joc.*) to be honoured (with), have the honour (of).

сподру́чник, а, *m.* 1. (*obs.*) assistant, right-hand man. 2. (*pejor.*) myrmidon.

сподру́ч|ный[1] (~ен, ~на), *adj.* (*coll.*) easy; convenient, handy.

сподру́чн|ый[2], ого, *m.* = ~ик.

спозара́нку, *adv.* (*coll.*) very early (in the morning).

спо|и́ть, ю́, и́шь, *pf.* (*of* спа́ивать[1]) 1. to give to drink. 2. to accustom to drinking; to make a drunkard (of).

споко́|йный (~ен, ~йна), *adj.* 1. quiet; calm, tranquil; placid, serene; ~йное мо́ре calm sea; с. о́браз жи́зни quiet life; ~йная со́весть clear conscience; ~йная улы́бка serene smile; бу́дьте ~йны! don't worry!, rest assured!; ~йной но́чи! good night! 2. quiet, composed. 3. comfortable; ~йное кре́сло easy chair.

споко́йстви|е, я, *n.* 1. quiet, tranquillity; calm, calmness. 2. order; наруше́ние обще́ственного ~я breach of the peace, breach of public order. 3. composure, serenity; с. ду́ха peace of mind.

споко́н: с. ве́ку, с. веко́в (*coll.*) from time immemorial.

спола́скива|ть, ю, *impf. of* сполосну́ть.

сполз|а́ть, а́ю, *impf. of* ~ти́.

сполз|ти́, у́, ёшь, *past* ~, ~ла́, *pf.* (*of* ~а́ть) 1. (с+*g.*) to climb down (from). 2. (в+ *a.*, к; *fig.*, *coll.*) to slip (into), fall away (into).

сполна́, *adv.* completely, in full; де́ньги полу́чены с. 'received in full'.

сполосн|у́ть, у́, ёшь, *pf.* (*of* спола́скивать) to rinse (out).

споло́х|и, ов, *no sing.* (*dial.*) 1. northern lights. 2. lightning.

спонде́ический, *adj.* (*lit.*) spondaic.

спонде́|й, я, *m.* (*lit.*) spondee.

спонта́нност|ь, и, *f.* spontaneity.

спонта́нный, *adj.* spontaneous.

спонти́р|овать, ую, *pf. of* понти́ровать.

спор, а, *m.* 1. argument; controversy; debate; зате́ять с. to start an argument; ~у

нет indisputably, undoubtedly; there's no denying. 2. (*leg.*) dispute.

спо́р|а, ы, *f.* (*biol.*) spore.

споради́ческий, *adj.* sporadic.

спора́нги|й, я, *m.* (*biol.*) sporangium, spore-case.

спо́р|ить, ю, ишь, *impf.* (*of* по~) (о+*p.*) 1. to argue (about); to dispute (about), debate; с. о слова́х to quibble over words; о вку́сах не ~ят tastes differ. 2. to dispute; с. о насле́дстве to dispute a legacy. 3. to bet (on), have a bet (on).

спор|и́ться, и́тся, *impf.* (*coll.*) to succeed, go well; у него́ всё ~и́тся he can't put a finger wrong.

спо́р|ный (~ен, ~на), *adj.* disputable, debatable, questionable; disputed, at issue; с. вопро́с moot point, vexed question; с. мяч (*in basketball*) jump ball, held ball; ~ное насле́дство disputed legacy.

спор|о́ть, ю́, ~ешь, *pf.* (*of* спа́рывать) to unstitch, take off (*by cutting stitches*).

спорт, а, *m.* sport.

спорти́вн|ый, *adj.* sports, sporting; с. зал gymnasium; с. инвента́рь sports goods, sports kit; ~ая площа́дка sports ground, playing-field; ~ые состяза́ния sports, sporting competitions.

спортсме́н, а, *m.* sportsman.

спортсме́нк|а, и, *f.* 1. sportswoman. 2. (*coll.*) gym-shoe.

спортсме́нский, *adj.* sportsmanlike.

спорхн|у́ть, у́, ёшь, *pf.* (*of* спа́рхивать) to flutter off; to flutter away.

спо́рщик, а, *m.* debater, wrangler.

спо́р|ый (~, ~а́, ~о), *adj.* (*coll.*) successful, profitable; ~ая рабо́та good work.

спорынь|я́, и́, *f.* (*bot.*) ergot, spur.

спо́соб, а, *m.* way, mode, method; means; таки́м ~ом in this way; сле́дующим ~ом as follows; с. употребле́ния лека́рства 'directions for use' of a medicine.

спосо́бност|ь, и, *f.* 1. (*usu. pl.*; к) ability (for); talent (for); aptitude (for), flair (for); челове́к с больши́ми ~ями person of great abilities; с. к языка́м facility for languages, linguistic ability. 2. capacity; покупа́тельная с. purchasing power; purchasing capacity; пропускна́я с. capacity.

спосо́б|ный (~ен, ~на), *adj.* 1. able, talented, gifted, clever; с. к матема́тике good at mathematics, with a gift for mathematics. 2. (на+*a. or* +*inf.*) capable (of), able (to); они́ ~ны на всё they are capable of anything.

спосо́бств|овать, ую, *impf.* (*of* по~) (+*d.*) 1. to assist. 2. to be conducive (to), further, promote, make (for); с. успе́ху бра́ка to make for the success of a marriage.

споткн|у́ться, у́сь, ёшься, *pf.* (*of* спотыка́ться) **1.** (o+*a*.) to stumble (against, over). **2.** (на+*p*. *or* o+*a*.; *fig*., *coll*.) to get stuck (on); в перево́де я ~у́лся на сло́ве „наро́дность" in my translation I got stuck on the word наро́дность.

спотыка́|ться, юсь, *impf. of* споткну́ться.

спохва|ти́ться, чу́сь, ~ти́шься, *pf.* (*of* ~тываться) (*coll*.) to remember suddenly, think suddenly; я написа́л бы́ло вам на ста́рый а́дрес, но ~ти́лся во́ время I was on the point of writing to you at your old address but remembered just in time (*sc.* that you had moved).

спра́ва, *adv.* (от) to the right (of).

справедли́вост|ь, и, *f.* **1.** justice; equity, fairness; по ~и (говоря́) in (all) fairness, by rights; отда́ть с. (+*d*.) to do justice (to). **2.** truth, correctness.

справедли́в|ый (~, ~a), *adj.* **1.** (*in var. senses*) just; equitable, fair; с. судья́ impartial judge; ~ая война́ just war. **2.** justified, true, correct; на́ши подозре́ния оказа́лись ~ыми our suspicions proved to be justified.

справ|ить[1], лю, ишь, *pf.* (*of* ~ля́ть) (*coll*.) to celebrate; с. сва́дьбу to celebrate one's wedding.

справ|ить[2], лю, ишь, *pf.* (*of* ~ля́ть) (себе́; *coll*.) to get, procure, acquire.

справ|иться[1], люсь, ишься, *pf.* (*of* ~ля́ться) (c+*i*.) **1.** to cope (with), manage; с. с зада́чей to cope with a task, be equal to a task. **2.** to manage, deal (with), get the better (of); я с ним ~люсь! I'll deal with him!

справ|иться[2], люсь, ишься, *pf.* (*of* ~ля́ться) (o+*p*.) to ask (about), inquire (about); об э́том вам сле́дует с. в бухгалте́рии you must inquire about this in the accounts department; с. в словаре́ to look up (*a word*) in the dictionary, consult a dictionary.

спра́вк|а, и, *f.* **1.** information; навести́ ~y (o+*p*.) to inquire (about); обрати́ться за ~ой (в+*a*., к) to apply for information (to). **2.** certificate; с. с ме́ста рабо́ты reference.

справля́|ть(ся), ю(сь), *impf. of* спра́вить(ся).

спра́вочник, a, *m.* reference book, handbook, vade-mecum, guide; телефо́нный с. telephone directory.

спра́вочн|ый, *adj.* inquiry, information; ~ое бюро́, с. стол inquiries office, information bureau; ~ая кни́га = ~ик.

спра́шива|ть, ю, *impf. of* спроси́ть.

спра́шива|ться, юсь, *impf.* **1.** *impf. of* спро-си́ться. **2.** *impf. only* ~ется the question is, arises.

спресс|ова́ть, у́ю, *pf. of* прессова́ть.

спринт, a, *m.* (*sport*) sprint.

спри́нтер, a, *m.* (*sport*) sprinter.

принц|ева́ть, у́ю, *impf.* to syringe.

спринцо́вк|а, и, *f.* **1.** syringing. **2.** syringe.

спрова|ди́ть, жу, ди́шь, *pf.* (*of* ~живать) (*coll*.) to show out, show the door, send on his way.

спрова́жива|ть, ю, *impf. of* спрова́дить.

спровоци́р|овать, ую, *pf. of* провоци́ровать.

спроекти́р|овать, ую, *pf. of* проекти́ровать[1].

спрос, a, *m.* **1.** (*econ*.) demand; (на+*a*.) demand (for), run (on); с. и предложе́ние supply and demand; по́льзоваться больши́м ~ом to be much in demand. **2.** без ~a (~y) (*coll*.) without permission, without asking leave.

спро|си́ть, шу́, ~сишь, *pf.* (*of* спра́шивать) **1.** (o+*p*.) to ask (about), inquire (about). **2.** (+*a*. *or g*.) to ask (for); to ask to see, desire to speak (to); с. рези́нку to ask for a rubber; с. сове́та to ask (for) advice; ~си́те хозя́йку ask to see the landlady. **3.** (c+*g*.) to make answer (for), make responsible (for).

спро|си́ться, шу́сь, ~сишься, *pf.* (*of* спра́шиваться) **1.** (+*g*. *or* y) to ask permission (of). **2.** (*impers*.) ~сится с него́, *etc.*, he, *etc.*, will be answerable.

спросо́нок, *adv.* (*coll*.) being only half-awake.

спроста́, *adv.* (*coll*.) without reflection; off the reel.

спрут, a, *m.* octopus.

спры́гива|ть, ю, *impf. of* спры́гнуть.

спры́г|нуть, ну, нешь, *pf.* (*of* ~ивать) (c+*g*.) to jump off (from), leap off (from); to jump down (from), leap down (from).

спры́скива|ть, ю, *impf. of* спры́сн ть.

спры́с|нуть, ну, нешь, *pf.* (*of* ~к вать) **1.** to sprinkle. **2.** (*coll*.) to celeb ate, drink (to); с. сде́лку to wet a bargain.

спряга́|ть[1], ю, *impf.* (*of* про~) (*gram*.) to conjugate.

спряга́|ть[2], ю, *impf. of* спрячь.

спряга́|ться, ется, *impf.* (*gram*.) to conjugate, be conjugated.

спряже́ни|е, я, *n.* (*gram*.) conjugation.

спря|сть, ду́, дёшь, *past* ~л, ~ла́, ~ло, *pf. of* прясть.

спря́та|ть(ся), ю(сь), *pf. of* пря́тать(ся).

спря|чь, гу́, жёшь, гу́т, *past* ~г, ~гла́, *pf.* (*of* ~га́ть) to harness together.

спу́гива|ть, ю, *impf. of* спугну́ть.

спуг|ну́ть, ну́, нёшь, *pf.* (*of* ~ивать) to frighten off, scare off.

спуд, a, *m.* (*arch*.) bushel; *now only used in phrases* (*i*) под ~ом under a bushel; держа́ть под ~ом (*fig*.) to hide under a bushel, keep back, (*ii*) из-под ~a from hiding; вы́тащить, извле́чь из-под ~a to bring into the light of day, put to use.

спуск, a, *m.* **1.** lowering, hauling down; с.

корабля́ launch(ing). 2. descent, descending. 3. release; draining. 4. slope, descent. 5. (*in fire-arms*) sear. 6. (*typ.*) imposition. 7. (*coll.*) quarter; не давáть ~у (+*d.*) to give no quarter, not to let off.

спускá|ть, ю, *impf. of* спустúть; не с. глаз (с+*g.*) not to take one's eyes (off), keep one's eyes glued (on); not to let out of one's sight.

спускá|ться, юсь, *impf. of* спустúться.

спускн|óй, *adj.* drain; с. кран drain-cock; ~áя трубá drain-pipe.

спусков|óй, *adj.* trigger; с. крючóк trigger; с. механúзм trigger mechanism, trigger guard group; ~áя скобá trigger guard.

спу|стúть, щý, ~стишь, *pf.* (*of* ~скáть) 1. to let down, lower; to haul down; с. корáбль (на вóду) to launch a ship; с. флаг to lower a flag; (*naut.*) to haul down the ensign; (*fig.*) to strike the colours; ~стя́ рукавá (*coll.*) in a slipshod fashion, carelessly; с. с лéстницы (*fig.*, *coll.*) to kick downstairs. 2. to let go, let loose, release; с. курóк to pull, release the trigger; с. затвóр (*phot.*) to release the shutter; с. пéтлю to drop a stitch; с. собáку с привязи to unleash a dog. 3. to let out, drain; с. вóду из бассéйна для плáвания to drain a swimming-bath; с. вóду в убóрной to flush a water closet. 4. to send down, send out; с. директúву в райсовéты to send down a directive to the district soviets. 5. (*of objects inflated with air*) to go down; однá из зáдних шин ~стúла one of the back tyres has gone down. 6. (*coll.*) to pardon, let off, let go, let pass. 7. (*coll.*) to lose (*weight*). 8. (*coll.*) to lose, throw away, squander; за одúн вéчер он ~стúл в кáрты всю полýчку he lost the whole of his pay--packet at cards in an evening.

спу|стúться, щýсь, ~стишься, *pf.* (*of* ~скáться) 1. to descend; to come down, go down; to go downstream; (*of darkness*) to fall; с. с лéстницы to come downstairs; ~стúлась мгла a mist came down; на её чулкé ~стúлась пéтля she has laddered her stocking. 2. *pass. of* ~стúть.

спустя́, *prep.+a.* after; later; с. дней дéсять after about ten days; с. год a year later.

спýта|ть(ся), ю(сь), *pf. of* пýтать(ся).

спýтник, а, *m.* 1. (travelling) companion; fellow-traveller. 2. concomitant. 3. (*astron.*) satellite; искýсственный с. землú artificial earth satellite, sputnik.

спýщенный, *p.p.p. of* спустúть *and adj.* (*of a flag*) at half-mast.

спья́на, *adv.* in a state of drunkenness, in one's cups.

спья́н|у, *adv.* = ~a.

спя́|тить, чу, тишь, *pf.*; с. с умá (*coll.*) to go balmy, go off one's rocker.

спя́чк|а, и, *f.* 1. (*of animals*) hibernation. 2. (*coll.*) sleepiness, lethargy.

срабáтыва|ться, юсь, *impf. of* срабóтаться.

срабóтанност|ь¹, и, *f.* harmony in work, harmonious team-work.

срабóтанност|ь², и, *f.* wear.

срабóтанный, *adj.* worn (out).

срабóта|ть, ю, *pf.* (*coll.*) 1. to make. 2. (+*i.*) to work, operate.

срабóта|ться¹, юсь, *pf.* to achieve harmony in work, work well together.

срабóта|ться², ется, *pf.* to wear out.

сравнéни|е, я, *n.* 1. comparison; по ~ю (с+*i.*) by comparison (with), as compared (with), as against; вне ~я beyond comparison; не идёт в с. (с+*i.*) it cannot be compared (with). 2. (*lit.*) simile.

срáвнива|ть, ю, *impf. of* сравнúть *and* сравня́ть.

сравнúтельно, *adv.* 1. (с+*i.*) by comparison (with). 2. comparatively.

сравнúтельн|ый, *adj.* comparative; ~ая стéпень (*gram.*) comparative (degree).

сравн|úть, ю, úшь, *pf.* (*of* ~ивать) (с+*i.*) to compare (to, with).

сравн|úться, юсь, úшься, *pf.* (с+*i.*) to compare (with), come up (to), touch; в знáнии Áрктики никтó не мóжет с ним с. for a knowledge of the Arctic no one can touch him.

сравн|я́ть, я́ю, *pf.* (*of* равня́ть *and* ~ивать) to make even; с. счёт (*sport*) to equalize, bring the score level.

сравня́|ться, юсь, *pf. of* равня́ться.

сража́|ть, ю, *impf. of* сразúть.

сража́|ться, юсь, *impf.* (*of* сразúться) (с+*i.*) to fight; to join battle (with).

сражéни|е, я, *n.* battle, engagement; дать с. to give battle.

сра|зúть, жý, зúшь, *pf.* (*of* ~жáть) 1. (*obs.*) to slay, strike down, fell. 2. (*fig.*) to overwhelm, crush; её ~зúла весть о катастрóфе в шáхте she was crushed by the news of the pit disaster.

сра|зúться, жýсь, зúшься, *pf. of* ~жáться.

срáзу, *adv.* 1. at once. 2. straight away, right away; straight off.

срам, а, *m.* 1. shame; какóй с.! for shame! 2. (*coll.*) privy parts.

срам|úть, лю́, úшь, *impf.* (*of* о~) to shame, put to shame.

срам|úться, лю́сь, úшься, *impf.* (*of* о~) to cover oneself with shame.

срамнúк, á, *m.* (*coll.*) shameless person.

срамн|óй, *adj.* 1. (*coll.*) shameless. 2. ~ые гýбы (*anat.*) labia; ~áя часть (*obs.*) privy parts.

срамот|á, ы́, *f.* (*coll.*) shame.

срастáни|е, я, *n.* (*physiol.*, *med.*) growing together, inosculation; (*of bones*) knitting.

сраст|áться, áется, *impf. of* ~**йсь.**

сраст|йсь, ётся, *past* **срóсся, срослáсь,** *pf.* (*of* ~**áться**) (*physiol.*, *med.*) to grow together, inosculate; (*of bones*) to knit.

сра|стйть, щý, стйшь, *pf.* (*of* ~**щивать**) 1. to join, joint. 2. to splice.

сращéни|е, я, *n.* union.

срáщивани|е, я, *n.* 1. joining; splicing. 2. (*fig.*) fusion, merging.

срáщива|ть, ю, *impf. of* срастйть.

срéбреник, а, *m.* silver coin, piece of silver; продáть за трйдцать ~ов to sell for thirty pieces of silver.

сребролюб|ец, ца, *m.* (*obs.*) money-grubber.

сребролюбйв|ый (~, ~a), *adj.* (*obs.*) money--grubbing.

сребролюби|е, я, *n.* (*obs.*) greed for money.

сребронóс|ный (~ен, ~на), *adj.* argenti-ferous.

сред|á¹, ы́, *a.* ~ý, *pl.* ~ы, *f.* 1. environment, surroundings; milieu; (*biol.*) habitat; в нáшей ~é in our midst, among us. 2. (*phys.*) medium.

сред|á², ы́, *a.* ~у, *pl.* ~ы, ~áм, *f.* Wednesday; по ~áм on Wednesdays, every Wednesday.

средактйр|овать, ую, *pf. of* редактйровать.

среди́, *prep.*+*g.* 1. among, amongst; amidst; с. них among them, in their midst. 2. in the middle (of); с. бéла дня in broad daylight.

средиземномóрский, *adj.* Mediterranean.

средйн|а, ы, *f.* (*obs.*) middle.

средйнн|ый, *adj.* middle; ~ое отклонéние (*mil.*) probable error (*in artillery firing*).

срéдне, *adv.* (*coll.*) middling, so-so.

среднеазиáтский, *adj.* Central Asian (*of Soviet Central Asia*).

среднеанглййский, *adj.* с. язык Middle English.

средневекóвый, *adj.* medieval.

средневекóвь|е, я, *n.* the Middle Ages.

среднегодовóй, *adj.* average annual.

среднекалйберный, *adj.* (*mil.*) medium (-calibre).

среднемéсячный, *adj.* average monthly.

среднесýточный, *adj.* average daily.

среднеязычный, *adj.* (*ling.*) medio-lingual.

срéдн|ий, *adj.* 1. middle; medium; с. бомбардирóвщик medium bomber; ~ие векá the Middle Ages; ~яя истóрия history of the Middle Ages; с. залóг (*gram.*) middle voice; ~их лет middle-aged; ~его рóста of medium height; ~ее ýхо (*anat.*) middle ear. 2. mean, average; ~ее врéмя mean time; с. зáработок average earnings; ~яя ошйбка mean error, standard deviation; ~ее пропорционáльное (*math.*) the mean

proportional; *as noun* ~**ее,** ~**его,** *n.* mean, average; в ~ем on average; выше ~его above (the) average. 3. (*coll.*) middling, average; ~ие способности average abilities. 4. (*in education*) secondary; ~яя шкóла secondary school. 5. с. род (*gram.*) neuter (gender). 6. (*aeron.*) waist, belly; с. стрелóк waist gunner.

средостéни|е, я, *n.* 1. (*anat.*) mediastinum. 2. (*fig.*) partition, barrier.

средотóчи|е, я, *n.* focus, centre point.

срéдств|о, а, *n.* 1. means; facilities; ~a передвижéния means of conveyance; ~a сообщéния means of communication; ~a к существовáнию means of subsistence; пустйть в ход все ~a to move heaven and earth. 2. (от) remedy (for); с. от кáшля cough medicine, something for a cough; с. от насекóмых insecticide. 3. (*pl.*) resources; credits. 4. (*pl.*) means; человéк со ~ами man of means; жить не по ~ам to live beyond one's means.

средь, *prep.*+*g.* = среди́.

срез, а, *m.* 1. cut; microscopic section. 2. (*tech.*) shear, shearing; плóскость ~a shear plane. 3. (*sport*) slice, slicing.

срé|зать, жу, жешь, *pf.* 1. (*impf.* ~зáть) to cut off; с. ýгол (*fig.*) to cut off a corner; с. на экзáмене (*school sl.*) to plough. 2. (*impf.* рéзать) (*sport*) to slice, cut, chop.

срезá|ть, ю, *impf. of* срéзать.

срé|заться, жусь, жешься, *pf.* (*of* ~зáться) (*school sl.*) to fail, be ploughed.

срезá|ться, юсь, *impf. of* срéзаться.

срепетйр|овать, ую, *pf. of* репетйровать.

срéтени|е, я, *n.* 1. (*arch.* or *poet.*) meeting. 2. С. (*eccl.*) Candlemas Day; Feast of the Purification.

срис|овáть, ýю, *pf.* (*of* ~óвывать) to copy.

срисóвыва|ть, ю, *impf. of* срисовáть.

сровня́|ть, ю, *pf. of* ровня́ть.

сродни́, *adv.* akin; быть, приходйться с. (+*d.*) to be related (to).

сродн|и́ть, ю́, и́шь, *pf.* (с+*i.*) to link (with).

сродн|и́ться, ю́сь, и́шься, *pf.* (с+*i.*) to become closely linked (with); to get used (to); с. с рабóтой to get the hang of a job.

срóд|ный (~ен, ~на), *adj.* (+*d.* or с+*i.*) related (to).

сродств|ó, á, *n.* relationship, affinity; химйческое с. chemical affinity.

срóду, *adv.* (*coll.*) in one's life; с. я не видáл такóй огрóмной кóшки I have never seen such a huge cat (in all my life).

срок, а (у), *m.* 1. time, period; term; мéсячный с. a period of one month; в кратчáйший с. in the shortest possible time; с. воéнной слýжбы call-up period; с. дéйствия period of validity; с. полномóчий term of office; с. рабóты life (*of* machine, *etc.*); по истече́нии ∼а when the time is up, when the time expires; продли́ть с. ви́зы to extend a visa; ∼ом до трёх ме́сяцев within three months; да́й(те) с. (*coll.*) wait a minute!, give us time!; ни о́тдыху, ни ∼у не дава́ть (+*d.*) to give no peace. **2.** date, term; кра́йний с. closing date; с. аре́нды term of lease; с. да́вности (*leg.*) prescription; с. платежа́ date of payment; пропусти́ть с. платежа́ to fail to pay by the date fixed; в ука́занный с., к устано́вленному ∼у by the date fixed, by a specified date; в с., к ∼у in time, to time.

сро́ст|ок, ка, *m.* joint, splice.

сро́чно, *adv.* urgently; quickly.

сро́чност|ь, и, *f.* urgency; hurry; что за с.? what's the hurry?

сро́ч|ный (∼ен, ∼на́, ∼но), *adj.* **1.** urgent, pressing; с. зака́з rush order. **2.** at a fixed date; for a fixed period; ∼ная слу́жба (*mil.*) service for a fixed period. **3.** periodic, routine; ∼ное донесе́ние (*mil.*) routine report.

сруб, а, *m.* **1.** felling; на с. for timber. **2.** frame(work), shell (*of an izba, well, etc.*). **3.** (*hist.*) framework.

сруб|а́ть, а́ю, *impf. of* ∼и́ть.

сруб|и́ть, лю́, ∼ишь, *pf.* (*of* ∼а́ть) **1.** to fell, cut down. **2.** to build (*of logs*).

срыв, а, *m.* disruption; derangement, frustration; с. перегово́ров break-down of talks; с. рабо́ты derangement of work, stoppage.

срыва́|ть¹, ю, *impf. of* сорва́ть.

срыва́|ть², ю, *impf. of* срыть.

срыва́|ться, юсь, *impf. of* сорва́ться.

срыть, сро́ю, сро́ешь, *pf.* (*of* срыва́ть²) to raze, level to the ground.

сря́ду, *adv.* (*coll.*) running; два ра́за с. twice running.

сса́дин|а, ы, *f.* scratch, abrasion.

сса|ди́ть¹, жу́, ∼дишь, *pf.* (*of* ∼жива́ть) (*coll.*) to scratch.

сса|ди́ть², жу́, ∼дишь, *pf.* (*of* ∼жива́ть) **1.** to help down, help to alight; с. кого́-н. с ло́шади to help someone down from a horse. **2.** to put off, make get off (*from public transport*).

сса́жива|ть, ю, *impf. of* ссади́ть.

сседа́|ться, ется, *impf. of* ссе́сться.

ссел|и́ть, ю́, и́шь, *pf.* (*of* ∼я́ть) to settle collectively.

ссел|я́ть, я́ю, *impf. of* ∼и́ть.

ссе́|сться, ссядется, *past* ∼лся, ∼лась, *pf.* (*of* ∼да́ться) (*coll.*) **1.** (*of materials*) to shrink. **2.** (*of milk*) to turn.

ссо́р|а, ы, *f.* **1.** quarrel; falling-out; они́ в ∼е друг с дру́гом they have fallen out. **2.** slanging-match.

ссо́р|ить, ю, ишь, *impf.* (*of* по∼) to cause to quarrel, cause to fall out.

ссо́р|иться, юсь, ишься, *impf.* (*of* по∼) (с+*i.*) to quarrel (with), fall out (with).

ссо́х|нуться, нется, *past* ∼ся, ∼лась, *pf.* (*of* ссыха́ться) **1.** to shrink, shrivel, warp. **2.** to harden out, dry out.

ссу́д|а, ы, *f.* loan, grant.

ссу|ди́ть, жу́, ∼дишь, *pf.* (*of* ∼жа́ть) (+*a.* and *i.* or +*d.* and *a.*) to lend, loan.

ссу́д|ный, *adj. of* ∼а; с. проце́нт interest on a loan.

ссу́до-сберега́тельн|ый, *adj.* ∼ая ка́сса savings bank.

ссужа́|ть, ю, *impf. of* ссуди́ть.

ссуту́л|ить(ся), ю(сь), ишь(ся), *pf. of* сутули́ть(ся).

ссуч|и́ть, у́, ∼ишь, *pf. of* сучи́ть.

ссыла́|ть(ся), ю(сь), *impf. of* сосла́ть(ся).

ссы́лк|а¹, и, *f.* exile, banishment; deportation.

ссы́лк|а², и, *f.* reference.

ссы́л|очный, *adj. of* ∼ка²; ∼очное примеча́ние reference note.

ссыльнопоселе́н|ец, ца, *m.* (*hist.*) deportee, convict settler (*ex-convict obliged by court order to settle in remote area after completing prison sentence*).

ссы́льн|ый, ого, *m.* exile.

ссып|а́ть, а́ю, *impf. of* ∼а́ть.

ссы́п|ать, лю, лешь, *pf.* (*of* ∼а́ть) to pour.

ссыпно́й, *adj.* с. пункт grain-collecting station.

ссыха́|ться, ется, *impf. of* ссо́хнуться.

стабилиза́тор, а, *m.* (*tech.*) stabilizer; (*aeron.*) tail-plane.

стабилиза́ци|я, и, *f.* stabilization.

стабилизи́р|овать, ую, *impf. and pf.* to stabilize.

стабилизи́р|оваться, уюсь, *impf. and pf.* to become stable.

стабилиз|ова́ть(ся), у́ю(сь), *impf. and pf.* = ∼и́ровать(ся).

стаби́льност|ь, и, *f.* stability.

стаби́л|ьный (∼ен, ∼ьна), *adj.* stable, firm; с. уче́бник standard text-book.

ста́в|ень, ня, *g. pl.* ∼ней, *m.* shutter (*on window*).

ста́в|ить, лю, ишь, *impf.* (*of* по∼) **1.** to put, place, set; to stand; to station; с. цветы́ в ва́зу to put flowers in a vase; с. буты́лки в ряд to stand bottles in a row; с. го́лос кому́-н. to train someone's voice; с. диа́гноз to diagnose; с. реко́рд to set up, create a record; с. то́чку to put a full stop; с. то́чки на „и" to dot one's 'i's' (and cross one's 't's'); с. часы́ to set a clock; с. самова́р to put a samovar on; с. в вину́ что-н. кому́-н. to accuse someone of something; с. в изве́стность to let know, inform; с. кого́-н. в нело́вкое положе́ние to put someone in an awkward position; с. в тупи́к to nonplus; с. в у́гол to stand in the corner; с. что-н. в упрёк кому́-н. to reproach someone with something; ни во что не с. to hold of no account; с. за пра́вило to make it a rule; с. кого́-н. на коле́ни to force someone to his knees; с. кого́-н. на ме́сто to put someone in his place; с. пе́ред соверши́вшимся фа́ктом to present with a fait accompli. 2. to put up, erect; to install; с. па́мятник to erect a monument; с. телефо́н to install the telephone. 3. (coll.) to put in, install; с. но́вого гла́вного инжене́ра to put in a new chief engineer; с. кого́-н. в архиере́и to make someone a bishop. 4. to apply, put on; с. горчи́чник to apply a mustard plaster; с. кому́-н. термо́метр to take someone's temperature. 5. to put, present; to put on, stage; с. резолю́цию to put a resolution; с. мелодра́му to stage a melodrama. 6. (на+а.) to place, stake (money on); с. на ло́шадь to back a horse.

ста́вк|а¹, и, f. 1. rate; с. зарпла́ты wage rate; ~и нало́га tax rates. 2. stake; де́лать ~у (на+а.) to stake (on); (fig.) to count (on), gamble (on).

ста́вк|а², и, f. (mil.) headquarters; с. главнокома́ндующего General Head-quarters.

ста́вк|а³, и, f. о́чная с. (leg.) confrontation.

ста́вленник, а, m. protégé.

ста́влен|ый, adj. ~ая гра́мота (eccl.) certificate of ordination.

ста́вн|я, и, f. = ста́вень.

стадиа́льный, adj. taking place by stages.

стадио́н, а, m. stadium.

ста́ди|я, и, f. stage.

ста́дност|ь, и, f. herd instinct, gregarious instinct.

ста́дный, adj. gregarious.

ста́д|о, а, pl. ~а́, n. herd; flock.

стаж, а, m. 1. length of service; record. 2. (испыта́тельный) с. probation; проходи́ть с. to work on probation.

стажёр, а, m. 1. probationer. 2. stazher (student on special course not leading to degree).

стажи́р|овать, ую, impf. to work on probation.

ста́ива|ть, ю, impf. of ста́ять.

ста́ива|ть², ю, impf., freq. of стоя́ть.

ста́йер, а, m. (sport) long-distance runner.

стака́н, а, m. 1. glass, tumbler, beaker. 2. (mil.) body (of projectile).

стакка́то, adv. or indecl., n. (mus.) staccato.

сталагми́т, а, m. stalagmite.

сталакти́т, а, m. stalactite.

сталева́р, а, m. steel founder.

сталели́тейный, adj. с. заво́д steel mill, steel works.

сталели́тейщик, а, m. steel founder.

сталеплави́льн|ый, adj. ~ая печь steel furnace.

сталепрока́тный, adj. с. заво́д, с. стан steel-rolling mill.

ста́линск|ий, adj. Stalin's, of Stalin; ~ая пре́мия (hist.) Stalin Prize.

ста́лкива|ть(ся), ю(сь), impf. of столкну́ть-(ся).

ста́ло быть, conj. (coll.) consequently, therefore, accordingly.

стал|ь, и, f. steel; нержаве́ющая с. stainless steel.

стальн|о́й, adj. steel; ~о́го цве́та steel-blue; ~ые во́лосы iron-grey hair; ~а́я во́ля iron will; ~ые не́рвы nerves of steel.

стаме́ск|а, и, f. (tech.) chisel.

стан¹, а, m. figure, torso.

стан², а, m. camp (also fig.); в ~е врага́ in the enemy's camp.

стан³, а, m. (tech.) mill.

станда́рт, а, m. (in var. senses) standard.

стандартиза́ци|я, и, f. standardization.

стандартиз|ова́ть, у́ю, impf. and pf. to standardize.

станда́рт|ный (~ен, ~на), adj. standard.

стани́н|а, ы, f. (tech.) mounting, bed (plate); боковая с. side plate, cheek; с. лафе́та cheek, side plate of gun-carriage.

станио́л|ь, я, m. tin foil.

стани́ц|а¹, ы, f. stanitsa (large Cossack village).

стани́ц|а², ы, f. (obs.) flock.

стани́чник, а, m. (Cossack) inhabitant of stanitsa.

стани́|чный, adj. of ~ца¹.

станко́в|ый, adj. 1. adj. of стано́к; с. пулемёт (mil.) heavy machine-gun. 2. ~ая жи́вопись easel (as opp. to mural) painting.

станкострое́ни|е, я, n. machine-tool construction.

станов|и́ться, лю́сь, ~ишься, impf. of стать.

становле́ни|е, я, n. (philos.) coming-to-be, coming into being; в проце́ссе ~я in the making.

станово́й¹, adj. main, chief, basic; с. хребе́т (fig.) backbone.

станов|о́й², adj. of стан²; с. при́став (hist.) district police-officer; as noun с., ~о́го, m. = при́став.

стан|о́к¹, ка́, m. 1. (tech.) machine-tool, machine; bench; печа́тный с. printing--press; столя́рный с. joiner's bench; тка́цкий с. loom; тока́рный с. lathe; рабо́чий от ~ка́ bench worker. 2. (mil.) mount, mounting.

стан|о́к², ка́, m. stall (for one horse).

стано́чник, а, m. machine operator, machine minder.

станс, а, m. (lit.) stanza.

станцио́нный, adj. of ста́нция; с. зал

waiting-room; с. смотри́тель (*obs.*) post-master.

ста́нци|я, и, *f.* (*in var. senses*) station; гидро-электри́ческая с. hydro-electric power station; межпланéтная с. inter-planetary station; телефóннаяс. telephone exchange; с. снабжéния (*mil.*) railhead.

ста́пел|ь, я, *m.* (*naut.*) building slip(s), stocks; на ~e, на ~ях on the stocks.

ста́плива|ть, ю, *impf. of* стопи́ть.

ста́птыва|ть(ся), ю(сь), *impf. of* стоптáть-(ся).

старáни|е, я, *n.* effort, endeavour; dili-gence; приложи́ть с. to make an effort; приложи́ть все ~я to do one's utmost, do one's best.

старáтел|ь, я, *m.* gold prospector, gold--digger.

старáтельност|ь, и, *f.* application, assi-duity, diligence, painstakingness.

старáтел|ьный (~ен, ~ьна), *adj.* assiduous, diligent, painstaking.

старá|ться, юсь, *impf.* (*of* по~) to try, endeavour, seek; to make an effort; с. изо всех сил to do one's utmost, try one's hardest.

стар|éе (*and* (*obs.*) стáре), *comp. of* ~ый.

старéйшин|а, ы, *m.* 1. (*hist., ethnol.*) elder. 2. Совéт ~ Council of Elders (*of U.S.S.R. Supreme Soviet*).

старé|ть, ю, *impf.* (*of* по~) to grow old, age.

стáр|ец, ца, *m.* 1. elder, (venerable) old man. 2. elderly monk. 3. spiritual adviser.

стари́к, á, *m.* old man.

старикáн, а, *m.* (*coll.*) old boy, old chap.

старикáшк|а, и, *m.* (*coll., pejor.*) old man, old chap.

старикóвский, *adj. of* стари́к; senile.

стáрин|а, ы, *f.* (*lit.*) bylina.

старин|á¹, ы́, *f.* 1. antiquity, olden times; в ~ý in olden times, in days of old. 2. (*collect.*) antiques.

старин|á², ы́, *m.* (*coll.*) old fellow, old chap.

стари́нк|а, и, *f.* (*coll.*) old fashion, old custom(s); держáться ~и to keep up the old customs; по ~e in the old fashion, in the old way.

стари́нный, *adj.* 1. ancient, old; antique; с. обы́чай time-honoured custom. 2. old, of long standing; с. друг old friend.

стáр|ить, ю, ишь, *impf.* (*of* со~) to age; to make look old(er).

стáр|иться, юсь, ишься, *impf.* (*of* со~) to grow old, age.

стáриц|а, ы, *f.* 1. elderly nun. 2. (*dial.*) old bed (*of river*).

старич|óк, кá, *m.* 1. little old man. 2. (*sport*) 'veteran' (*competitor in contest for age--group 35 and over*).

старовéр, а, *m.* 1. (*rel.*) Old Believer. 2. (*fig., joc.*) conservative, laudator temporis acti.

стародáвний, *adj.* ancient.

стародáвност|ь, и, *f.* antiquity.

старожи́л, а, *m.* old inhabitant, old resident.

старозавéт|ный (~ен, ~на), *adj.* 1. (*of per-sons*) old-fashioned, conservative. 2. (*pejor.*) old, antiquated; ~ные взгля́ды antiquated views.

старомóд|ный (~ен, ~на), *adj.* old--fashioned, outmoded; out-of-date.

старообрáз|ный (~ен, ~на), *adj.* old-look-ing.

старообря́д|ец, ца, *m.* (*rel.*) Old Believer.

старообря́д|ческий, *adj. of* ~ец *and* ~чество.

старообря́дчеств|о, а, *n.* (*rel.*) Old Belief.

старопечáтн|ый, *adj.* ~ые кни́ги early printed books (*books published in Russia before the 18th century*).

старорýсский, *adj.* old Russian.

старосвéтский, *adj.* old-world; old--fashioned.

старославя́нский, *adj.* (*ling.*) Old Church Slavonic.

стáрост|а, ы, *m.* (*elected*) head; senior (man); сéльский с. (*hist.*) village headman, elder; церкóвный с. churchwarden; с. клáсса (*in school*) form prefect, monitor; с. кýрса (*in college, etc.*) senior student of year.

стáрост|ь, и, *f.* old age; на ~и лет, под с. in one's old age.

старт, а, *m.* 1. (*sport*) start; дать с. to start; на с.! .on your marks! 2. (*aeron.*) take-off point; взять с. to take off.

стáртер *and* (*coll.*) стартёр, а, (*sport and tech.*) starter.

старт|овáть, ýю, *impf. and pf.* 1. (*sport*) to start. 2. (*aeron.*) to take off.

стáртовый, *adj.* starting.

старýх|а, и, *f.* old woman, old lady.

старý|шечий, *adj. of* ~ха; old-womanish.

старýшк|а, и, *f.* (little) old lady, old woman.

стáрческий, *adj.* old man's; senile.

старшеклáссник, а, *m.* senior (pupil).

старшекýрсник, а, *m.* senior student.

стáрше, *comp. of* стáрый; онá с. меня́ нá три гóда she is three years older than me.

стáрш|ий, *adj.* 1. elder; *as noun* ~ие, ~их (one's) elders. 2. oldest, eldest. 3. senior, superior; chief, head; с. врач head physi-cian; ~ая медсестрá sister; *as noun* с., ~его, *m.* chief; (*mil.*) man in charge, senior man. 4. senior, upper, higher; ~ая кáрта higher card; с. класс (*in school*) higher form.

старшин|á, ы́, *m.* 1. (*mil.*) sergeant-major; (*naut.*) petty officer. 2. войсковóй с. (*hist.*) lieutenant-colonel (*of Cossack troops*). 3. leader, senior representative (*of social group*, *professional organization, etc.*); с. дипломати́ческого ко́рпуса doyen of the diplomatic corps; с. прися́жных заседа́телей foreman of the jury.

старшинств|о́, á, *n.* seniority; по ~ý by seniority.

стáр|ый (~, ~á, ~ó), adj. (*in var. senses*) old; с. стиль the Old Style (*of the Julian calendar*); ~ая де́ва old maid, spinster; по ~ой па́мяти for old times' sake; from force of habit; *as noun* ~ые, ~ых the old, old people; ~ое, ~ого, *n.* the old, the past; кто ~ое помя́нет, тому́ глаз вон (*prov.*) let bygones be bygones.

старь|ё, я, *n.* (*collect.*; *coll.*) old things, old clothes.

старьёвщик, а, *m.* old-clothes dealer; junk dealer.

стáскива|ть, ю, *impf. of* стащи́ть.

стас|овáть, ýю, *pf. of* тасовáть.

стáтик|а, и, *f.* statics.

стати́ст, а, *m.* (*theatr.*) super, extra, mute.

стати́стик, а, *m.* statistician.

стати́стик|а, и, *f.* statistics.

статисти́ческий, adj. statistical.

стати́ческий, adj. static.

стáт|ный (~ен, ~на), adj. stately.

стáтор, а, *m.* (*tech.*) stator.

стáточн|ый, adj. ~ое ли де́ло? (*coll., obs.*) is it possible?, can it be?

статс-дáм|а, ы, *f.* lady-in-waiting.

стáтский, adj. 1. (*obs.*) = штáтский. 2. (*hist.*; *as part of titles of ranks in tsarist Russian civil service*) State; с. сове́тник Councillor of State.

статс-секретáр|ь, я, *m.* Secretary of State.

стáтус-квó, indecl., m. status quo.

статýт, а, *m.* statute.

статуэ́тк|а, и, *f.* statuette, figurine.

стáту|я, и, *f.* statue.

стать¹, стáну, стáнешь, *pf.* (*of* станови́ться) 1. to stand; с. на коле́ни to kneel; с. в о́чередь to queue (up); с. в по́зу to strike an attitude; с. на цы́почки to stand on tip-toe; с. на чью-н. сто́рону to take someone's side, stand up for someone; с. на защи́ту угнетённых to stand up for the oppressed. 2. to take up position; с. ла́герем to camp, encamp; с. в карау́л to mount guard; с. на рабо́ту to start work; с. на я́корь to anchor, come to anchor. 3. to stop, come to a halt; мои́ часы́ стáли my watch has stopped; рекá стáла the river has frozen over; за чем де́ло стáло? (*coll.*) what's holding things up?, what's the hitch? 4. (в+a.; *coll.*) to cost; во что бы то ни стáло at any price, at all costs. 5. (*impers.*; *coll.*) to suffice; с него́ э́то стáнет it is what one might expect of him.

стать², стáну, стáнешь, *pf.* (*of* станови́ться)

1. (+*inf.*) to begin (to), start; онá стáла говори́ть во сне she began talking in her sleep; он, слов нет, стáнет ворчáть he will start grousing, it goes without saying. 2. (+*i.*) to become, get, grow; он стал маши́нистом he became an engine-driver; стáло темно́ it got dark; ей стáло лýчше she was better, she had got better. 3. (с+*i.*) to become (of), happen (to); что с нúми стáло? what has become of them? 4. не с. (*impers.*+*g.*) to cease to be; to disappear, be gone; её отцá давно́ не стáло her father passed away long ago.

стат|ь³, и, pl. ~и, ~éй, f. 1. figure, build; (*pl.*) points (*of a horse*). 2. character, type; быть под с. (+*d.*) to be (well) matched (with).

стат|ь⁴, и, f. (*coll., obs.*) need, necessity; к э́той ме́стности нам не привыкáть с. this area is familiar ground to us; с какóй ~и? (*coll.*) why?, what for?

стá|ться, нется, pf. (*coll.*) to happen, become; что с нáми ~нется? what will become of us?; мóжет с. perhaps, it may be; вполне́ мóжет с. it is quite possible.

стат|ья́, ьи́, g. pl. ~éй, f. 1. article; передовáя с. leading article, leader, editorial. 2. clause; item; с. договóра clause of a treaty; расхóдная с. debit item; э́то осóбая с. that is another matter. 3. (*coll.*) matter, job; э́то не бýдет хи́трая с. that will not be difficult. 4. (*naut.*) class, rating; матрóс пéрвой ~ьи́ able seaman; старшинá пéрвой ~ьи́ chief petty officer. 5. (*pl.*) points (*of a horse*).

стафилокóкк, а, *m.* (*med., biol.*) staphylococcus.

стахáнов|ец, ца, *m.* (*hist.*) stakhanovite.

стахáновский, adj. (*hist.*) stakhanovite.

стационáр, а, *m.* permanent establishment; (лече́бный) с. hospital.

стационáрн|ый, adj. 1. stationary; с. объéкт (*mil.*) stationary target. 2. permanent, fixed; ~ая библиотéка permanent library; ~ая устанóвка (*mil.*) fixed mount. 3. с. больнóй in-patient; ~ое лечéние hospitalization.

стационéр, а, *m.* (*naut.*) station ship, guard ship.

стáчечник, а, *m.* striker.

стáч|ечный, adj. of ~ка¹.

стáчива|ть, ю, *impf. of* сточи́ть.

стáчк|а¹, и, f. strike; свобóда стáчек freedom to strike.

стáчк|а², и, f.; войти́ в ~y (с+*i.*; *coll., pejor.*) to come to terms (with), make a compact (with).

стащ|и́ть, ý, ~ишь, pf. (*of* стáскивать) 1. to drag off, pull off; to drag down. 2. (*coll.*) to pinch, swipe, whip.

ста́|я, и, *f.* (*of birds*) flock, flight; (*of fish*) school, shoal; (*of dogs or wolves*) pack.

ста́|ять, ет, *pf.* (*of* ~ивать) to melt.

ствол, á, m. 1. (*of tree*) trunk; stem; bole. 2. (*of firearm*) barrel. 3. (*anat.*) tube, pipe. 4. (*mining*) shaft.

стволов|о́й, о́го, m. (*in mine*) hanger-on; cager.

стволо́вый, *adj. of* ствол.

ство́льн|ый, *adj.* barrel; ~ая гру́ппа barrel assembly; с. кожу́х barrel housing.

створ, а, m. 1. = ~ка. 2. range, alignment.

створк|а, и, *f.* leaf, fold; door, gate, shutter (*one of a pair*).

створо́ж|иться, ится, *pf.* to curdle.

ство́рчатый, *adj.* folding; valved.

стеари́н, а, m. stearin.

стеари́н|овый, *adj. of* ~; ~овая свеча́ stearin candle.

стéб|ель, ля, *pl.* ~ли, ~лéй, *m.* stem, stalk.

стебéльчатый, *adj.* с. шов feather stitch.

стёганк|а, и, *f.* (*coll.*) quilted jacket.

стёган|ый, *adj.* quilted; ~ое одея́ло quilt.

стегá|ть¹, ю, *impf.* (*of* от~ *and* стегнýть) to whip, lash.

стегá|ть², ю, *impf.* (*of* вы~) to quilt.

стег|нýть, нý, нёшь, *pf. of* ~áть¹.

стёжк|а¹, и, *f.* quilting.

стёжк|а², и, *f.* (*dial.*) path.

стеж|óк, кá, m. stitch.

стез|я́, и́, g. pl. ~éй, *f.* (*rhet.*) path, way.

стек, а, m. riding-crop.

стекá|ть(ся), ю(сь), *impf. of* стéчь(ся).

стеклене́|ть, ет, *impf.* (*of* о~) to become glassy.

стек|ло́, лá, *pl.* ~лá, ~о́л, *n.* glass; ~лá lenses (*for spectacles*); ла́мповое с. lamp--chimney; око́нное с. window-pane; передне́е с. wind-screen.

стекло́вид|ный (~ен, ~на), *adj.* 1. glassy. 2. (*anat.*) hyaline, hyaloid; ~ное тéло hyaloid (membrane).

стеклодýв, а, m. glass-blower.

стеклодýвный, *adj.* glass-blowing.

стеклоплави́льный, *adj.* с. заво́д glass--foundry.

стёклыш|ко, ка, *pl.* ~ки, ~ек, ~кам, *n.* 1. *dim. of* стекло́. 2. piece of glass.

стекля́нн|ый, *adj.* 1. glass; ~ая бумáга glass-paper; ~ые издéлия glassware. 2. (*fig.*) glassy.

стекля́рус, а, m. (*collect.*) bugles (*tube-shaped glass beads*).

стеко́льный, *adj.* glass; vitreous; с. заво́д glass-works, glass-factory.

стеко́льщик, а, m. glazier.

стел|и́ть(ся), ю́(сь), ~ишь(ся), *impf.* = стлáть(ся).

стеллáж, á, m. 1. shelves. 2. rack, stand.

стéльк|а, и, *f.* insole, sock; пьян как с. (*coll.*) drunk as a lord.

стéльная, *adj.* с. коро́ва cow with calf.

стемне́|ть, ю, *pf. of* темне́ть.

стен|á, ы́, a. ~у, *pl.* ~ы, ~áм, *f.* wall (*also fig.*); обнести́ ~о́й to wall in; жить с. в ~у (с+*i.*) to live right on top (of); в ~áх (+*g.*) within the precincts (of); в четырёх ~áх within four walls; лезть на ~у (*coll.*) to climb up the wall; как об ~у горо́х (*coll.*) pointless, useless.

стенá|ть, ю, *impf.* (*obs.*) to groan, moan.

стенгазéт|а, ы, *f.* (*abbr. of* стеннáя газéта) wall newspaper.

стенд, а, m. 1. stand (*at exhibition, etc.*). 2. testing ground.

стéндер, а, m. stand-pipe.

стéнк|а, и, *f.* 1. wall; гимнасти́ческая с. wall-bars. 2. (*anat., etc.*) side, wall.

стенн|о́й, *adj.* wall; mural; ~áя жи́вопись mural painting.

стеноби́тный, *adj.* с. тарáн battering-ram.

стеногрáмм|а, ы, *f.* shorthand report.

стеногрáф, а, m. stenographer.

стенографи́р|овать, ую, *impf. and pf.* to take down in shorthand.

стенографи́ст, а, m. = стено́граф.

стенографи́ст|ка, ки, *f. of* ~.

стенографи́ческий, *adj.* stenographic, shorthand.

стеногрáфи|я, и, *f.* stenography, shorthand.

стéнопис|ь, и, *f.* mural (painting).

стéньг|а, и, *f.* (*naut.*) topmast.

степéн|ный (~ен, ~на), *adj.* 1. staid, steady. 2. middle-aged.

стéпен|ь, и, g. pl. ~éй, *f.* 1. degree, extent; в вы́сшей ~и in the highest degree; до извéстной ~и, до нéкоторой ~и to some degree, to some extent, to a certain extent; ~и сравнéния (*gram.*) degrees of comparison. 2. (*math.*) power; возвести́ в трéтью с. to raise to the third power. 3. (учёная) с. (academic) degree.

степ|но́й, *adj. of* ~ь.

степня́к, á, m. 1. inhabitant of steppe. 2. steppe horse.

степ|ь, и, о ~и, в ~и́, *pl.* ~и, ~éй, *f.* steppe.

стéрв|а, ы, *f.* 1. (*obs.*) dead animal, carrion. 2. (*vulg.; as term of abuse*) shit, stinker.

стервенé|ть, ю, *impf.* (*of* о~) (*coll.*) to become furious, get mad.

стерв|éц, ецá, m. = ~а 2.

стервя́тник, а, m. carrion-crow (*also fig., of enemy aircraft in Second World War*).

стереогрáфи|я, и, *f.* stereography.

стереодальномéр, а, m. (*mil.*) stereoscopic range-finder.

стереокино́, *indecl., n.* stereoscopic cinema.

стереомéтри|я, и, *f.* stereometry, solid geometry.

стереоско́п, а, *m.* stereoscope.

стереоскопи́ческий, *adj.* stereoscopic.

стереоти́п, а, *m.* stereotype.

стереоти́п|ный, *adj.* **1.** stereotype. **2.** (*fig.*) stereotyped; ～ая фра́за stock phrase.

стереотруб|а́, ы́, *f.* stereoscopic telescope; (*mil.*) battery commander's telescope.

стереофони́ческий, *adj.* stereophonic.

стереохи́ми|я, и, *f.* stereochemistry.

стер|е́ть, сотру́, сотрёшь, *past* ～, ～ла, *pf.* (*of* стира́ть[1]) **1.** to rub out, erase; to wipe off; с. с лица́ земли́ to wipe off the face of the earth. **2.** to rub sore. **3.** to grind (down).

стер|е́ться, сотрётся, *past* ～ся, ～лась, *pf.* (*of* стира́ться[1]) **1.** to rub off; (*fig.*) to fade; с. в па́мяти to sink into oblivion. **2.** to become worn down.

стере́|чь, гу́, жёшь, гу́т, *past* ～г, ～гла́, *impf.* **1.** to guard, watch (over). **2.** to watch (for).

стёрж|ень, ня, *m.* **1.** (*tech.*) pivot; shank, rod; поршнево́й с. piston rod. **2.** (*fig.*) core.

стержнев|о́й, *adj.* pivoted; ～а́я анте́нна rod aerial; с. вопро́с key question.

стерилиза́тор, а, *m.* sterilizer.

стерилиза́ци|я, и, *f.* sterilization.

стерилиз|ова́ть, у́ю, *impf. and pf.* to sterilize.

стери́льност|ь, и, *f.* sterility.

стери́л|ьный (～ен, ～ьна), *adj.* sterile.

стёрлинг, а, *m.* (*fin.*) sterling; фунт ～ов pound sterling.

стёрлинг|овый, *adj. of* ～; ～овая зо́на sterling area.

стёрляд|ь, и, *f.* sterlet.

стерн|ь, и, *f.* **1.** harvest-field. **2.** (*collect.*) stubble.

стерн|я́, и́, *f.* = ～ь.

стерп|е́ть, лю́, ～ишь, *pf.* to bear, suffer, endure.

стерп|е́ться, ～ишься, *pf.* (с + *i.*; *coll.*) to get used (to), accept; ～ится — слю́бится you will like it when you get used to it.

стёр|тый, *p.p.p. of* ～е́ть *and adj.* worn, effaced.

стесне́ни|е, я, *n.* constraint; без вся́ких ～й quite uninhibitedly.

стесн|ённый, *p.p.p. of* ～и́ть *and adj.;* ～ённые обстоя́тельства straitened circumstances.

стесни́тельност|ь, и, *f.* **1.** shyness; inhibition(s). **2.** difficulty, inconvenience.

стесни́тел|ьный (～ен, ～ьна), *adj.* **1.** shy; inhibited. **2.** difficult, inconvenient.

стесн|и́ть, ю́, и́шь, *pf.* (*of* ～я́ть) to constrain; to hamper; to inhibit.

стесн|и́ться, ю́сь, и́шься, *pf.* (*of* тесни́ться) to crowd together.

стесн|я́ть, я́ю, *impf. of* ～и́ть.

стесня́|ться, юсь, *impf.* (*of* по～) (+*inf.*) to feel too shy (to), be ashamed (to); (+*g.*) to feel shy (before, of); не ～йтесь! don't be shy!

стетоско́п, а, *m.* (*med.*) stethoscope.

стече́ни|е, я, *n.* confluence; с. наро́да concourse; с. обстоя́тельств coincidence.

сте|чь, чёт, ку́т, *past* ～к, ～кла́, *pf.* (*of* ～ка́ть) to flow down.

сте́|чься, чётся, ку́тся, *past* ～кся, ～кла́сь, *pf.* (*of* ～ка́ться) to flow together; to gather, throng.

сти́бр|ить, ю, ишь, *pf. of* ти́брить.

стиви́дор, а, *m.* stevedore.

стил|ево́й, *adj. of* ～ь; ～евы́е катего́рии stylistic categories.

стиле́т, а, *m.* stiletto.

стилиза́ци|я, и, *f.* stylization.

стилиз|ова́ть, у́ю, *impf. and pf.* to stylize.

стили́ст, а, *m.* stylist.

стили́стик|а, и, *f.* (study of) style, stylistics.

стилисти́ческий, *adj.* stylistic.

стил|ь, я, *m.* (*in var. senses*) style; но́вый с. New Style (*Gregorian calendar*); ста́рый с. Old Style (*Julian calendar*).

сти́л|ьный (～ен, ～ьна), *adj.* stylish; ～ьная ме́бель period furniture.

стиля́г|а, и, *m. and f.* stilyaga (*young person given to uncritical display of extravagant fashions in dress and manners*).

сти́мул, а, *m.* stimulus, incentive.

стимули́р|овать, ую, *impf. and pf.* to stimulate.

стипендиа́т, а, *m.* grant-aided student, scholarship holder.

стипе́нди|я, и, *f.* grant, scholarship.

стира́льн|ый, *adj.* washing; ～ая маши́на washing machine.

стира́|ть[1], ю, *impf. of* стере́ть.

стира́|ть[2], ю, *impf.* (*of* вы́～) to wash, launder.

стира́|ться[1], юсь, *impf. of* стере́ться.

стира́|ться[2], ется, *impf.* to wash; хорошо́ с. to wash well.

сти́рк|а, и, *f.* washing, laundering; отда́ть в ～у to send to the wash, send to the laundry.

сти́скива|ть, ю, *impf. of* сти́снуть.

сти́с|нуть, ну, нешь, *pf.* (*of* ～кивать) to squeeze; с. зу́бы to clench one's teeth; с. в объя́тиях to hug.

стих[1], а́, *m.* **1.** verse; line (*of poetry*); бе́лый с. blank verse; во́льный с. free verse; разме́р ～а́ metre. **2.** (*pl.*) verses; poetry.

стих[2], indecl., *m.* (*coll.*) mood; на него́ угрю́мый с. нашёл he was in a gloomy mood.

стих[3], *see* ～нуть.

стиха́р|ь, я́, *m.* (*eccl.*) surplice, alb.

стих|а́ть, а́ю, *impf. of* ～нуть.

стихи́йност|ь, и, *f.* spontaneity.

стихи́|йный (～ен, ～йна), *adj.* **1.** elemental; ～йное бе́дствие natural calamity. **2.** (*fig.*) spontaneous, uncontrolled.

стихи́р|а, ы, *f.* hymn, canticle.

стихи́|я, и, *f.* element; борьба́ со ~ями struggle with the elements; быть в свое́й ~и to be in one's element.

сти́х|нуть, ну, нешь, *past* ~, ~ла, *pf.* (*of* ~а́ть) to abate, subside; to die down; to calm down.

стихове́дени|е, я, *n.* (study of) prosody.

стихопле́т, а, *m.* (*coll.*) rhymester, versifier.

стихосложе́ни|е, я, *n.* versification; prosody.

стихотворе́ни|е, я, *n.* poem.

стихотво́р|ец, ца, *m.* (*obs.*) poet.

стихотво́рн|ый, *adj.* in verse form; с. разме́р metre; ~ая речь poetic diction.

стихотво́рчеств|о, а, *n.* poetry-writing.

стиш|о́к, ка́, *m.* (*coll.*) verse, rhyme.

стлать, стелю́, сте́лешь, *impf.* (*of* по~) to spread; с. посте́ль to make a bed; с. ска́терть to lay a table-cloth.

стла́ться, сте́лется, *impf.* to spread; с. по земле́ (*of mist, smoke, etc.*) to creep; to hang about.

сто¹, ста, *pl.* ста, сот, стам, ста́ми, стах, *num.* hundred; не́сколько сот рубле́й several hundred roubles; на все сто (*coll.*) in first-rate fashion.

сто², *indecl., n.* (*hist.*) merchant guild.

стог, а, *pl.* ~а́, *m.* (*agric.*) stack, rick.

стогова́ни|е, я, *n.* (*agric.*) stacking.

стогра́дусный, *adj.* centigrade.

стоеро́сов|ый, *adj. only in phrases* (*coll.*) дуби́на ~ая!, дура́к (болва́н) с.! damned fool!

сто́ик, а, *m.* (*philos. and fig.*) stoic.

сто́имост|ь, и, *f.* 1. cost; с. перево́зки carriage. 2. (*econ.*) value; менова́я с. exchange value; приба́вочная с. surplus value.

сто́|ить, ю, ишь, *impf.* 1. to cost (*also fig.*); ско́лько ~ит э́то пла́тье? how much is this dress?; отсю́да до грани́цы ~ит сто рубле́й from here to the frontier costs one hundred roubles; до́рого с. to cost dear; э́то ему́ ничего́ не ~ило it cost him nothing. 2. (+*g.*) to be worth; to deserve; ~ит (*impers.*) it is worth while; ~ит посмотре́ть э́тот фильм this film is worth seeing; ~ит ли он её? is he worthy of her?, does he deserve her?; не ~ит того́ (*coll.*) it is not worth while; не ~ит (благода́рности) don't mention it. 3. ~ит то́лько (*impers.+inf.*) one has only (to); ~ит то́лько упомяну́ть её и́мя, (как) он вы́йдет из себя́ you have only to mention her name for him to fly off the handle.

стоици́зм, а, *m.* (*philos. and fig.*) stoicism.

стои́ческий, *adj.* (*philos.*) stoic; (*fig.*) stoical.

сто́йбищ|е, а, *n.* nomad camp.

сто́йк|а, и, *f.* 1. (*sport*) stand, stance; с. на кистя́х hand-stand. 2. (*hunting*) set;

сде́лать ~у to point. 3. (*tech.*) support, prop; stanchion, upright; (*aeron.*) strut. 4. bar, counter.

сто́|йкий (~ек, ~йка́, ~йко), *adj.* 1. firm, stable; (*phys., chem.*) stable; (*of poisonous substances*) persistent. 2. (*fig.*) stable; steadfast, staunch, steady.

сто́йкост|ь, и, *f.* 1. firmness, stability. 2. (*fig.*) steadfastness, staunchness; determination.

сто́йл|о, а, *n.* stall.

сто́йло|вый, *adj.* of ~; ~вое содержа́ние скота́ keeping cattle stalled.

стоймя́, *adv.* upright.

сток, а, *m.* 1. flow; drainage, outflow. 2. drain, gutter; sewer.

сто́кер, а, *m.* (*tech.*) (mechanical) stoker.

стокра́т, *adv.* (*obs.*) a hundred times, an hundredfold.

стокра́тный, *adj.* hundredfold, centuple.

стол, а́, *m.* 1. table; пи́сьменный с. writing-table, desk; сесть за с. to sit down to table; за ~о́м at table. 2. board; cooking, cuisine; диети́ческий с. invalid dietary; ры́бный с. fish diet; держа́ть с. (*obs.*) to provide board; с. и кварти́ра board and lodging. 3. department; office, bureau; с. ли́чного соста́ва personnel department; с. нахо́док lost property office. 4. (*hist.*) throne.

столб, а́, *m.* post, pole, pillar, column; телегра́фный с. telegraph pole; пыль ~о́м a cloud of dust; стоя́ть ~о́м (*coll.*) to stand rooted to the ground.

столбене́|ть, ю, *impf.* (*of* о~) (*coll.*) to be rooted to the ground.

столб|е́ц, ца́, *m.* 1. column (*in dictionary, newspaper, etc.*). 2. (*pl.*) parchment roll.

сто́лбик, а, *m.* 1. *dim. of* столб; с. ртути mercury (column). 2. (*bot.*) style.

столбня́к, а́, *m.* 1. (*med.*) tetanus. 2. (*coll.*) stupor; на неё нашёл с. she was stunned.

столбов|о́й, *adj. of* столб; (*fig., coll.*) main, chief; с. дворяни́н (*hist.*) member of long-established family of (Russian) gentry; ~а́я доро́га high road, highway (*also fig.*).

столе́ти|е, я, *n.* 1. century. 2. centenary.

столе́тн|ий, *adj.* 1. of a hundred years' duration; ~яя война́ the Hundred Years' War. 2. a hundred years old; centennial; ~яя годовщи́на centenary; с. стари́к centenarian.

столе́тник, а, *m.* (*bot.*) agave.

столи́ц|а, ы, *f.* capital; metropolis.

столи́|чный, *adj. of* ~ца; с. го́род capital (city).

столкнове́ни|е, я, *n.* collision; (*mil. and fig.*) clash; вооружённое с. armed conflict, hostilities; с. интере́сов clash of interests.

столкн|у́ть, у́, ёшь, *pf.* (*of* ста́лкивать) 1. to push off, push away; с. ло́дку в во́ду to push a boat off (into the water). **2.** to cause to collide; to knock together. **3.** (*coll.*) to bring together.

столкн|у́ться, у́сь, ёшься, *pf.* (*of* ста́лкиваться) **1.** (c+*i.*) to collide (with), come into collision (with) (*also fig.*); (*fig.*) to clash (with), conflict (with); здесь на́ши интере́сы ~у́лись our interests clashed at this point. **2.** (c+*i.*; *fig., coll.*) to run (into), bump (into); c. со ста́рым ученико́м to bump into an old pupil.

столк|ова́ться, у́юсь, *pf.* (*of* ~о́вываться) (c+*i.*; *coll.*) to come to an agreement (with).

столко́выва|ться, юсь, *impf. of* столкова́ться.

стол|ова́ться, у́юсь, *impf.* to have meals, receive board; to mess; он ~у́ется у друзе́й he has meals with friends.

столо́в|ая, ой, *f.* **1.** dining-room; dining--hall; mess. **2.** dining-room(s); canteen.

столоверче́ни|е, я, *n.* (*coll., iron.*) table--turning.

столо́в|ый, *adj.* **1.** table; ~ое вино́ table wine; ~ая ло́жка table-spoon; c. прибо́р cover; ~ое серебро́ (*collect.*) silver, plate; ~ая соль table-salt. **2.** feeding, catering, messing; ~ые де́ньги dinner money; (*mil.*) ration allowance, messing allowance; ~ые расхо́ды catering expenses; (*mil.*) messing expenses. **3.** ~ые го́ры (*geogr.*) mesa, table-land.

столонача́льник, а, *m.* (*obs.*) head of a 'desk' (*in civil service*).

стол|о́чь, ку́, чёшь, ку́т, *past* ~о́к, ~ла́, *pf.* (*of* толо́чь) to pound, grind.

столп, á, *m.* (*arch. or fig.*) pillar, column; ~ы́ о́бщества pillars of society.

столп|и́ться, и́тся, *pf.* to crowd.

столпотворе́ни|е, я, *n.* вавило́нское c. babel.

столь, *adv.* so; э́то не c. ва́жно it is of no particular importance.

сто́лько, *adv.* so much; so many; ещё c. же as much again, as many again; не c. ...ско́лько not so much . . . as; где ты был c. вре́мени? where have you been all this time?; сто́лько-то so much, some.

сто́льник, а, *m.* (*hist.*) stolnik (*Russian courtier inferior in rank to boyar*).

сто́льный, *adj.* c. го́род, c. град (*hist.*) capital (city).

столя́р, á, *m.* joiner.

столя́рнича|ть, ю, *impf.* to be a joiner.

столя́рн|ый, *adj.* joiner's; ~ое де́ло joinery; c. клей carpenter's glue.

стомати́т, а, *m.* (*med.*) stomatitis.

стоматоло́ги|я, и, *f.* stomatology.

стон, а, *m.* moan, groan.

стон|а́ть, у́, ~ешь *and* ~а́ю, ~а́ешь, *impf.* to moan, groan (*also fig.*).

стоп, *interj.* stop!; сигна́л c. stop signal.

стоп|á¹, ы́, *f.* **1.** (*pl.* ~ы́) foot (*also fig.*); напра́вить свой ~ы́ to direct, bend one's steps; идти́ по чьим-н. ~а́м to follow in someone's footsteps. **2.** (*pl.* ~ы) (*lit.*) foot.

стоп|á², ы́, *pl.* ~ы, *f.* **1.** ream. **2.** pile, heap.

стоп|á³, ы́, *pl.* ~ы, *f.* (*obs.*) winebowl.

стоп|и́ть, лю́, ~ишь, *pf.* (*of* ста́пливать) **1.** to fuse, melt. **2.** (*of* топи́ть) (*coll.*) to heat.

сто́пк|а¹, и, *f.* pile, heap.

сто́пк|а², и, *f.* small drinking vessel.

сто́пор, а, *m.* **1.** (*tech.*) stop, catch, locking device. **2.** (*naut.*) stopper.

сто́пор|ить, ю, ишь, *impf.* (*tech.*) to stop, lock; (*fig., coll.*) to bring to a standstill.

сто́пор|иться, ится, *impf.* (*coll.*) to come to a standstill.

**сто́пор|ный, *adj.* of* ~; c. кла́пан stop-valve; c. кран stopcock; c. механи́зм stop gear, locking device; ~ное приспособле́ние, ~ное устро́йство lock, catch; c. у́зел (*naut.*) stopper-knot.

стопоходя́щий, *adj.* (*zool.*) plantigrade.

стопроце́нтный, *adj.* hundred per cent.

стоп-сигна́л, а, *m.* brake-light (*on car*).

стоп|та́ть, чу́, ~чешь, *pf.* (*of* ста́птывать) **1.** to wear down (*footwear*). **2.** (*coll.*) to trample.

стоп|та́ться, ~чется, *pf.* (*of* ста́птываться) to wear down, be worn down (*of footwear*).

сторг|ова́ть(ся), у́ю(сь), *pf. of* торгова́ть(ся).

стори́цею, *adv.* (*obs.*) a hundredfold; возда́ть c. (+*d.*) to return a hundredfold, repay with interest.

сто́рож, а, *pl.* ~á, ~е́й, *m.* watchman, guard; ночно́й c. night-watchman.

сторожеви́к, á, *m.* patrol-boat.

сторожев|о́й, *adj.* watch; ~а́я бу́дка sentry--box; ~а́я вы́шка watch-tower; c. кора́бль escort vessel; c. пёс watch-dog; c. пост sentry post; ~ы́е огни́ (*naut.*) warning lights.

сторож|и́ть, у́, и́шь, *impf.* to guard, watch, keep watch (over).

сторожи́х|а, и, *f.* **1.** female watchman. **2.** watchman's wife.

сторо́жк|а, и, *f.* lodge.

сторо́ж|кий (~ек, ~ка), *adj.* (*coll.*) watchful (*of animals and fig.*).

сторож|о́к, ка́, *m.* (*tech.*) **1.** catch. **2.** tongue, cock (*of scales*).

сторон|á, ы́, *a.* сто́рону, *pl.* сто́роны, сторо́н, ~а́м, *f.* **1.** (*in var. senses*) side; quarter; hand (*also fig.*); feature, aspect; в сто́рону (*theatr.*) aside; шу́тки в сто́рону (*coll.*) joking aside; в ~é aside; держа́ться в ~é to keep aloof; на ~é (*coll.*) elsewhere, not on the spot; он рабо́тает на ~é he does not work on the spot; продава́ть на́ сторону sell on the black market; по ту сто́рону

(+g.) across, on the other side (of), on the
far side (of); с пра́вой, с ле́вой ~ы́ on the
right, left side; с како́й ~ы́ ве́тер? from
what quarter is the wind blowing?; с мое́й
~ы́ for my part; э́то о́чень любе́зно с
ва́шей ~ы́ it is very kind of you; со ~ы́
(+g.) (indicating line of descent) on the side
(of); дед со ~ы́ ма́тери maternal grandfather; с одно́й ~ы́..., с друго́й ~ы́ on the
one hand . . ., on the other hand; узна́ть
~о́й to find out indirectly. 2. side, party;
вы на чьей ~е́? whose side are you on?;
взять чью-н. сто́рону to take someone's
part, side with someone; Высо́кие Дого-
ва́ривающиеся Сто́роны (dipl.) the High
Contracting Parties. 3. land, place; parts;
на чужо́й ~е́ in foreign parts.

сторон|и́ться, ю́сь, ~и́шься, impf. (of по~)
1. to stand aside, make way. 2. (+g.) to
shun, avoid.

сторо́нний, adj. 1. strange, foreign; с.
наблюда́тель detached observer. 2. indirect.

сторо́нник, а, m. supporter, adherent, advocate.

стоск|ова́ться, у́юсь, pf. (по+p., о+p.) to
pine (for), yearn (for).

сточ|и́ть, у́, ~ишь, pf. (of ста́чивать) to
grind off.

сто́чн|ый, adj. sewage, drainage; ~ые во́ды
sewage; ~ая труба́ sewer pipe.

стошн|и́ть, и́т, pf. (impers.) to be sick,
vomit; меня́ ~и́ло I was sick.

сто́я, adv. upright.

стоя́к, а́, m. 1. post, stanchion, upright.
2. stand-pipe, rising pipe. 3. chimney.

стоя́лый, adj. stagnant; stale, old.

стоя́ни|е, я, n. standing.

стоя́нк|а, и, f. 1. stop; parking; с. запре-
щена́! 'no parking!'; во вре́мя ~и (по́езда)
на ста́нции while the train is standing at
a station. 2. stopping place, halting place;
parking space; moorage; с. такси́ taxi-
rank. 3. (archaeol.) site.

сто|я́ть, ю́, и́шь, impf. 1. to stand; с. в
о́череди to stand in a queue; с. на коле́нях
to kneel; с. на четвере́ньках to be on all
fours. 2. to be, to be situated, lie; село́ ~и́т
на возвы́шенности the village is situated on
rising ground; стака́ны ~я́т в шкафу́ the
glasses are in the cupboard; с. во главе́
(+g.) to be at the head (of), head; с. на
часа́х to stand guard; с. на я́коре to be at
anchor; с. над душо́й у кого́-н. (coll.) to
plague someone, worry the life out of someone; с. у вла́сти to be in power, be in
office; с. у прича́ла (naut.) to lie alongside,
be moored; с. у руля́ to be at the helm.
3. (of weather conditions, etc.) to be; to continue; ~и́т моро́з there is a frost; ~я́ла

хоро́шая пого́да the weather continued
fine; а́кции ~я́т высоко́ shares continue
high. 4. to stay, put up; (mil.) to be sta-
tioned; с. на кварти́рах, по кварти́рам
(mil.) to be billeted; с. ла́герем to be en-
camped, be under canvas. 5. (за+a.) to
stand up (for); (на+p.) to stand (on),
insist (on); с. горо́й за кого́-н. (coll.) to stand
up for someone with all one's might, be
whole-heartedly behind someone; с. на
чьей-н. то́чке зре́ния to share someone's
point of view. 6. to stop; to come to a halt,
come to a standstill; мои́ часы́ ~я́т my
watch has stopped; рабо́та ~и́т work has
come to a standstill; ~й(те)! stop!, halt!

стоя́ч|ий, adj. 1. standing; upright, verti-
cal; с. воротничо́к stand-up collar; ~ая
ла́мпа standard lamp; ~ая труба́ stand-
-pipe. 2. stagnant.

сто́|ящий, pres. part. act. of ~ить and adj.
deserving; worth-while.

страв|и́ть, лю́, ~ишь, pf. (of ~ли́вать and
~ля́ть) 1. to set on (to fight); с. одного́ с
други́м to play off one against another.
2. to use up in feeding (cattle). 3. (of cattle)
to spoil (by eating and trampling). 4. to
remove by chemical means. 5. (naut.) to
let steam. 6. (naut.) to veer, pay out
(rope).

стра́влива|ть, ю, impf. of страви́ть.

стравля́|ть, ю, impf. = стра́вливать.

стра́гива|ть(ся), ю(сь), impf. of стро́нуть-
(ся).

стра́гива|ть, ю, impf. of стро́нуть.

страд|а́, ы́, pl. ~ы, f. hard work at harvest-
-time; period of hard work; (fig.) toil,
drudgery.

страда́л|ец, ьца, m. sufferer.

страда́льческ|ий, adj. full of suffering; с.
вид an air of suffering, a martyr's air; ~ая
жизнь life of suffering.

страда́ни|е, я, n. suffering.

страда́тельн|ый¹, adj. suffering; ~ое лицо́
sufferer.

страда́тельный², adj. (gram.) passive.

страда́|ть, ю, and (arch.) стра́жду, стра́ж-
дешь, impf. 1. impf. only (+i.) to suffer
(from); to be subject (to); с. бессо́нницей
to suffer from insomnia. 2. impf. only (от)
to suffer (from), be in pain (with); с. от
зубно́й бо́ли to have (a) toothache; с. от
любви́ to be in love. 3. impf. only с. за
кого́-н. to feel for someone. 4. impf. only
(по+d. or p.; coll.) to miss; to long (for),
pine (for). 5. (pf. по~) to suffer; с. за ве́ру
to suffer for one's faith; с. от за́сухи to
suffer from the drought; с. от бомбёжки
to be a victim of bombing; с. по свое́й
вине́ to suffer through one's own fault.
6. impf. only (coll.) to be weak, be poor; to

be at a low ebb; у неё па́мять ~ет she has a poor memory.

стра́д|ный 1. *adj. of* ~á; ~ная пора́ busy period. **2.** (*obs.*) suffering.

страж, а, *m.* (*obs., now only rhet.*) guard, custodian.

стра́ж|а, и, *f.* guard, watch; пограни́чная с. (*obs.*) frontier guard(s); быть, стоя́ть на ~e (+*g.*) to guard; под ~ей under arrest, in custody; взять, заключи́ть под ~y to take into custody.

стра́ждущ|ий, *pres. part. act.* (*obs.*) *of* страда́ть; ~ее челове́чество suffering humanity.

стра́жник, а, *m.* (*obs.*) **1.** police constable (*in rural areas*). **2.** берегово́й с. coastguard; лесно́й с. forest warden.

страз, а, *m.* paste (jewel); strass.

стран|á, ы́, *pl.* ~ы, *f.* **1.** country; land. **2.** с. све́та cardinal point (*of compass*).

страни́ц|а, ы, *f.* page (*also fig., rhet.*).

стра́нник, а, *m.* wanderer (*esp.* religious pilgrim).

стра́нниц|а, ы, *f. of* стра́нник.

стра́нно, *adv.* **1.** strangely, in a strange way. **2.** *as pred.* it is strange, it is funny, it is odd, it is queer.

странноприи́мный, *adj.* (*obs.*) hospitable to strangers; с. дом almshouse, old people's home.

стра́нност|ь, и, *f.* **1.** strangeness. **2.** oddity, eccentricity; за ним води́лись ~и he was an odd person, he had his quirks.

стра́н|ный (~ен, ~на́, ~но), *adj.* strange; funny, odd, queer.

страно́веде́ни|е, я, *n.* regional geography, area studies.

стра́нстви|е, я, *n.* (*obs.*) wandering, journeying, travelling.

стра́нствовани|е, я, *n.* wandering, journeying, travelling.

стра́нств|овать, ую, *impf.* to wander, travel.

стра́нств|ующий, *pres. part. act. of* ~овать *and adj.*; с. актёр strolling player; с. ры́царь knight-errant.

страстн|о́й, *adj.* of Holy Week; ~а́я неде́ля Holy Week; ~а́я пя́тница Good Friday; С. четве́рг Maundy Thursday.

стра́стност|ь, и, *f.* passion.

стра́ст|ный (~ен, ~на́, ~но), *adj.* passionate; impassioned; ardent; он — с. авиамоде́лист he is mad about making model aircraft.

страстоцве́т, а, *m.* passion flower.

страст|ь[1], и, *g. pl.* ~е́й, *f.* **1.** (к) passion (for); до ~и (*coll.*) passionately; люби́ть до ~и to be passionately fond (of); со ~ью with fervour; у неё с. к о́перам Мо́царта she is mad about Mozart's operas. **2.** ~и Христо́вы (*rel.*) the Passion; Стра́сти по

Матфе́ю (*title of oratorio*) St. Matthew Passion. **3.** (*coll.*) horror; расска́зывать (про) вся́кие ~и to recount all manner of horrors.

страсть[2], *adv.* (*coll.*) **1.** (как, како́й) awfully, frightfully; мне с. как хо́чется ви́деть э́тот фильм I want awfully to see this film; она́ с. кака́я на́глая she is frightfully brazen. **2.** an awful lot, a terrific number.

стратаге́м|а, ы, *f.* stratagem.

страте́г, а, *m.* strategist.

стратеги́ческий, *adj.* strategic.

стратеги|я, и, *f.* strategy; с. измо́ра проти́вника strategy of attrition.

стратифика́ци|я, и, *f.* stratification.

стратона́вт, а, *m.* stratosphere flier.

стратоста́т, а, *m.* stratosphere balloon.

стратосфе́р|а, ы, *f.* stratosphere.

стратосфе́рный, *adj.* stratospheric.

стра́ус, а, *m.* ostrich.

стра́ус|овый, *adj. of* ~; ~овое перо́ ostrich feather.

страх[1], а, *m.* **1.** fear; terror; с. Бо́жий, с. Госпо́день the fear of God; с. пе́ред неизве́стностью fear of the unknown; держа́ть в ~e to keep in awe; под ~ом сме́рти on pain of death; ~а ра́ди for fear, from fear; со ~ом и тре́петом with fear and trembling; у ~а глаза́ велики́ fear hath a hundred eyes. **2.** (*pl.*) terrors. **3.** risk, responsibility; на свой с. at one's own risk.

страх[2], *adv.* (*coll.*) (как) terribly; им с. хо́чется побыва́ть во Фра́нции they want terribly to go to France.

страхка́сс|а, ы, *f.* (*abbr. of* страхова́я ка́сса) insurance office.

страхова́ни|е, я, *n.* insurance; с. жи́зни life insurance; с. от несча́стных слу́чаев insurance against accidents; с. от огня́ fire insurance.

страхова́тел|ь, я, *m.* insurant.

страх|ова́ть, у́ю, *impf.* **1.** (*pf.* за~) (от) to insure (against); с. себя́ (от; *fig.*) to insure (against), safeguard oneself (against). **2.** (*sport*) to stand by (*in case of accident*).

страх|ова́ться, у́юсь, *impf.* (*of* за~) (от) to insure oneself (against) (*also fig.*).

страхови́к, á, *m.* (*coll.*) insurance man.

страхо́вк|а, и, *f.* **1.** insurance. **2.** (*fig., coll.*) insurance, guarantee.

страхо́вщик, а, *m.* insurer.

страше́нный, *adj.* (*coll.*) terrible.

страши́лищ|е, а, *m. and n.* fright (*object inspiring fear*); (*coll.*) monster; scarecrow.

страш|и́ть, у́, и́шь, *impf.* to frighten, scare.

страш|и́ться, у́сь, и́шься, *impf.* (+*g.*) to be afraid (of), fear.

стра́шно, *adv.* **1.** terribly, awfully. **2.** *as pred.* it is terrible; it is terrifying; нам бы́ло с. we were terrified.

стра́ш|ный (~ен, ~на́, ~но), *adj.* terrible,

awful, dreadful, frightful, fearful; terrifying, frightening; с. рассказ terrifying story; с. сон bad dream; с. шум (coll.) awful din; С. суд the Day of Judgement, Doomsday.

стращá|ть, ю, impf. (of по~) (coll.) to frighten, scare.

стре́ж|ень, ня, m. channel, main stream (of river).

стреж|невой, adj. of ~ень; ~невы́е во́ды channel, navigable waters (of a river).

стрекáв|ить, лю, ишь, impf. (of о~) (dial.) to sting (with a nettle).

стрекá|ть, ю, impf. (dial.) 1. (pf. об~) = ~вить. 2. (coll.) to take to one's heels, run for it.

стрекáч, á, m. now only in phrase (за)дáть ~á (coll.) to take to one's heels, run for it.

стреко́з|á, ы́, pl. ~ы, f. dragon-fly (also of a fidgety or lively girl).

стре́кот, а, m. chirr (of grasshoppers); (fig.) rattle, chatter (of machine-gun fire, etc.).

стрекотáни|е, я, n. chirring; (fig.) rattle, chatter.

стреко|тáть, чу́, ~чешь, impf. to chirr (of grasshoppers); (fig.) to rattle, chatter (of machine-guns, etc.).

стрел|á, ы́, pl. ~ы, f. 1. arrow (also fig.); (fig.) shaft, dart; пусти́ть ~у́ to shoot an arrow; мчáться ~о́й to fly like an arrow from the bow. 2. (bot.) shaft. 3. (archit.) rise; с. (подъёма) сво́да rise of vault. 4. (tech.) arm (of crane), boom, jib; (pl.; naut.) sheer-legs. 5. с. мо́ста cantilever. 6. с. прогиба (tech.) sag.

стрел|éц, ьцá, m. 1. (hist.) strelets (in Muscovite Russia in the 16th and 17th centuries; member of military corps instituted by Ivan the Terrible and enjoying special privileges). 2. С. (astron.) Sagittarius (constellation).

стрелéц|кий, adj. of ~ 1.

стрелк|а, и, f. 1. pointer, indicator; hand (of clock or watch); needle (of compass, etc.). 2. arrow (on diagram, etc.). 3. (railways) point(s), switch; перевести́ ~у to change the points. 4. (geogr.) spit. 5. shoot, blade (of grass, etc.).

стрелко́в|ый, adj. 1. rifle, shooting; small arms; ~ое мастерство́ marksmanship; ~ое ору́жие small arms; с. спорт shooting; с. тир rifle range. 2. (mil.) rifle, infantry; с. баталько́н rifle battalion, infantry battalion; ~ые войскá infantry; с. око́п fire trench; ~ая цепь riflemen in extended fire positions.

стрелови́дность|ь, и, f. (aeron.) angle (of wing); самолёт с изменя́емой ~ью крылá variable geometry aircraft.

стрелови́д|ный (~ен, ~на), adj. arrow-shaped; (bot., zool.) sagittate; ~ное крыло́ (aeron.) swept-back wing; с. шов че́репа (med.) sagittate suture of skull.

стрел|о́к, ка́, m. 1. shot; иску́сный с., отли́чный с. good shot, marksman. 2. (mil.) rifleman; (aeron.) gunner.

стре́лочник, а, m. (railways) pointsman, switchman; с. виновáт (iron.) the little man is always blamed, muggins!

стре́лочниц|а, ы, f. of стре́лочник.

стре́л|очный, adj. of ~ка 3.

стрельб|á, ы́, pl. ~ы, f. shooting, firing; shoot; ружéйная с. rifle fire, small arms fire; учéбная с. practice shoot; с. на поражéние fire for effect; с. по кáрте predicted shoot, shooting by the map; с. по плóщади area shoot, zone fire.

стрéльбищ|е, а, n. shooting range, target range.

стрельн|у́ть, у́, ёшь, pf. (coll.) 1. to fire a shot. 2. у меня́ ~у́ло в у́хе (impers.) I had a stab of pain in my ear. 3. to rush away. 4. (sl.) to cadge.

стрéльчат|ый, adj. 1. (archit.) lancet. 2. arched, pointed; ~ые бро́ви arched eyebrows.

стрéлян|ый, adj. (coll.) 1. shot; ~ая дичь shot game (as opp. to killed by strangling). 2. that has been under fire; он — солдáт с. he has had his baptism of fire; с. воробéй old hand. 3. used, fired, spent; ~ая ги́льза used cartridge, empty case.

стреля́|ть, ю, impf. 1. (в+a., по+d.) to shoot (at), fire (at); хорошо́ с. to be a good shot; с. из револьвéра, из ружья́ to fire a revolver, a gun; с. в цель to shoot at a target; с. по самолёту to fire at an aeroplane; с. из пу́шек по воробья́м (coll.) to use a sledgehammer to smash walnuts. 2. to shoot (= to hunt, kill by shooting); с. куропáток to go partridge-shooting. 3. с. глазáми (coll.) to dart glances (at); to make eyes (at). 4. (sl.) to cadge. 5. (impers.) to have a shooting pain. 6. to produce a sharp sound; стреля́ть кнуто́м crack a whip.

стреля́|ться, юсь, impf. 1. (coll.) to shoot oneself. 2. to fight a duel (with firearms). 3. pass. of ~ть 2.

стремглáв, adv. headlong.

стрем|енно́й, adj. = ~я́нный.

стреми́тел|ьный (~ен, ~ьна), adj. swift, headlong; impetuous.

стрем|и́ть, лю́, и́шь, impf. to urge.

стрем|и́ться, лю́сь, и́шься, impf. 1. (obs.) to rush, speed, charge. 2. (к) to strive (for), seek, aspire (to); (+inf.) to strive (to), try (to); с. к совершéнству to strive for perfection.

стремлéни|е, я, n. (к) striving (for), aspiration (to).

стремни́н|а, ы, f. 1. rapid (in a river). 2. (obs.) precipice.

стремни́н|ный, adj. of ~a (obs.).

стремни́ст|ый (~, ~а), adj. (obs.) steep, precipitous.

стрём|я, g., d., and p. ~ени, i. ~енем, pl. ~ена́, ~я́н, ~ена́м, n. 1. stirrup; е́хать стре́мя в стре́мя ride side by side (on horseback). 2. (anat.) stirrup-bone, stapedial bone, stapes.

стремя́нк|а, и, f. step-ladder, steps.

стремя́нн|ый, adj. of стре́мя; as noun (hist.) с., ~ого, m. groom.

стре́нг|а, и, f. (naut., tech.) strand (of cable).

стрено́ж|ить, у, ишь, pf. of трено́жить.

стре́пет, а, m. (orn.) little bustard.

стрептоко́кк, а, m. (biol., med.) streptococcus.

стрептоко́кк|овый, adj. of ~.

стрептомици́н, а, m. (med.) streptomycin.

стрех|а́, и́, pl. ~и, f. eaves.

стреч|о́к, ка́, m. now only in phrase (за)да́ть ~ка́ (coll.) to take to one's heels, run for it.

стрига́льн|ый, adj. ~ая маши́на (text.) cloth-shearing machine.

стрига́льщик, а, m. (text. and agric.) shearer.

стрига́льщиц|а, ы, f. of стрига́льщик.

стри|гу́, жёшь, гу́т, see ~чь.

стригу́н, á, m. yearling (foal).

стригун|о́к, ка́, m. = стригу́н.

стригу́щий, pres. part. act. of стричь; с. лиша́й (med.) ring-worm.

стриж, а́, m. (orn.) martin, swift; берегово́й с. sand-martin; ка́менный с. stone-martin.

стри́женый, adj. 1. short-haired, close--cropped. 2. (of hair) short; (of sheep) sheared; (of tree) clipped.

стри́жк|а, и, f. 1. hair-cutting; shearing; clipping. 2. cut, hair-style, hair-do.

стри́нгер, а, m. (naut., aeron.) stringer.

стрихни́н, а, m. (med.) strychnine.

стри|чь, гу́, жёшь, гу́т, past ~г, ~гла, impf. (of о~) 1. to cut, clip (hair or nails). 2. с. кого́-н. to cut someone's hair; с. ове́ц to shear sheep; с. пу́деля to clip a poodle; всех под одну́ гребёнку to treat all alike, reduce all to the same level. 3. (coll.) to cut into pieces, into strips.

стри́|чься, гу́сь, жёшься, гу́тся, past ~гся, ~гла́сь, impf. (of о~) 1. to cut one's hair; to have one's hair cut. 2. to have one's hair cut short, wear one's hair short. 3. pass. of ~чь.

стробоско́п, а, m. (phys.) stroboscope.

строга́л|ь, я́, m. (coll.) = ~ьщик.

строга́льный, adj. (tech.) с. стано́к planing machine, planer; с. резе́ц planer cutter.

строга́льщик, а, m. plane operator, planer.

строга́|ть, ю, impf. (of вы́~) (tech.) to plane, shave.

стро́г|ий (~, ~а́, ~о), adj. (in var. senses) strict; severe; ~ая дие́та strict diet; ~ие ме́ры strong measures; с. пригово́р severe

sentence; под ~им секре́том in strict confidence; в ~ом смы́сле сло́ва in the strict sense of the word; с. стиль severe, austere style; ~ие черты́ лица́ regular features.

стро́го, adv. strictly; severely; с. говоря́ strictly speaking; с. воспреща́ется 'strictly forbidden'.

стро́го-на́строго, adv. (coll.) very strictly.

стро́гост|ь, и, f. 1. (in var. senses) strictness; severity. 2. (pl.) (coll.) strong measures.

строеви́к, á, m. combatant soldier.

строево́й¹, adj. building; с. лес timber.

строев|о́й², adj. (mil.) 1. combatant, line; с. офице́р officer serving in line; ~а́я слу́жба (front-)line service, combatant service; ~а́я часть line unit. 2. drill; ~а́я подгото́вка drill; с. уста́в drill regulations, drill manual; с. шаг ceremonial step.

строе́ни|е, я, n. 1. building, structure. 2. (fig.; in var. senses) structure, composition; (biol.) texture; с. земно́й коры́ (geol.) structure of the earth's crust.

строжа́йший, superl. of стро́гий.

стро́же, comp. of стро́гий and стро́го.

строи́тел|ь, я, m. 1. builder (also fig.). 2. (eccl.) Father Superior (in some monasteries).

строи́тельн|ый, adj. building, construction; ~ая брига́да construction gang; ~ое иску́сство civil engineering; architecture; с. лес building timber; ~ая площа́дка building site; с. раство́р lime mortar.

строи́тельств|о, а, n. 1. building, construction (also fig.); доро́жное с. road-building, road-making; жили́щное с. house-building; зелёное с. laying out of parks, etc.; хозя́йственное с. building-up of the economy. 2. building site, construction project. 3. (fig.) organization, structuring.

стро́|ить, ю, ишь, impf. 1. (pf. по~) to build, construct; с. плоти́ну to build a dam; с. но́вую жизнь to make a new life; с. возду́шные за́мки to build castles in the air. 2. (pf. по~) (math., etc.) to construct; to formulate; to express; с. многоуго́льник to construct a polygon; с. у́гол to plot an angle; с. фра́зу to construct a sentence; с. мысль to express a thought. 3. (pf. со~) (in phrases denoting facial expressions, etc.) to make; с. гла́зки to make eyes; с. грима́сы, с. ро́жу to make, pull faces; с. из себя́ дурака́ to make a fool of oneself. 4. (на+p.) to base (on). 5. (impf. only) с. пла́ны to make plans, plan; с. себе́ иллю́зии to create illusions for oneself. 6. (pf. по~) (mil.) to draw up, form (up).

стро́|иться, юсь, ишься, impf. (of по~) 1. to build (a house, etc.) for oneself. 2. (mil.) to draw up, form up; стро́йся! (mil.) fall in! 3. pass. of ~ить.

стро|й, я, о ~е, в ~ю́, *pl.* ~и́, ~ев, *m.* 1. system, order, régime; общéственный с. social system, social order; феодáльный с. feudal system. 2. (*ling.*) system, structure. 3. (*mus.*) pitch. 3. (*pl.* ~и́, ~ёв) (*mil., naut., aeron.*) formation; развёрнутый с. (extended) line; разóмкнутый с. extended order; сóмкнутый с. close order; расчленённый с. deployed formation; пéленга (*naut.*) line of bearing; с. фрóнта (*naut.*) line abreast; в кóнном ~ю́ mounted; в пéшем ~ю́ dismounted. 4. (*mil.*) unit in formation; пéред ~ем in front of the ranks. 5. (*mil. and fig.*) service, commission; ввести́ в с. to put into commission; вы́вести из ~я to disable; to put out of action; вступи́ть в с. to come into service, come into operation; вы́йти из ~я to be disabled; to become unserviceable; остáться в ~ю́ (*mil.*) to remain in the ranks; (*fig.*) to remain at one's post.

стрóйк|а, и, *f.* 1. building, construction. 2. building-site.

стрóйност|ь, и, *f.* 1. proportion. 2. (*mus., etc.*) harmony; balance; order.

стрó|йный (~ен, ~йнá, ~йно), *adj.* 1. (*of the human figure*) well-proportioned; (*of a woman*) shapely, having a good figure; svelte. 2. (*mus., etc.*) harmonious; well-balanced; orderly; well put together.

строк|á, и́, *pl.* ~и, ~, ~áм, *f.* line; крáсная с., абзáцная с. (*typ.*) break line; с. в ~ý line by line; начáть с нóвой ~и́ to begin a new paragraph; читáть мéжду ~ to read between the lines.

строн|уть, у, ешь, *pf.* (*of* стрáгивать) (*coll.*) to move out, shift.

строн|уться, усь, ешься, *pf.* (*of* стрáгиваться) (*intrans.*; *coll.*) to move (out).

стрóнци|й, я, *m.* (*chem.*) strontium.

строп, а, *m.* sling (rope); shroud line (*of parachute*).

стропи́л|о, а, *n.* rafter, truss, beam.

стропти́в|ец, ца, *m.* obstinate person.

стропти́виц|а, ы, *f. of* стропти́вец.

стропти́вост|ь, и, *f.* obstinacy, refractoriness.

стропти́в|ый (~, ~а), *adj.* obstinate, refractory; shrewish.

строф|á, ы́, *pl.* ~ы, *f.* (*lit.*) stanza, strophe.

строфáнт, а, *m.* (*bot. and pharm.*) strophanthus.

строфи́ческий, *adj.* (*lit.*) strophic.

строчёный, *adj.* stitched.

строч|и́ть, ý, ~и́шь, *impf.* (*of* на~[1]) 1. to stitch. 2. (*coll.*) to scribble, dash off. 3. (*coll.*) to bang away (*with automatic weapons*).

стрóчк|а[1], и, *f.* stitch.

стрóчк|а[2], и, *f.* = строкá; списáть с. в ~у to copy out verbatim.

строчн|óй, *adj.* ~áя бýква small letter, lower-case letter; писáть с ~óй бýквы to write with a small letter.

струбци́н|а, ы, *f.* (*tech.*) (screw) clamp, cramp.

струг[1], а, *m.* (*tech.*) plane.

струг[2], а, *m.* (*obs.*) boat.

стрýжк|а, и, *f.* shaving, filing; снять ~у с кого́-н. (*sl.*) to tear someone off a strip.

стру|и́ть, и́т, *impf.* to pour, shed.

стру|и́ться, и́тся, *impf.* to stream, flow.

структýр|а, ы, *f.* structure.

структурали́зм, а, *m.* (*ling.*) structuralism.

структурали́ст, а, *m.* (*ling.*) structuralist.

структýрный, *adj.* structural; structured.

струн|á, ы́, *pl.* ~ы, *f.* string (*of mus. instrument, tennis racket, etc.*); слáбая с. weak point.

стрýн|ка, ки, *f.* *dim. of* ~á; вы́тянуться в ~ку, стать в ~ку to stand at attention; ходи́ть по ~ке (у, пéред) to be at the beck and call (of), dance attendance (on).

стрýнник, а, *m.* player on stringed instrument.

стрýнный, *adj.* (*mus.*); с. инструмéнт stringed instrument; с. оркéстр string orchestra.

струп, а, *pl.* ~ья, ~ьев, *m.* scab.

стру́|сить, шу, сишь, *pf. of* трýсить.

стручкóвый, *adj.* leguminous; с. пéрец capsicum; с. горóшек peas in the pod.

струч|óк, кá, *m.* pod.

стру|я́, и́, *pl.* ~и́, *f.* 1. jet, spurt, stream; current (*of air*); бить ~ёй to spurt. 2. (*fig.*) spirit; impetus; внести́ свéжую ~ю (в+*a.*) to infuse a fresh spirit (into). 3. (*obs., poet.*) water.

стряпа|ть, ю, *impf.* (*of* со~) (*coll.*) to cook; (*fig.*) to cook up, concoct.

стряпн|я́, и́, *f.* (*coll.*) cooking; (*fig., pejor.*) concoction.

стряпýх|а, и, *f.* (*coll.*) cook.

стряпч|ий, его, *m.* 1. (*hist.*) officer of tsar's household (*in Muscovite Russia*). 2. (*hist.*) scrivener, attorney. 3. (*obs.*) solicitor.

стряс|áть, áю, *impf. of* ~ти́.

стряс|ти́, ý, ~ёшь, *past* ~, ~лá, *pf.* (*of* ~áть) to shake off, shake down.

стряс|ти́сь, ётся, *past* ~ся, ~лáсь, *pf.* (над, с+*i.*; *coll.*) to befall; бедá ~лáсь с нáми a disaster befell us.

стря́хива|ть, ю, *impf. of* стряхнýть.

стрях|нýть, нý, нёшь, *pf.* (*of* ~ивать) to shake off.

студенé|ть, ет, *impf.* (*coll.*) to thicken, acquire the consistency of jelly.

студени́ст|ый (~, ~а), *adj.* jelly-like.

студéнт, а, *m.* student, undergraduate; с.-мéдик medical student; с.-юри́ст law student.

студéнт|ка, ки, *f. of* ~.

студéнческ|ий, *adj. of* студéнт; с. коллекти́в

the student body; ~ое общежи́тие student hostel, hall of residence.

студéнчеств|о, а, n. 1. (collect.) students. 2. student days.

студён|ый (~, ~a), adj. (coll.) very cold, bitter, freezing; as pred. ~о it is freezing.

сту́д|ень, ня, m. galantine; aspic; (meat- or fish-)jelly.

студи́|ец, йца, m. (coll.) student (of art school, drama school, music school, etc.).

студи́|йка, йки, f. of ~ец.

студи́йн|ый, adj. of сту́дия; ~ая радио- переда́ча studio broadcast.

сту|ди́ть, жу́, ~дишь, impf. (of о~) to cool.

сту́ди|я, и, f. 1. (artist's or broadcasting) studio, workshop. 2. (art, drama, music, etc.) school.

сту́ж|а, и, f. severe cold, hard frost.

стук¹, а, m. knock; tap; thump; с. в дверь knock at the door; с. колёс rumble of wheels; с. копы́т clatter of hooves; с.! с.! (onomat.) knock!, knock!

стук² (coll.) as pred. = ~нул.

сту́к|ать(ся), аю(сь), impf. of ~нуть(ся).

стука́ч, á, m. (sl.) knocker (= informer).

сту́к|нуть, ну, нешь, pf. (of ~ать) 1. to knock; to bang; to tap; to rap; с. в дверь to knock, bang, tap, rap at (on) the door; с. кулако́м по́ столу́ to bang one's fist on the table. 2. to bang, hit, strike; с. кого́-н. по спине́ to bang someone on the back. 3. (sl.) to bash (= to kill). 4. (sl.) to knock back (= to drink). 5. pf. only (impers.+d.; coll.) ему́ пятьдеся́т ско́ро ~нет he will soon be fifty. 6. (coll.) ему́ вдруг ~нуло в го́лову he suddenly had a bright idea.

сту́к|нуться, нусь, нешься, pf. (of ~аться) (о, обо+a.) to knock oneself (against), bang oneself (against), bump oneself (against).

стукотн|я́, и́, f. (coll.) knocking, banging, tapping, rapping.

стул, а, pl. ~ья, ~ьев, m. 1. chair; сиде́ть ме́жду двух ~ьев to fall between two stools. 2. (med.) stool.

сту́лик, а, m. small chair.

стульча́к, á, m. (lavatory) seat.

сту́льчик, а, m. stool.

ступ|á, ы, f. mortar.

ступ|а́ть, а́ю, impf. of ~и́ть; ~а́й(те) сюда́! come here!; ~а́й(те)! be off!, clear out!

ступе́нчатый, adj. stepped, graduated, graded.

ступ|е́нь, éни, f. 1. (g. pl. ~éней) step (of stairs); rung (of ladder). 2. (g. pl. ~éней) stage, grade, level, phase.

ступе́нь|ка, ки, f. = ~ 1.

ступ|и́ть, лю́, ~ишь, pf. (of ~а́ть) to step, take a step; to tread; тяжело́ с. to tread heavily; с. че́рез поро́г to cross the threshold

ступи́ц|а, ы, f. nave, hub (of a wheel).

ступн|я́, и́, pl. ~и́, ~éй, f. 1. foot. 2. sole (of foot).

стуч|а́ть, у́, и́шь, impf. 1. (pf. по~) to knock; to bang; to tap; to rap; (of teeth) to chatter. 2. impf. (3rd person only) to hammer, pulse, thump, pound; ~и́т в виска́х blood hammers in the temples; се́рдце у неё ~а́ло her heart was pounding.

стуч|а́ться, у́сь, и́шься, impf. (of по~) (в+a.) to knock (at); с. в дверь to knock at the door (also fig.).

стуш|ева́ть, у́ю, pf. (of ~ёвывать) 1. (art) to shade off. 2. (fig., coll.) to smooth over, efface.

стуш|ева́ться, у́юсь, pf. (of ~ёвываться) 1. (art) to shade off. 2. (coll.) to retire to the background, efface oneself. 3. to be covered with confusion.

стушёвыва|ть(ся), ю(сь), impf. of стуше- ва́ть(ся).

стыд, á, m. shame; к на́шему ~у́ to our shame; сгоре́ть со ~á to burn with shame; с. и срам! for shame!, it's a sin and a shame!

сты|ди́ть, жу́, ди́шь, impf. (of при~) to shame, put to shame.

сты|ди́ться, жу́сь, ди́шься, impf. (of по~) (+g.) to be ashamed (of).

стыдли́в|ый (~, ~a), adj. bashful.

сты́дно, as pred. it is a shame; ему́, etc., с. he, etc., is ashamed; как тебе́ не с.! you ought to be ashamed of yourself!

сты́дный, adj. shameful.

стык, а, m. 1. (tech.) joint, junction, butt. 2. (mil.) meeting-point of flanks of adjacent units. 3. (fig.) junction, meeting-point; с. доро́г road junction; на ~е двух веко́в at the turn of the century.

стык|ова́ть, у́ю, impf. (of со~) (tech.) to join.

стык|ова́ться, у́юсь, impf. (of со~) (tech.) to join (intrans.); (of space vehicles) to dock, rendezvous.

стыко́вк|а, и, f. (of space vehicles) docking, rendezvous.

стыков|о́й, adj. of стык 1; (railways) ~а́я на- кла́дка fish-plate; ~о́е соедине́ние, с. шов butt-weld, butt-joint.

сты́н|уть, у, ешь, past стыл, сты́ла, impf. 1. to cool, grow cold. 2. to become frozen over. 3. (fig.) кровь ~ет в жи́лах one's blood freezes.

стыть = сты́нуть.

сты́чк|а, и, f. 1. skirmish, clash. 2. (coll.) squabble.

стюарде́сс|а, ы, f. stewardess; (on aeroplane) air hostess.

стяг, а, m. (rhet.) banner.

стя́гива|ть(ся), ю(сь), impf. of стяну́ть(ся).

стяжа́тель, я, m. grasping person, person on the make; money-grubber.

стяжа́тел|ьный (~ен, ~ьна), *adj.* greedy, grasping, on the make.

стяжа́|ть, ю, *impf. and pf.* 1. to gain, win. 2. (*impf. only*) to seek, court; с. сла́ву to court fame.

стя|ну́ть[1], ну́, ~нешь, *pf.* (*of* ~ги́вать) 1. to tighten; to pull together; с. на себе́ по́яс to tighten one's belt; с. шине́ль ремнём to strap in a greatcoat. 2. (*mil.*) to gather, assemble (*trans.*) 3. (*impers.*; *coll.*) to have cramp; но́гу у меня́ ~ну́ло I have cramp in my leg.

стя|ну́ть[2], ну́, ~нешь, *pf.* (*of* ~ги́вать) 1. to pull off. 2. (*coll.*) to pinch, steal.

стя|ну́ться, ну́сь, ~нешься, *pf.* (*of* ~ги́ваться) 1. to tighten (*intrans.*). 2. to gird oneself tightly. 3. (*mil.*) to gather, assemble (*intrans.*).

су, *indecl.*, *n.* sou (*French coin*).

субалте́рн-офице́р, а, *m.* (*obs.*) subaltern.

субаре́нд|а, ы, *f.* sub-lease.

субарендáтор, а, *m.* sub-tenant.

суббо́т|а, ы, *f.* Saturday; Вели́кая с. Holy Saturday.

суббо́т|ний, *adj.* of ~а.

суббо́тник, а, *m.* subbotnik (*in U.S.S.R. voluntary unpaid work on days off, originally esp. on Saturdays*).

субве́нци|я, и, *f.* grant, subsidy, subvention.

сублима́т, а, *m.* (*chem.*) sublimate.

сублима́ци|я, и, *f.* (*chem.*) sublimation.

сублими́р|овать, ую, *impf. and pf.* (*chem.*) to sublimate, sublime.

субмари́н|а, ы, *f.* (*naut.*; *obs.*) submarine.

субордина́ци|я, и, *f.* (system of) seniority.

субре́тк|а, и, *f.* soubrette.

субсиди́р|овать, ую, *impf. and pf.* to subsidize.

субси́ди|я, и, *f.* subsidy, grant(-in-aid).

субстанти́в|ировать, ую, *impf. and pf.* (*ling.*) to substantivize.

субста́нци|я, и, *f.* (*philos.*) substance.

субстра́т, а, *m.* 1. (*philos.*) substance. 2. (*biol., geol., and ling.*) substratum.

субти́льност|ь, и, *f.* tenuousness; delicateness; frailty.

субти́л|ьный (~ен, ~ьна), *adj.* (*coll.*) tenuous; delicate; frail; (*obs.*) subtle, delicate.

субти́тр, а, *m.* subtitle (*in film*).

субтро́пик|и, ов, *no sing.* subtropics.

субтропи́ческий, *adj.* subtropical.

субъе́кт, а, *m.* 1. (*philos., gram.*) subject; (*philos.*) the self, the ego. 2. (*med., leg.*) subject; истери́чный с. hysterical subject. 3. (*coll.*) fellow, character, type; подозри́тельный с. suspicious character.

субъективи́зм, а, *m.* 1. (*philos.*) subjectivism. 2. subjectivity.

субъективи́ст, а, *m.* (*philos.*) subjectivist.

субъективисти́ческий, *adj.* (*philos.*) subjectivist.

субъективи́ст|ский, *adj.* = ~и́ческий.

субъекти́вност|ь, и, *f.* subjectivity.

субъекти́в|ный (~ен, ~на), *adj.* subjective.

субъе́кт|ный, *adj.* of ~.

сувени́р, а, *m.* souvenir.

сувере́н, а, *m.* (*polit., leg.*) sovereign.

суверените́т, а, *m.* (*polit., leg*). sovereignty.

сувере́нный, *adj.* (*polit., leg.*) sovereign.

суво́ров|ец, ца, *m.* pupil of Suvorov military school.

сугли́нистый, *adj.* loamy; argillaceous.

сугли́н|ок, ка, *m.* loam, loamy soil.

сугро́б, а, *m.* snow-drift.

сугу́бо, *adv.* especially, particularly; exclusively.

сугу́б|ый (~, ~а), *adj.* 1. (*obs.*) double, twofold. 2. especial, particular; exclusive.

суд, á, *m.* 1. court, law-court; с. Бо́жий (*hist.*) trial by single combat *or* by ordeal; с. че́сти court of honour; зал ~á court-room; заседа́ние ~á sitting of the court; се́ссия ~á court session; на ~é in court. 2. (*fig.*) court; trial, legal proceedings; ~да де́ло (*coll.*) hearing (of a case); (*fig.*) long-drawn-out proceedings; вы́звать в с. to summons, subpoena; пода́ть в с. на кого́-н. to bring an action against someone; отда́ть под с., преда́ть ~у́ to prosecute; быть под ~óм to be under trial; на тебя́ и ~á нет no one can blame you. 3. (*collect.*) the judges; the bench. 4. judgement, verdict; отда́ть на с. пото́мства to submit to the verdict of posterity.

суда́к, á, *m.* pike-perch (*fish*).

суда́н|ец, ца, *m.* Sudanese.

суда́н|ка, ки, *f.* 1. Sudanese (woman). 2. = ~ская трава́.

суда́нск|ий, *adj.* Sudanese; ~ая трава́ Sudan grass (*Sorghum halepense*).

суда́рын|я, и, *f.* (*obs.*; *mode of address*) madam, ma'am.

су́дар|ь, я, *m.* (*obs.*; *mode of address*) sir.

суда́ч|ить, у, ишь, *impf.* (*coll.*) to gossip, tittle-tattle.

суде́бник, а, *m.* (*hist.*) code of laws.

суде́бн|ый, *adj.* judicial; legal; forensic; ~ые изде́ржки costs; с. исполни́тель officer of the court; ~ая медици́на forensic medicine; ~ая оши́бка miscarriage of justice; ~ым поря́дком, в ~ом поря́дке in legal form; с. при́став (*obs.*) bailiff; ~ое разбира́тельство legal proceedings, hearing of a case; ~ое реше́ние court decision, court order; с. сле́дователь investigator; coroner; ~ое сле́дствие investigation in court, inquest.

суде́йск|ая, ой, *f.* 1. judge's room; judge's quarters. 2. referees' room.

суде́йск|ий, *adj.* 1. judge's; *as noun* (*obs.*) с., ~ого, *m.* officer of the court. 2. (*sport*) referee's, umpire's; с. свисток referee's whistle.

судейств|о, а, *n.* (*sport*) refereeing, umpiring; judging.

судёныш|ко, ка, *pl.* ~ки, ~ек, *n.* (*coll.*) tub (*vessel, ship*).

судилищ|е, а, *n.* (*obs. or joc.*) court of law.

судимост|ь, и, *f.* (*leg.*) conviction(s); снять с кого-н. с. to expunge someone's previous convictions.

су|дить, жу, ~дишь, *impf.* **1.** to judge; to form an opinion; насколько мы могли с. as far as we could judge; ~дите сами judge for yourself; ~дя (по+*d.*) judging (by), to judge (from); ~дя по всему to all appearances; с. да (и) рядить (*coll.*) to lay down the law, expatiate. **2.** (*leg.*) to try. **3.** to judge, pass judgement (upon); не ~дите их строго don't be hard on them. **4.** (*sport*) to referee, umpire. **5.** (*also pf.*) to predestine, preordain; но Бог ~дил иное but God decreed a different fate.

су|диться, жусь, ~дишься, *impf.* (с+*i.*) to be at law (with).

суд|но¹, на, *pl.* ~а, ~ов, *n.* vessel, craft; с. на воздушной подушке hovercraft; с. на подводных крыльях hydrofoil.

суд|но², на, *pl.* ~на, ~ен, *n.* chamber-pot; подкладное с. bed-pan.

судный, *adj.* (*obs.*) **1.** court; judicial. **2.** С. день (*rel.*) Day of Judgement.

судоверф|ь, и, *f.* shipyard.

судовладёл|ец, ьца, *m.* shipowner.

судоводитель, я, *m.* navigator.

судовождёни|е, я, *n.* navigation.

судов|ой, *adj.* ship's; marine; ~ая команда ship's crew; ~ое свидетельство ship's certificate of registry.

судоговорёни|е, я, *n.* (*leg.*) pleading(s).

суд|ок, ка, *m.* **1.** sauce-boat, gravy-boat. **2.** cruet(-stand). **3.** (*usually pl.*) set of dishes with covers (*for carrying food*).

судомойк|а, и, *f.* kitchen-maid, scullery maid, washer-up.

судопроизводств|о, а, *n.* legal proceedings.

судоремонт, а, *m.* ship repair.

судоремонт|ный, *adj.* of ~.

судорог|а, и, *f.* cramp, convulsion, spasm.

судорож|ный (~ен, ~на), *adj.* convulsive, spasmodic (*also fig.*).

судостроёни|е, я, *n.* shipbuilding.

судострои́тел|ь, я, *m.* shipbuilder, shipwright.

судостройтельный, *adj.* shipbuilding.

судоустройств|о, а, *n.* judicial system.

судоход|ный (~ен, ~на), *adj.* **1.** navigable; с. канал shipping canal. **2.** ~ная компания shipping company.

судоходств|о, а, *n.* navigation, shipping.

суд|ьба́, ьбы́, *pl.* ~ьбы, ~еб, ~ьбам, *f.* fate,

fortune, destiny, lot; ~ьбы страны the fortunes of the country; благодарить ~ьбу to thank one's lucky stars; искушать ~ьбу to tempt fate, tempt providence; какими ~ьбами? (*coll.*) fancy meeting you here!, how did you get here?; не с. нам (+*inf.*) we are not fated (to).

судьбин|а, ы, *f.* (*folk poet.*) fate, lot.

суд|ья́, ьи́, *pl.* ~ьи, ~ей, ~ьям, *m.* **1.** judge; мировой с. (*obs.*) Justice of the Peace; третейский с. arbitrator; я вам не с. who am I to judge you? **2.** (*sport*) referee, umpire.

суд|я́, see ~ить.

суд|я́, *pres. gerund of* ~ить.

суевёр, а, *m.* superstitious person.

суевёри|е, я, *n.* superstition.

суевёр|ный (~ен, ~на), *adj.* superstitious.

суеслови|е, я, *n.* (*obs.*) idle talk.

сует|а́, ы́, *f.* **1.** vanity; с. суёт vanity of vanities. **2.** bustle, fuss.

суе|ти́ться, чусь, ти́шься, *impf.* to bustle, fuss.

суетли́в|ый (~, ~а), *adj.* fussy, bustling.

суётност|ь, и, *f.* vanity.

суёт|ный (~ен, ~на), *adj.* vain, empty.

суетн|я́, и́, *f.* fuss, bustle.

суждёни|е, я, *n.* opinion; judgement (*in logic*).

суждён|ный (~, ~а́), *p.p.p. of* судить; нам было ~о встретиться we were fated to meet.

сужен|ая, ой, *f.* (*folk poet.*) intended (*bride*).

сужен|ый, ого, *m.* (*folk poet.*) intended (*bridegroom*).

суживá|ть(ся), ю, ет(ся), *impf. of* сузить(ся).

су|зить, жу, зишь, *pf.* (*of* ~живать) to narrow (*trans.*).

су|зиться, зится, *pf.* (*of* ~живаться) to narrow (*intrans.*), get narrow; to taper.

сук, а́, о ~е́, **на** ~у́, *pl.* ~и, ~ов *and* сучья, сучьев, *m.* **1.** bough. **2.** knot (*in wood*).

сук|а, и, *f.* bitch (*also as term of abuse*).

сук|ин, *adj. of* ~а; с. сын (*as term of abuse*) son of a bitch.

сукн|о́, на́, *pl.* ~на, ~он, *n.* (heavy, coarse) cloth; положить под с. (*fig.*) to shelve.

сукновáл, а, *m.* fuller.

сукновáльн|ый, *adj.* fulling; ~ая глина fuller's earth.

сукновáльн|я, и, *f.* fullery, fulling mill.

суковáт|ый (~, ~а), *adj.* with many boughs.

суконк|а, и, *f.* piece of cloth, rag.

сукóнн|ый, *adj.* **1.** cloth; ~ая фабрика cloth mill. **2.** (*fig.*) rough, clumsy, crude; с. язык rough tongue, clumsy way of speaking; ~ое рыло (*obs.*) merchant.

сукрóвиц|а, ы, *f.* **1.** (*physiol.*) lymph, serum. **2.** (*med.*) ichor, pus.

сулем|а́, ы́, *f.* (*chem.*, *med.*) corrosive sublimate, mercuric chloride.

сулем|о́вый, *adj. of* ~а́.

суле|я́, и́, *f.* (*obs.*) flask.

сул|и́ть, ю́, и́шь, *impf.* (*of* по~) to promise; с. золоты́е го́ры to promise the earth; э́то не ~и́т ничего́ хоро́шего this does not bode well.

султа́н[1], а, *m.* sultan.

султа́н[2], а, *m.* plume (*on headdress, etc.*).

султана́т, а, *m.* sultanate.

султа́н|ский, *adj. of* ~[1].

султа́нш|а, и, *f.* sultana (*sultan's wife*).

сульфа́т, а, *m.* (*chem.*) sulphate.

сульфи́д, а, *m.* (*chem.*) sulphide.

сульфо- (*chem.*) sulpho-.

сум|а́, ы́, *f.* bag, pouch; с. переметная (*fig.*) weathercock; пусти́ть с ~о́й to ruin, reduce to beggary; ходи́ть с ~о́й to beg, go a-begging.

сумасбро́д, а, *m.* madcap.

сумасбро́д|ка, ки, *f. of* ~.

сумасбро́|дить, жу, дишь, *impf.* (*coll.*) to behave wildly, extravagantly.

сумасбро́днича|ть, ю, *impf.* (*coll.*) = сумасбро́дить.

сумасбро́д|ный (~ен, ~на), *adj.* wild, extravagant.

сумасбро́дств|о, а, *n.* wild, extravagant behaviour.

сумасше́дш|ий, *adj.* 1. mad; *as noun* с., ~его, *m.* madman, lunatic; ~ая, ~ей, *f.* madwoman; бу́йный с. raving, violent lunatic; объяви́ть кого́-н. ~им to certify someone. 2. с. дом (*coll.*) lunatic asylum, madhouse. 3. (*fig.*) mad, lunatic; ~ая ско́рость lunatic speed; э́то бу́дет сто́ить ~их де́нег it will cost the earth.

сумасше́стви|е, я, *n.* madness, lunacy.

сумасше́ств|овать, ую, *impf.* (*coll.*) to act like a madman.

сумато́х|а, и, *f.* confusion, chaos, turmoil, hurly-burly.

сумато́шлив|ый (~, ~а), *adj.* (*coll.*) given to fussing.

сумато́ш|ный (~ен, ~на), *adj.* = ~ливый.

сумбу́р, а, *m.* confusion, chaos.

сумбу́р|ный (~ен, ~на), *adj.* confused, chaotic.

су́меречник, а, *m.* crepuscular animal.

су́мереч|ный (~ен, ~на), *adj.* 1. twilight, dusk. 2. (*zool.*) crepuscular.

су́мер|ки, ек, *no sing.* twilight, dusk.

су́мернича|ть, ю, *impf.* (*coll.*) to sit in the twilight.

суме́|ть, ю, *pf.* (*of* уме́ть) (+*inf.*) to be able (to), manage (to).

су́мк|а, и, *f.* 1. bag, handbag; satchel. 2. (*biol.*) pouch.

су́мм|а, ы, *f.* sum; вся с., о́бщая с. sum

total; в ~е in sum, all in all.

сумма́р|ный (~ен, ~на), *adj.* 1. total. 2. summary.

сумми́р|овать, ую, *impf.* 1. to sum up. 2. to summarize.

су́мнича|ть, ю, *pf. of* у́мничать.

сумня́ся, *only in phrase* (*obs. or joc.*) ничто́же с., ничто́же сумня́шеся without a second's hesitation, not batting an eyelid.

су́мрак, а, *m.* dusk, twilight.

су́мрач|ный (~ен, ~на), *adj.* gloomy (*also fig.*); murky.

су́мчат|ый, *adj.* 1. (*zool.*) marsupial. 2. ~ые грибы́ (*bot.*) Ascomycetes.

сумя́тиц|а, ы, *f.* confusion, chaos.

сунду́к, а́, *m.* trunk, box, chest.

су́н|уть(ся), у(сь), ешь(ся), *pf. of* сова́ть(ся).

суп, а, *pl.* ~ы́, *m.* soup.

суперарби́тр, а, *m.* chief arbitrator.

суперобло́жк|а, и, *f.* dust-cover, jacket (*of book*).

суперфосфа́т, а, *m.* (*chem.*) superphosphate.

су́пес|ный, *adj. of* ~ь.

су́пес|ок, ка, *m.* = ~ь.

супесча́ный, *adj.* = су́песный.

су́пес|ь, и, *f.* sandy soil, sandy loam.

супи́н, а, *m.* (*ling.*) supine.

су́п|ить, лю, ишь, *impf.* (*of* на~) с. бро́ви to knit one's brows, frown.

су́п|иться, люсь, ишься, *impf.* (*of* на~) = су́пить бро́ви.

супово́й, *adj. of* суп; ~а́я ло́жка soup-spoon; ~а́я ми́ска soup tureen.

супо́н|ь, и, *f.* hame-strap.

супоро́с(н)ая, *adj.* с. свинья́ sow in farrow.

супоста́т, а, *m.* (*arch. or rhet.*) adversary, foe; satan.

супроти́в (*coll.*) 1. *prep.*+*g.* against. 2. *adv. and prep.*+*g.* opposite.

супру́г, а, *m.* 1. husband, spouse. 2. (*pl.*) husband and wife, married couple.

супру́г|а, и, *f.* wife, spouse.

супру́жеский, *adj.* conjugal, matrimonial.

супру́жеств|о, а, *n.* conjugal state, matrimony, wedlock.

супря́г|а, и, *f.* (*dial.*) 1. yoke (*of draught cattle*). 2. joint tilling of land. 3. в ~е (с+*i.*) together (with).

сургу́ч, а́, *m.* sealing-wax.

сургу́ч|ный, *adj. of* ~.

сурди́нк|а, и, *f.* (*mus.*) mute, sordine; под ~у (*coll.*) on the quiet.

суре́пиц|а, ы, *f.* (*bot.*) 1. cole-seed, rape. 2. charlock.

суре́п|ный, *adj. of* ~ица; ~ное ма́сло rape-oil, colza oil.

су́рик, а, *m.* (*chem.*) minium, red lead.

су́рик|овый, *adj. of* ~.

суро́вост|ь, и, *f.* severity, sternness.

суро́в|ый (~, ~a), *adj.* 1. (*in var. senses*) severe, stern; rigorous; bleak. 2. (*text.*) unbleached, brown; ~ое полотно́ crash; brown Holland.

сур|о́к, ка́, *m.* marmot; спать как с. to sleep like a log.

суррога́т, а, *m.* substitute.

суррога́тный, *adj.* substitute, ersatz.

сурьм|а́, ы́, *f.* 1. (*chem.*) antimony. 2. hair-dye (*containing antimony*), kohl.

сурьм|и́ть, лю́, и́шь, *impf.* (*of* на~) (*obs.*) to dye, darken (*hair, eye-brows, etc.*).

сурьм|и́ться, лю́сь, и́шься, *impf.* (*of* на~) (*obs.*) to dye, darken one's hair, eye-brows, etc.

сурьмяно́й, *adj.* antimony.

сурьмя́н|ый, *adj.* = ~о́й.

суса́л|ить, ю, ишь, *impf.* (*obs.*) to tinsel.

суса́л|ь, и, *f.* (*obs.*) tinsel.

суса́льн|ый, *adj.* 1. tinsel; ~ое зо́лото gold leaf. 2. (*fig., coll.*) sugary.

су́слик, а, *m.* (*zool.*) gopher.

сусл|и́ть, ю, ишь, *impf.* (*of* за~) (*coll.*) to beslobber; to spatter.

су́сл|о, а, *n.* 1. виногра́дное с. must; пивно́е с. wort. 2. grape-juice.

сусо́л|ить, ю, ишь, *impf.* (*of* за~) (*coll.*) = сусли́ть.

суста́в, а, *m.* (*anat.*) joint, articulation; неподви́жность ~ов (*med.*) anchylosis.

суставно́й, *adj.* of суста́в.

сута́н|а, ы, *f.* soutane.

сутенёр, а, *m.* souteneur, ponce.

су́т|ки, ок, *no sing.* twenty-four hours; twenty-four-hour period; це́лые с. for days and nights.

су́толок|а, и, *f.* commotion, hubbub, hurly-burly; предпра́здничная с. pre-holiday rush.

су́точн|ый, *adj.* 1. twenty-four-hour; daily; round-the-clock; ~ые де́ньги per diem subsistence allowance; *as noun* ~ые, ~ых = ~ые де́ньги. 2. с. цыплёнок day-old chick.

сату́л|ить, ю, ишь, *impf.* (*of* с~) с. спи́ну to stoop.

сату́л|иться, ю́сь, ишься, *impf.* (*of* с~) to stoop.

сату́лост|ь, и, *f.* с. фигу́ры round shoulders, stoop.

сату́л|ый (~, ~a), *adj.* round-shouldered, stooping.

сут|ь¹, и, *f.* essence; с. де́ла the heart, crux of the matter; по ~и де́ла as a matter of fact, in point of fact.

суть², (*arch.*) 3rd pl. pres. of быть; э́то не с. ва́жно (*coll.*) this is not so important.

сутя́г|а, и, *m. and f.* (*coll., obs.*) litigious person.

сутя́жник, а, *m.* (*obs.*) = сутя́га.

сутя́жнича|ть, ю, *impf.* (*obs.*) to engage in (malicious) litigation.

сутя́жн|ый, *adj.* (*obs.*) litigious; ~ое де́ло malicious litigation.

суфле́, *indecl., n.* (*cul.*) soufflé.

суфлёр, а, *m.* (*theatr.*) prompter.

суфлёр|ский, *adj. of* ~; ~ская бу́дка prompt-box.

суфли́р|овать, ую, *impf.* (+*d.*) (*theatr.*) to prompt.

суфражи́зм, а, *m.* suffragette movement.

суфражи́стк|а, и, *f.* suffragette.

су́ффикс, а, *m.* (*gram.*) suffix.

суффикса́льный, *adj. of* су́ффикс.

суха́рниц|а, ы, *f.* biscuit dish; biscuit barrel.

суха́р|ь, я́, *m.* 1. rusk. 2. (*fig., coll.*) dried-up person.

сух|а́я, о́й, *f.* (*sport*) whitewash (*game in which loser fails to score a single point*); сде́лать ~у́ю кому́-н. to whitewash someone.

сухме́н|ь, и, *f.* (*dial.*) 1. dry weather, drought. 2. dry soil.

су́хо, *adv.* 1. drily; coldly; нас при́няли с. we were received coldly. 2. *as pred.* it is dry; на у́лице с. it is dry out of doors; у меня́ в го́рле с. my throat is parched.

сухова́т|ый (~, ~a), *adj.* dryish.

сухове́|й, я, *m.* hot dry wind.

сухове́й|ный, *adj. of* ~.

сухадо́л, а, *m.* waterless valley.

сухожи́ли|е, я, *n.* (*anat.*) tendon, sinew.

сухожи́л|ьный, *adj. of* ~ие.

сух|о́й (~, ~а́, ~о), *adj.* 1. dry; dried-up; arid; ~и́е дрова́ dry firewood; ~о́е ру́сло реки́ dried-up river-bed; ~и́м путём by land, overland; вы́йти ~и́м из воды́ to come out unscathed. 2. (*of foodstuffs, etc.*) dry, dried; ~о́е молоко́ dried milk. 3. (*of part of body*) dried-up, withered (*also fig.*; *of persons*). 4. (*in var. senses*) dry (= unconnected with, opp. to liquid); с. док dry-dock; с. зако́н (*hist.*) 'dry law' (*e.g. in U.S.A.*); с. ка́шель dry cough; ~а́я мо́лния summer lightning; ~а́я перего́нка dry, destructive distillation; с. тума́н fog of dust, smoke, etc.; с. элеме́нт (*electr.*) dry pile. 5. (*fig.*) dry (= dull, boring). 6. (*fig.*) chilly, cold; с. приём chilly reception.

сухолюби́в|ый (~, ~a), *adj.* (*bot.*) xerophilous.

сухомя́тк|а, и, *f.* (*coll.*) dry food (*without any beverage*).

сухопа́рник, а, *m.* (*tech.*) steam dome.

сухопа́р|ый (~, ~a), *adj.* (*coll.*) lean, skinny.

сухопу́тн|ый, *adj.* land (*as opp. to marine*, air); ~ые си́лы (*mil.*) ground forces.

сухору́к|ий (~, ~a), *adj.* without the use of one arm; having a withered arm.

сухосто́|й¹, я, *m.* (*collect.*) dead wood, dead standing trees.

сухостó|й², я, *m.* period before calving (*when cow ceases to give milk*).

сухост|ь, и, *f.* **1.** (*in var. senses*) dryness; aridity. **2.** (*fig.*) chilliness, coldness.

сухот|á, ы́, *f.* **1.** dryness; у меня́ в го́рле с. my throat is parched. **2.** dry spell (*of weather*). **3.** (*folk poet.*; *dial.*) longing, yearning.

сухо́тк|а, и, *f.* **1.** (*dial.*) wasting, emaciation. **2.** с. спинно́го мо́зга (*med.*) dorsal tabes, locomotor ataxia.

сухо́точный, *adj.* (*med.*) tabetic.

сухофру́кт|ы, ов, *no sing.* dried fruits.

сухоща́в|ый (~, ~а), *adj.* lean, skinny.

сухояде́ни|е, я, *n.* dry food.

сучёный, *adj.* twisted.

суч|и́ть, у́, ∼ишь, *impf.* (*of* с∼) **1.** to twist, spin; to throw (*silk*). **2.** (*cul.*) to roll out (*dough*).

сучкова́т|ый (~, ~а), *adj.* knotty; gnarled.

суч|о́к, ка́, *m.* **1.** twig. **2.** knot (*in wood*); без ∼ка́, без задо́ринки (*coll.*) without a hitch.

су́ш|а, и, *f.* (dry) land (*as opp. to sea*).

су́ше, *comp. of* сухо́й *and* су́хо.

суше́ни|е, я, *n.* **1.** drying. **2.** (*coll.*) dried fruit.

сушёный, *adj.* dried.

суши́лк|а, и, *f.* (*agric.*) **1.** drying apparatus, dryer. **2.** drying-room.

суши́льный, *adj.* (*tech.*) drying; с. бараба́н desiccator.

суши́л|ьня, ьни, *g. pl.* ∼ен, *f.* drying-room.

суш|и́ть, у́, ∼ишь, *impf.* to dry (out, up); с. вёсла (*naut.*; *not fig.*) to rest on one's oars.

суш|и́ться, у́сь, ∼ишься, *impf.* to dry (*intrans.*), get dry.

су́шк|а, и, *f.* **1.** drying. **2.** (*cul.*) dry (ring-shaped) cracker.

суш|ь, и, *f.* **1.** dry spell (*of weather*). **2.** dry place. **3.** dry object.

существен|ный (~, ~на), *adj.* essential, vital; material; important; ∼ное замеча́ние remark of material significance; ∼ная попра́вка important amendment; игра́ть ∼ную роль to play a vital part.

существи́тельн|ое, *adj.*, *only in phrase* и́мя с. *or as noun* с., ∼ого, *n.* noun, substantive.

существ|о́, á, *n.* **1.** essence; по ∼у́ in essence, essentially; говори́ть по ∼у́ to speak to the point; не по ∼у́ off the point, beside the point. **2.** being, creature; люби́мое с. loved one; нигде́ не́ было ви́дно ни одного́ живо́го ∼á there was nowhere a living creature in sight.

существова́ни|е, я, *n.* existence; сре́дства к ∼ю livelihood; отрави́ть кому́-н. (всё) с. to make someone's life a misery.

существ|ова́ть, у́ю, *impf.* to exist (= (*i*) to be, be in existence, (*ii*) to live, subsist).

су́щ|ий, *adj.* **1.** (*obs.*) existing. **2.** (*coll.*) real; absolute, utter, downright; с. ад absolute hell; ∼ие пустяки́ utter rubbish.

су́щност|ь, и, *f.* essence; с. де́ла the point; в ∼и in essence, at bottom; в ∼и говоря́ really and truly.

суя́гная, *adj.* с. овца́ ewe in yean.

сфабрик|ова́ть, у́ю, *pf. of* фабрикова́ть.

сфа́гновый, *adj.* sphagnum.

сфа́гнум, а, *m.* (*bot.*) sphagnum, bog-moss.

сфальц|ева́ть, у́ю, *pf. of* фальцева́ть.

сфальши́в|ить, лю, ишь, *pf. of* фальши́вить.

сфантази́р|овать, ую, *pf. of* фантази́ровать.

сфе́р|а, ы, *f.* **1.** (*in var. senses*) sphere; realm; с. влия́ния (*polit.*) sphere of influence; вы́сшие ∼ы the upper crust, influential circles; быть в свое́й ∼е to be on one's own ground. **2.** (*mil.*) zone, area; с. огня́ zone of fire.

сфери́ческий, *adj.* spherical.

сферо́ид, а, *m.* (*math.*) spheroid.

сфероида́льный, *adj.* (*math.*) spheroidal.

сфинкс, а, *m.* sphinx.

сфи́нктер, а, *m.* (*anat.*) sphincter.

сформир|ова́ть(ся), у́ю(сь), *pf. of* формирова́ть(ся).

сформ|ова́ть, у́ю, *pf. of* формова́ть.

сформули́р|овать, ую, *pf. of* формули́ровать.

сфотографи́р|овать(ся), ую(сь), *pf. of* фотографи́ровать(ся).

схва|ти́ть, чу́, ∼тишь, *pf.* **1.** *pf. of* хвата́ть¹. **2.** (*impf.* ∼тывать) (*coll.*) to catch (*a cold, etc.*). **3.** (*impf.* ∼тывать) (*coll.*) to grasp, comprehend; с. смысл to grasp the meaning, catch on. **4.** (*impf.* ∼тывать) (*tech.*) to clamp together.

схва|ти́ться, чу́сь, ∼тишься, *pf.* **1.** *pf. of* хвата́ться. **2.** (*impf.* ∼тываться) (с+*i.*) to grapple (with), come to grips (with) (*also fig.*). **3.** (*impf.* ∼тываться) (с+*g.*; *coll.*) to leap (out of, from).

схва́тк|а, и, *f.* **1.** skirmish, fight, encounter. **2.** (*coll.*) squabble.

схва́т|ки, ок, *no sing.* contractions (*of muscles*); fit, spasm; родовы́е с. labour, birth pangs.

схва́тыва|ть(ся), ю(сь), *impf. of* схвати́ть(ся).

схе́м|а, ы, *f.* **1.** diagram, chart; с. обстано́вки situation map; с. ориенти́ров range card. **2.** sketch, outline, plan; с. рома́на plan of a novel. **3.** (*electr.*, *radio*) circuit.

схематизи́р|овать, ую, *impf. and pf.* to present in sketchy form, over-simplify.

схемати́зм, а, *m.* sketchiness, over-simplification; employment of ready-made categories.

схемати́ческий, *adj.* **1.** diagrammatic, schematic. **2.** sketchy, over-simplified.

схемати́ч|ный (~ен, ~на), *adj.* sketchy, over-simplified.

схи́зм|а, ы, *f.* (*eccl.*) schism.

схизма́тик, а, *m.* (*eccl.*) schismatic.

схизмати́ческий, *adj.* (*eccl.*) schismatic.

схи́м|а, ы, *f.* (*eccl.*) schema (*strictest monastic rule in Orthodox Church*).

схи́мник, а, *m.* (*eccl.*) monk having taken vows of schema.

схи́мниц|а, ы, *f.* (*eccl.*) nun having taken vows of schema.

схи́мничес|кий, *adj.* of ~тво.

схи́мничеств|о, а, *n.* (*eccl.*) profession and practice of schema.

схитр|и́ть, ю́, и́шь, *pf.* of хитри́ть.

схлы́н|уть, у, ешь, *pf.* **1.** (*of waves*) to break and flow back. **2.** (*of a crowd*) to break up; to dwindle. **3.** (*of emotions*) to subside.

сход¹, а, *m.* **1.** coming off, alighting. **2.** descent.

сход², а, *m.* (*obs.*) gathering, assembly.

схо|ди́ть¹, жу́, ~дишь, *impf.* of сойти́.

схо|ди́ть², жу́, ~дишь, *pf.* **1.** to go (*and come back*); (за+*i.*) to go to fetch; с. посмотре́ть to go to see; ~ди́ за до́ктором! go and fetch a doctor! **2.** *pf.* of ходи́ть 11.

схо|ди́ться, жу́сь, ~дишься, *impf.* of сойти́сь.

схо́дк|а, и, *f.* (*obs.*) gathering, assembly.

схо́дн|и, ей, *sing.* ~я, ~и, *f.* gangway, gang-plank.

схо́д|ный (~ен, ~на́, ~но), *adj.* **1.** similar. **2.** (*coll.*) reasonable, fair (*of prices, etc.*).

схо́дств|о, а, *n.* likeness, similarity, resemblance.

схо́дств|овать, ую, *impf.* (с+*i.*; *obs.*) to resemble.

схо́жест|ь, и, *f.* likeness, similarity.

схо́ж|ий (~, ~а), *adj.* like, similar.

схола́ст, а, *m.* scholastic.

схола́стик, а, *m.* = схола́ст.

схола́стик|а, и, *f.* scholasticism.

схоласти́ческий, *adj.* scholastic (*of scholasticism*).

схорон|и́ть(ся), ю́(сь), ~ишь(ся), *pf.* of хорони́ть(ся).

сца́па|ть, ю, *pf.* (*coll.*) to catch hold (of), lay hold (of).

сцара́п|ать, аю, *pf.* (*of* ~ывать) to scratch off.

сцара́пыва|ть, ю, *impf.* of сцара́пать.

сце|ди́ть, жу́, ~дишь, *pf.* (*of* ~живать) to pour off, strain off, decant.

сце́жива|ть, ю, *impf.* of сцеди́ть.

сце́н|а, ы, *f.* **1.** (*theatr.*) stage, boards (*also fig.*); ста́вить на ~е to stage, put on the stage; сойти́ со ~ы to go off the scene, make one's exit (*also fig.*). **2.** (*theatr., lit.*)

scene. **3.** (*coll.*) scene; устра́ивать ~ы to make scenes.

сцена́ри|й, я, *m.* **1.** scenario. **2.** film script; (по+*d.*) screen version (of).

сцена́рист, а, *m.* scenario writer; script writer.

сцена́риус, а, *m.* (*theatr.; obs.*) producer's assistant.

сцени́ческ|ий, *adj.* stage; ~ая рема́рка stage direction; с. шёпот stage whisper.

сцени́ч|ный (~ен, ~на), *adj.* suitable for the theatre, effective on the stage; э́та пье́са не ~на this play is not good theatre.

сцеп, а, *m.* **1.** coupling; drawbar. **2.** couple (*two goods trucks, agric. implements, etc., coupled together*).

сцеп|и́ть, лю́, ~ишь, *pf.* (*of* ~ля́ть) to couple.

сцеп|и́ться, лю́сь, ~ишься, *pf.* (*of* ~ля́ться) **1.** to be coupled. **2.** (с+*i.; coll.*) to grapple (with), come to grips (with).

сце́пк|а, и, *f.* coupling.

сцепле́ни|е, я, *n.* **1.** coupling. **2.** (*phys.*) adhesion; cohesion. **3.** (*tech.*) clutch; выключе́ние ~я clutch release. **4.** (*fig.*) accumulation; с. обстоя́тельств chain of events.

сцепля́|ть(ся), ю(сь), *impf.* of сцепи́ть(ся).

сцепн|о́й, *adj.* (*tech.*) coupling; ~о́е ды́шло, с. шату́н coupling rod; с. крюк, ~а́я тя́га drawbar.

сце́пщик, а, *m.* (*railways*) coupler.

сча́лива|ть, ю, *impf.* of сча́лить.

сча́л|ить, ю, ишь, *pf.* (*of* ~ивать) to lash together.

счастли́в|ец, ца, *m.* lucky man.

счастли́виц|а, ы, *f.* lucky woman.

счастли́вчик, а, *m.* (*coll.*) = счастли́вец.

сча́стливо, *adv.* happily; with luck; с. отде́латься (от) to have a lucky escape (from); счастли́во (остава́ться)! good luck!

счастли́в|ый (сча́стлив, ~а), *adj.* **1.** happy. **2.** lucky, fortunate. **3.** successful; ~ого пути́!, ~ого пла́вания! bon voyage!

сча́сть|е, я, *n.* **1.** happiness. **2.** luck, good fortune; к ~ю, на с., по ~ю luckily, fortunately; на на́ше с. luckily for us; попыта́ть ~я to try one's luck.

счерп|а́ть, а́ю, *pf.* (*of* ~ывать) to skim (off).

счёрпыва|ть, ю, *impf.* of счерпа́ть.

счер|ти́ть, чу́, ~тишь, *pf.* (*of* ~чивать) (*coll.*) to copy, run off.

счёрчива|ть, ю, *impf.* of счерти́ть.

счесть(ся), сочту́(сь), сочтёшь(ся), *past* счёл(ся), сочла́(сь), *pf.* of счита́ть(ся)¹.

счёт, а (у), *pl.* ~ы and ~а́, *m.* **1.** *sing. only* counting, calculation, reckoning; вести́ с. (+*d.*) to keep count (of); потеря́ть с. (+*d.*) to lose count (of); он не в с. he does not count; в два ~а in a jiffy, in a trice; без

~у, ~у нет countless, without number.
2. *sing. only* (*sport*) score. **3.** (*pl.* ~á) bill,
account; подáть с. to present a bill. **4.** (*pl.*
~á) (*book-keeping*) account; откры́ть с. to
open an account; за с. (+*g.*) at the expense
(of); на с. on account; на с. (+*g.*) on the
account (of), to the account (of). **5.** (*fig.*)
account, expense; в с. (+*g.*) on the strength
(of); в конéчном ~е, в послéднем ~е in
the end; за с. (+*g.*) at the expense (of);
owing (to); на свой с. on one's own
account; на чужóй с. at others' expense;
на э́тот с. (*i*) on this score, (*ii*) in this
respect, in this department; предъяви́ть с.
to present a claim; приня́ть на свой с. to
take as referring to oneself; быть на хорó-
шем, дурнóм ~ý to be in good, bad (re-
pute); to stand well, badly; имéть на
своём ~ý to have to one's credit; сбрóсить
со ~ов to dismiss, rule out. **6.** ~ы (*no sing.*;
fig.) accounts, score(s); стáрые ~ы old
scores; свести́ ~ы (с+*i.*) to settle a score
(with), get even (with). **7.** *see* ~ы.

счётн|ый, *adj.* **1.** counting, calculating,
computing; ~ая линéйка slide-rule; ~ая
маши́на calculator, calculating machine.
2. accounts, accounting; с. рабóтник
accounts clerk; ~ая часть accounts department.

счетовóд, а, *m.* accountant; accounts clerk,
ledger clerk.

счетовóдн|ый, *adj.* accounting; ~ая кни́га
account book.

счетовóдств|о, а, *n.* accounting.

счётчик[1], а, *m.* teller; counter (*person*).

счётчик[2], а, *m.* meter; counter (*instrument*);
гáзовый с. gas meter.

счётчиц|а, ы, *f.* of счётчик[1].

счёт|ы[1], ов, *no sing.* abacus, counting frame.

счёт|ы[2], *see* ~ 6.

счислéни|е, я, *n.* **1.** numeration, counting;
систéма ~я (*math.*) scale of notation. **2.** с.
пути́ (*naut.*) dead reckoning.

счи́|стить, щу, стишь, *pf.* (*of* ~щáть) to
clean off; to clear away.

счи́|ститься, стится, *pf.* (*of* ~щáться) (*of
dirt, etc.*) to come off.

счи́тан|ный (~, ~а), *p.p.p.* of счита́ть;
остаю́тся ~ные дни (до) one can count
the days (until).

счита́|ть[1], ю, *impf.* (*of* счесть) **1.** (*pf. also*
со~) to count; to compute, reckon; с.
до ста to count up to a hundred; не ~я
not counting; с. звёзды, с. мух (*coll.*) to be
dreaming. **2.** (+*i. or* за+*a.*) to count, consider, think; to regard (as); я ~ю егó
надёжным наблюдáтелем, я ~ю егó за
надёжного наблюдáтеля I consider him
a reliable observer; с. ну́жным, с. за ну́ж-
ное to consider it necessary; с. за счáстье

to count it one's good fortune. **3.** (что) to
consider (that), hold (that); они́ ~ют, что
я не в состоя́нии об э́том суди́ть they consider that I am not in a position to be a
judge of this.

счита́|ть[2], áю, *pf.* (*of* ~ывать) (с+*i.*) to
compare (with), check (against).

счита́|ться[1], юсь, *impf.* (*of* счéсться) (с+*i.*)
to settle accounts (with) (*also fig.*).

счита́|ться[2], юсь, *impf.* (*no pf.*) **1.** (+*i.*) to
be considered, be thought, be reputed; to be
regarded (as); он ~ется первоклáссным
собесéдником he is considered a first-rate
conversationalist. **2.** (с+*i.*) to consider,
take into consideration, to take into account, reckon (with); с шéфом ещё нáдо с.
the boss has still to be reckoned with.

счи́тк|а, и, *f.* **1.** comparison, checking; с.
грáнок с рýкописью comparison of proofs
with manuscript. **2.** (*theatr.*) reading (*of a
part in a play*).

счища́|ть(ся), ю(сь), *impf.* of счи́стить(ся).

сшиба́|ть(ся), áю(сь), *impf.* of ~и́ть(ся).

сшиб|и́ть, ý, ёшь, *past* ~, ~ла, *pf.* (*of* ~áть)
(*coll.*) to knock off; с. с ног to knock down,
knock over; с. с когó-н. спесь to take someone down a peg.

сшиб|и́ться, ýсь, ёшься, *past* ~ся, ~лась,
pf. (*of* ~áться) (*coll.*) **1.** to collide; to come
to blows. **2.** *pass.* of ~и́ть.

сшива́|ть, ю, *impf.* of сшить.

сши́вк|а, и, *f.* sewing together.

сшить, сошью́, сошьёшь, *pf.* **1.** *pf.* o,
шить. **2.** (*impf.* сшивáть) to sew together;
(*med.*) to suture.

съеда́|ть, ю, *impf.* to eat (up).

съедéни|е, я, *n.,* *only in phrase* отдáть на с.
(+*d.*) to put at the mercy (of).

съедóб|ный (~ен, ~на), *adj.* **1.** edible; с.
гриб edible mushroom. **2.** eatable, nice.

съёжива|ться, юсь, *impf.* of съёжиться.

съёж|иться, усь, ишься, *pf.* (*of* ёжиться *and*
~иваться) to huddle up; to shrivel, shrink.

съезд[1], а, *m.* **1.** congress; conference, convention. **2.** arrival, gathering.

съезд[2], а, *m.* descent.

съéз|дить, жу, дишь, *pf.* **1.** to go (*and come
back*); с. в Ри́гу (*vulg.*) to spew (*when drunk*).
2. (*coll.*) to bash.

съéздовский, *adj.* congress.

съезжá|ть(ся), ю(сь), *impf.* of съéхать(ся).

съéзж|ая, ей, *f.* (*obs.*) cell (*in police station*).

съéзж|ий, *adj.* (*obs.*) **1.** of assembly; ~ая из-
бá assembly house. **2.** с. нарóд assembled
multitude.

съел, *see* съесть.

съём, а, *m.* removal.

съёмк|а, и, *f.* **1.** removal. **2.** survey, survey-
ing; plotting. **3.** (*phot.*) exposure; shooting.

съёмный, *adj.* detachable, removable.

съём|очный, *adj. of* ~ка; с. люк camera hatch (*in aircraft*); ~очные работы surveying.

съёмщик, а, *m.* 1. tenant, lessee. 2. surveyor.

съёмщиц|а, ы, *f. of* съёмщик.

съестн|о́й, *adj.* food; ~ы́е припа́сы food supplies, provisions; ~ы́е проду́кты foodstuffs, victuals; *as noun* ~о́е, ~о́го, *n.* = ~ы́е припа́сы.

съе|сть, м, шь, ст, ди́м, ди́те, дя́т, *past* ~л, ~ла, *pf. of* есть[1]; с. соба́ку (на+*p.*; *coll.*) to have at one's finger-tips, know inside out.

съе́|хать, ду, дешь, *pf.* (*of* ~зжа́ть) 1. to go down, come down. 2. с. на́ берег (*naut.*) to go ashore. 3. to move (*house*). 4. (*fig., coll.*) to come down, slip; га́лстук у тебя́ ~хал на́бок your tie is on one side. 5. (*fig., coll.*) to come down (= to lower one's price).

съе́|хаться, дусь, дешься, *pf.* (*of* ~зжа́ться) 1. to meet. 2. to arrive, gather, assemble.

съехи́днича|ть, ю, *pf. of* ехи́дничать.

съязв|и́ть, лю́, и́шь, *pf. of* язви́ть.

сы́воротк|а, и, *f.* 1. whey. 2. (*biol., med.*) serum.

сы́ворот|очный, *adj. of* ~ка; serous.

сы́гранност|ь, и, *f.* team-work.

сыгра́|ть, ю, *pf. of* игра́ть; с. шу́тку (с+*i.*) to play a practical joke (on).

сыгра́|ться, юсь, *pf.* to achieve team-work; to play well together.

сы́змала, *adv.* (*coll.*) from a child, ever since one was a child.

сы́знова, *adv.* (*coll.*) anew, afresh; нача́ть с. to make a fresh start, begin all over again.

сымпровизи́р|овать, ую, *pf. of* импровизи́ровать.

сын, а, *pl.* ~овья́, ~ове́й *and* ~ы́, ~о́в, *m.* 1. (*pl.* ~овья́) son. 2. (*pl.* ~ы́) (*fig., rhet.*) son, child; с. своего́ вре́мени child, product of one's time.

сыни́шк|а, и, *m.* (*coll.*) *dim. of* сын.

сыно́вний, *adj.* filial.

сын|о́к, ка́, *m. dim. of* ~; (*as mode of address*) sonny.

сы́п|ать, лю, лешь, *impf.* 1. to pour, strew. 2. (+*a. or i.*; *fig., coll.*) to pour forth; с. жа́лобами to pour forth complaints; с. деньга́ми to squander money.

сы́п|аться, лется, *impf.* 1. to fall; to pour out, run out; to scatter; мука́ ~алась из мешка́ flour poured out of the bag. 2. (*of sounds, etc.; coll.*) to pour forth (*intrans.*), rain down; уда́ры ~ались гра́дом blows were raining down, falling thick and fast. 3. (*of plaster, etc.*) to flake off. 4. (*of fabrics*) to fray out.

сыпно́й, *adj.* с. тиф (*med.*) typhus, spotted fever.

сыпнотифо́зный, *adj.* с. больно́й typhus patient.

сыпня́к, а́, *m.* (*coll.*) = сыпно́й тиф.

сыпу́ч|ий (~, ~а), *adj.* friable, free-flowing; с. грунт shifting ground; с. песо́к quicksand; ~ие тела́ dry substances; ме́ры ~их тел dry measures.

сып|ь, и, *f.* (*med.*) rash, eruption.

сыр, а, *pl.* ~ы́, *m.* cheese; как с. в ма́сле ката́ться (*coll.*) to live on the fat of the land.

сыр-бо́р, *now only in phrase* вот отку́да с. загоре́лся (*coll.*) that was the spark that set the forest on fire.

сыре́|ть, ю, *impf.* (*of* от~) to become damp.

сыр|е́ц, ца́, *m.* product in raw state; кирпи́ч-с. adobe; шёлк-с. raw silk.

сы́рник, а, *m.* curd fritter.

сы́р|ный, *adj. of* ~; caseous; ~ная неде́ля Shrovetide.

сы́ро, *as pred.* it is damp.

сырова́р, а, *m.* cheese-maker.

сыроваре́ни|е, я, *n.* cheese-making.

сырова́р|ня, ни, *g. pl.* ~ен, *f.* cheese dairy, creamery.

сырова́т|ый (~, ~а), *adj.* 1. dampish. 2. not quite ripe. 3. (*cul.*) underdone, undercooked.

сыроде́льный, *adj.* cheese-processing.

сырое́жк|а, и, *f.* Russula (*mushroom*).

сыр|о́й (~, ~а́, ~о), *adj.* 1. damp. 2. raw, uncooked; ~а́я вода́ unboiled water; ~о́е мя́со raw meat. 3. green; unripe. 4. raw; unfinished; ~ы́е материа́лы raw materials. 5. (*coll.*) fat, podgy.

сыр|о́к, ка́, *m.* cheese curds.

сыромя́тн|ый, *adj.* dressed, tawed; ~ая ко́жа rawhide.

сыромя́т|ь, и, *f.* tawed leather.

сы́рост|ь, и, *f.* dampness, humidity.

сыр|цо́вый, *adj. of* ~е́ц; ~цо́вая сталь natural steel.

сырь|ё, я́, *no pl., n.* raw material(s).

сырьев|о́й, *adj. of* сырьё; ~а́я ба́за raw material supply.

сырьём, *adv.* (*coll.*) raw; есть морко́вь с. to eat carrots raw.

сыск, а, *m.* (*obs.*) investigation, detection (*of criminals*).

сы|ска́ть, щу́, ~щешь, *pf.* (*coll.*) to find.

сы|ска́ться, щу́сь, ~щешься, *pf.* (*coll.*) to be found, come to light.

сыск|но́й, *adj. of* ~; ~на́я поли́ция (*obs.*) criminal investigation department.

сыте́|ть, ю, *impf.* (*coll.*) to become fuller.

сы́тно, *adv.* well; с. поза́втракать to have a good breakfast.

сы́т|ный (~ен, ~на́, ~но), *adj.* (*of a meal*)

substantial, copious; ~ное ме́сто)*fig.*, *joc.*, *obs.*) fat job.

сы́тост|ь, и, *f.* satiety, repletion.

сы́т|ый (~, ~а́, ~о), *adj.* 1. satisfied, replete, full; я ~ по го́рло I have eaten my fill, I am full up. 2. fat; с. скот fat stock.

сыч, а́, *m.* little owl (*Athene noctua*); ~о́м сиде́ть (*coll.*) to look glum.

сычу́г, а́, *m.* (*anat.*) abomasum, rennet bag.

сычу́жин|а, ы, *f.* rennet.

сы́щик, а, *m.* detective.

сы́щиц|а, ы, *f. of* сы́щик.

сэконо́м|ить, лю, ишь, *pf. of* эконо́мить.

сэр, а, *m.* sir.

сюда́, *adv.* here, hither.

сюже́т, а, *m.* subject; topic.

сюже́т|ный, *adj. of* ~.

сюзере́н, а, *m.* (*hist.*) suzerain.

сюзере́н|ный, *adj. of* ~.

сюи́т|а, ы, *f.* (*mus.*) suite.

сюрпри́з, а, *m.* surprise.

сюрреали́зм, а, *m.* surrealism.

сюрреали́ст, а, *m.* surrealist.

сюрту́к, а́, *m.* frock-coat.

сюсю́ка|ть, ю, *impf.* to lisp.

сяк, *adv.*; (*coll.*) и так и с., *see* так.

сям, *adv.*; и там и с., ни там ни с., *see* там.

Т

таба́к, а́ (у́), *m.* 1. tobacco-plant. 2. tobacco; ню́хательный т. snuff; де́ло — т.! (*coll.*) things are in a bad way.

табака́, *indecl.*, *only in phrase* (*cul.*) цыплёнок т. chicken tabak (*chicken flattened and grilled on charcoal*).

табаке́рк|а, и, *f.* snuff-box.

табаково́д, а, *m.* tobacco-grower.

табаково́дств|о, а, *n.* tobacco-growing.

табаково́д|ческий, *adj. of* ~ство.

таба́н|ить, ю, ишь, *impf.* to back water (*in rowing*).

таба́чник, а, *m.* 1. tobacco-worker. 2. (*obs.*) tobacco-user.

таба́чниц|а, ы, *f. of* таба́чник.

таба́чный, *adj.* 1. tobacco; т. кисе́т tobacco-pouch; т. лист tobacco leaf. 2. т. цве́т snuff colour.

та́бел|ь, я, *m. also* т., ~и, *f.* 1. (*m. and f.*) table; т. о ра́нгах (*hist.*) Table of Ranks (*introduced by Peter the Great*). 2. (*m.*) time-board (*in factory, etc.*). 3. (*m.*) number (*removed on arrival at work and replaced on leaving*).

та́бель|ный, *adj. of* ~; ~ная доска́ time-board; ~ные часы́ time-clock.

та́бельщик, а, *m.* timekeeper.

та́бельщиц|а, ы, *f. of* та́бельщик.

та́бес, а, *m.* (*med.*) tabes.

табле́тк|а, и, *f.* tablet, pill.

табли́ц|а, ы, *f.* table; plate (*with illustrations or diagrams*); т. умноже́ния multiplication table; ~ы логари́фмов logarithm tables; т. Менделе́ева (*chem.*) periodic table; т. прили́вов tide table; т. стрельбы́ (*mil.*) firing tables; т. вы́игрышей prize-list; т. (ро́зыгрыша) пе́рвенства (*sport*) (score-)table; пе́рвый, после́дний в ~е top, bottom of the table; внести́ в ~у to tabulate.

табли́чный, *adj.* 1. tabular. 2. standard, as per the tables.

табло́, *indecl.*, *n.* indicator board, scoreboard (*with neon-lit figures*).

табльдо́т, а, *m.* table d'hôte.

та́бор, а, *m.* 1. camp. 2. gipsy encampment.

та́бор|ный, *adj.* 1. *adj. of* ~. 2. gipsy.

табу́, *indecl.*, *n.* taboo.

табу́н, а́, *m.* herd (*usu. of horses, also of reindeer and some other animals*).

табу́н|ный, *adj. of* ~.

табу́нщик, а, *m.* horse-herd.

табуре́т, а, *m.* = ~ка.

табуре́т|ка, ки, *f.* stool.

таве́рн|а, ы, *f.* tavern, inn.

та́волг|а, и, *f.* (*bot.*) meadow-sweet.

таво́т, а, *m.* (*tech.*) axle grease, lubricating grease.

таво́тниц|а, ы, *f.* (*tech.*) grease gun, grease cup.

таврёный, *adj.* branded.

тавр|и́ть, ю́, и́шь, *impf.* (*of* за~) to brand.

тавр|о́, а́, *pl.* ~а, ~, ~а́м, *n.* brand (*on cattle, etc.*).

тавро́|вый, *adj.* 1. *adj. of* ~. 2. (*tech.*) T-shaped; ~вая ба́лка T-beam.

тавтологи́ческий, *adj.* tautological.

тавтоло́ги|я, и, *f.* tautology.

тага́н, а́, *m.* trivet.

таджи́к, а, *m.* Tadzhik.

таджи́кский, *adj.* Tadzhik.

таджи́чк|а, и, *f.* Tadzhik (woman).

таёжник, а, *m.* taiga dweller.

таёжный, *adj. of* тайга́.

таз¹, а, в ~у́, *pl.* ~ы́, *m.* basin; wash-basin.

таз², а, в ~е and в ~у́, *pl.* ~ы́, *m.* (*anat.*) pelvis.

тазобéдренный, *adj.* (*anat.*) hip, coxal; т. сустáв hip joint.

тáзовый, *adj.* (*anat.*) pelvic.

тайнственност|ь, и, *f.* mystery. ◄

тайнствен|ный (~, ~на), *adj.* **1.** mysterious; enigmatic. **2.** secret; егó т. отъéзд меня удивил his secret departure amazed me. **3.** secretive; т. вид secretive look.

тáинств|о, а, *n.* **1.** (*rel.*) sacrament. **2.** (*obs.*) mystery, secret.

та|и́ть, ю, и́шь, *impf.* to hide, conceal (*emotions, etc.*); to harbour; т. в себé to be fraught (with); т. злóбу (прóтив) to harbour a grudge (against); нéчего грехá т. it must be owned.

та|и́ться, ю́сь, и́шься, *impf.* **1.** (*coll.*) to be (in) hiding, lurk. **2.** (*fig.*) to lurk, be lurking; что за э́тим ~и́тся? what lies behind this? **3.** (*coll.*) to hold back (= to decline to reveal).

тайг|á, и́, *f.* (*geogr.*) taiga.

тайкóм, *adv.* in secret, surreptitiously, by stealth; on the quiet, on the sly; behind someone's back.

тайм, а, *m.* (*sport*) half, period (*of game*).

тáйн|а, ы, *f.* **1.** mystery. **2.** secret; держáть в ~e to keep secret, keep dark; хранить ~у to keep a secret; не т., что it is no secret that.

тайни́к, á, *m.* hiding-place; cache; в ~áх души́ in the inmost recesses of the heart.

тайнобрáчн|ый, *adj.* (*bot.*) cryptogamous, cryptogamic; *as noun* ~ые, ~ых Cryptogamia.

тайнопи́сный, *adj.* cryptographic.

тайнопи́с|ь, и, *f.* cryptographic writing.

тáйн|ый, *adj.* secret; clandestine; ~ое голосовáние secret ballot; т. совéт (*hist.*) Privy Council.

тайфýн, а, *m.* typhoon.

так 1. *adv.* so; thus, in this way, like this; in such a way; т. мнóго so many; мы сдéлали т. this is what we did, we did as follows; т. бы(и)... (*expressing strong desire to do something*; *coll.*) how I, *etc.*, should like ...; т. вот (*in proceeding with narration after digression*) and so, so then; т. же in the same way; т. и быть (*coll.*) all right, right you are, right-ho; т. и есть (*coll.*) so it is; т. и знáй(те) (*expressing warning*; *coll.*) get this clear; т. емý, *etc.*, и нáдо serves him, *etc.*, right; т. и́ли инáче (*i*) in any event, whatever happens, (*ii*) one way or another; т. называемый so-called; т. себé so-so, middling, not too good; т. сказáть so to speak; за т. (*coll.*) for nothing; и т. even so; as it is, as it stands; и т. дáлее and so on, and so forth; и т. и сяк this way and that; когдá т. (*coll.*) if so; (не) т. ли? isn't it so? **2.** *adv.* as it should be; не т. amiss, wrong;

т. ли я говорю́? am I right?; чтó-то бы́ло не совсéм т. something was amiss, something was not quite right. **3.** *adv.* just like that (= without further action or consequences); болéзнь не пройдёт т. the illness will not pass just like that; т. емý э́то не пройдёт he won't get away with it like that. **4.** *adv.*; т. (тóлько), прóсто т. for no special reason, for no reason in particular; just for fun, for the sake of it; т. какóй-то, т. какóй-н. (*coll.*, *pejor.*) some sort of. **5.** *particle* (*in answer to a question*) nothing in particular, nothing special; что тебé не понрáвилось там? — т., óбщее положéние what did you not like there? — Nothing in particular, just the set-up in general. **6.** т. и (*as emphatic particle*) simply, just; её глазá т. и сверкáли гнéвом her eyes were simply blazing with anger; я т. и забы́л принести́ кни́гу I clean forgot, I have gone and forgotten to bring the book. **7.** *conj.* then (*or not translated*); ты не спрóсишь егó, т. я спрошý if you won't ask him, then I will; éхать, т. éхать if we are going, let's go; не сегóдня, т. зáвтра if not today, then tomorrow. **8.** *conj.* so; т. вы знáете друг дрýга? so you know one another? **9.** т. как *conj.* as, since. **10.** *affirmative or emphatic particle* yes; т. тóчно (*in mil. parlance*) yes.

тáка|ть, ю, *impf.* (*coll.*) to rattle, chatter (*o machine-gun fire, etc.*).

такелáж, а, *m.* (*naut.*) rigging.

такелáжник, а, *m.* rigger, scaffolder.

такелáжн|ый, *adj.* **1.** (*naut.*) rigging. **2.** scaffolding; ~ые рабóты erection of scaffolding.

тáкже, *adv.* also, too, as well.

-таки after all; всё-т. nevertheless; опя́ть-т. again.

**такóв, ** *f.* ~á, *n.* ~ó, *pl.* ~ы́, *pron.* such; все они́ ~ы́ they are all the same; ~ы́ нáши свéдения so we are informed; и был т. (*coll.*) and that was the last we saw of him.

такóв|óй, *adj.* **1.** (*obs.*) such; éсли ~ые имéются if any. **2.** как т. as such.

такóвский, *adj.* (*coll.*) of such a kind.

так|óй, *pron.* **1.** such; so; т. же the same; он т. дóбрый! he is such a kind man! ~óе пальтó мне нýжно I need a coat like that; ~им óбразом thus, in this way; в ~óм слýчае in that case; до ~óй стéпени to such an extent. **2.** (*coll.*) a kind of; блинчик т. a kind of pancake. **3.** кто он т.? who is he?; что э́то ~óе? what is this?; что ~óе „кисéль"? what is 'kissel'?; что-~óе? what's that?, what did you say?; что ж тут ~óго? what is there so wonderful about that?; кудá ~óе он пошёл? (*coll.*) wherever has he gone?

такóй-сякóй, *pron.* (*coll.*) (a) so-and-so.

такóй-то, *pron.* so-and-so; such-and-such.

тáкс|а¹, ы, *f.* statutory price; tariff; по чёрной ~е at the black-market rate.

тáкс|а², ы, *f.* dachshund.

таксáтор, а, *m.* 1. price-fixer; valuer. 2. afforestation inspector.

таксáци|я, и, *f.* 1. price-fixing; valuation. 2. afforestation inspection.

таксú, *indecl.*, *n.* taxi.

тáксик, а, *m. dim. of* тáкса².

таксúр|овать, ую, *impf. and pf.* to fix the price (of), price.

таксúст, а, *m.* taxi-driver.

таксóметр, а, *m.* (taxi)meter.

таксомотóр, а, *m.* taxi.

таксомотóр|ный, *adj. of* ~; т. парк fleet of taxis.

таксомотóрщик, а, *m.* taxi-driver.

таксофóн, а, *m.* automatic telephone.

так-ся́к, *adv. as pred.* (*coll.*) it is tolerable, it is passable.

такт¹, а, *m.* 1. (*mus., etc.*) time; measure; bar; отбивáть т. to beat time; в т. in time. 2. (*tech.*) stroke (*of engine*).

такт², а, *m.* tact.

тáк-таки, *particle* (*coll.*) after all; really.

тáктик, а, *m.* tactician.

тáктик|а, и, *f.* tactics.

тактúческий, *adj.* tactical.

тактúчност|ь, и, *f.* tact.

тактúч|ный (~ен, ~на), *adj.* tactful.

тáк-то, *adv.* (*coll.*) so; он не т. скрóмен he's not all that humble; т. так that's as it may be.

тáкт|овый, *adj. of* ~¹; ~овая чертá bar.

талáн, а, *m.* (*folklore*) luck, good fortune.

талáнт, а, *m.* 1. talent, gift(s). 2. man of talent, gifted person. 3. (*hist.*) talent (*ancient coin and measure*).

талáнтливост|ь, и, *f.* talent, gifts.

талáнтлив|ый (~, ~a), *adj.* talented, gifted.

тáлер, а, *m.* thaler (*coin*).

тáл|и, ей, *no sing.* block and tackle.

талисмáн, а, *m.* talisman, charm, mascot.

тáли|я¹, и, *f.* waist; плáтье в ~ю dress fitting at the waist; обня́ть когó-н. за ~ю to put one's arm round someone's waist.

тáли|я², и, *f.* two packs of playing cards.

тáлли|й, я, *m.* (*chem.*) thallium.

талмýд, а, *m.* (*rel.*) Talmud.

талмудúст, а, *m.* Talmudist; (*fig.*) pedant, doctrinaire.

талмудúстский, *adj.* Talmudistic; (*fig.*) pedantic, doctrinaire.

талмудúческий, *adj.* = талмудúстский.

талóн, а, *m.* coupon; stub (*of cheque, etc.*).

талóнчик, а, *m. dim. of* талóн.

тáлреп, а, *m.* (*naut.*) lanyard; винтовóй т. turn-buckle.

тáл|ый, *adj.* thawed, melted; ~ая водá water from melted snow.

тальк, а, *m.* talc; talcum powder.

тáльк|овый, *adj. of* ~; т. слáнец (*min.*) talc schist.

тáльм|а, ы, *f.* (*obs.*) talma (*sleeveless cloak*).

тальнúк, á, *m.* willow.

там, *adv.* 1. there; т. же in the same place; (*in footnotes, etc.*) ibidem; и т. и сям here, there and everywhere. 2. (*coll.*) later, by and by. 3. *as particle* (*coll.*) expresses disregard, indifference, *etc.*, вся́кие т. глýпости говорúт he talks all kinds of nonsense; какóе т.! nothing of the kind!; not a bit of good!; чегó т.! go on!, go ahead!

тамад|á, ы́, *m.* master of ceremonies, toast-master.

тáмбур¹, а, *m.* 1. (*archit.*) tambour. 2. lobby. 3. platform (*of railway carriage*).

тáмбур², а, *m.* chain-stitch.

тамбýр, а, *m.* (*mus.*) 1. tambourine. 2. (*obs.*) tambour (= drum).

тамбурúн, а, *m.* 1. tambourine. 2. tambourin.

тамбурмажóр, а, *m.* (*mil.; obs.*) drum major.

тáмбур|ный, *adj. of* ~²; т. шов chain-stitch.

тамóженник, а, *m.* customs official.

тамóженн|ый, *adj.* customs; ~ые пóшлины, ~ые сбóры customs (*duties*).

тамóжн|я, и, *f.* custom-house.

тáмошн|ий, *adj.* (*coll.*) of that place; ~ие жúтели the local inhabitants.

тампóн, а, *m.* (*med.*) tampon, plug.

тампонáж, а, *m.* (*tech.*) tamping.

тампонáци|я, и, *f.* (*med.*) tamponade.

тампонúр|овать, ую, *impf. and pf.* (*med.*) to tampon, plug.

тамтáм, а, *m.* tom-tom.

тáнгенс, а, *m.* (*math.*) tangent.

тангенциáльный, *adj.* (*math.*) tangential.

тáнго, *indecl.*, *n.* tango.

тáн|ец, ца, *m.* 1. dance; dancing; урóки ~цев dancing lessons. 2. (*pl.*) a dance, dancing; пойтú на ~цы to go to a dance, go dancing.

танúн, а, *m.* tannin.

танк¹, а, *m.* (*mil.*) tank.

танк², а, *m.* container (*for transportation of liquids*).

тáнкер, а, *m.* (*naut.*) tanker.

танкéтк|а¹, и, *f.* tankette, small tank.

танкéтк|а², и, *f.* (*coll.*) (*ladies'*) wedge-heeled shoe, slipper.

танкúст, а, *m.* member of tank crew.

тáнковый, *adj.* tank, armoured.

танкодрóм, а, *m.* tank training area.

танкостроéни|е, я, *n.* tank-building, tank construction.

танк-паровóз, а, *m.* (*railways*) tank (engine).

тантáл, а, *m.* (*chem.*) tantalum.

тантьéм|а, ы, *f.* bonus.

танцевáльный, *adj.* dancing; т. вéчер a dance, party with dancing.

танц|евáть, ýю, *impf.* to dance.

танцклáсс, а, *m.* (*obs.*) school of dancing; dancing-classes.

танцмéйстер, а, *m.* (*obs.*) dancing-master.

танцóвщик, а, *m.* (ballet) dancer.

танцóвщиц|а, ы, *f. of* танцóвщик.

танцóр, а, *m.* dancer.

танцóрк|а, и, *f. of* танцóр.

танцýльк|а, и, *f.* (*coll.*) dance, hop.

тапёр, а, *m.* ballroom pianist.

тапёрш|а, ы, *f. of* тапёр.

тапиóк|а, и, *f.* tapioca.

тапи́р, а, *m.* tapir.

тáпочк|а, и, *f.* (*coll.*) slipper; спорти́вная т. sports shoe, gym shoe, plimsoll.

тáр|а, ы, *f.* 1. packing, packaging. 2. (*comm.*) tare.

тарабáн|ить, ю, ишь, *impf.* (*coll.*) to clatter.

тарабáрск|ий, *adj.* 1. (*obs.*) cryptographic. 2. ~ая грáмота (*coll.*) double Dutch.

тарабáрщин|а, ы, *f.* (*coll.*) double Dutch, gibberish.

таракáн, а, *m.* cockroach.

таракáн|ий, *adj. of* ~.

тарáн, а, *m.* 1. (*hist.*) battering ram. 2. (*mil.*) ram; ramming.

тарáн|ить, ю, ишь, *impf.* (*of* про~) to ram.

тарáн|ный, *adj.* 1. *adj. of* ~. 2. ~ная кость (*anat.*) astragalus.

тарантáс, а, *m.* tarantass (*springless carriage*).

тарантéлл|а, ы, *f.* tarantella.

таран|ти́ть, чý, ти́шь, *impf.* (*coll.*) to jabber, natter.

тарáнтул, а, *m.* tarantula.

тарáн|ь, и, *f.* sea-roach (*Rutilus rutilus Heckeli*).

тарарáм, а, *m.* (*coll.*) row, racket, hullaba-loo.

тарарáх|ать, аю, *impf. of* ~нуть.

тарарáх|нуть, ну, нешь, *pf.* (*of* ~ать) (*coll.*) to bang; to crash.

таратáйк|а, и, *f.* cabriolet, gig.

таратóр|а, ы, *m. and f.* (*coll.*) chatterbox, gabbler.

таратóр|ить, ю, ишь, *impf.* (*coll.*) to jabber, natter; to gabble.

тарах|тéть, чý, ти́шь, *impf.* (*coll.*) to rattle, rumble.

тарáщ|ить, у, ишь, *impf.* т. глазá (на+*a.*) to goggle (at).

тарбагáн, а, *m.* Siberian marmot.

тарéлк|а, и, *f.* 1. plate; глубóкая т. soup--plate; быть не в своéй ~е to be not quite oneself. 2. (*tech.*) plate, disc. 3. (*pl.*) cymbals.

тарéл|очный, *adj. of* ~ка; т. бýфер plate buffer; ~очная ми́на (*mil.*) flat anti-tank mine; ~очная печь (*tech.*) revolving hearth.

тарéльчат|ый, *adj.* (*tech.*) plate, disc; т. клáпан disc valve; ~ая мýфта plate coupling; т. тóрмоз disc brake.

тари́ф, а, *m.* tariff, rate.

тарификáци|я, и, *f.* tariffing.

тарифици́р|овать, ую, *impf. and pf.* to tariff.

тари́ф|ный, *adj. of* ~.

тартáни|е, я, *n.* (*tech.*) (oil-)bailing.

тартарары́: провали́ться в т. (*coll.*) I'll be damned.

тарти́нк|а, и, *f.* slice of bread and butter.

тархáн, а, *m.* (*hist.*) landowner enjoying special privileges.

тархáн|ный, *adj. of* ~.

тáры-бáры, *indecl.* (*coll.*) tittle-tattle.

таскá|ть, ю, *impf.* (*indet. of* тащи́ть) 1. *see* тащи́ть. 2. (*pf.* от~) (*coll.*) to pull (*as punishment*); т. когó-н. зá волосы to pull someone's hair. 2. (*coll.*) to wear.

таскá|ться, юсь, *impf.* (*indet. of* тащи́ться) 1. *see* тащи́ться. 2. (*coll., pejor.*) to roam about; to hang about.

тас|овáть, ýю, *impf.* (*of* с~) to shuffle (*cards in a pack*).

тасóвк|а, и, *f.* shuffle, shuffling (*of playing cards*).

татáрв|á, ы́, *f.* (*collect., obs., pejor.*) the Tatars.

татáр|ин, ина, *pl.* ~ы, ~, *m.* Tatar.

татáрк|а¹, и, *f.* Tatar (woman).

татáрк|а², и, *f.* spring onion.

татáрник, а, *m.* thistle.

татáрский, *adj.* Tatar.

тату́и́р|овать, ую, *impf. and pf.* to tattoo.

тату́и́р|оваться, уюсь, *impf. and pf.* to tattoo oneself; to have oneself tattooed.

татуирóвк|а, и, *f.* tattooing.

тат|ь, я, *m.* (*arch.*) thief, robber.

тафт|á, ы́, *f.* taffeta.

тахикарди́|я, и, *f.* (*med.*) tachycardia.

тахóметр, а, *m.* tachometer.

тахт|á, ы́, *f.* ottoman.

тачáнк|а, и, *f.* cart (*used in Ukraine and Caucasus*).

тачá|ть, ю, *impf.* (*of* вы́~) to stitch.

тáчк|а, и, *f.* wheelbarrow.

тащ|и́ть, ý, ~ишь, *impf.* (*det. of* таскáть) 1. to pull; to drag, lug; to carry. 2. (*coll.*) to take; to drag off; (*fig.*) т. когó-н. в кинó to drag someone off to the cinema. 3. to pull out. 4. (*coll.*) to pinch, swipe.

тащ|и́ться, ýсь, ~ишься, *impf.* (*det. of* таскáться) 1. to drag oneself along. 2. to drag, trail.

тáяни|е, я, *n.* thaw, thawing.

тá|ять, ю, ешь, *impf.* (*of* рас~) 1. to melt; to thaw; ~ет it is thawing. 2. (*fig.*) to melt away, dwindle, wane; нáши запáсы ~ют our stocks are dwindling; егó си́лы ~яли his strength was ebbing. **3.** (от; *fig.*) to melt (with), languish (with). **4.** (*impf. only*) to waste away.

твар|ь, и, *f.* creature; (*collect.*) creatures; all creation (*also pejor.*); вся́кой ~и по па́ре (*coll.*) all sorts and kinds of people.

тверде́ни|е, я, *n.* hardening.

тверде́|ть, ю, *impf.* to harden, become hard.

твер|ди́ть, жу́, ди́шь, *impf.* **1.** (+*a.* or о+*p.*) to repeat, say over and over again. **2.** to memorize, learn by rote.

тве́рдо, *adv.* hard; firmly, firm.

твердока́менный, *adj.* (*rhet.*) steadfast, staunch.

твердоло́б|ый (~, ~а), *adj.* **1.** thick-skulled. **2.** (*polit.*) diehard.

тве́рдост|ь, и, *f.* hardness; (*fig.*) firmness.

твёрд|ый (~, ~а́, ~о), *adj.* **1.** hard. **2.** firm; solid; т. грунт firm soil; т. переплёт stiff binding; ~ое те́ло (*phys., chem.*) solid; фи́зика ~ого те́ла solid state physics. **3.** (*fig. in var. senses*) firm; stable; steadfast; ~ое зада́ние specified task; ~ые зна́ния sound knowledge; ~ое реше́ние firm decision; т. срок fixed time-limit; ~ые це́ны stable, fixed prices. **4.** (*ling.*) hard; т. знак hard sign (*name of Russian letter 'ъ'*).

тверды́н|я, и, *f.* (*obs.*) stronghold (*also fig.*).

тверд|ь, и, *f.* (*arch.*) т. земна́я the earth; т. небе́сная the firmament, the heavens.

тво|й, его́, *f.* **~я́, ~е́й,** *n.* **~ё, ~его́,** *pl.* **~и́, ~и́х,** *possessive pron.* your, yours (thy, thine); ~его́ (*after comp. adv.*; *coll.*) than you; я зна́ю лу́чше ~его́ I know better than you; что т. (*coll.*) just like; гора́ — что т. Эльбру́с the mountain is just like Mt. Elbruz; *as noun* ~й, ~и́х your people.

творе́ни|е, я, *n.* **1.** creation; work. **2.** creature, being.

твор|е́ц, ца́, *m.* creator.

твори́л|о¹, а, *n.* hatch; aperture; water-gate (*in dam*).

твори́л|о², а, *n.* lime-pit.

твори́тельный, *adj.* т. паде́ж (*gram.*) instrumental case.

твор|и́ть¹, ю́, и́шь, *impf.* (*of* со~) **1.** to create. **2.** to do; to make; т. добро́ to do good; т. суд и распра́ву (*obs.*) to deal out justice; т. чудеса́ to work wonders.

твор|и́ть², ю́, и́шь, *impf.* (*obs.*) to knead; т. и́звесть to slake lime.

твор|и́ться¹, и́тся, *impf.* (*coll.*) to happen, go on; что тут ~и́тся? what is going on here?

твор|и́ться², и́тся, *impf., pass. of* ~и́ть².

творо́г, а́ and тво́рог, а, *m.* curds, cottage cheese.

творо́жист|ый (~, ~а), *adj.* curdled, clotted.

творо́жник, а, *m.* curd pancake.

творо́жн|ый, *adj.* curd; ~ая ма́сса curds; т. сыро́к cottage cheese.

тво́рческ|ий, *adj.* creative; ~ая си́ла creative power, creativeness; т. путь Толсто́го Tolstoy's career as a writer.

тво́рчеств|о, а, *n.* **1.** creation; creative work. **2.** (*collect.*) works.

теа́тр, а, *m.* **1.** (*in var. senses*) theatre; т. вое́нных де́йствий (*mil.*) theatre of operations; анатоми́ческий т. dissecting-room. **2.** (*fig.*) the stage. **3.** (*collect.*) (the) plays; т. Шекспи́ра the plays of Shakespeare.

театра́л, а, *m.* theatre-goer, playgoer; drama-lover.

театрализа́ци|я, и, *f.* adaptation for the stage.

театрализ|ова́ть, у́ю, *impf. and pf.* to adapt for the stage.

театра́льност|ь, и, *f.* theatricality.

театра́л|ьный (~ен, ~ьна), *adj.* **1.** theatre; theatrical; т. биле́т theatre ticket; т. зал auditorium; ~ьная ка́сса box-office; ~ьная шко́ла drama school. **2.** (*fig.*) theatrical, stagy.

театрове́дени|е, я, *n.* drama study.

тевто́н, а, *m.* Teuton.

тевто́нский, *adj.* Teutonic.

тёз|а, ы, *f.* = ~ис 1.

те́зис, а, *m.* **1.** thesis, proposition, point; вы́двинуть т. to advance a thesis. **2.** thesis (*in Hegelian philosophy*).

тёзк|а, и, *m. and f.* namesake; мы с ва́ми ~и you and I share the same name.

тейзм, а, *m.* theism.

тейст, а, *m.* theist.

теисти́ческий, *adj.* theistic.

тёк, ла́, *see* течь.

теки́н|ец, ца, *m.* Turkmen.

теки́нк|а, и, *f.* Turkmen (woman).

теки́нский, *adj.* Turkmen; т. ковёр Turkoman carpet.

текст, а, *m.* **1.** text. **2.** words, libretto.

тексти́л|ь, я, *no pl., m.* (*collect.*) textiles.

тексти́льный, *adj.* textile.

тексти́льщик, а, *m.* textile worker.

тексти́льщи|ца, цы, *f. of* ~к.

текстови́к, а́, *m.* librettist.

тексто́лог, а, *m.* textual critic.

текстоло́ги|я, и, *f.* textual study, textual criticism.

текстуа́л|ьный (~ен, ~ьна), *adj.* **1.** verbatim, word-for-word. **2.** (*philol.*) textual.

текто́ник|а, и, *f.* (*geol.*) tectonics.

тектони́ческий, *adj.* (*geol.*) tectonic.

теку́чест|ь, и, *f.* **1.** (*phys.*) fluidity. **2.** fluctuation, instability; т. рабо́чей си́лы fluctuation of manpower, labour fluidity.

теку́ч|ий (~, ~а), *adj.* **1.** (*phys.*) fluid. **2.** fluctuating, unstable.

теку́щ|ий, *pres. part. act. of* течь *and adj.* **1.**

current; of the present moment; в ~ем году́ in the current year; 2-го числа́ ~его ме́сяца the second instant; ~ие собы́тия current events, current affairs; т. счёт current áccount. 2. routine, ordinary; ~ие дела́ routine business; т. ремóнт routine repairs.

теле- tele-.

телеавтома́тик|а, и, *f.* wireless control.

телевеща́ни|е, я, *n.* television broadcasting.

телеви́дени|е, я, *n.* television.

телеви́зи|я, и, *f.* = телеви́дение.

телеви́зор, а, *m.* television set.

телеви́зор|ный, *adj.* of ~.

телéг|а, и, *f.* cart, waggon.

телегра́мм|а, ы, *f.* telegram.

телегра́ф, а, *m.* 1. telegraph. 2. telegraph office.

телеграфи́р|овать, ую, *impf. and pf.* to telegraph, wire.

телеграфи́ст, а, *m.* telegraphist.

телеграфи́ст|ка, ки, *f.* of ~.

телеграфи́|я, и, *f.* telegraphy.

телегра́фн|ый, *adj.* telegraph; telegraphic; т. áдрес telegraphic address; ~ая ле́нта telegraph tape, ticker-tape; т. стиль telegraphic style, telegraphese; т. столб telegraph-pole.

телéжк|а, и, *f.* 1. small cart, hand-cart. 2. bogie, trolley.

телé|жный, *adj.* of ~га; ~жное колесó cart-wheel.

телезри́тел|ь, я, *m.* (television) viewer.

тéлекс, а, *m.* telex.

телеметри́|ческий, *adj.* telemetric.

телеметри́|я, и, *f.* telemetry.

телеизмере́ни|е, я, *n.* telemetry.

телемеха́ник|а, и, *f.* telemechanics, remote control.

тел|ёнок, ёнка, *pl.* ~я́та, ~я́т, *m.* calf.

телеобъекти́в, а, *m.* (*phot.*) telescopic lens, telephoto lens.

телеологи́ческий, *adj.* teleological.

телеоло́ги|я, и, *f.* teleology.

телепати́ческий, *adj.* telepathic.

телепа́ти|я, и, *f.* telepathy.

телепереда́ч|а, и, *f.* television transmission.

телеприёмник, а, *m.* television set.

телес|á, телéс, ~а́м, *no sing.* (*coll., joc.*) frame (*of a stout person*).

телеско́п, а, *m.* telescope.

телескопи́ческий, *adj.* telescopic; т. прице́л telescopic sight (*of firearm*).

телескопи́|я, и, *f.* telescopy.

телеско́пи|ный, *adj.* of ~.

телéсн|ый, *adj.* 1. bodily; corporal; somatic; physical; ~ое наказа́ние corporal punishment; ~ого цве́та flesh-coloured. 2. corporeal.

телесту́ди|я, и, *f.* television studio.

телета́йп, а, *m.* teletype.

телеуправле́ни|е, я, *n.* remote control.

телефика́ци|я, и, *f.* equipping with television.

телефóн, а, *m.* telephone; позвони́ть по ~у (+*d.*) to telephone, phone, ring up; вы́зов по ~у telephone call; т.-автома́т public telephone, public call-box.

телефониза́ци|я, и, *f.* installation of the telephone (in).

телефони́р|овать, ую, *impf. and pf.* to telephone.

телефони́ст, а, *m.* telephone operator, telephonist.

телефони́ст|ка, ки, *f.* of ~.

телефони́|я, и, *f.* telephony.

телефóн|ный, *adj.* of ~.

телефоногра́мм|а, ы, *f.* telephoned telegram.

телефотогра́фи|я, и, *f.* telephotography.

тел|éц, ьца́, *m.* 1. (*obs.*) calf; золотóй т. the golden calf. 2. Т. (*astron.*) Taurus.

телеце́нтр, а, *m.* television centre.

тел|и́ться, ~и́тся, *impf.* (*of* о~) to calve.

тёлк|а, и, *f.* heifer.

теллу́р, а, *m.* (*chem.*) tellurium.

тéл|о, а, *pl.* ~á, ~, ~áм, *n.* (*in var. senses*) body; (*coll.*) быть в ~е to be stout; войти́ в т. to put on weight; спасть с ~а to grow thin; держа́ть в чёрном ~е to ill-treat, maltreat.

телогрéйк|а, и, *f.* (*woman's*) padded jacket (*usu. sleeveless*).

телодвиже́ни|е, я, *n.* movement, motion.

тел|óк, ка́, *m.* (*coll.*) calf.

телосложе́ни|е, я, *n.* build, frame.

телохрани́тел|ь, я, *m.* bodyguard.

тéльник, а, *m.* (knitted) vest.

тéл|ьный, *adj.* (*coll.*) of ~о; ~ьного цве́та flesh-coloured.

тельня́шк|а, и, *f.* (*coll.*) (*sailor's*) striped vest.

теля́тин|а, ы, *f.* veal.

теля́тник[1], а, *m.* calf-house.

теля́тник[2], а, *m.* calf-herd.

теля́ч|ий, *adj.* 1. *adj. of* телёнок; ~ья кóжа calf(skin). 2. (*cul.*) veal. 3. т. востóрг (*coll.*) foolish raptures; ~ьи не́жности (*coll.*) sloppy sentimentality.

тем 1. *i. sing. m. and n., d. pl. of* тот. 2. *conj.* (so much) the; чем вы́ше, т. лу́чше the taller, the better; т. лу́чше so much the better; т. бóлее, что the more so as, especially as; т. не ме́нее none the less, nevertheless.

тéм|а, ы, *f.* 1. subject, topic, theme; перейти́ к другóй ~е to change the subject; сочине́ние на ~у Наполеóновских войн a work on the subject of the Napoleonic Wars. 2. (*mus.*) theme; т. с вариа́циями theme and variations.

тема́тик|а, и, *f.* (*collect.*) subject-matter, themes, subjects.

темати́ческий, *adj.* **1.** *adj. of* тема́тика; т. план plan of subjects, plan of subject--matter (*e.g. of forthcoming publications*). **2.** (*mus.*) thematic.

тембр, а, *m.* timbre.

тéмбр|овый, *adj. of* ~.

теменн|о́й, *adj.* (*anat.*) sincipital; ~а́я кость parietal bone.

тéмен|ь, и, *f.* (*coll.*) darkness.

тéми, *i. pl. of* тот.

темля́к, а́, *m.* (*mil.*) sword-knot.

тёмн|ая, ой, *f.* (*obs.*) (*police*) cell.

темне́|ть, ю, *impf.* **1.** (*pf.* по~) to grow dark, become dark; to darken. **2.** (*pf.* с~) ~ет (*impers.*) it gets dark, it is getting dark. **3.** (*impf. only*) to show up darkly.

темне́|ться, ется, *impf.* to show up darkly.

темн|и́ть, ю́, и́шь, *impf.* to darken; to make darker.

темни́ц|а, ы, *f.* (*obs.*) dungeon.

темно́, *as pred.* it is dark; у меня́ в глаза́х ста́ло т. everything went dark before my eyes.

темно- dark-.

темноко́жий, *adj.* dark-skinned, swarthy.

темноси́ний, *adj.* dark blue; navy blue.

темнот|а́, ы́, *f.* **1.** dark, darkness; в ~é in the dark; до ~ы́ before dark, before it gets dark. **2.** (*coll.*) ignorance; backwardness.

тём|ный (~ен, ~на́, ~но́), *adj.* **1.** dark; ~ное пятно́ (*fig.*) dark stain, blemish; ~ная вода́ (*med.*) amaurosis; ~на́ вода́ во о́блацех the matter is wrapped in mystery. **2.** obscure, vague; ~ное ме́сто (*philol.*) obscure passage; ~ное пятно́ obscure place. **3.** sombre. **4.** shady, fishy, suspicious; ~ное де́ло shady business. **5.** ignorant, benighted.

темны́м-темно́, *adv.* (*coll.*) pitch-dark.

темп, а, *m.* **1.** (*mus.*) tempo. **2.** (*fig.*) tempo; rate, speed, pace; заме́длить т. to slacken one's pace; ускóрить т. to accelerate.

тéмпер|а, ы, *f.* **1.** distemper (*paint*). **2.** tempera (*painting*).

темпера́мент, а, *m.* temperament; челове́к с ~ом energetic person, spirited person.

темпера́мент|ный (~ен, ~на), *adj.* energetic; spirited, vigorous.

температу́р|а, ы, *f.* **1.** temperature; т. кипе́ния boiling-point; т. замерза́ния freezing-point; крива́я ~ы temperature curve; ме́рить кому́-н. ~у to take someone's temperature. **2.** (*coll.*) (heightened) temperature; ходи́ть с ~ой to go about with a temperature.

температу́р|ить, ю, ишь, *impf.* (*coll.*) to have a temperature.

температу́р|ный, *adj. of* ~а; ~ная крива́я temperature curve; т. шов (*tech.*) heat crack, expansion joint.

темпера́ци|я, и, *f.* (*mus.*) temperament.

темпери́р|овать, ую, *impf. and pf.* (*mus.*) to temper.

тем|ь, и, *f.* (*coll.*) dark, darkness.

тéм|я, ени, *no pl., n.* (*anat.*) sinciput; crown, top of the head.

тенденцио́з|ный (~ен, ~на), *adj.* (*pejor.*) tendentious, biased.

тенде́нци|я, и, *f.* **1.** (к) tendency (to, towards); у него́ т. (к) he has a tendency (to), he tends (to). **2.** (*pejor.*) bias; с ~ей tendentious, biased.

тéндер, а, *m.* **1.** (*railways*) tender. **2.** (*naut.*) cutter.

тéндер|ный, *adj. of* ~.

тенев|о́й, *adj.* shady (*also fig.*); ~а́я сторона́ shady side; (*fig.*) bad side, seamy side.

тенелюби́в|ый (~, ~а), *adj.* (*bot.*) requiring shade.

тенёт|а, ~, *no sing.* snare.

тени́ст|ый (~, ~а), *adj.* shady.

тéннис, а, *m.* tennis.

тенниси́ст, а, *m.* tennis-player.

тенниси́ст|ка, ки, *f. of* ~.

тéнниск|а, и, *f.* (*coll.*) tennis shirt, short--sleeved shirt.

тéннисн|ый, *adj.* tennis; т. корт, ~ая площа́дка tennis-court.

тéнор, а, *pl.* ~а́, ~о́в, *m.* (*mus.*) tenor.

тенорóвый, *adj. of* тéнор.

тент, а, *m.* awning.

тен|ь, и, в ~и́, *pl.* ~и, ~éй, *f.* **1.** shade; сиде́ть в ~и́ to sit in the shade; держа́ться в ~и́ (*fig.*) to keep in the background. **2.** shadow; дава́ть т. to cast a shadow; от него́ оста́лась одна́ т. he is but a shadow of his former self; навести́ т. (*coll.*) to confuse the issue. **3.** shadow, phantom, ghost; бле́ден, как т. pale as a ghost. **4.** (*fig.*) shadow, particle, vestige, atom; нет ни ~и сомне́ния there is not a shadow of doubt; в его́ расска́зе нет ни ~и пра́вды there is not a particle of truth in his story. **5.** suspicion; бро́сить т. на кого́-н. to cast suspicion on someone.

теогóни|я, и, *f.* theogony.

теодицé|я, и, *f.* theodicy.

теодоли́т, а, *m.* theodolite.

теократи́ческий, *adj.* theocratic.

теокра́ти|я, и, *f.* theocracy.

теологи́ческий, *adj.* theological.

теоло́ги|я, и, *f.* theology.

теорéм|а, ы, *f.* theorem.

теоретизи́р|овать, ую, *impf.* to theorize.

теорéтик, а, *m.* theorist.

теорети́ческий, *adj.* theoretical.

теорети́ч|ный (~ен, ~на), *adj.* (*pejor.*) theoretical, abstract, abstruse.

тео́ри|я, и, *f.* theory.

теософи́ческий, *adj.* theosophical.

теосо́фи|я, и, *f.* theosophy.

тепе́решн|ий, *adj.* (*coll.*) present; ~ие лю́ди people (of) today; в ~ее вре́мя at the present time, nowadays.

тепе́рь, *adv.* now; nowadays, today.

тепле́ньк|ий, *adj.* (*coll.*) (nice and) warm; ~ое месте́чко cushy job.

тепле́|ть, ет, *impf.* (*of* по~) to get warm.

те́пл|иться, ится, *impf.* to flicker, glimmer (*also fig.*); ~ится наде́жда there is still a glimmer of hope, a ray of hope.

тепли́ц|а, ы, *f.* greenhouse, hothouse, conservatory.

тепли́|чный, *adj. of* ~ца; ~чное расте́ние hothouse plant (*also fig.*).

тепло́[1], *adv.* 1. warmly. 2. *as pred.* it is warm.

тепл|о́[2], а́, *n.* heat; warmth; де́сять гра́дусов ~а́ ten degrees above zero (*centigrade*); держа́ть в ~е́ to keep (in the) warm.

теплово́з, а, *m.* diesel locomotive.

теплово́зный, *adj.* diesel.

теплов|о́й, *adj.* heat; thermal; т. дви́гатель heat-engine; ~а́я едини́ца heat unit, thermal unit; т. ожо́г flashburn; т. уда́р (*med.*) heat stroke; ~а́я электроста́нция thermal electric power station; ~а́я эне́ргия heat energy, thermal energy.

теплоёмкост|ь, и, *f.* (*phys.*) heat capacity, thermal capacity; уде́льная т. specific heat.

теплокро́вный, *adj.* (*zool.*) warm-blooded.

теплолюби́в|ый (~, ~а), *adj.* (*bot.*) heat-loving.

тепломе́р, а, *m.* (*phys.*) calorimeter.

теплообме́н, а, *m.* (*phys.*) heat exchange.

теплопрово́д, а, *m.* hot-water system.

теплопрово́дност|ь, и, f. heat conductivity.

теплопрово́дный, *adj.* heat-conducting.

теплопрозра́чный, *adj.* (*phys.*) diathermic.

теплосто́йкий, *adj.* heat-proof, heat-resistant.

теплот|а́, ы́, *f.* 1. (*phys.*) heat; едини́ца ~ы́ thermal unit. 2. warmth (*also fig.*); душе́вная т. warm-heartedness.

теплотво́рност|ь, и, *f.* (*phys.*) heating value, calorific value.

теплотво́рн|ый, *adj.* (*phys.*) calorific; ~ая спосо́бность = ~ость.

теплоте́хник, а, *m.* heating engineer.

теплоте́хник|а, и, *f.* heating engineering.

теплофика́ци|я, и, *f.* introduction of a heating system.

теплофици́р|овать, ую, *impf. and pf.* to introduce a heating system (in).

теплохо́д, а, *m.* motor ship.

теплоцентра́л|ь, и, f. heating plant.

теплу́шк|а, и, f. (*coll.*) heated goods van (*for transportation of human beings*).

тёп|лый (~ел, ~ла́, ~ло́, ~лы), *adj.* 1. (*in var. senses*) warm; ~лая оде́жда warm clothing; ~лые кра́ски warm colours; ~лое месте́чко (*coll.*) cushy job. 2. warmed, heated. 3. (*fig.*) warm, cordial; kindly, affectionate; т. приём warm welcome. 4. heartfelt. 5. (*coll.*) roguish; ~лая компа́ния bunch of rogues.

теплы́н|ь, и, f. (*coll.*) warm weather.

тепля́к, а́, *m.* temporary covered and heated enclosure on building site.

терапе́вт, а, *m.* therapeutist.

терапевти́ческий, *adj.* therapeutic.

терапи́|я, и, f. therapy.

тератоло́ги|я, и, f. (*biol.*) teratology.

те́рби|й, я, *m.* (*chem.*) terbium.

тереби́льщик, а, *m.* flax-puller.

тереб|и́ть, лю́, и́шь, *impf.* 1. to pull (at), pick (at). 2. т. лён to pull flax. 3. (*fig., coll.*) to pester, bother.

те́рем, а, pl. ~а́, *m.* (*hist.*) (tower-)chamber; tower.

тере́ть, тру, трёшь, past тёр, тёрла, *impf.* 1. to rub. 2. to grate, grind. 3. to rub, chafe.

тере́ться, трусь, трёшься, past тёрся, тёрлась, *impf.* 1. to rub oneself; (о, обо+а.) to rub (against). 2. (о́коло) (*fig., coll.*) to hang (about, round). 3. (среди́) (*fig., coll.*) to mix (with), hobnob (with).

терза́|ть, ю, *impf.* 1. to tear to pieces; to pull about. 2. to torment, torture; меня́ ~ли сомне́ния I was a prey to doubts.

терза́|ться, юсь, *impf.* (+i.) to suffer; to be a prey (to).

тёрк|а, и, f. grater.

те́рмин, а, *m.* term.

терминологи́ческий, *adj.* terminological.

терминоло́ги|я, и, f. terminology.

терми́т[1], а, *m.* (*chem.*) thermite.

терми́т[2], а, *m.* (*zool.*) termite.

терми́т|ный, *adj. of* ~[1].

терми́ческ|ий, *adj.* (*phys., tech.*) thermic, thermal; ~ая обрабо́тка thermal treatment.

термодина́мик|а, и, f. thermodynamics.

термодинами́ческий, *adj.* thermodynamic.

термо́метр, а, *m.* thermometer; т. Це́льсия centigrade thermometer; поста́вить т. кому́-н. to take someone's temperature.

термообрабо́тк|а, и, f. (*tech.*) heat treatment, thermal treatment.

термопа́р|а, ы, f. (*phys.*) thermocouple.

те́рмос, а, *m.* thermos (flask).

термоста́т, а, *m.* thermostat.

термоэлектри́ческий, *adj.* thermo-electrical; т. столб thermopile.

термоэлектро́нный, *adj.* thermionic.

термоя́дерный, *adj.* thermonuclear.

те́рм|ы, ~, *no sing.* (*hist.*) thermae, (hot) baths.

тёрн, а, *m.* (*bot.*) 1. blackthorn. 2. sloe(s).

те́рни|е, я, *n.* (*obs.*) 1. prickly plant. 2. prickle, thorn.

терно́вник, а, *m.* (*bot.*) blackthorn.

терно́в|ый, *adj.* 1. *adj. of* тёрн *and* ~ник. 2. thorny, prickly; т. вене́ц crown of thorns.

терпели́вост|ь, и, *f.* patience.

терпели́в|ый (~, ~а), *adj.* patient.

терпе́ни|е, я, *n.* patience; endurance, perseverance; вы́вести из ~я to exasperate; вы́йти из ~я to lose patience; запасти́сь, вооружи́ться ~ем to summon up patience, have patience.

терпенти́н, а, *m.* turpentine.

терпенти́н|ный, *adj. of* ~.

терпенти́н|овый, *adj.* = ~ный.

терп|е́ть, лю́, ~ишь, *impf.* 1. (*pf.* по~) to suffer, undergo; т. пораже́ние to suffer a defeat, be defeated. 2. to bear, endure, stand; мы не могли́ бо́льше т. тако́го хо́лода we could bear the cold no longer. 3. to have patience. 4. to tolerate, suffer, put up (with); не (мочь) т. to be unable to bear, endure, stand, support; т. не могу́ I can't stand it, I hate it; вре́мя ~ит there is plenty of time; вре́мя не ~ит there is no time to be lost, time is getting short; де́ло не ~ит the matter is urgent; де́ло не ~ит отлага́тельства the matter brooks no delay.

терп|е́ться, ~ится, *impf.* (*impers.*) ему́, *etc.,* не ~ится (+*inf.*) he, *etc.,* is impatient (to).

терпи́мост|ь, и, *f.* tolerance; indulgence; дом ~и (*obs., euph.*) brothel.

терпи́м|ый (~, ~а), *adj.* 1. tolerant; indulgent, forbearing. 2. tolerable, bearable, supportable.

те́рп|кий (~ок, ~ка́), *adj.* astringent; tart, sharp.

те́рпкост|ь, и, *f.* astringency; tartness, sharpness, acerbity.

те́рпн|уть, ет, *impf.* (*of* за~) (*coll.*) to grow numb.

терпу́г, а́, *m.* (*tech.*) rasp.

террако́т|а, ы, *f.* terracotta.

террако́т|овый, *adj. of* ~а.

терра́ри|й, я, *m.* animal case (*for keeping small animals, esp. reptiles and amphibians*).

терра́риум, а, *m.* = терра́рий.

терра́с|а, ы, *f.* (*in var. senses*) terrace.

террасир|овать, ую, *impf. and pf.* to terrace.

территориа́ль|ный, *adj.* territorial; ~ая а́рмия territorial army; ~ые во́ды territorial waters.

террито́ри|я, и, *f.* territory, confines; area.

терро́р, а, *m.* terror.

терроризи́р|овать, ую, *impf. and pf.* to terrorize.

террори́зм, а, *m.* terrorism.

террориз|ова́ть, у́ю, *impf. and pf.* = ~и́ровать.

террори́ст, а, *m.* terrorist.

террористи́ческий, *adj.* terrorist.

террори́ст|ка, ки, *f. of* ~.

тёрт|ый (~, ~а), *p.p.p. of* тере́ть *and adj.* (*full form only*) 1. ground; grated. 2. (*fig., coll.*) hardened, experienced; т. кала́ч old stager, old hand.

терце́т, а, *m.* 1. (*mus.*) terzetto. 2. (*lit.*) tercet, triplet.

терци́н|а, ы, *f.* (*lit.*) terza rima.

те́рци|я, и, *f.* 1. (*mus.*) mediant; third; бо́льшая т. major third; ма́лая т. minor third. 2. (*math.*) third (= *one sixtieth of a second*). 3. (*typ.*) 16-point type.

терье́р, а, *m.* terrier (*dog*).

теря́|ть, ю, *impf.* (*of* по~) (*in var. senses*) to lose; т. наде́жду to lose hope; не т. головы́ to keep one's head; т. си́лу to become invalid; т. си́лу за да́вностью (*leg.*) to be lost by limitation; т. по́чву под нога́ми to feel the ground slipping away from under one's feet; т. вре́мя на что-н. to waste time on something; т. в ве́се to lose weight; т. в чьём-н. мне́нии to sink in someone's estimation; не т. и́з виду to keep in sight; (*fig.*) to remember, bear in mind; нам не́чего т. we have nothing to lose.

теря́|ться, юсь, *impf.* (*of* по~) 1. to get lost; to disappear, vanish. 2. to fail, decline, decrease, weaken; па́мять у него́ ~ется his memory is failing, is going. 3. to pass unnoticed; to fail to attract notice; ре́плика не ~лась the retort did not pass unnoticed. 4. to lose one's self-possession; to become flustered; ~юсь, ума́ не приложу́ I am at my wits' end. 5. т. в дога́дках, т. в предположе́ниях to be lost in conjecture.

тёс, а (у), *m.* (*collect.*) boards, planks.

теса́к, а́, *m.* 1. broadsword; cutlass. 2. chopper, hatchet.

те|са́ть, шу́, ~шешь, *impf.* 1. to cut, hew. 2. to trim, square.

тесёмк|а, и, *f.* tape, ribbon, lace, braid.

тесём|очный, *adj. of* ~ка.

тесёмчатый, *adj.* tape-like; т. глист tapeworm.

тесн|а́, ы, *f.* board, plank.

тес|ло́, ла́, *pl.* ~ла, ~ел, *n.* adze.

тесни́н|а, ы, *f.* gorge, ravine.

тесн|и́ть, ю́, и́шь, *impf.* 1. (*pf.* по~) to press, crowd. 2. to squeeze, constrict; (*of clothing*) to be too tight; мне грудь ~и́т I have a tightness in my chest.

тесн|и́ться, ю́сь, и́шься, *impf.* 1. (*pf.* по~) to press through, push a way through. 2. (*pf.* с~) to crowd, cluster, jostle one another (*also fig.; of thoughts, etc.*).

тéсно, *adv.* 1. closely (*also fig.*); tightly; narrowly; идти́ т. в ряд to march shoulder to shoulder; быть т. свя́зано (c+*i.*) to be closely linked (with). 2. *as pred.* it is crowded, it is cramped; it is (too) tight; в трамва́е бы́ло о́чень т. the tram was very crowded; мне т. под мы́шками it feels tight in the arm-pits.

теснот|á, ы́, *f.* 1. crowded state; narrowness, narrow dimensions; tightness; closeness. 2. crush, squash; жить в ~é to live cooped up; в ~é, да не в оби́де the more the merrier.

тéс|ный (~ен, ~на́, ~но), *adj.* 1. crowded, cramped; мир ~ен! it's a small world. 2. narrow; т. прохо́д narrow passage. 3. (too) tight. 4. close, compact; ~ные ряды́ close ranks. 5. (*fig.*) close, tight; ~ная дру́жба close friendship. 6. (*fig., obs.*) hard, difficult; ~ные обстоя́тельства straitened circumstances. 7. в ~ном смы́сле сло́ва in the narrow sense of the word.

тесо́вый, *adj.* board, plank.

тéст|о, а, *n.* 1. dough; pastry; т. для блино́в batter. 2. paste; viscous mass.

тестообра́з|ный (~ен, ~на), *adj.* doughy, dough-like, paste-like.

тест|ь, я, *m.* father-in-law (*wife's father*).

тесьм|á, ы́, *f.* tape, ribbon, lace, braid (*as adornment or for tying something*).

тéтеньк|а, и, *f.* (*affect. form of* тётя, *also used by children in addressing an unknown woman*) aunty.

тéтерев, а, *pl.* ~á, ~о́в, *m.* (*orn.*) black grouse (blackcock); глухо́й т. (*i*) capercailzie, (*ii*) (*coll.*) deaf person.

тетёрк|а, и, *f.* grey-hen (*f. of* black grouse).

тетéр|я, и, *f.* 1. (*dial.*) = тéтерев. 2. (*coll., joc.*) chap, fellow; глуха́я т. deaf fellow; лени́вая т. lazybones; со́нная т. sleepyhead.

тетив|á, ы́, *f.* 1. bowstring. 2. taut rope. 3. (*tech.*) string-board, stringer.

тётк|а, и, *f.* 1. aunt. 2. (*as term of address to any elderly woman; coll.*) ma, lady.

тетра́д|ка, ки, *f.* = ~ь.

тетра́д|ь, и, *f.* 1. exercise book; copy-book; т. для рисова́ния drawing-book; sketch-book. 2. т. пи́счей бума́ги packet of notepaper. 3. part, fascicule (*of publication*). 4. quire (*of manuscript*).

тетрало́ги|я, и, *f.* tetralogy.

тетра́эдр, а, *m.* (*math.*) tetrahedron.

тётушк|а, и, *f.* (*affect. form of* тётка) aunty.

тёт|я, и, *g. pl.* ~ей, *f.* 1. aunt. 2. (*used by children to any unknown woman*) lady. 3. (*joc.*) woman.

тéфтел|и, ей, *no sing.* (*cul.*) meat-balls.

тех, *g., a., p. pl. of* тот.

тех- *abbr. of* техни́ческий.

техми́нимум, а, *m.* (*abbr. of* техни́ческий ми́нимум) required minimum of technical knowledge.

тéхник, а, *m.* 1. technician; зубно́й т. dental mechanic. 2. technically qualified person.

тéхник|а, и, *f.* 1. engineering; technics, technology. 2. technique, art; э́то — де́ло ~и it is a matter of technique; т. стихосложе́ния the technique of versification; овладе́ть ~ой to master the art. 3. (*collect.*) technical devices; т. безопа́сности safety devices. 4. (*collect.*) technical equipment, machinery; (*mil.*) matériel.

техникум, а, *m.* technical college, training college.

техници́зм, а, *m.* preoccupation with technical aspect of something.

техни́чески, *adv.* technically.

техни́ческ|ий, *adj.* 1. (*in var. senses*) technical; engineering; ~ие нау́ки engineering sciences; т. персона́л technical staff; т. реда́ктор technical editor; т. те́рмин technical term; ~ие усло́вия specifications. 2. (*mil.*) maintenance; ~ое обслу́живание maintenance. 3. ~ие культу́ры (*agric.*) industrial crops. 4. ~ая ско́рость (*tech.*) maximum speed. 5. assistant, subordinate (= not having powers of decision); т. сотру́дник junior member of staff.

технокра́т, а, *m.* technocrat.

технократи́ческий, *adj.* technocratic.

техно́лог, а, *m.* technologist.

технологи́ческий, *adj.* technological.

технологи|я, и, *f.* technology.

технору́к, а, *m.* (*abbr. of* техни́ческий руководи́тель) technical director.

техрéд, а, *m.* (*abbr. of* техни́ческий реда́ктор) technical editor.

течéни|е, я, *n.* 1. flow. 2. (*fig.*) course; с. ~ем вре́мени in the course of time, in time. 3. current, stream (*also fig.*); по ~ю, про́тив ~я with the stream, against the stream (*also fig.*). 4. (*fig.*) trend, tendency. 5. в т. (+*g.*) during, in the course (of).

тéчк|а, и, *f.* heat (*in animals*).

теч|ь¹, и, *f.* leak; дать т. to spring a leak; заде́лать т. to stop a leak.

течь², теку́, течёшь, теку́т, *past* тёк, текла́, *impf.* 1. to flow (*also fig.*); to stream; (*fig.*) (*of time*) to pass; у тебя́ кровь течёт из но́су your nose is bleeding; у него́ из но́су течёт his nose is running; у меня́ слю́нки текли́ my mouth was watering. 2. to leak, be leaky.

тéш|ить, у, ишь, *impf.* (*of* по~) 1. to amuse, entertain. 2. to gratify, please.

тéш|иться, усь, ишься, *impf.* (*of* по~) 1. (+*i.*) to amuse oneself (with), play (with); чем бы дитя́ ни ~илось, лишь бы не пла́кало anything for a quiet life. **2.** (над) to make fun (of).

тёшк|а, и, *f.* tyoshka (*abdomen of fish as food-stuff*).

тёщ|а, и, *f.* mother-in-law (*wife's mother*).

тиа́р|а, ы, *f.* tiara.

тибе́т|ец, ца, *m.* Tibetan.

тибе́тк|а, и, *f.* Tibetan (woman).

тибе́тский, *adj.* Tibetan.

тибр|ить, ю, ишь, *impf.* (*of* с~) (*coll.*) to pinch, snaffle.

ти́г|ель, ля, *m.* (*tech.*) crucible.

ти́гель|ный, *adj. of* ~.

тигр, а, *m.* tiger.

тигр|ёнок, ёнка, *pl.* ~я́та, ~я́т, *m.* tiger cub.

тигри́ц|а, ы, *f.* tigress.

тигро́в|ый, *adj. of* тигр; ~ая шку́ра tiger-skin.

тик¹, а, *m.* (*med.*) tic.

тик², а, *m.* tick, ticking (*material*).

тик³, а, *m.* (*bot.*) teak.

ти́кани|е, я, *n.* tick, ticking (*of a clock*).

ти́ка|ть, ю, *impf.* (*coll.*) to tick.

ти́ккер, а, *m.* (*radio*) ticker.

ти́ковый¹, *adj. of* тик².

ти́ков|ый², *adj. of* тик³; ~ое де́рево teak tree, teak wood.

тик-та́к, *onomat.* tick-tock.

ти́льд|а, ы, *f.* (*typ.*) tilde, swung dash.

ти́мберс, а, *m.* (*naut.*) beam, timber.

тимиа́н, а, *m.* = тимья́н.

тимо́л, а, *m.* (*chem.*) thymol.

тимофе́евк|а, и, *f.* (*bot.*) timothy-grass.

тимпа́н, а, *m.* **1.** (*mus.*) timbrel. **2.** (*archit.*) tympanum.

тимья́н, а. *m.* (*bot.*) thyme.

ти́н|а, ы, *no pl.,* *f.* slime, mud; mire (*also fig.*).

ти́нистый, *adj.* slimy, muddy.

тинкту́р|а, ы, *f.* tincture.

тип, а, *m.* **1.** (*in var. senses*) type; model. **2.** (*coll.*) type (= person); chap; strange character.

типа́ж, а, *m.* (*lit., art*) type.

типиза́ци|я, и, *f.* typification.

типизи́р|овать, ую, *impf. and pf.* to typify.

ти́пик¹, а, *m.* (*eccl.*) typicon (*manual of Orthodox Church containing order of services*).

ти́пик², а, *m.* (*coll., pejor.*) = тип 2.

типи́ческий, *adj.* **1.** typical (= constituting a type). **2.** model, standard.

типи́чност|ь, и, *f.* typicalness, typical nature.

типи́ч|ный (~ен, ~на), *adj.* typical (= characteristic).

типов|о́й, *adj.* model; standard; ~а́я моде́ль standard model; ~о́е изде́лие standard product.

типо́граф, а, *m.* **1.** printer. **2.** printing-house owner. **3.** printing machine.

типогра́фи|я, и, *f.* printing-house, printing-office, press.

типогра́фск|ий, *adj.* typographical; ~ое иску́сство typography.

типогра́фщик, а, *m.* (*obs.*) printer.

типолитогра́фи|я, и, *f.* typolithography.

типолитогра́фский, *adj.* typolithographical.

типологи́ческий, *adj.* typological.

типоло́ги|я, и, *f.* typology.

типу́н, а́, *m.* pip (*disease of birds*); т. тебе́ на язы́к! keep your trap shut!

тир¹, а, *m.* shooting-range; shooting-gallery.

тир², а, *m.* (*naut.*) pitch, tar.

тира́д|а, ы, *f.* tirade; sally.

тира́ж, а́, *m.* **1.** drawing (*of loan or lottery*); вы́йти в т. to be drawn; (*fig.*) to retire from the scene, take a back seat. **2.** circulation; edition; т. э́той газе́ты полтора́ миллио́на this newspaper has a circulation of a million and a half; т. в сто ты́сяч экземпля́ров an edition of a hundred thousand copies.

тира́н, а, *m.* tyrant.

тира́н|ить, ю, ишь, *impf.* to tyrannize (over), torment.

тирани́ческий, *adj.* tyrannical.

тирани́|я, и, *f.* (*hist. and fig.*) tyranny.

тира́нств|о, а, *n.* tyranny.

тира́нств|овать, ую, *impf.* (над) to tyrannize (over).

тире́, *indecl.,* *n.* dash.

тир|ова́ть, у́ю, *impf.* (*naut.*) to pitch, tar.

тиро́льский, *adj.* Tyrolese, Tyrolean.

тис, а, *m.* yew(-tree).

ти́ска|ть, ю, *impf.* (*of* ти́снуть) **1.** to press, squeeze. **2.** (*typ.*) to pull.

тиск|и́, о́в, *no sing.* (*tech.*) vice; зажа́ть в т. to grip in a vice; в ~а́х (+*g.*) in the grip (of), in the clutches (of).

тисне́ни|е, я, *n.* **1.** stamping, printing. **2.** imprint; design.

тиснёный, *adj.* stamped, printed; т. шрифт raised (Braille) type.

ти́с|нуть, ну, нешь, *pf. of* ~кать.

ти́с|овый, *adj. of* ~.

тита́н¹, а, *m.* (*myth. and fig.*) titan.

тита́н², а, *m.* (*chem.*) titanium.

тита́н³, а, *m.* boiler.

титани́ческий, *adj.* titanic.

тита́н|овый, *adj. of* ~²; titanic.

ти́тл|о, а, *n.* **1.** (*obs.*) title; под ~ом entitled. **2.** (*philol.*) titlo, tilde (*mark above letter in medieval texts indicating abbreviation of word*).

ти́тло|вый, *adj. of* ~; т. знак titlo.

титр¹, а, *m.* (*cinema*) caption, credit.

титр², а, *m.* (*chem.*) titre.

титрова́ни|е, я, *n.* (*chem.*) titration.

титр|ова́ть, у́ю, *impf. and pf.* (*chem.*) to titrate.

ти́тул, а, *m.* **1.** (*in var. senses*) title. **2.** title-page.

титуло́в|анный, *p.p.p. of* ~а́ть *and adj.* titled.

титул|ова́ть, **у́ю**, *impf. and pf.* to style, call by one's title.

ти́тул|ьный, *adj.* 1. *of* ~; т. лист title-page. 2. ~ьные спи́ски itemised lists (*of approved building projects*).

титуля́рный, *adj.* т. сове́тник (*hist.*) titular counsellor (*civil servant of 9th grade in tsarist Russia*).

тиу́н, **а**, *m.* (*hist.*) tiun (*title of various officials in mediaeval Russia*).

тиф, **а**, *m.* typhus; брюшно́й т. typhoid (fever); сыпно́й т. typhus, spotted fever.

ти́фдрук, **а**, *m.* (*typ.*) mezzotint.

тифлопедаго́гик|а, **и**, *f.* methods of teaching the blind.

тифо́зн|ый, *adj.* typhus; typhoid; ~ая лихора́дка typhoid fever; *as noun* т., ~ого, *m.* typhus patient.

ти́х|ий (~, ~а́, ~о), *adj.* 1. quiet; (*of sounds*) low, soft, gentle, faint; т. го́лос low voice. 2. silent, noiseless; still; ~ая ночь still night. 3. (*fig.*) quiet, calm; gentle; still; ~ая жизнь quiet life; т. нрав gentle disposition; ~ая пого́да calm weather; в ~ом о́муте че́рти во́дятся (*prov.*) still waters run deep. 4. slow, slow-moving; т. ход slow speed, slow pace; ~ая торго́вля slack trade.

ти́хо[1], *adv.* 1. quietly; softly, gently; т. постуча́ть to knock gently. 2. silently, noiselessly. 3. (*fig.*) quietly, calmly; still; сиде́ть т. to sit still; т.! gently!, careful! 4. slowly; дела́ иду́т т. things are slack.

ти́хо[2], *as pred.* 1. it is quiet, there is not a sound; ста́ло т. it became quiet, the noise died away. 2. (*fig.*) it is quiet; it is calm; на душе́ у меня́ ста́ло т. my mind is at rest. 3. (*comm.*) it is slack; с хло́пком т. cotton is slack.

тихомо́лком, *adv.* (*coll.*) quietly, without a sound.

тихо́нько, *adv.* (*coll.*) quietly; softly, gently.

тихо́н|я, **и**, *g. pl.* ~ей, *m. and f.* demure person; prig; прики́дываться ~ей, смотре́ть ~ей to look as if butter would not melt in one's mouth.

тихоокеа́н|ец, **ца**, *m.* sailor of Pacific fleet.

тихоокеа́нский, *adj.* Pacific.

тихохо́д, **а**, *m.* (*zool.*) sloth.

тихохо́д|ный (~ен, ~на), *adj.* slow.

ти́ше 1. *comp. of* ти́хий *and* ти́хо. 2. т.! (*i*) (be) quiet!, silence! (*ii*) gently!, careful!

тишин|а́, **ы́**, *f.* quiet, silence; stillness; нару́шить ~у́ to break the silence; соблюда́ть ~у́ to keep quiet.

тишко́м, *adv.* (*coll.*) quietly; imperceptibly.

тиш|ь, **и**, в ~и́, *f.* quiet, silence; stillness; т. да гладь peace and quiet.

ткан|евый, *adj. of* ~ь 1, 2.

тка́ный, *adj.* woven.

ткан|ь, **и**, *f.* 1. fabric, cloth; льняны́е ~и linen(s); шёлковые ~и silks. 2. (*anat.*) tissue. 3. (*fig.*) substance, essence; т. расска́за gist of a story.

тканьё|ё, **я́**, *n.* 1. weaving. 2. woven fabrics, cloth.

тканьёвый, *adj.* woven.

ткать, **тку**, **ткёшь**, *past* ткал, ткала́, тка́ло, *impf.* (*of* со~) to weave; т. паути́ну to spin a web.

тка́цк|ий, *adj.* weaver's, weaving; ~ое де́ло weaving; т. стано́к loom; т. челно́к shuttle.

ткач, **а́**, *m.* weaver.

тка́честв|о, **а**, *n.* weaving.

ткачи́х|а, **и**, *f. of* ткач.

ткн|у́ть(ся), **у́(сь)**, **ёшь(ся)**, *pf. of* ты́кать(ся).

тлен, **а**, *m.* (*obs.*) decay.

тле́ни|е, **я**, *n.* 1. decay, decomposition, putrefaction. 2. smouldering.

тле́н|ный (~ен, ~на), *adj.* (*obs.*) liable to decay.

тлетво́р|ный (~ен, ~на), *adj.* 1. putrefactive; putrid. 2. (*fig.*) pernicious, noxious.

тле́|ть, **ет**, *impf.* 1. to rot, decay, decompose, putrefy; to moulder. 2. to smoulder (*also fig.*); ещё ~ет наде́жда there is still a glimmer of hope.

тле́|ться, **ется**, *impf.* to smoulder.

тл|я, **и**, *g. pl.* ~ей, *f.* 1. plant-louse, aphis. 2. (*fig., pejor.*) louse.

тмин, **а**, *m.* 1. caraway. 2. (*collect.*) caraway-seeds.

тми́н|ный, *adj. of* ~; ~ная во́дка kümmel.

то[1], *pron.* (*nom. and a. sing. n. of* тот) that; то, что... the fact that...; то, что́ that which; то был, была́, бы́ло that was; то бы́ли those were; то́ есть that is (to say); то бишь that is to say; то ли де́ло (*coll.*) what a difference, how different (= how much better); а то, *see* а; (да) то and that, at that; там лишь оди́н мужчи́на, и то восьмидесятиле́тний стари́к there is only one man there, and that an old man of eighty.

то[2], *conj.* 1. (*in apodosis of conditional sentence*) then (*or not translated*); е́сли вас там не бу́дет, то и я не пойду́ if you won't be there, (then) I shan't go either. 2. то..., то now..., now; то тут, то там now here, now there. 3. не то..., не то either... or; whether... or; half..., half; не то по глу́пости, не то по зло́бе either through stupidity or through malice; не то удивле́ние, не то доса́да half surprise, half annoyance. 4. не то, что́бы..., но it is not, it was not that... (but); не то, что́бы я не хоте́л слу́шать радиопереда́чу, но я про́сто забы́л о ней it was not that I did not want to hear the broadcast: I simply forgot about it. **5.** то и де́ло, то и знай (*coll.*) time and again; incessantly, perpetually.

-то[1], *emphatic particle* (*in coll. Russian often merely adds familiar tone*) just, precisely, exactly (*or not translated*); в то́м-то и де́ло that's just it; чего́ же ва́м-то боя́ться? what have *you* to be afraid of?; вот ведь беда́-то где! that's where the whole trouble lies.

-то[2], *particle forming indef. pronouns and advs.* (кто́-то, како́й-то, когда́-то, etc.).

тобо́ю, *i. of* ты.

това́р, а, *m.* goods; wares; article; commodity; ~ы широ́кого потребле́ния consumer goods; показа́ть т. лицо́м (*coll.*) to show something to good effect.

това́рищ, а, *m.* **1.** comrade; friend; companion; colleague; т. де́тства childhood friend; т. по несча́стью fellow-sufferer, companion in distress; т. по ору́жию comrade-in-arms; т. по рабо́те colleague; mate; т. по шко́ле school-friend. **2.** (*as style and as term of address in U.S.S.R.*) Comrade. **3.** person; э́тот т. прие́хал из Москвы́ this man has come from Moscow; вот т. из Министе́рства here is the man from the Ministry. **4.** (*obs.*) assistant, deputy, vice-; т. председа́теля vice-president.

това́рищеск|**ий**, *adj.* **1.** comradely; friendly; с ~им приве́том (*epistolary formula*) with fraternal greetings. **2.** of equals; т. суд Comrades' Court (*tribunal of fellow-citizens or fellow-workers—before 1917, of fellow-members of a profession— empowered to pass censure in cases of misconduct*). **3.** (*sport*) friendly, unofficial; ~ое состяза́ние, ~ая встре́ча friendly (match).

това́риществ|**о**, а, *n.* **1.** comradeship, fellowship; чу́вство ~а a feeling of solidarity. **2.** company; association, society; т. на пая́х joint-stock company. **3.** companionship, partnership.

това́рк|**а**, и, *f.* (*coll., obs.*) friend.

това́рност|**ь**, и, *f.* (*econ.*) marketability.

това́рн|**ый**, *adj.* **1.** goods; т. знак trade mark; т. склад warehouse. **2.** (*railways*) goods, freight; т. ваго́н goods truck; т. парк goods yard; т. соста́в goods train. **3.** (*econ.*) commodity; ~ая проду́кция commodity output; ~ое хозя́йство commodity economy. **4.** (*econ.*) marketable; ~ое зерно́ marketable grain.

товарове́д, а, *m.* commodity researcher.

товарове́дени|**е**, я, *n.* commodity research.

товарообме́н, а, *m.* (*econ.*) barter.

товарооборо́т, а, *m.* commodity circulation.

товароотправи́тел|**ь**, я, *m.* consignor, forwarder of goods.

това́ро-пассажи́рский, *adj.* т.-п. по́езд mixed train.

товарополуча́тел|**ь**, я, *m.* consignee.

товаропроводя́щ|**ий**, *adj.* ~ая сеть commodity distribution network.

то́г|**а**, и, *f.* (*hist.*) toga; ряди́ться в ~у (+*g.*) (*rhet.*) to don the garb (of), array oneself (as).

тогда́ 1. *adv.* then (= (*i*) at that time, (*ii*) in that case). **2.** когда́..., т. (*conj.*) when; когда́ решу́сь, т. тебе́ напишу́ I will write to you when I have decided. **3.** т. как (*conj.*) whereas, while.

тогда́шний, *adj.* (*coll.*) of that time, of those days; the then.

того́[1], *interj.* (*filling pause in utterance*) er . . ., um . . . .

того́[2], *as pred.* you know (*coll., euph.* = (*i*) abnormal, simple, (*ii*) drunk, (*iii*) mediocre); к десяти́ часа́м он был совсе́м т. by ten o'clock he was completely—you know.

того́[3], *g. sing. m. and n. of* тот.

тожде́ственност|**ь**, и, *f.* identity.

тожде́ствен|**ный** (~, ~на), *adj.* identical, one and the same.

тожде́ств|**о**, а, *n.* identity.

то́же[1], *adv.* also, as well, too.

то́же[2], *particle* (*coll., iron.*) *expressing disapproval of someone's conduct or scepticism with regard to someone's pretensions to knowledge, etc.*: ты т. хоро́ш! you're a fine one, I must say; т. знато́к нашёлся! since when is he an expert!, as if he were an expert!

тоже́ственност|**ь**, и, *f.* = тожде́ственность.

тоже́ственный, *adj.* = тожде́ственный.

тоже́ств|**о**, а, *n.* = тожде́ство.

ток[1], а, *m.* (*in var. senses*) current; т. высо́кого напряже́ния (*electr.*) high-tension current; т. подогре́ва (*radio*) heater current; т. уте́чки leakage current; переме́нный т. alternating current; постоя́нный т. direct current.

ток[2], а, о ~е, на ~у́, *pl.* ~а́, ~о́в, *m.* (*birds'*) mating-place.

ток[3], а, о ~е́, на ~у́, *pl.* ~а́ *and* ~и, ~о́в, *m.* threshing-floor.

ток[4], а, *m.* toque.

тока́|**й**, я, *m.* Tokay (wine).

тока́йск|**ое**, ого, *n.* = тока́й.

тока́рн|**ый**, *adj.* (*tech.*) turning; ~ая мастерска́я turnery; т. резе́ц lathe tool; т. стано́к lathe; автомати́ческий т. стано́к engine lathe; т. цех turning shop; *as noun* ~ая, ~ой, *f.* = ~ая мастерска́я.

то́кар|**ь**, я, *pl.* ~и *and* ~я́, *m.* turner, lathe operator.

токка́т|**а**, ы, *f.* (*mus.*) toccata.

то́кмо, *adv.* (*arch. or coll.*) only.

ток|**ова́ть**, у́ет, *impf.* (*of birds*) to utter the mating-call.

токоприёмник, а, *m.* (*electr.*) current collector, trolley (*of electr. locomotive, trolley-bus, etc.*).

токсикологи́ческий, *adj.* toxicological.

токсиколо́ги|я, и, *f.* toxicology.

токси́н, а, *m.* (*med.*) toxin.

токси́ческий, *adj.* toxic.

тол, а, *m.* (*chem.*) tolite.

то́л|евый, *adj. of* ~ь.

толи́к|а, и, *f.* (*coll.*) ма́лая т., не́которая т. a little, a small quantity; a few.

толк¹, а (у), *m.* 1. sense; understanding; без ~у senselessly, wildly; с ~ом sensibly, intelligently; сбить с ~у to confuse, muddle; взять в т. (*coll.*) to understand, grasp, get, see; от него́ ~у не добьёшься you'll get no sense out of him. 2. (*coll.*) use, profit; из э́того не вы́йдет ~у nothing will come of it; понима́ть, знать т. (в+*p.*) to know what one is talking about (in), know one's onions (in). 3. (*obs.*) persuasion (= sect, grouping).

толк², *as pred.* (*coll.*) = ~ну́л.

толка́тел|ь, я, *m.* (*tech.*) pusher, push rod, tappet.

толк|а́ть, а́ю, *impf.* (*of* ~ну́ть) 1. to push, shove; to jog; т. ло́ктем to nudge. 2. (*sport*) т. шта́нгу to weight-lift; т. ядро́ to put the shot. 3. (на+*a.*) to push (into), incite (to), instigate (to).

толк|а́ться, а́юсь, *impf.* 1. (*impf. only*) to push (one another). 2. (*pf.* ~ну́ться) т. в дверь to knock on the door. 3. (*pf.* ~ну́ться) (к) to try to see, try to get access (to). 4. (*impf. only*) (*coll.*) to knock about.

толка́ч, á, *m.* 1. (*railways*) pusher. 2. pestle, pounder. 3. (*fig., coll.*) pusher, go-getter, fixer (*in Soviet industrial enterprises*).

то́лк|и, ов (*coll.*) talk; rumours, gossip; иду́т т. о том, что it is said that, it is rumoured that.

толк|ну́ть, ну́, нёшь, *pf. of* ~а́ть.

толк|ну́ться, ну́сь, нёшься, *pf. of* ~а́ться 2, 3.

толкова́ни|е, я, *n.* 1. interpretation; exegesis. 2. (*pl.*) commentary.

толкова́тел|ь, я, *m.* interpreter, commentator, expounder.

толк|ова́ть, у́ю, *impf.* 1. to interpret; ло́жно т. чьи-н. слова́ to misinterpret, misconstrue someone's words. 2. (+*d.*; *coll.*) to explain (to); ско́лько ему́ ни ~у́й, он ничего́ не понима́ет it's a waste of time trying to explain things to him. 3. (*coll.*) to talk; to say; т. де́ло to talk sense; он всё своё ~у́ет he keeps on about the same thing; ~у́ют, бу́дто people say that, they say that.

толко́в|ый (~, ~а), *adj.* 1. intelligent, sensible. 2. intelligible, clear. 3. (*full form only*) т. слова́рь explanatory dictionary.

то́лком, *adv.* (*coll.*) 1. plainly, clearly; поговори́ть т. to talk straight. 2. seriously, in all seriousness.

толкотн|я́, и́, f. (*coll.*) crush, scrum, squash; crowding.

тол|ку́, ку́т, *see* ~о́чь.

толку́чий, *adj.* т. ры́нок (*coll.*) second-hand goods market.

толку́ч|ка, ки, f. (*coll.*) 1. crush, scrum, squash; crowded place. 2. = ~ий ры́нок.

толма́ч, á, *m.* (*obs.*) interpreter.

то́л|овый, *adj. of* ~.

толокн|о́, á, *n.* oat flour.

толокня́нк|а, и, f. (*bot.*) bearberry (*Arctostaphylos*).

толоко́нный, *adj. of* ~о́; т. лоб blockhead.

тол|о́чь, ку́, чёшь, ку́т, *past* ~о́к, ~кла́, *impf.* (*of* рас~ *and* с~) to pound, crush; т. во́ду в сту́пе to beat the air, mill the wind.

тол|о́чься, ку́сь, чёшься, ку́тся, *past* ~о́кся, ~кла́сь, *impf.* (*coll.*) to knock about; to gad about.

толп|á, ы́, *pl.* ~ы, *f.* crowd; throng; multitude.

толп|и́ться, и́тся, *impf.* to crowd; to throng; to cluster.

толсте́нный, *adj.* (*coll.*) very fat.

толсте́|ть, ю, *impf.* (*of* по~) to grow fat, grow stout; to put on weight.

толст|и́ть, и́т, *impf.* (*coll.*) to make (look) fat; хлеб о́чень ~и́т bread is very fattening; шу́ба её о́чень ~и́ла the fur coat made her look very fat.

толстобрю́х|ий (~, ~а), *adj.* (*coll.*) fat-bellied.

толсто́в|ец, ца, *m.* Tolstoyan.

толсто́вк|а¹, и, f. *of* толсто́вец.

толсто́вк|а², и, f. tolstovka (*long belted blouse*).

толсто́вств|о, а, n. Tolstoyism.

толстогу́б|ый (~, ~а), *adj.* thick-lipped.

толстоко́ж|ий (~, ~а), *adj.* 1. thick-skinned (*also fig.*). 2. (*zool.*) pachydermatous; ~ее живо́тное pachyderm.

толстомо́рдый, *adj.* (*coll.*) fat-faced.

толстопу́з|ый (~, ~а), *adj.* pot-bellied (*hist.*, *esp. as term of abuse applied to merchants*).

толстосте́нный, *adj.* (*tech.*) thick-walled.

толстосу́м, а, *m.* (*obs.*, *coll.*) money-bags.

толсту́х|а, и, f. (*coll.*) fat woman; fat girl.

толсту́шк|а, и, f. *affect. form of* толсту́ха.

то́лст|ый (~, ~á, ~о), *adj.* 1. fat; stout; corpulent; т. нос big nose. 2. thick; heavy; stout; т. слой thick layer; ~ая бума́га thick paper; т. про́вод heavy-gauge wire; т. журна́л 'fat magazine' (= literary monthly, *etc.*); ~ая кишка́ (*anat.*) large intestine.

толстя́к, á, *m.* fat man; fat boy.

толуо́л, а, *m.* (*chem.*) toluene.

толче́ни|е, я, n. pounding, crushing.

толчёный, *adj.* pounded, crushed; ground.

тол|чёт, *see* ~о́чь.

толче|я́¹, и́, *f.* (*coll.*) crush, scrum, squash.

толче|я́², и́, *f.* (*tech.*) mill.

толч|о́к¹, ка́, *m.* **1.** push, shove; (*sport*) put. **2.** jolt, bump; (earthquake) shock, tremor. **3.** (*fig.*) push, shove; incitement, stimulus; послужи́ть мо́щным ~ко́м (к) to serve as a powerful spur (to).

толчо́к² = толку́чий ры́нок.

то́лщ|а, и, *f.* **1.** thickness; т. сне́га depth of snow. **2.** в ~е наро́да in the (thick of the) people.

то́лще, *comp. of* то́лстый.

толщин|а́, ы́, *f.* **1.** fatness, stoutness, corpulence. **2.** thickness.

тол|ь, я, *m.* (tarred) roofing paper.

то́лько 1. *adv.* only, merely; solely; just; не т...., но и not only . . ., but also; поду́май(те) т.! just think!; т. и всего́, да и т. (*coll.*) that's all; (and) that's that; т. что не (*coll.*) the only thing lacking (is, was); она́ и бога́та и краси́ва, т. что не благоразу́мна she has money and looks, the only thing she lacks is sense; не т. что (*coll.*) not to mention, let alone. **2.** т. что (*adv. and conj.*) just, only just; он т. что позвони́л he has just rung up; т. что мы дое́хали до ста́нции, про́било шесть we had just reached the station when it struck six. **3.** *conj.* (+как, лишь) as soon as; one has only to . . .; т. ска́жешь, я уйду́ you have only to say (the word) and I will go. **4.** *conj.* only, but; с удово́льствием, т. не сего́дня with pleasure, only not today. **5.** т. бы (+*inf.*) (*particle*) if only; т. бы получи́ть о нём ве́сточку if only we could hear news of him. **6.** *particle intensifying interrog. pronouns and advs.*: заче́м т.? why on earth?, whatever for?; кого́ т. он не зна́ет? whom does he *not* know?; где т. они́ не быва́ли? where have they *not* been?

то́лько-то́лько, *adv.* (*coll.*) only just.

том, а, *pl.* ~а́, ~о́в, *m.* volume.

томага́вк, а, *m.* tomahawk.

тома́совский, *adj.* (*tech.*) Thomas; т. чугу́н Thomas pig iron, basic pig iron.

тома́т, а, *m.* **1.** tomato. **2.** tomato purée.

тома́тный, *adj.* tomato; т. сок tomato juice.

то́мик, а, *m.* *dim. of* том.

томи́льн|ый, *adj.* (*tech.*) т. коло́дец soaking pit; ~ая печь soaking furnace.

томи́тел|ьный (~ен, ~ьна), *adj.* wearisome, tedious, wearing; tiresome, trying; agonizing; т. зной trying heat; ~ьное ожида́ние agonizing suspense; tedious wait; ~ьная ску́ка deadly boredom.

том|и́ть, лю́, и́шь, *impf.* (*of* ис~) **1.** to tire, wear, weary; to torment; to wear down; т. в тюрьме́ to leave to languish in prison;

меня́ ~и́т жа́жда I am parched. **2.** (*cul.*) to stew; to braise. **3.** (*tech.*) to render malleable.

том|и́ться, лю́сь, и́шься, *impf.* **1.** to pine; to languish; т. жа́ждой to be parched with thirst; т. ожида́нием to be in an agony of suspense; т. в плену́, в тюрьме́ to languish in captivity. **2.** *pass. of* ~и́ть.

томле́ни|е, я, *n.* **1.** languor. **2.** (*tech.*) malleablizing, cementation.

томлён|ый, *adj.* **1.** (*cul.*) stewed; braised. **2.** (*tech.*) malleablized; ~ая сталь converted steel, cement steel.

то́мност|ь, и, *f.* languor.

то́м|ный (~ен, ~на́), *adj.* languid, languorous.

томпа́к, а́, *m.* tombac (*copper and zinc alloy*).

тон, а, *pl.* ~ы and ~а́, *m.* **1.** (*pl.* ~ы) (*mus. and fig.*) tone; ~ом вы́ше, ни́же a tone higher, lower; хоро́ший, дурно́й т. good, bad form; зада́ть т. to set the tone; перемени́ть т. to change one's tone; попа́сть в т. to hit the right note. **2.** (*pl.* ~а́) (colour) tone, tint.

тона́льност|ь, и, *f.* (*mus.*) key.

то́ненький, *adj.* thin; slender, slim.

тонзу́р|а, ы, *f.* tonsure.

тонизи́р|овать, ую, *impf. and pf.* (*physiol.*) to tone up.

то́ник|а, и, *f.* (*mus.*) tonic, keynote.

тонин|а́, ы́, *f.* fineness.

тони́ческий¹, *adj.* (*mus., lit.*) tonic.

тони́ческий², *adj.* (*physiol., med.*) tonic.

то́н|кий (~ок, ~ка́, ~ко), *adj.* **1.** thin; slender, slim; т. ло́мтик thin slice; ~кая кишка́ (*anat.*) small intestine. **2.** fine; delicate; refined; dainty; ~кое бельё fine linen; т. за́пах delicate perfume; ~кая рабо́та fine workmanship; т. у́жин dainty supper; ~кие черты́ лица́ refined features. **3.** т. го́лос thin voice. **4.** (*fig.*) subtle, delicate; fine, nice; т. вопро́с nice point; т. знато́к connoisseur; т. кри́тик shrewd critic; ~кая лесть subtle flattery; т. намёк gentle hint; ~кое разли́чие subtle, fine, nice distinction; т. ум subtle intellect. **5.** (*of the senses*) keen. **6.** т. сон light sleep. **7.** (*coll., pejor.*) sharp; crafty, sly.

то́нко, *adv.* **1.** thinly. **2.** subtly, delicately, finely, nicely.

тонковолокни́ст|ый (~, ~а), *adj.* fine-fibred.

тонкозерни́ст|ый (~, ~а), *adj.* fine-grained.

тонкоко́ж|ий (~, ~а), *adj.* thin-skinned.

тонколистов|о́й, *adj.* (*tech.*) sheet; ~о́е желе́зо sheet iron; т. стан sheet rolling mill.

тонконтро́л|ь, я, *m.* (*radio*) tone control.

тонкопряди́льн|ый, *adj.*; ~ая маши́на fine-spinning frame.

тонкору́нный, *adj.* fine-fleeced.

тонкосте́нный, *adj.* (*tech.*) thin-walled.

то́нкост|ь, и, *f.* **1.** thinness; slenderness, slimness. **2.** fineness. **3.** subtlety. **4.** nice point, nicety, subtle point; до ~ей to a nicety; вдава́ться в ~и to split hairs.

тонкосуко́нный, *adj.* (*text.*) fine-cloth.

тонкошёрстный, *adj.* fine-wool, fine woollen.

тонкошёрст|ый = ~ный.

тонме́йстер, а, *m.* (*radio*) sound director.

то́нн|а, ы, *f.* ton.

тонна́ж, а, *m.* tonnage.

тонне́л|ь, я, *m.* = тунне́ль.

то́нн|ый (~а, ~о), *adj.* (*coll., iron.*) (*obs.*) grand; comme il faut.

то́нус, а, *m.* (*physiol., med.*) tone.

тон|у́ть, у́, ~ешь, *impf.* **1.** (*pf.* по~) to sink, go down. **2.** (*pf.* у~) to drown. **3.** (*pf.* у~) (в+*p.*) to sink (in); to be lost (in); to be hidden (in, by), be covered (in, by); т. в поду́шках to sink in the pillows; т. в дела́х to be up to one's eyes in work; надгро́бный па́мятник ~ет в высо́кой траве́ the tomb--stone is hidden from view by the long grass.

тонфи́льм, а, *m.* sound film; (*radio*) recording.

то́ньше, *comp. of* то́нкий *and* то́нко.

тон|я́, и, *f.* **1.** fishery, fishing-ground. **2.** haul (*of fish*).

топ, *as pred.* (*coll.*) = ~нул.

топа́з, а, *m.* (*min.*) topaz.

топа́з|овый, *adj. of* ~.

то́п|ать, аю, *impf.* **1.** (*pf.* ~нуть) to stamp; т. нога́ми to stamp one's feet. **2.** (*impf. only*) (*coll.*) to go, walk.

топинамбу́р, а, *m.* Jerusalem artichoke.

топ|и́ть¹, лю́, ~ишь, *impf.* **1.** to stoke (*a boiler, a stove, etc.*). **2.** to heat.

топ|и́ть², лю́, ~ишь, *impf.* **1.** to melt (down), render. **2.** т. молоко́ to bake milk.

топ|и́ть³, лю́, ~ишь, *impf.* **1.** (*pf.* по~) to sink. **2.** (*pf.* у~) to drown; (*fig., coll.*) to wreck, ruin; т. го́ре в вине́ to drown one's sorrows in drink.

топ|и́ться¹, ~ится, *impf.* (*of a stove, etc.*) to burn, be alight.

топ|и́ться², ~ится, *impf.* **1.** to melt. **2.** *pass. of* ~и́ть².

топ|и́ться³, лю́сь, ~ишься, *impf.* (*of* у~) to drown oneself.

то́пк|а¹, и, *f.* **1.** stoking. **2.** heating. **3.** furnace; (*on locomotive*) fire-box.

то́пк|а², и, *f.* melting (down).

то́п|кий (~ок, ~ка́, ~ко), *adj.* boggy, marshy, swampy.

топлён|ый, *adj.* melted; ~ое молоко́ baked milk.

то́плив|ный, *adj. of* ~о; ~ная нефть fuel oil.

то́плив|о, а, *n.* fuel; жи́дкое т. fuel oil; твёрдое т. solid fuel.

то́п|нуть, ну, нешь, *pf. of* ~ать.

топо́граф, а, *m.* topographer.

топографи́ческий, *adj.* topographical.

топогра́фи|я, и, *f.* topography.

то́пол|евый, *adj. of* ~ь.

то́пол|ь, я, *pl.* ~и *and* ~я́, *m.* poplar; пирами́дальный т. Lombardy poplar.

топони́ми|ка, ки, *f.* (*collect.*) place-names (*of a region*).

топони́ми|я, и, *f.* toponymy.

топо́р, а́, *m.* axe; хоть т. ве́шай (*of close atmosphere; coll.*) you could cut it with a knife.

топо́рик, а, *m.* hatchet.

топори́щ|е¹, а, *n.* axe-handle, axe helve.

топори́щ|е², а, *n.* large axe.

топо́р|ный (~ен, ~на), *adj.* clumsy, crude; uncouth.

топо́рщ|ить, ит, *impf.* (*coll.*) to bristle.

топо́рщ|иться, ится, *impf.* (*coll.*) **1.** to bristle (*intrans.*). **2.** to puff up.

то́пот, а, *m.* tread; tramp; ко́нский т. clatter of horses' hoofs.

топо|та́ть, чу́, ~чешь, *impf.* (*coll.*) to stamp; (*of horses*) to clatter.

то́почн|ый, *adj.* furnace; ~ая коро́бка fire--box; ~ое простра́нство combustion chamber; ~ая труба́ furnace flue.

то́псел|ь, я, *m.* (*naut.*) topsail.

топ|та́ть, чу́, ~чешь, *impf.* **1.** to trample (down). **2.** to make dirty (*with one's feet*). **3.** to trample out (*grapes, etc.*); т. гли́ну to knead clay.

топ|та́ться, чу́сь, ~чешься, *impf.* to stamp; т. на ме́сте to mark time (*also fig.*).

Топты́гин, а, *m.* (*joc.*) Bruin.

топча́к, а́, *m.* treadmill.

топча́н, а́, *m.* trestle-bed.

топы́р|ить, ю, ишь, *impf.* (*coll.*) to bristle; to spread wide.

топы́р|иться, ится, *impf.* (*coll.*) to bristle (*intrans.*).

топ|ь, и, *f.* bog, marsh, swamp.

то́р|а, ы, *f.* (*rel.*) Torah, Pentateuch.

то́рб|а, ы, *f.* bag; носи́ться (с+*i.*) как (дура́к) с пи́саной ~ой (*coll.*) to make a great song and dance (about).

торг¹, а, о ~е, на ~у́, *pl.* ~и́, *m.* **1.** trading; bargaining, haggling. **2.** (*obs.*) market. **3.** (*pl.*) auction; прода́ть с ~о́в to sell by auction. **4.** (*pl.*) competition for a contract.

торг², а, *m.* (*abbr. of* торго́вое учрежде́ние, торго́вая организа́ция) trading organization.

торга́ш, а́, *m.* (*pejor.*) **1.** (small) tradesman. **2.** mercenary-minded person.

торга́ш|еский, *adj. of* ~.

торга́шеств|о, а, *n.* **1.** small trading. **2.** mercenary-mindedness.

торг|ова́ть, у́ю, *impf.* **1.** (*impf. only*) (+*i.*) to trade (in), deal (in), sell. **2.** (*impf. only*) (*of a shop or business*) to be open. **3.** (*pf.* c~) (*coll.*) to bargain (for).

торг|ова́ться, у́юсь, *impf.* **1.** (*pf.* c~) (c+*i.*) to bargain (with), haggle (with). **2.** (*impf. only*) (*coll.*) to argue.

торго́в|ец, ца, *m.* merchant; trader, dealer; tradesman.

торго́вк|а, и, *f.* market-woman, stall-holder; woman street-trader.

торго́вл|я, и, *f.* trade, commerce.

торго́в|ый, *adj.* trade, commercial; mercantile; т. бала́нс balance of trade; т. дом business house, firm; ~ая пала́та chamber of commerce; т. представи́тель trade representative; ~ая сеть (*collect.*) shops; ~ая то́чка shop; ~ое су́дно merchant ship; т. флот merchant navy, mercantile marine.

торгпре́д, а, *m.* (*abbr. of* торго́вый представи́тель) trade representative.

торгпре́дств|о, а, *n.* (*abbr. of* торго́вое представи́тельство) trade delegation.

тореадо́р, а, *m.* toreador.

тор|е́ц, ца́, *m.* **1.** butt-end, face (*of beam, plank*). **2.** wooden paving-block. **3.** pavement of wooden blocks.

торже́ственност|ь, и, *f.* solemnity.

торже́ствен|ный (~, ~на), *adj.* **1.** ceremonial; festive; gala; т. въезд ceremonial entry; т. день red-letter day; ~ная оде́жда ceremonial attire. **2.** solemn; ~ная кля́тва solemn vow; т. слу́чай solemn occasion.

торжеств|о́, а́, *n.* **1.** celebration; (*pl.*) festivities, rejoicings. **2.** triumph (= victory). **3.** triumph, exultation; сказа́ть с ~о́м to say triumphantly; to say gloatingly.

торжеств|ова́ть, у́ю, *impf.* **1.** to celebrate; т. побе́ду to celebrate a victory; (*fig.*) to be victorious. **2.** (над) to triumph (over); to exult (over).

торжеств|у́ющий, *pres. part. act. of* ~ова́ть *and adj.* triumphant, exultant.

то́ржищ|е, а, *n.* (*obs.*) market, bazaar.

то́ри, *indecl., m.* (*polit.*) tory.

то́ри|й, я, *m.* (*chem.*) thorium.

торкре́т, а, *m.* т.(-бето́н) (*tech.*) gunite.

торма́шк|и: вверх т., вверх ~ами (*coll.*) head over heels, upside down, topsy-turvy.

торможе́ни|е, я, *n.* **1.** (*tech.*) braking. **2.** (*psych.*) inhibition.

то́рмоз, а, *m.* **1.** (*pl.* ~а́) brake; т. отка́та (*mil.*) recoil brake; т. нака́та (*mil.*) counter-recoil brake. **2.** (*pl.* ~ы) (*fig.*) brake; drag, hindrance, obstacle.

тормо|зи́ть, жу́, зи́шь, *impf.* (*of* за~) **1.** (*tech.*) to brake, apply the brake (to). **2.** (*fig.*) to hamper, impede, be a drag (on),

be an obstacle in the way (of). **3.** (*psych.*) to inhibit.

тормозн|о́й, *adj.* (*tech.*) brake, braking; т. башма́к brake-shoe; ~а́я площа́дка (*railways*) brake-platform.

тормош|и́ть, у́, и́шь, *impf.* (*coll.*) **1.** to pull about. **2.** (*fig.*) to pester, plague.

то́рн|ый, *adj.* smooth, even; пойти́ по ~ой доро́ге (*fig.*) to stick to the beaten track.

торова́т|ый (~, ~а), *adj.* (*coll.*) liberal, generous.

торо́к|а, о́в, *no sing.* saddle-bow straps.

тороп|и́ть, лю́, ~ишь, *impf.* (*of* по~) **1.** to hurry, hasten; to press; меня́ ~ят с оконча́нием рабо́ты I am being pressed to finish my work. **2.** to precipitate.

тороп|и́ться, лю́сь, ~ишься, *impf.* (*of* по~) to hurry, be in a hurry, hasten.

торопли́во, *adv.* hurriedly, hastily; in a hurry, in haste.

торопли́вост|ь, и, *f.* hurry, haste.

торопли́в|ый (~, ~а), *adj.* hurried, hasty.

торопы́г|а, и, *m. and f.* (*coll.*) person always in a hurry.

торо́с, а, *m.* ice-hummock.

торо́сист|ый (~, ~а), *adj.* hummocky; т. лёд pack ice.

торпе́д|а, ы, *f.* torpedo.

торпеди́р|овать, ую, *impf. and pf.* to torpedo.

торпеди́ст, а, *m.* (*mil., naut.*) torpedo artificer.

торпе́дник, а, *m.* (*mil., naut.*) member of MTB crew.

торпе́д|ный, *adj. of* ~а; т. аппара́т torpedo-tube; т. ка́тер motor torpedo boat (MTB).

торпедоно́с|ец, ца, *m.* **1.** torpedo bomber. **2.** torpedo bomber pilot.

торпедоно́сный, *adj.* (*naut., aeron.*) torpedo-carrying.

торс, а, *m.* trunk; torso.

торт, а, *m.* cake.

торф, а, *m.* peat.

торфобрике́т, а, *m.* (a) peat, peat briquette.

торфодобы́ч|а, и, *f.* peat-extraction, peat-cutting.

торфоразрабо́т|ки, ок, *no sing.* peatbog.

торфяни́к, а́, m. **1.** peatbog. **2.** peat-cutter.

торфяни́ст|ый (~, ~а), *adj.* peaty.

торфян|о́й, *adj.* peat; ~о́е боло́то peatbog; т. мох (*bot.*) peatmoss.

торц|ева́ть, у́ю, *impf.* to pave with wood blocks.

торцо́в|ый, *adj. of* торе́ц; ~ая мостова́я wood pavement.

торч|а́ть, у́, и́шь, *impf.* **1.** to stick up, stick out; to stand on end. **2.** (*coll.*) to hang about, stick around; т. перед чьи́ми-н. глаза́ми to be under someone's feet; он ~и́т це́лый день при бассе́йне для

пла́вания he hangs about at the swimming-
-pool the entire day.

торчко́м, *adv.* (*coll.*) on end, sticking up.

торч|мя́ = ∼ко́м.

торше́р, **а**, *m.* standard lamp.

тоск|а́, **и́**, *f.* **1.** melancholy; anguish; pangs;
у неё т. на се́рдце she is sick at heart; т.
любви́ pangs of love. **2.** depression; ennui,
boredom; одна́ т., сплошна́я т. a frightful
bore; навести́ ∼у́ (на+*a.*) to depress, bore;
т. берёт (*coll.*) it makes one sick, it is sickening. **3.** (по+*d. or p.*) longing (for), yearning
(for), nostalgia (for); т. по ро́дине home-
-sickness.

тоскли́в|ый (∼, ∼а), *adj.* **1.** melancholy;
depressed, miserable. **2.** dull, dreary, depressing; ∼ая пого́да depressing weather.

тоск|ова́ть, **у́ю**, *impf.* **1.** to be melancholy,
be depressed, be miserable. **2.** (по+*d. or
p.*) to long (for), yearn (for), pine (for),
miss.

тост, **а**, *m.* toast; провозгласи́ть, предло-
жи́ть т. (за+*a.*) to toast, drink (to); to
propose a toast (to).

тот, *f.* **та**, *n.* **то**, *pl.* **те**, *pron.* **1.** (*as opp. to*
э́тот) that; (*pl.*) those; мне бо́льше нра́-
вится та карти́на I like that picture better;
в тот раз on that occasion; в то вре́мя then,
at that time, in those days; в том слу́чае in
that case. **2.** (*as opp. to* э́тот) the former;
(*replacing 3rd sing. pron.*) he; she; it; я пе́ре-
дал корректу́ру профе́ссору, тот до́лжен
был вам верну́ть её I passed the proofs on
to the professor, he was supposed to return
them to you. **3.** (*as opp. to* э́тот) the other;
the opposite; на той стороне́ on the other
side; по ту сто́рону (+*g.*) beyond, on the
other side (of); с того́ бе́рега from the other
shore. **4.** (*as opp. to* сей *in certain set phrases*)
that, the other; то да сё one thing and
another; ни то ни сё neither one thing nor
another; поговори́ть о том, о сём to talk
about this and that, about one thing and
another; ни с того́ ни с сего́ for no reason
at all; without rhyme or reason. **5.** (*as opp.
to* друго́й, ино́й) the one; и тот и друго́й
both; ни тот ни друго́й neither; не тот,
так друго́й if not one, then the other. **6.**
тот..., (кото́рый) the . . . (which); тот,
(кто) the one (who), the person (who); тот
фильм, кото́рый вы ви́дели вчера́ the film
(which) you saw yesterday; та, кто но́сит
ту́фли на высо́ких каблука́х the one wearing high-heeled shoes; тот факт, что the
fact that (*see also* то¹). **7.** тот (же), тот (же)
са́мый the same; одно́ и то же one and the
same thing, the same thing over again; в
то же са́мое вре́мя at the same time, on the
other hand; он тепе́рь не тот he is not the
man he was. **8.** the right; не тот the wrong;

э́то не та дверь that's the wrong door; э́то
тот но́мер? is this the (right) room?; э́то
Федо́т, да не тот that's a horse of another
colour. **9.** +*preps. forms the following conjs.*:
для того́, что́бы in order that, in order to;
до того́, что (*i*) until, (*ii*) to such an extent
that; ме́жду тем, как whereas; несмотря́
на то, что in spite of the fact that; пе́ред
тем, как before; по́сле того́, как after; по
ме́ре того́, как in proportion as; с тем,
что́бы (*i*) in order to, with a view to, (*ii*) on
condition that, provided that. **10.** *forms
part of various adverbial phrases and particles*
(*see also* то¹): вме́сте с тем at the same time;
к тому́ же moreover; кро́ме того́ besides;
ме́жду тем, тем вре́менем meanwhile; со
всем тем notwithstanding all this; тем
са́мым hereby; тому́ наза́д ago; и тому́
подо́бное (и т. п.) and so forth; того́ и
гляди́ any minute now; before you know
where you are; и без того́ as it is; (да) и
то сказа́ть and indeed; не без того́ that's
about it; it can't altogether be denied.

тоталитари́зм, **а**, *m.* (*polit.*) totalitarianism.

тоталита́рный, *adj.* (*polit.*) totalitarian.

тота́льный, *adj.* total.

тоте́м, **а**, *m.* totem.

тотеми́зм, **а**, *m.* totemism.

то́-то, *particle* (*coll.*) **1.** *emphasizes point of
utterance*: (вот) то́-то, (вот) то́-то и оно́,
(вот) то́-то и есть that's just it; precisely,
exactly. **2.** *in exclamations, expressing emotion
or emotional judgement*: то́-то прекра́сно!
there, isn't that lovely! **3.** *expresses reproach,
or recalls warning or threat conveyed in previous
utterance*: ну, то́-то же! there you are, you
see!; well, what did I tell you!

то́тчас, *adv.* at once; immediately (*also of
spatial relations*).

тоха́рский, *adj.* (*ling.*) Tokharian.

точёный, *adj.* **1.** sharpened. **2.** (*tech.*)
turned. **3.** (*fig.; of bodily features*) finely-
-moulded, chiselled.

то́чечн|ый, *adj.* **1.** consisting of points. **2.**
∼ая сва́рка (*tech.*) spot welding.

точи́лк|а, **и**, *f.* (*coll.*) steel, knife-sharpener;
pencil-sharpener.

точи́л|о, **а**, *n.* whetstone, grindstone.

точи́льный, *adj.* grinding, sharpening; т.
ка́мень whetstone, grindstone; т. материа́л
abrasive; т. реме́нь strop; т. стано́к grinding lathe.

точи́льщик, **а**, *m.* grinder.

точ|и́ть¹, **у́**, ∼**ишь**, *impf.* **1.** (*pf.* на∼) to
sharpen; to grind; to whet, hone; т. зу́бы
на кого́-н. to have a grudge against someone. **2.** (*impf. only*) to turn (*on a lathe*).

точ|и́ть², **у́**, ∼**ишь**, *impf.* to eat away, gnaw
away; to corrode; (*fig.*) to gnaw (at), prey
(upon).

точ|и́ть³, у́, ~ишь, *impf.* (*obs.*) to secrete; т. слёзы to shed tears.

точ|и́ться¹, ~ится, *impf.*, *pass. of* ~и́ть¹,².

точ|и́ться², ~ится, *impf.* (*obs.*) to ooze.

то́чк|а¹, и, *f.* 1. spot, dot; бе́лое пла́тье в ро́зовых ~ах white dress with pink spots; „i“ с ~ой *name of letter* 'i' *in old Russian orthography*; ста́вить ~и на „и“ to dot one's 'i's' (*and cross one's 't's'*). 2. (*gram.*) full stop; т. с запято́й semicolon; поста́вить ~у to place a full stop; (*fig.*) to finish, come to the end. 3. (*mus.*) dot. 4. (*math.*, *phys.*, *tech.*) point; т. опо́ры fulcrum, point of support; (*fig.*) rallying-point; мёртвая т. dead point, dead centre; (*fig.*) dead stop, standstill; дойти́ до мёртвой ~и to come to a standstill, to a full stop. 5. (*mil.*) point; т. встре́чи, т. попада́ния point of impact; т. наво́дки aiming point; т. прице́ливания point of aim. 6. т. замерза́ния, кипе́ния, плавле́ния freezing, boiling, melting point; т. росы́ dew-point. 7. (*fig.*) point; т. зре́ния point of view; т. соприкоснове́ния point of contact, meeting-ground; т. в ~у (*coll.*) exactly; to the letter, word for word; попа́сть в (са́мую) ~у (*coll.*) to hit the nail on the head; до ~и (*coll.*) to the limit, to the extreme point; дойти́ до ~и (*coll.*) to come to the end of one's tether.

то́чк|а², и, *f.* 1. sharpening; grinding; whetting; stropping. 2. (*tech.*) turning (*on a lathe*).

то́чно¹, *adv.* 1. exactly, precisely; punctually; т. переписа́ть to make an exact copy; приходи́те, пожа́луйста, т. в час please, come at one o'clock sharp, punctually at one. 2. т. так just so, exactly, precisely; т. тако́й (же) just the same. 3. (*obs.*) indeed.

то́чно², *particle* (*coll.*) yes; true; так т. (*in mil. parlance*) yes.

то́чно³, *conj.* as though, as if; like; он там стоя́л т. окамене́лый he stood there as if turned to stone.

то́чност|ь, и, *f.* exactness; precision; accuracy; punctuality; в ~и exactly, precisely; accurately; to the letter; вы́числить с ~ью до... to calculate to within . . .; с приближённой ~ью approximately; с ~ью часово́го механи́зма like clockwork.

то́ч|ный (~ен, ~на́, ~но), *adj.* exact, precise; accurate; punctual; ~ная бомбарди́ровка precision bombing; ~ные нау́ки exact sciences; т. перево́д accurate translation; т. прибо́р precision instrument; ~ная устано́вка sensitive adjustment; т. челове́к punctual person.

то́чь-в-то́чь, *adv.* (*coll.*) exactly; to the letter; word for word; он — т.-в-т. оте́ц he is the spit and image of his father.

тошн|и́ть, и́т, *impf.* (*impers.*) меня́, *etc.*, ~и́т

I, *etc.*, feel sick; меня́ от э́того ~и́т (*fig.*) it makes me sick, it sickens me.

то́шно, *as pred.* (*coll.*) 1. мне, *etc.*, т. I. *etc.*, feel sick; (*fig.*) I, *etc.*, feel wretched, awful. 2. (+*inf.*) it is sickening, it makes one sick, it is nauseating.

тошнот|а́, ы́, *f.* sickness, nausea (*also fig.*); испы́тывать ~у́ to feel sick; мне э́то надое́ло до ~ы́ I am sick to death of it.

тошнотво́р|ный (~ен, ~на), *adj.* sickening, sick-making, nauseating (*also fig.*).

то́ш|ный (~ен, ~на́, ~но), *adj.* (*coll.*) 1. tiresome, tedious. 2. sickening, nauseating.

тоща́|ть, ю, *impf.* (*of* о~) (*coll.*) to become thin.

то́щ|ий (~, ~а́, ~е), *adj.* 1. gaunt, emaciated; scraggy, skinny. 2. empty; на т. желу́док on an empty stomach; т. карма́н (*fig.*) empty pocket. 3. poor (= with low content of some substance); ~ее мя́со lean meat; ~ая по́чва poor soil; т. сыр skim-milk cheese; т. у́голь hard coal.

тпру, *interj.* (*to horses*) wo!, whoa!; ни т., ни ну (*fig.*, *coll.*) he, *etc.*, won't budge.

трав|а́, ы́, *pl.* ~ы, *f.* grass; (a) grass, herb; лека́рственные ~ы medicinal herbs; морска́я т. sea-weed; со́рная т. weed; т. ~о́й, как т. (*coll.*) it has no taste at all; хоть т. не расти́ (*coll.*) (everything else) can go to hell.

травене́|ть, ет, *impf.* (*of* за~) to become overgrown (with grass).

тра́верз, а, *m.* (*naut.*) beam; на ~e on the beam, abeam.

тра́верс, а, *m.* 1. (*mil.*) traverse; ты́льный т. parados. 2. (*tech.*) traverse, cross-beam, cross-arm; cross member, transverse member; cross head.

тра́верс|а, ы, *f.* = ~ 2.

травести́, *indecl.*, *n.* travesty.

трави́нк|а, и, *f.* blade of grass.

трав|и́ть¹, лю́, ~ишь, *impf.* 1. (*pf.* вы́~) to exterminate, destroy (*by poisoning*). 2. (*coll.*) to poison. 3. (*pf.* вы́~) to etch. 4. (*pf.* по~) (*of cattle*, *etc.*) to trample down; to damage (*crops*, *etc.*). 5. (*pf.* за~) to hunt; (*fig.*) to persecute, torment; to badger; to worry the life out of.

трав|и́ть², лю́, ~ишь, *impf.* (*naut.*) to pay out, ease out, slacken out; (*of anchor chain*) to veer.

трав|и́ться¹, лю́сь, ~ишься, *impf.* (*coll.*) to poison oneself.

трав|и́ться², лю́сь, ~ишься, *impf.*, *pass. of* ~и́ть¹,².

тра́в|ка¹, ки, *f.* dim of ~а́.

тра́вк|а², и, *f.* (*naut.*) paying out.

травле́ни|е, я, *n.* 1. extermination, destruction. 2. etching.

тра́вленый¹, *adj.* etched.

тра́вленый², *adj.* hunted; т. зверь (*fig.*, *coll.*) old hand.

тра́вл|я, и, *f.* hunting; (*fig.*) persecution, tormenting; badgering.

тра́вм|а, ы, *f.* (*med.*) trauma, injury; психи́ческая т. (*psych.*) shock, trauma.

травмати́зм, а, *m.* (*med.*) traumatism; (*collect.*) injuries; произво́дственный т. industrial injuries.

травмати́ческий, *adj.* (*med.*, *psych.*) traumatic.

тра́вник¹, а, *m.* 1. (*obs.*) herb-tea, herb-water. 2. (*hist.*, *lit.*) herbal. 3. (*obs.*) herbarium.

тра́вник², а, *m.* (*orn.*) redshank.

травопо́л|е, я, *n.* grassland agriculture, ley farming.

травопо́ль|ный, *adj. of* ~е; т. севооборо́т grassland crop rotation.

травосе́яни|е, я, *n.* fodder-grass cultivation.

травосто́|й, я, *m.* (*collect.*; *agric.*) grass, herbage.

травоя́дный, *adj.* herbivorous.

травяни́ст|ый (~, ~а), *adj.* 1. grass; herbaceous. 2. grassy. 3. (*coll.*) tasteless, insipid.

травян|о́й, *adj.* 1. grass; herbaceous; т. покро́в grass, herbage; ~ы́е расте́ния grasses, herbs; ~ы́е уго́дья grasslands. 2. grassy; т. за́пах grassy smell; т. цвет grass-green. 3. ~а́я насто́йка herb-tea, herb-water.

трагеди́йный, *adj.* (*theatr.*) tragic.

траге́ди|я, и, *f.* tragedy.

траги́зм, а, *m.* tragic element.

тра́гик, а, *m.* 1. tragic actor. 2. tragedian.

трагикоме́ди|я, и, *f.* tragicomedy.

трагикоми́ческий, *adj.* tragicomic.

траги́ческ|ий, *adj.* (*in var. senses*) tragic; т. актёр tragic actor; ~ое зре́лище tragic sight; приня́ть т. оборо́т to take a tragic turn.

траги́чност|ь, и, *f.* tragedy, tragic nature, tragic character.

траги́ч|ный (~ен, ~на), *adj.* tragic (= sad, terrible; *not in theatr. sense*).

традицио́нност|ь, и, *f.* traditional character.

традицио́н|ный (~ен, ~на), *adj.* traditional.

тради́ци|я, и, *f.* tradition.

траекто́ри|я, и, *f.* trajectory.

трак, а, *m.* track (*of caterpillar tractor*).

тракт, а, *m.* 1. high road, highway; почто́вый т. (*obs.*) post road; желу́дочно-кише́чный т. (*anat.*) alimentary canal. 2. route.

тракта́т, а, *m.* 1. treatise. 2. treaty.

тракти́р, а, *m.* (*obs.*) inn, eating-house.

тракти́р|ный, *adj. of* ~.

тракти́рщик, а, *m.* (*obs.*) innkeeper.

тракти́рщиц|а, ы, *f. of* тракти́рщик.

тракт|ова́ть, у́ю, *impf.* 1. (о+*p.*) to treat (of), discuss. 2. to interpret (*a part in a play, etc.*).

тракт|ова́ться, у́ется, *impf.* to be treated, be discussed; о чём ~у́ется в э́том рома́не? what is the subject of this novel.

тракто́вк|а, и, *f.* 1. treatment; interpretation; э́то любопы́тная т. вопро́са this is a curious treatment of the subject.

тра́ктор, а, *m.* tractor; т. на колёсном ходу́, колёсный т. wheeler tractor; т. на гу́сеничном ходу́, гу́сеничный т. caterpillar tractor.

тракториза́ци|я, и, *f.* introduction of tractors.

трактори́ст, а, *m.* tractor driver.

трактори́ст|ка, ки, *f. of* ~.

тра́ктор|ный, *adj. of* ~; т. парк fleet of tractors; на ~ной тя́ге tractor-drawn.

тракторострое́ни|е, я, *n.* tractor-making.

тракторострои́тельный, *adj.*; т. заво́д tractor works.

трал, а, *m.* 1. trawl. 2. (*mil.*) mine-sweep.

тра́лени|е, я, *n.* 1. trawling. 2. mine-sweeping.

тра́лер, а, *m.* (*obs.*) trawler.

трал|и́ть, ю, ишь, *impf.* 1. to trawl. 2. (*mil.*) to sweep.

тра́ловый, *adj.* 1. trawling; т. лов trawling. 2. (*mil.*) mine-sweeping.

тра́л|ьный = ~овый.

тра́льщик, а, *m.* 1. trawler. 2. (*mil.*) mine-sweeper.

трамб|ова́ть, у́ю, *impf.* to ram.

трамбо́вк|а, и, *f.* 1. ramming. 2. rammer, beetle.

трамва́|й, я, *m.* 1. tramway, tram-line. 2. tram(-car); речно́й т. river bus.

трамва́й|ный, *adj. of* ~; т. ваго́н tram-car; ~ные ре́льсы tram-lines.

трамва́йщик, а, *m.* tram worker.

трампли́н, а, *m.* (*sport and fig.*) spring-board; jumping-off place, ski-jump.

транжи́р, а, *m.* (*coll.*) spendthrift, squander-bug.

транжи́р|а, ы, *m. and f.* = ~.

транжи́р|ить, ю, ишь, *impf.* (*of* рас~) (*coll.*) to blow, squander.

транжи́р|ка, ки, *f. of* ~.

транзи́т, а, *m.* transit; пойти́ ~ом to go as transit goods.

транзи́т|ный, *adj. of* ~; ~ная ви́за transit visa; ~ная та́кса transit dues.

транс, а, *m.* trance.

транс- trans-.

трансатланти́ческий, *adj.* transatlantic.

трансгре́сси|я, и, f. (geol.) transgression.

транскриби́р|овать, ую, impf. and pf. to transcribe.

транскри́пци|я, и, f. transcription.

трансли́р|овать, ую, impf. and pf. to broadcast, transmit (by radio); to relay.

транслитера́ци|я, и, f. transliteration.

трансляцио́нн|ый, adj. (radio) relaying; ~ая сеть relaying system, relay network; т. у́зел relaying station.

трансля́ци|я, и, f. broadcast, transmission; relay.

трансми́сс|ио́нный, adj. of ~ия.

трансми́сси|я, и, f. (tech.) transmission.

транспара́нт, а, m. 1. black-lined paper (placed under unruled writing-paper). 2. transparency; banner.

транспланта́ци|я, и, f. (med.) transplantation.

транспози́ци|я, и, f. transposition.

транспони́р|овать, ую, impf. and pf. (mus.) to transpose.

транспониро́вк|а, и, f. (mus.) transposition.

тра́нспорт, а, m. 1. transport. 2. transportation, conveyance. 3. consignment. 4. (mil.) train, transport. 5. (naut.) transport, supply ship; troopship.

транспо́рт, а, m. (book-keeping) carrying forward.

транспорта́бел|ьный (~ен, ~ьна), adj. transportable, mobile.

транспортёр, а, m. 1. (tech.) conveyer. 2. (mil.) carrier.

транспорти́р, а, m. protractor.

транспорти́ровать¹, ую, impf. and pf. to transport.

транспорти́р|овать², ую, impf. and pf. (book-keeping) to carry forward.

транспортиро́вк|а, и, f. transport, transportation.

тра́нспортник, а, m. 1. transport worker. 2. transport plane.

тра́нспорт|ный, adj. of ~; ~ная ве́домость (mil.) table of movements; т. парк transport pool; т. самолёт transport plane; (mil.) troop-carrier; ~ное су́дно = ~ 5.

транссиби́рский, adj. Trans-Siberian; т. магистра́ль the Trans-Siberian railway.

трансформа́тор¹, а, m. (electr.) transformer.

трансформа́тор², а, m. 1. quick-change actor. 2. conjurer, illusionist.

трансформа́ци|я, и, f. transformation.

трансформи́р|овать, ую, impf. and pf. to transform.

трансцендента́льный, adj. (philos.) transcendental.

трансценде́нт|ный (~ен, ~на), adj. (philos., math.) transcendental.

транше́|йный, adj. of ~я.

транше́|я, и, f. (mil.) trench.

трап, а, m. (naut.) ladder; (aeron.) gangway.

тра́пез|а, ы, f. 1. dining-table (esp. in a monastery). 2. meal; дели́ть ~у (c+i.) to share a meal (with). 3. refectory.

тра́пез|ный, adj. of ~а; as noun ~ная, ~ной, f. refectory.

трапециеви́д|ный (~ен, ~на), adj. 1. trapeziform, trapezoid. 2. tapered; ~ное крыло́ (aeron.) tapered wing.

трапе́ци|я, и, f. 1. (math.) trapezium. 2. trapeze.

тра́сс|а, ы, f. 1. line, course; direction; возду́шная т. airway. 2. route. 3. plan, draft, sketch.

трасса́нт, а, m. (fin.) drawer.

трасса́т, а, m. (fin.) drawee.

трасси́р|овать, ую, impf. and pf. to mark out, trace.

трасси́р|ующий, pres. part. act. of ~овать and adj. (mil.) tracer; ~ующая пу́ля tracer bullet.

тра́т|а, ы, f. expenditure; пуста́я т. вре́мени waste of time.

тра́|тить, чу, тишь, impf. (of ис~ and по~) to spend, expend, use up; to waste.

тра́|титься, чусь, тишься, impf. (of ис~ and по~) (на+a.; coll.) to spend one's money (on), spend up (on).

тра́тт|а, ы, f. (fin.) bill of exchange.

тра́улер, а, m. trawler; т. с кормовы́м тра́лением stern-trawler.

тра́ур, а, m. mourning; обле́чься в т. to go into mourning.

тра́урн|ый, adj. 1. mourning; funeral; т. марш funeral march, dead march; ~ая повя́зка (mourning) crape band; ~ое ше́ствие funeral procession. 2. mournful, sorrowful; funeral.

трафаре́т, а, m. 1. stencil; раскра́сить, расписа́ть по ~у to stencil. 2. engraved inscription. 3. (fig.) conventional, stereotyped pattern; cliché; мы́слить по ~у to think along conventional lines.

трафаре́тност|ь, и, f. conventionality; stereotyped character.

трафаре́т|ный, adj. 1. stencilled; т. рису́нок stencil drawing. 2. (~ен, ~на) (fig.) conventional, stereotyped; trite, hackneyed.

тра́ф|ить, лю, ишь, impf. (coll.) to please, oblige.

трах, interj. bang! (also as pred. = ~нул).

тра́х|ать, аю, impf. of ~нуть.

трахеи́т, а, m. (med.) tracheitis.

трахе́йный, adj. (anat.) tracheal.

трахеотоми́|я, и, f. (med.) tracheotomy.

трахе́|я, и, f. (anat.) trachea, windpipe.

тра́х|нуть, ну, нешь, pf. (of ~ать) (coll.) to bang, crash; т. кого́-н. по спине́ to bang someone on the back; т. из ружья́ to loose off with a gun.

трахо́м|а, ы, *f.* (*med.*) trachoma.

тре́б|а¹, ы, *f.* occasional religious rite (*christening, marriage, funeral, etc.*).

тре́ба², as *pred.* (*dial.*) it is necessary.

тре́бник, а, *m.* prayer-book (*containing order of service of all ceremonies and rites except the Eucharist and the ordination of priests*).

тре́бовани|е, я, *n.* 1. demand, request; по ~ю on demand, by request; остано́вка по ~ю request stop; по ~ю (+*g.*) at the request (of), at the instance (of); по ~ю суда́ by order of the court. 2. demand, claim; согласи́ться на чьи-н. ~я to agree to someone's demands; вы́двинуть т. to put in a claim. 3. requirement, condition; отвеча́ть ~ям to meet requirements. 4.(*pl.*) aspirations; needs. 5. requisition, order; т. на то́пливо fuel requisition.

тре́бовател|ьный (~ен, ~ьна), *adj.* 1. demanding, exacting; particular. 2. ~ьная ве́домость requisition sheet, order form.

тре́б|овать, ую, *impf.* 1. (+*g. or* +что́бы) to demand, request, require; т. извине́ния у кого́-н. to demand an apology from someone; они́ ~уют, что́бы мы извини́лись they demand that we apologize. 2. (+*g.* от) to expect (from), ask (of); вы ~уете сли́шком мно́го от ва́ших ученико́в you expect too much from your pupils. 3. (*pf.* по~) (+*g.*) to require, need, call (for); т. неме́дленного реше́ния to require an immediate decision. 4. (*pf.* по~) to send for, call, summons; её ~уют к умира́ющему де́ду she is being sent for to her grandfather's bedside.

тре́б|оваться, уется, *impf.* (*of* по~) 1. to be needed, be required; на э́то ~уется мно́го вре́мени it takes a lot of time; ~уется приходя́щая домрабо́тница 'daily woman required'; что и ~овалось доказа́ть (*math.*) Q.E.D. 2. *pass. of* ~овать.

требух|а́, и́, *no pl.,* *f.* 1. entrails; (*cul.*) offal, tripe. 2. (*fig., coll.*) tripe, rubbish.

трево́г|а, и, *f.* 1. alarm, anxiety; uneasiness, disquiet. 2. alarm, alert; возду́шная т. air-raid warning, alert; пожа́рная т. fire-alarm; бить ~у to sound the alarm (*also fig.*).

трево́ж|ить, у, ишь, *impf.* 1. (*of* вс~) to alarm; to disturb; worry, trouble. 2. (*pf.* по~) to disturb, interrupt; нас всё вре́мя ~ат посети́тели we are continually disturbed by callers. 3. to annoy, bait; не т. to leave alone. 4. т. ра́ну to re-open a wound.

трево́ж|иться, усь, ишься, *impf.* 1. to worry, be anxious, be alarmed, be uneasy. 2. (*pf.* по~) to worry oneself, trouble oneself, put oneself out; не ~ьтесь! don't bother (yourself)!

трево́ж|ный (~ен, ~на), *adj.* 1. worried, anxious, uneasy, troubled. 2. alarming, disturbing, disquieting; ~ные слу́хи alarming reports. 3. alarm; т. звоно́к alarm (bell).

треволне́ни|е, я, *n.* (*now coll., joc.*) agitation, disquiet.

трегла́вый, *adj.* 1. with three cupolas. 2. (*poet.*) three-headed.

тред-юнио́н, а, *m.* trade union.

тред-юниони́зм, а, *m.* trade-unionism.

тред-юниони́ст, а, *m.* trade unionist.

тре́звенник, а, *m.* teetotaller, abstainer.

трезве́|ть, ю, *impf.* (*of* о~) to sober (up), become sober.

трезво́н, а, *m.* 1. peal (of bells). 2. (*coll., joc.*) rumours, gossip. 3. (*coll., pejor.*) row, shindy; подня́ть т., зада́ть ~у to kick up a row.

трезво́н|ить, ю, ишь, *impf.* 1. to ring (a peal). 2. (о+*p.*; *coll.*) to noise abroad; т. по всему́ го́роду to proclaim from the housetops.

тре́звост|ь, и, *f.* 1. soberness, sobriety (*also fig.*). 2. abstinence; temperance.

трезву́чи|е, я, *n.* (*mus.*) triad.

тре́зв|ый (~, ~а́, ~о), *adj.* 1. sober (*also fig.*); име́ть т. взгляд на собы́тия to take a sober view of events. 2. teetotal, abstinent.

трезу́б|ец, ца, *m.* trident.

трек, а, *m.* (*sport*) track.

трекля́тый, *adj.* (*coll.*) accursed.

трел|ь, и, *f.* (*mus.*) trill, shake; warble.

трелья́ж, а, *m.* 1. trellis. 2. three-leaved mirror.

тре́моло, *indecl., n.* (*mus.*) tremolo.

трен, а, *m.* (*obs.*) train (*of dress*).

тре́нер, а, *m.* (*sport*) trainer, coach.

тре́нер|ский, *adj. of* ~.

трензел|ь, я, *pl.* ~и and ~я́, *m.* snaffle.

тре́ни|е, я, *n.* 1. friction, rubbing. 2. (*pl.*) (*fig.*) friction.

трениp|ова́ть, у́ю, *impf.* (*of* на~) to train, coach.

трениp|ова́ться, у́юсь, *impf.* (*of* на~) to train oneself, coach oneself; to be in training.

трениро́вк|а, и, *f.* training, coaching.

трениро́вочный, *adj.* training; practice.

трено́г|а, и, *f.* tripod.

трено́гий, *adj.* three-legged.

трено́ж|ить, у, ишь, *impf.* (*of* с~) to hobble.

трено́жник, а, *m.* tripod.

тре́нька|ть, ю, *impf.* (*coll.*) to strum.

трепа́к, а́, *m.* trepak (*Russian folk-dance*).

трепа́л|о, а, *n.* (*tech.*) swingle, scutcher.

трепа́льный, *adj.* scutching.

трепа́льщик, а, *m.* scutcher.

трепа́льщи|ца, цы, *f. of* ~к.

трепа́н, а, *m.* (*med.*) trepan.

трепана́ци|я, и, *f.* (*med.*) trepanation.

трепа́нг, а, *m.* (*zool.*) trepang.

трепа́ни|е, я, *n.* scutching.

трепани́р|овать, ую, *impf. and pf.* (*med.*) to trepan.

трёпаный, *adj.* 1. (*of flax, etc.*) scutched. 2. torn, tattered. 3. dishevelled.

треп|а́ть, лю́, ~лешь, *impf.* 1. (*impf. only*) to scutch, swingle (*flax, hemp, etc.*). 2. (*pf.* по~) to pull about; (*of the wind*) to blow about; to dishevel, tousle; т. кого́-н. за во́лосы to pull someone's hair; т. чьи-н. во́лосы to tousle someone's hair; т. язы-ко́м (*coll.*) to prattle, blather; т. чьи-н. не́рвы to get on someone's nerves; его́ ~лет лихора́дка he is feverish; т. чьё-н. и́мя to bandy someone's name about. 3. (*pf.* по~) (*coll.*) to tear; to wear out. 4. (*pf.* по~) to pat.

треп|а́ться, лю́сь, ~лешься, *impf.* 1. (*pf.* по~) to tear, fray; to wear out. 2. (*impf. only*) to flutter, blow about. 3. (*impf. only*) т. по земле́ to trail along the ground. 4. (*impf. only*) (*coll., pejor.*) to go round; to hang out. 5. (*impf. only*) (c+*i.*; *fig., coll.*) to go (with) (*someone of the opposite sex*). 6. (*impf. only*) (*coll.*) to blather, talk rubbish; to play the fool.

трепа́ч, а́, *m.* (*coll.*) boaster, blétherer; good-for-nothing.

тре́пет, а, *m.* trembling, quivering (*from fear, etc., or from pleasurable sensation*); trepi-dation; быть в ~e to be a-tremble, be in a dither.

трепе|та́ть, щу́, ~щешь, *impf.* 1. to tremble, quiver; to flicker; to palpitate. 2. (*fig.*) to tremble; to thrill, palpitate; т. за челове́-чество to tremble for humanity; т. от восто́рга to thrill with joy; т. при мы́сли (о+*p.*) to tremble at the thought (of). 3. (пе́ред *or* (*obs.*) +*a.*; *fig.*) to tremble (before).

тре́петный, *adj.* 1. trembling; flickering; palpitating. 2. anxious. 3. timid.

трёпк|а, и,*f.* 1. scutching. 2. (*coll.*) dressing--down, scolding. 3. т. не́рвов nervous strain.

трепыха́|ться, юсь, *impf.* (*coll.*) to flutter, quiver.

треск, а, *m.* 1. crack, crash; crackle, crack-ling; т. руже́йных вы́стрелов crackle of gun-fire; т. огня́ crackling of a fire; т. лома́ющихся су́чьев snapping of twigs; т. мото́ра popping of an engine; с ~ом про-вали́ться (*fig., coll.*) to come a crasher, flop. 2. (*fig., coll.*) noise, fuss.

треск|а́, и́,*f.* cod.

тре́ска|ть, ю, *impf.* (*coll.*) to guzzle.

тре́ска|ться¹, ется, *impf.* (*of* по~) to crack; to chap.

тре́ска|ться², юсь, *impf. of* тре́снуться.

треск|о́вый, *adj. of* ~а́; т. жир cod-liver oil.

трескотн|я́, и́,*f.* (*coll.*) 1. crackle, crackling; chirring (*of grasshoppers*). 2. (*fig.*) chatter, blather.

треску́ч|ий (~, ~а), *adj.* 1. (*pejor.*) high--faluting, high-flown. 2. т. моро́з hard frost, ringing frost.

тре́сн|уть, у, ешь, *pf.* 1. to snap, crackle, pop. 2. to crack; to chap; (*fig., coll.*) to crash, flop; хоть ~и (*coll.*) for the life of me. 3. (+*i.* по+*d. or* +*a.* по+*d.; coll.*) to bring down with a crash (on); to hit, bang; т. кулако́м по столу́ to bang one's fist on the table; т. кого́-н. по заты́лку to bang someone on the back of the head.

тре́с|нуться, нусь, нешься, *pf.* (*of* ~кать-ся²) (+*i.* о+*a.; coll.*) to bang (against); т. голово́й о две́рцу шка́фа to bang one's head against the door of a cupboard.

трест, а, *m.* (*econ.*) trust (*in U.S.S.R., a group of industrial or commercial enterprises with centralized direction*).

трест|а́, ы́, *f.* flax *or* hemp straw.

трести́р|овать, ую, *impf. and pf.* to combine into a trust.

тре́ст|овский, *adj. of* ~.

трете́йск|ий, *adj.* arbitration; ~ое реше́ние конфли́кта arbitration; т. суд arbitration tribunal; т. судья́ arbitrator.

тре́т|ий, ья, ье, *adj.* 1. third; глава́ ~ья chapter three; т. но́мер number three; полови́на ~ьего half past two; в ~ьем часу́ between two and three; ~ьего дня the day before yesterday; до ~ьих петухо́в until dawn; ~ье лицо́ (*gram.*) third person; ~ье сосло́вие (*hist.*) third estate; ~ья сто-рона́ third party; т. такт (*tech.*) power stroke; из ~ьих рук indirectly; уволь-не́ние по ~ьему пу́нкту (*hist.*) summary dismissal. 2. *as noun* ~ье, ~ьего, *n.* sweet, dessert.

трети́р|овать, ую, *impf.* to slight.

трети́чный, *adj.* (*geol., chem., etc.*) tertiary, ternary.

трет|ь, и, *pl.* ~и, ~е́й,*f.* third.

тре́тьево́дни, *adv.* (*dial.*) the day before yesterday.

третьекла́ссник, а, *m.* third-former.

третьекла́ссный, *adj.* third-class (*also fig.*).

третьеочередно́й, *adj.* of third-rate impor-tance.

третьесо́ртный, *adj.* third-rate.

третьестепе́нный, *adj.* 1. insignificant, minor. 2. mediocre, third-rate.

треуго́лк|а, и,*f.* cocked hat.

треуго́льник, а, *m.* triangle.

треугóльный, *adj.* three-cornered, triangular.

треýх, **а**, *m.* (*obs.*) 'three-eared' cap (*cap with ear-flaps and back flap*).

треф, **а**, *m.* food forbidden by the Jewish faith.

треф|а, **ы**, *f.* (*cards*) 1. see ∼ы. 2. (*coll.*) a club.

трефнóй, *adj.* (*of food*) forbidden by the Jewish faith.

трéфовый, *adj.* (*cards*) of clubs.

треф|ы, ∼, *sing.* ∼а, ∼ы, *f.* (*cards*) clubs; дáма ∼ queen of clubs.

трёх- three-, tri-.

трёхвалéнтный, *adj.* (*chem.*) trivalent.

трёхвёрст|ка, **ки**, *f.* = ∼ная кáрта.

трёхвёрстн|ый, *adj.* 1. three versts in length. 2. ∼ая кáрта map on scale of three versts to an inch.

трёхгодúчный, *adj.* three-year.

трёхгодовáлый, *adj.* three-year-old.

трёхголóс(н)ый, *adj.* (*mus.*) three-part.

трёхгрáнный, *adj.* three-edged; (*math.*) trihedral.

трёхднéвн|ый, *adj.* three-day; ∼ая лихорáдка tertian ague.

трёхдюймóвк|а, **и**, *f.* 1. (*obs.*) three-inch field-gun. 2. three-inch board.

трёхдюймóвый, *adj.* three-inch.

трёхзнáчный, *adj.* three-digit, three-figure.

трёхколёсный, *adj.* three-wheeled; т. велосипéд tricycle.

трёхлéти|е, **я**, *n.* 1. period of three years. 2. third anniversary.

трёхлéтний, *adj.* 1. three-year. 2. three-year-old. 3. (*bot.*) triennial.

трёхлéт|ок, **ка**, *m.* three-year-old (*animal*).

трёхлинéй|ка, **ки**, *f.* = ∼ная винтóвка.

трёхлинéйн|ый, *adj.* of three eighths of an inch calibre; ∼ая винтóвка .375 rifle.

трёхлúстный, *adj.* (*bot.*) trifoliate.

трёхмéрный, *adj.* three-dimensional.

трёхмéстный, *adj.* three-seater.

трёхмéсячный, *adj.* 1. three-month; quarterly. 2. three-month-old.

трёхнедéльный, *adj.* 1. three-week. 2. three-week-old.

трёхóсный, *adj.* triaxial.

трёхпáл|ый, *adj.* (*zool.*) tridactylous; ∼ая чáйка (*orn.*) kittiwake.

трёхпóль|е, **я**, *n.* (*agric.*) three-field system.

трёхпóль|ный, *adj.* of ∼e.

трёхпроцéнтный, *adj.* three per cent.

трёхрублёвк|а, **и**, *f.* (*coll.*) three-rouble note.

трёхслóжный, *adj.* trisyllabic.

трёхслóйный, *adj.* three-layered; three-ply.

трёхсотлéти|е, **я**, *n.* 1. three hundred years. 2. tercentenary.

трёхсотлéтний, *adj.* 1. of three hundred years. 2. tercentennial.

трёхсóтый, *adj.* three-hundredth.

трёхствóльный, *adj.* three-barrelled.

трёхствóрчатый, *adj.* three-leaved.

трёхсторóнний, *adj.* 1. three-sided; (*math.*) trilateral. 2. tripartite.

трёхтóнк|а, **и**, *f.* (*coll.*) three-ton lorry.

трёхфáзный, *adj.* (*electr.*) three-phase.

трёхходов|óй, *adj.* 1. (*tech.*) three-way, three-pass. 2. ∼áя задáча (*chess*) three-move problem.

трёхцвéтный, *adj.* three-coloured; tricolour(ed); (*phot.*) trichromatic.

трёхчасовóй, *adj.* 1. three-hour. 2. three o'clock.

трёхчлéн, **а**, *m.* (*math.*) trinomial.

трёхчлéн|ный, *adj.* of ∼.

трёхъязы́чный, *adj.* trilingual.

трёхэтáжный, *adj.* three-storeyed.

трёшк|а, **и**, *f.* (*coll.*) three-rouble note.

трёшниц|а, **ы**, *f.* = трёшка.

трещ|áть, **ý**, **úшь**, *impf.* 1. to crack; (*fig.*) to crack up; у меня́ головá ∼úт I have a splitting headache; т. по всем швам (*fig.*) to go to pieces. 2. to crackle; (*of furniture*) to creak; (*of grasshoppers*) to chirr; ∼áт морóзы there is a ringing frost. 3. (*coll.*) to jabber, chatter.

трещин|а, **ы**, *f.* crack, split (*also fig.*); cleft, fissure; chap (*of skin*); дать ∼у to crack, split; (*fig.*) to show signs of cracking.

трещóтк|а, **и**, *f.* 1. rattle. 2. *m. and f.* (*fig., coll.*) chatterbox. 3. (*tech.*) ratchet-drill.

три, **трёх**, **трём**, **тремя́**, **о трёх**, *num.* three.

триáд|а, **ы**, *f.* triad.

триангуля́ци|я, **и**, *f.* (*math., geod.*) triangulation.

триáсовый, *adj.* (*geol.*) triassic.

трибрáхи|й, **я**, *m.* (*lit.*) tribrach.

трибýн, **а**, *m.* (*hist. or rhet.*) tribune.

трибýн|а, **ы**, *f.* 1. platform, rostrum; tribune. 2. stand (*at sports stadiums*).

трибунáл, **а**, *m.* tribunal.

тривиáльност|ь, **и**, *f.* triviality, banality; triteness.

тривиáл|ьный (∼ен, ∼ьна), *adj.* trivial, banal; trite, hackneyed.

триглúф, **а**, *m.* (*archit.*) triglyph.

тригонометрúческий, *adj.* trigonometric(al).

тригономéтри|я, **и**, *f.* trigonometry.

тридевя́т|ый, *adj.* в ∼ом цáрстве = за тридевять земéль.

тридевять: за т. земéль (*in legends and fig., coll.*) at the other end of the world.

тридцатилéти|е, **я**, *n.* 1. thirty years. 2. thirtieth anniversary.

тридцатилéтний, *adj.* 1. thirty-year. 2. thirty-year-old.

тридцáт|ый, *adj.* thirtieth; ∼ые гóды the thirties.

три́дцат|ь, и́, *i.* ью, *num.* thirty.

три́дцатью, *adv.* thirty times.

триеди́ный, *adj.* (*theol. and fig.*) triune.

три́ер, а, *m.* (*agric.*) separator, grader, sifter; grain cleaner.

три́жды, *adv.* three times, thrice.

три́зн|а, ы, *f.* (*hist.*) funeral feast.

трико́, *indecl.*, *n.* 1. tricot (*woollen fabric*). 2. tights. 3. (*women's stockinet*) knickers, pants.

трико́вый, *adj.* tricot.

трикота́ж, а, *m.* 1. stockinet, jersey. 2. (*collect.*) knitted wear, knitted garments.

трикота́жн|ый, *adj.* stockinet, jersey; knitted; ~ые изде́лия knitted wear; ~ая фа́брика knitted-goods factory.

триктра́к, а, *m.* backgammon.

трили́стник, а, *m.* (*bot.*) trefoil.

триллио́н, а, *m.* trillion.

трило́ги|я, и, *f.* trilogy.

триме́стр, а, *m.* term (*at educational establishment*).

триме́тр, а, *m.* (*lit.*) trimeter.

три́ммер, а, *m.* (*aeron. and electr.*) trimmer.

тринадцатиле́тний, *adj.* 1. thirteen-year. 2. thirteen-year-old.

трина́дцатый, *adj.* thirteenth.

трина́дцат|ь, и, *num.* thirteen.

трино́м, а, *m.* (*math.*) trinomial.

три́о, *indecl.*, *n.* (*mus.*) trio.

трио́д, а, *m.* (*radio*) triode.

трио́д|ь, и, *f.* (*eccl.*) service-book; по́стная т. book containing liturgy from Septuagesima to Easter; цветна́я т. book containing liturgy from Easter to All Saints' week.

триоле́т, а, *m.* (*lit.*) triolet.

трио́л|ь, и, *f.* (*mus.*) triplet.

трип, а, *m.* velveteen.

трипла́н, а, *m.* triplane.

три́плекс, а, *m.* triplex (*safety glass*).

три́ппер, а, *m.* (*med.*) gonorrhoea.

трипси́н, а, *m.* (*biol.*) trypsin.

трире́м|а, ы, *f.* trireme.

три́сел|ь, я, *m.* (*naut.*) trysail.

три́ста, трёхсо́т, трёмста́м, тремяста́ми, трёхста́х, *num.* three hundred.

трито́н, а, *m.* (*zool.*) triton.

триумвира́т, а, *m.* triumvirate.

триу́мф, а, *m.* triumph; с ~ом triumphantly, in triumph.

триумфа́льный, *adj.* triumphal.

триумфа́тор, а, *m.* triumpher; victor.

трифто́нг, а, *m.* triphthong.

трихи́н|а, ы, *f.* trichina (*parasitical worm*).

трихино́з, а, *m.* (*med.*) trichinosis.

троака́р, а, *m.* (*med.*) trocar.

тро́гател|ьный (~ен, ~ьна), *adj.* touching; moving, affecting.

тро́га|ть¹, ю, *impf.* (*of* тро́нуть) 1. to touch. 2. to disturb, trouble; не ~й его́! don't

disturb him!, leave him be! 3. to touch, move, affect; т. до слёз to move to tears.

тро́га|ть², ю, *impf.* (*of* тро́нуть) (*coll.*) to start; ну ~й! go ahead!, get going!

тро́га|ться¹, юсь, *impf.* (*of* тро́нуться¹) *pass.* *of* ~ть¹; to be touched, be moved, be affected.

тро́га|ться², юсь, *impf. of* тро́нуться².

троглоди́т, а, *m.* troglodyte (*also fig. of a person*).

тро́е, трои́х, *num.* (*preceding m. nouns denoting living beings and pluralia tantum*) three; т. су́ток seventy-two hours.

троебо́рь|е, я, *n.* (*sport*) triathlon.

троекра́тный, *adj.* thrice-repeated.

троепе́рсти|е, я, *n.* (*eccl.*) making the sign of the cross with three fingers.

тро|и́ть, ю́, и́шь, *impf.* 1. (*obs.*) to treble. 2. to divide into three.

тро|и́ться, и́тся, *impf.* 1. to be trebled. 2. to appear treble.

Тро́иц|а, ы, *f.* 1. (*theol.*) Trinity. 2. (*eccl.*) Trinity; Whitsun(day). 3. (*coll.*) trio.

Тро́ицын, *adj.* Т. день Trinity; Whitsun(day).

тро́йк|а, и, *f.* 1. three. 2. (*school mark*) three (*out of five*). 3. (*cards*) the three (*of a suit*). 4. troika. 5. (*coll.*) three-piece suit. 6. No. 3 'bus, tram, *etc.* 7. three-man commission.

тройни́к, а́, *m.* 1. object *or* measure containing three units. 2. (*tech.*) tee; T-joint, T-pipe, T-bend. 3. (*electr.*) branch box, T-junction box.

тройни́чный, *adj.* 1. triple. 2. (*anat.*) trigeminal, trifacial.

тройн|о́й, *adj.* triple, threefold, treble; т. кана́т three-ply rope; ~о́е пра́вило (*math.*) the rule of three; в ~о́м разме́ре threefold, treble.

тро́йн|я, и, *f.* triplets.

тро́йственн|ый, *adj.* triple; ~ое согла́сие (*hist.*) Triple Entente (*of England, France and Russia, concluded in 1907*).

трок, а, *m.* surcingle.

тролле́|й, я, *m.* (*tech.*) trolley.

тролле́йбус, а, *m.* trolley-bus.

тролле́йбус|ный, *adj. of* ~.

тромб, а, *m.* (*med.*) clot of blood.

тромбо́з, а, *m.* (*med.*) thrombosis.

тромбо́н, а, *m.* trombone.

тромбони́ст, а, *m.* trombonist.

тромбофлеби́т, а, *m.* (*med.*) thrombo-phlebitis.

трон, а, *m.* throne.

тро́нк|а, и, *f.* (*dial.*) sheep-bell.

тро́н|ный, *adj. of* ~; т. зал throne-room; ~ная речь king's speech.

тро́|нуть, ну, нешь, *pf. of* ~гать.

тро́|нуться¹, нусь, нешься, *pf.* 1. *pf. of*

~га́ться¹. 2. (*pf. only*) (*fig., coll.*) to be touched (= to lose one's mind); он немно́го ~ну́лся he is a bit touched, he is a bit cracked.

тро́|нуться², нусь, нешься, *pf.* (*of* ~га́ться²) 1. to start, set out; т. с ме́ста to make a move, get going; по́езд ~ну́лся the train started; лёд ~ну́лся the ice has begun to break (*also fig.*). 2. (*coll.*) to go bad.

троп, а, *m.* (*lit.*) trope.

троп|а́, ы́, *f.* path.

тропа́р|ь, я́, *m.* (*eccl.*) anthem (*for festival or saint's day*).

тро́пик, а, *m.* (*geogr.*) 1. tropic; т. Ра́ка tropic of Cancer; т. Козеро́га tropic of Capricorn. 2. (*pl.*) the tropics.

тропи́нк|а, и, *f.* path.

тропи́ческ|ий, *adj.* tropical; ~ая лихора́дка jungle fever; т. по́яс torrid zone.

тропосфе́р|а, ы, *f.* (*meteor.*) troposphere.

трос, а, *m.* rope, cable, hawser.

трости́нк|а, и, *f.* thin reed.

тростни́к, а́, *m.* reed; rush; са́харный т. sugar-cane.

тростнико́вый, *adj.* reed; т. са́хар cane-sugar.

тро́сточк|а, и, *f.* = трость.

трост|ь, и, *f.* cane, walking-stick.

троти́л, а, *m.* (*chem., mil.*) trotyl, trinitrotoluol (T.N.T.).

тротуа́р, а, *m.* pavement.

трофе́|й, я, *m.* trophy (*also fig.*); (*pl.*) spoils of war, booty; captured material.

трофе́йн|ый, *adj.* (*mil.*) captured; ~ая пу́шка captured gun; ~ое отделе́ние captured (enemy) материел section.

трофи́ческий, *adj.* (*anat.*) trophic.

трохеи́ческий, *adj.* (*lit.*) trochaic.

трохе́|й, я, *m.* (*lit.*) trochee.

троцки́зм, а, *m.* Trotskyism.

троцки́ст, а, *m.* Trotskyist, Trotskyite.

троцки́стский, *adj.* Trotskyist, Trotskyite.

трою́родн|ый, *adj.* т. брат, ~ая сестра́ second cousin; т. племя́нник second cousin once removed (*son of second cousin*).

троя́кий, *adj.* threefold, triple.

троя́ко, *adv.* in three (different) ways.

труб|а́, ы́, *pl.* ~ы, *f.* 1. (*in var. senses*) pipe; conduit; т. орга́на organ-pipe; подзо́рная т. telescope. 2. chimney, flue; funnel, smoke-stack. 3. (*mus.*) trumpet; игра́ть на ~е́ to play the trumpet. 4. (*anat.*) tube; duct. 5. *as symbol of failure or ruin*: де́ло т. (*coll.*) things are in a bad way; it's a wash-out; вы́лететь в ~у́ (*coll.*) to go bust, go smash; пусти́ть в ~у́ (*coll.*) to blow, squander.

трубаду́р, а, *m.* troubadour.

труба́ч, а́, *m.* trumpeter; trumpet-player.

труб|и́ть, лю́, и́шь, *impf.* 1. (в+*a.*; *mus.*) to

blow. 2. (*of trumpets, etc.*) to sound; to blare. 3. to sound (*by blast of trumpet, etc.*); т. сбор (*mil.*) to sound assembly. 4. (o+*p.*; *coll.*) to trumpet, proclaim from the house-tops.

тру́бк|а, и, *f.* 1. tube; pipe; сверну́ть ~ой to roll up. 2. (tobacco-)pipe; наби́ть ~у to fill a pipe. 3. (*mil., etc.*) fuse; т. уда́рного де́йствия instantaneous fuse; т. с замедли́телем delayed action fuse. 4. (*telephone*) receiver.

тру́бный, *adj.* trumpet; т. сигна́л trumpet-call; т. глас (*rel., lit.*) the last trump.

трубокла́д, а, *m.* pipe-installer.

тр穂олите́йный, *adj.* pipe-casting, tube-casting.

трубонарезно́й, *adj.* (*tech.*) pipe-threading.

трубопрово́д, а, *m.* pipe-line; piping, tubing; manifold.

трубопрока́тный, *adj.* (*tech.*) tube-rolling.

трубочи́ст, а, *m.* chimney-sweep.

трубочн|ый, *adj. of* тру́бка; т. таба́к pipe tobacco; ~ая гли́на pipeclay.

тру́бчатый, *adj.* tubular.

труве́р, а, *m.* (*hist. lit.*) trouvère.

труд, а́, *m.* 1. labour, work; лю́ди ~а́ the workers. 2. difficulty, trouble; взять на себя́ т., дать себе́ т. (+*inf.*) to take the trouble (to); не сто́ит ~а́ it is not worth the trouble; с ~о́м with difficulty, hardly. 3. (scholarly) work; (*pl., in titles of scholarly periodicals, etc.*) transactions.

тру|ди́ться, жу́сь, ~дишься, *impf.* to toil, labour, work; не ~ди́тесь! (please) don't trouble.

тру́дно, *as pred.* it is hard, it is difficult; т. сказа́ть it is hard to say; т. мне суди́ть it is hard for me to tell.

трудновоспиту́ем|ый (~, ~а), *adj.* т. ребёнок difficult child.

трудендоступ|ный (~ен, ~на), *adj.* difficult of access.

труднопроходи́мый, *adj.* difficult (to traverse).

тру́дност|ь, и, *f.* difficulty; obstacle.

тру́д|ный (~ен, ~на́, ~но), *adj.* 1. (*in var. senses*) difficult, hard; arduous. 2. difficult, awkward. 3. (*coll.; of illness*) serious, grave; т. больно́й patient seriously ill.

трудов|о́й, *adj.* 1. labour, work; т. день day's work; ~ая кни́жка work-book, work record; т. ко́декс Labour Code; ~ая пови́нность labour conscription; ~ое уве́чье industrial disablement. 2. working; living on one's own earnings; т. наро́д working people. 3. earned; hard-earned.

трудод|ень, ня, *m.* work-day (*unit of payment on collective farms*).

трудоём|кий (~ок, ~ка), *adj.* labour-consuming; labour-intensive.

трудолюби́в|ый (~, ~a), *adj.* hard-working, industrious.

трудолюби|е, я, *n.* industry; liking for hard work.

трудоспосо́бност|ь, и, *f.* ability to work, capacity for work.

трудоспосо́б|ный (~ен, ~на), *adj.* able--bodied; capable of working.

трудоустро́йств|о, а, *n.* placing in a job; resettlement (*of demobilized servicemen in civilian occupations*).

труд|я́щийся, *pres. part. of* ~и́ться *and adj.* working; *as noun* ~я́щиеся, ~я́щихся the working people, the workers.

тру́женик, а, *m.* toiler.

тру́жениц|а, ы, *f. of* тру́женик.

тру́жени|ческий, *adj. of* ~к; ~ческая жизнь life of toil.

трун|и́ть, ю́, и́шь, *impf.* (над; *coll.*) to make fun (of), mock.

труп, а, *m.* dead body, corpse; carcass.

тру́п|ный, *adj. of* ~; т. за́пах putrid smell; ~ное разложе́ние putrefaction; т. яд ptomaine; отравле́ние ~ным я́дом ptomaine poisoning.

тру́пп|а, ы, *f.* troupe, company.

трус, а, *m.* coward; ~а пра́здновать (*coll.*) to show the white feather.

тру́сик|и, ов, *no sing.* shorts; swimming trunks.

тру́|сить, шу, сишь, *impf.* (*of* с~) 1. to be a coward; to funk; to have cold feet. 2. (пе́ред *or* +а.) to be afraid (of), be frightened (of).

тру|си́ть¹, шу́, си́шь, *impf.* (*of* на~) to shake out, scatter.

тру|си́ть², шу́, си́шь, *impf.* to trot, jog.

труси́х|а, и, *f. of* трус.

трусли́в|ый (~, ~a), *adj.* 1. cowardly. 2. faint-hearted, timorous; apprehensive.

тру́сост|ь, и, *f.* cowardice.

трусц|а́, ы́, *f.* (*coll.*) jog-trot.

трус|ы́, о́в, *no sing.* = ~ики.

трут, а, *m.* tinder; amadou.

тру́т|ень, ня, *m.* drone (*also fig.*).

тру́тник, а, *m.* tinder-fungus, punk.

трутови́к, а́, *m.* (*bot.*) polyporus, tree--fungus.

трух|а́, и́, *f.* dust (*of rotted wood*); hay-dust; (*fig.*) trash.

трухля́ве|ть, ет, *impf.* to moulder.

трухля́в|ый (~, ~a), *adj.* mouldering; rotten.

трущо́б|а, ы, *f.* 1. overgrown place (*in forest, etc.*). 2. (*fig.*) hole, out-of-the-way place. 3. slum. 4. (*coll.*) thieves' den.

трын-трава́, *as pred.* (+*d.*; *coll.*) it makes no odds, it's all the same.

трюи́зм, а, *m.* truism, platitude.

трюк, а, *m.* 1. feat, stunt. 2. (*fig., pejor.*) trick.

трюка́ч, а́, *m.* crafty, wily person.

трюка́чес|кий, *adj. of* ~тво; т. приём crafty trick, stunt.

трюка́честв|о, а, *n.* (*pejor.*) craft, wiliness.

трю́к|овый, *adj. of* ~ 1; т. но́мер turn.

трюм, а, *m.* (*naut.*) hold.

трю́м|ный, *adj. of* ~.

трюмо́, *indecl., n.* 1. cheval-glass, pier-glass. 2. (*archit.*) pier.

трю́фел|ь, я, *pl.* ~и, ~е́й, *m.* truffle.

тряпи́ц|а, ы, *f.* (*coll.*) rag.

тряпи́чник, а, *m.* rag (-and-bone) merchant.

тряпи́чниц|а, ы, *f. of* тряпи́чник.

тряпи́чный, *adj.* 1. rag. 2. (*coll., pejor.*) soft, spineless.

тря́пк|а, и, *f.* 1. rag; duster. 2. (*pl., coll.*) finery, glad rags. 3. (*coll., pejor.*) milksop, spineless creature.

тряпь|ё, я́, *n.* (*collect.*) rags; (*coll.*) clothes, things.

тряси́н|а, ы, *f.* quagmire.

тря́ск|а, и, *f.* shaking, jolting.

тря́с|кий (~ок, ~ка), *adj.* 1. shaky, jolty. 2. bumpy.

трясогу́зк|а, и, *f.* (*orn.*) wagtail.

тряс|ти́, у́, ёшь, *past* ~, ~ла́, *impf.* 1. to shake; т. кому́-н. ру́ку to shake someone's hand. 2. to shake out. 3. to cause to shake, cause to shiver (*usu. impers.*); его́ ~ла́ лихора́дка he was in the grip of a fever; её ~ло́ от стра́ха she was trembling with fear. 4. (+*i.*) to swing; to shake; т. гри́вой (*of an animal*) to toss its mane. 5. (*coll.*) to jolt, be jolty.

тряс|ти́сь, у́сь, ёшься, *past* ~ся, ~ла́сь, *impf.* 1. to shake; to tremble, shiver; т. от сме́ха to shake with laughter; т. от хо́лода to shiver with cold. 2. (*coll.*) to bump along, jog along; to be jolted. 3. (над; *coll.*) to watch (over) (= to fear to lose); они́ ~у́тся над ка́ждой копе́йкой they watch every penny.

тряхн|у́ть, у́, ёшь, *impf.* 1. to shake. 2. т. старино́й (*coll.*) to hark back to days of yore, revive the customs of the (good) old days; т. мо́лодостью (*coll.*) to hark back to (the days of) one's youth. 3. (+*i.*; *coll.*) to make free (with); т. мошно́й, карма́ном to throw one's money about, open one's purse-strings.

тсс, *interj.* ssh!, hush!

туале́т, а, *m.* 1. dress; toilet. 2. toilet, dressing; соверша́ть т. (*obs.*) to make one's toilet, dress. 3. dressing-table. 4. lavatory, toilet; public convenience.

туале́т|ный, *adj. of* ~; ~ная бума́га toilet--paper; ~ное мы́ло toilet-soap; ~ные принадле́жности toilet articles; т. сто́лик dressing-table.

туалéтчик, а, *m.* lavatory attendant.

туалéтчиц|а, ы, *f. of* туалéтчик.

тýб|а¹, ы, *f.* (*mus.*) tuba.

тýб|а², ы, *f.* tube.

туберкулёз, а, *m.* tuberculosis; т. лёгких pulmonary tuberculosis, consumption.

туберкулёзник, а, *m.* (*coll.*) 1. tuberculosis specialist. 2. tubercular patient; consumptive.

туберкулёз|ный, *adj. of* ~; т. больнóй tubercular patient; consumptive; ~ная пáлочка tuberculosis bacillus; *as noun* **т.,** ~**ного,** *m.*; ~**ная,** ~**ной,** *f.* = т. больнóй; ~ная больнáя.

туберóз|а, ы, *f.* (*bot.*) tuberose.

тувúн|ец, ца, *m.* Tuvinian.

тувúн|ка, ки, *f.* Tuvinian (woman).

тувúнский, *adj.* Tuvinian.

тýго, *adv.* 1. tight(ly), taut; т. набúть чемодáн to pack a suitcase tight; т. натянýть to stretch tight, taut. 2. with difficulty; т. продвигáться вперёд to make slow progress. 3. *as pred.* т. прихóдиться (+*d.*; *coll.*) to have difficulties, be in straits, be in a spot; с деньгáми у нас т. we are in a tight spot financially.

тугодýм, а, *m.* (*coll.*) slow-witted person.

туг|óй (~, ~á, ~о), *adj.* 1. tight; taut; т. ýзел tight knot; т. воротничóк tight collar. 2. tightly-filled; т. кошелёк tightly-stuffed purse. 3. т. нá ухо hard of hearing. 4.(*fig., coll.*) tight, close (*with money*); т. на распла́ту close-fisted. 5. (*fig., coll.*) difficult; делá у них ~úе they are in a (tight) spot.

тугоплáв|кий (~ок, ~ка), *adj.* (*tech.*) refractory.

тугоýздый, *adj.* (*of a horse*) hard-mouthed.

тýгрик, а, *m.* tugrik (*unit of currency of Mongolian People's Republic*).

тудá, *adv.* there, thither; that way; to the right place; т. и обрáтно there and back; билéт т. и обрáтно return ticket; не т.! not that way!; ни т. ни сюдá neither one way nor the other; вы не т. попáли (*on telephone*) you have got the wrong number; т. емý и дорóга (*coll.*) it serves him right; т. же (*coll.*) the same, likewise, following suit (*of someone attempting something of which he is not capable or to which he has not the right; also as interj.*).

тудá-сюдá, *adv.* (*coll.*) 1. hither and thither. 2. *as pred.* it will do, it will pass muster.

тý|евый, *adj. of* ~я.

тýер, а, *m.* (*naut.*) chain-tug.

тýже, *comp. of* тугóй *and* тýго.

туж|úть, ý, ~ишь, *impf.* (о, по+*p.*; *coll.*) to grieve (for).

тýж|иться, усь, ишься, *impf.* (*coll.*) to make an effort.

тужýрк|а, и, *f.* (*man's*) double-breasted jacket.

туз¹, á, *m.* 1. (*cards*) ace; пойтú с ~á to lead an ace; т. к мáсти (*coll.*) just the job. 2. (*coll.*) bigwig, big pot; big shot.

туз², а, *m.* two-oar dinghy.

тузéм|ец, ца, *m.* native.

тузéм|ка, ки, *f. of* ~ец.

тузéмный, *adj.* native, indigenous.

ту|зúть, жý, зúшь, *impf.* (*of* от~) (*coll.*) to punch; to pummel.

тук¹, а, *m.* 1. (*obs.*) fat. 2. (*pl.*) mineral fertilizers.

тук², *as pred.* = ~нул.

тýк|ать, аю, *impf.* (*of* ~нуть) (*coll.*) to bash, bonk.

тýк|нуть, ну, нешь, *pf. of* ~ать.

тýк|нуться, нусь, нешься, *pf.* (о+*a.*; *coll.*) to bang oneself (against, on).

тýковый, *adj.* fertilizer.

тук-тýк, *interj.* (*coll.*) rat-tat (*also as pred.*).

тýлли|й, я, *m.* (*chem.*) thulium.

тýловищ|е, а, *n.* trunk; torso.

тулумбáс, а, *m.* 1. big drum, bass drum. 2. (*coll., joc.*) punch; дать комý-н. ~а to punch someone.

тулýп, а, *m.* sheepskin (*or* hareskin) coat.

тул|ья́, ьи́, *g. pl.* ~éй, *f.* crown (*of headgear*).

туляремú|я, и, *f.* (*med.*) tularaemia.

тумáк¹, á, *m.* (*coll.*) cuff, punch.

тумáк², á, *m.* tunny(-fish).

тумáн, а, *m.* fog; mist, haze; у негó был т. в глазáх there was a mist before his eyes; у меня т. в головé (*fig.*) I see no light, I am groping in the dark; напустúть ~у (*coll.*) to obscure the issue.

тумáн|ить, ит, *impf.* to dim, cloud, obscure (*also fig.*).

тумáн|иться, ится, *impf.* 1. to grow misty, grow hazy; to become enveloped in mist. 2. (*fig., coll.*) to be in a fog, be befogged.

тумáнно, *as pred.* it is foggy, it is misty.

тумáнност|ь, и, *f.* 1. fog, mist. 2. (*astron.*) nebula. 3. haziness, obscurity.

тумáн|ный (~ен, ~на), *adj.* 1. foggy; misty; hazy; ~ная полосá fog patch. 2. (*fig.*) dull, lacklustre. 3. (*fig.*) hazy, obscure, vague. 4. (*obs.*) ~ные картúны (magic) lantern slides.

тýмб|а, ы, *f.* 1. curbstone; post; причáльная т. (*naut.*) bollard. 2. pedestal. 3. advertisement hoarding (*of cylindrical shape*). 4. (*fig., joc.*; *of a person*) lump.

тýмбочк|а, и, *f.* 1. bedside table. 2. *dim. of* тýмба.

тунг, а, *m.* tung-tree.

тýнг|овый, *adj. of* ~; ~овое мáсло tung-oil.

тýндр|а, ы, *f.* (*geogr.*) tundra.

тýндр|еный, *adj.* = ~овый.

тýндр|овый, *adj. of* ~а.

тун|е́ц, ца́, *m.* tunny(-fish).

тунея́д|ец, ца, *m.* parasite, sponger.

тунея́дств|о, а, *n.* parasitism, sponging.

тунея́дств|овать, ую, *impf.* to be a parasite; to sponge.

туннѐ́л|ь, я, *m.* tunnel; subway.

туннѐ́ль|ный, *adj. of* ~.

тупе́|й, я, *m.* (*obs.*) tuft of hair.

тупе́|ть, ю, *impf.* (*of* о~) to become blunt; to grow dull.

ту́пик, а, *m.* (*orn.*) puffin.

тупи́к, а́, *m.* 1. blind alley, cul-de-sac. 2. (*railways*) siding. 3. (*fig.*) impasse, deadlock; зайти́ в т. to reach a deadlock. 4. поста́вить в т. to stump, nonplus; стать в т. to be stumped, be nonplussed, be at a loss.

туп|и́ть, лю́, ~ишь, *impf.* to blunt.

туп|и́ться, ~ится, *impf.* to become blunt.

тупи́ц|а, ы, *m. and f.* (*coll.*) dolt, blockhead, dimwit.

тупоголо́в|ый (~, ~a), *adj.* (*coll.*) dim-witted.

туп|о́й (~, ~а́, ~о), *adj.* 1. blunt. 2. т. у́гол (*math.*) obtuse angle. 3. (*fig.*) dull (*pain, sensation, etc.*). 4. (*fig.*) vacant, stupid, meaningless; ~а́я улы́бка vacant smile. 5. (*fig.*) dull, obtuse; slow; dim; т. ум dull wits. 6. (*fig.*) blind, unquestioning; ~а́я поко́рность blind submission.

тупоконе́чн|ый, *adj.* blunt-pointed; ~ая пу́ля blunt-nosed bullet.

туполо́б|ый (~, ~а), *adj.* (*coll.*) dull, dim-witted.

тупоно́с|ый (~, ~а), *adj.* blunt-nosed (*also fig.*).

ту́пост|ь, и, f. 1. bluntness. 2. (*fig.*) vacancy. 3. (*fig.*) dullnesss, slowness.

тупоу́ми|е, я, *n.* dullness, obtuseness.

тупоу́м|ный (~ен, ~на), *adj.* dull, obtuse.

тур¹, а, *m.* 1. turn (*in a dance*). 2. (*at sports and games; also fig.*) round.

тур², а, *m.* (*obs.*) gabion.

тур³, а, *m.* (*zool.*) 1. aurochs. 2. Caucasian goat (*Capra caucasica*).

тур|а́, ы́, f. (*chess*) castle, rook.

турба́з|а, ы, f. tourist centre.

турби́н|а, ы, f. (*tech.*) turbine.

турби́нный, *adj.* turbine.

турбовинтово́й, *adj.* (*tech., aeron.*) turbo-prop.

турбово́з, а, *m.* turbine locomotive.

турбогенера́тор, а, *m.* (*tech.*) turbo-alternator.

турбореакти́вный, *adj.* (*tech., aeron.*) turbo-jet.

туре́л|ь, и, f. (*mil.*) (gun-)turret; ring mount(ing).

туре́цк|ий, *adj.* Turkish; т. бараба́н big drum, bass drum; ~ие бобы́ haricot beans;

т. горо́х chick pea; ~ая му́зыка (*mus.*; *obs.*) percussion instruments; ~ая пшени́ца (*obs.*) maize; гол, как т. свято́й (*coll.*) poor as a church mouse.

тури́зм, а, *m.* tourism; во́дный т. boating; го́рный т. mountaineering.

ту́рий, *adj. of* тур³.

тури́ст, а, *m.* tourist, hiker.

туристи́ческ|ий, *adj.* tourist; т. похо́д walking tour; ~ие путеше́ствия travels.

тури́ст|ка, ки, f. of ~.

тури́стск|ий, *adj.* tourist; ~ая ба́за tourist centre.

тур|и́ть, ю́, и́шь, *impf.* (*coll.*) to throw out, chuck out.

туркме́н, а, *m.* Turkmen.

туркме́нк|а, и, f. Turkmen (woman).

туркме́нский, *adj.* Turkmen.

ту́рман, а, *m.* tumbler-pigeon; полете́ть ~ом (*coll.*) to fall down head over heels.

турне́, *indecl.*, *n.* tour (*esp. of troupe of artistes or of sportsmen*).

турне́пс, а, *m.* swede.

турни́к, а́, *m.* (*sport*) horizontal bar.

турнике́т, а, *m.* 1. turnstile. 2. (*med.*) tourniquet.

турни́р, а, *m.* tournament (*at chess, etc., also hist.*).

турн|у́ть, у́, ёшь, *pf.* (*coll.*) to chuck out.

турню́р, а, *m.* bustle.

ту́р|ок, ка, g. pl. т., m. Turk.

турпа́н, а, *m.* (*orn.*) scoter.

туру́с|ы, ов, no sing. (*coll.*) idle gossip; т. на колёсах nonsense, rubbish, twaddle.

турухта́н, а, *m.* (*orn.*) ruff (*Philomachus pugnax*).

турча́нк|а, и, f. Turkish woman.

ту́скл|ый (~, ~а́, ~о), *adj.* 1. dim, dull; matt; tarnished. 2. wan; lacklustre. 3. (*fig.*) dim, dull; colourless; tame; т. го́лос flat voice; т. стиль colourless style.

тускне́|ть, ет, *impf.* (*of* по~) 1. to grow dim, grow dull; to tarnish; to grow wan, lose its lustre. 2. (пе́ред; *fig.*) to pale (before, by the side of).

ту́скн|уть, ет, *impf.* (*coll.*) = ~е́ть.

тут, *adv.* 1. here; кто т.? who's there?; и всё т. (*coll.*) and that's it, and that was that; т. как т. (*coll.*) there he is, there they are. 2. now; т. же there and then.

ту́товник, а, *m.* 1. mulberry (tree). 2. mulberry grove.

ту́тов|ый, *adj.* mulberry; ~ое де́рево mulberry (tree); т. шелкопря́д silkworm.

ту́т-то, *adv.* (*coll.*) 1. right here. 2. there and then. 3. не т.-то бы́ло! nothing of the sort!, far from it!

туф, а, *m.* (*geol., min.*) tufa; tuff.

ту́фл|я, и, f. shoe; slipper.

ту́ф|овый, *adj. of* ~.

тухли́нк|а, и, *f.* (*coll.*) bad smell.

ту́хл|ый (~, ~á, ~о), *adj.* rotten, bad; ~ое мя́со tainted meat.

тухля́тин|а, ы, *f.* (*coll.*) bad food; tainted meat.

ту́х|нуть¹, нет, *past* ~, ~ла, *impf.* (*of* по~) (*of source of light or heat*) to go out.

ту́х|нуть², нет, *past* ~, ~ла, *impf.* to go bad, become rotten.

ту́ч|а, и, *f.* 1. (rain) cloud; storm-cloud (*also fig.*); не из ~и гром a bolt from the blue; ~и собрали́сь, нави́сли (над) (*fig.*) the clouds are gathering (over). 2. *as symbol of sombre appearance or gloomy mood*: смотре́ть ~ей to look black, scowl, lour; сиде́ть т.-~ей to be in a black mood. 3. cloud, swarm, host; т.-~ей in a swarm.

ту́ч|ево́й, *adj. of* ~а.

ту́чк|а, и, *f. dim. of* ту́ча.

тучне́|ть, ю, *impf.* (*of* по~) 1. to grow stout, grow fat. 2. (*of soil*) to become fertile.

ту́чност|ь, и, *f.* 1. fatness, stoutness, obesity, corpulence. 2. (*of soil*) richness, fertility.

ту́ч|ный (~ен, ~на́, ~но), *adj.* 1. fat, stout, obese, corpulent. 2. (*of soil*) rich, fertile. 3. (*of grass*) succulent.

туш, а, *m.* (*mus.*) flourish.

ту́ш|а, и, *f.* carcass. 2. (*fig.*; *of a fat man*) hulk.

туше́, *indecl., n.* 1. (*mus.*) touch. 2. (*fencing*) touché.

туш|ева́ть, у́ю, *impf.* (*of* за~) to shade.

туше́вк|а, и, *f.* shading.

тушёный, *adj.* (*cul.*) braised, stewed.

туш|и́ть¹, у́, ~ишь, *impf.* (*of* по~) 1. to extinguish, put out. 2. (*fig.*) to suppress, stifle, quell.

туш|и́ть², у́, ~ишь, *impf.* (*cul.*) to braise, stew.

тушка́нчик, а, *m.* jerboa.

туш|ь, и, *f.* Indian ink.

ту́|я, и, *f.* (*bot.*) thuya.

тща́ни|е, я, *n.* (*obs.*) zeal, assiduity.

тща́тельност|ь, и, *f.* thoroughness, carefulness; care.

тща́тел|ьный (~ен, ~ьна), *adj.* thorough, careful; painstaking.

тщеду́ши|е, я, *n.* feebleness, frailty; debility.

тщеду́ш|ный (~ен, ~на), *adj.* feeble, frail, weak; puny.

тщесла́ви|е, я, *n.* vanity, vainglory.

тщесла́в|ный (~ен, ~на), *adj.* vain, vainglorious.

тщет|а́, ы́, *f.* vanity.

тще́тно, *adv.* vainly, in vain.

тще́тност|ь, и, *f.* futility, vainness.

тще́т|ный (~ен, ~на), *adj.* vain, futile; unavailing.

тщ|и́ться, усь, и́шься, *impf.* (+*inf.*; *obs.*) to try (to), endeavour (to).

ты, тебя́, тебе́, тобо́й (*and* тобо́ю), о тебе́, *2nd sing. personal pron.* you; thou; быть „на ты" (с+*i.*), говори́ть „ты" (+*d.*) to be on familiar terms (with).

ты́|кать¹, чу, чешь, *impf.* (*of* ткнуть) 1. (+*i.* в+*a.* or +*a.* в+*a.*) to stick (into) (*also fig.*); to poke (into); to prod; to jab (into); т. була́вкой во что-н. to stick a pin into something; т. па́лкой to prod with a stick; т. ко́лья в зе́млю to stick stakes into the ground; т. (свой) нос (в+*a.*; *fig., pejor.*) to stick, poke one's nose (into); т. в нос кому́-н. чем-н. (*fig., coll.*) to cast something in someone's teeth; т. кого́-н. но́сом во что-н. (*fig., coll.*) to rub someone's nose in something. 2. т. па́льцем (на+*a.*; *coll.*) to point (at), poke one's finger (at).

ты́|кать², ю, *impf.* (*coll.*) to address as „ты"; to be on familiar terms (with).

ты́|каться, чусь, чешься, *impf.* (*of* ткну́ться) (*coll.*) 1. (в+*a.*) to knock (against, into). 2. to rush about, fuss about.

ты́кв|а, ы, *f.* pumpkin; gourd.

ты́кв|енный, *adj. of* ~а; *as noun* ~енные, ~енных (*bot.*) gourd family, Cucurbitaceae.

тыл, а, о ~е, в ~у́, *pl.* ~ы́, *m.* 1. back, rear. 2. (*mil.*) rear; home front; напа́сть с ~а to attack in the rear. 3. (*pl.*; *mil.*) rear services, rear organizations. 4. the (whole) country (*as opp. to front or frontier areas*), the interior.

тылови́к, а́, *m.* (*mil.*) man serving in rear.

тылово́|й, *adj.* (*mil.*) rear; ~ая часть service element (*of unit.*); т. го́спиталь base hospital.

ты́льн|ый, *adj.* 1. back, rear; ~ая пове́рхность руки́ back of the hand. 2. (*mil.*) rear; ~ая заста́ва, ~ая часть rear party; т. тра́верс parados.

тын, а, *m.* paling; palisade, stockade.

ты́сяцк|ий, ого, *m.* 1. (*hist.*) captain, leader. 2. (*obs. or dial.*) master of ceremonies (*at peasant wedding ceremony*).

ты́сяч|а, и, *i.* ~ей *and* ~ью, *num. and noun, f.* thousand; в ~у раз a thousand times (*also fig.*).

тысячеле́ти|е, я, *n.* 1. a thousand years; millennium. 2. thousandth anniversary.

тысячеле́тний, *adj.* thousand-year; millennial.

ты́сячник, а, *m.* (*coll.*) 1. record-breaking worker (*with production figures of so many thousand units*). 2. person with capital amounting to thousands.

ты́сячн|ый, *adj.* 1. thousandth; *as noun* ~ая, ~ой, *f.* thousandth. 2. of many thousands. 3. worth a thousand, many thousand roubles.

тычи́нк|а, и, *f.* (*bot.*) stamen.

тыч|о́к, ка́, *m.* 1. sharp object sticking up; быть, сиде́ть на ~ке́ (*i*) to be in an uncomfortable position, (*ii*) (*fig.*) to be conspicuously perched. **2.** (*tech.*) bond-stone; header. **3.** hit, prod, jab.

тьм|а¹, ы, *no pl., f.* darkness (*also fig.* = *ignorance*); т. еги́петская, т. кроме́шная outer darkness (*bibl.*), pitch darkness.

тьм|а², ы, *g. pl.* **тем,** *f.* **1.** (*arch.*) ten thousand. **2.** (*coll.*) host, swarm, multitude; т.-тьму́щая countless multitudes.

тьфу, *interj.* (*coll.*) pah!; т., про́пасть! confound it!

тюбете́йк|а, и, tyubeteyka (*embroidered skull-cap worn in Central Asia*).

тю́бик, а, *m.* tube (*of tooth-paste, etc.*).

тю́бинг, а, *m.* (*tech.*) tubing.

тюк, а́, *m.* bale, package.

тюк|ать, аю, *impf.* (*of* ~нуть) (*coll.*) to chop, hack.

тюк|нуть, ну, нешь, *pf. of* ~ать.

тю́левый, *adj.* (*text.*) tulle.

тюле́невый, *adj.* sealskin.

тюле́н|ий, *adj. of* ~ь; т. про́мысел sealing, seal-fishery.

тюле́нин|а, ы, *f.* seal-meat.

тюле́н|ь, я, *m.* **1.** (*zool.*) seal, **2.** (*fig., coll.*) clumsy clot.

тюл|ь, я, *m.* (*text.*) tulle.

тюльпа́н, а, *m.* **1.** tulip. **2.** (*obs.*) (glass) lamp-shade.

тюльпа́н|ный, *adj. of* ~; ~ное де́рево tulip-tree.

тюни́к|а, и, *f.* **1.** (*obs.*) over-skirt. **2.** ballerina's dress.

тюрба́н, а, *m.* turban.

тюр|е́мный, *adj. of* ~ьма́; ~е́мное заключе́ние imprisonment.

тюрк, а, *m.* (*ethnol.*) Turki (*member of ethnic group having Turkic language*).

тю́ркский, *adj.* (*ethnol., ling.*) Turkic.

тюр|ьма́, ьмы́, *pl.* ~ьмы, ~ем, *f.* **1.** prison; jail, gaol; заключи́ть в ~ьму́ to put into prison, imprison, jail; сиде́ть в ~ьме́ to be in prison. **2.** imprisonment.

тюр|я, и, *f.* (*cul.*) tyurya (*a pulp of bread and milk, water, or kvass*).

тю́тельк|а, и, *f.* т. в ~у (*coll.*) exactly, to a T.

тю́тька|ться, юсь, *impf.* (с+*i.*; *coll., pejor.*) to nursemaid.

тю-тю́, *as pred.* (*coll., joc.*) it's all gone; we've (you've, they've) had it.

тютю́н, а́, *m.* (*dial.*) shag (tobacco).

тюфя́к, а́, *m.* **1.** mattress (*filled with straw, hay, etc.*). **2.** (*fig., coll.*) flabby fellow.

тюфя́|чный, *adj. of* ~к.

тя́вк|ать, аю, *impf.* (*of* ~нуть) to yap, yelp.

тя́вк|нуть, ну, нешь, *pf. of* ~ать.

тяг, у, *m.*; дать ~у (*coll.*) to take to one's heels, show a clean pair of heels.

тя́г|а¹, и, *f.* **1.** traction; locomotion; си́ла ~и tractive force; на ко́нной ~е horse-drawn. **2.** (*collect.*) locomotives. **3.** (*aeron.*) thrust. **4.** (*in boiler chimney, etc.*) draught; регуля́тор ~и damper. **5.** (к, на+*a*; *fig.*) pull (towards), attraction (towards), thirst (for), craving (for), taste (for); bent (for), inclination (to, for); т. к зна́нию thirst for knowledge; он испы́тывает си́льную ~у к Восто́ку he is strongly drawn towards the East.

тя́г|а², и, *f.* flight (*esp. of woodcock*) at mating-season, *etc.*

тяга́|ть, ю, *impf.* (*coll.*) to pull (up, out); т. лён to pull flax.

тяга́|ться, юсь, *impf.* (*of* по~) (с+*i.*) **1.** (*obs.*) to be at law (with). **2.** to have a tug-of-war (with). **3.** (*coll.*) to contend (with), vie (with), measure one's strength (with).

тяга́ч, а́, *m.* tractor (*for pulling train of trailers*).

тя́гл|о¹, а, *n.* (*collect.*) draught animals.

тя́гл|о², а, *g. pl.* **тя́гол,** *n.* (*hist.*) **1.** tax, impost. **2.** household (*as unit for tax assessment*). **3.** dues (*corvée, quit-rent, etc.*). **4.** strip of land (*worked by one household*).

тя́гловый¹, *adj.* = тя́глый.

тя́гловый², *adj.* (*hist.*) taxed, liable to tax.

тя́глый, *adj.* draught (*of cattle*).

тя́гов|ый, *adj.* traction, tractive; т. кана́т hauling rope; т. крюк trace hook, towing hook, drawbar hook; т. сте́ржень drawbar; ~ая си́ла tractive force.

тягоме́р, а, *m.* (*tech.*) draught gauge; suction gauge; blast meter.

тя́гост|ный (~ен, ~на), *adj.* **1.** burdensome, onerous. **2.** painful, distressing; ~ное зре́лище painful spectacle.

тя́гост|ь, и, *f.* **1.** weight, burden; быть кому́-н. в т. to be a burden to someone, weigh on someone. **2.** fatigue.

тягот|а́, ы́, *pl.* **тя́готы,** *f.* weight, burden.

тяготе́ни|е, я, *n.* **1.** (*phys.*) gravity, gravitation; зако́н (всеми́рного) ~я law of gravity. **2.** (к) attraction (towards), taste (for); bent (for), inclination (to, for); т. к детекти́вным рома́нам taste for detective stories.

тяготе́|ть, ю, *impf.* **1.** (к) (*phys.*) to gravitate (towards). **2.** (к) (*fig.*) to gravitate (towards), be drawn (by, towards); be attracted (by, towards). **3.** (над) to hang (over), threaten; стра́шный рок ~ет над на́ми a terrible fate hangs over us.

тяго|ти́ть, щу́, ти́шь, *impf.* to burden, be a burden (on, to); to lie heavy (on), oppress.

тягу́чест|ь, и, *f.* **1.** malleability, ductility. **2.** viscosity.

тягу́ч|ий (~, ~а), *adj.* **1.** malleable, ductile. **2.** viscous. **3.** (*fig.*) slow, leisurely, unhurried.

тягча́йш|ий, *superl. of* тя́жкий; ~ее преступле́ние very serious crime.

тяж, а́, *m.* **1.** (*tech.*) drawing rod; т. то́рмозного ва́ла brake rod. **2.** shaft brace.

тя́жб|а, ы, *f.* **1.** (*obs.*) (civil) suit, lawsuit; litigation. **2.** (*fig., coll.*) competition, rivalry.

тя́ж|ебный, *adj. of* ~ба 1.

тяжел|е́е, *comp. of* ~ый *and* ~о́.

тяжеле́|ть, ю, *impf.* **1.** to become heavier; to put on weight. **2.** to become heavy with sleep (*of eyes*).

тяжело́[1], *adv.* **1.** heavily. **2.** seriously, gravely; т. бо́лен seriously ill. **3.** with difficulty.

тяжело́[2], *as pred.* **1.** it is hard; it is painful, it is distressing. **2.** ему́, *etc.*, т. he, *etc.*, feels miserable, wretched.

тяжелоатле́т, а, *m.* weight-lifter; athlete competing in weight-lifting and/or wrestling.

тяжелоатлети́ческ|ий, *adj.* ~ое состяза́ние meeting, competition comprising weight-lifting and/or wrestling.

тяжелове́с[1], а, *m.* (*sport*) heavyweight.

тяжелове́с[2], а, *m.* (*min.*) Siberian topaz.

тяжелове́с|ный (~ен, ~на), *adj.* **1.** heavily-loaded; т. соста́в heavy goods train. **2.** (*fig., pejor.*) heavy, ponderous; clumsy, unwieldy; heavy-handed; ~ная остро́та ponderous witticism.

тяжелово́з, а, *m.* **1.** heavy draught-horse. **2.** heavy lorry.

тяжелогру́зный, *adj.* heavy(-load).

тяжелоду́м, а, *m.* (*coll.*) slow-witted person.

тяжёл|ый (~, ~а́), *adj.* **1.** (*in var. senses*) heavy; т. чемода́н heavy suitcase; ~ая артилле́рия heavy artillery; ~ая вода́ (*chem.*) heavy water; ~ое дыха́ние heavy breathing; ~ая промы́шленность heavy industry; ~ое то́пливо heavy fuel (*oil, petrol*); т. шаг heavy step, tread. **2.** *expresses idea of excessive, disagreeable heaviness*: т. во́здух close air; т. за́пах oppressive, strong smell; ~ая пи́ща heavy, indigestible food. **3.** hard, difficult; ~ая зада́ча hard task; ~ые ро́ды difficult confinement. **4.** slow; т. ум slow brain, wits; т. на подъём hard to move, sluggish. **5.** heavy, severe; ~ые поте́ри heavy casualties; ~ое наказа́ние severe punishment; т. уда́р severe blow. **6.** (*of illness, etc.*) serious, grave, bad; seriously ill; ~ое ране́ние serious injury, wound. **7.** heavy, hard, painful; ~ое чу́вство heavy heart; misgivings; ~ые времена́ hard times; ~ая обя́занность painful duty; т. день bad (= unsuccessful) day. **8.** (*of character*) difficult. **9.** (*of lit. style, etc.*) heavy, ponderous unwieldy.

тя́жест|ь, и, *f.* **1.** (*phys.*) gravity; центр ~и

centre of gravity (*also fig.*); (*fig.*) gravamen. **2.** weight, heavy object; подня́тие ~ей (*sport*) weight-lifting. **3.** weight, heaviness; вся т. чего́-н. (*fig.*) the whole weight, the brunt of something; т. ули́к weight of evidence. **4.** difficulty. **5.** heaviness, severity.

тя́ж|кий (~ек, ~ка́, ~ко), *adj.* **1.** (*fig.*) heavy, hard. **2.** severe; serious, grave; ~кая боле́знь dangerous illness; ~кое преступле́ние grave crime; т. уда́р severe blow. **3.** пусти́ться во все ~кие (*coll.*) to plunge into dissipation.

тяжкоду́м, а, *m.* (*coll.*) slow-witted person.

тя́жущийся, *adj.* litigant.

тяну́льный, *adj.* (*tech.*) stretching.

тян|у́ть, у́, ~ешь, *impf.* **1.** to pull, draw; to haul; to drag; т. на букси́ре to tow; т. кого́-н. за рука́в to pull someone by the sleeve, tug at someone's sleeve; т. кого́-н. за́ душу to torment someone; т. ля́мку (*coll.*) to drudge, toil. **2.** (*tech.*) to draw (*wire*). **3.** to lay; to put up (*wire, cable, etc.*); т. телефо́нную ли́нию to lay a telephone cable. **4.** т. жре́бий to draw lots. **5.** (*fig.*) to draw, attract; меня́, *etc.*, ~ет I long, I want; его́ ~ет домо́й he wants to go home; меня́ ~ет ко сну I feel sleepy; нас ~ет на Юг we are drawn towards, attracted by the South; меня́ ~ет купа́ться I'm dying for a swim. **6.** to drawl, drag out; т. слова́ to drawl; т. но́ту to sustain a note. **7.** to drag out, protract, delay; т. с отве́том to delay one's answer, delay over answering. **8.** to weigh (*intrans.*). **9.** to draw up; to take in, suck in; т. в себя́ во́здух to inhale deeply; т. че́рез соло́минку to suck through a straw. **10.** (из, с) to extract (from); to extort (from), squeeze (out of); т. все си́лы из кого́-н. to exhaust all the strength from someone. **11.** (*of a chimney, etc.*) to draw; печь пло́хо ~ет the stove is not drawing well. **12.** *impers.* +*i.*; *of a stream of air, of a smell*: ~ет хо́лодом из-под две́ри there is a draught coming from beneath the door; от поле́й ~у́ло за́пахом се́на a smell of hay was wafted from the fields. **13.** (*usu. impers.*) to press, be tight; ~ет в плеча́х it feels tight in the shoulders.

тян|у́ться, у́сь, ~ешься, *impf.* **1.** (*of rubber, etc.*) to stretch. **2.** (*pf.* по~) to stretch out, stretch oneself. **3.** (*of landscape features, etc.*) to stretch, extend; по ту сто́рону на со́тни киломе́тров ~ется тайга́ on that side for hundreds of kilometres stretches the taiga. **4.** (*of time*) to drag on; to crawl, hang heavy. **5.** (*coll.*) to last out, hold out; запа́сы ещё ~нутся supplies are still holding out. **6.** (к) to reach (for), reach out (for); to strive (after); т. к сла́ве to strive after fame. **7.** (за+*i.*; *fig., coll.*) to try to keep up (with), try to equal. **8.** to move one after the other. **9.** (*of clouds, smoke, etc.*) to drift.

тянучк|а, и, *f.* toffee, caramel.

тян|ущий, *pres. part. act. of* ~у́ть *and adj.*; ~у́щая боль nagging, persistent pain.

тяп|ать, а́ю, *impf.* (*of* ~нуть) (*coll.*) **1.** to hit; to chop (at), hack (at). **2.** to grab,

snatch; (*fig.*) to pinch. **3.** to knock back (= to drink off).

тя́пк|а, и, *f.* chopper.

тяп-ля́п, *adv. or as pred.* (*coll.*) anyhow (*o careless, slipshod work*).

тя́п|нуть, ну, нешь, *pf. of* ~ать.

тя́т|я, и, *m.* (*dial.*) dad, daddy.

У

у¹, *interj.* (*expressing reproach or fear*) oh.

у², *prep.+g.* **1.** by; at; у окна́ by the window; у воро́т at the gate; у мо́ря by the sea; у роя́ля at the piano; у руля́ at the helm (*also fig.*); у вла́сти in power. **2.** at; with (*often = French* chez); у нас (*i*) at our place, with us, (*ii*) in our country; у себя́ at one's (own) place, at home; я был у парикма́хера I was at the hairdresser's; она́ учи́лась у знамени́того испа́нского скрипача́ she was taught by a celebrated Spanish violinist; он шьёт костю́м у хоро́шего портно́го he is having a suit made by a good tailor; ты у меня́ смотри́! (you) watch out! **3.** *expresses relationship of possession, of part to whole, etc.*: зуб у меня́ боли́т my tooth aches; ши́на у пере́днего колеса́ ло́пнула there is a puncture in (the tyre of) the front wheel; мать у неё больна́ her mother is ill. **4.** (*indicating source, place of origin, etc.*, *of something obtained*) from, of; я за́нял де́сять рубле́й у сосе́да I borrowed ten roubles from a neighbour; спроси́те у него́ о́ттиск ask him to let you have an offprint; он вы́играл у меня́ три па́ртии в ша́хматы he won three games of chess from me. **5.** у меня́, *etc.*, I, *etc.*, have; у них великоле́пный дог they have a magnificent Great Dane; есть у вас радиоприёмник? have you a wireless?; у меня́ к вам ма́ленькая про́сьба I have a small favour to ask of you.

у- *verbal prefix indicating* **1.** *movement away from a place, as* улете́ть to fly away. **2.** *insertion in something, as* умести́ть to put in. **3.** *covering of something all over, as* усе́ять to strew. **4.** *reduction, curtailment, etc., as* уба́вить to reduce. **5.** *achievement of aim sought, as* уговори́ть to persuade; *with adjectival roots forms verbs expressing comparative degree, as* уско́рить to accelerate.

убав|ить, лю, ишь, *pf.* (*of* ~ля́ть) **1.** (+*a. or g.*) to reduce, lessen, diminish; у. ход to reduce speed; у. рука́в to shorten a sleeve. **2.** у. в ве́се to lose weight.

уба́в|иться, ится, *pf.* (*of* ~ля́ться) to diminish, decrease; дни ~ились the days

are shorter; воды́ ~илось the water(-level) has fallen.

убавля́|ть(ся), ю(сь), *impf. of* уба́вить(ся).

убаю́к|ать, аю, *pf.* (*of* ~ивать) to lull (*also fig.*).

убаю́кива|ть, ю, *impf. of* убаю́кать.

убега́|ть, ю, *impf. of* убежа́ть.

убеди́тельност|ь, и, *f.* persuasiveness, cogency.

убеди́тел|ьный (~ен, ~ьна), *adj.* **1.** convincing, persuasive, cogent; быть ~ьным to carry conviction. **2.** pressing; earnest; ~ьная про́сьба pressing request, earnest entreaty.

убе|ди́ть, *1st person sing. not used,* **ди́шь,** *pf.* (*of* ~жда́ть) **1.** (в+*p.*) to convince (of). **2.** (+*inf.*) to persuade (to), prevail on (to).

убе|ди́ться, *1st person sing. not used,* **ди́шься,** *pf.* (*of* ~жда́ться) **1.** (в+*p.*) to make certain (of), satisfy oneself (of). **2.** *pass. of* ~жда́ть.

убе|жа́ть, гу́, жи́шь, гу́т, *pf.* (*of* ~га́ть) **1.** to run away, run off, make off. **2.** to escape. **3.** (*coll.*) to boil over.

убежда́|ть(ся), ю(сь), *impf. of* убеди́ть(ся).

убежде́ни|е, я, *n.* **1.** persuasion, attempt to persuade; путём ~я by means of persuasion. **2.** conviction, belief.

убеждённо, *adv.* with conviction.

убеждённост|ь, и, *f.* conviction.

убеждён|ный, *p.p.p. of* убеди́ть *and adj.* **1.** (~, ~á) (в+*p.*) convinced (of), persuaded (of); я в э́том соверше́нно ~ I am absolutely convinced of this. **2.** convinced, confirmed; staunch, stalwart; у. пацифи́ст convinced pacifist; у. сторо́нник staunch supporter.

убе́жищ|е, а, *n.* **1.** refuge, asylum; sanctuary; иска́ть ~a to seek refuge, asylum; пра́во ~a right of asylum. **2.** (air-raid, *etc.*) shelter; (*mil.*) dug-out.

убел|ённый, *p.p.p. of* ~и́ть; у. седино́й, седи́нами hoary with age.

убел|и́ть, ю́, и́шь, *pf.* to whiten.

уберега́|ть(ся), ю(сь), *impf. of* убере́чь(ся).

убере́|чь, гу́, жёшь, гу́т, *past* ~г, ~гла́, *pf.*

(*of* ~га́ть) (от) to protect (against), guard (against), keep safe (from), preserve (from); у. шу́бу от мо́ли to protect a fur coat against moth.

убере́|чься, гу́сь, жёшься, гу́тся, *past* ~гся, ~гла́сь, *pf.* (*of* ~га́ться) (от) to protect oneself (against), guard (*intrans.*) (against).

убива́|ть, ю, *impf. of* уби́ть.

убива́|ться, юсь, *impf.* 1. (*impf. only*) (о+*p.*; *coll.*) to grieve (over). 2. *impf. of* уби́ться.

уби́йствен|ный (~, ~на), *adj.* 1. (*obs.*) death-dealing; ~ная стрела́ deadly arrow. 2. (*fig., coll.*) killing, murderous; у. кли́мат killing climate; у. взгляд murderous look.

уби́йств|о, а, *n.* murder; assassination.

уби́йц|а, ы, *m. and f.* murderer; assassin; killer.

убира́|ть(ся), ю(сь), *impf. of* убра́ть(ся); ~йся! clear off!, beat it!, hop it!

убира́|ющийся, *pres. part. of* ~ться; ~ющееся шасси́ (*aeron.*) retractable undercarriage.

уби́т|ый (~, ~а) 1. *p.p.p. of* ~ь; неприя́тель потеря́л две ты́сячи ~ыми the enemy lost two thousand killed; *as noun* у., ~ого, *m.* dead man; спать, как у. to sleep like a log; молча́ть, как у. to be silent as the grave; ходи́ть, как у. to be dazed (with grief, *etc.*). 2. у. Бо́гом (*coll.*) simple, dumb. 3. *adj.* (*fig.*) crushed, broken.

уб|и́ть, ью́, ьёшь, *pf.* (*of* ~ива́ть) 1. to kill; to murder; to assassinate; хоть ~е́й (*coll.*) for the life of me, to save my life; у. бобра́ *see* бобр. 2. (*fig.*) to kill, finish; to break, smash; её отка́з ~и́л его́ her refusal finished him; у. чьи-н. наде́жды to smash someone's hopes. 3. (*coll.*) to expend; to waste; у. вре́мя to kill time; у. мо́лодость to waste one's youth. 4. (*cards; coll.*) to cover.

уб|и́ться, ью́сь, ьёшься, *pf.* (*of* ~ива́ться) 1. (*coll.*) to hurt oneself, bruise oneself. 2. *pass. of* ~и́ть.

ублаготвор|и́ть, ю́, и́шь, *pf.* (*of* ~я́ть) (*obs. or coll., joc.*) to satisfy.

ублаготвор|я́ть, я́ю, *impf. of* ~и́ть.

ублаж|а́ть, а́ю, *impf. of* ~и́ть.

ублаж|и́ть, у́, и́шь, *pf.* (*of* ~а́ть) (*coll.*) to indulge; to gratify.

ублю́д|ок, ка, *m.* mongrel (*also fig.*).

ублю́дочный, *adj.* 1. mongrel, cross-bred. 2. (*fig., pejor.*) compromise; half-hearted.

убо́г|ий (~, ~а), *adj.* 1. poverty-stricken, beggarly (*also fig.*); wretched, squalid; ~ое воображе́ние poverty-stricken imagination; ~ое жили́ще wretched habitation; *as noun* у., ~ого, *m.* pauper, beggar. 2. (*obs.*) crippled; *as noun* у., ~ого, *m.*; ~ая, ~ой, *f.* cripple.

убо́гост|ь, и, *f.* poverty, penury (*also fig.*); wretchedness, squalor.

убо́жеств|о, а, *n.* 1. (*obs.*) physical disability; infirmity. 2. (*fig.*) poverty; lack ⌣ distinction; mediocrity; у. иде́й poverty of ideas.

убо́|й, я, *m.* slaughter (*of livestock*); корми́ть на у. to fatten (*livestock*); (*fig.*) to feed up, stuff with food.

убо́йност|ь, и, *f.* (*mil.*) effectiveness, destructive power (*of missile, weapon*).

убо́йн|ый, *adj.* 1. у. скот livestock for slaughter. 2. (*mil.*) killing, destructive, lethal; ~ая диста́нция killing range; ~ая мо́щность destructive power.

убо́р, а, *m.* 1. (*obs.*) dress, attire. 2. головно́й у. headgear, head-dress.

убо́рист|ый (~, ~а), *adj.* close, small (*of handwriting, etc.*).

убо́рк|а, и, *f.* 1. harvesting, reaping, gathering in; picking. 2. (*mil.*) collection, removal (*of casualties from field of battle*). 3. clearing up, tidying up.

убо́рн|ая, ой, *f.* 1. (*theatr.*) dressing-room. 2. lavatory; public convenience.

убо́рочн|ый, *adj.* harvest(ing); ~ая маши́на harvester.

убо́рщик, а, *m.* cleaner.

убо́рщиц|а, ы, *f.* cleaner (*in offices, etc.*); charwoman, charlady.

убра́нств|о, а, *n.* furniture, appointments; (*poet.*) attire.

убра́|ть, уберу́, уберёшь, *past* ~л, ~ла́, ~ло, *pf.* (*of* убира́ть) 1. to remove, take away; у. с доро́ги to put out of the way (*also fig.*); у. со стола́ to clear the table. 2. (*fig., coll.*) to kick out, chuck out; to sack; у. кого́-н. из ко́мнаты to chuck someone out of the room. 3. to put away; to store; у. я́корь to stow the anchor. 4. to harvest, reap, gather in. 5. to clear up, tidy up; у. ко́мнату to do a room; у. посте́ль to make the bed. 6. to decorate, adorn.

убра́|ться, уберу́сь, уберёшься, *past* ~лся, ~ла́сь, ~ло́сь, *pf.* (*of* убира́ться) 1. (*coll.*) to clear up, tidy up, clean up. 2. (*obs. or poet.*) to attire oneself. 3. (*coll.*) to clear off, beat it.

убыва́|ть, ю, *impf. of* убы́ть.

у́был|ь, и, *f.* 1. diminution, decrease; subsidence (*of water*); идти́ на у. to decrease; to subside, fall, go down, recede. 2. (*mil.*) losses, casualties.

убыстр|и́ть, ю́, и́шь, *pf.* (*of* ~я́ть) to speed up; to hasten.

убыстр|я́ть, я́ю, *impf. of* ~и́ть.

убы́т|ок, ка, *m.* 1. loss; терпе́ть, нести́ ~ки to incur losses; в у., с ~ком at a loss; быть в ~ке to lose, be down. 2. (*pl.*) damages;

взыска́ть ~ки to claim damages; компенси́ровать ~ки to pay damages; определи́ть ~ки to assess damages.

убы́точно, *adv.* at a loss.

убы́точ|ный (~ен, ~на), *adj.* unprofitable; ~ная торго́вля trading at a loss.

убы́ть, убу́ду, убу́дешь, *past* у́был, убыла́, у́было, *pf.* (*of* убыва́ть) **1.** to decrease, diminish; (*of water*) to subside, fall, go down; (*of the moon*) to wane, be on the wane (*also fig.*). **2.** тебя́, *etc.,* не убу́дет (от) (*coll.*) you, *etc.,* won't be any the worse (for); nothing will happen to you, *etc.* (as a result of). **3.** to go away, leave; у. в командиро́вку to go away on business; у. в о́тпуск to go on leave; у. по боле́зни to go sick.

уважа́|емый, *pres. part. pass. of* ~ть *and adj.* respected; (*in opening formal letter*) dear.

уважа́|ть, ю, *impf.* to respect, esteem.

уваже́ни|е, я, *n.* respect, esteem; внуша́ть у. to command respect; пита́ть глубо́кое у. к кому́-н. to have a profound respect for someone; из ~я (к) out of respect (for), in deference (to); с уваже́нием (*in letters*) yours sincerely.

уважи́тельност|ь, и, *f.* **1.** validity. **2.** respectfulness.

уважи́тел|ьный (~ен, ~ьна), *adj.* **1.** valid; ~ьная причи́на valid cause, good reason. **2.** respectful, deferential.

ува́ж|ить, у, ишь, *pf.* **1.** to comply (with). **2.** (*coll.*) to humour.

ува́л, а, *m.* steep slope.

ува́лист|ый (~, ~а), *adj.* steeply-sloping.

у́вал|ень, ьня, *m.* (*coll.*) bumpkin, clodhopper.

ува́рива|ться, ется, *impf. of* увари́ться.

увар|и́ться, ~ится, *pf.* (*of* ~ива́ться) (*coll.*) **1.** to be thoroughly cooked. **2.** to boil away.

уведоми́тельн|ый, *adj.* ~ое письмо́ letter of advice, notice.

уве́дом|ить, лю, ишь, *pf.* (*of* ~ля́ть) to inform, notify.

уведомле́ни|е, я, *n.* information, notification.

уведомля́|ть, ю, *impf. of* уве́домить.

увез|ти́, у́, ёшь, *past* ~, ~ла́, *pf.* (*of* увози́ть) **1.** to take (away); to take with one. **2.** to abduct, kidnap.

увекове́чива|ть, ю, *impf. of* увекове́чить.

увекове́ч|ить, у, ишь, *pf.* (*of* ~ивать) **1.** to immortalize. **2.** to perpetuate.

увеличе́ни|е, я, *n.* **1.** increase; augmentation; extension. **2.** magnification (*by means of an optical instrument*); (*phot.*) enlargement.

увели́чива|ть(ся), ю(сь), *impf. of* увели́чить(ся).

увеличи́тельн|ый, *adj.* **1.** magnifying; ~ое стекло́ magnifying glass; у. аппара́т (*phot.*) enlarger. **2.** (*gram.*) augmentative.

увели́ч|ить, у, ишь, *pf.* (*of* ~ивать) **1.** to increase; to augment; to extend; to enhance. **2.** to magnify; (*phot.*) to enlarge.

увели́ч|иться, ится, *pf.* (*of* ~иваться) to increase, grow, rise.

увенч|а́ть, а́ю, *pf.* (*of* венча́ть 1, 2, *and* ~ивать) to crown.

увенч|а́ться, а́ется, *pf.* (*of* ~ива́ться) (+*i.*; *fig., rhet.*) to be crowned (with); у. успе́хом to be crowned with success.

уве́нчива|ть(ся), ю(сь), *impf. of* увенча́ть(ся).

увере́ни|е, я, *n.* assurance; protestation.

увере́нност|ь, и, *f.* **1.** confidence; у. в себе́ self-confidence. **2.** confidence, certitude, certainty; мо́жно с ~ью сказа́ть one can say with confidence, it is safe to say; я был в по́лной ~и, что пойдёт дождь I was quite certain that it would rain.

уве́рен|ный (~, ~на), *adj.* **1.** confident, sure; ~ная рука́ sure hand. **2.** confident, sure, certain; быть ~ным to be sure, be certain; бу́дь(те) ~(ы)! you may be sure, you may rely on it.

уве́р|ить, ю, ишь, *pf.* (*of* ~я́ть) to assure; to convince, persuade.

уве́р|иться, юсь, ишься, *pf.* (*of* ~я́ться) to assure oneself, satisfy oneself; to become convinced.

увер|ну́ться, ну́сь, нёшься, *pf.* (*of* ~ты́ваться) (от) to dodge; to evade (*also fig.*); у. от прямо́го отве́та to avoid giving a direct answer.

уве́р|овать, ую, *pf.* (в+*a.*) to come to believe (in).

увёртк|а, и, *f.* dodge, evasion; subterfuge; (*pl.*) wiles.

увёртлив|ый (~, ~а), *adj.* evasive, shifty.

увёртыва|ться, юсь, *impf. of* увернуться.

увертю́р|а, ы, *f.* (*mus.*) overture.

увер|я́ть(ся), я́ю(сь), *impf. of* ~ить(ся).

увеселе́ни|е, я, *n.* entertainment, amusement.

увесели́тельн|ый, *adj.* pleasure, entertainment, amusement; ~ая пое́здка pleasure-trip, jaunt.

увесел|и́ть, ю, и́шь, *pf.* (*of* ~я́ть) to entertain, amuse.

увесел|я́ть, я́ю, *impf. of* ~и́ть.

уве́сист|ый (~, ~а), *adj.* (*coll.*) weighty; у. уда́р heavy blow (*also fig.*).

уве|сти́, ду́, дёшь, *past* ~л, ~ла́, *pf.* (*of* уводи́ть) **1.** to take (away); to take with one. **2.** (*coll.*) to carry off, lift, walk off with (= to steal).

уве́т, а, *m.* (*obs.*) = увеща́ние.

увеч|ить, у, ишь, *impf.* to maim, mutilate, cripple.

увеч|ный, *adj.* maimed, mutilated,

crippled; *as noun* у., ~ого, *m.*; ~ая, ~ой, *f.* cripple.

увéчь|е, я, *n.* maiming, mutilation.

увéш|ать, аю, *pf.* (*of* ~ивать) to cover (*with objects suspended*); у. стéну картúнами to cover a wall with pictures.

увéшива|ть, ю, *impf.* *of* увéшать.

увещáни|е, я, *n.* exhortation, admonition.

увещá|ть, ю, *impf.* (*obs.*) = увещевáть.

увещевá|ть, ю, *impf.* to exhort, admonish.

увивá|ть, ю, *impf.* *of* увúть.

увивá|ться, юсь, *impf.* (за+*i.*; *coll.*, *pejor.*) to hang round; to try to get round.

увидá|ть, ю, *pf.* (*of* видáть) (*coll.*) to see.

увидá|ться, юсь, *pf.* (*coll.*) to see one another.

увú|деть, жу, дишь, *pf.* 1. *pf. of* вúдеть. 2. to catch sight of.

увú|деться, жусь, дишься, *pf.* *of* вúдеться.

увúлива|ть, ю, *impf.* (от) 1. *impf. of* увильнýть. 1. (*impf. only*) to try to get out (of).

увильн|ýть, ý, ёшь, *pf.* (*of* увúливать) (от) *coll.*) 1. to dodge. 2. (*fig.*) to evade, shirk; to get out (of); у. от отвéта to get out of replying.

ув|úть, ью, ьёшь, *past* ~úл, ~илá, ~úло, *pf.* (*of* ~ивáть) to twine all over.

увлажн|úть, ю, úшь, *pf.* (*of* ~я́ть) to moisten, damp, wet.

увлажн|я́ть, я́ю, *impf.* *of* ~úть.

увлекáтел|ьный (~ен, ~ьна), *adj.* fascinating; absorbing.

увлекá|ть(ся), ю(сь), *impf.* *of* увлéчь(ся).

увлечéни|е, я, *n.* 1. animation. 2. (+*i.*) passion (for); enthusiasm (for), keenness (on); crush (on). 3. (object of) passion; планерúзм — егó у. gliding is his passion, he is mad about gliding; стáрое у. old flame.

увлé|чь, кý, чёшь, кýт, *past* ~к, ~клá, *pf.* (*of* ~кáть) 1. to carry along. 2. (*fig.*) to carry away, distract. 3. to captivate, fascinate. 4. to entice, allure.

увлé|чься, кýсь, чёшься, кýтся, *past* ~кся, ~клáсь, *pf.* (*of* ~кáться) (+*i.*) 1. to be carried away (by); to become keen (on), become mad (about); орáтор ~кся the speaker got carried away; онá ~клáсь ездóй верхóм she is mad about riding. 2. to become enamoured (of), become keen (on), fall (for).

увóд, а, *m.* 1. taking away; у. войск withdrawal of troops. 2. (*coll.*) carrying off; lifting (= stealing); женúтьба ~ом (*obs.*) elopement.

уво|дúть, жý, ~дишь, *impf.* *of* увестú.

увóз, а, *m.* (*coll.*) abduction; carrying off, lifting; женúтьба ~ом (*obs.*) elopement.

уво|зúть, жý, ~зишь, *pf.* *of* увезтú.

уволáкива|ть, ю, ю, *impf.* *of* уволóчь.

увóл|ить, ю, ишь, *pf.* (*of* ~ьня́ть) 1. to discharge, dismiss; to sack, fire; у. в отстáвку to retire, pension off; у. в запáс (*mil.*) to transfer to the reserve; у. в óтпуск to give a holiday, grant leave (of absence). 2. (*pf. only*) (от; *obs.*) to spare; ~ьте нас от подрóбного расскáза spare us the details.

увóл|иться, юсь, ишься, *pf.* (*of* ~ьня́ться) 1. to retire; (*mil.*) to leave the service, get one's discharge; у. в отстáвку to retire, go into retirement. 2. *pass. of* ~ить.

увол|óчь, окý, очёшь, окýт, *past* ~óк, ~оклá, *pf.* (*of* ~áкивать) (*coll.*) 1. to drag away; éле нóги у. to have a narrow escape. 2. to carry off, make off with.

увольнéни|е, я, *n.* discharge, dismissal; retiring, pensioning off; у. в запáс (*mil.*) transfer to the reserve; предупреждéние об ~и notice (of dismissal).

увольнúтельн|ый, *adj.* discharge, dismissal; у. билéт, ~ая запúска (*mil.*) leave-pass.

увольня́|ть(ся), ю(сь), *impf.* *of* увóлить(ся).

увор|овáть, ýю, *pf.* (*coll.*) to pinch, swipe.

уврач|евáть, ýю, *pf.* *of* врачевáть.

увуля́рный, *adj.* (*ling.*) uvular.

увы́, *interj.* alas!

увядá|ть, ю, *impf.* *of* увя́нуть.

увя|зáть[1], жý, ~жешь, *pf.* (*of* ~зывать) 1. to tie up; to pack up. 2. to co-ordinate.

увя|зáть[2], áю, *impf.* *of* ~нуть.

увя|зáться, жýсь, ~жешься, *pf.* (*of* ~зываться) (*coll.*) 1. to pack. 2. (за кем-н.) to dog (someone's footsteps).

увя́зк|а, и, *f.* 1. tying up, roping, strapping. 2. co-ordination.

увя́з|нуть, ну, нешь, *past* ~, ~ла, *pf.* (*of* ~áть[2]) (в+*p.*) to get stuck (in); to get bogged down (in) (*also fig.*).

увя́зыва|ть, ю, *impf.* *of* увязáть[1].

увя́зыва|ться, юсь, *impf.* *of* увязáться.

увя́|нуть, ну, нешь, *pf.* (*of* ~дáть) to fade, wither, wilt, droop (*also fig.*).

угадá|ть[1], áю, *pf.* (*of* ~ывать) to guess (right), divine.

угадá|ть[2], áю, *pf.* (в+*a.*; *coll.*) to get (into), fall (into).

угáдыва|ть, ю, *impf.* *of* угадáть[1].

угáр[1], а, *m.* 1. carbon monoxide fumes, charcoal fumes. 2. carbon monoxide poisoning; у них у. they are suffering from carbon monoxide poisoning. 3. (*fig.*) ecstasy, intoxication; в ~е (+*g.*) carried away (by), blinded (by); в ~е страстéй in the heat of passion.

угáр[2], а, *m.* (*tech.*, *text.*) waste (*from metal smelting, etc., or from cotton spinning*).

угáрно, *as pred.*; здесь у. there is a smell of fumes here.

угáрный[1], *adj.* full of (monoxide) fumes; (*tech.*) у. газ coal-gas, carbon monoxide.

угáрный[2], *adj.* (*tech., text.*) waste.

угас|áть, áет, *impf.* **1.** *impf. of* ∼нуть. **2.** (*impf. only*) to die down (*of a fire and fig.*); сúлы у негó ∼áли his strength was failing.

угáс|нуть, нет, *pf.* (*of* ∼áть) to go out.

углевóд, а, *m.* (*chem.*) carbohydrate.

углеводорóд, а, *m.* (*chem.*) hydrocarbon.

углевыжигáтельн|ый, *adj.* ∼ая печь charcoal kiln.

угледобы́ч|а, и, *f.* coal extraction, coal output.

углежжéни|е, я, *n.* charcoal burning.

углежóг, а, *m.* charcoal-burner.

углекислот|á, ы́, *f.* (*chem.*) carbonic acid, carbon dioxide.

углеки́слый, *adj.* (*chem.*) carbonate (of); у. газ carbonic acid gas; у. аммóний ammonium carbonate.

углекóп, а, *m.* (*obs.*) coal-miner, collier.

углепромы́шленност|ь, и, *f.* coal-mining, coal industry.

углерóд, а, *m.* (*chem.*) carbon.

углерóдист|ый, *adj.* (*chem.*) carbonaceous; ∼ое желéзо iron carbide.

углговáт|ый (∼, ∼а), *adj.* **1.** angular. **2.** (*fig., coll.*) awkward.

углов|óй, *adj.* **1.** (*math., phys., tech.*) angle; angular; ∼áя скóрость angular velocity; ∼áя частотá angular frequency. **2.** angle; corner; у. дом corner house, house on the corner.

угломéр, а, *m.* **1.** (*tech.*) goniometer, azimuth instrument, protractor, clinometer. **2.** (*mil.*) deflection.

углуб|и́ть, лю́, и́шь, *pf.* (*of* ∼ля́ть) **1.** to deepen, make deeper. **2.** to drive in deeper, sink deeper. **3.** (*fig.*) to extend; у. свой знáния to extend one's knowledge.

углуб|и́ться, лю́сь, и́шься, *pf.* (*of* ∼ля́ться) **1.** to deepen, become deeper. **2.** (*fig.*) to become intensified. **3.** (в+*a.*) to go deep (into); to delve deeply (into) (*also fig.*); у. в кóрень вещéй to go to the root of the matter. **4.** (в+*a.; fig.*) to become absorbed (in); у. в кни́гу to become absorbed in a book; у. в себя́ to become introspective.

углублéни|е, я, *n.* **1.** deepening. **2.** (*fig.*) extending; intensification; для ∼я свои́х знáний in order to extend one's knowledge. **3.** (*geogr.*) hollow, depression, dip. **4.** (*naut.*) draught (*of a vessel*).

углубля́|ть(ся), ю(сь), *impf. of* углуби́ть(ся).

угль, у́гля, *m.* (*arch. or poet.*) = ýголь.

угля|дéть, жý, ди́шь, *pf.* (*coll.*) **1.** to espy, spot. **2.** (за+*i.*) to look after; не у. (за+*i.*) to fail to take proper care (of).

угнá|ть, угоню́, угóнишь, *past* ∼л, ∼лá, ∼ло, *pf.* (*of* угоня́ть) **1.** to drive away.

2. (*coll.*) to send off, despatch. **3.** (*coll.*) to steal, lift.

угнá|ться, угоню́сь, угóнишься, *past* ∼лся, ∼лáсь, ∼лóсь, *pf.* (за+*i.*) to keep pace (with); to keep up (with) (*also fig., coll.*).

угнезд|и́ться, и́шься, *pf.* (*coll.*) to nestle, settle down (*in a confined space*).

угнетáтел|ь, я, *m.* oppressor.

угнетáтельский, *adj.* oppressive.

угнетá|ть, ю, *impf.* **1.** to oppress. **2.** to depress, dispirit.

угнетéни|е, я, *n.* **1.** oppression. **2.** depression; быть в ∼и to be depressed.

угнетённост|ь, и, *f.* depression, low spirits.

угнетённ|ый, *adj.* **1.** oppressed. **2.** depressed; быть в ∼ом состоя́нии to be depressed, be in low spirits.

угова́рива|ть, ю, *impf.* **1.** *impf. of* уговори́ть. **2.** (*impf. only*) to try to persuade, urge.

угова́рива|ться, юсь, *impf. of* уговори́ться.

угово́р, а, *m.* **1.** persuasion. **2.** agreement, compact; с ∼ом... on condition . . ., with the proviso . . . .

угово́р|и́ть, ю́, и́шь, *pf.* (*of* угова́ривать) (+*inf.*) to persuade (to), induce (to); to talk (into).

угово́р|и́ться, ю́сь, и́шься, *pf.* (*of* угова́риваться) (+*inf.*) to arrange (to), agree (to).

уго́д|а, ы, f. в ∼у (+*d.*) to please.

уго|ди́ть[1]**, жý, ди́шь,** *pf.* (*of* ∼жда́ть) (+*d. or* на+*a.*) to please, oblige.

уго|ди́ть[2]**, жý, ди́шь,** *pf.* (*coll.*) **1.** (в+*a.*) to fall (into), get (into); to bang (against); у. в западню́ to fall into a trap; у. в тюрьмý to land up in prison. **2.** (+*d.* в+*a.*) to hit (in, on), get (in, on); у. комý-н. в глаз кáмнем to hit someone in the eye with a stone.

уго́длив|ый (∼, ∼а), *adj.* obsequious.

уго́дник, а, *m.* **1.** (*obs., coll.*) person anxious to please. **2.** святóй у. saint.

уго́днича|ть, ю, *impf.* (пéред; *coll.*) to cringe (to).

уго́дничеств|о, а, *n.* subservience, servility.

уго́дно 1. *as pred.* (+*d.*) что вам у.? what would you like?, what can I do for you?; как вам у. as you wish, as you please; please yourself; скóлько дýше у. to one's heart's content; не у. ли вам? (*i*) (*as polite invitation*) would you like?, (*ii*) (*iron.; expressing request*) would you be good enough, would you mind; не у. ли (*iron.*) if you please. **2.** *forms indef. pronouns and adverbs*: кто у. anyone (you like), whoever you like; что у. anything (you like), whatever you like; скóлько у. as much as you like; any amount.

уго́д|ный (∼ен, ∼на), *adj.* pleasing, welcome.

угóд|ье, ья, *g. pl.* **~ий,** *n.* **1.** object *or* area of economic significance; лесны́е ~ья forests; полевы́е ~ья arable land; ры́бные ~ья fishing-ground. **2.** (*obs.*) advantage, favourable side, good point.

угождá|ть, ю, *impf. of* угоди́ть[1].

ýг|ол, лá, *об* ~лé, *в* ~лý, *m.* **1.** (*в* ~лé) (*math., phys.*) angle; у. встре́чи angle of impact; angle of incidence; у. засе́чки angle of intersection; у. зре́ния visual angle; (*fig.*) point of view; у. пока́тости angle of slope, gradient; под ~лóм (*в*+*a.*) at an angle (of); под прямы́м ~лóм at right angles. **2.** corner; *в* ~лý in the corner; *на* ~лý at the corner; *за* ~лóм round the corner; поста́вить в у. to put in the corner, make stand in the corner; из-за ~лá (from) round the corner; (*fig.*) on the sly, behind someone's back; загна́ть в у. to drive into a corner; сре́зать у. to cut off a corner. **3.** part of a room. **4.** place; име́ть свой у. to have a place of one's own; глухóй у., медве́жий у. remote part, God-forsaken spot.

угол|ёк, ькá, *m.* small piece of coal.

уголóвник, а, *m.* (*coll.*) criminal.

уголóвн|ый, *adj.* criminal; ~ое де́ло criminal case; у. кóдекс criminal code; ~ое пра́во criminal law; у. престу́пник criminal; у. рóзыск Criminal Investigation Department.

уголóвщин|а, ы, *f.* (*coll.*) criminal act, activity.

угол|óк, кá, *m. dim. of* ýгол; corner; у. приро́ды nature study corner; живóй у. pets' corner; кра́сный у. recreation and reading room.

ýголь, угля́, *m.* **1.** (*pl.* ýгли, ýгле́й) coal; ка́менный у. coal; бу́рый у. lignite; древе́сный у. charcoal. **2.** (*pl.* ýгли, ýгле́й *and* ~я́, ~ев) a coal; piece of coal; сиде́ть как на ~ях to be on thorns. **3.** (*art*) charcoal.

угóльник, а, *m.* **1.** set square. **2.** (*tech.*) corner iron; стыковóй у. angle bracket.

ýгольн|ый, *adj.* **1.** coal; у. бассе́йн coal-field; у. райóн coal-mining area. **2.** carbon; ~ая дуговáя ла́мпа carbon arc lamp. **3.** (*chem.*) carbonic; ~ая кислотá carbonic acid.

угóльный, *adj.* (*coll.*) corner.

ýгольщик[1], а, *m.* **1.** coal-miner, collier. **2.** charcoal-burner.

ýгольщик[2], а, *m.* collier (*ship*).

угомóн, а (*у*), *m.* (*coll.*) peace (and quiet); на них ~у нет they give one no peace; не знать ~у to have no peace.

угомон|и́ть, ю́, и́шь, *pf.* (*coll.*) to calm.

угомон|и́ться, ю́сь, и́шься, *pf.* (*coll.*) to calm down.

угóн, а, *m.* **1.** driving away. **2.** (*coll.*) lifting, stealing; hi-jacking. **3.** (*railways*) creep (*of lines*).

угоня́|ть, ю, *impf. of* угна́ть.

угора́зд|ить, ит, *pf.* (+*inf., usu. impers.*; *coll.*) to urge, make; как э́то егó ~ило жени́ться на ней? what on earth made him marry her?

угор|а́ть, а́ю, *impf. of* ~е́ть.

угоре́лый, *adj.* **1.** (*obs.*) burnt away. **2.** как у. like a madman, like one possessed.

угор|е́ть[1], ю́, и́шь, *pf.* (*of* ~а́ть) **1.** to be poisoned by charcoal fumes, get carbon monoxide poisoning. **2.** (*coll.*) to be mad, be crazy; что ты, ~е́л? are you out of your mind?

угор|е́ть[2], ю́, и́шь, *pf.* (*of* ~а́ть) to burn away, burn down.

угóрский, *adj.* (*ethnol., ling.*) Ugrian.

ýг|орь[1], ря́, *m.* eel; живóй как у. as lively as a cricket.

ýг|орь[2], ря́, *m.* blackhead.

уго|сти́ть, щу́, сти́шь, *pf.* (*of* ~ща́ть) (+*i.*) to entertain (to), treat (to); у. когó-н. обе́дом to have someone to dinner.

уготóван|ный, *p.p.p. as pred. adj.* (*obs.*) prepared, in store; им ~о све́тлое бу́дущее a splendid future is in store for them.

уготóв|ить, лю, ишь, *pf.* (*obs.*) to prepare.

угоща́|ть, ю, *impf. of* угости́ть.

угоще́ни|е, я, n. **1.** (+*i.*) entertaining (to, with), treating (to). **2.** refreshments; fare.

угр, а, *m.* (*ethnol.*) Ugrian (*member of ethnic group comprising Hungarians, Ostyaks and Voguls*).

угрева́т|ый (~, ~a), *adj.* covered with black-heads; pimply.

угроб|ить, лю, ишь, *pf.* (*sl.*) **1.** to do in. **2.** (*fig.*) to ruin, wreck; у. чью-н. репута́цию to ruin someone's reputation.

угрожа́|ть, ю, *impf.* to threaten.

угрожа́|ющий, *pres. part. act. of* ~ть *and adj.* threatening, menacing; ~ющая катастрóфа impending disaster.

угрóз|а, ы, *f.* threat, menace; под ~ой (+*g.*) under threat (of); поста́вить под ~у to threaten, endanger, imperil, jeopardize.

угрóзыск, а, *m.* (*abbr. of* уголóвный рóзыск) Criminal Investigation Department.

ýгро-фи́нский, *adj.* Finno-Ugrian.

угрызе́ни|е, я, n. pangs; ~я сóвести remorse; чу́вствовать ~я сóвести to feel pangs of conscience.

угрю́м|ый (~, ~a), *adj.* sullen, morose, gloomy.

удáв, а, *m.* (*zool.*) boa, boa constrictor.

уда|ва́ться, ётся, *impf. of* ~́ться.

удав|и́ть, лю́, ~ишь, *pf.* to strangle.

удав|и́ться, лю́сь, ~ишься, *pf.* (*of* дави́ться 2) to hang oneself.

удáвк|а, и, *f.* running knot, half hitch, timber hitch.

удавле́ни|е, я, *n.* strangling, strangulation.

уда́вленник, а, *m.* (*coll.*) person who has hanged himself; victim of strangling.

удале́ни|е, я, *n.* 1. removal; у. зу́ба extraction of a tooth. 2. sending away; у. с по́ля (*sport*) sending off the field. 3. moving off.

удалённост|ь, и, *f.* remoteness, distance.

удал|ённый, *p.p.p. of* ~и́ть *and adj.* remote.

удал|е́ц, ьца́, *m.* daring person.

удал|и́ть, ю́, и́шь, *pf.* (*of* ~я́ть) 1. to remove; у. зуб to extract a tooth. 2. to remove, send away; у. с рабо́ты to dismiss, sack. 3. to move away.

удал|и́ться, ю́сь, и́шься, *pf.* (*of* ~я́ться) 1. to move off, move away; поспе́шно у. to beat a hasty retreat. 2. to leave, withdraw, retire; у. на поко́й to retire to a quiet life; у. от о́бщества to withdraw from society.

удал|о́й (уда́л, ~а́, уда́ло), *adj.* daring, bold.

уда́л|ый, *adj.* = ~о́й.

у́дал|ь, и, *f.* daring, boldness.

удальств|о́, а́, *n.* (*coll.*) = у́даль.

удал|я́ть(ся), я́ю(сь), *impf. of* ~и́ть(ся).

уда́р, а, *m.* 1. (*in var. senses*) blow; stroke; одни́м ~ом at one stroke; нанести́ у. to strike a blow; у. в спи́ну (*fig.*) stab in the back; у. гро́ма thunder-clap; у. гро́ма средь я́сного не́ба bolt from the blue. 2. stroke (*sound*); ~ы пу́льса stroke of the pulse. 3. (*mil.*) blow; attack; thrust; у. в штыки́ bayonet charge; у. с во́здуха air strike; под ~ом exposed (to attack). 4. быть в ~е (*coll.*) to be in good form; не быть в ~е to be off one's stroke. 5. (*med.*) stroke, seizure; со́лнечный у. sun-stroke.

ударе́ни|е, я, *n.* 1. (*ling.*) stress, accent; (*fig.*) stress, emphasis; поста́вить у. to stress, accent; сде́лать у. (на+*p. or* на+*a.*) to stress, emphasize. 2. stress(-mark).

уда́р|енный, *p.p.p. of* ~ить *and adj.* (*ling.*) stressed, accented.

уда́р|ить, ю, ишь, *pf.* (*of* ~я́ть *and, in some senses, of* бить) 1. (+*a.* по+*d. or* в+*a.*) to strike; to hit; у. кого́-н. по лицу́ to slap someone's face; у. кулако́м по́ столу to bang on the table with one's fist; мо́лния ~ила в де́рево the tree was struck by lightning. 2. (в+*a. or* +*a.*) to strike; to sound; to beat; у. в бараба́н to beat a drum; у. в наба́т, у. трево́гу to sound the alarm; часы́ ~или по́лночь the clock struck midnight; у. в смычки́ (*mus.*) to strike up. 3. у. в го́лову (*of blood*) to rush to one's head; (*of wine, etc.*) to go to one's head. 4. (на+*a. or* по+*d.*) (*mil.*) to strike (against), attack. 5. (по+*d.*) to strike (at), hit (at); to combat; у. по кумовству́ to combat nepotism; у. по карма́ну (*coll.*) to hit one's pocket, set one back. 6. (*of weather conditions, etc.*; *coll.*)

to strike; to set in; ну и моро́зец ~ил the frosts have really set in. 7. у. по рука́м to strike a bargain. 8. па́лец о па́лец не у. (*coll.*) not to raise, lift a finger.

уда́р|иться, юсь, ишься, *pf.* (*of* ~я́ться) 1. (о+*a. or* в+*a.*) to strike (against), hit; у. о подво́дный ка́мень to strike a reef. 2. (в+*a. or* +*inf.*) to break (into); у. в бе́гство, у. бежа́ть to break into a run; у. в слёзы to burst into tears. 3. (в+*a.*) to become addicted (to), become keen (on). 4. у. в кра́йность to run to an extreme; у. из одно́й кра́йности в другу́ю to run from one extreme to another.

уда́рник¹, а, *m.* 1. shock-worker, udarnik. 2. (*mil.*) member of striking force.

уда́рник², а, *m.* (*in fire-arm*) striker, firing pin; (*in detonator*) plunger.

уда́рниц|а, ы, *f. of* уда́рник¹.

уда́рн|ый, *adj.* 1. (*tech. and mil.*) percussive; percussion; ~ая возду́шная волна́ blast wave; у. ка́псюль percussion cap; ~ая ми́на (*naut.*) contact mine; ~ая сва́рка percussive welding; ~ая си́ла striking power, force of impact; ~ая тру́бка percussion tube, percussion primer. 2. (*mus.*) percussion. 3. (*mil.*) striking, shock; ~ая гру́ппа striking force, main attack force; ~ые ча́сти shock troops. 4. shock(-working); ~ая рабо́та shock work; ~ые те́мпы accelerated tempo (*of work*). 5. urgent; ~ое зада́ние urgent task, rush job; в ~ом поря́дке with great despatch.

удар|я́ть(ся), я́ю(сь), *impf. of* ~ить(ся).

уда́|ться, стся, ду́тся, *past* ~лся, ~ла́сь, *pf.* (*of* ~ва́ться) 1. to succeed, be a success, be successful, work (well); опера́ция ~ла́сь the operation was a success. 2. (*impers.*+*d. and inf.*) to succeed, manage; мне не ~ло́сь прису́тствовать на их сва́дьбе I did not manage to attend their wedding.

уда́ч|а, и, *f.* success; good luck, good fortune; жела́ть ~и to wish good luck; им всегда́ у. they are always lucky.

уда́чливост|ь, и, *f.* success, luck.

уда́члив|ый (~, ~а), *adj.* successful, lucky.

уда́чник, а, *m.* (*coll.*) lucky person.

уда́ч|ный (~ен, ~на), *adj.* 1. successful. 2. felicitous, apt, good; у. перево́д felicitous translation; у. оборо́т apt turn of phrase; у. вы́бор happy choice.

удва́ива|ть, ю, *impf. of* удво́ить.

удвое́ни|е, я, *n.* doubling, redoubling; (*ling.*) reduplication.

удво́|енный, *p.p.p. of* ~ить *and adj.* doubled, redoubled; (*ling.*) reduplicated; (*of letter of the alphabet*) double.

удво́|ить, ю, ишь, *pf.* (*of* удва́ивать) to double, redouble; (*ling.*) to reduplicate; у. свои́ уси́лия to redouble one's efforts.

удéл, а, *m.* **1.** lot, destiny; достáться в у. комý-н. to fall to one's lot. **2.** (*hist.*) apanage principality (*in Kievan Russia*). **3.** (*hist.*) crown domain, crown landed property.

удел|и́ть, ю́, и́шь, *pf.* (*of* ~я́ть) to give, spare, devote; у. часть из полýчки на что-н. to give up part of one's wage-packet for something; у. врéмя чемý-н. to spare the time for something; нам нáдо у. внимáние э́тому вопрóсу we must give the matter thought.

удéльн|ый¹, *adj.* (*phys.*) specific; у. вес specific gravity; (*fig.*) proportion, share; ~ая мóщность horse power per pound of weight.

удéльн|ый², *adj.* (*hist.*) **1.** apanage; у. князь apanage prince (*in Kievan Russia*); у. перíод period of apanage principalities. **2.** crown; ~ые зéмли crown lands, crown domains.

удел|я́ть, я́ю, *impf. of* ~и́ть.

у́держ, у, *m.* без ~у (*coll.*) uncontrollably, unrestrainedly, without restraint; плáкать без ~у to weep uncontrollably; ~у нет емý, на негó (*coll.*) there's no holding him; ~у не знать (*coll.*) to be immoderate, know no bounds.

удержáни|е, я, *n.* **1.** keeping, holding, re-retention. **2.** deduction; у. из зарплáты money stopped from wages.

удерж|áть, ý, ~ишь, *pf.* (*of* ~ивать) **1.** to hold, hold on to, not let go. **2.** to keep, retain; у. своё мéсто в чемпионáте to retain one's place in a championship competition; у. в пáмяти to retain in one's memory. **3.** to hold back, keep back, restrain; у. лошадéй to hold horses back; у. когó-н. от опромéтчивого постýпка to restrain some from a headstrong action. **4.** to keep down, suppress; у. слёзы to stifle one's tears. **5.** to deduct, keep back; у. из зарплáты to stop from wages.

удерж|áться, ýсь, ~ишься, *pf.* (*of* ~иваться) **1.** to hold one's ground, hold on, hold out; to stand firm; у. на ногáх to remain on one's feet. **2.** (от) to keep (from), refrain (from); у. от соблáзна to resist a temptation; мы не моглú у. от смéха we couldn't help laughing.

удéржива|ть(ся), ю(сь), *impf. of* удержáть(ся).

удесятер|и́ть, ю́, и́шь, *pf.* (*of* ~я́ть) to increase tenfold.

удесятер|и́ться, и́тся, *pf.* (*of* ~я́ться) to increase (*intrans.*) tenfold.

удесятер|я́ть(ся), я́ю, я́ет(ся), *impf. of* ~и́ть(ся).

удешев|и́ть, лю́, и́шь, *pf.* (*of* ~ля́ть) to reduce the price (of).

удешев|и́ться, и́тся, *pf.* (*of* ~ля́ться) to become cheaper.

удешевлéни|е, я, *n.* reduction of prices.

удешевля́|ть(ся), ю, ет(ся), *impf. of* удешеви́ть(ся).

удиви́тельно, *adv.* **1.** astonishingly, surprisingly. **2.** wonderfully, marvellously. **3.** very, extremely.

удиви́тел|ьный (~ен, ~ьна), *adj.* **1.** astonishing, surprising, amazing; ~ьно (*as pred.*) it is astonishing, it is surprising, it is amazing; it is funny; не ~ьно, что no wonder that. **2.** wonderful, marvellous.

удив|и́ть, лю́, и́шь, *pf.* (*of* ~ля́ть) to astonish, surprise, amaze.

удив|и́ться, лю́сь, и́шься, *pf.* (*of* ~ля́ться) (+*d.*) to be astonished (at), be surprised (at), be amazed (at); to marvel (at).

удивлéни|е, я, *n.* astonishment, surprise, amazement; к моемý вели́кому ~ю to my great surprise; на у. (*as pred.; coll.*) excellent(ly), splendid(ly), marvellous(ly); приём вы́шел на у. the reception went off splendidly.

удивля́|ть(ся), ю(сь), *impf. of* удиви́ть(ся).

удил|á, уди́л, ~áм, *no sing.* bit; закуси́ть у. to take the bit between one's teeth (*also fig.*).

уди́лищ|е, а, *n.* fishing-rod.

уди́льн|ый, *adj.* ~ые принадлéжности fishing tackle.

уди́льщик, а, *m.* angler.

уди́льщиц|а, ы, *f. of* уди́льщик.

удира́|ть, ю, *impf. of* удрáть.

уди́ть, ужý, ýдишь, *impf.* у. ры́бу to fish, angle.

уди́ться, ýдится, *impf.* (*of fish*) to bite.

удлинéни|е, я, *n.* lengthening; у. срóка extension (of time).

удлин|и́ть, ю́, и́шь, *pf.* (*of* ~я́ть) to lengthen; to extend, prolong.

удлин|и́ться, и́тся, *pf.* (*of* ~и́ться) to become longer; to be extended, be prolonged.

удлин|я́ть(ся), я́ю(сь), *impf. of* ~и́ть(ся).

удмýрт, а, *m.* Udmurt.

удмýртк|а, и, *f.* Udmurt (woman).

удмýртский, *adj.* Udmurt.

удóбно¹, *adv.* **1.** comfortably. **2.** conveniently.

удóбно², *as pred.* **1.** (+*d.*) to feel, be comfortable; to be at one's ease; нам здесь вполнé у. we are very comfortable here. **2.** (+*d.*) it is convenient (for), it suits; у. ли вам срáзу же приéхать? is it convenient for you to come at once? **3.** it is proper, it is in order; у. ли задáть такóй вопрóс? is it proper to ask such a question?

удóб|ный (~ен, ~на), *adj.* **1.** comfortable; cosy. **2.** convenient, suitable, opportune; пóльзоваться ~ным слýчаем to take an opportunity. **3.** proper, in order.

удобовари́м|ый (∼, ∼а), *adj.* digestible.

удобоисполни́м|ый (∼, ∼а), *adj.* easy to carry out; ∼ая про́сьба simple request.

удобообтека́емый, *adj.* streamlined.

удобопоня́т|ный (∼ен, ∼на), *adj.* comprehensible, intelligible.

удобопроизноси́м|ый (∼, ∼а), *adj.* easy to pronounce.

удобочита́ем|ый (∼, ∼а), *adj.* easy to read; legible.

удобре́ни|е, я, *n.* (*agric.*) 1. fertilization, manuring. 2. fertilizer.

удо́бр|ить, ю, ишь, *pf.* (*of* ∼я́ть) to fertilize, manure.

удобр|я́ть, я́ю, *impf. of* ∼ить.

удо́бств|о, а, *n.* comfort. 2. конvenience; кварти́ра со все́ми ∼ами flat with all conveniences.

удовлетворе́ни|е, я, *n.* satisfaction, gratification; тре́бовать ∼я у кого́-н. to demand satisfaction from someone; отмеча́ть с ∼ем to note with satisfaction.

удовлетворённост|ь, и, *f.* satisfaction, contentment.

удовлетвор|ённый, *p.p.p. of* ∼и́ть *and adj.* satisfied, contented.

удовлетвори́тельно, *adv.* 1. satisfactorily. 2. *as noun, indecl.* 'satisfactory', 'fair' (*as school mark*).

удовлетвори́тел|ьный (∼ен, ∼ьна), *adj.* satisfactory.

удовлетвор|и́ть, ю́, и́шь, *pf.* (*of* ∼я́ть) 1. to satisfy; to give satisfaction (to); to comply (with); у. запро́сы to satisfy requirements; у. про́сьбу to comply with a request. 2. (+*d.*) to answer, meet; у. тре́бованиям to answer requirements. 3. (+*i.*) to supply (with), furnish (with); у. провиа́нтом to victual.

удовлетвор|и́ться, ю́сь, и́шься, *pf.* (*of* ∼я́ться) 1. (+*i.*) to content oneself (with), be satisfied (with). 2. *pass. of* ∼и́ть.

удовлетвор|я́ть(ся), я́ю(сь), *impf. of* ∼и́ть(ся).

удово́льстви|е, я, *n.* 1. (*sing. only*) pleasure; доста́вить у. (+*d.*) to give pleasure. 2. amusement; мно́го ∼й a lot of fun.

удово́льств|оваться, уюсь, *pf. of* дово́льствоваться.

удо́д, а, *m.* (*orn.*) hoopoe.

удо́|й, я, *m.* 1. yield of milk. 2. milking.

удо́йлив|ый (∼, ∼а), *adj.* yielding much milk; ∼ая коро́ва good milker.

удо́йност|ь, и, *f.* yield of milk; milking capacity.

удо́й|ный, *adj.* 1. *adj. of* ∼. 2. = ∼ливый.

удорожа́ни|е, я, *n.* rise in price(s).

удорож|а́ть, а́ю, *impf. of* ∼и́ть.

удорож|и́ть, у́, и́шь, *pf.* (*of* ∼а́ть) to raise the price (of).

удоста́ива|ть(ся), ю(сь), *impf. of* удосто́ить(ся).

удостовере́ни|е, я, *n.* 1. certification, attestation; в у. (+*g.*) in witness (of). 2. certificate; у. ли́чности identity card; у. пра́ва вожде́ния автомоби́ля driving licence; у. о сме́рти death certificate.

удостове́р|ить, ю, ишь, *pf.* (*of* ∼я́ть) to certify, attest, witness; у. по́дпись to witness a signature; у. ли́чность кого́-н. to identify someone.

удостове́р|иться, юсь, ишься, *pf.* (*o* ∼я́ться) (в+*p.*) to make sure (of), assure oneself (*of*); у. в по́длинности докуме́нта to assure oneself of the genuineness of a document.

удостовер|я́ть(ся), я́ю(сь), *impf. of* ∼и́ть(ся).

удосто́|ить, ю, ишь, *pf.* (*of* удоста́ивать) 1. (+*a. and g.*) to award (to), confer (on); у. кого́-н. ле́нинской пре́мии to award someone a Lenin prize. 2. (+*i.*; *usu. iron.*) to favour (with), vouchsafe; у. улы́бкой to favour with a smile.

удосто́|иться, юсь, ишься, *pf.* (*of* удоста́иваться) (+*g.*) 1. to receive, be awarded (*an honour, a prize, etc.*). 2. (*usu. iron.*) to be favoured (with), be vouchsafed.

удосу́жива|ться, юсь, *impf. of* удосу́житься.

удосу́ж|иться, усь, ишься, *pf.* (*of* ∼иваться) (+*inf.*; *coll.*) to find time (to), to manage.

удочер|и́ть, ю́, и́шь, *pf.* (*of* ∼я́ть) to adopt (*as a daughter*).

удочер|я́ть, я́ю, *impf. of* ∼и́ть.

у́дочк|а, и, *f.* (fishing-)rod (*also in fig., coll. phrases*); заки́нуть ∼у to cast a line; to put a line out (= to try to discover something); пойма́ть, подде́ть на ∼у to catch out; попа́сться на ∼у to swallow the bait.

удра́|ть, удеру́, удерёшь, *past* ∼л, ∼ла́, ∼ло, *pf.* (*of* удира́ть) (*coll.*) to make off; to do a bunk, flit.

удруж|и́ть, у́, и́шь, *pf.* (+*d.*; *coll.*) to do a good turn (*also iron.*, = to do a bad turn).

удруч|а́ть, а́ю, *impf. of* ∼и́ть.

удручённост|ь, и, *f.* depression, despondency.

удруч|и́ть, у́, и́шь, *pf.* (*of* ∼а́ть) to depress, dispirit.

уду́м|ать, аю, *pf.* (*of* ∼ывать) (*coll.*) to think up.

уду́мыва|ть, ю, *impf. of* уду́мать.

удуш|а́ть, а́ю, *impf. of* ∼и́ть.

удуше́ни|е, я, *n.* smothering, suffocation; asphyxiation.

удуш|и́ть, у́, ∼ишь, *pf.* (*of* ∼а́ть) to smother, stifle, suffocate; to asphyxiate.

удУ́шлив|ый (∼, ∼а), *adj.* stifling, suffocating; asphyxiating; ∼ая жара́ stifling heat; у. газ asphyxiating gas.

удушь|е, я, *n.* asthma; asphyxia.

уединени|е, я, *n.* solitude; seclusion.

уединённост|ь, и, *f.* solitariness, seclusion.

уединён|ный (~, ~на), *p.p.p.* of уединить and *adj.* solitary, secluded; lonely.

един|ить, ю, ишь, *pf.* (*of* ~ять) to seclude, set apart.

уедин|иться, юсь, ишься, *pf.* (*of* ~яться) (от) to retire (from), withdraw (from); to go off (by oneself); у. в свою комнату to retire to one's room.

уедин|ять(ся), яю(сь), *impf.* of ~ить(ся).

уезд, а, *m.* (*hist.*) uyezd (*lowest administrative division, now* район).

уезд|ный, *adj.* of ~; у. город chief town of uyezd.

уеть, уебу, уебёшь, *past* уёб, уебли, *pf.* (*of* еть *and* ебать) (*vulg.*) to fuck.

уехать, уеду, уедешь, *imp.* уезжай(те), *pf.* (*of* уезжать) to go away, leave, depart.

уж[1], а, *m.* grass-snake.

уж[2] 1. *adv.* = уже. 2. *emphatic particle* (*coll.*) to be sure, indeed, certainly; уж он узнает he is sure to find out; уж мы искали, искали we searched all over the place. 3. *particle emphasizing certain pronouns and adverbs* very; это не так уж сложно it's not so very complicated, it's not all that complicated.

ужал|ить, ю, ишь, *pf.* of жалить.

ужарива|ться, ется, *impf.* of ужариться.

ужар|иться, ится, *pf.* (*of* ~иваться) (*coll.*) 1. to be thoroughly roasted, fried. 2. to roast away, be roasted up.

ужас, а, *m.* 1. horror, terror; внушить у. (+*d.*) to inspire with horror, horrify; навести у. (на+*a.*) to instil terror (into); объятый ~ом horror-struck, terror-stricken; к моему ~у to my horror. 2. (*usu. pl.*) horror; ~ы осады the horrors of a siege. 3. *as pred.* (*coll.*) it is awful, it is terrible. 4. у. (как) *as adv.* (*coll.*) awfully, terribly; у. как громко awfully loud.

ужас|аться(ся), аю(сь), *impf.* of ~нуть(ся).

ужасно[1], *adv.* 1. horribly, terribly; у. себя чувствовать to feel awful. 2. (*coll.*) awfully, terribly, frightfully; он у. плохо играет he plays terribly badly.

ужасно[2], *as pred.* (*coll.*) it is awful, it is terrible, it is ghastly.

ужас|нуть, ну, нёшь, *pf.* (*of* ~ать) to horrify, terrify.

ужас|нуться, нусь, нёшься, *pf.* (*of* ~аться) to be horrified, be terrified.

ужас|ный (~ен, ~на), *adj.* (*in var. senses*) awful, terrible, ghastly, frightful; у. вид awful sight; у. насморк awful cold.

уже, *comp.* of узкий *and* узко.

уже 1. *adv.* already; now; by now; у. не longer; они у. прибыли they are here already; он, должно-быть, у. уехал he must have gone by now; она у. не ребёнок she is no longer a child. 2. *emphatic particle* = уж; это у. другое дело that's quite a different matter.

ужели, ужель, *adv.* (*obs.*) = неужели.

ужени|е, я, *n.* fishing, angling.

ужива|ться, юсь, *impf.* of ужиться.

уживчив|ый (~, ~а), *adj.* easy to get on with.

ужимк|а, и, *f.* grimace.

ужин, а, *m.* supper.

ужина|ть, ю, *impf.* (*of* по~) to have supper.

ужи|ться, вусь, вёшься, *past* ~лся, ~лась, *pf.* (*of* ~ваться) (с+*i.*) to get on (with); мы с ней так и не ~лись she and I simply couldn't get on.

ужо, *adv.* (*coll.*) 1. later, by and by. 2. *as threat*: у. тебе! just you wait!; я тебя у. проучу! just you wait—I'll show you!

ужовый, *adj.* of уж[1].

узаконени|е, я, *n.* 1. legalization, legitimization. 2. statute.

узаконива|ть, ю, *impf.* of узаконить.

узакон|ить, ю, ишь, *pf.* (*of* ~ивать *and* ~ять) to legalize, legitimize.

узакон|ять, яю, *impf.* = ~ивать.

узбек, а, *m.* Uzbek.

узбекский, *adj.* Uzbek.

узбечк|а, и, *f.* Uzbek (woman).

узд|а, ы, *pl.* ~ы, *f.* bridle (*also fig.*); держать в ~е to keep in check, restrain.

уздечк|а, и, *f.* 1. bridle. 2. (*anat.*) fraenum.

уздцы: под у. by the bridle.

уз|ел, ла, *m.* 1. knot (*also fig. and naut. measurement of speed*); bend, hitch; завязать у. to tie a knot; завязать ~лом to knot; у. противоречий knot of contradictions. 2. junction; centre; у. дорог road junction; промышленный у. industrial centre; у. сопротивления (*mil.*) centre of resistance. 3. нервный у. (*anat.*) nerve-centre, ganglion. 4. (*bot.*) node. 5. (*tech.*) group, assembly. 6. bundle, pack.

узел|ок, ка, *m.* 1. small knot. 2. (*bot.*) nodule. 3. small bundle.

уз|кий (~ок, ~ка, ~ко), *adj.* 1. narrow; ~кая колея (*railways*) narrow gauge; ~кое место (*fig.*) bottleneck. 2. tight. 3. (*fig.*) narrow, limited; в ~ком смысле слова in the narrow sense of the word. 4. (*fig.*) narrow, narrow-minded; у. человек narrow-minded person.

узковат|ый (~, ~а), *adj.* rather narrow; rather tight.

узкогорлый, *adj.* (*of a vessel*) narrow-necked.

узкоколейный, *adj.* narrow-gauge.

узколоб|ый (~, ~а), *adj.* 1. having a narrow forehead. 2. (*fig.*) narrow-minded.

узлист|ый (~, ~а), *adj.* knotty; nodose.

узловáт|ый (~, ~а), *adj.* knotty; nodose; gnarled.

узлов|óй, *adj.* **1.** junction; ~áя стáнция (*railways*) junction. **2.** main, principal, central, key; у. вопрóс central question. **3.** (*bot.*) nodal.

узна|вáть, ю, ёшь, *impf. of* ~ть.

узнá|ть, ю, *pf.* (*of* ~вáть) **1.** to recognize. **2.** to get to know, become familiar with. **3.** to learn, find out.

ýзник, а, *m.* (*obs. or rhet.*) prisoner.

ýзниц|а, ы, *f. of* ýзник.

узóр, а, *m.* pattern, design.

узóр|ный, *adj.* **1.** *adj. of* ~. **2.** decorated with a pattern, design.

узóрчат|ый (~, ~а), *adj.* decorated with a pattern, design.

ýзост|ь, и, *f.* narrowness (*also fig.*); tightness.

узр|éть, ю, ~ишь, *pf.* **1.** *pf. of* зреть². **2.** (*fig.*) to see; to take (as); онá ~éла в моём замечáнии обúду she took my remark as an insult.

узурпáтор, а, *m.* usurper.

узурпáци|я, и, *f.* usurpation.

узурпúр|овать, ую, *impf. and pf.* to usurp.

ýзус, а, *m.* (*leg.*) usage.

ýз|ы, ~, *no sing.* (*fig.*) bonds, ties.

уйгýр, а, *m.* Uighur.

уйгýрк|а, и, *f.* Uighur (woman).

уйгýрский, *adj.* Uighur.

уй|дý, дёшь, *see* ~тú.

ýйм|а, ы, *no pl.,f.* (*coll.*) lots (of), masses (of), heaps (of).

уйм|ý, ёшь, *see* унять.

уй|тú, дý, дёшь, *past* ушёл, ушлá, *pf.* (*of* уходúть) **1.** to go away, go off, leave; у. из кóмнаты to leave the room; у. ни с чем to go away empty-handed; у. в монастырь to go into a monastery. **2.** (от, из) to escape (from), get away (from); to evade. **3.** (от, из, с) to retire (from), give up; у. от политики to retire from politics; у. от жизни to retire from life; у. из жизни to pass away (= to die); у. со сцéны to quit the stage. **4.** (в+*a.*) to sink (into); (*fig.*) to bury oneself (in); у. в себя to retire into one's shell. **5.** to be used up, be spent. **6.** (*of time, youth, etc.*) to pass away, slip away. **7.** (*coll.*) to boil over; to spill. **8.** (*obs.*) to pass, outdistance. **9.** (вперёд) (*of a timepiece*) to gain, be fast.

укáз, а, *m.* **1.** decree; edict, ukase. **2.** (*as pred.+neg.*) (it is) not an order, not obligatory; ты мне не у. I'm not obliged to do as *you* say.

указáни|е, я, *n.* **1.** indication, pointing out. **2.** instruction, direction; дать ~я to give instructions.

укáз|анный, *p.p.p. of* ~áть *and adj.* fixed, appointed, stated; на ~анном мéсте at the place appointed.

указáтел|ь, я, *m.* **1.** indicator; marker; у. направлéния road sign; у. (воздýшной) скóрости airspeed indicator; у. оборóтов (*tech.*) revolution counter; у. кольцá угломéра azimuth scale index; у. ýровня водý water gauge. **2.** index; у. сóбственных имён index of proper names. **3.** guide, directory.

указáтельн|ый, *adj.* **1.** indicating; ~ая пластúнка dial; ~ая стрéлка pointer; у. пáлец, у. перст forefinger, index finger; у. столб road sign. **2.** ~ое местоимéние (*gram.*) demonstrative pronoun.

ука|зáть, жý, ~жешь, *pf.* (*of* ~зывать) **1.** to show, indicate. **2.** (на+*a.*) to point (at, to); (*fig.*) to point out; у. на ошúбку to point out a mistake. **3.** to explain; to give directions. **4.** (*obs. or coll.*) to give orders.

укáзк|а, и, *f.* **1.** pointer, fescue. **2.** (*coll., pejor.*) orders; по чужóй ~е at someone else's bidding.

укáз|ный, *adj.* (*obs.*) **1.** *adj. of* ~. **2.** established by decree.

указýющий, *adj.* у. перст (*obs.*) forefinger, index finger.

укáзчик, а, *m.* (*coll.*) person who gives orders; ты нам не у. you can't give us orders.

укáзыва|ть, ю, *impf. of* указáть.

укáлыва|ть, ю, *impf. of* уколóть.

укараýл|ить, ю, ишь, *pf.* (*coll.*) to guard, watch.

укат|áть, áю, *pf.* (*of* ~ывать¹) **1.** to roll (out); у. дорóгу to roll, make smooth a road. **2.** (*coll.*) to wear out, tire out.

укат|áться, áется, *pf.* (*of* ~ываться¹) (*of a road surface, etc.*) to become smooth.

ука|тúть, чý, ~тишь, *pf.* (*of* ~тывать²) **1.** to roll away. **2.** (*coll.*) to drive off.

ука|тúться, чýсь, ~тишься, *pf.* (*of* ~тываться) to roll away (*intrans.*).

укáтыва|ть(ся)¹, ю, ет(ся), *impf. of* укатáть(ся).

укáтыва|ть(ся)², ю(сь), *impf. of* укатúть(ся).

укач|áть, áю, *pf.* (*of* ~ивать) **1.** to rock to sleep. **2.** (*of motion of sea or of means of transport*) to make sick; меня ~áло (*impers.*) на парохóде the motion of the boat made me sick, I was (sea-)sick on the boat.

укáчива|ть, ю, *impf. of* укачáть.

укип|áть, áю, *impf. of* ~éть.

укип|éть, лю, úшь, *pf.* (*of* ~áть) (*coll.*) to boil away.

уклáд, а, *m.* structure; у. жúзни style of life; общéственно-экономúческий у. social and economic structure.

уклáдк|а, и, *f.* **1.** packing; stacking, piling;

stowing. **2.** laying (*of rails, sleepers, pipes, etc.*).

укла́дчик, а, *m.* **1.** packer. **2.** layer (*of rails, sleepers, etc.*).

укла́дыва|ть, ю, *impf. of* уложи́ть.

укла́дыва|ться[1]**, юсь,** *impf. of* уложи́ться.

укла́дыва|ться[2]**, юсь,** *impf. of* уле́чься.

укле́йк|а, и, *f.* (*fish*) bleak (*Alburnus alburnus*).

укло́н, а, *m.* **1.** slope, declivity; inclination; gradient. **2.** (*fig.*) bias, tendency. **3.** (*polit.*) deviation.

уклоне́ни|е, я, *n.* deviation; у. от те́мы digression; у. от вое́нной слу́жбы evasion of military service.

уклони́зм, а, *m.* (*polit.*) deviationism.

уклони́ст, а, *m.* (*polit.*) deviationist.

уклон|и́ть, ю́, ∼ишь, *pf.* (*of* ∼я́ть) to turn, fend off.

уклон|и́ться, ю́сь, ∼ишься, *pf.* (*of* ∼я́ться) **1.** (от) to avoid; to evade; у. от уда́ра to dodge a blow; у. от прямо́го отве́та to avoid giving a direct answer. **2.** to turn off, turn aside.

укло́нчив|ый (∼, ∼а), *adj.* **1.** evasive. **2.** (*obs.*) meek; compliant.

уклон|я́ть(ся), я́ю(сь), *impf. of* ∼и́ть(ся).

уключин|а, ы, *f.* rowlock.

укоко́ш|ить, у, ишь, *pf.* (*sl.*) to bump off.

уко́л, а, *m.* **1.** prick; jab. **2.** (*mil.*) thrust. **3.** injection; 'jab'.

уко́л|о́ть, ю́, ∼ешь, *pf.* (*of* ука́лывать) **1.** to prick. **2.** (*fig.*) to sting, wound; у. чьё-н. самолю́бие to touch someone's pride.

укомплектова́ни|е, я, *n.* bringing up to strength.

укомплекто́в|анный, *p.p.p. of* ∼а́ть *and adj.* complete, at full strength.

укомплект|ова́ть, у́ю, *pf.* (*of* комплектова́ть *and* ∼о́вывать) **1.** to complete; to bring up to (full) strength; to man. **2.** (+*i.*) to equip (with), furnish (with).

укомплекто́выва|ть, ю, *impf. of* укомплектова́ть.

уко́р, а, *m.* reproach; ∼ы со́вести pangs of conscience.

укора́чива|ть, ю, *impf. of* укороти́ть.

укорене́ни|е, я, *n.* **1.** implanting, inculcation. **2.** taking root, striking root.

укорен|и́ть, ю́, и́шь, *pf.* (*of* ∼я́ть) to implant, inculcate.

укорен|и́ться, ю́сь, и́шься, *pf.* (*of* ∼я́ться) to take, strike root (*also fig.*).

укорен|я́ть(ся), я́ю(сь), *impf. of* ∼и́ть(ся).

укори́зн|а, ы, *f.* reproach.

укори́зненный, *adj.* reproachful.

укор|и́ть, ю́, и́шь, *pf.* (*of* ∼я́ть) (+*a.* в+*p.*) to reproach (with).

укоро|ти́ть, чу́, ти́шь, *pf.* (*of* укора́чивать) to shorten.

укор|я́ть, я́ю, *impf. of* ∼и́ть.

уко́с[1]**, а,** *m.* hay-harvest, hay crop.

уко́с[2]**, а,** *m.* = ∼и́на.

уко́син|а, ы, *f.* (*tech.*) strut, brace; cantilever; (crane) jib.

укра́дкой, *adv.* stealthily, furtively, by stealth.

украи́н|ец, ца, *m.* Ukrainian.

украи́нк|а[1]**, и,** *f.* Ukrainian (woman).

украи́нк|а[2]**, и,** *f.* Ukrainka (*variety of winter wheat*).

украи́нский, *adj.* Ukrainian.

укра́|сить, шу, сишь, *pf.* (*of* ∼ша́ть) to adorn, decorate, ornament (*also fig.*).

укра́|ситься, шусь, сишься, *pf.* (*of* ∼ша́ться) **1.** *pass. of* ∼сить. **2.** to adorn oneself.

укра́|сть, ду́, дёшь, *past* ∼л, *pf.* (*of* красть) to steal.

украша́|ть(ся), ю(сь), *impf. of* укра́сить(ся).

украше́ни|е, я, *n.* **1.** adorning, decoration. **2.** adornment, decoration, ornament.

укреп|и́ть, лю́, и́шь, *pf.* (*of* ∼ля́ть) **1.** to strengthen; to reinforce; to make fast. **2.** (*mil.*) to fortify. **3.** (*fig.*) to fortify, brace. **4.** (*fig.*) to strengthen; to enhance; у. дисципли́ну to tighten up discipline.

укреп|и́ться, лю́сь, и́шься, *pf.* (*of* ∼ля́ться) **1.** to become stronger. **2.** (*mil.*) to fortify one's position. **3.** (*fig.*) to become firmly established.

укрепле́ни|е, я, *n.* **1.** strengthening, reinforcing. **2.** (*mil.*) fortification; work.

укреп|лённый, *p.p.p. of* ∼и́ть *and adj.* (*mil.*) fortified.

укрепля́|ть(ся), ю(сь), *impf. of* укрепи́ть(ся).

укрепля́ющ|ее, его, *n.* tonic, restorative.

укро́м|ный (∼ен, ∼на), *adj.* secluded; sheltered; cosy.

укро́п, а, *m.* (*bot.*) dill (*Anethum graveolens*); воло́шский у. fennel (*Foeniculum vulgare*); морско́й у. samphire (*Crithmum maritimum*).

укро́п|ный, *adj. of* ∼; ∼ное ма́сло dill oil.

укроти́тел|ь, я, *m.* (animal-)tamer.

укро|ти́ть, щу́, ти́шь, *pf.* (*of* ∼ща́ть) **1.** to tame. **2.** to curb, subdue, check; у. свои́ стра́сти to curb one's passions.

укро|ти́ться, щу́сь, ти́шься, *pf.* (*of* ∼ща́ться) **1.** to become tame. **2.** to calm down, die down.

укроща́|ть(ся), ю(сь), *impf. of* укроти́ть(ся).

укрупне́ни|е, я, *n.* enlargement, extension; amalgamation (*of collective farms, etc.*).

укрупн|и́ть, ю́, и́шь, *pf.* (*of* ∼я́ть) to enlarge, extend; to amalgamate.

укрупн|я́ть, я́ю, *impf. of* ∼и́ть.

укрыва́тел|ь, я, *m.* (*leg.*) concealer, harbourer; у. кра́деного receiver (of stolen goods).

укрыва́тельств|о, а, *n.* (*leg.*) concealment, harbouring; **у. кра́деного** receiving (of stolen goods).

укрыва́|ть(ся), ю(сь), *impf. of* укры́ть(ся).

укры́ти|е, я, *n.* (*mil.,* etc.) cover, concealment; shelter; **у. от огня́** cover (from fire); **у. от взоров** concealment; **стреля́ть из ~й** to fire from covered positions.

укры́т|ый, *p.p.p. of* **~ь** *and adj.* (*mil.*) concealed, covered.

укр|ы́ть, о́ю, о́ешь, *pf.* (*of* ~ыва́ть) **1.** to cover (up). **2.** to conceal, harbour; to give shelter; to receive (*stolen goods*); **у. уби́йцу** to harbour a murderer; **у. от дождя́** to give shelter from the rain.

укр|ы́ться, о́юсь, о́ешься, *pf.* (*of* ~ыва́ться) **1.** to cover oneself (up). **2.** to take cover; to seek shelter. **3.** to escape notice; **от меня́ не ~ы́лось** it has not escaped my notice.

у́ксус, а (у), *m.* vinegar.

у́ксусник, а, *m.* vinegar-cruet.

у́ксусниц|а, ы, *f.* = у́ксусник.

уксуснокис́л|ый, *adj.* (*chem.*) acetate (of); **~ая соль** acetate.

у́ксусн|ый, *adj.* **1.** *adj. of* у́ксус. **2.** acetic; **~ая кислота́** acetic acid; **~ая плёнка** flower of vinegar; **~ая эссе́нция** vinegar essence.

уку́порива|ть, ю, *impf. of* уку́порить.

уку́пор|ить, ю, ишь, *pf.* (*of* ~ивать) **1.** to cork (up). **2.** (*coll.*) to pack (up), crate.

уку́порк|а, и, *f.* **1.** corking. **2.** packing, crating.

уку́с, а, *m.* bite; sting.

уку|си́ть, шу́, ~сишь, *pf.* to bite; to sting; **кака́я му́ха его́ ~си́ла?** (*coll.*) what's bitten him?, what's got into him?

уку́т|ать, аю, *pf.* (*of* ~ывать) (**в**+*a.*) to wrap up (in).

уку́т|аться, аюсь, *pf.* (*of* ~ываться) to wrap oneself up.

уку́тыва|ть(ся), ю(сь), *impf. of* уку́тать(ся).

ула́вливател|ь, я, *m.* = улови́тель.

ула́влива|ть, ю, *impf. of* улови́ть.

ула́|дить, жу, дишь, *pf.* (*of* ~живать) **1.** to settle, arrange. **2.** (*obs.*) to reconcile.

ула́жива|ть, ю, *impf. of* ула́дить.

ула́мыва|ть, ю, *impf. of* уломать.

ула́н, а, *g. pl.* (*in collect. sense*) **ула́н,** *m.* (*mil.*) uhlan.

ула́н|ский, *adj. of* ~.

улеж|а́ть, у́, и́шь, *pf.* (*coll.*) to lie down (*for a certain length of time*).

у́л|ей, ья, *m.* (bee)hive.

улепет|ну́ть, ну́, нёшь, *pf. of* ~ывать.

улепётыва|ть, ю, *impf.* (*of* улепетну́ть) (*coll.*) to make off, bolt; **~й! hop it!**

улет|а́ть, а́ю, *impf. of* ~е́ть.

уле|те́ть, чу́ ти́шь, *pf.* (*of* ~та́ть) **1.** to fly

(away). **2.** (*fig.*) to fly; to vanish; **вре́мя ~те́ло** the time had flown by.

улету́чива|ться, юсь, *impf. of* улету́читься.

улету́ч|иться, усь, ишься, *pf.* (*of* ~иваться) **1.** to evaporate, volatilize. **2.** (*coll.*) to vanish, disappear.

ул|е́чься, я́гусь, я́жешься, я́гутся, *past* **~ёгся, ~егла́сь,** *pf.* **1.** (*impf.* укла́дываться[2]) to lie down. **2.** (*impf.* укла́дываться[2]) to find room (*lying down*). **3.** (*of dust, etc.*) to settle. **4.** (*fig.*) to subside; to calm down; **ве́тер ~ёгся** the wind dropped.

улизн|у́ть, у́, ёшь, *pf.* (*coll.*) to slip away, steal away.

ули́к|а, и, *f.* (piece of) evidence.

ули́тк|а, и, *f.* **1.** (*zool.*) snail; (*pl.*) gastropoda. **2.** (*anat.*) cochlea.

у́лиц|а, ы, *f.* street; (*fig.; pejor.*) 'the streets'; **на ~е** (*i*) in the street, (*ii*) out of doors, outside; **оказа́ться на ~е** (*fig.*) to find oneself in the street; **бу́дет и на на́шей ~е пра́здник** our day will come; **с ~ы** from out of doors; **челове́к с ~ы** anyone (who happens to be about).

улич|а́ть, а́ю, *impf. of* ~и́ть.

улич|и́ть, у́, и́шь, *pf.* (*of* ~а́ть) (**в**+*p.*) to establish the guilt (of).

у́личк|а, и, *f.* *dim. of* у́лица.

у́личн|ый, *adj.* street (*also fig., pejor.*); **у. бой** street fighting; **~ая де́вка** (*coll.*) streetwalker; **у. мальчи́шка** street urchin; **~ая пре́сса** gutter press.

уло́в, а, *m.* catch (*of fish*).

улов|и́мый, *pres. part. pass. of* ~и́ть *and adj.* perceptible; audible.

улови́тел|ь, я, *m.* (*tech.*) detector, locator.

улов|и́ть, лю́, ~ишь, *pf.* (*of* ула́вливать) **1.** (*tech.*) to catch, pick up, locate (*a sound wave, etc.*). **2.** to detect, perceive; **у. но́тку нетерпе́ния в чьём-н. го́лосе** to detect a note of impatience in someone's voice. **3.** (*coll.*) to seize (*an opportunity, etc.*).

уло́вк|а, и, *f.* trick, ruse, subterfuge.

уложе́ни|е, я, *n.* (*leg.*) code.

улож|и́ть, у́, ~ишь, *pf.* (*of* укла́дывать) **1.** to lay; **у. в посте́ль, у. спать** to put to bed; **у. в гроб** (*fig.*) to be the death (of). **2.** to pack; to stow; to pile, stack. **3.** (+*i.*) to cover (with), lay (with). **4.** to lay (*rails, sleepers, etc.*). **5.** (*pf. only*) (*coll.*) to lay out (= to kill).

улож|и́ться, у́сь, ~ишься, *pf.* (*of* укла́дываться[1]) **1.** to pack (up). **2.** (**в**+*a.*) to go (in), fit (in); **шу́ба не ~ится в э́тот чемода́н** a fur coat won't go into that case **3.** (**в**+*a.*) *coll.*) to keep (within), confine oneself (to); **у. в стипе́ндию** to keep within the bounds of, manage on a scholarship; **у. в полчаса́** to confine oneself to half an hour. **4. у. в голове́, в созна́нии** to sink in, go in.

уломá|ть, ю, *pf.* (*of* улáмывать) (*coll.*) to talk round; (+*inf.*) to talk into, prevail upon (to).

ýлочк|а, и, *f. dim. of* ýлица.

улýс, а, *m.* ulus (= (*i*) *settlement or nomad camp in some parts of Siberia,* (*ii*) *former administrative division in Yakut A.S.S.R., etc.*).

улуч|áть, áю, *impf. of* ~и́ть.

улуч|и́ть, ý, и́шь, *pf.* (*of* ~áть) (*coll.*) to find, seize, catch; у. момéнт для разговóра to find a moment for a talk; у. удóбный слýчай to seize an opportunity.

улучш|áть(ся), áю(сь), *impf. of* ~и́ть(ся).

улучшéни|е, я, *n.* improvement, amelioration.

улýчш|ить, у, ишь, *pf.* (*of* ~áть) to improve; to ameliorate, make better; to better.

улýчш|иться, усь, ишься, *pf.* (*of* ~áться) to improve; to get better.

улыб|áться, áюсь, *impf.* (*of* ~нýться) 1. to smile. 2. (+*d.*; *fig.*) to smile (upon). 3. (*impf. only*) (+*d.*; *coll.*) to please; задáча э́та мне вóвсе не ~áется I don't like the idea of this task at all.

улы́бк|а, и, *f.* smile.

улыб|нýться, нýсь, нёшься, *pf.* 1. *pf. of* ~áться. 2. (*coll.*) to fail to materialize; to fall through; to vanish, disappear; нáша нóвая квартúра ~нýлась our new flat failed to materialize, our hopes of a new flat were dashed.

улы́бчив|ый (~, ~а), *adj.* (*coll.*) smiling; happy.

ультиматúв|ный (~ен, ~на), *adj.* categorical, having the nature of an ultimatum.

ультимáтум, а, *m.* ultimatum

ультра- ultra-.

ультразвуковóй, *adj.* (*phys., aeron.*) supersonic.

ультракорóткий, *adj.* (*radio*) ultra-short.

ультрамарúн, а, *m.* ultramarine.

ультрамарúн|овый, *adj. of* ~.

ультрафиолéтовый, *adj.* ultra-violet.

улюлю́ка|ть, ю, *impf.* 1. (*hunting*) to halloo. 2. (*coll., pejor.*) to whoop (*in mockery*).

ум, á, *m.* mind, intellect; wits; склад ~á mentality; ~á не приложý (*coll.*) it's beyond me, I give up; у меня́ ум за рáзум захóдит (*coll.*) I am at my wits' end; быть без ~á (от) to be out of one's mind (about), be mad, crazy (about); (считáть, *etc.*) в ~é (to count, *etc.*) in one's head; в умé ли ты? (*coll.*) are you in your right mind?; и в ~é у меня́ нé было (*coll.*) the thought never even entered my head; взя́ться за ум (*coll.*) to come to one's senses; э́то у меня́ из ~á нейдёт (*coll.*) I can't get it out of my head; прийтú на ум (+*d.*) (*coll.*) to occur to one, cross one's mind; быть на ~é (*coll.*)

to be on one's mind; от большóго ~á (*coll., iron.*) in one's infinite wisdom; свести́ с ~á (*coll.*) to drive mad; (*fig.*) to make wild (*with delight, admiration*), send; сойти́ с ~á to go mad; (по+*d. or p.*; *fig.*) to go crazy (about); с ~óм (*coll.*) sensibly, intelligently; с умá сойти́! (*coll.*) incredible!

умалéни|е, я, *n.* belittling, disparagement.

умалúть, ю, и́шь, *pf.* (*of* ~я́ть) 1. (*obs.*) to decrease, lessen. 2. to belittle, disparage.

умалишённ|ый, *adj.* mad, lunatic; *as noun* у., ~ого, *m.*; ~ая, ~ой, *f.* madman, madwoman; lunatic; дом ~ых lunatic asylum.

умáлчива|ть, ю, *impf. of* умолчáть.

умал|я́ть, я́ю, *impf. of* ~и́ть.

умáслива|ть, ю, *impf. of* умáслить.

умáсл|ить, ю, ишь, *pf.* (*of* ~ивать) (*coll.*) to butter up.

ума|сти́ть, щý, сти́шь, *pf.* (*of* ~щáть) (*obs.*) to anoint.

умащá|ть, ю, *impf. of* умасти́ть.

умá|ять, ю, *pf.* (*coll.*) to tire out.

ýмбр|а, ы, *f.* umbre.

умéл|ец, ьца, *m.* skilled craftsman.

умéл|ый, *adj.* able, skilful; capable; у. рабóтник able workman; ~ая полúтика astute policy.

умéни|е, я, *n.* ability, skill; know-how.

уменьшáем|ое, ого, *n.* (*math.*) minuend.

уменьш|áть(ся), áю(сь), *impf. of* ~и́ть(ся).

уменьшéни|е, я, *n.* reduction, diminution, decrease, lessening, abatement; у. скóрости deceleration.

уменьши́тельн|ый, *adj.* 1. diminishing. 2. (*gram.*) diminutive. 3. ~ое úмя familiar variant of first name (*as* Kolya *for* Nikolai).

умéньш|ить, ~ý, ~и́шь, *pf.* (*of* ~áть) to reduce, diminish, decrease, lessen; у. ход to reduce speed; у. цéны to reduce prices; у. расхóды to cut down expenditure.

умéньш|иться, ~ýсь, ~и́шься, *pf.* (*of* ~áться) 1. to diminish, decrease, drop, dwindle; to abate. 2. *pass. of* ~и́ть.

умéренност|ь, и, *f.* moderation, moderateness; temperance.

умéр|енный, *p.p.p. of* ~ить *and adj.* 1. (~ен, ~енна) moderate (*polit.*; *also fig.*); у. аппетúт moderate appetite; ~енная полúтика moderate policy. 2. (*geogr., meteor.*) temperate; moderate; у. пояс temperate zone; у. вéтер moderate breeze (*on Beaufort scale*).

умер|éть, умрý, умрёшь, *past* ýмер, ~лá, ýмерло, *pf.* (*of* умирáть) to die; у. естéственной, насúльственной смéртью to die a natural, a violent death; у. от, со скýки to be bored to death.

умéр|ить, ю, ишь, *pf.* (*of* ~я́ть) to moderate; to restrain.

умéр|иться, юсь, ишься, *pf.* (*of* ~я́ться)

1. to become more moderate; to abate, die down. **2.** *pass. of* ~ить.

умер|твить, щвлю, твишь, *pf.* (*of* ~щвля́ть) to kill, destroy (*also fig.*); to mortify; у. все свои творческие побуждения to stifle all one's creative impulses.

умерщвле́ни|е, я, *n.* killing, destruction (*also fig.*); mortification.

умерщвля́|ть, ю, *impf. of* умертвить.

умер|я́ть(ся), я́ю(сь), *impf. of* ~ить(ся).

уме|сти́ть, щу́, сти́шь, *pf.* (*of* ~ща́ть) to get in, fit in, find room (for); она́ не могла́ у. все поку́пки в су́мку she could not get all her purchases into her bag.

уме|сти́ться, щу́сь, сти́шься, *pf.* (*of* ~ща́ться) to go in, fit in, find room.

уме́стно¹, *adv.* appropriately; opportunely.

уме́стно², *as pred.* it is appropriate; it is in order, it is proper, it is not out of place; у. бы́ло бы сде́лать намёк it would not be out of place to drop a hint.

уме́ст|ный (~ен, ~на), *adj.* appropriate; pertinent, to the point; opportune, timely; у. вопро́с pertinent question; ва́ше предложе́ние вполне́ ~но your suggestion is quite in order.

уме́|ть, ю, *impf.* (*of* с~) (+ *inf.*) to be able (to), know how (to).

умеща́|ть(ся), ю(сь), *impf. of* умести́ть(ся).

уме́ючи, *adv.* (*coll.*) skilfully.

умиле́ни|е, я, *n.* emotion; tenderness; прийти́ в у. to be moved; лить слёзы ~я to shed tears of emotion, weep with emotion.

умили́тел|ьный (~ен, ~ьна), *adj.* moving, touching, affecting.

умил|и́ть, ю, и́шь, *pf.* (*of* ~я́ть) to move, touch.

умил|и́ться, ю́сь, и́шься, *pf.* (*of* ~я́ться) to be moved, be touched.

умилосе́рд|ить, ишь, *pf.* to propitiate, mollify.

умилостив|ить, лю, ишь, *pf.* = умилосе́рдить.

уми́л|ьный (~ен, ~ьна), *adj.* **1.** touching, affecting; ~ьное ли́чико nice face. **2.** (*pejor.*) ingratiating, smarmy.

умил|я́ть(ся), я́ю(сь), *impf. of* ~и́ть(ся).

умина́|ть, ю, *impf. of* умя́ть.

умира́ни|е, я, *n.* dying.

умира́|ть, ю, *impf. of* умере́ть.

умир|и́ть, ю, и́шь, *pf.* (*of* ~я́ть) (*obs.*) to calm.

умиротворе́ни|е, я, *n.* pacification; conciliation; appeasement.

умиротворён|ный (~, ~на), *adj.* tranquil; contented.

умиротвор|и́ть, ю, и́шь, *pf.* (*of* ~я́ть) to pacify; to appease.

умиротвор|я́ть, я́ю, *impf. of* ~и́ть.

умир|я́ть, я́ю, *impf. of* ~и́ть.

умла́ут, а, *m.* (*ling.*) umlaut.

умн|е́е, *comp. of* ~ый *and* ~о.

умне́|ть, ю, *impf.* (*of* по~) to grow wiser.

у́мник, а, *m.* **1.** good boy; (*coll.*) clever person. **2.** (*iron.*) know-all, smart Alec.

у́мниц|а, ы, (*coll.*) **1.** (*f.*) good girl. **2.** (*m. and f.*) clever person.

у́мнича|ть, ю, *impf.* (*of* с~) (*coll.*) **1.** (*iron.*) to show off one's intelligence. **2.** (*pejor.*) to try to be clever.

умнож|а́ть(ся), а́ю(сь), *impf. of* ~и́ть(ся).

умноже́ни|е, я, *n.* **1.** increase, rise. **2.** (*math.*) multiplication.

умно́жител|ь, я, *m.* у. частоты́ (*radio*) frequency multiplier.

умно́ж|ить, у, ишь, *pf.* (*of* мно́жить *and* ~а́ть) **1.** to increase, augment. **2.** (*math.*) to multiply.

умно́ж|иться, усь, ишься, *pf.* (*of* мно́житься *and* ~а́ться) **1.** to increase, multiply (*intrans.*). **2.** *pass. of* ~ить.

у́мно¹, *adv.* cleverly, wisely; sensibly.

у́мно², *as pred.* it is wise; it is sensible.

у́м|ный (~ён, ~на́, ~но), *adj.* clever, wise, intelligent; sensible.

умозаключ|а́ть, а́ю, *impf. of* ~и́ть.

умозаключе́ни|е, я, *n.* deduction; conclusion, inference.

умозаключ|и́ть, у́, и́шь, *pf.* (*of* ~а́ть) to deduce; to conclude, infer.

умозре́ни|е, я, *n.* (*philos.*) speculation.

умозри́тел|ьный (~ен, ~ьна), *adj.* (*philos.*) speculative.

умоисступле́ни|е, я, *n.* delirium; де́йствовать в ~и to act while the balance of one's mind is disturbed.

умол|и́ть, ю, и́шь, *pf.* (*of* ~я́ть) to move by entreaties.

у́молк: без ~у (*to talk, etc.*) unceasingly, incessantly.

умолк|а́ть, а́ю, *impf. of* ~нуть.

умо́лк|нуть, ну, нешь, *past* ~, ~ла, *pf.* (*of* ~а́ть) to fall silent, lapse into silence; (*of noises*) to cease, stop.

умоло́т, а, *m.* (*agric.*) yield (*of threshed grain*).

умолча́ни|е, я, *n.* **1.** passing over in silence, failure to mention, suppression. **2.** (*lit.*) aposiopesis.

умолча́|ть, ю, *pf.* (*of* ума́лчивать) (о+*p.*) to pass over in silence, fail to mention, suppress, hush up.

умол|я́ть, я́ю, *impf.* **1.** *impf. of* ~и́ть. **2.** to entreat, implore.

умоля́|ющий, *pres. part. act. of* ~ть *and adj.* imploring, pleading, suppliant.

умонастрое́ни|е, я, *n.* frame of mind.

умопомеша́тельств|о, а, *n.* derangement of mind.

умопомраче́ни|е, я, *n.* (*obs.*) derangement

of mind; fit of insanity; до ~я (coll.) stupendously, tremendously.

умопомрачи́тел|ьный (~ен, ~ьна), adj. (coll.) stupendous, tremendous, terrific.

умо́р|а, ы, f. 1. (dial.) exhaustion. 2. (as pred.) (coll.) it's killing, it's incredibly funny.

умори́тельн|о¹, adv. of ~ый.

умори́тельно², as pred. = умо́ра 2.

умори́тел|ьный (~ен, ~ьна), adj. (coll.) killing, incredibly funny.

умор|и́ть, ю́, и́шь, pf. (of мори́ть¹) (coll.) 1. to kill; (fig.) to be the death (of); у. кого́-н. со́ смеху to make someone die of laughing. 2. to tire out, exhaust.

умр|у́, ёшь, see умере́ть.

у́мственн|о, adv. of ~ый; у. отста́лый retarded, backward.

у́мственн|ый, adj. mental, intellectual; у. бага́ж mental equipment, store of knowledge; у. труд brainwork; рабо́тник ~ого труда́ brainworker.

у́мствовани|е, я, n. (pejor.) theorizing, philosophizing.

у́мств|овать, ую, impf. (pejor.) to theorize, philosophize.

умудр|и́ть, ю́, и́шь, pf. (of ~я́ть) to teach, make wiser.

умудр|и́ться, ю́сь, и́шься, pf. (of ~я́ться) (coll.) to contrive, manage (also, iron., to do something which might easily have been avoided).

умудр|я́ть(ся), я́ю(сь), impf. of ~и́ть(ся).

умфо́рмер, а, m. (electr.) transformer.

умч|а́ть, у́, и́шь, pf. to whirl away, hurtle away.

умч|а́ться, у́сь, и́шься, pf. 1. to whirl away, hurtle away (intrans.). 2. (fig.) to fly away.

умыва́льн|ая, ой, f. wash-room.

умыва́льник, а, m. wash-(hand-)stand; wash-basin.

умыва́льн|ый, adj. wash, washing; ~ая ко́мната wash-room; у. таз wash-basin.

умыва́|ть(ся), ю(сь), impf. of умы́ть(ся).

умыка́ни|е, я, n. (ethnol.) abduction (of bride from her parents).

у́мыс|ел, ла, m. design, intention; со злым ~лом with malicious intent; (leg.) of malice prepense.

умы́сл|ить, ю, ишь, pf. (of умышля́ть) (+inf.) to intend, design; (+a.) to plan, plot.

ум|ы́ть, о́ю, о́ешь, pf. (of ~ыва́ть) to wash; у. ру́ки to wash one's hands (also fig.).

ум|ы́ться, о́юсь, о́ешься, pf. (of ~ыва́ться) to wash (oneself).

умы́шленно, adv. purposely, intentionally.

умы́|шленный, p.p.p. of ~слить and adj. intentional, deliberate, premeditated.

умышля́|ть, ю, impf. of умы́слить.

умягч|а́ть, а́ю, impf. of ~и́ть.

умягч|и́ть, у́, и́шь, pf. (of ~а́ть) to soften; to mollify.

умя́ть, умну́, умнёшь, pf. (of умина́ть) 1. to knead well. 2. (coll.) to press down; to tread down. 3. (sl.) to stuff down (= to eat).

унава́живать = унаво́живать.

унаво́жива|ть, ю, impf. of унаво́зить.

унаво́|зить, жу, зишь, pf. (of наво́зить and ~живать) to manure.

унасле́д|овать, ую, pf. of насле́довать 1.

унди́н|а, ы, f. undine, water-sprite.

унес|ти́, у́, ёшь, past ~, ~ла́, pf. (of уноси́ть) 1. to take away. 2. (coll.) to carry off, make off with. 3. to carry away, remove; ло́дку ~ло́ (impers.) тече́нием the boat was carried away by the current; ~й ты моё го́ре! (interj. expressing disapproval) heaven help us! 4. (fig.) to carry (in thought).

унес|ти́сь, у́сь, ёшься, past ~ся, ~ла́сь, pf. (of уноси́ться) 1. to whirl away (intrans.). 2. (fig.) to fly away, fly by; го́ды ~ли́сь the years flew by. 3. (fig.) to travel (in thought).

униа́т, а, m. (rel.) member of Uniat(e) Church.

униа́тк|а, и, f. of униа́т.

униа́тский, adj. (rel.) Uniat(e).

универма́г, а, m. (abbr. of универса́льный магази́н) department store.

универса́л, а, m. 1. all-round craftsman. 2. (geod.) theodolite.

универса́л|ьный (~ен, ~ьна), adj. 1. universal; all-round; ~ное сре́дство panacea; у. магази́н department store; ~ные зна́ния encyclopaedic knowledge. 2. many-sided; versatile; ~ьное образова́ние many-sided education; у. челове́к versatile person. 3. (tech.) multi-purpose, all-purpose; у. инструме́нт (astron. and geod.) theodolite; у. ключ universal wrench.

университе́т, а, m. university; у. культу́ры 'university of culture' (institution providing lecture courses, etc., on general and political topics for adults); поступи́ть в у. to enter, go up to university; око́нчить у. to graduate (from a university).

университе́т|ский, adj. of ~.

унижа́|ть(ся), ю(сь), impf. of уни́зить(ся).

униже́ни|е, я, n. humiliation, degradation, abasement.

уни́жен|ный, p.p.p. of уни́зить and adj. (~, ~на) humble.

унижён|ный (~, ~на), adj. oppressed, degraded.

уни|за́ть, жу́, ~жешь, pf. (of ~зывать) (+i.) to cover (with), stud (with).

унизи́тел|ьный (~ен, ~ьна), adj. humiliating, degrading.

уни|зить, жу, зишь, pf. (of ~жа́ть) to humble, humiliate; to lower, degrade.

уни́|зиться, жусь, зишься, *pf.* (*of* ~жа́ться) to debase oneself, demean oneself; у. до шанта́жа to stoop to blackmail.

уни́зыва|ть, ю, *impf. of* униза́ть.

уника́л|ьный (~ен, ~ьна), *adj.* unique.

у́никум, а, *m.* unique object (*of its kind*).

унима́|ть(ся), ю(сь), *impf. of* уня́ть(ся).

унисо́н, а, *m.* (*mus. and phys.*) unison; в у. in unison; (*fig.*) in unison, in concert.

унита́з, а, *m.* lavatory pan.

унита́рный, *adj.* unitary; у. патро́н (*mil.*) fixed round.

унифика́ци|я, и, *f.* unification; standardization.

унифици́р|овать, ую, *impf. and pf.* to unify; to standardize.

унифо́рм|а, ы, *f.* 1. (*obs.*) uniform. 2. (*collect.*) circus staff (*in the ring*).

униформи́ст, а, *m.* circus hand (*in the ring*).

уничижа́|ть, ю, *impf.* (*obs.*) to disparage.

уничиже́ни|е, я, *n.* disparaging, disparagement.

уничижи́тел|ьный (~ен, ~ьна), *adj.* 1. (*obs.*) disparaging. 2. (*gram.*) pejorative.

уничтож|а́ть, а́ю, *impf. of* ~и́ть.

уничтожа́|ющий, *pres. part. act. of* ~ть *and adj.* destructive; у. взгляд murderous look; ~ющее замеча́ние scathing comment.

уничтоже́ни|е, я, *n.* 1. destruction, annihilation; extermination, obliteration. 2. abolition, elimination.

уничто́ж|ить, у, ишь, *pf.* (*of* ~а́ть) 1. to destroy, annihilate; to wipe out; to exterminate, obliterate; у. си́лы проти́вника to wipe out the enemy's forces. 2. to abolish; to do away with, eliminate; to cancel (out); у. крепостно́е пра́во to abolish serfdom. 3. (*fig.*) to crush, make mincemeat (of), tear to shreds (*with an argument, etc.*).

у́ни|я, и, *f.* (*hist., eccl.*) union (*esp. of the act of 1596 by which the Uniat(e) Church was set up*).

уно́с, а, *m.* 1. taking away, carrying away. 2. (*obs.*) pair (*of a team of horses*).

уно|си́ть(ся), шу́(сь), ~сишь(ся), *impf. of* унести́(сь).

у́нтер, а, *m.* = ~-офице́р.

у́нтер-офице́р, а, *m.* non-commissioned officer.

унт|ы́, о́в, *sing.* ~, ~а́, *m.* (*and* у́нт|ы, *sing.* ~а, ~ы, *f.*) high boots (*of inverted pelt or goatskin*).

у́нци|я, и, *f.* ounce (*measure*).

унынва́|ть, ю, *impf.* to be depressed, be dejected.

уны́л|ый (~, ~а), *adj.* 1. (*of persons*) depressed, dejected, despondent, downcast. 2. (*of thoughts, looks, etc.*) melancholy, doleful, cheerless.

уны́ни|е, я, *n.* depression, dejection, despon-

dency; впасть в у. to become depressed; навести́ у. to depress.

уня́|ть, уйму́, уймёшь, *past* ~л, ~ла́, ~ло, *pf.* (*of* унима́ть) 1. to calm, soothe, pacify; у. деру́щихся to stop a fight. 2. (*coll.*) to stop, check; у. пожа́р to stop a fire. 3. to suppress (*feelings*).

уня́|ться, уйму́сь, уймёшься, *past* ~лся, ~ла́сь, *pf.* (*of* унима́ться) 1. to calm down. 2. (*coll.*) to stop, abate, die down; кровоте́чение ~ло́сь the bleeding has stopped.

упа́|вший, *past part. act. of* ~сть *and adj.* fallen; (*of voice or tone*) weak (*from emotion or fear*).

упа́д: до ~у to the point of exhaustion, till one drops.

упада́|ть, ю, *impf.* (*obs.*) to fall.

упа́д|ок, ка, *m.* 1. decline (*of polit. system, culture, etc.*); в состоя́нии ~ка on the decline. 2. decline, decay, collapse (*of physical or spiritual faculties*); у. ду́ха depression; у. сил breakdown.

упа́дочнический, *adj.* decadent.

упа́дочничеств|о, а, *n.* decadence.

упа́доч|ный (~ен, ~на), *adj.* 1. *adj. of* упа́док 1; decadent. 2. depressive; ~ное настрое́ние depression.

упак|ова́ть, у́ю, *pf.* (*of* накова́ть *and* ~о́вывать) to pack (up), wrap (up), bale.

упако́вк|а, и, *f.* 1. packing (*action*), wrapping, baling. 2. packing (*material*), package.

упако́воч|ный, *adj.* packing; ~ая клеть packing crate; у. материа́л packing material; *as noun* ~ая, ~ой, *f.* packing-house.

упако́вщик, а, *m.* packer.

упако́выва|ть, ю, *impf. of* упакова́ть.

упа́рива|ть, ю, *impf. of* упа́рить.

упа́р|ить, ю, ишь, *pf.* (*of* ~ивать) to boil down, concentrate.

упас|ти́, у́, ёшь, *past* ~, ~ла́, *pf.* (*coll.*) to save, preserve; ~й Бог, Бо́же ~й (*i*) (*expressing warning not to do something*) God preserve you!, heaven help you!, (*ii*) (*expressing vigorous denial*) good God, no!; God forbid!

упа́|сть, ду́, дёшь, *past* ~л, *pf.* (*of* па́дать 1) (*in var. senses*) to fall.

упёк[1], а, *m.* loss of weight in baking.

упёк[2], *see* упе́чь.

упер|е́ть, упру́, упрёшь, *past* ~, ~ла, *pf.* (*of* упира́ть) 1. (*a.* в+*a.*) to rest (against), prop (against), lean (against); у. ле́стницу в сте́ну to rest a ladder against the wall; у. глаза́ в кого́-н. (*coll.*) to fasten one's gaze upon someone. 2. (*sl.*) to pinch, filch.

упер|е́ться, упру́сь, упрёшься, *past* ~ся, ~лась, *pf.* (*of* упира́ться) 1. (+*i.* в+*a.*) to rest (against), prop (against), lean (against); у. ло́ктем в стол to rest one's elbow on the table; у. нога́ми в зе́млю to dig one's heels in the ground. **2.** (в+*a.*; *coll.*) to come up (against), bump (into) (*an obstacle*). **3.** (*coll.*) to jib; (*fig.*) to dig one's heels in.

упе́|чь, ку́, чёшь, ку́т, *past* **~к, ~кла́,** *pf.* (*of* **~ка́ть**) **1.** to bake thoroughly. **2.** (*coll.*) to drag off (*against one's will*); у. под суд to drag into court, through the courts.

упива́|ться, юсь, *impf. of* упи́ться.

упира́|ть, ю, *impf.* **1.** *impf. of* упере́ть. **2.** (*impf. only*) (на+*a.*; *coll.*) to stress, insist (on).

упира́|ться, юсь, *impf.* **1.** *impf. of* упере́ться. **2.** (*impf. only*) (в+*a.*; *coll.*) to come up (against), be held up (by), be stuck (on account of); прое́кт экспеди́ции ~ется в недоста́ток де́нег the plan for an expedition is held up for want of funds.

упи|са́ть¹, шу́, ~шешь, *pf.* (*of* ~сывать) to get in, fit in (*something written*); у. всё письмо́ на одно́м листе́ to get the whole letter on one sheet (*of paper*).

упи|са́ть², шу́, ~шешь, *pf.* (*of* ~сывать) (*coll.*) to get through, consume (= to eat up).

упи|са́ться, ~шется, *pf.* (*of* ~сываться) (*of something written*) to go in, fit in.

упи́сыва|ть(ся), ю(сь), *impf. of* уписа́ть(ся).

упи́танност|ь, и, *f.* nutritional state.

упи́танный, *p.p.p. of* упита́ть *and adj.* (**~, ~на**) well-fed; fattened, fatted; plump.

упит|а́ть, а́ю, *pf.* (*of* ~ывать) to fatten (up).

упи́тыва|ть, ю, *impf. of* упита́ть.

упи́|ться, упью́сь, упьёшься, *past* **~лся, ~ла́сь,** *pf.* (*of* ~ва́ться) (+*i.*) **1.** (*coll.*) to get drunk (on). **2.** (*fig.*) to revel (in), be intoxicated (by) (*sights, sounds, etc.*).

упла́т|а, ы, *f.* payment, paying; в ~у on account, in payment; подлежа́щий ~е payable.

упла|ти́ть, чу́, ~тишь, *pf.* (*of* ~чивать) to pay; у. чле́нский взнос to pay a (membership) subscription; у. по счёту to pay a bill, settle an account.

упла́тный, *adj.* relating to payment.

упле|сти́, ту́, тёшь, *past* **~л, ~ла́,** *pf.* (*of* ~та́ть) (*coll.*) to tuck in (to).

уплета́|ть, ю, *impf. of* уплести́.

уплотне́ни|е, я, *n.* **1.** consolidation, concentration, compression; packing (in); у. кварти́ры reduction of space per person in living accommodation; у. рабо́чего дня tightening up time-schedules to increase amount of work done. **2.** (*tech.*) sealing, luting. **3.** (*med.*) hardening (*of skin*).

уплотн|и́ть, ю́, и́шь, *pf.* (*of* ~я́ть) **1.** to consolidate, concentrate, compress; to pack (in); у. кварти́ру to reduce space per person in living accommodation, increase number of occupants per flat; у. рабо́чий день to plan the working day to increase

amount of work done. **2.** (*tech.*) to seal, lute.

уплотн|и́ться, ю́сь, и́шься, *pf.* (*of* ~я́ться) **1.** (*med.*) to harden. **2.** (+*i.*) to take in, give up part of one's accommodation (to). **3.** to condense, thicken; (*of fuel in combustion*) to sinter, clinker.

уплотн|я́ть(ся), я́ю(сь), *impf. of* ~и́ть(ся).

уплыва́|ть, ю, *impf. of* уплы́ть.

уплы́|ть, ву́, вёшь, *past* **~л, ~ла́, ~ло,** *pf.* (*of* ~ва́ть) **1.** to swim away; to sail, steam away. **2.** to be lost to sight. **3.** (*fig., coll.*) to fly away, pass, elapse; нема́ло вре́мени ~ло much water has flowed beneath the bridges. **4.** (*fig., coll.*) to vanish, ebb; наде́жда ~ла́ hope faded.

упова́ни|е, я, *n.* (*obs.*) hope; возлага́ть все ~я (на+*a.*) to set all one's hopes (upon).

упова́|ть, ю, *impf.* (*obs.*) (на+*a.*) to put one's trust (in); (+*inf.*) to hope to.

уподо́б|ить, лю, ишь, *pf.* (*of* ~ля́ть) to liken.

уподо́б|иться, люсь, ишься, *pf.* (*of* ~ля́ться) (+*d.*) **1.** to become like. **2.** (*ling.*) to become assimilated (to).

уподобле́ни|е, я, *n.* **1.** likening, comparison. **2.** (*ling.*) assimilation.

уподобля́|ть(ся), ю(сь), *impf. of* уподо́бить(ся).

упое́ни|е, я, *n.* ecstasy, rapture, thrill; с ~ем ecstatically.

упоённый, *part. as adj.* (+*i.*) intoxicated (with), thrilled (by), in raptures (about, over).

упои́тел|ьный (~ен, ~ьна), *adj.* intoxicating, ravishing.

упокое́ни|е, я, *n.* rest, repose; ме́сто ~я resting-place (= grave).

упоко́|ить, ю, ишь, *pf.* (*obs.*) to lay to rest (= to bury).

упоко́|иться, юсь, ишься, *pf.* (*obs.*) to find repose; to find one's resting-place (= to be buried).

уполз|а́ть, а́ю, *impf. of* ~ти́.

уполз|ти́, у́, ёшь, *past* **~, ~ла́,** *pf.* (*of* ~а́ть) to creep, crawl away.

уполномо́ч|енный, *p.p.p. of* ~ить; *as noun* у., ~енного, *m.* plenipotentiary, representative, person authorized.

уполномо́чива|ть, ю, *impf. of* уполномо́чить.

уполномо́чи|е, я, *n.* authorization; подписа́ть докуме́нт по ~ю кого́-н. to sign a document on someone's authority.

уполномо́ч|ить, у, ишь, *pf.* (*of* ~ивать) to authorize, empower.

уполо́вник, а, *m.* (*dial.*) ladle.

упомина́ни|е, я, *n.* mentioning; (о+*p.*) mention (of), reference (to).

упомина́|ть, ю, *impf. of* упомяну́ть.

упо́мн|ить, ю, ишь, *pf.* (*coll.*) to remember.

упомя́н|у́ть, у́, ~ешь, pf. (of упомина́ть) (+a. or o+p.) to mention, refer (to).

упо́р, а, m. **1.** rest, prop, support; (tech.) stay, brace. **2.** (tech.) stop, lug; arresting device. **3.** в у. (mil.) point-blank (also fig.); сказа́ть кому́-н. в у. to tell someone point-blank, flat(ly); смотре́ть на кого́-н. в у. to stare straight at someone. **4.** сде́лать у. (на+a. or p.) to lay special stress, emphasis (on).

упо́р|ный (~ен, ~на), adj. **1.** stubborn, unyielding, obstinate; dogged, persistent; sustained; у. челове́к stubborn person; у. ка́шель persistent cough; ~ная оборо́на sustained defence. **2.** (tech.) supporting; у. като́к bogie wheel; у. подши́пник thrust bearing. **3.** (tech.) stop; у. болт stop; у. рыча́г stop lever.

-упо́рный -resistant.

упо́рств|о, а, n. stubbornness, obstinacy; doggedness, persistence.

упо́рств|овать, ую, impf. to be stubborn, unyielding; (в+p.) to persist (in).

упорхн|у́ть, у́, ёшь, pf. to fly, flit away.

упоря́дочива|ть(ся), ю(сь), impf. of упоря́дочить(ся).

упоря́доч|ить, у, ишь, pf. (of ~ивать) to regulate, put in (good) order, set to rights.

упоря́доч|иться, ится, pf. (of ~иваться) to come right.

употреби́тельност|ь, и, f. (frequency of) use.

употреби́тел|ьный (~ен, ~ьна), adj. (widely-)used; common, generally accepted, usual; у. эвфеми́зм widely-used euphemism.

употреб|и́ть, лю́, и́шь, pf. (of ~ля́ть) (in var. senses) to use; to make use (of); to take (drink, medicine, etc.); у. все уси́лия to make every effort, do one's utmost; у. чьё-н. дове́рие во зло to abuse someone's confidence.

употребле́ни|е, я, n. use; application; спо́соб ~я direction for use (of medicine, etc.); для вну́треннего ~я to be taken internally; не для вну́треннего ~я not to be taken; вы́йти из ~я to go out of use, fall into disuse; вы́шедший из ~я out of use, obsolete.

употребля́|ть, ю, impf. of употреби́ть.

упра́в|а, ы, f. **1.** (coll.) control. **2.** (coll.) justice, satisfaction; иска́ть ~ы to seek justice; найти́ на кого́-н. ~у to obtain satisfaction from someone. **3.** (hist.) office, board, authority.

управде́л, а, m. (abbr. of управля́ющий дела́ми) office manager, business manager.

управдо́м, а, m. (abbr. of управля́ющий до́мом) manager of block of flats, house manager.

упра́в|иться, люсь, ишься, pf. (of ~ля́ться) (c+i.; coll.) **1.** to cope (with), manage. **2.** to deal (with) (= to get the better of).

управле́ни|е, я, n. **1.** management, administration; direction; у. госуда́рством government; орке́стр под ~ем Мрави́нского orchestra conducted by Mravinsky. **2.** (tech.) control; driving; piloting; steering; у. на расстоя́нии remote control; по ра́дио radio control; у. автомоби́лем driving (a car); теря́ть у. to get out of control. **3.** government; о́рганы ме́стного ~я local government organs. **4.** (governmental organ) administration, authority, directorate, board; гла́вное у. ры́бного хозя́йства chief administration of fisheries. **5.** (tech.) controls; steering; щит ~я control panel. **6.** (gram.) government.

управле́н|ческий, adj. of ~ие 3, 4; у. аппара́т government apparatus.

управл|я́емый, pres. part. pass. of ~я́ть and adj.; у. снаря́д guided missile.

управля́|ть, ю, impf. (+i.) **1.** to manage, administer, direct, run; to govern; to be in charge (of); у. канцеля́рией to manage an office. **2.** (tech.) to control, operate (a machine); to drive (a car, etc.); to pilot; to steer; у. су́дном (naut.) to navigate a vessel; у. весло́м to row. **3.** (gram.) to govern.

управл|я́ющий, pres. part. act. of ~я́ть and adj. control, controlling; у. вал (tech.) camshaft; as noun у., ~я́ющего, m. manager; bailiff, steward; у. по́ртом harbour master.

упражне́ни|е, я, n. exercise.

упражня́|ть, ю, impf. to exercise, train; у. му́скулы to exercise one's muscles; у. па́мять to train one's memory.

упражня́|ться, юсь, impf. (в+p., на+p., с+i.) to practise, train (at); у. в стрельбе́ в цель to practise marksmanship.

упраздне́ни|е, я, n. abolition; cancellation; annulment.

упраздн|и́ть, ю́, и́шь, pf. (of ~я́ть) to abolish; to cancel, annul.

упраздн|я́ть, я́ю, impf. of ~и́ть.

упра́шива|ть, ю, impf. of упроси́ть.

упрева́|ть, ю, impf. of упре́ть.

упре|ди́ть, жу́, ди́шь, pf. (of ~жда́ть) (obs.) **1.** to warn. **2.** to forestall, anticipate.

упрежда́|ть, ю, impf. of упреди́ть.

упрежде́ни|е, я, n. **1.** (obs.) warning. **2.** (obs.) forestalling, anticipation. **3.** (mil.) range correction, lead (for firing at moving target).

упрёк, а, m. reproach, reproof; бро́сить у. кому́-н. to reproach, reprove someone; ста́вить кому́-н. что-н. в у. to hold something against someone.

упрек|а́ть, а́ю, *impf.* (*of* ~ну́ть) to reproach, reprove; (в+*p.*) to accuse (of), charge (with).

упрек|ну́ть, ну́, нёшь, *pf. of* ~а́ть.

упре́|ть, ю, *pf.* (*of* ~ва́ть) (*coll.*) **1.** to be well stewed. **2.** to be covered with sweat.

упро|си́ть, шу́, ~сишь, *pf.* (*of* упра́шивать) **1.** to beg, entreat. **2.** (*pf. only*) to prevail upon.

упро|сти́ть, щу́, сти́шь, *pf.* (*of* ~ща́ть) **1.** to simplify; (до) to reduce (to). **2.** (*pejor.*) to oversimplify.

упро|сти́ться, сти́тся, *pf.* (*of* ~ща́ться) to become simpler, be simplified.

упроче́ни|е, я, *n.* strengthening, consolidation; fixing, securing.

упро́чива|ть(ся), ю(сь), *impf. of* упро́чить(ся).

упро́ч|ить, у, ишь, *pf.* (*of* ~ивать) **1.** to strengthen, consolidate; to fix, secure; to establish firmly, place on firm foundations. **2.** (за+*i.*) to grant permanent possession (to), leave (to); у. за кем-н. всё своё состоя́ние to leave one's entire estate to someone. **3.** (за+*i.*) to ensure; его́ Пе́рвая симфо́ния ~ила за ним репута́цию выдаю́щегося компози́тора his First Symphony ensured his reputation as an outstanding composer.

упро́ч|иться, усь, ишься, *pf.* (*of* ~иваться) **1.** to be strengthened, consolidated; to become firmer; to be firmly established; на́ше положе́ние ~илось our position is firmly established. **2.** to establish oneself (firmly), settle oneself. **3.** (за+*i.*) (*of property, etc.*) to be settled (upon). **4.** (за+*i.*) to be ensured; to become firmly attached (to); за ним ~илась сла́ва ко́мика his name as a comic actor was made; про́звище ~илось за ней the nickname stuck to her.

упроща́|ть(ся), ю(сь), *impf. of* упрости́ть(ся).

упроще́н|ец, ца, *m.* (*coll.*) oversimplifier.

упроще́ни|е, я, *n.* simplification.

упрощённост|ь, и, f. **1.** simplified character. **2.** oversimplification.

упро|щённый, p.p.p. of ~сти́ть and adj. **1.** simplified. **2.** oversimplified.

упроще́нческий, adj. (*pejor.*) oversimplified.

упроще́нчеств|о, а, *n.* (*pejor.*) oversimplification.

упру́г|ий (~, ~а), adj. **1.** elastic, resilient; ~ая похо́дка springy gait. **2.** (*phys.*) expansible, extensible (*of gases*).

упру́гост|ь, и, f. **1.** elasticity, resilience; spring, bound; преде́л ~и (*phys.*) elastic limit. **2.** (*phys.*) expansibility, extensibility.

упру́|же, *comp. of* ~гий.

упряжк|а, и, f. **1.** team, relay (*of horses, dogs, etc.*). **2.** harness, gear. **3.** (*obs., coll.*) shift, stint.

упряжн|о́й, adj. draught; ~а́я ло́шадь draught-horse, carriage-horse; ~а́я тя́га draw-bar.

у́пряж|ь, и, f. harness, gear.

упря́м|ец, ца, *m.* (*coll.*) obstinate person.

упря́м|иться, люсь, ишься, *impf.* to be obstinate; (в+*p.*) to persist (in).

упря́миц|а, ы, f. *of* упря́мец.

упря́мств|о, а, *n.* obstinacy, stubbornness.

упря́мств|овать, ую, *impf.* = упря́миться.

упря́м|ый (~, ~а), adj. **1.** obstinate, stubborn. **2.** persistent.

упря́|тать, чу, чешь, *pf.* (*of* ~тывать) **1.** to hide, conceal. **2.** (*fig., coll.*) to put away, banish.

упря́|таться, чусь, чешься, *pf.* (*of* ~тываться) (*coll.*) to hide (*intrans.*).

упря́тыва|ть(ся), ю(сь), *impf. of* упря́тать(ся).

упуска́|ть, ю, *impf. of* упусти́ть.

упу|сти́ть, щу́, ~стишь, *pf.* (*of* ~ска́ть) **1.** to let go, let slip, let fall; у. пово́дья to let the reins go. **2.** (*fig.*) to let go, let slip; to miss; to lose; у. возмо́жность to miss an opportunity; у. и́з виду to overlook, fail to take account (of). **3.** (*coll.*) to neglect.

упуще́ни|е, я, *n.* **1.** omission. **2.** (careless) slip; negligence; у. по слу́жбе neglect of duty, dereliction of duty.

упы́р|ь, я́, m. (*coll.*) vampire.

упятер|и́ть, ю́, и́шь, *pf.* (*of* ~я́ть) to increase fivefold.

упятер|я́ть, я́ю, *impf. of* ~и́ть.

ура́, *interj.* hurrah!, hurray! (*exclamation* (*i*) *expressing exultation or approbation*, (*ii*) *of troops going in to attack*); на у. (*i*) (*mil.*) by storm, (*ii*) (*iron.*) by luck (= without due preparation).

ура́- blind, unthinking (*e.g.* ура́-патриоти́зм, а, *m.* jingoism).

уравне́ни|е, я, *n.* **1.** equalization. **2.** (*math.*) equation; у. пе́рвой сте́пени simple equation.

ура́внива|ть¹, ю, *impf. of* уравня́ть.

ура́внива|ть², ю, *impf. of* уровня́ть.

уравни́ловк|а, и, f. (*coll.*) (*pejor. in Soviet usage*) egalitarianism; у. в опла́те труда́ wage-levelling.

уравни́тел|ь, я, m. **1.** (*tech.*) equalizer, leveller; regulator; у. хо́да governor. **2.** (*polit.*) egalitarian.

уравни́тельн|ый, adj. (*in var. senses*) equalizing, levelling; ~ая переда́ча (*tech.*) differential gear.

уравнове́|сить, шу, сишь, *pf.* (*of* ~шивать) **1.** to balance; (*tech.*) to equilibrate. **2.** (*fig.*) to counterbalance; to neutralize.

уравнове́шенност|ь, и, f. (*fig.*) balance, steadiness, composure.

уравнове́|шенный, *p.p.p. of* ~сить *and adj.* (*fig.*) balanced, steady, composed.

уравнове́шивани|е, я, *n.* balancing; (*tech.*) equilibration.

уравнове́шива|ть, ю, *impf. of* уравнове́сить.

уравня́|ть, ю, *pf.* (*of* ура́внивать¹) to equalize, make equal, make level.

урага́н, а, *m.* hurricane; (*fig.*) storm.

урага́н|ный, *adj. of* ~; у. ого́нь (*mil.*) drum--fire.

уразумева́|ть, ю, *impf. of* уразуме́ть.

уразуме́|ть, ю, *pf.* (*of* ~ва́ть) to comprehend.

ура́льский, *adj.* (*geogr.*) Ural(s).

ура́н, а, *m.* 1. У. (*astron.*) Uranus. 2. (*chem.*) uranium.

уранини́т, а, *m.* (*min.*) uraninite, pitchblende.

ура́новый, *adj.* uranium, uranic.

урв|а́ть, у́, ёшь, *past* ~а́л, ~ала́, ~а́ло, *pf.* (*of* урыва́ть) (*coll.*) to snatch (*also fig.*), grab; у. мину́ту-две для бесе́ды to snatch a minute or two for a chat.

урв|а́ться, у́сь, ёшься, *past* ~а́лся, ~ала́сь, ~а́лось, *pf.* (*of* урыва́ться) (*coll.*) to break loose; (*fig.*) to get away, snatch a free minute.

урду́, *indecl., m.* Urdu (*language*).

урегули́ровани|е, я, *n.* regulation; settlement, adjustment.

урегули́р|овать, ую, *pf.* (*of* регули́ровать) to regulate; to settle, adjust; у. спо́рную пробле́му to settle a dispute.

уре́з, а, *m.* (*coll.*) reduction, cut.

уре́|зать, жу, жешь, *pf.* (*of* ~за́ть *and* ~зыва́ть) 1. (*coll.*) to cut off; to shorten. 2. to cut down, reduce; to axe; у. шта́ты to cut down the staff.

уреза́|ть, а́ю, *impf. of* ~ать.

урезо́нива|ть, ю, *impf. of* урезо́нить.

урезо́н|ить, ю, ишь, *pf.* (*of* ~ивать) (*coll.*) to make to see reason, bring to reason.

уре́зыва|ть, ю, *impf.* = уреза́ть.

урем|а́, ы́ (and уре́м|а, ы), *f.* (*dial.*) woods along a river.

уреми́ческий, *adj.* (*med.*) uraemic.

уреми́|я, и, *f.* (*med.*) uraemia.

уре́тр|а, ы, *f.* (*anat.*) urethra.

уретри́т, а, *m.* (*med.*) urethritis.

уретроско́п, а, *m.* (*med.*) urethroscope.

ури́льник, а, *m.* (*obs.*) chamber-pot.

ури́н|а, ы, *f.* (*med.*) urine.

у́рк|а, и, *m. and f.* (*prison sl.*) 'urka' (*criminal serving time as opp. to political prisoner*).

у́рн|а, ы, *f.* 1. urn. 2. избира́тельная у. ballot-box. 3. refuse bin, litter receptacle.

у́ров|ень, ня, *m.* 1. (*in var. senses*) level, plane; standard; у. мо́ря sea level; высота́ над ~нем мо́ря altitude above sea level; в у. (c+i.) (*i*) level (with), at the height (of); flush (with), (*ii*) (*fig.*) abreast (of), in pace

(with); на ~не земли́ at ground level; быть на ~не to satisfy requirements; совеща́ние на высо́ком ~не (*polit.*) high-level conference. 2. (*tech.*) level, gauge.

уровнеме́р, а, *m.* (*tech.*) water-level.

уровня́|ть, ю, *pf.* (*of* ура́внивать²) to level, make even.

уро́д, а, *m.* 1. freak, monster; deformed person. 2. ugly person; (*morally*) depraved person.

уро́дин|а, ы, *m. and f.* (*coll.*) = уро́д.

уро|ди́ть, жу́, ди́шь, *pf.* (*coll.*) to bear, bring forth.

уро|ди́ться, жу́сь, ди́шься, *pf.* 1. (*of crops, etc.*) to ripen; (*of a human being*) to be born. 2. (в+a.; *coll.*) to take after.

уро́дливост|ь, и, *f.* 1. deformity. 2. ugliness.

уро́длив|ый (~, ~а), *adj.* 1. deformed, misshapen. 2. ugly. 3. (*fig.*) ugly, bad; abnormal; faulty; distorting, distorted; ~ое воспита́ние bad upbringing; у. перево́д faulty translation.

уро́д|овать, ую, *impf.* (*of* из~) 1. to deform, disfigure, mutilate. 2. to make ugly. 3. (*fig.*) to distort.

уро́д|ский, *adj.* (*coll.*) 1. *adj. of* ~. 2. distorted.

уро́дств|о, а, *n.* 1. deformity; disfigurement. 2. ugliness. 3. (*fig.*) abnormality.

урожа́|й, я, *m.* 1. harvest; crop, yield; собра́ть у. to gather in the harvest. 2. bumper crop, abundance (*also fig., coll.*); в э́том году́ был урожа́й на детекти́вные рома́ны this year there has been a bumper crop of detective stories.

урожа́йност|ь, и, *f.* productivity (*of crops*), (level of) yield.

урожа́|йный (~ен, ~йна), *adj.* 1. *adj. of* ~й. 2. producing high yield, productive; у. год good year (*for a crop*).

урождённ|ый, *p.p.p. of* уроди́ть *and adj.* 1. ~ая (*before maiden name*) née. 2. (*obs.*) inborn, born.

урожде́н|ец, ца, *m.* (+*g.*) native (of).

урожде́н|ка, ки, *f. of* ~ец.

уро́к, а, *m.* 1. lesson (*also fig.*); брать ~и (+*g.*) to have, take lessons, tuition (in); дава́ть ~и (+*g.*) to teach, give lessons, give tuition (in); дать кому́-н. у. (*fig.*) to teach someone a lesson; жить на ~е (*obs.*) to be, earn one's living as a (private) tutor. 2. homework; lesson, task; зада́ть у. to set homework; отвеча́ть у. to repeat one's lesson. 3. (*obs.*) task, work.

уро́лог, а, *m.* (*med.*) urologist.

урологи́ческий, *adj.* (*med.*) urological.

уроло́ги|я, и, *f.* (*med.*) urology.

уро́н, а, *no pl., m.* losses, casualties; нанести́ у. to inflict casualties.

урон|и́ть, ю́, ~ишь, *pf.* 1. *pf. of* роня́ть. 2. (*obs., coll.*) to ruin, cause to collapse.

уро́чищ|е, а, *n.* (*geogr.*) 1. natural boundary. 2. isolated terrain feature (*e.g. wood in swamp country*).

уро́чн|ый, *adj.* 1. (*obs.*) fixed, agreed; ~ая рабо́та piece-work; ~ая цена́ fixed price. 2. usual, established.

уругва́|ец, йца, *m.* Uruguayan.

уругва́йк|а, и, *f.* Uruguayan (woman).

уругва́йский, *adj.* Uruguayan.

урча́ни|е, я, *n.* rumbling; у. в желу́дке (*coll.*) tummy-rumbling.

урч|а́ть, у́, и́шь, *impf.* to rumble.

урыва́|ть(ся), ю(сь), *impf. of* урва́ть(ся).

уры́вками, *adv.* (*coll.*) in snatches, by fits and starts; at odd moments.

уры́воч|ный (~ен, ~на), *adj.* (*coll.*) fitful; occasional.

урю́к, а (у), *no pl., m.* (*collect.*) dried apricots.

урю́к|овый, *adj. of* ~.

уря́д, а, *m.* (*obs.*) 1. rule; customs, observances. 2. rank.

уря|ди́ть, жу́, ~ди́шь, *pf.* (*of* ~жа́ть) (*obs.*) to arrange, put in order.

уря́дник, а, *m.* (*hist.*) 1. Cossack N.C.O. (*in tsarist Russian army*). 2. village constable.

уряжа́|ть, ю, *impf. of* уряди́ть.

ус, а, *m.* 1. (*see also* ~ы́) moustache hair; и в ус (себе́) не дуть (*coll.*) not to give a damn; мота́ть (себе́) на ус (*coll.*) to take good note (of). 2. whisker (*of an animal*). 3. antenna, feeler (*of an insect*). 4. (*bot.*) tendril; awn. 5. кито́вый ус whalebone, baleen.

уса́д|ебный, *adj. of* ~ьба; у. быт life of country gentry.

уса|ди́ть, жу́, ~дишь, *pf.* (*of* ~живать) 1. to seat, help sit down; to make sit down; у. в тюрьму́ (*coll.*) to throw into jail; у. в печь (*coll.*) to put into the oven. 2. (за+*a. or* +*inf.*) to set (to, at); у. кого́-н. за роя́ль to set someone to (play at) the piano. 3. (+*i.*) to plant (with). 4. (+*i.*) to cover (with); стена́, ~женная пя́тнами a wall covered with stains.

уса́дк|а, и, *f.* shrinking; shrinkage; contraction.

уса́дьб|а, ы, *g. pl.* ~ *and* уса́деб, *f.* 1. (*hist.*) country estate; country-seat. 2. farmstead; farm centre (*of collective or State farm*).

уса́жива|ть, ю, *impf. of* усади́ть.

уса́жива|ться, юсь, *impf. of* усе́сться.

уса́ст|ый (~), *adj.* (*coll.*) with a big moustache.

уса́т|ый (~, ~а), *adj.* 1. moustached; with a big moustache. 2. (*of animals*) whiskered.

уса́хар|ить, ю, ишь, *pf.* (*coll.*) 1. to sugar plentifully. 2. to win over by flattery. 3. (*obs.*) to beat to death.

уса́ч, а́, *m.* 1. (*coll.*) man with a (big) moustache. 2. barbel (*fish*). 3. capricorn beetle (*Agapanthia dahli*).

усва́ива|ть, ю, *impf. of* усво́ить.

усвое́ни|е, я, *n.* mastering; assimilation.

усво́|ить, ю, ишь, *pf.* (*of* усва́ивать) 1. to adopt, acquire (*a habit, etc.*); to imitate; у. чужо́й вы́говор to pick up someone else's accent. 2. to master (= to learn); to assimilate; у. пра́вила у́личного движе́ния to master the traffic regulations. 3. (+*d.*; *obs.*) to inculcate (in). 4. to assimilate (*food, medicine, etc.*).

усвоя́емост|ь, и, *f.* 1. comprehensibility; хоро́шая у. ease of comprehension, easiness. 2. (*chem.*) assimilability.

усе́ива|ть, ю, *impf. of* усе́ять.

усека́|ть, ю, *impf. of* усе́чь.

усекнове́ни|е, я, *n.* (*rel.*) у. главы́ beheading (*of St. John Baptist*).

усе́рди|е, я, *n.* zeal; diligence, painstakingness.

усе́рд|ный (~ен, ~на), *adj.* zealous; diligent, painstaking.

усе́рдств|овать, ую, *impf.* to be zealous; to take pains.

усе́|сться, уся́дусь, уся́дешься, *past* ~лся, ~лась, *pf.* (*of* уса́живаться) 1. to take a seat; to settle (down). 2. (за+*a. or* +*inf.*) to set (to), settle down (to); у. за ка́рты to settle down to (a game of) cards.

усеч|ённый, *p.p.p. of* ~ь *and adj.* (*math.*) truncated.

усе́|чь, ку́, чёшь, ку́т, *past* ~к, ~кла́, *pf.* (*of* ~ка́ть) to cut off, truncate.

усе́|ять, ю, ешь, *pf.* (*of* ~ивать) (+*i.*) 1. to sow (with). 2. to cover (with), dot (with), stud (with), litter (with), strew (with); лицо́, ~янное весну́шками face covered with freckles; бе́рег мо́ря, ~янный меду́зами sea-shore littered with jelly-fish.

уси|де́ть, жу́, ди́шь, *pf.* 1. to keep one's place, remain sitting; он так волнова́лся, что е́ле мог у. he was so excited that he could hardly sit still. 2. (*coll.*) to hold down a job, keep a job. 3. (*sl.*) to guzzle; to knock back (*drink*).

усидчивост|ь, и, *f.* assiduity.

уси́дчив|ый (~, ~а), *adj.* assiduous; painstaking.

у́сик, а, *m.* 1. (*pl.*) small moustache. 2. (*bot.*) tendril; awn; runner (*of strawberry, etc.*). 3. (*zool.*) antenna, feeler.

усиле́ни|е, я, *n.* 1. strengthening; reinforcement. 2. intensification; aggravation; (*radio*) amplification.

уси́л|енный, *p.p.p. of* ~ить *and adj.* 1. reinforced; ~енное пита́ние high-caloric diet. 2. intensified, increased; ~енная рабо́та high pressure of work. 3. earnest, urgent, importunate; ~енные про́сьбы earnest entreaties.

усилива|ть, ю, *impf. of* уси́лить.

усилива|ться, юсь, *impf.* 1. *impf. of* уси́литься. 2. (+*inf.*; *obs.*) to try (to), make an effort (to).

усили|е, я, *n.* effort; exertion; приложи́ть все ~я to make every effort, spare no effort.

усили́тел|ь, я, *m.* 1. (*tech.*) booster. 2. (*radio*) amplifier. 3. (*chem.*) active filler (*of rubber*).

усили́тельный, *adj.* 1. (*tech.*) booster. 2. (*radio*) amplifying.

уси́л|ить, ю, ишь, *pf.* (*of* ~ивать) 1. to strengthen, reinforce. 2. to intensify, increase, heighten; to aggravate; (*radio*) to amplify.

уси́л|иться, ится, *pf.* (*of* ~иваться) to become stronger; to intensify, increase (*intrans.*); to become aggravated; (*of sound*) to swell, grow louder.

уси́льный, *adj.* (*obs.*) earnest, urgent, importunate.

уска|ка́ть, чу́, ~чешь, *pf.* 1. to bound away; (*coll.*) to skip off, slip off. 2. to gallop off.

ускольз|а́ть, а́ю, *impf. of* ~ну́ть.

ускольз|ну́ть, ну́, нёшь, *pf.* (*of* ~а́ть) 1. to slip off. 2. (*coll.*; *of a person*) to slip off, steal away; to get away. 3. (*fig.*) to disappear; to escape; у. от внима́ния to escape one's notice. 4. (от; *coll.*) to evade, avoid; у. от прямо́го отве́та to avoid giving a direct answer.

ускоре́ни|е, я, *n.* acceleration; speeding-up.

уско́р|енный, *p.p.p. of* ~ить *and adj.* accelerated; rapid; hasty; у. аллю́р increased gait.

ускори́тел|ь, я, *m.* (*tech.*) accelerator.

уско́р|ить, ю, ишь, *pf.* (*of* ~я́ть) 1. to quicken; to speed up, accelerate; у. шаг to quicken one's pace. 2. to hasten; to precipitate.

уско́р|иться, ится, *pf.* (*of* ~я́ться) 1. to quicken; to accelerate. 2. *pass. of* ~ить.

ускор|я́ть, я́ю, *impf. of* ~ить.

ускор|я́ться, я́ется, *impf. of* ~иться.

усла́вливаться = усло́вливаться.

усла́д|а, ы, *f.* (*obs.*) joy, delight; enjoyment.

услади́тел|ьный (~ен, ~ьна), *adj.* (*obs.*) pleasing, delightful.

усла|ди́ть, жу́, ди́шь, *pf.* (*of* ~жда́ть) (*obs. or poet.*) 1. to delight, charm. 2. to soften, mitigate.

усла|ди́ться, жу́сь, ди́шься, *pf.* (*of* ~жда́ться (+*i.*; *obs. or poet.*) to delight (in).

услажда́|ть(ся), ю(сь), *impf. of* услади́ть(ся).

усла|сти́ть, щу́, сти́шь, *pf.* (*of* ~ща́ть) to sweeten.

усла́ть, ушлю́, ушлёшь, *pf.* (*of* усыла́ть) to send away, despatch; у. на ка́торгу (*coll.*) to send away to (do) hard labour.

услаща́|ть, ю, *impf. of* усласти́ть.

усле|ди́ть, жу́, ди́шь, *pf.* (за+*i.*) 1. to keep an eye (on), mind. 2. to follow; у. за хо́дом расска́за to follow a story.

усло́ви|е, я, *n.* 1. condition; clause, term; stipulation, proviso; поста́вить ~ем to make it a condition, stipulate; под ~ем, что; при ~и, что; с ~ем, что on condition that, provided that, providing. 2. (*obs.*) agreement; заключи́ть у. to conclude an agreement. 3. (*pl.*) conditions; ~я пого́ды weather conditions; ~я приёма (*radio*) reception; при про́чих ра́вных ~ях other things being equal.

усло́в|иться, люсь, ишься, *pf.* (*of* ~ливаться) to agree, settle; to arrange, make arrangements; мы ~ились о ме́сте свида́ния we agreed on a meeting-place.

усло́вленный, *adj.* agreed, fixed, stipulated; в у. час at the hour agreed.

усло́влива|ться, юсь, *impf. of* усло́виться.

усло́вност|ь, и, *f.* 1. conditional character. 2. convention, conventionality.

усло́в|ный, *adj.* 1. conventional; agreed, pre-arranged; у. знак conventional sign; ~ное назва́ние code name; у. жест conventional gesture. 2. (~ен, ~на) conditional; у. пригово́р (*leg.*) suspended sentence; ~ное согла́сие conditional consent. 3. (~ен, ~на) relative. 4. theoretical; ~ное то́пливо ideal fuel, comparison fuel. 5. (*gram.*) conditional. 6. у. рефле́кс (*physiol.*) conditioned reflex.

усложне́ни|е, я, *n.* complication.

усложн|ённый, *p.p.p. of* ~и́ть *and adj.* complicated.

усложн|и́ть, ю, и́шь, *pf.* (*of* ~я́ть) to complicate.

усложн|и́ться, и́тся, *pf.* (*of* ~я́ться) to become complicated.

усложн|я́ть, я́ю, *impf. of* ~и́ть.

усложн|я́ться, я́ется, *impf. of* ~и́ться.

услу́г|а, и, *f.* 1. service; good turn; до́брые ~и (*dipl.*) good offices; оказа́ть ~у to do a service; предложи́ть свои́ ~и to offer one's services; к ва́шим ~ам at your service. 2. (*pl.*) service(s); ко́мната со все́ми ~ами room with service; коммуна́льные ~и public utilities. 3. (*collect.*; *obs.*) servants, domestics.

услуже́ни|е, я, *n.* (*obs.*) service; быть в ~и (у) to be in service (with); (*fig.*, *iron.*) to be a lackey (of).

услу́жива|ть, ю, *impf.* (*obs.*) 1. *impf. of* услужи́ть. 2. to serve, act as a servant.

услуж|и́ть, у́, ~ишь, *pf.* (*of* ~ивать) (+*d.*) to do a service, good turn.

услу́жлив|ый (~, ~а), *adj.* obliging.

услыха́ть = услы́шать.

услы́ш|ать, у, ишь, *pf.* (*of* слы́шать) **1.** to hear. **2.** (*coll.*) to perceive, sense; (*of animals*) to scent.

усма́трива|ть, ю, *impf. of* усмотре́ть.

усмех|а́ться, а́юсь, *impf. of* ~ну́ться.

усмех|ну́ться, ну́сь, нёшься, *pf.* (*of* ~а́ться) to smile; to grin.

усме́шк|а, и, *f.* smile; grin.

усмире́ни|е, я, *n.* suppression, putting down; pacification.

усмир|и́ть, ю́, и́шь, *pf.* (*of* ~я́ть) **1.** to pacify; to calm, quieten; (*fig.*) to tame. **2.** to suppress, put down (*a mutiny, etc.*).

усмир|я́ть, я́ю, *impf. of* ~и́ть.

усмотре́ни|е, я, *n.* discretion, judgement; предоста́вить чьему́-н. ~ю, на чье́й-н. to leave to someone's discretion; поступи́ть по своему́ ~ю to use one's own discretion, act as one thinks best.

усмотр|е́ть, ю́, ~ишь, *pf.* (*of* усма́тривать) **1.** (за+*i.*) to keep an eye (on). **2.** (*coll.*) to perceive, observe. **3.** (в+*p.*) to see (in); to regard (as), interpret (as); у. угро́зу в заявле́нии to interpret the statement as a threat.

усна|сти́ть, щу́, сти́шь, *pf.* (*of* ~ща́ть) (+*i.*; *coll.*) **1.** to rig (*a boat*). **2.** (*fig.*) to adorn (with); to stuff (with), lard (with); у. речь ци́фрами to stuff a speech with figures.

усна|ща́ть, ю, *impf. of* усна́сти́ть.

усн|у́ть, у́, ёшь, *pf.* **1.** to go to sleep, fall asleep (*also fig.*); у. ве́чным сном, наве́ки (*rhet.*) to pass to one's eternal rest. **2.** (*of fish*) to die.

усо́биц|а, ы, *f.* (*hist.*) intestine strife.

усоверше́нствовани|е, я, *n.* **1.** finishing, qualifying; ку́рсы ~я finals course(s). **2.** improvement, refinement.

усоверше́нствов|анный, *p.p.p. of* ~ать *and adj.* **1.** finished, complete (*education, etc.*). **2.** improved (*model of machine, etc.*).

усоверше́нств|овать(ся), ую(сь), *pf. of* соверше́нствовать(ся).

усове|сти́ть, щу́, сти́шь, *pf.* (*of* ~щивать) to appeal to the conscience (of); to make ashamed.

усове|сти́ться, щу́сь, сти́шься, *pf.* (*of* ~щиваться) to be sorry, be conscience-stricken.

усове́щива|ть(ся), ю(сь), *impf. of* усове́стить(ся).

усомн|и́ться, ю́сь, и́шься, *pf.* (в+*p.*) to doubt.

усо́пш|ий, *adj.* (*obs.*) deceased; *as noun* у., ~его, *m.*; ~ая, ~ей, *f.* the deceased.

усо́х|нуть, ну, past ~, ~ла, *pf.* (*of* усыха́ть) to dry up, dry out.

успева́емост|ь, и, *f.* progress (*in studies*).

успева́|ть, ю, *impf.* **1.** *impf. of* успе́ть. **2.**
(*impf. only*) (в+*p. or* по+*d.*) to make progress (in), get on well (in, at) (*of studies*).

успе́ется, *impers.*, *pf.* (*coll.*) there is still time, there is no need to hurry.

успе́ни|е, я, *n.* (*eccl.*) **1.** death, passing. **2.** У. (Feast of) the Assumption.

успе́н|ский, *adj. of* ~ие 2.

успе́|ть, ю, *pf.* (*of* ~ва́ть) **1.** to have time; to manage; у. написа́ть to have time to write; у. на заседа́ние to be in time for the meeting; у. к по́езду to manage to catch the train; не у. сде́лать что́-н., как... not to have time to do something before . . . **2.** (в+*p.*) to succeed (in), be successful (in).

успе́х, а, *m.* **1.** success; име́ть большо́й у. to be a great success; по́льзоваться ~ом to be a success; с тем же ~ом equally well, with the same result. **2.** (*pl.*) success, progress; как ва́ши ~и? how are you getting on?; де́лать ~и (в+*p.*) to make progress (in), get on (at).

успе́шност|ь, и, *f.* success; progress.

успе́ш|ный (~ен, ~на), *adj.* successful.

успока́ива|ть(ся), ю(сь), *impf. of* успоко́ить-(ся).

успока́ив|ающий, *pres. part. act. of* ~ать *and adj.* sedative; ~ающее сре́дство sedative.

успокое́ни|е, я, *n.* **1.** calming, quieting, soothing. **2.** calm; peace, tranquillity.

успоко́енност|ь, и, *f.* calmness; tranquility.

успокойте́л|ь, я, *m.* **1.** soother. **2.** (*tech.*) vibration damper.

успокойте́л|ьный (~ен, ~ьна), *adj.* calming, soothing; reassuring; *as noun* ~ьное, ~ьного, *n.* sedative.

успоко́|ить, ю, ишь, *pf.* (*of* успока́ивать) **1.** to calm, quiet, soothe; to reassure, set at rest, set one's mind at rest. **2.** to assuage, deaden (*pain, etc.*); у. чьи-н. подозре́ния to still someone's suspicions. **2.** (*coll.*) to reduce to order, control; у. дете́й to make children be quiet.

успоко́|иться, юсь, ишься, *pf.* (*of* успока́иваться) **1.** to calm down; to compose oneself. **2.** (на дости́гнутом) to rest content (with what has been achieved). **3.** (*of pain, etc.*) to abate; (*of the sea*) to become still; (*of the wind*) to drop. **4.** *pass. of* ~ить.

уст|а́, ~, ~а́м, *no sing.* (*obs. or poet.*) mouth, lips; вложи́ть в чьи-н. у. (*fig.*) to put into someone's mouth; из ~ в у. by word of mouth; узна́ть из пе́рвых, вторы́х ~ to learn at first, second hand; э́то у всех на ~а́х everyone's talking about it; твои́ми бы ~а́ми мёд пить if only you were right.

уста́в¹, а, *m.* regulations, rules, statutes; (*mil.*) service regulations; (*monastic*) rule; у. университе́та university statutes; У. КПСС Rules of the C.P.S.U.; У. ООН U.N.O Charter.

уста́в², а, *m.* (*philol.*) uncial (writing).

уста|ва́ть, ю, ёшь, *impf. of* ∼ть; не ∼ва́я (*as adv.*) incessantly, uninterruptedly.

уста́в|ить, лю, ишь, *pf.* (*of* ∼ля́ть) (*coll.*) 1. to set, arrange, dispose; у. ме́бель в ко́мнате to arrange furniture about the room. 2. (+*i.*) to cover (with), fill (with), pile (with); у. стол буты́лками to cover a table with bottles. 3. (глаза́, *etc.*, на+*a.*) to direct, fix (one's gaze, *etc.*, upon).

уста́в|иться, люсь, ишься, *pf.* (*of* ∼ля́ться) (*coll.*) 1. to find room, go in. 2. (на+*a.*) to fix one's gaze (upon), stare (at). 3. (*obs.*) to become fixed, become steady.

уставля́|ть(ся), ю(сь), *impf. of* уста́вить-(ся).

уста́вный¹, *adj.* regulation, statutory, pre-scribed.

уста́в|ный², *adj. of* ∼².

уста́лост|ь, и, *f.* fatigue, tiredness, weari-ness; у. мета́лла (*tech.*) metal fatigue; испыта́ние на у. fatigue test.

уста́лый, *adj.* tired, weary, fatigued.

у́стал|ь, и, *f.* (*obs. or coll.*) = ∼ость; без ∼и tirelessly, untiringly, unceasingly.

устана́влива|ть(ся), ю(сь), *impf. of* устано-ви́ть(ся).

устано́в|ить, лю, ∼ишь, *pf.* (*of* устана́вли-вать) 1. to place, put, set up; (*tech.*) to install, mount, rig up. 2. (на+*a.*; по+*d.*) to adjust, regulate, set (to; by); у. часы́ по ра́дио to set one's watch by the radio. 3. to establish, institute; у. связь (с+*i.*; *mil.*) to establish communication (with). 4. to fix, prescribe, establish; у. сро́ки о́тдыха to fix holidays. 5. to secure, obtain; у. тиши-ну́ to secure quiet. 6. to establish, deter-mine; to ascertain; у. причи́ну ава́рии to establish the cause of a crash.

устано́в|иться, люсь, ∼ишься, *pf.* (*of* устана́вливаться) 1. (*coll.*) to take position, dispose oneself. 2. to be settled, be estab-lished; to set in; ∼и́лся обы́чай it has become a custom; пого́да ∼и́лась the weather has become settled. 3. (*of character*, *etc.*) to be formed, be fixed.

устано́вк|а, и, *f.* 1. placing, putting, setting up, arrangement; (*tech.*) installation, mounting, rigging. 2. adjustment, regula-tion, setting; у. взрыва́теля fuse setting. 3. (*tech.*) plant, unit, installation. 4. aim, purpose; име́ть ∼у (на+*a.*) to aim (at). 5. directions, directive.

установле́ни|е, я, *n.* 1. (*in var. senses*) estab-lishment. 2. (*obs.*) statute; institution.

устано́в|ленный, *p.p.p. of* ∼ить *and adj.* established, fixed, prescribed, regulation; в ∼ленном поря́дке in prescribed manner; по ∼ленной фо́рме in due form, in accord-ance with set form.

устано́в|очный, *adj.* 1. (*tech.*) *adj. of* ∼ка 1, 2; у. винт adjusting screw; у. кронште́йн mounting bracket. 2. *adj. of* ∼ка 5; у. вопро́с fundamental question.

устано́вщик, а, *m.* fitter, mounter; (*mil.*) (instrument) setter.

устарева́|ть, ю, *impf. of* устаре́ть.

устаре́|вший, *past part. act. of* ∼ть *and adj.* obsolete.

устаре́лый, *adj.* obsolete; antiquated, out of date.

устаре́|ть, ю, *pf.* (*of* ∼ва́ть) 1. (*obs.*) to grow old. 2. to become obsolete; to become antiquated, out of date.

уста́|ть, ну, нешь, *pf.* (*of* ∼ва́ть) to become tired; я ∼л I am tired.

устерега́|ть, ю, *impf. of* устере́чь.

устере́|чь, гу́, жёшь, гу́т, *past* ∼г, ∼гла́, *pf.* (*of* ∼га́ть) (от; *coll.*) to guard (against); to keep watch over.

устила́|ть, ю, *impf. of* устла́ть.

устла́ть, устелю́, усте́лешь, *pf.* (*of* устила́ть) (+*i.*) to cover (with); to pave (with).

у́стно, *adv.* orally, by word of mouth.

у́стн|ый, *adj.* oral, verbal; ∼ая речь spoken language; ∼ая слове́сность oral literature, folk poetry (*orally transmitted*); у. экза́мен oral (examination).

усто́|й¹, я, *m.* 1. (*tech.*) abutment, buttress, pier (*of bridge*). 2. foundation, support. 3. (*pl.*; *fig.*) foundations, bases.

усто́|й², я, *m.* (*coll.*) thickened layer on sur-face of liquid; у. молока́ cream.

усто́йчивост|ь, и, *f.* stability, steadiness, firmness.

усто́йчив|ый (∼, ∼а), *adj.* stable, steady, firm (*also fig.*); ∼ая валю́та stable currency; ∼ая пого́да settled weather; ∼ое соеди-не́ние (*chem.*) stable compound.

усто|я́ть, ю́, и́шь, *pf.* 1. to keep one's balance, remain standing. 2. (*fig.*) to stand one's ground. 3. to resist, hold out; у. пе́ред собла́зном to resist a temptation.

усто|я́ться, и́тся, *pf.* 1. (*esp. of liquids*) to settle. 2. (*coll.*; *of beer, etc.*) to have stood (*sufficient time*). 3. (*coll.*) to become fixed, become permanent.

устра́ива|ть(ся), ю(сь), *impf. of* устро́ить-(ся).

устране́ни|е, я, *n.* removal, elimination, clearing.

устран|и́ть, ю́, и́шь, *pf.* (*of* ∼я́ть) 1. to re-move, eliminate, clear; у. прегра́ды to re-move obstacles. 2. to remove (*from office*), dismiss.

устран|и́ться, ю́сь, и́шься, *pf.* (*of* ∼я́ться) 1. to resign, retire, withdraw. 2. *pass. of* ∼и́ть.

устран|я́ть(ся), я́ю(сь), *impf. of* ∼и́ть(ся).

устраш|а́ть(ся), а́ю(сь), *impf. of* ∼и́ть(ся).

устраша́|ющий, *pres. part. act. of* ~ть *and adj.* frightening, appalling.

устраше́ни|е, я, *n.* **1.** frightening; сре́дство ~я (*mil., polit.*) deterrent. **2.** fright, fear.

устраш|и́ть, у́, и́шь, *pf.* (*of* ~а́ть) to frighten, scare, inspire fear (in).

устраш|и́ться, у́сь, и́шься, *pf.* (*of* ~а́ться) to be afraid, take fright, be scared.

устрем|и́ть, лю́, и́шь, *pf.* (*of* ~ля́ть) (на+*a.*) **1.** (*obs.*) to throw (*troops, etc.*) (against). **2.** to direct (to, at); у. глаза́ на что-н. to fasten one's gaze upon something.

устрем|и́ться, лю́сь, и́шься, *pf.* (*of* ~ля́ться) **1.** (на+*a.*) to rush (upon, at); to head (for). **2.** (на+*a.*; к) to be directed (at, towards), be fixed (upon), be concentrated (on); (*of a person*) to concentrate (on).

устремле́ни|е, я, *n.* **1.** rush. **2.** striving, aspiration.

устремлённост|ь, и, *f.* tendency.

устремля́|ть(ся), ю(сь), *impf. of* устреми́ть(ся).

у́стриц|а, ы, *f.* oyster.

у́стри|чный, *adj. of* ~ца; ~чная ра́ковина oyster shell; у. заво́д oyster farm.

устрое́ни|е, я, *n.* **1.** arranging, organization. **2.** (*obs.*) apparatus, mechanism.

устрои́тел|ь, я, *m.* organizer.

устро́|ить, ю, ишь, *pf.* (*of* устра́ивать) **1.** to make, construct. **2.** to arrange, organize; to establish; у. конце́рт to arrange a concert. **3.** (*fig., coll.*) to make, cause, create; у. сканда́л to make a scene. **4.** to settle, order, put in (good) order; у. свои́ дела́ to put one's affairs in order. **5.** to place, fix up; to get, secure; у. кого́-н. на рабо́ту to fix someone up with work, find someone a job; у. кому́-н. ко́мнату (*coll.*) to get someone a room. **6.** (*impers.; coll.*) to suit, be convenient (to, for).

устро́|иться, юсь, ишься, *pf.* (*of* устра́иваться) **1.** to work out (well); to come right. **2.** to manage, make arrangements. **3.** to settle down, get settled. **4.** to get fixed up (*in a job*); он ~ился на желе́зную доро́гу кочега́ром he has got a job on the railway as a fireman.

устро́йств|о, а, *n.* **1.** arrangement, organization. **2.** (mode of) construction; layout; (*tech.*) working principle(s). **3.** apparatus, mechanism, device. **4.** structure, system; обще́ственное у. social structure.

усту́п, а, *m.* **1.** shelf, ledge (*of wall or cliff*); spur (*of hill*); terrace; (*geol.*) bench; расположенный ~ами terraced. **2.** (*mil.*) echelon formation (*of artillery*).

уступ|а́ть, а́ю, *impf. of* ~и́ть.

уступи́тельный, *adj.* (*gram.*) concessive.

уступ|и́ть, лю́, ~ишь, *pf.* (*of* ~а́ть) **1.** (+*d.*) to let have, give up (to); to cede (to); to concede (to); у. кому́-н. ме́сто to give up one's place to someone; у. доро́гу (+*d.*) to make way (for), let pass. **2.** (+*d.*) to yield (to), give in (to). **3** (+*d.*) to be inferior (to); как забавник, он никому́ не ~ит as an entertainer he is second to none. **4.** (*coll.*) to let have (= to sell). **5.** (*coll.*) to take off, knock off (= to reduce the price by).

усту́пк|а, и, *f.* **1.** concession, compromise; сде́лать ~и to make concessions, compromise. **2.** reduction (*of price*).

усту́пчат|ый (~, ~а), *adj.* ledged, stepped, terraced.

усту́пчивост|ь, и, *f.* pliancy; compliance, tractability.

усту́пчив|ый (~, ~а), pliant, pliable; compliant, tractable.

усты|ди́ть, жу́, ди́шь, *pf.* to shame, put to shame.

усты|ди́ться, жу́сь, ди́шься, *pf.* (+*g.*) to be ashamed (of); to feel embarrassed (for).

у́сть|е, я, *g. pl.* ~ев, *n.* **1.** mouth, estuary (*of a river*). **2.** mouth, orifice (*of furnace, pipe, etc.*).

у́стье|вый (*and* устьево́й), *adj. of* ~.

у́стьиц|е, а, *n.* **1.** *dim. of* у́стье. **2.** (*bot.*) stoma.

усугу́б|ить, ~лю́, ~ишь, *pf.* (*of* ~ля́ть) to increase; to intensify; to aggravate.

усугубля́|ть, ю, *impf. of* усугуби́ть.

усуш|а́ться, а́ется, *impf. of* ~и́ться.

усуш|и́ться, ~ится, *pf.* (*of* ~а́ться) **1.** (*coll.*) to shrink (*in drying*). **2.** to lose weight (*in drying*).

усу́шк|а, и, *f.* **1.** (*coll.*) shrinkage (*in drying*). **2.** (*comm.*) wastage, loss of weight (*through drying*).

ус|ы́, о́в, *sing.* ус, а, *m.* moustache (*see also* ус); мы́, *etc.*, са́ми с ~а́ми (*coll.*) we, *etc.*, weren't born yesterday.

усыла́|ть, ю, *impf. of* усла́ть.

усынов|и́ть, лю́, и́шь, *pf.* (*of* ~ля́ть) to adopt.

усыновле́ни|е, я, *n.* adoption.

усыновля́|ть, ю, *impf. of* усынови́ть.

усыпа́льниц|а, ы, *f.* burial-vault.

усы́п|ать, лю, лешь, *pf.* (*of* ~а́ть) (+*i.*) to strew (with), scatter (with); (*fig.*) to cover (with).

усып|а́ть, а́ю, *impf. of* ~а́ть.

усыпи́тел|ьный (~ен, ~ьна), *adj.* soporific (*also fig.*); ~ьное сре́дство sleeping-draught.

усып|и́ть, лю́, и́шь, *pf.* (*of* ~ля́ть) **1.** to put to sleep (*by means of narcotics, etc.*); to lull to sleep. **2.** (*fig.*) to lull; to weaken, undermine, neutralize; у. со́весть to lull one's conscience; у. боль to deaden pain. **3.** to put (*an animal*) to sleep.

усыпле́ни|е, я, *n.* **1.** putting to sleep; lulling (to sleep). **2.** (*obs.*) sleep.

усыпля́|ть, ю, *impf. of* усыпи́ть.

усыха́|ть, ю, *impf. of* усо́хнуть.

у́ська|ть, ю, *impf.* (*hunting and fig.*; *coll.*) to set on.

ута́ива|ть, ю, *impf. of* утаи́ть.

ута́|и́ть, ю́, и́шь, *pf.* (*of* ⌣ивать) **1.** to conceal; to keep to oneself, keep secret. **2.** to appropriate.

ута́йк|а, и, *f.* (*coll.*) **1.** concealment; без ⌣и frankly, openly. **2.** appropriation.

ута́птыва|ть, ю, *impf. of* утопта́ть.

ута́скива|ть, ю, *impf. of* утащи́ть.

утащ|и́ть, у́, ⌣ишь, *pf.* (*of* ута́скивать) **1.** to drag away, off (*also fig.*); у. кого́-н. в кино́ (*coll.*) to drag someone off to the cinema. **2.** (*coll.*) to make off with (= to steal).

у́твар|ь, и, *no pl., f.* (*collect.*) utensils, equipment.

утверди́тел|ьный (⌣ен, ⌣ьна), *adj.* affirmative.

утвер|ди́ть, жу́, ди́шь, *pf.* (*of* ⌣жда́ть) **1.** (*obs.*) to fix, secure. **2.** to establish (*securely, firmly*); у. диктату́ру to establish a dictatorship; у. за кем-н. пра́во на име́ние to establish someone's right to an estate. **3.** (в+*p.*) to confirm (in) (*intention, opinion, etc.*). **4.** to approve; to confirm; to sanction, ratify; у. пове́стку дня to approve an agenda; у. завеща́ние to prove a will; у. кого́-н. в до́лжности to confirm someone's tenure of an office.

утвер|ди́ться, жу́сь, ди́шься, *pf.* (*of* ⌣жда́ться) **1.** to gain a foothold, gain a firm hold (*also fig.*); to become firmly established. **2.** (в+*p.*) to be confirmed (in) (*one's resolve, etc.*); у. в мы́сли to become firmly convinced.

утвержда́|ть, ю, *impf.* **1.** *impf. of* утверди́ть. **2.** (*impf. only*) to assert, affirm, hold, maintain, claim, allege.

утвержда́|ться, юсь, *impf. of* утверди́ться.

утвержде́ни|е, я, *n.* **1.** assertion, affirmation, claim, allegation. **2.** approval; confirmation; ratification; (*leg.*) probate. **3.** establishment.

утека́|ть, ю, *impf. of* уте́чь.

ут|ёнок, ёнка, *pl.* ⌣я́та, ⌣я́т, *m.* duckling.

утепле́ни|е, я, *n.* warming, heating.

утепл|ённый, *p.p.p. of* ⌣и́ть *and adj.* heated; insulated.

утепли́тел|ь, я, *m.* (*tech.*) **1.** heater. **2.** insulator (*building material*).

утепл|и́ть, ю́, и́шь, *pf.* (*of* ⌣я́ть) to warm, heat.

утепл|я́ть, я́ю, *impf. of* ⌣и́ть.

утер|е́ть, утру́, утрёшь, *past* ⌣, ⌣ла, *pf.* (*of* утира́ть) to wipe (off); to wipe dry; у. пот со лба to wipe the sweat off one's brow; у. кому́-н. нос (*coll.*) to score off someone.

утер|е́ться, утру́сь, утрёшься, *past* ⌣ся, ⌣ла́сь, *pf.* (*of* утира́ться) to wipe oneself, dry oneself.

утерп|е́ть, лю́, ⌣ишь, *pf.* to restrain oneself.

уте́р|я, и, *f.* loss.

утеря́|ть, ю, *pf.* to lose, mislay; to forfeit.

утёс, а, *m.* cliff, crag.

утёсист|ый (⌣, ⌣а), *adj.* steep, precipitous.

утесне́ни|е, я, *n.* oppression.

утесн|и́ть, ю́, и́шь, *pf.* (*of* ⌣я́ть) **1.** (в+*a.*; *coll.*) to stuff (into), squeeze (into). **2.** (*obs.*) to oppress, persecute.

утесн|я́ть, я́ю, *impf. of* ⌣и́ть.

уте́х|а, и, *f.* (*coll.*) **1.** pleasure; delight; для ⌣и for fun. **2.** comfort, consolation.

уте́чк|а, и, *f.* leak, leakage (*also fig.*); loss, wastage, dissipation; у. га́за gas escape.

уте́|чь, ку́, чёшь, ку́т, *past* ⌣к, ⌣кла́, *pf.* (*of* ⌣ка́ть) **1.** to flow away; to leak; (*of gas, etc.*) to escape; мно́го воды́ ⌣кло́ (*fig.*) much water has flowed (under the bridges). **2.** (*of time*) to pass, go by. **3.** (*coll.*) to run away.

утеш|а́ть(ся), а́ю(сь), *impf. of* ⌣ить(ся).

утеше́ни|е, я, *n.* comfort, consolation.

утеши́тел|ь, я, *m.* comforter.

утеши́тел|ьный (⌣ен, ⌣ьна), *adj.* comforting, consoling.

уте́ш|ить, у, ишь, *pf.* (*of* ⌣а́ть) to comfort, console.

уте́ш|иться, усь, ишься, *pf.* (*of* ⌣а́ться) **1.** to console oneself. **2.** (+*i.*) to take comfort (in).

утилизацио́нный, *adj.* у. заво́д salvage factory, by-products factory; у. цех salvage department.

утилиза́ци|я, и, *f.* **1.** utilization. **2.** salvaging; melting-down (*of scrap, etc., for re-use*).

утилизи́р|овать, ую, *impf. and pf.* to utilize.

утилитари́зм, а, *m.* utilitarianism.

утилитари́ст, а, *m.* utilitarian.

утилита́рност|ь, и, *f.* utilitarian attitude.

утилита́рный, *adj.* utilitarian.

ути́л|ь, я, *no pl., m.* (*collect.*) salvage, utility waste (*metal scrap, waste paper, etc.*).

ути́ль|ный, *adj. of* ⌣; ⌣ное желе́зо scrap iron.

утильсырь|ё, я́, *no pl., n.* (*collect.*) = ути́ль; сбо́рщик ⌣я́ salvage collector.

ути́льщик, а, *m.* salvage collector.

ути́ный, *adj. of* у́тка 1.

утира́льник, а, *m.* (*coll.*) hand-towel.

утира́|ть(ся), ю(сь), *impf. of* утере́ть(ся).

ути́рк|а, и, *f.* **1.** (*coll.*) wiping (off). **2.** (*dial.*) handkerchief; hand-towel.

утих|а́ть, а́ю, *impf. of* ⌣нуть.

ути́х|нуть, ну, нешь, *past* ⌣, ⌣ла, *pf.* (*o,* ⌣а́ть) **1.** to become quiet, still; (*of sounds*) to cease, die away. **2.** to abate, subside, slacken; (*of wind*) to drop. **3.** to become calm, calm down.

утихоми́рива|ть(ся), ю(сь), *impf. of* утихоми́рить(ся).

утихоми́р|ить, ю, ишь, *pf.* (*of* ~ивать) (*coll.*) to calm down; to pacify, placate.

утихоми́р|иться, юсь, ишься, *pf.* (*of* ~иваться) (*coll.*) to calm down; to abate, subside.

у́тк|а, и, *f.* 1. duck. 2. canard, false report; пусти́ть ~y to start a canard. 3. bed-pan.

уткн|у́ть, у́, ёшь, *pf.* (*coll.*) to bury; to fix; у. нос в кни́гу to bury oneself in a book; у. глаза́ (в+*a.*) to fix one's gaze (upon), stare steadily (at).

уткн|у́ться, у́сь, ёшься, *pf.* (в+*a.*; *coll.*) 1. to bury oneself (in), one's head (in); у. в па́пку to bury one's head in a file. 2. to bump (into), come to rest (upon), come up (against); ло́дка ~у́лась в бе́рег the boat bumped into the bank.

утконо́с, а, *m.* (*zool.*) duck-billed platypus.

утле́гар|ь, я, *m.* (*naut.*) jib-boom.

у́тлый, *adj.* 1. frail; unsound, unseaworthy. 2. poor, wretched.

ут|о́к, ка́, *m.* (*text.*) woof, weft.

утол|и́ть, ю́, и́шь, *pf.* (*of* ~я́ть) 1. to quench, slake (*thirst*); to satisfy (*hunger*). 2. to relieve, alleviate, soothe.

утол|сти́ть, щу́, сти́шь, *pf.* (*of* ~ща́ть) to thicken, make thicker.

утол|сти́ться, щу́сь, сти́шься, *pf.* (*of* ~ща́ться) to become thicker.

утолща́|ть(ся), ю(сь), *impf. of* утолсти́ть(ся).

утолще́ни|е, я, *n.* 1. thickening. 2. thickened part, bulge; (*tech.*) reinforcement, rib, boss.

утол|щённый, *p.p.p. of* ~сти́ть *and adj.* reinforced.

утол|я́ть, я́ю, *impf. of* ~и́ть.

утоми́тел|ьный (~ен, ~ьна́), *adj.* 1. wearisome, tiring, fatiguing. 2. tiresome; tedious.

утом|и́ть, лю́, и́шь, *pf.* (*of* ~ля́ть) to tire, weary, fatigue.

утом|и́ться, лю́сь, и́шься, *pf.* (*of* ~ля́ться) to get tired.

утомле́ни|е, я, *n.* tiredness, weariness, fatigue.

утом|лённый, *p.p.p. of* ~и́ть *and adj.* tired, weary, fatigued.

утомля́|ть(ся), ю(сь), *impf. of* утоми́ть(ся).

утон|у́ть, у́, ~ешь, *pf.* (*of* тону́ть *and* утопа́ть) 1. to drown, be drowned, sink. 2. (в+*p.*; *fig.*) to be lost (in).

утонча́|ть(ся), а́ю(сь), *impf. of* ~и́ть(ся).

утончённост|ь, и, *f.* refinement.

утонч|ённый, *p.p.p of* ~и́ть *and adj.* refined; exquisite, subtle.

утонч|и́ть, у́, и́шь, *pf.* (*of* ~а́ть) 1. to make

thinner; to taper. 2. (*fig.*) to refine, make refined.

утонч|и́ться, у́сь, и́шься, *pf.* (*of* ~а́ться) 1. to become thinner; to taper (*intrans.*). 2. (*fig.*) to become refined.

утопа́|ть, ю, *impf.* 1. *impf. of* утону́ть. 2. (*impf. only*) (в+*p.*; *fig.*) to roll (in), wallow (in).

утопи́зм, а, *m.* Utopianism.

утопи́ст, а, *m.* Utopian.

утоп|и́ть, лю́, ~ишь, *pf.* (*of* топи́ть) 1. to drown. 2. (*fig., coll.*) to ruin. 3. to bury, embed, countersink.

утоп|и́ться, лю́сь, ~ишься, *pf.* (*of* топи́ться) to drown oneself.

утопи́ческий, *adj.* Utopian.

уто́пи|я, и, *f.* Utopia.

уто́пленник, а, *m.* drowned man.

уто́пленниц|а, ы, *f. of* уто́пленник.

уто́п|ленный, *p.p.p. of* ~и́ть *and adj.* (*tech.*) built-in; ~ленная голо́вка countersink.

утоп|та́ть, чу́, ~чешь, *pf.* (*of* ута́птывать) to trample down, pound.

у́точк|а, и, *f. dim. of* у́тка; ходи́ть ~ой to waddle along.

уточне́ни|е, я, *n.* more precise definition, amplification, elaboration.

уточн|и́ть, ю́, и́шь, *pf.* (*of* ~я́ть) to make more precise, define more precisely; to amplify, elaborate.

уто́чный, *adj. of* уто́к.

уточн|я́ть, я́ю, *impf. of* ~и́ть.

утра́ива|ть, ю, *impf. of* утро́ить.

утрамб|ова́ть, у́ю, *pf.* (*of* ~о́вывать) to ram, tamp (*road material, etc.*).

утрамб|ова́ться, у́ется, *pf.* (*of* ~о́вываться) 1. to become flat, level (*also fig.*). 2. *pass. of* ~ова́ть.

утрамбо́выва|ть(ся), ю(сь), *impf. of* утрамбова́ть(ся).

утра́т|а, ы, *f.* (*in var. senses*) loss; у. трудоспосо́бности disablement.

утра́|тить, чу, тишь, *pf.* (*of* ~чивать) to lose.

утра́чива|ть, ю, *impf. of* утра́тить.

у́тренн|ий, *adj.* morning, early; ~ие за́морозки morning frost; ~яя заря́ dawn, daybreak; (*mil.*) reveille.

у́тренник, а, *m.* 1. morning frost. 2. morning performance, matinée.

у́трен|я, и, *f.* (*eccl.*) matins.

у́тречком, *adv.* (*coll.*) in the morning.

утри́р|овать, ую, *impf. and pf.* to exaggerate; to overplay.

утриро́вк|а, и, *f.* exaggeration.

у́тр|о, а (до ~а́, с ~а́), *d.* у (к ~у́), *pl.* ~а, ~, ~ам (по ~а́м),** *n.* 1. morning; в семь часо́в ~а́ at 7 a.m.; на у. next morning, in the morning; с ~а́ до ве́чера from morn till night; до́брое у.!, с до́брым ~ом! good morning! **2.** (*obs.*) morning performance, matinée.

утро́б|а, ы, *f.* **1.** womb. **2.** (*coll.*) belly; напиха́ть свою́ ~y to stuff one's belly. **3.** ~ой (*coll.*) by instinct.

утро́бист|ый (~, ~а), *adj.* (*coll.*) big-bellied.

утро́бный, *adj.* **1.** uterine, foetal; у. плод foetus; у. пери́од разви́тия period of gestation. **2.** internal; (*of sounds*) deep, hollow; у. смех belly-laugh.

утро́|ить, ю, ишь, *pf.* (*of* утра́ивать) to treble.

у́тром, *adv.* in the morning; сего́дня у. this morning.

утру|ди́ть, жу́, ди́шь, *pf.* (*of* ~жда́ть) to trouble, to tire.

утру|ди́ться, жу́сь, ди́шься, *pf.* (*of* ~жда́ться) (*coll.*) to trouble oneself, take trouble.

утружда́|ть(ся), ю(сь), *impf.* *of* утруди́ть(ся).

утру́ск|а, и, *f.* (*comm.*) spillage.

утряс|а́ть, а́ю, *impf.* *of* ~ти́.

утряс|ти́, у́, ёшь, *pf.* (*of* ~а́ть) (*coll.*) **1.** to shake down. **2.** to shake up, give a shaking. **3.** to settle; у. вопро́с to have a matter out.

утучн|и́ть, ю, и́шь, *pf.* (*of* ~я́ть) **1.** to fatten. **2.** to enrich, manure (*soil*).

утучн|я́ть, я́ю, *impf.* *of* ~и́ть.

утуш|а́ть, а́ю, *impf.* *of* ~а́ть.

утуш|и́ть, у́, ~ишь, *pf.* (*of* ~а́ть) (*coll.*) **1.** to put out, extinguish. **2.** (*fig.*) to suppress.

уты́к|ать, аю, *pf.* (*of* ~а́ть *and* ~ивать) (*coll.*) **1.** to stick (in) all over. **2.** to stop up, caulk.

утык|а́ть, а́ю, *impf.* *of* ~а́ть.

уты́кива|ть, ю, *impf.* = утыка́ть.

утю́г, а́, *m.* (flat) iron.

утюж|ить, у, ишь, *impf.* (*of* вы́~) **1.** to iron, press. **2.** (*coll.*) to smooth. **3.** (*coll.*) to beat; to lambast (*also fig.*).

утю́жк|а, и, *f.* ironing, pressing.

утя́гива|ть, ю, *impf.* *of* утяну́ть.

утяжели́тел|ь, я, *m.* (*tech.*) weighting compound.

утяжел|и́ть, ю, и́шь, *pf.* (*of* ~я́ть) to make heavier, increase the weight (of).

утяжел|и́ться, и́тся, *pf.* (*of* ~я́ться) to become heavier.

утяжел|я́ть(ся), я́ю, я́ет(ся), *impf.* *of* ~и́ть(ся).

утян|у́ть, у́, ~ешь, *pf.* (*of* утя́гивать) to drag away, off.

утя́тин|а, ы, *f.* (*cul.*) duck.

уф, *interj.* (*expressing* (i) *relief,* (ii) *fatigue, physical discomfort, etc.*) ooh!, ee!, gosh!

ух, *interj.* **1.** (*expresses various strong feelings*) ooh!, gosh! **2.** bang!

ух|а́, и́, *f.* ukha (*fish-soup*).

уха́б, а, *m.* pot-hole, pit (*in road*).

уха́бист|ый (~, ~а), *adj.* full of pot-holes; bumpy.

ухажёр, а, *m.* (*coll.*) ladies' man; admirer.

уха́жива|ть, ю, *impf.* (за+*i.*) **1.** to nurse, tend; to look after. **2.** to court (*a woman*); to pay court (to), make advances (to). **3.** to make up (to), try to get round.

у́харский, *adj.* (*coll.*) smart, 'fancy'; dashing; rakish.

у́харств|о, а, *n.* (*coll.*) bravado.

у́хар|ь, я, *m.* (*coll.*) 'lad', smart fellow; dashing fellow.

у́ха|ть(ся), ю(сь), *impf.* *of* у́хнуть(ся).

ухва́т, а, *m.* **1.** oven fork. **2.** (*tech.*) clip.

ухва́тист|ый (~, ~а), *adj.* (*coll.*) adroit, sure, strong.

ухва|ти́ть, чу́, ~тишь, *pf.* **1.** to lay hold (of); (*fig.*) to seize. **2.** (*fig., coll.*) to grasp.

ухва|ти́ться, чу́сь, ~тишься, *pf.* (за+*a.*) **1.** to grasp, lay hold (of); у. за ве́тку to grasp a branch. **2.** (*coll.*) to set (to, about); у. за но́вую рабо́ту to get stuck in to a new job. **3.** (*fig., coll.*) to seize; to jump (at); to take up; у. за предложе́ние to jump at an offer.

ухва́тк|а, и, *f.* (*coll.*) **1.** grip. **2.** (*fig.*) grasp; (a) skill; trick. **3.** manner.

ухитр|и́ться, ю́сь, и́шься, *pf.* (*of* ~я́ться) (+*inf.*; *coll.*) to manage (to), contrive (to).

ухитр|я́ться, я́юсь, *impf.* *of* ~и́ться.

ухищре́ни|е, я, *n.* contrivance, shift, device, trick, dodge.

ухищрённый, *adj.* cunning, artful.

ухищря́|ться, юсь, *impf.* to contrive; to resort to contrivance.

ухлоп|ать, аю, *pf.* (*of* ~ывать) (*coll.*) **1.** to kill, do for. **2.** to squander.

ухло́пыва|ть, ю, *impf.* *of* ухло́пать.

ухмы́лк|а, и, *f.* (*coll.*) smirk, grin.

ухмыльн|у́ться, у́сь, ёшься, *pf.* (*of* ухмыля́ться) (*coll.*) to smirk, grin.

ухмыл|я́ться, я́юсь, *impf.* *of* ~ну́ться.

у́хн|уть, у, ешь, *pf.* (*of* у́хать) (*coll.*) **1.** to cry out (*from surprise, pleasure, pain, fatigue, etc.*); (*of owls*) to hoot. **2.** to crash, bang, rumble; to ring out with a bang; вдруг ~ул гром there was a sudden crash of thunder; слы́шно бы́ло, как ~ула бо́мба the thud of a bomb (exploding) could be heard. **3.** to slip, fall; to come a cropper (*also fig.*). **4.** (*fig.*) to come to grief; to go for a Burton. **5.** to drop. **6.** to lose, squander, spend up. **7.** to bang, slap; у. кулако́м по столу́ to bang one's fist on the table.

у́хн|уться, усь, ешься, *pf.* (*of* у́хаться) (*coll.*) to fall with a bang.

у́х|о, а, *pl.* у́ши, уше́й, *n.* **1.** ear; нару́жное у. auricle; сре́днее у. middle ear; воспале́ние ~а (*med.*) otitis; у́ши вя́нут (от) (*coll.*)

it makes one sick to hear; и ~ом не вести not to listen (= to pay no heed); кра́ем ~а слу́шать to listen with half an ear; прожужжа́ть, прокрича́ть кому́-н. у́ши to talk someone's head off; у. в у. (с+*i.*) level (with), alongside; дать, зае́хать, съе́здить кому́-н. в у. (*coll.*) to box someone's ears; дуть, петь в у́ши кому́-н. to whisper (= to pass on scandal) to someone; во все у́ши слу́шать to be all ears; за́ уши тащи́ть кого́-н. (*fig.*) to give someone a leg-up; пропусти́ть ми́мо уше́й (*coll.*) to turn a deaf ear (to), pay no heed (to); говори́ть кому́-н. на́ у. to have a word in someone's ear, have a private word with someone; по́ уши up to one's eyes (*in work, etc.*), over head and ears, head over heels (*in love, etc.*). 2. ear-flap, ear-piece (*of cap, etc.*). 3. (*tech.*) ear, lug, hanger.

уховёртк|а, и, *f.* (*zool.*) earwig.

ухо́д[1], а, *m.* going away, leaving, departure; withdrawal; вы́йти ~ом (за́муж), взять ~ом (жену́) (*obs.*) to marry in secret, elope with.

ухо́д[2], а, *m.* (за+*i.*) nursing, tending, looking after; care (of); maintenance.

ухо|ди́ть[1], жу́, ~дишь, *impf.* 1. *impf. of* уйти́. 2. *impf. only* to stretch, extend.

ухо|ди́ть[2], жу́, ~дишь, *pf.* (*coll.*) 1. to wear out, tire out. 2. to remove, rid oneself (of); to do in.

ухо|ди́ться, жу́сь, ~дишься, *pf.* (*coll.*) 1. to be worn out, be tired out. 2. to calm down; to be rested.

ухоре́з, а, *m.* (*coll.*) desperate fellow.

ухуджа́|ть(ся), а́ю, а́ет(ся), *impf. of* ~ить(ся).

ухудше́ни|е, я, *n.* worsening, deterioration.

уху́дш|енный, *p.p.p. of* ~ить *and adj.* inferior.

уху́дш|ить, у, ишь, *pf.* (*of* ~а́ть) to make worse, worsen, deteriorate.

уху́дш|иться, ится, *pf.* (*of* ~а́ться) to become worse, worsen, deteriorate (*intrans.*).

уцеле́|ть, ю, *pf.* to remain intact, escape destruction; to remain alive, survive; to remain at liberty, escape.

уцен|ённый, *p.p.p. of* ~и́ть *and adj.* reduced (-price).

уцени́ва|ть, ю, *impf. of* уцени́ть.

уцен|и́ть, ю́, ~ишь, *pf.* (*of* ~ивать) to reduce the price (of).

уцеп|и́ть, лю́, ~ишь, *pf.* (*coll.*) to catch hold (of), grasp, seize.

уцеп|и́ться, лю́сь, ~ишься, *pf.* (за+*a.*) 1. to catch hold (of), grasp, seize. 2. (*fig., coll.*) to jump (at).

уча́ств|овать, ую, *impf.* 1. (в+*p.*) to take part (in), participate (in). 2. (в+*p.*) to have a share (in), have shares (in); у. в ак-

ционе́рном о́бществе to have shares in a (joint-stock) company. 3. (+*d.*; *obs.*) to sympathize (with), extend sympathy (to).

уча́ств|ующий, *pres. part. act. of* ~овать; *as noun* у., ~ующего, *m.* participant.

участи|е, я, *n.* 1. taking part, participation; при ~и, с ~ем (+*g.*) with the participation (of), with the assistance (of), including, featuring; принима́ть у. (в+*p.*) to take part (in), participate (in), take a hand (in). 2. share, sharing. 3. sympathy, concern; принима́ть у. в ком-н. to extend sympathy to someone, display concern for someone.

уча|сти́ть, щу́, сти́шь, *pf.* (*of* ~ща́ть) to make more frequent.

участ|и́ться, и́тся, *pf.* (*of* учаща́ться) to become more frequent; (*of pulse*) to quicken.

участко́в|ый, *adj. of* уча́сток; у. уполномо́ченный divisional inspector (*of police*); у. при́став (*hist.*) = у. уполномо́ченный (*in tsarist Russia*); *as noun* у., ~ого, *m.* = у. уполномо́ченный, у. при́став.

уча́стлив|ый (~, ~а), *adj.* sympathetic.

уча́стник, а, *m.* (+*g.*) participant (in), member (of); у. состяза́ния participant in a competition, competitor; у. литерату́рного кружка́ member of a literary society.

уча́ст|ок, ка, *m.* 1. (*of land*) plot, strip; lot, parcel. 2. part, section, portion; length (*of road, etc.*); (*railways*) division. 3. (*mil.*) sector (*area occupied by one regiment of Army*); area, zone; у. гла́вного уда́ра area of main strike; у. проры́ва breakthrough area. 4. district, area, zone (*as administrative unit*); избира́тельный у. (*i*) electoral district, ward, (*ii*) polling station. 5. (*fig.*) field, sphere (*of activity*). 6. (*hist.*) (*i*) police division, district, (*ii*) police-station.

у́част|ь, и, *f.* lot, fate, portion.

уча́|ть, учну́, учнёшь, *past* ~л, ~ла́, ~ло, *pf.* (*coll.*) to begin.

учаща́|ть(ся), ю, ет(ся), *impf. of* участи́ть(ся).

уча|щённый, *p.p.p. of* ~сти́ть *and adj.* quickened; faster; у. пульс quickened pulse.

уча́щ|ийся, *pres. part. of* учи́ться; *as noun* у., ~егося, *m.* student; pupil.

учёб|а, ы, *f.* 1. studies; studying, learning; за ~ой at one's studies. 2. drill, training.

учёбник, а, *m.* text-book; manual, primer.

учёбно- educational-.

учёбн|ый, *adj.* 1. educational; school; ~ое вре́мя school-hours, instruction, term-time; у. год academic year, school year; ~ое заведе́ние educational institution; у. план curriculum; у. предме́т subject; ~ая часть instructional side (*of school*); заве́дующий ~ой ча́стью director of studies. 2. (*mil.*) training, practice; у. патро́н dummy cartridge (*used in training*); ~ое пóле training ground; у. самолёт training aircraft, trainer; у. сбор reserve training period; ~ая стрельбá practice shoot; ~ое сýдно training ship.

учéни|е, я, *n.* 1. learning; studies; apprenticeship; отдáть в у. (+*d.*) to apprentice (to). **2.** teaching, instruction. **3.** (*mil.*) exercise; (*pl.*) training. **4.** teaching, doctrine.

ученúк, á, *m.* 1. pupil; у.-лётчик student pilot. **2.** apprentice. **3.** disciple, follower.

ученúц|а, ы, *f.* *of* ученúк.

ученú|ческий, *adj.* 1. *adj. of* ~к. **2.** raw, crude, immature.

ученúчеств|о, а, *n.* 1. period spent as a pupil, student. **2.** apprenticeship. **3.** rawness, immaturity.

учёност|ь, и, *f.* learning, erudition (*also iron.*).

учён|ый (~, ~a), *adj.* 1. learned, erudite; (*coll.*) educated. **2.** scholarly; academic; ~ая статья́ scholarly article; ~ая стéпень (university) degree. **3.** *forms part of title of certain academic posts and institutions in U.S.S.R.*: у. секретáрь academic secretary; у. совéт academic council. **4.** (*of animals*) trained, performing. **5.** *as noun* у., ~ого, *m.* scholar.

уч|éсть, учтý, учтёшь, *past* ~ёл, ~лá, *pf.* (*of* ~ы́тывать**) 1.** to take into account, consideration; to allow (for); to bear in mind. **2.** to take stock (of), make an inventory (of). **3.** (*fin.*) to discount.

учёт, а, *m.* 1. stock-taking, inventory-making; reckoning, calculation; вести́ у. (+*g.*) to take stock (of). **2.** taking into account; без ~а (+*g.*) disregarding. **3.** registration; взять на у. to register; встать, стать на у. to be registered; состоя́ть на ~е to be on the books; снять с ~а to strike off the register, take off the books. **4.** (*fin.*) discount, discounting.

учетвер|úть, ю́, úшь, *pf.* (*of* ~я́ть**)** to quadruple.

учетвер|я́ть, я́ю, *impf.* *of* ~úть.

учётно-вóинский, *adj.* у.-в. докумéнт (*mil.*) discharge papers (*also document indicating military service-liability status*).

учётно-медицúнск|ий, *adj.*; ~ая кáрточка medical record, medical card.

учётн|ый, *adj.* 1. registration; ~ая кáрточка registration form; ~ое отделéние records section. **2.** (*fin.*) discount; у. процéнт, ~ая стáвка бáнковского процéнта rate of discount; bank rate.

учётчик, а, *m.* tally clerk.

учúлищ|е, а, *n.* school, college (*now = institution providing specialist instruction at secondary level*); воéнное у. military school; ремéсленное у. trade school.

учúлищ|ный, *adj. of* ~е.

учин|úть, ю́, úшь, *pf.* (*of* ~я́ть**)** to make, commit; у. скандáл (*coll.*) to make a scene.

учин|я́ть, я́ю, *impf.* *of* ~úть.

учúтел|ь, я, *m.* 1. (*pl.* ~я́) teacher. **2.** (*pl.* ~и) (*fig.*) teacher, master (= *authority*).

учúтельниц|а, ы, *f.* *of* учúтель.

учúтельный, *adj.* (*obs.*) 1. skilled in teaching. **2.** edifying, instructive.

учúтель|ский, *adj. of* ~; as noun ~ская, ~ской, *f.* teachers' common room, staff (common) room.

учúтыва|ть, ю, *impf.* *of* учéсть.

уч|úть, у́, ~úшь, *impf.* 1. (*pf.* об~) (+*a. and d. or* +*inf.*) to teach; у. когó-н. немéцкому языкý to teach someone German; у. игрáть на скрúпке to teach to play the violin. **2.** to be a teacher. **3.** (что) (*of a theory, etc.*) to teach (that), say (that). **4.** (*pf.* вы́~) (+*a.*) to learn; to memorize.

уч|úться, у́сь, ~úшься, *impf.* 1. (*pf.* об~) (+*d. or* +*inf.*) to learn, study. **2.** to be a student; у. в шкóле to go to, be at school. **3.** (на когó-н.; *coll.*) to study (to be, become), learn (to be); он ~úтся на перевóдчика he is studying to be an interpreter.

учредúтел|ь, я, *m.* founder.

учредúтельниц|а, ы, *f.* foundress.

учредúтельн|ый, *adj.* constituent; ~ое собрáние (*polit.*) constituent assembly.

учре|дúть, жý, дúшь, *pf.* (*of* ~ждáть**)** to found, establish, set up; to introduce, institute.

учрежда́|ть, ю, *impf.* *of* учредúть.

учреждéни|е, я, *n.* 1. founding, establishment (*action*), setting up; introduction. **2.** establishment, institution (*object*).

учреждéн|ческий, *adj. of* ~ие 2.

учтúвост|ь, и, *f.* civility, courtesy.

учтúв|ый (~, ~a), *adj.* civil, courteous.

учу́|ять, ю, ешь, *pf.* (*coll.*) 1. to smell, nose out; (*fig.*) to sense.

ушáнк|а, и, *f.* (*coll.*) cap with ear-flaps.

ушáст|ый (~, ~a), *adj.* (*coll.*) big-eared.

ушáт, а, *m.* tub (*carried on pole slung through handles*).

ýши, *see* ýхо.

ушúб, а, *m.* 1. injury; knock; bruise; (*med.*) contusion. **2.** injured place.

ушиб|áть(ся), áю(сь), *impf.* of* ~úть(ся).

ушиб|úть, ý, ёшь, *past* ~, ~ла, *pf.* (*of* ~áть**) 1.** to injure (*by knocking*); to bruise. **2.** (*fig., coll.*) to hurt, shock.

ушиб|úться, ýсь, ёшься, *past* ~ся, ~лась, *pf.* (*of* ~áться**)** to hurt oneself, give oneself a knock; to bruise oneself.

ушивá|ть, ю, *impf.* *of* ушúть.

уш|úть, ью́, ьёшь, *pf.* (*of* ~ивáть**) (*dressmaking*)** to take in.

ушка́н, а, *m.* (*dial.*) hare.

у́шк|о, а, *pl.* **~и, у́шек,** *n. dim. of* у́хо; **у него́ ~и на маку́шке** he is on the qui-vive.

ушк|о́, а́, *pl.* **~и́, ~о́в,** *n.* **1.** (*tech.*) eye, lug. **2.** tab, tag (*of boot*). **3.** eye (*of needle*). **4.** (*pl.*) (*cul.*) noodles.

ушку́|й, я, *m.* (*hist.*) flat-bottomed boat (*propelled by sail or oars*).

ушку́йник, а, *m.* (*hist.*) river-pirate.

ушни́к, а́, *m.* (*coll.*) ear-specialist.

ушн|о́й, *adj.* ear, aural; **~а́я боль** ear-ache; **у. врач** ear-specialist; **~а́я ра́ковина** (*anat.*) auricle; **~а́я се́ра** ear-wax.

ущели́ст|ый (~, ~а), *adj.* abounding in ravines.

ущел|ье, ья, g. pl. ~ий, *n.* ravine, gorge, canyon.

ущем|и́ть, лю́, и́шь, *pf.* (*of* **~ля́ть**) **1.** to pinch, jam, nip; **у. себе́ па́лец две́рью** to pinch one's finger in the door. **2.** (*fig.*) to limit; to encroach (upon). **3.** (*fig.*) to wound, hurt; **у. чьё-н. самолю́бие** to hurt someone's pride.

ущемле́ни|е, я, *n.* **1.** pinching, jamming, nipping; **у. гры́жи** (*med.*) strangulation of hernia. **2.** (*fig.*) limitation. **3.** (*fig.*) wounding, hurting; frustration.

ущемля́|ть, ю, *impf. of* ущеми́ть.

ущем|лённый, p.p.p. of ~и́ть *and adj.* (*fig.*) wounded, hurt; frustrated.

ущерб, а, *m.* **1.** detriment; loss; damage, injury; **без ~а (для)** without prejudice (to); **в у.** (+*d.*) to the detriment (of), to the prejudice (of). **2.** weakening, decline. **3. на ~е** (*of the moon*) on the wane; (*fig.*) on the decline.

ущерб|и́ть, лю́, и́шь, *pf.* **1.** to injure, damage. **2.** (*fig.*) to limit.

ущербный, *adj.* (*of the moon*) waning; (*fig.*) on the decline.

ущипн|у́ть, у́, ёшь, *pf.* to pinch, tweak.

ую́т, а, *m.* comfort, cosiness.

ую́т|ный (~ен, ~на), *adj.* comfortable, cosy.

уязви́мост|ь, и, *f.* vulnerability.

уязви́м|ый (~, ~а), *adj.* vulnerable (*also fig.*); **~ое ме́сто** (*fig.*) weak spot, sensitive spot.

уязв|и́ть, лю́, и́шь, *pf.* (*of* **~ля́ть**) to wound, hurt.

уязвля́|ть, ю, *impf. of* уязви́ть.

уясне́ни|е, я, *n.* explanation, elucidation.

уясн|и́ть, ю́, и́шь, *pf.* (*of* **~я́ть**) **1.** (себе́) to understand, make out. **2.** (*obs.*) to explain.

уясн|я́ть, я́ю, *impf. of* **~и́ть.**

Ф

фа, *indecl., n.* (*mus.*) fa.

фаб- *abbr. of* фабри́чный.

фабза́вуч, а, *m.* (*abbr. of* фабри́чно-заводско́е учи́лище) factory workshop-school.

фа́брик|а, и, *f.* factory, mill.

фа́брика-ку́хня, фа́брики-ку́хни, *f.* (*large-scale*) canteen, municipal restaurant.

фабрика́нт, а, *m.* (*obs.*) manufacturer, factory-owner, mill-owner.

фабрика́т, а, *m.* finished product.

фабрика́ци|я, и, *f.* fabrication (*also fig.*).

фабрик|ова́ть, у́ю, *impf.* **1.** (*obs.*) to manufacture, make. **2.** (*pf.* **с~**) (*fig., coll.*) to fabricate, forge.

фа́бр|ить, ю, ишь, *impf.* (*of* **на~**) (*obs.*) to dye (*moustache or beard*).

фабри́чно-заводско́й (*and* **ф.-заво́дский**), *adj.* factory, works, industrial.

фабри́чн|ый, *adj.* **1.** factory; industrial, manufacturing; **ф. го́род** manufacturing town; **~ая ма́рка** trade mark; **~ое произво́дство** manufacturing; *as noun* **ф., ~ого,** *m.*; **~ая, ~ой,** *f.* factory worker. **2.** factory-made.

фа́бул|а, ы, *f.* (*lit.*) plot, story.

фавн, а, *m.* (*myth.*) faun.

фаво́р, а, *m.* (*obs.*) **быть в ~е (у), по́льзо**ваться **~ом (у)** to be in favour (with); **быть не в ~е у кого́-н.** to be in someone's bad books.

фавори́т, а, *m.* favourite (*also sport*).

фавори́ти́зм, а, *m.* favouritism.

фаго́т, а, *m.* (*mus.*) bassoon.

фаготи́ст, а, *m.* bassoon-player.

фагоци́т, а, *m.* (*biol.*) phagocyte.

фа́з|а, ы, *f.* (*in var. senses*) phase; stage.

фаза́н, а, *m.* pheasant.

фаза́н|ий, *adj. of* **~.**

фаза́них|а, и, *f.* hen pheasant.

фа́зис, а, *m.* phase.

фа́зн|ый, *adj.* (*tech.*) phase; **~ая обмо́тка** phase winding.

фа́з|овый, *adj.* = **~ный;** (*phys., tech.*) **ф. сдвиг** phase shift; **~овая ско́рость** phase velocity; **ф. у́гол** phase angle.

фазотро́н, а, *m.* (*phys.*) synchro-cyclotron.

фай, фа́я, *m.* (*text.*) faille.

файдеши́н, а, *m.* (*text.*) faille de Chine.

фа́кел, а, *m.* torch, flare; **ф.-ло́цман** pilot flame.

фа́кел|ьный, *adj. of* **~; ~ьное ше́ствие** torch-light procession.

фа́кельщик, а, *m.* **1.** torch-bearer. **2.** (*fig., pejor.*) incendiary, fire-bug.

факи́р, а, *m.* fakir.

факси́миле, *indecl.,* *n.* (*also as indecl. adj.*) facsimile.

факт, а, *m.* **1.** fact; соверши́вшийся ф. fait accompli; показа́ть на ~ах to show proof; факт, что (*coll.*) it is a fact that; ф. остаётся ~ом the fact remains.

факти́чески, *adv.* in fact, actually; practically, virtually, to all intents and purposes.

факти́ческ|ий, *adj.* actual; real; virtual; ~ие да́нные the facts.

факти́ч|ный (~ен, ~на), *adj.* factual, authentic.

фактографи́ч|ный (~ен, ~на), *adj.* factual, based on fact, authentic.

фактогра́фи|я, и, *f.* factual account.

фа́ктор, а, *m.* factor.

факто́ри|я, и, *f.* trading station.

факту́р|а, ы, *f.* **1.** (*arts and lit.*) style; manner of execution; texture. **2.** (*comm.*) invoice, bill.

факту́р|ный, *adj of* ~a.

факультати́в|ный (~ен, ~на), *adj.* optional.

факульте́т, а, *m.* faculty, department (*of higher education institution*).

факульте́т|ский, *adj. of* ~.

фал, а, *m.* (*naut.*) halyard.

фала́нг|а, и, *f.* **1.** (*hist.; fig.*) phalanx. **2.** (*polit.*) Falange. **3.** (*anat.*) phalanx, phalange.

фаланги́ст, а, *m.* (*polit.*) Falangist.

фаланстёр, а, *m.* (*polit. philos.*) phalanstery.

фа́лд|а, ы, *f.* tail, skirt (*of coat*).

фа́лин|ь, я, *m.* (*naut.*) painter.

фалли́ческий, *adj.* phallic.

фалло́пиев, *adj.* ~а труба́ (*med.*) Fallopian tube.

фа́ллос, а, *m.* phallus.

фалре́п, а, *m.* (*naut.*) side-rope, side-boy.

фальсифика́тор, а, *m.* falsifier; forger.

фальсифика́ци|я, и, *f.* **1.** falsification; forging. **2.** adulteration. **3.** forgery, fake, counterfeit.

фальсифици́р|овать, ую, *impf. and pf.* **1.** to falsify; to forge. **2.** to adulterate.

фальц, а, *m.* **1.** (*tech.*) rabbet; groove. **2.** (*typ.*) fold (*of printed sheet*).

фальцго́бел|ь, я, *m.* (*tech.*) fillister, rabbeting plane.

фальц|ева́ть, у́ю, *impf.* (*of* с~) **1.** (*tech.*) to rabbet, groove. **2.** to fold, crease.

фальце́т, а, *m.* (*mus.*) falsetto.

фальцо́вочный, *adj.* (*tech.*) rabbeting, grooving; ф. стано́к rabbeting machine.

фальшбо́рт, а, *m.* (*naut.*) bulwark, rails.

фальши́в|ить, лю, ишь, *impf.* **1.** to be a hypocrite; to act insincerely. **2.** (*pf.* с~) (*mus.*) to sing, play out of tune.

фальши́вк|а, и, *f.* (*coll.*) forged document.

фальшивомоне́тчик, а, *m.* counterfeiter, coiner (*of false money*).

фальши́в|ый (~, ~а), *adj.* **1.** false; spurious; forged, fake; artificial, imitation; ф. докуме́нт forged document; ~ые зу́бы false teeth; ф. же́мчуг imitation pearl. **2.** false; hypocritical, insincere; ф. комплиме́нт insincere compliment; попа́сть в ~ое положе́ние to put oneself into a false position. **3.** (*mus.*) false (= *out of tune*). **4.** (*naut.*) temporary, jury-; ~ая ма́чта jury-mast.

фальшки́л|ь, я, *m.* (*naut.*) false keel.

фальш|ь, и, *f.* **1.** deception, trickery. **2.** falsity; hypocrisy, insincerity. **3.** (*mus.*) singing, playing out of tune.

фами́ли|я, и, *f.* **1.** surname. **2.** family, kin.

фами́льный, *adj.* family.

фамилья́рнича|ть, ю, *impf.* (*coll.*) to be (too) familiar.

фамилья́рность, и, *f.* (excessive) familiarity; unceremoniousness.

фамилья́р|ный (~ен, ~на), *adj.* (excessively) familiar; unceremonious, off-hand.

фанабе́ри|я, и, *f.* (*coll.*) arrogance, bumptiousness.

фанати́зм, а, *m.* fanaticism.

фана́тик, а, *m.* fanatic.

фанати́ческий, *adj.* fanatical.

фанати́ч|ный (~ен, ~на), *adj.* fanatic(al).

фане́р|а, ы, *f.* **1.** veneer. **2.** plywood.

фане́р|ный, *adj. of* ~а; ф. лист plywood sheet; ~ная рабо́та veneering.

фа́нз|а́, ы-ы́, *f.* fanza (*peasant domicile in China or Korea*).

фанз|а́, ы́, *f.* (*text.*) foulard.

фа́нов|ый, *adj.* waste, sewage; ~ая труба́ waste pipe.

фант, а, *m.* forfeit (*in game 'forfeits'*); игра́ть в ~ы to play forfeits.

фантазёр, а, *m.* dreamer, visionary.

фантази́р|овать, ую, *impf.* **1.** (*impf. only*) to dream, indulge in fantasies. **2.** (*pf.* с~) to make up, dream up. **3.** (*impf. only*) to improvise (*on piano, etc.*).

фанта́зи|я, и, *f.* **1.** fantasy; imagination; бога́тая ф. fertile imagination. **2.** fantasy, fancy; предава́ться ~ям to indulge in fantasies. **3.** fabrication. **4.** (*coll.*) fancy, whim. **5.** (*mus.*) fantasia.

фантасмаго́ри|я, и, *f.* phantasmagoria.

фанта́ст, а, *m.* **1.** fantasy-monger; person with powerful imagination; dreamer, visionary. **2.** writer, artist treating the fantastic.

фанта́стик|а, и, *f.* **1.** the fantastic; (*collect.; lit.*) fantastic tales. **2.** fantasy, fiction (*as opp. to* reality); нау́чная ф. science fiction.

фантасти́ческий, *adj.* **1.** fantastical. **2.** (*in var. senses*) fantastic; fabulous; imaginary.

фантасти́ч|ный (~ен, ~на), *adj.* = ~еский.

фанто́м, а, *m.* phantom.

фанто́мный, *adj.* 1. (*physiol.*) imaginary, false. 2. (*electr.*) phantom.

фанфа́р|а, ы, *f.* (*mus.*) 1. bugle. 2. fanfare.

фанфаро́н, а, *m.* (*coll.*) braggart.

фанфаро́н|ить, ю, ишь, *impf.* (*coll.*) to brag.

фанфаро́нств|о, а, *n.* (*coll.*) bragging.

фа́р|а, ы, *f.* headlight (*on motor vehicle, locomotive, etc.*); поса́дочные ~ы landing lights (*on aircraft*).

фара́д|а, ы, *f.* (*electr.*) farad.

фарао́н, а, *m.* 1. (*hist.*) pharaoh (*also nickname for policeman*). 2. faro (*card-game*).

фарао́нов, *adj.* pharaoh's; ~а мышь (*zool.*) ichneumon.

фарва́тер, а, *m.* (*naut.*) fairway, channel; плыть, быть в чьём-н. ~е (*fig.*) to follow someone's lead, side with someone.

Фаренге́йт, а, *m.* Fahrenheit (thermometer); 80° по ~у 80° Fahrenheit.

фаринги́т, а, *m.* (*med.*) pharyngitis.

фарисе́|й, я, *m.* Pharisee (*also fig.*).

фарисе́йский, *adj.* pharisaical (*also fig.*).

фарисе́йств|о, а, *n.* pharisaism.

фарисе́йств|овать, ую, *impf.* to act pharisaically.

фармазо́н, а, *m.* (*coll., obs.*) freemason.

фарма́колог, а, *m.* pharmacologist.

фармакологи́ческий, *adj.* pharmacological.

фармаколо́ги|я, и, *f.* pharmacology.

фармакопе́|я, и, *f.* pharmacopoeia.

фармаце́вт, а, *m.* pharmaceutical chemist.

фармаце́втик|а, и, *f.* pharmaceutics.

фармацевти́ческий, *adj.* pharmaceutical.

фармаци́|я, и, *f.* pharmacy.

фарс, а, *m.* (*theatr.*) farce (*also fig.*).

фарт, а, *m.* (*sl.*) luck.

фарт|и́ть, и́т, *impf.* (*impers.+d.*; *sl.*) to be in luck.

фарто́вый, *adj.* (*sl.*) 1. lucky. 2. fine, smashing.

фа́ртук, а, *m.* 1. apron. 2. carriage-rug.

фарфо́р, а, *m.* 1. porcelain, china. 2. (*collect.*) china.

фарфо́р|овый, *adj. of* ~; ~овая гли́на china clay, kaolin; ~овая посу́да china(-ware).

фарцо́вщик, а, *m.* (*sl.*) currency speculator.

фарш, а, *m.* (*cul.*) force-meat; sausage-meat; stuffing.

фарширо́в|анный, *p.p.p. of* ~а́ть *and adj.* (*cul.*) stuffed, farci.

фарши́р|ова́ть, у́ю, *impf* (*of* за~) (*cul.*) to stuff.

фас, а, *m.* 1. front, façade; в ф. en face. 2. (*mil.*) face (*of salient*); ф. про́волочного загражде́ния straight leg of barbed-wire entanglement.

фаса́д, а, *m.* façade, front.

фасе́т, а, *m.* facet.

фасе́т|очный, *adj. of* ~; ~очные глаза́ (*zool.*) compound eyes.

фа́ск|а, и, *f.* (*tech.*) face, facet; (bevel) edge.

фас|ова́ть, у́ю, *impf.* (*comm.*) to pre-pack (*in measured quantities*).

фасо́вк|а, и, *f.* (*comm.*) pre-packing.

фасо́вочн|ый, *adj.* (*comm.*) (pre-)packing, packaging; *as noun* ~ая, ~ой, *f.* packing department.

фасо́л|евый, *adj. of* ~ь.

фасо́л|ь, и, *f.* haricot bean, French bean.

фасо́н, а, *m.* 1. cut (*of dress, etc.*); fashion, style; не ф. (*coll.*) it's not done. 2. (*coll.*) style, manner, way. 3. (*coll.*) swank, showing off; держа́ть ф. to swank, show off.

фасо́нист|ый (~, ~а), *adj.* (*coll.*) fashionable, stylish.

фасо́нн|ый, *adj.* (*tech.*) 1. fashioned, shaped; ~ое желе́зо shaped iron, profile iron, section iron. 2. form(ing), shape, shaping; ~ая накова́льня die block; ~ая обрабо́тка profiling; ф. резе́ц form tool, shaper tool; ~ая фрезеро́вка form milling.

фат, а, *m.* fop.

фат|а́, ы́, *f.* (*bridal*) veil.

фатали́зм, а, *m.* fatalism.

фатали́ст, а, *m.* fatalist.

фаталисти́ческий, *adj.* 1. fatalistic. 2. fatal.

фата́льность, и, *f.* fatality, fate.

фата́л|ьный (~ен, ~ьна), *adj.* 1. fatal, fated. 2. resigned (to one's fate); ф. вид resigned appearance.

фатова́т|ый (~, ~а), *adj.* foppish.

фа́тум, а, *m.* fate.

фа́ун|а, ы, *f.* fauna.

фауспатро́н, а, *m.* (*mil.*) 'panzer-faust' (*bazooka-type weapon*).

фахве́рк, а, *m.* frame building.

фахве́рковый, *adj.* frame-built.

фашизи́р|овать, ую, *impf. and pf.* to run on Fascist lines; to impose Fascism (upon).

фашизи́р|оваться, уюсь, *impf. and pf.* 1. to become Fascist. 2. *pass. of* ~овать.

фаши́зм, а, *m.* Fascism.

фаши́н|а, ы, *f.* fascine, faggot.

фаши́н|ный, *adj. of* ~а; ф. нож fascine-cutting knife.

фаши́ст, а, *m.* Fascist.

фаши́ст|ка, ки, *f. of* ~.

фаши́стский, *adj.* Fascist.

фаэто́н, а, *m.* phaeton.

фая́нс, а, *m.* faience, pottery, glazed earthenware.

фая́нс|овый, *adj. of* ~.

февра́л|ь, я́, *m.* February.

февра́ль|ский, *adj. of* ~.

федерали́зм, а, *m.* federalism.

федерали́ст, а, *m.* federalist.

федера́льный, *adj.* federal.

федерати́вный, *adj.* federative, federal.

федера́ци|я, и, *f.* federation.

фееpи́ческий, *adj.* 1. (*theatr.*) (based on a) fairytale. 2. fairy-like; magical.

фее́pи|я, и, *f.* 1. play, ballet, *etc.*, based on a fairytale. 2. magical sight.

фейеpве́pк, а, *m.* firework(s).

фейеpве́pкеp, а, *m.* (*hist.*) bombardier (*artillery N.C.O. in tsarist Russian army*).

фека́л|ии, ий, *sing.* ∼ия, ∼ии, *f.* faeces.

фека́льный, *adj.* faecal.

фелла́х, а, *m.* fellah.

фельдма́pшал, а, *m.* field-marshal.

фельдфе́бел|ь, я, *m.* (*hist.*) sergeant-major.

фельдшеp, а, *pl.* ∼а́, *m.* doctor's assistant, medical attendant (*medical practitioner lacking graduate qualification*).

фельдшеpи́ц|а, ы, *f. of* фе́льдшеp.

фе́льдшеp|ский, *adj. of* ∼.

фельдъе́геp|ский, *adj. of* ∼ь; ∼ская связь communication by courier.

фельдъе́геp|ь, я, *m.* (*hist.*) courier, special messenger.

фельето́н, а, *m.* feuilleton; satirical article.

фельетони́ст, а, *m.* feuilletonist; composer of satirical articles.

фельето́н|ный, *adj. of* ∼.

фелю́г|а, и, *f.* (*naut.*) felucca.

фемини́зм, а, *m.* feminism.

фемини́ст, а, *m.* feminist.

фемини́ст|ка, ки, *f. of* ∼.

фен, а, *m.* (hair-)drier.

фён, а, *m.* föhn (*wind*).

фе́никс, а, *m.* 1. (*mythol.*) phoenix. 2. (*obs.*) marvel, prodigy.

фено́л, а, *m.* (*chem.*) phenol, carbolic acid.

феноло́ги|я, и, *f.* (*biol.*) phenology.

фено́мен, а, *m.* phenomenon; phenomenal occurrence, person.

феноменали́зм, а, *m.* (*philos.*) phenomenalism.

феномена́л|ьный (∼ен, ∼ьна), *adj.* phenomenal.

феноменоло́ги|я, и, *f.* (*philos.*) phenomenology.

фе́нхел|ь, я, *m.* (*bot.*) fennel.

фео́д, а, *m.* (*hist.*) feud, fief.

феода́л, а, *m.* (*hist.*) feudal lord.

феодали́зм, а, *m.* feudalism.

феода́льный, *adj.* feudal.

фе́pз|евый, *adj. of* ∼ь.

феpз|ь, я́, *pl.* ∼и́, ∼е́й, *m.* (*chess*) queen.

фе́pм|а¹, ы, *f.* farm.

фе́pм|а², ы, *f.* (*tech.*) girder.

феpма́т|а, ы, *f.* (*mus.*) fermata.

фе́pм|енный, *adj. of* ∼а²; lattice.

феpме́нт, а, *m.* (*biol., chem.*) ferment.

феpменти́p|овать, ую, *impf.* to ferment.

фе́pмеp, а, *m.* farmer.

фе́pмеp|ский, *adj. of* ∼; ф. дом farm-house.

фе́pмеpств|о, а, *n.* 1. (*private*) farming. 2. (*collect.*) farmers.

фе́pмеp|ша, ши, *f.* (*coll.*) 1. *f. of* ∼. 2. farmer's wife.

фе́pм|овый, *adj. of* ∼а².

феpмуа́p, а, *m.* (*obs.*) 1. clasp (*on necklace, purse, etc.*). 2. necklace.

феpнамбу́к, а, *m.* (*bot.*) Brazil wood (*Caesalpinia brasiliensis*).

феpонье́pк|а, и, *f.* (*obs.*) frontlet, coronet.

феppо- ferro-.

феppоспла́в, а, *m.* ferro-alloy.

феpт, а, *m.* 1. old name of letter 'ф'; ∼ом стоя́ть to stand with arms akimbo. 2. (*coll.*) fop; smug person; ∼ом гляде́ть to look smug; ∼ом ходи́ть to strut about.

феpу́л|а, ы, *f.* 1. (*obs.*) ruler, ferula (*as instrument of punishment in school*). 2. surveillance.

фе́pяз|ь, и, *f.* (*hist.*) feryaz (*loose tunic formerly worn by Russians*).

фес, а, *m.* fez.

фе́с|ка, ки, *f.* = ∼.

фестива́л|ь, я, *m.* festival.

фесто́н, а, *m.* (*dressmaking*) scallops (*decoration on fabrics*).

фети́ш, а, *m.* fetish.

фетишизи́p|овать, ую, *impf.* to make a fetish (of).

фетиши́зм, а, *m.* fetishism.

фетиши́ст, а, *m.* fetishist.

фетp, а, *m.* felt.

фе́тp|овый, *adj. of* ∼.

фефёл|а, ы, *f.* (*coll.*) slattern.

фе́феp, а(у), *m. only in phrases* (*coll.*) зада́ть, показа́ть ∼y (+*d.*) to give it hot (to).

фехтова́льный, *adj.* fencing.

фехтова́льщик, а, *m.* fencer; ф. papи́pой foil fencer; ф. шпа́гой épée fencer.

фехтова́ни|е, я, *n.* fencing.

фехт|ова́ть, у́ю, *impf.* to fence.

фешене́бел|ьный (∼ен, ∼ьна), *adj.* fashionable.

фе́|я, и, *f.* fairy.

фи, *interj.* fie!, pah!

фиа́л, а, *m.* phial; (*poet.*) goblet, beaker.

фиа́лк|а, и, *f.* violet.

фиа́лк|овый, *adj. of* ∼а; ф. ко́pень orris-root; *as noun* ∼овые, ∼овых (*bot.*) Violaceae.

фи́бp|а, ы, *f.* 1. (*anat., bot.*) fibre (*also fig.*); все́ми ∼ами души́ in every fibre (of one's being). 2. fibre (*leather-substitute material*).

фи́бp|овый, *adj. of* ∼а 2.

фибpо́зный, *adj.* (*anat., bot.*) fibrous.

фибpо́м|а, ы, *f.* (*med.*) fibroma.

фи́г|а, и, *f.* 1. fig(-tree). 2. (*coll.*) = ку́киш.

фигаpо́, *indecl., n.* bolero (*short jacket*).

фи́гли-ми́гли, фи́глей-ми́глей, *no sing.* (*coll.*) tricks.

фигля́р, а, *m.* **1.** (*obs.*) (circus) acrobat; clown. **2.** poseur; (*pejor.*) actor.

фигля́р|ить, ю, ишь, *impf.* (*coll.*) to put on an act.

фигля́рнича|ть, ю, *impf.* = фигля́рить.

фи́г|овый, *adj. of* ∼а; ∼овое де́рево fig-tree; ф. листо́к fig-leaf (*also fig.* = pretence).

фигу́р|а, ы, *f.* **1.** (*in var. senses*) figure. **2.** (*cards*) court-card, picture-card. **3.** chess--man (*excluding pawns*).

фигура́л|ьный (∼ен, ∼ьна), *adj.* **1.** figurative, metaphorical. **2.** (*of lit. style*) ornate, involved.

фигура́нт, а, *m.* (*theatr.*) **1.** figurant (*in ballet*). **2.** super, extra.

фигури́р|овать, ую, *impf.* to figure, appear.

фигури́ст, а, *m.* figure skater.

фигури́ст|ка, ки, *f. of* ∼.

фигу́р|ка, ки, *f.* **1.** *dim. of* ∼а. **2.** figurine, statuette.

фигу́рн|ый, *adj.* **1.** figured; ornamented; irregularly shaped. **2.** ф. резе́ц (*tech.*) form tool. **3.** ∼ое ката́ние на конька́х figure skating; ф. пило́таж aerobatics.

фидеи́зм, а, *m.* (*philos.*) fideism.

фи́жм|ы, ∼, *no sing.* farthingale.

физ- physical.

фи́зик, а, *m.* physicist.

фи́зик|а, и, *f.* physics.

физио́лог, а, *m.* physiologist.

физиологи́ческий, *adj.* physiological.

физиоло́ги|я, и, *f.* physiology.

физионо́ми|я, и, *f.* physiognomy (*also joc.*).

физиотерапе́вт, а, *m.* physiotherapist.

физиотерапи́|я, и, *f.* physiotherapy.

физи́ческ|ий, *adj.* **1.** physical; ∼ая культу́ра physical training, gymnastics; ф. труд manual labour. **2.** *adj. of* фи́зика; ф. кабине́т physics laboratory.

физкульту́р|а, ы, *f.* (*abbr. of* физи́ческая культу́ра) physical training, gymnastics.

физкульту́рник, а, *m.* gymnast, athlete.

физкульту́рни|ца, цы, *f. of* ∼к.

физкульту́рн|ый, *adj.* gymnastic; athletic, sports; ф. зал gymnasium; ∼ая подгото́вка physical training.

фикс¹, а, *m.* **1.** fixed price. **2.** fixed sum.

фикс², а, *m.* (*coll.*) false gold tooth-capping.

фикса́ж, а, *m.* (*phot.*) fixing solution, fixer.

фиксати́в, а, *m.* (*art*) fixative.

фикса́тор, а, *m.* (*tech.*) **1.** stop; index pin. **2.** fixing solution.

фиксатуа́р, а, *m.* fixative, hair-grease.

фикси́р|овать, ую, *impf. and pf.* (*pf. also* за∼) **1.** to record (*in writing, etc.*). **2.** (*in var. senses*) to fix; ф. день свида́ния to fix a date to meet, make a date.

фикти́в|ный (∼ен, ∼на), *adj.* fictitious.

фи́кус, а, *m.* (*bot.*) ficus.

фи́кци|я, и, *f.* fiction.

филантро́п, а, *m.* philanthropist.

филантропи́ческий, *adj.* philanthropic.

филантро́пи|я, и, *f.* philanthropy.

филармо́ни|я, и, *f.* philharmonic society.

филатели́ст, а, *m.* philatelist, stamp collector.

филатели́|я, и, *f.* philately.

филе́¹, *indecl., n.* (*cul.*) **1.** sirloin. **2.** fillet (*of meat or fish*).

филе́², *indecl., n.* (*dressmaking*) drawn-thread work.

филе́|й, я, *m.* = ∼¹.

филе́йный, *adj. of* ∼¹, ².

филёнк|а, и, *f.* panel, slat.

филёр, а, *m.* detective, sleuth.

филиа́л, а, *m.* branch (*of an institution*).

филиа́л|ьный, *adj. of* ∼; ∼ьное отделе́ние branch (office).

филигра́нный, *adj.* **1.** filigree. **2.** (*fig.*) meticulous.

филигра́н|ь, и, *f.* **1.** filigree. **2.** water-mark.

фи́лин, а, *m.* eagle owl (*Bubo bubo*).

фили́ппик|а, и, *f.* philippic.

филиппи́нский, *adj.* Philippine.

фили́стер, а, *m.* philistine.

фили́стер|ский, *adj. of* ∼.

фили́стерств|о, а, *n.* philistinism.

филогене́з, а, *m.* (*biol.*) phylogenesis.

фило́лог, а, *m.* philologist, student of language and literature.

филологи́ческий, *adj.* philological; ф. факульте́т faculty of languages and literature.

филоло́ги|я, и, *f.* philology; study of language and literature.

филомени́ст, а, *m.* phillumenist (*collector of matchbox labels*).

филосо́ф, а, *m.* philosopher.

филосо́фи|я, и, *f.* philosophy.

филосо́фский, *adj.* philosophic(al).

филосо́фств|овать, ую, *impf.* to philosophize.

фильдеко́с, а, *m.* Lisle thread.

филье́р|а, ы, *f.* (*tech.*) draw plate; die; spinneret.

фи́лькин, *adj.* ∼а гра́мота invalid, crudely--written, obscure document.

фильм, а, *m.* (*cinema*) film.

фи́льм|а, ы, *f.* (*obs.*) = ∼.

фильмоте́к|а, и, *f.* film library.

фильтр, а, *m.* filter.

фильтра́т, а, *m.* filtrate.

фильтра́ци|я, и, *f.* filtration.

фильтрова́льный, *adj.* ф. насо́с filter pump; ф. слой filter-bed.

фильтр|ова́ть, у́ю, *impf.* (*of* про∼) **1.** to filter. **2.** (*fig., coll.*) to screen, check.

фимиа́м, а, *m.* incense; кури́ть ф. (+*d.*) to praise to the skies, sing the praises (of).

фин- *abbr. of* фина́нсовый.

фина́л, а, *m.* 1. finale. 2. (*sport*) final.

фина́льный, *adj.* final; ф. аккόрд (*mus.*) final chord; ф. матч (*sport*) final.

финанси́р|овать, ую, *impf. and pf.* to finance.

финанси́ст, а, *m.* 1. financier. 2. financial expert.

фина́нсовый, *adj.* financial; ф. год fiscal year; ф. отде́л finance department.

фина́нс|ы, ов, *no sing.* 1. finance(s). 2. (*coll.*) money.

фи́ник, а, *m.* date (*fruit*).

фи́ник|овый, *adj.* of ~; ~овая па́льма date--palm.

фини́фтевый, *adj.* (*obs.*) enamelled.

фининспе́ктор, а, *m.* (*abbr. of* фина́нсовый инспе́ктор) inspector of finance(s).

фини́фт|ь, и, *f.* (*obs.*) enamel.

фини́фт|яный = ~евый.

фи́ниш, а, *m.* (*sport*) 1. finish; finishing post. 2. final lap.

фи́нишер, а, *m.* (*naut.*) batsman (*on aircraft carrier*).

финиши́р|овать, ую, *impf. and pf.* (*sport*) to finish, come in.

фи́ниш|ный, *adj. of* ~; ~ная ле́нточка finishing tape.

фи́нк|а¹, и, *f. of* финн.

фи́нк|а², и, *f.* 1. Finnish knife. 2. Finnish cap (*round, flat cap with fur band*). 3. Finnish pony. 4. = фи́нна.

финля́ндский, *adj.* Finnish.

финн, а, *m.* Finn.

фи́нн|а, ы, *f.* (*zool.*) pork tapeworm.

финно́з, а, *m.* measles (*disease of swine*).

фи́нно-уго́рский, *adj.* (*ling.*) Finno-Ugric.

финотде́л, а, *m.* (*abbr. of* фина́нсовый отде́л) finance department.

фи́нский, *adj.* Finnish, Finnic; Ф. зали́в Gulf of Finland; ф. нож Finnish knife.

финт, а, *m.* (*sport*) feint.

фин|ти́ть, чу́, ти́шь, *impf.* (*coll.*) to be crafty, resort to ruses.

финтифа́нт|ы, ов, *no sing.* (*coll., obs.*) 1. вы́делывать, выки́дывать ф. to display finesse. 2. trifles.

финтифлю́шк|а, и, *f.* (*coll.*) 1. bagatelle. 2. (*pl.*) trifles. 3. flibbertigibbet.

фиоле́товый, *adj.* violet.

фио́рд, а, *m.* (*geogr.*) fiord, fjord.

фиориту́р|а, ы, *f.* (*mus.*) grace(-note).

фи́рм|а, ы, *f.* 1. (*econ.*) firm. 2. (*obs.*) sign, mark, signature; под ~ой (+*g.*) under the sign (of). 3. (*coll.*) appearance, pretext.

фи́рм|енный, *adj. of* ~а 1; ~енная этике́тка proprietary label.

фирн, а, *m.* (*geogr.*) névé, glacier snow.

фи́рн|овый, *adj. of* ~; ф. склон glacier slope.

фисгармо́ни|я, и, *f.* (*mus.*) harmonium.

фиск, а, *m.* fisc.

фиска́л, а, *m.* (*hist.*) fiscal, finance inspector; (*coll.*) sneak, tale-bearer.

фиска́л|ить, ю, ишь, *impf.* (*coll.*) to (be a) sneak.

фиска́льный, *adj.* (*leg.*) fiscal.

фиста́шк|а, и, *f.* pistachio(-tree).

фиста́шков|ый, *adj.* 1. pistachio; ф. лак mastic varnish; ~ая смола́ mastic. 2. pistachio-green.

фи́стул|а́, ы-ы́, *f.* 1. (*mus.*) pipe, flute. 2. falsetto. 3. (*med.*) fistula.

фити́л|ь, я́, *m.* 1. wick; fuse. 2. (*naut. sl.*) rocket (= reprimand).

фито- (*biol.*) phyto-.

фитю́льк|а, и, *f.* (*coll.*) little thing; (*of a person*) midget.

фиф|а, ы, *f.* (*coll.*) flibbertigibbet.

фи́шк|а, и, *f.* 1. counter, chip (*for scoring, recording stake, etc., in games*). 2. (*sl.*) face.

флаг, а, *m.* flag; вы́кинуть ф. to put out a flag; держа́ть (свой) ф. (на+*p.*; *naut.*) to sail (in), be (in); спусти́ть ф. to lower a flag; оста́ться за ~ом (*sport*; *fig.*) to fail to make the distance; под ~ом (+*g.*) (*i*) flying the flag (of), (*ii*) (*fig.*) under the guise (of).

фла́гдук, а, *m.* (*naut.*) bunting.

фла́гман, а, *m.* (*naut.*) 1. flag-officer. 2. flagship; (*aeron.*) leader's plane of bomber squadron. 3. (*fig.*) leader.

фла́гман|ский, *adj. of* ~; ф. кора́бль = ~ 2.

флаг-офице́р, а, *m.* flag-officer.

флагшто́к, а, *m.* flagstaff.

флажко́в|ый, *adj. of* флажо́к; ~ая сигнализа́ция flag signalling.

фла́жный, *adj.* flag.

флаж|о́к, ка́, *m.* (*small*) flag; signal flag.

флажоле́т, а, *m.* (*mus.*) flageolet.

флако́н, а, *m.* (scent-)bottle, flask.

флама́нд|ец, ца, *m.* Fleming.

флама́нд|ка, ки, *f. of* ~ец.

флама́ндский, *adj.* Flemish.

флами́нго, *indecl., m.* flamingo.

фланг, а, *m.* (*mil.*) flank; wing.

фланго́в|ый, *adj.* (*mil.*) flank; ф. охва́т flanking movement, envelopment; *as noun* ф., ~ого, *m.* flank man.

фланеле́вк|а, и, *f.* (*coll.*) flannel (*sailor's blouse*).

фране́левый, *adj.* flannel.

фране́л|ь, и, *f.* flannel.

фране́р, а, *m.* flâneur, idler.

фла́н|ец, ца, *m.* (*tech.*) flange.

флани́р|овать, ую, *impf.* (*coll.*) to idle; to mooch.

фланки́р|овать, ую, *impf. and pf.* (*mil.*) to flank.

фла́н|цевый, *adj. of* ~ец.

фла́тов|ый, *adj.* ~ая бума́га (*typ.*) flat paper.

флеби́т, а, *m.* (*med.*) phlebitis.

флѐгм|а, ы, *f.* **1.** (*fig.*) phlegm. **2.** (*coll.*) phlegmatic person.

флегма́тик, а, *m.* phlegmatic person.

флегмати́ч|ный (~ен, ~на), *adj.* phlegmatic.

флѐйт|а, ы, *f.* flute.

флейти́ст, а, *m.* flautist.

флѐйт|овый, *adj. of* ~а.

флѐкси|я, и, *f.* (*ling.*) inflexion.

флекти́вный, *adj.* (*ling.*) inflected.

флёр, а, *m.* crêpe; наки́нуть ф. (на+*a.*; *fig.*) to draw a veil (over).

флёрдора́нж, а, *m.* orange blossom.

флибустьёр, а, *m.* filibuster.

флѝгел|ь, я, *pl.* ~я́, ~е́й, *m.* **1.** wing (*of building*). **2.** outhouse, outbuilding.

флѝгель-адъюта́нт, а, *m.* (*hist.*) aide-de-camp.

флирт, а, *m.* flirtation.

флирт|ова́ть, у́ю, *impf.* (с+*i.*) to flirt (with).

флѐр|а, ы, *f.* flora.

флори́н, а, *m.* florin.

флори́ст, а, *m.* specialist in study of flora.

флори́стик|а, и, *f.* (study of) flora.

флот, а, *m.* **1.** fleet; вое́нно-морско́й ф. navy. **2.** возду́шный ф. air force.

флота́ци|я, и, *f.* (*min.*) flotation.

флоти́ли|я, и, *f.* flotilla.

флотово́д|ец, ца, *m.* naval commander.

флотск|ий, *adj.* naval; *as noun* ф., ~ого., *m.* sailor.

флуоресце́нци|я, и, *f.* fluorescence.

флуоресци́р|овать, ует, *impf.* (*phys.*) to fluoresce; ~ующий fluorescent.

флюга́рк|а, и, *f.* **1.** (*naut.*) pennant; distinguishing plate (*of boat*). **2.** (*chimney*) cowl. **3.** weather-vane.

флю́гер, а, *pl.* ~а́, *m.* **1.** weather-vane; weathercock (*also of a person*). **2.** (*mil.; obs.*) pennant.

флюйд|ы, ов, *sing.* ~, ~а, *m.* ectoplasm; (*fig.*) emanations.

флюс¹, а, *pl.* ~ы, *m.* dental abscess, gumboil.

флюс², а, *pl.* ~ы́, *m.* (*tech.*) flux.

фля́г|а, и, *f.* **1.** flask; (*mil.*) water bottle. **2.** churn.

фля́жк|а, и, *f. dim. of* фля́га.

фок, а, *m.* (*naut.*) foresail.

фок- (*naut.*) fore-.

фока́льный, *adj.* (*phys.*) focal.

фокстерьёр, а, *m.* fox-terrier.

фокстро́т, а, *m.* foxtrot.

фо́кус¹, а, *m.* (*math., phys., med., and fig.*) focus.

фо́кус², а, *m.* **1.** (conjuring) trick; пока́зывать ~ы to do conjuring tricks. **2.** trick, secret (*of mechanism, etc.*); в том-то и ф. that's the whole point, that's just it. **3.** (*coll.*) whim, caprice.

фокуси́р|овать, ую, *impf.* (*phys., phot.*) to focus.

фо́кусник, а, *m.* ·**1.** conjurer, juggler. **2.** (*coll.*) rogue, tricky customer.

фо́куснича|ть, ю, *impf.* **1.** (*obs.*) to do conjuring tricks. **2.** (*coll.*) to play tricks.

фо́кусный, *adj.* (*phys., phot.*) focal.

фолиа́нт, а, *m.* folio.

фолли́кул, а, *m.* (*anat.*) follicle.

фольва́рк, а, *m.* farm (*in West Russia, Poland, and Lithuania*).

фо́льг|а, и, *f.* foil.

фолькло́р, а, *m.* folklore.

фольклори́ст, а, *m.* student of folklore.

фон, а, *m.* background (*also fig.*).

фона́рик, а, *m.* small lamp; torch, flash-light.

фона́р|ный, *adj. of* ~ь; ф. столб lamppost.

фона́рщик, а, *m.* (*obs.*) **1.** lamplighter. **2.** torch-bearer.

фона́р|ь, я́, *m.* **1.** lantern; lamp; light. **2.** (*archit.*) light; skylight; ф. каби́ны (*aeron.*) cockpit canopy. **3.** (*coll.*) black eye.

фонд, а, *m.* **1.** (*fin.*) fund; stock, resources; валю́тный ф. currency reserves; земе́льный ф. available land; золото́й ф. gold reserves. **2.** (*pl.*) (*fin.*) stocks; (*fig.*) stock; ~ы его́ повы́сились his stock has risen. **3.** fund, foundation (*in U.S.S.R., organization serving as channel for State subsidies to writers, artists, etc.*). **4.** archive.

фо́нд|овый, *adj. of* ~; ~овая би́ржа stock exchange.

фоне́м|а, ы, *f.* (*ling.*) phoneme.

фонендоско́п, а, *m.* (*med.*) phonendoscope.

фоне́тик|а, и, *f.* phonetics.

фонети́ст, а, *m.* phonetician.

фонети́ческий, *adj.* phonetic.

фони́ческий, *adj.* **1.** phonic. **2.** ф. аппара́т (*mil.*) telephone with voice frequency signalling.

фоно́граф, а, *m.* phonograph.

фоноло́ги|я, и, *f.* phonemics.

фоноте́к|а, и, *f.* gramophone record library.

фонта́н, а, *m.* fountain; (*fig.*) stream; нефтяно́й ф. oil gusher; бить ~ом to gush forth.

фонтани́р|овать, ует, *impf.* to gush forth.

фо́р|а, ы, *f.* дать ~у (+*d.*) to give odds, give a start (*in a game*).

фо́рвард, а, *m.* (*sport.; obs.*) forward.

фордеви́нд, а, *m.* (*naut.*) following wind; идти́ на ф. to run before the wind.

фордыба́ч|ить, у, ишь, *impf.* (*coll.*) to contradict obstinately, object.

форе́йтор, а, *m.* (*obs.*) postilion.

форе́л|ь, и, *f.* trout.

фо́рзац, а, *m.* fly-leaf (*of a book*).

фо́ринт, а, *m.* forint (*Hungarian currency unit*).

фо́рм|а, ы, *f.* **1.** (*in var. senses*) form; по ~е,

...по содержа́нию in form, ... in content; по (всей) ~е in due form, properly. **2.** shape; (*pl.*) contours (*of human body*). **3.** (*tech.*) mould, cast; отли́ть в ~y to mould, cast. **4.** uniform. **5.** быть в ~е (*coll.*) to be in (good) form.

формали́зм, а, *m.* formalism (*pejor. in Marxist criticism of bourgeois art, etc.*).

формали́н, а, *m.* formalin.

формали́ст, а, *m.* formalist.

формали́стик|а, и, *f.* **1.** formalism. **2.** formalities.

формальдеги́д, а, *m.* (*chem.*) formaldehyde.

форма́льность|ь, и, *f.* formality.

форма́л|ьный (~ен, ~ьна), *adj.* (*in var. senses*) formal; ~ьное доказа́тельство formal proof; ~ьная ло́гика formal logic.

фор-ма́рс, а, *m.* (*naut.*) foretop.

форма́т, а, *m.* size, format.

форма́ци|я, и, *f.* **1.** structure; stage (of development). **2.** stamp, mentality. **3.** (*geol.*) formation.

фо́рменк|а, и, *f.* (*coll.*) (*sailor's*) duck blouse.

фо́рменный, *adj.* **1.** uniform. **2.** (*obs.*) formal. **3.** (*coll.*) proper, regular, positive.

формирова́ни|е, я, *n.* **1.** forming; organizing. **2.** (*mil.*) unit, formation.

формир|ова́ть, у́ю, *impf.* (*of* с~) to form; to organize; ф. хара́ктер to form character; ф. батальо́н to raise a battalion; ф. по́езд to make up a train.

формир|ова́ться, у́юсь, *impf.* (*of* с~) **1.** to form, shape, develop (*intrans.*). **2.** *pass. of* ~ова́ть.

форм|ова́ть, у́ю, *impf.* (*of* с~) to form, shape; to model; (*tech.*) to mould, cast.

формо́вк|а, и, *f.* forming, shaping; (*tech.*) moulding, casting.

формо́вочн|ый, *adj.* (*tech.*) moulding, casting; ~ая гли́на foundry loam; ~ые черни́ла (foundry) blacking.

формо́вщик, а, *m.* moulder.

фо́рмул|а, ы, *f.* formula; formulation.

формули́р|овать, ую, *impf. and pf.* (*pf. also* с~) to formulate.

формулиро́вк|а, и, *f.* **1.** formulation. **2.** formula.

формуля́р, а, *m.* **1.** (*obs.*) record of service. **2.** (*tech.*) logbook (*of installation, machine, etc.*). **3.** library card (*card inserted in book recording details thereof*); reader's record card (*card kept by library for each reader, recording details of books loaned*).

форпо́ст, а, *m.* (*mil.*) advanced post; outpost (*also fig.*).

форс, а (у), *m.* (*coll.*) swank; для ~а to show off; сбить кому́-н. ф. to take someone down a peg.

форси́ров|анный, *p.p.p. of* ~ать *and adj.* forced; accelerated; ф. марш forced march.

форси́р|овать, ую, *impf. and pf.* **1.** to force; to speed up. **2.** (*mil.*) to force (*a crossing of*).

фор|си́ть, шу́, си́шь, *impf.* (*coll.*) to swank, show off.

форс-мажо́р, а, *m.* force majeur.

форсу́нк|а, и, *f.* (*tech.*) sprayer, atomizer, jet; fuel injector.

форт, а, о ~е, в ~у́, *pl.* ~ы́, *m.* (*mil.*) fort.

фо́ртел|ь, я, *m.* (*coll.*) trick, stunt.

фортепьяни́ст, а, *m.* (*obs.*) pianist.

фортепья́нный, *adj.* piano; ф. конце́рт piano concerto.

фортепья́но, *indecl.,* *n.* piano.

фортификацио́нный, *adj.* fortification.

фортифика́ци|я, и, *f.* fortification.

фо́рточк|а, и, *f.* fortochka (*small hinged pane for ventilation in window of Russian houses*).

фо́рум, а, *m.* forum.

форшла́г, а, *m.* (*mus.*) grace-note.

форшма́к, а́, *m.* (*cul.*) forshmak (*baked hashed meat or herring with sliced potatoes and onions*).

форште́в|ень, ня, *m.* (*naut.*) stem.

фосге́н, а, *m.* (*chem.*) phosgene.

фосфа́т, а, *m.* (*chem.*) phosphate.

фо́сфор, а, *m.* (*chem.*) phosphorus.

фосфоресце́нци|я, и, *f.* phosphorescence.

фосфоресци́р|овать, ую, *impf.* to phosphoresce; ~ующая кра́ска luminous paint.

фо́сфорист|ый, *adj.* (*chem.*) phosphorous; ~ая бро́нза phosphor bronze.

фосфори́ческий, *adj.* phosphoric.

фосфорноки́смый, *adj.* (*chem.*) phosphate (*of*).

фо́сфорный, *adj.* (*chem.*) phosphorous, phosphoric.

фота́ри|й, я, *m.* (*med.*) radiation therapy room.

фо́то, *indecl.,* *n.* (*coll.*) photo.

фото- photo-.

фотоальбо́м, а, *m.* photograph album.

фотоаппара́т, а, *m.* camera.

фотобума́г|а, и, *f.* photographic paper.

фотогени́ч|ный (~ен, ~на), *adj.* photogenic.

фотограмметри́ческий, *adj.* photogrammetric.

фотограмме́три|я, и, *f.* photogrammetry, photographic survey.

фото́граф, а, *m.* photographer.

фотографи́р|овать, ую, *impf.* (*of* с~) to photograph.

фотографи́р|оваться, уюсь, *impf.* (*of* с~) to be photographed, have one's photo taken.

фотографи́ческ|ий, *adj.* photographic; ~ая плёнка photographic film.

фотогра́фи|я, и, *f.* **1.** photography. **2.** photograph. **3.** photographer's studio.

фотодешифро́вщик, а, *m.* aerial photograph interpreter.

фотодонесéни|е, я, *n.* (*mil.*) intelligence photograph.

фотокáрточк|а, и, *f.* photograph.

фотокóпи|я, и, *f.* photostat (copy).

фотолáмп|а, ы, *f.* **1.** dark room lamp. **2.** (*electr.*) photoelectric cell.

фотолюбѝтел|ь, я, *m.* amateur photographer.

фотóн, а, *m.* (*phys.*) photon.

фотообъектѝв, а, *m.* (camera) lens.

фоторепортáж, а, *m.* picture story.

фоторепортёр, а, *m.* press photographer.

фотосѝнтез, а, *m.* (*bot.*) photosynthesis.

фотостáт, а, *m.* photostat (apparatus).

фототéк|а, и, *f.* photograph library, photograph collection.

фототѝпи|я, и, *f.* phototype.

фотоувеличѝтел|ь, я, *m.* photographic enlarger.

фотохрóник|а, и, *f.* news in pictures.

фотоэлемéнт, а, *m.* (*electr.*) photoelectric cell.

фóфан, а, *m.* (*coll.*) dim-wit.

фрагмéнт, а, *m.* fragment.

фрагментáр|ный (~ен, ~на), *adj.* fragmentary.

фрáз|а, ы, *f.* **1.** sentence. **2.** phrase.

фразеологѝческий, *adj.* phraseological.

фразеолóги|я, и, *f.* **1.** phraseology. **2.** mere verbiage.

фразёр, а, *m.* phrase-monger.

фразёрств|о, а, *n.* mere verbiage, love of flowery language.

фразѝр|овать, ую, *impf.* **1.** to use empty phrases. **2.** (*mus.*) to observe the phrasing (of).

фрак, а, *m.* tail-coat, tails.

фракѝйский, *adj.* Thracian.

фрактýр|а, ы, *f.* (*typ.*) Gothic type, black letter.

фракционѝр|овать, ую, *impf. and pf.* (*chem.*) to fractionate.

фракциóнност|ь, и, *f.* (*polit.*) fractionalism.

фракциóнный¹, *adj.* (*polit.*) fractional; factional.

фракциóнный², *adj.* (*chem.*) fractional.

фрáкци|я¹, и, *f.* (*polit.*) fraction; faction, group.

фрáкци|я², и, *f.* (*chem.*) fraction.

фрамýг|а, и, *f.* upper part of window *or* door; casement.

франк¹, а, *m.* (*hist.*) Frank.

франк², а, *m.* franc.

франкѝр|овать, ую, *impf. and pf.* to prepay, pay the postage (of).

франкирóвк|а, и, *f.* prepayment.

франкмасóн, а, *m.* freemason.

франкмасóн|ский, *adj.* of ~.

фрáнко- (*comm.*) free, prepaid; ф.-борт, ф.-сýдно free on board.

фрáнковый, *adj.* costing, worth a franc.

фрáнкский, *adj.* (*hist.*) Frankish.

франт, а, *m.* dandy.

фран|тѝть, чý, тѝшь, *impf.* (*coll.*) to play the dandy, dress foppishly.

франтѝх|а, и, *f.* of франт.

франтовáт|ый (~, ~а), *adj.* (*coll.*) **1.** dandyish. **2.** fussy, pernickety.

франтовскóй, *adj.* dandyish, dandyfied.

франтовств|ó, á, *n.* dandyism.

француженк|а, и, *f.* Frenchwoman.

францýз, а, *m.* Frenchman.

францýзский, *adj.* French; ф. ключ (*tech.*) monkey wrench.

фраппѝр|овать, ую, *impf. and pf.* (*obs.*) to shock.

фрахт, а, *m.* freight.

фрахт|овáть, ýю, *impf.* (of за~) to charter.

фрáчн|ый, *adj.* of фрак; *as noun* ф., ~ого, *m.* (*obs.*) person not wearing uniform (*i.e. not in Government service*).

фрегáт, а, *m.* **1.** (*naut.*) frigate. **2.** frigate-bird.

фрéз|а, ы, *f.* (*tech.*) mill, milling cutter, cutter; ф.-барабáн drum shredder (*for cutting peat*).

фрéзер, а, *m.* = фрéза.

фрéзерный, *adj.* (*tech.*) milling; ф. станóк milling machine; ф. торф peat cut with drum shredder.

фрезер|овáть, ýю, *impf. and pf.* (*tech.*) to mill, cut.

фрезерóвк|а, и, *f.* (*tech.*) milling, cutting.

фрезерóвщик, а, *m.* milling-machine operator.

фрéйлин|а, ы, *f.* (*hist.*) maid of honour.

френóлог, а, *m.* phrenologist.

френологѝческий, *adj.* phrenological.

френолóги|я, и, *f.* phrenology.

френч, а, *m.* service jacket.

фрéск|а, и, *f.* fresco.

фривóльност|ь, и, *f.* frivolity.

фривóл|ьный (~ен, ~ьна), *adj.* frivolous.

фриз, а, *m.* (*archit.*) frieze.

фрикадéльк|а, и, *f.* meat-ball, fish-ball (*in soup*).

фрикассé, *indecl.*, *n.* fricassé.

фрикатѝвный, *adj.* (*ling.*) fricative.

фрикциóн, а, *m.* (*tech.*) friction clutch.

фрикциóнн|ый, *adj.* (*tech.*) friction; ~ое колесó friction wheel, adhesion wheel.

фрóнд|а, ы, *f.* (*hist.*) Fronde (*also fig.*).

фрондёр, а, *m.* (*hist.*) Frondeur (*also fig.*).

фрондѝр|овать, ую, *impf.* to express discontent.

фронт, а, *pl.* ~ы, ~óв, *m.* (*mil.*; *fig.*) front; на два ~а on two fronts; стать во ф. to stand to attention.

фронтáльн|ый, *adj.* frontal; ~ая атáка frontal attack.

фронтиспи́с, а, *m.* (*archit., typ.*) frontispiece.

фронтови́к, а́, *m.* front-line soldier.

фронтов|о́й, *adj.* (*mil.*) front(-line); ~а́я полоса́ zone of action of a front; ~ы́е пи́сьма letters from the front.

фронто́н, а, *m.* (*archit.*) pediment.

фрукт, а, *m.* **1.** fruit. **2.** (*coll., pejor.*) fellow, type.

фрукто́вый, *adj.* fruit; ф. нож fruit knife; ф. сад orchard; ф. са́хар fruit sugar, fructose.

фрукто́з|а, ы, *f.* fructose.

фр|я, и, *f.* (*coll.*) personage.

фря́жский, *adj.* (*obs.*) western European, foreign.

фтор, а, *m.* (*chem.*) fluorine.

фто́ристый, *adj.* fluorine; fluoride (of).

фу, *interj.* **1.** (*expressing contempt, revulsion, etc.*) ugh! **2.** (*expressing fatigue, etc.*) oh!, ooh! **3.** фу́-ты (*expressing surprise or annoyance*) my word!, my goodness!

фу́г|а, и, *f.* (*mus.*) fugue.

фуга́н|ок, ка, *m.* (*tech.*) smoothing-plane.

фуга́с, а, *m.* (*mil.*) landmine, fougasse.

фуга́ск|а, и, *f.* (*coll.*) **1.** landmine. **2.** high--explosive bomb.

фуга́с|ный, *adj.* **1.** adj. of ~. **2.** high-explosive; ~ная бо́мба high-explosive bomb.

фуг|ова́ть, у́ю, *impf.* (*tech.*) to joint, mortise.

фуже́р, а, *m.* tall wine glass.

фузе́|я, и, *f.* (*hist.*) flint-lock rifle.

фу́к|ать, аю, *impf. of* ~нуть.

фу́к|нуть, ну, нешь, *pf.* (*of* ~ать) (*coll.*) **1.** to blow; to blow out. **2.** to snort. **3.** (*at draughts*) to huff. **4.** (*sl.*) to chuck out.

фу́кси|я, и, *f.* fuchsia.

фуля́р, а, *m.* (*text.*) foulard.

фунда́мент, а, *m.* foundation, base (*also fig.*); substructure; seating (*of boiler, etc.*).

фундамента́л|ьный (~ен, ~ьна), *adj.* **1.** solid, sound; (*fig.*) thorough(-going). **2.** main, basic; ~ьная библиоте́ка main library.

фунди́рованный, *adj.* (*fin.*) funded, consolidated.

фуникулёр, а, *m.* funicular (railway), cable railway.

функциона́льный, *adj.* functional.

функциони́р|овать, ую, *impf.* to function.

фу́нкци|я, и, *f.* (*in var. senses*) function.

фунт, а, *m.* **1.** pound (*measure of weight*). **2.** (сте́рлингов) pound (sterling).

фу́нтик, а, *m.* (*cone-shaped*) paper bag.

фу́ра, ы, *f.* (baggage-)waggon.

фура́ж, а́, *m.* forage, fodder.

фуражи́р, а, *m.* **1.** fodder storeman. **2.** (*mil.*) forager.

фуражи́р|овать, ую, *impf.* (*mil.*) to forage.

фуражиро́вк|а, и, *f.* (*mil.*) foraging.

фура́жк|а, и, *f.* peak-cap; (*mil.*) service cap.

фура́ж|ный, *adj.* of ~; ~ное зерно́ fodder grain; ~ная да́ча forage ration.

фурго́н, а, *m.* **1.** van; estate car. **2.** caravan.

фу́ри|я, и, *f.* **1.** (*myth.*) Fury. **2.** (*fig.*) fury, termagant, virago.

фу́рман, а, *m.* (*obs.*) driver.

фу́рм|енный, *adj.* of ~а; ~енная коро́бка tuyère box, blast box (*in cupola furnace*).

фурниту́р|а, ы, *f.* accessories.

фуру́нкул, а, *m.* (*med.*) furuncle.

фурункулёз, а, *m.* (*med.*) furunculosis.

фурьери́зм, а, *m.* (*polit., philos.*) Fourierism.

фут, а, *m.* **1.** foot (*measure of length*). **2.** foot rule.

футбо́л, а, *m.* football, soccer.

футболи́ст, а, *m.* football-player, footballer.

футбо́лк|а, и, *f.* (*coll.*) football jersey, sports shirt.

футбо́л|ьный, *adj.* of ~; ~ьные бу́тсы football boots; ф. мяч football.

футер|ова́ть, у́ю, *impf.* (*tech.*) to line, fettle.

футеро́вк|а, и, *f.* (*tech.*) (brick-)lining, fettling.

футля́р, а, *m.* case; container; (*tech.*) casing, housing; ф. для очко́в spectacle--case.

фу́товый, *adj.* one-foot.

футури́зм, а, *m.* futurism.

футури́ст, а, *m.* futurist.

футуристи́ческий, *adj.* futuristic.

футшто́к, а, *m.* (*naut.*) tide-gauge; sounding rod.

фуфа́йк|а, и, *f.* jersey.

фуфу́; на ф. (*coll.*) anyhow, carelessly.

фьорд, а, *m.* = фио́рд.

фы́рк|ать, аю, *impf.* (*of* ~нуть) **1.** to snort (*also fig., of a machine*). **2.** (*coll.*) to chuckle. **3.** (*coll.*) to grouse.

фы́рк|нуть, ну, нешь, *pf. of* ~ать.

фюзеля́ж, а, *m.* (*aeron.*) fuselage.

X

хаба́р, а, *m.* (*and* ~а́, ~ы́, *f.*) (*coll., obs.*) bribe.

ха́вбек, а, *m.* (*sport; obs.*) half(-back).

хавро́нь|я, и, *f.* (*coll.*) sow.

хаджи́, *indecl., m.* Hadji (*title of Mohammedan pilgrim who has been to Mecca*).

ха́живать, *pres. tense not used, impf.* (*coll.*) *freq. of* ходи́ть.

хайл|о́, а́, *pl.* **~а,** *n.* **1.** (*coll.*) aperture. **2.** (*sl.*) gob.

хака́с, а, *m.* Khakas (*indigenous inhabitant of Khakas Autonomous Oblast in Siberia*).

хака́с|ка, ки, *f. of* ~.

хака́сский, *adj.* Khakas.

ха́ки, *indecl. adj. and noun, n.* khaki.

хала́т, а, *m.* **1.** dressing-gown. **2.** overall; до́кторский х. doctor's smock. **3.** (*oriental*) robe.

хала́тност|ь, и, *f.* carelessness, negligence.

хала́т|ный, *adj.* **1.** *adj. of* ~. **2.** (**~ен, ~на**) careless, negligent.

халв|а́, ы́, *f.* (*cul.*) halva (*Eastern sweet made from ground nuts and caramel*).

халде́|й, я, *m.* Chaldean.

халде́й|ский, *adj. of* ~.

хали́ф, а, *m.* (*hist.*) caliph.

халифа́т, а, *m.* (*hist.*) caliphate.

халту́р|а, ы, *f.* (*coll.*) **1.** pot-boiler; (*collect.*) hack-work. **2.** extra work; money made on the side.

халту́р|ить, ю, ишь, *impf.* (*coll.*) **1.** to turn out pot-boilers; to do hack-work. **2.** to make money on the side (*by doing extra work*).

халту́р|ный, *adj. of* ~a.

халту́рщик, а, *m.* (*coll.*) **1.** person turning out pot-boilers; hack(-worker). **2.** person making money on the side (*by extra work*).

халу́п|а, ы, *f.* peasant house (*in Ukraine and Byelorussia*).

халцедо́н, а, *m.* (*min.*) chalcedony.

хам, а, *m.* (*coll.*) boor, lout.

хамелео́н, а, *m.* chameleon (*also fig.*).

хам|и́ть, лю́, и́шь, *impf.* (+*d.*) to be rude (to).

хамс|а́, ы́, *f.* khamsa (*small fish of anchovy family*).

ха́мский, *adj.* (*coll.*) boorish, loutish.

ха́мств|о, а, *n.* (*coll.*) boorishness, loutishness.

хан, а, *m.* khan.

хандр|а́, ы́, *f.* depression.

хандр|и́ть, ю́, и́шь, *impf.* to be depressed.

ханж|а́, и́, *g. pl.* **~е́й,** *m. and f.* sanctimonious person; canting hypocrite.

ха́нжеск|ий (and ~о́й), *adj.* sanctimonious; hypocritical.

ханжеств|о́, а́, *n.* sanctimoniousness; hypocrisy.

ханж|и́ть, у́, и́шь, *impf.* (*coll.*) to display sanctimoniousness; to play the hypocrite.

ха́н|ский, *adj. of* ~.

ха́нств|о, а, *n.* khanate.

ханты́, *indecl., m. and f.* Khanty (*formerly Ostyak(s), inhabitant(s) of Khanty-Mansi National Region*).

ханты́йский, *adj.* Khanty.

ха́ос, а, *m.* (*myth.*) Chaos.

хао́с, а, *m.* chaos (*disorder*).

хаоти́ческий, *adj.* chaotic.

хаоти́чност|ь, и, *f.* chaotic character; state of chaos.

хаоти́ч|ный (~ен, ~на), *adj.* = ~еский.

ха́п|ать, аю, *impf. of* ~нуть.

ха́п|нуть, ну, нешь, *pf.* (*of* ~ать) (*coll.*) **1.** to seize, grab. **2.** (*fig.*) to nab, pinch, scrounge.

хапу́г|а, и, *m. and f.* (*coll.*) thief, scrounger.

хара́ктер, а, *m.* character, personality, nature, disposition (*of a human being*); они́ не сошли́сь ~ами they could not get on (together); э́то не в его́ ~е it's not like him. **2.** (strong) character; челове́к с ~ом determined person, strong character. **3.** character, nature, type; х. рабо́ты type of work.

характериз|ова́ть, у́ю, *impf. and pf.* **1.** to describe. **2.** to characterize, be characteristic (*of*).

характериз|ова́ться, у́юсь, *impf.* (+*i.*) to be characterized (by).

характери́стик|а, и, *f.* **1.** description. **2.** reference; х. с ме́ста пре́жней слу́жбы reference from former place of work. **3.** (*math.*) characteristic (*of logarithm*). **4.** (*tech.*) characteristic curve; performance graph.

хара́ктерно, *as pred.* it is characteristic, it is typical.

хара́ктерный, *adj.* (*obs. or coll.*) having a strong character; strong-willed; temperamental.

хара́ктер|ный (~ен, ~на), *adj.* **1.** characteristic; typical; э́то для него́ ~но it is typical of him. **2.** distinctive. **3.** (*theatr.*) character; х. актёр character actor.

ха́риус, а, *m.* (*fish*) grayling, umber.

ха́рканъ|е, я, *n.* (*coll.*) expectoration.

ха́рк|ать, аю, *impf.* (*of* ~нуть) (*coll.*) to spit, expectorate; х. кро́вью to spit blood.

ха́рк|нуть, ну, нешь, *pf. of* ~ать.

ха́рти|я, и, *f.* charter.

харче́вн|я, и, *f.* (*obs.*) eating-house.

харч|и́, е́й, *sing.* ~, **~а,** *m.* (*coll.*) grub.

харчо́, *indecl., n.* kharcho (*Caucasian mutton soup*).

ха́р|я, и, *f.* (*sl.*) mug (= face).

ха́т|а, ы, *f.* peasant house (*in S. Russia, Ukraine, and Byelorussia*); моя́ х. с кра́ю it's no concern of mine; that's your, their, *etc.,* funeral.

ха́хал|ь, я, *m.* (*sl.*) fancy man.

ха́|ять, ю, ешь, *impf.* (*of* о~) (*coll.*) to play down, run down.

хвал|а́, ы́, *f.* praise; х. Бо́гу! thank God!

хвале́б|ный (~ен, ~на), *adj.* laudatory, eulogistic, complimentary.

хвалёный, *adj.* (*iron.*) much-vaunted, celebrated.

хвал|и́ть, ю́, ~ишь, *impf.* (*of* по~) to praise, compliment.

хвал|и́ться, ю́сь, ~ишься, *impf.* (*of* по~) (+*i.*) to boast (of).

хва́стать = ~ся.

хва́ста|ться, юсь, *impf.* (*of* по~) (+*i.*) to boast (of).

хвастли́в|ый (~, ~a), *adj.* boastful.

хвастовств|о́, а́, *n.* boasting, bragging.

хвасту́н, а́, *m.* (*coll.*) boaster, braggart.

хват, а, *m.* (*coll.*) successful fellow.

хват|а́ть¹, а́ю, *impf.* (*of* ~и́ть¹ *and* схвати́ть) **1.** to snatch, seize, catch hold (of); to grab, grasp; x. что попа́ло to seize up whatever comes to hand. **2.** (*impf. only*) (*coll.*) to bite (*of fish*). **3.** (*impf. only*) (*coll.*) to pick up (= to detain).

хват|а́ть², а́ет, *impf.* (*of* ~и́ть²) *impers.* **1.** (+*g.*) to suffice, be sufficient, enough; to last out; у меня́, *etc.*, не ~а́ет I, *etc.*, am short (of); вре́мени не ~а́ло there was not long enough; у нас не ~а́ет де́нег we have not enough money; э́того ещё не ~а́ло! that's the last straw! **2.** (+*g.* на+*a.*) to be up to, be capable (of); его́ не ~а́ет на тако́й посту́пок he is not up to such an act.

хват|а́ться, а́юсь, *impf.* (*of* ~и́ться *and* схвати́ться) (за+*a.*) **1.** to snatch (at), catch (at), pluck (at); x. за соло́минку to reach for a straw; x. за́ ум to come to one's senses. **2.** to take up, try out.

хва|ти́ть¹, чу́, ~тишь, *pf.* (*coll.*) **1.** *pf. of* ~та́ть¹. **2.** to drink up, knock back; x. ли́шнего to have one too many. **3.** to suffer, endure. **4.** to stick one's neck out; to blurt out; x. че́рез край to go too far. **5.** (*in var. senses*) to strike; to hit; to smash; его́ ~ти́л уда́р he has had a stroke; моро́зом ~ти́ло посе́в (*impers.*) the frost hit the crops. **6.** to strike up, start up; x. плясову́ю to strike up a tune for dancing.

хват|и́ть², ~ит, *pf.* (*of* ~а́ть²); ~ит that will do!, that's enough!; с меня́ ~ит! I've had enough!; ~ит тебе́ хны́кать! that's enough of your whining!

хва|ти́ться, чу́сь, ~тишься, *pf.* **1.** *pf. of* ~та́ться. **2.** (+*g.*; *coll.*) to notice the absence (of), remember (*that one has left behind*); по́здно ~ти́лись! you thought of it too late! **3.** (о+*a.*; *coll.*) to hit, bump (into).

хва́тк|а, и, *f.* **1.** grasp, grip, clutch. **2.** (*coll.*) method, technique. **3.** skill.

хва́т|кий (~ок, ~ка́, ~ко), *adj.* (*coll.*) **1.** strong (*of hands, grip, etc.*); tenacious. **2.** skilful, crafty.

хвать (*coll.*) *used in place of various forms of* хвати́ть¹ *and* хвати́ться 2 (*also as interj.*); я x. его́ за воротни́к I grabbed him by the collar; я чуть бы́ло не сел на по́езд, а — x.! — биле́та нет I was just about to board

the train when suddenly I found I had not got my ticket.

хво́йн|ый, *adj.* **1.** *adj. of* хвоя́; x. покро́в covering of (pine) needles; x. дёготь pine--tar. **2.** coniferous; *as noun* ~ые, ~ых (*bot.*) conifers.

хвора́|ть, ю, *impf.* (*coll.*) to be ill, sick.

хво́рост, а (у), *m.* (*collect.*) **1.** brushwood. **2.** (*cul.*) (pastry) straws, twiglets.

хворости́н|а, ы, *f.* stick, switch (*for driving cattle, etc.*).

хво́рост|ь, и, *f.* (*coll.*) illness, ailment.

хворостяно́й, *adj. of* хворост 1.

хво́р|ый (~, ~а́, ~о), *adj.* (*coll.*) ill, sick.

хвор|ь, и, *f.* (*coll.*) illness, ailment.

хвост, а́, *m.* **1.** tail (*also fig.; of aircraft, comet, etc.*); tail-feathers; маха́ть ~о́м to wag one's tail; задра́ть x. to get on one's high horse; поджа́ть x. to draw in one's horns; показа́ть x. (*coll.*) to show a clean pair of heels; (и) в x. и в гри́ву (*coll.*) neck and crop. **2.** (*fig.*) tail, rear, end, tail-end; x. по́езда rear (coaches) of train; быть, плести́сь в ~е́ to get behind, lag behind. **3.** (*coll.*) train (*of dress*); наступи́ть на x. кому́-н. (*coll.*) to tread on someone's toes, corns. **4.** (*coll.*) throng, following. **5.** (*coll.*) queue, line; x. за хле́бом bread queue. **6.** (*coll.*) unfinished portion (*of work, etc.*). **7.** (*tech.*) shank, shaft (*of tool*). **8.** (*pl.*) (*min.*) tails, tailings.

хвоста́т|ый (~, ~а), *adj.* **1.** having a tail; caudate. **2.** having a large tail.

хвости́зм, а, *m.* (*polit.*) 'tailism' (*limitation of revolutionary aims to those intelligible to backward masses*).

хво́стик, а, *m. dim. of* хвост; с ~ом and a little more; сто с ~ом a hundred odd.

хвости́ст, а, *m.* **1.** (*polit.*) 'tailist' (*see* хвости́зм). **2.** (*coll.*) student failing to obtain required number of passes in examination.

хвосто́в|о́й, *adj. of* хвост; ~а́я ве́на (*anat.*) caudal vein; x. ого́нь (*aeron.*) tail light; ~о́е опере́ние (*aeron.*) tail unit; x. патро́н (*mil.*) ignition charge, cartridge.

хвощ, а́, *m.* (*bot.*) horse-tail, mare's tail (*Equisetum*).

хво́|я, и, *f.* **1.** needle(s) (*of conifer*). **2.** (*collect.*) branches (*of conifer*).

хе́рес, а (у), *m.* sherry.

хе́р|ить, ю, ишь, *impf.* (*coll., obs.*) to cross out.

херуви́м, а, *m.* cherub.

херуви́м|ский, *adj.* **1.** *adj. of* ~. **2.** (*coll.*) cherubic.

хе́ттский, *adj.* (*hist. and ling.*) Hittite.

хиба́р|а, ы, *f.* (*coll.*) shack, hovel.

хиба́р|ка, ки, *f. dim. of* ~a.

хи́жин|а, ы, *f.* shack, hut.

хилé|ть, ю, *impf.* (*of* за~) (*coll.*) to become weak, sickly.

хи́л|ый (~, ~á, ~о), *adj.* weak, sickly; puny; decrepit.

хим- *abbr. of* хими́ческий.

химéр|а, ы, *f.* chimera.

химери́ческий, *adj.* chimerical.

химиза́ци|я, и, *f.* 'chemicalisation' (*intensified development of chemical industry and utilization of its products*).

хими́зм, а, *m.* chemistry (= chemical composition).

хи́мик, а, *m.* 1. chemist. 2. chemical industry worker.

химика́л|ии, ий, *no sing.* chemicals.

химика́т|ы, ов, *sing.* ~, ~а, = химика́лии.

хими́ческ|ий, *adj.* 1. chemical; х. каранда́ш indelible pencil; ~ие препара́ты chemicals; ~ая чи́стка (одéжды) dry--cleaning; х. элемéнт chemical element. 2. chemistry; х. кабинéт chemistry laboratory. 3. (*mil.*) chemical warfare, gas; ~ая бóмба gas bomb; ~ая войнá chemical warfare; ~ое подразделéние chemical warfare unit.

хи́ми|я, и, *f.* chemistry.

химчи́стк|а, и, *f.* dry-cleaning.

хи́нди, *indecl.*, *m.* Hindi (*language*).

хини́н, а, *m.* cinchona, quinine.

хи́нн|ый, *adj.* cinchona; ~ое дéрево cinchona (tree); ~ая кóрка Peruvian bark.

хин|ь, и, *f.*; идёт ~ью (*coll.*, *obs.*) it is in vain, to no purpose.

хирé|ть, ю, *impf.* (*of* за~) to grow sickly; (*of plants*) to wither; (*fig.*) to decay.

хиромáнт, а, *m.* chiromancer, palmist.

хиромáнти|я, и, *f.* chiromancy, palmistry.

хиротóни|я, и, *f.* (*eccl.*) consecration, ordination (*to bishopric, priesthood, diaconate*).

хиру́рг, а, *m.* surgeon.

хирурги́ческ|ий, *adj.* surgical; ~ие нóжницы forceps; ~ая сестрá theatre nurse.

хирурги́|я, и, *f.* surgery.

хити́н, а, *m.* (*biol.*) chitin.

хити́новый, *adj.* (*biol.*) chitinous.

хитóн, а, *m.* tunic.

хитрéц, á, *m.* sly, cunning person.

хитрец|á, ы́, *f.* (*coll.*) cunning, guile; говори́ть с ~ой to speak disingenuously.

хитри́нк|а, и, *f.* = хитрецá.

хитр|и́ть, ю́, и́шь, *impf.* (*of* с~) to use cunning, guile; to dissemble.

хитросплетéни|е, я, *n.* 1. cunning trick, stratagem. 2. (*pl.*) fanciful construction; hair-splitting.

хитросплетённый, *adj.* intricate, contrived.

хи́трост|ь, и, *f.* 1. cunning, guile, craft, wiles. 2. ruse, stratagem. 3. (*coll.*) skill, resource. 4. (*coll.*) intricacy, subtlety.

хитроу́ми|е, я, *n.* cunning; resourcefulness.

хитроу́м|ный (~ен, ~на), *adj.* 1. cunning; resourceful. 2. intricate, complicated.

хи́т|рый (~ёр, ~рá, ~ро), *adj.* 1. cunning, sly, crafty, wily. 2. (*coll.*) skilful, resourceful. 3. (*coll.*) intricate, subtle; complicated.

хихи́к|ать, аю, *impf.* (*of* ~нуть) to giggle, titter, snigger.

хихи́к|нуть, ну, нешь, *pf. of* ~ать.

хищéни|е, я, *n.* theft; embezzlement, misappropriation.

хи́щник, а, *m.* 1. beast, bird of prey. 2. (*fig.*) plunderer, despoiler.

хи́щническ|ий, *adj.* 1. *adj. of* хи́щник. 2. predatory, rapacious. 3. destructive; injurious (*to the economy*).

хи́щничеств|о, а, *n.* 1. preying. 2. predatoriness. 3. injurious exploitation of natural resources. 4. embezzlement, misappropriation.

хи́щ|ный (~ен, ~на), *adj.* 1. predatory; ~ные звéри, пти́цы beasts, birds of prey. 2. rapacious, grasping, greedy.

хлад, а, *m.* (*obs. or poet.*) cold.

хладнокрóви|е, я, *n.* coolness, composure, presence of mind, sang-froid.

хладнокрóв|ный (~ен, ~на), *adj.* cool, composed.

хладнолóмкий, *adj.* (*tech.*) cold-short, brittle at atmospheric temperature.

хлáд|ный (~ен, ~на), *adj.* (*obs. or poet.*) cold.

хладостó|йкий, (~ек, ~йка), *adj.* (*tech.*) cold-resistant; х. состáв anti-freeze.

хлам, а, *m.* (*collect.*) rubbish, trash.

хлами́д|а, ы, *f.* 1. (*hist.*) chlamys. 2. (*coll.*) long, loose-fitting garment.

хлеб, а, *pl.* ~ы and ~á, *m.* 1. (*sing. only*) bread (*also fig.*); х. насу́щный daily bread; добывáть х. (*fig.*) to win one's bread; отби́ть у когó-н. х. to take the bread out of someone's mouth; перебивáться с ~а на квас to live from hand to mouth. 2. (*pl.* ~ы) loaf. 3. (*pl.* ~á) bread-grain; (*pl.*) corn, crops; cereals. 4. (*pl.* ~á) (*coll.*) food; жить на ~áх у когó-н. (*i*) to board with someone, (*ii*) to be dependent on someone, live off someone; идти́ на ~á к комý-н. to become dependent on someone.

хлебá|ть, ю, *impf.* 1. to gulp (down). 2. (*coll.*) to eat, drink (*liquids*) with a spoon.

хлéб|ец, ца, *m.* small loaf.

хлéбин|а, ы, *f.* bee-bread.

хлéбник, а, *m.* (*obs.*) baker.

хлéбниц|а, ы, *f.* bread-plate; bread-basket.

хлебн|у́ть, у́, ёшь, *pf.* (*coll.*) 1. to drink down. 2. (+*g.*) to go through, endure, experience.

хлéб|ный, *adj.* 1. *adj. of* хлеб 1; ~ые дрóжжи baker's yeast; ~ые запáсы bread supplies; x. магази́н baker's shop; ~ое де́рево bread-fruit tree. **2.** *adj. of* хлеб 3; x. амба́р granary; ~ое вино́ (*obs.*) vodka; ~ые зла́ки bread-grains, cereals; x. спирт grain alcohol, ethyl alcohol. **3.** rich (*in grain*), abundant; grain-producing. **4.** (*coll.*) lucrative, profitable.

хлёбов|о, а, *n.* (*coll.*) gruel.

хлебозаво́д, а, *m.* bread-baking plant, bakery.

хлебо|заготови́тельный, *adj. of* ~загото́вка.

хлебозагото́вк|а, и, *f.* (State) grain procurement.

хлебозаку́пк|а, и, *f.* (State) grain-purchase.

хлеб|о́к, ка́, *m.* (*coll.*) mouthful (*of liquid food*).

хлебопа́шеств|о, а, *n.* (*obs.*) tillage, cultivation, arable farming.

хлебопа́ш|ец, ца, *m.* (*obs.*) tiller of the soil.

хлебопа́шный, *adj.* ploughing; arable.

хлебопёк, а, *m.* baker.

хлебопека́рный, *adj.* baking.

хлебопека́рн|я, и, *f.* bakery, bake-house.

хлебопоста́вк|а, и, *f.* grain delivery (*to State*).

хлеборо́б, а, *m.* peasant (engaged in arable farming); (*rhet.*) corn-producer.

хлеборо́д|ный (~ен, ~на), *adj.* rich (in grain crops), abundant; x. год good year (for grain crops).

хлебосо́л, а, *m.* hospitable person.

хлебосо́л|ьный (~ен, ~ьна), *adj.* hospitable.

хлебосо́льств|о, а, *n.* hospitality.

хлеботорго́в|ец, ца, *m.* corn-merchant, grain-merchant.

хлеботорго́вл|я, и, *f.* corn-trade.

хлебоубо́рк|а, и, *f.* (corn-)harvest.

хлебоубо́рочный, *adj.* harvest(ing); x. комба́йн combine harvester.

хлеб-со́ль, хле́ба-со́ли bread and salt (*offered to guest as symbol of hospitality*); hospitality.

хлев, а, в ~е *or* в ~у́, *pl.* ~а́, *m.* cow-house, cattle-shed, byre; (*fig., coll.*) pig-sty.

хлестако́вщин|а, ы, *f.* shameless bragging (*in the manner of Khlestakov, hero of Gogol's comedy 'The Inspector-General'*).

хле|ста́ть, щу́, ~щешь, *impf.* (*of* ~стну́ть) **1.** (+*a. or* по+*d.*) to lash; to whip. **2.** (*of rain, etc.*) to lash (down), beat (down), pour; to stream, gush. **3.** (*coll.*) to swill (= to drink in large quantities).

хлёст|кий (~ок, ~ка́, ~ко), *adj.* **1.** biting. **2.** (*fig.*) biting, scathing; trenchant. **3.** (*of sounds, etc.*) sharp. **4.** (*coll.*) lively, gay.

хлест|ну́ть, ну́, нёшь, *pf. of* ~а́ть.

хлёст|че, *comp. of* ~кий

хле́ще, *comp. of* хлёсткий

хли́па|ть, ю, *impf.* (*coll.*) to sob.

хли́п|кий (~ок, ~ка́, ~ко), *adj.* (*coll.*) **1.** rickety, shaky. **2.** (*fig.*) weak, fragile. **3.** watery, slushy.

хлобы|ста́ть, щу́, ~щешь, *impf.* (*of* ~стну́ть) (*coll.*) to lash.

хлобыст|ну́ть, ну, нёшь, *inst. pf. of* ~а́ть.

хлоп¹, *interj.* bang! (*as pred.*; *stands for pres. and past tenses of* ~ать, ~нуть, *and* ~аться).

хлоп², а, *m.* (*coll.*) bang, clatter.

хло́па|ть, ю, *impf.* (*of* хло́пнуть) **1.** (+*i. or* по+*d.*) to bang; to slap; x. кали́ткой to bang the gate; x. кого́-н. по спине́ to slap someone on the back; x. глаза́ми (*i*) to look blank, (*ii*) to be at a loss what to say (*in answer to a question*); x. уша́ми (*coll.*) to look dumb. **2.** (в ладо́ши) (+*d.*) to clap, applaud. **3.** (*coll.*) to shoot. **4.** (*coll.*) to knock back (= to drink).

хло́па|ться, юсь, *impf.* (*of* хло́пнуться) (*coll.*) to flop down.

хло́п|ец, ца, *m.* (*coll. or dial.*) lad.

хлопково́д, а, *m.* cotton-grower.

хлопково́дств|о, а, *n.* cotton-growing.

хлопково́дческий, *adj.* cotton-growing.

хло́пков|ый, *adj.* cotton; ~ое ма́сло cotton-seed oil; ~ые очёски cotton waste; ~ая пря́жа cotton yarn.

хлопкопряди́льный, *adj.* cotton-spinning.

хлопкоро́б, а, *m.* cotton-grower.

хлопкоубо́рочный, *adj.* cotton-picking.

хло́п|нуть(ся), ну(сь), нешь(ся), *pf. of* ~ать(ся).

хло́п|ок, ка, *m.* cotton; x.-сыре́ц cotton-wool.

хлоп|о́к, ка́, *m.* **1.** clap. **2.** bang.

хлопо|та́ть, чу́, ~чешь, *impf.* (*of* по~) **1.** (*impf. only*) to busy oneself; to bustle about, toil. **2.** (о+*p. or* + чтобы) to make efforts; to take trouble, go to pains; to solicit, petition (for); x., чтобы привести́ кого́-н. в чу́вство to endeavour to bring someone round. **3.** (за+*a. or* о+*p.*) to plead (for), make efforts on behalf (of).

хлопотли́в|ый (~, ~а), *adj.* **1.** troublesome, bothersome; involving (much) trouble, requiring (great) pains, exacting. **2.** busy, bustling, restless.

хло́пот|ный (~ен, ~на), *adj.* (*coll.*) involving (much) trouble, exacting.

хлопотн|я́, и́, *f.* (*coll.*) efforts, labour, toil.

хлопоту́н, а́, *m.* (*coll.*) busy, restless person.

хло́пот|ы, хлопо́т, ~ам, *no sing.* **1.** trouble. **2.** (о+*p.*) efforts (on behalf of, for); pains.

хлопу́шк|а, и, *f.* **1.** fly-swatter. **2.** (Christmas) cracker. **3.** (*bot.*) catchfly (*Silene venosa*). **4.** (*tech.*) gate valve.

хлопча́тк|а, и, *f.* (*coll.*) cotton (*fabric*).

хлопча́тник, а, *m.* cotton(-plant).

хлопчатобума́жный, *adj.* cotton; x. по́рох gun-cotton.

хлопча́т|ый¹, adj. ~ая бума́га (obs.) (i) cotton-plant, (ii) cotton (fabric, thread).

хлопча́тый², adj. flaky.

хло́пчик, а, m. (coll. or dial.) boy.

хлопьеви́д|ный (~ен, ~на), adj. flaky, flocculent.

хло́пь|я, ев, no sing. flakes (of snow, etc., or as component of name of certain cereal foods); кукуру́зные х., пшени́чные х. corn flakes.

хлор, а, m. (chem.) chlorine.

хлора́тор, а, m. chlorinator.

хлори́р|овать, ую, impf. and pf. to chlorinate.

хлористоводоро́дный, adj. (chem.) hydrochloride (of).

хло́ристый, adj. (chem.) chlorine; chloride (of); х. водоро́д hydrogen chloride.

хлори́т, а, m. (min.) chlorite.

хло́рк|а, и, f. (coll.) bleaching powder (of calcium hypochlorite).

хло́р|ный, adj. of ~.

хлоро́з, а, m. (bot. and med.) chlorosis.

хлорофи́лл, а, m. (bot.) chlorophyll.

хлорофо́рм, а, m. chlorophorm.

хлороформи́р|овать, ую, impf. and pf. (pf. also за~) to chloroform.

хлорпикри́н, а, m. (chem. and agric.) chloropicrin.

хлы́н|уть, у, ешь, pf. 1. (of blood, rain, etc.) to gush, pour. 2. (fig.) to pour, rush, surge; на пло́щадь ~ула толпа́ наро́ду a crowd poured into the square.

хлыст¹, а́, m. 1. whip, switch. 2. trunk (of felled tree).

хлыст², а́, m. Khlyst (member of sect).

хлысто́вств|о, а, n. Khlysts (Russian religious sect).

хлыщ, а́, m. (coll.) fop.

хлю́па|ть, ю, impf. (coll.) 1. to squelch. 2. to flounder (through mud, etc.). 3. to snivel; х. но́сом to sniff.

хлю́пик, а, m. (coll.) sniveller, milksop.

хлю́п|кий (~ок, ~ка́, ~ко), adj. (coll.) 1. soggy. 2. rickety. 3. (fig.) frail, feeble.

хлюст¹, а́, m. (coll.) smart Alec.

хлюст², а́, m. (coll.) suit (in a hand at cards).

хляб|ь, и, f. 1. (obs. or poet.) abyss; ~и небе́сные разве́рзлись (joc.) the heavens opened (of heavy rain). 2. (coll.) mud, muddy ground.

хля́стик, а, m. half-belt (sewn or buttoned on to back of coat).

хмелево́д, а, m. hop-grower.

хмелево́дств|о, а, n. hop-growing.

хмел|ево́й, adj. of ~ь.

хмел|ёк, ька́, m. dim. of ~ь; под ~ько́м tipsy, tight.

хмеле́|ть, ю, impf. (of за ~ and о ~) to become tipsy, get tight.

хмел|ь, я, m. 1. (bot.) hop(s); hop-plant.

2. (о ~е, во ~ю́) drunkenness, tipsiness; под ~ем, во ~ю́, tipsy, tight.

хмел|ьно́й (~ён, ~ьна́), adj. 1. drunken, tipsy. 2. intoxicating; as noun ~ьно́е, ~ьно́го, n. intoxicating liquor, alcohol.

хму́р|ить, ю, ишь, impf. (of на~) х. лицо́ to frown; х. бро́ви to knit one's brows.

хму́р|иться, юсь, ишься, impf. (of на~) 1. to frown. 2. to become gloomy. 3. to be overcast, cloudy.

хму́рост|ь, и, f. 1. gloom. 2. cloudiness.

хму́р|ый (~, ~а́, ~о), adj. 1. gloomy, sullen. 2. overcast, cloudy; lowering; х. день dull day; ~ое не́бо lowering sky.

хмы́ка|ть, ю, impf. (coll.) to hem (expressing surprise, annoyance, doubt, etc.).

хн|а, ы, f. henna.

хны́ка|ть, ю (and хны́ч|у, ешь), impf. (coll.) to whimper, snivel; (fig.) to whine.

хо́бот, а, m. 1. (zool.) trunk, proboscis. 2. (tech.) tool-holder. 3. х. лафе́та (mil.) trail of gun-carriage.

хоботно́й, adj. of хо́бот 1.

хо́бот|овый, adj. of ~ 2, 3.

хобот|о́к, ка́, m. proboscis (of insects).

ход, а (у), о ~е, в (на) ~е and ~у́, m. 1. (в ~е, на ~у́) motion, movement, travel, going; speed, pace; три часа́ ~у three hours' going; за́дний х. backing, reversing; ма́лый х., ти́хий х. slow speed; по́лный х. full speed; по́лный х.! full speed ahead!; по́лным ~ом (fig.) in full swing; свобо́дный х. free-wheeling, coasting; сре́дний х. half-speed; дать х. (+d.) to set in motion, set going; д. ~у (i) (coll.) to increase pace, go faster, (ii) (coll.) to take to one's heels; не дать ~у кому́-н. not to give someone a chance, hold someone back; идти́ свои́м ~ом (i) to travel under one's own steam, (ii) to take its course; пойти́ в х. to come to be widely used, acquire a vogue; пусти́ть в х. to start, set in motion, set going (also fig.), put into operation, put into service; быть в ~у́ to be in demand, be in vogue; на ~у́ (i) in transit, on the move, without halting, (ii) in motion, in operation; на по́лном ~у́ at full speed, full blast; с ~у (coll.) without a pause, straight off. 2. (eccl.) procession. 3. (в, на ~е) (fig.) course, progress; х. мы́слей train of thought; х. собы́тий course of events. 4. (в ~е, на ~е and ~у́) (tech.) work, operation, running; на холосто́м ~у́ idling. 5. (в, на ~е; pl. ~ы, ~ов) (tech.) stroke (of piston), blow (of press); cycle; travel; х. вверх, х. вниз, х. сжа́тия (of piston) upstroke, downstroke, compression stroke. 6. (на ~е; pl. ~ы́) (chess, draughts) move; (cards) lead; х. бе́лых white's move. 7. (в ~е; pl. ~ы) (fig.) move, gambit, manœuvre;

ло́вкий x. shrewd move. **8.** (в ~е and ~ý; *pl.* ~ы́) entrance (*to building*); знать все ~ы́ и вы́ходы to know all the ins and outs. **9.** (в, на ~е and ~ý; *pl.* ~ы́, ~óв) passage, covered way, thoroughfare; ~ы́ сообщéния (*mil.*) communication trench. **10.** (в, на ~ý; *pl.* ~ы́ and ~á, ~óв) (*tech.*) wheel-base; runners (*of sledge*); гýсеничный x. caterpillar tracks.

ходáта|й, я, *m.* **1.** intercessor, mediator. **2.** (*obs.*) (по делáм) solicitor.

ходáтайств|о, а, *n.* **1.** petitioning; entreaty, pleading. **2.** petition; application.

ходáтайств|овать, ую, *impf.* (*of* по~) **1.** (о+*p.* or за+*a.*) to petition (for); to apply (for). **2.** (за+*a.*) to defend, intercede (for), plead (for).

ходéбщик, а, *m.* (*obs.*) hawker, pedlar.

хо́дик|и, ов, *no sing.* (*coll.*) grandfather clock (*worked by weights*).

хо|ди́ть, жу́, ~дишь, *impf.* **1.** to (be able to) walk. **2.** (*indet. of* идти́) to go (*on foot*); x. в го́сти to be invited out, visit (friends); x. в кино́ to go to the cinema; x. в атáку to go into the attack; x. на парусáх to go sailing; x. по́ миру to be a beggar. **3.** (*of trains, etc.*) to run. **4.** to pass, go round; x. из рук в ру́ки, по рукáм to pass from hand to hand; недóбрые вéсти ~дят bad news is going round. **5.** (*cards*) to lead, play; (*chess, etc.*) to move; x. с пик to lead a spade; x. ферзём to move one's queen. **6.** (*indet. only*) (за+*i.*) to look after, take care of, tend. **7.** to sway, shake, wobble. **8.** (*coll., obs.*) to cost; to pass, be current. **9.** (в+*p.*; *coll.*) to be (= to occupy the post of, work as). **10.** (в+*p.*) to wear. **11.** (*pf.* с~) (*coll.*) to go (= to excrete).

хо́д|кий (~ок, ~кá, ~ко), *adj.* (*coll.*) **1.** fast, fleet. **2.** saleable, marketable; popular, in great demand, much sought after; x. товáр popular line; ~кое выражéние popular phrase.

ходов|óй, *adj.* **1.** (*tech.*) running, working; ~óе врéмя working time; x. золотни́к throttle valve; ~ы́е испытáния running tests; x. механи́зм running gear; x. рóлик traveller. **2.** in (good) working order. **3.** (*tech., naut.*) free, running (= not secured). **4.** (*coll.*) popular; current; x. анекдóт (currently) popular story. **5.** (*coll.*) smart, clever.

ходóк, á, *m.* **1.** walker. **2.** быть ~óм (кудá-н.) (*coll.*) to make regular visits (to). **3.** envoy, petition-bearer. **4.** (на+*a.*, по+*d.*) (*coll.*) person clever (at). **5.** (*tech.*) passage (*in mine*).

ходýл|и, ей, *sing.* ~я, ~и, *f.* stilts.

ходýл|ьный (~ен, ~ьна), *adj.* stilted; pompous.

ходýн, á, *m.* *now only in phrase* ~óм ходи́ть (*coll.*) to shake, rock; (*fig.*) to rush about.

ходьб|á, ы́, *f.* walking; цéрковь нахóдится в пяти́ мину́тах ~ы́ отсю́да the church is five minutes' walk from here.

ходя́ч|ий, *adj.* **1.** walking; able to walk. **2.** (*fig., coll., iron.*) the personification (of); ~ая добродéтель virtue personified. **3.** popular; current; ~ее выражéние current phrase.

хождéни|е, я, *n.* **1.** walking; going; x. по мýкам (*fig.*) (going through) purgatory. **2.** имéть x. to be in circulation, pass current.

хозрасчёт, а, *m.* (*abbr. of* хозя́йственный расчёт) (*econ.*) self-supporting running, self-financing (*system whereby an industrial undertaking, etc., in the U.S.S.R. finances itself without the aid of central State funds*).

хозрасчёт|ный, *adj. of* ~.

хозя́|ин, ина, *pl.* ~ева, ~ев, *m.* **1.** owner, proprietor. **2.** master; boss. **3.** landlord (*in relation to tenant*). **4.** host; ~ева пóля (*sport*) the home team. **5.** хорóший, плохóй x. good, bad manager. **6.** (*coll.*) husband. **7.** (*biol.*) host.

хозя́йк|а, и, *g. pl.* хозя́ек, *f.* **1.** owner, proprietress. **2.** mistress. **3.** landlady. **4.** (*coll.*) wife.

хозя́йнича|ть, ю, *impf.* **1.** to manage, carry on management. **2.** to keep house. **3.** (*fig., pejor.*) to lord it; to throw one's weight about.

хозя́йский, *adj.* **1.** *adj. of* хозя́ин. **2.** solicitous, careful. **3.** (*pejor.*) proprietary; imperious.

хозя́йственник, а, *m.* economic planner.

хозя́йствен|ный (~, ~на), *adj.* **1.** economic, of the economy; ~ная жизнь страны́ the country's economy. **2.** x. расчёт *see* хозрасчёт. **3.** household; home management; x. инвентáрь household equipment. **4.** economical, thrifty. **5.** commanding; confident.

хозя́йств|о, а, *n.* **1.** economy; сéльское x. agriculture; домáшнее x. housekeeping; вести́ x. to manage, carry on management. **2.** equipment. **3.** (*agric.*) farm, holding. **4.** housekeeping; хлопотáть по ~у to be busy about the house.

хозя́йств|овать, ую, *impf.* to manage, carry on management.

хозя́йчик, а, *m.* (*coll.*) small proprietor.

хоккеи́ст, а, *m.* hockey-player.

хоккé|й, я, *m.* hockey; x. с шáйбой ice hockey.

хоккéй|ный, *adj. of* ~; ~ная клю́шка hockey-stick.

хóленый, *adj.* well-groomed, carefully tended; sleek.

холéр|а, ы, *f.* (*med.*) cholera (*also as expletive*).

холе́рик, а, *m.* **1.** choleric person. **2.** (*coll.*) person suffering from cholera.

холери́ческий, *adj.* choleric.

холе́р|ный, *adj. of* ~а; х. вибрио́н cholera bacillus.

хо́л|ить, ю, ишь, *impf.* to tend, care for.

хо́лк|а, и, *f.* withers; намы́лить ~у кому́-н. (*coll.*) to give someone a dressing-down.

холл, а, *m.* hall, vestibule, foyer.

холм, а́, *m.* hill.

холми́ст|ый (~, ~а), *adj.* hilly.

хо́лод, а (у), *pl.* ~а́, ~о́в, *m.* **1.** cold; coldness (*also fig.*). **2.** cold (spell of) weather.

холода́|ть, ю, *impf.* **1.** (*pf.* по~; *impers.*) to become cold, turn cold. **2.** (*coll.*) to endure cold.

холоде́|ть, ю, *impf.* (*of* по~) to grow cold; (*impers.*) to turn cold.

холод|е́ц, ца́, *m.* (*coll.*) meat *or* fish in jelly.

холоди́льник, а, *m.* **1.** refrigerator; ваго́н-х. refrigerator van. **2.** (*tech.*) condenser.

холоди́льн|ый, *adj.* refrigeration, refrigeratory; ~ая те́хника refrigeration engineering; ~ая устано́вка cold storage plant.

холо|ди́ть, жу́, ди́шь, *impf.* **1.** (*pf.* на~) (*coll.*) to cool. **2.** to cause a cold sensation (*also impers.*).

хо́лодно¹, *adv.* (*fig.*) coldly.

хо́лодно², *as pred.* it is cold; мне, *etc.*, х. I, *etc.*, am cold, feel cold.

холоднова́т|ый (~, ~а), *adj.* rather cold, chilly.

холоднока́таный, *adj.* (*tech.*) cold-rolled.

холоднокро́вный, *adj.* (*zool.*) cold-blooded.

холодноло́мкий, *adj.* (*tech.*) cold-short.

хо́лодност|ь, и, *f.* coldness.

холо́д|ный (хо́лоден, ~на́, хо́лодно), *adj.* **1.** (*in var. senses*) cold; х. ве́тер cold wind; х. отве́т cold reply; х. по́яс (*geogr.*) frigid zone; ~ная война́ cold war; ~ное ору́жие side-arms, cold steel; *as noun* ~ная, ~ной, *f.* (*obs., coll.*) 'the cooler' (= place of detention); ~ное, ~ного, *n.* meat *or* fish in jelly. **2.** inadequate (*of clothing, etc.*; = not affording protection against cold).

холод|о́к, ка́, *m.* **1.** coolness, chill (*also fig.*). **2.** cool breeze. **3.** cool place. **4.** cool of the day.

холодосто́|йкий (~ек, ~йка), *adj.* (*agric.*) cold-resistant.

холо́п, а, *m.* **1.** (*hist.*) villein, bond slave. **2.** serf. **3.** (*fig., pejor.*) lackey.

холо́п|ий, *adj. of* ~ I.

холо́п|ский, *adj. of* ~. **2.** servile.

холо́пств|о, а, *n.* **1.** (*hist.*) villeinage, bond slavery. **2.** servility.

холо́пств|овать, ую, *impf.* to display servility.

холостёж|ь, и, *f.* (*collect.*) (*coll.*) bachelors.

холо|сти́ть, щу́, сти́шь, *impf.* to castrate, geld (*an animal*).

холост|о́й (хо́лост, ~а́), *adj.* **1.** unmarried, single; bachelor. **2.** (*tech.*) idle, free-running; на ~о́м ходу́ idling. **3.** (*mil.*) blank, dummy; х. патро́н blank cartridge.

холостя́к, а́, *m.* bachelor.

холостя́|цкий, *adj. of* ~к.

холоще́ни|е, я, *n.* castration, gelding.

холощёный, *adj.* castrated, gelded.

холст, а́, *m.* **1.** canvas; sackcloth. **2.** (*art*) canvas.

холсти́н|а, ы, *f.* **1.** = холст. **2.** piece of canvas.

холсти́нк|а, и, *f.* (*text.*) gingham.

холу́|й, я́, *m.* (*obs. and fig.*) lackey.

холщо́вый, *adj. of* холст I.

хо́л|я, и, *f.* (*coll.*) care, attention; жить в ~е to be well cared for.

хому́т, а́, *m.* **1.** (horse's) collar; (*fig.*) burden. **2.** (*tech.*) clamp, ring.

хомя́к, а́, *m.* hamster.

хонинг|ова́ть, у́ю, *impf.* (*tech.*) to hone.

хор, а, *pl.* ~ы́ (*and* ~ы), *m.* **1.** choir. **2.** (*mus. and fig.*) chorus; ~ом all together.

хора́л, а, *m.* chorale.

хорва́т, а, *m.* Croat.

хорва́т|ка, ки, *f. of* ~.

хорва́тский, *adj.* Croatian.

хо́рд|а, ы, *f.* **1.** (*math.*) chord. **2.** (*biol.*) notochord.

хо́рд|овый, *adj. of* ~а 2; *as noun* ~овые, ~овых (*zool.*) chordata.

хор|ёвый, *adj. of* ~ь.

хореи́ческий, *adj.* (*lit.*) trochaic.

хоре́|й, я, *m.* (*lit.*) trochee.

хор|ёк, ька́, *m.* polecat, ferret.

хореографи́ческий, *adj.* choreographic.

хореогра́фи|я, и, *f.* choreography.

хоре́|я, и, *f.* (*med.*) chorea, St. Vitus' dance.

хори́ст, а, *m.* **1.** member of a choir, chorister. **2.** member of a chorus.

хорме́йстер, а, *m.* **1.** choir master. **2.** chorus master.

хорово́д, а, *m.* round dance (*traditional Slavonic folk dance*).

хорово́|диться, жусь, дишься, *impf.* (с+*i.*) (*coll.*) **1.** to be occupied (with), take up one's time (with). **2.** to carry on (with) (= to have a sexual liaison).

хорово́й, *adj.* **1.** choral. **2.** (*obs.*) joint, collective.

хоро́м|ы, ~, *no sing.* (*obs.*) mansion.

хорон|и́ть, ю́, ~ишь, *impf.* (*of* по~) **1.** (*pf.* also за~ *and* с~) to bury (*also fig.*); to inter. **2.** (*obs. or coll.*) to hide, conceal; х. концы́ to cover up one's tracks.

хорон|и́ться, ю́сь, ~ишься, *impf.* (*of* с~) **1.** (*coll.*) to hide, conceal oneself. **2.** *pass. of* ~и́ть I.

хорохо́р|иться, юсь, ишься, *impf.* (*coll.*) to swagger; to boast.

хоро́шенький, *adj.* pretty, nice (*also iron.*).

хороше́нько, *adv.* (*coll.*) properly, thoroughly, well and truly.

хороше́|ть, ю, *impf.* (*of* по~) to grow prettier.

хоро́ш|ий (~, ~а́, ~о́), *adj.* 1. (*in var. senses*) good. 2. nice (*often iron.*). 3. (*short forms*) pretty, good looking.

хорошо́¹, *adv.* 1. well; nicely. 2. (*as particle expressing agreement, acceptance*) all right!, very well! 3. *as noun* (*indecl.*) good (*mark*).

хорошо́², *as pred.* it is good; it is nice, pleasant; х., что вы успе́ли прие́хать it is good that you managed to come; им х. — ведь у них своя́ маши́на it is all right for them, they have a car of their own.

хорт, а, *m.* (*hunting*) greyhound.

хо́ртый, *adj.* smooth-haired (*of a dog*).

хору́гв|ь, и, *f.* 1. (*mil.*; *obs.*) ensign, standard. 2. (*eccl.*) banner.

хору́нж|ий, его, *m.* (*hist.*) 1. (*mil.*) standard--bearer. 2. cornet (*junior commissioned rank in Cossack cavalry*).

хо́р|ы, ~ and ~ов (musicians') gallery.

хор|ь, я́, *m.* polecat.

хор|ько́вый, *adj. of* ~ёк.

хоте́ни|е, я, *n.* desire, wish.

хоте́|ть, хочу́, хо́чешь, хо́чет, хоти́м, хоти́те, хотя́т, *impf.* (*of* за~) (+*g.*, *inf. or* чтобы) to want, desire; я ~л бы I should like; х. пить to be thirsty; х. сказа́ть to mean; е́сли хоти́те if you like (*also* = perhaps).

хоте́|ться, хо́чется, *impf.* (*of* за~) (*impers.* +*d.*) to want; мне хо́чется I want; мне ~лось бы I should like.

хоть, *conj. and particle* 1. *conj.* although. 2. *conj.* even if (*esp. in set phrases*); у него́ де́нег х. отбавля́й he has money enough and to spare; х. убе́й, не скажу́ I couldn't tell you to save my life; х. бы и так (*coll.*) even so, even at that. 3. *particle* (*also* х. бы) at least, if only; ты бы посмотре́л х. на мину́точку you should take a look, if only for a minute. 4. *particle* (*coll.*) for example, to take only, even; вот, х. его́ семиле́тняя сестрёнка, ведь, догада́лась why, even his little seven-year-old sister had guessed it. 5. х. бы if only. 6. + *relat. pron. forms indefinite pron.*: х. кто anyone; х. где anywhere, everywhere; х. куда́ (*as pred.*; *coll.*) first-rate, terrific. 7. х. бы что (+*d.*; *coll.*) it does not affect, does not bother.

хотя́, *conj.* 1. although, though. 2. х. бы even if. 3. *as particle* х. бы if only; э́то я́вствует х. бы из заключи́тельной фра́зы его́ ре́чи this is evident if only from the final sentence of his speech.

хохла́т|ый (~, ~а), *adj.* crested, tufted; cristate.

хох|о́л, ла́, *m.* 1. crest; topknot, tuft of hair. 2. (*joc.*) Ukrainian (*from custom of shaving head except for single tuft of hair*).

хо́хот, а, *m.* guffaw, loud laugh.

хохо|та́ть, чу́, ~чешь, *impf.* to guffaw, laugh loudly.

хохоту́н, а́, *m.* (*coll.*) laughter, joker.

хохоту́н|ья, ьи, *f. of* ~.

храбре́ц, а́, *m.* brave person.

храбр|и́ться, юсь, и́шься, *impf.* (*coll.*) to try not to appear afraid; to make a show of bravery.

хра́брост|ь, и, *f.* bravery, courage, valour.

хра́бр|ый (~, ~а́, ~о), *adj.* brave, courageous, valiant.

храм, а, *m.* temple, church, place of worship.

храмо́вник, а, *m.* (*hist.*) knight Templar.

храм|ово́й, *adj. of* ~; х. пра́здник patronal festival.

хране́ни|е, я, *n.* keeping, custody; storage, conservation; ка́мера ~я cloakroom, left luggage office; сдать на х. to store, deposit, leave in a cloakroom.

храни́лищ|е, а, *n.* storehouse, depository.

храни́тел|ь, я, *m.* 1. keeper, custodian; (*fig.*) repository. 2. curator.

хран|и́ть, ю́, и́шь, *impf.* (*in var. senses*) to keep; to preserve, maintain; to store; х. молча́ние to keep silence; х. в та́йне to keep secret.

храни́т|ься, ~ся, *impf.* 1. to be, be kept. 2. to be preserved.

храп, а, *m.* snore; snoring.

храпан|у́ть, у, ёшь, *pf.* (*coll.*) to have a good kip.

храп|е́ть, лю́, и́шь, *impf.* 1. to snore. 2. (*of an animal*) to snort.

храпови́к, а́, *m.* (*tech.*) ratchet.

храпови́цк|ий: *only in phrase* зада́ть ~ого (*coll.*) to fall fast asleep (and snore).

храпово́й, *adj.* (*tech.*) ratchet; х. механи́зм ratchet gear.

храпу́н, а́, *m.* (*coll.*) snorer.

хреб|е́т, та́, *m.* 1. (*anat.*) spine, spinal column; (*fig.*, *coll.*) back. 2. (mountain) range; ridge; (*fig.*) crest, peak.

хреб|то́вый, *adj. of* ~е́т.

хрен, а(у), *m.* horseradish; говя́дина под ~ом roast beef with horseradish sauce; х. ре́дьки не сла́ще (*fig.*) it's six of one to half a dozen of the other; ста́рый х. (*fig.*, *coll.*) old fogey, old sod; х. с(+*i.*) to hell (with).

хре́н|овый, *adj. of* ~; (*sl.*) rotten, lousy.

хрестома́т|ийный, *adj. of* ~ия.

хрестома́ти|я, и, *f.* reader (= selections of literature, etc. for study); х. по дре́вней ру́сской литерату́ре medieval Russian literature reader.

хризанте́м|а, ы, *f.* chrysanthemum.

хризоли́т, а, *m.* (*min.*) chrysolite.

хрип, а, *m.* wheeze, wheezing sound.

хрип|е́ть, лю́, и́шь, *impf.* to wheeze.

хрипли́в|ый (~, ~а), *adj.* (rather) hoarse; wheezy.

хри́пл|ый (~, ~а́, ~о), *adj.* hoarse; wheezy.

хри́п|нуть, ну, нешь, *past* ~, ~ла, *impf.* (*of* о~) to become hoarse, lose one's voice.

хрипот|а́, ы́, *f.* hoarseness.

христара́дник, а, *m.* (*obs.*) beggar, mendicant.

христара́днича|ть, ю, *impf.* (*obs.*) to beg; to be a beggar, mendicant.

христианиза́ци|я, и, *f.* 1. conversion to Christianity. 2. adaptation to Christianity.

христианизи́р|овать, ую, *impf. and pf.* to convert to Christianity.

христианизи́р|оваться, уюсь, *impf. and pf.* become Christian; to adopt Christianity.

христи|ани́н, ани́на, *pl.* ~а́не, ~а́н, *m.* Christian.

христиа́нк|а, и, *f.* Christian (woman).

христиа́нский, *adj.* Christian; провести́ в х. вид, прида́ть (+*d.*) х. вид (*joc.*) to give an air of respectability.

христиа́нств|о, а, *n.* 1. Christianity. 2. (*collect.*) Christendom.

христ|о́в, *adj.* of ~о́с; Х. день (*obs. or eccl.*) Easter day; жить ~о́вым и́менем (*obs.*) to live by begging, on alms.

христопрода́в|ец, ца, *m.* (*obs.*) traitor.

Христо́с, Христа́, *m.* Christ; жить Христа́ ра́ди (*obs., coll.*) (*i*) to live on alms, (*ii*) (у кого́-н.) to live on (someone's) charity; вот тебе́ (те) Х. (*obs., coll.*) it's the very truth.

христо́с|оваться, уюсь, *impf.* (*of* по~) to exchange a triple kiss (*as Easter salutation*).

хром¹, а, *m.* (*chem.*) chromium; chrome.

хром², а, *m.* box-calf.

хромати́зм, а, *m.* 1. (*phys.*) chromatism. 2. (*mus.*) chromatic scale.

хромат|и́ческий, *adj.* of ~и́зм; ~и́ческая га́мма (*mus.*) chromatic scale.

хрома́|ть, ю, *impf.* 1. to limp, be lame; х. на о́бе ноги́ (*fig., coll.*) to be in a poor way. 2. (*fig., coll.*) to be weak, unsatisfactory; арифме́тика у тебя́ ~ет your arithmetic is very shaky.

хроме́|ть, ю, *impf.* (*of* о~) to go lame.

хроми́ровани|е, я, *n.* chromium-plating.

хроми́р|овать, ую, *impf. and pf.* to chromium-plate.

хро́м|истый, *adj.* of ~¹.

хро́мовый¹, *adj.* (*chem.*) chromium, chromic.

хро́м|овый², *adj.* of ~².

хром|о́й (~, ~а́, ~о), *adj.* 1. lame, limping; х. на ле́вую но́гу lame in the left leg; *as noun* х., ~о́го, *m.*; ~а́я, ~о́й, *f.* lame man, woman. 2. (*of leg; coll.*) lame. 3. (*of article of furniture; coll.*) shaky (*having one leg broken or shorter than others*).

хромоно́г|ий (~, ~а), *adj.* lame, limping.

хромоно́жк|а, и, *f.* (*coll.*) lame woman.

хромосо́м|а, ы, *f.* (*biol.*) chromosome.

хромот|а́, ы́, *f.* lameness.

хро́ник, а, *m.* (*coll.*) chronic invalid.

хро́ник|а, и, *f.* 1. (*hist. and lit.*) chronicle. 2. (*section of newspaper or radio news service*) chronicle (of events), news items. 3. (*cinema*) (*i*) newsreel, (*ii*) historical film.

хроника́льный, *adj.* of хро́ника 2, 3; х. фильм = хро́ника 3.

хроникёр, а, *m.* news-snippets man (*reporter supplying material for chronicle section of newspaper*).

хрони́ческ|ий, *adj.* (*med. and fig.*) chronic; х. больно́й chronic invalid; ~ая безрабо́тица chronic unemployment.

хроно́граф¹, а, *m.* (*hist.*) chronicle.

хроно́граф², а, *m.* stopwatch.

хронологи́ческий, *adj.* chronological.

хроноло́ги|я, и, *f.* chronology.

хроно́метр, а, *m.* chronometer.

хронометра́ж, а, *m.* time study, time-keeping.

хронометражи́ст, а, *m.* time study specialist, timekeeper.

хру́п|кий (~ок, ~ка́, ~ко), *adj.* 1. fragile, brittle. 2. (*fig.*) fragile, frail; delicate.

хру́пкост|ь, и, *f.* 1. fragility, brittleness. 2. (*fig.*) fragility, frailness.

хруст, а, *m.* crunch; crackle.

хруста́лик, а, *m.* (*anat.*) crystalline lens.

хруста́л|ь, я́, *m.* cut glass, crystal; го́рный х. rock crystal.

хруста́льный, *adj.* 1. cut-glass, crystal. 2. (*fig.*) crystal-clear.

хру|сте́ть, щу́, сти́шь, *impf.* (*of* ~стнуть) to crunch (*of snow, etc.*); to crackle.

хру́ст|нуть, ну, нешь, *pf.* of ~е́ть.

хруст|я́щий, *pres. part.* of ~е́ть *and adj.*; х. карто́фель potato crisps.

хрущ, а́, *m.* cockchafer, may bug.

хрыч, а́, *m.* ста́рый х. (*coll.*) old fogey, old sod.

хрычо́вк|а, и, *f.* ста́рая х. (*coll.*) old hag, old bag.

хрю́кань|е, я, *n.* grunting (*of a pig*).

хрю́к|ать, аю, *impf.* (*of* ~нуть) to grunt (*of a pig*).

хрю́к|нуть, ну, нешь, *pf.* (*of* ~ать) to give a grunt (*of a pig*).

хряк, а́, *m.* (*dial.*) hog.

хря́стн|уть, у, ешь, *pf.* (*coll.*) 1. (*dial.*) to snap (off). 2. to bash.

хрящ¹, á, *m.* (*anat.*) cartilage, gristle.
хрящ², á, *m.* gravel, grit.
хрящевáт|ый¹ (~, ~a), *adj.* cartilaginous, gristly.
хрящевáт|ый² (~, ~a), *adj.* of хрящ².
хрящ|евóй¹, ², adj. of ~¹, ².
худ|ée, *comp.* of ~óй¹, ³.
худé|ть, ю, *impf.* (*of* по~) to grow thin.
худ|о¹, a, *n.* harm, ill, evil; нет ~a без добрá every cloud has a silver lining.
хýдо², *adv.* ill, badly.
хýдо³, *as pred.* (*impers.*+*d.*) емý, etc., x. (*i*) he, *etc.*, feels poorly, unwell, (*ii*) he, *etc.*, is in a bad way, is having a bad time.
худоб|á, ы́, *f.* thinness, leanness.
худóжественность|, и, *f.* artistry, artistic merit.
худóжествен|ный (~, ~на), *adj.* 1. of art, of the arts; ~ная литератýра belles-lettres, fiction; ~ная самодéятельность amateur art (and dramatic) activities, amateur theatricals; X. теáтр Arts Theatre (*in Moscow*); x. фильм feature film; ~ная шкóла art school. 2. artistic; tasteful; aesthetically satisfying.
худóжеств|о, a, *n.* 1. art; *pl.* (*obs.*) the arts; Акадéмия ~ Academy of Arts. 2. (*obs.*) artistry. 3. (*coll.*) trick, escapade.
худóжник, a, *m.* artist (*practitioner of fine arts*; *also fig., of writers, craftsmen, etc.*).
худ|óй¹ (~, ~á, ~o), *adj.* thin, lean.
худ|óй² (~, ~á, ~o), *adj.* bad; на x. конéц if the worst comes to the worst; не говоря ~óго слóва (*coll.*) without a word, without warning.

худ|óй³ (~, ~á, ~o), *adj.* (*coll.*) in holes, full of holes; worn; tumbledown.
худорóд|ный (~ен, ~на), *adj.* (*obs.*) of humble birth.
худорóдств|о, a, *n.* (*obs.*) humble birth.
худощáвост|ь, и, *f.* thinness, leanness.
худощáв|ый (~, ~а), *adj.* thin, lean.
хýд|ший, *superl.* of ~óй² *and* плохóй, (the) worst.
ху|ёвый, *adj.* of ~й; (*vulg.*) rotten, lousy.
хý|же, *comp.* of ~дóй² *and* ~до², плохóй *and* плóхо; worse.
хуй, хýя, *m.* (*vulg.*) prick, tool (= penis); ни хуя́ (*vulg.*) not a bloody thing.
хул|á, ы́, *f.* abuse, (hostile) criticism.
хулигáн, a, *m.* hooligan.
хулигáн|ить, ю, ишь, *impf.* to engage in hooliganism; to behave like a hooligan.
хулигáн|ский, *adj.* of ~.
хулигáнств|о, a, *n.* hooliganism.
хули́тел|ьный (ен, ~ьна), *adj.* abusive.
хул|и́ть, ю, и́шь, *impf.* to abuse, criticize (*from a hostile position*).
хýнт|а, ы, *f.* (*polit.*) junta.
хурáл, a, *m.* hural (*name of national and local organs of government in Mongolian People's Republic*).
хурм|á, ы́, *f.* (*bot.*) persimmon (*Diospyros*).
хýтор, a, *pl.* ~á, *m.* 1. farm; farmstead. 2. small village (*in the Ukraine and areas of Cossack settlement in S. Russia*).
хуторск|óй, *adj.* of хýтор; ~и́е казаки́ Cossack farmers; ~óе хозяйство individual (*as opp. to* collective *or* State) farm.
хуторя́н|ин, ина, *pl.* ~е, ~, *m.* farmer.

Ц

цáнг|и, ~, *no sing.* (*tech.*) pliers, tongs.
цáнг|овый, *adj.* of ~и; ц. патрóн draw-in attachment.
цап *as pred.* (*coll.*) = ~нул.
цáп|ать, аю, *impf.* (*of* ~нуть) 1. to seize, snatch, grab. 2. to scratch. 3. (за+*a.*) to snatch, grab.
цáп|аться, аюсь, *impf* (*of* ~нуться) (*coll.*) 1. to scratch one another. 2. (*pf. also* по~) (*fig.*) to bicker, squabble.
цáпк|а, и, *f.* hoe.
цáп|ля, ли, *g. pl.* ~ель, *f.* heron.
цáп|нуть(ся), ну(сь), нешь(ся), *pf.* of ~ать(ся).
цáпф|а, ы, *f.* 1. (*tech.*) pin, pivot, journal (*of shaft*). 2. (*mil.*) trunnion.
цап-царáп, *as pred.* (*coll.*) he, *etc.*, grabbed, made a grab.

царáп|ать, аю, *impf.* 1. (*pf.* о~ *and* ~нуть) to scratch. 2. (*coll.*) to scribble.
царáпа|ться, юсь, *impf.* 1. to scratch (*intrans.*); to scratch one another. 2. to scramble (along).
царáпин|а, ы, *f.* scratch; abrasion.
царáп|нуть, ну, нешь, *pf.* of ~ать.
царéвич, a, *m.* tsarevich, czarevitch (*son of a tsar*).
царéв|на, ны, *g. pl.* ~ен, *f.* tsarevna, czarevna (*daughter of a tsar*).
царедвóр|ец, ца, *m.* (*obs.*) courtier.
цар|ёк, ька́, *m.* princeling, ruler.
цареуби́йств|о, a, *n.* regicide (*action*).
цареуби́йц|а, ы, *m. and f.* regicide (*agent*).
цари́зм, a, *m.* tsarism, czarism.
цари́стский, *adj.* tsarist, czarist.
цар|и́ть, ю, и́шь, *impf.* 1. (*obs.*) to be tsar.

2. to hold sway. **3.** (*fig.*) to reign, prevail; ~и́ла тишина́ silence reigned.

цари́ц|а, ы, *f.* **1.** tsarina, czarina (*empress in own right or wife of tsar*). **2.** (*fig.*) queen.

ца́рск|ий, *adj.* **1.** tsar's, of the tsar; royal; ц. двор tsar's court; ~ая во́дка aqua regia; ~ие врата́ (*eccl.*) royal gates (*central doors in iconostasis in Orthodox churches*); ц. ко́рень (*bot.*) masterwort. **2.** tsarist, czarist. **3.** (*fig.*) regal, kingly; ~ая ро́скошь regal splendour.

ца́рствен|ный (~, ~на), *adj.* **1.** (*obs.*) of the tsar. **2.** (*fig.*) regal, kingly.

ца́рств|о, а, *n.* **1.** kingdom, realm. **2.** reign. **3.** (*fig.*) realm, domain; живо́тное ц. animal kingdom; со́нное ц. land of Nod.

ца́рствовани|е, я, *n.* reign; в ц. (+*g.*) during the reign (of).

ца́рств|овать, ую, *impf.* to reign (*also fig.*).

цар|ь, я́, *m.* **1.** tsar, czar; он с ~ём (без ~я́) в голове́ (*coll.*) he is wise (stupid). **2.** (*fig.*) king, ruler.

ца́ц|а, ы, *f.* (*coll.*) someone with an exaggerated opinion of himself.

ца́цка|ться, юсь, *impf.* (с кем-н.; *coll.*) to make a fuss (of someone).

цвель, и, *f.* (*dial.*) mould (*on foodstuffs or on walls, rocks, pond surfaces, etc.*).

цве|сти́, ту́, тёшь, *past* ~л, ~ла́, ~ло́, *impf.* **1.** to flower, bloom, blossom (*also fig.*); ц. здоро́вьем to be radiant with health. **2.** (*fig.*) to prosper, flourish. **3.** to be covered with mould. **4.** (*dial.*) to be covered with spots.

цвет¹, а, *pl.* ~а́, *m.* colour; ц. лица́ complexion.

цвет², а, *m.* **1.** (*pl.* ~ы́) (*coll.*) flower. **2.** (*fig.*) flower, cream, pick (*best part*). **3.** blossom-time; (*fig.*) prime; в цвету́ in blossom; дать ц. to blossom, flower; во ~е сил in one's prime, at the height of one's powers. **4.** blossom.

цвете́ни|е, я, *n.* (*bot.*) flowering, florescence, blossoming.

цве́т|ень, ня, *m.* (*coll.*) pollen.

цвети́ст|ый (~, ~а), *adj.* **1.** multi-coloured, variegated. **2.** (*fig.*) flowery, florid.

цветко́в|ый, *adj.* ~ые расте́ния (*bot.*) flowering plants, phanerogams.

цветни́к¹, а́, *m.* **1.** flower-bed. **2.** (*fig.*) array, galaxy.

цветни́к², а́, *m.* (*coll.*) worker in non-ferrous metals industry.

цветн|о́й, *adj.* **1.** coloured; colour; ~о́е стекло́ stained glass; ~а́я литогра́фия chromolithography; ~а́я капу́ста cauliflower; *as noun* ц., ~о́го, *m.* coloured person. **2.** (*tech.*) non-ferrous; ~ы́е мета́ллы non-ferrous metals.

цветово́д, а, *m.* flower-grower.

цветово́дств|о, а, *n.* flower-growing, floriculture.

цветов|о́й, *adj. of* цвет¹; ~а́я га́мма colour spectrum; ~а́я слепота́ colour-blindness.

цвет|о́к, ка́, *pl.* ~ы́, ~о́в, *m.* flower; (*pl. also* ~ки́, ~ко́в) flower (*as opp. to other parts of plant*).

цветоло́ж|е, а, *n.* (*bot.*) receptacle.

цветоно́ж|а, и, *f.* (*bot.*) peduncle.

цветоно́сный, *adj.* flower-bearing.

цвето́ч|ек, ка, *m. dim. of* цвето́к.

цвето́чник, а, *m.* florist; flower-seller.

цвето́чниц|а, ы, *f. of* цвето́чник.

цвето́чн|ый, *adj. of* цвето́к; ~ая клу́мба flower-bed; ц. магази́н flower-shop, florist's; ц. чай flower tea.

цвету́щий, *pres. part. act. of* цвести́ *and adj.* **1.** flowering, blossoming, blooming (*also fig.*). **2.** (*fig.*) prosperous, flourishing.

це́вк|а, и, *f.* (*tech.*) bobbin, spool.

цевни́ц|а, ы, *f.* (*obs.*) pipe (*musical instrument*).

цевь|ё, я́, *n.* **1.** fore-end (*of rifle stock*). **2.** pivot.

цеди́лк|а, и, *f.* (*coll.*) strainer, filter.

цеди́льн|ый, *adj.* filter, filtering; ~ая бума́га filter paper; ~ая поду́шка filter pad.

це|ди́ть, жу́, ~дишь, *impf.* **1.** to strain, filter; to percolate. **2.** to decant (*liquids*). **3.** (*coll.*) to say (speaking through set teeth); to mutter (*often of a person barely containing anger*).

це́др|а, ы, *f.* (dried) lemon *or* orange peel.

цежёный, *adj.* (*coll.*) strained.

це́зи|й, я, *m.* (*chem.*) caesium.

цезу́р|а, ы, *f.* (*lit.*) caesura.

цейло́н|ец, ца, *m.* Ceylonese.

цейло́нк|а, и, *f.* Ceylonese (woman).

цейло́нский, *adj.* of Ceylon, Cingalese, Sinhalese.

цейтно́т, а, *m.* находи́ться в ~е to exceed the time permitted for a move (*at chess*).

цейхга́уз, а, *m.* (*mil.*; *obs.*) armoury, stores.

целе́бность|ь, и, *f.* curative, healing properties.

целе́б|ный (~ен, ~на), *adj.* curative, healing, medicinal.

цел|ево́й, *adj.* **1.** *adj. of* ~ь. **2.** having a special purpose; ~евы́е сбо́ры funds earmarked for a special purpose.

целенапра́вленность|ь, и, *f.* purposefulness, single-mindedness.

целенапра́влен|ный (~, ~на), *adj.* purposeful, single-minded.

целесообра́зност|ь, и, *f.* expediency.

целесообра́з|ный (~ен, ~на), *adj.* expedient.

целеустремлённост|ь, и, *f.* purposefulness.

целеустремлён|ный (~, ~а́), *adj.* purposeful.

це́лик, а, *m.* (*mil.*) sight (*on fire-arm*).

цели́к, а́, *m.* **1.** (*coll.*) virgin land, forest, *etc.* **2.** (*min.*) pillar, block (*of untouched ore*).

целико́м, *adv.* **1.** whole; проглоти́ть ц. to swallow whole. **2.** wholly, entirely; ц. и по́лностью utterly and completely.

целин|а́, ы́, *f.* virgin lands, virgin soil (*esp. of the steppe lands of Kazakhstan and Western Siberia, extensively cultivated since 1954*).

цели́нник, а, *m.* worker in the virgin lands (*of Kazakhstan and W. Siberia*).

цели́н|ный, *adj. of* ~á; ~ные зе́мли virgin lands.

цели́тел|ьный (~ен, ~ьна), *adj.* curative, healing, medicinal.

цел|и́ть, ю, ишь, *impf.* (*of* на~) **1.** to take aim; (в+*a.*) to aim (at). **2.** (*obs.*) to mean, intend. **3.** (+*inf.*; *coll.*) to aim (to).

цел|и́ть, ю, и́шь, *impf.* (*obs.*) to heal, cure.

цел|и́ться, ю́сь, ишься, *impf.* (*of* на~) = ~и́ть.

целко́в|ый, ого, *m.* (*coll.*) one rouble (*obs., silver coin*).

целлофа́н, а, *m.* cellophane.

целлуло́ид, а, *m.* celluloid.

целлюло́з|а, ы, *f.* cellulose.

целова́льник, а, *m.* **1.** (*hist.*) tax-collector. **2.** (*obs.*) inn-keeper, publican.

цел|ова́ть, у́ю, *impf.* (*of* по~) to kiss

цел|ова́ться, у́юсь, *impf.* (*of* по~) to kiss (one another).

це́л|ое, ого, *n.* **1.** whole. **2.** (*math.*) integer.

целому́дрен|ный (~, ~на), *adj.* chaste.

целому́дри|е, я, *n.* chastity.

це́лостност|ь, и, *f.* integrity.

це́лост|ный (~ен, ~на), *adj.* integral; entire, complete.

це́лост|ь, и, *f.* **1.** safety; в ~и и сохра́нности intact. **2.** unity.

це́л|ый, *adj.* **1.** whole, entire; ~ое число́ whole number, integer; в ~ом as a whole; по ~ым неде́лям for weeks on end. **2.** (~, ~á, ~о) safe, intact; ~ и невреди́м safe and sound.

цел|ь, и, *f.* **1.** target; бить в ц., попа́сть в ц. to hit the target; бить ми́мо ~и to miss. **2.** aim, object, goal, end, purpose; с ~ью (+*inf.*) with the object (of), in order (to); отвеча́ть ~и to answer the purpose; пресле́довать ц. to pursue an object; ста́вить себе́ ~ью (+*inf.*) to set oneself (to).

цельнометалли́ческий, *adj.* all-metal.

це́л|ьный, *adj.* **1.** of one piece, solid. **2.** (~ен, ~ьна́, ~ьно) entire, integral; single. **3.** undiluted. **4.** (*coll.*) = ~ый.

це́льност|ь, и, *f.* wholeness, entirety, integrity.

Це́льси|й, я, *m.* Celsius, centigrade (thermometer); 10° по ~ю 10° centigrade.

цеме́нт, а, *m.* cement.

цемента́ци|я, и, *f.* (*tech.*) **1.** cementation. **2.** carbonization (*of wrought iron*), case--hardening.

цементи́р|овать, ую, *impf. and pf.* **1.** (*tech.*) to cement; to case-harden. **2.** (*fig.*) to cement.

цеме́нт|ный, *adj. of* ~.

цен|а́, ы́, *a.* ~у, *pl.* ~ы, *f.* **1.** price, cost; ~о́ю (+*g.*) at the price (of), at the cost (of); любо́й ~о́й at any price; э́тому ~ы́ нет it is invaluable; э́то в ~é it is very costly. **2.** worth, value; знать ~у (+*d.*) to know the worth (of); знать себе́ ~у to be self-assured, self-possessed.

ценз, а, *m.* qualification (*for enjoyment of political rights, etc.*).

це́нз|овый, *adj. of* ~.

це́нзор, а, *m.* censor.

цензу́р|а, ы, *f.* censorship.

цензу́р|ный, *adj.* **1.** *adj. of* ~a. **2.** (~ен, ~на) decent (*of words or phrases*).

цензур|ова́ть, у́ю, *impf.* (*obs.*) to censor.

цени́тел|ь, я, *m.* judge, connoisseur, expert.

цен|и́ть, ю́, ~ишь, *impf.* **1.** (*coll.*) to fix a price for; (*fig.*) to assess, evaluate. **2.** to value, appreciate; высоко́ ц. to rate highly.

це́нник, а, *m.* price-list.

це́нност|ь, и, *f.* **1.** price, value. **2.** (*fig.*) value, importance. **3.** (*pl.*) valuables; values.

це́н|ный (~ен, ~на), *adj.* **1.** containing valuables; representing a stated value; ~ная бандеро́ль registered postal packet (*with statement of value of contents*); ~ные бума́ги (*fin.*) securities. **2.** valuable, costly; ц. пода́рок costly present. **3.** (*fig.*) valuable; precious; important; ц. докуме́нт important document.

цент, а, *m.* cent (*unit of currency*).

це́нтнер, а, *m.* centner (= 100 kg).

центр, а, *m.* (*in var. senses*) centre; ц. тя́жести centre of gravity.

центра́л, а, *m.* (*hist.*) central prison.

централиза́ци|я, и, *f.* centralization.

централи́зм, а, *m.* (*polit.*) centralism.

централиз|ова́ть, у́ю, *impf. and pf.* to centralize.

центра́л|ь, и, *f.* (*tech.*) main (*in electricity transmission network, etc.*).

центра́ль|ный, *adj.* (*in var. senses*) central; ~ые газе́ты national newspapers (*newspapers published in the capital*); ц. напада́ющий (*sport*) centre forward; ~ая не́рвная систе́ма central nervous system; ~ое отопле́ние central heating.

центри́р|овать, ую, *impf. and pf.* (*tech.*) to centre.

центрифу́г|а, и, *f.* **1.** (*tech.*) centrifuge. **2.** spin drier.

центробе́жный, *adj.* centrifugal; ц. насо́с rotary pump.

центрово́й, *adj.* (*tech.*) central, centre.

центростреми́тельный, *adj.* centripetal.

цеп, **á**, *m.* (*agric.*) flail.

цепене́|ть, **ю**, *impf.* (*of* o∼) to become rigid, freeze (up), be rooted to the spot (*from cold or from strong emotion*).

цеп|кий (∼ок, ∼ка́, ∼ко), *adj.* **1.** tenacious, strong (*also fig.*); prehensile. **2.** (*of soil, mud, etc.*) sticky, tacky, loamy. **3.** (*coll.*) obstinate, persistent, strong-willed.

це́пкост|ь, **и**, *f.* **1.** tenacity, strength. **2.** (*coll.*) obstinacy, persistence, strength of will.

цепля́|ть, **ю**, *impf.* (*coll.*) **1.** (за+*a.*) = ∼ться. **2.** to clutch (at), try to grasp.

цепля́|ться, **юсь**, *impf.* **1.** (за+*a.*) to clutch (at), try to grasp. **2.** (за+*a.*; *coll.*) to cling (to); to stick (to). **3.** (к, за+*a.*; *coll.*) to pick (on) (= *to carp at, complain of*).

цеп|но́й, *adj. of* ∼ь; ∼на́я соба́ка watchdog, house-dog; ∼но́е колесо́ sprocket wheel; ∼на́я ли́ния (*math.*) catenary; ц. мост chain bridge, suspension bridge; ∼на́я реа́кция (*chem.*, *phys.*; *fig.*) chain reaction; ∼на́я тя́га (*tech.*) chain traction.

цепо́чк|а, **и**, *f.* **1.** (small) chain. **2.** file, series; идти́ ∼ой to walk in file.

цеп|ь, **и**, o ∼и, на ∼и́, *pl.* ∼и, ∼е́й, *f.* **1.** chain; (*pl.*) chains (= *fetters*; *also fig.*); посади́ть на ц. (*or* на це́пь) to chain (up), shackle. **2.** row, series; range (*of mountains*). **3.** (*mil.*) line, file. **4.** (*fig.*) series, succession; ц. катастро́ф succession of disasters. **5.** (*electr.*) circuit; вести́ в ц. to connect.

Це́рбер, **а**, *m.* (*myth.*; *fig.*) Cerberus.

церемониа́л, **а**, *m.* **1.** ceremonial, ritual; order, procedure. **2.** пройти́ ∼ом (*mil.*; *obs.*) to march past.

церемониа́л|ьный, *adj.* **1.** *adj. of* ∼. **2.** solemn, ceremonial; ц. марш (*mil.*) march-past.

церемониймейстер, **а**, *m.* (*obs.*) master of ceremonies.

церемо́н|иться, **юсь**, *impf.* (*of* по∼) **1.** to stand upon ceremony. **2.** (с кем-н.) to treat excessively considerately.

церемо́ни|я, **и**, *f.* **1.** ceremony. **2.** (*pl.*) ceremony (*pejor.*), exaggerated observation of convention, etiquette.

церемо́н|ный (∼ен, ∼на), *adj.* **1.** ceremonious. **2.** (*pejor.*) excessively strict in observing etiquette, protocolaire.

це́ри|й, **я**, *m.* (*chem.*) cerium; за́кись ∼я cerous oxide; о́кись ∼я ceric oxide.

церко́вник, **а**, *m.* **1.** churchman, church-goer. **2.** clergyman, minister of religion.

церковноприхо́дский, *adj.* (*eccl.*) parish.

церковнославя́нский, *adj.* (*ling.*) Church Slavonic.

церковнослужи́тел|ь, **я**, *m.* clergyman, minister.

церко́вн|ый, *adj.* church; ∼ое пра́во ecclesiastical law, canon law; ц. ста́роста churchwarden; ц. сто́рож sexton.

це́рк|овь, **ви**, *i.* ∼овью, *pl.* ∼ви, ∼ве́й, ва́м, *f.* church (*building and organization*).

цесаре́вич, **а**, *m.* cesarevitch (*heir to throne in tsarist Russia*).

цеса́рк|а, **и**, *f.* guinea-fowl.

цех, **а**, в ∼е and (*coll.*) в ∼у́, *pl.* ∼и and (*coll.*) ∼á, *m.* **1.** shop, section (*in factory*). **2.** (*hist.*) guild, corporation.

цех|ово́й, *adj.* **1.** *adj. of* ∼. **2.** (*pejor.*) limited, parochial.

цеховщи́н|а, **ы**, *f.* (*pejor.*) narrow professionalism.

цеце́, *indecl.*, *f.* tsetse (fly).

циа́н, **а**, *m.* (*chem.*) cyanogen.

циа́нистый, *adj.* (*chem.*) cyanogen; cyanide (*of*); ц. ка́лий potassium cyanide.

циа́нов|ый, *adj.* (*chem.*) cyanic; ∼ая кислота́ cyanic acid; ∼ая ртуть mercuric cyanide.

циано́з, **а**, *m.* (*med.*) cyanosis.

ци́бик, **а**, *m.* (*obs.*) tea-chest.

цивилиза́тор, **а**, *m.* (*usu. iron.*) civilizer.

цивилиза́ци|я, **и**, *f.* civilization.

цивилизо́в|анный, *p.p.p. of* ∼а́ть and *adj.* civilized.

цивилизо́в|ать, **у́ю**, *impf. and pf.* to civilize.

цивили́ст, **а**, *m.* (*leg.*) specialist in civil law.

циви́льный, *adj.* (*obs.*) civil, civilian; ц. лист civil list.

цига́рк|а, **и**, *f.* (*coll.*) home-rolled cigarette.

циге́йк|а, **и**, *f.* beaver lamb.

циге́йковый, *adj.* beaver-lamb.

циду́лк|а, **и**, *f.* (*coll.*, *obs.*) note; billet-doux.

цика́д|а, **ы**, *f.* cicada.

цикл, **а**, *m.* (*in var. senses*) cycle.

цикламе́н, **а**, *m.* cyclamen.

цикли́ческий, *adj.* cyclic(al).

цикли́ч|ный (∼ен, ∼на), *adj.* = ∼еский.

цикло́ид|а, **ы**, *f.* (*math.*) cycloid.

цикло́н, **а**, *m.* (*meteor.*) cyclone.

циклони́ческий, *adj.* (*meteor.*) cyclonic.

циклопи́ческий, *adj.* (*archit.*) cyclopean.

циклотро́н, **а**, *m.* (*phys.*) cyclotron.

ци́кл|я, **и**, *f.* (*tech.*) scraper.

цико́ри|й, **я**, *m.* chicory.

цико́р|ный, *adj. of* ∼ий.

цику́т|а, **ы**, *f.* (*bot.*) water hemlock (*Cicuta virosa*).

цили́ндр, **а**, *m.* **1.** (*math.*) cylinder. **2.** (*tech.*) cylinder, drum. **3.** top hat.

цилиндри́ческий, *adj.* cylindrical.

цили́ндр|овый, *adj. of* ∼ 2.

цимбали́ст, **а**, *m.* cymbalist.

цимба́л|ы, ∼, *no sing.* (*mus.*) cymbals.

цинг|á, **и́**, *f.* (*med.*) scurvy.

цинг|о́тный, *adj. of* ∼á; scorbutic.

цини́зм, а, *m.* cynicism.
ци́ник, а, *m.* cynic.
цини́ческий, *adj.* cynical.
цини́ч|ный (~ен, ~на), *adj.* cynical.
цинк, а, *m.* (*chem.*) zinc.
цинк|ова́ть, у́ю, *impf.* (*tech.*) to zinc-plate.
ци́нковый, *adj.* zinc.
цино́вк|а, и, *f.* mat.
цино́в|очный, *adj. of* ~ка.
цирк, а, *m.* circus.
циркя́ч, а́, *m.* (*coll.*) circus artiste.
циркя́чес|кий, *adj. of* ~тво.
циркя́честв|о, а, *n.* (*fig., pejor.*) playing to the gallery, exhibitionism.
цирк|ово́й, *adj. of* ~.
цирко́н, а, *m.* (*min.*) zircon.
цирко́ни|й, я, *m.* (*chem.*) zirconium.
циркора́м|а, ы, *f.* (*cinema*) circorama.
циркули́р|овать, ую, *impf.* 1. to circulate (*of liquids, etc.; also fig.*); ~ова́ли слу́хи rumours were circulating. 2. (*coll.*) to pass, go to and fro.
ци́ркул|ь, я, *m.* (pair of) compasses; dividers.
ци́ркуль|ный, *adj. of* ~.
циркуля́р, а, *m.* (*official*) instruction.
циркуля́рн|ый¹, *adj.* circulated; ~ое письмо́ circular (letter).
циркуля́рный², *adj.* circular; circulating; ц. нож knife with circular action.
циркуляцио́нный, *adj.* (*tech.*) circulating, circulation; ц. насо́с circulation pump.
циркуля́ци|я, и, *f.* (*in var. senses*) circulation; (*naut.*) gyration.
цирро́з, а, *m.* (*med.*) cirrhosis.
цирю́льник, а, *m.* (*obs.*) barber.
цирю́л|ьня, ьни, *g. pl.* ~ен, *f.* (*obs.*) barber's shop.
цисте́рн|а, ы, *f.* cistern, tank; ваго́н-ц. tank-truck (*rail or road transport*).
цитаде́л|ь, и, *f.* citadel; (*fig.*) bulwark, stronghold.
цита́т|а, ы, *f.* quotation.
цита́тничеств|о, а, *n.* (*pejor.*) quotation-mongering (*in political argumentation*).
цитва́р|ный, *adj.* (*bot.*) santonic, wormseed; ~ая полы́нь santonin; ~ое се́мя santonin, wormseed (*med.; used as anthelmintic*).
цити́р|овать, ую, *impf.* (*of* про~) to quote.
цитоло́ги|я, и, *f.* (*biol.*) cytology.

ци́тр|а, ы, *f.* (*mus.*) zither.
ци́трус, а, *m.* citrus.
цитрусово́дств|о, а, *n.* citrus-growing.
ци́трус|овый, *adj. of* ~; *as noun* ~овые, ~овых citrus plants.
циферблá́т, а, *m.* dial, face (*of clocks, watches, and measuring instruments*).
цифи́р|ь, и, *f.* (*obs.*) 1. (*collect.*) figures. 2. counting, calculation; arithmetic.
ци́фр|а, ы, *f.* 1. figure; number, numeral. 2. (*pl.*) figures (= statistical data).
цифр|ова́ть, у́ю, *impf.* to number.
цифр|ово́й, *adj. of* ~а; numerical.
ци́церо, *indecl., n.* (*typ.*) pica.
цо́к|ать¹, аю, *impf.* (*of* ~нуть) to clatter (*of the sound of metal against stone*).
цо́к|ать², аю, *impf.* to pronounce 'ч' as 'ц' (*as in some North Russian dialects*).
цо́к|нуть, ну, *pf. of* ~ать¹.
цо́кол|ь, я, *m.* 1. (*archit.*) socle, plinth, pedestal. 2. (*electr.*) cap (*metal extremity of light bulb which is fitted into socket*).
цо́коль|ный, *adj. of* ~; ц. эта́ж ground floor.
цо́кот, а, *m.* clatter (*as of horses' hoofs on paving-stones*).
цоко|та́ть, чу́, ~чешь, *impf.* (*coll.*) to clatter.
цуг, а, *m.* team (*of horses harnessed tandem or in pairs*).
цу́гом, *adv.* 1. (*of horses in harness*) tandem. 2. (*coll.*) in file.
цука́т, а, *m.* candied peel.
цыга́н, а, *pl.* ~е, ~ (*obs.* ~ы, ~ов), *m.* Gipsy.
цыга́н|ка, ки, *f. of* ~.
цыга́нский, *adj.* gipsy.
цы́к|ать, аю, *impf.* (*of* ~нуть) (на кого́-н.; *coll.*) to shut up.
цы́к|нуть, ну, *pf. of* ~ать.
цы́пк|а, и, *f.* (*coll.*) chicken, chick (*also used as affectionate mode of address to women*).
цы́п|ки, ок, *sing.* ~ка, ~ки, *f.* (*coll.*) red spots (*on hands, etc.*).
цыпл|ёнок, ёнка, *pl.* ~я́та, ~я́т, *m.* chicken; chick.
цыпля́тник, а, *m.* chicken-house.
цыпл|я́чий, *adj. of* ~ёнок.
цы́почк|и; на ц., на ~ах on tiptoe.
цып-цы́п, *interj.*, cry made in calling chicken.
цыц, *interj.* (*coll.*) cry indicating prohibition or enjoining silence.

Ч

чабáн, á, *m.* shepherd.
чабáн|ский, *adj. of* ~.
чабёр, рá, *m.* (*bot.*) savory (*Satureia*).
чабрéц, á, *m.* (*bot., cul.*) thyme (*Satureia hortensis*).
чáвк|ать, аю, *impf.* (*of* ~нуть) 1. to champ, smack one's lips (*whilst eating*); to munch noisily. 2. to tramp, tread noisily; to make a crunching, squelching noise.
чáвк|нуть, ну, нешь, *pf. of* ~ать.
чад, а (у), о ~е, в~у́, *m.* 1. fumes. 2. (*fig.*) intoxication.

ча|ди́ть, жу́, ди́шь, *impf.* (*of* на~) to smoke, emit fumes.

ча́д|ный (~ен, ~на, ~но), *adj.* 1. smoky, smoke-laden; ~но (*as pred.*) it is smoky, full of smoke. 2. (*fig.*) doped, drugged, stupefied; stupefying.

ча́д|о, а, *n.* 1. (*obs. or joc.*) child, offspring, progeny. 2. (*fig.*) child, product, creature; ч. двадца́того ве́ка product of the twentieth century.

чадолюби́в|ый (~, ~а), *adj.* (*obs. or joc.*) fond of one's child(ren).

чадра́|а, ы́, *f.* veil, yashmak (*worn by Moslem women*).

чае́вник, а, *m.* (*coll.*) tea-drinker (*person partial to tea-drinking*).

чае́внича|ть, ю, *impf.* (*coll.*) to drink tea, indulge in tea-drinking.

чаево́д, а, *m.* tea-grower.

чаево́дств|о, а, *n.* tea-growing.

чаево́д|ческий, *adj. of* ~ство.

чаев|ы́е, ы́х, *no sing.* tip, gratuity.

ча|ёк, ~йка́ (у́), *m.* = чай.

чаепи́ти|е, я, *n.* tea-drinking.

ча́йнк|а, и, *f.* tea-leaf.

ча|й¹, я (ю), *pl.* ~й, ~ёв, *m.* 1. tea. 2. tea (-drinking); за ~ем, за ча́шкой ~я over (a cup of) tea; пригласи́ть на ч., на ча́шку ~я to invite to tea. 3. дать (+*d.*) на ч. to tip.

чай², *as adv. or conj.* (*coll.*) 1. probably, maybe; no doubt; вам тут, ч., ску́чно you must find it dull here. 2. (= ведь) after all, for.

ча́йк|а, и, *g. pl.* ча́ек, *f.* (sea-)gull.

ча́йн|ая, ой, *f.* tea-room, tea-shop.

ча́йник, а, *m.* teapot; kettle.

ча́йниц|а, ы, *f.* tea-caddy.

ча́йнича|ть, ю, *impf.* (*coll.*) to drink tea, have tea.

ча́йн|ый, *adj.* (*in var. senses*) tea; ~ая колбаса́ bologna sausage; ч. куст tea-plant; ~ая ло́жка tea-spoon; ~ая ро́за tea-rose; ~ая ча́шка teacup.

чайхан|а́, ы́, *f.* chaikhana (*tea-drinking establishment in Central Asia*).

чако́н|а, ы, *f.* (*mus.*) chaconne.

чалдо́н, а, *m.* native of Siberia (*of Russian extraction*).

чалдо́н|ский, *adj. of* ~.

ча́л|ить, ю, ишь, *impf.* (*naut.*) to tie up, moor.

ча́лк|а, и, *f.* (*naut.*) 1. tieing up, mooring. 2. tie-rope, mooring rope.

чалм|а́, ы́, *f.* turban.

ча́лый, *adj.* (*of colour of horse's coat*) roan.

чан, а, в ~е *or* в ~у́, *pl.* ~ы́, *m.* vat, tub, tank.

чапы́г|а, и, *f.* (*dial.*) plough-handle.

ча́р|а, ы, *f.* (*arch. or folk poet.*) cup, goblet.

ча́р|ка, ки, *f.* = ~а.

чар|ова́ть, у́ю, *impf.* 1. (*obs.*) to bewitch. 2. (*fig.*) to charm, captivate, enchant.

чароде́|й, я, *m.* magician, enchanter, wizard (*also fig.*).

чароде́йств|о, а, *n.* magic, charms.

ча́р|ы, ~, *no sing.* magic, charms (*also fig.*).

час, а, о ~е, в ~у́ *and* в ~е, *pl.* ~ы́, *m.* 1. hour (*also fig.*); че́тверть ~а́ a quarter of an hour; ч. проби́л the hour has struck, has come; ч. в ч. at the time appointed, on the dot; ч. от ~у with every passing hour; с ~у на ч. (*i*) hourly, with every passing hour, (*ii*) any moment; че́рез ч. (*i*) in an hour, (*ii*) at hourly intervals; в до́брый ч.! good luck! 2. (*in time measurement: g. sing.* ~а́ *after numerals* 2, 3, 4) o'clock; час о́дно ч.; два ~а́ two o'clock; во второ́м ~у́ between one and two (o'clock); кото́рый ч.? what is the time? 3. (*usually pl.*) hours, time, period; ч. пик, ~ы́ пик rush hour; ~ы́ заня́тий working hours; ч. рисова́ния (*in school, etc.*) drawing period. 4. ~ы́ (*mil.*) guard-duty; стоя́ть на ~а́х to stand guard. 5. ~ы́ (*eccl.*) (canonical) hours.

часа́ми, *adv.* for hours.

часо́в|ня, ни, *g. pl.* ~ен, *f.* chapel.

часов|о́й¹, о́го, *m.* sentry, sentinel, guard.

часов|о́й², *adj.* (*of* час) 1. of one hour's duration; ч. переры́в one hour's interval. 2. (measured) by the hour; ~а́я опла́та payment by the hour; ч. по́яс time zone. 3. one o'clock; ч. по́езд one o'clock train.

часов|о́й³, *adj. of* часы́; ч. замыка́тель clockwork fuse; ч. магази́н watch shop, watchmaker's, watch repair shop; ~ы́х дел ма́стер watchmaker; ч. механи́зм clockwork; ~а́я стре́лка clock hand, hour hand; по ~о́й стре́лке clockwise.

часовщи́к, а́, *m.* watchmaker.

ча́сом, *adv.* (*coll.*) 1. sometimes, at times. 2. by chance, by the way.

часосло́в, а, *m.* (*eccl.*) Book of Hours.

часте́нько, *adv.* (*coll.*) quite often, fairly often.

части́к, а́, *m.* 1. thick net. 2. fish caught in such a net.

ча|сти́ть, щу́, сти́шь, *impf.* (*coll.*) 1. to do something *or* speak rapidly, hurriedly. 2. (к) to visit frequently, see much (of).

части́ц|а, ы, *f.* 1. small part, element. 2. (*phys.*) particle. 3. (*gram.*) particle.

части́чно, *adv.* partly, partially.

части́ч|ный (~ен, ~на), *adj.* partial.

ча́стник, а, *m.* (*coll.*) private trader; private medical practitioner.

частновладе́льческий, *adj.* privately--owned.

ча́стн|ое, ого, *n.* (*math.*) quotient.

частнособственнический, *adj.* private-
-ownership.

ча́стност|ь, и, *f.* detail; в ~и in particular.

ча́стн|ый, *adj.* **1.** private, personal; ~ым
о́бразом privately; ~ая пра́ктика private
(*medical*) practice. **2.** (*econ.*) private, privately-owned; ~ая со́бственность private
property. **3.** particular, individual; *as noun*
~ое, ~ого, *n.* the particular. **4.** (*mil.*) local;
ч. успе́х local gain. **5.** (*hist.*) district; ч.
дом district police station.

ча́сто, *adv.* often, frequently.

частоко́л, а, *m.* fence, paling; palisade.

частот|а́, ы́, *pl.* ~ы, *f.* (*in var. senses*) fre-
quency.

частот|ный, *adj.* (*tech.*) of ~а́.

часту́шк|а, и, *f.* chastushka (*two-line or
four-line rhymed poem or ditty on some topical or
humorous theme*).

част|ый (~, ~а́, ~о), *adj.* **1.** frequent; он у
нас ч. гость he is a frequent visitor at our
house. **2.** close (together); dense, thick;
close-woven; ч. гре́бень fine-tooth comb;
~ые дере́вни villages close together; ч.
дождь steady rain; ~ая и́згородь thick
hedge; ~ое си́то fine sieve. **3.** quick,
rapid; ч. ого́нь (*mil.*) rapid fire.

част|ь, и, *pl.* ~и, ~е́й, *f.* **1.** part; portion; ~и
ре́чи (*gram.*) parts of speech; разобра́ть на
~и to take to pieces, dismantle; бо́льшей
~ью, по бо́льшей ~и for the most part,
mostly; рвать кого́-н. на ~и to give someone no peace. **2.** section, department, side;
уче́бная ч. teaching (*as opp. to administrative*)
side (*in educational institution*). **3.** sphere,
field; э́то не по мое́й ~и this is not my province; по ~и (+*g.*) in connexion (with).
4. (*coll.*) share; войти́, вступи́ть в ч. с кем-н.
to join forces with someone (*usually in commerce*). **5.** (*mil.*) unit. **6.** (в ~й) (*hist.*) administrative region (*of city*); police station
(*responsible for such region*); fire brigade. **7.**
(*obs.*) fate.

ча́стью, *adv.* partly, in part.

час|ы́[1], о́в, *no sing.* clock, watch.

часы́[2], *see* час 4, 5.

ча́хл|ый (~, ~а), *adj.* **1.** (*of vegetation*)
stunted; poor, sorry. **2.** weakly, sickly, puny.

ча́х|нуть, ну, нешь, *past* ~, ~ла, *impf.* (*of
за*~) **1.** (*of vegetation*) to wither away. **2.** to
become weak, (go into a) decline; (*fig.*) to
tire oneself out, become exhausted.

чахо́тк|а, и, *f.* (*coll.*) consumption; кар-
ма́нная ч. (*joc.*) an empty pocket.

чахо́точный, *adj.* (*coll.*) **1.** consumptive.
2. poor, sorry, feeble.

ча́ш|а, и, *f.* cup, bowl (*also fig.*); (*eccl.*)
chalice; ч. весо́в scale, pan; ч. на́шего
терпе́ния перепо́лнилась our patience was
exhausted; сия́ ч. минова́ла его́ he has

survived the ordeal.

чашели́стик, а, *m.* (*bot.*) sepal.

ча́шечк|а, и, *f.* **1.** *dim. of* ча́шка. **2.** (*bot.*)
calyx.

ча́ш|ечный, *adj.* **1.** *adj. of* ~ка. **2.** cup-
-shaped.

ча́шк|а, и, *f.* **1.** cup; bowl, pan. **2.** ч. весо́в
pan (*of scales*). **3.** (коле́нная) knee-cap.
4. (*tech.*) housing.

ча́шник, а, *m.* (*hist.*) cellarer.

ча́щ|а, и, *f.* thicket.

ча́ще, *comp. of* ча́стый *and* ча́сто more often,
more frequently; ч. всего́ most often, mostly.

ча́яни|е, я, *n.* expectation; aspiration;
па́че ~я, сверх ~я unexpectedly, contrary
to expectation.

ча́|ять, ю, ешь, *impf.* (*obs. or coll.*) **1.** to
think, suppose. **2.** (+*g. or inf.*) to hope (for),
expect.

чва́н|иться, юсь, ишься, *impf.* to boast.

чванли́вост|ь, и, *f.* boastfulness, arrogance.

чванли́в|ый (~, ~а), *adj.* boastful, arro-
gant, conceited.

чва́нный, *adj.* conceited, arrogant, proud
(*pejor.*).

чва́нств|о, а, *n.* conceit, arrogance, pride
(*pejor.*).

чебота́р|ь, я́, *m.* (*dial.*) cobbler, shoemaker.

чёбот|ы, ов, *sing.* ~, ~а, *m.* (*dial.*) boots,
shoes.

чебура́хн|уть, у, ешь, *pf.* (*coll.*) to crash
down (*trans.*).

чебура́хн|уться, усь, ешься, *pf.* (*coll.*) to
crash down (*intrans.*).

чебуре́к, а, *m.* cheburek (*kind of meat pasty
eaten in the Crimea and the Caucasus*).

чебуре́чн|ая, ой, *f.* stall selling chebureki.

чего́[1] *interrog. adv.* (*coll.*) why? what for?

чего́[2], *g. of* что.

чей, чья, чьё, *interrog. and relat. pron.* whose.

че́й-либо, *pron.* anyone's.

че́й-нибудь, *pron.* anyone's.

че́й-то, *pron.* someone's.

чек, а, *m.* **1.** cheque; вы́писать ч. to draw a
cheque. **2.** (*in shops, etc.*) bill, chit (*indicating
amount to be paid*); receipt (*for payment, to be
presented at counter when claiming purchase*).

чек|а́[1], и́, *f.* pin, linchpin, cotter-pin.

Чек|а́[2], *indecl. or* (*coll.*) *g.* ~и́, *f.* (*coll.*) Cheka
(*abbr. of* Чрезвыча́йная Коми́ссия по
борьбе́ с контрреволю́цией, сабота́жем
и спекуля́цией *the Soviet security organ, 1918–
1922*).

чека́н, а, *m.* **1.** stamp, die. **2.** caulking-
iron. **3.** (*orn.*) chat; лугово́й ч. whinchat;
черного́рлый ч. stonechat.

чека́н|ить, ю, ишь, *impf.* **1.** (*pf.* вы́~, от~)
to mint, coin; to stamp, engrave, emboss,
chase. **2.** (*pf.* от~) to do, make with precision; ч. слова́ to enunciate one's words

clearly, speak abruptly; ч. шаг to measure out one's pace, step out. **3.** (*pf.* рас~) (*tech.*) to caulk. **4.** (*agric., hort.*) to prune.

чека́нк|а, и, *f*. 1. coinage, coining, minting; stamping, engraving, embossing, chasing. **2.** (*tech.*) caulking. **3.** (*agric., hort.*) pruning. **4.** stamp, engraving, relief work.

чека́нн|ый, *adj.* **1.** stamping, engraving, embossing; ~ая рабо́та = чека́нка 4. **2.** stamped, engraved, embossed, chased. **3.** (*fig.*) precise, expressive, sharp.

чека́н|очный, *adj.* = ~ный 1; ч. пресс stamping press; ч. штамп die.

чека́нщик, а, *m*. coiner; stamper, engraver; caulker.

чеки́ст, а, *m*. official of Cheka (*hist.*); official of Soviet security service, security officer.

чекма́р|ь, я́, *m*. (*dial.*) rammer, beetle.

чекме́н|ь, я́, *m*. (cloth) jacket.

чек|овый, *adj. of* ~; ~овая кни́жка cheque book.

челе́ст|а, ы, *f*. (*mus.*) glockenspiel.

чёлк|а, и, *f*. fringe (*of hair or as name of hair-style*); forelock.

чёлн, á, *pl*. ~ы́ *or* ~ы, *m*. **1.** dug-out (canoe). **2.** (*obs. or poet.*) boat.

челно́к, á, *m*. 1. = чёлн. **2.** shuttle.

челно́|чный, *adj. of* ~к 2; ч. полёт (*aeron.*) shuttle flight.

чел|ó¹, á, *n*. forehead, brow; бить ~о́м кому́-н. (*hist. or iron.*) (*i*) to bow to someone (*in greeting*), (*ii*) to petition someone, (*iii*) to offer someone humble thanks.

чел|ó², á, *pl*. ~а, *n*. (*tech.*) stoking hole (*in furnace*).

челоби́тн|ая, ой, *f*. (*hist.*) petition.

челоби́тчик, а, *m*. (*hist.*) petitioner.

челоби́ть|е, я, *n*. (*hist.*) **1.** low bow. **2.** petition.

челове́к, а, *pl*. лю́ди (*g. pl., etc.*, **челове́к,** ~ам, ~ами, о ~ах *only in combination with numerals*) *m*. **1.** man, person, human being. **2.** (*obs.*) servant, man; waiter.

челове́ко-де́нь, ч. -дня́, *m*. (*econ.*) man-day.

человеколюби́в|ый (~, ~а), *adj.* philanthropic.

человеколюби|е, я, *n*. philanthropy, love of fellow-men.

человеконави́стник, а, *m*. misanthrope.

человеконенави́стнический, *adj.* misanthropic.

человеконенави́стничеств|о, а, *n*. misanthropy.

человекообра́з|ный (~ен, ~на), *adj.* anthropomorphous; (*zool.*) anthropoid.

человекоподо́б|ный (~ен, ~на), *adj.* resembling a human being.

челове́ко-ча́с, а, *m*. (*econ.*) man-hour.

челове́ч|ек, ка, *m*. little man.

челове́ческий, *adj.* **1.** human. **2.** humane.

челове́честв|о, а, *n*. humanity, mankind.

челове́|чий, *adj. of* ~к.

челове́чин|а, ы, (*coll.*) **1.** (*m. and f.*) human being, man. **2.** (*f.*) human flesh (*as meat*).

челове́чност|ь, и, *f*. humaneness, humanity.

челове́ч|ный (~ен, ~на), *adj.* humane.

челюстно́й, *adj.* jaw; (*anat.*) maxillary.

че́люст|ь, и, *f*. 1. jaw, jaw-bone; (*anat.*) maxilla. **2.** dental plate, set of false teeth.

че́ляд|ь, и, *f*. (*collect.; hist.*) servants, retainers, men.

чем, *conj.* **1.** than. **2.** (+*comp.*) ч...., тем... the more ..., the more ...; ч. скоре́е, тем лу́чше the sooner, the better. **3.** (+*inf.*) rather than, instead of; чем писа́ть, ты бы лу́чше позвони́л you'd do better to ring up rather than write.

чембу́р, а, *m*. halter.

чемери́ц|а, ы, *f*. (*bot.*) hellebore.

чемода́н, а, *m*. suitcase.

чемпио́н, а, *m*. champion.

чемпиона́т, а, *m*. championship.

чемпио́н|ка, ки, *f. of* ~.

чемпио́нств|о, а, *n*. champion's title.

чеп|е́ц, ца́, *m*. (*woman's*) cap.

чепра́к, á, *m*. saddle-cloth.

чепух|а́, и́, *f*. (*coll.*) **1.** nonsense, rubbish. **2.** a trifle, trifling matter; trivialities.

чепухо́вый, *adj.* (*coll.*) **1.** nonsensical. **2.** trifling; trivial; insignificant.

че́пчик, а, *m*. 1. = чепе́ц. **2.** (*child's*) bonnet.

че́рв|а, ы, *f*. (*collect.*) larvae (*of bees*).

червеобра́зный, *adj.* vermiform, vermicular; ч. отро́сток (*anat.*) appendix.

черв|и́¹, е́й *and* ~и, ~ *sing*. ~а, ~ы, hearts (*card suit*); коро́ль ~е́й king of hearts.

че́рв|и², *pl. of* ~ь.

черви́ве|ть, ет, *impf.* (*of* о~) to become worm-eaten.

черви́в|ый (~, ~а), *adj.* worm-eaten.

червлёный, *adj.* (*obs.*) dark red.

черв|о́вый, *adj. of* ~и́¹.

черво́н|ец, ца, *m*. 1. (*hist.*) chervonets (*gold coin of 3, 5, or 10 roubles' denomination; or 10-rouble bank-note in circulation 1922–47*). **2.** (*pl.*) (*coll., obs.*) money.

черво́нн|ый¹, *adj.* **1.** (*obs. or dial.*) red, dark red; ~ое зо́лото pure gold (*as having a reddish tint*). **2.** *adj. of* черво́нец 1.

черв|о́нный², *adj. of* ~и́¹; ч. туз ace of hearts.

червото́чин|а, ы, *f*. 1. worm-hole, maggot hole. **2.** (*fig.*) rottenness.

черв|ь, я́, *pl*. ~и, ~е́й, *m*. 1. worm; maggot. **2.** (*fig.*) bug, virus, germ; его́ то́чит ч. сомне́ния he is nagged by doubts.

червя́к, á, *m*. 1. = червь. **2.** (*tech.*) worm.

червя́чн|ый, *adj. of* червя́к 2; ~ое колесо́, ~ая шестерня́ worm wheel; ~ая переда́ча worm gearing.

червяч|о́к, ка́, *m. dim. of* червя́к 1; замори́ть ~ка́ (*coll.*) to have a bite to eat.

черда́к, а́, *m.* attic, loft.

черда́|чный, *adj. of* ~к.

черевик|и, ов, (*sing.* ~, ~а), *m.* chereviki (*high-heeled leather boots worn by women in the Ukraine*).

черёд, а́, о ~е́, **в** ~у́, *m.* **1.** turn; идти́ свои́м ~о́м to take its course. **2.** (*coll.*) queue.

черед|а́¹, ы́, *f.* **1.** (*obs.*) = черёд 1. **2.** sequence. **3.** file (*of people*).

черед|а́², ы́, *f.* (*bot.*) bur-marigold (*Bidens*).

чередова́ни|е, я, *n.* alternation, interchange, rotation; ч. гла́сных (*ling.*) vowel interchange.

черед|ова́ть, у́ю, *impf.* (c+*i.*) to alternate (with).

черед|ова́ться, у́юсь, *impf.* to alternate; to take turns.

чередо́м, *adv.* (*coll.*) properly.

че́рез, *prep.*+*a.* **1.** (*of place*) across; over; through. **2.** via. **3.** through (= *by means of, with the aid of*); ч. печа́ть through the press; ч. перево́дчика through an interpreter. **4.** (*coll.*) through (= *due to, in consequence of*); ч. боле́знь through illness. **5.** (*of time*) in; ч. полчаса́ in half an hour's time; я верну́сь ч. год I shall be back in a year's time. **6.** (*of space*) after; (further) on; ч. три киломе́тра three kilometres (further) on. **7.** (*i*) *indicates repetition at stated unit of time or space*: принима́ть ч. час по столо́вой ло́жке to take one tablespoonful every hour; ч. ка́ждые три страни́цы every three pages, (*ii*) *indicates repetition alternating at stated unit of time or space*: дежу́рить ч. день to be on duty every other day, on alternate days; печа́тать ч. строку́ to double-space.

череми́с, а, *m.* Cheremis(*former name of Mari*).

черёмух|а, и, *f.* bird cherry (*Padus*).

черёмух|овый, *adj. of* ~а.

черемш|а́, и́, *f.* (*bot.*) ramson.

черенк|ова́ть, у́ю, *impf.* (*of* от~) (*hort.*) **1.** to graft. **2.** to take a cutting (of).

черен|о́к, ка́, *m.* **1.** handle, haft (*of implement*). **2.** (*hort.*) graft, cutting, slip.

че́реп, а, *pl.* ~а́, *m.* skull, cranium.

черепа́х|а, и, *f.* **1.** tortoise; turtle; идти́ ~ой to go at a crawl, at a snail's pace. **2.** tortoise-shell.

черепа́ховый, *adj.* tortoise, turtle; tortoise-shell.

черепа́|ший, *adj.* **1.** *adj. of* ~ха 1. **2.** (*fig.*) very slow.

черепи́ц|а, ы, *f.* tile.

черепи́чный, *adj.* tile; tiled.

череп|о́й, *adj. of* че́реп; ~а́я коро́бка cranium.

череп|о́к, ка́, *m.* broken piece of pottery.

чересполо́сиц|а, ы, *f.* strip farming.

чересседе́льник, а, *m.* saddle girth.

чересчу́р, *adv.* too; too much.

чере́шн|евый, *adj. of* ~я.

чере́шн|я, и, *f.* cherry(-tree) (*Cerasus avium*).

черка́|ть, ю, (and **чёрка|ть, ю),** *impf.* (*coll.*) to cross out, cross through.

черке́с, а, *m.* Circassian.

черке́ск|а, и, *f.* Circassian coat (*long, narrow, collar-less coat worn by Caucasian highlanders*).

черке́сский, *adj.* Circassian.

черке́шенк|а, и, *f. of* черке́с.

черкн|у́ть, у́, ёшь, *pf.* (*coll.*) **1.** to make, leave a line on. **2.** to dash off, scribble.

че́рнет|ь, и, *f.* (*orn.*) морска́я ч. scaup; хохла́тая ч. tufted duck..

черне́|ть, ю, *impf.* **1.** (*pf.* по~) to turn black, grow black. **2.** to show up black.

черне́ц, а́, *m.* (*hist.*) monk.

черни́к|а, и, *f.* bilberry, blaeberry, whortleberry (*Vaccinium myrtillus*).

черни́л|а, ~, *no sing.* ink.

черни́льниц|а, ы, *f.* ink-pot, ink-well.

черни́|льный, *adj.* **1.** *adj. of* ~а; ч. каранда́ш indelible pencil; ч. оре́шек oak-gall, nut-gall. **2.** (*iron.*) paper, verbal; ~ьная война́ war of words.

черн|и́ть, ю́, и́шь, *impf.* **1.** (*pf.* за~ *and* на~) to blacken, paint black. **2.** (*pf.* о~) (*fig.*) to blacken, slander. **3.** to burnish.

черни́ц|а, ы, *f.* (*hist.*) nun.

черни́|чный, *adj. of* ~ка.

черновиќ, а́, *m.* rough copy, draft.

чернов|о́й, *adj.* **1.** rough, draft; preparatory. **2.** ~а́я рабо́та (*coll.*) heavy, rough, dirty work. **3.** (*tech.*; *of metals*) crude.

черноволо́с|ый (~, ~а), *adj.* black-haired.

черногла́з|ый (~, ~а), *adj.* black-eyed.

черного́р|ец, ца, *m.* Montenegrin.

черного́р|ка, ки, *f. of* ~ец.

черного́рский, *adj.* Montenegrin.

чернозём, а, *m.* (*agric., geol.*) chernozem, black earth.

чернозём|ный, *adj. of* ~.

чернозо́бик, а, *m.* (*orn.*) dunlin.

чернокни́жи|е, я, *n.* (*obs.*) black magic.

чернокни́жник, а, *m.* (*obs.*) practitioner of black magic.

черноко́ж|ий (~, ~а), *adj.* black, coloured; *as noun* ч., ~его, *m.* negro, black (man).

чернолес́|е, я, *n.* deciduous forest.

черномаз|ый (~, ~а), *adj.* (*coll.*) swarthy.

черномо́р|ец, ца, *m.* sailor of Black Sea fleet.

черномо́рский, *adj.* Black Sea.

чернорабо́ч|ий, его, *m.* unskilled labourer.

чернори́з|ец, ца, *m.* (*hist.*) monk.

чернослив, а (у), *m.* (*collect.*) prunes.

черносморо́динный, *adj.* blackcurrant.

черносо́тен|ец, ца, *m.* (*hist. or iron.*) member

of 'Black Hundred' (*name of armed anti-*
-revolutionary groups in Russia, active 1905–7).
черносо́тен|ный, *adj. of* ~ец.
чернот|а́, ы́, *f.* blackness (*also fig.*); dark-
ness.
чернота́л, а, *m.* (*bot.*) bay-leaf willow (*Salix
pentandra*).
черну́шк|а, и, *f.* **1.** (*bot.*) nutmeg flower
(*Nigella sativa*). **2.** (*coll.*) swarthy, dark-
-haired *or* dark-eyed woman.
чёр|ный (~ен, ~на́, ~но́), *adj.* **1.** (*in var.
senses*) black; ~ная би́ржа, ч. ры́нок black
market; ч. глаз (*coll.*) evil eye; (отложи́ть
на) ч. день (to put by for) a rainy day; ~ное
де́рево ebony; ~ное духове́нство regular
clergy, monks; ~ное зо́лото 'black gold'
(= oil); ч. лес deciduous forest; ч. наро́д
(*hist.*) common people; ~ное сло́во (*dial.*)
bad language; держа́ть в ~ном те́ле to
ill-treat; ~ным по бе́лому in black and
white; *as noun* ч., ~ного, *m.* negro, black
(man). **2.** (*as opp. to* пара́дный) back; ч.
ход back entrance, back door. **3.** (*of work*)
heavy; unskilled. **4.** (*hist.*) State (*as opp. to
privately-owned*). **5.** (*tech.*) ferrous (*as opp.
to* цветно́й). **6.** (*fig.*) gloomy, melancholy.
черн|ь¹, и, *f.* mob, common people.
черн|ь², и, *f.* niello; black enamel.
черпа́к, а́, *m.* scoop; bucket; grab.
черпа́лк|а, и, *f.* scoop; ladle.
че́рп|ать, аю, *impf.* (*of* ~ну́ть) **1.** to draw
(up); to scoop; to ladle. **2.** (*fig.*) to extract,
derive, draw.
черп|ну́ть, ну́, нёшь. *pf. of* ~ать.
черстве́|ть, ю, *impf.* **1.** (*pf.* за~) to become
stale. **2.** (*pf.* о~) to grow hardened, become
hard (*fig.*).
чёрств|ый (~, ~а́, ~о), *adj.* **1.** stale. **2.** (*fig.*)
hard, callous.
чёрт, а, *pl.* **че́рти, ~éй,** *m.* devil; ч. (его́)
возьми́! the devil take it!; ч. его́ зна́ет! the
devil only knows!; до ~а̇ devilishly, hell-
ishly; на кой ч.? why the hell?; ~а с два
like hell!; у ~а на рога́х, на кули́чках at
the back of beyond.
черт|а́, ы́, *f.* **1.** line; провести́ ~у́ to draw
a line; подвести́ ~у́ (под) (*fig.*) to draw a
line (under), put an end (to), dispose (of). **2.**
boundary; ч. осе́длости (*hist.*) the (Jewish)
Pale. **3.** trait, characteristic; ~ы́ лица́
features; в о́бщих ~а́х in general outline.
чертёж, а́, *m.* draught, drawing, sketch;
blueprint, plan, scheme; ч. на ка́льке trac-
ing.
чертёжн|ая, ой, *f.* drawing office.
чертёжник, а, *m.* draughtsman.
чертёжн|ый, *adj.* drawing; ~ая доска́ draw-
ing board; ~ая мастерска́я drawing office;
~ое перо́ lettering pen.
чертён|ок, ка, *pl.* ~я́та, ~я́т, *m.* (*coll.*) imp.

чер|ти́ть¹, чу́, ~тишь, *impf.* (*of* на~) to
draw; to draw up.
чер|ти́ть², чу́, ти́шь, *impf.* (*coll.*) to go on
a binge, on the booze.
чёртов, *adj.* **1.** devil's; ~а дю́жина baker's
dozen. **2.** (*coll.*) devilish, hellish.
черто́вк|а, и, *f.* she-devil; (*as term of abuse*)
bitch.
черто́вский, *adj.* (*coll.*) devilish, damnable.
чертовщи́н|а, ы, *f.* **1.** (*collect.*) devils,
demons. **2.** (*fig., coll.*) devilry; idiocy.
черто́г, а, *m.* (*obs.*) hall, mansion.
чертополо́х, а, *m.* thistle.
чёрточк|а, и, *f.* **1.** *dim. of* черта́ 1. **2.**
hyphen.
чертых|а́ться, а́юсь, *impf.* (*of* ~ну́ться)
(*coll.*) to swear.
чертых|ну́ться, ну́сь, нёшься, *pf. of* ~а́ться.
черче́ни|е, я, *n.* drawing; sketching.
чёс, а, *m.* (*coll.*) itch(ing); зада́ть ~у (*i*)
кому́-н. to tick someone off, (*ii*) to make off.
чеса́лк|а, и, *f.* (*text.*) comb, combing
machine.
чеса́льный, *adj.* (*text.*) combing, carding.
чеса́льщик, а, *m.* (*text.*) comber, carder.
чёсаный, *adj.* (*text.*) combed, carded.
че|са́ть, шу́, ~шешь, *impf.* (*of* по~) **1.** to
scratch; ч. заты́лок, в заты́лке to scratch
one's head (*also fig.*); ч. язы́к to wag one's
tongue. **2.** (*coll.*) to comb (*hair*). **3.** (*text.*) to
comb, card. **4.** (*coll.*) *expresses rapid or vigorous action* (*translated in accordance with context*).
че|са́ться, шу́сь, ~шешься, *impf.* (*of* по~)
1. to scratch oneself. **2.** (*impf. only*) to itch;
ру́ки у него́, *etc.*, ~шутся (+*inf.*) he is, *etc.*,
itching to ... **3.** (*coll.*) to comb one's hair.
чесно́к, а́ (у́), *m.* garlic.
чесно́|чный, *adj. of* ~к.
чесо́тк|а, и, *f.* **1.** (*med.*) scab; rash; mange.
2. itch.
чесо́т|очный, *adj. of* ~ка; ч. клещ itch-mite.
че́ствовани|е, я, *n.* (кого́-н.) celebration (in
honour of someone).
че́ств|овать, ую, *impf.* to celebrate (*an
occasion, etc.*); to honour, arrange a celebration in honour of (*someone*)).
че|сти́ть, щу́, сти́шь, *impf.* **1.** (*coll.*) to
abuse. **2.** (*obs.*) to honour.
честн|о́й, *adj.* (*obs.*) **1.** (*eccl.*) sanctified,
sainted; saintly; мать ~а́я! (*coll.*) my
sainted aunt! **2.** worthy, honoured; ~а́я
компа́ния (*iron.*) gang, network.
че́стност|ь, и, *f.* honesty, integrity.
че́ст|ный (~ен, ~на́, ~но), *adj.* honest, up-
right; ~ное сло́во! honestly!, upon my
honour!
честолю́б|ец, ца, *m.* ambitious person.
честолюби́в|ый (~, ~а), *adj.* ambitious.
честолюби|е, я, *n.* ambition.

чест|ь¹, и, *f.* **1.** honour; в ч. (+*g.*) in honour (of); по ~и сказа́ть to say in all honesty; счита́ть за ч. to consider (it) an honour; отда́ть ч. (+*d.*) (*i*) to salute, (*ii*) (*joc.*) to do honour (to); потеря́ть ч. (*euph.*) to lose one's honour; проси́ть ~ью to urge; пора́ и ч. знать (*coll.*) it is time to go (*joc. formula used on taking leave of host, etc.*); ч. ~ью (*coll.*) fittingly, properly; ч. и ме́сто! (*coll., obs.*) please be seated! **2.** regard, respect; быть в ~й to be in favour.

честь², чту, чтёшь, *impf.* (*obs.*) **1.** to consider. **2.** to read.

чесуч|а́, и́, *f.* tussore.

чесуч|о́вый, *adj.* of ~а́.

чёт, а, *m.* even number.

чет|а́, ы́, *f.* pair, couple; счастли́вая ч. (the) happy couple; не ч. кому́-н. no match for someone (*as being, by implication, either worse or better*).

четве́рг, а́, *m.* Thursday.

четвере́ньк|и (*coll.*) на ч., на ~ах on all fours, on one's hands and knees; стать на ч. to go down on all fours.

четвери́к, а́, *m.* chetverik (*old Russian dry measure, equivalent to 26·239 litres*).

четвёрк|а, и, *f.* (*coll.*) **1.** number '4'; No. 4 (*bus, tram, etc.*). **2.** 'four' (*as school mark—out of five, hence* = 'good'). **3.** four (*at cards*; team *of horses*; *rowing-boat, etc.*).

четверно́й, *adj.* fourfold, quadruple.

четверн|я́, и́, *f.* **1.** team of four horses. **2.** quadruplets.

че́твер|о, ы́х, *num.* four; нас бы́ло ч. there were four of us.

четвероно́г|ий, *adj.* four-legged; *as noun* ~ое, ~ого, *n.* quadruped.

четверости́ши|е, я, *n.* (*lit.*) quatrain.

четверта́к, а́, *m.* (*obs*) 25 kopecks.

четверти́нк|а, и, *f.* (*coll.*) quarter-litre bottle (*of vodka or wine*).

четверти́чный, *adj.* (*geol.*) quaternary.

четвёртк|а, и, *f.* (*coll.*) quarter.

четвертно́й, *adj.* **1.** quarter. **2.** (*obs.*) costing, worth 25 roubles.

четверт|ова́ть, у́ю, *impf. and pf.* to quarter (*as means of execution; hist.*).

четвёртый, *adj.* fourth.

че́тверт|ь, и, *g. pl.* ~е́й, *f.* **1.** (*in var. senses*) quarter (*as measure, approx. equivalent to 3 litres*). **2.** quarter (*of an hour*); без ~и час a quarter to one; ч. деся́того a quarter past nine. **3.** (*mus.*) fourth. **4.** term.

четвертьфина́л, а, *m.* (*sport*) quarter-final.

чёт|ки, ок, *no sing.* (*eccl.*) rosary.

чёт|кий (~ок, ~ка́, ~ко), *adj.* **1.** precise; clear-cut; ~кое движе́ние precise movement. **2.** clear, well-defined (*of handwriting*) legible; (*of sound*) plain, distinct; (*of speech*) articulate.

чёткост|ь, и, *f.* **1.** precision, preciseness. **2.** clarity, clearness, definition; legibility; distinctness.

чётный, *adj.* even (*of numbers*).

четы́р|е, ёх, ём, ьмя́, о ~ёх, *num.* four.

четы́режды, *adv.* four times.

четы́р|еста, ёхсо́т, ёмста́м, ьмяста́ми, о ~ёхста́х, *num.* four hundred.

четырёх- four-, quadri-, tetra-.

четырёхгоди́чный, *adj.* four-year.

четырёхголо́сный, *adj.* (*mus.*) four-part.

четырёхгра́нник, а, *m.* (*math.*) tetrahedron.

четырёхгра́нный, *adj.* (*math.*) tetrahedral.

четырёхкра́тный, *adj.* fourfold.

четырёхле́ти|е, я, *n.* **1.** four-year period. **2.** fourth anniversary.

четырёхле́тний, *adj.* **1.** four years', of four years' duration. **2.** four-year-old.

четырёхме́стный, *adj.* four-seater.

четырёхме́сячный, *adj.* **1.** four-month, four months', of four months' duration. **2.** four-month-old.

четырёхмото́рный, *adj.* four-engined.

четырёхпо́ль|е, я, *n.* (*agric.*) four-field system.

четырёхсотле́ти|е, я, *n.* **1.** four hundred years. **2.** quatercentenary.

четырёхсотле́тний, *adj.* **1.** four hundred years', of four hundred years' duration. **2.** quatercentenary.

четырёхсо́тый, *adj.* fourhundredth.

черыре́хсто́пный, *adj.* (*lit.*) tetrameter.

четырёхсторо́нний, *adj.* **1.** quadrilateral. **2.** (*polit., etc.*) quadripartite.

четырёхта́ктный, *adj.* **1.** (*tech.*) four-stroke. **2.** (*mus.*) four-beat.

четырёхуго́льник, *adj.* quadrangle.

четырёхуго́льный, *adj.* quadrangular.

четырёхчасово́й, *adj.* **1.** four hours', of four hours' duration. **2.** four o'clock.

четы́рнадцатый, *adj.* fourteenth.

четы́рнадцат|ь, и, *num.* fourteen.

чех, а, *m.* Czech.

чехард|а́, ы́, *f.* leap-frog (*also fig.*; *of rapid changes in governmental appointments, etc.*).

чехл|и́ть, ю́, йшь, *impf.* (*of* за~) to cover.

чех|о́л, ла́, *m.* **1.** cover, case; ч. для кре́сла chair-cover. **2.** underdress.

чехослова́к, а, *m.* Czechoslovak.

чехослова́цкий, *adj.* Czechoslovak.

чехослова́чк|а, и, *f.* Czechoslovak (woman).

чечеви́ц|а¹, ы, *f.* lentil.

чечеви́ц|а², ы, *f.* (*obs.*) lens.

чечеви́|чный, *adj.* of ~ца¹; прода́ть за ~чную похлёбку to sell for a mess of pottage.

чечётк|а, и, *f.* **1.** (*orn.*) redpoll. **2.** chechotka (*kind of tap-dance*).

чéшк|а, и, f. of чех.

чéшский, adj. Czech.

чешýйк|а, и, f. scale (of fish).

чешýйчат|ый, adj. scaly; squamose, lamellar; ~ые, ~ых (zool.) Squamata.

чешу|я́, й, no pl., f. (zool.) scales.

чńбис, а, m. (orn.) lapwing.

чń|в|ый (~, ~а), adj. (dial.) generous.

чиж, á, m. (orn.) siskin.

чńжик, а, m. 1. = чиж. 2. ~и tip-cat (children's game).

чилибýх|а, и, f. (bot.) Nux vomica.

чилń|ец, йца, m. Chilean.

чилń|йка, йки, f. of ~ец.

чилńйск|ий, adj. Chilean; ~ая селńтра (chem.) Chile saltpetre, sodium nitrate.

чилńка|ть, ю, impf. = чирńкать.

чилńм, а, m. (bot.) water chestnut (Trapa natans).

чин, а, pl. ~ы́, m. 1. rank; быть в ~áх to hold, be of high rank. 2. official. 3. rite, ceremony, order; ч. ~ом properly, fittingly; без ~óв without ceremony; держáть ч. (obs.) to conduct a ceremony.

чинáр, а, m. plane (tree).

чинáр|а, ы, f. = ~.

чинёный, adj. (coll.) old, patched (of clothing, etc.).

чин|ńть[1], ю, ~ишь, impf. (of по~) to repair, mend.

чин|ńть[2], ю, ~ишь, impf. (of о~) to sharpen.

чин|ńть[3], ю, ńшь, impf. to carry out, execute; to cause; ч. препя́тствия (+d.) to impede; ч. распрáву to carry out reprisals.

чин|ńться, юсь, ńшься, impf. (obs.) to stand on ceremony, hold back, be shy.

чńнност|ь, и, f. decorum, propriety, orderliness.

чńн|ный (~ен, ~ná, ~но), adj. decorous, proper, orderly; well-ordered.

чинóвник, а, m. 1. official, functionary (not used of officials of U.S.S.R.). 2. (pejor.) bureaucrat.

чинóвни|ческий, adj. 1. adj. of ~к. 2. (pejor.) bureaucratic.

чинóвничеств|о, а, n. 1. (collect.) officials, officialdom. 2. (pejor.) red tape.

чинóвнич|ий, adj. = ~еский.

чинóвный, adj. (obs.) 1. official, holding an official post. 2. of high rank.

чинýш|а, и, m. (pejor.) bureaucrat.

чńр|ей, ья, m. (coll.) boil.

чирńка|ть, ю, impf. to chirp, twitter.

чńрик|и, ов or чирńк|и, óв, (dial.) shoes.

чирńкн|уть, у, ешь, pf. to give a chirp.

чńрк|ать, аю, impf. (of ~нуть) (о+a., по+d.) to strike sharply (against, on); ч. спńчкой to strike a match.

чńрк|нуть, ну, нешь, pf. of ~ать.

чир|óк, ká, m. (orn.) teal.

чńсленност|ь, и, f. numbers; (mil.) strength.

чńсленный, adj. numerical.

числńтел|ь, я, m. (math.) numerator.

числńтельн|ое, ого, n. (gram.) numeral.

числńтельн|ый, adj. ńмя ~ое (gram.) numeral.

чńсл|ить, ю, ишь, impf. to count, reckon.

чńсл|иться, юсь, ишься, impf. 1. to be (in context of calculation or official records); в нáшей дерéвне ~ится трńста жńтелей there are three hundred inhabitants in our village; ч. в отпускý to be (recorded as) on leave; он ~ится в кóнкурсе his name is down for the competition. 2. (+i.) to be reckoned, be on paper; он ещё ~ился завéдующим отдéлом, а все обя́занности исполня́ли егó заместńтели he was still head of the department on paper, but all the duties were being performed by his deputies. 3. (за+i.) to be attributed (to), have; за ним ~ится мнóго недостáтков he has many failings.

чис|лó, лá, pl. ~ла, ~ел, n. 1. number; теóрия ~ел theory of number; ~лóм in number; нет им ~лá they are innumerable; без ~лá without number, in great numbers; в ~лé (+g.) among; в том ~лé including. 2. date, day (of month); какóе сегóдня ч.? what is the date today?; какóго ~лá вы уезжáете? what is the date of your departure, which day are you leaving?; без ~лá undated; помéтить (зáдним) ~лóм to date (antedate). 3. (gram.) number; едńнственное, мнóжественное ч. singular, plural.

числовóй, adj. numerical.

чистńлищ|е, а, n. (rel.) purgatory.

чńстильщик, а, m. cleaner; ч. сапóг shoeblack, bootblack.

чń|стить, щу, стишь, impf. 1. (pf. по~, вы~) to clean; (щёткой) to brush; to scour; ч. посýду to wash dishes, wash up; ч. трýбу to sweep a chimney. 2. (pf. по~, вы~) to clear; to dredge. 3. (pf. о~) to peel (vegetables, fruit); to shell (nuts); to clean (fish). 4. (pf. по~) (polit.) to purge. 5. (coll.) to clean out (= to rob). 6. (coll.) to swear at; to beat up.

чń|ститься, щусь, стишься, impf. 1. (pf. по~, вы~) to clean oneself (up). 2. pass. of ~стить.

чńстк|а, и, f. 1. cleaning; отдáть в ~у to have cleaned, send to be cleaned. 2. (polit.) purge.

чńсто[1], as pred. it is clean.

чńст|о[2], adv. 1. adv. of ~ый; ч.-нáчисто spotlessly clean. 2. purely, merely; completely; я ч. случáйно егó нашёл it was by mere chance that I found it. 3. as conj. (coll.) just like, just as if.

чистовńк, á, m. (coll.) fair copy.

чистово́й, *adj.* 1. fair, clean; ч. экземпля́р fair copy. 2. (*tech.*) finishing, planishing.

чистога́н, а, *m.* (*coll.*) cash, ready money.

чистокро́вный, *adj.* thorough-bred, pure-blooded.

чистописа́ни|е, я, *n.* calligraphy.

чистопло́т|ный (~ен, ~на), *adj.* 1. clean, cleanly; neat, tidy. 2. (*fig.*) clean, decent, upright.

чистоплю́|й, я, *m.* (*coll.*) cissy; fastidious person.

чистопо́ль|е, я, *n.* (*coll.*) open country.

чистопоро́д|ный (~ен, ~на), *adj.* thorough-bred.

чистопро́бный, *adj.* pure (*of gold or silver*).

чистосерде́ч|ие, ия, *n.* = ~ность.

чистосерде́чност|ь, и, *f.* frankness, sincerity, candour.

чистосерде́ч|ный (~ен, ~на), *adj.* frank, sincere, candid.

чистот|а́, ы́, *f.* 1. cleanness, cleanliness; neatness, tidiness. 2. (*in var. senses*) purity.

чистоте́л, а, *m.* (*bot.*) celandine.

чи́ст|ый (~, ~а́, ~о), *adj.* 1. clean; neat, tidy; (*of speech, voice, etc.*) pure. 2. (*fig.*) pure, upright, unsullied; ч. понеде́льник (*eccl.*) first Monday in Lent; от ~ого се́рдца, с ~ой со́вестью with a clear conscience. 3. pure; undiluted, neat; ~ое зо́лото, ~ая шерсть pure gold, wool; ~ое иску́сство art for art's sake; ч. спирт pure, neat alcohol; ~ой воды́ (*min.*) of the first water; (*fig.*) pure, first-class; вы́вести на ~ую во́ду to expose, unmask; за ~ые де́ньги for cash; приня́ть что-н. за ~ую моне́ту to take something at its face value. 4. clear, open; ~ое не́бо clear sky; на ~ом во́здухе in the open air; ч. лист blank sheet; ~ое по́ле open field. 5. (*fin., etc.*) net, clear; ~ая при́быль clear profit. 6. (*obs.*) main; special, ceremonial, show; ч. вход front entrance. 7. (*of work or product of work*) skilled; finished; ~ая рабо́та craftsmanship. 8. (*obs.*; *as social criterion*) better-class, 'best'. 9. (*coll.*) pure, utter; mere, sheer; complete, absolute; ч. вздор utter nonsense; ~ая беста́ктность sheer tactlessness; ~ая случа́йность pure chance; ~ая отста́вка (*obs.*) final retirement; по ~ой (*coll.*) finally, once and for all.

чистю́л|я, и, *m. and f.* (*coll.*) person with passion for cleanliness *or* tidiness.

чита́емост|ь, и, *f.* popularity, wide circulation (*of literature*).

чита́|емый 1. *pres. part. pass. of* ~ть *and adj.* widely-read, popular.

чита́льн|ый, *adj.* ч. зал = ~я.

чита́|льня, ьни, g. pl. ~ен, *f.* reading-room.

чита́тел|ь, я, *m.* reader.

чита́тель|ский, *adj. of* ~.

чита́|ть, ю, *impf.* (*of* про~, прочесть) 1. to read. 2. ч. ле́кции to lecture, give lectures; ч. стихи́ to recite poetry; ч. кому́-н. наставле́ния, нравоуче́ния to lecture someone.

чита́|ться, ется, *impf.* 1. *pass. of* ~ть. 2. to be legible. 3. (*fig.*) to be visible, be discernible. 4. (*impers.*) мне, *etc.*, не ~ется I, *etc.*, don't feel like reading.

чи́тк|а, и, *f.* 1. reading (*usually of documents, etc., by a group*). 2. (*theatr.*) (first) reading, reading through.

чи́тывать, *pres. tense not used, impf., freq. of* чита́ть.

чих, а, *m.* (*coll.*) sneeze; *as interj., onomat. of sound of sneezing.*

чиха́нь|е, я, *n.* sneezing; на вся́кое ч. не наздра́вствуешься you can't please everyone.

чиха́тельный, *adj.* causing sneezing, sternutatory; ч. газ sneezing gas.

чих|а́ть, а́ю, *impf.* (*of* ~ну́ть) 1. to sneeze. 2. (на+*a.*; *coll.*) to scorn; ч. мне на него́! I don't give a damn for him!

чих|ну́ть, ну́, нёшь, *pf. of* ~а́ть.

чихо́т|а, ы, *f.* (*coll.*) sneezing (fit).

чи́ще, *comp. of* чи́стый, чи́сто.

чи́|щу, *see* ~стить.

член, а, *m.* 1. (*in var. senses*) member; ч.-корреспонде́нт corresponding member (*of an Academy*). 2. (*math.*) term; (*gram.*) part (*of sentence*). 3. limb, member. 4. (*gram.*) article.

члене́ни|е, я, *n.* articulation.

чле́ник, а, *m.* (*zool.*) segment.

членистоно́г|ие, их (*zool.*) arthropoda.

чле́нистый, *adj.* (*zool.*) articulated, segmented.

член|и́ть, ю́, и́шь, *impf.* (*of* рас~) to divide into parts, articulate.

членовреди́тельств|о, а, *n.* maiming, mutilation; self-mutilation.

членоразде́л|ьный (~ен, ~ьна), *adj.* articulate.

член|ский, *adj. of* ~; ~ские взно́сы membership fee, dues.

чле́нств|о, а, *n.* membership.

чмо́к|ать, аю, *impf.* (*of* ~нуть) 1. to make a smacking sound with one's lips. 2. (*coll.*) to give a smacking kiss. 3. to squelch, make a squelching sound.

чмо́к|нуть, ну, нешь, *pf. of* ~ать.

чо́глок, а, *m.* hobby (*bird of falcon family*).

чо́кань|е, я, *n.* clinking of glasses.

чо́к|аться, аюсь, *impf.* (*of* ~нуться) to clink glasses (*when drinking toasts*).

чо́к|нуться, нусь, нешься, *pf. of* ~аться.

чо́порност|ь, и, *f.* primness; standoffishness, stiffness.

чо́пор|ный (~ен, ~на), *adj.* prim; stuck-up; standoffish, stiff.

чох = чих.

чо́хом, *adv.* (*coll.*) wholesale.

чрева́т|ый (~, ~а), *adj.* 1. (+*i.*) fraught (with). 2. ~ая (*obs.*) pregnant.

чрев|о́, а, **n. (*obs. or rhet., fig.*) belly; womb.

чревовеща́ни|е, я, **n. ventriloquy.

чревовеща́тел|ь, я, **m. ventriloquist.

чревоуго́ди|е, я, **n. gluttony.

чревоуго́дник, а, **m. glutton, gourmand.

чред|а́, ы́, **f. (*obs.*) 1. (*poet.*) turn, succession. 2. sphere (*of activity*).

чрез = че́рез.

чрезвыча́йно, *adv.* extremely, extraordinarily, exceedingly.

чрезвыча́|йный (~ен, ~йна), *adj.* 1. extraordinary (= exceptional, unusual). 2. special, extreme, extraordinary; ~йные ме́ры emergency measures; ~йное положе́ние state of emergency; ч. и полномо́чный посо́л ambassador extraordinary and plenipotentiary.

чрезме́рно, *adv.* excessively, to excess.

чрезме́р|ный (~ен, ~на), *adj.* excessive, inordinate, extreme.

чре́сл|а, ~, **no sing. (*arch. or poet.*) hips, loins.

чте́ни|е, я, **n. 1. reading; ч. карт map-reading; ч. ле́кций lecturing. 2. reading-matter.

чтец, а́, **m. reader; (*professional*) reciter.

чти́в|о, а, **n. (*coll., pejor.*) reading-matter.

чтить, чту, чтишь, чтят (*and* **чтут**), *impf.* to honour.

чти́ц|а, ы, **f. of чтец.

что¹, чего́, чему́, о чём, *interrog. pron.* 1. what?; что с тобо́й? what's the matter (with you)?; что де́лать, что поде́лаешь? it can't be helped; для чего́? why?, what ... for?; к чему́? why?; с чего́? whence?, on what grounds?; что ему́, *etc.*, до...? what does it matter to him, *etc.*? 2. how?; что сего́дня На́дя? how is Nadya today? 3. why?; что вы не пьёте? why aren't you drinking? 4. (*coll.*) how much?; что сто́ит? how much does it cost?; что то́лку? what is the sense?

что² (*sometimes printed* что), *relat. pron.* which, that; (*coll.*) who; я зна́ю, что вы име́ете в виду́ I know what you mean; па́рень, что стоя́л ря́дом со мной the fellow (who was) standing next to me; он всё молча́л, что для него́ не характе́рно he said nothing the whole time, which is unlike him.

что³, (*coll.*) = что́-нибудь; е́сли что случи́тся if anything happens.

что⁴, as far as; что есть мо́чи with all one's might; что до, что каса́ется (+*g.*) as far, with regard (to), as far as ... is concerned.

что⁵, *conj.* that; то, что... the fact that ...

чтоб = что́бы.

что́бы, *conj.* 1. (*expressing purpose*) in order to, in order that; ч....не lest. 2. (*after neg.*) (that); я никогда́ не вида́л, ч. он яви́лся пья́ным на рабо́ту I have never seen him turn up drunk for work; сомнева́юсь, ч. вам э́то понра́вилось I doubt whether you will like it. 3. (*as particle*) *expresses wish*: ч. я тебя́ бо́льше не ви́дел! may I never see your face again!

что ж (*coll.*) *expresses admission, acceptance of argument*: yes; all right, right you are.

что за (*coll.*) 1. (*interrog.*) what? what sort of ...?; что э́то за пти́ца? what sort of bird is that? 2. (*interj.*) что за день! what a (marvellous) day!; что за ерунда́! what (utter) nonsense!

что ли (*coll.*) *expresses uncertainty or hesitation*: пора́ нам идти́, что ли? perhaps we should be going?; позвони́ть тебе́, что ли? do you want me to ring you, then?

что-либо, чего́-либо, *indef. pron.* anything.

что ни, *indef. pron.*; что ни день every day, not a day that passes but ...; что ни говори́ no matter what you may say, say what you like; во что бы то ни ста́ло at whatever cost.

что́-нибудь, чего́-нибудь, *indef. pron.* anything.

что́-то¹, чего́-то, *indef. pron.* something.

что́-то², *adv.* (*coll.*) 1. somewhat, slightly; на слу́шателей его́ выступле́ние произвело́ что́-то не о́чень прия́тное впечатле́ние his speech made a somewhat disagreeable impression on the audience. 2. somehow, for no obvious reason; что́-то мне не хо́чется идти́ I don't feel like going for some reason; тепе́рь что́-то я припомина́ю now I vaguely remember.

чу, *interj.* hark!

чуб, а, **pl. ~ы́, **m.** forelock (*hist.; single lock on otherwise shaven head, as worn formerly by Ukrainian Cossacks*).

чуба́рый, *adj.* (*of a horse's coat*) dappled.

чубу́к, а́, **m. 1. stem (*of smoking pipe*); chibouk. 2. grape stalk.

чува́л, а, **m. (*dial.*) pannier, basket.

чува́ш, а (*and* **а́**), *pl.* ~и, ~ей (*and* ~й, ~ей), *m.* Chuvash.

чува́шк|а, и, **f. Chuvash (woman).

чува́шский, *adj.* Chuvash.

чуви́х|а, и, **f. (*sl.*) bird (= girl).

чу́вственност|ь, и, **f. sensuality.

чу́вствен|ный, *adj.* 1. (~, ~на) sensual. 2. (*philos.*) perceptible, sensible; ~ное восприя́тие perception.

чувстви́тельност|ь, и, **f. 1. (*in var. senses*) sensitivity, sensitiveness; (*of phot. film*) speed. 2. perceptibility, sensibility. 3. sentimentality. 4. tenderness; (deep) feeling.

чувстви́тел|ьный (~ен, ~ьна), *adj.* **1.** (*in var. senses*) sensitive. **2.** perceptible, sensible. **3.** sentimental. **4.** tender; (*of feelings*) deep.

чу́вств|о, а, *n.* **1.** (*physiol.*) sense; ч. вку́са sense of taste; о́рганы ~ senses, organs of sense; обма́н ~ delusion. **2.** (*sing. or pl.*) senses (= consciousness); без ~ unconscious; лиши́ться ~, упа́сть без ~ to faint, lose consciousness; привести́ в ч. to bring round; прийти́ в ч. to come round, regain consciousness, come to one's senses. **3.** (*in var. senses*) feeling; sense; ч. ло́ктя feeling of comradeship, of solidarity; ч. ю́мора sense of humour; пита́ть к кому́-н. не́жные ~а to have a soft spot for someone.

чу́вств|овать, ую, *impf.* **1.** to feel, sense; ч. себя́ to feel (*intrans.*); ч. го́лод to feel hungry; дава́ть себя́ ч. to make itself felt; как вы себя́ ~уете? how do you feel? **2.** to appreciate, have a feeling (for) (*music, etc.*).

чу́вств|оваться, уется, *impf.* **1.** to be perceptible; to make itself felt. **2.** *pass. of* ~овать.

чувя́к|и, ов, *sing.* ~, ~а, *m.* slippers (*worn mainly in the Caucasus and Crimea*).

чугу́н, а́, *m.* **1.** cast iron; ч. в болва́нках pig-iron. **2.** cast-iron pot, vessel.

чугу́нк|а, и, *f.* (*coll.*) **1.** (cast-iron) stove. **2.** (*obs.*) railway.

чугу́нный, *adj.* cast-iron (*also fig.*).

чугунолите́йный, *adj.* ч. заво́д iron foundry.

чуда́к, а́, *m.* eccentric, crank.

чуда́ческий, *adj.* eccentric.

чуда́честв|о, а, *n.* eccentricity, crankiness.

чуда́ч|ить, у, ишь, *impf.* (*coll.*) = чуди́ть.

чуда́чк|а, и, *f. of* чуда́к.

чуде́с|ный (~ен, ~на), *adj.* **1.** miraculous; ~ное исцеле́ние miraculous healing. **2.** marvellous, wonderful.

чуд|и́ть, *1st person not used,* и́шь, *impf.* (*coll.*) **1.** to behave eccentrically, oddly. **2.** to clown, act the fool.

чу́д|иться, ится, *impf.* (*of* по~ *and* при~) (*coll.*) to seem.

чуд|но́й (~ён, ~на́, ~но́), *adj.* strange, odd; ~но́ *as pred.* it is strange, it is odd.

чу́д|ный (~ен, ~на), *adj.* **1.** magic. **2.** (*fig.*) magical; marvellous, wonderful; lovely; ~но *as pred.* it is marvellous, wonderful, lovely.

чу́д|о, а, *pl.* ~еса́, ~е́с, *n.* **1.** miracle. **2.** wonder, marvel; ~еса́ те́хники wonders of engineering; ч. как *as adv.* marvellously; ч., что... *as pred.* it is a marvel that . . .

чу́до-богаты́р|ь, я́, *m.* hero.

чудо́вищ|е, а, *n.* monster.

чудо́вищ|ный (~ен, ~на), *aaj.* **1.** monstrous (*also fig., pejor.*). **2.** enormous.

чудоде́|й, я, *m.* **1.** (*obs.*) miracle-worker. **2.**

(*coll.*) crank.

чудоде́йствен|ный (~, ~на), *adj.* miracle-working; miraculous.

чу́дом, *adv.* miraculously; ч. спасти́сь to be saved by a miracle.

чудотво́р|ец, ца, *m.* miracle-worker.

чудотво́рный, *adj.* miracle-working; (*fig.*) marvellous.

чу́до-ю́до, *indecl., n.* (*folk poet.*) monster.

чужа́к, а́, *m.* (*coll.*) stranger; (*pejor.*) alien, interloper.

чужа́н|ин, и́на, *pl.* ~е, ~, *m.* (*folk poet. or coll.*) stranger.

чужби́н|а, ы, *f.* foreign land, country.

чужда́|ться, юсь, *impf.* (+*g.*) to shun, avoid; to stand aloof (from), remain unaffected (by).

чу́жд|ый (~, ~а́, ~о), *adj.* **1.** (+*d.*) alien (to); extraneous. **2.** (+*g.*) free (from), devoid (of); он ~ зло́бы he is devoid of malice.

чужезе́м|ец, ца, *m.* (*obs.*) foreigner, stranger.

чужезе́м|ка, ки, *f. of* ~ец.

чужезе́мный, *adj.* (*obs.*) foreign.

чужеро́д|ный, (~ен, ~на), *adj.* alien, foreign.

чужестра́н|ец, ца, *m.* (*obs.*) = чужезе́мец.

чужестра́н|ка, ки, *f. of* ~ец.

чужестра́нный, *adj.* (*obs.*) = чужезе́мный.

чужея́дный, *adj.* (*bot.*) parasitic.

чуж|о́й, *adj.* **1.** someone else's, another's, others'; на ч. счёт at someone else's expense; с ~и́х слов at second-hand; *as noun* ~о́е, ~о́го, *n.* someone else's belongings, what belongs to others. **2.** strange, alien; foreign; ~и́е края́ = ~би́на; попа́сть в ~и́е ру́ки to fall into strange hands; *as noun* ч., ~о́го, *m.* stranger.

чу́йк|а, и, *f.* (*obs.*) chuyka (*knee-length cloth jacket formerly worn by men as outer garment*).

чуко́тский, *adj.* Chukchi.

чу́кч|а, и, *m.* Chukchi (man).

чукча́нк|а, и, *f.* Chukchi (woman).

чула́н, а, *m.* **1.** store-room, lumber-room. **2.** larder.

чул|о́к, ка́, *g. pl.* ч., *m.* stocking.

чуло́чник, а, *m.* stocking-maker.

чуло́чно-носо́чн|ый, *adj.* ~ые изде́лия hosiery.

чуло́чный, *adj. of* чуло́к.

чум|а́, ы́, *f.* plague (*also as form of abuse*).

чума́з|ый (~, ~а), *adj.* (*coll.*) grubby, dirty; *as noun* (*obs., pejor.*) ч., ~ого, *m.* upstart, parvenu, kulak.

чума́к, а́, *m.* (*obs.*) chumak (*in Ukraine, ox-cart driver transporting fish, salt, and grain*).

чума́|цкий, *adj. of* ~к.

чуми́чк|а, и, *f.* **1.** (*dial.*) ladle. **2.** (*coll., obs.*) servant-girl. **3.** (*coll.*) slut, slattern.

чум|но́й, *adj. of* ~а́; plague-stricken; ~на́я па́лочка plague bacillus.

чумово́й, *adj.* (*sl.*) crazy, half-witted.

чу́н|и, ей, *sing.* ~я, ~и, *f.* (*dial.*) **1.** rope shoes. **2.** galoshes.

чупри́н|а, ы, *f.* (*dial.*) = чуб.

чур, *interj.* (*coll.*) keep away!; mind!; ч. меня́ (*in children's games, etc.*) keep away from me!

чура́|ться, юсь, *impf.* (+*g.*; *coll.*) to shun, avoid, steer clear (of).

чурба́н, а, *m.* **1.** block, log. **2.** (*coll.*) block-head.

чу́рк|а, и, *f.* block, lump, chock.

чу́т|кий (~ок, ~ка́, ~ко), *adj.* **1.** (*of senses of hearing and smell*) keen, sharp, quick; ч. нюх keen sense of smell; ~кая соба́ка keen-nosed dog; ч. сон light sleep. **2.** (*fig.*) sensitive; sympathetic; tactful.

чу́ткост|ь, и, *f.* **1.** keenness, sharpness, quickness. **2.** sensitivity; sympathetic attitude; tactfulness.

чуто́к, *adv.* (*coll.*) a little.

чу́точк|а, и, *f.* ни ~и (*coll.*) not in the least.

чу́точку, *adv.* (*coll.*) a little, a wee bit.

чу́точный, *adj.* (*coll.*) tiny, wee.

чу́т|че, *comp. of* ~кий.

чуть (*coll.*) **1.** *adv.* hardly, scarcely; just; ч. (бы́ло) не, ч. ли не almost, nearly, all but. **2.** *adv.* (just) a little, very slightly. **3.** *conj.* as soon as; ч. свет at daybreak, at first light; ч. что at the slightest provocation.

чуть|ё, я́, *n.* **1.** (*of animals*) scent. **2.** (*fig.*) flair, feeling (for).

чуть-чу́ть, *adv.* (*coll.*) a tiny bit; ч.-ч. не= чуть не.

чухо́н|ец, ца, *m.* (*obs., pejor.*) Finn.

чухо́н|ка, ки, *f. of* ~ец.

чухо́нск|ий, *adj.* (*obs., pejor.*) Finnish; ~ое ма́сло butter.

чу́чел|о, а, *n.* **1.** stuffed animal. **2.** scarecrow (*also fig.*).

чу́шк|а, и, *f.* **1.** (*coll.*) piglet. **2.** (*tech.*) pig, ingot, bar.

чуш|ь, и, *f.* (*coll.*) nonsense, rubbish.

чу́|ять, ю, ешь, *impf.* to scent, smell; (*fig.*) to sense, feel.

чу́|яться, ется, *impf.* (*impers.*) to make itself felt.

Ш

ша́баш, а, *m.* (*rel.*) sabbath; ш. ведьм witches' sabbath; (*fig.*) orgy.

шаба́ш, а, *m.* **1.** (*obs., coll.*) end of work, knocking-off time. **2.** *as pred.* that's enough!, that'll do!; (*naut.*) ship oars!

шаба́ш|ить, у, ишь, *impf.* (*coll.*) (*trans. and intrans.*) to stop (work); to knock off, down tools.

ша́бер, а, *m.* (*tech.*) scraper.

шаб|ёр, ра́, *m.* (*dial.*) neighbour; жить в ~ра́х to live next door.

шабло́н, а, *m.* **1.** (*tech.*) template, pattern; mould, form; stencil. **2.** (*fig., pejor.*) cliché; (fixed) pattern; routine; рабо́тать по ~у to work by rote, work mechanically.

шабло́нност|ь, и, *f.* triteness, banality.

шабло́н|ный, *adj.* **1.** *adj. of* ~. **2.** (~ен, ~на) trite, banal; stereotyped; routine.

ша́вк|а, и, *f.* (*coll.*) (small) dog.

шаг, а (у) (*after numerals* 2, 3, 4 ~а́), о ~е, в (на) ~у́, *pl.* ~й, ~о́в, *m.* **1.** step (*also fig.*); pace; stride; ш. на ме́сте marking time; ни ~у да́льше! not a step further!, stay where you are!; идти́ бы́стрыми ~а́ми to make rapid strides; ~у ступи́ть нельзя́ (не даю́т) one can't do anything; заме́длить ш. to slow down; приба́вить ~у to quicken one's pace; ши́ре ш.! (*i*) step out, take bigger strides!, (*ii*) (*fig.*) get a move on!; в двух ~а́х, в не́скольких ~а́х a stone's throw away; у́зки в ~у́ (*of cut of trousers*)

tight in the seat; на ка́ждом ~у́ everywhere, at every turn, continually; с пе́рвого ~у (*obs.*) from the outset. **2.** (*tech.*) pitch, spacing.

шаг|а́ть, а́ю, *impf.* (*of* ~ну́ть) **1.** to step; to walk, stride; to pace. **2.** (*coll.*) to go, come.

шага́|ющий, *pres. part. act. of* ~ть; ш. экскава́тор self-propelled excavator.

шаги́стик|а, и, *f.* (*pejor.*) square-bashing (*as part of military training*).

шаг|ну́ть, ну́, нёшь, *pf.* (*of* ~а́ть) to take a step; (*fig.*) to make progress; ш. нельзя́ (не даю́т) one can't do anything, there's no scope for action.

ша́гом, *adv.* at a walk, at walking pace; slowly; ш. марш! (*mil. word of command*) quick march!

шагоме́р, а, *m.* pedometer.

шагре́н|евый, *adj. of* ~ь.

шагре́н|ь, и, *f.* shagreen leather.

шажко́м, *adv.* (*coll.*) taking short steps.

шаж|о́к, ка́, *m., dim. of* шаг.

ша́йб|а, ы, *f.* **1.** (*tech.*) washer. **2.** (*sport*) puck; хокке́й с ~ой ice hockey.

ша́йк|а¹, и, *g. pl.* ша́ек, *f.* tub (*two-handled, of wood or metal*).

ша́йк|а², и, *g. pl.* ша́ек, *f.* gang, band.

шайта́н, а, *m.* (*in Moslem theology*) evil spirit; (*coll.*; *as term of abuse*) devil.

шака́л, а, *m.* jackal.

шала́нд|а, ы, *f.* (*flat-bottomed*) barge, lighter.

шала́ш, á, *m.* (*hunter's or fisherman's*) cabin (*made of branches and straw, etc.*).

шале́|ть, ю, *impf.* (*of* о~) (*coll.*) to go crazy.

шал|и́ть, ю́, и́шь, *impf.* **1.** to be naughty (*of children*); to play up, play tricks (*also of inanimate objects*); ~и́шь! (*as rebuke*) don't try that on!, don't come that with me! **2.** (*obs., coll.*) to carry out robberies.

шаловли́в|ый (~, ~а), *adj.* **1.** (*of children*) naughty, apt to get into mischief. **2.** mischievous; flirtatious.

шалопа́|й, я, *m.* (*coll.*) good-for-nothing, idler, skiver.

ша́лост|ь, и, *f.* (*childish*) prank, game; (*pl.*) mischief, naughtiness. **2.** (*obs., coll.*) robbery.

шалу́н, á, *m.* naughty child.

шалу́н|ья, ьи, *f. of* ~.

шалфе́|й, я, *m.* (*bot.*) sage.

ша́лый, *adj.* (*coll.*) mad, crazy.

шал|ь, и, *f.* shawl.

шальн|о́й, *adj.* mad, crazy; wild; ~ы́е де́ньги easy money; ~а́я пу́ля stray bullet.

шама́н, а, *m.* (*rel.*) shaman.

шама́н|ский, *adj. of* ~.

шама́нств|о, а, *n.* (*rel.*) shamanism.

ша́ма|ть, ю, *impf.* (*sl.*) to eat.

ша́мка|ть, ю, *impf.* to mumble.

шамо́вк|а, и, *f.* (*sl.*) grub (*food*).

шамо́т, а, *m.* (*tech.*) fire-clay.

шамо́т|ный, *adj. of* ~; ш. кирпи́ч fire-brick, refractory brick.

шампа́нск|ое, ого, *n.* champagne.

шампиньо́н, а, *m.* field mushroom (*Agaricus campestris* or *Psalliota campestris*).

шампу́н|ь, я, *m.* shampoo.

шанда́л, а, *m.* (*obs.*) candlestick.

ша́н|ец, ца, *m.* (*hist.*) field-work; entrenchment.

шанкр, а, *m.* (*med.*) chancre.

шанс, а, *m.* chance; име́ть мно́го ~ов, больши́е ~ы (на+*a.*) to have a good chance (of).

шансоне́тк|а, и, *f.* **1.** (*music-hall*) song. **2.** singer (*in music-hall or café chantant*).

шанта́ж, á, *m.* blackmail.

шантажи́р|овать, ую, *impf.* to blackmail.

шантажи́ст, а, *m.* blackmailer.

шантрап|а́, ы́, *m. and f.* (*coll.*) worthless individual; scum, riff-raff.

ша́н|цевый, *adj. of* ~ец; ш. инструме́нт entrenching tool.

ша́пк|а, и, *f.* **1.** cap; заломи́ть ~у to wear one's cap at a rakish angle; лома́ть ~у (пе́ред; *obs., coll.*) to touch one's forelock (to); дать по ~е (+*d.*; *coll.*) (*i*) to hit, strike, (*ii*) to sack, fire (= dismiss); получи́ть по ~е (*coll.*) (*i*) to receive a blow, (*ii*) to be sacked, fired; ~ами закида́ем it's in the bag (= we expect to win without diffi-

culty); на во́ре ш. гори́т he's given the game away; по Се́ньке ш. he's got his deserts. **2.** banner headline(s). **3.** (*fig.; of something covering or crowning other objects*) cap, crown, head, cupola; ш. ды́ма wreath of smoke, smoke-haze.

шапова́л, а, *m.* (*obs.*) fuller.

шапокля́к, а, *m.* opera-hat.

ша́почк|а, и, *f.*, *dim. of* ша́пка.

ша́почн|ый, *adj. of* ша́пка; ~ое знако́мство nodding acquaintance; прийти́ к ~ому разбо́ру (*fig., coll.*) to miss the bus.

шар, а (*after numerals* 2, 3, 4 ~á), *pl.* ~ы́, *m.* **1.** (*math.*) sphere; земно́й ш. the Earth, globe. **2.** spherical object; ball; возду́шный ш. balloon; хоть ~о́м покати́ completely empty. **3.** (*obs.*) ballot; vote. **4.** (*pl.*) (*sl.*) eyes.

шара́х|ать, аю, *impf.* (*of* ~нуть) (*coll.*) to strike; to hit, shoot.

шара́х|аться, аюсь, *impf.* (*of* ~нуться) (*coll.*) **1.** to shy (*of a horse*); to start (up); to rush, dash. **2.** (о+*a.*) to hit, strike.

шара́х|нуть(ся), ну(сь), нешь(ся), *pf. of* ~ать(ся).

шарж, а, *m.* caricature, cartoon; дру́жеский ш. harmless, well-meant caricature.

шаржи́р|овать, ую, *impf.* to caricature.

ша́рик, а, *m.* *dim. of* шар; (кровяно́й) ш. (blood) corpuscle.

ша́рик|овый, *adj. of* ~; ~овая (авто)ру́чка ball-point pen; ш. подши́пник (*tech.*) ball--bearing.

шарикоподши́пник, а, *m.* (*tech.*) ball--bearing.

шарикоподши́пник|овый, *adj. of* ~.

ша́р|ить, ю, ишь, *impf.* (в+*p.*, по+*d.*) to grope about, feel, fumble (in, through); (*of machine-gun fire, searchlight beams, etc.*) to sweep (*in order to locate a target*).

ша́ркань|е, я, *n.* shuffling (*of the feet or footwear*).

ша́рк|ать, аю, *impf.* (*of* ~нуть) **1.** (+*i.*) to shuffle. **2.** (ного́й; *obs.*) to click one's heels. **3.** (*coll.*) to hit, strike.

ша́рк|нуть, ну, нешь, *pf. of* ~ать.

шарлата́н, а, *m.* charlatan, fraud; quack.

шарлата́н|ить, ю, ишь, *impf.* to be a charlatan.

шарлата́н|ский, *adj. of* ~.

шарлата́нств|о, а, *n.* charlatanism.

шарло́тк|а, и, *f.* (*cul.*) charlotte.

шарма́нк|а, и, *f.* barrel-organ, street organ.

шарма́нщик, а, *m.* organ-grinder.

шарни́р, а, *m.* (*tech.*) hinge, joint; на ~ах hinged; быть как на ~ах (*fig.*) to be on edge, be restless, fidget.

шарни́р|ный, *adj. of* ~; ш. болт link bolt; ш. кла́пан flap valve; ~ная опо́ра rocker bearing, tip bearing; ~ное соедине́ние hinge joint, ball and socket joint, toggle joint.

шаровар|ы, ~, *no sing.*, wide trousers (*as worn by certain Eastern peoples, or for certain sports*).

шаровид|ный (~ен, ~на), *adj.* spherical, globe-shaped.

шар|овой, *adj.* of ~; globular; ш. клапан ball-cock; ш. шарнир, ~овое шарнирное соединение ball and socket joint.

шаромы́г|а, и, *m. and f.* (*coll.*) parasite; rogue, scoundrel.

шаромы́жник, а, *m.* = шаромы́га.

шарообра́з|ный (~ен, ~на), *adj.* spherical, ball-shaped.

шартрёз, а, *m.* Chartreuse (*liqueur*).

шарф, а, *m.* scarf.

шасси́, *indecl., n.* 1. chassis. 2. (*aeron.*) undercarriage.

ша́ста|ть, ю, *impf.* (*coll.*) to roam, hang about.

шата́ни|е, я, *n.* 1. swaying, reeling. 2. roaming, wandering. 3. (*fig.*) vacillation; instability.

шата́|ть, ю, *impf.* to rock, shake, cause to reel.

шата́|ться, юсь, *impf.* 1. (*intrans.*) to rock, sway, reel. 2. to be, come loose; to be unsteady. 3. (*coll.*) to roam; to loaf, lounge about.

шата́|ющийся, *pres. part. of* ~ться *and adj.* loose (*of a screw, tooth, etc.*).

шате́н, а, *m.* person with auburn, brown hair.

шате́н|ка, ки, *f. of* ~.

шат|ёр, ра́, *m.* 1. tent, marquee. 2. (*archit.*) hipped roof.

ша́ти|я, и, *f.* (*coll., pejor.*) gang, crowd, 'mob'.

ша́т|кий (~ок, ~ка), *adj.* 1. unsteady; shaky; loose. 2. (*fig.*) unstable, insecure, shaky; unreliable; vacillating; ш. в убеждениях lacking the courage of one's convictions.

ша́ткост|ь, и, *f.* 1. unsteadiness; shakiness. 2. (*fig.*) instability; vacillation.

шатро́в|ый, *adj. of* шатёр; ~ая крыша hipped roof.

шату́н¹, а́, *m.* (*tech.*) connecting rod.

шату́н², а́, *m.* (*coll.*) loafer, idler.

ша́фер, а, *pl.* ~а́, *m.* best man (*at wedding*).

шафра́н, а, *m.* (*bot.*) saffron.

шафра́н|ный, *adj. of* ~.

шах¹, а, *m.* Shah.

шах², а, *m.* (*chess*) check; ш. и мат checkmate; объяви́ть ш. (+*d.*) to put in check; под ~ом in check.

ша́хер-ма́хер, а, *m.* (*coll.*) shady deal.

шахмати́ст, а, *m.* chess-player.

ша́хматн|ый, *adj.* 1. chess; ш. дебют chess

opening, opening gambit; ~ая доска́ chess-board; ~ая па́ртия game of chess. 2. chess-board, checkered; staggered; ~ая ска́терть check table-cloth; в ~ом поря́дке staggered.

ша́хмат|ы, ~, *no sing.* 1. chess. 2. chessmen.

ша́хт|а, ы, *f.* 1. mine, pit. 2. (*tech.*) shaft.

шахтёр, а, *m.* miner.

шахтёр|ский, *adj. of* ~.

ша́хт|ный, *adj. of* ~а; ш. ствол pit-shaft.

ша́хт|овый, *adj. of* ~а.

ша́шечниц|а, ы, *f.* draught-board, chess-board.

ша́шк|а¹, и, *f.* 1. block (*of stone or wood plank, for paving*). 2. charge (*of explosive*).

ша́шк|а², и, *f.* 1. draught, draughtsman (*piece in game of draughts*). 2. (*pl.*) draughts (*game*).

ша́шк|а³, и, *f.* sabre, cavalry sword.

шашлы́к, а́, *m.* (*cul.*) shashlik, kebab.

шашлы́чн|ая, ой, *f.* shashlik-house.

ша́шн|и, ей, *no sing.* (*coll., pejor.*) 1. tricks. 2. amorous intrigues; affair; завести́ ш. с(+*i.*) to take up with.

шва, *g. sing. of* шов.

шва́бр|а, ы, *f.* mop, swab.

швал|ь, и, *f.* (*coll.*) 1. (*collect.*) rubbish, worthless stuff. 2. good-for-nothing.

шва́льн|я, и, *f.* (*obs.*) tailor's shop.

шва́ркн|уть, у, ешь, *pf.* (*coll.*) to hurl.

швартов, а, *m.* (*naut.*) hawser, mooring line; отда́ть ~ы to cast off.

шварт|ова́ть, у́ю, *impf.* (*of* при~) (*naut.*) to moor.

шварт|ова́ться, у́юсь, *impf.* (*of* при~) (*naut.*) to moor, make fast.

швах, *as pred.* (*coll.*) poor, bad; in a bad way.

швед, а, *m.* Swede.

шве́д|ка, ки, *f. of* ~.

шве́дский, *adj.* Swedish.

шве́йник, а, *m.* sewer, sewing industry worker.

шве́йн|ый, *adj.* sewing; ~ые изде́лия ready-made garments; ~ая маши́на sewing-machine; ~ая фа́брика garment factory.

швейца́р, а, *m.* porter, door-keeper, commissionaire.

швейца́р|ец, ца, *m.* Swiss.

швейца́р|ка, ки, *f. of* ~ец.

швейца́рск|ая, ой, *f.* porter's lodge.

швейца́рский¹, *adj.* Swiss.

швейца́р|ский², *adj. of* ~.

швермер, а, *m.* squib (*firework*).

швец, а́, *m.* 1. (*obs.*) tailor; и ш., и жнец, и в ду́ду игре́ц (*fig..*) jack of all trades. 2. (*dial.*) cobbler.

шве|я́, й, *f.* seamstress; ш.-мотори́стка electric sewing-machine operator; ш.-ру́чница (*coll.*) hand finisher.

шво́р|ень, ня, *m.* = шкво́рень.

швырко́в|ый, *adj.* ~ые дрова́ logs, firewood.

швыр|ну́ть, ну́, нёшь, *pf. of* ~я́ть.

швыр|о́к, ка́, *m.* 1. throw. 2. (*collect.*) logs, firewood. 3. (*moving*) practice target.

швыр|я́ть, я́ю, *impf.* (*of* ~ну́ть) (+*a. or i.*; *coll.*) to throw, fling, chuck, hurl; ш. де́ньги (деньга́ми) to fling one's money about.

швыря́|ться, юсь, *impf.* (*coll.*) (+*i.*) 1. to throw, fling, hurl (at one another). 2. to make light (of), trifle (with).

шевел|и́ть, ю́, и́шь, *impf.* (*of* ~ьну́ть *and* по~) 1. to turn over. 2. (+*i.*) to move, stir, budge; ш. мозга́ми (*coll., joc.*) to use one's wits, use one's loaf.

шевел|и́ться, ю́сь, и́шься, *impf.* (*of* ~ьну́ть-ся *and* по~) 1. to move, stir, budge; у него́ ~я́тся де́ньги (*coll.*) he has a tidy bank balance. 2. (*fig.*) to stir (*of hopes, fears, etc.*). 3. ~и́сь, ~и́тесь! (*coll.*) get a move on!, get cracking!

шевел|ьну́ть, ьну́, ьнёшь, *pf.* (*of* ~и́ть); бро́вью не ш. not to bat an eyelid; па́льцем не ш. not to lift a finger.

шевел|ьну́ться, ьну́сь, ьнёшься, *pf. of* ~и́ться.

шевелю́р|а, ы, *f.* (head of) hair.

шевио́т, а, *m.* (*text.*) cheviot (*cloth*).

шевио́т|овый, *adj. of* ~.

шевро́, *indecl., n.* kid (*leather*).

шевро́|вый, *adj. of* ~.

шевро́н, а, *m.* (*mil.*) long-service stripe.

шеде́вр, а, *m.* masterpiece, chef d'œuvre.

ше́йк|а, и, *g. pl.* ше́ек, *f.* 1. *dim. of* ше́я. 2. (*narrow part of various objects*) neck; (*tech.*) pin, journal; ш. ги́льзы cartridge neck; ш. ре́льса web (*of rail*). 3. (*anat.*) cervix.

ше́йный, *adj. of* ше́я; (*anat.*) jugular, cervical.

шейх, а, *m.* sheikh.

шёл, *see* идти́.

ше́лест, а, *m.* rustle, rustling.

шелест|е́ть, *1st person not used,* и́шь, *impf.* to rustle.

шёлк, а (у), о ~е, на (в) ~у́, *pl.* ~а́, *m.* silk (*also fig. of an object resembling silk in softness, etc., or of a gentle-natured person*); ш.-сыре́ц raw silk; ходи́ть в ~а́х to wear silks; в долгу́ как в ~у́ up to the eyes in debt.

шелкови́нк|а, и, *f.* silk thread.

шелкови́ст|ый (~, ~а), *adj.* silky.

шелкови́ц|а, ы, *f.* mulberry (tree).

шелкови́|чный, *adj. of* ~ца; ш. червь silkworm.

шелково́д, а, *m.* silkworm breeder.

шелково́дств|о, а, *n.* silkworm breeding, seri(ci)culture.

шелково́д|ческий, *adj. of* ~ство.

шёлковый, *adj.* 1. silk. 2. (*fig., coll.*) meek, good (= tractable).

шелкопря́д, а, *m.* silkworm.

шёлкопряде́ни|е, я, *n.* silk-spinning.

шёлкопряд|и́льный, *adj. of* ~е́ние.

шёлкотка́цкий, *adj.* silk-weaving.

шелла́к, а, *m.* shellac.

шело́м, а, *m.* (*arch. or poet.*) = шлем.

шелохн|у́ть, у́, ёшь, *pf.* to stir, agitate.

шелохн|у́ться, у́сь, ёшься, *pf.* to stir, move.

шелуди́в|ый (~, ~а), *adj.* (*coll.*) mangy.

шелух|а́, и́, *f.* skin (*of vegetables or fruit*); peel; pod; scale (*of fish*).

шелуше́ни|е, я, *n.* 1. peeling, shelling (*action*). 2. peeling (*of human skin*).

шелуш|и́ть, у́, и́шь, *impf.* to peel; to shell.

шелуш|и́ться, и́тся, *impf.* 1. (*of skin*) to peel. 2. (*of paint, etc.*) to come off, peel off.

ше́льм|а, ы, *m. and f.* (*coll.*) rascal, scoundrel.

шельмова́т|ый (~, ~а), *adj.* (*coll.*) rascally, sly, wily.

шельм|ова́ть, у́ю, *impf.* (*of* о~) (*coll.*) to abuse; to run down; to defame.

шельф, а, *m.* (*geogr.*) shelf.

шемя́кин, *adj., only in phrase* ш. суд unjust trial.

ше́нкел|ь, я, *pl.* ~я́, ~е́й, *m.* (*horsemanship*) leg (*of rider*).

шепеля́в|ить, лю, ишь, *impf.* to lisp, hiss (*pronounce 's', 'z' as 'sh', 'zh'*).

шепеля́в|ый (~, ~а), *adj.* lisping, hissing.

шеп|ну́ть, ну́, нёшь, *pf. of* ~та́ть.

шёпот, а, *m.* whisper (*also fig. = rumour*).

шёпотом, *adv.* in a whisper.

шептал|а́, ы́, *f.* (*collect.*) dried apricots *or* peaches.

шеп|та́ть, чу́, ~чешь, *impf.* (*of* ~ну́ть) to whisper.

шеп|та́ться, чу́сь, ~чешься, *impf.* to whisper, converse in whispers.

шепту́н; а́, *m.* (*coll.*) 1. one who speaks in a whisper. 2. (*fig.*) whisperer, tell-tale, informer.

шербе́т, а, *m.* sherbet.

шере́нг|а, и, *f.* rank (= row); file, column.

шери́ф, а, *m.* sheriff.

шерохова́тост|ь, и, *f.* roughness (*also fig.*); unevenness.

шерохова́т|ый (~, ~а), *adj.* rough (*also fig.*); uneven; rugged.

шерсте- wool-.

шерсти́нк|а, и, *f.* strand of wool.

шерсти́ст|ый (~, ~а), *adj.* woolly, fleecy.

шерст|и́ть, и́т, *impf.* 1. to irritate, tickle (*of a woollen garment*). 2. (*fig., coll.*) to blow up, tear a strip off.

шерсто- wool-.

шерстоби́т, а, *m.* wool-beater.

шерстобо́йн|я, и, *f.* wool-beating mill.

шерстопряде́ни|е, я, n. wool-spinning.

шерстопряд|и́льный, adj. of ~е́ние.

шерстоткáчеств|о, а, n. wool-weaving.

шерсточесáльный, adj. wool-carding.

шерст|ь, и, pl. ~и, ~е́й, f. 1. hair (of animals); глáдить кого́-н. про́тив ~и (fig.) to rub someone up the wrong way. 2. wool. 3. woollen material; worsted.

шерстян|о́й, adj. wool, woollen; ш. пот suint; ~áя пря́жа wool yarn.

шерхéбел|ь, я, m. (tech.) rough plane.

шершáве|ть, ет, impf. to become rough.

шершáв|ый (~, ~а), adj. rough; ~ые ру́ки horny hands.

шéрш|ень, ня, m. hornet.

шест, á, m. pole; staff.

шéстви|е, я, n. procession.

шéств|овать, ую, impf. to walk (as in procession).

шестерёнк|а, и, f. dim. of шестерня́².

шестерён|очный, adj. of ~ка; ~очная коро́бка gear-box.

шестёрк|а, и, f. 1. figure '6'; six, group of six. 2. (cards) six. 3. six-in-hand. 4. six-oar (boat).

шестерно́й, adj. sixfold, sextuple.

шестерн|я́¹, й, g. pl. ~éй, f. (obs.) six-in-hand.

шестер|ня́², ни́, g. pl. ~ён, f. (tech.) gear (wheel), cogwheel, pinion.

шéстер|о, ы́х, collect. num. six.

шести- six-.

шестигрáнник, а, m. (math.) hexahedron.

шестидесятилéти|е, я, n. 1. sixty years, sixty-year period. 2. sixtieth anniversary.

шестидесятилéтний, adj. 1. of sixty years, sixty-year. 2. sixty-year-old.

шестидеся́тник, а, m. (hist.) 'man of the sixties' (of Russian public figures and social thinkers who flourished in the 1860's—e.g., Chernyshevsky and Dobrolyubov).

шестидеся́тый, adj. sixtieth.

шестиклáссник, а, m. sixth-former.

шестисотлéти|е, я, n. 1. six hundred years. 2. six-hundred anniversary, sexcentenary.

шестисо́тый, adj. six-hundredth.

шестиуго́льник, а, m. (math.) hexagon.

шестиуго́льный, adj. hexagonal.

шестичасово́й, adj. 1. lasting six hours. 2. (coll.) occurring at, timed for six o'clock.

шестнадцати- sixteen-.

шестнадцатилéтний, adj. 1. of sixteen years, sixteen-year. 2. sixteen-year-old.

шестнáдцатый, adj. sixteenth.

шестнáдцат|ь, и, num. sixteen.

шест|ово́й, adj. of ~.

шест|о́й, adj. sixth; одна́ ~áя one sixth.

шест|о́к, кá, m. 1. hearth (in Russian stove). 2. roost.

шест|ь, и́, ью́, num. six.

шестьдеся́т, шести́десяти, шестью́десятью, о шести́десяти, num. sixty.

шест|ьсо́т, ~исо́т, ~истáм, ~ьюстáми, о ~истáх, num. six hundred.

шéстью, adv. six times.

шеф, а, m. 1. (coll.) boss, chief. 2. (of an organization) patron, sponsor.

шеф-по́вар, а, pl. ~á, ~о́в, m. chef.

шéф|ский, adj. of ~ство.

шéфств|о, а, n. patronage, sponsorship (in the U.S.S.R., relationship between two organizations—e.g. a factory and a collective farm—in which one 'adopts' the other, or arrangement by which an organization takes a special interest in a priority construction project); взять ш. (над) to take under one's patronage.

шéфств|овать, ую, impf. (над) to act as patron, sponsor (to).

шé|я, и, f. neck; бросáться на ~ю кому́-н. to throw one's arms around someone's neck; на свою́ ~ю (coll.) to one's own detriment; бить по ~я́м (coll.) to beat up, knock the daylight out of; вéшаться на ~ю кому́-н. (fig., coll.) to hang round someone's neck; прогнáть, вы́толкать кого́-н. в ~ю, в три ~и (coll.) to throw someone out on his ear; сидéть на ~е у кого́-н. (coll.) to live off someone; сломáть, сверну́ть (себé) ~ю на чём-н. (coll.) to come a cropper over something.

шибá|ть, ю, impf. (coll.) 1. (+a. or i.) to throw, chuck. 2. to hit (also, impers., of smells, etc.).

ши́бер, а, m. (tech.) damper; gate (valve), slide (valve).

ши́б|кий (~ок, ~кá, ~ко), adj. (coll.) fast, quick.

ши́бк|о, adv. (coll.) 1. adv. of ~ий. 2. hard; much, very; ш. испугáться to be scared stiff.

ши́б|че, comp. of ~кий and ~ко.

ши́ворот, а, m. (coll.) за ш. by the collar, by the scruff of the neck; ш.-навы́ворот (adv.) topsy-turvy, upside down, haywire.

шизофрéник, а, m. (med.) schizophrenic.

шизофрени|я, и, f. (med.) schizophrenia.

шик, а (у), m. ostentatious smartness, stylishness; style.

шикáрн|о¹, adv. of ~ый.

шикáрно², as pred. it is splendid, magnificent.

шикáр|ный (~ен, ~на), adj. 1. chic, smart, stylish. 2. ostentatious, done for effect. 3. (coll.) splendid, magnificent.

ши́к|ать, аю, impf. (of ~нуть) (coll.) 1. (на+a.) to hush (by crying 'sh'). 2. (+d.) to hiss (at), boo, catcall.

ши́к|нуть, ну, нешь, pf. of ~ать.

шик|ну́ть, ну, нёшь, pf. of ~овáть.

шик|ова́ть, у́ю, *impf.* (*of* ~**ну́ть**) (+*i. or intrans.*; *coll.*) to parade; to show off.

ши́л|о, а, *pl.* ~**ья, ~ьев,** *n.* awl.

шилохво́ст|ь, и, *f.* (*orn.*) pintail.

шимпанзе́, *indecl., m.* chimpanzee.

ши́н|а, ы, *f.* 1. tyre. 2. (*med.*) splint. 3. (*electr.*) bus-bar.

шине́л|ь, и, *f.* (*mil. or uniform*) greatcoat.

шине́ль|ный, *adj. of* ~.

шинка́р|ка, ки, *f. of* ~**ь.**

шинка́рств|о, а, *n.* (*obs.*) bootlegging.

шинка́р|ь, я́, *m.* (*obs.*) 1. tavern-keeper, publican. 2. bootlegger.

шинко́в|анный, *p.p.p. of* ~**а́ть** *and adj.* (*cul.*) shredded, chopped.

шинк|ова́ть, у́ю, *impf.* (*cul.*) to shred, chop.

ши́н|ный, *adj. of* ~**а;** ~**ое желе́зо** band iron, hoop-iron; ш. заво́д tyre factory.

шин|о́к, ка́, *m.* (*obs.*) 1. tavern. 2. (*coll.*) bootlegging establishment.

шиншилл|а, ы, *f.* chinchilla.

шип¹, а́, *m.* 1. (*bot.*) thorn, spine. 2. spike, crampon, nail (*on running shoes, mountaineering boots, etc., to prevent slipping*). 3. (*tech.*) pin, tenon; lug; ш. и гнездо́ mortise and tenon.

шип², а, *m.* (*coll.*) hissing (sound).

шипе́ни|е, я, *n.* hissing; sizzling; sputtering.

шип|е́ть, лю́, и́шь, *impf.* 1. to hiss; to sizzle; to fizz; to sputter. 2. to make the sound 'sh' (*to comfort a child, etc., or to enjoin silence*).

шипо́вник, а, *m.* (*bot.*) dogrose.

шипу́чий, *adj.* (*of drinks*) sparkling; fizzy.

шипу́чк|а, и, *f.* (*coll.*) fizzy drink.

шип|я́щий, *pres. part. act. of* ~**е́ть** *and adj.* (*ling.*) hushing.

шир|е, *comp. of* ~**о́кий** *and* ~**око́;** ш. шаг, *see* шаг.

ширин|а́, ы́, *f.* width, breadth; gauge (*of railway track*); ш. фро́нта (*mil.*) frontage.

шири́нк|а, и, *f.* 1. (*coll.*) fly (*of trousers*). 2. (*dial.*) (piece of) cloth.

шир|ить, ю, ишь, *impf.* to extend, expand.

шир|иться, ится, *impf.* to spread, expand (*intrans.*).

ши́рм|а, ы, *f.* screen (*also fig.*).

широ́к|ий (~, ~а́, ~о́, *pl.* ~**и́),** *adj.* 1. wide, broad (*also fig.*); ~**ая колея́** (*railways*) broad gauge; ш. экра́н (*cinema*) wide screen; в ~**ом смы́сле** in a broad sense. 2. (*fig.*) big, extensive, large-scale, general; ~**ие пла́ны** big plans; ~**ие ма́ссы** the general public; ш. чита́тель the average reader, the general reading public; това́ры ~**ого потребле́ния** (*econ.*) consumer goods; жить на ~**ую но́гу** to live in grand style; у него́ ~**ая нату́ра** he likes to do things in a big way (*not pejor.*).

широко́, *adv.* 1. wide, widely, broadly (*also fig.*); ш. раскры́ть глаза́ to open one's eyes

wide; ш. толкова́ть to interpret loosely. 2. extensively, on a large scale.

широко- wide-, broad-.

широковеща́ни|е, я, *n.* (*radio*) broadcasting.

широковеща́тельный, *adj.* 1. broadcasting. 2. (*pejor.*) loud, loud-mouthed; containing large promises.

ширококоле́йный, *adj.* (*railways*) broad-gauge.

ширококо́стный, *adj.* big-boned.

широкопле́ч|ий (~, ~а), *adj.* broad-shouldered.

широкопо́лый, *adj.* wide-brimmed (*of hats*); full-skirted (*of clothes*).

широкоэкра́нный, *adj.* wide-screen.

широт|а́, ы́, *pl.* ~**ы, ~,** *f.* 1. width, breadth. 2. (*geogr.*) latitude.

широ́тный, *adj.* (*geogr.*) latitudinal, of latitude.

широча́йший, *superl. of* широ́кий.

широче́нный, *adj.* (*coll.*) very wide, broad.

ширпотре́б, а, *m.* (*econ.; coll.*) consumption; (*collect.*) consumer goods.

шир|ь, и, *f.* (wide) expanse; во всю ш. to full width; (*fig.*) to the full extent.

ши́то-кры́то, *adv.* (*coll.*) всё ш.-к. it's all being kept dark.

ши́т|ый, *p.p.p. of* ~**ь** *and adj.* embroidered.

шить, шью, шьёшь, *impf.* (*of* с~) 1. to sew. 2. make (*by sewing*); ш. себе́ что-н. to have something made. 3. (*impf. only*) to embroider.

шить|ё, я́, *n.* 1. sewing, needlework. 2. embroidery.

ши́фер, а, *m.* slate.

ши́фер|ный, *adj. of* ~; ~**ое ма́сло** shale oil.

шифо́н, а, *m.* (*text.*) chiffon.

шифонье́рк|а, и, *f.* chest of drawers.

шифр, а, *m.* 1. cypher, cipher; code. 2. pressmark. 3. (*obs.*) monogram.

шифрова́льщик, а, *m.* cypher clerk.

шифро́в|анный, *p.p.p. of* ~**а́ть** *and adj.* (in) cypher.

шифр|ова́ть, у́ю, *impf.* (*of* за~) to encipher.

шифро́вк|а, и, *f.* 1. enciphering. 2. (*coll.*) cipher communication.

ши́хт|а, ы, *f.* (*tech.*) (*furnace*) charge, batch, burden.

шиш, а́, *m.* (*coll.*) 1. (*vulg.*) fig; показа́ть ш. to pull a long nose. 2. nothing; ни ~**а́** damn all. 3. (*hist.*) ruffian, brigand.

шиша́к, а́, *m.* (*hist.*) spiked helmet.

ши́шк|а, и, *f.* 1. (*bot.*) cone. 2. bump; lump. 3. (*tech.*) (mould) core. 4. (*coll., joc.*) big-wig, big wheel.

шишкова́т|ый (~, ~а), *adj.* knobby, knobbly; bumpy.

шишкови́д|ный (~ен, ~на), *adj.* cone-shaped.

шишконо́сный, *adj.* (*bot.*) coniferous.

шкал|а́, ы́, *pl.* **~ы,** *f.* scale; dial.

шка́лик, а, *m.* (*obs.*) **1.** shkalik (*old Russian unit of liquid volume, equivalent to* 0·06 *litres*). **2.** bottle *or* glass (*containing above measure*).

шка́н|ечный, *adj. of* **~цы;** ш. журна́л log (book).

шка́нц|ы, ев, *no sing.* (*naut.*) quarterdeck.

шкап, а, *m.* (*arch. or dial.*) = шкаф.

шкату́лк|а, и, *f.* box, casket, case.

шкаф, а, о ~е, в ~у́, *pl.* **~ы́,** *m.* cupboard, wardrobe; dresser; вытяжно́й ш. (*tech.*) exhaust hood; духово́й ш. oven; кни́жный ш. bookcase (*with doors*); несгора́емый ш. safe.

шкафу́т, а, *m.* (*naut.*) waist (*of ship*).

шка́фчик, а, *m.* closet, locker.

шквал, а, *m.* squall (*also, fig., of artillery fire*).

шква́листый, *adj.* squally.

шква́льный, *adj.* ш. ого́нь (*mil.*) heavy fire, mass barrage.

шква́р|ки, ок, *sing.* **~ка, ~ки,** *f.* (*cul.*) crackling.

шкво́р|ень, ня, *m.* (*tech.*) pintle, kingpin, kingbolt, draw-bolt.

шкив, а, *pl.* **~ы́,** *m.* (*tech.*) pulley; sheave.

шки́пер, а, *pl.* **~ы** *and* **~а́,** *m.* (*naut.*) skipper, master.

шкод|а, ы, *f.* (*coll.*) **1.** harm, damage. **2.** trick, mischief.

шкодли́в|ый (~, ~а), *adj.* (*coll.*) **1.** harmful. **2.** mischievous.

шко́л|а, ы, *f.* **1.** (*in var. senses*) school; ходи́ть в ~у to go to school; око́нчить ~у to leave school; ш.-интерна́т boarding school; вы́сшая ш. university, college; (*in abstract sense*) higher education. **2.** schooling, training.

шко́л|ить, ю, ишь, *impf.* (*of* вы́~) (*coll.*) to train, discipline.

шко́льник, а, *m.* schoolboy.

шко́льниц|а, ы, *f.* schoolgirl.

шко́льнический, *adj.* schoolboy(ish).

шко́льничеств|о, а, *n.* schoolboyish behaviour, schoolboy tricks.

шко́льн|ый, *adj.* school; ш. во́зраст school age; со ~ой скамьи́ since one's schooldays; ш. учи́тель school-teacher, schoolmaster.

школя́р, á, *m.* (*obs.*) schoolboy.

школя́рств|о, а, *n.* scholasticism, pedantry.

шкот, а, *m.* (*naut.*) sheet.

шко́т|овый, *adj. of* **~;** ш. у́зел sheet bend.

шку́р|а, ы, *f.* **1.** skin (*also fig.*), hide, pelt; волк в ове́чьей ~e wolf in sheep's clothing; быть в чьей-н. ~e to be in someone's shoes; драть ~у (с кого́-н.) to fleece someone; дрожа́ть за свою́ ~y to be concerned for one's own skin; чу́вствовать что-н. на свое́й ~e to know what something feels like. **2.** (*coll., pejor.*) = ~ник.

шку́рк|а, и, *f.* **1.** skin. **2.** (*coll.*) rind. **3.** emery paper, sandpaper.

шку́рник, а, *m.* (*coll., pejor.*) person concerned only with self-advantage.

шку́рный, *adj.* (*pejor.*) selfish, self-seeking.

шла, *see* идти́.

шлагба́ум, а, *m.* barrier (*of swing-beam type, at road or rail crossing*).

шлак, а, *m.* slag; dross; cinder; clinker.

шлакобето́н, а, *m.* slag concrete (*made of slag, cement, and sand*).

шлакобло́к, а, *m.* breeze block (*building material made of cinder with addition of cement*).

шла́к|овый, *adj. of* **~.**

шланг, а, *m.* hose.

шлаф|о́р, а, *m.* = **~ро́к.**

шлафро́к, а, *m.* (*obs.*) housecoat, dressing-gown.

шлейф, а, *m.* train (*of dress*).

шлем[1], а, *m.* helmet.

шлем[2], а, *m.* (*cards*) slam; большо́й, ма́лый ш. grand, little slam.

шлемофо́н, а, *m.* (*mil.*) helmet with ear-phones, intercom head-set.

шлёпан|цы, цев, *sing.* **~ец, ~ца,** *m.* bedroom slippers.

шлёп|ать, аю, *impf.* (*of* ~нуть) **1.** to smack, spank. **2.** (*coll.*) to shuffle; to tramp.

шлёп|аться, аюсь, *impf.* (*of* ~нуться) (*coll.*) to fall with a plop, thud.

шлёп|нуть(ся), ну(сь), нешь(ся), *pf. of* ~ать(ся).

шлеп|о́к, ка́, *m.* smack, slap.

шле|я́, и́, *f.* breech-band, breast-band (*part of harness*).

шли, *see* идти́.

шлифова́льный, *adj.* (*tech.*) polishing, burnishing; grinding; ш. материа́л abrasive(s); ш. стано́к grinding-machine.

шлифова́ни|е, я, *n.* (*tech.*) polishing, burnishing; grinding.

шлиф|ова́ть, у́ю, *impf.* (*of* от~) **1.** (*tech.*) to polish, burnish; to grind. **2.** (*fig.*) to polish, perfect.

шлифо́вк|а, и, *f.* (*tech.*) **1.** polishing, burnishing; grinding. **2.** polish (*result of action*).

шли́хт|а, ы, *f.* (*tech.*) size.

шлихт|ова́ть, у́ю, *impf.* (*tech.*) to smooth, finish; to size, dress.

шло, *see* идти́.

шлюз, а, *m.* lock, sluice, floodgate.

шлюз|ова́ть, у́ю, *impf. and pf.* **1.** to construct locks (on). **2.** to lock through, convey through a lock.

шлюз|ово́й, *adj. of* **~;** ~ова́я ка́мера lock chamber.

шлюпба́лк|а, и, *f.* (*naut.*) davit.

шлю́пк|а, и, *f.* launch, boat; спаса́тельная ш. lifeboat.

шлюх|а, и, *f.* (*vulg.*) streetwalker, tart.

шля́п|а, ы, *f.* 1. hat; дéло в ~e (*coll.*) it's in the bag, all is well. 2. *coll.*, *pejor.*; *of a feeble, helpless person.*

шля́пк|а, и, *f.* 1. (*woman's*) hat. 2. head (*of nail, etc.*); cap (*of mushroom*).

шля́пник, а, *m.* milliner, hatter.

шля́пн|ица, ицы, *f.* of ~ик.

шля́п|ный, *adj.* of ~а.

шля́|ться, юсь, *impf.* (*coll.*) to loaf about.

шлях, а, о ~е, на ~ý, *m.* highway, high road (*in the Ukraine and S. Russia*).

шляхе́т|ский, *adj.* of ~ство and шля́хта.

шляхе́тств|о, а, *n.* 1. = шля́хта. 2. (*hist.*) (Russian) nobility, gentry (*designation used in early 18th century,* = дворя́нство).

шля́хт|а, ы, *f.* (*hist.*) szlachta (*Polish gentry*).

шля́хтич, а, *m.* (*hist.*) member of szlachta.

шмат|о́к, ка́, *m.* (*coll.*) bit, piece.

шмел|ь, я́, *m.* bumble-bee.

шмона́|ть, ю, *impf.* (*sl.*) to frisk.

шмуцти́тул, а, *m.* (*typ.*) bastard-title.

шмы́г|ать, аю, *impf.* (*of* ~ну́ть) (*coll.*) 1. (+*i.*) to rub, brush; ш. но́сом to sniff. 2. to rush up and down.

шмыг|ну́ть, ну́, нёшь, *pf.* (*coll.*) 1. *inst. pf.* of ~ать. 2. to dart, nip, sneak (= to move rapidly, in order to escape notice).

шмя́к|ать, аю, *impf.* (*of* ~нуть) (*coll.*) to drop with a thud.

шмя́к|нуть, ну, нешь, *pf.* of ~ать.

шни́цел|ь, я, *m.* (*cul.*) schnitzel.

шнур, á, *m.* 1. cord; lace. 2. (*electr.*) flex, cable.

шнур|ова́ть, у́ю, *impf.* 1. (*pf.* за~) to lace up. 2. (*pf.* про~) to tie (*leaves of a document, etc.*).

шнур|ова́ться, у́юсь, *impf.* (*of* за~) 1. to lace oneself up. 2. *pass.* of ~ова́ть.

шнуро́вк|а, и, *f.* 1. lacing, tying. 2. (*obs.*) corset.

шнур|ово́й, *adj.* of ~.

шнур|о́к, ка́, *m.* lace.

шныр|ну́ть, ну́, нёшь, *pf.* of ~я́ть.

шныр|я́ть, я́ю, *impf.* (*of* ~ну́ть) (*coll.*) to dart about, dart in and out.

шов, шва, *m.* 1. seam; без шва seamless; держа́ть ру́ки по швам to stand to attention; треща́ть по всем швам (*fig.*) to burst at the seams, fall to pieces, crack up, collapse. 2. stitch (*in embroidery*). 3. (*med.*) stitch, suture; наложи́ть, снять швы to put in, remove stitches. 4. (*tech.*) joint, junction.

шовини́зм, а, *m.* chauvinism.

шовини́ст, а, *m.* chauvinist.

шовинисти́ческий, *adj.* chauvinistic.

шок, а, *m.* (*med.*) shock.

шоки́р|овать, ую, *impf.* to shock.

шокола́д, а, *m.* chocolate.

шокола́дк|а, и, *f.* (*coll.*) bar of chocolate, a chocolate (sweet).

шокола́д|ный, *adj.* 1. *adj.* of ~. 2. chocolate-coloured.

шо́мпол, а, *pl.* ~á, *m.* (*mil.*) 1. cleaning rod. 2. (*obs.*) ramrod.

шо́мпол|ьный, *adj.* of ~; ~ьное ружьё muzzle-loading gun.

шо́рник, а, *m.* saddler, harness-maker.

шо́рн|ый, *adj.* harness; ~ая мастерска́я = ~я.

шо́рн|я, и, *f.* saddler's shop, saddle-maker's, harness-maker's.

шо́рох, а, *m.* rustle.

шо́рт|ы, ~, *no sing.* shorts.

шо́р|ы, ~, *no sing.* 1. blinkers (*also fig.*); держа́ть кого-н. в ~ах (*fig.*) to keep someone in blinkers. 2. harness (*with breech-band, but without collar*).

шоссе́, *indecl.*, *n.* highway; surfaced road.

шоссе́|йный, *adj.* of ~; ~йная доро́га = ~.

шосси́р|овать, ую, *impf. and pf.* to metal, surface (*a road*).

шотла́нд|ец, ца, *m.* Scotsman, Scot.

шотла́нд|ка[1], ки, *f.* of ~ец.

шотла́нд|ка[2], ки, *f.* (*text.*) tartan, plaid.

шотла́ндский, *adj.* Scottish, Scots.

шофёр, а, *m.* driver (*of a motor vehicle*), chauffeur.

шофёр|ский, *adj.* of ~; ~ское свиде́тельство, ~ские права́ driver's, driving licence.

шпа́г|а, и, *f.* sword; обнажи́ть ~y to draw one's sword; скрести́ть ~и to cross swords (*also fig.*); взять на ~y (*obs.*) to gain by the sword; отда́ть ~y (*obs.*) to surrender.

шпага́т, а, *m.* 1. string, cord; (*agric.*) binder twine. 2. (*gymnastics*) the splits.

шпагоглота́тел|ь, я, *m.* sword-swallower.

шпа́жник, а, *m.* (*bot.*) gladiolus.

шпак, а, *m.* (*obs.*, *pejor.*) civilian.

шпакл|ева́ть, юю, юешь, *impf.* (*of* за~) to fill, putty, stop (*holes*); (*naut.*) to caulk.

шпаклёвк|а, и, *f.* 1. filling, puttying, stopping up. 2. putty.

шпа́л|а, ы, *f.* (*railways*) sleeper.

шпале́р|а, ы, *f.* 1. trellis, lattice-work. 2. hedge, line of trees (*lining road*). 3. (*mil.*) line (*of soldiers along ceremonial route*); стоя́ть ~ами to line the route. 4. *pl.* (*obs.*) wall-paper.

шпан|а́, ы́, *f.* (*coll.*) hooligan, ruffian; (*also collect.*) rabble.

шпанго́ут, а, *m.* (*tech.*) frame (*of aircraft*); ribs (*of ship*).

шпа́н|ка, ки, *f.* 1. black cherry. 2. = ~ская му́шка.

шпа́нск|ий, *adj.* ~ая ви́шня black cherry; ~ая му́шка (*zool.*, *med.*) Spanish fly, cantharides.

шпарга́лк|а, и, *f.* (*coll.*) crib (*in school*).

шпа́р|ить, ю, ишь, *impf.* (*of* о~) (*coll.*) 1. to scald, pour boiling water on. 2. to go, speak, read, *etc.*, in a rush.

шпат, а, *m.* (*min.*) spar; полево́й ш. feld-spar.

шпа́тел|ь, я, *m.* 1: (*tech.*, *art*) palette-knife. 2. (*med.*) spatula.

шпа́ци|я, и, *f.* (*typ.*) space.

шпен|ёк, ька́, *m.* pin, peg, prong.

шпига́т, а, *m.* (*naut.*) scupper.

шпиг|ова́ть, у́ю, *impf.* (*of* на~) 1. (*cul.*) to lard. 2. (*coll.*) ш. кого́-н. to suggest to someone, work upon someone, put it into someone's head.

шпик¹, а (у), *m.* (*cul.*) lard.

шпик², а́, *m.* (*coll.*) secret agent; plain--clothes detective.

шпил|ь, я, *m.* 1. spire, steeple. 2. (*naut.*) capstan, windlass.

шпи́льк|а, и, *f.* 1. hairpin; hat-pin. 2. (*tech.*) peg, dowel, cotter pin; tack, brad. 3. (*fig.*) caustic remark; подпусти́ть ~и (кому́-н.) to get at, have a dig at (someone).

шпина́т, а, *m.* spinach.

шпингале́т, а, *m.* 1. catch, latch (*of door or window*). 2. (*coll.*) urchin, boy.

шпио́н, а, *m.* spy.

шпиона́ж, а, *m.* espionage.

шпио́н|ить, ю, ишь, *impf.* (за+*i.*) to spy (on), engage in espionage.

шпио́н|ский, *adj. of* ~.

шпиц¹, а, *m.* (*obs.*) spire, steeple.

шпиц², а, *m.* Pomeranian (*dog*).

шплинт, а, *m.* (*tech.*) split pin, cotter-pin.

шпон, а, *m.* 1. (*typ.*) lead. 2. veneer sheet (*of wood*).

шпо́н|а, ы, *f.* = ~.

шпо́нк|а, и, *f.* (*tech.*) bushing key, dowel.

шпо́р|а, ы, *f.* spur; дать ~ы (+*d.*) to spur on.

шприц, а, *m.* (*med.*) syringe.

шпро́т|ы, ~, *sing.* ~а, ~ы, *f. and* ~, ~а, *m.* sprats.

шпу́льк|а, и, *f.* spool, bobbin.

шпунт, а́, *m.* (*tech.*) groove, tongue, rabbet.

шпур, а, *m.* (*min.*) blast-hole, bore-hole.

шпыня́|ть, ю, *impf.* (*coll.*) to needle, nag.

шрам, а, *m.* scar.

шрапне́л|ь, и, *f.* shrapnel.

шрифт, а, *pl.* ~ы́, *m.* 1. type, type face; курси́вный ш. cursive; прямо́й ш. upright. 2. script.

шрифт|ово́й, *adj. of* ~.

штаб, а, *pl.* ~ы́, *m.* (*mil.*) staff; headquarters.

шта́бел|ь, я, *pl.* ~я́, ~е́й, *m.* stack, pile.

штаби́ст, а, *m.* (*coll.*) staff officer.

штаб-кварти́р|а, ы, *f.* (*mil.*) headquarters.

штабни́к, а́, *m.* (*coll.*) staff officer.

штаб|но́й, *adj. of* ~; ~на́я рабо́та staff work; ~но́е подразделе́ние headquarters unit.

штаб-офице́р, а, *m.* (*mil.*, *hist.*) officer of field rank.

штабс-капита́н, а, *m.* (*hist.*; *in tsarist army*) staff-captain (*officer of rank intermediate between lieutenant and captain*).

штаг, а, *m.* (*naut.*) stay.

штаке́тник, а, *m.* fence, fencing.

шталме́йстер, а, *m.* (*hist.*) equerry.

штамб, а, *m.* (*bot.*) stem, trunk (*of tree*).

штамм, а, *m.* (*biol.*) culture.

штамп, а, *m.* 1. (*tech.*) die, punch. 2. stamp, impress; letter-head. 3. (*fig.*, *pejor.*) cliché, stock phrase.

штампова́льный, *adj.* (*tech.*) punching, stamping, pressing.

штампо́в|анный, *p.p.p. of* ~а́ть *and adj.* 1. (*tech.*) punched, stamped, pressed. 2. (*fig.*) trite, hackneyed; stock, standard.

штамп|ова́ть, у́ю, *impf.* 1. (*tech.*) to punch, press. 2. to stamp, die. 3. (*fig.*) to carry out, go through mechanically; to rubber--stamp.

штампо́вк|а, и, *f.* 1. (*tech.*) punching, pressing; горя́чая ш. drop forging. 2. (die-)stamping.

штампо́|вочный, *adj.* = ~ва́льный.

штампо́вщик, а, *m.* puncher; stamp operator.

шта́нг|а, и, *f.* 1. (*tech.*) bar, rod, beam. 2. (*sport*) weight. 3. (*sport*) crossbar (*of goal*).

штангенци́ркул|ь, я, *m.* (*tech.*) sliding calipers, slide gauge.

штанги́ст, а, *m.* (*sport*) weight-lifter.

штанда́рт, а, *m.* (*obs.*) standard.

штани́н|а, ы, *f.* (*coll.*) trouser-leg.

штани́ш|ки, ек, *no sing.*, *dim. of* штаны́.

штан|ы́, о́в, *no sing.* trousers, breeches.

шта́пел|ь, я, *m.* (*text.*) staple.

шта́пельный, *adj.* (*text.*) staple.

штат¹, а, *m.* state (*administrative unit*); Соединённые ~ы Аме́рики United States of America.

штат², а, *m.* (*sing or pl.*) staff, establishment; ~ы ми́рного вре́мени peace-time establishment; сокраще́ние ~ов reduction of staff; зачи́слить в ш. to take on the staff, establish; оста́ться за ~ом (*i*) (*obs.*) to be disestablished, declared supernumerary, (*ii*) (*fig.*) to be superfluous.

штати́в, а, *m.* tripod, base, support, stand.

шта́т|ный, *adj. of* ~²; ~ная до́лжность established post; ш. рабо́тник permanent member of staff; ~ное расписа́ние list of members of staff.

шта́тск|ий, *adj.* civilian; ~ое (пла́тье) civilian clothes, civvies, mufti; *as noun* ш., ~ого, *m.* civilian.

штафи́рк|а, и, *f.* (*coll.*, *pejor.*) civilian.

штевен|ь, ня, *m.* (*naut.*) stem- or stern-post.

штейгер, а, *m.* foreman miner.

штемпел|ева́ть, юю, юешь, *impf.* (*of* за~) to stamp; to frank, postmark.

штéмпел|ь, я, *pl.* ~я́, *m.* stamp; почто́вый ш. postmark.

штéмпель|ный, *adj. of* ~.

штéпсел|ь, я, *pl.* ~я́, *m.* (*electr.*) plug, socket.

штéпсель|ный, *adj. of* ~; ~ная ви́лка plug; ~ная розéтка socket.

штиблéт|ы, ~, *sing.* ~а, ~ы, *f.* 1. (*lace-up*) boots, shoes. 2. (*obs.*) gaiters.

штил|ево́й, *adj. of* ~ь.

штил|ь, я, *m.* (*naut.*) calm.

штифт, á, *m.* (*tech.*) (joint-)pin, dowel, sprig.

шток, а, *m.* 1. (*tech.*) (coupling) rod; ш. по́ршня piston rod. 2. (*geol.*) stock, shoot.

штокро́з|а, ы, *f.* (*bot.*) hollyhock.

што́льн|я, и, *g. pl.* што́лен, *f.* (*mining*) gallery.

што́пальный, *adj.* darning.

што́паный, *adj.* darned.

што́па|ть, ю, *impf.* (*of* за~) to darn.

што́пк|а, и, *f.* 1. darning. 2. darning thread, wool. 3. (*coll.*) darn (*darned place*).

што́пор, а, *m.* 1. corkscrew. 2. (*aeron.*) spin; ~ом (*as adv.*) in a spin.

што́пор|ить, ю, ишь, *impf.* (*aeron.*) to descend in a spin.

што́р|а, ы, *f.* blind.

шторм, а, *m.* (*naut.*) strong gale; си́льный ш. whole gale (*wind force 9*); жесто́кий ш. storm (*wind force 11*).

шторм|ова́ть, у́ет, *impf.* (*naut.*) to ride out a storm.

шторм|ово́й, *adj. of* ~; вéтер ~ово́й си́лы wind of gale force; ш. костю́м weatherproof clothing.

штормтра́п, а, *m.* (*naut.*) jacob's ladder.

што́р|ный, *adj. of* ~a.

штоф¹, а, *m.* shtof (*old Russian unit of liquid measure* (= 1·23 *litres*) *or bottle of this measure*).

штоф², а, *m.* (*text.*) damask, brocade.

што́ф|ный¹, *adj. of* ~¹; ~ная ла́вка drinking-shop.

што́ф|ный², *adj. of* ~².

штраф, а, *m.* fine; взима́ть ш. (с+*g.*) to fine; наложи́ть ш. to impose a fine.

штрафни́к, á, *m.* (*coll.*) soldier in the 'glass-house'.

штраф|но́й, *adj.* 1. *adj. of* ~. 2. penal, penalty; ш. батальо́н (*mil.*) penal battalion; ш. журна́л (*obs.*) penalties book; ~на́я площа́дка (*sport*) penalty area; ш. уда́р (*sport*) penalty kick.

штраф|ова́ть, у́ю, *impf.* (*of* о~) to fine.

штрейкбрéхер, а, *m.* strike-breaker, black-leg.

штрейкбрéхерств|о, а, *n.* strike-breaking, blacklegging.

штрек, а, *m.* (*mining*) drift.

штри́пк|а, и, *f.* strap.

штрих, á, *m.* 1. stroke (*in drawing*); hachure (*on map*). 2. (*fig.*) feature, trait.

штрих|ова́ть, у́ю, *impf.* (*of* за~) to shade, hatch.

штрих|ово́й, *adj. of* ~; ш. рису́нок line drawing; ш. пункти́р dash line.

штуди́р|овать, ую, *impf.* (*of* про~) to study.

шту́к|а, и, *f.* 1. item, one of a kind (*often not translated*); по рублю́ ш. one rouble each; пять ~ яи́ц five eggs; я возьму́ шесть ~ I'll have six (*of item in question*). 2. piece (*of cloth, fabric*). 3. (*coll.*) thing; вот так ш.! well I'll be damned! 4. (*coll.*) trick; сыгра́ть ~у to play a trick; не ш. it's not too hard, it doesn't take much.

штука́р|ь, я́, *m.* (*coll.*) joker; rogue.

штукату́р, а, *m.* plasterer.

штукату́р|ить, ю, ишь, *impf.* (*of* о~ *and* от~) to plaster.

штукату́рк|а, и, *f.* 1. plastering. 2. plaster. 3. stucco.

штукату́р|ный, *adj. of* ~ка.

штук|ова́ть, у́ю, *impf.* to mend invisibly.

штурва́л, а, *m.* steering-wheel; controls; стоя́ть за ~ом to be at the wheel, helm, controls.

штурва́л|ьный, *adj. of* ~; *as noun* ш., ~ьного, *m.* helmsman, pilot.

штурм, а, *m.* (*mil.*) storm, assault.

шту́рман, а, *pl.* ~ы *and* ~á, *m.* (*naut., aeron.*) navigator.

шту́рман|ский, *adj. of* ~; ~ская ру́бка (*naut.*) chart house.

штурм|ова́ть, у́ю, *impf.* to storm, assault.

штурмови́к, á, *m.* low-flying attack air-craft.

штурмо́вк|а, и, *f.* low-flying air attack.

штурм|ово́й, *adj. of* ~ *and* ~о́вка; ~ова́я авиа́ция ground support aircraft; ~овы́е дéйствия ground support action; ~ова́я лéстница (*hist.*) scaling ladder; ~ова́я ло́дка assault craft; ~ова́я полоса́ assault course; ш. самолёт = ~ови́к.

штурмовщи́н|а, ы, *f.* (*pejor.*) rushed work, production spurt, sporadic effort.

штуф, а, *m.* (*min.*) piece of ore.

шту́цер, а, *pl.* ~á, *m.* 1. carbine. 2. (*tech.*) connecting pipe.

шту́чн|ый, *adj.* (by the) piece; ш. пол parquet floor; ~ая рабо́та piece-work; ш. това́р goods sold by the piece (*and not by weight*); ш. хлеб bread rolls.

штык, á, *m.* 1. bayonet; идти́ в ~й to fight at bayonet point; встрéтить, приня́ть в ~й (*fig.*) to give a hostile reception (to), oppose adamantly. 2. (*mil.*) = man, soldier. 3. (*naut.*) bend. 4. spade's depth. 5. (*min.*) bar, ingot.

штык|овóй, *adj. of* ~; ш. удáр bayonet thrust.

штыр|ь, я́, *m.* (*tech.*) pin, dowel, pintle.

шýб|а, ы, *f.* fur coat.

шýб|ный, *adj.* 1. *adj. of* ~a. 2. fur-bearing. 3. ш. клей (*obs.*) carpenter's glue.

шуг|á, и́, *f.* sludge ice.

шуг|áть, áю, *impf.* (*of* ~нýть) (*coll.*) to scare off.

шуг|нýть, нý, нёшь, *pf. of* ~áть.

шýйц|а, ы, *f.* (*arch.*) left hand.

шýлер, а, *pl.* ~á, *m.* card-sharper, cheat.

шýлер|ский, *adj. of* ~.

шýлерств|о, а, *n.* card-sharping, sharp practice.

шум, а (у), *m.* 1. noise. 2. din, uproar, racket; поднять ш. to kick up a racket. 3. (*fig.*) sensation, stir.

шум|éть, лю́, и́шь, *impf.* 1. to make a noise. 2. (*coll.*) to row, wrangle. 3. (*coll.*) to make a stir, fuss; to cause a sensation, stir.

шуми́х|а, и, *f.* (*coll.*) sensation, stir.

шумли́в|ый (~, ~а), *adj.* noisy.

шýм|ный (~ен, ~нá, ~но), *adj.* 1. noisy; loud. 2. sensational.

шумови́к, á, *m.* (*theatr.*) sound effects man.

шумóвк|а, и, *f.* (*cul.*) perforated spoon, straining spoon.

шум|овóй, *adj. of* ~; ш. оркéстр percussion band; ш. фон (*radio*) background noise; ~овы́е эффéкты sound effects.

шум|óк, кá, *m.* (*coll.*) noise; под ш. on the quiet.

шýр|ин, ина, *pl.* ~ья́, ~ьёв *m.* brother-in-law (*wife's brother*).

шур|овáть, ýю, *impf.* to stoke, poke (*a furnace*).

шурýп, а, *m.* (*tech.*) screw.

шурф, а, *m.* (*mining*) prospecting shaft.

шурф|овáть, ýю, *impf.* (*mining*) to excavate, make a prospecting dig.

шурш|áть, ý, и́шь, *impf.* to rustle (*also* +*i.*, *trans.*), crackle.

шýры-мýры, *indecl. pl.* (*coll.*) love affair(s).

шýст|рый (~ёр, ~рá, ~ро), *adj.* (*coll.*) smart, bright, sharp.

шут, á, *m.* 1. (*hist.*) fool, jester. 2. fool, buffoon, clown; разыгрáть ~á to play the fool. 3. (*coll.*) *in certain phrases* devil; на кой ш.?, какóго ~a? why the devil?

шу|ти́ть, чý, ~тишь, *impf.* (*of* по~) 1. to joke, jest; я же не ~чý but I'm not joking; чем чёрт не ~тит! (*coll.*) we can but see (what will happen)! 2. (с+*i.*) to play with), trifle (with); ш. с огнём to play with fire. 3. (над) to laugh (at), make fun (of).

шути́х|а, и, *f.* 1. *f. of* шут. 2. firecracker, rocket.

шýтк|а, и, *f.* 1. joke, jest; не ш. it's no joke; ш. (ли) +*inf.* it's not so easy, it's no laughing matter (to); с ней ~и плóхи she is not to be trifled with; ~и в стóрону, ~и прочь let's get down to business; без шýток joking apart; сказáть в ~у to say as a joke; не на ~у in earnest. 2. trick; сыгрáть ~у (с+*i.*) to play a trick (on). 3. (*theatr.*) farce.

шутли́в|ый (~, ~а), *adj.* 1. humorous. 2. joking, light-hearted.

шутни́к, á, *m.* joker, wag.

шут|овскóй, *adj. of* шут; ш. колпáк fool's cap; ~овски́е вы́ходки clowning, buffoon-ery.

шутовств|ó, á, *n.* buffoonery.

шýточ|ный (~ен, ~на), *adj.* comic; joking; дéло не ~ное it's no joke, no laughing matter.

шут|я́, *pres. gerund of* ~и́ть *and adv.* 1. easily, lightly; ш. отдéлаться to get off lightly. 2. for fun, in jest; не ш. in earnest.

шýшер|а, ы, *f.* (*coll.*) rubbish; riff-raff.

шушýка|ться, юсь, *impf.* (*coll.*) to whisper; (*fig.*) to gossip.

шхéр|ный, *adj. of* ~ы.

шхéр|ы, ~, *no sing.* (*geogr.*) skerries.

шхýн|а, ы, *f.* schooner.

Щ

щавéл|евый, *adj.* 1. *adj. of* ~ь. 2. (*chem.*) oxalic; соль ~евой кислоты́ oxalate.

щавéл|ь, я́, *m.* (*bot.*) sorrel (*Rumex*).

щавéльник, а, *m.* (*coll.*) sorrel soup.

ща|ди́ть, жý, ди́шь, *impf.* (*of* по~) to spare; to have mercy (on); щ. чьи-н. чýвства to spare someone's feelings; не щ. врагóв to give one's enemies no quarter.

щебёнк|а, и, *f.* = щéбень.

щéб|ень, ня, *m.* 1. crushed stone, ballast (*as road surfacing*). 2. (*geol.*) detritus.

щéбет, а, *m.* twitter, chirp.

щебетáни|е, я, *n.* twittering, chirping.

щебе|тáть, чý, ~чешь, *impf.* to twitter, chirp.

щегл|ёнок, ёнка, *pl.* ~я́та, *m.* 1. young goldfinch. 2. = щегóл.

щег|óл, лá, *m.* goldfinch.

щеголевáт|ый (~, ~а), *adj.* foppish, dandified.

щёгол|ь, я, *m.* fop, dandy.

щегол|ьнýть, ьнý, ьнёшь, *pf. of* ~я́ть 2.

щегольскóй, *adj.* foppish, dandified.

щегольств|ó, á, *n.* foppishness, dandyism.

щего́л|я́ть, я́ю, *impf.* 1. to dress ultra-fashionably, foppishly; to strut around. 2. (*pf.* ~ьну́ть) (+*i.*; *coll.*) to show off, parade, flaunt.

щедрост|ь, и, *f.* generosity.

щедро́т|ы, ~, *sing.* ~а, ~ы, *f.* (*obs.*) munificence; подари́ть от свои́х ~ (*iron.*) to donate generously.

ще́др|ый (~, ~а́, ~о), *adj.* 1. generous. 2. lavish, liberal; щ. на похвалы́ lavish in praises.

щек|а́, и́, *a.* ~у, *pl.* ~и, ~, ~а́м, *f.* 1. cheek; уда́рить кого́-н. по ~е́ to slap someone's face; упи́сывать, уплета́ть за о́бе ~и́ (*coll.*) to eat ravenously, guzzle. 2. (*tech.*) side, sidepiece, stock.

щеко́лд|а, ы, *f.* latch; catch, pawl.

щеко|та́ть, чу́, ~чешь, *impf.* (*of* по~) 1. to tickle (*also fig.*) 2. (*impers.*) у меня́ в го́рле, *etc.*, ~чет I have a tickle in my throat, *etc.*

щеко́тк|а, и, *f.* tickling; боя́ться ~и to be ticklish.

щекотли́в|ый (~, ~а), *adj.* 1. ticklish, delicate; ~ая те́ма delicate topic. 2. (*obs.*) = щепети́льный.

щеко́тно, *as pred.* (*impers.*; +*i.*) it tickles.

щел|ево́й, *adj.* 1. *adj. of* ~ь. 2. = ~и́нный.

щели́нный, *adj.* (*ling.*) fricative.

щели́ст|ый (~, ~а), *adj.* (*coll.*) full of chinks.

щёлк, а, *m.* snap, crack.

щёлк|а, и, *f.* chink.

щёлкань|е, я, *n.* 1. flicking. 2. clicking, snapping, cracking, popping. 3. trilling (*of some birds*).

щёлк|ать, аю, *impf.* (*of* ~нуть) 1. to flick. 2. (+*i.*) to click, snap, crack, pop; щ. затво́ром to click the shutter (*of a camera*); щ. па́льцами to snap one's fingers; щ. кнуто́м to crack a whip. 3. (*impf. only*) to crack (*nuts*). 4. (*impf. only*) to trill (*of some birds*).

щёлк|нуть, ну, нешь, *pf. of* ~ать.

щелкопёр, а, *m.* (*obs., pejor.*) scribbler, hack.

щелку́нчик, а, *m.* nutcracker.

щёлок, а, *m.* alkaline solution, lye.

щелочно́й, *adj.* (*chem.*) alkaline.

щёлочност|ь, и, *f.* (*chem.*) alkalinity.

щёлоч|ь, и, *pl.* ~и, ~е́й, *f.* (*chem.*) alkali.

щелч|о́к, ка́, *m.* 1. flick (of the fingers). 2. (*fig., coll.*) insult, slight, blow.

щел|ь, и, *pl.* ~и, ~е́й, *f.* 1. crack; chink; slit; fissure, crevice. 2. (*mil.*) slit trench. 3. голосова́я щ. (*anat.*) glottis.

щем|и́ть, и́т, *impf.* 1. (*coll.*) to press, pinch. 2. to oppress, grieve (*also impers.*).

щем|я́щий, *pres. part. act. of* ~и́ть *and adj.* 1. aching, nagging; ~я́щая боль ache. 2. (*fig.*) painful, melancholy, oppressive.

щен|и́ться, и́тся, *impf.* (*of* о~) to whelp cub.

щен|о́к, ка́, *pl.* ~ки́, ~ко́в *and* ~я́та, ~я́т, *m.* puppy, pup (*also fig.*); whelp, cub.

щеп|а́, ы́, *pl.* ~ы, ~, ~а́м, *f.* (*wood*) splinter, chip; (*collect.*) kindling.

щеп|а́ть, лю́, ~лешь, *impf.* to chip, chop (*wood*).

щепети́л|ьный (~ен, ~ьна), *adj.* punctilious, correct; (over-)scrupulous, fussy, finicky.

ще́пк|а, и, *f.* = щепа́; худо́й как щ. thin as a rake; лес ру́бят — ~и летя́т (*prov.*) you can't make omelettes without breaking eggs.

щепо́т|ка, ки, *f.* = щепо́ть.

щепо́т|ь, и, *f.* pinch (*of salt, snuff, etc.*).

щерба́т|ый (~, ~а), *adj.* 1. dented; chipped. 2. (*coll.*) pock-marked. 3. (*coll.*) gap-toothed.

щерби́н|а, ы, *f.* 1. indentation; gap, hole. 2. pock-mark.

щети́н|а, ы, *f.* bristle; (*coll.*) stubble (*of beard*).

щети́нист|ый (~, ~а), *adj.* bristly, bristling; (*coll.*) stubble-covered.

щети́н|иться, ится, *impf.* (*of* о~) to bristle (*also fig.*).

щётк|а, и, *f.* 1. brush (*also electr.*); зубна́я щ. toothbrush; щ. для воло́с hairbrush. 2. fetlock.

щёт|очный, *adj. of* ~ка; щ. па́лец (*electr.*) brush-holder arm.

щёчный, *adj. of* щека́.

щи, щей (*coll.* щец), щам, ща́ми, о щах, *no sing.* shchi (*cabbage soup*); попа́сть как кур во́ щи to get into hot water.

щи́колотк|а, и, *f.* ankle.

щип|а́ть, лю́, ~лешь, *impf.* 1. (*pf.* ~ну́ть) to pinch, nip, tweak. 2. (*impf. only*) to sting, bite (*of frost, etc.*); to burn (*of condiments, hot liquids, etc.*). 3. (*impf. only*) to nibble, munch, browse (on). 4. (*pf.* об~ *and* о~) to pluck.

щип|а́ться, лю́сь, ~лешься, *impf.* (*coll.*) 1. to pinch (each other). 2. *pass. of* ~а́ть.

щип|е́ц, ца́, *m.* 1. (*archit.*) gable. 2. (*hunting*) muzzle (*of dog*).

щипко́в|ый, *adj.* ~ые музыка́льные инструме́нты (*mus.*) stringed instruments played by plucking.

щипко́м, *adv.* (*mus.*) pizzicato.

щип|ну́ть, ну́, нёшь, *pf. of* ~а́ть 1.

щип|о́к, ка́, *m.* pinch, nip, tweak.

щипц|ы́, о́в, *no sing.* tongs, pincers, pliers; forceps; щ. для зави́вки воло́с curling-irons; щ. для са́хара sugar-tongs.

щи́пчик|и, ов, *no sing.* tweezers.

щит, а́, *m.* 1. (*in var. senses*) shield; подня́ть на щ. to extol, eulogize, boost; верну́ться на ~е́ to suffer defeat; верну́ться со ~о́м to be triumphant, victorious. 2. (*tech.*) shield, screen. 3. sluice-gate. 4. (*zool.*) (tortoise-)shell; scutum. 5. (display) board.

6. (*tech.*) panel; распредели́тельный щ. switchboard.

щитови́дный, *adj.* (*anat.*) thyroid.

щит|о́к, ка́, *m.* **1.** *dim. of* ~ 2–6; dashboard (*of motor vehicle*). **2.** (*zool.*) thorax. **3.** (*bot.*) cyme, corymb.

щу́к|а, и, *f.* pike (*fish*).

щуп, а, *m.* (*tech.*) **1.** probe, sounding borer. **2.** (*mil.*) probing rod (*in mine detection*). **3.** clearance gauge.

щу́пальц|е, а, *g. pl.* **щу́палец**, *n.* (*zool.*) tentacle; antenna.

щу́па|ть, ю, *impf.* (*of* по~) to feel (for),

touch; to probe; щ. глаза́ми to scan; щ. пульс (*med.*) to feel the pulse.

щу́пл|ый (~, ~á, ~o), *adj.* weak, puny, frail.

щур[1], а, *m.* (*ethnol.*) ancestor.

щур[2], á, *m.* (*orn.*) pine grosbeak.

щу́р|ить, ю, ишь, *impf.* (*of* со~); щ. глаза́ = ~иться.

щу́р|иться, юсь, ишься, *impf.* (*of* со~) **1.** to screw up one's eyes. **2.** (*of the eyes*) to narrow.

щу́рк|а, и, *f.* (*orn.*) bee-eater.

щу́|чий, *adj. of* ~ка; как по ~чьему веле́нью as if of its own volition, as if by magic.

Э

эбе́новый, *adj.* ebony.

эбони́т, а, *m.* ebonite.

э́ва[1], *particle* (*coll. or dial.*) there is, here is.

э́ва[2], *interj.* (*coll.*) **1.** (*expressing surprise, incredulity, etc.*) what's that!; you don't mean to say so! **2.** (*expressing disagreement*) nonsense!

эвако- = эвакуацио́нный.

эвакуацио́нный, *adj. of* эвакуа́ция; э. пункт evacuation centre; э. райо́н evacuation area.

эвакуа́ци|я, и, *f.* evacuation.

эвакуи́ров|анный, *p.p.p. of* ~ать; *as noun* э., ~анного, *m. and* ~анная, ~анной, *f.* evacuee.

эвакуи́р|овать, ую, *impf. and pf.* to evacuate (*trans.*).

эвакуи́р|оваться, уюсь, *impf. and pf.* **1.** to evacuate (*intrans.*). **2.** *pass. of* ~овать.

эвентуа́л|ьный (~ен, ~ьна), *adj.* possible.

эвкали́пт, а, *m.* (*bot.*) eucalyptus.

эвкали́пт|овый, *adj. of* ~; ~овое ма́сло eucalyptus oil.

эволюциони́р|овать, ую, *impf. and pf.* to evolve.

эволюциони́ст, а, *m.* evolutionist.

эволюцио́нн|ый, *adj.* evolutionary; ~ое уче́ние (*biol.*) doctrine of evolution.

эволю́ци|я, и, *f.* **1.** evolution. **2.** (*mil.*) manœuvre.

эвристи́ческий, *adj.* (*philos.*) heuristic.

эвфеми́зм, а, *m.* euphemism.

эвфемисти́ческий, *adj.* euphemistic.

эвфони́ческий, *adj.* euphonious.

эвфони́|я, и, *f.* euphony.

эги́д|а, ы, *f.* aegis; под ~ой (+*g.*) under the aegis (of).

эгои́зм, а, *m.* egoism, selfishness.

эгои́ст, а, *m.* egoist.

эгоисти́ческий, *adj.* egoistic, selfish.

эгоисти́ч|ный (~ен, ~на), *adj.* = ~еский.

эгре́т, а, *m.* egret-plume.

э́дак(ий) = э́так(ий).

эдельве́йс, а, *m.* (*bot.*) edelweiss.

эзо́пов = ~ский.

эзо́повский, *adj.* Aesopian; э. язык 'Aesopian language' (*especially of allegorical language used by Russian non-conformist publicists to conceal anti-régime sentiments*).

эй, *interj.* heigh!, hi!

эк[1], *adv.* (*coll.*) how.

эк[2] (and э́ко, э́ка), *particle* (*coll.*) *expressing surprise, indignation, etc.* my goodness!

эквадо́р|ец, ца, *m.* Ecuadorian.

эквадо́р|ка, ки, *f. of* ~ец.

эквадо́рский, *adj.* Ecuadorian.

эква́тор, а, *m.* equator.

экваториа́льный, *adj.* equatorial.

эквивале́нт, а, *m.* equivalent.

эквивале́нт|ный (~ен, ~на), *adj.* equivalent.

эквилибри́ст, а, *m.* tightrope-walker.

эквилибри́стик|а, и, *f.* tightrope-walking (*also fig.*).

экзальта́ци|я, и, *f.* exaltation; excitement.

экзальти́рован|ный (~, ~на), *adj.* in a state of exaltation, exalté, excited.

экза́мен, а, *m.* examination; держа́ть, сдава́ть э. to take, sit an examination; вы́держать, сдать э. to pass an examination; провали́ться на ~e to fail an examination.

экзамена́тор, а, *m.* examiner.

экзамен|ацио́нный, *adj. of* экза́мен; э. биле́т examination question(-paper); ~ацио́нная се́ссия examination period, exams.

экзамен|ова́ть, у́ю, *impf.* (*of* про~) to examine.

экзамен|ова́ться, у́юсь, *impf.* (*of* про~) **1.** to go in for an examination. **2.** *pass. of* ~ова́ть.

экзамен|у́ющийся, *pres. part. of* ~ова́ться; *as noun* э., ~у́ющегося, *m.* examinee.

экза́рх, а, *m.* (*eccl.*) exarch.

экзарха́т, а, *m.* (*eccl.*) exarchate.

экзеку́тор, а, *m.* (*obs.*) administrator.

экзеку́ци|я, и, *f.* (*obs.*) 1. corporal punishment. 2. (*leg.*) execution.

экзе́м|а, ы, *f.* (*med.*) eczema.

экземпля́р, а, *m.* 1. copy; в двух, трёх ~ах in duplicate, in triplicate; переписа́ть в двух ~ах to make two copies. 2. specimen, example.

экзистенциали́зм, а, *m.* existentialism.

экзистенциали́ст, а, *m.* existentialist.

экзо- exo-.

экзо́тик|а, и, *f.* exotica, exotic objects.

экзоти́ческий, *adj.* exotic.

экивóк|и, ов, *sing.* ~, ~а, *m.* 1. double entendre. 2. quibbling, evasion, hedging; говори́ть без ~ов to call a spade a spade. 3. subtleties, intricacies.

э́кий, *pron.* (*coll.*) what (a).

экипа́ж¹, а, *m.* carriage.

экипа́ж², а, *m.* crew (*of ship, aircraft, tank*); ship's company.

экипир|ова́ть, у́ю, *impf. and pf.* to equip.

экипирóвк|а, и, *f.* 1. equipping. 2. equipment.

э́ккер, а, *m.* (*geod.*) cross-staff (*instrument for erecting a perpendicular*).

эклекти́зм, а, *m.* eclecticism.

экле́ктик, а, *m.* eclectic.

эклекти́ч|ный (~ен, ~на), *adj.* eclectic.

экли́птик|а, и, *f.* (*astron.*) ecliptic.

эклóг|а, и, *f.* (*lit.*) eclogue.

э́ко, *see* эк².

экологи́ческий, *adj.* ecological.

эколóги|я, и, *f.* ecology.

эконóм, а, *m.* (*obs.*) 1. steward, housekeeper. 2. economist.

экономáйзер, а, *m.* (*tech.*) economiser, waste gas heater.

экономи́зм, а, *m.* (*hist., polit.*) economism.

эконóмик|а, и, *f.* 1. economics. 2. economy (*of a country, etc.*).

экономи́ст, а, *m.* economist.

эконóм|ить, лю, ишь, *impf.* (*of* с~) 1. to use sparingly, husband; to save. 2. (на+*p.*) to economise (on), save (on).

экономи́ческ|ий, *adj.* economic; э. райóн economic region; э. журна́л economics journal; ~ая горе́лка pilot burner; ~ая скóрость cruising speed.

экономи́ч|ный (~ен, ~на), *adj.* economical.

экономи|я, и, *f.* 1. economy, saving; режи́м ~и economy effort; соблюда́ть ~ю to economize. 2. полити́ческая э. political economy. 3. (*obs.*) estate.

эконóмк|а, и, *f.* housekeeper.

эконóмнича|ть, ю, *impf.* (*coll.*) to be (excessively) economical.

эконóм|ный (~ен, ~на), *adj.* economical; careful, thrifty.

экра́н, а, *m.* 1. (*cinema*) screen. 2. (*fig.*) screen (= cinema industry, cinema art). 3. (*phys., tech.*) screen, shield, shade.

экраниза́ци|я, и, *f.* (*cinema*) filming, screening; film version (*of novel, etc.*).

экранизи́р|овать, ую, *impf. and pf.* (*cinema*) to film, screen.

экрани́р|овать, ую, *impf. and pf.* (*tech.*) to screen, shield.

экс-, ех-.

экскава́тор, а, *m.* (*tech.*) excavator, earth-moving machine.

экскава́торщик, а, *m.* excavator operator.

экскремéнт|ы, ов, *no sing.* excrement.

э́кскурс, а, *m.* excursus, digression.

экскурса́нт, а, *m.* tourist; participant in (conducted) tour *or* excursion.

экскурс|иóнный, *adj. of* ~ия.

экскýрси|я, и, *f.* 1. excursion, (conducted) tour, trip; outing. 2. tourist group, excursion party.

экскурсовóд, а, *m.* guide.

экслибрис, а, *m.* book-plate.

экспанси́в|ный (~ен, ~на), *adj.* effusive.

экспансиони́зм, а, *m.* (*polit.*) expansionism.

экспа́нси|я, и, *f.* (*polit.*) expansion.

экспеди́р|овать, ую, *impf. and pf.* to despatch.

экспеди́тор, а, *m.* 1. forwarding agent, shipping clerk. 2. (*obs.*) head clerk (*head of a section in a large office*).

экспедициóнный, *adj.* 1. despatch, forwarding. 2. expeditionary.

экспеди́ци|я, и, *f.* 1. despatch, forwarding. 2. despatch office. 3. (*obs.*) section, department (*of an office*). 4. expedition.

эксперимéнт, а, *m.* experiment.

экспериментáльный, *adj.* experimental.

экспериментáтор, а, *m.* experimenter.

эксперименти́р|овать, ую, *impf.* (над, с+*i.*) to experiment (on, with).

экспéрт, а, *m.* expert.

эксперти́з|а, ы, *f.* (*leg., med.*) 1. (expert) examination, expert opinion; произвести́ ~у to make an examination. 2. commission of experts.

экспéрт|ный, *adj. of* ~; ~ная комиссия commission of experts.

эксплози́вный, *adj.* (*ling.*) plosive.

эксплуата́тор, а, *m.* exploiter.

эксплуатац|иóнный, *adj. of* ~ия 2; ~иóнные ка́чества operating characteristics; ~иóнные расхóды running costs; ~иóнные услóвия working conditions.

эксплуата́ци|я, и, *f.* 1. (*polit.; pejor.*) exploitation. 2. exploitation (*econ.*); utilization; operation, running; сдать в ~ю to commission, put into operation.

эксплуати́р|овать, ую, *impf.* **1.** (*polit.*; *pejor.*) to exploit. **2.** to exploit (*econ.*); to operate, run, work.

экспози́ци|я, и, *f.* **1.** layout (*of an exhibition, etc.*). **2.** (*lit.*) exposition. **3.** (*phot.*) exposure.

экспона́т, а, *m.* exhibit.

экспоне́нт, а, *m.* **1.** exhibitor. **2.** (*math.*) exponent, index.

экспони́р|овать, ую, *impf. and pf.* **1.** to exhibit. **2.** (*phot.*) to expose.

экспоно́метр, а, *m.* (*phot.*) exposure meter.

э́кспорт, а, *m.* export.

экспортёр, а, *m.* exporter.

экспорти́р|овать, ую, *impf. and pf.* to export.

э́кспорт|ный, *adj.* of ~.

экспре́сс, а, *m.* express (*train, motor coach, etc.*).

экспресси́в|ный (~ен, ~на), *adj.* expressive.

экспрессиони́зм, а, *m.* (*art*) expressionism.

экспре́сси|я, и, *f.* expression.

экспре́сс|ный, *adj.* of ~.

экспро́мт, а, *m.* impromptu, improvisation, extemporisation.

экспро́мтом, *adv.* **1.** impromptu; петь, игра́ть, *etc.*, э. to extemporise, improvise. **2.** suddenly, without warning.

экспроприа́тор, а, *m.* expropriator.

экспроприа́ци|я, и, *f.* expropriation.

экспроприи́р|овать, ую, *impf. and pf.* to expropriate, dispossess.

экста́з, а, *m.* ecstasy.

экстенси́в|ный (~ен, ~на), *adj.* extensive.

экстерн, а, *m.* **1.** external student; око́нчить университе́т ~ом to take an external degree. **2.** (*obs.*) externe (*unpaid hospital doctor*).

экстерна́т, а, *m.* external studies.

экстерриториа́льност|ь, и, *f.* extraterritoriality, exterritoriality.

экстерриториа́л|ьный (~ен, ~ьна), *adj.* extraterritorial, exterritorial.

экстерье́р, а, *m.* form, figure (*of an animal*).

экстравага́нт|ный (~ен, ~на), *adj.* eccentric, bizarre, preposterous.

экстраги́р|овать, ую, *impf. and pf.* (*chem., med.*) to extract.

экстради́ци|я, и, *f.* (*leg.*) extradition.

экстра́кт, а, *m.* **1.** (*cul.*) extract. **2.** resumé, précis.

экстра́кци|я, и, *f.* (*chem., med.*) extraction.

экстраордина́р|ный (~ен, ~на), *adj.* extraordinary; э. профе́ссор (*obs.*) professor extraordinary.

э́кстрен|ный (~, ~на), *adj.* **1.** urgent; emergency; э. вы́зов urgent summons; в ~ном слу́чае in case of emergency. **2.** extra, special; ~ное заседа́ние extraordinary session; ~ное изда́ние special edition.

эксце́нтрик¹, а, *m.* **1.** clown. **2.** (*obs.*) eccentric (person).

эксце́нтрик², а, *m.* (*tech.*) cam, eccentric.

эксце́нтрик|а, и, *f.* clowning.

эксцентрицте́т, а, *m.* (*tech.*) eccentricity, off-centre.

эксцентри́ческий, *adj.* (*tech.*) eccentric.

эксцентри́чност|ь, и, *f.* eccentricity.

эксцентри́ч|ный (~ен, ~на), *adj.* eccentric.

эксце́сс, а, *m.* excess.

экумени́ческий, *adj.* ecumenical, oecumenical.

эласти́ч|ный (~ен, ~на), *adj.* **1.** elastic (*also fig.*). **2.** (*fig.*) springy, resilient.

элева́тор, а, *m.* **1.** (*agric.*) elevator. **2.** (*tech.*) hoist.

элега́нтност|ь, и, *f.* elegance.

элега́нт|ный (~ен, ~на), *adj.* elegant, smart.

элеги́ческий, *adj.* (*lit., mus.*) elegiac.

элеги́ч|ный (~ен, ~на), *adj.* melancholy.

эле́ги|я, и, *f.* (*lit., mus.*) elegy.

электриза́ци|я, и, *f.* (*phys., med.*) electrification; treatment by electric charge(s).

электриз|ова́ть, у́ю, *impf.* **1.** (*phys., med.*) to electrify, subject to electric charge(s). **2.** (*fig.*) to electrify.

эле́ктрик, а, *m.* electrician.

электри́к, *adj.*, *indecl.* electric blue.

электрифика́ци|я, и, *f.* electrification.

электрифици́р|овать, ую, *impf. and pf.* (*tech.*) to electrify.

электри́ческий, *adj.* electric(al).

электри́честв|о, а, *n.* **1.** electricity. **2.** electric light; заже́чь э. to turn on the light.

электри́чк|а, и, *f.* (*coll.*) (suburban) electric train.

электро- electro-.

электробытов|о́й, *adj.* electrical; ~ы́е прибо́ры electrical appliances (*irons, cleaners, etc.*).

электрово́з, а, *m.* electric locomotive.

электро́д, а, *m.* (*phys.*) electrode.

электродви́гател|ь, я, *m.* electric motor.

электродви́жущий, *adj.* (*phys.*) electromotive.

электродина́мик|а, и, *f.* electrodynamics.

электродои́льный, *adj.* electric milking.

электродо́йк|а, и, *f.* **1.** electric milking. **2.** electric milking machine.

электродугов|о́й, *adj.* ~а́я сва́рка electric arc welding.

электроёмкост|ь, и, *f.* (*phys.*) capacity.

электрока́р, а, *m.* electric trolley, float.

электрола́мп|а, ы, *f.* electric light bulb.

электролече́ни|е, я, *n.* (*med.*) electrical treatment.

электро́лиз, а, *m.* (*phys.*) electrolysis.

электромагни́т, а, *m.* electromagnet.

электромагни́тный, *adj.* electromagnetic.

электромеха́ник|а, и, *f.* electromechanics.
электромонтёр, а, *m.* electrician.
электро́н, а, *m.* (*phys.*) electron.
электро́ник|а, и, *f.* electronics.
электро́нно- electronic-.
электро́н|ный, *adj.* 1. *adj. of* ~; ~ная ла́мпа electron tube, thermionic valve; э. микроско́п electron microscope. 2. electronic; ~ная вычисли́тельная маши́на electronic computer.
электропереда́ч|а, и, *f.* electricity transmission.
электропе́ч|ь, и, *f.* electric furnace.
электропо́езд, а, *m.* electric train.
электроприбо́р, а, *m.* electrical appliance.
электропро́вод, а, *m.* electricity cable.
электропрово́дк|а, и, *f.* electric wiring.
электропромы́шленност|ь, и, *f.* electrical industry.
электросва́рк|а, и, *f.* electric welding.
электросилово́й, *adj.* electric power.
электроста́л|ь, и, *f.* electric steel.
электроста́нци|я, и, *f.* electric power station.
электроте́хник, а, *m.* electrical engineer.
электроте́хник|а, и, *f.* electrical engineering.
электротех|ни́ческий, *adj. of* ~ника.
электротя́г|а, и, *f.* electric traction.
электрохими́ческий, *adj.* electrochemical.
электрохи́ми|я, и, *f.* electro-chemistry.
электроцентра́л|ь, и, *f.* electric power plant.
электрочайник, а, *m.* electric kettle.
электроэне́рги|я, и, *f.* electrical energy, electric power.
элеме́нт, а, *m.* 1. (*in var. senses*) element. 2. (*coll.*) type, character; подозри́тельный э. suspicious type. 3. (*electr.*) cell; сухо́й э. dry cell.
элемента́р|ный (~ен, ~на), *adj.* (*in var. senses*) elementary.
элеро́н, а, *m.* (*aeron.*) aileron.
эли́зи|я, и, *f.* elision.
эли́т|а, ы, *f.* 1. (*collect.*; *agric.*) best specimens; э. карто́феля highest-quality potatoes. 2. élite.
эли́т|ный, *adj. of* ~а.
э́ллин, а, *m.* ancient Greek, Hellene.
э́ллинг, а, *m.* 1. (*naut.*) slipway. 2. (*aeron.*) shed, hangar (*for airships or balloons*).
эллини́зм, а, *m.* 1. Hellenism. 2. (*hist.*) the Hellenistic period.
эллини́ст, а, *m.* Hellenist.
эллинисти́ческий, *adj.* (*hist.*) Hellenistic.
э́ллин|ка, ки, *f. of* ~.
э́ллинский, *adj.* ancient Greek, Hellenic.
э́ллипс, а, *m.* (*math.*, *lit.*) ellipse.
э́ллипс|ис, а, *m.* = ~.
эллипти́ческий, *adj.* elliptic(al).

эл|ь, я, *m.* ale.
эльф, а, *m.* elf.
элю́ви|й, я, *m.* (*geol.*) eluvium.
эма́левый, *adj.* enamel.
эмалиро́в|анный, *p.p.p. of* ~а́ть *and adj.* enamelled; ~анная посу́да enamel ware.
эмалир|ова́ть, у́ю, *impf.* to enamel.
эмалиро́вк|а, и, *f.* 1. enamelling. 2. enamel.
эма́л|ь, и, *f.* enamel.
эмана́ци|я, и, *f.* emanation.
эмансипа́ци|я, и, *f.* emancipation.
эмансипи́р|овать, ую, *impf. and pf.* to emancipate.
эмба́рго, *indecl.*, *n.* (*econ.*) embargo; наложи́ть э. (на + *a.*) to embargo, place an embargo (on).
эмбле́м|а, ы, *f.* 1. emblem. 2. (*mil.*) insignia.
эмбо́ли|я, и, *f.* (*med.*) embolism.
эмбриоло́ги|я, и, *f.* embryology.
эмбрио́н, а, *m.* (*biol.*) embryo.
эмерита́льн|ый, *adj.* ~ая ка́сса old age insurance scheme.
эмериту́р|а, ы, *f.* (*obs.*) old age benefit (*secured by voluntary contributions*).
эмигра́нт, а, *m.* emigré, emigrant.
эмигра́нт|ский, *adj. of* ~.
эмигра|цио́нный, *adj. of* ~ция.
эмигра́ци|я, и, *f.* 1. emigration. 2. (*collect.*) emigration, emigrés.
эмигри́р|овать, ую, *impf. and pf.* to emigrate.
эмисса́р, а, *m.* emissary.
эмисс|ио́нный, *adj. of* ~ия.
эми́сси|я, и, *f.* (*fin.*, *phys.*) emission.
эмоциона́л|ьный (~ен, ~ьна), *adj.* emotional.
эмо́ци|я, и, *f.* emotion.
эмпире́|й, я, *m.* empyrean; вита́ть в ~ях to have one's head in the clouds.
эмпири́зм, а, *m.* empiricism.
эмпи́рик, а, *m.* empiricist.
эмпириокритици́зм, а, *m.* (*philos.*) empirio-criticism.
эмпири́ческий, *adj.* 1. (*philos.*) empiricist. 2. empirical.
эмпири́ч|ный (~ен, ~на), *adj.* = ~еский 2.
э́му, *indecl.*, *m.* emu.
эму́льси|я, и, *f.* emulsion.
эмфа́з|а, ы, *f.* (*ling.*) emphasis.
эмфати́ческий, *adj.* (*ling.*) emphatic.
эндокри́нн|ый, *adj.* (*physiol.*) endocrine; ~ые же́лезы endocrine glands, ductless glands.
эндокриноло́ги|я, и, *f.* endocrinology.
э́ндшпил|ь, я, *m.* (*chess*) end-game.
энерге́тик, а, *m.* power engineering specialist.
энерге́тик|а, и, *f.* power engineering.
энергет|и́ческий, *adj. of* ~ика; ~и́ческая ба́за (*econ.*) power supply sources, power base.

энерги́ч|ный (~ен, ~на), *adj.* energetic, vigorous, forceful.

эне́рги|я, и, *f.* 1. (*phys.*) energy; затра́та ~и energy consumption; растра́та ~и energy loss. 2. (*fig.*) energy; vigour, effort.

энерго-, power-.

энергоёмкий, *adj.* power-consuming.

энергосисте́м|а, ы, *f.* power (supply) system.

энкли́тик|а, и, *f.* (*ling.*) enclitic.

энклити́ческий, *adj.* (*ling.*) enclitic.

э́нн|ый, *adj.* (*expressing indefinite quantity, size, duration of time, etc.*) 'N', 'X'; any, unspecified; в ~ой сте́пени to the *n*th degree; ~ое коли́чество вре́мени *n* hours, an inordinate length of time.

э́нск|ий, *adj.* (*denoting a military unit, establishment, etc., which cannot be identified for reasons of security*) 'N', an unspecified; ~ая заста́ва погранво́йск frontier guards' post 'N'.

энтомо́лог, а, *m.* entomologist.

энтомологи́ческий, *adj.* entomological.

энтомоло́ги|я, и, *f.* entomology.

энтропи́|я, и, *f.* (*phys.*) entropy.

энтузиа́зм, а, *m.* enthusiasm.

энтузиа́ст, а, *m.* (+*g.*) enthusiast (about, for), devotee (of); э. футбо́ла football enthusiast.

энцефали́т, а, *m.* (*med.*) encephalitis.

энци́клик|а, и, *f.* (*eccl.*) encyclical.

энциклопеди́зм, а, *m.* encyclopaedic learning.

энциклопеди́ст, а, *m.* 1. (*hist.*) Encyclopaedist. 2. person of encyclopaedic learning.

энциклопеди́ческий, *adj.* encyclopaedic; э. слова́рь encyclopaedia; э. ум encyclopaedic brain.

энциклопе́ди|я, и, *f.* encyclopaedia; ходя́чая э. (*joc.*) walking encyclopaedia.

эоли́т, а, *m.* (*archaeol.*) eolithic period.

э́олов, *adj.* ~а а́рфа Aeolian harp.

эоце́н, а, *m.* (*geol.*) eocene period.

эпати́р|овать, ую, *impf. and pf.* to shock.

эпиго́н, а, *m.* (*pejor.*) imitator, unoriginal follower.

эпиго́н|ский, *adj.* of ~.

эпиго́нств|о, а, *n.* (*pejor.*) imitation, unoriginal following (*of another's work*).

эпигра́мм|а, ы, *f.* epigram.

эпи́граф, а, *m.* epigraph.

эпигра́фик|а, и, *f.* epigraphy.

эпиде́ми|я, и, *f.* epidemic.

эпиде́рм|а, ы, *f.* (*obs.*) = ~ис.

эпиде́рмис, а, *m.* (*biol.*) epidermis.

эпизо́д, а, *m.* episode.

эпизоди́ческий, *adj.* episodic; occasional, sporadic.

эпизооти́|я, и, *f.* epizootic (*of cattle diseases*).

э́пик, а, *m.* epic poet.

э́пик|а, и, *f.* epic poetry.

эпикуре́|ец, йца, *m.* epicurean.

эпикуре́йский, *adj.* epicurean.

эпикуре́йств|о, а, *n.* epicureanism.

эпиле́пси|я, и, *f.* (*med.*) epilepsy.

эпиле́птик, а, *m.* epileptic (person).

эпилепти́ческий, *adj.* epileptic.

эпило́г, а, *m.* epilogue.

эпистоля́рный, *adj.* epistolary.

эпита́фи|я, и, *f.* epitaph.

эпите́ли|й, я, *m.* (*anat.*) epithelium.

эпи́тет, а, *m.* epithet.

эпице́нтр, а, *m.* (*geol.*) epicentre.

эпици́кл, а, *m.* (*math.*) epicycle.

эпи́ческий, *adj.* epic.

эполе́т|ы, ~, *sing.* ~а, ~ы, *f.* epaulettes.

эпопе́|я, и, *f.* (*lit. or fig.*) epic.

э́пос, а, *m.* epos, epic literature.

эпо́х|а, и, *f.* epoch, age, era.

эпоха́льный, *adj.* epoch-making.

эпю́р, а, *m.* diagram, drawing.

э́р|а, ы, *f.* era; до на́шей ~ы в.с.; на́шей ~ы A.D.

эрг, а, *m.* erg (*unit of work*).

э́ре, *indecl., n.* öre, øre (*Scandinavian unit of currency*).

эре́кци|я, и, *f.* (*physiol.*) erection.

эрза́ц, а, *m.* ersatz.

эритроци́т, а, *m.* (*physiol.*) red corpuscle.

эроди́р|овать, ую, *impf.* to erode.

эро́зи|я, и, *f.* erosion.

эроти́зм, а, *m.* eroticism.

эро́тик|а, и, *f.* sensuality.

эроти́ческий, *adj.* erotic, sensual.

эроти́ч|ный (~ен, ~на), *adj.* = ~еский.

эротома́н, а, *m.* erotomaniac, sexual maniac.

эротома́ни|я, и, *f.* erotomania.

эрсте́д, а, *m.* oersted (*unit of magnetism*).

эруди́рован|ный (~, ~на), *adj.* erudite.

эруди́т, а, *m.* erudite person.

эруди́ци|я, и, *f.* erudition.

эрцге́рцог, а, *m.* archduke.

эрцгерцоги́н|я, и, *f.* archduchess.

эрцгерцогств|о, а, *n.* archduchy, archdukedom.

эсде́к, а, *m.* (*hist.*) S.D. (*member of Social Democratic Party*).

эсе́р, а, *m.* (*hist.*) S.R. (*member of Socialist Revolutionary Party*).

эсе́ровский, *adj.* (*hist.*) S.R. (*Socialist Revolutionary*).

эска́др|а, ы, *f.* (*naut.*) squadron.

эска́др|енный, *adj.* of ~а; э. бронено́сец (*obs.*) battleship; э. миноно́сец destroyer.

эскадри́л|ьный, *adj.* of ~ья.

эскадри́л|ья, ьи, *g. pl.* ~ий, *f.* (*aeron.*) squadron.

эскадрóн, а, *m.* (*mil.*) (*cavalry*) squadron, troop.

эскадрóн|ный, *adj. of* ~.

эскалáтор, а, *m.* escalator.

эскалáци|я, и, *f.* (*mil.*) escalation.

эскалóп, а, *m.* (*cul.*) cutlet(s).

эскáрп, а, *m.* (*mil.*) scarp, escarpment.

эскúз, а, *m.* sketch, study; draft, outline.

эскúз|ный, *adj. of* ~; э. чертёж draft, outline sketch.

эскимó, *indecl., n.* choc(olate) ice.

эскимóс, а, *m.* Eskimo.

эскимóс|ка, ки, *f. of* ~.

эскимóсский, *adj.* Eskimo.

эскóрт, а, *m.* (*mil.*) escort.

эскортúр|овать, ую, *impf. and pf.* (*mil.*) to escort.

эскулáп, а, *m.* (*obs. or joc.*) doctor.

эсмúн|ец, ца, *m.* (*abbr. of* эскáдренный миноносец) (*naut.*) destroyer.

эспадрóн, а, *m.* (*fencing*) cutting-sword, back-sword.

эспаньóлк|а, и, *f.* imperial (*beard*).

эспарцéт, а, *m.* (*bot.*) sainfoin.

эссéнци|я, и, *f.* (*in var. senses*) essence.

эстакáд|а, ы, *f.* **1.** viaduct, platform (*carrying elevated railway*); gantry. **2.** overpass. **3.** (*naut.*) pier. **4.** (*naut.*) boom (*of harbour*).

эстакáд|ный, *adj. of* ~а; ~ная желéзная дорóга elevated railway; э. кран gantry crane.

эстáмп, а, *m.* (*art*) print, engraving, plate.

эстафéт|а, ы, *f.* **1.** (*sport*) relay race. **2.** baton (*in relay race*); приня́ть у когó-н. ~у (*fig.*) to carry on someone's work, maintain someone's tradition. **3.** (*obs.*) mail (*carried by relays of horsemen*).

эстéт, а, *m.* aesthete.

эстетúзм, а, *m.* aestheticism.

эстéтик|а, и, *f.* **1.** aesthetics. **2.** design; промы́шленная э. industrial design.

эстетúческий, *adj.* aesthetic.

эстéт|ский, *adj. of* ~.

эстéтств|о, а, *n.* aestheticism.

эстóн|ец, ца, *m.* Estonian.

эстóн|ка, ки, *f. of* ~ец.

эстóнский, *adj.* Estonian.

эстрагóн, а, *m.* (*bot.*) tarragon.

эстрáд|а, ы, *f.* **1.** stage, platform; вы́йти на ~у to come on stage. **2.** variety (*art*); артúст ~ы variety performer, artiste.

эстрáд|ный, *adj. of* ~а; э. концéрт variety show.

эстуáри|й, я, *m.* estuary.

эсэсóв|ец, ца, *m.* (*hist.*) SS man.

эсэсóвский, *adj.* (*hist.*) SS.

этáж, á, *m.* storey, floor; пéрвый, вторóй, *etc.*, э. ground floor, first floor, *etc.*

этажéрк|а, и, *f.* bookcase, shelves.

этáжност|ь, и, *f.* number of storeys.

этак, *adv.* (*coll.*) **1.** so, thus; мóжно э́то сдéлать и так и э. you can do it like this or like that. **2.** about, approximately.

этакий, *pron.* (*coll.*) such (a), what (a).

эталóн, а, *m.* standard (*of weights and measures*).

этáн, а, *m.* (*chem.*) ethane.

этáп, а, *m.* **1.** stage, phase. **2.** (*sport*) lap. **3.** halting-place, stage (*for troops*; *formerly, for groups of deported convicts in transit*); отпрáвить по ~у, ~ом to transport, deport (*under guard*).

этáпник, а, *m.* (*hist.*) convict in transit.

этáп|ный, *adj. of* ~; ~ное собы́тие (*fig.*) landmark, turning-point; отпрáвить ~ным поря́дком (*hist.*) to transport, deport (*under guard*).

этик|а, и, *f.* ethics.

этикéт, а, *m.* etiquette.

этикéтк|а, и, *f.* label.

этúл, а, *m.* (*chem.*) ethyl.

этилéн, а, *m.* (*chem.*) ethylene.

этúл|овый, *adj. of* ~; э. спирт ethyl alcohol.

этимóлог, а, *m.* etymologist.

этимологúческий, *adj.* etymological.

этимолóги|я, и, *f.* etymology; нарóдная э. popular etymology.

этúческий, *adj. of* э́тика.

этúч|ный (~ен, ~на), *adj.* ethical.

этнúческий, *adj.* ethnic.

этнóграф, а, *m.* ethnographer, social anthropologist.

этнографúческий, *adj.* ethnographic(al).

этногрáфи|я, и, *f.* ethnography, social anthropology.

э́то¹, *see* э́тот.

э́то², *emphatic particle* (*coll.*); кудá э. он дéлся? wherever has he got to?; что э. ты не готóв? why on earth aren't you ready?; э. вы спрáшивали? was it *you* who was asking?

э́то³, *pron.* (*as noun*) this (is), that (is); э. наш дом this is our house; э. вам помóжет this will help you; э. вéрно that is true; не в э́том дéло that's not the point; об э́том я вам потóм расскажу́ I will tell you about it later; э. я ви́жу so I can see.

э́тот, э́та, э́то, *pl.* э́ти, *pron.* this (these); *as noun* (*i*) this one, (*ii*) the latter.

этрýск, а, *m.* Etruscan.

этрýсский, *adj.* Etruscan.

этю́д, а, *m.* **1.** (*art, lit.*) study, sketch. **2.** (*mus.*) étude. **3.** (*mus.*) exercise; (*chess*) problem.

эфемерúд|ы, ~, *sing.* ~а, ~ы, *f.* **1.** (*zool.*) ephemeridae. **2.** (*astron.*) ephemerides.

эфемéр|ный (~ен, ~на), *adj.* ephemeral.

эфéс, а, *m.* hilt, handle (*of sword, sabre, etc.*).

эфиóп, а, *m.* Ethiopian.

эфиóп|ка, ки, *f. of* ~.

эфио́пский, *adj.* Ethiopian.

эфи́р, а, *m.* **1.** ether; (*fig.*) air; передава́ть в э. to put on the air, broadcast. **2.** (*chem.*) ether; просто́й э. ether; сло́жный э. ester.

эфи́р|ный (~ен, ~на), *adj.* **1.** ethereal. **2.** (*chem.*) ether, ester; ~ное ма́сло essential oil, volatile oil.

эфироно́с, а, *m.* volatile-oil-bearing plant.

эфироно́сный, *adj.* volatile-oil-bearing.

эффе́кт, а, *m.* **1.** effect, impact; произвести́ э. (на + *a.*) to have an effect (on), make an impression (on). **2.** (*econ.*) result, consequences. **3.** (*pl.*) (*theatr.*) effects; шумовы́е ~ы sound effects.

эффекти́в|ный (~ен, ~на), *adj.* effective, efficacious.

эффе́кт|ный (~ен, ~на), *adj.* **1.** effective (= *making an impact*), striking. **2.** done for effect.

эх, *interj.* *expressing regret, reproval, amazement, etc.*; eh!, oh!

эхма́, *interj.* = эх.

э́х|о, а, *n.* echo.

эхоло́т, а, *m.* (*naut.*) sonic depth finder, echo sounder.

эшафо́т, а, *m.* scaffold; взойти́ на э. to mount the scaffold.

эшело́н, а, *m.* **1.** (*mil.*) échelon. **2.** special train.

эшелони́р|овать, ую, *impf. and pf.* (*mil.*) to échelon; э. оборо́ну to dispose defence in depth.

Ю

юа́н|ь, я, *m.* yuan (*Chinese currency unit*).

юбиле́|й, я, *m.* **1.** anniversary; jubilee. **2.** anniversary celebrations.

юбиле́й|ный, *adj.* of ~.

юбиля́р, а, *m.* person (*or* institution) whose anniversary is celebrated.

ю́бк|а, и, *f.* skirt; держа́ться за чью-н. ~у to cling to someone's apron-strings.

ю́бочк|а, и, *f.* short skirt.

ю́бочник, а, *m.* (*coll.*) womanizer.

ю́б|очный, *adj.* of ~ка.

ювели́р, а, *m.* jeweller.

ювели́р|ный, *adj.* **1.** *adj.* of ~; ~ные изде́лия gold and silver ware, jewelry; ю. магази́н jeweller's. **2.** (*fig.*) fine, intricate.

юг, а, *m.* south; the South (*of Russia, etc.*); на ю́ге in the south; к ю́гу от to the south of.

юго-восто́к, а, *m.* south-east.

юго-восто́чный, *adj.* south-east(ern).

юго-за́пад, а, *m.* south-west.

юго-за́падный, *adj.* south-west(ern).

югосла́в, а, *m.* Yugoslav.

югосла́в|ка, ки, *f.* of ~.

югосла́вский, *adj.* Yugoslav.

юдо́л|ь, и, *f.* (*arch.*) valley; ю. пла́ча, ю. печа́ли, земна́я ю. 'vale of tears'.

юдофо́б, а, *m.* anti-Semite.

юдофо́бств|о, а, *n.* anti-Semitism.

южа́н|ин, ина, *pl.* ~е, ~, *m.* southerner.

южне́е, *comp.* of ~ый; ю. Ло́ндона to the south of London.

ю́жный, *adj.* south, southern; Ю. по́люс South Pole; Ю. поля́рный круг antarctic circle; ю. темпера́мент (*fig.*) southern temperament.

ю́зом, *adv.* skidding, in a skid.

ю́кк|а, и, *f.* (*bot.*) yucca.

юл|а́, ы́, *f.* **1.** top (*child's toy*). **2.** (*coll.*) fidget. **3.** (*orn.*) wood lark.

юл|и́ть, ю́, и́шь, *impf.* (*coll.*) **1.** to fuss, fidget. **2.** (пе́ред) to play up (to).

ю́мор, а, *m.* humour; чу́вство ~а a sense of humour.

юморе́ск|а, и, *f.* (*mus., lit.*) humoresque.

юмори́ст, а, *m.* humourist.

юмори́стик|а, и, *f.* **1.** (*collect.*) humour. **2.** (*coll.*) something funny.

юмористи́ческий, *adj.* humorous, comic, funny.

ю́нг|а, и, *m.* ship's boy; sea cadet.

юн|е́ц, ца́, *m.* (*coll.*) youth.

ю́нкер, а, *m.* (*hist.*) **1.** (*pl.* ~а́, ~о́в) cadet. **2.** (*pl.* ~ы, ~ов) Junker (*Prussian landowner*).

ю́нкер|ский, *adj.* of ~.

юннáт, а, *m.* abbr. of ю́ный натурали́ст.

ю́ност|ь, и, *f.* youth (*age*).

ю́нош|а, и, *m.* youth (*person*).

ю́ношеский, *adj.* youthful.

ю́ношеств|о, а, *n.* **1.** youth (*age*). **2.** (*collect.*) youth, young people.

ю́н|ый (~, ~á, ~о), *adj.* **1.** young; теа́тр ~ого зри́теля young people's theatre; ю. натурали́ст member of junior natural history study group. **2.** youthful.

юпи́тер, а, *m.* floodlight.

юр, а, *m.* only in phrase на ~у́ (*i*) in a high, exposed place, (*ii*) (*fig.*) in the limelight, in the forefront.

ю́р|а, ы, *f.* (*geol.*) Jurassic period.

юр|а́, ы́, *f.* (*dial.*) large shoal (*of fish*); school (*of marine animals*).

юриди́ческ|ий, *adj.* legal, juridical; ~ая консульта́ция legal advice office; ~ое лицо́ juridical person; ~ие нау́ки jurisprudence, law; ю. факульте́т faculty of law.

юрисди́кци|я, и, *f.* jurisdiction.

юриско́нсульт, а, *m.* legal adviser.

юриспруде́нц|я, и, *f.* jurisprudence, law (*as an academic discipline*).

юри́ст, а, *m.* legal expert, lawyer.

ю́р|кий (~ок, ~ка́, ~ко), *adj.* 1. quick-moving, brisk. 2. (*fig., coll.*) clever, sharp, smart.

юркн|у́ть, у́, ёшь, *pf.* to scamper away, dart away, plunge.

юро́див|ый, *adj.* 1. crazy, simple, touched. 2. *as noun* ю., ~ого, *m.* 'God's fool' (*idiot believed to possess divine gift of prophecy*).

юро́дств|о, а, *n.* 1. craziness, idiocy. 2. idiotic action.

юро́дств|овать, ую, *impf.* to behave like an idiot.

ю́рский, *adj.* (*geol.*) Jurassic.

ю́рт|а, ы, *f.* yurt, yurta (*nomad's tent in Central Asia*).

ю́рьев, *adj.* Ю. день St. George's Day; вот тебе́ и Ю. день! here's a fine how d'ye do!

юс, а, *pl.* ~ы́, *m.* (*ling.*) yus (*name of two letters originally representing nasal vowels in Old Church Slavonic*); юс большо́й large 'yus' (Ѫ); юс ма́лый little 'yus' (Ѧ).

юстир|ова́ть, у́ю, *impf. and pf.* to adjust, regulate (*instruments*).

юсти́ци|я, и, *f.* justice.

ют, а, *m.* (*naut.*) quarter-deck.

ю|ти́ться, чу́сь, ти́шься, *impf.* to huddle (together); to take shelter.

юфт|евый, *adj. of* ~ь.

юфт|ь, и, *f.* yuft, Russia leather.

юфт|яно́й = ~евый.

Я

я, меня́, мне, мной (мно́ю), обо мне, *personal pron.* I (me); я не я (*coll.*) it's nothing to do with me; (я) не я бу́ду, е́сли не добью́сь от него́ извине́ния I'll damn well see that I get an apology from him; *as noun, n., indecl.* the self, the ego; второ́е я alter ego.

я́бед|а, ы, *f.* 1. (*obs.*) information, slander. 2. (*m. and f.*) = ~ник.

я́бедник, а, *m.* (*coll.*) informer, sneak.

я́беднича|ть, ю, *impf.* (*of* на~) (на + a.; *coll.*) to inform (on), tell tales (about).

я́блок|о, а, *pl.* ~и, ~, *n.* apple; глазно́е я. eyeball; в ~ах (*of a horse's coat*) dappled; я. раздо́ра bone of contention; ~y не́где упа́сть there's not room to swing a cat.

я́блон|евый, *adj. of* ~я.

я́блон|ный = ~евый.

я́блон|я, и, *f.* apple-tree.

я́блочк|о, а, *n.* *dim. of* я́блоко.

я́бло|чный, *adj. of* ~ко.

яв|и́ть, лю́, ~ишь, *pf.* (*of* ~ля́ть) to show, display; я. (собо́й) приме́р (+ *g.*) to give an example (of), display.

яв|и́ться, лю́сь, ~ишься, *pf.* (*of* ~ля́ться) 1. to appear, present oneself; to report; я. в суд to appear before the court; я. на слу́жбу to report for duty; я. с пови́нной to give oneself up. 2. to turn up, arrive, show up. 3. to arise, occur; у меня́ ~и́лась блестя́щая мысль I had a brilliant idea; ~и́лся удо́бный слу́чай a suitable opportunity presented itself.

я́вк|а, и, *f.* 1. appearance, attendance; я. в суд appearance in court. 2. secret

rendezvous; signal for secret rendezvous. 3. (*obs.*) information.

явле́ни|е, я, *n.* 1. phenomenon; occurrence, happening. 2. (*theatr.*) scene.

явле́нный, *adj.* (*rel.*) appearing miraculously (*esp. of icons*).

явля́|ть, ю, *impf. of* яви́ть.

явля́|ться, юсь, *impf.* 1. *impf. of* яви́ться. 2. (*impf. only*) (+ *i.*) to be; to serve (as); э́то ~ется кощу́нством this is blasphemy.

я́вно¹, *adv.* manifestly, patently; obviously.

я́вно², *as pred.* it is manifest, patent; it is obvious.

я́в|ный (~ен, ~на), *adj.* 1. manifest, patent; overt, explicit. 2. obvious.

я́вор, а, *m.* sycamore (*tree*).

я́вор|овый, *adj. of* ~.

я́вочн|ый, *adj.* 1. *adj. of* я́вка 2; ~ая кварти́ра secret rendezvous. 2. (*mil.*) reporting; recruiting; я. пункт reporting point (*for conscripts*); я. уча́сток recruiting office. 3. ~ым поря́дком on the spur of the moment, without prior arrangement.

я́вствен|ный (~, ~на), *adj.* clear, distinct.

я́вств|овать, ует, *impf.* to appear; to be clear, apparent, obvious; to follow (*logically*).

яв|ь, и, *f.* reality.

ягдта́ш, а, *m.* game-bag.

я́гел|ь, я, *m.* (*bot.*) Iceland moss, reindeer moss.

ягн|ёнок, ёнка, *pl.* ~я́та, ~я́т, *m.* lamb.

ягн|и́ться, и́тся, *impf.* (*of* о~) to lamb.

ягня́тник, а, *m.* lammergeier (*vulture*).

я́год|а, ы, *f.* berry; (*collect.*) soft fruit (*strawberries, blackcurrants, etc.*); ви́нная я. dried fig; пойти́ по ~ы to go berry-picking; одного́ по́ля я. a soul-mate.

я́годиц|а, ы, *f.* buttock(s).

я́годи|чный, *adj. of* ~ца.

я́годник, а, *m.* **1.** berry plantation. **2.** berry bush. **3.** (*coll.*) berry-picker.

я́год|ный, *adj. of* ~а.

ягуа́р, а, *m.* jaguar.

яд, а (у), *m.* poison; venom (*also fig.*).

я́дерн|ый, *adj.* **1.** (*phys.*) nuclear; ~ое расщепле́ние nuclear fission; я. реа́ктор nuclear reactor; ~ая фи́зика nuclear physics. **2.** *adj. of* ядро́.

ядови́т|ый (~, ~а), *adj.* **1.** poisonous; toxic; я. газ poison gas; ~ая змея́ poisonous snake. **2.** (*fig.*) venomous, malicious.

ядохимика́т, а, *m.* (*agric.*) chemical weed-and/or pest-killer.

ядрён|ый (~, ~а), *adj.* (*coll.*) **1.** having a large kernel (*of nuts*); juicy (*of fruit*); hearty (*of cabbages*). **2.** (*fig.*) healthy, vigorous. **3.** (*fig.*) fresh, bracing.

ядр|о́, а́, *pl.* ~а, я́дер, ~ам, *n.* **1.** kernel; core. **2.** (*phys.*) nucleus. **3.** (*mil., etc.*) main body (*of a unit, group*). **4.** (*hist., mil.*) ball, shot. **5.** (*sport*) shot; толка́ние ~а́ putting the shot.

ядро́|вый, *adj. of* ~ 1; ~вое мы́ло high-grade soap.

я́дрышк|о, а, *pl.* ~и, *n.* **1.** *dim. of* ядро́. **2.** (*biol.*) nucleolus.

я́зв|а, ы, *f.* **1.** ulcer, sore; я. желу́дка stomach ulcer; морова́я я. plague; сиби́р-ская я. malignant anthrax. **2.** (*fig.*) harm; plague, curse. **3.** (*fig., coll.*) malicious person; (*as term of abuse*) scum.

я́звенн|ый, *adj.* ulcerous; ~ая боле́знь stomach ulcer.

я́звин|а, ы, *f.* **1.** indentation, pit. **2.** (*coll.*) large ulcer.

язви́тел|ьный (~ен, ~ьна), *adj.* caustic, biting, sarcastic.

язв|и́ть, лю́, и́шь, *impf.* (*of* съ~) **1.** (*obs.*) to wound; to sting. **2.** to say sarcastically; to mock; я. на чей-н. счёт to be sarcastic at someone's expense.

язы́к¹, а́, *pl.* ~и́, *m.* **1.** tongue; у него́ я. без косте́й he is too fond of talking; у него́ что на уме́, то и на ~е́ (*coll.*) he cannot keep his thoughts to himself; держа́ть я. за зуба́ми, придержа́ть я. to hold one's tongue; прикуси́ть я. (*coll.*) to shut up; я. у него́ хорошо́ подве́шен (*coll.*) he has a glib tongue; распусти́ть я. (*coll.*) to talk too glibly; дёргать, тяну́ть кого́-н. за я. (*coll.*) to make someone talk; сорвало́сь с ~á (*fig.*) it slipped out; лиши́ться ~á (*fig.*) to lose one's tongue; я. у меня́ не поверну́лся э́то сказа́ть (*coll.*) I could not bring myself to say it; чеса́ть, болта́ть ~о́м (*coll.*) to natter, blather; я. у меня́ чеса́лся (*coll.*) I was itching to speak; я. прогло́тишь (*coll.*)

it makes one's mouth water. **2.** (*cul.*) tongue; копчёный я. smoked tongue. **3.** clapper (*of a bell*). **4.** (*mil.; coll.*) prisoner who will talk (*will provide information when interrogated*).

язы́к², а́, *pl.* ~и́, *m.* **1.** language (*also fig.*); владе́ть мно́гими ~а́ми to know many languages; говори́ть на ло́маном ру́сском ~е́ to talk in broken Russian; найти́ о́бщий я. (*fig.*) to find a common language. **2.** (*pl.* ~и́) (*obs.*) people, nationality, nation.

языка́ст|ый (~, ~а), *adj.* (*coll.*) sharp--tongued.

языкове́д, а, *m.* linguist, specialist on linguistics.

языкове́дени|е, я, *n.* linguistics.

языкове́д|ческий, *adj. of* ~ение.

языково́й, *adj.* linguistic.

языко́вый, *adj.* **1.** (*anat.*) tongue, lingual. **2.** (*cul.*) tongue.

языкозна́ни|е, я, *n.* linguistics, science of language.

язы́ческий, *adj.* heathen, pagan.

язы́честв|о, а, *n.* heathenism, paganism.

языч|ко́вый, *adj. of* ~о́к; я. инструме́нт (*mus.*) reed instrument.

язы́чник, а, *m.* heathen, pagan.

язы́|чный, *adj. of* ~к¹ 1.

языч|о́к, ка́, *m.* **1.** (*anat.*) uvula. **2.** (*mus.*) reed. **3.** (*tech.*) catch, lug. **4.** *dim. of* язы́к.

яз|ь, я́, *m.* ide (*fish of carp family*).

яи́чк|о, а, *pl.* ~и, *n.* **1.** (*anat.*) testicle. **2.** *dim. of* яйцо́.

яи́чник, а, *m.* (*anat.*) ovary.

яи́чниц|а, ы, *f.* (*cul.*) fried eggs (*also* я.-глазу́нья); я.-болту́нья scrambled eggs.

яи́чн|ый, *adj. of* яйцо́; я. бело́к white of egg; я. желто́к yolk of egg; я. порошо́к dried egg(s); ~ая скорлупа́ egg-shell.

яйл|а́, ы́, *f.* (*dial.*) mountain pasture (*in Crimea*).

яйцеви́д|ный (~ен, ~на), *adj.* egg-shaped, oval, oviform, ovoid.

яйцево́д, а, *m.* (*anat.*) oviduct.

яйцекла́д, а, *m.* (*zool.*) ovipositor.

яйцекле́тк|а, и, *f.* (*biol.*) ovule.

яйцено́ск|ий, *adj.* (*agric.*) ~ие ку́ры good laying hens.

яйцено́скост|ь, и, *f.* (*agric.*) egg-laying qualities.

яйцеро́дный, *adj.* (*zool.*) oviparous.

яйц|о́, а́, *pl.* ~а, яйц, ~ам, *n.* egg; (*biol.*) ovum; нести́ ~a to lay eggs; я. всмя́тку lightly-boiled egg; я. вкруту́ю hard-boiled egg; я. в мешо́чек medium-timed egg.

як, а, *m.* yak.

якоби́н|ец, ца, *m.* (*hist., polit.*) Jacobin.

якоби́н|ский, *adj. of* ~ец.

я́кобы **1.** *conj.* (*expressing doubt about validity of another's statement*) that; говоря́т, я. он у́мер they say (= they claim) that he has died. **2.** *conj.* as if, as though; он вообрази́л, я. его́ произвели́ в генера́лы he imagined he had been made a general. **3.** *particle* supposedly, ostensibly, allegedly, purportedly; мы посмотре́ли э́ту я. стра́шную карти́ну we have seen this supposedly dreadful film.

я́кор|ный, *adj. of* ~ь; ~ная лебёдка capstan; ~ное ме́сто, ~ная стоя́нка anchorage.

я́кор|ь, я, *pl.* ~я́, ~е́й, *m.* **1.** (*naut.*) anchor; я. спасе́ния (*fig.*) sheet-anchor; стать на я. to anchor; бро́сить я. to cast, drop anchor; стоя́ть на ~e to ride at anchor; сня́ться с ~я to weigh anchor. **2.** (*electr.*) armature; rotor.

яку́т, а, *m.* Yakut.

яку́т|ка, ки, *f. of* ~.

яку́тский, *adj.* Yakut.

якша́|ться, юсь, *impf.* (c+*i.*; *coll.*) to consort (with), hob-nob (with).

ял, а, *m.* whaler, pinnace; yawl.

я́лик, а, *m.* skiff, dinghy; yawl.

я́личник, а, *m.* ferryman.

я́ли|чный, *adj. of* ~к.

я́лове|ть, ет, *impf.* to be barren, dry (*of cows*).

я́ловк|а, и, *f.* barren cow, dry cow.

я́ловост|ь, и, *f.* barrenness, dryness (*in cows*).

я́ловый, *adj.* barren, dry (*of cows*).

ям, а, *m.* (*hist.*) mail staging-post.

я́м|а, ы, *f.* **1.** pit, hole; возду́шная я. air pocket; выгребна́я я. cesspit; у́гольная я. coal bunker; рыть кому́-н. ~у (*fig.*) to lay a trap for someone. **2.** (*geogr.*; *coll.*) depression, hollow. **3.** (*obs.*) prison.

яма́йский, *adj.* Jamaican.

ямб, а, *m.* (*lit.*) iambus, iambic verse.

ямби́ческий, *adj.* iambic.

я́мк|а, и, *f. dim. of* я́ма; я. на щека́х dimple.

ямщи́к, а́, *m.* coachman.

янва́р|ский, *adj. of* ~ь.

янва́р|ь, я́, *m.* January.

я́нки, *indecl.,* *m.* Yankee.

янта́рн|ый, *adj.* **1.** amber; ~ая кислота́ succinic acid. **2.** amber-coloured.

янта́р|ь, я́, *m.* amber.

яныча́р, а, *m.* (*hist.*) janissary.

япо́н|ец, ца, *m.* Japanese.

япо́н|ка, ки, *f. of* ~ец.

япо́нский, *adj.* Japanese; я. лак Japan lacquer, japan.

яр¹, а, о ~е, на ~у́, *m.* **1.** steep bank (*of river, lake, etc.*); slope (*of ravine*). **2.** ravine.

яр², а, *m.* (*physiol.*) heat.

ярд, а, *m.* yard (*measure*).

яре́мн|ый, *adj. of* ярмо́; ~ая ве́на (*anat.*) jugular vein.

яр|и́ться, ю́сь, и́шься, *impf.* **1.** (*obs.*) to

rage, be in a fury. **2.** (*physiol.*) to be in heat.

я́рк|а, и, *f.* young ewe (*up to first lambing*).

я́р|кий (~ок, ~ка́, ~ко), *adj.* **1.** bright (*of light, colours, etc.*). **2.** (*fig.*) colourful, striking; vivid, graphic; ~кая карти́на graphic picture; я. приме́р striking, glaring example. **3.** (*fig.*) brilliant, outstanding; impressive; ~кая речь brilliant speech; я. тала́нт outstanding gifts.

я́ркост|ь, и, *f.* **1.** brightness. **2.** (*fig.*) brilliance.

ярлы́к, а́, *m.* **1.** (*hist.*) yarlyk, edict (*of khans of Golden Horde*). **2.** label, tag. **3.** (*fig.*) label; прикле́ить я. кому́-н. to pin a label on someone.

я́рмарк|а, и, *f.* (trade) fair.

я́рмар|очный, *adj. of* ~ка.

ярм|о́, а́, *pl.* ~а, *n.* yoke (*also fig.*); сбро́сить с себя́ я. (*fig.*) to cast off the yoke.

яровиза́ци|я, и, *f.* (*agric.*) vernalization.

яровизи́р|овать, ую, *impf. and pf.* (*agric.*) to vernalize.

яров|о́й, *adj.* (*agric.*) spring; ~а́я пшени́ца spring wheat; *as noun* ~о́е, ~о́го, *n.* spring crop.

я́рост|ный (~ен, ~на), *adj.* furious, fierce, savage, frenzied.

я́рост|ь, и, *f.* fury, rage, frenzy.

я́рус, а, *m.* **1.** (*theatr.*) circle. **2.** tier. **3.** (*geol.*) stage, layer.

я́рус|ный, *adj.* **1.** *adj. of* ~. **2.** tiered; stepped; graduated.

ярча́йший, *superl. of* я́ркий.

я́р|че, *comp. of* ~кий *and* ~ко.

ярь́|га, и, *m.* **1.** (*hist.*) constable. **2.** (*obs.*) drunkard.

я́р|ый¹ (~, ~а), *adj.* **1.** furious, raging; violent. **2.** vehement, fervent.

я́рый², *adj.* (*obs.*) light; bright.

я́рь-медя́нка, я́ри-медя́нки, *f.* (*chem.*) verdigris.

я́с|ельный, *adj. of* ~ли.

я́сен|евый, *adj. of* ~ь.

я́сен|ь, я, *m.* ash-tree.

я́сл|и, ей, *no sing.* **1.** manger, crib (*for cattle*). **2.** crèche, day nursery.

ясне́|ть, ет, *impf.* to become clear(er).

я́сн|о¹, *adv. of* ~ый.

я́сно², *as pred.* **1.** (*of weather*) it is fine. **2.** (*fig.*) it is clear. **3.** (*as affirmative particle*) yes, of course.

яснови́дени|е, я, *n.* clairvoyance.

яснови́д|ец, ца, *m.* clairvoyant.

яснови́дящий, *adj.* (*also as noun*) clairvoyant.

я́сност|ь, и, *f.* clearness, clarity; lucidity; внести́ я. во что-н. to clarify something.

я́сн|ый (~ен, ~на́, ~но), *adj.* **1.** clear; bright; (*of weather*) fine; ~ное не́бо clear sky; гром средь ~ного не́ба a bolt from the blue. **2.** distinct. **3.** serene. **4.** (*fig.*) clear, plain; сде́лать ~ным to make it clear; ~ное де́ло of course. **5.** lucid; precise, logical; я. ум precise mind.

я́ств|а, ~, *sing.* ~о, ~а, *n.* viands, victuals.

я́стреб, а, *pl.* ~á *and* ~ы, *m.* hawk.

ястреби́н|ый, *adj. of* я́стреб; ~ая охо́та falconry; с ~ым взгля́дом hawk-eyed; я. нос hawk nose.

ястреб|о́к, ка́, m. 1. *dim. of* я́стреб. **2.** (*coll.*) fighter (*plane*).

ятага́н, а, *m.* yataghan.

ятры́шник, а, *m.* (*bot.*) orchis.

ят|ь, я, *m.* yat′ (*name of old Russian letter* ‘ѣ’ *replaced by* ‘е’ *in 1918*); на я. (*coll.*) first-class; splendid(ly).

яфети́ческий, *adj.* (*ling.*) Japhetic.

я́хонт, а, *m.* (кра́сный) ruby; (си́ний) sapphire.

я́хонт|овый, *adj. of* ~.

я́хт|а, ы, *f.* yacht.

я́хт-клу́б, а, *m.* yacht club.

яхтсме́н, а, *m.* yachtsman.

яче́ист|ый (~, ~а), *adj.* cellular, porous.

яче́йк|а, и, *g. pl.* яче́ек, *f.* **1.** (*biol., polit.*) cell. **2.** (*mil.*) foxhole; slit trench.

яче́йк|овый, *adj. of* ~а.

я́ честв|о, а, *n.* (*pejor.*) individualism, egocentrism.

яче|я́, и́, *f.* (*biol.*) cell.

я́чий, *adj. of* як.

ячме́н|ный, *adj. of* ~ь¹; ~ное зерно́ barley-corn; я. отва́р barley-water; я. са́хар barley-sugar, malt-sugar.

ячме́н|ь¹, я́, *m.* barley.

ячме́н|ь², я́, *m.* sty (*in the eye*).

я́чневый, *adj.* of crushed, coarse barley.

я́шм|а, ы, *f.* (*min.*) jasper.

я́шм|овый, *adj. of* ~а.

я́щериц|а, ы, *f.* lizard.

я́щик, а, *m.* **1.** box, chest, case; cabinet; му́сорный я. dustbin; почто́вый я. letter-box, pillar-box; откла́дывать в до́лгий я. (*fig.*) to shelve, put off. **2.** drawer.

я́щи|чный, *adj. of* ~к.

я́щур, а, *m.* foot-and-mouth disease.

я́щур|ный, *adj.* **1.** *adj. of* ~. **2.** infected with foot-and-mouth disease.

APPENDIX

PRINCIPAL ABBREVIATIONS

(a) *Official abbreviations*

Note. This select list comprises only abbreviations made up of initial letters of words. A very much larger group is that of words formed by compounding entire syllables: the most important of these are found in the body of the Dictionary (*see* исполко́м, колхо́з, etc.), while the meaning of many others may be deduced from prefixes (e.g. авиа-, гос-) and entries for the relevant component words.

АМН	Акаде́мия медици́нских нау́к	Academy of Medical Sciences
АН	Акаде́мия нау́к	Academy of Sciences
АН-	Анто́нов-	Antonov- (*make of aircraft*)
АО	автоно́мная о́бласть	autonomous oblast
АПН	Аге́нтство печа́ти «Но́вости»	Novosti news agency
АССР	Автоно́мная Сове́тская Социалисти́ческая Респу́блика	Autonomous Soviet Socialist Republic
АТС	автомати́ческая телефо́нная ста́нция	automatic telephone exchange
АЭС	а́томная электроста́нция	atomic electric power-station.
БССР	Белору́сская Сове́тская Социалисти́ческая Респу́блика	Byelorussian Soviet Socialist Republic
БСЭ	Больша́я Сове́тская Энциклопе́дия	the Large Soviet Encyclopedia
ВАО	Всесою́зное акционе́рное о́бщество	All-Union joint-stock company
ВАСХНИЛ	Всесою́зная Акаде́мия сельскохозя́йственных нау́к и́мени Ле́нина	All-Union Lenin Academy of Agricultural Sciences
ВВС	Вое́нно-Возду́шные Си́лы	Air Force
ВГИК	Всесою́зный госуда́рственный институ́т кинематогра́фии	All-Union State Cinematography Institute
ВДНХ	Вы́ставка достиже́ний наро́дного хозя́йства	Exhibition of Economic Achievements (*in Moscow*)
ВИНИТИ	Всесою́зный институ́т нау́чной и техни́ческой информа́ции	All-Union Scientific and Technical Information Institute
ВКП(б)	Всесою́зная Коммунисти́ческая па́ртия (большевико́в) (*hist.*)	All-Union Communist Party (Bolsheviks)
ВЛКСМ	Всесою́зный Ле́нинский Коммунисти́ческий Сою́з Молодёжи	All-Union Leninist Communist Youth League
ВМФ	Вое́нно-Морско́й Флот	Navy
ВНИИ	всесою́зный нау́чно-иссле́довательский институ́т	All-Union scientific research institute
ВНР	Венге́рская Наро́дная Респу́блика	Hungarian People's Republic
ВО	вое́нный о́круг	military district
ВОКС	Всесою́зное о́бщество культу́рных свя́зей с заграни́цей (*hist.*)	All-Union Society for Cultural Relations with Foreign Countries
ВПШ	Вы́сшая парти́йная шко́ла	Higher Party School
ВСМ	Всеми́рный Сове́т Ми́ра	World Peace Council
ВЦИК	Всероссийский Центра́льный Исполни́тельный Комите́т (*hist.*)	All-Russian Central Executive Committee
ВЦСПС	Всесою́зный Центра́льный Сове́т Профессиона́льных Сою́зов	All-Union Central Trade Union Council

ВЧК	Всероссийская чрезвычайная комиссия по борьбе с контрреволюцией, саботажем и спекуляцией (*hist.*) All-Russian Special Commission for Combatting Counter-revolution, Sabotage, and Speculation ('Cheka')
ГАБТ	Государственный академический большой театр (State Academic) Bolshoi Theatre
ГАЗ	Горьковский автомобильный завод (vehicle produced by) Gorky motor-vehicle factory
ГАИ	Государственная автомобильная инспекция State motor-vehicle inspectorate
ГДР	Германская Демократическая Республика German Democratic Republic
ГИТИС	Государственный институт театрального искусства State Institute of Dramatic Art
ГК	Гражданский кодекс Civil Law Code
ГКО	Государственный Комитет Обороны (*hist.*) State Defence Committee
ГОСТ	государственный общесоюзный стандарт State All-Union standard
ГОЭЛРО	Государственная комиссия по электрификации России (*hist.*) State Commission for Electrification of Russia
ГПК	Гражданско-процессуальный кодекс Civil Law Procedure Code
ГПУ	Государственное политическое управление (*hist.*) State Political Directorate ('GPU')
ГРУ	Главное разведывательное управление (*mil.*) Main Intelligence Directorate
ГРЭС	государственная районная электростанция State regional electric power-station
ГТО	Готов к труду и обороне! Ready for labour and defence! (*inscription on physical efficiency badge*)
ГУМ	Государственный универсальный магазин State department store
ГЭС	гидроэлектростанция hydro-electric power-station
ДОСААФ	Добровольное общество содействия армии, авиации и флоту Voluntary Society for Collaboration with the Army, Air Force, and Navy
ДРВ	Демократическая Республика Вьетнам Democratic Republic of Vietnam
ЖАКТ	жилищно-арендное кооперативное общество housing lease cooperative society
ЖЭК	жилищно-эксплуатационная контора housing office
ЗАГС	(отдел) записи актов гражданского состояния register office.
ЗИЛ	Завод имени Лихачёва (vehicle produced by) Likhachev motor-vehicle factory
ЗИМ	Завод имени Молотова (*hist.*) (vehicle produced by) Molotov motor-vehicle factory
ЗИС	Завод имени Сталина (*hist.*) (vehicle produced by) Stalin motor-vehicle factory
ИККИ	Исполнительный комитет Коммунистического Интернационала (*hist.*) Executive Committee of the Communist International
ИЛ-	Ильюшин- Ilyushin- (*make of aircraft*)
ИМЛ	Институт марксизма-ленинизма Institute of Marxism-Leninism
ИМЭЛС	Институт Маркса, Энгельса, Ленина и Сталина (*hist.*) Institute (for study) of Marx, Engels, Lenin, and Stalin
КГБ	Комитет государственной безопасности State Security Committee
КЗоБиС	Кодекс законов о браке и семье Marriage and Family Law Code
КЗоТ	Кодекс законов о труде Labour Law Code
КМО	Комитет молодёжных организаций Youth Organisations' Committee
КНДР	Корейская Народно-Демократическая Республика Korean People's Democratic Republic

КНР	Китáйская Нарóдная Респýблика	Chinese People's Republic
КП	Коммунистѝческая пáртия	Communist Party
КПСС	Коммунистѝческая пáртия Совéтского Сою́за	Communist Party of the Soviet Union
КУТВ	Коммунистѝческий университéт трудя́щихся Востóка	(hist.) Communist University of the Toilers of the East
ЛГУ	Ленингрáдский госудáрственный университéт	Leningrad State University
МАЗ	Мѝнский автомобѝльный завóд	(vehicle produced by) Minsk motor-vehicle factory
МАИ	Москóвский авиациóнный институ́т	Moscow Aeronautical Institute
МВТ	Министéрство внéшней торгóвли	Ministry of Foreign Trade
МВТУ	Москóвское вы́сшее технѝческое учѝлище	Moscow Technical High School
МВД	Министéрство внýтренних дел	Ministry of Internal Affairs
МГК	Москóвский городскóй комитéт	Moscow City Committee (*of Communist Party, etc.*)
МГУ	Москóвский госудáрственный университéт	Moscow State University
МИГ	Микоя́н и Гурéвич	Mikoyan and Gurevich ('Mig') (*make of aircraft*)
МИД	Министéрство инострáнных дел	Ministry of Foreign Affairs
МК	Москóвский комитéт	Moscow (Oblast) Committee (*of Communist Party, etc.*)
МНР	Монгóльская Нарóдная Респýблика	Mongolian People's Republic
МТС	машѝнно-трáкторная стáнция	(hist.) machinery and tractor station
МХАТ	Москóвский худóжественный академѝческий теáтр	Moscow Arts Theatre
МЭИ	Москóвский энергетѝческий институ́т	Moscow Power Engineering Institute
НИИ-	наýчно-исслéдовательский институ́т	scientific research institute
НКВД	Нарóдный комиссариáт внýтренних дел	(hist.) People's Commissariat for Internal Affairs
НО	Национáльный óкруг	National Area.
НОТ	наýчная организáция трудá	scientific organization of work, work study
НРБ	Нарóдная Респýблика Болгáрии	People's Republic of Bulgaria
НЭП	Нóвая экономѝческая полѝтика	(hist.) New Economic Policy ('Nep')
ОАР	Объединённая Арáбская Респýблика	United Arab Republic
ОВиР	отдéл виз и регистрáции	visa and registration department
ОГИЗ	Объединéние госудáрственных издáтельств	Central State Publishing House
ОГПУ	Объединённое госудáрственное политѝческое управлéние	(hist.) Unified State Political Directorate ('Ogpu')
ОЗЕТ	Óбщество землеустрóйства еврéев трудя́щихся	(hist.) Society for Settlement of Working Jews on the Land
ОИЯИ .	Объединённый институ́т я́дерных исслéдований	Joint Nuclear Research Institute
ОНО	отдéл нарóдного образовáния	education department (*of local authority*)
ООН	Организáция Объединённых Нáций	United Nations Organisation
ОРС	отдéл рабóчего снабжéния	workers' supply department
ОРУД	отдéл регулѝрования ýличного движéния	street traffic control department (*traffic police*)
ОТК	отдéл технѝческого контрóля	technical inspection department (*of factories, etc.*)
ПВО	противовоздýшная оборóна	(mil.) anti-aircraft defences
ПНР	Пóльская Нарóдная Респýблика	Polish People's Republic

РАПП	Росси́йская ассоциа́ция пролета́рских писа́телей (*hist.*) Russian Proletarian Writers' Association
РВС	революцио́нно-вое́нный сове́т (*hist.*) Revolutionary Military Council
РЖ	реферати́вный журна́л Journal of Abstracts
РКИ	Рабо́че-крестья́нская инспе́кция (Рабкри́н) (*hist.*) Workers' and Peasants' Inspectorate
РККА	Рабо́че-Крестья́нская Кра́сная А́рмия (*hist.*) Workers' and Peasants' Red Army
РОСТА	Росси́йское телегра́фное аге́нтство (*hist.*) Russian Telegraph Agency
РСДРП	Росси́йская социа́л-демократи́ческая рабо́чая па́ртия (*hist.*) Russian Social Democratic Workers' Party
РСФСР	Росси́йская Сове́тская Федерати́вная Социалисти́ческая Респу́блика Russian Soviet Federal Socialist Republic
РТС	ремо́нтно-техни́ческая ста́нция (*agric.*) repairs and engineering station
СЗ	сбо́рник зако́нов collection of laws
СМУ	строи́тельно-монта́жное управле́ние building and erection directorate
СНК	Сове́т Наро́дных Комисса́ров (*hist.*) Council of People's Commissars
СНХ	сове́т наро́дного хозя́йства Council of National Economy
СОБЕС	(отде́л) социа́льного обеспе́чения social security department (*of local authority*)
СП	сбо́рник постановле́ний collection of decrees
СП-	Се́верный по́люс- North Pole- (No. 1, 2, 3, *etc.*) (*designation of Soviet Arctic research stations*)
СПБ, СПб	Санкт-Петербу́рг St. Petersburg
СРР	Социалисти́ческая Респу́блика Румы́нии Socialist Republic of Rumania
ССР	Сове́тская Социалисти́ческая Респу́блика Soviet Socialist Republic
СССР	Сою́з Сове́тских Социалисти́ческих Респу́блик Union of Soviet Socialist Republics (USSR)
СУ	(*i*) сбо́рник ука́зов collection of decrees (*ii*) строи́тельное управле́ние building directorate
СФРЮ	Социалисти́ческая Федерати́вная Респу́блика Югосла́вии Socialist Federal Republic of Yugoslavia
США	Соединённые Шта́ты Аме́рики United States of America
СЭВ	Сове́т Экономи́ческой Взаимопо́мощи Council for Mutual Economic Aid ('Comecon')
ТАСС	Телегра́фное аге́нтство Сове́тского Сою́за Telegraph Agency of the Soviet Union
ТОЗ	това́рищество по обрабо́тке земли́ (*hist.*) association for tilling the soil
ТУ-	Ту́полев- Tupolev (*make of aircraft*)
ТЭЦ	теплова́я электроцентра́ль thermal electric power-station
УК	Уголо́вный ко́декс Criminal Law Code
УПК	Уголо́вно-процессуа́льный ко́декс Criminal Law Procedure Code
УССР	Украи́нская Сове́тская Социалисти́ческая Респу́блика Ukrainian Soviet Socialist Republic
ФРГ	Федерати́вная Респу́блика Герма́нии Federal Republic of Germany
ЦАГИ	Центра́льный аэрогидродинами́ческий институ́т Central Aero- and Hydro-dynamics Institute (*in Moscow*)
ЦГАДА	Центра́льный госуда́рственный архи́в дре́вних а́ктов Central State Archive of Ancient Documents
ЦДСА	Центра́льный дом Сове́тской А́рмии Central Club of the Soviet Army
ЦИК	Центра́льный Исполни́тельный Комите́т (*hist.*) Central Executive Committee
ЦК	Центра́льный Комите́т Central Committee
ЦКК	Центра́льная контро́льная коми́ссия (*hist.*) Central Control Commission

ЦРУ	Центра́льное разве́дывательное управле́ние	Central Intelligence Agency (*U.S.A.*)
ЦСКА	Центра́льный спорти́вный клуб А́рмии	Central Army Sports Club
ЦСУ	Центра́льное статисти́ческое управле́ние	Central Statistical Board
ЦУМ	Центра́льный универса́льный магази́н	Central department store
ЧССР	Чехослова́цкая Социалисти́ческая Респу́блика	Czechoslovak Socialist Republic
ЭВМ	электро́нно-вычисли́тельная маши́на	electronic computer

(b) *Common abbreviations*

в.	век century		оз.	о́зеро lake
г.	(*i*) год year, (*ii*) го́род city, town, (*iii*) гора́ mountain, (*iv*) господи́н Mr.		пл.	пло́щадь square.
			п. о.	почто́вое отделе́ние post office
га	гекта́р hectare		р.	(*i*) река́ river, (*ii*) рубль rouble
г-жа	госпожа́ Mrs., Miss		р-н	райо́н raion
г-н	господи́н Mr.		с.	(*i*) село́ village, (*ii*) страни́ца page
гр.	граждани́н, гражда́нка citizen			
д.	дом house		с. г.	сего́ го́да of this year
до н. э.	до на́шей э́ры в.с.		см.	смотри́ see, *vide*
ж. д.	желе́зная доро́га railway		соч.	сочине́ния works (*of an author*)
и др.	и други́е & co.; *et al.*		ср.	сравни́ compare, cf.
и пр.	и про́чие & co.; *et al.*		ст.	(*i*) статья́ article (*of law, etc.*), (*ii*) столе́тие century
и т. д.	и так да́лее etc., and so on			
и т. п.	и тому́ подо́бное etc., and so on		ст. ст.	ста́рый стиль Old Style (*of calendar*)
им.	и́мени named after		стр.	страни́ца page
к.	копе́йка kopeck		с.-х.	сельскохозя́йственный agricultural
кв.	кварти́ра flat, apartment			
м.	(*i*) мину́та minute, (*ii*) мыс (*geogr.*) cape		т.	(*i*) това́рищ Comrade, (*ii*) том volume (*of printed work*)
напр.	наприме́р for example		т. е.	то есть that is, *i.e.*
н. ст.	но́вый стиль New Style (*of calendar*)		т. к.	так как as, since
			тов.	това́рищ Comrade
н. э.	на́шей э́ры A.D.		тт.	(*i*) това́рищи Comrades, (*ii*) тома́ volumes (*of printed work*)
о.	о́стров island, isle			
обл.	о́бласть oblast		ул.	у́лица street, road
о-во	о́бщество society		ч.	час hour; ~а́, ~о́в o'clock